53rd Annual Meeting of the Association for Computational Linguistics and 7th International Joint Conference on Natural Language Processing of the Asian Federation of Natural Language Processing

(ACL-IJCNLP 2015)

Short Papers

Beijing, China
26 – 31 July 2015

ISBN: 978-1-5108-0846-1

Printed from e-media with permission by:

Curran Associates, Inc.
57 Morehouse Lane
Red Hook, NY 12571

Some format issues inherent in the e-media version may also appear in this print version.

Printed by Curran Associates, Inc. (2015)

For permission requests, please contact the Association for Computational Linguistics at the address below.

Association for Computational Linguistics
209 N. Eighth Street
Stroudsburg, Pennsylvania 18360

Phone: 1-570-476-8006
Fax: 1-570-476-0860

acl@aclweb.org

Additional copies of this publication are available from:

Curran Associates, Inc.
57 Morehouse Lane
Red Hook, NY 12571 USA
Phone: 845-758-0400
Fax: 845-758-2634
Email: curran@proceedings.com
Web: www.proceedings.com

ACL-IJCNLP 2015

The 53rd Annual Meeting of the Association for Computational Linguistics and the 7th International Joint Conference on Natural Language Processing of the Asian Federation of Natural Language Processing

Proceedings of the Conference
Short Papers

ACL 2015
July 26-31
Beijing, China

Platinum Sponsors:

Gold Sponsors:

Silver Sponsors:

Bronze Sponsor:

Best Paper Sponsor:

Table of Contents

Conference Program

Monday, July 27

17:00–18:00 Session 4: Short Papers

Session 4A: 17:00–18:00 Semantics

A Framework for the Construction of Monolingual and Cross-lingual Word Similarity Datasets
José Camacho-Collados, Mohammad Taher Pilehvar and Roberto Navigli

On metric embedding for boosting semantic similarity computations
Julien Subercaze, Christophe Gravier and Frédérique Laforest

Improving Distributed Representation of Word Sense via WordNet Gloss Composition and Context Clustering
Tao Chen, Ruifeng Xu, Yulan He and Xuan Wang

A Multitask Objective to Inject Lexical Contrast into Distributional Semantics
Nghia The Pham, Angeliki Lazaridou and Marco Baroni

Session 4B: 17:00–18:00 Sentiment Analysis

Semi-Stacking for Semi-supervised Sentiment Classification
Shoushan Li, Lei Huang, Jingjing Wang and Guodong Zhou

Deep Markov Neural Network for Sequential Data Classification
Min Yang

Semantic Analysis and Helpfulness Prediction of Text for Online Product Reviews
Yinfei Yang, Yaowei Yan, Minghui Qiu and Forrest Bao

Document Classification by Inversion of Distributed Language Representations
Matt Taddy

Semantic Interpretation of Superlative Expressions via Structured Knowledge Bases
Sheng Zhang, Yansong Feng, Songfang Huang, Kun Xu, Zhe Han and Dongyan Zhao

Grounding Semantics in Olfactory Perception
Douwe Kiela, Luana Bulat and Stephen Clark

Session 5D: 10:30–12:00 Parsing, Tagging

Word-based Japanese typed dependency parsing with grammatical function analysis
Takaaki Tanaka and Masaaki Nagata

KLcpos3 - a Language Similarity Measure for Delexicalized Parser Transfer
Rudolf Rosa and Zdenek Zabokrtsky

CCG Supertagging with a Recurrent Neural Network
Wenduan Xu, Michael Auli and Stephen Clark

An Efficient Dynamic Oracle for Unrestricted Non-Projective Parsing
Carlos Gómez-Rodríguez and Daniel Fernández-González

Synthetic Word Parsing Improves Chinese Word Segmentation
Fei Cheng, Kevin Duh and Yuji Matsumoto

If all you have is a bit of the Bible: Learning POS taggers for truly low-resource languages
Željko Agić, Dirk Hovy and Anders Søgaard

Session 5E: 10:30–12:00 Information Extraction

Improving distant supervision using inference learning
Roland Roller, Eneko Agirre, Aitor Soroa and Mark Stevenson

A Lexicalized Tree Kernel for Open Information Extraction
Ying Xu, Christoph Ringlstetter, Mi-young Kim, Grzegorz Kondrak, Randy Goebel and Yusuke Miyao

A Dependency-Based Neural Network for Relation Classification
Yang Liu, Furu Wei, Sujian Li, Heng Ji, Ming Zhou and Houfeng WANG

Embedding Methods for Fine Grained Entity Type Classification
Dani Yogatama, Daniel Gillick and Nevena Lazic

Sieve-Based Entity Linking for the Biomedical Domain
Jennifer D'Souza and Vincent Ng

Open IE as an Intermediate Structure for Semantic Tasks
Gabriel Stanovsky and Ido Dagan

16:30–19:30 **Poster and Dinner Session 2: Short Papers, Student Research Workshop Papers**

Session P2.01: 16:30–19:30 Poster: Discourse, Pragmatics

Recovering dropped pronouns from Chinese text messages
Yaqin Yang, Yalin Liu and Nianwen Xue

The Users Who Say 'Ni': Audience Identification in Chinese-language Restaurant Reviews
Rob Voigt and Dan Jurafsky

Chinese Zero Pronoun Resolution: A Joint Unsupervised Discourse-Aware Model Rivaling State-of-the-Art Resolvers
Chen Chen and Vincent Ng

Session P2.02: 16:30–19:30 Poster: Information Retrieval

Co-Simmate: Quick Retrieving All Pairwise Co-Simrank Scores
Yu Weiren and Julie McCann

Retrieval of Research-level Mathematical Information Needs: A Test Collection and Technical Terminology Experiment
Yiannos Stathopoulos and Simone Teufel

Learning to Mine Query Subtopics from Query Log
Zhenzhong Zhang, Le Sun and Xianpei Han

Session P2.03: 16:30–19:30 Poster: Information Extraction and Text Mining

Learning Topic Hierarchies for Wikipedia Categories
Linmei Hu, Xuzhong Wang, Mengdi Zhang, Juanzi Li, Xiaoli Li, Chao Shao, Jie Tang and Yongbin Liu

Semantic Clustering and Convolutional Neural Network for Short Text Categorization
Peng Wang, Jiaming Xu, Bo Xu, Chenglin Liu, Heng Zhang, Fangyuan Wang and Hongwei Hao

Document Level Time-anchoring for TimeLine Extraction
Egoitz Laparra, Itziar Aldabe and German Rigau

Event Detection and Domain Adaptation with Convolutional Neural Networks
Thien Huu Nguyen and Ralph Grishman

Seed-Based Event Trigger Labeling: How far can event descriptions get us?
Ofer Bronstein, Ido Dagan, Qi Li, Heng Ji and Anette Frank

An Empirical Study of Chinese Name Matching and Applications
Nanyun Peng, Mo Yu and Mark Dredze

Language Identification and Modeling in Specialized Hardware
Kenneth Heafield, Rohan Kshirsagar and Santiago Barona

Cross-lingual Transfer of Named Entity Recognizers without Parallel Corpora
Ayah Zirikly

Robust Multi-Relational Clustering via ℓ_1-Norm Symmetric Nonnegative Matrix Factorization
Kai Liu and Hua Wang

Session P2.05: 16:30–19:30 Poster: Language Resources

Painless Labeling with Application to Text Mining
Sajib Dasgupta

FrameNet+: Fast Paraphrastic Tripling of FrameNet
Ellie Pavlick, Travis Wolfe, Pushpendre Rastogi, Chris Callison-Burch, Mark Dredze and Benjamin Van Durme

IWNLP: Inverse Wiktionary for Natural Language Processing
Matthias Liebeck and Stefan Conrad

TR9856: A Multi-word Term Relatedness Benchmark
Ran Levy, Liat Ein-Dor, Shay Hummel, Ruty Rinott and Noam Slonim

PPDB 2.0: Better paraphrase ranking, fine-grained entailment relations, word embeddings, and style classification
Ellie Pavlick, Pushpendre Rastogi, Juri Ganitkevitch, Benjamin Van Durme and Chris Callison-Burch

Automatic Discrimination between Cognates and Borrowings
Alina Maria Ciobanu and Liviu P. Dinu

The Media Frames Corpus: Annotations of Frames Across Issues
Dallas Card, Amber E. Boydstun, Justin H. Gross, Philip Resnik and Noah A. Smith

deltaBLEU: A Discriminative Metric for Generation Tasks with Intrinsically Diverse Targets
Michel Galley, Chris Brockett, Alessandro Sordoni, Yangfeng Ji, Michael Auli, Chris Quirk, Margaret Mitchell, Jianfeng Gao and Bill Dolan

Tibetan Unknown Word Identification from News Corpora for Supporting Lexicon-based Tibetan Word Segmentation
Minghua Nuo, Huidan Liu, Congjun Long and Jian Wu

Session P2.06: 16:30–19:30 Poster: Lexical Semantics

Learning Lexical Embeddings with Syntactic and Lexicographic Knowledge
Tong Wang, Abdelrahman Mohamed and Graeme Hirst

Non-distributional Word Vector Representations
Manaal Faruqui and Chris Dyer

Early and Late Combinations of Criteria for Reranking Distributional Thesauri
Olivier Ferret

Session P2.07: 16:30–19:30 Poster: Linguistic and Psycholinguistic Aspects of CL

Dependency length minimisation effects in short spans: a large-scale analysis of adjective placement in complex noun phrases
Kristina Gulordava, Paola Merlo and Benoit Crabbé

Tagging Performance Correlates with Author Age
Dirk Hovy and Anders Søgaard

Session P2.08: 16:30–19:30 Poster: Machine Learning and Topic Models

User Based Aggregation for Biterm Topic Model
Weizheng Chen, Jinpeng Wang, Yan Zhang, Hongfei Yan and Xiaoming Li

The Fixed-Size Ordinally-Forgetting Encoding Method for Neural Network Language Models
ShiLiang Zhang, Hui Jiang, MingBin Xu, JunFeng Hou and LiRong Dai

Unsupervised Decomposition of a Multi-Author Document Based on Naive-Bayesian Model
Khaled Aldebei, Xiangjian He and Jie Yang

Extended Topic Model for Word Dependency
Tong Wang, Vish Viswanath and Ping Chen

Dependency Recurrent Neural Language Models for Sentence Completion
Piotr Mirowski and Andreas Vlachos

Point Process Modelling of Rumour Dynamics in Social Media
Michal Lukasik, Trevor Cohn and Kalina Bontcheva

Learning Hidden Markov Models with Distributed State Representations for Domain Adaptation
Min Xiao and Yuhong Guo

Session P2.09: 16:30–19:30 Poster: Machine Translation

MT Quality Estimation for Computer-assisted Translation: Does it Really Help?
Marco Turchi, Matteo Negri and Marcello Federico

Context-Dependent Translation Selection Using Convolutional Neural Network
Baotian Hu, Zhaopeng Tu, Zhengdong Lu, Hang Li and Qingcai Chen

Learning Word Reorderings for Hierarchical Phrase-based Statistical Machine Translation
jingyi zhang, Masao Utiyama, Eiichro Sumita and Hai Zhao

UNRAVEL—A Decipherment Toolkit
Malte Nuhn, Julian Schamper and Hermann Ney

Multi-Pass Decoding With Complex Feature Guidance for Statistical Machine Translation
Benjamin Marie and Aurélien Max

What's in a Domain? Analyzing Genre and Topic Differences in Statistical Machine Translation
Marlies van der Wees, Arianna Bisazza, Wouter Weerkamp and Christof Monz

Learning Cross-lingual Word Embeddings via Matrix Co-factorization
Tianze Shi, Zhiyuan Liu, Yang Liu and Maosong Sun

Session P2.10: 16:30–19:30 Poster: NLP Applications

Session P2.11: 16:30–19:30 Poster: NLP for the Web and Social Media

Automatic Keyword Extraction on Twitter
Luis Marujo, Wang Ling, Isabel Trancoso, Chris Dyer, Alan W Black, Anatole Gershman, David Martins de Matos, João Neto and Jaime Carbonell

Towards a Contextual Pragmatic Model to Detect Irony in Tweets
Jihen Karoui, Benamara Farah, Véronique MORICEAU, Nathalie Aussenac-Gilles and Lamia Hadrich-Belguith

Annotation and Classification of an Email Importance Corpus
Fan Zhang and Kui Xu

Lexical Comparison Between Wikipedia and Twitter Corpora by Using Word Embeddings
Luchen Tan, Haotian Zhang, Charles Clarke and Mark Smucker

Session P2.12: 16:30–19:30 Poster: Morphology, Word Segmentation

The Discovery of Natural Typing Annotations: User-produced Potential Chinese Word Delimiters
Dakui Zhang, Yu Mao, Yang Liu, Hanshi Wang, Chuyuan Wei and Shiping Tang

One Tense per Scene: Predicting Tense in Chinese Conversations
Tao Ge, Heng Ji, Baobao Chang and Zhifang Sui

A Language-Independent Feature Schema for Inflectional Morphology
John Sylak-Glassman, Christo Kirov, David Yarowsky and Roger Que

Session P2.13: 16:30–19:30 Poster: Question Answering

Rhetoric Map of an Answer to Compound Queries
Boris Galitsky, Dmitry Ilvovsky and Sergey O. Kuznetsov

Thread-Level Information for Comment Classification in Community Question Answering
Alberto Barrón-Cedeño, Simone Filice, Giovanni Da San Martino, Shafiq Joty, Lluís Màrquez, Preslav Nakov and Alessandro Moschitti

Learning Hybrid Representations to Retrieve Semantically Equivalent Questions
Cicero dos Santos, Luciano Barbosa, Dasha Bogdanova and Bianca Zadrozny

Machine Comprehension with Syntax, Frames, and Semantics
Hai Wang, Mohit Bansal, Kevin Gimpel and David McAllester

A Long Short-Term Memory Model for Answer Sentence Selection in Question Answering
Di Wang and Eric Nyberg

Answer Sequence Learning with Neural Networks for Answer Selection in Community Question Answering
Xiaoqiang Zhou, Baotian Hu, Qingcai Chen, Buzhou Tang and Xiaolong Wang

Session P2.14: 16:30–19:30 Poster: Semantics

Bilingual Word Embeddings from Non-Parallel Document-Aligned Data Applied to Bilingual Lexicon Induction
Ivan Vulić and Marie-Francine Moens

How Well Do Distributional Models Capture Different Types of Semantic Knowledge?
Dana Rubinstein, Effi Levi, Roy Schwartz and Ari Rappoport

Low-Rank Tensors for Verbs in Compositional Distributional Semantics
Daniel Fried, Tamara Polajnar and Stephen Clark

Constrained Semantic Forests for Improved Discriminative Semantic Parsing
Wei Lu

Automatic Identification of Rhetorical Questions
Shohini Bhattasali, Jeremy Cytryn, Elana Feldman and Joonsuk Park

Session P2.15: 16:30–19:30 Poster: Sentiment Analysis

Lifelong Learning for Sentiment Classification
Zhiyuan Chen, Nianzu Ma and Bing Liu

Harnessing Context Incongruity for Sarcasm Detection
Aditya Joshi, Vinita Sharma and Pushpak Bhattacharyya

Emotion Detection in Code-switching Texts via Bilingual and Sentimental Information
Zhongqing Wang, Sophia Lee, Shoushan Li and Guodong Zhou

Model Adaptation for Personalized Opinion Analysis
Mohammad Al Boni, Keira Zhou, Hongning Wang and Matthew S. Gerber

Session P2.16: 16:30–19:30 Poster: Spoken Language Processing and Dialogue Systems

Session P2.17: 16:30–19:30 Poster: Summarization and Generation

A Deeper Exploration of the Standard PB-SMT Approach to Text Simplification and its Evaluation
Sanja Štajner, Hannah Bechara and Horacio Saggion

Learning Summary Prior Representation for Extractive Summarization
Ziqiang Cao, Furu Wei, Sujian Li, Wenjie Li, Ming Zhou and Houfeng WANG

A Methodology for Evaluating Timeline Generation Algorithms based on Deep Semantic Units
Sandro Bauer and Simone Teufel

Unsupervised extractive summarization via coverage maximization with syntactic and semantic concepts
Natalie Schluter and Anders Søgaard

Session P2.18: 16:30–19:30 Poster: Parsing

Low Resource Dependency Parsing: Cross-lingual Parameter Sharing in a Neural Network Parser
Long Duong, Trevor Cohn, Steven Bird and Paul Cook

Semantic Structure Analysis of Noun Phrases using Abstract Meaning Representation
Yuichiro Sawai, Hiroyuki Shindo and Yuji Matsumoto

Boosting Transition-based AMR Parsing with Refined Actions and Auxiliary Analyzers
Chuan Wang, Nianwen Xue and Sameer Pradhan

Generative Incremental Dependency Parsing with Neural Networks
Jan Buys and Phil Blunsom

Labeled Grammar Induction with Minimal Supervision
Yonatan Bisk, Christos Christodoulopoulos and Julia Hockenmaier

On the Importance of Ezafe Construction in Persian Parsing
Alireza Nourian, Mohammad Sadegh Rasooli, Mohsen Imany and Heshaam Faili

Day Date

Session Ses Code: Ses Time–Ses End Time Ses Title

Gen *Time–Gen End Time Gen Title*
Gen Presenter

A Framework for the Construction of Monolingual and Cross-lingual Word Similarity Datasets

José Camacho-Collados, Mohammad Taher Pilehvar and **Roberto Navigli**
Department of Computer Science
Sapienza University of Rome
{collados,pilehvar,navigli}@di.uniroma1.it

Abstract

Despite being one of the most popular tasks in lexical semantics, word similarity has often been limited to the English language. Other languages, even those that are widely spoken such as Spanish, do not have a reliable word similarity evaluation framework. We put forward robust methodologies for the extension of existing English datasets to other languages, both at monolingual and cross-lingual levels. We propose an automatic standardization for the construction of cross-lingual similarity datasets, and provide an evaluation, demonstrating its reliability and robustness. Based on our procedure and taking the RG-65 word similarity dataset as a reference, we release two high-quality Spanish and Farsi (Persian) monolingual datasets, and fifteen cross-lingual datasets for six languages: English, Spanish, French, German, Portuguese, and Farsi.

1 Introduction

Semantic similarity is a field of Natural Language Processing which measures the extent to which two linguistic items are similar. In particular, word similarity is one of the most popular benchmarks for the evaluation of word or sense representations. Applications of word similarity range from Word Sense Disambiguation (Patwardhan et al., 2003) to Machine Translation (Lavie and Denkowski, 2009), Information Retrieval (Hliaoutakis et al., 2006), Question Answering (Mohler et al., 2011), Text Summarization (Mohammad and Hirst, 2012), Ontology Alignment (Pilehvar and Navigli, 2014), and Lexical Substitution (McCarthy and Navigli, 2009).

However, due to the lack of standard multilingual benchmarks, word similarity systems had in the main been limited to the English language (Mihalcea and Moldovan, 1999; Agirre and Lopez, 2003; Agirre and de Lacalle, 2004; Strube and Ponzetto, 2006; Gabrilovich and Markovitch, 2007; Mihalcea, 2007; Pilehvar et al., 2013; Baroni et al., 2014), up until the recent creation of datasets built by translating the English RG-65 dataset (Rubenstein and Goodenough, 1965) into French (Joubarne and Inkpen, 2011), German (Gurevych, 2005), and Portuguese (Granada et al., 2014). And what is more, cross-lingual applications have grown in importance over the last few years (Hassan and Mihalcea, 2009; Navigli and Ponzetto, 2012; Franco-Salvador et al., 2014; Camacho-Collados et al., 2015b). Unfortunately, very few reliable datasets exist for evaluating cross-lingual systems.

This paper provides two contributions: Firstly, we construct Spanish and Farsi versions of the standard RG-65 dataset scored by twelve annotators with high inter-annotator agreements of 0.83 and 0.88, respectively, in terms of Pearson correlation, and secondly, we create fifteen cross-lingual word similarity datasets based on RG-65, covering six languages, by proposing an improved version of the approach of Kennedy and Hirst (2012) for the automatic construction of cross-lingual datasets from aligned monolingual datasets.

The paper is structured as follows. We first briefly review some of the major monolingual and cross-lingual word similarity datasets in Section 2. We then discuss the details of our procedure for the construction of the Spanish and Farsi word similarity datasets in Section 3. Section 4 provides the details of our algorithm for the automatic construction of the cross-lingual datasets. We report the results of the evaluation performed on the generated datasets in Section 5. Finally, we specify the released resources in Section 6, followed by concluding remarks in Section 7.

Proceedings of the 53rd Annual Meeting of the Association for Computational Linguistics and the 7th International Joint Conference on Natural Language Processing (Short Papers), pages 1–7,
Beijing, China, July 26-31, 2015.

2 Related Work

Multiple word similarity datasets have been constructed for the English language: MC-30 (Miller and Charles, 1991), WordSim-353 (Finkelstein et al., 2002), MEN (Bruni et al., 2014), and Simlex-999 (Hill et al., 2014). The RG-65 dataset (Rubenstein and Goodenough, 1965) is one of the oldest and most popular word similarity datasets, and has been used as a standard benchmark for measuring the reliability of word and sense representations (Agirre and de Lacalle, 2004; Gabrilovich and Markovitch, 2007; Hassan and Mihalcea, 2011; Pilehvar et al., 2013; Baroni et al., 2014; Camacho-Collados et al., 2015a). The original RG-65 dataset was constructed with the aim of evaluating the degree to which contextual information is correlated with semantic similarity for the English language. Rubenstein and Goodenough (1965) reported an inter-annotator agreement of 0.85 for a subset of fifteen judges (no final inter-annotator agreement for the total fifty-one judges was calculated). The original English RG-65 has also been used as a base for different languages: French (Joubarne and Inkpen, 2011), German (Gurevych, 2005), and Portuguese (Granada et al., 2014). No inter-annotator agreement was calculated for the French version, while the German and Portuguese were reported to have the respective inter-annotator agreements of 0.81 and 0.71 in terms of average pairwise Pearson correlation. Our Spanish version of the RG-65 dataset reports a high inter-annotator agreement of 0.83, while the Farsi version achieves 0.88.

A few works have also focused on the construction of cross-lingual resources. Hassan and Mihalcea (2009) built two sets of cross-lingual datasets by translating the English MC-30 (Miller and Charles, 1991) and the WordSim-353 (Finkelstein et al., 2002) datasets into three languages. However, these datasets have several issues due to their construction procedure. The main problem arises from keeping the original scores from the English dataset in the translated datasets. For instance, the Spanish dataset contains the identical pair *mediodia-mediodia* with a similarity score of 3.42 (in the 0-4 scale). Furthermore, the datasets contain orthographic errors such as *despliege* and the previously mentioned *mediodia* (instead of *despliegue* and *mediodía*), and nouns translated into words with a different part of speech (e.g., *implement* from the English noun dataset MC-30 translated to the Spanish verb *implementar*). Additionally, the selection of the datasets was not ideal: MC-30 is a small subset of RG-65 and WordSim-353 has been criticized for its annotation scheme, which conflates similarity and relatedness (Hill et al., 2014).

Kennedy and Hirst (2012) proposed an automatic procedure for the construction of a French-English version of RG-65. We refine their approach by also dealing with some issues that may arise in the automatic process. Additionally, we provide an evaluation of the automatic procedure on different languages.

3 Building Monolingual Word Similarity Datasets

In this section we explain our methodology for the construction of the Spanish and Farsi versions of the English RG-65 dataset (Rubenstein and Goodenough, 1965). The methodology is divided into two main steps: First, the original English dataset is translated into the target language (Section 3.1) and then, the newly translated pairs are scored by human annotators (Section 3.2).

3.1 Translating from English to Spanish/Farsi

The translation of RG-65 from English to Spanish and Farsi was performed by, respectively, three English-Spanish and three English-Farsi annotators who were fluent English speakers and native speakers of the target language. The translation procedure was as follows. First, two annotators translated each English pair in the dataset into the target language. Then a third annotator checked for disagreements between the first two translators and picked the more appropriate translation among the two options.

Finally, all three translators met and performed a final check, with specific focus on the following two cases: (1) duplicate pairs in the dataset, and (2) pairs with repeated words. Our goal was to reduce these two cases as much as possible. A final adjudication was performed accordingly. We note that there remain three pairs with identical words in both Spanish and Farsi datasets, as no suitable translation could be found to distinguish the words in the English pair. For instance, the two words in the pair *midday-noon* translate to the same Spanish word *mediodía*.

English			Spanish			Farsi		
noon	string	0.04	mediodía	cuerda	0.00	ظهر	نخ	0.00
cemetery	woodland	0.79	cementerio	bosque	1.18	قبرستان	جنگل	0.50
mound	shore	0.97	loma	orilla	1.21	ماهور	ساحل	1.17
food	rooster	1.09	comida	gallo	1.54	غذا	خروس	1.00
bird	woodland	1.24	pájaro	bosque	1.67	پرنده	بیشه زار	1.79
glass	jewel	1.78	cristal	joya	1.96	شیشه	جواهر	1.29
bird	crane	2.63	pájaro	grulla	2.92	پرنده	درنا	2.83
autograph	signature	3.59	autógrafo	firma	3.46	امضا	امضا	4.00
automobile	car	3.92	automóvil	coche	3.92	خودرو	ماشین	3.88

Table 1: Sample word pairs from the English and the newly created Spanish and Farsi RG-65 datasets.

3.2 Scoring the dataset

Twelve native Spanish speakers were asked to evaluate the similarity for the Spanish translations. In order to obtain a more global distribution of judges, we included judges both both Spain and Latin America. As far as the Farsi dataset was concerned, twelve Farsi native speakers scored the newly translated pairs. The guidelines provided to the annotators were based on the recent SemEval task on Cross-Level Semantic Similarity (Jurgens et al., 2014), which provides clear indications in order to distinguish similarity and relatedness. The annotators were allowed to give scores from 0 to 4, with a step size of 0.5.

Table 1 shows example pairs with their corresponding scores from the English and the newly created Spanish and Farsi versions of the RG-65 dataset. As we can see from the table, the scores across languages are not necessarily identical, with small, in a few cases significant, differences between the corresponding scores. This is due to the fact that associated senses with words do not hold one-to-one correspondence across different languages. This renders the approach of Hassan and Mihalcea (2009) insufficiently accurate for handling these differences.

4 Automatic Creation of Cross-lingual Similarity Datasets

In this section we present our automatic method for building cross-lingual datasets. Although being targeted at building semantic similarity datasets, the algorithm is task-independent, so it may also be used for any task which measures any kind of relation between two linguistic items in a numerical way.

Kennedy and Hirst (2012) proposed a method which exploits two aligned monolingual word similarity datasets for the construction of a French-English cross-lingual dataset. We followed their initial idea and proposed a generalization of the approach which would be capable of automatically constructing reliable cross-lingual similarity datasets for any pair of languages.

Algorithm. Algorithm 1 shows our procedure for constructing a cross-lingual dataset starting from two monolingual datasets. Note that the pairs in the two monolingual datasets should be previously aligned. Specifically, we refer to each dataset D as $\{P_D, S_D\}$, where P_D is the set of pairs and S_D is a function mapping each pair in P_D to a value on a similarity scale (0-4 for RG-65). For each two aligned pairs *a*-*b* and *a'*-*b'* across the two datasets, if the difference in the corresponding scores is greater than a quarter of the similarity scale size (1.0 in RG-65), the pairs are not considered (line 7) and therefore discarded. Otherwise, two new pairs *a*-*b'* and *a'*-*b* are created with a score equal to the average of the two original pairs' scores (lines 8-11 and 15-18). In the case of repeated pairs, we merge them into a single pair with a similarity equal to their average score (lines 12-14 and lines 19-21).

By following this procedure we created fifteen cross-lingual datasets based on the RG-65 word similarity datasets for English, French, German, Spanish, Portuguese, and Farsi. Table 2 shows

Algorithm 1 Automatic construction of cross-lingual similarity datasets

Input: two aligned datasets $D = \{P_D, S_D\}$ and $D' = \{P_{D'}, S_{D'}\}$, where P_X is the set of pairs in dataset X and S_X is the mapping of these pairs to their corresponding scores.

Output: a cross-lingual semantic similarity dataset $C = \{P_C, S_C\}$

$P_C \leftarrow \emptyset$
Define *Cnt*, which counts how many times an output cross-lingual pair is repeated
for each aligned pairs $(a, b) \in P_D, (a', b') \in P_{D'}$
  $score = S_D(a, b)$
  $score' = S_{D'}(a', b')$
  $avg\_score = (score + score')/2$
  if $|score - score'| \leq size(sim\_scale)/4$ **then**
    if $(a, b') \notin P_C$ **then**
      $P_C \leftarrow P_C \cup \{(a, b')\}$
      $S_C(a, b') = avg\_score$
      $Cnt(a, b') = 1$
    else
      $S_C(a, b') = \frac{(S_C(a,b') \times Cnt(a,b')) + avg\_score}{Cnt(a,b')+1}$
      $Cnt(a, b') + +$
    if $(a', b) \notin P_C$ **then**
      $P_C \leftarrow P_C \cup \{(a', b)\}$
      $S_C(a', b) = avg\_score$
      $Cnt(a', b) = 1$
    else
      $S_C(a', b) = \frac{(S_C(a',b) \times Cnt(a',b)) + avg\_score}{Cnt(a',b)+1}$
      $Cnt(a', b) + +$
return $\{P_C, S_C\}$

the number of word pairs for each cross-lingual dataset. Note that there is not a single pair of languages whose total count reaches the maximum number of possible word pairs, i.e., 130. This is due, on the one hand, to language peculiarities resulting in some pairs having significant score difference across languages (higher than 1 on the 0-4 scale), and, on the other hand, to the repetition of some pairs occurring as a result of the automatic creation process, a problem which is handled by our algorithm.

Table 3 shows sample pairs with their corresponding similarity scores from four of the cross-lingual datasets: Spanish-English, Spanish-French, Spanish-German, and English-Farsi. These cross-lingual datasets are constructed on the basis of our newly-generated Spanish and Farsi monolingual datasets (see Section 3). The quality of these four datasets is evaluated in Section 5.2.

	FR	DE	ES	PT	FA
EN	100	125	126	120	120
FR	-	96	103	92	100
DE	-	-	125	118	122
ES	-	-	-	113	122
PT	-	-	-	-	122

Table 2: Number of word pairs for each cross-lingual dataset (EN: English, FR: French, DE: German, ES: Spanish, PT: Portuguese, FA: Farsi).

5 Evaluation

5.1 Spanish and Farsi Monolingual Datasets

The inter-annotator agreements according to the average pairwise Pearson correlation among the judges for the newly created Spanish and Farsi datasets are, respectively, 0.83 and 0.88, which may be used as upper bounds for evaluating automatic systems. Our further analysis revealed that for both datasets no annotator obtained an average Pearson correlation with the rest of the annotators lower than 0.80, which attests to the reliability of our judges and guidelines. The German (Gurevych, 2005) and Portuguese (Granada et al., 2014) versions of the RG-65 dataset reported a lower inter-annotator agreement of 0.81 and 0.71, respectively, whereas the original English RG-65 (Rubenstein and Goodenough, 1965) reported an inter-annotator agreement of 0.85 for a subset of fifteen judges. As also mentioned earlier, the French version (Joubarne and Inkpen, 2011) did not report any inter-annotator agreement.

5.2 Cross-lingual Datasets

Along with the monolingual evaluation, we also performed an evaluation on four of the automatically created cross-lingual datasets. The evaluated language pairs were Spanish-English, Spanish-French, Spanish-German, and English-Farsi. In each case a proficient speaker of both languages was selected to carry out the evaluation. The Pearson correlations of the human judges with the automatically generated scores were 0.89 for Spanish-English, 0.94 for Spanish-French, 0.91 for Spanish-German, and 0.92 for English-Farsi, showing the reliability of our cross-lingual dataset creation process and reinforcing the quality of the newly created monolingual datasets.

ES	EN		ES	FR	
monje	assylum	0.41	cuerda	midi	0.00
bosque	bird	1.46	chico	sage	0.54
viaje	car	1.74	comida	coq	1.08
hermano	monk	2.25	hermano	gars	1.71
pollo	rooster	3.36	grulla	oiseau	2.67
cementerio	graveyard	3.94	chaval	garçon	3.88

ES	DE		EN	FA	
orilla	autogramm	0.02	mound	اجاق	0.07
caldera	werkzeug	1.04	coast	جنگل	1.03
pájaro	wald	1.65	journey	ماشین	1.53
coche	fahrt	2.34	food	میوه	2.56
cojín	kissen	3.21	stove	کوره	3.10
colina	berg	3.61	car	خودرو	3.90

Table 3: Example pairs from the Spanish-English, Spanish-French, Spanish-German, and English-Farsi cross-lingual word similarity datasets (EN: English, FR: French, DE: German, ES: Spanish, FA: Farsi).

6 Release of the Resources

All the resources obtained as a result of this work are freely downloadable and available to the research community at `http://lcl.uniroma1.it/similarity-datasets/`.

Among these resources we include the newly created Spanish and Farsi word similarity datasets, together with the annotation guidelines used during the creation of the datasets. Our algorithm for the automatic creation of cross-lingual datasets (Algorithm 1) is provided as an easy-to-use Python script. Finally, we also release the fifteen cross-lingual datasets built by using this algorithm, including Spanish, English, French, German, Portuguese, and Farsi languages.

7 Conclusion

We developed two versions of the standard RG-65 dataset in Spanish and Farsi. We also proposed and evaluated an automatic method for creating cross-lingual semantic similarity datasets. Thanks to this method, we release fifteen cross-lingual datasets for pairs of languages including English, Spanish, French, German, Portuguese, and Farsi. All these datasets are intended for use as a standard benchmark (as RG-65 already is for the English language) for evaluating word or sense representations and, more specifically, word similarity systems, not only for languages other than English, but also across different languages.

Acknowledgments

The authors gratefully acknowledge the support of the ERC Starting Grant MultiJEDI No. 259234.

We would like to thank Leyli Badiei, Núria Bel, Alicia Burga, Marcos Camacho, Ángela Collados, José Cuenca, Luis Espinosa, Darío Garigliotti, Afsaneh Hojjat, Ignacio Iacobacci, Amin Lak, Montserrat Marimon, Javier Martínez, Ali Orang, Ana Osorio, Lluís Padró, Abdolhamid, Razieh, and Zahra Pilehvar, Mohammad Sadegh Rasooli, Molood Sadat Safavi, Mohammad Shojafar, Hossein Soleimani, and Fatemeh Torabi Asr for their help in the construction and evaluation of the word similarity datasets. We would also like to thank Jim McManus for his comments on the manuscript.

References

Eneko Agirre and Oier Lopez de Lacalle. 2004. Publicly available topic signatures for all WordNet nominal senses. In *Proceedings of LREC*, pages 1123–1126, Lisbon, Portugal.

Eneko Agirre and Oier Lopez. 2003. Clustering WordNet word senses. In *Proceedings of Recent Advances in Natural Language Processing*, pages 121–130, Borovets, Bulgaria.

Marco Baroni, Georgiana Dinu, and Germán Kruszewski. 2014. Don't count, predict! a systematic comparison of context-counting vs. context-predicting semantic vectors. In *Proceedings of ACL*, pages 238–247, Baltimore, Maryland.

Elia Bruni, Nam-Khanh Tran, and Marco Baroni. 2014. Multimodal distributional semantics. *Journal of Artificial Intelligence Research*, 49:1–47.

José Camacho-Collados, Mohammad Taher Pilehvar, and Roberto Navigli. 2015a. NASARI: a Novel Approach to a Semantically-Aware Representation of Items. In *Proceedings of NAACL*, pages 567–577, Denver, USA.

José Camacho-Collados, Mohammad Taher Pilehvar, and Roberto Navigli. 2015b. A unified multilingual semantic representation of concepts. In *Proceedings of ACL*, Beijing, China.

Lev Finkelstein, Gabrilovich Evgenly, Matias Yossi, Rivlin Ehud, Solan Zach, Wolfman Gadi, and Ruppin Eytan. 2002. Placing search in context: The concept revisited. *ACM Transactions on Information Systems*, 20(1):116–131.

Marc Franco-Salvador, Paolo Rosso, and Roberto Navigli. 2014. A knowledge-based representation for cross-language document retrieval and categorization. In *Proceedings of the 14th Conference on European chapter of the Association for Computational Linguistics (EACL)*, pages 414–423, Gothenburg, Sweden.

Evgeniy Gabrilovich and Shaul Markovitch. 2007. Computing semantic relatedness using Wikipedia-based explicit semantic analysis. In *Proceedings of IJCAI*, pages 1606–1611, Hyderabad, India.

Roger Granada, Cassia Trojahn, and Renata Vieira. 2014. Comparing semantic relatedness between word pairs in Portuguese using Wikipedia. In *Computational Processing of the Portuguese Language*, pages 170–175. São Carlos/SP, Brazil.

Iryna Gurevych. 2005. Using the structure of a conceptual network in computing semantic relatedness. In *Proceedings of IJCNLP*, pages 767–778. Jeju Island, Korea.

Samer Hassan and Rada Mihalcea. 2009. Cross-lingual semantic relatedness using encyclopedic knowledge. In *Proceedings of EMNLP*, pages 1192–1201, Singapore.

Samer Hassan and Rada Mihalcea. 2011. Semantic Relatedness Using Salient Semantic Analysis. In *Proceedings of AAAI*, pages 884–889, San Francisco, USA.

Felix Hill, Roi Reichart, and Anna Korhonen. 2014. Simlex-999: Evaluating semantic models with (genuine) similarity estimation. arXiv:1408.3456.

Angelos Hliaoutakis, Giannis Varelas, Epimenidis Voutsakis, Euripides GM Petrakis, and Evangelos Milios. 2006. Information retrieval by semantic similarity. *International Journal on Semantic Web and Information Systems*, 2(3):55–73.

Colette Joubarne and Diana Inkpen. 2011. Comparison of semantic similarity for different languages using the Google n-gram corpus and second-order co-occurrence measures. In *Advances in Artificial Intelligence*, pages 216–221. Perth, Australia.

David Jurgens, Mohammad Taher Pilehvar, and Roberto Navigli. 2014. Semeval-2014 task 3: Cross-level semantic similarity. In *Proceedings of the 8th International Workshop on Semantic Evaluation (SemEval 2014), in conjunction with COLING 2014*, pages 17–26, Dublin, Ireland.

Alistair Kennedy and Graeme Hirst. 2012. Measuring semantic relatedness across languages. In *Proceedings of xLiTe: Cross-Lingual Technologies Workshop at the Neural Information Processing Systems Conference*, pages 1–6, Lake Tahoe, USA.

Alon Lavie and Michael J. Denkowski. 2009. The Meteor metric for automatic evaluation of Machine Translation. *Machine Translation*, 23(2-3):105–115.

Diana McCarthy and Roberto Navigli. 2009. The English lexical substitution task. *Language Resources and Evaluation*, 43(2):139–159.

Rada Mihalcea and Dan Moldovan. 1999. An automatic method for generating sense tagged corpora. In *Proceedings of AAAI*, pages 461–466, Orlando, Florida, USA.

Rada Mihalcea. 2007. Using Wikipedia for automatic Word Sense Disambiguation. In *Proc. of NAACL-HLT-07*, pages 196–203, Rochester, NY.

George A. Miller and Walter G. Charles. 1991. Contextual correlates of semantic similarity. *Language and Cognitive Processes*, 6(1):1–28.

Saif Mohammad and Graeme Hirst. 2012. Distributional measures of semantic distance: A survey. *CoRR*, abs/1203.1858.

Michael Mohler, Razvan Bunescu, and Rada Mihalcea. 2011. Learning to grade short answer questions using semantic similarity measures and dependency graph alignments. In *Proceedings of ACL*, pages 752–762, Portland, Oregon.

Roberto Navigli and Simone Paolo Ponzetto. 2012. BabelRelate! a joint multilingual approach to computing semantic relatedness. In *Proceedings of AAAI*, pages 108–114, Toronto, Canada.

Siddharth Patwardhan, Satanjeev Banerjee, and Ted Pedersen. 2003. Using measures of semantic relatedness for Word Sense Disambiguation. In *Proceedings of CICLing*, pages 241–257, Mexico City, Mexico.

Mohammad Taher Pilehvar and Roberto Navigli. 2014. A robust approach to aligning heterogeneous lexical resources. In *Proceedings of ACL*, pages 468–478, Baltimore, USA.

Mohammad Taher Pilehvar, David Jurgens, and Roberto Navigli. 2013. Align, Disambiguate and Walk: a Unified Approach for Measuring Semantic Similarity. In *Proceedings of ACL*, pages 1341–1351, Sofia, Bulgaria.

Herbert Rubenstein and John B. Goodenough. 1965. Contextual correlates of synonymy. *Communications of the ACM*, 8(10):627–633.

Michael Strube and Simone Paolo Ponzetto. 2006. WikiRelate! Computing semantic relatedness using Wikipedia. In *Proceedings of AAAI*, pages 1419–1424, Boston, USA.

On metric embedding for boosting semantic similarity computations

Julien Subercaze, Christophe Gravier, Frederique Laforest
Université de Lyon, F-42023, Saint-Etienne, France,
CNRS, UMR5516, Laboratoire Hubert Curien, F-42000, Saint-Etienne, France,
Université de Saint-Etienne, Jean Monnet, F-42000, Saint-Etienne, France.
firstname.lastname@univ-st-etienne.fr

Abstract

Computing pairwise word semantic similarity is widely used and serves as a building block in many tasks in NLP. In this paper, we explore the embedding of the shortest-path metrics from a knowledge base (Wordnet) into the Hamming hypercube, in order to enhance the computation performance. We show that, although an isometric embedding is untractable, it is possible to achieve good non-isometric embeddings. We report a speedup of three orders of magnitude for the task of computing Leacock and Chodorow (LCH) similarity while keeping strong correlations ($r = .819, \rho = .826$).

1 Introduction

Among semantic relatedness measures, semantic similarity encodes the conceptual distance between two units of language – this goes beyond lexical ressemblance. When words are the speech units, semantic similarity is at the very core of many NLP problems. It has proven to be essential for word sense disambiguation (Mavroeidis et al., 2005; Basile et al., 2014), open domain question answering (Yih et al., 2014), and information retrieval on the Web (Varelas et al., 2005), to name a few. Two established strategies to estimate pairwise word semantic similarity includes knowledge-based and distributional semantics.

Knowledge-based approaches exploit the structure of the taxonomy ((Leacock and Chodorow, 1998; Hirst and St-Onge, 1998; Wu and Palmer, 1994)), its content ((Banerjee and Pedersen, 2002)), or both (Resnik, 1995; Lin, 1998). In the earliest applications, Wordnet-based semantic similarity played a predominant role so that semantic similarity measures reckon with information from the lexical hierarchy. It therefore ignores contextual information on word occurrences and relies on humans to encode such hierarchies – a tedious task in practice. In contrast, well-known distributional semantics strategies encode semantic similarity using the correlation of statistical observations on the occurrences of words in a textual corpora (Lin, 1998).

While providing a significant impact on a broad range of applications, (Herbelot and Ganesalingam, 2013; Lazaridou et al., 2013; Beltagy et al., 2014; Bernardi et al., 2013; Goyal et al., 2013; Lebret et al., 2013), distributional semantics – similarly to knowledge-based strategies – struggle to process the ever-increasing size of textual corpora in a reasonable amount of time. As an answer, embedding high-dimensional distributional semantics models for words into low-dimensional spaces (henceforth *word embedding* (Collobert and Weston, 2008)) has emerged as a popular method. Word embedding utilizes deep learning to learn a real-valued vector representation of words so that any vector distance – usually the cosine similarity – encodes the word-to-word semantic similarity. Although word embedding was successfully applied for several NLP tasks (Hermann et al., 2014; Andreas and Klein, 2014; Clinchant and Perronnin, 2013; Xu et al., 2014; Li and Liu, 2014; Goyal et al., 2013), it implies a slow training phase – measured in days (Collobert and Weston, 2008; Mnih and Kavukcuoglu, 2013; Mikolov et al., 2013), though re-embedding words seems promising (Labutov and Lipson, 2013). There is another usually under-considered issue: the tractability of the pairwise similarity computation in the vector space for large volume of data. Despite these limitations, the current enthusiasm for word embedding certainly echoes the need for lightning fast word-to-word semantic similarity computation.

In this context, it is surprising that embedding semantic similarity of words in low dimensional

Proceedings of the 53rd Annual Meeting of the Association for Computational Linguistics and the 7th International Joint Conference on Natural Language Processing (Short Papers), pages 8–14,
Beijing, China, July 26-31, 2015.

spaces for knowledge-based approaches is understudied. This oversight may well condemn the word-to-word semantic similarity task to remain corpus-dependant – i.e. ignoring the background knowledge provided by a lexical hierarchy.

In this paper, we propose an embedding of knowledge base semantic similarity based on the shortest path metric (Leacock and Chodorow, 1998), into the Hamming hypercube of size n (the size of targeted binary codes). The Leacock and Chodorow semantic similarity is one of the most meaningful measure. It yields the second rank for highest correlation with the data collected by (Miller and Charles, 1991), and the first one within edge centric approaches, as shown by (Seco et al., 2004). This method is only surpassed by the information theoretic based similarity from (Jiang and Conrath, 1997). A second study present similar result (Budanitsky and Hirst, 2006), while a third one ranks this similarity measure at the first rank for precision in paraphrase identification (Mihalcea et al., 2006).

The hypercube embedding technique benefits from the execution of Hamming distance within a few cycles on modern CPUs. This allows the computation of several millions distances per second. Multi-index techniques allows the very fast computation of top-k queries (Norouzi et al., 2012) on the Hamming space. However, the dimension of the hypercube (i.e. the number of bits used to represent an element) should obey the threshold of few CPU words (64, 128 ..., bits) to maintain such efficiency (Heo et al., 2012).

An isometric embedding requires a excessively high number of dimensions to be feasible. However, in this paper we show that practical embeddings exist and present a method to construct them. The best embedding presents very strong correlations ($r = .819, \rho = .829$) with the Leacock & Chodorow similarity measure (LCH in the rest of this paper). Our experiments against the state-of-the art implementation including caching techniques show that performance is increased by up to three orders of magnitude.

2 Shortest path metric embedding

Let us first introduce few notations. We denote H_2^n as an n-dimensional hypercube whose nodes are labeled by the 2^n binary n-tuples. The nodes are adjacent if and only if their corresponding n-tuples differ in exactly one position, i.e. their Hamming distance (ℓ_1) is equal to one. In what follows, Q^n denotes the metric space composed of H_2^n with ℓ_1.

We tackle the following problem: We aim at defining a function f that maps every node w of the taxonomy (Wordnet for Leacock & Chodorow) into Q^n so that for every pair of nodes: $\forall(w_i, w_j), d(w_i, w_j) = \lambda \cdot \ell_1(f(w_i), f(w_j))$, where λ is a scalar. For practical purposes, the construction of the mapping should also be reasonable in terms of time complexity.

Theoretical limitations Wordnet with its hypernym relation forms a partially ordered set (poset). The first approach is to perform an isometric embedding from the poset with shortest path distance into the Hamming hypercube. Such a mapping would exactly preserve the original distance in the embedding. As proven by (Deza and Laurent, 1997), poset lattices, with their shortest path metric, can be isometrically embedded into the hypercube, but the embedding requires 2^n dimensions. The resulting embedding would not fit in the memory of any existing computer, for a lattice having more than 60 nodes. Using Wordnet, with tens of thousands synsets, this embedding is untractable. The bound given by Deza et al. is not tight, however it would require a more than severe improvement to be of any practical interest.

Tree embedding To reduce the dimensionality, we weaken the lattice into a tree. We build a tree from the Wordnet's Hyponyms/Hypernyms poset by cutting 1,300 links, which correspond to roughly one percent of the edges in the original lattice. The nature of the cut to be performed can be subject to discussion. In this preliminary research, we used a simple approach. Since hypernyms are ordered, we decided to preserve only the first hypernym – semantically more relevant, or at least statistically – and to cut edges to other hypernyms.

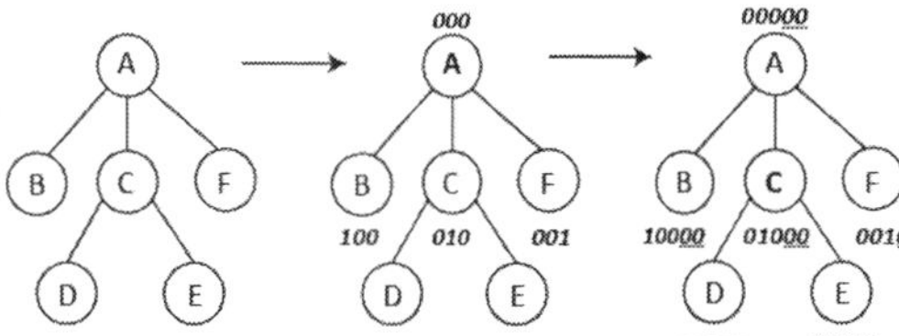

Figure 1: Construction of isometric embedding on a sample tree. For this six nodes tree, the embedding requires five bits.

Our experiments in Table 1 shows that using the obtained tree instead of the lattice keeps a high correlation ($r = .919, \rho = .931$) with the original LCH distance, thus validating the approach.

(Wilkeit, 1990) showed that any k-ary tree of size n can be embedded into Q^{n-1}. We give an isometric embedding algorithm, which is linear in time and space, exhibiting a much better time complexity than Winkler's generic approach for graphs, running in $O(n^5)$ (Winkler, 1984). Starting with an empty binary signature, the algorithm is the following: at each step of a depth-first pre-order traversal: if the node has k children, we set the signature for the i-th child by appending k zeroes to the parent's signature and by setting the i-th of the k bits to one. An example is given in Figure 1. However, when using real-world datasets such as Wordnet, the embedding still requires several thousands of bits to represent a node. This dimension reduction to tens of kilobits per node remains far from our goal of several CPU words, and calls for a task-specific approach.

Looking at the construction of the isometric embedding, the large dimension results from the appending of bits to all nodes in the tree. This results in a large number of bits that are rarely set to one. At the opposite, the optimal embedding in terms of dimension is given by the approach of (Chen and Stallmann, 1995) that assigns gray codes to each node. However, the embedding is not isometric and introduces a very large error. As shown in Table 1, this approach gives the most compact embedding with $\lceil log_2(87{,}000) \rceil = 17$ bits, but leads to poor correlations ($r = .235$ and $\rho = .186$).

An exhaustive search is also out of reach: for a fixed dimension n and r nodes in the tree, the number of combinations C is given by:

$$C = \frac{(2^n)!}{(n-r)!}$$

Even with the smallest value of $n = 17$ and $r = 87{,}000$, we have $C > 10^{10{,}000}$. With $n = 64$, to align to a CPU word, $C > 10^{100{,}000}$.

3 Non-isometric Embedding

Our approach is a trade-off between the isometric embedding and the pre-order gray code solution. When designing our algorithm, we had to decide which tree distance we will preserve, either between parent and children, or among siblings.

Therefore, we take into account the nature of the tree that we aim to embed into the hypercube. Let

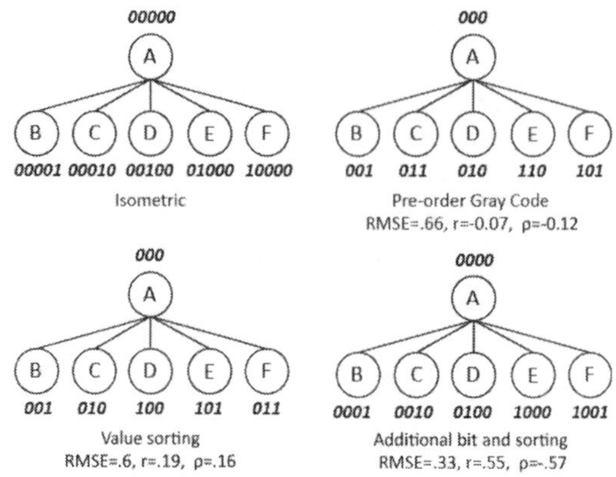

Figure 2: Approaches to reduce the tree embedding dimensions.

first analyse the characteristics of the tree obtained from the cut. The tree has an average branching factor of 4.9, with a standard deviation of 14 and 96% of the nodes have a branching factor lesser than 20. At the opposite, the depth is very stable with an average of 8.5, a standard deviation of 2, and a maximum of 18. Consequently, we decide to preserve the parent-children distance over the very unstable siblings distance. To lower the dimensions, we aim at allocating less than k bits for a node with k children, thus avoiding the signature extension taking place for every node in the isometric approach. Our approach uses the following principles.

Branch inheritance: each node inherits the signature from its father, but contrary to isometric embedding, the signature extension does not apply to all the nodes in the tree. This guarantees the compactness of the structure.

Parentship preservation: when allocating less bits than required for the isometric embedding, we introduce an error. Our allocation favours as much as possible the parentship distance at the expense of the sibling distance. As a first allocation, for a node with k children, we allocate $\lceil log_2(k+1) \rceil$ bits for the signatures, in order to guarantee the unicity of the signature. Each child node is assigned a signature extension using a gray code generation on the $\lceil log_2(k+1) \rceil$ bits. The parent node simply extends its signature with $\lceil log_2(k+1) \rceil$ zeroes, which is much more compact than the k bits from the isometric embedding algorithm.

Word alignment: The two previous techniques give a compact embedding for low-depth trees, which is the case of Wordnet. The dimension D

of the embedding is not necessarily aligned to a CPU word size W: $kW \leq D \leq (k+1)W$. We want to exploit the potential $(k+1)W - D$ bits that are unused but still processed by the CPU. For this purpose we rank the nodes along a value $v(i), i \in N$ to decide which nodes are allowed to use extra bits. Since our approach favours parent/child distance, we want to allow additional bits for nodes that are both close to the root and the head of a large branch. To balance the two values, we use the following formula: $v(i) = (max_{depth} - depth(i)) \cdot log(size_{branch}(i))$ We therefore enable our approach to take full advantage of the otherwise unused bits.

In order to enhance the quality of the embedding, we also introduce two potential optimizations:

The first is called *Children-sorting*: we allocate a better preserving signature to children having larger descents. A better signature is among the available the $2^{\lceil log_2(k+1) \rceil}$ available, the one that reduces the error with the parent node. We rank the children by the size of their descent and assign the signatures accordingly.

The second optimization is named *Value-sorting* and is depicted in Figure 2. Among the $2^{\lceil log_2(k+1) \rceil}$ available signatures, only $k+1$ will be assigned (one for the parent and k for the children). For instance in the case of 5 children as depicted in Figure 2, we allocate 3 bits for 6 signatures. We favor the parentship distance by selecting first the signatures where one bit differs from the parent's one.

4 Experiments

In this section, we run two experiments to evaluate both the soundness and the performance of our approach. In the first experiment, we test the quality of our embedding against the tree distance and the LCH similarity. The goal is to assess the soundness of our approach and to measure the correlation between the approximate embedding and the original LCH similarity.

In the second experiment we compare the computational performance of our approach against an optimized in-memory library that implements the LCH similarity.

Our algorithm called `FSE` for Fast Similarity Embedding, is implemented in Java and available publicly[1]. Our testbed is an Intel Xeon E3 1246v3 with 16GB of memory, a 256Go PCI Express SSD. The system runs a 64-bit Linux 3.13.0 kernel with Oracle's JDK 7u67.

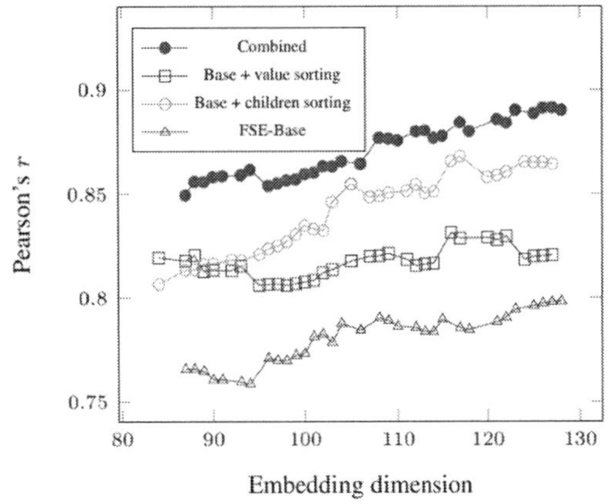

Figure 3: FSE: influence of optimizations and dimensions on the correlation over the tree distance on Wordnet.

The `FSE` algorithm is implemented in various flavours. `FSE-Base` denotes the basic algorithm, containing none of the optimizations detailed in the previous section. `FSE-Base` can be augmented with either or both of the optimizations. This latter version is denoted `FSE-Best`.

4.1 Embedding

We first measure the correlation of the embedded distance with the original tree distance, to validate the approach and to determine the gain induced by the optimizations. Figure 3 shows the influence of dimensions and optimizations on the Pearson's product moment correlation r. The base version reaches $r = .77$ for an embedding of dimension 128. Regarding the optimizations, children sorting is more efficient than value sorting, excepted for dimensions under 90. Finally, combined optimizations (FSE-Best) exhibit a higher correlation ($r = .89$) than the other versions.

We then measure the correlation with the Leacock & Chodorow similarity measure. We compare our approach to the gray codes embedding from (Chen and Stallmann, 1995) as well as the isometric embedding. We compute the correlation on 5 millions distances from the Wordnet-Core noun pairs[2] (Table 1). As expected, the embed-

[1]Source code, binaries and instructions to reproduce the experiments are available at `http://demo-satin.telecom-st-etienne.fr/FSE/`

[2]`https://wordnet.princeton.edu/wordnet/download/standoff/`

Embedding	Bits	Pearson's r	Spearman's ρ
Chen et al.	17	.235	.186
FSE-Base	84	.699	.707
FSE-Best	**128**	**.819**	**.829**
Isometric	84K	.919	.931

Table 1: Correlations between LCH, isometric embedding, and FSE for all distances on all Wordnet-Core noun pairs (p-values $\leq 10^{-14}$).

Algorithm	Measure	Amount of pairs (n)				
		10^3	10^4	10^5	10^6	10^7
WS4J	$10^3 \cdot$ ms	0.156	1.196	11.32	123.89	1,129.3
FSE-Best	ms	0.04	0.59	14.15	150.58	1,482
speedup		×3900	×2027	×800	×822	×762

Table 2: Running time in milliseconds for pairwise similarity computations.

ding obtained using gray codes present a very low correlation with the original distance.

Similarly to the results obtained on the tree distance correlation, `FSE-Best` exhibits the highest scores with $r = .819$ and $\rho = .829$, not far from the theoretical bound of $r = .919$ and $\rho = .931$ for the isometric embedding of the same tree. Our approach requires 650 times less bits than the isometric one, while keeping strong guarantees on the correlation with the original LCH distance.

4.2 Speedup

Table 4.2 presents the computation time of the LCH similarity. This is computed using WS4J[3], an efficient library that enables in-memory caching.

Because of the respective computational complexities of the Hamming distance and the shortest path algorithms, FSE unsurprisingly boosts LCH similarity computation by orders of magnitudes. When the similarity is computed on a small number of pairs (a situation of the utmost practical interest), the factor of improvement is three orders of magnitude. This factor decreases to an amount of 800 times for very large scale applications. The reason of the decrease is that WS4J caching mechanism becomes more efficient for larger numbers of comparisons. As the caching system stores shortest path between nodes, these computed values are more likely to be a subpath of another query when the number of queries grows.

[3]`https://code.google.com/p/ws4j/`

5 Conclusion

We proposed in this paper a novel approach based on metric embedding to boost the computation of shortest-path based similarity measures such as the one of Leacock & Chodorow. We showed that an isometric embedding of the Wordnet's hypernym/hyponym lattice does not lead to a practical solution. To tackle this issue, we weaken the lattice structure into a tree by cutting less relevant edges. We then devised an algorithm and several optimizations to embed the tree shortest-path distance in a word-aligned number of bits. Such an embedding can be used to boost NLP core algorithms – this was demonstrated here on the computation of LCH for which our approach offers a factor of improvement of three orders of magnitude, with a very strong correlation.

Acknowledgements

This work is supported by the OpenCloudware project. OpenCloudware is funded by the French FSN (Fond national pour la Société Numérique), and is supported by Pôles Minalogic, Systematic and SCS.

References

Jacob Andreas and Dan Klein. 2014. How much do word embeddings encode about syntax. In *Association for Computational Linguistics (ACL)*.

Satanjeev Banerjee and Ted Pedersen. 2002. An adapted lesk algorithm for word sense disambiguation using wordnet. In *Computational linguistics and intelligent text processing*, pages 136–145. Springer.

Pierpaolo Basile, Annalina Caputo, and Giovanni Semeraro. 2014. An enhanced lesk word sense disambiguation algorithm through a distributional semantic model. In *Proceedings of COLING*, pages 1591–1600.

Islam Beltagy, Katrin Erk, and Raymond Mooney. 2014. Semantic parsing using distributional semantics and probabilistic logic. *Association for Computational Linguistics (ACL)*, page 7.

Raffaella Bernardi, Georgiana Dinu, Marco Marelli, and Marco Baroni. 2013. A relatedness benchmark to test the role of determiners in compositional distributional semantics. In *Association for Computational Linguistics (ACL)*, pages 53–57.

Alexander Budanitsky and Graeme Hirst. 2006. Evaluating wordnet-based measures of lexical semantic relatedness. *Computational Linguistics*, 32(1):13–47.

Woei-Kae Chen and Matthias FM Stallmann. 1995. On embedding binary trees into hypercubes. *Journal of Parallel and Distributed Computing*, 24(2):132–138.

Stéphane Clinchant and Florent Perronnin. 2013. Aggregating continuous word embeddings for information retrieval. *Association for Computational Linguistics (ACL)*.

Ronan Collobert and Jason Weston. 2008. A unified architecture for natural language processing: Deep neural networks with multitask learning. In *Proceedings of the 25th international conference on Machine learning*, pages 160–167. ACM.

M. Deza and M. Laurent. 1997. *Geometry of Cuts and Metrics*. Springer, 588 pages.

Kartik Goyal, Sujay Kumar Jauhar, Huiying Li, Mrinmaya Sachan, Shashank Srivastava, and Eduard H Hovy. 2013. A structured distributional semantic model for event co-reference. In *Association for Computational Linguistics (ACL)*, pages 467–473.

Jae-Pil Heo, Youngwoon Lee, Junfeng He, Shih-Fu Chang, and Sung-Eui Yoon. 2012. Spherical hashing. In *Computer Vision and Pattern Recognition (CVPR), 2012 IEEE Conference on*, pages 2957–2964. IEEE.

Aurélie Herbelot and Mohan Ganesalingam. 2013. Measuring semantic content in distributional vectors. In *Association for Computational Linguistics (ACL)*, pages 440–445.

Karl Moritz Hermann, Dipanjan Das, Jason Weston, and Kuzman Ganchev. 2014. Semantic frame identification with distributed word representations. In *Association for Computational Linguistics (ACL)*.

Graeme Hirst and David St-Onge. 1998. Lexical chains as representations of context for the detection and correction of malapropisms. *WordNet: An electronic lexical database*, 305:305–332.

Jay J Jiang and David W Conrath. 1997. Semantic similarity based on corpus statistics and lexical taxonomy. *Proceedings of the 10th Research on Computational Linguistics International Conference*.

Igor Labutov and Hod Lipson. 2013. Re-embedding words. In *ACL (2)*, pages 489–493.

Angeliki Lazaridou, Marco Marelli, Roberto Zamparelli, and Marco Baroni. 2013. Compositional-ly derived representations of morphologically complex words in distributional semantics. In *Association for Computational Linguistics (ACL)*, pages 1517–1526.

Claudia Leacock and Martin Chodorow. 1998. Combining local context and wordnet similarity for word sense identification. *WordNet: An electronic lexical database*, 49(2):265–283.

Rémi Lebret, Joël Legrand, and Ronan Collobert. 2013. Is Deep Learning Really Necessary for Word Embeddings? Technical report, Idiap.

Chen Li and Yang Liu. 2014. Improving text normalization via unsupervised model and discriminative reranking. *Association for Computational Linguistics (ACL)*, page 86.

Dekang Lin. 1998. An information-theoretic definition of similarity. In *ICML*, volume 98, pages 296–304.

Dimitrios Mavroeidis, George Tsatsaronis, Michalis Vazirgiannis, Martin Theobald, and Gerhard Weikum. 2005. Word sense disambiguation for exploiting hierarchical thesauri in text classification. In *Knowledge Discovery in Databases: PKDD 2005*, pages 181–192. Springer.

Rada Mihalcea, Courtney Corley, and Carlo Strapparava. 2006. Corpus-based and knowledge-based measures of text semantic similarity. In *AAAI*, volume 6, pages 775–780.

Tomas Mikolov, Kai Chenand, Greg Corradoand, and Jeffrey Dean. 2013. Efficient estimation of word representations in vector space. In *Proceedings of the International Conference on Learning Representations*.

George A Miller and Walter G Charles. 1991. Contextual correlates of semantic similarity. *Language and cognitive processes*, 6(1):1–28.

Andriy Mnih and Koray Kavukcuoglu. 2013. Learning word embeddings efficiently with noise-contrastive estimation. In C.J.C. Burges, L. Bottou, M. Welling, Z. Ghahramani, and K.Q. Weinberger, editors, *Advances in Neural Information Processing Systems 26*, pages 2265–2273. Curran Associates, Inc.

Mohammad Norouzi, Ali Punjani, and David J Fleet. 2012. Fast search in hamming space with multi-index hashing. In *Computer Vision and Pattern Recognition (CVPR), 2012 IEEE Conference on*, pages 3108–3115. IEEE.

Philip Resnik. 1995. Using information content to evaluate semantic similarity in a taxonomy. In *Proceedings of the 14th International Joint Conference on Artificial Intelligence - Volume 1*, IJCAI'95, pages 448–453, San Francisco, CA, USA. Morgan Kaufmann Publishers Inc.

Nuno Seco, Tony Veale, and Jer Hayes. 2004. An intrinsic information content metric for semantic similarity in wordnet. In *ECAI*, volume 16, page 1089.

Giannis Varelas, Epimenidis Voutsakis, Paraskevi Raftopoulou, Euripides GM Petrakis, and Evangelos E Milios. 2005. Semantic similarity methods in wordnet and their application to information retrieval on the web. In *Proceedings of the 7th annual ACM international workshop on Web information and data management*, pages 10–16. ACM.

Elke Wilkeit. 1990. Isometric embeddings in hamming graphs. *Journal of Combinatorial Theory, Series B*, 50(2):179–197.

Peter M Winkler. 1984. Isometric embedding in products of complete graphs. *Discrete Applied Mathematics*, 7(2):221–225.

Zhibiao Wu and Martha Palmer. 1994. Verbs semantics and lexical selection. In *Proceedings of the 32nd annual meeting on Association for Computational Linguistics*, pages 133–138. Association for Computational Linguistics.

Liheng Xu, Kang Liu, Siwei Lai, and Jun Zhao. 2014. Product feature mining: Semantic clues versus syntactic constituents. In *Association for Computational Linguistics (ACL)*, pages 336–346.

Wen-tau Yih, Xiaodong He, and Christopher Meek. 2014. Semantic parsing for single-relation question answering. In *Proceedings of ACL*.

Improving Distributed Representation of Word Sense via WordNet Gloss Composition and Context Clustering

Tao Chen[1] **Ruifeng Xu**[1*] **Yulan He**[2] **Xuan Wang**[1]
[1]Shenzhen Engineering Laboratory of Performance Robots at Digital Stage,
Harbin Institute of Technology Shenzhen Graduate School, Shenzhen, China
[2]School of Engineering and Applied Science, Aston University, UK
chentao1999@gmail.com {xuruifeng,wangxuan}@hitsz.edu.cn
y.he9@aston.ac.uk

Abstract

In recent years, there has been an increasing interest in learning a distributed representation of word sense. Traditional context clustering based models usually require careful tuning of model parameters, and typically perform worse on infrequent word senses. This paper presents a novel approach which addresses these limitations by first initializing the word sense embeddings through learning sentence-level embeddings from WordNet glosses using a convolutional neural networks. The initialized word sense embeddings are used by a context clustering based model to generate the distributed representations of word senses. Our learned representations outperform the publicly available embeddings on 2 out of 4 metrics in the word similarity task, and 6 out of 13 sub tasks in the analogical reasoning task.

1 Introduction

With the rapid development of deep neural networks and parallel computing, distributed representation of knowledge attracts much research interest. Models for learning distributed representations of knowledge have been proposed at different granularity level, including word sense level (Huang et al., 2012; Chen et al., 2014; Neelakantan et al., 2014; Tian et al., 2014; Guo et al., 2014), word level (Rummelhart, 1986; Bengio et al., 2003; Collobert and Weston, 2008; Mnih and Hinton, 2009; Mikolov et al., 2010; Mikolov et al., 2013), phrase level (Socher et al., 2010; Zhang et al., 2014; Cho et al., 2014), sentence level (Mikolov et al., 2010; Socher et al., 2013; Kalchbrenner et al., 2014; Kim, 2014; Le and Mikolov, 2014), discourse level (Ji and Eisenstein, 2014) and document level (Le and Mikolov, 2014).

In distributed representations of word senses, each word sense is usually represented by a dense and real-valued vector in a low-dimensional space which captures the contextual semantic information. Most existing approaches adopted a cluster-based paradigm, which produces different sense vectors for each polysemy or homonymy through clustering the context of a target word. However, this paradigm usually has two limitations: (1) The performance of these approaches is sensitive to the clustering algorithm which requires the setting of the sense number for each word. For example, Neelakantan et al. (2014) proposed two clustering based model: the Multi-Sense Skip-Gram (MSSG) model and Non-Parametric Multi-Sense Skip-Gram (NP-MSSG) model. MSSG assumes each word has the same k-sense (e.g. $k = 3$), i.e., the same number of possible senses. However, the number of senses in WordNet (Miller, 1995) varies from 1 such as "*ben*" to 75 such as "*break*". As such, fixing the number of senses for all words would result in poor representations. NP-MSSG can learn the number of senses for each word directly from data. But it requires a tuning of a hyperparameter λ which controls the creation of cluster centroids during training. Different λ needs to be tuned for different datasets. (2) The initial value of sense representation is critical for most statistical clustering based approaches. However, previous approaches usually adopted random initialization (Neelakantan et al., 2014) or the mean average of candidate words in a gloss (Chen et al., 2014). As a result, they may not produce optimal clustering results for word senses.

Focusing on the aforementioned two problems, this paper proposes to learn distributed representations of word senses through WordNet gloss composition and context clustering. The basic idea is that a word sense is represented as a synonym set (*synset*) in WordNet. In this way, instead of assigning a fixed sense number to each word as in the

Proceedings of the 53rd Annual Meeting of the Association for Computational Linguistics and the 7th International Joint Conference on Natural Language Processing (Short Papers), pages 15–20,
Beijing, China, July 26-31, 2015.

previous methods, different word will be assigned with different number of senses based on their corresponding entries in WordNet. Moreover, we notice that each synset has a textual definition (named as *gloss*). Naturally, we use a convolutional neural network (CNN) to learn distributed representations of these glosses (a.k.a. sense vectors) through sentence composition. Then, we modify MSSG for context clustering by initializing the sense vectors with the representations learned by our CNN-based sentence composition model. We expect that word sense vectors initialized in this way would potentially lead to better representations of word senses generated from context clustering.

The obtained word sense representations are evaluated on two tasks. One is word similarity task, the other is analogical reasoning task provided by WordRep (Gao et al., 2014). The results show that our approach attains comparable performance on learning distributed representations of word senses. In specific, our learned representation outperforms publicly available embeddings on the globalSim and localSim metrics in word similarity task, and 6 in 13 subtasks in the analogical reasoning task.

2 Our Approach

Our proposed approach first train a Continuous Bag-Of-Words (CBOW) model (Mikolov et al., 2013) from a large collection of raw text to generate word embeddings. These word embeddings are then used by a *Sentence Composition Model*, which takes glosses in WordNet as positive training data and randomly replaces part of the sentences as negative training data to construct the corresponding word sense vectors based on a one-dimensional CNN. For example, a WordNet gloss of word *star* is "*an actor who plays a principal role*". This is taken as a positive training example when learning the word sense vector for "*star*". We concatenate the word embedding generated by the CBOW model for each of the words in the gloss, take the concatenated word embeddings as an input to CNN, and get the output vector as one sense vector of word *star*.

The learned sense vectors are fed into a variant of the previously proposed *Multi-Sense Skip-Gram Model* (MSSG) to generates distributed representations of word senses from a text corpus. We name our approach as CNN-VMSSG.

2.1 Training Sense Vectors From WordNet Glosses Using CNN

In this step, we learn the distributed representation of each gloss sentence as the representation of the corresponding synset. The training objective is to minimize the ranking loss below:

$$G_s = \sum_{s \in P} \max\{0, 1 - f(s) + f(s')\} \quad (1)$$

Given a gloss sentence s as a positive training sample, we randomly replace some words (controlled by a parameter λ) in s to construct a negative training sample s'. We compute the scores $f(s)$ and $f(s')$ where $f(\cdot)$ is the scoring function representing the whole CNN architecture without the softmax layer. We expect $f(s)$ and $f(s')$ to be close to 1 and 0 respectively, and $f(s)$ to be larger than $f(s')$ by a margin of 1 for all the sentence in positive training set P.

The CNN architecture used in this component follows the architecture proposed by (Kim, 2014)[1] which is a slight variant of the architecture proposed by (Collobert and Weston, 2008)[2]. It takes a gloss matrix s as input where each column corresponds to the distributed representation $v_{w_i} \in \mathbb{R}^d$ of a word w_i in the sentence.

The idea behind the one-dimensional convolution is to take the dot product of the vector w with each n-gram in the sentence to obtain another sequence c, where n is the width of filter in the convolutional layer. In order to make c to cover different words in the negative sample corresponding a positive sample, in this work, we randomly replace half of the words in a positive training sample to construct a negative training sample ($\lambda = 0.5$). For example, take the WordNet gloss "*an actor who plays a principal role*" as a positive sample, a negative training sample constructed by this method may be "x_1 *actor who* x_2 x_3 *principal* x_4", where x_1 to x_4 are randomly selected words in a vocabulary collected from a large corpus.

In the pooling layer, a max-overtime pooling operation (Collobert et al., 2011), which forces the network to capture the most useful local features produced by the convolutional layers, is applied. The model uses multiple filters (with varying window sizes) to obtain multiple features. These features form the penultimate layer and are passed to a fully connected softmax layer whose output is

[1] https://github.com/yoonkim/CNN_sentence

[2] http://ronan.collobert.com/senna/

the probability distribution over labels. The training error propagates back to fine-tune the parameters of the CNN and the input word vectors. The vector generated in the penultimate layer of the CNN architecture is regarded as the sense vector which captures the semantic content of the input gloss to a certain degree.

2.2 Context Clustering and VMSSG Model

Neelakantan et al. (2014) proposed the MSSG model which extends the skip-gram model to learn multi-prototype word embeddings by clustering the word embeddings of context words around each word. In this model, for each word w, the corresponding word embedding $v_w \in \mathbb{R}^d$, k-sense vector $v_{s_k} \in \mathbb{R}^d$ $(k = 1, 2, \ldots, K)$ and k-context cluster with center $\mu_k \in \mathbb{R}^d$ $(k = 1, 2, \ldots, K)$ are initialized randomly. The sense number K of each word is a fixed parameter in the training algorithm.

We improve the MSSG model by using the learned CBOW word embedding to initialize v_w and the sense vector trained by the sentence composition model to initialize v_{s_k}. We also use the sense number of each word in WordNet K_w to replace K. We named this model as a variant of the MSSG (VMSSG) model.

Algorithm 1 Algorithm of VMSSG model

```
Input: D, d, K_1, ..., K_w, ..., K_|V|, M.
Initialize: ∀w ∈ V, k ∈ {1, ..., K_w}, initialize v_w to a pre-trained word vector, v_{s_k^w} to a pre-trained sense vector for word w with sense k, and μ_k^w to a vector of random real value ∈ (−1, 1)^d.
for each w in D do
    r ← random number ∈ [1, M]
    C ← {w_{i−r}, ..., w_{i−1}, w_{i+1}, ..., w_{i+r}}
    v_c ← (1 / 2×r) Σ_{w∈C} v_w
    k̂ = arg max_k {sim(μ_k^w, v_c)}
    Assign C to context cluster k̂.
    Update μ_k̂.
    C′ = NoisySamples(C)
    Gradient update on v_{s_k^w}, v_w in C, C′.
end for
Output: v_{s_k^w}, v_w, ∀w ∈ V, k ∈ {1, ..., K_w}
```

The training algorithm of the VMSSG model is shown as Algorithm 1, where D is a text corpus, V is the vocabulary of D, $|V|$ is the vocabulary size, M is the size of context window, v_w is the word embedding for w, s_k^w is a kth context cluster of word w, μ_k^w is the centroid of cluster k for word w. The function NoisySamples(C) randomly replaces context words with noisy words from V.

3 Evaluation and Discussion

3.1 Experimental Setup

In all experiments, we train word vectors and sense vectors on a snapshot of Wikipedia in April 2010[3] (Shaoul, 2010), previously used in (Huang et al., 2012; Neelakantan et al., 2014). WordNet 3.1 is used for training the sentence composition model. A publicly available word vectors trained by CBOW from Google News[4] are used as pre-trained word vectors for CNN.

For training CNN, we use: rectified linear units, filter windows of 3, 4, 5 with 100 feature maps each, AdaDelta decay parameter of 0.95, the dropout rate of 0.5. For training VMSSG, we use *MSSG-KMeans* as the clustering algorithm, and CBOW for learning sense vectors. We set the size of word vectors to 300, using boot vectors and sense vectors. For other parameter, we use default parameter settings for MSSG.

3.2 Word Similarity Task

We evaluate our embeddings on the Contextual Word Similarities (SCWS) dataset (Huang et al., 2012). It contains 2,003 pairs of words and their sentential contexts. Each pair is associated with 10 to 16 human judgments of similarity on a scale from 0 to 10. We use the same metrics in (Neelakantan et al., 2014) to measure the similarity between two words given their respective context. The *avgSim* metric computes the average similarity of all pairs of prototype vectors for each word, ignoring context. The *avgSimC* metric weights each similarity term in avgSim by the likelihood of the word context appearing in its respective cluster. The *globalSim* metric computes each word vector ignoring senses. The *localSim* metric chooses the most similar sense in context to estimate the similarity of a words pair.

We report the Spearman's correlation $\rho \times 100$ between a model's similarity scores and the human judgments in Table 1.[5]

[3] http://www.psych.ualberta.ca/westburylab/downloads/westburylab.wikicorp.download.html

[4] https://drive.google.com/file/d/0B7XkCwpI5KDYNlNUTTlSS21pQmM/edit?usp=sharing

[5] The localSim metric of *Unified-WSR* is not reported in (Chen et al., 2014).

Model	avgSim	avgSimC	globalSim	localSim
Huang et al. 50d	62.8	65.7	58.6	26.1
Unified-WSR 200d	66.2	68.9	64.2	-
MSSG 300d	67.2	**69.3**	65.3	57.3
NP-MSSG 300d	**67.3**	69.1	65.5	59.8
CNN-VMSSG 300d	65.7	66.4	**66.3**	**61.1**

Table 1: Experimental results in the SCWS task.

Subtask	Word Pairs	C&W	CBOW	MSSG	NP-MSSG	CNN-VMSSG
Antonym	973	0.28	**4.57**	0.25	0.10	1.01
Attribute	184	0.22	1.18	0.03	0.15	**1.63**
Causes	26	0.00	1.08	0.31	0.31	**1.23**
DerivedFrom	6,119	0.05	**0.63**	0.09	0.05	0.17
Entails	114	0.05	0.38	0.49	0.34	**1.29**
HasContext	1,149	0.12	0.35	**1.73**	1.56	1.41
InstanceOf	1,314	0.08	0.58	**2.52**	2.34	2.46
IsA	10,615	0.07	0.67	0.15	0.08	**0.86**
MadeOf	63	0.03	0.72	0.80	0.48	**1.28**
MemberOf	406	0.08	**1.06**	0.14	0.86	0.90
PartOf	1,029	0.31	1.27	**1.50**	0.73	0.48
RelatedTo	102	0.00	0.05	0.12	0.11	**1.28**
SimilarTo	3,489	0.02	**0.29**	0.03	0.01	0.12

Table 2: Experimental results in the analogical reasoning task.

It is observed that our model achieves the best performance on the *globalSim* and *localSim* metrics. It indicates that the use of pre-trained word vectors and initializing sense vectors with the embeddings learned from WordNet glosses are indeed helpful in improving the quality of both global word vectors and sense-level word vectors. Our approach performs worse on *avgSim* and *avgSimC*. One possible reason is that we set the number of context clusters for each word to be the same as the number of its corresponding senses in WordNet. However, not all senses appear in the our experimented corpus which could lead to fragmented context clustering results. One possible way to alleviate this problem is to perform post-processing to merge clusters which have smaller inter-cluster differences or to remove sense clusters which are under-represented in our data. We will leave it as our future work.

3.3 Analogical Reasoning Task

The analogical reasoning task introduced by (Mikolov et al., 2013) consists of questions of the form "a is to b is as c is to _", where (a, b) and (c, _) are two word pairs. The goal is to find a word d^* in vocabulary V whose representation vector is the closest to $v_b - v_a + v_c$.

WordRep is a benchmark collection for the research on learning distributed word representations, which expands the Mikolov et al.'s analogical reasoning questions. In our experiments, we use one evaluation set in WordRep, the WordNet collection which consists of 13 sub tasks.

We use the precision $p \times 100$ as metric for each sub task. Table 2 shows the results on the 13 sub tasks. The *Word Pair* column is the number of word pairs of each sub task. The results of C&W were obtained using the 50-dimensional word embeddings that were made publicly available by Turian et al. (2010).[6] The CBOW results were previously reported in (Gao et al., 2014).

It can be observed that among 13 subtasks, our model outperforms the others by a good margin in 6 subtasks, *Attribute*, *Causes*, *Entails*, *IsA*, *MadeOf* and *RelatedTo*.

3.4 Discussion

Although our evaluation results on the word similarity task and the analogical reasoning task show that our proposed approach outperforms a number of existing word representation methods in some

[6] http://metaoptimize.com/projects/wordreprs/

of the subtasks, it is worth noting that both tasks do not consider the full spectrum of senses. In specific, the analogical reasoning task was originally designed for evaluating single-prototype word representations which ignore that a word could have multiple meanings. Compared to single-prototype word vectors, evaluating sense vectors requires a significantly larger search space since each word could be represented by multiple sense vectors depending on the context. One may also argue that the analogical reasoning task may not be the most appropriate one in evaluating multiple-prototype word vectors since the context information is not available. In the future, we plan to evaluate our learned multiple-prototype word vectors in more relevant NLP tasks such as word sense disambiguation and question answering.

Our proposed approach initializes sense vectors using the learned sentence embeddings from WordNet glosses. In other low resourced languages, it is still possible to intialize sense vectors based on, for example, the word meanings found in language-specific dictionaries.

4 Conclusion and Future Work

This paper presents a method of incorporating WordNet glosses composition and context clustering based model for learning distributed representations of word senses. By initializing sense vectors using the embeddings learned by a sentence composition from WordNet glosses, the context clustering method is able to generate better distributed representations of word senses. The obtained word sense representations achieve state-of-the-art results on the globalSim and localSim metrics in the word similarity task and in 6 sub tasks of the analogical reasoning task. It shows the effectiveness of our proposed learning algorithm for generating word sense distributed representations.

Considering the coverage of word senses in our training data, in future work we plan to filter out those sense vectors which are under-represented in the training corpus. We will also further investigate the feasibility of applying the multi-prototype word embeddings in a wide range of NLP tasks.

Acknowledgments

This work is supported by the National Natural Science Foundation of China (No. 61370165, 61203378), National 863 Program of China 2015AA015405, the Natural Science Foundation of Guangdong Province (No. S2013010014475), Shenzhen Development and Reform Commission Grant No.[2014]1507, Shenzhen Peacock Plan Research Grant KQCX20140521144507925 and Baidu Collaborate Research Funding.

References

Yoshua Bengio, Rejean Ducharme, and Pascal Vincent. 2003. A neural probabilistic language model. *Journal of Machine Learning Research*, 3:1137–1155.

Xinxiong Chen, Zhiyuan Liu, and Maosong Sun. 2014. A unified model for word sense representation and disambiguation. In *Proceedings of the 2014 Conference on Empirical Methods in Natural Language Processing (EMNLP)*, pages 1025–1035.

Kyunghyun Cho, Bart van Merrienboer, Caglar Gulcehre, Fethi Bougares, Holger Schwenk, and Yoshua Bengio. 2014. Learning phrase representations using RNN encoder-decoder for statistical machine translation. *Proceedings of the 2014 Conference on Empirical Methods in Natural Language Processing (EMNLP)*, pages 1724–1734.

Ronan Collobert and Jason Weston. 2008. A unified architecture for natural language processing: Deep neural networks with multitask learning. In *Proceedings of the 25th International Conference on Machine Learning (ICML)*, pages 160–167. ACM.

Ronan Collobert, Jason Weston, Léon Bottou, Michael Karlen, Koray Kavukcuoglu, and Pavel Kuksa. 2011. Natural language processing (almost) from scratch. *The Journal of Machine Learning Research*, 12:2493–2537.

Bin Gao, Jiang Bian, and Tie-Yan Liu. 2014. Wordrep: A benchmark for research on learning word representations. In *ICML 2014 Workshop on Knowledge-Powered Deep Learning for Text Mining (KPDLTM2014)*.

Jiang Guo, Wanxiang Che, Haifeng Wang, and Ting Liu. 2014. Learning sense-specific word embeddings by exploiting bilingual resources. In *Proceedings of the 25th International Conference on Computational Linguistics (COLING)*, pages 497–507.

Eric H Huang, Richard Socher, Christopher D Manning, and Andrew Y Ng. 2012. Improving word representations via global context and multiple word prototypes. In *Proceedings of the 50th Annual Meeting of the Association for Computational Linguistics (ACL)*, pages 873–882. Association for Computational Linguistics.

Yangfeng Ji and Jacob Eisenstein. 2014. Representation learning for text-level discourse parsing. In *Proceedings of the 52nd Annual Meeting of the Association for Computational Linguistics (ACL)*, pages 13–24, Baltimore, Maryland, June. Association for Computational Linguistics.

Nal Kalchbrenner, Edward Grefenstette, and Phil Blunsom. 2014. A convolutional neural network for modelling sentences. In *Proceedings of the 52nd Annual Meeting of the Association for Computational Linguistics (ACL)*, pages 655–665, Baltimore, Maryland, June. Association for Computational Linguistics.

Yoon Kim. 2014. Convolutional neural networks for sentence classification. In *Proceedings of the 2014 Conference on Empirical Methods in Natural Language Processing (EMNLP)*, pages 1746–1751, October.

Quoc V Le and Tomas Mikolov. 2014. Distributed representations of sentences and documents. In *Proceedings of the 31th International Conference on Machine Learning (ICML)*, pages 1188–1196.

Tomas Mikolov, Martin Karafiát, Lukas Burget, Jan Cernockỳ, and Sanjeev Khudanpur. 2010. Recurrent neural network based language model. In *Proceedings of INTERSPEECH*, pages 1045–1048.

Tomas Mikolov, Kai Chen, Greg Corrado, and Jeffrey Dean. 2013. Efficient estimation of word representations in vector space. In *Proceedings of Workshop at the International Conference on Learning Representations (ICLR)*.

George A Miller. 1995. Wordnet: a lexical database for english. *Communications of the ACM*, 38(11):39–41.

Andriy Mnih and Geoffrey E Hinton. 2009. A scalable hierarchical distributed language model. In *Advances in neural information processing systems*, pages 1081–1088.

Arvind Neelakantan, Jeevan Shankar, Alexandre Passos, and Andrew McCallum. 2014. Efficient non-parametric estimation of multiple embeddings per word in vector space. In *Proceedings of the 2014 Conference on Empirical Methods in Natural Language Processing (EMNLP)*, pages 1059–1069.

DE Rummelhart. 1986. Learning representations by back-propagating errors. *Nature*, 323(9):533–536.

Cyrus Shaoul. 2010. The westbury lab wikipedia corpus. *Edmonton, AB: University of Alberta*.

Richard Socher, Christopher D Manning, and Andrew Y Ng. 2010. Learning continuous phrase representations and syntactic parsing with recursive neural networks. In *Proceedings of the NIPS-2010 Deep Learning and Unsupervised Feature Learning Workshop*, pages 1–9.

Richard Socher, Alex Perelygin, Jean Y Wu, Jason Chuang, Christopher D Manning, Andrew Y Ng, and Christopher Potts. 2013. Recursive deep models for semantic compositionality over a sentiment treebank. In *Proceedings of the Conference on Empirical Methods in Natural Language Processing (EMNLP)*, pages 1631–1642. Citeseer.

Fei Tian, Hanjun Dai, Jiang Bian, Bin Gao, Rui Zhang, Enhong Chen, and Tie-Yan Liu. 2014. A probabilistic model for learning multi-prototype word embeddings. In *Proceedings of the 25th International Conference on Computational Linguistics (COLING)*, pages 151–160.

Joseph Turian, Lev Ratinov, and Yoshua Bengio. 2010. Word representations: a simple and general method for semi-supervised learning. In *Proceedings of the 48th annual meeting of the association for computational linguistics (ACL)*, pages 384–394.

Jiajun Zhang, Shujie Liu, Mu Li, Ming Zhou, and Chengqing Zong. 2014. Bilingually-constrained phrase embeddings for machine translation. In *Proceedings of the 52nd Annual Meeting of the Association for Computational Linguistics (ACL)*, pages 111–121, Baltimore, Maryland, June. Association for Computational Linguistics.

A Multitask Objective to Inject Lexical Contrast into Distributional Semantics

Nghia The Pham Angeliki Lazaridou Marco Baroni
Center for Mind/Brain Sciences
University of Trento
{thenghia.pham|angeliki.lazaridou|marco.baroni}@unitn.it

Abstract

Distributional semantic models have trouble distinguishing strongly contrasting words (such as antonyms) from highly compatible ones (such as synonyms), because both kinds tend to occur in similar contexts in corpora. We introduce the multitask Lexical Contrast Model (mLCM), an extension of the effective Skip-gram method that optimizes semantic vectors on the joint tasks of predicting corpus contexts and making the representations of WordNet synonyms closer than that of matching WordNet antonyms. mLCM outperforms Skip-gram both on general semantic tasks and on synonym/antonym discrimination, even when no direct lexical contrast information about the test words is provided during training. mLCM also shows promising results on the task of learning a compositional negation operator mapping adjectives to their antonyms.

1 Introduction

Distributional semantic models (DSMs) extract vectors representing word meaning by relying on the *distributional hypothesis*, that is, the idea that words that are related in meaning will tend to occur in similar contexts (Turney and Pantel, 2010). While extensive work has shown that contextual similarity is an excellent proxy to semantic similarity, a big problem for DSMs is that both words with very compatible meanings (e.g., near synonyms) and words with strongly contrasting meanings (e.g., antonyms) tend to occur in the same contexts. Indeed, Mohammad et al. (2013) have shown that synonyms and antonyms are indistinguishable in terms of their average degree of distributional similarity.

This is problematic for the application of DSMs to reasoning tasks such as entailment detection (*black* is very close to both *dark* and *white* in distributional semantic space, but it implies the former while contradicting the latter). Beyond word-level relations, the same difficulties make it challenging for compositional extensions of DSMs to capture the fundamental phenomenon of negation at the phrasal and sentential levels (the distributional vectors for *good* and *not good* are nearly identical) (Hermann et al., 2013; Preller and Sadrzadeh, 2011).

Mohammad and colleagues concluded that DSMs alone cannot detect semantic contrast, and proposed an approach that couples them with other resources. Pure-DSM solutions include isolating contexts that are expected to be more discriminative of contrast, tuning the similarity measure to make it more sensitive to contrast or training a supervised contrast classifier on DSM vectors (Adel and Schütze, 2014; Santus et al., 2014; Schulte im Walde and Köper, 2013; Turney, 2008). We propose instead to induce word vectors using a multitask cost function combining a traditional DSM context-prediction objective with a term forcing words to be closer to their WordNet synonyms than to their antonyms. In this way, we make the model aware that contrasting words such as *hot* and *cold*, while still semantically related, should not be nearest neighbours in the space.

In a similar spirit, Yih et al. (2012) devise a DSM in which the embeddings of the antonyms of a word are pushed to be the vectors that are farthest away from its representation. While their model is able to correctly pick the antonym of a target item from a list of candidates (since it is the most dissimilar element in the list), we conjecture that their radical strategy produces embeddings with poor performance on general semantic tasks.[1] Our method has instead a beneficial global

[1]Indeed, by simulating their strategy, we were able to inject lexical contrast into word embeddings, but performance on a general semantic relatedness task decreased dramati-

Proceedings of the 53rd Annual Meeting of the Association for Computational Linguistics and the 7th International Joint Conference on Natural Language Processing (Short Papers), pages 21–26,
Beijing, China, July 26-31, 2015.

effect on semantic vectors, leading to state-of-the-art results in a challenging similarity task, and enabling better learning of a compositional negation function.

Our work is also closely related to Faruqui et al. (2015), who propose an algorithm to adapt pre-trained DSM representations using semantic resources such as WordNet. This post-processing approach, while extremely effective, has the disadvantage that changes only affect words that are present in the resource, without propagating to the whole lexicon. Other recent work has instead adopted multitask objectives similar to ours in order to directly plug in knowledge from structured resources at DSM induction time (Fried and Duh, 2015; Xu et al., 2014; Yu and Dredze, 2014). Our main novelties with respect to these proposals are the focus on capturing semantic contrast, and explicitly testing the hypothesis that the multitask objective is also beneficial to words that are not directly exposed to WordNet evidence during training.[2]

2 The multitask Lexical Contrast Model

Skip-gram model The multitask Lexical Contrast Model (mLCM) extends the Skip-gram model (Mikolov et al., 2013). Given an input text corpus, Skip-gram optimizes word vectors on the task of approximating, for each word, the probability of other words to occur in its context. More specifically, its objective function is:

$$\frac{1}{T}\sum_{t=1}^{T}\left(\sum_{-c\leq j\leq c, j\neq 0} \log p(w_{t+j}|w_t)\right) \quad (1)$$

where $w_1, w_2, ..., w_T$ is the training corpus, consisting of a list of target words w_t, for which we want to learn the vector representations (and serving as contexts of each other), and c is the window size determining the span of context words to be considered. $p(w_{t+j}|w_t)$, the probability of a context word given the target word is computed using softmax:

$$p(w_{t+j}|w_t) = \frac{e^{{v'_{w_{t+j}}}^T v_{w_t}}}{\sum_{w'=1}^{W} e^{{v'_{w'}}^T v_{w_t}}} \quad (2)$$

cally, with a 25% drop in terms of Spearman correlation.

[2]After submitting this work, we became aware of Ono et al. (2015), that implement very similar ideas. However, one major difference between their work and ours is that their strategy is in the same direction of (Yih et al., 2012), which might result in poor performance on general semantic tasks.

where v_w and v'_w are respectively the target and context vector representations of word w, and W is the number of words in the vocabulary. To avoid the $O(|W|)$ time complexity of the normalization term in Equation (2), Mikolov et al. (2013) use either hierarchical softmax or negative sampling. Here, we adopt the negative sampling method.

Injecting lexical contrast information We account for lexical contrast by implementing a 2-task strategy, combining the Skip-gram context prediction objective with a new term:

$$\frac{1}{T}\sum_{t=1}^{T}(J_{skipgram}(w_t) + J_{lc}(w_t)) \quad (3)$$

The *lexical contrast* objective $J_{lc}(w_t)$ tries to enforce the constraint that contrasting pairs should have lower similarity than compatible ones within a max-margin framework. Our formulation is inspired by Lazaridou et al. (2015), who use a similar multitask strategy to induce multimodal embeddings. Given a target word w, with sets of antonyms $A(w)$ and synonyms $S(w)$, the max-margin objective for lexical contrast is:

$$-\sum_{s\in S(w), a\in A(w)} \max(0, \Delta - cos(v_w, v_s) + cos(v_w, v_a)) \quad (4)$$

where Δ is the margin and $cos(x, y)$ stands for cosine similarity between vectors x and y. Note that, by equation (3), the $J_{lc}(w_t)$ term is evaluated each time a word is encountered in the corpus. We extract antonym and synonym sets from WordNet (Miller, 1995). If a word w_t is not associated to synonym/antonym information in WordNet, we set $J_{lc}(w_t) = 0$.

3 Experimental setup

We compare the performance of mLCM against Skip-gram. Both models' parameters are estimated by backpropagation of error via stochastic gradient descent. Our text corpus is a Wikipedia[3] 2009 dump comprising approximately 800M tokens and 200K distinct word types.[4] Other hyper-parameters, selected without tuning, include: vector size (300), window size (5), negative samples (10), sub-sampling to disfavor frequent words (10^{-3}). For mLCM, we use 7500 antonym pairs

[3]`https://en.wikipedia.org`

[4]We only consider words that occur more than 50 times in the corpus

	MEN	SimLex
Skip-gram	0.73	0.39
mLCM	**0.74**	**0.52**

Table 1: Relatedness/similarity tasks

	AUC
Skip-gram	0.62
mLCM	**0.78**
mLCM-propagate	0.66

Table 2: Synonym vs antonym task

and 15000 synonym pairs; on average, 2.5 pairs per word and 9000 words are covered.

Both models are evaluated in four tasks: two lexical tasks testing the general quality of the learned embeddings and one focusing on antonymy, and a negation task which verifies the positive influence of lexical contrast in a compositional setting.

4 Lexical tasks

4.1 Relatedness and similarity

In classic semantic relatedness/similarity tasks, the models provide cosine scores between pairs of word vectors that are then compared to human ratings for the same pairs. Performance is evaluated by Spearman correlation between system and human scores. For general relatedness, we use the **MEN** dataset of Bruni et al. (2014), which consists of 3,000 word pairs comprising 656 nouns, 57 adjectives and 38 verbs. The **SimLex** dataset from Hill et al. (2014b), comprising 999 word pairs (666 noun, 222 verb and 111 adjective pairs) was explicitly built to test a tighter notion of strict "semantic" similarity.

Table 1 reports model performance. On MEN, mLCM outperforms Skip-gram by a small margin, which shows that the new information, at the very least, does not have any negative effect on general semantic relatedness. On the other hand, lexical contrast information has a strong positive effect on measuring strict semantic similarity, leading mLCM to achieve state-of-the-art SimLex performance (Hill et al., 2014a).

4.2 Distinguishing antonyms and synonyms

Having shown that capturing lexical contrast information results in higher-quality representations for general purposes, we focus next on the specific task of distinguishing contrasting words from highly compatible ones. We use the adjective part of dataset of Santus et al. (2014), that contains 262 antonym and 364 synonym pairs. We compute cosine similarity of all pairs and use the area under the ROC curve (AUC) to measure model performance. Moreover, we directly test mLCM's ability to propagate lexical contrast across the vocabulary by retraining it without using WordNet information for any of the words in the dataset, i.e. the words in the dataset are removed from the synonym or antonym sets of all the adjectives used in training (**mLCM-propagate** in the results table).

The results, in Table 2, show that mLCM can successfully learn to distinguish contrasting words from synonyms. The performance of the mLCM model trained without explicit contrast information about the dataset words proves moreover that lexical contrast information is indeed propagated through the lexical network.

4.3 Vector space structure

To further investigate the effect of lexical contrast information, we perform a qualitative analysis of how it affects the space structure. We pick 20 scalar adjectives denoting spatial or weight-related aspects of objects and living beings, where 10 indicate the presence of the relevant property to a great degree (*big, long, heavy*...), whereas the remaining 10 suggest that the property is present in little amounts (*little, short, light*...). We project the 300-dimensional vectors of these adjectives onto a 2-dimensional plane using the t-SNE toolkit,[5] which attempts to preserve the structure of the original high-dimensional word neighborhoods. Figure 1 shows that, in Skip-gram space, pairs at the extreme of the same scale (*light* vs *heavy*, *narrow* vs *wide*, *fat* vs *skinny*) are very close to each other compared to other words; whereas for mLCM the extremes are farther apart from each other, as expected. Moreover, the adjectives at the two ends of the scales are grouped together. This is a very nice property, since many adjectives in one group will tend to characterize the same objects. Within the two clusters, words that are more similar (e.g., *wide* and *broad*) are still closer to each other, just as we would expect them to be.

[5] http://lvdmaaten.github.io/tsne/

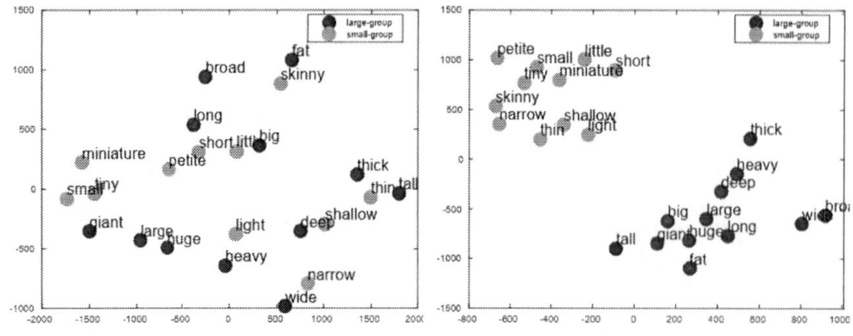

(a) Skip-gram space (b) mLCM space

Figure 1: Arrangement of some scalar adjectives in Skip-gram vs mLCM spaces

5 Learning Negation

Having shown that injecting lexical contrast information into word embeddings is beneficial for lexical tasks, we further explore if it can also help composition. Since mLCM makes contrasting and compatible words more distinguishable from each other, we conjecture that it would be easier for compositional DSMs to capture negation in mLCM space. We perform a proof-of-concept experiment where we represent *not* as a function that is trained to map an adjective to its antonym (*good* to *bad*). That is, by adopting the framework of Baroni et al. (2014), we take *not* to be a matrix that, when multiplied with an adjective-representing vector, returns the vector of an adjective with the opposite meaning. We realize that this is capturing only a tiny fraction of the linguistic uses of negation, but it is at least a concrete starting point.

First, we select a list of adjectives and antonyms from WordNet; for each adjective, we only pick the antonym of its first sense. This yields a total of around 4,000 antonym pairs. Then, we induce the *not* matrix with least-squares regression on training pairs. Finally, we assess the learned negation function by applying it to an adjective and computing accuracy in the task of retrieving the correct antonym as nearest neighbour of the *not*-composed vector, searching across all WordNet adjectives (10K items). The results in Table 3 are obtained by using 10-fold cross-validation on the 4,000 pairs. We see that mLCM outperforms Skip-gram by a large margin.

Figure 2 shows heatmaps of the weight matrices learnt for *not* by the two models. Intriguingly, for mLCM, the *not* matrix has negative values on the diagonal, that is, it will tend to flip the values in the input vector, not unlike what arithmetic negation would do. On the other hand, the Skip-gram-based *not* matrix is remarkably identity-like, with large positive values concentrated on the diagonal. Thus, under this approach, an adjective will be almost identical to its antonym, which explains why it fails completely on the test set data: the nearest neighbour of *not-X* will typically be X itself.

	train	test
Skip-gram	0.44	0.02
mLCM	**0.87**	**0.27**

Table 3: Average accuracy in retrieving antonym as nearest neighbour when applying the *not* composition function to 4,000 adjectives.

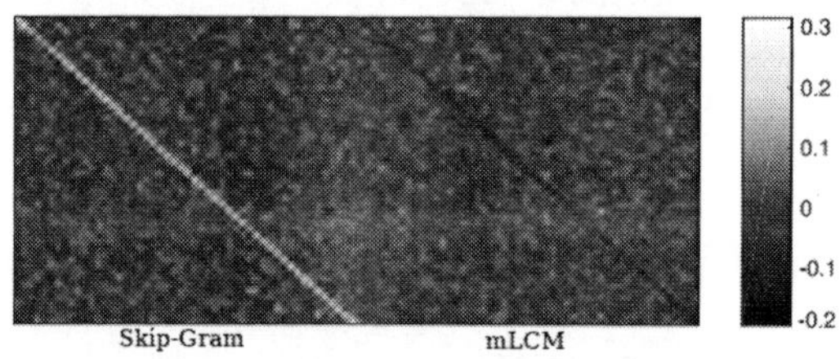

Figure 2: Heatmaps of *not*-composition matrices.

6 Conclusion

Given the promise shown by mLCM in the experiments reported here, we plan to test it next on a range of linguistically interesting phenomena that are challenging for DSMs and where lexical contrast information might help. These include modeling a broader range of negation types (de Swart, 2010), capturing lexical and phrasal inference (Levy et al., 2015), deriving adjectival scales (Kim and de Marneffe, 2013) and distinguishing semantic similarity from referential compatibility

(Kruszewski and Baroni, 2015).

7 Acknowledgments

This research was supported by the ERC 2011 Starting Independent Research Grant n. 283554 (COMPOSES).

References

Heike Adel and Hinrich Schütze. 2014. Using mined coreference chains as a resource for a semantic task. In *Proceedings of EMNLP*, pages 1447–1452, Doha, Qatar.

Marco Baroni, Raffaella Bernardi, and Roberto Zamparelli. 2014. Frege in space: A program for compositional distributional semantics. *Linguistic Issues in Language Technology*, 9(6):5–110.

Elia Bruni, Nam Khanh Tran, and Marco Baroni. 2014. Multimodal distributional semantics. *Journal of Artificial Intelligence Research*, 49:1–47.

Henriette de Swart. 2010. *Expression and Interpretation of Negation: an OT Typology*. Springer, Dordrecht, Netherlands.

Manaal Faruqui, Jesse Dodge, Sujay Jauhar, Chris Dyer, Ed Hovy, and Noah Smith. 2015. Retrofitting word vectors to semantic lexicons. In *Proceedings of NAACL*, Denver, CO. In press.

Daniel Fried and Kevin Duh. 2015. Incorporating both distributional and relational semantics in word representations. In *Proceedings of ICLR Workshop Track*, San Diego, CA. Published online: `http://www.iclr.cc/doku.php?id=iclr2015:main#accepted_papers`.

Karl Moritz Hermann, Edward Grefenstette, and Phil Blunsom. 2013. "Not not bad" is not "bad": A distributional account of negation. In *Proceedings of ACL Workshop on Continuous Vector Space Models and their Compositionality*, pages 74–82, Sofia, Bulgaria.

Felix Hill, KyungHyun Cho, Sebastien Jean, Coline Devin, and Yoshua Bengio. 2014a. Not all neural embeddings are born equal. *arXiv preprint arXiv:1410.0718*.

Felix Hill, Roi Reichart, and Anna Korhonen. 2014b. Simlex-999: Evaluating semantic models with (genuine) similarity estimation. *arXiv preprint arXiv:1408.3456*.

Joo-Kyung Kim and Marie-Catherine de Marneffe. 2013. Deriving adjectival scales from continuous space word representations. In *Proceedings of EMNLP*, pages 1625–1630, Seattle, WA.

Germán Kruszewski and Marco Baroni. 2015. So similar and yet incompatible: Toward automated identification of semantically compatible words. In *Proceedings of NAACL*, pages 64–969, Denver, CO.

Angeliki Lazaridou, Nghia The Pham, and Marco Baroni. 2015. Combining language and vision with a multimodal skip-gram model. In *Proceedings of NAACL*, pages 153–163, Denver, CO.

Omer Levy, Steffen Remus, Chris Biemann, , and Ido Dagan. 2015. Do supervised distributional methods really learn lexical inference relations? In *Proceedings of NAACL*, Denver, CO. In press.

Tomas Mikolov, Wen-tau Yih, and Geoffrey Zweig. 2013. Linguistic regularities in continuous space word representations. In *Proceedings of NAACL*, pages 746–751, Atlanta, Georgia.

George A Miller. 1995. Wordnet: a lexical database for english. *Communications of the ACM*, 38(11):39–41.

Saif Mohammad, Bonnie Dorr, Graeme Hirst, and Peter Turney. 2013. Computing lexical contrast. *Computational Linguistics*, 39(3):555–590.

Masataka Ono, Makoto Miwa, and Yutaka Sasaki. 2015. Word embedding-based antonym detection using thesauri and distributional information. In *Proceedings of the 2015 Conference of the North American Chapter of the Association for Computational Linguistics: Human Language Technologies*, pages 984–989, Denver, Colorado, May–June. Association for Computational Linguistics.

Anne Preller and Mehrnoosh Sadrzadeh. 2011. Bell states and negative sentences in the distributed model of meaning. *Electr. Notes Theor. Comput. Sci.*, 270(2):141–153.

Enrico Santus, Qin Lu, Alessandro Lenci, and Chu-Ren Huang. 2014. Taking antonymy mask off in vector space. In *Proceedings of PACLIC*, pages 135–144, Phuket,Thailand.

Sabine Schulte im Walde and Maximilian Köper. 2013. Pattern-based distinction of paradigmatic relations for German nouns, verbs, adjectives. In *Proceedings of GSCL*, pages 184–198, Darmstadt, Germany.

Peter Turney and Patrick Pantel. 2010. From frequency to meaning: Vector space models of semantics. *Journal of Artificial Intelligence Research*, 37:141–188.

Peter Turney. 2008. A uniform approach to analogies, synonyms, antonyms and associations. In *Proceedings of COLING*, pages 905–912, Manchester, UK.

Chang Xu, Yalong Bai, Jiang Bian, Bin Gao, Gang Wang, Xiaoguang Liu, and Tie-Yan Liu. 2014. RC-NET: A general framework for incorporating knowledge into word representations. In *Proceedings of CIKM*, pages 1219–1228, Shanghai, China.

Wen-tau Yih, Geoffrey Zweig, and John Platt. 2012. Polarity inducing latent semantic analysis. In *Proceedings of EMNLP-CONLL*, pages 1212–1222.

Mo Yu and Mark Dredze. 2014. Improving lexical embeddings with semantic knowledge. In *Proceedings of ACL*, pages 545–550, Baltimore, MD.

Semi-Stacking for Semi-supervised Sentiment Classification

Shoushan Li[†‡], **Lei Huang**[†], **Jingjing Wang**[†], **Guodong Zhou**[†*]

[†]Natural Language Processing Lab, Soochow University, China

[‡] Collaborative Innovation Center of Novel Software Technology and Industrialization

{shoushan.li, lei.huang2013, djingwang}@gmail.com, gdzhou@suda.edu.cn

Abstract

In this paper, we address semi-supervised sentiment learning via semi-stacking, which integrates two or more semi-supervised learning algorithms from an ensemble learning perspective. Specifically, we apply *meta*-learning to predict the unlabeled data given the outputs from the member algorithms and propose *N*-fold cross validation to guarantee a suitable size of the data for training the *meta*-classifier. Evaluation on four domains shows that such a semi-stacking strategy performs consistently better than its member algorithms.

1 Introduction

The past decade has witnessed a huge exploding interest in sentiment analysis from the natural language processing and data mining communities due to its inherent challenges and wide applications (Pang et al., 2008; Liu, 2012). One fundamental task in sentiment analysis is sentiment classification, which aims to determine the sentimental orientation a piece of text expresses (Pang et al., 2002). For instance, the sentence "*I absolutely love this product.*" is supposed to be determined as a *positive* expression in sentimental orientation.

While early studies focus on supervised learning, where only labeled data are required to train the classification model (Pang et al., 2002), recent studies devote more and more to reduce the heavy dependence on the large amount of labeled data by exploiting semi-supervised learning approaches, such as co-training (Wan, 2009; Li et al., 2011), label propagation (Sindhwani and Melville, 2008), and deep learning (Zhou et al., 2013), to sentiment classification. Empirical evaluation on various domains demonstrates the effectiveness of the unlabeled data in enhancing the performance of sentiment classification. However, semi-supervised sentiment classification remains challenging due to the following reason.

Although various semi-supervised learning algorithms are now available and have been shown to be successful in exploiting unlabeled data to improve the performance in sentiment classification, each algorithm has its own characteristic with different pros and cons. It is rather difficult to tell which performs best in general. Therefore, it remains difficult to pick a suitable algorithm for a specific domain. For example, as shown in Li et al. (2013), the co-training algorithm with personal and impersonal views yields better performances in two product domains: Book and Kitchen, while the label propagation algorithm yields better performances in other two product domains: DVD and Electronic.

In this paper, we overcome the above challenge above by combining two or more algorithms instead of picking one of them to perform semi-supervised learning. The basic idea of our algorithm ensemble approach is to apply *meta*-learning to re-predict the labels of the unlabeled data after obtaining their results from the member algorithms. First, a small portion of labeled samples in the initial labeled data, namely *meta*-samples, are picked as unlabeled samples and added into the initial unlabeled data to form a new unlabeled data. Second, we use the remaining labeled data as the new labeled data to perform semi-supervised learning with each member algorithm. Third, we collect the *meta*-samples' probability results from all member algorithms to train a *meta*-learning classifier (called *meta*-classifier). Forth and finally, we utilize the *meta*-classifier to re-predict the unlabeled samples as new automatically-labeled samples. Due to the limited number of labeled data in semi-supervised learning, we use *N*-fold cross validation to obtain more *meta*-samples for better learning the *meta*-classifier. In principle, the above ensemble learning approach could be

* Corresponding author

Proceedings of the 53rd Annual Meeting of the Association for Computational Linguistics and the 7th International Joint Conference on Natural Language Processing (Short Papers), pages 27–31,
Beijing, China, July 26-31, 2015. ©2015 Association for Computational Linguistics

seen as an extension of the famous stacking approach (Džeroski and Ženko, 2004) to semi-supervised learning. For convenience, we call it semi-stacking.

The remainder of this paper is organized as follows. Section 2 overviews the related work on semi-supervised sentiment classification. Section 3 proposes our semi-stacking strategy to semi-supervised sentiment classification. Section 4 proposes the data filtering approach to filter low-confident unlabeled samples. Section 5 evaluates our approach with a benchmark dataset. Finally, Section 6 gives the conclusion and future work.

2 Related Work

Early studies on sentiment classification mainly focus on supervised learning methods with algorithm designing and feature engineering (Pang et al., 2002; Cui et al., 2006; Riloff et al., 2006; Li et al., 2009). Recently, most studies on sentiment classification aim to improve the performance by exploiting unlabeled data in two main aspects: semi-supervised learning (Dasgupta and Ng, 2009; Wan, 2009; Li et al., 2010) and cross-domain learning (Blitzer et al. 2007; He et al. 2011; Li et al., 2013). Specifically, existing approaches to semi-supervised sentiment classification could be categorized into two main groups: bootstrapping-style and graph-based.

As for bootstrapping-style approaches, Wan (2009) considers two different languages as two views and applies co-training to conduct semi-supervised sentiment classification. Similarly, Li et al. (2010) propose two views, named personal and impersonal views, and apply co-training to use unlabeled data in a monolingual corpus. More recently, Gao et al. (2014) propose a feature subspace-based self-training to semi-supervised sentiment classification. Empirical evaluation demonstrates that subspace-based self-training outperforms co-training with personal and impersonal views.

As for graph-based approaches, Sindhwani and Melville (2008) first construct a document-word bipartite graph to describe the relationship among the labeled and unlabeled samples and then apply label propagation to get the labels of the unlabeled samples.

Unlike above studies, our research on semi-supervised sentiment classification does not merely focus on one single semi-supervised learning algorithm but on two or more semi-supervised learning algorithms with ensemble learning. To the best of our knowledge, this is the first attempt to combine two or more semi-supervised learning algorithms in semi-supervised sentiment classification.

3 Semi-Stacking for Semi-supervised Sentiment Classification

In semi-supervised sentiment classification, the learning algorithm aims to learn a classifier from a small scale of labeled samples, named initial labeled data, with a large number of unlabeled samples. In the sequel, we refer the labeled data as $L=\{(x_i,y_i)\}_{i=1}^{n_L}$ where $x_i \in \mathbf{R}^d$ is the d dimensional input vector, and y_i is its output label. The unlabeled data in the target domain is denoted as $U=\{(x_k)\}_{k=1}^{n_U}$. Suppose l^{semi} is a semi-supervised learning algorithm. The inputs of l^{semi} are L and U, and the output is $U'=\{(x_k,y_k)\}_{k=1}^{n_U}$ which denotes the unlabeled data with automatically assigned labels. Besides the labeled results, it is always possible to obtain the probability results, denoted as $P^{U'}$, which contains the posterior probabilities belonging to the positive and negative categories of each unlabeled sample, i.e., $< p(pos \mid x_k), p(neg \mid x_k) >$. For clarity, some important symbols are listed in Table 1.

Table 1: Symbol definition

Symbol	Definition
L	Labeled data
U	Unlabeled data
U'	Unlabeled data with automatically assigned labels
$P^{U'}$	The probability result of unlabeled data
l^{super}	A supervised learning algorithm
l^{semi}	A semi-supervised learning algorithm
c_{meta}	The *meta*-classifier obtained from *meta*-learning
c_{test}	The test classifier for classifying the test data

3.1 Framework Overview

In our approach, two member semi-supervised learning algorithm are involved, namely, l_1^{semi} and l_2^{semi} respectively, and the objective is to leverage both of them to get a better-performed semi-supervised learning algorithm. Our basic idea is to apply *meta*-learning to re-predict the labels of the unlabeled data given the outputs from the member algorithms. Figure 1 shows the framework of our implementation of the basic idea. The core component in semi-stacking is the *meta*-classifier learned from the *meta*-learning process, i.e., c_{meta}. This classifier aims to make a better prediction on the unlabeled samples by combining two different probability results from the two member algorithms.

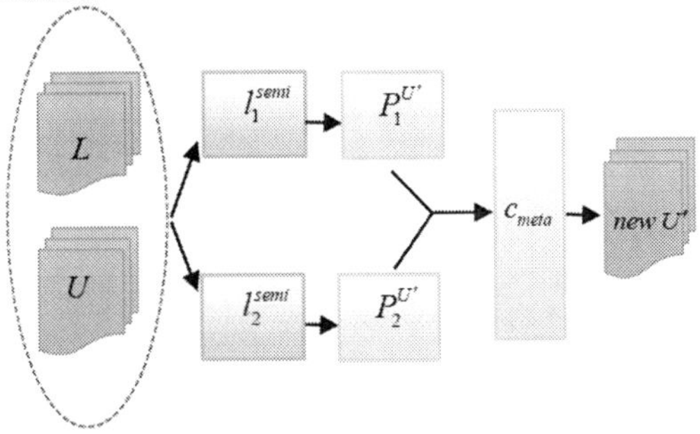

Figure 1: The framework of *semi-stacking*

3.2 *Meta*-learning

As shown above, *meta*-classifier is the core component in *semi-stacking*, trained through the *meta*-learning process. Here, *meta*- means the learning samples are not represented by traditional descriptive features, e.g., bag-of-words features, but by the result features generated from member algorithms. In our approach, the learning samples in *meta*-learning are represented by the posterior probabilities of the unlabeled samples belonging to the *positive* and *negative* categories from member algorithms, i.e.,

$$x^{meta} = < p_1(pos \mid x_k), p_1(neg \mid x_k), p_2(pos \mid x_k), p_2(neg \mid x_k) > \quad (1)$$

Where $p_1(pos \mid x_k)$ and $p_1(neg \mid x_k)$ are the posterior probabilities from the first semi-supervised learning algorithm while $p_2(pos \mid x_k)$ and $p_2(neg \mid x_k)$ are the posterior probabilities from the second semi-supervised learning algorithm.

The framework of the *meta*-learning process is shown in Figure 2. In detail, we first split the initial labeled data into two partitions, L_{new} and L_{un} where L_{new} is used as the new initial labeled data while L_{un} is merged into the unlabeled data U to form a new set of unlabeled data $L_{un}+U$. Then, two semi-supervised algorithms are performed with the labeled data L_{new} and the unlabeled data $L_{un}+U$. Third and finally, the probability results of L_{un}, together with their real labels are used as *meta*-learning samples to train the *meta*-classifier. The feature representation of each *meta*-sample is defined in Formula (1).

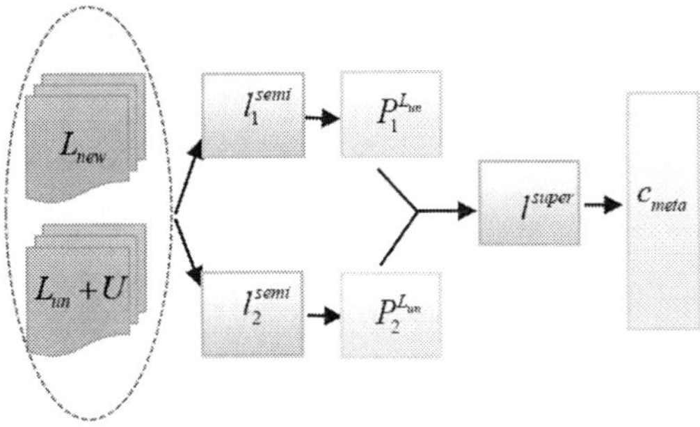

Figure 2: The framework of *meta*-learning

3.3 *Meta*-learning with *N*-fold Cross Validation

Input: Labeled data L, Unlabeled data U

Output: The *meta*-classifier c_{meta}

Procedure:

(a) Initialize the *meta*-sample set $S_{meta} = \varnothing$

(b) Split L into N folds, i.e., $L = L_1 + L_2 + \ldots L_N$

(c) For i in $1:N$:

c1) $L_{new} = L - L_i$, $L_{un} = L_i$

c2) Perform l_1^{semi} on L_{new} and $L_{un}+U$

c3) Perform l_2^{semi} on L_{new} and $L_{un}+U$

c4) Generate the *meta*-samples, S_{meta}^{i}, from the probability results of L_{un} in the above two steps.

c5) $S_{meta} = S_{meta} + S_{meta}^{i}$

(d) Train the *meta*-classifier c_{meta} with S_{meta} and l^{super}

Figure 3: The algorithm description of meta-learning with *N*-fold cross validation

One problem of *meta*-learning is that the data size of L_{un} might be too small to learn a good meta-classifier. To better use the labeled samples in the initial labeled data, we employ *N*-fold cross validation to generate more meta- samples. Specifically, we first split L into N folds. Then, we select one of them as L_{un} and consider the others as L_{new} and generate the *meta*-learning samples as described in Section 3.2; Third and finally, we repeat the above step $N-1$ times by selecting a different fold as L_{un} in each time. In this way, we can obtain the *meta*-learning samples with the same size as the initial labeled data. Figure 3 presents the algorithm description of *meta*-learning with *N*-fold cross validation. In our implementation, we set N to be 10.

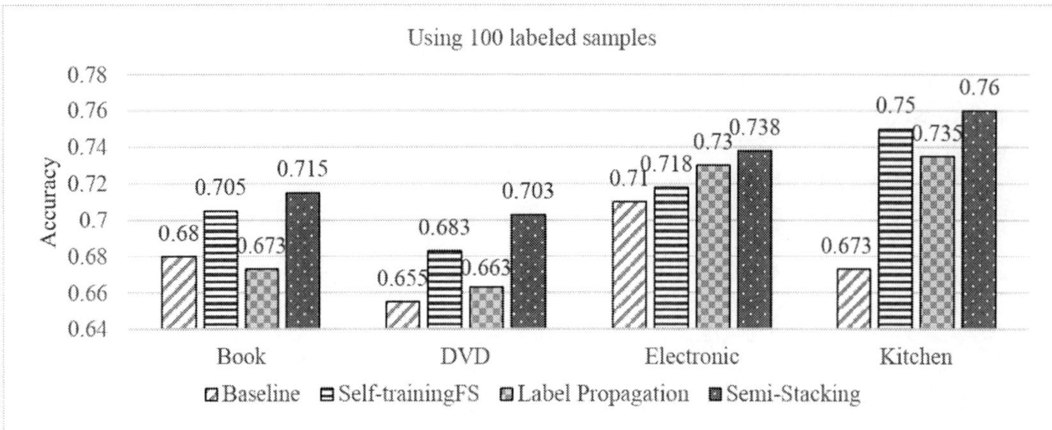

Figure 4: Performance comparison of baseline and three semi-supervised learning approaches

4 Experimentation

Dataset: The dataset contains product reviews from four different domains: Book, DVD, Electronics and Kitchen appliances (Blitzer et al., 2007), each of which contains 1000 *positive* and 1000 *negative* labeled reviews. We randomly select 100 instances as labeled data, 400 instances are used as test data and remaining 1500 instances as unlabeled data.

Features: Each review text is treated as a bag-of-words and transformed into binary vectors encoding the presence or absence of word unigrams and bigrams.

Supervised learning algorithm: The maximum entropy (ME) classifier implemented with the public tool, Mallet Toolkits (http://mallet.cs.umass.edu/), where probability outputs are provided.

Semi-supervised learning algorithms: (1) The first member algorithm is called self-trainingFS, proposed by Gao et al. (2014). This approach can be seen as a special case of self-training. Different from the traditional self-training, self-trainingFS use the feature-subspace classifier to make the prediction on the unlabeled samples instead of using the whole-space classifier. In our implementation, we use four random feature subspaces. (2) The second member algorithm is called label propagation, a graph-based semi-supervised learning approach, proposed by Zhu and Ghahramani (2002). In our implementation, the document-word bipartite graph is adopted to build the document-document graph (Sindhwani and Melville, 2008).

Significance testing: We perform *t*-test to evaluate the significance of the performance difference between two systems with different approaches (Yang and Liu, 1999)

Figure 4 compares the performances of the baseline approach and three semi-supervised learning approaches. Here, the baseline approach is the supervised learning approach by using only the initial labeled data (i.e. no unlabeled data is used). From the figure, we can see that both Self-trainingFS and label propagation are successful in exploiting unlabeled data to improve the performances. Self-trainingFS outperforms label propagation in three domains including Book, DVD, and Kitchen but it performs worse in Electronic. Our approach (semi-stacking) performs much better than baseline with an impressive improvement of 4.95% on average. Compared to the two member algorithms, semi-stacking always yield a better performance, although the improvement over the better-performed member algorithm is slight, only around 1%-2%. Significance test shows that our approach performs significantly better than worse-performed member algorithm (p-value<0.01) in all domains and it also performs significantly better than better-performed member algorithm (p-value<0.05) in three domains, i.e., Book, DVD, and Kitchen.

5 Conclusion

In this paper, we present a novel ensemble learning approach named semi-stacking to semi-supervised sentiment classification. Semi-stacking is implemented by re-predicting the labels of the unlabeled samples with *meta*-learning after two or more member semi-supervised learning approaches have been performed. Experimental evaluation in four domains demonstrates that semi-stacking outperforms both member algorithms.

Acknowledgments

This research work has been partially supported by three NSFC grants, No.61273320, No.61375073, No.61331011, and Collaborative Innovation Center of Novel Software Technology and Industrialization.

References

Blitzer J., M. Dredze and F. Pereira. 2007. Biographies, Bollywood, Boom-boxes and Blenders: Domain Adaptation for Sentiment Classification. In *Proceedings of ACL-07*, pp.440-447.

Blum A. and T. Mitchell. 1998. Combining Labeled and Unlabeled Data with Co-training. In *Proceedings of COLT-98*,pp. 92-100.

Cui H., V. Mittal and M. Datar. 2006. Comparative Experiments on Sentiment Classification for Online Product Reviews. In *Proceedings of AAAI-06*, pp.1265-1270.

Dasgupta S. and V. Ng. 2009. Mine the Easy, Classify the Hard: A Semi-Supervised Approach to Automatic Sentiment Classification. In *Proceedings of ACL-IJCNLP-09*, pp.701-709, 2009.

Džeroski S. and B. Ženko. 2004. Is Combining Classifiers with Stacking Better than Selecting the Best One? *Machine Learning*, vol.54(3), pp.255-273, 2004.

Gao W., S. Li, Y. Xue, M. Wang, and G. Zhou. 2014. Semi-supervised Sentiment Classification with Self-training on Feature Subspaces. In *Proceedings of CLSW-14*, pp.231-239.

He Y., C. Lin and H. Alani. 2011. Automatically Extracting Polarity-Bearing Topics for Cross-Domain Sentiment Classification. In *Proceedings of ACL-11*, pp.123-131.

Li S., C. Huang, G. Zhou and S. Lee. 2010. Employing Personal/Impersonal Views in Supervised and Semi-supervised Sentiment Classification. In *Proceedings of ACL-10*, pp.414-423.

Li S., R. Xia, C. Zong, and C. Huang. 2009. A Framework of Feature Selection Methods for Text Categorization. In *Proceedings of ACL-IJCNLP-09*, pp.692-700.

Li S., Y. Xue, Z. Wang, and G. Zhou. 2013. Active Learning for Cross-Domain Sentiment Classification. In *Proceedings of IJCAI-13*, pp.2127-2133.

Li S., Z. Wang, G. Zhou and S. Lee. 2011. Semi-supervised Learning for Imbalanced Sentiment Classification. In *Proceedings of IJCAI-11*, pp.1826-1831.

Liu B. 2012. *Sentiment Analysis and Opinion Mining (Introduction and Survey)*. Morgan & Claypool Publishers, May 2012.

Pang B. and L. Lee. 2008. Opinion Mining and Sentiment Analysis: Foundations and Trends. *Information Retrieval*, vol.2(12), pp.1-135.

Pang B., L. Lee, and S. Vaithyanathan. 2002. Thumbs up? Sentiment Classification using Machine Learning Techniques. In *Proceedings of EMNLP-02*, pp.79-86.

Riloff E., S. Patwardhan and J. Wiebe. 2006. Feature Subsumption for Opinion Analysis. In *Proceedings of EMNLP-06*, pp.440-448.

Sindhwani V. and P. Melville. 2008. Document-Word Co-Regularization for Semi-supervised Sentiment Analysis. In *Proceedings of ICDM-08*, pp.1025-1030.

Wan X. 2009. Co-Training for Cross-Lingual Sentiment Classification. In *Proceedings of ACL-IJCNLP-09*, pp.235-243.

Yang Y. and X. Liu. 1999. A Re-Examination of Text Categorization Methods. In *Proceedings of SIGIR-99*.

Zhu X. and Z. Ghahramani. 2002. Learning from Labeled and Unlabeled Data with Label Propagation. *CMU CALD Technical Report*. CMU-CALD-02-107.

Deep Markov Neural Network for Sequential Data Classification

Min Yang[1] **Wenting Tu**[1] **Wenpeng Yin**[2] **Ziyu Lu**[1]
[1]Department of Computer Science, The University of Hong Kong, Hong Kong
{myang,wttu,zylu}@cs.hku.hk
[2]Center for Information and Language Processing, University of Munich, Germany
wenpeng@cis.lmu.de

Abstract

We present a general framework for incorporating sequential data and arbitrary features into language modeling. The general framework consists of two parts: a hidden Markov component and a recursive neural network component. We demonstrate the effectiveness of our model by applying it to a specific application: predicting topics and sentiments in dialogues. Experiments on real data demonstrate that our method is substantially more accurate than previous methods.

1 Introduction

Processing sequential data is a significant research challenge for natural language processing. In the past decades, numerous studies have been conducted on modeling sequential data. Hidden Markov Models (HMMs) and its variants are representative statistical models of sequential data for the purposes of classification, segmentation, and clustering (Rabiner, 1989). For most aforementioned methods, only the dependencies between consecutive hidden states are modeled. In natural language processing, however, we find there are dependencies locally and at a distance. Conservatively using the most recent history to perform prediction yields overfitting to short-term trends and missing important long-term effects. Thus, it is crucial to explore in depth to capture long-term temporal dynamics in language use.

Numerous real world learning problems are best characterized by interactions between multiple causes or factors. Taking sentiment analysis for dialogues as an example, the topic of the document and the author's identity are both valuable for mining user's opinions in the conversation. Specifically, each participant in the dialogue usually has specific sentiment polarities towards different topics. However, most existing sequential data modeling methods are not capable of incorporating the information from both the topic and the author's identity. More generally, there is no sufficiently flexible sequential model that allows incorporating an arbitrary set of features.

In this paper, we present a Deep Markov Neural Network (DMNN) for incorporating sequential data and arbitrary features into language modeling. Our method learns from general sequential observations. It is also capable of taking the ordering of words into account, and collecting information from arbitrary features associated with the context. Comparing to traditional HMM-based method, it explores deeply into the structure of sentences, and is more flexible in taking external features into account. On the other hand, it doesn't suffer from the training difficulties of recurrent neural networks, such as the vanishing gradient problem.

The general framework consists of two parts: a hidden Markov component and a neural network component. In the training phase, the hidden Markov model is trained on the sequential observation, resulting in transition probabilities and hidden states at each time step. Then, the neural network is trained, taking words, features and hidden state at the previous time step as input, to predict the hidden states at the present time step. The procedure is reversed in the testing phase: the neural network predicts the hidden states using words and features, then the hidden Markov model predicts the observation using hidden states.

A key insight of our method is to use hidden states as an intermediate representation, as a bridge to connect sentences and observations. By using hidden states, we can deal with arbitrary observation, without worrying about the issue of discretization and normalization. Hidden states are robust with respect to the random noise in the observation. Unlike recurrent neural net-

Proceedings of the 53rd Annual Meeting of the Association for Computational Linguistics and the 7th International Joint Conference on Natural Language Processing (Short Papers), pages 32–37,
Beijing, China, July 26-31, 2015.

work which connects networks between consecutive time steps, the recursive neural network in our framework connects to the previous time step by using its hidden states. In the training phase, since hidden states are inferred by the hidden Markov model, the training of recursive neural networks at each time step can be performed separately, preventing the difficulty of learning an extremely deep neural network.

We demonstrate the effectiveness of our model by applying it to a specific application: predicting topics and sentiments in dialogues. In this example, the sequential observation includes topics and sentiments. The feature includes the identity of the author. Experiments on real data demonstrate that our method is substantially more accurate than previous methods.

2 Related work

Modeling sequential data is an active research field (Lewis and Gale, 1994; Jain et al., 2000; Rabiner, 1989; Baldi and Brunak, 2001; Kum et al., 2005). The paper proposed by Kum et al. (2005) describes most of the existing techniques for sequential data modeling. Hidden Markov Models (HMMs) is one of the most successful models for sequential data that is best known for speech recognition (Rabiner, 1989). Recently, HMMs have been applied to a variety of applications outside of speech recognition, such as handwriting recognition (Nag et al., 1986; Kundu and Bahl, 1988) and fault-detection (Smyth, 1994). The variants and extensions of HMMs also include language models (Guyon and Pereira, 1995) and econometrics (Garcia and Perron, 1996).

In order to properly capture more complex linguistic phenomena, a variety of neural networks have been proposed, such as neural probabilistic language model (Bengio et al., 2006), recurrent neural network (Mikolov et al., 2010) and recursive neural tensor network (Socher et al., 2013). As opposed to the work that only focuses on the context of the sequential data, some studies have been proposed to incorporate more general features associated with the context. Ghahramani and Jordan (1997) proposes a factorial HMMs method and it has been successfully utilized in natural language processing (Duh, 2005), computer vision (Wang and Ji, 2005) and speech processing (Gael et al., 2009). However, exact inference and parameter estimation in factorial HMMs is intractable, thus the learning algorithm is difficult to implement and is limited to the study of real-valued data sets.

3 The DMNN Model

In this section, we describe our general framework for incorporating sequential data and an arbitrary set of features into language modeling.

3.1 Generative model

Given a time sequence $t = 1, 2, 3, \ldots, n$, we associate each time slice with an observation (s_t, u_t) and a state label y_t. Here, s_t represents the sentence at time t, and u_t represents additional features. Additional features may include the author of the sentence, the bag-of-word features and other semantic features. The label y_t is the item that we want to predict. It might be the topic of the sentence, or the sentiment of the author.

Given tuples (s_t, u_t, y_t), it is natural to build a supervised classification model to predict y_t. Recurrent neural networks have been shown effective in modeling temporal NLP data. However, due to the depth of the time sequence, training a single RNN is difficult. When the time sequence length n is large, the RNN model suffers from many practical problems, including the vanishing gradient issue which makes the training process inefficient.

We propose a Deep Markov Neural Network (DMNN) model. The DMNN model introduces a hidden state variable H_t for each time slice. It serves as an intermediate layer connecting the label y_t and the observation (s_t, u_t). These hidden variables disentangle the correlation between neural networks for each sentence, but preserving time series dependence. The time series dependence is modeled by a Markov chain. In particular, we assume that there is a labeling matrix L such that

$$P(y_t = i | H_t = j) = L_{ij} \tag{1}$$

and a transition matrix T such that

$$P(H_{t+1} = i | H_t = j) = T_{ij} \tag{2}$$

These two equations establish the relation between the hidden state and the labels. On the other hand, we use a neural network model M to model the relation between the hidden states and the observations. The neural network model takes (H_{t-1}, s_t, u_t) as input, and predict H_t as its output. In particular, we use a logistic model to define the probability:

$$P(H_t = i | H_{t-1}, s_t, u_t) \propto \qquad (3)$$
$$\exp(\langle w_h^i, \phi(H_{t-1})\rangle + \langle w_u^i, \varphi(u_t)\rangle + \langle w_s^i N(s_t) + b\rangle)$$

The vectors w_h, w_u, w_s are linear combination coefficients to be estimated. The functions ϕ, φ and function N turn H_{t-1}, u_t and s_t into featurized vectors. Among these functions, we recommend choosing $\phi(H_{t-1})$ to be a binary vector whose H_{t-1}-th coordinate is one and all other coordinates are zeros. Both function φ and function N are modeled by deep neural networks.

Since the sentence s_t has varied lengths and distinct structures, choosing an appropriate neural network to extract the sentence-level feature is a challenge task. In this paper, we choose N to be the recursive autoencoder (Socher et al., 2011a), which explicitly takes structure of the sentence into account. The network for defining φ can be a standard fully connect neural network.

3.2 Estimating Model Parameters

There are two sets of parameters to be estimated: the parameters L, T for the Markov chain model, and the parameters $w_h, w_u, w_s, \varphi, N$ for the deep neural networks. The training is performed in two phases. In the first phase, the hidden states $\{H_t\}$ are estimated based on the labels $\{y_t\}$. The emission matrix L and the transition matrix T are estimated at the same time. This step can be done by using the Baum-Welch algorithm (Baum et al., 1970; Baum, 1972) for learning hidden Markov models.

When the hidden states $\{H_t\}$ are obtained, the second phase estimates the remaining parameters for the neural network model in a supervised prediction problem. First, we use available sentences to train the structure of the recursive neural network N. This step can be done without using other information besides $\{s_t\}$. After the structure of N is given, the remaining task is to train a supervised prediction model to predict the hidden state H_t for each time slice. In this final step, the parameters to be estimated are $w_h, w_u, w_s$and the weight coefficients in neural networks N and φ. By maximizing the log-likelihood of the prediction, all model parameters can be estimated by stochastic gradient descent.

3.3 Prediction

The prediction procedure is a reverse of the training procedure. For prediction, we only have the sentence s_t and the additional feature u_t. By equation (3), we use (s_1, u_1) to predict H_1, then use (H_1, s_2, u_2) to predict H_2. This procedure continues until we have reached H_n. Note that each H_t is a random variable. Equation (3) yields

$$P(H_t = i|s,u) = \sum_j P(H_t = i|s_t, u_t, H_{t-1} = j) \cdot P(H_{t-1} = j|s,u) \qquad (4)$$

This recursive formula suggests inferring the probability distribution $P(H_t|s,u)$ one by one, starting from $t = 1$ and terminate at $t = n$. After $P(H_t|s,u)$ is available, we can infer the probability distribution of y_t as

$$P(y_t = i|s,u) = \sum_j P(y_t = i|H_t = j)P(H_t = j|s,u) = \sum_j L_{i,j} P(H_t = j|s,u) \qquad (5)$$

which gives the prediction for the label of interest.

3.4 Application: Sentiment analysis in conversation

Sentiment analysis for dialogues is a typical sequential data modeling problem.The sentiments and topics expressed in a conversation affect the interaction between dialogue participants (Suin Kim, 2012). For example, given a user say that "I have had a high fever for 3 days", the user may write back positive-sentiment response like "I hope you feel better soon", or it could be negative-sentiment content when the response is "Sorry, but you cannot join us today" (Hasegawa et al., 2013). Incorporating the session's sequential information into sentiment analysis may improve the prediction accuracy. Meanwhile, each participate in the dialogue usually has specific sentiment polarities towards different topics.

In this paper, the sequential labels available to the framework include topics and sentiments. In the training dataset, topics are obtained by running an LDA model, while the sentiment labels are manually labeled. The feature includes the identity of the author. In the training phase, the hidden Markov model is trained on the sequential labels, resulting in transition probabilities and hidden states at each time step. Then, the recursive autoencoders (Socher et al., 2011a) is trained, taking words, the identity of the author and hidden state at the previous time step as input, to predict the hidden states at the present time step. The procedure is reversed in the testing phase: the neural network predicts the hidden states using words and the identity of the author, then the hidden Markov model predicts the observation using hidden states.

4 Experiments

To evaluate our model, we conduct experiments for sentiment analysis in conversations.

4.1 Datasets

We conduct experiments on both English and Chinese datasets. The detailed properties of the datasets are described as follow.

Twitter conversation (Twitter): The original dataset is a collection of about 1.3 million conversations drawn from Twitter by Ritter et al. (2010). Each conversation contains between 2 and 243 posts. In our experiments, we filter the data by keeping only the conversations of five or more tweets. This results in 64,068 conversations containing 542,866 tweets.

Sina Weibo conversation (Sina): since there is no authoritative publicly available Chinese short-text conversation corpus, we write a web crawler to grab tweets from Sina Weibo, which is the most popular Twitter-like microblogging website in China[1]. Following the strategy used in (Ritter et al., 2010), we crawled Sina Weibo for a 3 months period from September 2013 to November 2013. Filtering the conversations that contain less than five posts, we get a Chinese conversation corpus with 5,921 conversations containing 37,282 tweets.

For both datasets, we set the ground truth of sentiment classification of tweets by using human annotation. Specifically, we randomly select 1000 conversations from each datasets, and then invite three researchers who work on natural language processing to label sentiment tag of each tweet (i.e., positive, negative or neutral) manually. From 3 responses for each tweet, we measure the agreement as the number of people who submitted the same response. We measure the performance of our framework using the tweets that satisfy at least 2 out of 3 agreement.

For both datasets, data preprocessing is performed. The words about time, numeral words, pronoun and punctuation are removed as they are unrelated to the sentiment analysis task.

[1]http://weibo.com

Dataset	SVM	NBSVM	RAE	Mesnil's	DMNN
Twitter	0.572	0.624	0.639	0.650	0.682
Sina	0.548	0.612	0.598	0.626	0.652

Table 1: Three-way classification accuracy

4.2 Baseline methods

To evaluate the effectiveness of our framework on the application of sentiment analysis, we compare our approach with several baseline methods, which we describe below:

SVM: Support Vector Machine is widely-used baseline method to build sentiment classifiers (Pang et al., 2002). In our experiment, 5000 words with greatest information gain are chosen as features, and we use the LibLinear[2] to implement SVM.

NBSVM: This is a state-of-the-art performer on many sentiment classification datasets (Wang and Manning, 2012). The model is run using the publicly available code[3].

RAE: Recursive Autoencoder (Socher et al., 2011b) has been proven effective in many sentiment analysis tasks by learning compositionality automatically. The RAE model is run using the publicly available code[4] and we follow the same setting as in (Socher et al., 2011b).

Mesnil's method: This method is proposed in (Mesnil et al., 2014), which achieves the strongest results on movie reviews recently. It is a ensemble of the generative technique and the discriminative technique. We run this algorithm with publicly available code [5].

4.3 Experiment results

In our HMMs component, the number of hidden states is 80. We randomly initialize the matrix of state transition probabilities and the initial state distribution between 0 and 1. The emission probabilities are determined by Gaussian distributions. In our recursive autoencoders component, we represent each words using 100-dimensional vectors. The hyperparameter used for weighing reconstruction and cross-entropy error is 0.1.

For each dataset, we use 800 conversations as the training data and the remaining are used for testing. We summarize the experiment results in

[2]http://www.csie.ntu.edu.tw/~cjlin/liblinear/

[3]http://nlp.stanford.edu/~sidaw

[4]https://github.com/sancha/jrae/zipball/stable

[5]https://github.com/mesnilgr/iclr15.

Table 1. According to Table 1, the proposed approach significantly and consistently outperforms other methods on both datasets. This verifies the effectiveness of the proposed approach. For example, the overall accuracy of our algorithm is 3.2% higher than Mesnil's method and 11.0% higher than SVM on Twitter conversations dataset. For the Sina Weibo dataset, we observe similar results. The advantage of our model comes from its capability of exploring sequential information and incorporating an arbitrary number of factors of the corpus.

5 Conclusion and Future Work

In this paper, we present a general framework for incorporating sequential data into language modeling. We demonstrate the effectiveness of our method by applying it to a specific application: predicting topics and sentiments in dialogues. Experiments on real data demonstrate that our method is substantially more accurate than previous methods.

References

Pierre Baldi and Søren Brunak. 2001. *Bioinformatics: the machine learning approach*. MIT press.

Leonard E Baum, Ted Petrie, George Soules, and Norman Weiss. 1970. A maximization technique occurring in the statistical analysis of probabilistic functions of markov chains. *The annals of mathematical statistics*, pages 164–171.

Leonard E Baum. 1972. An equality and associated maximization technique in statistical estimation for probabilistic functions of markov processes. *Inequalities*, 3:1–8.

Yoshua Bengio, Holger Schwenk, Jean-Sébastien Senécal, Fréderic Morin, and Jean-Luc Gauvain. 2006. Neural probabilistic language models. In *Innovations in Machine Learning*, pages 137–186. Springer.

Kevin Duh. 2005. Jointly labeling multiple sequences: A factorial hmm approach. In *Proceedings of the ACL Student Research Workshop*, pages 19–24. Association for Computational Linguistics.

Jurgen V Gael, Yee W Teh, and Zoubin Ghahramani. 2009. The infinite factorial hidden markov model. In *Advances in Neural Information Processing Systems*, pages 1697–1704.

René Garcia and Pierre Perron. 1996. An analysis of the real interest rate under regime shifts. *The Review of Economics and Statistics*, pages 111–125.

Zoubin Ghahramani and Michael I Jordan. 1997. Factorial hidden markov models. *Machine learning*, 29(2-3):245–273.

Isabelle Guyon and Fernando Pereira. 1995. Design of a linguistic postprocessor using variable memory length markov models. In *Document Analysis and Recognition, 1995., Proceedings of the Third International Conference on*, volume 1, pages 454–457. IEEE.

Takayuki Hasegawa, Nobuhiro Kaji, Naoki Yoshinaga, and Masashi Toyoda. 2013. Predicting and eliciting addressee's emotion in online dialogue. In *ACL (1)*, pages 964–972.

Anil K Jain, Robert P. W. Duin, and Jianchang Mao. 2000. Statistical pattern recognition: A review. *Pattern Analysis and Machine Intelligence, IEEE Transactions on*, 22(1):4–37.

Hye-Chung Monica Kum, Susan Paulsen, and Wei Wang. 2005. Comparative study of sequential pattern mining models. In *Foundations of Data Mining and knowledge Discovery*, pages 43–70. Springer.

Amlan Kundu and Paramrir Bahl. 1988. Recognition of handwritten script: a hidden markov model based approach. In *Acoustics, Speech, and Signal Processing, 1988. ICASSP-88., 1988 International Conference on*, pages 928–931. IEEE.

David D Lewis and William A Gale. 1994. A sequential algorithm for training text classifiers. In *Proceedings of the 17th annual international ACM SIGIR conference on Research and development in information retrieval*, pages 3–12. Springer-Verlag New York, Inc.

Grégoire Mesnil, Marc'Aurelio Ranzato, Tomas Mikolov, and Yoshua Bengio. 2014. Ensemble of generative and discriminative techniques for sentiment analysis of movie reviews. *arXiv preprint arXiv:1412.5335*.

Tomas Mikolov, Martin Karafiát, Lukas Burget, Jan Cernockỳ, and Sanjeev Khudanpur. 2010. Recurrent neural network based language model. In *INTERSPEECH*, pages 1045–1048.

R Nag, K Wong, and Frank Fallside. 1986. Script recognition using hidden markov models. In *Acoustics, Speech, and Signal Processing, IEEE International Conference on ICASSP'86.*, volume 11, pages 2071–2074. IEEE.

Bo Pang, Lillian Lee, and Shivakumar Vaithyanathan. 2002. Thumbs up?: sentiment classification using machine learning techniques. In *Proceedings of the ACL-02 conference on Empirical methods in natural language processing-Volume 10*, pages 79–86. Association for Computational Linguistics.

Lawrence Rabiner. 1989. A tutorial on hidden markov models and selected applications in speech recognition. *Proceedings of the IEEE*, 77(2):257–286.

Alan Ritter, Colin Cherry, and Bill Dolan. 2010. Unsupervised modeling of twitter conversations.

Padhraic Smyth. 1994. Hidden markov models for fault detection in dynamic systems. *Pattern recognition*, 27(1):149–164.

Richard Socher, Jeffrey Pennington, Eric H Huang, Andrew Y Ng, and Christopher D Manning. 2011a. Semi-supervised recursive autoencoders for predicting sentiment distributions. In *Proceedings of the Conference on Empirical Methods in Natural Language Processing*, pages 151–161. Association for Computational Linguistics.

Richard Socher, Jeffrey Pennington, Eric H. Huang, Andrew Y. Ng, and Christopher D. Manning. 2011b. Semi-Supervised Recursive Autoencoders for Predicting Sentiment Distributions. In *Proceedings of the 2011 Conference on Empirical Methods in Natural Language Processing (EMNLP)*.

Richard Socher, Alex Perelygin, Jean Y Wu, Jason Chuang, Christopher D Manning, Andrew Y Ng, and Christopher Potts. 2013. Recursive deep models for semantic compositionality over a sentiment treebank. In *Proceedings of the Conference on Empirical Methods in Natural Language Processing (EMNLP)*, pages 1631–1642. Citeseer.

Alice Oh Suin Kim, JinYeong Bak. 2012. Discovering emotion influence patterns in online social network conversations. In *SIGWEB ACM Special Interest Group on Hypertext, Hypermedia, and Web*. ACM.

Peng Wang and Qiang Ji. 2005. Multi-view face tracking with factorial and switching hmm. In *Application of Computer Vision, 2005. WACV/MOTIONS'05 Volume 1. Seventh IEEE Workshops on*, volume 1, pages 401–406. IEEE.

Sida Wang and Christopher D Manning. 2012. Baselines and bigrams: Simple, good sentiment and topic classification. In *Proceedings of the 50th Annual Meeting of the Association for Computational Linguistics: Short Papers-Volume 2*, pages 90–94. Association for Computational Linguistics.

Semantic Analysis and Helpfulness Prediction of Text for Online Product Reviews

Yinfei Yang
Amazon Inc.
Seattle, WA 98121
yangyin7@ gmail.com

Yaowei Yan
Dept. of Electrical & Computer Engineering
University of Akron
Akron, OH 44325-3904
yy28@ uakron.edu

Minghui Qiu
Alibaba Group
Hangzhou, China 311121
minghuiqiu@ gmail.com

Forrest Sheng Bao
Dept. of Electrical & Computer Engineering
University of Akron
Akron, OH 44325-3904
forrest.bao@ gmail.com

Abstract

Predicting the helpfulness of product reviews is a key component of many e-commerce tasks such as review ranking and recommendation. However, previous work mixed review helpfulness prediction with those outer layer tasks. Using non-text features, it leads to less transferable models. This paper solves the problem from a new angle by hypothesizing that helpfulness is an internal property of text. Purely using review text, we isolate review helpfulness prediction from its outer layer tasks, employ two interpretable semantic features, and use human scoring of helpfulness as ground truth. Experimental results show that the two semantic features can accurately predict helpfulness scores and greatly improve the performance compared with using features previously used. Cross-category test further shows the models trained with semantic features are easier to be generalized to reviews of different product categories. The models we built are also highly interpretable and align well with human annotations.

1 Introduction

Product reviews have influential impact to online shopping as consumers tend to read product reviews when finalizing purchase decisions (Duan et al., 2008). However, a popular product usually has too many reviews for a consumer to read. Therefore, reviews need to be ranked and recommended to consumers. In particular, review helpfulness plays a critical role in review ranking and recommendation (Ghose and Ipeirotis, 2011; Mudambi and Schuff, 2010; Danescu-Niculescu-Mizil et al., 2009). The simple question "Was this review helpful to you?" increases an estimated $2.7B revenue to Amazon.com annually[1].

However, existing literature solves helpfulness prediction together with its outer layer task, the review ranking (Kim et al., 2006; O'Mahony and Smyth, 2010; Liu et al., 2008; Martin and Pu, 2014). Those studies use features not contributing to helpfulness, such as date (Liu et al., 2008), or features making the model less transferable, such as product type (Mudambi and Schuff, 2010). Models built in these ways are also difficult to interpret from linguistic perspective.

Therefore, it is necessary to isolate review helpfulness prediction from its outer layer tasks and formulate it as a new problem. In this way, models can be more robust and generalizable. Beyond predicting *whether* a review is helpful, we can also understand *why* it is helpful. In our approach, the results can also facilitate many other tasks, such as review summarization (Xiong and Litman, 2014) and sentiment extraction (Hu and Liu, 2004).

Recent NLP studies reveal the connection between text style and its properties, include readability (Agichtein et al., 2008), informativeness (Yang and Nenkova, 2014) and trustworthiness (Pasternack and Roth, 2011) of text. Hence, we hypothesize that helpfulness is also an underlying property of text.

To understand the essence of review text, we leverage existing linguistic and psychological dictionaries and represent reviews in semantic dimensions. Two semantic features that are new to solving this problem, LIWC (Pennebaker et al., 2007) and INQUIRER (Stone et al., 1962), are employed in this work. The intuition behind is that people usually embed semantic meanings, such as emotion and reasoning, into text. For example, the re-

[1] http://www.uie.com/articles/magicbehindamazon/

Proceedings of the 53rd Annual Meeting of the Association for Computational Linguistics and the 7th International Joint Conference on Natural Language Processing (Short Papers), pages 38–44,
Beijing, China, July 26-31, 2015.

view *"With the incredible brightness of the main LED, this light is visible from a distance on a sunny day at noon."* is more helpful than the review *"I ordered an iPad, I received an iPad. I got exactly what I ordered which makes me satisfied. Thanks!"* because the former mentions user experience and functionality of the product while the latter has emotional statements only.

Previous work approximates the ground truth of helpfulness from users' votes using "X of Y approach": if X of Y users think a review is helpful, then the helpfulness score of the review is the ratio X/Y. However, not many reviews have statistically abundant votes, i.e., a very small Y. Fewer than 20% of the reviews in Amazon Review Dataset (McAuley and Leskovec, 2013) have at least 5 votes (Table 1) while only 0.44% have 100+ votes. In addition, the review voting itself may be biased (Danescu-Niculescu-Mizil et al., 2009; Cao et al., 2011). Therefore, we proactively recruited human annotators and let them score the helpfulness of reviews in our dataset.

We model the problem of predicting review helpfulness score as a regression problem. Experimental results show that it is feasible to use text-only features to accurately predict helpfulness scores. The two semantic features significantly outperform baseline features used in previous work. In cross-category test, the two semantic features show good transferability. To interpret the models, we analyze the semantic features and find that Psychological Process plays an important role in review text helpfulness. Words reflecting thinking and understanding are more related to helpful reviews while emotional words are not. Lastly, we validate the models trained on "X of Y approach" data on human annotated data and achieve highly correlated prediction.

2 Dataset

Two subsets of reviews are constructed from Amazon Review Dataset (McAuley and Leskovec, 2013), which includes nearly 35 million reviews from Amazon.com between 1995 and 2013. A subset of 696,696 reviews from 4 categories: Books, Home (home and kitchen), Outdoors and Electronics, are chosen in this research. For each category, we select the top 100 products with the most reviews and then include all reviews related to the selected products for analysis. Each review comes with users' helpfulness votes and hence helpfulness score can be approximated using "X of Y approach." Finally, 115,880 reviews, each of which has at least 5 votes, form the **automatic labeled** dataset (Table 1).

Table 1: Number of Reviews for Each Category

Category	Total number of reviews	Number of reviews with at least 5 votes, selected for experiments
Books	391,666	81,014 (20.7%)
Home	116,194	13,331 (11.5%)
Outdoors	52,838	6,158 (11.7%)
Electronics	135,998	15,377 (11.3%)
Overall	696,696	115,880 (16.6%)

In addition, we also create the **human labeled** dataset. As mentioned earlier, the X of Y approach may not be a good approximation to helpfulness. A better option is human scoring. We randomly select 400 reviews outside of the automatic labeled dataset, 100 from each category. Eight students annotated these reviews in a fashion similar to that in (Bard et al., 1996) by assigning real-value scores ($\in [0, 100]$) to each review. Review text was the only information given to them. The average helpfulness score of all valid annotations is used as the ground truth for each review. We have released the human annotation data at `https://sites.google.com/site/forrestbao/acl_data.tar.bz2`.

3 Features

Driven by the hypothesis that helpfulness is an underlying feature of text itself, we consider text-based features only. Features used in previous related work, namely Structure (STR) (Kim et al., 2006; Xiong and Litman, 2011), Unigram (Kim et al., 2006; Xiong and Litman, 2011; Agarwal et al., 2011) and GALC emotion (Martin and Pu, 2014), are considered as baselines.

We then introduce two semantic features LIWC and General Inquirer (INQUIRER) for easy mapping from text to human sense, including emotions, writing styles, etc. Our rationale for the two semantic features is that a helpful review includes opinions, analyses, emotions and personal experiences, etc. These two features have been proven effective in other semantic analysis tasks and hence we are here giving them a try for studying review helpfulness. We leave the study of using more sophisticated features like syntactic and discourse representations to future work. All features except UGR are independent of training data.

STR Following the (Xiong and Litman, 2011), we use the following structural features: total number of tokens, total number of sentences, average length of sentences, number of exclamation marks, and the percentage of question sentences.

UGR Unigram feature has been demonstrated as a very reliable feature for review helpfulness prediction in previous work. We build a vocabulary with all stopwords and non-frequent words ($df < 3$) removed. Each review is represented by the vocabulary with $tf - idf$ weighting for each appeared term.

GALC (Geneva Affect Label Coder) (Scherer, 2005) proposes to recognize 36 effective states commonly distinguished by words. Similar to (Martin and Pu, 2014), we construct a feature vector with the number of occurrences of each emotion plus one additional dimension for non-emotional words.

LIWC (Linguistic Inquiry and Word Count) (Pennebaker et al., 2007) is a dictionary which helps users to determine the degree that any text uses positive or negative emotions, self-references and other language dimensions. Each word in LIWC is assigned 1 or 0 for each language dimension. For each review, we sum up the values of all words for each dimension. Eventually each review is represented by a histogram of language dimensions. We employ the LIWC2007 English dictionary which contains 4,553 words with 64 dimensions in our experiments.

INQUIRER General Inquirer (Stone et al., 1962) is a dictionary in which words are grouped in categories. It is basically a mapping tool which maps each word to some semantic tags, e.g., *absurd* is mapped to tags NEG and VICE. The dictionary contains 182 categories and a total of 7,444 words. Like for LIWC representation, we compute the histogram of categories for each review.

4 Experiments

Up to this point, we are very interested in first whether a prediction model learned for one category can be generalized to a new category, and second what elements make a review helpful. In other words, we want to know the robustness of our approach and the underlying reasons.

In this section we will evaluate the effectiveness of each of the features as well as the combination of them. For convenience, we use $\text{Fusion}_{Semantic}$ to denote the combination of GALC, LIWC and INQUIRER, and Fusion_{All} to denote the combination of all features. Because STR and UGR are widely used in previous work, we use them as two baselines. GALC has been introduced for this task as an emotion feature before, so we use it as the third baseline. STR, URG and GALC are used as 3 baselines. For predicting helpfulness scores, we use SVM regressor with RBF kernel provided by LibSVM (Chang and Lin, 2011).

Two kinds of labels are used: automatic labels obtained in "X of Y approach" from votes, and human labels made by human annotators. Performance is evaluated by Root Mean Square Error (RMSE) and Pearson's correlation coefficients. Ten-fold cross-validation is performed for all experiments.

4.1 Results using Automatic Labels

Before studying the transferability of models, we first need to make sure that models work well on reviews of products of the same category.

4.1.1 RMSE

RMSE and correlation coefficient using automatic labels are given in Table 2 and Table 3 respectively. Each row corresponds to the model trained by a feature or a combination of features, while each column corresponds to one product category. The lowest RMSE achieved using every single feature in each category is marked in bold.

The two newly employed semantic features, LIWC and INQUIRER, have 8% lower RMSE on average than UGR, the best baseline feature. Fusion_{All} has the best overall RMSE, ranging from 0.200 to 0.265. $\text{Fusion}_{Semantic}$ has the second best performance on average. It achieves the lowest RMSE in Books category.

Table 2: RMSE (the lower the better) using automatic labels

	Books	Home	Outdoors	Electro.	Average
STR	0.239	0.289	0.314	0.307	0.287
UGR	0.242	0.260	0.284	0.286	0.268
GALC	0.266	0.290	0.310	0.308	0.365
LIWC	**0.188**	0.256	0.279	0.278	0.250
INQUIRER	0.193	**0.248**	**0.274**	**0.273**	**0.247**
$\text{Fusion}_{Semantic}$	0.187	0.248	0.272	0.268	0.244
Fusion_{All}	0.200	0.247	0.261	0.265	0.243

Table 3: Correlation coefficients (the higher the better) using automatic labels. All correlations are highly significant, with $p < 0.001$.

	Books	Home	Outdoors	Electronics
STR	0.500	0.280	0.333	0.351
UGR	0.507	0.467	**0.458**	0.471
GALC	0.239	0.216	0.255	0.274
LIWC	**0.742**	0.439	0.424	0.475
INQUIRER	0.720	**0.487**	0.455	**0.498**
$\text{Fusion}_{Semantic}$	0.744	0.490	0.467	0.527
Fusion_{All}	0.682	0.525	0.535	0.539

4.1.2 Correlation Coefficient

In line with RMSE measurements, the semantic feature based models outperform the baseline features in terms of correlation coefficient (Table 3). In each category, the highest correlation coefficient is achieved by using LIWC or INQUIRER, with only one exception (Outdoors). The two fusion models further improve the results. $\text{Fusion}_{Semantic}$ has the highest coefficients in Books category while Fusion_{All} has the highest coefficients in other 3 categories.

4.2 Cross Category Test

One motivation of introducing semantic features is that, unlike UGR which is category-dependent, they can be more transferable. To validate the transferability of semantic features, we perform cross category test by using the model trained from one category to predict the helpfulness scores of reviews in other categories. GALC is excluded in this analysis due to its poor performance earlier.

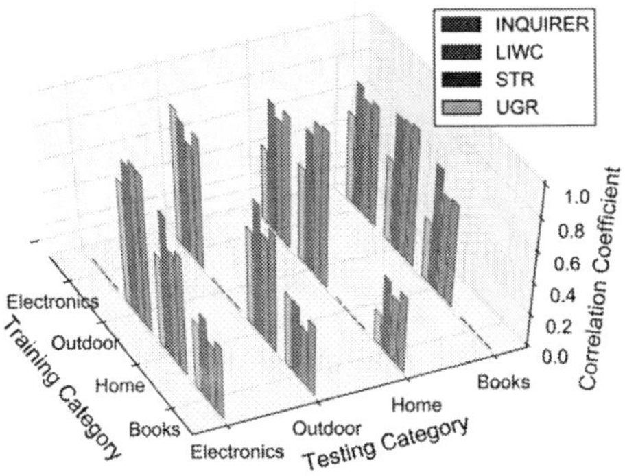

Figure 1: Normalized cross-category correlation coefficients

Model transferability from Category A to Category B cannot be measured simply by the performance when using A as the training set and B as the test set. Instead, it should be compared relatively with the performance when using A as both the training and test sets. There are 4 categories in our dataset, and the performances on the 4 categories vary (Tables 2 and 3). In order to provide a fair comparison, we normalize cross-category correlation coefficients by the corresponding same-category ones, i.e., cross-category correlation coefficient / correlation coefficient on training category. For example, the 3 cross-category correlation coefficients of using Books category as training set are all normalized by the correlation coefficient when using Books as both training and test sets earlier. A normalized correlation coefficient of 0 means the prediction on the test category is random, and thus the model has no transferability, while 1 means as accurate as predicting on the training category, and thus the model is fully transferable.

Results on transferrability are visualized in Figure 1 with same-category correlation coefficients ignored as they are always 1. Correlation coefficients of 4 features are clustered for each pair of training and testing categories and are color-coded.

It is shown that INQUIRER and STR are two best features in cross category test, leading in most of the category pairs. LIWC follows, achieving at least 70% of the same-category correlation coefficients in most cases. The UGR feature, however, performs poorly in this test. In most cases, the correlation coefficients have been halved, compared with same-category results.

According to the results, we can conclude that semantic features are accurate and transferable, UGR is accurate but is not transferable, and STR is transferable but not accurate enough (Figure 2).

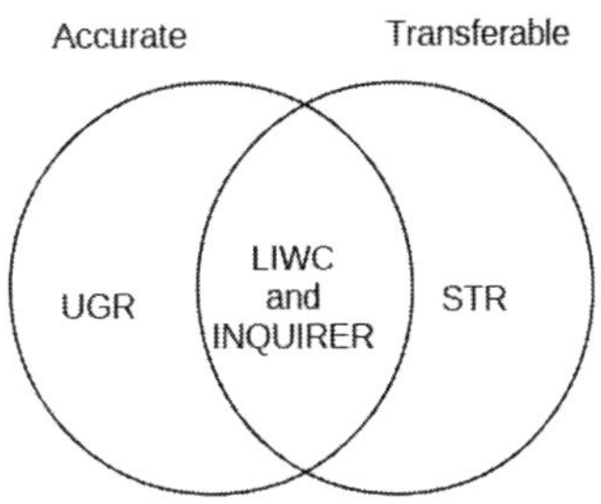

Figure 2: Classification of features based on experimental results

4.3 What Makes a Review Helpful: A Semantic Interpretation

LIWC and INQUIRER not only have better performances than previously used features but also provide us a good semantic interpretation to what makes a review helpful. We analyze the correlation coefficients between helpfulness and each language dimension in the two dictionaries. The top 5 language dimensions that are mostly correlated to helpfulness from LIWC and INQUIRER are given in Figure 3.

The top 5 dimensions from LIWC are: Relativ (Relativity), Time, Incl (Inclusive), Posemo (Positive Emotion), and Cogmech (Cognitive Processes). All of them belong to *Psychological Processes* categories in LIWC, indicating that people are more thoughtful when writing a helpful review.

The top 5 dimensions from INQUIRER are: Vary, Begin, Exert, Vice and Undrst. Words with

Vary, Begin or Exert tags belong to *process or change words*, such as *start, happen* and *break.* Vice tag contains words indicating an assessment of moral disapproval or misfortune.Undrst (Understated) tag contains words indicating de-emphasis and caution in these realms, which often reflects the lack of emotional expressiveness. Accordingly, we can infer that consumers perfer critical reviews with personal experience and a lack of emotion.

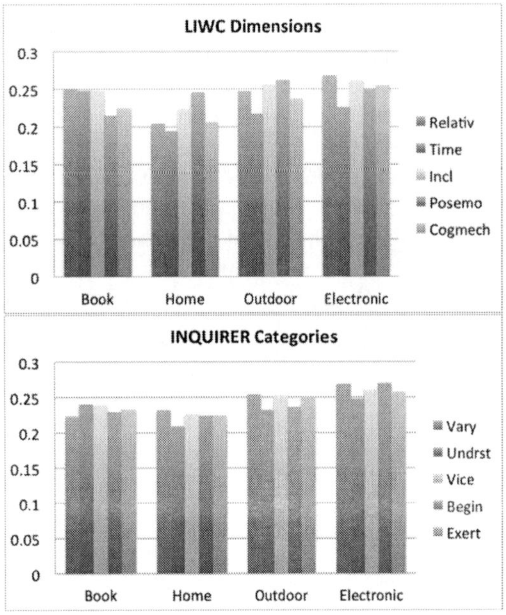

Figure 3: Language dimensions with highest correlation coefficients. Top: LIWC's; Bottom: INQUIRER's.

The discovery that helpful reviews are less emotional is consistent with the weak performance of GALC (Tables 2, 3 and 4), which is emotion focused. However, we notice that one of the top 5 dimensions in LIWC, PosEmo, is an emotional feature. This is partially because some words appear in both emotional and rational expressions, such as LIWC PosEmo words: *love, nice, sweet.* For example, the sentence *"I used to love linksys, but my experience with several of their products makes me seriously think that their quality is suspect"* is a rational statement. But the word "love" appears in it.

4.4 Prediction Results on Human Labels

A better ground truth for helpfulness is human rating. We further evaluate the prediction models on human annotated data to evaluate whether the predictions indeed align with human perceptions of review helpfulness by reading text only.

The model we built indeed aligns with human perceptions of review helpfulness when text is the only data. Table 4 shows the correlation coefficients between the predicted scores and human annotated scores. INQUIRER is the best feature, leading in 3 of 4 categories. It is followed by UGR and LIWC, which show comparable results.

Table 4: Correlation coefficients between predicted scores and human annotation, *: $p < 0.001$.

	Books	Home	Outdoors	Electronics
STR	0.539*	0.522*	0.471*	0.635*
UGR	0.607*	0.560*	0.579*	0.626*
GALC	0.214	0.405*	0.156	0.418*
LIWC	0.524*	0.553*	0.517*	**0.702***
INQUIRER	**0.620***	**0.662***	**0.620***	0.676*
$\text{Fusion}_{Semantic}$	0.556*	0.680*	0.569*	0.603*
Fusion_{All}	0.610*	0.801*	0.698*	0.768*

For Fusion_{All} models, correlation coefficients are about or over 0.7 in 3 of 4 categories, indicating the successful prediction. The only exception is on Books category. We notice that reviews in Books are more subjective. Therefore, in Books reviews, consumers are more influenced by factors outside of the text, e.g., personal preference on the book. In this case, the approximate scores used in training may not reflect the real text helpfulness. This observation echoes with our speculation that the "X of Y approach" may not always be a good approximation for helpfulness due to the subjectivity. We will leave the analysis to this as a future work.

5 Conclusion

In this paper, we formulate a new problem which is an important component of many tasks about online product reviews: predicting the helpfulness of review text. We hypothesize that helpfulness is an underlying property of text and isolate helpfulness prediction from its outer layer problems, such as review ranking. Introducing two semantic features, which have been shown effective in other NLP tasks, we achieve more accurate and transferable prediction than using features used in existing related work. The ground truth is provided by votes on massive Amazon product reviews. We further explore a semantic interpretation to reviews' helpfulness that helpful reviews exhibit more reasoning and experience and less emotion. The results are further validated on human scoring to helpfulness.

References

[Agarwal et al.2011] Deepak Agarwal, Bee-Chung Chen, and Bo Pang. 2011. Personalized recommendation of user comments via factor models. In *Proceedings of the Conference on Empirical Methods in Natural Language Processing*, EMNLP '11, pages 571–582, Stroudsburg, PA, USA. Association for Computational Linguistics.

[Agichtein et al.2008] Eugene Agichtein, Carlos Castillo, Debora Donato, Aristides Gionis, and Gilad Mishne. 2008. Finding high-quality content in social media. In *Proceedings of the 2008 International Conference on Web Search and Data Mining*, WSDM '08, pages 183–194. ACM.

[Bard et al.1996] Ellen Gurman Bard, Dan Robertson, and Antonella Sorace. 1996. Magnitude estimation of linguistic acceptability. *Language*, 72(1):pp. 32–68.

[Cao et al.2011] Qing Cao, Wenjing Duan, and Qiwei Gan. 2011. Exploring determinants of voting for the "helpfulness" of online user reviews: A text mining approach. *Decis. Support Syst.*, 50(2):511–521, January.

[Chang and Lin2011] Chih-Chung Chang and Chih-Jen Lin. 2011. LIBSVM: A library for support vector machines. *ACM Transactions on Intelligent Systems and Technology*, 2:27:1–27:27. Software available at `http://www.csie.ntu.edu.tw/~cjlin/libsvm`.

[Danescu-Niculescu-Mizil et al.2009] Cristian Danescu-Niculescu-Mizil, Gueorgi Kossinets, Jon Kleinberg, and Lillian Lee. 2009. How opinions are received by online communities: A case study on amazon.com helpfulness votes. In *Proceedings of the 18th International Conference on World Wide Web*, WWW '09, pages 141–150, New York, NY, USA. ACM.

[Duan et al.2008] Wenjing Duan, Bin Gu, and Andrew B. Whinston. 2008. The dynamics of online word-of-mouth and product sales-an empirical investigation of the movie industry. *Journal of Retailing*, 84:233242.

[Ghose and Ipeirotis2011] A. Ghose and P.G. Ipeirotis. 2011. Estimating the helpfulness and economic impact of product reviews: Mining text and reviewer characteristics. volume 23, pages 1498–1512, Oct.

[Hu and Liu2004] Minqing Hu and Bing Liu. 2004. Mining opinion features in customer reviews. In *Proceedings of the 19th National Conference on Artifical Intelligence*, AAAI'04, pages 755–760. AAAI Press.

[Kim et al.2006] Soo-Min Kim, Patrick Pantel, Tim Chklovski, and Marco Pennacchiotti. 2006. Automatically assessing review helpfulness. In *Proceedings of the 2006 Conference on Empirical Methods in Natural Language Processing*, EMNLP '06, pages 423–430, Stroudsburg, PA, USA. Association for Computational Linguistics.

[Liu et al.2008] Yang Liu, Xiangji Huang, Aijun An, and Xiaohui Yu. 2008. Modeling and predicting the helpfulness of online reviews. In *Proceedings of the 2008 Eighth IEEE International Conference on Data Mining*, ICDM '08, pages 443–452, Washington, DC, USA. IEEE Computer Society.

[Martin and Pu2014] Lionel Martin and Pearl Pu. 2014. Prediction of helpful reviews using emotions extraction. In *Twenty-Eighth AAAI Conference on Artificial Intelligence*, AAAI '14.

[McAuley and Leskovec2013] Julian McAuley and Jure Leskovec. 2013. Hidden factors and hidden topics: Understanding rating dimensions with review text. In *Proceedings of the 7th ACM Conference on Recommender Systems*, RecSys '13, pages 165–172, New York, NY, USA. ACM.

[Mudambi and Schuff2010] Susan M. Mudambi and David Schuff. 2010. What makes a helpful online review? a study of customer reviews on amazon.com. *MIS Quarterly*, pages 185–200.

[O'Mahony and Smyth2010] Michael P. O'Mahony and Barry Smyth. 2010. Using readability tests to predict helpful product reviews. In *Adaptivity, Personalization and Fusion of Heterogeneous Information*, RIAO '10, pages 164–167, Paris, France, France. LE CENTRE DE HAUTES ETUDES INTERNATIONALES D'INFORMATIQUE DOCUMENTAIRE.

[Pasternack and Roth2011] Jeff Pasternack and Dan Roth. 2011. Making better informed trust decisions with generalized fact-finding. In *Proceedings of the Twenty-Second International Joint Conference on Artificial Intelligence - Volume Three*, IJCAI'11, pages 2324–2329. AAAI Press.

[Pennebaker et al.2007] J. W. Pennebaker, Roger J. Booth, and M. E. Francis. 2007. Linguistic inquiry and word count: Liwc.

[Scherer2005] Klaus R. Scherer. 2005. What are emotions? and how can they be measured? *Social Science Information*, 44(4):695–729.

[Stone et al.1962] P. J. Stone, R. F. Bales, J. Z. Namenwirth, and D. M. Ogilvie. 1962. The general inquirer: a computer system for content analysis and retrieval based on the sentence as a unit of information. In *Behavioral Science*, pages 484–498.

[Xiong and Litman2011] Wenting Xiong and Diane Litman. 2011. Automatically predicting peer-review helpfulness. In *Proceedings of the 49th Annual Meeting of the Association for Computational Linguistics: Human Language Technologies: Short Papers - Volume 2*, HLT '11, pages 502–507, Stroudsburg, PA, USA. Association for Computational Linguistics.

[Xiong and Litman2014] Wenting Xiong and Diane Litman. 2014. Empirical analysis of exploiting review helpfulness for extractive summarization of online reviews. In *Proceedings of COLING 2014, the 25th International Conference on Computational Linguistics: Technical Papers*, pages 1985–1995.

[Yang and Nenkova2014] Yinfei Yang and Ani Nenkova. 2014. Detecting information-dense texts in multiple news domains. In *Proceedings of Twenty-Eighth AAAI Conference on Artificial Intelligence*.

Document Classification by Inversion of Distributed Language Representations

Matt Taddy
University of Chicago Booth School of Business
taddy@chicagobooth.edu

Abstract

There have been many recent advances in the structure and measurement of *distributed* language models: those that map from words to a vector-space that is rich in information about word choice and composition. This vector-space is the distributed language representation.

The goal of this note is to point out that any distributed representation can be turned into a classifier through inversion via Bayes rule. The approach is simple and modular, in that it will work with any language representation whose training can be formulated as optimizing a probability model. In our application to 2 million sentences from Yelp reviews, we also find that it performs as well as or better than complex purpose-built algorithms.

1 Introduction

Distributed, or vector-space, language representations $\mathcal{V}$ consist of a location, or embedding, for every vocabulary *word* in $\mathbb{R}^K$, where K is the dimension of the latent representation space. These locations are learned to optimize, perhaps approximately, an objective function defined on the original text such as a likelihood for word occurrences.

A popular example is the Word2Vec machinery of Mikolov et al. (2013). This trains the distributed representation to be useful as an input layer for prediction of words from their neighbors in a Skip-gram likelihood. That is, to maximize

$$\sum_{j \neq t,\, j=t-b}^{t+b} \log \mathrm{p}_{\mathcal{V}}(w_{sj} \mid w_{st}) \qquad (1)$$

summed across all words w_{st} in all sentences $\mathbf{w}_s$, where b is the skip-gram window (truncated by the ends of the sentence) and $\mathrm{p}_{\mathcal{V}}(w_{sj}|w_{st})$ is a neural network classifier that takes vector representations for w_{st} and w_{sj} as input (see Section 2).

Distributed language representations have been studied since the early work on neural networks (Rumelhart et al., 1986) and have long been applied in natural language processing (Morin and Bengio, 2005). The models are generating much recent interest due to the large performance gains from the newer systems, including Word2Vec and the Glove model of Pennington et al. (2014), observed in, e.g., word prediction, word analogy identification, and named entity recognition.

Given the success of these new models, researchers have begun searching for ways to adapt the representations for use in document classification tasks such as sentiment prediction or author identification. One naive approach is to use aggregated word vectors across a document (e.g., a document's average word-vector location) as input to a standard classifier (e.g., logistic regression). However, a document is actually an *ordered* path of locations through $\mathbb{R}^K$, and simple averaging destroys much of the available information.

More sophisticated aggregation is proposed in Socher et al. (2011; 2013), where recursive neural networks are used to combine the word vectors through the estimated parse tree for each sentence. Alternatively, Le and Mikolov's Doc2Vec (2014) adds document labels to the conditioning set in (1) and has them influence the skip-gram likelihood through a latent input vector location in $\mathcal{V}$. In each case, the end product is a distributed representation for every sentence (or document for Doc2Vec) that can be used as input to a generic classifier.

1.1 Bayesian Inversion

These approaches all add considerable model and estimation complexity to the original underlying distributed representation. We are proposing a simple alternative that turns fitted distributed language representations into document classifiers

Proceedings of the 53rd Annual Meeting of the Association for Computational Linguistics and the 7th International Joint Conference on Natural Language Processing (Short Papers), pages 45–49,
Beijing, China, July 26-31, 2015.

without any additional modeling or estimation.

Write the probability model that the representation $\mathcal{V}$ has been trained to optimize (likelihood maximize) as $\mathrm{p}_{\mathcal{V}}(d)$, where document $d = \{\mathbf{w}_1, ...\mathbf{w}_S\}$ is a set of sentences – ordered vectors of word identities. For example, in Word2Vec the skip-gram likelihood in (1) yields

$$\log \mathrm{p}_{\mathcal{V}}(d) = \sum_s \sum_t \sum_{j \neq t,\, j=t-b}^{t+b} \log \mathrm{p}_{\mathcal{V}_y}(w_{sj} \mid w_{st}). \tag{2}$$

Even when such a likelihood is not explicit it will be implied by the objective function that is optimized during training.

Now suppose that your training documents are grouped by class label, $y \in \{1 \ldots C\}$. We can train *separate* distributed language representations for each set of documents as partitioned by y; for example, fit Word2Vec independently on each sub-corpus $D_c = \{d_i : y_i = c\}$ and obtain the labeled distributed representation map $\mathcal{V}_c$. A new document d has probability $\mathrm{p}_{\mathcal{V}_c}(d)$ if we treat it as a member of class c, and Bayes rule implies

$$\mathrm{p}(y|d) = \frac{\mathrm{p}_{\mathcal{V}_y}(d)\pi_y}{\sum_c \mathrm{p}_{\mathcal{V}_c}(d)\pi_c} \tag{3}$$

where π_c is our prior probability on class label c.

Thus distributed language representations trained separately for each class label yield directly a document classification rule via (3). This approach has a number of attractive qualities.

Simplicity: The inversion strategy works for any model of language that can (or its training can) be interpreted as a probabilistic model. This makes for easy implementation in systems that are already engineered to fit such language representations, leading to faster deployment and lower development costs. The strategy is also interpretable: whatever intuition one has about the distributed language model can be applied directly to the inversion-based classification rule. Inversion adds a plausible model for reader understanding on top of any given language representation.

Scalability: when working with massive corpora it is often useful to split the data into blocks as part of distributed computing strategies. Our model of classification via inversion provides a convenient top-level partitioning of the data. An efficient system could fit separate by-class language representations, which will provide for document classification as in this article as well as class-specific answers for NLP tasks such as word prediction or analogy. When one wishes to treat a document as unlabeled, NLP tasks can be answered through ensemble aggregation of the class-specific answers.

Performance: We find that, in our examples, inversion of Word2Vec yields lower misclassification rates than both Doc2Vec-based classification and the multinomial inverse regression (MNIR) of Taddy (2013b). We did not anticipate such outright performance gain. Moreover, we expect that with calibration (i.e., through cross-validation) of the many various tuning parameters available when fitting both Word and Doc 2Vec the performance results will change. Indeed, we find that all methods are often outperformed by phrase-count logistic regression with rare-feature up-weighting and carefully chosen regularization. However, the out-of-the-box performance of Word2Vec inversion argues for its consideration as a simple default in document classification.

In the remainder, we outline classification through inversion of a specific Word2Vec model and illustrate the ideas in classification of Yelp reviews. The implementation requires only a small extension of the popular `gensim` python library (Rehurek and Sojka, 2010); the extended library as well as code to reproduce all of the results in this paper are available on `github`. In addition, the yelp data is publicly available as part of the corresponding data mining contest at `kaggle.com`. See `github.com/taddylab/deepir` for detail.

2 Implementation

Word2Vec trains $\mathcal{V}$ to maximize the skip-gram likelihood based on (1). We work with the Huffman softmax specification (Mikolov et al., 2013), which includes a pre-processing step to encode each vocabulary word in its representation via a binary Huffman tree (see Figure 1).

Each individual probability is then

$$\mathrm{p}_{\mathcal{V}}(w|w_t) = \prod_{j=1}^{L(w)-1} \sigma\left(\mathrm{ch}\left[\eta(w, j+1)\right] \mathbf{u}_{\eta(w,j)}^{\top} \mathbf{v}_{w_t}\right) \tag{4}$$

where $\eta(w, i)$ is the ith node in the Huffman tree path, of length $L(w)$, for word w; $\sigma(x) = 1/(1 + \exp[-x])$; and $\mathrm{ch}(\eta) \in \{-1, +1\}$ translates from whether η is a left or right child to +/- 1. Every word thus has both input and output vector coordinates, $\mathbf{v}_w$ and $[\mathbf{u}_{\eta(w,1)} \cdots \mathbf{u}_{\eta(w,L(w))}]$. Typically,

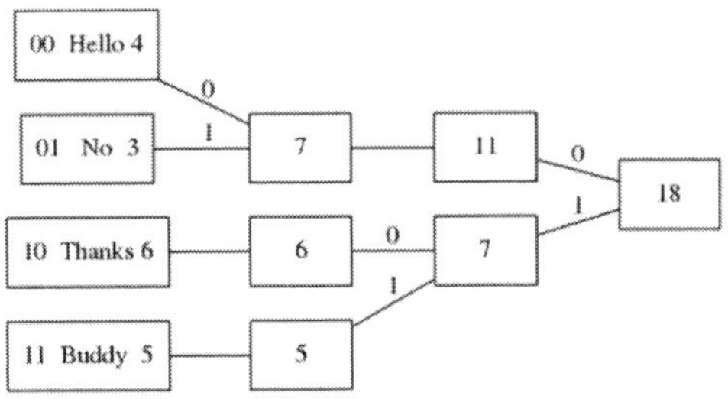

Figure 1: Binary Huffman encoding of a 4 word vocabulary, based upon 18 total utterances. At each step proceeding from left to right the two nodes with lowest count are combined into a parent node. Binary encodings are read back off of the splits moving from right to left.

only the input space $\mathbf{V} = [\mathbf{v}_{w_1} \cdots \mathbf{v}_{w_p}]$, for a p-word vocabulary, is reported as the language representation – these vectors are used as input for NLP tasks. However, the full representation $\mathcal{V}$ includes mapping from each word to both $\mathbf{V}$ and $\mathbf{U}$.

We apply the `gensim` python implementation of Word2Vec, which fits the model via stochastic gradient descent (SGD), under default specification. This includes a vector space of dimension $K = 100$ and a skip-gram window of size $b = 5$.

2.1 Word2Vec Inversion

Given Word2Vec trained on each of C class-specific corpora $D_1 \dots D_C$, leading to C distinct language representations $\mathcal{V}_1 \dots \mathcal{V}_C$, classification for new documents is straightforward. Consider the S-sentence document d: each sentence $\mathbf{w}_s$ is given a probability under each representation $\mathcal{V}_c$ by applying the calculations in (1) and (4). This leads to the $S \times C$ matrix of sentence probabilities, $\mathrm{p}_{\mathcal{V}_c}(\mathbf{w}_s)$, and document probabilities are obtained

$$\mathrm{p}_{\mathcal{V}_c}(d) = \frac{1}{S}\sum_s \mathrm{p}_{\mathcal{V}_c}(\mathbf{w}_s). \quad (5)$$

Finally, class probabilities are calculated via Bayes rule as in (3). We use priors $\pi_c = 1/C$, so that classification proceeds by assigning the class

$$\hat{y} = \mathrm{argmax}_c \ \mathrm{p}_{\mathcal{V}_c}(d). \quad (6)$$

3 Illustration

We consider a corpus of reviews provided by Yelp for a contest on `kaggle.com`. The text is tokenized simply by converting to lowercase before splitting on punctuation and white-space. The training data are 230,000 reviews containing more than 2 million sentences. Each review is marked by a number of *stars*, from 1 to 5, and we fit separate Word2Vec representations $\mathcal{V}_1 \dots \mathcal{V}_5$ for the documents at each star rating. The validation data consist of 23,000 reviews, and we apply the inversion technique of Section 2 to score each validation document d with class probabilities $\mathbf{q} = [q_1 \cdots q_5]$, where $q_c = \mathrm{p}(c|d)$.

The probabilities will be used in three different classification tasks; for reviews as

a. negative at 1-2 stars, or positive at 3-5 stars;

b. negative 1-2, neutral 3, or positive 4-5 stars;

c. corresponding to each of 1 to 5 stars.

In each case, classification proceeds by summing across the relevant sub-class probabilities. For example, in task a, $\mathrm{p}(\texttt{positive}) = q_3 + q_4 + q_5$. Note that the same five fitted Word2Vec representations are used for each task.

We consider a set of related comparator techniques. In each case, some document representation (e.g., phrase counts or Doc2Vec vectors) is used as input to logistic regression prediction of the associated review rating. The logistic regressions are fit under L_1 regularization with the penalties weighted by feature standard deviation (which, e.g., up-weights rare phrases) and selected according to the corrected AICc criteria (Flynn et al., 2013) via the `gamlr` R package of Taddy (2014). For multi-class tasks *b-c*, we use distributed Multinomial regression (DMR; Taddy 2015) via the `distrom` R package. DMR fits multinomial logistic regression in a factorized representation wherein one estimates independent Poisson linear models for each response category. Document representations and logistic regressions are always trained using only the training corpus.

Doc2Vec is also fit via `gensim`, using the same latent space specification as for Word2Vec: $K = 100$ and $b = 5$. As recommended in the documentation, we apply repeated SGD over 20 reorderings of each corpus (for comparability, this was also done when fitting Word2Vec). Le and Mikolov provide two alternative Doc2Vec specifications: distributed memory (DM) and distributed bag-of-words (DBOW). We fit both. Vector representations for validation documents are trained without updating the word-vector elements, leading to 100 dimensional vectors for each document for each of DM and DCBOW. We input

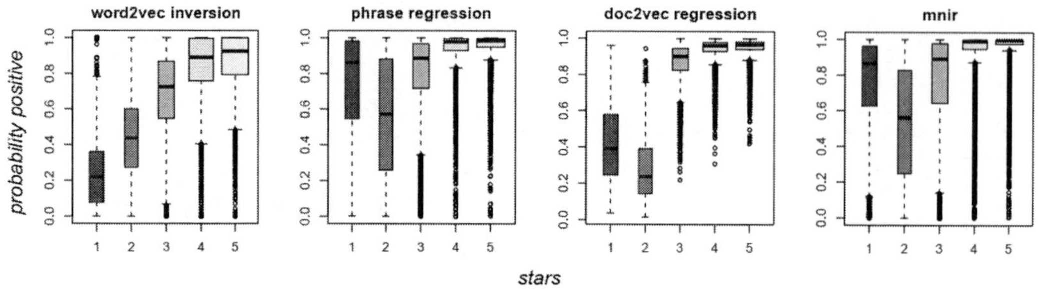

Figure 2: Out-of-Sample fitted probabilities of a review being *positive* (having greater than 2 stars) as a function of the true number of review stars. Box widths are proportional to number of observations in each class; roughly 10% of reviews have each of 1-3 stars, while 30% have 4 stars and 40% have 5 stars.

each, as well as the combined 200 dimensional DM+DBOW representation, to logistic regression.

Phrase regression applies logistic regression of response classes directly onto counts for short 1-2 word 'phrases'. The phrases are obtained using `gensim`'s phrase builder, which simply combines highly probable pairings; e.g., `first_date` and `chicken_wing` are two pairings in this corpus.

MNIR, the multinomial inverse regression of Taddy (2013a; 2013b; 2015) is applied as implemented in the `textir` package for R. MNIR maps from text to the class-space of interest through a multinomial logistic regression of phrase counts onto variables relevant to the class-space. We apply MNIR to the same set of 1-2 word phrases used in phrase regression. Here, we regress phrase counts onto stars expressed numerically and as a 5-dimensional indicator vector, leading to a 6-feature multinomial logistic regression. The MNIR procedure then uses the $6 \times p$ matrix of feature-phrase regression coefficients to map from phrase-count to feature space, resulting in 6 dimensional 'sufficient reduction' statistics for each document. These are input to logistic regression.

Word2Vec aggregation averages fitted word representations for a single Word2Vec trained on all sentences to obtain a fixed-length feature vector for each review ($K = 100$, as for inversion). This vector is then input to logistic regression.

	a (NP)	b (NNP)	c (1-5)
W2V inversion	.099	**.189**	.435
Phrase regression	**.084**	.200	**.410**
D2V DBOW	.144	.282	.496
D2V DM	.179	.306	.549
D2V combined	.148	. 284	.500
MNIR	.095	.254	.480
W2V aggregation	.118	.248	.461

Table 1: Out-of-sample misclassification rates.

3.1 Results

Misclassification rates for each task on the validation set are reported in Table 1. Simple phrase-count regression is consistently the strongest performer, bested only by Word2Vec inversion on task b. This is partially due to the relative strengths of discriminative (e.g., logistic regression) vs generative (e.g., all others here) classifiers: given a large amount of training text, asymptotic efficiency of logistic regression will start to work in its favor over the finite sample advantages of a generative classifier (Ng and Jordan, 2002; Taddy, 2013c). However, the comparison is also unfair to Word2Vec and Doc2Vec: both phrase regression and MNIR are optimized exactly under AICc selected penalty, while Word and Doc 2Vec have only been approximately optimized under a single specification. The distributed representations should improve with some careful engineering.

Word2Vec inversion outperforms the other document representation-based alternatives (except, by a narrow margin, MNIR in task a). Doc2Vec under DBOW specification and MNIR both do worse, but not by a large margin. In contrast to Le and Mikolov, we find here that the Doc2Vec DM model does much worse than DBOW. Regression onto simple within- document aggregations of Word2Vec perform slightly better than any Doc2Vec option (but not as well as the Word2Vec inversion). This again contrasts the results of Le and Mikolov and we suspect that the more complex Doc2Vec model would benefit from a careful tuning of the SGD optimization routine.[1]

Looking at the fitted probabilities in detail we see that Word2Vec inversion provides a more useful document *ranking* than any comparator (including phrase regression). For example, Figure 2 shows the probabilities of a review being 'positive' in task a as a function of the true star rating for each validation review. Although phrase regression does slightly better in terms of misclassification rate, it does so at the cost of classifying many terrible (1 star) reviews as positive. This occurs because 1-2 star reviews are more rare than 3-5 star reviews and because words of emphasis (e.g. `very`, `completely`, and `!!!`) are used both in very bad and in very good reviews. Word2Vec inversion is the *only* method that yields positive-document probabilities that are clearly increasing in distribution with the true star rating. It is not difficult to envision a misclassification cost structure that favors such nicely ordered probabilities.

4 Discussion

The goal of this note is to point out inversion as an option for turning distributed language representations into classification rules. We are not arguing for the supremacy of Word2Vec inversion in particular, and the approach should work well with alternative representations (e.g., Glove). Moreover, we are not even arguing that it will always outperform purpose-built classification tools. However, it is a simple, scalable, interpretable, and effective option for classification whenever you are working with such distributed representations.

References

Cheryl Flynn, Clifford Hurvich, and Jefferey Simonoff. 2013. Efficiency for Regularization Parameter Selection in Penalized Likelihood Estimation of Misspecified Models. *Journal of the American Statistical Association*, 108:1031–1043.

Quoc V. Le and Tomas Mikolov. 2014. Distributed representations of sentences and documents. In *Proceedings of the 31 st International Conference on Machine Learning*.

Tomas Mikolov, Ilya Sutskever, Kai Chen, Greg S. Corrado, and Jeff Dean. 2013. Distributed representations of words and phrases and their compositionality. In *Advances in Neural Information Processing Systems*, pages 3111–3119.

Frederic Morin and Yoshua Bengio. 2005. Hierarchical probabilistic neural network language model. In *Proceedings of the International Workshop on Artificial Intelligence and Statistics*, pages 246–252.

Andrew Y. Ng and Michael I. Jordan. 2002. On Discriminative vs Generative Classifiers: A Comparison of Logistic Regression and naive Bayes. In *Advances in Neural Information Processing Systems (NIPS)*.

Jeffrey Pennington, Richard Socher, and Christopher D. Manning. 2014. Glove: Global vectors for word representation. *Proceedings of the Empiricial Methods in Natural Language Processing (EMNLP 2014)*, 12.

Radim Rehurek and Petr Sojka. 2010. Software Framework for Topic Modelling with Large Corpora. In *Proceedings of the LREC 2010 Workshop on New Challenges for NLP Frameworks*, pages 45–50.

David Rumelhart, Geoffrey Hinton, and Ronald Williams. 1986. Learning representations by back-propagating errors. *Nature*, 323:533–536.

Richard Socher, Cliff C. Lin, Chris Manning, and Andrew Y. Ng. 2011. Parsing natural scenes and natural language with recursive neural networks. In *Proceedings of the 28th international conference on machine learning (ICML-11)*, pages 129–136.

Richard Socher, Alex Perelygin, Jean Y. Wu, Jason Chuang, Christopher D. Manning, Andrew Y. Ng, and Christopher Potts. 2013. Recursive deep models for semantic compositionality over a sentiment treebank. In *Proceedings of the conference on empirical methods in natural language processing (EMNLP)*, volume 1631, page 1642.

Matt Taddy. 2013a. Measuring Political Sentiment on Twitter: Factor Optimal Design for Multinomial Inverse Regression. *Technometrics*, 55(4):415–425, November.

Matt Taddy. 2013b. Multinomial Inverse Regression for Text Analysis. *Journal of the American Statistical Association*, 108:755–770.

Matt Taddy. 2013c. Rejoinder: Efficiency and structure in MNIR. *Journal of the American Statistical Association*, 108:772–774.

Matt Taddy. 2014. One-step estimator paths for concave regularization. arXiv:1308.5623.

Matt Taddy. 2015. Distributed Multinomial Regression. *Annals of Applied Statistics*, To appear.

[1]Note also that the unsupervised document representations – Doc2Vec or the single Word2Vec used in Word2Vec aggregation – could be trained on larger unlabeled corpora. A similar option is available for Word2Vec inversion: one could take a single Word2Vec model trained on a large unlabeled corpora as a shared baseline (prior) and update separate models with additional training on each labeled sub-corpora. The representations will all be shrunk towards a baseline language model, but will differ according to distinctions between the language in each labeled sub-corpora.

Using Tweets to Help Sentence Compression for News Highlights Generation

Zhongyu Wei[1], Yang Liu[1], Chen Li[1], Wei Gao[2]
[1]Computer Science Department, The University of Texas at Dallas
Richardson, Texas 75080, USA
[2]Qatar Computing Research Institute, Hamad Bin Khalifa University, Doha, Qatar
{zywei,yangl,chenli}@hlt.utdallas.edu[1]
wgao@qf.org.qa[2]

Abstract

We explore using relevant tweets of a given news article to help sentence compression for generating compressive news highlights. We extend an unsupervised dependency-tree based sentence compression approach by incorporating tweet information to weight the tree edge in terms of informativeness and syntactic importance. The experimental results on a public corpus that contains both news articles and relevant tweets show that our proposed tweets guided sentence compression method can improve the summarization performance significantly compared to the baseline generic sentence compression method.

1 Introduction

"Story highlights" of news articles are provided by only a few news websites such as CNN.com. The highlights typically consist of three or four succinct itemized sentences for readers to quickly capture the gist of the document, and can dramatically reduce reader's information load. A highlight sentence is usually much shorter than its original corresponding news sentence; therefore applying extractive summarization methods directly to sentences in a news article is not enough to generate high quality highlights.

Sentence compression aims to retain the most important information of an original sentence in a shorter form while being grammatical at the same time. Previous research has shown the effectiveness of sentence compression for automatic document summarization (Knight and Marcu, 2000; Lin, 2003; Galanis and Androutsopoulos, 2010; Chali and Hasan, 2012; Wang et al., 2013; Li et al., 2013; Qian and Liu, 2013; Li et al., 2014). The compressed summaries can be generated through a pipeline approach that combines a generic sentence compression model with a summary sentence pre-selection or post-selection step. Prior studies have mostly used the generic sentence compression approaches, however, a generic compression system may not be the best fit for the summarization purpose because it does not take into account the summarization task in the compression module. Li et al. (2013) thus proposed a summary guided compression method to address this problem and showed the effectiveness of their method. But this approach relied heavily on the training data, thus has the limitation of domain generalization.

Instead of using a manually generated corpus, we investigate using existing external sources to guide sentence compression for the purpose of compressive news highlights generation. Nowadays it becomes more and more common that users share interesting news content via Twitter together with their comments. The availability of cross-media information provides new opportunities for traditional tasks of Natural Language Processing (Zhao et al., 2011; Subašić and Berendt, 2011; Gao et al., 2012; Kothari et al., 2013; Štajner et al., 2013). In this paper, we propose to use relevant tweets of a news article to guide the sentence compression process in a pipeline framework for generating compressive news highlights. This is a pioneer study for using such parallel data to guide sentence compression for document summarization.

Our work shares some similar ideas with (Wei and Gao, 2014; Wei and Gao, 2015). They also attempted to use tweets to help news highlights generation. Wei and Gao (2014) derived external features based on the relevant tweet collection to assist the ranking of the original sentences for extractive summarization in a fashion of supervised machine learning. Wei and Gao (2015) proposed a graph-based approach to simultaneously rank the

Proceedings of the 53rd Annual Meeting of the Association for Computational Linguistics and the 7th International Joint Conference on Natural Language Processing (Short Papers), pages 50–56,
Beijing, China, July 26-31, 2015.

original news sentences and relevant tweets in an unsupervised way. Both of them focused on using tweets to help sentence extraction while we leverage tweet information to guide sentence compression for compressive summary generation.

We extend an unsupervised dependency-tree based sentence compression approach to incorporate tweet information from the aspects of both informativeness and syntactic importance to weight the tree edge. We evaluate our method on a public corpus that contains both news articles and relevant tweets. The result shows that generic compression hurts the performance of highlights generation, while sentence compression guided by relevant tweets of the news article can improve the performance.

2 Framework

We adopt a pipeline approach for compressive news highlights generation. The framework integrates a sentence extraction component and a post-sentence compression component. Each is described below.

2.1 Tweets Involved Sentence Extraction

We use LexRank (Erkan and Radev, 2004) as the baseline to select the salient sentences in a news article. This baseline is an unsupervised extractive summarization approach and has been proved to be effective for the summarization task.

Besides LexRank, we also use Heterogeneous Graph Random Walk (HGRW) (Wei and Gao, 2015) to incorporate relevant tweet information to extract news sentences. In this model, an undirected similarity graph is created, similar to LexRank. However, the graph is heterogeneous, with two types of nodes for the news sentences and tweets respectively.

Suppose we have a sentence set S and a tweet set T. By considering the similarity between the same type of nodes and cross types, the score of a news sentence s is computed as follows:

$$\begin{aligned} p(s) = \frac{d}{N+M} &+ (1-d)\left[\epsilon \sum_{m \in T} \frac{sim(s,m)}{\sum_{v \in T} sim(s,v)} p(m)\right] \\ &+(1-d)\left[(1-\epsilon) \sum_{n \in S \setminus \{s\}} \frac{sim(s,n)}{\sum_{v \in S \setminus \{s\}} sim(s,v)} p(n)\right] \end{aligned} \quad (1)$$

where N and M are the size of S and T, respectively, d is a damping factor, $sim(x,y)$ is the similarity function, and the parameter ϵ is used to control the contribution of relevant tweets. For a tweet node t, its score can be computed similarly. Both d and $sim(x,y)$ are computed following the setup of LexRank, where $sim(x,y)$ is computed as cosine similarity:

$$sim(x,y) = \frac{\sum_{w \in x,y} tf_{w,x} tf_{w,y} (idf_w)^2}{\sqrt{\sum_{w_i \in x} (tf_{w_i,x} idf_{w_i})^2} \times \sqrt{\sum_{w_i \in y} (tf_{w_i,y} idf_{w_i})^2}} \quad (2)$$

where $tf_{w,x}$ is the number of occurrences of word w in instance x, idf_w is the inverse document frequency of word w in the dataset. In our task, each sentence or tweet is treated as a document to compute the IDF value.

Although both types of nodes can be ranked in this framework, we only output the top news sentences as the highlights, and the input to the subsequent compression component.

2.2 Dependency Tree Based Sentence Compression

We use an unsupervised dependency tree based compression framework (Filippova and Strube, 2008) as our baseline. This method achieved a higher F-score (Riezler et al., 2003) than other systems on the Edinburgh corpus (Clarke and Lapata, 2006). We will introduce the baseline in this part and describe our extended model that leverages tweet information in the next subsection.

The sentence compression task can be defined as follows: given a sentence s, consisting of words $w_1, w_2, ..., w_m$, identify a subset of the words of s, such that it is grammatical and preserves essential information of s. In the baseline framework, a dependency graph for an original sentence is first generated and then the compression is done by deleting edges of the dependency graph. The goal is to find a subtree with the highest score:

$$f(X) = \sum_{e \in E} x_e \times w_{info}(e) \times w_{syn}(e) \quad (3)$$

where x_e is a binary variable, indicating whether a directed dependency edge e is kept (x_e is 1) or removed (x_e is 0), and E is the set of edges in the dependency graph. The weighting of edge e considers both its syntactic importance ($w_{syn}(e)$) as well as the informativeness ($w_{info}(e)$). Suppose edge e is pointed from head h to node n with dependency label l, both weights can be computed from a background news corpus as:

$$w_{info}(e) = \frac{P_{summary}(n)}{P_{article}(n)} \quad (4)$$

$$w_{syn}(e) = P(l|h) \quad (5)$$

where $P_{summary}(n)$ and $P_{article}(n)$ are the unigram probabilities of word n in the two language models trained on human generated summaries and the original articles respectively. $P(l|h)$ is the conditional probability of label l given head h. Note that here we use the formula in (Filippova and Altun, 2013) for $w_{info}(e)$, which was shown to be more effective for sentence compression than the original formula in (Filippova and Strube, 2008).

The optimization problem can be solved under the tree structure and length constraints by integer linear programming[1]. Given that L is the maximum number of words permitted for the compression, the length constraint is simply represented as:

$$\sum_{e \in E} x_e \leq L \quad (6)$$

The surface realizatdion is standard: the words in the compression subtree are put in the same order they are found in the source sentence. Due to space limit, we refer readers to (Filippova and Strube, 2008) for a detailed description of the baseline method.

2.3 Leverage Tweets for Edge Weighting

We then extend the dependency-tree based compression framework by incorporating tweet information for dependency edge weighting. We introduce two new factors, $w^T_{info}(e)$ and $w^T_{syn}(e)$, for informativeness and syntactic importance respectively, computed from relevant tweets of the news. These are combined with the weights obtained from the background news corpus defined in Section 2.2, as shown below:

$$w_{info}(e) = (1-\alpha) \cdot w^N_{info}(e) + \alpha \cdot w^T_{info}(e) \quad (7)$$

$$w_{syn}(e) = (1-\beta) \cdot w^N_{syn}(e) + \beta \cdot w^T_{syn}(e) \quad (8)$$

where α and β are used to balance the contribution of the two sources, and $w^N_{info}(e)$ and $w^N_{syn}(e)$ are based on Equation 4 and 5.

The new informative weight $w^T_{info}(e)$ is calculated as:

$$w^T_{info}(e) = \frac{P_{relevantT}(n)}{P_{backgroundT}(n)} \quad (9)$$

$P_{relevantT}(n)$ and $P_{backgroundT}(n)$ are the unigram probabilities of word n in two language models trained on the relevant tweet dataset and a background tweet dataset respectively.

The new syntactic importance score is:

$$w^T_{syn}(e) = \frac{NT(h,n)}{NT} \quad (10)$$

$NT(h,n)$ is the number of tweets where n and head h appear together within a window frame of K, and NT is the total number of tweets in the relevant tweet collection. Since tweets are always noisy and informal, traditional parsers are not reliable to extract dependency trees. Therefore, we use co-occurrence as pseudo syntactic information here. Note $w^N_{info}(e)$, $w^T_{info}(e)$, $w^N_{syn}(e)$ and $w^T_{syn}(e)$ are normalized before combination.

3 Experiment

3.1 Setup

We evaluate our pipeline news highlights generation framework on a public corpus based on CNN/USAToday news (Wei and Gao, 2014). This corpus was constructed via an event-oriented strategy following four steps: 1) 17 salient news events taking place in 2013 and 2014 were manually identified. 2) For each event, relevant tweets were retrieved via Topsy[2] search API using a set of manually generated core queries. 3) News articles explicitly linked by URLs embedded in the tweets were collected. 4) News articles from CNN/USAToday that have more than 100 explicitly linked tweets were kept. The resulting corpus contains 121 documents, 455 highlights and 78,419 linking tweets.

We used tweets explicitly linked to a news article to help extract salience sentences in *HGRW* and to generate the language model for computing $w^T_{info}(e)$. The co-occurrence information computed from the set of explicitly linked tweets is very sparse because the size of the tweet set is small. Therefore, we used all the tweets retrieved for the event related to the target news article to compute the co-occurrence information for $w^T_{syn}(e)$. Tweets retrieved for events were not published in (Wei and Gao, 2014). We make it available here[3]. The statistics of the dataset can be found in Table. 1.

[1]In our implementation we use GNU Linear Programming Kit (GULP) (`https://www.gnu.org/software/glpk/`)

[2]`http://topsy.com`

[3]`http://www.hlt.utdallas.edu/~zywei/data/CNNUSATodayEvent.zip`

Event	Doc #	HLight #	Linked Tweet #	Retrieved Tweet #	Event	Doc #	HLight #	Linked Tweet #	Retrieved Tweet #
Aurora shooting	14	54	12,463	588,140	African runner murder	8	29	9,461	303,535
Boston bombing	38	147	21,683	1,650,650	Syria chemical weapons use	1	4	331	11,850
Connecticut shooting	13	47	3,021	213,864	US military in Syria	2	7	719	619,22
Edward Snowden	5	17	1,955	379,349	DPRK Nuclear Test	2	8	3,329	103,964
Egypt balloon crash	3	12	836	36,261	Asiana Airlines Flight 214	11	42	8,353	351,412
Hurricane Sandy	4	15	607	189,082	Moore Tornado	5	19	1,259	1,154,656
Russian meteor	3	11	6,841	239,281	Chinese Computer Attacks	2	8	507	28,988
US Flu Season	7	23	6,304	1,042,169	Williams Olefins Explosion	1	4	268	14,196
Super Bowl blackout	2	8	482	214,775	Total	121	455	78,419	6,890,987

Table 1: Distribution of documents, highlights and tweets with respect to different events

Method	ROUGE-1			Compr. Rate(%)
	F(%)	P(%)	R(%)	
LexRank	26.1	19.9	**39.1**	100
LexRank + SC	25.2	22.4	29.6	63.0
LexRank + SC+w^T_{info}	25.7	22.8	30.1	62.0
LexRank + SC+w^T_{syn}	26.2	23.5	30.4	63.7
LexRank + SC+*both*	**27.5**	**25.0**	31.4	61.5
HGRW	28.1	22.6	**39.5**	100
HGRW + SC	26.4	24.9	29.5	66.1
HGRW + SC+w^T_{info}	27.5	25.7	30.8	65.4
HGRW + SC+w^T_{syn}	27.0	25.3	30.2	66.7
HGRW + SC+*both*	**28.4**	**26.9**	31.2	64.8

Table 2: Overall Performance. **Bold**: the best value in each group in terms of different metrics.

Following (Wei and Gao, 2014), we output 4 sentences for each news article as the highlights and report the ROUGE-1 scores (Lin, 2004) using human-generated highlights as the reference.

The sentence compression rates are set to 0.8 for short sentences containing fewer than 9 words, and 0.5 for long sentences with more than 9 words, following (Filippova and Strube, 2008). We empirically use 0.8 for α, β and ϵ such that tweets have more impact for both sentence selection and compression. We leveraged The New York Times Annotated Corpus (LDC Catalog No: LDC2008T19) as the background news corpus. It has both the original news articles and human generated summaries. The Stanford Parser[4] is used to obtain dependency trees. The background tweet corpus is collected from Twitter public timeline via Twitter API, and contains more than 50 million tweets.

3.2 Results

Table 2 shows the overall performance[5]. For summaries generated by both *LexRank* and *HGRW*, "+*SC*" means generic sentence compression baseline (Section. 2.2) is used, "+w^T_{info}" and "+w^T_{syn}" indicate tweets are used to help edge weighting for sentence compression in terms of informativeness and syntactic importance respectively, and "+*both*" means both factors are used. We have several findings.

- The tweets involved sentence extraction model *HGRW* can improve *LexRank* by 8.8% relatively in terms of ROUGE-1 F score, showing the effectiveness of relevant tweets for sentence selection.
- With generic sentence compression, the ROUGE-1 F scores for both *LexRank* and *HGRW* drop, mainly because of a much lower recall score. This indicates that generic sentence compression without certain guidance removes salient content of the original sentence that may be important for summarization and thus hurts the performance. This is consistent with the finding of (Chali and Hasan, 2012).
- By adding either w^T_{info} or w^T_{syn}, the performance of summarization increases, showing that relevant tweets can be used to help the scores of both informativeness and syntactic importance.
- *+SC+both* improves the summarization performance significantly[6] compared to the corresponding compressive summarization baseline *+SC*, and outperforms the corresponding original baseline, *LexRank* and *HGRW*.
- The improvement obtained by *LexRank+SC+both* compared to *LexRank* is more promising than that obtained by *HGRW+SC+both* compared to *HGRW*. This may be because *HGRW* has used tweet information already, and leaves limited room for improvement for the sentence compression model when using the same source of information.

[4]http://nlp.stanford.edu/software/lex-parser.shtml

[5]The performance of HGRW reported here is different from (Wei and Gao, 2015) because the setup is different. We use all the explicitly linked tweets in the ranking process here without considering redundancy while a redundancy filtering process was applied in (Wei and Gao, 2015).

[6]Significance throughout the paper is computed by two tailed t-test and reported when $p < 0.05$.

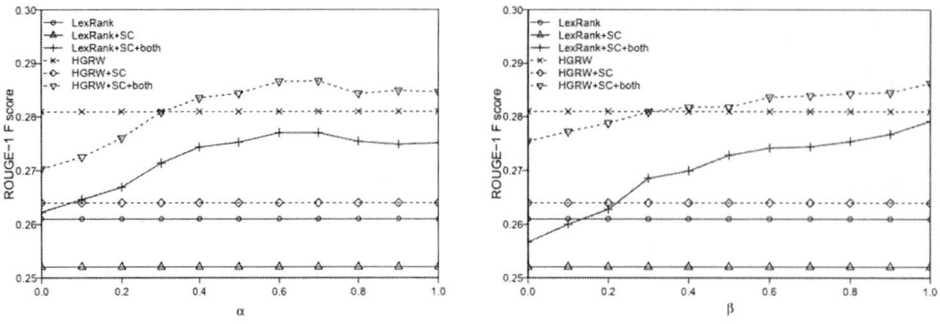

(a) Impact of α (b) Impact of β

Figure 1: The influence of α and β. Solid lines are used for approaches based on LexRank; Dotted lines are used for HGRW based approaches.

Method	Example 1	Example 2
LexRank	Boston bombing suspect Tamerlan Tsarnaev, killed in a shootout with police days after the blast, has been buried at an undisclosed location, police in Worcester, Mass., said.	Three people were hospitalized in critical condition, according to information provided by hospitals who reported receiving patients from the blast.
LexRank+SC	suspect Tamerlan Tsarnaev, killed in a shootout after the blast, has been buried at an location, police in Worcester Mass. said.	Three people were hospitalized, according to information provided by hospitals who reported receiving from the blast.
LexRank+SC+both	**Boston bombing** suspect Tamerlan Tsarnaev, killed in a shootout after the blast, has been buried at an location police said.	Three people were hospitalized in **critical condition**, according to information provided by hospitals.
Ground Truth	**Boston bombing** suspect Tamerlan Tsarnaev has been buried at an undisclosed location	Hospitals report three people in **critical condition**

Table 3: Example highlight sentences from different systems

- By incorporating tweet information for both sentence selection and compression, the performance of *HGRW+SC+both* outperforms *LexRank* significantly.

Table 3 shows some examples. As we can see in Example 1, with the help of tweet information, our compression model keeps the valuable part "Boston bombing" for summarization while the generic one abandons it.

We also investigate the influence of α and β. To study the impact of α, we fix β to 0.8, and vice versa. As shown in Figure 1, it is clear that larger α or β, i.e., giving higher weights to tweets related information, is generally helpful.

4 Conclusion and Future Work

In this paper, we showed that the relevant tweet collection of a news article can guide the process of sentence compression to generate better story highlights. We extended a dependency-tree based sentence compression model to incorporate tweet information. The experiment results on a public corpus that contains both news articles and relevant tweets showed the effectiveness of our approach. With the popularity of Twitter and increasing interaction between social media and news media, such parallel data containing news and related tweets is easily available, making our approach feasible to be used in a real system.

There are some interesting future directions. For example, we can explore more effective ways to incorporate tweets for sentence compression; we can study joint models to combine both sentence extraction and compression with the help of relevant tweets; it will also be interesting to use the parallel dataset of the news articles and the tweets for timeline generation for a specific event.

Acknowledgments

We thank the anonymous reviewers for their detailed and insightful comments on earlier drafts of this paper. The work is partially supported by NSF award IIS-0845484 and DARPA Contract No. FA8750-13-2-0041. Any opinions, findings, and conclusions or recommendations expressed are those of the authors and do not necessarily reflect the views of the funding agencies.

References

YLlias Chali and Sadid A Hasan. 2012. On the effectiveness of using sentence compression models for query-focused multi-document summarization. In *Proceedings of the 25th International Conference on Computational Linguistics*, pages 457–474.

James Clarke and Mirella Lapata. 2006. Models for sentence compression: A comparison across domains, training requirements and evaluation measures. In *Proceedings of the 21st International Conference on Computational Linguistics and the 44th annual meeting of the Association for Computational Linguistics*, pages 377–384. Association for Computational Linguistics.

Günes Erkan and Dragomir R Radev. 2004. Lexrank: Graph-based lexical centrality as salience in text summarization. *Journal of Artificial Intelligence Research*, 22:457–479.

Katja Filippova and Yasemin Altun. 2013. Overcoming the lack of parallel data in sentence compression. In *Proceedings of the 2013 Conference on Empirical Methods in Natural Language Processing*, pages 1481–1491. Association for Computational Linguistics.

Katja Filippova and Michael Strube. 2008. Dependency tree based sentence compression. In *Proceedings of the Fifth International Natural Language Generation Conference*, pages 25–32. Association for Computational Linguistics.

Dimitrios Galanis and Ion Androutsopoulos. 2010. An extractive supervised two-stage method for sentence compression. In *Human Language Technologies: The 2010 Annual Conference of the North American Chapter of the Association for Computational Linguistics*, pages 885–893. Association for Computational Linguistics.

Wei Gao, Peng Li, and Kareem Darwish. 2012. Joint topic modeling for event summarization across news and social media streams. In *Proceedings of the 21st ACM International Conference on Information and Knowledge Management*, pages 1173–1182.

Kevin Knight and Daniel Marcu. 2000. Statistics-based summarization-step one: Sentence compression. In *Proceedings of The 7th National Conference on Artificial Intelligence*, pages 703–710.

Alok Kothari, Walid Magdy, Ahmed Mourad Kareem Darwish, and Ahmed Taei. 2013. Detecting comments on news articles in microblogs. In *Proceedings of The 7th International AAAI Conference on Weblogs and Social Media*, pages 293–302.

Chen Li, Fei Liu, Fuliang Weng, and Yang Liu. 2013. Document summarization via guided sentence compression. In *Proceedings of the 2013 Conference on Empirical Methods in Natural Language Processing*, pages 490–500. Association for Computational Linguistics.

Chen Li, Yang Liu, Fei Liu, Lin Zhao, and Fuliang Weng. 2014. Improving multi-documents summarization by sentence compression based on expanded constituent parse trees. In *Proceedings of the 2014 Conference on Empirical Methods in Natural Language Processing*, pages 691–701. Association for Computational Linguistics.

Chin-Yew Lin. 2003. Improving summarization performance by sentence compression: a pilot study. In *Proceedings of the sixth international workshop on Information retrieval with Asian languages-Volume 11*, pages 1–8. Association for Computational Linguistics.

Chin-Yew Lin. 2004. Rouge: A package for automatic evaluation of summaries. In *Text Summarization Branches Out: Proceedings of the ACL-04 Workshop*, pages 74–81.

Xian Qian and Yang Liu. 2013. Fast joint compression and summarization via graph cuts. In *Proceedings of the 2013 Conference on Empirical Methods in Natural Language Processing*, pages 1492–1502. Association for Computational Linguistics.

Stefan Riezler, Tracy H King, Richard Crouch, and Annie Zaenen. 2003. Statistical sentence condensation using ambiguity packing and stochastic disambiguation methods for lexical-functional grammar. In *Proceedings of the 2003 Conference of the North American Chapter of the Association for Computational Linguistics on Human Language Technology*, pages 118–125. Association for Computational Linguistics.

Tadej Štajner, Bart Thomee, Ana-Maria Popescu, Marco Pennacchiotti, and Alejandro Jaimes. 2013. Automatic selection of social media responses to news. In *Proceedings of the 19th ACM International Conference on Knowledge Discovery and Data Mining*, pages 50–58. ACM.

Ilija Subašić and Bettina Berendt. 2011. Peddling or creating? investigating the role of twitter in news reporting. In *Advances in Information Retrieval*, pages 207–213. Springer.

Lu Wang, Hema Raghavan, Vittorio Castelli, Radu Florian, and Claire Cardie. 2013. A sentence compression based framework to query-focused multi-document summarization. In *Proceedings of the 48th Annual Meeting of the Association for Computational Linguistics*, pages 1384–1394. Association for Computational Linguistics.

Zhongyu Wei and Wei Gao. 2014. Utilizing microblog for automatic news highlights extraction. In *Proceedings of the 25th International Conference on Computational Linguistics*, pages 872–883.

Zhongyu Wei and Wei Gao. 2015. Gibberish, assistant, or master? using tweets linking to news for extractive single-document summarization. In *Proceedings of the 38th International ACM SIGIR Conference on Research and Development in Information Retrieval*.

Wayne Xin Zhao, Jing Jiang, Jianshu Weng, Jing He, Ee-Peng Lim, Hongfei Yan, and Xiaoming Li. 2011. Comparing twitter and traditional media using topic models. In *Advances in Information Retrieval*, pages 338–349. Springer.

Domain-Specific Paraphrase Extraction

Ellie Pavlick[1] Juri Ganitkevitch[2] Tsz Ping Chan[3] Xuchen Yao[4]
Benjamin Van Durme[2,5] Chris Callison-Burch[1]
[1]Computer and Information Science Department, University of Pennsylvania
[2]Center for Language and Speech Processing, Johns Hopkins University
[3]Bloomberg L.P., New York, NY
[4]kitt.ai,* Seattle, WA
[5]Human Language Technology Center of Excellence, Johns Hopkins University

Abstract

The validity of applying paraphrase rules depends on the domain of the text that they are being applied to. We develop a novel method for extracting domain-specific paraphrases. We adapt the bilingual pivoting paraphrase method to bias the training data to be more like our target domain of biology. Our best model results in higher precision while retaining complete recall, giving a 10% relative improvement in AUC.

1 Introduction

Many data-driven paraphrase extraction algorithms have been developed in recent years (Madnani and Dorr, 2010; Androutsopoulos and Malakasiotis, 2010). These algorithms attempt to learn paraphrase rules, where one phrase can be replaced with another phrase which has equivalent meaning in at least some context. Determining whether a paraphrase is appropriate for a specific context is a difficult problem (Bhagat and Hovy, 2013), encompassing issues of syntax (Callison-Burch, 2008), word sense (Apidianaki et al., 2014), and style (Xu et al., 2012; Pavlick and Nenkova, 2015). To date, the question of how domain effects paraphrase has been left unexplored.

Although most paraphrase extraction algorithms attempt to estimate a confidence with which a paraphrase rule might apply, these scores are not differentiated by domain, and instead correspond to the general domain represented by the model's training data. As illustrated by Table 1, paraphrases that are highly probable in the general domain (e.g. *hot* = *sexy*) can be extremely improbable in more specialized domains like biology. Dominant word senses change depending on domain: the verb *treat* is used in expressions like *treat you to dinner* in conversational domains versus *treat an infection* in biology. This domain shift changes the acceptability of its paraphrases.

	General	Biology
hot	warm, sexy, exciting	heated, warm, thermal
treat	address, handle, buy	cure, fight, kill
head	leader, boss, mind	skull, brain, cranium

Table 1: Examples of domain-sensitive paraphrases. Most paraphrase extraction techniques learn paraphrases for a mix of senses that work well in general. But in specific domains, paraphrasing should be sensitive to specialized language use.

We address the problem of customizing paraphrase models to specific target domains. We explore the following ideas:

1. We sort sentences in the training corpus based on how well they represent the target domain, and then extract paraphrases from a subsample of the most domain-like data.

2. We improve our domain-specific paraphrases by weighting each training example based on its domain score, instead of treating each example equally.

3. We dramatically improve recall while maintaining precision by combining the subsampled in-domain paraphrase scores with the general-domain paraphrase scores.

2 Background

The paraphrase extraction algorithm that we customize is the bilingual pivoting method (Bannard and Callison-Burch, 2005) that was used to create PPDB, the paraphrase database (Ganitkevitch et al., 2013). To perform the subsampling, we adapt and improve the method that Moore and Lewis (2010) originally developed for domain-specific language models in machine translation.

*Incubated by the Allen Institute for Artificial Intelligence.

Proceedings of the 53rd Annual Meeting of the Association for Computational Linguistics and the 7th International Joint Conference on Natural Language Processing (Short Papers), pages 57–62,
Beijing, China, July 26-31, 2015.

2.1 Paraphrase extraction

Paraphrases can be extracted via bilingual pivoting. Intuitively, if two English phrases e_1 and e_2 translate to the same foreign phrase f, we can assume that e_1 and e_2 have similar meaning, and thus we can "pivot" over f and extract $\langle e_1, e_2 \rangle$ as a paraphrase pair. Since many possible paraphrases are extracted in this way, and since they vary in quality (in PPDB, the verb *treat* has 1,160 potential paraphrases, including *address, handle, deal with, care for, cure him, 'm paying*, and *'s on the house*), it is necessary to assign some measure of confidence to each paraphrase rule. Bannard and Callison-Burch (2005) defined a conditional paraphrase probability $p(e_2|e_1)$ by marginalizing over all shared foreign-language translations f:

$$p(e_2|e_1) \approx \sum_f p(e_2|f)p(f|e_1) \tag{1}$$

where $p(e_2|f)$ and $p(f|e_1)$ are translation model probabilities estimated from the bilingual data.

Equation 1 approximates the probability with which e_1 can paraphrase as e_2, but its estimate inevitably reflects the domain and style of the bilingual training text. If e_1 is a polysemous word, the highest probabilities will be assigned to paraphrases of the most frequently occurring sense of e_1, and lower probabilities to less frequent senses. This results in inaccurate probability estimates when moving to a domain with different sense distributions compared to the training corpus.

2.2 Sorting by domain specificity

The crux of our method is to train a paraphrase model on data from the same domain as the one in which the paraphrases will be used. In practice, it is unrealistic that we will be able to find bilingual parallel corpora precompiled for each domain of interest. We instead subsample from a large bitext, biasing the sample towards the target domain.

We adapt and extend a method developed by Moore and Lewis (2010) (henceforth M-L), which builds a domain-specific sub-corpus from a large, general-domain corpus. The M-L method assigns a score to each sentence in the large corpus based on two language models, one trained on a sample of target domain text and one trained on the general domain. We want to identify sentences which are similar to our target domain and dissimilar from the general domain. M-L captures this notion using the difference in the cross-entropies according to each language model (LM). That is, for a sentence s_i, we compute

$$\sigma_i = H_{tgt}(s_i) - H_{gen}(s_i) \tag{2}$$

where H_{tgt} is the cross-entropy under the in-domain language model and H_{gen} is the cross-entropy under the general domain LM. Cross-entropy is monotonically equivalent to LM perplexity, in which lower scores imply a better fit. Lower σ_i signifies greater domain-specificity.

3 Domain-Specific Paraphrases

To apply the M-L method to paraphrasing, we need a sample of in-domain monolingual text. This data is not directly used to extract paraphrases, but instead to train an n-gram LM for the target domain. We compute σ_i for the English side of every sentence pair in our bilingual data, using the target domain LM and the general domain LM. We sort the entire bilingual training corpus so that the closer a sentence pair is to the top of the list, the more specific it is to our target domain.

We can apply Bannard and Callison-Burch (2005)'s bilingual pivoting paraphrase extraction algorithm to this sorted bitext in several ways:

1. By choosing a threshold value for σ_i and discarding all sentence pairs that fall outside of that threshold, we can extract paraphrases from a subsampled bitext that approximates the target domain.

2. Instead of simply extracting from a subsampled corpus (where each training example is equally weighted), we can weight each training example proportional to σ_i when computing the paraphrase scores.

3. We can combine multiple paraphrase scores: one derived from the original corpus and one from the subsample. This has the advantage of producing the full set of paraphrases that can be extracted from the entire bitext.

4 Experimental Conditions

Domain data We evaluate our domain-specific paraphrasing model in the target domain of biology. Our monolingual in-domain data is a combination of text from the GENIA database (Kim et al., 2003) and text from an introductory biology textbook. Our bilingual general-domain data is the 10^9 word parallel corpus (Callison-Burch et al.,

2009), a collection of French-English parallel data covering a mix of genres from legal text (Steinberger et al., 2006) to movie subtitles (Tiedemann, 2012). We use 5-gram language models with Kneser-Ney discounting (Heafield et al., 2013).

Evaluation We measure the precision and recall of paraphrase pairs produced by each of our models by collecting human judgments of what paraphrases are acceptable in sentences drawn from the target domain and in sentences drawn from the general domain. We sample 15K sentences from our biology data, and 10K general-domain sentences from Wikipedia. We select a phrase from each sentence, and show the list of candidate paraphrases[1] to 5 human judges. Judges make a binary decision about whether each paraphrase is appropriate given the domain-specific context. We consider a paraphrase rule to be good in the domain if it is judged to be good in least one context by the majority of judges. See Supplementary Materials for a detailed description of our methodology.

Baseline We run normal paraphrase extraction over the entire 10^9 word parallel corpus (which has 828M words on the English side) without any attempt to bias it toward the target domain. We refer this system as **General**.

Subsampling After sorting the 10^9 word parallel corpus by Equation 2, we chose several threshold values for subsampling, keeping only top-ranked τ words of the bitext. We train models on for several values of τ (1.5M, 7M, 35M, and 166M words). We refer to these model as **M-L,T=**τ.

M-L Change Point We test a model where τ is set at the point where σ_i switches from negative to positive. This includes all sentences which look more like the target domain than the general. This threshold is equivalent to sampling 20M words.

Weighted Counts Instead of weighting each subsampled sentence equally, we test a novel extension of M-L in which we weight each sentence proportional to σ_i when computing $p(e_2|e_1)$.

Combined Models We combine the subsampled models with the general model, using binary logistic regression to combine the $p(e_2|e_1)$ estimate of the general model and that of the domain-specific model. We use 1,000 labeled pairs from the target domain to set the regression weights. This tuning set is disjoint from the test set.

[1]The candidates paraphrases constitute the full set of paraphrases that can be extracted from our training corpus.

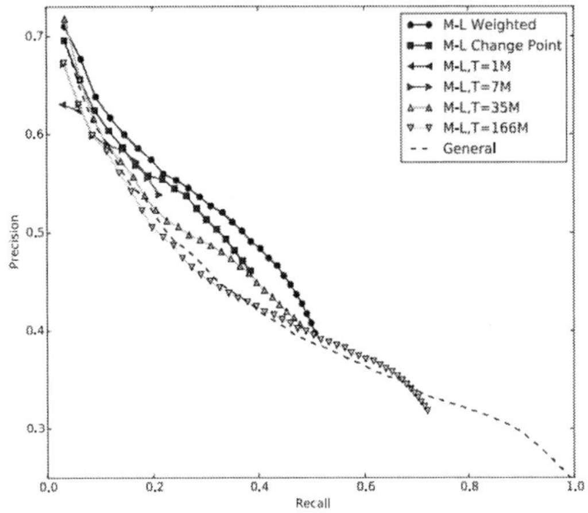

Figure 1: Precision-recall curves for paraphrase pairs extracted by models trained on data from each of the described subsampling methods. These curves are generated using the 15k manually annotated sentences in the biology domain.

5 Experimental Results

What is the effect of subsampling? Figure 1 compares the precision and recall of the different subsampling methods against the baseline of training on everything, when they are evaluated on manually labeled test paraphrases from the biology domain. All of subsampled models have a higher precision than the baseline **General** model, except for the largest of the subsampled models (which was trained on sentence pairs with 166M words - many of which are more like the general domain than the biology domain).

The subsampled models have reduced recall since many of the paraphrases that occur in the full 10^9 word bilingual training corpus do not occur in the subsamples. As we increase τ we improve recall at the expense of precision, since we are including training data that is less and less like our target domain. The highest precision model based on the vanilla M-L method is **M-L Change Point**, which sets the subsample size to include exactly those sentence pairs that look more like the target domain than the general domain.

Our novel extension of the M-L model (**M-L Weighted**) provides further improvements. Here, we weight each sentence pair in the bilingual training corpus proportional to σ_i when computing the paraphrase scores. Specifically, we weight the counting during the bilingual pivoting so that

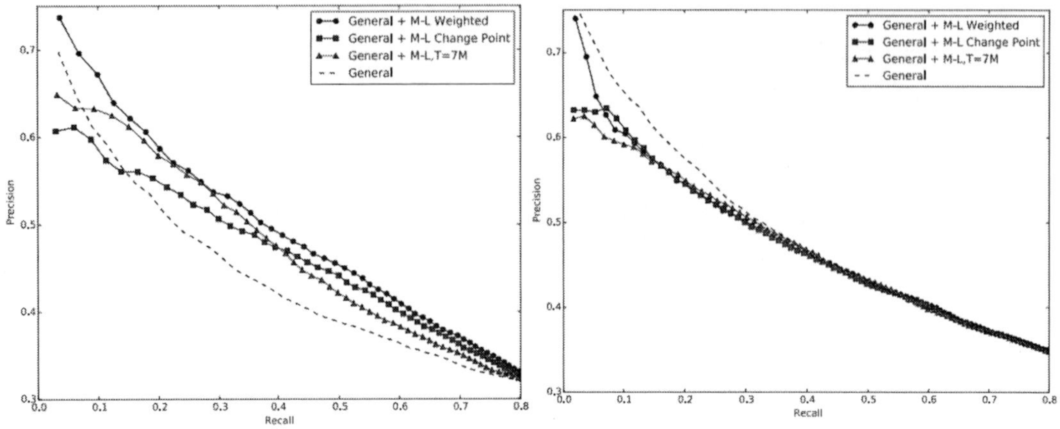

(a) Biology domain

(b) General domain

Figure 2: Performance of models build by combining small domain-specific models trained on subsampled data with general domain models trained on all the data. Performance in the general domain are shown as a control.

rather than each occurrence counting as 1, each occurrence counts as the ratio of the sentence's cross-entropies: $\frac{H_{gen}}{H_{tgt}}$. The top-ranked sentence pairs receive an exaggerated count of 52, while the bottom ones receive a tiny factional count of 0.0068. Thus, paraphrases extracted from sentence pairs that are unlike the biology domain receive very low scores. This allows us to achieve higher recall by incorporating more training data, while also improving the precision.

What is the benefit of combining models? We have demonstrated that extracting paraphrases from subsampled data results in higher precision domain-specific paraphrases. But these models extract only a fraction of the paraphrases that are extracted by a general model trained on the full bitext, resulting in a lower recall.

We dramatically improve the recall of our domain-specific models by combining the small subsampled models with the large general-domain model. We use binary logistic regression to combine the $p(e_2|e_1)$ estimate of the general model with that of each domain-specific model. Figure 2(a) shows that we are able to extend the recall of our domain-specific models to match the recall of the full general-domain model. The precision scores remain higher for the domain-specific models. Our novel **M-L Weighted** model performs the best. Table 3 gives the area under the curve (AUC). The best combination improves AUC by more than 4 points absolute (>10 points relative) in the biology domain. Table 2 provides examples of paraphrases extracted using our domain-specific

	general / bio-spec.		general / bio-spec.
air	aerial / atmosphere	fruit	result / fruiting
balance	pay / equilibrate	heated	lively / hot
breaks	pauses / ruptures	motion	proposal / movement

Table 2: Top paraphrase under the general and the best domain-specific model, General+M-L Weighted.

	AUC	$\Delta_{absolute}$	$\Delta_{relative}$
General	39.5	–	–
Gen.+M-L,T=1	40.8	+1.3	+3.3
Gen.+M-L,T=145	40.8	+1.3	+3.3
Gen.+M-L,T=29	41.2	+1.7	+4.3
Gen.+M-L CP	41.9	+2.4	+6.1
Gen.+M-L,T=6	42.3	+2.8	+7.1
Gen.+M-L Weighted	**43.7**	**+4.2**	**+10.6**

Table 3: AUC (× 100) for each model in the biology domain from Figure 2(a).

model for biology versus the baseline model.

6 Related Work

Domain-specific paraphrasing has not received previous attention, but there is relevant prior work on domain-specific machine translation (MT). We build on the Moore-Lewis method, which has been used for language models (Moore and Lewis, 2010) and translation models (Axelrod et al., 2011). Similar methods use LM perplexity to rank sentences (Gao et al., 2002; Yasuda et al., 2008), rather than the difference in cross-entropy. Within MT, Foster and Kuhn (2007) used log-linear weightings of translation probabilities to combine models trained in different domains, as we do here. Relevant to our proposed method of fractional counting, (Madnani et al., 2007) used introduced a count-centric approach to paraphrase probability estimation. Matsoukas et al. (2009) and Foster et al. (2010) explored weighted training sentences for MT, but set weights discriminatively based on sentence-level features.

7 Conclusion

We have discussed the new problem of extracting domain-specific paraphrases. We adapt a method from machine translation to the task of learning domain-biased paraphrases from bilingual corpora. We introduce two novel extensions to this method. Our best domain-specific model dramatically improves paraphrase quality for the target domain.

Acknowledgements This research was supported by the Allen Institute for Artificial Intelligence (AI2), the Human Language Technology Center of Excellence (HLTCOE), and by gifts from the Alfred P. Sloan Foundation, Google, and Facebook. This material is based in part on research sponsored by the NSF under grant IIS-1249516 and DARPA under agreement number FA8750-13-2-0017 (the DEFT program). The U.S. Government is authorized to reproduce and distribute reprints for Governmental purposes. The views and conclusions contained in this publication are those of the authors and should not be interpreted as representing official policies or endorsements of DARPA or the U.S. Government.

We would like to thank Luke Orland for his contributions to this research, and to thank the anonymous reviewers for their thoughtful comments.

References

Ion Androutsopoulos and Prodromos Malakasiotis. 2010. A survey of paraphrasing and textual entailment methods. *JAIR*, pages 135–187.

Marianna Apidianaki, Emilia Verzeni, and Diana McCarthy. 2014. Semantic clustering of pivot paraphrases. In *LREC*.

Amittai Axelrod, Xiaodong He, and Jianfeng Gao. 2011. Domain adaptation via pseudo in-domain data selection. In *EMNLP*, pages 355–362.

Colin Bannard and Chris Callison-Burch. 2005. Paraphrasing with bilingual parallel corpora. In *ACL*, pages 597–604.

Rahul Bhagat and Eduard Hovy. 2013. What is a paraphrase? *Computational Linguistics*, 39(3):463–472.

Chris Callison-Burch, Philipp Koehn, Christof Monz, and Josh Schroeder. 2009. Findings of the 2009 Workshop on Statistical Machine Translation. In *Proceedings of the Fourth Workshop on Statistical Machine Translation*.

Chris Callison-Burch. 2008. Syntactic constraints on paraphrases extracted from parallel corpora. In *EMNLP*, pages 196–205. Association for Computational Linguistics.

George Foster and Roland Kuhn. 2007. Mixture-model adaptation for smt.

George Foster, Cyril Goutte, and Roland Kuhn. 2010. Discriminative instance weighting for domain adaptation in statistical machine translation. In *EMNLP*, pages 451–459.

Juri Ganitkevitch, Benjamin Van Durme, and Chris Callison-Burch. 2013. PPDB: The paraphrase database. In *NAACL-HLT*, pages 758–764, Atlanta, Georgia, June.

Jianfeng Gao, Joshua Goodman, Mingjing Li, and Kai-Fu Lee. 2002. Toward a unified approach to statistical language modeling for chinese. *ACM Transactions on Asian Language Information Processing (TALIP)*, 1(1):3–33.

Kenneth Heafield, Ivan Pouzyrevsky, Jonathan H Clark, and Philipp Koehn. 2013. Scalable modified kneser-ney language model estimation. In *ACL*.

J-D Kim, Tomoko Ohta, Yuka Tateisi, and Junichi Tsujii. 2003. Genia corpusa semantically annotated corpus for bio-textmining. *Bioinformatics*, 19(suppl 1):i180–i182.

Nitin Madnani and Bonnie J. Dorr. 2010. Generating phrasal and sentential paraphrases: A survey of data-driven methods. *Computational Linguistics*, 36.

Nitin Madnani, Necip Fazil Ayan, Philip Resnik, and Bonnie Dorr. 2007. Using paraphrases for parameter tuning in statistical machine translation. In *Proceedings of the Workshop on Machine Translation*.

Spyros Matsoukas, Antti-Veikko I Rosti, and Bing Zhang. 2009. Discriminative corpus weight estimation for machine translation. In *EMNLP*, pages 708–717.

Robert C Moore and William Lewis. 2010. Intelligent selection of language model training data. In *ACL*, pages 220–224.

Ellie Pavlick and Ani Nenkova. 2015. Inducing lexical style properties for paraphrase and genre differentiation. In *NAACL*.

Ralf Steinberger, Bruno Pouliquen, Anna Widiger, Camelia Ignat, Tomaz Erjavec, Dan Tufis, and Dániel Varga. 2006. The jrc-acquis: A multilingual aligned parallel corpus with 20+ languages. *arXiv preprint*.

Jörg Tiedemann. 2012. Parallel data, tools and interfaces in opus. In *LREC*, pages 2214–2218.

Wei Xu, Alan Ritter, Bill Dolan, Ralph Grishman, and Colin Cherry. 2012. Paraphrasing for style. In *COLING*, pages 2899–2914.

Keiji Yasuda, Ruiqiang Zhang, Hirofumi Yamamoto, and Eiichiro Sumita. 2008. Method of selecting training data to build a compact and efficient translation model. In *IJCNLP*, pages 655–660.

Simplifying Lexical Simplification: Do We Need Simplified Corpora?

Goran Glavaš
University of Zagreb
Faculty of Electrical Engineering and Computing
goran.glavas@fer.hr

Sanja Štajner
University of Wolverhampton
Research Group in Computational Linguistics
SanjaStajner@wlv.ac.uk

Abstract

Simplification of lexically complex texts, by replacing complex words with their simpler synonyms, helps non-native speakers, children, and language-impaired people understand text better. Recent lexical simplification methods rely on manually simplified corpora, which are expensive and time-consuming to build. We present an unsupervised approach to lexical simplification that makes use of the most recent word vector representations and requires only regular corpora. Results of both automated and human evaluation show that our simple method is as effective as systems that rely on simplified corpora.

1 Introduction

Lexical complexity makes text difficult to understand for various groups of people: non-native speakers (Petersen and Ostendorf, 2007), children (De Belder and Moens, 2010), people with intellectual disabilities (Feng, 2009; Saggion et al., 2015), and language-impaired people such as autistic (Martos et al., 2012), aphasic (Carroll et al., 1998), and dyslexic (Rello, 2012) people. Automatic simplification that replaces complex words with their simpler synonyms is thus needed to make texts more understandable for everyone.

Lexical simplification systems still predominantly use a set of rules for substituting long and infrequent words with their shorter and more frequent synonyms (Devlin and Tait, 1998; De Belder and Moens, 2010). In generating the substitution rules (i.e., finding simple synonyms of a complex word), most systems refer to lexico-semantic resources like WordNet (Fellbaum, 1998). The nonexistence of lexicons like WordNet for a vast number of languages diminishes the impact of these simplification methods.

The emergence of the Simple Wikipedia[1] shifted the focus towards the data-driven approaches to lexical simplification, ranging from unsupervised methods leveraging either the metadata (Yatskar et al., 2010) or co-occurrence statistics of the simplified corpora (Biran et al., 2011) to supervised methods learning substitutions from the sentence-aligned corpora (Horn et al., 2014). Using simplified corpora improves the simplification performance, but reduces method applicability to the few languages for which such corpora exist.

The research question motivating this work relates to achieving comparable simplification performance without resorting to simplified corpora or lexicons like WordNet. Observing that "simple" words appear in regular (i.e., "complex", not simplified) text as well, we exploit recent advances in word vector representations (Pennington et al., 2014) to find suitable simplifications for complex words. We evaluate the performance of our resource-light approach (1) automatically, on two existing lexical simplification datasets and (2) manually, via human judgements of grammaticality, simplicity, and meaning preservation. The obtained results support the claim that effective lexical simplification can be achieved without using simplified corpora.

2 Related Work

Systems for lexical simplification are still dominantly rule-based, i.e., they rely on a set of substitutions, each consisting of a complex word and its simpler synonym, which are in most cases applied regardless of the context in which the complex word appears. Constructing substitution rules involves identifying synonyms, usually in Word-

[1] https://simple.wikipedia.org

Proceedings of the 53rd Annual Meeting of the Association for Computational Linguistics and the 7th International Joint Conference on Natural Language Processing (Short Papers), pages 63–68, Beijing, China, July 26-31, 2015.

Net, for a predefined set of complex words (Carroll et al., 1998; Bautista et al., 2009), and then choosing the "simplest" of these synonyms, typically using some frequency-based (Devlin and Tait, 1998; De Belder and Moens, 2010) or length-based heuristics (Bautista et al., 2009). The main shortcomings of the rule-based systems include low recall (De Belder and Moens, 2010) and misclassification of simple words as complex (and vice versa) (Shardlow, 2014).

The paradigm shift from knowledge-based to data-driven simplification came with the creation of Simple Wikipedia, which, aligned with the "original" Wikipedia, constitutes a large comparable corpus to learn from. Yatskar et al. (2010) used the edit history of Simple Wikipedia to recognize lexical simplifications. They employed a probabilistic model to discern simplification edits from other types of content changes. Biran et al. (2011) presented an unsupervised method for learning substitution pairs from a corpus of comparable texts from Wikipedia and Simple Wikipedia, although they exploited the (co-)occurrence statistics of the simplified corpora rather than its metadata. Horn et al. (2014) proposed a supervised framework for learning simplification rules. Using a sentence-aligned simplified corpus, they generated the candidate rules for lexical simplification. A context-aware binary classifier, trained and evaluated on 500 Wikipedia sentences (annotated via crowdsourcing), then decides whether a candidate rule should be applied or not in a certain context.

The main limitation of the aforementioned methods is the dependence on simplified corpora and WordNet. In contrast, we propose a resource-light approach to lexical simplification that requires only a sufficiently large corpus of regular text, making it applicable to the many languages lacking these resources.

3 Resource-Light Lexical Simplification

At the core of our lexical simplification method, which we name LIGHT-LS, is the observation that "simple" words, besides being frequent in simplified text, are also present in abundance in regular text. This would mean that we can find simpler synonyms of complex words in regular corpora, provided that reliable methods for measuring (1) the "complexity" of the word and (2) semantic similarity of words are available. LIGHT-LS simplifies only single words, but we fully account for this in the evaluation, i.e., LIGHT-LS is penalised for not simplifying multi-word expressions. In this work, we associate word complexity with the commonness of the word in the corpus, and not with the length of the word.

3.1 Simplification Candidate Selection

We employ GloVe (Pennington et al., 2014), a state-of-the-art model of distributional lexical semantics to obtain vector representations for all corpus words. The semantic similarity of two words is computed as the cosine of the angle between their corresponding GloVe vectors. For each content word (noun, verb, adjective, or adverb) w, we select as simplification candidates the top n words whose GloVe vectors are most similar to that of word w. In all experiments, we used 200-dimensional GloVe vectors pretrained on the merge of the English Wikipedia and Gigaword 5 corpus.[2] For each content word w, we select $n = 10$ most similar candidate words, excluding the morphological derivations of w.

3.2 Goodness-of-Simplification Features

We rank the simplification candidates according to several features. Each of the features captures one aspect of the suitability of the candidate word to replace the original word. The following are the descriptions for each of the features.

Semantic similarity. This feature is computed as the cosine of the angle between the GloVe vector of the original word and the GloVe vector of the simplification candidate.

Context similarity. Since type-based distributional lexico-semantic models do not discern senses of polysemous words, considering only semantic similarity between the original and candidate word may lead to choosing a synonym of the wrong sense as simplification of the complex word. The simplification candidates that are synonyms of the correct sense of the original word should be more semantically similar to the context of the original word. Therefore, we compute this feature by averaging the semantic similarities of the simplification candidate and each content word from the context of the original word:

$$csim(w, c) = \frac{1}{|C(w)|} \sum_{w' \in C(w)} \cos(\mathbf{v_w}, \mathbf{v_{w'}})$$

[2]http://www-nlp.stanford.edu/data/glove.6B.200d.txt.gz

where $C(w)$ is the set of context words of the original word w and $\mathbf{v_w}$ is the GloVe vector of the word w. We use as context a symmetric window of size three around the content word.

Difference of information contents. The primary purpose of this feature is to determine whether the simplification candidate is more informative than the original word. Under the hypothesis that the word's informativeness correlates with its complexity (Devlin and Unthank, 2006), we choose the candidate which is less informative than the original word. The complexity of the word is estimated by its information content (*ic*), computed as follows:

$$ic(w) = -\log \frac{\mathit{freq}(w) + 1}{\sum_{w' \in C} \mathit{freq}(w') + 1}$$

where $\mathit{freq}(w)$ is the frequency of the word w in a large corpus C, which, in our case, was the Google Book Ngrams corpus (Michel et al., 2011). The final feature value is the difference between the information contents of the original word and the simplification candidate, approximating the complexity reduction (or gain) that would be introduced should the simplification candidate replace the original word.

Language model features. The rationale for having language model features is obvious – a simplification candidate is more likely to be a compatible substitute if it fits into the sequence of words preceding and following the original word. Let $w_{-2}w_{-1}ww_1w_2$ be the context of the original word w. We consider a simplification candidate c to be a good substitute for w if $w_{-2}w_{-1}cw_1w_2$ is a likely sequence according to the language model. We employed the Berkeley language model (Pauls and Klein, 2011) to compute the likelihoods. Since Berkeley LM contains only bigrams and trigrams, we retrieve the likelihoods for ngrams $w_{-1}c$, cw_1, $w_{-2}w_{-1}c$, cw_1w_2, and $w_{-1}cw_1$, for each simplification candidate c.

3.3 Simplification Algorithm

The overall simplification algorithm is given in Algorithm 1. Upon retrieving the simplification candidates for each content word (line 4), we compute each of the features for each of the simplification candidates (lines 5–8) and rank the candidates according to feature scores (line 9). We choose as the best candidate the one with the highest average rank over all features (line 12). One important thing to notice is, that even though LIGHT-LS has no dedicated component for deciding whether simplifying a word is necessary, it accounts for this implicitly by performing the simplification only if the best candidate has lower information content than the original word (lines 13–15). Since simplification candidates need not have the same POS tag as the original word, to preserve grammaticality, we transform the chosen candidate into the morphological form that matches the POS-tag of the original word (line 14) using the NodeBox Linguistics tool.[3]

Algorithm 1: Simplify(*tt*)

```
1:  subst ← ∅
2:  for each content token t ∈ tt do
3:    all_ranks ← ∅
4:    scs ← most_similar(t)
5:    for each feature f do
6:      scores ← ∅
7:      for each sc ∈ scs do
8:        scores ← scores ∪ f(sc)
9:      rank ← rank_numbers(scores)
10:     all_ranks ← all_ranks ∪ rank
11:   avg_rank ← average(all_ranks)
12:   best ← argmax_sc(avg_rank)
13:   if ic(best) < ic(tt) do
14:     bpos ← in_pos(best, pos(tt))
15:     subst ← subst ∪ (tt, bpos)
16: return subst
```

4 Evaluation

We evaluate the effectiveness of LIGHT-LS automatically on two different datasets but we also let humans judge the quality of LIGHT-LS's simplifications.

4.1 Replacement Task

We first evaluated LIGHT-LS on the dataset crowdsourced by Horn et al. (2014) where manual simplifications for each target word were collected from 50 people. We used the same three evaluation metrics as Horn et al. (2014): (1) *precision* is the percentage of correct simplifications (i.e., the system simplification was found in the list of manual simplifications) out of all the simplifications made by the system; (2) *changed* is the percentage of target words changed by the system; and (3) *accuracy* is the percentage of correct simplifications out of all words that should have been simplified.

[3]`https://www.nodebox.net`

Table 1: Performance on the replacement task

Model	Precision	Accuracy	Changed
Biran et al. (2011)	71.4	3.4	5.2
Horn et al. (2014)	**76.1**	66.3	86.3
LIGHT-LS	71.0	**68.2**	**96.0**

LIGHT-LS's performance on this dataset is shown in Table 1 along with the performance of the supervised system by Horn et al. (2014) and the unsupervised system by Biran et al. (2011), which both used simplified corpora. The results show that LIGHT-LS significantly outperforms the unsupervised system of Biran et al. (2011) and performs comparably to the supervised system of Horn et al. (2014), which requires sentence-aligned simplified corpora. The unsupervised system of Biran et al. (2011) achieves precision similar to that of LIGHT-LS but at the cost of changing only about 5% of complex words, which results in very low accuracy. Our method numerically outperforms the supervised method of Horn et al. (2014), but the difference is not statistically significant.

4.2 Ranking Task

We next evaluated LIGHT-LS on the SemEval-2012 lexical simplification task for English (Specia et al., 2012), which focused on ranking a target word (in a context) and three candidate replacements, from the simplest to the most complex. To account for the peculiarity of the task where the target word is also one of the simplification candidates, we modified the features as follows (otherwise, an unfair advantage would be given to the target word): (1) we excluded the *semantic similarity* feature, and (2) we used the information content of the candidate instead of the difference of information contents.

We used the official SemEval task evaluation script to compute the Cohen's kappa index for the agreement on the ordering for each pair of candidates. The performance of LIGHT-LS together with results of the best-performing system (Jauhar and Specia, 2012) from the SemEval-2012 task and two baselines (random and frequency-based) is given in Table 2. LIGHT-LS significantly outperforms the supervised model by Jauhar and Specia (2012) with $p < 0.05$, according to the non-parametric stratified shuffling test (Yeh, 2000). An interesting observation is that the competitive frequency-based baseline highly correlates with our information content-based feature (the higher the frequency, the lower the information content).

Table 2: SemEval-2012 Task 1 performance

Model	κ
baseline-random	0.013
baseline-frequency	0.471
Jauhar and Specia (2012)	0.496
LIGHT-LS	**0.540**

4.3 Human Evaluation

Although automated task-specific evaluations provide useful indications of a method's performance, they are not as reliable as human assessment of simplification quality. In line with previous work (Woodsend and Lapata, 2011; Wubben et al., 2012), we let human evaluators judge the grammaticality, simplicity, and meaning preservation of the simplified text. We compiled a dataset of 80 sentence-aligned pairs from Wikipedia and Simple Wikipedia and simplified the original sentences with LIGHT-LS and the publicly available system of Biran et al. (2011). We then let two annotators (with prior experience in simplification annotations) grade grammaticality and simplicity for the manual simplification from Simple Wikipedia and simplifications produced by each of the two systems (total of 320 annotations per annotator). We also paired the original sentence with each of the three simplifications (manual and two systems') and let annotators grade how well the simplification preserves the meaning of the original sentence (total of 240 annotations per annotator). We averaged the grades of the two annotators for the final evaluation. All grades were assigned on a Likert (1–5) scale, with 5 being the highest grade, i.e., all fives indicate a very simple and completely grammatical sentence which fully preserves the meaning of the original text. The inter-annotator agreement, measured by Pearson correlation coefficient, was the highest for grammaticality (0.71), followed by meaning preservation (0.62) and simplicity (0.57), which we consider to be a fair agreement, especially for inherently subjective notions of simplicity and meaning preservation.

The results of human evaluation are shown in Table 3. In addition to grammaticality (Gr), simplicity (Smp), and meaning preservation (MP), we measured the percentage of sentences with at least one change made by the system (Ch). The results imply that the sentences produced by LIGHT-

Table 4: Example simplifications

Source	Sentence
Original sentence	*The contrast between a high level of education and a low level of political rights was particularly great in Aarau, and the city refused to send troops to defend the Bernese border.*
Biran et al. (2011) simpl.	*The **separate** between a high level of education and a low level of political rights was particularly great in Aarau , and the city refused to send troops to defend the Bernese border.*
LIGHT-LS simpl.	*The contrast between a high level of education and a low level of political rights was **especially** great in Aarau, and the city **asked** to send troops to **protect** the Bernese border.*

Table 3: Human evaluation results

Source	Gr	Smp	MP	Ch
Original sentence	4.90	3.36	–	–
Manual simplification	4.83	3.95	4.71	76.3%
Biran et al. (2011)	**4.63**	3.24	**4.65**	17.5%
LIGHT-LS	4.60	**3.76**	4.13	**68.6%**
Biran et al. (2011) Ch.	3.97	2.86	3.57	–
LIGHT-LS Ch.	4.57	3.55	3.75	–

LS are significantly simpler ($p < 0.01$; paired Student's t-test) than both the original sentences and sentences produced by the system of Biran et al. (2011). The system of Biran et al. (2011) produces sentences which preserve meaning better than the sentences produced by LIGHT-LS, but this is merely because their system performs no simplifications in over 80% of sentences, which is something that we have already observed on the replacement task evaluation. Furthermore, annotators found the sentences produced by this system to be more complex than the original sentences. On the contrary, LIGHT-LS simplifies almost 70% of sentences, producing significantly simpler text while preserving grammaticality and, to a large extent, the original meaning.

In order to allow for a more revealing comparison of the two systems, we additionally evaluated each of the systems only on sentences on which they proposed at least one simplification (in 70% of sentences for LIGHT-LS and in only 17.5% of sentences for the system of Biran et al. (2011)). These results, shown in the last two rows of Table 3, demonstrate that, besides simplicity and grammaticality, LIGHT-LS also performs better in terms of meaning preservation. In Table 4 we show the output of both systems for one of the few example sentences in which both systems made at least one change.

Since LIGHT-LS obtained the lowest average grade for meaning preservation, we looked deeper into the causes of changes in meaning introduced by LIGHT-LS. Most changes in meaning stem from the inability to discern synonymy from relatedness (or even antonymy) using GloVe vectors. For example, the word "cool" was the best simplification candidate found by LIGHT-LS for the target word *"warm"* in the sentence *"Water temperatures remained warm enough for development"*.

5 Conclusion

We presented LIGHT-LS, a novel unsupervised approach to lexical simplification that, unlike existing methods, does not rely on Simple Wikipedia and lexicons like WordNet, which makes it applicable in settings where such resources are not available. With the state-of-the-art word vector representations at its core, LIGHT-LS requires nothing but a large regular corpus to perform lexical simplifications.

Three different evaluation settings have shown that LIGHT-LS's simplifications based on multiple features (e.g., information content reduction, contextual similarity) computed on regular corpora lead to performance comparable to that of systems using lexicons and simplified corpora.

At the moment, LIGHT-LS supports only single-word simplifications but we plan to extend it to support multi-word expressions. Other lines of future research will focus on binding LIGHT-LS with methods for syntax-based (Zhu et al., 2010) and content-based (Glavaš and Štajner, 2013) text simplification.

Acknowledgements

This work has been partially supported by the Ministry of Science, Education and Sports, Republic of Croatia under the Grant 036-1300646-1986. We thank the anonymous reviewers for their useful comments.

References

Susana Bautista, Pablo Gervás, and R. Ignacio Madrid. 2009. Feasibility analysis for semi-automatic conversion of text to improve readability. In *Proceedings of the Second International Conference on Information and Communication Technology and Accessibility (ICTA)*, pages 33–40.

Or Biran, Samuel Brody, and Noémie Elhadad. 2011. Putting it simply: A context-aware approach to lexical simplification. In *Proceedings of the ACL-HLT 2011*, pages 496–501. ACL.

John Carroll, Guido Minnen, Yvonne Canning, Siobhan Devlin, and John Tait. 1998. Practical simplification of english newspaper text to assist aphasic readers. In *Proceedings of AAAI-98 Workshop on Integrating Artificial Intelligence and Assistive Technology*, pages 7–10.

Jan De Belder and Marie-Francine Moens. 2010. Text simplification for children. In *Proceedings of the SIGIR Workshop on Accessible Search Systems*, pages 19–26.

Siobhan Devlin and John Tait. 1998. The use of a psycholinguistic database in the simplification of text for aphasic readers. *Linguistic Databases*, pages 161–173.

Siobhan Devlin and Gary Unthank. 2006. Helping aphasic people process online information. In *Proceedings of the 8th International ACM SIGACCESS Conference on Computers and Accessibility (ASSETS)*, pages 225–226. ACM.

Christiane Fellbaum. 1998. *WordNet*. Wiley Online Library.

Lijun Feng. 2009. Automatic readability assessment for people with intellectual disabilities. In *ACM SIGACCESS Accessibility and Computing*, number 93, pages 84–91. ACM.

Goran Glavaš and Sanja Štajner. 2013. Event-centered simplification of news stories. In *Proceedings of the Student Workshop held in conjunction with RANLP*, pages 71–78.

Colby Horn, Cathryn Manduca, and David Kauchak. 2014. Learning a lexical simplifier using wikipedia. In *Proceedings of ACL 2014 (Short Papers)*, pages 458–463.

Sujay Kumar Jauhar and Lucia Specia. 2012. UOW-SHEF: SimpLex – lexical simplicity ranking based on contextual and psycholinguistic features. In *Proceedings of the SemEval-2012*, pages 477–481. ACL.

Juan Martos, Sandra Freire, Ana González, David Gil, and Maria Sebastian. 2012. D2.1: Functional requirements specifications and user preference survey. Technical report, FIRST project.

Jean-Baptiste Michel, Yuan Kui Shen, Aviva Presser Aiden, Adrian Veres, Matthew K. Gray, Joseph P. Pickett, Dale Hoiberg, Dan Clancy, Peter Norvig, and Jon Orwant. 2011. Quantitative analysis of culture using millions of digitized books. *Science*, 331(6014):176–182.

Adam Pauls and Dan Klein. 2011. Faster and smaller n-gram language models. In *Proceedings of ACL-HLT 2011*, pages 258–267. ACL.

Jeffrey Pennington, Richard Socher, and Christopher D Manning. 2014. GloVe: Global vectors for word representation. In *Proceedings of EMNLP 2014*, pages 1532–1543.

Sarah E. Petersen and Mari Ostendorf. 2007. Text simplification for language learners: A corpus analysis. In *Proceedings of Workshop on Speech and Language Technology for Education (SLaTE)*.

Luz Rello. 2012. DysWebxia: A Model to Improve Accessibility of the Textual Web for Dyslexic Users. In *ACM SIGACCESS Accessibility and Computing.*, number 102, pages 41–44. ACM, New York, NY, USA, January.

Horacio Saggion, Sanja Štajner, Stefan Bott, Simon Mille, Luz Rello, and Biljana Drndarevic. 2015. Making it simplext: Implementation and evaluation of a text simplification system for spanish. *ACM Transactions on Accessible Computing*, 6(4):14.

Matthew Shardlow. 2014. Out in the open: Finding and categorising errors in the lexical simplification pipeline. In *Proceedings of LREC 2014*, pages 1583–1590.

Lucia Specia, Sujay Kumar Jauhar, and Rada Mihalcea. 2012. SemEval-2012 Task 1: English lexical simplification. In *Proceedings of the SemEval 2012*, pages 347–355. ACL.

Kristian Woodsend and Mirella Lapata. 2011. Learning to simplify sentences with quasi-synchronous grammar and integer programming. In *Proceedings of EMNLP 2011*, pages 409–420. ACL.

Sander Wubben, Antal Van Den Bosch, and Emiel Krahmer. 2012. Sentence simplification by monolingual machine translation. In *Proceedings of ACL 2012 (Long Papers)*, pages 1015–1024. ACL.

Mark Yatskar, Bo Pang, Cristian Danescu-Niculescu-Mizil, and Lillian Lee. 2010. For the sake of simplicity: unsupervised extraction of lexical simplifications from Wikipedia. In *Proceedings of NAACL 2010*, pages 365–368. ACL.

Alexander Yeh. 2000. More accurate tests for the statistical significance of result differences. In *Proceedings of COLING 2000*, pages 947–953. ACL.

Zhemin Zhu, Delphine Bernhard, and Iryna Gurevych. 2010. A monolingual tree-based translation model for sentence simplification. In *Proceedings of the COLING 2010*, pages 1353–1361. ACL.

Zoom: a corpus of natural language descriptions of map locations

Romina Altamirano
FaMAF
Nat.Univ. of Córdoba
Córdoba, Argentina
ialtamir@famaf.unc.edu.ar

Thiago C. Ferreira
EACH-USP
Univ. of São Paulo
São Paulo, Brazil
thiago.castro.ferreira@usp.br

Ivandré Paraboni
EACH-USP
Univ. of São Paulo
São Paulo, Brazil
ivandre@usp.br

Luciana Benotti
FaMAF
Nat.Univ. of Córdoba
Córdoba, Argentina
benotti@famaf.unc.edu.ar

Abstract

This paper describes an experiment to elicit referring expressions from human subjects for research in natural language generation and related fields, and preliminary results of a computational model for the generation of these expressions. Unlike existing resources of this kind, the resulting data set - the Zoom corpus of natural language descriptions of map locations - takes into account a domain that is significantly closer to real-world applications than what has been considered in previous work, and addresses more complex situations of reference, including contexts with different levels of detail, and instances of singular and plural reference produced by speakers of Spanish and Portuguese.

1 Introduction

Referring Expression Generation (REG) is the computational task of producing adequate natural language descriptions (e.g., pronouns, definite descriptions, proper names, etc.) of domain entities. In particular, the issue of how to determine the semantic contents of definite descriptions (e.g., 'the Indian restaurant on 5th street', 'the restaurant we went to last night', etc.) has received significant attention in the field, and it is also the focus of the present work.

The input to a REG algorithm is a context set C containing an intended referent r and a number of distractor objects. All objects are represented as attribute-value pairs representing either *atomic* (*type-restaurant*) or *relational* (*on-5thstreet*) properties (Krahmer and Theune, 2002; Krahmer et al., 2003; Kelleher and Kruijff, 2006; Viethen et al., 2013). The expected output is a *uniquely identifying* list L of properties known to be true of r so that L distinguishes r from all distractors in C (Dale and Reiter, 1995).

Properties are selected for inclusion in L according to multiple - and often conflicting - criteria, including discriminatory power (i.e., the ability to rule out distractors) as in (Dale, 2002; Gardent, 2002), domain preferences (Pechmann, 1989; Gatt et al., 2013) and many others. A description that conveys more information than what is strictly required for disambiguation is said to be *overspecified* (Arts et al., 2011; Koolen et al., 2011; van Gompel et al., 2012; Engelhardt and Ferreira, 2006; Engelhardt et al., 2011). For a review of the research challenges in REG, see (Krahmer and van Deemter, 2012).

Existing approaches to REG largely consist of algorithmic solutions, many of which have been influenced by, or adapted from, the Dale & Reiter Incremental algorithm in (Dale and Reiter, 1995). The use of machine learning (ML) techniques, by contrast, seems to be less frequent than in other NLG tasks, although a number of exceptions do exist (e.g., (Jordan and Walker, 2005; Viethen and Dale, 2010; Viethen, 2011; Garoufi and Koller, 2013; Ferreira and Paraboni, 2014)).

A possible explanation for the small interest in ML for REG may be the relatively low availability of data. While research in many fields may benefit from the wide availability of text corpora (e.g., obtainable from the web), research in REG usually requires highly specialised data - hereby called REG corpora - conveying not only referring expressions produced by human speakers, but also a fully-annotated representation of the context (i.e., all objects and their semantic properties) within which the expressions have been produced.

REG corpora such as TUNA (Gatt et al., 2007) and GRE3D3 (Dale and Viethen, 2009) are useful both to gain general insights on human language production, and to benefit from data-intensive computational techniques such as ML. However, being usually the final product of controlled experiments involving human subjects, REG cor-

Proceedings of the 53rd Annual Meeting of the Association for Computational Linguistics and the 7th International Joint Conference on Natural Language Processing (Short Papers), pages 69–75,
Beijing, China, July 26-31, 2015.

pora tend to address highly specific research questions. For instance, GRE3D3 is largely devoted to the investigation of relational referring expressions (Kelleher and Kruijff, 2006) in simple visual scenes involving geometric shapes, as in 'the large ball next to the red cube'. As a result, and despite the usefulness of these resources to a large body of work in REG, further research questions will usually require the collection of new data.

In this paper we introduce the Zoom corpus of referring expressions. Zoom addresses a domain that is considerably closer to real-world applications (namely, city maps in different degrees of detail represented by zoom levels) than what has been considered in previous work, involving both singular and plural reference, and making extensive use of relational properties. Moreover, Zoom descriptions were produced by both Spanish and Portuguese speakers, which will allow (to the best of our knowledge, for the first time) a comprehensive study of the REG surface realisation subtask in these languages, and enable research on the issues of human variation in REG (Fabbrizio et al., 2008; Altamirano et al., 2012; Gatt et al., 2011).

2 Related work

TUNA (Gatt et al., 2007) was the first prominent REG corpus to be made publicly available for research purposes. The corpus was developed in a series of controlled experiments, containing 2280 atomic descriptions produced by 60 speakers of English in two domains (1200 descriptions of furniture items and 1080 descriptions of people's photographs). TUNA has been used in a series of REG shared tasks (Gatt et al., 2009).

GRE3D3 and its extension GRE3D7 (Dale and Viethen, 2009; Viethen and Dale, 2011) were developed in a series of web-based experiments primarily focussed on the study of relational descriptions. GRE3D3 contains 630 descriptions produced by 63 speakers, and GRE3D7 contains 4480 descriptions produced by 287 speakers. In both cases, the language of the experiment was English. The domain consists of simple visual scenes conveying boxes and spheres.

Stars (Teixeira et al., 2014) and its extension Stars2 were collected for the study of referential overspecification. Stars contains 704 descriptions produced by 64 speakers in a web-based experiment. Stars2 was produced in dialogue situations involving subject pairs, and it contains 884 descriptions produced by 56 speakers. Both domains make use of simple visual scenes containing up to four object types (e.g., stars, boxes, cones and spheres) and include atomic and relational descriptions alike. The language of both experiments was Brazilian Portuguese.

3 Experiment

We designed a web-based experiment to collect natural language descriptions of map locations in both Spanish and Portuguese. The collected data set comprises a corpus of referring expressions for research in REG and related fields. The situations of reference under consideration make use of map scenes in two degrees of detail (represented by low and high zoom levels), and address instances of singular and plural reference. A fragment of the experiment interface is shown in Fig. 1.

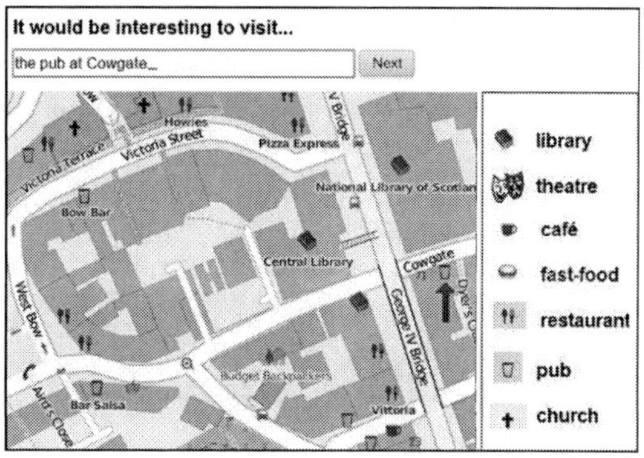

Figure 1: Experiment interface

3.1 Subjects

Volunteers were recruited upon invitation sent by email. The Portuguese data had 93 participants, being 66 (71.0%) male and 27 (29.0%) female. The Spanish data had 80 participants, being 59 male (69.4%) and 26 female (30.6%).

3.2 Procedure

Subjects received a web link to the on-line experiment interface (cf. Fig. 1) with self-contained instructions. Age and gender details were collected for statistical purposes. The experiment consisted of a series of map images presented in random order, one by one. Each map scene showed a particular location (e.g., a restaurant, pub, theatre etc.) pointed by an arrow. For each scene, subjects were required to imagine that they were giving travel advice to a friend, and to complete the sentence 'It would be interesting to visit...' with a description of the location pointed by the arrow. After pressing a 'Next' button, another stimulus was selected, until the end of the experiment. The first two images were fillers solely intended to make subjects familiar with the experiment setting, and the corresponding responses were not recorded. Incomplete trials, and ill-formed descriptions, were also discarded.

3.3 Materials

The experiment made use of the purpose-built interface illustrated in Fig. 1, and a set of map images obtained from OpenStreetMap[1], which consisted of selected portions of maps of Madrid and Lisbon to be presented to Spanish and Portuguese speakers, respectively. For each city, 10 map locations were used. Each location was shown in low and high zoom levels, making 20 images in total. In both cases, the intended target was kept the same, but the more detailed version would display a larger number of distractors and additional details in general. In addition to that, certain street and landmark names might not be depicted at different zoom levels. Half images showed a single arrow pointing to one map location (i.e., requiring a single description as 'the restaurant on Baker street'), whereas the other half showed two arrows pointed to two different locations (and hence requiring a reference to a set, as in 'the two restaurants near the museum').

3.4 Data collection

Upon manual verification, 602 ill-formed Portuguese descriptions and 366 Spanish descriptions were discarded. Thus, the Portuguese subcorpus consists of 1358 descriptions, and the Spanish subcorpus consists of 1234 descriptions. In the Portuguese subcorpus, 78.6% of the descriptions include relational properties. In addition to that, 36.4% were minimally distinguishing, 44.3% were overspecified, and 19.3% were underspecified. In the Spanish subcorpus, 70% of the descriptions include relational properties, 35% were minimally distinguishing, 40% were overspecified, and 25% were underspecified. Underspecified descriptions are not common in existing REG corpora (i.e., certainly not in this proportion), which may reflect the complexity of the domain and/or limitations of the web-based setting.

[1]openstreetmap.org

3.5 Annotation

Each referring expression was modelled as conveying a description of the main target object and, optionally, up to four descriptions of related landmarks. The annotation scheme consisted of three target attributes, four landmark attributes for each of the four possible landmark objects, and seven relational properties. This makes 26 possible attributes for each referring expression. In the case of plural descriptions (i.e., those involving two target objects), this attribute set is doubled.

Every object was annotated with the atomic attributes *type*, *name* and *others* and, in the case of landmark objects, also with their *id*. In addition to that, seven relational properties were considered: *in/on/at*[2], *next-to*, *right-of*, *left-of*, *in-front-of*, *behind-of*, and the multivalue relation *between* intended to represent 'corner' relations.

Possible values for the *type* and *name* attributes are predefined by each referential context. The *others* attribute may be assigned any string value, and it is intended to represent any non-standard piece of information conveyed by the expression. For the spatial relations, possible values are the object identifiers available from each scene.

The collected descriptions were fully annotated by two independent annotators. After completion, a third annotator assumed the role of judge and provided the final annotation. Since the annotation scheme was fairly straightforward (i.e., largely because all non-standard responses were simply assigned to the *others* attribute), agreement between judges as measured by Kappa (Cohen, 1960) was 84% at the attribute level. Both referential contexts and referring expressions were represented in XML format using a relational version of the format adopted in TUNA (Gatt et al., 2007).

3.6 Comparison with previous work

Table 1 presents a comparison between the collected data and existing REG corpora[3]: the number of referring expressions (REs), the number of subjects in each experiment, the number of possible atomic attributes (Attrib.) and possible landmarks (LMs) in a description, the average description size (in number of annotated properties), and the proportion of property usage, which is taken to

[2]The three prepositions were aggregated as a single attribute because they have approximately the same meaning in the languages under consideration

[3]The information on TUNA and Zoom descriptions is based on the singular portion of each corpus only

be the proportion of properties that appear in the description over the total number of possible attributes and landmarks. From a REG perspective, larger description sizes and lower usage rates may suggest more complex situations of reference.

Table 1: Comparison with existing REG corpora

Corpus	REs	Subj.	Attrib.	LMs	Avg.size	Usage
TUNA-F	1200	60	4	0	3.1	0.8
TUNA-P	1080	60	10	0	3.1	0.3
GRE3D3	630	63	9	1	3.4	0.3
GRE3D7	4480	287	6	1	3.0	0.4
Stars	704	64	8	2	4.4	0.4
Stars2	884	56	9	2	3.3	0.3
Zoom-Pt	1358	93	19	4	6.7	0.3
Zoom-Sp	1234	80	19	4	7.2	0.3

4 REG evaluation

In what follows we illustrate the use of the Zoom corpus as training and test data for a simple machine learning approach to REG adapted from (Ferreira and Paraboni, 2014). The goal of this evaluation is to provide reference results for future comparison with purpose-built REG algorithms, and not to present a complete REG solution for the Zoom domain or others.

The present model consists of 12 binary classifiers representing whether individual referential attributes should be selected for inclusion in an output description. The classifiers correspond to atomic attributes of the target and first landmark object (*type*, *name* and *others*), and relations. Referential attributes of other landmark objects were not modelled due to data sparsity and also to reduce computational costs. For similar reasons, the multivalue *between* relation is also presently disregarded, and 'corner' relations involving two landmarks (e.g., two streets) will be modelled as two independent classification tasks.

Only two learning features are considered by each classifier: *landmarkCount*, which represents the number of landmark objects near the main target, and *distractorCount*, which represents the number of objects of the same type as the target within the relevant context in the map. For other possible features applicable to this task, see, for instance, (dos Santos Silva and Paraboni, 2015).

From the outcome of the 12 binary classifiers, a description is built by considering atomic target attributes in the first place. All attributes that correspond to a positive prediction are selected for inclusion in the output description. Next, relations are considered. If no relation is predicted, the algorithm terminates by returning an atomic description of the main target object. If the description includes a relation, the corresponding landmark object is selected, and the algorithm is called recursively to describe it as well. Since every attribute that corresponds to a positive prediction is always selected, the algorithm does not regard uniqueness as a stop condition. As a result, the output description may convey a certain amount of overspecification.

For evaluation purposes, we used the subset of singular descriptions from the Portuguese portion of the corpus, comprising 821 descriptions. Evaluation was carried out by comparing the corpus description with the system output to measure overall accuracy (i.e., the number of exact matches between the two descriptions), Dice (Dice, 1945) and MASI (Passonneau, 2006) coefficients.

Following (Ferreira and Paraboni, 2014), we built a REG model using support vector machines with radial basis function kernel. The classifiers were trained and tested using 6-fold cross validation. Optimal parameters were selected using grid search as follows: for each step in the main k-fold validation, one fold was reserved for testing, and the remaining $k - 1$ folds were subject to a secondary cross-validation procedure in which different parameter combinations were attempted. The C parameter was assigned the values 1, 10, 100 and 1000, and γ was assigned 1, 0.1, 0.001 and 0.0001. The best-performing parameter set was selected to build a classifier trained from the $k - 1$ fold, and tested on the test data. This was repeated for every iteration of the main cross-validation procedure.

Table 2 summarises the results obtained by the REG algorithm built from SVM classifiers, those obtained by a baseline system representing a relational extension of the Dale & Reiter Incremental Algorithm, and by a Random selection strategy.

Table 2: REG results

Algorithm	Acc.	Dice	MASI
SVM	0.15	0.51	0.28
Incremental	0.04	0.53	0.21
Random selection	0.03	0.45	0.15

We compare accuracy scores obtained by every algorithm pair using the chi-square test, and we compare *Dice* scores using *Wilcoxon's* signed-rank test. In terms of overall accuracy, the SVM approach outperforms both alternatives. The difference from the second best-performing algorithm (i.e., the Incremental approach) is significant ($\chi^2 = 79.87$, df=1, p<0.0001). Only in terms of Dice scores a small effect in the opposite direction is observed (T=137570.5, p= 0.01413).

We also assessed the performance of the individual classifiers. Table 3 shows these results as measured by precision (P), recall (R), F1-measure (F1) and area under the ROC curve (AUC).

Table 3: Classifier results

Classifier	P	R	F_1	AUC
tg_type	0.95	1.00	0.98	0.25
tg_name	0.09	0.05	0.07	0.41
tg_other	0.00	0.00	0.00	0.05
lm_type	0.93	1.00	0.96	0.44
lm_name	0.97	1.00	0.98	0.35
lm_other	0.00	0.00	0.00	0.43
next-to	0.50	0.24	0.32	0.63
right-of	0.00	0.00	0.00	0.28
left-of	0.00	0.00	0.00	0.27
in-front-of	0.00	0.00	0.00	0.42
behind-of	0.00	0.00	0.00	0.17
in/on/at	0.60	0.60	0.60	0.61

From these results we notice that highly frequent attributes (e.g., target type and landmark name) were classified with high accuracy, whereas others (e.g., multivalue attributes and relations) were not.

5 Discussion

This paper has introduced the Zoom corpus of natural language descriptions of map locations, a resource intended to support future research in REG and related fields. Preliminary results of a SVM-based approach to REG - which were solely presented for the future assessment of REG algorithms based on Zoom data - hint at the actual complexity of the REG task in this domain in a number of ways. First, we notice that a similar approach in (Ferreira and Paraboni, 2014) on GRE3D3 and GRE3D7 data has obtained considerably higher mean accuracy. This is partially explained by the increased complexity of the Zoom domain, but also by the currently simple annotation scheme.

Second, we notice that Zoom descriptions are prone to convey relations between a single target and multiple landmark objects, as in 'the restaurant between the 5th and 6th streets'. Although common in language use, the use of multiple relational properties in this way has been little investigated in the REG field.

Finally, we notice that the Zoom domain contains two descriptions for every target object, which are based on different - but related - models corresponding to the same map location seen at different zoom levels. Interestingly, the referring expression in a 1X situation may or may not be the same as in a 2X situation. Consider a map with higher zoom level (2X) as illustrated in the previous Fig. 2, and the same map location as seen with lower zoom level in the previous Fig. 1.

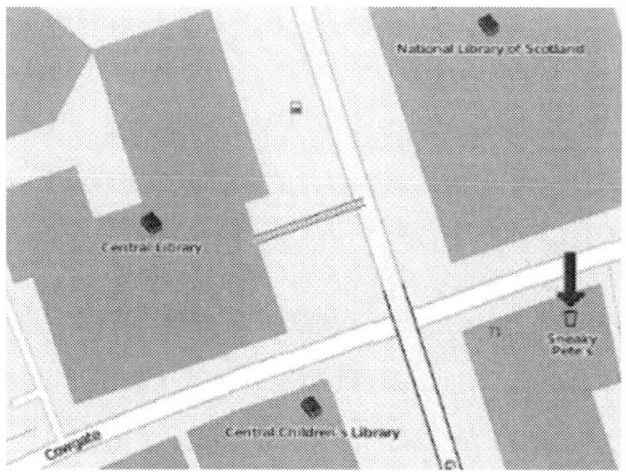

Figure 2: Map with a more detailed zoom level

The underlying models for these two maps are certainly different, but not unrelated. The map with 2X zoom contains fewer objects but may include more properties due to the added level of detail. The referring expression for the target in the 1X map may or may not be the same as in the 2X map. For instance, the referring expression "the pub at Cowgate" is underspecified on the 1X map, but it is minimally distinguishing on the 2X map.

Differences of this kind are common in interactive applications (e.g., in which the context of reference may change in structure or in the number of objects and referable properties), and the challenge for REG algorithms would be to produce an appropriate description for the modified context without starting from scratch. REG algorithms based on local context partitioning (Areces et al., 2008) may have an advantage in this respect, but further investigation is still required.

Acknowledgements

This work has been supported by FAPESP and CAPES. The authors are also grateful to the annotators Adriano S. R. da Silva, Jefferson S. F. da Silva and Alan K. Yamasaki.

References

Romina Altamirano, Carlos Areces, and Luciana Benotti. 2012. Probabilistic refinement algorithms for the generation of referring expressions. In *COLING (Posters)*, pages 53–62.

Carlos Areces, Alexander Koller, and Kristina Striegnitz. 2008. Referring expressions as formulas of description logic. In *Proceedings of the Fifth International Natural Language Generation Conference*, INLG '08, pages 42–49, Stroudsburg, PA, USA. Association for Computational Linguistics.

A. Arts, A. Maes, L. G. M. Noordman, and C. Jansen. 2011. Overspecification facilitates object identification. *Journal of Pragmatics*, 43(1):361–374.

J. Cohen. 1960. A coeficient of agreement for nominal scales. *Educational and Psychological Measurement*, 20(1):37–46.

Robert Dale and Ehud Reiter. 1995. Computational interpretations of the Gricean maxims in the generation of referring expressions. *Cognitive Science*, 19(2):233–263.

Robert Dale and Jette Viethen. 2009. Referring expression generation through attribute-based heuristics. In *Proceedings of ENLG-2009*, pages 58–65.

Robert Dale. 2002. Cooking up referring expressions. In *Proceedings of the 27th Annual Meeting of the Association for Computational Linguistics*, pages 68–75.

L. R. Dice. 1945. Measures of the amount of ecologic association between species. *Ecology*, 26(3):297–302.

Diego dos Santos Silva and Ivandré Paraboni. 2015. Generating spatial referring expressions in interactive 3D worlds. *Spatial Cognition and Computation*.

P. E. Engelhardt and K. Baileyand F. Ferreira. 2006. Do speakers and listeners observe the Gricean maxim of quantity? *Journal of Memory and Language*, 54(4):554–573.

P. E. Engelhardt, S. B. Demiral, and Fernanda Ferreira. 2011. Over-specified referring expressions impair comprehension: An ERP study. *Brain and Cognition*, 77(2):304–314.

Giuseppe Di Fabbrizio, Amanda J. Stent, and Srinivas Bangalore. 2008. Trainable speaker-based referring expression generation. In *Proceedings of the Twelfth Conference on Computational Natural Language Learning*, CoNLL '08, pages 151–158, Stroudsburg, PA, USA.

Thiago Castro Ferreira and Ivandré Paraboni. 2014. Classification-based referring expression generation. *Lecture Notes in Computer Science*, 8403:481–491.

C. Gardent. 2002. Generating minimal definite descriptions. In *Proceedings of the 40th Annual Meeting of the Association for Computational Linguistics*, pages 96–103.

Konstantina Garoufi and Alexander Koller. 2013. Generation of effective referring expressions in situated context. *Language and Cognitive Processes*, 29(8):986–1001.

Albert Gatt, Ilka van der Sluis, and Kees van Deemter. 2007. Evaluating algorithms for the generation of referring expressions using a balanced corpus. In *Proceedings of ENLG-07*.

Albert Gatt, Anja Belz, and Eric Kow. 2009. The TUNA challenge 2009: Overview and evaluation results. In *Proceedings of the 12nd European Workshop on Natural Language Generation*, pages 174–182.

Albert Gatt, R. van Gompel, E. Krahmer, and K. van Deemter. 2011. Non-deterministic attribute selection in reference production. In *Workshop on the Production of Referring Expressions (PRE-CogSci 2011)*, pages 1–7.

Albert Gatt, E. Krahmer, R. van Gompel, and K. van Deemter. 2013. Production of referring expressions: Preference trumps discrimination. In *35th Meeting of the Cognitive Science Society*, pages 483–488.

Pamela W. Jordan and Marilyn A. Walker. 2005. Learning content selection rules for generating object descriptions in dialogue. *J. Artif. Int. Res.*, 24(1):157–194.

J. D. Kelleher and G. Kruijff. 2006. Incremental generation of spatial referring expressions in situated dialog. In *Proceedings of the 21st International Conference on Computational Linguistics and 44th Annual Meeting of the ACL*, pages 1041–1048.

Ruud Koolen, Albert Gatt, Martijn Goudbeek, and Emiel Krahmer. 2011. Factors causing overspecification in definite descriptions. *Journal of Pragmatics*, 43(13):3231–3250.

Emiel Krahmer and Mariet Theune. 2002. Efficient context-sensitive generation of referring expressions. In Kees van Deemter and Rodger Kibble, editors, *Information Sharing: Reference and Presupposition in Language Generation and Interpretation*, pages 223–264. CSLI Publications, Stanford, CA.

Emiel Krahmer and Kees van Deemter. 2012. Computational generation of referring expressions: A survey. *Computational Linguistics*, 38(1):173–218.

Emiel Krahmer, Sebastiaan van Erk, and Andre Verleg. 2003. Graph-based generation of referring expressions. *Computational Linguistics*, 29(1):53–72.

Rebecca Passonneau. 2006. Measuring agreement on set-valued items (MASI) for semantic and pragmatic annotation. In *Proceedings of the International Conference on Language Resources and Evaluation (LREC)*.

T. Pechmann. 1989. Incremental speech production and referential overspecification. *Linguistics*, 27(1):98–110.

Caio V. M. Teixeira, Ivandré Paraboni, Adriano S. R. da Silva, and Alan K. Yamasaki. 2014. Generating relational descriptions involving mutual disambiguation. *Lecture Notes in Computer Science*, 8403:492–502.

R. van Gompel, Albert Gatt, E. Krahmer, and K. van Deemter. 2012. PRO: A computational model of referential overspecification. In *Proceedings of AMLAP-2012*.

Jette Viethen and Robert Dale. 2010. Speaker-dependent variation in content selection for referring expression generation. In *Proceedings of the Australasian Language Technology Association Workshop 2010*, pages 81–89, Melbourne, Australia.

Jette Viethen and Robert Dale. 2011. GRE3D7: A corpus of distinguishing descriptions for objects in visual scenes. In *Proceedings of UCNLG+Eval-2011*, pages 12–22.

Jette Viethen, Margaret Mitchell, and Emiel Krahmer. 2013. Graphs and spatial relations in the generation of referring expressions. In *Proceedings of the 14th European Workshop on Natural Language Generation*, pages 72–81, Sofia, Bulgaria, August. Association for Computational Linguistics.

Jette Viethen. 2011. *The Generation of Natural Descriptions: Corpus-Based Investigations of Referring Expressions in Visual Domains*. Ph.D. thesis, Macquarie University, Sydney, Australia.

Generating overspecified referring expressions: the role of discrimination

Ivandré Paraboni, Michelle Reis Galindo, Douglas Iacovelli
School of Arts, Sciences and Humanities (EACH)
University of São Paulo (USP)
Av. Arlindo Bettio, 1000 - São Paulo, Brazil
{ivandre,michelle.galindo,douglas.iacovelli}@usp.br

Abstract

We present an experiment to compare a standard, minimally distinguishing algorithm for the generation of relational referring expressions with two alternatives that produce overspecified descriptions. The experiment shows that discrimination - which normally plays a major role in the disambiguation task - is also a major influence in referential overspecification, even though disambiguation is in principle not relevant.

1 Introduction

In Natural Language Generation (NLG) systems, Referring Expression Generation (REG) is the computational task of providing natural language descriptions of domain entities (Levelt, 1989; Dale and Reiter, 1995), as in 'the second street on the left', 'the money that I found in the kitchen' etc. In this paper we will focus on the issue of content selection of *relational* descriptions, that is, those in which the intended target is described *via* another object, hereby called a *landmark*. Consider the example of context in Fig. 1.

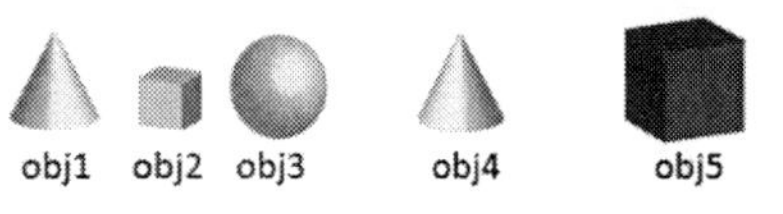

Figure 1: A simple visual context. All objects are grey except for $obj5$, which is red.

Let us consider the goal of uniquely identifying the target $obj1$ in the context in Fig.1. Since the target shares most atomic properties (e.g., type, colour and size) with other distractor objects in the context (and particularly so with respect to $obj4$), using a relational property (*near-obj2*) may help prevent ambiguity. The following (a)-(c) are examples of descriptions of this kind produced from the above context.

(a)The cone near the box
(b)The cone near the *grey* box
(c)The cone near the *small* box

As in example (a), existing REG algorithms will usually pay regard to the Gricean maxim of quantity (Grice, 1975), and avoid the inclusion of properties that are not strictly required for disambiguation. In the case of relational reference, this means that both target and landmark portions of the description may be left *underspecified*, and uniqueness will follow from the fact that they mutually disambiguate each other (Teixeira et al., 2014). In other words, example (a) may be considered felicitous even though both 'cone' and 'box' are ambiguous if interpreted independently.

Minimally distinguishing descriptions as in (a) are the standard output of many REG algorithms that handle relational descriptions as in (Dale and Haddock, 1991; Krahmer and Theune, 2002; Krahmer et al., 2003). Human speakers, on the other hand, are largely redundant (Engelhardt et al., 2006; Arts et al., 2011; Koolen et al., 2011; Engelhardt et al., 2011), and will often produce so-called *overspecified* descriptions as in (b-c) above.

In this paper we will focus on the issue of generating overspecified relational descriptions as in examples (b-c), discussing which properties should be selected by a REG algorithm assuming that the decision to overspecify has already been made. More specifically, we will discuss whether the algorithm should include colour as in (b), size as in (c), or other alternatives, and we will assess the impact of a referential overspecification strategy that favours highly discriminatory properties over preferences that are well-established in the literature. Although this may in principle seem as a narrow research topic, the generation of relational descriptions is still subject of considerable debate in the field (e.g., (Viethen and Dale, 2011) and

Proceedings of the 53rd Annual Meeting of the Association for Computational Linguistics and the 7th International Joint Conference on Natural Language Processing (Short Papers), pages 76–82, Beijing, China, July 26-31, 2015.

the issue of landmark under/full-specification has a number of known consequences for referential identification (e.g., (Paraboni and van Deemter, 2014)).

2 Related work

2.1 Relational REG

One of the first REG algorithms to take relations into account is the work in (Dale and Haddock, 1991), which generates descriptions that may include relational properties only as a last resort, that is, only when it is not possible to obtain a uniquely identifying descriptions by making use of a set of atomic properties. The algorithm prevents circularity (e.g., 'the cup on the table that supports a cup that...') and avoids the inclusion of redundant properties with the aid of consistency networks. As a result, the algorithm favours the generation of minimally distinguishing relational descriptions as example (a) in the previous section.

In the Graph algorithm described in (Krahmer et al., 2003), the referential context is modelled as a labelled directed graph with vertices representing domain entities and edges representing properties that can be either relational (when connecting two entities) or atomic (when forming self-loops). The task of obtaining a uniquely identifying description is implemented as a subgraph construction problem driven by domain-dependent cost functions associated with the decisions made by the algorithm. The work in (Krahmer et al., 2003) does not make specific assumptions about the actual attribute selection policy, and by varying the cost functions it is possible to implement a wide range of referential strategies. The use of the algorithm for the generation of relational descriptions is discussed in (Viethen et al., 2013).

The work in (Paraboni et al., 2006) discusses the issue of ease of search by focussing on the particular case of relational description in hierarchically-ordered domains (e.g., books divided into sections and subsections etc.) Descriptions that may arguably make search difficult, as in 'the section that contains a picture' are prevented by producing fully-specified descriptions of each individual object (i.e., picture, section etc.). As in (Dale and Haddock, 1991), atomic properties are always attempted first, and each target (e.g., a subsection) holds only one relation (e.g., to its parent section). Descriptions of this kind are similar to the examples (b-c) in the previous section. However, hierarchical structures are highly specialised domains, and it is less clear to which extent these findings are applicable to more general situations of reference as in, e.g., spatial domains (Byron et al., 2007; dos Santos Silva and Paraboni, 2015).

2.2 Referential overspecification

Assuming that we would like to add a redundant property to overspecify a certain description, which property should be selected? Research on REG, cognitive sciences and related fields has investigated a number of factors that may play a role in referential overspecification. First of all, it has been widely observed that some properties are simply preferred to others. This seems to be the case, for instance, of the colour attribute. Colour is ubiquitously found in both redundant and non-redundant use (Pechmann, 1989), and empirical evidence suggests that colour is overspecified more frequently than size (Belke and Meyer, 2002).

The inherent preference for colour has however been recently challenged. The work in (van Gompel et al., 2014), for instance, points out that when perceptual salience is manipulated so that a high contrast between target and distractors is observed, the size attribute may be preferred to colour. In other words, a highly preferred property may not necessarily match the choices made by human speakers when producing overspecified descriptions. Results along these lines are also reported in (Tarenskeen et al., 2014).

Redundant and non-redundant uses of colour (and possibly other preferred properties) may also be influenced by the difficulty in encoding visual properties. In (Viethen et al., 2012), for instance, it is argued that the colour property is more likely to be selected when it is maximally different from the other colours in the context. For instance, a red object is more likely to be described as 'red' when none of the distractors is red, and less so when a modifier (e.g., 'light red') would be required for disambiguation.

Closer to our present discussion, we notice that the issue of discrimination as proposed in (Olson, 1970) has been considered by most REG algorithms to date (e.g., (Dale and Reiter, 1995; Krahmer and van Deemter, 2012)), and it has even motivated a number of greedy or minimally distinguishing REG strategies (Gardent, 2002; Dale, 2002; Areces et al., 2011). Interestingly, the work in (Gatt et al., 2013) has suggested that small differences in discriminatory power do not seem to influence content selection, but large differences do, a notion that has been applied to the design of REG algorithms on at least two occasions: in (de Lucena et al., 2010) properties are selected in order of preference regardless of their discriminatory power and, if necessary, an additional, highly discriminatory property is included; in (van Gompel et al., 2012), a fully distinguishing property is attempted first and, if necessary for disambiguation, further properties are considered based on both preference and discrimination.

Discrimination clearly plays a major role in the disambiguation task, but it less clear whether it is still relevant when disambiguation is not an issue, that is, in the case of referential overspecification. The present work is an attempt to shed light on this particular issue.

3 Current work

Following (Pechmann, 1989) and others, we may assume that colour should be generally (or perhaps always) preferred to size. Moreover, as in (Kelleher and Kruijff, 2006), we may follow the principle of minimal effort (Clark and Wilkes-Gibbs, 1986) and assume that atomic properties such as colour or size should be preferred to relations that lead to more complex descriptions. In our current work, however, we will argue that neither needs to be the case: under the right circumstances, a wide range of properties - colour, size and even spatial relations - may be overspecified depending on their *discriminatory power* alone. Thus, it may be the case that size is preferred to colour (unlike, e.g., (Pechmann, 1989)), and that longer, relational descriptions are preferred to shorter ones (unlike, e.g., (Kelleher and Kruijff, 2006)).

The possible preference for highly discriminatory properties in referential overspecification is easily illustrated by the examples in the introduction section. Following (Pechmann, 1989), one might assume that, if a speaker decides to overspecify the landmark portion of description (a), she may add the colour attribute, as in (b). This strategy, however, turns out to be far less common in language use if a more discriminatory property is available, as in the example. More specifically, the availability of a highly discriminatory landmark property (*size-small*) makes (c) much more likely than (b). This observation gives rise to the following research hypothesis:

> *h1: Given the goal of overspecifying a relational description by using an additional landmark property p, p should correspond to the most discriminatory property available in the context.*

The idea that speakers may take discriminatory power into account when referring is of course not novel. What is less obvious, however, is that discrimination may also play a significant role in situations that do not involve ambiguity, as in the above examples. To illustrate this, let us consider a basic REG algorithm - hereby called *Baseline* - consisting of a relational implementation of an Incremental-like algorithm as proposed in (Dale and Reiter, 1995).

Given the goal of producing a uniquely identifying description L of a target object r, the *Baseline* algorithm works as follows: first, an atomic description is attempted by examining a list of preferred attributes P and by selecting those that help disambiguate the reference, as in the standard Incremental approach (Dale and Reiter, 1995). If the description is uniquely identifying, the algorithm terminates. If not, a relational property relating r to a landmark object o is included in L, and the algorithm is called recursively to describe o using an atomic description if possible.

Since *Baseline* terminates as soon as a uniquely identifying description is obtained, the landmark description will be usually left underspecified as in example (a) in Section 1. This behaviour is consistent with existing relational REG algorithms (e.g., (Dale and Haddock, 1991; Krahmer et al., 2003)).

Using the *Baseline* descriptions as a starting point, however, we may decide to fully-specify the landmark description (e.g., in order to facilitate search, as in (Paraboni and van Deemter, 2014)) by selecting an additional property p from the remainder P list, hereby called P_0.

There are of course many ways of defining p. In corpus-based REG, for instance, a plausible strategy would be to assume that the definition of p is domain-dependent, and simply select the most frequent (but still discriminatory) property in P_0 as seen in training data. We will call this variation the *Most Frequent* overspecification strategy.

Choosing the most frequent property p may lead to descriptions that closely resemble those observed in the data. However, we predict that the availability of a highly discriminatory property may change this preference. To illustrate this, we will also consider a *Proposal* strategy in which p is taken to be the most discriminatory property available in P_0. In case of a tie, the most frequent property that appears in P_0 is selected. If P_0 does not contain any discriminatory properties, none will be selected and the landmark description will remain underspecified as in the standard *Baseline* approach.

The context in the previous Fig.1 and the accompanying examples (a-c) in Section 1 illustrate the expected output of each of the three algorithms under consideration. As in previous work on relational REG, the *Baseline* approach would produce the minimally distinguishing description (a); the *Most Frequent* strategy would overspecify the landmark portion of the description by adding the preferred property in the relevant domain (e.g., colour) as in (b); and the *Proposal* strategy would overspecify by adding the highly discriminatory property (in this particular example, size) as in (c).

The relation between the three algorithms and our research hypothesis $h1$ is straightforward. We would like to show that the predictions made by *Proposal* are more accurate than those made by *Baseline* and *Most Frequent*. An experiment to verify this claim is described in the next section.

4 Experiment

For evaluation purposes we will make use the Stars2 corpus of referring expressions[1]. Stars2 is an obvious choice for our experiment since these data convey visual scenes in which objects will usually have one highly discriminatory property available for reference. Moreover, descriptions in this domain may convey up to two relations (e.g., 'the cone next to the ball, near the cone'), which gives rise to multiple opportunities for referential overspecification.

In addition to this, we will also make use of the subset of relational descriptions available from the GRE3D3 (Dale and Viethen, 2009) and GRE3D7 (Viethen and Dale, 2011) corpora. Situations of reference in the GRE3D3/7 domain are in many ways simpler than those in Stars2 (i.e., by containing at most one possible relation in each scene, by not presenting any property whose discriminatory power is substantially higher than others etc.), but the comparison is still useful since GRE3D3/7 are among the very few annotated relational REG corpora made publicly available for research purposes, and which have been extensively used in previous work.

From the three domains - Stars2, GRE3D3 and GRE3D7 - we selected all instances of relational descriptions in which the landmark object was described by making use of the *type* attribute and exactly one additional property p. This amounts to three *Reference* sets containing 725 descriptions in total: 367 descriptions from Stars2, 114 from GRE3D3 and 244 from GRE3D7.

In the situations of reference available from these domains, the use of p is never necessary for disambiguation, and p will never be selected by a standard REG algorithm as the *Baseline* strategy described in the previous section. Thus, our goal is to investigate which overspecification strategy - *Proposal* or *Most Frequent*, cf. previous section - will select the correct p, and the corresponding impact of this decision on the overall results of each algorithm.

From the unused portion of each corpus, we estimate attribute frequencies to create the preference list P required by the algorithms. The following preference orders were obtained:

$P(Stars2)$ ={*type, colour, size, near, in-front-of, right, left, below, above, behind*}

$P(GRE3D)$ ={*type, colour, size, above, in-front-of, hpos, vpos, near, right, left*}

In the case of the GRE3D3/7 corpora, we notice that not all attributes appear in both data sets. Moreover, the attributes *hpos* and *vpos* were computed from the existing *pos* attribute, which was originally intended to model both horizontal and vertical screen coordinates as a single property in (Dale and Viethen, 2009).

Each of the three REG strategies - *Baseline*, *Proposal* and *Most Frequent* - received as an input the 725 situations of reference represented in the *Reference* data and the corresponding P list for each domain. As a result, three sets of output descriptions were obtained, hereby called *System* sets.

Evaluation was carried out by comparing each *System* set to the corresponding *Reference* corpus descriptions and measuring *Dice* scores (Dice, 1945) and overall accuracy (that is, the number of exact matches between each *System-Reference* description pair).

[1]Some of the corpus features are described in (Ferreira and Paraboni, 2014)

Table 1: Results

Algorithm	*Baseline*				*Most frequent*				*Proposal*			
	Dice		Accuracy		Dice		Accuracy		Dice		Accuracy	
Dataset	mean	sdv	mean	sdv	mean	sdv	mean	sdv	mean	sdv	mean	sdv
Stars2	0.63	0.14	0.00	0.00	0.62	0.18	0.11	0.31	**0.76**	0.18	**0.27**	0.45
GRE3D3	0.81	0.06	0.00	0.00	0.87	0.10	0.25	0.43	**0.90**	0.09	**0.36**	0.48
GRE3D7	0.84	0.07	0.00	0.00	**0.92**	0.10	**0.47**	0.50	0.89	0.10	0.34	0.48
Overall	0.73	0.15	0.00	0.00	0.76	0.21	0.25	0.43	**0.82**	0.16	**0.31**	0.46

5 Results

Table 1 shows descriptive statistics for the evaluation of our three algorithms - *Baseline*, *Proposal* and *Most Frequent* - applied to each corpus - Stars2, GRE3D3 and GRE3D7. Best results are highlighted in boldface.

Following (Gatt and Belz, 2007) and many others, we compare *Dice* scores obtained by the three algorithms applied to the generation of the selected descriptions of each domain using *Wilcoxon's* signed-rank test. In the Overall evaluation, *Proposal* outperforms both alternatives. The difference is significant (W(338)=-34327, Z=-9.55, $p < 0.0001$). Highly discriminatory properties are indeed those that are normally selected by human speakers when they decide to overspecify a landmark description. This supports our research hypothesis $h1$.

Individual results are as follows. In the case of the Stars2 domain, *Proposal* outperforms both alternatives. The difference is significant (W(241)=-26639, Z=-12.29, $p < 0.0001$). In the case of GRE3D3, once again *Proposal* outperforms the alternatives. The difference is also significant (W(27)=-248, Z=-2.97, $p < 0.03$). Finally, in the case of GRE3D7, an effect in the opposition direction was observed, i.e., the *Most Frequent* algorithm outperforms the alternatives. The difference is significant (W(70)=1477, Z=4.32, $p < 0.0001$).

The differences across domains are explained by the proportion of highly discriminatory landmark properties in each corpus. In Stars2, the nearest landmark has at least one highly discriminatory property in all scenes involving relational reference. In GRE3D3, the nearest landmark has a highly discriminatory property in 80% of the scenes, and in GRE3D7 this is the case in only 50% of the scenes. Thus, given the opportunity, the use of a highly discriminatory property seems to be preferred. The absence of a property that 'stands out', by contrast, appears to make the choice among them a matter of preference, an observation that is consistent with the findings in (Gatt et al., 2013).

6 Final remarks

This paper has presented a practical REG experiment to illustrate the impact of discrimination on the generation of overspecified relational descriptions. The experiment shows that discrimination - which normally plays a major role in the disambiguation task - is also a considerable influence in referential overspecification, that is, even when discrimination is in principle not an issue. Our findings correlate with previous empirical work in the field, and show that discrimination may effectively trump the inherent preference for absolute properties and for those that are easier to realise in surface form. For instance, contrary to (Pechmann, 1989) and many others, speakers would generally prefer referring to size as in (b), despite evidence suggesting that colour is overspecified more frequently than size. Moreover, contrary to (Kelleher and Kruijff, 2006), speakers would also prefer referring to a spatial relation as in (c) even though the resulting descriptions turns out to be more complex.

We are aware that the present work has focussed on extreme situations in which a highly discriminatory property is available for overspecification. As future work, it is necessary to further this investigation by taking into account various degrees of discrimination. As suggested in (Gatt et al., 2013), the effect of discrimination may be perceived as a continuum, and in that case a practical REG algorithm should be able to make more complex decisions that those presently implemented.

Acknowledgements

This work has been supported by FAPESP and by the University of São Paulo.

References

C. Areces, S. Figueira, and D. Gorín. 2011. Using logic in the generation of referring expressions. In *Proceedings of the 6th International Conference on Logical Aspects of Computational Linguistics (LACL 2011)*, pages 17–32, Montpelier. Springer.

A. Arts, A. Maes, L. G. M. Noordman, and C. Jansen. 2011. Overspecification facilitates object identification. *Journal of Pragmatics*, 43(1):361–374.

E. Belke and A. Meyer. 2002. Tracking the time course of multidimensional stimulus discrimination. *European Journal of Cognitive Psychology*, 14(2):237–266.

D. Byron, A. Koller, J. Oberlander, L. Stoia, and K. Striegnitz. 2007. Generating instructions in virtual environments (GIVE): A challenge and evaluation testbed for NLG. In *Workshop on Shared Tasks and Comparative Evaluation in Natural Language Generation.*

H. Clark and D. Wilkes-Gibbs. 1986. Referring as a collaborative process. *Cognition*, 22:1–39.

R. Dale and N. J. Haddock. 1991. Content determination in the generation of referring expressions. *Computational Intelligence*, 7(4):252–265.

R. Dale and E. Reiter. 1995. Computational interpretations of the Gricean maxims in the generation of referring expressions. *Cognitive Science*, 19(2):233–263.

Robert Dale and Jette Viethen. 2009. Referring expression generation through attribute-based heuristics. In *Proceedings of ENLG-2009*, pages 58–65.

Robert Dale. 2002. Cooking up referring expressions. In *Proceedings of the 27th Annual Meeting of the Association for Computational Linguistics*, pages 68–75.

Diego Jesus de Lucena, Ivandré Paraboni, and Daniel Bastos Pereira. 2010. From semantic properties to surface text: The generation of domain object descriptions. *Inteligencia Artificial. Revista Iberoamericana de Inteligencia Artificial*, 14(45):48–58.

L. R. Dice. 1945. Measures of the amount of ecologic association between species. *Ecology*, 26(3):297–302.

Diego dos Santos Silva and Ivandré Paraboni. 2015. Generating spatial referring expressions in interactive 3D worlds. *Spatial Cognition and Computation.*

P. E. Engelhardt, K. Baileyand, and F. Ferreira. 2006. Do speakers and listeners observe the Gricean maxim of quantity? *Journal of Memory and Language*, 54(4):554–573.

P. E. Engelhardt, S. B. Demiral, and Fernanda Ferreira. 2011. Over-specified referring expressions impair comprehension: An ERP study. *Brain and Cognition*, 77(2):304–314.

Thiago Castro Ferreira and Ivandré Paraboni. 2014. Referring expression generation: taking speakers' preferences into account. *Lecture Notes in Artificial Intelligence*, 8655:539–546.

C. Gardent. 2002. Generating minimal definite descriptions. In *Proceedings of the 40th Annual Meeting of the Association for Computational Linguistics*, pages 96–103.

Albert Gatt and Anja Belz. 2007. The attribute selection for GRE challenge: Overview and evaluation results. In *UCNLG+MT: Language Generation and Machine Translation.*

Albert Gatt, E. Krahmer, R. van Gompel, and K. van Deemter. 2013. Production of referring expressions: Preference trumps discrimination. In *35th Meeting of the Cognitive Science Society*, pages 483–488.

H. P. Grice. 1975. Logic and conversation. In Peter Cole and Jerry L. Morgan, editors, *Syntax and semantics*, volume 3. New York: Academic Press.

J. D. Kelleher and G. Kruijff. 2006. Incremental generation of spatial referring expressions in situated dialog. In *Proceedings of the 21st International Conference on Computational Linguistics and 44th Annual Meeting of the ACL*, pages 1041–1048.

Ruud Koolen, Albert Gatt, Martijn Goudbeek, and Emiel Krahmer. 2011. Factors causing overspecification in definite descriptions. *Journal of Pragmatics*, 43(13):3231–3250.

Emiel Krahmer and Mariet Theune. 2002. Efficient context-sensitive generation of referring expressions. In Kees van Deemter and Rodger Kibble, editors, *Information Sharing: Reference and Presupposition in Language Generation and Interpretation*, pages 223–264. CSLI Publications, Stanford, CA.

E. Krahmer and Kees van Deemter. 2012. Computational generation of referring expressions: A survey. *Computational Linguistics*, 38(1):173–218.

Emiel Krahmer, Sebastiaan van Erk, and Andre Verleg. 2003. Graph-based generation of referring expressions. *Computational Linguistics*, 29(1):53–72.

W. Levelt. 1989. *Speaking: From intention to articulation.* MIT press, Cambridge, Ma.

D. R. Olson. 1970. Language and thought: aspects of a cognitive theory of semantics. *Psychological Review*, 77(4):257–273.

Ivandré Paraboni and Kees van Deemter. 2014. Reference and the facilitation of search in spatial domains. *Language, Cognition and Neuroscience*, 29(8):1002–1017.

Ivandré Paraboni, Judith Masthoff, and Kees van Deemter. 2006. Overspecified reference in hierarchical domains: measuring the benefits for readers. In *Proc. of INLG-2006*, pages 55–62, Sydney.

T. Pechmann. 1989. Incremental speech production and referential overspecification. *Linguistics*, 27(1):98–110.

Sammie Tarenskeen, Mirjam Broersma, and Bart Geurts. 2014. Referential overspecification: Colour is not that special. In *RefNet Workshop on Psychological and Computational Models of Reference Comprehension and Production*, Edinburgh, Scotland.

Caio V. M. Teixeira, Ivandré Paraboni, Adriano S. R. da Silva, and Alan K. Yamasaki. 2014. Generating relational descriptions involving mutual disambiguation. *Lecture Notes in Computer Science*, 8403:492–502.

R. van Gompel, Albert Gatt, E. Krahmer, and K. van Deemter. 2012. PRO: A computational model of referential overspecification. In *Proceedings of AMLAP-2012*.

Roger van Gompel, Albert Gatt, Emiel Krahmer, and Kees Van Deemter. 2014. Testing computational models of reference generation as models of human language production: The case of size contrast. In *RefNet Workshop on Psychological and Computational Models of Reference Comprehension and Production*, Edinburgh, Scotland.

Jette Viethen and Robert Dale. 2011. GRE3D7: A corpus of distinguishing descriptions for objects in visual scenes. In *Proceedings of UCNLG+Eval-2011*, pages 12–22.

Jette Viethen, Martijn Goudbeek, and Emiel Krahmer. 2012. The impact of colour difference and colour codability on reference production. In *Proceedings of CogSci-2012*, pages 1084–1098.

Jette Viethen, Margaret Mitchell, and Emiel Krahmer. 2013. Graphs and spatial relations in the generation of referring expressions. In *Proceedings of the 14th European Workshop on Natural Language Generation*, pages 72–81, Sofia, Bulgaria, August. Association for Computational Linguistics.

Using prosodic annotations to improve coreference resolution of spoken text

Ina Rösiger and Arndt Riester
Institute for Natural Language Processing
University of Stuttgart, Germany
Pfaffenwaldring 5b, 70569 Stuttgart
roesigia|arndt@ims.uni-stuttgart.de

Abstract

This paper is the first to examine the effect of prosodic features on coreference resolution in spoken discourse. We test features from different prosodic levels and investigate which strategies can be applied. Our results on the basis of manual prosodic labelling show that the presence of an accent is a helpful feature in a machine-learning setting. Including prosodic boundaries and determining whether the accent is the nuclear accent further increases results.

1 Introduction

Noun phrase coreference resolution is the task of determining which noun phrases (NPs) in a text or dialogue refer to the same discourse entities (Ng, 2010). Coreference resolution has been extensively addressed in NLP research, e.g. in the CoNLL shared task 2012 (Pradhan et al., 2012) or in the SemEval shared task 2010 (Recasens et al., 2010). Amoia et al. (2012) have shown that there are differences between written and spoken text wrt coreference resolution and that the performance typically drops when systems that have been developed for written text are applied on spoken text. There has been considerable work on coreference resolution in written text, but comparatively little work on spoken text, with a few exceptions of systems for pronoun resolution in transcripts of spoken text e.g. Strube and Müller (2003), Tetreault and Allen (2004). However, so far, prosodic information has not been taken into account. The interaction between prosodic prominence and coreference has been investigated in several experimental and theoretical analyses (Terken and Hirschberg, 1994; Schwarzschild, 1999; Cruttenden, 2006); for German (Baumann and Riester, 2013; Baumann and Roth, 2014; Baumann et al., 2015).

There is a tendency for coreferent items, i.e. entities that have already been introduced into the discourse, to be deaccented, as the speaker assumes the entity to be salient in the listener's discourse model. We can exploit this by including prominence features in the coreference resolver.

Our prosodic features mainly aim at definite descriptions, where it is difficult for the resolver to decide whether the potential anaphor is actually anaphoric or not. In these cases, accentuation is an important means to distinguish between given entities (often deaccented) and other categories (i.e. bridging anaphors, see below) that are typically accented, particularly for entities whose heads have a different lexeme than their potential antecedent. Pronouns are not the case of interest here, as they are (almost) always anaphoric. To make the intuitions clearer, Example (1), taken from Umbach (2002), shows the difference prominence can make:

(1) John has <u>an old cottage</u>.[1]

a. Last year he reconstructed the SHED.
b. Last year he reconSTRUCted **the shed**.

Due to the pitch accent on *shed* in (1a), it is quite obvious that *the shed* and *the cottage* refer to different entities; they exemplify a bridging relation, where the shed is a part of the cottage. In (1b), however, *the shed* is deaccented, which has the effect that *the shed* and *the cottage* corefer.

We present a pilot study on German spoken text that uses manual prominence marking to show the principled usefulness of prosodic features for coreference resolution. In the long run and for application-based settings, of course, we do not want to rely on manual annotations. This work is investigating the potential of prominence information and is meant to motivate the use of automatic

[1]Anaphors are typed in boldface, their antecedents are underlined. Accented syllables are capitalised.

Proceedings of the 53rd Annual Meeting of the Association for Computational Linguistics and the 7th International Joint Conference on Natural Language Processing (Short Papers), pages 83–88,
Beijing, China, July 26-31, 2015.

prosodic features. Our study deals with German data, but the prosodic properties are comparable to other West Germanic languages, like English or Dutch. To the best of our knowledge, this is the first work on coreference resolution in spoken text that tests the theoretical claims regarding the interaction between coreference and prominence in a general, state-of-the-art coreference resolver, and shows that prosodic features improve coreference resolution.

2 Prosodic features for coreference resolution

The prosodic information used for the purpose of our research results from manual annotations that follow the GToBI(S) guidelines by Mayer (1995), which stand in the tradition of autosegmental-metrical phonology, cf. Pierrehumbert (1980), Gussenhoven (1984), Féry (1993), Ladd (2008), Beckman et al. (2005). We mainly make use of *pitch accents* and *prosodic phrasing*. The annotations distinguish *intonation phrases*, terminated by a major boundary (%), and *intermediate phrases*, closed by a minor boundary (-), as shown in Examples (2) and (3).

The available pitch accent and boundary annotations allow us to automatically derive a secondary layer of prosodic information which represents a mapping of the pitch accents onto a prominence scale in which the nuclear (i.e. final) accents of an intonation phrase *(n2)* rank as the most prominent, followed by the nuclear accents of intermediate phrases *(n1)* and prenuclear (i.e. non-final) accents which are perceptually the least prominent. To put it simply, the nuclear accent is the most prominent accent in a prosodic phrase while prenuclear accents are less prominent.

While we expect the difference between the presence or absence of pitch accents to influence the classification of short NPs like in Example (1), we do not expect complex NPs to be fully deaccented. For complex NPs, we nevertheless hope that the prosodic structure of coreferential NPs will turn out to significantly differ from the structure of discourse-new NPs such as to yield a measurable effect. Examples (2) and (3) show the prosodic realisation of two expressions with different information status. In Example (2), the complex NP *the text about the aims and future of the EU* refers back to *the Berlin Declaration*, whereas in Example (3), the complex NP *assault with lethal consequences and reckless homicide* is not anaphoric. The share of prenuclear accents is higher in the anaphoric case, which indicates lower overall prominence. The features described in Section 2.1 only take into account the absence or type of the pitch accent; those in Section 2.2 additionally employ prosodic phrasing. To get a better picture of the effect of these features, we implement, for each feature, one version for all noun phrases and a second version only for short noun phrases (<=4 words).

2.1 Prosodic features ignorant of phrase boundaries

Pitch accent type corresponds to the following pitch accent types that are present in the GToBI(S) based annotations.

Fall	H*L
Rise	L*H
Downstep fall	!H*L
High target	H*
Low target	L*
Early peak	HH*L
Late peak	L*HL

For complex NPs, the crucial label is the last label in the mention. For short NPs, this usually matches the label on the syntactic head.

Pitch accent presence focuses on the presence of a pitch accent, disregarding its type. If one accent is present in the markable, the boolean feature gets assigned the value *true*, and *false* otherwise.

2.2 Prosodic features including phrase boundary information

The following set of features takes into account the degree of prominence of pitch accents as presented at the beginning of Section 2, which at the same time encodes information about prosodic phrasing.

Nuclear accent type looks at the different degrees of accent prominence. The markable gets assigned the type *n2*, *n1*, *pn* if the last accent in the phrase matches one of the types (and *none* if it is deaccented).

Nuclear accent presence is a Boolean feature comparable to pitch accent presence. It gets assigned the value *true* if there is some kind of accent present in the markable. To be able to judge the helpfulness of the distinction between the categories that are introduced above, we experiment with two different versions:

(2) Anaphoric complex NP (DIRNDL sentences 9/10):

9: Im Mittelpunkt steht eine von der Ratspräsidentin, Bundeskanzlerin Merkel, vorbereitete "Berliner Erklärung".

10: Die Präsidenten [...] wollen	**[den**	**TEXT**	**über die**	**ZIEle**	**und**	**ZUkunft**	**der**	**EU]**	unterzeichnen.
the presidents [...] want	[the	text	about the	aims	and	future	the	EU]	sign
	((	L*H		L*H-)	(	H*L		H*L	H*L -)%)
		pn		n1		pn		pn	

Central is the 'Berlin Declaration' that was prepared by the president of the Council of the EU, Chancellor Merkel. The presidents want to sign ***[the text about the aims and future of the EU.]***

(3) Non-anaphoric complex NP (DIRNDL sentences 2527/2528):

2527: Der Prozess um den Tod eines Asylbewerbers aus Sierra Leone in Polizeigewahrsam ist [...] eröffnet worden.

2528: [Wegen	KÖRperverletzung	mit	TOdesfolge	und	fahrlässiger	TÖtung]	MÜSsen	...
[Due	assault	with	lethal consequence,	and	reckless	homicide]	must	
((	H*L		L*H -)	(		H*L -)%)		
	pn		n1			n2		

The trial about the death of an asylum seeker from Sierra Leone during police custody has started. Charges include [assault with lethal consequence, and reckless homicide], ...

1. Only *n2* accents get assigned *true*
2. *n2* and *n1* accents get assigned *true*

Note that a version where all accents get assigned *true*, i.e. *pn* and *n1* and *n2*, is not included as this equals the feature *Pitch accent presence*.

Nuclear bag of accents treats accents like a bag-of-words approach treats words: if one accent type is present once (or multiple times), the accent type is considered present. This means we get a number of different combinations ($2^3 = 8$ in total) of accent types that are present in the markable, e.g. *pn* and *n1* but no *n2* for Example (2), and *pn, n1* and *n2* for Example (3).

Nuclear: first and last includes linear information while avoiding an explosion of combinations. It only looks at the (degree of the) first pitch accent present in the markable and combines it with the last accent.

3 Experimental setup

We perform our experiments using the IMS HotCoref system (Björkelund and Kuhn, 2014), a state-of-the-art coreference resolution system for English. As German is not a language that is featured in the standard resolver, we first had to adapt it. These adaptations include gender and number agreement, lemma-based (sub)string match and a feature that addresses German compounds, to name only a few.[2]

For our experiments on prosodic features, we use the DIRNDL corpus[3] (ca. 50.000 tokens, 3221 sentences), a radio news corpus annotated with both manual coreference and manual prosody labels (Eckart et al., 2012; Björkelund et al., 2014)[4]. We adopt the official train, test and development split. We decided to remove abstract anaphors (e.g. anaphors that refer to events or facts), which are not resolved by the system. In all experiments, we only use predicted annotations and no gold mention boundary (GB) information as we aim at real end-to-end coreference resolution. On DIRNDL, our system achieves a CoNLL score of 47.93, which will serve as a baseline in our experiments. To put the baseline in context, we also report performance on the German reference corpus TüBa-D/Z[5] (Naumann, 2006), which consists

[2]To download the German coreference system, visit: www.ims.uni-stuttgart.de/forschung/ressourcen/werkzeuge/HOTCorefDe.html

[3]http://www.ims.uni-stuttgart.de/forschung/ressourcen/korpora/dirndl.html

[4]In this work, we have focused on improvements within the clearly defined field of coreference resolution, using prosodic features. As one of the reviewers pointed out, the DIRNDL corpus additionally features manual two-level information status annotations according to the *RefLex* scheme (Baumann and Riester, 2012), which additionally distinguishes bridging anaphors, deictic expressions, and more. Recent work on smaller datasets of read text has shown that there is a meaningful correspondence between information status classes and degrees of prosodic prominence, with regard to both pitch accent type and position (Baumann and Riester, 2013; Baumann et al., 2015). Moreover, information status classification has been identified as a task closely related to coreference resolution (Cahill and Riester, 2012; Rahman and Ng, 2012). Integrating these approaches is a promising, though rather complex task, which we reserve for future work. It might, furthermore, require more detailed prosodic analyses than are currently available in DIRNDL.

[5]http://www.sfs.uni-tuebingen.de/de/ascl/ressourcen/corpora/tueba-dz.html

System	CoNLL (+singl.)	CoNLL (-singl.)
IMS HotCoref DE (open)	60.35	48.61
CorZu (open)	60.27	45.82
BART (open)	57.72	39.07
SUCRE (closed)	51.23	36,32
TANL-1 (closed)	38.48	14.17

Table 1: SemEval Shared Task 2010 post-task evaluation for track *regular* (on TüBa 8), including and excluding singletons

System	CoNLL
IMS HOTCoref DE (no GB matching)	51.61
CorZu (no GB matching)	53.07

Table 2: IMS HotCoref performance on TüBa 9 (no singletons), using regular preprocessing

of newspaper text. In a post-task SemEval 2010 evaluation[6] our system achieves a CoNLL score of 60.35 in the *open, regular* track[7] (cf. Table 1). On the newest dataset available (TüBa-D/Z v9), our resolver currently achieves a CoNLL score of 51.61.[8] Table 2 compares the performance of our system against CorZu (Klenner and Tuggener, 2011; Tuggener and Klenner, 2014), a rule-based state-of-the-art system for German[9](on the newest TüBa dataset).

4 Experiments using prosodic features

Table 3 shows the effect of the respective features which are not informed about intonation boundaries (Table 3a) and those that are (Table 3b). Features that achieved a significant improvement over the baseline are marked in boldface.[10]

The best-performing feature in Table 3a is the presence of a pitch accent in short NPs. It can be seen that this feature has a negative effect when being applied on all NPs. Presumably, this is because the system is misled to classify a higher number of complex anaphoric expressions as non-anaphoric, due to the presence of pitch accents. This confirms our conjecture that long NPs will always contain *some* kind of accent and we cannot distinguish nuclear from prenuclear accents. Features based on GToBI(S) accent type did not result in any improvements.

(a) No boundary information

Baseline	47.93	
+ Feature applied to ...	... short NPs only	... all NPs
PitchAccentType	45.31	46.23
PitchAccentPresence	**48.30**	46.57

(b) Including boundary information

Baseline	47.93	
+ Feature applied to ...	... short NPs only	... all NPs
NuclearType (*n1* vs. *n2* vs. *pn* vs. *none*)	47.17	46.79
NuclearType (*n1*/*n2* vs. *pn* vs. *none*)	**48.55**	45.24
NuclearPresence (*n2*)	46.69	**48.88**
NuclearPresence (*n1*/*n2*)	**48.76**	47.47
NuclearBagOfAccents	46.09	**48.45**
NuclearFirst+Last	46.41	46.74

Table 3: CoNLL metric scores on DIRNDL for different prosodic features (no singletons, significant results in boldface)

Table 3b presents the performance of the features that are phonologically more informed. Distinguishing between prenuclear and nuclear accents *(NuclearType)* is a feature that works best for short NPs where there is only one accent, while having a negative effect on all NPs. Nuclear presence, however, works well for both versions (not distinguishing between *n1* or *n2* works for short NPs while *n2* accents only works best for all NPs). This feature achieves the overall best performance for both short NPs (48.76) and all NPs (48.88).

The *NuclearBagOfAccents* feature works quite well, too: this is a feature designed for NPs that have more than one accent and so it works best for complex NPs. Combining the features did not lead to any improvements.

Overall, it becomes clear that one has to be very careful in terms of how the prosodic information is used. In general, the presence of an accent works better than the distinction between certain accent types, and including intonation boundary information also contributes to the system's performance. When including this information, we can observe that when we look at the presence of a pitch accent (the best-performing feature), the distinction between prenuclear and nuclear is an important one: not distinguishing between prenuclear and nuclear deteriorates results. The results also seem to sug-

[6] `http://stel.ub.edu/semeval2010-coref/`

[7] Using the official CoNLL scorer v8.01, including singletons as they are part of TüBa 8

[8] Using the official CoNLL scorer v8.01, not including singletons as TüBa 9 does not contain them.

[9] CorZu performance: Don Tuggener, personal communication. We did not use CorZu for our experiments as the integration of prosodic information in a rule-based system is non-trivial.

[10] We compute significance using the Wilcoxon signed rank test (Siegel and Castellan, 1988) at the 0.01 level.

gest that simpler features (like the presence or absence of a certain type of pitch accent) work best for simple (i.e. short) phrases. For longer markables this effect turns into the negative. This probably means that simple features cannot do justice to the complex prosody of longer NPs, which gets blurred. The obvious solution is to define more complex features that approximate the rhythmic pattern (or even the prosodic contour) found on longer phrases, which however will require more data and, ideally, automatic prosodic annotation.

5 Conclusion

We have tested a set of features that include different levels of prosodic information and investigated which strategies can be successfully applied for coreference resolution. Our results on the basis of manual prosodic labelling show that including prosody improves performance. While information on pitch accent types does not seem beneficial, the presence of an accent is a helpful feature in a machine-learning setting. Including prosodic boundaries and determining whether the accent is the nuclear accent further increases results. We interpret this as a promising result, which motivates further research on the integration of coreference resolution and spoken language.

Acknowledgements

We would like to thank Anders Björkelund for his valuable comments on an earlier version of this paper, as well as Kerstin Eckart for her help with the preparation of DIRNDL data. This work was funded by the German Science Foundation (DFG), Sonderforschungsbereich 732 *Incremental Specification in Context*, Project A6, at the University of Stuttgart.

References

Marilisa Amoia, Kerstin Kunz, and Ekaterina Lapshinova-Koltunski. 2012. Coreference in spoken vs. written texts: a corpus-based analysis. In *Proceedings of LREC*, Istanbul.

Stefan Baumann and Arndt Riester. 2012. Referential and Lexical Givenness: semantic, prosodic and cognitive aspects. In Gorka Elordieta and Pilar Prieto, editors, *Prosody and Meaning*, pages 119–162. Mouton de Gruyter, Berlin.

Stefan Baumann and Arndt Riester. 2013. Coreference, Lexical Givenness and Prosody in German. *Lingua*, 136:16–37.

Stefan Baumann and Anna Roth. 2014. Prominence and coreference – On the perceptual relevance of F0 movement, duration and intensity. In *Proceedings of Speech Prosody*, pages 227–231, Dublin.

Stefan Baumann, Christine Röhr, and Martine Grice. 2015. Prosodische (De-)Kodierung des Informationsstatus im Deutschen. *Zeitschrift für Sprachwissenschaft*, 34(1):1–42.

Mary Beckman, Julia Hirschberg, and Stefanie Shattuck-Hufnagel. 2005. The original ToBI system and the evolution of the ToBI framework. In Sun-Ah Jun, editor, *Prosodic Typology – The Phonology of Intonation and Phrasing*, pages 9–54. Oxford University Press.

Anders Björkelund and Jonas Kuhn. 2014. Learning structured perceptrons for coreference resolution with latent antecedents and non-local features. In *Proceedings of the 52nd Annual Meeting of the Association for Computational Linguistics (Volume 1: Long Papers)*, pages 47–57, Baltimore.

Anders Björkelund, Kerstin Eckart, Arndt Riester, Nadja Schauffler, and Katrin Schweitzer. 2014. The extended DIRNDL corpus as a resource for automatic coreference and bridging resolution. In *Proceedings of LREC*, pages 3222–3228, Reykjavík.

Aoife Cahill and Arndt Riester. 2012. Automatically Acquiring Fine-Grained Information Status Distinctions. In *Proceedings of the 13th Annual SIGdial Meeting on Discourse and Dialog*, pages 232–236, Seoul.

Alan Cruttenden. 2006. The de-accenting of given information: a cognitive universal? In Giuliano Bernini and Marcia Schwartz, editors, *Pragmatic Organization of Discourse in the Languages of Europe*, pages 311–355. De Gruyter, Berlin.

Kerstin Eckart, Arndt Riester, and Katrin Schweitzer. 2012. A Discourse Information Radio News Database for Linguistic Analysis. In Sebastian Nordhoff Christian Chiarcos and Sebastian Hellmann, editors, *Linked Data in Linguistics: Representing and Connecting Language Data and Language Metadata*, pages 65–76. Springer.

Caroline Féry. 1993. *German Intonational Patterns*. Niemeyer, Tübingen.

Carlos Gussenhoven. 1984. *On the Grammar and Semantics of Sentence Accents*. Foris, Dordrecht.

Manfred Klenner and Don Tuggener. 2011. An incremental entity-mention model for coreference resolution with restrictive antecedent accessibility. In *Proceedings of RANLP*, pages 178–185, Hissar, Bulgaria.

D. Robert Ladd. 2008. *Intonational Phonology (2nd ed.)*. Cambridge University Press.

Jörg Mayer. 1995. Transcription of German Intonation. The Stuttgart System. University of Stuttgart.

Karin Naumann. 2006. Manual for the annotation of in-document referential relations. University of Tübingen.

Vincent Ng. 2010. Supervised noun phrase coreference research: The first fifteen years. In *Proceedings of the 48th Annual Meeting of the Association for Computational Linguistics*, pages 1396–1411.

Janet Pierrehumbert. 1980. *The Phonology and Phonetics of English Intonation*. Ph.D. thesis, Massachusetts Institute of Technology.

Sameer Pradhan, Alessandro Moschitti, Nianwen Xue, Olga Uryupina, and Yuchen Zhang. 2012. Conll-2012 shared task: Modeling multilingual unrestricted coreference in ontonotes. In *Joint Conference on EMNLP and CoNLL-Shared Task*, pages 1–40. Association for Computational Linguistics.

Altaf Rahman and Vincent Ng. 2012. Learning the fine-grained information status of discourse entities. In *Proceedings of the 13th Conference of the European Chapter of the Association for Computational Linguistics*, pages 798–807. Association for Computational Linguistics.

Marta Recasens, Lluís Màrquez, Emili Sapena, M. Antònia Martí, Mariona Taulé, Véronique Hoste, Massimo Poesio, and Yannick Versley. 2010. Semeval-2010 task 1: Coreference resolution in multiple languages. In *Proceedings of the 5th International Workshop on Semantic Evaluation*, SemEval '10, pages 1–8, Stroudsburg, PA, USA.

Roger Schwarzschild. 1999. GIVENness, AvoidF, and Other Constraints on the Placement of Accent. *Natural Language Semantics*, 7(2):141–177.

Michael Strube and Christoph Müller. 2003. A machine learning approach to pronoun resolution in spoken dialogue. In *Proceedings of the 41st Annual Meeting on Association for Computational Linguistics*, pages 168–175.

Jacques Terken and Julia Hirschberg. 1994. Deaccentuation of words representing 'given' information: Effects of persistence of grammatical function and surface position. *Language and Speech*, 37(2):125–145.

Joel Tetreault and James Allen. 2004. Dialogue structure and pronoun resolution. In *Proceedings of the 5th Discourse Anaphora and Anaphor Resolution Colloquium*, S. Miguel, Portugal.

Don Tuggener and Manfred Klenner. 2014. A hybrid entity-mention pronoun resolution model for german using markov logic networks. In *Proceedings of KONVENS 2014*, pages 21–29.

Carla Umbach. 2002. (De)accenting definite descriptions. *Theoretical Linguistics*, 2/3:251–280.

Spectral Semi-Supervised Discourse Relation Classification

Robert Fisher
Carnegie Mellon University
5000 Forbes Ave
Pittsburgh, PA 15213
rwfisher@cs.cmu.edu

Reid Simmons
Carnegie Mellon University
5000 Forbes Ave
Pittsburgh, PA 15213
reids@cs.cmu.edu

Abstract

Discourse parsing is the process of discovering the latent relational structure of a long form piece of text and remains a significant open challenge. One of the most difficult tasks in discourse parsing is the classification of implicit discourse relations. Most state-of-the-art systems do not leverage the great volume of unlabeled text available on the web–they rely instead on human annotated training data. By incorporating a mixture of labeled and unlabeled data, we are able to improve relation classification accuracy, reduce the need for annotated data, while still retaining the capacity to use labeled data to ensure that specific desired relations are learned. We achieve this using a latent variable model that is trained in a reduced dimensionality subspace using spectral methods. Our approach achieves an F_1 score of 0.485 on the implicit relation labeling task for the Penn Discourse Treebank.

1 Introduction

Discourse parsing is a fundamental task in natural language processing that entails the discovery of the latent relational structure in a multi-sentence piece of text. Unlike semantic and syntactic parsing, which are used for single sentence parsing, discourse parsing is used to discover intersentential relations in longer pieces of text. Without discourse, parsing methods can only be used to understand documents as sequences of unrelated sentences.

Unfortunately, manual annotation of discourse structure in text is costly and time consuming. Multiple annotators are required for each relation to estimate inter-annotator agreement. The Penn Discourse Treebank (PDTB) (Prasad et al., 2008). is one of the largest annotated discourse parsing datasets, with 16,224 implicit relations. However, this pales in comparison to unlabeled datasets that can include millions of sentences of text. By augmenting a labeled dataset with unlabeled data, we can use a bootstrapping framework to improve predictive accuracy, and reduce the need for labeled data–which could make it much easier to port discourse parsing algorithms to new domains. On the other hand, a fully unsupervised parser may not be desirable because in many applications specific discourse relations must be identified, which would be difficult to achieve without the use of labeled examples.

There has recently been growing interest in a breed of algorithms based on spectral decomposition, which are well suited to training with unlabeled data. Spectral algorithms utilize matrix factorization algorithms such as Singular Value Decomposition (SVD) and rank factorization to discover *low-rank decompositions* of matrices or tensors of empirical moments. In many models, these decompositions allow us to identify the subspace spanned by a group of parameter vectors or the actual parameter vectors themselves. For tasks where they can be applied, spectral methods provide statistically consistent results that avoid local maxima. Also, spectral algorithms tend to be much faster—sometimes orders of magnitude faster—than competing approaches, which makes them ideal for tackling large datasets. These methods can be viewed as inferring something about the latent structure of a domain—for example, in a hidden Markov model, the number of latent states and the sparsity pattern of the transition matrix are forms of latent structure, and spectral methods can recover both in the limit.

This paper presents a semi-supervised spectral model for a sequential relation labeling task for discourse parsing. Besides the theoretically desirable properties mentioned above, we also demon-

Proceedings of the 53rd Annual Meeting of the Association for Computational Linguistics and the 7th International Joint Conference on Natural Language Processing (Short Papers), pages 89–93,
Beijing, China, July 26-31, 2015. ©2015 Association for Computational Linguistics

strate the practical advantages of the model with an empirical evaluation on the Penn Discourse Treebank (PDTB) (Prasad et al., 2008) dataset, which yields an F_1 score of 0.485. This accuracy shows a 7-9 percentage point improvement over approaches that do not utilize unlabeled training data.

2 Related Work

There has been quite a bit of work concerning fully supervised relation classification with the PDTB (Lin et al., 2014; Feng and Hirst, 2012; Webber et al., 2012). Semi-supervised relation classification is much less common however. One recent example of an attempt to leverage unlabeled data appears in (Hernault et al., 2011), which showed that moderate classification accuracy can be achieved with very small labeled datasets. However, this approach is not competitive with fully supervised classifiers when more training data is available. Recently there has also been some work to use Conditional Random Fields (CRFs) to represent the global properties of a parse sequence (Joty et al., 2013; Feng and Hirst, 2014), though this work has focused on the RST-DT corpus, rather than the PDTB.

In addition to requiring a fully supervised training set, most existing discourse parsers use non-spectral optimization that is often slow and inexact. However, there has been some work in other parsing tasks to employ spectral methods in both supervised and semi-supervised settings (Parikh et al., 2014; Cohen et al., 2014). Spectral methods have also been applied very successfully in many non-linguistic domains (Hsu et al., 2012; Boots and Gordon, 2010; Fisher et al., 2014).

3 Problem Definition and Dataset

This section defines the discourse parsing problem and discusses the characteristics of the PDTB. The PDTB consists of annotated articles from the Wall Street Journal and is used in our empirical evaluations. This is combined with the New York Times Annotated Corpus (Sandhaus, 2008), which includes 1.8 million New York Times articles printed between 1987 and 2007.

Discourse parsing can be reduced to three separate tasks. First, the text must be decomposed into *elementary discourse units* (EDUs), which may or may not coincide with sentence boundaries. The EDUs are often independent clauses that may be connected with conjunctions. After the text has been partitioned into EDUs, the discourse structure must be identified. This requires us to identify all pairs of EDUs that will be connected with *some* discourse relation. These relational links induce the skeletal structure of the discourse parse tree. Finally, each connection identified in the previous step must be labeled using a known set of relations. Examples of these discourse relations include concession, causal, and instantiation relations. In the PDTB, only adjacent discourse units are connected with a discourse relation, so with this dataset we are considering parse sequences rather than parse trees.

In this work, we focus on the relation labeling task, as fairly simple methods perform quite well at the other two tasks (Webber et al., 2012). We use the ground truth parse structures provided by the PDTB dataset, so as to isolate the error introduced by relation labeling in our results, but in practice a greedy structure learning algorithm can be used if the parse structures are not known *a priori*.

Some of the relations in the dataset are induced by specific connective words in the text. For example, a contrast relation may be explicitly revealed by the conjunction *but*. Simple classifiers using only the text of the discourse connective with POS tags can find explicit relations with high accuracy (Lin et al., 2014). The following sentence shows an example of a more difficult implicit relation. In this sentence, two EDUs are connected with an explanatory relation, shown in bold, although the connective word does not occur in the text.

> "But a few funds have taken other defensive steps. Some have raised their cash positions to record levels. **[BECAUSE]** High cash positions help buffer a fund when the market falls."

We focus on the more difficult implicit relations that are not induced by coordinating connectives in the text. The implicit relations have been shown to require more sophisticated feature sets including syntactic and linguistic information (Lin et al., 2009). The PDTB dataset includes 16,053 examples of implicit relations.

A full list of the PDTB relations is available in (Prasad et al., 2008). The relations are organized hierarchically into top level, types, and subtypes. Our experiments focus on learning only up

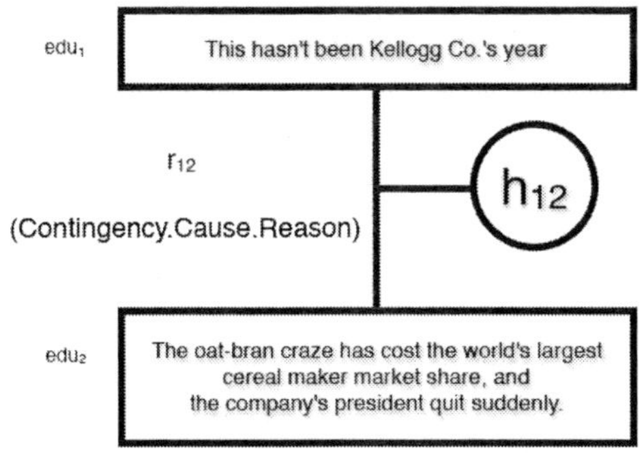

Figure 1: An example of the latent variable discourse parsing model taken from the Penn Discourse Treebank Dataset. The relation here is an example of a cause attribution relation.

to level 2, as the level 3 (sub-type) relations are too specific and show only 80% inter-annotator agreement. There are 16 level 2 relations in the PDTB, but the 5 least common relations only appear a handful of times in the dataset and are omitted from our tests, yielding 11 possible classes.

4 Approach

We incorporate unlabeled data into our spectral discourse parsing model using a bootstrapping framework. The model is trained over several iterations, and the most useful unlabeled sequences are added as labeled training data after each iteration. Our method also utilizes Markovian latent states to compactly capture global information about a parse sequence, with one latent variable for each relation in the discourse parsing sequence. Most discourse parsing frameworks will label relations independently of the rest of the accompanying parse sequence, but this model allows for information about the global structure of the discourse parse to be used when labeling a relation. A graphical representation of one link in the parsing model is shown in Figure 1.

Specifically, each potential relation r_{ij} between elementary discourse units e_i and e_j is accompanied by a corresponding latent variable as h_{ij}. According to the model assumptions, the following equality holds:

$$P(r_{ij} = r | r_{1,2}, r_{2,3}...r_{n+1,n}) = P(r_{ij} = r | h_{ij})$$

To maintain notational consistency with other latent variable models, we will denote these relation variables as $x_1...x_n$, keeping in mind that there is one possible relation for each adjacent pair of elementary discourse units.

For the Penn Discourse Treebank Dataset, the discourse parses behave like sequence of random variables representing the relations, which allows us to use an HMM-like latent variable model based on the framework presented in (Hsu et al., 2012). If the discourse parses were instead trees, such as those seen in Rhetorical Structure Theory (RST) datasets, we can modify the standard model to include separate parameters for left and right children, as demonstrated in (Dhillon et al., 2012).

4.1 Spectral Learning

This section briefly describes the process of learning a spectral HMM. Much more detail about the process is available in (Hsu et al., 2012). Learning in this model will occur in a subspace of dimensionality m, but system dynamics will be the same if m is not less than the rank of the observation matrix. If our original feature space has dimensionality n, we define a transformation matrix $U \in \mathbb{R}^{n \times m}$, which can be computed using Singular Value Decomposition. Given the matrix U, coupled with the empirical unigram (P_1), bigram ($P_{2,1}$), and trigram matrices ($P_{3,x,1}$), we are able to estimate the subspace initial state distribution ($\hat{\pi}_U$) and observable operator ($\hat{A}_U$) using the following equalities (wherein the Moore-Penrose pseudo-inverse of matrix X is denoted by X^+):

$$\hat{\pi}_U = U^T P_1$$
$$\hat{A}_U = U^T P_{3,x,1} (U^T P_{2,1})^+ \ \forall x$$

For our original feature space, we use the rich linguistic discourse parsing features defined in (Feng and Hirst, 2014), which includes syntactic and linguistic features taken from dependency parsing, POS tagging, and semantic similarity measures. We augment this feature space with a vector space representation of semantics. A term-document co-occurrence matrix is computed using all of Wikipedia and Latent Dirichlet Analysis was performed using this matrix. The top 200 concepts from the vector space representation for each pair of EDUs in the dataset are included in the feature space, with a concept regularization parameter of 0.01.

4.2 Semi-Supervised Training

To begin semi-supervised training, we perform a syntactic parse of the unlabeled data and extract EDU segments using the method described in (Feng and Hirst, 2014). The model is then trained using the labeled dataset, and the unlabeled relations are predicted using the Viterbi algorithm. The most informative sequences in the unlabeled training set are added to the labeled training set as labeled examples. To measure how informative a sequence of relations is, we use *density-weighted certainty sampling* (DCS). Specifically for a sequence of relations $r_1 ... r_n$ taken from a document, d, we use the following formula:

$$DCS(d) = \frac{1}{n} \sum_{i=1}^{n} \frac{\hat{p}(r_i)}{H(r_i)}$$

In this equation, $H(r_i)$ represented the entropy of the distribution of label predictions for the relation r_i generated by the current spectral model, which is a measure of the model's uncertainty for the label of the given relation. Density is denoted $\hat{p}(r_i)$, and this quantity measures the extent to which the text corresponding to this relation is representative of the labeled corpus. To compute this measure, we create a Kernel Density Estimate (KDE) over a 100 dimensional LDA vector space representation of all EDU's in the labeled corpus. We then compute the density of the KDE for the text associated with relation r_i, which gives us $\hat{p}(r_i)$. All sequences of relations in the unlabeled dataset are ranked according to their average density-weighted certainty score, and all sequences scoring above a parameter ψ are added to the training set. The model is then retrained, the unlabeled data re-scored, and the process is repeated for several iterations. In iteration i, the labeled data in the training set is weighted w_i^l, and the unlabeled data is weighted w_i^u, with the unlabeled data receiving higher weight in subsequent iterations. The KDE kernel bandwidth and the parameters ψ, w_i^l, w_i^u, and the number of hidden states are chosen in experiments using 10-fold cross validation on the labeled training set, coupled with a subset of the unlabeled data.

5 Results

Figure 2 shows the F_1 scores of the model using various sizes of labeled training sets. In all cases, the entirety of the unlabeled data is made available, and 7 rounds of bootstrapping is conducted. Sections 2-22 of the PDTB are used for training, with section 23 being withheld for testing, as recommended by the dataset guidelines (Prasad et al.,

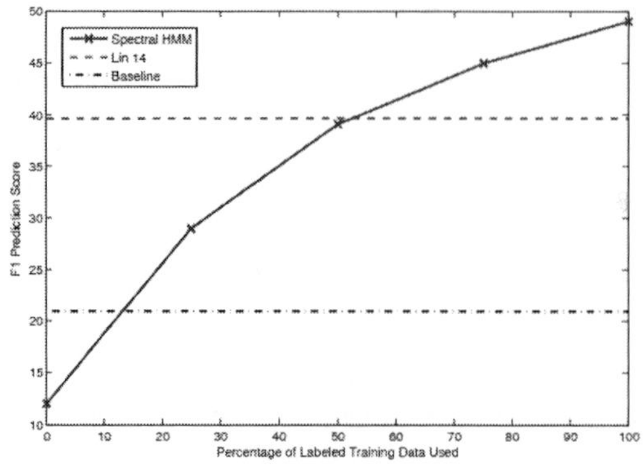

Figure 2: Empirical results for labeling of implicit relations.

2008). The results are compared against those reported in (Lin et al., 2014), as well as a simple baseline classifier that labels all relations with the most common class, *EntRel*. Compared to the semi-supervised method described in (Hernault et al., 2011), we show significant gains in accuracy at various sizes of dataset, although the unlabeled dataset used in our experiments is much larger.

When the spectral HMM is trained using only the labeled dataset, with no unlabeled data, it produces an F_1 score of 41.1%, which is comparable to the results reported in (Lin et al., 2014). By comparison, the semi-supervised classifier is able to obtain similar accuracy when using approximately 50% of the labeled training data. When given access to the full labeled dataset, we see an improvement in the F_1 score of 7-9 percentage points. Recent work has shown promising results using CRFs for discourse parsing (Joty et al., 2013; Feng and Hirst, 2014), but the results reported in this work were taken from the RST-DT corpus and are not directly comparable. However, supervised CRFs and HMMs show similar accuracy in other language tasks (Ponomareva et al., 2007; Awasthi et al., 2006).

6 Conclusions

In this work, we have shown that we are able to outperform fully-supervised relation classifiers by augmenting the training data with unlabeled text. The spectral optimization used in this approach makes computation tractable even when using over one million documents. In future work, we would like to further improve the performance of this method when very small labeled training sets are available, which would allow discourse analysis to be applied in many new and interesting domains.

Acknowledgements

We give thanks to Carolyn Penstein Rosé and Geoff Gordon for their helpful discussions and suggestions. We also gratefully acknowledge the National Science Foundation for their support through EAGER grant number IIS1450543. This material is also based upon work supported by the Quality of Life Technology Center and the National Science Foundation under Cooperative Agreement EEC-0540865.

References

Pranjal Awasthi, Delip Rao, and Balaraman Ravindran. 2006. Part of speech tagging and chunking with hmm and crf. *Proceedings of NLP Association of India (NLPAI) Machine Learning Contest 2006.*

Byron Boots and Geoffrey J Gordon. 2010. Predictive state temporal difference learning. *arXiv preprint arXiv:1011.0041.*

Shay B Cohen, Karl Stratos, Michael Collins, Dean P Foster, and Lyle Ungar. 2014. Spectral learning of latent-variable pcfgs: Algorithms and sample complexity. *The Journal of Machine Learning Research*, 15(1):2399–2449.

Paramveer S Dhillon, Jordan Rodu, Michael Collins, Dean P Foster, and Lyle H Ungar. 2012. Spectral dependency parsing with latent variables. In *Proceedings of the 2012 joint conference on empirical methods in natural language processing and computational natural language learning*, pages 205–213. Association for Computational Linguistics.

Vanessa Wei Feng and Graeme Hirst. 2012. Text-level discourse parsing with rich linguistic features. In *Proceedings of the 50th Annual Meeting of the Association for Computational Linguistics: Long Papers-Volume 1*, pages 60–68. Association for Computational Linguistics.

Vanessa Wei Feng and Graeme Hirst. 2014. A linear-time bottom-up discourse parser with constraints and post-editing. In *Proceedings of The 52nd Annual Meeting of the Association for Computational Linguistics (ACL 2014), Baltimore, USA, June.*

Robert Fisher, Reid Simmons, Cheng-Shiu Chung, Rory Cooper, Garrett Grindle, Annmarie Kelleher, Hsinyi Liu, and Yu Kuang Wu. 2014. Spectral machine learning for predicting power wheelchair exercise compliance. In *Foundations of Intelligent Systems*, pages 174–183. Springer.

Hugo Hernault, Danushka Bollegala, and Mitsuru Ishizuka. 2011. Semi-supervised discourse relation classification with structural learning. In *Computational Linguistics and Intelligent Text Processing*, pages 340–352. Springer.

Daniel Hsu, Sham M Kakade, and Tong Zhang. 2012. A spectral algorithm for learning hidden markov models. *Journal of Computer and System Sciences*, 78(5):1460–1480.

Shafiq R Joty, Giuseppe Carenini, Raymond T Ng, and Yashar Mehdad. 2013. Combining intra-and multi-sentential rhetorical parsing for document-level discourse analysis. In *ACL (1)*, pages 486–496.

Ziheng Lin, Min-Yen Kan, and Hwee Tou Ng. 2009. Recognizing implicit discourse relations in the penn discourse treebank. In *Proceedings of the 2009 Conference on Empirical Methods in Natural Language Processing: Volume 1-Volume 1*, pages 343–351. Association for Computational Linguistics.

Ziheng Lin, Hwee Tou Ng, and Min-Yen Kan. 2014. A pdtb-styled end-to-end discourse parser. *Natural Language Engineering*, pages 1–34.

Ankur Parikh, Shay B Cohen, and Eric Xing. 2014. Spectral unsupervised parsing with additive tree metrics. In *Proceedings of the 52nd Annual Meeting of the Association for Computational Linguistics: Long Papers*. Association for Computational Linguistics.

Natalia Ponomareva, Paolo Rosso, Ferrán Pla, and Antonio Molina. 2007. Conditional random fields vs. hidden markov models in a biomedical named entity recognition task. In *Proc. of Int. Conf. Recent Advances in Natural Language Processing, RANLP*, pages 479–483.

Rashmi Prasad, Nikhil Dinesh, Alan Lee, Eleni Miltsakaki, Livio Robaldo, Aravind K Joshi, and Bonnie L Webber. 2008. The penn discourse treebank 2.0. In *LREC*. Citeseer.

Evan Sandhaus. 2008. The new york times annotated corpus ldc2008t19. *Linguistic Data Consortium.*

Bonnie Webber, Markus Egg, and Valia Kordoni. 2012. Discourse structure and language technology. *Natural Language Engineering*, 18(4):437–490.

I do not disagree: Leveraging monolingual alignment to detect disagreement in dialogue

Ajda Gokcen and **Marie-Catherine de Marneffe**
Linguistics Department
The Ohio State University
gokcen.2@osu.edu, mcdm@ling.ohio-state.edu

Abstract

A wide array of natural dialogue discourse can be found on the internet. Previous attempts to automatically determine disagreement between interlocutors in such dialogue have mostly relied on n-gram and grammatical dependency features taken from respondent text. Agreement-disagreement classifiers built upon these baseline features tend to do poorly, yet have proven difficult to improve upon. Using the Internet Argument Corpus, which comprises quote and response post pairs taken from an online debate forum with human-annotated agreement scoring, we introduce semantic environment features derived by comparing quote and response sentences which align well. We show that this method improves classifier accuracy relative to the baseline method namely in the retrieval of disagreeing pairs, which improves from 69% to 77%.

1 Introduction

To achieve robust text understanding, natural language processing systems need to automatically extract information that is expressed indirectly. Here we focus on identifying agreement and disagreement in online debate posts. Previous work on this task has used very shallow linguistic analysis: features are surface-level ones, such as n-grams, post initial unigrams, bigrams and trigrams (which aim at learning the discourse functions of discourse markers, e.g., *well*, *really*, *you know*), repeated sequential use of punctuation signs (e.g., *!!*, *?!*). When automatically detecting (dis)agreement, these features fall short, reaching around 65% accuracy on a balanced dataset (Abbott et al., 2011; Misra and Walker, 2013). Adding extra-linguistic features, such as the structure of the post threads and stance of the post's author on other subjects, boosts performance to 75% (Hasan and Ng, 2013). In this work, we leverage richer linguistic models to increase performance.

Agreement may be explicitly marked. In example (1) in Table 2, the response-initial bigram *I agree* is a strong cue of agreement that surface features can learn, but there are more complex examples that surface features cannot capture. In example (2), the response-initial word *Yes* is not indicating agreement, despite being in general a good cue for it. Instead it is necessary to capture the polarity mismatch between the first sentence in the quote and the first sentence in the response (*God doesn't take away sinful desires* vs. *Yes, God does take away sinful desires*) to infer that the response disagrees with the quote. There may also be mismatches of modality, as demonstrated in the third example (*saw* vs. *may have believed*). Here we also see an example of an explicit agreement word which is negated *(that does **not** make it **true**)* in a way that most surface features fail to capture.

Some discourse-level parsing (Joty et al., 2013) has been utilized in agreement detection, but most previous work does not take discourse structure into account: the response post is simply taken *as a whole* as the reply to the quote. To overcome this issue, we take advantage of the considerable progress in monolingual alignment (e.g., Thadani et al. 2012, Yao et al. 2013, Sultan et al. 2014) which allows us to align sentences of the quote to sentences in the response. This approach is reminiscent of the one used for Recognizing Textual Entailment (RTE, Dagan et al. 2006, Giampiccolo et al. 2007) where, given two short passages, systems identify whether the second passage follows from the first one according to the intuitions of an intelligent human reader. One common approach used in RTE was to align the two passages, and reason based on the alignment obtained.

Proceedings of the 53rd Annual Meeting of the Association for Computational Linguistics and the 7th International Joint Conference on Natural Language Processing (Short Papers), pages 94–99,
Beijing, China, July 26-31, 2015.

	Quote	Response	Score
1	CCW LAWS ARE FOR TRACKING GUN OWNERS WHO EXERCISE THIER RIGHTS!!!	I agree. What is the point? Felons with firearms do not bother with CCW licenses.	2.5
2	God doesn't take away sinful desires. You've never had sinful desires? I know I have. People assume that when you become a Christian some manner of shield gets put up around you and shields you from "worldly" things. I believe that's wrong, I actually believe that life as a Christian is very hard. We often pawn it off as the end of our troubles to "convert" people. I don't believe it.	Yes, God does take away sinful desires. (If you ask Him.) I'm not saying that it doesn't take any work on your part, though. When you have a sinful desire, you allow a thought to become more than just a stray idea. You foster and encourage the thought and it becomes a desire. God takes away the desires, helps you deal with your "stray thoughts", and shows you how to keep them from becoming desires.	-1.7
3	Your idea about science is a philosophy of science. [...] *The Apostles saw Jesus walk on water.* There was no 'measure' by your version of science, but what they saw remains true.	Many people once believed that the earth is flat: perhaps some still do. [...] *The apostles may have believed that Jesus walked on water: that does NOT make it true.*	-2
4	*does life end here?*	*end where?* ambiguously phrased. if "here" = "death", then yes! by definition, yes!	-1.4
5	*Is even 'channel' sufficiently ateleological a verb?*	Yes. It describes an action without ascribing its form to its end result, outcome, whatever but strictly to a cause's force's in action. [...] *But since it is understood that mechanical forces can also 'channel', unintentional, out of simple mechanics, the word channel cannot be called teleological.* In the same way, 'sorting' can be considered non-teleological, hence mechanical, and thus suited to your glossary, because things can be sorted by mechanical forces alone.	2.8

Table 1: QR pairs from the Internet Argument Corpus.

Here, similarly, once we have identified sentences in the response which align well with sentences in the quote, it becomes easier to extract deep semantic features such as polarity and modality mismatch between sentences as well as embeddings under modality, negation, or attitude verbs. For instance, in example (2) in Table 1, the first sentence in the quote gets aligned with high probability to the first sentence in the response, which enables us to identify the polarity mismatch (*doesn't* vs. *does*). In example (3), the italicized sentences are the most well-aligned, enabling us to identify that the response's author embeds under modality the event of Jesus walking on water and thus does not take it as a fact, whereas the quote's author does take it as a fact.

Our experiments demonstrate that our linguistic model based on alignment significantly outperforms a baseline bag-of-words model in the recall of disagreeing quote-response (QR) pairs. Such linguistic models will transfer more easily to any debate dialogue, independent of the structural information of post threads and author's stance which might not always be recoverable.

	Full Data Set	Balanced Training Set
Disagree	5741	779
Neutral	3125	0
Agree	1113	779
Total	9980	1158

Table 2: Category counts in the training set.

2 Data

We used the Internet Argument Corpus (IAC), a corpus of quote-response pairs annotated for agreement via Mechanical Turk (Walker et al., 2012). Agreement scores span from -5 (strong disagreement) and +5 (strong agreement). The distribution is shown in Figure 2. Because the original data skews toward disagreement, following Abbott et al. (2011), we created a balanced set, discarding "neutral" pairs between -1 and +1. We split the data into training, development and test sets. [1] Table 2 shows the category counts in the training set.

[1] We could not obtain the training-development-test split from Abbott et al. (2011). Our split is available at `www.ling.ohio-state.edu/~mcdm/data/2015/Balanced_IAC.zip`.

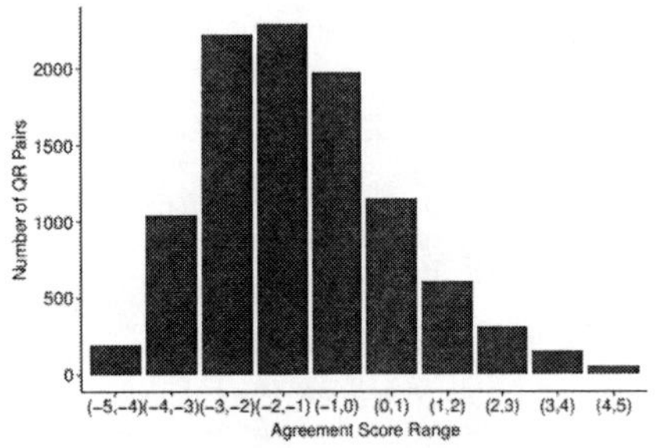

(a) Full dataset.

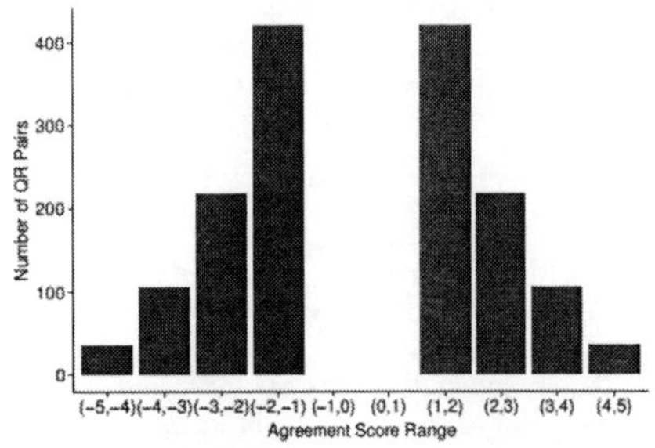

(b) Balanced training set.

Figure 1: Agreement score distribution of the dataset, before and after balancing. -5 is high disagreement, +5 is high agreement.

3 Features

In this section, we detail the features of our model. We use the maximum entropy model as implemented in the Stanford CoreNLP toolset (Manning and Klein, 2003). Many of the features make use of the typed dependencies from the CoreNLP toolset (de Marneffe et al., 2006). For comparison, the baseline features attempt to replicate Abbott et al. (2011).

3.1 Baseline Features from Abbott et al. 2011

N-Grams. All unigrams, bigrams, and trigrams were taken from each response.

Discourse Markers. In lieu of tracking discourse markers such as *oh* and *so really*, Abbott et al. (2011) tracked response-initial unigrams, bigrams, and trigrams.

Typed Dependencies and MPQA. In addition to all dependencies from the response being used as features, dependencies were supplemented with MPQA sentiment values (Wilson et al., 2005). A dependency like *(agree,I)* would also yield the sentiment-dependency feature *(positive,I)*, whereas *(wrong, you)* would also yield *(negative,you)*.

Punctuation. The presence of special punctuation such as repeated exclamation points *(!!)*, question marks *(??)*, and interrobang strings *(?!)* were tracked as binary features.

3.2 Alignment+ Features

Our features utilize focal sentences: not only well-aligned sentences from the quote and response, but also the first sentence of the response in general. Tracking certain features in initial and aligned sentences proved more informative than doing the same without discerning location.

Alignment scoring comes from running the Jacana aligner (Yao et al., 2013) pairwise on every sentence from each QR pair. Pairs of quote and response sentences with alignment scores above a threshold tuned on the development set are then analyzed for feature extraction. The sentence pair with the maximum alignment score for each post pair is also analyzed regardless of its meeting the threshold.

Post Length. Following Misra and Walker (2013), we track various length features such as word count, sentence count, and average sentence length, including differentials of these measures between quote and response. Short responses (relative to both word-wise and sentence-wise counts) tend to correlate with agreement, while longer responses tend to correlate with disagreement.

Emoticons. Emoticons are a popular way of communicating sentiment in internet text. Many emoticons in the corpus are in forum-specific code, such as *emoticon_rolleyes*. We also detect a wider array of common emoticons as regular expressions beginning with colons, semicolons, or equals signs, such as *:-D*, *;)*, and *=)*.

Speech Acts. To account for phenomena such as commands (e.g., *please read carefully*, *try again*, and *define evil*) and the rhetorical use of multiple questions in a row, we use punctuation, dependencies, and phrase-level analysis to automatically detect and count interrogative and imperative sentences. A phrase-structure tree headed by SQ or a sentence-final question mark means a sentence is considered interrogative; if a sentence's root is labeled VB and has no subject relation, it is deemed an imperative. The features in the classifier are counts of the instances of interrogatives and imperatives in the response.

	Accuracy	Agreement			Disagreement		
		P	R	F1	P	R	F1
Baseline	71.85	70.64	74.77	72.65	73.21	68.92	71.00
Alignment+	75.45	76.04	74.32	75.17	74.89	76.58	75.73

Table 3: Accuracy, precision (P), recall (R) and F1 scores for both categories (agreement and disagreement) on the test set.

Personal Pronouns. The presence of first, second, and third person pronouns in the response are each tracked as binary features. The inclusion of personal pronouns in a post tends to indicate a more emotional or personal argument, especially second person pronouns.

Explicit Truth Values. Rather than simply relying on n-gram-based tracking of explicit statements of agreement, we include as features polar (positive or negative) and modal (modal or non-modal) context of instances of the words *agree*, *disagree*, *true*, *false*, *right*, and *wrong* found in the response, parallel to the agreement and denial tracking in Misra and Walker (2013). Polar context is determined by the presence or absence of negation modifiers (e.g., *not*, *never*) in the dependencies; modal context is determined by the presence of modal auxiliaries (e.g., *might*, *could*) and adverbs (e.g., *possibly*).

Sentiment Scoring. Expanding on the use of MPQA sentiment values, we use the *positive/negative/neutral* and *strong/weak* classifications of the words in the MPQA lexicon to calculate sentiment scores of the posts and focal sentences (well-aligned sentences from the quote and response as well as the first sentence of the response). The scoring assigns a value to each MPQA word in the quote or response: the *positive/negative* label of a word means a positive or negative score and the *strong/weak* label determines the weight: whether the word is worth +/-2 or +/-1. The sum of these values is computed as the sentiment score. A score is generated for both the response and quote in their entireties as well as for focal sentences.

Discourse Markers. Initial 1, 2 and 3-grams are tracked relative to focal sentences. This picks up on discourse markers (such as *well* and *but*) without having to explicitly code for each marker we want to track.

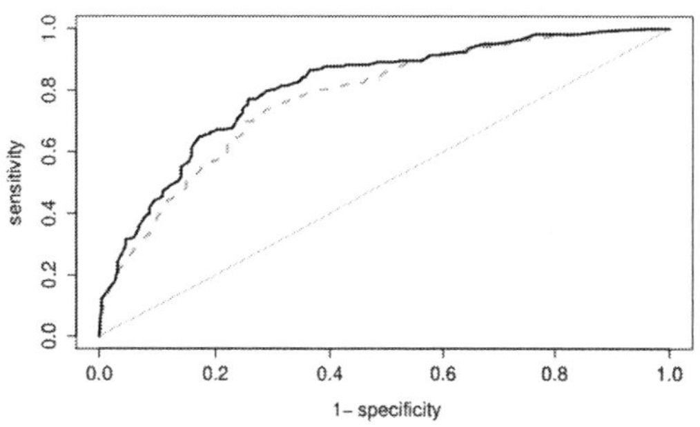

Figure 2: ROC curves. The gray dotted line represents the baseline feature set, while the solid black line represents the alignment+ feature set.

Punctuation. As in the baseline, the presence of special punctuation like *!!* and *?!* are used as binary features.

Factuality Comparison. Given aligned words from well-aligned sentences in the quote and response (e.g., *God doesn't **take** away sinful desires* and *Yes, God does **take** away sinful desires*), we analyze the polarity, modality, and any subsequent contradiction of both the quote and response instances. As with the analysis of explicit truth value words, polarity and modality are determined according to the presence or absence of negation and modal modifiers (auxiliaries and adverbs) in the dependencies. Contradictions are tracked as phrases marked with known contradictory adverbs and conjunctions (e.g., *however...*, *but...*). An aligned word pair is analyzed if it involves content words, or if the words serve as the root of their sentence's dependency structure regardless of part of speech. The features generated indicate the part of speech of the word in the quote and whether there is (1) a polarity match/clash, (2) a modality match/clash, or (3) any contradiction phrases immediately following the word or sentence in the quote or response.

4 Results and Discussion

Table 3 compares the results obtained with the baseline features and the alignment+ features. The alignment+ features lead to an overall improvement, but a statistically significant improvement ($p < 0.05$, McNemar's test) is only achieved for classifying disagreeing pairs. The baseline model underclassifies for disagreement and overclassifies for agreement, but the alignment+ model does well on both. As most cases of high alignment do, indeed, correspond with disagreement, these features are better in picking up on disagreement in general. The ROC curve in Figure 3 shows that the alignment+ classifier consistently has a higher sensitivity (true-positive) rate than the baseline.

Figure 4 shows for both feature sets (baseline and alignment+) the correct (gray bar) and incorrect (black bar) classifications on the test set, by agreement score. The agreement score is predictive of the correctness of the system (confirmed by a logistic regression predicting system accuracy given strength of agreement score, $p < 0.001$): the stronger the (dis)agreement score, the more accurate the system is. The alignment+ features help classify accurately the less strong (dis)agreements.

Examples (4) and (5) in Table 1 are incorrectly classified by the baseline but correctly by the alignment+ classifier. In (4), the strongest feature in the baseline is the unigram *yes*, but the alignment+ features compare *does life end here?* to *end where?*, and the fact that the aligned sentence in the response is a question suggests disagreement. Example (5) shows that superficial features like a response-initial *yes* are not always enough, even when the pair is indeed in agreement. Here the alignment+ model aligns the italic sentences (*Is even 'channel' sufficiently ateleological a verb?* and *[...]the word channel cannot be called teleological*), finding them to be in agreement and thus getting the correct classification.

5 Conclusion

The incorporation of alignment-based features shows promise in improving agreement classification. Further ablation testing is needed to determine the full extent to which alignment features contribute, and not only better whole-post features on their own. However, given that many pairs do not have sentences which align at all, alignment features cannot classify on their own without some more basic features to fill in the gaps.

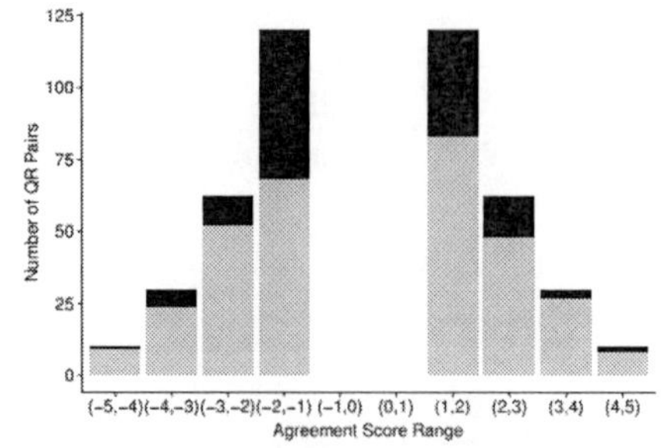

(a) Baseline feature set classifications.

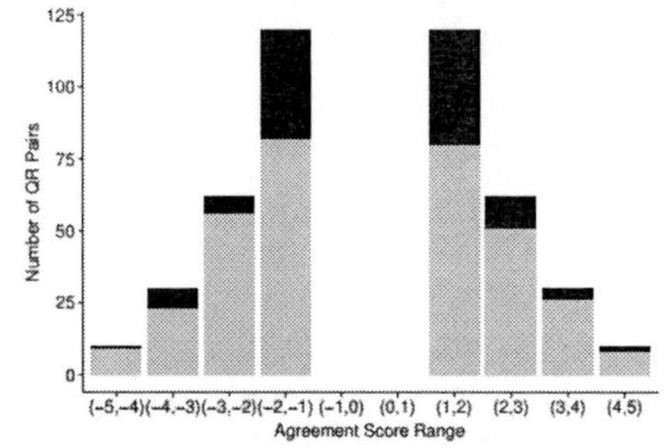

(b) Alignment+ feature set classifications.

Figure 3: Correct and incorrect classifications on the test set given the corpus agreement scores, for both feature sets. The gray area represents correct classifications, while the black area represents incorrect classifications.

Following previous work, we focused on pairs judged as being in strong (dis)agreement. How do systems fare when uncertain cases are present in the training data? This has not been investigated. One aspect of language interpretation, however, is its inherent uncertainty. In future work, we will use the full IAC corpus, and instead of drawing a binary distinction between strong agreements and disagreements, have a three-way classification where unclear instances are also categorized.

Acknowledgments

We thank Christopher Potts and the members of the Clippers group at The Ohio State University for productive discussions about this work, as well as our anonymous reviewers for their helpful comments. We also thank Xuchen Yao for his tremendous help with the Jacana aligner. This research is supported in part by the NSF under Grant No. 1464252. Any opinions, findings, and conclusions or recommendations expressed in this paper are those of the authors and do not necessarily reflect the views of the NSF.

References

Rob Abbott, Marilyn Walker, Pranav Anand, Jean E. Fox Tree, Robeson Bowmani, and Joseph King. 2011. How can you say such things?!?: Recognizing disagreement in informal political argument. In *Proceedings of the Workshop on Languages in Social Media*, pages 2–11.

Ido Dagan, Oren Glickman, and Bernardo Magnini. 2006. The PASCAL recognising textual entailment challenge. In J. Quinonero-Candela, I. Dagan, B. Magnini, and F. d'Alché-Buc, editors, *Machine Learning Challenges, Lecture Notes in Computer Science*, volume 3944, pages 177–190. Springer-Verlag.

Marie-Catherine de Marneffe, Bill McCartney, and Christopher D. Manning. 2006. Generating typed dependency parses from phrase structure parses. In *Proceedings of LREC*.

Danilo Giampiccolo, Ido Dagan, Bernardo Magnini, and Bill Dolan. 2007. The third PASCAL recognizing textual entailment challenge. In *Proceedings of the ACL-PASCAL Workshop on Textual Entailment and Paraphrasing*, pages 1–9.

Kazi Saidul Hasan and Vincent Ng. 2013. Extra-linguistic constraints on stance recognition in ideological debates. In *Proceedings of the 51st Annual Meeting of the Association for Computational Linguistics*, pages 816–821.

Shafiq Joty, Giuseppe Carenini, Raymond T. Ng, and Yashar Mehdad. 2013. Combining intra-and multi-sentential rhetorical parsing for document-level discourse analysis. In *ACL (1)*, pages 486–496.

Christopher D. Manning and Dan Klein. 2003. Optimization, maxent models, and conditional estimation without magic. In *Tutorial at HLT-NAACL 2003 and ACL 2003*. http://nlp.stanford.edu/software/classifier.shtml.

Amita Misra and Marilyn A. Walker. 2013. Topic independent identification of agreement and disagreement in social media dialogue. In *Conference of the Special Interest Group on Discourse and Dialogue*, pages 41–50.

Md Arafat Sultan, Steven Bethard, and Tamara Sumner. 2014. Back to basics for monolingual alignment: Exploiting word similarity and contextual evidence. *Transactions of the Association for Computational Linguistics*, 2:219–230.

Kapil Thadani, Scott Martin, and Michael White. 2012. A joint phrasal and dependency model for paraphrase alignment. In *Proceedings of COLING 2012*, pages 1229–1238. The COLING 2012 Organizing Committee.

Marilyn A. Walker, Jean E. Fox Tree, Pranav Anand, Rob Abbott, and Joseph King. 2012. A corpus for research on deliberation and debate. In *Proceedings of the 8th Language Resources and Evaluation Conference*, pages 812–817.

Theresa Wilson, Paul Hoffmann, Swapna Somasundaran, Jason Kessler, Janyce Wiebe, Yejin Choi, Claire Cardie, Ellen Riloff, and Siddharth Patwardhan. 2005. OpinionFinder: A system for subjectivity analysis. In *Demonstration Description in Conference on Empirical Methods in Natural Language Processing*, pages 34–35.

Xuchen Yao, Benjamin Van Durme, Chris Callison-Burch, and Peter Clark. 2013. A lightweight and high performance monolingual word aligner. In *Proceedings of the 51st Annual Meeting of the Association for Computational Linguistics*, pages 702–707.

Language Models for Image Captioning: The Quirks and What Works

Jacob Devlin★, Hao Cheng♠, Hao Fang♠, Saurabh Gupta♣,
Li Deng, Xiaodong He★, Geoffrey Zweig★, Margaret Mitchell★

Microsoft Research

★ Corresponding authors: {jdevlin,xiaohe,gzweig,memitc}@microsoft.com
♠ University of Washington
♣ University of California at Berkeley

Abstract

Two recent approaches have achieved state-of-the-art results in image captioning. The first uses a pipelined process where a set of candidate words is generated by a convolutional neural network (CNN) trained on images, and then a maximum entropy (ME) language model is used to arrange these words into a coherent sentence. The second uses the penultimate activation layer of the CNN as input to a recurrent neural network (RNN) that then generates the caption sequence. In this paper, we compare the merits of these different language modeling approaches for the first time by using the same state-of-the-art CNN as input. We examine issues in the different approaches, including linguistic irregularities, caption repetition, and data set overlap. By combining key aspects of the ME and RNN methods, we achieve a new record performance over previously published results on the benchmark COCO dataset. However, the gains we see in BLEU do not translate to human judgments.

1 Introduction

Recent progress in automatic image captioning has shown that an image-conditioned language model can be very effective at generating captions. Two leading approaches have been explored for this task. The first decomposes the problem into an initial step that uses a convolutional neural network to predict a bag of words that are likely to be present in a caption; then in a second step, a maximum entropy language model (ME LM) is used to generate a sentence that covers a minimum number of the detected words (Fang et al., 2015). The second approach uses the activations from final hidden layer of an object detection CNN as the input to a recurrent neural network language model (RNN LM). This is referred to as a Multimodal Recurrent Neural Network (MRNN) (Karpathy and Fei-Fei, 2015; Mao et al., 2015; Chen and Zitnick, 2015). Similar in spirit is the the log-bilinear (LBL) LM of Kiros et al. (2014).

In this paper, we study the relative merits of these approaches. By using an identical state-of-the-art CNN as the input to RNN-based and ME-based models, we are able to empirically compare the strengths and weaknesses of the language modeling components. We find that the approach of directly generating the text with an MRNN[1] outperforms the ME LM when measured by BLEU on the COCO dataset (Lin et al., 2014),[2] but this recurrent model tends to reproduce captions in the training set. In fact, a simple k-nearest neighbor approach, which is common in earlier related work (Farhadi et al., 2010; Mason and Charniak, 2014), performs similarly to the MRNN. In contrast, the ME LM generates the most novel captions, and does the best at captioning images for which there is no close match in the training data. With a Deep Multimodal Similarity Model (DMSM) incorporated,[3] the ME LM significantly outperforms other methods according to human judgments. In sum, the contributions of this paper are as follows:

1. We compare the use of discrete detections and continuous valued CNN activations as the conditioning information for language models trained to generate image captions.
2. We show that a simple k-nearest neighbor retrieval method performs at near state-of-the-art for this task and dataset.
3. We demonstrate that a state-of-the-art

[1]In our case, a gated recurrent neural network (GRNN) is used (Cho et al., 2014), similar to an LSTM.

[2]This is the largest image captioning dataset to date.

[3]As described by Fang et al. (2015).

Proceedings of the 53rd Annual Meeting of the Association for Computational Linguistics and the 7th International Joint Conference on Natural Language Processing (Short Papers), pages 100–105,
Beijing, China, July 26-31, 2015.

MRNN-based approach tends to reconstruct previously seen captions; in contrast, the two stage ME LM approach achieves similar or better performance while generating relatively novel captions.

4. We advance the state-of-the-art BLEU scores on the COCO dataset.
5. We present human evaluation results on the systems with the best performance as measured by automatic metrics.
6. We explore several issues with the statistical models and the underlying COCO dataset, including linguistic irregularities, caption repetition, and data set overlap.

2 Models

All language models compared here are trained using output from the same state-of-the-art CNN. The CNN used is the 16-layer variant of VGGNet (Simonyan and Zisserman, 2014) which was initially trained for the ILSVRC2014 classification task (Russakovsky et al., 2015), and then fine-tuned on the Microsoft COCO data set (Fang et al., 2015; Lin et al., 2014).

2.1 Detector Conditioned Models

We study the effect of leveraging an explicit detection step to find key objects/attributes in images before generation, examining both an ME LM approach as reported in previous work (Fang et al., 2015), and a novel LSTM approach introduced here. Both use a CNN trained to output a bag of words indicating the words that are likely to appear in a caption, and both use a beam search to find a top-scoring sentence that contains a subset of the words. This set of words is dynamically adjusted to remove words as they are mentioned.

We refer the reader to Fang et al. (2015) for a full description of their ME LM approach, whose 500-best outputs we analyze here.[4] We also include the output from their ME LM that leverages scores from a Deep Multimodal Similarity Model (DMSM) during n-best re-ranking. Briefly, the DMSM is a non-generative neural network model which projects both the image pixels and caption text into a comparable vector space, and scores their similarity.

In the LSTM approach, similar to the ME LM approach, we maintain a set of likely words $\mathcal{D}$ that have not yet been mentioned in the caption under construction. This set is initialized to all the words predicted by the CNN above some threshold α.[5] The words already mentioned in the sentence history h are then removed to produce a set of conditioning words $\mathcal{D} \setminus \{\mathbf{h}\}$. We incorporate this information within the LSTM by adding an additional input encoded to represent the remaining visual attributes $\mathcal{D} \setminus \{\mathbf{h}\}$ as a continuous valued auxiliary feature vector (Mikolov and Zweig, 2012). This is encoded as $f(\mathbf{s}_{h_{-1}} + \sum_{v \in \mathcal{D}\setminus\{\mathbf{h}\}} \mathbf{g}_v + \mathbf{U}\mathbf{q}_{\mathbf{h},\mathcal{D}})$, where $\mathbf{s}_{h_{-1}}$ and $\mathbf{g}_v$ are respectively the continuous-space representations for last word h_{-1} and detector $v \in \mathcal{D} \setminus \{\mathbf{h}\}$, $\mathbf{U}$ is learned matrix for recurrent histories, and $f(\cdot)$ is the sigmoid transformation.

2.2 Multimodal Recurrent Neural Network

In this section, we explore a model directly conditioned on the CNN activations rather than a set of word detections. Our implementation is very similar to captioning models described in Karpathy and Fei-Fei (2015), Vinyals et al. (2014), Mao et al. (2015), and Donahue et al. (2014). This joint vision-language RNN is referred to as a Multimodal Recurrent Neural Network (MRNN).

In this model, we feed each image into our CNN and retrieve the 4096-dimensional final hidden layer, denoted as `fc7`. The `fc7` vector is then fed into a hidden layer H to obtain a 500-dimensional representation that serves as the initial hidden state to a gated recurrent neural network (GRNN) (Cho et al., 2014). The GRNN is trained jointly with H to produce the caption one word at a time, conditioned on the previous word and the previous recurrent state. For decoding, we perform a beam search of size 10 to emit tokens until an END token is produced. We use a 500-dimensional GRNN hidden layer and 200-dimensional word embeddings.

2.3 k-Nearest Neighbor Model

Both Donahue et al. (2015) and Karpathy and Fei-Fei (2015) present a 1-nearest neighbor baseline. As a first step, we replicated these results using the cosine similarity of the `fc7` layer between each test set image t and training image r. We randomly emit one caption from t's most similar training image as the caption of t. As reported in previous results, performance is quite poor, with a BLEU

[4]We will refer to this system as D-ME.

[5]In all experiments in this paper, α=0.5.

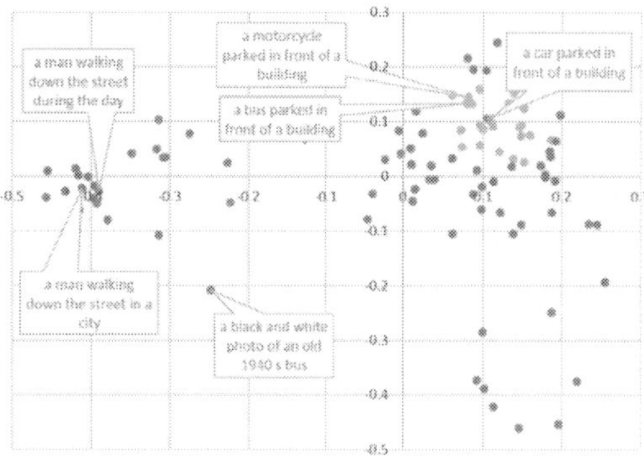

Figure 1: Example of the set of candidate captions for an image, the highest scoring m captions (green) and the consensus caption (orange). This is a real example visualized in two dimensions.

score of 11.2%.

However, we explore the idea that we may be able to find an optimal k-nearest neighbor *consensus caption*. We first select the $k = 90$ nearest training images of a test image t as above. We denote the union of training captions in this set as $C = c_1, ..., c_{5k}$.[6] For each caption c_i, we compute the n-gram overlap F-score between c_i and each other caption in C. We define the consensus caption c^* to be caption with the highest mean n-gram overlap with the other captions in C. We have found it is better to only compute this average among c_i's $m = 125$ most similar captions, rather than all of C. The hyperparameters k and m were obtained by a grid search on the validation set.

A visual example of the consensus caption is given in Figure 1. Intuitively, we are choosing a single caption that may describe *many* different images that are similar to t, rather than a caption that describes the *single* image that is most similar to t. We believe that this is a reasonable approach to take for a retrieval-based method for captioning, as it helps ensure incorrect information is not mentioned. Further details on retrieval-based methods are available in, e.g., (Ordonez et al., 2011; Hodosh et al., 2013).

3 Experimental Results

3.1 The Microsoft COCO Dataset

We work with the Microsoft COCO dataset (Lin et al., 2014), with 82,783 training images, and the validation set split into 20,243 validation images and 20,244 testval images. Most images contain multiple objects and significant contextual information, and each image comes with 5 human-annotated captions. The images create a challenging testbed for image captioning and are widely used in recent automatic image captioning work.

[6]Each training image has 5 captions.

LM	PPLX	BLEU	METEOR
D-ME†	18.1	23.6	22.8
D-LSTM	14.3	22.4	22.6
MRNN	13.2	25.7	22.6
k-Nearest Neighbor	-	26.0	22.5
1-Nearest Neighbor	-	11.2	17.3

Table 1: Model performance on testval. †: From (Fang et al., 2015).

	D-ME+DMSM	a plate with a sandwich and a cup of coffee
	MRNN	a close up of a plate of food
	D-ME+DMSM+MRNN	a plate of food and a cup of coffee
	k-NN	a cup of coffee on a plate with a spoon
	D-ME+DMSM	a black bear walking across a lush green forest
	MRNN	a couple of bears walking across a dirt road
	D-ME+DMSM+MRNN	a black bear walking through a wooded area
	k-NN	a black bear that is walking in the woods
	D-ME+DMSM	a gray and white cat sitting on top of it
	MRNN	a cat sitting in front of a mirror
	D-ME+DMSM+MRNN	a close up of a cat looking at the camera
	k-NN	a cat sitting on top of a wooden table

Table 2: Example generated captions.

3.2 Metrics

The quality of generated captions is measured automatically using BLEU (Papineni et al., 2002) and METEOR (Denkowski and Lavie, 2014). BLEU roughly measures the fraction of N-grams (up to 4 grams) that are in common between a hypothesis and one or more references, and penalizes short hypotheses by a brevity penalty term.[7] METEOR (Denkowski and Lavie, 2014) measures unigram precision and recall, extending exact word matches to include similar words based on WordNet synonyms and stemmed tokens. We also report the perplexity (PPLX) of studied detection-conditioned LMs. The PPLX is in many ways the natural measure of a statistical LM, but can be loosely correlated with BLEU (Auli et al., 2013).

3.3 Model Comparison

In Table 1, we summarize the generation performance of our different models. The discrete detection based models are prefixed with "D". Some example generated results are show in Table 2.

We see that the detection-conditioned LSTM LM produces much lower PPLX than the detection-conditioned ME LM, but its BLEU score is no better. The MRNN has the lowest PPLX, and highest BLEU among all LMs stud-

[7]We use the length of the reference that is closest to the length of the hypothesis to compute the brevity penalty.

Re-Ranking Features	BLEU	METEOR
D-ME †	23.6	22.8
+ DMSM †	25.7	23.6
+ MRNN	26.8	23.3
+ DMSM + MRNN	**27.3**	23.6

Table 3: Model performance on testval after re-ranking. †: previously reported and reconfirmed BLEU scores from (Fang et al., 2015). +DMSM had resulted in the highest score yet reported.

ied in our experiments. It significantly improves BLEU by 2.1 absolutely over the D-ME LM baseline. METEOR is similar across all three LM-based methods.

Perhaps most surprisingly, the k-nearest neighbor algorithm achieves a higher BLEU score than all other models. However, as we will demonstrate in Section 3.5, the generated captions perform significantly better than the nearest neighbor captions in terms of human quality judgements.

3.4 n-best Re-Ranking

In addition to comparing the ME-based and RNN-based LMs independently, we explore whether combining these models results in an additive improvement. To this end, we use the 500-best list from the D-ME and add a score for each hypothesis from the MRNN.[8] We then re-rank the hypotheses using MERT (Och, 2003). As in previous work (Fang et al., 2015), model weights were optimized to maximize BLEU score on the validation set. We further extend this combination approach to the D-ME model with DMSM scores included during re-ranking (Fang et al., 2015).

Results are show in Table 3. We find that combining the D-ME, DMSM, and MRNN achieves a 1.6 BLEU improvement over the D-ME+DMSM.

3.5 Human Evaluation

Because automatic metrics do not always correlate with human judgments (Callison-Burch et al., 2006; Hodosh et al., 2013), we also performed human evaluations using the same procedure as in Fang et al. (2015). Here, human judges were presented with an image, a system generated caption, and a human generated caption, and were asked which caption was "better".[9] For each condition, 5 judgments were obtained for 1000 images from the testval set.

[8]The MRNN does not produce a diverse n-best list.

[9]The captions were randomized and the users were not informed which was which.

Results are shown in Table 4. The D-ME+DMSM outperforms the MRNN by 5 percentage points for the "Better Or Equal to Human" judgment, despite both systems achieving the same BLEU score. The k-Nearest Neighbor system performs 1.4 percentage points worse than the MRNN, despite achieving a slightly higher BLEU score. Finally, the combined model does not outperform the D-ME+DMSM in terms of human judgments despite a 1.6 BLEU improvement.

Although we cannot pinpoint the exact reason for this mismatch between automated scores and human evaluation, a more detailed analysis of the difference between systems is performed in Sections 4 and 5.

	Human Judgements		
Approach	Better	Better or Equal	BLEU
D-ME+DMSM	7.8%	34.0%	25.7
MRNN	8.8%	29.0%	25.7
D-ME+DMSM+MRNN	5.7%	34.2%	**27.3**
k-Nearest Neighbor	5.5%	27.6%	26.0

Table 4: Results when comparing produced captions to those written by humans, as judged by humans. These are the percent of captions judged to be "better than" or "better than or equal to" a caption written by a human.

4 Language Analysis

Examples of common mistakes we observe on the testval set are shown in Table 5. The D-ME system has difficulty with anaphora, particularly within the phrase "on top of it", as shown in examples (1), (2), and (3). This is likely due to the fact that is maintains a local context window. In contrast, the MRNN approach tends to generate such anaphoric relationships correctly.

However, the D-ME LM maintains an explicit coverage state vector tracking which attributes have already been emitted. The MRNN *implicitly* maintains the full state using its recurrent layer, which sometimes results in multiple emission mistakes, where the same attribute is emitted more than once. This is particularly evident when coordination ("and") is present (examples (4) and (5)).

4.1 Repeated Captions

All of our models produce a large number of captions seen in the training and repeated for different images in the test set, as shown in Table 6 (also observed by Vinyals et al. (2014) for their LSTM-based model). There are at least two potential causes for this repetition.

	D-ME+DMSM	MRNN
1	a slice of pizza sitting on top of it	a bed with a red blanket on top of it
2	a black and white bird perched on top of it	a birthday cake with candles on top of it
3	a little boy that is brushing his teeth with a toothbrush in her mouth	a little girl brushing her teeth with a toothbrush
4	a large bed sitting in a bedroom	a bedroom with a bed and a bed
5	a man wearing a bow tie	a man wearing a tie and a tie

Table 5: Example errors in the two basic approaches.

System	Unique Captions	Seen In Training
Human	99.4%	4.8%
D-ME+DMSM	47.0%	30.0%
MRNN	33.1%	60.3%
D-ME+DMSM+MRNN	28.5%	61.3%
k-Nearest Neighbor	36.6%	100%

Table 6: Percentage unique (Unique Captions) and novel (Seen In Training) captions for testval images. For example, 28.5% unique means 5,776 unique strings were generated for all 20,244 images.

First, the systems often produce generic captions such as "a close up of a plate of food", which may be applied to many publicly available images. This may suggest a deeper issue in the training and evaluation of our models, which warrants more discussion in future work. Second, although the COCO dataset and evaluation server[10] has encouraged rapid progress in image captioning, there may be a lack of diversity in the data. We also note that although caption duplication is an issue in all systems, it is a greater issue in the MRNN than the D-ME+DMSM.

5 Image Diversity

The strong performance of the k-nearest neighbor algorithm and the large number of repeated captions produced by the systems here suggest a lack of diversity in the training and test data.[11]

We believe that one reason to work on image captioning is to be able to caption *compositionally* novel images, where the individual *components* of the image may be seen in the training, but the entire composition is often not.

In order to evaluate results for only compositionally novel images, we bin the test images based on visual overlap with the training data. For each test image, we compute the `fc7` cosine similarity with each training image, and the mean value of the 50 closest images. We then compute BLEU on the 20% least overlapping and 20% most overlapping subsets.

[10]http://mscoco.org/dataset/

[11]This is partially an artifact of the manner in which the Microsoft COCO data set was constructed, since each image was chosen to be in one of 80 pre-defined object categories.

Condition	Train/Test Visual Overlap BLEU		
	Whole Set	20% Least	20% Most
D-ME+DMSM	25.7	20.9	29.9
MRNN	25.7	18.8	32.0
D-ME+DMSM+MRNN	27.3	21.7	32.0
k-Nearest Neighbor	26.0	18.4	33.2

Table 7: Performance for different portions of testval, based on visual overlap with the training.

Results are shown in Table 7. The D-ME+DMSM outperforms the k-nearest neighbor approach by 2.5 BLEU on the "20% Least" set, even though performance on the whole set is comparable. Additionally, the D-ME+DMSM outperforms the MRNN by 2.1 BLEU on the "20% Least" set, but performs 2.1 BLEU *worse* on the "20% Most" set. This is evidence that D-ME+DMSM generalizes better on novel images than the MRNN; this is further supported by the relatively low percentage of captions it generates seen in the training data (Table 6) while still achieving reasonable captioning performance. We hypothesize that these are the main reasons for the strong human evaluation results of the D-ME+DMSM shown in Section 3.5.

6 Conclusion

We have shown that a gated RNN conditioned directly on CNN activations (an MRNN) achieves better BLEU performance than an ME LM or LSTM conditioned on a set of discrete activations; and a similar BLEU performance to an ME LM combined with a DMSM. However, the ME LM + DMSM method significantly outperforms the MRNN in terms of human quality judgments. We hypothesize that this is partially due to the lack of novelty in the captions produced by the MRNN. In fact, a k-nearest neighbor retrieval algorithm introduced in this paper performs similarly to the MRNN in terms of both automatic metrics and human judgements.

When we use the MRNN system alongside the DMSM to provide additional scores in MERT reranking of the n-best produced by the image-conditioned ME LM, we advance by 1.6 BLEU points on the best previously published results on the COCO dataset. Unfortunately, this improvement in BLEU does not translate to improved human quality judgments.

References

Michael Auli, Michel Galley, Chris Quirk, and Geoffrey Zweig. 2013. Joint language and translation modeling with recurrent neural networks. In *Proc. Conf. Empirical Methods Natural Language Process. (EMNLP)*, pages 1044–1054.

Chris Callison-Burch, Miles Osborne, and Philipp Koehn. 2006. Re-evaluation the role of bleu in machine translation research. In *EACL*, volume 6, pages 249–256.

Xinlei Chen and C. Lawrence Zitnick. 2015. Mind's eye: A recurrent visual representation for image caption generation. In *Proc. Conf. Comput. Vision and Pattern Recognition (CVPR)*.

Kyunghyun Cho, Bart van Merrienboer, Caglar Gulcehre, Fethi Bougares, Holger Schwenk, and Yoshua Bengio. 2014. Learning phrase representations using RNN encoder-decoder for statistical machine translation. *CoRR*.

Michael Denkowski and Alon Lavie. 2014. Meteor universal: language specific translation evaluation for any target language. In *Proc. EACL 2014 Workshop Statistical Machine Translation*.

Jeff Donahue, Lisa Anne Hendricks, Sergio Guadarrama, Marcus Rohrbach, Subhashini Venugopalan, Kate Saenko, and Trevor Darrell. 2014. Long-term recurrent convolutional networks for visual recognition and description. *arXiv:1411.4389 [cs.CV]*.

Jeffrey Donahue, Lisa Anne Hendricks, Sergio Guadarrama, Marcus Rohrbach, Subhashini Venugopalan, Kate Saenko, and Trevor Darrell. 2015. Long-term recurrent convolutional networks for visual recognition and description. In *Proc. Conf. Comput. Vision and Pattern Recognition (CVPR)*.

Hao Fang, Saurabh Gupta, Forrest Iandola, Rupesh Srivastava, Li Deng, Piotr Dollá, Margaret Mitchell, John C. Platt, C. Lawrence Zitnick, and Geoffrey Zweig. 2015. From captionons to visual concepts and back. In *Proc. Conf. Comput. Vision and Pattern Recognition (CVPR)*.

Ali Farhadi, Mohsen Hejrati, Mohammad Amin Sadeghi, Peter Young, Cyrus Rashtchian, Julia Hockenmaier, and David Forsyth. 2010. Every picture tells a story: generating sentences from images. In *Proc. European Conf. Comput. Vision (ECCV)*, pages 15–29.

Micah Hodosh, Peter Young, and Julia Hockenmaier. 2013. Framing image description as a ranking task: data models and evaluation metrics. *J. Artificial Intell. Research*, pages 853–899.

Andrej Karpathy and Li Fei-Fei. 2015. Deep visual-semantic alignments for generating image descriptions. In *Proc. Conf. Comput. Vision and Pattern Recognition (CVPR)*.

Ryan Kiros, Ruslan Salakhutdinov, and Richard Zemel. 2014. Multimodal neural language models. In *Proc. Int. Conf. Machine Learning (ICML)*.

Tsung-Yi Lin, Michael Maire, Serge Belongie, James Hays, Pietro Perona, Deva Ramanan, Piotr Dollár, and C. Lawrence Zitnick. 2014. Microsoft COCO: Common objects in context. *arXiv:1405.0312 [cs.CV]*.

Junhua Mao, Wei Xu, Yi Yang, Jiang Wang, and Alan L. Yuille. 2015. Deep captioning with multimodal recurrent neural networks (m-RNN). In *Proc. Int. Conf. Learning Representations (ICLR)*.

Rebecca Mason and Eugene Charniak. 2014. Domain-specific image captioning. In *CoNLL*.

Tomas Mikolov and Geoffrey Zweig. 2012. Context dependent recurrent neural network language model. In *SLT*, pages 234–239.

Franz Josef Och. 2003. Minimum error rate training in statistical machine translation. In *ACL*, ACL '03.

Vicente Ordonez, Girish Kulkarni, and Tamara L. Berg. 2011. Im2Text: Describing images using 1 million captioned photogrphs. In *Proc. Annu. Conf. Neural Inform. Process. Syst. (NIPS)*.

Kishore Papineni, Salim Roukos, Todd Ward, and Wei-Jing Zhu. 2002. BLEU: a method for automatic evaluation of machine translation. In *Proc. Assoc. for Computational Linguistics (ACL)*, pages 311–318.

Olga Russakovsky, Jia Deng, Hao Su, Jonathan Krause, Sanjeev Satheesh, Sean Ma, Zhiheng Huang, Andrej Karpathy, Aditya Khosla, Michael Bernstein, Alexander C. Berg, and Li Fei-Fei. 2015. ImageNet Large Scale Visual Recognition Challenge. *International Journal of Computer Vision (IJCV)*.

Karen Simonyan and Andrew Zisserman. 2014. Very deep convolutional networks for large-scale image recognition. *arXiv preprint*.

Oriol Vinyals, Alexander Toshev, Samy Bengio, and Dumitru Erhan. 2014. Show and tell: a neural image caption generator. In *Proc. Conf. Comput. Vision and Pattern Recognition (CVPR)*.

A Distributed Representation Based Query Expansion Approach for Image Captioning

Semih Yagcioglu[1] **Erkut Erdem**[1] **Aykut Erdem**[1] **Ruket Çakıcı**[2]
[1] Hacettepe University Computer Vision Lab (HUCVL)
Dept. of Computer Engineering, Hacettepe University, Ankara, TURKEY
semih.yagcioglu@hacettepe.edu.tr, {erkut,aykut}@cs.hacettepe.edu.tr
[2] Dept. of Computer Engineering, Middle East Technical University, Ankara, TURKEY
ruken@ceng.metu.edu.tr

Abstract

In this paper, we propose a novel query expansion approach for improving transfer-based automatic image captioning. The core idea of our method is to translate the given visual query into a distributional semantics based form, which is generated by the average of the sentence vectors extracted from the captions of images visually similar to the input image. Using three image captioning benchmark datasets, we show that our approach provides more accurate results compared to the state-of-the-art data-driven methods in terms of both automatic metrics and subjective evaluation.

1 Introduction

Automatic image captioning is a fast growing area of research which lies at the intersection of computer vision and natural language processing and refers to the problem of generating natural language descriptions from images. In the literature, there are a variety of image captioning models that can be categorized into three main groups as summarized below.

The first line of approaches attempts to generate novel captions directly from images (Farhadi et al., 2010; Kulkarni et al., 2011; Mitchell et al., 2012). Specifically, they borrow techniques from computer vision such as object detectors and scene/attribute classifiers, exploit their outputs to extract the visual content of the input image and then generate the caption through surface realization. More recently, a particular set of generative approaches have emerged over the last few years, which depends on deep neural networks (Chen and Zitnick., 2015; Karpathy and Fei-Fei, 2015; Xu et al., 2015; Vinyals et al., 2015). In general, these studies combine convolutional neural networks (CNNs) with recurrent neural networks (RNNs) to generate a description for a given image.

The studies in the second group aim at learning joint representations of images and captions (Hodosh et al., 2013; Socher et al., 2014; Karpathy et al., 2014). They employ certain machine learning techniques to form a common embedding space for the visual and textual data, and perform cross-modal (image-sentence) retrieval in that intermediate space to accordingly score and rank the pool of captions to find the most proper caption for a given image.

The last group of works, on the other hand, follows a data-driven approach and treats image captioning as a caption transfer problem (Ordonez et al., 2011; Kuznetsova et al., 2012; Patterson et al., 2014; Mason and Charniak, 2014). For a given image, these methods first search for visually similar images and then use the captions of the retrieved images to provide a description, which makes them much easier to implement compared to the other two classes of approaches.

The success of these data-driven approaches depends directly on the amount of data available and the quality of the retrieval set. Clearly, the image features and the corresponding similarity measures used in retrieval play a significant role here but, as investigated in (Berg et al., 2012), what makes this particularly difficult is that while describing an image humans do not explicitly mention every detail. That is, some parts of an image are more salient than the others. Hence, one also needs to bridge the semantic gap between what is there in the image and what people say when describing it.

As a step towards achieving this goal, in this paper, we introduce a novel automatic query expansion approach for image captioning to retrieve semantically more relevant captions. As illustrated in Fig. 1, we swap modalities at our query expan-

Proceedings of the 53rd Annual Meeting of the Association for Computational Linguistics and the 7th International Joint Conference on Natural Language Processing (Short Papers), pages 106–111, Beijing, China, July 26-31, 2015.

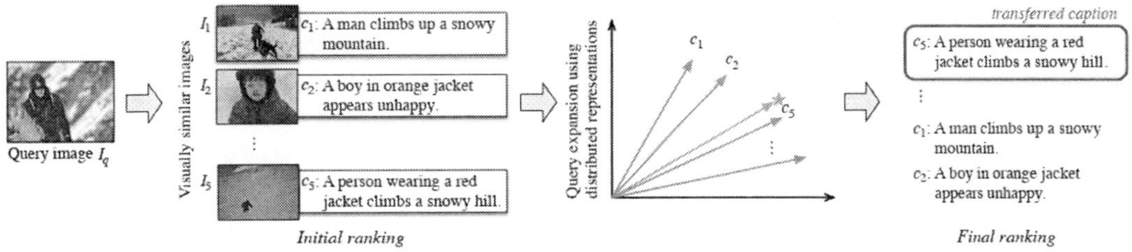

Figure 1: A system overview of the proposed query expansion approach for image captioning.

sion step and synthesize a new query, based on distributional representations (Baroni and Lenci, 2010; Turney and Pantel, 2010; Mikolov et al., 2013; Pennington et al., 2014) of the captions of the images visually similar to the input image. Through comprehensive experiments over three benchmark datasets, we show that our model improves upon existing methods and produces captions more appropriate to the query image.

2 Related Work

As mentioned earlier, a number of studies pose image captioning as a caption transfer problem by relying on the assumption that visually similar images generally contain very similar captions. The pioneering work in this category is the im2text model by Ordonez et al. (2011), which suggests a two-step retrieval process to transfer a caption to a given query image. The first step, which provides a baseline for the follow-up caption transfer approaches, is to find visually similar images in terms of some global image features. In the second step, according to the retrieved captions, specific detectors and classifiers are applied to images to construct a semantic representation, which is then used to re-rank the associated captions.

Kuznetsova et al. (2012) proposed performing multiple retrievals for each detected visual element in the query image and then combining the relevant parts of the retrieved captions to generate the output caption. Patterson et al. (2014) extended the baseline model by replacing global features with automatically extracted scene attributes, and showed the importance of scene information in caption transfer. Mason and Charniak (2014) formulated caption transfer as an extractive summarization problem and proposed to perform the re-ranking step by means of a word frequency-based representations of captions. More recently, Mitchell et al. (2015) proposed to select the caption that best describes the remaining descriptions of the retrieved similar images wrt an n-gram overlap-based sentence similarity measure.

In this paper, we take a new perspective to data-driven image captioning by proposing a novel query expansion step based on compositional distributed semantics to improve the results. Our approach uses the weighted average of the distributed representations of retrieved captions to expand the original query in order to obtain captions that are semantically more related to the visual content of the input image.

3 Our Approach

In this section, we describe the steps of the proposed method in more detail.

3.1 Retrieving Visually Similar Images

Representing Images. Data-driven approaches such as ours rely heavily on the quality of the initial retrieval, which makes having a good visual feature of utmost importance. In our study, we use the recently proposed Caffe deep learning features (Jia et al., 2014), trained on ImageNet, which have been proven to be effective in many computer vision problems. Specifically, we use the activations from the seventh hidden layer (fc7), resulting in a 4096-dimensional feature vector.

Adaptive Neighborhood Selection. We create our expanded query by using the distributed representations of the captions associated with the retrieved images, and thus, having no outliers is also an important factor for the effectiveness of the approach. For this, instead of using a fixed neighborhood, we adopt an adaptive strategy to select the initial candidate set of image-caption pairs $\{(I_i, c_i)\}$.

For a query image I_q, we utilize a ratio test and only consider the candidates that fall within a radius defined by the distance score of the query image to the nearest training image $I_{closest}$, as

$$\mathcal{N}(I_q) = \{(I_i, c_i) \mid dist(I_q, I_i) \le (1+\epsilon) dist(I_q, I_{closest}), \\ I_{closest} = \arg\min \; dist(I_q, I_i), I_i \in \mathcal{T}\} \quad (1)$$

where $dist$ denotes the Euclidean distance between two feature vectors, $\mathcal{N}$ represents the candidate set based on the adaptive neighborhood, $\mathcal{T}$ is the training set, and ϵ is a positive scalar value[1].

3.2 Query Expansion Based on Distributed Representations

Representing Words and Captions. In this study, we build our query expansion model on the distributional models of semantics where the meanings of words are represented with vectors that characterize the set of contexts they occur in a corpus. Existing approaches to distributional semantics can be grouped into two, as count and predict-based models (Baroni et al., 2014). In our experiments, we tested our approach using two recent models, namely *word2vec* (Mikolov et al., 2013) and *GloVe* (Pennington et al., 2014), and found out that the predict-based model of Mikolov et al. (2013) performs better in our case.

To move from word level to caption level, we take the simple addition based compositional model described in (Blacoe and Lapata, 2012) and form the vector representation of a caption as the sum of the vectors of its constituent words. Note that here we only use the non-stop words in the caption.

Query Expansion. For a query image I_q, we first retrieve visually similar images from a large dataset of captioned images. In our query expansion step, we swap modalities and construct a new query based on the distributed representations of captions. In particular, we expand the original visual query with a new textual query based on the weighted average of the vectors of the retrieved captions as follows:

$$q = \frac{1}{NM} \sum_{i=1}^{N} \sum_{j=1}^{M} sim(I_q, I_i) \cdot c_i^j \quad (2)$$

where N and M respectively denote the total number of image-caption pairs in the candidate set $\mathcal{N}$ and the number of reference captions associated with each training image, and $sim(I_q, I_i)$ refers to the visual similarity score of the image I_i to the query image I_q[2] which is used to give more importance to the captions of images visually more close to the query image.

Then, we re-rank the candidate captions by estimating the cosine distance between the distributed representation of the captions and the expanded query vector q, and finally transfer the closest caption as the description of the input image.

4 Experimental Setup and Evaluation

In the following, we give the details about our experimental setup.

Corpus. We estimated the distributed representation of words based on the captions of the MS COCO (Lin et al., 2014) dataset, containing 620K captions. As a preprocessing step, all captions in the corpus were lowercased, and stripped from punctuation.

In the training of word vectors, we used 500 dimensional vectors obtained with both *GloVe* (Pennington et al., 2014) and *word2vec* (Mikolov et al., 2013) models. The minimum word count was set to 5, and the window size was set to 10. Although these two methods seem to produce comparable results, we found out that *word2vec* gives better results in our case, and thus we only report our results with *word2vec* model.

Datasets. In our experiments, we used the popular Flickr8K (Hodosh et al., 2013), Flickr30K (Young et al., 2014), MS COCO (Lin et al., 2014) datasets, containing 8K, 30K and 123K images, respectively. Each image in these datasets comes with 5 captions annotated by different people. For each dataset, we utilized the corresponding validation split to optimize the parameters of our method, and used the test split for evaluation where we considered all the image-caption pairs in the training and the validation splits as our knowledge base.

Although Flickr8K, and Flickr30K datasets have been in use for a while, MS COCO dataset is under active development and might be subject to change. Here, we report our results with version 1.0 of MS COCO dataset where we used the train, validation and test splits provided by (Karpathy et al., 2014).

We compared our proposed approach against the adapted baseline model (VC) of *im2text* (Ordonez et al., 2011) which corresponds to using the caption of the nearest visually similar im-

[1]The adaptive neighborhood parameter ϵ was emprically set to 0.15.

[2]We define $sim(I_q, I_i) = 1 - dist(I_q, I_i)/Z$ where Z is a normalization constant.

MC-KL	a black and white dog is playing or fighting with a brown dog in grass	a man is sitting on a blue bench with a blue blanket covering his face	a man in a white shirt and sunglasses is holding hands with a woman wearing a red shirt outside	one brown and black pigmented bird sitting on a tree branch
MC-SB	a dog looks behind itself	a girl looks at a woman s face	a woman and her two dogs are walking down the street	a tree with many leaves around it
VC	a brown and white dog jumping over a red yellow and white pole	a father feeding his child on the street	a girl is skipping across the road in front of a white truck	a black bear climbing a tree in forest area
OURS	a brown and white dog jumps over a dog hurdle	a man in a black shirt and his little girl wearing orange are sharing a treat	a girl jumps rope in a parking lot	a bird standing on a tree branch in a wooded area
HUMAN	a brown and white sheltie leaping over a rail	a man and a girl sit on the ground and eat	a girl is in a parking lot jumping rope	a painted sign of a blue bird in a tree in the woods

Figure 2: Some example input images and the generated descriptions.

	Flickr8K			Flickr30K			MS COCO		
	BLEU	METEOR	CIDEr	BLEU	METEOR	CIDEr	BLEU	METEOR	CIDEr
OURS	**3.78**	**11.57**	**0.31**	**3.22**	**10.06**	0.20	**5.36**	**13.17**	**0.58**
MC-KL	2.71	10.95	0.15	2.02	9.92	0.07	4.04	12.56	0.37
MC-SB	3.08	9.06	0.27	2.76	8.06	**0.20**	5.02	11.78	0.56
VC	2.79	8.91	0.19	2.33	7.53	0.14	3.71	10.07	0.35
HUMAN	7.59	17.72	2.67	6.52	15.70	2.53	7.42	16.73	2.70

Table 1: Comparison of the methods on the benchmark datasets based on automatic evaluation metrics.

age, and the word frequency-based approaches of Mason and Charniak (2014) (MC-SB and MC-KL). We also provide the human agreement results (HUMAN) by comparing one groundtruth caption against the rest.

For a fair comparison with the MC-SB and MC-KL models (Mason and Charniak, 2014) and the baseline approach VC, we used the same image similarity metric and training splits in retrieving visually similar images for all models. For human agreement, we had five groundtruth image captions, thus we determine the human agreement score by following a leave-one-out strategy. For display purposes, we selected one description randomly from the available five groundtruth captions in the figures.

Automatic Evaluation. We evaluated our approach with a range of existing metrics, which are thoroughly discussed in (Elliott and Keller, 2014; Vedantam et al., 2015). We used smoothed BLEU (Papineni et al., 2002) for benchmarking purposes. We also provided the scores of METEOR (Denkowski and Lavie, 2014) and the recently proposed CIDEr metric (Vedantam et al., 2015), which has been shown to correlate well with the human judgments in (Elliott and Keller, 2014) and (Vedantam et al., 2015), respectively[3].

Human Evaluation. We designed a subjective experiment to measure how relevant the transferred caption is to a given image using a setup similar to those of (Kuznetsova et al., 2012; Mason and Charniak, 2014)[4]. In this experiment, we provided human annotators an image and a candidate description where it is rated according to a scale of 1 to 5 (5: perfect, 4: almost perfect, 3: 70-80% good, 2: 50-70% good, 1: totally bad) for its relevancy. We experimented on a randomly selected set of 100 images from our test set and evaluated our captions as well as those of the competing approaches.

[3]We collected METEOR and BLEU scores via MultEval (Clark et al., 2011) and for CIDEr scores we used the authors' publicly available code.

[4]We used CrowdFlower and at least 5 different human annotators for each question.

	Rate	Variance
OURS	**2.73**	0.65
MC-SB	2.38	0.58
VC	2.27	0.66
MC-KL	2.03	0.62
HUMAN	4.84	0.26

Table 2: Human judgment scores on a scale of 1 to 5.

a man wearing a santa hat holding a dog posing for a picture — a boy is holding a dog that is wearing a hat

Figure 3: Limitation. A query image on the left and its actual caption, a proposed caption on the right along with its actual image.

5 Results and Discussion

In Figure 2, we present sample results obtained with our framework, MC-SB, MC-KL and VC models along with the groundtruth caption. We provide the quantitative results based on automatic evaluation measures and human judgment scores in Table 1 and Table 2, respectively.

Our findings indicate that our query expansion approach which is based on distributed representations of captions gives results better than those of VC, MC-SB and MC-KL models. Although our method makes a modest improvement compared to the human scores we believe that there is still a big gap between the human baseline, which align well with the recently held MS COCO 2015 Captioning Challenge results.

One limitation in this work is the Out-of-Vocabulary (OOV) words, which is around 1% on average for the benchmark datasets. We omit them in our calculations, since there is no practical way to map word vectors for the OOV words, as they are not included in the training of the word embeddings. Another limitation is that this approach currently does not incorporate the syntactic structures in captions, therefore the position of a word in a caption does not make any difference in the representation, i.e. *"a man with a hat is holding a dog"* and *"a man is holding a dog with a hat"* are represented with the same vector. This limitation is illustrated in Fig. 3, where the closest caption from retrieval set contains similar scene elements but does not depict the scene well.

6 Conclusion

In this paper, we present a novel query expansion approach for image captioning, in which we utilize a distributional model of meaning for sentences. Extensive experimental results on three well-established benchmark datasets have demonstrated that our approach outperforms the state-of-the art data-driven approaches. Our future plans focus on incorporating other cues in images, and considering the syntactic structures in image descriptions.

Acknowledgments

This study was supported in part by The Scientific and Technological Research Council of Turkey (TUBITAK), with award no 113E116.

References

Marco Baroni and Alessandro Lenci. 2010. Distributional Memory: A General Framework for Corpus-Based Semantics. *Computational Linguistics*, 36(4):673–721. 2

Marco Baroni, Georgiana Dinu, and Germán Kruszewski. 2014. Don't count, predict! A systematic comparison of context-counting vs. context-predicting semantic vectors. In *Proc. of ACL*. 3

Alexander C Berg, Tamara L Berg, Hal Daume, Jesse Dodge, Amit Goyal, Xufeng Han, Alyssa Mensch, Margaret Mitchell, Aneesh Sood, Karl Stratos, et al. 2012. Understanding and Predicting Importance in Images. In *Proc. of CVPR*. 1

William Blacoe and Mirella Lapata. 2012. A Comparison of Vector-based Representations for Semantic Composition. In *Proc. of EMNLP-CoNLL*. 3

Xinlei Chen and C. Lawrence Zitnick. 2015. Mind's Eye: A Recurrent Visual Representation for Image Caption Generation. In *Proc. of CVPR*. 1

Jonathan H Clark, Chris Dyer, Alon Lavie, and Noah A Smith. 2011. Better hypothesis testing for statistical machine translation: Controlling for optimizer instability. In *Proc. of ACL*. 4

Michael Denkowski and Alon Lavie. 2014. Meteor Universal: Language Specific Translation Evaluation for Any Target Language. In *Proc. of EACL Workshop on Statistical Machine Translation*. 4

Desmond Elliott and Frank Keller. 2014. Comparing Automatic Evaluation Measures for Image Description. In *Proc. of ACL*. 4

Ali Farhadi, M Hejrati, Mohammad Amin Sadeghi, P Young, C Rashtchian, J Hockenmaier, and David Forsyth. 2010. Every Picture Tells a Story: Generating Sentences from Images. In *Proc. of ECCV*. 1

Micah Hodosh, Peter Young, and Julia Hockenmaier. 2013. Framing Image Description as a Ranking Task: Data, Models and Evaluation Metrics. *Journal of Artificial Intelligence Research*. 1, 3

Yangqing Jia, Evan Shelhamer, Jeff Donahue, Sergey Karayev, Jonathan Long, Ross Girshick, Sergio Guadarrama, and Trevor Darrell. 2014. Caffe: Convolutional Architecture for Fast Feature Embedding. In *Proc. of ACM MM*. 2

Andrej Karpathy and Li Fei-Fei. 2015. Deep Visual-semantic Alignments for Generating Image Descriptions. In *Proc. of CVPR*. 1

Andrej Karpathy, Armand Joulin, and Li Fei-Fei. 2014. Deep Fragment Embeddings for Bidirectional Image Sentence Mapping. In *Proc. of NIPS*. 1, 3

Girish Kulkarni, Visruth Premraj, Sagnik Dhar, Siming Li, Yejin Choi, Alexander C Berg, and Tamara L Berg. 2011. Baby Talk: Understanding and Generating Simple Image Descriptions. In *Proc. of CVPR*. 1

Polina Kuznetsova, Vicente Ordonez, Alexander C Berg, Tamara L Berg, and Yejin Choi. 2012. Collective Generation of Natural Image Descriptions. In *Proc. of ACL*. 1, 2, 4

Tsung-Yi Lin, Michael Maire, Serge Belongie, James Hays, Pietro Perona, Deva Ramanan, Piotr Dollár, and C Lawrence Zitnick. 2014. Microsoft COCO: Common Objects in Context. In *Proc. of ECCV*. 3

Rebecca Mason and Eugene Charniak. 2014. Nonparametric Method for Data-driven Image Captioning. In *Proc. of ACL*. 1, 2, 4

Tomas Mikolov, Ilya Sutskever, Kai Chen, Greg S Corrado, and Jeff Dean. 2013. Distributed Representations of Words and Phrases and their Compositionality. In *Proc. of NIPS*. 2, 3

Margaret Mitchell, Xufeng Han, Jesse Dodge, Alyssa Mensch, Amit Goyal, Alex Berg, Kota Yamaguchi, Tamara Berg, Karl Stratos, and Hal Daumé III. 2012. Midge: Generating Image Descriptions from Computer Vision Detections. In *Proc. of EACL*. 1

Margaret Mitchell, Hao Fang, Hao Cheng, Saurabh Gupta, Jacob Devlin, and Geoffrey Zweig. 2015. Language Models for Image Captioning: The Quirks and What Works. In *Proc. of ACL*. 2

Vicente Ordonez, Girish Kulkarni, and Tamara L Berg. 2011. Im2text: Describing Images using 1 Million Captioned Photographs. In *Proc. of NIPS*. 1, 2, 3

Kishore Papineni, Salim Roukos, Todd Ward, and Wei-Jing Zhu. 2002. BLEU: a Method for Automatic Evaluation of Machine Translation. In *Proc. of ACL*. 4

Genevieve Patterson, Chen Xu, Hang Su, and James Hays. 2014. The SUN Attribute Database: Beyond Categories for Deeper Scene Understanding. *International Journal of Computer Vision*, 108(1-2):59–81. 1, 2

Jeffrey Pennington, Richard Socher, and Christopher D Manning. 2014. GloVe: Global Vectors for Word Representation. *Proc. of EMNLP*. 2, 3

Richard Socher, Andrej Karpathy, Quoc V. Le, Christopher D. Manning, and Andrew Y. Ng. 2014. Grounded Compositional Semantics for Finding and Describing Images with Sentences. *Transactions of the Association for Computational Linguistics*. 1

Peter Turney and Patrick Pantel. 2010. From Frequency to Meaning: Vector Space Models of Semantics. *Journal of Artificial Intelligence Research*. 2

Ramakrishna Vedantam, C Lawrence Zitnick, and Devi Parikh. 2015. CIDEr: Consensus-based Image Description Evaluation. In *Proc. of CVPR*. 4

Oriol Vinyals, Alexander Toshev, Samy Bengio, and Dumitru Erhan. 2015. Show and Tell: A Neural Image Caption Generator. In *Proc. of CVPR*. 1

Kelvin Xu, Jimmy Ba, Ryan Kiros, Kyunghyun Cho, Aaron Courville, Ruslan Salakhutdinov, Richard Zemel, and Yoshua Bengio. 2015. Show, Attend and Tell: Neural Image Caption Generation with Visual attention. In *Proc. of ICML*. 1

Peter Young, Alice Lai, Micah Hodosh, and Julia Hockenmaier. 2014. From Image Descriptions to Visual Denotations: New similarity Metrics for Semantic Inference over Event Descriptions. *Transactions of the Association for Computational Linguistics*. 3

Learning language through pictures

Grzegorz Chrupała
g.chrupala@uvt.nl

Ákos Kádár
a.kadar@uvt.nl

Afra Alishahi
a.alishahi@uvt.nl

Tilburg Center for Cognition and Communication
Tilburg University

Abstract

We propose IMAGINET, a model of learning visually grounded representations of language from coupled textual and visual input. The model consists of two Gated Recurrent Unit networks with shared word embeddings, and uses a multi-task objective by receiving a textual description of a scene and trying to concurrently predict its visual representation and the next word in the sentence. Mimicking an important aspect of human language learning, it acquires meaning representations for individual words from descriptions of visual scenes. Moreover, it learns to effectively use sequential structure in semantic interpretation of multi-word phrases.

1 Introduction

Vision is the most important sense for humans and visual sensory input plays an important role in language acquisition by grounding meanings of words and phrases in perception. Similarly, in practical applications processing multimodal data where text is accompanied by images or videos is increasingly important. In this paper we propose a novel model of learning visually-grounded representations of language from paired textual and visual input. The model learns language through comprehension and production, by receiving a textual description of a scene and trying to "imagine" a visual representation of it, while predicting the next word at the same time.

The full model, which we dub IMAGINET, consists of two Gated Recurrent Unit (GRU) networks coupled via shared word embeddings. IMAGINET uses a multi-task Caruana (1997) objective: both networks read the sentence word-by-word in parallel; one of them predicts the feature representation of the image depicting the described scene after reading the whole sentence, while the other one predicts the next word at each position in the word sequence. The importance of the visual and textual objectives can be traded off, and either of them can be switched off entirely, enabling us to investigate the impact of visual vs textual information on the learned language representations.

Our approach to modeling human language learning has connections to recent models of image captioning (see Section 2). Unlike in many of these models, in IMAGINET the image is the target to predict rather then the input, and the model can build a visually-grounded representation of a sentence independently of an image. We can directly compare the performance of IMAGINET against a simple multivariate linear regression model with bag-of-words features and thus quantify the contribution of the added expressive power of a recurrent neural network.

We evaluate our model's knowledge of word meaning and sentence structure through simulating human judgments of word similarity, retrieving images corresponding to single words as well as full sentences, and retrieving paraphrases of image captions. In all these tasks the model outperforms the baseline; the model significantly correlates with human ratings of word similarity, and predicts appropriate visual interpretations of single and multi-word phrases. The acquired knowledge of sentence structure boosts the model's performance in both image and caption retrieval.

2 Related work

Several computational models have been proposed to study early language acquisition. The acquisition of word meaning has been mainly modeled using connectionist networks that learn to associate word forms with semantic or perceptual features (e.g., Li et al., 2004; Coventry et al., 2005; Regier, 2005), and rule-based or probabilistic implementations which use statistical reg-

Proceedings of the 53rd Annual Meeting of the Association for Computational Linguistics and the 7th International Joint Conference on Natural Language Processing (Short Papers), pages 112–118,
Beijing, China, July 26-31, 2015.

ularities observed in the input to detect associations between linguistic labels and visual features or concepts (e.g., Siskind, 1996; Yu, 2008; Fazly et al., 2010). These models either use toy languages as input (e.g., Siskind, 1996), or child-directed utterances from the CHILDES database (MacWhinney, 2014) paired with artificially generated semantic information. Some models have investigated the acquisition of terminology for visual concepts from simple videos (Fleischman and Roy, 2005; Skocaj et al., 2011). Lazaridou et al. (2015) adapt the skip-gram word-embedding model (Mikolov et al., 2013) for learning word representations via a multi-task objective similar to ours, learning from a dataset where some words are individually aligned with corresponding images. All these models ignore sentence structure and treat inputs as bags of words.

A few models have looked at the concurrent acquisition of words and some aspect of sentence structure, such as lexical categories (Alishahi and Chrupała, 2012) or syntactic properties (Howell et al., 2005; Kwiatkowski et al., 2012), from utterances paired with an artificially generated representation of their meaning. To our knowledge, no existing model has been proposed for concurrent learning of grounded word meanings and sentence structure from large scale data and realistic visual input.

Recently, the engineering task of generating captions for images has received a lot of attention (Karpathy and Fei-Fei, 2014; Mao et al., 2014; Kiros et al., 2014; Donahue et al., 2014; Vinyals et al., 2014; Venugopalan et al., 2014; Chen and Zitnick, 2014; Fang et al., 2014). From the point of view of modeling, the research most relevant to our interests is that of Chen and Zitnick (2014). They develop a model based on a context-dependent recurrent neural network (Mikolov and Zweig, 2012) which simultaneously processes textual and visual input and updates two parallel hidden states. Unlike theirs, our model receives the visual target only at the end of the sentence and is thus encouraged to store in the final hidden state of the visual pathway all aspects of the sentence needed to predict the image features successfully. Our setup is more suitable for the goal of learning representations of complete sentences.

3 Models

IMAGINET consists of two parallel recurrent pathways coupled via shared word embeddings. Both pathways are composed of Gated Recurrent Units (GRU) first introduced by Cho et al. (2014) and Chung et al. (2014). GRUs are related to the Long Short-Term Memory units (Hochreiter and Schmidhuber, 1997), but do not employ a separate memory cell. In a GRU, activation at time t is the linear combination of previous activation, and candidate activation:

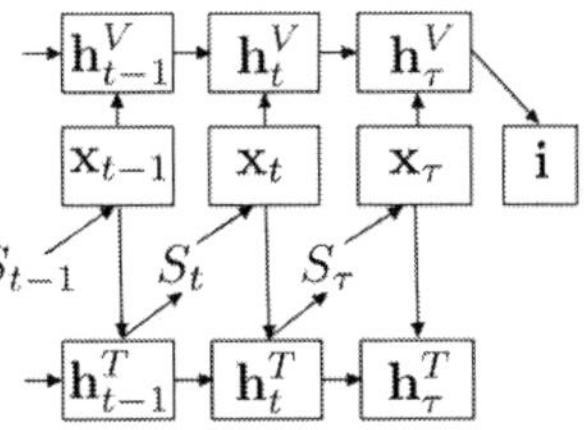

Figure 1: Structure of IMAGINET

$$\mathbf{h}_t = (1 - \mathbf{z}_t) \odot \mathbf{h}_{t-1} + \mathbf{z}_t \odot \tilde{\mathbf{h}}_t \quad (1)$$

where $\odot$ is elementwise multiplication. The update gate determines how much the activation is updated:

$$\mathbf{z}_t = \sigma_s(\mathbf{W}_z \mathbf{x}_t + \mathbf{U}_z \mathbf{h}_{t-1}) \quad (2)$$

The candidate activation is computed as:

$$\tilde{\mathbf{h}}_t = \sigma(\mathbf{W}\mathbf{x}_t + \mathbf{U}(\mathbf{r}_t \odot \mathbf{h}_{t-1})) \quad (3)$$

The reset gate is defined as:

$$\mathbf{r}_t = \sigma_s(\mathbf{W}_r \mathbf{x}_t + \mathbf{U}_r \mathbf{h}_{t-1}) \quad (4)$$

Our gated recurrent units use steep sigmoids for gate activations:

$$\sigma_s(z) = \frac{1}{1 + \exp(-3.75z)}$$

and rectified linear units clipped between 0 and 5 for the unit activations:

$$\sigma(z) = \mathrm{clip}(0.5(\mathrm{z} + \mathrm{abs}(\mathrm{z})), 0, 5)$$

Figure 1 illustrates the structure of the network. The word embeddings is a matrix of learned parameters $\mathbf{W}_e$ with each column corresponding to a vector for a particular word. The input word symbol S_t of sentence S at each step t indexes into the embeddings matrix and the vector $\mathbf{x}_t$ forms input to both GRU networks:

$$\mathbf{x}_t = \mathbf{W}_e[:, S_t] \quad (5)$$

This input is mapped into two parallel hidden states, $\mathbf{h}_t^V$ along the visual pathway, and $\mathbf{h}_t^T$ along the textual pathway:

$$\mathbf{h}_t^V = \mathrm{GRU}^V(\mathbf{h}_{t-1}^V, \mathbf{x}_t) \quad (6)$$

$$\mathbf{h}_t^T = \mathrm{GRU}^T(\mathbf{h}_{t-1}^T, \mathbf{x}_t) \quad (7)$$

The final hidden state along the visual pathway $\mathbf{h}_\tau^V$ is then mapped to the predicted target image representation $\hat{\mathbf{i}}$ by the fully connected layer with parameters $\mathbf{V}$ and the clipped rectifier activation:

$$\hat{\mathbf{i}} = \sigma(\mathbf{V}\mathbf{h}_\tau^V) \quad (8)$$

Each hidden state along the textual pathway $\mathbf{h}_t^T$ is used to predict the next symbol in the sentence S via a softmax layer with parameters $\mathbf{L}$:

$$p(S_{t+1}|S_{1:t}) = \mathrm{softmax}(\mathbf{L}\mathbf{h}_t^T) \quad (9)$$

The loss function whose gradient is backpropagated through time to the GRUs and the embeddings is a composite objective with terms penalizing error on the visual and the textual targets simultaneously:

$$L(\theta) = \alpha L^T(\theta) + (1-\alpha)L^V(\theta) \quad (10)$$

where θ is the set of all IMAGINET parameters. L^T is the cross entropy function:

$$L^T(\theta) = -\frac{1}{\tau}\sum_{t=1}^{\tau} \log p(S_t|S_{1:t}) \quad (11)$$

while L^V is the mean squared error:

$$L^V(\theta) = \frac{1}{K}\sum_{k=1}^{K}(\hat{i}_k - i_k)^2 \quad (12)$$

By setting α to 0 we can switch the whole textual pathway off and obtain the VISUAL model variant. Analogously, setting α to 1 gives the TEXTUAL model. Intermediate values of α (in the experiments below we use 0.1) give the full MULTITASK version. Finally, as baseline for some of the tasks we use a simple linear regression model LINREG with a bag-of-words representation of the sentence:

$$\hat{\mathbf{i}} = \mathbf{A}\mathbf{x} + b \quad (13)$$

where $\hat{\mathbf{i}}$ is the vector of the predicted image features, $\mathbf{x}$ is the vector of word counts for the input sentence and $(\mathbf{A}, b)$ the parameters of the linear model estimated via L_2-penalized sum-of-squared-errors loss.

	SimLex	MEN 3K
VISUAL	0.32	0.57
MULTITASK	0.39	0.63
TEXTUAL	0.31	0.53
LINREG	0.18	0.23

Table 1: Word similarity correlations with human judgments measured by Spearman's ρ (all correlations are significant at level $p < 0.01$).

4 Experiments

Settings The model was implemented in Theano (Bastien et al., 2012; Bergstra et al., 2010) and optimized by Adam (Kingma and Ba, 2014).[1] The fixed 4096-dimensional target image representation come from the pre-softmax layer of the 16-layer CNN (Simonyan and Zisserman, 2014). We used 1024 dimensions for the embeddings and for the hidden states of each of the GRU networks. We ran 8 iterations of training, and we report either full learning curves, or the results for each model after iteration 7 (where they performed best for the image retrieval task). For training we use the standard MS-COCO training data. For validation and test, we take a sample of 5000 images each from the validation data.

4.1 Word representations

We assess the quality of the learned embeddings for single words via two tasks: (i) we measure similarity between embeddings of word pairs and compare them to elicited human ratings; (ii) we examine how well the model learns visual representations of words by projecting word embeddings into the visual space, and retrieving images of single concepts from ImageNet.

Word similarity judgment For similarity judgment correlations, we selected two existing benchmarks that have the largest vocabulary overlap with our data: MEN 3K (Bruni et al., 2014) and SimLex-999 (Hill et al., 2014). We measure the similarity between word pairs by computing the cosine similarity between their embeddings from three versions of our model, VISUAL, MULTITASK and TEXTUAL, and the baseline LINREG.

Table 1 summarizes the results. All IMAGINET models significantly correlate with human similarity judgments, and outperform LINREG. Examples of word pairs for which MULTITASK cap-

[1]Code available at github.com/gchrupala/imaginet.

VISUAL	MULTITASK	LINREG
0.38	0.38	0.33

Table 2: Accuracy@5 of retrieving images with compatible labels from ImageNet.

tures human similarity judgments better than VISUAL include antonyms (*dusk*, *dawn*), collocations (*sexy*, *smile*), or related but not visually similar words (*college*, *exhibition*).

Single-word image retrieval In order to visualize the acquired meaning for individual words, we use images from the ILSVRC2012 subset of ImageNet (Russakovsky et al., 2014) as benchmark. Labels of the images in ImageNet are synsets from WordNet, which identify a single concept in the image rather than providing descriptions of its full content. Since the synset labels in ImageNet are much more precise than the descriptions provided in the captions in our training data (e.g., *elkhound*), we use synset hypernyms from WordNet as substitute labels when the original labels are not in our vocabulary.

We extracted the features from the 50,000 images of the ImageNet validation set. The labels in this set result in 393 distinct (original or hypernym) words from our vocabulary. Each word was projected to the visual space by feeding it through the model as a one-word sentence. We ranked the vectors corresponding to all 50,000 images based on their similarity to the predicted vector, and measured the accuracy of retrieving an image with the correct label among the top 5 ranked images (Accuracy@5). Table 2 summarizes the results: VISUAL and MULTITASK learn more accurate word meaning representations than LINREG.

4.2 Sentence structure

In the following experiments, we examine the knowledge of sentence structure learned by IMAGINET, and its impact on the model performance on image and paraphrase retrieval.

Image retrieval We retrieve images based on the similarity of their vectors with those predicted by IMAGINET in two conditions: sentences are fed to the model in their original order, or scrambled. Figure 2 (left) shows the proportion of sentences for which the correct image was in the top 5 highest ranked images for each model, as a function of the number of training iterations: both models out-

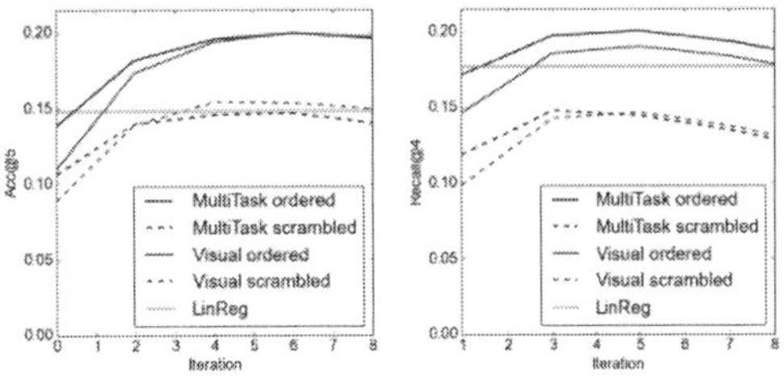

Figure 2: Left: Accuracy@5 of **image retrieval** with original versus scrambled captions. Right: Recall@4 of **paraphrase retrieval** with original vs scrambled captions.

perform the baseline. MULTITASK is initially better in retrieving the correct image, but eventually the gap disappears. Both models perform substantially better when tested on the original captions compared to the scrambled ones, indicating that models learn to exploit aspects of sentence structure. This ability is to be expected for MULTITASK, but the VISUAL model shows a similar effect to some extent. In the case of VISUAL, this sensitivity to structural aspects of sentence meaning is entirely driven by how they are reflected in the image, as this models only receives the visual supervision signal.

Qualitative analysis of the role of sequential structure suggests that the models are sensitive to the fact that periods terminate a sentence, that sentences tend not to start with conjunctions, that topics appear in sentence-initial position, and that words have different importance as modifiers versus heads. Figure 3 shows an example; see supplementary material for more.

IMAGINET vs captioning systems While it is not our goal to engineer a state-of-the-art image retrieval system, we want to situate IMAGINET's performance within the landscape of image retrieval results on captioned images. As most of these are on Flickr30K (Young et al., 2014), we ran MULTITASK on it and got an accuracy@5 of 32%, within the range of numbers reported in previous work: 29.8% (Socher et al., 2014), 31.2% (Mao et al., 2014), 34% (Kiros et al., 2014) and 37.7% (Karpathy and Fei-Fei, 2014). Karpathy and Fei-Fei (2014) report 29.6% on MS-COCO, but with additional training data.

Original	a couple of horses UNK their head over a rock pile
rank 1	two brown horses hold their heads above a rocky wall .
rank 2	two horses looking over a short stone wall .
Scrambled	rock couple their head pile a a UNK over of horses
rank 1	an image of a man on a couple of horses
rank 2	looking in to a straw lined pen of cows
Original	a cute baby playing with a cell phone
rank 1	small baby smiling at camera and talking on phone .
rank 2	a smiling baby holding a cell phone up to ear .
Scrambled	phone playing cute cell a with baby a
rank 1	someone is using their phone to send a text or play a game .
rank 2	a camera is placed next to a cellular phone .

Table 3: Examples of two nearest neighbors retrieved by MULTITASK for original and scrambled captions.

Figure 3: For the original caption MULTITASK understands *kitchen* as a modifier of headword *utensils*, which is the topic. For the scrambled sentence, the model thinks *kitchen* is the topic.

Paraphrase retrieval In our dataset each image is paired with five different captions, which can be seen as paraphrases. This affords us the opportunity to test IMAGINET's sentence representations on a non-visual task. Although all models receive one caption-image pair at a time, the co-occurrence with the same image can lead the model to learn structural similarities between captions that are different on the surface. We feed the whole set of validation captions through the trained model and record the final hidden visual state $\mathbf{h}_\tau^V$. For each caption we rank all others according to cosine similarity and measure the proportion of the ones associated with the same image among the top four highest ranked. For the scrambled condition, we rank original captions against a scrambled one. Figure 2 (right) summarizes the results: both models outperform the baseline on ordered captions, but not on scrambled ones. As expected, MULTITASK is more affected by manipulating word order, because it is more sensitive to structure. Table 3 shows concrete examples of the effect of scrambling words in what sentences are retrieved.

5 Discussion

IMAGINET is a novel model of grounded language acquisition which simultaneously learns word meaning representations and knowledge of sentence structure from captioned images. It acquires meaning representations for individual words from descriptions of visual scenes, mimicking an important aspect of human language learning, and can effectively use sentence structure in semantic interpretation of multi-word phrases. In future we plan to upgrade the current word-prediction pathway to a sentence reconstruction and/or sentence paraphrasing task in order to encourage the formation of representations of full sentences. We also want to explore the acquired structure further, especially for generalizing the grounded meanings to those words for which visual data is not available.

Acknowledgements

The authors would like to thank Angeliki Lazaridou and Marco Baroni for their many insightful comments on the research presented in this paper.

References

Afra Alishahi and Grzegorz Chrupała. 2012. Concurrent acquisition of word meaning and lexical categories. In *Proceedings of the 2012 Joint Conference on Empirical Methods in Natural Language Processing and Computational Natural Language Learning*, pages 643–654. Association for Computational Linguistics.

Frédéric Bastien, Pascal Lamblin, Razvan Pascanu, James Bergstra, Ian J. Goodfellow, Arnaud Bergeron, Nicolas Bouchard, and Yoshua Bengio. 2012. Theano: new features and speed improvements. Deep Learning and Unsupervised Feature Learning NIPS 2012 Workshop.

James Bergstra, Olivier Breuleux, Frédéric Bastien, Pascal Lamblin, Razvan Pascanu, Guillaume Desjardins, Joseph Turian, David Warde-Farley, and Yoshua Bengio. 2010. Theano: a CPU and GPU math expression compiler. In *Proceedings of the Python for Scientific Computing Conference (SciPy)*. Oral Presentation.

Elia Bruni, Nam-Khanh Tran, and Marco Baroni. 2014. Multimodal distributional semantics. *Journal of Artificial Intelligence Research (JAIR)*, 49:1–47.

Rich Caruana. 1997. Multitask learning. *Machine learning*, 28(1):41–75.

Xinlei Chen and C Lawrence Zitnick. 2014. Learning a recurrent visual representation for image caption generation. *arXiv preprint arXiv:1411.5654*.

Kyunghyun Cho, Bart van Merriënboer, Dzmitry Bahdanau, and Yoshua Bengio. 2014. On the properties of neural machine translation: Encoder-decoder approaches. In *Eighth Workshop on Syntax, Semantics and Structure in Statistical Translation (SSST-8)*.

Junyoung Chung, Caglar Gulcehre, KyungHyun Cho, and Yoshua Bengio. 2014. Empirical evaluation of gated recurrent neural networks on sequence modeling. In *NIPS 2014 Deep Learning and Representation Learning Workshop*.

Kenny R. Coventry, Angelo Cangelosi, Rohanna Rajapakse, Alison Bacon, Stephen Newstead, Dan Joyce, and Lynn V. Richards. 2005. Spatial prepositions and vague quantifiers: Implementing the functional geometric framework. In Christian Freksa, Markus Knauff, Bernd Krieg-Brückner, Bernhard Nebel, and Thomas Barkowsky, editors, *Spatial Cognition IV. Reasoning, Action, Interaction*, volume 3343 of *Lecture Notes in Computer Science*, pages 98–110. Springer Berlin Heidelberg.

Jeff Donahue, Lisa Anne Hendricks, Sergio Guadarrama, Marcus Rohrbach, Subhashini Venugopalan, Kate Saenko, and Trevor Darrell. 2014. Long-term recurrent convolutional networks for visual recognition and description. *arXiv preprint arXiv:1411.4389*.

Hao Fang, Saurabh Gupta, Forrest Iandola, Rupesh Srivastava, Li Deng, Piotr Dollár, Jianfeng Gao, Xiaodong He, Margaret Mitchell, John Platt, et al. 2014. From captions to visual concepts and back. *arXiv preprint arXiv:1411.4952*.

Afsaneh Fazly, Afra Alishahi, and Suzanen Stevenson. 2010. A probabilistic computational model of cross-situational word learning. *Cognitive Science: A Multidisciplinary Journal*, 34(6):1017–1063.

Michael Fleischman and Deb Roy. 2005. Intentional context in situated natural language learning. In *Proceedings of the Ninth Conference on Computational Natural Language Learning*, pages 104–111. Association for Computational Linguistics.

Felix Hill, Roi Reichart, and Anna Korhonen. 2014. Simlex-999: Evaluating semantic models with (genuine) similarity estimation. *arXiv preprint arXiv:1408.3456*.

Sepp Hochreiter and Jürgen Schmidhuber. 1997. Long short-term memory. *Neural computation*, 9(8):1735–1780.

Steve R Howell, Damian Jankowicz, and Suzanna Becker. 2005. A model of grounded language acquisition: Sensorimotor features improve lexical and grammatical learning. *Journal of Memory and Language*, 53(2):258–276.

Andrej Karpathy and Li Fei-Fei. 2014. Deep visual-semantic alignments for generating image descriptions. *arXiv preprint arXiv:1412.2306*.

Diederik P. Kingma and Jimmy Ba. 2014. Adam: A method for stochastic optimization. *CoRR*, abs/1412.6980.

Ryan Kiros, Ruslan Salakhutdinov, and Richard S Zemel. 2014. Unifying visual-semantic embeddings with multimodal neural language models. *arXiv preprint arXiv:1411.2539*.

Tom Kwiatkowski, Sharon Goldwater, Luke Zettlemoyer, and Mark Steedman. 2012. A probabilistic model of syntactic and semantic acquisition from child-directed utterances and their meanings. In *Proceedings of the 13th Conference of the European Chapter of the Association for Computational Linguistics*, pages 234–244. Association for Computational Linguistics.

Angeliki Lazaridou, Nghia The Pham, and Marco Baroni. 2015. Combining language and vision with a multimodal skip-gram model. In *Proceedings of NAACL HLT 2015 (2015 Conference of the North American Chapter of the Association for Computational Linguistics - Human Language Technologies)*.

Ping Li, Igor Farkas, and Brian MacWhinney. 2004. Early lexical development in a self-organizing neural network. *Neural Networks*, 17:1345–1362.

Brian MacWhinney. 2014. *The CHILDES project: Tools for analyzing talk, Volume I: Transcription format and programs*. Psychology Press.

Junhua Mao, Wei Xu, Yi Yang, Jiang Wang, and Alan L Yuille. 2014. Explain images with multimodal recurrent neural networks. In *NIPS 2014 Deep Learning Workshop*.

Tomas Mikolov, Ilya Sutskever, Kai Chen, Greg S Corrado, and Jeff Dean. 2013. Distributed representations of words and phrases and their compositionality. In *Advances in Neural Information Processing Systems*, pages 3111–3119.

Tomas Mikolov and Geoffrey Zweig. 2012. Context dependent recurrent neural network language model. In *SLT*, pages 234–239.

Terry Regier. 2005. The emergence of words: Attentional learning in form and meaning. *Cognitive Science: A Multidisciplinary Journal*, 29:819–865.

Olga Russakovsky, Jia Deng, Hao Su, Jonathan Krause, Sanjeev Satheesh, Sean Ma, Zhiheng Huang, Andrej Karpathy, Aditya Khosla, Michael Bernstein, Alexander C. Berg, and Li Fei-Fei. 2014. ImageNet Large Scale Visual Recognition Challenge.

K. Simonyan and A. Zisserman. 2014. Very deep convolutional networks for large-scale image recognition. *CoRR*, abs/1409.1556.

Jeffrey M. Siskind. 1996. A computational study of cross-situational techniques for learning word-to-meaning mappings. *Cognition*, 61(1-2):39–91.

Danijel Skocaj, Matej Kristan, Alen Vrecko, Marko Mahnic, Miroslav Janicek, Geert-Jan M Kruijff, Marc Hanheide, Nick Hawes, Thomas Keller, Michael Zillich, et al. 2011. A system for interactive learning in dialogue with a tutor. In *Intelligent Robots and Systems (IROS), 2011 IEEE/RSJ International Conference on*, pages 3387–3394. IEEE.

Richard Socher, Andrej Karpathy, Quoc V Le, Christopher D Manning, and Andrew Y Ng. 2014. Grounded compositional semantics for finding and describing images with sentences. *Transactions of the Association for Computational Linguistics*, 2:207–218.

Subhashini Venugopalan, Huijuan Xu, Jeff Donahue, Marcus Rohrbach, Raymond Mooney, and Kate Saenko. 2014. Translating videos to natural language using deep recurrent neural networks. *arXiv preprint arXiv:1412.4729*.

Oriol Vinyals, Alexander Toshev, Samy Bengio, and Dumitru Erhan. 2014. Show and tell: A neural image caption generator. *arXiv preprint arXiv:1411.4555*.

Peter Young, Alice Lai, Micah Hodosh, and Julia Hockenmaier. 2014. From image descriptions to visual denotations: New similarity metrics for semantic inference over event descriptions. *Transactions of the Association for Computational Linguistics*, 2:67–78.

Chen Yu. 2008. A statistical associative account of vocabulary growth in early word learning. *Language Learning and Development*, 4(1):32–62.

Exploiting Image Generality for Lexical Entailment Detection

Douwe Kiela
Computer Laboratory
University of Cambridge
douwe.kiela@cl.cam.ac.uk

Laura Rimell
Computer Laboratory
University of Cambridge
laura.rimell@cl.cam.ac.uk

Ivan Vulić
Department of Computer Science
KU Leuven
ivan.vulic@cs.kuleuven.be

Stephen Clark
Computer Laboratory
University of Cambridge
stephen.clark@cl.cam.ac.uk

Abstract

We exploit the visual properties of concepts for lexical entailment detection by examining a concept's *generality*. We introduce three unsupervised methods for determining a concept's generality, based on its related images, and obtain state-of-the-art performance on two standard semantic evaluation datasets. We also introduce a novel task that combines hypernym detection and directionality, significantly outperforming a competitive frequency-based baseline.

1 Introduction

Automatic detection of lexical entailment is useful for a number of NLP tasks including search query expansion (Shekarpour et al., 2013), recognising textual entailment (Garrette et al., 2011), metaphor detection (Mohler et al., 2013), and text generation (Biran and McKeown, 2013). Given two semantically related words, a key aspect of detecting lexical entailment, or the hyponym-hypernym relation, is the *generality* of the hypernym compared to the hyponym. For example, *bird* is more general than *eagle*, having a broader intension and a larger extension. This property has led to the introduction of lexical entailment measures that compare the entropy of distributional word representations, under the assumption that a more general term has a higher-entropy distribution (Herbelot and Ganesalingam, 2013; Santus et al., 2014).

A strand of distributional semantics has recently emerged that exploits the fact that meaning is often grounded in the perceptual system, known as multi-modal distributional semantics (Bruni et al., 2014). Such models enhance purely linguistic models with extra-linguistic perceptual information, and outperform language-only models on a range of tasks, including modelling semantic similarity and conceptual relatedness (Silberer and Lapata, 2014). In fact, under some conditions uni-modal visual representations outperform traditional linguistic representations on semantic tasks (Kiela and Bottou, 2014).

We hypothesize that visual representations can be particularly useful for lexical entailment detection. Deselaers and Ferrari (2011) have shown that sets of images corresponding to terms at higher levels in the WordNet hierarchy have greater visual variability than those at lower levels. We exploit this tendency using sets of images returned by Google's image search. The intuition is that the set of images returned for *animal* will consist of pictures of different kinds of animals, the set of images for *bird* will consist of pictures of different birds, while the set for *owl* will mostly consist only of images of owls, as can be seen in Figure 1.

Here we evaluate three different vision-based methods for measuring term generality on the semantic tasks of hypernym detection and hypernym directionality. Using this simple yet effective unsupervised approach, we obtain state-of-the-art results compared with supervised algorithms which use linguistic data.

2 Related Work

In the linguistic modality, the most closely related work is by Herbelot and Ganesalingam (2013) and Santus et al. (2014), who use unsupervised distributional generality measures to identify the hypernym in a hyponym-hypernym pair. Herbelot and Ganesalingam (2013) use KL divergence to compare the probability distribution of context words, given a term, to the background probability distribution of context words. Santus et al. (2014) use the median entropy of the probability distributions associated with a term's top-weighted con-

Proceedings of the 53rd Annual Meeting of the Association for Computational Linguistics and the 7th International Joint Conference on Natural Language Processing (Short Papers), pages 119–124,
Beijing, China, July 26-31, 2015.

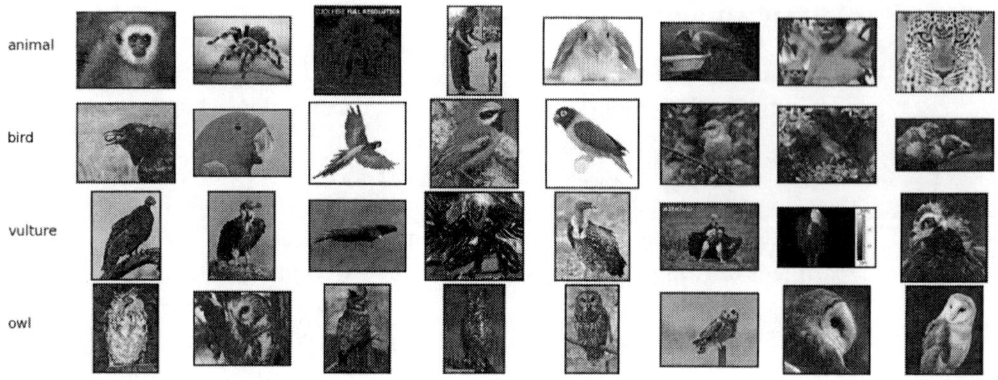

Figure 1: Example of how *vulture* and *owl* are less dispersed concepts than *bird* and *animal*, according to images returned by Google image search.

text words as a measure of information content.

In the visual modality, the intuition that visual representations may be useful for detecting lexical entailment is inspired by Deselaers and Ferrari (2011). Using manually annotated images from ImageNet (Deng et al., 2009), they find that concepts and categories with narrower intensions and smaller extensions tend to have less visual variability. We extend this intuition to the unsupervised setting of Google image search results and apply it to the lexical entailment task.

3 Approach

We use two standard evaluations for lexical entailment: hypernym directionality, where the task is to predict which of two words is the hypernym; and hypernym detection, where the task is to predict whether two words are in a hypernym-hyponym relation (Weeds et al., 2014; Santus et al., 2014). We also introduce a third, more challenging, evaluation that combines detection and directionality.

For the directionality experiment, we evaluate on the hypernym subset of the well-known BLESS dataset (Baroni and Lenci, 2011), which consists of 1337 hyponym-hypernym pairs. In this case, it is known that the words are in an entailment relation and the task is to predict the directionality of the relation. BLESS data is always presented with the hyponym first, so we report how often our measures predict that the second term in the pair is more general than the first.

For the detection experiment, we evaluate on the BLESS-based dataset of Weeds et al. (2014), which consists of 1168 word pairs and which we call WBLESS. In this dataset, the positive examples are hyponym-hypernym pairs. The negative examples include pairs in the reversed hypernym-hyponym order, as well as holonym-meronym pairs, co-hyponyms, and randomly matched nouns. Accuracy on WBLESS reflects the ability to distinguish hypernymy from other relations, but does not require detection of directionality, since reversed pairs are grouped with the other negatives.

BLESS	turtle—animal	1
WBLESS	owl—creature	1
	owl—vulture	0
	animal—owl	0
BIBLESS	owl—creature	1
	owl—vulture	0
	animal—owl	-1

Table 1: Examples for evaluation datasets.

For the combined experiment, we assign reversed hyponym-hypernym pairs a value of -1 instead of 0. We call this more challenging dataset BIBLESS. Examples of pairs in the respective datasets can be found in Table 1.

3.1 Image representations

Following previous work in multi-modal semantics (Bergsma and Goebel, 2011; Kiela et al., 2014), we obtain images from *Google Images*[1] for the words in the evaluation datasets. It has been shown that images from Google yield higher-quality representations than comparable resources such as Flickr and are competitive with "hand prepared datasets" (Bergsma and Goebel, 2011; Fergus et al., 2005).

[1] www.google.com/imghp. Images were retrieved on 10 April, 2015 from Cambridge in the United Kingdom.

For each image, we extract the pre-softmax layer from a forward pass in a convolutional neural network (CNN) that has been trained on the ImageNet classification task using Caffe (Jia et al., 2014). As such, this work is an instance of deep transfer learning; that is, a deep learning representation trained on one task (image classification) is used to make predictions on a different task (image generality). We chose to use CNN-derived image representations because they have been found to be of higher quality than the traditional bag of visual words models (Sivic and Zisserman, 2003) that have previously been used in multi-modal distributional semantics (Bruni et al., 2014; Kiela and Bottou, 2014).

3.2 Generality measures

We propose three measures that can be used to calculate the generality of a set of images. The image *dispersion* d of a concept word w is defined as the average pairwise cosine distance between all image representations $\{\vec{w_1} \ldots \vec{w_n}\}$ of the set of images returned for w:

$$d(w) = \frac{2}{n(n-1)} \sum_{i<j\leq n} 1 - cos(\vec{w_i}, \vec{w_j}) \quad (1)$$

This measure was originally introduced to account for the fact that perceptual information is more relevant for e.g. *elephant* than it is for *happiness*. It acts as a substitute for the concreteness of a word and can be used to regulate how much perceptual information should be included in a multi-modal model (Kiela et al., 2014).

Our second measure follows Deselaers and Ferrari (2011), who take a similar approach but instead of calculating the pairwise distance calculate the distance to the *centroid* $\vec{\mu}$ of $\{\vec{w_1} \ldots \vec{w_n}\}$:

$$c(w) = \frac{1}{n} \sum_{1\leq i\leq n} 1 - cos(\vec{w_i}, \vec{\mu}) \quad (2)$$

For our third measure we follow Lazaridou et al. (2015), who try different ways of modulating the inclusion of perceptual input in their multi-modal skip-gram model, and find that the *entropy* of the centroid vector $\vec{\mu}$ works well (where $p(\mu_j) = \frac{\mu_j}{||\vec{\mu}||}$ and m is the vector length):

$$H(w) = -\sum_{j=1}^{m} p(\mu_j) \log_2(p(\mu_j)) \quad (3)$$

3.3 Hypernym Detection and Directionality

We calculate the directionality of a hyponym-hypernym pair with a measure f using the following formula for a word pair (p, q). Since even co-hyponyms will not have identical values for f, we introduce a threshold α which sets a minimum difference in generality for hypernym identification:

$$s(p, q) = 1 - \frac{f(p) + \alpha}{f(q)} \quad (4)$$

In other words, $s(p, q) > 0$ iff $f(q) > f(p) + \alpha$, i.e. if the second word (q) is (sufficiently) more general. To avoid false positives where one word is more general but the pair is not semantically related, we introduce a second threshold θ which sets f to zero if the two concepts have low cosine similarity. This leads to the following formula:

$$s_\theta(p, q) = \begin{cases} 1 - \frac{f(p)+\alpha}{f(q)} & \text{if } \cos(\vec{\mu_p}, \vec{\mu_q}) \geq \theta \\ 0 & \text{otherwise} \end{cases} \quad (5)$$

We experimented with different methods for obtaining the mean vector representations for cosine (hereafter μ_c) in Equation (5), and found that multi-modal representations worked best. We concatenate an L2-normalized linguistic vector with the L2-normalized centroid of image vectors to obtain a multi-modal representation, following Kiela and Bottou (2014). For a word p with image representations $\{p_1^{img} \ldots p_n^{img}\}$, we thus set $\mu_c = p^{ling} \mid\mid \frac{1}{n}\sum_i^n p_i^{img}$, after normalizing both representations. For comparison, we also report results for a visual-only μ_c.

For BLESS, we know the words in a pair stand in an entailment relation, so we set $\alpha = \theta = 0$ and evaluate whether $s(p, q) > 0$, indicating that q is a hypernym of p. For WBLESS, we set $\alpha = 0.02$ and $\theta = 0.2$ without tuning, and evaluate whether $s_\theta(p, q) > 0$ (hypernym relation) or $s_\theta(p, q) \leq 0$ (no hypernym relation). For BIBLESS, we set $\alpha = 0.02$ and $\theta = 0.25$ without tuning, and evaluate whether $s_\theta(p, q) > 0$ (hyponym-hypernym), $s(p, q) = 0$ (no relation), or $s(p, q) \leq 0$ (hypernym-hyponym).

4 Results

The results can be found in Table 2. We compare our methods with a frequency baseline, setting $f(p) = \text{freq}(p)$ in Equation 4 and using the frequency scores from Turney et al. (2011). Frequency has been proven to be a surprisingly

	BLESS	WBLESS	BIBLESS
Frequency	0.58	0.57	0.39
WeedsPrec	0.63	—	—
WeedsSVM	—	0.75	—
WeedsUnSup	—	0.58	—
SLQS	0.87	—	—
Dispersion	0.88	0.75 (0.74)	0.57 (0.55)
Centroid	0.87	0.74 (0.74)	0.57 (0.54)
Entropy	0.83	0.71 (0.71)	0.56 (0.53)

Table 2: Accuracy. For WBLESS and BIBLESS we report results for multi-modal μ_c, with visual-only μ_c in brackets.

challenging baseline for hypernym directionality (Herbelot and Ganesalingam, 2013; Weeds et al., 2014). In addition, we compare to the reported results of Santus et al. (2014) for WeedsPrec (Weeds et al., 2004), an early lexical entailment measure, and SLQS, the entropy-based method of Santus et al. (2014). Note, however, that these are on a subsampled corpus of 1277 word pairs from BLESS, so the results are indicative but not directly comparable. On WBLESS we compare to the reported results of Weeds et al. (2014): we include results for the highest-performing supervised method (WeedsSVM) and the highest-performing unsupervised method (WeedsUnSup).

For BLESS, both dispersion and centroid distance reach or outperform the best other measure (SLQS). They beat the frequency baseline by a large margin (+30% and +29%). Taking the entropy of the mean image representations does not appear to do as well as the other two methods but still outperforms the baseline and WeedsPrec (+25% and +20% respectively).

In the case of WBLESS and BIBLESS, we see a similar pattern in that dispersion and centroid distance perform best. For WBLESS, these methods outperform the other unsupervised approach, WeedsUnsup, by +17% and match the best-performing support vector machine (SVM) approach in Weeds et al. (2014). In fact, Weeds et al. (2014) report results for a total of 6 supervised methods (based on SVM and k-nearest neighbor (k-NN) classifiers): our unsupervised image dispersion method outperforms all of these except for the highest-performing one, reported here.

We can see that the task becomes increasingly difficult as we go from directionality to detection to the combination: the dispersion-based method goes from 0.88 to 0.75 to 0.57, for example. BIBLESS is the most difficult, as shown by the frequency baseline obtaining only 0.39. Our methods do much better than this baseline (+18%). Image dispersion appears to be the most robust measure.

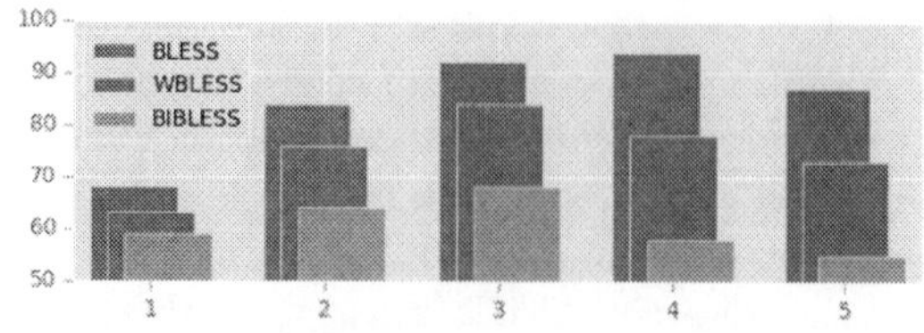

Figure 2: Accuracy by WordNet shortest path bucket (1 is shortest, 5 is longest).

To examine our results further, we divided the test data into buckets by the shortest WordNet path connecting word pairs (Miller, 1995). We expect our method to be less accurate on word pairs with short paths, since the difference in generality may be difficult to discern. It has also been suggested that very abstract hypernyms such as *object* and *entity* are difficult to detect because their linguistic distributions are not supersets of their hyponyms' distributions (Rimell, 2014), a factor that should not affect the visual modality. We find that concept comparisons with a very short path (bucket 1) are indeed the least accurate. We also find some drop in accuracy on the longest paths (bucket 5), especially for WBLESS and BIBLESS, perhaps because semantic similarity is difficult to detect in these cases. For a histogram of the accuracy scores according to WordNet similarity, see Figure 2.

5 Conclusions

We have evaluated three unsupervised methods for determining the generality of a concept based on its visual properties. Our best-performing method, image dispersion, reaches the state-of-the-art on two standard semantic evaluation datasets. We introduced a novel, more difficult task combining hypernym detection and directionality, and showed that our methods outperform a frequency baseline by a large margin.

We believe that image generality may be particularly suited to entailment detection because it does not suffer from the same issues as linguistic distributional generality. Herbelot and Ganesalingam (2013) found that general terms like *liquid* do not always have higher entropy distributions than their hyponyms, since speakers use them in very specific contexts, e.g. *liquid* is often coordinated with *gas*.

We also acknowledge that our method depends

to some degree on Google's search result diversification, but do not feel this detracts from the utility of the method, since the fact that general concepts achieve greater maximum image dispersion than specific concepts is not dependent on any particular diversification algorithm. In future work, we plan to explore more sophisticated visual generality measures, other semantic relations and different ways of fusing visual representations with linguistic knowledge.

Acknowledgments

DK and LR are supported by EPSRC grant EP/I037512/1. IV is supported by the PARIS project (IWT-SBO 110067) and the PDM Kort postdoctoral fellowship from KU Leuven. SC is supported by ERC Starting Grant DisCoTex (306920) and EPSRC grant EP/I037512/1. We thank the anonymous reviewers for their helpful comments.

References

Marco Baroni and Alessandro Lenci. 2011. How we BLESSed distributional semantic evaluation. In *Proceedings of the GEMS 2011 Workshop*, pages 1–10.

Shane Bergsma and Randy Goebel. 2011. Using visual information to predict lexical preference. In *Proceedings of RANLP*, pages 399–405.

Or Biran and Kathleen McKeown. 2013. Classifying taxonomic relations between pairs of wikipedia articles. In *Proceedings of IJCNLP*, pages 788–794.

Johan Bos and Katja Markert. 2005. Recognising textual entailment with logical inference. In *Proceedings of EMNLP*, pages 628–635.

Elia Bruni, Nam-Khanh Tran, and Marco Baroni. 2014. Multimodal distributional semantics. *Journal of Artificial Intelligence Research*, 49:1–47.

Daoud Clarke. 2009. Context-theoretic semantics for natural language: An overview. In *Proceedings of the GEMS 2009 Workshop*, pages 112–119.

Jia Deng, Wei Dong, Richard Socher, Li-Jia Li, Kai Li, and Fei-Fei Li. 2009. ImageNet: A large-scale hierarchical image database. In *Proceedings of CVPR*, pages 248–255.

Thomas Deselaers and Vittorio Ferrari. 2011. Visual and semantic similarity in imagenet. In *Proceedings of CVPR*, pages 1777–1784.

Robert Fergus, Li Fei-Fei, Pietro Perona, and Andrew Zisserman. 2005. Learning object categories from Google's image search. In *Proceedings of ICCV*, pages 1816–1823.

Dan Garrette, Katrin Erk, and Raymond Mooney. 2011. Integrating logical representations with probabilistic information using Markov logic. In *Proceedings of IWCS*, pages 105–114.

M. Geffet and I. Dagan. 2005. The distributional inclusion hypotheses and lexical entailment. In *Proceedings of ACL*, pages 107–114.

Aurélie Herbelot and Mohan Ganesalingam. 2013. Measuring semantic content in distributional vectors. In *Proceedings of ACL*, pages 440–445.

Yangqing Jia, Evan Shelhamer, Jeff Donahue, Sergey Karayev, Jonathan Long, Ross Girshick, Sergio Guadarrama, and Trevor Darrell. 2014. Caffe: Convolutional architecture for fast feature embedding. *arXiv preprint arXiv:1408.5093*.

Hongyan Jing. 1998. Usage of wordnet in natural language generation. In *Proceedings of COLING-ACL'98 Workshop on Usage of WordNet in Natural Language Processing Systems*.

Douwe Kiela and Léon Bottou. 2014. Learning image embeddings using convolutional neural networks for improved multi-modal semantics. In *Proceedings of EMNLP*, pages 36–45.

Douwe Kiela, Felix Hill, Anna Korhonen, and Stephen Clark. 2014. Improving multi-modal representations using image dispersion: Why less is sometimes more. In *Proceedings of ACL*, pages 835–841.

Lili Kotlerman, Ido Dagan, Idan Szpektor, and Maayan Zhitomirsky-Geffet. 2010. Directional distributional similarity for lexical inference. *Natural Language Engineering*, 16(4):359–389.

Angeliki Lazaridou, Nghia The Pham, and Marco Baroni. 2015. Combining language and vision with a multimodal skip-gram model. In *Proceedings of NAACL-HLT*.

Alessandro Lenci and Giulia Benotto. 2012. Identifying hypernyms in distributional semantic spaces. In *Proceedings of *SEM*, pages 75–79.

Omer Levy, Steffen Remus, Chris Biemann, and Ido Dagan. 2015. Do supervised distributional methods really learn lexical inference relations? In *Proceedings of NAACL*.

J.H. Martin. 1990. *A Computational Model of Metaphor Interpretation*. Academic Press Professional, Inc.

George A. Miller. 1995. WordNet: A lexical database for English. In *Communications of the ACM*, volume 38, pages 39–41.

Michael Mohler, David Bracewell, Marc Tomlinson, and David Hinote. 2013. Semantic signatures for example-based linguistic metaphor detection. In *Proceedings of the 1st Workshop on Metaphor in NLP*.

Laura Rimell. 2014. Distributional lexical entailment by topic coherence. In *Proceedings of EACL*, pages 511–519.

Enrico Santus, Alessandro Lenci, Qin Lu, and Sabine Schulte im Walde. 2014. Chasing hypernyms in vector spaces with entropy. In *Proceedings of EACL*, pages 38–42.

Saeedeh Shekarpour, Konrad Höffner, Jens Lehmann, and Sören Auer. 2013. Keyword query expansion on linked data using linguistic and semantic features. In *Proceedings of the 7th IEEE International Conference on Semantic Computing*, pages 191–197.

Carina Silberer and Mirella Lapata. 2014. Learning grounded meaning representations with autoencoders. In *Proceedings of ACL*, pages 721–732.

Josef Sivic and Andrew Zisserman. 2003. Video Google: A text retrieval approach to object matching in videos. In *Proceedings of ICCV*, pages 1470–1477.

Peter D. Turney, Yair Neuman, Dan Assaf, and Yohai Cohen. 2011. Literal and metaphorical sense identification through concrete and abstract context. In *Proceedings of EMNLP*, pages 680–690.

Julie Weeds, David Weir, and Diana McCarthy. 2004. Characterising measures of lexical distributional similarity. In *Proceedings of COLING*.

Julie Weeds, Daoud Clarke, Jeremy Reffin, David Weir, and Bill Keller. 2014. Learning to distinguish hypernyms and co-hyponyms. In *Proceedings of COLING*, pages 2249–2259.

W. A. Woods, Stephen Green, Paul Martin, and Ann Houston. 2001. Aggressive morphology and lexical relations for query expansion. In *Proceedings of TREC*.

M. Zhitomirsky-Geffet and I. Dagan. 2009. Bootstrapping distributional feature vector quality. *Computational Linguistics*, 35(3):435461.

Lexicon Stratification for Translating Out-of-Vocabulary Words

Yulia Tsvetkov
Language Technologies Institute
Carnegie Mellon University
Pittsburgh, PA, 15213, USA
ytsvetko@cs.cmu.edu

Chris Dyer
Language Technologies Institute
Carnegie Mellon University
Pittsburgh, PA, 15213, USA
cdyer@cs.cmu.edu

Abstract

A language lexicon can be divided into four main strata, depending on origin of words: core vocabulary words, fully- and partially-assimilated foreign words, and unassimilated foreign words (or transliterations). This paper focuses on translation of fully- and partially-assimilated foreign words, called "borrowed words". Borrowed words (or loanwords) are content words found in nearly all languages, occupying up to 70% of the vocabulary. We use models of lexical borrowing in machine translation as a pivoting mechanism to obtain translations of out-of-vocabulary loanwords in a low-resource language. Our framework obtains substantial improvements (up to 1.6 BLEU) over standard baselines.

1 Introduction

Out-of-vocabulary (OOV) words are a ubiquitous and difficult problem in statistical machine translation (SMT). When a translation system encounters an OOV—a word that was not observed in the training data, and the trained system thus lacks its translation variants—it usually outputs the word just as it is in the source language, producing erroneous and disfluent translations.

All SMT systems, even when trained on billion-sentence-size parallel corpora, are prone to OOVs. These are often named entities and neologisms. However, OOV problem is much more serious in low-resource scenarios: there, OOVs are primarily not lexicon-peripheral items such as names and specialized/technical terms, but regular content words.

Procuring translations for OOVs has been a subject of active research for decades. Translation of named entities is usually generated using transliteration techniques (Al-Onaizan and Knight, 2002; Hermjakob et al., 2008; Habash, 2008). Extracting a translation lexicon for recovering OOV content words and phrases is done by mining bi-lingual and monolingual resources (Rapp, 1995; Callison-Burch et al., 2006; Haghighi et al., 2008; Marton et al., 2009; Razmara et al., 2013; Saluja et al., 2014; Zhao et al., 2015). In addition, OOV content words can be recovered by exploiting cognates, by transliterating and then pivoting via a closely-related resource-richer language, when such a language exists (Hajič et al., 2000; Mann and Yarowsky, 2001; Kondrak et al., 2003; De Gispert and Marino, 2006; Durrani et al., 2010; Wang et al., 2012; Nakov and Ng, 2012; Dholakia and Sarkar, 2014). Our work is similar in spirit to the latter line of research, but we show how to curate translations for OOV content words by pivoting via an unrelated, often typologically distant resource-rich languages. To achieve this goal, we replace transliteration by a new technique that captures more complex morpho-phonological transformations of historically-related words.

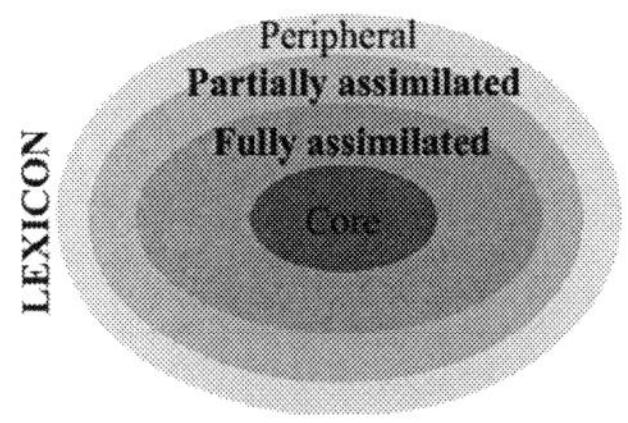

Figure 1: A language lexicon can be divided into four main strata, depending on origin of words. This work focuses on fully- and partially-assimilated foreign words, called borrowed words. Borrowed words (or loanwords) are content words found in all languages, occupying up to 70% of the vocabulary.

Our method is inspired by prior research in constraint-based phonology, advocating "lexicon stratification," i.e., splitting the language lexicon into separate strata, depending on origin of words and degree of their assimilation in the language (Itô and Mester, 1995). As shown in figure 1, there are four main strata: core vocabulary, foreign words that are fully assimilated, partially-assimilated for-

Proceedings of the 53rd Annual Meeting of the Association for Computational Linguistics and the 7th International Joint Conference on Natural Language Processing (Short Papers), pages 125–131, Beijing, China, July 26-31, 2015.

eign words, and named entities which belong to the peripheral stratum. Our work focuses on the fully- and partially-assimilated foreign words, i.e., words that historically were *borrowed* from another language. Borrowing is the pervasive linguistic phenomenon of transferring and adapting linguistic constructions (lexical, phonological, morphological, and syntactic) from a "donor" language into a "recipient" language (Thomason and Kaufman, 2001). In this work, we advocate a pivoting mechanism exploiting lexical borrowing to bridge between resource-rich and resource-poor languages.

Our method (§2) employs a model of lexical borrowing to obtain cross-lingual links from loanwords in a low-resource language to their donors in a resource-rich language (§2.1). The donor language is used as pivot to obtain translations via triangulation of OOV loanwords (§2.2). We conduct experiments with two resource-poor setups: Swahili–English, pivoting via Arabic, and Romanian–English,pivoting via French (§3). We provide a systematic quantitative analysis of contribution of integrated OOV translations, relative to baselines and upper bounds, and on corpora of varying sizes (§4). The proposed approach yields substantial improvement (up to +1.6 BLEU) in Swahili–Arabic–English translation, and a small but statistically significant improvement (+0.2 BLEU) in Romanian–French–English.

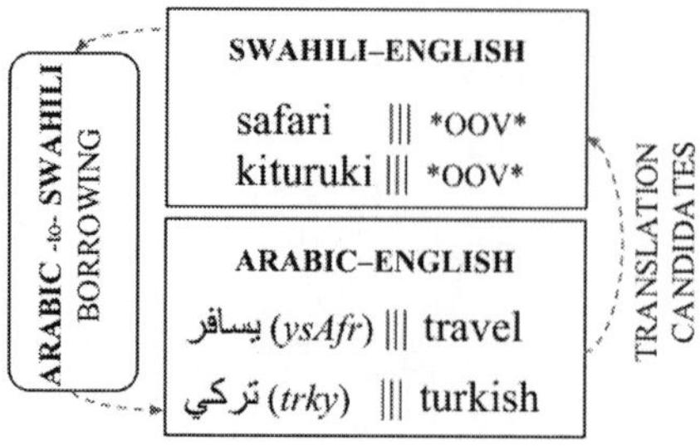

Figure 2: To improve a resource-poor Swahili–English SMT system, we extract translation candidates for OOV Swahili words borrowed from Arabic using the Swahili-to-Arabic borrowing system and Arabic–English resource-rich SMT.

2 Methodology

Our high-level solution is depicted in figure 2. Given an OOV word in resource-poor SMT, we plug it into a borrowing system (§2.1) that identifies the list of plausible donor words in the donor language. Then, using the resource-rich SMT, we translate the donor words to the same target language as in the resource-poor SMT (here, English). Finally, we integrate translation candidates in the resource-poor system (§2.2).

2.1 Models of Lexical Borrowing

Borrowed words (also called loanwords) are found in nearly all languages, and routinely account for 10–70% of the vocabulary (Haspelmath and Tadmor, 2009). Borrowing occurs across genetically and typologically unrelated languages, for example, about 40% of Swahili's vocabulary is borrowed from Arabic (Johnson, 1939). Importantly, since resource-rich languages are (historically) geopolitically important languages, borrowed words often bridge between resource-rich and resource-limited languages; we use this observation in our work.

Transliteration and cognate discovery models perform poorly in the task of loanword generation/identification (Tsvetkov et al., 2015). The main reason is that the recipient language, in which borrowed words are fully or partially assimilated, may have very different morpho-phonological properties from the donor language (e.g., 'orange' and 'sugar' are not perceived as foreign by native speakers, but these are English words borrowed from Arabic نارنج (*nArnj*)[1] and السكر (*Alskr*), respectively). Therefore, morpho-phonological loanword adaptation is more complex than is typically captured by transliteration or cognate models.

We employ a discriminative cross-lingual model of lexical borrowing to identify plausible donors given a loanword (Tsvetkov et al., 2015). The model is implemented in a cascade of finite-state transducers that first maps orthographic word forms in two languages into a common space of their phonetic representation (using IPA—the International Phonetic Alphabet), and then performs morphological and phonological updates to the input word in one language to identify its (donor/loan) counterpart in another language. Transduction operations include stripping donor language prefixes and suffixes, appending recipient affixes, insertion, deletion, and substitution of consonants and vowels. The output of the model, given an input loanword, is a n-best list of donor candidates, ranked by linguistic constraints of the donor and recipient languages.[2]

[1] We use Buckwalter notation to write Arabic glosses.

[2] In this work, we give as input into the borrowing system all OOV words, although, clearly, not all OOVs are loanwords, and not all loanword OOVs are borrowed from the donor language. However, an important property of the borrowing model is that its operations are not general, but specific to

2.2 Pivoting via Borrowing

We now discuss integrating translation candidates acquired via borrowing plus resource-rich translation. For each OOV, the borrowing system produces the n-best list of plausible donors; for each donor we then extract the k-best list of its translations.[3] Then, we pair the OOV with the resulting $n \times k$ translation candidates. The translation candidates are noisy: some of the generated donors may be erroneous, the errors are then propagated in translation. To allow the low-resource system to leverage good translations that are missing in the default phrase inventory, while being stable to noisy translation hypotheses, we integrate the acquired translation candidates as *synthetic phrases* (Tsvetkov et al., 2013; Chahuneau et al., 2013). Synthetic phrases is a strategy of integrating translated phrases directly in the MT translation model, rather than via pre- or post-processing MT inputs and outputs. Synthetic phrases are phrasal translations that are not directly extractable from the training data, generated by auxiliary translation and postediting processes (for example, extracted from a borrowing model). An important advantage of synthetic phrases is that they are recall-oriented, allowing the system to leverage good translations that are missing in the default phrase inventory, while being stable to noisy translation hypotheses.

To let the translation model learn whether to trust these phrases, the translation options obtained from the borrowing model are augmented with a boolean translation feature indicating that the phrase was generated externally. Additional features annotating the integrated OOV translations correspond to properties of the donor–loan words' relation; their goal is to provide an indication of plausibility of the pair (to mark possible errors in the outputs of the borrowing system).

We employ two types of features: phonetic and semantic. Since borrowing is primarily a phonological phenomenon, phonetic features will provide an indication of how typical (or atypical) pronunciation of the word in a language; loanwords are expected to be less typical than core vocabulary words. The goal of semantic features is to measure semantic similarity between donor and loan words: erroneous candidates and borrowed words that changed meaning over time are expected to have different meaning from the OOV.

Phonetic features. To compute phonetic features we first train a (5-gram) language model (LM) of IPA pronunciations of the donor/recipient language vocabulary (phoneLM). Then, we re-score pronunciations of the donor and loanword candidates using the LMs.[4] We hypothesize that in donor–loanword pairs the donor phoneLM score is higher but the loanword score is lower (i.e., the loanword phonology is atypical in the recipient language). We capture this intuition in three features: $f_1 = P_{phoneLM}(donor)$, $f_2 = P_{phoneLM}(loanword)$, and the harmonic mean between the two scores $f_3 = \frac{2 f_1 f_2}{f_1 + f_2}$.

Semantic features. We compute a semantic similarity feature between the candidate donor and the OOV loanword as follows. We first train, using large monolingual corpora, 100-dimensional word vector representations for donor and recipient language vocabularies.[5] Then, we employ canonical correlation analysis (CCA) with small donor–loanword dictionaries (training sets in the borrowing models) to project the word embeddings into 50-dimensional vectors with maximized correlation between their dimensions. The semantic feature annotating the synthetic translation candidates is cosine distance between the resulting donor and loanword vectors. We use the `word2vec` tool (Mikolov et al., 2013) to train monolingual vectors,[6] and the CCA-based tool (Faruqui and Dyer, 2014) for projecting word vectors.[7]

3 Experimental Setup

Datasets and software. The Swahili–English parallel corpus was crawled from the Global Voices project website[8]. To simulate resource-poor scenario for the Romanian–English language pair, we sample a parallel corpus of same size from the transcribed TED talks (Cettolo et al., 2012). To evalu-

the language-pair and reduced only to a small set of plausible changes that the donor word can undergo in the process of assimilation in the recipient language. Thus, the borrowing system only *minimally* overgenerates the set of output candidates given an input. If the borrowing system encounters an input word that was not borrowed from the target donor language, it usually (but not always) produces an empty output.

[3] We set n and k to 5, we did not experiment with other values.

[4] For Arabic and French we use the `GlobalPhone` pronunciation dictionaries (Schultz et al., 2013) (we manually convert them to IPA). For Swahili and Romanian we automatically construct pronunciation dictionaries using the Omniglot grapheme-to-IPA conversion rules at `www.omniglot.com`.

[5] We assume that while parallel data is limited in the recipient language, monolingual data is available.

[6] `code.google.com/p/word2vec`

[7] `github.com/mfaruqui/eacl14-cca`

[8] `sw.globalvoicesonline.org`

ate translation improvement on corpora of different sizes we conduct experiments with sub-sampled 4K, 8K, and 14K parallel sentences from the training corpora (the smaller the training corpus, the more OOVs it has). Corpora sizes along with statistics of source-side OOV tokens and types are given in tables 1 and 2. Statistics of the held-out dev and test sets used in all translation experiments are given in table 3.

	SW–EN		RO–EN	
	dev	test	dev	test
Sentences	1,552	1,732	2,687	2,265
Tokens	33,446	35,057	24,754	19,659
Types	7,008	7,180	5,141	4,328

Table 3: Dev and test corpora sizes.

In all the MT experiments, we use the `cdec`[9] toolkit (Dyer et al., 2010), and optimize parameters with MERT (Och, 2003). English 4-gram language models with Kneser-Ney smoothing (Kneser and Ney, 1995) are trained using KenLM (Heafield, 2011) on the target side of the parallel training corpora and on the Gigaword corpus (Parker et al., 2009). Results are reported using case-insensitive BLEU with a single reference (Papineni et al., 2002). We train three systems for each MT setup; reported BLEU scores are averaged over systems.

Upper bounds. The goal of our experiments is not only to evaluate the contribution of the OOV dictionaries that we extract when pivoting via borrowing, but also to understand the potential contribution of the lexicon stratification. What is the overall improvement that can be achieved if we correctly translate all OOVs that were borrowed from another language? What is the overall improvement that can be achieved if we correctly translate all OOVs? We answer this question by defining "upper bound" experiments. In the upper bound experiment we word-align all available parallel corpora, including dev and test sets, and extract from the alignments oracle translations of OOV words. Then, we append the extracted OOV dictionaries to the training corpora and re-train SMT setups without OOVs. Translation scores of the resulting system provide an upper bound of an improvement from correctly translating all OOVs. When we append oracle translations of the subset of OOV dictionaries, in particular translations of all OOVs for which the output of the borrowing system is not empty, we obtain an upper bound that can be achieved using our method (if the borrowing system provided perfect outputs). Understanding the upper bounds is relevant not only for our experiments, but for any experiments that involve augmenting translation dictionaries; however, we are not aware of prior work providing similar analysis of upper bounds, and we recommend this as a calibrating procedure for future work on OOV mitigation strategies.

Borrowing-augmented setups. As described in §2.2, we integrate translations of OOV loanwords in the translation model. Due to data sparsity, we conjecture that non-OOVs that occur only few times in the training corpus can also lack appropriate translation candidates, i.e., these are target-language OOVs. We therefore run the borrowing system on OOVs and non-OOV words that occur less than 3 times in the training corpus. We list in table 4 sizes of translated lexicons that we integrate in translation tables.

	4K	8K	14K
Loan OOVs in SW–EN	5,050	4,219	3,577
Loan OOVs in RO–EN	347	271	216

Table 4: Sizes of translated lexicons extracted using pivoting via borrowing and integrated in translation models.

Transliteration-augmented setups. In addition to the standard baselines, we evaluate transliteration-augmented setups, where we replace the borrowing model by a transliteration model (Ammar et al., 2012). The model is a linear-chain CRF where we label each source character with a sequence of target characters. The features are label unigrams and bigrams, separately or conjoined with a moving window of source characters. We employ the Swahili–Arabic and Romanian–French transliteration systems that were used as baselines in (Tsvetkov et al., 2015). As in the borrowing system, transliteration outputs are filtered to contain only target language lexicons. We list in table 5 sizes of obtained translated lexicons.

	4K	8K	14K
Translit. OOVs in SW–EN	49	32	22
Translit. OOVs in RO–EN	906	714	578

Table 5: Sizes of translated lexicons extracted using pivoting via transliteration and integrated in translation models.

[9] `www.cdec-decoder.org`

	4K	8K	14K
Tokens	84,764	170,493	300,648
Types	14,554	23,134	33,288
OOV tokens	4,465 (12.7%)	3,509 (10.0%)	2,965 (8.4%)
OOV types	3,610 (50.3%)	2,950 (41.1%)	2,523 (35.1%)

Table 1: Statistics of the Swahili–English corpora and source-side OOV for 4K, 8K, 14K parallel training sentences.

	4K	8K	14K
Tokens	35,978	71,584	121,718
Types	7,210	11,144	15,112
OOV tokens	3,268 (16.6%)	2,585 (13.1%)	2,177 (11.1%)
OOV types	2,382 (55.0%)	1,922 (44.4%)	1,649 (38.1%)

Table 2: Statistics of the Romanian–English corpora and source-side OOV for 4K, 8K, 14K parallel training sentences.

4 Results

Translation results are shown in tables 6 and 7. We evaluate separately the contribution of the integrated OOV translations, and the same translations annotated with phonetic and semantic features. We also provide upper bound scores for integrated loanword dictionaries as well as for recovering all OOVs.

	4K	8K	14K
Baseline	13.2	15.1	17.1
+ Translit. OOVs	13.4	15.3	17.2
+ Loan OOVs	14.3	15.7	18.2
+ Features	**14.8**	**16.4**	**18.4**
Upper bound loan	18.9	19.1	20.7
Upper bound all OOVs	19.2	20.4	21.1

Table 6: Swahili–English MT experiments.

	4K	8K	14K
Baseline	15.8	18.5	20.7
+ Translit. OOVs	15.8	**18.7**	**20.8**
+ Loan OOVs	**16.0**	**18.7**	20.7
+ Features	**16.0**	18.6	20.6
Upper bound loan	16.6	19.4	20.9
Upper bound all OOVs	28.0	28.8	30.4

Table 7: Romanian–English MT experiments.

Swahili–English MT performance is improved by up to +1.6 BLEU when we augment it with translated OOV loanwords leveraged from the Arabic–Swahili borrowing and then Arabic–English MT. The contribution of the borrowing dictionaries is +0.6–1.1 BLEU, and phonetic and semantic features contribute additional half BLEU. More importantly, upper bound results show that the system can be improved more substantially with better dictionaries of OOV loanwords. This result confirms that OOV borrowed words is an important type of OOVs, and with proper modeling it has the potential to improve translation by a large margin. Romanian–English systems obtain only small (but significant for 4K and 8K, $p < .01$) improvement. However, this is expected as the rate of borrowing from French into Romanian is smaller, and, as the result, the integrated loanword dictionaries are small. Transliteration baseline, conversely, is more effective in Romanian–French language pair, as two languages are related typologically, and have common cognates in addition to loanwords. Still, even with these dictionaries the translations with pivoting via borrowing/transliteration improve, and even almost approach the upper bounds results.

5 Conclusion

This paper focuses on fully- and partially-assimilated foreign words in the source lexicon—borrowed words—and a method for obtaining their translations. Our results substantially improve translation and confirm that OOV loanwords are important and merit further investigation. In addition, we propose a simple technique to calculate an upper bound of improvements that can be obtained from integrating OOV translations in SMT.

Acknowledgments

This work was supported by the U.S. Army Research Laboratory and the U.S. Army Research Office under contract/grant number W911NF-10-1-0533. Computational resources were provided by Google Cloud Computing grant. We are grateful to Waleed Ammar for his help with transliteration, and to the anonymous reviewers.

References

Yaser Al-Onaizan and Kevin Knight. 2002. Machine transliteration of names in Arabic text. In *Proc. the ACL workshop on Computational Approaches to Semitic Languages*, pages 1–13.

Waleed Ammar, Chris Dyer, and Noah A. Smith. 2012. Transliteration by sequence labeling with lattice encodings and reranking. In *Proc. NEWS workshop at ACL*.

Chris Callison-Burch, Philipp Koehn, and Miles Osborne. 2006. Improved statistical machine translation using paraphrases. In *Proc. NAACL*, pages 17–24.

Mauro Cettolo, Christian Girardi, and Marcello Federico. 2012. WIT^3: Web inventory of transcribed and translated talks. In *Proc. EAMT*, pages 261–268.

Victor Chahuneau, Eva Schlinger, Noah A Smith, and Chris Dyer. 2013. Translating into morphologically rich languages with synthetic phrases. In *Proc. EMNLP*, pages 1677–1687.

Adrià De Gispert and Jose B Marino. 2006. Catalan-English statistical machine translation without parallel corpus: bridging through Spanish. In *Proc. LREC*, pages 65–68.

Rohit Dholakia and Anoop Sarkar. 2014. Pivot-based triangulation for low-resource languages. In *Proc. AMTA*, pages 315–328.

Nadir Durrani, Hassan Sajjad, Alexander Fraser, and Helmut Schmid. 2010. Hindi-to-Urdu machine translation through transliteration. In *Proc. ACL*, pages 465–474.

Chris Dyer, Adam Lopez, Juri Ganitkevitch, Johnathan Weese, Ferhan Ture, Phil Blunsom, Hendra Setiawan, Vladimir Eidelman, and Philip Resnik. 2010. cdec: A decoder, alignment, and learning framework for finite-state and context-free translation models. In *Proc. ACL System Demonstrations*, pages 7–12.

Manaal Faruqui and Chris Dyer. 2014. Improving vector space word representations using multilingual correlation. In *Proc. EACL*, pages 462–471.

Nizar Habash. 2008. Four techniques for online handling of out-of-vocabulary words in Arabic-English statistical machine translation. In *Proc. ACL*, pages 57–60.

Aria Haghighi, Percy Liang, Taylor Berg-Kirkpatrick, and Dan Klein. 2008. Learning bilingual lexicons from monolingual corpora. In *Proc. ACL*, pages 771–779.

Jan Hajič, Jan Hric, and Vladislav Kuboň. 2000. Machine translation of very close languages. In *Proc. ANLP*, pages 7–12.

Martin Haspelmath and Uri Tadmor, editors. 2009. *Loanwords in the World's Languages: A Comparative Handbook*. Max Planck Institute for Evolutionary Anthropology, Leipzig.

Kenneth Heafield. 2011. KenLM: Faster and smaller language model queries. In *Proc. WMT*, pages 187–197.

Ulf Hermjakob, Kevin Knight, and Hal Daumé III. 2008. Name translation in statistical machine translation-learning when to transliterate. In *Proc. ACL*, pages 389–397.

Junko Itô and Armin Mester. 1995. The core-periphery structure of the lexicon and constraints on reranking. *Papers in Optimality Theory*, 18:181–209.

Frederick Johnson. 1939. *Standard Swahili-English dictionary*. Oxford University Press.

Reinhard Kneser and Hermann Ney. 1995. Improved backing-off for m-gram language modeling. In *Proc. ICASSP*, volume 1, pages 181–184.

Grzegorz Kondrak, Daniel Marcu, and Kevin Knight. 2003. Cognates can improve statistical translation models. In *Proc. HLT-NAACL*, pages 46–48.

Gideon S Mann and David Yarowsky. 2001. Multipath translation lexicon induction via bridge languages. In *Proc. HLT-NAACL*, pages 1–8.

Yuval Marton, Chris Callison-Burch, and Philip Resnik. 2009. Improved statistical machine translation using monolingually-derived paraphrases. In *Proc. EMNLP*, pages 381–390.

Tomas Mikolov, Ilya Sutskever, Kai Chen, Greg S. Corrado, and Jeff Dean. 2013. Distributed representations of words and phrases and their compositionality. In *Proc. NIPS*, pages 3111–3119.

Preslav Nakov and Hwee Tou Ng. 2012. Improving statistical machine translation for a resource-poor language using related resource-rich languages. *Journal of Artificial Intelligence Research*, pages 179–222.

Franz Josef Och. 2003. Minimum error rate training in statistical machine translation. In *Proc. ACL*, pages 160–167.

Kishore Papineni, Salim Roukos, Todd Ward, and Wei-Jing Zhu. 2002. BLEU: a method for automatic evaluation of machine translation. In *Proc. ACL*, pages 311–318.

Robert Parker, David Graff, Junbo Kong, Ke Chen, and Kazuaki Maeda. 2009. English Gigaword fourth edition.

Reinhard Rapp. 1995. Identifying word translations in non-parallel texts. In *Proc. ACL*, pages 320–322.

Majid Razmara, Maryam Siahbani, Reza Haffari, and Anoop Sarkar. 2013. Graph propagation for paraphrasing out-of-vocabulary words in statistical machine translation. In *Proc. ACL*, pages 1105–1115.

Avneesh Saluja, Hany Hassan, Kristina Toutanova, and Chris Quirk. 2014. Graph-based semi-supervised learning of translation models from monolingual data. In *Proc. ACL*, pages 676–686.

Tanja Schultz, Ngoc Thang Vu, and Tim Schlippe. 2013. GlobalPhone: A multilingual text & speech database in 20 languages. In *Proc. ICASSP*, pages 8126–8130.

Sarah Grey Thomason and Terrence Kaufman. 2001. *Language contact*. Edinburgh University Press Edinburgh.

Yulia Tsvetkov, Chris Dyer, Lori Levin, and Archna Bhatia. 2013. Generating English determiners in phrase-based translation with synthetic translation options. In *Proc. WMT*, pages 271–280.

Yulia Tsvetkov, Waleed Ammar, and Chris Dyer. 2015. Constraint-based models of lexical borrowing. In *Proc. NAACL*, pages 598–608.

Pidong Wang, Preslav Nakov, and Hwee Tou Ng. 2012. Source language adaptation for resource-poor machine translation. In *Proc. EMNLP*, pages 286–296.

Kai Zhao, Hany Hassan, and Michael Auli. 2015. Learning translation models from monolingual continuous representations. In *Proc. NAACL*.

Recurrent Neural Network based Rule Sequence Model for Statistical Machine Translation

Heng Yu, Xuan Zhu

Samsung R&D Institute of China, Beijing, China
{h0517.yu, xuan.zhu}@samsung.com

Abstract

The inability to model long-distance dependency has been handicapping SMT for years. Specifically, the context independence assumption makes it hard to capture the dependency between translation rules. In this paper, we introduce a novel recurrent neural network based rule sequence model to incorporate arbitrary long contextual information during estimating probabilities of rule sequences. Moreover, our model frees the translation model from keeping huge and redundant grammars, resulting in more efficient training and decoding. Experimental results show that our method achieves a 0.9 point BLEU gain over the baseline, and a significant reduction in rule table size for both phrase-based and hierarchical phrase-based systems.

1 Introduction

Modeling long-distance dependency has always been a bottleneck for statistical machine translation (SMT). While lots of efforts have been made in solving long-distance reordering (Xiong et al., 2006; Zens and Ney, 2006; Kumar and Byrne, 2005), long-span n-gram matching (Charniak et al., 2003; Shen et al., 2008; Yu et al., 2014), much less attention has been concentrated on capturing translation rule dependency, which is not explicitly modeled in most translation systems (Wu et al., 2014).

SMT systems typically model the translation process as a sequence of translation steps, each of which uses a translation rule. These rules are usually applied independently of each other, which violates the conventional wisdom that translation should be done in context (Giménez and Màrquez, 2007). However, it is not an easy task to capture the rule dependency, which entails much longer context and more severe data sparsity. There are two major solutions: the first one is breaking the rules into bilingual word-pairs and use a n-gram translation model to incorporate lexical dependencies that span rule boundaries (Marino et al., 2006; Durrani et al., 2013). These n-gram models (also known as tuple sequence model) could help phrase-based translation models to overcome the phrasal independence assumption, but they rely on word alignment to extract bilingual tuples, which brings in additional alignment error (Wu et al., 2014). The other direction lies in utilizing the rule Markov model (Vaswani et al., 2011; Quirk and Menezes, 2006), which directly explores dependencies in rule derivation history and achieves both good performance and slimmer translation model in syntax-based SMT systems. However, the sparsity of translation rules entails aggressive pruning of the training data and constrains the model from scaling to high order grams, significantly limiting the ability of the model.

In this paper we follow the second line and propose a novel recurrent neural network based rule sequence model (RNN-RSM), which utilizes the representational power of recurrent neural network (RNN) to capture arbitrary distance of contextual information in estimating the probability of rule sequences, rather than constrained to n-gram local context limited by Markov assumption. Compared with previous studies, our contributions are as follows:

First, we lift the Markov assumption in rule sequence model and use RNN to capture arbitrary-length of contextual information, which is proven to be more accurate in estimating sequential probabilities (Mikolov et al., 2010).

Second, to alleviate the sparsity of translation rules, we extend our model to factorized RNN-RSM, which incorporates both the source and target side phrase embedding in addition to the translation rule

Proceedings of the 53rd Annual Meeting of the Association for Computational Linguistics and the 7th International Joint Conference on Natural Language Processing (Short Papers), pages 132–138,
Beijing, China, July 26-31, 2015.

history.

Lastly, we apply our model to both phrase-based and hierarchical phrase-based (HPB) systems and achieve an average improvement of 0.9 BLEU points with much slimmer translation models in hypergraph reranking task (Huang, 2008).

2 Rule Sequence Model

We will first brief our rule sequence model with an example from phrase-based system (Koehn et al., 2007). Consider the following translation from Chinese to English:

Bùshí yǔ Shālóng jǔxíng le huìtán
Bush with Sharon hold -ed meeting

'Bush held a meeting with Sharon'

So one possible rule derivation of the above example could be:

$$\dfrac{\dfrac{\dfrac{(_0\text{\_ \_ \_ \_ \_ \_}) : (s_0, \text{``''})}{(\bullet_1\text{\_ \_ \_ \_ \_}) : (s_1, \text{``Bush''})}\,r_1}{(\bullet\text{\_ \_}\bullet\bullet\bullet_6) : (s_2, \text{``Bush held talks''})}\,r_2}{(\bullet\bullet\bullet_3\bullet\bullet\bullet) : (s_3, \text{``Bush held talks with Sharon''})}\,r_3$$

r_1: *Bùshí* → Bush
r_2: *jǔxíng le huìtán* → held talks
r_3: *yǔ Shālóng* → with Sharon

Each row is a derivation step, where s_n denotes a hypothesis with a coverage vector capturing the source language words translated so far, and a $\bullet$ in the coverage vector indicates the source word at this position is "covered". Each hypothesis s_{n-1} can be extended into a longer hypothesis s_n by a rule r_n translating an uncovered segment. Note that in phrase-based translation we need to set a distortion limit to prohibit long distance reordering, so the ending position of last phrase is maintained (e.g., $_1$ and $_6$ in the coverage vector).

In our example, translation rules r_1, r_2, r_3 form a *derivation* T which leads to a complete translation. So for rule sequence model, the probability of r_n depends on its derivation history $H(r_n)$:

$$P(r_n) = P(r_n | H(r_n)) \quad (1)$$

and the probability of a rule derivation T is

$$P(T) = \prod_{r_i \in T} P(r_i | H(r_i)) \quad (2)$$

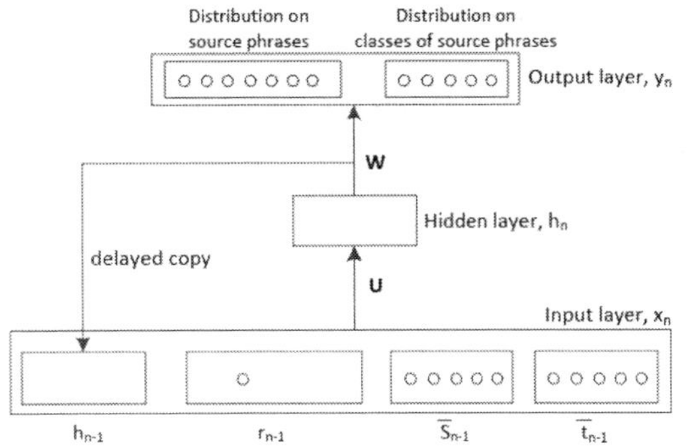

Figure 1: Factorized recurrent neural network with source and target side phrase embeddings.

So the rule sequence model does not make any context independence assumption and generate a rule by looking at a context of previous rules.

2.1 Training

The rule sequence model can then be trained on the path set of rule derivations. To obtain golden derivations of translation rules for each sentence pair, We follow Yu et al. (2013) to utilize force decoding to get golden rule derivations. Specifically, we define a new forced decoding LM which only accepts two consecutive words (denote as p, q) in the reference translation (y_i):

$$P_{forced}(q \mid p) = \begin{cases} 1 & \text{if } \exists j, \text{s.t. } p = y_j \text{ and } q = y_{j+1} \\ 0 & \text{otherwise} \end{cases}$$

For each hypothesis, we keep the bourndary words as its signiture (only right side for phrase-based model and both sides for HPB). If a boundary word does not occur in the reference, its language model score will be set to $-\infty$; if a boundary word occurs more than once in the reference, the hypothesis is split into multiple hypotheses, one for each index of occurance.

According to the definition, we can see that the rule sequence $[r_1, r_2, r_3]$ in the example could produce the exact reference translation, which is ideal for the training of rule sequence model.

3 Recurrent Neural Network based Rule Sequence Model

In order to capture long-span context, we introduce recurrent neural network based rule sequence model to estimate the probability $P(r_n|H(r_n))$. Our RNN-RSM can potentially capture arbitrary long context rather than n-1 previous rules limited by Markov assumption. Following Mikolov et al. (2010), we adopt the standard RNN architecture: the input layer encodes previous translation rule using one-hot coding, the output layer produces a probability distribution over all translation rules, and the hidden layer maintains a representation of rule derivation history. However, the standard implementation has severe data sparsity problem due to the large size of rule table couple with the limited training data.

3.1 Factorized RNN-RSM

To solve the sparsity problem, we extend the RNN-RSM model with factorizing rules in the input layer, as shown in Figure 1. It consists of an input layer x, a hidden layer h (state layer), and an output layer y. The connection weights among layers are denoted by matrixes **U** and **W** respectively. Unlike the RNN-RSM, which predicts probability $P(r_n|r_{n-1}, H(r_{n-1}))$, the factorized RNN-RSM predicts probability $P(r_n|r_{n-1}, H(r_{n-1}), \bar{s}_{n-1}, \bar{t}_{n-1})$ to generate following rule r_n, where $\bar{s}_{n-1}$/$\bar{t}_{n-1}$ are the source/target side of r_{n-1}, However, $\bar{s}_{n-1}$ and $\bar{t}_{n-1}$ are still too sparse considering the huge vocabulary size and the diversity in forming phrases, so here we use recursive auto-encoder (Socher et al., 2011; Li et al., 2013) to learn phrase embeddings on both source and target side in an unsupervised mannner, minimizing the reconstruction error.

For those rules that are not contained in the training data, the factorized RNN-RSM backs off to the source/target side embedding $E_{s_{i-1}}$/$E_{t_{i-1}}$. In the special case that $E_{s_{i-1}}$ and $E_{t_{i-1}}$ are dropped, the factorized RNN-RSM goes back to RNN-RSM. Finally, the input layer x_n is formed by concatenating the input vectors and hidden layer h_{n-1} at the preceding time step, as shown in the following equation.

$$x_n = [v^u_{n-1}, v^{\bar{s}}_{n-1}, v^{\bar{t}}_{n-1}, h_{n-1}] \quad (3)$$

The neurons in the hidden and output layers are computed as follows:

$$h_n = f(\mathbf{U} \times x_n), y_n = g(\mathbf{w} \times h_n) \quad (4)$$

$$f(z) = \frac{1}{1+e^{-z}}, g(z) = \frac{e^{z_m}}{\sum_k e^{z_k}} \quad (5)$$

3.2 Factorized RNN-RSM on source and target phrases

The above factorized RNN-RSM is conditioned on the previous context during computing the probability of rule r_n. Since r_n may still suffer from sparsity, we further factorize r_n into its source side phrase $\bar{s}_n$ and target side phrase $\bar{t}_n$. So the probability formula could be rewrite as:

$$\begin{aligned} P(r_n|H(r_n)) &= P(s_n, t_n|H(r_n)) \\ &= P(s_n|H(r_n)) \times P(t_n|s_n, H(r_n)) \quad (6) \end{aligned}$$

The first sub-model $P(s_n, |H(r_n))$ computes the probability distribution over source phrases. Then the second sub-model $P(t_n|s_n, H(r_n))$ computes the probability distribution over t_n that are translated from s_n. The two sub-models are computed with the similar recurrent network shown in Figure 1 except adding the source side information s_n of the current rule r_n into the input layer. This method share the same spirit with the RNN-based translation model (Sundermeyer et al., 2014; Cho et al., 2014), except that we focus on capturing rule dependencies which has a much small search space. Noted that this new factorize model provides richer information for prediction, and actually is faster to train since the vocabulary of source/target phrases are much small than that of the translation rules.

4 Experiments

4.1 Setup

The training corpus consists of 1M sentence pairs with 25M/21M words of Chinese/English respectively. Our development and test set are NIST 2006 and 2008 (newswire portion) respectively.

We obtained alignments by running GIZA++ (Och and Ney, 2004) and used the SRILM toolkit (Stolcke, 2002) to train a 4-gram language model with KN-smoothing on the English side of the training data. Case-insensitive BLEU (Papineni et al., 2002) and MERT (Och, 2003) were used for evaluation and tuning.

We test our method on both phrase-based and hierarchical phrase-based translation models. For phrase-based system, we use Moses with standard features (Koehn et al., 2007). While for hierarchical phrase-based model, we use a in-house implementation of Hiero (Chiang, 2005). We set phrase-limit

System	Moses		Hiero	
	dev-set	test-set	dev-set	test-set
Baseline	28.4	27.7	30.4	30.0
+RMM	28.7	28.3	30.7	30.2
+fRNN-RSM (1)	28.9	**28.6**	30.9	**30.6**
+fRNN-RSM$_{st}$ (2)	**29.3**	**28.5**	**31.2**	**30.7**
+(1)+(2)	**29.6**	**28.7**	**31.4**	**30.8**

Table 1: Main results. RMM is the re-implementation of Vaswani et al. (2011), fRNN-RSM denotes for factorized RNN-RSM describe in Section 3.1, fRNN-RSM$_{st}$ denotes for RNN-RSM factorized by source/target side in Section 3.2. Results in bold mean that the improvements over "Baseline" are statistically significant ($p < 0.05$) (Koehn, 2004).

to 5 for the extraction of both phrase-based rule and SCFG rule, as well as beam size to 100 and distortion limit to 7 in decoding.

Since the rule sequence model belongs to the family of non-local feature (Huang, 2008), traditional testing methods like nbest reranking are not suitable for our experiments. So we adopt *hypergraph reranking* (Huang and Chiang, 2007; Huang, 2008), which proves to be effective for integrating nonlocal features into dynamic programming. The decoding process is divided into two passes. In the first pass, only standard features (i.e., standard features for phrase-based or HPB model) are used to produce a hypergraph. In the second pass, we use the hypergraph reranking algorithm (Huang, 2008) to find promising translations using additional rule sequence feature.

For RNN training, we set the hidden layer size to 512 and classes in the output layer to 256. To obtain phrase-embedding, we use open source tool str2vec[1] (Li et al., 2013) to train two autoencoders on the source and target side of rule-table respectively.

4.2 Results

Table 1 presents the main results of our paper. To show the merits of our RNN-RSM, we also re-implement Vaswani et al. (2011)'s work, denote as rule Markov model (RMM). It utilize tri-gram rule derivation history for prediction, whereas our RNN-RSM could capture arbitrary length of contextual information. We can see that RMM provides a modest improvement over the baseline, 0.6/0.2 points over Moses/Hiero, thanks to the positive guidance

[1]https://github.com/pengli09/str2vec

System	w/o monotone		Full	
	Moses	Hiero	Moses	Hiero
Baseline	27.4	29.8	27.7	30.0
+RMM	27.6	29.9	28.3	30.2
+fRNN-RSM	28.0	30.4	28.6	30.6
+fRNN-RSM$_{st}$	28.2	30.6	28.5	30.7

Table 2: BLEU score comparison on different rule-set, "w/o monotone" denotes we filter out monotone composed rules in both rule table and our RNN-RSM, full denotes we use the total rule-set.

of short-span rule dependency. On the other hand, our factorized RNN-RSM with phrase embeddings (fRNN-RSM) provides a more significant BLEU score improvement (0.9 for Moses, 0.6 for Hiero), which exemplifies that the long-span rule dependency captured by RNN could provides additional boost in translation quality. At the same time, factorized RNN-RSM on source and target phrases (fRNN-RSM$_{st}$) alleviate the data sparse problem in RNN training, resulting in slightly better performance. Finally, when we combine both factorized model, we get the best performance at 28.7 for Moses and 30.8 for Hiero, both significantly better than baseline systems.

Also, we conduct an interesting experiment to see if our fRNN-RSM could somehow replace the role of composed rules (rules that can be formed out of smaller rules in the grammar) and guides more fine-grained rule-set to produce better translation results. We re-implement He et al. (2009)'s work to filter out monotone composed rules for both Hiero and Moses. We are able to filter out a large number of monotone composed rules, about 50% rules for Hiero and 31% for Moses. The results are shown in Table 2. Interestingly the performance of slimmer translation model with fRNN-RSM exceeds baseline with full rule-table, and catches up with the original fRNN-RSM. The reason is two-folded: first, deleting monotone composed rules doesn't effect the overall coverage of the rule-set, making limited harm to the system. Second, with less rules, the data sparse problem of RNN training is further alleviated, resulting in a better fRNN-RSM for probability prediction.

5 Related Work

Besides the work of Vaswani et al. (2011) discussed in Section 1, there are several other works using a rule bigram or trigram model in machine translation, Ding and Palmer (2005) use n-gram rule Markov model in the dependency treelet model, Liu and Gildea (2008) applies the same method in a tree-to-string model. Our work is different from theirs in that we lift the Markov assumption and use recurrent neural network to capture much longer contextual information to help probability prediction.

Our work is also in the same spirit with tuple sequence models (Marino et al., 2006; Durrani et al., 2013; Hui Zhang, 2013; Wu et al., 2014), which break the translation sequence into bilingual tuples and use a Markov model to capture the dependency of tuples. Comparing to them, we take a more direct approach to use translation rule dependency to guide translation process, rather than rely on tuples which will be significant affected by word alignment errors.

Outside of machine translation, the idea of weakening independence assumption by modeling the derivation history is also found in parsing (Johnson, 1998), where rule probabilities are conditioned on parent and grand-parent nonterminals. Inspired by it, we successfully find a solution for the translation field.

6 Conclusion

In this paper, we have presented a novel recurrent neural network based rule sequence model to estimate the probability of translation rule sequences. One of the major advantages of our model is its potential to capture long-span dependency compared with n-gram Markov models. In addition, our factorized model with phrase embedding could further alleviate the data sparse problem in RNN training. Finally we conduct experiments on both phrase-based and hierarchical phrase-based models and get an average improvement of 0.9 BLEU points over the baseline. In the future we will investigate stronger network structure such as LSTM to further improve the prediction power of our model.

References

Eugene Charniak, Kevin Knight, and Kenji Yamada. 2003. Syntax-based language models for statistical machine translation. In *Proceedings of MT Summit IX*, pages 40–46. Citeseer.

David Chiang. 2005. A hierarchical phrase-based model for statistical machine translation. In *Proceedings of the 43rd ACL*, Ann Arbor, MI.

Kyunghyun Cho, Bart van Merrienboer, Caglar Gulcehre, Fethi Bougares, Holger Schwenk, and Yoshua Bengio. 2014. Learning phrase representations using rnn encoder-decoder for statistical machine translation. *arXiv preprint arXiv:1406.1078*.

Yuan Ding and Martha Palmer. 2005. Machine translation using probabilistic synchronous dependency insertion grammars. In *Proceedings of the 43rd Annual Meeting on Association for Computational Linguistics*, pages 541–548. Association for Computational Linguistics.

Nadir Durrani, Alexander Fraser, Helmut Schmid, Hieu Hoang, and Philipp Koehn. 2013. Can markov models over minimal translation units help phrase-based smt? In *ACL (2)*, pages 399–405.

Jesús Giménez and Lluís Màrquez. 2007. Context-aware discriminative phrase selection for statistical machine translation. In *Proceedings of the Second Workshop on Statistical Machine Translation*, pages 159–166. Association for Computational Linguistics.

Zhongjun He, Yao Meng, and Hao Yu. 2009. Discarding monotone composed rule for hierarchical phrase-based statistical machine translation. In *Proceedings of the 3rd International Universal Communication Symposium*, pages 25–29. ACM.

Liang Huang and David Chiang. 2007. Forest rescoring: Fast decoding with integrated language models. In *Proceedings of ACL*, Prague, Czech Rep., June.

Liang Huang. 2008. Forest reranking: Discriminative parsing with non-local features. In *Proceedings of the ACL: HLT*, Columbus, OH, June.

Chris Quirk Jianfeng Gao Hui Zhang, Kristina Toutanova. 2013. Beyond left-to-right: Multiple decomposition structures for smt. In *NAACL*.

Mark Johnson. 1998. Pcfg models of linguistic tree representations. *Computational Linguistics*, 24(4):613–632.

P. Koehn, H. Hoang, A. Birch, C. Callison-Burch, M. Federico, N. Bertoldi, B. Cowan, W. Shen, C. Moran, R. Zens, C. Dyer, O. Bojar, A. Constantin, and E. Herbst. 2007. Moses: open source toolkit for statistical machine translation. In *Proceedings of ACL: Demonstrations*.

Philipp Koehn. 2004. Statistical significance tests for machine translation evaluation. In *EMNLP*, pages 388–395. Citeseer.

Shankar Kumar and William Byrne. 2005. Local phrase reordering models for statistical machine translation. In *Proceedings of the conference on Human Language Technology and Empirical Methods in Natural Language Processing*, pages 161–168. Association for Computational Linguistics.

Peng Li, Yang Liu, and Maosong Sun. 2013. Recursive autoencoders for itg-based translation. In *EMNLP*, pages 567–577.

Ding Liu and Daniel Gildea. 2008. Improved tree-to-string transducer for machine translation. In *Proceedings of the Third Workshop on Statistical Machine Translation*, pages 62–69. Association for Computational Linguistics.

José B Marino, Rafael E Banchs, Josep M Crego, Adria de Gispert, Patrik Lambert, José AR Fonollosa, and Marta R Costa-Jussà. 2006. N-gram-based machine translation. *Computational Linguistics*, 32(4):527–549.

Tomas Mikolov, Martin Karafiát, Lukas Burget, Jan Cernockỳ, and Sanjeev Khudanpur. 2010. Recurrent neural network based language model. In *INTERSPEECH 2010, 11th Annual Conference of the International Speech Communication Association, Makuhari, Chiba, Japan, September 26-30, 2010*, pages 1045–1048.

Franz Joseph Och and Hermann Ney. 2004. The alignment template approach to statistical machine translation. *Computational Linguistics*, 30:417–449.

Franz Joseph Och. 2003. Minimum error rate training in statistical machine translation. In *Proceedings of ACL*, pages 160–167.

Kishore Papineni, Salim Roukos, Todd Ward, and Wei-Jing Zhu. 2002. Bleu: a method for automatic evaluation of machine translation. In *Proceedings of ACL*, pages 311–318, Philadephia, USA, July.

Chris Quirk and Arul Menezes. 2006. Do we need phrases?: challenging the conventional wisdom in statistical machine translation. In *Proceedings of the main conference on human language technology conference of the north american chapter of the association of computational linguistics*, pages 9–16. Association for Computational Linguistics.

Libin Shen, Jinxi Xu, and Ralph M Weischedel. 2008. A new string-to-dependency machine translation algorithm with a target dependency language model. In *ACL*, pages 577–585.

Richard Socher, Jeffrey Pennington, Eric H Huang, Andrew Y Ng, and Christopher D Manning. 2011. Semi-supervised recursive autoencoders for predicting sentiment distributions. In *Proceedings of the Conference on Empirical Methods in Natural Language Processing*, pages 151–161. Association for Computational Linguistics.

Andreas Stolcke. 2002. Srilm - an extensible language modeling toolkit. In *Proceedings of ICSLP*, volume 30, pages 901–904.

Martin Sundermeyer, Tamer Alkhouli, Joern Wuebker, and Hermann Ney. 2014. Translation modeling with bidirectional recurrent neural networks. In *Proceedings of the Conference on Empirical Methods on Natural Language Processing, October*.

Ashish Vaswani, Haitao Mi, Liang Huang, and David Chiang. 2011. Rule markov models for fast tree-to-string translation. In *Proceedings of ACL 2011*, Portland, OR.

Youzheng Wu, Taro Watanabe, and Chiori Hori. 2014. Recurrent neural network-based tuple sequence model for machine translation. In *Proc. COLING*, pages 1908–1917.

Deyi Xiong, Qun Liu, and Shouxun Lin. 2006. Maximum entropy based phrase reordering model for statistical machine translation. In *Proceedings of the 21st International Conference on Computational Linguistics and the 44th annual meeting of the Association for Computational Linguistics*, pages 521–528. Association for Computational Linguistics.

Heng Yu, Liang Huang, Haitao Mi, and Kai Zhao. 2013. Max-violation perceptron and forced decoding for scalable mt training. In *EMNLP*, pages 1112–1123.

Heng Yu, Haitao Mi, Liang Huang, and Qun Liu. 2014. A structured language model for incremental tree-to-string translation.

Richard Zens and Hermann Ney. 2006. Discriminative reordering models for statistical machine translation. In *Proceedings of the Workshop on Statistical Machine Translation*, pages 55–63. Association for Computational Linguistics.

Discriminative Preordering Meets Kendall's τ Maximization

Sho Hoshino **Yusuke Miyao**
National Institute of Informatics / The Graduate University for Advanced Studies, Japan
{hoshino,yusuke}@nii.ac.jp

Katsuhito Sudoh **Katsuhiko Hayashi** **Masaaki Nagata**
NTT Communication Science Laboratories, NTT Corporation
{sudoh.katsuhito,hayashi.katsuhiko,nagata.masaaki}@lab.ntt.co.jp

Abstract

This paper explores a simple discriminative preordering model for statistical machine translation. Our model traverses binary constituent trees, and classifies whether children of each node should be reordered. The model itself is not extremely novel, but herein we introduce a new procedure to determine oracle labels so as to maximize Kendall's τ. Experiments in Japanese-to-English translation revealed that our simple method is comparable with, or superior to, state-of-the-art methods in translation accuracy.

1 Introduction

Current statistical machine translation systems suffer from major accuracy degradation in distant languages, primarily because they utilize exceptionally dissimilar word orders. One promising solution to this problem is *preordering*, in which source sentences are reordered to resemble the target language word orders, after which statistical machine translation is applied to reordered sentences (Xia and McCord, 2004; Collins et al., 2005). This is particularly effective for distant language pairs such as English and Japanese (Isozaki et al., 2010b).

Among such preordering, one of the simplest and straightforward model is a discriminative preordering model (Li et al., 2007), which classifies whether children of each constituent node should be reordered, given binary trees.[1] This simple model has, however, difficulty to find oracle labels. Yang et al. (2012) proposed a method to approximate oracle labels along dependency trees.

The present paper proposes a new procedure to find oracle labels. The main idea is simple: we determine reordering decisions in a way that maximizes Kendall's τ of word alignments. We prove that our procedure guarantees the optimal solution for word alignments given as an integer list; in a way that local decisions on each node reach global maximization of Kendall's τ in total. Any reordering methods that utilize word alignments along constituency benefit from this proof.

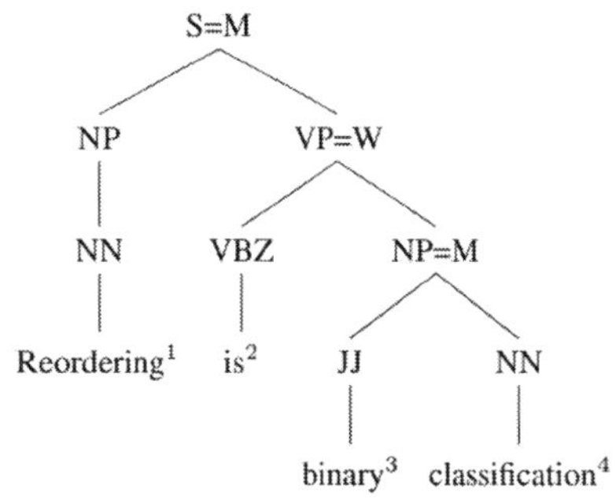

Figure 1: Discriminative preordering model.

Empirical study in Japanese-to-English translation demonstrate that our simple method outperforms a rule-based preordering method, and is comparable with, or superior to, state-of-the-art methods that rely on language-specific heuristics.

Our contributions are summarized as follows:

- We define a method for obtaining oracle labels in discriminative preordering as the maximization of Kendall's τ.
- We give a theoretical background to Kendall's τ based reordering for binary constituent trees.
- We achieve state-of-the-art accuracy in Japanese-to-English translation with a simple method without language-specific heuristics.

[1] It is also possible to use n-ary trees (Li et al., 2007; Yang et al., 2012), but we keep this binary model for simplicity.

Proceedings of the 53rd Annual Meeting of the Association for Computational Linguistics and the 7th International Joint Conference on Natural Language Processing (Short Papers), pages 139–144,
Beijing, China, July 26-31, 2015. ©2015 Association for Computational Linguistics

2 Preordering Method

2.1 Discriminative Preordering Model

The discriminative preordering model (Li et al., 2007) is a reordering model that determines whether children of each node should be reordered, given a binary constituent tree. For a sentence with n words, a node in a binary constituent tree is expressed as $v(i, p, j)$, where $1 \leq i \leq p < p+1 \leq j \leq n$. This indicates that the node takes the left span from i-th to p-th words and the right span from $(p+1)$-th to j-th words. Then we define whether a node should be reordered as $P(x \mid \theta(v(i,p,j)))$, where $x \in \{W, M\}$. W represents a reverse action (reorder the child nodes), M represents a monotonic action (do not reorder the child nodes), and θ is a feature function that is described at Section 2.4.

For instance, Figure 1 shows a sentence ($n = 4$) that has three binary nodes S, VP, and NP, which are our reordering candidates. We examine the NP node $v(3,3,4)$ that has a left ($binary^3$) and a right ($classification^4$) spans, of which reordering is determined by $P(x \mid \theta(v(3,3,4)))$, and is classified $x = M$ in this example. The actions for the VP node $v(2,2,4)$ and the S root node $v(1,1,4)$ are determined in a similar fashion.

Once all classifications are finished, the children of the nodes with W are reversed. From the constituent tree in Figure 1, this reordering produces a new tree in Figure 2 that represents a reordered sentence *Reordering binary classification is*, which is used in statistical machine translation.

2.2 Oracle Labels Maximizing Kendall's τ

In order to train such a classifier, we need an oracle label, W or M, for each node. Since we cannot rely on manual label annotation, we define a procedure to obtain oracle labels from word alignments. The principal idea is that we determine an oracle label of each node $v(i,p,j)$ so that it maximizes Kendall's τ under $v(i,p,j)$. This is intuitively a straightforward idea, because our objective is to find a monotonic order, which indicates maximization of Kendall's τ.

In the context of statistical machine translation, Kendall's τ is used as an evaluation metric for monotonicity of word orderings (Birch and Osborne, 2010; Isozaki et al., 2010a; Talbot et al., 2011). Given an integer list $\mathbf{x} = x_1, \ldots, x_n$, $\tau(\mathbf{x})$

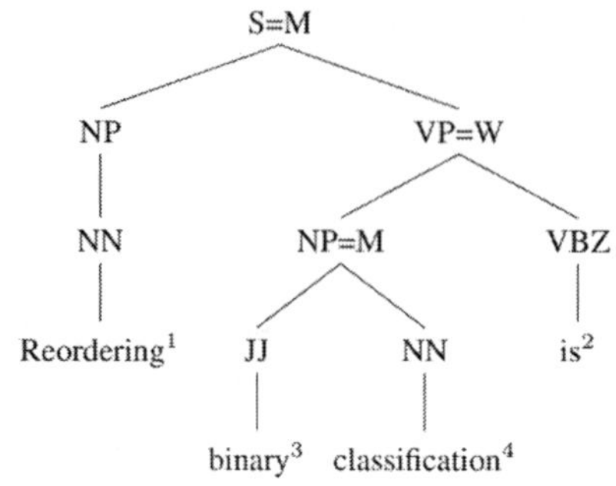

Figure 2: Output of discriminative preordering.

measures a similarity between $\mathbf{x}$ and sorted $\mathbf{x}$ as:

$$\tau(\mathbf{x}) = \frac{4c(\mathbf{x})}{n(n-1)} - 1,$$

where $c(\mathbf{x})$ is the number of concordant pairs between $\mathbf{x}$ and sorted $\mathbf{x}$, which is defined as:

$$c(\mathbf{x}) = \sum_{i,j \in [1,n], i<j} \delta(x_i < x_j),$$

where $\delta(x_i < x_j) = 1$ if $x_i < x_j$, and 0 otherwise. The τ function expresses that $\mathbf{x}$ is completely monotonic when $\tau(\mathbf{x}) = 1$, and in contrast, $\mathbf{x}$ is completely reversed when $\tau(\mathbf{x}) = -1$. Since $\tau(\mathbf{x})$ is proportional to $c(\mathbf{x})$, only $c(\mathbf{x})$ is considered in the course of our maximization.

Suppose that word alignments are given in the form $\mathbf{a} = a_1, \ldots, a_n$, where $a_x = y$ indicates that the x-th word in a source sentence corresponds to the y-th word in a target sentence.[2] We also assume that a binary constituent tree is given, and alignment for the span (i,j) is denoted as $\mathbf{a}(i,j)$. For each node $v(i,p,j)$, we define the score as:

$$s(v(i,p,j)) = c(\mathbf{a}(i,p) \cdot \mathbf{a}(p+1,j)) - c(\mathbf{a}(p+1,j) \cdot \mathbf{a}(i,p)),$$

where $\cdot$ indicates a concatenation of vectors. Then, a node that has $s(v(i,p,j)) < 0$ is assigned W, and a node that has $s(v(i,p,j)) > 0$ is assigned M. All the nodes scored as $s = 0$ are excluded from the training data, because they are noisy and ambiguous in terms of binary classification.

2.3 Proof of Independency over Constituency

The question then arises: *Can oracle labels achieve the best reordering in total?* We see this

[2]We used median values to approximate this y-th word in the target sentence for simplicity.

$t_{i:p}, t_{p+1:j}, w_{i:p}, w_{p+1:j}$,	$\sigma(v(i,p,j))$,
$t_{i:p} \circ t_{p+1:j}, w_{i:p} \circ w_{p+1:j}$,	$\sigma_r(v(i,p,j))$,
$t_{i:p} \circ t_{p+1:j} \circ w_{i:p} \circ w_{p+1:j}$,	$\sigma_t(v(i,p,j))$,
$t_{l:p}, t_{p+1:r}, w_{l:p}, w_{p+1:r}$,	$\sigma_w(v(i,p,j))$
$t_{l:p} \circ t_{p+1:r}, w_{l:p} \circ w_{p+1:r}$,	
$t_{l:p} \circ t_{p+1:r} \circ w_{l:p} \circ w_{p+1:r}$	

Table 1: Templates for the node $v(i,p,j)$: where integers l and r satisfy $i \leq l \leq p < p+1 \leq r \leq j$.

Template	Instance	Template	Instance
$t_{2:2}$	VBZ	$w_{2:2}$	is
$t_{3:4}$	JJ_NN	$w_{3:4}$	binary_classification
$t_{3:3}$	JJ	$w_{3:3}$	binary

Template	Instance
$\sigma(v(2,2,4))$	(VP(VBZis)(NP(JJbinary)(NNclassification)))
$\sigma_r(v(2,2,4))$	VP VBZ NP JJ NN VP_VBZ VP_NP NP_JJ NP_NN
$\sigma_t(v(2,2,4))$	(VP(VBZ)(NP(JJ)(NN)))
$\sigma_w(v(2,2,4))$	((is)((binary)(classification)))

Table 2: Examples in $v(2,2,4)$ from Figure 1.

Proposed	Accuracy	Previous	Accuracy
Full	**90.91**	Li et al. (2007)	84.43
w/o the first set	87.50		
w/o $\sigma(v(i,p,j))$	90.76		
w/o $\sigma_r(v(i,p,j))$	90.85		
w/o $\sigma_t(v(i,p,j))$	90.90		
w/o $\sigma_w(v(i,p,j))$	90.88		

Table 3: Ablation tests on binary classification accuracy (%).

is true, because $c(\mathbf{a}(i,j))$ can be computed in a recursive manner. See $c(\mathbf{a}(i,j))$ is decomposed as:

$$c(\mathbf{a}(i,j)) = c(\mathbf{a}(i,p)) + c(\mathbf{a}(p+1,j)) + \sum_{k \in [i,p], l \in [p+1,j]} \delta(a_k < a_l).$$

The three terms in this formula are mutually independent. That is, any reordering of $\mathbf{a}(i,p)$ changes only the first term and the others are unchanged. We maximize $c(\mathbf{a}(i,j))$ by maximizing each term. Since the first and the second terms are maximized recursively, our method directly maximizes the third term, which corresponds to our oracle labels, hence $c(\mathbf{a})$ and $\tau(\mathbf{a})$ of entire sentence.[3]

Essentially, our decisions on each node are equivalent to sorting a list consists of left and right points, while the order of the points inside of left and right lists are left untouched. We determine oracle labels for a given constituent tree by computing $s(v(i,p,j))$ for every $v(i,p,j)$ independently.

[3]Oracle labels guarantee $\tau(\mathbf{a}) \geq 0$, but not $\tau(\mathbf{a}) = 1$, because parsed trees will not correspond to word alignments.

		test9		test10	
Settings	DL	RIBES	BLEU	RIBES	BLEU
Baseline w/o preordering					
Moses	0	66.95	26.36	67.50	27.17
Moses	10	68.95	29.41	69.64	30.20
Moses	20	69.88	30.12	70.22	30.51
Proposed preordering					
Giza	0	77.49	33.08	77.49	33.65
Giza	10	77.44	**33.28**	77.42	33.77
Nile	0	77.74	32.97	77.89	**33.91**
Nile	10	**77.97**	**33.55**	**78.07**	**34.13**

Table 4: Results in Japanese-to-English translation. Boldfaces denote the highest scores and the insignificant difference ($p < 0.01$) from the highest scores in bootstrap resampling (Koehn, 2004).

2.4 Features

Table 1 shows the templates for the node $v(i,p,j)$ of the feature function θ in Section 2.1. To tell the differences between the left span $\mathbf{a}(i,p)$ and the right span $\mathbf{a}(p+1,j)$, such as whether the head word of the node is in left or right, the first set of templates considers individual indices $x{:}y$ that denote the span from x-th to y-th words: where t_x represents a part-of-speech feature; w_x represents a lexical feature; and $\circ$ represents feature combination. The second set of templates considers constituent structures of the node by supplying three S-expressions and parent-child relations: where $\sigma(v(i,p,j))$ represents a constituent structure under the node $v(i,p,j)$; $\sigma_r(v(i,p,j))$ represents part-of-speech tags of the node and their parent-child relations; $\sigma_t(v(i,p,j))$ represents the constituent structure including only part-of-speech tags; and $\sigma_w(v(i,p,j))$ represents the constituent structure including only surface words.

Table 2 shows instances of features for the VP node $v(2,2,4)$ in Figure 1, which has the left (is^2) and the right ($binary^3$ $classification^4$) spans.

Table 3 shows ablation test results on binary classification, which indicate that our templates performed better than that of Li et al. (2007).

3 Experiment

3.1 Experimental Settings

We perform experiments over the NTCIR patent corpus (Goto et al., 2011) that consists of more than 3 million sentences in English and Japanese. Following conventional literature settings (Goto et al., 2012; Hayashi et al., 2013), we used all 3 million sentences from the NTCIR-7 and NTCIR-

Reordering Methods	DL	test9 RIBES	Δ	BLEU	Δ	test10 RIBES	Δ	BLEU	Δ
Moses	20	69.88		30.12		70.22		30.51	
Proposed preordering	10	**77.97**	**+8.09**	**33.55**	**+3.43**	**78.07**	+7.85	**34.13**	**+3.62**
Moses (Hoshino et al., 2013)	20	68.08		27.57					
Preordering (Hoshino et al., 2013)	10	72.37	+4.29	30.56	+2.99				
Moses (Goto et al., 2012)	20	68.28		30.20					
Moses-chart (Goto et al., 2012)		70.64	+2.36	30.69	+0.49				
Postordering (Goto et al., 2012)		75.48	+7.20	33.04	+2.84				
Moses (Hayashi et al., 2013)	20	69.31		29.43		68.90		29.99	
Postordering (Hayashi et al., 2013)	0	76.46	+7.15	32.59	+3.16	76.76	**+7.86**	33.14	+3.15

Table 5: Comparison with previous systems in Japanese-to-English translation, of which scores are retrieved from their papers. Boldfaces indicate the highest scores and differences.

8 training sets, used the first 1000 sentences in NTCIR-8 development set, and then fetched both the NTCIR-9 and NTCIR-10 testing sets. The machine translation experiments pipelined Moses 3 (Koehn et al., 2007) with lexicalized reordering, SRILM 1.7.0 (Stolcke et al., 2011) in 6-gram order, MGIZA (Gao and Vogel, 2008), and RIBES (Isozaki et al., 2010a) and BLEU (Papineni et al., 2002) for evaluation. Binary constituent parsing in Japanese used Haruniwa (Fang et al., 2014), Berkeley parser 1.7 (Petrov and Klein, 2007), Comainu 0.7.0 (Kozawa et al., 2014), MeCab 0.996 (Kudo et al., 2004), and Unidic 2.1.2.

We explore two types of word alignment data for training our preordering model. The first data (*Giza*) is created by running an unsupervised aligner Giza (Och and Ney, 2003) on the training data (3 million sentences). The second data (*Nile*) is developed by training a supervised aligner Nile (Riesa et al., 2011) with manually annotated 8,000 sentences, then applied the trained alignment model to remaining training data. In the evaluation on manually annotated 1,000 sentences[4], Giza achieved F1 50.1 score, while Nile achieved F1 86.9 score, for word alignment task.

3.2 Result

Table 4 shows the performance of our method, which indicates that our preordering significantly improved translation accuracy in both RIBES and BLEU scores, from the baseline result attained by Moses without preordering. In particular, the preordering model trained with the Giza data revealed a substantial improvement, while the use of the Nile data further improves accuracy. This suggests that our method is particularly effective when high-accuracy word alignments are given. In addition, we achieved modest improvements even with *DL=0* (no distortion allowed), which indicates the monotonicity of our reordered sentences.

Table 5 shows a comparison of the proposed method with a rule-based preordering method (Hoshino et al., 2013) and two postordering methods (Goto et al., 2012; Hayashi et al., 2013).[5] One complication is that each work reports different baseline accuracy, although Moses is shared as a baseline, because these systems differ in various settings in data preprocessing, tokenization criteria, etc. Since this makes a fair comparison difficult, we additionally put a score difference (Δ) of each system from its own baseline.

Our proposed method showed translation accuracy comparable with, or superior to, state-of-the-art methods. This highlights the importance of Kendall's τ maximization in the simple discriminative preordering model. In contrast to a substantial gain in RIBES, we attained a rather comparable gain in BLEU. The investigation of our translation suggests that insufficient generation of English articles caused a significant degradation in the BLEU score. Previous systems listed in Table 5 incorporated article generation and demonstrated its positive effect (Goto et al., 2012; Hayashi et al., 2013). While we achieved state-of-the-art accuracy without language-specific techniques, it is also a promising direction to integrate our preordering method with language-specific techniques such as article generation and subject generation (Kudo et al., 2014).

[4]This testing data is excluded from latter experiments.

[5]We could not find a comparable report using tree-based machine translation systems apart from Moses-chart; nevertheless, Neubig and Duh (2014) reported that their forest-to-string system on the same corpus, which is unfortunately evaluated on the different testing data (test7), showed RIBES +6.19 (75.94) and BLEU +2.93 (33.70) improvements. Although not directly comparable, our method achieves a comparable or superior improvement.

4 Related Work

Li et al. (2007) proposed a simple discriminative preordering model as described in Section 2.1. They employed heuristics that utilize Giza to align their training sentences, then sort source words to resemble target word indices. After that, sorted source sentences without overlaps are used to train the model. They gained BLEU +1.54 improvement in Chinese-to-English evaluation. Our proposal follows their model, while we do not rely on their heuristics for preparing training data.

Lerner and Petrov (2013) proposed another discriminative preordering model along dependency trees, which classifies whether the parent of each node should be the head in target language. They reported BLEU +3.7 improvement in English-to-Japanese translation. Hoshino et al. (2013) proposed a similar but rule-based method for Japanese-to-English dependency preordering.

Yang et al. (2012) proposed a method to produce oracle reordering in the discriminative preordering model along dependency trees. Their idea behind is to minimize word alignment crossing recursively, which is essentially the same reordering objective as our Kendall's τ maximization. Since they targeted complex n-ary dependency instead of simple binary trees, their method only calculates approximated oracle reordering in practice by ranking principle. We did not take n-ary trees into consideration to follow the simple discriminative preordering model along constituency, while the use of binary trees enabled us to produce strict oracle reordering as a side effect.

Another research direction called postordering (Sudoh et al., 2011; Goto et al., 2012; Hayashi et al., 2013) has been explored in Japanese-to-English translation. They first translate Japanese input into head final English texts obtained by the method of Isozaki et al. (2010b), then reorder head final English texts into English word orders.

5 Conclusion

We proposed a simple procedure to train a discriminative preordering model. The main idea is to obtain oracle labels for each node by maximizing Kendall's τ of word alignments. Experiments in Japanese-to-English translation demonstrated that our procedure, without language-specific heuristics, achieved state-of-the-art translation accuracy.

Acknowledgments

We would like to thank Kevin Duh, Atsushi Fujita, Taku Kudo, Shinsuke Mori, Toshiaki Nakazawa, Graham Neubig, Hiroshi Noji, and anonymous reviewers for their insightful comments.

References

Alexandra Birch and Miles Osborne. 2010. LRscore for evaluating lexical and reordering quality in MT. In *Proceedings of the Joint Fifth Workshop on Statistical Machine Translation and MetricsMATR*, pages 327–332.

Michael Collins, Philipp Koehn, and Ivona Kucerova. 2005. Clause restructuring for statistical machine translation. In *Proceedings of the 43rd Annual Meeting of the Association for Computational Linguistics*, pages 531–540.

Tsaiwei Fang, Alastair Butler, and Kei Yoshimoto. 2014. Parsing Japanese with a PCFG treebank grammar. In *Proceedings of the Twentieth Meeting of the Association for Natural Language Processing*, pages 432–435.

Qin Gao and Stephan Vogel. 2008. Parallel implementations of word alignment tool. In *Software Engineering, Testing, and Quality Assurance for Natural Language Processing*, pages 49–57.

Isao Goto, Bin Lu, Ka Po Chow, Eiichiro Sumita, and Benjamin K. Tsou. 2011. Overview of the patent machine translation task at the NTCIR-9 workshop. In *Proceedings of the NTCIR-9 Workshop Meeting*, pages 559–578.

Isao Goto, Masao Utiyama, and Eiichiro Sumita. 2012. Post-ordering by parsing for Japanese-English statistical machine translation. In *Proceedings of the 50th Annual Meeting of the Association for Computational Linguistics*, pages 311–316.

Katsuhiko Hayashi, Katsuhito Sudoh, Hajime Tsukada, Jun Suzuki, and Masaaki Nagata. 2013. Shift-reduce word reordering for machine translation. In *Proceedings of the 2013 Conference on Empirical Methods in Natural Language Processing*, pages 1382–1386.

Sho Hoshino, Yusuke Miyao, Katsuhito Sudoh, and Masaaki Nagata. 2013. Two-stage pre-ordering for Japanese-to-English statistical machine translation. In *Proceedings of the Sixth International Joint Conference on Natural Language Processing*, pages 1062–1066.

Hideki Isozaki, Tsutomu Hirao, Kevin Duh, Katsuhito Sudoh, and Hajime Tsukada. 2010a. Automatic evaluation of translation quality for distant language pairs. In *Proceedings of the 2010 Conference on Empirical Methods in Natural Language Processing*, pages 944–952.

Hideki Isozaki, Katsuhito Sudoh, Hajime Tsukada, and Kevin Duh. 2010b. Head finalization: A simple reordering rule for SOV languages. In *Proceedings of the Joint Fifth Workshop on Statistical Machine Translation and MetricsMATR*, pages 244–251.

Philipp Koehn, Hieu Hoang, Alexandra Birch, Chris Callison-Burch, Marcello Federico, Nicola Bertoldi, Brooke Cowan, Wade Shen, Christine Moran, Richard Zens, Chris Dyer, Ondrej Bojar, Alexandra Constantin, and Evan Herbst. 2007. Moses: Open source toolkit for statistical machine translation. In *Proceedings of the 45th Annual Meeting of the Association for Computational Linguistics*, pages 177–180.

Philipp Koehn. 2004. Statistical significance tests for machine translation evaluation. In *Proceedings of the 2004 Conference on Empirical Methods in Natural Language Processing*, pages 388–395.

Shunsuke Kozawa, Kiyotaka Uchimoto, and Yasuharu Den. 2014. Adaptation of long-unit-word analysis system to different part-of-speech tagset (in Japanese). *Journal of Natural Language Processing*, 21(2):379–401.

Taku Kudo, Kaoru Yamamoto, and Yuji Matsumoto. 2004. Applying conditional random fields to japanese morphological analysis. In *Proceedings of the 2004 Conference on Empirical Methods in Natural Language Processing*, pages 230–237.

Taku Kudo, Hiroshi Ichikawa, and Hideto Kazawa. 2014. A joint inference of deep case analysis and zero subject generation for Japanese-to-English statistical machine translation. In *Proceedings of the 52nd Annual Meeting of the Association for Computational Linguistics*, pages 557–562.

Uri Lerner and Slav Petrov. 2013. Source-side classifier preordering for machine translation. In *Proceedings of the 2013 Conference on Empirical Methods in Natural Language Processing*, pages 513–523.

Chi-Ho Li, Minghui Li, Dongdong Zhang, Mu Li, Ming Zhou, and Yi Guan. 2007. A probabilistic approach to syntax-based reordering for statistical machine translation. In *Proceedings of the 45th Annual Meeting of the Association of Computational Linguistics*, pages 720–727.

Graham Neubig and Kevin Duh. 2014. On the elements of an accurate tree-to-string machine translation system. In *Proceedings of the 52nd Annual Meeting of the Association for Computational Linguistics*, pages 143–149.

Franz Josef Och and Hermann Ney. 2003. A systematic comparison of various statistical alignment models. *Computational Linguistics*, 29(1):19–51.

Kishore Papineni, Salim Roukos, Todd Ward, and Wei-Jing Zhu. 2002. BLEU: a method for automatic evaluation of machine translation. In *Proceedings of 40th Annual Meeting of the Association for Computational Linguistics*, pages 311–318.

Slav Petrov and Dan Klein. 2007. Improved inference for unlexicalized parsing. In *Human Language Technologies 2007: The Conference of the North American Chapter of the Association for Computational Linguistics; Proceedings of the Main Conference*, pages 404–411.

Jason Riesa, Ann Irvine, and Daniel Marcu. 2011. Feature-rich language-independent syntax-based alignment for statistical machine translation. In *Proceedings of the 2011 Conference on Empirical Methods in Natural Language Processing*, pages 497–507.

Andreas Stolcke, Jing Zheng, Wen Wang, and Victor Abrash. 2011. SRILM at sixteen: Update and outlook. In *Proceedings of the IEEE Automatic Speech Recognition and Understanding Workshop*.

Katsuhito Sudoh, Xianchao Wu, Kevin Duh, Hajime Tsukada, and Masaaki Nagata. 2011. Post-ordering in statistical machine translation. In *Proceedings of the Machine Translation Summit XIII*, pages 316–323.

David Talbot, Hideto Kazawa, Hiroshi Ichikawa, Jason Katz-Brown, Masakazu Seno, and Franz Och. 2011. A lightweight evaluation framework for machine translation reordering. In *Proceedings of the Sixth Workshop on Statistical Machine Translation*, pages 12–21.

Fei Xia and Michael McCord. 2004. Improving a statistical MT system with automatically learned rewrite patterns. In *Proceedings of the 20th International Conference on Computational Linguistics*, pages 508–514.

Nan Yang, Mu Li, Dongdong Zhang, and Nenghai Yu. 2012. A ranking-based approach to word reordering for statistical machine translation. In *Proceedings of the 50th Annual Meeting of the Association for Computational Linguistics*, pages 912–920.

Evaluating Machine Translation Systems with Second Language Proficiency Tests

Takuya Matsuzaki[†‡] **Akira Fujita**[‡] **Naoya Todo**[‡] **Noriko H. Arai**[‡]
[†]Dept. of Electrical Engineering and Computer Science, Nagoya University
matuzaki@nuee.nagoya-u.ac.jp
[‡]Information and Society Research Division, National Institute of Informatics
{a-fujita, ntodo, arai}@nii.ac.jp

Abstract

A lightweight, human-in-the-loop evaluation scheme for machine translation (MT) systems is proposed. It extrinsically evaluates MT systems using human subjects' scores on second language ability test problems that are machine-translated to the subjects' native language. A large-scale experiment involving 320 subjects revealed that the context-unawareness of the current MT systems severely damages human performance when solving the test problems, while one of the evaluated MT systems performed as good as a human translation produced in a context-unaware condition. An analysis of the experimental results showed that the extrinsic evaluation captured a different dimension of translation quality than that captured by manual and automatic intrinsic evaluation.

1 Introduction

Automatic evaluation metrics, such as the BLEU score (Papineni et al., 2002), were crucial ingredients for the advances of machine translation technology in the last decade. Meanwhile, the shortcomings of BLEU and similar n-gram proximity-based metrics have been pointed out by many authors including Callison-Burch et al. (2006). The main criticisms include: 1) unreliability in evaluating short translations, 2) non-interpretability of the scores beyond numerical comparison, and 3) bias towards statistical MT systems.

Manual evaluation of translation quality is more reliable in many regards, but it is costly. Furthermore, it is not necessarily easy to *analyze* the characteristics of MT systems based solely on the evaluation results such as a 5-point scale evaluation of adequacy/fluency and a ranking of the outputs of different systems.

A remedy for some of the above-raised issues is task-based evaluation of MT systems (Jones et al., 2005; Voss and Tate, 2006; Laoudi et al., 2006; Jones et al., 2007; Schneider et al., 2010; Berka et al., 2011), which measures the human performance in a task such as information extraction from a machine-translated text. The main burden of conducting task-based evaluation is also its cost; the development of a sizable amount of test materials and the gathering of appropriate human subjects is time consuming and expensive.

This paper proposes to utilize second-language proficiency tests (SLPTs), such as TOEIC, as the source of the specimens for extrinsic evaluation of MT systems. For evaluating, e.g., English-to-Japanese MT systems, a set of English test problems is translated by the systems and the translation qualities are evaluated by the test scores achieved by native Japanese speakers on the translated problems.

In many languages, a large collection of SLPT problems is available. More than 130 standardized tests for 32 languages are listed in the English Wikipedia page for 'List of language proficiency tests' as of April 30, 2015. They are carefully designed to evaluate various aspects of language ability with objective criteria. We can thus obtain an easy-to-use test set that focuses on a certain aspect of MT system performance by appropriately choosing the problem types and levels. Moreover, SLPTs are primarily designed to assess the test-takers' language ability but not their general intelligence. Hence, as evidenced later in the paper, the proposed scheme is expected to be robust against the heterogeneity of the subjects, as long as they are native speakers of the target language. This is a desirable property for conducting a large-scale experiment, possibly with crowdsourcing.

In the current paper, we utilize a typical format of multiple-choice dialogue completion problems (Figure 1). The subjects are given a machine-

Proceedings of the 53rd Annual Meeting of the Association for Computational Linguistics and the 7th International Joint Conference on Natural Language Processing (Short Papers), pages 145–149,
Beijing, China, July 26-31, 2015.

INSTRUCTION
Choose the most suitable utterance for the blank in the following dialogue from choices 1, 2, 3, and 4.
DIALOGUE
A: Hello. Can I help you? **B**: Yes. **[BLANK]** **A**: I'm sorry, I can't find that name on the reservation list. **B**: Oh, really? Then give me a new reservation, please.
OPTIONS
1. I'd like to make a reservation for Flight 502. 2. I have a reservation under the name Hashimoto. 3. I'm sure you can find my name on the list. 4. I wonder if you could tell me how to make a reservation.

Figure 1: Example of multiple-choice dialogue completion problem

translated conversation and asked to choose an appropriate utterance from several options, which are also machine-translated, to fill in a blank in the conversation.

We evaluated four translation methods in the experiment including both machine-translation and manual-translation. The extrinsic evaluation revealed that one of the MT systems is comparable to the human translation produced by randomly presenting the individual sentences to the translator without any context, but the translation produced by the best MT system is still far worse than that produced by a human translator working on the entire dialogue at once. Furthermore, we examined the relations between the extrinsic metric based on the subjects' scores and various intrinsic metrics including automatic scores such as the BLEU score and manual evaluation. The test material is available on request for research purposes.

2 Method

2.1 Overview of Experiment

We extrinsically evaluated four different translations of the same material, namely multiple-choice dialogue completion problems taken from second language ability tests. The original problems were in English, and we translated them into Japanese. Two of the translations were produced by MT systems, and the other two were produced by a human translator with and without considering the contexts of the individual sentences in the dialogues. The human subjects solved the translated problems without knowing whether a machine or a human produced them. Finally, the translation quality was evaluated based on the rate of correct answers given by the human subjects.

2.2 Participants

The subjects of the experiment included 320 Japanese junior high school students (12-15 years old) from two schools (schools A and B). The participants from school A consisted of 80 first-year students, 80 second-year students, and 78 third-year students. All the students from school B (82 students) were first-year students. Thus, the participants had varying levels of English and scholastic abilities. We will examine the effect of these factors on the experimental results later in the paper.

2.3 Materials

All the problems used in the experiment consisted of a short conversation between two people, where part of an utterance is hidden. The subject was presented with four options and asked to complete the dialogue with the most appropriate one.

We randomly extracted 40 English dialogue completion problems from mock National Center Test for University Admissions conducted by one of the largest preparatory schools in Japan. In the extracted problems, the number of utterances in one dialogue ranged from two to four, with each utterance consisting of one to three sentences, and an option including one or two sentences. All 40 problems contained 327 sentences.

2.4 Translation Systems

The English dialogue completion problems were translated by four methods: [1]

G: Automatic translation by Google Translate[2]

Y: Automatic translation by Yahoo Translate[3]

H_S: Human translation produced by providing individual sentences from the problems to a translator in random order

H_O: Human translation produced by a translator working on the entire dialogue at once

The subscripts of H_S and H_O stand for the translations of the sentences in "<u>s</u>huffled order" and "<u>o</u>riginal order", respectively. The translations by H_S were created by first preparing a file containing all the sentences from the 40 problems in a randomized order and then asking a translator to translate the file sentence-by-sentence, without assuming any specific context. H_S thus provides

[1] The two MT results were produced on June 11th, 2014.
[2] https://translate.google.co.jp/?hl=ja
[3] http://honyaku.yahoo.co.jp/

an estimate of the performance upper-bound of the current MT systems since most current systems translate each sentence individually.

We asked three native Japanese speakers who are fluent in English to first produce the sentence-by-sentence translations by method H_S and then translate all the dialogue problems in the normal way (i.e., by H_O). We randomly chose one of the translators and used his translations as the test material that the subjects solved. The other human translations were used as the reference translations for the automatic evaluation.

2.5 Procedure

Each subject was given 12 different problems that consisted of an equal number (3) of translated problems produced by the four translation methods. Although the sets of problems were different among the subjects, they were designed such that the number of subjects who solve each translated problem was roughly the same. Each subject was given 12 sheets of paper, each of which showed a problem and its answer choices, and was given one minute to complete each problem.

2.6 Extrinsic Evaluation Metric

The translation systems were evaluated by the average of the rate of correct answers made on the translated problems. Let $P = \{p_i\}$ be the set of original problems and $M(p)$ be the translation of problem p produced by method M. The correct answer rate (CAR) on $M(p)$ is defined as:

$$\mathrm{CAR}_M(p) = \frac{\text{\# of subjects that correctly answered } M(p)}{\text{\# of subjects who solved } M(p)}.$$

The extrinsic evaluation score of translation method M is the average of CAR over P:

$$\text{Avg-CAR}_M = \frac{1}{|P|}\sum_{p \in P} \mathrm{CAR}_M(p).$$

2.7 Intrinsic Evaluations

Automatic Evaluation Metrics We also evaluated the translation quality using BLEU, BLEU+1 (Lin and Och, 2004), RIBES (Isozaki et al., 2010), and TER (Snover et al., 2006). We prepared two sorts of reference translations: Ref_S and Ref_O. Ref_S consisted of two manual translations of the 40 problems produced by method H_S. Ref_O consisted of three manual translations produced in the normal way, i.e., by H_O.

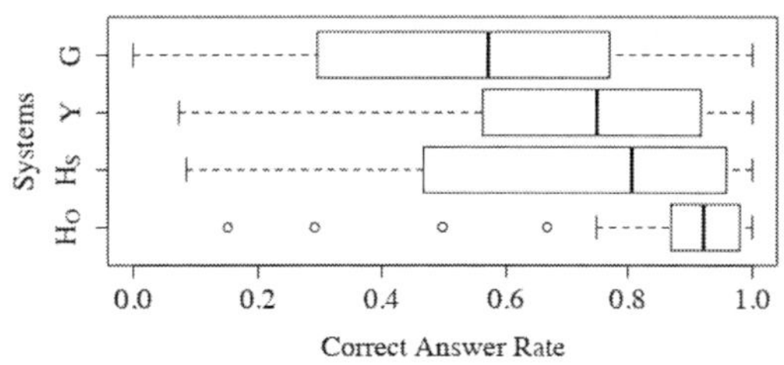

Figure 2: Boxplots of Correct Answer Rates for 40 Problems

Human Evaluation Five native Japanese speakers ranked the translations by the four systems for each of the 40 problems. They were shown the translations of a problem by the four methods with its source problem in English and asked to give a relative ranking among them, such as "$G < Y < H_S = H_O$." This method was adapted from the manual evaluation conducted in the recent WMT workshops (Callison-Burch et al., 2010). The relative ranking was broken down into six ($= {}_4C_2$) binary relations. For each relation "$A > B$" found in the broken-down relations, one point was added to system A. The final ranking among the systems for a problem was determined by the total points.

3 Results and Discussion

3.1 Preliminary Analysis: Robustness against the Heterogeneity of the Human Subjects

We divided the participants from school A into three groups according to grade level, and then examined the differences in the rate of correct answers for each problem among each group. We also compared the correct answer rates between the participants in the 1st grade at schools A and B. The two-way analysis of variance (ANOVA) revealed that the grades and schools had no significant effect on the correct answer rate for 38 out of the 40 problems ($p > 0.05$). The results showed that the participants' grade levels and scholastic abilities (including English ability) did not affect the test results.

3.2 System-level Evaluation

We first present the system-level evaluation results for the four translation methods. Figure 2 shows the min/max and the quartiles of the correct answer rates (CARs) for the 40 problems translated by each system. The averages of the correct answer rates are 0.524, 0.696, 0.693, and 0.875 for each translation system G, Y, H_S, and H_O, re-

Reference	Metrics	G	Y	H_S	H_O
Ref$_O$	BLEU	22.04	20.33	40.30	47.43
	BLEU+1	22.08	20.37	40.33	47.46
	RIBES	67.80	69.43	78.16	82.42
	TER	41.72	43.66	27.47	24.14
Ref$_S$	BLEU	27.53	23.63	41.24	30.69
	BLEU+1	27.56	23.67	41.27	30.73
	RIBES	73.61	73.63	80.18	70.59
	TER	36.51	39.52	27.60	31.51
Avg-CAR		0.524	0.696	0.693	0.875

Table 1: Automatic Evaluation Scores and Average Correct Answer Rate

spectively. We conducted a pairwise t-test on each adjacent set (G-Y, Y-H_S, and H_S-H_O) for the CARs and found a statistically significant difference ($p < 0.05$) between G and Y and H_S and H_O but not between Y and H_S ($p = 0.954$).

Table 1 lists the five automatic evaluation scores for each translation method measured against the two reference translation sets. The averages of the CARs over the 40 problems are also listed in the bottom row of the table. There are several noticeable facts. First, despite the significantly better average CAR for Y over G, BLEU, BLEU+1, and TER prefer G to Y. Second, while the average CARs for Y and H_S are almost equal, there are large differences between their automatic evaluation scores across all metrics. Third, a comparison of the corresponding automatic evaluation scores using Ref$_S$ and Ref$_O$ reveals that G, Y, and H_S are more similar to the manual translations that were produced without referring to the contexts of the individual sentences than those produced taking the contexts into consideration. This is not surprising. However, the large difference in the correct answer rates for H_S and H_O suggests that ignorance of the context in the current MT systems severely degrades the comprehensibility of the translations of texts like daily conversations.

3.3 Agreement between Intrinsic and Extrinsic Evaluation Metrics

We examined how often an intrinsic metric correctly predicts the difference of the subjects' test performance on a problem. Specifically, for two translation methods A and B, we say an intrinsic metric M agrees with the CAR by the subjects on problem p_i iff metric M scores A's translation of p_i (= $A(p_i)$) better than B's translation (= $B(p_i)$) and the CAR is higher on $A(p_i)$ than on $B(p_i)$. The rate of agreements is the fraction of the problems on which M and CAR agree. The agreement

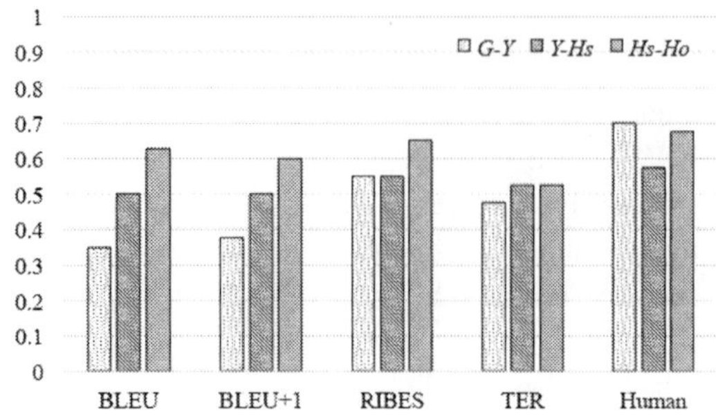

Figure 3: Agreement Rates between Intrinsic Evaluation Metrics and Correct Answer Rate

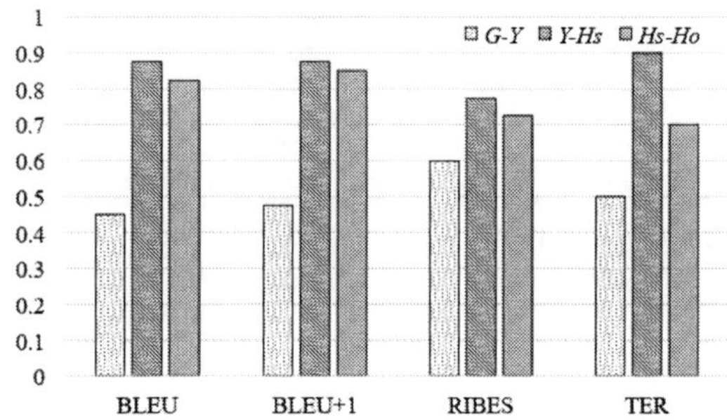

Figure 4: Agreement Rates between Automatic Evaluation Metrics and Human Evaluation

between two intrinsic metrics is defined similarly.

Figure 3 shows the rates of agreements between the automatic metrics and CARs and between the human evaluation and CARs. As Figure 3 shows, all the agreement rates between the automatic metrics and CARs were less than 0.65. When considering a random baseline of 0.5, we may conclude that the automatic metrics are not very good predictors of the CARs. This is unfortunate since the CARs directly indicate the comprehensibility of the translated dialogues. The disagreements cannot be attributed only to the unreliability of automatic metrics on short translations. Figure 4 shows the rate of agreements between the automatic metrics and the human evaluation. As Figure 4 shows, BLEU, BLEU+1, and TER agree with human evaluation on nearly 90% of the problems when comparing Y and H_S.

The human evaluation agrees with the CAR slightly better than the automatic metrics. However, the agreement rates are still less than 0.7 for all pairs of compared systems. These findings suggest that there is an inherent discrepancy between the assessment of the overall translation quality of a problem and the CAR. It is presumably because the CAR can be critically damaged by a subtle translation mistake that spoils a coherent understanding of a dialogue.

4 Conclusion and Future Work

We have presented the results of an experiment, in which machine- and human-translated second language proficiency test (SLPT) problems were used for extrinsic evaluation of the translation quality. Comparison of four translation methods revealed, most notably, the crucial importance of considering contexts of individual sentences in translating dialogues. The analysis on the experimental results suggests that the extrinsic evaluation based on SLPT problems captures a different dimension of translation quality than the manual/automatic intrinsic metrics. The robustness against the heterogeneity of human subjects and the abundance of existing SLPT problems enable easy adaption of the proposed evaluation scheme in addition to the traditional intrinsic evaluations. Our future work includes experiments with other types of SLPT problems that focus on different aspects of translation quality and language understanding.

Acknowledgments

The authors are grateful to all the participants in the experiments for their time and patience and also grateful to Yoyogi Seminar for their allowance to use their problems in the experiments. This study is conducted as a part of the Todai Robot Project (`http://21robot.org/?lang=english`).

References

Jan Berka, Martin Černý, and Ondřej Bojar. 2011. Quiz-based evaluation of machine translation. *The Prague Bulletin of Mathematical Linguistics*, 95:77–86.

Chris Callison-Burch, Miles Osborne, and Philipp Koehn. 2006. Re-evaluation the role of bleu in machine translation research. In *11th Conference of the European Chapter of the Association for Computational Linguistics (EACL-2006)*, pages 249–256.

Chris Callison-Burch, Philipp Koehn, Christof Monz, Kay Peterson, Mark Przybocki, and Omar F. Zaidan. 2010. Findings of the 2010 joint workshop on statistical machine translation and metrics for machine translation. In *Proceedings of the Joint 5th Workshop on Statistical Machine Translation and MetricsMATR*, pages 17–53.

Hideki Isozaki, Tsutomu Hirao, Kevin Duh, Katsuhito Sudoh, and Hajime Tsukada. 2010. Automatic evaluation of translation quality for distant language pairs. In *Proceedings of the 2010 Conference on Empirical Methods in Natural Language Processing (EMNLP-2010)*, pages 944–952.

Douglas Jones, Wade Shen, Neil Granoien, Martha Herzog, and Clifford Weinstein. 2005. Measuring translation quality by testing english speakers with a new defense language proficiency test for arabic. In *Proceedings of the 2005 International Conference on Intelligence Analysis*.

Douglas Jones, Martha Herzog, Hussny Ibrahim, Arvind Jairam, Wade Shen, Edward Gibson, and Michael Emonts. 2007. Ilr-based mt comprehension test with multi-level questions. In *Human Language Technologies 2007: The Conference of the North American Chapter of the Association for Computational Linguistics (HLT-NAACL 2007); Companion Volume, Short Papers*, pages 77–80.

Jamal Laoudi, Calandra R. Tate, and Clare R. Voss. 2006. Task-based mt evaluation: From who/when/where extraction to event understanding. In *Proceedings of the Fifth International Conference on Language Resources and Evaluation (LREC-2006)*, pages 2048–2053.

Chin-Yew Lin and Franz Josef Och. 2004. Orange: A method for evaluating automatic evaluation metrics for machine translation. In *Proceedings of the 20th International Conference on Computational Linguistics (COLING-2004)*, pages 501–507.

Kishore Papineni, Salim Roukos, Todd Ward, and Wei-Jing Zhu. 2002. Bleu: A method for automatic evaluation of machine translation. In *Proceedings of the 40th Annual Meeting of the Association for Computational Linguistics (ACL-2002)*, pages 311–318.

Anne H. Schneider, Ielka van der Sluis, and Saturnino Luz. 2010. Comparing intrinsic and extrinsic evaluation of mt output in a dialogue system. In *Proceedings of the International Workshop on Spoken Language Translation (IWSLT-2010)*, pages 329–336.

Matthew Snover, Bonnie Dorr, Richard Schwaltz, Linnea Micciulla, and John Makhoul. 2006. A study of translation edit rate with targeted human annotation. In *Proceedings of Association for Machine Translation in the Americas (AMTA-2006)*, pages 223–231.

Clare R. Voss and Calandra R. Tate. 2006. Task-based evaluation of machine translation (mt) engines: Measuring how well people extract who, when, where-type elements in mt output. In *In Proceedings of 11th Annual Conference of the European Association for Machine Translation (EAMT-2006)*, pages 203–212.

Representation Based Translation Evaluation Metrics

Boxing Chen and Hongyu Guo
National Research Council Canada
first.last@nrc-cnrc.gc.ca

Abstract

Precisely evaluating the quality of a translation against human references is a challenging task due to the flexible word ordering of a sentence and the existence of a large number of synonyms for words. This paper proposes to evaluate translations with distributed representations of words and sentences. We study several metrics based on word and sentence representations and their combination. Experiments on the WMT metric task shows that the metric based on the combined representations achieves the best performance, outperforming the state-of-the-art translation metrics by a large margin. In particular, training the distributed representations only needs a reasonable amount of monolingual, unlabeled data that is not necessary drawn from the test domain.

1 Introduction

Automatic machine translation (MT) evaluation metrics measure the quality of the translations against human references. They allow rapid comparisons between different systems and enable the tuning of parameter values during system training. Many machine translation metrics have been proposed in recent years, such as BLEU (Papineni et al., 2002), NIST (Doddington, 2002), TER (Snover et al., 2006), Meteor (Banerjee and Lavie, 2005) and its extensions, and the MEANT family (Lo and Wu, 2011), amongst others.

Precisely evaluating translation, however, is not easy. This is mainly caused by the flexible word ordering and the existence of the large number of synonyms for words. One straightforward solution to improve the evaluation quality is to increase the number of various references. Nevertheless, it is expensive to create multiple references. In order to catch synonym matches between the translations and references, synonym dictionaries or paraphrasing tables have been used. For example, Meteor (Banerjee and Lavie, 2005) uses WordNet (Miller, 1995); TER-Plus (Snover et al., 2009) and Meteor Universal (Denkowski and Lavie, 2014) deploy paraphrasing tables. These dictionaries have helped to improve the accuracy of the evaluation; however, not all languages have synonym dictionaries or paraphrasing tables, especially for those low resource languages.

This paper leverages recent developments on distributed representations to address the above mentioned two challenges. A distributed representation maps each word or sentence to a continuous, low dimensional space, where words or sentences having similar syntactic and semantic properties are close to one another (Bengio et al., 2003; Socher et al., 2011; Socher et al., 2013; Mikolov et al., 2013). For example, the words *vacation* and *holiday* are close to each other in the vector space, but both are far from the word *business* in that space.

We propose to evaluate the translations with different word and sentence representations. Specifically, we investigate the use of three widely deployed representations: one-hot representations, distributed word representations learned from a neural network model, and distributed sentence representations computed with recursive autoencoder. In particular, to leverage the different advantages and focuses, in terms of benefiting evaluation, of various representations, we concatenate the three representations to form one vector representation for each sentence. Our experiments on the WMT metric task show that the metric based on the concatenated representation outperforms several state-of-the-art machine translation metrics, by a large margin on both segment and system-level. Furthermore, our results also indicate that the representation based metrics are robust to a variety of training conditions, such as the data volume and domain.

Proceedings of the 53rd Annual Meeting of the Association for Computational Linguistics and the 7th International Joint Conference on Natural Language Processing (Short Papers), pages 150–155,
Beijing, China, July 26-31, 2015.

2 Representations

A representation, in the context of NLP, is a mathematical object associated with each word, sentence, or document. This object is typically a vector where each element's value describes, to some degree, the semantic or syntactic properties of the associated word, sentence, or document. Using word or phrase representations as extra features has been proven to be an effective and simple way to improve the predictive performance of an NLP system (Turian et al., 2010; Cherry and Guo, 2015). Our evaluation metrics are based on three widely used representations, as discussed next.

2.1 One-hot Representations

Conventionally, a word is represented by a one-hot vector. In a one-hot representation, a vocabulary is first defined, and then each word in the vocabulary is assigned a symbolic ID. In this scenario, for each word, the feature vector has the same length as the size of the vocabulary, and only one dimension that corresponds to the word is on, such as a vector with one element set to 1 and all others set to 0. This feature representation has been traditionally used for many NLP systems. On the other hand, recent years have witnessed that simply plugging in distributed word vectors as real-valued features is an effective way to improve a NLP system (Turian et al., 2010).

2.2 Distributed Word Representations

Distributed word representations, also called word embeddings, map each word deterministically to a real-valued, dense vector (Bengio et al., 2003). A widely used approach for generating useful word vectors is developed by (Mikolov et al., 2013). This method scales very well to very large training corpora. Their skip-gram model, which we adopt here, learns word vectors that are good at predicting the words in a context window surrounding it. A very promising perspective of such distributed representation is that words that have similar contexts, and therefore similar syntactic and semantic properties, will tend to be near one another in the low-dimensional vector space.

2.3 Sentence Vector Representations

Word level representation often cannot properly capture more complex linguistic phenomena in a sentence or multi-word phrase. Therefore, we adopt an effective and efficient method for multi-word phrase distributed representation, namely the greedy unsupervised recursive auto-encoder strategy (RAE) (Socher et al., 2011). This method works under an unsupervised setting. In particular, it does not rely on a parsing tree structure in order to generate sentence level vectors. This characteristic makes it very desirable for applying it to the outputs of machine translation systems. This is because the outputs of translation systems are often not syntactically correct sentences; parsing them is possible to introduce unexpected noise.

For a given sentence, the greedy unsupervised RAE greedily searches a pair of words that results in minimal reconstruction error by an auto-encoder. The corresponding hidden vector of the auto-encoder (denoted as the two children's parent vector), which has the same size as that of the two child vectors, is then used to replace the two children vectors. This process repeats and treats the new parent vector like any other word vectors. In such a recursive manner, the parent vector generated from the word pool with only two vectors left will be used as the vector representation for the whole sentence. Interested readers are referred to (Socher et al., 2011) for detailed discussions of the strategy.

2.4 Combined Representations

Each of the above mentioned representations has a different strength in terms of encoding syntactic and semantic contextual information for a given sentence. Specifically, the one-hot representation is able to reflect the particular words that occur in the sentence. The word embeddings can recognize synonyms of words appearing in the sentence, through the co-occurrence information encoded in the vector's representation. Finally, the RAE vector can encode the composed semantic information of the given sentence. These observations suggest that it is beneficial to take various types of representations into account.

The most straightforward way to integrate multiple vectors is using concatenation. In our studies here, we first compute the sentence-level one-hot, word embedding, and RAE representations. Next, we concatenate the three sentence-level representations to form one vector for each sentence.

3 Representations Based Metrics

Our translation evaluation metrics are built on the four representations as discussed in Section 2.

Consider we have the sentence representations for the translations (t) and references (r), the translation quality is measured with a similarity score computed with Cosine function and a length penalty. Suppose the size of the vector is N, we calculate the quality as follows.

$$\text{Score}(t, r) = \text{Cos}^{\alpha}(t, r) \times P_{len} \quad (1)$$

$$\text{Cos}(t, r) = \frac{\sum_{i=1}^{i=N} v_i(t) \cdot v_i(r)}{\sqrt{\sum_{i=1}^{i=N} v_i^2(t)} \sqrt{\sum_{i=1}^{i=N} v_i^2(r)}} \quad (2)$$

$$P_{len} = \begin{cases} exp(1 - l_r/l_t) & \text{if } (l_t < l_r) \\ exp(1 - l_t/l_r) & \text{if } (l_t \geq l_r) \end{cases} \quad (3)$$

where α is a free parameter, $v_i(.)$ is the value of the vector element, P_{len} is the length penalty, and l_r, l_t are length of the translation and reference, respectively.

In the scenarios of there exist multiple references, we compute the score with each reference, then choose the highest one. Also, we treat the document-level score as the weighted average of sentence-level scores, with the weights being the reference lengths, as follows.

$$\text{Score}_d = \frac{\sum_{i=1}^{D} \text{len}(r_i)\text{Score}_i}{\sum_{i=1}^{D} \text{len}(r_i)} \quad (4)$$

where Score_i denotes the score of sentence i, and D is the size of the document in sentences. With these score equations, we then can formulate our five presentations based metrics as follows.

For the one-hot representation metric, once we have the representations of the words and n-grams, we sum all the vectors to obtain the representation of the sentence. For efficiency, we only keep the entries which are not both zero in the reference and translation vectors. After we generate the two vectors for both translation and reference, we then compute the score using Equation 1.

For the word embedding based metric, we first learn the word vector representation using the code provided by (Mikolov et al., 2013) [1]. Next, following (Zou et al., 2013), we average the word embeddings of all words in the sentence to obtain the representation of the sentence.

As discussed in Section 2.4, the three sentence-level one-hot, word embedding and RAE representations have different strength when they are used to compare two sentences. In our metric here, each of the three vectors is first scaled with a particular weight (learned on dev data) and then the vectors are concatenated. With these concatenation vectors, we then calculate the similarity score using Equation 1.

For comparison, we also combine the strength of the three representations using weighted average of the three metrics computed. Weights are tuned using development data.

4 Experiments

We conducted experiments on the WMT metric task data. Development sets include WMT 2011 all-to-English, and English-to-all submissions. Test sets contain WMT 2012, and WMT 2013 all-to-English, plus 2012, 2013 English-to-all submissions. The languages "all" include French, Spanish, German and Czech. For training the word embedding and recursive auto-encoder model, we used WMT 2013 training data [2].

We compared our metrics with smoothed BLEU (mteval-v13a), TER [3], Meteor v1.0 [4], and Meteor Universal (i.e. v1.5) [5]. We used the default settings for all these four metrics.

When considering the representation based metrics, we tuned all the parameters to maximize the system-level γ score for all representation based metrics on the dev sets. We tuned the weights for combining the three vectors automatically, using the downhill simplex method as described in (Press et al., 2002). The weights are 1 for the RAE vector, about 0.1 for the word embedding vector, and around 0.01 for the one-hot vector, respectively. We tuned other parameters manually. Specifically, we set n equal to 2 for the one-hot n-gram representation, the vector size of the recursive auto-encoder to 10, and the vector size of word embeddings to 80.

Following WMT 2013's metric task (Macháček and Bojar, 2013), to measure the correlation with human judgment, we use Kendall's rank correlation coefficient τ for the segment level, and Pearson's correlation coefficient (γ in the below tables and figures) for the system-level respectively.

[1] https://code.google.com/p/word2vec/

[2] http://www.statmt.org/wmt13/translation-task.html

[3] http://www.cs.umd.edu/ snover/tercom/

[4] http://www.cs.cmu.edu/ alavie/METEOR/

[5] Meteor universal package does not include paraphrasing table for other target language except English, so we did not run Out-of-English experiments for this metric.

	Into-Eng		Out-of-Eng	
metric	seg τ	sys γ	seg τ	sys γ
BLEU	0.220	0.751	0.179	0.736
TER	0.211	0.742	0.175	0.745
Meteor	0.228	0.824	0.180	0.778
Met. Uni.	0.249	0.808	–	–
One-hot	0.235	0.795	0.183	0.773
Word emb.	0.212	0.818	0.175	0.788
RAE vec.	0.203	0.856	0.171	0.780
Comb. rep.	**0.259**	**0.874**	**0.191**	**0.832**
Wghted avg.	0.247	0.863	0.185	0.798

Table 1: Correlations with human judgment on WMT data for Into-English and Out-of-English task. Results are averaged on all test sets.

4.1 General Performance

We first report the main experimental results conducted on the Into-English and Out-of-English tasks. Results in Tables 1 suggest that metrics based on three single representations all obtained comparable or better performance than BLEU, TER and Meteor. In particular, the metric based on recursive auto-encoder outperformed the other testing metrics on system-level. When combining the strengths of the three representations, our experimental results show that the metric based on the combined representation outperformed all state-of-the-art metrics by a large margin on both segment- and system-level.

Regarding the evaluation speed of the representation metrics, it took around 1 minute to score about 2000 sentences with the above settings on a machine with a 2.33GHz Intel CPU. It is worth noting that if we increase the vector size of the RAE model and word embeddings, longer execution time is expected for the scoring processes.

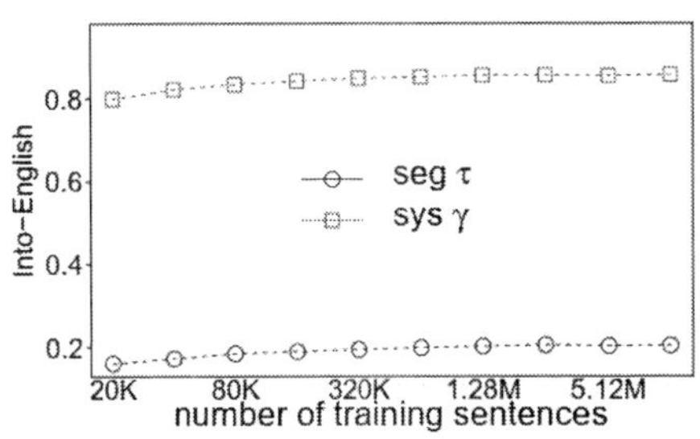

Figure 1: Correlations with human judgment on WMT data for Into-English task for combined representation based metric when increasing the size of the training data.

4.2 Effect of the Training Data Size

In our second experiment, we measure the performance on the Into-English task and increase the training data from 20K sentences to 11 million sentences. The sentences are randomly selected from the whole training data, which include the English side of WMT 2013 French-to-English parallel data ("Europarl v7", "News Commentary" and "UN Corpus"). The results are reported in Figure 1. From this figure, one can conclude that the performance improves with the increasing of the training data, however, when more than 1.28M sentences are used, the performance stabilizes. This result indicates that training a stable and good model for our metric does not need a huge amount of training data.

4.3 Sensitivity to Data Across Domains

The last experiment aimed at the following question: should the test domain be consistent with the training domain? In this experiment, we sampled three training sets from different domain data sets in equal number (136K) of sentences: Europarl (EP), News Commentary (NC), and United Nation proceedings (UN), while the test domain remains the same, i.e., the news domain. The metric trained on NC domain data achieved slightly higher segment-level τ score (0.181 vs 0.178 for EP, 0.176 for UN) and system-level Pearson's correlation score γ (0.821 vs 0.820 for EP, 0.817 for UN). Nevertheless, the results are consistent across domains. This is explainable: although the same test sentence may have different representations w.r.t. the training domain, the distance between the translation and its reference may stay consistent. Practically, the training and test data not necessary being in the same domain is a very attractive characteristic for the translation metrics. It means that we do not have to train the word embeddings and RAE model for each testing domain.

4.4 Cope with Word Ordering and Synonym

In order to better understand why metrics based on combined representations can achieve better correlation with human judgment than other metrics, we select, in Table 2, some interesting examples for further analysis.

Consider, for instance, the first reference (denoted as "1 R" in Table 2) and their translations. If we replace the word *vacation* in the reference with words *business* and *holiday*, respectively, then we

id	sentence	BLEU	rep.
1 R	i had a wonderful vacation in italy	–	–
1 H1	i had a wonderful business in italy	0.489	0.555
1 H2	i had a wonderful holiday in italy	0.489	0.865
1 H3	in italy i had a wonderful vacation	0.707	0.804
1 H4	vacation in i had a wonderful italy	0.508	0.305
2 R	but the decision was not his to make	–	–
2 H1	but it is not up to him to decide	0.063	0.652
2 H2	but the decision not him to take	0.241	0.620
2 H3	but the decision was not the to make	0.595	0.612
3 R	they were set to go on trial in jan	–	–
3 H1	they should appear in court in jan	0.109	0.498
3 H2	the trial was scheduled in jan	0.109	0.454
3 H3	the procedures were prepared in jan	0.109	0.445

Table 2: Examples evaluated with smoothed BLEU and combined representation based metric. Examples 2-3 are picked up from the real test sets; human judgment ranks H1 better than H2, and H2 better than H3 for each of these example sentences. The combined representation based metric better matches human judgment than BLEU does.

have hypothesis 1 and hypothesis 2, denoted as "1 H1" and "1 H2", respectively, in Table 2 . In this scenario, the metric BLEU assigns the same score of 0.489 for these two translations. In contrast, the representation based metric associates hypothesis 2 with a much higher score than that of hypothesis 1, namely 0.865 and 0.555, respectively. In other words, the score for hypothesis 2 is close to one, suggesting that the RAE based metric considers this translation is almost identical to the reference. The reason here is that the vector representations for the two words are very near to one another in the vector space. Consequently, the representation based metric treats the *holiday* as a synonym of *vacation*, which matches human's judgment perfectly.

Let us continue with this example. Suppose, in hypothesis 3, we reorder the phrase *in italy*. The representation based metric still considers this to be a good translation with respect to the reference, thus associating a very close score as that of the reference, namely 0.804. The reason for representation metric's correct judgment is that H3 and the reference, in the vector space, embed very similar semantic knowledge, although they have different word orderings. Now let us take this example a bit further. We randomly mess up the words in the reference, resulting in hypothesis 4 (denoted as "1 H4" as shown in Table 2). In such scenario, the representation metric score drops sharply because the syntactic and semantic information embedded in the vector space is very different from the reference. Interestingly, the BLEU metric still consider this translation is not a very bad translation.

We made up the first example sentence for illustrative purpose, however, the examples 2-3 are picked up from the real test sets. According to the human judgment, hypothesis 1 (H1) is better than hypothesis 2 (H2); hypothesis 2 is better than hypothesis 3 (H3) for each of these example sentences. These results indicate that the combined representation based metric better matches the human judgment than BLEU does.

5 Conclusion

We studied a series of translation evaluation metrics based on three widely used representations. Experiments on the WMT metric task indicate that the representation metrics obtain better correlations with human judgment on both system-level and segment-level, compared to popular translation evaluation metrics such as BLEU, Meteor, Meteor Universal, and TER. Also, the representation-based metrics use only monolingual, unlabeled data for training; such data are easy to obtain. Furthermore, the proposed metrics are robust to various training conditions, such as the data size and domain.

Acknowledgements

The authors would like to thank Colin Cherry and Roland Kuhn for useful discussions.

References

Satanjeev Banerjee and Alon Lavie. 2005. METEOR: An automatic metric for MT evaluation with improved correlation with human judgments. In *Proceedings of the ACL Workshop on Intrinsic and Extrinsic Evaluation Measures for Machine Translation and/or Summarization*, pages 65–72, Ann Arbor, Michigan, June. Association for Computational Linguistics.

Yoshua Bengio, Réjean Ducharme, Pascal Vincent, and Christian Janvin. 2003. A neural probabilistic language model. *J. Mach. Learn. Res.*, 3:1137–1155, March.

Colin Cherry and Hongyu Guo. 2015. The unreasonable effectiveness of word representations for twitter named entity recognition. In *Proceedings of the 2012 Conference of the North American Chapter of the Association for Computational Linguistics: Human Language Technologies*.

Michael Denkowski and Alon Lavie. 2014. Meteor universal: Language specific translation evaluation for any target language. In *Proceedings of the Ninth Workshop on Statistical Machine Translation*, pages 376–380, Baltimore, Maryland, USA, June. Association for Computational Linguistics.

G. Doddington. 2002. Authomatic evaluation of machine translation quality using n-gram cooccurrence statistics. In *Proceedings of the Human Language Technology Conference*, page 128132, San Diego, CA.

Chi-kiu Lo and Dekai Wu. 2011. Meant: An inexpensive, high-accuracy, semi-automatic metric for evaluating translation utility based on semantic roles. In *Proceedings of the 49th Annual Meeting of the Association for Computational Linguistics: Human Language Technologies*, pages 220–229, Portland, Oregon, USA, June. Association for Computational Linguistics.

Matouš Macháček and Ondřej Bojar. 2013. Results of the WMT13 metrics shared task. In *Proceedings of the Eighth Workshop on Statistical Machine Translation*, pages 45–51, Sofia, Bulgaria, August. Association for Computational Linguistics.

Tomas Mikolov, Ilya Sutskever, Kai Chen, Gregory S. Corrado, and Jeffrey Dean. 2013. Distributed representations of words and phrases and their compositionality. In *Advances in Neural Information Processing Systems 26: 27th Annual Conference on Neural Information Processing Systems 2013. Proceedings of a meeting held December 5-8, 2013, Lake Tahoe, Nevada, United States.*, pages 3111–3119.

George A. Miller. 1995. Wordnet: A lexical database for english. *Comunications of the ACM*, 38:39–41.

Kishore Papineni, Salim Roukos, Todd Ward, and Wei-Jing Zhu. 2002. BLEU: A method for automatic evaluation of Machine Translation. In *Proceedings of the 40th Annual Meeting of the Association for Computational Linguistics (ACL)*, pages 311–318, Philadelphia, July. ACL.

W. Press, S. Teukolsky, W. Vetterling, and B. Flannery. 2002. *Numerical Recipes in C++*. Cambridge University Press, Cambridge, UK.

Matthew Snover, Bonnie Dorr, Richard Schwartz, Linnea Micciulla, and John Makhoul. 2006. A study of translation edit rate with targeted human annotation. In *Proceedings of Association for Machine Translation in the Americas*.

Matthew G. Snover, Nitin Madnani, Bonnie Dorr, and Richard Schwartz. 2009. Ter-plus: Paraphrase, semantic, and alignment enhancements to translation edit rate. In *Machine Translation*, volume 23, pages 117–127.

Richard Socher, Jeffrey Pennington, Eric H. Huang, Andrew Y. Ng, and Christopher D. Manning. 2011. Semi-supervised recursive autoencoders for predicting sentiment distributions. In *Proceedings of the Conference on Empirical Methods in Natural Language Processing*, EMNLP '11, pages 151–161, Stroudsburg, PA, USA. Association for Computational Linguistics.

Richard Socher, Alex Perelygin, Jean Y Wu, Jason Chuang, Christopher D Manning, Andrew Y Ng, and Christopher Potts Potts. 2013. Recursive deep models for semantic compositionality over a sentiment treebank. In *EMNLP*.

J. Turian, L. Ratinov, and Y. Bengio. 2010. Word representations: A simple and general method for semi-supervised learning. In *ACL*, pages 384–394.

Will Y. Zou, Richard Socher, Daniel Cer, and Christopher D. Manning. 2013. Bilingual word embeddings for phrase-based machine translation. In *Proceedings of the 2013 Conference on Empirical Methods in Natural Language Processing*, pages 1393–1398, Seattle, Washington, USA, October. Association for Computational Linguistics.

Exploring the Planet of the APEs: a Comparative Study of State-of-the-art Methods for MT Automatic Post-Editing

Rajen Chatterjee[1,2], **Marion Weller**[3], **Matteo Negri**[2], **Marco Turchi**[2]
[1] University of Trento
[2] FBK - Fondazione Bruno Kessler
[3] IMS, University of Stuttgart
{chatterjee,negri,turchi}@fbk.eu
{wellermn@ims.uni-stuttgart.de}

Abstract

Downstream processing of machine translation (MT) output promises to be a solution to improve translation quality, especially when the MT system's internal decoding process is not accessible. Both rule-based and statistical automatic post-editing (APE) methods have been proposed over the years, but with contrasting results. A missing aspect in previous evaluations is the assessment of different methods: *i)* under comparable conditions, and *ii)* on different language pairs featuring variable levels of MT quality. Focusing on statistical APE methods (more portable across languages), we propose the first systematic analysis of two approaches. To understand their potential, we compare them in the same conditions over six language pairs having English as source. Our results evidence consistent improvements on all language pairs, a relation between the extent of the gain and MT output quality, slight but statistically significant performance differences between the two methods, and their possible complementarity.

1 Introduction

Automatic post-editing (APE) aims to correct systematic machine translation (MT) errors. The problem is appealing for several reasons. On one side, as pointed out by Parton et al. (2012), APE systems can improve MT output by exploiting information unavailable to the decoder, or by performing deeper text analysis that is too expensive at decoding stage. On the other side, and to our view more importantly, APE represents the only way to recover errors produced in "black-box" conditions in which the MT system is unknown or its internal decoding process is not accessible.

The task, firstly proposed by Knight and Chander (1994) to cope with article selection in Japanese to English translation, has been later addressed in various ways. On one side, rule-based methods (Rosa et al., 2012) gained limited attention, probably due to the extensive manual work they involve and their scarce portability across languages. On the other side, the statistical approach proposed by Allen and Hogan (2000) reached maturity in the work by Simard et al. (2007) and inspired a number of further investigations (Isabelle et al., 2007; Dugast et al., 2007; Dugast et al., 2009; Lagarda et al., 2009; Béchara et al., 2011; Béchara et al., 2012; Rubino et al., 2012; Rosa et al., 2013; Lagarda et al., 2014, inter alia).

Such prior works address orthogonal aspects like: *i)* performance variations when APE is applied to correct the output of *rule-based vs. statistical MT*, *ii)* the use of APE for *error correction vs. domain adaptation*, *iii)* the difference between training on *general domain vs. domain-specific data*, *iv)* performance variations when learning from *reference translations vs. human post-edits*. Their common trait is that the reported results are difficult to generalise. Indeed, most of the works focus on evaluating a specific method,[1] which is typically applied to one single dataset for a given language pair. As a result, the global landscape of the "planet of the APEs" is still blurred and open to more systematic explorations.

To shed light on the potential of statistical post-editing, in this paper we examine two alternative approaches. One is the method proposed in (Simard et al., 2007), which to date is the most widely used. The other is the "context-aware" solution proposed in (Béchara et al., 2011) which, to the best of our knowledge, represents the most significant variant of (Simard et al., 2007).

The major contribution of our work is the first systematic analysis of different APE approaches,

[1] Typically the same of (Simard et al., 2007).

Proceedings of the 53rd Annual Meeting of the Association for Computational Linguistics and the 7th International Joint Conference on Natural Language Processing (Short Papers), pages 156–161,
Beijing, China, July 26-31, 2015.

which are tested in controlled conditions over several language pairs. To ensure the soundness of the analysis, our experimental setup consists of a dataset composed of the same English source sentences with automatic translations into six languages and respective manual post-edits by professional translators. Overall, this represents the ideal condition to complement prior research with the missing answers to questions like:

Q1: *Does APE yield consistent MT quality improvements across different language pairs?*

Q2: *What is the relation between the original MT output quality and the APE results?*

Q3: *Which of the two analysed APE methods has the highest potential?*

2 Statistical APE methods

The two methods we analyse follow the same "statistical phrase-based post-editing" strategy outlined by Simard et al. (2007), but differ in the way data is represented. Let's give them a closer look.

2.1 Method 1 (Simard et al., 2007)

The underlying idea is that APE components can be trained in the same way in which statistical MT systems are developed – *i.e.* starting from "parallel data". Since the goal is to transform rough MT output into its correct version, parallel data consists of MT output as source texts and correct (human quality) sentences as target. In (Simard et al., 2007) these are used to train a phrase-based MT system, which is then applied to correct the output of a commercial rule-based MT system.

Positive evaluation results are reported on English-French, and even better ones on French-English data. In both cases, statistical APE yields significant BLEU and TER improvements over the original MT output. However, since training and test data for the two language directions are different (in content and size), the measured performance variations cannot be directly ascribed to the effectiveness of the method in the two settings.

2.2 Method 2 (Béchara et al., 2011)

One limitation of the "monolingual translation" approach proposed in (Simard et al., 2007) is that the basic statistical APE pipeline is only trained on data in the target language (F), disregarding information about the source language (E): Correction rules learned from (f', f) pairs[2] lose the connection between the translated words (or phrases) and the corresponding source terms (e). This implies that information lost or distorted in the translation process is out of the reach of the APE component, and the resulting errors are impossible to recover.

To cope with this issue, Béchara et al. (2011) propose a "context-aware" variant to represent the data. For each word f', the corresponding source word (or phrase) e is identified through word alignment and used to obtain a joint representation $f'\#e$. The result is an intermediate language $F'\#E$ that represents the new source side of the parallel data used to train the statistical APE component. Though in principle more precise, this method can be affected by two problems. First, preserving the source context comes at the cost of a larger vocabulary size and, consequently, higher data sparseness. While the basic statistical APE pipeline combines and exploits the counts of all the co-occurrences of f' and f in the parallel data, its context-aware variant considers each $f'\#e_i$ as a separate term, thus breaking down the co-occurrence counts of f' and f into smaller numbers. Second, all these counts can be influenced by word alignment errors. To cope with data sparseness and unreliable word alignment, Béchara et al. (2011) experiment with different thresholds set on word alignment strengths to filter context information. In particular, they discard the $(f'\#e, f)$ pairs in which the $f'\#e$ alignment score is smaller than the threshold.

The approach, applied to correct the output of a statistical phrase-based MT system, achieves ambiguous evaluation results. On French-English, significant improvements up to 2 BLEU points are observed both over the baseline (the original MT output) and the basic method of Simard et al. (2007). On English-French, however, performance slightly drops. Moreover, follow-up experiments with the same method (Béchara, 2014) did not confirm these results. *In light of these ambiguous results and the lack of a systematic comparison between the two APE methods, our objective is to replicate them[3] for a fair comparison in a controlled evaluation setting involving different lan-*

[2]Here, f' and f respectively stand for the rough MT output and its correct version in the foreign language F.

[3]This is done based on the description provided by the published works. Discrepancies with the actual methods are possible, due to our misinterpretation or to wrong guesses about details that are missing in the papers.

guage pairs.

2.3 Reimplementing the two methods

To obtain the statistical APE pipeline that represents the backbone of both methods we used a phrase-based Moses system (Koehn et al., 2007). Our training data (see Section 3) consists of (*source, MT output, post-edition*) triplets for six language pairs having English as source. While Method 1 uses only the last two elements of the triplet, all of them play a role in the context-aware Method 2. Apart from the different data representation, the training process is identical.

Translation and reordering models were estimated following the Moses protocol with default setup using MGIZA++ (Gao and Vogel, 2008) for word alignment.[4] For language modeling we used the KenLM toolkit (Heafield, 2011) for standard n-gram modeling with an n-gram length of 5. The APE system for each target language was tuned on comparable development sets (see below), optimizing TER with Minimum Error Rate Training (Och, 2003) using the post-edited sentences as references.

3 Experiments

Some lessons learned from prior works on statistical APE methods (Béchara, 2014) include: *i)* learning from human post-edits is more effective than learning from (independent) reference translations, *ii)* learning from (and applying APE to) domain-specific data is more promising than working on general-domain data, *iii)* correcting the output of rule-based MT systems is easier than improving translations from statistical MT. Our work capitalizes on these findings (we learn from domain-specific post-edited data and apply APE to statistical MT), but fills a gap of previous research: a fair comparative study between different methods in controlled conditions. The key enabling factor is the availability, for the first time, of data consisting of the *same source sentences*, *machine-translated in several languages* and *post-edited by professional translators.*

Data. We experiment with the Autodesk Post-Editing Data corpus,[5] which predominantly covers the domain of software user manuals. English sentences are translated into several languages (30K to 410K translations per language) with Autodesk's in-house MT system (Zhechev, 2012) and post-edited by professional translators.

Lang.	No. tokens	Vocab. Size	No. Lemmas
En	210,491	10,727	8,260
Cs	202,475	16,716	10,137
De	211,149	17,563	14,368
Es	252,020	11,075	6,683
Fr	263,690	10,928	7,213
It	239,912	10,703	6,549
Pl	206,016	17,027	10,430

Table 1: Data statistics for each language.

Our experiments are run on six language pairs having English as source and Czech, German, Spanish, French, Italian and Polish as target. To set up our controlled environment, we extract all the (*source, MT output, post-edition*) triplets sharing the same source (En) sentences across all language pairs. Table 1 provides some statistics about the resulting *tri-parallel* corpora. After random shuffling the triplets, we create training (12.2K triplets), development (2K) and test data (2K) sharing exactly the same source sentences across languages. Training and evaluation of our APE systems are performed on true-case data.

To guarantee similar experimental conditions in the six language settings, we also train comparable target language models from external data (indeed, the 12.2K post-edits would not be enough to train reliable LMs). We build our LMs from approximately 2.5M translations of the same English sentences collected from Europarl (Koehn, 2005), DGT-Translation Memory (Steinberger et al., 2012), JRC Acquis (Steinberger et al., 2006), OPUS IT (Tiedemann,) and other Autodesk data common to all languages.

Evaluation metric. We evaluate the APE methods based on their capability to reduce the distance between the MT output and a correct (fluent and adequate) translation. As a measure of the amount of the editing operations needed for the correction, TER and HTER (Snover et al., 2006) fit for our purpose. TER and HTER measure the minimum edit distance between the MT output and its cor-

[4]In Method 1, MGIZA++ is used to align f' and f. In Method 2 it is used to align f' and e, and then $f'\#e$ and f.

[5]`https://autodesk.app.box.com/Autodesk-PostEditing`

	MT Baseline	Method 1			Method 2			Oracle
	TER	*TER*	Δ	*% Reduction*	*TER*	Δ	*% Reduction*	*TER*
En-De	46.46	43.07	-3.39	7.3	42.79*	-3.67	7.9	40.17
En-Cs	44.06	39.38	-4.68	10.62	39.10*	-4.96	11.25	36.32
En-Pl	43.02	38.24	-4.78	11.11	37.75*	-5.27	12.25	35.05
En-It	34.44	30.43	-4.01	11.64	30.13*	-4.31	12.55	28.33
En-Fr	32.76	29.70	-3.06	9.34	29.51	-3.25	9.92	27.12
En-Es	30.90	26.69	-4.21	13.62	26.35*	-4.55	14.72	24.34

Table 2: Performance of the MT baseline and the APE methods for each language pair. Results for Method 2 marked with the "*" symbol are statistically significant compared to Method 1.

rect version.[6] This can be either a reference translation created independently from the MT output (TER) or a human post-edition obtained by manually correcting the MT output (HTER). For the sake of simplicity, henceforth we will use the term TER to refer to both situations (though, when measuring the distance between the MT output and its human post-edition the actual metric is the HTER).

Baseline. Similar to all previous works on APE, our baseline is the MT output *as is*. Hence, baseline scores for each language pair correspond to the TER computed between the original MT output (produced by the "black-box" Autodesk in-house system) and the human post-edits.

4 Results

Table 2 lists our results, with language pairs ordered according to the respective baseline TER. The positive answer to **Q1** (*"Does APE yield consistent improvements to MT output?"*) is evident: both APE methods consistently improve MT quality on all language pairs. TER reductions range from 3.06 to 5.27 points. Quality improvements are statistically significant at $p < 0.05$, measured by bootstrap test (Koehn, 2004).

In answer to **Q2** (*"What is the relation between original MT quality and APE results?"*), our controlled experiments evidence for the first time in APE research that the higher the MT quality, the higher is the improvement, *i.e.* percentage of error reduction, yielded by the APE methods. On one side, this interesting result may seem counter-intuitive because a larger room for improvement is expected for sentences of poor quality. On the other side, it reveals that learning from (and correcting) noisy data affected by many errors is particularly difficult for statistical APE methods. This finding is violated by En-Fr, for which a reasonably good MT quality does not induce a gain in performance comparable to language pairs featuring similar MT TER (En-It and En-Es). On further analysis of the data, we notice that all the target languages except French keep a coherent behaviour with respect to the domain-specific English terms, which are always either preserved (It) or translated (other languages). Instead, French shows an alternation between the two conducts. One example is the English word "*workflow*", which appears in the French post-editions both *as is* (21 sentences) and translated into "*flux de travail*" (34 sentences). In contrast, in the other language directions all the occurrences of '*workflow*" are either translated or kept in English. These frequent ambiguities are difficult to manage (especially if the two forms occur a similar number of times in the training data), and might motivate the smaller quality gains observed on En-Fr compared to the other language pairs.

In answer to **Q3** (*"Which method has the highest potential?"*), we observe slight TER reductions when moving from Method 1 to its "context-aware" variant.[7] Although small (from 0.19 to 0.49 TER points), such gains are statistically significant ($p < 0.05$), except for En-Fr ($p < 0.07$). This suggests that linking the MT words to the source terms can help to recover adequacy errors that are out of the reach of Method 1.

To better understand to what extent the two methods behave differently, we calculated the results of an *Oracle* system, similar to the one pro-

[6]Edit distance is calculated as the number of edits (word insertions, deletions, substitutions, and shifts) divided by the number of words in the correct translation. Lower TER/HTER values indicate better MT quality.

[7]Filtering the context information with thresholds between 0.6 and 0.8 leads to the best results for all languages.

posed by Rubino et al. (2012), defined by selecting for each test sentence the best post-edit (lower TER) produced by two approaches. As shown in the last column of Table 2, such an oracle achieves a significant TER reduction (from 1.8 to 2.78 points) for all the language pairs. We interpret such gains as clues of a possible complementarity between the two methods, which is worth to investigate.

As mentioned in Section 2.2, an advantage of Method 1 is its robust estimation of translation parameters. In contrast, by exploiting contextual information from the source, Method 2 is more precise but potentially affected by data sparsity issues due to its highly increased vocabulary. In an attempt to use a less sparse model at the level of word alignment, we trained a SMT system based on the context-aware representation of Method 2 ($f'\#e$), but with word alignment computed on the representation of Method 1 (f'). Applying this method to the three language pairs for which the two original methods achieved the lowest TER reductions (*i.e.* En-De, En-Fr and En-Cs) shows that this simple way to combine Methods 1 and 2 is able to produce a TER decrement of 0.75 (42.04) for En-De, 0.60 (38.50) for En-Cs and 0.53 (28.98) for En-Fr. This seems to validate our intuition about the possible complementarity of Methods 1 and 2, suggesting a promising direction for future work.

5 Conclusions

We explored the "planet of the APEs" in ideal conditions (quantity and quality of data) and with the right equipment (state-of-the-art methods). The data available (the same English sentences, machine-translated in six languages and post-edited by professional translators) allowed us to compare for the first time different approaches in a fair setting (*our first contribution*). The two methods we analysed allowed us to measure consistent improvements on all language pairs (TER reductions from 7.3% to 14.7% – *second contribution*), and to observe interesting relations between the extent of the gain and the original MT output quality (the higher the quality, the higher the gain yield by APE – *third contribution*). This first study represents a good starting point for future quests. A promising direction to explore is the possible complementarity between the two methods and the room for mutual improvement. Now we just have a glimpse of the path (higher oracle results, slight gains with a first combination method – *fourth contribution*), but positive preliminary results confirm its existence.

To encourage the replication of our experiments by other researchers and the reuse of the selected Autodesk data for benchmarking purposes in the same setting, the scripts developed in this work have been publicly released. They can be downloaded from: `https://bitbucket.org/turchmo/apeatfbk/src/master/papers/ACL2015/`.

Acknowledgements

This work has been partially supported by the EC-funded H2020 project QT21 (grant agreement no. 645452). The work of Marion Weller was supported by the FBK-HLT Summer Internship Program 2014. The authors would like to thank Dr. Ventsislav Zhechev for his support with the Autodesk Post-Editing Data corpus.

References

Jeffrey Allen and Christopher Hogan. 2000. Toward the Development of a Post Editing Module for Raw Machine Translation Output: A Controlled Language Perspective. In *Third International Controlled Language Applications Workshop (CLAW-00)*, pages 62–71.

Hanna Béchara, Yanjun Ma, and Josef van Genabith. 2011. Statistical Post-Editing for a Statistical MT System. In *Proceedings of the 13th Machine Translation Summit*, pages 308–315, Xiamen, China, September.

Hanna Béchara, Raphaël Rubino, Yifan He, Yanjun Ma, and Josef Genabith. 2012. An Evaluation of Statistical Post-Editing Systems Applied to RBMT and SMT Systems. In *Proceedings of COLING 2012*, pages 215–230, Mumbai, India.

Hanna Béchara. 2014. Statistical Post-editing and Quality Estimation for Machine Translation Systems. *M.Sc. Thesis, Dublin City University, Dublin.*

Loïc Dugast, Jean Senellart, and Philipp Koehn. 2007. Statistical Post-editing on SYSTRAN's Rule-based Translation System. In *Proceedings of the Second Workshop on Statistical Machine Translation*, StatMT '07, pages 220–223, Stroudsburg, PA, USA.

Loïc Dugast, Jean Senellart, and Philipp Koehn. 2009. Statistical Post Editing and Dictionary Extraction: Systran/Edinburgh Submissions for ACL-WMT2009. In *Proceedings of the Fourth Workshop on Statistical Machine Translation*, pages 110–114, Athens, Greece.

Qin Gao and Stephan Vogel. 2008. Parallel Implementations of Word Alignment Tool. In *Proceedings of the ACL 2008 Software Engineering, Testing, and Quality Assurance Workshop*, pages 49–57, Columbus, Ohio.

Kenneth Heafield. 2011. KenLM: Faster and Smaller Language Model Queries. In *Proceedings of the EMNLP 2011 Sixth Workshop on Statistical Machine Translation*, pages 187–197, Edinburgh, Scotland, United Kingdom.

Pierre Isabelle, Cyril Goutte, and Michel Simard. 2007. Domain Adaptation of MT Systems through Automatic Post-editing. In *Proceedings of the Eleventh Machine Translation Summit (MT Summit XI)*, pages 255–261, Copenhagen, Denmark.

Kevin Knight and Ishwar Chander. 1994. Automated Postediting of Documents. In *Proceedings of the 12th National Conference on Artificial Intelligence*, pages 779–784, Seattle, WA, USA.

Philipp Koehn, Hieu Hoang, Alexandra Birch, Chris Callison-Burch, Marcello Federico, Nicola Bertoldi, Brooke Cowan, Wade Shen, Christine Moran, Richard Zens, Chris Dyer, Ondrej Bojar, Alexandra Constantin, and Evan Herbst. 2007. Moses: Open Source Toolkit for Statistical Machine Translation. In *Proceedings of the 45th Annual Meeting of the Association for Computational Linguistics Companion Volume Proceedings of the Demo and Poster Sessions*, pages 177–180, Prague, Czech Republic.

Philipp Koehn. 2004. Statistical Significance Tests for Machine Translation Evaluation. In *Proceedings of EMNLP 2004*, pages 388–395, Barcelona, Spain.

Philipp Koehn. 2005. Europarl: A Parallel Corpus for Statistical Machine Translation. In *Proceedings of the Tenth Machine Translation Summit (MT Summit X)*, pages 79–86, Phuket, Thailand, September.

Antonio L. Lagarda, Vicent Alabau, Francisco Casacuberta, Roberto Silva, and Enrique Díaz-de Liaño. 2009. Statistical Post-editing of a Rule-based Machine Translation System. In *Proceedings of Human Language Technologies: The 2009 Annual Conference of the North American Chapter of the Association for Computational Linguistics*, pages 217–220.

Antonio L. Lagarda, Daniel Ortiz-Martínez, Vicent Alabau, and Francisco Casacuberta. 2014. Translating without in-domain Corpus: Machine Translation Post-editing with Online Learning Techniques. *Computer Speech & Language*.

Franz Josef Och. 2003. Minimum Error Rate Training in Statistical Machine Translation. In *Proceedings of the 41st Annual Meeting on Association for Computational Linguistics - Volume 1*, ACL '03, pages 160–167, Sapporo, Japan.

Kristen Parton, Nizar Habash, Kathleen McKeown, Gonzalo Iglesias, and Adrià de Gispert. 2012. Can Automatic Post-Editing Make MT More Meaningful? In *Proceedings of the 16th Conference of the European Association for Machine Translation (EAMT)*, pages 111–118, Trento, Italy.

Rudolf Rosa, David Mareček, and Ondřej Dušek. 2012. DEPFIX: A System for Automatic Correction of Czech MT Outputs. In *Proceedings of the Seventh Workshop on Statistical Machine Translation*, WMT '12, pages 362–368, Montreal, Canada.

Rudolf Rosa, David Marecek, and Ales Tamchyna. 2013. Deepfix: Statistical Post-editing of Statistical Machine Translation Using Deep Syntactic Analysis. In *Proceedings of the ACL 2013 Student Research Workshop*, pages 172–179, Sofia, Bulgaria.

Raphaël Rubino, Stéphane Huet, Fabrice Lefèvre, and Georges Lenarés. 2012. Statistical Post-Editing of Machine Translation for Domain Adaptation. In *Proceedings of the European Association for Machine Translation (EAMT)*, pages 221–228, Trento, Italy.

Michel Simard, Cyril Goutte, and Pierre Isabelle. 2007. Statistical Phrase-Based Post-Editing. In *Proceedings of the Annual Conference of the North American Chapter of the Association for Computational Linguistics (NAACL HLT)*, pages 508–515, Rochester, New York.

Matthew Snover, Bonnie Dorr, Richard Schwartz, Linnea Micciulla, and John Makhoul. 2006. A Study of Translation Edit Rate with Targeted Human Annotation. In *Proceedings of Association for Machine Translation in the Americas*, pages 223–231, Cambridge, Massachusetts, USA.

Ralf Steinberger, Bruno Pouliquen, Anna Widiger, Camelia Ignat, Tomaz Erjavec, Dan Tufis, and Dniel Varga. 2006. The JRC-Acquis: A Multilingual Aligned Parallel Corpus with 20+ Languages. In *Proceedings of the 5th International Conference on Language Resources and Evaluation (LREC'2006)*, Genoa, Italy.

Ralf Steinberger, Andreas Eisele, Szymon Klocek, Spyridon Pilos, and Patrick Schlüter. 2012. DGT-TM: A Freely Available Translation Memory in 22 Languages. In *Proceedings of the Eight International Conference on Language Resources and Evaluation (LREC'12)*, Istanbul, Turkey.

Jörg Tiedemann. Parallel Data, Tools and Interfaces in OPUS. In *Proceedings of the Eight International Conference on Language Resources and Evaluation (LREC'12)*, pages 2214–2218, Istanbul, Turkey.

Ventsislav Zhechev. 2012. Machine Translation Infrastructure and Post-Editing Performance at Autodesk. In *AMTA 2012 Workshop on Post-Editing Technology and Practice (WPTP 2012)*, pages 87–96, San Diego, CA, USA.

Efficient Learning for Undirected Topic Models

Jiatao Gu and Victor O.K. Li
Department of Electrical and Electronic Engineering
The University of Hong Kong
{jiataogu, vli}@eee.hku.hk

Abstract

Replicated Softmax model, a well-known undirected topic model, is powerful in extracting semantic representations of documents. Traditional learning strategies such as Contrastive Divergence are very inefficient. This paper provides a novel estimator to speed up the learning based on Noise Contrastive Estimate, extended for documents of variant lengths and weighted inputs. Experiments on two benchmarks show that the new estimator achieves great learning efficiency and high accuracy on document retrieval and classification.

1 Introduction

Topic models are powerful probabilistic graphical approaches to analyze document semantics in different applications such as document categorization and information retrieval. They are mainly constructed by directed structure like pLSA (Hofmann, 2000) and LDA (Blei et al., 2003). Accompanied by the vast developments in deep learning, several undirected topic models, such as (Salakhutdinov and Hinton, 2009; Srivastava et al., 2013), have recently been reported to achieve great improvements in efficiency and accuracy.

Replicated Softmax model (RSM) (Hinton and Salakhutdinov, 2009), a kind of typical undirected topic model, is composed of a family of Restricted Boltzmann Machines (RBMs). Commonly, RSM is learned like standard RBMs using approximate methods like Contrastive Divergence (CD). However, CD is not really designed for RSM. Different from RBMs with binary input, RSM adopts softmax units to represent words, resulting in great inefficiency with sampling inside CD, especially for a large vocabulary. Yet, NLP systems usually require vocabulary sizes of tens to hundreds of thousands, thus seriously limiting its application.

Dealing with the large vocabulary size of the inputs is a serious problem in deep-learning-based NLP systems. Bengio et al. (2003) pointed this problem out when normalizing the softmax probability in the neural language model (NNLM), and Morin and Bengio (2005) solved it based on a hierarchical binary tree. A similar architecture was used in word representations like (Mnih and Hinton, 2009; Mikolov et al., 2013a). Directed tree structures cannot be applied to undirected models like RSM, but stochastic approaches can work well. For instance, Dahl et al. (2012) found that several Metropolis Hastings sampling (MH) approaches approximate the softmax distribution in CD well, although MH requires additional complexity in computation. Hyvärinen (2007) proposed Ratio Matching (RM) to train unnormalized models, and Dauphin and Bengio (2013) added stochastic approaches in RM to accommodate high-dimensional inputs. Recently, a new estimator Noise Contrastive Estimate (NCE) (Gutmann and Hyvärinen, 2010) is proposed for unnormalized models, and shows great efficiency in learning word representations such as in (Mnih and Teh, 2012; Mikolov et al., 2013b).

In this paper, we propose an efficient learning strategy for RSM named α-NCE, applying NCE as the basic estimator. Different from most related efforts that use NCE for predicting single word, our method extends NCE to generate noise for documents in variant lengths. It also enables RSM to use weighted inputs to improve the modelling ability. As RSM is usually used as the first layer in many deeper undirected models like Deep Boltzmann Machines (Srivastava et al., 2013), α-NCE can be readily extended to learn them efficiently.

2 Replicated Softmax Model

RSM is a typical undirected topic model, which is based on bag-of-words (BoW) to represent documents. In general, it consists of a series of RBMs,

Proceedings of the 53rd Annual Meeting of the Association for Computational Linguistics and the 7th International Joint Conference on Natural Language Processing (Short Papers), pages 162–167,
Beijing, China, July 26-31, 2015.

each of which contains variant softmax visible units but the same binary hidden units.

Suppose K is the vocabulary size. For a document with D words, if the ith word in the document equals the kth word of the dictionary, a vector $\boldsymbol{v}_i \in \{0,1\}^K$ is assigned, only with the kth element $v_{ik} = 1$. An RBM is formed by assigning a hidden state $\boldsymbol{h} \in \{0,1\}^H$ to this document $\boldsymbol{V} = \{\boldsymbol{v}_1, ..., \boldsymbol{v}_D\}$, where the energy function is:

$$E_{\boldsymbol{\theta}}(\boldsymbol{V}, \boldsymbol{h}) = -\boldsymbol{h}^T \boldsymbol{W} \hat{\boldsymbol{v}} - \boldsymbol{b}^T \hat{\boldsymbol{v}} - D \cdot \boldsymbol{a}^T \boldsymbol{h} \quad (1)$$

where $\boldsymbol{\theta} = \{\boldsymbol{W}, \boldsymbol{b}, \boldsymbol{a}\}$ are parameters shared by all the RBMs, and $\hat{\boldsymbol{v}} = \sum_{i=1}^{D} \boldsymbol{v}_i$ is commonly referred to as the word count vector of a document. The probability for the document $\boldsymbol{V}$ is given by:

$$\begin{aligned} P_{\boldsymbol{\theta}}(\boldsymbol{V}) &= \frac{1}{Z_D} e^{-F_{\boldsymbol{\theta}}(\boldsymbol{V})}, Z_D = \sum\nolimits_{\boldsymbol{V}} e^{-F_{\boldsymbol{\theta}}(\boldsymbol{V})} \\ F_{\boldsymbol{\theta}}(\boldsymbol{V}) &= \log \sum\nolimits_{\boldsymbol{h}} e^{-E_{\boldsymbol{\theta}}(\boldsymbol{V}, \boldsymbol{h})} \end{aligned} \quad (2)$$

where $F_{\boldsymbol{\theta}}(\boldsymbol{V})$ is the "free energy", which can be analytically integrated easily, and Z_D is the "partition function" for normalization, only associated with the document length D. As the hidden state and document are conditionally independent, the conditional distributions are derived:

$$P_{\boldsymbol{\theta}}(v_{ik} = 1 | \boldsymbol{h}) = \frac{\exp\left(\boldsymbol{W}_k^T \boldsymbol{h} + b_k\right)}{\sum_{k=1}^{K} \exp\left(\boldsymbol{W}_k^T \boldsymbol{h} + b_k\right)} \quad (3)$$

$$P_{\boldsymbol{\theta}}(h_j = 1 | \boldsymbol{V}) = \sigma\left(\boldsymbol{W}_j \hat{\boldsymbol{v}} + D \cdot a_j\right) \quad (4)$$

where $\sigma(x) = \frac{1}{1+e^{-x}}$. Equation (3) is the softmax units describing the multinomial distribution of the words, and Equation (4) serves as an efficient inference from words to semantic meanings, where we adopt the probabilities of each hidden unit "activated" as the topic features.

2.1 Learning Strategies for RSM

RSM is naturally learned by minimizing the negative log-likelihood function (ML) as follows:

$$L(\boldsymbol{\theta}) = -\mathbb{E}_{\boldsymbol{V} \sim P_{data}}\left[\log P_{\boldsymbol{\theta}}(\boldsymbol{V})\right] \quad (5)$$

However, the gradient is intractable for the combinatorial normalization term Z_D. Common strategies to overcome this intractability are MCMC-based approaches such as Contrastive Divergence (CD) (Hinton, 2002) and Persistent CD (PCD) (Tieleman, 2008), both of which require repeating Gibbs steps of $\boldsymbol{h}^{(i)} \sim P_{\boldsymbol{\theta}}(\boldsymbol{h}|\boldsymbol{V}^{(i)})$ and $\boldsymbol{V}^{(i+1)} \sim P_{\boldsymbol{\theta}}(\boldsymbol{V}|\boldsymbol{h}^{(i)})$ to generate model samples to approximate the gradient. Typically, the performance and consistency improve when more steps are adopted. Notwithstanding, even one Gibbs step is time consuming for RSM, since the multinomial sampling normally requires linear time computations. The "alias method" (Kronmal and Peterson Jr, 1979) speeds up multinomial sampling to constant time while linear time is required for processing the distribution. Since $P_{\boldsymbol{\theta}}(\boldsymbol{V}|\boldsymbol{h})$ changes at every iteration in CD, such methods cannot be used.

3 Efficient Learning for RSM

Unlike (Dahl et al., 2012) that retains CD, we adopted NCE as the basic learning strategy. Considering RSM is designed for documents, we further modified NCE with two novel heuristics, developing the approach "Partial Noise Uniform Contrastive Estimate" (or α-NCE for short).

3.1 Noise Contrastive Estimate

Noise Contrastive Estimate (NCE), similar to CD, is another estimator for training models with intractable partition functions. NCE solves the intractability through treating the partition function Z_D as an additional parameter Z_D^c added to $\boldsymbol{\theta}$, which makes the likelihood computable. Yet, the model cannot be trained through ML as the likelihood tends to be arbitrarily large by setting Z_D^c to huge numbers. Instead, NCE learns the model in a proxy classification problem with noise samples.

Given a document collection (data) $\{\boldsymbol{V}_d\}_{T_d}$, and another collection (noise) $\{\boldsymbol{V}_n\}_{T_n}$ with $T_n = kT_d$, NCE distinguishes these $(1+k)T_d$ documents simply based on Bayes' Theorem, where we assumed data samples matched by our model, indicating $P_{\boldsymbol{\theta}} \simeq P_{\boldsymbol{data}}$, and noise samples generated from an artificial distribution P_n. Parameters are learned by minimizing the cross-entropy function:

$$\begin{aligned} J(\boldsymbol{\theta}) = &-\mathbb{E}_{\boldsymbol{V}_d \sim P_{\boldsymbol{\theta}}}\left[\log \sigma_k(X(\boldsymbol{V}_d))\right] \\ &-k\mathbb{E}_{\boldsymbol{V}_n \sim P_n}\left[\log \sigma_{k^{-1}}(-X(\boldsymbol{V}_n))\right] \end{aligned} \quad (6)$$

and the gradient is derived as follows,

$$\begin{aligned} -\nabla_{\boldsymbol{\theta}} J(\boldsymbol{\theta}) = &\mathbb{E}_{\boldsymbol{V}_d \sim P_{\boldsymbol{\theta}}}\left[\sigma_{k^{-1}}(-X) \nabla_{\boldsymbol{\theta}} X(\boldsymbol{V}_d)\right] \\ &-k\mathbb{E}_{\boldsymbol{V}_n \sim P_n}\left[\sigma_k(X) \nabla_{\boldsymbol{\theta}} X(\boldsymbol{V}_n)\right] \end{aligned} \quad (7)$$

where $\sigma_k(x) = \frac{1}{1+ke^{-x}}$, and the "log-ratio" is:

$$X(\boldsymbol{V}) = \log\left[P_{\boldsymbol{\theta}}(\boldsymbol{V}) / P_n(\boldsymbol{V})\right] \quad (8)$$

$J(\boldsymbol{\theta})$ can be optimized efficiently with stochastic gradient descent (SGD). Gutmann and Hyvärinen (2010) showed that the NCE gradient $\nabla_{\boldsymbol{\theta}} J(\boldsymbol{\theta})$ will reach the ML gradient when $k \to \infty$. In practice, a larger k tends to train the model better.

3.2 Partial Noise Sampling

Different from (Mnih and Teh, 2012), which generates noise per word, RSM requires the estimator to sample the noise at the document level. An intuitive approach is to sample from the empirical distribution $\tilde{\boldsymbol{p}}$ for D times, where the log probability is computed: $\log P_n(\boldsymbol{V}) = \sum_{\boldsymbol{v}\in\boldsymbol{V}} \left[\boldsymbol{v}^T \log \tilde{\boldsymbol{p}}\right]$.

For a fixed k, Gutmann and Hyvärinen (2010) suggested choosing the noise close to the data for a sufficient learning result, indicating full noise might not be satisfactory. We proposed an alternative "Partial Noise Sampling (PNS)" to generate noise by replacing part of the data with sampled words. See Algorithm 1, where we fixed the

Algorithm 1 Partial Noise Sampling

```
Initialize: k, α ∈ (0,1)
for each V_d = {v}_D ∈ {V_d}_{T_d} do
    Set: D_r = ⌈α · D⌉
    Draw: V_r = {v_r}_{D_r} ⊆ V uniformly
    for j = 1, ..., k do
        Draw: V_n^(j) = {v_n^(j)}_{D-D_r} ~ p̃
        V_n^(j) = V_n^(j) ∪ V_r
    end for
    Bind: (V_d, V_r), (V_n^(1), V_r), ..., (V_n^(k), V_r)
end for
```

proportion of remaining words at α, named "noise level" of PNS. However, traversing all the conditions to guess the remaining words requires $O(D!)$ computations. To avoid this, we simply bound the remaining words with the data and noise in advance and the noise $\log P_n(\boldsymbol{V})$ is derived readily:

$$\log P_{\boldsymbol{\theta}}(\boldsymbol{V}_r) + \sum_{\boldsymbol{v}\in\boldsymbol{V}\setminus\boldsymbol{V}_r} \left[\boldsymbol{v}^T \log \tilde{\boldsymbol{p}}\right] \quad (9)$$

where the remaining words $\boldsymbol{V}_r$ are still assumed to be described by RSM with a smaller document length. In this way, it also strengthens the robustness of RSM towards incomplete data.

Sampling the noise normally requires additional computational load. Fortunately, since $\tilde{\boldsymbol{p}}$ is fixed, sampling is efficient using the "alias method". It also allows storing the noise for subsequent use, yielding much faster computation than CD.

3.3 Uniform Contrastive Estimate

When we initially implemented NCE for RSM, we found the document lengths terribly biased the log-ratio, resulting in bad parameters. Therefore "Uniform Contrastive Estimate (UCE)" was proposed to accommodate variant document lengths by adding the uniform assumption:

$$\bar{X}(\boldsymbol{V}) = D^{-1} \log\left[P_{\boldsymbol{\theta}}(\boldsymbol{V})/P_n(\boldsymbol{V})\right] \quad (10)$$

where UCE adopts the uniform probabilities $\sqrt[D]{P_{\boldsymbol{\theta}}}$ and $\sqrt[D]{P_n}$ for classification to average the modelling ability at word-level. Note that D is not necessarily an integer in UCE, and allows choosing a real-valued weights on the document such as *idf*-weighting (Salton and McGill, 1983). Typically, it is defined as a weighting vector $\boldsymbol{w}$, where $w_k = \log \frac{T_d}{|\boldsymbol{V}\in\{\boldsymbol{V}_d\}: v_{ik}=1, \boldsymbol{v}_i\in\boldsymbol{V}|}$ is multiplied to the kth word in the dictionary. Thus for a weighted input $\boldsymbol{V}^w$ and corresponding length D^w, we derive:

$$\bar{X}(\boldsymbol{V}^w) = D^{w-1} \log\left[P_{\boldsymbol{\theta}}(\boldsymbol{V}^w)/P_n(\boldsymbol{V}^w)\right] \quad (11)$$

where $\log P_n(\boldsymbol{V}^w) = \sum_{\boldsymbol{v}^w\in\boldsymbol{V}^w} \left[\boldsymbol{v}^{wT} \log \tilde{\boldsymbol{p}}\right]$. A specific $Z^c_{D^w}$ will be assigned to $P_{\boldsymbol{\theta}}(\boldsymbol{V}^w)$.

Combining PNS and UCE yields a new estimator for RSM, which we simply call α-NCE[1].

4 Experiments

4.1 Datasets and Details of Learning

We evaluated the new estimator to train RSMs on two text datasets: 20 Newsgroups and IMDB.

The 20 Newsgroups[2] dataset is a collection of the Usenet posts, which contains 11,345 training and 7,531 testing instances. Both the training and testing sets are labeled into 20 classes. Removing stop words as well as stemming were performed.

The IMDB dataset[3] is a benchmark for sentiment analysis, which consists of 100,000 movie reviews taken from IMDB. The dataset is divided into 75,000 training instances (1/3 labeled and 2/3 unlabeled) and 25,000 testing instances. Two types of labels, positive and negative, are given to show sentiment. Following (Maas et al., 2011), no stop words are removed from this dataset.

For each dataset, we randomly selected 10% of the training set for validation, and the *idf*-weight vector is computed in advance. In addition, replacing the word count $\hat{\boldsymbol{v}}$ by $\lceil\log(1+\hat{\boldsymbol{v}})\rceil$ slightly improved the modelling performance for all models.

We implemented α-NCE according to the parameter settings in (Hinton, 2010) using SGD in minibatches of size 128 and an initialized learning rate of 0.1. The number of hidden units was fixed

[1] α comes from the noise level in PNS, but UCE is also the vital part of this estimator, which is absorbed in α-NCE.

[2] Available at http://qwone.com/~jason/20Newsgroups

[3] Available at http://ai.stanford.edu/~amaas/data/sentiment

at 128 for all models. Although learning the partition function Z_D^c separately for every length D is nearly impossible, as in (Mnih and Teh, 2012) we also surprisingly found freezing Z_D^c as a constant function of D without updating never harmed but actually enhanced the performance. It is probably because the large number of free parameters in RSM are forced to learn better when Z_D^c is a constant. In practise, we set this constant function as $Z_D^c = 2^H \cdot \left(\sum_k e^{b_k}\right)^D$. It can readily extend to learn RSM for real-valued weighted length D^w.

We also implemented CD with the same settings. All the experiments were run on a single GPU GTX970 using the library *Theano* (Bergstra et al., 2010). To make the comparison fair, both α-NCE and CD share the same implementation.

4.2 Evaluation of Efficiency

To evaluate the efficiency in learning, we used the most frequent words as dictionaries with sizes ranging from 100 to 20,000 for both datasets, and test the computation time both for CD of variant Gibbs steps and α-NCE of variant noise sample sizes. The comparison of the mean running

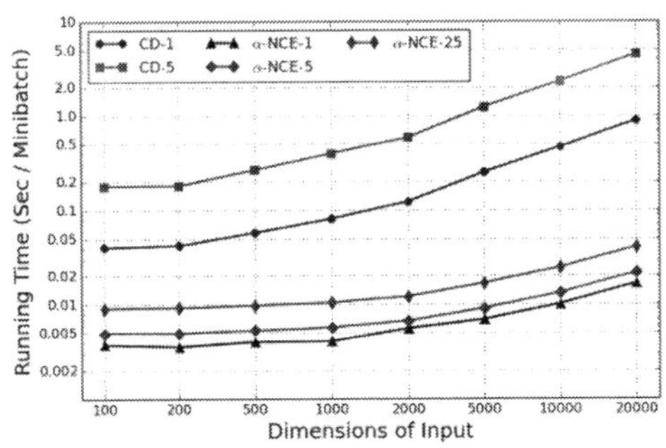

Figure 1: Comparison of running time

time per minibatch is clearly shown in Figure 1, which is averaged on both datasets. Typically, α-NCE achieves 10 to 500 times speed-up compared to CD. Although both CD and α-NCE run slower when the input dimension increases, CD tends to take much more time due to the multinomial sampling at each iteration, especially when more Gibbs steps are used. In contrast, running time stays reasonable in α-NCE even if a larger noise size or a larger dimension is applied.

4.3 Evaluation of Performance

One direct measure to evaluate the modelling performance is to assess RSM as a generative model to estimate the log-probability per word as *perplexity*. However, as α-NCE learns RSM by distinguishing the data and noise from their respective features, parameters are trained more like a feature extractor than a generative model. It is not fair to use *perplexity* to evaluate the performance. For this reason, we evaluated the modelling performance with some indirect measures.

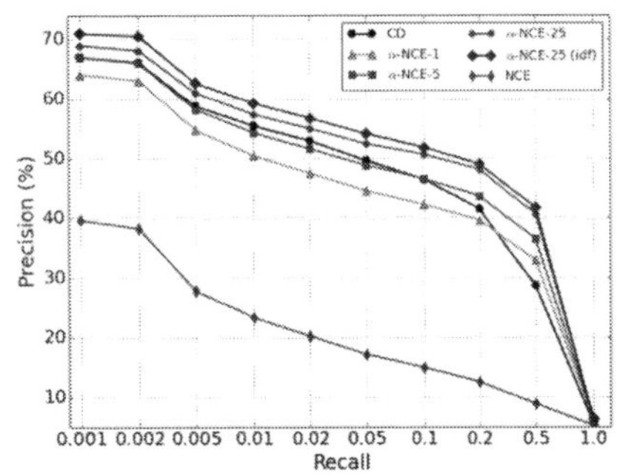

Figure 2: Precision-Recall curves for the retrieval task on the 20 Newsgroups dataset using RSMs.

For 20 Newsgroups, we trained RSMs on the training set, and reported the results on document retrieval and document classification. For retrieval, we treated the testing set as queries, and retrieved documents with the same labels in the training set by *cosine-similarity*. Precision-recall (P-R) curves and mean average precision (MAP) are two metrics we used for evaluation. For classification, we trained a softmax regression on the training set, and checked the accuracy on the testing set. We use this dataset to show the modelling ability of RSM with different estimators.

For IMDB, the whole training set is used for learning RSMs, and an L2-regularized logistic regression is trained on the labeled training set. The error rate of sentiment classification on the testing set is reported, compared with several BoW-based baselines. We use this dataset to show the general modelling ability of RSM compared with others.

We trained both α-NCE and CD, and naturally NCE (without UCE) at a fixed vocabulary size (2000 for 20 Newsgroups, and 5000 for IMDB). Posteriors of the hidden units were used as topic features. For α-NCE , we fixed noise level at 0.5 for 20 Newsgroups and 0.3 for IMDB. In comparison, we trained CD from 1 up to 5 Gibbs steps.

Figure 2 and Table 1 show that a larger noise size in α-NCE achieves better modelling perfor-

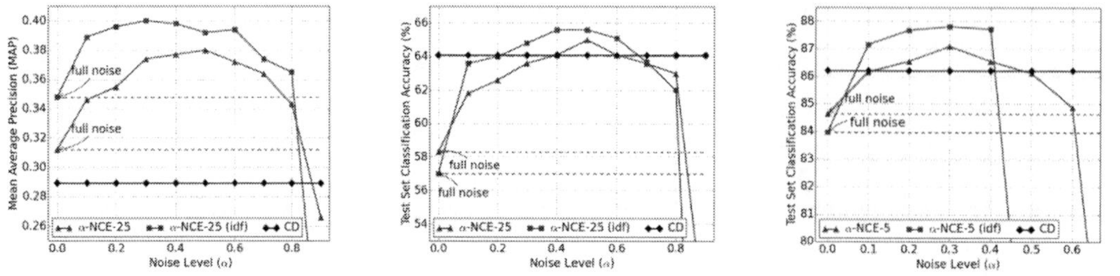

(a) MAP for document retrieval (b) Document classification accuracy (c) Sentiment classification accuracy

Figure 3: Tracking the modelling performance with variant α using α-NCE to learn RSMs. CD is also reported as the baseline. (a) (b) are performed on 20 Newsgroups, and (c) is performed on IMDB.

mance, and α-NCE greatly outperforms CD on retrieval tasks especially around large recall values. The classification results of α-NCE is also comparable or slightly better than CD. Simultaneously, it is gratifying to find that the *idf*-weighting inputs achieve the best results both in retrieval and classification tasks, as *idf*-weighting is known to extract information better than word count. In addition, naturally NCE performs poorly compared to others in Figure 2, indicating variant document lengths actually bias the learning greatly.

CD	α-NCE			
	k=1	k=5	k=25	k=25 (idf)
64.1%	61.8%	63.6%	**64.8%**	**65.6%**

Table 1: Comparison of classification accuracy on the 20 Newsgroups dataset using RSMs.

Models	Accuracy
Bag of Words (BoW) (Maas and Ng, 2010)	86.75%
LDA (Maas et al., 2011)	67.42%
LSA (Maas et al., 2011)	83.96%
Maas et al. (2011)'s "full" model	87.44%
WRRBM (Dahl et al., 2012)	87.42%
RSM:CD	86.22%
RSM:α-NCE-5	**87.09%**
RSM:α-NCE-5 (idf)	**87.81%**

Table 2: The performance of sentiment classification accuracy on the IMDB dataset using RSMs compared to other BoW-based approaches.

On the other hand, Table 2 shows the performance of RSM in sentiment classification, where model combinations reported in previous efforts are not considered. It is clear that α-NCE learns RSM better than CD, and outperforms BoW and other BoW-based models[4] such as LDA. The *idf*-weighting inputs also achieve the best performance. Note that RSM is also based on BoW, indicating α-NCE has arguably reached the limits of learning BoW-based models. In future work, RSM can be extended to more powerful undirected topic models, by considering more syntactic information such as word-order or dependency relationship in representation. α-NCE can be used to learn them efficiently and achieve better performance.

[4]Accurately, WRRBM uses "bag of *n*-grams" assumption.

4.4 Choice of Noise Level-α

In order to decide the best noise level (α) for PNS, we learned RSMs using α-NCE with different noise levels for both word count and *idf*-weighting inputs on the two datasets. Figure 3 shows that α-NCE learning with partial noise ($\alpha > 0$) outperforms full noise ($\alpha = 0$) in most situations, and achieves better results than CD in retrieval and classification on both datasets. However, learning tends to become extremely difficult if the noise becomes too close to the data, and this explains why the performance drops rapidly when $\alpha \to 1$. Furthermore, curves in Figure 3 also imply the choice of α might be problem-dependent, with larger sets like IMDB requiring relatively smaller α. Nonetheless, a systematic strategy for choosing optimal α will be explored in future work. In practise, a range from $0.3 \sim 0.5$ is recommended.

5 Conclusions

We propose a novel approach α-NCE for learning undirected topic models such as RSM efficiently, allowing large vocabulary sizes. It is new a estimator based on NCE, and adapted to documents with variant lengths and weighted inputs. We learn RSMs with α-NCE on two classic benchmarks, where it achieves both efficiency in learning and accuracy in retrieval and classification tasks.

References

Yoshua Bengio, Réjean Ducharme, Pascal Vincent, and Christian Janvin. 2003. A neural probabilistic language model. *The Journal of Machine Learning Research*, 3:1137–1155.

James Bergstra, Olivier Breuleux, Frédéric Bastien, Pascal Lamblin, Razvan Pascanu, Guillaume Desjardins, Joseph Turian, David Warde-Farley, and Yoshua Bengio. 2010. Theano: a CPU and GPU math expression compiler. In *Proceedings of the Python for Scientific Computing Conference (SciPy)*, June. Oral Presentation.

David M Blei, Andrew Y Ng, and Michael I Jordan. 2003. Latent dirichlet allocation. *the Journal of machine Learning research*, 3:993–1022.

George E Dahl, Ryan P Adams, and Hugo Larochelle. 2012. Training restricted boltzmann machines on word observations. *arXiv preprint arXiv:1202.5695*.

Yann Dauphin and Yoshua Bengio. 2013. Stochastic ratio matching of rbms for sparse high-dimensional inputs. In *Advances in Neural Information Processing Systems*, pages 1340–1348.

Michael Gutmann and Aapo Hyvärinen. 2010. Noise-contrastive estimation: A new estimation principle for unnormalized statistical models. In *International Conference on Artificial Intelligence and Statistics*, pages 297–304.

Geoffrey E Hinton and Ruslan R Salakhutdinov. 2009. Replicated softmax: an undirected topic model. In *Advances in neural information processing systems*, pages 1607–1614.

Geoffrey Hinton. 2002. Training products of experts by minimizing contrastive divergence. *Neural computation*, 14(8):1771–1800.

Geoffrey Hinton. 2010. A practical guide to training restricted boltzmann machines. *Momentum*, 9(1):926.

Thomas Hofmann. 2000. Learning the similarity of documents: An information-geometric approach to document retrieval and categorization.

Aapo Hyvärinen. 2007. Some extensions of score matching. *Computational statistics & data analysis*, 51(5):2499–2512.

Richard A Kronmal and Arthur V Peterson Jr. 1979. On the alias method for generating random variables from a discrete distribution. *The American Statistician*, 33(4):214–218.

Andrew L Maas and Andrew Y Ng. 2010. A probabilistic model for semantic word vectors. In *NIPS Workshop on Deep Learning and Unsupervised Feature Learning*.

Andrew L Maas, Raymond E Daly, Peter T Pham, Dan Huang, Andrew Y Ng, and Christopher Potts. 2011. Learning word vectors for sentiment analysis. In *Proceedings of the 49th Annual Meeting of the Association for Computational Linguistics: Human Language Technologies-Volume 1*, pages 142–150. Association for Computational Linguistics.

Tomas Mikolov, Kai Chen, Greg Corrado, and Jeffrey Dean. 2013a. Efficient estimation of word representations in vector space. *arXiv preprint arXiv:1301.3781*.

Tomas Mikolov, Ilya Sutskever, Kai Chen, Greg S Corrado, and Jeff Dean. 2013b. Distributed representations of words and phrases and their compositionality. In *Advances in Neural Information Processing Systems*, pages 3111–3119.

Andriy Mnih and Geoffrey E Hinton. 2009. A scalable hierarchical distributed language model. In *Advances in neural information processing systems*, pages 1081–1088.

Andriy Mnih and Yee Whye Teh. 2012. A fast and simple algorithm for training neural probabilistic language models. *arXiv preprint arXiv:1206.6426*.

Frederic Morin and Yoshua Bengio. 2005. Hierarchical probabilistic neural network language model. In *Proceedings of the international workshop on artificial intelligence and statistics*, pages 246–252. Citeseer.

Ruslan Salakhutdinov and Geoffrey Hinton. 2009. Semantic hashing. *International Journal of Approximate Reasoning*, 50(7):969–978.

Gerard Salton and Michael J McGill. 1983. Introduction to modern information retrieval.

Nitish Srivastava, Ruslan R Salakhutdinov, and Geoffrey E Hinton. 2013. Modeling documents with deep boltzmann machines. *arXiv preprint arXiv:1309.6865*.

Tijmen Tieleman. 2008. Training restricted boltzmann machines using approximations to the likelihood gradient. In *Proceedings of the 25th international conference on Machine learning*, pages 1064–1071. ACM.

A Hassle-Free Unsupervised Domain Adaptation Method Using Instance Similarity Features

Jianfei Yu
School of Information Systems
Singapore Management University
jfyu.2014@phdis.smu.edu.sg

Jing Jiang
School of Information Systems
Singapore Management University
jingjiang@smu.edu.sg

Abstract

We present a simple yet effective unsupervised domain adaptation method that can be generally applied for different NLP tasks. Our method uses unlabeled target domain instances to induce a set of instance similarity features. These features are then combined with the original features to represent labeled source domain instances. Using three NLP tasks, we show that our method consistently outperforms a few baselines, including SCL, an existing general unsupervised domain adaptation method widely used in NLP. More importantly, our method is very easy to implement and incurs much less computational cost than SCL.

1 Introduction

Domain adaptation aims to use labeled data from a source domain to help build a system for a target domain, possibly with a small amount of labeled data from the target domain. The problem arises when the target domain has a different data distribution from the source domain, which is often the case. In NLP, domain adaptation has been well studied in recent years. Existing work has proposed both techniques designed for specific NLP tasks (Chan and Ng, 2007; Daume III and Jagarlamudi, 2011; Yang et al., 2012; Plank and Moschitti, 2013; Hu et al., 2014; Nguyen et al., 2014; Nguyen and Grishman, 2014) and general approaches applicable to different tasks (Blitzer et al., 2006; Daumé III, 2007; Jiang and Zhai, 2007; Dredze and Crammer, 2008; Titov, 2011). With the recent trend of applying deep learning in NLP, deep learning-based domain adaptation methods (Glorot et al., 2011; Chen et al., 2012; Yang and Eisenstein, 2014) have also been adopted for NLP tasks (Yang and Eisenstein, 2015).

There are generally two settings of domain adaptation. We use *supervised domain adaptation* to refer to the setting when a small amount of labeled target data is available, and when no such data is available during training we call it *unsupervised domain adaptation*.

Although many domain adaptation methods have been proposed, for practitioners who wish to avoid implementing or tuning sophisticated or computationally expensive methods due to either lack of enough machine learning background or limited resources, simple approaches are often more attractive. A notable example is the frustratingly easy domain adaptation method proposed by Daumé III (2007), which simply augments the feature space by duplicating features in a clever way. However, this method is only suitable for supervised domain adaptation. A later semi-supervised version of this easy adaptation method uses unlabeled data from the target domain (Daumé III et al., 2010), but it still requires some labeled data from the target domain. In this paper, we propose a general unsupervised domain adaptation method that is almost equally hassle-free but does not use any labeled target data.

Our method uses a set of unlabeled target instances to induce a new feature space, which is then combined with the original feature space. We explain analytically why the new feature space may help domain adaptation. Using a few different NLP tasks, we then empirically show that our method can indeed learn a better classifier for the target domain than a few baselines. In particular, our method performs consistently better than or competitively with Structural Correspondence Learning (SCL) (Blitzer et al., 2006), a well-known unsupervised domain adaptation method in NLP. Furthermore, compared with SCL and other advanced methods such as the marginalized structured dropout method (Yang and Eisenstein, 2014) and a recent feature embedding method (Yang and

Proceedings of the 53rd Annual Meeting of the Association for Computational Linguistics and the 7th International Joint Conference on Natural Language Processing (Short Papers), pages 168–173,
Beijing, China, July 26-31, 2015.

Eisenstein, 2015), our method is much easier to implement.

In summary, our main contribution is a simple, effective and theoretically justifiable unsupervised domain adaptation method for NLP problems.

2 Adaptation with Similarity Features

We first introduce the necessary notation needed for presenting our method. Without loss of generality, we assume a binary classification problem where each input is represented as a feature vector $\boldsymbol{x}$ from an input vector space $\mathcal{X}$ and the output is a label $y \in \{0, 1\}$. This assumption is general because many NLP tasks such as text categorization, NER and relation extraction can be cast into classification problems and our discussion below can be easily extended to multi-class settings. We further assume that we have a set of labeled instances from a source domain, denoted by $D^{\text{s}} = \{(\boldsymbol{x}_i^{\text{s}}, y_i^{\text{s}})\}_{i=1}^{N}$. We also have a set of unlabeled instances from a target domain, denoted by $D^{\text{t}} = \{\boldsymbol{x}_j^{\text{t}}\}_{j=1}^{M}$. We assume a general setting of learning a linear classifier, which is essentially a weight vector $\boldsymbol{w}$ such that $\boldsymbol{x}$ is labeled as 1 if $\boldsymbol{w}^\top \boldsymbol{x} \geq 0$.[1]

A naive method is to simply learn a classifier from D^{s}. The goal of unsupervised domain adaptation is to make use of both D^{s} and D^{t} to learn a good $\boldsymbol{w}$ for the target domain. It has to be assumed that the source and the target domains are similar enough such that adaptation is possible.

2.1 The Method

Our method works as follows. We first randomly select a subset of target instances from D^{t} and normalize them. We refer to the resulting vectors as *exemplar vectors*, denoted by $\mathcal{E} = \{\boldsymbol{e}^{(k)}\}_{k=1}^{K}$. Next, we transform each source instance $\boldsymbol{x}$ into a new feature vector by computing its similarity with each $\boldsymbol{e}^{(k)}$, as defined below:

$$g(\boldsymbol{x}) = [s(\boldsymbol{x}, \boldsymbol{e}^{(1)}), \ldots, s(\boldsymbol{x}, \boldsymbol{e}^{(K)})]^\top, \quad (1)$$

where $\top$ indicates transpose and $s(\boldsymbol{x}, \boldsymbol{x}')$ is a similarity function between $\boldsymbol{x}$ and $\boldsymbol{x}'$. In our work we use dot product as s.[2] Once each labeled source domain instance is transformed into a K-dimensional vector by Equation 1, we can append this vector to the original feature vector of the source instance and use the combined feature vectors of all labeled source instances to train a classifier. To apply this classifier to the target domain, each target instance also needs to add this K-dimensional induced feature vector.

It is worth noting that the exemplar vectors are randomly chosen from the available target instances and no special trick is needed. Overall, the method is fairly easy to implement, and yet as we will see in Section 3, it performs surprisingly well. We also want to point out that our instance similarity features bear strong similarity to what was proposed by Sun and Lam (2013), but their work addresses a completely different problem and we developed our method independently of their work.

2.2 Justification

In this section, we provide some intuitive justification for our method without any theoretical proof.

Learning in the Target Subspace

Blitzer et al. (2011) pointed out that the hope of unsupervised domain adaptation is to "couple" the learning of weights for target-specific features with that of common features. We show our induced feature representation is exactly doing this.

First, we review the claim by Blitzer et al. (2011). We note that although the input vector space $\mathcal{X}$ is typically high-dimensional for NLP tasks, the actual space where input vectors lie can have a lower dimension because of the strong feature dependence we observe with NLP tasks. For example, binary features defined from the same feature template such as the previous word are mutually exclusive. Furthermore, the actual low-dimensional spaces for the source and the target domains are usually different because of domain-specific features and distributional difference between the domains. Borrowing the notation used by Blitzer et al. (2011), define subspace $\mathcal{X}_{\text{s}}$ to be the (lowest dimensional) subspace of $\mathcal{X}$ spanned by all source domain input vectors. Similarly, a subspace $\mathcal{X}_{\text{t}}$ can be defined. Define $\mathcal{X}_{\text{s,t}} = \mathcal{X}_{\text{s}} \bigcap \mathcal{X}_{\text{t}}$, the shared subspace between the two domains. Define $\mathcal{X}_{\text{s},\perp}$ to be the subspace that is orthogonal to $\mathcal{X}_{\text{s,t}}$ but together with $\mathcal{X}_{\text{s,t}}$ spans $\mathcal{X}_{\text{s}}$, that is, $\mathcal{X}_{\text{s},\perp} + \mathcal{X}_{\text{s,t}} = \mathcal{X}_{\text{s}}$. Similarly we can define $\mathcal{X}_{\perp,\text{t}}$. Essentially $\mathcal{X}_{\text{s,t}}$, $\mathcal{X}_{\text{s},\perp}$ and $\mathcal{X}_{\perp,\text{t}}$ are the shared

[1] A bias feature that is always set to be 1 can be added to allow a non-zero threshold.

[2] We find that normalizing the exemplar vectors results in better performance empirically. On the other hand, if we normalize both the exemplar vectors and each instance $\boldsymbol{x}$, i.e. if we use cosine similarity as s, the performance is similar to not normalizing $\boldsymbol{x}$.

subspace and the domain-specific subspaces, and they are mutually orthogonal.

We can project any input vector $\boldsymbol{x}$ into the three subspaces defined above as follows:

$$\boldsymbol{x} = \boldsymbol{x}_{\text{s,t}} + \boldsymbol{x}_{\text{s},\perp} + \boldsymbol{x}_{\perp,\text{t}}.$$

Similarly, any linear classifier $\boldsymbol{w}$ can be decomposed into $\boldsymbol{w}_{\text{s,t}}$, $\boldsymbol{w}_{\text{s},\perp}$ and $\boldsymbol{w}_{\perp,\text{t}}$, and

$$\boldsymbol{w}^\top \boldsymbol{x} = \boldsymbol{w}_{\text{s,t}}^\top \boldsymbol{x}_{\text{s,t}} + \boldsymbol{w}_{\text{s},\perp}^\top \boldsymbol{x}_{\text{s},\perp} + \boldsymbol{w}_{\perp,\text{t}}^\top \boldsymbol{x}_{\perp,\text{t}}.$$

For a naive method that simply learns $\boldsymbol{w}$ from D^{s}, the learned component $\boldsymbol{w}_{\perp,\text{t}}$ will be $\mathbf{0}$, because the component $\boldsymbol{x}_{\perp,\text{t}}$ of any source instance is $\mathbf{0}$, and therefore the training error would not be reduced by any non-zero $\boldsymbol{w}_{\perp,\text{t}}$. Moreover, any non-zero $\boldsymbol{w}_{\text{s},\perp}$ learned from D^{s} would not be useful for the target domain because for all target instances we have $\boldsymbol{x}_{\text{s},\perp} = \mathbf{0}$. So for a $\boldsymbol{w}$ learned from D^{s}, only its component $\boldsymbol{w}_{\text{s,t}}$ is useful for domain transfer.

Blitzer et al. (2011) argues that with unlabeled target instances, we can hope to "couple" the learning of $\boldsymbol{w}_{\perp,\text{t}}$ with that of $\boldsymbol{w}_{\text{s,t}}$. We show that if we use only our induced feature representation without appending it to the original feature vector, we can achieve this. We first define a matrix $M_{\mathcal{E}}$ whose column vectors are the exemplar vectors from $\mathcal{E}$. Then $g(\boldsymbol{x})$ can be rewritten as $M_{\mathcal{E}}^\top \boldsymbol{x}$. Let $\boldsymbol{w}'$ denote a linear classifier learned from the transformed labeled data. $\boldsymbol{w}'$ makes prediction based on $\boldsymbol{w}'^\top M_{\mathcal{E}}^\top \boldsymbol{x}$, which is the same as $(M_{\mathcal{E}}\boldsymbol{w}')^\top \boldsymbol{x}$. This shows that the learned classifier $\boldsymbol{w}'$ for the induced features is equivalent to a linear classifier $\overline{\boldsymbol{w}} = M_{\mathcal{E}}\boldsymbol{w}'$ for the original features.

It is not hard to see that $M_{\mathcal{E}}\boldsymbol{w}'$ is essentially $\sum_k w'_k \boldsymbol{e}^{(k)}$, i.e. a linear combination of vectors in $\mathcal{E}$. Because $\boldsymbol{e}^{(k)}$ comes from $\mathcal{X}_{\text{t}}$, we can write $\boldsymbol{e}^{(k)} = \boldsymbol{e}_{\text{s,t}}^{(k)} + \boldsymbol{e}_{\perp,\text{t}}^{(k)}$. Therefore we have

$$\overline{\boldsymbol{w}} = \underbrace{\sum_k w'_k \boldsymbol{e}_{\text{s,t}}^{(k)}}_{\overline{\boldsymbol{w}}_{\text{s,t}}} + \underbrace{\sum_k w'_k \boldsymbol{e}_{\perp,\text{t}}^{(k)}}_{\overline{\boldsymbol{w}}_{\perp,\text{t}}}.$$

There are two things to note from the formula above. (1) The learned classifier $\overline{\boldsymbol{w}}$ does not have any component in the subspace $\mathcal{X}_{\text{s},\perp}$, which is good because such a component would not be useful for the target domain. (2) The learned $\overline{\boldsymbol{w}}_{\perp,\text{t}}$ will unlikely be zero because its learning is "coupled" with the learning of $\overline{\boldsymbol{w}}_{\text{s,t}}$ through $\boldsymbol{w}'$. In effect, we pick up target specific features that correlate with useful common features.

In practice, however, we need to append the induced features to the original features to achieve good adaptation results. One may find this counter-intuitive because this results in an expanded instead of restricted hypothesis space. Our explanation is that because of the typical L_2 regularizer used during training, there is an incentive to shift the weight mass to the additional induced features. The need to combine the induced features with original features was also reported in previous domain adaptation work such as SCL (Blitzer et al., 2006) and marginalized denoising autoencoders (Chen et al., 2012).

Reduction of Domain Divergence

Another theory on domain adaptation developed by Ben-David et al. (2010) essentially states that we should use a hypothesis space that can achieve low error on the source domain while at the same time making it hard to separate source and target instances. If we use only our induced features, then $\mathcal{X}_{\text{s},\perp}$ is excluded from the hypothesis space. This is likely to make it harder to distinguish source and target instances. To verify this, in Table 1 we show the following errors based on three feature representations: (1) The training error on the source domain ($\hat{\varepsilon}_{\text{s}}$). (2) The classification error when we train a classifier to separate source and target instances. (3) The error on the target domain using the classifier trained from the source domain ($\hat{\varepsilon}_{\text{t}}$). ISF- means only our induced instance similarity features are used while ISF uses combined feature vectors. The results show that ISF achieves relatively low $\hat{\varepsilon}_{\text{s}}$ and increases the domain separation error. These two factors lead to a reduction in $\hat{\varepsilon}_{\text{t}}$.

features	$\hat{\varepsilon}_{\text{s}}$	domain separation error	$\hat{\varepsilon}_{\text{t}}$
Original	0.000	0.011	0.283
ISF-	0.120	0.129	0.315
ISF	0.006	0.062	**0.254**

Table 1: Three errors of different feature representations on a spam filtering task. K is 200 for ISF- and ISF. We expect a low $\hat{\varepsilon}_{\text{t}}$ when $\hat{\varepsilon}_{\text{s}}$ is low and domain separation error is high.

Difference from EA++

The easy domain adaptation method EA proposed by Daumé III (2007) has later been extended to a semi-supervised version EA++ (Daumé III et al., 2010), where unlabeled data from the target domain is also used. Theoretical justifications for both EA and EA++ are given by Kumar et al.

(2010). Here we briefly discuss how our method is different from EA++ in terms of using unlabeled data. In both EA and EA++, since labeled target data is available, the algorithms still learn two classifiers, one for each domain. In our algorithm, we only learn a single classifier using labeled data from the source domain. In EA++, unlabeled target data is used to construct a regularizer that brings the two classifiers of the two domains closer. Specifically, the regularizer defines a penalty if the source classifier and the target classifier make different predictions on an unlabeled target instance. However, with this regularizer, EA++ does not strictly restrict either the source classifier or the target classifier to lie in the target subspace $\mathcal{X}_t$. In contrast, as we have pointed out above, when only the induced features are used, our method leverages the unlabeled target instances to force the learned classifier to lie in $\mathcal{X}_t$.

3 Experiments

3.1 Tasks and Data Sets

We consider the following NLP tasks.

Personalized Spam Filtering (Spam): The data set comes from ECML/PKDD 2006 discovery challenge. The goal is to adapt a spam filter trained on a common pool of 4000 labeled emails to three individual users' personal inboxes, each containing 2500 emails. We use bag-of-word features for this task, and we report classification accuracy.

Gene Name Recognition (NER): The data set comes from BioCreAtIvE Task 1B (Hirschman et al., 2005). It contains three sets of Medline abstracts with labeled gene names. Each set corresponds to a single species (fly, mouse or yeast). We consider domain adaptation from one species to another. We use standard NER features including words, POS tags, prefixes/suffixes and contextual features. We report F1 scores for this task.

Relation Extraction (Relation): We use the ACE2005 data where the annotated documents are from several different sources such as broadcast news and conversational telephone speech. We report the F1 scores of identifying the 7 major relation types. We use standard features including entity types, entity head words, contextual words and other syntactic features derived from parse trees.

3.2 Methods for Comparison

Naive uses the original features.

Common uses only features commonly seen in both domains.

SCL is our implementation of Structural Correspondence Learning (Blitzer et al., 2006). We set the number of induced features to 50 based on preliminary experiments. For pivot features, we follow the setting used by Blitzer et al. (2006) and select the features with a term frequency more than 50 in both domains.

PCA uses principal component analysis on D^t to obtain K-dimensional induced feature vectors and then appends them to the original feature vectors.

ISF is our method using instance similarity features. We first transform each training instance to a K-dimensional vector according to Equation 1 and then append the vector to the original vector.

For all the three NLP tasks and the methods above that we compare, we employ the logistic regression (a.k.a. maximum entropy) classification algorithm with L_2 regularization to train a classifier, which means the loss function is the cross entropy error. We use the L-BFGS optimization algorithm to optimize our objective function.

3.3 Results

In Table 2, we show the comparison between our method and Naive, Common and SCL. For ISF, the parameter K is set to 100 for Spam, 50 for NER and 500 for Relation after tuning. As we can see from the table, Common, which removes source domain specific features during training, can sometimes improve the classification performance, but this is not consistent and the improvement is small. SCL can improve the performance in most settings for all three tasks, which confirms the general effectiveness of this method. For our method ISF, we can see that on average it outperforms both Naive and SCL significantly. When we zoom into the different source-target domain pairs of the three tasks, we can see that ISF outperforms SCL in most of the cases. This shows that our method is competitive despite its simplicity. It is also worth pointing out that SCL incurs much more computational cost than ISF.

We next compare ISF with PCA. Because PCA is also expensive, we only managed to run it on the Spam task. Table 3 shows that ISF also outperforms PCA significantly.

Method	Spam				NER							Relation
	u00	u01	u02	**average**	f→y	f→m	m→y	m→f	y→f	y→m	**average**	**average**
Naive	0.678	0.710	0.816	0.735	0.396	0.379	0.526	0.222	0.050	0.339	0.319	0.398
Common	0.697	0.732	0.781	0.737	0.409	0.388	0.559	0.208	0.059	0.344	0.328	0.401
SCL	0.699	0.717	0.824	0.747	0.405	0.380	0.525	**0.239**	0.063	0.35	0.327	0.403
ISF	**0.720**	**0.769**	**0.884**	**0.791****	**0.415**	**0.395**	**0.566**	0.212	**0.079**	**0.360**	**0.338****	**0.416****

Method	Relation									
	bc→bn	bc→cts	bc→nw	bc→un	bc→wl	bn→bc	bn→cts	bn→nw	bn→un	bn→wl
Naive	0.455	0.400	0.445	0.376	0.397	0.528	0.430	0.482	0.469	0.454
Common	**0.484**	0.408	0.446	0.373	0.400	0.536	0.452	0.478	0.465	0.444
SCL	0.467	0.395	0.453	0.391	**0.415**	0.531	0.434	**0.484**	0.461	**0.461**
ISF	0.474	**0.434**	**0.455**	**0.446**	0.405	**0.537**	**0.454**	**0.484**	**0.504**	0.460
	cts→bc	cts→bn	cts→nw	cts→un	cts→wl	nw2bc	nw→bn	nw→cts	nw→un	nw→wl
Naive	0.358	0.355	0.307	0.446	0.358	0.476	0.433	0.360	0.394	0.420
Common	0.345	0.336	0.292	0.432	0.339	0.475	**0.441**	**0.363**	0.399	0.429
SCL	0.361	0.359	0.314	0.448	0.357	0.480	0.439	0.354	**0.405**	0.426
ISF	**0.387**	**0.377**	**0.333**	**0.449**	**0.361**	**0.488**	0.439	0.342	0.401	**0.431**
	un→bc	un→bn	un→cts	un→nw	un→wl	wl→bc	wl→bn	wl→cts	wl→nw	wl→un
Naive	0.373	0.394	0.423	0.357	0.375	0.355	0.338	0.282	0.373	0.316
Common	0.399	**0.409**	0.416	0.370	0.370	0.351	0.364	**0.298**	0.379	**0.335**
SCL	0.379	0.399	0.423	0.356	0.377	0.361	0.355	0.288	0.381	0.330
ISF	**0.442**	0.404	**0.436**	**0.381**	**0.380**	**0.389**	**0.368**	**0.298**	**0.395**	0.329

Table 2: Comparison of performance on three NLP tasks. For each source-target pair of each task, the performance shown is the average of 5-fold cross validation. We also report the overall average performance for each task. We tested statistical significance only for the overall average performance and found that ISF was significantly better than both Naive and SCL with $p < 0.05$ (indicated by **) based on the Wilcoxon signed-rank test.

Method	Spam			
	u00	u01	u02	**average**
Naive	0.678	0.710	0.816	0.735
PCA	0.700	0.718	0.818	0.745
ISF	**0.720**	**0.769**	**0.884**	**0.791****

Table 3: Comparison between ISF and PCA.

4 Conclusions

We presented a hassle-free unsupervised domain adaptation method. The method is simple to implement, fast to run and yet effective for a few NLP tasks, outperforming SCL, a widely-used unsupervised domain adaptation method. We believe the proposed method can benefit a large number of practitioners who prefer simple methods than sophisticated domain adaptation methods.

Acknowledgment

We would like to thank the reviewers for their valuable comments.

References

Shai Ben-David, John Blitzer, Koby Crammer, Alex Kulesza, Fernando Pereira, and Jennifer Wortman Vaughan. 2010. A theory of learning from different domains. *Machine Learning*, 79(1-2):151–175.

John Blitzer, Ryan McDonald, and Fernando Pereira. 2006. Domain adaptation with structural correspondence learning. In *Proceedings of the 2006 Conference on Empirical Methods in Natural Language Processing*, pages 120–128. Association for Computational Linguistics.

John Blitzer, Sham Kakade, and Dean P. Foster. 2011. Domain adaptation with coupled subspaces. In *Proceedings of the Fourteenth International Conference on Artificial Intelligence and Statistics*, pages 173–181.

Yee Seng Chan and Hwee Tou Ng. 2007. Domain adaptation with active learning for word sense disambiguation. In *Proceedings of the 45th Annual Meeting of the Association of Computational Linguistics*, pages 49–56.

Minmin Chen, Zhixiang Eddie Xu, Kilian Q. Weinberger, and Fei Sha. 2012. Marginalized denoising autoencoders for domain adaptation. In *Proceedings of the 29th International Conference on Machine Learning*.

Hal Daume III and Jagadeesh Jagarlamudi. 2011. Domain adaptation for machine translation by mining unseen words. In *Proceedings of the 49th Annual Meeting of the Association for Computational Linguistics: Human Language Technologies*, pages 407–412.

Hal Daumé III, Abhishek Kumar, and Avishek Saha. 2010. Frustratingly easy semi-supervised domain adaptation. In *Proceedings of the 2010 Workshop on Domain Adaptation for Natural Language Processing*, pages 53–59.

Hal Daumé III. 2007. Frustratingly easy domain adaptation. In *Proceedings of the 45th Annual Meeting of the Association of Computational Linguistics*, pages 256–263.

Mark Dredze and Koby Crammer. 2008. Online methods for multi-domain learning and adaptation. In *Proceedings of the Conference on Empirical Methods in Natural Language Processing*, pages 689–697.

Xavier Glorot, Antoine Bordes, and Yoshua Bengio. 2011. Domain adaptation for large-scale sentiment classification: A deep learning approach. In *In Proceedings of the Twenty-eight International Conference on Machine Learning*.

Lynette Hirschman, Marc Colosimo, Alexander Morgan, and Alexander Yeh. 2005. Overview of BioCreAtIvE task 1B: normailized gene lists. *BMC Bioinformatics*, 6(Suppl 1):S11.

Yuening Hu, Ke Zhai, Vladimir Eidelman, and Jordan Boyd-Graber. 2014. Polylingual tree-based topic models for translation domain adaptation. In *Proceedings of the 52nd Annual Meeting of the Association for Computational Linguistics*, pages 1166–1176.

Jing Jiang and ChengXiang Zhai. 2007. Instance weighting for domain adaptation in nlp. In *Proceedings of the 45th Annual Meeting of the Association of Computational Linguistics*, pages 264–271.

Abhishek Kumar, Avishek Saha, and Hal Daume. 2010. Co-regularization based semi-supervised domain adaptation. In *Advances in neural information processing systems*, pages 478–486.

Thien Huu Nguyen and Ralph Grishman. 2014. Employing word representations and regularization for domain adaptation of relation extraction. In *Proceedings of the 52nd Annual Meeting of the Association for Computational Linguistics*, pages 68–74.

Minh Luan Nguyen, Ivor W. Tsang, Kian Ming A. Chai, and Hai Leong Chieu. 2014. Robust domain adaptation for relation extraction via clustering consistency. In *Proceedings of the 52nd Annual Meeting of the Association for Computational Linguistics*, pages 807–817.

Barbara Plank and Alessandro Moschitti. 2013. Embedding semantic similarity in tree kernels for domain adaptation of relation extraction. In *Proceedings of the 51st Annual Meeting of the Association for Computational Linguistics*, pages 1498–1507.

Chensheng Sun and Kin-Man Lam. 2013. Multiple-kernel, multiple-instance similarity features for efficient visual object detection. *IEEE Transactions on Image Processing*, 22(8):3050–3061.

Ivan Titov. 2011. Domain adaptation by constraining inter-domain variability of latent feature representation. In *Proceedings of the 49th Annual Meeting of the Association for Computational Linguistics: Human Language Technologies*, pages 62–71.

Yi Yang and Jacob Eisenstein. 2014. Fast easy unsupervised domain adaptation with marginalized structured dropout. In *Proceedings of the 52nd Annual Meeting of the Association for Computational Linguistics*, pages 538–544.

Yi Yang and Jacob Eisenstein. 2015. Unsupervised multi-domain adaptation with feature embeddings. In *Proceedings of the North American Chapter of the Association for Computational Linguistics*, pages 672–682.

Pei Yang, Wei Gao, Qi Tan, and Kam-Fai Wong. 2012. Information-theoretic multi-view domain adaptation. In *Proceedings of the 50th Annual Meeting of the Association for Computational Linguistics*, pages 270–274.

Dependency-based Convolutional Neural Networks for Sentence Embedding*

Mingbo Ma[†] **Liang Huang**[† ‡] **Bing Xiang**[‡] **Bowen Zhou**[‡]

[†]Graduate Center & Queens College
City University of New York
{mma2,lhuang}gc.cuny.edu

[‡]IBM Watson Group
T. J. Watson Research Center, IBM
{lhuang,bingxia,zhou}@us.ibm.com

Abstract

In sentence modeling and classification, convolutional neural network approaches have recently achieved state-of-the-art results, but all such efforts process word vectors sequentially and neglect long-distance dependencies. To combine deep learning with linguistic structures, we propose a dependency-based convolution approach, making use of tree-based n-grams rather than surface ones, thus utlizing nonlocal interactions between words. Our model improves sequential baselines on all four sentiment and question classification tasks, and achieves the highest published accuracy on TREC.

1 Introduction

Convolutional neural networks (CNNs), originally invented in computer vision (LeCun et al., 1995), has recently attracted much attention in natural language processing (NLP) on problems such as sequence labeling (Collobert et al., 2011), semantic parsing (Yih et al., 2014), and search query retrieval (Shen et al., 2014). In particular, recent work on CNN-based sentence modeling (Kalchbrenner et al., 2014; Kim, 2014) has achieved excellent, often state-of-the-art, results on various classification tasks such as sentiment, subjectivity, and question-type classification. However, despite their celebrated success, there remains a major limitation from the linguistics perspective: CNNs, being invented on pixel matrices in image processing, only consider sequential n-grams that are consecutive on the surface string and neglect long-distance dependencies, while the latter play an important role in many linguistic phenomena such as negation, subordination, and *wh*-extraction, all of which might dully affect the sentiment, subjectivity, or other categorization of the sentence.

* This work was done at both IBM and CUNY, and was supported in part by DARPA FA8750-13-2-0041 (DEFT), and NSF IIS-1449278. We thank Yoon Kim for sharing his code, and James Cross and Kai Zhao for discussions.

Indeed, in the sentiment analysis literature, researchers have incorporated long-distance information from syntactic parse trees, but the results are somewhat inconsistent: some reported small improvements (Gamon, 2004; Matsumoto et al., 2005), while some otherwise (Dave et al., 2003; Kudo and Matsumoto, 2004). As a result, syntactic features have yet to become popular in the sentiment analysis community. We suspect one of the reasons for this is data sparsity (according to our experiments, tree n-grams are significantly sparser than surface n-grams), but this problem has largely been alleviated by the recent advances in word embedding. Can we combine the advantages of both worlds?

So we propose a very simple dependency-based convolutional neural networks (DCNNs). Our model is similar to Kim (2014), but while his sequential CNNs put a word in its sequential context, ours considers a word and its parent, grand-parent, great-grand-parent, and siblings on the dependency tree. This way we incorporate long-distance information that are otherwise unavailable on the surface string.

Experiments on three classification tasks demonstrate the superior performance of our DCNNs over the baseline sequential CNNs. In particular, our accuracy on the TREC dataset outperforms all previously published results in the literature, including those with heavy hand-engineered features.

Independently of this work, Mou et al. (2015, unpublished) reported related efforts; see Sec. 3.3.

2 Dependency-based Convolution

The original CNN, first proposed by LeCun et al. (1995), applies convolution kernels on a series of continuous areas of given images, and was adapted to NLP by Collobert et al. (2011). Following Kim (2014), one dimensional convolution operates the convolution kernel in sequential order in Equation 1, where $\mathbf{x}_i \in \mathbb{R}^d$ represents the d dimensional word representation for the i-th word in

Proceedings of the 53rd Annual Meeting of the Association for Computational Linguistics and the 7th International Joint Conference on Natural Language Processing (Short Papers), pages 174–179,
Beijing, China, July 26-31, 2015. ©2015 Association for Computational Linguistics

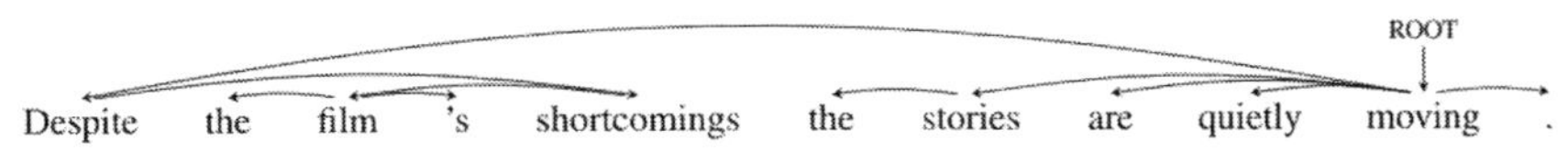

Figure 1: Dependency tree of an example sentence from the Movie Reviews dataset.

the sentence, and $\oplus$ is the concatenation operator. Therefore $\widetilde{\mathbf{x}}_{i,j}$ refers to concatenated word vector from the i-th word to the $(i+j)$-th word:

$$\widetilde{\mathbf{x}}_{i,j} = \mathbf{x}_i \oplus \mathbf{x}_{i+1} \oplus \cdots \oplus \mathbf{x}_{i+j} \qquad (1)$$

Sequential word concatenation $\widetilde{\mathbf{x}}_{i,j}$ works as n-gram models which feeds local information into convolution operations. However, this setting can not capture long-distance relationships unless we enlarge the window indefinitely which would inevitably cause the data sparsity problem.

In order to capture the long-distance dependencies we propose the dependency-based convolution model (DCNN). Figure 1 illustrates an example from the Movie Reviews (MR) dataset (Pang and Lee, 2005). The sentiment of this sentence is obviously positive, but this is quite difficult for sequential CNNs because many n-gram windows would include the highly negative word "shortcomings", and the distance between "Despite" and "shortcomings" is quite long. DCNN, however, could capture the tree-based bigram "Despite – shortcomings", thus flipping the sentiment, and the tree-based trigram "ROOT – moving – stories", which is highly positive.

2.1 Convolution on Ancestor Paths

We define our concatenation based on the dependency tree for a given modifier $\mathbf{x}_i$:

$$\mathbf{x}_{i,k} = \mathbf{x}_i \oplus \mathbf{x}_{p(i)} \oplus \cdots \oplus \mathbf{x}_{p^{k-1}(i)} \qquad (2)$$

where function $p^k(i)$ returns the i-th word's k-th ancestor index, which is recursively defined as:

$$p^k(i) = \begin{cases} p(p^{k-1}(i)) & \text{if } k > 0 \\ i & \text{if } k = 0 \end{cases} \qquad (3)$$

Figure 2 (left) illustrates ancestor paths patterns with various orders. We always start the convolution with x_i and concatenate with its ancestors. If the root node is reached, we add "ROOT" as dummy ancestors (vertical padding).

For a given tree-based concatenated word sequence $\mathbf{x}_{i,k}$, the convolution operation applies a filter $\mathbf{w} \in \mathbb{R}^{k\times d}$ to $\mathbf{x}_{i,k}$ with a bias term b described in equation 4:

$$c_i = f(\mathbf{w} \cdot \mathbf{x}_{i,k} + b) \qquad (4)$$

where f is a non-linear activation function such as rectified linear unit (ReLu) or sigmoid function. The filter $\mathbf{w}$ is applied to each word in the sentence, generating the feature map $\mathbf{c} \in \mathbb{R}^l$:

$$\mathbf{c} = [c_1, c_2, \cdots, c_l] \qquad (5)$$

where l is the length of the sentence.

2.2 Max-Over-Tree Pooling and Dropout

The filters convolve with different word concatenation in Eq. 4 can be regarded as pattern detection: only the most similar pattern between the words and the filter could return the maximum activation. In sequential CNNs, max-over-time pooling (Collobert et al., 2011; Kim, 2014) operates over the feature map to get the maximum activation $\hat{c} = \max \mathbf{c}$ representing the entire feature map. Our DCNNs also pool the maximum activation from feature map to detect the strongest activation over the whole tree (i.e., over the whole sentence). Since the tree no longer defines a sequential "time" direction, we refer to our pooling as "max-over-tree" pooling.

In order to capture enough variations, we randomly initialize the set of filters to detect different structure patterns. Each filter's height is the number of words considered and the width is always equal to the dimensionality d of word representation. Each filter will be represented by only one feature after max-over-tree pooling. After a series of convolution with different filter with different heights, multiple features carry different structural information become the final representation of the input sentence. Then, this sentence representation is passed to a fully connected soft-max layer and outputs a distribution over different labels.

Neural networks often suffer from overtraining. Following Kim (2014), we employ random dropout on penultimate layer (Hinton et al., 2014). in order to prevent co-adaptation of hidden units. In our experiments, we set our drop out rate as 0.5 and learning rate as 0.95 by default. Following Kim (2014), training is done through stochastic gradient descent over shuffled mini-batches with the Adadelta update rule (Zeiler, 2012).

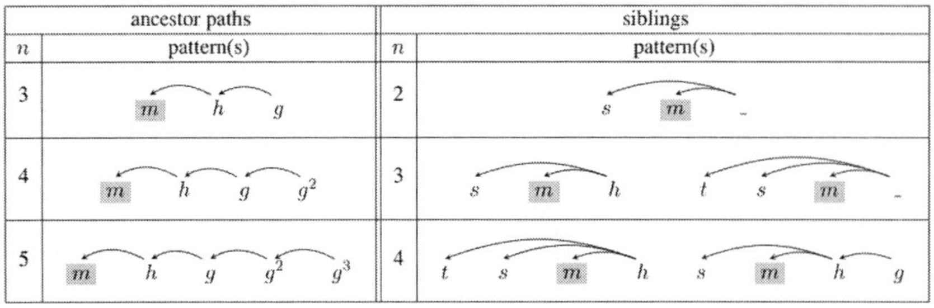

Figure 2: Convolution patterns on trees. Word concatenation always starts with m, while h, g, and g^2 denote parent, grand parent, and great-grand parent, etc., and "_" denotes words excluded in convolution.

2.3 Convolution on Siblings

Ancestor paths alone is not enough to capture many linguistic phenomena such as conjunction. Inspired by higher-order dependency parsing (McDonald and Pereira, 2006; Koo and Collins, 2010), we also incorporate siblings for a given word in various ways. See Figure 2 (right) for details.

2.4 Combined Model

Powerful as it is, structural information still does not fully cover sequential information. Also, parsing errors (which are common especially for informal text such as online reviews) directly affect DCNN performance while sequential n-grams are always correctly observed. To best exploit both information, we want to combine both models. The easiest way of combination is to concatenate these representations together, then feed into fully connected soft-max neural networks. In these cases, combine with different feature from different type of sources could stabilize the performance. The final sentence representation is thus:

$$\hat{\mathbf{c}} = [\underbrace{\hat{c}_a^{(1)}, ..., \hat{c}_a^{(N_a)}}_{\text{ancestors}}; \underbrace{\hat{c}_s^{(1)}, ..., \hat{c}_s^{(N_s)}}_{\text{siblings}}; \underbrace{\hat{c}^{(1)}, ..., \hat{c}^{(N)}}_{\text{sequential}}]$$

where N_a, N_s, and N are the number of ancestor, sibling, and sequential filters. In practice, we use 100 filters for each template in Figure 2 . The fully combined representation is 1,100-dimensional by contrast to 300-dimensional for sequential CNN.

3 Experiments

Table 1 summarizes results in the context of other high-performing efforts in the literature. We use three benchmark datasets in two categories: sentiment analysis on both Movie Review (MR) (Pang and Lee, 2005) and Stanford Sentiment Treebank (SST-1) (Socher et al., 2013) datasets, and question classification on TREC (Li and Roth, 2002).

For all datasets, we first obtain the dependency parse tree from Stanford parser (Manning et al., 2014).[1] Different window size for different choice of convolution are shown in Figure 2. For the dataset without a development set (MR), we randomly choose 10% of the training data to indicate early stopping. In order to have a fare comparison with baseline CNN, we also use 3 to 5 as our window size. Most of our results are generated by GPU due to its efficiency, however CPU could potentially get better results.[2] Our implementation, on top of Kim (2014)'s code,[3] will be released.[4]

3.1 Sentiment Analysis

Both sentiment analysis datasets (MR and SST-1) are based on movie reviews. The differences between them are mainly in the different numbers of categories and whether the standard split is given. There are 10,662 sentences in the MR dataset. Each instance is labeled positive or negative, and in most cases contains one sentence. Since no standard data split is given, following the literature we use 10 fold cross validation to include every sentence in training and testing at least once. Concatenating with sibling and sequential information obviously improves DCNNs, and the final model outperforms the baseline sequential CNNs by 0.4, and ties with Zhu et al. (2015).

Different from MR, the Stanford Sentiment Treebank (SST-1) annotates finer-grained labels, very positive, positive, neutral, negative and very negative, on an extension of the MR dataset. There are 11,855 sentences with standard split. Our model achieves an accuracy of 49.5 which is second only to Irsoy and Cardie (2014).

[1] The phrase-structure trees in SST-1 are actually automatically parsed, and thus can not be used as gold-standard trees.

[2] GPU only supports `float32` while CPU supports `float64`.

[3] `https://github.comw/yoonkim/CNN_sentence`

[4] `https://github.com/cosmmb/DCNN`

Category	Model	MR	SST-1	TREC	TREC-2
This work	DCNNs: ancestor	80.4†	47.7†	95.4†	88.4†
	DCNNs: ancestor+sibling	81.7†	48.3†	**95.6**†	89.0†
	DCNNs: ancestor+sibling+sequential	**81.9**	49.5	95.4†	88.8†
CNNs	CNNs-non-static (Kim, 2014) – baseline	81.5	48.0	93.6	86.4*
	CNNs-multichannel (Kim, 2014)	81.1	47.4	92.2	86.0*
	Deep CNNs (Kalchbrenner et al., 2014)	-	48.5	93.0	-
Recursive NNs	Recursive Autoencoder (Socher et al., 2011)	77.7	43.2	-	-
	Recursive Neural Tensor (Socher et al., 2013)	-	45.7	-	-
	Deep Recursive NNs (Irsoy and Cardie, 2014)	-	**49.8**	-	-
Recurrent NNs	LSTM on tree (Zhu et al., 2015)	**81.9**	48.0	-	-
Other deep learning	Paragraph-Vec (Le and Mikolov, 2014)	-	48.7	-	-
Hand-coded rules	SVM_S (Silva et al., 2011)	-		95.0	**90.8**

Table 1: Results on Movie Review (MR), Stanford Sentiment Treebank (SST-1), and TREC datasets. TREC-2 is TREC with fine grained labels. †Results generated by GPU (all others generated by CPU). *Results generated from Kim (2014)'s implementation.

3.2 Question Classification

In the TREC dataset, the entire dataset of 5,952 sentences are classified into the following 6 categories: abbreviation, entity, description, location and numeric. In this experiment, DCNNs easily outperform any other methods even with ancestor convolution only. DCNNs with sibling achieve the best performance in the published literature. DCNNs combined with sibling and sequential information might suffer from overfitting on the training data based on our observation. One thing to note here is that our best result even exceeds SVM_S (Silva et al., 2011) with 60 hand-coded rules.

The TREC dataset also provides subcategories such as numeric:temperature, numeric:distance, and entity:vehicle. To make our task more realistic and challenging, we also test the proposed model with respect to the 50 subcategories. There are obvious improvements over sequential CNNs from the last column of Table 1. Like ours, Silva et al. (2011) is a tree-based system but it uses constituency trees compared to ours dependency trees. They report a higher fine-grained accuracy of 90.8 but their parser is trained *only* on the QuestionBank (Judge et al., 2006) while we used the standard Stanford parser trained on both the Penn Treebank and QuestionBank. Moreover, as mentioned above, their approach is rule-based while ours is automatically learned.

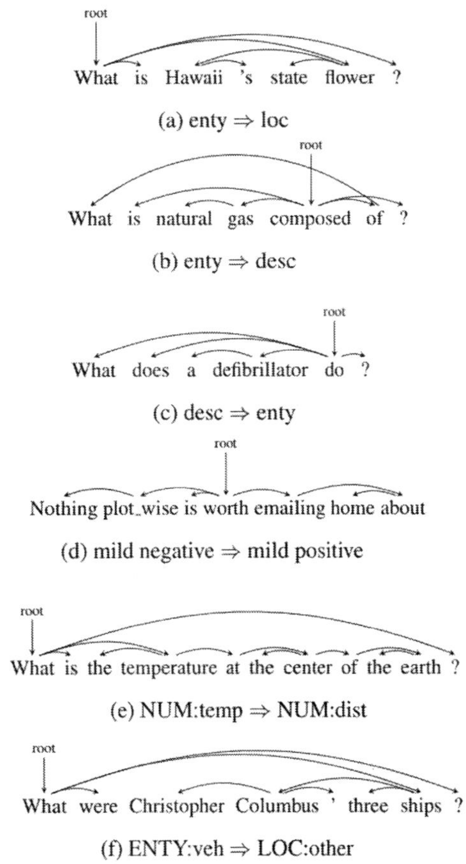

Figure 3: Examples from TREC (a–c), SST-1 (d) and TREC with fine-grained label (e–f) that are misclassified by the baseline CNN but correctly labeled by our DCNN. For example, (a) should be *entity* but is labeled *location* by CNN.

3.3 Discussions and Examples

Compared with sentiment analysis, the advantage of our proposed model is obviously more substantial on the TREC dataset. Based on our error analysis, we conclude that this is mainly due to the

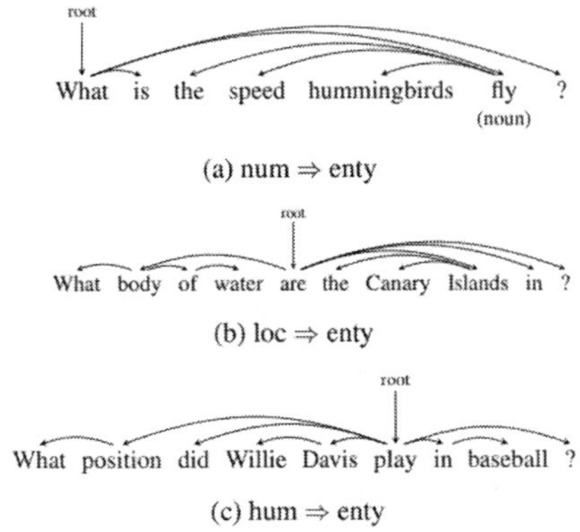

(a) num ⇒ enty

(b) loc ⇒ enty

(c) hum ⇒ enty

Figure 4: Examples from TREC datasets that are misclassified by DCNN but correctly labeled by baseline CNN. For example, (a) should be *numerical* but is labeled *entity* by DCNN.

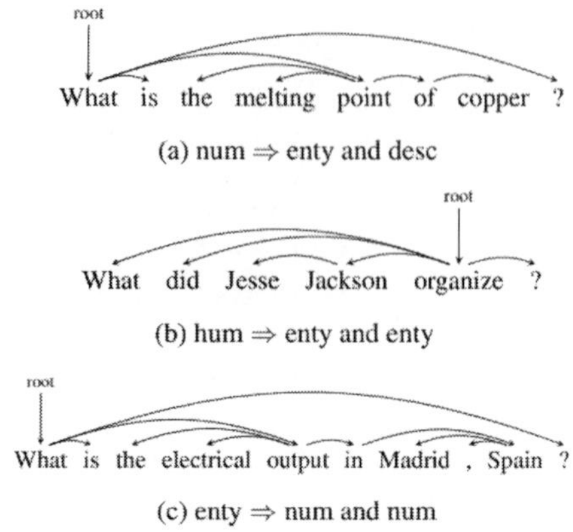

(a) num ⇒ enty and desc

(b) hum ⇒ enty and enty

(c) enty ⇒ num and num

Figure 5: Examples from TREC datasets that are misclassified by both DCNN and baseline CNN. For example, (a) should be *numerical* but is labeled *entity* by DCNN and *description* by CNN.

difference of the parse tree quality between the two tasks. In sentiment analysis, the dataset is collected from the *Rotten Tomatoes* website which includes many irregular usage of language. Some of the sentences even come from languages other than English. The errors in parse trees inevitably affect the classification accuracy. However, the parser works substantially better on the TREC dataset since all questions are in formal written English, and the training set for Stanford parser[5] already includes the QuestionBank (Judge et al., 2006) which includes 2,000 TREC sentences.

Figure 3 visualizes examples where CNN errs while DCNN does not. For example, CNN labels (a) as *location* due to "Hawaii" and "state", while the long-distance backbone "What – flower" is clearly asking for an *entity*. Similarly, in (d), DCNN captures the obviously negative tree-based trigram "Nothing – worth – emailing". Note that our model also works with non-projective dependency trees such as the one in (b). The last two examples in Figure 3 visualize cases where DCNN outperforms the baseline CNNs in fine-grained TREC. In example (e), the word "temperature" is at second from the top and is root of a 8 word span "the ... earth". When we use a window of size 5 for tree convolution, every words in that span get convolved with "temperature" and this should be the reason why DCNN get correct.

Figure 4 showcases examples where baseline CNNs get better results than DCNNs. Example (a) is misclassified as *entity* by DCNN due to parsing/tagging error (the Stanford parser performs its own part-of-speech tagging). The word "fly" at the end of the sentence should be a verb instead of noun, and "hummingbirds fly" should be a relative clause modifying "speed".

There are some sentences that are misclassified by both the baseline CNN and DCNN. Figure 5 shows three such examples. Example (a) is not classified as *numerical* by both methods due to the ambiguous meaning of the word "point" which is difficult to capture by word embedding. This word can mean location, opinion, etc. Apparently, the numerical aspect is not captured by word embedding. Example (c) might be an annotation error.

Shortly before submitting to ACL 2015 we learned Mou et al. (2015, unpublished) have independently reported concurrent and related efforts. Their constituency model, based on their unpublished work in programming languages (Mou et al., 2014),[6] performs convolution on pretrained recursive *node* representations rather than *word* embeddings, thus baring little, if any, resemblance to our dependency-based model. Their dependency model is related, but always includes a node and all its children (resembling Iyyer et al. (2014)), which is a variant of our sibling model and always flat. By contrast, our ancestor model looks at the vertical path from any word to its ancestors, being linguistically motivated (Shen et al., 2008).

4 Conclusions

We have presented a very simple dependency-based convolution framework which outperforms sequential CNN baselines on modeling sentences.

[5] `http://nlp.stanford.edu/software/parser-faq.shtml`

[6] Both their 2014 and 2015 reports proposed (independently of each other and independently of our work) the term "tree-based convolution" (TBCNN).

References

R. Collobert, J. Weston, L. Bottou, M. Karlen, K. Kavukcuoglu, and P. Kuksa. 2011. Natural language processing (almost) from scratch. *Journal of Machine Learning Research*, 12.

Kushal Dave, Steve Lawrence, and David M Pennock. 2003. Mining the peanut gallery: Opinion extraction and semantic classification of product reviews. In *Proceedings of World Wide Web*.

Michael Gamon. 2004. Sentiment classification on customer feedback data: noisy data, large feature vectors, and the role of linguistic analysis. In *Proceedings of COLING*.

Geoffrey E. Hinton, Nitish Srivastava, Alex Krizhevsky, Ilya Sutskever, and Ruslan Salakhutdinov. 2014. Improving neural networks by preventing co-adaptation of feature detectors. *Journal of Machine Learning Research*, 15.

Ozan Irsoy and Claire Cardie. 2014. Deep recursive neural networks for compositionality in language. In *Advances in Neural Information Processing Systems*, pages 2096–2104.

Mohit Iyyer, Jordan Boyd-Graber, Leonardo Claudino, Richard Socher, and Hal Daumé III. 2014. A neural network for factoid question answering over paragraphs. In *Proceedings of EMNLP*.

John Judge, Aoife Cahill, and Josef van Genabith. 2006. Questionbank: Creating a corpus of parse-annotated questions. In *Proceedings of COLING*.

Nal Kalchbrenner, Edward Grefenstette, and Phil Blunsom. 2014. A convolutional neural network for modelling sentences. In *Proceedings of ACL*.

Yoon Kim. 2014. Convolutional neural networks for sentence classification. In *Proceedings of EMNLP*.

Terry Koo and Michael Collins. 2010. Efficient third-order dependency parsers. In *Proceedings of ACL*.

Taku Kudo and Yuji Matsumoto. 2004. A boosting algorithm for classification of semi-structured text. In *Proceedings of EMNLP*.

Quoc V Le and Tomas Mikolov. 2014. Distributed representations of sentences and documents. In *Proceedings of ICML*.

Y. LeCun, L. Jackel, L. Bottou, A. Brunot, C. Cortes, J. Denker, H. Drucker, I. Guyon, U. Mller, E. Sckinger, P. Simard, and V. Vapnik. 1995. Comparison of learning algorithms for handwritten digit recognition. In *Int'l Conf. on Artificial Neural Nets*.

Xin Li and Dan Roth. 2002. Learning question classifiers. In *Proceedings of COLING*.

Christopher D. Manning, Mihai Surdeanu, John Bauer, Jenny Finkel, Steven J. Bethard, and David McClosky. 2014. The Stanford CoreNLP natural language processing toolkit. In *Proceedings of ACL: Demonstrations*, pages 55–60.

Shotaro Matsumoto, Hiroya Takamura, and Manabu Okumura. 2005. Sentiment classification using word sub-sequences and dependency sub-trees. In *Proceedings of PA-KDD*.

Ryan McDonald and Fernando Pereira. 2006. Online learning of approximate dependency parsing algorithms. In *Proceedings of EACL*.

Lili Mou, Ge Li, Zhi Jin, Lu Zhang, and Tao Wang. 2014. TBCNN: A tree-based convolutional neural network for programming language processing. *Unpublished manuscript*: `http://arxiv.org/abs/1409.5718`.

Lili Mou, Hao Peng, Ge Li, Yan Xu, Lu Zhang, and Zhi Jin. 2015. Discriminative neural sentence modeling by tree-based convolution. *Unpublished manuscript*: `http://arxiv.org/abs/1504.01106v5`. Version 5 dated June 2, 2015; Version 1 ("Tree-based Convolution: A New Architecture for Sentence Modeling") dated Apr 5, 2015.

Bo Pang and Lillian Lee. 2005. Seeing stars: Exploiting class relationships for sentiment categorization with respect to rating scales. In *Proceedings of ACL*, pages 115–124.

Libin Shen, Lucas Champollion, and Aravind K Joshi. 2008. LTAG-spinal and the treebank. *Language Resources and Evaluation*, 42(1):1–19.

Yelong Shen, Xiaodong he, Jianfeng Gao, Li Deng, and Gregoire Mesnil. 2014. Learning semantic representations using convolutional neural networks for web search. In *Proceedings of WWW*.

J. Silva, L. Coheur, A. C. Mendes, and Andreas Wichert. 2011. From symbolic to sub-symbolic information in question classification. *Artificial Intelligence Review*, 35.

Richard Socher, Jeffrey Pennington, Eric H. Huang, Andrew Y. Ng, and Christopher D. Manning. 2011. Semi-Supervised Recursive Autoencoders for Predicting Sentiment Distributions. In *Proceedings of EMNLP 2011*.

Richard Socher, Alex Perelygin, Jean Wu, Jason Chuang, Christopher D. Manning, Andrew Y. Ng, and Christopher Potts. 2013. Recursive deep models for semantic compositionality over a sentiment treebank. In *Proceedings of EMNLP 2013*.

Wen-tau Yih, Xiaodong He, and Christopher Meek. 2014. Semantic parsing for single-relation question answering. In *Proceedings of ACL*.

Mattgew Zeiler. 2012. Adadelta: An adaptive learning rate method. *Unpublished manuscript*: `http://arxiv.org/abs/1212.5701`.

Xiaodan Zhu, Parinaz Sobhani, and Hongyu Guo. 2015. Long short-term memory over tree structures. In *Proceedings of ICML*.

Non-Linear Text Regression with a Deep Convolutional Neural Network

Zsolt Bitvai
University of Sheffield, UK
z.bitvai@shef.ac.uk

Trevor Cohn
University of Melbourne, Australia
t.cohn@unimelb.edu.au

Abstract

Text regression has traditionally been tackled using linear models. Here we present a non-linear method based on a deep convolutional neural network. We show that despite having millions of parameters, this model can be trained on only a thousand documents, resulting in a 40% relative improvement over sparse linear models, the previous state of the art. Further, this method is flexible allowing for easy incorporation of side information such as document meta-data. Finally we present a novel technique for interpreting the effect of different text inputs on this complex non-linear model.

1 Introduction

Text regression involves predicting a real world phenomenon from textual inputs, and has been shown to be effective in domains including election results (Lampos et al., 2013), financial risk (Kogan et al., 2009) and public health (Lampos and Cristianini, 2010). Almost universally, the text regression problem has been framed as linear regression, with the modelling innovation focussed on effective regression, e.g., using Lasso penalties to promote feature sparsity (Tibshirani, 1996).[1] Despite their successes, linear models are limiting: text regression problems will often involve complex interactions between textual inputs, thus requiring a non-linear approach to properly capture such phenomena. For instance, in modelling movie revenue conjunctions of features are likely to be important, e.g., a movie described as 'scary' is likely to have different effects for children's versus adult movies. While these kinds of features can be captured using explicit feature engineering, this process is tedious, limited in scope (e.g., to conjunctions) and – as we show here – can be dramatically improved by representational learning as part of a non-linear model.

In this paper, we propose an artificial neural network (ANN) for modelling text regression. In language processing, ANNs were first proposed for probabilistic language modelling (Bengio et al., 2003), followed by models of sentences (Kalchbrenner et al., 2014) and parsing (Socher et al., 2013) *inter alia.* These approaches have shown strong results through automatic learning dense low-dimensional distributed representations for words and other linguistic units, which have been shown to encode important aspects of language syntax and semantics. In this paper we develop a convolutional neural network, inspired by their breakthrough results in image processing (Krizhevsky et al., 2012) and recent applications to language processing (Kalchbrenner et al., 2014; Kim, 2014). These works have mainly focused on 'big data' problems with plentiful training examples. Given their large numbers of parameters, often in the millions, one would expect that such models can only be effectively learned on very large datasets. However we show here that a complex deep convolution network can be trained on about a thousand training examples, although careful model design and regularisation is paramount.

We consider the problem of predicting the future box-office takings of movies based on reviews by movie critics and movie attributes. Our approach is based on the method and dataset of Joshi et al. (2010), who presented a linear regression model over uni-, bi-, and tri-gram term frequency counts extracted from reviews, as well as movie and reviewer metadata. This problem is especially interesting, as comparatively few instances are available for training (see Table 1) while each in-

[1] Some preliminary work has shown strong results for non-linear text regression using Gaussian Process models (Lampos et al., 2014), however this approach has not been shown to scale to high dimensional inputs.

Proceedings of the 53rd Annual Meeting of the Association for Computational Linguistics and the 7th International Joint Conference on Natural Language Processing (Short Papers), pages 180–185,
Beijing, China, July 26-31, 2015.

	train	dev	test	total
# movies	1147	317	254	1718
# reviews per movie	4.2	4.0	4.1	4.1
# sentences per movie	95	84	82	91
# words per movie	2879	2640	2605	2794

Table 1: Movie review dataset (Joshi et al., 2010).

stance (movie) includes a rich array of data including the text of several critic reviews from various review sites, as well as structured data (genre, rating, actors, etc.) Joshi et al. found that regression purely from movie meta-data gave strong predictive accuracy, while text had a weaker but complementary signal. Their best results were achieved by domain adaptation whereby text features were conjoined with a review site identifier. Inspired by Joshi et al. (2010) our model also operates over n-grams, $1 \leq n \leq 3$, and movie metadata, albeit using an ANN in place of their linear model. We use word embeddings to represent words in a low dimensional space, a convolutional network with max-pooling to represent documents in terms of n-grams, and several fully connected hidden layers to allow for learning of complex non-linear interactions. We show that including non-linearities in the model is crucial for accurate modelling, providing a relative error reduction of 40% (MAE) over their best linear model. Our final contribution is a novel means of model interpretation. Although it is notoriously difficult to interpret the parameters of an ANN, we show a simple method of quantifying the effect of text n-grams on the prediction output. This allows for identification of the most important textual inputs, and investigation of non-linear interactions between these words and phrases in different data instances.

2 Model

The outline of the convolutional network is shown in Figure 1. We have n training examples of the form $\{\mathbf{b}_i, \mathbf{r}_i, y_i\}_{i=1}^{n}$, where $\mathbf{b}_i$ is the meta data associated with movie i, y_i is the target gross weekend revenue, and $\mathbf{r}_i$ is a collection of u_i number of reviews, $\mathbf{r}_i = \{\mathbf{x}_j, t_j\}_{j=1}^{u_i}$ where each review has review text $\mathbf{x}_j$ and a site id t_j. We concatenate all the review texts $d_i = (\mathbf{x}_1, \mathbf{x}_2, ..., \mathbf{x}_u)$ to form our text input (see part **I** of Figure 1).

To acquire a distributed representation of the text, we look up the input tokens in a pretrained word embedding matrix $\mathbf{E}$ with size $|V| \times e$, where

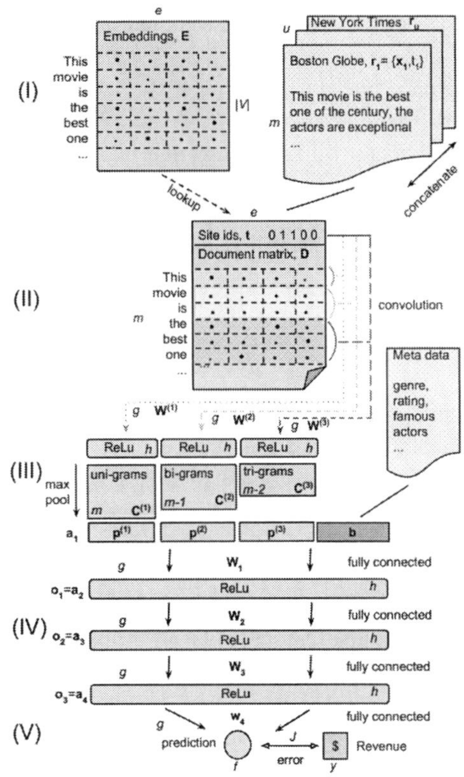

Figure 1: Outline of the network architecture.

$|V|$ is the size of our vocabulary and e is the embedding dimensionality. This gives us a dense document matrix $D_{i,j} = E_{d_i,j}$ with dimensions $m \times e$ where m is the number of tokens in the document.

Since the length of text documents vary, in part **II** we apply convolutions with width one, two and three over the document matrix to obtain a fixed length representation of the text. The n-gram convolutions help identify local context and map that to a new higher level feature space. For each feature map, the convolution takes adjacent word embeddings and performs a feed forward computation with shared weights over the convolution window. For a convolution with width $1 \leq q \leq m$ this is

$$\mathbf{S}_{i,\cdot}^{(q)} = (\mathbf{D}_{i,\cdot}, \mathbf{D}_{i+1,\cdot}, ..., \mathbf{D}_{i+q-1,\cdot})$$
$$\mathbf{C}_{i,\cdot}^{(q)} = \langle \mathbf{S}_{i,\cdot}^{(q)}, \mathbf{W}^{(q)} \rangle$$

where $\mathbf{S}_{i,\cdot}^{(q)}$ is q adjacent word embeddings concatenated, and $\mathbf{C}^{(q)}$ is the convolution output matrix with $(m-q+1)$ rows after a linear transformation with weights $\mathbf{W}^{(q)}$. To allow for a non-linear transformation, we make use of rectified linear activation units, $\mathbf{H}^{(q)} = \max(\mathbf{C}^{(q)}, 0)$, which are universal function approximators. Finally, to compress the representation of text to a fixed dimensional vector while ensuring that important information is preserved and propagated throughout the network, we apply max pooling over time, i.e. the sequence of words, for each dimension, as shown in part **III**,

$$p_j^{(q)} = \max \mathbf{H}_{\cdot,j}^{(q)}$$

where $p_j^{(q)}$ is dimension j of the pooling layer for convolution q, and $\mathbf{p}$ is the concatenation of all pooling layers, $\mathbf{p} = (\mathbf{p}^{(1)}, \mathbf{p}^{(2)}, ..., \mathbf{p}^{(q)})$.

Next, we perform a series of non-linear transformations to the document vector in order to progressively acquire higher level representations of the text and approximate a linear relationship in the final output prediction layer. Applying multiple hidden layers in succession can require exponentially less data than mapping through a single hidden layer (Bengio, 2009). Therefore, in part **IV**, we apply densely connected neural net layers of the form $\mathbf{o}_k = h(g(\mathbf{a}_k, \mathbf{W}_k))$ where $\mathbf{a}_k$ is the input and $\mathbf{o}_k = \mathbf{a}_{k+1}$ is the output vector for layer k, g is a linear transformation function $\langle \mathbf{a}_k, \mathbf{W}_k \rangle$, and h is the activation function, i.e. rectified linear seen above. $l = 3$ hidden layers are applied before the final regression layer to produce the output $f = g(\mathbf{o}_l, \mathbf{w}_{l+1})$ in part **V**.

The mean absolute error is measured between the predictions $\mathbf{f}$ and the targets $\mathbf{y}$, which is more permissible to outliers than the squared error. The cost J is defined as

$$J = \frac{1}{n} \sum_{v=1}^{n} |f_v - y_v|.$$

The network is trained with stochastic gradient descent and the Ada Delta (Zeiler, 2012) update rule using random restarts. Stochastic gradient descent is noisier than batch training due to a local estimation of the gradient, but it can start converging much faster. Ada Delta keeps an exponentially decaying history of gradients and updates in order to adapt the learning rate for each parameter, which partially smooths out the training noise. Regularisation and hyperparmeter selection are performed by early stopping on the development set. The size of the vocabulary is 90K words. Note that 10% of our lexicon is not found in the embeddings pretrained on Google News. Those terms are initialised with random small weights. The model has around 4 million weights plus 27 million tunable word embedding parameters.

Model Description	**MAE($M)**
Baseline mean	11.7
Linear Text	8.0
Linear Text+Domain+POS	7.4
Linear Meta	6.0
Linear Text+Meta	5.9
Linear Text+Meta+Domain+Deps	5.7
ANN Text	6.3
ANN Text+Domain	6.0
ANN Meta	3.9
ANN Text+Meta	**3.4**
ANN Text+Meta+Domain	**3.4**

Table 2: Experiment results on test set. Linear models by (Joshi et al., 2010).

Structured data Besides text, injecting meta data and domain information into the model likely provides additional predictive power. Combining text with structured data early in the network fosters joint non-linear interaction in subsequent hidden layers. Hence, if meta data $\mathbf{b}$ is present, we concatenate that with the max pooling layer $\mathbf{a}_1 = (\mathbf{p}, \mathbf{b})$ in part **III**. Domain specific information $\mathbf{t}$ is appended to each n-gram convolution input $(\mathbf{S}_{i,\cdot}^{(q)}, \mathbf{t})$ in part **II**, where $\mathbf{t}_z = \mathbf{1}_z$ indicates whether domain z has reviewed the movie.[2] This helps the network bias the convolutions, and thus change which features get propagated in the pooling layer.

3 Results

The results in Table 2 show that the neural network performs very well, with around 40% improvement over the previous best results (Joshi et al., 2010). Our dataset splits are identical, and we have accurately reproduced the results of their linear model. Non-linearities are clearly helpful as evidenced by the ANN Text model beating the bag of words Linear Text model with a mean absolute test error of 6.0 vs 8.0. Moreover, simply using structured data in the ANN Meta beats all the Linear models by a sizeable margin. Further improvements are realised through the inclusion of text, giving the lowest error of 3.4. Note that Joshi et al. (2010) preprocessed the text by stemming, down-

[2]Alternatively, site information can be encoded with one-hot categorical variables.

Model Description	MAE($M)
fixed word2vec embeddings	**3.4***
tuned word2vec embeddings	3.6
fixed random embeddings	3.6
tuned random embeddings	3.8
uni-grams	3.6
uni+bi-grams	3.5
uni+bi+tri-grams	**3.4***
uni+bi+tri+four-grams	3.6
0 hidden layer	6.3
1 hidden layer	3.9
2 hidden layers	3.5
3 hidden layers	**3.4***
4 hidden layers	3.6

Table 3: Various alternative configurations, based on the ANN Text+Meta model. The asterisk ($*$) denotes the settings in the ANN Text+Meta model.

casing, and discarding feature instances that occurred in fewer than five reviews. In contrast, we did not perform any processing of the text or feature engineering, apart from tokenization, instead learning this automatically.[3]

We find that both text and meta data contain complementary signals with some information overlap between them. This confirms the finding of Bitvai and Cohn (2015) on another text regression problem. The meta features alone almost achieve the best results whereas text alone performs worse but still well above the baseline. For the combined model, the performance improves slightly. In Table 3 we can see that contrary to expectations, fine tuning the word embeddings does not help significantly compared to keeping them fixed. Moreover, randomly initialising the embeddings and fixing them performs quite well. Fine tuning may be a challenging optimisation due to the high dimensional embedding space and the loss of monolingual information. This is further exacerbated due to the limited supervision signal.

One of the main sources of improvement appears to come from the non-linearity applied to the neural network activations. To test this, we try using linear activation units in parts **II** and **IV** of the network. Composition of linear functions yields a linear function, and therefore we recover the linear model results. This is much worse than the model with non-linear activations. Changing the network depth, we find that the model performs much better with a single hidden layer than without any, while three hidden layers are optimal. For the weight dimensions we find square 1058 dimensional weights to perform the best. The ideal number of convolutions are three with uni, bi and trigrams, but unigrams alone perform only slightly worse, while taking a larger n-gram window $n > 3$ does not help. Average and sum pooling perform comparatively well, while max pooling achieves the best result. Note that sum pooling recovers a non-linear bag-of-words model. With respect to activation functions, both ReLU and sigmoid work well.

Model extensions Multi task learning with task identifiers, ANN Text+Domain, does improve the ANN Text model. This suggests that the tendency by certain sites to review specific movies is in itself indicative of the revenue. However this improvement is more difficult to discern with the ANN Text+Meta+Domain model, possibly due to redundancy with the meta data. An alternative approach for multi-task learning is to have a separate convolutional weight matrix for each review site, which can learn site specific characteristics of the text. This can also be achieved with site specific word embedding dimensions. However neither of these methods resulted in performance improvements. In addition, we experimented with applying a hierarchical convolution over reviews in two steps with k-max pooling (Kalchbrenner et al., 2014), as well as parsing sentences recursively (Socher et al., 2013), but did not observe any improvements.

For optimisation, both Ada Grad and Steepest Gradient Descent had occasional problems with local minima, which Ada Delta was able to escape more often. In contrast to earlier work (Kim, 2014), applying dropout on the final layer did not improve the validation error. The optimiser mostly found good parameters after around 40 epochs which took around 30 minutes on a NVidia Kepler Tesla K40m GPU.

Model interpretation Next we perform analysis to determine which words and phrases influenced the output the most in the ANN Text model. To do so, we set each phrase input to zeros in turn and measure the prediction difference for each movie across the test set. We report the min/max/average/count values in Table 4. We isolate the effect of each n-gram by making sure the uni, bi and trigrams are independent,

[3]Although we do make use of pretrained word embeddings in our text features.

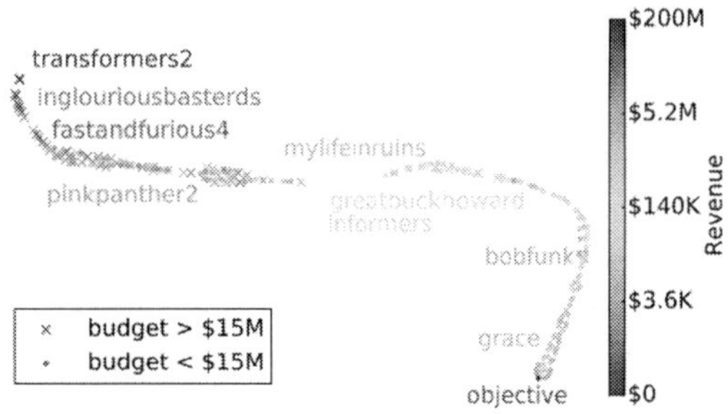

Figure 2: Projection of the last hidden layer of test movies using t-SNE. Red means high and blue means low revenue. The cross vs dot symbols indicate a production budget above or below $15M.

i.e. we process "Hong Kong" without zeroing "Hong" or "Kong". About 95% of phrases result in no output change, including common sentiment words, which shows that text regression is a different problem to sentiment analysis. We see that words related to series "# 2", effects, awards "praise", positive sentiment "intense", locations, references "Batman", body parts "chest", and others such as "plot twist", "evil", and "cameo" result in increased revenue by up to $5 million. On the other hand, words related to independent films "vérité", documentaries "the period", foreign film "English subtitles" and negative sentiment decrease revenue. Note that the model has identified structured data in the unstructured text, such as related to revenue of prequels "39 million", crew members, duration "15 minutes in", genre "[sci] fi", ratings, sexuality, profanity, release periods "late 2008 release", availability "In selected theaters" and themes. Phrases can be composed, such as "action unfolds" amplifies "action", and "cautioned" is amplified by "strongly cautioned". "functional" is neutral, but "functional at best" is strongly negative. Some words exhibit both positive and negative impacts depending on the context. This highlights the limitation of a linear model which is unable to discover these non-linear relationships. "13 - year [old]" is positive in New in Town, a romantic comedy and negative in Zombieland, a horror. The character strings "k /" (mannerism of reviewer), "they're" (unique apostrophe), "&#39" (encoding error) are high impact and unique to specific review sites, showing that the model indirectly uncovers domain information. This can explain the limited gain that can be achieved via multi task learning. Last, we have

Top 5 positive phrases	min	max	avg	#
sequel	20	4400	2300	28
flick	0	3700	1600	22
k /	1500	3600	2200	3
product	10	3400	1800	27
predecessor	22	3400	1400	13
Top 5 negative phrases	**min**	**max**	**avg**	**#**
Mildly raunchy lang.	-3100	-3100	-3100	1
(Under 17	-2500	1	-570	75
Lars von	-2400	-900	-1500	3
talk the language	-2200	-2200	-2200	1
. their English	-2200	-2200	-2200	1
Selected phrases	**min**	**max**	**avg**	**#**
CGI	145	3000	1700	28
action	-7	1500	700	105
summer	3	1200	560	42
they're	3	1300	530	68
1950s	10	1600	500	17
hit	8	950	440	72
fi	-15	340	160	26
Cage	7	95	45	28
Hong Kong	-440	40	-85	11
requires acc. parent	-780	1	-180	77
English	-850	6	-180	41
Sundance Film Festival	-790	3	-180	10
written and directed	-750	-3	-220	19
independent	-990	-2	-320	12
some strong language	-1600	6	-520	13

Table 4: Selected phrase impacts on the predictions in $ USD(K) in the test set, showing min, max and avg change in prediction value and number of occurrences (denoted #). Periods denote abbreviations (language, accompanying).

plotted the last hidden layer of each test set movie with t-SNE (Van der Maaten and Hinton, 2008). This gives a high level representation of a movie. In Figure 2 it is visible that the test set movies can be discriminated into high and low revenue groups and this also correlates closely with their production budget.

4 Conclusions

In this paper, we have shown that convolutional neural networks with deep architectures greatly outperform linear models even with very little supervision, and they can identify key textual and numerical characteristics of data with respect to predicting a real world phenomenon. In addition, we have demonstrated a way to intuitively interpret the model. In the future, we will investigate ways for automatically optimising the hyperparameters of the network (Snoek et al., 2012) and various extensions to recursive or hierarchical convolutions.

References

Yoshua Bengio, Réjean Ducharme, Pascal Vincent, and Christian Janvin. 2003. A neural probabilistic language model. *The Journal of Machine Learning Research*, 3:1137–1155.

Yoshua Bengio. 2009. Learning deep architectures for AI. *Foundations and Trends in Machine Learning*, 2(1):1–127.

Zsolt Bitvai and Trevor Cohn. 2015. Predicting peer-to-peer loan rates using Bayesian non-linear regression. In *Proceedings of the 29th AAAI conference on Artificial Intelligence*, pages 2203–2210.

Mahesh Joshi, Dipanjan Das, Kevin Gimpel, and Noah A Smith. 2010. Movie reviews and revenues: An experiment in text regression. In *Human Language Technologies: The 2010 Annual Conference of the North American Chapter of the Association for Computational Linguistics*, pages 293–296.

Nal Kalchbrenner, Edward Grefenstette, and Phil Blunsom. 2014. A convolutional neural network for modelling sentences. *Proceedings of the 52nd Annual Meeting of the Association for Computational Linguistics*.

Yoon Kim. 2014. Convolutional neural networks for sentence classification. In *Proceedings of the Conference on Empirical Methods in Natural Language Processing*.

Shimon Kogan, Dimitry Levin, Bryan R Routledge, Jacob S Sagi, and Noah A Smith. 2009. Predicting risk from financial reports with regression. In *Proceedings of Human Language Technologies: The 2009 Annual Conference of the North American Chapter of the Association for Computational Linguistics*, pages 272–280.

Alex Krizhevsky, Ilya Sutskever, and Geoffrey E Hinton. 2012. ImageNet classification with deep convolutional neural networks. In *Advances in Neural Information Processing Systems*, pages 1097–1105.

Vasileios Lampos and Nello Cristianini. 2010. Tracking the flu pandemic by monitoring the social web. In *Cognitive Information Processing*, pages 411–416.

Vasileios Lampos, Daniel Preotiuc-Pietro, and Trevor Cohn. 2013. A user-centric model of voting intention from social media. In *Proc 51st Annual Meeting of the Association for Computational Linguistics*, pages 993–1003.

Vasileios Lampos, Nikolaos Aletras, D Preoţiuc-Pietro, and Trevor Cohn. 2014. Predicting and characterising user impact on twitter. In *Proceedings of the 14th Conference of the European Chapter of the Association for Computational Linguistics*, pages 405–-413.

Jasper Snoek, Hugo Larochelle, and Ryan P Adams. 2012. Practical Bayesian optimization of machine learning algorithms. In *Advances in Neural Information Processing Systems*, pages 2951–2959.

Richard Socher, Alex Perelygin, Jean Y Wu, Jason Chuang, Christopher D Manning, Andrew Y Ng, and Christopher Potts. 2013. Recursive deep models for semantic compositionality over a sentiment treebank. In *Proceedings of the Conference on Empirical Methods in Natural Language Processing*, pages 1631–1642.

Robert Tibshirani. 1996. Regression shrinkage and selection via the lasso. *Journal of the Royal Statistical Society. Series B (Methodological)*, pages 267–288.

Laurens Van der Maaten and Geoffrey Hinton. 2008. Visualizing data using t-SNE. *Journal of Machine Learning Research*, 9(2579-2605):85.

Matthew D Zeiler. 2012. Adadelta: an adaptive learning rate method. *arXiv preprint arXiv:1212.5701*.

A Unified Learning Framework of Skip-Grams and Global Vectors

Jun Suzuki and **Masaaki Nagata**
NTT Communication Science Laboratories, NTT Corporation
2-4 Hikaridai, Seika-cho, Soraku-gun, Kyoto, 619-0237 Japan
{suzuki.jun, nagata.masaaki}@lab.ntt.co.jp

Abstract

Log-bilinear language models such as SkipGram and GloVe have been proven to capture high quality syntactic and semantic relationships between words in a vector space. We revisit the relationship between SkipGram and GloVe models from a machine learning viewpoint, and show that these two methods are easily merged into a unified form. Then, by using the unified form, we extract the factors of the configurations that they use differently. We also empirically investigate which factor is responsible for the performance difference often observed in widely examined word similarity and analogy tasks.

$\mathcal{V}$	: set of vocabulary (set of words)
$\lvert\mathcal{V}\rvert$	: vocabulary size, or number of words in $\mathcal{V}$
i	: index of the input vector, where $i \in \{1, \dots, \lvert\mathcal{V}\rvert\}$
j	: index of the output vector, where $j \in \{1, \dots, \lvert\mathcal{V}\rvert\}$
$\mathbf{e}_i$	: input vector of the i-th word in $\mathcal{V}$
$\mathbf{o}_j$	: output vector of the j-th word in $\mathcal{V}$. If $i = j$, then $\mathbf{e}_i$ and $\mathbf{o}_j$ are the input and output vectors of the same word in $\mathcal{V}$, respectively.
D	: number of dimensions in input and output vectors
$m_{i,j}$	: (i, j)-factor of matrix M
$s_{i,j}$	: dot product of input and output vectors, $s_{i,j} = \mathbf{e}_i \cdot \mathbf{o}_j$
$\mathcal{D}$	: training data, $\mathcal{D} = \{(i_n, j_n)\}_{n=1}^N$
$\Psi(\cdot)$	: objective function
$\sigma(\cdot)$	: sigmoid function, $\sigma(x) = \frac{1}{1+\exp(-x)}$
$c_{i,j}$	: co-occurrence of the i-th and j-th words in $\mathcal{D}$
$\mathcal{D}'$	: (virtual) negative sampling data
$c'_{i,j}$	: co-occurrence of the i-th and j-th words in $\mathcal{D}'$
k	: hyper-parameter of the negative sampling
$\beta(\cdot)$	: 'weighting factor' of loss function
$\Phi(\cdot)$	: loss function

Table 1: List of notations used in this paper.

1 Introduction

Neural-network-inspired word embedding methods such as Skip-Gram (**SkipGram**) have been proven to capture high quality syntactic and semantic relationships between words in a vector space (Mikolov et al., 2013a). A similar embedding method, called 'Global Vector (**GloVe**)', was recently proposed. It has demonstrated significant improvements over SkipGram on the widely used 'Word Analogy' and 'Word Similarity' benchmark datasets (Pennington et al., 2014). Unfortunately, a later deep re-evaluation has revealed that GloVe does not consistently outperform SkipGram (Levy et al., 2015); both methods provided basically the same level of performance, and SkipGram even seems 'more robust (not yielding very poor results)' than GloVe. Moreover, some other papers, *i.e.*, (Shi and Liu, 2014), and some researchers in the community have discussed a relationship, and/or which is superior, SkipGram or GloVe.

From this background, we revisit the relationship between SkipGram and GloVe from a machine learning viewpoint. We show that it is natural to think that these two methods are essentially identical, with the chief difference being their learning configurations.

The final goal of this paper is to provide a unified learning framework that encompasses the configurations used in SkipGram and GloVe to gain a deeper understanding of the behavior of these embedding methods. We also empirically investigate which learning configuration most clearly elucidates the performance difference often observed in word similarity and analogy tasks.

2 SkipGram and GloVe

Table 1 shows the notations used in this paper.

2.1 Matrix factorization view of SkipGram

SkipGram can be categorized as one of the simplest neural language models (Mnih and Kavukcuoglu, 2013). It generally assigns two distinct D-dimensional vectors to each word in vocabulary $\mathcal{V}$; one is 'input vector', and the other is 'output vector'[1].

[1]These two vectors are generally referred to as 'word (or target) vector' and 'context vector'. We use the terms 'in-

Proceedings of the 53rd Annual Meeting of the Association for Computational Linguistics and the 7th International Joint Conference on Natural Language Processing (Short Papers), pages 186–191, Beijing, China, July 26-31, 2015. ©2015 Association for Computational Linguistics

Roughly speaking, SkipGram models word-to-word co-occurrences, which are extracted within the predefined context window size, by the input and output vectors. Recently, SkipGram has been interpreted as implicitly factorizing the matrix, where the factors are calculated from co-occurrence information (Levy and Goldberg, 2014). Let $m_{i,j}$ be the (i,j)-factor of matrix $\mathbf{M}$ to be 'implicitly' factorized by SkipGram. SkipGram approximates each $m_{i,j}$ by the inner product of the corresponding input and output vectors, that is:

$$m_{i,j} \approx \mathbf{e}_i \cdot \mathbf{o}_j, \tag{1}$$

2.1.1 SkipGram with negative sampling

The primitive training sample for SkipGram is a pair of a target word and its corresponding context word. Thus, we can represent the training data of SkipGram as a list of input and output index pairs, that is, $\mathcal{D} = \{(i_n, j_n)\}_{n=1}^{N}$. Thus the estimation problem of 'SkipGram with negative sampling (**SGNS**)' is defined as the minimization problem of objective function Ψ:

$$\begin{aligned}\Psi = -&\sum_{(i_n,j_n)\in\mathcal{D}} \log\left(\sigma(\mathbf{e}_{i_n}\cdot\mathbf{o}_{j_n})\right)\\ -&\sum_{(i_n,j_n)\in\mathcal{D}'} \log\left(1-\sigma(\mathbf{e}_{i_n}\cdot\mathbf{o}_{j_n})\right),\end{aligned} \tag{2}$$

where the optimization parameters are $\mathbf{e}_i$ and $\mathbf{o}_j$ for all i and j. Note that we explicitly represent the negative sampling data $\mathcal{D}'$ (Goldberg and Levy, 2014).

Let us assume that, in a preliminary step, we count all co-occurrences in $\mathcal{D}$. Then, the SGNS objective in Eq. 2 can be rewritten as follows by a simple reformulation:

$$\begin{aligned}\Psi = -\sum_i\sum_j\Big(&c_{i,j}\log\left(\sigma(\mathbf{e}_i\cdot\mathbf{o}_j)\right)\\ &+c'_{i,j}\log\left(1-\sigma(\mathbf{e}_i\cdot\mathbf{o}_j)\right)\Big).\end{aligned} \tag{3}$$

Here, let us substitute $\mathbf{e}_i \cdot \mathbf{o}_j$ in Eq. 3 for $s_{i,j}$, and then assume that all $s_{i,j}$ are free parameters. Namely, we can freely select the value of $s_{i,j}$ independent from any other $s_{i',j'}$, where $i \neq i'$ and $j \neq j'$, respectively. The partial derivatives of Ψ with respect to $s_{i,j}$ take the following form:

$$\partial_{s_{i,j}}\Psi = -\Big(c_{i,j}\left(1-\sigma(s_{i,j})\right) - c'_{i,j}\sigma(s_{i,j})\Big). \tag{4}$$

The minimizer can be obtained when $\partial_{s_{i,j}}\Psi = 0$ for all $s_{i,j}$. By using this relation, we can obtain the following closed form solution:

$$s_{i,j} = \log\left(\frac{c_{i,j}}{c'_{i,j}}\right). \tag{5}$$

Overall, SGNS approximates the log of the co-occurrence ratio between 'real' training data $\mathcal{D}$ and 'virtual' negative sampling data $\mathcal{D}'$ by the inner product of the corresponding input and output vectors in terms of minimizing the SGNS objective written in Eq. 2, and Eq. 3 as well. Therefore, we can obtain the following relation for SGNS:

$$m_{i,j} = \log\left(\frac{c_{i,j}}{c'_{i,j}}\right) \approx \mathbf{e}_i \cdot \mathbf{o}_j. \tag{6}$$

Note that the expectation of $c'_{i,j}$ is $\frac{kc_ic_j}{|\mathcal{D}|}$ if the negative sampling is assumed to follow unigram probability $\frac{c_j}{|\mathcal{D}|}$, and the negative sampling data is k-times larger than the training data $\mathcal{D}$, where $c_i = \sum_j c_{i,j}$ and $c_j = \sum_i c_{i,j}$[2]. The above matches 'shifted PMI' as described in (Levy and Goldberg, 2014) when we substitute $c'_{i,j}$ for $\frac{kc_ic_j}{|\mathcal{D}|}$ in Eq. 6,

In addition, the `word2vec` implementation uses a smoothing factor α to reduce the selection of high-occurrence-frequency words during the negative sampling. The expectation of $c'_{i,j}$ can then be written as: $kc_i\frac{(c_j)^\alpha}{\sum_{j'}(c_{j'})^\alpha}$. We refer to $\log\left(c_{i,j}\frac{\sum_{j'}(c_{j'})^\alpha}{kc_i(c_j)^\alpha}\right)$ as 'α-parameterized shifted PMI ($\text{SPMI}_{k,\alpha}$)'.

2.2 Matrix factorization view of GloVe

The GloVe objective is defined in the following form (Pennington et al., 2014):

$$\Psi = \sum_i\sum_j \beta(c_{i,j})\Big(\mathbf{e}_i\cdot\mathbf{o}_j - \log(c_{i,j})\Big)^2, \tag{7}$$

where $\beta(\cdot)$ represent a 'weighting function'. In particular, $\beta(\cdot)$ satisfies the relations $0 \leq \beta(x) < \infty$, and $\beta(x) = 0$ if $x = 0$. For example, the following weighting function has been introduced in (Pennington et al., 2014):

$$\beta(x) = \min\Big(1, \big(x/x_{\max}\big)^\gamma\Big). \tag{8}$$

This is worth noting here that the original GloVe introduces two bias terms, b_i and b_j, and defines

put' and 'output' to reduce the ambiguity since 'word' and 'context' are exchangeable by the definition of model (*i.e.*, SkipGram or CBoW).

[2]Every input of the i-th word samples k words. Therefore, the negative sampling number is kc_i. Finally, the expectation can be obtained by multiplying count kc_i by probability $\frac{c_j}{|\mathcal{D}|}$.

configuration	SGNS	GloVe
training unit	sample-wise	co-occurrence
loss function	logistic (Eq. 11)	squared (Eq. 12)
neg. sampling	explicit	no sampling
weight. func. $\beta(\cdot)$	fixed to 1	Eq. 8
fitting function	$\text{SPMI}_{k,\alpha}$	$\log(c_{i,j})$
bias	none	b_i and b_j

Table 2: Comparison of the different configurations used in SGNS and GloVe.

$\mathbf{e}_i \cdot \mathbf{o}_j + b_i + b_j$ instead of just $\mathbf{e}_i \cdot \mathbf{o}_j$ in Eq. 7. For simplicity and ease of discussion, we do not explicitly introduce bias terms in this paper. This is because, without loss of generality, we can embed the effect of the bias terms in the input and output vectors by introducing two additional dimensions for all $\mathbf{e}_i$ and $\mathbf{o}_j$, and fixing parameters $e_{i,D+1} = 1$ and $o_{j,D+2} = 1$.

According to Eq. 7, GloVe can also be viewed as a matrix factorization method. Different from SGNS, GloVe approximates the log of co-occurrences:

$$m_{i,j} = \log(c_{i,j}) \approx \mathbf{e}_i \cdot \mathbf{o}_j, \tag{9}$$

3 Unified Form of SkipGram and GloVe

An examination of the differences between Eqs. 6 and 9 finds that Eq. 6 matches Eq. 9 if $c'_{i,j} = 1$. Recall that $c'_{i,j}$ is the number of co-occurrences of (i,j) in negative sampling data $\mathcal{D}'$. Therefore, what GloVe approximates is SGNS when the negative sampling data $\mathcal{D}'$ is constructed as 1 for all co-occurrences. From the viewpoint of matrix factorization, GloVe can be seen as a special case of SGNS, in that it utilizes a sort of uniform negative sampling method.

Our assessment of the original GloVe paper suggests that the name "Global Vector" mainly stands for the architecture of the two stage learning framework. Namely, it first counts all the co-occurrences in $\mathcal{D}$, and then, it leverages the gathered co-occurrence information for estimating (possibly better) parameters. In contrast, the name "SkipGram" stands mainly for the model type; how it counts the co-occurrences in $\mathcal{D}$. The key points of these two methods seems different and do not conflict. Therefore, it is not surprising to treat these two similar methods as one method; for example, SkipGram model with two-stage global vector learning. The following objective function is a generalized form that subsumes Eqs. 3 and 7:

$$\Psi = \sum_i \sum_j \beta(c_{i,j}) \Phi(\mathbf{e}_i, \mathbf{o}_j, c_{i,j}, c'_{i,j}). \tag{10}$$

hyper-parameter	selected value	
	`word2vec`	`glove`
context window (W)	10	
`sub` (Levy et al., 2015)	dirty, $t = 10^{-5}$	–
`del` (Levy et al., 2015)	use 400,000 most frequent words	
`cds` (Levy et al., 2015)	$\alpha = 3/4$	–
`w+c` (Levy et al., 2015)	$\mathbf{e} + \mathbf{o}$	
weight. func. ($\gamma, x_{\max}$)	–	3/4, 100
initial learning rate (η)	0.025	0.05
# of neg. sampling (k)	5	–
# of iterations (T)	5	20
# of threads	56	
# of dimensions (D)	300	

Table 3: Hyper-parameters in our experiments.

In particular, the original SGNS uses $\beta(c_{i,j}) = 1$ for all (i,j), and logistic loss function:

$$\Phi(\mathbf{e}_i, \mathbf{o}_j, c_{i,j}, c'_{i,j}) = c_{i,j} \log\left(\sigma(\mathbf{e}_i \cdot \mathbf{o}_j)\right) + c'_{i,j} \log\left(1 - \sigma(\mathbf{e}_i \cdot \mathbf{o}_j)\right). \tag{11}$$

In contrast, GloVe uses a least squared loss function:

$$\Phi(\mathbf{e}_i, \mathbf{o}_j, c_{i,j}, c'_{i,j}) = \left(\mathbf{e}_i \cdot \mathbf{o}_j - \log\left(\frac{c_{i,j}}{c'_{i,j}}\right)\right)^2. \tag{12}$$

Table 2 lists the factors of each configuration used differently in SGNS and GloVe.

Note that this unified form also includes SkipGram with noise contrastive estimation (SGNCE) (Mnih and Kavukcuoglu, 2013), which approximates $m_{i,j} = \log(\frac{c_{i,j}}{kc_j})$ in matrix factorization view. This paper omits a detailed discussion of SGNCE for space restrictions.

4 Experiments

Following the series of neural word embedding papers, our training data is taken from a Wikipedia dump (Aug. 2014). We tokenized and lowercased the data yielding about 1.8B tokens.

For the hyper-parameter selection, we mostly followed the suggestion made in (Levy et al., 2015). Table 3 summarizes the default values of hyper-parameters used consistently in all our experiments unless otherwise noted.

4.1 Benchmark datasets for evaluation

We prepared eight word similarity benchmark datasets (**WSimilarity**), namely, R&G (Rubenstein and Goodenough, 1965), M&C (Miller and Charles, 1991), WSimS (Agirre et al., 2009), WSimR (Agirre et al., 2009), MEM (Bruni et al., 2014), MTurk (Radinsky et al., 2011), SCWS (Huang et al., 2012), and RARE (Luong

method	time	WSimilarity	WAnalogy
SGNS (original)	8856	**65.4** (65.2, 65.7)	63.0 (62.2, 63.8)
GloVe (original)	8243	57.6 (57.5, 57.9)	64.8 (64.6, 65.0)
w/o bias terms	8027	57.6 (57.5, 57.7)	64.8 (64.5, 65.0)
fitting=SPMI$_{k,\alpha}$	8332	57.5 (57.2, 57.8)	**65.0** (64.8. 65.1)

Table 4: Results: the micro averages of Spearman's rho (WSimilarity) and accuracy (WAnalogy) for all benchmark datasets.

et al., 2013). Moreover, we also prepared three analogy benchmark datasets (**WAnalogy**), that is, GSEM (Mikolov et al., 2013a), GSYN (Mikolov et al., 2013a), and MSYN (Mikolov et al., 2013b).

4.2 SGNS and GloVe Results

Table 4 shows the training time and performance results gained from our benchmark data. The column 'time' indicates average elapsed time (second) for model learning. All the results are the **average performance of ten runs**. This is because the comparison methods have some randomized factors, such as initial value (since they are non-convex optimization problems) and (probabilistic) sampling method, which significantly impact the results.

At first, we compared the original SGNS as implemented in the `word2vec` package[3] and the original GloVe as implemented in the `glove` package[4]. These results are shown in the first and second rows in Table 4. In our experiments, SGNS significantly outperformed GloVe in WSimilarity while GloVe significantly outperformed SGNS in WAnalogy. As we explained, these two methods can be easily merged into a unified form. Thus, there must be some differences in their configurations that yields such a large difference in the results. Next, we tried to determine the clues as the differences.

4.3 Impact of incorporating bias terms

The third row (w/o bias terms) in Table 4 shows the results of the configuration without using the bias terms in the `glove` package. A comparison with the results of the second row, finds no meaningful benefit to using the bias terms. In contrast, obviously, the elapsed time for model learning is consistently shorter since we can discard the bias term update.

[3]https://code.google.com/p/word2vec/

[4]http://nlp.stanford.edu/projects/glove/

(a) WSimilarity

method	W=2	3	5	10	20
SGNS (original)	64.9	65.1	**65.4**	**65.4**	64.9
GloVe (original)	53.6	55.7	57.0	57.6	**57.8**
w/o harmonic func.	54.6	56.9	57.8	**58.2**	57.9

(b) WAnalogy

method	W=2	3	5	10	20
SGNS (original)	62.8	63.5	**63.9**	63.0	61.3
GloVe (original)	51.7	58.4	62.3	64.8	**66.1**
w/o harmonic func.	52.6	58.0	60.5	**61.6**	60.7

Table 5: Impact of the context window size, and harmonic function.

	W=2	3	5	10	20
(1) $0 < c_{i,j} < 1$	104M	213M	377M	649M	914M
(2) $1 \le c_{i,j}$	167M	184M	207M	234M	251M
non-zero $c_{i,j}$	271M	398M	584M	883M	1165M
ratio of (1)	38.5%	53.6%	64.5%	73.5%	78.4%

Table 6: The ratio of entries less than one in co-occurrence matrix.

4.4 Impact of fitting function

The fourth row (fitting=SPMI$_{k,\alpha}$) in Table 4 shows the performance when we substituted the fitting function of GloVe, namely, $\log(c_{i,j})$, for SPMI$_{k=5,\alpha=3/4}$ used in SGNS. Clearly, the performance becomes nearly identical to the original GloVe. Accordingly, the selection of fitting function has only a small impact.

4.5 Impact of context window size and harmonic function

Table 5 shows the impact of context window size W. The results of SGNS seem more stable against W than those of GloVe.

Additionally, we investigated the impact of the 'harmonic function' used in GloVe. The 'harmonic function' uses the inverse of context distance, *i.e.*, $1/a$ if the context word is a-word away from the target word, instead of just count 1 regardless of the distance when calculating the co-occurrences. Clearly, GloVe without using the harmonic function shown in the third row of Table 5 yielded significantly degraded performance on WAnalogy, and slight improvement on WSimilarity. This fact may imply that the higher WAnalogy performance of GloVe was derived by the effect of this configuration.

4.6 Link between harmonic function and negative sampling

This section further discusses a benefit of harmonic function.

Recall that GloVe does not explicitly consider 'negative samples'. It fixes $c'_{i,j} = 1$ for all (i, j) as shown in Eq. 7. However, the co-occurrence count given by using the harmonic function can take values less than 1, *i.e.*, $c_{i,j} = 2/3$, if the i-th word and the j-th word co-occurred twice with distance 3. As a result, the value of the fitting function of GloVe becomes $\log(2/3)$. Interestingly, this is essentially equivalent to co-occur 3 times in the negative sampling data and 2 times in the real data since the fitting function of the unified form shown in Eq. 12 is $\log(c_{i,j}/c'_{i,j}) = \log(2/3)$ when $c_{i,j} = 2$ and $c'_{i,j} = 3$. It is not surprising that rare co-occurrence words that occur only in long range contexts may have almost no correlation between them. Thus treating them as negative samples will not create a problem in most cases. Therefore, the harmonic function seems to 'unexpectedly' mimic a kind of a negative sampling method; it is interpreted as 'implicitly' generating negative data.

Table 6 shows the ratio of the entries $c_{i,j}$ whose value is less than one in matrix $\mathbf{M}$. Remember that vocabulary size was 400,000 in our experiments. Thus, we had a total of 400K×400K=160B elements in $\mathbf{M}$, and most were 0. Here, we consider only non-zero entries. It is clear that longer context window sizes generated many more entries categorized in $0 < c_{i,j} < 1$ by the harmonic function. One important observation is that the ratio of $0 < c_{i,j} < 1$ is gradually increasing, which offers a similar effect to increasing the number of negative samples. This can be a reason why GloVe demonstrated consistent improvements in WAnalogy performance as context window increased since larger negative sampling size often improves performance (Levy et al., 2015). Note also that the number of $0 < c_{i,j} < 1$ always becomes 0 in the configuration without the harmonic function. This is equivalent to using uniform negative sampling $c'_{i,j} = 1$ as described in Sec. 3. This fact also indicates the importance of the negative sampling method.

4.7 Impact of weighting function

Table 7 shows the impact of weighting function used in GloVe, namely, Eq 8. Note that '$\beta(\cdot)$=1' column shows the results when we fixed 1 for all non-zero entries[5]. This is also clear that the weighting function Eq 8 with appropriate parameters significantly improved the performance of both WSimilarity and WAnalogy tasks. However unfortunately, the best parameter values for WSimilarity and WAnalogy tasks looks different.

(a) WSimilarity

hyper param.	$\beta(\cdot)$=1	$x_{\max} = 1$	10	100	10000
$\gamma = 0.75$	59.4	60.1	**60.9**	57.7	49.5
w/o harmonic func.	58.2	58.0	**60.7**	58.2	56.0
$\gamma = 1.0$	(59.4)	**60.1**	59.4	55.9	36.1
w/o harmonic func.	(58.2)	58.3	**60.7**	57.7	46.7

(b) WAnalogy

hyper param.	$\beta(\cdot)$=1	$x_{\max} = 1$	10	100	10000
$\gamma = 0.75$	55.7	61.1	64.3	**64.8**	28.4
w/o harmonic func.	53.4	52.6	60.3	**61.6**	42.5
$\gamma = 1.0$	(55.7)	61.0	**63.8**	59.1	7.5
w/o harmonic func.	(53.4)	54.1	**60.8**	60.1	20.3

Table 7: Impact of the weighting function.

We emphasize that harmonic function discussed in the previous sub-section was still a necessary condition to obtain the best performance, and better performance in the case of '$\beta(\cdot)$=1' as well.

5 Conclusion

This paper reconsidered the relationship between SkipGram and GloVe models in machine learning viewpoint. We showed that SGNS and GloVe can be easily merged into a unified form. We also extracted the factors of the configurations that are used differently. We empirically investigated which learning configuration is responsible for the performance difference often observed in widely examined word similarity and analogy tasks. Finally, we found that at least two configurations, namely, the weighting function and harmonic function, had significant impacts on the performance. Additionally, we revealed a relationship between harmonic function and negative sampling. We hope that our theoretical and empirical analyses will offer a deeper understanding of these neural word embedding methods[6].

Acknowledgment

We thank three anonymous reviewers for their helpful comments.

References

Eneko Agirre, Enrique Alfonseca, Keith Hall, Jana Kravalova, Marius Paşca, and Aitor Soroa. 2009. A study on similarity and relatedness using distributional and wordnet-based approaches. In *Proceedings of Human Language Technologies: The 2009 Annual Conference of the North American Chapter of the Association for Computational Linguistics*, NAACL '09, pages 19–27, Stroudsburg, PA, USA. Association for Computational Linguistics.

[5]This is equivalent to set 0 to `-x-max` option in `glove` implementation.

[6]The modified codes for our experiments will be available in author's homepage

Elia Bruni, Nam Khanh Tran, and Marco Baroni. 2014. Multimodal distributional semantics. *J. Artif. Int. Res.*, 49(1):1–47, January.

Yoav Goldberg and Omer Levy. 2014. word2vec Explained: Deriving Mikolov et al.'s Negative-sampling Word-embedding Method. *CoRR*, abs/1402.3722.

Eric H. Huang, Richard Socher, Christopher D. Manning, and Andrew Y. Ng. 2012. Improving word representations via global context and multiple word prototypes. In *Proceedings of the 50th Annual Meeting of the Association for Computational Linguistics: Long Papers - Volume 1*, pages 873–882. Association for Computational Linguistics.

Omer Levy and Yoav Goldberg. 2014. Neural Word Embedding as Implicit Matrix Factorization. In Z. Ghahramani, M. Welling, C. Cortes, N.D. Lawrence, and K.Q. Weinberger, editors, *Advances in Neural Information Processing Systems 27*, pages 2177–2185. Curran Associates, Inc.

Omer Levy, Yoav Goldberg, and Ido Dagan. 2015. Improving Distributional Similarity with Lessons Learned from Word Embeddings. *Transactions of the Association for Computational Linguistics*, 3.

Thang Luong, Richard Socher, and Christopher Manning. 2013. Better word representations with recursive neural networks for morphology. In *Proceedings of the Seventeenth Conference on Computational Natural Language Learning*, pages 104–113, Sofia, Bulgaria, August. Association for Computational Linguistics.

Tomas Mikolov, Kai Chen, Greg Corrado, and Jeffrey Dean. 2013a. Efficient estimation of word representations in vector space. *CoRR*, abs/1301.3781.

Tomas Mikolov, Wen-tau Yih, and Geoffrey Zweig. 2013b. Linguistic Regularities in Continuous Space Word Representations. In *Proceedings of the 2013 Conference of the North American Chapter of the Association for Computational Linguistics: Human Language Technologies*, pages 746–751, Atlanta, Georgia, June. Association for Computational Linguistics.

George A. Miller and Walter G. Charles. 1991. Contextual Correlates of Semantic Similarity. *Language & Cognitive Processes*, 6(1):1–28.

Andriy Mnih and Koray Kavukcuoglu. 2013. Learning word embeddings efficiently with noise-contrastive estimation. In C.J.C. Burges, L. Bottou, M. Welling, Z. Ghahramani, and K.Q. Weinberger, editors, *Advances in Neural Information Processing Systems 26*, pages 2265–2273. Curran Associates, Inc.

Jeffrey Pennington, Richard Socher, and Christopher Manning. 2014. Glove: Global vectors for word representation. In *Proceedings of the 2014 Conference on Empirical Methods in Natural Language Processing (EMNLP)*, pages 1532–1543, Doha, Qatar, October. Association for Computational Linguistics.

Kira Radinsky, Eugene Agichtein, Evgeniy Gabrilovich, and Shaul Markovitch. 2011. A word at a time: Computing word relatedness using temporal semantic analysis. In *Proceedings of the 20th International Conference on World Wide Web*, WWW '11, pages 337–346, New York, NY, USA. ACM.

Herbert Rubenstein and John B. Goodenough. 1965. Contextual correlates of synonymy. *Commun. ACM*, 8(10):627–633, October.

Tianze Shi and Zhiyuan Liu. 2014. Linking GloVe with word2vec. *CoRR*, abs/1411.5595.

Pre-training of Hidden-Unit CRFs

Young-Bum Kim[†] **Karl Stratos**[‡] **Ruhi Sarikaya**[†]

[†]Microsoft Corporation, Redmond, WA
[‡]Columbia University, New York, NY
{ybkim, ruhi.sarikaya}@microsoft.com
stratos@cs.columbia.edu

Abstract

In this paper, we apply the concept of pre-training to hidden-unit conditional random fields (HUCRFs) to enable learning on unlabeled data. We present a simple yet effective pre-training technique that learns to associate words with their clusters, which are obtained in an unsupervised manner. The learned parameters are then used to initialize the supervised learning process. We also propose a word clustering technique based on canonical correlation analysis (CCA) that is sensitive to multiple word senses, to further improve the accuracy within the proposed framework. We report consistent gains over standard conditional random fields (CRFs) and HUCRFs without pre-training in semantic tagging, named entity recognition (NER), and part-of-speech (POS) tagging tasks, which could indicate the task independent nature of the proposed technique.

1 Introduction

Despite the recent accuracy gains of the deep learning techniques for sequence tagging problems (Collobert and Weston, 2008; Collobert et al., 2011; Mohamed et al., 2010; Deoras et al., 2012; Xu and Sarikaya, 2013; Yao et al., 2013; Mesnil et al., 2013; Wang and Manning, 2013; Devlin et al., 2014), conditional random fields (CRFs) (Lafferty et al., 2001; Sutton and McCallum, 2006) still have been widely used in many research and production systems for the problems due to the effectiveness and simplicity of training, which does not involve task specific parameter tuning (Collins, 2002; McCallum and Li, 2003; Sha and Pereira, 2003; Turian et al., 2010; Kim and Snyder, 2012; Celikyilmaz et al., 2013; Sarikaya et al., 2014; Anastasakos et al., 2014; Kim et al., 2014; Kim et al., 2015a; Kim et al., 2015c; Kim et al., 2015b). The objective function for CRF training operates globally over sequence structures and can incorporate arbitrary features. Furthermore, this objective is convex and can be optimized relatively efficiently using dynamic programming.

Pre-training has been widely used in deep learning (Hinton et al., 2006) and is one of the distinguishing advantages of deep learning models. The best results obtained across a wide range of tasks involve unsupervised pre-training phase followed by the supervised training phase. The empirical results (Erhan et al., 2010) suggest that unsupervised pre-training has the regularization effect on the learning process and also results in a model parameter configuration that places the model near the basins of attraction of minima that support better generalization.

While pre-training became a standard steps in many deep learning model training recipes, it has not been applied to the family of CRFs. There were several reasons for that; (i) the shallow and linear nature of basic CRF model topology, which limits their expressiveness to the inner product between data and model parameters, and (ii) Lack of a training criterion and configuration to employ pre-training on unlabeled data in a task independent way.

Hidden-unit CRFs (HUCRFs) of Maaten et al. (2011) provide a deeper model topology and improve the expressive power of the CRFs but it does not address how to train them in a task independent way using unlabeled data. In this paper, we present an effective technique for pre-training of HUCRFs that can potentially lead to accuracy gains over HUCRF and basic linear chain CRF models. We cluster words in the text and treat clusters as pseudo-labels to train an HUCRF. Then we transfer the parameters corresponding to observations to initialize the training process on labeled

Proceedings of the 53rd Annual Meeting of the Association for Computational Linguistics and the 7th International Joint Conference on Natural Language Processing (Short Papers), pages 192–198, Beijing, China, July 26-31, 2015.

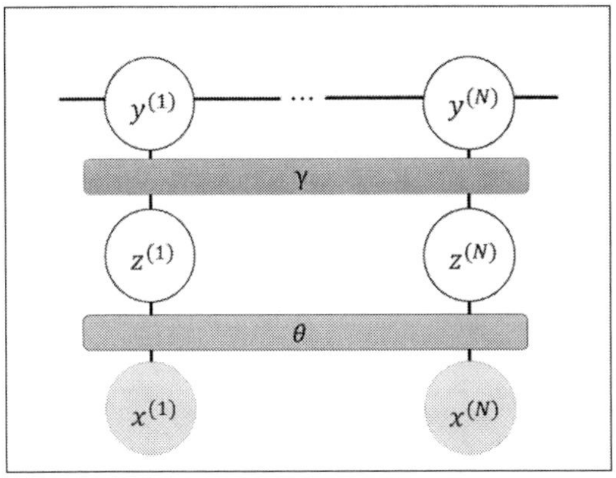

Figure 1: Graphical representation of hidden unit CRFs.

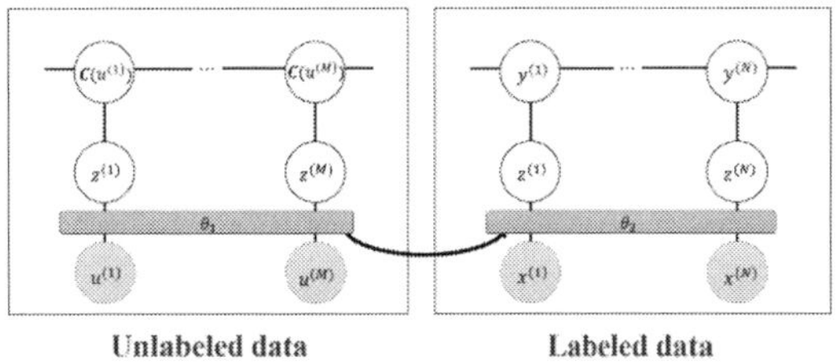

Figure 2: Illustration of a pre-training scheme for HUCRFs.

data. The intuition behind this is that words that are clustered together tend to assume the same labels. Therefore, learning the model parameters to assign the correct cluster ID to each word should accrue to assigning the correct task specific label during supervised learning.

This pre-training step significantly reduces the challenges in training a high-performance HUCRF by (i) acquiring a broad feature coverage from unlabeled data and thus improving the generalization of the model to unseen events, (ii) finding a good a initialization point for the model parameters, and (iii) regularizing the parameter learning by minimizing variance and introducing a bias towards configurations of the parameter space that are useful for unsupervised learning.

We also propose a word clustering technique based on canonical correlation analysis (CCA) that is sensitive to multiple word senses. For example, the resulting clusters can differentiate the instance of "bank" in the sense of financial institutions and the land alongside the river. This is an important point as different senses of a word are likely to have a different task specific tag. Putting them in different clusters would enable the HUCRF model to learn the distinction in terms of label assignment.

2 Model

2.1 HUCRF definition

A HUCRF incorporates a layer of binary-valued hidden units $z = z_1 \dots z_n \in \{0, 1\}$ for each pair of observation sequence $x = x_1 \dots x_n$ and label sequence $y = y_1 \dots y_n$. It is parameterized by $\theta \in \mathbb{R}^d$ and $\gamma \in \mathbb{R}^{d'}$ and defines a joint probability of y and z conditioned on x as follows:

$$p_{\theta,\gamma}(y, z|x) = \frac{\exp(\theta^\top \Phi(x, z) + \gamma^\top \Psi(z, y))}{\sum_{\substack{z' \in \{0,1\}^n \\ y' \in \mathcal{Y}(x,z')}} \exp(\theta^\top \Phi(x, z') + \gamma^\top \Psi(z', y'))}$$

where $\mathcal{Y}(x, z)$ is the set of all possible label sequences for x and z, and $\Phi(x, z) \in \mathbb{R}^d$ and $\Psi(z, y) \in \mathbb{R}^{d'}$ are global feature functions that decompose into local feature functions: $\Phi(x, z) = \sum_{j=1}^n \phi(x, j, z_j)$ and $\Psi(z, y) = \sum_{j=1}^n \psi(z_j, y_{j-1}, y_j)$.

HUCRF forces the interaction between the observations and the labels at each position j to go through a latent variable z_j: see Figure 1 for illustration. Then the probability of labels y is given by marginalizing over the hidden units,

$$p_{\theta,\gamma}(y|x) = \sum_{z \in \{0,1\}^n} p_{\theta,\gamma}(y, z|x)$$

As in restricted Boltzmann machines (Larochelle and Bengio, 2008), hidden units are conditionally independent given observations and labels. This allows for efficient inference with HUCRFs despite their richness (see Maaten et al. (2011) for details). We use a perceptron-style algorithm of Maaten et al. (2011) for training HUCRFs.

2.2 Pre-training HUCRFs

How parameters are initialized for training is important for HUCRFs because the objective function is non-convex. Instead of random initialization, we use a simple and effective initialization scheme (in a similar spirit to the pre-training methods in neural networks) that can leverage a large body of unlabeled data. This scheme is a simple two-step approach.

In the first step, we cluster observed tokens in M unlabeled sequences and treat the clusters as labels to train an intermediate HUCRF. Let $C(u^{(i)})$ be the "cluster sequence" of the i-th unlabeled sequence $u^{(i)}$. We compute:

$$(\theta_1, \gamma_1) \approx \arg\max_{\theta,\gamma} \sum_{i=1}^{M} \log p_{\theta,\gamma}(C(u^{(i)})|u^{(i)}))$$

In the second step, we train a final model on the labeled data $\{(x^{(i)}, y^{(i)})\}_{i=1}^{N}$ using θ_1 as an initialization point:

$$(\theta_2, \gamma_2) \approx \arg\max_{\substack{\theta,\gamma: \\ \textbf{init}(\theta,\theta_1)}} \sum_{i=1}^{N} \log p_{\theta,\gamma}(y^{(i)}|x^{(i)})$$

While we can use γ_1 for initialization as well, we choose to only use θ_1 since the label space is task-specific. This process is illustrated in Figure 2.

In summary, the first step is used to find generic parameters between observations and hidden states; the second step is used to specialize the parameters to a particular task. Note that the first step also generates additional feature types absent in the labeled data which can be useful at test time.

3 Multi-Sense Clustering via CCA

The proposed pre-training method requires assigning a cluster to each word in unlabeled text. Since it learns to associate the words to their clusters, the quality of clusters becomes important. A straightforward approach would be to perform Brown clustering (Brown et al., 1992), which has been very effective in a variety of NLP tasks (Miller et al., 2004; Koo et al., 2008).

However, Brown clustering has some undesirable aspects for our purpose. First, it assigns a single cluster to each word type. Thus a word that can be used very differently depending on its context (e.g., "bank") is treated the same across the corpus. Second, the Brown model uses only unigram and bigram statistics; this can be an issue if we wish to capture semantics in larger contexts. Finally, the algorithm is rather slow in practice for large vocabulary size.

To mitigate these limitations, we propose multi-sense clustering via canonical correlation analysis (CCA). While there are previous work on inducing multi-sense representations (Reisinger and Mooney, 2010; Huang et al., 2012; Neelakantan et al., 2014), our proposed method is simpler and is shown to perform better in experiments.

CCA-PROJ
Input: samples $(x^{(1)}, y^{(1)}) \dots (x^{(n)}, y^{(n)}) \in \{0,1\}^d \times \{0,1\}^{d'}$, dimension k
Output: projections $A \in \mathbb{R}^{d \times k}$ and $B \in \mathbb{R}^{d' \times k}$

- Calculate $B \in \mathbb{R}^{d \times d'}$, $u \in \mathbb{R}^d$, and $v \in \mathbb{R}^{d'}$:

$$B_{i,j} = \sum_{l=1}^{n} [[x_i^{(l)} = 1]][[y_j^{(l)} = 1]]$$

$$u_i = \sum_{l=1}^{n} [[x_i^{(l)} = 1]] \qquad v_i = \sum_{l=1}^{n} [[y_i^{(l)} = 1]]$$

- Define $\hat{\Omega} = \text{diag}(u)^{-1/2} B \text{diag}(v)^{-1/2}$.
- Calculate rank-k SVD $\hat{\Omega}$. Let $U \in \mathbb{R}^{d \times k}$ ($V \in \mathbb{R}^{d' \times k}$) be a matrix of the left (right) singular vector corresponding to the largest k singular values.
- Let $A = \text{diag}(u)^{-1/2} U$ and $B = \text{diag}(v)^{-1/2} V$.

Figure 3: Algorithm for deriving CCA projections from samples of two variables.

3.1 Review of CCA

CCA is a general technique that operates on a pair of multi-dimensional variables. CCA finds k dimensions (k is a parameter to be specified) in which these variables are maximally correlated. Let $x^{(1)} \dots x^{(n)} \in \mathbb{R}^d$ and $y^{(1)} \dots y^{(n)} \in \mathbb{R}^{d'}$ be n samples of the two variables. For simplicity, assume that these variables have zero mean. Then CCA computes the following for $i = 1 \dots k$:

$$\arg\max_{\substack{a_i \in \mathbb{R}^d,\, b_i \in \mathbb{R}^{d'}: \\ a_i^\top a_{i'} = 0 \ \forall i' < i \\ b_i^\top b_{i'} = 0 \ \forall i' < i}} \frac{\sum_{l=1}^{n} (a_i^\top x^{(l)})(b_i^\top y^{(l)})}{\sqrt{\sum_{l=1}^{n} (a_i^\top x^{(l)})^2} \sqrt{\sum_{l=1}^{n} (b_i^\top y^{(l)})^2}}$$

In other words, each (a_i, b_i) is a pair of projection vectors such that the *correlation* between the projected variables $a_i^\top x^{(l)}$ and $b_i^\top y^{(l)}$ (now scalars) is maximized, under the constraint that this projection is *uncorrelated* with the previous $i - 1$ projections. A method based on singular value decomposition (SVD) provides an efficient and exact solution to this problem (Hotelling, 1936). The resulting solution $A \in \mathbb{R}^{d \times k}$ (whose i-th column is a_i) and $B \in \mathbb{R}^{d' \times k}$ (whose i-th column is b_i) can be used to project the variables from

Input: word-context pairs from a corpus of length n: $D = \{(w^{(l)}, c^{(l)})\}_{l=1}^{n}$, dimension k

Output: cluster $C(l) \leq k$ for $l = 1 \ldots n$

- Use the algorithm in Figure 3 to compute projection matrices $(\Pi_W, \Pi_C) = \textbf{CCA-PROJ}(D, k)$.
- For each word type w, perform k-means clustering on $C_w = \{\Pi_C^\top c^{(l)} \in \mathbb{R}^k : w^{(l)} = w\}$ to partition occurrences of w in the corpus into at most k clusters.
- Label each word $w^{(l)}$ with the cluster obtained from the previous step. Let $\bar{D} = \{(\bar{w}^{(l)}, \bar{c}^{(l)})\}_{l=1}^{n}$ denote this new dataset.
- $(\Pi_{\bar{W}}, \Pi_{\bar{C}}) = \textbf{CCA-PROJ}(\bar{D}, k)$
- Perform k-means clustering on $\{\Pi_{\bar{W}}^\top \bar{w}^{(l)} \in \mathbb{R}^k\}$.
- Let $C(l)$ be the cluster corresponding to $Pi_{\bar{W}}^\top v^{(l)}$.

Figure 4: Algorithm for clustering of words in a corpus sensitive to multiple word senses.

the original d- and d'-dimensional spaces to a k-dimensional space:

$$x \in \mathbb{R}^d \longrightarrow A^\top x \in \mathbb{R}^k$$
$$y \in \mathbb{R}^{d'} \longrightarrow B^\top y \in \mathbb{R}^k$$

The new k-dimensional representation of each variable now contains information about the other variable. The value of k is usually selected to be much smaller than d or d', so the representation is typically also low-dimensional. The CCA algorithm is given in Figure 3: we assume that samples are 0-1 indicator vectors. In practice, calculating the CCA projections is fast since there are many efficient SVD implantations available. Also, CCA can incorporate arbitrary context definitions unlike the Brown algorithm.

3.2 Multi-sense clustering

CCA projections can be used to obtain vector representations for both words and contexts. If we wished for only single-sense clusters (akin to Brown clusters), we could simply perform k-means on word embeddings.

However, we can exploit context embeddings to infer word senses. For each word type, we create a set of context embeddings corresponding to all occurrences of that word type. Then we cluster these embeddings; we use an implementation of k-means which automatically determines the number of clusters upper bounded by k. The number of word senses, k, is set to be the number of label types occurring in labeled data (for each task-specific training set).

We use the resulting context clusters to determine the sense of each occurrence of that word type. For instance, an occurrence of "bank" might be labeled as "bank_1" near "financial" or "Chase" and "bank_2" near "shore" or "edge".

This step is for disambiguating word senses, but what we need for our pre-training method is the partition of words in the corpus. Thus we perform a second round of CCA on these disambiguated words to obtain corresponding word embeddings. As a final step, we perform k-means clustering on the disambiguated word embeddings to obtain the partition of words in the corpus. The algorithm is shown in Table 4.

4 Experiments

To validate the effectiveness of our pre-training method, we experiment on three sequence labeling tasks: semantic tagging, named entity recognition (NER), and part-of-speech (POS) tagging. We used L-BFGS for training CRFs [1] and the averaged perceptron for training HUCRFs. The number of hidden variables was set to 500.

4.1 Semantic tagging

The goal of semantic tagging is to assign the correct semantic tag to a words in a given utterance. We use a training set of 50-100k queries across domains and the test set of 5-10k queries. For pre-training, we collected 100-200k unlabeled text from search log data and performed a standard preprocessing step. We use n-gram features up to $n = 3$, regular expression features, domain specific lexicon features and Brown clusters. We present the results for various configurations in Table 1. HUCRF with random initialization from Gaussian distribution (HUCRF_G) boosts the average performance up to 90.52% (from 90.39% of CRF). HUCRF with pre-training with Brown clusters (HUCRF_B) and CCA-based clusters (HUCRF_C) further improves performance to 91.36% and 91.37%, respectively.

Finally, when we use multi-sense cluster (HUCRF_{C+}), we obtain an F1-score of 92.01%. We also compare other alternative pre-training methods. HUCRF with pre-training RBM

[1] For CRFs, we found that L-BFGS had higher performance than SGD and the average percetpron.

	alarm	calendar	comm.	note	ondevice	places	reminder	weather	home	avg
CRF	92.8	89.59	92.13	88.02	88.21	89.64	87.72	96.93	88.51	90.39
HUCRF$_G$	91.79	89.56	92.08	88.42	88.64	90.99	89.21	96.38	87.63	90.52
HUCRF$_R$	91.64	89.6	91.77	88.64	87.43	88.54	88.83	95.88	88.17	90.06
HUCRF$_B$	92.86	90.58	92.8	88.72	89.37	91.14	90.05	97.63	89.08	91.36
HUCRF$_C$	92.82	90.61	92.84	88.69	88.94	91.45	90.31	97.62	89.04	91.37
HUCRF$_S$	91.2	90.53	92.43	88.7	88.09	90.91	89.54	97.24	88.91	90.84
HUCRF$_{NS}$	90.8	89.88	91.54	87.83	88.15	91.02	88.2	96.77	89.02	90.36
HUCRF$_{C+}$	**92.86**	**91.94**	**93.72**	**89.18**	**89.97**	**93.22**	**91.51**	**97.95**	**89.66**	**92.22**

Table 1: Comparison of slot F1 scores on nine personal assistant domains. The numbers in boldface are the best performing method. Subscripts mean the following: G = random initialization from a Gaussian distribution with variance 10^{-4}, R = pre-training with Restricted Boltzmann Machine (RBM) using contrastive divergence of (Hinton, 2002), C = pre-training with CCA-based clusters, B = pre-training with Brown clusters, S = pre-training with skip-ngram multi-sense clusters with fixed cluster size 5, NS = pre-training with non-parametric skip-ngram multi-sense clusters, $C+$ = pre-training with CCA-based multi-sense clusters.

(HUCRF$_R$) does not perform better than with random initialization. The skip-gram clusters (HUCRF$_S$, HUCRF$_{SN}$) do not perform well either. Some examples of disambiguated word occurrences are shown below, demonstrating that the algorithm in Figure 3 yields intuitive clusters.

	NER		POS	
	Test-A	Test-B	Test-A	Test-B
CRF	90.75	86.37	95.51	94.99
HUCRF$_G$	89.99	86.72	95.14	95.08
HUCRF$_R$	90.12	86.43	95.42	94.14
HUCRF$_B$	90.27	87.24	95.55	95.33
HUCRF$_C$	90.9	86.89	95.67	95.23
HUCRF$_S$	90.18	86.84	95.48	95.07
HUCRF$_{NS}$	90.14	85.66	95.35	94.82
HUCRF$_{C+}$	**92.04**	**88.41**	**95.88**	**95.48**

Table 2: F1 Score for NER task and Accuracy for POS task.

word	**context**
Book	a **book(1)** store within 5 miles of my address find comic **book(1)** stores in novi michigan **book(2)** restaurant for tomorrow **book(2)** taxi to pizza hut look for **book(3)** chang dong tofu house in pocono find **book(3)** bindery seattle
High	restaurant nearby with **high(1)** ratings show me **high(1)** credit restaurant nearby the address for shelley **high(2)** school directions to leota junior **high(2)** school what's the distance to kilburn **high(3)** road domino's pizza in **high(3)** ridge missouri

Table 3: Examples of disambiguated word occurrences.

4.2 NER & POS tagging

We use CoNLL 2003 dataset for NER and POS with the standard train/dev/test split. For pre-training, we used the Reuters-RCV1 corpus. It contains 205 millions tokens with 1.6 million types. We follow same preprocessing steps as in semantic tagging. Also, we use the NER features used in Turian et al. (2010) and POS features used in Maaten et al. (2011).

We present the results for both tasks in Table 2. In both tasks, the HUCRF$_{C+}$ yields the best performance, achieving error reduction of 20% (Test-A) and 13% (Test-B) for NER as well as 15% (Test-A) and 8% (Test-B) for POS over HUCRF$_R$. Note that HUCRF does not always perform better than CRF when initialized randomly. However, However, HUCRF consistently outperforms CRF with the pre-training methods proposed in this work.

5 Conclusion

We presented an effective technique for pre-training HUCRFs. Our method transfers observation parameters trained on clustered text to initialize the training process. We also proposed a word clustering scheme based on CCA that is sensitive to multiple word senses. Using our pre-training method, we reported significant improvement over several baselines in three sequence labeling tasks.

References

Tasos Anastasakos, Young-Bum Kim, and Anoop Deoras. 2014. Task specific continuous word representations for mono and multi-lingual spoken language understanding. In *ICASSP*, pages 3246–3250. IEEE.

Peter F Brown, Peter V Desouza, Robert L Mercer, Vincent J Della Pietra, and Jenifer C Lai. 1992.

Class-based n-gram models of natural language. *Computational linguistics*, 18(4):467–479.

Asli Celikyilmaz, Dilek Z Hakkani-Tür, Gökhan Tür, and Ruhi Sarikaya. 2013. Semi-supervised semantic tagging of conversational understanding using markov topic regression. In *ACL*, pages 914–923. Association for Computational Linguistics.

Michael Collins. 2002. Discriminative training methods for hidden markov models: Theory and experiments with perceptron algorithms. In *Proceedings of the ACL-02 conference on Empirical methods in natural language processing-Volume 10*, pages 1–8. Association for Computational Linguistics.

Ronan Collobert and Jason Weston. 2008. A unified architecture for natural language processing: Deep neural networks with multitask learning. In *ICML*, pages 160–167. ACM.

Ronan Collobert, Jason Weston, Léon Bottou, Michael Karlen, Koray Kavukcuoglu, and Pavel Kuksa. 2011. Natural language processing (almost) from scratch. *The Journal of Machine Learning Research*, 12:2493–2537.

Anoop Deoras, Ruhi Sarikaya, Gökhan Tür, and Dilek Z Hakkani-Tür. 2012. Joint decoding for speech recognition and semantic tagging. In *INTERSPEECH*.

Jacob Devlin, Rabih Zbib, Zhongqiang Huang, Thomas Lamar, Richard Schwartz, and John Makhoul. 2014. Fast and robust neural network joint models for statistical machine translation. In *ACL*, volume 1, pages 1370–1380.

Dumitru Erhan, Yoshua Bengio, Aaron Courville, Pierre-Antoine Manzagol, Pascal Vincent, and Samy Bengio. 2010. Why does unsupervised pre-training help deep learning? *The Journal of Machine Learning Research*, 11:625–660.

Geoffrey Hinton, Simon Osindero, and Yee-Whye Teh. 2006. A fast learning algorithm for deep belief nets. *Neural computation*, 18(7):1527–1554.

Geoffrey Hinton. 2002. Training products of experts by minimizing contrastive divergence. *Neural computation*, 14(8):1771–1800.

Harold Hotelling. 1936. Relations between two sets of variates. *Biometrika*, 28(3/4):321–377.

Eric H. Huang, Richard Socher, Christopher D. Manning, and Andrew Y. Ng. 2012. Improving Word Representations via Global Context and Multiple Word Prototypes. In *ACL*. Association for Computational Linguistics.

Young-Bum Kim and Benjamin Snyder. 2012. Universal grapheme-to-phoneme prediction over latin alphabets. In *EMNLP*, pages 332–343. Association for Computational Linguistics.

Young-Bum Kim, Heemoon Chae, Benjamin Snyder, and Yu-Seop Kim. 2014. Training a korean srl system with rich morphological features. In *ACL*, pages 637–642. Association for Computational Linguistics.

Young-Bum Kim, Minwoo Jeong, Karl Stratos, and Ruhi Sarikaya. 2015a. Weakly supervised slot tagging with partially labeled sequences from web search click logs. In *HLT-NAACL*, pages 84–92. Association for Computational Linguistics.

Young-Bum Kim, Karl Stratos, Xiaohu Liu, and Ruhi Sarikaya. 2015b. Compact lexicon selection with spectral methods. In *ACL*. Association for Computational Linguistics.

Young-Bum Kim, Karl Stratos, Ruhi Sarikaya, and Minwoo Jeong. 2015c. New transfer learning techniques for disparate label sets. In *ACL*. Association for Computational Linguistics.

Terry Koo, Xavier Carreras, and Michael Collins. 2008. Simple semi-supervised dependency parsing.

John Lafferty, Andrew McCallum, and Fernando CN Pereira. 2001. Conditional random fields: Probabilistic models for segmenting and labeling sequence data. In *ICML*, pages 282–289.

Hugo Larochelle and Yoshua Bengio. 2008. Classification using discriminative restricted boltzmann machines. In *ICML*.

Laurens van der Maaten, Max Welling, and Lawrence K Saul. 2011. Hidden-unit conditional random fields. In *AISTAT*.

Andrew McCallum and Wei Li. 2003. Early results for named entity recognition with conditional random fields, feature induction and web-enhanced lexicons. In *HLT-NAACL*, pages 188–191. Association for Computational Linguistics.

Grégoire Mesnil, Xiaodong He, Li Deng, and Yoshua Bengio. 2013. Investigation of recurrent-neural-network architectures and learning methods for spoken language understanding. In *INTERSPEECH*, pages 3771–3775.

Scott Miller, Jethran Guinness, and Alex Zamanian. 2004. Name tagging with word clusters and discriminative training. In *HLT-NAACL*, volume 4, pages 337–342. Citeseer.

Abdel-rahman Mohamed, Dong Yu, and Li Deng. 2010. Investigation of full-sequence training of deep belief networks for speech recognition. In *INTERSPEECH*, pages 2846–2849.

Arvind Neelakantan, Jeevan Shankar, Alexandre Passos, and Andrew McCallum. 2014. Efficient non-parametric estimation of multiple embeddings per word in vector space. In *EMNLP*. Association for Computational Linguistics.

Joseph Reisinger and Raymond J Mooney. 2010. Multi-prototype vector-space models of word meaning. In *Human Language Technologies: The 2010 Annual Conference of the North American Chapter of the Association for Computational Linguistics*, pages 109–117. Association for Computational Linguistics.

Ruhi Sarikaya, Asli Celikyilmaz, Anoop Deoras, and Minwoo Jeong. 2014. Shrinkage based features for slot tagging with conditional random fields. In *Proc. of Interspeech*.

Fei Sha and Fernando Pereira. 2003. Shallow parsing with conditional random fields. In *Proceedings of the 2003 Conference of the North American Chapter of the Association for Computational Linguistics on Human Language Technology-Volume 1*, pages 134–141. Association for Computational Linguistics.

Charles Sutton and Andrew McCallum. 2006. An introduction to conditional random fields for relational learning. *Introduction to statistical relational learning*, pages 93–128.

Joseph Turian, Lev Ratinov, and Yoshua Bengio. 2010. Word representations: a simple and general method for semi-supervised learning. In *Proceedings of the 48th annual meeting of the association for computational linguistics*, pages 384–394. Association for Computational Linguistics.

Mengqiu Wang and Christopher D Manning. 2013. Effect of non-linear deep architecture in sequence labeling. In *ICML Workshop on Deep Learning for Audio, Speech and Language Processing*.

Puyang Xu and Ruhi Sarikaya. 2013. Convolutional neural network based triangular crf for joint intent detection and slot filling. In *IEEE Workshop on Automatic Speech Recognition and Understanding (ASRU)*, pages 78–83. IEEE.

Kaisheng Yao, Geoffrey Zweig, Mei-Yuh Hwang, Yangyang Shi, and Dong Yu. 2013. Recurrent neural networks for language understanding. In *INTERSPEECH*, pages 2524–2528.

Distributional Neural Networks for Automatic Resolution of Crossword Puzzles

Aliaksei Severyn*, Massimo Nicosia, Gianni Barlacchi, Alessandro Moschitti†
DISI - University of Trento, Italy
†Qatar Computing Research Institute, Hamad Bin Khalifa University, Qatar
*Google Inc.
{aseveryn,gianni.barlacchi,m.nicosia,amoschitti}@gmail.com

Abstract

Automatic resolution of Crossword Puzzles (CPs) heavily depends on the quality of the answer candidate lists produced by a retrieval system for each clue of the puzzle grid. Previous work has shown that such lists can be generated using Information Retrieval (IR) search algorithms applied to the databases containing previously solved CPs and reranked with tree kernels (TKs) applied to a syntactic tree representation of the clues. In this paper, we create a labelled dataset of 2 million clues on which we apply an innovative Distributional Neural Network (DNN) for reranking clue pairs. Our DNN is computationally efficient and can thus take advantage of such large datasets showing a large improvement over the TK approach, when the latter uses small training data. In contrast, when data is scarce, TKs outperform DNNs.

1 Introduction

Automatic solvers of CPs require accurate list of answer candidates to find good solutions in little time. Candidates can be retrieved from the DBs of previously solved CPs (CPDBs) since clues are often reused, and thus querying CPDBs with the target clue allows us to recuperate the same (or similar) clues.

In this paper, we propose for the first time the use of Distributional Neural Networks to improve the ranking of answer candidate lists. Most importantly, we build a very large dataset for clue retrieval, composed of 2,000,493 clues with their associated answers, i.e., this is a supervised corpus where large scale learning models can be developed and tested. This dataset is an interesting resource that we make available to the research community[1]. To assess the effectiveness of our DNN model, we compare it with the current state of the art model (Nicosia et al., 2015) in reranking CP clues, where tree kernels (Moschitti, 2006) are used to rerank clues according to their syntactic/semantic similarity with the query clue.

The experimental results on our dataset demonstrate that:

(i) DNNs are efficient and can greatly benefit from large amounts of data;

(ii) when DNNs are applied to large-scale data, they largely outperform traditional feature-based rerankers as well as kernel-based models; and

(iii) if limited training data is available for training, tree kernel-based models are more accurate than DNNs

2 Clue Reranking Models for CPs

In this section, we briefly introduce the general idea of CP resolution systems and the state-of-the-art models for reranking answer candidates.

2.1 CP resolution systems

The main task of a CP resolution system is the generation of candidate answer lists for each clue of the target puzzle (Littman et al., 2002). Then a solver for Probabilistic-Constraint Satisfaction Problems, e.g., (Pohl, 1970), tries combinations of letters that satisfy the crossword constraints. The combinations are derived from words found in dictionaries or in the lists of answer candidates. The latter can be generated using large crossword databases as well as several expert modules accessing domain-specific databases (e.g., movies, writers and geography). WebCrow, one of the

*Work done when student at University of Trento

[1] http://ikernels-portal.disi.unitn.it/projects/webcrow/

Proceedings of the 53rd Annual Meeting of the Association for Computational Linguistics and the 7th International Joint Conference on Natural Language Processing (Short Papers), pages 199–204,
Beijing, China, July 26-31, 2015.

Rank	Clue	Answer
1	Actress Pflug who played Lt. Dish in "MASH"	Jo Ann
2	Actress Pflug who played in "MASH" (1970)	Jo Ann
3	Actress Jo Ann	Pflug
4	MASH Actress Jo Ann	Pflug
5	MASH	Crush

Table 1: Candidate list for the query clue: *Jo Ann who played Lt. "Dish" in 1970's "MASH"* (answer: Pflug)

best systems (Ernandes et al., 2005), incorporates knowledge sources and an effective clue retrieval model from DB. It carries out basic linguistic analysis such as part-of-speech tagging and lemmatization and takes advantage of semantic relations contained in WordNet, dictionaries and gazetteers. It also uses a Web module constituted by a search engine (SE), which can retrieve text snippets related to the clue.

Clearly, lists of better quality, i.e., many correct candidates in top positions, result in higher accuracy and speed of the solver. Thus the design of effective answer rankers is extremely important.

2.2 Clue retrieval and reranking

One important source of candidate answers is the DB of previously solved clues. In (Barlacchi et al., 2014a), we proposed the BM25 retrieval model to generate clue lists, which were further refined by applying our reranking models. The latter promote the most similar, which are probably associated with the same answer of the query clue, to the top. The reranking step is important because SEs often fail to retrieve the correct clues in the first position. For example, Table 1 shows the first five clues retrieved for the query clue: *Jo Ann who played Lt. "Dish" in 1970's "MASH"*. BM25 retrieved the wrong clue, *Actress Pflug who played Lt. Dish in "MASH"*, at the top since it has a larger bag-of-words overlap with the query clue.

2.3 Reranking with Kernels

We applied our reranking framework for question answering systems (Moschitti, 2008; Severyn and Moschitti, 2012; Severyn et al., 2013a; Severyn et al., 2013b; Severyn and Moschitti, 2013). This retrieves a list of related clues by using the target clue as a query in an SE (applied to the Web or to a DB). Then, both query and candidates are represented by shallow syntactic structures (generated by running a set of NLP parsers) and traditional similarity features which are fed to a kernel-based reranker. Hereafter, we give a brief description of our models for clue reranking whereas the reader can refer to our previous work (Barlacchi et al., 2014a; Nicosia et al., 2015; Barlacchi et al., 2014b) for more specific details.

Given a query clue q_c and two retrieved clues c_1, c_2, we can rank them by using a classification approach: the two clues c_1 and c_2 are reranked by comparing their classification scores: SVM($\langle q, c_1\rangle$) and SVM($\langle q, c_2\rangle$). The SVM classifier uses the following kernel applied to two pairs of query/clues, $p = \langle q, c_i\rangle$ and $p' = \langle q', c'_j\rangle$:

$$K(p,p') = TK(q,q') + TK(c_i,c'_j) + FV(q,c_i) \cdot FV(q',c'_j),$$

where TK can be any tree kernel, e.g., the syntactic tree kernel (STK) also called SST by Moschitti (2006), and FV is the feature vector representation of the input pair, e.g., $\langle q, c_i\rangle$ or $\langle q', c'_j\rangle$. STK maps trees into the space of all possible tree fragments constrained by the rule that the sibling nodes from their parents cannot be separated. It enables the exploitation of structural features, which can be effectively combined with more traditional features (described hereafter).

Feature Vectors (FV). We compute the following similarity features between clues: (i) tree kernel similarity applied to intra-pairs, i.e., between the query and the retrieved clues; (ii) DKPro Similarity, which defines features used in the context of the Semantic Textual Similarity (STS) challenge (Bär et al., 2013); and (iii) WebCrow features (WC), which are the similarity measures computed on the clue pairs by WebCrow (using the Levenshtein distance) and the SE score.

3 Distributional models for clue reranking

The architecture of our distributional matching model for measuring similarity between clues is presented in Fig. 1. Its main components are:

(i) sentence matrices $\mathbf{s}_{c_i} \in \mathbb{R}^{d \times |\mathbf{c}_i|}$ obtained by the concatenation of the word vectors $\mathbf{w}_j \in \mathbb{R}^d$ (with d being the size of the embeddings) of the corresponding words w_j from the input clues $\mathbf{c}_i$;

(ii) a distributional sentence model $f : \mathbb{R}^{d \times |\mathbf{c}_i|} \rightarrow \mathbb{R}^m$ that maps the sentence

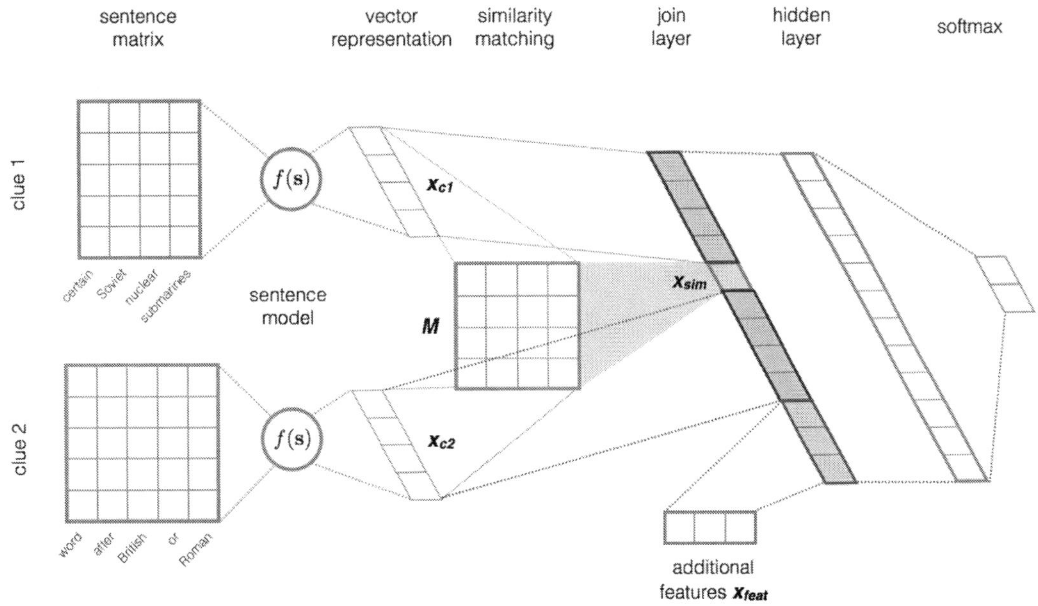

Figure 1: Distributional sentence matching model for computing similarity between clues.

matrix of an input clue $\mathbf{c}_i$ to a fixed-size vector representations $\mathbf{x}_{c_i}$ of size m;

(iii) a layer for computing the similarity between the obtained intermediate vector representations of the input clues, using a similarity matrix $\mathbf{M} \in \mathbb{R}^{m \times m}$ – an intermediate vector representation $\mathbf{x}_{c_1}$ of a clue $\mathbf{c}_1$ is projected to a $\tilde{\mathbf{x}}_{c_1} = \mathbf{x}_{c_1}\mathbf{M}$, which is then matched with $\mathbf{x}_{c_2}$ (Bordes et al., 2014), i.e., by computing a dot-product $\tilde{\mathbf{x}}_{c_1}\mathbf{x}_{c_2}$, thus resulting in a single similarity score x_{sim};

(vi) a set of fully-connected hidden layers that models the similarity between clues using their vector representations produced by the sentence model (also integrating the single similarity score from the previous layer); and

(v) a *softmax* layer that outputs probability scores reflecting how well the clues match with each other.

The choice of the sentence model plays a crucial role as the resulting intermediate representations of the input clues will affect the successive step of computing their similarity. Recently, distributional sentence models, where $f(\mathbf{s})$ is represented by a sequence of convolutional-pooling feature maps, have shown state-of-the-art results on many NLP tasks, e.g., (Kalchbrenner et al., 2014; Kim, 2014). In this paper, we opt for a simple solution where $f(\mathbf{s}_{\mathbf{c}_i}) = \sum_i \mathbf{w}_i/|\mathbf{c}_i|$, i.e., the word vectors, are averaged to a single fixed-sized vector $\mathbf{x} \in \mathbb{R}^d$. Our preliminary experiments revealed that this simpler model works just as well as more complicated single or multi-layer convolutional architectures. We conjecture that this is largely due to the nature of the language used in clues, which is very dense and where the syntactic information plays a minor role.

Considering recent deep learning models for matching sentences, our network is most similar to the models in Hu et al. (2014) applied for computing sentence similarity and in Yu et al.(2014) (answer sentence selection in Question Answering) with the following differences:

(i) In contrast to more complex *convolutional* sentence models explored in (Hu et al., 2014) and in (Yu et al., 2014), our sentence model is composed of a single averaging operation.

(ii) To compute the similarity between the vector representation of the input sentences, our network uses two methods: (i) computing the similarity score obtained by transforming one clue into another using a similarity matrix $\mathbf{M}$ (explored in (Yu et al., 2014)), and (ii) directly modelling interactions between intermediate vector representations of the input clues via fully-connected hidden layers (used by (Hu et al., 2014)).

4 Experiments

Our experiments compare different ranking models, i.e., BM25 as the IR baseline, and several rerankers, and our distributional neural network (DNN) for the task of clue reranking.

4.1 Experimental setup

Data. We compiled our crossword corpus combining (i) CPs downloaded from the Web[2] and (ii) the clue database provided by Otsys[3]. We removed duplicates, fill-in-the-blank clues (which are better solved by using other strategies) and clues representing anagrams or linguistic games.

We collected over 6.3M pairs of clue/answer and after removal of duplicates, we obtained a compressed dataset containing 2M unique and standard clues, with associated answers, which we called CPDB. We used these clues to build a Small Dataset (SD) and a Large Dataset (LD) for reranking. The two datasets are based on pairs of clues: query and retrieved clues. Such clues are retrieved using a BM25 model on CPDB.

For creating SD, we used 8k clues that (i) were randomly extracting from CPDB and (ii) satisfying the property that at least one correct clue (i.e., having the same answer of the query clue) is in the first retrieved 10 clues (of course the query clue is eliminated from the ranked list provided by BM25). In total we got about 120K examples, 84,040 negative and 35,960 positive clue[4].

For building LD, we collected 200k clues with the same property above. More precisely we obtained 1,999,756 pairs (10×200k minus few problematic examples) with 599,025 positive and 140,0731 negative pairs of queries with their retrieved clues. Given the large number of examples, we only used such dataset in classification modality, i.e., we did not form reranking examples (pairs of pairs).

[2]http://www.crosswordgiant.com

[3]http://www.otsys.com/clue

[4]A true reranker should be built using pairs of clue pairs, where the positive pairs are those having the correct pair as the first member. This led to form 127,109 reranking examples, with 66,011 positive and 61,098 negative pairs. However, in some experiments, which we do not report in the paper, we observed that the performance both of the simple classifier as well as the true reranker were similar, thus we decided to use the simpler classifier.

Structural model. We use SVM-light-TK[5], which enables the use of structural kernels (Moschitti, 2006). We applied structural kernels to shallow tree representations and a polynomial kernel of degree 3 to feature vectors (FV).

Distributional neural network model. We pre-initialize the word embeddings by running the `word2vec` tool (Mikolov et al., 2013) on the English Wikipedia dump. We opt for a skipgram model with window size 5 and filtering words with frequency less than 5. The dimensionality of the embeddings is set to 50. The input sentences are mapped to fixed-sized vectors by computing the average of their word embeddings. We use a single non-linear hidden layer (with rectified linear (ReLU) activation function) whose size is equal to the size of the previous layer.

The network is trained using SGD with shuffled mini-batches using the Adagrad update rule (Duchi et al., 2011). The batch size is set to 100 examples. We used 25 epochs with early stopping, i.e., we stop the training if no update to the best accuracy on the `dev` set (we create the dev set by allocating 10% of the training set) is made for the last 5 epochs. The accuracy computed on the `dev` set is the Mean Average Precision (MAP) score. To extract the DNN features we simply take the output of the hidden layer just before the softmax.

Evaluation. We used standard metrics widely used in QA: the Mean Reciprocal Rank (MRR) and Mean Average Precision (MAP).

4.2 Results

Table 2 summarizes the results of our different reranking models trained on a small dataset (SD) of 120k examples and a large dataset (LD) with 2M examples.

The first column reports the BM25 result; the second column shows the performance of SVM perf (SVM_p), which is a very fast variant of SVM, using FV; the third column reports the state-of-the-art model for crossword clue reranking (Nicosia et al., 2015), which uses FV vector and tree kernels, i.e., SVM(TK).

Regarding the other systems: $DNNM_{SD}$ is the DNN model trained on the small data (SD) of 120k training pairs; SVMp($DNNF_{LD}$) is SVM perf trained with (i) the features derived from

[5]`http://disi.unitn.it/moschitti/Tree-Kernel.htm`

	BM25	SVMp	SVM(TK)	DNNM_{SD}	$\text{SVMp(DNNF}_{LD})$	$\text{SVM(DNNF}_{LD}\text{,TK)}$
Training classifiers with the Small Dataset (SD) (120K instances)						
MRR	37.57	41.95	43.59	40.08	46.12	45.50
MAP	27.76	30.06	31.79	28.25	33.75	33.71

	BM25	SVMp	SVM(TK)	DNNM_{LD}	$\text{SVMp(DNNF}_{LD},-\text{FV)}$	$\text{SVMp(DNNF}_{LD})$
Training classifiers with the Large Dataset (LD) (2 million instances)						
MRR	37.57	41.47	–	46.10	46.36	46.27
MAP	27.76	29.95	–	33.81	34.07	33.86

Table 2: SVM models and DNN trained on 120k (small dataset) and 2 millions (large dataset) examples. Feature vectors are used with all models except when indicated by −FV

DNN trained on a large clue dataset LD and (ii) the FV; and finally, SVM(DNNF$_{LD}$,TK) is SVM using DNN features (generated from LD), FV and TK. It should be noted that:

(i) SVM$_p$ is largely improved by TK;

(ii) DNNM$_{SD}$ on relatively small data delivers an accuracy lower than FV;

(iii) if SVM$_p$ is trained with DNNM$_{LD}$, i.e., features derived from the dataset of 2M clues, the accuracy greatly increases; and

(iv) finally, the combination with TK, i.e., SVM(DNNF$_{LD}$,TK), does not significantly improve the previous results.

In summary, when a dataset is relatively small DNNM fails to deliver any noticeable improvement over the SE baseline even when combined with additional similarity features. SVM and TK models generalize much better on the smaller dataset.

Additionally, it is interesting to see that training an SVM on a small number of examples enriched with the features produced by a DNN trained on large data gives us the same results of DNN trained on the large dataset. Hence, it is desired to use larger training collections to build an accurate distributional similarity matching model that can be then effectively combined with other feature-based or tree kernel models, although at the moment the combination does not significantly improve TK models.

Regarding the LD training setting it can be observed that:

(i) the second column shows that adding more training examples to SVM$_p$ does not increase accuracy (compared with SD result);

(ii) DNNM$_{LD}$ delivers high accuracy suggesting that a large dataset is essential to its training; and

(iii) again SVM$_p$ using DNN features deliver state-of-the-art accuracy independently of using or not additional features (i.e., see −FV, which excludes the latter).

5 Conclusions

In this paper, we have explored various reranker models to improve automatic CP resolution. The most important finding is that our distributional neural network model is very effective in establishing similarity matching between clues. We combine the features produced by our DNN model with other rerankers to greatly improve over the previous state-of-the-art results. Finally, we collected a very large dataset composed of 2 millions clue/answer pairs that can be useful to the NLP community for developing semantic textual similarity models.

Future research will be devoted to find models to effectively combine TKs and DNN. In particular, our previous model exploiting Linked Open Data in QA (Tymoshenko et al., 2014) seems very promising to find correct answer to clues. This as well as further research will be integrated in our CP system described in (Barlacchi et al., 2015).

Acknowledgments

This work was supported by the EC project CogNet, 671625 (H2020-ICT-2014-2). The first author was supported by the Google Europe Doctoral Fellowship Award 2013.

References

Daniel Bär, Torsten Zesch, and Iryna Gurevych. 2013. DKPro similarity: An open source framework for text similarity. In *Proceedings of ACL (System Demonstrations)*.

Gianni Barlacchi, Massimo Nicosia, and Alessandro Moschitti. 2014a. Learning to rank answer candidates for automatic resolution of crossword puzzles. In *Proceedings of the Eighteenth Conference on Computational Natural Language Learning*. Association for Computational Linguistics.

Gianni Barlacchi, Massimo Nicosia, and Alessandro Moschitti. 2014b. A retrieval model for automatic resolution of crossword puzzles in italian language. In *The First Italian Conference on Computational Linguistics CLiC-it 2014*.

Gianni Barlacchi, Massimo Nicosia, and Alessandro Moschitti. 2015. SACRY: Syntax-based automatic crossword puzzle resolution system. In *Proceedings of 53nd Annual Meeting of the Association for Computational Linguistics: System Demonstrations*, Beijing, China, July. Association for Computational Linguistics.

Antoine Bordes, Sumit Chopra, and Jason Weston. 2014. Question answering with subgraph embeddings. In *Proceedings of the 2014 Conference on Empirical Methods in Natural Language Processing (EMNLP)*, pages 615–620, Doha, Qatar, October. Association for Computational Linguistics.

John Duchi, Elad Hazan, and Yoram Singer. 2011. Adaptive subgradient methods for online learning and stochastic optimization. *J. Mach. Learn. Res.*, 12:2121–2159.

Marco Ernandes, Giovanni Angelini, and Marco Gori. 2005. Webcrow: A web-based system for crossword solving. In *In Proc. of AAAI 05*, pages 1412–1417. Menlo Park, Calif., AAAI Press.

Baotian Hu, Zhengdong Lu, Hang Li, and Qingcai Chen. 2014. Convolutional neural network architectures for matching natural language sentences. In *NIPS*.

Nal Kalchbrenner, Edward Grefenstette, and Phil Blunsom. 2014. A convolutional neural network for modelling sentences. *Proceedings of the 52nd Annual Meeting of the Association for Computational Linguistics*, June.

Yoon Kim. 2014. Convolutional neural networks for sentence classification. Doha, Qatar.

Michael L. Littman, Greg A. Keim, and Noam Shazeer. 2002. A probabilistic approach to solving crossword puzzles. *Artificial Intelligence*, 134(12):23 – 55.

Tomas Mikolov, Ilya Sutskever, Kai Chen, Greg S Corrado, and Jeff Dean. 2013. Distributed representations of words and phrases and their compositionality. In *Advances in Neural Information Processing Systems 26*, pages 3111–3119.

Alessandro Moschitti. 2006. Efficient convolution kernels for dependency and constituent syntactic trees. In *ECML*, pages 318–329.

Alessandro Moschitti. 2008. Kernel methods, syntax and semantics for relational text categorization. In *Proceedings of the 17th ACM Conference on Information and Knowledge Management*, CIKM '08, pages 253–262, Napa Valley, California, USA.

Massimo Nicosia, Gianni Barlacchi, and Alessandro Moschitti. 2015. Learning to rank aggregated answers for crossword puzzles. In Allan Hanbury, Gabriella Kazai, Andreas Rauber, and Norbert Fuhr, editors, *Advances in Information Retrieval - 37th European Conference on IR Research, ECIR, Vienna, Austria. Proceedings*, volume 9022 of *Lecture Notes in Computer Science*, pages 556–561.

Ira Pohl. 1970. Heuristic search viewed as path finding in a graph. *Artificial Intelligence*, 1(34):193 – 204.

Aliaksei Severyn and Alessandro Moschitti. 2012. Structural relationships for large-scale learning of answer re-ranking. In *Proceedings of ACM SIGIR*, New York, NY, USA.

Aliaksei Severyn and Alessandro Moschitti. 2013. Automatic feature engineering for answer selection and extraction. In *Proceedings of the 2013 Conference on Empirical Methods in Natural Language Processing*, pages 458–467, Seattle, Washington, USA, October. Association for Computational Linguistics.

Aliaksei Severyn, Massimo Nicosia, and Alessandro Moschitti. 2013a. Building structures from classifiers for passage reranking. In *CIKM*.

Aliaksei Severyn, Massimo Nicosia, and Alessandro Moschitti. 2013b. Learning adaptable patterns for passage reranking. In *Proceedings of the Seventeenth Conference on Computational Natural Language Learning*, pages 75–83, Sofia, Bulgaria, August. Association for Computational Linguistics.

Kateryna Tymoshenko, Alessandro Moschitti, and Aliaksei Severyn. 2014. Encoding semantic resources in syntactic structures for passage reranking. In *Proceedings of the 14th Conference of the European Chapter of the Association for Computational Linguistics*, pages 664–672, Gothenburg, Sweden, April. Association for Computational Linguistics.

Lei Yu, Karl Moritz Hermann, Phil Blunsom, and Stephen Pulman. 2014. Deep learning for answer sentence selection. *CoRR*.

Word Order Typology through Multilingual Word Alignment

Robert Östling
Department of Linguistics
Stockholm University
SE-106 91 Stockholm, Sweden
robert@ling.su.se

Abstract

With massively parallel corpora of hundreds or thousands of translations of the same text, it is possible to automatically perform typological studies of language structure using very large language samples. We investigate the domain of word order using multilingual word alignment and high-precision annotation transfer in a corpus with 1144 translations in 986 languages of the New Testament. Results are encouraging, with 86% to 96% agreement between our method and the manually created WALS database for a range of different word order features. Beyond reproducing the categorical data in WALS and extending it to hundreds of other languages, we also provide quantitative data for the relative frequencies of different word orders, and show the usefulness of this for language comparison. Our method has applications for basic research in linguistic typology, as well as for NLP tasks like transfer learning for dependency parsing, which has been shown to benefit from word order information.

1 Introduction

Since the work of Greenberg (1963), word order features have played a central role in linguistic typology research. There is a great deal of variation across languages, and interesting interactions between different features which may hint at cognitive constraints in the processing of human language. A full theoretical discussion on word order typology is beyond the scope of this paper, but the interested reader is referred to e.g. Dryer (2007) for an overview of the field.

This study uses multilingual word alignment (Östling, 2014) and high-precision annotation projection of part-of-speech (PoS) tags and dependency parse trees to investigate five different word order properties in 986 different languages, through a corpus of New Testament translations. The results are validated through comparison to relevant chapters in the World Atlas on Language Structures, WALS (Dryer and Haspelmath, 2013), and we find a very high level of agreement between this database and our method.

We identify two primary applications of this method. First, it provides a new tool for basic research in linguistic typology. Second, it has been shown that using these word order features leads to increased accuracy during dependency parsing model transfer (Täckström et al., 2013). These benefits can now be extended to hundreds of more languages. The quantified word order characteristics computed for each of the 986 languages in the New Testament corpus, including about 600 not in the WALS samples for these features, are available for download.[1]

2 Related work

Using parallel texts for linguistic typology has become increasingly popular recently, as massively parallel texts with hundreds or thousands of languages have become easily accessible through the web (Cysouw and Wälchli, 2007; Dahl, 2007; Wälchli, 2014). Specific applications include data-driven language classification (Mayer and Cysouw, 2012) and lexical typology (Wälchli and Cysouw, 2012). However, unlike our work, none of these authors developed automatic methods for studying syntactic properties like word order, nor did they utilize recent advances in the field of word alignment algorithms.

[1] http://www.ling.su.se/acl2015-wordorder.zip

Proceedings of the 53rd Annual Meeting of the Association for Computational Linguistics and the 7th International Joint Conference on Natural Language Processing (Short Papers), pages 205–211,
Beijing, China, July 26-31, 2015. ©2015 Association for Computational Linguistics

3 Method

The first step consists of using supervised systems for annotating the source texts with Universal PoS Tags (Petrov et al., 2012) and dependency structure in the Universal Dependency Treebank format (McDonald et al., 2013). For PoS tagging, we use the Stanford Tagger (Toutanova et al., 2003) followed by a conversion step from the Penn Treebank tagset to the "universal" PoS tags using the tables published by Petrov et al. Next, we use the MaltParser dependency parser (Nivre et al., 2007) trained on the Universal Dependency Treebank using MaltOptimizer (Ballesteros and Nivre, 2012).

The corpus is then aligned using the multilingual alignment tool of Östling (2014). This model learns an "interlingua" representation of the text, in this case the New Testament, to which all translations are then aligned independently. An interlingua sentence $\boldsymbol{e}$ is assumed to generate the corresponding sentences $\boldsymbol{f}^{(l)}$ for each of the L languages through a set of alignment variables $\boldsymbol{a}^{(l)}$ for each language. This can be seen as a multilingual extension of the IBM model 1 (Brown et al., 1993) with Dirichlet priors (Mermer and Saraçlar, 2011), where not only the alignment variables are hidden but also the source $\boldsymbol{e}$. The probability of a sentence and its alignments (in L languages) under this model is

$$P(\boldsymbol{a}^{(1...L)}, \boldsymbol{f}^{(1...L)}|\boldsymbol{e}) = \prod_{l=1}^{L}\prod_{j=1}^{J} p_t(f_j^{(l)}|e_{a_j^{(l)}}) \cdot \prod_{i=1}^{I} p_c(e_i) \quad (1)$$

where the translation distributions p_t are assumed to have symmetric Dirichlet priors and the source token distribution p_c a Chinese Restaurant Process prior. Given the parallel sentences $\boldsymbol{f}^{(1...L)}$, then $\boldsymbol{a}^{(1...L)}$ and $\boldsymbol{e}$ are sampled using Gibbs sampling. The advantage of this method is that the multi-source transfer can be done once, to the interlingua representation, then transferred in a second step to all of the 986 languages investigated. It would be possible to instead perform 986 separate multi-source projection steps, but at the expense of having to perform a large number of bitext alignments.

From the annotated source texts, PoS and dependency annotations are transferred to the interlingua representation. Since alignments are noisy and low recall is acceptable in this task, we use an aggressive filtering scheme: dependency links must be transferred from at least 80% of source texts in order to be included. For PoS tags, which are only used to double-check grammatical relations and should not impact precision negatively, the majority tag among aligned words is used. Apart from compensating for noisy alignments and parsing errors, this method also helps to catch violations against the direct correspondence assumption (Hwa et al., 2002) by filtering out instances where different source texts use different constructions, favoring the most prototypical cases. Each word order feature is coded in terms of dependency relations, with additional constraints on the parts of speech that can be involved. For instance, when investigating the order between nouns and their modifying adjectives we look for an AMOD dependency relation between an ADJ-tagged and a NOUN-tagged word, and note the order between the adjective and the noun. This method rests on the assumption that translation equivalents have the same grammatical functions across translations, which is not always the case. For instance, if one language uses a passive construction where the source texts all use the active voice, we would obtain the wrong order between subject and object.

To summarize, our algorithm consists of the following steps:

1. Compute an interlingua representation of the parallel text, as well as word alignments linking it to each of the translations.
2. Annotate a subset of translations with PoS tags and dependency structure.
3. Use multi-source annotation projection from this subset to the interlingua representation, including only dependency links where the same link is projected from at least 80% of the source translations.
4. Use single-source annotation projection from the interlingua representation to each of the 986 translations.
5. For each construction of interest, and for each language, count the frequency of each ordering of its constituents.

4 Evaluation

We evaluate our method through comparison to the WALS database (Dryer and Haspelmath,

SOV	SVO	OSV	OVS	VSO	VOS
Polynesian (Hawaiian, Maori)					
3	31	2	2	70	3
6	26	5	4	76	18
Sinitic (Mandarin, Hakka)					
54	235	6	0	3	5
18	84	1	2	5	3
Turkic (Kara-Kalpak, Kumyk)					
114	2	8	7	0	0
89	1	12	11	4	1

Table 1: Number of transitive clauses with a given order of subject/object/verb, according to our algorithm, for six languages (from three families).

2013), by manual analysis of selected cases, and by cluster analysis of the word order properties computed for each language by our method.

4.1 Data and methodology

A corpus of web-crawled translations of the New Testament was used, comprising 1144 translations in 986 different languages. Of these, we used five English translations as source texts for annotation projection. Ideally more languages should be used as sources, but since we only had access to complete annotation pipelines for English and German we only considered these two languages, and preliminary experiments using some German translations in addition to the English ones did not lead to significantly different results. A typologically more diverse set of source languages would help to identify those instances in the text which are most consistently translated across languages, in order to reduce the probability that peculiarities of the source language(s) will bias the results.

In order to evaluate our method automatically, we used data from the WALS database (Dryer and Haspelmath, 2013) which classifies languages according to a large number of features. Several features concern word order, and we focused on five of these (listed in Table 2). Only languages which are represented both in the New Testament corpus and the WALS data were used for the evaluation. In addition, we exclude languages for which WALS does not indicate a particular word order. This might be due to e.g. lacking adpositions altogether (which makes the adposition/noun order of that language undefined), or because no specific order is considered dominant.

The frequencies of all possible word orders for a feature are then counted, and for the purpose of evaluation the most common order is chosen as the algorithm's output. Although the relative frequencies of the different possible word orders are discarded for the sake of comparability with WALS, these frequencies are themselves an important result of our work and tell a much richer story of the word order properties (see Table 1 and Figure 1).

Counting the number of instances (token frequency) of each word order is the most straightforward way to estimate the relative proportions of each ordering, but the results are biased towards the behavior of the most frequent words, which often have idiosyncratic, non-productive features. Therefore, we also compute the corresponding statistics where each type is counted only once for each word order it participates in, disregarding its frequency. The type-based counts should better capture the behavior of productive patterns in the language. For the purpose of this study, we define the type of our relations as follows:

- **adjective-noun**: the form of the adjective
- **adposition-noun**: the forms of both adposition and noun
- **verb-(subject)-(object)**: the form of the verb

For instance, given the following three sentences: "we see him," "I see her" and "them I see", we would increase the count by one for SVO order and for OVS order, because these are the orders in which the verb *see* has been observed to participate.

In cases where there are multiple translations into a particular language, information is aggregated from all these translations into a single profile for the language. This is problematic in some cases, such as when a very long time separates two translations and word order characteristics have evolved, or simply due to different translators or source texts. However, since the typical case is a single translation per language, and WALS only contains one data point per language, we leave inter-language comparison to future research.

4.2 Results and Discussion

Table 1 shows how the output of our token-based algorithm looks for three pairs of languages selected from different families. The absolute counts vary due to our filtering procedure and differing numbers of translations, but as we might expect

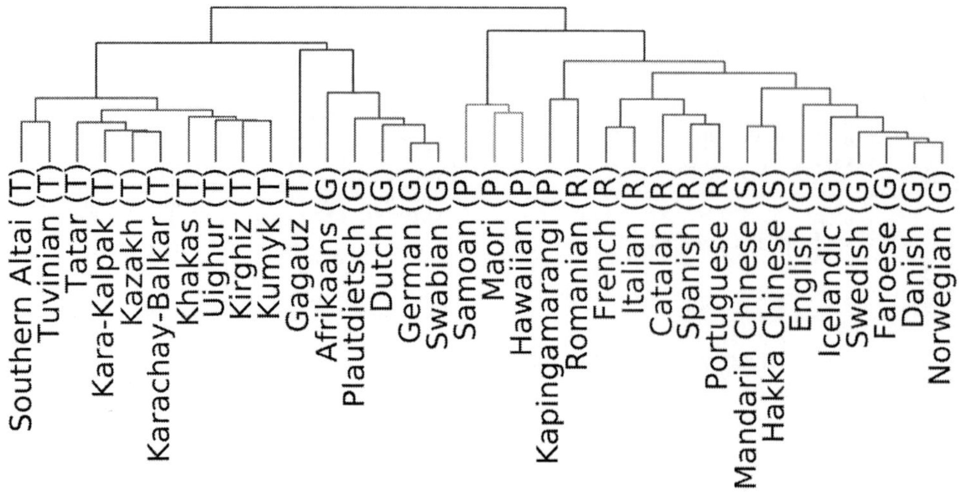

Figure 1: Hierarchical clustering based on word order statistics from our algorithm. Language families represented are (G)ermanic, (R)omance, (T)urkic, (P)olynesian and (S)initic.

the relative numbers are quite similar within each pair.

As a way of visualizing our data, we also tried performing hierarchical clustering of languages, by normalizing the word order count vectors and treating them (together) as a single 14-dimensional vector. The result confirmed that languages can be grouped remarkably well on basis of these five automatically extracted word order features. A subset of the clustering containing all languages from five language families represented in the New Testament corpus can be found in Figure 1. While the clustering mostly follows traditional genealogical boundaries, it is perhaps more interesting to look at the cases where it does not. The most glaring case is the wide split between the West Germanic and the North Germanic languages, which in spite of their shared ancestry have widely different word order characteristics. Interestingly, English is not grouped with the West Germanic languages, but rather with the North Germanic languages which it has been in close contact with.[2] One can also note that the Sinitic languages, with respect to word order, are quite close to the North Germanic languages.

Table 2 shows the agreement between the algorithm's output and the corresponding WALS chapter for each feature. The level of agreement is high, even though the sample consists mainly of languages unrelated to English, from which the dependency structure and PoS annotations were transferred. The **most common** column gives the ratio of the most common ordering for each feature (according to WALS), which can serve as a naive baseline.

As expected, the lowest level of agreement is observed for WALS chapter 81A, which has a lower baseline since it allows six permutations of the verb, subject and object, whereas all the other features are binary. In addition, this feature requires that *two* dependency relations (subject-verb and object-verb) have been correctly transferred, which substantially reduces the number of relations available for comparison.

The fact that sources sometimes differ as to the basic word order of a given language makes it evident that the disagreement reported in Table 2 is not necessarily due to errors made by our algorithm. Another example of this can be found when looking at the order of adjective and noun in some Romance languages (Spanish, Catalan, Portuguese, French and Italian), which are all classified as having noun-adjective order (Dryer, 2013a). It turns out that adjective-noun order in fact dominates in all of these languages, narrowly when using type counts and by a fairly large margin when using token counts. This result was confirmed by manual inspection, which leads us

[2] One reviewer pointed us to the controversial claim of Emonds (2011), that modern English in fact *is* a North Germanic language, albeit with strong influence from the extinct West Germanic language of Old English.

Table 2: Agreement between WALS and our results, on languages present in both datasets. The relative frequency of the most common ordering is given for comparison. **Types** is the agreement using type-based counts (see text for details), whereas **Tokens** uses token-based counts.

Feature	Languages	Types	Tokens	Most common
81A: Subject, Object, Verb (Dryer, 2013e)	342	85.4%	85.7%	SOV: 43.3%
82A: Subject, Verb (Dryer, 2013d)	376	89.4%	90.4%	SV: 79.8%
83A: Object, Verb (Dryer, 2013c)	387	96.4%	96.4%	VO: 54.8%
85A: Adposition, Noun Phrase (Dryer, 2013b)	329	94.8%	95.1%	Prep: 50.4%
87A: Adjective, Noun (Dryer, 2013a)	334	85.9%	88.0%	AdjN: 68.9%

to search further for an explanation for the discrepancy.[3] The Universal Dependency Treebank (McDonald et al., 2013) version 2 contains subcorpora in French, Italian, Spanish and Brazilian Portuguese. In all of these, noun-adjective order is dominant, which casts further doubts on our result. The key difference turns out to be the genre: whereas the modern texts used for the Universal Dependency Treebank have mainly noun-adjective order, we used our supervised annotation pipeline to confirm that the French translations of the New Testament indeed are dominated by adjective-noun order. This should serve as a warning about extrapolating too far from results obtained in one very specific genre, let alone in a single text.

5 Conclusions and future directions

The promising results from this study show that high-precision annotation transfer is a realistic way of exploring word order features in very large language samples, when a suitable parallel text is available. Although the WALS features on word order already use very large samples (over a thousand languages), using our method with the New Testament corpus contributes about 600 additional data points per feature, and adds quantitative data for all of the 986 languages contained in the corpus.

There are many other structural properties of languages that could be investigated with high-precision annotation transfer in massively parallel corpora, not just regarding word order but also within in domains such as negation, comparison and tense/aspect systems. While there are limits to the quality and types of answers obtainable, our work demonstrates that for some problems it is possible to obtain quick, quantitative answers that can be used to guide more traditional and thorough typological research.

On the technical side, the alignment model used is based on a non-symmetrized IBM model 1, and more elaborate methods for alignment and annotation projection could potentially lead to more accurate results. Preliminary results however indicate that adding a HMM-based word order model akin to Vogel et al. (1996) actually leads to somewhat reduced agreement with the WALS classification, because the projections become biased towards the word order characteristics of the source language(s), in our case English. This indicates that using the less accurate but also less biased IBM model 1 is in fact an advantage, when aggressive high-precision filtering is used.

Acknowledgments

Thanks to Calle Börstell, Östen Dahl, Francesca Di Garbo, Joakim Nivre, Janet B. Pierrehumbert, Jörg Tiedemann, Bernhard Wälchli, Mats Wirén and the anonymous reviewers for helpful comments and discussions.

[3]Thanks to Francesca Di Garbo for helping with this.

References

Miguel Ballesteros and Joakim Nivre. 2012. MaltOptimizer: An optimization tool for MaltParser. In *Proceedings of the Demonstrations at the 13th Conference of the European Chapter of the Association for Computational Linguistics*, EACL '12, pages 58–62, Stroudsburg, PA, USA. Association for Computational Linguistics.

Peter F. Brown, Vincent J. Della Pietra, Stephen A. Della Pietra, and Robert L. Mercer. 1993. The mathematics of statistical machine translation: Parameter estimation. *Computational Linguistics*, 19(2):263–311, June.

Michael Cysouw and Bernhard Wälchli. 2007. Parallel texts: Using translational equivalents in linguistic typology. *STUF - Language Typology and Universals*, 60(2):95–99.

Östen Dahl. 2007. From questionnaires to parallel corpora in typology. *STUF - Language Typology and Universals*, 60(2):172–181.

Matthew S. Dryer and Martin Haspelmath. 2013. *The World Atlas of Language Structures Online*. `http://wals.info`.

Matthew S. Dryer. 2007. Word order. In Timothy Shopen, editor, *Language Typology and Syntactic Description*, volume I, chapter 2, pages 61–131. Cambridge University Press.

Matthew S. Dryer. 2013a. Order of adjective and noun. In Matthew S. Dryer and Martin Haspelmath, editors, *The World Atlas of Language Structures Online*. Max Planck Institute for Evolutionary Anthropology, Leipzig.

Matthew S. Dryer. 2013b. Order of adposition and noun phrase. In Matthew S. Dryer and Martin Haspelmath, editors, *The World Atlas of Language Structures Online*. Max Planck Institute for Evolutionary Anthropology, Leipzig.

Matthew S. Dryer. 2013c. Order of object and verb. In Matthew S. Dryer and Martin Haspelmath, editors, *The World Atlas of Language Structures Online*. Max Planck Institute for Evolutionary Anthropology, Leipzig.

Matthew S. Dryer. 2013d. Order of subject and verb. In Matthew S. Dryer and Martin Haspelmath, editors, *The World Atlas of Language Structures Online*. Max Planck Institute for Evolutionary Anthropology, Leipzig.

Matthew S. Dryer. 2013e. Order of subject, object and verb. In Matthew S. Dryer and Martin Haspelmath, editors, *The World Atlas of Language Structures Online*. Max Planck Institute for Evolutionary Anthropology, Leipzig.

Joseph Emonds. 2011. English as a North Germanic language: From the Norman conquest to the present. In Roman Trušník, Katarína Nemčoková, and Gregory Jason Bell, editors, *Proceedings of the Second International Conference on English and American Studies*, pages 13–26, Zlín, Czech Republic, September.

Joseph H. Greenberg. 1963. Some universals of grammar with particular reference to the order of meaningful elements. In Joseph H. Greenberg, editor, *Universals of Human Language*, pages 73–113. MIT Press, Cambridge, Massachusetts.

Rebecca Hwa, Philip Resnik, Amy Weinberg, and Okan Kolak. 2002. Evaluating translational correspondence using annotation projection. In *Proceedings of the 40th Annual Meeting on Association for Computational Linguistics*, ACL '02, pages 392–399, Stroudsburg, PA, USA. Association for Computational Linguistics.

Thomas Mayer and Michael Cysouw. 2012. Language comparison through sparse multilingual word alignment. In *Proceedings of the EACL 2012 Joint Workshop of LINGVIS & UNCLH*, EACL 2012, pages 54–62, Stroudsburg, PA, USA. Association for Computational Linguistics.

Ryan McDonald, Joakim Nivre, Yvonne Quirmbach-Brundage, Yoav Goldberg, Dipanjan Das, Kuzman Ganchev, Keith Hall, Slav Petrov, Hao Zhang, Oscar Täckström, Claudia Bedini, Núria Bertomeu Castelló, and Jungmee Lee. 2013. Universal dependency annotation for multilingual parsing. In *Proceedings of the 51st Annual Meeting of the Association for Computational Linguistics (Volume 2: Short Papers)*, pages 92–97, Sofia, Bulgaria, August. Association for Computational Linguistics.

Coşkun Mermer and Murat Saraçlar. 2011. Bayesian word alignment for statistical machine translation. In *Proceedings of the 49th Annual Meeting of the Association for Computational Linguistics: Human Language Technologies: short papers - Volume 2*, HLT '11, pages 182–187, Stroudsburg, PA, USA. Association for Computational Linguistics.

Joakim Nivre, Johan Hall, Jens Nilsson, Atanas Chanev, Gülsen Eryigit, Sandra Kübler, Svetoslav Marinov, and Erwin Marsi. 2007. MaltParser: A language-independent system for data-driven dependency parsing. *Natural Language Engineering*, 13:95–135, 6.

Robert Östling. 2014. Bayesian word alignment for massively parallel texts. In *Proceedings of the 14th Conference of the European Chapter of the Association for Computational Linguistics, volume 2: Short Papers*, pages 123–127, Gothenburg, Sweden, April. Association for Computational Linguistics.

Slav Petrov, Dipanjan Das, and Ryan McDonald. 2012. A universal part-of-speech tagset. In *Proceedings of the Eight International Conference on Language Resources and Evaluation (LREC'12)*, Istanbul, Turkey, may. European Language Resources Association (ELRA).

Oscar Täckström, Dipanjan Das, Slav Petrov, Ryan McDonald, and Joakim Nivre. 2013. Token and type constraints for cross-lingual part-of-speech tagging. *Transactions of the Association for Computational Linguistics*, 1:1–12.

Kristina Toutanova, Dan Klein, Christopher D. Manning, and Yoram Singer. 2003. Feature-rich part-of-speech tagging with a cyclic dependency network. In *Proceedings of the 2003 Conference of the North American Chapter of the Association for Computational Linguistics on Human Language Technology - Volume 1*, NAACL '03, pages 173–180, Stroudsburg, PA, USA. Association for Computational Linguistics.

Stephan Vogel, Hermann Ney, and Christoph Tillmann. 1996. HMM-based word alignment in statistical translation. In *Proceedings of the 16th Conference on Computational Linguistics - Volume 2*, COLING '96, pages 836–841, Stroudsburg, PA, USA. Association for Computational Linguistics.

Bernhard Wälchli and Michael Cysouw. 2012. Lexical typology through similarity semantics: Toward a semantic map of motion verbs. *Linguistics*, 50(3):671–710.

Bernhard Wälchli. 2014. Algorithmic typology and going from known to similar unknown categories within and across languages. In Benedikt Szmrecsanyi and Bernhard Wälchli, editors, *Linguistic Variation in Text and Speech*, number 28 in Linguae & Litterae, pages 355–393. De Gruyter.

Measuring idiosyncratic interests in children with autism

Masoud Rouhizadeh[†], Emily Prud'hommeaux[°], Jan van Santen[†], Richard Sproat[§]
[†]Oregon Health & Science University
[°]Rochester Institute of Technology
[§] Google, Inc.
{rouhizad,vansantj}@ohsu.edu, emilypx@rit.edu, rws@xoba.com

Abstract

A defining symptom of autism spectrum disorder (ASD) is the presence of restricted and repetitive activities and interests, which can surface in language as a perseverative focus on idiosyncratic topics. In this paper, we use semantic similarity measures to identify such idiosyncratic topics in narratives produced by children with and without ASD. We find that neurotypical children tend to use the same words and semantic concepts when retelling the same narrative, while children with ASD, even when producing accurate retellings, use different words and concepts relative not only to neurotypical children but also to other children with ASD. Our results indicate that children with ASD not only stray from the target topic but do so in idiosyncratic ways according to their own restricted interests.

1 Introduction

Autism spectrum disorder (ASD) is a neurodevelopmental disorder characterized by impaired communication and social behavior. One of the core symptoms is a preoccupation with specific restricted interests (American Psychiatric Association, 2013), and several commonly used diagnostic instruments for ASD instruct examiners to evaluate the degree to which subjects display this characteristic (Lord et al., 2002; Rutter et al., 2003). In verbal individuals with ASD, such a preoccupation can be expressed as a tendency to fixate on a particular idiosyncratic topic.

Previous research relying on expert annotation of spoken language in children with ASD has found that their spoken narratives and conversations include significantly more instances of irrelevant content and more topic digressions (Loveland et al., 1990; Losh and Capps, 2003; Lam et al., 2012). Similar results at the lexical level have been reported using automated annotations (Prud'hommeaux and Rouhizadeh, 2012; Rouhizadeh et al., 2013). There has been little work, however, in characterizing the precise direction of the departure from a target topic, leaving open the question of whether children with ASD are instigating similar, potentially reasonable topic changes or whether they are introducing idiosyncratic topics consistent with their own restricted interests.

In this paper, we attempt to automatically identify topic digressions in the narrative retellings of children with ASD and to determine whether these digressions are influenced by their idiosyncratic or restricted interests. From a corpus of spoken retellings of the same brief narrative, we extract several measures designed to capture different facets of semantic similarity between a pair of retellings. We find that the retellings of children with typical development (TD) semantically resemble one another much more than they resemble retellings by children with ASD. This indicates that TD children are adhering to a common target topic, while children with ASD are introducing topic changes. More strikingly, the similarity between pairs of ASD retellings is even lower, suggesting that children with ASD are straying from the target topic in individual and idiosyncratic ways. Although we do not yet have manual annotations to confirm that these topic shifts correspond to the particular restricted interests of each study participant, our methods and results show the potential of using automated analysis for revealing diagnostically relevant linguistic features.

2 Data

Thirty-nine children with typical development (TD) and 21 high-functioning children with ASD,

Proceedings of the 53rd Annual Meeting of the Association for Computational Linguistics and the 7th International Joint Conference on Natural Language Processing (Short Papers), pages 212–217,
Beijing, China, July 26-31, 2015.

ranging in age from 4 to 9 years, participated in this study. ASD was diagnosed via clinical consensus according to the DSM-IV-TR criteria (American Psychiatric Association, 2000) and the established thresholds on two widely-used diagnostic instruments: the Autism Diagnostic Observation Schedule (Lord et al., 2002) and the Social Communication Questionnaire (Rutter et al., 2003). No children met the criteria for a language impairment, and there were no significant between-group differences in age or full-scale IQ.

To elicit retellings, we used the Narrative Memory subtest of the NEPSY (Korkman et al., 1998), a large battery of tasks testing neurocognitive functioning in children. In the NEPSY Narrative Memory (NNM) subtest, the subject listens to a brief narrative about a boy and his dog and then must retell the narrative to the examiner. Figure 1 shows two sample retellings from our corpus. The NNM was administered by a trained clinician to each study participant, and each participant's retelling was recorded, transcribed, and evaluated according to the published scoring guidelines.

Under standard administration of the NNM, a retelling is scored according to how many story elements from a predetermined list it contains. The guidelines for scoring do not require verbatim recall for most elements and generally allow the use of synonyms and paraphrases. As is typically reported when comparing matched groups (Diehl et al., 2006), we observed no significant difference in the standard NNM free recall score between the TD group (mean = 6.25, sd = 3.43) and the ASD group (mean = 4.90, sd = 3.72). It might seem that a low similarity score between two retellings simply indicates that one retelling includes fewer story elements. However, given the equivalent number of story elements recalled by the two groups, we can assume that a low similarity score indicates a difference in the quality rather than the quantity of information in the retellings.

3 Semantic similarity measures

We expect that two different retellings of the same narrative will lie in the same lexico-semantic space and will thus have high similarity scores. In this work we use well-known similarity measures with two modifications. Children with autism tend to use more off-topic and unexpected words. Such words always have high inverse document frequency (IDF) scores since they are very specific to a particular retelling. By including IDF weights, a similarity measure would be biased toward off-topic words rather than actual content words in the story elements. Conventional IDF weights are therefore not useful for our particular purpose. Instead, we remove closed-class function words to avoid their bias in our similarity measures. In addition, we lemmatize our narrative corpus to reduce the sparsity due to inflectional variation.

3.1 Word overlap measures

3.1.1 Jaccard similarity coefficient

The Jaccard similarity coefficient (Sim_{Jac}) (Jaccard, 1912) is a simple word overlap measure between a pair of narratives n and m defined as the size of intersection of the words in narratives n and m, relative to the size of word union of n and m:

$$Sim_{Jacc}(n,m) = \frac{|n \cap m|}{|n \cup m|} \quad (1)$$

3.1.2 Cosine similarity score

Cosine similarity score Sim_{Cos} is the similarity between two narratives by cosine of the angle between their vector. We use a non-weighted cosine similarity based on the following formula, where $tf_{w,n}$ is the term frequency of word w in narrative n:

$$Sim_{Cos}(n,m) = \frac{\sum_{w \in n \cap m} tf_{w,n} \times tf_{w,m}}{\sqrt{\sum_{w_i \in n} (tf_{w_i,n})^2} \sqrt{\sum_{w_j \in m} (tf_{w_j,m})^2}} \quad (2)$$

3.1.3 Relative frequency measure

Relative frequency measure (Sim_{RF}) (Hoad and Zobel, 2003) is an author identity measure for identifying plagiarism at the document level. This measure normalizes the frequency of the words appearing in both narratives n and m by the overall length of the two narratives, as well as the relative frequency of the words common to the two narratives. We used a simplified variation of this measure, described by Metzler et al. (2005) and formulated as follows:

$$Sim_{RF}(n,m) = \frac{1}{1 + \frac{max(|n|,|m|)}{min(|m|,|m|)}} \times \sum_{w \in n \cap m} \frac{1}{1 + |tf_{w,n} - tf_{w,m}|} \quad (3)$$

Jim went up a tree with a ladder. He lost his shoe he got stuck he hung from a branch. Pepper took his shoe. He showed it to his sister and she helped him down. Let me look at this picture with my trusty vision gadget.

The boy got stuck and someone rescued him and pepper was a really smart dog. Dogs have a great sense of smell too, like T-rex. T-rex could smell things that were really far away. T-rex could be over there and the meat could be way back there under the couch Well, that guy got stuck on the tree and then he, and then Pepper, his shoe fell out of the tree. Anna rescued it. Pepper brought his shoe back and Anna rescued them.

Figure 1: Two topically different NNM retellings with similar free recall scores (6 and 5, respectively).

3.1.4 BLEU

BLEU (Papineni et al., 2002) is commonly used measure of n-gram overlap for automatically evaluating machine translation output. Because it is a precision metric, the BLEU score for any pair of narratives n and m will depend on which narrative is considered the "reference". To create a single BLEU-based overlap score for each pair of narratives, we calculate $Sim_{BLEU(n,m)}$ as the mean of $BLEU(m, n)$ and $BLEU(n, m)$.

3.2 Knowledge-based measures

It is reasonable to expect people to use synonyms or semantically similar words in their narratives retellings. It is therefore possible that children with autism are discussing the appropriate topic but choosing unusual words within that topic space in their retellings. We therefore use a set of measures that consider the semantic overlap of two narratives using WordNet (Fellbaum, 1998) similarities (Achananuparp et al., 2008), in order to distinguish instances of atypical but semantically appropriate language from true examples of poor topic maintenance. Because WordNet-based similarity measures only consider word pairs with the same part-of-speech, we POS-tagged the data using a perceptron tagger (Yarmohammadi, 2014).

3.2.1 WordNet-based vector similarity

In a modified version ofWordNet-based vector similarity, Sim_{WV}), (Li et al., 2006), we first create vectors v_n and v_m for each narrative n and m, where each element corresponds to a word in the type union of n and m. We assign values to each element e in v_n using the following formulation:

$$S(e, n) = \begin{cases} 1 & \text{if } e \in n \\ \max_{w_i \in n} LS(e, w_i) & \text{otherwise} \end{cases} \quad (4)$$

where LS is Lin's universal similarity (Lin, 1998). In other words, if the element e is present in n, $S(e, n)$ will be 1. If not, the most similar word to e will be chosen from words in n using Lin's universal similarity and $S(e, n)$ will be that maximum score. The same procedure is applied to v_m, and finally the similarity score between n and m is derived from the cosine score between v_n and v_m.

3.2.2 WordNet-based mutual similarity

In a modified version of WordNet-based mutual similarity (Sim_{WM}) (Mihalcea et al., 2006), we find the maximum similarity score $S(w_i, m)$ for each word w_i in narrative n with words in narrative m as described in Equation 4. The same procedure is applied to narrative m, and Sim_{WM} is calculated as follows:

$$Sim_{WM}(n, m) = \frac{1}{2}\left(\frac{\sum_{w_i \in n} S(w_i, m)}{|n|} + \frac{\sum_{w_j \in m} S(w_j, n)}{|m|}\right) \quad (5)$$

4 Results

For each of the semantic similarity measures, we build a similarity matrix comparing every possible pair of children. Because this pairwise similarity matrix is diagonally symmetrical, we need only consider the top right section of the matrix above the diagonal in our analyses. Table 1 shows the mean semantic overlap scores between the narratives for each of the three sub-matrices described above. We see that for both the word-overlap and the knowledge-based semantic similarity measures described in Section 3, TD children are most similar to other TD children. ASD children are less similar to TD children than TD children are to one another; and children with ASD are even less similar to other ASD children than to TD children.

Our goal is to explore the degree of similarity, as measured by the semantic overlap measures, within and across diagnostic groups. With this in mind, we consider the following three sub-matrices for each similarity matrix: one in which each TD child is compared with every other

	TD.TD	TD.ASD	ASD.ASD
Sim_{Jac}	0.19	0.14	0.11
Sim_{Cos}	0.42	0.34	0.28
Sim_{RF}	2.07	1.52	1.08
Sim_{BLEU}	0.36	0.29	0.24
Sim_{WV}	0.54	0.47	0.42
Sim_{WM}	0.80	0.69	0.59

Table 1: Average semantic overlap scores for each group.

measure	*statistic*	***p-values***		
		TD.TD vs ASD.ASD	TD.TD vs TD.ASD	TD.ASD vs ASD.ASD
Sim_{Jac}	t	.014	.022	.022
	w	.012	.002	.002
Sim_{Cos}	t	.025	.043	.027
	w	.025	.001	.001
Sim_{RF}	t	.056	.072	.046
	w	.012	.002	.002
Sim_{BLEU}	t	.032	.039	.034
	w	.036	.002	.002
Sim_{WV}	t	.014	.008	.028
	w	.01	.01	.01
Sim_{WM}	t	.018	.007	.042
	w	.018	.002	.002

Table 2: Monte Carlo significance test p-values for each similarity measure.

TD child (the TD.TD sub-matrix); one in which each ASD child is compared with every other ASD child (the ASD.ASD sub-matrix); and one in which each child is compared with the children in the diagnostic group to which he does not belong (the TD.ASD sub-matrix).

Note that we have no a priori reason to assume that the similarity scores are from any particular distribution. In order to calculate the statistical significance of these between-group differences, we therefore apply a Monte Carlo permutation method, a non-parametric procedure commonly used in non-standard significance testing situations. For each pair of sub-matrices (e.g., TD.TD vs ASD.ASD) we calculate two statistics that compare the cells in one sub-matrix with the cells in other sub-matrices: the t-statistic, using the Welch Two Sample t-test; and the w-statistic, using the Wilcoxon rank sum test. We next take a large random sample with replacement from all possible permutations of the data by shuffling the diagnosis labels of the children 1000 times. We then calculate two above statistics for each shuffle and count the number of times the observed values exceed the values produced by the 1000 shuffles.

Applying the Monte Carlo permutation method, we calculate the statistical significance of the following comparisons: TD.TD vs ASD.ASD; TD.TD vs TD.ASD; and TD.ASD vs ASD.ASD. Table 2 summarizes the results of these significance tests. In all cases, the differences are significant at $p < 0.05$ except for the first two comparisons in the t-test permutation of Sim_{RF}, which narrowly eluded significance.

5 Conclusions and future work

High-functioning children with ASD have long been described as "little professors", using pedantic or overly-adult language (Asperger, 1944). Low lexical overlap similarity measures by themselves might indicate that children with ASD are using semantically appropriate but infrequent or sophisticated words that were not used by other children. We note, however, that the knowledge-based overlap measures follow the same pattern as the purely lexical overlap measures. This suggests that it not the case that children with ASD are simply using rare synonyms of the more common words used by TD children. Instead, it seems that the children with ASD are moving away from the target topic and following their own individual and idiosyncratic semantic paths. These findings provide additional quantitative evidence not only for the common qualitative observation that young children with ASD have difficulty with topic maintenance but also for the more general behavioral symptom of idiosyncratic and restricted interests.

The overlap measures presented in this paper could be used as features for machine learning classification of ASD in combination with other linguistic features we have explored, including the use of off-topic lexical items (Rouhizadeh et al., 2013), features associated with poor pragmatic competence (Prud'hommeaux et al., 2014), and repetitive language measures (van Santen et al., 2013). Recall, however, that a clinician must consider a wide range of social, communication, and behavioral criteria when making a diagnosis of ASD, making it unlikely that language features alone could perfectly predict a diagnosis of ASD. The more significant potential in our approaches is more likely to lie in the area of language deficit detection and remediation.

A focus of our future work will be to manually annotate the data to determine the frequency and nature of the topic excursions. It is our expectation that children with ASD do not only veer from the target topic more frequently than typically developing children but also pursue topics of their own individual specific interests. We also plan to apply our methods to ASR output rather than manual transcripts. Despite the high word error rates typically observed with this sort of audio data, we anticipate that our methods, which rely primarily on content words, will be relatively robust.

The work presented here demonstrates the utility of applying automated analysis methods to spoken language collected in a clinical settings for diagnostic and remedial purposes. Carefully designed tools using such methods could provide helpful information not only to clinicians and therapists working with children with ASD but also to researchers exploring the specific linguistic and behavioral deficits associated with ASD.

Acknowledgments

This work was supported in part by NSF grant #BCS-0826654, and NIH NIDCD grants #R01-DC007129 and #1R01DC012033-01. Any opinions, findings, conclusions or recommendations expressed in this publication are those of the authors and do not necessarily reflect the views of the NSF or the NIH.

References

Palakorn Achananuparp, Xiaohua Hu, and Xiajiong Shen. 2008. The evaluation of sentence similarity measures. In *Data Warehousing and Knowledge Discovery*, pages 305–316. Springer.

American Psychiatric Association. 2000. *DSM-IV-TR: Diagnostic and Statistical Manual of Mental Disorders*. American Psychiatric Publishing, Washington, DC.

American Psychiatric Association. 2013. *Diagnostic and statistical manual of mental disorders (5th ed.)*. American Psychiatric Publishing, Washington, DC.

Hans Asperger. 1944. Die "autistischen psychopathe" im kindesalter. *Archiv fur Psychiatrie und Nervenkrakheiten*, 117:76–136.

Joshua J. Diehl, Loisa Bennetto, and Edna Carter Young. 2006. Story recall and narrative coherence of high-functioning children with autism spectrum disorders. *Journal of Abnormal Child Psychology*, 34(1):87–102.

Christian Fellbaum. 1998. *WordNet: An Electronic Lexical Database*. MIT Press, Cambridge, MA.

Timothy C Hoad and Justin Zobel. 2003. Methods for identifying versioned and plagiarized documents. *Journal of the American society for information science and technology*, 54(3):203–215.

Paul Jaccard. 1912. The distribution of the flora in the alpine zone. 1. *New phytologist*, 11(2):37–50.

Marit Korkman, Ursula Kirk, and Sally Kemp. 1998. *NEPSY: A developmental neuropsychological assessment*. The Psychological Corporation, San Antonio.

Yan Grace Lam, Siu Sze, and Susanna Yeung. 2012. Towards a convergent account of pragmatic language deficits in children with high-functioning autism: Depicting the phenotype using the pragmatic rating scale. *Research in Autism Spectrum Disorders*, 6(2):792–797.

Yuhua Li, David McLean, Zuhair A Bandar, James D O'shea, and Keeley Crockett. 2006. Sentence similarity based on semantic nets and corpus statistics. *Knowledge and Data Engineering, IEEE Transactions on*, 18(8):1138–1150.

Dekang Lin. 1998. An information-theoretic definition of similarity. In *ICML*, volume 98, pages 296–304.

Catherine Lord, Michael Rutter, Pamela DiLavore, and Susan Risi. 2002. *Autism Diagnostic Observation Schedule (ADOS)*. Western Psychological Services, Los Angeles.

Molly Losh and Lisa Capps. 2003. Narrative ability in high-functioning children with autism or asperger's syndrome. *Journal of Autism and Developmental Disorders*, 33(3):239–251.

Katherine Loveland, Robin McEvoy, and Belgin Tunali. 1990. Narrative story telling in autism and down's syndrome. *British Journal of Developmental Psychology*, 8(1):9–23.

Donald Metzler, Yaniv Bernstein, W Bruce Croft, Alistair Moffat, and Justin Zobel. 2005. Similarity measures for tracking information flow. In *Proceedings of the ACM International Conference on Information and Knowledge Management*, pages 517–524.

Rada Mihalcea, Courtney Corley, and Carlo Strapparava. 2006. Corpus-based and knowledge-based measures of text semantic similarity. In *AAAI*, volume 6, pages 775–780.

Kishore Papineni, Salim Roukos, Todd Ward, and Wei-Jing Zhu. 2002. Bleu: A method for automatic evaluation of machine translation. In *Proceedings of the 40th Annual Meeting of the Association for Computational :inguistics*, pages 311–318.

Emily Prud'hommeaux and Masoud Rouhizadeh. 2012. Automatic detection of pragmatic deficits in children with autism. In *Proceedings of the 3rd Workshop on Child, Computer and Interaction (WOCCI)*, pages 1–6.

Emily Prud'hommeaux, Eric Morley, Masoud Rouhizadeh, Laura Silverman, Jan van Santen, Brian Roark, Richard Sproat, Sarah Kauper, and Rachel DeLaHunta. 2014. Computational analysis of trajectories of linguistic development in autism. In *Proceedings of the IEEE Spoken Language Technology Workshop (SLT)*, pages 266–271.

Masoud Rouhizadeh, Emily Prud'hommeaux, Brian Roark, and Jan van Santen. 2013. Distributional semantic models for the evaluation of disordered language. In *Proceedings of the Conference of the North American Chapter of the Association for Computational Linguistics: Human Language Technologies*.

Michael Rutter, Anthony Bailey, and Catherine Lord. 2003. *Social Communication Questionnaire (SCQ)*. Western Psychological Services, Los Angeles.

Jan van Santen, Richard Sproat, and Alison Presmanes Hill. 2013. Quantifying repetitive speech in autism spectrum disorders and language impairment. *Autism Research*, 6(5):372–383.

Mahsa Yarmohammadi. 2014. Discriminative training with perceptron algorithm for pos tagging task. Technical Report CSLU-2014-001, Center for Spoken Language Understanding, Oregon Health & Science University.

Frame-Semantic Role Labeling with Heterogeneous Annotations

Meghana Kshirsagar* **Sam Thomson*** **Nathan Schneider**[†]
Jaime Carbonell* **Noah A. Smith*** **Chris Dyer***
*School of Computer Science, Carnegie Mellon University, Pittsburgh, PA, USA
[†]School of Informatics, University of Edinburgh, Edinburgh, Scotland, UK

Abstract

We consider the task of identifying and labeling the semantic arguments of a predicate that evokes a FrameNet frame. This task is challenging because there are only a few thousand fully annotated sentences for supervised training. Our approach augments an existing model with features derived from FrameNet and PropBank and with partially annotated exemplars from FrameNet. We observe a 4% absolute increase in F_1 versus the original model.

1 Introduction

Paucity of data resources is a challenge for semantic analyses like frame-semantic parsing (Gildea and Jurafsky, 2002; Das et al., 2014) using the FrameNet lexicon (Baker et al., 1998; Fillmore and Baker, 2009).[1] Given a sentence, a frame-semantic parse maps word tokens to **frames** they evoke, and for each frame, finds and labels its **argument** phrases with frame-specific **roles**. An example appears in figure 1.

In this paper, we address this **argument identification** subtask, a form of semantic role labeling (SRL), a task introduced by Gildea and Jurafsky (2002) using an earlier version of FrameNet. Our contribution addresses the paucity of annotated data for training using standard domain adaptation techniques. We exploit three annotation sources:

- the frame-to-frame relations in FrameNet, by using hierarchical features to share statistical strength among related roles (§3.2),
- FrameNet's corpus of partially-annotated **exemplar** sentences, by using "frustratingly easy" domain adaptation (§3.3), and

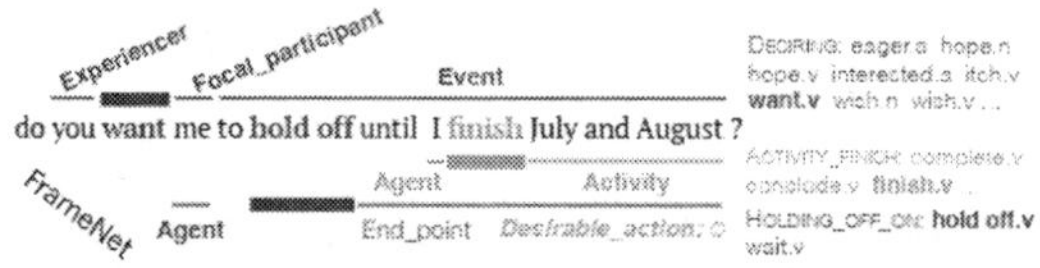

Figure 1: Part of a sentence from FrameNet full-text annotation. 3 frames and their arguments are shown: DESIRING is evoked by *want*, ACTIVITY_FINISH by *finish*, and HOLDING_OFF_ON by *hold off*. Thin horizontal lines representing argument spans are labeled with role names. (Not shown: *July* and *August* evoke CALENDRIC_UNIT and fill its **Unit** role.)

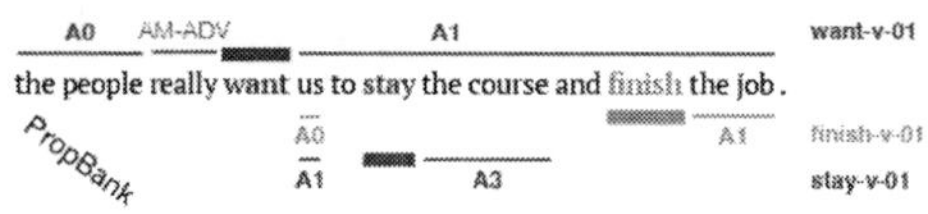

Figure 2: A PropBank-annotated sentence from OntoNotes (Hovy et al., 2006). The PB lexicon defines rolesets (verb sense–specific frames) and their core roles: e.g., `finish-v-01` 'cause to stop', `A0` 'intentional agent', `A1` 'thing finishing', and `A2` 'explicit instrument, thing finished with'. (`finish-v-03`, by contrast, means 'apply a finish, as to wood'.) Clear similarities to the FrameNet annotations in figure 1 are evident, though PB uses lexical frames rather than deep frames and makes some different decisions about roles (e.g., `want-v-01` has no analogue to **Focal_participant**).

- a PropBank-style SRL system, by using guide features (§3.4).[2]

These expansions of the *training corpus* and the *feature set* for supervised argument identification are integrated into SEMAFOR (Das et al., 2014), the leading open-source frame-semantic parser for English. We observe a 4% F_1 improvement in argument identification on the FrameNet test set, leading to a 1% F_1 improvement on the full frame-semantic parsing task. Our code and models are available at `http://www.ark.cs.cmu.edu/SEMAFOR/`.

2 FrameNet

FrameNet represents events, scenarios, and relationships with an inventory of **frames** (such as

[‡] Corresponding author: `mkshirsa@cs.cmu.edu`

[1] `http://framenet.icsi.berkeley.edu`

[2] Preliminary experiments training on PropBank annotations mapped to FrameNet via SemLink 1.2.2c (Bonial et al., 2013) hurt performance, likely due to errors and coverage gaps in the mappings.

Proceedings of the 53rd Annual Meeting of the Association for Computational Linguistics and the 7th International Joint Conference on Natural Language Processing (Short Papers), pages 218–224,
Beijing, China, July 26-31, 2015.

SHOPPING and SCARCITY). Each frame is associated with a set of **roles** (or **frame elements**) called to mind in order to understand the scenario, and lexical **predicates** (verbs, nouns, adjectives, and adverbs) capable of evoking the scenario. For example, the BODY_MOVEMENT frame has **Agent** and **Body_part** as its core roles, and lexical entries including verbs such as bend, blink, crane, and curtsy, plus the noun use of curtsy. In FrameNet 1.5, there are over 1,000 frames and 12,000 lexical predicates.

2.1 Hierarchy

The FrameNet lexicon is organized as a network, with several kinds of **frame-to-frame relations** linking pairs of frames and (subsets of) their arguments (Ruppenhofer et al., 2010). In this work, we consider two kinds of frame-to-frame relations:

Inheritance: E.g., ROBBERY inherits from COMMITTING_CRIME, which inherits from MISDEED. Crucially, roles in inheriting frames are mapped to corresponding roles in inherited frames: ROBBERY.**Perpetrator** links to COMMITTING_CRIME.**Perpetrator**, which links to MISDEED.**Wrongdoer**, and so forth.

Subframe: This indicates a subevent within a complex event. E.g., the CRIMINAL_PROCESS frame groups together subframes ARREST, ARRAIGNMENT and TRIAL. CRIMINAL_PROCESS.**Defendant**, for instance, is mapped to ARREST.**Suspect**, TRIAL.**Defendant**, and SENTENCING.**Convict**.

We say that a *parent* of a role is one that has either the **Inheritance** or **Subframe** relation to it. There are 4,138 **Inheritance** and 589 **Subframe** links among role types in FrameNet 1.5.

Prior work has considered various ways of grouping role labels together in order to share statistical strength. Matsubayashi et al. (2009) observed small gains from using the **Inheritance** relationships and also from grouping by the role name (SEMAFOR already incorporates such features). Johansson (2012) reports improvements in SRL for Swedish, by exploiting relationships between both frames and roles. Baldewein et al. (2004) learn latent clusters of roles and role-fillers, reporting mixed results. Our approach is described in §3.2.

2.2 Annotations

Statistics for the annotations appear in table 1.

Full-text (FT): This portion of the FrameNet corpus consists of documents and has about 5,000 sentences for which annotators assigned frames and arguments to as many words as possible. Beginning with the SemEval-2007 shared task on FrameNet analysis, frame-semantic parsers have been trained and evaluated on the full-text data (Baker et al., 2007; Das et al., 2014).[3] The full-text documents represent a mix of genres, prominently including travel guides and bureaucratic reports about weapons stockpiles.

	Full-Text		Exemplars	
	train	*test*	*train*	*test*
Sentences	2,780	2,420	137,515	4,132
Frames	15,019	4,458	137,515	4,132
Overt arguments	25,918	7,210	278,985	8,417
TYPES				
Frames	642	470	862	562
Roles	2,644	1,420	4,821	1,224
Unseen frames *vs. train:*		46		0
Roles in unseen frames *vs. train:*		178		0
Unseen roles *vs. train:*		289		38
Unseen roles *vs. combined train:*		103		32

Table 1: Characteristics of the training and test data. (These statistics exclude the development set, which contains 4,463 frames over 746 sentences.)

Exemplars: To document a given predicate, lexicographers manually select corpus examples and annotate them *only with respect to the predicate in question.* These singly-annotated sentences from FrameNet are called lexicographic **exemplars**. There are over 140,000 sentences containing argument annotations and relative to the FT dataset, these contain an order of magnitude more frame annotations and over two orders of magnitude more sentences. As these were manually selected, the rate of overt arguments per frame is noticeably higher than in the FT data. The exemplars formed the basis of early studies of frame-semantic role labeling (e.g., Gildea and Jurafsky, 2002; Thompson et al., 2003; Fleischman et al., 2003; Litkowski, 2004; Kwon et al., 2004). Exemplars have not yet been exploited successfully to improve role labeling performance on the more realistic FT task.[4]

2.3 PropBank

PropBank (PB; Palmer et al., 2005) is a lexicon and corpus of predicate–argument structures that takes a shallower approach than FrameNet. FrameNet frames cluster lexical predicates that evoke sim-

[3]Though these were *annotated* at the document level, and train/development/test splits are by document, the frame-semantic parsing is currently restricted to the sentence level.

[4]Das and Smith (2011, 2012) investigated semi-supervised techniques using the exemplars and WordNet for frame identification. Hermann et al. (2014) also improve frame identification by mapping frames and predicates into the same continuous vector space, allowing statistical sharing.

ilar kinds of scenarios In comparison, PropBank frames are purely lexical and there are no formal relations between different predicates or their roles. PropBank's sense distinctions are generally coarser-grained than FrameNet's. Moreover, FrameNet lexical entries cover many different parts of speech, while PropBank focuses on verbs and (as of recently) eventive noun and adjective predicates. An example with PB annotations is shown in figure 2.

3 Model

We use the model from SEMAFOR (Das et al., 2014), detailed in §3.1, as a starting point. We experiment with techniques that augment the model's training data (§3.3) and feature set (§3.2, §3.4).

3.1 Baseline

In SEMAFOR, the argument identification task is treated as a structured prediction problem. Let the classification input be a dependency-parsed sentence $\mathbf{x}$, the token(s) p constituting the predicate in question, and the frame f evoked by p (as determined by frame identification). We use the heuristic procedure described by (Das et al., 2014) for extracting candidate argument spans for the predicate; call this $spans(\mathbf{x}, p, f)$. $spans$ always includes a special span denoting an empty or non-overt role, denoted $\varnothing$. For each candidate argument $a \in spans(\mathbf{x}, p, f)$ and each role r, a binary feature vector $\boldsymbol{\phi}(a, \mathbf{x}, p, f, r)$ is extracted. We use the feature extractors from (Das et al., 2014) as a baseline, adding additional ones in our experiments (§3.2–§3.4). Each a is given a real-valued score by a linear model:

$$score_{\mathbf{w}}(a \mid \mathbf{x}, p, f, r) = \mathbf{w}^{\top}\boldsymbol{\phi}(a, \mathbf{x}, p, f, r) \quad (1)$$

The model parameters $\mathbf{w}$ are learned from data (§4).

Prediction requires choosing a joint assignment of all arguments of a frame, respecting the constraints that a role may be assigned to at most one span, and spans of overt arguments must not overlap. Beam search, with a beam size of 100, is used to find this arg max.[5]

3.2 Hierarchy Features

We experiment with features shared between related roles of related frames in order to capture statistical generalizations about the kinds of arguments seen in those roles. Our hypothesis is that this will be beneficial given the small number of training examples for individual roles.

All roles that have a common parent based on the **Inheritance** and **Subframe** relations will share a set of features in common. Specifically, for each base feature ϕ which is conjoined with the role r in the baseline model ($\phi \wedge$ "role=r"), and for each parent r' of r, we add a new copy of the feature that is the base feature conjoined with the parent role, ($\phi \wedge$ "parent_role=r'"). We experimented with using more than one level of the hierarchy (e.g., grandparents), but the additional levels did not improve performance.

3.3 Domain Adaptation and Exemplars

Daumé (2007) proposed a feature augmentation approach that is now widely used in supervised domain adaptation scenarios. We use a variant of this approach. Let $\mathcal{D}_{\text{ex}}$ denote the exemplars training data, and $\mathcal{D}_{\text{ft}}$ denote the full text training data. For every feature $\phi(a, \mathbf{x}, p, f, r)$ in the base model, we add a new feature $\phi_{\text{ft}}(\cdot)$ that fires only if $\phi(\cdot)$ fires and $\mathbf{x} \in \mathcal{D}_{\text{ft}}$. The intuition is that each base feature contributes both a "general" weight and a "domain-specific" weight to the model; thus, it can exhibit a general preference for specific roles, but this general preference can be fine-tuned for the domain. Regularization encourages the model to use the general version over the domain-specific, if possible.

3.4 Guide Features

Another approach to domain adaptation is to train a supervised model on a source domain, make predictions using that model on the target domain, then use those predictions as additional features while training a new model on the target domain. The source domain model is effectively a form of preprocessing, and the features from its output are known as **guide features** (Johansson, 2013; Kong et al., 2014).[6]

In our case, the full text data is our target domain, and PropBank and the exemplars data are our source domains, respectively. For PropBank, we run the SRL system of Illinois Curator 1.1.4 (Pun-

[5] Recent work has improved upon global decoding techniques (Das et al., 2012; Täckström et al., 2015). We expect such improvements to be complementary to the gains due to the added features and data reported here.

[6] This is related to the technique of model stacking, where successively richer models are trained by cross-validation on the same dataset (e.g., Cohen and Carvalho, 2005; Nivre and McDonald, 2008; Martins et al., 2008).

yakanok et al., 2008)[7] on verbs in the full-text data. For the exemplars, we train baseline SEMAFOR on the exemplars and run it on the full-text data.

We use two types of guide features: one encodes the role label predicted by the source model, and the other indicates that a span a was assigned *some* role. For the exemplars, we use an additional feature to indicate that the predicted role matches the role being filled.

4 Learning

Following SEMAFOR, we train using a **local** objective, treating each role and span pair as an independent training instance. We have made two modifications to training which had negligible impact on full-text accuracy, but decreased training time significantly:[8]

- We use the online optimization method AdaDelta (Zeiler, 2012) with minibatches, instead of the batch method L-BFGS (Liu and Nocedal, 1989). We use minibatches of size 4,000 on the full text data, and 40,000 on the exemplar data.
- We minimize squared structured hinge loss instead of a log-linear loss. Let $((\mathbf{x}, p, f, r), a)$ be the ith training example. Then the squared hinge loss is given by $L_{\mathbf{w}}(i)$ =

$$\left(\max_{a'}\left\{\begin{matrix}\mathbf{w}^\top \boldsymbol{\phi}(a', \mathbf{x}, p, f, r) \\ +\mathbf{1}\{a' \neq a\}\end{matrix}\right\} - \mathbf{w}^\top \boldsymbol{\phi}(a, \mathbf{x}, p, f, r)\right)^2$$

We learn $\mathbf{w}$ by minimizing the ℓ_2-regularized average loss on the dataset:

$$\mathbf{w}^* = \arg\min_{\mathbf{w}} \frac{1}{N} \sum_{i=1}^{N} L_{\mathbf{w}}(i) + \frac{1}{2}\lambda \|\mathbf{w}\|_2^2 \quad (2)$$

5 Experimental Setup

We use the same FrameNet 1.5 data and train/test splits as Das et al. (2014). Automatic syntactic dependency parses from MSTParserStacked (Martins et al., 2008) are used, as in Das et al. (2014).

Preprocessing. Out of 145,838 exemplar sentences, we removed 4,191 sentences which had no role annotations. We removed sentences that appeared in the full-text data. We also merged spans which were adjacent and had the same role label.

[7] http://cogcomp.cs.illinois.edu/page/software_view/SRL

[8] With SEMAFOR's original features and training data, the result of the above changes is that full-text F_1 decreases from 59.3% to 59.1%, while training time (running optimization to convergence) decreases from 729 minutes to 82 minutes.

Training Configuration (Features)	Model Size	P (%)	R (%)	F_1 (%)
FT (Baseline)	1.1	65.6	53.8	59.1
FT (Hierarchy)	1.9	67.2	54.8	60.4
Exemplars $\xrightarrow{\text{guide}}$ FT	1.2	65.2	55.9	60.2
FT+Exemplars (Basic)	5.0	66.0	58.2	61.9
FT+Exemplars (DA)	5.8	65.7	59.0	62.2
PB-SRL $\xrightarrow{\text{guide}}$ FT	1.2	65.0	54.8	59.5
Combining the best methods				
PB-SRL $\xrightarrow{\text{guide}}$ FT+Exemplars	5.5	67.4	58.8	62.8
FT+Exemplars (Hierarchy)	9.3	66.0	60.4	**63.1**

Table 2: Argument identification results on the full-text test set. Model size is in millions of features.

Hyperparameter tuning. We determined the stopping criterion and the ℓ_2 regularization parameter λ by tuning on the FT development set, searching over the following values for λ: 10^{-5}, 10^{-7}, 10^{-9}, 10^{-12}.

Evaluation. A complete frame-semantic parsing system involves frame identification and argument identification. We perform two evaluations: one assuming gold-standard frames are given, to evaluate argument identification alone; and one using the output of the system described by Hermann et al. (2014), the current state-of-the-art in frame identification, to demonstrate that our improvements are retained when incorporated into a full system.

6 Results

Argument Identification. We present precision, recall, and F_1-measure microaveraged across the test instances in table 2, for all approaches. The evaluation used in Das et al. (2014) assesses both frames and arguments; since our focus is on SRL, we only report performance for arguments, rendering our scores more interpretable. Under our argument-only evaluation, the system of Das et al. (2014) gets 59.3% F_1.

The first block shows baseline performance. The next block shows the benefit of FrameNet hierarchy features (+1.2% F_1). The third block shows that using exemplars as training data, especially with domain adaptation, is preferable to using them as guide features (2.8% F_1 vs. 0.9% F_1). PropBank SRL as guide features offers a small (0.4% F_1) gain.

The last two rows of table 2 show the performance upon combining the best approaches. Both use full-text and exemplars for training; the first uses PropBank SRL as guide features, and the second adds hierarchy features. The best result is the

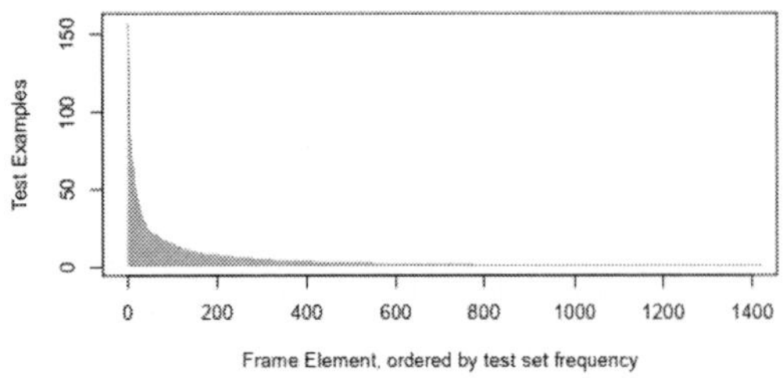

(a) Frequency of each role appearing in the test set.

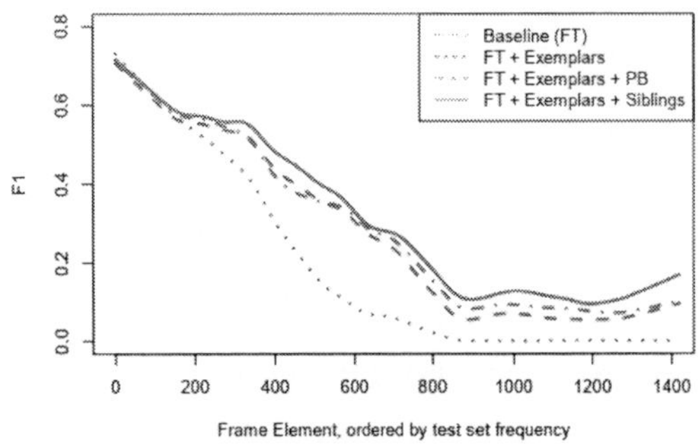

(b) F_1 of the best methods compared with the baseline.

Figure 3: F_1 for each role appearing in the test set, ranked by frequency. F_1 values have been smoothed with `loess`, with a smoothing parameter of 0.2. "Siblings" refers to hierarchy features.

latter, gaining 3.95% F_1 over the baseline.

Role-level evaluation. Figure 3(b) shows F_1 per frame element, for the baseline and the three best models. Each x-axis value is one role, sorted by decreasing frequency (the distribution of role frequencies is shown in figure 3(a)). For frequent roles, performance is similar; our models achieve gains on rarer roles.

Full system. When using the frame output of Hermann et al. (2014), F_1 improves by 1.1%, from 66.8% for the baseline, to 67.9% for our combined model (from the last row in table 2).

7 Conclusion

We have empirically shown that auxiliary semantic resources can benefit the challenging task of frame-semantic role labeling. The significant gains come from the FrameNet exemplars and the FrameNet hierarchy, with some signs that the PropBank scheme can be leveraged as well.

We are optimistic that future improvements to lexical semantic resources, such as crowdsourced lexical expansion of FrameNet (Pavlick et al., 2015) as well as ongoing/planned changes for PropBank (Bonial et al., 2014) and SemLink (Bonial et al., 2013), will lead to further gains in this task. Moreover, the techniques discussed here could be further explored using semi-automatic mappings between lexical resources (such as UBY; Gurevych et al., 2012), and correspondingly, this task could be used to extrinsically validate those mappings.

Ours is not the only study to show benefit from heterogeneous annotations for semantic analysis tasks. Feizabadi and Padó (2015), for example, successfully applied similar techniques for SRL of *implicit* arguments.[9] Ultimately, given the diversity of semantic resources, we expect that learning from heterogeneous annotations in different corpora will be necessary to build automatic semantic analyzers that are both accurate and robust.

Acknowledgments

The authors are grateful to Dipanjan Das for his assistance, and to anonymous reviewers for their helpful feedback. This research has been supported by the Richard King Mellon Foundation and DARPA grant FA8750-12-2-0342 funded under the DEFT program.

References

Collin Baker, Michael Ellsworth, and Katrin Erk. 2007. SemEval-2007 Task 19: frame semantic structure extraction. In *Proc. of SemEval*, pages 99–104. Prague, Czech Republic.

Collin F. Baker, Charles J. Fillmore, and John B. Lowe. 1998. The Berkeley FrameNet project. In *Proc. of COLING-ACL*, pages 86–90. Montreal, Quebec, Canada. URL `http://framenet.icsi.berkeley.edu`.

Ulrike Baldewein, Katrin Erk, Sebastian Padó, and Detlef Prescher. 2004. Semantic role labelling with similarity-based generalization using EM-based clustering. In Rada Mihalcea and Phil Edmonds, editors, *Proc. of SENSEVAL-3, the Third International Workshop on the Evaluation of Systems for the Semantic Analysis of Text*, pages 64–68. Barcelona, Spain.

Claire Bonial, Julia Bonn, Kathryn Conger, Jena D. Hwang, and Martha Palmer. 2014. PropBank: semantics of new predicate types. In Nicoletta Calzolari, Khalid Choukri, Thierry Declerck, Hrafn Loftsson, Bente Maegaard, Joseph Mariani, Asuncion Moreno, Jan Odijk, and Stelios Piperidis, editors, *Proc. of LREC*, pages 3013–3019. Reykjavík, Iceland.

Claire Bonial, Kevin Stowe, and Martha Palmer. 2013. Renewing and revising SemLink. In *Proc. of the*

[9] They applied frustratingly easy domain adaptation to learn from FrameNet along with a PropBank-like dataset of nominal frames.

2nd Workshop on Linked Data in Linguistics (LDL-2013): Representing and linking lexicons, terminologies and other language data, pages 9–17. Pisa, Italy.

William W. Cohen and Vitor R. Carvalho. 2005. Stacked sequential learning. In *Proc. of IJCAI*, pages 671–676. Edinburgh, Scotland, UK.

Dipanjan Das, Desai Chen, André F. T. Martins, Nathan Schneider, and Noah A. Smith. 2014. Frame-semantic parsing. *Computational Linguistics*, 40(1):9–56. URL http://www.ark.cs.cmu.edu/SEMAFOR.

Dipanjan Das, André F. T. Martins, and Noah A. Smith. 2012. An exact dual decomposition algorithm for shallow semantic parsing with constraints. In *Proc. of *SEM*, pages 209–217. Montréal, Canada.

Dipanjan Das and Noah A. Smith. 2011. Semi-supervised frame-semantic parsing for unknown predicates. In *Proc. of ACL-HLT*, pages 1435–1444. Portland, Oregon, USA.

Dipanjan Das and Noah A. Smith. 2012. Graph-based lexicon expansion with sparsity-inducing penalties. In *Proc. of NAACL-HLT*, pages 677–687. Montréal, Canada.

Hal Daumé, III. 2007. Frustratingly easy domain adaptation. In *Proc. of ACL*, pages 256–263. Prague, Czech Republic.

Parvin Sadat Feizabadi and Sebastian Padó. 2015. Combining seemingly incompatible corpora for implicit semantic role labeling. In *Proc. of *SEM*, pages 40–50. Denver, Colorado, USA.

Charles J. Fillmore and Collin Baker. 2009. A frames approach to semantic analysis. In Bernd Heine and Heiko Narrog, editors, *The Oxford Handbook of Linguistic Analysis*, pages 791–816. Oxford University Press, Oxford, UK.

Michael Fleischman, Namhee Kwon, and Eduard Hovy. 2003. Maximum entropy models for FrameNet classification. In Michael Collins and Mark Steedman, editors, *Proc. of EMNLP*, pages 49–56.

Daniel Gildea and Daniel Jurafsky. 2002. Automatic labeling of semantic roles. *Computational Linguistics*, 28(3):245–288.

Iryna Gurevych, Judith Eckle-Kohler, Silvana Hartmann, Michael Matuschek, Christian M. Meyer, and Christian Wirth. 2012. UBY - a large-scale unified lexical-semantic resource based on LMF. In *Proc. of EACL*, pages 580–590. Avignon, France.

Karl Moritz Hermann, Dipanjan Das, Jason Weston, and Kuzman Ganchev. 2014. Semantic frame identification with distributed word representations. In *Proc. of ACL*, pages 1448–1458. Baltimore, Maryland, USA.

Eduard Hovy, Mitchell Marcus, Martha Palmer, Lance Ramshaw, and Ralph Weischedel. 2006. OntoNotes: the 90% solution. In *Proc. of HLT-NAACL*, pages 57–60. New York City, USA.

Richard Johansson. 2012. Non-atomic classification to improve a semantic role labeler for a low-resource language. In *Proc. of *SEM*, pages 95–99. Montréal, Canada.

Richard Johansson. 2013. Training parsers on incompatible treebanks. In *Proc. of NAACL-HLT*, pages 127–137. Atlanta, Georgia, USA.

Lingpeng Kong, Nathan Schneider, Swabha Swayamdipta, Archna Bhatia, Chris Dyer, and Noah A. Smith. 2014. A dependency parser for tweets. In *Proc. of EMNLP*, pages 1001–1012. Doha, Qatar.

Namhee Kwon, Michael Fleischman, and Eduard Hovy. 2004. FrameNet-based semantic parsing using maximum entropy models. In *Proc. of Coling*, pages 1233–1239. Geneva, Switzerland.

Ken Litkowski. 2004. SENSEVAL-3 task: Automatic labeling of semantic roles. In Rada Mihalcea and Phil Edmonds, editors, *Proc. of SENSEVAL-3, the Third International Workshop on the Evaluation of Systems for the Semantic Analysis of Text*, pages 9–12. Barcelona, Spain.

Dong C. Liu and Jorge Nocedal. 1989. On the Limited Memory BFGS Method for Large Scale Optimization. *Math. Program.*, 45(3):503–528.

André F. T. Martins, Dipanjan Das, Noah A. Smith, and Eric P. Xing. 2008. Stacking dependency parsers. In *Proc. of EMNLP*, pages 157–166. Honolulu, Hawaii.

Yuichiroh Matsubayashi, Naoaki Okazaki, and Jun'ichi Tsujii. 2009. A comparative study on generalization of semantic roles in FrameNet. In *Proc. of ACL-IJCNLP*, pages 19–27. Suntec, Singapore.

Joakim Nivre and Ryan McDonald. 2008. Integrating graph-based and transition-based dependency parsers. In *Proc. of ACL-HLT*, pages 950–958. Columbus, Ohio, USA.

Martha Palmer, Daniel Gildea, and Paul Kingsbury. 2005. The Proposition Bank: an annotated corpus of semantic roles. *Computational Linguistics*, 31(1):71–106.

Ellie Pavlick, Travis Wolfe, Pushpendre Rastogi, Chris Callison-Burch, Mark Drezde, and Benjamin Van Durme. 2015. FrameNet+: Fast paraphrastic tripling of FrameNet. In *Proc. of ACL-IJCNLP*. Beijing, China.

Vasin Punyakanok, Dan Roth, and Wen-tau Yih. 2008. The importance of syntactic parsing and inference in semantic role labeling. *Computational Linguistics*, 34(2):257–287. URL http://cogcomp.cs.illinois.edu/page/software_view/SRL.

Josef Ruppenhofer, Michael Ellsworth, Miriam R. L. Petruck, Christopher R. Johnson, and Jan Scheffczyk. 2010. FrameNet II: extended theory and practice. URL https://framenet2.icsi.berkeley.edu/docs/r1.5/book.pdf.

Oscar Täckström, Kuzman Ganchev, and Dipanjan Das. 2015. Efficient inference and structured learning for semantic role labeling. *Transactions of the Association for Computational Linguistics*, 3:29–41.

Cynthia A. Thompson, Roger Levy, and Christopher D. Manning. 2003. A generative model for semantic role labeling. In *Machine Learning: ECML 2003*, pages 397–408.

Matthew D. Zeiler. 2012. ADADELTA: An adaptive learning rate method. *arXiv:1212.5701 [cs]*. URL `http://arxiv.org/abs/1212.5701`, arXiv: 1212.5701.

Semantic Interpretation of Superlative Expressions via Structured Knowledge Bases

Sheng Zhang[1], **Yansong Feng**[1*], **Songfang Huang**[2], **Kun Xu**[1], **Zhe Han**[1] and **Dongyan Zhao**[1]
[1]ICST, Peking University, Beijing, China
[2]IBM China Research Lab, Beijing, China
{evancheung, fengyansong, xukun, zhehan1992, zhaodongyan}@pku.edu.cn
huangsf@cn.ibm.com

Abstract

This paper addresses a novel task of semantically analyzing the comparative constructions inherent in attributive superlative expressions against structured knowledge bases (KBs). The task can be defined in two-fold: first, selecting the comparison dimension against a KB, on which the involved items are compared; and second, determining the ranking order, in which the items are ranked (ascending or descending). We exploit Wikipedia and Freebase to collect training data in an unsupervised manner, where a neural network model is then learnt to select, from Freebase predicates, the most appropriate comparison dimension for a given superlative expression, and further determine its ranking order heuristically. Experimental results show that it is possible to learn from coarsely obtained training data to semantically characterize the comparative constructions involved in attributive superlative expressions.

1 Introduction

Superlatives are fairly common in natural languages and play an essential role in daily communications, when in conveying comparisons among a set of items or degrees of certain properties. Properly analyzing superlative expressions holds the promise for many applications such as question answering (QA), text entailment, sentiment analysis and so on. In literature, analysis of superlatives has drawn more interests from both formal linguistics and semantics(Szabolcsi, 1986; Gawron, 1995; Heim, 1999; Farkas and Kiss, 2000), but relatively less attention from the computational linguistics and NLP communities(Bos and Nissim, 2006; Jindal and Liu, 2006; Scheible, 2007; Scheible, 2009).

Earlier computational treatments to superlatives focus on the categorizations of superlatives(Bos and Nissim, 2006; Scheible, 2009), where the most common but important type is being part of a noun phrase or describing certain properties or attributes of the subjects, named as *attributive superlatives* or *ISA-superlatives*, accounting for around 90% of appearances in newswire. A typical example is *Nile is the longest river in the world*.

In most cases, the gist behind such superlative expressions is the comparative constructions that the utterance intends to convey to readers, e.g., in the *Nile* example, *Nile* is *longer* than any other rivers in the world. Semantically understanding such attributive superlative expressions boils down to interpreting the comparative construction involved in the utterance in the following four aspects:

1. **Target**: one or more items that work as the protagonist of the utterance, and are being compared within the comparative construction, e.g., *Nile*;

2. **Comparison set**: the set of items that are being compared against in the utterance(Bos and Nissim, 2006), e.g., *all rivers in the world*;

3. **Comparison dimension**: the attribute or property that the items are compared upon, e.g., *the length of a river*;

4. **Ranking order**: the order in which the items in the comparison set are sorted according to the dimension, in an ascending or descending order, e.g., we should rank all rivers regarding their lengths in a *descending* order to get the *longest* at the top.

So far, there have been only a few computational treatments for superlatives, addressing the

Proceedings of the 53rd Annual Meeting of the Association for Computational Linguistics and the 7th International Joint Conference on Natural Language Processing (Short Papers), pages 225–230,
Beijing, China, July 26-31, 2015.

importance of categorizing superlatives, identifying the target and comparison set(Bos and Nissim, 2006; Jindal and Liu, 2006; Scheible, 2009), while putting less attention on other aspects.

In fact, grounding the comparison dimension into a canonical predicate of a KB can help provide more accurate interpretations for the involved comparative constructions. In question answering over structured KBs, accurate treatments for superlatives will not only help build more precise of structured queries, but also support shallow functional reasoning, e.g., formally analyzing *the fifth longest river in the world*, will explore the most of the structured nature of KBs, and is advantageous to traditional IR based methods.

However, selecting an appropriate comparison dimension against a structured KB is not a trivial task. Usually, the numbers of adjective superlatives and gradable KB predicates are large, so that it is impossible to craft mapping rules to cover every pair of adjective superlative and predicate. Consequently, preparing wide-coverage annotated data to help automate this procedure is also labor-intensive and time consuming. Moreover, some adjectives are widely used, but often vague to decide a dimension by themselves(Bos and Nissim, 2006). One may need to draw support from their context and even common sense knowledge.

In this paper, we propose a novel task, semantically interpreting the comparative constructions inherent in attributive superlative expressions again structured KBs, e.g., Freebase(Google, 2013), specifically, focusing on selecting appropriate comparison dimensions and corresponding ranking orders. To this end, we collect training data from roughly aligned Wikipedia resources and knowledge facts in Freebase, from which we build a neural network model to reveal the underlying correspondence between the comparative construction, as well as its context, and a Freebase predicate. Our method leverages the potentials of structured KBs and large amount of text resources in Wikipedia without relying on human annotated data.

We evaluate our interpretation of superlatives in two tasks, and experimental results show that it is possible to learn the comparison dimensions in form of canonical knowledge bases predicates from roughly collected training data, which is noisy in nature but provides the essentials to semantically characterize superlative expressions.

2 The Task

Given a sentence with an attributive superlative expression, our task is to find on which dimension the comparison happens against a KB and how the comparison results are arranged, i.e., (1) **Dimension Selection:** decide the *dimension* on which the involved items are compared, and ground the selected dimension into Freebase predicates. (2) **Ranking Order Determination:** given the comparison set and the selected dimension, determine the *order* in which the involved items are ranked within the comparisons, in an **ascending** or **descending** order? For superlatives coupled with ordinals, we also need to assign the standing in the rankings.

In the *Nile* example, we expect to interpret *the longest river* into a vector <*fb:geography.river.length*, *descending*, **1**>, where all *rivers in the world* are compared upon Freebase predicate *fb:geography.river.length*, sorted in a *descending* order and the referred target ranks the ***first***.

3 The WikiDiF Dataset

Previous superlative datasets are built to facilitate superlative extraction, classification, and comparison set identification(Bos and Nissim, 2006; Scheible, 2012). There are currently no available datasets that can be used directly for our task, especially no annotations against structured KBs.

We therefore present a distantly supervised method to collect annotated training data from rich text resources of Wikipedia and the help of Freebase, without much human involvement. The **key assumption** behind our method is that if a superlative expression frequently appears in a context that may describe a KB predicate, then this predicate probably plays an important role in the comparative construction triggered by this superlative. Inspired by recent advances in relation extraction(Mintz et al., 2009), given a Freebase predicate, we are able to collect many sentences from Wikipedia pages, which more or less describe this predicate, without extra human annotation. These sentences in turn can be used to collect the co-occurrences between a superlative expression and this predicate.

In more detail, we first find all Freebase predicates that may involve in comparative constructions, i.e., all *gradable* predicates, e.g., *fb:geography.river.length*, on which different rivers can be compared with each other. In practice, we simply treat all Freebase predicates that take objects of type $\in$ {*/type/int, /type/float, /type/datetime*} as *gradable* predicates. In total, we collect 8,968,383 <*subj, rel, obj*> triples covering all 1,795 *gradable* predicates from Freebase dump.

Next, we extract, from Wikipedia pages, all sentences containing superlative expressions, as well as their ± 3 context sentences[1]. To detect superlatives, we rely on part-of-speech tags (*JJS, RBS*) which can achieve a high recall in practice according to (Jindal and Liu, 2006). By doing so, we collect 7,734,006 sentences with superlative expressions from Wikipedia.

Finally, for each collected triple <*subj, rel, obj*> , we match *subj* and *obj* into our sentence collection, including those contextual sentences. This gives us 20,609 sentences with superlative expressions that potentially describe our collected knowledge triples with *gradable* predicates. For example, the following sentences from the page of *Nile* in Wikipedia may describes a Freebase fact <*Nile, fb:geography.river.length, 6,853*>:

> "*The Nile is a major north-flowing river in northeastern Africa, generally regarded as the longest river in the world. It is 6,853 km (4,258 miles) long.* "

where we can see that *longest* has implied a comparative construction among all *rivers in the world* and *fb:geography.river.length* is the involved hidden comparison dimension.

Our resulting dataset, WikiDiF, contains **20,609** sentences paired with Freebase predicates, covering **2,335** superlative words and **340** Freebase predicates[2]. In WikiDiF, there are on average 8.8 sentences per superlative word targeting for about 2 predicates, and for commonly seen superlatives, e.g., largest or biggest, there are on average 70 sentences per superlative word targeting for 30 predicates. Compared to other human annotated datasets, WikiDiF is admittedly noisy in nature, but exploits the underlying connections between knowledge facts and their possibly corresponding textual descriptions, where the pseudo co-occurrences of superlative expressions and Freebase predicates will work as a proxy for us to formally analyze the involved comparative constructions.

[1]In Wikipedia, sentences with superlative expressions may not always contain the knowledge facts that support the superlative constructions, which often appear in their neighbouring sentences. For example, *highest*, and its supporting fact, (*Everest, 8,848 metres*), are not in the same sentence, but indeed very near: *Mount Everest, also known ..., is Earth's* ***highest*** *mountain. It is located in ... of the Himalayas. Its peak is* ***8,848 metres*** *(29,029 ft) above sea level.*

[2]We also filter out predicates whose objects are very common in the documents, e.g., 1 or 2, which is difficult to collect training data.

4 Comparison Dimension Selection

Our WikiDiF dataset contains utterances with roughly annotated *superlative-predicate* pairs, which helps us to model the dimension selection task as a classification problem. Given a superlative word S and its context C, our goal is to find a *gradable* Freebase predicate R that maximizes the conditional probability $P(R \mid C, S)$:

$$R^* = \underset{R \in cands_S}{\arg\max}\, P(R \mid C, S)$$

where we can limit our search space to a candidate set $cands_S$ according to the domain and type constraints regarding the comparison set.

Currently, our WikiDiF covers limited predicates and training instances for each superlative S, traditional classification models may suffer from the coverage and data sparsity issues. Here, we adopt a classic one-layer neural network (NN) model with the help of word embeddings to predict how likely a predicate R can work as the comparison dimension given S and its context vector.

We start by constructing vector representations of words and store them in a table L. We use the publicly available word embeddings trained by SENNA (Collobert et al., 2011), with 50 dimensions throughout our experiments.

We construct the context vector for each instance by concatenating the vectors of context words within a window of $\pm k$. If there are not enough words within the window, special filling vectors will be used.

$$V = (w_{j_S-k}, ..., w_{j_S-1}, w_{j_S+1}, ..., w_{j_S+k})$$

where j_S is the index of superlative S in the sentence, and w is the vector of context word or special filling parameter.

The output layer of the NN model is a standard *softmax* function, which takes a *sigmoid* nonlinearity of the context vectors as input. Therefore, the probability of ith predicate in Freebase is chosen as the comparison dimension given superlative S and its context C can be written as:

$$P(R_i \mid C, S) = \frac{e^{z_i}}{\sum_n^{q=1} e^{z_q}}$$

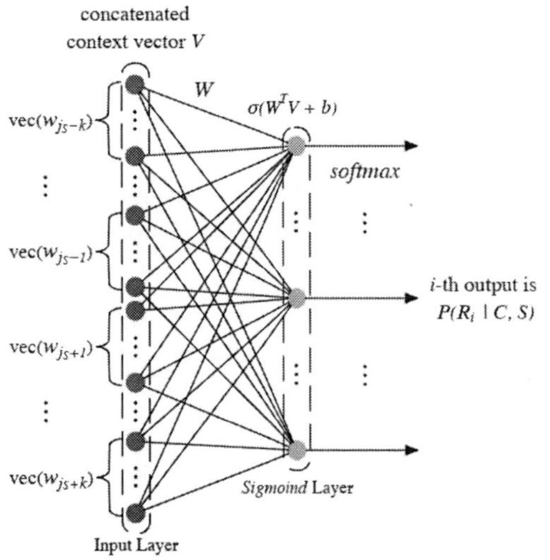

Figure 1: Neural network for dimension selection.

where z_i is estimated using a *sigmoid* function:

$$z_i = \sigma_i(W^T_{m \times n} V + b)$$

where n is the number of candidate predicates for superlative S, m is the length of concatenated vector V, $W_{m \times n}$ is the parameter matrix, b is the bias vector, and σ_i is the *sigmoid* function that applies to the i-th element of argument vector.

Training this standard one-layer neural network model can be straightforward, and the parameters W, b and filling vectors can be updated using stochastic gradient descent (SGD).

5 Ranking Order Determination

To exploit the most from a structured KB, we use an effective heuristic method to decide the ranking order when a superlative expression S triggers a comparative construction regarding a KB predicate R. For each pair of (S, R), we first find from R's supporting sentences the ones that contain superlative S, and further trace the $<subj^*, R, obj^*>$ tuples from the KB which these sentences are assumed to describe. We next look up into the KB, and find other tuples $<subj^o, R, obj^o>$ with the same predicate R. If $subj^o$ and $subj^*$ are of the same type, and most $obj^o < obj^*$, we will say the ranking order for expression S is **descending** when implying predicate R, otherwise, **ascending** order.

In the *Nile* example, if we find in our KB that nearly all other entities of type *river* have smaller values than *6,853* in *fb:geography.river.length* , we can conclude that the ranking order for *longest* regarding *fb:geography.river.length* is *descending* , i.e., we should rank all rivers *descendingly* to get the *longest* one at the top.

Ordinals are processed as a post-processing step to interpret ordinals into a numerical values.

6 Experiments

The main purposes of this work is to answer the following two questions: (1) can we learn from noisy training data without much human involvement to semantically interpret attributive superlative expressions via structured KBs? (2) can our semantic analysis help better understand utterances with superlative expressions?

6.1 Interpreting Superlative Comparisons

We first evaluate our models in the vanilla setup defined in Section 2[3], in terms of accuracy of dimension selection (Acc_d), precision of predicates covered by WikiDiF (P_d), and precision of ranking order determination (P_o).

Datasets: We manually annotate superlative expressions from QALD-4 evaluation dataset(Unger et al., 2014) and TREC QA (2002, 2003) datasets(NIST, 2003), and guarantee that all the labeled superlative instances can be grounded to gradable Freebase predicates. The resulting question dataset contains 135 questions covering 44 Freebase predicates. Additionally, we manually annotate 77 declarative sentences covering 24 Freebase predicates from WSJ and Wikipedia as the declarative dataset.

We build a Naïve Bayes model using co-occurrences as a baseline to predict proper *dimensions*. We further implement a simple baseline to decide the ranking order, by measuring the relatedness between a superlative word and two sets of seed words using word embeddings. The two seed sets, {*most, more, much, many*} and {*least, less, few, little*}, potentially indicate two ranking orders, respectively.

We can see in Table 1 that our method can better capture the underlying connections between superlative expressions and KB predicates. Comparing with the baseline, our model benefits from the NN architecture and distributional word representations and avoids data sparsity to some ex-

[3]We assume that the domain and type constraints regarding the comparison set are known

	Questions			Declaratives		
Model	Acc_d	P_d	P_o	Acc_d	P_d	P_o
Baselines	40.7	81.7	95.5	25.9	78.5	97.4
Ours	48.9	92.9	99.2	33.8	92.8	100

Table 1: Performances of superlative interpretations on two datasets

tent. Our model achieves over 90% of precision on the predicates covered by our training data, showing that it is possible to learn from noisy training data to characterize comparison dimensions against a KB. However, the relatively lower accuracy is mainly due to that some predicates in the testing data are not covered by our WikiDiF, which only covers 19% of gradable Freebase predicates. Regarding the ranking order determination, our simple heuristic method makes the most of Freebase triples, and outperforms the relatedness based baseline, which does not take Freebase into account.

By looking at the different performances on question and declarative sentences, we can see that our method performs better on relatively simpler and shorter questions, while a slightly worse on longer declarative sentences. This is not surprising, since questions are often simple in structure and ask for a straightforward property about the target, while declarative sentences are usually complicated in syntax, which a ± 5 context words window may not be able to capture. Another reason is that for newswire, there are many predicates that are similar in definitions but with tiny differences, which often confuse our methods, e.g., *fb:business.business_operation.assets* and *fb:business.business_operation.current_assets*.

6.2 Question Answering over Freebase

We also investigate how our semantic analysis for superlatives can help improve question answering on two benchmark datasets, Free917(Cai and Yates, 2013) and WebQuestions(Berant et al., 2013), which contain 35 questions with attributive superlative expressions in total. We inject our formal analysis as superlative-triggered aggregation operations into an existing system, Xu14(Xu et al., 2014). Note that we leave the *comparison_set* to be decided by Xu14's parser.

The 35 superlative-triggered complex questions can not be correctly answered by most state-of-the-art systems(Berant et al., 2013; Yao and Van Durme, 2014; Xu et al., 2014), since they can not properly analyze the superlative-triggered functions. When integrated with our analysis, Xu14 is able to correctly answer **14 out of 35** such questions (**40%**), significantly outperforming other systems. The remaining 21 questions are mainly idiomatic usage, e.g., *the Best Actor Award*, or with predicates not covered by WikiDiF.

The result shows that our analysis can help QA systems better handle superlative-triggered aggregation functions, which previous works fail to do. This also gives a good reason to introduce the analysis for comparison constructions into the QA community, which will leverage the potentials of structured KBs to better deal with complex questions.

7 Conclusion

In this paper, we present a novel attempt to semantically analyze the comparisons involved in attributive superlative expressions by investigating on which dimension the comparative construction works and how the comparison results are arranged. We leverage Freebase and their roughly aligned textural descriptions from Wikipedia, and learn from such training data to characterize a comparative construction in two aspects, the dimension of the comparison and its ranking order.

Currently, our analysis suffers from the limited coverage of our WikiDiF. In the future, it would be interesting to improve our method to cover more KB predicates, and extend our NN model with more advanced structures to further improve the performances and also simultaneously characterize the target and comparison set involved.

Acknowledgments

We would like to thank Heng Ji, Benjamin Van Durme, Liwei Chen and Bingfeng Luo for their helpful discussions and three anonymous reviewers for their insightful comments that greatly improved the work. This work was supported by National High Technology R&D Program of China (Grant No. 2015AA015403, 2014AA015102), Natural Science Foundation of China (Grant No. 61202233, 61272344, 61370055) and the joint project with IBM Research. Any correspondence please refer to Yansong Feng.

References

Jonathan Berant, Andrew Chou, Roy Frostig, and Percy Liang. 2013. Semantic parsing on freebase from question-answer pairs. In *EMNLP*, pages 1533–1544.

Johan Bos and Malvina Nissim. 2006. An empirical approach to the interpretation of superlatives. In *EMNLP 2007, Proceedings of the 2006 Conference on Empirical Methods in Natural Language Processing, 22-23 July 2006, Sydney, Australia*, pages 9–17.

Qingqing Cai and Alexander Yates. 2013. Semantic Parsing Freebase: Towards Open-domain Semantic Parsing. In *Proceedings of the Second Joint Conference on Lexical and Computational Semantics (*SEM)*.

Ronan Collobert, Jason Weston, Léon Bottou, Michael Karlen, Koray Kavukcuoglu, and Pavel Kuksa. 2011. Natural language processing (almost) from scratch. *The Journal of Machine Learning Research*, 12:2493–2537.

Donka F Farkas and Katalin É Kiss. 2000. On the comparative and absolute readings of superlatives. *Natural Language & Linguistic Theory*, 18(3):417–455.

Jean Mark Gawron. 1995. Comparatives, superlatives, and resolution. *Linguistics and Philosophy*, 18(4):333–380.

Google. 2013. Freebase data dumps. `https://developers.google.com/freebase/data`.

Irene Heim. 1999. Notes on superlatives.

Nitin Jindal and Bing Liu. 2006. Mining comparative sentences and relations. In *Proceedings, The Twenty-First National Conference on Artificial Intelligence and the Eighteenth Innovative Applications of Artificial Intelligence Conference, July 16-20, 2006, Boston, Massachusetts, USA*, pages 1331–1336.

Mike Mintz, Steven Bills, Rion Snow, and Dan Jurafsky. 2009. Distant supervision for relation extraction without labeled data. In *Proceedings of the Joint Conference of the 47th Annual Meeting of the ACL and the 4th IJCNLP of the AFNLP: Volume 2 - Volume 2*, ACL '09, pages 1003–1011.

NIST. 2003. Text retrieval conference question answering track.

Silke Scheible. 2007. Towards a computational treatment of superlatives. In *Proceedings of the 45th Annual Meeting of the ACL: Student Research Workshop*, ACL '07, pages 67–72, Stroudsburg, PA, USA. Association for Computational Linguistics.

Silke Scheible. 2009. *A Computational Treatment of Superlatives*. Ph.D. thesis, University of Edinburgh.

Silke Scheible. 2012. Textwiki: a superlative resource. *Language Resources and Evaluation*, 46(4):635–666.

Anna Szabolcsi. 1986. Comparative superlatives. *MIT Working papers in Linguistics*, 8:245–265.

Christina Unger, Corina Forascu, Vanessa Lopez, Axel Cyrille Ngonga Ngomo, Elena Cabrio, Philipp Cimiano, and Sebastian Walter. 2014. Question answering over linked data (qald-4). In *Proceedings of the CLEF 2014*, pages 1172–1180.

Kun Xu, Sheng Zhang, Yansong Feng, and Dongyan Zhao. 2014. Answering natural language questions via phrasal semantic parsing. In *Proceedings of the 2014 Conference on Natural Language Processing and Chinese Computing (NLPCC)*, pages 333–344.

Xuchen Yao and Benjamin Van Durme. 2014. Information extraction over structured data: Question answering with freebase. In *Proceedings of ACL*.

Grounding Semantics in Olfactory Perception

Douwe Kiela, Luana Bulat and Stephen Clark
Computer Laboratory
University of Cambridge
douwe.kiela,ltf24,stephen.clark@cl.cam.ac.uk

Abstract

Multi-modal semantics has relied on feature norms or raw image data for perceptual input. In this paper we examine grounding semantic representations in olfactory (smell) data, through the construction of a novel bag of chemical compounds model. We use standard evaluations for multi-modal semantics, including measuring conceptual similarity and cross-modal zero-shot learning. To our knowledge, this is the first work to evaluate semantic similarity on representations grounded in olfactory data.

1 Introduction

Distributional semantics represents the meanings of words as vectors in a "semantic space", relying on the *distributional hypothesis*: the idea that words that occur in similar contexts tend to have similar meanings (Turney and Pantel, 2010; Clark, 2015). Although these models have been successful, the fact that the meaning of a word is represented as a distribution over other words implies they suffer from the *grounding problem* (Harnad, 1990); i.e. they do not account for the fact that human semantic knowledge is grounded in physical reality and sensori-motor experience (Louwerse, 2008).

Multi-modal semantics attempts to address this issue and there has been a surge of recent work on perceptually grounded semantic models. These models learn semantic representations from both textual and perceptual input and outperform language-only models on a range of tasks, including modelling semantic similarity and relatedness, and predicting compositionality (Silberer and Lapata, 2012; Roller and Schulte im Walde, 2013; Bruni et al., 2014). Perceptual information is obtained from either feature norms (Silberer and Lapata, 2012; Roller and Schulte im Walde, 2013; Hill and Korhonen, 2014) or raw data sources such as images (Feng and Lapata, 2010; Leong and Mihalcea, 2011; Bruni et al., 2014; Kiela and Bottou, 2014). The former are elicited from human annotators and thus tend to be limited in scope and expensive to obtain. The latter approach has the advantage that images are widely available and easy to obtain, which, combined with the ready availability of computer vision methods, has led to raw visual information becoming the de-facto perceptual modality in multi-modal models.

However, if our objective is to ground semantic representations in perceptual information, why stop at image data? The meaning of *lavender* is probably more grounded in its smell than in the visual properties of the flower that produces it. Olfactory (smell) perception is of particular interest for grounded semantics because it is much more primitive compared to the other perceptual modalities (Carmichael et al., 1994; Krusemark et al., 2013). As a result, natural language speakers might take aspects of olfactory perception "for granted", which would imply that text is a relatively poor source of such perceptual information. A multi-modal approach would overcome this problem, and might prove useful in, for example, metaphor interpretation (*the sweet smell of success; rotten politics*) and cognitive modelling, as well as in real-world applications such as automatically retrieving smells or even producing smell descriptions. Here, we explore grounding semantic representations in olfactory perception.

We obtain olfactory representations by constructing a novel bag of chemical compounds (BoCC) model. Following previous work in multi-modal semantics, we evaluate on well known conceptual similarity and relatedness tasks and on zero-shot learning through induced cross-modal mappings. To our knowledge this is the first work to explore using olfactory perceptual data for grounding linguistic semantic models.

Proceedings of the 53rd Annual Meeting of the Association for Computational Linguistics and the 7th International Joint Conference on Natural Language Processing (Short Papers), pages 231–236,
Beijing, China, July 26-31, 2015.

Olfactory-Relevant Examples					
MEN		sim	SimLex-999		sim
bakery	bread	0.96	steak	meat	0.75
grass	lawn	0.96	flower	violet	0.70
dog	terrier	0.90	tree	maple	0.55
bacon	meat	0.88	grass	moss	0.50
oak	wood	0.84	beach	sea	0.47
daisy	violet	0.76	cereal	wheat	0.38
daffodil	rose	0.74	bread	flour	0.33

Table 1: Examples of pairs in the evaluation datasets where olfactory information is relevant, together with the gold-standard similarity score.

2 Tasks

Following previous work in grounded semantics, we evaluate performance on two tasks: conceptual similarity and cross-modal zero-shot learning.

2.1 Conceptual similarity

We evaluate the performance of olfactory multi-modal representations on two well-known similarity datasets: SimLex-999 (Hill et al., 2014) and the MEN test collection (Bruni et al., 2014). These datasets consist of concept pairs together with a human-annotated similarity score. Model performance is evaluated using the Spearman ρ_s correlation between the ranking produced by the cosine of the model-derived vectors and that produced by the gold-standard similarity scores.

Evidence suggests that the inclusion of visual representations only improves performance for certain concepts, and that in some cases the introduction of visual information is detrimental to performance on similarity and relatedness tasks (Kiela et al., 2014). The same is likely to be true for other perceptual modalities: in the case of a comparison such as *lily-rose*, the olfactory modality certainly is meaningful, while this is probably not the case for *skateboard-swimsuit*. Some examples of relevant pairs can be found in Table 1.

Hence, we had two annotators rate the two datasets according to whether smell is relevant to the pairwise comparison. The annotation criterion was as follows: if both concepts in a pairwise comparison have a distinctive associated smell, then the comparison is relevant to the olfactory modality. Only if both annotators agree is the comparison deemed olfactory-relevant. This annotation leads to a total of four evaluation sets: the MEN test collection **MEN** (3000 pairs) and its olfactory-relevant subset **OMEN** (311 pairs); and the SimLex-999 dataset **SLex** (999 pairs) and its olfactory-relevant subset **OSLex** (65 pairs). The inter-annotator agreement on the olfactory relevance judgments was high ($\kappa = 0.94$ for the MEN test collection and $\kappa = 0.96$ for SimLex-999).[1]

2.2 Cross-modal zero-shot learning

Cross-modal semantics, instead of being concerned with improving semantic representations through grounding, focuses on the problem of reference. Using, for instance, mappings between visual and textual space, the objective is to learn which words refer to which objects (Lazaridou et al., 2014). This problem is very much related to the object recognition task in computer vision, but instead of using just visual data and labels, these cross-modal models also utilize textual information (Socher et al., 2014; Frome et al., 2013). This approach allows for *zero-shot learning*, where the model can predict how an object relates to other concepts just from seeing an image of the object, but without ever having seen the object previously (Lazaridou et al., 2014).

We evaluate cross-modal zero-shot learning performance through the average percentage correct at N (P@N), which measures how many of the test instances were ranked within the top N highest ranked nearest neighbors. A chance baseline is obtained by randomly ranking a concept's nearest neighbors. We use partial least squares regression (PLSR) to induce cross-modal mappings from the linguistic to the olfactory space and vice versa.[2]

Due to the nature of the olfactory data source (see Section 3), it is not possible to build olfactory representations for all concepts in the test sets. However, cross-modal mappings yield an additional benefit: since linguistic representations have full coverage over the datasets, we can project from linguistic space to perceptual space to also obtain full coverage for the perceptual modalities. This technique has been used to increase coverage for feature norms (Fagarasan et al., 2015). Consequently, we are in a position to compare perceptual spaces directly to each other, and to linguistic

[1] To facilitate further work in multi-modal semantics beyond vision, our code and data have been made publicly available at http://www.cl.cam.ac.uk/~dk427/aroma.html.

[2] To avoid introducing another parameter, we set the number of latent variables in the cross-modal PLSR map to a third of the number of dimensions of the perceptual representation.

Smell label	Phenethyl acetate	Isoamyl butyrate	Anisyl butyrate	Myrcene	Syringaldehyde
Melon	✓	✓			
Pineapple	✓				✓
Licorice			✓		
Anise			✓	✓	
Beer				✓	✓

(Column group heading: Chemical Compound)

Table 2: A BoCC model.

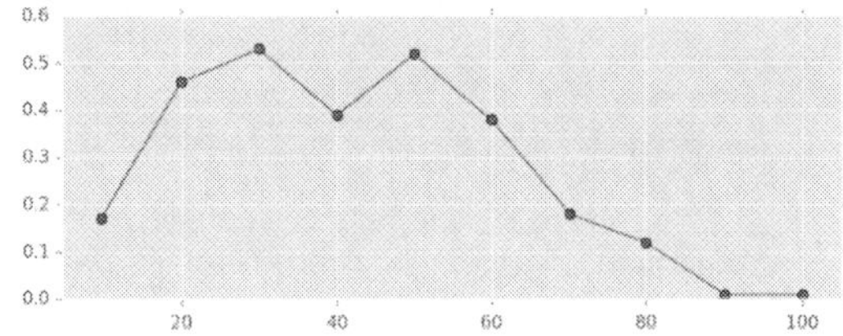

Figure 1: Performance of olfactory representations when using SVD to reduce the number of dimensions.

Dataset	Linguistic	BoCC-Raw	BoCC-SVD
OMEN (35)	0.40	0.42	0.53

Table 3: Comparison of olfactory representations on the covered OMEN dataset.

space, over the entire dataset, as well as on the relevant olfactory subsets. When projecting into such a space and reporting results, the model is prefixed with an arrow (→) in the corresponding table.

3 Olfactory Perception

The Sigma-Aldrich Fine Chemicals flavors and fragrances catalog[3] (henceforth SAFC) is one of the largest publicly accessible databases of semantic odor profiles that is used extensively in fragrance research (Zarzo and Stanton, 2006). It contains organoleptic labels and the chemical compounds—or more accurately the perfume raw materials (PRMs)—that produce them. By automatically scraping the catalog we obtained a total of 137 organoleptic smell labels from SAFC, with a total of 11,152 associated PRMs. We also experimented with Flavornet[4] and the LRI and odour database[5], but found that the data from these were more noisy and generally of lower quality.

For each of the smell labels in SAFC we count the co-occurrences of associated chemical compounds, yielding a bag of chemical compounds (BoCC) model. Table 2 shows an example subspace of this model. Although the SAFC catalog is considered sufficiently comprehensive for fragrance research (Zarzo and Stanton, 2006), the fact that PRMs usually occur only once per smell label means that the representations are rather sparse. Hence, we apply dimensionality reduction to the original representation to get denser vectors. We call the model without any dimensionality reduction BoCC-Raw and use singular value decomposition (SVD) to create an additional BoCC-SVD model with reduced dimensionality. Positive pointwise mutual information (PPMI) weighting is applied to the raw space before performing dimensionality reduction.

The number of dimensions in human olfactory space is a hotly debated topic in the olfactory chemical sciences (Buck and Axel, 1991; Zarzo and Stanton, 2006). Recent studies involving multi-dimensional scaling on the SAFC catalog revealed approximately 32 dimensions in olfactory perception space (Mamlouk et al., 2003; Mamlouk and Martinetz, 2004). We examine this finding by evaluating the Spearman ρ_s correlation on the pairs of **OMEN** that occur in the SAFC database (35 pairs). The coverage on SimLex was not sufficient to also try that dataset (only 5 pairs). Figure 1 shows the results. It turns out that the best olfactory representations are obtained with 30 dimensions. In other words, our findings appear to corroborate recent evidence suggesting that olfactory space (at least when using SAFC as a data source) is best modeled using around 30 dimensions.

3.1 Linguistic representations

For the linguistic representations we use the continuous vector representations from the log-linear skip-gram model of Mikolov et al. (2013), specifically the 300-dimensional vector representations trained on part of the Google News dataset (about 100 billion words) that have been released on the

[3]http://www.sigmaaldrich.com/industries/flavors-and-fragrances.html

[4]http://www.flavornet.org

[5]http://www.odour.org.uk

	MEN	OMEN	SLex	OSLex
Linguistic	0.78	0.38	0.44	0.30
→BoCC-Raw	0.38	0.36	0.19	0.23
→BoCC-SVD	0.46	0.51	0.23	0.48
Multi-modal	0.69	0.53	0.40	0.49

Table 4: Comparison of linguistic, olfactory and multi-modal representations.

Mapping	P@1	P@5	P@20	P@50
Chance	0.0	3.76	13.53	36.09
Olfactory ⇒ Ling.	1.51	8.33	24.24	47.73
Ling. ⇒ Olfactory	4.55	15.15	43.18	67.42

Table 5: Zero-shot learning performance for BoCC-SVD.

Word2vec website.[6]

3.2 Conceptual Similarity

Results on the 35 covered pairs of **OMEN** for the two BoCC models are reported in Table 3. Olfactory representations outperform linguistic representations on this subset. In fact, linguistic representations perform poorly compared to their performance on the whole of **MEN**. The SVD model performs best, improving on the linguistic and raw models with a 33% and 26% relative increase in performance, respectively.

We use a cross-modal PLSR map, trained on all available organoleptic labels in SAFC, to extend coverage and allow for a direct comparison between linguistic representations and cross-modally projected olfactory representations on the entire datasets and relevant subsets. The results are shown in Table 4. As might be expected, linguistic performs better than olfactory on the full datasets. On the olfactory-relevant subsets, however, the projected BoCC-SVD model outperforms linguistic for both datasets. Performance increases even further when the two representations are combined into a multi-modal representation by concatenating the L2-normalized linguistic and olfactory (→BoCC-SVD) vectors.

3.3 Zero-shot learning

We learn a cross-modal mapping between the two spaces and evaluate zero-shot learning. We use all 137 labels in the SAFC database that have corresponding linguistic vectors for the training data.

[6]https://code.google.com/p/word2vec/

apple	bacon	brandy	cashew
pear	smoky	rum	hazelnut
banana	roasted	whiskey	peanut
melon	coffee	wine-like	almond
apricot	mesquite	grape	hawthorne
pineapple	mossy	fleshy	jam
chocolate	**lemon**	**cheese**	**caramel**
cocoa	citrus	grassy	nutty
sweet	geranium	butter	roasted
coffee	grapefruit	oily	maple
licorice	tart	creamy	butterscotch
roasted	floral	coconut	coffee

Table 6: Example nearest neighbors for BoCC-SVD representations.

For each term, we train the map on all other labels and measure whether the correct instance is ranked within the top N neighbors. We use the BoCC-SVD model for the olfactory space, since it performed best on the conceptual similarity task. Table 5 shows the results. It appears that mapping linguistic to olfactory is easier than mapping olfactory to linguistic, which may be explained by the different number of dimensions in the two spaces. One could say that it is easier to find the chemical composition of a "smelly" word from its linguistic representation, than it is to linguistically represent or describe a chemical composition.

3.4 Qualitative analysis

We also examined the BoCC representations qualitatively. As Table 6 shows, the nearest neighbors are remarkably semantically coherent. The nearest neighbors for *bacon* and *cheese*, for example, accurately sum up how one might describe those smells. The model also groups together nuts and fruits, and expresses well what *chocolate* and *caramel* smell (or taste) like.

4 Conclusions

We have studied grounding semantic representations in raw olfactory perceptual information. We used a bag of chemical compounds model to obtain olfactory representations and evaluated on conceptual similarity and cross-modal zero-shot learning, with good results. It is possible that the olfactory modality is well-suited to other forms of evaluation, but in this initial work we chose to follow standard practice in multi-modal semantics to allow for a direct comparison.

This work opens up interesting possibilities in analyzing smell and even taste. It could be applied in a variety of settings beyond semantic similarity, from chemical information retrieval to metaphor interpretation to cognitive modelling. A speculative blue-sky application based on this, and other multi-modal models, would be an NLG application describing a wine based on its chemical composition, and perhaps other information such as its color and country of origin.

Acknowledgements

DK is supported by EPSRC grant EP/I037512/1. LB is supported by an EPSRC Doctoral Training Grant. SC is supported by ERC Starting Grant DisCoTex (306920) and EPSRC grant EP/I037512/1. We thank the anonymous reviewers for their helpful comments and Flaviu Bulat for providing useful feedback.

References

Elia Bruni, Nam-Khanh Tran, and Marco Baroni. 2014. Multimodal distributional semantics. *Journal of Artifical Intelligence Research*, 49:1–47.

Linda Buck and Richard Axel. 1991. A novel multigene family may encode odorant receptors: a molecular basis for odor recognition. *Cell*, 65(1):175–187.

S. Thomas Carmichael, M.-C. Clugnet, and Joseph L. Price. 1994. Central olfactory connections in the macaque monkey. *Journal of Comparative Neurology*, 346(3):403–434.

Stephen Clark. 2015. Vector Space Models of Lexical Meaning. In Shalom Lappin and Chris Fox, editors, *Handbook of Contemporary Semantics*, chapter 16. Wiley-Blackwell, Oxford.

Luana Fagarasan, Eva Maria Vecchi, and Stephen Clark. 2015. From distributional semantics to feature norms: grounding semantic models in human perceptual data. In *Proceedings of the 11th International Conference on Computational Semantics (IWCS 2015)*, pages 52–57, London, UK.

Yansong Feng and Mirella Lapata. 2010. Visual information in semantic representation. In *Proceedings of NAACL*, pages 91–99.

Andrea Frome, Gregory S. Corrado, Jonathon Shlens, Samy Bengio, Jeffrey Dean, Marc'Aurelio Ranzato, and Tomas Mikolov. 2013. DeViSE: A Deep Visual-Semantic Embedding Model. In *Proceedings of NIPS*, pages 2121–2129.

Stevan Harnad. 1990. The symbol grounding problem. *Physica D*, 42:335–346.

Felix Hill and Anna Korhonen. 2014. Learning abstract concept embeddings from multi-modal data: Since you probably can't see what I mean. In *Proceedings of EMNLP*, pages 255–265.

Felix Hill, Roi Reichart, and Anna Korhonen. 2014. SimLex-999: Evaluating semantic models with (genuine) similarity estimation. *CoRR*, abs/1408.3456.

Douwe Kiela and Léon Bottou. 2014. Learning image embeddings using convolutional neural networks for improved multi-modal semantics. In *Proceedings of EMNLP*, pages 36–45.

Douwe Kiela, Felix Hill, Anna Korhonen, and Stephen Clark. 2014. Improving multi-modal representations using image dispersion: Why less is sometimes more. In *Proceedings of ACL*, pages 835–841.

Elizabeth A Krusemark, Lucas R Novak, Darren R Gitelman, and Wen Li. 2013. When the sense of smell meets emotion: anxiety-state-dependent olfactory processing and neural circuitry adaptation. *The Journal of Neuroscience*, 33(39):15324–15332.

Angeliki Lazaridou, Elia Bruni, and Marco Baroni. 2014. Is this a wampimuk? Cross-modal mapping between distributional semantics and the visual world. In *Proceedings of ACL*, pages 1403–1414.

Chee Wee Leong and Rada Mihalcea. 2011. Going beyond text: A hybrid image-text approach for measuring word relatedness. In *Proceedings of IJCNLP*, pages 1403–1407.

Max M. Louwerse. 2008. Symbol interdependency in symbolic and embodied cognition. *Topics in Cognitive Science*, 59(1):617–645.

Amir Madany Mamlouk and Thomas Martinetz. 2004. On the dimensions of the olfactory perception space. *Neurocomputing*, 58:1019–1025.

Amir Madany Mamlouk, Christine Chee-Ruiter, Ulrich G Hofmann, and James M Bower. 2003. Quantifying olfactory perception: Mapping olfactory perception space by using multidimensional scaling and self-organizing maps. *Neurocomputing*, 52:591–597.

Tomas Mikolov, Kai Chen, Greg Corrado, and Jeffrey Dean. 2013. Efficient estimation of word representations in vector space. In *Proceedings of ICLR*, Scottsdale, Arizona, USA.

Stephen Roller and Sabine Schulte im Walde. 2013. A multimodal LDA model integrating textual, cognitive and visual modalities. In *Proceedings of EMNLP*, pages 1146–1157.

Carina Silberer and Mirella Lapata. 2012. Grounded models of semantic representation. In *Proceedings of EMNLP*, pages 1423–1433.

Richard Socher, Andrej Karpathy, Quoc V. Le, Christopher D. Manning, and Andrew Y. Ng. 2014. Grounded compositional semantics for finding and describing images with sentences. *Transactions of ACL*, 2:207–218.

Peter D. Turney and Patrick Pantel. 2010. From Frequency to Meaning: vector space models of semantics. *Journal of Artifical Intelligence Research*, 37(1):141–188, January.

Manuel Zarzo and David T. Stanton. 2006. Identification of latent variables in a semantic odor profile database using principal component analysis. *Chemical Senses*, 31(8):713–724.

Word-based Japanese typed dependency parsing with grammatical function analysis

Takaaki Tanaka **Nagata Masaaki**
NTT Communication Science Laboratories, NTT Corporation
2-4, Hikaridai, Seika-cho, Soraku-gun, Kyoto, 619-0237, Japan
{tanaka.takaaki,nagata.masaaki}@lab.ntt.co.jp

Abstract

We present a novel scheme for word-based Japanese typed dependency parser which integrates syntactic structure analysis and grammatical function analysis such as predicate-argument structure analysis. Compared to bunsetsu-based dependency parsing, which is predominantly used in Japanese NLP, it provides a natural way of extracting syntactic constituents, which is useful for downstream applications such as statistical machine translation. It also makes it possible to jointly decide dependency and predicate-argument structure, which is usually implemented as two separate steps. We convert an existing treebank to the new dependency scheme and report parsing results as a baseline for future research. We achieved a better accuracy for assigning function labels than a predicate-argument structure analyzer by using grammatical functions as dependency label.

1 Introduction

The goal of our research is to design a Japanese typed dependency parsing that has sufficient linguistically derived structural and relational information for NLP applications such as statistical machine translation. We focus on the Japanese-specific aspects of designing a kind of Stanford typed dependencies (de Marneffe et al., 2008).

Syntactic structures are usually represented as dependencies between chunks called *bunsetsus*. A bunsetsu is a Japanese grammatical and phonological unit that consists of one or more content words such as a noun, verb, or adverb followed by a sequence of zero or more function words such as auxiliary verbs, postpositional particles, or sentence-final particles. Most publicly available Japanese parsers, including CaboCha [1] (Kudo et al., 2002) and KNP [2] (Kawahara et al., 2006), return bunsetsu-based dependency as syntactic structure. Such parsers are generally highly accurate and have been widely used in various NLP applications.

However, bunsetsu-based representations also have two serious shortcomings: one is the discrepancy between syntactic and semantic units, and the other is insufficient syntactic information (Butler et al., 2012; Tanaka et al., 2013).

Bunsetsu chunks do not always correspond to constituents (e.g. NP, VP), which complicates the task of extracting semantic units from bunsetsu-based representations. This kind of problem often arises in handling such nesting structures as coordinating constructions. For example, there are three dependencies in a sentence (1): a coordinating dependency $b2 - b3$ and ordinary dependencies $b1 - b3$ and $b3 - b4$. In extracting predicate-argument structures, it is not possible to directly extract a coordinated noun phrase ワインと酒 "wine and sake" as a direct object of the verb 飲んだ "drank". In other words, we need an implicit interpretation rule in order to extract NP in coordinating construction: head bunsetsu $b3$ should be divided into a content word 酒 and a function word の, then the content word should be merged with the dependent bunsetsu $b2$.

(1) $_{b1}$ 飲んだ | $_{b2}$ ワイン と | $_{b3}$ 酒 の | $_{b4}$ リスト

nonda	*wain*	*to*	*sake*	*no*	*risuto*
drank	wine	CONJ	sake	GEN	list

'A list of wine and sake that (someone) drank'

Therefore, predicate-argument structure analysis is usually implemented as a post-processor of bunsetsu-based syntactic parser, not just for assigning grammatical functions, but for identifying constituents, such as an analyzer SynCha [3] (Iida

[1] http://taku910.github.io/cabocha/.
[2] http://nlp.ist.i.kyoto-u.ac.jp/EN/index.php?KNP.
[3] http://www.cl.cs.titech.ac.jp/~ryu-i/syncha/.

Proceedings of the 53rd Annual Meeting of the Association for Computational Linguistics and the 7th International Joint Conference on Natural Language Processing (Short Papers), pages 237–242,
Beijing, China, July 26-31, 2015.

	魚 / フライ	を	食べ	た	か / も / しれ / ない	三毛 / 猫
	fish / fry	-ACC	eat	-PAST	may	calico / cat
	“the calico cat that may have eaten fried fish”					
SUW	NN / NN	PCS	VB	AUX	P / P / VB / AUX	NN / NN
LUW	NN	PCS	VB	AUX	AUX	NN

Figure 1: A tokenized and chunked sentence.

et al., 2011), which uses the parsing results from CaboCha. We assume that using a word as a parsing unit instead of a bunsetsu chunk helps to maintain consistency between syntactic structure analysis and predicate-argument structure analysis.

Another problem is that linguistically different constructions share the same representation. The difference of a gapped relative clause and a gapless relative clause is a typical example. In sentences (2) and (3), we cannot discriminate the two relations between bunsetsus *b*2 and *b*3 using unlabeled dependency: the former is a subject-predicate construction of the noun 猫 “cat” and the verb 食べる “eat” (subject gap relative clause) while the latter is not a predicate-argument construction (gapless relative clause).

(2) *b*1 魚 を |*b*2 食べた |*b*3 猫
sakana o *tabe ta* *neko*
fish ACC eat PAST cat
‘the cat that ate fish’

(3) *b*1 魚 を |*b*2 食べた |*b*3 話
sakana o *tabe ta* *hanashi*
fish ACC eat PAST story
‘the story about having eaten fish’

We aim to build a Japanese typed dependency scheme that can properly deal with syntactic constituency and grammatical functions in the same representation without implicit interpretation rules. The design of Japanese typed dependencies is described in Section 3, and we present our evaluation of the dependency parsing results for a parser trained with a dependency corpus in Section 4.

2 Related work

Mori et al. (2014) built word-based dependency corpora in Japanese. The reported parsing achieved an unlabeled attachment score of over 90%; however, there was no information on the syntactic relations between the words in this corpus. Uchimoto et al. (2008) also proposed the criteria and definitions of word-level dependency structure mainly for annotation of a spontaneous speech corpus, the Corpus of Spontaneous Japanese (CSJ) (Maekawa et al., 2000), and they do not make a distinction between detailed syntactic functions either.

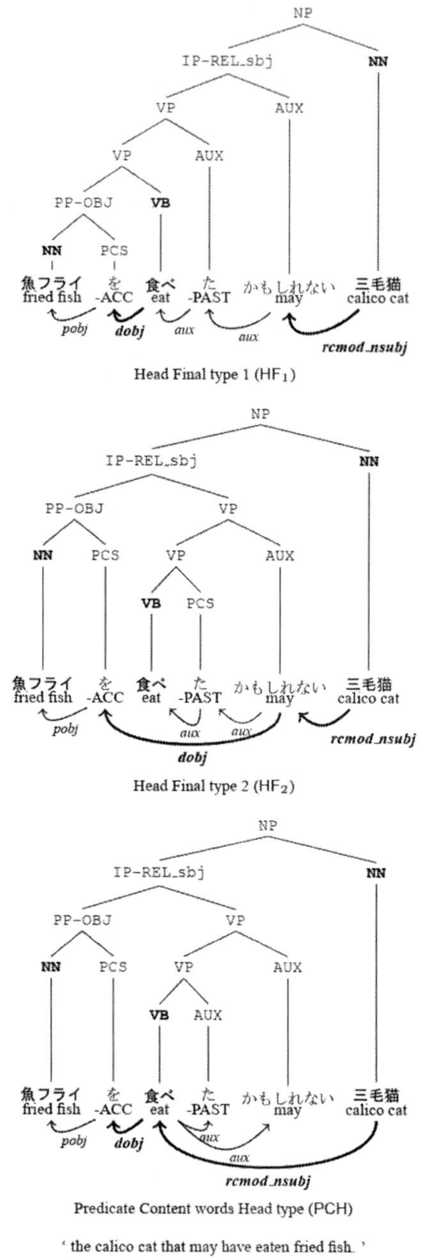

Figure 2: Example structures in three dependency schemes. Boldface words are content words that may be predicates or arguments. Thick lines denote dependencies with types related to predicate-argument structures.

Category	Dep. type	
case (argument)	*nsubj*	subject
	dobj	direct object
	iobj	indirect object
case (adjunct)	*tmod*	temporal
	lmod	locative
gapped relative clause	*rcmod_nsubj*	subject gap relative clause
	rcmod_dobj	direct object gap relative clause
	rcmod_iobj	indirect object gap relative clause
adnominal clause	*ncmod*	gapless relative clause
adverbial clause	*advcl*	
coordinating construction	*conj*	
apposition	*appos*	
function word relation	*aux*	relation between an auxiliary verb and other word
	pobj	relation between a particle and other word

Table 1: Dependency types (excerpt).

We proposed a typed dependency scheme based on the well-known and widely used Stanford typed dependencies (SD), which originated in English and has since been extended to many languages, but not to Japanese. The Universal dependencies (UD) (McDonald et al., 2013; de Marneffe et al., 2014) has been developed based on SD in order to design the cross-linguistically consistent treebank annotation [4]. The UD for Japanese has also been discussed, but no treebanks have been provided yet. We focus on the feasibility of word-based Japanese typed dependency parsing rather than on cross-linguistic consistency. We plan to examine the conversion between UD and our scheme in the future.

3 Typed dependencies in Japanese

To design a scheme of Japanese typed dependencies, there are three essential points: what should be used as parsing units, which dependency scheme is appropriate for Japanese sentence structure, and what should be defined as dependency types.

3.1 Parsing unit

Defining a word unit is indispensable for word-based dependency parsing. However, this is not a trivial question, especially in Japanese, where words are not segmented by white spaces in its orthography. We adopted two types of word units defined by NINJL [5] for building the Balanced Corpus of Contemporary Written Japanese (BCCWJ) (Maekawa et al., 2014; Den et al., 2008): Short unit word (SUW) is the shortest token conveying morphological information, and the long unit word (LUW) is the basic unit for parsing, consisting of one or more SUWs. Figure 1 shows example results from the preprocessing of parsing. In the figure, "/" denotes a border of SUWs in an LUW, and "||" denotes a bunsetsu boundary.

[4] `http://universaldependencies.github.io/docs/`.

[5] National Institute for Japanese Language and Linguistics.

3.2 Dependency scheme

Basically, Japanese dependency structure is regarded as an aggregation of pairs of a left-side dependent word and a right-side head word, i.e. right-headed dependency, since Japanese is a head-final language. However, how to analyze a predicate constituent is a matter of debate. We define two types of schemes depending on the structure related to the predicate constituent: first conjoining predicate and arguments, and first conjoining predicate and function words such as auxiliary verbs.

As shown in sentence (4), a predicate bunsetsu consists of a main verb followed by a sequence of auxiliary verbs in Japanese. We consider two ways of constructing a verb phrase (VP). One is first conjoining the main verb and its arguments to construct VP as in sentence (4a), and the other is first conjoining the main verb and auxiliary verbs as in sentence (4b). These two types correspond to sentences (5a) and (5b), respectively, in English.

(4) 猫 が 魚 を 食べた かもしれない
cat NOM fish ACC eat PAST may
'the cat may have eaten the fish'
a. [[[$_{VP}$ 猫が 魚を 食べ] た] かもしれない]
S O V aux aux
b. [猫が [魚を [$_{VP}$ 食べ た かもしれない]]]
S O V aux aux

(5) a. [The cat [may have [$_{VP}$ eaten the fish]]] .
S aux aux V O
b. [The cat [[$_{VP}$ may have eaten] the fish]] .
S aux aux V O

The structures in sentences (4a) and (5a) are similar to a structure based on generative grammar. On the other hand, the structures in sentences (4b) and (5b) are similar to the bunsetsu structure.

We defined two dependency schemes **Head Final type 1** (HF_1) and **Head Final type 2** (HF_2) as shown in Figure 2, which correspond to structures of sentences (4a) and (4b), respectively. Additionally, we introduced **Predicate Content word Head type** (PCH), where a content word (e.g. verb) is treated as a head in a predicate phrase so as to link the predicate to its argument more directly.

3.3 Dependency type

We defined 35 dependency types for Japanese based on SD, where 4-50 types are assigned for syntactic relations in English and other languages.

LUW (Long Unit Word)		source
l_FORM	form	LUW chunker
l_LEMMA	lemma	LUW chunker
l_UPOS	POS	LUW chunker
l_INFTYPE	inflection type	LUW chunker
l_INFFORM	inflection form	LUW chunker
l_CPOS	non-terminal symbol	*
l_SEMCLASS	semantic class	thesaurus**
l_PNCLASS	NE class	thesaurus**
SUW (Short Unit Word)		
s_FORM_R	form (rightmost)	tokenizer
s_FORM_L	form (leftmost)	tokenizer
s_LEMMA_R	lemma (rightmost)	tokenizer
s_LEMMA_L	lemma (leftmost)	tokenizer
s_UPOS_R	POS	tokenizer
s_CPOS_R	non-terminal symbol	*
s_SEMCLASS_R	semantic class	thesaurus**
s_PNCLASS_R	NE class	thesaurus**

Table 2: Word attributes used for parser features. * 26 non-terminal symbols (e.g. NN, VB) are employed as coarse POS tags (CPOS) from an original treebank. ** Semantic classes SEMCLASS and PNCLASS are used for general nouns and proper nouns, respectively from a Japanese thesaurus (Ikehara et al., 1997) to generalize the nouns.

Table 1 shows the major dependency types. To discriminate between a gapped relative clause and a gapless relative clause as described in Section 1, we assigned two dependency types *rcmod* and *ncmod* respectively. Moreover, we introduced gap information by subdividing *rcmod* into three types to extract predicate-argument relations, while the original SD make no distinction between them.

The labels of case and gapped relative clause enable us to extract predicate-argument structures by simply tracing dependency paths. In the case of HF_1 in Figure 2, we find two paths between content words: 魚フライ "fried fish"(NN)←*pobj*←***dobj***← 食べ "eat"(VB) and 食べ (VB)←*aux*←*aux*←***rcmod_nsubj***← 三毛猫 "calico cat"(NN). By marking the dependency types *dobj* and *rcmod_nsubj*, we can extract the arguments for predicate 食べる, i.e., 魚フライ as a direct object and 三毛猫 as a subject.

4 Evaluation

We demonstrated the performance of the typed dependency parsing based on our scheme by using the dependency corpus automatically converted from a constituent treebank and an off-the-self parser.

4.1 Resources

We used a dependency corpus that was converted from the Japanese constituent treebank (Tanaka et al., 2013) built by re-annotating the Kyoto University Text Corpus (Kurohashi et al., 2003) with phrase structure and function labels. The Kyoto corpus consists of approximately 40,000 sentences from newspaper articles, and from these 17,953 sentences have been re-annotated. The treebank is designed to have complete binary trees, which can be easily converted to dependency trees by adapting head rules and dependency-type rules for each partial tree. We divided this corpus into 15,953 sentences (339,573 LUWs) for the training set and 2,000 sentences (41,154 LUWs) for the test set.

4.2 Parser and features

In the analysis process, sentences are first tokenized into SUW and tagged with SUW POS by the morphological analyzer MeCab (Kudo et al., 2004). The LUW analyzer Comainu (Kozawa et al., 2014) chunks the SUW sequences into LUW sequences. We used the MaltParser (Nivre et al., 2007), which marked over 81 % in labeled attachment score (LAS), for English SD. Stack algorithm (projective) and LIBLINEAR were chosen as the parsing algorithm and the learner, respectively. We built and tested the three types of parsing models with the three dependency schemes.

Features of the parsing model are made by combining word attributes as shown in Table 2. We employed SUW-based attributes as well as LUW-based attributes because LUW contains many multiword expressions such as compound nouns, and features combining LUW-based attributes tend to be sparse. The SUW-based attributes are extracted by using the leftmost or rightmost SUW of the target LUW. For instance, for LUW 魚フライ in Figure 1, the SUW-based attributes are s_LEMMA_L (the leftmost SUW's lemma 魚 "fish") and s_LEMMA_R (the rightmost SUW's lemma フライ "fry").

4.3 Results

The parsing results for the three dependency schemes are shown in Table 3 (a). The dependency schemes HF_1 and HF_2 are comparable, but PCH is slightly lower than them, which is probably because PCH is a more complicated structure, having left-to-right dependencies in the predicate phrase, than the head-final types HF_1 and HF_2. The performances of the LUW-based parsings are considered to be comparable to the results of a bunsetsu-dependency parser CaboCha on the same data set, i.e. a UAS of 92.7%, although we cannot directly compare them due to the difference in parsing units. Table 3 (b) shows the results for each dependency type. The argument types (*nsubj*,

Scheme	UAS	LAS
HF_1	94.09	89.49
HF_2	**94.21**	**89.66**
PCH	93.53	89.22

(a) Overall results

dep. type	F_1 score		
	HF_1	HF_2	PCH
nsubj	80.47	**82.12**	81.08
dobj	92.06	90.28	**92.29**
iobj	**82.05**	80.22	81.89
tmod	55.54	**56.01**	54.09
lmod	52.10	**53.56**	48.48
rcmod_nsubj	60.38	61.10	**62.95**
rcmod_dobj	28.07	33.33	**39.46**
rcmod_iobj	32.65	33.90	**36.36**
ncmod	82.81	**83.07**	82.94
advcl	65.28	**66.70**	60.69
conj	**70.78**	70.68	69.53
appos	51.11	**57.45**	46.32

(b) Results for each dependency type

Table 3: Parsing results.

Scheme	Precision	Recall	F_1 score
HF_1	82.1	71.4	76.4
HF_2	81.9	67.0	73.7
PCH	**82.5**	**72.4**	**77.1**
SynCha	76.6	65.3	70.5

Table 4: Predicate-argument structure analysis.

dobj and *iobj*) resulted in relatively high scores in comparison to the temporal (*tmod*) and locative (*lmod*) cases. These types are typically labeled as belonging to the postpositional phrase consisting of a noun phrase and particles, and case particles such as が "ga", を "o" and に "ni" strongly suggest an argument by their combination with verbs, while particles に and で "de" are widely used outside the temporal and locative cases.

Predicate-argument structure We extracted predicate-argument structure information as triplets, which are pairs of predicates and arguments connected by a relation, i.e. $(pred, rel, arg)$, from the dependency parsing results by tracing the paths with the argument and gapped relative clause types. $pred$ in a triplet is a verb or an adjective, arg is a head noun of an argument, and rel is nsubj, dobj or iobj.

The gold standard data is built by converting predicate-argument structures in NAIST Text Corpus (Iida et al., 2007) into the above triples. Basically, the cases "ga", "o" and "ni" in the corpus correspond to "nsubj", "dobj" and "iobj", respectively, however, we should apply the alternative conversion to passive or causative voice, since the annotation is based on active voice. The conversion for case alternation was manually done for each triple. We filtered out the triples including zero pronouns or arguments without the direct dependencies on their predicates from the converted triples, finally 6,435 triplets remained.

Table 4 shows the results of comparing the extracted triples with the gold data. PCH marks the highest score here in spite of getting the lowest score in the parsing results. It is assumed that the characteristics of PCH, where content words tend to be directly linked, are responsible. The table also contains the results of the predicate-argument structure analyzer SynCha. Note that we focus on only the relations between a predicate and its dependents, while SynCha is designed to deal with zero anaphora resolution in addition to predicate-argument structure analysis over syntactic dependencies. Since SynCha uses the syntactic parsing results of CaboCha in a cascaded process, the parsing error may cause conflict between syntactic structure and predicate-argument structure. A typical example is that case where a gapped relative clause modifies a noun phrase A の B "B of A", e.g., [$_{VP}$ 庭 から 逃げ た] [$_{NP}$ 猫 の 足跡] "footprints of the cat that escaped from a garden." If the noun A is an argument of a main predicate in a relative clause, the predicate is a dependent of the noun A; however, this is not actually reliable because two analyses are separately processed. There are 75 constructions of this type in the test set; the LUW-based dependency parsing captured 42 correct predicate-argument relations (and dependencies), while the cascaded parsing was limited to obtaining 6 relations.

5 Conclusion

We proposed a scheme of Japanese typed-dependency parsing for dealing with constituents and capturing the grammatical function as a dependency type that bypasses the traditional limitations of bunsetsu-based dependency parsing. The evaluations demonstrated that a word-based dependency parser achieves high accuracies that are comparable to those of a bunsetsu-based dependency parser, and moreover, provides detailed syntactic information such as predicate-argument structures. Recently, discussion has begun toward Universal Dependencies, including Japanese. The work presented here can be viewed as a feasibility study of UD for Japanese. We are planning to port our corpus and compare our scheme with UD to contribute to the improvement of UD for Japanese.

References

Alastair Butler, Zhen Zhou and Kei Yoshimoto. 2012. Problems for successful bunsetsu based parsing and some solutions. In *Proceedings of the Eighteenth Annual Meeting on the Association for Natural Language Processing*, pp. 951–954.

Marie-Catherine de Marneffe and Christopher D. Manning. 2008. The Stanford typed dependencies representation. In *Proceedings of COLING 2008 Workshop on Cross-framework and Cross-domain Parser Evaluation*.

Marie-Catherine de Marneffe, Natalia Silveira, Timothy Dozat, Katri Haverinen, Filip Ginter, Joakim Nivre, and Christopher D. Manning. 2014. Universal Stanford Dependencies: A cross-linguistic typology. In *Proceedings of the Ninth International Conference on Language Resources and Evaluation (LREC-2014)*.

Yasuharu Den, Junpei Nakamura, Toshinobu Ogiso and Hideki Ogura. 2008. A proper approach to Japanese morphological analysis: Dictionary, model and evaluation. In *Proceedings of the Sixth International Conference on Language Resources and Evaluation (LREC-2008)*.

Ryu Iida, Mamoru Komachi, Kentaro Inui and Yuji Matsumoto. 2007. Annotating a Japanese Text Corpus with Predicate-argument and Coreference Relations. In *Proceedings of the the Linguistic Annotation Workshop (LAW '07)*, pp. 132–139.

Ryu Iida and Massimo Poesio. 2011. A Cross-Lingual ILP Solution to Zero Anaphora Resolution. In *Proceedings of the 49th Annual Meeting of the Association for Computational Linguistics: Human Language Technologies (ACL-HLT 2011)*, pp. 804-813.

Satoru Ikehara, Masahiro Miyazaki, Satoshi Shirai, Akio Yokoo, Kentaro Ogura, Yoshifumi Ooyama and Yoshihiko Hayashi. 1998. Nihongo Goitaikei. Iwanami Shoten, In Japanese.

Daisuke Kawahara and Sadao Kurohashi. 2006. A fully-lexicalized probabilistic model for Japanese syntactic and case structure analysis. In *Proceedings of the Human Language Technology Conference of the North American Chapter of the Association of Computational Linguistics (HLT-NAACL 2006)*, pp. 176–183.

Shunsuke Kozawa, Kiyotaka Uchimoto and Yasuharu Den. 2014. Adaptation of long-unit-word analysis system to different part-of-speech tagset. In *Journal of Natural Language Processing*, Vol. 21, No. 2, pp. 379–401 (in Japanese).

Taku Kudo, Kaoru Yamamoto and Yuji Matsumoto. 2004. Applying conditional random fields to Japanese morphological analysis. In *Proceedings of the Conference on Empirical Methods in Natural Language Processing (EMNLP-2004)*, pp. 230–237.

Taku Kudo and Yuji Matsumoto. 2002. Japanese dependency analysis using cascaded chunking. In *Proceedings of the 6th Conference on Natural Language Learning (CoNLL-2002)*, Volume 20, pp. 1–7.

Sadao Kurohashi and Makoto Nagao. 2003. Building a Japanese parsed corpus – while improving the parsing system. In Abeille (ed.), *Treebanks: Building and Using Parsed Corpora*, Chap. 14, pp. 249–260. Kluwer Academic Publishers.

Kikuo Maekawa, Hanae Koiso, Sasaoki Furui, Hitoshi Isahara. 2000. Spontaneous Speech Corpus of Japanese. In *Proceedings of the Second International Conference on Language Resources and Evaluation (LREC-2000)*, pp. 947–952.

Kikuo Maekawa, Makoto Yamazaki, Toshinobu Ogiso, Takehiko Maruyama, Hideki Ogura, Wakako Kashino, Hanae Koiso, Masaya Yamaguchi, Makiro Tanaka and Yasuharu Den. 2014. Balanced Corpus of Contemporary Written Japanese. *Language Resources and Evaluation*, Vol. 48, pp. 345–371.

Ryan McDonald, Joakim Nivre, Yvonne Quirmbach-Brundage, Yoav Goldberg, Dipanjan Das, Kuzman Ganchev, Keith Hall, Slav Petrov, Hao Zhang, Oscar Täckström, Claudia Bedini, Núria Bertomeu Castelló, and Jungmee Lee. 2013. Universal Dependency Annotation for Multilingual Parsing. In *Proceedings of the 51st Annual Meeting of the ACL (ACL 2013)*.

Shunsuke Mori, Hideki Ogura and Teturo Sasada. 2014. A Japanese word dependency corpus. In *Proceedings of the Ninth International Conference on Language Resources and Evaluation (LREC-2014)*, pp. 753–758.

Joakim Nivre, Johan Hall, Jens Nilsson, Atanas Chanev, Gülşen Eryiğit, Sandra Kübler, Svetoslav Marinov and Erwin Marsi. 2007. MaltParser: A language-independent system for data-driven dependency parsing, In Journal of Natural Language Engineering, Vol. 13, No. 2, pp. 95–135.

Takaaki Tanaka and Masaaki Nagata. 2013. Constructing a Practical Constituent Parser from a Japanese Treebank with Function Labels. In *Proceedings of the Fourth Workshop on Statistical Parsing of Morphologically-Rich Languages*, pp. 108–118.

Kiyotaka Uchimoto and Yasuharu Den . 2008. Word-level Dependency-structure Annotation to Corpus of Spontaneous Japanese and its Application. In *Proceedings of the International Conference on Language Resources and Evaluation (LREC 2008)*, pp.3118–3122.

KL_{cpos^3} – a Language Similarity Measure for Delexicalized Parser Transfer

Rudolf Rosa and **Zdeněk Žabokrtský**
Charles University in Prague, Faculty of Mathematics and Physics
Institute of Formal and Applied Linguistics
Malostranské náměstí 25, Prague, Czech Republic
{rosa, zabokrtsky}@ufal.mff.cuni.cz

Abstract

We present KL_{cpos^3}, a language similarity measure based on Kullback-Leibler divergence of coarse part-of-speech tag trigram distributions in tagged corpora. It has been designed for multilingual delexicalized parsing, both for source treebank selection in single-source parser transfer, and for source treebank weighting in multi-source transfer. In the selection task, KL_{cpos^3} identifies the best source treebank in 8 out of 18 cases. In the weighting task, it brings +4.5% UAS absolute, compared to unweighted parse tree combination.

1 Introduction

The approach of delexicalized dependency parser transfer is to train a parser on a treebank for a source language (*src*), using only non-lexical features, most notably part-of-speech (POS) tags, and to apply that parser to POS-tagged sentences of a target language (*tgt*) to obtain dependency parse trees. Delexicalized transfer yields worse results than a supervised lexicalized parser trained on a target language treebank. However, for languages with no treebanks available, it may be useful to obtain at least a lower-quality parse tree for tasks such as information retrieval.

Usually, multiple source treebanks are available, and it is non-trivial to select the best one for a given target language. As a solution, we present a language similarity measure based on KL divergence (Kullback and Leibler, 1951) of distributions of coarse POS tag trigrams in POS-tagged corpora, which we call KL_{cpos^3}. The measure has been designed and tuned specifically for multilingual delexicalized parser transfer, and it often succeeds in selecting the best source treebank in a single-source setting, as well as in appropriately weighting the source treebanks by similarity to the target language in a multi-source parse tree combination approach.

2 Related Work

Delexicalized parser transfer was conceived by Zeman and Resnik (2008), who also introduced two important preprocessing steps – mapping treebank-specific POS tagsets to a common set using Interset (Zeman, 2008), and harmonizing treebank annotation styles into a common style, which later developed into the HamleDT harmonized treebank collection (Zeman et al., 2012).

McDonald et al. (2011) applied delexicalized transfer in a setting with multiple source treebanks available, finding that the problem of selecting the best source treebank without access to a target language treebank for evaluation is non-trivial. They combined all source treebanks by concatenating them but noted that this yields worse results than using only the best source treebank.

An alternative is the (monolingual) parse tree combination method of Sagae and Lavie (2006), who apply several independent parsers to the input sentence and combine the resulting parse trees using a maximum spanning tree algorithm. Surdeanu and Manning (2010) enrich tree combination with weighting, assigning each parser a weight based on its Unlabelled Attachment Score (UAS). In our work, we introduce an extension of this method to a crosslingual setting by combining parsers for different languages and using source-target language similarity to weight them.

Several authors (Naseem et al., 2012; Søgaard and Wulff, 2012; Täckström et al., 2013b) employed WALS (Dryer and Haspelmath, 2013) to estimate source-target language similarity for delexicalized transfer, focusing on genealogy distance and word-order features. Søgaard and Wulff (2012) also introduced weighting into the treebank concatenation approach, using a POS n-gram model trained on a target-language corpus

Proceedings of the 53rd Annual Meeting of the Association for Computational Linguistics and the 7th International Joint Conference on Natural Language Processing (Short Papers), pages 243–249,
Beijing, China, July 26-31, 2015.

to weight source sentences in a weighted perceptron learning scenario (Cavallanti et al., 2010). KL divergence (Kullback and Leibler, 1951) of POS tag distributions, as well as several other measures, was used by Plank and Van Noord (2011) to estimate monolingual domain similarity.

As is quite common in parsing papers, including those dealing with semi-supervised and unsupervised parsing, we use gold POS tags in all our experiments. This enables us to evaluate the effectiveness of our parsing method alone, not influenced by errors stemming from the POS tagging. Based on the published results, it seems to be considerably easier to induce POS tags than syntactic structure for under-resourced languages, as there are several high-performance weakly-supervised POS taggers. Das and Petrov (2011) report an average accuracy of 83% using word-aligned texts, compared to 97% reached by a supervised tagger. Täckström et al. (2013a) further improve this to 89% by leveraging Wiktionary. For some languages, there are even less resources available; Agić et al. (2015b) were able to reach accuracies around 70% by using partial or full Bible translation. Our methods could thus be applied even in a more realistic scenario, where gold POS tags are not available for the target text, by using a weakly-supervised POS tagger. We intend to evaluate the performance of our approach in such a setting in future.

3 Delexicalized Parser Transfer

Throughout this work, we use MSTperl (Rosa, 2015b), an implementation of the unlabelled single-best MSTParser of McDonald et al. (2005b), with first-order features and non-projective parsing, trained using 3 iterations of MIRA (Crammer and Singer, 2003).[1]

Our delexicalized feature set is based on the set of McDonald et al. (2005a) with lexical features removed. It consists of combinations of signed edge length (distance of head and parent, bucketed for values above 4 and for values above 10) with POS tag of the head, dependent, their neighbours, and all nodes between them.[2] We use the Universal POS Tagset (UPOS) of Petrov et al. (2012).

3.1 Single-source Delexicalized Transfer

In the single-source parser transfer, the delexicalized parser is trained on a single source treebank, and applied to the target corpus. The problem thus reduces to selecting a source treebank that will lead to a high performance on the target language.

3.2 Multi-source Delexicalized Transfer

In our work, we extend the monolingual parse tree combination method to a multi-source crosslingual delexicalized parser transfer setting:

1. Train a delexicalized parser on each source treebank.
2. Apply each of the parsers to the target sentence, obtaining a set of parse trees.
3. Construct a weighted directed graph as a complete graph over all tokens of the target sentence, where each edge is assigned a score equal to the number of parse trees in which it appears (each parse tree contributes by either 0 or 1 to the edge score). In the weighted variant of the method, the contribution of each parse tree is multiplied by its weight.
4. Find the final dependency parse tree as the maximum spanning tree over the graph, using the algorithm of Chu and Liu (1965) and Edmonds (1967).

4 KL_{cpos^3} Language Similarity

We introduce KL_{cpos^3}, a language similarity measure based on distributions of coarse POS tags in source and target POS-tagged corpora. This is motivated by the fact that POS tags constitute a key feature for delexicalized parsing.

The distributions are estimated as frequencies of UPOS trigrams[3] in the treebank training sections:

$$f(cpos_{i-1}, cpos_i, cpos_{i+1}) = \\ = \frac{\text{count}(cpos_{i-1}, cpos_i, cpos_{i+1})}{\sum_{\forall cpos_{a,b,c}} \text{count}(cpos_a, cpos_b, cpos_c)}; \quad (1)$$

we use a special value for $cpos_{i-1}$ or $cpos_{i+1}$ if $cpos_i$ appears at sentence beginning or end.

We then apply the Kullback-Leibler divergence

[1]Note that while our approach does not depend in principle on the actual parser used, our results and conclusions may not be valid for other parsers.

[2]The feature set, as well as scripts and configuration files for the presented experiments, are available in (Rosa, 2015a).

[3]Bigrams and tetragrams performed comparably on the weighting task, but worse on the selection task. Using more fine-grained POS tags led to worse results as fine-grained features tend to be less shared across languages.

$D_{\mathrm{KL}}(tgt||src)$ to compute language similarity:[4]

$$KL_{cpos^3}(tgt, src) = = \sum_{\forall cpos^3 \in tgt} f_{tgt}(cpos^3) \cdot \log \frac{f_{tgt}(cpos^3)}{f_{src}(cpos^3)}, \quad (2)$$

where $cpos^3$ is a coarse POS tag trigram. For the KL divergence to be well-defined, we set the source count of each unseen trigram to 1.

4.1 KL_{cpos^3} for Source Selection

For the single-source parser transfer, we compute KL_{cpos^3} distance of the target corpus to each of the source treebanks and choose the closest source treebank to use for the transfer.

4.2 $KL^{-4}_{cpos^3}$ for Source Weighting

To convert KL_{cpos^3} from a negative measure of language similarity to a positive source parser weight for the multi-source tree combination method, we take the fourth power of its inverted value.[5] The parse tree produced by each source parser is then weighted by $KL^{-4}_{cpos^3}(tgt, src)$.

5 Dataset

We carry out our experiments using HamleDT 2.0 of Rosa et al. (2014), a collection of 30 treebanks converted into Universal Stanford Dependencies (de Marneffe et al., 2014), with POS tags converted into UPOS; we use gold-standard POS tags in all experiments. We use the treebank training sections for parser training and language similarity estimation, and the test sections for evaluation.[6]

5.1 Tuning

To avoid overfitting the exact definition of KL_{cpos^3} and $KL^{-4}_{cpos^3}$ to the 30 treebanks, we used only 12 *development treebanks* for hyperparameter tuning: ar, bg, ca, el, es, et, fa, fi, hi, hu, it, ja.[7]

Measure	Avg	SD	Best
$KL^{-4}_{cpos^3}(tgt, src)$	**51.0**	**16.7**	**6**
$KL^{-4}_{cpos^3}(src, tgt)$	50.6	17.4	4
$JS^{-4}_{cpos^3}(tgt, src)$	49.6	18.0	2
$cos_{cpos^3}(tgt, src)$	49.0	17.7	1

Table 1: Weighted multi-source transfer using various similarity measures. Evaluation using average UAS on the development set.
Avg = Average UAS.
SD = Standard sample deviation of UAS, serving as an indication of robustness of the measure.
Best = Number of targets for which the measure scored best.

Table 1 contains evaluation of several language similarity measures considered in the tuning phase, applied to weighted multi-source transfer and evaluated using average UAS on the development set. We evaluated KL divergences computed in both directions, as well as Jenses-Shannon divergence (Lee, 2001) and cosine similarity. Based on the results, $KL^{-4}_{cpos^3}$ was selected, as it performed best in all aspects.

Once the hyperparameters were fixed, we applied the parser transfer methods to the full set of 30 treebanks; our final evaluation is based on the results on the 18 test treebanks as targets.

5.2 Other datasets

Additionally, we also report preliminary results on the Prague style conversion of HamleDT, which loosely follows the style of the Prague Dependency Treebank of Böhmová et al. (2003), and on the subset of CoNLL 2006 and 2007 shared tasks (Buchholz and Marsi, 2006; Nilsson et al., 2007) that was used by McDonald et al. (2011).[8]

6 Evaluation

6.1 Results

Table 2 contains the results of our methods both on the test languages and the development languages.

[4]The KL divergence is non-symmetric; $D_{\mathrm{KL}}(P||Q)$ expresses the amount of information lost when a distribution Q is used to approximate the true distribution P. Thus, in our setting, we use $D_{\mathrm{KL}}(tgt||src)$, as we try to minimize the loss of using a *src* parser as an approximation of a *tgt* parser.

[5]A high value of the exponent strongly promotes the most similar source language, giving minimal power to the other languages, which is good if there is a *very* similar source language. A low value enables combining information from a larger number of source languages. We chose a compromise value of 4 based on performance on the development data.

[6]Contrary to the motivation, we do not evaluate our method on truly underresourced languages, since automatic intrinsic evaluation is not possible on languages without treebanks. Still, e.g., Bengali and Telugu can be considered low-resourced, since their treebanks are very small.

[7]We tuned the choice of the similarity measure, POS n-gram length, and the way of turning KL_{cpos^3} into $KL^{-4}_{cpos^3}$. To tune our method to perform well in many different situations, we chose the development set to contain both smaller and larger treebanks, a pair of very close languages (ca, es), a very solitary language (ja), multiple members of several language families (Uralic, Romance), and both primarily left-branching (bg, el) and right-branching (ar, ja) languages.

[8]The CoNLL subset is: da, de, el, en, es, it, nl, pt, sv.

For each target language, we used all remaining 29 source languages for training (in the single-source method, only one of them is selected and applied).

Our baseline is the treebank concatenation method of McDonald et al. (2011), i.e., a single delexicalized parser trained on the concatenation of the 29 source treebanks.

As an upper bound,[9] we report the results of the oracle single-source delexicalized transfer: for each target language, the oracle source parser is the one that achieves the highest UAS on the target treebank test section.[10] For space reasons, we do not include results of a higher upper bound of a supervised delexicalized parser (trained on the target treebank), which has an average UAS of 68.5%. It was not surpassed by our methods for any target language, although it was reached for Telugu, and approached within 5% for Czech and Latin.

6.2 Discussion

The results show that KL_{cpos^3} performs well both in the selection task and in the weighting task, as both the single-source and the weighted multi-source transfer methods outperform the unweighted tree combination on average, as well as the treebank concatenation baseline. In 8 of 18 cases, KL_{cpos^3} is able to correctly identify the oracle source treebank for the single-source approach. In two of these cases, weighted tree combination further improves upon the result of the single-source transfer, i.e., surpasses the oracle; in the remaining 6 cases, it performs identically to the single-source method. This proves KL_{cpos^3} to be a successful language similarity measure for delexicalized parser transfer, and the weighted multi-source transfer to be a better performing approach than the single-source transfer.

The weighted tree combination is better than its unweighted variant only for half of the target languages, but it is more stable, as indicated by its lower standard deviation, and achieves an average UAS higher by 4.5% absolute. The unweighted tree combination, as well as treebank concatenation, perform especially poorly for English, German, Tamil, and Turkish, which are rich in determiners, unlike the rest of the treebanks;[11] there-

Tgt lang	TB conc	Oracle del trans		Single-src KL			Multi-src ×1	Multi-src $\times w$
bn	61.0	te	**66.7**	0.5	**te**	**66.7**	63.2	**66.7**
cs	60.5	sk	**65.8**	0.3	**sk**	**65.8**	60.4	**65.8**
da	**56.2**	en	**55.4**	0.5	sl	42.1	**54.4**	50.3
de	12.6	en	**56.8**	0.7	**en**	**56.8**	27.6	**56.8**
en	12.3	de	**42.6**	0.8	**de**	**42.6**	21.1	**42.6**
eu	**41.2**	da	**42.1**	0.7	tr	29.1	**40.8**	30.6
grc	43.2	et	42.2	1.0	sl	34.0	**44.7**	42.6
la	38.1	grc	40.3	1.2	cs	35.0	**40.3**	39.7
nl	55.0	da	57.9	0.7	**da**	57.9	56.2	**58.7**
pt	62.8	en	64.2	0.2	es	62.7	**67.2**	62.7
ro	44.2	it	**66.4**	1.6	la	30.8	**51.2**	50.0
ru	55.5	sk	57.7	0.9	la	40.4	**57.8**	57.2
sk	52.2	cs	**61.7**	0.2	sl	58.4	**59.6**	58.4
sl	45.9	sk	**53.9**	0.2	**sk**	**53.9**	47.1	**53.9**
sv	45.4	de	**61.6**	0.6	da	49.8	**52.3**	50.8
ta	27.9	hi	**53.5**	1.1	tr	31.1	28.0	**40.0**
te	67.8	bn	**77.4**	0.4	**bn**	**77.4**	68.7	**77.4**
tr	18.8	ta	40.3	0.7	**ta**	40.3	23.2	**41.1**
Test	44.5		**55.9**	0.7		48.6	48.0	**52.5**
SD	16.9		10.8			14.4	15.0	11.8
ar	37.0	ro	**43.1**	1.7	sk	41.2	35.3	**41.3**
bg	64.4	sk	66.8	0.4	**sk**	66.8	66.0	**67.4**
ca	56.3	es	**72.4**	0.1	**es**	**72.4**	61.5	**72.4**
el	63.1	sk	61.4	0.7	cs	60.7	62.3	**63.8**
es	59.9	ca	**72.7**	0.0	**ca**	**72.7**	64.3	**72.7**
et	67.5	hu	71.8	0.9	da	64.9	70.5	**72.0**
fa	30.9	ar	**35.6**	1.1	cs	**34.7**	32.5	33.3
fi	41.9	et	44.2	1.1	**et**	44.2	41.7	**47.1**
hi	24.1	ta	**56.3**	1.1	fa	20.8	24.6	**27.2**
hu	55.1	et	52.0	0.7	cs	46.0	**56.5**	51.2
it	52.5	ca	**59.8**	0.3	pt	54.9	59.5	**59.6**
ja	29.2	tr	**49.2**	2.2	ta	**44.9**	28.8	34.1
Dev	48.5		**57.1**	0.9		52.0	50.3	**53.5**
SD	15.2		12.5			16.1	16.5	16.7
All	46.1		**56.4**	0.8		50.0	48.9	**52.9**
SD	16.1		11.3			15.0	15.4	13.7
PRG test			**60.0**			49.7	55.7	**58.1**
PRG dev			**64.0**			57.5	58.0	**61.1**
PRG all			**61.5**			52.8	56.6	**59.3**
CoNLL			**58.3**			53.1	**58.1**	55.7

Table 2: Evaluation using UAS on test target treebanks (upper part of the table) and development target treebanks (lower part).

For each target language, all 29 remaining non-target treebanks were used for training the parsers. The best score among our transfer methods is marked in bold; the baseline and upper bound scores are marked in bold if equal to or higher than that.

Legend:
Tgt lang = Target treebank language.
TB conc = Treebank concatenation.
Oracle del trans = Single-source delexicalized transfer using the oracle source language.
Single-src = Single-source delexicalized transfer using source language with lowest KL_{cpos^3} distance to the target language (language bold if identical to oracle).
Multi-src = Multi-source delexicalized transfer, unweighted ($\times 1$) and $KL_{cpos^3}^{-4}$ weighted ($\times w$).
Test, Dev, All, SD = Average on test/development/all, and its standard sample deviation.
PRG, CoNLL = Preliminary results (average UAS) on Prague conversion of HamleDT, and on subset of CoNLL used by McDonald et al. (2011).

[9] This is a hard upper-bound for the single-source transfer, but can be surpassed by the multi-source transfer.

[10] We do not report the matrix of all source/target combination results, as this amounts to 870 numbers.

[11] In the treebanks for these four languages, determiners constitute around 5-10% of all tokens, while most other treebanks contain no determiners at all; in some cases, this is

fore, determiners are parsed rather randomly.[12] In the weighted methods, this is not the case anymore, as for a determiner-rich target language, determiner-rich source languages are given a high weight.

For target languages for which KL_{cpos^3} of the closest source language was lower or equal to its average value of 0.7, the oracle treebank was identified in 7 cases out of 12 and a different but competitive one in 2 cases; when higher than 0.7, an appropriate treebank was only chosen in 1 case out of 6. When KL_{cpos^3} failed to identify the oracle, weighted tree combination was always better or equal to single-source transfer but mostly worse than unweighted tree combination. This shows that for distant languages, KL_{cpos^3} does not perform as good as for close languages.

We believe that taking multiple characteristics of the languages into account would improve the results on distant languages. A good approach might be to use an empirical measure, such as KL_{cpos^3}, combined with supervised information from other sources, such as WALS. Alternatively, a backoff approach, i.e. combining KL_{cpos^3} with e.g. KL_{cpos^2}, might help to tackle the issue.

Still, for target languages dissimilar to any source language, a better similarity measure will not help much, as even the oracle results are usually poor. More fine-grained resource combination methods are probably needed there, such as selectively ignoring word order, or using different sets of weights based on POS of the dependent node.

6.3 Evaluation on Other Datasets

In (Rosa, 2015c), we show that the accuracies obtained when parsing HamleDT treebanks in the Universal Stanford Dependencies annotation style are significantly lower than when using the Prague style. Preliminary experiments using the Prague style conversion of HamleDT generally show our methods to be effective even on that dataset, although the performance of KL_{cpos^3} is lower in source selection – it achieves lower UAS than unweighted tree combination, and only identifies the oracle source treebank in 30% cases. This may be due to us having used only the Stanfordized treebanks for tuning the exact definition of the measure.

Preliminary trials on the subset of CoNLL used by McDonald et al. (2011) indicated that our methods do not perform well on this dataset. The best results by far are achieved by the unweighted combination, i.e., it is best not to use KL_{cpos^3} at all on this dataset. We believe this to be a deficiency of the dataset rather than of our methods – it is rather small, and there is low diversity in the languages involved, most of them being either Germanic or Romanic. The HamleDT dataset is larger and more diverse, and we believe it to correspond better to the real-life motivation for our methods, thus providing a more trustworthy evaluation.

In the near future, we intend to reevaluate our methods using the Universal Dependencies treebank collection (Nivre et al., 2015; Agić et al., 2015a), which currently contains 18 languages of various types and seems to be steadily growing. A potential benefit of this collection is the fact that the annotation style harmonization seems to be done with more care and in a more principled way than in HamleDT, presumably leading to a higher quality of the dataset.

7 Conclusion

We presented KL_{cpos^3}, an efficient language similarity measure designed for delexicalized dependency parser transfer. We evaluated it on a large set of treebanks, and showed that it performs well in selecting the source treebank for single-source transfer, as well as in weighting the source treebanks in multi-source parse tree combination.

Our method achieves good results when applied to similar languages, but its performance drops for distant languages. In future, we plan to explore combinations of KL_{cpos^3} with other language similarity measures, so that similarity of distant languages is estimated more reliably.

In this work, we only used the unlabelled first-order MSTParser. We intend to also employ other parsers in future, possibly in combination, and in a labelled as well as unlabelled setting.

Acknowledgments

This research was supported by the grants GAUK 1572314, SVV 260 224, and FP7-ICT-2013-10-610516 (QTLeap). This work has been using language resources developed, stored and distributed by the LINDAT/CLARIN project of the Ministry of Education, Youth and Sports of the Czech Republic (project LM2010013).

related to properties of the treebank annotation or its harmonization rather than properties of the language.

[12] UAS of determiner attachment tends to be lower than 5%, which is several times less than for any other POS.

References

Željko Agić, Maria Jesus Aranzabe, Aitziber Atutxa, Cristina Bosco, Jinho Choi, Marie-Catherine de Marneffe, Timothy Dozat, Richárd Farkas, Jennifer Foster, Filip Ginter, Iakes Goenaga, Koldo Gojenola, Yoav Goldberg, Jan Hajič, Anders Trærup Johannsen, Jenna Kanerva, Juha Kuokkala, Veronika Laippala, Alessandro Lenci, Krister Lindén, Nikola Ljubešić, Teresa Lynn, Christopher Manning, Héctor Alonso Martínez, Ryan McDonald, Anna Missilä, Simonetta Montemagni, Joakim Nivre, Hanna Nurmi, Petya Osenova, Slav Petrov, Jussi Piitulainen, Barbara Plank, Prokopis Prokopidis, Sampo Pyysalo, Wolfgang Seeker, Mojgan Seraji, Natalia Silveira, Maria Simi, Kiril Simov, Aaron Smith, Reut Tsarfaty, Veronika Vincze, and Daniel Zeman. 2015a. Universal Dependencies 1.1. `http://hdl.handle.net/11234/LRT-1478`.

Željko Agić, Dirk Hovy, and Anders Søgaard. 2015b. If all you have is a bit of the bible: Learning POS taggers for truly low-resource languages. In *The 53rd Annual Meeting of the Association for Computational Linguistics and the 7th International Joint Conference of the Asian Federation of Natural Language Processing (ACL-IJCNLP 2015)*. Hrvatska znanstvena bibliografija i MZOS-Svibor.

Alena Böhmová, Jan Hajič, Eva Hajičová, and Barbora Hladká. 2003. The Prague dependency treebank. In *Treebanks*, pages 103–127. Springer.

Sabine Buchholz and Erwin Marsi. 2006. CoNLL-X shared task on multilingual dependency parsing. In *Proceedings of the Tenth Conference on Computational Natural Language Learning*, pages 149–164. Association for Computational Linguistics.

Giovanni Cavallanti, Nicolo Cesa-Bianchi, and Claudio Gentile. 2010. Linear algorithms for online multitask classification. *The Journal of Machine Learning Research*, 11:2901–2934.

Yoeng-Jin Chu and Tseng-Hong Liu. 1965. On shortest arborescence of a directed graph. *Scientia Sinica*, 14(10):1396.

Koby Crammer and Yoram Singer. 2003. Ultraconservative online algorithms for multiclass problems. *The Journal of Machine Learning Research*, 3:951–991.

Dipanjan Das and Slav Petrov. 2011. Unsupervised part-of-speech tagging with bilingual graph-based projections. In *Proceedings of the 49th Annual Meeting of the Association for Computational Linguistics: Human Language Technologies-Volume 1*, pages 600–609. Association for Computational Linguistics.

Marie-Catherine de Marneffe, Natalia Silveira, Timothy Dozat, Katri Haverinen, Filip Ginter, Joakim Nivre, and Christopher D. Manning. 2014. Universal Stanford dependencies: A cross-linguistic typology. In *Proc. of LREC'14*, Reykjavík, Iceland. ELRA.

Matthew S. Dryer and Martin Haspelmath, editors. 2013. *WALS Online*. Max Planck Institute for Evolutionary Anthropology, Leipzig.

Jack Edmonds. 1967. Optimum branchings. *Journal of Research of the National Bureau of Standards B*, 71(4):233–240.

Solomon Kullback and Richard A Leibler. 1951. On information and sufficiency. *The annals of mathematical statistics*, pages 79–86.

Lillian Lee. 2001. On the effectiveness of the skew divergence for statistical language analysis. In *Artificial intelligence and statistics*, volume 2001, pages 65–72.

Ryan McDonald, Koby Crammer, and Fernando Pereira. 2005a. Online large-margin training of dependency parsers. In *Proceedings of the 43rd annual meeting on ACL*, pages 91–98. ACL.

Ryan McDonald, Fernando Pereira, Kiril Ribarov, and Jan Hajič. 2005b. Non-projective dependency parsing using spanning tree algorithms. In *Proceedings of the conference on Human Language Technology and Empirical Methods in Natural Language Processing*, pages 523–530. ACL.

Ryan McDonald, Slav Petrov, and Keith Hall. 2011. Multi-source transfer of delexicalized dependency parsers. In *Proceedings of the Conference on Empirical Methods in Natural Language Processing*, EMNLP '11, pages 62–72, Stroudsburg, PA, USA. ACL.

Tahira Naseem, Regina Barzilay, and Amir Globerson. 2012. Selective sharing for multilingual dependency parsing. In *Proceedings of the 50th Annual Meeting of the ACL: Long Papers - Volume 1*, ACL '12, pages 629–637, Stroudsburg, PA, USA. ACL.

Jens Nilsson, Sebastian Riedel, and Deniz Yuret. 2007. The CoNLL 2007 shared task on dependency parsing. In *Proceedings of the CoNLL shared task session of EMNLP-CoNLL*, pages 915–932. sn.

Joakim Nivre, Cristina Bosco, Jinho Choi, Marie-Catherine de Marneffe, Timothy Dozat, Richárd Farkas, Jennifer Foster, Filip Ginter, Yoav Goldberg, Jan Hajič, Jenna Kanerva, Veronika Laippala, Alessandro Lenci, Teresa Lynn, Christopher Manning, Ryan McDonald, Anna Missilä, Simonetta Montemagni, Slav Petrov, Sampo Pyysalo, Natalia Silveira, Maria Simi, Aaron Smith, Reut Tsarfaty, Veronika Vincze, and Daniel Zeman. 2015. Universal Dependencies 1.0. `http://hdl.handle.net/11234/1-1464`.

Slav Petrov, Dipanjan Das, and Ryan McDonald. 2012. A universal part-of-speech tagset. In *Proc. of LREC-2012*, pages 2089–2096, Istanbul, Turkey. ELRA.

Barbara Plank and Gertjan Van Noord. 2011. Effective measures of domain similarity for parsing. In *Proceedings of the 49th Annual Meeting of the ACL: Human Language Technologies-Volume 1*, pages 1566–1576. ACL.

Rudolf Rosa, Jan Mašek, David Mareček, Martin Popel, Daniel Zeman, and Zdeněk Žabokrtský. 2014. HamleDT 2.0: Thirty dependency treebanks Stanfordized. In *Proceedings of the 9th International Conference on Language Resources and Evaluation (LREC 2014)*, pages 2334–2341, Reykjavík, Iceland. ELRA.

Rudolf Rosa. 2015a. MSTperl delexicalized parser transfer scripts and configuration files. http://hdl.handle.net/11234/1-1485.

Rudolf Rosa. 2015b. MSTperl parser (2015-05-19). http://hdl.handle.net/11234/1-1480.

Rudolf Rosa. 2015c. Multi-source cross-lingual delexicalized parser transfer: Prague or Stanford? In Eva Hajičová and Joakim Nivre, editors, *Proceedings of the Third International Conference on Dependency Linguistics, Depling 2015*, Uppsala, Sweden. Uppsala University.

Kenji Sagae and Alon Lavie. 2006. Parser combination by reparsing. In *Proceedings of the Human Language Technology Conference of the NAACL, Companion Volume: Short Papers*, pages 129–132. ACL.

Anders Søgaard and Julie Wulff. 2012. An empirical study of non-lexical extensions to delexicalized transfer. In *COLING (Posters)*, pages 1181–1190.

Mihai Surdeanu and Christopher D. Manning. 2010. Ensemble models for dependency parsing: Cheap and good? In *Human Language Technologies: The 2010 Annual Conference of the North American Chapter of the ACL*, HLT '10, pages 649–652, Stroudsburg, PA, USA. ACL.

Oscar Täckström, Dipanjan Das, Slav Petrov, Ryan McDonald, and Joakim Nivre. 2013a. Token and type constraints for cross-lingual part-of-speech tagging. *Transactions of the Association for Computational Linguistics*, 1:1–12.

Oscar Täckström, Ryan McDonald, and Joakim Nivre. 2013b. Target language adaptation of discriminative transfer parsers. In *Proceedings of NAACL-HLT 2013*, pages 1061–1071.

Daniel Zeman and Philip Resnik. 2008. Cross-language parser adaptation between related languages. In *IJCNLP 2008 Workshop on NLP for Less Privileged Languages*, pages 35–42, Hyderabad, India. Asian Federation of Natural Language Processing, International Institute of Information Technology.

Daniel Zeman, David Mareček, Martin Popel, Loganathan Ramasamy, Jan Štěpánek, Zdeněk Žabokrtský, and Jan Hajič. 2012. HamleDT: To parse or not to parse? In *Proceedings of the Eight International Conference on Language Resources and Evaluation (LREC'12)*, Istanbul, Turkey, May. ELRA.

Daniel Zeman. 2008. Reusable tagset conversion using tagset drivers. In *Proceedings of the 6th International Conference on Language Resources and Evaluation (LREC 2008)*, pages 213–218, Marrakech, Morocco. ELRA.

CCG Supertagging with a Recurrent Neural Network

Wenduan Xu
University of Cambridge
Computer Laboratory
wx217@cam.ac.uk

Michael Auli*
Facebook AI Research
michaelauli@fb.com

Stephen Clark
University of Cambridge
Computer Laboratory
sc609@cam.ac.uk

Abstract

Recent work on supertagging using a feed-forward neural network achieved significant improvements for CCG supertagging and parsing (Lewis and Steedman, 2014). However, their architecture is limited to considering local contexts and does not naturally model sequences of arbitrary length. In this paper, we show how directly capturing sequence information using a recurrent neural network leads to further accuracy improvements for both supertagging (up to 1.9%) and parsing (up to 1% F1), on CCGBank, Wikipedia and biomedical text.

1 Introduction

Combinatory Categorial Grammar (CCG; Steedman, 2000) is a highly lexicalized formalism; the standard parsing model of Clark and Curran (2007) uses over 400 lexical categories (or *supertags*), compared to about 50 POS tags for typical CFG parsers. This makes accurate disambiguation of lexical types much more challenging. However, the assignment of lexical categories can still be solved reasonably well by treating it as a sequence tagging problem, often referred to as supertagging (Bangalore and Joshi, 1999). Clark and Curran (2004) show that high tagging accuracy can be achieved by leaving some ambiguity to the parser to resolve, but with enough of a reduction in the number of tags assigned to each word so that parsing efficiency is greatly increased.

In addition to improving parsing efficiency, supertagging also has a large impact on parsing accuracy (Curran et al., 2006; Kummerfeld et al., 2010), since the derivation space of the parser is determined by the supertagger, at both training and test time. Clark and Curran (2007) enhanced supertagging using a so-called adaptive strategy, such that additional categories are supplied to the parser only if a spanning analysis cannot be found. This strategy is used in the de facto C&C parser (Curran et al., 2007), and the two-stage CCG parsing pipeline (supertagging and parsing) continues to be the choice for most recent CCG parsers (Zhang and Clark, 2011; Auli and Lopez, 2011; Xu et al., 2014).

Despite the effectiveness of supertagging, the most widely used model for this task (Clark and Curran, 2007) has a number of drawbacks. First, it relies too heavily on POS tags, which leads to lower accuracy on out-of-domain data (Rimell and Clark, 2008). Second, due to the sparse, indicator feature sets mainly based on raw words and POS tags, it shows pronounced performance degradation in the presence of rare and unseen words (Rimell and Clark, 2008; Lewis and Steedman, 2014). And third, in order to reduce computational requirements and feature sparsity, each tagging decision is made without considering any potentially useful contextual information beyond a local context window.

Lewis and Steedman (2014) introduced a feed-forward neural network to supertagging, and addressed the first two problems mentioned above. However, their attempt to tackle the third problem by pairing a conditional random field with their feed-forward tagger provided little accuracy improvement and vastly increased computational complexity, incurring a large efficiency penalty.

We introduce a recurrent neural network-based (RNN) supertagging model to tackle all the above problems, with an emphasis on the third one. RNNs are powerful models for sequential data, which can potentially capture long-term dependencies, based on an *unbounded* history of previous words (§2); similar to Lewis and Steedman (2014) we only use distributed word representa-

*All work was completed before the author joined Facebook.

Proceedings of the 53rd Annual Meeting of the Association for Computational Linguistics and the 7th International Joint Conference on Natural Language Processing (Short Papers), pages 250–255,
Beijing, China, July 26-31, 2015.

tions (§2.2). Our model is highly accurate, and by integrating it with the C&C parser as its adaptive supertagger, we obtain substantial accuracy improvements, outperforming the feed-forward setup on both supertagging and parsing.

2 Supertagging with a RNN

2.1 Model

We use an Elman recurrent neural network (Elman, 1990) which consists of an input layer x_t, a hidden state (layer) h_t with a recurrent connection to the previous hidden state h_{t-1} and an output layer y_t. The input layer is a vector representing the surrounding context of the current word at position t, whose supertag is being predicted.[1] The hidden state h_{t-1} keeps a representation of all context history up to the current word. The current hidden state h_t is computed using the current input x_t and hidden state h_{t-1} from the previous position. The output layer represents probability scores of all possible supertags, with the size of the output layer being equal to the size of the lexical category set.

The parameterization of the network consists of three matrices which are learned during supervised training. Matrix $\mathbf{U}$ contains weights between the input and hidden layers, $\mathbf{V}$ contains weights between the hidden and output layers, and $\mathbf{W}$ contains weights between the previous hidden state and the current hidden state. The following recurrence[2] is used to compute the activations of the hidden state at word position t:

$$h_t = f(x_t \mathbf{U} + h_{t-1} \mathbf{W}), \quad (1)$$

where f is a non-linear activation function; here we use the sigmoid function $f(z) = \frac{1}{1+e^{-z}}$. The output activations are calculated as:

$$y_t = g(h_t \mathbf{V}), \quad (2)$$

where g is the softmax activation function $g(z_i) = \frac{e^{z_i}}{\sum_j e^{z_j}}$ that squeezes raw output activations into a probability distribution.

2.2 Word Embeddings

Our RNN supertagger only uses continuous vector representations for features and each feature type has an associated look-up table, which maps a feature to its distributed representation. In total, three feature types are used. The first type is word embeddings: given a sentence of N words, $(w_1, w_2, \ldots, w_N)$, the embedding feature of w_t (for $1 \leq t \leq N$) is obtained by projecting it onto a n-dimensional vector space through the look-up table $L_w \in \mathbb{R}^{|w| \times n}$, where $|w|$ is the size of the vocabulary. Algebraically, the projection operation is a simple vector-matrix product where a one-hot vector $b_j \in \mathbb{R}^{1 \times |w|}$ (with zeros everywhere except at the jth position) is multiplied with L_w:

$$e_{w_t} = b_j L_w \in \mathbb{R}^{1 \times n}, \quad (3)$$

where j is the look-up index for w_t.

In addition, as in Lewis and Steedman (2014), for every word we also include its 2-character suffix and capitalization as features. Two more look-up tables are used for these features. $L_s \in \mathbb{R}^{|s| \times m}$ is the look-up table for suffix embeddings, where $|s|$ is the suffix vocabulary size. $L_c \in \mathbb{R}^{2 \times m}$ is the look-up table for the capitalization embeddings. L_c contains only two embeddings, representing whether or not a given word is capitalized.

We extract features from a context window surrounding the current word to make a tagging decision. Concretely, with a context window of size k, $\lfloor k/2 \rfloor$ words either side of the target word are included. For a word w_t, its continuous feature representation is:

$$f_{w_t} = [e_{w_t}; s_{w_t}; c_{w_t}], \quad (4)$$

where $e_{w_t} \in \mathbb{R}^{1 \times n}$, $s_{w_t} \in \mathbb{R}^{1 \times m}$ and $c_{w_t} \in \mathbb{R}^{1 \times m}$ are the output vectors from the three different look-up tables, and $[e_{w_t}; s_{w_t}; c_{w_t}]$ denotes the concatenation of three vectors and hence $f_{w_t} \in \mathbb{R}^{1 \times (n+2m)}$. At word position t, the input layer of the network x_t is:

$$x_t = [f_{w_{t-\lfloor k/2 \rfloor}}; \ldots f_{w_t}; \ldots; f_{w_{t+\lfloor k/2 \rfloor}}], \quad (5)$$

where $x_t \in \mathbb{R}^{1 \times k(n+2m)}$ and the right-hand side is the concatenation of all feature representations in a size k context window.

We use pre-trained word embeddings from Turian et al. (2010) to initialize look-up table L_w, and we apply a set of word pre-processing techniques at both training and test time to reduce sparsity. All words are first lower-cased, and all numbers are collapsed into a single digit '0'. If a lower-cased hyphenated

[1] This is different from some RNN models (e.g., Mikolov et al. (2010)) where the input is a one-hot vector.

[2] We assume the input to any layer is a row vector unless otherwise stated.

word does not have an entry in the pre-trained word embeddings, we attempt to back-off to the substring after the last hyphen. For compound words and numbers delimited by "\/", we attempt to back-off to the substring after the delimiter. After pre-processing, the Turian embeddings have a coverage of 94.25% on the training data; for out-of-vocabulary words, three separate randomly initialized embeddings are used for lower-case alphanumeric words, upper-case alphanumeric words, and non-alphanumeric symbols. For padding at the start and end of a sentence, the "unknown" entry from the pre-trained embeddings is used. Look-up tables L_s and L_c are also randomly initialized, and all look-up tables are modified during supervised training using backpropagation.

3 Experiments

Datasets and Baseline. We follow the standard splits of CCGBank (Hockenmaier and Steedman, 2007) for all experiments using sections 2-21 for training, section 00 for development and section 23 as in-domain test set. The Wikipedia corpus from Honnibal et al. (2009) and the Bioinfer corpus (Pyysalo et al., 2007) are used as two out-of-domain test sets. We compare supertagging accuracy with the MaxEnt C&C supertagger and the neural network tagger of Lewis and Steedman (2014) (henceforth NN), and we also evaluate parsing accuracy using these three supertaggers as a front-end to the C&C parser. We use the same 425 supertag set used in both C&C and NN.

Hyperparameters and Training. For L_w, we use the scaled 50-dimensional Turian embeddings ($n = 50$ for L_w) as initialization. We have experimented during development with using 100-dimensional embeddings and found no improvements in the resulting model. Out-of-vocabulary embedding values in L_w and all embedding values in L_s and L_c are initialized with a uniform distribution in the interval $[-2.0, 2.0]$. The embedding dimension size m of L_s and L_c is set to 5. Other parameters of the network $\{\mathbf{U}, \mathbf{V}, \mathbf{W}\}$ are initialized with values drawn uniformly from the interval $[-2.0, 2.0]$, and are then scaled by their corresponding input vector size. We experimented with context window sizes of 3, 5, 7, 9 and 11 during development and found a window size of 7 gives the best performing model on the dev set. We use a fixed learning rate of 0.0025 and a hidden state size of 200.

Model	Accuracy	Time
C&C (gold POS)	92.60	-
C&C (auto POS)	91.50	0.57
NN	91.10	21.00
RNN	92.63	-
RNN+dropout	93.07	2.02

Table 1: 1-best tagging accuracy and speed comparison on CCGBank Section 00 with a single CPU core (1,913 sentences), tagging time in secs.

To train the model, we optimize cross-entropy loss with stochastic gradient descent using mini-batched backpropagation through time (BPTT; Rumelhart et al., 1988; Mikolov, 2012); the mini-batch size for BPTT, again tuned on the dev set, is set to 9.

Embedding Dropout Regularization. Without any regularization, we found cross-entropy error on the dev set started to increase while the error on the training set was continuously driven to a very small value (Fig. 1a). With the suspicion of overfitting, we experimented with l_1 and l_2 regularization and learning rate decay but none of these techniques gave any noticeable improvements for our model. Following Legrand and Collobert (2014), we instead implemented word embedding dropout as a regularization for all the look-up tables, since the capacity of our tagging model mainly comes from the look-up tables, as in their system. We observed more stable learning and better generalization of the trained model with dropout. Similar to other forms of droput (Srivastava et al., 2014), we randomly drop units and their connections to other units at training time. Concretely, we apply a binary dropout mask to x_t, with a dropout rate of 0.25, and at test time no mask is applied, but the input to the network, x_t, at each word position is scaled by 0.75. We experimented during development with different dropout rates, but found the above choice to be optimal in our setting.

3.1 Supertagging Results

We use the RNN model which gives the highest 1-best supertagging accuracy on the dev set as the final model for all experiments. Without any form of regularization, the best model was obtained at the 20th epoch, and it took 35 epochs for the dropout model to peak (Fig. 1b). We use the dropout model for all experiments and, unlike the C&C supertagger, no tag dictionaries are used.

Table 1 shows 1-best supertagging accuracies on the dev set. The accuracy of the C&C supertag-

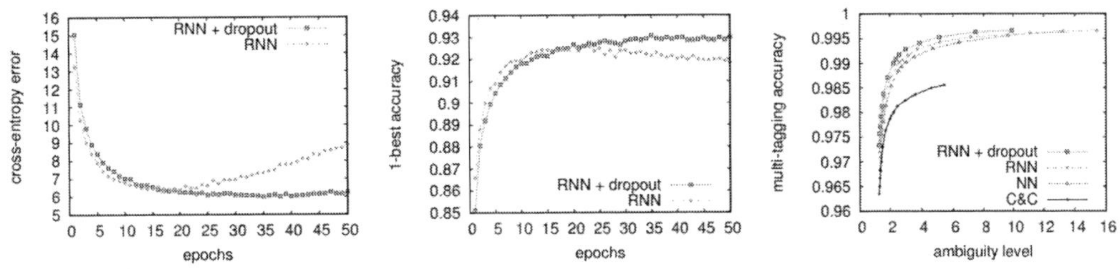

(a) learning curve on dev set (b) 1-best accuracy on dev set (c) multi-tagging accuracy on dev set

Figure 1: Learning curve and 1-best tagging accuracy of the RNN model on CCGBank Section 00. Plot (c) shows ambiguity vs. multi-tagging accuracy for all supertaggers (auto POS).

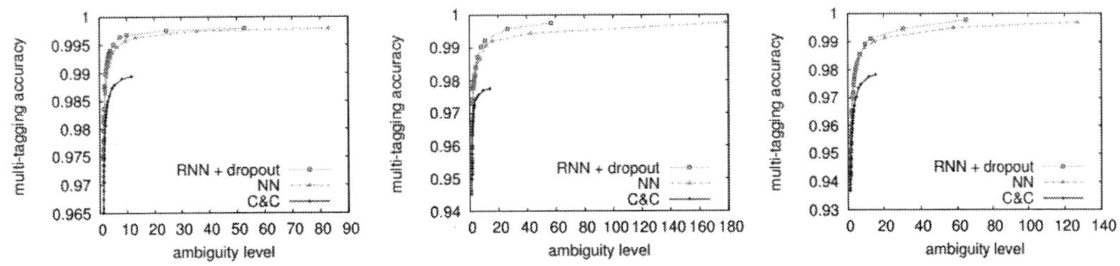

(a) CCBBank Section 23 (b) wikipedia (c) bio-GENIA

Figure 2: Multi-tagging accuracy for all supertagging models on CCGBank Section 23, Wikipedia and Bio-GENIA data (auto POS).

	RNN			NN			C&C (auto pos)			C&C (gold pos)		
β	WORD	SENT	amb.	WORD	SENT	amb.	WORD	SENT	amb.	WORD	SENT	amb.
0.075	97.33	66.07	1.27	96.83	61.27	1.34	96.34	60.27	1.27	**97.34**	**67.43**	1.27
0.030	**98.12**	**74.39**	1.46	97.81	70.83	1.58	97.05	65.50	1.43	97.92	72.87	1.43
0.010	**98.71**	**81.70**	1.84	98.54	79.25	2.06	97.63	70.52	1.72	98.37	77.73	1.72
0.005	**99.01**	**84.79**	2.22	98.84	83.38	2.55	97.86	72.24	1.98	98.52	79.25	1.98
0.001	**99.41**	**90.54**	3.90	99.29	89.07	4.72	98.25	80.24	3.57	99.17	87.19	3.00

Table 2: Multi-tagging accuracy and ambiguity comparison (supertags/word) at the default C&C β levels on CCGBank Section 00.

Model	Section 23	Wiki	Bio
C&C (gold POS)	93.32	88.80	91.85
C&C (auto POS)	92.02	88.80	89.08
NN	91.57	89.00	88.16
RNN	93.00	90.00	88.27

Table 3: 1-best tagging accuracy comparison on CCGBank Section 23 (2,407 sentences), Wikipedia (200 sentences) and Bio-GENIA (1,000 sentences).

ger drops about 1% with automatically assigned POS tags, while our RNN model gives higher accuracy (+0.47%) than the C&C supertagger with gold POS tags. All timing values are obtained on a single Intel i7-4790k core, and all implementations are in C++ except NN which is implemented using Torch and Java, and therefore we believe the efficiency of NN could be vastly improved with an implementation with a lower-level language.

Table 2 compares different supertagging models for multi-tagging accuracy at the default β levels used by the C&C parser on the dev set. The β parameter determines the average number of supertags assigned to each word (ambiguity) by a supertagger when integrated with the parser; categories whose probabilities are not within β times the probability of the 1-best category are pruned. At the first β level (0.075), the three supertagging models give very close ambiguity levels, but our RNN model clearly outperforms NN and C&C (auto POS) in both word (WORD) and sentence (SENT) level accuracies, giving similar word-level accuracy as C&C (gold POS). For other β levels (except $\beta = 0.001$), the RNN model gives comparable ambiguity levels to the C&C model which uses a tagdict, while being much more accurate than both the other two models.

	LP	LR	LF	SENT	CAT	cov.
C&C (normal)	85.18	82.53	83.83	31.42	92.39	100
C&C (hybrid)	86.07	82.77	84.39	32.62	92.57	100
C&C (normal + RNN)	86.74	84.58	85.65	34.13	93.60	100
C&C (hybrid + RNN)	**87.73**	**84.83**	**86.25**	**34.97**	**93.84**	100
C&C (normal)	85.18	84.32	84.75	31.73	92.83	99.01 (C&C cov)
C&C (hybrid)	86.07	84.49	85.28	32.93	93.02	99.06 (C&C cov)
C&C (normal + RNN)	86.81	86.01	86.41	34.37	93.80	99.01 (C&C cov)
C&C (hybrid + RNN)	**87.77**	**86.25**	**87.00**	**35.20**	**94.04**	99.06 (C&C cov)
C&C (normal + RNN)	86.74	86.15	86.45	34.33	93.81	**99.42**
C&C (hybrid + RNN)	87.73	86.41	87.06	35.17	94.05	**99.42**

Table 4: Parsing development results on CCGBank Section 00 (auto POS).

	CCGBank Section 23				Wikipedia				Bioinfer			
	LP	LR	LF	cov.	LP	LR	LF	cov.	LP	LR	LF	cov.
C&C	86.24	84.85	85.54	99.42	81.58	80.08	80.83	99.50	77.78	76.07	76.91	95.40
C&C (+ NN)	86.71	85.56	86.13	99.92	82.65	81.36	82.00	**100**	79.77	**78.62**	**79.19**	97.40
C&C (+ RNN)	**87.68**	**86.47**	**87.07**	**99.96**	**83.22**	**81.78**	**82.49**	**100**	**80.10**	78.21	79.14	**97.80**
C&C	86.24	84.17	85.19	100	81.58	79.48	80.52	100	77.78	71.44	74.47	100
C&C (+ NN)	86.71	85.40	86.05	100	-	-	-	-	79.77	75.35	77.50	100
C&C (+ RNN)	**87.68**	**86.41**	**87.04**	100	-	-	-	-	**80.10**	**75.52**	**77.74**	100

Table 5: Parsing test results on all three domains (auto POS). We evaluate on all sentences (100% coverage) as well as on only those sentences that returned spanning analyses (% cov.). RNN and NN both have 100% coverage on the Wikipedia data.

Fig. 1c compares multi-tagging accuracies of all the models on the dev set. For all models, the same β levels are used (ranging from 0.075 to 10^{-4}, and all C&C default values are included). The RNN model consistently outperforms other models across different ambiguity levels.

Table 3 shows 1-best accuracies of all models on the test data sets (Bio-GENIA gold-standard CCG lexical category data from Rimell and Clark (2008) are used, since no gold categories are available in the Bioinfer data). With gold-standard POS tags, the C&C model outperforms both the NN and RNN models on CCGBank and Bio-GENIA; with auto POS, the accuracy of the C&C model drops significantly, due to its high reliance on POS tags.

Fig. 2 shows multi-tagging accuracies on all test data (using β levels ranging from 0.075 to 10^{-6}, and all C&C default values are included). On CCGBank, the RNN model has a clear accuracy advantage, while on the other two data sets, the accuracies given by the NN model are closer to the RNN model at some ambiguity levels, representing these data sets are still more challenging than CCGBank. However, both the NN and RNN models are more robust than the C&C model on the two out-of-domain data sets.

3.2 Parsing Results

We integrate our supertagging model into the C&C parser, at both training and test time, using all default parser settings; C&C hybrid model is used for CCGBank and Wikipedia; the normal-form model is used for the Bioinfer data, in line with Lewis and Steedman (2014) and Rimell and Clark (2008). Parsing development results are shown in Table 4; for out-of-domain data sets, no separate development experiments were done. Final results are shown in Table 5, and we substantially improve parsing accuracies on CCGBank and Wikipedia. The accuracy of our model on CCGBank represents a F1 score improvement of $1.53\%/1.85\%$ over the C&C baseline, which is comparable to the best known accuracy reported in Auli and Lopez (2011). However, our RNN-supertagging-based model is conceptually much simpler, with no change to the parsing model required at all.

4 Conclusion

We presented a RNN-based model for CCG supertagging, which brings significant accuracy improvements for supertagging and parsing, on both in- and out-of-domain data sets. Our supertagger is fast and well-suited for large scale processing.

Acknowledgements

The first author acknowledges the Carnegie Trust for the Universities of Scotland and the Cambridge Trusts for providing funding. SC is supported by ERC Starting Grant DisCoTex (306920) and EPSRC grant EP/I037512/1. We also thank the anonymous reviewers for their helpful comments.

References

Michael Auli and Adam Lopez. 2011. Training a log-linear parser with loss functions via softmax-margin. In *Proceedings of the Conference on Empirical Methods in Natural Language Processing*, pages 333–343. Association for Computational Linguistics.

Srinivas Bangalore and Aravind K Joshi. 1999. Supertagging: An approach to almost parsing. *Computational linguistics*, 25(2):237–265.

Stephen Clark and James R Curran. 2004. The importance of supertagging for wide-coverage CCG parsing. In *Proceedings of the 20th international conference on Computational Linguistics*, page 282. Association for Computational Linguistics.

Stephen Clark and James R. Curran. 2007. Wide-coverage efficient statistical parsing with CCG and log-linear models. *Computational Linguistics*, 33(4):493–552.

James R Curran, Stephen Clark, and David Vadas. 2006. Multi-tagging for lexicalized-grammar parsing. In *Proceedings of the 21st International Conference on Computational Linguistics and the 44th annual meeting of the Association for Computational Linguistics*, pages 697–704. Association for Computational Linguistics.

James R Curran, Stephen Clark, and Johan Bos. 2007. Linguistically motivated large-scale NLP with C&C and Boxer. In *Proceedings of the 45th Annual Meeting of the ACL on Interactive Poster and Demonstration Sessions*, pages 33–36. Association for Computational Linguistics.

Jeffrey L Elman. 1990. Finding structure in time. *Cognitive science*, 14(2):179–211.

Julia Hockenmaier and Mark Steedman. 2007. CCGbank: A corpus of CCG derivations and dependency structures extracted from the Penn Treebank. *Computational Linguistics*, 33(3):355–396.

Matthew Honnibal, Joel Nothman, and James R Curran. 2009. Evaluating a statistical CCG parser on wikipedia. In *Proceedings of the 2009 Workshop on The People's Web Meets NLP: Collaboratively Constructed Semantic Resources*, pages 38–41. Association for Computational Linguistics.

Jonathan K Kummerfeld, Jessika Roesner, Tim Dawborn, James Haggerty, James R Curran, and Stephen Clark. 2010. Faster parsing by supertagger adaptation. In *Proceedings of the 48th Annual Meeting of the Association for Computational Linguistics*, pages 345–355. Association for Computational Linguistics.

Joël Legrand and Ronan Collobert. 2014. Joint RNN-based greedy parsing and word composition. *arXiv preprint arXiv:1412.7028*.

Mike Lewis and Mark Steedman. 2014. Improved CCG parsing with semi-supervised supertagging. *Transactions of the Association for Computational Linguistics*, 2:327–338.

Tomas Mikolov, Martin Karafiát, Lukas Burget, Jan Cernockỳ, and Sanjeev Khudanpur. 2010. Recurrent neural network based language model. In *INTERSPEECH 2010, 11th Annual Conference of the International Speech Communication Association, Makuhari, Chiba, Japan, September 26-30, 2010*, pages 1045–1048.

Tomáš Mikolov. 2012. *Statistical Language Models Based on Neural Networks*. Ph.D. thesis, Brno University of Technology.

Sampo Pyysalo, Filip Ginter, Juho Heimonen, Jari Björne, Jorma Boberg, Jouni Järvinen, and Tapio Salakoski. 2007. Bioinfer: a corpus for information extraction in the biomedical domain. *BMC bioinformatics*, 8(1):50.

Laura Rimell and Stephen Clark. 2008. Adapting a lexicalized-grammar parser to contrasting domains. In *Proceedings of the Conference on Empirical Methods in Natural Language Processing*, pages 475–484. Association for Computational Linguistics.

David E Rumelhart, Geoffrey E Hinton, and Ronald J Williams. 1988. Learning representations by back-propagating errors. *Cognitive modeling*, 5.

Nitish Srivastava, Geoffrey Hinton, Alex Krizhevsky, Ilya Sutskever, and Ruslan Salakhutdinov. 2014. Dropout: A simple way to prevent neural networks from overfitting. *The Journal of Machine Learning Research*, 15(1):1929–1958.

Mark Steedman. 2000. *The Syntactic Process*. The MIT Press, Cambridge, Mass.

Joseph Turian, Lev Ratinov, and Yoshua Bengio. 2010. Word representations: a simple and general method for semi-supervised learning. In *Proceedings of the 48th annual meeting of the association for computational linguistics*, pages 384–394. Association for Computational Linguistics.

Wenduan Xu, Stephen Clark, and Yue Zhang. 2014. Shift-reduce CCG parsing with a dependency model. In *Proceedings of the 2014 ACL Conference*.

Yue Zhang and Stephen Clark. 2011. Shift-reduce CCG parsing. In *Proc. ACL 2011*, pages 683–692, Portland, OR.

An Efficient Dynamic Oracle for Unrestricted Non-Projective Parsing

Carlos Gómez-Rodríguez
Departamento de Computación
Universidade da Coruña
Campus de Elviña, s/n
15071 A Coruña, Spain
carlos.gomez@udc.es

Daniel Fernández-González
Departamento de Informática
Universidade de Vigo
Campus As Lagoas, s/n
32004 Ourense, Spain
danifg@uvigo.es

Abstract

We define a dynamic oracle for the Covington non-projective dependency parser. This is not only the first dynamic oracle that supports arbitrary non-projectivity, but also considerably more efficient ($O(n)$) than the only existing oracle with restricted non-projectivity support. Experiments show that training with the dynamic oracle significantly improves parsing accuracy over the static oracle baseline on a wide range of treebanks.

1 Introduction

Greedy transition-based dependency parsers build analyses for sentences incrementally by following a sequence of transitions defined by an automaton, using a scoring model to choose the best transition to take at each state (Nivre, 2008). While this kind of parsers have become very popular, as they achieve competitive accuracy with especially fast parsing times; their raw accuracy is still behind that of slower alternatives like transition-based parsers that use beam search (Zhang and Nivre, 2011; Choi and McCallum, 2013). For this reason, a current research challenge is to improve the accuracy of greedy transition-based parsers as much as possible without sacrificing efficiency.

A relevant recent advance in this direction is the introduction of dynamic oracles (Goldberg and Nivre, 2012), an improvement in the training procedure of greedy parsers that can boost their accuracy without any impact on parsing speed. An oracle is a training component that selects the best transition(s) to take at a given configuration, using knowledge about the gold tree. Traditionally, transition-based parsers were trained to follow a so-called static oracle, which is only defined on the configurations of a canonical computation that generates the gold tree, returning the next transition in said computation. In contrast, dynamic oracles are non-deterministic (not limited to one sequence, but supporting all the possible computations leading to the gold tree), and complete (also defined for configurations where the gold tree is unreachable, choosing the transition(s) that lead to a tree with minimum error). This extra robustness in training provides higher parsing accuracy.

However, defining a usable dynamic oracle for a given parser is non-trivial in general, due to the need of calculating the loss of each configuration, i.e., the minimum Hamming loss to the gold tree from a tree reachable from that configuration. While it is always easy to do this in exponential time by simulating all possible computations in the algorithm to obtain all reachable trees, it is not always clear how to achieve this calculation in polynomial time. At the moment, this problem has been solved for several projective parsers exploiting either arc-decomposability (Goldberg and Nivre, 2013) or tabularization of computations (Goldberg et al., 2014). However, for parsers that can handle crossing arcs, the only known dynamic oracle (Gómez-Rodríguez et al., 2014) has been defined for a variant of the parser by Attardi (2006) that supports a restricted set of non-projective trees. To our knowledge, no dynamic oracles are known for any transition-based parser that can handle unrestricted non-projectivity.

In this paper, we define such an oracle for the Covington non-projective parser (Covington, 2001; Nivre, 2008), which can handle arbitrary non-projective dependency trees. As this algorithm is not arc-decomposable and its tabularization is NP-hard (Neuhaus and Bröker, 1997), we do not use the existing techniques to define dynamic oracles, but a reasoning specific to this parser. It is worth noting that, apart from being the first dynamic oracle supporting unrestricted non-projectivity, our oracle is very efficient, solving the loss calculation in $O(n)$. In contrast, the restricted non-projective oracle of Gómez-Rodríguez et al.

Proceedings of the 53rd Annual Meeting of the Association for Computational Linguistics and the 7th International Joint Conference on Natural Language Processing (Short Papers), pages 256–261,
Beijing, China, July 26-31, 2015.

(2014) has $O(n^8)$ time complexity.

The rest of the paper is organized as follows: after a quick outline of Covington's parser in Sect. 2, we present the oracle and prove its correctness in Sect. 3. Experiments are reported in Sect. 4, and Sect. 5 contains concluding remarks.

2 Preliminaries

We will define a dynamic oracle for the non-projective parser originally defined by Covington (2001), and implemented by Nivre (2008) under the transition-based parsing framework. For space reasons, we only sketch the parser very briefly, and refer to the above reference for more details.

Parser configurations are of the form $c = \langle \lambda_1, \lambda_2, B, A \rangle$, where λ_1 and λ_2 are lists of partially processed words, B is another list (called the buffer) with currently unprocessed words, and A is the set of dependencies built so far. Suppose that we parse a string $w_1 \cdots w_n$, whose word occurrences will be identified with their indices $1 \cdots n$ for simplicity. Then, the parser starts at an initial configuration $c_s(w_1 \ldots w_n) = \langle [], [], [1 \ldots n], \emptyset \rangle$, and executes transitions chosen from those in Figure 1 until a terminal configuration of the form $\{\langle \lambda_1, \lambda_2, [], A \rangle \in C\}$ is reached, and the sentence's parse tree is obtained from A.[1]

The transition semantics is very simple, mirroring the double nested loop traversing word pairs in the formulation by Covington (2001). When the algorithm is in a configuration $\langle \lambda_1|i, \lambda_2, j|B, A \rangle$, we will say that it is considering the **focus words** i and j, located at the end of the first list and at the beginning of the buffer. A decision is then made about whether these two words should be linked with a rightward arc $i \rightarrow j$ (Right-Arc transition), a leftward arc $i \leftarrow j$ (Left-Arc transition) or not linked (No-Arc transition). The first two choices will be unavailable in configurations where the newly-created arc would violate the **single-head constraint** (a node cannot have more than one incoming arc) or the **acyclicity constraint** (cycles are not allowed). In any of these three transitions, i is then moved to the second list to make $i-1$ and j the focus words for the next step. Alternatively, we can choose to read a new word from the string with a Shift transition, so that the focus words in the resulting configuration will be j and $j+1$.

The result is a parser that can generate any possible dependency tree for the input, and runs in quadratic worst-case time. Although in theory this complexity can seem like a drawback compared to linear-time transition-based parsers (e.g. (Nivre, 2003; Gómez-Rodríguez and Nivre, 2013)), it has been shown by Volokh and Neumann (2012) to actually outperform linear algorithms in practice, as it allows for relevant optimizations in feature extraction that cannot be implemented in other parsers. In fact, one of the fastest dependency parsers to date uses this algorithm (Volokh, 2013).

3 The oracle

As sketched in Sect. 1, a dynamic oracle is a training component that, given a configuration c and a gold tree t_G, provides the set of transitions that are applicable in c and lead to trees with minimum Hamming loss with respect to t_G. The Hamming loss between a tree t and t_G, written $\mathcal{L}(t, t_G)$, is the number of nodes that have a different head in t than in t_G. Following Goldberg and Nivre (2013), we say that a set of arcs A is **reachable** from configuration c, written $c \rightsquigarrow A$, if there is some (possibly empty) path of transitions from c to some configuration $c' = \langle \lambda_1, \lambda_2, B, A' \rangle$, with $A \subseteq A'$. Then, we can define the loss of a configuration as

$$\ell(c) = \min_{t | c \rightsquigarrow t} \mathcal{L}(t, t_G),$$

and the set of transitions that must be returned by a correct dynamic oracle is then

$$o_d(c, t_G) = \{\tau \mid \ell(c) - \ell(\tau(c)) = 0\},$$

i.e., the transitions that do not increase configuration loss, and hence lead to the best parse (in terms of loss) reachable from c. Therefore, implementing a dynamic oracle reduces to computing the loss $\ell(c)$ for each configuration c.

Goldberg and Nivre (2013) show that the calculation of the loss is easy for parsers that are **arc-decomposable**, i.e., those where for every configuration c and arc set A that is **tree-compatible** (i.e. that can be a part of a well-formed parse[2]), $c \rightsquigarrow A$ is entailed by $c \rightsquigarrow (i \rightarrow j)$ for every $i \rightarrow j \in A$. That is, if each arc in a tree-compatible set is individually reachable from configuration c, then that

[1]The arcs in A form a forest, but we convert it to a tree by linking any node without a head as a dependent of an artificial node at position 0 that acts as a dummy root. From now on, when we refer to some dependency graph as a tree, we assume that this transformation is being implicitly made.

[2]In the cited paper, tree-compatibility required projectivity, as the authors were dealing with projective parsers. In our case, since the parser is non-projective, tree-compatibility only consists of the single-head and acyclicity constraints.

Shift:	$\langle\lambda_1, \lambda_2, j\|B, A\rangle \Rightarrow \langle\lambda_1 \cdot \lambda_2\|j, [], B, A\rangle$
No-Arc:	$\langle\lambda_1\|i, \lambda_2, B, A\rangle \Rightarrow \langle\lambda_1, i\|\lambda_2, B, A\rangle$
Left-Arc:	$\langle\lambda_1\|i, \lambda_2, j\|B, A\rangle \Rightarrow \langle\lambda_1, i\|\lambda_2, j\|B, A \cup \{j \rightarrow i\}\rangle$ only if $\nexists k \mid k \rightarrow i \in A$ (single-head) and $i \rightarrow^* j \notin A$ (acyclicity).
Right-Arc:	$\langle\lambda_1\|i, \lambda_2, j\|B, A\rangle \Rightarrow \langle\lambda_1, i\|\lambda_2, j\|B, A \cup \{i \rightarrow j\}\rangle$ only if $\nexists k \mid k \rightarrow j \in A$ (single-head) and $j \rightarrow^* i \notin A$ (acyclicity).

Figure 1: Transitions of the Covington non-projective dependency parser.

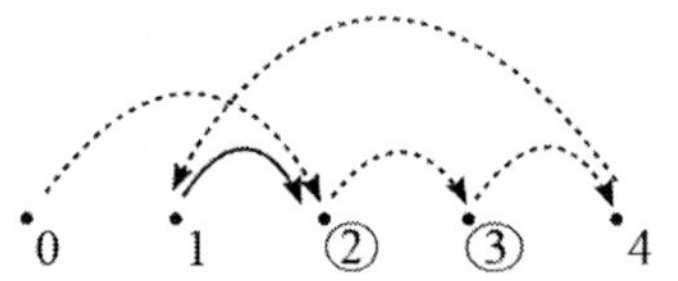

Figure 2: An example of non-arc-decomposability of the Covington parser: graphical representation of configuration $c = \langle[1,2], [], [3,4], A = \{1 \rightarrow 2\}\rangle$. The solid arc corresponds to the arc set A, and the circled indexes mark the focus words. The dashed arcs represent the gold tree t_G.

set of arcs is reachable from c. If this holds, then computing the loss of a configuration c reduces to determining and counting the gold arcs that are *not* reachable from c, which is easy in most parsers.

Unfortunately, the Covington parser is not arc-decomposable. This can be seen in the example of Figure 2: while any of the gold arcs $2\rightarrow3$, $3\rightarrow4$, $4\rightarrow1$ can be reachable individually from the depicted configuration, they are not jointly reachable as they form a cycle with the already-built arc $1\rightarrow2$. Thus, the configuration has only one individually unreachable arc ($0\rightarrow2$), but its loss is 2.

However, it is worth noting that non-arc-decomposability in the parser is exclusively due to cycles. If a set of individually reachable arcs do not form a cycle together with already-built arcs, then we can show that the set will be reachable. This idea is the basis for an expression to compute loss based on counting individually unreachable arcs, and then correcting for the effect of cycles:

Theorem 1 *Let $c = \langle\lambda_1, \lambda_2, B, A\rangle$ be a configuration of the Covington parser, and t_G the set of arcs of a gold tree. We call $\mathcal{I}(c, t_G) = \{x \rightarrow y \in t_G \mid c \rightsquigarrow (x \rightarrow y)\}$ the set of **individually reachable arcs** of t_G; note that this set may overlap A. Conversely, we call $\mathcal{U}(c, t_G) = t_G \setminus \mathcal{I}(c, t_G)$ the set of **individually unreachable arcs** of t_G from c. Finally, let $n_c(G)$ denote the number of cycles in a graph G.*

Then $\ell(c) = |\mathcal{U}(c, t_G)| + n_c(A \cup \mathcal{I}(c, t_G))$. □

We now sketch the proof. To prove Theorem 1, it is enough to show that (1) there is at least one tree reachable from c with exactly that Hamming loss to t_G, and (2) there are no trees reachable from c with a smaller loss. To this end, we will use some properties of the graph $A \cup \mathcal{I}(c, t_G)$. First, we note that no node in this graph has in-degree greater than 1. In particular, each node except for the dummy root has exactly one head, either explicit or (if no head has been assigned in A or in the gold tree) the dummy root. No node has more than one head: a node cannot have two heads in A because the parser transitions enforce the single-head constraint, it cannot have two heads in $\mathcal{I}(c, t_G)$ because t_G must satisfy this constraint as well, and it cannot have one head in A and another in $\mathcal{I}(c, t_G)$ because the corresponding arc in $\mathcal{I}(c, t_G)$ would be unreachable due to the single-head constraint.

This, in turn, implies that the graph $A \cup \mathcal{I}(c, t_G)$ has no overlapping cycles, as overlapping cycles can only appear in graphs with in-degree greater than 1. This is the key property enabling us to exactly calculate loss using the number of cycles.

To show (1), consider the graph $A \cup \mathcal{I}(c, t_G)$. In each of its cycles, there is at least one arc that belongs to $\mathcal{I}(c, t_G)$, as A must satisfy the acyclicity constraint. We arbitrarily choose one such arc from each cycle, and remove it from the graph. Note that this results in removing exactly $n_c(A \cup \mathcal{I}(c, t_G))$ arcs, as we have shown that the cycles in $A \cup \mathcal{I}(c, t_G)$ are disjoint. We call the resulting graph $\mathcal{B}(c, t_G)$. As it has maximum in-degree 1 and it is acyclic (because we have broken all the cycles), $\mathcal{B}(c, t_G)$ is a tree, modulo our standard assumption that headless nodes are assumed to be linked to the dummy root.

This tree $\mathcal{B}(c, t_G)$ is reachable from c and has loss $\ell(c) = |\mathcal{U}(c, t_G)| + n_c(A \cup \mathcal{I}(c, t_G))$. Reachability is shown by building a sequence of transitions that will visit the pairs of words corresponding to remaining arcs in order, and intercalating the corresponding Left-Arc or Right-Arc transitions, which cannot violate the acyclicity or single-head constraints. The term $\mathcal{U}(c, t_G)$ in the loss stems from the fact that $A \cup \mathcal{I}(c, t_G)$ cannot contain arcs in $\mathcal{U}(c, t_G)$, and the term $n_c(A \cup \mathcal{I}(c, t_G))$ from not including the $n_c(A \cup \mathcal{I}(c, t_G))$ arcs that we discarded to break cycles.

Finally, from these observations, it is easy to see that $\mathcal{B}(c, t_G)$ has the best loss among reachable trees, and thus prove (2): the arcs in $\mathcal{U}(c, t_G)$ are always unreachable by definition, and for each cycle in $n_c(A \cup \mathcal{I}(c, t_G))$, the acyclicity constraint forces us to miss at least one arc. As the cycles are disjoint, this means that we necessarily miss at least $n_c(A \cup \mathcal{I}(c, t_G))$ arcs, hence $|\mathcal{U}(c, t_G)| + n_c(A \cup \mathcal{I}(c, t_G))$ is indeed the minimum loss among reachable trees. □

Thus, to calculate the loss of a configuration c, we only need to compute both of the terms in Theorem 1. For the first term, note that if c has focus words i and j (i.e., $c = \langle \lambda_1 | i, \lambda_2, j | B, A \rangle$), then an arc $x \rightarrow y$ is in $\mathcal{U}(c, t_G)$ if it is not in A, and at least one of the following holds:

- $j > \max(x, y)$, as in this case we have read too far in the string and will not be able to get x and y as focus words,
- $j = \max(x, y) \wedge i < \min(x, y)$, as in this case we have $\max(x, y)$ as the right focus word but the left focus word is to the left of $\min(x, y)$, and we cannot move it back,
- there is some $z \neq 0, z \neq x$ such that $z \rightarrow y \in A$, as in this case the single-head constraint prevents us from creating $x \rightarrow y$,
- x and y are on the same weakly connected component of A, as in this case the acyclicity constraint will not let us create $x \rightarrow y$.

All of these arcs can be trivially enumerated in $O(n)$ time (in fact, they can be updated in $O(1)$ if we start from the configuration that preceded c). The second term of the loss, $n_c(A \cup \mathcal{I}(c, t_G))$, can be computed by obtaining $\mathcal{I}(c, t_G)$ as $t_G \setminus \mathcal{U}(c, t_G)$ to then apply a standard cycle-finding algorithm (Tarjan, 1972) which, for a graph with maximum in-degree 1, runs in $O(n)$ time.

Algorithm 1 presents the resulting loss calculation algorithm in pseudocode form, where CountCycles is a function that counts the number of cycles in the given graph in linear time as mentioned above. Note that the for loop runs in

Algorithm 1 Computation of the loss of a configuration.

1: **function** Loss($c = \langle \lambda_1 | i, \lambda_2, j | B, A \rangle, t_G$)
2: $\quad U \leftarrow \emptyset$ ▷ Variable U is for $\mathcal{U}(c, t_G)$
3: $\quad$**for each** $x \rightarrow y \in (t_G \setminus A)$ **do**
4: $\quad\quad$ $left \leftarrow \min(x, y)$
5: $\quad\quad$ $right \leftarrow \max(x, y)$
6: $\quad\quad$ **if** $j > right \vee$
7: $\quad\quad$ $(j = right \wedge i < left) \vee$
8: $\quad\quad$ $(\exists z > 0, z \neq x : z \rightarrow y \in A) \vee$
9: $\quad\quad$ WeaklyConnected(A, x, y) **then**
10: $\quad\quad\quad$ $U \leftarrow u \cup \{x \rightarrow y\}$
11: $\quad I \leftarrow t_G \setminus U$ ▷ Variable I is for $\mathcal{I}(c, t_G)$
12: $\quad$**return** $|U|$ + CountCycles($A \cup I$)

linear time: the condition on line 8 can be computed in constant time by recovering the head of y. The call to WeaklyConnected in line 9 finds out whether the two given nodes are weakly connected in A, and can also be resolved in $O(1)$, by querying the disjoint set data structure that implementations of the Covington algorithm commonly use for the parser's acyclicity checks (Nivre, 2008).

It is worth noting that the linear-time complexity can also be achieved by a standalone implementation of the loss calculation algorithm, without recurse to the parser's auxiliary data structures (although this is dubiously practical). To do so, we can implement WeaklyConnected so that the first call computes the connected components of A in linear time (Hopcroft and Tarjan, 1973) and subsequent calls use this information to find out if two nodes are weakly connected in constant time.

On the other hand, a more efficient implementation than the one shown in Algorithm 1 (which we chose for clarity) can be achieved by more tightly coupling the oracle to the parser, as the relevant sets of arcs associated with a configuration can be obtained incrementally from those of the previous configuration.

4 Experiments

To evaluate the performance of our approach, we conduct experiments on both static and dynamic Covington non-projective oracles. Concretely, we train an averaged perceptron model for 15 iterations on nine datasets from the CoNLL-X shared task (Buchholz and Marsi, 2006) and all data-

Unigrams
L_0w; L_0p; L_0wp; L_0l; $L_{0h}w$; $L_{0h}p$; $L_{0h}l$; $L_{0l'}w$; $L_{0l'}p$; $L_{0l'}l$; $L_{0r'}w$; $L_{0r'}p$; $L_{0r'}l$; $L_{0h2}w$; $L_{0h2}p$; $L_{0h2}l$; $L_{0l}w$; $L_{0l}p$; $L_{0l}l$; $L_{0r}w$; $L_{0r}p$; $L_{0r}l$; L_0wd; L_0pd; L_0wv_r; L_0pv_r; L_0wv_l; L_0pv_l; L_0ws_l; L_0ps_l; L_0ws_r; L_0ps_r; L_1w; L_1p; L_1wp; R_0w; R_0p; R_0wp; $R_{0l'}w$; $R_{0l'}p$; $R_{0l'}l$; $R_{0l}w$; $R_{0l}p$; $R_{0l}l$; R_0wd; R_0pd; R_0wv_l; R_0pv_l;R_0ws_l; R_0ps_l; R_1w; R_1p; R_1wp; R_2w; R_2p; R_2wp; CLw; CLp; $CLwp$; CRw; CRp; $CRwp$;
Pairs
L_0wp+R_0wp; L_0wp+R_0w; L_0w+R_0wp; L_0wp+R_0p; L_0p+R_0wp; L_0w+R_0w; L_0p+R_0p;R_0p+R_1p; L_0w+R_0wd; L_0p+R_0pd;
Triples
R_0p+R_1p+R_2p; L_0p+R_0p+R_1p; $L_{0h}p$+L_0p+R_0p; L_0p+$L_{0l'}p$+R_0p; L_0p+$L_{0r'}p$+R_0p; L_0p+R_0p+$R_{0l'}p$; L_0p+$L_{0l'}p$+$L_{0l}p$; L_0p+$L_{0r'}p$+$L_{0r}p$; L_0p+$L_{0h}p$+$L_{0h2}p$; R_0p+$R_{0l'}p$+$R_{0l}p$;

Table 1: Feature templates. L_0 and R_0 denote the left and right focus words; $L_1, L_2, \ldots$ are the words to the left of L_0 and $R_1, R_2, \ldots$ those to the right of R_0. X_{ih} means the head of X_i, X_{ih2} the grandparent, X_{il} and $X_{il'}$ the farthest and closest left dependents, and X_{ir} and $X_{ir'}$ the farthest and closest right dependents, respectively. CL and CR are the first and last words between L_0 and R_0 whose head is not in the interval $[L_0, R_0]$. Finally, w stands for word form; p for PoS tag; l for dependency label; d is the distance between L_0 and R_0; v_l, v_r are the left/right valencies (number of left/right dependents); and s_l, s_r the left/right label sets (dependency labels of left/right dependents).

	s-Covington		d-Covington	
Language	UAS	LAS	UAS	LAS
Arabic	80.03	71.32	**81.47***	**72.77***
Basque	75.76	69.70	**76.49***	**70.27***
Catalan	88.66	83.92	**89.28**	**84.26**
Chinese	83.94	79.59	**84.68***	**80.16***
Czech	77.38	71.21	**78.58***	**72.59***
English	84.64	83.72	**86.14***	**84.96***
Greek	79.33	72.65	**80.52***	**73.67***
Hungarian	77.70	74.32	**78.22**	**74.61**
Italian	83.39	79.66	**83.66**	**79.91**
Turkish	82.14	76.00	**82.38**	**76.15**
Bulgarian	87.68	84.55	**88.48***	**85.32***
Danish	84.07	79.99	**84.98***	**80.85***
Dutch	80.28	77.55	**81.17***	**78.54***
German	86.12	83.93	**87.47***	**85.15***
Japanese	**93.92**	**92.51**	93.79	92.42
Portuguese	85.70	82.78	**86.23**	**83.27**
Slovene	75.31	68.97	**76.76***	**70.35***
Spanish	78.82	75.84	**79.87***	**76.97***
Swedish	**86.78**	**81.29**	86.66	81.21
Average	82.72	78.39	**83.52**	**79.13**

Table 2: Parsing accuracy (UAS and LAS, including punctuation) of Covington non-projective parser with static (s-Covington) and dynamic (d-Covington) oracles on CoNLL-XI (first block) and CoNLL-X (second block) datasets. For each language, we run five experiments with the same setup but different seeds and report the averaged accuracy. Best results for each language are shown in boldface. Statistically significant improvements ($\alpha = .05$) (Yeh, 2000) are marked with *.

sets from the CoNLL-XI shared task (Nivre et al., 2007). We use the same feature templates for all languages, which result from adapting the features described by Zhang and Nivre (2011) to the data structures of the Covington non-projective parser, and are listed in detail in Table 1.

Table 2 reports the accuracy obtained by the Covington non-projective parser with both oracles. As we can see, the dynamic oracle implemented in the Covington algorithm improves over the accuracy of the static version on all datasets except Japanese and Swedish, and most improvements are statistically significant at the .05 level.[3]

In addition, the Covington dynamic oracle achieves a greater average improvement in accuracy than the Attardi dynamic oracle (Gómez-Rodríguez et al., 2014) over their respective static versions. Concretely, the Attardi oracle accomplishes an average improvement of 0.52 percentage points in UAS and 0.71 in LAS, while our approach achieves 0.80 in UAS and 0.74 in LAS.

[3]Note that the loss of accuracy in Japanese and Swedish is not statistically significant.

5 Conclusion

We have defined the first dynamic oracle for a transition-based parser supporting unrestricted non-projectivity. The oracle is very efficient, computing loss in $O(n)$, compared to $O(n^8)$ for the only previously known dynamic oracle with support for a subset of non-projective trees (Gómez-Rodríguez et al., 2014).

Experiments on the treebanks from the CoNLL-X and CoNLL-XI shared tasks show that the dynamic oracle significantly improves accuracy on many languages over a static oracle baseline.

Acknowledgments

Research partially funded by the Spanish Ministry of Economy and Competitiveness/ERDF (grants FFI2014-51978-C2-1-R, FFI2014-51978-C2-2-R), Ministry of Education (FPU grant program) and Xunta de Galicia (grant R2014/034).

References

Giuseppe Attardi. 2006. Experiments with a multilanguage non-projective dependency parser. In *Proceedings of the 10th Conference on Computational Natural Language Learning (CoNLL-X)*, pages 166–170, Morristown, NJ, USA. Association for Computational Linguistics.

Sabine Buchholz and Erwin Marsi. 2006. CoNLL-X shared task on multilingual dependency parsing. In *Proceedings of the 10th Conference on Computational Natural Language Learning (CoNLL)*, pages 149–164.

Jinho D. Choi and Andrew McCallum. 2013. Transition-based dependency parsing with selectional branching. In *Proceedings of the 51st Annual Meeting of the Association for Computational Linguistics (Volume 1: Long Papers)*, pages 1052–1062, Sofia, Bulgaria.

Michael A. Covington. 2001. A fundamental algorithm for dependency parsing. In *Proceedings of the 39th Annual ACM Southeast Conference*, pages 95–102, New York, NY, USA. ACM.

Yoav Goldberg and Joakim Nivre. 2012. A dynamic oracle for arc-eager dependency parsing. In *Proceedings of COLING 2012*, pages 959–976, Mumbai, India, December. Association for Computational Linguistics.

Yoav Goldberg and Joakim Nivre. 2013. Training deterministic parsers with non-deterministic oracles. *Transactions of the Association for Computational Linguistics*, 1:403–414.

Yoav Goldberg, Francesco Sartorio, and Giorgio Satta. 2014. A tabular method for dynamic oracles in transition-based parsing. *Transactions of the Association for Computational Linguistics*, 2:119–130.

Carlos Gómez-Rodríguez and Joakim Nivre. 2013. Divisible transition systems and multiplanar dependency parsing. *Computational Linguistics*, 39(4):799–845.

Carlos Gómez-Rodríguez, Francesco Sartorio, and Giorgio Satta. 2014. A polynomial-time dynamic oracle for non-projective dependency parsing. In *Proceedings of the 2014 Conference on Empirical Methods in Natural Language Processing (EMNLP)*, pages 917–927. Association for Computational Linguistics.

John Hopcroft and Robert Endre Tarjan. 1973. Algorithm 447: Efficient algorithms for graph manipulation. *Commun. ACM*, 16(6):372–378, June.

Peter Neuhaus and Norbert Bröker. 1997. The complexity of recognition of linguistically adequate dependency grammars. In *Proceedings of the 35th Annual Meeting of the Association for Computational Linguistics (ACL) and the 8th Conference of the European Chapter of the Association for Computational Linguistics (EACL)*, pages 337–343.

Joakim Nivre, Johan Hall, Sandra Kübler, Ryan McDonald, Jens Nilsson, Sebastian Riedel, and Deniz Yuret. 2007. The CoNLL 2007 shared task on dependency parsing. In *Proceedings of the CoNLL Shared Task Session of EMNLP-CoNLL 2007*, pages 915–932, June.

Joakim Nivre. 2003. An efficient algorithm for projective dependency parsing. In *Proceedings of the 8th International Workshop on Parsing Technologies (IWPT 03)*, pages 149–160. ACL/SIGPARSE.

Joakim Nivre. 2008. Algorithms for Deterministic Incremental Dependency Parsing. *Computational Linguistics*, 34(4):513–553.

Robert Endre Tarjan. 1972. Depth-first search and linear graph algorithms. *SIAM J. Comput.*, 1(2):146–160.

Alexander Volokh and Günter Neumann. 2012. Dependency parsing with efficient feature extraction. In Birte Glimm and Antonio Krüger, editors, *KI*, volume 7526 of *Lecture Notes in Computer Science*, pages 253–256. Springer.

Alexander Volokh. 2013. *Performance-Oriented Dependency Parsing*. Doctoral dissertation, Saarland University, Saarbrücken, Germany.

Alexander Yeh. 2000. More accurate tests for the statistical significance of result differences. In *Proceedings of the 18th International Conference on Computational Linguistics (COLING)*, pages 947–953.

Yue Zhang and Joakim Nivre. 2011. Transition-based dependency parsing with rich non-local features. In *Proceedings of the 49th Annual Meeting of the Association for Computational Linguistics: Human Language Technologies: short papers - Volume 2*, pages 188–193.

Synthetic Word Parsing Improves Chinese Word Segmentation

Fei Cheng Kevin Duh Yuji Matsumoto
Graduate School of Information Science
Nara Institute of Science and Technology
8916-5 Takayama, Ikoma, Nara, 630-0192, Japan
{fei-c,kevinduh,matsu}@is.naist.jp

Abstract

We present a novel solution to improve the performance of Chinese word segmentation (CWS) using a synthetic word parser. The parser analyses the internal structure of words, and attempts to convert out-of-vocabulary words (OOVs) into in-vocabulary fine-grained sub-words. We propose a pipeline CWS system that first predicts this fine-grained segmentation, then chunks the output to reconstruct the original word segmentation standard. We achieve competitive results on the PKU and MSR datasets, with substantial improvements in OOV recall.

1 Introduction

Since Chinese has no spaces between words to indicate word boundaries, Chinese word segmentation is a task to determine word boundaries between characters. In recent years, research in Chinese word segmentation has progressed significantly, with state-of-the-art performing at around 96% in precision and recall (Xue, 2003; Zhang and Clark, 2007; Li and Sun, 2009).

However, frequent OOVs are still a crucial issue that causes low accuracy in word segmentation. Li and Zhou (2012) defined those words that are OOVs but consisting of frequent internal parts as pseudo-OOV words and estimated that over 60% of OOVs are pseudo-OOVs in five common Chinese corpora. For instance, PKU corpus does not contain the word 陈列室 (exhibition room), even though the word 陈列 (exhibit) and 室 (room) appear hundreds of times. Goh et al. (2006) also claimed that most OOVs are proper nouns taking the form of Chinese synthetic words.

These previous works suggest that by analysing the internal structure of the synthetic words, we can transform pseudo-OOVs into in-vocabulary words (IVs). By running a synthetic word parser on each of the words in a CWS training set, we can generate a fine-grained segmentation standard that contains more IVs. Since the current conditional random field (CRF) word segmenters (Tseng et al., 2005; Sun and Xu, 2011) perform well on IVs, this transforming process can conceivably improve the handling of pseudo-OOV words, as long as we can recover the original word segmentation standard from the fine-grained sub-word segmentation.

In recent years, some related works about improving OOV problem in CWS have been ongoing. Sun et al. (2012) presented a joint model for Chinese word segmentation and OOVs detection. Their models achieved fast training speed, high accuracies and increase on OOV recall. Sun (2011) proposed a similar sub-word structure which is generated by merging the segmentations provided by different segmenters (a word-based segmenter, a character-based segmenter and a local character classifier). However, her models does not predict the sub-words of all the synthetic words, but those words with different segmented results of the three segmenters. Her work maximizes the agreement of different models to improve CWS performance. Different from her work, we aim to provide an unified way to incorporate morphological information of the synthetic words into the CWS task.

In this paper, we propose a pipeline word segmentation system to address the pseudo-OOV problem. Our word segmentation system first converts the original training data into a fine-grained standard by parsing all words with a synthetic word parser (Section 2.1), then trains a CRF-based sub-word segmenter (Section 2.2). A second CRF chunker is trained to recover the original word segmentation given the fine-grained results of the first CRF. The intuition is that fine-grained sub-word segmentations resolve pseudo-OOVs into IVs, which are easier to predict correctly by the first CRF. Secondly, by training an-

Proceedings of the 53rd Annual Meeting of the Association for Computational Linguistics and the 7th International Joint Conference on Natural Language Processing (Short Papers), pages 262–267,
Beijing, China, July 26-31, 2015.

other CRF that predicts the original word segmentation given the fine-grained segmentation as input, we can recover the fine-grained output into original word segmentation standard (Section 2.3). The flow chart of our word segmentation system is shown in Figure 1.

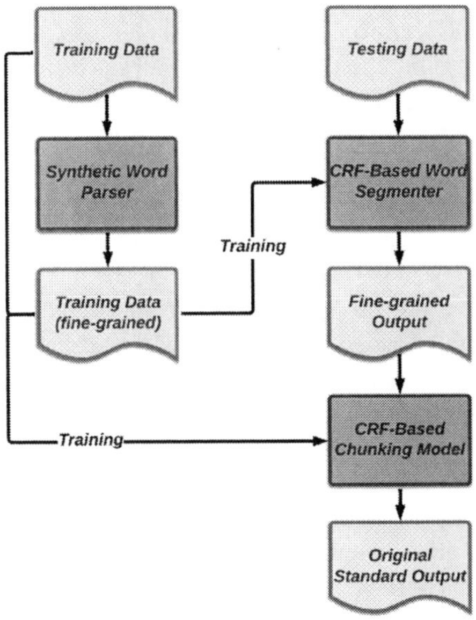

Figure 1: The Flow Chart of the Chinese Word Segmentation System.

2 System Components

2.1 Synthetic Word Parser

Intuitively, Chinese synthetic words contain internal morphological information that is helpful to recognize OOVs. Cheng et al. (2014) proposed a character-based parser to parse the internal tree structure of words. For instance, the tree and flat segmented result of the word 市政府 (municipal government) are shown in Figure 2. In this work, we train a graph-based parser (McDonald, 2006) on the data released by Cheng et al. (2014) and include the dictionary (NAIST Chinese Dictionary[1]) features and Brown clustering features extracted from a large unlabeled corpus (Chinese Gigaword Second Edition[2]) as described in Cheng et al. (2014).

For native Chinese speakers, single character and two character words are usually treated as the smallest units. In this work, we parse all the words in the PKU and MSR training data with character length greater than two. By replacing the words with the flat segmented results, we convert the training data into a fine-grained word segmentation standard as shown in Figure 3.

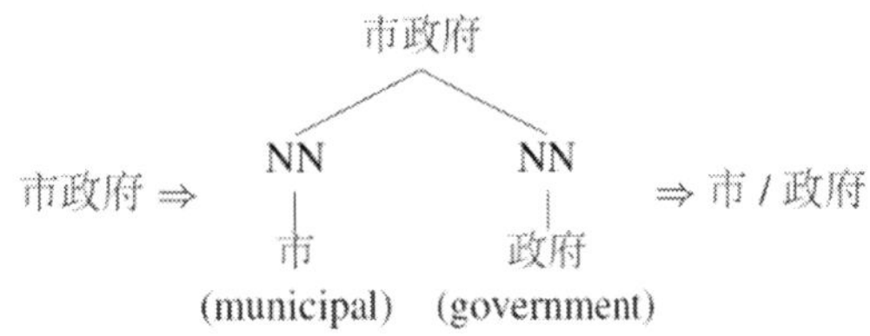

Figure 2: The Tree Structure of a Sample Word and the Flat Segmented Result.

Original CWS tags	市政府 / 办公厅 / 等 / 单位 B I E / B I E / S / B E
Fine-grained CWS tags	市 / 政府 / 办公 / 厅 / 等 / 单位 S / B E / B E / S / S / B E

Figure 3: A Sample Sentence of Labeling Chinese word segmentation tags on the Original and Fine-grained Standard. In this work, we adopt 4-tag set for word segmentation. "B" denotes the beginning character of a word. "I" denotes the middle character of a word. "E" denotes the end character of a word. "S" denotes a single character word.

2.2 CRF-based Word Segmenter

Xue et al. (2003) proposed a method which treated Chinese word segmentation as a character-based sequential labeling problem and exploited several discriminative learning algorithms. Tseng et al. (2005) adopted the CRFs as the learning method and obtained the best results in the second international Chinese word segmentation bakeoff-2005. Moreover, Sun and Xu (2011) attempted to extract information from large unlabeled data to enhance the Chinese word segmentation results.

In this work, we train a traditional CRF-based supervised model on the fine-grained training data, include the dictionary (NAIST Chinese Dictionary) features and access variety features extracted from a large unlabeled corpus (Chinese Gigaword Second Edition) as described in Sun and Xu (2011).

[1] http://cl.naist.jp/index.php?%B8%F8%B3%AB%A5%EA%A5%BD%A1%BC%A5%B9%2FNCD

[2] https://catalog.ldc.upenn.edu/LDC2005T14

2.3 CRF-based Chunking Model

In order to obtain the word segmentation result with original word segmentation standard, we train a CRF-based chunking model on the original and fine-grained training data. We show a sample sentence of labeling chunking tags in Figure 4. Comparing two sentences, we label all common units with the tag "S". The words 市 and 政府 are tagged as "B" and "E", since 市 is the beginning part of the synthetic word 市政府 and 政府 is the ending part. In the chunking process, the frequent prefix 市 is coordinated with neighbouring units to compose the synthetic word 市政府.

For each labeling, we include previous, current and next word as the features for the chunking model.

Original	市政府 / 办公厅 / 等 / 单位
Fine-grained	市 / 政府 / 办公 / 厅 / 等 / 单位
Chunking tags	B / E / B / E / S / S

Figure 4: A Sample Sentence of Labeling Chunking Tags. In this work, we adopt 4-tag set for chunking. "B" denotes the beginning part of a synthetic word. "I" denotes the middle part. "E" denotes the end part. "S" denotes a single word.

3 Experiments

3.1 Settings

Cheng et al. (2014) released a dictionary of 31,849 synthetic words with internal structure annotated. Since transliteration words (e.g. 贝克汉姆 Becham) exist in Chinese, our synthetic word parser should perform well not only on synthetic words but also on transliteration words. We extracted 6,574 transliteration words from the NAIST Chinese Dictionary and automatically assigned flat structures for these words. As a result, we obtained 38,423 words as the training data for our parser.

The second international Chinese word segmentation bakeoff-2005 provided two annotated simplified Chinese corpora: PKU and MSR. We conducted all word segmentation experiments on these two corpora.

We used CRF++[3] (version 0.58) as the implementation of CRFs in our experiments with the default regularization algorithm L2.

[3]The CRF++ package can be found in the following website: http://taku910.github.io/crfpp/

3.2 Word Segmentation Results

Table 1 summarizes the word segmentation results on PKU and MSR corpora. For comparison, we give a baseline result by training a CRF word segmenter on the original PKU and MSR data sets with the same features. Our proposed system is expected to improve the word segmentation performance on pseudo-OOVs. Compared to the baseline, there are significant increases on OOV recall from 0.792 to 0.822 on PKU and 0.682 to 0.717 on MSR. We also evaluated the pseudo-OOV recall and observed 4% increases from the baseline to the proposed system. Our proposed system achieves higher F-score with 0.961 on PKU and 0.971 on MSR. Comparing to other systems, our proposed method obtains the state-of-the-art F-score as the results of Zhang et al. (2013) who extracted dynamic statistical features from both in-domain and out-domain corpus and our OOV recall significantly outperforms theirs with a 9% lead. In MSR, we obtain very close OOV recall and slightly lower F-score than the state-of-the-art system (Sun et al., 2009), which adopted a latent variable CRF model. However, our system significantly outperforms their system in PKU. In both corpora, our proposed system outperforms the best "Bakeoff-2005" results.

We also test the statistical significance of the results by using the criterion (Sproat and Emerson, 2003; Emerson, 2005). The 95% confidence interval is given as $\pm 2\sqrt{p(1-p)/n}$, where n is the number of words in the test data. They treat two systems as significantly different (at the 95% confidence level), if at least one of their precision-based confidences "C_p" or recall-based "C_r" are different. As the results shown in Table 2, the baseline and proposed method are significantly different on precision and recall in both PKU and MSR corpus. In conclusion, our proposed method significantly outperforms the baseline.

3.3 Additional Experiments

We conducted additional experiments to evaluate the performance of the synthetic word parser and CRF-based chunking model.

First, we are interested in how much parsing accuracy is needed for good results. Figure 5 displays the OOV recall results of our word segmentation system when the synthetic word parser is trained with amounts of labeled synthetic words data. As the data size increases, our word segmen-

System	PKU					MSR				
	P	**R**	**F**	**R_{oov}**	**R_{pseudo}**	**P**	**R**	**F**	**R_{oov}**	**R_{pseudo}**
Baseline	0.957	0.960	0.959	0.792	0.797	0.971	0.968	0.970	0.682	0.689
Proposed method	0.960	**0.962**	**0.961**	**0.822**	0.838	0.972	0.970	0.971	0.717	0.73
Zhang et al. (2013)	**0.965**	0.958	**0.961**	0.731	-	-	-	-	-	-
Sun et al. (2009)	0.956	0.948	0.952	0.778	-	**0.973**	**0.973**	**0.973**	**0.722**	-
Bakeoff-2005	0.953	0.946	0.950	0.636	-	0.962	0.966	0.964	0.717	-

Table 1: Comparison of the Proposed Method to the Baseline and Previous works on PKU and MSR Corpora. Here, "R_{pseudo}" denotes the recall of pseudo-OOV words. "Bakeoff-2005" denotes the best results of the second international Chinese word segmentation bakeoff-2005 on two corpora. Since we use extra resources and our proposed method replies on the synthetic word parser trained on an dictionary with internal structure annotated, the results cannot be directly compared with the state-of-the-art systems.

System	PKU					MSR				
	Words	**P**	**C_p**	**R**	**C_r**	**Words**	**P**	**C_p**	**R**	**C_r**
Baseline	104372	0.957	±0.00126	0.960	±0.00121	106873	0.971	±0.00103	0.968	±0.00108
Proposed	104372	0.960	±0.00121	0.962	±0.00118	106873	0.972	±0.00101	0.970	±0.00104

Table 2: The Statistical Significance Test of the Word Segmentation Results on PKU and MSR Corpora.

tation system obtains consistent gains on OOV recall on both corpora. On the whole 38K words training data, our system reaches the highest OOV recall. An interesting observation is that the OOV recall on MSR is more sensitive on data size changing. The main reason is the different annotation standard of the two corpus. PKU is a correspondingly fine-grained annotated corpus with shorter average word length than MSR. Our synthetic word parser reaches high parsing accuracy on short length words (three-character and four-character words) even with a small training data size. With the increase of word length, the parser needs more training data. These factors cause that our system reaches high OOV recall on PKU starting from a small training data size and obtains more OOV recall gains on MSR when increasing the training data size.

Our pipeline system adopts a chunking model to recover the original standard from the fine-grained standard. One question is how difficult is this task. Unfortunately, we do not have the gold fine-grained input to evaluate the performance of our chunking model directly; i.e. it is not clear whether a segmentation error is due to mis-predictions in the first or second CRF. Therefore, we use the synthetic word parser to parse all the words in the gold testing data and generate an artificial gold fine-grained input for the chunking model. This data keeps the original word bound-

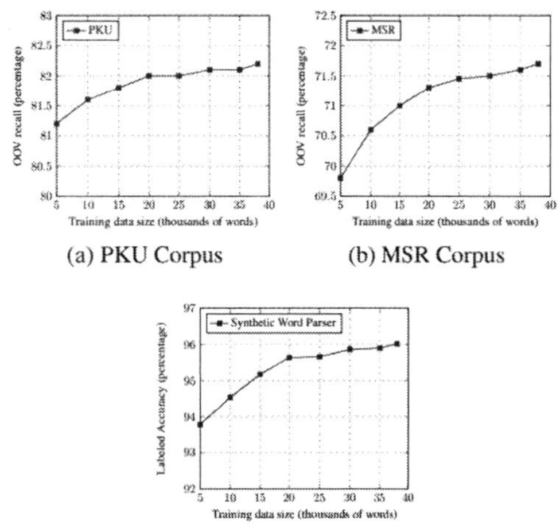

(a) PKU Corpus (b) MSR Corpus

(c) Parsing Performance

Figure 5: The OOV Recall Evaluation and the Character Labeled Accuracy (5-fold cross-validation) of the Synthetic Word Parser on Training Data Size.

aries and can be used to observe the chunking performance. Table 3 shows that the chunking model on the artificial data obtains a 0.822 to 0.847 improvement in OOV recall. We can interpret this to mean that 0.025 improvement is possible if the first CRF was perfect; on the other hand, the gap between 0.847 and 1.0 shows that potentially the second CRF is a harder task. However, the real gap is less for the lose of the parsing step and the existence of non-pseudo OOVs.

System	PKU		MSR	
	F	**R_{oov}**	**F**	**R_{oov}**
Proposed	0.961	0.822	0.971	0.717
Artifical gold	0.965	0.847	0.973	0.743

Table 3: The Word Segmentation evaluation of the Chunking Model. "Artificial gold" denotes the word segmentation result when the chunking model runs on the artificial gold input.

3.4 Analysis

As we expected, the proposed method obtains significant improvement on OOV recall. In both corpora, we observed a number of OOVs are segmented correctly. For instance, 管理法 (management law) is an OOV word in PKU corpus. In this word, 管理 (management) appears frequently and 法 (law) is a common suffix in Chinese synthetic words, such as 行政法 (administrative law) or 国际法 (international law). This type of pseudo-OOVs share a major contribution to upgrade the system performance. We also observed that some polysemous words bring ambiguities to the chunking step. The character 会 carries the meanings "will" as an auxiliary verb or "meeting" in a synthetic word 运动会 (sports meeting).

4 Conclusion

In this paper, we presented a series processes to reduce OOV rate and extract morphological information inside Chinese synthetic words on a fine-grained word segmentation standard. As a result, we can improve the Chinese word segmentation performance (especially on pseudo-OOVs) without introducing any new feature types. Our proposed method achieved the state-of-the-art F-score and OOV recall on two common corpus PKU and MSR. However, note that we only exploited the flat segmented results of internal word structure here. As future work, we plan to exploit the full tree structure of synthetic words to improve not only CWS but also additional downstream tasks such as sentence parsing.

References

Fei Cheng, Kevin Duh, and Yuji Matsumoto. 2014. Parsing chinese synthetic words with a character-based dependency model. In *Proceedings of the Ninth International Conference on Language Resources and Evaluation (LREC'14)*, Reykjavik, Iceland, may. European Language Resources Association (ELRA).

Thomas Emerson. 2005. The second international chinese word segmentation bakeoff. In *Proceedings of the fourth SIGHAN workshop on Chinese language Processing*, volume 133.

Chooi-Ling Goh, Masayuki Asahara, and Yuji Matsumoto. 2006. Machine learning-based methods to chinese unknown word detection and pos tag guessing. *Journal of Chinese Language and Computing*, 16(4):185–206.

Zhongguo Li and Maosong Sun. 2009. Punctuation as implicit annotations for chinese word segmentation. *Computational Linguistics*, 35(4):505–512.

Zhongguo Li and Guodong Zhou. 2012. Unified dependency parsing of chinese morphological and syntactic structures. In *Proceedings of the 2012 Joint Conference on Empirical Methods in Natural Language Processing and Computational Natural Language Learning*, pages 1445–1454. Association for Computational Linguistics.

Ryan McDonald. 2006. *Discriminative learning and spanning tree algorithms for dependency parsing*. Ph.D. thesis, PhD Thesis. University of Pennsylvania.

Richard Sproat and Thomas Emerson. 2003. The first international chinese word segmentation bakeoff. In *Proceedings of the second SIGHAN workshop on Chinese language processing-Volume 17*, pages 133–143. Association for Computational Linguistics.

Weiwei Sun and Jia Xu. 2011. Enhancing chinese word segmentation using unlabeled data. In *Proceedings of the Conference on Empirical Methods in Natural Language Processing*, pages 970–979. Association for Computational Linguistics.

Xu Sun, Yaozhong Zhang, Takuya Matsuzaki, Yoshimasa Tsuruoka, and Jun'ichi Tsujii. 2009. A discriminative latent variable chinese segmenter with hybrid word/character information. In *Proceedings of Human Language Technologies: The 2009 Annual Conference of the North American Chapter of the Association for Computational Linguistics*, pages 56–64. Association for Computational Linguistics.

Xu Sun, Houfeng Wang, and Wenjie Li. 2012. Fast online training with frequency-adaptive learning rates for chinese word segmentation and new word detection. In *Proceedings of the 50th Annual Meeting of the Association for Computational Linguistics: Long Papers-Volume 1*, pages 253–262. Association for Computational Linguistics.

Weiwei Sun. 2011. A stacked sub-word model for joint chinese word segmentation and part-of-speech tagging. In *Proceedings of the 49th Annual Meeting of the Association for Computational Linguistics: Human Language Technologies-Volume 1*, pages 1385–1394. Association for Computational Linguistics.

Huihsin Tseng, Pichuan Chang, Galen Andrew, Daniel Jurafsky, and Christopher Manning. 2005. A conditional random field word segmenter for sighan bakeoff 2005. In *Proceedings of the fourth SIGHAN workshop on Chinese language Processing*, volume 171.

Nianwen Xue. 2003. Chinese word segmentation as character tagging. *Computational Linguistics and Chinese Language Processing*, 8(1):29–48.

Yue Zhang and Stephen Clark. 2007. Chinese segmentation with a word-based perceptron algorithm. In *ANNUAL MEETING-ASSOCIATION FOR COMPUTATIONAL LINGUISTICS*, volume 45, page 840.

Longkai Zhang, Houfeng Wang, Xu Sun, and Mairgup Mansur. 2013. Exploring representations from unlabeled data with co-training for Chinese word segmentation. In *Proceedings of the 2013 Conference on Empirical Methods in Natural Language Processing*, pages 311–321, Seattle, Washington, USA, October. Association for Computational Linguistics.

If all you have is a bit of the Bible: Learning POS taggers for truly low-resource languages

Željko Agić, Dirk Hovy, and Anders Søgaard
Center for Language Technology
University of Copenhagen, Denmark
Njalsgade 140
{zeljko.agic|dirk.hovy|soegaard}@hum.ku.dk

Abstract

We present a simple method for learning part-of-speech taggers for languages like Akawaio, Aukan, or Cakchiquel – languages for which nothing but a translation of parts of the Bible exists. By aggregating over the tags from a few annotated languages and spreading them via word-alignment on the verses, we learn POS taggers for 100 languages, using the languages to bootstrap each other. We evaluate our cross-lingual models on the 25 languages where test sets exist, as well as on another 10 for which we have tag dictionaries. Our approach performs much better (20-30%) than state-of-the-art unsupervised POS taggers induced from Bible translations, and is often competitive with weakly supervised approaches that assume high-quality parallel corpora, representative monolingual corpora with perfect tokenization, and/or tag dictionaries. We make models for all 100 languages available.

1 Introduction

Most previous work in cross-lingual NLP has been limited to training and evaluating on no more than a dozen languages, typically all from the major Indo-European languages. While it has been observed repeatedly that using multiple source languages improves performance (Yarowsky et al., 2001; Yarowsky and Ngai, 2001; Fossum and Abney, 2005; McDonald et al., 2011), most available techniques work best for closely related languages.

In contrast, this paper presents an effort to learn POS taggers for truly low-resource languages, with minimum assumptions about the available language resources. Most low-resource languages are non-Indo-European, and typically, their typological and geographic neighbors have sparse resources as well. However, for a surprisingly large number of languages, translations of the Bible (or parts of it) exist. Due to the canonical nature and the verse format, these translations are viable parallel data, albeit lacking annotation. In our experiments, we use word alignments across all pairs of 100 parallel Bible translations to bootstrap annotation projections for those languages without any (even just weakly) supervised taggers. The projections provide both pseudo-annotated data as well as tag dictionaries for all languages. We use both resources to train semi-supervised POS taggers following Garrette and Baldridge (2013).

Our contribution We present a novel approach to learning POS taggers for truly low-resource languages, where only a translation of (parts of) the Bible is available. We obtain results competitive with approaches that assume the availability of larger volumes of more representative parallel corpora, perfectly tokenized monolingual corpora, and/or tag dictionaries for the target languages. Additionally, we make the POS tagging models for 100 languages publicly available and extend the mappings in Petrov et al. (2011) for six new languages (Hindi, Croatian, Icelandic, Norwegian, Persian, and Serbian). The models, mappings, as well as a complete list of all the resources used in these experiments, are available at https://bitbucket.org/lowlands/.

2 Experiments

Our approach is a combination of simple techniques. Part of the process is depicted in Figure 1, and the algorithm is presented in Algorithm 1. Assume we have n languages for which we assume the availability of m verses of the Bible. We run IBM-2[1] on all $n(n-1)$ pairs of languages. Assume also manually POS-annotated training data

[1] github.com/clab/fast_align

Proceedings of the 53rd Annual Meeting of the Association for Computational Linguistics and the 7th International Joint Conference on Natural Language Processing (Short Papers), pages 268–272,
Beijing, China, July 26-31, 2015.

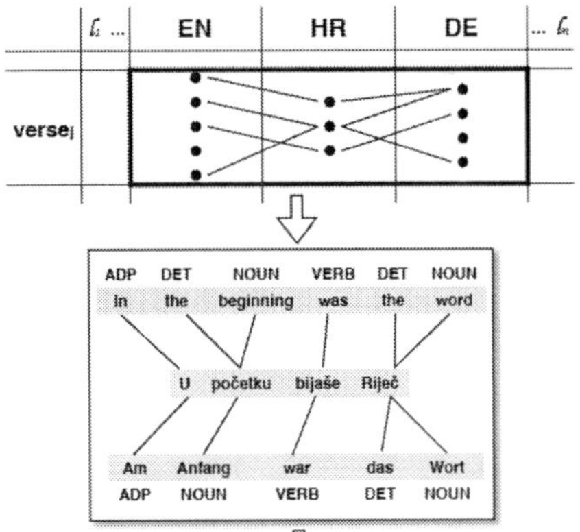

HR	EN	DE	...	voted	confidence
U	ADP	ADP	...	ADP	0.8667
početku	NOUN, DET	NOUN	...	NOUN	0.7448
bijaše	VERB	VERB	...	VERB	0.8560
Riječ	DET, NOUN	DET, NOUN	...	NOUN	0.6307

Figure 1: An illustration of our approach.

is available for the first k of these languages. We then run taggers for these languages on the corresponding translations of the Bible to predict tags for all tokens in these translations.

We can think of this partially annotated multi-parallel corpus as a tensor object. Each column is a language l_i, and each row a verse v_j (trivially sentence-aligned to the corresponding verses in the other columns). In each cell of this matrix $M(i, j, \cdot)$, we have a sequence of word tokens. For two languages, l_1 and l_2, the word tokens in $M(1, j, \cdot)$ can be aligned (by IBM-2) to multiple word tokens in $M(2, j, \cdot)$, but not all words need to be aligned.

After running supervised POS taggers on the k languages for which we have training data, we have POS-annotated the word tokens in k columns of our tensor object. We then project the POS tag of each word token w to all other word tokens aligned to w. In our experiments, $k = 17$ or 18 (if the target language is not one of the languages for which we have training data), which means each word token will potentially have many POS tags projected onto it. Note that the number of tags can exceed 18, since many-to-many word alignments are allowed.

We now use these projections to train POS taggers for the remaining $n - k$ languages. We use aggregated projected annotations as token-level supervision. We aggregate from the incoming projected POS tags by majority voting. We also use the complete set of projections onto each word type in the target language as a type-level tag dictionary. We combine the tag dictionary and the token-level projections to train discriminative, type-constrained POS taggers (Collins, 2002; Täckström et al., 2013). Below we refer to these POS taggers as using k sources (k-SRC).

These n many POS taggers can now also be used to obtain predictions for all word tokens in our tensor object. This corresponds to doing the second loop over lines 8–17 in Algorithm 1. For each of our n languages, we thus complete the tensor by projecting tags into word tokens from the $n - 1$ remaining source languages. For the k supervised languages, we project the tags produced by the supervised POS taggers rather than the tags obtained by projection. We can then train our final POS taggers for all n languages – 100, in our case – using projections from 99 languages (n-1-SRC). Note that we also train projected taggers for those languages for which we have annotated data. This is to enable us to evaluate our methodology on more languages.

Algorithm 1 Train n taggers with supervision for k

1: Let M be a tensor with $M(i, j, \cdot)$ the word-aligned token sequence in the jth verse of the Bible in language i
2: **for** $i \leq k$ **do**
3: Train TNT tagger for l_i using manually annotated data
4: **for** $j \leq m$ **do**
5: Obtain POS predictions for $M(i, j, \cdot)$
6: **end for**
7: **end for**
8: **for** $I \in \{0, 1\}$ **do**
9: **if** $i > k, I = 1$ **then**
10: Train TNT tagger for l_i using projected annotations in $M(i, \cdot, \cdot)$
11: **end if**
12: Populate $M(i, \cdot, \cdot)$ by propagating tags across alignments
13: **for** $i \leq n$ **do**
14: Use majority voting to obtain one tag per word
15: Obtain type-level tag dictionary from all the data
16: Train TNT/GAR tagger for l_i using projected annotations in $M(i, \cdot, \cdot)$ and tag dictionary
17: **end for**
18: **end for**

Data We use the 100 translations of (parts of) the Bible available as part of the Edinburgh Multilingual Parallel Bible Corpus (Christodouloupoulos and Steedman, 2014).[2] This dataset includes translations into languages such as Akawaio, Aukan or Cakchiquel. The majority of these languages are non-Indoeuropean, and 39 of them have less than one million speakers. For 54 of

[2] homepages.inf.ed.ac.uk/s0787820/bible/

			Unsupervised						Upper bounds			
			Baselines		Our Systems				Weakly Sup		Supervised	
		OOV	Brown	2HMM	TnT-k-Src	TnT-n-1-Src	Gar-k-Src	Gar-n-1-Src	Das	Li	Gar	TnT
bul	YT	31.8	54.5	71.8	**78.0**	77.7	75.7	75.7	-	-	83.1	96.9
ces	YT	44.3	51.9	66.3	71.7	**73.3**	70.9	71.4	-	-	-	98.7
dan	YT	28.6	58.6	69.6	78.6	**79.0**	73.7	73.3	83.2	83.3	78.8	96.7
deu	YT	36.8	45.3	70.0	**80.5**	80.2	77.6	77.6	82.8	85.8	87.1	98.1
eng	YT	38.0	58.2	62.6	72.4	**73.0**	72.2	72.6	-	87.1	80.8	96.7
eus	NT	64.6	46.0	41.6	**63.4**	62.8	57.3	56.9	-	-	66.9	93.7
fra	YT	26.1	42.0	76.5	76.1	76.6	78.6	**80.2**	-	-	85.5	95.1
ell	YT	63.7	43.0	49.8	51.9	52.3	57.9	**59.0**	82.5	79.2	64.4	-
hin	Y	36.1	59.5	69.2	**70.9**	67.6	70.8	71.5	-	-	-	-
hrv	Y	34.7	52.8	65.6	**67.8**	67.1	67.2	66.7	-	-	-	-
hun	YT	41.2	45.9	57.4	70.0	70.4	71.3	**72.0**	-	-	77.9	95.6
isl	Y	19.7	42.6	65.9	**70.6**	69.0	68.7	68.3	-	-	-	-
ind	YT	29.4	52.6	73.1	76.6	**76.8**	74.9	76.0	-	-	87.1	95.1
ita	YT	24.0	45.1	78.3	76.5	76.9	78.5	**79.2**	86.8	86.5	83.5	95.8
plt	Y	35.0	48.9	44.3	56.4	56.6	62.0	**64.6**	-	-	-	-
mar	Y	33.0	**55.8**	45.8	52.0	52.9	52.8	52.3	-	-	-	-
nor	YT	27.5	56.1	73.0	**77.0**	76.7	75.4	76.0	-	-	84.3	97.7
pes	Y	33.6	57.9	**61.5**	59.3	59.6	59.1	60.8	-	-	-	-
pol	YT	36.4	52.2	68.7	**75.6**	75.1	70.8	74.0	-	-	-	95.7
por	YT	27.9	54.5	74.3	82.9	**83.8**	81.1	82.0	87.9	84.5	87.3	96.8
slv	Y	15.8	42.1	78.1	79.5	**80.5**	68.7	70.1	-	-	-	-
spa	YT	21.9	52.6	47.3	81.1	81.4	**82.6**	**82.6**	84.2	86.4	88.7	96.2
srp	Y	41.7	59.3	47.3	**69.6**	69.2	67.9	67.2	-	-	-	94.7
swe	YT	31.5	58.5	68.4	74.7	**75.2**	71.4	71.9	80.5	86.1	76.1	94.7
tur	YT	41.6	53.7	46.8	60.5	**61.3**	56.5	57.9	-	-	72.2	89.1
average		≤ 50	52.2	64.4	72.1	72.2	70.8	71.5				

Table 1: Results on 25 test languages. Y=entire Bible available. N=only New Testament available. T=manually annotated data available for training (but not used to obtain results for the language itself). Unsupervised baselines are evaluated using optimal 1:1 mappings.

these languages, we have a translation of the entire Bible. For 42, we only have the New Testament, and for the remaining four we only have parts of the New Testament. We note that Bible translations typically have fewer POS-unambiguous words than newswire (Christodouloupoulos and Steedman, 2014). We also note that in rare cases sentences span multiple verses, which means, we sometimes train POS taggers on partial sentences. See Christodouloupoulos and Steedman (2014) for further discussion of the resource. Most of the manually annotated resources were obtained from the CoNLL 2006-2007 releases of various treebanks, the NLTK corpora, the HamleDT resources, and the Universal Dependencies project. We provide a complete overview of the resources at `https://bitbucket.org/lowlands/`

ModelsWe train TnT POS taggers (Brants, 2000) using only token-level projections. We also train semi-supervised POS taggers using the approach in Garrette and Baldridge (2013) (Gar), using both projections and dictionaries, as well as the unlabelled Bible translations.[3] We use the English data as development data. We train TnT and Gar using k or $n-1$ source languages, leading to four taggers in total.

Baselines Our baselines are two standard unsupervised POS induction algorithms: Brown clustering using the implementation by Percy Liang[4] and second-order unsupervised HMMs using logistic regression for emission probabilities (Berg-Kirkpatrick et al., 2010; Li et al., 2012), with and without our Bible tag dictionaries.[5]

Upper bounds The weakly supervised system in Das and Petrov (2011) (Das) relies on larger volumes of more representative and perfectly tokenized parallel data than we assume, as well as a representative sample of unlabeled data. Such data is simply not available for many of the languages considered here. The weakly supervised system in Li et al. (2012) (Li) also relies on crowd-sourced type-level tag dictionaries, not available for most of the languages of concern to us. We present their reported results. Finally, we train the two base POS taggers (Gar and TnT) on the manually annotated data available for 17 of our languages, to be able to compare against state-of-the-art performance of supervised POS taggers.

[3] `github.com/dhgarrette/low-resource-pos-tagging-2014/`

[4] `github.com/percyliang/brown-cluster`

[5] `code.google.com/p/wikily-supervised-pos-tagger/`

Results Our results on the 25 test languages are consistently better than the unsupervised baselines, with the exceptions of Marathi and Persian, and by a very large margin. Our average performance across the languages with OOV rates smaller than 50% is above 70%. While previous papers on weakly supervised POS tagging (e.g., DAS and LI) have presented slightly better results for the small set of Indo-European languages in the CoNLL 2006–7 shared tasks, we emphasize again that our set-up requires fewer resources and does *not* rely on perfectly tokenized training data. Our parallel data also suffers from a severe, but more realistic domain bias. Note that doing the second round of projections (n-1-SRC) often improves performance by about a percentage point, but this improvement is not consistent across languages. We observe that most errors are due to our systems predicting too many nouns. Note that for the two languages with underlined OOV rates ($\geq$ 50), performance is very low. This is due to differences in orthography and tokenization. We leave out those results in the averages, but leave them in the results table.

To evaluate on more low-resource languages, we also extracted tag dictionaries from Wiktionary for another 10 languages, from Afrikaans to Swahili. Figure 2 presents the type-level in-vocabulary tag errors of the projected tags in the Bible. This figure is similar to the ones used in Li et al. (2012). We also computed token-level accuracies, where every tag assignment licensed by Wiktionary counts as correct. For three languages, results were 80-90%: Afrikaans, Lithuanian, and Russian. For another three languages, results were 50-70%: Hebrew, Romanian, and Swahili. Results were 35-50% for the remaining four languages: Latin, Maori, Albanian, and Ewe.

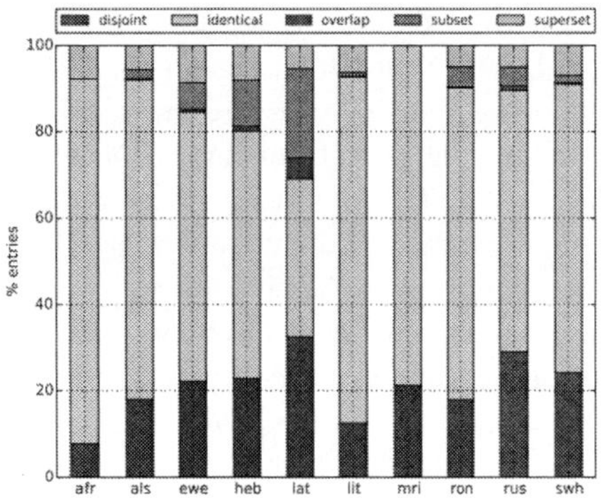

Figure 2: Type-level in-vocabulary tag errors as the percentage of word types assigned a set of tags that is disjoint, identical to, overlaps, is a subset, or is a superset of the Wiktionary tags.

3 Related work

The Bible has been used as a resource for machine translation and multi-lingual information retrieval before, e.g., (Chew et al., 2006). It has also been used in cross-lingual POS tagging (Yarowsky et al., 2001; Fossum and Abney, 2005), NP-chunking (Yarowsky et al., 2001; Yarowsky and Ngai, 2001) and cross-lingual dependency parsing (Sukhareva and Chiarcos, 2014) before. Yarowsky et al. (2001) and Fossum and Abney (2005) use word-aligned parallel translations of the Bible to project the predictions of POS taggers for several language pairs, including English, German, and Spanish to Czech and French. The resulting annotated target language corpora enable them to train POS taggers for these languages. Yarowsky and Ngai (2001) showed similar results using just the Hansards corpus on English to French and Chinese. Our work is inspired by these approaches, yet broader in scope on both the source and target side.

Das and Petrov (2011) use word-aligned text to automatically create type-level tag dictionaries. Earlier work on building tag dictionaries from word-aligned text includes Probst (2003). Their tag dictionaries contain target language trigrams to be able to disambiguate ambiguous target language words. To handle the noise in the automatically obtained dictionaries, they use label propagation on a similarity graph to smooth and expand the label distributions. Our approach is similar to theirs in using projections to obtain type-level tag dictionaries, but we keep the token supervision and type supervision apart and end up with a model more similar to that of Täckström et al. (2013), who combine word-aligned text with crowdsourced type-level tag dictionaries. Täckström et al. (2013) constrain Viterbi search via type-level tag dictionaries, pruning all tags not licensed by the dictionary. For the remaining tags, they use high-confidence word alignments to further prune the Viterbi search. We follow Täckström et al. (2013) in using our automatically created, *not* crowdsourced, tag dictionaries to prune tags during search, but we use word alignments to obtain token-level annotations that we use as annotated training data, similar to Fossum and Abney (2005), Yarowsky et al. (2001), and Yarowsky and Ngai (2001).

Duong et al. (2013) use word-alignment probabilities to select training data for their cross-lingual POS models. They consider a simple single-source training set-up. We also tried ranking projected training data by confidence, using an ensemble of projections from 17–99 source languages and majority voting to obtain probabilities for the token-level target-language projections, but this did not lead to improvements on the English development data.

4 Conclusions

We present a novel approach to learning POS taggers, assuming only that parts of the Bible are available for the target language. Our approach combines annotation projection, bootstrapping, and label propagation to learn POS taggers that perform significantly better than unsupervised baselines, and often competitive to state-of-the-art weakly supervised POS taggers that assume more and better resources are available.

Acknowledgements

This research is funded by the ERC Starting Grant LOWLANDS No. 313695.

References

Taylor Berg-Kirkpatrick, Alexandre Bouchard-Cote, John DeNero, , and Dan Klein. 2010. Painless unsupervised learning with features. In *Proceedings of NAACL*.

Thorsten Brants. 2000. Tnt: a statistical part-of-speech tagger. In *ANLP*.

Peter Chew, Steve Verzi, Travis Bauer, and Jonathan McClain. 2006. Evaluation of the bible as a resource for cross-language information retrieval. In *ACL Workshop on n Multilingual Language Resources and Interoperability*.

Cristos Christodouloupoulos and Mark Steedman. 2014. A massively parallel corpus: the bible in 100 languages. *Language Resources and Evaluation*.

Michael Collins. 2002. Discriminative Training Methods for Hidden Markov Models: Theory and Experiments with Perceptron Algorithms. In *EMNLP*.

Dipanjan Das and Slav Petrov. 2011. Unsupervised part-of-speech tagging with bilingual graph-based projections. In *ACL*.

Long Duong, Paul Cook, Steven Bird, and Pavel Pecina. 2013. Simpler unsupervised pos tagging with bilingual projections. In *Proceedings of ACL*.

Victoria Fossum and Steven Abney. 2005. Automatically inducing a part-of-speech tagger by projecting from multiple source languages across aligned corpora. In *IJCNLP*.

Dan Garrette and Jason Baldridge. 2013. Learning a part-of-speech tagger from two hours of annotation. In *NAACL*.

Shen Li, João Graça, and Ben Taskar. 2012. Wiki-ly supervised part-of-speech tagging. In *EMNLP*.

Ryan McDonald, Slav Petrov, and Keith Hall. 2011. Multi-source transfer of delexicalized dependency parsers. In *EMNLP*.

Slav Petrov, Dipanjan Das, and Ryan McDonald. 2011. A universal part-of-speech tagset. CoRR abs/1104.2086.

Katharina Probst. 2003. Using 'smart' bilingual projection to feature-tag a monolingual dictionary. In *CoNLL*.

Maria Sukhareva and Christian Chiarcos. 2014. Diachronic proximity vs. data sparsity in cross-lingual parser projection. In *COLING Workshop on Applying NLP Tools to Similar Languages, Varieties and Dialects*.

Oscar Täckström, Dipanjan Das, Slav Petrov, Ryan McDonald, and Joakim Nivre. 2013. Token and type constraints for cross-lingual part-of-speech tagging. *TACL*, 1:1–12.

David Yarowsky and Grace Ngai. 2001. Inducing multilingual pos taggers and np brackets via robust projection across aligned corpora. In *Proceedings of NAACL*.

David Yarowsky, Grace Ngai, and Richard Wicentowski. 2001. Inducing multilingual text analysis tools via robust projection across aligned corpora. In *Proceedings of the first international conference on Human language technology research*.

Improving distant supervision using inference learning

Roland Roller[1], **Eneko Agirre**[2], **Aitor Soroa**[2] and **Mark Stevenson**[1]
[1] Department of Computer Science, University of Sheffield
roland.roller,mark.stevenson@sheffield.ac.uk
[2] IXA NLP group, University of the Basque Country
e.agirre,a.soroa@ehu.eus

Abstract

Distant supervision is a widely applied approach to automatic training of relation extraction systems and has the advantage that it can generate large amounts of labelled data with minimal effort. However, this data may contain errors and consequently systems trained using distant supervision tend not to perform as well as those based on manually labelled data. This work proposes a novel method for detecting potential false negative training examples using a knowledge inference method. Results show that our approach improves the performance of relation extraction systems trained using distantly supervised data.

1 Introduction

Distantly supervised relation extraction relies on automatically labelled data generated using information from a knowledge base. A sentence is annotated as a positive example if it contains a pair of entities that are related in the knowledge base. Negative training data is often generated using a closed world assumption: pairs of entities not listed in the knowledge base are assumed to be unrelated and sentences containing them considered to be negative training examples. However this assumption is violated when the knowledge base is incomplete which can lead to sentences containing instances of relations being wrongly annotated as negative examples.

We propose a method to improve the quality of distantly supervised data by identifying possible wrongly annotated negative instances. Our proposed method includes a version of the Path Ranking Algorithm (PRA) (Lao and Cohen, 2010; Lao et al., 2011) which infers relation paths by combining random walks though a knowledge base. We use this knowledge inference to detect possible false negatives (or at least entity pairs closely connected to a target relation) in automatically labelled training data and show that their removal can improve relation extraction performance.

2 Related Work

Distant supervision is widely used to train relation extraction systems with Freebase and Wikipedia commonly being used as knowledge bases, e.g. (Mintz et al., 2009; Riedel et al., 2010; Krause et al., 2012; Zhang et al., 2013; Min et al., 2013; Ritter et al., 2013). The main advantage is its ability to automatically generate large amounts of training data automatically. On the other hand, this automatically labelled data is noisy and usually generates lower performance than approaches trained using manually labelled data. A range of filtering approaches have been applied to address this problem including multi-class SVM (Nguyen and Moschitti, 2011) and Multi-Instance learning methods (Riedel et al., 2010; Surdeanu et al., 2012). These approaches take into account the fact that entities might occur in different relations at the same time and may not necessarily express the target relation. Other approaches focus directly on the noise in the data. For instance Takamatsu et al. (2012) use a generative model to predict incorrect data while Intxaurrondo et al. (2013) use a range of heuristics including PMI to remove noise. Augenstein et al. (2014) apply techniques to detect highly ambiguous entity pairs and discard them from their labelled training set.

This work proposes a novel approach to the problem by applying an inference learning method to identify potential false negatives in distantly labelled data. Our method makes use of a modified version of PRA to learn relation paths from a knowledge base and uses this information to identify false negatives.

Proceedings of the 53rd Annual Meeting of the Association for Computational Linguistics and the 7th International Joint Conference on Natural Language Processing (Short Papers), pages 273–278,
Beijing, China, July 26-31, 2015.

3 Data and Methods

We chose to apply our approach to relation extraction tasks from the biomedical domain since this has proved to be an important problem within these documents (Jensen et al., 2006; Hahn et al., 2012; Cohen and Hunter, 2013; Roller and Stevenson, 2014). In addition, the first application of distant supervision was to biomedical journal articles (Craven and Kumlien, 1999). In addition, the most widely used knowledge source in this domain, the UMLS Metathesaurus (Bodenreider, 2004), is an ideal resource to apply inference learning given its rich structure.

We develop classifiers to identify relations found in two subsets of UMLS: the National Drug File-Reference Terminology (ND-FRT) and the National Cancer Institute Thesaurus (NCI). A corpus of approximately 1,000,000 publications is used to create the distantly supervised training data. The corpus contains abstracts published between 1990 and 2001 annotated with UMLS concepts using MetaMap (Aronson and Lang, 2010).

3.1 Distantly labelled data

Distant supervision is carried out for a target UMLS relation by identifying instance pairs and using them to create a set of positive instance pairs. Any pairs which also occur as an instance pair of another UMLS relation are removed from this set. A set of negative instance pairs is then created by forming new combinations that do not occur within the positive instance pairs. Sentences containing a positive or negative instance pair are then extracted to generate positive and negative training examples for the relation. These candidate sentences are then stemmed (Porter, 1997) and PoS tagged (Charniak and Johnson, 2005).

The sets of positive and negative training examples are then filtered to remove sentences that meet any of the following criteria: contain the same positive pair more than once; contain both a positive and negative pair; more than 5 words between the two elements of the instance pair; contain very common instance pairs.

3.2 PRA-Reduction

PRA (Lao and Cohen, 2010; Lao et al., 2011) is an algorithm that infers new relation instances from knowledge bases. By considering a knowledge base as a graph, where nodes are connected through typed relations, it performs random walks over it and finds bounded-length relation paths that connect graph nodes. These paths are used as features in a logistic regression model, which is meant to predict new relations in the graph. Although initially conceived as an algorithm to discover new links in the knowledge base, PRA can also be used to learn relevant relation paths for any given relation. For instance, if x and y are related via *sibling* relation, the model trained by PRA would learn that the relation path *parent(x,a)* $\wedge$ *_parent(a,y)*[1] is highly relevant, as siblings share the same parents.

Knowledge graphs were extracted from the ND-FRT and NCI vocabularies generating approximately $200,000$ related instance pairs for ND-FRT and $400,000$ for NCI. PRA is then run on both graphs in order to learn paths for each target relation. Table 1 shows examples of the paths PRA generated for the relation *biological-process-involves-gene-product* together with their weights. We only make use of relation paths with positive weights generated by PRA.

path	weight
gene-encodes-gene-product(x,a) $\wedge$ _gene-plays-role-in-process(a,y)	10.53
_isa(x,a) $\wedge$ biological-process-involves-gene-product(a,y)	6.17
isa(x,a) $\wedge$ biological-process-involves-gene-product(a,y)	2.80
gene-encodes-gene-product(x,a) $\wedge$ _gene-plays-role-in-process(a,b) $\wedge$ isa(b,y)	-0.06

Table 1: Example PRA-induced paths and weights for the NCI relation *biological-process-involves-gene-product*.

The paths induced by PRA are used to identify potential false negatives in the negative training examples (Section 3.1). Each negative training example is examined to check whether the entity pair is related in UMLS by following any of the relation paths extracted by PRA for the relevant target relation. Examples containing related entity pairs are assumed to be false negatives, since the relation can be inferred from the knowledge base, and removed from the set of negatives training examples. For instance, using the path in the top row of Table 1, sentences containing the entities x and y would be removed if the path *gene-encodes-gene-product*(x,a) $\wedge$ *_gene-plays-role-in-process*(a,y) could be identified within UMLS.

[1]An underline ('_') prefix represents the inverse of a relation while $\wedge$ represents path composition.

3.3 Evaluation

Relation Extraction system: The MultiR system (Hoffmann et al., 2010) with features described by Surdeanu et al. (2011) was used for the experiments.

Datasets: Three datasets were created to train MultiR and evaluate performance. The first (**Unfiltered**) uses the data obtained using distant supervision (Section 3.1) without removing any examples identified by PRA. The overall ratio of positive to negative sentences in this dataset was 1:5.1. However, this changes to 1:2.3 after removing examples identified by PRA. Consequently the bias in the distantly supervised data was adjusted to 1:2 to increase comparability across configurations. Reducing bias was also found to increase relation extraction performance, producing a strong baseline. The **PRA-reduced** dataset is created by applying PRA reduction (Section 3.2) to the *Unfiltered* dataset to remove a portion of the negative training examples. Removing these examples produces a dataset that is smaller than *Unfiltered* and with a different bias. Changing the bias of the training data can influence the classification results. Consequently the **Random-reduced** dataset was created by removing randomly selected negative examples from *Unfiltered* to produce a dataset with the same size and bias as *PRA-reduced*. The *Random-reduced* dataset is used to show that randomly removing negative instances leads to lower results than removing those suggested by PRA.

Evaluation: Two approaches were used to evaluate performance.

The **Held-out** datasets consist of the *Unfiltered*, *PRA-reduced* and *Random-reduced* data sets. The set of entity pairs obtained from the knowledge base is split into four parts and a process similar to 4-fold cross validation applied. In each fold the automatically labelled sentences obtained from the pairs in 3 of the quarters are used as training data and sentences obtained from the remaining quarter used for testing.

The **Manually labelled** dataset contains 400 examples of the relation *may-prevent* and 400 of *may-treat* which were manually labelled by two annotators who were medical experts. Both relations are taken from the ND-FRT subset of UMLS. Each annotator was asked to label every sentence and then re-examine cases where there was disagreement. This process lead to inter-annotator agreement of 95.5% for *may-treat* and 97.3% for *may-prevent*. The annotated data set is publicly available[2]. Any sentences in the training data containing an entity pair that occurs within the manually labelled dataset are removed. Although this dataset is smaller than the held-out dataset, its annotations are more reliable and it is therefore likely to be a more accurate indicator of performance accuracy. This dataset is more balanced than the held-out data with a ratio of 1:1.3 for *may-treat* and 1:1.8 for *may-prevent*.

Evaluation metric: Our experiments use entity level evaluation since this is the most appropriate approach to determine suitability for database population. Precision and recall are computed based on the proportion of entity pairs identified. For the held-out data the set of correct entity pairs are those which occur in sentences labeled as positive examples of the relation and which are also listed as being related in UMLS. For the manually labelled data it is simply the set of entity pairs that occur in positive examples of the relation.

4 Results

4.1 Held-out data

Table 2 shows the results obtained using the held-out data. Overall results, averaged across all relations with maximum recall, are shown in the top portion of the table and indicate that applying PRA improves performance. Although the highest precision is obtained using the *Unfiltered* classifier, the *PRA-reduced* classifier leads to the best recall and F1. Performance of the *Random-reduced* classifier indicates that the improvement is not simply due to a change in the bias in the data but that the examples it contains lead to an improved model.

The lower part of Table 2 shows results for each relation. The *PRA-reduced* classifier produces the best results for the majority of relations and always increases recall compared to *Unfiltered*.

It is perhaps surprising that removing false negatives from the training data leads to an increase in recall, rather than precision. False negatives cause the classifier to generate an overly restrictive model of the relation and to predict positive examples of a relation as negative. Removing them leads to a less constrained model and higher recall.

There are two relations where there is also an increase in precision (*contraindicating-class-of* and *mechanism-of-action-of*) and these are also the ones for which the fewest training examples are

[2] https://sites.google.com/site/umlscorpus/home

	Unfiltered			Random-reduced			PRA-reduced		
	Prec.	Rec.	F1	Prec.	Rec.	F1	Prec.	Rec.	F1
Overall	62.30	51.82	56.58	44.49	74.26	55.64	56.85	77.10	**65.44**
	NCI relations								
biological_process_involves_gene_product	89.61	43.18	57.86	65.67	78.79	71.38	70.63	84.85	**76.97**
disease_has_normal_cell_origin	60.20	83.86	**69.95**	43.2	95.21	58.85	42.80	91.88	57.91
gene_product_has_associated_anatomy	41.65	64.04	**49.96**	29.22	74.63	41.81	37.94	65.28	47.82
gene_product_has_biochemical_function	86.43	72.00	78.33	60.66	91.57	72.90	70.58	95.80	**81.17**
process_involves_gene	78.92	50.71	61.54	51.38	80.64	62.73	68.16	87.34	**76.47**
	ND-FRT relations								
contraindicating_class_of	40.00	20.83	26.14	28.48	72.50	39.58	41.30	82.50	**54.33**
may_prevent	27.48	14.69	18.87	20.61	44.79	27.94	38.11	35.63	**36.64**
may_treat	48.66	39.63	43.14	39.57	50.00	43.84	50.88	57.93	**54.11**
mechanism_of_action_of	47.15	40.63	43.12	40.25	59.38	47.62	52.85	59.38	**55.82**

Table 2: Evaluation using held-out data

	Unfiltered			Random-reduced			PRA-reduced		
relation	Prec.	Rec.	F1	Prec.	Rec.	F1	Prec.	Rec.	F1
may_prevent	54.17	21.67	30.95	53.57	25.00	34.09	39.66	38.33	**38.98**
may_treat	40.00	47.48	43.42	43.21	50.36	46.51	41.05	67.63	**51.09**

Table 3: Evaluation using manually labelled data

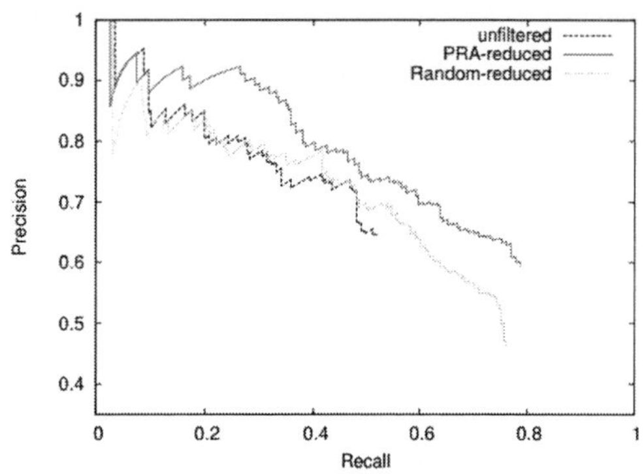

Figure 1: Precision/Recall Curve for Held-out data

available. The classifier has access to such a limited amount of data for these relations that removing the false negatives identified by PRA allows it to learn a more accurate model.

Figure 1 presents a precision/recall curve computed using MultiR's output probabilities. Results for the *PRA-reduced* and the *Random-reduced* classifiers show that reducing the amount of negative training data increases recall. However, using *PRA-reduced* generally leads to higher precision, indicating that PRA is able to identify suitable instances for removal from the training set. The *Unfiltered* classifier produces good results but precision and recall are lower than *PRA-reduced*.

4.2 Manually labelled

Table 3 shows results of evaluation on the more reliable manually labelled data set. The best overall performance is once again obtained using the *PRA-reduced* classifier. There is an increase in recall for both relations and a slight increase in precision for *may_treat*. Performance of the *Random-reduced* classifier also improves due to an increasing recall but remains below *PRA-reduced*. Performance of the *Random-reduced* classifier is also better than *Unfiltered*, with the overall improvement largely resulting from increased recall, but below *PRA-reduced*. These results confirm that removing examples identified by PRA improves the quality of training data.

Further analysis indicated that the *PRA-reduced* classifier produces the fewest false negatives in its predictions on the manually annotated dataset. It incorrectly labels 82 entity pairs (45 *may-treat*, 37 *may-prevent*) as negative while *Unfiltered* predicts 120 (73, 47) and *Random-reduced* 114 (69, 45). This supports our initial hypothesis that removing potential false negatives from training data improves classifier predictions.

5 Conclusions and Future Work

This paper proposes a novel approach to identifying incorrectly labelled instances generated using distant supervision. Our method applies an inference learning method to detect and discard possible false negatives from the training data. We show that our method improves performance for a range of relations in the biomedical domain by making use of information from UMLS.

In future we would like to explore alternative

methods for selecting PRA relation paths to identify false negatives. Furthermore we would like to examine the PRA-reduced data in more detail. We would like to find which kind of entity pairs are detected by our proposed method and whether the reduced data can also be used to extend the positive training data. We would also like to apply the approach to other domains and alternative knowledge bases. Finally it would be interesting to compare our approach to other state of the art relation extraction systems for distant supervision or biased-SVM approaches such as Liu et al. (2003).

Acknowledgements

The authors are grateful to the Engineering and Physical Sciences Research Council for supporting the work described in this paper (EP/J008427/1).

References

A. Aronson and F. Lang. 2010. An overview of MetaMap: historical perspective and recent advances. *Journal of the American Medical Association*, 17(3):229–236.

Isabelle Augenstein, Diana Maynard, and Fabio Ciravegna. 2014. Relation extraction from the web using distant supervision. In *Proceedings of the 19th International Conference on Knowledge Engineering and Knowledge Management (EKAW 2014)*, Linköping, Sweden, November.

Olivier Bodenreider. 2004. The unified medical language system (umls): integrating biomedical terminology. *Nucleic acids research*, 32(suppl 1):D267–D270.

Eugene Charniak and Mark Johnson. 2005. Coarse-to-fine n-best parsing and maxent discriminative reranking. In *Proceedings of the 43rd Annual Meeting on Association for Computational Linguistics*, ACL '05, pages 173–180, Stroudsburg, PA, USA. Association for Computational Linguistics.

K Bretonnel Cohen and Lawrence E Hunter. 2013. Text mining for translational bioinformatics. *PLoS computational biology*, 9(4):e1003044.

Mark Craven and Johan Kumlien. 1999. Constructing biological knowledge bases by extracting information from text sources. In *In Proceedings of the Seventh International Conference on Intelligent Systems for Molecular Biology (ISMB)*, pages 77–86. AAAI Press.

Udo Hahn, K Bretonnel Cohen, Yael Garten, and Nigam H Shah. 2012. Mining the pharmacogenomics literaturea survey of the state of the art. *Briefings in bioinformatics*, 13(4):460–494.

Raphael Hoffmann, Congle Zhang, and Daniel S. Weld. 2010. Learning 5000 relational extractors. In *Proceedings of the 48th Annual Meeting of the Association for Computational Linguistics*, ACL '10, pages 286–295, Stroudsburg, PA, USA. Association for Computational Linguistics.

Ander Intxaurrondo, Mihai Surdeanu, Oier Lopez de Lacalle, and Eneko Agirre. 2013. Removing noisy mentions for distant supervision. *Procesamiento del Lenguaje Natural*, 51:41–48.

Lars Juhl Jensen, Jasmin Saric, and Peer Bork. 2006. Literature mining for the biologist: from information retrieval to biological discovery. *Nature reviews genetics*, 7(2):119–129.

Sebastian Krause, Hong Li, Hans Uszkoreit, and Feiyu Xu. 2012. Large-scale learning of relation-extraction rules with distant supervision from the web. In *Proceedings of the 11th International Conference on The Semantic Web - Volume Part I*, ISWC'12, pages 263–278, Berlin, Heidelberg. Springer-Verlag.

Ni Lao and William W. Cohen. 2010. Relational retrieval using a combination of path-constrained random walks. *Mach. Learn.*, 81(1):53–67, October.

Ni Lao, Tom Mitchell, and William W. Cohen. 2011. Random walk inference and learning in a large scale knowledge base. In *Proceedings of the 2011 Conference on Empirical Methods in Natural Language Processing*, pages 529–539, Edinburgh, Scotland, UK., July. Association for Computational Linguistics.

Bing Liu, Yang Dai, Xiaoli Li, Wee Sun Lee, and Philip S. Yu. 2003. Building text classifiers using positive and unlabeled examples. In *Intl. Conf. on Data Mining*, pages 179–188.

Bonan Min, Ralph Grishman, Li Wan, Chang Wang, and David Gondek. 2013. Distant supervision for relation extraction with an incomplete knowledge base. In *Proceedings of the 2013 Conference of the North American Chapter of the Association for Computational Linguistics: Human Language Technologies*, pages 777–782, Atlanta, Georgia, June. Association for Computational Linguistics.

Mike Mintz, Steven Bills, Rion Snow, and Dan Jurafsky. 2009. Distant supervision for relation extraction without labeled data. In *Proceedings of the Joint Conference of the 47th Annual Meeting of the ACL and the 4th International Joint Conference on Natural Language Processing of the AFNLP: Volume 2 - Volume 2*, ACL '09, pages 1003–1011, Stroudsburg, PA, USA. Association for Computational Linguistics.

Truc-Vien T. Nguyen and Alessandro Moschitti. 2011. End-to-end relation extraction using distant supervision from external semantic repositories. In *Proceedings of the 49th Annual Meeting of the Association for Computational Linguistics: Human Language Technologies: short papers - Volume 2*, HLT

'11, pages 277–282, Stroudsburg, PA, USA. Association for Computational Linguistics.

M. F. Porter. 1997. Readings in information retrieval. chapter An Algorithm for Suffix Stripping, pages 313–316. Morgan Kaufmann Publishers Inc., San Francisco, CA, USA.

Sebastian Riedel, Limin Yao, and Andrew McCallum. 2010. Modeling relations and their mentions without labeled text. In *Proceedings of the European Conference on Machine Learning and Knowledge Discovery in Databases (ECML PKDD '10)*.

Alan Ritter, Luke Zettlemoyer, Oren Etzioni, et al. 2013. Modeling missing data in distant supervision for information extraction. *Transactions of the Association for Computational Linguistics*, 1:367–378.

Roland Roller and Mark Stevenson. 2014. Self-supervised relation extraction using umls. In *Proceedings of the Conference and Labs of the Evaluation Forum 2014*, Sheffield, England.

Mihai Surdeanu, David McClosky, Mason Smith, Andrey Gusev, and Christopher Manning. 2011. Customizing an information extraction system to a new domain. In *Proceedings of the ACL 2011 Workshop on Relational Models of Semantics*, pages 2–10, Portland, Oregon, USA, June. Association for Computational Linguistics.

Mihai Surdeanu, Julie Tibshirani, Ramesh Nallapati, and Christopher D. Manning. 2012. Multi-instance multi-label learning for relation extraction. In *Proceedings of the 2012 Joint Conference on Empirical Methods in Natural Language Processing and Computational Natural Language Learning*, EMNLP-CoNLL '12, pages 455–465, Stroudsburg, PA, USA. Association for Computational Linguistics.

Shingo Takamatsu, Issei Sato, and Hiroshi Nakagawa. 2012. Reducing wrong labels in distant supervision for relation extraction. In *Proceedings of the 50th Annual Meeting of the Association for Computational Linguistics: Long Papers - Volume 1*, ACL '12, pages 721–729, Stroudsburg, PA, USA. Association for Computational Linguistics.

Xingxing Zhang, Jianwen Zhang, Junyu Zeng, Jun Yan, Zheng Chen, and Zhifang Sui. 2013. Towards accurate distant supervision for relational facts extraction. In *Proceedings of the 51st Annual Meeting of the Association for Computational Linguistics (Volume 2: Short Papers)*, pages 810–815, Sofia, Bulgaria, August. Association for Computational Linguistics.

A Lexicalized Tree Kernel for Open Information Extraction

Ying Xu†, Christoph Ringlstetter‡, Mi-Young Kim†, Randy Goebel†,
Grzegorz Kondrak†, Yusuke Miyao§
†Department of Computing Science, University of Alberta
‡Gini, Muenchen
§National Institute of Informatics / JST, PRESTO
†{yx2,miyoung2,rgoebel,gkondrak}@ualberta.ca
‡c.ringlstetter@gini.net
§yusuke@nii.ac.jp

Abstract

In contrast with traditional relation extraction, which only considers a fixed set of relations, Open Information Extraction (Open IE) aims at extracting all types of relations from text. Because of data sparseness, Open IE systems typically ignore lexical information, and instead employ parse trees and Part-of-Speech (POS) tags. However, the same syntactic structure may correspond to different relations. In this paper, we propose to use a lexicalized tree kernel based on the word embeddings created by a neural network model. We show that the lexicalized tree kernel model surpasses the unlexicalized model. Experiments on three datasets indicate that our Open IE system performs better on the task of relation extraction than the state-of-the-art Open IE systems of Xu et al. (2013) and Mesquita et al. (2013).

1 Introduction

Relation Extraction (RE) is the task of recognizing relationships between entities mentioned in text. In contrast with traditional relation extraction, for which a target set of relations is fixed a priori, Open Information Extraction (Open IE) is a generalization of RE that attempts to extract all relations (Banko et al., 2007). Although Open IE models that extract N-ary relations have been proposed, here we concentrate on binary relations.

Most Open IE systems employ syntactic information such as parse trees and part of speech (POS) tags, but ignore lexical information. However, previous work suggests that Open IE would benefit from lexical information because the same syntactic structure may correspond to different relations. For instance, the relation <Annacone, coach of, Federer> is correct for the sentence "Federer hired Annacone as a coach", but not for the sentence "Federer considered Annacone as a coach," even though they have the same dependency path structure (Mausam et al., 2012). Lexical information is required to distinguish the two cases.

Here we propose a lexicalized tree kernel model that combines both syntactic and lexical information. In order to avoid lexical sparsity issues, we investigate two smoothing methods that use word vector representations: Brown clustering (Brown et al., 1992) and word embeddings created by a neural network model (Collobert and Weston, 2008). To our knowledge, we are the first to apply word embeddings and to use lexicalized tree kernel models for Open IE.

Experiments on three datasets demonstrate that our Open IE system achieves absolute improvements in F-measure of up to 16% over the current state-of-the-art systems of Xu et al. (2013) and Mesquita et al. (2013). In addition, we examine alternative approaches for including lexical information, and find that excluding named entities from the lexical information results in an improved F-score.

2 System Architecture

The goal of the Open IE task is to extract from text a set of triples $\{< E_1, R, E_2 >\}$, where E_1 and E_2 are two named entities, and R is a textual fragment that indicates the semantic relation between the two entities. We concentrate on binary, single-word relations between named entities. The candidate relation words are extracted from dependency structures, and then filtered by a supervised tree kernel model.

Our system consists of three modules: entity extraction, relation candidate extraction, and tree

Proceedings of the 53rd Annual Meeting of the Association for Computational Linguistics and the 7th International Joint Conference on Natural Language Processing (Short Papers), pages 279–284,
Beijing, China, July 26-31, 2015.

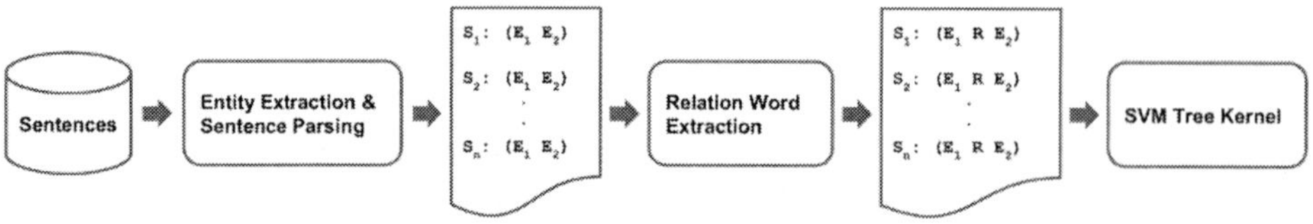

Figure 1: Our Open IE system structure.

kernel filtering. The system structure is outlined in Figure 1. We identify named entities, parse sentences, and convert constituency trees into dependency structures using the Stanford tools (Manning et al., 2014). Entities within a fixed token distance (set to 20 according to development results) are extracted as pairs $\{< E_1, E_2 >\}$. We then identify relation candidates R for each entity pair in a sentence, using dependency paths. Finally, the candidate triples $\{< E_1, R, E_2 >\}$ are paired with their corresponding tree structures, and provided as input to the SVM tree kernel. Our Open IE system outputs the triples that are classified as positive. In the following sections, we describe the components of the system in more detail.

3 Relation Candidates

Relation candidates are words that may represent a relation between two entities. We consider only lemmatized nouns, verbs and adjectives that are within two dependency links from either of the entities. Following Wu and Weld (2010) and Mausam et al. (2012), we use dependency patterns rather than POS patterns, which allows us to identify relation candidates which are farther away from entities in terms of token distance.

We extract the first two content words along the dependency path between E_1 and E_2. In the following example, the path is $E_1 \rightarrow$ encounter $\rightarrow$ build $\rightarrow E_2$, and the two relation word candidates between "Mr. Wathen" and "Plant Security Service" are *encounter* and *build*, of which the latter is the correct one.

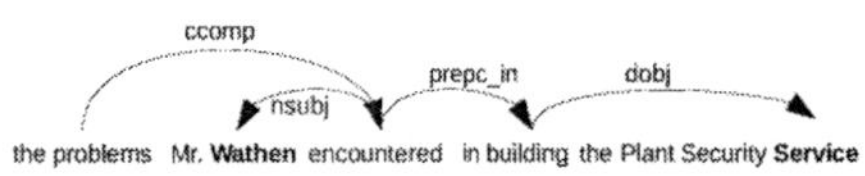

If there are no content words on the dependency path between the two entities, we instead consider words that are directly linked to either of them. In the following example, the only relation candidate is the word *battle*, which is directly linked to "Edelman."

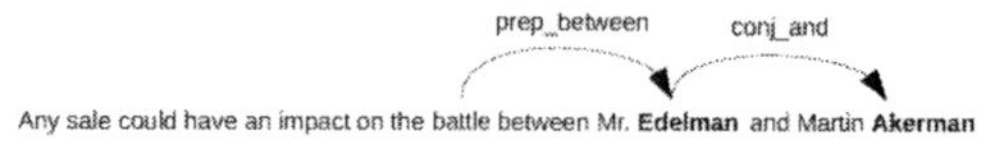

The relation candidates are manually annotated as correct/incorrect in the training data for the tree kernel models described in the following section.

4 Lexicalized Tree Kernel

We use a supervised lexicalized tree kernel to filter negative relation candidates from the results of the candidate extraction module. For semantic tasks, the design of input structures to tree kernels is as important as the design of the tree kernels themselves. In this section, we introduce our tree structure, describe the prior basic tree kernel, and finally present our lexicalized tree kernel function.

4.1 Tree Structure

In order to formulate the input for tree kernel models, we need to convert the dependency path to a tree-like structure with unlabelled edges. The target dependency path is the shortest path that includes the triple and other content words along the path. Consider the following example, which is a simplified representation of the sentence *"Georgia-Pacific Corp.'s unsolicited \$3.9 billion bid for Great Northern Nekoosa Corp. was hailed by Wall Street."* The candidate triple identified by the relation candidate extraction module is *<Georgia-Pacific Corp., bid, Great Northern Nekoosa Corp.>*.

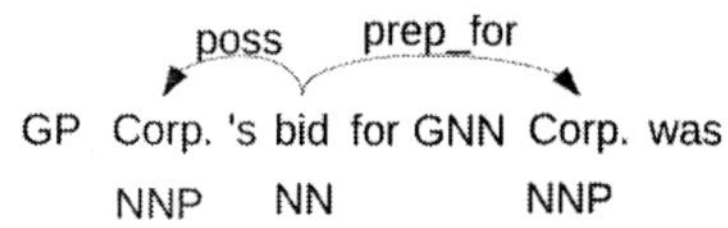

Our unlexicalized tree representation model is similar to the unlexicalized representations of Xu et al. (2013), except that instead of using the POS tag of the path's head word as the root, we create an abstract *Root* node. We preserve the dependency labels, POS tags, and entity information as tree nodes: (a) the top dependency labels are in-

(a) An un-lexicalized dependency tree.

(b) A lexicalized dependency tree.

Figure 2: An unlexicalized tree and the corresponding lexicalized tree.

cluded as children of the abstract *Root* node, other labels are attached to the corresponding parent labels; (b) the POS tag of the head word of the dependence path is a child of the *Root*; (c) other POS tags are attached as children of the dependency labels; and (d) the relation tag 'R' and the entity tags 'NE' are the terminal nodes attached to their respective POS tags. Figure 2(a) shows the unlexicalized dependency tree for our example sentence.

Our lexicalized tree representation is derived from the unlexicalized representation by attaching words as terminal nodes. In order to reduce the number of nodes, we collapse the relation and entity tags with their corresponding POS tags. Figure 2(b) shows the resulting tree for the example sentence.

4.2 Tree Kernels

Tree kernel models extract features from parse trees by comparing pairs of tree structures. The essential distinction between different tree kernel functions is the Δ function that calculates similarity of subtrees. Our modified kernel is based on the SubSet Tree (SST) Kernel proposed by Collins and Duffy (2002). What follows is a simplified description of the kernel; a more detailed description can be found in the original paper.

The general function for a tree kernel model over trees T_1 and T_2 is:

$$K(T_1, T_2) = \sum_{n_1 \in T_1} \sum_{n_2 \in T_2} \Delta(n_1, n_2), \quad (1)$$

where n_1 and n_2 are tree nodes. The Δ function of SST kernel is defined recursively:

1. $\Delta(n_1, n_2) = 0$ if the productions (context-free rules) of n_1 and n_2 are different.

2. Otherwise, $\Delta(n_1, n_2) = 1$ if n_1 and n_2 are matching pre-terminals (POS tags).

3. Otherwise,
$\Delta(n_1, n_2) = \prod_j (1 + \Delta(c(n_1, j), c(n_2, j)))$,

where $c(n, j)$ is the jth child of n.

4.3 Lexicalized Tree Kernel

Since simply adding words to lexicalize a tree kernel leads to sparsity problems, a type of smoothing must be applied. Bloehdorn and Moschitti (2007) measure the similarity of words using WordNet. Croce et al. (2011) employ word vectors created by Singular Value Decomposition (Golub and Kahan., 1965) from a word co-occurrence matrix. Plank and Moschitti (2013) use word vectors created by Brown clustering algorithm (Brown et al., 1992), which is another smoothed word representation that represents words as binary vectors. Srivastava et al. (2013) use word embeddings of Collobert and Weston (2008), but their tree kernel does not incorporate POS tags or dependency labels.

We propose using word embeddings created by a neural network model (Collobert and Weston, 2008), in which words are represented by n-dimensional real valued vectors. Each dimension represents a latent feature of the word that reflects its semantic and syntactic properties. Next, we describe how we embed these vectors into tree kernels.

Our lexicalized tree kernel model is the same as SST, except in the following case: if n_1 and n_2 are matching pre-terminals (POS tags), then

$$\Delta(n_1, n_2) = 1 + G(c(n_1), c(n_2)), \quad (2)$$

where $c(n)$ denotes the word w that is the unique child of n, and $G(w_1, w_2) = exp(-\gamma \|w_1 - w_2\|^2)$ is a Gaussian function for two word vectors, which is a valid kernel.

We examine the contribution of different types of words by comparing three methods of including lexical information: (1) relation words only; (2) all words (relation words, named entities, and other words along the dependency path fragment); and (3) all words, except named entities. The words that are excluded are assumed to be different; for example, in the third method, $G(E_1, E_2)$ is always zero, even if the entities, E_1 and E_2, are the same.

5 Experiments

Here we evaluate alternative tree kernel configurations, and compare our Open IE system to previous work.

We perform experiments on three datasets (Table 1): the Penn Treebank set (Xu et al., 2013), the New York Times set (Mesquita et al., 2013), and the ClueWeb set which we created for this project from a large collection of web pages.[1] The models are trained on the Penn Treebank training set and tested on the three test sets, of which the Penn Treebank set is in-domain, and the other two sets are out-of-domain. For word embedding and Brown clustering representations, we use the data provided by Turian et al. (2010). The SVM parameters, as well as the Brown cluster size and code length, are tuned on the development set.

Set	train	dev	test
Penn Treebank	750	100	100
New York Times	—	300	500
ClueWeb	—	450	250

Table 1: Data sets and their size (number of sentences).

Table 2 shows the effect of different smoothing and lexicalization techniques on the tree kernels. In order to focus on tree kernel functions, we use the relation candidate extraction (Section 3) and tree structure (Section 4.1) proposed in this paper. The results in the first two rows indicate that adding unsmoothed lexical information to the method of Xu et al. (2013) is not helpful, which we attribute to data sparsity. On the other hand, smoothed word representations do improve F-measure. Surprisingly, a neural network approach of creating word embeddings actually achieves a lower recall than the method of Plank and Moschitti (2013) that uses Brown clustering; the difference in F-measure is not statistically significant according to compute-intensive randomization test (Padó, 2006).

With regards to lexicalization, the inclusion of relation words is important. However, unlike Plank and Moschitti (2013), we found that it is better to exclude the lexical information of entities themselves, which confirms the findings of Riedel et al. (2013). We hypothesize that the correctness of a relation triple in Open IE is not closely related to entities. Consider the example mentioned in (Riedel et al., 2013): for relations like "X visits Y", X could be a person or organization, and Y could be a location, organization, or person.

[1]The Treebank set of (Xu et al., 2013), with minor corrections, and the ClueWeb set are appended to this publication.

Smoothing	Lexical info	P	R	F_1
none (Xu13)	none	85.7	72.7	78.7
none	all words	89.8	66.7	76.5
Brown (PM13)	relation only	88.7	71.2	79.0
Brown (PM13)	all words	84.5	74.2	79.0
Brown (PM13)	excl. entities	86.2	75.8	80.7
embedding	relation only	93.9	69.7	80.0
embedding	all words	93.8	68.2	79.0
embedding	excl. entities	95.9	71.2	**81.7**

Table 2: The results of relation extraction with alternative smoothing and lexicalization techniques on the Penn Treebank set (with our relation candidate extraction and tree structure).

Our final set of experiments evaluates the best-performing version of our system (the last row in Table 2) against two state-of-the-art Open IE systems: Mesquita et al. (2013), which is based on several hand-crafted dependency patterns; and Xu et al. (2013), which uses POS-based relation candidate extraction and an unlexicalized tree kernel. Tree kernel systems are all trained on the Penn Treebank training set, and tuned on the corresponding development sets.

The results in Table 3 show that our system consistently outperforms the other two systems, with absolute gains in F-score between 4 and 16%. We include the reported results of (Xu et al., 2013) on the Penn Treebank set, and of (Mesquita et al., 2013) on the New York Times set. The ClueWeb results were obtained by running the respective systems on the test set, except that we used our relation candidate extraction method for the tree kernel of (Xu et al., 2013). We conclude that the substantial improvement on the Penn Treebank set can be partly attributed to a superior tree kernel, and not only to a better relation candidate extraction method. We also note that word embeddings statistically outperform Brown clustering on the ClueWeb set, but not on the other two sets.

The ClueWeb set is quite challenging because it contains web pages which can be quite noisy. As a result we've found that a number of Open IE errors are caused by parsing. Conjunction structures are especially difficult for both parsing and relation extraction. For example, our system extracts the relation triple <Scotland, base, Scott> from the sentence "Set in 17th century Scotland

	P	R	F_1
	Penn Treebank set		
Xu et al. (2013)*	66.1	50.7	57.4
Brown (PM13)	82.8	65.8	73.3
Ours (embedding)	91.8	61.6	**73.8**
	New York Times set		
Mesquita et al. (2013)*	72.8	39.3	51.1
Brown (PM13)	83.5	44.0	**57.6**
Ours (embedding)	85.9	40.7	55.2
	ClueWeb set		
Xu et al. (2013)	54.3	35.8	43.2
Mesquita et al. (2013)	63.3	29.2	40.0
Brown (PM13)	54.1	31.1	39.5
Ours (embedding)	45.8	51.9	**48.7**

Table 3: Comparison of complete Open IE systems. The asterisks denote results reported in previous work.

and based on a novel by Sir Walter Scott, its high drama..." with the wrong dependency path *Scotland* $\stackrel{conj\_and}{\rightarrow}$ *based* $\stackrel{prep\_by}{\rightarrow}$ *Scott*. In the future, we will investigate whether adding information from context words that are not on the dependency path between two entities may alleviate this problem.

6 Conclusion

We have proposed a lexicalized tree kernel model for Open IE, which incorporates word embeddings learned from a neural network model. Our system combines a dependency-based relation candidate extraction method with a lexicalized tree kernel, and achieves state-of-the-art results on three datasets. Our experiments on different configurations of the smoothing and lexicalization techniques show that excluding named entity information is a better strategy for Open IE.

In the future, we plan to mitigate the performance drop on the ClueWeb set by adding information about context words around relation words. We will also investigate other ways of collapsing different types of tags in the lexicalized tree representation.

Acknowledgments

We would like to thank the anonymous reviewers for their helpful suggestions. This work was funded in part by Alberta Innovates Center for Machine Learning (AICML), Natural Sciences and Engineering Research Council of Canada (NSERC), Alberta Innovates Technology Futures (AITF), and National Institute of Informatics (NII) International Internship Program.

References

Michele Banko, Michael J Cafarella, Stephen Soderl, Matt Broadhead, and Oren Etzioni. 2007. Open information extraction from the web. In *International Joint Conference on Artificial Intelligence*, pages 2670–2676.

Stephan Bloehdorn and Alessandro Moschitti. 2007. Structure and semantics for expressive text kernels. In *Proceedings of the Sixteenth ACM Conference on Conference on Information and Knowledge Management*, CIKM '07, pages 861–864, New York, NY, USA. ACM.

Peter F. Brown, Peter V. deSouza, Robert L. Mercer, Vincent J. Della Pietra, and Jenifer C. Lai. 1992. Class-based n-gram models of natural language. *Comput. Linguist.*, 18(4):467–479, December.

Michael Collins and Nigel Duffy. 2002. New ranking algorithms for parsing and tagging: kernels over discrete structures, and the voted perceptron. In *Proceedings of the 40th Annual Meeting on Association for Computational Linguistics*, ACL '02, pages 263–270, Stroudsburg, PA, USA. Association for Computational Linguistics.

Ronan Collobert and Jason Weston. 2008. A unified architecture for natural language processing: Deep neural networks with multitask learning. In *International Conference on Machine Learning, ICML*.

Danilo Croce, Alessandro Moschitti, and Roberto Basili. 2011. Structured lexical similarity via convolution kernels on dependency trees. In *Proceedings of the Conference on Empirical Methods in Natural Language Processing*, EMNLP '11, pages 1034–1046, Stroudsburg, PA, USA. Association for Computational Linguistics.

G. Golub and W. Kahan. 1965. Calculating the singular values and pseudo-inverse of a matrix. *Journal of the Society for Industrial and Applied Mathematics: Series B, Numerical Analysis*, page 205224.

Christopher D. Manning, Mihai Surdeanu, John Bauer, Jenny Finkel, Steven J. Bethard, and David McClosky. 2014. The Stanford CoreNLP natural language processing toolkit. In *Proceedings of 52nd Annual Meeting of the Association for Computational Linguistics: System Demonstrations*, pages 55–60.

Mausam, Michael Schmitz, Robert Bart, Stephen Soderland, and Oren Etzioni. 2012. Open language learning for information extraction. In *Proceedings of the 2012 Joint Conference on Empirical Methods in Natural Language Processing and Computational Natural Language Learning*, pages 523–534. Association for Computational Linguistics.

Filipe Mesquita, Jordan Schmidek, and Denilson Barbosa. 2013. Effectiveness and efficiency of open relation extraction. In *Proceedings of the 2013 Conference on Empirical Methods in Natural Language Processing*, pages 447–457. Association for Computational Linguistics.

Sebastian Padó, 2006. *User's guide to* `sigf`*: Significance testing by approximate randomisation.*

Barbara Plank and Alessandro Moschitti. 2013. Embedding semantic similarity in tree kernels for domain adaptation of relation extraction. In *Proceedings of the 51st Annual Meeting of the Association for Computational Linguistics (Volume 1: Long Papers)*, pages 1498–1507, Sofia, Bulgaria, August. Association for Computational Linguistics.

Sebastian Riedel, Limin Yao, Benjamin M. Marlin, and Andrew McCallum. 2013. Relation extraction with matrix factorization and universal schemas. In *Joint Human Language Technology Conference/Annual Meeting of the North American Chapter of the Association for Computational Linguistics (HLT-NAACL '13)*, June.

Shashank Srivastava, Dirk Hovy, and Eduard Hovy. 2013. A walk-based semantically enriched tree kernel over distributed word representations. In *Proceedings of the 2013 Conference on Empirical Methods in Natural Language Processing*, pages 1411–1416, Seattle, Washington, USA, October. Association for Computational Linguistics.

Joseph Turian, Lev Ratinov, and Yoshua Bengio. 2010. Word representations: a simple and general method for semi-supervised learning. In *Proceedings of the 48th Annual Meeting of the Association for Computational Linguistics*, ACL '10, pages 384–394, Stroudsburg, PA, USA. Association for Computational Linguistics.

Fei Wu and Daniel S. Weld. 2010. Open information extraction using wikipedia. In *Proceedings of the 48th Annual Meeting of the Association for Computational Linguistics*, ACL '10, pages 118–127, Stroudsburg, PA, USA. Association for Computational Linguistics.

Ying Xu, Mi-Young Kim, Kevin Quinn, Randy Goebel, and Denilson Barbosa. 2013. Open information extraction with tree kernels. In *Proceedings of the 2013 Conference of the North American Chapter of the Association for Computational Linguistics: Human Language Technologies*, pages 868–877, Atlanta, Georgia, June. Association for Computational Linguistics.

A Dependency-Based Neural Network for Relation Classification

Yang Liu[1,2*] Furu Wei[3] Sujian Li[1,2] Heng Ji[4] Ming Zhou[3] Houfeng Wang[1,2]
[1]Key Laboratory of Computational Linguistics, Peking University, MOE, China
[2]Collaborative Innovation Center for Language Ability, Xuzhou, Jiangsu, China
[3]Microsoft Research, Beijing, China
[4]Computer Science Department, Rensselaer Polytechnic Institute, Troy, NY, USA
{cs-ly, lisujian, wanghf}@pku.edu.cn
{furu, mingzhou}@microsoft.com jih@rpi.edu

Abstract

Previous research on relation classification has verified the effectiveness of using dependency shortest paths or subtrees. In this paper, we further explore how to make full use of the combination of these dependency information. We first propose a new structure, termed augmented dependency path (ADP), which is composed of the shortest dependency path between two entities and the subtrees attached to the shortest path. To exploit the semantic representation behind the ADP structure, we develop dependency-based neural networks (DepNN): a recursive neural network designed to model the subtrees, and a convolutional neural network to capture the most important features on the shortest path. Experiments on the SemEval-2010 dataset show that our proposed method achieves state-of-art results.

1 Introduction

Relation classification aims to classify the semantic relations between two entities in a sentence. It plays a vital role in robust knowledge extraction from unstructured texts and serves as an intermediate step in a variety of natural language processing applications. Most existing approaches follow the machine learning based framework and focus on designing effective features to obtain better classification performance.

The effectiveness of using dependency relations between entities for relation classification has been reported in previous approaches (Bach and Badaskar, 2007). For example, Suchanek et al. (2006) carefully selected a set of features from tokenization and dependency parsing, and extended some of them to generate high order features in different ways. Culotta and Sorensen (2004) designed a dependency tree kernel and attached more information including Part-of-Speech tag, chunking tag of each node in the tree. Interestingly, Bunescu and Mooney (2005) provided an important insight that the shortest path between two entities in a dependency graph concentrates most of the information for identifying the relation between them. Nguyen et al. (2007) developed these ideas by analyzing multiple subtrees with the guidance of pre-extracted keywords. Previous work showed that the most useful dependency information in relation classification includes the shortest dependency path and dependency subtrees. These two kinds of information serve different functions and their collaboration can boost the performance of relation classification (see Section 2 for detailed examples). However, how to uniformly and efficiently combine these two components is still an open problem. In this paper, we propose a novel structure named Augmented Dependency Path (ADP) which attaches dependency subtrees to words on a shortest dependency path and focus on exploring the semantic representation behind the ADP structure.

Recently, deep learning techniques have been widely used in exploring semantic representations behind complex structures. This provides us an opportunity to model the ADP structure in a neural network framework. Thus, we propose a dependency-based framework where two neural networks are used to model shortest dependency paths and dependency subtrees separately. One convolutional neural network (CNN) is applied over the shortest dependency path, because CNN is suitable for capturing the most useful features in a flat structure. A recursive neural network (RNN) is used for extracting semantic representations from the dependency subtrees, since RNN is good at modeling hierarchical structures. To connect these two networks, each word on the shortest

*Contribution during internship at Microsoft Research.

Proceedings of the 53rd Annual Meeting of the Association for Computational Linguistics and the 7th International Joint Conference on Natural Language Processing (Short Papers), pages 285–290,
Beijing, China, July 26-31, 2015.

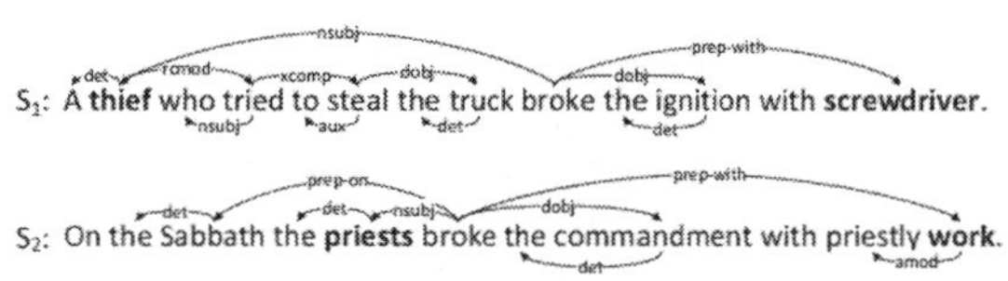

Figure 1: Sentences and their dependency trees.

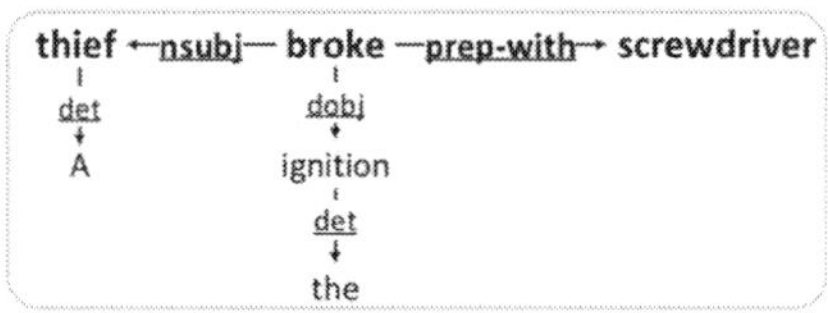

(a) Augmented dependency path in S_1.

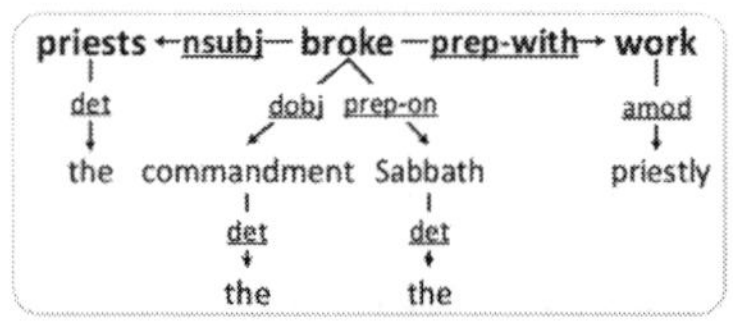

(b) Augmented dependency path in S_2.

Figure 2: Augmented dependency paths.

path is combined with a representation generated from its subtree, strengthening the semantic representation of the shortest path. In this way, the augmented dependency path is represented as a continuous semantic vector which can be further used for relation classification.

2 Problem Definition and Motivation

The task of relation classification can be defined as follows. Given a sentence S with a pair of entities e_1 and e_2 annotated, the task is to identify the semantic relation between e_1 and e_2 in accordance with a set of predefined relation classes (e.g., *Content-Container, Cause-Effect*). For example, in Figure 2, the relation between two entities e_1=*thief* and e_2=*screwdriver* is *Instrument-Agency*.

Bunescu and Mooney (2005) first used shortest dependency paths between two entities to capture the predicate-argument sequences (e.g., "thief←broke→screwdriver" in Figure 2), which provide strong evidence for relation classification. As we observe, the shortest paths contain more information and the subtrees attached to each node on the shortest path are not exploited enough. For example, Figure 2a and 2b show two instances which have similar shortest dependency paths but belong to different relation classes. Methods only using the path will fail in this case. However, we can distinguish these two paths by virtue of the attached subtrees such as "dobj→commandment" and "dobj→ignition". Based on many observations like this, we propose the idea that combines the subtrees and the shortest path to form a more precise structure for classifying relations. This combined structure is called "**augmented dependency path** (ADP)", as illustrated in Figure 2.

Next, our goal is to capture the semantic representation of the ADP structure between two entities. We first adopt a recursive neural network to model each word according to its attached dependency subtree. Based on the semantic information of each word, we design a convolutional neural network to obtain salient semantic features on the shortest dependency path.

3 Dependency-Based Neural Networks

In this section, we will introduce how we use neural network techniques and dependency information to explore the semantic connection between two entities. We dub our architecture of modeling ADP structures as dependency-based neural networks (DepNN). Figure 3 illustrates DepNN with a concrete example. First, we associate each word w and dependency relation r with a vector representation $\boldsymbol{x}_w, \boldsymbol{x}_r \in \mathbb{R}^{dim}$. For each word w on the shortest dependency path, we develop an RNN from its leaf words up to the root to generate a subtree embedding $\boldsymbol{c}_w$ and concatenate $\boldsymbol{c}_w$ with $\boldsymbol{x}_w$ to serve as the final representation of w. Next, a CNN is designed to model the shortest dependency path based on the representation of its words and relations. Finally our framework can efficiently represent the semantic connection between two entities with consideration of more comprehensive dependency information.

3.1 Modeling Dependency Subtree

The goal of modeling dependency subtrees is to find an appropriate representation for the words on the shortest path. We assume that each word w can be interpreted by itself and its children on the dependency subtree. Then, for each word w on the subtree, its word embedding $\boldsymbol{x}_w \in \mathbb{R}^{dim}$ and subtree representation $\boldsymbol{c}_w \in \mathbb{R}^{dim_c}$ are concatenated to form its final representation $\boldsymbol{p}_w \in \mathbb{R}^{dim+dim_c}$. For a word that does not have a subtree, we set its subtree representation as $\boldsymbol{c}_{LEAF}$. The subtree representation of a word is derived through transforming the representations of its children words.

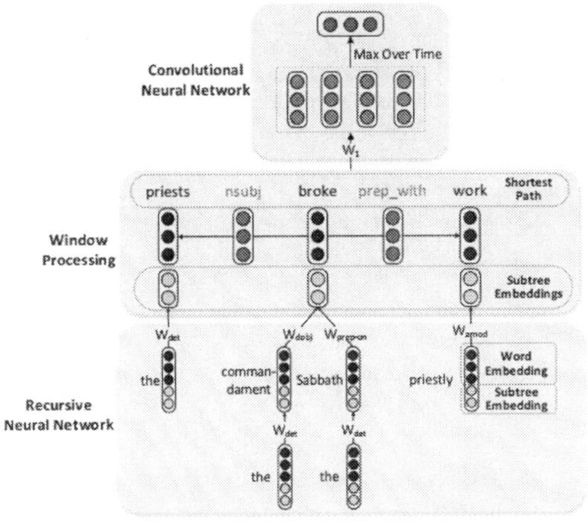

Figure 3: Illustration of Dependency-based Neural Networks.

During the bottom-up construction of the subtree, each word is associated with a dependency relation such as *dobj* as in Figure 3. For each dependency relation r, we set a transformation matrix $\boldsymbol{W}_r \in \mathbb{R}^{dim_c \times (dim+dim_c)}$ which is learned during training. Then we can get,

$$\boldsymbol{c}_w = f(\sum_{q \in Children(w)} \boldsymbol{W}_{R_{(w,q)}} \cdot \boldsymbol{p}_q + \boldsymbol{b}) \quad (1)$$

$$\boldsymbol{p}_q = [\boldsymbol{x}_q, \boldsymbol{c}_q] \quad (2)$$

where $R_{(w,q)}$ denotes the dependency relation between word w and its child word q. This process continues recursively up to the root word on the shortest path.

3.2 Modeling Shortest Dependency Path

To classify the semantic relation between two entities, we further explore the semantic representation behind their shortest dependency path, which can be seen as a sequence of words and dependency relations as the bold-font part in Figure 2. As the convolutional neural network (CNN) is good at capturing the salient features from a sequence of objects, we design a CNN to tackle the shortest dependency path.

A CNN contains a convolution operation over a window of object representations, followed by a pooling operation. As we know, a word w on the shortest path is associated with the representation p_w through modeling the subtree. For a dependency relation r on the shortest path, we set its representation as a vector $x_r \in \mathbb{R}^{dim}$. As a sliding window is applied on the sequence, we set the window size as k. For example, when $k = 3$, the sliding windows of a shortest dependency path with n words are: $\{[r_s\ w_1\ r_1], [r_1\ w_2\ r_2], \ldots, [r_{n-1}\ w_n\ r_e]\}$ where r_s and r_e are used to denote the beginning and end of a shortest dependency path between two entities.

We concatenate k neighboring words (or dependency relations) representations into a new vector. Assume $\boldsymbol{X}_i \in \mathbb{R}^{dim \cdot k + dim_c \cdot n_w}$ as the concatenated representation of the i-th window, where n_w is the number of words in one window. A convolution operation involves a filter $\mathbf{W}_1 \in \mathbb{R}^{l \times (dim \cdot k + dim_c \cdot n_w)}$, which operates on $\boldsymbol{X}_i$ to produce a new feature vector $\boldsymbol{L}_i$ with l dimensions,

$$\boldsymbol{L}_i = \boldsymbol{W}_1 \boldsymbol{X}_i \quad (3)$$

where the bias term is ignored for simplicity.

Then $\mathbf{W}_1$ is applied to each possible window in the shortest dependency path to produce a feature map: $[L_0, L_1, L_2, \cdots]$. Next, we adopt the widely-used max-over-time pooling operation (Collobert et al., 2011), which can retain the most important features, to obtain the final representation $\boldsymbol{L}$ from the feature map. That is, $\boldsymbol{L} = max(\boldsymbol{L}_0, \boldsymbol{L}_1, \boldsymbol{L}_2, \ldots)$.

3.3 Learning

Like other relation classification systems, we also incorporate some lexical level features such as named entity tags and WordNet hypernyms, which prove useful to this task. We concatenate them with the ADP representation $\boldsymbol{L}$ to produce a combined vector $\boldsymbol{M}$. We then pass $\boldsymbol{M}$ to a fully connected $softmax$ layer whose output is the probability distribution $\boldsymbol{y}$ over relation labels.

$$\boldsymbol{M} = [\boldsymbol{L}, \boldsymbol{LEX}] \quad (4)$$

$$\boldsymbol{y} = softmax(\boldsymbol{W}_2 \boldsymbol{M} + \boldsymbol{b}_2) \quad (5)$$

Then, the optimization objective is to minimize the cross-entropy error between the ground-truth label vector and the $softmax$ output. Parameters are learned using the back-propagation method (Rumelhart et al., 1988).

4 Experiments

We compare DepNN against multiple baselines on SemEval-2010 dataset (Hendrickx et al., 2010).

The training set includes 8000 sentences, and the test set includes 2717 sentences. There are 9 relation types, and each type has two directions. Instances which don't fall in any of these classes are labeled as *Other*. The official evaluation metric is the macro-averaged F1-score (excluding *Other*) and the direction is considered. We use dependency trees generated by the Stanford Parser (Klein and Manning, 2003) with the *collapsed* option.

4.1 Contributions of different components

We first show the contributions from different components of DepNN. Two different kinds of word embeddings for initialization are used in the experiments. One is the 50-*d* embeddings provided by SENNA (Collobert et al., 2011). The second is the 200-*d* embeddings used in (Yu et al., 2014), trained on Gigaword with word2vec[1]. All the hyperparameters are set with 5-fold cross-validation.

Model	F1	
	50-*d*	200-*d*
baseline (Path words)	73.8	75.5
+Depedency relations	80.3	81.8
+Attached subtrees	81.2	82.8
+Lexical features	82.7	83.6

Table 1: Performance of DepNN with different components.

We start with a baseline model using a CNN with only the words on the shortest path. We then add dependency relations and attached subtrees. The results indicate that both parts are effective for relation classification. The rich linguistic information embedded in the dependency relations and subtrees can on one hand, help distinguish different functions of the same word, and on the other hand infer an unseen word's role in the sentence. Finally, the lexical features are added and DepNN achieves state-of-the-art results.

4.2 Comparison with Baselines

In this subsection, we compare DepNN with several baseline relation classification approaches. Here, DepNN and the baselines are all based on the 200-*d* embeddings trained on Gigaword due to the larger corpus and higher dimensions.

SVM (Rink and Harabagiu, 2010): This is the top performed system in SemEval-2010. It utilizes many external corpora to extract features from the sentence to build an SVM classifier.

[1]https://code.google.com/p/word2vec/

Model	Additional Features	F1
SVM	POS, PropBank, morphological WordNet, TextRunner, FrameNet dependency parse, etc.	82.2
MV-RNN	POS, NER, WordNet	81.8[2]
CNN	WordNet	82.7
FCM	NER	83.0
DT-RNN	NER	73.1
DepNN	WordNet	83.0
	NER	**83.6**

Table 2: Results on SemEval-2010 dataset with Gigaword embeddings.

MV-RNN (Socher et al., 2012): This model finds the path between the two entities in the constituent parse tree and then learns the distributed representation of its highest node with a matrix for each word to make the compositions specific.

CNN: Zeng et al. (2014) build a convolutional model over the tokens of a sentence to learn the sentence level feature vector. It uses a special position vector that indicates the relative distances of current input word to two marked entities.

FCM (Yu et al., 2014): FCM decomposes the sentence into substructures and extracts features for each of them, forming substructure embeddings. These embeddings are combined by sum-pooling and input into a $softmax$ classifier.

DT-RNN (Socher et al., 2014) : This is an RNN for modeling dependency trees. It combines node's word embedding with its children through a linear combination but not a subtree embedding. We adapt the augmented dependency path into a dependency subtree and apply DT-RNN.

As shown in Table 2, DepNN achieves the best result (83.6) using NER features. WordNet features can also improve the performance of DepN-N, but not as obvious as NER. Yu et al. (2014) had similar observations, since the larger number of WordNet tags may cause overfitting. SVM achieves a comparable result, though the quality of feature engineering highly relies on human experience and external NLP resources. MV-RNN models the constituent parse trees with a recursive procedure and its F1-score is about 1.8 percent lower than DepNN. Meanwhile, MVR-NN is very slow to train, since each word is associated with a matrix. Both CNN and FCM use features from the whole sentence and achieve similar performance. DT-RNN is the worst of all baselines, though it

[2]MV-RNN achieves a higher F1-score (82.7) on SENNA embeddings reported in the original paper.

also considers the information from shortest dependency paths and attached subtrees. As we analyze, shortest dependency paths and subtrees play different roles in relation classification. However, we can see that DT-RNN does not distinguish the modeling processes of shortest paths and subtrees. This phenomenon is also seen in a kernel-based method (Wang, 2008), where the tree kernel performs worse than the shortest path kernel. We also look into the DepNN model and find it can identify different patterns of words and the dependency relations. For example, in the *Instrument-Agency* relation, the word "using" and the dependency relation "prep_with" are found playing a major role.

5 Conclusion

In this paper, we propose to classify relations between entities by modeling the augmented dependency path in a neural network framework. We present a novel approach, DepNN, to taking advantages of both convolutional neural network and recursive neural network to model this structure. Experiment results demonstrate that DepNN achieves state-of-the-art performance.

Acknowledgments

We thank all the anonymous reviewers for their insightful comments. This work was partially supported by National Key Basic Research Program of China (No. 2014CB340504), National Natural Science Foundation of China (No. 61273278 and 61370117), and National Social Science Fund of China (No: 12&ZD227). The correspondence author of this paper is Sujian Li.

References

Nguyen Bach and Sameer Badaskar. 2007. A survey on relation extraction. *Language Technologies Institute, Carnegie Mellon University*.

Razvan C. Bunescu and Raymond J. Mooney. 2005. A Shortest Path Dependency Kernel for Relation Extraction. In *North American Chapter of the Association for Computational Linguistics*.

Ronan Collobert, Jason Weston, Léon Bottou, Michael Karlen, Koray Kavukcuoglu, and Pavel Kuksa. 2011. Natural language processing (almost) from scratch. *The Journal of Machine Learning Research*, 12:2493–2537.

Aron Culotta and Jeffrey S. Sorensen. 2004. Dependency Tree Kernels for Relation Extraction. In *Meeting of the Association for Computational Linguistics*, pages 423–429.

Iris Hendrickx, Zornitsa Kozareva, Preslav Nakov, Sebastian Pad ok, Marco Pennacchiotti, Lorenza Romano, and Stan Szpakowicz. 2010. SemEval-2010 Task 8: Multi-Way Classification of Semantic Relations Between Pairs of Nominals.

Dan Klein and Christopher D. Manning. 2003. Accurate Unlexicalized Parsing. In *Meeting of the Association for Computational Linguistics*, pages 423–430.

Dat PT Nguyen, Yutaka Matsuo, and Mitsuru Ishizuka. 2007. Relation extraction from wikipedia using subtree mining. In *Proceedings of the National Conference on Artificial Intelligence*, volume 22, page 1414. Menlo Park, CA; Cambridge, MA; London; AAAI Press; MIT Press; 1999.

Bryan Rink and Sanda Harabagiu. 2010. Utd: Classifying semantic relations by combining lexical and semantic resources. In *Proceedings of the 5th International Workshop on Semantic Evaluation*, pages 256–259, Uppsala, Sweden, July. Association for Computational Linguistics.

David E Rumelhart, Geoffrey E Hinton, and Ronald J Williams. 1988. Learning representations by back-propagating errors. *Cognitive modeling*, 5.

Richard Socher, Brody Huval, Christopher D. Manning, and Andrew Y. Ng. 2012. Semantic compositionality through recursive matrix-vector spaces. In *Proceedings of the 2012 Joint Conference on Empirical Methods in Natural Language Processing and Computational Natural Language Learning*, pages 1201–1211, Jeju Island, Korea, July. Association for Computational Linguistics.

Richard Socher, Andrej Karpathy, Quoc V Le, Christopher D Manning, and Andrew Y Ng. 2014. Grounded compositional semantics for finding and describing images with sentences. *Transactions of the Association for Computational Linguistics*, 2:207–218.

Fabian M Suchanek, Georgiana Ifrim, and Gerhard Weikum. 2006. Combining linguistic and statistical analysis to extract relations from web documents. In *Proceedings of the 12th ACM SIGKDD international conference on Knowledge discovery and data mining*, pages 712–717. ACM.

Mengqiu Wang. 2008. A re-examination of dependency path kernels for relation extraction. In *IJCNLP*, pages 841–846.

Mo Yu, Matthew Gormley, and Mark Dredze. 2014. Factor-based compositional embedding models. In *NIPS Workshop on Learning Semantics*.

Daojian Zeng, Kang Liu, Siwei Lai, Guangyou Zhou, and Jun Zhao. 2014. Relation classification via convolutional deep neural network. In *Proceedings of COLING 2014, the 25th International Conference on Computational Linguistics: Technical Papers*, pages 2335–2344, Dublin, Ireland, August. Dublin City University and Association for Computational Linguistics.

Embedding Methods for Fine Grained Entity Type Classification

Dani Yogatama
Language Technologies Institute
Carnegie Mellon University
Pittsburgh, PA 15213
`dyogatama@cs.cmu.edu`

Dan Gillick, Nevena Lazic
Google Research
1600 Amphitheatre Parkway
Mountain View, CA 94043
`{dgillick,nevena}@google.com`

Abstract

We propose a new approach to the task of fine grained entity type classifications based on label embeddings that allows for information sharing among related labels. Specifically, we learn an embedding for each label and each feature such that labels which frequently co-occur are close in the embedded space. We show that it outperforms state-of-the-art methods on two fine grained entity-classification benchmarks and that the model can exploit the finer-grained labels to improve classification of standard coarse types.

1 Introduction

Entity type classification is the task of assigning type labels (e.g., `person`, `location`, `organization`) to mentions of entities in documents. These types are useful for deeper natural language analysis such as coreference resolution (Recasens et al., 2013), relation extraction (Yao et al., 2010), and downstream applications such as knowledge base construction (Carlson et al., 2010) and question answering (Lin et al., 2012).

Standard entity type classification tasks use a small set of coarse labels, typically fewer than 20 (Hirschman and Chinchor, 1997; Sang and Meulder, 2003; Doddington et al., 2004). Recent work has focused on a much larger set of fine grained labels (Ling and Weld, 2012; Yosef et al., 2012; Gillick et al., 2014). Fine grained labels are typically subtypes of the standard coarse labels (e.g., `artist` is a subtype of `person` and `author` is a subtype of `artist`), so the label space forms a tree-structured *is-a* hierarchy. See Figure 1 for the label sets used in our experiments. A mention labeled with type `artist` should also be labeled with all ancestors of `artist`. Since we allow mentions to have multiple labels, this is a multi-label classification task. Multiple labels typically correspond to a single path in the tree (from root to a leaf or internal node).

An important aspect of context-dependent fine grained entity type classification is that mentions of an entity can have different types depending on the context. Consider the following example: *Madonna starred as Breathless Mahoney in the film Dick Tracy*. In this context, the most appropriate label for the mention *Madonna* is `actress`, since the sentence talks about her role in a film. In the majority of other cases, *Madonna* is likely to be labeled as a `musician`.

The main difficulty in fine grained entity type classification is the absence of labeled training examples. Training data is typically generated automatically (e.g. by mapping Freebase labels of resolved entities), without taking context into account, so it is common for mentions to have noisy labels. In our example, the labels for the mention *Madonna* would include `musician`, `actress`, `author`, and potentially others, even though not all of these labels apply here. Ideally, a fine grained type classification system should be robust to such noisy training data, as well as capable of exploiting relationships between labels during learning. We describe a model that uses a ranking loss—which tends to be more robust to label noise—and that learns a joint representation of features and labels, which allows for information sharing among related labels.[1] A related idea to learn output representations for multiclass document classification and part-of-speech tagging was considered in Srikumar and Manning (2014). We show that it outperforms state-of-the-art methods on two fine grained entity-classification benchmarks. We also evaluate our model on standard coarse type classification and find that training embedding models on all fine grained labels gives better results than training it on just the coarse

[1] Turian et al. (2010), Collobert et al. (2011), and Qi et al. (2014) consider representation learning for *coarse* label named entity recognition.

Proceedings of the 53rd Annual Meeting of the Association for Computational Linguistics and the 7th International Joint Conference on Natural Language Processing (Short Papers), pages 291–296,
Beijing, China, July 26-31, 2015.

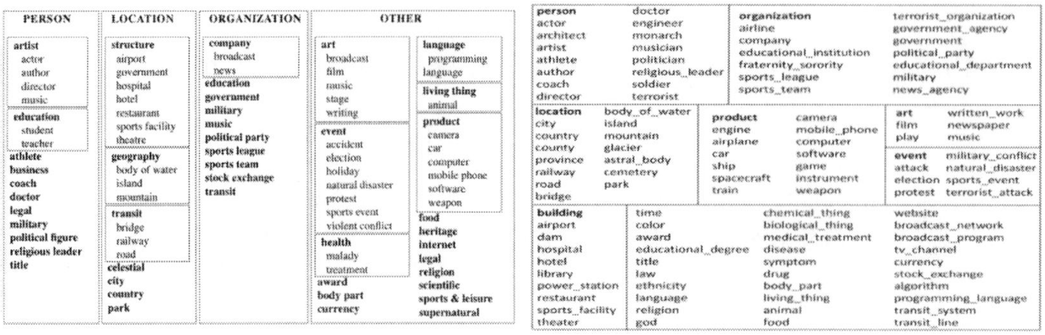

Figure 1: Label sets for Gillick et al. (2014)—left, GFT—and Ling and Weld (2012)—right, FIGER.

types of interest.

2 Models

In this section, we describe our approach, which is based on the WSABIE (Weston et al., 2011) model.

Notation We use lower case letters to denote variables, bold lower case letters to denote vectors, and bold upper case letters to denote matrices. Let $\mathbf{x} \in \mathbb{R}^D$ be the feature vector for a mention, where D is the number of features and x_d is the value of the d-th feature. Let $\mathbf{y} \in \{0,1\}^T$ be the corresponding binary label vector, where T is the number of labels. $y_t = 1$ if and only if the mention is of type t. We use $\mathbf{y}_t$ to denote a one-hot binary vector of size T, where $y_t = 1$ and all other entries are zero.

Model To leverage the relationships among the fine grained labels, we would like a model that can learn an embedding space for labels. Our model, based on WSABIE, learns to map both feature vectors and labels to a low dimensional space $\mathbb{R}^H$ (H is the embedding dimension size) such that each instance is close to its label(s) in this space; see Figure 2 for an illustration. Relationships between labels are captured by their distances in the embedded space: co-occurring labels tend to be closer, whereas mutually exclusive labels are further apart.

Formally, we are interested in learning the mapping functions:

$$\begin{aligned} f(\mathbf{x}) : \mathbb{R}^D &\rightarrow \mathbb{R}^H \\ \forall t \in \{1, 2, \ldots, T\}, g(\mathbf{y}_t) : \{0,1\}^T &\rightarrow \mathbb{R}^H \end{aligned}$$

In this work, we parameterize them as linear functions $f(\mathbf{x}, \mathbf{A}) = \mathbf{A}\mathbf{x}$ and $g(\mathbf{y}_t, \mathbf{B}) = \mathbf{B}\mathbf{y}_t$, where $\mathbf{A} \in \mathbb{R}^{H \times D}$ and $\mathbf{B} \in \mathbb{R}^{H \times T}$ are parameters.

The score of a label t (represented as a one-hot label vector $\mathbf{y}_t$) and a feature vector $\mathbf{x}$ is the dot product between their embeddings:

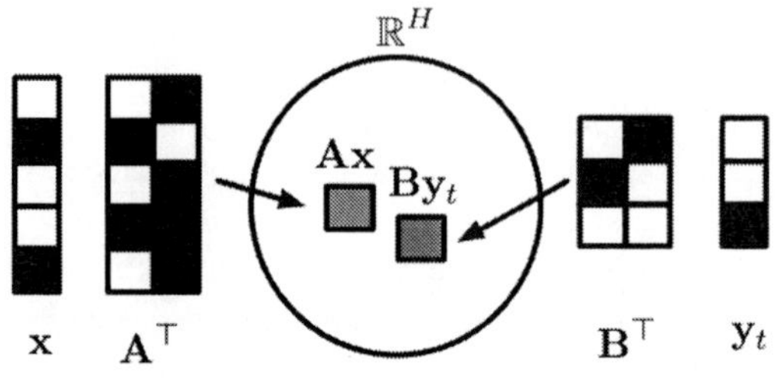

Figure 2: An illustration of the standard WSABIE model. $\mathbf{x}$ is the feature vector extracted from a mention, and $\mathbf{y}_t$ is its label. Here, black cells indicate non-zero and white cells indicate zero values. The parameters are matrices $\mathbf{A}$ and $\mathbf{B}$ which are used to map the feature vector $\mathbf{x}$ and the label vector $\mathbf{y}_t$ into an embedding space.

$$s(\mathbf{x}, \mathbf{y}_t; \mathbf{A}, \mathbf{B}) = f(\mathbf{x}, \mathbf{A}) \cdot g(\mathbf{y}_t, \mathbf{B}) = \mathbf{A}\mathbf{x} \cdot \mathbf{B}\mathbf{y}_t$$

For brevity, we denote this score by $s(\mathbf{x}, \mathbf{y}_t)$. Note that the total number of parameters is $(D+T) \times H$, which is typically less than the number of parameters in standard classification models that use regular conjunctions of input features with label classes (e.g., logistic regression) when $H < T$.

Learning Since we expect the training data to contain some extraneous labels, we use a ranking loss to encourage the model to place positive labels above negative labels without competing with each other. Let $\mathcal{Y}$ denote the set of positive labels for a mention, and let $\bar{\mathcal{Y}}$ denote its complement. Intuitively, we try to rank labels in $\mathcal{Y}$ higher than labels in $\bar{\mathcal{Y}}$. Specifically, we use the weighted approximate pairwise (WARP) loss of Weston et al. (2011). For a mention $\{\mathbf{x}, \mathbf{y}\}$, the WARP loss is:

$$\sum_{t \in \mathcal{Y}} \sum_{\bar{t} \in \bar{\mathcal{Y}}} \mathcal{R}(\text{rank}(\mathbf{x}, \mathbf{y}_t)) \max(1 - s(\mathbf{x}, \mathbf{y}_t) + s(\mathbf{x}, \mathbf{y}_{\bar{t}}), 0)$$

where $\text{rank}(\mathbf{x}, \mathbf{y}_t)$ is the margin-infused rank of label t: $\text{rank}(\mathbf{x}, \mathbf{y}_t) = \sum_{\bar{t} \in \bar{\mathcal{Y}}} \mathbb{I}(1 + s(\mathbf{x}, \mathbf{y}_{\bar{t}}) > s(\mathbf{x}, \mathbf{y}_t))$, $\mathcal{R}(\text{rank}(\mathbf{x}, \mathbf{y}_t))$ is a function that transforms this rank into a weight. In this work, since each mention can have multiple positive labels, we choose to optimize precision at k by setting $\mathcal{R}(k) = \sum_{i=1}^{k} \frac{1}{i}$. Favoring precision over recall in fine grained entity type classification makes sense because if we are not certain about a particular fine grained label for a mention, we should use its ancestor label in the hierarchy.

In order to learn the parameters with this WARP loss, we use stochastic (sub)gradient descent.

Inference During inference, we consider the top-k predicted labels, where k is the maximum depth of the label hierarchy, and greedily remove labels that are not consistent with other labels (i.e., not on the same path of the tree). For example, if the (ordered) top-k labels are `person`, `artist`, and `location`, we output only `person` and `artist` as the predicted labels. We use a threshold δ such that $\hat{y}_t = 1$ if $s(\mathbf{x}, \mathbf{y}_t) > \delta$ and $\hat{y}_t = 0$ otherwise.

Kernel extension We extend the WSABIE model to include a weighting function between each feature and label, similar in spirit to Weston et al. (2014). Recall that the WSABIE scoring function is: $s(\mathbf{x}, \mathbf{y}_t) = \mathbf{Ax} \cdot \mathbf{By}_t = \sum_d (\mathbf{A}_d x_d)^\top \mathbf{B}_t$, where $\mathbf{A}_d$ and $\mathbf{B}_t$ denote the column vectors of $\mathbf{A}$ and $\mathbf{B}$. We can weight each (feature, label) pair by a kernel function prior to computing the embedding:

$$s(\mathbf{x}, \mathbf{y}_t) = \sum_d K_{d,t} (\mathbf{A}_d x_d)^\top \mathbf{B}_t,$$

where $\mathbf{K} \in \mathbb{R}^{D \times T}$ is the kernel matrix. We use a N-nearest neighbor kernel[2] and set $K_{d,t} = 1$ if $\mathbf{A}_d$ is one of N-nearest neighbors of the label vector $\mathbf{B}_t$, and $K_{d,t} = 0$ otherwise. In all our experiments, we set $N = 200$.

To incorporate the kernel weighting function, we only need to make minor modifications to the learning procedure. At every iteration, we first compute the similarity between each feature embedding and each label embedding. For each label t, we then set the kernel values for the N most similar features to 1, and the rest to 0 (update $\mathbf{K}$). We can then follow the learning algorithm for the standard WSABIE model described above. At inference time, we fix $\mathbf{K}$ so this extension is only slightly slower than the standard model.

[2]We explored various kernels in preliminary experiments and found that the nearest neighbor kernel performs the best.

The nearest-neighbor kernel introduces nonlinearities to the embedding model. It implicitly plays the role of a label-dependent feature selector, learning which features can interact with which labels and turns off potentially noisy features that are not in the relevant label's neighborhood.

3 Experiments

Setup and Baselines We evaluate our methods on two publicly available datasets that are manually annotated with gold labels for fine grained entity type classification: GFT (Google Fine Types; Gillick et al., 2014) and FIGER (Ling and Weld, 2012). On the GFT dataset, we compare with state-of-the-art baselines from Gillick et al. (2014): flat logistic regression (FLAT), an extension of multiclass logistic regression for multilabel classification problems; and multiple independent binary logistic regression (BINARY), one per label $t \in \{1, 2, \ldots, T\}$. On the FIGER dataset, we compare with a state-of-the-art baseline from Ling and Weld (2012).

We denote the standard embedding method by WSABIE and its extension by K-WSABIE. We fix our embedding size to $H = 50$. We report micro-averaged precision, recall, and F1-score for each of the competing methods (this is called *Loose Micro* by Ling and Weld). When development data is available, we use it to tune δ by optimizing F1-score.

Training data Because we have no manually annotated data, we create training data using the technique described in Gillick et al. (2014). A set of 133,000 news documents are automatically annotated by a parser, a mention chunker, and an entity resolver that assigns Freebase types to entites, which we map to fine grained labels. This approach results in approximately 3 million training examples which we use to train all the models evaluated below. The only difference between models trained for different tasks is the mapping from Freebase types. See Gillick et al. (2014) for details.

Table 1 lists the features we use—the same set as used by Gillick et al. (2014), and very similar to those used by Ling and Weld. String features are randomly hashed to a value in 0 to 999,999, which simplifies feature extraction and adds some additional regularization (Ganchev and Dredze, 2008).

Feature	Description	Example
Head	The syntactic head of the mention phrase	"Obama"
Non-head	Each non-head word in the mention phrase	"Barack", "H."
Cluster	Word cluster id for the head word	"59"
Characters	Each character trigram in the mention head	":ob", "oba", "bam", "ama", "ma:"
Shape	The word shape of the words in the mention phrase	"Aa A. Aa"
Role	Dependency label on the mention head	"subj"
Context	Words before and after the mention phrase	"B:who", "A:first"
Parent	The head's lexical parent in the dependency tree	"picked"
Topic	The most likely topic label for the document	"politics"

Table 1: List of features used in our experiments, similar to features in Gillick et al. (2014). Features are extracted from each mention. The example mention in context is ... *who Barack H. Obama first picked* ....

	GFT Dev	GFT Test	FIGER
Total mentions	6,380	11,324	778
at Level 1	3,934	7,975	568
at Level 2	2,215	2,994	210
at Level 3	251	335	–

Table 2: Mention counts in our datasets.

GFT evaluation There are $T = 86$ fine grained labels in the GFT dataset, as listed in Figure 1. The four top-level labels are: `person`, `location`, `organization`, and `other`; the remaining labels are subtypes of these labels. The maximum depth of a label is 3. We split the dataset into a development set (for tuning hyperparameters) and test set (see Table 2).

The overall experimental results are shown in Table 3. Embedding methods performed well. Both WSABIE and K-WSABIE outperformed the baselines by substantial margins in F1-score, though the advantage of the kernel version over the linear version is only marginally significant.

To visualize the learned embeddings, we project label embeddings down to two dimensions using PCA in Figure 3. Since there are only 4 top-level labels here, the fine grained labels are color-coded according to their top-level labels for readability. We can see that related labels are clustered together, and the four major clusters correspond to to the top-level labels. We note that these first two components only capture 14% of the total variance of the full 50-dimensional space.

Method	P	R	F1
FLAT	79.22	60.18	68.40
BINARY	80.05	62.20	70.01
WSABIE	**80.58**	66.20	72.68
K-WSABIE	80.11	**67.01**	**72.98**

Table 3: Precision (P), Recall (R), and F1-score on the GFT test dataset for four competing models. The improvements for WSABIE and K-WSABIE over both baselines are statistically significant ($p < 0.01$).

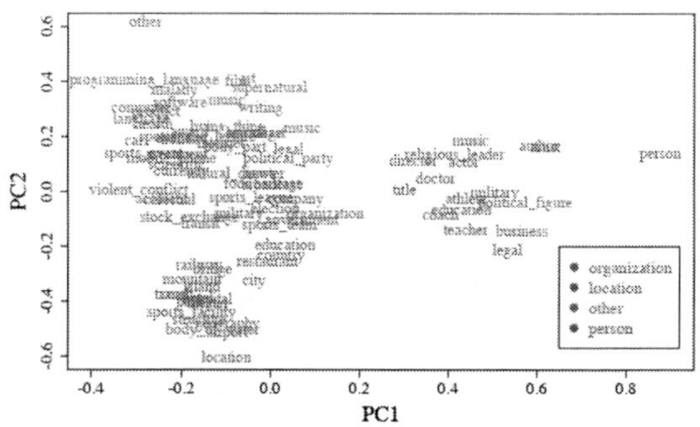

Figure 3: Two-dimensional projections of label embeddings for GFT dataset. See text for details.

FIGER evaluation Our second evaluation dataset is FIGER from Ling and Weld (2012). In this dataset, there are $T = 112$ labels organized in a two-level hierarchy; however, only 102 appear in our training data (see Figure 1, taken from their paper, for the complete set of labels). The training labels include 37 top-level labels (e.g., `person`, `location`, `product`, `art`, etc.) and 75 second-level labels (e.g., `actor`, `city`, `engine`, etc.) The FIGER dataset is much smaller than the GFT dataset (see Table 2).

Our experimental results are shown in Table 4. Again, K-WSABIE performed the best, followed by the standard WSABIE model. Both of these methods significantly outperformed Ling and Weld's best result.

Method	P	R	F1
Ling and Weld (2012)	–	–	69.30
WSABIE	81.85	63.75	71.68
K-WSABIE	**82.23**	**64.55**	**72.35**

Table 4: Precision (P), Recall (R), and F1-score on the FIGER dataset for three competing models. We took the F1 score from Ling and Weld's best result (no precision and recall numbers were reported). The improvements for WSABIE and K-WSABIE over the baseline are statistically significant ($p < 0.01$).

Feature learning We investigate whether having a large fine grained label space is helpful in learning a good representation for *feature vectors* (recall that WSABIE learns representations for both feature vectors and labels). We focus on the task of coarse type classification, where we want to classify a mention into one of the four top-level GFT labels. We fix the training mentions and learn WSABIE embeddings for feature vectors and labels by (1) training only on coarse labels and (2) training on all labels; we evaluate the models only on coarse labels. Training with all labels gives an improvement of about 2 points (F1 score) over training with just coarse labels, as shown in Table 5. This suggests that including additional subtype labels can help us learn better feature embeddings, even if we are not explicitly interested in the deeper labels.

Training labels	P	R	F1
Coarse labels only	82.41	77.87	80.07
All labels	85.18	79.28	82.12

Table 5: Comparison of two WSABIE models on coarse type classification for GFT. The first model only used coarse top-level labels, while the second model was trained on all 86 labels.

4 Discussion

Design of fine grained label hierarchy Results at different levels of the hierarchies in Table 6 show that it is more difficult to discriminate among deeper labels. However, it appears that the depth-2 FIGER types are easier to discriminate than the depth-2 (and depth-3) GFT labels. This may simply be an artifact of the very small FIGER dataset, but it suggests it may be worthwhile to flatten the `other` subtree ini GFT since many of its subtypes do not obviously share any information.

GFT	P	R	F1
LEVEL 1	85.22	80.55	82.82
LEVEL 2	56.02	37.14	44.67
LEVEL 3	65.12	7.89	14.07

FIGER	P	R	F1
LEVEL 1	82.82	70.42	76.12
LEVEL 2	68.28	47.14	55.77

Table 6: WSABIE model's Precision (P), Recall (R), and F1-score at each level of the label hierarchies for GFT (top) and FIGER (bottom).

5 Conclusion

We introduced embedding methods for fine grained entity type classifications that outperforms state-of-the-art methods on benchmark entity-classification datasets. We showed that these methods learned reasonable embeddings for fine-type labels which allowed information sharing across related labels.

Acknowledgements

We thank Andrew McCallum for helpful discussions and anonymous reviewers for feedback on an earlier draft of this paper.

References

Andrew Carlson, Justin Betteridge, Richard C. Wang, Estevam R. Hruschka Jr., and Tom M. Mitchell. 2010. Coupled semi-supervised learning for information extraction. In *Proc. of WSDM*.

R. Collobert, J. Weston, L. Bottou, M. Karlen, K. Kavukcuoglu, and P. Kuksa. 2011. Natural language processing (almost) from scratch. *Journal of Machine Learning Research*, 12:2493–2537.

George Doddington, Alexis Mitchell, Mark Przybocki, Lance Ramshaw, Stephanie Strassel, and Ralph Weischedel. 2004. The automatic content extraction (ACE) program tasks, data, and evaluation. In *Proc. of LREC*.

Kuzman Ganchev and Mark Dredze. 2008. Small statistical models by random feature mixing. In *Proceedings of the ACL08 HLT Workshop on Mobile Language Processing*, pages 19–20.

Dan Gillick, Nevena Lazic, Kuzman Ganchev, Jesse Kirchner, and David Huynh. 2014. Context-dependent fine-grained entity type tagging. In *arXiv*.

Lynette Hirschman and Nancy Chinchor. 1997. MUC-7 named entity task definition. In *Proc. of MUC-7*.

Thomas Lin, Mausam, and Oren Etzioni. 2012. No noun phrase left behind: Detecting and typing unlinkable entities. In *Proc. of EMNLP-CoNLL*.

Xiao Ling and Daniel S. Weld. 2012. Fine-grained entity recognition. In *Proc. of AAAI*.

Yanjun Qi, Sujatha Das G, Ronan Collobert, and Jason Weston. 2014. Deep learning for character-based information extraction. In *Proc. of ECIR*.

Marta Recasens, Marie-Catherine de Marneffe, and Christopher Potts. 2013. The life and death of discourse entities: Identifying singleton mentions. In *Proc. of NAACL*.

Erik F. Tjong Kim Sang and Fien De Meulder. 2003. Introduction to the conll-2003 shared task: language-independent named entity recognition. In *Proc. of HLT-NAACL*.

Vivek Srikumar and Christopher D. Manning. 2014. Learning distributed representations for structured output prediction. In *Proc. of NIPS*.

Joseph Turian, Lev Ratinov, and Yoshua Bengio. 2010. Word representations: A simple and general method for semi-supervised learning. In *Proc. of ACL.*

Jason Weston, Samy Bengio, and Nicolas Usunier. 2011. Wsabie: Scaling up to large vocabulary image annotation. In *Proc. of IJCAI.*

Jason Weston, Ron Weiss, and Hector Yee. 2014. Affinity weighted embedding. In *Proc. of ICML.*

Limin Yao, Sebastian Riedel, and Andrew McCallum. 2010. Collective cross-document relation extraction without labelled data. In *Proc. of EMNLP.*

Mohamed Amir Yosef, Sandro Bauer, Johannes Hoffart, Marc Spaniol, and Gerhard Weikum. 2012. HYENA: Hierarchical type classification for entity names. In *Proc. of COLING.*

Sieve-Based Entity Linking for the Biomedical Domain

Jennifer D'Souza and **Vincent Ng**
Human Language Technology Research Institute
University of Texas at Dallas
Richardson, TX 75083-0688
{jld082000,vince}@hlt.utdallas.edu

Abstract

We examine a key task in biomedical text processing, normalization of disorder mentions. We present a multi-pass sieve approach to this task, which has the advantage of simplicity and modularity. Our approach is evaluated on two datasets, one comprising clinical reports and the other comprising biomedical abstracts, achieving state-of-the-art results.

1 Introduction

Entity linking is the task of mapping an entity mention in a text document to an entity in a knowledge base. This task is challenging because (1) the same word or phrase can be used to refer to different entities, and (2) the same entity can be referred to by different words or phrases. In the biomedical text processing community, the task is more commonly known as normalization, where the goal is to map a word or phrase in a document to a unique concept in an ontology (based on the description of that concept in the ontology) after disambiguating potential ambiguous surface words or phrases. Unlike in the news domain, in the biomedical domain it is rare for the same word or phrase to refer to multiple different concepts. However, different words or phrases often refer to the same concept. Given that mentions in biomedical text are relatively unambiguous, normalizing them involves addressing primarily the second challenge mentioned above.

The goal of this paper is to advance the state of the art in normalizing *disorder mentions* in documents from two genres, clinical reports and biomedical abstracts. For example, given the disorder mention *swelling of abdomen*, a normalization system should map it to the concept in the ontology associated with the term *abdominal distention*. Not all disorder mentions can be mapped to a given ontology, however. The reason is that the ontology may not include all of the possible concepts. Hence, determining whether a disorder mention can be mapped to a concept in the given ontology is part of the normalization task. Note that disorders have been the target of many research initiatives in the biomedical domain, as one of its major goals is to alleviate health disorders.

	ShARe (Clinical Reports)		**NCBI (Biomedical Abstracts)**	
	Train	**Test**	**Train**	**Test**
Documents	199	99	692	100
Disorder mentions	5816	5351	5921	964
Mentions w/ ID	4178	3615	5921	964
ID-less mentions	1638	1736	0	0

Table 1: Corpus statistics.

Our contributions are three-fold. First, we propose a simpler and more modular approach to normalization than existing approaches: a multi-pass sieve approach. Second, our system achieves state-of-the-art results on datasets from two genres, clinical reports and biomedical abstracts. To our knowledge, we are the first to present normalization results on two genres. Finally, to facilitate comparison with future work on this task, we release the source code of our system.[1]

2 Corpora

We evaluate our system on two standard corpora (see Table 1 for their statistics):

The **ShARe/CLEF eHealth Challenge corpus** (Pradhan et al., 2013) contains 298 de-identified clinical reports from US intensive care partitioned into 199 reports for training and 99 reports for testing. In each report, each disorder mention is manually annotated with either the unique identifier of the concept in the reference ontology to which it refers, or "CUI-less" if it cannot be mapped to any

[1]The code is available from http://www.hlt.utdallas.edu/~jld082000/normalization/.

Proceedings of the 53rd Annual Meeting of the Association for Computational Linguistics and the 7th International Joint Conference on Natural Language Processing (Short Papers), pages 297–302,
Beijing, China, July 26-31, 2015.

(1) C0000731| |swollen abdomen|abdominal distension|abdomen distended|abdominal distention|abdominal swelling

(2) D008288| |Malaria|Fever, Marsh|Fever, Remittent|Infection, Plasmodium|MALS|Plasmodium Infection|Remittent Fever

Figure 1: Example concepts in the ontologies. The first one is taken from SNOMED-CT and the second one is taken from MEDIC ontologies. In each concept, only its ID and the list of terms associated with it are shown.

concept in the reference ontology. The reference ontology used is the SNOMED-CT resource of the UMLS Metathesaurus (Campbell et al., 1998), which contains 128,430 disorder concepts.

The **NCBI disease corpus** (Doğan et al., 2014) contains 793 biomedical abstracts partitioned into 693 abstracts for training and development and 100 abstracts for testing. Similar to the ShARe corpus, a disorder mention in each abstract is manually annotated with the identifier of the concept in the reference ontology to which it refers. The reference ontology used is the MEDIC lexicon (Davis et al., 2012), which contains 11,915 disorder concepts. Unlike in the ShARe corpus, in NCBI only those disorder mentions that can be mapped to a concept in MEDIC are annotated. As a result, all the annotated disorder mentions in the NCBI corpus have a concept identifier. Unlike in ShARe, in NCBI there exist *composite* disorder mentions, each of which is composed of more than one disorder mention. A composite disorder mention is annotated with the set of the concept identifiers associated with its constituent mentions.

We note that each concept in the two ontologies (the UMLS Metathesaurus and MEDIC) is not only identified by a concept ID, but also associated with a number of attributes, such as the list of *terms* commonly used to refer to the concept, the preferred term used to refer to the concept, and its definition. In our approach, we use only the list of terms associated with each concept ID in the normalization process. Figure 1 shows two example concepts taken from these two ontologies.

3 A Multi-Pass Approach to Normalization

Despite the simplicity and modularity of the multi-pass sieve approach and its successful application to coreference resolution (Raghunathan et al., 2010), it has not been extensively applied to other NLP tasks. In this section, we investigate its application to normalization.

3.1 Overview of the Sieve Approach

A sieve is composed of one or more heuristic rules. In the context of normalization, each rule *normalizes* (i.e., assigns a concept ID to) a disorder mention in a document. Sieves are ordered by their precision, with the most precise sieve appearing first. To normalize a set of disorder mentions in a document, the normalizer makes multiple passes over them: in the i-th pass, it uses only the rules in the i-th sieve to normalize a mention. If the i-th sieve cannot normalize a mention *unambiguously* (i.e., the sieve normalizes it to more than one concept in the ontology), the sieve will leave it unnormalized. When a mention is normalized, it is added to the list of terms associated with the ontology concept to which it is normalized. This way, later sieves can exploit the normalization decisions made in earlier sieves. Note that a normalization decision made earlier cannot be overridden later.

3.2 Normalization Sieves

In this subsection, we describe the ten sieves we designed for normalization. For convenience, we use the word *concept* to refer to a concept in the ontology, and we say that a disorder mention has an exact match with a concept if it has an exact match with one of the *terms* associated with it.

Sieve 1: Exact Match. This sieve normalizes a disorder mention m to a concept c if m has an exact match with c.

Sieve 2: Abbreviation Expansion. This sieve first expands all abbreviated disorder mentions using Schwartz and Hearst's (2003) algorithm and the Wikipedia list of disorder abbreviations.[2] Then, it normalizes a disorder mention m to a concept c if the unabbreviated version of m has an exact match with c.

For each unnormalized mention, we pass both its original form and its new (i.e., unabbreviated) form, if applicable, to the next sieve. As we will see, we keep expanding the set of possible forms of an unnormalized mention in each sieve. Whenever a subsequent sieve processes an unnormalized mention, we mean that it processes each form of the mention created by the preceding sieves.

Sieve 3: Subject $\Leftrightarrow$ Object Conversion. This

[2] http://en.wikipedia.org/wiki/List_of_abbreviations_for_diseases_and_disorders

sieve normalizes a mention to a concept c if any of its new forms has an exact match with c. New forms of a mention m are created from its original and unabbreviated forms by: (1) replacing any preposition(s) in m with other prepositions (e.g., "changes on ekg" converted to "changes in ekg"); (2) dropping a preposition from m and swapping the substrings surrounding it (e.g., "changes on ekg" converted to "ekg changes"); (3) bringing the last token to the front, inserting a preposition as the second token, and shifting the remaining tokens to the right by two (e.g., "mental status alteration" converted to "alteration in mental status"); and (4) moving the first token to the end, inserting a preposition as the second to last token, and shifting the remaining tokens to the left by two (e.g., "leg cellulitis" converted to "cellulitis of leg"). As in Sieve 2, for each unnormalized mention in this and all subsequent sieves, both its original and new forms are passed to the next sieve.

Sieve 4: Numbers Replacement. For a disorder mention containing numbers between one to ten, new forms are produced by replacing each number in the mention with other forms of the same number. Specifically, we consider the numeral, roman numeral, cardinal, and multiplicative forms of a number for replacement. For example, three new forms will be created for "three vessel disease": {"3 vessel disease", "iii vessel disease", and "triple vessel disease"}. This sieve normalizes a mention m to a concept c if one of the new forms of m has an exact match with c.

Sieve 5: Hyphenation. A disorder mention undergoes either hyphenation (if it is not already hyphenated) or dehyphenation (if it is currently hyphenated). Hyphenation proceeds as follows: the consecutive tokens of a mention are hyphenated one pair at a time to generate a list of hyphenated forms (e.g., "ventilator associated pneumonia" becomes {"ventilator-associated pneumonia", "ventilator associated-pneumonia"}). Dehyphenation proceeds as follows: the hyphens in a mention are removed one at a time to generate a list of dehyphenated forms (e.g., "saethre-chotzen syndrome" becomes "saethre chotzen syndrome"). This sieve normalizes a mention m to a concept c if one of the new forms of m has an exact match with c.

Sieve 6: Suffixation. Disorder mentions satisfying suffixation patterns manually observed in the training data are suffixated. For example, "infectious source" becomes "source of infectious" in Sieve 3, which then becomes "source of infection" in this sieve. This sieve normalizes a mention m to a concept c if the suffixated form of m has an exact match with c.

Sieve 7: Disorder Synonyms Replacement. For mentions containing a disorder term, new forms are created by replacing the disorder term with its synonyms.[3] For example, "presyncopal events" becomes {"presyncopal disorders", "presyncopal episodes", etc.}. In addition, one more form is created by dropping the disorder modifier term (e.g., "iron-overload disease" becomes "iron overload disease" in Sieve 5, which becomes "iron overload" in this sieve). For mentions that do not contain a disorder term, new forms are created by appending the disorder synonyms to the mention. E.g., "crohns" becomes {"crohns disease", "crohns disorder", etc.}. This sieve normalizes a mention m to a concept c if any of the new forms of m has an exact match with c.

Sieve 8: Stemming. Each disorder mention is stemmed using the Porter (1980) stemmer, and the stemmed form is checked for normalization by exact match with the stemmed concept terms.

Sieve 9: Composite Disorder Mentions/Terms. A disorder mention/concept term is *composite* if it contains more than one concept term. Note that composite concept terms only appear in the UMLS ontology (i.e., the ontology for the ShARe dataset), and composite disorder mentions only appear in the NCBI corpus. Hence, different rules are used to handle the two datasets in this sieve. In the ShARe corpus, we first split each composite term associated with each concept in the UMLS ontology (e.g., "common eye and/or eyelid symptom") into separate phrases (e.g., {"common eye symptom", "common eyelid symptom"}), so each concept may now be associated with additional terms (i.e., the split terms). This sieve then normalizes a mention to a concept c if it has an exact match with c. In the NCBI corpus, we consider each disorder mention containing "and", "or", or "/" as composite, and split each such composite mention into its constituent mentions (e.g., "pineal and retinal tumors" is split into {"pineal tumors", "retinal tumors"}). This sieve then normalizes a composite mention m to a concept c as follows. First, it normalizes each of its split mentions to a concept c if the split mention has an exact match

[3]A list of the disorder word synonyms is manually created by inspection of the training data.

with c. The normalized form of m will be the union of the concepts to which each of its split mentions is normalized.[4]

Sieve 10: Partial Match. Owing to the differences in the ontologies used for the two domains, the partial match rules for the ShARe corpus are different from those for the NCBI corpus. In ShARe, a mention m is normalized to a concept c if one of the following ordered set of rules is applicable: (1) m has more than three tokens and has an exact match with c after dropping its first token or its second to last token; (2) c has a term with exactly three tokens and m has an exact match with this term after dropping its first or middle token; and (3) all of the tokens in m appear in one of the terms in c and vice versa. In NCBI, a mention is normalized to the concept with which it shares the most tokens. In the case of ties, the concept with the fewest tokens is preferred.

Finally, the disorder mentions not normalized in any of the sieves are classified as "CUI-less".

4 Related Work

In this section, we focus on discussing the two systems that have achieved the best results reported to date on our two evaluation corpora. We also discuss a state-of-the-art open-domain entity-linking system whose underlying approach is similar in spirit to ours.

DNorm (Leaman et al., 2013), which adopts a pairwise learning-to-rank approach, achieves the best normalization result on NCBI. The inputs to their system are linear vectors of paired query mentions and candidate concept terms, where the linear vectors are obtained from a tf-idf vector space representation of all unique tokens from the training disorder mentions and the candidate concept terms. Among all the candidate concepts that a given query disorder mention is paired with, the system normalizes the query mention to the highest ranked candidate. Similarity scores for ranking the candidates are computed by multiplying the linear tf-idf vectors of the paired query-candidate mentions and a learned weight matrix. The weight matrix represents all possible pairs of the unique tokens used to create the tf-idf vector. At the beginning of the learning phase, the weight matrix is initialized as an identity matrix. The matrix weights are then iteratively adjusted by stochastic gradient descent for all the concept terms, their matched training data mentions, and their mismatched training data mentions. After convergence, the weight matrix is then employed in the scoring function to normalize the test disorder mentions.

Ghiasvand and Kate's (Ghiasvand and Kate, 2014) system has produced the best results to date on ShARe. It first generates variations of a given disorder word/phrase based on a set of learned edit distance patterns for converting one word/phrase to another, and then attempts to normalize these query phrase variations by performing exact match with a training disorder mention or a concept term.

Rao et al.'s (2013) open-domain entity-linking system adopts an approach that is similar in spirit to ours. It links organizations, geo-political entities, and persons to the entities in a Wikipedia-derived knowledge base, utilizing heuristics for matching mention strings with candidate concept phrases. While they adopt a learning-based approach where the outcomes of the heuristics are encoded as features for training a ranker, their heuristics, like ours, employ syntactic transformations of the mention strings.

5 Evaluation

In this section, we evaluate our multi-pass sieve approach to normalization of disorder mentions. Results on normalizing gold disorder mentions are shown in Table 2, where performance is reported in terms of accuracy (i.e., the percentage of gold disorder mentions correctly normalized).

Row 1 shows the baseline results, which are the best results reported to date on the ShARe and NCBI datasets by Leaman et al. (2013) and Ghiasvand and Kate (2014), respectively. As we can see, the baselines achieve accuracies of 89.5 and 82.2 on ShARe and NCBI, respectively.

The subsequent rows show the results of our approach when our ten sieves are added incrementally. In other words, each row shows the results obtained after adding a sieve to the sieves in the previous rows. Our best system results, highlighted in bold in Table 2, are obtained when all our ten sieves are employed. These results are significantly better than the baseline results (paired t-tests, $p < 0.05$).

To better understand the usefulness of each sieve, we apply paired t-tests on the results in adjacent rows. We find that among the ten sieves,

[4]Note that a composite mention in NCBI may be associated with multiple concepts in the ontology.

	ShARe	NCBI
BASELINE	89.5	82.2
OUR SYSTEM		
Sieve 1 (Exact Match)	84.04	69.71
+ Sieve 2 (Abbrev.)	86.13	74.17
+ Sieve 3 (Subj/Obj)	86.40	74.27
+ Sieve 4 (Numbers)	86.45	75.00
+ Sieve 5 (Hyphen)	86.62	75.21
+ Sieve 6 (Affix)	88.11	75.62
+ Sieve 7 (Synonyms)	88.45	76.56
+ Sieve 8 (Stemming)	90.47	77.70
+ Sieve 9 (Composite)	90.53	78.00
+ Sieve 10 (Partial)	**90.75**	**84.65**

Table 2: Normalization accuracies on the test data from the ShARe corpus and the NCBI corpus.

Sieve 2 improves the results on both datasets at the lowest significance level ($p < 0.02$), while Sieves 6, 7, 8, and 10 improve results on both datasets at a slightly higher significance level ($p < 0.05$). Among the remaining four sieves (3, 4, 5, 9), Sieve 3 improves results only on the clinical reports ($p < 0.04$), Sieve 4 improves results only on the biomedical abstracts dataset ($p < 0.02$), and Sieves 5 and 9 do not have any significant impact on either dataset ($p > 0.05$). The last finding can be ascribed to the low proportions of hyphenated (Sieve 5) and composite (Sieve 9) disorder mentions found in the test datasets. After removing Sieves 5 and 9, accuracies drop insignificantly ($p > 0.05$) by 0.3% and 1.14% on the clinical reports and biomedical abstracts, respectively.

6 Error Analysis

In this section, we discuss the two major types of error made by our system.

Failure to unambiguously resolve a mention. Errors due to ambiguous normalizations where a disorder mention is mapped to more than one concept in the Partial Match sieve comprise 11–13% of the errors made by our system. For example, "aspiration" can be mapped to "pulmonary aspiration" and "aspiration pneumonia", and "growth retardation" can be mapped to "fetal growth retardation" and "mental and growth retardation with amblyopia". This ambiguity typically arises when the disorder mention under consideration is anaphoric, referring to a previously mentioned entity in the associated text. In this case, context can be used to disambiguate the mention. Specifically, a coreference resolver can first be used to identify the coreference chain to which the ambiguous mention belongs, and then the ambiguous mention can be normalized by normalizing its coreferent yet unambiguous counterparts instead.

Normalization beyond syntactic transformations. This type of error accounts for about 64–71% of the errors made by our system. It occurs when a disorder mention's string is so lexically dissimilar with the concept terms that none of our heuristics can syntactically transform it into any of them. For example, using our heuristics, "bleeding vessel" cannot be matched with any of the terms representing its associated concept, such as "vascular hemorrhage", "rupture of blood vessel", and "hemorrhage of blood vessel". Similarly, "dominantly inherited neurodegeneration" cannot be matched with any of the terms representing its associated concept, such as "hereditary neurodegenerative disease". In this case, additional information beyond a disorder mention's string and the concept terms is needed to normalize the mention. For example, one can exploit the contexts surrounding the mentions in the training set. Specifically, given a test disorder mention, one may first identify a disorder mention in the training set that is "sufficiently" similar to it based on context, and then normalize it to the concept that the training disorder mention is normalized to. Another possibility is to exploit additional knowledge bases such as Wikipedia. Specifically, one can query Wikipedia for the test mention's string, then employ the titles of the retrieved pages as alternate mention names.

7 Conclusion

We have presented a multi-pass sieve approach to the under-studied task of normalizing disorder mentions in the biomedical domain. When normalizing the gold disorder mentions in the ShARe and NCBI corpora, our approach achieved accuracies of 90.75 and 84.65, respectively, which are the best results reported to date on these corpora. Above all, to facilitate comparison with future work, we released the source code of our normalization system.

Acknowledgments

We thank the three anonymous reviewers for their detailed and insightful comments on an earlier draft of this paper. This work was supported in part by NSF Grants IIS-1147644 and IIS-1219142.

References

Keith E. Campbell, Diane E. Oliver, and Edward H. Shortliffe. 1998. The Unified Medical Language System: Towards a collaborative approach for solving terminologic problems. *Journal of the American Medical Informatics Assocication*, 5(1):12–16.

Allan Peter Davis, Thomas C. Wiegers, Michael C. Rosenstein, and Carolyn J. Mattingly. 2012. MEDIC: A practical disease vocabulary used at the Comparative Toxicogenomics Database. *Database*, 2012:bar065.

Rezarta Islamaj Doğan, Robert Leaman, and Zhiyong Lu. 2014. NCBI disease corpus: A resource for disease name recognition and concept normalization. *Journal of Biomedical Informatics*, 47:1–10.

Omid Ghiasvand and Rohit Kate. 2014. UWM: Disorder mention extraction from clinical text using CRFs and normalization using learned edit distance patterns. In *Proceedings of the 8th International Workshop on Semantic Evaluation*, pages 828–832.

Robert Leaman, Rezarta Islamaj Doğan, and Zhiyong Lu. 2013. DNorm: Disease name normalization with pairwise learning to rank. *Bioinformatics*, pages 2909–2917.

Martin F. Porter. 1980. An algorithm for suffix stripping. *Program*, 14(3):130–137.

Sameer Pradhan, Noemie Elhadad, B South, David Martinez, Lee Christensen, Amy Vogel, Hanna Suominen, W Chapman, and Guergana Savova. 2013. Task 1: ShARe/CLEF eHealth Evaluation Lab 2013. *Online Working Notes of CLEF*, 230.

Karthik Raghunathan, Heeyoung Lee, Sudarshan Rangarajan, Nathanael Chambers, Mihai Surdeanu, Dan Jurafsky, and Christopher Manning. 2010. A multipass sieve for coreference resolution. In *Proceedings of the 2010 Conference on Empirical Methods in Natural Language Processing*, pages 492–501.

Delip Rao, Paul McNamee, and Mark Dredze. 2013. Entity linking: Finding extracted entities in a knowledge base. In *Multi-source, Multi-lingual Information Extraction and Summarization*, pages 93–115.

Ariel Schwartz and Marti Hearst. 2003. A simple algorithm for identifying abbreviation definitions in biomedical text. In *Proceedings of the 8th Pacific Symposium on Biocomputing*, pages 451–462.

Open IE as an Intermediate Structure for Semantic Tasks

Gabriel Stanovsky[†] **Ido Dagan**[‡] **Mausam**[§]
[†,‡]Department of Computer Science, Bar-Ilan University
[§]Department of Computer Science & Engg, Indian Institute of Technology, Delhi
[†]gabriel.satanovsky@gmail.com
[‡]dagan@cs.biu.ac.il
[§]mausam@cse.iitd.ac.in

Abstract

Semantic applications typically extract information from intermediate structures derived from sentences, such as dependency parse or semantic role labeling. In this paper, we study Open Information Extraction's (Open IE) output as an additional intermediate structure and find that for tasks such as text comprehension, word similarity and word analogy it can be very effective. Specifically, for word analogy, Open IE-based embeddings surpass the state of the art. We suggest that semantic applications will likely benefit from adding Open IE format to their set of potential sentence-level structures.

1 Introduction

Semantic applications, such as QA or summarization, typically extract sentence features from a derived intermediate structure. Common intermediate structures include: (1) Lexical representations, in which features are extracted from the original word sequence or the bag of words, (2) Stanford dependency parse trees (De Marneffe and Manning, 2008), which draw syntactic relations between words, and (3) Semantic role labeling (SRL), which extracts frames linking predicates with their semantic arguments (Carreras and Màrquez, 2005). For instance, a QA application can evaluate a question and a candidate answer by examining their lexical overlap (Pérez-Coutiño et al., 2006), by using short dependency paths as features to compare their syntactic relationships (Liang et al., 2013), or by using SRL to compare their predicate-argument structures (Shen and Lapata, 2007).

In a seemingly independent research direction, Open Information Extraction (Open IE) extracts coherent propositions from a sentence, each comprising a relation phrase and two or more argument phrases (Etzioni et al., 2008; Fader et al., 2011; Mausam et al., 2012). We observe that while Open IE is primarily used as an end goal in itself (e.g., (Fader et al., 2014)), it also makes certain structural design choices which differ from those made by dependency or SRL. For example, Open IE chooses different predicate and argument boundaries and assigns different relations between them.

Given the differences between Open IE and other intermediate structures (see Section 2), a research question arises: Can certain downstream applications gain additional benefits from utilizing Open IE structures? To answer this question we quantitatively evaluate the use of Open IE output against other dominant structures (Sections 3 and 4). For each of text comprehension, word similarity and word analogy tasks, we choose a state-of-the-art algorithm in which we can easily *swap* the intermediate structure while preserving the algorithmic computations over the features extracted from it. We find that in several tasks Open IE substantially outperforms other structures, suggesting that it can provide an additional set of useful sentence-level features.

2 Intermediate Structures

In this section we review how intermediate structures differ from each other, in terms of their imposed structure, predicate and argument boundaries, and the type of relations that they introduce. We include Open IE in this analysis, along with lexical, dependency and SRL representations, and highlight its unique properties. As we show in Section 4, these differences have an impact on the overall performance of certain downstream applications.

Lexical representations introduce little or no structure over the input text. Features for following computations are extracted directly from the original word sequence, e.g., word count statistics or lexical overlap (see Figure 1a).

Proceedings of the 53rd Annual Meeting of the Association for Computational Linguistics and the 7th International Joint Conference on Natural Language Processing (Short Papers), pages 303–308,
Beijing, China, July 26-31, 2015.

Syntactic dependencies impose a tree structure (see Figure 1b), and use words as atomic elements. This structure implies that predicates are generally composed of a single word and that arguments are computed either as single words or as entire spans of subtrees subordinate to the predicate word.

In SRL (see Figure 1c), several non-connected frames are extracted from the sentence. The atomic elements of each frame consist of a single-word predicate (e.g., the different frames for *visit* and *refused*), and a list of its semantic arguments, without marking their internal structure. Each argument is listed along with its semantic relation (e.g., *agent*, *instrument*, etc.) and usually spans several words.

Open IE (see Figure 1d) also extracts non-connected propositions, consisting of a predicate and its arguments. In contrast to SRL, argument relations are not analyzed, and predicates (as well as arguments) may consist of several consecutive words. Since Open IE focuses on human-readability, infinitive constructions (e.g., *refused to visit*), and multi-word predicates (e.g., *took advantage*) are grouped in a single predicate slot. Additionally, arguments are truncated in cases such as prepositional phrases and reduced relative clauses. The resulting structure can be understood as an extension of shallow syntactic chunking (Abney, 1992), where chunks are labeled as either predicates or arguments, and are then interlinked to form a complete proposition.

It is not clear apriory whether the differences manifested in Open IE's structure could be beneficial as intermediate structures for downstream applications. Although a few end tasks have made use of Open IE's output (Christensen et al., 2013; Balasubramanian et al., 2013), there has been no systematic comparison against other structures. In the following sections, we quantitatively study and analyze the value of Open IE structures against the more common intermediate structures – lexical, dependency and SRL, for three downstream NLP tasks.

3 Tasks and Algorithms

Comparing the effectiveness of intermediate structures in semantic applications is hard for several reasons: (1) extracting the underlying structure depends on the accuracy of the specific system used, (2) the overall performance in the task depends heavily on the computations carried on top of these

S: John refused [**to visit a Vegas casino**]
CA: John **visited a Vegas casino**

(a) Lexical matching of a 5 words window (marked with a box). Current window yields a score of 4 - words contributing to the score are marked in bold.

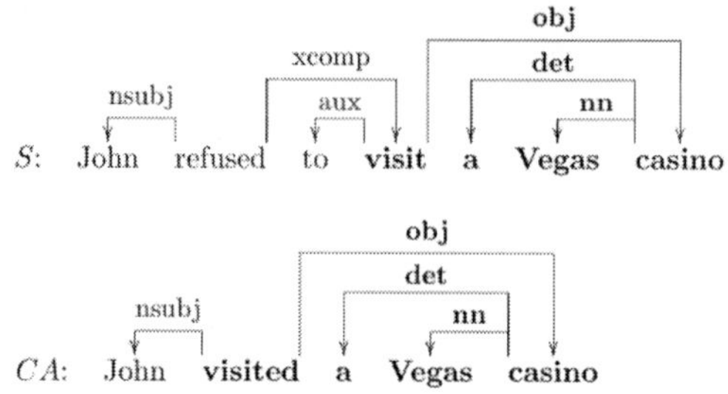

(b) Dependency matching yields a score of 3. Contributing triplets are marked in bold.

S:	refused$_{0.1}$:	**A$_0$: John**	A$_1$: to visit a Vegas casino
	visit$_{0.1}$:	**A$_0$: John**	**A$_1$: a Vegas casino**
CA:	**visit$_{0.1}$:**	**A$_0$: John**	**A$_1$: a Vegas casino**

(c) SRL frames matching yields a score of 4, frame elements contributing to the score marked in bold.

S: (**John**, refused to visit, **a Vegas casino**)
CA: (**John**, visited, **a Vegas casino**)

(d) Open IE matching yields a score of 2, contributing entries marked in bold.

Figure 1: Different intermediate structures used to compute the modified text comprehension matching score (Section 3), when answering a question *"Where did John visit?"*, given an input sentence S: *"John refused to visit a Vegas casino"*, and a *wrong* candidate answer CA: *"John visited a Vegas casino"*.

structures, and (3) different structures may be suitable for different tasks. To mitigate these complications, and comparatively evaluate the effectiveness of different types of structures, we choose three semantic tasks along with state-of-the-art algorithms that make a clear separation between feature extraction and subsequent computation. We then compare performance by using features from four intermediate structures – lexical, dependency, SRL and Open IE. Each of these is extracted using state-of-the-art systems. Thus, while our comparisons are valid only for the tested tasks and systems, they do provide valuable evidence for the general question of effective intermediate structures.

3.1 Text Comprehension Task

Text comprehension tasks extrinsically test natural language understanding through question answer-

Target	Lexical	Dependency	SRL	Open IE
	John	nsubj_John	A0_John	0_John
	to	xcomp_visit	A1_to	1_to
refused	visit		A1_visit	1_visit
	Vegas		A1_Vegas	2_Vegas

Table 1: Some of the different contexts for the target word "refused" in the sentence *"John refused to visit Vegas"*. SRL and Open IE contexts are preceded by their element (predicate or argument) index. See figure 1 for the different representations of this sentence.

ing. We use the MCTest corpus (Richardson et al., 2013), which is composed of short stories followed by multiple choice questions. The MCTest task does not require extensive world knowledge, which makes it ideal for testing underlying sentence representations, as performance will mostly depend on accuracy and informativeness of the extracted structures.

We adapt the unsupervised lexical matching algorithm from the original MCTest paper. It counts lexical matches between an assertion obtained from a candidate answer (CA) and a sliding window over the story. The selected answer is the one for which the maximum number of matches are found. Our adaptation changes the algorithm to compute a modified *matching score* by counting matches between *structure units*. The corresponding units are either dependency edges, SRL frame elements or Open IE tuple elements. Figure 1 illustrates computations for a sentence - candidate answer pair.

3.2 Similarity and Analogy Tasks

Word similarity tasks deal with assessing the degree of "similarity" between two input words. Turney (2012) classifies two types of similarity: (1) domain similarity, e.g., *carpenter* is similar to *wood, hammer*, and *nail*, (2) functional similarity, in which *carpenter* will be similar to other professions, e.g., *shoemaker, brewer, miner* etc. Several evaluation test sets exist for this task, each targeting a slightly different aspect of similarity. While Bruni (2012), Luong (2013), Radinsky (2011), and ws353 (Finkelstein et al., 2001) can be largely categorized as targeting domain similarity, simlex999 (Hill et al., 2014) specifically targets functional aspects of similarity (e.g., *coast* will be similar to *shore*, while *closet* will not be similar to *clothes*). A related task is *word analogy*, in which systems take three input words (A:A^*, B:?) and output a word B^*, such that the relation between B and B^* is closest to the relation between A and A^*. For instance, *queen* is the desired answer for the triple (*man:king, woman*:?).

Some recent state-of-the-art approaches to these two tasks derive a similarity score via arithmetic computations on word embeddings (Mikolov et al., 2013b). While original training of word embeddings used lexical contexts (n-grams), recently Levy and Goldberg (2014) generalized this to arbitrary contexts, such as dependency paths. We use their software[1] and recompute the word embeddings using contexts from our four structures: lexical context, dependency paths, SRL's semantic relations, and Open IE's surrounding tuple elements. Table 1 shows the different contexts for a sample word.

4 Evaluation

In our experiments we use MaltParser (Nivre et al., 2007) for dependency parsing, and ClearNLP (Choi and Palmer, 2011) for SRL.

To obtain Open-IE structures, we use the recent Open IE-4 system[2] which produces n-ary extractions of both verb-based relation phrases using SRLIE (an improvement over (Christensen et al., 2011)) and nominal relations using regular expressions. SRLIE first processes sentences using SRL and then uses hand-coded rules to convert SRL frames and associated dependency parses to open extractions.

We choose these tools as they are on par with state-of-the-art in their respective fields, and therefore represent the current available off-the-shelf intermediate structures for semantic applications. Furthermore, Open IE-4 is based on ClearNLP's SRL, allowing for a direct comparison. For SRL systems, we take argument boundaries as their complete parse subtrees.[3]

Results on Text Comprehension Task We report results (in percentage of correct answers) on the whole of MC500 dataset (ignoring train-dev-test split) since all our methods are unsupervised. Figure 2 shows the accuracies obtained on the multiple-choice questions, categorized by *single* (the question can be answered based on a sin-

[1] *https://bitbucket.org/yoavgo/word2vecf*

[2] *http://knowitall.github.io/openie/*

[3] We tried an alternative approach which takes only the heads as arguments, but that performed much worse.

	Open IE	Lexical	Deps	SRL
bruni	**.757**	.735	.618	.491
luong	**.288**	.229	.197	.171
radinsky	**.681**	.674	.592	.433
simlex	.39	.365	**.447**	.306
ws353-rel	**.647**	.64	.492	.551
ws353-sym	**.77**	.763	.759	.439
ws353-full	**.711**	.703	.629	.693

Table 2: Performance in word similarity tasks (Spearman's ρ)

	Google		MSR	
	Add	Mul	Add	Mul
Open IE	**.714**	**.719**	**.529**	**.55**
Lexical	.651	.656	.438	.455
Deps	.34	.367	.4	.434
SRL	.352	.362	.389	.406

Table 3: Performance in word analogy tasks (percentage of correct answers)

gle story sentence) , *multiple* (multiple sentences needed) and *all* (*single* + *multiple*).[4]

In this task, we find that Open IE and dependency edges substantially outperform lexical and SRL. We conjecture that SRL's weak performance is due to its treatment of infinitives and multi-word predicates as different propositions (see Section 2). This adds noise by wrongly counting partial matching between predications, as exemplified in Figure 1c. The gain over the lexical approach can be explained by the ability to capture longer range relations than the fixed size window.[5] In our results Open IE slightly improves over dependency. This can be traced back to the different structural choices depicted in Section 2 – Open IE counts matches at the proposition level while the dependency variant may count path matches over unrelated sentence parts. The differences between the performance of Open IE and all other systems were found to be statistically significant ($p < 0.01$).

Results on Similarity and Analogy Tasks For these tasks, we train the various word embeddings on a Wikipedia dump (August 2013 dump), containing 77.5M sentences and 1.5B tokens. We used the default hyperparameters from Levy and Goldberg (2014): 300 dimensions, skip gram with negative sampling of size 5. Lexical embeddings were trained with 5-gram contexts. Performance is measured using Spearman's ρ, in order to assess the correlation of the predictions to the gold annotations, rather than comparing their values directly. Table 2 compares the results on the *word similarity task* using cosine similarity between embeddings as the similarity predictor. For the *ws353* test set we report results on the whole corpus (*full*) as well as on the partition suggested by (Agirre et al., 2009) into *relatedness* (mainly meronym-holonym) and *similarity* (synonyms, antonyms, or hyponym-hypernym).

We find that Open IE-based embeddings consistently do well; performing best across all test sets, except for simlex999. Analysis reveals that Open IE's ability to represent multi-word predicates and arguments allows it to naturally incorporate *both* notions of similarity. Context words originating from the same Open IE slot (either predicate or argument) are lexically close and indicate domain-similarity, whereas context words from other elements in the tuple express semantic relationships, and target functional similarity.

Thus, Open IE performs better on word-pairs which exhibit both topical and functional similarity, such as *(latinist, classicist)*, or *(provincialism, narrow-mindedness)*, which were taken from the Luong test set. Table 4 further illustrates this dual capturing of both types of similarity in Open IE space.

Our results also reiterate previous findings – lexical contexts do well on domain-similarity test sets (Mikolov et al., 2013b). The results on the simlex999 test set can be explained by its focus on functional similarity, previously identified as better captured by dependency contexts (Levy and Goldberg, 2014).

For the *Word analogy task* we use the Google (Mikolov et al., 2013a) and the Microsoft corpora (Mikolov et al., 2013b), which are composed of $\sim 195K$ and $8K$ instances respectively. We obtain the analogy vectors using both the additive and multiplicative measures (Mikolov et al., 2013b; Levy and Goldberg, 2014). Table 3 shows the results – Open IE obtains the best accuracies by vast margins ($p < 0.01$), for reasons simi-

[4]As expected, all sentence-level intermediate structures perform best on the *single* partition, yet results show that some of the questions from the *multiple* partition may also be answered correctly using information from a single sentence.

[5]We experimented with various window sizes and found that window size of the length of the current candidate-answer performed best.

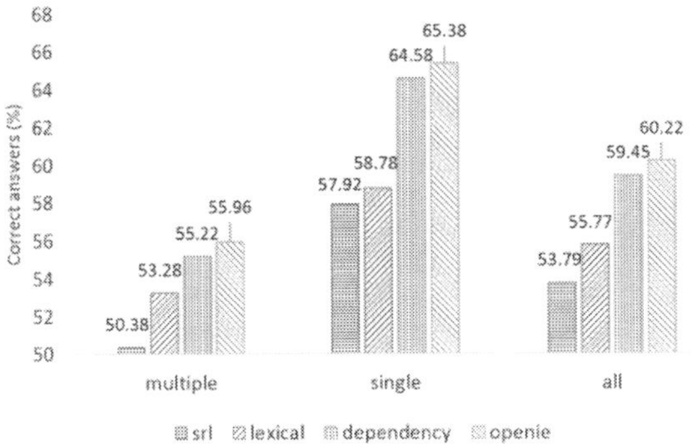

Figure 2: Performance in MCTest (percentage of correct answers).

lar to the word similarity tasks. To our knowledge, Open IE results on both analogy datasets surpass the state of the art. An example (from the Microsoft test set) which supports the observation regarding Open IE embeddings space is (*gentlest:gentler, loudest:*?), for which only Open IE answers correctly as *louder*, while lexical respond with *higher-pitched* (domain similar to *loudest*), and dependency with *thinnest* (functionally similar to *loudest*). Our Open-IE embeddings are freely available[6] and we note that these can serve as plug-in features for other NLP applications, as demonstrated in (Turian et al., 2010).

5 Conclusions

We studied Open IE's output compared with other dominant structures, highlighting their main differences. We then conduct experiments and analysis suggesting that these structural differences prove beneficial for certain downstream semantic applications. A key strength is Open IE's ability to balance lexical proximity with long range dependencies in a single representation. Specifically, for the word analogy task, Open IE-based embeddings surpass all prior results. We conclude that an NLP practitioner will likely benefit from adding Open IE to their toolkit of potential sentence representations.

[6] *http://www.cs.bgu.ac.il/~gabriels*

Target Word	Lexical	Dependency	Open IE
	dog	feline	dog
	incisor	bovine	carnassial
canine	dentition	equine	feline
	parvovirus	porcine	fang-like
	dysplasia	murine	bovine

Table 4: Closest words to *canine* in various word embeddings. Illustrating domain similarity (Lexical), functional similarity (Dependency), and a mixture of both (Open IE).

Acknowledgments

This work was partially supported by the Israel Science Foundation grant 880/12, the German Research Foundation through the German-Israeli Project Cooperation (DIP, grant DA 1600/1-1), a Google Research Award to Ido Dagan, and Google's Language Understanding and Knowledge Discovery Focused Research Award to Mausam.

References

Steven P Abney. 1992. Parsing by chunks. *Principle-based parsing*, pages 257–278.

Eneko Agirre, Enrique Alfonseca, Keith Hall, Jana Kravalova, Marius Paşca, and Aitor Soroa. 2009. A study on similarity and relatedness using distributional and wordnet-based approaches. In *Proceedings of Human Language Technologies: The 2009 Annual Conference of the North American Chapter of the Association for Computational Linguistics*, pages 19–27. Association for Computational Linguistics.

Niranjan Balasubramanian, Stephen Soderland, Mausam, and Oren Etzioni. 2013. Generating coherent event schemas at scale. In *Conference on Empirical Methods in Natural Language Processing*, pages 1721–1731.

Elia Bruni, Gemma Boleda, Marco Baroni, and Nam-Khanh Tran. 2012. Distributional semantics in technicolor. In *Proceedings of the 50th Annual Meeting of the Association for Computational Linguistics: Long Papers-Volume 1*, pages 136–145. Association for Computational Linguistics.

Xavier Carreras and Lluís Màrquez. 2005. Introduction to the conll-2005 shared task: Semantic role labeling. In *Proceedings of The SIGNLL Conference on Computational Natural Language Learning (CoNLL)*, pages 152–164.

Jinho D Choi and Martha Palmer. 2011. Transition-based semantic role labeling using predicate argument clustering. In *Proceedings of the ACL 2011 Workshop on Relational Models of Semantics*, pages 37–45. Association for Computational Linguistics.

Janara Christensen, Mausam, Stephen Soderland, and Oren Etzioni. 2011. An analysis of open information extraction based on semantic role labeling. In *Proceedings of the 6th International Conference on Knowledge Capture (K-CAP '11)*.

Janara Christensen, Mausam, Stephen Soderland, and Oren Etzioni. 2013. Towards coherent multi-document summarization. In *Conference of the North American Chapter of the Association for Computational Linguistics Human Language Technologies*, pages 1163–1173.

Marie-Catherine De Marneffe and Christopher D Manning. 2008. The stanford typed dependencies representation. In *Coling 2008: Proceedings of the workshop on Cross-Framework and Cross-Domain Parser Evaluation*, pages 1–8.

Oren Etzioni, Michele Banko, Stephen Soderland, and Daniel S Weld. 2008. Open information extraction from the Web. *Communications of the ACM*, 51(12):68–74.

Anthony Fader, Stephen Soderland, and Oren Etzioni. 2011. Identifying relations for open information extraction. In *Proceedings of the Conference on Empirical Methods in Natural Language Processing*, pages 1535–1545. Association for Computational Linguistics.

Anthony Fader, Luke Zettlemoyer, and Oren Etzioni. 2014. Open question answering over curated and extracted knowledge bases. In *The 20th ACM SIGKDD International Conference on Knowledge Discovery and Data Mining, KDD '14, New York, NY, USA - August 24 - 27, 2014*, pages 1156–1165.

Lev Finkelstein, Evgeniy Gabrilovich, Yossi Matias, Ehud Rivlin, Zach Solan, Gadi Wolfman, and Eytan Ruppin. 2001. Placing search in context: The concept revisited. In *Proceedings of the 10th international conference on World Wide Web*, pages 406–414. ACM.

Felix Hill, Roi Reichart, and Anna Korhonen. 2014. Simlex-999: Evaluating semantic models with (genuine) similarity estimation. *arXiv preprint arXiv:1408.3456*.

Omer Levy and Yoav Goldberg. 2014. Dependency-based word embeddings. In *Proceedings of the 52nd Annual Meeting of the Association for Computational Linguistics*, volume 2.

Percy Liang, Michael I. Jordan, and Dan Klein. 2013. Learning dependency-based compositional semantics. *Computational Linguistics*, 39(2):389–446.

Minh-Thang Luong, Richard Socher, and Christopher D. Manning. 2013. Better word representations with recursive neural networks for morphology. *The SIGNLL Conference on Computational Natural Language Learning (CoNLL)*, 104.

Mausam, Michael Schmitz, Stephen Soderland, Robert Bart, and Oren Etzioni. 2012. Open language learning for information extraction. In *Proceedings of the 2012 Joint Conference on Empirical Methods in Natural Language Processing and Computational Natural Language Learning*, pages 523–534, Jeju Island, Korea, July. Association for Computational Linguistics.

Tomas Mikolov, Kai Chen, Greg Corrado, and Jeffrey Dean. 2013a. Efficient estimation of word representations in vector space. In *Workshop at The International Conference on Learning Representations (ICLR)*.

Tomas Mikolov, Wen-tau Yih, and Geoffrey Zweig. 2013b. Linguistic regularities in continuous space word representations. In *Conference of the North American Chapter of the Association for Computational Linguistics Human Language Technologies*, pages 746–751.

Joakim Nivre, Johan Hall, Jens Nilsson, Atanas Chanev, Gülsen Eryigit, Sandra Kübler, Svetoslav Marinov, and Erwin Marsi. 2007. Maltparser: A language-independent system for data-driven dependency parsing. *Natural Language Engineering*, 13(02):95–135.

Manuel Pérez-Coutiño, Manuel Montes-y Gómez, Aurelio López-López, and Luis Villaseñor-Pineda. 2006. *The role of lexical features in Question Answering for Spanish*. Springer.

Kira Radinsky, Eugene Agichtein, Evgeniy Gabrilovich, and Shaul Markovitch. 2011. A word at a time: computing word relatedness using temporal semantic analysis. In *Proceedings of the 20th international conference on World wide web*, pages 337–346. ACM.

Matthew Richardson, Christopher JC Burges, and Erin Renshaw. 2013. Mctest: A challenge dataset for the open-domain machine comprehension of text. In *Conference on Empirical Methods in Natural Language Processing*, pages 193–203.

Dan Shen and Mirella Lapata. 2007. Using semantic roles to improve question answering. In *EMNLP-CoNLL 2007, Proceedings of the 2007 Joint Conference on Empirical Methods in Natural Language Processing and Computational Natural Language Learning, June 28-30, 2007, Prague, Czech Republic*, pages 12–21.

Joseph Turian, Lev Ratinov, and Yoshua Bengio. 2010. Word representations: a simple and general method for semi-supervised learning. In *Proceedings of the 48th annual meeting of the association for computational linguistics*, pages 384–394. Association for Computational Linguistics.

Peter D Turney. 2012. Domain and function: A dual-space model of semantic relations and compositions. *Journal of Artificial Intelligence Research*, 44:533–585.

Recovering dropped pronouns from Chinese text messages

Yaqin Yang
Paypal Inc.
yaqin276@gmail.com

Yalin Liu
Brandeis University
yalin@brandeis.edu

Nianwen Xu
Brandeis University
xuen@brandeis.edu

Abstract

Pronouns are frequently dropped in Chinese sentences, especially in informal data such as text messages. In this work we propose a solution to recover dropped pronouns in SMS data. We manually annotate dropped pronouns in 684 SMS files and apply machine learning algorithms to recover them, leveraging lexical, contextual and syntactic information as features. We believe this is the first work on recovering dropped pronouns in Chinese text messages.

1 Introduction

Text messages generated by users via SMS or Chat have distinct linguistic characteristics that pose unique challenges for existing natural language processing techniques. Since such text messages are often generated via mobile devices in informal settings and are limited in length, abbreviations and omissions are commonplace. In this paper, we report work on detecting one particular type of omission in Chinese text messages, namely dropped pronouns.

It is well-known that Chinese is a pro-drop language, meaning pronouns can be dropped from a sentence without causing the sentence to become ungrammatical or incomprehensible when the identity of the pronoun can be inferred from the context. Pronouns can be dropped even in formal text genres like newswire, but the extent to which this happens and the types of pronouns that are dropped in text messages and formal genres like newswire are very different. For example, the most frequently dropped pronouns in Chinese newswire is the third person singular 它("it") (Baran et al. 2012), and one reason is that first and second person pronouns are rarely used in newswire in the first place. In contrast, in text messages, the first person singular 我 and the second person singular 你 are commonly found in text messages due to their conversational style, and they are often dropped as well when their referent is understood in the context. This is illustrated in (1), where there are instances of dropped first person singular, second person singular and third person singular pronouns. There is also an instance where the dropped pronoun in Chinese does not have any actual referent, translating to the English pleonastic "it". Dropped pronouns are in parentheses:

(1) A 你们那 下雪 了 ，你 怎么去 上班
your area snow ASP , you how go work

"It snowed in your area. How do you go to work?"

B (我) 步行 或坐车
(I) walk or take the bus

"(I) walk or take the bus."

A (pleonastic) 看来 交通业 还是
(it) look like transportation
比较 发达 的.
relatively developed

"(It) looks like you have a relatively developed transportation system."

B (pleonastic) 下雪 (我) 就 不 能
(it) snow (I) then not can
上班 了
go to work ASP

"When (it) snows, (I) cannot go to work."

B (它) 还可以
(it) OK

"(It) is OK."

Detecting dropped pronouns involves first of all determining where in the sentence pronouns are

Proceedings of the 53rd Annual Meeting of the Association for Computational Linguistics and the 7th International Joint Conference on Natural Language Processing (Short Papers), pages 309–313,
Beijing, China, July 26-31, 2015.

dropped and then determining what the dropped pronoun is, i.e., whether the dropped pronoun should be 我, 你, 他, etc. The dropped pronoun could either correspond to one of possible pronouns in Chinese, or it can be an abstract pronoun that does not correspond to any of the Chinese pronouns. For example, Chinese does not have a pronoun that is the equivalent of the pleonastic "it" in English, but there are sentences in which a dropped pronoun occurs in a context that is similar to where "it" occurs. In this case we label the dropped pronoun as a type of abstract pronoun. Note that we do not attempt to resolve these pronouns to an antecedent in this work. We think there is value in just detecting these pronouns. For example, if we translate Chinese sentences with dropped pronouns into English, they may have to be made explicit.

We approach this as a supervised learning problem, so first we need a corpus annotated with the location and type of dropped pronouns to train machine learning models. We annotated 292,455 words of Chinese SMS/Chat data with dropped pronouns and we describe our annotation in more detail in Section 2. We then present our machine learning approach in Section 3. Experimental results are presented in Section 4, and related work is described in Section 5. Finally we conclude in Section 6.

2 Dropped pronoun annotation

We annotated 684 Chinese SMS/Chat files following the dropped pronoun annotation guidelines described in (Baran et al. 2012). The original guidelines are mainly designed for annotating dropped pronouns in newswire text, and we had to extend the guidelines to accommodate SMS/Chat data. For example, (Baran et al. 2012) identify 14 types of pronouns, which include four *abstract pronouns* which do not correspond to any actual pronouns in Chinese. To accommodate SMS/Chat data, we add one more type of abstract pronoun that refers to the previous utterance. The full list of pronouns that we use are listed below:

1. 我(I): first person singular
2. 我们(we): first person plural
3. 你(you): second person singular
4. 你们(you): second person plural
5. 他(he): third person masculine singular
6. 他们(they): third person masculine plural
7. 她(she): third person feminine singular
8. 她们(they): third person feminine plural
9. 它(it): third person inanimate singular
10. 它们(they): third person inanimate plural
11. Event: abstract pronoun that refers to an event
12. Existential: abstract pronoun that refers to existential subject
13. Pleonastic: abstract pronoun that refers to pleonastic subject
14. generic: abstract pronoun that refers to something generic or unspecific
15. Previous Utterance: abstract pronoun that refers to previous utterance
16. Other: cases where it is unclear what the correct pronoun should be

3 Learning

We have formulated dropped pronoun recovery as a sequential tagging problem, following (Yang and Xue. 2010). We check each word token in a sentence and decide if there is a pronoun dropped before this word. If there is one, then we further identify what type of pronoun it should be. Instead of doing this in two separate steps, we trained a 17-class Maximum Entropy classifier with the Mallet (McCallum et al. 2002) machine learning package to tag each word token with one of the pronouns or *None* in one run. *None* indicates that there is no dropped pronoun before this word.

We leveraged a set of lexical features from previous work (Yang and Xue. 2010). To our knowledge, the work we report here represents the first effort on dropped pronoun recovery on Chinese SMS/Chat data. As described in Section 2, SMS data is different from newswire data which is commonly used in previous work (Converse. 2006; Zhao and Ng. 2007; Peng and Araki. 2007; Kong and Zhou. 2010; Chung and Gildea 2010; Cai et al. 2011; Xiang et al. 2013) in many aspects. The frequency of pronoun being dropped is much higher in SMS/Chat data compared to newswire data. The distribution of dropped pronoun types in SMS data is also very different from that of newswire data. In SMS/Chat data, the identities of the participants who send the messages are critical in identifying the dropped pronoun type, while there is no participant information in newswire data. Thus, we also design a new set of context based features to capture the stylistic properties of text messages.

Lexical Features: Information embedded in the target and surrounding words provide clues for identifying dropped pronouns, e.g.,

(2) (它) 坏 了 .
(it) broken ASP .
"(It) is broken."

In (2), a pronoun is dropped at the beginning of the sentence. The follwing words "坏了" means "is broken", and it indicates that the subject refers to a thing, not a person. Part-of-speech tags are also crucial in finding the location of a dropped pronoun. Just like pronouns are usually located before verbs, it is more likely to have a pronoun dropped before an verb than a noun. We implemented a set of lexical features along with part-of-speech tags within a sliding window of five words to capture such information. The contextual features are listed below:

- unigrams within current window;
- previous and following (including current word) bigrams;
- POS tags of unigrams within current window;
- POS tags of the previous and following (including current word) bigrams;
- POS tags of the following (including current word) trigram;
- combination previous word and POS tag of current word;
- combination of POS tag of previous word and current word;
- POS tag sequence from the previous word to the beginning of a sentence or a punctuation mark.

Context-based Features: It is hard to recover dropped pronouns without understanding the context. In SMS data, one sometimes needs to trace back a few sentences to figure out what a dropped pronoun refers to.

(3) a. 我想 买 个 单反 .
I want buy CL SLR camera .
"I want to buy a SLR camera."

b. (我) 国庆节 出去 玩 啊.
(I) Independent Day go out travel .
"(I) will travel on Independent Day."

In (3), the two sentences are attributed to the same person, and a pronoun is dropped at the beginning of the second sentence. While we could easily understand the dropped pronoun refers to "我(I)" from the previous sentence, it is difficult to make this determination by just looking at the second sentence independently. Thus, we propose a list of novel context-based features tailored towards SMS/Chat data to capture such information:

- previous pronoun used by the same participant;
- previous pronoun used by the other participant;
- all previous pronouns till the beginning of a sentence or a punctuation mark used;
- next punctuation mark;
- if it is a question;
- if the POS tag of the last word is SP;
- for the first word in a sentence, use first two nouns/pronouns from the previous sentence.

Syntactic Features: Syntactic features have been shown to be useful in previous work (**?**). We also implemented the following syntactic features:

- if it is the left frontier of the lowest IP antecedent;
- if current word is "有", then find it's subject;
- path from current word to the root node.

4 Experiments and discussion

4.1 Data split

Table 1 presents the data split used in our experiments.

data set	# of words	# of files
Train	235,184	487
Dev	24,769	98
Test	32,502	99

Table 1: Training, development and test data on SMS data set.

4.2 Results

As mentioned in Section 3, we extract lexical, context and syntactic features from SMS data and train a 17-class classifier to automatically recover dropped pronouns. To obtain syntactic features, we divided 684 SMS files into 10 portions, and parsed each portion with a model trained on other portions, using the Berkeley parser (Petrov and Klein 2007). The parsing accuracy stands at 82.11% (F-score), with a precision of 82.57% and a recall of 81.65%. The results of our experiments are presented in Table 2.

tag	pre.(%)	rec.(%)	f.	count
NE	99.1	95.7	97.3	28963
我	48	53.1	50.4	1155
你	34.4	48.1	40.1	787
它	12.1	54.6	19.8	488
prev_utterance	87.6	65.3	74.8	314
pleonastic	7	10.2	8.3	172
她	4.3	27.8	7.4	117
他	11	22.2	14.7	109
我们	24	41	30.3	104
generic	6.6	17.1	9.5	91
他们	2.7	11.1	4.4	73
event	4.3	25	7.3	47
它们	4.7	100	8.9	43
other	0	0	0	16
你们	0	0	0	13
existential	12.5	2	3.4	8
她们	0	0	0	2

Table 2: precision, recall and f-score for different dropped pronoun categories on test set. The combination of "我(I)", "你(singular you)" and "utterance" accounts for 63.7% of the overall dropped pronoun population. The overall accuracy is 92.1%. "NE" stands for None, meaning there is no dropped pronoun.

	NE	我	你	它	ut	pl	她	他	我们	ge	他们	ev	它们	ot	你们	ex	她们
NE	28695	130	77	9	8	7	2	10	9	8	1	.	.	.	1	6	.
我	433	554	101	11	5	13	2	5	10	4	1	1	.	.	1	14	.
你	327	135	271	6	3	16	1	6	6	9	1	1	.	.	.	5	.
它	199	85	49	59	23	42	1	10	1	3	5	1	.	.	1	9	.
utterance	23	7	1	4	275	4	.	.	.	.	.	.	.	.	.	.	.
pleonastic	36	17	5	5	88	12	1	1	1	.	1	.	.	.	.	5	.
她	47	21	21	5	1	6	5	5	1	.	3	1	.	.	.	1	.
他	46	23	10	2	6	5	1	12	.	1	.	.	.	.	.	3	.
我们	47	17	5	2	.	.	2	2	25	.	1	1	.	.	.	2	.
generic	52	20	5	.	.	.	.	2	2	6	.	.	.	.	.	4	.
他们	38	15	7	2	.	3	2	.	1	2	2	1	.	.	.	.	.
event	16	4	3	2	11	6	1	1	.	.	1	2	.	.	.	.	.
它们	14	11	4	.	1	3	.	.	3	2	2	.	2	.	.	1	.
other	15	.	.	.	.	1	.	.	.	.	.	.	.	.	.	.	.
你们	6	2	4	1	.	.	.	.	.	.	.	.	.	.	.	.	.
existential	4	2	.	.	.	.	.	.	1	.	.	.	.	.	.	1	.
她们	1	.	.	.	.	.	.	.	1	.	.	.	.	.	.	.	.

Table 3: Confusion matrix for each annotation category. Columns correspond to Maxent predicted values and rows refer to annotated values.

4.3 Error Analysis

From Table 3, which is a confusion matrix generated from results on the test set, showing the classification errors among different types, we can see that the classifier did a better job of recovering "我(I)", "你(singular you)" and "previous utterance", the combination of which accounts for 63.7% of the total dropped pronoun instances. However, it is hard for the classifier to recover "它(it)", e.g.,

"*pro* 这种? (*pro* that kind?)"

SMS sentences are usually short. To understand what the dropped pronoun stands for, one needs to look at its previous context. But it is hard for machine to capture such long distance information.

5 Related Work

One line of work that is closely related to ours is zero pronoun resolution. In zero pronoun resolution (Converse. 2006; Zhao and Ng. 2007; Peng and Araki. 2007; Kong and Zhou. 2010), pronouns are typically resolved in three steps: zero pronoun detection, anaphoricity determination, and antecedent resolution. In the work we report here, we are more interested in detecting dropped pronouns and determining what types of pronoun they are.

Dropped pronoun detection is also related to Empty Category (EC) detection and resolution (Chung and Gildea 2010; Cai et al. 2011; Xiang et al. 2013), the aim of which is to recover long-distance dependencies, discontinuous constituents, and certain dropped elements in phrase structure treebanks (Marcus et al. 1993; Xue et al. 2005). In previous work on EC detection (Chung and Gildea 2010; Cai et al. 2011; Xiang et al. 2013), ECs are recovered from newswire data by leveraging lexical and syntactic information from each sentence. Context information beyond the current sentence is typically not used. When recovering dropped pronouns in SMS/Chat messages, it is crucially important to make use of information beyond the current sentence.

6 Conclusion and Future Work

In this paper we report work on recovering dropped pronouns in Chinese SMS/Chat messages. Based on the properties of SMS data, we designed a set of lexical, contextual and syntactic features, and trained a Maxent classifier to recover dropped pronouns in Chinese SMS/Chat messages. We believe this is the first work on recovering dropped pronouns in Chinese text messages. This proves to be a very challenging task, and much remains to be done. In future work, we plan to experiment with applying more expressive machine learning techniques to this task.

Acknowledgments

We want to thank the anonymous reviewers for their suggestions. This work was partially supported by the National Science Foundation via Grant No.0910532 entitled "Richer Representations for Machine Translation". All views expressed in this paper are those of the authors and do not necessarily represent the view of the National Science Foundation.

References

Zhao, Shanheng and Ng, Hwee Tou 2007 *Identification and Resolution of Chinese Zero Pronouns: A Machine Learning Approach.*. Proceedings of the 2007 Joint Conference on Empirical Methods in Natural Language Processing and Computational Natural Language Learning (EMNLP-CoNLL).

Kong, Fang and Zhou, Guodong 2010 *A tree kernel-based unified framework for Chinese zero anaphora resolution.*. Proceedings of the 2010 Conference on Empirical Methods in Natural Language Processing.

Fang Kong and Hwee Tou Ng 2013 *Exploiting Zero Pronouns to Improve Chinese Coreference Resolution.*. Proceedings of the 2013 Conference on Empirical Methods in Natural Language Processing.

Shu Cai, David Chiang, and Yoav Goldberg. 2011 *Language-independent parsing with empty elements.*. In Proceedings of the 49th Annual Meeting of the Association for Computational Linguistics: Human Language Technologies, pages 212–216, Portland, Oregon, USA, June. Association for Computational Linguistics.

Tagyoung Chung and Daniel Gildea. 2010. *Effects of empty categories on machine translation.* In Proceedings of the 2010 Conference on Empirical Methods in Natural Language Processing.

Elizabeth Baran, Yaqin Yang and Nianwen Xue. 2012 *Annotating dropped pronouns in Chinese newswire text.*. In Proceedings of the 8th International Conference on Language Resources and Evaluation (LREC), Istanbul, Turkey.

Andrew Kachites McCallum. 2002 *Mallet: A machine learning for language toolkit.*. http://mallet.cs.umass.edu.

Nianwen Xue and Yaqin Yang. 2013 *Dependency-based empty category detection via phrase structure trees.*. In Proceedings of NAACL HLT. Atlanta, Georgia.

Yaqin Yang and Nianwen Xue. 2010 *Chasing the ghost: recovering empty categories in the Chinese Treebank.*. In Proceedings of the 23rd International Conference on Computational Linguistics (COLING). Beijing, China.

Bing Xiang, Xiaoqiang Luo, Bowen Zhou. 2013. *Enlisting the Ghost: Modeling Empty Categories for Machine Translation.* In Proceedings of the ACL.

Converse, Susan 2006 *Pronominal anaphora resolution for Chinese.*. Ph.D. thesis.

Mitchell P. Marcus, Beatrice Santorini, and Mary Ann Marcinkiewicz. 1993 *Building a large annotated corpus of english: The penn treebank.*. Computational Linguistics, 19(2):313–330.

Nianwen Xue, Fei Xia, Fu dong Chiou, and Martha Palmer. 2005 *The Penn Chinese TreeBank: Phrase Structure Annotation of a Large Corpus.* Natural Language Engineering, 11(2):207–238.

Slav Petrov and Dan Klein. 2007. *Improved Inferencing for Unlexicalized Parsing.* In Proceedings of HLT-NAACL 2007.

Jing Peng and Kenji Araki. 2007 *Zero-Anaphora Resolution in Chinese Using Maximum Entropy.*. IEICE Transactions.

The Users Who Say 'Ni':
Audience Identification in Chinese-language Restaurant Reviews

Rob Voigt **Dan Jurafsky**
Stanford University
{robvoigt, jurafsky}@stanford.edu

Abstract

We give an algorithm for disambiguating generic versus referential uses of second-person pronouns in restaurant reviews in Chinese. Reviews in this domain use the 'you' pronoun 你 either generically or to refer to shopkeepers, readers, or for self-reference in reported conversation. We first show that linguistic features of the local context (drawn from prior literature) help in disambigation. We then show that document-level features (n-grams and document-level embeddings)— not previously used in the referentiality literature— actually give the largest gain in performance, and suggest this is because pronouns in this domain exhibit 'one-sense-per-discourse'. Our work highlights an important case of discourse effects on pronoun use, and may suggest practical implications for audience extraction and other sentiment tasks in online reviews.

1 Introduction and Task Description

Detecting whether a given entity is referential is an important question in computational discourse processing. Linguistic features in the local context of a given mention have been successfully used for determining whether a second-person pronoun (you) in dialogue is referential (Gupta et al., 2007b; Frampton et al., 2009; Purver et al., 2009). The related task of anaphoricity detection is an important subtask of coreference resolution (Ng and Cardie, 2002; Ng, 2004; Luo, 2007; Zhou and Kong, 2009; Recasens et al., 2013).

In this paper we consider the task of audience identification in review texts, using restaurant reviews written in Chinese. Our task is to disambiguate a mention of the Chinese second-person pronoun 你 (*ni*, "you") into the following four labels that we found to occur commonly in reviews:

Generic
饮品只有雪碧和可乐，而且要点才拿给你
For drinks they only have Sprite and Coke, and you have to order before they'll give them to you.

Referential - Shop
这么好的服务下次还来你家哦
With such good service, I'll definitely come back to your shop next time!

Referential - Reader
不信你们去试你们会终身遗憾！
Go and try it if you don't believe me - your whole body will feel regret!

Referential - Writer / Self
店员说 "你们就只要钵钵鸡？"
The shop employee said, "You only want the stone-bowl chicken?"

We aim to gain insight into the linguistics of narrative by distinguishing the types of discourse contexts in which different referential senses are found. Restaurant reviews provide an important new test case, and resolving who a reviewer wants to address could have important implications for coreference resolution or sentiment analysis of reviews, as well as downstream tasks like information extraction.

2 Related Work

A number of closely related earlier papers have focused on disambiguating 'you' in English. Gupta et al. (2007b) annotated the Switchboard corpus of telephone dialogue, showing that features based on specific lexical patterns, adjacent parts-of-speech, punctuation, and dialog acts are sufficient to achieve performance of 84.39% at the binary generic/referential prediction task. Gupta et al. (2007a) show that similar features generalize to addressee prediction for multi-party in-

Proceedings of the 53rd Annual Meeting of the Association for Computational Linguistics and the 7th International Joint Conference on Natural Language Processing (Short Papers), pages 314–319,
Beijing, China, July 26-31, 2015.

teractions significantly better than a simple baseline. Frampton et al. (2009) combine discourse features with acoustic and visual information for four-way interactions to resolve participant reference, and in the same setting Purver et al. (2009) employ cascaded classifiers that first establish referentiality and then attempt to resolve the referent. They show that utterance-level lexical features help, suggesting that different uses of 'you' are associated with distinct vocabularies.

Reiter and Frank (2010) investigate the more general question of identifying genericity for noun phrases, showing the usefuleness of linguistic features such as syntactic dependency relations. Similar local structural cues like phrase-structure positioning, head word identity, and distance to surrounding clauses have been used as features in machine learning approaches for anaphoricity detection as one stage in a coreference resolution (Kong and Zhou, 2010; Zhou and Kong, 2011; Kong and Ng, 2013).

Prior work has also shown improvements in performance in the dialogue domain from incorporating features having to do with acoustic prosody, gaze, and head movements (Jovanović et al., 2006; Takemae and Ozawa, 2006; Gupta et al., 2007b; Frampton et al., 2009). Of course in the review domain we have no access to such information; as we'll see, however, we can exploit other unique properties of reviews to make up for this lack.

3 Data

We scrape reviews from *dianping.com*, a Chinese-language restaurant review site, from the ten cities with the most reviews. We randomly sample 750 restaurants within each city and randomly sample reviews of those restaurants.

We scraped 346,381 reviews, including all associated metadata (city, restaurant category, and cost) for each restaurant, as well as the provided ratings (service, taste, ambience, and overall stars) for each review. Of these reviews only 6,704 (less than 2%) have the second-person pronominal character *ni*, highlighting another particular interest of this task: explicit second-person pronominals are quite rare in Chinese, at least in this genre, making the reviews in which they appear linguistically marked.

Summary statistics for this dataset are given in Table 1. We release all our data and annotations at `nlp.stanford.edu/robvoigt/nis`.

3.1 Preprocessing

We apply the Stanford CRF Word Segmenter (Tseng et al., 2005) to segment the text of each review into words, and use simple heuristics based on whitespace and punctuation to extract sentences or sentence fragments. The Stanford Parser (Klein and Manning, 2003; Levy and Manning, 2003) is then run on each extracted sentence or fragment containing a *ni* to produce a dependency graph and set of part-of-speech (POS) tags for later use in feature extraction.

3.2 Annotation

We hand-annotated 701 examples of *ni* tokens (including both singular and plural cases), placing them into one of seven categories: generic, writer-referential, reader-referential, shop-referential, idiomatic, non-"you", and other. The idiomatic and non-"you" cases are commonly comprised of set phrases such as 你好 (*nihao*, "hello") or 迷你 (*mini*, "mini") and are therefore relatively trivial to filter; and the "other" class is both rare and varied, including cases such as direct reference to prior review-writers.

We therefore only consider the generic and large-class referential cases, leaving us with 636 examples for our task; the distribution of annotated *nis* is shown in Table 2.

The approximately half-and-half split between generic and referential tokens is surprisingly similar to that found by studies on English dialogue like Gupta et al. (2007b), in spite of the large divergence in language and genre.

We also found an unexpected word-sense property of second-person pronouns in this genre: of the 122 annotated reviews which contain more than one *ni*, 83.6% use *ni* with the same sense in each occurrence in the review, recalling the *one-sense-per-discourse* hypothesis of Gale et al. (1992). Finding that this discourse property—normally predicated of word-sense in common nouns—occurs in pronouns suggests the use of features of the entire discourse in this task.

4 Features

We consider two primary types of features: *"local"* and *"discourse"*.

4.1 Local Features

"Local" features model textual and linguistic properties of the immediate context of a given *ni*

SUBSET	small REVIEWS	CHARACTERS	WORDS	CHARS / REVIEW	WORDS / REVIEW
Total	346,381	15,010,375	10,112,722	43.33	29.20
Containing *ni*	6,704	1,099,597	748,683	164.02	111.68

Table 1: Summary statistics for the dataset collected for this paper; 701 cases of *ni* in 472 documents were annotated.

TYPE	ADDRESSEE	COUNT
Generic	-	296
Referential	Shop	256
Referential	Reader	48
Referential	Writer	36
Idiomatic	-	25
Non-"you"	-	26
Other	-	14

Table 2: Distribution of relevant types of 你 (*ni*, "you") in our annotated data.

mention, and were drawn from the large literature on referentiality, anaphoricity, and singleton-detection:

Word Identity This feature simply encodes the word-segmented identity of the word in which the current *ni* token is found, capturing cases such as the second-person plural 你们 (*nimen*, "you [plural]").

Adjacent POS Tags Following Gupta et al. (2007b), we include POS tag features for the single words immediately following and preceeding the *ni* token.

Dependencies We include binary features for the presence or absence of lexicalized dependency relations in which the given *ni* participates. As an example, for the phrase 你要推销菜 ("if you want to sell dishes"), we extract a feature for NSUBJ(推销, 你) – *you* is the subject of the verb *sell*.

Lexical Context This feature set fires binary features for the presence or absence of words in the vocabulary within a three-word window on either side of the given *ni* token.

4.2 Discourse Features

The *"discourse"* category considers features that characterize the entire review, capturing the intuition that the classic one-sense-per-discourse property is likely to hold for a given review, so we expect that features on the entire text of the review will be relevant for prediction.

This is a novel contribution of this work: we propose that in certain contexts (such as reviews), referentiality resolution can be interpreted in part as a text classification task.

Review N-grams These are binary features for the presence or absence of n-grams in the entire text of the review. We found that using a larger n than 1 caused overfitting on our relatively small dataset and reduced performance; therefore, results are reported using unigram features.

Review Vector Embedding To see if we can induce higher-level representations of the review text than simply binary n-gram features, we also train a document-level distributed vector representation (Le and Mikolov, 2014) on the entire corpus of reviews using the "doc2vec" implementation in GENSIM (Řehůřek and Sojka, 2010), and include 200 vector features per review: a 100-dimensional embedding learned on the entire document, as well as a 100-dimensional average embedding calculated by averaging the vectors for each word in the document. In experiments we found using both the document and the average vectors combined resulted in higher performance than either alone, so we report results in this setting.

Metadata In addition to discourse features, we also included features that encode the category, city, and estimated cost for each restaurant, as well as the service, taste, environment, and overall star rank ratings associated with a given review on a 5-point scale.

5 Experiments

We tested the effectiveness of these features at predicting genericity and reference for each *ni* token with multinomial logistic regression, as implemented in SCIKIT-LEARN (Pedregosa et al., 2011). We used two classification settings: a binary prediction of whether a given *ni* is referential or not, and a four-way prediction including distinctions between the three annotated referential targets. The results for each task are shown in Table 3.

In each case, we compare the performance of all local and discourse features, as well as several relevant subsets. One question we aim to address is whether our discourse-level n-gram and embed-

	Features	Binary	Four-way
	Baseline	53.44%	46.56%
Local	Word ID	67.19%	62.19%
	+ POS	74.84%	64.38%
	+ Deps	75.00%	69.38%
	+ Context	78.44%	72.19%
Discourse	N-grams	81.72%	77.03%
	Vectors	74.84%	66.56%
	N-grams + Vectors	81.25%	76.72%
Mixed	Local + N-grams	84.38%	79.84%
	Local + Vectors	86.56%	78.91%
	Local + Discourse	85.78%	80.63%
All	Local + Discourse + Meta	**88.21%**	**81.45%**

Table 3: Average ten-fold cross-validation classification accuracy for different feature sets on two tasks. "Local" refers to all feature sets described in Section 4.1. BINARY distinguishes generic and referential *ni*, FOUR-WAY distinguishes between generic and three referential senses.

Feature	Binary		Four-way	
	estimate	*p*	*estimate*	*p*
ID	2.5%	***	1.9%	***
POS	1.0%	.	1.0%	.
Deps	0.2%		0.6%	
Context	4.2%	***	4.2%	***
N-grams	6.6%	***	7.8%	***
Vectors	3.8%	***	3.8%	***
Metadata	2.7%	***	2.6%	***

Table 4: Meta-analysis results for both tasks: effect size estimates from linear regressions ($n = 127$) predicting cross-validation scores from feature set. the p column denotes statistical significance; . is $p < 0.1$ and *** is $p < 0.001$.

ding features contribute similar information, so we test them both separately and together. We compare our results to a baseline of choosing the most common class for either task.

We train and test models with ten-fold cross-validation. In each fold, we use 80% of the data for training, 10% for development, and 10% for testing. For each feature set, we set the $l2$ regularization strength as a hyperparameter based on average cross-validation accuracy on the development data in each fold. All reported results are average cross-validation accuracy at that regularization strength on the test set in each fold.

5.1 Meta-analysis

To better understand the effectiveness of each feature set for this task, we perform a full ablation study by training a classifier on all 127 ($2^7 - 1$, ignoring the empty set) possible combinations of our 7 feature sets, and run a linear regression predicting the classification score from the feature sets used. This allows us to obtain estimates of the effect size and statistical significance for each set of features with reference to all the others. These results are shown in Table 4.

6 Discussion

These results show that on the task of detecting genericity and reference for second-person pronouns in our annotated set of Chinese-language restaurant reviews, both discourse-level features as well as local, contextual features significantly impact classification performance.

Simple word identity features alone already provide surprising performance: the classifier learns that the singular *ni* is more likely to be generic while the plural 你们 often refers to people affiliated with the shop.

While local features alone achieve respectable performance (78.44% for binary genericity detection and 72.19% for four-way classification), we show that in the review context significant gains can be made from using a combination of local and discourse-level features, exploiting discourse-level indicators of referentiality and the fact that a one-sense-per-discourse assumption tends to hold with regards to the use of *ni*.

Analysis of learned feature weights in our highest-performing model also provides some interesting social insights. Reviews with a high overall star rank were more likely to use generic *ni*, and reviewers who thought highly of the restaurant's service as indicated by their quality-of-service rating were more likely to use reader-directed referential *ni*.

Reviews with shop-directed referential *ni* were likely to use emotive sentence-final particles like 啊 (*a*), exclamation points, and question marks, just as question marks were among the strongest indicators of referential uses in the English "you"s in Gupta et al. (2007b). We also found that other pronouns like 我 (*wo*, "I") and 我们 (*women*, "we"), as well as words of temporal sequencing 第一 (*diyi*, "the first"), 又 (*you*, "again"), and 次 (*ci*, "[one] time") receive high weights for referential classes.

Combined with the observation that reviews containing *ni* simply tend to be much longer than those without (see Table 1), these results suggest a link to the narrative work of Jurafsky et al. (2014), who characterize negative reviews as narrative expositions of an individual bad experience.

For example, consider the following review containing a referential *ni*:

> 菜品，份量都不错。环境更没得说。但我们中午去的晚，没想到人家先关灯，后又关空调。想问下你们省电了，是想证明我们吃饭可以不用给钱吗？
>
> The food and quantity was fine. The ambience need not be mentioned. But in spite of having been a bit late for lunch, we wouldn't have imagined you'd first turn off the lights, and then turn off the air conditioner. I'd like to ask: saving money on electricity like this, do you mean to imply that there's no need for us to pay for our meal?

While the immediate context suggests a referential interpretation (想问下你们省电了, literally "want to ask you [plural], saving electricity"), it is only when this mention is connected to elements of the entire discourse (the sequence of events, the first-person pronouns) that it becomes completely clear first that the mention is referential and second that it refers to the shop owner.

Furthermore, we found that when combined with local features, features derived from distributed representations of each document perform at least as well for this task as document-level n-grams, but at a much lower dimensionality. This suggests that these embeddings do successfully encode the information necessary to reproduce document-level distinctions in discourse types, such as between the personal narratives that often surround referential uses of *ni* and the abstract descriptions of generic uses.

Our meta-analysis shows that more linguistically motivated local features such as POS tags and dependency relations are substantially overshadowed in effectiveness by lexical and discourse features, although this may be due in part to reduced performance of these automatic taggers on the more colloquial language in online reviews.

Finally, this work challenges prior claims that spoken language is "more complex" than other genres with regards to referentiality. On the contrary: whereas in a spoken discourse the potential addressees are by default the participants, web texts such as the reviews studied here have no such default, and may include complex, creative, and domain-specific deictic reference that can be important for computational systems to address.

References

Matthew Frampton, Raquel Fernández, Patrick Ehlen, Mario Christoudias, Trevor Darrell, and Stanley Peters. 2009. Who is you?: combining linguistic and gaze features to resolve second-person references in dialogue. In *Proceedings of the 12th Conference of the European Chapter of the Association for Computational Linguistics*, pages 273–281. Association for Computational Linguistics.

William A Gale, Kenneth W Church, and David Yarowsky. 1992. One sense per discourse. In *Proceedings of the workshop on Speech and Natural Language*, pages 233–237. Association for Computational Linguistics.

Surabhi Gupta, John Niekrasz, Matthew Purver, and Daniel Jurafsky. 2007a. Resolving "you" in multiparty dialog. In *Proceedings of the 8th SIGdial Workshop on Discourse and Dialogue*, pages 227–30.

Surabhi Gupta, Matthew Purver, and Dan Jurafsky. 2007b. Disambiguating between generic and referential you in dialog. In *Proceedings of the 45th Annual Meeting of the ACL on Interactive Poster and Demonstration Sessions*, pages 105–108. Association for Computational Linguistics.

Natasa Jovanović, Anton Nijholt, et al. 2006. Addressee identification in face-to-face meetings. Association for Computational Linguistics.

Dan Jurafsky, Victor Chahuneau, Bryan R Routledge, and Noah A Smith. 2014. Narrative framing of consumer sentiment in online restaurant reviews. *First Monday*, 19(4).

Dan Klein and Christopher D Manning. 2003. Accurate unlexicalized parsing. In *Proceedings of the 41st Annual Meeting on Association for Computational Linguistics-Volume 1*, pages 423–430. Association for Computational Linguistics.

Fang Kong and Hwee Tou Ng. 2013. Exploiting zero pronouns to improve chinese coreference resolution. In *EMNLP*, pages 278–288.

Fang Kong and Guodong Zhou. 2010. A tree kernel-based unified framework for chinese zero anaphora resolution. In *Proceedings of the 2010 Conference on Empirical Methods in Natural Language Processing*, pages 882–891. Association for Computational Linguistics.

Quoc V Le and Tomas Mikolov. 2014. Distributed representations of sentences and documents. *arXiv preprint arXiv:1405.4053*.

Roger Levy and Christopher Manning. 2003. Is it harder to parse chinese, or the chinese treebank? In *Proceedings of the 41st Annual Meeting on Association for Computational Linguistics-Volume 1*, pages 439–446. Association for Computational Linguistics.

Xiaoqiang Luo. 2007. Coreference or not: A twin model for coreference resolution. In *HLT-NAACL*, pages 73–80.

Vincent Ng and Claire Cardie. 2002. Identifying anaphoric and non-anaphoric noun phrases to improve coreference resolution. In *Proceedings of the 19th international conference on Computational linguistics-Volume 1*, pages 1–7. Association for Computational Linguistics.

Vincent Ng. 2004. Learning noun phrase anaphoricity to improve coreference resolution: Issues in representation and optimization. In *Proceedings of the 42nd Annual Meeting on Association for Computational Linguistics*, page 151. Association for Computational Linguistics.

F. Pedregosa, G. Varoquaux, A. Gramfort, V. Michel, B. Thirion, O. Grisel, M. Blondel, P. Prettenhofer, R. Weiss, V. Dubourg, J. Vanderplas, A. Passos, D. Cournapeau, M. Brucher, M. Perrot, and E. Duchesnay. 2011. Scikit-learn: Machine learning in Python. *Journal of Machine Learning Research*, 12:2825–2830.

Matthew Purver, Raquel Fernández, Matthew Frampton, and Stanley Peters. 2009. Cascaded lexicalised classifiers for second-person reference resolution. In *Proceedings of the SIGDIAL 2009 Conference: The 10th Annual Meeting of the Special Interest Group on Discourse and Dialogue*, pages 306–309. Association for Computational Linguistics.

Marta Recasens, Marie-Catherine de Marneffe, and Christopher Potts. 2013. The life and death of discourse entities: Identifying singleton mentions. In *HLT-NAACL*, pages 627–633.

Radim Řehůřek and Petr Sojka. 2010. Software Framework for Topic Modelling with Large Corpora. In *Proceedings of the LREC 2010 Workshop on New Challenges for NLP Frameworks*, pages 45–50, Valletta, Malta, May. ELRA. `http://is.muni.cz/publication/884893/en`.

Nils Reiter and Anette Frank. 2010. Identifying generic noun phrases. In *Proceedings of the 48th Annual Meeting of the Association for Computational Linguistics*, pages 40–49. Association for Computational Linguistics.

Yoshinao Takemae and Shinji Ozawa. 2006. Automatic addressee identification based on participants' head orientation and utterances for multiparty conversations. In *Multimedia and Expo, 2006 IEEE International Conference on*, pages 1285–1288. IEEE.

Huihsin Tseng, Pichuan Chang, Galen Andrew, Daniel Jurafsky, and Christopher Manning. 2005. A conditional random field word segmenter. In *Proceedings of the fourth SIGHAN workshop on Chinese language Processing*, volume 171.

Guodong Zhou and Fang Kong. 2009. Global learning of noun phrase anaphoricity in coreference resolution via label propagation. In *Proceedings of the 2009 Conference on Empirical Methods in Natural Language Processing: Volume 2-Volume 2*, pages 978–986. Association for Computational Linguistics.

Guodong Zhou and Fang Kong. 2011. Learning noun phrase anaphoricity in coreference resolution via label propagation. *Journal of Computer Science and Technology*, 26(1):34–44.

Chinese Zero Pronoun Resolution: A Joint Unsupervised Discourse-Aware Model Rivaling State-of-the-Art Resolvers

Chen Chen and **Vincent Ng**
Human Language Technology Research Institute
University of Texas at Dallas
Richardson, TX 75083-0688
{yzcchen,vince}@hlt.utdallas.edu

Abstract

We propose an unsupervised probabilistic model for zero pronoun resolution. To our knowledge, this is the first such model that (1) is trained on zero pronouns in an unsupervised manner; (2) jointly identifies and resolves anaphoric zero pronouns; and (3) exploits discourse information provided by a salience model. Experiments demonstrate that our unsupervised model significantly outperforms its state-of-the-art unsupervised counterpart when resolving the Chinese zero pronouns in the OntoNotes corpus.

1 Introduction

A zero pronoun (ZP) is a gap in a sentence that is found when a phonetically null form is used to refer to a real-world entity. An anaphoric zero pronoun (AZP) is a ZP that corefers with one or more preceding mentions in the associated text. Below is an example taken from the Chinese TreeBank (CTB), where the ZP (denoted as *pro*) refers to 俄罗斯 (Russia).

[俄罗斯] 作为米洛舍夫维奇一贯的支持者，*pro* 曾经提出调停这场政治危机。

([Russia] is a consistent supporter of Milošević, *pro* has proposed to mediate the political crisis.)

As we can see, ZPs lack grammatical attributes that are useful for overt pronoun resolution such as NUMBER and GENDER. This makes ZP resolution more challenging than overt pronoun resolution.

Automatic ZP resolution is typically composed of two steps. The first step, AZP identification, involves extracting ZPs that are anaphoric. The second step, AZP resolution, aims to identify an antecedent of an AZP. State-of-the-art ZP resolvers have tackled both of these steps in a supervised manner, training one classifier for AZP identification and another for AZP resolution (e.g., Zhao and Ng (2007), Kong and Zhou (2010)).

More recently, we have proposed an unsupervised AZP resolution model (henceforth the CN14 model) that rivals its supervised counterparts in performance (Chen and Ng, 2014). The idea is to resolve AZPs by using a probabilistic pronoun resolution model trained on *overt* pronouns in an *unsupervised* manner. This is an appealing approach, as its language-independent generative process enables it to be applied to languages where data annotated with ZP links are not available.

In light of the advantages of unsupervised models, we examine in this paper the possibility of advancing the state of the art in unsupervised AZP resolution. The design of our unsupervised model is motivated by a key question: can we resolve AZPs by using a probabilistic model trained on *zero* pronouns in an *unsupervised* manner? As mentioned above, the CN14 model was trained on overt pronouns, but it is not clear how much this helped its resolution performance. In particular, the contexts in which overt and zero pronouns occur may not statistically resemble each other. For example, a ZP is likely to be closer to its antecedent than its overt counterpart. As another example, the verbs governing a ZP and its antecedent are more likely to be identical than the verbs governing an overt pronoun and its antecedent. Given such differences, it is not clear whether the knowledge learned from overt pronouns is always applicable to the resolution of AZPs. For this reason, we propose to train an *unsupervised* AZP resolution model directly on *zero* pronouns. Moreover, while we previously employed a *pipeline* architecture where we (1) used a set of heuristic rules for AZP identification, and then (2) applied their probabilistic model to all and only those ZPs that were determined to be anaphoric (Chen and Ng, 2014), in this work we identify and resolve AZPs in a *joint* fashion. To our knowledge, the model we are

Proceedings of the 53rd Annual Meeting of the Association for Computational Linguistics and the 7th International Joint Conference on Natural Language Processing (Short Papers), pages 320–326, Beijing, China, July 26-31, 2015. ©2015 Association for Computational Linguistics

proposing here is the first unsupervised model for joint AZP identification and resolution.[1]

In addition, motivated by work on *overt* pronoun resolution, we hypothesize that AZP resolution can be improved by exploiting *discourse* information. Specifically, we design a model of salience and incorporate salience information into our model as a feature. Inspired by traditional work on discourse-based anaphora resolution (e.g., Lappin and Leass (1994)), we compute salience based on the coreference clusters constructed so far using a rule-based coreference resolver. While ZPs have been exploited to improve coreference resolution (Kong and Ng, 2013), we are the first to improve AZP resolution using coreference information.

When evaluated on the Chinese portion of the OntoNotes corpus, our AZP resolver outperforms the CN14 model, achieving state-of-the-art results.

2 Related Work

Early approaches to AZP resolution employed *heuristic* rules to resolve AZPs in Chinese (e.g., Converse (2006), Yeh and Chen (2007)) and Spanish (e.g., Ferrández and Peral (2000)). More recently, *supervised* approaches have been extensively employed to resolve AZPs in Chinese (e.g., Zhao and Ng (2007), Kong and Zhou (2010), Chen and Ng (2013)), Korean (e.g., Han (2006)), Japanese (e.g., Seki et al. (2002), Isozaki and Hirao (2003), Iida et al. (2003; 2006; 2007), Imamura et al. (2009), Iida and Poesio (2011), Sasano and Kurohashi (2011)), and Italian (e.g., Iida and Poesio (2011)). As mentioned before, in order to reduce reliance on annotated data, we recently proposed an *unsupervised* probabilistic model for Chinese AZP resolution that rivaled its supervised counterparts in performance (Chen and Ng, 2014).

3 The Generative Model

Next, we present our model for jointly identifying and resolving AZPs in an unsupervised manner.

3.1 Notation

Let z be a ZP. C, the set of candidate antecedents of z, contains (1) the maximal or modifier NPs that precede z in the associated text that are at most two sentences away from it; and (2) a dummy candidate antecedent d (to which z will be resolved if it is non-anaphoric). k is the context surrounding z as well as every candidate antecedent c in C; k_c is the context surrounding z and candidate antecedent c; and l is a binary variable indicating whether c is the correct antecedent of z.

3.2 Training

Our model estimates $P(z, k, c, l)$, the probability of seeing (1) the ZP z; (2) the context k surrounding z and its candidate antecedents; (3) a candidate antecedent c of z; and (4) whether c is the correct antecedent of z. Since we estimate this probability from a raw, unannotated corpus, we are treating z, k, and c as observed data[2] and l as hidden data.

Motivated in part by previous work on English overt pronoun resolution (e.g., Cherry and Bergsma (2005) and Charniak and Elsner (2009)), we estimate the model parameters using the Expectation-Maximization algorithm (Dempster et al., 1977). Specifically, we use EM to iteratively (1) estimate the model parameters from data in which each ZP is labeled with the probability that it corefers with each of its candidate antecedents, and (2) apply the resulting model to re-label each ZP with the probability that it corefers with each of its candidate antecedents. Below we describe the details of the E-step and the M-step.

3.2.1 E-Step

The goal of the E-step is to compute $P(l{=}1|z, k, c)$, the probability that a candidate antecedent c is the correct antecedent of z given context k. Applying the definition of conditional probability and the Theorem of Total Probability, we can rewrite $P(l{=}1|z, k, c)$ as follows:

$$P(l{=}1|z,k,c) = \frac{P(z,k,c,l{=}1)}{P(z,k,c,l{=}1) + P(z,k,c,l{=}0)} \quad (1)$$

Assuming that exactly one of z's candidate antecedents is its correct antecedent, we can rewrite $P(z, k, c, l{=}0)$ as follows:

$$P(z,k,c,l{=}0) = \sum_{c' \in C, c' \neq c} P(z,k,c',l{=}1) \quad (2)$$

Given Equation (2), we can rewrite

[1] Note that Iida and Poesio (2011) perform joint *inference* over an AZP identification model and an AZP resolution model trained separately, not joint *learning* of the two tasks.

[2] Here, we treat z as observed data because we assume that the set of ZPs has been identified by a separate process. We adopt the heuristics for ZP identification that we introduced in Chen and Ng (2014).

$P(l{=}1|z,k,c)$ as follows:

$$P(l{=}1|z,k,c) = \frac{P(z,k,c,l{=}1)}{\sum_{c' \in C} P(z,k,c',l{=}1)} \quad (3)$$

Applying the Chain Rule, we can rewrite $P(z,k,c,l{=}1)$ as follows:

$$P(z,k,c,l{=}1) = P(z|k,c,l{=}1) * P(l{=}1|k,c) * P(c|k) * P(k) \quad (4)$$

Next, since z is a phonetically null form (and therefore is not represented by any linguistic attributes), we assume that each of its candidate antecedents and the associated context has the same probability of generating it. So we can rewrite $P(z|k,c,l{=}1)$ as follows:

$$P(z|k,c,l{=}1) = P(z|k,c',l{=}1) \;\; \forall\, c,c' \in C \quad (5)$$

Moreover, we assume that (1) given z and c's context, the probability of c being the antecedent of z is not affected by the context of the other candidate antecedents; and (2) k_c is sufficient for determining whether c is the antecedent of z. So,

$$P(l{=}1|k,c) \approx P(l{=}1|k_c,c) \approx P(l{=}1|k_c) \quad (6)$$

Next, applying Bayes Rule to $P(l{=}1|k_c)$, we get:

$$\frac{P(k_c|l{=}1)P(l{=}1)}{P(k_c|l{=}1)P(l{=}1) + P(k_c|l{=}0)P(l{=}0)} \quad (7)$$

Representing k_c as a set of n features $f_c^1, \ldots f_c^n$ and assuming that each f_c^i is conditionally independent given l, we can approximate Expression (7) as:

$$\frac{\prod_i P(f_c^i|l{=}1)P(l{=}1)}{\prod_i P(f_c^i|l{=}1)P(l{=}1) + \prod_i P(f_c^i|l{=}0)P(l{=}0)} \quad (8)$$

Furthermore, we assume that given context k, each candidate antecedent of z is generated with equal probability. In other words,

$$P(c|k) = P(c'|k) \;\; \forall\, c,c' \in C \quad (9)$$

Given Equations (4), (5), (8) and (9), we can rewrite $P(l{=}1|z,k,c)$ as:

$$P(l{=}1|z,k,c) = \frac{P(z,k,c,l{=}1)}{\sum_{c' \in C} P(z,k,c',l{=}1)}$$
$$= \frac{P(z|k,c,l{=}1) * P(l{=}1|k,c) * P(c|k)}{\sum_{c' \in C} P(z|k,c',l{=}1) * P(l{=}1|k,c') * P(c'|k)}$$
$$\approx \frac{P(l{=}1|k_c)}{\sum_{c' \in C} P(l{=}1|k_{c'})} \approx \frac{\frac{\prod_i P(f_c^i|l=1)}{Z_c}}{\sum_{c' \in C} \frac{\prod_i P(f_{c'}^i|l=1)}{Z_{c'}}} \quad (10)$$

where

$$Z_x = \prod_i P(f_x^i|l{=}1)P(l{=}1) + \prod_i P(f_x^i|l{=}0)P(l{=}0) \quad (11)$$

As we can see from Equation (10), our model has one group of parameters, namely $P(f_c^i|l{=}1)$. Using Equation (10) and the current parameter estimates, we can compute $P(l{=}1|z,k,c)$.

A point deserves mention before we describe the M-step. By including d as a dummy candidate antecedent for each z, we effectively model AZP identification and resolution in a joint fashion. If the model resolves z to d, it means that the model posits z as non-anaphoric; on the other hand, if the model resolves z to a non-dummy candidate antecedent c, it means that the model posits z as anaphoric and c as z's correct antecedent.

3.2.2 M-Step

Given $P(l{=}1|z,k,c)$, the goal of the M-step is to (re)estimate the model parameters, $P(l{=}1|k_c)$, using maximum likelihood estimation. Specifically, $P(l{=}1|k_c)$ is estimated as follows:

$$P(l{=}1|k_c) = \frac{Count(k_c,l{=}1) + \theta}{Count(k_c) + \theta * 2} \quad (12)$$

where $Count(k_c)$ is the number of times k_c appears in the training data, $Count(k_c,l{=}1)$ is the expected number of times k_c is the context surrounding an AZP and its antecedent c, and θ is the Laplace smoothing parameter, which we set to 1. Given context k'_c, we compute $Count(k'_c,l{=}1)$ as follows:

$$Count(k'_c,l{=}1) = \sum_{k:k_c=k'_c} P(l{=}1|z,k,c) \quad (13)$$

To start the induction process, we initialize all parameters with uniform values. Specifically, $P(l{=}1|k_c)$ is set to 0.5. Then we iteratively run the E-step and the M-step until convergence.

There is an important question we have not addressed: what features should we use to represent context k_c, which we need to estimate $P(l{=}1|k_c)$? We answer this question in Section 4.

3.3 Inference

After training, we can apply the resulting model to resolve ZPs. Given a test document, we process its ZPs in a left-to-right manner. For each ZP z enountered, we determine its antecedent as follows:

$$\hat{c} = \arg\max_{c \in C} P(l{=}1|z,k,c) \quad (14)$$

where C is the set of candidate antecedents of z. If we resolve a ZP to a preceding NP c, we fill its gap with c. Hence, when we process a ZP z, all of its preceding AZPs in the associated text have already been resolved, having had their gaps filled with their associated NPs. To resolve z, we create test instances between z and its candidate antecedents in the same way we described before. The only difference is that z's candidate antecedents may now include the NPs to which previous AZPs were resolved. In other words, this incremental resolution procedure may increase the number of candidate antecedents of each ZP z. Some of these additional candidate antecedents are closer to z than were their parent NPs, thus facilitating the resolution of z to the NPs in the following way: If the model resolves z to the additional candidate antecedent that fills the gap left behind by, say, AZP z', we postprocess the output by resolving z to the NP that z' is resolved to.[3]

4 Context Features

To fully specify our model, we need to describe how to represent k_c, which is needed to compute $P(l{=}1|k_c)$. Recall that k_c encodes the context surrounding candidate antecedent c and the associated ZP z. As described below, we represent k_c using eight features. Note that (1) all but feature 1 are computed based on syntactic parse trees, and (2) features 2, 3, and 6 are ternary-valued features.

1. the sentence distance between c and z;
2. whether the node spanning c has an ancestor NP node; if so, whether this NP node is a descendant of c's lowest ancestor IP node;
3. whether the node spanning c has an ancestor VP node; if so, whether this VP node is a descendant of c's lowest ancestor IP node;
4. whether vp has an ancestor NP node, where vp is the VP node spanning the VP that follows z;
5. whether vp has an ancestor VP node;
6. whether z is the first word of a sentence; if not, whether z is the first word of an IP clause;
7. whether c is a subject whose governing verb is lexically identical to the verb governing z;
8. c's salience rank (see Section 5).

[3]This postprocessing step is needed because the additional candidate antecedents are only gap fillers.

	Training	Test
Documents	1,391	172
Sentences	36,487	6,083
Words	756,063	110,034
AZPs	–	1,713

Table 1: Statistics on the training and test sets.

Note that features 1, 2, 3 and 7 are not directly applicable to the dummy candidate. To compute the feature values of the dummy candidate, we first find the highest ranking non-dummy entity E in the salience list, and then set the values of these four features of the dummy candidate to the corresponding feature values of the rightmost mention of E. The motivation is that we want the dummy candidate to compete with the most salient non-dummy candidate.

5 Adding Salience

Recall from Section 4 that feature 8 requires the computation of salience. Intuitively, salient entities are more likely to contain the antecedent of an AZP.

We model salience as follows. For each ZP z, we compute the salience score for each (partial) entity preceding z.[4] To reduce the size of the list of preceding entities, we only consider a partial entity *active* if one of its mentions appears within two sentences of the active ZP z. We compute the salience score of each active entity w.r.t. z using the following equation:

$$\sum_{m \in E} g(m) * decay(m) \quad (15)$$

where m is a mention belonging to active entity E, $g(m)$ is a grammatical score which is set to 4, 2, or 1 depending on whether m's grammatical role is SUBJECT, OBJECT, or OTHER, respectively, and $decay(m)$ is decay factor that is set to 0.5^{dis} (where dis is the sentence distance between m and z). After computing the scores, we first sort the list of the active entities in descending order of salience. Then, within each active entity, we sort the mentions in increasing order of distance from z. Finally, we set the salience rank of each mention m to its position in the sorted list, but cap the rank

[4]We compute the list of preceding entities automatically using SinoCoreferencer, a publicly available Chinese entity coreference resolver. See `http://www.hlt.utdallas.edu/~yzcchen/coreference/`.

	Setting 1: Gold Parses, Gold AZPs						Setting 2: Gold Parses, System AZPs						Setting 3: System Parses, System AZPs					
	Baseline			Our Model			Baseline			Our Model			Baseline			Our Model		
Source	R	P	F	R	P	F	R	P	F	R	P	F	R	P	F	R	P	F
Overall	47.5	47.9	47.7	50.0	50.4	50.2	35.4	21.0	26.4	35.7	26.2	30.3	19.9	12.9	15.7	19.6	15.5	17.3
NW	41.7	41.7	41.7	46.4	46.4	46.4	29.8	24.8	27.0	32.1	28.1	30.0	11.9	13.0	12.4	11.9	14.3	13.0
MZ	34.0	34.2	34.1	38.9	39.1	39.0	24.1	14.5	18.1	29.6	19.6	23.6	6.2	5.2	5.7	4.9	4.7	4.8
WB	47.9	47.9	47.9	51.8	51.8	51.8	37.3	18.7	24.9	39.1	22.9	28.9	19.0	11.3	14.2	20.1	14.3	16.7
BN	52.8	52.8	52.8	53.8	53.8	53.8	31.5	28.1	29.7	30.8	30.7	30.7	18.2	19.5	18.8	18.2	22.3	20.0
BC	49.8	50.3	50.0	49.2	49.6	49.4	38.0	21.0	27.0	35.9	26.6	30.6	20.6	12.4	15.5	19.4	14.6	16.7
TC	45.2	46.7	46.0	51.9	53.5	52.7	42.4	20.3	27.4	43.5	28.7	34.6	32.2	13.3	18.8	31.8	17.0	22.2

Table 2: AZP resolution results of the baseline and our model on the test set.

at 5 in order to reduce sparseness during parameter estimation.

Note that the above list contains only non-dummy entities. We model the salience of a dummy entity D, which contains only the dummy candidate for z, as follows. Intuitively, if z is non-anaphoric, D should be the most salient entity. Hence, we put D at the top of the list if z satisfies any of the following three conditions, all of which are strong indicators of non-anaphoricity: (1) z appears at the beginning of a document; (2) the verb following z is 有 (there is) or 没有 (there is not) with part of speech VE; or (3) the VP node in the syntactic parse tree following z does not span any verb. If none of these conditions is satisfied, we put D at the bottom of the list.

6 Evaluation

6.1 Experimental Setup

Datasets. We employ the Chinese portion of the OntoNotes 5.0 corpus that was used in the official CoNLL-2012 shared task (Pradhan et al., 2012). In the CoNLL-2012 data, the training set and development set contain ZP coreference annotations, but the test set does not. Therefore, we train our models on the training set and perform evaluation on the development set. Statistics on the datasets are shown in Table 1. The documents in these datasets come from six sources, namely Broadcast News (BN), Newswires (NW), Broadcast Conversations (BC), Telephone Conversations (TC), Web Blogs (WB), and Magazines (MZ).

Evaluation measures. We express results in terms of recall (R), precision (P), and F-score (F) on resolving AZPs, considering an AZP z correctly resolved if it is resolved to any NP in the same coreference chain as z.

Evaluation settings. Following Chen and Ng (2014), we evaluate our model in three settings. In Setting 1, we assume the availability of gold syntactic parse trees and gold AZPs.[5] In Setting 2, we employ gold syntactic parse trees and system (i.e., automatically identified) AZPs. Finally, in Setting 3 (the end-to-end setting), we employ system syntactic parse trees and system AZPs. The gold and system syntactic parse trees, as well as the gold AZPs, are obtained from the CoNLL-2012 shared task dataset, while the system AZPs are identified by our generative model.

6.2 Results

As our baseline, we employ the CN14 system, which has achieved the best result to date on our test set. Table 2 shows results obtained using both the baseline system and our model on the entire test set as well as on each of the six sources. As we can see, our model significantly[6] outperforms the baseline under all three settings by 2.5%, 3.9% and 1.6% respectively in terms of overall F-score.

7 Conclusion

We proposed a novel unsupervised model for Chinese zero pronoun resolution by (1) training on zero pronouns; (2) jointly identifying and resolving anaphoric zero pronouns; and (3) exploiting salience information. Experiments on the OntoNotes 5.0 corpus showed that our unsupervised model achieved state-of-the-art results.

Acknowledgments

We thank the three anonymous reviewers for their detailed and insightful comments on an earlier draft of this paper. This work was supported in part by NSF Grants IIS-1147644 and IIS-1219142. Any opinions, findings, conclusions or recommendations expressed in this paper are those of the authors and do not necessarily reflect the views or official policies, either expressed or implied, of NSF.

[5]When gold AZPs are used (i.e., Setting 1), we simply remove the dummy candidate antecedent from the list of candidate antecedents during inference.

[6]All significance tests are paired t-test, with $p < 0.05$.

References

Eugene Charniak and Micha Elsner. 2009. EM works for pronoun anaphora resolution. In *Proceedings of the 12th Conference of the European Chapter of the Association for Computational Linguistics*, pages 148--156.

Chen Chen and Vincent Ng. 2013. Chinese zero pronoun resolution: Some recent advances. In *Proceedings of the 2013 Conference on Empirical Methods in Natural Language Processing*, pages 1360--1365.

Chen Chen and Vincent Ng. 2014. Chinese zero pronoun resolution: An unsupervised probabilistic model rivaling supervised resolvers. In *Proceedings of the 2014 Conference on Empirical Methods in Natural Language Processing*, pages 763--774.

Colin Cherry and Shane Bergsma. 2005. An expectation maximization approach to pronoun resolution. In *Proceedings of the Ninth Conference on Natural Language Learning*, pages 88--95.

Susan Converse. 2006. *Pronominal Anaphora Resolution in Chinese*. Ph.D. thesis, University of Pennsylvania.

Arthur P. Dempster, Nan M. Laird, and Donald B. Rubin. 1977. Maximum likelihood from incomplete data via the EM algorithm. *Journal of the Royal Statistical Society. Series B (Methodological)*, 39:1--38.

Antonio Ferrández and Jesús Peral. 2000. A computational approach to zero-pronouns in Spanish. In *Proceedings of the 38th Annual Meeting on Association for Computational Linguistics*, pages 166--172.

Barbara J. Grosz, Aravind K. Joshi, and Scott Weinstein. 1995. Centering: A framework for modeling the local coherence of discourse. *Computational Linguistics*, 21(2):203--226.

Na-Rae Han. 2006. *Korean zero pronouns: analysis and resolution*. Ph.D. thesis, University of Pennsylvania.

Jerry Hobbs. 1978. Resolving pronoun references. *Lingua*, 44:311--338.

Ryu Iida and Massimo Poesio. 2011. A cross-lingual ILP solution to zero anaphora resolution. In *Proceedings of the 49th Annual Meeting of the Association for Computational Linguistics: Human Language Technologies-Volume 1*, pages 804--813.

Ryu Iida, Kentaro Inui, Hiroya Takamura, and Yuji Matsumoto. 2003. Incorporating contextual cues in trainable models for coreference resolution. In *Proceedings of the EACL Workshop on The Computational Treatment of Anaphora*, pages 23--30.

Ryu Iida, Kentaro Inui, and Yuji Matsumoto. 2006. Exploting syntactic patterns as clues in zero-anaphora resolution. In *Proceedings of the 21st International Conference on Computational Linguistics and the 44th Annual Meeting of the Association for Computational Linguistics*, pages 625--632.

Ryu Iida, Kentaro Inui, and Yuji Matsumoto. 2007. Zero-anaphora resolution by learning rich syntactic pattern features. *ACM Transactions on Asian Language Information Processing*, 6(4).

Kenji Imamura, Kuniko Saito, and Tomoko Izumi. 2009. Discriminative approach to predicate-argument structure analysis with zero-anaphora resolution. In *Proceedings of the ACL-IJCNLP 2009 Conference Short Papers*, pages 85--88.

Hideki Isozaki and Tsutomu Hirao. 2003. Japanese zero pronoun resolution based on ranking rules and machine learning. In *Proceedings of the 2003 Conference on Empirical methods in natural language processing*, pages 184--191.

Fang Kong and Hwee Tou Ng. 2013. Exploiting zero pronouns to improve chinese coreference resolution. In *Proceedings of the 2013 Conference on Empirical Methods in Natural Language Processing*, pages 278--288.

Fang Kong and Guodong Zhou. 2010. A tree kernel-based unified framework for Chinese zero anaphora resolution. In *Proceedings of the 2010 Conference on Empirical Methods in Natural Language Processing*, pages 882--891.

Shalom Lappin and Herbert Leass. 1994. An algorithm for pronominal anaphora resolution. *Computational Linguistics*, 20(4):535--562.

Sameer Pradhan, Alessandro Moschitti, Nianwen Xue, Olga Uryupina, and Yuchen Zhang. 2012. CoNLL-2012 shared task: Modeling multilingual unrestricted coreference in OntoNotes. In *Proceedings of 2012 Joint Conference on Empirical Methods in Natural Language Processing and Computational Natural Language Learning: Shared Task*, pages 1--40.

Ryohei Sasano and Sadao Kurohashi. 2011. A discriminative approach to Japanese zero anaphora resolution with large-scale lexicalized case frames. In *Proceedings of the 5th International Joint Conference on Natural Language Processing*, pages 758--766.

Kazuhiro Seki, Atsushi Fujii, and Tetsuya Ishikawa. 2002. A probabilistic method for analyzing Japanese anaphora integrating zero pronoun detection and resolution. In *Proceedings of the 19th International Conference on Computational linguistics*.

Ching-Long Yeh and Yi-Chun Chen. 2007. Zero anaphora resolution in Chinese with shallow parsing. *Journal of Chinese Language and Computing*, 17(1):41--56.

Shanheng Zhao and Hwee Tou Ng. 2007. Identification and resolution of Chinese zero pronouns: A machine learning approach. In *Proceedings of the 2007 Joint Conference on Empirical Methods on Natural Language Processing and Computational Natural Language Learning*, pages 541--550.

GuoDong Zhou, Fang Kong, and Qiaoming Zhu. 2008. Context-sensitive convolution tree kernel for pronoun resolution. In *Proceedings of the 3rd International Joint Conference on Natural Language Processing*, pages 25--31.

Co-Simmate: Quick Retrieving All Pairwise Co-Simrank Scores

Weiren Yu, Julie A. McCann
Department of Computing,
Imperial College London, UK
{weiren.yu, j.mccann}@imperial.ac.uk

Abstract

Co-Simrank is a useful Simrank-like measure of similarity based on graph structure. The existing method iteratively computes each pair of Co-Simrank score from a dot product of two Pagerank vectors, entailing $\mathcal{O}(\log(1/\epsilon)n^3)$ time to compute all pairs of Co-Simranks in a graph with n nodes, to attain a desired accuracy ϵ. In this study, we devise a model, Co-Simmate, to speed up the retrieval of all pairs of Co-Simranks to $\mathcal{O}(\log_2(\log(1/\epsilon))n^3)$ time. Moreover, we show the optimality of Co-Simmate among other hop-(u^k) variations, and integrate it with a matrix decomposition based method on singular graphs to attain higher efficiency. The viable experiments verify the superiority of Co-Simmate to others.

1 Introduction

Many NLP applications require a pairwise graph-based similarity measure. Examples are bilingual lexicon extraction (Laws et al., 2010), sentiment analysis (Scheible and Schütze, 2013), synonym extraction (Minkov and Cohen, 2014), named entity disambiguation (Alhelbawy and Gaizauskas, 2014), acronym expansion (Zhang et al., 2011). Recently, Co-Simrank (Rothe and Schütze, 2014) becomes an appealing graph-theoretical similarity measure that integrates both features of Simrank (Jeh and Widom, 2002) and Pagerank (Berkhin, 2005). Co-Simrank works by weighing all the number of connections between two nodes to evaluate how similar two nodes are. The intuition behind Co-Simrank is that *"more similar nodes are likely to be pointed to by other similar nodes"*.

Co-Simrank is defined in a recursive style:

$$\mathbf{S} = c\mathbf{A}^T\mathbf{S}\mathbf{A} + \mathbf{I}, \qquad (1)$$

where $\mathbf{S}$ is *the exact Co-Simrank matrix*, $\mathbf{A}$ is the column-normalised adjacency matrix of the graph, c is a decay factor, and $\mathbf{I}$ is an identity matrix.

The best-known method by (Rothe and Schütze, 2014) computes a single element of $\mathbf{S}$ iteratively from a dot product $\langle *, * \rangle$ of two Pagerank vectors:

$$\mathbf{S}_k(a,b) = c^k\langle \mathbf{p}_k(a), \mathbf{p}_k(b)\rangle + \mathbf{S}_{k-1}(a,b) \qquad (2)$$

where $\mathbf{p}_k(a)$ is *a Pagerank vector*, defined as

$$\mathbf{p}_k(a) = \mathbf{A}^T\mathbf{p}_{k-1}(a) \;\; \text{with} \;\; \mathbf{p}_0(a) = \mathbf{I}(*, a) \qquad (3)$$

This method is highly efficient when only a small fraction of pairs of Co-Simranks need computing because there is no need to access the entire graph for computing only a single pair score. However, partial pairs retrieval is insufficient for many real-world applications (Zhou et al., 2009; Yu et al., 2012a; Zwick, 2002; Leicht et al., 2006) which require all-pairs scores. Let us look at two examples.

a) Co-Citation Analysis. In a co-citation network, one wants to retrieve the relevance between *any* two given documents *at any moment* based on their references. To answer such an *ad-hoc* query, quantifying scores of all document-pairs provides a comprehensive way to show where low and high relevance of pairwise documents may exist (Li et al., 2010; Yu et al., 2014; Haveliwala, 2002).

b) Water Burst Localization. In a water network, nodes denote deployed pressure sensor locations, and edges are pipe sections that connect the nodes. To determine the burst location, one needs to evaluate "proximities" of all pairs of sensor nodes first, and then compare all these "proximities" with the difference in the arrival times of the burst transient at sensor locations, to find the sensor node nearest to the burst event. (Srirangarajan and Pesch, 2013; Srirangarajan et al., 2013; Stoianov et al., 2007)

Hence, the retrieval of all pairwise Co-Simranks is very useful in many applications. Unfortunately, when it comes to *all pairs* computation of $\mathbf{S}(*, *)$, the way of (2) has no advantage over the naive way

$$\mathbf{S}_k = c\mathbf{A}^T\mathbf{S}_{k-1}\mathbf{A} + \mathbf{I} \;\; \text{with} \;\; \mathbf{S}_0 = \mathbf{I} \qquad (4)$$

Proceedings of the 53rd Annual Meeting of the Association for Computational Linguistics and the 7th International Joint Conference on Natural Language Processing (Short Papers), pages 327–333,
Beijing, China, July 26-31, 2015.

as both entail $\mathcal{O}(\log(1/\epsilon)n^3)$ time to compute all pairs of Co-Simranks to attain desired accuracy ϵ.

The complexity $\mathcal{O}(\log(1/\epsilon)n^3)$ has two parts: The first part $\mathcal{O}(n^3)$ is for matrix multiplications $(\mathbf{A}^T\mathbf{S}_{k-1}\mathbf{A})$ at each step. A careful implementation, *e.g.,* partial sums memoisation (Lizorkin et al., 2010) or fast matrix multiplications (Yu et al., 2012b),[1] can optimise this part further to $\mathcal{O}(dn^2)$ or $\mathcal{O}(n^{\log_2 7})$, with d the average graph degree. The second part $\mathcal{O}(\log(1/\epsilon))$ is the total number of steps required to guarantee a given accuracy ϵ, because, as implied by (Rothe and Schütze, 2014),

$$|\mathbf{S}_k(a,b) - \mathbf{S}(a,b)| \le c^{k+1}. \quad \forall a, b, \quad \forall k \quad (5)$$

To the best of our knowledge, there is a paucity of work on optimising the second part $\mathcal{O}(\log(1/\epsilon))$. Yu et al. (2012b) used a successive over-relaxation (SOR) method to reduce the number of steps for Simrank, which is also applicable to Co-Simrank. However, this method requires a judicious choice of an internal parameter (*i.e.,* relaxation factor ω), which is hard to determine a-priori. Most recently, Yu et al. (2015) propose an exponential model to speed up the convergence of Simrank:

$$\bar{\mathbf{S}}_0 = \exp(-c)\cdot\mathbf{I}, \qquad \mathrm{d}\bar{\mathbf{S}}_t/\mathrm{d}t = \mathbf{A}^T\cdot\mathbf{S}\cdot\mathbf{A}.$$

However, $\bar{\mathbf{S}}$ and $\mathbf{S}$ do not produce the same results. Thus, this exponential model, if used to compute Co-Simrank, will lose some ranking accuracy.

Contributions. In this paper, we propose an efficient method, Co-Simmate, that computes all pairs of Co-Simranks in just $\mathcal{O}(\log_2(\log(1/\epsilon))n^3)$ time, without any compromise in accuracy. In addition, Co-Simmate is parameter-free, and easy to implement. It can also integrate the best-of-breed matrix decomposition based method by Yu and McCann (2014) to achieve even higher efficiency.

2 Co-Simmate Model

First, we provide the main idea of Co-Simmate.

We notice that Co-Simrank solution $\mathbf{S}$ in (1) is expressible as a matrix series:

$$\begin{aligned}\mathbf{S} = \mathbf{I} + c\mathbf{A}^T\mathbf{A} + c^2(\mathbf{A}^T)^2\mathbf{A}^2 \\ + c^3(\mathbf{A}^T)^3\mathbf{A}^3 + c^4(\mathbf{A}^T)^4\mathbf{A}^4 + \cdots\end{aligned} \quad (6)$$

The existing iterative method (4) essentially uses the following association to compute (6):

$$\mathbf{S} = \Big(c\mathbf{A}^T\overbrace{\Big(c\mathbf{A}^T\underbrace{(c\mathbf{A}^T\mathbf{A}+\mathbf{I})}_{=\mathbf{S}_1}\mathbf{A}+\mathbf{I}\Big)}^{=\mathbf{S}_2}\mathbf{A}+\mathbf{I}\Big) + \cdots \quad (7)$$

The downside of this association is that the resulting $\mathbf{S}_{k-1}$ of the last step can be reused only *once* to compute $\mathbf{S}_k$. Thus, after k iterations, $\mathbf{S}_k$ in (4) grasps only the first k-th partial sums of $\mathbf{S}$ in (6).

To speed up the computation, we observe that (6) can be reorganised as follows:

$$\begin{aligned}\mathbf{S} =& \Big(\mathbf{I} + c\mathbf{A}^T\mathbf{A}\Big) + \Big(c^2(\mathbf{A}^T)^2\mathbf{A}^2 + c^3(\mathbf{A}^T)^3\mathbf{A}^3\Big) + \\ &+ \Big(c^4(\mathbf{A}^T)^4\mathbf{A}^4 + \cdots + c^7(\mathbf{A}^T)^7\mathbf{A}^7\Big) + \cdots \\ =& \Big(\mathbf{I} + c\mathbf{A}^T\mathbf{A}\Big) + \Big(c^2(\mathbf{A}^T)^2(\mathbf{I} + c\mathbf{A}^T\mathbf{A})\mathbf{A}^2\Big) + \\ &+ \Big(c^4(\mathbf{A}^T)^4\Big(\mathbf{I} + c\mathbf{A}^T\mathbf{A} + \cdots + c^3(\mathbf{A}^T)^3\mathbf{A}^3\Big)\mathbf{A}^4\Big) + \cdots\end{aligned}$$

Thereby, we can derive the following novel association, referred to as Co-Simmate, to compute (6):

$$\begin{aligned}\mathbf{S} =& \underbrace{\Big(\overbrace{(\mathbf{I} + c\mathbf{A}^T\mathbf{A})}^{=\mathbf{R}_1} + (c\mathbf{A}^T)^2\overbrace{(\mathbf{I} + c\mathbf{A}^T\mathbf{A})}^{=\mathbf{R}_1}\mathbf{A}^2\Big)}_{=\mathbf{R}_2} + \quad (8) \\ & (c\mathbf{A}^T)^4\underbrace{\Big((\mathbf{I} + c\mathbf{A}^T\mathbf{A}) + (c\mathbf{A}^T)^2(\mathbf{I} + c\mathbf{A}^T\mathbf{A})\mathbf{A}^2\Big)}_{=\mathbf{R}_2}\mathbf{A}^4 + \cdots\end{aligned}$$

There are two advantages of our association: one is that the resulting $\mathbf{R}_{k-1}$ from the last step can be reused *twice* to compute $\mathbf{R}_k$. Hence, $\mathbf{R}_k$ can grasp the first $(2^k - 1)$-th partial sums[2] of $\mathbf{S}$ in (6). Another merit is that $\mathbf{A}^{2^k}$ can be obtained from the result of squaring $\mathbf{A}^{2^{k-1}}$, *e.g.,* $\mathbf{A}^4 = (\mathbf{A}^2)^2$. With these advantages, Co-Simmate can compute all pairs of scores much faster.

Next, let us formally introduce Co-Simmate:

Definition 1. *We call* $\mathbf{R}_k$ *a Co-Simmate matrix at* k*-th step if it is iterated as*

$$\begin{cases}\mathbf{R}_0 = \mathbf{I}, \qquad \mathbf{A}_0 = \mathbf{A} \\ \mathbf{R}_{k+1} = \mathbf{R}_k + c^{2^k}({\mathbf{A}_k}^T\mathbf{R}_k\mathbf{A}_k) \\ \mathbf{A}_{k+1} = {\mathbf{A}_k}^2\end{cases} \quad (9)$$

By successive substitution in (9), one can verify that $\lim_{k\to\infty}\mathbf{R}_k$ is the exact solution of $\mathbf{S}$ in (6). More precisely, the following theorem shows that, at step k, how many first terms of $\mathbf{S}$ in (6) can be grasped by $\mathbf{R}_k$, showing the fast speedup of (9).

Theorem 1. *Let* $\mathbf{R}_k$ *be the Co-Simmate matrix in* (9)*, and* $\mathbf{S}_k$ *the Co-Simrank matrix in* (4)*. Then,*

$$\mathbf{R}_k = \mathbf{S}_{2^k-1} \qquad \forall k = 0, 1, 2, \cdots \quad (10)$$

[1]These Simranks methods also suit Co-Simranks.

[2]This amount of the first partial sums will be proved later.

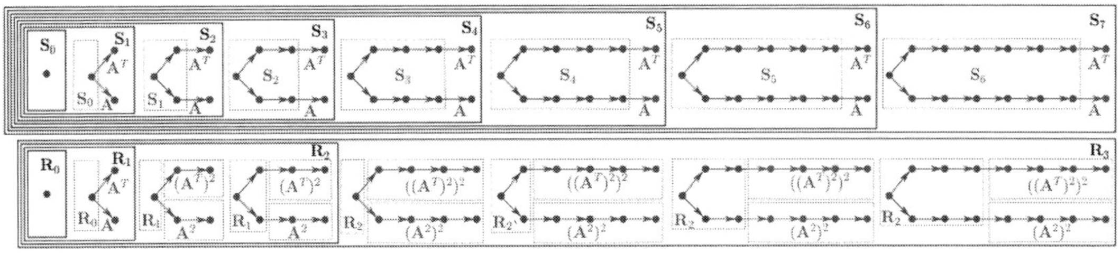

Figure 1: Co-Simmate speeds up Co-Simrank by aggregating more first terms of $\mathbf{S}$ in (6) at each step

Proof. Successive substitution in (4) produces

$$\mathbf{S}_k = \sum_{i=0}^{k} c^i (\mathbf{A}^i)^T \mathbf{A}^i \tag{11}$$

Thus, proving (10) is equivalent to showing that

$$\mathbf{R}_k = \sum_{i=0}^{2^k-1} c^i (\mathbf{A}^i)^T \mathbf{A}^i \tag{12}$$

To show (12), we will use induction on k.

1. For $k = 0$, we have $\mathbf{R}_0 = \mathbf{I} = c^0 (\mathbf{A}^0)^T \mathbf{A}^0$.
2. When $k > 0$, we assume that (12) holds for k, and want to prove that (12) holds for $k+1$.
   From $\mathbf{A}_{k+1} = \mathbf{A}_k{}^2$ and $\mathbf{A}_0 = \mathbf{A}$ follows that

$$\mathbf{A}_k = \mathbf{A}_{k-1}{}^2 = \mathbf{A}_{k-2}{}^{2^2} = \cdots = \mathbf{A}^{2^k} \tag{13}$$

Plugging $\mathbf{R}_k$ (12) and $\mathbf{A}_k$ (13) into (9) yields

$$\begin{aligned}
&\mathbf{R}_{k+1} = \{\text{using (12) and (13)}\} \\
&= \mathbf{R}_k + c^{2^k} (\mathbf{A}^{2^k})^T \Big(\sum_{i=0}^{2^k-1} c^i (\mathbf{A}^i)^T \mathbf{A}^i\Big) \mathbf{A}^{2^k} \\
&= \mathbf{R}_k + \sum_{i=0}^{2^k-1} c^{i+2^k} (\mathbf{A}^{i+2^k})^T \mathbf{A}^{i+2^k} \\
&= \mathbf{R}_k + \sum_{j=2^k}^{2^k-1+2^k} c^j (\mathbf{A}^j)^T \mathbf{A}^j \\
&= \sum_{j=0}^{2^{k+1}-1} c^j (\mathbf{A}^j)^T \mathbf{A}^j
\end{aligned}$$

Lastly, coupling (11) and (12) concludes (10). □

Theorem 1 implies that, at each step k, $\mathbf{R}_k$ in (9) can grasp the first $(2^k - 1)$-th terms of $\mathbf{S}$, whereas $\mathbf{S}_k$ in (4) can grasp only the first k-th terms of $\mathbf{S}$. Thus, given the number of steps K, Co-Simmate is always more accurate than Co-Simrank because $\mathbf{R}_K$ is exponentially closer to $\mathbf{S}$ than $\mathbf{S}_K$ to $\mathbf{S}$.

Convergence Rate. We next provide a quantitative result on how closer $\mathbf{R}_k$ is to $\mathbf{S}$ than $\mathbf{S}_k$ to $\mathbf{S}$.

Theorem 2. *For any given step k, the difference between $\mathbf{R}_k$ and $\mathbf{S}$ can be bounded by*

$$|\mathbf{R}_k(a,b) - \mathbf{S}(a,b)| \le c^{2^k}, \qquad \forall a, b \tag{14}$$

Proof. The Co-Simrank result in (5) implies that

$$|\mathbf{S}_{2^k-1}(a,b) - \mathbf{S}(a,b)| \le c^{2^k}, \qquad \forall a, b$$

Plugging (10) into this inequality yields (14). □

Theorem 2 implies that, to attain a desired accuracy ϵ, Co-Simmate (9) takes exponentially fewer steps than Co-Simrank (4) since the total number of steps required for $\mathbf{R}_K$, as implied by (14), is

$$K = \max\{0, \lceil \log_2 \log_c \epsilon \rceil + 1\},$$

in contrast to the $\lceil \log_c \epsilon \rceil$ steps required for $\mathbf{S}_K$.

Total Computational Cost. Though Co-Simmate takes fewer steps than Co-Simrank for a desired ϵ, in each step Co-Simmate (9) performs one more matrix multiplication than Co-Simrank (4). Next, we compare their total computational time.

Theorem 3. *To guarantee a desired accuracy ϵ, the total time of Co-Simmate (9) is exponentially faster than that of Co-Simrank (4).*

Proof. For $k = 1$, both Co-Simmate (9) and Co-Simrank (4) take 2 matrix multiplications.

For $k > 1$, Co-Simmate (9) takes 3 matrix multiplications (2 for $\mathbf{A}_k^T \mathbf{R}_k \mathbf{A}_k$ and 1 for $\mathbf{A}_k^2$), whilst Co-Simrank (4) takes 2 (only for $\mathbf{A}_k^T \mathbf{S}_k \mathbf{A}_k$).

Let $|\mathfrak{M}|$ be the number of operations for one matrix multiplication. Then, for Co-Simmate (9),

$$(\text{total \# of operations for } \mathbf{R}_k) = 3k|\mathfrak{M}|,$$

whereas for Co-Simrank (4), by Theorem 1,

$$(\text{total \# of operations for } \mathbf{S}_k) = 2(2^k - 1)|\mathfrak{M}|.$$

Since $3k|\mathfrak{M}| \le 2(2^k-1)|\mathfrak{M}|, \forall k = 2, 3, \cdots$, we can conclude that the total time of Co-Simmate is exponentially faster than that of Co-Simrank. □

Example. Figure 1 pictorially visualises how Co-Simmate accelerates Co-Simrank computation by aggregating more first terms of $\mathbf{S}$ in (6) each step.

Algorithm 1: Co-Simmate on Singular Graphs

Input : $\mathbf{A}$ – column-normalised adjacency matrix, c – decay factor, ϵ – desired accuracy.

Decompose $\mathbf{A}$ *s.t.* $[\mathbf{V}_r, \mathbf{H}_r^T] \leftarrow$ Gram-Schmidt($\mathbf{A}$).
Compute $\mathbf{P} \leftarrow \mathbf{H}_r^T \mathbf{V}_r$.
Initialise $K \leftarrow \max\{0, \lceil \log_2 \log_c \epsilon \rceil + 1\}$.
Initialise $\mathbf{S}_0 \leftarrow \mathbf{I}_r, \quad \mathbf{P}_0 \leftarrow \mathbf{P}$.
for $k \leftarrow 0, 1, \cdots, K-1$ **do**
  Compute $\mathbf{S}_{k+1} \leftarrow c^{2^k} (\mathbf{P}_k)^T \mathbf{S}_k (\mathbf{P}_k) + \mathbf{S}_k$.
  Compute $\mathbf{P}_{k+1} \leftarrow (\mathbf{P}_k)^2$.
return $\mathbf{S} \leftarrow c\mathbf{H}_r \mathbf{S}_K \mathbf{H}_r^T + \mathbf{I}$.

At k-th step, Co-Simrank $\mathbf{S}_k$ connects only two new *hop-1* paths with the old retrieved paths $\mathbf{S}_{k-1}$, whereas Co-Simmate $\mathbf{R}_k$ connects two new *hop-*(2^k) paths (by squaring the old hop-(2^{k-1}) paths) with the old retrieved paths $\mathbf{R}_{k-1}$. Consequently, in each step of Co-Simrank, Co-Simmate is exponential steps faster than Co-Simrank. Moreover, the speedup is more obvious as k grows. □

Optimality of Co-Simmate. To compute $\mathbf{S}$ in (6), besides the prior association methods (7) and (8), the following association can also be adopted:

$$\mathbf{S} = \overbrace{\left(\mathbf{I} + c\mathbf{A}^T\mathbf{A} + c^2(\mathbf{A}^T)^2\mathbf{A}^2\right)}^{=\mathbf{T}_1} + \quad (15)$$
$$c^3(\mathbf{A}^T)^3 \underbrace{\left(\mathbf{I} + c\mathbf{A}^T\mathbf{A} + c^2(\mathbf{A}^T)^2\mathbf{A}^2\right)}_{=\mathbf{T}_1} \mathbf{A}^3 + \cdots$$

More generally, we can write the following model that covers (8) and (15) as special cases:

$$\begin{cases} \mathbf{R}_0^{(u)} = \mathbf{I}, \quad \mathbf{A}_0 = \mathbf{A} \\ \mathbf{R}_{k+1}^{(u)} = \mathbf{R}_k^{(u)} + c^{u^k} \cdot \mathbf{A}_k^T \cdot \mathbf{R}_k^{(u)} \cdot \mathbf{A}_k \\ \qquad + c^{2 \cdot u^k} \cdot ({\mathbf{A}_k}^2)^T \cdot \mathbf{R}_k^{(u)} \cdot {\mathbf{A}_k}^2 + \cdots + \\ \qquad + c^{(u-1) \cdot u^k} \cdot ({\mathbf{A}_k}^{u-1})^T \cdot \mathbf{R}_k^{(u)} \cdot {\mathbf{A}_k}^{u-1} \\ \mathbf{A}_{k+1} = {\mathbf{A}_k}^u \quad (u = 2, 3, \cdots) \end{cases}$$

$\mathbf{R}_k^{(u)}$ is *a hop-*(u^k) *Co-Simmate matrix* at step k. $\mathbf{R}_k^{(u)}$ becomes Co-Simmate $\mathbf{R}_k$ in (8) when $u = 2$; and reduces to $\mathbf{T}_k$ in (15) when $u = 3$. For all u, it is easy to verify that $\lim_{k \to \infty} \mathbf{R}_k^{(u)} = \mathbf{S}$. Below, we show that Co-Simmate (8) $(u = 2)$ is optimal.

Theorem 4. *To attain a desired accuracy* ϵ*, the total time of Co-Simmate* (8) *is minimum among all hop-*(u^k) *Co-Simmate models* $\mathbf{R}_k^{(u)} (u = 2, 3, \cdots)$.

Proof. Similar to Theorem 1, we can show that

$$|\mathbf{R}_k^{(u)}(a,b) - \mathbf{S}(a,b)| \leq c^{u^k}, \quad \forall a, b, \ \forall u \quad (16)$$

Thus, given ϵ, the total number of steps for $\mathbf{R}_K^{(u)}$ is

$$K = \max\{0, \lceil \log_u \log_c \epsilon \rceil + 1\}.$$

For each step k, for hop-(u^k) Co-Simmate $\mathbf{R}_k^{(u)}$,

$$(\text{\# of operations}) = ((u-1) + \textstyle\sum_{i=0}^{u-2} i)|\mathfrak{M}| = \frac{(u-1)u}{2}|\mathfrak{M}|.$$

Therefore, the total time of computing $\mathbf{R}_k^{(u)}$ is

$$\mathcal{O}(\max\{0, \lceil \log_u \log_c \epsilon \rceil + 1\}(u-1)u|\mathfrak{M}|).$$

This complexity is increasing with $u = 2, 3, \cdots$. Thus, Co-Simmate (8) $(u = 2)$ is minimum. □

Incorporate Co-Simmate into Singular Graphs. Co-Simmate (9) can also be combined with other factorisation methods, *e.g.*, Sig-SR, a Co-Simrank algorithm proposed by (Yu and McCann, 2014), to speed up all pairs of Co-Simrank computation from $\mathcal{O}(rn^2 + Kr^3)$ to $\mathcal{O}(rn^2 + (\log_2 K)r^3)$ time further on a singular graph with rank r for K steps. The enhanced Sig-SR is shown in Algorithm 1.

3 Experiments

3.1 Experimental Settings

Datasets. We use both real and synthetic datasets. Three real graphs (Twitter, Email, Facebook) are taken from SNAP (Leskovec and Sosič, 2014).

1) Twitter is a who-follows-whom social graph crawled from the entire Twitter site. Each node is a user, and each edge represents a social relation.

2) Email is an Email communication network from Enron. If an address i sent at least one email to address j, there is a link from i to j.

3) FB contains 'circles' (or 'friends lists') from Facebook. This dataset is collected from the survey participants using the Facebook app, including node features (profiles), circles, and ego networks.

The statistics of these datasets are as follows:

Datasets	# edges	# nodes	ave degree
Twitter	1,768,149	81,306	21.70
Email	183,831	36,692	5.01
FB	88,234	4,039	21.84

To build synthetic data, we use Boost toolkit (Lee et al., 2001).We control the number of nodes n and edges m to follow densification power laws (Leskovec et al., 2005; Faloutsos et al., 1999).

Baselines. We compare our Co-Simmate with 1) Ite-Mat (Rothe and Schütze, 2014), a Co-Simrank method using the dot product of Pagerank vectors. 2) K-Sim (Kusumoto et al., 2014), a linearized method modified to Co-Simrank. 3) Sig-SR (Yu and McCann, 2014), a SVD Co-Simrank method.

All experiments are on 64bit Ubuntu 14.04 with Intel Xeon E2650 2.0GHz CPU and 16GB RAM.

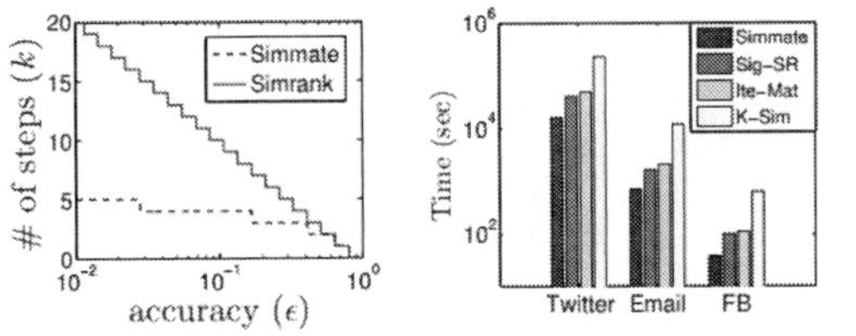

(a) Rate of Convergence (on FB dataset, $c = 0.8$)

(b) Total Computational Time (on three real datasets, $c = 0.8$)

ϵ	$c = 0.6$ SM	$c = 0.6$ SR	$c = 0.7$ SM	$c = 0.7$ SR	$c = 0.8$ SM	$c = 0.8$ SR
0.1	3	4	3	6	4	10
0.01	4	9	4	12	5	20
0.001	4	13	5	19	5	30
0.0001	5	18	5	25	6	41
0.00001	5	22	6	32	6	51

(c) Effect of Damping Factor c on Iterations k (on FB)

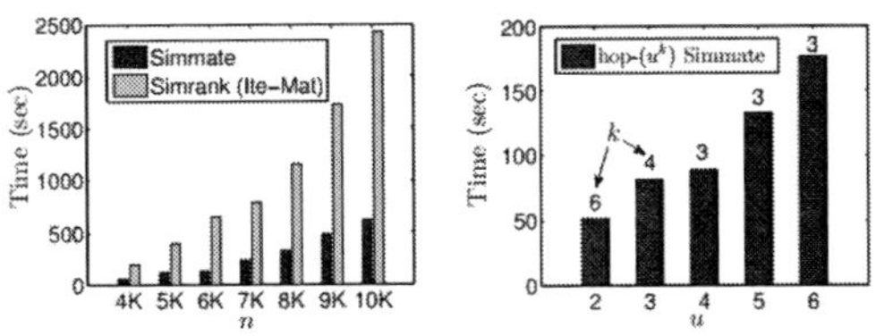

(d) Scalability *w.r.t.* # nodes (on 7 synthetic datasets)

(e) Effect of Hop-(u^k) (on FB dataset, $c = 0.8$)

Figure 2: Compare Co-Simmate with Baselines

3.2 Experimental Results

Exp-I. Convergence Rate. We compare the number of steps k needed for Co-Simmate and Co-Simrank (Ite-Mat) to attain a desired accuracy ϵ on Twitter, Email, FB. The results on all the datasets are similar. Due to space limits, Figure 2(a) only reports the result on FB. We can discern that, when ϵ varies from 0.01 to 1, k increases from 1 to 5 for Co-Simmate, but from 1 to 20 for Co-Simrank. The fast convergence rate of Co-Simmate is due to our model that *twice* reuses $\mathbf{R}_{k-1}$ of the last step.

Exp-II. Total Computational Time. Figure 2(b) compares the total computational time of Co-Simmate with 3 best-known methods on real data. The result shows Co-Simmate runs 10x, 5.6x, 4.3x faster than K-Sim, Ite-Mat, Sig-SR, respectively. This is because 1) K-Sim is efficient only when a fraction pair of scores are computed, whereas Co-Simmate can efficiently handle all pairs scores, by twice sharing $\mathbf{R}_{k-1}$ and repeated squaring $\mathbf{A}^{2^{k-1}}$. 2) Co-Simmate grasps exponential new terms of $\mathbf{S}$ per step, but Ite-Mat grasps just 1 new term of $\mathbf{S}$. 3) Sig-SR does not adopt association tricks in the subspace, unlike our methods that integrate (9).

Exp-III. Effect of Damping Factor c. Using real datasets (Twitter, Email, FB), we next evaluate the effect of damping factor c on the number of iterations k to guarantee a given accuracy ϵ. We vary ϵ from 0.1 to 0.00001 and c from 0.6 to 0.8, the results of k on all the datasets are similar. For the interests of space, Figure 2(c) tabularises only the results on FB, where 'SM' columns list the number of iterations required for Co-Simmate, and 'SR' columns lists that for Co-Simrank. From the results, we can see that, for any given ϵ and c, the number of iterations for Co-Simmate is consistently smaller than that for Co-Simrank. Their gap is more pronounced when ϵ becomes smaller or c is increased. This is because, at each iteration, Co-Simmate can grasp far more first terms of $\mathbf{S}$ than Co-Simrank. Thus, for a fixed accuracy, Co-Simmate requires less iterations than Co-Simrank. This is consistent with our analysis in Theorem 2.

Exp-IV. Scalability. By using synthetic datasets, we fix $\epsilon = 0.0001$ and vary n from 4,000 to 10,000. Figure 2(d) depicts the total time of Co-Simmate and Ite-Mat. We can notice that, as n grows, the time of Co-Simmate does not increase so fast as Co-Simrank. The reason is that the number of steps of Co-Simmate is greatly cut down by twice $\mathbf{R}_{k-1}$ sharing and $\mathbf{A}^{2^{k-1}}$ memoisation.

Exp-V. Effect of Hop-u^k. Finally, we test the impact of u on the total time of our hop-(u^k) Co-Simmate variations on real datasets. Due to similar results, Figure 2(e) merely reports the results on FB. It can be observed that, as u grows from 2 to 6, the total number of steps for hop-(u^k) Co-Simmate decreases, but their total time still grows. This is because, in each step, the cost of hop-(u^k) Co-Simmate is increasing with u. Thus, the lowest cost is Co-Simmate when $u = 2$.

4 Conclusions

We propose an efficient algorithm, Co-Simmate, to speed up all pairs Co-Simranks retrieval from $\mathcal{O}(\log(1/\epsilon)n^3)$ to $\mathcal{O}(\log_2(\log(1/\epsilon))n^3)$ time, to attain a desired accuracy ϵ. Besides, we integrate Co-Simmate with Sig-SR on singular graphs to attain higher efficacy. The experiments show that Co-Simmate can be 10.2x faster than the state-of-the-art competitors. As future work, we will incorporate our partial-pairs Simrank (Yu and McCann, 2015) into partial-pairs Co-Simmate search.

Acknowledgement. This research is supported by NEC Smart Water Network research project.

References

Ayman Alhelbawy and Robert J. Gaizauskas. 2014. Graph ranking for collective named entity disambiguation. In *Proceedings of the 52nd Annual Meeting of the Association for Computational Linguistics (ACL 2014)*, pages 75–80.

Pavel Berkhin. 2005. Survey: A survey on PageRank computing. *Internet Mathematics*, 2(1):73–120.

Michalis Faloutsos, Petros Faloutsos, and Christos Faloutsos. 1999. On power-law relationships of the internet topology. In *Proceedings of the Conference on Applications, Technologies, Architectures, and Protocols for Computer Communication (SIGCOMM 1999)*, pages 251–262.

Taher H Haveliwala. 2002. Topic-sensitive PageRank. In *Proceedings of the 11th International Conference on World Wide Web (WWW 2002)*, pages 517–526. ACM.

Glen Jeh and Jennifer Widom. 2002. SimRank: A measure of structural-context similarity. In *Proceedings of the 8th ACM SIGKDD International Conference on Knowledge Discovery and Data Mining (SIGKDD 2002)*, pages 538–543.

Mitsuru Kusumoto, Takanori Maehara, and Ken-ichi Kawarabayashi. 2014. Scalable similarity search for SimRank. In *Proceedings of the 2014 ACM SIGMOD International Conference on Management of Data (SIGMOD 2014)*, pages 325–336.

Florian Laws, Lukas Michelbacher, Beate Dorow, Christian Scheible, Ulrich Heid, and Hinrich Schütze. 2010. A linguistically grounded graph model for bilingual lexicon extraction. In *Proceedings of the 23rd International Conference on Computational Linguistics (COLING 2010, Poster)*, pages 614–622.

Lie-Quan Lee, Andrew Lumsdaine, and Jeremy G Siek. 2001. The boost graph library. `http://www.boost.org/`.

E. A. Leicht, Petter Holme, and M. E. J. Newman. 2006. Vertex similarity in networks. *Physical Review E*, 73(2):026120.

Jure Leskovec and Rok Sosič. 2014. SNAP: A general purpose network analysis and graph mining library in C++. `http://snap.stanford.edu/snap`, June.

Jure Leskovec, Jon Kleinberg, and Christos Faloutsos. 2005. Graphs over time: Densification laws, shrinking diameters and possible explanations. In *Proceedings of the 11th ACM SIGKDD International Conference on Knowledge Discovery in Data Mining (SIGKDD 2005)*, pages 177–187. ACM.

Cuiping Li, Jiawei Han, Guoming He, Xin Jin, Yizhou Sun, Yintao Yu, and Tianyi Wu. 2010. Fast computation of SimRank for static and dynamic information networks. In *Proceedings of the 13th International Conference on Extending Database Technology (EDBT 2010)*, pages 465–476.

Dmitry Lizorkin, Pavel Velikhov, Maxim N. Grinev, and Denis Turdakov. 2010. Accuracy estimate and optimization techniques for SimRank computation. *The VLDB Journal (The International Journal on Very Large Data Bases)*, 19(1):45–66.

Einat Minkov and William W. Cohen. 2014. Adaptive graph walk-based similarity measures for parsed text. *Natural Language Engineering*, 20(3):361–397.

Sascha Rothe and Hinrich Schütze. 2014. CoSimRank: A flexible & efficient graph-theoretic similarity measure. In *Proceedings of the 52nd Annual Meeting of the Association for Computational Linguistics (ACL 2014)*, pages 1392–1402.

Christian Scheible and Hinrich Schütze. 2013. Sentiment relevance. In *Proceedings of the 51st Annual Meeting of the Association for Computational Linguistics (ACL 2013)*, pages 954–963.

Seshan Srirangarajan and Dirk Pesch. 2013. Source localization using graph-based optimization technique. In *IEEE Wireless Communications and Networking Conference (WCNC 2013)*, pages 1127–1132.

Seshan Srirangarajan, Michael Allen, Ami Preis, Mudasser Iqbal, HockBeng Lim, and AndrewJ. Whittle. 2013. Wavelet-based burst event detection and localization in water distribution systems. *Journal of Signal Processing Systems*, 72(1):1–16.

Ivan Stoianov, Lama Nachman, Steve Madden, Timur Tokmouline, and M Csail. 2007. PIPENET: A wireless sensor network for pipeline monitoring. In *The 6th International Symposium on Information Processing in Sensor Networks (IPSN 2007)*, pages 264–273.

Weiren Yu and Julie A. McCann. 2014. Sig-SR: SimRank search over singular graphs. In *Proceedings of the 37th ACM SIGIR International Conference on Research & Development in Information Retrieval (SIGIR 2014)*, pages 859–862.

Weiren Yu and Julie A McCann. 2015. Efficient partial-pairs SimRank search on large networks. *Proceedings of the VLDB Endowment (PVLDB 2015)*, 8(5):569–580.

Weiren Yu, Xuemin Lin, Wenjie Zhang, Ying Zhang, and Jiajin Le. 2012a. SimFusion+: Extending SimFusion towards efficient estimation on large and dynamic networks. In *Proceedings of the 35th ACM SIGIR International Conference on Research & Development in Information Retrieval (SIGIR 2012)*, pages 365–374.

Weiren Yu, Wenjie Zhang, Xuemin Lin, Qing Zhang, and Jiajin Le. 2012b. A space and time efficient algorithm for SimRank computation. *World Wide Web*, 15(3):327–353.

Weiren Yu, Xuemin Lin, and Wenjie Zhang. 2014. Fast incremental SimRank on link-evolving graphs. In *Proceedings of the 30th IEEE International Conference on Data Engineering (ICDE 2014)*, pages 304–315.

Weiren Yu, Xuemin Lin, Wenjie Zhang, and Julie A. McCann. 2015. Fast all-pairs SimRank assessment on large graphs and bipartite domains. *IEEE Transactions on Knowledge and Data Engineering (TKDE)*, 27(7):1810–1823.

Wei Zhang, Yan Chuan Sim, Jian Su, and Chew Lim Tan. 2011. Entity linking with effective acronym expansion, instance selection and topic modeling. In *Proceedings of the 22nd International Joint Conference on Artificial Intelligence (IJCAI 2011)*, pages 1909–1914.

Yang Zhou, Hong Cheng, and Jeffrey Xu Yu. 2009. Graph clustering based on structural / attribute similarities. *Proceedings of the VLDB Endowment (PVLDB)*, 2(1):718–729.

Uri Zwick. 2002. All pairs shortest paths using bridging sets and rectangular matrix multiplication. *Journal of the ACM (JACM)*, 49(3):289–317.

Retrieval of Research-level Mathematical Information Needs: A Test Collection and Technical Terminology Experiment

Yiannos A. Stathopoulos **Simone Tuefel**
Computer Laboratory, University of Cambridge
15 JJ Thomson Avenue, Cambridge, UK
{yiannos.stathopoulos,simone.teufel}@cl.cam.ac.uk

Abstract

In this paper, we present a test collection for mathematical information retrieval composed of real-life, research-level mathematical information needs. Topics and relevance judgements have been procured from the on-line collaboration website MathOverflow by delegating domain-specific decisions to experts on-line. With our test collection, we construct a baseline using Lucene's vector-space model implementation and conduct an experiment to investigate how prior extraction of technical terms from mathematical text can affect retrieval efficiency. We show that by boosting the importance of technical terms, statistically significant improvements in retrieval performance can be obtained over the baseline.

1 Introduction

Since their introduction through the Cranfield experiments (Cleverdon, 1960; Cleverdon, 1962; Cleverdon et al., 1966a; Cleverdon et al., 1966b), test collections have become the foundation of information retrieval (IR) evaluation.

Recent interest in Mathematical information retrieval (MIR) has prompted the construction of the NTCIR Math IR test collection (Aizawa et al., 2013). Like many general-purpose, domain-specific IR test collections, the NTCIR collection is composed of broad queries intended to test systems over a wide spectrum of query complexity.

In this paper we present a test collection composed of real-life, research-level mathematical topics and associated relevance judgements procured from the online collaboration web-site MathOverflow[1]. The resulting test collection contains 160 atomic questions - material derived from 120 MathOverflow discussion threads.

Topics in our test collection capture specialised information needs that are complex to resolve and often demand collective effort from multiple domain experts. For example[2]:

> The "most symmetric" Mukai-Umemura 3-fold with automorphism group $PGL(2, C)$ admits a Kaehler-Einstein metric according to Donaldson's result. On the contrary, there are some arbitrarily small complex deformations of the above 3-fold which do not admit Kaehler-Einstein metrics, as shown by Tian. All examples considered by Tian seem to have no symmetries at all. *Is it possible to find similarly arbitrarily small complex deformations with C^*-action and which do not admit any Kaehler-Einstein metric?*

Due to their specialised nature, our topics have a relatively small number of relevant documents. Fortunately, there is precedent of this from IR tasks such as QA (Ishikawa et al., 2010) and known-item search (Craswell et al., 2003).

With our test collection, we construct a baseline using Lucene's default implementation of the vector space model (VSM). Additionally, we conduct an experiment designed to investigate the hypothesis that technical terms in mathematics have elevated retrieval significance.

Information in mathematics is communicated by defining, manipulating and otherwise operating on mathematical structures and objects which can be instantiated in the mathematical discourse. In this sense, technical terminology in mathematics has an elevated role. This hypothesis stems from the observation that the mathematical discourse is dense with named mathematical objects, structures, properties and results.

[1] http://mathoverflow.net/

[2] Adapted from MathOverflow post 68096, http://mathoverflow.net/questions/68096/

Proceedings of the 53rd Annual Meeting of the Association for Computational Linguistics and the 7th International Joint Conference on Natural Language Processing (Short Papers), pages 334–340,
Beijing, China, July 26-31, 2015.

In the next section, we present our test collection and discuss the procedure for its construction from crowd-sourced expertise on MathOverflow. In section 3, we discuss related material in the literature and compare it to our work. Our experimental setup and results are discussed in section 4, with a brief summary of our work presented in section 5.

2 The Test Collection

The main motivation behind this work comes from our long-term goal to develop and evaluate MIR models intended to satisfy research-level mathematical information needs. Evaluation is an important final step in the development of IR models and is preconditioned on the availability of a test collection.

A test collection is a resource composed of (1) a *document collection* (or corpus) with uniquely identifiable documents (e.g., scientific papers, news articles), (2) a set of *topics* from which search queries can be produced and (3) a set of *relevance judgements*: pairs connecting individual topics to documents (in the corpus) known to satisfy the corresponding information need.

General-purpose MIR test collections, such as the one produced for NTCIR-10 (Aizawa et al., 2013), are expected to contain both broad and narrow topics capturing a wide range of retrieval complexity. In contrast, we require a collection of topics characterised by a higher lower bound on topic complexity with individual topics capturing highly-specialised, real-world information needs.

Unfortunately, research-level mathematical information needs are hard to source from documents in a way that would not render them artificial. Furthermore, manual construction of topics and relevance judgements is unrealistic due to the large number of experts required to cover the various specialised sub-fields of mathematics. This, coupled with limited access to numerous MIR systems, makes TREC-like pooling (Harman, 1993; Voorhees and Harman, 2005) impractical.

We propose that topics and relevance judgements be procured from the on-line collaboration website MathOverflow (MO), an online QA site for research mathematicians. A user (information seeker) can post a question on the site, usually relating to a small niche field in mathematics. Colleagues can either post a candidate answer, comment on the question, comment on and/or upvote existing answers. Ultimately, the information seeker decides which answer satisfies the underlying information need by marking it as "accepted".

Prelude	1) Apparently, physicist can calculate the GW invariants of quintic CY 3-fold up to genus 51. 2) For each genus g, there is a lower bound $d(g)$ such that for every $d < d(g)$, all genus g degree d invariants of quintic are zero.
MT-1	I am looking for a reference that has a table of these number for some low degrees (say up to degree 5) and low genera (at least until $g = 3$).
MT-2	Where can I found this lower bound?

Table 1: MO post 14655, prelude and micro-topics

Material on MO is closely aligned with our requirements. Specifically, Tausczik et al. (2014) and Martin and Pease (2013) agree that MO questions (information needs) *arise from doing mathematics research* and are novel to the mathematician involved. The authors conclude that, having been produced by experts, MO answers are *authoritative* and partially credit the website's reward system for their strong *reliability*.

MO questions often have multiple sub-parts, which we refer to as *micro-topics* since they encode atomic information needs. Furthermore, information in MO questions is carried by two types of sentences: *prelude* sentences, which are used to set the mathematical context (introduce mathematical constructs and results) and *query* sentences, which transcribe the information need itself and are semantically bound to the accompanying prelude.

As the underlying document collection, we have used the Mathematical Retrieval Corpus (MREC)[3] (Líška et al., 2011), which contains more than 439,000 mathematical publications, complete with mathematical formulae converted to machine-readable MathML. Similarly, we have made mathematical expressions in our topics accessible to MIR systems by converting all LaTeX embedded in MO questions into MathML using the LaTeXML tool-kit.

For the purpose of constructing our test collection we have adopted a multi-step process. All steps in the process are systematically applicable regardless of the subject material of the topic being considered for inclusion. As such, our test collection can be as diverse, in terms of mathematical subject and sub-fields, as MathOverflow.

[3]version 2011.4.439

Decisions relating to relevance of material to a given topic (MO question) are delegated to experts on the website. However, the information seeker (MO user posting the question) remains the ultimate judge of relevance. This authority is typically exercised by either accepting an answer directly or, by explicitly commenting on the relevance of posted material.

In the first step, all MO discussion threads[4] with at least one citation to the MREC in their accepted answer were collected. Each identified thread was examined by one of the authors for conformance to two ideal-standard criteria: (1) Useful MO questions should not be too broad or vague but rather express an information need that is clear and can be satisfied by describing objects or properties, stating conditions and/or producing examples or counter-examples. (2) MREC documents cited in MO accepted answers should address all sub-parts of the question in a manner that requires minimal deduction and do not synthesise mathematical results from multiple resources.

Subsequently, relevance of documents for each micro-topic is decided using two criteria: *totality* and *directness*. A cited resource is *total* if it contains all necessary information to derive the answer for the micro-topic and *partial* if it only addresses a special case. A cited resource is also said to be *direct*, if the answer can be derived with little intellectual effort from its text, or *indirect* if the same information requires considerable effort (such as mathematical deduction or reasoning) for the information seeker to reproduce.

Making these determinations involves matching the language of arguments and the symbolic context of the answer to the cited resource. As part of this step, we also examine the post-answer (PA) comments for expressions of confirmation of the usefulness of a cited resource from the information seeker.

The completed test collection contains 160 micro-topics with 184 associated relevance judgements (involving 224 unique MREC documents) organised in 120 topics. Topic text in our test collection is sentence tokenised, with relevance judgements being represented conceptually as tuples of the form:

```
(Topic ID, sentenceID, Micro-topic ID,
    relevant MREC document ID)
```

From Table 2 we observe that the vast majority of

[4]from MathOverflow data-dump of 20/01/2014

Micro-topics	1	2	3	≥ 4
Instances (topics)	88	24	8	0
Percentage	73.33%	20.00 %	6.67%	0%

Table 2: Topic/Micro-topic break-down

topics (93.33%) have either 1 or 2 micro-topics, with the average being close to 1 (1.33). The majority of topics (97,80.83%) have only one relevant document while a further 21 (17.5%) have two relevant documents. Two topics have more than 2 relevant documents: one with 3 and another with 4. In terms of micro-topics, this corresponds to 140 micro-topics (87.50%) with 1 relevant document, 17 (10.625%) with 2, 2 micro-topics (1.25%) with 3 and just one (0.625%) with 4 relevant documents.

3 Related Work

Test collections over scientific publications were first introduced for the Cranfield experiments (Cleverdon, 1960; Cleverdon, 1962; Cleverdon et al., 1966a; Cleverdon et al., 1966b). Despite criticism for sourcing queries from collection documents, the Cranfield experiments highlighted the importance of jointly reporting recall and precision, pioneered the practice of using authors and citations for augmenting relevance judgements and established the test collection paradigm.

Expert citations have already been exploited for procuring relevance judgements. For example, Ritchie et al. (2006) elicited relevance judgements for citations in papers accepted in a scientific conference from their authors and used these judgements as part of their test collection of scientific publications.

In terms of domain, our work is related to the NTCIR-10 Math IR test collection (Aizawa et al., 2013). Furthermore, the topics in our collection are analogous to those in the NTCIR full-text search, in the sense that they take the form of coherent text interspersed with mathematical expressions. Rather than being focused on accommodating information needs of varying complexity, however, our test collection has been designed to facilitate retrieval of highly specialised, mathematical information needs of uniformly high complexity.

Similar use of crowd-sourced expertise has been proposed in the context of QA. For example, Gyongyi et al. (2008), examined 10 months-worth of "Yahoo! Answers" material as part of an investigation of QA data, which was later used for the

NTCIR-8 Community QA pilot task (Ishikawa et al., 2010; Sakai et al., 2011). Characterisation of crowd-sourced answers in terms of totality (section 2) has also been considered in the context of QA. In particular, Sakai et al. (2011) describe a relevance grading scheme of crowd-sourced answers based on the total/partial/irrelevant scale, but highlight that answers on "Yahoo! Answers" vary in quality (e.g., due to instances of bias or obscenity).

Finally, the idea of sourcing relevance judgements from expert citations is an established practice in IR. In the context of patent search, for example, Graf and Azzopardi (2008) utilised citations in patent office expert reports as relevance judgements, while Fujii et al. (2006) automatically extracted patent office expert citations used to reject patent applications.

4 Experiments

In this section we conduct an experiment to demonstrate the usefulness of our test collection by investigating the impact of terminology boosting on MIR effectiveness. An important assumption of this experiment is that the retrieval of each micro-topic is dependent only on the attached prelude.

4.1 Experimental Setup

We first produced a Lucene index over all documents in the MREC. In order to normalise processing of XHTML+MathML, topics and MREC documents were passed through the Tika framework[5]. Lucene's `StandardAnalyzer` was modified to preserve stop-words since frequent words such as the preposition "of" can be important parts of technical terms (e.g., "set of vectors"). The analyzer was also modified to preserve dashes, which are common in technical terms (e.g., "Calabi-Yau manifold"). This analyzer is used during both indexing and query processing for consistency.

4.2 Building Queries

For each micro-topic in a given topic, we emit a query string by concatenating all sentences in the prelude with sentences associated with the micro-topic. For example, query string for micro-topic MT-1 in Table 1 is generated by concatenating its text with that of the prelude. Using this strategy, consistency with the assumption outlined at the beginning of the section is achieved since no overlap beyond the prelude is introduced between queries generated for micro-topics attached to a given topic.

[5]https://tika.apache.org/

4.3 Systems

Using Lucene as the indexing and searching backend, we compare the performance of two retrieval methods. Underpinning both methods is Lucene's default similarity (project, 2013), which is based on cosine similarity:

$$sim(q,d) = \frac{V(q).V(d)}{|V(q)||V(d)|}$$

where $V(q)$ and $V(d)$ are weighted vectors for the query and candidate document respectively. As a performance measure, we use mean average precision (MAP):

$$MAP(Q) = \frac{1}{|Q|}\sum_{j=1}^{|Q|}\frac{1}{m_j}\sum_{k=1}^{m_j} Precision(R_{jk})$$

4.3.1 Baseline

Lucene's VSM implementation with default TF-IDF weighting and scoring is used as the baseline. This is intended to emulate a general-purpose information retrieval scenario, which is the motivation behind the design of Lucene's default configuration.

4.3.2 Boosted Technical Terms

The alternative model is designed to give more weight to technical terminology common to both documents and queries. In order to construct this model, all technical terms are extracted from the document collection using an implementation of the C-Value multi-word technical term extraction method (Frantzi et al., 1996; Frantzi et al., 1998). Given an input corpus, the C-Value method extracts multi-word terms by making use of a linguistic and a statistical component.

The linguistic component is responsible for eliminating multi-term strings that are unlikely to be technical terms through the use of a stop-list (composed of high-frequency corpus terms) and linguistic filters (regular expressions) applied on sequences of part-of-speech tags. The statistical component assigns a "termhood" score to a candidate term sequence based on corpus-wide statistical characteristics of the sequence itself and those of term sequences that contain it. The output of

class/Form 1	Form 2 ...	Form 8	C-Value
riemannian manifold	Riemannian manifold	RIEMANNIAN MANIFOLDS	13236.6

Table 3: C-Value technical-term list entry

Original Text
a Riemannian manifold is a smooth manifold
Original Term vector
(a,2), (Riemannian,1),(manifold,2),(is,1),(smooth,1)
Technical terms
Riemannian manifold, smooth manifold
Re-Attributed Term Vector
(a,2), (Riemannian_manifold,1),(is,1),(smooth_manifold,1)
Re-generated delta index text
a a a a Riemannian_manifold Riemannian_manifold is is smooth_manifold smooth_manifold

Table 4: Example of re-attribution and delta index

the algorithm is a list of candidate technical terms in the corpus, ordered by their C-Value termhood score.

As shown in Table 3, each entry in the resulting list represents a single technical term (the class) and enumerates all forms of the candidate term as observed in the input corpus. In total, 3 million classes of technical terms have been detected in the MREC. Using Lucene's positional indexing mechanism, we retrieved the position of each technical term (all forms), recorded its term frequency (TF) and produced a new technical term index. This technical term index contains 426 million tuple entries of the form

```
<class , form , MREC docid , TF, position
    -of-occurrence list>
```

The same re-indexing process is repeated for the queries and the result is stored in a separate query table (10,433 entries).

Subsequently, the indexed document and query term vectors were modified by (1) adding new tokens to represent technical term phrases and (2) re-attributing the TF of component terms to the term vector of the phrase.

Finally, the text for each MREC document and query is re-generated from the term vectors and stored in a "delta index". At this stage, the number of technical term instances emitted is twice that recorded by the original term vector. This has the effect of boosting the significance of technical terms and phrases. An example of the application of this process, from original text to delta index generation is presented in Table 4. Rankings for the alternative model can be obtained by searching the delta index using the re-generated query.

	Baseline	Tech-Term boosting	Difference
MAP	0.0602	0.0732	**0.013*** (17.7%)

Table 5: Difference in MAP performance between models (* **statistically significant at** $\alpha = 0.05$)

Although the choice of boosting factor 2 is arbitrary, our intention is to demonstrate the presence of a difference in retrieval efficiency, rather than optimising the effect of boosting.

4.4 Results

The MAP scores obtained for the models are presented in Table 5. We observe that the difference in MAP is in favour of the alternative model. This difference is statistically significant at $\alpha = 0.05$ using the Wilcoxon signed-rank test ($p < 0.05$). Therefore, we have sufficient evidence to conclude that, in the context of the VSM, boosting technical terms improves retrieval efficiency of research mathematics.

When compared to MAP scores produced by the same systems in more traditional IR tasks, the scores in Table 5 may seem poor. We attribute this phenomenon to the fact that sense in written mathematics is communicated via a complex interaction of text and mathematical expressions and is thus hard to extract using shallow methods.

5 Conclusions and Further Work

We have constructed a Math IR test collection for real-life, research-level mathematical information needs. As part of the work of constructing our test collection, we have developed a methodology for compiling domain-specific test collections that requires minimal expertise in the domain itself.

Using 160 micro-topics in our test collection, we have shown experimentally that the performance of VSM-based retrieval models with research mathematics can be improved by boosting the importance of technical terminology. Furthermore, our experimental work suggests that our test collection can be used to identify statistically significant differences between MIR systems. It is our intention to make our collection available to the IR community.

As part of on-going and future work, we will be incorporating additional retrieval models, such as the Okapi BM25, in our evaluation framework. In addition, we are looking into investigating the statistical properties of our test collection along the lines of Harman (2011) and Soboroff et al. (2001).

References

Akiko Aizawa, Michael Kohlhase, and Iadh Ounis. 2013. Ntcir-10 math pilot task overview. In *Proceedings of the 10th NTCIR Conference*, June.

C.W. Cleverdon, J. Mills, M. Keen, and Aslib. Cranfield Research Project. 1966a. *Factors Determining the Performance of Indexing Systems, Vol. 1: Design*. Number v. 1 in Factors Determining the Performance of Indexing Systems. College of Aeronautics.

C.W. Cleverdon, J. Mills, M. Keen, and Aslib. Cranfield Research Project. 1966b. *Factors determining the performance of indexing systems, Vol 2: Test Results*. Number v. 2 in Factors Determining the Performance of Indexing Systems. College of Aeronautics.

C. W. Cleverdon. 1960. Report on the first stage of an investigation into the comparative efficiency of indexing systems. Technical report.

C. W. Cleverdon. 1962. Aslib cranfield research project: Report on the testing and analysis of an investigation into the comparative efficiency of indexing systems. Technical report, October.

Cyril W. Cleverdon. 1991. The significance of the cranfield tests on index languages. In *Proceedings of the 14th Annual International ACM SIGIR Conference on Research and Development in Information Retrieval*, SIGIR '91, pages 3–12, New York, NY, USA. ACM.

Nick Craswell, David Hawking, Ross Wilkinson, and Mingfang Wu. 2003. Overview of the trec-2003 web track. In *Proceedings of TREC-2003*, Gaithersburg, Maryland USA, November.

K. Frantzi, S. Ananiadou, and J. Tsujii. 1996. Extracting terminological expressions. In *The Special Interest Group Notes of Information Processing Society of Japan , IPSJ SIG Notes*, number 112 in Natural Language, page 8388.

Katerina T. Frantzi, Sophia Ananiadou, and Jun-ichi Tsujii. 1998. The c-value/nc-value method of automatic recognition for multi-word terms. In *Proceedings of the Second European Conference on Research and Advanced Technology for Digital Libraries*, ECDL '98, pages 585–604, London, UK, UK. Springer-Verlag.

Atsushi Fujii, Makoto Iwayama, and Noriko K. 2006. Test collections for patent retrieval and patent classification in the fifth ntcir workshop.

E. Graf and L. Azzopardi. 2008. A methodology for building a patent test collection for prior art search.

Zoltan Gyongyi, Georgia Koutrika, Jan Pedersen, and Hector Garcia-Molina. 2008. Questioning yahoo! answers.

Donna Harman. 1993. Overview of the first trec conference. In *Proceedings of the 16th Annual International ACM SIGIR Conference on Research and Development in Information Retrieval*, SIGIR '93, pages 36–47, New York, NY, USA. ACM.

Donna Harman. 2011. *Information Retrieval Evaluation*. Synthesis Lectures on Information Concepts, Retrieval, and Services. Morgan & Claypool Publishers.

Daisuke Ishikawa, Tetsuya Sakai, and Noriko Kando. 2010. Overview of the ntcir-8 community qa pilot task (part i): The test collection and the task.

Makoto Iwayama, Atsushi Fujii, Noriko Kando, and Akihiko Takano. 2003. Overview of patent retrieval task at ntcir-3. In *Proceedings of the ACL-2003 Workshop on Patent Corpus Processing - Volume 20*, PATENT '03, pages 24–32, Stroudsburg, PA, USA. Association for Computational Linguistics.

K.S. Jones. 1981. *Information retrieval experiment*. Butterworths.

Martin Líška, Petr Sojka, Michal Růžička, and Petr Mravec. 2011. Web interface and collection for mathematical retrieval: Webmias and mrec. In Petr Sojka and Thierry Bouche, editors, *Towards a Digital Mathematics Library.*, pages 77–84, Bertinoro, Italy, Jul. Masaryk University.

Ursula Martin and Alison Pease. 2013. What does mathoverflow tell us about the production of mathematics? *CoRR*, abs/1305.0904.

Lucene project. 2013. Lucene's tf-idf similarity function.

Anna Ritchie, Simone Teufel, and Stephen Robertson. 2006. Creating a test collection for citation-based ir experiments. In *Proceedings of the Human Language Technology Conference of the NAACL, Main Conference*, pages 391–398, New York City, USA, June. Association for Computational Linguistics.

Tetsuya Sakai, Daisuke Ishikawa, Noriko Kando, Yohei Seki, Kazuko Kuriyama, and Chin-Yew Lin. 2011. Using graded-relevance metrics for evaluating community qa answer selection. In *Proceedings of the Fourth ACM International Conference on Web Search and Data Mining*, WSDM '11, pages 187–196, New York, NY, USA. ACM.

Ian Soboroff, Charles Nicholas, and Patrick Cahan. 2001. Ranking retrieval systems without relevance judgments. In *Proceedings of the 24th Annual International ACM SIGIR Conference on Research and Development in Information Retrieval*, SIGIR '01, pages 66–73, New York, NY, USA. ACM.

K. Sprck Jones and C.J. Van Rijsbergen. 1975. Report on the need for and provision of an 'ideal' information retrieval test collection. Technical report, British Library Research and Development Report 5266, University Computer Laboratory, Cambridge.

K. Sprck Jones and C.J. Van Rijsbergen. 1976. Information retrieval test collections. *Journal of Documentation*, 32(1):59–75.

Heinrich Stamerjohanns and Michael Kohlhase. 2008. Transforming the ariv to xml. In Serge Autexier, John Campbell, Julio Rubio, Volker Sorge, Masakazu Suzuki, and Freek Wiedijk, editors, *Intelligent Computer Mathematics*, volume 5144 of *Lecture Notes in Computer Science*, pages 574–582. Springer Berlin Heidelberg.

Heinrich Stamerjohanns, Michael Kohlhase, Deyan Ginev, Catalin David, and Bruce R. Miller. 2010. Transforming large collections of scientific publications to xml. *Mathematics in Computer Science*, 3(3):299–307.

Yla R. Tausczik and James W. Pennebaker. 2011. Predicting the perceived quality of online mathematics contributions from users' reputations. In *Proceedings of the SIGCHI Conference on Human Factors in Computing Systems*, CHI '11, pages 1885–1888, New York, NY, USA. ACM.

Yla R. Tausczik and James W. Pennebaker. 2012. Participation in an online mathematics community: Differentiating motivations to add. In *Proceedings of the ACM 2012 Conference on Computer Supported Cooperative Work*, CSCW '12, pages 207–216, New York, NY, USA. ACM.

Yla R. Tausczik, Aniket Kittur, and Robert E. Kraut. 2014. Collaborative problem solving: A study of mathoverflow. In *Proceedings of the 17th ACM Conference on Computer Supported Cooperative Work & Social Computing*, CSCW '14, pages 355–367, New York, NY, USA. ACM.

Ellen M. Voorhees and Donna K. Harman. 2005. *TREC: Experiment and Evaluation in Information Retrieval (Digital Libraries and Electronic Publishing)*. The MIT Press.

Ellen M. Voorhees. 1998. Variations in relevance judgments and the measurement of retrieval effectiveness. In *Proceedings of the 21st Annual International ACM SIGIR Conference on Research and Development in Information Retrieval*, SIGIR '98, pages 315–323, New York, NY, USA. ACM.

Ellen M. Voorhees. 2004. Overview of the trec 2001 question answering track. In *Proceedings of the Thirteenth Text REtreival Conference (TREC 2004)*.

Learning to Mine Query Subtopics from Query Log

Zhenzhong Zhang, Le Sun, Xianpei Han
Institute of Software, Chinese Academy of Sciences, Beijing, China
{zhenzhong, sunle, xianpei}@nfs.iscas.ac.cn

Abstract

Many queries in web search are ambiguous or multifaceted. Identifying the major senses or facets of queries is very important for web search. In this paper, we represent the major senses or facets of queries as subtopics and refer to indentifying senses or facets of queries as query subtopic mining, where query subtopic are represented as a number of clusters of queries. Then the challenges of query subtopic mining are how to measure the similarity between queries and group them semantically. This paper proposes an approach for mining subtopics from query log, which jointly learns a similarity measure and groups queries by explicitly modeling the structure among them. Compared with previous approaches using manually defined similarity measures, our approach produces more desirable query subtopics by learning a similarity measure. Experimental results on real queries collected from a search engine log confirm the effectiveness of the proposed approach in mining query subtopics.

1 Introduction

Understanding the search intents of queries is essential for satisfying users' information needs and is very important for many search tasks such as personalized search, query suggestion, and search result presentation. However, it is not a trivial task because the underlying intents of the same query may be different for different users. Two well-known types of such queries are ambiguous queries and multifaceted queries. For example, the ambiguous query 'michael jordon' may refer to a basketball player or a professor of statistics in Berkeley. The multifaceted query 'harry potter' may refer to different search intents such as films, books, or games and so on.

Many approaches have been proposed to identify the search intents of a query which are represented by search goals, topics, or subtopics. For example, Broder (2002) classified query intents into three search goals: informational, navigational, and transactional. Broder et al. (2007) and Li et al. (2005) represented query intents by topics. Clarke et al. (2009) represented query intents by subtopics which denote different senses or multiple facets of queries.

Previous work on query subtopic mining is mostly based on clustering framework by manually defining a similarity measure with few factors. Hu et al. (2012) employed an agglomerative clustering algorithm with a similarity measure combining string similarities, click similarities, and keyword similarities linearly. Wang et al. (2013) applied affinity propagation algorithm (Frey and Dueck, 2009) with a sense-based similarity. Tsukuda et al. (2013) used a hierarchical clustering algorithm with the similarity measure based on search results.

In this paper, we argue that the similarity between queries is affected by many different factors and it could produce more desirable query subtopics by learning a similarity measure. To learn a similarity measure for query subtopic mining, a natural approach is to use a binary classifier, that is, the classifier targets pairs of queries and makes predictions about whether they belong to the same subtopic. However, because such pairwise classifiers assume that pairs are independent, they might make inconsistent predictions: e.g., predicting queries q_i and q_j, q_j and q_k to belong to the same subtopic, but q_i and q_k to belong to different subtopics. For example, given three queries, 'luxury car', 'sport car' and 'XJ sport', for the query 'jaguar', a lexicon-similarity-based classifier is easy to learn that 'luxury car' and 'sport car', and 'sport car' and 'XJ sport' belong to the same subtopic; but difficult to learn that 'luxury car' and 'XJ sport' belong to the same subtopic. From this example, we can see that a learner should exploit these transitive dependencies among queries to learn a more effective similarity measure. Hence, in this paper, our first contribution is that we learn a similarity measure by explicitly modeling the dependencies among queries in the same subtopic. The second contribution is that we analyze the performance of the proposed approach with different dependencies among queries. The third contribution is that we conduct experiments on

Proceedings of the 53rd Annual Meeting of the Association for Computational Linguistics and the 7th International Joint Conference on Natural Language Processing (Short Papers), pages 341–345,
Beijing, China, July 26-31, 2015.

real-world data and the experimental results confirm the effectiveness of the proposed approach in mining query subtopics.

2 Learning to Mine Query Subtopics

In this section, we present our approach in details. First, we collect queries as subtopic candidates from query log using a heuristic method. Then, we learn a similarity measure to mine query subtopics from these candidates.

2.1 Collecting Subtopic Candidates from Query Log

In web search, users usually add additional words to clarify the underlying intents of a query (Hu et al., 2012). For example, if the ambiguous query 'jaguar' does not satisfy a user's information need, he/she may submit 'jaguar sport car' as an expanded query to specify the subtopic. Therefore, for a given query q, we collect its reformulations with additional words from query log as query subtopic candidates, e.g., we collect {'jaguar sports car', 'jaguar XJ sport', 'jaguar diet', …} for query 'jaguar'. We say query q' is a subtopic candidate of q if (1) q' is superset of q (e.g. q' = 'jaguar sports car' and q = 'jaguar'), and (2) q' occurred at least five times in query log. In this way, we collect a series of subtopic candidates for each query. Many subtopic candidates, however, belong to the same subtopic, e.g., 'jaguar sports car' and 'jaguar XJ sport'. Thus, to obtain the subtopics of a query, we need to group its subtopic candidates into clusters, each of which corresponds to an individual subtopic.

2.2 Mining Query Subtopics

As we described above, we need to group the subtopic candidates of a query into clusters to obtain its subtopics. The key to producing desirable subtopics is how to measure the similarity between subtopic candidates. In this paper, we learn a similarity measure by exploiting the dependencies among subtopic candidates in the same subtopic.

We represent each pair of subtopic candidates q_i and q_j as a feature vector $\phi(q_i, q_j)$, each dimension of which describes a factor. The similarity measure Sim_w parameterized by w is defined as $Sim_w(q_i, q_j) = w^T \cdot \phi(q_i, q_j)$, which maps pairs of subtopic candidates to a real number indicating how similar the pair is: positive for similar and negative for dissimilar. As argued in the introduction, the dependencies among subtopic candidates within the same subtopic are useful for learning an effective similarity measure. We denote the dependencies among subtopic candidates as a graph h, whose vertices are subtopic candidates and edges connect two vertices belonging to the same subtopic. In this paper, we employ two different graphs. The first one is the all-connection structure, where all subtopic candidates belonging to the same subtopic associate with each other. Figure 1 gives an example of the all-connection structure. The second one is the strong-connection structure, where each subtopic candidate only associates with its 'most similar' subtopic candidate within the same subtopic. Figure 2 gives an example.

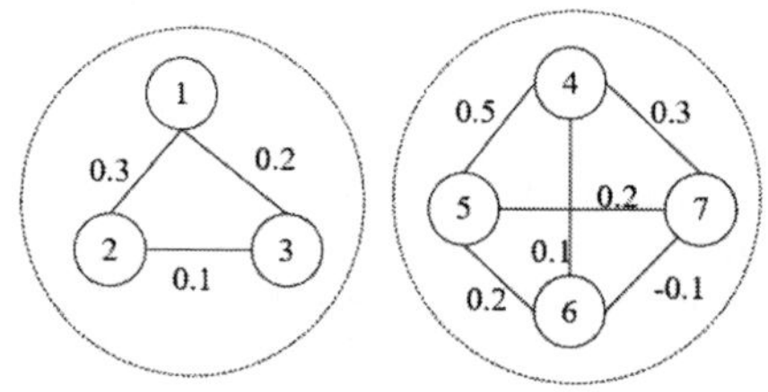

Figure 1. An example of the all-connection structure. The dashed circles denote the subtopics. The subtopic candidates (small solid circles) in the same dashed circle belong to the same subtopic. The weights indicate how similar the pair of two vertices is.

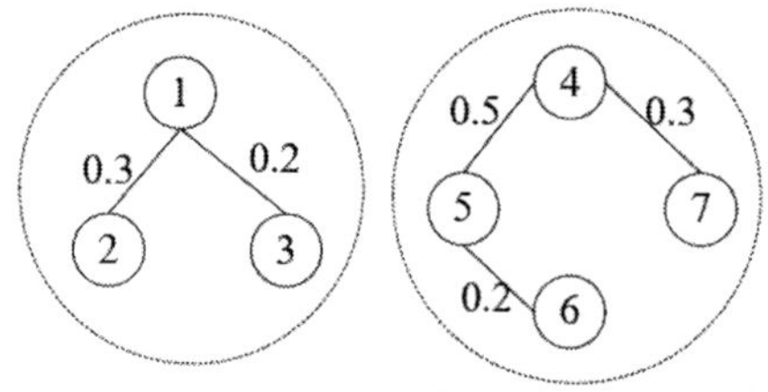

Figure 2. An example of the strong-connection structure.

Formally, we denote the set of subtopic candidates for a given query q as $S = \{q_1, q_2, \ldots, q_N\}$. The label y is a partition of the N subtopic candidates into subtopic clusters. h is the corresponding graph that is consistent with y. h is consistent with a clustering y if every cluster in y is a connected component in h, and there are no edges in h that connect two distinct clusters in y. Given S, our approach makes predictions by maximizing the sum of similarities for subtopic candidate pairs that are adjacent in h, that is,

$$\arg\max_{(y,h)\in Y\times H} \sum_{(i,j)\in h} Sim_w(q_i, q_j) = \arg\max_{(y,h)\in Y\times H} \sum_{(i,j)\in h} w^T \cdot \phi(q_i, q_j) \quad (1)$$

where Y and H are the sets of possible y and h respectively. (i, j) $\in h$ denotes q_i and q_j are directly connected in h.

To predict a partition y with the all-connection structure, we use the algorithm in (Bansal et al., 2002) with the objective function Eq (1). To predict a partition y with the strong-connection structure, we run Kruskal's algorithm on h and each tree corresponds to a subtopic, as shown in Algorithm 1.

Algorithm 1: Mining Query Subtopic with Strong-connection Structure

Input: the set of query subtopic candidates $S = \{q_1, q_2, \ldots, q_N\}$, feature vectors $\phi(q_i, q_j)$ ($1 \le i, j \le N, i \ne j$) and the weight w
Output: the partition y

```
//search for the strong-connection structure h, MST-KRUSKAL(G) denotes the Minimum Spanning Tree algorithm- Kruskal's algorithm

for i = 1...N-1 do
    for j = i+1...N do
        sim = w^T · φ(q_i, q_j);
        G(i, j)=−sim;
    end
end
h' = MST-KRUSKAL(G);
for i = 1...N-1 do
    for j = i+1...N do
        if h'(i, j)<0 then
            h(i, j) = 1;
        end
    end
end
// construct the partition y
t = 0;
y(1)=0;
for i = 2...N do
    j = 1;
    while j ≤ i-1 do
        if h(j, i) = 1 then
            y(i)= y(j);
            break;
        end
        j = j+1;
    end
    if j ≥ i then
        t = t + 1;
        y(i) = t;
    end
end
return y
```

2.3 Solving the Proposed Approach

For a given set of subtopic candidates with annotated subtopics, $\{(S_n, y_n)\}$ ($1 \le n \le N$), we need to estimate the optimal weight w. Empirically, the optimal weight w should minimize the error between the predicted partition y' and the true partition y, and it should also have a good generalization capability. Therefore, it is learnt by solving the following optimization problem (Yu and Joachims, 2009):

$$\begin{aligned} &\min_{w,\xi} \frac{1}{2}\|w\|^2 + C\sum_{n=1}^{N}\xi_n \\ &\text{s.t. } \forall n,\ \max_{h \in H} w^T \cdot \sum_{(i,j)\in h} \phi(q_i, q_j) \ge \\ &\qquad \max_{(y',h')\in Y\times H} [w^T \cdot \sum_{(i,j)\in h'} \phi(q_i, q_j) + \Delta(y_n, y', h')] - \xi_n \end{aligned} \quad (2)$$

where $\Delta(y_n, y', h')$ indicates a loss between a true partition y_n and the predicted partition y' specified by h', ξ_n ($1 \le n \le N$) is a set of slack variables to allow errors in the training data, and C controls the trade-off between empirical loss and model complexity.

Intuitively, the loss function $\Delta(y_n, y', h')$ should satisfy that $\Delta(y_n, y', h') = 0$ if $y_n = y'$, and rises as y_n and y' become more dissimilar. Because the all-connection structure is observable in the training data while the strong-connection structure is hidden, we define different loss functions for them. For the all-connection structure, we define the loss function as,

$$\Delta(y_n, y', h') = 10\frac{D}{T} \quad (3)$$

where T is the total number of pairs of subtopic candidates in the set partitioned by y_n and y', and D is the total number of pairs where y_n and y' disagree about their cluster membership.

Since the strong-connection structure h_n for y_n is hidden in the training data, we cannot measure the loss between (y_n, h_n) and (y', h'). According to (Yu and Joachims, 2009), we define the loss function based on the inferred structure h' as.

$$\Delta(y_n, y', h') = n(y_n) - k(y_n) - \sum_{(i,j)\in h'} l(y_n, (i,j)) \quad (4)$$

where $n(y_n)$ and $k(y_n)$ are the number of subtopic candidates and the number of clusters in the correct clustering y_n. $l(y_n, (i, j)) = 1$ if q_i and q_j are in the same cluster in y_n, otherwise $l(y_n, (i, j)) = -1$. Then the optimization problem introduced in Eq. (2) can be solved by the Concave-Convex Procedure (CCCP) (Yuille and Rangarajan, 2003).

2.4 Pairwise Similarity Features

The proposed approach requires a set of features to measure the similarity between two subtopic candidates. Table 1 lists the features employed in our approach. These features are categorized into two types: lexicon-based similarity and URL-based similarity. The lexicon-based similarity features are employed to measure the string similarity between two subtopic candidates. And the URL-based similarity features are used to measure the semantic similarity between two subtopic candidates. The basic idea is that if two queries share many clicked URLs, they have similar search intent to each other (Li et al., 2008). To make the features comparable with each other, we normalize them into range of [0, 1] accordingly.

Feature	Description
COS	cosine similarity between q_i and q_j
EUC	Euclidean distance between q_i and q_j
JAC	Jaccard coeff between q_i and q_j
EDIT	norm edit distance between q_i and q_j
LEN	$\|length(q_i)-length(q_j)\|$
SUBSET	whether one is a subset of the other
UCOS	cosine similarity between the clicked URL sets of q_i and q_j
UJAC	Jaccard coeff between the clicked URL sets of q_i and q_j

Table 1: pairwise similarity features employed in our approach

3 Experiments

3.1 Data Set

To illustrate the effectiveness of our approach, we use 100 ambiguous/multifaceted queries provided by the NTCIR-9 intent task as original queries and collect their subtopic candidates from SogouQ dataset (http://www.sogou.com) using the method mentioned in section 2.1. For the 100 queries, we totally collect 2,280 query subtopic candidates. Three annotators manually label these candidates with their subtopics according to the content words of these candidates and their clicked web pages (if there are clicked URLs for the candidate in query log). A candidate belongs to a specific subtopic if at least two annotators agree with it. At last we obtain 1,086 subtopics. We randomly split the original queries into two parts: half used for training and the rest for testing.

3.2 Evaluation Metrics and Baselines

To evaluate the performance of our approach, we employ the measures in (Luo, 2005), which are computed as follows,

$$p = \frac{\sum_i \pi(R_i', g(R_i'))}{\sum_i \pi(R_i', R_i')},\quad r = \frac{\sum_i \pi(R_i', g(R_i'))}{\sum_j \pi(R_j, R_j))}$$

where R' is the predicted partition and R is the ground-truth partition; $\pi(A, B)$ is a similarity measure between set A and B, which is Jaccard coefficient in this paper; and $g(.)$ is the optimal mapping between R' and R. Based on p and r, *f-measure* can be calculated as,

$$f-measure = \frac{2 \times p \times r}{p + r}$$

The higher the *f-measure* score is, the better performance an approach achieves.

We used the following approaches as baselines:

- K-means: we perform the standard k-means clustering algorithm with different manually defined similarity measures to mine query subtopics. COS, JAC, EUC, EDIT refer to cosine similarity, Jaccard similarity, Euclidean distance, and edit distance, respectively.
- Binary Classification Cluster with the all-connection structure (BCC-AC): BCC-AC uses a SVM classifier to learn the weight w and clusters with correlation clustering method.
- Binary Classification Cluster with the strong-connection structure (BCC-SC): BCC-SC uses a SVM classifier to learn the weight w and clusters with the method presented in Algorithm 1.

For the proposed methods, we denote the method with the all-connection structure as AC and the method with the strong-connection structure as SC. The parameter C in Eq. (2) is picked from10^{-2} to 10^4 using a 10-fold cross validation procedure.

3.3 Experimental Results

Methods	p	r	f-measure
K-Means-COS	0.6885	0.6589	0.6734
K-Means-JAC	0.6872	0.6616	0.6742
K-Means-EUC	0.6899	0.6652	0.6774
K-Means-EDIT	0.6325	0.6275	0.6300
BCC-AC	0.7347	0.7263	0.7305
BCC-SC	0.7406	0.7258	0.7331
AC	0.8027	0.7911	0.7968
SC	**0.8213***	**0.8187***	**0.8200***

Table2: the performance of all methods. "*" indicates significant difference at 0.05 level using a paired t-test.

Table 2 presents the experimental results. Compared with K-Means methods with different manually defined similarity measures, SC achieves at least **13.14%** precision improvement, **15.35%** recall improvement, and **14.26%** F-Measure improvement. And AC achieves at least **11.28%** precision improvement, **12.59%** recall improvement, and **11.94%** F-Measure improvement. These results confirm that the similarity between two subtopic candidates is affected by many factors and our methods can achieve more desirable query subtopics by learning a similarity measure.

Compared with BCC-AC and BCC-SC, SC achieves at least **8.07%** precision improvement, **9.29%** recall improvement, and **8.69%** F-Measure improvement. And AC achieves at least **6.21%** precision improvement, **6.53%** recall improvement, and **6.37%** F-Measure improvement. These results confirm that the dependencies among the subtopic candidates within the same subtopic are useful for learning a similarity measure for query subtopic mining.

Compared with AC, SC achieves **1.86%** precision improvement, **2.76%** recall improvement, and **2.32%** F-Measure improvement. These results confirm that a subtopic candidate belonging to a given query subtopic does not need to similar with all subtopic candidates within the given subtopic.

In order to understand which pairwise similarity feature is important for the problem of query subtopic mining, we list the features and their weights learned by SC, AC, and BCC (Binary Classification Cluster) in Table 3.

Method / Feature	SC	AC	BCC
COS	0.08	0.04	0.19
EUC	−1.74	−1.07	−0.73
JAC	4.44	4.73	4.90
EDIT	−1.60	−1.01	−0.48
LEN	−1.34	−0.91	−1.07
SUBSET	0.21	0.11	−0.05
UCOS	0.01	0.01	0.04
UJAC	0.06	0.07	0.09

Table 3: the features and their weights learned by the different methods.

As can be seen in Table 3, JAC has the largest importance weight for mining query subtopics in the three methods. The URL-based features (UCOS and UJAC) have small importance weight. The reason is that clicked URLs are sparse in our query log and many long-tail subtopic candidates in the same subtopic do not share any common URLs.

4 Conclusions

In this paper, we propose an approach for mining query subtopics from query log. Compared with previous approaches, our approach learns a similarity measure by explicitly modeling the dependencies among subtopic candidates within the same subtopic. Experimental results on real queries collected from a search engine log confirm our approach produces more desirable query subtopics by using the learned similarity measure.

Acknowledgments

The work is supported by the National Natural Science Foundation of China under Grants no. 61433015 and 61272324, and the National High Technology Development 863 Program of China under Grants no. 2015AA015405. Moreover, we sincerely thank the reviewers for their valuable comments.

References

N. Bansal, A. Blum, and S. Chawla. 2002. Correlation clustering. In *Machine Learning*, 56, 89-113.

A. Z. Broder. A taxonomy of web search. 2002. In *Sigir Forum*, 36:3-10.

A. Z. Broder, M. Fontoura, E. Gabrilovich, A. Joshi, V. Josifovski, and T. Zhang. 2007. Robust classification of rare queries using web knowledge. In *SIGIR*, pp. 231-238.

C. L. A. Clarke, N. Craswell, and I. Soboroff. 2009. Overview of the trec 2009 web track. In *TREC'09*, pp. 1-9.

Y. Hu, Y. Qian, H. Li, D. Jiang, J.Pei, and Q. Zheng. 2012. Ming query subtopics from search log data. In *SIGIR'12*, pp. 305-314.

T. Finley and T. Joachims. 2005. Supervised clustering with support vector machines. In *ICML*, pp. 217-224.

B. J. Frey and D. Dueck. 2007. Clustering by passing messages between data points. In *science*, 315(5814):972-976.

Y. Li, Z. Zheng, and H. K. Dai. 2005. Kdd cup-2005 report: facing a great challenge. In *SIGKDD Explor. Newsl.*, 7:91-99.

L. Li, Z. Yang, L. Liu, and M. Kitsuregawa. 2008. Query-url bipartite based approach to personalized query recommendation. In AAAI'08, pp. 1189-1194.

X. Luo. 2005. On Coreference resolution performance metrics. In *HLT&EMNLP*, pp. 25-32.

F. Radlinski, M. Szummer, and N. Craswell. 2010. Inferring Query Intent from Reformulations and Clicks. In *WWW*, pp. 1171-1172.

R. Song et, al. 2011. Overview of the ntcir-9 intent task, In *NTCIR-9*, pp.82-105.

K. Tsukuda, Z. Dou, and T. Sakai. 2013. Microsoft research asia at the ntcir-10 intent task. In *NTCIR-10*, pp. 152-158.

J. Wang, G. Tang, Y. Xia, Q. Hu, S. Na, Y. Huang, Q. Zhou, and F. Zheng. 2013. Understanding the query: THCIB and THUIS at ntcir-10 intent task. In *NTCIR-10*, pp. 132-139.

C. J. Yu and T. Joachims. 2009. Learning Structural SVMs with Latent Variables. In *ICML*, pp. 1169-1176

A. Yuille, and A. Rangarajan. 2003. The concave-convex procedure. In *Neural Computation*, 15, 915.

Learning Topic Hierarchies for Wikipedia Categories

Linmei Hu[†], Xuzhong Wang[§], Mengdi Zhang[†], Juanzi Li[†], Xiaoli Li[‡], Chao Shao[†], Jie Tang[†], Yongbin Liu[†]

[†] Dept. of Computer Sci. and Tech. Tsinghua University, China
[§] State Key Laboratory of Math. Eng. and Advanced Computing, China
[‡] Institute for Infocomm Research(I2R), A*STAR, Singapore
{hulinmei1991,koodoneko,mdzhangmd,lijuanzi2008}@gmail.com
xlli@i2r.a-star.edu.sg, birdlinux@gmail.com
jietang@tsinghua.edu.cn, yongbinliu03@gmail.com

Abstract

Existing studies have utilized Wikipedia for various knowledge acquisition tasks. However, no attempts have been made to explore multi-level topic knowledge contained in Wikipedia articles' *Contents* tables. The articles with similar subjects are grouped together into Wikipedia *categories*. In this work, we propose novel methods to automatically construct *comprehensive* topic hierarchies for given categories based on the structured *Contents* tables as well as corresponding unstructured *text* descriptions. Such a hierarchy is important for information browsing, document organization and topic prediction. Experimental results show our proposed approach, incorporating both the structural and textual information, achieves high quality category topic hierarchies.

1 Introduction

As a free-access online encyclopedia, written collaboratively by people all over the world, Wikipedia (abbr. to Wiki) offers a surplus of rich information. Millions of articles cover various concepts and instances [1]. Wiki has been widely used for various knowledge discovery tasks. Some good examples include knowledge mining from Wiki infoboxes (Lin et al., 2011; Wang et al., 2013), and *taxonomy deriving* from Wiki category system (Zesch and Gurevych, 2007).

We observe that, in addition to Wiki's infoboxes and category system, Wiki articles' Contents tables (CT for short) also provide valuable structured topic knowledge with different levels of granularity. For example, in the article "*2010 Haiti Earthquake*", shown in Fig.1, the left Contents zone is a CT formed in a topic hierarchy format. If we view "*2010 Haiti earthquake*" as the root topic, the first-level "*Geology*" and "*Damage to infrastructure*" tags can be viewed as its subtopics, and the second-level "*Tsunami*" and "*Aftershocks*" tags underneath "*Geology*" are the subtopics of "*Geology*". Clicking any of the tags in Contents, we can jump to the corresponding text description. Wiki articles contain a wealth of this kind of structured and unstructured information. However, to our best knowledge, little work has been done to leverage the knowledge in CT.

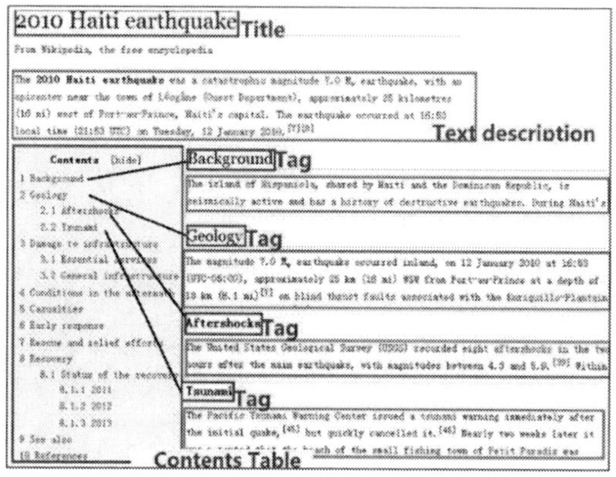

Figure 1: The Wiki article "2010 Haiti Earthquake" with structured *Contents* table and corresponding unstructured *text* descriptions.

In Wiki, similar articles (each with their own CT) belonging to the same subject are grouped together into a *Wiki category*. We aim to integrate multiple topic hierarchies represented by CT (from the articles under the same *Wiki category*) into a comprehensive *category topic hierarchy* (CTH). While there also exist manually built CTH represented by CT in corresponding Wiki articles, they are still too high-level and incomplete. Take the "*Earthquake*" category as an example, its corresponding Wiki article [2] only contains

[1]http://en.wikipedia.org/wiki/Encyclopedia

[2]http://en.wikipedia.org/wiki/Earthquake

Proceedings of the 53rd Annual Meeting of the Association for Computational Linguistics and the 7th International Joint Conference on Natural Language Processing (Short Papers), pages 346–351,
Beijing, China, July 26-31, 2015.

some major and common topics. It does not include the subtopic "*nuclear power plant*", which is an important subtopic of the "*2011 Japan earthquake*". A comprehensive CTH is believed to be more useful for information browsing, document organization and topic extraction in new text corpus (Veeramachaneni et al., 2005). Thus, we propose to investigate the Wiki articles of the same category to *automatically* build a comprehensive CTH to enhance the manually built CTH.

Clearly, it is very challenging to learn a CTH from multiple topic hierarchies in different articles due to the following 3 reasons: 1) A topic can be denoted by a variety of tags in different articles (e.g., "*foreign aids*" and "*aids from other countries*"); 2) Structural/hierarchical information can be inconsistent (or even opposite) across different articles (e.g., "response *subtopicOf* aftermath" and "aftermath *subtopicOf* response" in different earthquake event articles); 3) Intuitively, text descriptions of the topics in Wiki articles are supposed to be able to help determine *subtopic* relations between topics. However, how can we model the textual correlation?

In this study, we propose a novel approach to build a high-quality CTH for any given Wiki category. We use a Bayesian network to model a CTH, and map the CTH learning problem as a structure learning problem. We leverage both structural and textual information of topics in the articles to induce the optimal tree structure. Experiments on 3 category data demonstrate the effectiveness of our approach for CTH learning.

2 Preliminaries

Our problem is to learn a CTH for a Wiki category from multiple topic hierarchies represented by CT in the Wiki articles of the category. For example, consider the category "earthquake". There are a lot of Wikipedia articles about earthquake events which are manually created by human experts. In these articles, the CTs imply hierarchical topic knowledge in the events. However, due to crowdsourcing nature, these knowledge is heterogeneous across different articles. We want to integrate these knowledge represented by CTs in different earthquake event articles to form a comprehensive understanding of the category "earthquake" (CTH).

Specifically, our input consists of a set of Wiki articles $A_c = \{a\}$, belonging to a Wiki category c. As shown in Fig.1, each article $a \in A_c$ contains a CT (topic tree hierarchy) $H_a = \{T_a, R_a\}$, where T_a is a set of topics, each denoted by a tag g and associated with a text description d_g, and $R_a = \{(g_i, g_j)\}, g_i, g_j \in T_a$ is a set of subtopic relations (g_j is a subtopic of g_i). The output is an integrated comprehensive CTH $H_c = \{T_c, R_c\}$ where $T_c = \{t\}$ is a set of topics, each denoted by *a set of tags* $t = \{g\}$ and associated by a text description d_t *aggregated by* $\{d_g\}_{g \in t}$, and $R_c = \{(t_i, t_j)\}, t_i, t_j \in T_c$ is a set of subtopic relations (t_j is a subtopic of t_i).

We map the problem of learning the output H_c from the input $\{H_a\}, a \in A_c$, as a structure learning problem. We first find clusters of similar tags T_c (each cluster represents a topic) and then derive hierarchical relations R_c among these clusters.

Particularly, given a category c, we first collect relevant Wiki articles $A_c = \{a\}$. This can be done automatically since each Wiki article has links to its categories. We can also manually find the Wikipage which summarizes the links of A_c (e.g., `http://en.wikipedia.org/wiki/Lists_of_earthquakes`) and then collect A_c according to the links.

Then we can get a global tag set $G = \{g\}$ containing all the tags including titles in the articles A_c. We cluster the same or similar tags from different articles using single-pass incremental clustering (Hammouda and Kamel, 2003) to construct the topic set T_c, with cosine similarity computed based on the names of tags g and their text descriptions d_g. Note that titles of all the articles belonging to the same cluster corresponds to a root topic.

Next, the issue is how to induce a CTH $H_c = \{T_c, R_c\}$ from a set of topics T_c.

3 Topic Hierarchy Construction

We first present a basic method to learn H_c and then describe a principled probabilistic model incorporating both structural and textual information for CTH learning.

3.1 Basic Method

After replacing the tags in a CT (see Fig.1) with the topics they belong to, we can then get a topic hierarchy $H_a = \{T_a, R_a\}$ for each article a. For each subtopic relation $(t_i, t_j) \in R_a$, we can calculate a count/weight $n(t_i, t_j)$, representing the number of articles in A_c containing the relation. We then construct a directed complete graph with a weight $w(t_i, t_j) = n(t_i, t_j)$ on each edge (t_i, t_j). Finally, we apply the widely used Chu-Liu/Edmonds algorithm (Chu and Liu, 1965; Edmonds, 1967) to find an optimal tree with the largest sum of weights from our constructed graph, meaning that the overall subtopic relations in the tree is best supported by all the CT/articles. The Chu-Liu/Edmonds algorithm works as follows. First, it selects, for each node, the maximum-weight incoming edge. Next, it recursively breaks cycles with the following idea: nodes in a cycle are collapsed into a pseudo-node and the maximum-weight edge entering the pseudo-node is selected to replace the other incoming edge in the cycle. During backtracking, pseudo-nodes are expanded into an acyclic directed graph, i.e., our final category topic hierarchy H_c.

However, the basic method has a problem. Consider if *n*("*earthquake*", "*damages to hospitals*")=10 and *n*("*earthquake*") =100, while *n*("*damages*", "*damages to hospitals*")=5 and *n*("*damages*")=5. We would prefer "*damages*" to be the parent topic of "*damages to hospitals*" with a higher *confidence* level (5/5=1 vs 10/100=0.1). However, the above basic method will choose "*earthquake*" which maximizes the weight sum. An intuitive solution is to normalize the weights. In Subsection 3.2, we present our proposed principled probabilistic model which can derive normalized structure based weights. In addition, it can be easily used to incorporate and combine textual information of topics into CTH learning.

3.2 Probabilistic Model for CTH Learning

We first describe the principled probabilistic model for a CTH. Then we present how to encode structural dependency and textual correlation between topics. Last, we present our final approach combining both structural dependency and textual correlation for CTH construction.

3.2.1 Modeling a Category Topic Hierarchy

In a topic hierarchy, each node represents a topic. We consider each node as a variable and the topic hierarchy as a Bayesian network. Then the joint probability distribution of nodes N given a particular tree H is

$$P(N|H) = P(root) \prod_{n \in N \setminus root} P(n|par_H(n)),$$

where $P(n|par_H(n))$ is the conditional probability of node n given its parent node $par_H(n)$ in H. Given the nodes, this is actually the likelihood of H. Maximizing the likelihood with respect to the tree structure gives the optimal tree:

$$\begin{aligned} H^* &= \text{argmax}_H P(N|H) \\ &= \text{argmax}_H P(root) \prod_{n \in N \setminus root} P(n|par_H(n)) \\ &= \text{argmax}_H \sum_{n \in N} logP(n|par_H(n)) \end{aligned} \tag{1}$$

Encoding Structural Dependency. Considering t_j is a subtopic of t_i, we define the structural conditional probability:

$$P_{struc}(t_j|t_i) = \frac{n(t_i, t_j) + \alpha}{n(t_i) + \alpha \cdot |T_c - 1|}, \tag{2}$$

where $n(t_i, t_j)$ is the count of articles containing relation (t_i, t_j) and $n(t_i)$ is the count of articles containing topic t_i. The parameter $\alpha = 1.0$ is the Laplace smoothing factor, and $|T_c - 1|$ is the total number of possible relations taking t_i as their parent topic.

Encoding Textual Correlation. Considering a topic text description d_t as a bag of words, we use the normalized word frequencies $\phi_t = \{\phi_{t,w}\}_{w \in V} s.t. \sum_{w \in V} \phi_{t,w} = 1$ to represent a topic t. To capture the subtopic relationship (t_i, t_j), we prefer a model where the expectation of the distribution for the child is exactly same with the distribution for its parent, i.e., $E(\phi_{t_j}) = \phi_{t_i}$. This naturally leads to the hierarchical Dirichlet model (Wang et al., 2014; Veeramachaneni et al., 2005), formally, $\phi_{t_j}|\phi_{t_i} \sim Dir(\beta\phi_{t_i})$ in which β [3] is the concentration parameter which determines how concentrated the probability density is likely to be. Thus we have:

$$P_{text}(t_j|t_i) = \frac{1}{Z} \prod_{w \in V} \phi_{t_j,v}^{\beta\phi_{t_i,w}-1}, \tag{3}$$

where $Z = \frac{\prod_{w \in V} \Gamma(\alpha\phi_{t_i,w})}{\Gamma(\sum_{w \in V} \alpha\phi_{t_i,w})}$ is a normalization factor and $\Gamma(\cdot)$ is the standard Gamma distribution. We note that for the root node we have the uniform prior instead of the prior coming from the parent.

3.2.2 Combining Structural and Textual Information

Substituting Eq.2 into Eq.1, we can solve the optimal tree structure by applying Chu-

[3]Experimental results are insensitive to β, we set β=5

Liu/Edmonds algorithm to the directed complete graph with structure based weights w_{struc}=$log(P_{struc}(t_j|t_i) = log\frac{n(t_i,t_j)+\alpha}{n(t_i)+\alpha\cdot|T_c-1|}$ on the edges (t_i, t_j). While this solves the problem of the basic method, it only considers structural dependency and does not consider textual correlation which is supposed to be useful.

Therefore, we calculate text based weights w_{text}=$log(P_{text}(t_j|t_i) = \sum_{w\in V} log\phi_{t_j,v}^{\alpha\phi_{t_i,w}-1} - logZ$ similarly. Then we combine structural information and textual information by defining the weights $w(t_i, t_j)$ of the edges (t_i, t_j) as a simple weighted average of $w_{struc}(t_i, t_j)$ and $w_{text}(t_i, t_j)$. Specifically, we define:

$$w(t_i, t_j) = \lambda w_{text}(t_i, t_j) + (1 - \lambda) w_{struc}(t_i, t_j) ,$$

where λ controls the impacts of text correlation and structure dependency in optimal structure learning. Note that w_{text} and w_{struc} should be scaled [4] first before applying Chu-Liu/Edmonds algorithm to find an optimal topic hierarchy.

4 Experiments

We evaluate the CTH automatically generated by our proposed methods via comparing it with a manually constructed ground-truth CTH.

4.1 Data and Evaluation Metric

Data. We evaluate our methods on 3 categories, i.e., English "earthquake" and "election" categories containing 293 and 60 articles, and Chinese "earthquake" category containing 48 articles [5]. After removing noisy tags such as "references" and "see also", they contain 463, 79 and 426 unique tags respectively. After tag clustering [6], we can get 176, 57 and 112 topics for each category.

Evaluation Metric. We employ the *precision* measure to evaluate the performance of our methods. Let $\mathbf{R}$ and $\mathbf{R}_s$ be subtopic relation sets of our generated result and ground-truth result respectively, then *precison*=$|\mathbf{R} \cap \mathbf{R}_s|/|\mathbf{R}|$. Due to the number of relations $|\mathbf{R}|$=$|\mathbf{R}_s| = |T_c - 1|$, we have *precison=recall=F1*=$|\mathbf{R} \cap \mathbf{R}_s|/|\mathbf{R}|$.

We compare three methods, including our basic method (Basic) which uses only non-normalized structural information, our proposed probabilistic method considering only structural information ($\lambda = 0$) (Pro+S), and considering both structural and textual information ($0 < \lambda < 1$) (Pro+ST).

4.2 Results and Analysis

Quantitative Analysis. From Table 1, we observe that our approach Pro+ST (with best λ values as shown in Fig.2) significantly outperforms Basic and Pro+S which only utilize the structural information (+24.3% and +5.1% on average, p <0.025 with *t-test*). Pro+S which normalizes structural information also achieves significant higher precision than Basic (+19.2% on average, p <0.025).

	Earth.(En)	Elect.(En)	Earth.(Ch)
Basic	0.5965	0.7719	0.7143
Pro+S	0.8971	0.8596	0.9017
Pro+ST	0.9543	0.9298	0.9286

Table 1: Precision of different methods on 3 categories

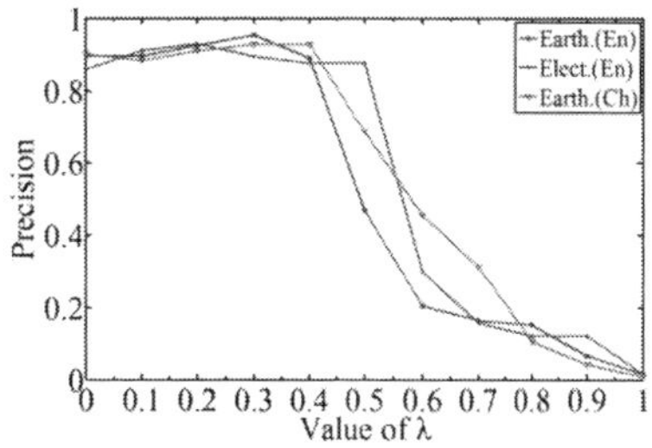

Figure 2: The precision of CTH with different λ values

To examine the influence of λ, we show the performance of our approach Pro+ST with different λ values on 3 categories in Fig.2. All the curves grow up first and then decrease dramatically as we emphasize more on textual information. They can always get consistent better results when $0.2 \leq \lambda \leq 0.3$. When λ approaches 1, the precision declines fast to near 0. The reason is that the topics with short (or null) text descriptions are likely to be a parent node of all other nodes and influence the results dramatically, but if we rely mostly on structural information and use the textual information as auxiliary for correcting minor errors in some ambiguous cases, we can improve the precision of the resultant topic hierarchy.

Qualitative Analysis. Due to space limitation, we only show the topic hierarchy for "Election" with smaller topic size in Fig.3. As we can see,

[4]We use min-max normalization $x^* = \frac{x-min}{max-min}$

[5]We filter articles with little information in Contents.

[6]We use an incremental clustering algorithm

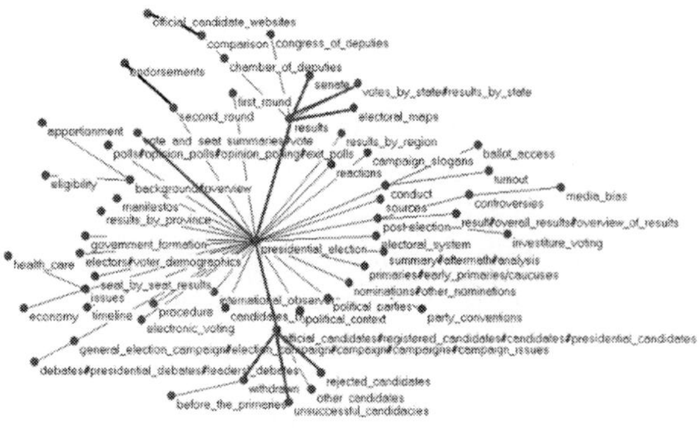

Figure 3: The category topic hierarchy for presidential elections. Topics are labeled by tags separated by "#".

the root topic "*presidential elections*" includes subtopics "*results*", "*vote*", "*official candidates*", etc. Furthermore, '*official candidates*" contains subtopics "*debates*, "*rejected candidates*", "*unsuccessful candidates*", etc. The above mentioned examples are shown with red edges. However, there are also a few (7%) mistaken relations (black edges) such as "*comparison*" (should be "*official candidates*" instead) → "*official candidate websites*". Overall, the above hierarchy aligns well with human knowledge.

5 Related Work

To our best knowledge, our overall problem setting is novel and there is no previous work using Wiki articles' *contents* tables to learn topic hierarchies for categories. Existing work mainly focused on learning topic hierarchies from *texts* only and used traditional hierarchical clustering methods (Chuang and Chien, 2004) or topic models such as HLDA (Griffiths and Tenenbaum, 2004), HPAM (Mimno et al., 2007), hHDP (Zavitsanos et al., 2011), and HETM (Hu et al., 2015). Differently, we focus on structured contents tables with corresponding text descriptions.

Our work is also different from ontology (taxonomy) construction (Li et al., 2007; Tang et al., 2009; Zhu et al., 2013; Navigli et al., 2011; Wu et al., 2012) as their focus is concept hierarchies (e.g. *isA* relation) rather than thematic topic hierarchies. For example, given the "*animals*" category, they may derive "*cats*" and "*dogs*", etc. as subcategories, while our work aims to derive thematic topics "*animal protection*" and "*animal extinction*", etc. as subtopics. Our work enables a fresher to quickly familiarize himself/herself with any new category, and is very useful for information browsing, organization and topic extraction.

6 Conclusion

In this paper, we propose an innovative problem, i.e., to construct high quality comprehensive topic hierarchies for different Wiki categories using their associated Wiki articles. Our novel approach is able to model a topic hierarchy and to incorporate both structural dependencies and text correlations into the optimal tree learning. Experimental results demonstrate the effectiveness of our proposed approach. In future work, we will investigate how to update the category topic hierarchy incrementally with the creation of new related articles.

Acknowledgments

The work is supported by 973 Program (No. 2014CB340504), NSFC-ANR (No. 61261130588), Tsinghua University Initiative Scientific Research Program (No. 20131089256), Science and Technology Support Program (No. 2014BAK04B00), China Postdoctoral Science Foundation (No. 2014M550733), National Natural Science Foundation of China (No. 61309007) and THU-NUS NExT Co-Lab.

References

Yoeng-Jin Chu and Tseng-Hong Liu. 1965. On shortest arborescence of a directed graph. *Scientia Sinica*, 14(10):1396.

Shui-Lung Chuang and Lee-Feng Chien. 2004. A practical web-based approach to generating topic hierarchy for text segments. In *Proceedings of the thirteenth ACM international conference on Information and knowledge management*, pages 127–136. ACM.

Jack Edmonds. 1967. Optimum branchings. *Journal of Research of the National Bureau of Standards B*, 71(4):233–240.

DMBTL Griffiths and MIJJB Tenenbaum. 2004. Hierarchical topic models and the nested chinese restaurant process. *Advances in NIPS*, 16:17.

Khaled M Hammouda and Mohamed S Kamel. 2003. Incremental document clustering using cluster similarity histograms. In *Web Intelligence, 2003. WI 2003. Proceedings. IEEE/WIC International Conference on*, pages 597–601. IEEE.

Linmei Hu, Juanzi Li, Jing Zhang, and Chao Shao. 2015. o-hetm: An online hierarchical entity topic model for news streams. In *Advances in Knowledge Discovery and Data Mining - 19th Pacific-Asia Conference, PAKDD 2015, Proceedings, Part I*, pages 696–707.

Rui Li, Shenghua Bao, Yong Yu, Ben Fei, and Zhong Su. 2007. Towards effective browsing of large scale social annotations. In *Proceedings of the 16th international conference on World Wide Web*, pages 943–952. ACM.

Wen-Pin Lin, Matthew Snover, and Heng Ji. 2011. Unsupervised language-independent name translation mining from wikipedia infoboxes. In *Proceedings of the First workshop on Unsupervised Learning in NLP*, pages 43–52. Association for Computational Linguistics.

David Mimno, Wei Li, and Andrew McCallum. 2007. Mixtures of hierarchical topics with pachinko allocation. In *Proceedings of the 24th ICML*, pages 633–640. ACM.

Roberto Navigli, Paola Velardi, and Stefano Faralli. 2011. A graph-based algorithm for inducing lexical taxonomies from scratch. In *IJCAI*, pages 1872–1877.

Jie Tang, Ho-fung Leung, Qiong Luo, Dewei Chen, and Jibin Gong. 2009. Towards ontology learning from folksonomies. In *IJCAI*, volume 9, pages 2089–2094.

Sriharsha Veeramachaneni, Diego Sona, and Paolo Avesani. 2005. Hierarchical dirichlet model for document classification. In *Proceedings of the 22nd ICML*, pages 928–935. ACM.

Zhigang Wang, Zhixing Li, Juanzi Li, Jie Tang, and Jeff Z Pan. 2013. Transfer learning based cross-lingual knowledge extraction for wikipedia. In *ACL (1)*, pages 641–650.

Jingjing Wang, Changsung Kang, Yi Chang, and Jiawei Han. 2014. A hierarchical dirichlet model for taxonomy expansion for search engines. In *Proceedings of the 23rd international conference on WWW*, pages 961–970. International World Wide Web Conferences Steering Committee.

Wentao Wu, Hongsong Li, Haixun Wang, and Kenny Q Zhu. 2012. Probase: A probabilistic taxonomy for text understanding. In *Proceedings of the 2012 ACM SIGMOD International Conference on Management of Data*, pages 481–492. ACM.

Elias Zavitsanos, Georgios Paliouras, and George A Vouros. 2011. Non-parametric estimation of topic hierarchies from texts with hierarchical dirichlet processes. *The Journal of Machine Learning Research*, 12:2749–2775.

Torsten Zesch and Iryna Gurevych. 2007. Analysis of the wikipedia category graph for nlp applications. In *Proceedings of the TextGraphs-2 Workshop (NAACL-HLT 2007)*, pages 1–8.

Xingwei Zhu, Zhao-Yan Ming, Xiaoyan Zhu, and Tat-Seng Chua. 2013. Topic hierarchy construction for the organization of multi-source user generated contents. In *Proceedings of the 36th international ACM SIGIR conference on Research and development in information retrieval*, pages 233–242. ACM.

Semantic Clustering and Convolutional Neural Network for Short Text Categorization

Peng Wang, Jiaming Xu, Bo Xu, Cheng-Lin Liu, Heng Zhang
Fangyuan Wang, Hongwei Hao
{peng.wang, jiaming.xu, boxu}@ia.ac.cn, liucl@nlpr.ia.ac.cn
{heng.zhang, fangyuan.wang, hongwei.hao}@ia.ac.cn
Institute of Automation, Chinese Academy of Sciences, Beijing, 100190, P.R. China

Abstract

Short texts usually encounter data sparsity and ambiguity problems in representations for their lack of context. In this paper, we propose a novel method to model short texts based on semantic clustering and convolutional neural network. Particularly, we first discover semantic cliques in embedding spaces by a fast clustering algorithm. Then, multi-scale semantic units are detected under the supervision of semantic cliques, which introduce useful external knowledge for short texts. These meaningful semantic units are combined and fed into convolutional layer, followed by max-pooling operation. Experimental results on two open benchmarks validate the effectiveness of the proposed method.

1 Introduction

Conventional texts mining methods based on bag-of-words (BoW) easily encounter data sparsity and ambiguity problems in short text modeling (Chen *et al.*, 2011), which ignore semantic relations between words (Sriram *et al.*, 2010). How to acquire effective representation for short text has been an active research issue (Chen *et al.*, 2011; Phan *et al.*, 2008).

In order to overcome the weakness of BoW, researchers have proposed to expand the representation of short text using latent semantics, where the words are mapped to distributional representations by Latent Dirichlet Allocation (LDA) (Blei *et al.*, 2003) and its extensions. Phan et al. (2008) presented a general framework to expand the short and sparse text by appending topic names discovered using LDA. Yan et al. (2013) presented a variant of LDA, dubbed Biterm Topic Model (BTM), especially for short text modeling to alleviate the problem of sparsity. However, the methods discussed above still view a piece of text as BoW. Therefore, they are not effective in capturing fine-grained semantic information for short texts modeling.

Recently, neural network related methods have received much attention, including learning word embeddings (Bengio *et al.*, 2003; Mikolov *et al.*, 2013a) and performing semantic composition to obtain phrase or sentence level representations (Collobert *et al.*, 2011; Le and Mikolov, 2014). For learning word embedding, the training objective of continuous Skip-gram model (Mikolov *et al.*, 2013b) is to predict its context. Thus, the co-occurrence information can be effectively used to describe a word, and each component of word embedding might have a semantic or grammatical interpretation.

In embedding spaces, semantically close words are likely to cluster together and form semantic cliques (or word embedding cliques). Moreover, the embedding spaces exhibit linear structure that the word vectors can be meaningfully combined using simple additive operation (Mikolov *et al.*, 2013b), for example:

$$vec(Germany) + vec(Capital) \approx vec(Berlin) \quad (1)$$

$$vec(Athlete) + vec(Football) \approx vec(Football\_Player) \quad (2)$$

The above examples indicate that the additive composition can often produce meaningful results. In Equation (1), the token $'Berlin'$ can be viewed that it has an embedding offset $vec(Capital)$ to the token $'Germany'$ in embedding spaces. Furthermore, the embedding offsets represent the syntactical and semantic relations among words.

In this paper, we propose a method to model short texts using semantic clustering and convolutional neural network (CNN). Firstly, the fast clustering algorithm (Rodriguez and Laio, 2014), based on searching density peaks, is utilized to cluster word embeddings and discover semantic cliques, as shown in Figure 1. Then semantic composition is performed over n-gram embeddings to

Proceedings of the 53rd Annual Meeting of the Association for Computational Linguistics and the 7th International Joint Conference on Natural Language Processing (Short Papers), pages 352–357,
Beijing, China, July 26-31, 2015.

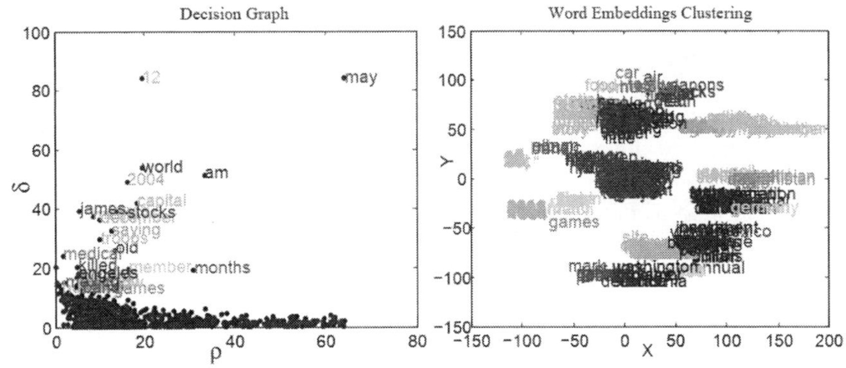

Figure 1: Fast clustering based on density peaks of embeddings

detect candidate Semantic Units[1](abbr. to SUs) appearing in short texts. The part of candidate SUs meeting the preset threshold are chosen to constitute semantic matrices, which are used as input for the CNN, otherwise dropout. In this stage, semantic cliques are used as supervision information, which guarantee meaningful SUs can be extracted.

The motivation of our work is to introduce extra knowledge by pre-trained word embeddings and fully exploit the contextual information of short texts to improve their representations. The main contributions include: (1) semantic cliques are discovered using fast clustering method based on searching density peaks; (2) for fine-tuning multi-scale SUs, the semantic cliques are used to supervise the selection stage.

The remainder of this paper is organized as follows. The related works are briefly reviewed in Section 2. Section 3 introduces the semantic clustering based on fast searching density peaks. Section 4 describes the architecture of the proposed method. Section 5 demonstrates the effectiveness of our method with experiments. Finally, concluding remarks are offered in Section 6.

2 Related Works

Traditional statistics-based methods usually fail to achieve satisfactory performance for short texts classification due to their sparsity of representations (Sriram *et al.*, 2010). Based on external Wikipedia corpus, Phan et al. (2008) proposed a method to discover hidden topics using LDA and expand short texts. Chen et al. (2011) proved that leveraging topics at multiple granularity can model short texts more precisely.

Neural networks have been used to model languages, and the word embeddings can be learned simultaneously (Mnih and Teh, 2012). Mikolov et al. (2013b) introduced the continuous Skip-gram model that is an efficient method for learning high quality word embeddings from large-scale unstructured text data. Recently, various pre-trained word embeddings are publicly available, and many composition-based methods are proposed to induce the semantic representation of texts. Le and Mikolov (2014) presented the Paragraph Vector algorithm to learn a fixed-size feature representation for documents.

Kalchbrenner et al. (2014) introduced the Dynamic Convolutional Neural Network (DCNN) for modeling sentences. Their work is closely related to our study in that k-max pooling is utilized to capture global feature vector and do not rely on parse tree. Kim (2014) proposed a simple improvement to the convolutional architecture that two input channels are used to allow the employment of task-specific and static word embeddings simultaneously.

Zeng et al. (2014) developed a deep convolutional neural network (DNN) to extract lexical and sentence level features, which are concatenated and fed into the softmax classifier. Socher et al. (2013) proposed the Recursive Neural Network (RNN) that has been proven to be efficient in terms of constructing sentences representations. In order to reduce the overfitting of neural network especially trained on small data set, Hinton et al. (2012) used random dropout to prevent

[1] Semantic units are defined as n-grams which have dominant meaning of text. With n varying, multi-scale contextual information can be exploited.

complex co-adaptations. To exploit more structure information of text, based on CNN and direct embedding of small text regions, an alternative mechanism for effective use of word order for text categorization was proposed (Johnson and Zhang, 2014).

Although the popular methods can capture high-order information and word relations to produce complex features, they cannot guarantee the classification performance for very short texts. In this paper, we design a method to exploit more contextual information for short text classification using semantic clustering and CNN.

3 Semantic Clustering

Since the neighbors of each word are semantically related in embedding space (Mikolov *et al.*, 2013b), clustering methods (Rodriguez and Laio, 2014) can be used to discover semantic cliques. For implementation, two quantities of data point i are computed, include: local density ρ_i, defined as follows,

$$\rho_i = \sum_j \chi(d_{ij} - d_c) \tag{3}$$

where d_{ij} is the distance between data points, d_c is a cutoff distance. Furthermore, distance δ_i from points of higher density is measured by,

$$\delta_i = \begin{cases} \min\limits_{j:\rho_j > \rho_i} (d_{ij}) \ , \ if \ \rho_i < \rho_{\max} \\ \max\limits_j (d_{ij}) \ , \ otherwise \end{cases} \tag{4}$$

An example of semantic clustering is illustrated in Figure 1. The decision graph shows the two quantities ρ and δ of each word embedding. According to the definitions above, these word embeddings with large ρ and δ simultaneously are chosen as cluster centers, which are labeled using the corresponding words.

4 Proposed Architecture

As shown in Figure 2, the proposed architecture use well pre-trained word embeddings to initialize the lookup table, and higher levels extract more complexity features.

For short text $S = \{w_1, w_2, \cdots, w_N\}$, its projected matrix $\mathbf{PM} \in \mathbf{R}^{d \times N}$ is obtained by table looking up in the first layer, where d is the dimension of word embedding. The second layer is used to obtain multi-scale SUs to constitute the semantic

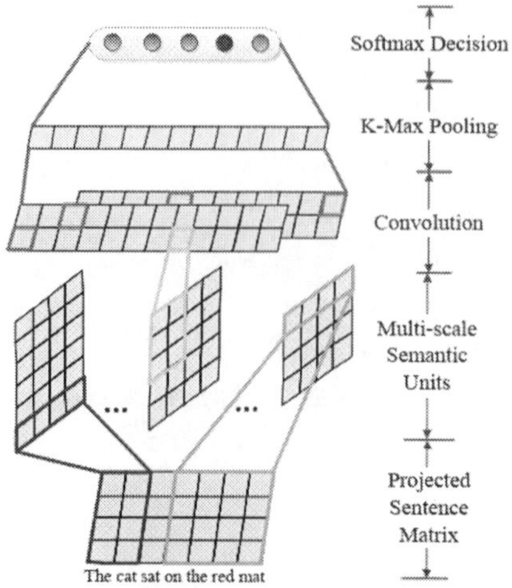

Figure 2: Architecture for short text modeling

matrices, which are combined and fed into convolutional layer, followed by k-max pooling operation. Finally, a softmax function is employed as classifier.

4.1 Detection for Multi-scale SUs

Methods for modeling short text S mainly have problem that its semantic meaning is determined by a few of key-phrases, however, these meaningful phrases may appear at any position of S. Thus, simply combining all words of S may introduce unnecessary divergence and hurt the overall semantic representation. Therefore, the detection for SUs are useful, which capture salient local information, as shown in Figure 2.

In particular, to obtain the representations of candidate SUs, multiple windows with variable width over word embeddings are used to perform element-wise additive composition, as follows:

$$[\mathbf{SU}_1, \mathbf{SU}_2, \cdots, \mathbf{SU}_{N-m+1}] = \mathbf{PM} \otimes \mathbf{E}_{win} \tag{5}$$

where, $E_{win} \in R^{d \times m}$ is a window matrix with all weights equal to one, and

$$\mathbf{SU}_i = \sum_{j=1}^{|\mathbf{PM}^{win,i}|} \mathbf{PM}_j^{win,i} \tag{6}$$

$\mathbf{PM}_j^{win,i}$ is the jth column from the sub-matrix $\mathbf{PM}^{win,i}$, which is windowed on projected matrix $\mathbf{PM}$ by E_{win} with the ith times sliding. m is the width of the window matrix E_{win}. With m varying, multi-scale contextual information can be exploited, which is helpful to reduce the impact of ambiguous words.

The meaningful SUs are assumed that they have one close neighbor at least in embedding space. Thus, we compute Euclidean distance between candidate SUs and semantic cliques. If the distance between candidate SUs and nearest word embeddings are smaller than the preset threshold, the candidate SUs are selected to constitute the semantic matrices, otherwise dropout.

4.2 Convolution Layer

In our network, the convolutional layer is used to extract local features. Kernel matrices $\mathbf{k}$ with certain width n are utilized to calculate convolution with the input matrices $\mathbf{M}$, as Equation (7).

$$C = [\mathbf{c}_1, \mathbf{c}_2, \cdots, \mathbf{c}_{d/2}]^{\mathrm{T}} = K^{\mathrm{T}} \otimes M \quad (7)$$

where,

$$K = [\mathbf{k}_1, \mathbf{k}_2, \cdots, \mathbf{k}_{d/2}] \quad (8)$$

$$M = [\mathbf{M}_1^{win}, \mathbf{M}_2^{win}, \cdots, \mathbf{M}_{d/2}^{win}] \quad (9)$$

$$c_i^j = \mathbf{k}_i \cdot (\mathbf{M}_i^{win,j})^T \quad (10)$$

The c_i^j is generated from the jth n-gram in $\mathbf{M}$. Equation (7) produce the feature maps of convolutional layer.

4.3 K-Max Pooling

This operator is a non-linear sub-sampling function that returns the sub-sequence of K maximum values (LeCun *et al.*, 1998), which is used to capture the most relevant global features with fixed-length. Then, tangent transformation over the results of K-max pooling is performed, the output of which is concatenated to used as representation for the input short texts.

4.4 Network Training

The last layer is fully connected, where a softmax classifier is applied to predict the probability distribution over categories. The network is trained with the objective that minimizes the cross-entropy of the predicted distributions and the actual distributions (Turian *et al.*, 2010),

$$J(\theta) = -\frac{1}{t}\sum_{i=1}^{t} \log p(c^{\dagger}|\mathbf{x}_i, \theta) + \alpha\|\theta\|^2 \quad (11)$$

where t is number of training examples $\mathbf{x}$, and θ is the parameters set which comprises the kernels of weights used in convolutional layer and the connective weights from the fully connected layer.

Embedding	Senna[2]	GloVe[3]	Word2Vec[4]
Corpus	Wikipedia	Wikipedia	Google News
Dimension	50	50	300
$\|Vocab.\|$	130,000	400,000	3,000,000

Table 1: Details of word embeddings

Methods		Google Snippets	TREC
Semantic-CNN	Senna	83.6	96.4
	GloVe	84.4	**97.2**
	Word2Vec	**85.1**	95.6
DCNN (Kalchbrenner et al,2014)		-	93
SVMS (Silva et al., 2011)		-	95
CNN-TwoChannel (Kim, 2014)		-	93.6
LDA+MaxEnt (Phan et al., 2008)		82.7	-
Multi-Topics+MaxEnt (Chen et al., 2011)		84.17	-

Table 2: The classification accuracy of proposed method against other models

5 Experiments

5.1 Datasets

Experiments are conducted on two benchmarks: Google Snippets (Phan *et al.*, 2008) and TREC (Li and Roth, 2002).

Google Snippets This dataset consists of 10,060 training snippets and 2,280 test snippets from 8 categories. On average, each snippet has 18.07 words.

TREC The TREC questions dataset contains 6 different question types. The training dataset consists of 5,452 labeled questions whereas the test dataset consists of 500 questions.

5.2 Experimental Setup

Three pre-trained word embeddings for initializing the lookup table are summarized in Table 1. To discover semantic cliques, we take $\rho_{\min} = 16$ and $\delta_{\min} = 1.54$. Through our experiments, 6 kernel matrices in convolutional layer, $K = 3$ for max pooling, and mini-batch size of 100 are used.

5.3 Results and Discussions

5.3.1 Comparison with state-of-the-art methods

As shown in Table 2, we introduce 5 popular methods as baselines, and the details are described:

DCNN Kalchbrenner et al. (2014) proposed DCNN for sentence modeling with dynamic k-max pooling.

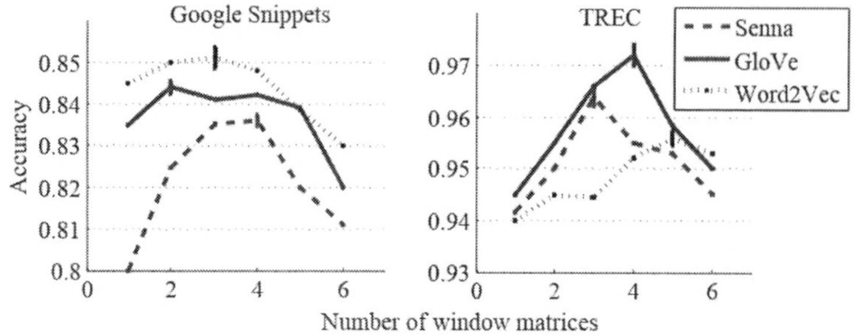

Figure 3: Number of windows for multi-scale SUs

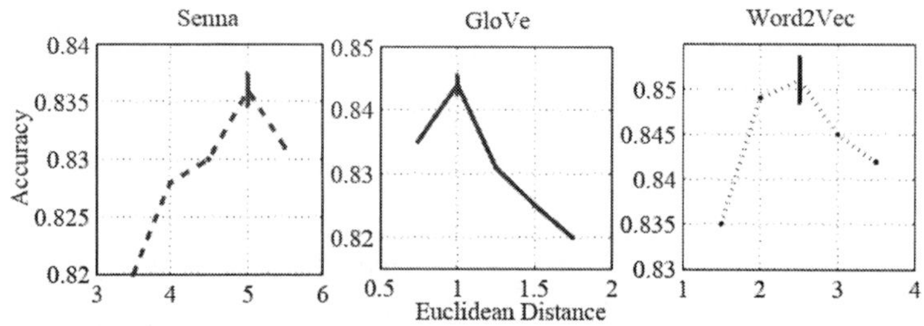

Figure 4: Influence of threshold in SUs detection

SVMs Parser, wh word, head word, POS, hypernyms, and 60 hand-coded rules were used as features to train SVMs (Silva *et al.*, 2011).

CNN-TwoChannel An improved CNN that allows task-specific and static word embeddings are used simultaneously (Kim, 2014).

LDA+MaxEnt LDA was used to discover hidden topics for expanding short texts (Phan *et al.*, 2008).

Multi-topics+MaxEnt Multiple granularity topics from LDA were utilized to model short texts (Chen *et al.*, 2011).

For valid comparisons, we respectively initialize the lookup table with the word embeddings in Table 1, and three experiments are conducted for each benchmark. As a whole, our method achieves the best performance, especially for TREC with 97.2% when the GloVe word embedding is employed. For Google snippets, our method achieves the highest result of 85.1% corresponding to the word embedding induced by Word2Vec.

5.3.2 Effect of Hyper-parameters

In Figure 2, for obtaining SUs with multi-scale, multiple window matrices with increasing width m are used. With respect to the variable m, the results are shown in Figure 3. We find small size of window may result in loss of critical information, however, the window with large size may introduce noise.

Figure 4 demonstrate how preset threshold d impact our method over benchmark Goggle snippets. We can draw a conclusion that when d is too small, only a few of SUs can be detected, whereas meaningless features are enrolled. The optimal threshold d can be chosen by cross-validation.

The impacts of other hyper-parameters like the number and size of the feature detectors in convolutional layer, and the variable k in k-max pooling layer are beyond the scope of this paper.

6 Conclusion

This paper proposes a novel semantic hierarchical model for short text classification. The model uses pre-trained word embeddings to introduce extra knowledge, and multi-scale SUs in short texts are detected.

Acknowledgement

This work is supported by the National Natural Science Foundation of China (No. 61203281, No. 61303172, No. 61403385) and Hundred Talents Program of Chinese Academy of Sciences (No. Y3S4011D31).

[2]http://ml.nec-labs.com/senna/

[3]http://nlp.stanford.edu/projects/glove/

[4]https://code.google.com/p/word2vec/

References

Ainur Yessenalina and Claire Cardie. Compositional matrix-space models for sentiment analysis. In *EMNLP*, pages 172–182. Association for Computational Linguistics, 2011.

Alex Rodriguez and Alessandro Laio. Clustering by fast search and find of density peaks. *Science*, 344(6191):1492–1496, 2014.

Andriy Mnih and Yee Whye Teh. A fast and simple algorithm for training neural probabilistic language models. *arXiv preprint arXiv:1206.6426*, 2012.

Bharath Sriram, Dave Fuhry, Engin Demir, Hakan Ferhatosmanoglu, and Murat Demirbas. Short text classification in twitter to improve information filtering. In *SIGIR*, pages 841–842. ACM, 2010.

Daojian Zeng, Kang Liu, Siwei Lai, Guangyou Zhou, and Jun Zhao. Relation classification via convolutional deep neural network. In *Proceedings of COLING*, pages 2335–2344, 2014.

David M Blei, Andrew Y Ng, and Michael I Jordan. Latent dirichlet allocation. *the Journal of machine Learning research*, 3:993–1022, 2003.

Geoffrey E Hinton, Nitish Srivastava, Alex Krizhevsky, Ilya Sutskever, and Ruslan R Salakhutdinov. Improving neural networks by preventing co-adaptation of feature detectors. *arXiv preprint arXiv:1207.0580*, 2012.

Jeff Mitchell and Mirella Lapata. Composition in distributional models of semantics. *Cognitive science*, 34(8):1388–1429, 2010.

John Duchi, Elad Hazan, and Yoram Singer. Adaptive subgradient methods for online learning and stochastic optimization. *The Journal of Machine Learning Research*, 12:2121–2159, 2011.

Joseph Turian, Lev Ratinov, and Yoshua Bengio. Word representations: a simple and general method for semi-supervised learning. In *ACL*, pages 384–394. Association for Computational Linguistics, 2010.

Mehran Sahami and Timothy D Heilman. A web-based kernel function for measuring the similarity of short text snippets. In *Proceedings of the 15th international conference on World Wide Web*, pages 377–386. AcM, 2006.

Mengen Chen, Xiaoming Jin, and Dou Shen. Short text classification improved by learning multi-granularity topics. In *IJCAI*, pages 1776–1781. Citeseer, 2011.

Nal Kalchbrenner, Edward Grefenstette, and Phil Blunsom. A convolutional neural network for modelling sentences. *arXiv preprint arXiv:1404.2188*, 2014.

Quoc V Le and Tomas Mikolov. Distributed representations of sentences and documents. *arXiv preprint arXiv:1405.4053*, 2014.

Richard Socher, Alex Perelygin, Jean Y Wu, Jason Chuang, Christopher D Manning, Andrew Y Ng, and Christopher Potts. Recursive deep models for semantic compositionality over a sentiment treebank. In *EMNLP*, volume 1631, page 1642. Citeseer, 2013.

Ronan Collobert, Jason Weston, Léon Bottou, Michael Karlen, Koray Kavukcuoglu, and Pavel Kuksa. Natural language processing (almost) from scratch. *The Journal of Machine Learning Research*, 12:2493–2537, 2011.

Tomas Mikolov, Kai Chen, Greg Corrado, and Jeffrey Dean. Efficient estimation of word representations in vector space. *arXiv preprint arXiv:1301.3781*, 2013.

Tomas Mikolov, Ilya Sutskever, Kai Chen, Greg S Corrado, and Jeff Dean. Distributed representations of words and phrases and their compositionality. In *Advances in Neural Information Processing Systems*, pages 3111–3119, 2013.

Tomas Mikolov, Wen-tau Yih, and Geoffrey Zweig. Linguistic regularities in continuous space word representations. In *HLT-NAACL*, pages 746–751, 2013.

Xiaohui Yan, Jiafeng Guo, Yanyan Lan, and Xueqi Cheng. A biterm topic model for short texts. In *WWW*, pages 1445–1456. International World Wide Web Conferences Steering Committee, 2013.

Xin Li and Dan Roth. Learning question classifiers. In *Proceedings of the 19th international conference on Computational linguistics-Volume 1*, pages 1–7. Association for Computational Linguistics, 2002.

Xuan-Hieu Phan, Le-Minh Nguyen, and Susumu Horiguchi. Learning to classify short and sparse text & web with hidden topics from large-scale data collections. In *Proceedings of the 17th international conference on World Wide Web*, pages 91–100. ACM, 2008.

Yann LeCun, Léon Bottou, Yoshua Bengio, and Patrick Haffner. Gradient-based learning applied to document recognition. *Proceedings of the IEEE*, 86(11):2278–2324, 1998.

Yoon Kim. Convolutional neural networks for sentence classification. *arXiv preprint arXiv:1408.5882*, 2014.

Yoshua Bengio, Réjean Ducharme, Pascal Vincent, and Christian Janvin. A neural probabilistic language model. *The Journal of Machine Learning Research*, 3:1137–1155, 2003.

Joao Silva, Luísa Coheur, Ana Cristina Mendes, and Andreas Wichert. From symbolic to sub-symbolic information in question classification. *Artificial Intelligence Review*, 35(2):137–154, 2011.

Rie Johnson and Tong Zhang. Effective use of word order for text categorization with convolutional neural networks. *arXiv preprint arXiv:1412.1058*, 2014.

Document Level Time-anchoring for TimeLine Extraction

Egoitz Laparra, Itziar Aldabe, German Rigau
IXA NLP group, University of the Basque Country (UPV/EHU)
{egoitz.laparra,itziar.aldabe,german.rigau}@ehu.eus

Abstract

This paper investigates the contribution of document level processing of time-anchors for TimeLine event extraction. We developed and tested two different systems. The first one is a baseline system that captures explicit time-anchors. The second one extends the baseline system by also capturing implicit time relations. We have evaluated both approaches in the SemEval 2015 task 4 *TimeLine: Cross-Document Event Ordering*. We empirically demonstrate that the document-based approach obtains a much more complete time anchoring. Moreover, this approach almost doubles the performance of the systems that participated in the task.

1 Introduction

Temporal relation extraction has been the topic of different SemEval tasks (Verhagen et al., 2007; Verhagen et al., 2010; UzZaman et al., 2013; Llorens et al., 2015) and other challenges as the 6th i2b2 NLP Challenge (Sun et al., 2013). These tasks focused mainly on the temporal relations of the events with respect to other events or time expressions, and their goals are to discover which of them occur before, after or simultaneously to others. Recently, SemEval 2015 included a novel task regarding temporal information extraction (Minard et al., 2015). The aim of SemEval 2015 task 4 is to order in a TimeLine the events in which a target entity is involved and presents some significant differences with respect to previous exercises. First, the temporal information must be recovered from different sources in a cross-document way. Second, the TimeLines are focused on the events involving just a given entity. Finally, unlike previous challenges, SemEval 2015 task 4 requires a quite complete time anchoring. This work focuses mainly on this latter point. We show that the temporal relations that explicitly connect events and time expressions are not enough to obtain a full time-anchor annotation and, consequently, produce incomplete TimeLines. We propose that for a complete time-anchoring the temporal analysis must be performed at a document level in order to discover implicit temporal relations. We present a preliminary approach that obtains, by far, the best results on the main track of SemEval 2015 task 4.

2 Related work

The present work is closely related to previous approaches involved in TempEval campaigns (Verhagen et al., 2007; Verhagen et al., 2010; UzZaman et al., 2013; Llorens et al., 2015). In these works, the problem can be seen as a classification task for deciding the type of the temporal link that connects two different events or an event and a temporal expression. For that reason, the task has been mainly addresed using supervised techniques. For example, (Mani et al., 2006; Mani et al., 2007) trained a MaxEnt classifier using training data which were bootstrapped by applying temporal closure. (Chambers et al., 2007) focused on event-event relations using previously learned event attributes. More recently, (DŚouza and Ng, 2013) combined hand-coded rules with some semantic and discourse features. (Laokulrat et al., 2013) obtained the best results on TempEval 2013 annotating sentences with predicate-role structures, while (Mirza and Tonelli, 2014) affirm that using a simple feature set results in better performances.

However, recent works like (Chambers et al., 2014) have pointed out that these tasks cover just a part of all the temporal relations that can be inferred from the documents. Furthermore, time-anchoring is just a part of the works presented above. Our approach aims to extend these strategies and it is based on other research lines

Proceedings of the 53rd Annual Meeting of the Association for Computational Linguistics and the 7th International Joint Conference on Natural Language Processing (Short Papers), pages 358–364,
Beijing, China, July 26-31, 2015.

involving the extraction of implicit information (Palmer et al., 1986; Whittemore et al., 1991; Tetreault, 2002). Particularly, we are inspired by recent works on Implicit Semantic Role Labelling (ISRL) (Gerber and Chai, 2012) and very specially on the work by (Blanco and Moldovan, 2014) who adapted the ideas about ISRL to focus on modifiers, including arguments of time, instead of core arguments or roles. As the SemEval 2015 task 4 does not include any training data we decided to develop a deterministic algorithm of the type of (Laparra and Rigau, 2013) for ISRL.

3 TimeLine: Cross-Document Event Ordering

In the SemEval task 4 *TimeLine: Cross-Document Event Ordering* (Minard et al., 2015), given a set of documents and a target entity, the aim is to build a TimeLine by detecting the events in which the entity is involved and anchoring these events to normalized times. Thus, a TimeLine is a collection of ordered events in time relevant for a particular entity. TimeLines contain relevant events in which the target entity participates as ARG0 (i.e agent) or ARG1 (i.e. patient) as defined in PropBank (Palmer et al., 2005).[1] The target entities can be *people*, *organization*, *product* or *financial* entities and the annotation of time anchors is based on TimeML.

For example, given the entity *Steve Jobs*, a TimeLine contains the events with the associated ordering in the TimeLine and the time anchor:

1	2004	18135-7-fighting
2	2005-06-05	1664-2-keynote
...		
4	2011-08-24	18315-2-step_down

The dataset used for the task is composed of articles from Wikinews. The trial data consists of 30 documents about "Apple Inc." and gold standard TimeLines for six target entities. The test corpus consists of 3 sets of 30 documents around three topics and 38 target entities. The topics are "Airbus and Boeing", "General Motors, Chrysler and Ford" and "Stock Market".

The evaluation used in the task is based on the metric previously introduced in TempEval-3 (UzZaman et al., 2013). The metric captures the temporal awareness of an annotation (UzZaman and Allen, 2011) based on temporal closure graphs. In order to calculate the precision, recall and F1 score, the TimeLines are first transformed into a graph representation. For that, the time anchors are represented as TIMEX3 and the events are related to the corresponding TIMEX3 by means of the SIMULTANEOUS relation type. In addition, BEFORE relation types are created to represent that one event happens before another one and SIMULTANEOUS relation types to refer to events happening at the same time. The official scores are based on the micro-average of F1 scores.

The main track of the task (Track A) consists of building TimeLines providing only the raw text sources. Two systems participated in the task. The organisers also defined a Track B where gold event mentions were given. In this case, two different systems sent results. For both tracks, a sub-track in which the events are not associated to a time anchor was also presented.

In this work, we focus on the main track of the task. We believe the main track is the most challenging one as no annotated data is provided. Indeed, WHUNLP 1 was the best run and achieved an F1 of 7.28%.

Three runs were submitted. The WHUNLP team used the Stanford CoreNLP and they applied a rule-based approach to extract the entities and their predicates. They also performed temporal reasoning.[2] The remaining two runs were submitted using the SPINOZA_VU system (Caselli et al., 2015). They performed entity resolution, event detection, event-participant linking, coreference resolution, factuality profiling and temporal processing at document and cross-document level. Then, the TimeLine extractor built a global timeline between all events and temporal expressions regardless of the target entities and then it extracted the target entities for the TimeLines. The participants also presented an out of the competition system which anchors events to temporal expressions appearing not only in the same sentence but also in the previous and following sentences.

4 Baseline TimeLine extraction

In this section we present a system that builds TimeLines which contain events with explicit time-anchors. We have defined a three step pro-

[1]For more information consult http://tinyurl.com/owyuybb

[2]Unfortunately, the task participants did not submit a paper with the description of the system.

cess to build TimeLines. Given a set of documents and a target entity, the system first obtains the events in which the entity is involved. Second, it obtains the time-anchors for each of these events. Finally, it sorts the events according to their time-anchors. For steps 1 and 2 we apply a pipeline of tools (cf. section 4.1) that provides annotations at different levels.

4.1 NLP processing

Detecting mentions of events, entities and time expressions in text requires the combination of various Natural Language Processing (NLP) modules. We apply a generic pipeline of linguistic tools that includes Named-Entity Recognition (NER) and Disambiguation (NED), Co-reference Resolution (CR), Semantic Role Labelling (SRL), Time Expressions Identification (TEI) and Normalization (TEN), and Temporal Relation Extraction (TRE). The NLP processing is based on the NewsReader pipeline (Agerri et al., 2014a), version 2.1. Next, we present the different tools in our pipeline.

Named-Entity Recognition (NER) and Disambiguation (NED): We perform NER using the ixa-pipe-nerc that is part of IXA pipes (Agerri et al., 2014b). The module provides very fast models with high performances, obtaining 84.53 in F1 on CoNLL tasks. Our NED module is based on DBpedia Spotlight (Daiber et al., 2013). We have created a NED client to query the DBpedia Spotlight server for the Named entities detected by the ixa-pipe-nerc module. Using the best parameter combination, the best results obtained by this module on the TAC 2011 dataset were 79.77 in precision and 60.67 in recall. The best performance on the AIDA dataset is 79.67 in precision and 76.94 in recall.

Coreference Resolution (CR): In this case, we use a coreference module that is loosely based on the Stanford Multi Sieve Pass sytem (Lee et al., 2011). The system consists of a number of rule-based sieves that are applied in a deterministic manner. The system scores 56.4 F1 on CoNLL 2011 task, around 3 points worse than the system by (Lee et al., 2011).

Semantic Role Labelling (SRL): SRL is performed using the system included in the MATE-tools (Björkelund et al., 2009). This system reported on the CoNLL 2009 Shared Task a labelled semantic F1 of 85.63 for English.

Time Expression Identification (TEI) and Normalization (TEN): We use the time module from TextPro suite (Pianta et al., 2008) to capture the tokens corresponding to temporal expressions and to normalize them following TIDES specification. This module is trained on TempEval3 data. The average results for English is: 83.81% precision, 75.94% recall and 79.61% F1 values.

Time Relation Extraction (TRE): We apply the temporal relation extractor module from TextPro to extract and classify temporal relations between an event and a time expression. This module is trained using yamcha tool on the TempEval3 data. The result for relation classification on the corpus of TempEval3 is: 58.8% precision, 58.2% recall and 58.5% F1.

4.2 TimeLine extraction

Our TimeLine extraction system uses the linguistic information provided by the pipeline. The process to extract the target entities, the events and time-anchors can be described as follows:

(1) Target entity identification: The target entities are identified by the NED module. As they can be expressed in several forms, we use the redirect links contained in DBpedia to extend the search of the events involving those target entities. For example, if the target entity is *Toyota* the system would also include events involving the entities *Toyota Motor Company* or *Toyota Motor Corp.* In addition, as the NED does not always provide a link to DBpedia, we also consider the matching of the wordform of the head of the argument with the head of the target entity.

(2) Event selection: We use the output of the SRL module to extract the events that occur in a document. Given a target entity, we combine the output of the NER, NED, CR and SRL to obtain those events that have the target entity as filler of their ARG0 or ARG1. We also set some constraints to select certain events according to the specification of the SemEval task. That is, we only return those events that are not negated and are not accompanied by modal verbs except *will*.

(3) Time-anchoring: We extract the time-anchors from the output of the TRE and SRL. From the TRE, we extract as time-anchors those relations between events and time-expressions identified as SIMULTANEOUS. From the SRL, we extract as time-anchors those ARG-TMP related to time expressions. In both cases we use the time-expression returned by the TEI module. The tests performed on the trial data show that the best choice for time-anchoring is combining both options. For each time anchor we normalize the time expression using the output of the TEN module.

The TimeLine extraction process described following this approach builds TimeLines for events with explicit time-anchors. We call this system **BTE** and it can be seen as a baseline since we believe that the temporal analysis should be carried out at document level. Section 5 presents our strategy for improving the time-anchoring carried out by our baseline system.

5 Document level time-anchoring

The explicit time anchors provided by the NLP tools presented in Section 4.1 do not cover the full set of events involving a particular entity. That is, most of the events do not have an explicit time anchor and therefore are not captured as part of the TimeLine of that entity. Thus, we need to recover the time-anchors that appear implicitly in the text. In this preliminary work, we propose a simple strategy that tries to capture implicit time-anchors while maintaining the coherence of the temporal information in the document. As said in Section 2, this strategy follows previous works on Implicit Semantic Role Labelling.

The rationale behind the algorithm 1 is that by default the events of an entity that appear in a document tend to occur at the same time as previous events involving the same entity, except stated explicitly. For example, in Figure 1 all the events involving *Steve Jobs*, like *gave* and *announced*, are anchored to the same time-expression *Monday* although this only happens explicitly for the first event *gave*. The example also shows how for other events that occur in different times the time-anchor is also mentioned explicitly, like for those events that involve the entities *Tiger* and *Mac OS X Leopard*.

Algorithm 1 starts from the annotation obtained by the tools described in Section 4.1. For a particular entity a list of events ($eventList$) is created sorted by its occurrence in the text. Then, for each event in this list the system checks if that event has already a time-anchor ($eAnchor$). If this is the case, the time-anchor is included in the list of default time-anchors ($defaultAnchor$) for the following events of the entity with the same verb tense ($eTense$). If the event does not have an explicit time-anchor but the system has found a time-anchor for a previous event belonging to the same tense ($defaultAnchor[eTense]$), this time-anchor is also assigned to the current event ($eAnchor$). If none of the previous conditions satisfy, the algorithm anchors the event to the **Document Creation Time** (DCT) and sets this time-expression as the default time-anchor for the following events with the same tense.

Algorithm 1 Implicit Time-anchoring

$eventList$ = sorted list of events of an entity
for $event$ in $eventList$ **do**
  $eAnchor$ = time anchor of $event$
  $eTense$ = verb tense of $event$
  if $eAnchor$ not $NULL$ **then**
    $defaultAnchor[eTense] = eAnchor$
  else if $defaultAnchor[eTense]$ not $NULL$ **then**
    $eAnchor = defaultAnchor[eTense]$
  else
    $eAnchor$ = DCT
    $defaultAnchor[eTense]$ = DCT
  end if
end for

Note that the algorithm 1 strongly depends on the tense of the events. As this information can be only recovered from verbal predicates, this strategy cannot be applied to events described by nominal predicates. For these cases just explicit time-anchors are taken into account.

The TimeLine is built ordering the events according to the time-anchors obtained both explicitly and implicitly. We call this system **DLT**.

6 Experiments

We have evaluated our two TimeLine extractors on the main track of the SemEval 2015 task 4. Two systems participated in this track, **WHUNLP** and **SPINOZAVU**, with three runs in total. Their performances in terms of Precision (P), Recall (R) and F1-score (F1) are presented in Table 6. We also present in italics additional results of both systems. On the one hand, the results of a corrected run of the WHUNLP system provided by the SemEval organizers. On the other hand, the results of an out of the competition version of the SPINOZAVU team explained in (Caselli et al., 2015). The best run is obtained by the corrected version of **WHUNLP_1** with an F1 of 7.85%. The low figures obtained show the intrinsic difficulty of the task, specially in terms of Recall.

Apple Computer CEO and co-founder **Steve Jobs** gave his annual opening keynote to the World Wide Developers Conference (WWDC) at Moscone Center in San Francisco, California on **Monday**...

Moving on, **Jobs** announced that there have been 2 million copies of Tiger sold in the 6 weeks that it has been available....

Steve announced that Mac OS X Leopard would be released in 2007 ....

Figure 1: Example of document-level time-anchoring.

Table 6 also contains the results obtained by our systems. We present two different runs. On the one hand, we present the results obtained using just the explicit time-anchors provided by **BTE**. As it can be seen, the results obtained by this run are similar to those obtained by **WHUNLP_1**. On the other hand, the results of the implicit time-anchoring approach (**DLT**) outperforms by far our baseline and all previous systems applied to the task. To check that these results are not biased by the time-relation extractor we use in our pipeline (TimePro), we reproduce the performances of BTE and DLT using another system to obtain the time-relations. For this purpose we have used CAEVO by (Chambers et al., 2014). The results obtained in this case show that the improvement obtained by our proposal is quite similar, regardless of the time-relation extractor chosen.

System	P	R	F1
SPINOZAVU-RUN-1	7.95	1.96	3.15
SPINOZAVU-RUN-2	8.16	0.56	1.05
WHUNLP_1	14.10	4.90	7.28
OC_SPINOZA_VU	-	-	7.12
WHUNLP_1	14.59	5.37	7.85
BTE	**26.42**	4.44	7.60
DLT	20.67	10.95	**14.31**
BTE_caevo	17.56	4.86	7.61
DLT_caevo	17.02	**12.09**	14.13

Table 1: Results on the SemEval-2015 task

The figures in Table 6 seem to prove our hypothesis. In order to obtain a full time-anchoring annotation, the temporal analysis must be carried out at a document level. The TimeLine extractor almost doubles the performance by just including a straightforward strategy as the one described in Section 5. As expected, Table 6 shows that this improvement is much more significant in terms of Recall.

7 Conclusion and future-work

In this work we have shown that explicit temporal relations are not enough to obtain a full time-anchor annotation of events. We have proved the need of a temporal analysis at document level. For that, we have proposed a simple strategy that acquires implicit relations and it obtains a more complete time-anchoring.[3] The approach has been evaluated on the TimeLine extraction task and the results show that the performance can be doubled when using implicit relations. As future work, we plan to explore in more detail this research line by applying more sophisticated approaches in the temporal analysis at document level.

However, this is not the only research line that we want to go in depth. The errors that the tools of the pipeline are producing have a direct impact on the final result of our TimeLine extractors. In a preliminary analysis, we have noticed that this is specially critical when detecting the events given a target entity. Our pipeline does not detect all mentions of the target entities. That is why we are planning an in-depth error analysis of the pipeline in order to find the best strategy to improve on the linguist analyses and the TimeLine extraction.

8 Acknowledgment

We are grateful to the anonymous reviewers for their insightful comments. This work has been partially funded by SKaTer (TIN2012-38584-C06-02) and NewsReader (FP7-ICT-2011-8-316404), as well as the READERS project with the financial support of MINECO (CHIST-ERA READERS project - PCIN-2013-002-C02-01).

[3]Publicly available at `http://adimen.si.ehu.es/web/DLT`

References

Rodrigo Agerri, Itziar Aldabe, Zuhaitz Beloki, Egoitz Laparra, Maddalen Lopez de Lacalle, German Rigau, Aitor Soroa, Antske Fokkens, Ruben Izquierdo, Marieke van Erp, Piek Vossen, Christian Girardi, and Anne-Lyse Minard. 2014a. Event detection, version 2. Newsreader Deliverable 4.2.2. http://www.newsreader-project.eu/files/2012/12/NWR-D4-2-2.pdf.

Rodrigo Agerri, Josu Bermudez, and German Rigau. 2014b. IXA pipeline: Efficient and Ready to Use Multilingual NLP tools. In *Proceedings of the Ninth International Conference on Language Resources and Evaluation (LREC-2014)*. 00013.

Anders Björkelund, Love Hafdell, and Pierre Nugues. 2009. Multilingual semantic role labeling. In *Proceedings of the Thirteenth Conference on Computational Natural Language Learning: Shared Task*, CoNLL '09, pages 43–48, Boulder, Colorado, USA.

Eduardo Blanco and Dan Moldovan. 2014. Leveraging verb-argument structures to infer semantic relations. In *Proceedings of the 14th Conference of the European Chapter of the Association for Computational Linguistics*, pages 145–154, Gothenburg, Sweden.

Tommaso Caselli, Antske Fokkens, Roser Morante, and Piek Vossen. 2015. SPINOZA_VU: An nlp pipeline for cross document timelines. In *Proceedings of the 9th International Workshop on Semantic Evaluation (SemEval 2015)*, pages 786–790, Denver, Colorado, June 4-5.

Nathanael Chambers, Shan Wang, and Dan Jurafsky. 2007. Classifying temporal relations between events. In *Proceedings of the 45th Annual Meeting of the ACL on Interactive Poster and Demonstration Sessions*, ACL'07, pages 173–176, Prague, Czech Republic.

Nathanael Chambers, Taylor Cassidy, Bill McDowell, and Steven Bethard. 2014. Dense event ordering with a multi-pass architecture. *Transactions of the Association for Computational Linguistics*, 2:273–284.

Joachim Daiber, Max Jakob, Chris Hokamp, and Pablo N. Mendes. 2013. Improving efficiency and accuracy in multilingual entity extraction. In *Proceedings of the 9th International Conference on Semantic Systems (I-Semantics)*.

Jennifer DŚouza and Vincent Ng. 2013. Classifying temporal relations with rich linguistic knowledge. In *Proceedings of the 2013 Conference of the North American Chapter of the Association for Computational Linguistics: Human Language Technologies*, NACL'13, pages 918–927, Atlanta, Georgia.

Matthew Gerber and Joyce Chai. 2012. Semantic role labeling of implicit arguments for nominal predicates. *Computational Linguistics*, 38(4):755–798, December.

Natsuda Laokulrat, Makoto Miwa, Yoshimasa Tsuruoka, and Takashi Chikayama. 2013. Uttime: Temporal relation classification using deep syntactic features. In *Second Joint Conference on Lexical and Computational Semantics (*SEM), Volume 2: Proceedings of the Seventh International Workshop on Semantic Evaluation (SemEval 2013)*, pages 88–92, Atlanta, Georgia, USA.

Egoitz Laparra and German Rigau. 2013. Impar: A deterministic algorithm for implicit semantic role labelling. In *Proceedings of the 51st Annual Meeting of the Association for Computational Linguistics (ACL 2013)*, pages 33–41.

Heeyoung Lee, Yves Peirsman, Angel Chang, Nathanael Chambers, Mihai Surdeanu, and Dan Jurafsky. 2011. Stanford's multi-pass sieve coreference resolution system at the conll-2011 shared task. In *Proceedings of the Fifteenth Conference on Computational Natural Language Learning: Shared Task*, CONLL Shared Task '11, Portland, Oregon.

Hector Llorens, Nathanael Chambers, Naushad UzZaman, Nasrin Mostafazadeh, James Allen, and James Pustejovsky. 2015. Semeval-2015 task 5: Qa tempeval - evaluating temporal information understanding with question answering. In *Proceedings of the 9th International Workshop on Semantic Evaluation (SemEval 2015)*, pages 792–800, Denver, Colorado, June.

Inderjeet Mani, Marc Verhagen, Ben Wellner, Chong Min Lee, and James Pustejovsky. 2006. Machine learning of temporal relations. In *Proceedings of the 21st International Conference on Computational Linguistics and the 44th Annual Meeting of the Association for Computational Linguistics*, ACL'06, pages 753–760, Sydney, Australia.

Inderjeet Mani, Ben Wellner, Marc Verhagen, and James Pustejovsky. 2007. Three approaches to learning tlinks in timeml. Technical report.

Anne-Lyse Minard, Manuela Speranza, Eneko Agirre, Itziar Aldabe, Marieke van Erp, Bernardo Magnini, German Rigau, and Ruben Urizar. 2015. Semeval-2015 task 4: Timeline: Cross-document event ordering. In *Proceedings of the 9th International Workshop on Semantic Evaluation (SemEval 2015)*, pages 778–786, Denver, Colorado, June 4–5.

Paramita Mirza and Sara Tonelli. 2014. Classifying temporal relations with simple features. In *Proceedings of the 14th Conference of the European Chapter of the Association for Computational Linguistics*, pages 308–317, Gothenburg, Sweden, April. Association for Computational Linguistics.

Martha S. Palmer, Deborah A. Dahl, Rebecca J. Schiffman, Lynette Hirschman, Marcia Linebarger, and John Dowding. 1986. Recovering implicit information. In *Proceedings of the 24th annual meeting on Association for Computational Linguistics*, ACL '86, pages 10–19, New York, New York, USA.

Martha Palmer, Daniel Gildea, and Paul Kingsbury. 2005. The proposition bank: An annotated corpus of semantic roles. *Computational Linguistics*, 31(1):71–106, March.

Emanuele Pianta, Christian Girardi, and Roberto Zanoli. 2008. The textpro tool suite. In *Proceedings of the Sixth International Conference on Language Resources and Evaluation (LREC'08)*, Marrakech, Morocco, may.

Weiyi Sun, Anna Rumshisky, and Ozlem Uzuner. 2013. Evaluating temporal relations in clinical text: 2012 i2b2 Challenge. *Journal of the American Medical Informatics Association*, 20(5):806–813, September.

Joel R. Tetreault. 2002. Implicit role reference. In *International Symposium on Reference Resolution for Natural Language Processing*, pages 109–115, Alicante, Spain.

Naushad UzZaman and James Allen. 2011. Temporal evaluation. In *Proceedings of the 49th Annual Meeting of the Association for Computational Linguistics: Human Language Technologies*, pages 351–356, Portland, Oregon, USA.

Naushad UzZaman, Hector Llorens, Leon Derczynski, James Allen, Marc Verhagen, and James Pustejovsky. 2013. Semeval-2013 task 1: Tempeval-3: Evaluating time expressions, events, and temporal relations. In *Second Joint Conference on Lexical and Computational Semantics (*SEM), Volume 2: Proceedings of the Seventh International Workshop on Semantic Evaluation (SemEval 2013)*, SemEval '13, pages 1–9, Atlanta, Georgia, USA.

Marc Verhagen, Robert Gaizauskas, Frank Schilder, Mark Hepple, Graham Katz, and James Pustejovsky. 2007. Semeval-2007 task 15: Tempeval temporal relation identification. In *Proceedings of the 4th International Workshop on Semantic Evaluations*, SemEval '07, pages 75–80, Prague, Czech Republic.

Marc Verhagen, Roser Saurí, Tommaso Caselli, and James Pustejovsky. 2010. Semeval-2010 task 13: Tempeval-2. In *Proceedings of the 5th International Workshop on Semantic Evaluation*, SemEval '10, pages 57–62, Los Angeles, California.

Greg Whittemore, Melissa Macpherson, and Greg Carlson. 1991. Event-building through role-filling and anaphora resolution. In *Proceedings of the 29th annual meeting on Association for Computational Linguistics*, ACL '91, pages 17–24, Berkeley, California, USA.

Event Detection and Domain Adaptation with Convolutional Neural Networks

Thien Huu Nguyen
Computer Science Department
New York University
New York, NY 10003 USA
thien@cs.nyu.edu

Ralph Grishman
Computer Science Department
New York University
New York, NY 10003 USA
grishman@cs.nyu.edu

Abstract

We study the event detection problem using convolutional neural networks (CNNs) that overcome the two fundamental limitations of the traditional feature-based approaches to this task: complicated feature engineering for rich feature sets and error propagation from the preceding stages which generate these features. The experimental results show that the CNNs outperform the best reported feature-based systems in the general setting as well as the domain adaptation setting without resorting to extensive external resources.

1 Introduction

We address the problem of event detection (ED): identifying instances of specified types of events in text. Associated with each event mention is a phrase, the event trigger (most often a single verb or nominalization), which evokes that event. Our task, more precisely stated, involves identifying event triggers and classifying them into specific types. For instance, according to the ACE 2005 annotation guideline[1], in the sentence "*A police **officer** was **killed** in **New Jersey today***", an event detection system should be able to recognize the word "*killed*" as a trigger for the event "*Die*". This task is quite challenging, as the same event might appear in the form of various trigger expressions and an expression might represent different events in different contexts. ED is a crucial component in the overall task of event extraction, which also involves event argument discovery.

Recent systems for event extraction have employed either a pipeline architecture with separate classifiers for trigger and argument labeling (Ji and Grishman, 2008; Gupta and Ji, 2009; Patwardhan and Rilof, 2009; Liao and Grishman, 2011; McClosky et al., 2011; Huang and Riloff, 2012; Li et al., 2013a) or a joint inference architecture that performs the two subtasks at the same time to benefit from their inter-dependencies (Riedel and McCallum, 2011a; Riedel and McCallum, 2011b; Li et al., 2013b; Venugopal et al., 2014). Both approaches have coped with the ED task by elaborately hand-designing a large set of features (*feature engineering*) and utilizing the existing supervised natural language processing (NLP) toolkits and resources (i.e name tagger, parsers, gazetteers etc) to extract these features to be fed into statistical classifiers. Although this approach has achieved the top performance (Hong et al., 2011; Li et al., 2013b), it suffers from at least two issues:

(i) The choice of features is a manual process and requires linguistic intuition as well as domain expertise, implying additional studies for new application domains and limiting the capacity to quickly adapt to these new domains.

(ii) The supervised NLP toolkits and resources for feature extraction might involve errors (either due to the imperfect nature or the performance loss of the toolkits on new domains (Blitzer et al., 2006; Daumé III, 2007; McClosky et al., 2010)), probably propagated to the final event detector.

This paper presents a convolutional neural network (LeCun et al., 1988; Kalchbrenner et al., 2014) for the ED task that automatically learns features from sentences, and minimizes the dependence on supervised toolkits and resources for features, thus alleviating the error propagation and improving the performance for this task. Due to the emerging interest of the NLP community in deep learning recently, CNNs have been studied extensively and applied effectively in various tasks: semantic parsing (Yih et al., 2014), search query retrieval (Shen et al., 2014), semantic matching (Hu et al., 2014), sentence modeling and classification (Kalchbrenner et al., 2014; Kim,

[1] https://www.ldc.upenn.edu/sites/www.ldc.upenn.edu/files/english-events-guidelines-v5.4.3.pdf

Proceedings of the 53rd Annual Meeting of the Association for Computational Linguistics and the 7th International Joint Conference on Natural Language Processing (Short Papers), pages 365–371,
Beijing, China, July 26-31, 2015.

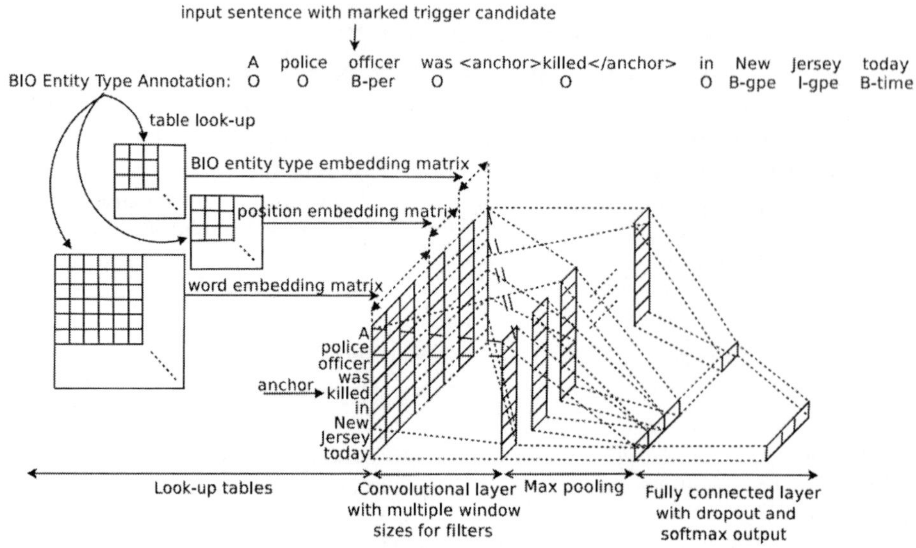

Figure 1: Convolutional Neural Network for Event Detection.

2014), name tagging and semantic role labeling (Collobert et al., 2011), relation classification and extraction (Zeng et al., 2014; Nguyen and Grishman, 2015). However, to the best of our knowledge, this is the first work on event detection via CNNs so far.

First, we evaluate CNNs for ED in the general setting and show that CNNs, though not requiring complicated feature engineering, can still outperform the state-of-the-art feature-based methods extensively relying on the other supervised modules and manual resources for features. Second, we investigate CNNs in a domain adaptation (DA) setting for ED. We demonstrate that CNNs significantly outperform the traditional feature-based methods with respect to generalization performance across domains due to: (i) their capacity to mitigate the error propagation from the preprocessing modules for features, and (ii) the use of word embeddings to induce a more general representation for trigger candidates. We believe that this is also the first research on domain adaptation using CNNs.

2 Model

We formalize the event detection problem as a multi-class classification problem. Given a sentence, for every token in that sentence, we want to predict if the current token is an event trigger: i.e, does it express some event in the pre-defined event set or not (Li et al., 2013b)? The current token along with its context in the sentence constitute an event trigger candidate or an example in multi-class classification terms. In order to prepare for the CNNs, we limit the context to a fixed window size by trimming longer sentences and padding shorter sentences with a special token when necessary. Let $2w + 1$ be the fixed window size, and $x = [x_{-w}, x_{-w+1}, \ldots, x_0, \ldots, x_{w-1}, x_w]$ be some trigger candidate where the current token is positioned in the middle of the window (token x_0). Before entering the CNNs, each token x_i is transformed into a real-valued vector by looking up the following embedding tables to capture different characteristics of the token:

- **Word Embedding Table** (initialized by some pre-trained word embeddings): to capture the hidden semantic and syntactic properties of the tokens (Collobert and Weston, 2008; Turian et al., 2010).

- **Position Embedding Table**: to embed the relative distance i of the token x_i to the current token x_0. In practice, we initialize this table randomly.

- **Entity Type Embedding Table**: If we further know the entity mentions and their entity types[2] in the sentence, we can also capture this information for each token by looking up the entity type embedding table (initialized randomly) using the entity type associated with each token. We employ the BIO annotation scheme to assign entity type labels to each token in the trigger candidate

[2]For convenience, when mentioning entities in this paper, we always include ACE timex and values.

using the heads of the entity mentions.

For each token x_i, the vectors obtained from the three look-ups above are concatenated into a single vector $\mathbf{x}_i$ to represent the token. As a result, the original event trigger x is transformed into a matrix $\mathbf{x} = [\mathbf{x}_{-w}, \mathbf{x}_{-w+1}, \ldots, \mathbf{x}_0, \ldots, \mathbf{x}_{w-1}, \mathbf{x}_w]$ of size $m_t \times (2w+1)$ (m_t is the dimensionality of the concatenated vectors of the tokens).

The matrix representation $\mathbf{x}$ is then passed through a convolution layer, a max pooling layer and a softmax at the end to perform classification (like (Kim, 2014; Kalchbrenner et al., 2014)). In the convolution layer, we have a set of feature maps (filters) $\{\mathbf{f}_1, \mathbf{f}_2, \ldots, \mathbf{f}_n\}$ for the convolution operation. Each feature map $\mathbf{f}_i$ corresponds to some window size k and can be essentially seen as a weight matrix of size $m_t \times k$. Figure 1 illustrates the proposed CNN.

The gradients are computed using back-propagation; regularization is implemented by a dropout (Kim, 2014; Hinton et al., 2012), and training is done via stochastic gradient descent with shuffled mini-batches and the AdaDelta update rule (Zeiler, 2012; Kim, 2014). During the training, we also optimize the weights of the three embedding tables at the same time to reach an effective state (Kim, 2014).

3 Experiments

3.1 Dataset, Hyperparameters and Resources

As the benefit of multiple window sizes in the convolution layer has been demonstrated in the previous work on sentence modeling (Kalchbrenner et al., 2014; Kim, 2014), in the experiments below, we use window sizes in the set {2, 3, 4, 5} to generate feature maps. We utilize 150 feature maps for each window size in this set. The window size for triggers is set to 31 while the dimensionality of the position embeddings and entity type embeddings is 50[3].We inherit the values for the other parameters from Kim (2014), i.e, the dropout rate $\rho = 0.5$, the mini-batch size = 50, the hyperparameter for the l_2 norms = 3. Finally, we employ the pre-trained word embeddings `word2vec` with 300 dimensions from Mikolov et al. (2013) for initialization.

We evaluate the presented CNN over the ACE 2005 corpus. For comparison purposes, we utilize the same test set with 40 newswire articles (672 sentences), the same development set with 30 other documents (836 sentences) and the same training set with the remaining 529 documents (14,849 sentences) as the previous studies on this dataset (Ji and Grishman, 2008; Liao and Grishman, 2010; Li et al., 2013b). The ACE 2005 corpus has 33 event subtypes that, along with one class "*None*" for the non-trigger tokens, constitutes a 34-class classification problem.

In order to evaluate the effectiveness of the position embeddings and the entity type embeddings, Table 1 reports the performance of the proposed CNN on the development set when these embeddings are either included or excluded from the systems. With the large margins of performance, it is very clear from the table that the position embeddings are crucial while the entity embeddings are also very useful for CNNs on ED.

Systems		P	R	F
-Entity Types	-Position	16.8	12.0	14.0
	+Position	75.0	63.0	**68.5**
+Entity Types	-Position	17.0	15.0	15.9
	+Position	75.6	66.4	**70.7**

Table 1: Performance on the Development Set.

For the experiments below, we examine the CNNs in two scenarios: excluding the entity type embeddings (CNN1) and including the entity type embeddings (CNN2). We always use position embeddings in these two scenarios.

3.2 Performance Comparison

The state-of-the-art systems for event detection on the ACE 2005 dataset have followed the traditional feature-based approach with rich hand-designed feature sets, and statistical classifiers such as MaxEnt and perceptron for structured prediction in a joint architecture (Hong et al., 2011; Li et al., 2013b). In this section, we compare the proposed CNNs with these state-of-the-art systems on the blind test set. Table 2 presents the overall performance of the systems with gold-standard entity mention and type information[4].

As we can see from the table, considering the systems that only use sentence level information, CNN1 significantly outperforms the MaxEnt classifier as well as the joint beam search with local features from Li et al. (2013b) (an improvement of 1.6% in F1 score), and performs comparably

[3]These values are chosen for their best performance on the development data.

[4]Entity mentions and types are used to introduce more features into the systems.

Methods	P	R	F
Sentence-level in Hong et al (2011)	67.6	53.5	59.7
MaxEnt with local features in Li et al. (2013b)	74.5	59.1	65.9
Joint beam search with local features in Li et al. (2013b)	73.7	59.3	65.7
Joint beam search with local and global features in Li et al. (2013b)	73.7	62.3	67.5
Cross-entity in Hong et al. (2011) †	72.9	64.3	68.3
CNN1: CNN without any external features	71.9	63.8	67.6
CNN2: CNN augmented with entity types	71.8	66.4	**69.0**

Table 2: Performance with Gold-Standard Entity Mentions and Types. † beyond sentence level.

with the joint beam search approach using both local and global features (Li et al., 2013b). This is remarkable since CNN1 does not require any external features[5], in contrast to the other feature-based systems that extensively rely on such external features to perform well. More interestingly, when the entity type information is incorporated into CNN1, we obtain CNN2 that still only needs sentence level information but achieves the state-of-the-art performance for this task (an improvement of 1.5% over the best system with only sentence level information (Li et al., 2013b)).

Except for CNN1, all the systems reported in Table 2 employ the gold-standard (perfect) entities mentions and types from manual annotation which might not be available in reality. Table 3 compares the performance of CNN1 and the feature-based systems in a more realistic setting, where entity mentions and types are acquired from an automatic high-performing name tagger and information extraction system (Li et al., 2013b). Note that CNN1 is eligible for this comparison as it does not utilize any external features, thus avoiding usage of the name tagger and the information extraction system to identify entity mentions and types.

3.3 Domain Adaptation Experiment

In this section, we aim to further compare the proposed CNNs with the feature-based systems under the domain adaptation setting for event detection.

The ultimate goal of domain adaptation research is to develop techniques taking training data in some *source domain* and learning models that can work well on *target domains*. The target domains are supposed to be so dissimilar from the source domain that the learning techniques would suffer from a significant performance loss when trained on the source domain and applied to the target domains. To make it clear, we address the unsupervised DA problem in this section, i.e no training data in the target domains (Blitzer et al., 2006; Plank and Moschitti, 2013). The fundamental reason for the performance loss of the feature-based systems on the target domains is twofold:

(i) The behavioral changes of features across domains: As domains differ, some features might be informative in the source domain but become less relevant in the target domains and vice versa.

(ii) The propagated errors of the pre-processing toolkits for lower-level tasks (POS tagging, name tagging, parsing etc) to extract features: These pre-processing toolkits are also known to degrade when shifted to target domains (Blitzer et al., 2006; Daumé III, 2007; McClosky et al., 2010), introducing noisy features into the systems for higher-level tasks in the target domains and eventually impairing the performance of these higher-level systems on the target domains.

For ED, we postulate that CNNs are more useful than the feature-based approach for DA for two reasons. First, rather than relying on the symbolic and concrete forms (i.e words, types etc) to construct features as the traditional feature-based systems (Ji and Grishman, 2008; Li et al., 2013b) do, CNNs automatically induce their features from word embeddings, the general distributed representation of words that is shared across domains. This helps CNNs mitigate the lexical sparsity, learn more general and effective feature representation for trigger candidates, and thus bridge the gap between domains. Second, as CNNs minimize the reliance on the supervised pre-processing toolkits for features, they can alleviate the error

[5]External features are the features generated from the supervised NLP modules and manual resources such as parsers, name tagger, entity mention extractors (either automatic or manual), gazetteers etc.

Methods	F
Sentence level in Ji and Grishman (2008)	59.7
MaxEnt with local features in Li et al. (2013b)	64.7
Joint beam search with local features in Li et al. (2013b)	63.7
Joint beam search with local and global features in Li et al. (2013b)	65.6
CNN1: CNN without any external features	**67.6**

Table 3: Performance with Predicted Entity Mentions and Types.

System	In-domain(bn+nw)			bc			cts			wl		
	P	R	F	P	R	F	P	R	F	P	R	F
MaxEnt	74.5	59.4	66.0	70.1	54.5	61.3	66.4	49.9	56.9	59.4	34.9	43.9
Joint beam search in Li et al. (2013b)												
Joint+Local	73.5	62.7	67.7	70.3	57.2	63.1	64.9	50.8	57.0	59.5	38.4	46.7
Joint+Local+Global	72.9	63.2	67.7	68.8	57.5	62.6	64.5	52.3	57.7	56.4	38.5	45.7
CNN1	70.9	64.0	67.3	71.0	61.9	66.1†	64.0	55.0	59.1	53.2	38.4	44.6
CNN2	69.2	67.0	**68.0**	70.2	65.2	**67.6**†	68.3	58.2	**62.8**†	54.8	42.0	**47.5**

Table 4: In-domain (first column) and Out-of-domain Performance (columns two to four). Cells marked with †designate CNN models that significantly outperform ($p < 0.05$) all the reported feature-based methods on the specified domain.

propagation and be more robust to domain shifts.

3.3.1 Dataset

We also do the experiments in this part over the ACE 2005 dataset but focus more on the difference between domains. The ACE 2005 corpus comes with 6 different domains: broadcast conversation (bc), broadcast news (bn), telephone conversation (cts), newswire (nw), usenet (un) and webblogs (wl). Following the common practice of domain adaptation research on this dataset (Plank and Moschitti, 2013; Nguyen and Grishman, 2014), we use **news** (the union of **bn** and **nw**) as the source domain and **bc**, **cts**, **wl** as three different target domains. We take half of bc as the development set and use the remaining data for testing. We note that the distribution of event subtypes and the vocabularies of the source and target domains are quite different (Plank and Moschitti, 2013).

3.3.2 Domain Adaptation Results

Table 4 presents the performance of five systems: the MaxEnt classifier with the local features from Li et al. (2013b) (called *MaxEnt*); the state-of-the-art joint beam search systems with: (i) only local features (called *Joint+Local*); and (ii) both local and global features (called *Joint+Local+Global*) in Li et al. (2013b) (the baseline systems); CNN1 and CNN2 via 5-fold cross validation. For each system, we train a model on the training set of the source domain and report the performance of this model on the test set of the source domain (in-domain performance) as well as the performance of the model on the three target domains bc, cts and wl (out-of-domain performance)[6].

The main conclusions from the table include: (i) The baseline systems *MaxEnt*, *Joint+Local*, *Joint+Local+Global* achieve high performance on the source domain, but degrade dramatically on the target domains due to the domain shifts. (ii) Comparing CNN1 and the baseline systems, we see that CNN1 performs comparably with the baseline systems on the source domain (in-domain performance) (as expected), substantially outperform the baseline systems on two of the three target domains (i.e, bc and cts), and is only less effective than the joint beam search approach on the wl domain; (iii) Finally and most importantly, we consistently achieve the best adaptation performance across all the target domains with CNN2 by only introducing entity type information into CNN1. In fact, CNN2 significantly outperforms the feature-based systems with $p < 0.05$ and large margins of about 5.0% on the domains bc and cts, clearly confirming our argument in Section 3.3 and testifying to the benefits of CNNs on DA for ED.

[6]The performance of the feature-based systems *MaxEnt*, *Joint+Local* and *Joint+Local+Global* are obtained from the actual systems in Li et al. (2013b).

4 Conclusion

We present a CNN for event detection that automatically learns effective feature representations from pre-trained word embeddings, position embeddings as well as entity type embeddings and reduces the error propagation. We conducted experiments to compare the proposed CNN with the state-of-the-art feature-based systems in both the general setting and the domain adaptation setting. The experimental results demonstrate the effectiveness as well as the robustness across domains of the CNN. In the future, our plans include: (i) to explore the joint approaches for event extraction with CNNs; (ii) and to investigate other neural network architectures for information extraction.

Acknowledgments

We would like to thank Qi Li for providing the performance of the feature-based systems on the domain adaptation experiments. Thank you to Yifan He, Kai Cao, and Xiang Li for useful discussions on the task as well as the anonymous reviewers for their valuable feedback.

References

John Blitzer, Ryan McDonald, and Fernando Pereira. 2006. *Domain Adaptation with Structural Correspondence Learning*. In Proceedings of EMNLP.

Ronan Collobert and Jason Weston. 2008. *A Unified Architecture for Natural Language Processing: Deep Neural Networks with Multitask Learning*. In Proceedings of ICML.

Ronan Collobert, Jason Weston, Léon Bottou, Michael Karlen, Koray Kavukcuoglu and Pavel Kuksa. 2011. *Natural Language Processing (Almost) from Scratch*. Journal of Machine Learning Research 12:24932537.

Hal Daumé III. 2007. *Frustratingly Easy Domain Adaptation*. In Proceedings of ACL.

Prashant Gupta and Heng Ji. 2009. *Predicting Unknown Time Arguments Based on Cross-Event Propagation*. In Proceedings of ACL-IJCNLP.

Geoffrey E. Hinton, Nitish Srivastava, Alex Krizhevsky, Ilya Sutskever, and Ruslan Salakhutdinov. 2012. *Improving Neural Networks by Preventing Co-Adaptation of Feature Detectors*. CoRR, abs/1207.0580.

Yu Hong, Jianfeng Zhang, Bin Ma, Jian-Min Yao, Guodong Zhou, and Qiaoming Zhu. 2011. *Using Cross-entity Inference to Improve Event Extraction*. In Proceedings of ACL.

Baotian Hu, Zhengdong Lu, Hang Li, Qingcai Chen. 2014. *Convolutional Neural Network Architectures for Matching Natural Language Sentences*. In Proceedings of NIPS.

Ruihong Huang and Ellen Riloff. 2012. *Modeling Textual Cohesion for Event Extraction*. In Proceedings of AAAI.

Heng Ji and Ralph Grishman. 2008. *Refining Event Extraction through Cross-Document Inference*. In Proceedings of ACL.

Nal Kalchbrenner, Edward Grefenstette and Phil Blunsom. 2014. *A Convolutional Neural Network for Modeling Sentences*. In Proceedings of ACL.

Yoon Kim. 2014. *Convolutional Neural Networks for Sentence Classification*. In Proceedings of EMNLP.

Yann LeCun, Léon Bottou, Yoshua Bengio and Patrick Haffner. 1988. *Gradient-based Learning Applied to Document Recognition*. In Proceedings of the IEEE, 86(11):22782324.

Peifeng Li, Qiaoming Zhu, and Guodong Zhou. 2013a. *Argument Inference from Relevant Event Mentions in Chinese Argument Extraction*. In Proceedings of ACL.

Qi Li, Heng Ji, and Liang Huang. 2013b. *Joint Event Extraction via Structured Prediction with Global Features*. In Proceedings of ACL.

Shasha Liao and Ralph Grishman. 2010. *Using Document Level Cross-event Inference to Improve Event Extraction*. In Proceedings of ACL.

Shasha Liao and Ralph Grishman. 2011. *Acquiring Topic Features to Improve Event Extraction: in Preselected and Balanced Collections*. In Proceedings RANLP.

David McClosky, Eugene Charniak, and Mark Johnson. 2010. *Automatic Domain Adaptation for Parsing*. In Proceedings of HLT-NAACL.

David McClosky, Mihai Surdeanu, and Chris Manning. 2011. *Event Extraction as Dependency Parsing*. In Proceedings of ACL-HLT.

Tomas Mikolov, Ilya Sutskever, Kai Chen, Greg Corrado, and Jeffrey Dean. 2013. *Distributed Representations of Words and Phrases and their Compositionality*. In Proceedings of NIPS.

Thien Huu Nguyen and Ralph Grishman. 2014. *Employing Word Representations and Regularization for Domain Adaptation of Relation Extraction*. In Proceedings of ACL.

Thien Huu Nguyen and Ralph Grishman. 2015. *Relation Extraction: Perspective from Convolutional Neural Networks*. In Proceedings of the NAACL Workshop on Vector Space Modeling for NLP (VSM).

Siddharth Patwardhan and Ellen Rilof. 2009. *A Unified Model of Phrasal and Sentential Evidence for Information Extraction*. In Proceedings of EMNLP.

Barbara Plank and Alessandro Moschitti. 2013. *Embedding Semantic Similarity in Tree Kernels for Domain Adaptation of Relation Extraction*. In Proceedings of ACL.

Sebastian Riedel and Andrew McCallum. 2011. *Fast and Robust Joint Models for Biomedical Event Extraction*. In Proceedings of EMNLP.

Sebastian Riedel and Andrew McCallum. 2011. *Robust Biomedical Event Extraction with Dual Decomposition and Minimal Domain Adaptation*. In Proceedings of the BioNLP Shared Task 2011 Workshop.

Yelong Shen, Xiaodong He, Jianfeng Gao, Li Deng and Grégoire Mesnil. 2014. *Learning Semantic Representations Using Convolutional Neural Networks for Web Search*. In Proceedings of WWW.

Joseph Turian, Lev Ratinov, and Yoshua Bengio. 2010. *Word Representations: A Simple and General Method for Semi-supervised Learning*. In Proceedings of ACL.

Deepak Venugopal, Chen Chen, Vibhav Gogate and Vincent Ng. 2014. *Relieving the Computational Bottleneck: Joint Inference for Event Extraction with High-Dimensional Features*. In Proceedings of EMNLP.

Wen-tau Yih, Xiaodong He, and Christopher Meek. 2014. *Semantic Parsing for Single-Relation Question Answering*. In Proceedings of ACL.

Matthew D. Zeiler. 2012. *ADADELTA: An Adaptive Learning Rate Method*. CoRR, abs/1212.5701.

Daojian Zeng, Kang Liu, Siwei Lai, Guangyou Zhou and Jun Zhao. 2014. *Relation Classification via Convolutional Deep Neural Network*. In Proceedings of COLING.

Seed-Based Event Trigger Labeling: How far can event descriptions get us?

Ofer Bronstein[1], **Ido Dagan**[1], **Qi Li**[2], **Heng Ji**[2], **Anette Frank**[3,4]
[1] Computer Science Department, Bar-Ilan University
[2] Department of Computer Science, Rensselaer Polytechnic Institute
[3] Department of Computational Linguistics, Heidelberg University
[4]Research Training Group AIPHES, Dept. of Computational Linguistics, Heidelberg University
oferbr@gmail.com dagan@cs.biu.ac.il
{liq7,jih}@rpi.edu frank@cl.uni-heidelberg.de

Abstract

The task of event trigger labeling is typically addressed in the standard supervised setting: triggers for *each* target event type are annotated as training data, based on annotation guidelines. We propose an alternative approach, which takes the example trigger terms mentioned in the guidelines as seeds, and then applies an event-independent similarity-based classifier for trigger labeling. This way we can skip manual annotation for new event types, while requiring only minimal annotated training data for few example events at system setup. Our method is evaluated on the ACE-2005 dataset, achieving 5.7% F_1 improvement over a state-of-the-art supervised system which uses the full training data.

1 Introduction

Event trigger labeling is the task of identifying the main word tokens that express mentions of prespecified event types in running text. For example, in "20 people were *wounded* in Tuesday's airport *blast*", "*wounded*" is a trigger of an *Injure* event and "*blast*" is a trigger of an *Attack*. The task both detects trigger tokens and classifies them to appropriate event types. While this task is often a component within the broader *event extraction* task, labeling both triggers and arguments, this paper focuses on trigger labeling.

Most state-of-the-art event trigger labeling approaches (Ji and Grishman, 2008; Liao and Grishman, 2010b; Hong et al., 2011; Li et al., 2013) follow the standard supervised learning paradigm. For each event type, experts first write annotation guidelines. Then, annotators follow them to label event triggers in a large dataset. Finally, a classifier is trained over the annotated triggers to label the target events.

The supervised paradigm requires major human efforts both in producing high-quality guidelines and in dataset annotation for each new event type. Given the rich information embedded in the guidelines, we raise in this paper the following research question: how well can we perform by leveraging *only* the lexical knowledge already available in quality guidelines for *new* event types, without requiring annotated training data for them?

To address this question, we propose a seed-based approach for the trigger labeling task (Section 2). Given the description for a new event type, which contains some examples of triggers, we first collect these triggers into a list of *seeds*. Then, at the labeling phase, we consider each text token as a candidate for a trigger and assess its similarity to the seed list. In the above example, given seeds such as "*explosion*" and "*fire*" for the *Attack* event type, we identify that the candidate token "*blast*" is a hyponym of "*explosion*" and synonym of "*fire*" and infer that "*blast*" is a likely *Attack* trigger.

In our method, such similarity indicators are encoded as a small set of event-independent classification features, based on lexical matches and external resources like WordNet. Using event-independent features allows us to train the system only once, at system setup phase, requiring annotated triggers in a training set for just a few preselected event types. Then, whenever a new event type is introduced for labeling, we only need to collect a seed list for it from its description, and provide it as input to the system.

We developed a seed-based system (Section 3), based on a state-of-the-art fully-supervised event extraction system (Li et al., 2013). When evaluated on the ACE-2005 dataset,[1] our system outperforms the fully-supervised one (Section 4), even though we don't utilize any annotated triggers of the test events during the labeling phase, and only

[1]http://projects.ldc.upenn.edu/ace

Proceedings of the 53rd Annual Meeting of the Association for Computational Linguistics and the 7th International Joint Conference on Natural Language Processing (Short Papers), pages 372–376,
Beijing, China, July 26-31, 2015.

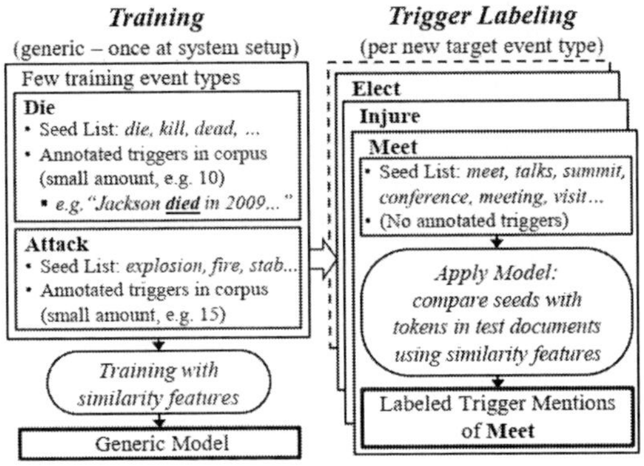

Figure 1: Flow of the seed-based approach

use the seed triggers appearing in the ACE annotation guidelines. This result contributes to the broader line of research on avoiding or reducing annotation cost in information extraction (Section 5). In particular, it suggests the potential utility of the seed-based approach in scenarios where manual annotation per each new event is too costly.

2 Seed-Based Problem Setup

This section describes our setup, as graphically illustrated in Figure 1.

Similarly to the supervised setting, our approach assumes that whenever a new event type is defined as target, an informative *event description* should be written for it. As a prominent example, we consider Section 5 of the ACE-2005 event annotation guidelines,[2] which provides a description for each event type. The description includes a short verbal specification plus several illustrating example sentences with marked triggers, spanning on average less than a page per event type.

As event descriptions specify the intended event scope, they inherently include representative examples for event triggers. For instance, the ACE-2005 guidelines include: *"MEET Events include talks, summits, conferences, meetings, visits,... "*, followed by an example: *"Bush and Putin met this week... "*. We thus collect triggers mentioned in each event description into a *seed list* for the event type, which is provided as input to our trigger labeling method. Triggers from the above quoted sentences are hence included in the *Meet* seed list, shown in Figure 1.

As mentioned in the Introduction, our method (Section 3) is based on event-independent features that identify similarities between a candidate trigger and a given seed list. To train such generic features, our training requires several arbitrary *training event types*, with a small amount of annotated triggers, from which it learns weights for the features. In our evaluation (Section 4) we use 5 training event types, with a total of 30 annotated trigger mentions (compared to roughly 5000 used by the baseline fully-supervised system). In this setting, the training phase is required only once during system setup, while no further training is required for each new target event type.

In summary, our setup requires: (1) a seed list per target event type; (2) a small number of annotated triggers for few training event types, along with their seed lists (at system setup).

3 Method

This section describes the method we designed to implement the *seed-based* approach. To assess our approach, we compare it (Section 4) with the common *fully-supervised* approach, which requires annotated triggers for each target event type. Therefore, we implemented our system by adapting the state-of-the-art fully-supervised event extraction system of Li et al. (2013), modifying mechanisms relevant for features and for trigger labels, as described below. Hence the systems are comparable with respect to using the same preprocessing and machine learning infrastructure.

3.1 The Fully-Supervised System

The event extraction system of Li et al. (2013) labels triggers and their arguments for a set of target event types $\mathcal{L}$, for which annotated training documents are provided. The system utilizes a structured perceptron with beam search (Collins and Roark, 2004; Huang et al., 2012). To label triggers, the system scans each sentence x, and creates candidate assignments y, that for each token x_i assign each possible label $y_i \in \mathcal{L} \cup \{\perp\}$ ($\perp$ meaning x_i is not a trigger at all). The score of an assignment (x_i, y_i) is calculated as $\mathbf{w} \cdot \mathbf{f}$, where f is the binary feature vector calculated for (x_i, y_i), and w is the learned feature weight vector.

The classifier's features capture various properties of x_i and its context, such as its unigram and its containing bigrams. These features are highly lexicalized, resulting in a very large feature space. Additionally, each feature is replicated and paired with each label y_i, allowing the system to learn

[2] https://www.ldc.upenn.edu/sites/www.ldc.upenn.edu/files/english-events-guidelines-v5.4.3.pdf

Feature	Description
Same Lemma	Do the candidate token and a seed share the same lemma?
Synonym	Is a seed a WN synonym of the candidate token?
Hypernym	Is a seed a WN hypernym or instance-hypernym of the candidate token?
Similarity Relations	Does one of these WN relations hold between a seed and a candidate token? Synonym, Hypernym, Instance Hypernym, Part Holonym, Member Holonym, Substance Meronym, Entailment

Table 1: Similarity features using WordNet (WN). For the last two features we allow up to 2 levels of transitivity (e.g. hypernym of hypernym), and consider also derivations of candidate tokens.

different weights for different labels, e.g., feature *(Unigram:"visited", Meet)* will have a different weight than *(Unigram:"visited", Attack)*.

3.2 The Seed-Based System

To implement the seed-based approach for trigger labeling, we adapt only the trigger classification part in the Li et al. (2013) fully-supervised system, ignoring arguments. Given a set of new target event types $\mathcal{T}$ we classify every test sentence once for each event type $t \in \mathcal{T}$. Hence, when classifying a sentence for t, the labeling of each token x_i is binary, where $y_i \in \{\top, \bot\}$ marks whether x_i is a trigger of type t ($\top$) or not ($\bot$). For instance x_i="visited" labeled as $\top$ when classifying for t=*Meet*, means x_i is labeled as a *Meet* trigger. To score the binary label assignment (x_i, y_i), we use a small set of features that assess the similarity between x_i and t's given seed list.

We implement our approach with a basic set of binary features (Table 1), which are turned on if similarity is found for at least one seed in the list. We use a single knowledge resource (WordNet (Fellbaum, 1998)) for expansion.[3] As in the fully-supervised system, each feature is replicated for each label in $\{\top, \bot\}$, learning separately how well a feature can predict a trigger ($\top$) and a non-trigger ($\bot$). As labels are event-independent, features are event-independent as well, and their weights can be learned generically (Figure 1).

Since we label each token independently for each event type t, multiple labels may be assigned to the same token. If a single-label setting is required, standard techniques can be applied, such as choosing a single random label, or the highest scoring one.

[3]This could be potentially extended, e.g. with paraphrase databases, like (Ganitkevitch et al., 2013).

4 Evaluation

4.1 Setting

We evaluate our seed-based approach (Section 2) in comparison to the fully-supervised approach implemented by Li et al. (2013) (Section 3). To maintain comparability, we use the ACE-2005 documents with the same split as in (Ji and Grishman, 2008; Liao and Grishman, 2010b; Li et al., 2013) to 40 test documents and 559 training documents. However, some evaluation settings differ: Li et al. (2013) train a multi-class model for all 33 ACE-2005 event types, and classify all tokens in the test documents into these event types. Our approach, on the other hand, trains an event-independent binary classifier, while testing on new event types that are different from those utilized for training. We next describe how this setup is addressed in our evaluation.

Per-Event Classification To label the test documents to all 33 event types, we classify each token in the test documents once for each *test event type*.[4]

Training Event Types When we label for a test event type t, we use a model that was trained on different pre-selected training event types. Since we need to label for all event types, we cannot use the same model for testing them all, since then the event types used to train this model could not be tested. Thus, for each t we use a model trained on 5 randomly chosen training event types, different than t.[5] Additionally, to avoid a bias caused by a particular random choice, we build 10 different models, each time choosing a different set of 5 training event types. Then, we label the test documents for t 10 times, once by each model. When measuring performance we compute the average of these 10 runs for each t, as well as the variance within these runs.

Annotated Triggers Training event types require annotated triggers from the training documents. To maintain consistency between different sets of training event types, we use a fixed total of 30 annotated trigger tokens for each set of

[4]To maintain comparability with the single-label classification results of Li et al. (2013), we randomly choose a single label for our classification in the few (7) cases where it yielded two labels for the same token.

[5]Li et al. (2013) internally split the training documents to "train" and "dev". Accordingly, our training event types are split to 3 "train" events and 2 "dev" events (with annotations taken from the "train" and "dev" documents respectively).

	Micro-Avg. (%)			*Var*
	Prec	*Rec*	F_1	*Avg*
Seed-Based	**80.6**	**67.1**	**73.2**	0.04
Li et al. (2013)	73.7	62.3	67.5	-
Ji and Grishman (2008)	67.6	53.5	59.7	-

Table 2: Seed-based performance compared to fully-supervised systems, plus average F_1 variance (%) over the 10 test runs per test event type.

training event types. The amounts of 5 training event types and 30 annotated triggers were chosen to demonstrate that such small amounts, requiring little manual effort at system setup, yield high performance (larger training didn't improve results, possibly due to the small number of features).

Seed Lists To build the seed lists for all event types, we manually extracted all triggers mentioned in Section 5 of the ACE-2005 guidelines, as described in Section 2.[6] This resulted in lists of 4.2 seeds per event type on average, which is fairly small. For comparison, each event type has an average of 46 distinct trigger terms in the training corpus used by the fully-supervised method.

4.2 Results

Table 2 shows our system's precision, recall and F_1,[7] and the average variance of F_1 within the 10 runs of each test event type. The very low variance indicates that the system's performance does not depend much on the choice of training event types.

We compare our system's performance to the published trigger classification results of the baseline system of (Li et al., 2013) (its globally optimized run, when labeling both triggers and arguments). We also compare to the sentence-level system in (Ji and Grishman, 2008) which uses the same dataset split. Our system outperforms the fully-supervised baseline by 5.7% F_1, which is statistically significant (two-tailed Wilcoxon test, $p < 0.05$). This shows that there is no performance hit for the seed-based method on this dataset, even though it does not require any annotated data for new tested events, thus saving costly annotation efforts.

[6]Our seed lists are publicly available for download at: `https://goo.gl/sErDW9`

[7]We report micro-average as typical for this task. Macro-average results are a few points lower for our system and for the system of Li et al. (2013), maintaining similar relative difference.

5 Related Work

Our work contributes to the broader research direction of reducing annotation for information extraction. One such IE paradigm, including Preemptive IE (Shinyama and Sekine, 2006), On-demand IE (Sekine, 2006; Sekine and Oda, 2007) and Open IE (Etzioni et al., 2005; Banko et al., 2007; Banko et al., 2008), focuses on unsupervised relation and event discovery. We, on the other hand, follow the same goal as fully-supervised systems in targeting pre-specified event types, but aim at minimal annotation cost.

Bootstrapping methods (such as (Yangarber et al., 2000; Agichtein and Gravano, 2000; Riloff, 1996; Greenwood and Stevenson, 2006; Liao and Grishman, 2010a; Stevenson and Greenwood, 2005; Huang and Riloff, 2012)) have been widely applied in IE. Most work started from a small set of seed patterns, and repeatedly expanded them from unlabeled corpora. Relying on unlabeled data, bootstrapping methods are scalable but tend to produce worse results (Liao and Grishman, 2010a) than supervised models due to semantic drift (Curran et al., 2007). Our method can be seen complementary to bootstrapping frameworks, since we exploit manually crafted linguistic resources which are more accurate but may not cover all domains and languages.

Our approach is perhaps closest to (Roth et al., 2009). They addressed a different IE task – relation extraction, by recognizing entailment between candidate relation mentions and seed patterns. While they exploited a supervised recognizing textual entailment (RTE) system, we show that using only simple WordNet-based similarity features and minimal training yields relatively high performance in event trigger labeling.

6 Conclusions and Future Work

In this paper we show that by utilizing the information embedded in annotation guidelines and lexical resources, we can skip manual annotation for new event types. As we match performance of a state-of-the-art fully-supervised system over the ACE-2005 benchmark (and even surpass it), we offer our approach as an appealing way of reducing annotation effort while preserving result quality. Future research may explore additional features and knowledge resources, investigate alternative approaches for creating effective seed lists, and extend our approach to argument labeling.

Acknowledgments

This work was partially supported by the European Commission (project EXCITEMENT, FP7 ICT-287923), and the U.S. DARPA DEFT Program No. FA8750-13-2-0041, ARL NS-CTA No. W911NF-09-2-0053, NSF CAREER IIS-1523198.

References

Eugene Agichtein and Luis Gravano. 2000. *Snowball*: extracting relations from large plain-text collections. In *Proc. Fifth ACM International Conference on Digital Libraries*, pages 85–94.

M. Banko, M. Cafarella, S. Soderland, M. Broadhead, and O. Etzioni. 2007. Open information extraction for the web. In *Proc. IJCAI*, pages 2670–2676.

M. Banko, O. Etzioni, and T. Center. 2008. The tradeoffs between open and traditional relation extraction. In *Proc. ACL*, pages 28–36.

Michael Collins and Brian Roark. 2004. Incremental parsing with the perceptron algorithm. In *Proc. ACL*, pages 111–118.

James R Curran, Tara Murphy, and Bernhard Scholz. 2007. Minimising semantic drift with mutual exclusion bootstrapping. In *Proc. PACLING*, pages 172–180.

O. Etzioni, M. Cafarella, D. Downey, A. Popescu, T. Shaked, S. Soderland, D. Weld, and A. Yates. 2005. Unsupervised named-entity extraction from the web: An experimental study. *Artificial Intelligence*, 165:91–134.

Christiane Fellbaum, editor. 1998. *WordNet: An Electronic Lexical Database*. The MIT Press.

Juri Ganitkevitch, Benjamin Van Durme, and Chris Callison-Burch. 2013. PPDB: The paraphrase database. In *Proc. NAACL-HLT*, pages 758–764.

Mark A. Greenwood and Mark Stevenson. 2006. Improving semi-supervised acquisition of relation extraction patterns. In *Proc. Workshop on Information Extraction Beyond The Document*, pages 29–35.

Yu Hong, Jianfeng Zhang, Bin Ma, Jian-Min Yao, Guodong Zhou, and Qiaoming Zhu. 2011. Using cross-entity inference to improve event extraction. In *Proc. ACL*, pages 1127–1136.

Ruihong Huang and Ellen Riloff. 2012. Bootstrapped training of event extraction classifiers. In *Proc. ACL*, pages 286–295.

Liang Huang, Suphan Fayong, and Yang Guo. 2012. Structured perceptron with inexact search. In *Proc. NAACL*, pages 142–151.

Heng Ji and Ralph Grishman. 2008. Refining event extraction through cross-document inference. In *Proc. ACL*, pages 254–262.

Qi Li, Heng Ji, and Liang Huang. 2013. Joint event extraction via structured prediction with global features. In *Proc. ACL*, pages 73–82.

Shasha Liao and Ralph Grishman. 2010a. Filtered ranking for bootstrapping in event extraction. In *Proc. COLING*, pages 680–688.

Shasha Liao and Ralph Grishman. 2010b. Using document level cross-event inference to improve event extraction. In *Proc. ACL*, pages 789–797.

Ellen Riloff. 1996. Automatically generating extraction patterns from untagged text. In *Proc. AAAI*, pages 1044–1049.

Dan Roth, Mark Sammons, and V. G. Vinod Vydiswaran. 2009. A framework for entailed relation recognition. In *Proc. ACL-IJCNLP Short Papers*, pages 57–60.

Satoshi Sekine and Akira Oda. 2007. System demonstration of on-demand information extraction. In *Proc. ACL Demo and Poster Sessions*, pages 17–20.

Satoshi Sekine. 2006. On-demand information extraction. In *Proc. COLING-ACL Poster Sessions*, pages 731–738.

Yusuke Shinyama and Satoshi Sekine. 2006. Preemptive information extraction using unrestricted relation discovery. In *Proc. NAACL*, pages 304–311.

Mark Stevenson and Mark A. Greenwood. 2005. A semantic approach to IE pattern induction. In *Proc. ACL*, pages 379–386.

Roman Yangarber, Ralph Grishman, Pasi Tapanainen, and Silja Huttunen. 2000. Automatic acquisition of domain knowledge for information extraction. In *Proc. COLING*, pages 940–946.

An Empirical Study of Chinese Name Matching and Applications

Nanyun Peng[1] and **Mo Yu**[2] and **Mark Dredze**[1]
[1]Human Language Technology Center of Excellence
Center for Language and Speech Processing
Johns Hopkins University, Baltimore, MD, 21218
[2]Machine Intelligence and Translation Lab
Harbin Institute of Technology, Harbin, China
npeng1@jhu.edu, gflfof@gmail.com, mdredze@cs.jhu.edu

Abstract

Methods for name matching, an important component to support downstream tasks such as entity linking and entity clustering, have focused on alphabetic languages, primarily English. In contrast, logogram languages such as Chinese remain untested. We evaluate methods for name matching in Chinese, including both string matching and learning approaches. Our approach, based on new representations for Chinese, improves both name matching and a downstream entity clustering task.

1 Introduction

A key technique in entity disambiguation is name matching: determining if two mention strings could refer to the same entity. The challenge of name matching lies in name variation, which can be attributed to many factors: nicknames, aliases, acronyms, and differences in transliteration, among others. In light of these issues, exact string match can lead to poor results. Numerous downstream tasks benefit from improved name matching: entity coreference (Strube et al., 2002), name transliteration (Knight and Graehl, 1998), identifying names for mining paraphrases (Barzilay and Lee, 2003), entity linking (Rao et al., 2013) and entity clustering (Green et al., 2012).

As a result, there have been numerous proposed name matching methods (Cohen et al., 2003), with a focus on person names. Despite extensive exploration of this task, most work has focused on Indo-European languages in general and English in particular. These languages use alphabets as representations of written language. In contrast, other languages use logograms, which represent a word or morpheme, the most popular being Chinese which uses hanzi (汉字). This presents challenges for name matching: a small number of hanzi represent an entire name and there are tens of thousands of hanzi in use. Current methods remain largely untested in this setting, despite downstream tasks in Chinese that rely on name matching (Chen et al., 2010; Cassidy et al., 2011). Martschat et al. (2012) point out errors in coreference resolution due to Chinese name matching errors, which suggests that downstream tasks can benefit from improvements in Chinese name matching techniques.

This paper presents an analysis of new and existing approaches to name matching in Chinese. The goal is to determine whether two Chinese strings can refer to the same entity (person, organization, location) based on the strings alone. The more general task of entity coreference (Soon et al., 2001), or entity clustering, includes the context of the mentions in determining coreference. In contrast, standalone name matching modules are context independent (Andrews et al., 2012; Green et al., 2012). In addition to showing name matching improvements on newly developed datasets of matched Chinese name pairs, we show improvements in a downstream Chinese entity clustering task by using our improved name matching system. We call our name matching tool Mingpipe, a Python package that can be used as a standalone tool or integrated within a larger system. We release Mingpipe as well as several datasets to support further work on this task.[1]

2 Name Matching Methods

Name matching originated as part of research into record linkage in databases. Initial work focused

[1]The code and data for this paper are available at: https://github.com/hltcoe/mingpipe

Proceedings of the 53rd Annual Meeting of the Association for Computational Linguistics and the 7th International Joint Conference on Natural Language Processing (Short Papers), pages 377–383,
Beijing, China, July 26-31, 2015.

on string matching techniques. This work can be organized into three major categories: 1) Phonetic matching methods, e.g. Soundex (Holmes and McCabe, 2002), double Metaphone (Philips, 2000) etc.; 2) Edit-distance based measures, e.g. Levenshtein distance (Levenshtein, 1966), Jaro-Winkler (Porter et al., 1997; Winkler, 1999), and 3) Token-based similarity, e.g. soft TF-IDF (Bilenko et al., 2003). Analyses comparing these approaches have not found consistent improvements of one method over another (Cohen et al., 2003; Christen, 2006). More recent work has focused on learning a string matching model on name pairs, such as probabilistic noisy channel models (Sukharev et al., 2014; Bilenko et al., 2003). The advantage of trained models is that, with sufficient training data, they can be tuned for specific tasks.

While many NLP tasks rely on name matching, research on name matching techniques themselves has not been a major focus within the NLP community. Most downstream NLP systems have simply employed a static edit distance module to decide whether two names can be matched (Chen et al., 2010; Cassidy et al., 2011; Martschat et al., 2012). An exception is work on training finite state transducers for edit distance metrics (Ristad and Yianilos, 1998; Bouchard-Côté et al., 2008; Dreyer et al., 2008; Cotterell et al., 2014). More recently, Andrews et al. (2012) presented a phylogenetic model of string variation using transducers that applies to pairs of names string (supervised) and unpaired collections (unsupervised).

Beyond name matching in a single language, several papers have considered cross lingual name matching, where name strings are drawn from two different languages, such as matching Arabic names (El-Shishtawy, 2013) with English (Freeman et al., 2006; Green et al., 2012). Additionally, name matching has been used as a component in cross language entity linking (McNamee et al., 2011a; McNamee et al., 2011b) and cross lingual entity clustering (Green et al., 2012). However, little work has focused on logograms, with the exception of Cheng et al. (2011). As we will demonstrate in § 3, there are special challenges caused by the logogram nature of Chinese. We believe this is the first evaluation of Chinese name matching.

3 Challenges

Numerous factors cause name variations, including abbreviations, morphological derivations, historical sound or spelling change, loanword formation, translation, transliteration, or transcription error (Andrews et al., 2012). In addition to all the above factors, Chinese name matching presents unique challenges (Table 1):

Examples	Notes
许历农 v.s. 許歷農	simplified v.s. traditional
東盟 v.s. 东南亚国家联盟	Abbreviation and traditional v.s. simplified
亚的斯亚贝巴 v.s. 阿迪斯阿貝巴 / iʌ·ti·si·iʌ·bei·bʌ / v.s. / ʌ·ti·si·ʌ·bei·bʌ /	Transliteration of Addis Ababa in Mainland and Taiwan. Different hanzi, similar pronunciations.
佛罗伦萨 v.s. 翡冷翠 / fo·luo·luən·sʌ / v.s. / fei·lɛŋ·tsʰɵʏ /	Transliteration of Florence in Mainland and Hong Kong. Different writing and dialects.
鲁弗斯·汉弗莱 v.s. 韓魯弗 / *lu·fu·sɯ·xan·fu·laɪ* / v.s. / xan·lu·fu /	Transliteration of Humphrey Rufus in Mainland and Hong Kong. The first uses a literal transliteration, while the second does not. Both reverse the name order (consistent with Chinese names) and change the surname to sound Chinese.

Table 1: Challenges in Chinese name matching.

- There are more than 50k Chinese characters. This can create a large number of parameters in character edit models, which can complicate parameter estimation.

- Chinese characters represent morphemes, not sounds. Many characters can share a single pronunciation[2], and many characters have similar sounds[3]. This causes typos (mistaking characters with the same pronunciation) and introduces variability in transliteration (different characters chosen to represent the same sound).

- Chinese has two writing systems (simplified, traditional) and two major dialects (Mandarin, Cantonese), with different pairings in different regions (see Table 2 for the three dominant regional combinations.) This has a significant impact on loanwords and transliterations.

[2]486 characters are pronounced / *tɕi* / (regardless of tone).

[3]e.g. 庄 and 张 (different orthography) are pronounced similar (/*tʂuaŋ*/ and /*tʂaŋ* /).

Region	Writing System	Dialect
Hong Kong	Traditional	Cantonese
Mainland	Simplified	Mandarin
Taiwan	Traditional	Mandarin

Table 2: Regional variations for Chinese writing and dialect.

4 Methods

We evaluate several name matching methods, representative of the major approaches to name matching described above.

String Matching We consider two common string matching algorithms: Levenshtein and Jaro-Winkler. However, because of the issues mentioned above we expect these to perform poorly when applied to Chinese strings. We consider several transformations to improve these methods.

First, we map all strings to a single writing system: simplified. This is straightforward since traditional Chinese characters have a many-to-one mapping to simplified characters. Second, we consider a pronunciation based representation. We convert characters to pinyin[4], the official phonetic system (and ISO standard) for transcribing Mandarin pronunciations into the Latin alphabet. While pinyin is a common representation used in Chinese entity disambiguation work (Feng et al., 2004; Jiang et al., 2007), the pinyin for an entire entity is typically concatenated and treated as a single string ("string-pinyin"). However, the pinyin string itself has internal structure that may be useful for name matching. We consider two new pinyin representations. Since each Chinese character corresponds to a pinyin, we take each pinyin as a token corresponding to the Chinese character. We call this "character-pinyin". Additionally, every Mandarin syllable (represented by a pinyin) can be spelled with a combination of an initial and a final segment. Therefore, we split each pinyin token further into the initial and final segment. We call this "segmented-pinyin"[5].

Transducers We next consider methods that can be trained on available Chinese name pairs. Transducers are common choices for learning edit distance metrics for strings, and they perform better than string similarity (Ristad and Yianilos, 1998; Andrews et al., 2012; Cotterell et al., 2014). We use the probabilistic transducer of Cotterell et al. (2014) to learn a stochastic edit distance. The model represent the conditional probability $p(y|x;\theta)$, where y is a generated string based on editing x according to parameters θ. At each position x_i, one of four actions (copy, substitute, insert, delete) are taken to generate character y_j. The probability of each action depends on the string to the left of x_i ($x_{(i-N_1):i}$), the string to the right of x_i ($x_{i:(i+N_2)}$), and generated string to the left of y_j ($y_{(j-N_3):j}$). The variables N_1, N_2, N_3 are the context size. Note that characters to the right of y_j are excluded as they are not yet generated. Training maximizes the observed data log-likelihood and EM is used to marginalize over the latent edit actions. Since the large number of Chinese characters make parameter estimation prohibitive, we only train transducers on the three pinyin representations: string-pinyin (28 characters), character-pinyin (384 characters), segmented-pinyin (59 characters).

Name Matching as Classification An alternate learning formulation considers name matching as a classification task (Mayfield et al., 2009; Zhang et al., 2010; Green et al., 2012). Each string pair is an instance: a positive classification means that two strings can refer to the same name. This allows for arbitrary and global features of the two strings. We use an SVM with a linear kernel.

To learn possible edit rules for Chinese names we add features for pairs of n-grams. For each string, we extract all n-grams (n=1,2,3) and align n-grams between strings using the Hungarian algorithm.[6] Features correspond to the aligned n-gram pairs, as well as the unaligned n-grams. To reduce the number of parameters, we only include features which appear in positive training examples. These features are generated for two string representations: the simplified Chinese string (**simplified n-grams**) and a pinyin representation (**pinyin n-grams**), so that we can incorporate both orthographic features and phonetic features. We separately select the best performing pinyin representation (string-pinyin, character-pinyin, segmented-pinyin) on development data

[4]Hong Kong has a romanization scheme more suitable for Cantonese, but we found no improvements over using pinyin. Therefore, for simplicity we use pinyin throughout.

[5]For example, the pinyin for 张 is segmented into */ zh /* and */ ang /*.

[6]We found this performed much better than directly aligning characters or tokens. We also tried n-gram TF-IDF cosine similarity, but it degraded results (Cohen et al., 2003).

Feature Type	Number of Features
Simplified n-grams	~10k
Pinyin n-grams	~9k
Jaccard similarity	6 × 10
TF-IDF similarity	2 × 10
Levenshtein distance	2 × 10
Other	7

Table 3: Features for SVM learning.

for each dataset.

We measure **Jaccard similarity** between the two strings separately for 1,2,3-grams for each string representation. An additional feature indicates no n-gram overlap. The best performing **Levenshtein** distance metric is included as a feature. Finally, we include **other** features for several name properties: the difference in character length and two indicators as to whether the first character of the two strings match and if its a common Chinese last name. Real valued features are binarized.

Table 3 lists the feature templates we used in our SVM model and the corresponding number of features.

5 Experiments

5.1 Dataset

We constructed two datasets from Wikipedia.

REDIRECT: We extracted webpage redirects from Chinese Wikipedia pages that correspond to entities (person, organization, location); the page type is indicated in the page's metadata. Redirect links indicate queries that all lead to the same page, such as "Barack Hussein Obama" and "Barack Obama". To remove redirects that are not entities (e.g. "44th president") we removed entries that contain numerals and Latin characters, as well as names that contain certain keywords.[7] The final dataset contains 13,730 pairs of person names, 10,686 organizations and 5,152 locations, divided into $\frac{3}{5}$ train, $\frac{1}{5}$ development and $\frac{1}{5}$ test.

NAME GROUPS: Chinese Wikipedia contains a handcrafted mapping between the entity name and various transliterations,[8] including for Mainland, Hong Kong and Taiwan. We created two datasets: Mainland-Hong Kong (1288 people pairs, 357 locations, 177 organizations), and Mainland-Taiwan (1500 people, 439 locations, 112 organizations). Data proportions are split as in REDIRECT.

[7]Entries that contain 列表(list), 代表(representative) , 运动 (movement), 问题 (issue) and 维基 (wikipedia).

[8]http://zh.wikipedia.org/wiki/Template:CGroup

Method	Character	prec@1	prec@3	MRR
Levenshtein	original	0.773	0.838	0.821
	simplified	0.816	0.872	0.856
	string-pinyin	0.743	0.844	0.811
	character-pinyin	**0.824**	**0.885**	**0.866**
	segment-pinyin	0.797	0.877	0.849
Jaro-Winkler	original	0.690	0.792	0.767
	simplified	0.741	0.821	0.803
	string-pinyin	0.741	0.818	0.800
	character-pinyin	**0.751**	**0.831**	**0.813**
	segment-pinyin	0.753	0.821	0.808

Table 4: String matching on development data.

5.2 Evaluation

We evaluated performance on a ranking task (the setting of Andrews et al. (2012)). In each instance, the algorithm was given a query and a set of 11 names from which to select the best match. The 11 names included a matching name as well as 10 other names with some character overlap with the query that are randomly chose from the same data split. We evaluate using precision@1,3 and mean reciprocal rank (MRR). Classifiers were trained on the true pairs (positive) and negative examples constructed by pairing a name with 10 other names that have some character overlap with it. The two SVM parameters (the regularizer co-efficient C and the instance weight w for positive examples), as well as the best pinyin representation, were selected using grid search on dev data.

Results For string matching methods, simplified characters improve over the original characters for both Levenshtein and Jaro-Winkler (Table 4). Surprisingly, pinyin does not help over the simplified characters. Segmented pinyin improved over pinyin but did not do as well as the simplified characters. Our method of character pinyin performed the best overall, because it utilizes the phonetic information the pinyin encodes: all the different characters that have the same pronunciation are reduced to the same pinyin representation. Over all the representations, Levenshtein outperformed Jaro-Winkler, consistent with previous work (Cohen et al., 2003).

Compared to the best string matching method (Levenshtein over pinyin characters), the transducer improves for the two name group datasets but does worse on REDIRECT (Table 5). The heterogeneous nature of REDIRECT, including variation from aliases, nicknames, and long-distance re-ordering, may confuse the transducer. The SVM does best overall, improving for all datasets over string matching and

Method	Dataset	prec@1	prec@3	MRR
	REDIRECT	0.820	0.868	0.859
Levenshtein	Mainland-Taiwan	0.867	0.903	0.897
	Mainland-Hong Kong	0.873	0.937	0.911
	REDIRECT	0.767	0.873	0.833
Transducer	Mainland-Taiwan	0.889	0.938	0.921
	Mainland-Hong Kong	**0.925**(*)	**0.989**(*)	**0.954**(*)
	REDIRECT	**0.888**(**)	**0.948**(**)	**0.924**(**)
SVM	Mainland-Taiwan	**0.926**	**0.966**(**)	**0.951**(*)
	Mainland-Hong Kongs	0.882	0.972	0.928

Table 5: Results on test data. * better than Levenshtein; ** better than all other methods ($p = 0.05$)

Features	Datasets	
	REDIRECT	Name Groups
ALL	0.921	0.966
- Jaccard similariy	0.908	0.929
- Levenshtein	0.919	0.956
- Simplified pairs	0.918	0.965
- Pinyin pairs	0.920	0.960
- Others	0.921	0.962

Table 6: Ablation experiments on SVM features

tying or beating the transducer. Different pinyin representations (combined with the simplified representation) worked best on different datasets: character-pinyin for REDIRECT, segmented-pinyin for Mainland-Hongkong and string-pinyin for Mainland-Taiwan. To understand how the features for SVM affect the final results, we conduct ablation tests for different group of features when trained on person names (only) for each dataset (Table 6). Overall, Jaccard features are the most effective.

Error Analysis We annotated 100 randomly sampled REDIRECT development pairs incorrectly classified by the SVM. We found three major types of errors. 1) Matches requiring external knowledge (43% of errors), where there were nicknames or aliases. In these cases, the given name strings are insufficient for determining the correct answer. These types of errors are typically handled using alias lists. 2) Transliteration confusions (13%) resulting from different dialects, transliteration versus translation, or only part of a name being transliterated. 3) Noisy data (19%): Wikipedia redirects include names in other languages (e.g. Japanese, Korean) or orthographically identical strings for different entities. Finally, 25% of the time the system simply got the wrong answer, Many of these cases are acronyms.

5.3 Entity Clustering

We evaluate the impact of our improved name matching on a downstream task: entity clustering

Method	Dev			Test		
	Precision	Recall	F1	Precision	Recall	F1
Exact match	84.55	57.46	68.42	63.95	65.44	64.69
Jaro-winkler	84.87	58.35	69.15	70.79	66.21	68.42
Levenshtein	83.16	61.13	70.46	69.56	67.27	68.40
Transducer	**90.33**	**74.92**	**81.90**	73.59	63.70	68.29
SVM	90.05	63.90	74.75	**74.33**	**67.60**	**70.81**

Table 7: Results on Chinese entity clustering.

(cross document coreference resolution), where the goal is identify co-referent named mentions across documents. Only a few studies have considered Chinese entity clustering (Chen and Martin, 2007), including the TAC KBP shared task, which has included clustering Chinese NIL mentions (Ji et al., 2011). We construct an entity clustering dataset from the TAC KBP entity linking data. All of the 2012 Chinese data is used as development, and the 2013 data as test. We use the system of Green et al. (2012), which allows for the inclusion of arbitrary name matching metrics. We follow their setup for training and evaluation (B^3) and use TF-IDF context features. We tune the clustering cutoff for their hierarchical model, as well as the name matching threshold on the development data. For the trainable name matching methods (transducer, SVM) we train the methods on the development data using cross-validation, as well as tuning the representations and model parameters. We include an exact match baseline.

Table 7 shows that on test data, our best method (SVM) improves over all previous methods by over 2 points. The transducer makes strong gains on dev but not test, suggesting that parameter tuning overfit. These results demonstrate the downstream benefits of improved name matching.

6 Conclusion

Our results suggest several research directions. The remaining errors could be addressed with additional resources. Alias lists could be learned from data or derived from existing resources. Since the best pinyin representation varies by dataset, work could automatically determine the most effective representation, which may include determining the type of variation present in the proposed pair, as well as the associated dialect.

Our name matching tool, Mingpipe, is implemented as a Python library. We make Mingpipe and our datasets available to aid future research on this topic.[9]

[9]`https://github.com/hltcoe/mingpipe`

References

Nicholas Andrews, Jason Eisner, and Mark Dredze. 2012. Name phylogeny: A generative model of string variation. In *Empirical Methods in Natural Language Processing (EMNLP)*, pages 344–355.

Regina Barzilay and Lillian Lee. 2003. Learning to paraphrase: An unsupervised approach using multiple-sequence alignment. In *North American Chapter of the Association for Computational Linguistics: Human Language Technologies (NAACL-HLT)*, pages 16–23.

Mikhail Bilenko, Raymond Mooney, William Cohen, Pradeep Ravikumar, and Stephen Fienberg. 2003. Adaptive name matching in information integration. *IEEE Intelligent Systems*, 18(5):16–23.

Alexandre Bouchard-Côté, Percy Liang, Dan Klein, and Thomas L Griffiths. 2008. A probabilistic approach to language change. In *Advances in Neural Information Processing Systems (NIPS)*, pages 169–176.

Taylor Cassidy, Zheng Chen, Javier Artiles, Heng Ji, Hongbo Deng, Lev-Arie Ratinov, Jing Zheng, Jiawei Han, and Dan Roth. 2011. Cuny-uiuc-sri tac-kbp2011 entity linking system description. In *Text Analysis Conference (TAC)*.

Ying Chen and James Martin. 2007. Towards robust unsupervised personal name disambiguation. In *Empirical Methods in Natural Language Processing (EMNLP)*, pages 190–198.

Ying Chen, Peng Jin, Wenjie Li, and Chu-Ren Huang. 2010. The chinese persons name disambiguation evaluation: Exploration of personal name disambiguation in chinese news. In *CIPS-SIGHAN Joint Conference on Chinese Language Processing*.

Gang Cheng, Fei Wang, Haiyang Lv, and Yinling Zhang. 2011. A new matching algorithm for chinese place names. In *International Conference on Geoinformatics*, pages 1–4. IEEE.

Peter Christen. 2006. A comparison of personal name matching: Techniques and practical issues. In *IEEE International Conference on Data Mining Workshops*, pages 290–294.

William Cohen, Pradeep Ravikumar, and Stephen Fienberg. 2003. A comparison of string metrics for matching names and records. In *KDD Workshop on Data Cleaning and Object Consolidation*, pages 73–78.

Ryan Cotterell, Nanyun Peng, and Jason Eisner. 2014. Stochastic contextual edit distance and probabilistic fsts. In *Association for Computational Linguistics (ACL)*, pages 625–630.

Markus Dreyer, Jason R Smith, and Jason Eisner. 2008. Latent-variable modeling of string transductions with finite-state methods. In *Empirical Methods in Natural Language Processing (EMNLP)*, pages 1080–1089.

Tarek El-Shishtawy. 2013. A hybrid algorithm for matching arabic names. *arXiv preprint arXiv:1309.5657*.

Donghui Feng, Yajuan Lü, and Ming Zhou. 2004. A new approach for english-chinese named entity alignment. In *Empirical Methods in Natural Language Processing (EMNLP)*, pages 372–379.

Andrew T Freeman, Sherri L Condon, and Christopher M Ackerman. 2006. Cross linguistic name matching in english and arabic: a one to many mapping extension of the levenshtein edit distance algorithm. In *North American Chapter of the Association for Computational Linguistics: Human Language Technologies (NAACL-HLT)*, pages 471–478.

Spence Green, Nicholas Andrews, Matthew R. Gormley, Mark Dredze, and Christopher D. Manning. 2012. Entity clustering across languages. In *North American Chapter of the Association for Computational Linguistics: Human Language Technologies (NAACL-HLT)*, pages 60–69.

David Holmes and M Catherine McCabe. 2002. Improving precision and recall for soundex retrieval. In *International Conference on Information Technology: Coding and Computing*, pages 22–26.

Heng Ji, Ralph Grishman, and Hoa Trang Dang. 2011. Overview of the tac 2011 knowledge base population track. In *Text Analytics Conference*.

Long Jiang, Ming Zhou, Lee-Feng Chien, and Cheng Niu. 2007. Named entity translation with web mining and transliteration. In *International Joint Conference on Artificial Intelligence (IJCAI)*, pages 1629–1634.

Kevin Knight and Jonathan Graehl. 1998. Machine transliteration. *Computational Linguistics*, 24(4):599–612.

A Levenshtein. 1966. Binary codes capable of correcting deletions, insertions and reversals. *Soviet Physics Doklady*, 10(8):707–710.

Sebastian Martschat, Jie Cai, Samuel Broscheit, Éva Mújdricza-Maydt, and Michael Strube. 2012. A multigraph model for coreference resolution. In *Empirical Methods in Natural Language Processing (EMNLP) and the Conference on Natural Language Learning (CONLL)*, pages 100–106.

James Mayfield, David Alexander, Bonnie J Dorr, Jason Eisner, Tamer Elsayed, Tim Finin, Clayton Fink, Marjorie Freedman, Nikesh Garera, Paul McNamee, et al. 2009. Cross-document coreference resolution: A key technology for learning by reading. In *AAAI Spring Symposium: Learning by Reading and Learning to Read*, pages 65–70.

Paul McNamee, James Mayfield, Dawn Lawrie, Douglas W Oard, and David S Doermann. 2011a. Cross-language entity linking. In *International Joint Conference on Natural Language Processing (IJCNLP)*, pages 255–263.

Paul McNamee, James Mayfield, Douglas W Oard, Tan Xu, Ke Wu, Veselin Stoyanov, and David Doermann. 2011b. Cross-language entity linking in maryland during a hurricane. In *Empirical Methods in Natural Language Processing (EMNLP)*.

L Philips. 2000. The double metaphone search algorithm. *C/C++ Users Journal*, 18(6).

Edward H Porter, William E Winkler, et al. 1997. Approximate string comparison and its effect on an advanced record linkage system. In *Advanced record linkage system. US Bureau of the Census, Research Report*.

Delip Rao, Paul McNamee, and Mark Dredze. 2013. Entity linking: Finding extracted entities in a knowledge base. In *Multi-source, Multilingual Information Extraction and Summarization*, pages 93–115. Springer.

Eric Sven Ristad and Peter N Yianilos. 1998. Learning string-edit distance. *IEEE Transactions on Pattern Analysis and Machine Intelligence*, 20(5):522–532.

Wee Meng Soon, Hwee Tou Ng, and Daniel Chung Yong Lim. 2001. A machine learning approach to coreference resolution of noun phrases. *Computational linguistics*, 27(4):521–544.

Michael Strube, Stefan Rapp, and Christoph Müller. 2002. The influence of minimum edit distance on reference resolution. In *Empirical Methods in Natural Language Processing (EMNLP)*, pages 312–319.

Jeffrey Sukharev, Leonid Zhukov, and Alexandrin Popescul. 2014. Learning alternative name spellings. *arXiv preprint arXiv:1405.2048*.

William E Winkler. 1999. The state of record linkage and current research problems. In *Statistical Research Division, US Census Bureau*.

Wei Zhang, Jian Su, Chew Lim Tan, and Wen Ting Wang. 2010. Entity linking leveraging: Automatically generated annotation. In *International Conference on Computational Linguistics (COLING)*, pages 1290–1298.

Language Identification and Modeling in Specialized Hardware

Kenneth Heafield[*,†] **Rohan Kshirsagar**[*] **Santiago Barona**[*]
[*] Bloomberg L.P.
731 Lexington Ave.
New York, NY 10022 USA
[†] University of Edinburgh
10 Crichton Street
Edinburgh EH8 9AB, UK
{kheafield, rkshirsagar2, sbarona}@bloomberg.net

Abstract

We repurpose network security hardware to perform language identification and language modeling tasks. The hardware is a deterministic pushdown transducer since it executes regular expressions and has a stack. One core is 2.4 times as fast at language identification and 1.8 to 6 times as fast at part-of-speech language modeling.

1 Introduction

Larger data sizes and more detailed models have led to adoption of specialized hardware for natural language processing. Graphics processing units (GPUs) are the most common, with applications to neural networks (Oh and Jung, 2004) and parsing (Johnson, 2011). Field-programmable gate arrays (FPGAs) are faster and more customizable, so grammars can be encoded in gates (Ciressan et al., 2000). In this work, we go further down the hardware hierarchy by performing language identification and language modeling tasks on an application-specific integrated circuit designed for network monitoring.

The hardware is programmable with regular expressions and access to a stack. It is therefore a deterministic pushdown transducer. Prior work used the hardware mostly as intended, by scanning hard drive contents against a small set of patterns for digital forensics purposes (Lee et al., 2008). The purposes of this paper are to introduce the natural language processing community to the hardware and evaluate performance.

We chose the related tasks of language identification and language modeling because they do not easily map to regular expressions. Fast language classification is essential to using the web as a corpus (Smith et al., 2013) and packages compete on speed (Lui and Baldwin, 2012). Extensive literature on fast language models comprises a strong baseline (Stolcke, 2002; Federico et al., 2008; Heafield, 2011; Yasuhara et al., 2013). In both cases, matches are frequent, which differs from network security and forensics applications where matches are rare.

2 Related Work

Automata have been emulated on CPUs with AT&T FSM (Mohri et al., 2000) and OpenFST (Allauzen et al., 2007), on GPUs (Rudomín et al., 2005; He et al., 2015), and on FPGAs (Sidhu and Prasanna, 2001; Lin et al., 2006; Korenek, 2010). These are candidates for the ASIC we use. In particular, gappy pattern matching (He et al., 2015) maps directly to regular expressions.

GPUs have recently been applied to the related problem of parsing (Johnson, 2011; Yi et al., 2011). These operate largely by turning a sparse parsing problem into a highly-parallel dense problem (Canny et al., 2013) and by clustering similar workloads (Hall et al., 2014). Since the hardware used in this paper is a deterministic pushdown automaton, parsing ambiguous natural language is theoretically impossible without using the CPU as an oracle. Hall et al. (2014) rely on communication between the CPU and GPU, albeit for efficiency reasons rather than out of necessity.

Work on efficiently querying backoff language models (Katz, 1987) has diverged from a finite state representation. DALM (Yasuhara et al., 2013) is an efficient trie-based representation using double arrays while KenLM (Heafield, 2011) has traditional tries and a linear probing hash table. We use the fastest baselines from both.

3 Programming Model

The fundamental programming unit is a POSIX regular expression including repetition, line boundaries, and trailing context. For example, `a[bc]` matches "ab" and "ac".

Proceedings of the 53rd Annual Meeting of the Association for Computational Linguistics and the 7th International Joint Conference on Natural Language Processing (Short Papers), pages 384–389,
Beijing, China, July 26-31, 2015.

When an expression matches, the hardware can output a constant to the CPU, output the span matched, push a symbol onto the stack, pop from the stack, or halt. There is little meaning to the order in which the expressions appear in the program. All expressions are able to match at any time, but can condition on the top of the stack. This is similar to the `flex` tool (Lesk and Schmidt, 1975), which refers to stack symbols as start conditions.

4 Language Identification

We exactly replicate the model of `langid.py` (Lui and Baldwin, 2012) to identify 97 languages. Their Naïve Bayes model has 7,480 features f_i, each of which is a string of up to four bytes (Lui and Baldwin, 2011). Inference amounts to collecting the count c_i of each feature and computing the most likely language l given model p.

$$l^* = \operatorname*{argmax}_l p(l) \prod_i p(f_i|l)^{c_i}$$

We use the hardware to find all instances of features in the input. Feature strings are converted to literal regular expressions. When the hardware matches the expression for feature f_i, it outputs the unique feature index i. Since the hardware has no user-accessible arithmetic, the CPU accumulates feature counts c_i in an array and performs subsequent modeling steps. The baseline emulates automata on the CPU (Aho and Corasick, 1975).

Often the input is a collection of documents, each of which should be classified independently. To separate documents, we have the hardware match document boundaries, such as newlines, and output a special value. Since the hardware natively reports matches in order by start position (then by end position), the special value acts as a delimiter between documents that the CPU can detect. This removes the need to reconcile document offsets on the CPU and saves bus bandwidth since the hardware can be configured to not report offsets.

5 Language Model Probability

The task is to compute the language model probability p of some text w. Backoff models (Katz, 1987) memorize probability for seen n–grams and charge a backoff penalty b for unseen n–grams.

$$p(w_n \mid w_1^{n-1}) = \begin{cases} p(w_n \mid w_1^{n-1}) \text{ if } w_1^n \text{ is seen} \\ p(w_n \mid w_2^{n-1}) b(w_1^{n-1}) \text{ o.w.} \end{cases}$$

5.1 Optimizing the Task

The backoff algorithm normally requires storing probability p and backoff b with each seen n–gram. However, Heafield et al. (2012) used telescoping series to prove that probability and backoff can be collapsed into a single function q

$$q(w_n|w_1^{n-1}) = p(w_n|w_1^{n-1}) \frac{\prod_{i=1}^{n} b(w_i^n)}{\prod_{i=1}^{n-1} b(w_i^{n-1})}$$

This preserves sentence-level probabilities.[1]

Because the hardware lacks user-accessible arithmetic, terms are sent to the CPU. Sending just q for each token instead of p and various backoffs b reduces communication and CPU workload. We also benefit from a simplified query procedure: for each word, match as much context as possible then return the corresponding value q.

5.2 Greedy Matching

Language models are greedy in the sense that, for every word, they match as much leading context as possible. We map this onto greedy regular expressions, which match as much trailing context as possible, by reversing the input and n–grams.[2]

Unlike language identification, we run the hardware in a greedy mode that scans until a match is found, reports the longest such match, and resumes scanning afterwards. The trailing context operator / allows fine-grained control over the offset where scanning resumes. Given two regular expressions r and s, the trailing context expression r/s matches rs as if they were concatenated, but scanning resumes after r. For example, if the language model contains n–gram "This is a", then we create regular expression

```
" a"/" is This "
```

where the quotes ensure that spaces are interpreted literally. Scanning resumes at the space before the next word: " is". Because greedy mode suppresses shorter matches, only the longest n–gram will be reported. The CPU can then sum $\log q$ values associated with each expression without regard to position.

Unknown words are detected by matching a space: `" "`. Vocabulary words will greedily

[1]Technically, q is off by the constant $b(\text{<s>})$ due to conditioning on <s>. We account for this at the end of sentence, re-defining $q(\text{</s>} \mid w_1^{n-1}) \leftarrow q(\text{</s>} \mid w_1^{n-1}) b(\text{<s>})$. Doing so saves one output per sentence.

[2]For exposition, we show words in reverse order. The implementation reverses bytes.

Rule	Value	Purpose
`" a"/" in "`	$q(\text{a} \mid \text{in})$	Normal query
`" "`	$q(<\text{unk}>)$	Unknown word
`" in"/" \n"`	$q(\text{in} \mid <\text{s}>)$	Sentence begin
`" \n"/" "`	$q(</\text{s}>)$	Sentence end
`" \n"/" in "`	$q(</\text{s}> \mid \text{in})$	Sentence end

Table 1: Example regular expressions, including the special rules for the unknown word and sentence boundaries. We rely on the newline `\n` in lieu of sentence boundary tokens <s> and </s>.

Model	Platform	1 core	5 cores
langid	Hardware	160.34	608.41
	C	64.57	279.18
	Java	25.53	102.72
	Python	2.90	12.63
CLD2	C++	12.39	30.15

Table 2: Language identification speed in MB/s.

match their own regular expression, which begins with a space. This space also prevents matching inside an unknown word (e.g. "Ugrasena" should not match "a"). The tokenizer is expected to remove duplicate spaces and add them at line boundaries. Table 1 shows key expressions.

Instead of strings, we can match vocabulary indices. Spaces are unnecessary since indices have fixed length and the unknown word has an index.

6 Experiments

We benchmarked a Tarari T2540 PCI express device from 2011 against several CPU baselines. It has 2 GB of DDR2 RAM and 5 cores. A single-threaded CPU program controls the device and performs arithmetic. The program scaled linearly to control four devices, so it is not a bottleneck. Wall clock time, except loading, is the minimum from three runs on an otherwise-idle machine. Models and input were in RAM before each run.

6.1 Language Identification

The `langid.py` model is 88.6–99.2% accurate (Lui and Baldwin, 2012). We tested the original Python, a Java implementation that "should be faster than anything else out there" (Weiss, 2013), a C implementation (Lui, 2014), and our replica in hardware. We also tested CLD2 (Sites, 2013) written in C++, which has a different model that was less accurate on 4 of 6 languages selected from Europarl (Koehn, 2005). Time includes the costs of feature extraction and modeling.

Lines	Tokens	Ken	DA	1 core	5 cores
100	$2.6 \cdot 10^3$	37.8	40.3	6.6	2.1
1000	$2.2 \cdot 10^4$	42.4	43.6	16.2	10.7
10000	$2.6 \cdot 10^5$	53.9	55.7	46.2	42.0
100000	$2.8 \cdot 10^6$	78.6	85.3	91.3	93.6
305263	$8.6 \cdot 10^6$	92.9	105.6	97.0	91.8

Table 3: Seconds to compute perplexity on strings. The hardware was tested with 1 core and 5 cores.

Table 2 reports speed measured on a 9.6 GB text file created by concatenating the 2013 News Crawl corpora for English, French, German, Hindi, Spanish, and Russian (Bojar et al., 2014). One hardware core is 2.48 times as fast as the fastest CPU program. Using five cores instead of one yielded speed improvements of 3.8x on hardware and 4.3x on a 16-core CPU. The hardware performs decently on this task, likely because the 1 MB binary transition table mostly fits in cache.

6.2 Language Modeling

We benchmarked against the fastest reported language models, DALM's reverse trie (Yasuhara et al., 2013) and KenLM's linear probing (Heafield, 2011). Both use stateful queries. For surface strings, time includes the cost of vocabulary lookup. For vocabulary identifiers, we converted words to bytes then timed custom query programs.

Unpruned models were trained on the English side of the French–English MultiUN corpus (Eisele and Chen, 2010). Perplexity was computed on 2.6 GB of tokenized text from the 2013 English News Crawl (Bojar et al., 2014).

6.2.1 Surface Strings

We tested trigram language models trained on various amounts of data before reaching a software-imposed limit of 4.2 million regular expressions.[3] Figure 1 and Table 3 show total query time as a function of training data size while Figure 2 shows model size. DALM model size includes the entire directory.

Cache effects are evident: the hardware binary format is much larger because it stores a generic table. Queries are fast for tiny models but become slower than the CPU. Multiple cores do not help for larger models because they share the cache and memory bus. Since the hardware operates at the byte level and there is an average of 5.34 bytes

[3]Intel is working to remove this restriction.

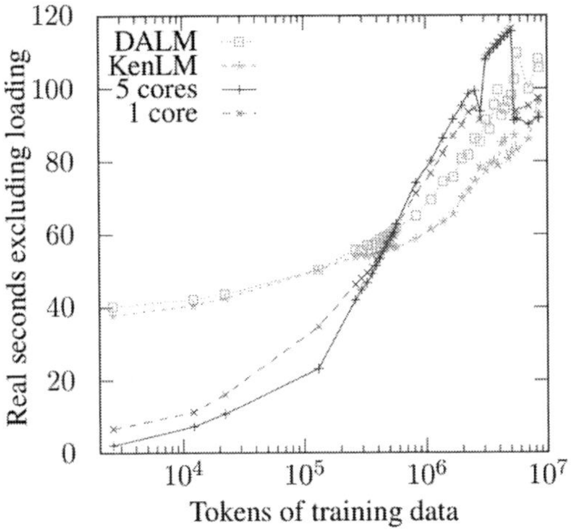

Figure 1: Time to compute perplexity on strings.

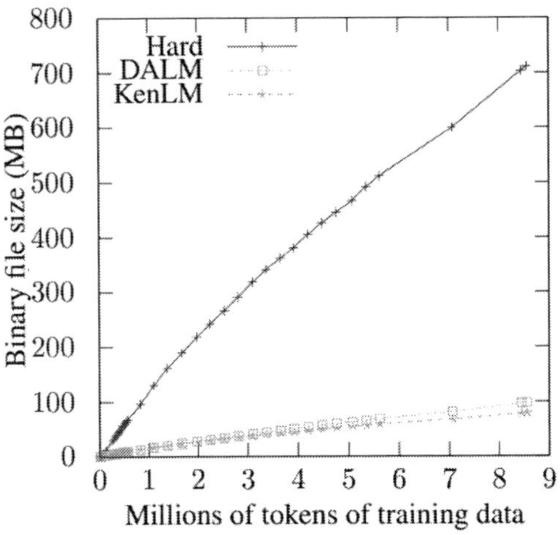

Figure 2: Size of the models on strings.

per word, random memory accesses happen more often than in CPU-based models that operate on words. We then set out to determine if the hardware runs faster when each word is a byte.

6.2.2 Vocabulary Indices

Class-based language models are often used alongside lexical language models to form generalizations. We tested a 5–gram language model over CoNLL part-of-speech tags from MITIE (King, 2014). There are fewer than 256 unique tags, fitting into a byte per word. We also created special KenLM and DALM query programs that read byte-encoded input. Figure 3 and Table 4 show total time while model sizes are shown in Figure 4. Performance plateaus for very small models, which is more clearly shown by plotting speed in Figure 5.

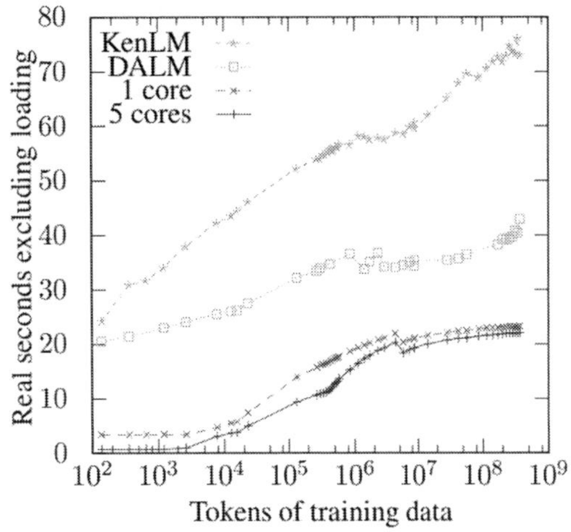

Figure 3: Time to compute perplexity on bytes.

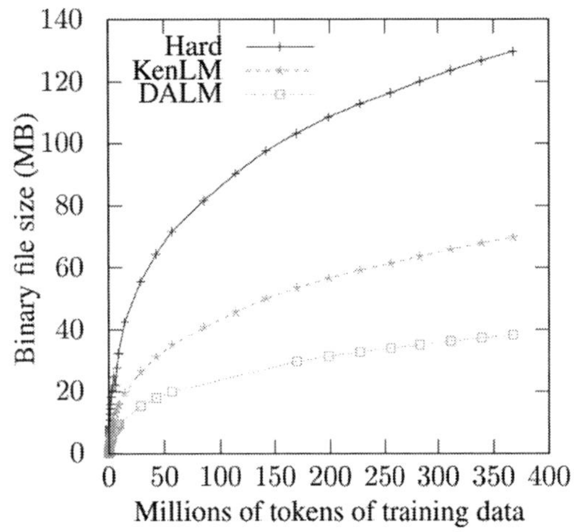

Figure 4: Size of the models on bytes.

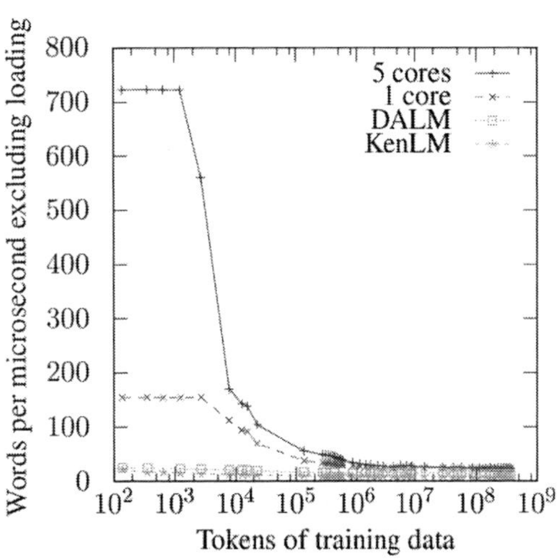

Figure 5: Speed, in words per microsecond, to compute perplexity on bytes.

Lines	Tokens	Ken	DA	1 core	5 cores
100	$2.6 \cdot 10^3$	38.0	24.1	3.4	0.9
1000	$2.3 \cdot 10^4$	46.1	27.5	7.5	5.0
10000	$2.7 \cdot 10^5$	53.9	33.4	15.7	10.7
100000	$2.9 \cdot 10^6$	57.5	34.2	21.1	19.3
1000000	$2.9 \cdot 10^7$	65.2	35.4	22.1	20.7
13000000	$3.7 \cdot 10^8$	73.0	42.9	23.3	22.0

Table 4: Seconds to compute perplexity on bytes. The hardware was tested with 1 core and 5 cores.

The hardware is faster for all training data sizes we tested. For tiny models, one core is initially 6 times as fast one CPU core while larger models are 1.8 times as fast as the CPU. For small models, the hardware appears to hitting another limit, perhaps the speed at which a core can output matches. This is not a CPU or PCI bus limitation because five cores are faster than one core, by a factor of 4.67.

Model growth is sublinear because novel POS n–grams are limited. The hardware binary image is 3.4 times as large as DALM, compared with 7.2 times as large for the lexical model. We attribute this to denser transition tables that result from model saturation.

Acknowledgements

We thank Intel and Xanadata for numerous consultations and for providing access to a machine with four devices. Intel markets the hardware as a regular expression processor, not a deterministic pushdown automaton.

7 Conclusion

Language identification and language modeling entail scanning that can be offloaded to regular expression hardware. The hardware works best for small models, such as those used in language identification. Like CPUs, random memory accesses are slow. We believe it will be useful for web-scale extraction problems, where language identification and coarse language modeling are used to filter large amounts of data. We plan to investigate a new hardware version that Intel is preparing.

References

Alfred V. Aho and Margaret J. Corasick. 1975. Efficient string matching: An aid to bibliographic search. *Commun. ACM*, 18(6):333–340, June.

Cyril Allauzen, Michael Riley, Johan Schalkwyk, Wojciech Skut, and Mehryar Mohri. 2007. Openfst: A general and efficient weighted finite-state transducer library. In *Implementation and Application of Automata*, pages 11–23. Springer.

Ondrej Bojar, Christian Buck, Christian Federmann, Barry Haddow, Philipp Koehn, Johannes Leveling, Christof Monz, Pavel Pecina, Matt Post, Herve Saint-Amand, Radu Soricut, Lucia Specia, and Aleš Tamchyna. 2014. Findings of the 2014 workshop on statistical machine translation. In *Proceedings of the Ninth Workshop on Statistical Machine Translation*, pages 12–58, Baltimore, Maryland, USA, June. Association for Computational Linguistics.

John Canny, David Hall, and Dan Klein. 2013. A multi-teraflop constituency parser using GPUs. In *Proceedings of EMNLP*, pages 1898–1907.

Cristian Ciressan, Eduardo Sanchez, Martin Rajman, and Jean-Cedric Chappelier. 2000. An fpga-based coprocessor for the parsing of context-free grammars. In *Field-Programmable Custom Computing Machines, Annual IEEE Symposium on*, pages 236–236. IEEE Computer Society.

Andreas Eisele and Yu Chen. 2010. MultiUN: A multilingual corpus from United Nation documents. In Daniel Tapias, Mike Rosner, Stelios Piperidis, Jan Odjik, Joseph Mariani, Bente Maegaard, Khalid Choukri, and Nicoletta Calzolari, editors, *Proceedings of the Seventh conference on International Language Resources and Evaluation*, pages 2868–2872. European Language Resources Association (ELRA), 5.

Marcello Federico, Nicola Bertoldi, and Mauro Cettolo. 2008. IRSTLM: an open source toolkit for handling large scale language models. In *Proceedings of Interspeech*, Brisbane, Australia.

David Hall, Taylor Berg-Kirkpatrick, John Canny, and Dan Klein. 2014. Sparser, better, faster GPU parsing. In *Proceedings of the 52nd Annual Meeting of the Association for Computational Linguistics*, pages 208–217, June.

Hua He, Jimmy Lin, and Adam Lopez. 2015. Gappy pattern matching on GPUs for on-demand extraction of hierarchical translation grammars. *Transactions of the Association for Computational Linguistics*, 3:87–100.

Kenneth Heafield, Philipp Koehn, and Alon Lavie. 2012. Language model rest costs and space-efficient storage. In *Proceedings of the 2012 Joint Conference on Empirical Methods in Natural Language Processing and Computational Natural Language Learning*, Jeju Island, Korea.

Kenneth Heafield. 2011. KenLM: Faster and smaller language model queries. In *Proceedings of the Sixth Workshop on Statistical Machine Translation*, Edinburgh, UK, July. Association for Computational Linguistics.

Mark Johnson. 2011. Parsing in parallel on multiple cores and GPUs. In *Proceedings of the Australasian Language Technology Association Workshop 2011*, pages 29–37, December.

Slava Katz. 1987. Estimation of probabilities from sparse data for the language model component of a speech recognizer. *IEEE Transactions on Acoustics, Speech, and Signal Processing*, ASSP-35(3):400–401, March.

Davis E. King. 2014. MITIE: MIT information extraction, January. `https://github.com/mit-nlp/MITIE`.

Philipp Koehn. 2005. Europarl: A parallel corpus for statistical machine translation. In *Proceedings of MT Summit*.

Jan Korenek. 2010. Fast regular expression matching using FPGA. *Information Sciences and Technologies Bulletin of the ACM Slovakia*, 2(2):103–111.

Jooyoung Lee, Sungkyong Un, and Dowon Hong. 2008. High-speed search using Tarari content processor in digital forensics. *Digital Investigation*, 5:S91–S95.

Michael E Lesk and Eric Schmidt. 1975. Lex: A lexical analyzer generator, July.

Cheng-Hung Lin, Chih-Tsun Huang, Chang-Ping Jiang, and Shih-Chieh Chang. 2006. Optimization of regular expression pattern matching circuits on FPGA. In *Design, Automation and Test in Europe, 2006. DATE'06. Proceedings*, volume 2, pages 1–6. IEEE.

Marco Lui and Timothy Baldwin. 2011. Cross-domain feature selection for language identification. In *Proceedings of the 5th International Joint Conference on Natural Language Processing*, pages 553–561, Chiang Mai, Thailand, November.

Marco Lui and Timothy Baldwin. 2012. `langid.py`: An off-the-shelf language identification tool. In *Proceedings of the 50th Annual Meeting of the Association for Computational Linguistics*, pages 25–30, Jeju, Republic of Korea, July.

Marco Lui. 2014. Pure C natural language identifier with support for 97 languages. `https://github.com/saffsd/langid.c`.

Mehryar Mohri, Fernando Pereira, and Michael Riley. 2000. The design principles of a weighted finite-state transducer library. *Theoretical Computer Science*, 231(1):17–32.

Kyoung-Su Oh and Keechul Jung. 2004. GPU implementation of neural networks. *Pattern Recognition*, 37(6):1311–1314.

Isaac Rudomín, Erik Millán, and Benjamín Hernández. 2005. Fragment shaders for agent animation using finite state machines. *Simulation Modelling Practice and Theory*, 13(8):741–751.

Reetinder Sidhu and Viktor K Prasanna. 2001. Fast regular expression matching using FPGAs. In *Field-Programmable Custom Computing Machines, 2001. FCCM'01. The 9th Annual IEEE Symposium on*, pages 227–238. IEEE.

Dick Sites. 2013. Compact language detection 2. `https://code.google.com/p/cld2/`.

Jason R. Smith, Herve Saint-Amand, Magdalena Plamada, Philipp Koehn, Chris Callison-Burch, and Adam Lopez. 2013. Dirt cheap web-scale parallel text from the common crawl. In *Proceedings of the 51st Annual Meeting of the Association for Computational Linguistics*, Sofia, Bulgaria, August.

Andreas Stolcke. 2002. SRILM - an extensible language modeling toolkit. In *Proceedings of the Seventh International Conference on Spoken Language Processing*, pages 901–904.

Dawid Weiss. 2013. Java port of langid.py (language identifier). `https://github.com/carrotsearch/langid-java`.

Makoto Yasuhara, Toru Tanaka, Jun-ya Norimatsu, and Mikio Yamamoto. 2013. An efficient language model using double-array structures. In *Proceedings of EMNLP*, pages 222–232, October.

Youngmin Yi, Chao-Yue Lai, Slav Petrov, and Kurt Keutzer. 2011. Efficient parallel CKY parsing on GPUs. In *Proceedings of the 12th International Conference on Parsing Technologies*, pages 175–185. Association for Computational Linguistics.

Cross-lingual Transfer of Named Entity Recognizers without Parallel Corpora

Ayah Zirikly*
Department of Computer Science
The George Washington University
Washington DC, USA
ayaz@gwu.edu

Masato Hagiwara
Duolingo, Inc.
Pittsburgh PA, USA
masato@duolingo.com

Abstract

We propose an approach to cross-lingual named entity recognition model transfer without the use of parallel corpora. In addition to global de-lexicalized features, we introduce multilingual gazetteers that are generated using graph propagation, and cross-lingual word representation mappings without the use of parallel data. We target the e-commerce domain, which is challenging due to its unstructured and noisy nature. The experiments have shown that our approaches beat the strong MT baseline, where the English model is transferred to two languages: Spanish and Chinese.

1 Introduction

Named Entity Recognition (NER) is usually solved by a supervised learning approach, where sequential labeling models are trained from a large amount of manually annotated corpora. However, such rich annotated data only exist for resource-rich languages such as English, and building NER systems for the majority of resource-poor languages, or specific domains in *any* languages, still poses a great challenge.

Annotation projection through parallel text (Yarowsky et al., 2001), (Das and Petrov, 2011), (Wang and Manning, 2014) has been traditionally used to overcome this issue, where the annotated tags in the source (resource-rich) language are projected via word-aligned bilingual parallel text (bitext) and used to train sequential labeling models in the (resource-poor) target language. However, this could lead to two issues: firstly, word alignment and projected tags are potentially noisy, making the trained models sub-optimal. Instead of projecting noisy labels explicitly, Wang and Manning (2014) project posterior marginals expectations as soft constraints. Das and Petrov (2011) projected POS tags from source language types to target language trigarms using graph propagation and used the projected label distribution to train robust POS taggers. Secondly, the availability of such bitext is limited especially for resource-poor languages and domains, where it is often the case that available resources are moderately-sized monolingual/comparable corpora and small bilingual dictionaries.

Instead, we seek a *direct transfer* approach (Figure 1) to cross-lingual NER (also classified as transductive transfer learning (Pan and Yang, 2010) and closely related to domain adaptation). Specifically, we only assume the availability of *comparable* corpora and small-sized bilingual dictionaries, and use the same sequential tagging model trained on the source corpus for tagging the target corpus. Direct transfer approaches are extensively studied for cross-lingual dependency parser transfer. For example, Zeman et al. (2008) built a constituent parser using direct transfer between closely related languages, namely, Danish and Swedish. McDonald et al. (2011) trained de-lexicalized dependency parsers in English and then "re-lexicalized" the parser. However, cross-lingual transfer of named entity taggers have not been studied enough, and this paper, to the best of the authors' knowledge, is the first to apply direct transfer learning to NER.

Transfer of NER taggers poses a difficult challenge that is different from syntax transfer: most of the past work deals with de-lexicalized parsers, yet one of the most important clues for NER, gazetteers, is inherently lexicalized. Also, various features used for dependency parsing (Universal POS tags, unsupervised clustering, etc.) are yet to

* This work has been performed while the authors were at Rakuten Institute of Technology, New York. The authors would like to thank Prof. Satoshi Sekine at New York University and other members of Rakuten Institute of Technology for their support during the project.

Proceedings of the 53rd Annual Meeting of the Association for Computational Linguistics and the 7th International Joint Conference on Natural Language Processing (Short Papers), pages 390–396,
Beijing, China, July 26-31, 2015.

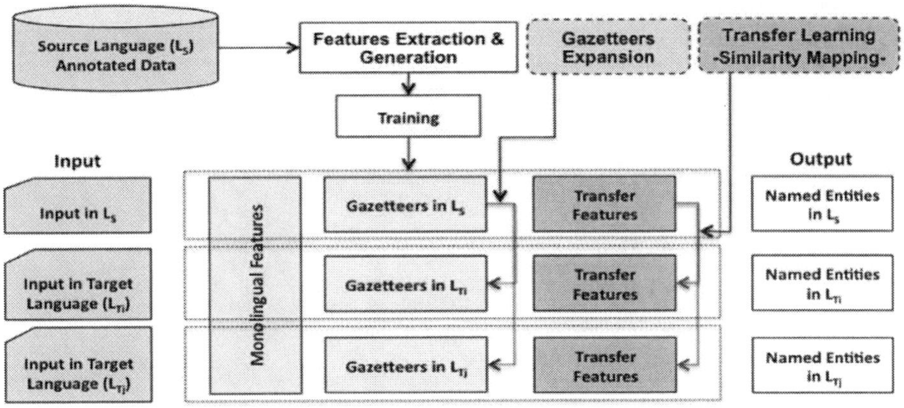

Figure 1: System Framework

be proven useful for direct transfer of NER. Therefore, the contributions of this paper is as follows:

1. We show that direct transfer approach for multilingual NER actually works and performs better than the strong MT baseline (Shah et al., 2010), where the system's output in the source language is simply machine translated into the target language.

2. We explore various non-lexical features, namely, Universal POS tags and Brown cluster mapping, which are deemed effective for multilingual NER transfer. Although brown cluster mapping (Täckström et al., 2012), Universal POS Tagset (Petrov et al., 2011), and re-lexicalization and self training (Täckström et al., 2013) are shown to be effective for direct transfer of dependency parsers, there have been no studies exploring these features for NER transfer.

3. We show that gazetteers can actually be generated only from the source language gazetteers and a comparable corpus, through a technique which we call *gazetteer expansion* based on semi-supervised graph propagation (Zhu et al., 2003). Gazetteer expansion has been used for various other purposes, including POS tagging (Alexandrescu and Kirchhoff, 2007) and dependency parsers (Durrett et al., 2012).

2 Approach

In this paper we propose a direct transfer learning approach to train NER taggers in a multilingual setting. Our goal is to identify named entities in a target language L_T, given solely annotated data in the source language L_S. Previous approaches rely on parallel data to transfer the knowledge from one language to another. However, parallel data is very expensive to construct and not available for all language pairs in all domains. Thus, our approach loosens the constraint and only requires in-domain comparable corpora.

2.1 Monolingual NER in Source Language

Our framework is based on *direct transfer* approach, where we extract abstract, language-independent and non lexical features F_S and F_T in L_S and L_T. A subset of F_T is generated using a mapping scheme discussed in Section 2.2, then, directly apply L_S NER model on L_T using F_T. We adopt Conditional Random Field (CRF) sequence labeling (Lafferty et al., 2001) to train our system and generate the English model.

Monolingual Features 1) *Token position*: Instead of using token exact position, we use token relative position in addition to position's binary features such as token is in: first, second, and last third of the sentence. These features are based on the observation that certain tokens, such as brand names in title or description of a product, tend to appear at the beginning of the sentence, while others toward the end.

2) *Word Shape*: We use a list of binary features: is-alphanumerical, is-number, is-alpha, is-punctuation, the number length (if is-num is true), pattern-based features (e.g. regular expressions to capture certain patterns such as products model numbers), latin-only features (first-is-capital, all-capitals, all-small);

3) *In-Title*: A binary feature that specifies whether the token is in the product's title or description. For instance, brand names mostly appear in the beginning of titles, while this does not hold in descriptions;

4) *Preceding/Proceeding keywords within window*: some NEs are often preceded by certain keywords. For instance, often a product size is preceded by certain keywords such as dimension, height or word"size." In our work we use a manually created list of keywords for two classes Color and Size. Although the keyword list is domain dependent, it is often short and can be easily updated.

5) *Universal Part of Speech Tags*: Part of Speech (POS) tags have been widely used in many NER systems. However, each language has its own POS tagset that often has limited overlap with other POS languages' tagsets. Thus, we use a coarse-grained layer of POS tags called Universal POS, as proposed in (Petrov et al., 2011).

6) *Token is a unit*: A binary feature that is set to true if it matches an entry in the units dictionary (e.g., "cm.")

7) *Gazetteers*: Building dictionaries for every L_T of interest is expensive; thus, we propose a method, described in Section 3, to generate gazetteers in L_T given ones in L_S.

8) *Brown Clustering (BC)*: Word representations, especially Brown Clustering (Brown et al., 1992), are used in many NLP tasks and are proven to improve NER performance (Turian et al., 2010). In this work, we use cluster IDs of variable prefix lengths in order to retrieve word similarities on different granularity levels.

2.2 Multilingual NER in Target Language

Our goal is to transfer each feature from L_S to L_T space. The main challenge resides in transferring features 7 and 8 without the use of external resources and parallel data for every target language.

2.2.1 Brown Clustering Mapping

Given i) Vocabulary in the source/target languages $V_S = \{w_1^S, w_2^S, ..., w_{N_S}^S\}$ and $V_T = \{w_1^T, w_2^T, ..., v_{N_T}^T\}$; ii) The output of brown clustering on L_S and L_T: $C_S = \{c_1^S, ..., c_{K_S}^S\}$ and $C_T = \{c_1^T, ..., c_{K_L}^T\}$, we aim to find the best mapping c^{S*} that maximizes the cluster similarity sim_C for each target cluster (Equation 1), and for each metric discussed in the following. We calculate the cluster similarity sim_C as the weighted average of the word similarity sim_W of the members of the two clusters (Equation 2).

$$c^{S*} = \arg\max_{c^S \in C_S} sim_C(c^S, c^T) \text{ for each } c_T \in C_T \quad (1)$$

$$sim_C(c_t, c_s) = \frac{1}{|c^S||c^T|} \sum_{w^S \in c^S, w^T \in c^T} sim_W(w^S, w^T) \quad (2)$$

Clusters Similarity Metrics The similarity metrics used can be summarized in:

a) *String Similarity* (external resources independent): This metric works only on languages that share the same alphabet, as it is based on the intuition that most NEs conserve the name's shape or present minor changes that can be identified using edit distance in closely related languages (we use Levenshtein distance (Levenshtein, 1966)). The two variations of string similarity metrics used are: i) *Exact match*: $sim_W(w_i, w_j) = 1$ if $w_i = w_j$; ii) *Edit distance*: $sim_W(w_i, w_j) = 1$ if levenshtein-distance$(w_i, w_j) < \theta$.

b) *Dictionary-based similarity*: We present two similarity metrics using BabelNet synsets (Navigli and Ponzetto, 2012): i) *Binary co-occurence*: $sim_W^{binary}(w_i, w_j) = 1$ if $w_j \in synset(w_i)$, where $synset(w_i)$ is the set of words in the BabelNet synset of w_i; ii) *Frequency weighted*: Weighted version of the binary similarity that is based on the observation that less frequent words tend to be less reliable in brown clustering: $sim_W^{weighted}(w_i, w_j) = [\log f(w_i) + \log f(w_j)] \times sim_W^{binary}(w_i, w_j)$ where $f(w)$ is the frequency of word w. Unlike String similarity metrics, this metric is not limited to similar languages due to the use of multilingual dictionaries i.e., BabelNet, which covers 271 languages.

3 Gazetteer expansion

In our approach, we use graph-based semi-supervised learning to expand the gazetteers in the source language to the target. Figure 2 illustrates the motivation of our approach. Suppose we have "New York" in the GPE gazetteer in L_S (English in this case), and we would like to bootstrap the corresponding GPE gazetteer in L_T (Spanish). Although there is no direct link between "New York" and "Nueva York," you can infer that "Puerto Rico" (in English) is similar to "New York" based on some intra-language semantic similarity model, then "Puerto Rico" is actually

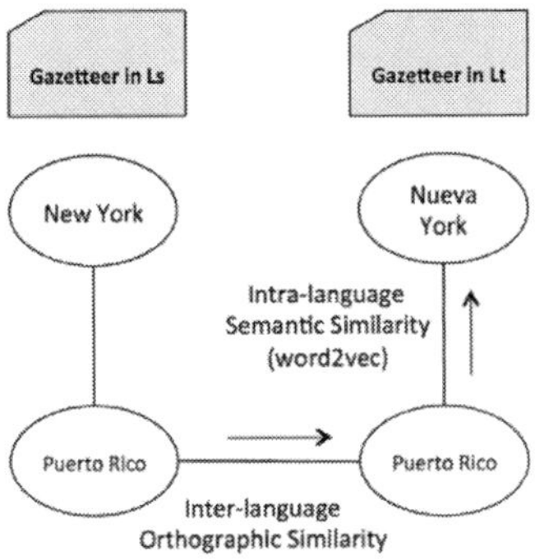

Figure 2: Gazeteer expansion

identical in both languages, then finally "Nueva York" is similar to "Puerto Rico" (in Spanish) again based on the Spanish intra-language similarity model. This indirect inference of beliefs from the source gazetteers to the target can be modeled by semi-supervised graph propagation (Zhu et al. 2003), where graph nodes are $V_S \cup V_T$, positive labels are entries in the L_S gazetteer (e.g., GPE) which we wish to expand to L_T, and negative labels are entries in other gazetteers (e.g., PERSON) in L_S. The edge weights between same-language nodes w_i and w_j are given by $\exp(-\sigma||\mathbf{w}_i - \mathbf{w}_j||)$ where $\mathbf{w}_i$ is the distributed vector representation of word w_i computed by word2vec (Mikolov et al., 2013). The edge weights between node $w_i \in V_S$ and $v_j \in V_T$ are defined 1 if the spelling of these two words are identical and 0 otherwise. Note that this spelling based similarity propagation is still available for language pairs with different writing systems such as English and Chinese, because major NEs (e.g., brand names) are often written in Roman alphabets even in Chinese products. Since the analytical solution to this propagation involves the computation of $n \times n$ (n is the number of unlabeled nodes) matrix, we approximated it by running three propagation steps iteratively, namely, $L_S \rightarrow L_S$, $L_S \rightarrow L_T$, and $L_T \rightarrow L_T$. After the propagation, we used all the nodes with their propagated values $f(w_i) > \theta$ as entities in the new gazetteer.

4 Experiments

4.1 Datasets

The targeted dataset contains a list of products (titles and descriptions). The titles of products are $\approx$ 10 words long and poorly structured, adding more difficulties to our task. On the other hand, the length of product descriptions ranges from 12-130 words. The e-commerce genre poses the need to introduce new NE tagset as opposed to the conventional ones, thus we introduce 6 tag types: 1) Color; 2) Brand names; 3) Size; 4) Type: e.g. "camera," "shirt"; 5) Material: e.g. "plastic", "cotton"; 6) Model: the model number of a product: e.g., "A1533.". For the rest of the experiments, English (EN) is the source language, whereas we experiment with Spanish (ES) and Chinese (ZH) as target languages. The datasets used are: i) Training data: 1800 annotated English products from Rakuten.com shopping (Rakuten, 2013a); ii) Test data: 300 ES products from Rakuten Spain (Rakuten, 2013b) and 500 products from Rakuten Taiwan (Rakuten, 2013c); iii) Brown clustering: *English*: Rakuten shopping 2013 dump (19m unique products with 607m tokens); *Spanish*: Rakuten Spain 2013 dump (700K unique products that contains 41m tokens) in addition to Spanish Wikipedia dump (Al-Rfou', 2013); *Chinese*: Wikipedia Chinese 2014 dump (147m tokens) plus 16k products crawled from Rakuten Taiwan. Table 1 shows the numbers of tags per category for each language.

	Color	Brand	Material	Model	Type	Size
EN	358	814	733	203	1238	427
ES	207	425	301	172	606	126
ZH	416	60	381	24	690	306

Table 1: Language-Tags Numbers Stats

4.2 Baseline

To the best of our knowledge, there is no previous work that proposes transfer learning for NER without the use of parallel data. Thus, we ought to generate a strong baseline to compare our results to. Given the language pair (L_S, L_T), we use Microsoft Bing Translate API to generate $L_T \rightarrow L_S$ translation. Then, we apply L_S NER model on the translated text and evaluate by mapping the tagged tokens back to L_T using the word alignments generated by Bing Translate. We choose Bing translate as opposed to Google translate due to its free-to-use API that provides word alignment information on the character level.

4.3 Results & Discussion

For each studied language we use Stanford CoreNLP (Manning et al., 2014) for EN and ZH, and TreeTagger (Schmid, 1994) for ES to produce

	Color	Brand	Material	Model	Type	Size	Micro-Avg
EN-Mono	68.45	71.91	50.94	59.78	53.73	45.42	61.12
ES-Baseline	24.23	3.44	13.08	14.51	12.5	6.61	13.79
ES-TL	18.00	9.37	8.05	16.99	18.26	10.64	**39.46**
ES-GT	38.49	13.31	33.5	2.27	36.43	1.16	30.20
ZH-Baseline	19.16	2.79	11.96	None	9.35	6.34	12.58
ZH-TL	9.36	1.02	1.81	None	17.28	17.74	**23.43**

Table 2: F-score Results

the tokens and the POS tags. However, we apply extra processing steps to the tokenizer due to the nature of the domain's data (e.g., avoid tokenizing models instances), in addition to normalizing URLs, numbers, and elongation. We also map POS tags for all the source and target languages to the universal POS tagset as explained in 2.1.

Based on Table 2, we note that English monolingual performance (80:20 train/test split and 5-folds cross variation) is considerably lower than state-of-the-art English NER systems, which is due to the nature of our targeted domain, the newly proposed NE tagset, and most importantly, the considerably small training data (1280 products). These factors also affects the baseline and our proposed system performance.

Table 2 illustrates the results for the English monolingual NER system (EN-Mono), baseline for ES and ZH (ES-Baseline and ZH-Baseline, respectively), our proposed transfer learning approach with the gazetteer expansion (ES-TL and ZH-TL). Additionally, we added the results of our proposed approach where the gazetteers used are machine translated using Google translate from the English gazetteers to Spanish (ES-MT), in order to evaluate our gazetteer expansion approach performance to the translated gazetteers.

We note that ES-Baseline and ZH-Baseline are considerably low due to the poor word alignment generated by Bing Translator, which results in incorrect tag projection. The quality of mapping is mainly due to the noisy nature of the domain's data, which can be very expensive to fix.

Although the performance of our proposed system is low (39.46% for ES and 23.43% for ZH), but it surpasses the baseline performance in most of the tag classes and yields an overall improvement on the micro-average F-score of $\approx$ 23% in ES and 11% in ZH. We note that one of the reasons behind ZH *Brand* low performance is that universal-POS for brands in EN are mostly proper noun as opposed to noun in ZH, additionally the considerably low number of brands in ZH test data (60). On the other hand, it is intuitive that *Model* yields one of the best performance among the tags, since it is the most language independent tag (as depicted in ES-TL). However, this does not hold true in ZH due to the very small number of *Model* instances (24). *Type* produces the best performance in ES and ZH, due to the high coverage of the new expanded gazetteer over *Type* instances, in addition to the large number of training instances (1238), in comparison to the other tags. After conducting leave-out experiments on Brown clustering and gazetteers features in ES, we note that both shows an improvement of $\approx$ 4% and $\approx$ 8% respectively.

Our system surpasses the MT-based gazetter expansion by $\approx$ 9%, when comparing ES-TL to ES-MT. However, as expected the main improvement is in *Model* and *Size* tags as opposed to other tags (e.g. *Brand* and *Color*) where MT provides more accurate gazetteers. In our system output, colors that are included in L_T expanded gazetteers (e.g. "azul" in ES) and have a high similarity score in our proposed BC mapping, are correctly tagged. On the other hand OOV Brand have a very large prediction error rate due to the small training data.

5 Conclusion and Future Works

In this paper, we propose a cross-lingual NER transfer learning approach which does not depend on parallel corpora. Our experiments showed the ability to transfer NER model to latin (ES) and non latin (ZH) languages. For the future work, we would like to investigate the generality of our approach in broader languages and domains.

References

Rami Al-Rfou'. 2013. Spanish wikipedia dump. url = https://sites.google.com/site/rmyeid/projects/polyglot.

Andrei Alexandrescu and Katrin Kirchhoff. 2007. Data-driven graph construction for semi-supervised graph-based learning in NLP. In *Human Language Technologies 2007: The Conference of the North American Chapter of the Association for Computational Linguistics; Proceedings of the Main Conference*, pages 204–211, Rochester, New York, April. Association for Computational Linguistics.

Peter F Brown, Peter V Desouza, Robert L Mercer, Vincent J Della Pietra, and Jenifer C Lai. 1992. Class-based n-gram models of natural language. *Computational linguistics*, 18(4):467–479.

Dipanjan Das and Slav Petrov. 2011. Unsupervised part-of-speech tagging with bilingual graph-based projections. In *Proceedings of the 49th Annual Meeting of the Association for Computational Linguistics: Human Language Technologies*, pages 600–609, Portland, Oregon, USA, June. Association for Computational Linguistics.

Greg Durrett, Adam Pauls, and Dan Klein. 2012. Syntactic transfer using a bilingual lexicon. In *Proceedings of the 2012 Joint Conference on Empirical Methods in Natural Language Processing and Computational Natural Language Learning*, pages 1–11. Association for Computational Linguistics.

John Lafferty, Andrew McCallum, and Fernando CN Pereira. 2001. Conditional random fields: Probabilistic models for segmenting and labeling sequence data.

VI Levenshtein. 1966. Binary Codes Capable of Correcting Deletions, Insertions and Reversals. *Soviet Physics Doklady*, 10:707.

Christopher D. Manning, Mihai Surdeanu, John Bauer, Jenny Finkel, Steven J. Bethard, and David McClosky. 2014. The Stanford CoreNLP natural language processing toolkit. In *Proceedings of 52nd Annual Meeting of the Association for Computational Linguistics: System Demonstrations*, pages 55–60.

Ryan McDonald, Slav Petrov, and Keith Hall. 2011. Multi-source transfer of delexicalized dependency parsers. In *Proceedings of the Conference on Empirical Methods in Natural Language Processing*, EMNLP '11, pages 62–72, Stroudsburg, PA, USA. Association for Computational Linguistics.

Tomas Mikolov, Ilya Sutskever, Kai Chen, Greg S Corrado, and Jeff Dean. 2013. Distributed representations of words and phrases and their compositionality. In *Advances in Neural Information Processing Systems*, pages 3111–3119.

Roberto Navigli and Simone Paolo Ponzetto. 2012. BabelNet: The automatic construction, evaluation and application of a wide-coverage multilingual semantic network. *Artificial Intelligence*, 193:217–250.

Sinno Jialin Pan and Qiang Yang. 2010. A survey on transfer learning. *IEEE Trans. on Knowl. and Data Eng.*, 22(10):1345–1359, October.

Slav Petrov, Dipanjan Das, and Ryan McDonald. 2011. A universal part-of-speech tagset. *arXiv preprint arXiv:1104.2086*.

Rakuten. 2013a. Rakuten shopping. url = http://www.rakuten.com/.

Rakuten. 2013b. Rakuten spanish.

Rakuten. 2013c. Rakuten taiwanese.

Helmut Schmid. 1994. Probabilistic part-of-speech tagging using decision trees.

Rushin Shah, Bo Lin, Anatole Gershman, and Robert Frederking. 2010. Synergy: A named entity recognition system for resource-scarce languages such as swahili using online machine translation. In *Proceedings of the Second Workshop on African Language Technology (AfLaT 2010)*, pages 21–26.

Oscar Täckström, Ryan McDonald, and Jakob Uszkoreit. 2012. Cross-lingual word clusters for direct transfer of linguistic structure. In *Proceedings of the 2012 Conference of the North American Chapter of the Association for Computational Linguistics: Human Language Technologies*, pages 477–487, Montréal, Canada, June. Association for Computational Linguistics.

Oscar Täckström, Ryan McDonald, and Joakim Nivre. 2013. Target language adaptation of discriminative transfer parsers. In *Proceedings of the 2013 Conference of the North American Chapter of the Association for Computational Linguistics: Human Language Technologies*, pages 1061–1071, Atlanta, Georgia, June. Association for Computational Linguistics.

Joseph Turian, Lev Ratinov, and Yoshua Bengio. 2010. Word representations: A simple and general method for semi-supervised learning. In *Proceedings of the 48th Annual Meeting of the Association for Computational Linguistics*, pages 384–394. Association for Computational Linguistics.

Mengqiu Wang and Christopher D Manning. 2014. Cross-lingual projected expectation regularization for weakly supervised learning.

David Yarowsky, Grace Ngai, and Richard Wicentowski. 2001. Inducing multilingual text analysis tools via robust projection across aligned corpora. In *Proceedings of the First International Conference on Human Language Technology Research*, HLT '01, pages 1–8, Stroudsburg, PA, USA. Association for Computational Linguistics.

Daniel Zeman, Univerzita Karlova, and Philip Resnik. 2008. Cross-language parser adaptation between related languages. In *In IJCNLP-08 Workshop on NLP for Less Privileged Languages*, pages 35–42.

Xiaojin Zhu, Zoubin Ghahramani, and John Lafferty. 2003. Semi-supervised learning using gaussian fields and harmonic functions. In *IN ICML*, pages 912–919.

Robust Multi-Relational Clustering via ℓ_1-Norm Symmetric Nonnegative Matrix Factorization

Kai Liu
Colorado school of Mines
Department of EECS
Golden, Colorado 80401
kaliu@mines.edu

Hua Wang
Colorado school of Mines
Department of EECS
Golden, Colorado 80401
HUAWANGCS@gmail.com

Abstract

In this paper, we propose an ℓ_1-norm Symmetric Nonnegative Matrix Tri-Factorization (ℓ_1 S-NMTF) framework to cluster multi-type relational data by utilizing their interrelatedness. Due to introducing the ℓ_1-norm distances in our new objective function, the proposed approach is robust against noise and outliers, which are inherent in multi-relational data. We also derive the solution algorithm and rigorously analyze its correctness and convergence. The promising experimental results of the algorithm applied to text clustering on IMDB dataset validate the proposed approach.

1 Introduction

Traditional clustering aims to partition data points into several groups, such that the data points in the same group can share some commonalities whilst those from different groups are dissimilar. With the recent progresses of Internet and computational technologies, data have started to appear in much richer structures. To be more specific, in many real-world problems a pair of object can be related in several different ways, which inevitably complicates the problem and calls for new clustering algorithms for better understanding to the data. To address this new challenge, Wang *et. al.* (Wang et al., 2011c; Wang et al., 2011d) proposed nonnegative matrix factorization (NMF) (Lee and Seung, 1999) based computational algorithms that have successfully solved the problems.

Due to its mathematical elegance and its equivalence to K-means clustering and spectral clustering (Ding et al., 2005), NMF (Lee and Seung, 1999) has been broadly studied in recent years and successfully solved a variety of practical problems in data mining and machine learning, such as those in computer vision (Wang et al., 2011b), bioinformatics (Wang et al., 2013), natural language understanding (Wang et al., 2011a), to name a few. Compared to many traditional clustering methods, such as K-means clustering, NMF has better mathematical interpretation, which usually lead to improved accuracy on clustering (Ding et al., 2010). Traditional clustering algorithms concentrate on dealing with homogeneous data, in which all the data belong to one single type (Wang et al., 2011d). To deal with the richer data structures in modern real-world applications, symmetric Nonnegative Matrix Tri-Factorization (NMTF)(Wang et al., 2011c) have demonstrated its effectiveness on simultaneous clustering of multi-type relational data by utilizing the interrelatedness among different data types.

Traditional NMF algorithms routinely use the least square error functions, which are notably known to be sensitive against outliers (Kong et al., 2011). However, at the era of big data outliers are inevitable due to the ever increasing data sizes. As a result, developing a more robust NMF model for multi-relational data clustering has become more and more important. In this paper, we further develop the symmetric NMF clustering model proposed in (Wang et al., 2011c) by using the ℓ_1-norm distances, such that our new clustering model is more robust against outliers, which is of particular importance in multi-relational data.

2 Robust Multi-Relational Clustering via ℓ_1-Norm Symmetric NMTF (S-NMTF)

In this section, we first introduce the backgrounds to use symmetric NMF to cluster multi-relational data. Then we develop our new ℓ_1-norm symmetric NMF model for better robustness against outlying data. The solution algorithm to our new model will be proposed and analyzed in the next section.

Notations. In this paper, we use upper case letters to denote matrices. Given a matrix M, its en-

Proceedings of the 53rd Annual Meeting of the Association for Computational Linguistics and the 7th International Joint Conference on Natural Language Processing (Short Papers), pages 397–401,
Beijing, China, July 26-31, 2015.

try at the i-th row and j-th column is denoted as $M_{(ij)}$. The Frobenius norm of a matrix M is denoted as $\|M\|_F = \left(\sum_i \sum_j M^2_{(ij)}\right)^{1/2}$ and its ℓ_1-norm is denoted as $\|M\|_1 = \sum_i \sum_j |M_{(ij)}|$.

2.1 Problem Formalization

K-type relational data set can be denoted as $\chi = \{\chi_1, \chi_2, \ldots, \chi_K\}$, where $\chi_k = \{x^k_1, x^k_2, \ldots, x^k_{n_k}\}$ represents the data set of k-th type. Suppose we are given a set of relationship matrices $\{R_{kl} \in \Re^{n_k \times n_l}\}_{(1\leq k\leq K, 1\leq l\leq K)}$ between different types of data objects, then we have $R_{kl} = R^T_{lk}$. Our goal is to simultaneously partition the data objects in $\chi_1, \chi_2, \ldots, \chi_K$ into $c_1, c_2, \ldots, c_K$ disjoint clusters respectively.

2.2 Our objective

To cluster multi-relation data, symmetric NMF has been taken advantage that solves the following optimization problem (Wang et al., 2008):

$$\begin{aligned} \min J = & \sum_{1\leq k<l\leq K} \|R_{kl} - G_k S_{kl} G_l^T\|^2_F, \\ s.t. \quad & G_k \geq 0, \ \forall\, 1 \leq k \leq K \ . \end{aligned} \tag{1}$$

It has also been shown that solving the above equation is equivalent to solve (Long et al., 2006):

$$\min J = \|R - GSG^T\|^2_F, \quad s.t. \quad G \geq 0, \tag{2}$$

in which

$$R = \begin{bmatrix} 0^{n_1\times n_1} & R_{12}^{n_1\times n_2} & \cdots & R_{1K}^{n_1\times n_K} \\ R_{21}^{n_2\times n_1} & 0^{n_2\times n_2} & \cdots & R_{2K}^{n_2\times n_K} \\ \vdots & \vdots & \ddots & \vdots \\ R_{K1}^{n_K\times n_1} & R_{K2}^{n_K\times n_2} & \cdots & 0^{n_K\times n_K} \end{bmatrix},$$

$$G = \begin{bmatrix} G_1^{n_1\times c_1} & 0^{n_1\times c_2} & \cdots & 0^{n_1\times c_K} \\ 0^{n_2\times c_1} & G_2^{n_2\times c_2} & \cdots & 0^{n_2\times c_K} \\ \vdots & \vdots & \ddots & \vdots \\ 0^{n_K\times c_1} & 0^{n_K\times c_2} & \cdots & G_K^{n_K\times c_K} \end{bmatrix},$$

$$S = \begin{bmatrix} 0^{c_1\times c_1} & S_{12}^{c_1\times c_2} & \cdots & S_{1K}^{c_1\times c_K} \\ S_{21}^{c_2\times c_1} & 0^{c_2\times c_2} & \cdots & S_{2K}^{c_2\times c_K} \\ \vdots & \vdots & \ddots & \vdots \\ S_{K1}^{c_K\times c_1} & S_{K2}^{c_K\times c_2} & \cdots & 0^{c_K\times c_K} \end{bmatrix}, \tag{3}$$

where $R_{ji} = R^T_{ij}$ and $S_{ij} = S^T_{ji}$.

Despite its successfulness of the method proposed in (Wang et al., 2011c) in multi-relational data clustering, the objectives in Equations (1—2) use the squared ℓ_2-norm distances to measure the matrix approximation errors, which, though, are prone to outliers. As a result, the clustering results could be heavily dominated by outlying data points with large approximation errors (Kong et al., 2011; Nie et al., 2011; Wang et al., 2014). To improve the robustness of the clustering model, following prior works (Kong et al., 2011; Nie et al., 2011; Wang et al., 2014) we propose to use the following ℓ_1-norm symmetric NMTF model for multi-relational data clustering:

$$\min J = \|R - GSG^T\|_1 \quad s.t. \quad G \geq 0, \tag{4}$$

In this new formulation, the approximation errors are measured by the ℓ_1-norm distances, which are expected to be more insensitive to outlying data points. As shown in Figure 1, when there exist outliers in the input data, traditional squared Frobenius-norm NMF are inclined to cluster incorrectly, while the ℓ_1-norm NMF are more robust and can cluster more accurately.

Algorithm 1: Algorithm to solve ℓ_1-norm S-NMTF

Data: Relationship matrices: $\{R_{ij}\}_{1\leq i<j\leq K}$
Result: Factor matrices: $\{G_k\}_{1\leq k\leq K}$
1. Construct R, G, S
2. Initialize G as in (Ding et al., 2006).
repeat
 3. Construct diagonal matrix D, where $D(i,i) = \frac{\sum |R-GSG^T|_i}{\|R-GSG^T\|_i^2}$.
 4. Compute $S = (G^TG)^{-1}G^TRG(G^TG)^{-1}$.
 5. Update $G_{(ij)} \leftarrow G_{(ij)} \left[\frac{(RDGS)_{(ij)}}{(GSG^TDGS)_{(ij)}}\right]^{\frac{1}{4}}$.
until *Converges*

3 Algorithm to Solve ℓ_1-Norm S-NMTF and its analysis

The computational algorithm for the proposed ℓ_1-norm S-NMTF approach is summarized in Algorithm 1 (Due to space limit, the derivation of the algorithm is skipped and will be provided in our journal version of the paper). Upon solution, the

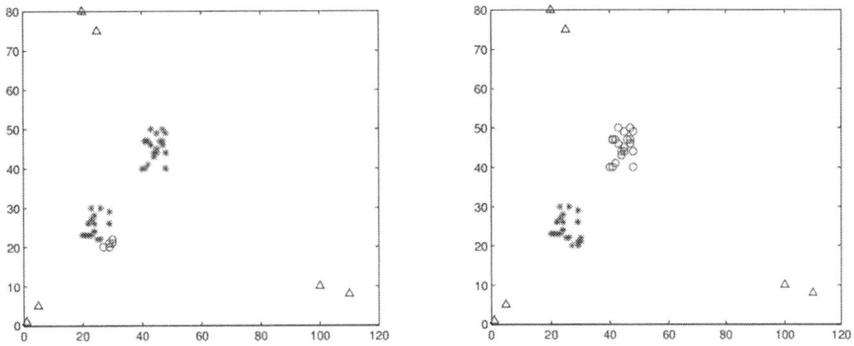

Figure 1: Clustering data in two clusters with some outliers (represented as triangle). **Left**: Clustering performance by using traditional squared Frobenius-norm NMF algorithm. **Right**: Clustering performance by using the proposed ℓ_1-norm NMF algorithm.

final cluster labels are obtained from the resulted G_k.

The following theorems guarantee the correctness of Algorithm 1 (Due to space limit, the derivation of the algorithm is skipped and will be provided in our journal version of the paper).

Theorem 3.1 *If the updating rules of G and S in Algorithm 1 converges, the final solution satisfies the KKT optimal condition.*

This is the fixed point relationships that the solution must satisfy.

The following lemmas and theorem guarantee the convergence of Algorithm 1 (Due to space limit, the derivation of the algorithm is skipped and will be provided in our journal version of the paper).

Lemma 3.2 *(Lee and Seung, 1999) $Z(h,h')$ is an auxiliary function of $F(h)$ if the conditions $Z(h,h') \geq F(h)$ and $Z(h,h') = F(h)$ are satisfied.*

Lemma 3.3 *(Lee and Seung, 1999) If Z is an auxiliary function for F, then F is non-increasing under the update $h^{(t+1)} = \arg\min_h Z(h,h')$.*

Theorem 3.4 *Let*

$$J(G) = \mathbf{tr}(-2RDGSG^T + GSG^TDGSG^T), \tag{5}$$

then the following function

$$Z(G,G') = -2\sum_{ijkl} G'_{(ji)}S_{(jk)}G'_{(kl)}D_{(ll)}R_{(li)}\left(1+\log\frac{G_{(ji)}G_{(kl)}}{G'_{(ij)}G'_{(kl)}}\right) + \sum_{ij}(G'SG'^TDG'S)_{(ij)}\frac{G^4_{(ij)}}{G'^3_{(ij)}} \tag{6}$$

is an auxiliary function of $J(G)$. Furthermore, it is a convex function in G and its global minimum is

$$G_{(ik)} = G_{(ik)}\left[\frac{(RDGS)_{(ik)}}{(GSG^TDGS)_{(ik)}}\right]^{\frac{1}{4}} \tag{7}$$

Based on the property of auxiliary function and convex function, by updating G, we can always get the optimal solution to the object function, thus determining the final cluster label.

4 Experiments Result

In this section, We test our proposed algorithm on IMDB dataset by using its inter-type relationship information.

4.1 Data set

We use the dataset from **ACL-IMDB** provided by (Maas et al., 2011). In this dataset, there is a subtraining set of 25000 highly polar movie reviews, in which positive and negative comments come up with one half(12500) each. The dataset also includes the following two important files: the content of each comment and the corresponding URL

where each comment comes from. There are also some other files but not related with the experiment we conduct, thus we skip them.

4.2 Experiments settings

In our experiment, we set the multi-type data as 3 types: author, comment and word. As it is discussed in the 3rd part, there are three relationships we need to find, which correspond to three matrices we need to construct the multi-type data matrix:comment-author, comment-word and author-word. By making use of the URL of every comment, we can find the author who posts the corresponding comment, thus we can build the author-comment matrix.Since each comment with content is given by the dataset file, we could therefore construct the matrix of comment-word, and the author-word matrix is the product of author-comment matrix and comment-word matrix.

We could find the first 1500 authors who post comments most, since the comments from the same person are more likely to have some correlations, such as similar sentence structures, same words and etc. We also rule out the stop-words since they may disturb the clustering and they are meaningless to the property of comments. To make our experiments to be more persuasive, we also add some noise to the three relationship matrices with a ratio of 25 percentage(1/5 in amplitude). By randomly choosing 500 authors from 1500, we could generate many sub-datasets to conduct our experiments.

4.3 Experiments Results

We compare the performance of our proposed ℓ_1-norm S-NMTF algorithm with other methods such as P-NMF, Frobenius norm S-NMTF, traditional NMF and K-means clustering. For simplicity, we only compare the clustering accuracy of comment-word matrix since its label (positive or negative) is fixed(the grounding label), thus could be compared with the clustering results by using the clustering algorithms.

Table 1 shows that when the data is pure, in many cases(more than the listed), ℓ_1-norm S-NMTF approach has better performance than others

Table 2 illustrates the situation when some noise is added to the data, it is easy to find that ℓ_1-norm S-NMTF algorithm is the best in terms of clustering accuracy. This meets our analysis in our Motivation part.

Alg	L11	L22	PMF	NMF	Kms
set 1	**0.578**	0.528	0.554	0.510	0.504
set 2	**0.583**	0.556	0.551	0.521	0.521
set 3	**0.584**	0.559	0.555	0.501	0.501
set 4	**0.551**	0.522	0.502	0.527	0.506
set 5	**0.566**	0.534	0.506	0.529	0.531
set 6	**0.558**	0.517	0.510	0.535	0.526

Table 1: Clustering Accuracy with Pure Data.

Alg	L11	L22	PMF	NMF	Kms
sub 1	**0.586**	0.545	0.508	0.530	0.530
sub 2	**0.575**	0.535	0.540	0.518	0.532
sub 3	**0.567**	0.528	0.520	0.500	0.500
sub 4	**0.574**	0.533	0.525	0.500	0.500
sub 5	**0.574**	0.537	0.530	0.519	0.518
sub 6	**0.556**	0.525	0.524	0.504	0.505

Table 2: Clustering Accuracy with Noise.

Careful examination in Table 3 reveals the fact that ℓ_1-norm S-NMTF algorithm performs more robust than any other algorithm. Though the clustering accuracy of ℓ_1-norm S-NMTF decreases when noise exists, still it reduces the least among the five algorithms. This result convincingly demonstrates the robustness of our proposed ℓ_1-norm S-NMTF method.

Alg	L11	L22	PMF	NMF	Kms
s.1(P)	**0.547**	0.546	0.521	0.546	0.546
s.1(N)	**0.546**	0.525	0.516	0.540	0.545
s.2(P)	**0.543**	0.543	0.534	0.543	0.543
s.2(N)	**0.543**	0.539	0.531	0.513	0.531
s.3(P)	**0.536**	0.536	0.524	0.536	0.536
s.3(N)	**0.536**	0.534	0.522	0.517	0.508

Table 3: Clustering Accuracy Contrast.

5 Conclusion

In this paper, we presented an ℓ_1-norm Symmetric Nonnegative Matrix Tri-Factorization Framework to cluster multi-type relational data simultaneously. Our proposed approach clusters different types of data, using its inter-type relationship by transforming the original problem into a symmetric NMTF problem. We also presented an auxiliary function and high order matrix inequality to derive the solution algorithm. The proposed algorithm not only makes use of the rich data structure to improve the clustering accuracy, but also remains robust when there is noise and outliers. Experimental results demonstrate the potential usage and advantage of ℓ_1-norm S-NMTF in clustering especially when there are outliers, which is in accordance with our theory analysis.

References

C. Ding, X. He, and H.D. Simon. 2005. On the equivalence of nonnegative matrix factorization and spectral clustering. In *SDM*.

C. Ding, T. Li, W. Peng, and H. Park. 2006. Orthogonal nonnegative matrix t-factorizations for clustering. In *SIGKDD*.

C. Ding, T. Li, and M.I. Jordan. 2010. Convex and semi-nonnegative matrix factorizations. *IEEE TPAMI*, 32(1):45–55.

Deguang Kong, Chris Ding, and Heng Huang. 2011. Robust nonnegative matrix factorization using l21-norm. In *Proceedings of the 20th ACM international conference on Information and knowledge management*, pages 673–682. ACM.

D.D. Lee and H.S. Seung. 1999. Learning the parts of objects by non-negative matrix factorization. *Nature*, 401(6755):788–791.

Bo Long, Zhongfei Mark Zhang, Xiaoyun Wu, and Philip S Yu. 2006. Spectral clustering for multi-type relational data. In *Proceedings of the 23rd international conference on Machine learning*, pages 585–592. ACM.

Andrew L. Maas, Raymond E. Daly, Peter T. Pham, Dan Huang, Andrew Y. Ng, and Christopher Potts. 2011. Learning word vectors for sentiment analysis. In *Proceedings of the 49th Annual Meeting of the Association for Computational Linguistics: Human Language Technologies*, pages 142–150, Portland, Oregon, USA, June. Association for Computational Linguistics.

Feiping Nie, Heng Huang, Chris Ding, Dijun Luo, and Hua Wang. 2011. Robust principal component analysis with non-greedy l1-norm maximization. In *IJCAI Proceedings-International Joint Conference on Artificial Intelligence*, volume 22, page 1433. Citeseer.

F. Wang, T. Li, and C. Zhang. 2008. Semi-supervised clustering via matrix factorization. In *SDM*.

H. Wang, H. Huang, F. Nie, and C. Ding. 2011a. Cross-language web page classification via dual knowledge transfer using nonnegative matrix tri-factorization. In *SIGIR*.

H. Wang, F. Nie, H. Huang, and C. Ding. 2011b. Dyadic transfer learning for cross-domain image classification. In *ICCV*.

Hua Wang, Heng Huang, and Chris Ding. 2011c. Simultaneous clustering of multi-type relational data via symmetric nonnegative matrix tri-factorization. In *Proceedings of the 20th ACM international conference on Information and knowledge management*, pages 279–284. ACM.

Hua Wang, Feiping Nie, Heng Huang, and Chris Ding. 2011d. Nonnegative matrix tri-factorization based high-order co-clustering and its fast implementation. In *Data Mining (ICDM), 2011 IEEE 11th International Conference on*, pages 774–783. IEEE.

Hua Wang, Heng Huang, Chris Ding, and Feiping Nie. 2013. Predicting protein–protein interactions from multimodal biological data sources via nonnegative matrix tri-factorization. *Journal of Computational Biology*, 20(4):344–358.

Hua Wang, Feiping Nie, and Heng Huang. 2014. Robust distance metric learning via simultaneous l1-norm minimization and maximization. In *Proceedings of the 31st International Conference on Machine Learning (ICML-14)*, pages 1836–1844.

Painless Labeling with Application to Text Mining

Sajib Dasgupta
Chittagong Indepedent University
Chittagong, Bangladesh
sdgnew@gmail.com

Abstract

Labeled data is not readily available for many natural language domains, and it typically requires expensive human effort with considerable domain knowledge to produce a set of labeled data. In this paper, we propose a simple unsupervised system that helps us create a labeled resource for categorical data (e.g., a document set) using only fifteen minutes of human input. We utilize the labeled resources to discover important insights about the data. The entire process is domain independent, and demands no prior annotation samples, or rules specific to an annotation.

1 Introduction

Consider the following two scenarios:

Scenario 1: We start processing a new language and we want to get an initial idea of the language before embarking on the expensive process of creating hand annotated resources. For instance, we may want to know how people express opinion in a language of interest, what characterizes the subjective content of the language and how expressions of opinion differ along opinion types. The question is how to acquire such first-hand insights of an unknown language in quick time and with minimal human effort?

Scenario 2: We have a set of blog articles and we are interested in learning how blogging differs across gender. In particular, we seek to learn the writing styles or other indicative patterns – topics of interest, word choices etc. – that can potentially distinguish writings across gender. A traditional NLP approach would be to collect a set of articles that are tagged with gender information, which we can then input to a learning system to learn patterns that can differentiate gender. What if no such annotation is available, as the bloggers don't reveal their gender information? Could we arrange a human annotation task to annotate the articles along gender? Often the articles contain explicit patterns (e.g., "my boyfriend", "as a woman" etc.) which help the annotators to annotate the articles. Often there are no indicative patterns in the written text, and it becomes impossible to annotate the articles reliably.

The above scenarios depict the cases when we are resource constrained and creating a new resource is nontrivial and time consuming. Given such difficulties, it would be helpful if we could design a system that requires less human input to create a labeled resource. In this paper, we present a simple unsupervised system that helps us create a labeled resource with minimal human effort. The key to our method is that instead of labeling the entire set of unlabeled instances the system labels a subset of data instances for which it is confident to achieve high level of accuracy. We experiment with several document labeling tasks and show that a high-quality labeled resource can be produced by a clustering-based labeling system that requires a mere fifteen minutes of human input. It achieves 85% and 78% accuracy for the task of sentiment and gender classification, showing its effectiveness on two nontrivial labeling tasks with distinct characteristics (see Section 3).

We also utilize the labeled resources created by our system to learn discriminative patterns that help us gain insights into a dataset. For instance, we learn how users generally express opinion in a language of interest, and how writing varies across gender. The next section describes the details of our main algorithm. We present experimental results in Section 3 and 4.

Proceedings of the 53rd Annual Meeting of the Association for Computational Linguistics and the 7th International Joint Conference on Natural Language Processing (Short Papers), pages 402–407, Beijing, China, July 26-31, 2015.

The sound from my system did seem to be a little better (the CD's were not skipping as much). But the bottom line is it didn't fix the problem as the CDs are still skipping noticeably, although not as bad as before. ..

Table 1: Snippet of an ambiguous CD Player review.

2 Problem Formulation

We consider a general classification framework. Let $X = \{x_1, \ldots, x_n\}$ represents a categorical dataset with n data points where $x_i \in \Re^d$. Let $c_x \in$ {1,-1} is the true label of x[1]. Our goal is label a subset of the data, $X' = \{C_1, C_2\} \subseteq X$, where C_1 and C_2 comprise data points of positive and negative class respectively. Note that, X' represents the subset of datapoints that are confidently labeled by the system.

To illustrate, we show a snippet of a CD player review taken from Amazon in Table 1. As you can see this review is highly ambiguous, as it describes both the positive and negative aspects of the product: while the phrases *a little better*, *not skipping*, and *not as bad* conveys a positive sentiment, the phrases *didn't fix* and *skipping noticeably* are negative sentiment-bearing. Any automated system would find it *hard* to correctly label this review, as the review is highly ambiguous. Our goal is to remove such ambiguous data points from the data space and label the remaining unambiguous data points. The fact that unambiguous data instances are easier to label allows us to use an automated system to label them quickly with minimal human effort (see the next section).

Now how could we set apart unambiguous data points from the ambiguous ones from a set of unlabeled data points? Note that we desire the system to be unsupervised. We also desire the system to be generic i.e., applicable to any application domain. Next we show how we extend spectral clustering to achieve this goal.

2.1 Ambiguity Resolution with Iterative Spectral Clustering

In spectral clustering, a set of n data points is represented as an undirected graph, where each node corresponds to a data point and the edge weight between two nodes is their similarity as defined by S. The goal is to induce a clustering, or equivalently, a *partitioning function* f, which is typically represented as a vector of length n such that $f(i) \in \{1, -1\}$ indicates which of the two clusters data point i should be assigned to.

[1]We present our system for binary classification task. It can be extended fairly easily to multi-way classification tasks.

In spectral clustering, the normalized cut partition of a similarity graph, S is derived from the solution of the following constrained optimization problem: $\text{argmin}_{f\in\Re^n} \sum_{i,j} S_{i,j}(\frac{f(i)}{\sqrt{d_i}} - \frac{f(j)}{\sqrt{d_j}})^2$ subject to $f^T D f = 1$ and $Df \perp \mathbf{1}$, where D is a diagonal matrix with $D_{i,i} = \sum_j S_{i,j}$ and $d_i = D_{i,i}$. The closed form solution to this optimization problem is the eigenvector corresponding to the second smallest eigenvalue of the Laplacian matrix, $L = D^{-1/2}(D - S)D^{-1/2}$ (Shi and Malik (2000)). Clustering using the second eigenvector, is trivial: since we have a linearization of the points, all we need to do is to determine a threshold for partitioning the data points.

Second eigenvector reveals useful information regarding the ambiguity of the individual data points. In the computation of eigenvectors each data point factors out orthogonal projections of each of the neighboring data points. Ambiguous data points factor out orthogonal projections from both the positive and negative data instances, and hence they have near zero values in the pivot eigenvectors. We exploit this important information. The basic idea is that the data points with near zero values in the second eigenvector are more ambiguous than those with large absolute values. Hence, to cluster only the unambiguous datapoints, we can therefore sort the data points according to second eigenvector, and keep only the top and bottom $m (m < n)$ datapoints. Finally, instead of removing $(n - m)$ datapoints at once, we remove them in iteration.

Here is our final algorithm:

1. Let $s : X \times X \rightarrow \Re$ be a similarity function defined over data X. Construct a similarity matrix S such that $S_{ij} = s(x_i, x_j)$.

2. Construct the Laplacian matrix $L = D^{-1/2}(D - S)D^{-1/2}$, where D is a diagonal matrix with $D_{i,i} = \sum_j S_{i,j}$.

3. Find *eigenvector* e_2 corresponding to second smallest eigenvalue of L.

4. Sort X according to e_2 and remove α points indexed from $(|X|/2 - \alpha/2 + 1)$ to $(|X|/2 + \alpha/2)$.

5. If $|X| = m$, goto Step 6; else goto Step 1.

Dataset	System	$m = \frac{1}{5}n$	$m = \frac{2}{5}n$	$m = \frac{3}{5}n$	$m = \frac{4}{5}n$	$m = n$	Fully Supervised
Gender	Kmeans++	52.3%	51.6%	52.3%	51.7%	51.2%	-
	TSVM	53.1%	53.6%	52.7%	52.6%	52.0%	**80.4%**
	OUR	**78.5%**	**73.7%**	**69.3%**	**66.8%**	**64.4%**	-
Spam	Kmeans++	67.6%	58.6%	54.9%	53.8%	52.4%	-
	TSVM	**87.8%**	**85.0%**	**82.7%**	**80.7%**	**78.9%**	**96.9%**
	OUR	83.8%	82.9%	80.4%	79.8%	78.4%	-
Sentiment	Kmeans++	64.5%	61.4%	60.5%	57.8%	56.5%	-
	TSVM	70.2%	65.1%	61.5%	61.8%	60.4%	**86.4%**
	OUR	**90.3%**	**85.4%**	**79.9%**	**74.9%**	**71.2%**	-

Table 2: Accuracy of automatically labeled data for each dataset. We also report 5-fold supervised classification result for each dataset.

6. Sort X according to e_2 and put top $\frac{m}{2}$ data points in cluster C_1 and bottom $\frac{m}{2}$ data points in cluster C_2.

In the algorithm stated above, we start with an initial clustering of all of the data points, and then iteratively remove the α most ambiguous points from the data space. We iterate the process of removing ambiguous data points and re-clustering until we have m data points remaining. It should not be difficult to see the advantage of removing the data points in an iterative fashion (as opposed to removing them in a single iteration): the clusters produced in a given iteration are supposed to be better than those in the previous iterations, as subsequent clusterings are generated from less ambiguous points. In all our experiments, we set α to 100. Finally, we label the clusters by inspecting 10 randomly sampled points from each cluster. We use the cluster labels to assign labels to the m unambiguous data points. Note that labeling the clusters is the only form of human input we require in our system.

3 Experiments

We use three text classification tasks for evaluation:

Gender Classification: Here we classify blog articles according to whether an article is written by a male or female. We employ the blog dataset as introduced by Schler et al. (2006) for this task. The dataset contains 19320 blog articles, out of which we randomly selected 5000 blog articles as our dataset.

Spam Classification: Here the goal is to determine whether an email is Spam or Ham (i.e., not spam). We use the Enron spam dataset as introduced by Metris et al. (Metsis et al. (2006)). We join together the BG section of Spam emails and kaminski section of Ham emails, and randomly selected 5000 emails as our dataset.

Sentiment Classification: Here the goal is to determine whether the sentiment expressed in a product review is positive or negative. We use Pang et al.'s movie review dataset for this task (Pang et al. (2002)). The dataset contains 2000 reviews annotated with the positive and negative sentiment label.

To preprocess a document, we first tokenize and downcase it, remove stop words, and represent it as a vector of unigrams, using frequency as presence. For spectral clustering, we use dot product as a measure of similarity between two documents vectors.

Dataset	Data points	Features	Pos:Neg
Gender	5000	75188	2751:2249
Spam	5000	23760	2492:2508
Sentiment	2000	24531	1000:1000

Table 3: Description of the datasets.

3.1 Accuracy of Automatically Labeled Data

For each dataset, given n unlabeled data points, we apply our system to label $m(m <= n)$ least ambiguous data points. We check the quality of labeled data by comparing the assigned (cluster) labels of m datapoints against their true labels, and show the accuracy. Table 2 shows the accuracy of automatically labeled data for five different values of m for each dataset. For example, when $m = n/5$, our system labels 1000 out of available 5000 data points with 78.5% accuracy for the gender dataset. These 1000 data points are the most unambiguous out of the 5000 data points, as selected by the algorithm. For $m = n$ the system labels the entire dataset.

As you can see, for all three datasets, the accuracy of labeling unambiguous data instances is much higher than the accuracy of labeling the entire dataset. For instance, the accuracy of top $n/5$ unambiguous labeled instances of the sentiment dataset is 90.3%, whereas the accuracy of labeling the entire dataset is 71.2%. The more unambiguous the data instances are the higher is the quality of labeled data (as shown by the fact that the accuracy of labeled instances increases as we increase m). Notice that our system labels 60% of the data points of the spam dataset with 80.4% accuracy; 40% of the data points of the sentiment dataset with 85.4% accuracy; and 20% of the data points of the gender dataset with 78.5% accuracy.

We also report 5-fold supervised classification result for each dataset. We used linear SVM for classification with all parameters set to their default values. As you can see, when $m = n/5$ our system achieves near supervised labeling performance for the gender and sentiment dataset. One of the reviewers asked how SVM performed when trained with unambiguous data instances alone. We refer to Dasgupta and Ng (2009) where the authors report that training SVM with unambiguous data alone produces rather inferior result. They, however, work on a small data sample. It would be interesting to know whether large number of unambiguous (or, semi-ambiguous) data instances could offset the need for ambiguous data in a general classification setting. Given that unlabeled data are abundantly available in many NLP tasks, one can employ our method to create decent size labeled data quickly from unlabeled data, and utilize them later in the process to build an independent classifier or augment the performance of an existing classifier (Fuxman et al. (2009)).

We employed two baseline algorithms, i.e., kmeans++ and a semi-supervised learning system, Transductive SVM. For kmeans++ we used the following as a measure of ambiguity for each data point: $1 - \frac{(\mathbf{x}-\mu_i)^2}{\sum_i^k (\mathbf{x}-\mu_i)^2}$, where $\mathbf{x}$ is a data vector and μ_i, $i = 1 : k$ are k mean vectors. It ranges from 0 to 1. Ambiguity score near 0.5 suggests that the data point is ambiguous. Following common practice in document clustering, we reduced the dimensions of the data to 100 using SVD before we apply kmeans++. For transductive SVM, we randomly selected 20 labeled data points as seeds. Table 2 shows the result for each baseline.

Notice that our system beat the baselines (one of them is a semisupervised system) by a big margin for the Gender and Sentiment dataset, whereas Transductive SVM performs the best for the Spam dataset. Interesting to point that our method of removing ambiguous data instances to get a qualitatively stronger clustering contrasts with the max-margin methods which use the ambiguous data instances to acquire the margin. Also important to mention that spectral clustering is a graph-based clustering algorithm, where similarity measure employed to construct the graph plays a crucial role in performance (Maier et al. (2013)). In fact, "right" construction of the feature space and a right similarity measure can considerably change the performance of a graph-based clustering algorithm. We have not tried different similarity measures in this initial study, but it provides us room for improvement for a dataset like Spam.

Implementation Details: On a machine with 3GHz of Intel Quad Core Processor and 4GB of RAM, the iterative spectral clustering algorithm takes less than 2 minutes in Matlab for a dataset comprising 5000 data points and 75188 features. This along with the fact that human labelers take on average 12 minutes to label the clusters suggests that the entire labeling process requires less than 15 minutes to complete.

4 Mining Patterns and Insights

In this section, we show that we can utilize the labeled resources created by our system to learn discriminative patterns that help us gain insights into a dataset (Don et al. (2007), Larsen and Aone (1999), Cheng et al. (2007), Maiya et al. (2013)). We utilize the top $n/5$ unambiguous labeled instances for this task, where n is size of the dataset. Note that the quality of unambiguous labeled instances is much higher than the entire set of labeled instances (see Section 3.1), so the statistics we collect from the unambiguous labeled instances to identify discriminative patterns are supposedly more reliable.

We learn our first category of discriminative patterns the following way: for each cluster, we rank all unigrams in the vocabulary by their weighted log-likelihood ratio:

$$P(w_t \mid c_j) \cdot \log \frac{P(w_t \mid c_j)}{P(w_t \mid \neg c_j)}$$

where w_t and c_j denote the t-th word in the vocabulary and the j-th cluster, respectively, and each conditional probability is add one smoothed. Informally, a unigram w will have a high rank with respect to a cluster c if it appears frequently in c and infrequently in $\neg c$. The higher the score the more discriminative the pattern is. We also learn the discriminative bigrams similarly: for each cluster, we rank all bigrams by their weighted

Dataset	Class	Top Discriminative Unigrams
Gender	**Female**	*haha, wanna, sooo, lol, ppl, omg, hahaha, ur, yay, soo, cuz, bye, soooo, hehe, ate, hurts, sucks.*
	Male	*provide, reported, policies, administration, companies, development, policy, services, nations.*
Spam	**Spam**	*vicodin, goodbye, utf, rolex, watches, loading, promotion, reproductions, nepel, fw, fwd, click.*
	Ham	*risk, securities, statements, exchange, terms, third, events, act, investing, objectives, assumptions.*
Sentiment	**Positive**	*relationship, husband, effective, mother, strong, perfect, tale, novel, fascinating, outstanding.*
	Negative	*stupid, worst, jokes, bunch, sequel, lame, guess, dumb, boring, maybe, guys, video, flick, oh.*

Table 4: Top discriminative unigram patterns identified by our system.

Dataset	Class	Top Discriminative Bigrams
Gender	**Female**	*wanna go, im so, im gonna, at like, don't wanna, was sooo, was gonna, soo much, so yeah.*
	Male	*to provide, york times, the issue, understanding of, the political, bush admin, the democratic.*
Spam	**Spam**	*promotional material, adobe photoshop, name it, choose from, you name, stop getting, office xp.*
	Ham	*investment advice, this report, respect to, current price, risks and, information provided.*
Sentiment	**Positive**	*story of, her husband, relationship with, begins to, love and, life of, the central, the perfect.*
	Negative	*the worst, bad movie, bunch of, got to, too bad, action sequences, waste of, than this, the bad.*

Table 5: Top discriminative bigram patterns identified by our system.

log-likelihood ratio score and select the top scoring bigrams as the most discriminative bigrams.

Table 4 and 5 show the most discriminative unigrams and bigrams learned by our system. Notice that the learned patterns are quite informative. For instance, in the case of blog dataset we learn that certain word usages (e.g., sooo, cuz etc.) are more common in women's writings, whereas men's writings often contain discussion of politics, news and technology. For sentiment data, the patterns correspond well to the generic sentiment lexicon manually created by the sentiment experts. The ability of our system to learn top sentiment features could be handy for a resource-scarce language, which may not have a general purpose sentiment lexicon. Note that the system is not limited to unigram and bigram patterns only. The labeled instances can be utilized similarly to gather statistics for other form of usage patterns including syntactic and semantic patterns for document collections.

5 Related Work

Automatic extraction of labeled data has gained momentum in recent years (Durme and Pasca (2008), Nakov and Hearst (2005), Fuxman et al. (2009)). Traditionally, researchers use task-specific heuristics to generate labeled data, e.g., searching for a specific pattern in the web to collect data instances of a particular category (Hearst (1992), Go et al. (2009), Hu et al. (2013)). Another line of research follows semi-supervised information extraction task, where given a list of seed instances of a particular category, a bootstrapping algorithm is applied to mine new instances from large corpora (Riloff and Jones (1999), Etzioni et al. (2005), Durme and Pasca (2008)).

There has also been a surge of interests in unsupervised approaches which primarily rely on clustering to induce psuedo labels from large amount of text (Clark (2000), Slonim and Tishby (2000), Sahoo et al. (2006), Christodoulopoulos et al. (2010)). We differ from existing unsupervised clustering algorithms in a way that we uncomplicate spectral clustering by forcing it to cluster unambiguous data points only, which ensures that the system makes less mistakes during clustering and the clustered data are qualitatively strong.

6 Conclusion

We have presented a system that helps us create a labeled resource for a given dataset with minimal human effort. We also utilize the labeled resources to discover important insights about the data. The ability of our system to learn and visualize top discriminative patterns facilitates exploratory data analysis for a dataset that might be unknown to us. Even if we have some knowledge of the data, the system may unveil additional characterisitcs that are unknown to us. The top features induced for each classification task can also be interpreted as our system's ability to discover new feature spaces, which can be utilized independently or along with a simpler feature space (e.g., *bag of words*) to learn a better classification model. Additional research is needed to further explore this idea.

Acknowledgements

We acknowledge three anonymous reviewers and Vincent Ng for their valuable feedback on an earlier draft of the paper.

References

H. Cheng, X. Yan, J. Han, and C. Hsu. 2007. Discriminative frequent pattern analysis for effective classification. In *International Conference on Data Engineering (ICDE)*.

C. Christodoulopoulos, S. Goldwater, and M. Steedman. 2010. Two decades of unsupervised pos induction: How far have we come? In *Empirical Methods in Natural Language Processing (EMNLP)*.

Alexander Clark. 2000. Inducing syntactic categories by context distributional clustering. In *the Conference on Natural Language Learning (CoNLL)*.

S. Dasgupta and V. Ng. 2009. Mine the easy, classify the hard: A semi-supervised approach to automatic sentiment classification. In *ACL-IJCNLP 2009: Proceedings of the Main Conference*.

A. Don, E. Zheleva, M. Gregory, S. Tarkan, L. Auvil, T. Clement, B. Shneiderman, and C. Plaisant. 2007. Discovering interesting usage patterns in text collections: integrating text mining with visualization. In *Proceedings of the ACM International Conference on Information and Knowledge Management (CIKM)*.

Benjamin Van Durme and Marius Pasca. 2008. Finding cars, goddesses and enzymes: Parametrizable acquisition of labeled instances for open-domain information extraction. In *the AAAI Conference on Artificial Intelligence (AAAI)*.

O. Etzioni, M. Cafarella, D. Downey, A. Popescu, T. Shaked, S. Soderland, D. Weld, and A. Yates. 2005. Unsupervised named-entity extraction from the web: an experimental study. In *Artificial Intelligence*.

A. Fuxman, A. Kannan, A. Goldberg, R. Agrawal, P. Tsaparas, and J. Shafer. 2009. Improving classification accuracy using automatically extracted training data. In *15th ACM Conference on Knowledge Discovery and Data Mining (SIGKDD)*.

A Go, R Bhayani, and L Huang. 2009. Twitter sentiment classification using distant supervision. In *Project Report, Stanford University*.

M. A. Hearst. 1992. Automatic acquisition of hyponyms from large text corpora. In *the International Conference on Computational Linguistics (COLING)*.

X. Hu, J. Tang, H. Gao, and H. Liu. 2013. Unsupervised sentiment analysis with emotional signals. In *In the Proceedings of the International World Wide Web Conference (WWW)*.

B. Larsen and C. Aone. 1999. Fast and effective text mining using linear-time document clustering. In *the Conference on Knowledge Discovery and Data Mining (SIGKDD)*.

M. Maier, U. von Luxburg, and M. Hein. 2013. How the result of graph clustering methods depends on the construction of the graph. In *ESAIM: Probability and Statistics, vol. 17*.

A. S. Maiya, J. P. Thompson, F. Loaiza-Lemos, and R. M. Rolfe. 2013. Exploratory analysis of highly heterogeneous document collections. In *the Conference on Knowledge Discovery and Data Mining (SIGKDD)*.

V. Metsis, I. Androutsopoulos, and G. Paliouras. 2006. Spam filtering with naive bayes - which naive bayes? In *3rd Conference on Email and Anti-Spam (CEAS)*.

Preslav Nakov and Marti Hearst. 2005. Using the web as an implicit training set: Application to structural ambiguity resolution. In *Empirical Methods in Natural Language Processing (EMNLP)*.

Bo Pang, Lillian Lee, and Shivakumar Vaithyanathan. 2002. Thumbs up? Sentiment classification using machine learning techniques. In *Proceedings of Empirical Methods in Natural Language Processing (EMNLP)*.

E. Riloff and R. Jones. 1999. Learning dictionaries for information extraction by multi-level bootstrapping. In *Proceedings of the ACM International Conference on Information and Knowledge Management (CIKM)*.

N. Sahoo, J. Callan, R. Krishnan, G. Duncan, and R. Padman. 2006. Incremental hierarchical clustering of text documents. In *the International Conference on Information and Knowledge Management (CIKM)*.

J. Schler, M. Koppel, S. Argamon, and J. Pennebaker. 2006. Effects of age and gender in blogging. In *AAAI Symposium on Computational Approaches for Analyzing Weblogs*.

Jianbo Shi and Jitendra Malik. 2000. Normalized cuts and image segmentation. *IEEE Transactions on Pattern Analysis and Machine Intelligence*.

Noam Slonim and Naftali Tishby. 2000. Document clustering using word clusters via the information bottleneck method. In *Proceedings of the ACM SIGIR Conference on Research and Development in Information Retrieval*.

FrameNet+: Fast Paraphrastic Tripling of FrameNet

Ellie Pavlick[1] **Travis Wolfe**[2,3] **Pushpendre Rastogi**[2]
Chris Callison-Burch[1] **Mark Dredze**[2,3] **Benjamin Van Durme**[2,3]
[1]Computer and Information Science Department, University of Pennsylvania
[2]Center for Language and Speech Processing, Johns Hopkins University
[3]Human Language Technology Center of Excellence, Johns Hopkins University

Abstract

We increase the lexical coverage of FrameNet through automatic paraphrasing. We use crowdsourcing to manually filter out bad paraphrases in order to ensure a high-precision resource. Our expanded FrameNet contains an additional 22K lexical units, a 3-fold increase over the current FrameNet, and achieves 40% better coverage when evaluated in a practical setting on New York Times data.

1 Introduction

Frame semantics describes a word in relation to real-world events, entities, and activities. Frame semantic analysis can improve natural language understanding (Fillmore and Baker, 2001), and has been applied to tasks like question answering (Shen and Lapata, 2007) and recognizing textual entailment (Burchardt and Frank, 2006; Aharon et al., 2010). FrameNet (Fillmore, 1982; Baker et al., 1998) is a widely-used lexical-semantic resource embodying frame semantics. It contains close to 1,000 manually defined *frames*, i.e. representations of concepts and their semantic properties, covering a wide array of concepts from Expensiveness to Obviousness.

Frames in FrameNet are characterized by a set of semantic roles and a set of lexical units (LUs), which are word/POS pairs that "evoke" the frame. For example, the following sentence contains a mention (i.e. *target*) of the Obviousness frame: *In late July, it was barely visible to the unaided eye.* This particular target instantiates several semantic roles of the Obviousness frame, including a Phenomenon (*it*) and a Perceiver (*the unaided eye*). Here, the LU `visible.a` evokes the frame. In total, the Obviousness frame has 13 LUs including `clarity.n`, `obvious.a`, and `show.v`.

accurate, **ambiguous**, **apparent**, **apparently**, audible, **axiomatic**, **blatant**, **blatantly**, **blurred**, **blurry**, **certainly**, **clarify**, clarity, clear, clearly, **confused**, **confusing**, **conspicuous**, **crystal-clear**, **dark**, **definite**, **definitely**, **demonstrably**, **discernible**, **distinct**, evident, **evidently**, **explicit**, **explicitly**, **flagrant**, **fuzzy**, **glaring**, **imprecise**, **inaccurate**, **lucid**, manifest, **manifestly**, **markedly**, **naturally**, **notable**, **noticeable**, **obscure**, **observable**, obvious, obviously, **opaque**, **openly**, **overt**, **patently**, **perceptible**, **plain**, **precise**, **prominent**, **self-evident**, show, show up, **significantly**, **soberly**, **specific**, **straightforward**, **strong**, **sure**, **tangible**, **transparent**, **unambiguous**, **unambiguously**, **uncertain**, unclear, **undoubtedly**, **unequivocal**, **unequivocally**, **unspecific**, **vague**, **viewable**, **visibility**, visible, **visibly**, **visual**, **vividly**, **well**,[1] **woolly**

Table 1: 81 LUs invoking the Obviousness frame according to the new FrameNet+. New LUs (bold) have been added using the method of paraphrasing and human-vetting described in Section 4.

The semantic information in FrameNet (FN) is broadly useful for problems such as entailment (Ellsworth and Janin, 2007; Aharon et al., 2010) and knowledge base population (Mohit and Narayanan, 2003; Christensen et al., 2010; Gregory et al., 2011), and is of general enough interest to language understanding that substantial effort has focused on building parsers to map natural language onto FrameNet frames (Gildea and Jurafsky, 2002; Das and Smith, 2012). In practice, however, FrameNet's usefulness is limited by its size. FN was built entirely manually by linguistic experts. As a result, despite many years of work, most of the words that one confronts in naturally occurring text do not appear at all in FN. For example, the word *blatant* is likely to evoke the Obviousness frame, but is not present in FN's list of LUs (Table 1). In fact, out of the targets we sample in this work (described in Section 4), fewer than 50% could be mapped to a correct frame using the LUs in FrameNet. This finding is consistent with what has been reported by Palmer and Sporleder (2010). Such low lexical coverage prevents FN from applying to many real-world applications.

[1]*well* received a rating of 3.67 as a paraphrase of *clearly* in the context *the intention to do so is clearly present.*

Proceedings of the 53rd Annual Meeting of the Association for Computational Linguistics and the 7th International Joint Conference on Natural Language Processing (Short Papers), pages 408–413,
Beijing, China, July 26-31, 2015.

Frame	Original	Paraphrase	Frame-annotated sentence
Quantity	amount	figure	It is not clear if this **figure** includes the munitions...
Expertise	expertise	specialization	... the technology, **specialization**, and infrastructure...
Labeling	called	dubbed	... eliminate who he **dubbed** Sheiks of sodomite...
Importance	significant	noteworthy	... assistance provided since the 1990s is **noteworthy**...
Mental_property	crazy	berserk	You know it's **berserk**.

Table 2: Examples paraphrases from FrameNet's annotated fulltext. The bolded words are automatically proposed rewrites from PPDB.

In this work, we triple the lexical coverage of FrameNet quickly and with high precision. We do this in two stages: 1) we use rules from the Paraphrase Database (Ganitkevitch et al., 2013) to automatically paraphrase FN sentences and 2) we apply crowdsourcing to manually verify that the automatic paraphrases are of high quality. While prior efforts have entertained the idea of expanding FN's coverage (Ferrández et al., 2010; Das and Smith, 2012; Fossati et al., 2013), none have resulted in a publicly available resource that can be easily used. As our main contribution, we release FrameNet+, a huge, manually-vetted extension to the current FrameNet. FrameNet+ provides over 22,000 new frame/LU mappings in a format that can be readily incorporated into existing systems. We demonstrate that the expanded resource provides a 40% improvement in lexical coverage in a practical setting.

2 Expanding FrameNet Automatically

The Paraphrase Database (PPDB) (Ganitkevitch et al., 2013) is an enormous collection of lexical, phrasal, and syntactic paraphrases. The database is released in six sizes (S to XXXL) ranging from highest precision/lowest recall to lowest average precision/highest recall. We focus on lexical (single word) paraphrases from the XL distribution, of which there are over 370K.

Our aim is to increase the type-level coverage of FN. We use the rules in PPDB along with a 5-gram Kneser-Ney smoothed language model (Heafield et al., 2013) to paraphrase FN's full frame-annotated sentences (called *fulltext*). We ignore paraphrase rules which are redundant with LUs already covered by FN. This method for automatic paraphrasing has been discussed previously by Rastogi and Van Durme (2014). However, whereas their work only discussed the idea as a hypothetical way of augmenting FN, we apply the method, vet the results, and release it as a public resource.

In total, we generate 188,061 paraphrased sentences, covering 686 frames. Table 2 shows some of the paraphrases produced.

3 Manual Refining with Crowdsourcing

Our automatic process produces a large number of good paraphrases, but does not address issues like word sense, and many of the paraphrased LUs alter the sentence so that it no longer evokes the intended frame. For example, PPDB proposes *free* as a paraphrase of *open*. This is a good paraphrase in the Secrecy_status frame but does not hold for the Openness frame (Table 3).

✓	Secrecy_status
	The facilities are **open** to public scrutiny
	The facilities are **free** to public scrutiny
X	Openness
	Museum (**open** Wednesday and Friday.)
	Museum (**free** Wednesday and Friday.)

Table 3: Turkers approved *free* as a paraphrase of *open* for the Secrecy_status frame (rating of 4.3) but rejected it in the Openness frame (rating of 1.6).

We therefore refine the automatic paraphrases manually to remove paraphrased LUs which do not evoke the same frame as the original LU. We show each sentence to three unique workers on Amazon Mechanical Turk (MTurk) and ask each to judge how well the paraphrase retains the meaning of the original phrase. We use the 5-point grading scale for paraphrase proposed by Callison-Burch (2008).

To ensure that annotators perform our task conscientiously, we embed gold-standard control sentences taken from WordNet synsets. Overall, workers were 76% accurate on our controls and showed good levels of agreement– the average correlation between two annotators' ratings was $\rho = 0.49$.

Figure 1 shows the distribution of Turkers' ratings for the 188K automatically paraphrased targets. In 44% of cases, the new LU was judged to retain the meaning of the original LU given the frame-specific context. These 85K sentences contain 22K unique frame/LU mappings which we are able to confidently add to FN, tripling the total number in the resource. Figure 1 shows 69 new LUs added to the Obviousness frame.

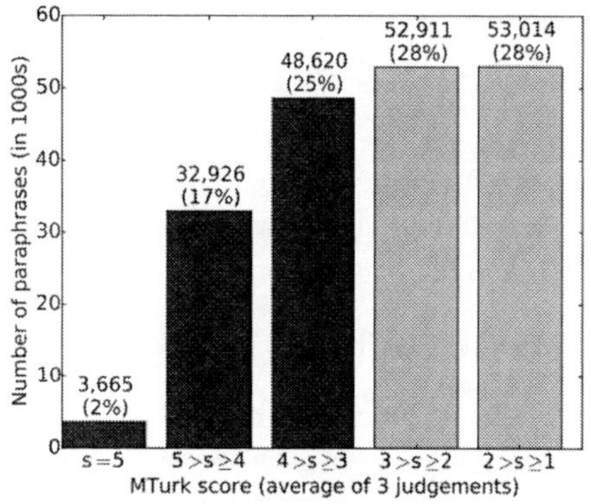

Figure 1: Distribution of MTurk ratings for paraphrased full-text sentences. 44% received an average rating ≥ 3, indicating the paraphrased LU was a good fit for the frame-specific context.

4 Evaluation

We aim to measure the type-level coverage improvements provided by our expanded FrameNet in a practical setting. Ideally, one would like to identify frames evoked by arbitrary sentences from natural text. To emulate this setting, we consider potentially frame-evoking LUs sampled from the New York Times. The question we ask is: does the resource contain an entry associating this LU with the frame that is actually evoked by this target?

FrameNet+ We refer to the expanded FrameNet, which contains the current FN's LUs as well as the proposed paraphrased LUs, as FrameNet+. The size and precision of FrameNet+ can be tuned by setting a threshold t and only including LU/frame mappings for which the average MTurk rating was at least t. Setting $t = 0$ includes all paraphrases, even those which human's judged to be incorrect, while setting $t > 5$ includes no paraphrases, and is equal to the current FN. Unless otherwise specified, we set $t = 3$. This includes all paraphrases which were judged minimally as "retaining the meaning of the original."

Sampling LUs We consider a word to be "potentially frame-evoking" if FN+ ($t = 0$) contains some entry for the word, i.e. the word is either an LU in the current FN or appears in PPDB-XL as a paraphrase of some LU in the current FN. We sample 300 potentially frame-evoking word types from the New York Times: 100 each nouns, verbs, and adjectives. We take a stratified sample: within each POS, types are divided into buckets based on their frequency, and we sample uniformly from each bucket.

Annotation For each of the potentially frame-evoking words in our sample, we have expert (non-MTurk) annotators determine the frame evoked. The annotator is given the candidate LU in the context of the NYT sentence in which it occurred, and is shown the list of frames which are potentially evoked by this LU according to FrameNet+. The annotator then chooses which of the proposed frames fits the target, or determines that none do. We measure agreement by having two experts label each target. On average, agreement was good (κ=0.56). In cases where they disagreed, the annotators discussed and came to a final consensus.

Results We compute the *coverage* of a resource as the percent of targets for which the resource contained a correct LU/frame mapping. Figure 2 shows the coverage computed for the current FN compared to FN+. By including the human-vetted paraphrases, FN+ is able to return a correct LU/frame mapping for 60% of the targets in our sample, 40% more targets than were covered by the current FN. Table 4 shows some sentences covered by FN+ that are missed by the current FN.

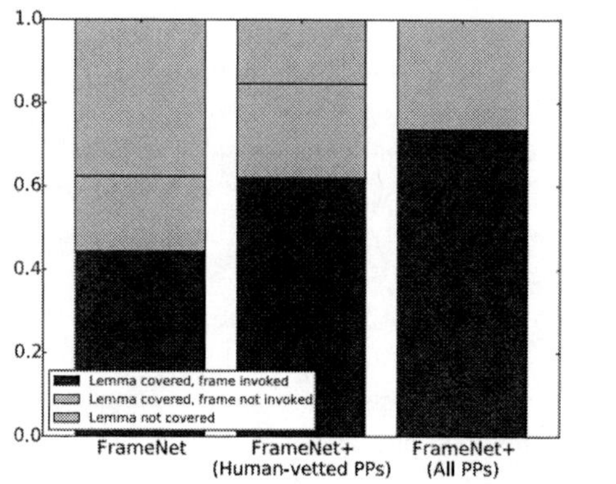

Figure 2: Number of LUs covered by the current FrameNet vs. two versions of FrameNet+: one including manually-approved paraphrases ($t = 3$), and one including all paraphrases ($t = 0$).

Figure 3 compares FN+'s coverage and number of LUs per frame using different paraphrase quality thresholds t. FN+ provides an average of more than 40 LUs per frame, compared to just over 10 LUs per frame in the current FN. Adding un-vetted

LU	Frame	NYT Sentence
outsider	Indigenous_origin	... I get more than my fair share because I 'm the ultimate **outsider**...
mini	Size	... a **mini** version of "The King and I" ...
prod	Attempt_suasion	He gently **prods** his patient to step out of his private world...
precious	Expensiveness	Keeping **precious** artwork safe.
sudden	Expectation	... on the **sudden** passing of David .

Table 4: Example sentences from the New York Times. The frame-invoking LUs in these sentences are not currently covered by FrameNet but are covered by the proposed FrameNet+.

LU paraphrases (setting $t = 0$) provides nearly 70 LUs per frame and offers 71% coverage.

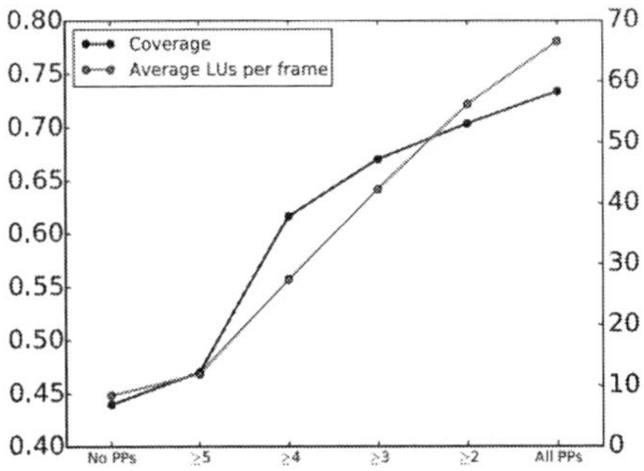

Figure 3: Overall coverage and average number of LUs per frame for varying values of t.

5 Data Release

The augmented FrameNet+ is available to download at `http://www.seas.upenn.edu/~nlp/resources/FN+.zip`. The resource contains over 22K new manually-verified LU/frame pairs, making it three times larger than the currently available FrameNet. Table 5 shows the distribution of FN+'s full set of LUs by part of speech.

Noun	12,786	Prep.	455	Conj.	14
Verb	10,862	Number	163	Wh-adv.	12
Adj.	6,195	Article	43	Particle	6
Adv.	749	Modal	22	Other	19

Table 5: Part of speech distribution for 31K LUs in FrameNet+.

The release also contains 85K human-approved paraphrases of FN's fulltext. This is a huge increase over the 4K fulltext sentences currently in FN, and the new data can be easily used to retrain existing frame semantic parsers, improving their coverage at application time.

6 Related Work

Several efforts have worked on expanding FN coverage. Most approaches align FrameNet's LUs to WordNet or other lexical resources (Shi and Mihalcea, 2005; Johansson and Nugues, 2007; Pennacchiotti et al., 2008; Ferrández et al., 2010).

Das and Smith (2011) and Das and Smith (2012) used graph based semi-supervised methods to improve frame coverage and Hermann et al. (2014) used word and frame embeddings to improve generalization. All of these improvements are restricted to their respective tool rather than a general-use resource. In principle one of these tools could be used to annotate a large corpus in search of new LUs, but their precision on unseen predicates/LUs (our focus here) is still below 50%, considerably lower than this work.

Fossati et al. (2013) added new frames to FN by collecting full frame annotations through crowdsourcing, a more complicated task that again did not result in a useable resource. Buzek et al. (2010) applied crowdsourced paraphrasing to expand training data for machine translation. Our approach differs in that we expand the number of LUs directly using automatic paraphrasing and use crowdsourcing to verify that the new LUs are correct. We apply our method in full, resulting in a large resource can be easily incorporated into existing systems.

7 Conclusion

We have applied automatic paraphrasing to greatly increase the type-level lexical coverage of FrameNet, a widely used resource embodying the theory of frame semantics. We use crowdsourcing to manually verify that the newly added lexical units are correct, resulting in FrameNet+, a high-precision resource that is three times as large as the existing resource. We demonstrate that in a practical setting, the expanded resource provides a 40% increase in the number of sentences for which FN is able to identify the correct frame. The data released will improve the applicability of FN to end-use applications with diverse vocabularies.

Acknowledgements This research was supported by the Allen Institute for Artificial Intelligence (AI2), the Human Language Technology Center of Excellence (HLTCOE), and by gifts from the Alfred P. Sloan Foundation, Google, and Facebook. This material is based in part on research sponsored by the NSF under grant IIS-1249516 and DARPA under agreement number FA8750-13-2-0017 (the DEFT program). The U.S. Government is authorized to reproduce and distribute reprints for Governmental purposes. The views and conclusions contained in this publication are those of the authors and should not be interpreted as representing official policies or endorsements of DARPA or the U.S. Government.

The authors would like to thank Nathan Schneider and the anonymous reviewers for their thoughtful suggestions.

References

Roni Ben Aharon, Idan Szpektor, and Ido Dagan. 2010. Generating entailment rules from framenet. In *ACL*, pages 241–246.

Collin F Baker, Charles J Fillmore, and John B Lowe. 1998. The Berkeley FrameNet Project. In *COLING*.

Aljoscha Burchardt and Anette Frank. 2006. Approaching textual entailment with LFG and FrameNet frames. In *Proceedings of the Second PASCAL RTE Challenge Workshop*. Citeseer.

Olivia Buzek, Philip Resnik, and Benjamin B Bederson. 2010. Error driven paraphrase annotation using mechanical turk. In *Proceedings of the NAACL HLT 2010 Workshop on Creating Speech and Language Data with Amazon's Mechanical Turk*, pages 217–221. Association for Computational Linguistics.

Chris Callison-Burch. 2008. Syntactic constraints on paraphrases extracted from parallel corpora. In *EMNLP*, pages 196–205. Association for Computational Linguistics.

Janara Christensen, Stephen Soderland, Oren Etzioni, et al. 2010. Semantic role labeling for open information extraction. In *Proceedings of the NAACL HLT 2010 First International Workshop on Formalisms and Methodology for Learning by Reading*, pages 52–60. Association for Computational Linguistics.

Dipanjan Das and Noah A Smith. 2011. Semi-supervised frame-semantic parsing for unknown predicates. In *ACL*, pages 1435–1444.

Dipanjan Das and Noah A Smith. 2012. Graph-based lexicon expansion with sparsity-inducing penalties. In *NAACL*.

Michael Ellsworth and Adam Janin. 2007. Mutaphrase: Paraphrasing with framenet. In *Proceedings of the ACL-PASCAL Workshop on Textual Entailment and Paraphrasing*, pages 143–150.

Oscar Ferrández, Michael Ellsworth, Rafael Munoz, and Collin F Baker. 2010. Aligning FrameNet and WordNet based on semantic neighborhoods. In *LREC*.

Charles J Fillmore and Collin F Baker. 2001. Frame semantics for text understanding. In *Proceedings of WordNet and Other Lexical Resources Workshop, NAACL*. Association for Computational Linguistics.

Charles Fillmore. 1982. Frame semantics. *Linguistics in the morning calm*.

Marco Fossati, Claudio Giuliano, and Sara Tonelli. 2013. Outsourcing FrameNet to the crowd. In *ACL*, pages 742–747.

Juri Ganitkevitch, Benjamin Van Durme, and Chris Callison-Burch. 2013. Ppdb: The paraphrase database. In *HLT-NAACL*.

Daniel Gildea and Daniel Jurafsky. 2002. Automatic labeling of semantic roles. *Computational linguistics*, 28(3):245–288.

Michelle L Gregory, Liam McGrath, Eric Belanga Bell, Kelly O'Hara, and Kelly Domico. 2011. Domain independent knowledge base population from structured and unstructured data sources. In *FLAIRS Conference*.

Kenneth Heafield, Ivan Pouzyrevsky, Jonathan H Clark, and Philipp Koehn. 2013. Scalable modified kneser-ney language model estimation. In *ACL*.

Karl Moritz Hermann, Dipanjan Das, Jason Weston, and Kuzman Ganchev. 2014. Semantic frame identification with distributed word representations. In *ACL*.

Richard Johansson and Pierre Nugues. 2007. Using WordNet to extend FrameNet coverage. In *Building Frame Semantics Resources for Scandinavian and Baltic Languages*, pages 27–30. Department of Computer Science, Lund University.

Behrang Mohit and Srini Narayanan. 2003. Semantic extraction with wide-coverage lexical resources. In *NAACL-HLT*, pages 64–66.

Alexis Palmer and Caroline Sporleder. 2010. Evaluating FrameNet-style semantic parsing: The role of coverage gaps in framenet. In *COLING*. Association for Computational Linguistics.

Marco Pennacchiotti, Diego De Cao, Roberto Basili, Danilo Croce, and Michael Roth. 2008. Automatic induction of FrameNet lexical units. In *EMNLP*.

Pushpendre Rastogi and Benjamin Van Durme. 2014. Augmenting FrameNet via PPDB. In *Proceedings of the 2nd Workshop on Events: Definition, Detection, Coreference, and Representation*. Association of Computational Linguistics.

Dan Shen and Mirella Lapata. 2007. Using semantic roles to improve question answering. In *EMNLP-CoNLL*.

Lei Shi and Rada Mihalcea. 2005. Putting pieces together: Combining FrameNet, VerbNet and WordNet for robust semantic parsing. In *Computational linguistics and intelligent text processing*. Springer.

IWNLP: Inverse Wiktionary for Natural Language Processing

Matthias Liebeck and **Stefan Conrad**
Institute of Computer Science
Heinrich-Heine-University Düsseldorf
D-40225 Düsseldorf, Germany
{liebeck,conrad}@cs.uni-duesseldorf.de

Abstract

Nowadays, there are a lot of natural language processing pipelines that are based on training data created by a few experts. This paper examines how the proliferation of the internet and its collaborative application possibilities can be practically used for NLP. For that purpose, we examine how the German version of Wiktionary can be used for a lemmatization task. We introduce IWNLP, an open-source parser for Wiktionary, that reimplements several MediaWiki markup language templates for conjugated verbs and declined adjectives. The lemmatization task is evaluated on three German corpora on which we compare our results with existing software for lemmatization. With Wiktionary as a resource, we obtain a high accuracy for the lemmatization of nouns and can even improve on the results of existing software for the lemmatization of nouns.

1 Introduction

Wiktionary is an internet-based dictionary and thesaurus that lists words, inflected forms and relations (e.g. synonyms) between words. Just as Wikipedia, Wiktionary uses MediaWiki as a platform but focuses on word definitions and their meaning, rather than explaining each word in detail, as Wikipedia does. The dictionary contains articles, which can each list multiple entries for different languages and multiple parts of speech. For instance, the English word *home* has entries as a noun, verb, adjective and as an adverb.

Each article is rendered by the MediaWiki engine from a text-based input, which uses the MediaWiki syntax and relies heavily on the use of templates. The articles are editable by everyone, even by unregistered users. Although vandalism is possible, most of the vandalized entries are identified by other users who watch a list of the latest changes and subsequently revert these entries to previously correct versions. All text content is licensed under the Creative Commons License, which makes it attractive for academic use.

Table 1: Declension of the German noun *Turm* (*tower*)

Case	Singular	Plural
Nominative	der Turm	die Türme
Genitive	des Turmes des Turms	der Türme
Dative	dem Turm dem Turme	den Türmen
Accusative	den Turm	die Türme

There are currently 111 localized versions of Wiktionary, which contain more than 1000 articles[1]. A localized version can establish own rules via majority votes and public opinion. For example, the German version of Wiktionary[2] currently enforces a 5-source-rule, which requires that each entry that is not listed in a common dictionary is documented by at least 5 different sources. The German version of Wiktionary has grown over the last years and currently contains almost 400000 articles[3]. Each word is listed with its part-of-speech tag, among other information. If a word is inflectable (nouns, verbs, adjectives, pronouns and articles are inflectable in the German language), all inflected forms are also enumerated. Table 1 shows the declension of the noun *Turm* (*tower*). Wiktionary provides information that can be used as a resource for Natural Language Processing (NLP), for instance for part-of-speech tagging, for lemmatization and as a thesaurus.

[1] https://meta.wikimedia.org/wiki/Wiktionary
[2] https://de.wiktionary.org
[3] https://de.wiktionary.org/wiki/Wiktionary:Meilensteine

Proceedings of the 53rd Annual Meeting of the Association for Computational Linguistics and the 7th International Joint Conference on Natural Language Processing (Short Papers), pages 414–418, Beijing, China, July 26-31, 2015.

The rest of the paper is structured as follows: Section 2 gives on overview of previous applications of Wiktionary for natural language processing purposes. Section 3 outlines the basic steps of parsing Wiktionary. The use of Wiktionary as a lemmatizer is evaluated in section 4 and compared with existing software for lemmatization. Finally, we conclude in chapter 5 and outline future work.

2 Related Work

The closest work to ours is JWKTL (Zesch et al., 2008). JWKTL is a Wiktionary parser that was originally developed for the English and the German version of Wiktionary, but it now also supports Russian. Our work differs from JWKTL, because we currently focus more on inflections in the German version than JWKTL. Therefore, we have a larger coverage of inflections, because we additionally reimplemented several templates from the namespace *Flexion*. Also, we have an improved handling of special syntactic cases, as compared to JWKTL.

Wiktionary has previously been used for several NLP tasks. The use of the German edition as a thesaurus has been investigated by Meyer and Gurevych (2010). The authors compared the semantic relations in Wiktionary with GermaNet (Hamp and Feldweg, 1997) and OpenThesaurus (Naber, 2005).

Smedt et al. (2014) developed a part-of-speech tagger based on entries in the Italian version of Wiktionary. They achieved an accuracy of 85,5 % with Wiktionary alone. By using morphological and contextual rules, they improve their tagging to an accuracy of 92,9 %. Li et al. (2012) also used Wiktionary to create a part-of-speech tagger, which is based on a hidden Markov model. Their evaluation of 9 different languages shows an average accuracy of 84,5 %, with English having the best result with an accuracy of 87,1 %.

3 Parsing Wiktionary

There are multiple ways to parse Wiktionary. It is possible to crawl all existing articles from the online servers. To reduce stress from the servers and to easily reproduce our parsing results, we parse the latest of the monthly XML dumps[4] from Wiktionary. For this paper, we use the currently latest dump *20150407*.

[4]http://dumps.wikimedia.org/dewiktionary/

We iterate over every article in the XML dump and parse articles which contain German word entries. These articles can be separated into two groups: the ones in the main namespace (without any preceding namespace, like *'namespace:'*) and the ones in the namespace *Flexion*. First, we describe how we parse the articles in the main namespace. An article can contain entries for multiple languages. Therefore, we divide its text content into language blocks (== heading ==) and skip non-German language blocks. Afterward, we extract one or more entries (=== heading ===) from each German language block. If an article lists more than one entry with the same name, its word forms will be different from each other. For instance, the German word *Mutter*[5], contains an entry for *mother* and for *nut*, which have different plural forms. We parse the part-of-speech tag for each entry. If a word is inflectable, we will also parse its inflections, which are listed in a key-value-pair template. Depending on the part-of-speech tag, different templates are used in Wiktionary for which we use different parsers. We provide parsers for nouns, verbs, adjective and pronouns. The key-value-template for the adjective *gelb* (*yellow*) is displayed in Figure 1.

```
== gelb ({{Language|German}}) ==
=== {{POS|Adjective|German}} ===
{{German Adjective Overview
|Positive=gelb
|Comparative=gelber
|Superlative=am gelbsten
}}
```

Figure 1: Adjective template for the word *gelb* (yellow), with keywords translated into English

At this point, we should point out that the inflections for verbs and adjectives in the main namespace are only a small portion of all possible inflections. For example, a verb in the main namespace only lists one inflection for the past tense (first person singular), while other possible past tense forms are not listed.

Fortunately, it is possible that a verb or an adjective has an additional article in the namespace *Flexion*, where all inflections are listed. However, the parsing of these inflections is more challenging, because the articles use complex templates.

[5]https://de.wiktionary.org/wiki/Mutter

Although the parsing of the parameters for the templates remains the same, it is more difficult to retrieve the rendered output by the MediaWiki engine (and thus the inflections) from these templates, because it is very rare that inflections are listed as a key-value-pair. Instead, these templates require principal parts, which are combined with suffixes. The users of Wiktionary have created templates, that take care of special cases, for instance for a verb conjugation, where the suffix 'est' is added to a verb stem instead of 'st', if the last character of a verb stem is a 't'. Wiktionary uses a MediaWiki extension called ParserFunctions, which allows the use of control flows, like if-statements and switch statements. Special cases for the conjugation of verbs and the declension of adjectives are covered by a nested control flow. We have analyzed these templates and reimplemented the template of the adjectives and the most frequently used templates for verbs into IWNLP as C# code. In total, Wiktionary currently contains 3705 verb conjugations in the *Flexion* namespace, which use several templates. We have limited our implementation to the three most used verb conjugation templates (weak inseparable (51,4 %), irregular (27,2 %), regular (12,4 %)).

Altogether, we have extracted 74254 different words and 281457 different word forms. To reduce errors while parsing, we have written more than 150 unit tests to ensure that our parser operates as accurate as possible on various notations and special cases. During the development of IWNLP, we have manually corrected more than 200 erroneous Wiktionary articles, which contained wrong syntax or false content. To guarantee that we didn't worsen the quality of these articles, we've consulted experienced Wiktionary users before performing these changes.

Our parser and its output will be made available under an open-source license.[6]

4 Lemmatization

Wiktionary can be used as a resource for multiple NLP tasks. Currently, we are interested in using Wiktionary as a resource for a lemmatization task, where we want to determine a lemma for a given inflected form. For each lemma, Wiktionary lists multiple inflected forms. As outlined in section 3, we have parsed the inflected forms for each lemma. For our lemmatization task, we inverse this mapping to retrieve a list of possible lemmas for a given inflection, hence our project name IWNLP. For example, we use the information presented in Table 1 to retrieve *Türme* $\mapsto$ *Turm*. For each lemma l in Wiktionary, we have also added a mapping $l \mapsto l$. Our mapping will also be available via download.

It is possible, that an inflected form maps to more than one lemma. For instance, the word *Kohle* maps to *Kohle* (*coal*) and *Kohl* (*cabbage*). In total, our mapping contains 2035 words, which map to more than one lemma.

With this paper, we want to evaluate how good Wiktionary performs in a lemmatization task. Additionally, we want to validate our assumption, that by first looking up word forms and their lemmas in Wiktionary, we should be able to improve the performance of existing software for lemmatization.

Therefore, we evaluate IWNLP and existing software on three German corpora, which list words and their lemmas: TIGER Corpus (Brants et al., 2004), Hamburg Dependency Treebank (HDT) (Foth et al., 2014) and TüBa-D/Z (Telljohann et al., 2012) release 9.1. The TIGER Corpus consists of 50472 sentences from the German newspaper *Frankfurter Rundschau*. The Hamburg Dependency Treebank (part A) contains 101981 sentences from the German IT news site Heise online. The TüBa-D/Z corpus comprises of 85358 sentences from the newspaper *die tageszeitung (taz)*. Each word in these corpora is listed with its part-of-speech tag from the STTS tagset (Schiller et al., 1999). We evaluate the lemmatization for nouns (POS tag *NN*), verbs (POS tags *V**) and adjectives (POS tags *ADJA* and *ADJD*). Due to the low amount of different articles and pronouns in the German language, we ignore them in our evaluation.

In our experiments, we look up the nouns, verbs and adjectives from each corpus in IWNLP. If we map a word form to more than one lemma in IWNLP, we treat this case as if there would be no entry for this particular word form in IWNLP. The same policy is applied in all of our experiments. We preserve case sensitivity, which worsens our results slightly. In a modification, that we name *keep*, we assume that a word w will be its own lemma, if w does not have an entry in the mapping. IWNLP is compared with a mapping[7] ex-

[6] http://www.iwnlp.com

[7] http://www.danielnaber.de/morphologie/index_en.html

Method	TIGER Corpus			TüBa-D/Z			HDT		
	Noun	Verb	Adj	Noun	Verb	Adj	Noun	Verb	Adj
IWNLP	0,734	0,837	0,633	0,720	0,809	0,567	0,607	0,864	0,613
IWNLP + keep	**0,894**	0,854	0,692	0,897	0,827	0,650	0,647	0,882	0,699
Morphy	0,196	0,713	0,531	0,181	0,671	0,490	0,163	0,675	0,475
Morphy + keep	0,857	0,962	0,763	0,860	0,916	0,744	0,619	0,963	0,735
Mate Tools	—	—	—	0,926	0,927	**0,852**	0,639	0,971	0,712
TreeTagger	0,860	**0,974**	0,867	0,848	0,930	0,832	0,611	**0,977**	0,687
IWNLP + Mate Tools	—	—	—	**0,943**	0,929	0,841	**0,653**	0,976	**0,751**
Morphy + Mate Tools	—	—	—	0,918	**0,932**	0,837	0,627	0,974	0,744
IWNLP + TreeTagger	0,888	0,969	**0,869**	0,879	0,927	0,795	0,641	0,973	0,724
Morphy + TreeTagger	0,859	0,970	0,810	0,843	0,926	0,787	0,602	0,968	0,713

Table 2: Lemmatization accuracy for nouns, verbs and adjectives in all three corpora

tracted from Morphy (Lezius et al., 1998), a tool for morphological analysis.

For our comparison with existing software, that can be used for lemmatization, we have chosen Mate Tools (Björkelund et al., 2010) and TreeTagger (Schmid, 1994), which both accept token-based input.

The results of our experiments are shown in Table 2. In a direct comparison between IWNLP and Morphy, IWNLP outperforms Morphy in the basic variant in all POS tags across all corpora. With the modification *keep*, the results of IWNLP and Morphy improve. IWNLP + keep is still superior for nouns, but Morphy + keep achieves better results for verbs and adjectives. The results from Mate Tools on the TIGER Corpus are excluded from Table 2 because Mate Tools was trained on the TIGER Corpus and, therefore, cannot be evaluated on it. The direct comparison of Mate Tools and TreeTagger shows that Mate Tools achieves an accuracy that is at least 2 % better in four of the six cases. In the other two cases, TreeTagger only performs slightly better.

For the lemmatization of nouns, IWNLP is able to improve on the results of Mate Tools and TreeTagger across all three corpora. In total, IWNLP enhances the results of Mate Tools in five of the six test cases. Surprisingly, the additional lookup of word forms in IWNLP and Morphy can impair the accuracy for verbs and adjectives. In our future work, we will systematically analyze which words are responsible for worsening the results, correct their Wiktionary articles and improve our lookup in IWNLP.

The overall bad performance for the lemmatization of nouns in the HDT corpus can be explained by the gold lemmas for compound nouns, which are often defined as the last word in the compound noun. For instance, HDT defines that *Freiheit* (*freedom*) is the gold lemma for *Meinungsfreiheit* (*freedom of speech*).

5 Conclusion

We have presented IWNLP, a parser for the German version of Wiktionary. The current focus of the parser lies in the extraction of inflected forms. They have been used to construct a mapping from inflected forms to lemmas, which can be utilized in a lemmatization task. We evaluated our IWNLP lemmatizer on three German corpora. The results for the lemmatization of nouns show that IWNLP outperforms existing software on the TIGER Corpus and can improve their results on the TüBa-D/Z and the HDT corpora. However, we have also discovered that we still need to improve IWNLP to get better results for the lemmatization of verbs and adjectives. We will try to resolve the correct lemma for an inflected form if multiple lemmas are possible.

Additionally, IWNLP will be extended to parse hyponyms and hypernyms for nouns. We plan to compare the use of Wiktionary as thesaurus with GermaNet (Hamp and Feldweg, 1997).

We expect that the presented results for the lemmatization task will improve with every new monthly dump if Wiktionary continues to grow and improve through a community effort.

Acknowledgments

This work is part of the graduate school *NRW Fortschrittskolleg Online-Partizipation*. We thank the Wiktionary user *Yoursmile* for his help.

References

Anders Björkelund, Bernd Bohnet, Love Hafdell, and Pierre Nugues. 2010. A High-Performance Syntactic and Semantic Dependency Parser. In *Proceedings of the 23rd International Conference on Computational Linguistics: Demonstrations*, COLING '10, pages 33–36. Association for Computational Linguistics.

Sabine Brants, Stefanie Dipper, Peter Eisenberg, Silvia Hansen-Schirra, Esther König, Wolfgang Lezius, Christian Rohrer, George Smith, and Hans Uszkoreit. 2004. TIGER: Linguistic Interpretation of a German Corpus. *Research on Language and Computation*, 2(4):597–620.

Kilian A. Foth, Arne Köhn, Niels Beuck, and Wolfgang Menzel. 2014. Because Size Does Matter: The Hamburg Dependency Treebank. In *Proceedings of the Ninth International Conference on Language Resources and Evaluation (LREC-2014)*, pages 2326–2333.

Birgit Hamp and Helmut Feldweg. 1997. GermaNet - a Lexical-Semantic Net for German. In *Proceedings of ACL workshop Automatic Information Extraction and Building of Lexical Semantic Resources for NLP Applications*, pages 9–15.

Wolfgang Lezius, Reinhard Rapp, and Manfred Wettler. 1998. A Freely Available Morphological Analyzer, Disambiguator and Context Sensitive Lemmatizer for German. In *Proceedings of the 17th International Conference on Computational Linguistics - Volume 2*, COLING '98, pages 743–748. Association for Computational Linguistics.

Shen Li, João V. Graça, and Ben Taskar. 2012. Wiki-ly Supervised Part-of-speech Tagging. In *Proceedings of the 2012 Joint Conference on Empirical Methods in Natural Language Processing and Computational Natural Language Learning*, EMNLP-CoNLL '12, pages 1389–1398. Association for Computational Linguistics.

Christian M. Meyer and Iryna Gurevych. 2010. Worth Its Weight in Gold or Yet Another Resource - A Comparative Study of Wiktionary, OpenThesaurus and GermaNet. In *Computational Linguistics and Intelligent Text Processing, 11th International Conference, CICLing 2010*, volume 6008 of *Lecture Notes in Computer Science*, pages 38–49. Springer.

Daniel Naber. 2005. OpenThesaurus: ein offenes deutsches Wortnetz. In *Sprachtechnologie, mobile Kommunikation und linguistische Ressourcen: Beiträge zur GLDV-Tagung 2005 in Bonn*, pages 422–433. Peter-Lang-Verlag.

Anne Schiller, Simone Teufel, Christine Stöckert, and Christine Thielen. 1999. Guidelines für das Tagging deutscher Textcorpora mit STTS (kleines und großes Tagset). Technical report, Universität Stuttgart, Universität Tübingen.

Helmut Schmid. 1994. Probabilistic Part-of-Speech Tagging Using Decision Trees. In *Proceedings of the International Conference on New Methods in Language Processing*.

Tom De Smedt, Fabio Marfia, Matteo Matteucci, and Walter Daelemans. 2014. Using Wiktionary to Build an Italian Part-of-Speech Tagger. In *Natural Language Processing and Information Systems - 19th International Conference on Applications of Natural Language to Information Systems, NLDB 2014*, volume 8455 of *Lecture Notes in Computer Science*, pages 1–8. Springer.

Heike Telljohann, Erhard W. Hinrichs, Sandra Kübler, Heike Zinsmeister, and Kathrin Beck. 2012. Stylebook for the Tübingen Treebank of Written German (TüBa-D/Z). Technical report, University of Tübingen.

Torsten Zesch, Christof Müller, and Iryna Gurevych. 2008. Extracting Lexical Semantic Knowledge from Wikipedia and Wiktionary. In *Proceedings of the Sixth International Conference on Language Resources and Evaluation (LREC'08)*. European Language Resources Association.

TR9856: A Multi-word Term Relatedness Benchmark

Ran Levy and **Liat Ein-Dor** and **Shay Hummel** and **Ruty Rinott** and **Noam Slonim**
IBM Haifa Research Lab, Mount Carmel, Haifa, 31905, Israel
{ranl,liate,shayh,rutyr,noams}@il.ibm.com

Abstract

Measuring word relatedness is an important ingredient of many NLP applications. Several datasets have been developed in order to evaluate such measures. The main drawback of existing datasets is the focus on single words, although natural language contains a large proportion of multi-word terms. We propose the new TR9856 dataset which focuses on multi-word terms and is significantly larger than existing datasets. The new dataset includes many real world terms such as acronyms and named entities, and further handles term ambiguity by providing topical context for all term pairs. We report baseline results for common relatedness methods over the new data, and exploit its magnitude to demonstrate that a combination of these methods outperforms each individual method.

1 Introduction

Many NLP applications share the need to determine whether two terms are semantically related, or to quantify their degree of "relatedness". Developing methods to automatically quantify term relatedness naturally requires benchmark data of term pairs with corresponding human relatedness scores. Here, we propose a novel benchmark data for term relatedness, that addresses several challenges which have not been addressed by previously available data. The new benchmark data is the first to consider relatedness between multi–word terms, allowing to gain better insights regarding the performance of relatedness assessment methods when considering such terms. Second, in contrast to most previous data, the new data provides a context for each pair of terms, allowing to disambiguate terms as needed. Third, we use a simple systematic process to ensure that the constructed data is enriched with "related" pairs, beyond what one would expect to obtain by random sampling. In contrast to previous work, our enrichment process does not rely on a particular relatedness algorithm or resource such as Wordnet (Fellbaum, 1998), hence the constructed data is less biased in favor of a specific method. Finally, the new data triples the size of the largest previously available data, consisting of $9,856$ pairs of terms. Correspondingly, it is denoted henceforth as **TR9856**. Each term pair was annotated by 10 human annotators, answering a binary question – related/unrelated. The relatedness score is given as the mean answer of annotators where related $= 1$ and unrelated $= 0$.

We report various consistency measures that indicate the validity of TR9856. In addition, we report baseline results over TR9856 for several methods, commonly used to assess term–relatedness. Furthermore, we demonstrate how the new data can be exploited to train an ensemble–based method, that relies on these methods as underlying features. We believe that the new TR9856 benchmark, which is freely available for research purposes, [1] along with the reported results, will contribute to the development of novel term relatedness methods.

2 Related work

Assessing the relatedness between single words is a well known task which received substantial attention from the scientific community. Correspondingly, several benchmark datasets exist. Presumably the most popular among these is the **WordSimilarity-353** collection (Finkelstein et al., 2002), covering 353 word pairs, each labeled by $13 - 16$ human annotators, that selected a continuous relatedness score in the range 0-10. These hu-

[1] https://www.research.ibm.com/haifa/dept/vst/mlta_data.shtml

Proceedings of the 53rd Annual Meeting of the Association for Computational Linguistics and the 7th International Joint Conference on Natural Language Processing (Short Papers), pages 419–424,
Beijing, China, July 26-31, 2015.

man results were averaged, to obtain a relatedness score for each pair. Other relatively small datasets include (Radinsky et al., 2011; Halawi et al., 2012; Hill et al., 2014).

A larger dataset is Stanford's Contextual Word Similarities dataset, denoted **SCWS** (Huang et al., 2012) with 2,003 word pairs, where each word appears in the context of a specific sentence. The authors rely on Wordnet (Fellbaum, 1998) for choosing a diverse set of words as well as to enrich the dataset with related pairs. A more recent dataset, denoted **MEN** (Bruni et al., 2014) consists of 3,000 word pairs, where a specific relatedness measure was used to enrich the data with related pairs. Thus, these two larger datasets are potentially biased in favor of the relatedness algorithm or lexical resource used in their development. TR9856 is much larger and potentially less biased than all these previously available data. Hence, it allows to draw more reliable conclusions regarding the quality and characteristics of examined methods. Moreover, it opens the door for developing term relatedness methods within the supervised machine learning paradigm as we demonstrate in Section 5.2.

It is also worth mentioning the existence of related datasets, constructed with more specific NLP tasks in mind. For examples, datasets constructed to assess lexical entailment (Mirkin et al., 2009) and lexical substitution (McCarthy and Navigli, 2009; Kremer et al., 2014; Biemann, 2013) methods. However, the focus of the current work is on the more general notion of term–relatedness, which seems to go beyond these more concrete relations. For example, the words *whale* and *ocean* are related, but are not similar, do not entail one another, and can not properly substitute one another in a given text.

3 Dataset generation methodology

In constructing the TR9856 data we aimed to address the following issues: (i) include terms that involve more than a single word; (ii) disambiguate terms, as needed; (iii) have a relatively high fraction of "related" term pairs; (iv) focus on terms that are relatively common as opposed to esoteric terms; (v) generate a relatively large benchmark data. To achieve these goals we defined and followed a systematic and reproducible protocol, which is described next. The complete details are included in the data release notes.

3.1 Defining topics and articles of interest

We start by observing that framing the relatedness question within a pre-specified context may simplify the task for humans and machines alike, in particular since the correct sense of ambiguous terms can be identified. Correspondingly, we focus on 47 topics selected from Debatabase [2]. For each topic, 5 human annotators searched Wikipedia for relevant articles as done in (Aharoni et al., 2014). All articles returned by the annotators – an average of 21 articles per topic – were considered in the following steps. The expectation was that articles associated with a particular topic will be enriched with terms related to that topic, hence with terms related to one another.

3.2 Identifying dominant terms per topic

In order to create a set of terms related to a topic of interest, we used the Hyper-geometric (HG) test. Specifically, given the number of sentences in the union of articles identified for all topics; the number of sentences in the articles identified for a specific topic, i.e., in the *topic articles*; the total number of sentences that include a particular term, t; and the number of sentences *within the topic articles*, that include t, denoted x; we use the HG test to assess the probability p, to observe $\geq x$ occurrences of t within sentences selected at random out of the total population of sentences. The smaller p is, the higher our confidence that t is related to the examined topic. Using this approach, for each topic we identify all n–gram terms, with $n = 1, 2, 3$, with a p-value ≤ 0.05, after applying Bonfferroni correction. We refer to this collection of n–gram terms as the *topic lexicon* and refer to n–gram terms as n–terms.

3.3 Selecting pairs for annotation

For each topic, we define S_{def} as the set of manually identified terms mentioned in the topic definition. E.g., for the topic "The use of performance enhancing drugs in professional sports should be permitted", $S_{def} = \{$"performance enhancing drugs","professional sports"$\}$. Given the topic lexicon, we anticipate that terms with a small p–value will be highly related to terms in S_{def}. Hence, we define $S_{top,n}$ to include the top 10 n–terms in the topic lexicon, and add to the dataset all pairs in $S_{def} \times S_{top,n}$ for $n = 1, 2, 3$. Similarly, we define $S_{misc,n}$ to include an additional set of 10

[2] http://idebate.org/debatabase

n–terms, selected at random from the remaining terms in the topic lexicon, and add to the dataset all pairs in $S_{def} \times S_{misc,n}$. We expect that the average relatedness observed for these pairs will be somewhat lower. Finally, we add to the dataset $60 \cdot |S_{def}|$ pairs – i.e., the same number of pairs selected in the two previous steps – selected at random from $\cup_{n,m} S_{top,n} \times S_{misc,m}$. We expect that the average relatedness observed for this last set of pairs will be even lower.

3.4 Relatedness labeling guidelines

Each annotator was asked to mark a pair of terms as "related", if she/he believes there is an immediate associative connection between them, and as "unrelated" otherwise. Although "relatedness" is clearly a vague notion, in accord with previous work – e.g., (Finkelstein et al., 2002), we assumed that human judgments relying on simple intuition will nevertheless provide reliable and reproducible estimates. As discussed in section 4, our results confirm this assumption.

The annotators were further instructed to consider antonyms as related, and to use resources such as Wikipedia to confirm their understanding regarding terms they are less familiar with. Finally, the annotators were asked to disambiguate terms as needed, based on the pair's associated topic. The complete labeling guidelines are available as part of the data release.

We note that in previous work, given a pair of words, the annotators were typically asked to determine a relatedness score within the range of 0 to 10. Here, we took a simpler approach, asking the annotators to answer a binary related/unrelated question. To confirm that this approach yields similar results to previous work we asked 10 annotators to re-label the **WS353** data using our guidelines – except for the context part. Comparing the mean binary score obtained via this re-labeling to the original scores provided for these data we observe a Spearman correlation of 0.87, suggesting that both approaches yield fairly similar results.

4 The TR9856 data – details and validation

The procedure described above led to a collection of 9,856 pairs of terms, each associated with one out of the 47 examined topics. Out of these pairs, 1,489 were comprised of single word terms (SWT) and 8,367 were comprised of at least one multi-word term (MWT). Each pair was labeled by 10 annotators that worked independently. The binary answers of the annotators were averaged, yielding a relatedness score between 0 to 1 – denoted henceforth as the *data score*.

Using the notations above, pairs from $S_{def} \times S_{top,n}$ had an average data score of 0.66; pairs from $S_{def} \times S_{misc,n}$ had an average data score of 0.51; and pairs from $S_{top,n} \times S_{misc,m}$ had an average relatedness score of 0.41. These results suggest that the intuition behind the pair selection procedure described in Section 3.3 is correct. We further notice that 31% of the labeled pairs had a relatedness score ≥ 0.8, and 33% of the pairs had a relatedness score ≤ 0.2, suggesting the constructed data indeed includes a relatively high fraction of pairs with related terms, as planned.

To evaluate annotator agreement we followed (Halawi et al., 2012; Snow et al., 2008) and divided the annotators into two equally sized groups and measured the correlation between the results of each group. The largest subset of pairs for which the same 10 annotators labeled all pairs contained roughly 2,900 pairs. On this subset, we considered all possible splits of the annotators to groups of size 5, and for each split measured the correlation of the relatedness scores obtained by the two groups. The average Pearson correlation was 0.80. These results indicate that in spite of the admitted vagueness of the task, the average annotation score obtained by different sets of annotators is relatively stable and consistent.

Several examples of term pairs and their corresponding dataset scores are given in Table 1. Note that the first pair includes an acronym – *wipo* – which the annotators are expected to resolve to *World Intellectual Property Organization*.

4.1 Transitivity analysis

Another way to evaluate the quality and consistency of a term relatedness dataset is by measuring the transitivity of its relatedness scores. Given a triplet of term pairs (a, b) , (b, c) and (a, c), the transitivity rule implies that if a is related to b, and b is related to c then a is related to c. Using this rule, transitivity can be measured by computing the relative fraction of pair triplets fulfilling it. Note that this analysis can be applied only if all the three pairs exist in the data. Here, we used the following intuitive transitivity measure: let (a, b), (b, c), and (a, c), be a triplet of term pairs in the

Term 1	Term 2	Score
copyright	wipo	1.0
grand theft auto	violent video games	1.0
video games sales	violent video games	0.7
civil rights	affirmative action	0.6
rights	public property	0.5
nation of islam	affirmative action	0.1
racial	sex discrimination	0.1

Table 1: Examples of pairs of terms and their associated dataset scores.

dataset, and let R_1, R_2, and R_3 be their relatedness scores, respectively. Then, for high values of R_2, R_1 is expected to be close to R_3. More specifically, on average, $|R_3 - R_1|$ is expected to decrease with R_2. Figure 1 shows that this behavior indeed takes place in our dataset. The p-value of the correlation between $mean(|R_3 - R_1|)$ and R_2 is $\approx 1e - 10$. Nevertheless, the curves of the WS353 data (both with the original labeling and with our labeling) do not show this behavior, probably due to the very few triplet term pairs existing in these data, resulting with a very poor statistics. Besides validating the transitivity behavior, these results emphasize the advantage of the relatively dense TR9856 data, in providing sufficient statistics for performing this type of analysis.

Figure 1: $mean(|R_3 - R_1|)$ vs. R_2.

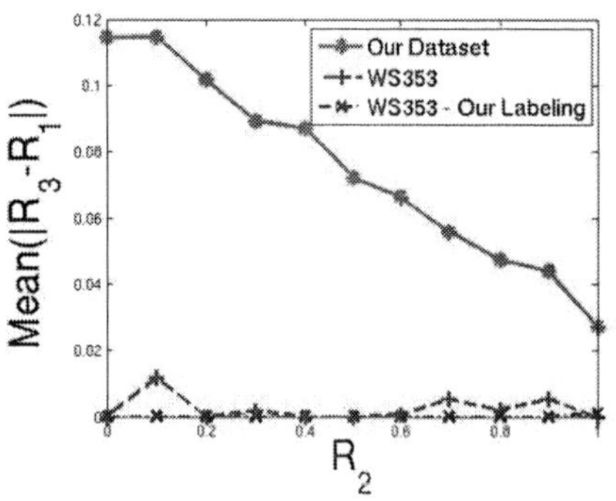

5 Results for existing techniques

To demonstrate the usability of the new TR9856 data, we present baseline results of commonly used methods that can be exploited to predict term relatedness, including ESA (Gabrilovich and Markovitch, 2007), Word2Vec (W2V) (Mikolov et al., 2013) and first–order positive PMI (PMI) (Church and Hanks, 1990). To handle MWTs, we used summation on the vector representations of W2V and ESA. For PMI, we tokenized each MWT and averaged the PMI of all possible single–word pairs. For all these methods we used the March 2015 Wikipedia dump and a relatively standard configuration of the relevant parameters. In addition, we report results for an ensemble of these methods using 10-fold cross validation.

5.1 Evaluation measures

Previous experiments on **WS353** and other datasets reported Spearman Correlation (ρ) between the algorithm predicted scores and the ground–truth relatedness scores. Here, we also report Pearson Correlation (r) results and demonstrate that the top performing algorithm becomes the worst performing algorithm when switching between these two correlation measures. In addition, we note that a correlation measure gives equal weight to all pairs in the dataset. However, in some NLP applications it is more important to properly distinguish related pairs from unrelated ones. Correspondingly, we also report results when considering the problem as a binary classification problem, aiming to distinguish pairs with a relatedness score ≥ 0.8 from pairs with a relatedness score ≤ 0.2.

5.2 Correlation results

The results of the examined methods are summarized in Table 2. Note that these methods are not designed for multi-word terms, and further do not exploit the topic associated with each pair for disambiguation. The results show that all methods are comparable except for ESA in terms of Pearson correlation, which is much lower. This suggest that ESA scores are not well scaled, a property that might affect applications using ESA as a feature.

Next, we exploit the relatively large size of TR9856 to demonstrate the potential for using supervised machine learning methods. Specifically, we trained a simple linear regression using the baseline methods as features, along with a *token*

Method	r	ρ
ESA	0.43	**0.59**
W2V	**0.57**	0.56
PMI	0.55	0.58

Table 2: Baseline results for common methods.

length feature, that counts the combined number of tokens per pair, in a 10-fold cross validation setup. The resulting model outperforms all individual methods, as depicted in Table 3.

Method	r	ρ
ESA	0.43	0.59
W2V	0.57	0.56
PMI	0.55	0.58
Lin. Reg.	**0.62**	**0.63**

Table 3: Mean results over 10-fold cross validation.

5.3 Single words vs. multi-words

To better understand the impact of MWTs, we divided the data into two subsets. If both terms are SWTs the pair was assigned to the SWP subset; otherwise it was assigned to the MWP subset. The SWP subset included $1,489$ pairs and the MWP subset comprised of $8,367$ pairs. The experiment in subsection 5.2 was repeated for each subset. The results are summarized in Table 4. Except for the Pearson correlation results of ESA, for all methods we observe lower performance over the MWP subset, suggesting that assessing term–relatedness is indeed more difficult when MWTs are involved.

Method	r		ρ	
	SWP	MWP	SWP	MWP
ESA	0.41	0.43	0.63	0.58
W2V	0.62	0.55	0.58	0.55
PMI	0.63	0.55	0.63	0.59

Table 4: Baseline results for SWP vs. MWP.

5.4 Binary classification results

We turn the task into binary classification task by considering the $3,090$ pairs with a data score ≥ 0.8 as positive examples, and the $3,245$ pairs with a data score ≤ 0.2 as negative examples. We use a 10-fold cross validation to choose an optimal threshold for the baseline methods as well as to learn a Logistic Regression (LR) classifier, that further used the token length feature. Again, the resulting model outperforms all individual methods, as indicated in Table 5.

Method	Mean Error
ESA	0.19
W2V	0.22
PMI	0.21
Log. Reg.	**0.18**

Table 5: Binary classification results.

6 Discussion

The new TR9856 dataset has several important advantages compared to previous datasets. Most importantly – it is the first dataset to consider the relatedness between multi–word terms; ambiguous terms can be resolved using a pre–specified context; and the data itself is much larger than previously available data, enabling to draw more reliable conclusions, and to develop supervised machine learning methods that exploit parts of the data for training and tuning.

The baseline results reported here for commonly used techniques provide initial intriguing insights. Table 4 suggests that the performance of specific methods may change substantially when considering pairs composed of unigrams vs. pairs in which at least one term is a MWT. Finally, our results demonstrate the potential of supervised–learning techniques to outperform individual methods, by using these methods as underlying features.

In future work we intend to further investigate the notion of term relatedness by manually labeling the type of the relation identified for highly related pairs. In addition, we intend to develop techniques that aim to exploit the context provided for each pair, and to consider the potential of more advanced – and in particular non–linear – supervised learning methods.

Acknowledgments

The authors thank Ido Dagan and Mitesh Khapra for many helpful discussions.

References

Ehud Aharoni, Anatoly Polnarov, Tamar Lavee, Daniel Hershcovich, Ran Levy, Ruty Rinott, Dan Gutfre-

und, and Noam Slonim. 2014. A benchmark dataset for automatic detection of claims and evidence in the context of controversial topics. *ACL 2014*, page 64.

Chris Biemann. 2013. Creating a system for lexical substitutions from scratch using crowdsourcing. *Language Resources and Evaluation*, 47(1):97–122.

Elia Bruni, Nam-Khanh Tran, and Marco Baroni. 2014. Multimodal distributional semantics. *J. Artif. Intell. Res.(JAIR)*, 49:1–47.

Kenneth Ward Church and Patrick Hanks. 1990. Word association norms, mutual information, and lexicography. *Computational linguistics*, 16(1):22–29.

Christiane Fellbaum. 1998. *WordNet*. Wiley Online Library.

Lev Finkelstein, Evgeniy Gabrilovich, Yossi Matias, Ehud Rivlin, Zach Solan, Gadi Wolfman, and Eytan Ruppin. 2002. Placing search in context: The concept revisited. *ACM Transactions on Information Systems*, 20(1):116–131.

Evgeniy Gabrilovich and Shaul Markovitch. 2007. Computing semantic relatedness using wikipedia-based explicit semantic analysis. In *IJCAI*, volume 7, pages 1606–1611.

Guy Halawi, Gideon Dror, Evgeniy Gabrilovich, and Yehuda Koren. 2012. Large-scale learning of word relatedness with constraints. In *Proceedings of the 18th ACM SIGKDD international conference on Knowledge discovery and data mining*, pages 1406–1414. ACM.

Felix Hill, Roi Reichart, and Anna Korhonen. 2014. Simlex-999: Evaluating semantic models with (genuine) similarity estimation. *arXiv preprint arXiv:1408.3456*.

Eric H. Huang, Richard Socher, Christopher D. Manning, and Andrew Y. Ng. 2012. Improving word representations via global context and multiple word prototypes. In *Annual Meeting of the Association for Computational Linguistics (ACL)*.

Gerhard Kremer, Katrin Erk, Sebastian Padó, and Stefan Thater. 2014. What substitutes tell us - analysis of an "all-words" lexical substitution corpus. In *Proceedings of the 14th Conference of the European Chapter of the Association for Computational Linguistics*, pages 540–549, Gothenburg, Sweden, April. Association for Computational Linguistics.

Diana McCarthy and Roberto Navigli. 2009. The english lexical substitution task. *Language resources and evaluation*, 43(2):139–159.

Tomas Mikolov, Kai Chen, Greg Corrado, and Jeffrey Dean. 2013. Efficient estimation of word representations in vector space. *arXiv preprint arXiv:1301.3781*.

Shachar Mirkin, Ido Dagan, and Eyal Shnarch. 2009. Evaluating the inferential utility of lexical-semantic resources. In *Proceedings of the 12th Conference of the European Chapter of the Association for Computational Linguistics*, pages 558–566. Association for Computational Linguistics.

Kira Radinsky, Eugene Agichtein, Evgeniy Gabrilovich, and Shaul Markovitch. 2011. A word at a time: computing word relatedness using temporal semantic analysis. In *Proceedings of the 20th international conference on World wide web*, pages 337–346. ACM.

Rion Snow, Brendan O'Connor, Daniel Jurafsky, and Andrew Y Ng. 2008. Cheap and fast—but is it good?: evaluating non-expert annotations for natural language tasks. In *Proceedings of the conference on empirical methods in natural language processing*, pages 254–263. Association for Computational Linguistics.

PPDB 2.0: Better paraphrase ranking, fine-grained entailment relations, word embeddings, and style classification

Ellie Pavlick[1] Pushpendre Rastogi[2] Juri Ganitkevitch[2]
Benjamin Van Durme[2,3] Chris Callison-Burch[1]
[1]Computer and Information Science Department, University of Pennsylvania
[2]Center for Language and Speech Processing, Johns Hopkins University
[3]Human Language Technology Center of Excellence, Johns Hopkins University

Abstract

We present a new release of the Paraphrase Database. PPDB 2.0 includes a discriminatively re-ranked set of paraphrases that achieve a higher correlation with human judgments than PPDB 1.0's heuristic rankings. Each paraphrase pair in the database now also includes fine-grained entailment relations, word embedding similarities, and style annotations.

1 Introduction

The Paraphrase Database (PPDB) is a collection of over 100 million paraphrases that was automatically constructed by Ganitkevitch et al. (2013). Although it is relatively new, it has been adopted by a large number of researchers, who have demonstrated that it is useful for a variety of natural language processing tasks. It has been used for recognizing textual entailment (Beltagy et al., 2014; Bjerva et al., 2014), measuring the semantic similarity of texts (Han et al., 2013; Ji and Eisenstein, 2013; Sultan et al., 2014b), monolingual alignment (Yao et al., 2013; Sultan et al., 2014a), natural language generation (Ganitkevitch et al., 2011), and improved lexical embeddings (Yu and Dredze, 2014; Rastogi et al., 2015; Faruqui et al., 2015).

For any given input phrase to PPDB, there are often dozens or hundreds of possible paraphrases. There are several interesting research questions that arise because of the number and variety of paraphrases in PPDB. How can we distinguish between correct and incorrect paraphrases? Within the paraphrase sets, are all of the paraphrases truly substitutable or do they sometimes exhibit other types of relationships (like directional entailment)? When the paraphrases share the same meaning, are there stylistic reasons why we should choose one versus another (e.g., is one paraphrase a less formal version of another)?

ranked paraphrases of *berries*				
	PPDB 1.0		PPDB 2.0	
1.	embayments	1.	strawberries	⊏
2.	strawberries	2.	raspberries	⊏
3.	racks	3.	blueberries	⊏
4.	grains	4.	blackberries	⊏
5.	raspberries	5.	fruits	⊐
6.	blueberries	6.	fruit	⊐
7.	fruits	7.	beans	#
8.	fruit	8.	grains	~
9.	blackberries	9.	seeds	#
10.	beans	10.	kernels	#

Figure 1: PPDB 2.0 includes an improved scoring model for ranking paraphrases. Shown are the top 10 ranked paraphrases for the word *berries* according to PPDB 1.0 (left) and PPDB 2.0 (right). PPDB 2.0 also contains an entailment relation for every pair. These relations capture asymmetries in the paraphrases, such as the fact that *strawberries* entails (⊏) *berries*, while *fruits* is entailed by (⊐) *berries*.

In this paper we describe several improvements to PPDB that address these questions. We release PPDB version 2.0, incorporating the following improvements:

- A completely re-ranked set of paraphrases that uses a regression model to fit the paraphrase scores to human judgments of paraphrase quality. Figure 1 shows the re-ranked paraphrases for the word *berries*.
- Each paraphrase pair is automatically labeled with an explicit entailment relationship. Instead of assuming all paraphrases are perfectly equivalent, we label some as one directional entailments (or other entailment types).
- Each paraphrase rule now has new features that indicate when its application is expected to result in a change in style.
- Each paraphrase entry in the database now has an associated word embedding learned using Multiview Latent Semantic Analysis.

Proceedings of the 53rd Annual Meeting of the Association for Computational Linguistics and the 7th International Joint Conference on Natural Language Processing (Short Papers), pages 425–430,
Beijing, China, July 26-31, 2015.

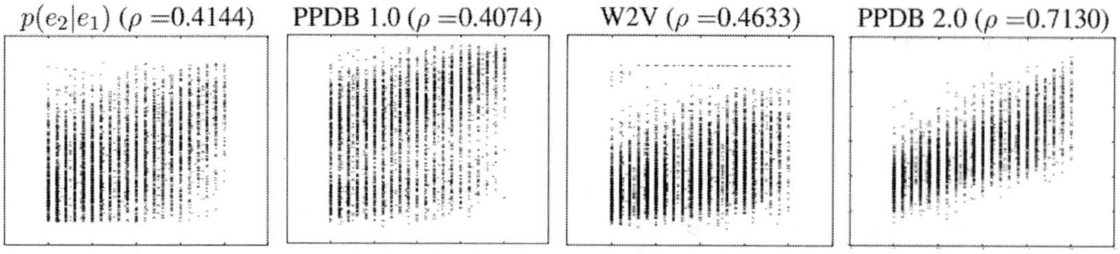

Figure 2: Scatterplots of automatic paraphrase scores (vertical axis) versus human scores (horizontal axis) for four ways of automatically ranking the paraphrases: $p(e_2|e_1)$ (far left), PPDB 1.0's heuristic ranking method (middle left), word2vec similarity (middle right), and our supervised model for PPDB 2.0 (far right). Our rankings achieve the highest correlation with human judgements with a Spearman's ρ of 0.71.

Upon publication of this paper, we will release PPDB 2.0 along with a set of 26K phrase pairs annotated with human similarity judgments.

2 Improved rankings of paraphrases

The notion of ranking paraphrases goes back to the original method that PPDB is based on. Bannard and Callison-Burch (2005) introduced the bilingual pivoting method, which extracts *incarcerated* as a potential paraphrase of *put in prison* since they are both aligned to *festgenommen* in different sentence pairs in an English-German bitext. Since *incarcerated* aligns to many foreign words (in many languages) the list of potential paraphrases is long. Paraphrases vary in quality since the alignments are automatically produced and noisy. In order to rank the paraphrases, Bannard and Callison-Burch (2005) define a paraphrase probability in terms of the translation model probabilities $p(f|e)$ and $p(e|f)$:

$$p(e_2|e_1) \approx \sum_f p(e_2|f)p(f|e_1). \quad (1)$$

Heuristic scoring in PPDB 1.0 Instead of ranking the paraphrases with a single score, Ganitkevitch et al. (2013) expanded the set of scores in PPDB. Each paraphrase rule in PPDB consists of four components: a phrase (e_1), a paraphrase (e_2), a syntactic category (LHS^1), and a feature vector. This feature vector contains 33 scores of paraphrase quality, which are described in full in the supplementary material to this paper. The rules in PPDB 1.0 were scored using an ad-hoc weighting of seven of these features, given by the following equation:

$$\begin{aligned} & 1.0 \times -log\ p(e_1|e_2) \\ + & 1.0 \times -log\ p(e_2|e_1) \\ + & 1.0 \times -log\ p(e_1|e_2, LHS) \\ + & 1.0 \times -log\ p(e_2|e_1, LHS) \\ + & 0.3 \times -log\ p(LHS|e_1) \\ + & 0.3 \times -log\ p(LHS|e_2) \\ + & 100 \times RarityPenalty \end{aligned}$$

where $-log\ p(e_2|e_1)$ is the paraphrase probability computed according to Equation 1 and $RarityPenalty$ is a real-valued feature that indicates how frequently the paraphrase was observed in the training data.

This heuristic linear combination of scores was used to divide PPDB into six increasingly large sizes– S, M, L, XL, XXL, and XXXL. PPDB-XXXL contains all of the paraphrase rules and has the highest recall, but the lowest average precision. The smaller sizes contain better average scores but offer lower coverage. Ganitkevitch et al. (2013) performed a small-scale analysis of how their heuristic score correlated with human judgments by collecting <2,000 judgments for PPDB paraphrases of verbs that occurred in Propbank.

Supervised scoring model For this paper, we rank the paraphrases using a supervised scoring model. To train the model, we collected human judgements for 26,455 paraphrase pairs sampled from PPDB. Each paraphrase pair was judged by 5 people who each assigned a score on a 5-point Likert scale, as described in Callison-Burch (2008). These 5 scores were averaged.

We used these human judgments to fit a regression to the 33 features available in the PPDB 1.0 feature vector, plus an additional 176 new features that we developed. Our features included the cosine similarity of the word embeddings that we generated for each PPDB phrase (described in Section 3.3), as well as lexical overlap features, features derived from WordNet, and distributional

[1]The name LHS is due to the fact that the syntactic category comes from the lefthand side of the synchronous CFG rule used to produce the paraphrase.

similarity features. We weighted the contribution of these features using ridge regression with its regularization parameter tuned using cross validation on the training data.

See the supplemental materials for a complete description of the features used in our model and our data collection methodology including inter-annotator agreement.

2.1 Evaluating the rankings

We evaluate the new rankings in two ways:

- We calculate the correlation of the different ways of automatically ranking the paraphrases against the 26k human judgments that we collected.
- We compute the goodness (in terms of mean reciprocal rank and averaged precision) of the ranked paraphrase lists for 100 phrases drawn randomly from Wikipedia.

Correlation Figure 2 plots the different automatic paraphrase scores against the 5-point human judgments for four different ways of ranking the paraphrases: 1) the original paraphrase probability defined by Bannard and Callison-Burch (2005), 2) the heuristic ranking that Ganitkevitch et al. (2013) defined for PPDB 1.0, 3) the cosine similarity of word2vec[2] embeddings[3], and 4) the new score predicted by our discriminative model. The paraphrase probability has a Spearman correlation of 0.41. The heuristic PPDB 1.0 ranking has a similar correlation of $\rho = 0.41$. The word2vec similarity improves correlation slightly to 0.46. To test our supervised method, we use cross validation: in each fold, we hold out 200 phrases along with all of their associated paraphrases for testing. Our rankings for PPDB 2.0 dramatically improve correlation with human judgments to $\rho = 0.71$.

Goodness of the top-ranked paraphrases In addition to calculating the correlation over the sample of paraphrases (where the human judgments were taken evenly over the range of $p(e_2|e_1)$ values), we also evaluated the full list of paraphrases as it is likely to be used by researchers who use PPDB. We took a sample of 100 unique phrase types from Wikipedia (constraining to types which appear in PPDB), and collected human judgments for their full list of paraphrases.

[2]https://code.google.com/p/word2vec/

[3]For phrases, we use the vector of the rarest word as an approximation of the vector for the phrase.

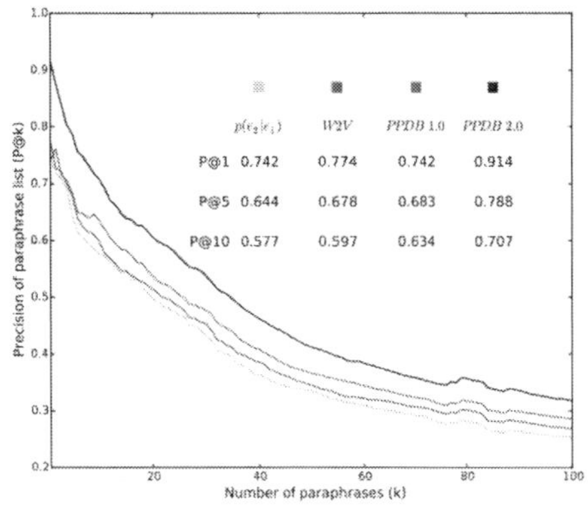

Figure 3: Averaged precision of paraphrases lists for 100 phrases randomly drawn from Wikipedia. Curves show precision @ k for varying values of k, up to 100. Here, "good" paraphrases are defined as having received an average human rating ≥ 3.

		MRR	AP
human rating $\geq$3	Random	0.56	0.46
(16% of judgments)	$p(e_2\|e_1)$	0.84	0.61
	W2V	0.85	0.64
	PPDB 1.0	0.86	0.64
	PPDB 2.0	**0.95**	**0.72**
human rating $\geq$4	Random	0.34	0.27
(4% of judgments)	$p(e_2\|e_1)$	0.69	0.46
	W2V	0.69	0.49
	PPDB 1.0	0.70	0.50
	PPDB 2.0	**0.80**	**0.59**
human rating $\geq$4.5	Random	0.25	0.20
(1% of judgments)	$p(e_2\|e_1)$	0.46	0.37
	W2V	0.46	0.36
	PPDB 1.0	0.53	0.42
	PPDB 2.0	**0.61**	**0.49**

Table 1: Quality of rankings using for the improved PPDB 2.0 score versus the current heuristic score. Both metrics (AP and MRR) range from 0 to 1 and higher is better. $\geq$t means that the statistics are computed by considering a paraphrase to be "good" if its human judgments averaged $\geq$t.

We compare the ranking produced by the proposed PPDB 2.0 model against the heuristic PPDB 1.0 ranking in terms of each one's ability to put good paraphrases at the top of its list. Figure 3 shows precision curves for the ranked paraphrases in PPDB 1.0 compared to PPDB 2.0. PPDB 2.0 achieves consistently higher precision, improving P@1 by 17 points and P@5 by 9 points.

We also analyzed the different rankings when we varied the criterion that we used for what constitutes a good paraphrase. Table 1 shows how the averaged precision (AP) and the mean reciprocal rank (MRR) change as we vary the human score for good paraphrases from $\geq$3 to $\geq$4.5. Depending on the threshold, our PPDB 2.0 ranking achieves a 9-12 point improvement in MRR over the PPDB 1.0 rankings. Similarly, it improves AP by 7-9 points.

3 Other Additions

In addition to dramatically improving the rankings of the paraphrases (novel to this publication), our PPDB 2.0 release adds several automatic annotations created in other research. Every paraphrase pair now has an entailment relation from Pavlick et al. (2015), style classifications from Pavlick and Nenkova (2015), and associated vector embedding from Rastogi et al. (2015). These are described briefly below.

3.1 Entailment relations

Although we typically think of paraphrases as equivalent or as bidirectionally entailing, a substantial fraction of the phrase pairs in PPDB exhibit different entailment relations. Figure 1 gives an example of how these relations capture the range or entailment present in the paraphrases of *berries*. We automatically annotate each paraphrase rule in PPDB with an explicit entailment relation based on *natural logic* (MacCartney, 2009). These relations include forward entailment/hyponym ($\sqsubset$), reverse entailment/hypernym ($\sqsupset$), non-entailing topical relatedness ($\sim$), unrelatedness ($\#$), and even exclusion/contradiction ($\neg$). For a complete evaluation of the entailment classifications, and the prevalence of each type in PPDB, see Pavlick et al. (2015).

3.2 Style scores

Some of the variation within paraphrase sets can be attributed to stylistic variations of language. We automatically induce style information on each rule in PPDB for two dimensions– complexity and formality. Table 2 shows some paraphrases of *the end*, sorted from most complex to most simple using these scores. These classifications could be useful for natural language generation tasks like text simplification (Xu et al., 2015). A complete evaluation of these scores is given in Pavlick and Nenkova (2015).

3.3 Multiview LSA vector embeddings

Recently there has been tremendous interest in representing words via vector embeddings (Dhillon et al., 2011; Mikolov et al., 2013; Pennington et al., 2014). Such representations can be used to measure word and phrase similarity, possibly to improve paraphrasing. Multiview Latent Semantic Analysis (MVLSA) is a state-of-the-art method for modeling word similarities. MVLSA can incorporate an arbitrary number of data views, such as monolingual signals, bilingual signals, and even signals from other embeddings. PPDB 2.0 contains new similarity features based on MVLSA embeddings for all phrases. A complete discussion is given in Rastogi et al. (2015).

1. the finalization	6. the latter part	11. the final analysis
2. the expiration	7. termination	12. the last
3. the demise	8. goal	13. the finish
4. the completion	9. the close	14. the final part
5. the closing	10. late	15. the last part

Table 2: Some paraphrases of *the end*, ranked from most complex to most simple according to the style scores included in PPDB 2.0.

4 Related Work

The most closely related work to our supervised re-ranking of PPDB is work by Zhao et al. (2008) and Malakasiotis and Androutsopoulos (2011). Zhao et al. (2008) improved Bannard and Callison-Burch (2005)'s paraphrase probability by converting it into log-linear model inspired by machine translation, allowing them to incorporate a variety of features. Malakasiotis and Androutsopoulos (2011) developed a similar model trained on human judgements. Both efforts apply their model to natural language generation by paraphrasing full sentences. We apply our model to the sub-sentential paraphrases directly, in order to improve the quality of the Paraphrase Database.

Also related is work by Chan et al. (2011) which reranked bilingually-extracted paraphrases using monolingual distributional similarities, but did not use a supervised model. Work that is relevant to our classification of semantic entailment types to each paraphrase, includes learning directionality of inference rules (Bhagat et al., 2007; Berant et al., 2011) and learning hypernyms rather than paraphrases (Snow et al., 2004). Our style annotations are related to Xu et al. (2012)'s efforts at learning stylistic paraphrases. Our word embeddings additions to the paraphrase database are related to many current projects on that topic, including projects that attempt to customize embeddings to lexical resources (Faruqui et al., 2015). However, the Rastogi et al. (2015) embeddings included here were shown to be state-of-the art in predicting human judgements.

5 Conclusion

We release PPDB 2.0 (`http://paraphrase.org/#/download`). The resource includes dramatically improved paraphrase rankings, explicit entailment relations, style information, and state-of-the-art distributional similarity measures for each paraphrase rule. The 2.0 release contains 100m+ paraphrases, and 26k manually rated phrase pairs, which will facilitate further research in modeling semantic similarity.

Acknowledgements This research was supported by the Allen Institute for Artificial Intelligence (AI2), the Human Language Technology Center of Excellence (HLTCOE), and by gifts from the Alfred P. Sloan Foundation, Google, and Facebook. This material is based in part on research sponsored by the NSF under grant IIS-1249516 and DARPA under agreement number FA8750-13-2-0017 (the DEFT program). The U.S. Government is authorized to reproduce and distribute reprints for Governmental purposes. The views and conclusions contained in this publication are those of the authors and should not be interpreted as representing official policies or endorsements of DARPA or the U.S. Government.

We would like to thank the anonymous reviewers for their thoughtful comments.

References

Colin Bannard and Chris Callison-Burch. 2005. Paraphrasing with bilingual parallel corpora. In *ACL*, pages 597–604.

Islam Beltagy, Stephen Roller, Gemma Boleda, Katrin Erk, and Raymond J Mooney. 2014. Utexas: Natural language semantics using distributional semantics and probabilistic logic. In *SemEval*.

Jonathan Berant, Ido Dagan, and Jacob Goldberger. 2011. Global learning of typed entailment rules. In *ACL*.

Rahul Bhagat, Patrick Pantel, Eduard H Hovy, and Marina Rey. 2007. LEDIR: An unsupervised algorithm for learning directionality of inference rules. In *EMNLP-CoNLL*, pages 161–170.

Johannes Bjerva, Johan Bos, Rob van der Goot, and Malvina Nissim. 2014. The meaning factory: Formal semantics for recognizing textual entailment and determining semantic similarity. In *SemEval*.

Chris Callison-Burch. 2008. Syntactic constraints on paraphrases extracted from parallel corpora. In *EMNLP*, pages 196–205.

Tsz Ping Chan, Chris Callison-Burch, and Benjamin Van Durme. 2011. Reranking bilingually extracted paraphrases using monolingual distributional similarity. In *GEMS*, pages 33–42.

Paramveer S. Dhillon, Dean Foster, and Lyle Ungar. 2011. Multi-view learning of word embeddings via CCA. In *NIPS*.

Manaal Faruqui, Jesse Dodge, Sujay K Jauhar, Chris Dyer, Eduard Hovy, and Noah A Smith. 2015. Retrofitting word vectors to semantic lexicons. In *NAACL*.

Juri Ganitkevitch, Chris Callison-Burch, Courtney Napoles, and Benjamin Van Durme. 2011. Learning sentential paraphrases from bilingual parallel corpora for text-to-text generation. In *EMNLP*, pages 1168–1179.

Juri Ganitkevitch, Benjamin Van Durme, and Chris Callison-Burch. 2013. PPDB: The paraphrase database. In *NAACL-HLT*, pages 758–764, Atlanta, Georgia, June.

Lushan Han, Abhay Kashyap, Tim Finin, James Mayfield, and Jonathan Weese. 2013. Umbc ebiquity-core: Semantic textual similarity systems. In *Proceedings of the Second Joint Conference on Lexical and Computational Semantics*, volume 1, pages 44–52.

Yangfeng Ji and Jacob Eisenstein. 2013. Discriminative improvements to distributional sentence similarity. In *EMNLP*, pages 891–896.

Bill MacCartney. 2009. *Natural language inference*. Ph.D. thesis, Citeseer.

Prodromos Malakasiotis and Ion Androutsopoulos. 2011. A generate and rank approach to sentence paraphrasing. In *EMNLP*, pages 96–106.

Tomas Mikolov, Kai Chen, Greg Corrado, and Jeffrey Dean. 2013. Efficient estimation of word representations in vector space. In *Workshop at ICLR*.

Ellie Pavlick and Ani Nenkova. 2015. Inducing lexical style properties for paraphrase and genre differentiation. In *NAACL*.

Ellie Pavlick, Johan Bos, Malvina Nissim, Charley Beller, Benjamin Van Durme, and Chris Callison-Burch. 2015. Adding semantics to data-driven paraphrasing. In *ACL*.

Jeffrey Pennington, Richard Socher, and Christopher D Manning. 2014. Glove: Global vectors for word representation. *Proceedings of the Empiricial Methods in Natural Language Processing (EMNLP 2014)*, 12.

Pushpendre Rastogi, Benjamin Van Durme, and Raman Arora. 2015. Multiview LSA: Representation learning via generalized CCA. In *NAACL*.

Rion Snow, Daniel Jurafsky, and Andrew Y Ng. 2004. Learning syntactic patterns for automatic hypernym discovery. In *NIPS*.

Md. Arafat Sultan, Steven Bethard, and Tamara Sumner. 2014a. Back to basics for monolingual alignment: Exploiting word similarity and contextual evidence. *Transactions of the Association for Computational Linguistics*, 2:219–230.

Md Arafat Sultan, Steven Bethard, and Tamara Sumner. 2014b. Dls@cu: Sentence similarity from word alignment. In *SemEval*.

Wei Xu, Alan Ritter, Bill Dolan, Ralph Grishman, and Colin Cherry. 2012. Paraphrasing for style. In *COLING*.

Wei Xu, Chris Callison-Burch, and Courtney Napoles. 2015. Problems in current text simplification research: New data can help. *TACL*.

Xuchen Yao, Benjamin Van Durme, Chris Callison-Burch, and Peter Clark. 2013. Semi-markov phrase-based monolingual alignment. In *EMNLP*, pages 590–600.

Mo Yu and Mark Dredze. 2014. Improving lexical embeddings with semantic knowledge. In *ACL*, volume 2, pages 545–550.

Shiqi Zhao, Cheng Niu, Ming Zhou, Ting Liu, and Sheng Li. 2008. Combining multiple resources to improve SMT-based paraphrasing model. In *ACL*.

Automatic Discrimination between Cognates and Borrowings

Alina Maria Ciobanu, Liviu P. Dinu
Faculty of Mathematics and Computer Science, University of Bucharest
Center for Computational Linguistics, University of Bucharest
alina.ciobanu@my.fmi.unibuc.ro, ldinu@fmi.unibuc.ro

Abstract

Identifying the type of relationship between words provides a deeper insight into the history of a language and allows a better characterization of language relatedness. In this paper, we propose a computational approach for discriminating between cognates and borrowings. We show that orthographic features have discriminative power and we analyze the underlying linguistic factors that prove relevant in the classification task. To our knowledge, this is the first attempt of this kind.

1 Introduction

Natural languages are living eco-systems. They are subject to continuous change due, in part, to the natural phenomena of language contact and borrowing (Campbell, 1998). According to Hall (1960), there is no such thing as a "pure language" – a language "without any borrowing from a foreign language". Although admittedly regarded as relevant factors in the history of a language (McMahon et al., 2005), borrowings bias the genetic classification of the languages, characterizing them as being closer than they actually are (Minett and Wang, 2003). Thus, the need for discriminating between cognates and borrowings emerges. Heggarty (2012) acknowledges the necessity and difficulty of the task, emphasizing the role of the "computerized approaches".

In this paper we address the task of automatically distinguishing between borrowings and cognates: given a pair of words, the task is to determine whether one is a historical descendant of the other, or whether they both share a common ancestor. A *borrowing* (also called *loanword*), is defined by Campbell (1998) as a "lexical item (a word) which has been 'borrowed' from another language, a word which originally was not part of the vocabulary of the recipient language but was adopted from some other language and made part of the borrowing language's vocabulary". The notion of *cognate* is much more relaxed, and various NLP tasks and applications use different definitions of the cognate pairs. In some situations, cognates and borrowings are considered together, and are referred to as *historically connected words* (Kessler, 2001) or denoted by the term *correlates* (Heggarty, 2012; McMahon et al., 2005). In some tasks, such as statistical machine translation (Kondrak et al., 2003) and sentence alignment, or when studying the similarity or intelligibility of the languages, cognates are seen as words that have similar spelling and meaning, their etymology being completely disregarded. However, in problems of language classification, distinguishing cognates from borrowings is essential. Here, we account for the etymology of the words, and we adopt the following definition: two words form a cognate pair if they share a common ancestor and have the same meaning. In other words, they derive directly from the same word, have a similar meaning and, due to various (possibly language-specific) changes across time, their forms might differ.

2 Related Work

In a natural way, one of the most investigated problems in historical linguistics is to determine whether similar words are related or not (Kondrak, 2002). Investigating pairs of related words is very useful not only in historical and comparative linguistics, but also in the study of language relatedness (Ng et al., 2010), phylogenetic inference (Atkinson et al., 2005) and in identifying how and to what extent languages changed over time or influenced each other.

Most studies in this area focus on automatically identifying pairs of cognates. For measuring the orthographic or phonetic proximity of the cognate candidates, string similarity metrics (Inkpen

Proceedings of the 53rd Annual Meeting of the Association for Computational Linguistics and the 7th International Joint Conference on Natural Language Processing (Short Papers), pages 431–437,
Beijing, China, July 26-31, 2015. ©2015 Association for Computational Linguistics

et al., 2005; Hall and Klein, 2010) and algorithms for string alignment (Delmestri and Cristianini, 2010) have been applied, both in cognate detection (Koehn and Knight, 2000; Mulloni and Pekar, 2006; Navlea and Todirascu, 2011) and in cognate production (Beinborn et al., 2013; Mulloni, 2007). Minett and Wang (2003) focus on identifying borrowings within a family of genetically related languages and propose, to this end, a distance-based and a character-based technique. Minett and Wang (2005) address the problem of identifying language contact, building on the idea that borrowings bias the lexical similarities among genetically related languages.

According to the regularity principle, the distinction between cognates and borrowings benefits from the regular sound changes that generate regular phoneme correspondences in cognates (Kondrak, 2002). In turn, sound correspondences are represented, to a certain extent, by alphabetic character correspondences (Delmestri and Cristianini, 2010).

3 Our Approach

In light of this, we investigate whether cognates can be automatically distinguished from borrowings based on their orthography. More specifically, our task is as follows: given a pair of words in two different languages (x, y), we want to determine whether x and y are cognates or if y is borrowed from x (in other words, x is the etymon of y).

Our starting point is a methodology that has previously proven successful in discriminating between related and unrelated words (Ciobanu and Dinu, 2014b). Briefly, the method comprises the following steps:

1) Aligning the pairs of related words using a string alignment algorithm;
2) Extracting orthographic features from the aligned words;
3) Training a binary classifier to discriminate between the two types of relationship.

To align the pairs of related words, we employ the Needleman-Wunsch global alignment algorithm (Needleman and Wunsch, 1970), which is equivalent to the weighted edit distance algorithm. We consider words as input sequences and we use a very simple substitution matrix[1], which assigns

[1]In our future work, we intend to also experiment with more informed language-specific substitution matrices.

Lang.	Cognates			Borrowings		
	len$_1$	**len$_2$**	**edit**	**len$_1$**	**len$_2$**	**edit**
IT-RO	7.95	8.78	0.26	7.58	8.41	0.29
ES-RO	7.91	8.33	0.26	5.78	6.14	0.52
PT-RO	7.99	8.35	0.28	5.35	5.42	0.52
TR-RO	7.35	6.88	0.31	6.49	6.09	0.44

Table 2: Statistics for the dataset of related words. Given a pair of languages (L_1, L_2), the **len$_1$** and **len$_2$** columns represent the average word length of the words in L_1 and L_2. The **edit** column represents the average normalized edit distance between the words. The values are computed only on the training data, to keep the test data unseen.

equal scores to all substitutions, disregarding diacritics (e.g., we ensure that *e* and *è* are matched). As features, we use characters n-grams extracted from the alignment[2]. We mark word boundaries with \$ symbols. For example, the Romanian word *funcţie* (meaning *function*) and its Spanish cognate pair *función* are aligned as follows:

```
$ f u n c ţ i e - $
$ f u n c - i ó n $
```

The features for n = 2 are:

```
$f≻$f,  fu≻fu,  un≻un,  nc≻nc,  cţ≻c-,
ţi≻-i,  ie≻ió,  e-≻ón,  -$≻n$.
```

For the prediction task, we experiment with two models, Naive Bayes and Support Vector Machines. We extend the method by introducing additional linguistic features and we conduct an analysis on their predictive power.

4 Experiments and Results

In this section we present and analyze the experiments we run for discriminating between cognates and borrowings.

4.1 Data

Our experiments revolve around Romanian, a Romance language belonging to the Italic branch of the Indo-European language family. It is surrounded by Slavic languages and its relationship with the big Romance kernel was difficult. Its geographic position, at the North of the Balkans, put

[2]While the original methodology proposed features extracted around mismatches in the alignment, we now compare two approaches: 1) features extracted around mismatches, and 2) features extracted from the entire alignment. The latter approach leads to better results, as measured on the test set.

Lang.	Borrowings			Cognates			
IT-RO	baletto	→	balet (ballet)	vittoria	-	victorie (victory)	↑ victoria (LAT)
PT-RO	selva	→	selvă(selva)	instinto	-	instinct (instinct)	↑ instinctus (LAT)
ES-RO	machete	→	macetă (machete)	castillo	-	castel (castle)	↑ castellum (LAT)
TR-RO	tütün	→	tutun (tobacco)	aranjman	-	aranjament (arrangement)	↑ arrangement (FR)

Table 1: Examples of borrowings and cognates. For cognates we also report the common ancestor.

it in contact not only with the Balkan area, but also with the vast majority of Slavic languages. Political and administrative relationships with the Ottoman Empire, Greece (the Phanariot domination) and the Habsburg Empire exposed Romanian to a wide variety of linguistic influences. We apply our method on four pairs of languages extracted from the dataset proposed by Ciobanu and Dinu (2014c):

- Italian - Romanian (IT-RO);
- Portuguese - Romanian (PT-RO);
- Spanish - Romanian (ES-RO);
- Turkish - Romanian (TR-RO).

For the first three pairs of languages, which are formed of *sister languages*[3], most cognate pairs have a Latin common ancestor, while for the fourth pair, formed of languages belonging to different families (Romance and Turkic), most of the cognate pairs have a common French etymology, and date back to the end of the 19th century, when both Romanian and Turkish borrowed massively from French. In Table 1 we provide examples of borrowings and cognates.

The dataset contains borrowings[4] and cognates that share a common ancestor. The words (and information about their origins) were extracted from electronic dictionaries and their relationships were determined based on their etymology. We use a stratified dataset of 2,600 pairs of related words for each pair of languages. In Table 2 we provide an initial analysis of our dataset. We report statistics regarding the length of the words and the edit distance between them. The difference in length between the related words shows what operations to expect when aligning the words. Romanian words are almost in all situations shorter, in average, than their pairs. For TR-RO $\mathbf{len_1}$ is higher than $\mathbf{len_2}$, so we expect more deletions for this pair of languages. The **edit** columns show how much words vary from one language to another based on their relationship (cognates or borrowings). For IT-RO both distances are small (0.26 and 0.29), as opposed to the other languages, where there is a more significant difference between the two (e.g., 0.26 and 0.52 for ES-RO). The small difference for IT-RO might make the discrimination between the two classes more difficult.

4.2 Baselines

Given the initial analysis presented above, we hypothesize that the distance between the words might be indicative of the type of relationship between them. Previous studies (Inkpen et al., 2005; Gomes and Lopes, 2011) show that related and non-related words can be distinguished based on the distance between them, but a finer-grained task, such as determining the type of relationship between the words, is probably more subtle. We compare our method with two baselines:

- A baseline which assigns a label based on the normalized edit distance between the words: given a test instance pair $word_1$ - $word_2$, we subtract the average normalized edit distance between $word_1$ and $word_2$ from the average normalized edit distance of the cognate pairs and from the average normalized edit distance between the borrowings and their etymons (computed on the training set; see Table 2), and assign the label which yields a smaller difference (in absolute value). In case of equality, the label is chosen randomly.

- A decision tree classifier, following the strategy proposed by Inkpen et al. (2005): we use the normalized edit distance as single feature, and we fit a decision tree classifier with the maximum tree depth set to 1. We perform 3-fold cross-validation in order to select the best threshold for discriminating between borrowings and cognates. Using the

[3]Sister languages are "languages which are related to one another by virtue of having descended from the same common ancestor (proto-language)" (Campbell, 1998).

[4]Romanian is always the recipient language in our dataset (i.e., the language that borrowed the words).

best threshold selected for each language, we further assign one of the two classes to the pairs of words in our test set.

4.3 Task Setup

We experiment with Naive Bayes and Support Vector Machines (SVMs) to learn orthographic changes. We put our system together using the Weka[5] workbench (Hall et al., 2009). For SVM, we employ the radial basis function kernel (RBF) and we use the wrapper provided by Weka for LibSVM (Chang and Lin, 2011). For each language pair, we split the dataset in two stratified subsets, for training and testing, with a 3:1 ratio. We experiment with different values for the n-gram size (n $\in \{1, 2, 3\}$) and we perform grid search and 3-fold cross validation over the training set in order to optimize hyperparameters c and γ for SVM. We search over $\{1, 2, ..., 10\}$ for c and over $\{10^{-2}, 10^{-1}, 10^{0}, 10^{1}, 10^{2}\}$ for γ.

4.4 Results Analysis

Table 3 and Table 4 show the results of our experiment. The two baselines produce comparable results. For all pairs of languages, our method significantly improves over the baselines (99% confidence level)[6] with values between 7% and 29% for the F_1 score, suggesting that the n-grams extracted from the alignment of the words are better indicators of the type of relationship than the edit distance between them. The best results are obtained for TR-RO, with an F_1 score of 92.1, followed closely by PT-RO with 90.1 and ES-RO with 85.5. These results show that, for these pairs of languages, the orthographic cues are different with regard to the relationship between the words. For IT-RO we obtain the lowest F_1 score, 69.0.

In this experiment, we know beforehand that there is a relationship between the words, and our aim is to identify the type of relationship. However, in many situations this kind of a-priori information is not available. In a real scenario, we would have either to add an intermediary classifier for discriminating between related and unrelated words, or to discriminate between three classes: cognates, borrowings, and unrelated. We augment our dataset with unrelated words (determined based on their etymology), building a stratified dataset annotated with three classes, and we repeat the previous experiment. The performance decreases[7], but the results are still significantly better than chance (99% confidence level).

Lang.	Baseline #1			Baseline #2		
	P	R	F_1	P	R	F_1
IT-RO	50.7	50.7	50.7	64.4	54.5	45.0
PT-RO	79.3	79.0	79.2	80.1	80.0	80.0
ES-RO	78.6	78.4	78.5	78.6	78.5	78.4
TR-RO	61.1	61.0	61.1	62.5	59.8	57.6

Table 3: Weighted average precision (P), recall (R) and F_1 score (F_1) for automatic discrimination between cognates and borrowings.

4.5 Linguistic Factors

To gain insight into the factors with high predictive power, we perform several further experiments.

Part of speech. We investigate whether adding knowledge about the part of speech of the words leads to performance improvements. Verbs, nouns, adverbs and adjectives have language-specific endings, thus we assume that part of speech might be useful when learning orthographic patterns. We obtain POS tags from the DexOnline[8] machine-readable dictionary. We employ the POS feature as an additional categorical feature for the learning algorithm. It turns out that, except for PT-RO (F_1 score 92.3), the additional POS feature does not improve the performance of our method.

Syllabication. We analyze whether the system benefits from using the syllabified form of the words as input to the alignment algorithm. We are interested to see if marking the boundaries between the syllables improves the alignment (and, thus, the feature extraction). We obtain the syllabication for the words in our dataset from the RoSyllabiDict dictionary (Barbu, 2008) for Romanian words and several available Perl modules[9] for the other languages. For PT-RO and ES-RO the F_1 score increases by about 1%, reaching a value of 93.4 for the former and 86.7 for the latter.

[5] www.cs.waikato.ac.nz/ml/weka

[6] All the statistical significance tests reported in this paper are performed on 1,000 iterations of paired bootstrap resampling (Koehn, 2004).

[7] Weighted average F_1 score on the test set for SVM: IT-RO 63.8, PT-RO 77.6, ES-RO 74.0, TR-RO 86.1.

[8] www.dexonline.ro

[9] Lingua::ID::Hyphenate modules where ID $\in$ {IT, PT, ES, TR}, available on the Comprehensive Perl Archive Network: www.cpan.org.

Lang.	Naive Bayes				SVM					
	P	R	F_1	n	P	R	F_1	n	c	γ
IT-RO	68.6	68.2	68.3	3	69.2	69.1	69.0	3	10	0.10
PT-RO	92.6	91.7	92.1	3	90.1	90.0	90.0	3	3	0.10
ES-RO	85.3	84.5	84.9	3	85.7	85.5	85.5	2	2	0.10
TR-RO	89.7	89.4	89.5	3	90.3	90.2	90.1	3	6	0.01

Table 4: Weighted average precision (P), recall (R), F_1 score (F_1) and optimal n-gram size for automatic discrimination between cognates and borrowings. For SVM we also report the optimal values for c and γ.

Consonants. We examine the performance of our system when trained and tested only on the aligned *consonant skeletons* of the words (i.e., a version of the words where vowels are discarded). According to Ashby and Maidment (2005), consonants change at a slower pace than vowels across time; while the former are regarded as reference points, the latter are believed to carry less information useful for identifying the words (Gooskens et al., 2008). The performance of the system decreases when vowels are removed (95% confidence level). We also train and test the decision tree classifier on this version of the dataset, and its performance is lower in this case as well (95% confidence level), indicating that, for our task, the information carried by the vowels is helpful.

Stems. We repeat the first experiment using stems as input, instead of lemmas. What we seek to understand is whether the aligned affixes are indicative of the type of relationship between the words. We use the Snowball Stemmer[10] and we find that the performance decreases when stems are used instead of lemmas. Performing a χ^2 feature ranking on the features extracted from mismatches in the alignment of the related words reveals further insight into this matter: for all pairs of languages, at least one feature containing the $ character (indicating the beginning or the end of a word) is ranked among the 10 most relevant features, and over 50 are ranked among the 500 most relevant features. This suggests that prefixes and suffixes (usually removed by the stemmer) vary with the type of relationship between the words.

Diacritics. We explore whether removing diacritics influences the performance of the system. Many words have undergone transformations by the augmentation of language-specific diacritics when entering a new language (Ciobanu and Dinu, 2014a). For this reason, we expect diacritics to play a role in the classification task. We observe that, when diacritics are removed, the F_1 score on the test set is lower in almost all situations. Analyzing the ranking of the features extracted from mismatches in the alignment provides even stronger evidence in this direction: for all pairs of languages, more than a fifth of the top 500 features contain diacritics.

[10]http://snowball.tartarus.org

5 Conclusions

In this paper, we propose a computational method for discriminating between cognates and borrowings based on their orthography. Our results show that it is possible to identify the type of relationship with fairly good performance (over 85.0 F_1 score) for 3 out of the 4 pairs of languages we investigate. Our predictive analysis shows that the orthographic cues are different for cognates and borrowings, and that underlying linguistic factors captured by our model, such as affixes and diacritics, are indicative of the type of relationship between the words. Other insights, such as the syllabication or the part of speech of the words, are shown to have little or no predictive power. We intend to further account for finer-grained characteristics of the words and to extend our experiments to more languages. The method we propose is language-independent, but we believe that incorporating language-specific knowledge might improve the system's performance.

Acknowledgements

We thank the anonymous reviewers for their helpful and constructive comments. The contribution of the authors to this paper is equal. Liviu P. Dinu was supported by UEFISCDI, PNII-ID-PCE-2011-3-0959.

References

Michael Ashby and John Maidment. 2005. *Introducing Phonetic Science*. Cambridge University Press.

Quentin D. Atkinson, Russell D. Gray, Geoff K. Nicholls, and David J. Welch. 2005. From Words to Dates: Water into Wine, Mathemagic or Phylogenetic Inference? *Transactions of the Philological Society*, 103(2):193–219.

Ana-Maria Barbu. 2008. Romanian Lexical Data Bases: Inflected and Syllabic Forms Dictionaries. In *Proceedings of the 6th International Conference on Language Resources and Evaluation, LREC 2008*, pages 1937–1941.

Lisa Beinborn, Torsten Zesch, and Iryna Gurevych. 2013. Cognate Production using Character-based Machine Translation. In *Proceedings of the 6th International Joint Conference on Natural Language Processing, IJCNLP 2013*, pages 883–891.

Lyle Campbell. 1998. *Historical Linguistics. An Introduction*. MIT Press.

Chih-Chung Chang and Chih-Jen Lin. 2011. LIBSVM: A Library for Support Vector Machines. *ACM Transactions on Intelligent Systems and Technology*, 2(3):27:1–27:27. Software available at `http://www.csie.ntu.edu.tw/~cjlin/libsvm`.

Alina Maria Ciobanu and Liviu P. Dinu. 2014a. An Etymological Approach to Cross-Language Orthographic Similarity. Application on Romanian. In *Proceedings of the 2014 Conference on Empirical Methods in Natural Language Processing, EMNLP 2014*, pages 1047–1058.

Alina Maria Ciobanu and Liviu P. Dinu. 2014b. Automatic Detection of Cognates Using Orthographic Alignment. In *Proceedings of the 52st Annual Meeting of the Association for Computational Linguistics, ACL 2014*, pages 99–105.

Alina Maria Ciobanu and Liviu P. Dinu. 2014c. Building a Dataset of Multilingual Cognates for the Romanian Lexicon. In *Proceedings of the 9th International Conference on Language Resources and Evaluation, LREC 2014*.

Antonella Delmestri and Nello Cristianini. 2010. String Similarity Measures and PAM-like Matrices for Cognate Identification. *Bucharest Working Papers in Linguistics*, 12(2):71–82.

Luís Gomes and José Gabriel Pereira Lopes. 2011. Measuring Spelling Similarity for Cognate Identification. In *Proceedings of the 15th Portugese Conference on Progress in Artificial Intelligence, EPIA 2011*, pages 624–633. Software available at `http://research.variancia.com/spsim`.

Charlotte Gooskens, Wilbert Heeringa, and Karin Beijering. 2008. Phonetic and Lexical Predictors of Intelligibility. *International Journal of Humanities and Arts Computing*, 2(1-2):63–81.

David Hall and Dan Klein. 2010. Finding Cognate Groups Using Phylogenies. In *Proceedings of the 48th Annual Meeting of the Association for Computational Linguistics, ACL 2010*, pages 1030–1039.

Mark Hall, Eibe Frank, Geoffrey Holmes, Bernhard Pfahringer, Peter Reutemann, and Ian H. Witten. 2009. The WEKA Data Mining Software: An Update. *SIGKDD Explorations*, 11(1):10–18.

Robert Anderson Hall. 1960. *Linguistics and Your Language*. Doubleday New York.

Paul Heggarty. 2012. Beyond Lexicostatistics: How to Get More out of "Word List" Comparisons. In *Quantitative Approaches to Linguistic Diversity: Commemorating the Centenary of the Birth of Morris Swadesh*, pages 113–137. Benjamins.

Diana Inkpen, Oana Frunza, and Grzegorz Kondrak. 2005. Automatic Identification of Cognates and False Friends in French and English. In *Proceedings of the International Conference on Recent Advances in Natural Language Processing, RANLP 2005*, pages 251–257.

Brett Kessler. 2001. *The Significance of Word Lists*. Stanford: CSLI Publications.

Philipp Koehn and Kevin Knight. 2000. Estimating Word Translation Probabilities from Unrelated Monolingual Corpora Using the EM Algorithm. In *Proceedings of the 17th National Conference on Artificial Intelligence and 12th Conference on Innovative Applications of Artificial Intelligence*, pages 711–715.

Philipp Koehn. 2004. Statistical Significance Tests for Machine Translation Evaluation. In *Proceedings of the 2004 Conference on Empirical Methods in Natural Language Processing, EMNLP 2004*, pages 388–395.

Grzegorz Kondrak, Daniel Marcu, and Keven Knight. 2003. Cognates Can Improve Statistical Translation Models. In *Proceedings of the 2003 Conference of the North American Chapter of the Association for Computational Linguistics on Human Language Technology, HLT-NAACL 2003*, pages 46–48.

Grzegorz Kondrak. 2002. *Algorithms For Language Reconstruction*. Ph.D. thesis, University of Toronto.

April McMahon, Paul Heggarty, Robert McMahon, and Natalia Slaska. 2005. Swadesh Sublists and the Benefits of Borrowing: an Andean Case Study. *Transactions of the Philological Society*, 103(2):147–170.

James W. Minett and William S.-Y. Wang. 2003. On Detecting Borrowing: Distance-based and Character-based Approaches. *Diachronica*, 20(2):289–331.

James W. Minett and William S.-Y. Wang. 2005. Vertical and Horizontal Transmission in Language Evolution. *Transactions of the Philological Society*, 103(2):121–146.

Andrea Mulloni and Viktor Pekar. 2006. Automatic Detection of Orthographic Cues for Cognate Recognition. In *In Proceedings of the 5th International Conference on Language Resources and Evaluation, LREC 2006*, pages 2387–2390.

Andrea Mulloni. 2007. Automatic Prediction of Cognate Orthography Using Support Vector Machines. In *Proceedings of the 45th Annual Meeting of the ACL: Student Research Workshop, ACL 2007*, pages 25–30.

Mirabela Navlea and Amalia Todirascu. 2011. Using Cognates in a French-Romanian Lexical Alignment System: A Comparative Study. In *Proceedings of the International Conference on Recent Advances in Natural Language Processing, RANLP 2011*, pages 247–253.

Saul B. Needleman and Christian D. Wunsch. 1970. A General Method Applicable to the Search for Similarities in the Amino Acid Sequence of Two Proteins. *Journal of Molecular Biology*, 48(3):443 – 453.

Ee-Lee Ng, Beatrice Chin, Alvin W. Yeo, and Bali Ranaivo-Malançon. 2010. Identification of Closely-Related Indigenous Languages: An Orthographic Approach. *International Journal of Asian Language Processing*, 20(2):43–62.

The Media Frames Corpus: Annotations of Frames Across Issues

Dallas Card[1] **Amber E. Boydstun**[2] **Justin H. Gross**[3] **Philip Resnik**[4] **Noah A. Smith**[1]
[1]School of Computer Science, Carnegie Mellon University, Pittsburgh, PA 15213, USA
[2]Department of Political Science, University of California, Davis, CA 95616, USA
[3]Department of Political Science, University of Massachusetts, Amherst, MA 01003, USA
[4]UMIACS, University of Maryland, College Park, MD 20742, USA
dcard@cmu.edu aboydstun@ucdavis.edu jhgross@polsci.umass.edu
resnik@umiacs.umd.edu nasmith@cs.cmu.edu

Abstract

We describe the first version of the Media Frames Corpus: several thousand news articles on three policy issues, annotated in terms of media *framing*. We motivate framing as a phenomenon of study for computational linguistics and describe our annotation process.

1 Introduction

An important part of what determines how information will be interpreted by an audience is how that information is *framed*. Framing is a phenomenon largely studied and debated in the social sciences, where, for example, researchers explore how news media shape debate around policy issues by deciding what aspects of an issue to emphasize, and what to exclude. Theories of framing posit that these decisions give rise to thematic sets of interrelated ideas, imagery, and arguments, which tend to cohere and persist over time.

Past work on framing includes many examples of issue-specific studies based on manual content analysis (Baumgartner et al., 2008; Berinsky and Kinder, 2006). While such studies reveal much about the range of opinions on an issue, they do not characterize framing at a level of abstraction that allows comparison *across* social issues.

More recently, there have also been a handful of papers on the computational analysis of framing (Nguyen et al., 2015; Tsur et al., 2015; Baumer et al., 2015). While these papers represent impressive advances, they are still focused on the problem of automating the analysis of framing along a single dimension, or within a particular domain.

We propose that framing can be understood as a general aspect of linguistic communication about facts and opinions on any issue. Empirical assessment of this hypothesis requires analyzing framing in real-world media coverage. To this end, we contribute an initial dataset of annotated news articles, the Media Frames Corpus (version 1). These annotations are based on 15 general-purpose metaframes (here called "framing dimensions") outlined below, which are intended to subsume all specific frames that might be encountered on any issue of public concern.

Several features of this annotation project distinguish it from linguistic annotation projects familiar to computational linguists:

- A degree of subjectivity in framing analysis is unavoidable. While some variation in annotations is due to mistakes and misunderstandings by annotators (and is to be minimized), much variation is due to valid differences in interpretation (and is therefore properly preserved in the coding process).
- Annotator skill appears to improve with practice; our confidence in the quality of the annotations has grown in later phases of the project, and this attribute is not suppressed in our data release.

All of the annotations and metadata in this corpus are publicly available, along with tools to acquire the original news articles usable by those who have an appropriate license to the texts from their source (Lexis-Nexis).[1] This dataset and planned future extensions will enable computational linguists and others to develop and empirically test models of framing.

2 What is Framing?

Consider a politically contested issue such as same-sex marriage. Conflicting perspectives on this issue compete to attract our attention and influence our opinions; any communications about

[1]https://github.com/dallascard/media_frames_corpus

Proceedings of the 53rd Annual Meeting of the Association for Computational Linguistics and the 7th International Joint Conference on Natural Language Processing (Short Papers), pages 438–444,
Beijing, China, July 26-31, 2015.

the issue—whether emanating from political parties, activist organizations, or media providers—will be fraught with decisions about how the issue should be defined and presented.

In a widely cited definition, Entman (1993) argues that "to frame is to select some aspects of a perceived reality and make them more salient in a communicating text, in such a way as to promote problem definition, causal interpretation, moral evaluation, and/or treatment recommendation for the item described." Further elaborations have emphasized how various elements of framing tend to align and cohere, eventually being deployed "packages" which can be evoked through particular phrases, images, or other synecdoches (Gameson and Modigliani, 1989; Benford and Snow, 2000; Chong and Druckman, 2007). These may take the form of simple slogans, such as *the war on terror*, or more complex, perhaps unstated, assumptions, such as the rights of individuals, or the responsibilities of government. The patterns that emerge from these decisions and assumptions are, in essence, what we refer to as framing.[2]

Traditionally, in the social sciences, framing is studied by developing an extensive codebook of frames specific to an issue, reading large numbers of documents, and manually annotating them for the presence of the frames in the codebook (e.g., Baumgartner et al., 2008; Terkildsen and Schnell, 1997). Computational linguists therefore have much to offer in formalizing and automating the analysis of framing, enabling greater scale and breadth of application across issues.

3 Annotation Scheme

The goal of our annotation process was to produce a corpus of examples demonstrating how the choice of language in a document relates to framing in a non-issue-specific way. To accomplish this task, we annotated news articles with a set of 15 cross-cutting framing dimensions, such as economics, morality, and politics, developed by Boydstun et al. (2014). These dimensions, summarized in Figure 1, were informed by the framing literature and developed to be general enough to be applied to any policy issue.

For each article, annotators were asked to identify any of the 15 framing dimensions present in the article and to label spans of text which cued them. Annotators also identified the dominant framing of the article headline (if present), as well as for the entire article, which we refer to as the "primary frame." Finally, newspaper corrections, articles shorter than four lines of text, and articles about foreign countries were marked as irrelevant. There were no constraints on the length or composition of annotated text spans, and annotations were allowed to overlap. The last framing dimension ("Other") was used to categorize any articles that didn't conform to any of the other options (used in $< 10\%$ of cases). An example of two independent annotations of the same article is shown in Figure 2.

Economic: costs, benefits, or other financial implications
Capacity and resources: availability of physical, human or financial resources, and capacity of current systems
Morality: religious or ethical implications
Fairness and equality: balance or distribution of rights, responsibilities, and resources
Legality, constitutionality and jurisprudence: rights, freedoms, and authority of individuals, corporations, and government
Policy prescription and evaluation: discussion of specific policies aimed at addressing problems
Crime and punishment: effectiveness and implications of laws and their enforcement
Security and defense: threats to welfare of the individual, community, or nation
Health and safety: health care, sanitation, public safety
Quality of life: threats and opportunities for the individual's wealth, happiness, and well-being
Cultural identity: traditions, customs, or values of a social group in relation to a policy issue
Public opinion: attitudes and opinions of the general public, including polling and demographics
Political: considerations related to politics and politicians, including lobbying, elections, and attempts to sway voters
External regulation and reputation: international reputation or foreign policy of the U.S.
Other: any coherent group of frames not covered by the above categories

Figure 1: Framing dimensions from Boydstun et al. (2014).

For the initial version of this corpus, three policy issues were chosen for their expected diversity of framing and their contemporary political relevance: immigration, smoking, and same-sex marriage. Lexis-Nexis was used to obtain all articles matching a set of keywords published by a set of 13 national U.S. newspapers between the years 1990 and 2012.[3] Duplicate and near-duplicate articles were removed and randomly selected articles were chosen for annotation for each issue (see supplementary material for additional details).

[2] A distinct though related usage, known as "equivalence framing" in psychology, refers to different phrasings of semantically equivalent expressions (e.g., is an 8-ounce glass containing 4 ounces of water *half empty* or *half full*?).

[3] The immigration articles extend back to 1969, though there are few before 1980.

Annotation guidelines for the project are documented in a codebook, which was used for training the annotators. The codebook for these issues was refined in an ongoing manner to include examples from each issue, and more carefully delineate the boundaries between the framing dimensions.

4 Annotation Process

Our annotation process reflects the less-than-ideal circumstances faced by academics requiring content analysis: relatively untrained annotators, high turnover, and evolving guidelines. Our process is delineated into three stages, summarized in Table 1 and discussed in detail below. Each stage involved 14–20-week-long rounds of coding; in each round, annotators were given approximately 100 articles to annotate, and the combinations of annotators assigned the same articles were rotated between rounds. Our annotators were undergraduates students at a U.S. research university, and a total of 19 worked on this project, with 8 being involved in more than one stage. The average number of frames identified in an article varied from 2.0 to 3.7 across annotators, whereas the average number of spans highlighted per article varied from 3.4 to 10.0. Additional detail is given in Table 1 in the supplementary material.

Stage	Issue	Articles	Av. annotators per article
1	Immigration	4,113	1.2
1	Smoking	4,077	1.2
2	Same-sex marriage	6,298	2.2
3	Immigration	5,549	2.2

Table 1: Summary of the number of articles annotated and average number of annotators per article

4.1 Stage 1

During the first stage, approximately 4,000 articles on each of immigration and smoking were annotated, with approximately 500 articles in each group annotated by multiple annotators to measure inter-annotator agreement. Our goals here were high coverage and ensuring that the guidelines were not too narrowly adapted to any single issue. Annotators received only minimal feedback on their agreement levels during this stage.

4.2 Stage 2

In the second stage, annotations shifted to same-sex marriage articles, again emphasizing general fit across issues. Beginning in stage 2, each article

[WHERE THE JOBS ARE]$_{\text{Economic}}$
[Critics of illegal immigration can make many cogent arguments to support the position that the U.S. Congress and the Colorado legislature must develop effective and well-enforced immigration policies that will restrict the number of people who migrate here legally and illegally.]$_{\text{Policy prescription}}$
[It's true that all forms of [immigration exert influence over our economic and cultural make-up.]$_{\text{Cultural identity}}$ **In some ways, immigration improves our economy by adding laborers, taxpayers and consumers, and in other ways immigration detracts from our economy by increasing the number of students, health care recipients and other beneficiaries of public services.]**$_{\text{Economic}}$
[Some economists say that immigrants, legal and illegal, produce a net economic gain, while others say that they create a net loss]$_{\text{Economic}}$. There are rational arguments to support both sides of this debate, and it's useful and educational to hear the varying positions.

[WHERE THE JOBS ARE]$_{\text{Economic}}$
[Critics of illegal immigration can make many cogent arguments to support the position that the U.S. Congress and the Colorado legislature must develop effective and well-enforced immigration policies that will restrict the number of people who migrate here legally and illegally.]$_{\text{Public opinion}}$
[It's true that all forms of immigration exert influence over our economic and [cultural make-up.]$_{\text{Cultural identity}}$ **In some ways, immigration improves our economy by adding laborers, taxpayers and consumers, and in other ways [immigration detracts from our economy by increasing the number of students, health care recipients and other beneficiaries of public services.]**$_{\text{Capacity}}$**]**$_{\text{Economic}}$
[Some economists say that immigrants, legal and illegal, produce a net economic gain, while others say that they create a net loss.]$_{\text{Economic}}$ There are rational arguments to support both sides of this debate, and it's useful and educational to hear the varying positions.

Figure 2: Two independent annotations of a 2006 editorial in the *Denver Post*. The annotators agree perfectly about which parts of the article make use of economic framing, but disagree about the first paragraph. Moreover, the second annotator identifies an additional dimension (capacity and resources). Although they both identify a reference to cultural identity, they annotated slightly different spans of text.

was assigned to at least two annotators, in order to track inter-annotator agreement more carefully, and to better capture the subjectivity inherent in this task. Since the guidelines had become more stable by this stage, we also focused on identifying good practices for annotator training. Annotators were informed of their agreement levels with each other, and pairs of framing dimensions on which annotators frequently disagreed were emphasized. This information was presented to annotators in weekly meetings.

4.3 Stage 3

The third stage revisited the immigration articles from stage 1 (plus an additional group of articles), with the now well-developed annotation guidelines. As in the second stage, almost all articles were annotated by two annotators, working independently. More detailed feedback was provided, including inter-annotator agreement for the use of each framing dimension anywhere in articles.

During stage 3, for each article where two annotators independently disagreed on the primary frame, the pair met to discuss the disagreement and attempt to come to a consensus.[4] Disagreements continue to arise, however, reflecting the reality that the same article can cue different frames more strongly for different annotators. We view these disagreements not as a weakness, but as a source of useful information about the diversity of ways in which the same text can be interpreted by different audiences (Pan and Kosicki, 1993; Rees et al., 2001).

The proportion of articles annotated with each framing dimension (averaged across annotators) is shown in Figure 3.

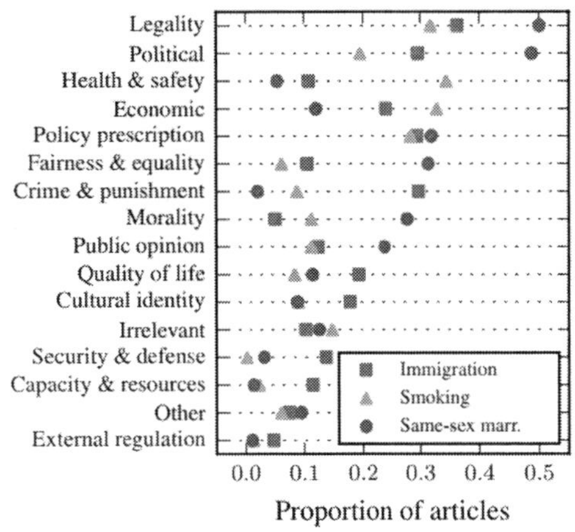

Figure 3: Proportion of articles annotated with each of the framing dimensions (averaging across annotators for each article).

Figure 4 shows the inter-annotator agreement on the primary frame per round. We observe first that difficulty varies by issue, with same-sex marriage the most difficult. Annotators do appear to improve with experience. Agreement on immigration articles in stage 3 are significantly higher ($p < 0.05$, permutation test) than agreement on the same articles in stage 1, even though only one annotator worked on both stages.[6]

These results demonstrate that consistent performance can be obtained from different groups of annotators, given sufficient training. Although we never obtain perfect agreement, this is not surprising, given that the same sentences can and do cue multiple types of framing, as illustrated by the example in Figure 2.

Inter-annotator agreement at the level of individually selected spans of text can be assessed using an extension of Krippendorff's α (α_U) which measures disagreement between two spans as the sum of the squares of the lengths of the parts which do not overlap.[7] As with the more common α statistic, α_U is a chance-corrected agreement metric scaled such that 1 represents perfect agreement and 0 represents the level of chance. This met-

5 Inter-annotator Agreement

Because our annotation task is complex (selecting potentially overlapping text spans and labeling them), there is no single comprehensive measure of inter-annotator agreement. The simplest aspect of the annotations to compare is the choice of primary frame, which we measure using Krippendorff's α (Krippendorff, 2012).[5]

[4]A small secondary experiment, described in supplementary material, was used to test the reliability of this process.

[5]Krippendorff's α is similar to Cohen's κ, but calculates expected agreement between annotators based on the combined pool of labels provided by all annotators, rather than considering each annotators's frequency of use separately. Moreover, it can be used for more than two annotators and accommodates missing values. See Passonneau and Carpenter (2014) for additional details.

[6]Note that this is not a controlled experiment on annotation procedures, but rather a difference observed between two stages of an evolving process.

[7]For example, in the example shown in Figure 2, the amount of disagreement on the two Cultural identity annotations would be the square of the length (in characters) of the non-overlapping part of the annotations ("immigration exert influence over our economic and") which is $50^2 = 2500$.

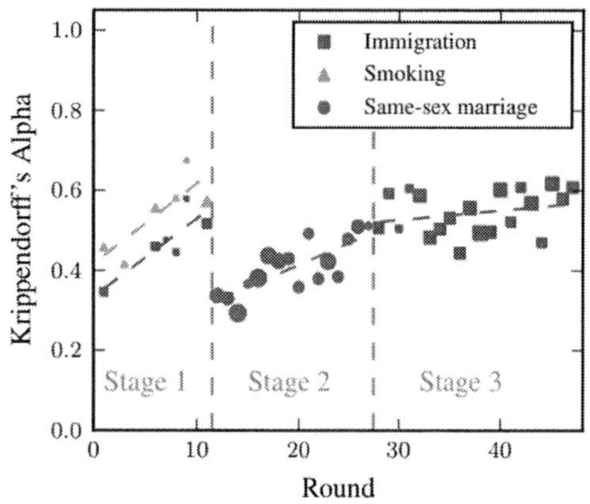

Figure 4: Chance-corrected inter-annotator agreement on the primary frame. Marker size indicates the number of annotations being compared; $\alpha = 1$ indicates perfect agreement.

ric has been previously recommended for tasks in computational linguistics that involve *unitizing* (Artstein and Poesio, 2008). For a more complete explanation, see Krippendorff (2004).

The pattern of α_U values across rounds is very similar to that shown in Figure 4, but not surprisingly, average levels of agreement are much lower. Arguably, this agreement statistic is overly harsh for our purposes. We do not necessarily expect annotators to agree perfectly about where to start and end each annotated span, or how many spans to annotate per article, and our codebook and guidelines offer relatively little guidance on these low-level decisions. Nevertheless, it is encouraging that in all cases, average agreement is greater than chance. The α_U values for all annotated spans of text (averaged across articles) are 0.16 for immigration (stage 1), 0.23 for tobacco, 0.08 for same-sex marriage, and 0.20 for immigration (stage 3).

6 Prior Work

Several previous papers in the computer science literature deal with framing, though usually in a more restricted sense. Perhaps the most common approach is to treat the computational analysis of framing as a variation on sentiment analysis, though this often involves reducing framing to a binary variable. Various models have been applied to news and social media datasets with the goal of identifying political ideology, or "perspective" (typically on a liberal to conservative scale) (Ahmed and Xing, 2010; Gentzkow and Shapiro, 2010; Lin et al., 2006; Hardisty et al., 2010; Klebanov et al., 2010; Sim et al., 2013; Iyyer et al., 2014), or "stance" (position for or against an issue) (Walker et al., 2012; Hasan and Ng, 2013). A related line of work is the analysis of subjective language or "scientific" language, which has also been posed in terms of framing (Wiebe et al., 2004; Choi et al., 2012). While the study of ideology, sentiment, and subjectivity are interesting in their own right, we believe that they fail to capture the more nuanced nature of framing, which is often more complex than positive or negative sentiment. In discussions of same-sex marriage, for example, both advocates and opponents may attempt to control whether the issue is perceived as primarily about politics, legality, or ethics. Moreover, we emphasize that framing is an important feature of even seemingly neutral or objective language.

A different but equally relevant line of work has focused on text re-use. Leskovec et al. (2009) perform clustering of quotations and their variations, uncovering patterns in the temporal dynamics of how memes spread through the media. On a smaller scale, others have examined text reuse in the development of legislation and the culture of reprinting in nineteenth-century newspapers (Smith et al., 2013; Smith et al., 2014). While not the same as framing, identifying this sort of text reuse is an important step towards analyzing the "media packages" that social scientists associate with framing.

7 Conclusion

Framing is a complex and difficult aspect of language to study, but as with so many aspects of modern NLP, there is great potential for progress through the use of statistical methods and public datasets, both labelled and unlabeled. By releasing the Media Frames Corpus, we seek to bring the phenomenon to the attention of the computational linguistics community, and provide a framework that others can use to analyze framing for additional policy issues. As technology progresses towards ever more nuanced understanding of natural language, it is important to analyze not just what is being said, but how, and with what effects. The Media Frames Corpus enables the next step in that direction.

Acknowledgments This research was supported by NSF grants 1211201, 1211266, 1211277, and 1211153.

References

Amr Ahmed and Eric P. Xing. 2010. Staying informed: Supervised and semi-supervised multi-view topical analysis of ideological perspective. In *Proc. of EMNLP*.

Ron Artstein and Massimo Poesio. 2008. Inter-coder agreement for computational linguistics. *Computational Linguistics*, 34(4):555–596.

Eric Baumer, Elisha Elovic, Ying Qin, Francesca Polletta, and Geri Gay. 2015. Testing and comparing computational approaches for identifying the language of framing in political news. In *Proc. of NAACL*.

Frank R. Baumgartner, Suzanna L. De Boef, and Amber E. Boydstun. 2008. *The decline of the death penalty and the discovery of innocence*. Cambridge University Press.

Robert D. Benford and David A. Snow. 2000. Framing processes and social movements: An overview and assessment. *Annual Review of Sociology*, 26:611–639.

Adam J. Berinsky and Donald R. Kinder. 2006. Making sense of issues through media frames: Understanding the Kosovo crisis. *Journal of Politics*, 68(3):640–656.

Amber E. Boydstun, Dallas Card, Justin H. Gross, Philip Resnik, and Noah A. Smith. 2014. Tracking the development of media frames within and across policy issues. *APSA 2014 Annual Meeting Paper*.

Eunsol Choi, Chenhao Tan, Lillian Lee, Cristian Danescu-Niculescu-Mizil, and Jennifer Spindel. 2012. Hedge detection as a lens on framing in the GMO debates: A position paper. In *Proc of. ACL Workshop on Extra-Propositional Aspects of Meaning in Computational Linguistics*, pages 70–79.

Dennis Chong and James N. Druckman. 2007. Framing theory. *Annual Review of Political Science*, 10(1):103–126.

Robert M. Entman. 1993. Framing: Toward clarification of a fractured paradigm. *Journal of Communication*, 43(4):51–58.

William A. Gameson and Andre Modigliani. 1989. Media discourse and public opinion on nuclear power: A constructionist approach. *American Journal of Sociology*, 95(1):1–37.

Matthew Gentzkow and Jesse M. Shapiro. 2010. What drives media slant? Evidence from U.S. daily newspapers. *Econometrica*, 78(1):35–71.

Eric Hardisty, Jordan L. Boyd-Graber, and Philip Resnik. 2010. Modeling perspective using adaptor grammars. In *Proc. of EMNLP*.

Kazi Saidul Hasan and Vincent Ng. 2013. Stance classification of ideological debates: Data, models, features, and constraints. In *Proc. of IJCNLP*.

Mohit Iyyer, Peter Enns, Jordan L. Boyd-Graber, and Philip Resnik. 2014. Political ideology detection using recursive neural networks. In *Proc. of ACL*.

Beata Beigman Klebanov, Eyal Beigman, and Daniel Diermeier. 2010. Vocabulary choice as an indicator of perspective. In *Proc. of ACL*.

Klaus Krippendorff. 2004. Measuring the reliability of qualitative text analysis data. *Quality and Quantity*, 38(6):787–800.

Klaus Krippendorff. 2012. *Content Analysis: An Introduction to its Methodology*. SAGE Publications.

Jure Leskovec, Lars Backstrom, and Jon Kleinberg. 2009. Meme-tracking and the dynamics of the news cycle. In *Proc. of KDD*.

Wei-Hao Lin, Theresa Wilson, Janyce Wiebe, and Alexander Hauptmann. 2006. Which side are you on? Identifying perspectives at the document and sentence levels. In *Proc. of CoNNL*.

Viet-An Nguyen, Jordan Boyd-Graber, Philip Resnik, and Kristina Miler. 2015. Tea party in the house: A hierarchical ideal point topic model and its application to Republican legislators in the 112th congress. In *Proc. of ACL*.

Zhongdang Pan and Gerald M. Kosicki. 1993. Framing analysis: An approach to news discourse. *Political communication*, 10(1):55–75.

Rebecca J. Passonneau and Bob Carpenter. 2014. The benefits of a model of annotation. In *Proc. of ACL*.

Stephen D. Rees, Oscar H. Gandy Jr., , and August E. Grant, editors. 2001. *Framing public life: Perspectives on media and our understanding of the social world*. Routledge.

Yanchuan Sim, Brice D. L. Acree, Justin H. Gross, and Noah A. Smith. 2013. Measuring ideological proportions in political speeches. In *Proc. of EMNLP*.

David A. Smith, Ryan Cordell, and Elizabeth Maddock Dillon. 2013. Infectious texts: modeling text reuse in nineteenth-century newspapers. In *IEEE International Conference on Big Data*.

David A. Smith, Ryan Cordel, Elizabeth Maddock Dillon, Nick Stramp, and John Wilkerson. 2014. Detecting and modeling local text reuse. In *IEEE/ACM Joint Conference on Digital Libraries*.

Nayda Terkildsen and Frauke Schnell. 1997. How media frames move public opinion: An analysis of the women's movement. *Political research quarterly*, 50(4):879–900.

Oren Tsur, Dan Calacci, and David Lazer. 2015. Frame of mind: Using statistical models for detection of framing and agenda setting campaigns. In *Proc. of ACL*.

Marilyn A. Walker, Pranav Anand, Robert Abbott, and Ricky Grant. 2012. Stance classification using dialogic properties of persuasion. In *Proc. of NAACL*.

Janyce Wiebe, Theresa Wilson, Rebecca Bruce, Matthew Bell, and Melanie Martin. 2004. Learning subjective language. *Computational Linguistics*, 30(3):277–308.

ΔBLEU: A Discriminative Metric for Generation Tasks with Intrinsically Diverse Targets

Michel Galley[1†] **Chris Brockett**[1] **Alessandro Sordoni**[2*] **Yangfeng Ji**[3*]
Michael Auli[4*] **Chris Quirk**[1] **Margaret Mitchell**[1] **Jianfeng Gao**[1] **Bill Dolan**[1]

[1]Microsoft Research, Redmond, WA, USA
[2]DIRO, Université de Montréal, Montréal, QC, Canada
[3]Georgia Institute of Technology, Atlanta, GA, USA
[4]Facebook AI Research, Menlo Park, CA, USA

Abstract

We introduce Discriminative BLEU (ΔBLEU), a novel metric for intrinsic evaluation of generated text in tasks that admit a diverse range of possible outputs. Reference strings are scored for quality by human raters on a scale of $[-1, +1]$ to weight multi-reference BLEU. In tasks involving generation of conversational responses, ΔBLEU correlates reasonably with human judgments and outperforms sentence-level and IBM BLEU in terms of both Spearman's ρ and Kendall's τ.

1 Introduction

Many natural language processing tasks involve the generation of texts where a variety of outputs are acceptable or even desirable. Tasks with intrinsically diverse targets range from machine translation, summarization, sentence compression, paraphrase generation, and image-to-text to generation of conversational interactions. A major hurdle for these tasks is automation of evaluation, since the space of plausible outputs can be enormous, and it is it impractical to run a new human evaluation every time a new model is built or parameters are modified.

In Statistical Machine Translation (SMT), the automation problem has to a large extent been ameliorated by metrics such as BLEU (Papineni et al., 2002) and METEOR (Banerjee and Lavie, 2005) Although BLEU is not immune from criticism (e.g., Callison-Burch et al. (2006)), its properties are well understood, BLEU scores have been shown to correlate well with human judgments (Doddington, 2002; Coughlin, 2003; Graham and Baldwin, 2014; Graham et al., 2015) in SMT, and it has allowed the field to proceed.

BLEU has been less successfully applied to non-SMT generation tasks owing to the larger space of plausible outputs. As a result, attempts have been made to adapt the metric. To foster diversity in paraphrase generation, Sun and Zhou (2012) propose a metric called iBLEU in which the BLEU score is discounted by a BLEU score computed between the source and paraphrase. This solution, in addition to being dependent on a tunable parameter, is specific only to paraphrase. In image captioning tasks, Vendantam et al. (2015), employ a variant of BLEU in which n-grams are weighted by *tf·idf*. This assumes the availability of a corpus with which to compute *tf·idf*. Both the above can be seen as attempting to capture a notion of target goodness that is not being captured in BLEU.

In this paper, we introduce Discriminative BLEU (ΔBLEU), a new metric that embeds human judgments concerning the quality of reference sentences directly into the computation of corpus-level multiple-reference BLEU. In effect, we push part of the burden of human evaluation into the automated metric, where it can be repeatedly utilized.

Our testbed for this metric is data-driven conversation, a field that has begun to attract interest (Ritter et al., 2011; Sordoni et al., 2015) as an alternative to conventional rule-driven or scripted dialog systems. Intrinsic evaluation in this field is exceptionally challenging because the semantic space of possible responses resists definition and is only weakly constrained by conversational inputs.

Below, we describe ΔBLEU and investigate its characteristics in comparison to standard BLEU in the context of conversational response generation. We demonstrate that ΔBLEU correlates well with human evaluation scores in this task and thus can

*The entirety of this work was conducted while at Microsoft Research.

†Corresponding author: mgalley@microsoft.com

Proceedings of the 53rd Annual Meeting of the Association for Computational Linguistics and the 7th International Joint Conference on Natural Language Processing (Short Papers), pages 445–450,
Beijing, China, July 26-31, 2015.

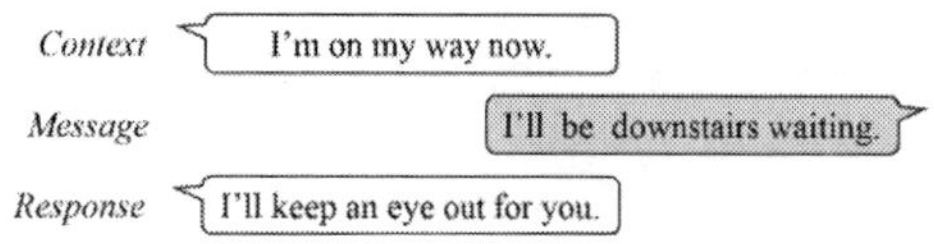

Figure 1: Example of consecutive utterances of a dialog.

provide a basis for automated training and evaluation of data-driven conversation systems—and, we ultimately believe, other text generation tasks with inherently diverse targets.

2 Evaluating Conversational Responses

Given an input message m and a prior conversation history c, the goal of a response generation system is to produce a hypothesis h that is both well-formed and a pertinent response to message m (example in Fig. 1). We assume that a set of J references $\{r_{i,j}\}$ is available for the context c_i and message m_i, where $i \in \{1 \dots I\}$ is an index over the test set. In the case of BLEU,[1] the automatic score of the system output $h_1 \dots h_I$ is defined as:

$$\text{BLEU} = \text{BP} \cdot \exp\left(\sum_n \log p_n\right) \quad (1)$$

with:

$$\text{BP} = \begin{cases} 1 & \text{if } \eta > \rho \\ e^{(1-\rho/\eta)} & \text{otherwise} \end{cases} \quad (2)$$

where ρ and η are respectively hypothesis and reference lengths.[2] Then corpus-level n-gram precision is defined as:

$$p_n = \frac{\sum_i \sum_{g \in n\text{-grams}(h_i)} \max_j \{\#_g(h_i, r_{i,j})\}}{\sum_i \sum_{g \in n\text{-grams}(h_i)} \#_g(h_i)}$$

where $\#_g(\cdot)$ is the number of occurrences of n-gram g in a given sentence, and $\#_g(u, v)$ is a shorthand for $\min\{\#_g(u), \#_g(v)\}$.

It has been demonstrated that metrics such as BLEU show increased correlation with human judgment as the number of references increases (Przybocki et al., 2008; Dreyer and Marcu, 2012). Unfortunately, gathering multiple references is difficult in the case of conversations. Data gathered from naturally occurring conversations offer only one response per message. One could search (c, m) pairs that occur multiple times in conversational data with the hope of finding distinct responses, but this solution is not feasible. Indeed, the larger the context, the less likely we are to find pairs that match exactly. Furthermore, while it is feasible to have writers create additional references when the downstream task is relatively unambiguous (e.g., MT), this approach is more questionable in the case of more subjective tasks such as conversational response generation. Our solution is to mine candidate responses from conversational data and have judges rate the quality of these responses. Our new metric thus naturally incorporates qualitative weights associated with references.

3 Discriminative BLEU

Discriminative BLEU, or ΔBLEU, extends BLEU by exploiting human qualitative judgments $w_{i,j} \in [-1, +1]$ associated with references $r_{i,j}$. It is discriminative in that it both rewards matches with "good" reference responses ($w > 0$) and penalizes matches with "bad" reference responses ($w < 0$). Formally, ΔBLEU is defined as in Equation 1 and 2, except that p_n is instead defined as:

$$\frac{\sum_i \sum_{g \in n\text{-grams}(h_i)} \max_{j: g \in r_{i,j}} \{w_{i,j} \cdot \#_g(h_i, r_{i,j})\}}{\sum_i \sum_{g \in n\text{-grams}(h_i)} \max_j \{w_{i,j} \cdot \#_g(h_i)\}}$$

In a nutshell, this is saying that each n-gram match is weighted by the highest scoring reference in which it occurs, and this weight can sometimes be negative. To ensure that the denominator is never zero, we assume that, for each i there exists at least one reference $r_{i,j}$ whose weight $w_{i,j}$ is strictly positive. In addition to its discriminative nature, this metric has two interesting properties. First, if all weights $w_{i,j}$ are equal to 1, then the metric score is identical to BLEU. As such, ΔBLEU admits BLEU as a special case. Second, as with IBM BLEU, the maximum theoretical score is also 1. If the hypothesis happens to match the highest weighted reference for each sentence, the numerator equals the denominator and the metric score becomes 1. While we find this metric particularly appropriate for response generation, the metric makes no assumption on the task and is applicable to other text generation tasks such as MT and image captioning.

4 Data

4.1 Multi-reference Datasets

To create the multi-reference BLEU dev and test sets used in this study, we adapted and extended the methodology of Sordoni et al. (2015). From a corpus of 29M Twitter context-message-response conversational triples, we randomly extracted approxi-

[1] Unless mentioned otherwise, BLEU refers to the original IBM BLEU as first described in (Papineni et al., 2002).

[2] In the case of multiple references, BLEU selects the reference whose length is closest to that of the hypothesis.

Context c	Message m	Response r	Score
i was about to text you and my two cousins got excited cause they thought you were "rihanna"	aww, i can imagine their disappointment	they were very disappointed!!!	0.6
yes. my ex-boyfriend, killed my cat. like i say, it was the start of a bad time...	*i can imagine!*	*yes. luckily, the whole thing feels very much of the past now.*	0.8
its good.. for some reason i can't name stand out tracks but i've been playing it since it dropped	*i can imagine, banks doesn't disappoint*	*na this is anything but a disappointment..*	0.6
at my lil cousins dancing to "dance for you". these kids are a mess.	*lmaoo i can imagine.*	*they were belly rolling, filarious.*	0.4
what's sick about it?? do you know how long it is?? no so how is it sick?	*i can imagine it*	*your imagination is wrong, very wrong at that.*	-0.1
it's saad oh yeah the snow is very beautiful	*yeah i can imagine*	*the weather in russia is very cool.*	-0.7
walking outside with lightning and thunder sounds 10x scarier than when you 're inside	play in the rain	haha i love listening to thunder! i would def be out there if i wasn't so sleepy	0.9
also rain(s)	*no play, rain(s)*	*i'm scared of the thunder*	0.5
no beach or running today, stupid weather.	*lets play in the rain. "yolo" isnt that the vibe??*	*i would but its thundering to*	0.2
then its raining...	*go outside and play in the rain lol!*	*if i had a buddy to go play in it with , i would . it's no fun alone*	0.1
my only official day off this week... now what to do	*play in the rain!*	*yeah right haha. i wan na go swimming*	0.1
now playing silence	*nice music i 'm playing rain*	*ohh i love that song*	-0.2
yeah it is, i just dont see the point of the first 2 laps	me either it would be sick if there was like 5 laps	exactly and if there were more riders so they drafted and crashed each other	0.3
yippee how many 711 are there	*like 5!*	*sweaarr i thought there were more*	0.8
i've got that muck off dry shower stuff to try out, hope it's muddy now.	*i think if we go for it we cud get 5 laps in an hour!*	*i've heard its a 30 min lap. but that was from a dh rider!*	0.6
how much are they ?	*like $5*	*i thought they were more then that but ok*	0.4
igot you, wen iroll up ill pass that shit. iaint stingy.	*me either!!*	*they more the marrier.*	-0.3
i dont eat gravy on biscuits.	*me either.*	*well then! why were the biscuits needed?*	-0.8

Table 1: Sample reference sets created by our multi-reference extraction algorithm, along with the weights used in ΔBLEU. Triples from which additional references are extracted are in italics. Boxed sentences are in our multi-reference dev set.

mately 33K candidate triples that were then judged for conversational quality on a 5-point Likert-type scale by 3 crowdsourced annotators. Of these, 4232 triples scored an average 4 or higher; these were randomly binned to create seed dev and test sets of 2118 triples and 2114 triples respectively. Note that the dev set is not used in the experiments of this paper, since ΔBLEU and IBM BLEU are metrics that do not require training. However, the dev set is released along with a test set in the dataset release accompanying this paper.

We then sought to identify candidate triples in the 29M corpus for which both message and response are similar to the original messages and responses in these seed sets. To this end, we employed an information retrieval algorithm with a bag-of-words BM25 similarity function (Robertson et al., 1995), as detailed in Sordoni et al. (2015), to extract the top 15 responses for each message-response pair. Unlike Sordoni et al. (2015), we further appended the original messages (as if parroted back). The new triples were then scored for quality of the response in light of both context and message by 5 crowdsourced raters each on a 5-point Likert-type scale.[3] Crucially, and again in contradistinction to Sordoni et al. (2015), we did not impose a score cutoff on these synthetic multi-reference sets. Instead, we retained all candidate responses and scaled their scores into $[-1, +1]$.

Table 1 presents representative multi-reference examples (from the dev set) together with their converted scores. The context and messages associated with the supplementary mined responses are also shown for illustrative purposes to demonstrate the range of conversations from which they were taken. In the table, negative-weighted mined responses are semantically orthogonal to the intent of their newly assigned context and message. Strongly negatively weighted responses are completely out of the ballpark ("the weather in Russia is very cool", "well then! Why were the biscuits needed?"); others are a little more plausible, but irrelevant or possibly topic changing ("ohh I love that song"). Higher-valued positive-weighted mined responses are typically reasonably appropriate and relevant (even though

[3]For this work, we sought 2 additional annotations of the seed responses for consistency with the mined responses. As a result, scores for some seed responses slipped below our initial threshold of 4. Nonetheless, these responses were retained.

extracted from a completely unrelated conversation), and in some cases can outscore the original response, as can be seen in the third set of examples.

4.2 Human Evaluation of System Outputs

Responses generated by the 7 systems used in this study on the 2114-triple test set were hand evaluated by 5 crowdsourced raters each on a 5-point Likert-type scale. From these 7 systems, 12 system pairs were evaluated, for a total of about pairwise 126K ratings ($12 \cdot 5 \cdot 2114$). Here too, raters were asked to evaluate responses in terms of their relevance to both context and message. Outputs from different systems were randomly interleaved for presentation to the raters. We obtained human ratings on the following systems:

Phrase-based MT: A phrase-based MT system similar to (Ritter et al., 2011), whose weights have been manually tuned. We also included four variants of that system, which we tuned with MERT (Och, 2003). These variants differ in their number of features, and augment (Ritter et al., 2011) with the following phrase-level features: edit distance between source and target, cosine similarity, Jaccard index and distance, length ratio, and DSSM score (Huang et al., 2013).
RNN-based MT: the log-probability according to the RNN model of (Sordoni et al., 2015).
Baseline: a random baseline.

While ΔBLEU relies on human qualitative judgments, it is important to note that human judgments on multi-references (§ 4.1) and those on system outputs were collected completely independently. We also note that the set of systems listed above specifically does not include a retrieval-based model, as this might have introduced spurious correlation between the two datasets (§ 4.1 and § 4.2).

5 Setup

We use two rank correlation coefficients—Kendall's τ and Spearman's ρ—to assess the level of correlation between human qualitative ratings (§4.2) and automated metric scores. More formally, we compute each correlation coefficient on a series of paired observations $(m_1, q_1), \cdots, (m_N, q_N)$. Here, m_i and q_i are respectively differences in automatic metric scores and qualitative ratings for two given systems A and B on a given subset of the test set.[4] While much prior work assesses automatic metrics for MT and other tasks (Lavie and Agarwal, 2007; Hodosh et al., 2013) by computing correlations on observations consisting of single-sentence system outputs, it has been shown (e.g., Przybocki et al. (2008)) that correlation coefficients significantly increase as observation units become larger. For instance, corpus-level or system-level correlations tend to be much higher than sentence-level correlations; Graham and Baldwin (2014) show that BLEU is competitive with more recent and advanced metrics when assessed at the system level.[5]

Therefore, we define our observation unit size to be $M = 100$ sentences (responses),[6] unless stated otherwise. We evaluate q_i by averaging human ratings on the M sentences, and m_i by computing metric scores on the same set of sentences.[7] We compare three different metrics: BLEU, ΔBLEU, and sentence-level BLEU (sBLEU). The last computes sentence-level BLEU scores (Nakov et al., 2012) and averages them on the M sentences (akin to macro-averaging). Finally, unless otherwise noted, all versions of BLEU use n-gram order up to 2 (BLEU-2), as this achieves better correlation for all metrics on this data.

6 Results

The main results of our study are shown in Table 2. ΔBLEU achieves better correlation with human than BLEU, when comparing the best configuration of each metric.[8] In the case of Spearman's ρ, the confidence intervals of BLEU $(.265, .416)$ and

[4] For each given observation pair (m_i, q_i), we randomize the order in which A and B are presented to the raters in order to avoid any positional bias.

[5] We do not intend to minimize the benefit of a metric that would be competitive at the sentence-level, which would be particularly useful for detailed error analyses. However, our main goal is to reliably evaluate generation systems on test sets of thousands of sentences, in which case any metric with good corpus-level correlation (such as BLEU, as shown in (Graham and Baldwin, 2014)) would be sufficient.

[6] Enumerating all possible ways of assigning sentences to observations would cause a combinatorial explosion. Instead, for all our results we sample 1K assignments and average correlations coefficients over them (using the same 1K assignments across all metrics). These assignments are done in such a way that all sentences within an observation belong to the same system pair.

[7] We refrained from using larger units, as creating larger observation units M reduces the total number of units N. This would have caused confidence intervals to be so wide as to make this study inconclusive.

[8] This is also the case on single reference. While ΔBLEU and BLEU would have the same correlation if original references all had the same score of 1, it is not unusual for original references to get ratings below 1.

Metric	refs.	Spearman's ρ	Kendall's τ
BLEU	single	.260 (.178, .337)	.171 (.087, .252)
BLEU	$w \geq 0.6$	.343 (.265, .416)	.232 (.150, .312)
BLEU	all	.318 (.239, .392)	.212 (.129, .292)
sBLEU	single	.265 (.183, .342)	.175 (.091, .256)
sBLEU	$w \geq 0.6$	.330 (.252, .404)	.222 (.140, .302)
sBLEU	all	.258 (.177, .336)	.167 (.083, .249)
ΔBLEU	single	.280 (.199,.357)	.187 (.103, .268)
ΔBLEU	$w \geq 0.6$	.405 (.331,.474)	.281 (.200, .357)
ΔBLEU	all	**.484** (.415,.546)	**.342** (.265, .415)

Table 2: Human correlations for IBM BLEU, sentence-level BLEU, and ΔBLEU with 95% confidence intervals. This compares 3 types of references: single only, high scoring references ($w \geq 0.6$), and all references.

ΔBLEU $(.415, .546)$ barely overlap, while interval overlap is more significant in the case of Kendall's τ. Correlation coefficients degrade for BLEU as we go from $w \geq 0.6$ to using all references. This is expected, since BLEU treats all references as equal and has no way of discriminating between them. On the other hand, correlation coefficients increase for ΔBLEU after adding lower scoring references. It is also worth noticing that BLEU and sBLEU obtain roughly comparable correlation coefficients. This may come as a surprise, because it has been suggested elsewhere that sBLEU has much worse correlation than BLEU computed at the corpus level (Przybocki et al., 2008). We surmise that (at least for this task and data) the differences in correlations between BLEU and sBLEU observed in prior work may be less the result of a difference between micro- and macro-averaging than they are the effect of different observation unit sizes (as discussed in §5).

Finally, Figure 2 shows how Spearman's ρ is affected along three dimensions of study. In particular, we see that ΔBLEU actually benefits from the references with negative ratings. While the improvement is not pronounced, we note that most references have positive ratings. Negatively-weighted references could have a greater effect if, for example, randomly extracted responses had also been annotated.

7 Conclusions

ΔBLEU correlates well with human quality judgments of generated conversational responses, outperforming both IBM BLEU and sentence-level BLEU in this task and demonstrating that it can serve as a plausible intrinsic metric for system de-

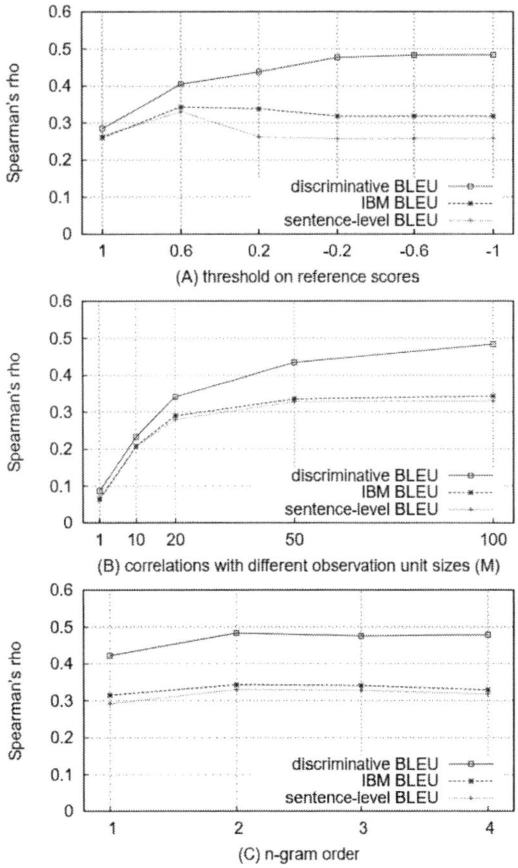

Figure 2: A comparison of BLEU, sentence-level BLEU, and ΔBLEU along three dimensions: (A) decreasing the threshold on reference scores $w_{i,j}$; (B) increasing the unit size for the correlation study from a single sentence (M=1) to a size of 100; (C) going from BLEU-1 to BLEU-4 for the different versions of BLEU.

velopment.[9] An upfront cost is paid for human evaluation of the reference set, but following that, the need for further human evaluation can be minimized during system development. ΔBLEU may help other tasks that use multiple references for intrinsic evaluation, including image-to-text, sentence compression, and paraphrase generation, and even statistical machine translation. Evaluation of ΔBLEU in these tasks awaits future work.

Acknowledgments

We thank the anonymous reviewers, Jian-Yun Nie, and Alan Ritter for their helpful comments and suggestions.

[9]An implementation of ΔBLEU, multi-reference dev and test sets, and human rated outputs are available at: `http://research.microsoft.com/convo`

References

Satanjeev Banerjee and Alon Lavie. 2005. METEOR: An automatic metric for MT evaluation with improved correlation with human judgments. In *Proc. of ACL Workshop on Intrinsic and Extrinsic Evaluation Measures for Machine Translation and/or Summarization*, pages 65–72.

Chris Callison-Burch, Miles Osborne, and Philipp Koehn. 2006. Re-evaluating the role of BLEU in machine translation research. In *EACL*, pages 249–256.

Deborah Coughlin. 2003. Correlating automated and human assessments of machine translation quality. In *Proc. of MT Summit IX*, pages 63–70.

George Doddington. 2002. Automatic evaluation of machine translation quality using n-gram co-occurrence statistics. In *Proc. of HLT*, pages 138–145.

Markus Dreyer and Daniel Marcu. 2012. HyTER: Meaning-equivalent semantics for translation evaluation. In *Proc. of HLT-NAACL*, pages 162–171.

Yvette Graham and Timothy Baldwin. 2014. Testing for significance of increased correlation with human judgment. In *Proc. of EMNLP*, pages 172–176.

Yvette Graham, Timothy Baldwin, and Nitika Mathur. 2015. Accurate evaluation of segment-level machine translation metrics. In *Proc. of NAACL-HLT*, pages 1183–1191.

Micah Hodosh, Peter Young, and Julia Hockenmaier. 2013. Framing image description as a ranking task: Data, models and evaluation metrics. *J. Artif. Int. Res.*, 47(1):853–899.

Po-Sen Huang, Xiaodong He, Jianfeng Gao, Li Deng, Alex Acero, and Larry Heck. 2013. Learning deep structured semantic models for web search using clickthrough data. In *Proc. of the 22nd ACM International Conference on Information & Knowledge Management*, pages 2333–2338.

Alon Lavie and Abhaya Agarwal. 2007. METEOR: An automatic metric for mt evaluation with high levels of correlation with human judgments. In *Proc. of the Workshop on Statistical Machine Translation (StatMT)*, pages 228–231.

Preslav Nakov, Francisco Guzman, and Stephan Vogel. 2012. Optimizing for Sentence-Level BLEU+1 Yields Short Translations. In *Proc. of COLING*.

Franz Josef Och. 2003. Minimum error rate training in statistical machine translation. In *Proc. of ACL*, pages 160–167.

Kishore Papineni, Salim Roukos, Todd Ward, and Wei-Jing Zhu. 2002. BLEU: a method for automatic evaluation of machine translation. In *Proc. of ACL*, pages 311–318.

M. Przybocki, K. Peterson, and S. Bronsart. 2008. Official results of the NIST 2008 "Metrics for MAchine TRanslation" challenge (MetricsMATR08). http://nist.gov/speech/tests/metricsmatr/2008/results/.

Alan Ritter, Colin Cherry, and William B. Dolan. 2011. Data-driven response generation in social media. In *Proc. of EMNLP*, pages 583–593.

Stephen E Robertson, Steve Walker, Susan Jones, et al. 1995. Okapi at TREC-3. In *TREC*.

Alessandro Sordoni, Michel Galley, Michael Auli, Chris Brockett, Yangfeng Ji, Meg Mitchell, Jian-Yun Nie, Jianfeng Gao, and Bill Dolan. 2015. A neural network approach to context-sensitive generation of conversational responses. In *Proc. of NAACL-HLT*.

Hong Sun and Ming Zhou. 2012. Joint learning of a dual SMT system for paraphrase generation. In *ACL*, pages 38–42.

Ramakrishna Vedantam, C. Lawrence Zitnick, and Devi Parikh. 2015. CIDEr: Consensus-based image description evaluation. In *CVPR*.

Tibetan Unknown Word Identification from News Corpora for Supporting Lexicon-based Tibetan Word Segmentation

Minghua Nuo[1]
minghua@iscas.ac.cn

Huidan Liu[1]
huidan@iscas.ac.cn

Congjun Long[1,2]
congjun@nfs.iscas.ac.cn

Jian Wu[1]
wujian@iscas.ac.cn

[1]Institute of Software, Chinese Academy of Sciences, Beijing, China; [2]Institute of Ethnology and Anthropology, Chinese Academy of Social Sciences, Beijing, China

Abstract

In Tibetan, as words are written consecutively without delimiters, finding unknown word boundary is difficult. This paper presents a hybrid approach for Tibetan unknown word identification for offline corpus processing. Firstly, Tibetan named entity is preprocessed based on natural annotation. Secondly, other Tibetan unknown words are extracted from word segmentation fragments using MTC, the combination of a statistical metric and a set of context sensitive rules. In addition, the preliminary experimental results on Tibetan News Corpus are reported. Lexicon-based Tibetan word segmentation system SegT with proposed unknown word extension mechanism is indeed helpful to promote the performance of Tibetan word segmentation. It increases the F-score of Tibetan word segmentation by 4.15% on random-selected test set. Our unknown word identification scheme can find new words in any length and in any field.

1 Introduction

Tibetan is a phonetic writing script; it is syllabic, like many of the alphabets of India and South East Asia. Tibetan sentences are strings of syllables with no delimiters to mark word boundaries. Therefore the initial step for Tibetan processing is word segmentation. However, occurrences of unknown words, which are not listed in the dictionary, degraded significantly the performances of most word segmentation methods.

Currently, the lexicon-based Tibetan word segmentation scheme is widely adopted. In general, any lexicon is limited and unable to cover all the words in real texts. According to our statistics on a 326,062,576-bytes news corpus from the website *Tibet Daily,* there are about 2.89% unknown words. Therefore, unknown word identification (UWI) became a key technology for Tibetan segmentation.

The rest of this paper is organized as follows. In Section 2 we recall related work on UWI methods. Semi-automatic Tibetan UWI method is provided in Section 3. Section 4 gives the description of experimental results for evaluation, and Section 5 offers concluding remarks.

2 Related Work

For unknown words with more regular morphological structures, such as personal names, morphological rules are commonly used for improving the performance by restricting the structures of extracted words (Chen et al. 1994, Sun et al. 1995, Lin et al. 1993, Ma & Chen 2003). However, it is not possible to list morphological rules for all kinds of unknown words, especially those words with very irregular structures. Therefore, statistical approaches usually play major roles on irregular UWI in most previous work (Sproat & Shih 1990, Chiang et al. 1992, Tung & Lee 1995, Palmer 1997, Chang et al. 1997, Sun et al. 1998, Ge et al. 1999).

Many statistical metrics have been proposed, including point-wise mutual information (MI) (Church et al., 1991), mean and variance, hypothesis testing (t-test, chi-square test, etc.), log-likelihood ratio (LR) (Dunning, 1993), statistic language model (Tomokiyo et al., 2003), context-entropy (on each side) and frequency ratio against background corpus (Luo & Song 2004), DCF (Hong et al., 2009), and so on. Point-wise MI is often used to find interesting bigrams (collocations). However, MI is actually better to think of it as a measure of independence than of dependence (Manning et al., 1999). LR is one of the most stable methods for automatic term extraction so far, and more appropriate for sparse data than other metrics. However, LR is still biased to two frequent words that are rarely adjacent, such as the pair (the, the) (Pantel et al., 2001). On the other aspect, MI and LR metrics

Proceedings of the 53rd Annual Meeting of the Association for Computational Linguistics and the 7th International Joint Conference on Natural Language Processing (Short Papers), pages 451–457, Beijing, China, July 26-31, 2015.

are difficult to extend to extract multi-word terms.

There are also many hybrid methods combined statistical metrics with linguistic knowledge and machine Learning algorithms, such as Part-of-Speech filters (Smadja, 1994; Asanee, 1997), roles tagging based (Zhang et al., 2002), syntactic discriminators (Chen & Ma 2002), max-margin Markov networks (Qiao and Sun, 2010; Li and Chang, 2010), Unsupervised Learning Strategy (Sun et al., 2004), Latent Discriminative Model(Sun et al., 2011), boosting-based ensemble learning (TeCho et al., 2012). But POS filters, roles tagging, machine learning algorithms does not work for Tibetan UWI. So far, there is no Tibetan POS tagger and Tibetan parser. We have built large scale Tibetan text resources recently, and we are tagging Part-Of-Speech and labeling role right now, these corpora can form training set in the near future.

Previous research and work in Tibetan word segmentation have made great progresses. However, cases with unknown words are not satisfactory. In recent years, researchers mainly use maximum-matching method accompanying with some grammar rules (Chen et al. 2003a, Chen et al. 2003b, Cai 2009a, Cai 2009b, Qi 2006, Dolha 2007, Zha 2007, Tashi 2009) to segment Tibetan text. Liu et al. (2012) designed and implemented a Tibetan word segmentation system named "SegT" which is lexicon-based practical system with a constant lexicon. However, it has the difficulty of identifying unknown words in newspaper articles and web documents which are highly changeable texts with time.

The research on Tibetan UWI is, however, still at its initial stage. There is no public report of performance of Tibetan new word or unknown word identification. This paper introduces Tibetan UWI work which is in progress.

3 Tibetan Unknown Word Identification from News Corpus

Generally, Tibetan location name and organization names are formed from a shorter word or proper noun adding a morpheme, river(ཀླུང), lake(མཚོ), beach(ཐང), gorge(འགག), ministry(པུའུ), bureau(ཅུའུ), association(ཁང), company(ཀུང་སི), province(ཞིང་ཆེན), city(གྲོང་ཁྱེར), county(རྫོང) etc.; some are also followed by modifiers, such as postposition, size, color, shape. We also observe that often, these morphemes are segmented separately during the first-time segmentation process. "Natural annotation" in our news articles also indicates the occurrence of unknown words. This section simply introduces Tibetan script first and then aims to detail the two key procedures in Tibetan UWI from Tibetan web resources, that is, detect unknown words based on natural annotation and based on context sensitive rules.

3.1 Characteristics of Tibetan Script

The Tibetan alphabet is syllabic; a syllable contains one or up to seven character(s). Syllables are separated by a marker known as intersyllabic marks (tsheg), which is simply a superscripted dot. Linguistic words are made up of one or more syllables and are also separated by the same symbol, "tsheg". Consonant clusters are written with special conjunct letters. Tibetan texts consists of a string of syllables without any blanks to mark word boundaries except for punctuation'།', called shad, at the end of each sentence, and '་', called tsheg, within syllables. Figure 1 shows the structure of a Tibetan word which is made up of two syllables and means "show" or "exhibition".

Figure 1. Structure of a Tibetan word

Tibetan sentence consists of one or more words, phrases or multi-word units. Another marker known as "shad" indicates the sentence boundary, which looks like a vertical pipe. Figure 2 shows a Tibetan sentence. It is segmented in line 2 and word by word translation is given in line 3.

ཁ་ས་མི་ཕྱུག་པོ་འདིའི་ཁང་པ་གོང་ཆེན་པོ་ཞིག་གཟིགས་སོང།									
ཁ་ས་	མི་	ཕྱུག་པོ་	འདིའི་	ཁང་པ	གོང་ཆེན་པོ་	ཞིག་	གཟིགས་	སོང་	।
Yesterday	man	rich	this	house	expensive	an	bought	did	.
Yesterday this rich man bought an expensive house.									

Figure 2. A Tibetan sentence and its translation

3.2 Natural Annotation based Identification

Tibetan unknown word covers both named entity and emerging new words in Tibetan web corpus. Special attention is paid to those noticeable named entities in order to suggest strong word candidates. "naturally annotated" means different type of annotations on varieties of Web resources which are "unconsciously handcrafted" by Web users for their own purposes, but can be used by computational linguists in a conscious and systematic way for various tasks of natural language processing, for examples, punctuation marks in Tibetan can benefit word boundaries identification, social tags in social media can benefit keyword extraction, "categories" given in News Corpus can benefit text categorization.

"Space", "punctuation" and "Tibetan auxiliary words" always appear next to a word. Hyperlink in web text is a useful explicit natural annotation too. In addition, <head> tag of html pages including meta data as keywords, author, source, description; these are also quite useful natural annotation for UWI. Meanwhile, in our Tibetan News Corpus, English and Chinese in brackets give the hints for their corresponding Tibetan translation words. Sentences including this kind of annotation are as follow.

- ༢༠༠༠འཛའ་ནེད་རྒྱ་མཚོ།(janet gyatso)རྩོམ་པ།
- འཇར་མེ་ནི(germany)རྒྱལ་ཁབ་ཀྱི་མུན་ཆེན(münchen)གྲོང་ཁྱེར་གྱི(schloss hohenkammer)མཐོ་སློབ་ཏུ་ཚོགས།
- ཕྱི་ལོ་༡༩༩༥ལོར་ཨེར་ནི་སི་ཏེ་སི་ཏེན་ཀེལ་ནར(Ernst Steinkellner)གྱིས་ཨོ་ཙི་སི་ཁྲི་རི་ཡ(Austria)རྒྱལ་ཁབ་ཀྱི་གྲེ་ར་ཛི(Graz)གྲོང་ཁྱེར་ཆེན་མོའི(Schloss Segau)མཐོ་སློབ་ཏུ་གོ་སྒྲིག་མཛད།
- ཕྱི་ལོ་༡༩༩༨ལོར་སློང་ཚོགས་པ་ཨེ་ལི་ཡོ་ཏི་སི་པར་ལིང(Elliot Sperling)གིས་ཨ་རིའི་གྲོང་ཁྱེར་བྷ་ལུ་མིང་ཏོན(Bloomington)གྱི་ཨིན་ཌི་ཡ་ན/ཡའི་མཐོ་སློབ(Indiana University)ཏུ་བཙུགས།
- ཕ་མེས་ཨེར (帕 米 尔) མཐོ་སྒང་ནས་ཤར་ཕྱོགས་ཀྱི་ཆིན་ལེན་རི་རྒྱུད (祁连山脉) བར་འཕྱེད་ཤིག་ཏུ་31ལྷག་ཡོད་ལ།

These brackets in news texts point out the right boundary of lots of location name and organization names. We confirm left boundaries relying on pre-established transliteration table. Thus following named entities such as གྲེ་ར་ཛི(Graz), བྷ་ལུ་མིང་ཏོན(Bloomington), ཨིན་ཌི་ཡ་ནའི་མཐོ་སློབ (Indiana University), ཕ་མེས་ཨེར(帕米尔) can be extracted from examples given above.

3.3 Contextual Rule based Identification

We will use a hybrid method MTC, that is, combination of statistical metric and context sensitive rules, to recognize the boundary of an unknown word. It is applied to segmented texts.

Beforehand, we analyse the lexicon-based pre-segmentation of a sentence. Unknown words in the text would be incorrectly segmented into pieces of single syllable or shorter words through pre- segmentation.

Figure 3 illustrates two possible pre-segmented results of syllable string, that is, explicit unknown words in above expression or hidden unknown word in below expression.

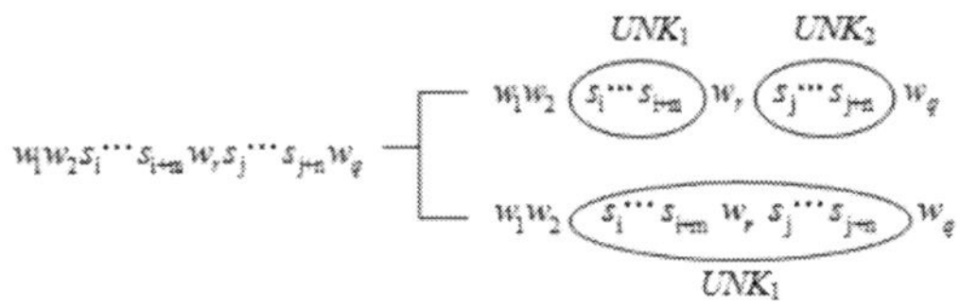

Figure 3. Categories of Tibetan unknown words

In Figure 3, *UNK*, *w* and *s* denotes unknown word, word and syllable respectively. Only explicit unknown words are discussed in this paper.

Assume *S* is a sentence; and the right side of following equation represents its pre-segmented result.

$$S = w_1 w_2 s_1 s_2 s_3 w_3 s_4 s_5 s_6 w_4$$

$$\text{where} \quad w_1, w_2, w_3, w_4 \quad \in \text{Lexibase}$$

$$s_1 s_2 s_3, s_4 s_5 s_6 \quad \notin \text{Lexibase}$$

We name consecutive monosyllables (i.e. $s_1 s_2 s_3$) after the first-time word segmentation as segmentation fragments. Table 1 gives examples of Tibetan word segmentation fragments.

segmentation fragments	Correct segmentation	Translation of terms
ཊུ་ཙུ་/ རལ་/ ཝེ་/ ལའི་/ ལི/	ཊུ་ཙུ་རལ་ཝེ་ལའི་ལི	Turrell wylie
ཏོ་/ ཀྱོ་/ ཡོ/	ཏོ་ཀྱོ་ཡོ	Tokyo
ཀོ་/ ལུམ་/ བྷི་/ ཡ་/ མཐོ་/ སློབ/	ཀོ་ལུམ་བྷི་ཡ་མཐོ་སློབ	Columbia university

Table 1: Example of segmentation fragments.

Column II in Table 1 is the correct segmentation of these unknown words. After maximum-matching word segmentation, it is segmented to the content in column I. Almost all these unknown words in our corpus are segmented into monosyllables because these words are not included in our Tibetan word segmentation lexicon.

At detection stages, the contextual rules were applied to detect fragments of unknown words, i.e. monosyllabic morphemes. Since it is hard to derive a set of morphological rules, which exactly cover all types of unknown words, statistical rules are designed without differentiate their extracted word types.

A corpus-based learning method is proposed to derive a set of rules for monosyllabic words and monosyllabic morphemes. The idea is that if two consecutive morphemes are highly associated then combines them to form a new word.

For each bi-seed-gram, the mutual information MI and t-score are calculated. These scores reflect the co-occurrence affinity between the two tokens of the bi-gram. These two scores are calculated by the following formulas:

$$MI^2 = \log_2 \frac{a^2}{(a+b)(a+c)} \tag{1}$$

$$t = \frac{P_r(w_a, w_b) - P_r(w_a) \times P_r(w_b)}{\sqrt{\frac{1}{N} P_r(w_a, w_b)}} = \sqrt{a} - \frac{(a+b)(a+c)}{\sqrt{a}(a+b+c+d)} \tag{2}$$

where, *a*, *b*, *c* and *d* are elements of a contingency table. For example, given a bi-gram containing tokens *x* and *y*,

a = number of bi-grams in which both *x* and *y* occur;

b = number of bi-grams in which only *x* occurs;

c = number of bi-grams in which only *y* occurs;

d = number of bi-grams in which neither *x* nor *y* occurs.

Another measure for Tibetan UWI is seed extension confidence. Denote Tibetan word (or syllable) grouping of n-grams as $S_T(n)$, where *n* indicates the length of current word; Extend it to an adjacent Tibetan syllable and get $S_T(n+1)$, so the seed extension confidence C_n defined as:

$$C_n = \lambda_1 \,|\, MI_{mean}(n) - MI_{mean}(n+1) \,| + \lambda_2 \,|\, T_{mean}(n) - T_{mean}(n+1) \,| \tag{3}$$

in which MI_{mean} and T_{mean} indicates the mean of *MI* and t-value in the scope of extended Tibetan word respectively.

To characterize Tibetan unknown words and their boundaries the extension step will be held. For each extension-ready Tibetan seed word, note the extension confidence C_n; if C_n is greater than the threshold, current Tibetan word is accepted, and extension continues; when C_n is less than the threshold extension stops. Boundary for Tibetan unknown word is obtained at the end of extension. Figure 4 shows the detail of extension process. High frequency bi-seed-gram can be extended to an unknown word (which is in brackets in Figure 4) using C_n.

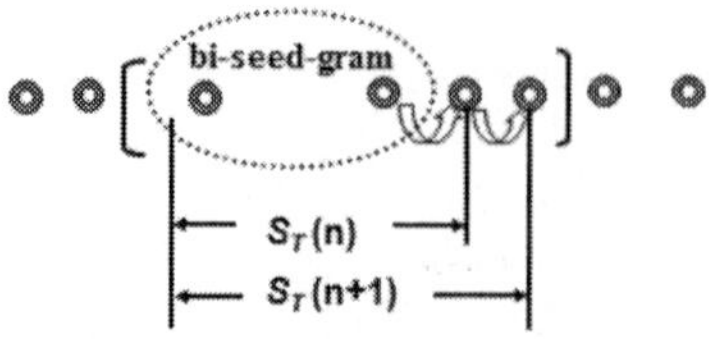

Figure 4. Concept of bi-seed-gram extension

4 Evaluation

In this section, we first evaluate performance of Tibetan unknown word identification; then present the performance of Tibetan word segmentation system SegT with unknown word discovery to show the positive effect of UWI.

4.1 Experimental Data

We have built the largest Tibetan text resources over the internet via an automatic crawler. They are from three web sites, that are, *Tibet Daily*, *People's Daily* and *Qinghai Daily*. This News Corpus includes different fields such as politics, science, technology, education, language and culture, religion, tourism, environment and Tibetan medicine. Presently, other types of text, especially informal discussion on social network like Twitter and Wikipedia in Tibetan is in small size. Thus, we will utilize above Tibetan News Corpus to extract likely new words in this paper. Our evaluation data contains 12,027 words from 737 randomly selected sentences which have word checking results (the proportion of unknown word is more than 1%).

4.2 Performance of Tibetan UWI

We will use the precision, recall, f-score of unknown word (P_{unk}, R_{unk}, F_{unk}) to evaluate the performance of Tibetan UWI. In our 3-fold cross validation, 70% of evaluation data is selected as training set, and the remainder is test set. Table 1 shows the Tibetan unknown word identification results on our evaluation dataset.

Method	P_{unk}	R_{unk}	F_{unk}
MT	0.8205	0.7091	0.7607
MTC	0.8323	0.7606	0.7948

Table 1. 3-fold cross validation Results of Tibetan unknown word identification.

In Table 1, MT denotes statistical metric, and MTC denotes the combination of MT and context sensitive rules; the given result is the average of 3-fold cross validation. As shown in Table 1, combination of contextual rules with statistical measure can promote the performance of Tibetan UWI; the f-score reaches 79.48%.

After analyzing the results, we find that wrongly identified words can be divided into two classes, i.e., Tibetan person name and transliterated names. We will add deictic words into context sensitive rule and supplement transliteration table to promote identification accuracy of these kinds of unknown words.

4.3 Evaluation for Tibetan Word Segmentation with the Extended Lexicon

In order to validate the effect of our unknown word identification on Tibetan word segmentation, we conduct following experiments.

In a typical word segmentation system, once a text is segmented using the available lexicon or heuristic rules, the segmentation process is finished. We observe that unknown words make up 0.5% to 4% of all the words in our Tibetan news articles. Therefore, UWI is an important issue for a word segmentation algorithm. We add a semi-automatic unknown word identification component to the back-end of the whole segmentation process.

We will evaluate the precision (P_{seg}), recall (R_{seg}), f-score (F_{seg}) of Tibetan word segmentation in this subsection.

$P_{seg} = N_{seg1} / N_{seg2}$

$R_{seg} = N_{seg1} / N_{seg3}$

$F_{seg} = 2P_{seg}R_{seg} / (P_{seg} + R_{seg})$

where N_{seg1} denotes the number of correctly segmented Tibetan words; N_{seg2} denotes total number of segmented Tibetan words; N_{seg3} denotes the total number of Tibetan words in the testing texts.

The segmentation of original web texts uses a basic Segmentor (SegT (Liu et al, 2012)) and a general lexicon (with 220,000 Tibetan entries). Unknown words (out of our lexicon) are segmented into pieces in this step. The following process is to detect possible unknown words from word segmentation fragment which are very likely to be words. We will compare lexicon-based Tibetan segmenter with and without unknown word identification component on our evaluation data. Presently, there is no Tibetan word segmentation specification and standard; in addition, there is no large and publicly available Tibetan training corpus. Thus make comparison with other research papers is difficult. We choose the best Tibetan word segmentation system Liu's SegT (Liu et al. 2012) as baseline.

Table 2 illustrates the results of Tibetan segmentation by SegT with general lexicon and SegT with lexicon extension on evaluation. SegT+MTC, denotes Tibetan word segmenter SegT with lexicon extension; the proposed method in section 3 has been applied to semi-automatically extend the lexicon of Tibetan word segmentation system SegT.

	P_{seg}	R_{seg}	F_{seg}
SegT	0.7769	0.8638	0.8181
SegT + MTC	0.8197	0.8872	0.8521

Table 2: Effects of Tibetan word segmentation.

Experimental results show that the maximum word segmentation performance is got using general lexicon extended by MTC. As we see from Table 2, the precision, recall and f-score are increased by 5.49%, 2.71%, 4.15% respectively compared with SegT. The score of SegT+MTC is increased significantly because of the higher proportion of unknown words. The experimental results demonstrate that the Tibetan word segmentation system SegT with proposed unknown word extension mechanism is indeed helpful to promote the accuracy and recall rates of Tibetan word segmentation.

5 Conclusion

In this paper, we present a hybrid method for Tibetan unknown word identification. Its f-score reaches around 80%. Compared with English or Chinese unknown word recognition work, the proposed methods doesn't achieve satisfactory results, however, preliminary experimental results demonstrate that SegT with proposed unknown word extension mechanism is indeed helpful to promote Tibetan word segmentation performance. In the future, the evaluation of proposed method needs to be extended to large-scale test corpus and detailed context sensitive rules are used to identify Tibetan unknown words.

Acknowledgements

We thank the reviewers for their critical and constructive comments and suggestions that helped us improve the quality of the paper. The research is partially supported by National Science Foundation (No.61303165, No.61202219, and No.61202220), Major Science and Technology Projects in Press and Publishing (No.0610-1041BJNF2328/23), and Informationization Project of the Chinese Academy of Sciences (No.XXH12504-1-10).

Reference

Kawtrakul Asanee, Thumkanon Chalatip, Poovorawan Yuen, Varasrai Patcharee, Suktarachan Mukda. 1997. Automatic Thai Unknown Word Recognition.

Rang-jia Cai. 2009. Research on the Word Categories and Its Annotation Scheme for Tibetan Corpus, *Journal of Chinese Information Processing*, 23(04):107-112.

Zhi-jie Cai. 2009a. Identification of Abbreviated Word in Tibetan Word Segmentation. *Journal of Chinese Information Processing*, 23(01):35-37.

Zhi-jie Cai. 2009b. The Design of Banzhida Tibetan word segmentation system. In: proceedings of *the 12th Symposium on Chinese Minority Information Processing*.

Jing-Shin Chang and Keh-Yih Su. 1997a. An Unsupervised Iterative Method for Chinese New Lexicon Extraction. *International Journal of Computational Linguistics & Chinese Language Processing.*

Hsin-Hsi Chen and Jen-Chang Lee. 1994. The Identification of Organization Names in Chinese Texts. *Communication of Chinese and Oriental Languages Information Processing Society*, 4(2), Singapore, 1994, pp131-142 (in Chinese).

Keh-Jiann Chen and Wei-Yun Ma, 2002. Unknown Word Extraction for Chinese Documents. In: Proceedings of *COLING 2002*, pp 169-175.

Yu-Zhong Chen, Bao-Li Li and Shi-Wen Yu. 2003a. The Design and Implementation of a Tibetan Word Segmentation System, *Journal of Chinese Information Processing*, 17(3): 15-20.

Yu-Zhong Chen, Bao-Li Li, Shi-Wen Yu and Lancuoji. 2003b. An Automatic Tibetan Segmentation Scheme Based on Case Auxiliary Words and Continuous Features, *Journal of Applied Linguistics*, (01): 75-82.

Tung-Hui Chiang, Jing-Shin Chang, Ming-Yu Lin and Keh-Yih Su. 1992. Statistical Models for Word Segmentation and Unknown Word Resolution. In: Proceedings of *ROCLING V*, pp 121-146.

Lee-Feng Chien. 1999. PAT-tree-based adaptive keyphrase extraction for intelligent Chinese information retrieval. *Information processing and management* 35:501-521.

Kenneth Church, William Gale, Patrick Hanks and Donald Hindle. 1991. Using Statistics in Lexical Analysis. In: *Zernik ed. Lexical Acquisition: Exploiting On-Line Resources to Build a Lexicon.* Hillsdale, N J: Erlbaum, pp 115-164.

Dolha, Zhaxijia, Losanglangjie, Ouzhu. 2007. The parts-of-speech and tagging set standards of Tibetan information process. In: proceedings of *the 11th Symposium on Chinese Minority Information Processing.*

Ted E. Dunning. 1993. Accurate methods for the statistics of surprise and coincidence. *Computational Linguistics*, 19 (1): 61-74.

Xian-Ping Ge, Wan-Da Pratt, and Padhraic Smyth. 1999. Discovering Chinese Words from Unsegmented Text. In: proceedings of *SIGIR '99*, pp 271-272.

Chin-ming Hong, Chih-ming Chen, Chao-yang Chiu. 2009. Automatic extraction of new words based on Google News corpora for supporting lexicon-based Chinese word segmentation systems. *Expert Systems with Applications*, 36:3641-3651.

Yun-Lun Li, Bao-Bao Chang. 2010. Maximum Margin Markov Networks-Based Chinese Word Segmentation Method. *Journal of Chinese Information Processing*, 24(1):8-14.

Ming-yu Lin, Tung-hui Chiang and Keh-Yih Su. 1993. A preliminary study on unknown word problem in Chinese word segmentation. In: Proceedings of *1993 R.O.C. Computational Linguistics Conference*, Taiwan, pp 119-137.

Hui-dan Liu, Wei-na Zhao, Ming-hua Nuo, Li Jiang, Jian Wu, Ye-ping He. 2010. Tibetan Number Identification Based on Classification of Number Components in Tibetan Word Segmentation. In: Proceedings of *the 23rd International Conference on Computational Linguistics - poster volume* (*COLING 2010*), pp 719-724.

Hui-dan Liu, Ming-hua Nuo, Wei-na Zhao, Jian Wu, Ye-ping He. 2012. SegT: A Practical Tibetan Word Segmentation System. *Journal of Chinese Information Processing*, 26(1):97-103.

Zhi-Yong Luo, Rou Song. 2004. An Integrated Method for Chinese Unknown Word Extraction. In: Proceedings of *3rd ACL SIGHAN Workshop*. Barcelona, Spain. pp 148-154.

Wei-Yun Ma and Keh Jiann Chen. 2003. A Bottom-up Merging Algorithm for Chinese Unknown Word Extraction. In: Proceedings of *the Second SIGHAN Workshop on Chinese Language Processing*, pp 31-38.

Christopher D. Manning, Hinrich Schutze. 1999. Foundations of Statistical Natural Language Processing, MIT Press.

Palmer D. David. 1997. A Trainable Rule-based Algorithm for Word Segmentation. In: Proceedings of *the 35th Annual Meeting of ACL and 8th Conference of the European Chapter of ACL*. Madrid.

Patrick Pantel and De-kang Lin. 2001. A statistical corpus based term extractor. In E. Stroulia and S.

Matwin, editors, *Lecture Notes in Artificial Intelligence*, pp 36-46. Springer-Verlag.

Kunyu Qi. 2006. On Tibetan Automatic Participate Research with the Aid of Information Treatment. *Journal of Northwest University for Nationalities (Philosophy and Social Science)*, (04):92-97.

Wei Qiao, Mao-song Sun. 2010. Joint Chinese word segmentation and named entity recognition based on max-margin Markov networks. *Journal of Tsinghua University (Science & Technology)*, 50(5): 758-762.

Richard Sproat and Chilin Shih. 1990. A Statistical Method for Finding Word Boundaries in Chinese Text. *Computer Processing of Chinese and Oriental Languages,* 4, 336-351.

Mao-song Sun, Chang-ning Huang, Benjamin K. Tsou, Fang Lu and Da-yang Shen.1997. Using Character Bigram for Ambiguity Resolution in Chinese Word Segmentation. *Computer Research & Development.* 34(5):332-339.

Mao-song Sun, Chang-ning Huang, Hai-yan Gao, Jie Fang. 1995. Identifying Chinese Names in Unrestricted Texts. *Journal of Chinese Information Processing*, 9(2):16-27.

Mao-song Sun, Da-yang Shen and Benjamin K. Tsou. 1998. Chinese Word Segmentation without Using Lexicon and Hand-crafted Training Data. In: Proceedings of *COLING-ACL '98*, pp1265-1271.

Xiao Sun, De-gen Huang, Hai-yu Song et al. 2011. Chinese new word identification: a latent discriminative model with global features. *Journal of computer science and technology*, 26(1): 14-24.

Yuan Sun, Luosangqiangba, Rui Yang and Xiao-Bing Zhao. 2009. Design of a Tibetan Automatic Segmentation Scheme. In: proceedings of *the 12th Symposium on Chinese Minority Information Processing.*

Yuan Sun, Xiao-Dong Yan, Xiao-Bing Zhao and Guo-Sheng Yang. 2010. A resolution of overlapping ambiguity in Tibetan word segmentation. In: Proceedings of *the 3rd International Conference on Computer Science and Information Technology*, pp 222-225.

Gyal Tashi and Zhujie. 2009. Research on Tibetan Segmentation Scheme for Information Processing, *Journal of Chinese Information Processing*, 23(04):113-117.

Jakkrit TeCho, Cholwich Nattee, Thanaruk Theeramunkong. 2012. Boosting-based ensemble learning with penalty profiles for automatic Thai unknown word recognition. *Computers and Mathematics with Applications* 63, pp 1117-1134.

T. Tomokiyo and M. Hurst. 2003. A Language Model Approach to Keyphrase Extraction. In: Proceedings of *ACL-2003 workshop on multiword expressions.* Sapporo, Japan. pp 33-40.

C.H. Tung and H. J. Lee. 1995. Identification of unknown words from corpus. *International Journal of Computer Processing of Chinese and Oriental Languages*, Vol. 8, Supplement, pp 131-146.

Xia-Jia Zha, Dolha, Losanglangjie, Ouzhu. 2007. The theoretical explanation on "the parts-of-speech and tagging set standards of Tibetan information process". In: proceedings of *the 11th Symposium on Chinese Minority Information Processing.*

Hua-ping Zhang, Qun Liu, Xue-qi Cheng. 2003. Chinese lexical analysis using hierarchical hidden Markov model. In: proceedings of *Second SIGHAN workshop affiliated with 41th ACL.* Sapporo Japan, pp 63-70.

Kevin Zhang (Hua-Ping Zhang), Qun Liu, Hao Zhang, Xue-qi Cheng. 2002. Automatic Recognition of Chinese Unknown Words Based on Role Tagging, In: Proceedings of *SigHan 2002 Workshop attached with the 19th International Conference on Computational Linguistics*, Taipei, September. pp 71-77.

Ying Zhang, Ralf D. Brown, Robert E. Frederking, Alon Lavie. 2001. Pre-processing of Bilingual Corpora for Mandarin-English EBMT. In: Proceedings of *MT Summit VIII*, Santiago de Compostela, Spain.

Learning Lexical Embeddings with Syntactic and Lexicographic Knowledge

Tong Wang
University of Toronto
tong@cs.toronto.edu

Abdel-rahman Mohamed
Microsoft Research
asamir@microsoft.com

Graeme Hirst
University of Toronto
gh@cs.toronto.edu

Abstract

We propose two improvements on lexical association used in embedding learning: factorizing individual dependency relations and using lexicographic knowledge from monolingual dictionaries. Both proposals provide low-entropy lexical co-occurrence information, and are empirically shown to improve embedding learning by performing notably better than several popular embedding models in similarity tasks.

1 Lexical Embeddings and Relatedness

Lexical embeddings are essentially real-valued distributed representations of words. As a vector-space model, an embedding model approximates semantic relatedness with the Euclidean distance between embeddings, the result of which helps better estimate the real lexical distribution in various NLP tasks. In recent years, researchers have developed efficient and effective algorithms for learning embeddings (Mikolov et al., 2013a; Pennington et al., 2014) and extended model applications from language modelling to various areas in NLP including lexical semantics (Mikolov et al., 2013b) and parsing (Bansal et al., 2014).

To approximate semantic relatedness with geometric distance, objective functions are usually chosen to correlate positively with the Euclidean similarity between the embeddings of related words. Maximizing such an objective function is then equivalent to adjusting the embeddings so that those of the related words will be geometrically closer.

The definition of relatedness among words can have a profound influence on the quality of the resulting embedding models. In most existing studies, relatedness is defined by co-occurrence within a window frame sliding over texts. Although supported by the *distributional hypothesis* (Harris, 1954), this definition suffers from two major limitations. Firstly, the window frame size is usually rather small (for efficiency and sparsity considerations), which increases the false negative rate by missing long-distance dependencies. Secondly, a window frame can (and often does) span across different constituents in a sentence, resulting in an increased false positive rate by associating unrelated words. The problem is worsened as the size of the window increases since each false-positive n-gram will appear in two subsuming false-positive $(n+1)$-grams.

Several existing studies have addressed these limitations of window-based contexts. Nonetheless, we hypothesize that lexical embedding learning can further benefit from (1) factorizing syntactic relations into individual relations for structured syntactic information and (2) defining relatedness using lexicographic knowledge. We will show that implementation of these ideas brings notable improvement in lexical similarity tasks.

2 Related Work

Lexical embeddings have traditionally been used in language modelling as distributed representations of words (Bengio et al., 2003; Mnih and Hinton, 2009) and have only recently been used in other NLP tasks. Turian et al. (2010), for example, used embeddings from existing language models (Collobert and Weston, 2008; Mnih and Hinton, 2007) as unsupervised lexical features to improve named entity recognition and chunking. Embedding models gained further popularity thanks to the simplicity and effectiveness of the `word2vec` model (Mikolov et al., 2013a), which implicitly factorizes the *point-wise mutual information* matrix shifted by biases consisting of marginal counts of individual words (Levy and Goldberg, 2014b). Efficiency is greatly improved by approximating the computationally costly softmax function with

Proceedings of the 53rd Annual Meeting of the Association for Computational Linguistics and the 7th International Joint Conference on Natural Language Processing (Short Papers), pages 458–463,
Beijing, China, July 26-31, 2015.

negative sampling (similar to that of Collobert and Weston 2008) or hierarchical softmax (similar to that of Mnih and Hinton 2007).

To address the limitation of contextual locality in many language models (including word2vec), Huang et al. (2012) added a "global context score" to the local n-gram score (Collobert and Weston, 2008). The concatenation of word vectors and a "document vector" (centroid of the composing word vectors weighted by *idf*) was used as model input. Pennington et al. (2014) proposed to explicitly factorize the global co-occurrence matrix between words, and the resulting log bilinear model achieved state-of-the-art performance in lexical similarity, analogy, and named entity recognition.

Several later studies addressed the limitations of window-based co-occurrence by extending the word2vec model to predict words that are *syntactically* related to target words. Levy and Goldberg (2014a) used syntactically related words *non-discriminatively* as syntactic context. Bansal et al. (2014) used a training corpus consisting of sequences of labels following certain manually compiled patterns. Zhao et al. (2014) employed coarse-grained classifications of contexts according to the hierarchical structures in a parse tree.

Semantic relations have also been explored as a form of lexical association. Faruqui et al. (2015) proposed to retrofit pre-trained embeddings (derived using window-based contexts) to semantic lexicons. The goal is to derive a set of embeddings to capture relatedness suggested by semantic lexicons while maintaining their resemblance to the corresponding window-based embeddings. Bollegala et al. (2014) trained an embedding model with lexical, part-of-speech, and dependency patterns extracted from sentences containing frequently co-occurring word pairs. Each relation was represented by a pattern representation matrix, which was combined and updated together with the word representation matrix (i.e., lexical embeddings) in a bilinear objective function.

3 The Proposed Models

3.1 Factorizing Dependency Relations

One strong limitation of the existing dependency-based models is that no distinctions are made among the many different types of dependency relations. This is essentially a compromise to avoid issues in model complexity and data sparsity, and it precludes the possibility of studying individual or interactive effects of individual dependency relations on embedding learning.

Consequently, we propose a *relation-dependent model* to predict dependents given a governor under *individual* dependency relations. For example, given a nominal governor *apple* of the *adjective modifier* relation (amod), an embedding model will be trained to assign higher probability to observed adjectival dependents (e.g., *red*, *sweet*, etc.) than to rarely or never observed ones (e.g., *purple*, *savoury*, etc.). If a model is able to accurately make such predictions, it can then be said to "understand" the meaning of *apple* by possessing semantic knowledge about its certain attributes. By extension, similar models can be trained to learn the meaning of the governors in other dependency relations (e.g., adjectival governors in the inverse relation amod^{-1}, etc.).

The basic model uses an objective function similar to that of Mikolov et al. (2013a):

$$\log\sigma(\mathbf{e}_g^T\mathbf{e}'_d)+\sum_{i=1}^{k}\mathbf{E}_{\hat{d}_i}[\log\sigma(-\mathbf{e}_g^T\mathbf{e}'_{\hat{d}_i})],$$

where $\mathbf{e}_*$ and $\mathbf{e}'_*$ are the target and the output embeddings for the corresponding words, respectively, and σ is the sigmoid function. The subscripts g and d indicate whether an embedding correspond to the governor or the dependent of a dependency pair, and $\hat{d}_*$ correspond to random samples from the dependent vocabulary (drawn by unigram frequency).

3.2 Incorporating Lexicographic Knowledge

Semantic information used in existing studies (Section 2) either relies on specialized lexical resources with limited availability or is obtained from complex procedures that are difficult to replicate. To address these issues, we propose to use monolingual dictionaries as a simple yet effective source of semantic knowledge. The defining relation has been demonstrated to have good performance in various semantic tasks (Chodorow et al., 1985; Alshawi, 1987). The inverse of the defining relation (also known as the *Olney Concordance Index*, Reichert et al. 1969) has also been proven useful in building lexicographic taxonomies (Amsler, 1980) and identifying synonyms (Wang and Hirst, 2011). Therefore, we use both the defining relation and its inverse as sources of semantic association in the proposed embedding models.

Lexicographic knowledge is represented by adopting the same terminology used in syntactic dependencies: definienda as governors and definientia as dependents. For example, *apple* is related to *fruit* and *rosaceous* as a governor under `def`, or to *cider* and *pippin* as a dependent under $\texttt{def}^{-1}$.

3.3 Combining Individual Knowledge Sources

Sparsity is a prominent issue in the relation-dependent models since each individual relation only receives a limited share of the overall co-occurrence information. We also propose a post-hoc, *relation-independent* model that combines the individual knowledge sources. The input of the model is the structured knowledge from relation-dependent models, for example, that *something* can be *red* or *sweet*, or it can *ripen* or *fall*, etc. The training objective is to predict the *original word* given the relation-dependent embeddings, with the intuition that if a model is trained to be able to "solve the riddle" and predict that this *something* is an *apple*, then the model is said to possess generic, relation-independent knowledge about the target word by learning from the relation-dependent knowledge sources.

Given input word w_I, its relation-independent embedding is derived by applying a linear model M on the concatenation of its relation-dependent embeddings ($\tilde{\mathbf{e}}_{w_I}$). The objective function of a relation-independent model is then defined as

$$\log \sigma(\mathbf{e}'^T_{w_I} M \tilde{\mathbf{e}}_{w_I}) + \sum_{i=1}^{k} \mathbf{E}_{\bar{w}_i}[\log \sigma(-\mathbf{e}'^T_{\bar{w}_i} M \tilde{\mathbf{e}}_{w_I})],$$

where $\mathbf{e}'_*$ are the context embeddings for the corresponding words. Since $\tilde{\mathbf{e}}_{w_I}$ is a real-valued vector (instead of a 1-hot vector as in relation-dependent models), M can no longer be updated one column at a time. Instead, updates are defined as:

$$\frac{\partial}{\partial M} = [1 - \sigma(\mathbf{e}'^T_{w_O} M \tilde{\mathbf{e}}_{w_I})]\mathbf{e}'_{w_O} \tilde{\mathbf{e}}^T_{w_I} - \sum_{i=1}^{k} [1 - \sigma(-\mathbf{e}'^T_{w_i} M \tilde{\mathbf{e}}_{w_I})]\mathbf{e}'_{w_i} \tilde{\mathbf{e}}^T_{w_I}.$$

Training is quite efficient in practice due to the low dimensionality of M; convergence is achieved after very few epochs.[1]

Note that this model is different from the non-factorized models that conflate multiple dependency relations because the proposed model is a deeper structure with pre-training on the factorized results (via the relation-dependent models) in the first layer.

4 Evaluations

4.1 Training Data and Baselines

The *Annotated English Gigaword* (Napoles et al., 2012) is used as the main training corpus. It contains 4 billion words from news articles, parsed by the Stanford Parser. A random subset with 17 million words is also used to study the effect of training data size (dubbed *17M*).

Semantic relations are derived from the definition text in the *Online Plain Text English Dictionary*[2]. There are approximately 806,000 definition pairs, 33,000 distinct definienda and 24,000 distinct defining words. The entire corpus has 1.25 million words in a 7.1MB file.

Three baseline systems are used for comparison, including one non-factorized dependency-based model `DEP` (Levy and Goldberg, 2014a) and two window-based embedding models `w2v` (or `word2vec`, Mikolov et al. 2013a) and `GloVe` (Pennington et al., 2014). Embedding dimension is 50 for all models (baselines as well as the proposed). Embeddings in the window-based models are obtained by running the published software for each of these systems on the Gigaword corpus with default values for all hyper-parameters except for vector size (50) and minimum word frequency (100 for the entire Gigaword corpus; 5 for the *17M* subset). For the `w2v` model, for example, we used the skip-gram model with the default value 5 as window size, negative sample size, and epoch size, and 0.025 as initial learning rate.

4.2 Lexical Similarity

Relation-Dependent Models

Table 1 shows the results on four similarity datasets: *MC* (Miller and Charles, 1991), *RG* (Rubenstein and Goodenough, 1965), *FG* (or *wordsim353*, Finkelstein et al. 2001), and *SL* (or *SimLex*, Hill et al. 2014b). The first three datasets consist of nouns, while the last one also includes verbs (SL_v) and adjectives (SL_a) in addition to nouns (SL_n). Semantically, *FG* contains many related pairs (e.g., *movie–popcorn*), whereas the other three datasets are purely similarity oriented.

[1]We also experimented with updating the relation-dependent embeddings together with M, but this worsened evaluation performance.

[2]`http://www.mso.anu.edu.au/~ralph/OPTED/`

Model	*MC*	*RG*	*FG*	SL_n	SL_v	SL_a
amod	**.766**	**.798**	.572	**.566**	.154	.466
amod^{-1}	.272	.296	.220	.218	.248	**.602**
nsubj	.442	.350	.376	.388	**.392**	.464
nn	.596	.620	.514	.486	.130	.068
Baselines						
DEP	.640	.670	.510	.400	.240	.350
w2v	.656	.618	**.600**	.382	.237	.560
GloVe	.609	.629	.546	.346	.142	.517

Table 1: Correlation between human judgement and *cosine* similarity of embeddings (trained on the Gigaword corpus) on six similarity datasets.

Model	*MC*	*RG*	*FG*	SL_n	SL_v	SL_a
Rel. Dep. #1	.512	.486	.380	.354	.222	.394
Rel. Dep. #2	.390	.380	.360	.304	.206	.236
Rel. Indep.	**.570**	.550	.392	**.360**	**.238**	.338
Baselines						
DEP	.530	**.558**	.506	.346	.138	.412
w2v	.563	.491	**.562**	.287	.065	.379
GloVe	.306	.368	.308	.132	−.007	.254

Table 2: Lexical similarity performance of relation-independent models (trained on the *17M* corpus) combining top two best-performing relations for each POS.

Performance is measured by *Spearman's* ρ between system scores and human judgements of similarity between the pairs that accompany each dataset.

When dependency information is factorized into individual relations, models using the best-performing relation for each dataset[3] out-perform the baselines by large margins on 5 out of the 6 datasets. In comparison, the advantage of the syntactic information is not at all obvious when they are used in a non-factorized fashion in the DEP model; it out-performs the window-based methods (below the dashed line) on only 3 datasets with limited margins. However, the window-based methods consistently outperform the dependency-based methods on the *FG* dataset, confirming our intuition that window-based methods are better at capturing relatedness than similarity.

When dependency relations are factorized into individual types, sparsity is a rather prominent issue especially when the training corpus is small. With sufficient training data, however, factorized models consistently outperform all baselines by very large margins on all but the *FG* dataset. Average correlation (weighted by the size of each sub-dataset corresponding to the three POS's) on the *SL* dataset is 0.531, outperforming the best reported result on the dataset (Hill et al., 2014a).

Although the co-occurrence data is sparse, it is nonetheless highly "focused" (Levy and Goldberg, 2014a) with much lower entropy. As a result, convergence is much faster when compared to the non-factorized models such as DEP, which takes up to 10 times more iterations to converge.

Among the individual dependency relations, the most effective relations for nouns, adjectives, and verbs are amod, amod^{-1}, and nsubj, respectively. For nouns, we observed a notable gap in performance between amod and nn. Data inspection reveals that a much higher proportion of nn modifiers are proper nouns (64.0% compared to about 0.01% in amod). The comparison suggests that, as noun modifiers, amod describes the attributes of nominal concepts while nn are more often instantiations, which apparently is semantically less informative. On the other hand, nn is the better choice if the goal is to train embeddings for proper nouns.

Relation-Independent Model

The relation-independent model (Section 3.3) is implemented by combining the top two best-performing relations for each POS: amod and dobj^{-1} for noun pairs, nsubj and dobj for verb pairs, and amod^{-1} and dobj^{-1} for adjective pairs.

Lexical similarity results on the *17M* corpus are listed in Table 2. The combined results improve over the best relation-dependent models for all categories except for SL_a (adjectives), where only the top-performing relation-dependent model (amod^{-1}) yielded statistically significant results and thus, results are worsened by combining the second-best relation-dependent source dobj^{-1} (which is essentially noise). Comparing to baselines, the relation-independent model achieves better results in four out of the six cat-

[3]We did not hold out validation data to choose the best-performing relations for each dataset. Our assumption is that the dominant part-of-speech of the words in each dataset is the determining factor of the top-performing syntactic relation for that dataset. Consequently, the choice of this relation should be relatively constant without having to rely on traditional parameter tuning. For the four noun datasets, for example, we observed that amod is consistently the top-performing relation, and we subsequently assumed similar consistency on the verb and the adjective datasets. The same observations and rationales apply for the relation-independent experiments.

Model	*MC*	*RG*	*FG*	SL_n	SL_v	SL_a
`def`	.640	.626	.378	.332	.320	.306
`def`$^{-1}$	.740	.626	.436	.366	.332	.376
Combined	**.754**	**.722**	.530	**.410**	**.356**	.412
`w2v`	.656	.618	**.600**	.382	.237	**.560**

Table 3: Lexical similarity performance of models using dictionary definitions and compared to `word2vec` trained on the Gigaword corpus.

egories.

Using Dictionary Definitions

Embeddings trained on dictionary definitions are also evaluated on the similarity datasets, and the results are shown in Table 3. The individual relations (defining and inverse) perform surprisingly well on the datasets when compared to `word2vec`. The relation-independent model brings consistent improvement by combining the relations, and the results compare favourably to `word2vec` trained on the entire Gigaword corpus. Similar to dependency relations, lexicographic information is also better at capturing similarity than relatedness, as suggested by the results.

5 Conclusions

This study explored the notion of relatedness in embedding models by incorporating syntactic and lexicographic knowledge. Compared to existing syntax-based embedding models, the proposed embedding models benefits from factorizing syntactic information by individual dependency relations. Empirically, syntactic information from individual dependency types brings about notable improvement in model performance at a much higher rate of convergence. Lexicographic knowledge from monolingual dictionaries also helps improve lexical embedding learning. Embeddings trained on a compact, knowledge-intensive resource rival state-of-the-art models trained on free texts thousands of times larger in size.

Acknowledgments

We thank Gerald Penn, Ruslan Salakhutdinov, Suzanne Stevenson, and Xiaodan Zhu for their insightful comments, as well as the anonymous reviewers for their valuable feedback. This study is financially supported by the Natural Sciences and Engineering Research Council of Canada.

References

Hiyan Alshawi. Processing dictionary definitions with phrasal pattern hierarchies. *Computational Linguistics*, 13(3-4):195–202, 1987.

Robert Amsler. *The structure of the Merriam-Webster Pocket Dictionary*. PhD thesis, The University of Texas at Austin, 1980.

Mohit Bansal, Kevin Gimpel, and Karen Livescu. Tailoring continuous word representations for dependency parsing. In *Proceedings of the Annual Meeting of the Association for Computational Linguistics*, 2014.

Yoshua Bengio, Holger Schwenk, Jean-Sébastien Senécal, Fréderic Morin, and Jean-Luc Gauvain. Neural probabilistic language models. In *Innovations in Machine Learning*, pages 137–186. Springer, 2003.

Danushka Bollegala, Takanori Maehara, Yuichi Yoshida, and Ken-ichi Kawarabayashi. Learning word representations from relational graphs. *arXiv preprint arXiv:1412.2378*, 2014.

Martin Chodorow, Roy Byrd, and George Heidorn. Extracting semantic hierarchies from a large on-line dictionary. In *Proceedings of the 23rd Annual Meeting of the Association for Computational Linguistics*, pages 299–304, Chicago, Illinois, USA, 1985.

Ronan Collobert and Jason Weston. A unified architecture for natural language processing: Deep neural networks with multitask learning. In *Proceedings of the 25th International Conference on Machine Learning*, pages 160–167. ACM, 2008.

Manaal Faruqui, Jesse Dodge, Sujay Kumar Jauhar, Chris Dyer, Eduard Hovy, and Noah A. Smith. Retrofitting word vectors to semantic lexicons. In *Proceedings of the 2015 Conference of the North American Chapter of the Association for Computational Linguistics: Human Language Technologies*, pages 1606–1615, Denver, Colorado, 2015. Association for Computational Linguistics.

Lev Finkelstein, Evgeniy Gabrilovich, Yossi Matias, Ehud Rivlin, Zach Solan, Gadi Wolfman, and Eytan Ruppin. Placing search in context: The concept revisited. In *Proceedings of the 10th International Conference on World Wide Web*, pages 406–414. ACM, 2001.

Zellig Harris. Distributional structure. *Word*, 10 (23):146–162, 1954.

Felix Hill, Kyunghyun Cho, Sebastien Jean, Coline Devin, and Yoshua Bengio. Embedding word similarity with neural machine translation. *arXiv preprint arXiv:1412.6448*, 2014a.

Felix Hill, Roi Reichart, and Anna Korhonen. Simlex-999: Evaluating semantic models with (genuine) similarity estimation. *arXiv preprint arXiv:1408.3456*, 2014b.

Eric Huang, Richard Socher, Christopher D Manning, and Andrew Ng. Improving word representations via global context and multiple word prototypes. In *Proceedings of the 50th Annual Meeting of the Association for Computational Linguistics: Long Papers-Volume 1*, pages 873–882. Association for Computational Linguistics, 2012.

Omer Levy and Yoav Goldberg. Dependency-based word embeddings. In *Proceedings of the 52nd Annual Meeting of the Association for Computational Linguistics*, volume 2, 2014a.

Omer Levy and Yoav Goldberg. Neural word embedding as implicit matrix factorization. In *Advances in Neural Information Processing Systems*, pages 2177–2185, 2014b.

Tomas Mikolov, Kai Chen, Greg Corrado, and Jeffrey Dean. Efficient estimation of word representations in vector space. In *Proceedings of the International Conference on Learning Representations*, 2013a.

Tomas Mikolov, Wen-tau Yih, and Geoffrey Zweig. Linguistic regularities in continuous space word representations. In *Proceedings of Human Language Technologies: The 2013 Annual Conference of the North American Chapter of the Association for Computational Linguistics*, pages 746–751, 2013b.

George Miller and Walter Charles. Contextual correlates of semantic similarity. *Language and Cognitive Processes*, 6(1):1–28, 1991.

Andriy Mnih and Geoffrey Hinton. Three new graphical models for statistical language modelling. In *Proceedings of the 24th International Conference on Machine Learning*, pages 641–648. ACM, 2007.

Andriy Mnih and Geoffrey E Hinton. A scalable hierarchical distributed language model. In *Advances in Neural Information Processing Systems*, pages 1081–1088, 2009.

Courtney Napoles, Matthew Gormley, and Benjamin Van Durme. Annotated Gigaword. In *Proceedings of the Joint Workshop on Automatic Knowledge Base Construction and Web-scale Knowledge Extraction*, pages 95–100. Association for Computational Linguistics, 2012.

Jeffrey Pennington, Richard Socher, and Christopher D Manning. GloVe: Global vectors for word representation. In *Proceedings of the Conference on Empirical Methods in Natural Language Processing*, 2014.

Richard Reichert, John Olney, and James Paris. *Two Dictionary Transcripts and Programs for Processing Them – The Encoding Scheme, Parsent and Conix.*, volume 1. DTIC Research Report AD0691098, 1969.

Herbert Rubenstein and John Goodenough. Contextual correlates of synonymy. *Communications of the ACM*, 8(10):627–633, 1965.

Joseph Turian, Lev Ratinov, and Yoshua Bengio. Word representations: a simple and general method for semi-supervised learning. In *Proceedings of the 48th Annual Meeting of the Association for Computational Linguistics*, pages 384–394, Uppsala, Sweden, July 2010.

Tong Wang and Graeme Hirst. Exploring patterns in dictionary definitions for synonym extraction. *Natural Language Engineering*, 17, 2011.

Yinggong Zhao, Shujian Huang, Xinyu Dai, Jianbing Zhang, and Jiajun Chen. Learning word embeddings from dependency relations. In *Proceedings of 2014 International Conference on Asian Language Processing (IALP)*, pages 123–127. IEEE, 2014.

Non-distributional Word Vector Representations

Manaal Faruqui and **Chris Dyer**
Language Technologies Institute
Carnegie Mellon University
Pittsburgh, PA, 15213, USA
{mfaruqui, cdyer}@cs.cmu.edu

Abstract

Data-driven representation learning for words is a technique of central importance in NLP. While indisputably useful as a source of features in downstream tasks, such vectors tend to consist of uninterpretable components whose relationship to the categories of traditional lexical semantic theories is tenuous at best. We present a method for constructing interpretable word vectors from hand-crafted linguistic resources like WordNet, FrameNet etc. These vectors are binary (i.e, contain only 0 and 1) and are 99.9% sparse. We analyze their performance on state-of-the-art evaluation methods for distributional models of word vectors and find they are competitive to standard distributional approaches.

1 Introduction

Distributed representations of words have been shown to benefit a diverse set of NLP tasks including syntactic parsing (Lazaridou et al., 2013; Bansal et al., 2014), named entity recognition (Guo et al., 2014) and sentiment analysis (Socher et al., 2013). Additionally, because they can be induced directly from unannotated corpora, they are likewise available in domains and languages where traditional linguistic resources do not exhaust. Intrinsic evaluations on various tasks are helping refine vector learning methods to discover representations that captures many facts about lexical semantics (Turney, 2001; Turney and Pantel, 2010).

Yet induced word vectors do not look anything like the representations described in most lexical semantic theories, which focus on identifying classes of words (Levin, 1993; Baker et al., 1998; Schuler, 2005; Miller, 1995). Though expensive to construct, conceptualizing word meanings symbolically is important for theoretical understanding and interpretability is desired in computational models.

Our contribution to this discussion is a new technique that constructs task-independent word vector representations using linguistic knowledge derived from pre-constructed linguistic resources like WordNet (Miller, 1995), FrameNet (Baker et al., 1998), Penn Treebank (Marcus et al., 1993) etc. In such word vectors every dimension is a linguistic feature and 1/0 indicates the presence or absence of that feature in a word, thus the vector representations are binary while being highly sparse ($\approx$ 99.9%). Since these vectors do not encode any word cooccurrence information, they are non-distributional. An additional benefit of constructing such vectors is that they are fully interpretable i.e, every dimension of these vectors maps to a linguistic feature unlike distributional word vectors where the vector dimensions have no interpretability.

Of course, engineering feature vectors from linguistic resources is established practice in many applications of discriminative learning; e.g., parsing (McDonald and Pereira, 2006; Nivre, 2008) or part of speech tagging (Ratnaparkhi, 1996; Collins, 2002). However, despite a certain common inventories of features that re-appear across many tasks, feature engineering tends to be seen as a task-specific problem, and engineered feature vectors are not typically evaluated independently of the tasks they are designed for. We evaluate the quality of our linguistic vectors on a number of tasks that have been proposed for evaluating distributional word vectors. We show that linguistic word vectors are comparable to current state-of-the-art distributional word vectors trained on billions of words as evaluated on a battery of semantic and syntactic evaluation benchmarks.[1]

[1]Our vectors can be downloaded at: https://github.com/mfaruqui/non-distributional

Proceedings of the 53rd Annual Meeting of the Association for Computational Linguistics and the 7th International Joint Conference on Natural Language Processing (Short Papers), pages 464–469,
Beijing, China, July 26-31, 2015.

Lexicon	Vocabulary	Features
WordNet	10,794	92,117
Supersense	71,836	54
FrameNet	9,462	4,221
Emotion	6,468	10
Connotation	76,134	12
Color	14,182	12
Part of Speech	35,606	20
Syn. & Ant.	35,693	75,972
Union	119,257	172,418

Table 1: Sizes of vocabualry and features induced from different linguistic resources.

2 Linguistic Word Vectors

We construct linguistic word vectors by extracting word level information from linguistic resources. Table 1 shows the size of vocabulary and number of features induced from every lexicon. We now describe various linguistic resources that we use for constructing linguistic word vectors.

WordNet. WordNet (Miller, 1995) is an English lexical database that groups words into sets of synonyms called synsets and records a number of relations among these synsets or their members. For a word we look up its synset for all possible part of speech (POS) tags that it can assume. For example, *film* will have SYNSET.FILM.V.01 and SYNSET.FILM.N.01 as features as it can be both a verb and a noun. In addition to synsets, we include the hyponym (for ex. HYPO.COLLAGEFILM.N.01), hypernym (for ex. HYPER:SHEET.N.06) and holonym synset of the word as features. We also collect antonyms and pertainyms of all the words in a synset and include those as features in the linguistic vector.

Supsersenses. WordNet partitions nouns and verbs into semantic field categories known as supsersenses (Ciaramita and Altun, 2006; Nastase, 2008). For example, *lioness* evokes the supersense SS.NOUN.ANIMAL. These supersenses were further extended to adjectives (Tsvetkov et al., 2014).[2] We use these supsersense tags for nouns, verbs and adjectives as features in the linguistic word vectors.

FrameNet. FrameNet (Baker et al., 1998; Fillmore et al., 2003) is a rich linguistic resource that contains information about lexical and predicate-argument semantics in English. Frames can be realized on the surface by many different word types, which suggests that the word types evoking the same frame should be semantically related. For every word, we use the frame it evokes along with the roles of the evoked frame as its features. Since, information in FrameNet is part of speech (POS) disambiguated, we couple these feature with the corresponding POS tag of the word. For example, since *appreciate* is a verb, it will have the following features: VERB.FRAME.REGARD, VERB.FRAME.ROLE.EVALUEE etc.

Emotion & Sentiment. Mohammad and Turney (2013) constructed two different lexicons that associate words to sentiment polarity and to emotions resp. using crowdsourcing. The polarity is either positive or negative but there are eight different kinds of emotions like anger, anticipation, joy etc. Every word in the lexicon is associated with these properties. For example, *cannibal* evokes POL.NEG, EMO.DISGUST and EMO.FEAR. We use these properties as features in linguistic vectors.

Connotation. Feng et al. (2013) construct a lexicon that contains information about connotation of words that are seemingly objective but often allude nuanced sentiment. They assign positive, negative and neutral connotations to these words. This lexicon differs from Mohammad and Turney (2013) in that it has a more subtle shade of sentiment and it extends to many more words. For example, *delay* has a negative connotation CON.NOUN.NEG, *floral* has a positive connotation CON.ADJ.POS and *outline* has a neutral connotation CON.VERB.NEUT.

Color. Most languages have expressions involving color, for example *green with envy* and *grey with uncertainly* are phrases used in English. The word-color associtation lexicon produced by Mohammad (2011) using crowdsourcing lists the colors that a word evokes in English. We use every color in this lexicon as a feature in the vector. For example, COLOR.RED is a feature evoked by the word *blood*.

Part of Speech Tags. The Penn Treebank (Marcus et al., 1993) annotates naturally occurring text for linguistic structure. It contains syntactic parse trees and POS tags for every word in the corpus. We collect all the possible POS tags that a word is annotated with and use it as features in the linguistic vectors. For example, *love* has PTB.NOUN,

[2] `http://www.cs.cmu.edu/~ytsvetko/adj-supersenses.tar.gz`

Word	POL.POS	COLOR.PINK	SS.NOUN.FEELING	PTB.VERB	ANTO.FAIR	···	CON.NOUN.POS
love	1	1	1	1	0		1
hate	0	0	1	1	0		0
ugly	0	0	0	0	1		0
beauty	1	1	0	0	0		1
refundable	0	0	0	0	0		1

Table 2: Some linguistic word vectors. 1 indicates presence and 0 indicates absence of a linguistic feature.

PTB.VERB as features.

Synonymy & Antonymy. We use Roget's thesaurus (Roget, 1852) to collect sets of synonymous words.[3] For every word, its synonymous word is used as a feature in the linguistic vector. For example, *adoration* and *affair* have a feature SYNO.LOVE, *admissible* has a feature SYNO.ACCEPTABLE. The synonym lexicon contains 25,338 words after removal of multiword phrases. In a similar manner, we also use antonymy relations between words as features in the word vector. The antonymous words for a given word were collected from Ordway (1913).[4] An example would be of *impartiality*, which has features ANTO.FAVORITISM and ANTO.INJUSTICE. The antonym lexicon has 10,355 words. These features are different from those induced from WordNet as the former encode word-word relations whereas the latter encode word-synset relations.

After collecting features from the various linguistic resources described above we obtain linguistic word vectors of length 172,418 dimensions. These vectors are 99.9% sparse i.e, each vector on an average contains only 34 non-zero features out of 172,418 total features. On average a linguistic feature (vector dimension) is active for 15 word types. The linguistic word vectors contain 119,257 unique word types. Table 2 shows linguistic vectors for some of the words.

3 Experiments

We first briefly describe the evaluation tasks and then present results.

3.1 Evaluation Tasks

Word Similarity. We evaluate our word representations on three different benchmarks to measure word similarity. The first one is the widely used WS-353 dataset (Finkelstein et al., 2001), which contains 353 pairs of English words that have been assigned similarity ratings by humans. The second is the RG-65 dataset (Rubenstein and Goodenough, 1965) of 65 words pairs. The third dataset is SimLex (Hill et al., 2014) which has been constructed to overcome the shortcomings of WS-353 and contains 999 pairs of adjectives, nouns and verbs. Word similarity is computed using cosine similarity between two words and Spearman's rank correlation is reported between the rankings produced by vector model against the human rankings.

Sentiment Analysis. Socher et al. (2013) created a treebank containing sentences annotated with fine-grained sentiment labels on phrases and sentences from movie review excerpts. The coarse-grained treebank of positive and negative classes has been split into training, development, and test datasets containing 6,920, 872, and 1,821 sentences, respectively. We use average of the word vectors of a given sentence as features in an ℓ_2-regularized logistic regression for classification. The classifier is tuned on the dev set and accuracy is reported on the test set.

NP-Bracketing. Lazaridou et al. (2013) constructed a dataset from the Penn TreeBank (Marcus et al., 1993) of noun phrases (NP) of length three words, where the first can be an adjective or a noun and the other two are nouns. The task is to predict the correct bracketing in the parse tree for a given noun phrase. For example, *local (phone company)* and *(blood pressure) medicine* exhibit *left* and *right* bracketing respectively. We append the word vectors of the three words in the NP in order and use them as features in an ℓ_2-regularized logistic regression classifier. The dataset contains 2,227 noun phrases split into 10 folds. The classifier is tuned on the first fold and cross-validation accuracy is reported on the remaining nine folds.

[3]http://www.gutenberg.org/ebooks/10681

[4]https://archive.org/details/synonymsantonyms00ordwiala

Vector	Length (D)	Params.	Corpus Size	WS-353	RG-65	SimLex	Senti	NP
Skip-Gram	300	$D \times N$	300 billion	65.6	72.8	43.6	**81.5**	80.1
Glove	300	$D \times N$	6 billion	60.5	76.6	36.9	77.7	77.9
LSA	300	$D \times N$	1 billion	**67.3**	77.0	49.6	81.1	79.7
Ling Sparse	172,418	–	–	44.6	**77.8**	56.6	79.4	**83.3**
Ling Dense	300	$D \times N$	–	45.4	67.0	**57.8**	75.4	76.2
Skip-Gram $\oplus$ Ling Sparse	172,718	–	–	67.1	80.5	55.5	82.4	82.8

Table 3: Performance of different type of word vectors on evaluation tasks reported by Spearman's correlation (first 3 columns) and Accuracy (last 2 columns). Bold shows the best performance for a task.

3.2 Linguistic Vs. Distributional Vectors

In order to make our linguistic vectors comparable to publicly available distributional word vectors, we perform singular value decompostion (SVD) on the linguistic matrix to obtain word vectors of lower dimensionality. If $\mathbf{L} \in \{0,1\}^{N \times D}$ is the linguistic matrix with N word types and D linguistic features, then we can obtain $\mathbf{U} \in \mathbb{R}^{N \times K}$ from the SVD of $\mathbf{L}$ as follows: $\mathbf{L} = \mathbf{U}\mathbf{\Sigma}\mathbf{V}^\top$, with K being the desired length of the lower dimensional space.

We compare both sparse and dense linguistic vectors to three widely used distributional word vector models. The first two are the pre-trained Skip-Gram (Mikolov et al., 2013)[5] and Glove (Pennington et al., 2014)[6] word vectors each of length 300, trained on 300 billion and 6 billion words respectively. We used latent semantic analysis (LSA) to obtain word vectors from the SVD decomposition of a word-word cooccurrence matrix (Turney and Pantel, 2010). These were trained on 1 billion words of Wikipedia with vector length 300 and context window of 5 words.

3.3 Results

Table 3 shows the performance of different word vector types on the evaluation tasks. It can be seen that although Skip-Gram, Glove & LSA perform better than linguistic vectors on WS-353, the linguistic vectors outperform them by a huge margin on SimLex. Linguistic vectors also perform better at RG-65. On sentiment analysis, linguistic vectors are competitive with Skip-Gram vectors and on the NP-bracketing task they outperform all distributional vectors with a statistically significant margin ($p < 0.05$, McNemar's test Dietterich (1998)). We append the sparse linguistic vectors to Skip-Gram vectors and evaluate the resultant vectors as shown in the bottom row of Table 3. The combined vector outperforms Skip-Gram on all tasks, showing that linguistic vectors contain useful information orthogonal to distributional information.

It is evident from the results that linguistic vectors are either competitive or better to state-of-the-art distributional vector models. Sparse linguistic word vectors are high dimensional but they are also sparse, which makes them computationally easy to work with.

4 Discussion

Linguistic resources like WordNet have found extensive applications in lexical semantics, for example, for word sense disambiguation, word similarity etc. (Resnik, 1995; Agirre et al., 2009). Recently there has been interest in using linguistic resources to enrich word vector representations. In these approaches, relational information among words obtained from WordNet, Freebase etc. is used as a constraint to encourage words with similar properties in lexical ontologies to have similar word vectors (Xu et al., 2014; Yu and Dredze, 2014; Bian et al., 2014; Fried and Duh, 2014; Faruqui et al., 2015a). Distributional representations have also been shown to improve by using experiential data in addition to distributional context (Andrews et al., 2009). We have shown that simple vector concatenation can likewise be used to improve representations (further confirming the established finding that lexical resources and cooccurrence information provide somewhat orthogonal information), but it is certain that more careful combination strategies can be used.

Although distributional word vector dimensions cannot, in general, be identified with linguistic properties, it has been shown that some vector construction strategies yield dimensions that are relatively more interpretable (Murphy et al., 2012; Fyshe et al., 2014; Fyshe et al., 2015; Faruqui et al., 2015b). However, such analysis is difficult to generalize across models of representation. In constrast to distributional word vectors, linguistic

[5] `https://code.google.com/p/word2vec`

[6] `http://www-nlp.stanford.edu/projects/glove/`

word vectors have interpretable dimensions as every dimension is a linguistic property.

Linguistic word vectors require no training as there are no parameters to be optimized, meaning they are computationally economical. While good quality linguistic word vectors may only be obtained for languages with rich linguistic resources, such resources do exist in many languages and should not be disregarded.

5 Conclusion

We have presented a novel method of constructing word vector representations solely using linguistic knowledge from pre-existing linguistic resources. These non-distributional, linguistic word vectors are competitive to the current models of distributional word vectors as evaluated on a battery of tasks. Linguistic vectors are fully interpretable as every dimension is a linguistic feature and are highly sparse, so they are computationally easy to work with.

Acknowledgement

We thank Nathan Schneider for giving comments on an earlier draft of this paper and the anonymous reviewers for their feedback.

References

Eneko Agirre, Enrique Alfonseca, Keith Hall, Jana Kravalova, Marius Paşca, and Aitor Soroa. 2009. A study on similarity and relatedness using distributional and wordnet-based approaches. In *Proc. of NAACL*.

Mark Andrews, Gabriella Vigliocco, and David Vinson. 2009. Integrating experiential and distributional data to learn semantic representations. *Psychological review*, 116(3):463.

Collin F. Baker, Charles J. Fillmore, and John B. Lowe. 1998. The berkeley framenet project. In *Proc. of ACL*.

Mohit Bansal, Kevin Gimpel, and Karen Livescu. 2014. Tailoring continuous word representations for dependency parsing. In *Proc. of ACL*.

Jiang Bian, Bin Gao, and Tie-Yan Liu. 2014. Knowledge-powered deep learning for word embedding. In *Proc. of MLKDD*.

Massimiliano Ciaramita and Yasemin Altun. 2006. Broad-coverage sense disambiguation and information extraction with a supersense sequence tagger. In *Proc. of EMNLP*.

Michael Collins. 2002. Discriminative training methods for hidden markov models: Theory and experiments with perceptron algorithms. In *Proc. of EMNLP*.

Thomas G. Dietterich. 1998. Approximate statistical tests for comparing supervised classification learning algorithms. *Neural Computation*.

Manaal Faruqui, Jesse Dodge, Sujay K. Jauhar, Chris Dyer, Eduard Hovy, and Noah A. Smith. 2015a. Retrofitting word vectors to semantic lexicons. In *Proc. of NAACL*.

Manaal Faruqui, Yulia Tsvetkov, Dani Yogatama, Chris Dyer, and Noah A. Smith. 2015b. Sparse overcomplete word vector representations. In *Proc. of ACL*.

Song Feng, Jun Seok Kang, Polina Kuznetsova, and Yejin Choi. 2013. Connotation lexicon: A dash of sentiment beneath the surface meaning. In *Proc. of ACL*.

Charles Fillmore, Christopher Johnson, and Miriam Petruck. 2003. Lexicographic relevance: selecting information from corpus evidence. *International Journal of Lexicography*.

Lev Finkelstein, Evgeniy Gabrilovich, Yossi Matias, Ehud Rivlin, Zach Solan, Gadi Wolfman, and Eytan Ruppin. 2001. Placing search in context: the concept revisited. In *Proc. of WWW*.

Daniel Fried and Kevin Duh. 2014. Incorporating both distributional and relational semantics in word representations. *arXiv preprint arXiv:1412.4369*.

Alona Fyshe, Partha P. Talukdar, Brian Murphy, and Tom M. Mitchell. 2014. Interpretable semantic vectors from a joint model of brain- and text- based meaning. In *Proc. of ACL*.

Alona Fyshe, Leila Wehbe, Partha P. Talukdar, Brian Murphy, and Tom M. Mitchell. 2015. A compositional and interpretable semantic space. In *Proc. of NAACL*.

Jiang Guo, Wanxiang Che, Haifeng Wang, and Ting Liu. 2014. Revisiting embedding features for simple semi-supervised learning. In *Proc. of EMNLP*.

Felix Hill, Roi Reichart, and Anna Korhonen. 2014. Simlex-999: Evaluating semantic models with (genuine) similarity estimation. *CoRR*, abs/1408.3456.

Angeliki Lazaridou, Eva Maria Vecchi, and Marco Baroni. 2013. Fish transporters and miracle homes: How compositional distributional semantics can help NP parsing. In *Proc. of EMNLP*.

Beth Levin. 1993. *English verb classes and alternations : a preliminary investigation*. University of Chicago Press.

Mitchell P Marcus, Mary Ann Marcinkiewicz, and Beatrice Santorini. 1993. Building a large annotated corpus of english: The penn treebank. *Computational linguistics*, 19(2):313–330.

Ryan T McDonald and Fernando CN Pereira. 2006. Online learning of approximate dependency parsing algorithms. In *Proc. of EACL*.

Tomas Mikolov, Kai Chen, Greg Corrado, and Jeffrey Dean. 2013. Efficient estimation of word representations in vector space. *arXiv preprint arXiv:1301.3781*.

George A Miller. 1995. Wordnet: a lexical database for english. *Communications of the ACM*.

Saif M. Mohammad and Peter D. Turney. 2013. Crowdsourcing a word-emotion association lexicon. *Computational Intelligence*, 29(3):436–465.

Saif Mohammad. 2011. Colourful language: Measuring word-colour associations. In *Proc. of the Workshop on Cognitive Modeling and Computational Linguistics*.

Brian Murphy, Partha Talukdar, and Tom Mitchell. 2012. Learning effective and interpretable semantic models using non-negative sparse embedding. In *Proc. of COLING*.

Vivi Nastase. 2008. Unsupervised all-words word sense disambiguation with grammatical dependencies. In *Proc. of IJCNLP*.

Joakim Nivre. 2008. Algorithms for deterministic incremental dependency parsing. *Computational Linguistics*, 34(4):513–553.

Edith Bertha Ordway. 1913. *Synonyms and Antonyms: An Alphabetical List of Words in Common Use, Grouped with Others of Similar and Opposite Meaning*. Sully and Kleinteich.

Jeffrey Pennington, Richard Socher, and Christopher D. Manning. 2014. Glove: Global vectors for word representation. In *Proc. of EMNLP*.

Adwait Ratnaparkhi. 1996. A maximum entropy model for part-of-speech tagging. In *Proc. of EMNLP*.

Philip Resnik. 1995. Using information content to evaluate semantic similarity in a taxonomy. In *Proc. of IJCAI*.

P. M. Roget. 1852. *Roget's Thesaurus of English words and phrases*. Available from Project Gutemberg.

Herbert Rubenstein and John B. Goodenough. 1965. Contextual correlates of synonymy. *Commun. ACM*, 8(10).

Karin Kipper Schuler. 2005. *Verbnet: A Broad-coverage, Comprehensive Verb Lexicon*. Ph.D. thesis, University of Pennsylvania.

Richard Socher, Alex Perelygin, Jean Wu, Jason Chuang, Christopher D. Manning, Andrew Y. Ng, and Christopher Potts. 2013. Recursive deep models for semantic compositionality over a sentiment treebank. In *Proc. of EMNLP*.

Yulia Tsvetkov, Nathan Schneider, Dirk Hovy, Archna Bhatia, Manaal Faruqui, and Chris Dyer. 2014. Augmenting english adjective senses with supersenses. In *Proc. of LREC*.

Peter D. Turney and Patrick Pantel. 2010. From frequency to meaning : Vector space models of semantics. *JAIR*, pages 141–188.

Peter D. Turney. 2001. Mining the web for synonyms: Pmi-ir versus lsa on toefl. In *Proc. of ECML*.

Chang Xu, Yalong Bai, Jiang Bian, Bin Gao, Gang Wang, Xiaoguang Liu, and Tie-Yan Liu. 2014. Rc-net: A general framework for incorporating knowledge into word representations. In *Proc. of CIKM*.

Mo Yu and Mark Dredze. 2014. Improving lexical embeddings with semantic knowledge. In *Proc. of ACL*.

Early and Late Combinations of Criteria for Reranking Distributional Thesauri

Olivier Ferret
CEA, LIST, Vision and Content Engineering Laboratory,
Gif-sur-Yvette, F-91191 France.
olivier.ferret@cea.fr

Abstract

In this article, we first propose to exploit a new criterion for improving distributional thesauri. Following a bootstrapping perspective, we select relations between the terms of similar nominal compounds for building in an unsupervised way the training set of a classifier performing the reranking of a thesaurus. Then, we evaluate several ways to combine thesauri reranked according to different criteria and show that exploiting the complementary information brought by these criteria leads to significant improvements.

1 Introduction

The work presented in this article aims at improving thesauri built following the distributional approach as implemented by (Grefenstette, 1994; Lin, 1998; Curran and Moens, 2002). A part of the work for improving such thesauri focuses on the filtering of the components of the distributional contexts of words (Padró et al., 2014; Polajnar and Clark, 2014) or their reweighting, either by turning the weights of these components into ranks (Broda et al., 2009) or by adapting them through a bootstrapping method from the thesaurus to improve (Zhitomirsky-Geffet and Dagan, 2009; Yamamoto and Asakura, 2010). The other part implies more radical changes, including dimensionality reduction methods such as Latent Semantic Analysis (Padó and Lapata, 2007), multi-prototype (Reisinger and Mooney, 2010) or exemplar-based models (Erk and Pado, 2010), neural approaches (Huang et al., 2012; Mikolov et al., 2013) or the adoption of a Bayesian viewpoint (Kazama et al., 2010; Dinu and Lapata, 2010).

Our work follows (Ferret, 2012), which proposed a different way from (Zhitomirsky-Geffet and Dagan, 2009) to exploit bootstrapping by selecting in an unsupervised way a set of semantically similar words from an initial thesaurus and training from them a classifier to rerank the semantic neighbors of the initial thesaurus entries. More precisely, we propose a new criterion for this selection, based on the similarity relations of the components of similar compounds, and we show two modes – early and late – of combination of thesauri reranked from different criteria, including ours, leading to significant further improvements.

2 Reranking a distributional thesaurus

Distributional thesauri are characterized by heterogeneous performance in their entries, even for high frequency entries. This is a favorable situation for implementing a bootstrapping approach in which the results for "good" entries are exploited for improving the results of the other ones. However, such idea faces two problems: first, detecting "good" entries; second, learning a model from them for improving the performance of the other entries.

The first issue consists in selecting without supervision a set of positive and negative examples of similar words that represents a good compromise between its error rate and its size. Straightforward solutions such as using the similarity value between an entry and its neighbors or relying on the frequency of entries are not satisfactory in terms of error rate. Hence, we propose in Section 3 a new method, based on the semantic compositionality hypothesis of compounds, for achieving this selection in a more indirect way and show the interest to combine it with the criterion of (Ferret, 2012) for building a large training set with a reasonable error rate.

We address the second issue by following (Hagiwara et al., 2009), which defined a Support Vector Machine (SVM) model for deciding whether two words are similar or not. In our context, a positive example is a pair of nouns that are

Proceedings of the 53rd Annual Meeting of the Association for Computational Linguistics and the 7th International Joint Conference on Natural Language Processing (Short Papers), pages 470–476,
Beijing, China, July 26-31, 2015.

semantically similar while a negative example is a pair of non similar nouns. The features of each pair of nouns are built by summing the weights of the elements shared by their distributional representations, which are vectors of weighted cooccurrents. Cooccurrents not shared by the two nouns are given a null weight.

This SVM model is used for improving a thesaurus by reranking its semantic neighbors as follows: for each entry E of the thesaurus, the representation as an example of the word pair (E, *neighbor*) is built for each of the neighbors of E and submitted to the SVM model in classification mode. Finally, all the neighbors of E are reranked according to the value of the decision function computed for each neighbor by the SVM model.

3 Unsupervised example selection

The evaluation of distributional thesauri shows that a true semantic neighbor is more likely to be found when the thesaurus entry is a high frequency noun and the neighbor has a low rank. However, relying only on these two criteria doesn't lead to a good enough set of positive examples. For instance, taking as positive examples from the initial thesaurus of Section 4 the first neighbor of its 2,148 most frequent entries, the number of positive examples of (Hagiwara et al., 2009), only leads to 44.3% of correct examples. Moreover, this percentage exceeds 50% only when the number of examples is less than 654, which represents a very small training set for this kind of task.

Hence, we propose a more selective approach for choosing positive examples among high frequency nouns to get a more balanced solution between the number of examples and their error rate. This approach exploits a form of semantic compositionality hypothesis of compounds. While much work has been done recently for defining the distributional representation of compounds by composing the distributional representations of their components (Mitchell and Lapata, 2010; Paperno et al., 2014), we adopt a kind of reverse viewpoint by exploiting the possibility to link the meaning of a compound to the meaning of its components. More precisely, we assume that the mono-terms of two semantically related compounds with the same syntactic role in their compound are likely to be semantically linked themselves.

In this work, we only consider compounds having one of these three term structures (with their percentage of the vocabulary of compounds):

(a) <noun>$_{mod}$ <noun>$_{head}$ (30)
(b) <adjective>$_{mod}$ <noun>$_{head}$ (58)
(c) <noun>$_{head}$ <preposition><noun>$_{mod}$ (12)

Each compound C_i is represented as a pair (H_i, M_i), where H_i stands for the head of the compound whereas M_i represents its modifier (*mod*). According to the assumption underlying our selection procedure, if a compound (H_2, M_2) is a semantic neighbor of a compound (H_1, M_1) (*i.e.* at most its cth neighbor in a distributional thesaurus of compounds), we can expect H_1 and H_2 on one hand and M_1 and M_2 on the other hand to be semantically similar. Since distributional thesauri of compounds are far from being perfect, we added constraints on the matching of the components of two compounds. More precisely, the positive examples of semantically similar nouns (noun pairs after $\rightarrow$) are selected by the three following rules, where $H_1 = H_2$ means that H_1 is the same word as H_2 and $H_1 \equiv H_2$ means that H_2 is at most the mth neighbor of H_1 in the initial thesaurus of mono-terms (but is different from H_1):

(1) $H_1 \equiv H_2$ & $M_1 = M_2 \rightarrow (H_1, H_2)$
(2) $M_1 \equiv M_2$ & $H_1 = H_2 \rightarrow (M_1, M_2)$
(3) $M_1 \equiv M_2$ & $H_1 \equiv H_2 \rightarrow (H_1, H_2), (M_1, M_2)$

The selection of negative examples is also an important issue but benefits from the fact that the number of semantic neighbors of an entry that are actually semantically linked to this entry in a distributional thesaurus quickly decreases as their rank increase. In the experiments of Section 4, we built negative examples from positive examples by turning each positive example (A,B) into two negative examples: (A, *rank 10 A neighbor*) and (B, *rank 10 B neighbor*). Choosing neighbors with a higher rank would have guaranteed fewer false negative examples but taking neighbors with a rather small rank for building negative examples is more useful in terms of discrimination.

4 Experiments and evaluation

4.1 Building of distributional thesauri

The first step of the work we present is the building of two distributional thesauri: the thesaurus of mono-terms to improve (A2ST) and a thesaurus of compounds (A2ST-comp). Similarly to (Ferret, 2012), they were both built from the AQUAINT-2 corpus, a 380 million-word corpus of news articles in English. The building procedure, defined by (Ferret, 2010), was also identical to (Ferret, 2012), with distributional contexts compared with the Cosine measure and made of window-based lemmatized cooccurrents (1 word before and after) weighted by Positive Pointwise Mutual Information (PPMI). For the thesaurus of compounds, a preprocessing step was added to identify nominal compounds in texts. This identification was done in two steps: first, a set of compounds were extracted from the AQUAINT-2 corpus by relying on a restricted set of morpho-syntactic patterns applied by the Multiword Expression Toolkit (`mwetoolkit`) (Ramisch et al., 2010); then, the most frequent compounds in this set (frequency > 100) were selected as reference and their occurrences in the AQUAINT-2 corpus were identified by applying the longest-match strategy to the output of the *TreeTagger* part-of-speech tagger (Schmid, 1994)[1]. Finally, distributional contexts made of mono-terms and compounds were built as stated above and neighbors were found for 29,174 compounds.

4.2 Example selection

We applied the three rules of Section 3 with all the entries of our thesaurus of compounds and the upper half in frequency of our mono-term entries. For mono-terms, we only took the first neighbor ($m = 1$) of each entry because of the rather low performance of the initial thesaurus while for compounds, a larger value ($c = 3$) was chosen for enlarging the number of selected examples since neighbors were globally more reliable (see results of Table 2). As the selection method makes the definition of a development set quite difficult, the values of these two parameters were chosen in a conservative way.

Table 1 gives for each rule and two combinations of them the number of selected positive examples (#pos. ex.) and the percentage of positive (%good pos.) and negative examples (%bad neg.) found in our Gold Standard resource for thesaurus evaluation. This resource results from the union of the synonyms of WordNet 3.0 and the associated words of the Moby thesaurus. Table 1 also gives the same data for examples selected by the method of (Ferret, 2012) (*symmetry* row, *sym.* for short), based on the fact that as similarity relations are symmetric, a pair of words (A,B) are more likely to be similar if the first neighbor of A is B and the first neighbor of B is A. The data for the union of the examples produced by the two methods also appear in Table 1.

[1] Longest-match strategy: if C1 is a reference compound that is part of a reference compound C2, the identification of an occurrence of C2 blocks out the identification of the associated occurrence of C1.

method	%good pos.	%bad neg.	#pos. ex.
symmetry	59.7	12.4	796
(1)	56.9	16.1	921
(2)	44.7	14.7	308
(3)	46.2	16.9	40
rules (1,2)	53.0	16.1	1,115
rules (1,2,3)	52.4	15.9	1,131
sym. + (1,2)	**54.3**	**15.0**	**1,710**
sym. + (1,2,3)	53.9	14.5	1,725

Table 1: Selection of examples.

Concerning the method we propose, Table 1 shows that rule (3), which is a priori the least reliable of the three rules as it only requires similarity and not equality for both heads and modifiers, actually produces a very small set of examples that tends to degrade global results. As a consequence, only the combination of rules (1) and (2) is used thereafter (row in bold). Table 1 also suggests that the heads of two semantically linked compounds are more likely to be actually linked themselves if they have the same modifier than the modifiers of two semantically linked compounds having the same head. This confirms our expectation that the head of a compound is more related to the meaning of the compound than its modifier. More globally, Table 1 shows that the *symmetry* method has higher results than the second one but their association produces an interesting compromise between the number of examples, 1,710, and its error rate, 45.7. The fact that the two methods only share 201 noun pairs also illustrates their complementarity.

4.3 Reranking evaluation

For our SVM models, we adopted the RBF kernel, as (Hagiwara et al., 2009), and a grid search strategy for optimizing both the γ and C parameters by applying a 5-fold cross validation procedure to our training set and adopting the precision measure as the evaluation function to optimize. The models were built with LIBSVM (Chang and Lin, 2001) and then applied to the neighbors of our initial thesaurus.

Table 2 gives the results of the reranking for both the method we propose, *compound* (*comp.* for short), with examples selected by rules (1) and

(2), and the one of (Ferret, 2012), *symmetry*. In either case, they correspond to an intrinsic evaluation achieved by comparing the semantic neighbors of each thesaurus entry with the synonyms and related words of our Gold Standard resource for that entry. 12,243 entries with frequency > 10 were present in this resource and evaluated in such a way. As the neighbors are ranked according to their similarity value with their entry, we adopted the classical evaluation measures of Information Retrieval by replacing documents with synonyms and queries with entries: R-precision (R-prec.), Mean Average Precision (MAP) and precision at different cut-offs (1, 5 and 10).

More precisely, the *initial* row of Table 2 gives the values of these measures for our initial thesaurus of mono-terms while its *A2ST-comp* row corresponds to the measures for our thesaurus of compounds. It should be note that in the case of the A2ST-comp thesaurus, the number of evaluated entries is very small, restricted to 813 entries, with also a very small number of reference synonyms by entry. Hence, the results of the evaluation of A2ST-comp have to be considered with caution even if their high level for the very first semantic neighbors tends to confirm the positive impact of the low level of ambiguity of compounds compared to mono-terms.

The two following rows gives the results of the thesauri built from the best models of (Baroni et al., 2014), *B14-count* for the count model, whose main parameters are close or identical to ours, and *B14-predict* for the predict model, built from (Mikolov et al., 2013). These results first illustrate the known importance of corpus size, as the (Baroni et al., 2014)'s corpus is more than 7 times larger than ours, and the fact that for building thesauri, the count model is superior to the predict model. This last observation is confirmed by the results of the skip-gram model of (Mikolov et al., 2013) with its best parameters[2] for our corpus (5th row), which clearly exhibits worst results than *initial*. For this *Mikolov* thesaurus and the following reranked ones, each value corresponds to the difference between the measure for the considered thesaurus and the measure for the initial thesaurus. All these differences were found statistically significant according to a paired Wilcoxon test with p-value < 0.05.

[2]word2vec -cbow 0 -size 600 -window 10 -negative 0 -hs 0 -sample 1e-5

Thesaurus	**R-prec.**	**MAP**	**P@1**	**P@5**	**P@10**
initial (A2ST)	7.7	5.6	22.5	14.1	10.8
A2ST-comp	32.7	39.5	34.9	12.3	7.1
B14-count	12.5	9.8	31.9	19.6	15.2
B14-pred	10.9	8.5	30.3	18.4	13.8
Mikolov	-2.2	-1.4	-6.2	-4.6	-3.8
symmetry	+0.3	+0.1	+2.1	+0.8	+0.6
compound	+0.1	+0.0	+2.0	+0.9	+0.6
sym.+comp.	+0.3	+0.2	+2.8	+1.2	+0.9
RRF	+0.7	+0.6	+3.7	+1.9	+1.4
borda	+0.7	+0.5	+3.6	+1.7	+1.3
condorcet	+0.5	+0.4	+3.4	+1.6	+1.2
CombSum	+0.9	+0.8	**+4.7**	**+2.2**	**+1.5**
CS-w-Mik	**+1.2**	**+1.4**	+4.2	+2.0	**+1.5**

Table 2: Evaluation of our initial thesaurus and its reranked versions (values = percentages).

The analysis of the next two rows of Table 2 first shows that each criterion used for reranking our initial thesaurus leads to a global increase of results. The extent of this increase is quite similar for the two criteria: *symmetry* slightly outperforms *compound* but the difference is not significant. This increase is higher for P@{1,5,10} than for R-precision and MAP, which can be explained by the high number of synonyms and related words, 38.7 on average, that an entry of our initial thesaurus has in our reference. Hence, even a significant increase of P@{1,5,10} may have a modest impact on R-precision and MAP as the overall recall, equal to 9.8%, is low.

4.4 Thesaurus fusion

Having several thesauri reranked according to different criteria offers the opportunity to apply ensemble methods. Such idea was already experimented in (Curran, 2002) for thesauri built with different parameters (window or syntactic based cooccurrents, etc). We tested more particularly two general strategies for data fusion (Atrey et al., 2010): early and late fusions. The first one consists in our case in fusing the training sets built from our two criteria. As for each criterion, a classifier is then built from the fused training set and applied for reranking the initial thesaurus (see the *sym.+comp.* row of Table 2).

Table 3 illustrates qualitatively the impact of this first strategy for the entry *esteem*. Its **WordNet** row gives all the synonyms for this entry in WordNet while its Moby row gives the first related words for this entry in Moby. In our *initial*

WordNet	respect, admiration, regard
Moby	admiration, appreciation, acceptance, dignity, regard, respect, account, adherence, consideration, estimate, estimation, fame, greatness, homage + 79 words more
initial	cordiality, gratitude, **admiration**, comradeship, back-scratching, perplexity, **respect**, ruination, appreciation, neighbourliness ...
sym.+comp.	**respect**, **admiration**, trust, recognition, gratitude, confidence, affection, understanding, solidarity, dignity, appreciation, **regard**, sympathy, acceptance ...

Table 3: Reranking for the entry *esteem* with the early fusion strategy.

thesaurus, the first two neighbors of *esteem* that are present in our reference resources are *admiration* (rank 3) and *respect* (rank 7). The reranking produces a thesaurus in which these two words appear as the first two neighbors of the entry while its third synonym in WordNet raises from rank 22 to rank 12. Moreover, the number of neighbors among the first 14 ones that are present in Moby increases from 3 to 6.

The late fusion strategy relies on the methods used in Information Retrieval for merging ranked lists of retrieved documents. More precisely, we experimented the Borda, Condorcet (Nuray and Can, 2006) and Reciprocal Rank (RRF) (Cormack et al., 2009) fusions based on ranks and the CombSum fusion based on similarity values, normalized in our case with the Zero-one method (Wu et al., 2006). The corresponding thesauri were built by fusing, entry by entry, the lists of neighbors coming from the *initial*, *symmetry* and *compound* thesauri.

Table 2 first shows that all the thesauri produced by our ensemble methods outperform our first three thesauri, which confirms that *initial*, *symmetry* and *compound* can bring complementary information, exploited by the fusion. It also shows that our late fusion methods are more effective than our early fusion method. However, no specific element advocates at this stage for a generalization of this observation. The evaluation reported by Table 2 also suggests that for fusing distributional thesauri, the similarity of a neighbor with its entry is a more relevant criterion than its rank. Among the rank based methods, we observe that *RRF* is clearly superior to *condorcet* but only weakly superior to *borda*. Finally, the last row of Table 2 – *CS-w-Mik* – illustrates one step further the interest of ensemble methods for distributional thesauri: whereas the "Mikolov thesaurus" gets the worst results among all the thesauri of Table 2, adding it to the *initial*, *symmetry* and *compound* thesauri in the *CombSum* method leads to improve both R-precision and MAP, with a only small decrease of P@1 and P@5. From a more global perspective, it is interesting to note that our best method, *CombSum*, clearly outperforms the reranking method of (Ferret, 2013) with the same initial starting point.

5 Conclusion and perspectives

In this article, we have presented a method based on bootstrapping for improving distributional thesauri. More precisely, we have proposed a new criterion, based on the relations of mono-terms in similar compounds, for the unsupervised selection of training examples used for reranking the semantic neighbors of a thesaurus. We have evaluated two different strategies for combining this criterion with an already existing one and showed that a late fusion approach based on the merging of lists of neighbors is particularly effective compared to an early fusion approach based on the merging of training sets.

We plan to extend this work by studying how the combination of the unsupervised selection of examples and their use for training supervised classifiers can be exploited for improving distributional thesauri through feature selection. We will also investigated the interest of taking into account word senses in this framework, as in (Huang et al., 2012) or (Reisinger and Mooney, 2010).

References

Pradeep K. Atrey, M. Anwar Hossain, Abdulmotaleb El Saddik, and Mohan S. Kankanhalli. 2010. Multimodal fusion for multimedia analysis: a survey. *Multimedia Systems*, 16(6):345–379.

Marco Baroni, Georgiana Dinu, and Germán Kruszewski. 2014. Don't count, predict! a systematic comparison of context-counting vs. context-predicting semantic vectors. In *52nd Annual Meeting of the Association for Computational Linguistics (ACL 2014)*, pages 238–247, Baltimore, Maryland.

Bartosz Broda, Maciej Piasecki, and Stan Szpakowicz. 2009. Rank-Based Transformation in Measuring Semantic Relatedness. In 22nd *Canadian Conference on Artificial Intelligence*, pages 187–190.

Chih-Chung Chang and Chih-Jen Lin. 2001. LIBSVM: a library for support vector machines. http://www.csie.ntu.edu.tw/~cjlin/libsvm.

Gordon V. Cormack, Charles L. A. Clarke, and Stefan Buettcher. 2009. Reciprocal rank fusion outperforms condorcet and individual rank learning methods. In 32nd *International ACM SIGIR Conference on Research and Development in Information Retrieval (SIGIR'09)*, pages 758–759.

James R. Curran and Marc Moens. 2002. Improvements in automatic thesaurus extraction. In *Workshop of the ACL Special Interest Group on the Lexicon (SIGLEX)*, pages 59–66, Philadelphia, USA.

James Curran. 2002. Ensemble methods for automatic thesaurus extraction. In *2002 Conference on Empirical Methods in Natural Language Processing (EMNLP 2002)*, pages 222–229.

Georgiana Dinu and Mirella Lapata. 2010. Measuring distributional similarity in context. In *2010 Conference on Empirical Methods in Natural Language Processing (EMNLP 2010)*, pages 1162–1172, MIT, Massachusetts, USA.

Katrin Erk and Sebastian Pado. 2010. Exemplar-based models for word meaning in context. In 48th*th Annual Meeting of the Association for Computational Linguistics (ACL 2010), short paper*, pages 92–97, Uppsala, Sweden, July.

Olivier Ferret. 2010. Testing semantic similarity measures for extracting synonyms from a corpus. In *Seventh conference on International Language Resources and Evaluation (LREC'10)*, Valletta, Malta.

Olivier Ferret. 2012. Combining bootstrapping and feature selection for improving a distributional thesaurus. In 20th *European Conference on Artificial Intelligence (ECAI 2012)*, pages 336–341, Montpellier, France.

Olivier Ferret. 2013. Identifying bad semantic neighbors for improving distributional thesauri. In 51st *Annual Meeting of the Association for Computational Linguistics (ACL 2013)*, pages 561–571, Sofia, Bulgaria.

Gregory Grefenstette. 1994. *Explorations in automatic thesaurus discovery*. Kluwer Academic Publishers.

Masato Hagiwara, Yasuhiro Ogawa, and Katsuhiko Toyama. 2009. Supervised synonym acquisition using distributional features and syntactic patterns. *Information and Media Technologies*, 4(2):59–83.

Eric H. Huang, Richard Socher, Christopher D. Manning, and Andrew Y. Ng. 2012. Improving word representations via global context and multiple word prototypes. In *50th Annual Meeting of the Association for Computational Linguistics (ACL'12)*, pages 873–882.

Jun'ichi Kazama, Stijn De Saeger, Kow Kuroda, Masaki Murata, and Kentaro Torisawa. 2010. A bayesian method for robust estimation of distributional similarities. In 48th *Annual Meeting of the Association for Computational Linguistics*, pages 247–256, Uppsala, Sweden.

Dekang Lin. 1998. Automatic retrieval and clustering of similar words. In 17th *International Conference on Computational Linguistics and* 36th *Annual Meeting of the Association for Computational Linguistics (ACL-COLING'98)*, pages 768–774, Montral, Canada.

Tomas Mikolov, Wen-tau Yih, and Geoffrey Zweig. 2013. Linguistic regularities in continuous space word representations. In *2013 Conference of the North American Chapter of the Association for Computational Linguistics: Human Language Technologies (NAACL HLT 2013)*, pages 746–751, Atlanta, Georgia.

Jeffrey Mitchell and Mirella Lapata. 2010. Composition in distributional models of semantics. *Cognitive Science*, 34(8):1388–1439.

Rabia Nuray and Fazli Can. 2006. Automatic ranking of information retrieval systems using data fusion. *Information Processing and Management*, 42(3):595–614.

Sebastian Padó and Mirella Lapata. 2007. Dependency-based construction of semantic space models. *Computational Linguistics*, 33(2):161–199.

Muntsa Padró, Marco Idiart, Aline Villavicencio, and Carlos Ramisch. 2014. Nothing like good old frequency: Studying context filters for distributional thesauri. In *2014 Conference on Empirical Methods in Natural Language Processing (EMNLP 2014)*, pages 419–424, Doha, Qatar.

Denis Paperno, Nghia The Pham, and Marco Baroni. 2014. A practical and linguistically-motivated approach to compositional distributional semantics. In 52nd *Annual Meeting of the Association for Computational Linguistics (ACL 2014)*, pages 90–99, Baltimore, Maryland.

Tamara Polajnar and Stephen Clark. 2014. Improving distributional semantic vectors through context selection and normalisation. In 14th *Conference of the European Chapter of the Association for Computational Linguistics (EACL 2014)*, pages 230–238, Gothenburg, Sweden.

Carlos Ramisch, Aline Villavicencio, and Christian Boitet. 2010. mwetoolkit: a Framework for Multiword Expression Identification. In *Seventh International Conference on Language Resources and Evaluation (LREC 2010)*, Valetta, Malta, May.

Joseph Reisinger and Raymond J. Mooney. 2010. Multi-prototype vector-space models of word meaning. In *Human Language Technologies: The 2010 Annual Conference of the North American Chapter of the Association for Computational Linguistics (HLT-NAACL 2010)*, pages 109–117, Los Angeles, California, June.

Helmut Schmid. 1994. Probabilistic part-of-speech tagging using decision trees. In *International Conference on New Methods in Language Processing*.

Shengli Wu, Fabio Crestani, and Yaxin Bi. 2006. Evaluating score normalization methods in data fusion. In *Third Asia Conference on Information Retrieval Technology (AIRS'06)*, pages 642–648. Springer-Verlag.

Kazuhide Yamamoto and Takeshi Asakura. 2010. Even unassociated features can improve lexical distributional similarity. In *Second Workshop on NLP Challenges in the Information Explosion Era (NLPIX 2010)*, pages 32–39, Beijing, China.

Maayan Zhitomirsky-Geffet and Ido Dagan. 2009. Bootstrapping Distributional Feature Vector Quality. *Computational Linguistics*, 35(3):435–461.

Dependency length minimisation effects in short spans: a large-scale analysis of adjective placement in complex noun phrases

Kristina Gulordava
University of Geneva
Kristina.Gulordava,

Paola Merlo
University of Geneva
Paola.Merlo@unige.ch

Benoit Crabbé
U. Paris Diderot/Inria/IUF
bcrabbe@
univ-paris-diderot.fr

Abstract

It has been extensively observed that languages minimise the distance between two related words. Dependency length minimisation effects are explained as a means to reduce memory load and for effective communication. In this paper, we ask whether they hold in typically short spans, such as noun phrases, which could be thought of being less subject to efficiency pressure. We demonstrate that minimisation does occur in short spans, but also that it is a complex effect: it is not only the length of the dependency that is at stake, but also the effect of the surrounding dependencies.

1 Introduction

One of the main goals in the study of language is to find explanations for those fundamental properties that are found in every human language. The observation that human languages appear to minimise the distance between any two related words – called the property of dependency length minimisation (DLM) — is a universal property that has been documented in sentence processing (Gibson, 1998; Hawkins, 1994; Hawkins, 2004; Demberg and Keller, 2008), in corpus properties of treebanks (Temperley, 2007; Futrell et al., 2015), in diachronic language change (Tily, 2010). Functional explanations have been proposed for this pervasive linguistic property. If speakers want to reduce memory load and maximise efficiency of processing, they will choose to produce and preferentially analyse constructions where words are linearised in such a way that minimises the total distance of related words.

The DLM principle can be stated as follows: if there exist possible alternative orderings of a phrase, the one with the shortest overall dependency length (DL) is preferred. We measure the length of a dependency as the number of words between the head and its dependent.

As an illustration, DLM principle is widely reported in the literature to explain the alternation of postverbal complements (Bresnan et al., 2007; Wasow, 2002). Consider, for example, the case when a verb has both a direct object (NP) and a prepositional complement or adjunct (PP). Two alternative orders of the verb complements are possible: VP_1 = V NP PP, whose length is DL_1 and VP_2 = V PP NP, whose length is DL_2. DL_1 is $DL(\text{V-NP}) + DL(\text{V-PP}) = |\text{NP}| + 1$; DL_2 is $DL(\text{V-NP}) + DL(\text{V-PP}) = |\text{PP}| + 1$. [1] If DL_1 is bigger than DL_2, then VP_2 is preferred over VP_1, despite the non-canonical V-PP-NP order.

While DLM has been demonstrated on a large scale and explanations have been proposed based on human sentence processing facts in the verbal domain, it is not clear what the effects of DLM are in the more limited nominal domain. If the explanations are really rooted in memory and efficiency, will they still hold in phrases that might span only a few words?

In this paper, we look at the structural factors that play a role in adjective-noun word order alternations in Romance languages. We choose Romance languages because they show a good amount of variation, making studies of DLM meaningful. This would not be the case in English, for instance, as English has no variation of word order placement in the noun phrase. Adjective placement in Romance is often studied in connection with semantic and lexical properties of adjectives (Bouchard, 1998; Cinque, 2010). There exists, however, a body of work which shows that structural syntactic properties like the size of adjective phrase also affect the adjective position (Abeillé and Godard, 2000; Thuilier, 2012).

We demonstrate that, unlike results for the ver-

[1] The minimal dependency length is equal to one when the head and its dependent are adjacent.

Proceedings of the 53rd Annual Meeting of the Association for Computational Linguistics and the 7th International Joint Conference on Natural Language Processing (Short Papers), pages 477–482,
Beijing, China, July 26-31, 2015.

	RightNP=Yes	RightNP=No
X=Left	$\|\beta\| - \|\alpha\|$	$2\|\beta\| + 1$
X=Right	$-3\|\alpha\| - 2$	$-2\|\alpha\| - 1$

Table 1: Dependency length difference for different types of noun phrases. By convention, we always calculate $DL_1 - DL_2$.

bal domain, it is not only the length of the dependency that is at stake, but also the effect of the surrounding dependencies.

2 Dependency length minimisation in the noun phrase

In applying the general principle of DLM to the dependency structure of noun phrases, our goal is to test to what extent the DLM principle predicts the observed adjective-noun word order alternation pattern in relatively short spans.

Consider a prototypical noun phrase with an adjective phrase as a modifier. We assume two possible placements for an adjective phrase: postnominal and prenominal. To simplify, we concentrate on noun phrases with only one adjective modifier adjacent to the noun. The adjective modifier can be a complex phrase with both left and right dependents (α and β, respectively, in Figure 1). The noun phrase can have parents and right modifiers (X and Y, respectively, in Figure 1). These alternative orderings yield different dependency lengths, as can be seen from Figure 1. By convention, we will always indicate the prenominal order as DL_1, and the postnominal order as DL_2. Their difference is always calculated as $DL_1 - DL_2$.

We consider all dependencies in a noun phrase and not only the length of the noun-adjective dependency. This is because we assume, as previously done, that DLM is global, and not a local, effect. Our analysis is a faithful interpretation of the very general DLM principle of Gildea and Temperley (2010) which is based on the overall dependency length of a sentence. We do no take other dependencies in the sentence into account, because their lengths are the same across DL_1 and DL_2. The difference $DL_1 - DL_2$ is therefore the difference between the overall dependency length of two sentences that differ only in their placement of one adjective.

The first panel, panel a, shows the case where the parent of the NP is on the left of it. The dependency length for the prenominal adjective structure is equal to $DL_1 = d'_1 + d'_2 = (|\alpha| + |\beta| + 1) + |\beta|$ and for the postnominal adjective structure is $DL_2 = d''_1 + d''_2 = |\alpha|$. The difference between these lengths is $2|\beta| + 1$, which means that $DL_1 > DL_2$ and suggests that the postnominal placement is always preferred.

Similarly, the second panel, panel b, in the figure shows how we calculate the dependency lengths when the parent of the NP is on its right. The difference of lengths is equal to $-2|\alpha| - 1$, yielding a preference for prenominal adjectives.

We also consider more complex noun phrases with at least one right dependent, which are very common in Romance languages (around 50% of noun phrases in our sample include, for instance, a complement, such as a relative clause). The third and fourth panels in Figure 1 illustrate the case where three dependencies should be taken into account. The calculations of these dependency lengths for the prenominal and postnominal alternatives yield the corresponding differences of $|\beta| - |\alpha|$ (in the case of a left external dependency) and $-3|\alpha| - 2$ (in the case of a right external dependency). These values are different from the dependency length differences for noun phrases without a right dependent (panel a and b). The comparison of the values, where RightNP=Yes is smaller than RightNP=No in both cases, suggests that the presence of a right dependent favours the prenominal placement of adjectives in comparison to the case of a simple noun phrase.

The differences in dependency lengths are summarized in Table 1. The expectations based on dependency length minimisation are as indicated in (1) below.

(1) a. the presence of a left dependent of an adjective favours the adjective's prenominal placement;

b. the presence of a right dependent of an adjective favours the adjective's postnominal placement;

c. when the external dependency is leftwards, X = right, (for canonical subjects, for example), then the adjective is prenominal, because the difference is negative and it is a function of α;

d. when the noun has a right dependent, the prenominal adjective position is more preferred than when there is no right dependent,

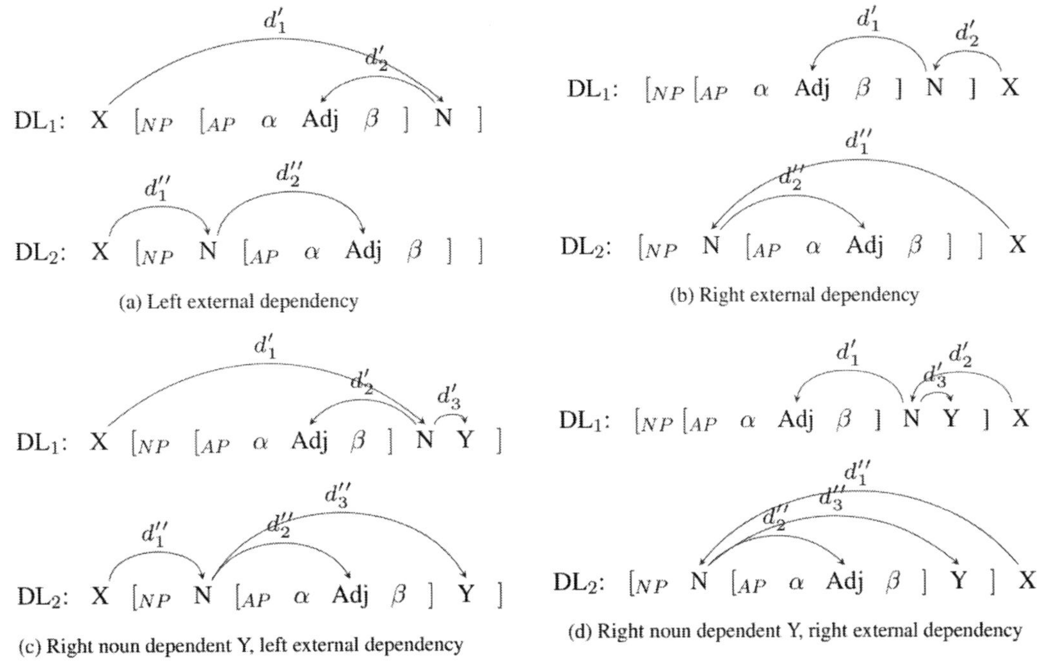

Figure 1: Noun phrase structure variants and the dependencies relevant for the DLM calculation.

as evinced by the fact that the RightNP = Yes column is always greater than the RightNP = No column.

The predictions (1a) and (1b) are formulated for an average case of adjective placement, across nouns phrases with different values of X and RightNP factors. Table 1 shows that for each combination of these context factors the weight of α is negative or zero and the weight of β is positive or zero. On average, therefore, we expect to see a negative effect of α (1a) and a positive effect of β (1b).

We develop a model to test which of the fine-grained predictions derived from DLM are confirmed by the data provided by the dependency annotated corpora of five of the main Romance languages.

3 Identifying dependency minimisation factors

3.1 Materials: Dependency treebanks

We use the dependency annotated corpora of five Romance languages: Catalan, Spanish, Italian (Hajič et al., 2009), French (Agić et al., 2015), and Portuguese (Buchholz and Marsi, 2006).

We use part-of-speech information and dependency arcs from the gold annotation to extract noun phrases containing adjectives. Specifically, we first convert all treebanks to coarse universal part-of-speech tags, using existing conventional mappings from the original tagset to the universal tagset (Petrov et al., 2012). We then identify all adjectives (tagged using the universal PoS tag 'ADJ') whose dependency head is a noun (tagged using the universal PoS tag 'NOUN'). In addition, we recover all elements of the noun phrase rooted in this noun, that is, its dependency subtree. For all languages where this information is available, we extract lemmas of adjective and noun tokens which are the features in our analysis. The only treebank without lemma annotation is French, for which we extract token forms.[2] We extract a total of around 64'000 instances of adjectives in noun phrases, ranging from 2'800 for Italian to 20'000 for Spanish.

The data present a substantial amount of variation in the placement of the adjective: the ratio of postnominal adjectives ranges from around 65%

[2] During preprocessing, we exclude all adjectives and nouns with non-lower case and non-alphabetic symbols which can include common names, compounds (in Spanish and Catalan treebanks), and English borrowings. In addition, we leave out noun phrases which have their elements separated by punctuation (for example, commas or parentheses) to ensure that the placement of adjective is not affected by an unusual structure of the noun phrase.

for Italian to 78% for Catalan. Among all adjective types, at least 10% in each language are observed both prenominally and postnominally (ranging between 147 types for Italian and 445 types for Spanish).

3.2 Method: Mixed Effects models

We analyse the interactions of several dependency factors, using a logit mixed effect models (Bates et al., 2014). Mixed-effect logistic regression models (logit models) are a type of Generalized Linear Mixed Models with the logit link function and are designed for binomially distributed outcomes such as $Order$ in our case.

More precisely, Generalized Linear Mixed Models describe an outcome as the linear combination of fixed effects X and conditional random effects Z associated with grouping of instances, where β and γ are the corresponding weights of the effects.

(2) $$y = X\beta + Z\gamma + \epsilon$$

In logistic regression models, this linear combination is then transformed with the logit link function to predict the binomial output:

(3) $$Order = \frac{1}{1 + \exp^{-y}}$$

In our model, $Order = 0$ codes the prenominal adjective order and $Order = 1$ codes the postnominal order.

3.3 Factors

We define and test the following factors, corresponding to the factors illustrated in Figure 1 and example (1), represented as binary or real-valued variables:

- *LeftAP* - the cumulative length (in words) of all left dependents of the adjective, indicated as α in Figure 1;
- *RightAP* - the cumulative length (in words) of all right dependents of the adjective, indicated as β in Figure 1;
- *RightNP* - the indicator variable representing the presence ($RightNP = 1$) or absence ($RightNP = 0$) of the right dependent of the noun, indicated as Y in Figure 1;
- *ExtDep* - the direction of the arc from the noun to its parent X, an indicator variable. $ExtDep = 0$ when X is on the left of the noun, $ExtDep = 1$ when X is on the right.

Predictor	β	SE	Z	p
Intercept	-0.17	(0.117)	-1.42	0.16
LeftAP	2.21	(0.101)	21.91	$< .001$
RightAP	0.76	(0.054)	14.08	$< .001$
ExtDep	-0.06	(0.071)	-0.85	0.40
RightNP	-0.77	(0.050)	-15.34	$< .001$

Random effects	Var
Adjective	1.989
Language	0.024

Table 2: Summary of the fixed and random effects in the mixed-effects logit model ($N = 15842$), shown in (4).

In addition, to account for lexical variation, we include adjective lemmas (for French, we include tokens) as grouping variables introducing random effects. For example, the instances of adjective-noun order for a particular adjective will share the same weight value γ for the adjective variable, but across different adjectives this value can vary.[3]

For a given example involving an adjective i and belonging to language j, the linear component of the model is shown in (4).

(4)
$$y_{ij} = LeftAP \cdot \beta_{LAP} + RightAP \cdot \beta_{RAP} + \\ + RightNP \cdot \beta_{RNP} + ExtDep \cdot \beta_{ED} + \\ + \gamma_{Adj_i} + \gamma_{Lang_j}$$

By fitting the logit mixed-effect model to our dataset, we find the fixed and random effects coefficients which best explain the data. To show that a factor has a statistically significant effect on adjective placement, we must show that its fixed effect coefficient is significantly different from zero.

3.4 Results

The logit mixed-effects model fitted to our data, shown in (4), reveals the following picture (Table 2).

Both the LeftAP and RightAP factors favour postnominal placement ($\beta_{LAP} = 2.21$, $\beta_{RAP} = 0.76, p < 0.001$), however there are important differences between the two.

[3]We include only random intercepts because the size of the data is not sufficient to estimate the slope variables. In addition, for a robust estimation of the random effects, we include in our dataset only adjectives that are observed both prenominally and postnominally.

LeftAP shows a complex behavior. When LeftAP is equal to one, it favors (slightly) the prenominal placement and when LeftAP is greater than one, it favors the postnominal placement. This result suggests that the adjective can behave differently depending on the size or type of its left periphery. For the moment it is not clear if the difference is due to length or type, as LeftAP of length one are almost always adverbs. It is important to notice that the results for LeftAP then do not entirely pattern with the predictions of dependency length minimisation, shown in (1a).

The RightAP factor shows a consistent postnominal preference, positively correlated to its length. Consequently, we can say that the RightAP is a stronger indicator of the postnominal placement than LeftAP, in agreement with the previously observed ordering patterns of adjective phrases (Abeillé and Godard, 2000) and the DLM prediction.

The external dependency factor is not significant ($p > 0.1$). Moreover, the log likelihood ratio between the full model and the model without *ExtDep* is χ^2 distributed with 1 degree of freedom with $\chi^2 = 3.8, p = 0.052$. This comparison confirms that the introduction of the external dependency does not help predicting the Order. At first sight, this result suggests that this dependency is not subject to the minimisation principle. A plausible explanation claims that only the dependencies between the head and the *edge* of the dependent phrase are minimised (Hawkins, 1994). In Romance languages, the majority of the noun phrases take an article which unambiguously defines the left edge of the noun phrase. There is no need therefore to minimize the external dependency to the noun, since the noun phrase can be entirely predicted based on its left corner.

The RightNP factor is significant in the fitted model ($\beta_{RNP} = -0.77, p < 0.001$).[4] The presence of a noun dependent on the right of the noun favours a prenominal placement, as predicted by DLM (1d). This is a result which, to our knowledge, was not previously observed in the literature, and that clearly answers our initial question, confirming that DLM also applies to very short spans. A much more detailed study of the lexical and structural properties of this effect is developed in (Gulordava and Merlo, 2015).

[4] A log-likelihood test of the model including RightAP, LeftAP and RightNP factors compared to the model including only RightAP and LeftAP factors yields $\chi^2 = 107$ and $p < .001$.

4 Conclusion

In this paper, we have developed a model of dependency length minimisation in the noun phrase and shown subtle interactions among its subcomponents. We show that most of DLM predictions are confirmed, and that DLM also apply to short spans. The fact that DLM effects also hold in such short spans casts doubts, in our opinion, on the grounding of this effect in memory limitations. The subtle interactions also raise questions on the exact definition of what dependencies are minimised and to what extent a given dependency annotation captures these distinctions, questions that we reserve for future work.

Acknowledgements

We gratefully acknowledge the partial funding of this work by the Swiss National Science Foundation, under grant 144362 to the second author. Thanks also to the Labex EFL (ANR-10-LABX-0083 EFL) in Paris for supporting the visit of the first author.

References

Anne Abeillé and Daniele Godard. 2000. French word order and lexical weight. In Robert D. Borsley, editor, *The nature and function of Syntactic Categories*, volume 32 of *Syntax and Semantics*, pages 325–360. BRILL.

Željko Agić, Maria Jesus Aranzabe, Aitziber Atutxa, Cristina Bosco, Jinho Choi, Marie-Catherine de Marneffe, Timothy Dozat, Richárd Farkas, Jennifer Foster, Filip Ginter, Iakes Goenaga, Koldo Gojenola, Yoav Goldberg, Jan Hajič, Anders Trærup Johannsen, Jenna Kanerva, Juha Kuokkala, Veronika Laippala, Alessandro Lenci, Krister Lindén, Nikola Ljubešić, Teresa Lynn, Christopher Manning, Héctor Alonso Martínez, Ryan McDonald, Anna Missilä, Simonetta Montemagni, Joakim Nivre, Hanna Nurmi, Petya Osenova, Slav Petrov, Jussi Piitulainen, Barbara Plank, Prokopis Prokopidis, Sampo Pyysalo, Wolfgang Seeker, Mojgan Seraji, Natalia Silveira, Maria Simi, Kiril Simov, Aaron Smith, Reut Tsarfaty, Veronika Vincze, and Daniel Zeman. 2015. Universal dependencies 1.1.

Douglas Bates, Martin Maechler, Ben Bolker, and Steven Walker, 2014. *lme4: Linear mixed-effects models using Eigen and S4*. R package version 1.1-7.

Denis Bouchard. 1998. The distribution and interpretation of adjectives in French: A consequence of Bare Phrase Structure. *Probus*, 10(2):139–184.

Joan Bresnan, Anna Cueni, Tatiana Nikitina, and Harald Baayen. 2007. Predicting the dative alternation. In G. Boume, I. Kraemer, and J. Zwarts, editors, *Cognitive Foundations of Interpretation*, pages 69–94. Royal Netherlands Academy of Science, Amsterdam.

Sabine Buchholz and Erwin Marsi. 2006. CoNLL-X Shared Task on Multilingual Dependency Parsing. In *Proceedings of the Tenth Conference on Computational Natural Language Learning*, CoNLL-X '06, pages 149–164, Stroudsburg, PA, USA. Association for Computational Linguistics.

Guglielmo Cinque. 2010. *The Syntax of Adjectives: A Comparative Study*. MIT Press.

Vera Demberg and Frank Keller. 2008. Data from eye-tracking corpora as evidence for theories of syntactic processing complexity. *Cognition*, 109(2):193–210, November.

Richard Futrell, Kyle Mahowald, and Edward Gibson. 2015. Large-Scale Evidence of Dependency Length Minimization in 37 Languages. (Submitted to Proceedings of the National Academy of Sciences of the United States of America).

Edward Gibson. 1998. Linguistic complexity: Locality of syntactic dependencies. *Cognition*, 68(1):1–76.

Daniel Gildea and David Temperley. 2010. Do Grammars Minimize Dependency Length? *Cognitive Science*, 34(2):286–310.

Kristina Gulordava and Paola Merlo. 2015. Structural and lexical factors in adjective placement in complex noun phrases across Romance languages. In *Proceedings of the Nineteenth Conference on Computational Natural Language Learning (CoNLL'15)*.

Jan Hajič, Massimiliano Ciaramita, Richard Johansson, Daisuke Kawahara, Maria Antònia Martí, Lluís Màrquez, Adam Meyers, Joakim Nivre, Sebastian Padó, Jan Štěpánek, Pavel Straňák, Mihai Surdeanu, Nianwen Xue, and Yi Zhang. 2009. The CoNLL-2009 shared task: syntactic and semantic dependencies in multiple languages. In *Proceedings of the Thirteenth Conference on Computational Natural Language Learning: Shared Task*, CoNLL '09, pages 1–18, Stroudsburg, PA, USA. Association for Computational Linguistics.

John A Hawkins. 1994. *A performance theory of order and constituency*. Cambridge University Press, Cambridge.

John A. Hawkins. 2004. *Efficiency and Complexity in Grammars*. Oxford linguistics. Oxford University Press, Oxford, UK.

Slav Petrov, Dipanjan Das, and Ryan T. McDonald. 2012. A Universal Part-of-Speech Tagset. In *Proceedings of the Eight International Conference on Language Resources and Evaluation (LREC'12)*, pages 2089–2096, Istanbul, Turkey.

David Temperley. 2007. Minimization of dependency length in written English. *Cognition*, 105(2):300–333.

Juliette Thuilier. 2012. *Contraintes préférentielles et ordre des mots en français*. Ph.D. Thesis, Université Paris-Diderot - Paris VII, Sep.

Harry Joel Tily. 2010. *The role of processing complexity in word order variation and change*. Ph.D. Thesis, Stanford University.

Thomas Wasow. 2002. *Postverbal Behavior*. CSLI Publications.

Tagging Performance Correlates with Author Age

Dirk Hovy[1] and Anders Søgaard[1]
Center for Language Technology
University of Copenhagen, Denmark
Njalsgade 140, DK-2300 Copenhagen S
{dirk.hovy,soegaard}@hum.ku.dk

Abstract

Many NLP tools for English and German are based on manually annotated articles from the Wall Street Journal and Frankfurter Rundschau. The average readers of these two newspapers are middle-aged (55 and 47 years old, respectively), and the annotated articles are more than 20 years old by now. This leads us to speculate whether tools induced from these resources (such as part-of-speech taggers) put older language users at an advantage. We show that this is actually the case in both languages, and that the cause goes beyond simple vocabulary differences. In our experiments, we control for gender and region.

1 Introduction

One of the main challenges in natural language processing (NLP) is to correct for biases in the manually annotated data available to system engineers. Selection biases are often thought of in terms of textual domains, motivating work in domain adaptation of NLP models (Daume III and Marcu, 2006; Ben-David et al., 2007; Daume III, 2007; Dredze et al., 2007; Chen et al., 2009; Chen et al., 2011, inter alia). Domain adaptation problems are typically framed as adapting models that were induced on newswire to other domains, such as spoken language, literature, or social media.

However, newswire is not just a domain with particular conventions. It is also a source of information written by and for particular people. The reader base of most newspapers is older, richer, and more well-educated than the average population. Also, many newspapers have more readers in some regions of their country. In addition, newswire text is much more canonical than other domains, and includes fewer neologisms and non-standard language. Both, however, are frequent in the language use of young adults, who are the main drivers of language change (Holmes, 2013; Nguyen et al., 2014).

In this paper, we focus on the most widely used manually annotated resources for English and German, namely the English Penn Treebank and the TIGER Treebank for German. The English treebank consists of manually annotated Wall Street Journal articles from 1989. The TIGER Treebank consists of manually annotated Frankfurter Rundschau articles from the early 1990s. Both newspapers have regionally and demographically biased reader bases, e.g., with more old than young readers. We discuss the biases in §2.

In the light of recent research (Volkova et al., 2013; Hovy, 2015; Jørgensen et al., 2015), we explore the hypothesis that these biases transfer to NLP tools induced from these resources. As a result, these models perform better on texts written by certain people, namely those whose language is closer to the training data. Language dynamics being what they are, we expect English and German POS taggers to perform better on texts written by older people. To evaluate this hypothesis, we collected English and German user reviews from a user review site used by representative samples of the English and German populations. We annotated reviews written by users whose age, gender, and location were known with POS tags. The resulting data set enables us to test whether there are significant performance differences between ages, genders, and regions, while controlling for the two respective other, potentially confounding, factors.

Contribution We show that age bias leads to significant performance differences in off-the-shelf POS taggers for English and German. We also analyze the relevant linguistic differences between the age groups, and show that they are *not*

[1] Both authors contributed equally to the paper, and flipped a heavily biased coin until they were both satisfied with the order.

Proceedings of the 53rd Annual Meeting of the Association for Computational Linguistics and the 7th International Joint Conference on Natural Language Processing (Short Papers), pages 483–488,
Beijing, China, July 26-31, 2015.

solely lexical, but instead extend to the grammatical level. As a corollary, we also present several new evaluation datasets for English and German that allow us to control for age, gender, and location.

2 Data

2.1 Wall Street Journal and Frankfurter Rundschau

The *Wall Street Journal* is a New York City-based newspaper, in print since 1889, with about two million readers. It employs 2,000 journalists in 85 news bureaus across 51 countries. Wall Street Journal is often considered business-friendly, but conservative. In 2007, Rupert Murdoch bought the newspaper. The English Penn Treebank consists of manually annotated articles from 1989, including both essays, letters and errata, but the vast majority are news pieces.[1]

Frankfurter Rundschau is a German language newspaper based in Frankfurt am Main. Its first issue dates back to 1945, shortly after the end of the second world war. It has about 120,000 readers. It is often considered a left-wing liberal newspaper. According to a study conducted by the newspaper itself,[2] its readers are found in "comfortable" higher jobs, well-educated, and on average in their mid-forties. While the paper is available internationally, most of its users come from the Rhine-Main region.

2.2 The Trustpilot Corpus

The Trustpilot Corpus (Hovy et al., 2015a) consists of user reviews scraped from the multilingual website `trustpilot.com`. The reviewer base has been shown to be representative of the populations in the countries for which large reviewer bases exist, at least wrt. age, gender, and geographical spread (Hovy et al., 2015a). The language is more informal than newswire, but less creative than social media posts. This is similar to the language in the reviews section of the English Web Treebank.[3] For the experiments below, we annotated parts of the British and German sections of the Trustpilot Corpus with the tag set proposed in Petrov et al. (2011).

2.3 POS annotations

We use an in-house interface to annotate the English and German data. For each of the two languages, we annotate 600 sentences. The data is sampled in the following way: we first extract all reviews associated with a location, split and tokenize the review using the NLTK tokenizer for the respective language, and discard any sentences with fewer than three or more than 100 tokens. We then map each review to the NUTS region corresponding to the location. If the location name is ambiguous, we discard it.

We then run two POS taggers (TreeTagger[4], and a model implemented in CRF++[5]) to obtain log-likelihoods for each sentence in the English and German sub corpora. We normalize by sentence length and compute the average score for each region under each tagger.

We single out the two regions in England and Germany with the highest, respectively lowest, average log-likelihoods from both taggers. We do this to be able to control for dialectal variation. In each region, we randomly sample 200 reviews written by women under 35, 200 reviews written by men under 35, 200 reviews written by women over 45, and 200 reviews written by men over 45. This selection enables us to study and control for gender, region, and age.

While sociolinguistics agrees on language change between age groups (Barke, 2000; Schler et al., 2006; Barbieri, 2008; Rickford and Price, 2013), it is not clear where to draw the line. The age groups selected here are thus solely based on the availability of even-sized groups that are separated by 10 years.

3 Experiments

3.1 Training data and models

As training data for our POS tagging models, we use manually annotated data from the Wall Street Journal (English Penn Treebank) and Frankfurter Rundschau (TIGER). We use the training and test sections provided in the CoNLL 2006–7 shared tasks, but we convert all tags to the universal POS tag set (Petrov et al., 2011).

[1] `http://www.let.rug.nl/~bplank/metadata/genre_files_updated.html`

[2] `http://www.fr-online.de/wir-ueber-uns/studie-wer-sind-unsere-leser-,4353508,4356262.html`

[3] `https://catalog.ldc.upenn.edu/LDC2012T13`

[4] `http://www.cis.uni-muenchen.de/~schmid/tools/TreeTagger/`

[5] `http://taku910.github.io/crfpp/`

Our POS taggers are trained using TreeTagger with default parameters, and CRF++ with default parameters and standard POS features (Owoputi et al., 2013; Hovy et al., 2015b). We use two different POS tagger induction algorithms in order to be able to abstract away from their respective inductive biases. Generally, TreeTagger (TREET) performs better than CRF++ on German, whereas CRF++ performs best on English.

3.2 Results

country	group	TREET	CRF++	avg.
DE	U35	87.42	85.93	86.68
	O45	**89.39**	87.04	88.22
	male	88.53	86.11	87.32
	female	88.21	**86.78**	87.50
	highest reg.	88.46	86.49	87.48
	lowest reg.	88.85	87.41	88.13
EN	U35	87.92	88.23	88.08
	O45	**88.26**	**88.40**	88.33
	male	88.19	88.55	88.37
	female	87.97	88.08	88.03
	highest reg.	88.27	88.57	88.42
	lowest reg.	88.24	88.52	88.38

Table 1: POS accuracy on different demographic groups for English and German. Significant differences per tagger in bold

Table 1 shows the accuracies for both algorithms on the three demographic groups (age, gender, region) for German and English. We see that there are some consistent differences between the groups. In both languages, results for both taggers are better for the older group than for the younger one. In three out of the four cases, this difference is statistically significant at $p < 0.05$, according to a bootstrap-sample test. The difference between the genders is less pronounced, although we do see CRF++ reaching a significantly higher accuracy for women in German. For regions, we find that while the models assign low log-likelihood scores to some regions, this is not reflected in the accuracy.

As common in NLP, we treat American (training) and British English (test data) as variants. It is possible that this introduces a confounding factor. However, since we do not see marked effects for gender or region, and since the English results closely track the German data, this seems unlikely. We plan to investigate this in future work.

4 Analysis

The last section showed the performance differences between various groups, but it does not tell us where the differences come from. In this section, we try to look into potential causes, and analyze the tagging errors for systematic patterns. We focus on age, since this variable showed the largest differences between groups.

Holmes (2013) argues that people between 30 and 55 years use standard language the most, because of societal pressure from their workplace. Nguyen et al. (2014) made similar observations for Twitter. Consequently, both young and retired people often depart from the standard linguistic norms, young people because of innovation, older people because of adherence to previous norms. Our data suggests, however, that young people do so in ways that are more challenging for off-the-shelf NLP models induced on age-biased data. But what exactly are the linguistic differences that lead to lower performance for this group?

The obvious cause for the difference between age groups would be *lexical* change, i.e., the use of neologisms, spelling variation, or linguistic change at the structural level in the younger group. The resulting vocabulary differences between age groups would result in an increased out-of-vocabulary (OOV) rate in the younger group, which in turn negatively affects model performance.

While we do observe an unsurprising correlation between sentence-level performance and OOV-rate, the young reviewers in our sample do *not* use OOV words more often than the older age group. Both groups differ from the training data roughly equally. This strongly suggests that age-related differences in performance are *not* a result of OOV items.

In order to investigate whether the differences extend beyond the vocabulary, we compare the *tag* bigram distributions, both between the two age groups and between each group and the training data. We measure similarity by KL divergence between the distributions, and inspect the 10 tag bigrams which are most prevalent for either group. We use Laplace smoothing to

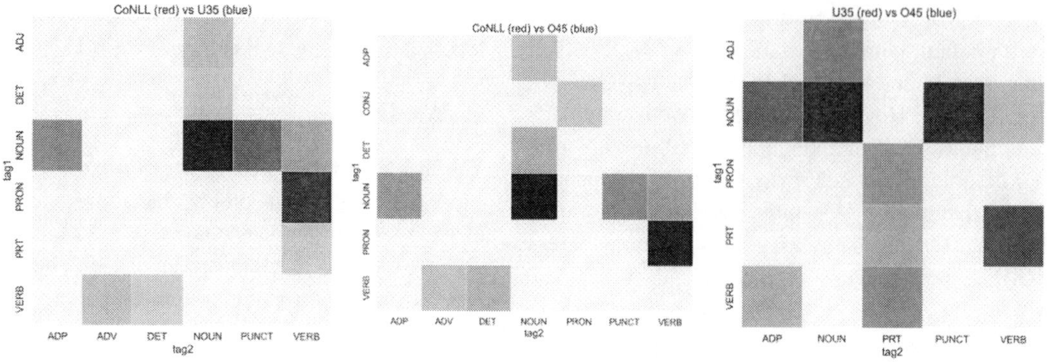

Figure 1: Tag bigrams with highest differences between distributions in English data.

account for missing bigrams and ensure a proper distribution.

For the English age groups, we find that a) the two Trustpilot data sets have a smaller KL divergence with respect to each other ($1.86e-6$) than either has with the training data (young: $3.24e-5$, old.: $2.36e-5$, respectively). We do note however, b), that the KL divergence for the older groups is much smaller than for the younger group. This means that there is a cross-domain effect, which is bigger, measured this way, than the difference in age groups. The age group difference in KL divergence, however, suggests that the two groups use different syntactic constructions.

Inspecting the bigrams which are most prevalent for each group, we find again that a) the Trustpilot groups show more instances involving verbs, such as PRON–VERB, VERB–ADV, and VERB–DET, while the English Penn Treebank data set has a larger proportion of instances of nominal constructions, such as NOUN–VERB, NOUN–ADP, and NOUN–NOUN.

On the other hand, we find that b) the younger group has more cases of verbal constructions and the use of particles, such as PRT–VERB, VERB–PRT, PRON–PRT, and VERB–ADP, while the older group–similar to the treebank–shows more instances of nominal constructions, i.e., again NOUN–VERB, ADJ–NOUN, NOUN–ADP, and NOUN–NOUN.

The heatmaps in Figure 1 show all pairwise comparisons between the three distributions. In the interest of space and visibility, we select the 10 bigrams that differ most from each other between the two distributions under comparison. The color indicates in which of the two distributions a bigram is more prevalent, and the degree of shading indicates the size of the difference.

For German, we see similar patterns. The Trustpilot data shows more instances of ADV–ADV, PRON–VERB, and ADV–VERB, while the TIGER treebank contains more NOUN–DET, NOUN–ADP, and NOUN–NOUN.

Again, the younger group is more dissimilar to the CoNLL data, but less so than for English, with CONJ–PRON, NOUN–VERB, VERB–VERB, and PRON–DET, while the older group shows more ADV–ADJ, ADP–NOUN, NOUN–ADV, and ADJ–NOUN.

In all of these cases, vocabulary does *not* factor into the differences, since we are at the POS level. The results indicate that there exist fundamental *grammatical* differences between the age groups, which go well beyond mere lexical differences. These findings are in line with the results in Johannsen et al. (2015), who showed that entire (delexicalized) dependency structures correlate with age and gender, often across several languages.

4.1 Tagging Error Analysis

Analyzing the tagging errors of our model can give us an insight into the constructions that differ most between groups.

In German, most of the errors in the younger group occur with adverbs, determiners, and verbs. Adverbs are often confused with adjectives, because adverbs and adjectives are used as modifiers in similar ways. The taggers also frequently confused adverbs with nouns, especially sentence-initially, presumably largely because they are capitalized. Sometimes, such errors are also due to spelling mistakes and/or English loanwords. Determiners are often incorrectly predicted to be pronouns, presumably due to homography: in German, *der*, *die*, *das*, etc. can be used as determiners, but also as relative pronouns, depending on the position. Verbs are often incorrectly predicted to be nouns. This last error is again mostly due to capitalization, homographs, and, again, English loanwords. Another interesting source is sentence-initial use of verbs, which is unusual in canonical German declarative sentences, but common in informal language, where pronouns are dropped, i.e, "[Ich] Kann mich nicht beschweren" (*[I] Can't complain*).

Errors involving verbs are much less frequent in the older group, where errors with adjectives and nouns are more frequent.

For English, the errors in the younger and older group are mostly on the same tags (nouns, adjectives, and verbs). Nouns often get mis-tagged as VERB, usually because of homography due to null-conversion (*ordering*, *face*, *needs*). Adjectives are also most commonly mis-tagged as VERB, almost entirely due to homography in participles (*-ed*, *-ing*). We see more emoticons (labeled X) in the younger group, and some of them end up with incorrect tags (NOUN or ADV). There are no mis-tagged emoticons in the older group, who generally uses fewer emoticons (see also Hovy et al. (2015a)).

5 Conclusion

In this position paper, we show that some of the common training data sets bias NLP tools towards the language of older people. I.e., there is a statistically significant correlation between tagging performance and age for models trained on CoNLL data. A study of the actual differences between age groups shows that they go beyond the vocabulary, and extend to the grammatical level.

The results suggest that NLP's focus on a limited set of training data has serious consequences for model performance on new data sets, but also demographic groups. Due to language dynamics and the age of the data sets, performance degrades significantly for younger speakers. Since POS tagging is often the first step in any NLP pipeline, performance differences are likely to increase downstream. As a result, we risk disadvantaging younger groups when it comes to the benefits of NLP.

The case study shows that our models are susceptible to the effects of language change and demographic factors. Luckily, the biases are not *inherent* to the models, but reside mostly in the data. The problem can thus mostly be addressed with more thorough training data selection that takes demographic factors into account. It does highlight, however, that we also need to develop more robust technologies that are less susceptible to data biases.

Acknowledgements

We would like to thank the anonymous reviewers for their comments, which helped improve the paper. This research is funded by the ERC Starting Grant LOWLANDS No. 313695.

References

Federica Barbieri. 2008. Patterns of age-based linguistic variation in American English. *Journal of sociolinguistics*, 12(1):58–88.

Andrew J Barke. 2000. The Effect of Age on the Style of Discourse among Japanese Women. In *Proceedings of the 14th Pacific Asia Conference on Language, Information and Computation*, pages 23–34.

Shai Ben-David, John Blitzer, Koby Crammer, and Fernando Pereira. 2007. Analysis of representations for domain adaptation. In *NIPS*.

Bo Chen, Wai Lam, Ivor Tsang, and Tak-Lam Wong. 2009. Extracting discriminative concepts for domain adaptation in text mining. In *KDD*.

Minmin Chen, Killiang Weinberger, and John Blitzer. 2011. Co-training for domain adaptation. In *NIPS*.

Hal Daume III and Daniel Marcu. 2006. Domain adaptation for statistical classifiers. *Journal of Artificial Intelligence Research*, 26:101–126.

Hal Daume III. 2007. Frustratingly easy domain adaptation. In *Proceedings of ACL*.

Mark Dredze, John Blitzer, Partha Pratim Talukdar, Kuzman Ganchev, João Graca, and Fernando Pereira. 2007. Frustratingly Hard Domain Adaptation for Dependency Parsing. In *EMNLP-CoNLL*.

Janet Holmes. 2013. *An introduction to sociolinguistics*. Routledge.

Dirk Hovy, Anders Johannsen, and Anders Søgaard. 2015a. User review-sites as a source for large-scale sociolinguistic studies. In *Proceedings of WWW*.

Dirk Hovy, Barbara Plank, Héctor Martínez Alonso, and Anders Søgaard. 2015b. Mining for unambiguous instances to adapt pos taggers to new domains. In *Proceedings of NAACL-HLT*.

Dirk Hovy. 2015. Demographic factors improve classification performance. In *Proceedings of ACL*.

Anders Johannsen, Dirk Hovy, and Anders Søgaard. 2015. Cross-lingual syntactic variation over age and gender. In *Proceedings of CoNLL*.

Anna Jørgensen, Dirk Hovy, and Anders Søgaard. 2015. Challenges of studying and processing dialects in social media. In *Workshop on Noisy User-generated Text (W-NUT)*.

Dong Nguyen, Dolf Trieschnigg, A. Seza Doğruöz, Rilana Gravel, Mariet Theune, Theo Meder, and Franciska De Jong. 2014. Predicting Author Gender and Age from Tweets: Sociolinguistic Theories and Crowd Wisdom. In *Proceedings of COLING 2014*.

Olutobi Owoputi, Brendan O'Connor, Chris Dyer, Kevin Gimpel, Nathan Schneider, and Noah A Smith. 2013. Improved part-of-speech tagging for online conversational text with word clusters. In *Proceedings of NAACL*.

Slav Petrov, Dipanjan Das, and Ryan McDonald. 2011. A universal part-of-speech tagset. CoRR abs/1104.2086.

John Rickford and Mackenzie Price. 2013. Girlz ii women: Age-grading, language change and stylistic variation. *Journal of Sociolinguistics*, 17(2):143–179.

Jonathan Schler, Moshe Koppel, Shlomo Argamon, and James W Pennebaker. 2006. Effects of age and gender on blogging. In *AAAI Spring Symposium: Computational Approaches to Analyzing Weblogs*, volume 6, pages 199–205.

Svitlana Volkova, Theresa Wilson, and David Yarowsky. 2013. Exploring demographic language variations to improve multilingual sentiment analysis in social media. In *Proceedings of EMNLP*, pages 1815–1827.

User Based Aggregation for Biterm Topic Model

Weizheng Chen, Jinpeng Wang, Yan Zhang , Hongfei Yan and Xiaoming Li

School of Electronic Engineering and Computer Science, Peking University, China
{cwz.pku,wjp.pku,yhf1029}@gmail.com, zhy@cis.pku.edu.cn, lxm@pku.edu.cn

Abstract

Biterm Topic Model (BTM) is designed to model the generative process of the word co-occurrence patterns in short texts such as tweets. However, two aspects of BTM may restrict its performance: 1) user individualities are ignored to obtain the corpus level words co-occurrence patterns; and 2) the strong assumptions that two co-occurring words will be assigned the same topic label could not distinguish background words from topical words. In this paper, we propose Twitter-BTM model to address those issues by considering user level personalization in BTM. Firstly, we use user based biterms aggregation to learn user specific topic distribution. Secondly, each user's preference between background words and topical words is estimated by incorporating a background topic. Experiments on a large-scale real-world Twitter dataset show that Twitter-BTM outperforms several state-of-the-art baselines.

1 Introduction

In recent years, short texts are increasingly prevalent due to the explosive growth of online social media. For example, about 500 million tweets are published per day on Twitter[1], one of the most popular online social networking services. Probabilistic topic models (Blei et al., 2003) are broadly used to uncover the hidden topics of tweets, since the low-dimensional semantic representation is crucial for many applications, such as product recommendation (Zhao et al., 2014), hashtag recommendation (Ma et al., 2014), user interest tracking (Sasaki et al., 2014), sentiment analysis (Si et al., 2013). However, the scarcity of context and the noisy words restrict LDA and its variations in topic modeling over short texts.

Previous works model topic distribution at three different levels for tweets: 1) document, the standard LDA assumes each document is associated with a topic distribution (Godin et al., 2013; Huang, 2012). LDA and its variations suffer from context sparsity in each tweet. 2) user, user based aggregation is utilized to alleviate the sparsity problem in short texts (Weng et al., 2010; Hong and Davison, 2010). In these models, all the tweets of the same user are aggregated together as a pseudo document based on the observation that the tweets written by the same user are more similar. 3) corpus, BTM (Yan et al., 2013) assumes that all the biterms (co-occurring word pairs) are generated by a corpus level topic distribution to benefit from the global rich word co-occurrence patterns.

As far as we know, how to incorporate user factor into BTM has not been studied yet. User based aggregation has proven effective for LDA. But unfortunately, our preliminary experiments indicate that simple user-based aggregation for BTM will generate incoherent topics. To distinguish between commonly used words (e.g., *good*, *people*, etc) and topical words (e.g., *food*, *travel*, etc), a background topic is often incorporated into the topic models. Zhao et al. (2011) use a background topic in Twitter-LDA to distill discriminative words in tweets. Sasaki et al. (2014) reduce the perplexity of Twitter-LDA by estimating the ratio between choosing background words and topical words for each user. They both make a very strong assumption that one tweet only covers one topic. Yan et al. (2015) use a background topic to distinguish between common biterms and bursty biterms, which need external data to evaluate the burstiness of each biterm as prior knowledge. Unlike those above, we incorporate a background

[1] See https://about.Twitter.com/company

Proceedings of the 53rd Annual Meeting of the Association for Computational Linguistics and the 7th International Joint Conference on Natural Language Processing (Short Papers), pages 489–494,
Beijing, China, July 26-31, 2015.

topic to absorb non-discriminative common words in each biterm. And we also estimate the user's preference between common words and topical words. Our new model is named as Twitter-BTM, which combines user based aggregation and the background topic in BTM. Finally, experiments on a Twitter dataset show that Twitter-BTM not only can discover more coherent topics but also can give more accurate topic representation of tweets compared with several state-of-the-art baselines.

We organize the rest of the paper as follows. Section 2 gives a brief review for BTM. Section 3 introduces our Twitter-BTM model and its implementation. Section 4 describes experimental results on a large-scale Twitter dataset. Finally, Section 5 contains a conclusion and future work.

2 BTM

There are two major differences between BTM and LDA (Yan et al., 2013). For one thing, considering a topic is a mixture of highly correlated words, which implies that they often occur together in the same document, BTM models the generative process of the word co-occurrence patterns directly. Thus a document made up of n words will be converted to C_n^2 biterms. For another, LDA and its variants suffer from the severe data sparsity in short documents. BTM uses global co-occurrence patterns to model the topic distribution over corpus level instead of document level.

The graphical representation of BTM (Yan et al., 2013) is shown in Figure 1(a). It assumes that the whole corpus is associated with a distributions θ over K topics drawn from a Dirichlet prior $Dir(\alpha)$. And each topic t is associated with a multinomial distribution ϕ^t over a vocabulary of V unique words drawn from a Dirichlet prior $Dir(\beta)$. The generative process for a corpus which consists of N_B biterms $\mathbb{B} = \{b_1, ..., b_{N_B}\}$, where $b_i = (w_{i_1}, w_{i_2})$, is as follows:

1 For each topic t=1,...,T
   (a) Draw $\phi^t \sim Dir(\beta)$
2 For the whole tweets collection
   (a) Draw $\theta \sim Dir(\alpha)$
3 For each biterm b = 1,...,N_B
   (a) Draw $z_b \sim Multi(\theta)$
   (b) Draw $w_{b,1}, w_{b,2} \sim Multi(\phi^{z_b})$

In the above process, z_b is the topic assignment latent variable of biterm b. To infer the parameters ϕ and θ, collapsed Gibbs sampling algorithm (Griffiths and Steyvers, 2004) is used for approximate inference.

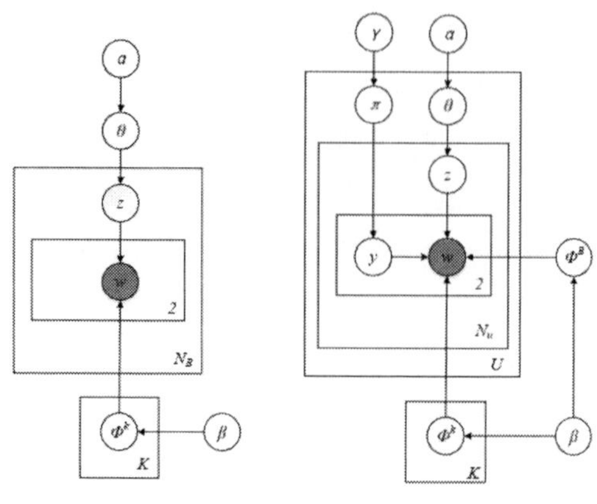

Figure 1: Graphical representation of (a) BTM, (b) Twitter-BTM

Compared with the strong assumption that a short document only covers a single topic (Diao et al., 2012; Ding et al., 2013), BTM makes a looser assumption that two words will be assigned the same topic label if they have co-occurred. Thus a short document could cover more than one topic, which is more close to the reality. But this assumption causes another issue, those commonly used words and those topical words are treated equally. Obviously it is inappropriate to assign same topic label to those words.

3 Twitter-BTM

In this Section, we introduce our Twitter-BTM model. Figure 1(b) shows the graphical representation of Twitter-BTM. The generative process of Twitter-BTM is as follows:

1 Draw $\phi^B \sim Dir(\beta)$
2 For each topic t=1,...,T
   (a) Draw $\phi^t \sim Dir(\beta)$
3 For each user u=1,...,U
   (a) Draw $\theta^u \sim Dir(\alpha), \pi^u \sim Beta(\gamma)$
   (b) For each biterm b = 1,...,N_u
      (i) Draw $z_{u,b} \sim Multi(\theta^u)$
      (ii) For each word n = 1,2
         (A) Draw $y_{u,b,n} \sim Bern(\pi^u)$
         (B) if $y_{u,b,n} = 0$ Draw $w_{u,b,n} \sim Multi(\phi^B)$
         if $y_{u,b,n} = 1$ Draw $w_{u,b,n} \sim Multi(\phi^{z_{u,b}})$

In the above process, user u's topic interest θ^u is a multinomial distribution over K topics drawn from a Dirichlet prior $Dir(\alpha)$. The background topic B is associated with a multinomial distribution ϕ^B drawn from a Dirichlet prior $Dir(\beta)$. The assumption that each user has a different preference between topical words and background words is shown to be effective in (Sasaki et al., 2014). We adopt this assumption in Twitter-BTM. User u's preference is represented as a Bernoulli distribution with parameter π^u drawn from a beta prior $Beta(\gamma)$. N_u is the number of biterms of user u, $z_{u,b}$ is the topic assignment latent variable of user u's biterm b. For user u and his/her biterm b, n=1 or 2, we use a latent variable $y_{u,b,n}$ to indicate the word type of the word $w_{b,n}$. When $y_{u,b,n} = 1$, $w_{b,n}$ is generated from topic $z_{u,b}$. When $y_{u,b,n} = 0$, $w_{b,n}$ is generated from the background topic B.

We adopt collapsed Gibbs Sampling to estimate the parameters. Because of the limitations of space, we leave out the details about the sampling algorithm. Since we can't get a document's distribution over topics from the parameters estimated by Twitter-BTM directly, we utilize the following formula (Yan et al., 2013) to infer the topic distribution of document d. Given a document d whose author is user u:

$$P(z = t|d) = \sum_{i}^{N_b} P(z = t|b_i)P(b_i|d) \quad (1)$$

Now the problem is converted to how to estimate $P(b_i|d)$ and $P(z = t|b_i)$. $P(b_i|d)$ is estimated by empirical distribution in d:

$$P(b_i|d) = \frac{N_{b_i}}{N_b} \quad (2)$$

where N_{b_i} is the number of biterm b_i occurred in d, N_b is the total number of biterms in d. We can apply Bayes' rule to compute $P(z = t|b_i)$ via following expression:

$$\frac{\theta_t^u \left[\pi^u \phi_{w_{i,1}}^B + (1-\pi^u)\phi_{w_{i,1}}^t\right] \left[\pi^u \phi_{w_{i,2}}^B + (1-\pi^u)\phi_{w_{i,2}}^t\right]}{\sum_k \theta_k^u \left[\pi^u \phi_{w_{i,1}}^B + (1-\pi^u)\phi_{w_{i,1}}^k\right] \left[\pi^u \phi_{w_{i,2}}^B + (1-\pi^u)\phi_{w_{i,2}}^k\right]} \quad (3)$$

4 Experiments

In this Section, we describe our experiments carried on a Twitter dataset collected form 10th Jun, 2009 to 31st Dec, 2009. Stop words and words occur less than 5 times are removed. We also filter tweets which only have one or two words. All letters are converted into lower case. The dataset is divided into two parts. The first part whose statistics is shown in Table 1 is used for training. The second part which consists of 22,496,107 tweets is used as the external dataset in topic coherence evaluation task in Section 4.1.

We compare the performance of Twitter-BTM with five baselines:

- LDA-U, user based aggregation is applied before training LDA.
- Twitter-LDA (Zhao et al., 2011), which makes a strong assumption that a tweet only covers one topic.
- TwitterUB-LDA (Sasaki et al., 2014), an improved version of Twitter-LDA, which models the user level preference between topical words and background words.
- BTM (Yan et al., 2013), the Biterm Topic Model.
- BTM-U, a simplified version of Twitter-BTM without background topic.

For all the above models, we use symmetric Dirichlet priors. The hyperparameters are set as follows: for all the models, we set $\alpha = 50/K$, $\beta = 0.01$; for Twitter-LDA, TwitterUB-LDA and Twitter-BTM, we set $\gamma = 0.5$. We run Gibbs sampling for 400 iterations.

DataSet	Twitter
#tweets	1,201,193
#users	12,006
#vocabulary	71,038
#avgTweetLen	7.04

Table 1: Summary of dataset

Perplexity metric is not used in our experiments since it is not a suitable evaluation metric for BTM (Cheng et al., 2014). The first reason is that BTM and LDA optimize different likelihood. The second reason is that topic models which have better perplexity may infer less semantically topics (Chang et al., 2009).

4.1 Topic Coherence

We use PMI-Score (Newman et al., 2010) to quantitatively evaluate the quality of topic component.

K	50			100		
method	Top5	Top10	Top20	Top5	Top10	Top20
LDA-U	2.83±0.07	1.93±0.06	1.40±0.04	3.11±0.09	1.89±0.09	1.15±0.04
Twitter-LDA	2.58±0.04	1.90±0.03	1.39±0.03	2.97±0.20	1.98±0.09	1.44±0.06
TwitterUB-LDA	2.57±0.05	1.87±0.07	1.45±0.04	3.07±0.11	2.05±0.05	1.45±0.05
BTM	2.88±0.14	2.01±0.09	1.44±0.08	3.25±0.14	2.13±0.06	**1.49±0.06**
BTM-U	2.92±0.10	1.89±0.05	1.33±0.04	3.03±0.07	1.95±0.05	1.34±0.07
Twitter-BTM	**3.04±0.10**	**2.05±0.08**	**1.47±0.05**	**3.27±0.12**	**2.15±0.08**	1.48±0.05

Table 2: PMI-Score of different topic models

Equation (4) defines PMI (Pointwise Mutual Information) for two words w_i and w_j:

$$PMI(w_i, w_j) = \log \frac{P(w_i, w_j) + \epsilon}{P(w_i)P(w_j)} \tag{4}$$

ϵ is an extremely small constant (Stevens et al., 2012), which is equal to 10^{-12} in this paper. The word probabilities and the co-occurrence probabilities are computed on the large-scale external dataset empirically. Here we use the second part Twitter dataset as the external dataset. Then for a topic t and its top T words ranked by topic-word probability ϕ_w^t, the PMI-Score of topic t is defined as follow:

$$PMI-Score(t) = \frac{1}{T(T-1)} \sum_{1 \le i < j \le T} PMI(w_i, w_j) \tag{5}$$

The model's PMI-Score is defined as the mean of all the topics' PMI-Score. Table 2 shows the average results over 10 runs of different models. When $K = 50$, Twitter-BTM outperforms all other models significantly. When $K = 100$, The PMI-Score of BTM and Twitter-BTM are very close. BTM-U is worse than BTM, the reason may be that each user's biterm sets provide extremely limited words co-occurring information.

Table 3 shows top 10 words of topic "food" learned by BTM, BTM-U and Twitter-BTM when $K = 50$. We use italic fonts to indicate background words labeled by human judgement. Compared with BTM and BTM-U, Twitter-BTM can rank those background words at lower level. It demonstrates that representative words learned by Twitter-BTM are more coherent and meaningful.

4.2 Document Representation

Topic models are powerful dimension reduction methods for texts. Given a tweet d, we can infer its probability distribution over K topics with

BTM	BTM-U	Twitter-BTM
food	food	vegan
eat	vegan	food
chicken	eat	eat
good	***good***	chicken
vegan	chicken	chocolate
lol	#vegan	cheese
cheese	cream	cream
chocolate	cheese	#vegan
love	chocolate	ice
dinner	ice	dinner

Table 3: Top 10 words of topic food

equation (1). Thus d can be represented as a topic probability vector:

$$d = [P(z = 1|d), ..., P(z = K|d)] \tag{6}$$

We use document classification task (Cheng et al., 2014) and document clustering task (Duan et al., 2012) to measure the quality of the documents' topic proportions. Tweets in Twitter have no explicit label information. But some tweets are labeled by one or more hashtags (a type of label whose form is "#keyword") manually by its author to indicate the topic the tweets involve. We follow previous works (Cheng et al., 2014; Wang et al., 2014) and use hashtags as the tweets' labels. Table 4 lists 38 frequent (at least appears in 100 tweets) hashtags relating to certain topic or event manually selected in our dataset.

We choose those tweets which contain only one of these hashtags appear in Table 4 from our original data in the following experiments. When we infer a tweet's topic distribution, the hashtag is ignored. Because it doesn't make sense to use the label information to construct the feature vector directly.

We classify these selected tweets by Random Forest classifier (Breiman, 2001) implemented in aaliyah afghanistan beatcancer birding blogtalkradio digguser dmv dontyouhate fact giladshalit gno gov green haiku healthcare honduras india iranelection jazz jesus krp lgbt mindsetshift nfl nn oink rhoa slaughterhouse socialmedia tech travel trueblood vegan vegas voss weeklyfitnesschallenge wordpress yyj

Table 4: Hashtags selected for evaluation

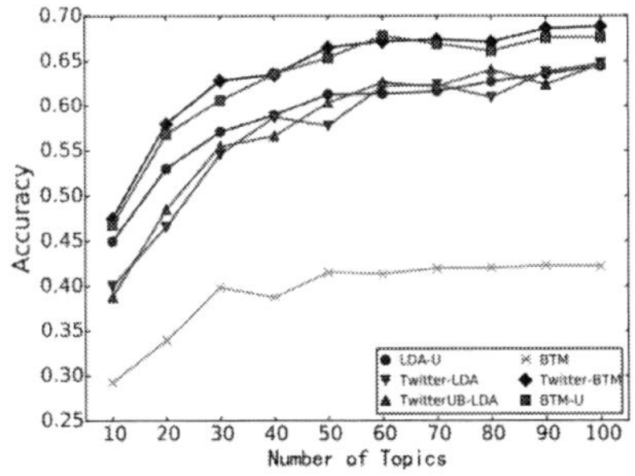

Figure 2: Performance of classification

sklearn [2] python module with 10-fold cross validation. Using accuracy as the evaluation metric, we report the classification performance of different topic models in Figure 2. With the increase of the topic number K, all the models' accuracies are tending to increase. BTM is worse than all other models, which confirms the effectiveness of user based aggregation. Twitter-BTM and BTM-U always outperform LDA-U, Twitter-LDA and TwitterUB-LDA. Twitter-BTM's accuracy is a little higher than BTM-U, which demonstrates that the background topic is helpful to capture more accurate topic representation of documents.

We adopt k-means algorithm implemented in sklearn python module as our clustering method. The number of cluster is set to 38. Considering we have the knowledge of ground truth class assignments of each tweet, and Adjusted Rand Index (ARI) and Normalized Mutual Information are used as cluster validation indices in our experiments. As shown in Figure 3 and Figure 4, The higher ARI and NMI value indicate that Twitter-BTM outperform other models. And BTM performs worse than all other models.

5 Conclusion

In this paper, we investigate the problem of topic modeling over short texts with user factor. User individualities are sacrificed to obtain the corpus level words co-occurrence patterns in BTM. However, unlike LDA, simple user based aggregation will reduce the topic coherence for BTM. To address this problem, we propose Twitter-BTM which loosens the inappropriate assumption that two co-occurring words must have same topic label made in BTM by leveraging user based aggregation and incorporating a background topic in BTM. The experimental results show that Twitter-BTM substantially outperforms BTM.

In the future, we plan to study the influence of other factors such as temporal information to BTM and its variants.

[2]See http://scikit-learn.org/stable/

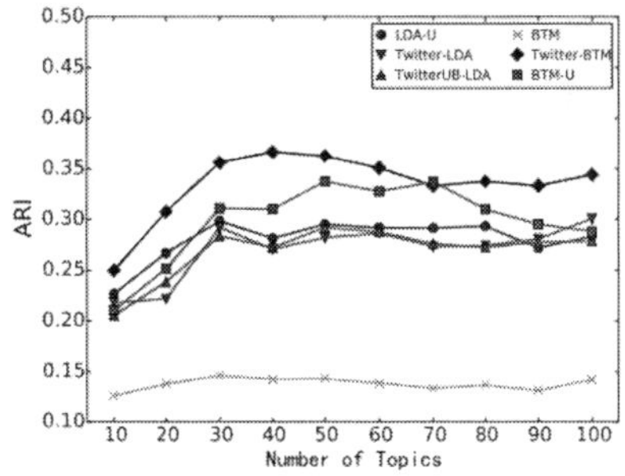

Figure 3: Performance of clustering (ARI)

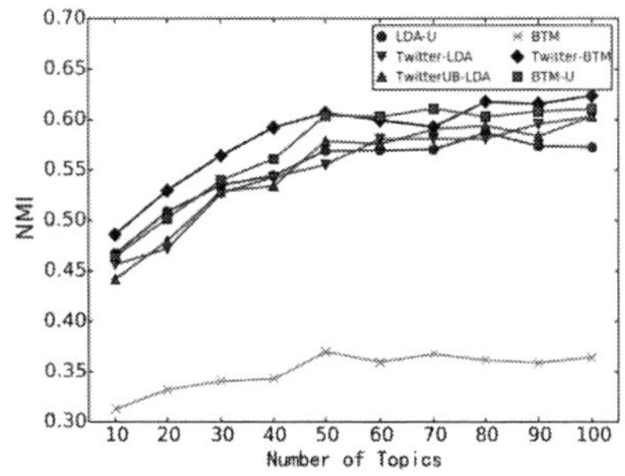

Figure 4: Performance of clustering (NMI)

Acknowledgments

This work is supported by 973 Program with Grant No.2014CB340405, NSFC with Grant No.61272340. Yan Zhang is supported by NSFC with Grant No.61370054. We thank the three anonymous reviewers for their comments and constructive criticism.

References

David M Blei, Andrew Y Ng, and Michael I Jordan. 2003. Latent dirichlet allocation. *the Journal of machine Learning research*, 3:993–1022.

Leo Breiman. 2001. Random forests. *Machine Learning*, 45(1):5–32.

Jonathan Chang, Sean Gerrish, Chong Wang, Jordan L Boyd-Graber, and David M Blei. 2009. Reading tea leaves: How humans interpret topic models. In *Advances in neural information processing systems*, pages 288–296.

Xueqi Cheng, Xiaohui Yan, Yanyan Lan, and Jiafeng Guo. 2014. Btm: Topic modeling over short texts. *IEEE TRANSACTIONS ON KNOWLEDGE AND DATA ENGINEERING*.

Qiming Diao, Jing Jiang, Feida Zhu, and Ee-Peng Lim. 2012. Finding bursty topics from microblogs. In *ACL (1)*, pages 536–544. The Association for Computer Linguistics.

Zhuoye Ding, Xipeng Qiu, Qi Zhang, and Xuanjing Huang. 2013. Learning topical translation model for microblog hashtag suggestion. In *IJCAI 2013, Proceedings of the 23rd International Joint Conference on Artificial Intelligence, Beijing, China, August 3-9, 2013*.

Dongsheng Duan, Yuhua Li, Ruixuan Li, Rui Zhang, and Aiming Wen. 2012. Ranktopic: Ranking based topic modeling. In *ICDM*, pages 211–220.

Fréderic Godin, Viktor Slavkovikj, Wesley De Neve, Benjamin Schrauwen, and Rik Van de Walle. 2013. Using topic models for twitter hashtag recommendation. In *Proceedings of the 22nd international conference on World Wide Web companion*, pages 593–596. International World Wide Web Conferences Steering Committee.

T. L. Griffiths and M. Steyvers. 2004. Finding scientific topics. *Proceedings of the National Academy of Sciences*, 101:5228–5235.

Liangjie Hong and Brian D. Davison. 2010. Empirical study of topic modeling in twitter. In *Proceedings of the First Workshop on Social Media Analytics*, SOMA '10, pages 80–88, New York, NY, USA. ACM.

Zhuoye Ding Qi Zhang XuanJing Huang. 2012. Automatic hashtag recommendation for microblogs using topic-specific translation model. In *24th International Conference on Computational Linguistics*, page 265. Citeseer.

Zongyang Ma, Aixin Sun, Quan Yuan, and Gao Cong. 2014. Tagging your tweets: A probabilistic modeling of hashtag annotation in twitter. In *Proceedings of the 23rd ACM International Conference on Conference on Information and Knowledge Management*, pages 999–1008. ACM.

David Newman, Jey Han Lau, Karl Grieser, and Timothy Baldwin. 2010. Automatic evaluation of topic coherence. In *Human Language Technologies: The 2010 Annual Conference of the North American Chapter of the Association for Computational Linguistics*, pages 100–108. Association for Computational Linguistics.

Kentaro Sasaki, Tomohiro Yoshikawa, and Takeshi Furuhashi. 2014. Online topic model for twitter considering dynamics of user interests and topic trends. In *Proceedings of the 2014 Conference on Empircal Methods in Natural Language Processing*, pages 1977–1985.

Jianfeng Si, Arjun Mukherjee, Bing Liu, Qing Li, Huayi Li, and Xiaotie Deng. 2013. Exploiting topic based twitter sentiment for stock prediction. In *ACL (2)*, pages 24–29.

Keith Stevens, Philip Kegelmeyer, David Andrzejewski, and David Buttler. 2012. Exploring topic coherence over many models and many topics. In *Proceedings of the 2012 Joint Conference on Empirical Methods in Natural Language Processing and Computational Natural Language Learning*, pages 952–961. Association for Computational Linguistics.

Yuan Wang, Jie Liu, Jishi Qu, Yalou Huang, Jimeng Chen, and Xia Feng. 2014. Hashtag graph based topic model for tweet mining. In *2014 IEEE International Conference on Data Mining, ICDM 2014, Shenzhen, China, December 14-17, 2014*, pages 1025–1030.

Jianshu Weng, Ee-Peng Lim, Jing Jiang, and Qi He. 2010. Twitterrank: finding topic-sensitive influential twitterers. In *WSDM*, pages 261–270. ACM.

Xiaohui Yan, Jiafeng Guo, Yanyan Lan, and Xueqi Cheng. 2013. A biterm topic model for short texts. In *Proceedings of the 22nd international conference on World Wide Web*, pages 1445–1456. International World Wide Web Conferences Steering Committee.

Xiaohui Yan, Jiafeng Guo, Yanyan Lan, Jun Xu, and Xueqi Cheng. 2015. A probabilistic model for bursty topic discovery in microblogs.

Wayne Xin Zhao, Jing Jiang, Jianshu Weng, Jing He, Ee-Peng Lim, Hongfei Yan, and Xiaoming Li. 2011. Comparing twitter and traditional media using topic models. In *Advances in Information Retrieval*, pages 338–349. Springer.

Xin Wayne Zhao, Yanwei Guo, Yulan He, Han Jiang, Yuexin Wu, and Xiaoming Li. 2014. We know what you want to buy: a demographic-based system for product recommendation on microblogs. In *Proceedings of the 20th ACM SIGKDD international conference on Knowledge discovery and data mining*, pages 1935–1944. ACM.

The Fixed-Size Ordinally-Forgetting Encoding Method for Neural Network Language Models

Shiliang Zhang[1], Hui Jiang[2], Mingbin Xu[2], Junfeng Hou[1], Lirong Dai[1]
[1]National Engineering Laboratory for Speech and Language Information Processing
University of Science and Technology of China, Hefei, Anhui, China
[2]Department of Electrical Engineering and Computer Science
York University, 4700 Keele Street, Toronto, Ontario, M3J 1P3, Canada
{zsl2008,hjf176}@mail.ustc.edu.cn, {hj,xmb}@cse.yorku.ca, lrdai@ustc.edu.cn

Abstract

In this paper, we propose the new fixed-size ordinally-forgetting encoding (FOFE) method, which can almost uniquely encode any variable-length sequence of words into a fixed-size representation. FOFE can model the word order in a sequence using a simple ordinally-forgetting mechanism according to the positions of words. In this work, we have applied FOFE to feedforward neural network language models (FNN-LMs). Experimental results have shown that without using any recurrent feedbacks, FOFE based FNN-LMs can significantly outperform not only the standard fixed-input FNN-LMs but also the popular recurrent neural network (RNN) LMs.

1 Introduction

Language models play an important role in many applications like speech recognition, machine translation, information retrieval and nature language understanding. Traditionally, the back-off n-gram models (Katz, 1987; Kneser, 1995) are the standard approach to language modeling. Recently, neural networks have been successfully applied to language modeling, yielding the state-of-the-art performance in many tasks. In neural network language models (NNLM), the feedforward neural networks (FNN) and recurrent neural networks (RNN) (Elman, 1990) are two popular architectures. The basic idea of NNLMs is to use a projection layer to project discrete words into a continuous space and estimate word conditional probabilities in this space, which may be smoother to better generalize to unseen contexts. FNN language models (FNN-LM) (Bengio and Ducharme, 2001; Bengio, 2003) usually use a limited history within a fixed-size context window to predict the next word. RNN language models (RNN-LM) (Mikolov, 2010; Mikolov, 2012) adopt a time-delayed recursive architecture for the hidden layers to memorize the long-term dependency in language. Therefore, it is widely reported that RNN-LMs usually outperform FNN-LMs in language modeling. While RNNs are theoretically powerful, the learning of RNNs needs to use the so-called back-propagation through time (BPTT) (Werbos, 1990) due to the internal recurrent feedback cycles. The BPTT significantly increases the computational complexity of the learning algorithms and it may cause many problems in learning, such as gradient vanishing and exploding (Bengio, 1994). More recently, some new architectures have been proposed to solve these problems. For example, the long short term memory (LSTM) RNN (Hochreiter, 1997) is an enhanced architecture to implement the recurrent feedbacks using various learnable gates, and it has obtained promising results on handwriting recognition (Graves, 2009) and sequence modeling (Graves, 2013).

Comparing with RNN-LMs, FNN-LMs can be learned in a simpler and more efficient way. However, FNN-LMs can not model the long-term dependency in language due to the fixed-size input window. In this paper, we propose a novel encoding method for discrete sequences, named *fixed-size ordinally-forgetting encoding* (FOFE), which can almost uniquely encode any variable-length word sequence into a fixed-size code. Relying on a constant forgetting factor, FOFE can model the word order in a sequence based on a simple ordinally-forgetting mechanism, which uses the position of each word in the sequence. Both the theoretical analysis and the experimental simulation have shown that FOFE can provide *almost* unique codes for variable-length word sequences as long as the forgetting factor is properly selected. In this work, we apply FOFE to

Proceedings of the 53rd Annual Meeting of the Association for Computational Linguistics and the 7th International Joint Conference on Natural Language Processing (Short Papers), pages 495–500,
Beijing, China, July 26-31, 2015.

neural network language models, where the fixed-size FOFE codes are fed to FNNs as input to predict next word, enabling FNN-LMs to model long-term dependency in language. Experiments on two benchmark tasks, Penn Treebank Corpus (PTB) and Large Text Compression Benchmark (LTCB), have shown that FOFE-based FNN-LMs can not only significantly outperform the standard fixed-input FNN-LMs but also achieve better performance than the popular RNN-LMs with or without using LSTM. Moreover, our implementation also shows that FOFE based FNN-LMs can be learned very efficiently on GPUs without the complex BPTT procedure.

2 Our Approach: FOFE

Assume vocabulary size is K, NNLMs adopt the 1-of-K encoding vectors as input. In this case, each word in vocabulary is represented as a one-hot vector $\mathbf{e} \in \mathbb{R}^K$. The 1-of-K representation is a context independent encoding method. When the 1-of-K representation is used to model a word in a sequence, it can not model its history or context.

2.1 Fixed-size Ordinally Forgetting Encoding

We propose a simple context-dependent encoding method for any sequence consisting of discrete symbols, namely *fixed-size ordinally-forgetting encoding* (FOFE). Given a sequence of words (or any discrete symbols), $S = \{w_1, w_2, \cdots, w_T\}$, each word w_t is first represented by a 1-of-K representation $\mathbf{e}_t$, from the first word $t = 1$ to the end of the sequence $t = T$, FOFE encodes each partial sequence (history) based on a simple recursive formula (with $\mathbf{z}_0 = \mathbf{0}$) as:

$$\mathbf{z}_t = \alpha \cdot \mathbf{z}_{t-1} + \mathbf{e}_t \quad (1 \leq t \leq T) \qquad (1)$$

where $\mathbf{z}_t$ denotes the FOFE code for the partial sequence up to w_t, and α $(0 < \alpha < 1)$ is a constant forgetting factor to control the influence of the history on the current position. Let's take a simple example here, assume we have three symbols in vocabulary, e.g., *A*, *B*, *C*, whose 1-of-K codes are $[1, 0, 0]$, $[0, 1, 0]$ and $[0, 0, 1]$ respectively. In this case, the FOFE code for the sequence $\{ABC\}$ is $[\alpha^2, \alpha, 1]$, and that of $\{ABCBC\}$ is $[\alpha^4, \alpha + \alpha^3, 1 + \alpha^2]$.

Obviously, FOFE can encode any variable-length discrete sequence into a fixed-size code. Moreover, it is a recursive context dependent encoding method that smartly models the order in-

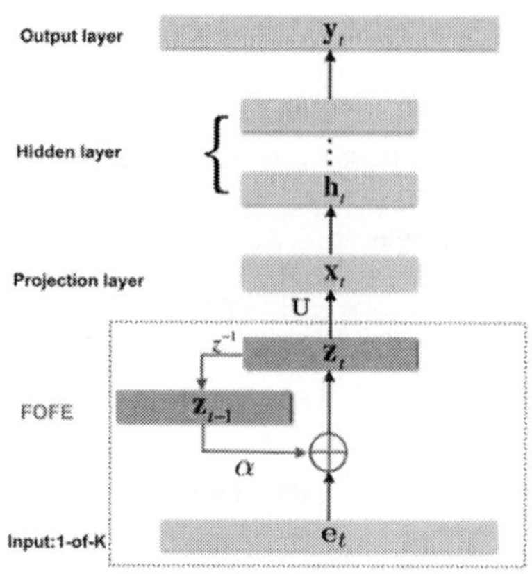

Figure 1: The FOFE-based FNN language model.

formation by various powers of the forgetting factor. Furthermore, FOFE has an appealing property in modeling natural languages that the far-away context will be gradually forgotten due to $\alpha < 1$ and the nearby contexts play much larger role in the resultant FOFE codes.

2.2 Uniqueness of FOFE codes

Given the vocabulary (of K symbols), for any sequence S with a length of T, based on the FOFE code $\mathbf{z}_T$ computed as above, if we can always decode the original sequence S unambiguously (perfectly recovering S from $\mathbf{z}_T$), we say FOFE is unique.

Theorem 1 *If the forgetting factor α satisfies $0 < \alpha \leq 0.5$,* FOFE *is unique for any K and T.*

The proof is simple because if the FOFE code has a value α^t in its i-th element, we may determine the word w_i occurs in the position t of S without ambiguity since no matter how many times w_i occurs in the far-away contexts ($< t$), they do not sum to α^t (due to $\alpha \leq 0.5$). If w_i appears in any closer context ($> t$), the i-th element must be larger than α^t.

Theorem 2 *For $0.5 < \alpha < 1$, given any finite values of K and T,* FOFE *is almost unique everywhere for $\alpha \in (0.5, 1.0)$, except only a finite set of countable choices of α.*

Refer to (Zhang et. al., 2015a) for the complete proof. Based on Theorem 2, FOFE is unique almost everywhere between $(0.5, 1.0)$ only except a countable set of isolated choices of α. In practice, the chance to exactly choose these isolated values between $(0.5, 1.0)$ is extremely slim, realistically

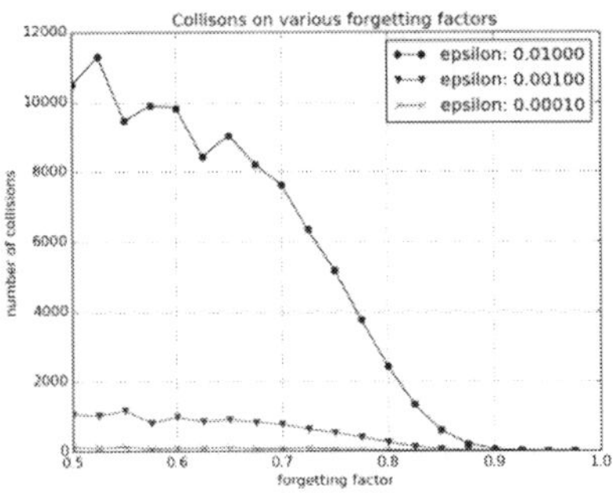

Figure 2: Numbers of collisions in simulation.

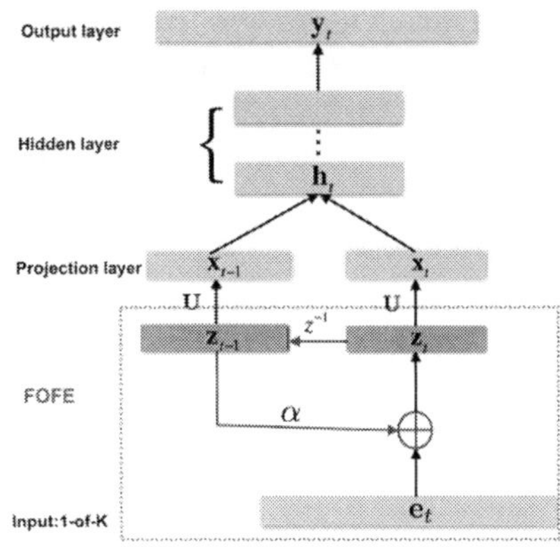

Figure 3: Diagram of 2nd-order FOFE FNN-LM.

almost impossible due to quantization errors in the system. To verify this, we have run simulation experiments for all possible sequences up to $T = 20$ symbols to count the number of collisions. Each collision is defined as the maximum element-wise difference between two FOFE codes (generated from two different sequences) is less than a small threshold ϵ. In Figure 2, we have shown the number of collisions (out of the total 2^{20} tested cases) for various α values when $\epsilon = 0.01$, 0.001 and 0.0001.[1] The simulation experiments have shown that the chance of collision is extremely small even when we allow a word to appear any times in the context. Obviously, in a natural language, a word normally does not appear repeatedly within a near context. Moreover, we have run the simulation to examine whether collisions actually occur in two real text corpora, namely PTB (1M words) and LTCB (160M words), using $\epsilon = 0.01$, we have not observed a single collision for nine different α values between $[0.55, 1.0]$ (incremental 0.05).

2.3 Implement FOFE for FNN-LMs

The architecture of a FOFE based neural network language model (FOFE-FNNLM) is shown in Figure 1. It is similar to regular bigram FNN-LMs except that it uses a FOFE code to feed into neural network LM at each time. Moreover, the FOFE can be easily scaled to higher orders like n-gram NNLMs. For example, Figure 3 is an illustration of a second order FOFE-based neural network language model.

FOFE is a simple recursive encoding method but a direct sequential implementation may not be efficient for the parallel computation platform like GPUs. Here, we will show that the FOFE computation can be efficiently implemented as sentence-by-sentence matrix multiplications, which are suitable for the mini-batch based stochastic gradient descent (SGD) method running on GPUs.

Given a sentence, $S = \{w_1, w_2, \cdots, w_T\}$, where each word is represented by a 1-of-K code as $\mathbf{e}_t$ $(1 \leq t \leq T)$. The FOFE codes for all partial sequences in S can be computed based on the following matrix multiplication:

$$\mathbf{S} = \begin{bmatrix} 1 & & & & \\ \alpha & 1 & & & \\ \alpha^2 & \alpha & 1 & & \\ \vdots & & \ddots & 1 & \\ \alpha^{T-1} & \cdots & & \alpha & 1 \end{bmatrix} \begin{bmatrix} \mathbf{e}_1 \\ \mathbf{e}_2 \\ \mathbf{e}_3 \\ \vdots \\ \mathbf{e}_T \end{bmatrix} = \mathbf{MV}$$

where $\mathbf{V}$ is a matrix arranging all 1-of-K codes of the words in the sentence row by row, and $\mathbf{M}$ is a T-th order lower triangular matrix. Each row vector of $\mathbf{S}$ represents a FOFE code of the partial sequence up to each position in the sentence.

This matrix formulation can be easily extended to a mini-batch consisting of several sentences. Assume that a mini-batch is composed of N sequences, $\mathcal{L} = \{S_1\ S_2 \cdots S_N\}$, we can compute the FOFE codes for all sentences in the mini-batch as follows:

$$\bar{\mathbf{S}} = \begin{bmatrix} \mathbf{M}_1 & & & \\ & \mathbf{M}_2 & & \\ & & \ddots & \\ & & & \mathbf{M}_N \end{bmatrix} \begin{bmatrix} \mathbf{V}_1 \\ \mathbf{V}_2 \\ \vdots \\ \mathbf{V}_N \end{bmatrix} = \bar{\mathbf{M}}\bar{\mathbf{V}}.$$

[1]When we use a bigger value for α, the magnitudes of the resultant FOFE codes become much larger. As a result, the number of collisions (as measured by a fixed absolute threshold ϵ) becomes smaller.

When feeding the FOFE codes to FNN as shown in Figure 1, we can compute the activation signals (assume f is the activation function) in the first hidden layer for all histories in S as follows:

$$\mathbf{H} = f\Big((\bar{\mathbf{M}}\bar{\mathbf{V}})\mathbf{U}\mathbf{W}+\mathbf{b}\Big) = f\Big(\bar{\mathbf{M}}(\bar{\mathbf{V}}\mathbf{U})\mathbf{W}+\mathbf{b}\Big)$$

where $\mathbf{U}$ denotes the word embedding matrix that projects the word indices onto a continuous low-dimensional continuous space. As above, $\bar{\mathbf{V}}\mathbf{U}$ can be done efficiently by looking up the embedding matrix. Therefore, for the computational efficiency purpose, we may apply FOFE to the word embedding vectors instead of the original high-dimensional one-hot vectors. In the backward pass, we can calculate the gradients with the standard back-propagation (BP) algorithm rather than BPTT. As a result, FOFE based FNN-LMs are the same as the standard FNN-LMs in terms of computational complexity in training, which is much more efficient than RNN-LMs.

3 Experiments

We have evaluated the FOFE method for NNLMs on two benchmark tasks: i) the Penn Treebank (PTB) corpus of about 1M words, following the same setup as (Mikolov, 2011). The vocabulary size is limited to 10k. The preprocessing method and the way to split data into training/validation/test sets are the same as (Mikolov, 2011). ii) The Large Text Compression Benchmark (LTCB) (Mahoney, 2011). In LTCB, we use the *enwik9* dataset, which is composed of the first 10^9 bytes of enwiki-20060303-pages-articles.xml. We split it into three parts: training (153M), validation (8.9M) and test (8.9M) sets. We limit the vocabulary size to 80k for LTCB and replace all out-of-vocabulary words by <UNK>. [2]

3.1 Experimental results on PTB

We have first evaluated the performance of the traditional FNN-LMs, taking the previous several words as input, denoted as n-gram FNN-LMs here. We have trained neural networks with a linear projection layer (of 200 hidden nodes) and two hidden layers (of 400 nodes per layer). All hidden units in networks use the rectified linear activation function, i.e., $f(x) = \max(0, x)$. The nets are initialized based on the normalized initialization

[2]Matlab codes are available at `https://wiki.eecs.yorku.ca/lab/MLL/projects:fofe:start` for readers to reproduce all results reported in this paper.

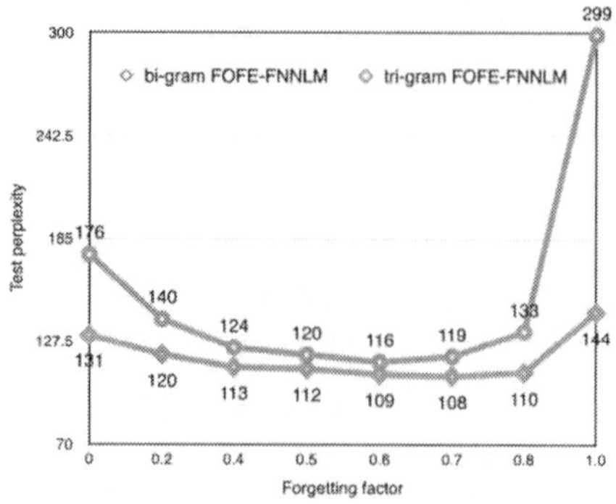

Figure 4: Perplexities of FOFE FNNLMs as a function of the forgetting factor.

in (Glorot, 2010), without using any pre-training. We use SGD with a mini-batch size of 200 and an initial learning rate of 0.4. The learning rate is kept fixed as long as the perplexity on the validation set decreases by at least 1. After that, we continue six more epochs of training, where the learning rate is halved after each epoch. The performance (in perplexity) of several n-gram FNN-LMs (from bigram to 6-gram) is shown in Table 1.

For the FOFE-FNNLMs, the net architecture and the parameter setting are the same as above. The mini-batch size is also 200 and each mini-batch is composed of several sentences up to 200 words (the last sentence may be truncated). All sentences in the corpus are randomly shuffled at the beginning of each epoch. In this experiment, we first investigate how the forgetting factor α may affect the performance of LMs. We have trained two FOFE-FNNLMs: i) 1st-order (using $\mathbf{z}_t$ as input to FNN for each time t; ii) 2nd-order (using both $\mathbf{z}_t$ and $\mathbf{z}_{t-1}$ as input for each time t, with a forgetting factor varying between $[0.0, 1.0]$. Experimental results in Figure 4 have shown that a good choice of α lies between $[0.5, 0.8]$. Using a too large or too small forgetting factor will hurt the performance. A too small forgetting factor may limit the memory of the encoding while a too large α may confuse LM with a far-away history. In the following experiments, we set $\alpha = 0.7$ for the rest experiments in this paper.

In Table 1, we have summarized the perplexities on the PTB test set for various models. The proposed FOFE-FNNLMs can significantly outperform the baseline FNN-LMs using the same architecture. For example, the perplexity of the baseline bigram FNNLM is 176, while the FOFE-

Table 1: Perplexities on PTB for various LMs.

Model	Test PPL
KN 5-gram (Mikolov, 2011)	141
FNNLM (Mikolov, 2012)	140
RNNLM (Mikolov, 2011)	123
LSTM (Graves, 2013)	117
bigram FNNLM	176
trigram FNNLM	131
4-gram FNNLM	118
5-gram FNNLM	114
6-gram FNNLM	113
1st-order FOFE-FNNLM	116
2nd-order FOFE-FNNLM	**108**

Table 2: Perplexities on LTCB for various language models. [M*N] denotes the sizes of the input context window and projection layer.

Model	Architecture	Test PPL
KN 3-gram	-	156
KN 5-gram	-	132
FNN-LM	[1*200]-400-400-80k	241
	[2*200]-400-400-80k	155
	[2*200]-600-600-80k	150
	[3*200]-400-400-80k	131
	[4*200]-400-400-80k	125
RNN-LM	[1*600]-80k	112
FOFE FNN-LM	[1*200]-400-400-80k	120
	[1*200]-600-600-80k	115
	[2*200]-400-400-80k	112
	[2*200]-600-600-80k	**107**

FNNLM can improve to 116. Moreover, the FOFE-FNNLMs can even overtake a well-trained RNNLM (400 hidden units) in (Mikolov, 2011) and an LSTM in (Graves, 2013). It indicates FOFE-FNNLMs can effectively model the long-term dependency in language without using any recurrent feedback. At last, the 2nd-order FOFE-FNNLM can provide further improvement, yielding the perplexity of 108 on PTB. It also outperforms all higher-order FNN-LMs (4-gram, 5-gram and 6-gram), which are bigger in model size. To our knowledge, this is one of the best reported results on PTB without model combination.

3.2 Experimental results on LTCB

We have further examined the FOFE based FNN-LMs on a much larger text corpus, i.e. LTCB, which contains articles from Wikipedia. We have trained several baseline systems: i) two n-gram LMs (3-gram and 5-gram) using the modified Kneser-Ney smoothing without count cutoffs; ii) several traditional FNN-LMs with different model sizes and input context windows (bigram, trigram, 4-gram and 5-gram); iii) an RNN-LM with one hidden layer of 600 nodes using the toolkit in (Mikolov, 2010), in which we have further used a spliced sentence bunch in (Chen et al. 2014) to speed up the training on GPUs. Moreover, we have examined four FOFE based FNN-LMs with various model sizes and input window sizes (two 1st-order FOFE models and two 2nd-order ones). For all NNLMs, we have used an output layer of the full vocabulary (80k words). In these experiments, we have used an initial learning rate of 0.01, and a bigger mini-batch of 500 for FNN-LMMs and of 256 sentences for the RNN and FOFE models. Experimental results in Table 2 have shown that the FOFE-based FNN-LMs can significantly outperform the baseline FNN-LMs (including some larger higher-order models) and also slightly overtake the popular RNN-based LM, yielding the best result (perplexity of 107) on the test set.

4 Conclusions

In this paper, we propose the fixed-size ordinally-forgetting encoding (FOFE) method to *almost* uniquely encode any variable-length sequence into a fixed-size code. In this work, FOFE has been successfully applied to neural network language modeling. Next, FOFE may be combined with neural networks (Zhang and Jiang, 2015; Zhang et. al., 2015b) for other NLP tasks, such as sentence modeling/matching, paraphrase detection, machine translation, question and answer and etc.

Acknowledgments

This work was supported in part by the Science and Technology Development of Anhui Province, China (Grants No. 2014z02006) and the Fundamental Research Funds for the Central Universities from China, as well as an NSERC Discovery grant from Canadian federal government. We appreciate Dr. Barlas Oguz at Microsoft for his insightful comments and constructive suggestions on Theorem 2.

References

Slava Katz. 1987. Estimation of probabilities from sparse data for the language model component of a speech recognizer. *IEEE Transactions on Acoustics, Speech and Signal Processing (ASSP)*, Volume 35, no 3, pages 400-401.

Reinhard Kneser and Hermann Ney. 1995. Improved backing-off for m-gram language modeling. In *Proc. of International Conference on Acoustics, Speech and Signal Processing (ICASSP)*, pages 181-184.

Paul Werbos. 1990. Back-propagation through time: what it does and how to do it. *Proceedings of the IEEE*, volume 78, no 10, pages 1550-1560.

Yoshua Bengio, Patrice Simard and Paolo Frasconi. 1994. Learning long-term dependencies with gradient descent is difficult. *IEEE Transactions on Neural Networks* volume 5, no 2, pages 157-166.

Yoshua Bengio and Rejean Ducharme. 2001. A neural probabilistic language model. In *Proc. of NIPS*, volume 13.

Yoshua Bengio, Rejean Ducharme, Pascal Vincent, and Christian Jauvin. 2003. A neural probabilistic language model. *Journal of Machine Learning Research*, volume 3, no 2, pages 1137-1155.

Jeffery Elman. 1990. Finding structure in time. *Cognitive science*, volume 14, no 2, pages 179-211.

Tomas Mikolov, Martin Karafiát, Lukas Burget, Jan Cernockỳ and Sanjeev Khudanpur. 2010. Recurrent neural network based language model. In *Proc. of Interspeech*, pages 1045-1048.

Tomas Mikolov, Stefan Kombrink, Lukas Burget, Jan Cernocky and Sanjeev Khudanpur. 2011. Extensions of recurrent neural network language model. In *Proc. of International Conference on Acoustics, Speech and Signal Processing (ICASSP)*, pages 5528-5531.

Tomas Mikolov and Geoffrey Zweig. 2012. Context dependent recurrent neural network language model. In *Proc. of SLT*, pages 234-239.

X. Chen, Y. Wang, X. Liu, et al. 2014. Efficient GPU-based training of recurrent neural network language models using spliced sentence bunch. In *Proc. of Interspeech*.

Ilya Sutskever and Geoffrey Hinton. 2010. Temporal-kernel recurrent neural networks. *Neural Networks*. pages 239-243.

Yong-Zhe Shi, Wei-Qiang Zhang, Meng Cai and Jia Liu. 2013. Temporal kernel neural network language model. In *Proc. of International Conference on Acoustics, Speech and Signal Processing (ICASSP)*. pages 8247-8251.

Sepp Hochreiter and Jurgen Schmidhuber. 1997. Long short-term memory. *Neural computation*, volume 9, no 8, pages 1735-1780.

Alex Graves and Jurgen Schmidhuber. 2009. Offline handwriting recognition with multidimensional recurrent neural networks. In *Proc. of NIPS*. pages 545-552.

Alex Graves. 2013. Generating sequences with recurrent neural networks. *arXiv preprint arXiv*:1308.0850.

Glorot Xavier and Yoshua Bengio. 2010. Understanding the difficulty of training deep feedforward neural networks. In *Proc. of AISTATS*.

Matt Mahoney. 2011. Large Text Compression Benchmark. In *http://mattmahoney.net/dc/textdata.html*.

Barlas Oguz. 2015. Personal Communications.

Shiling Zhang, Hui Jiang, Mingbin Xu, Junfeng Hou and LiRong Dai. 2015a. A Fixed-Size Encoding Method for Variable-Length Sequences with its Application to Neural Network Language Models. *arXiv:1505.01504*.

Shiliang Zhang and Hui Jiang. 2015. Hybrid Orthogonal Projection and Estimation (HOPE): A New Framework to Probe and Learn Neural Networks. *arXiv:1502.00702*.

Shiliang Zhang, Hui Jiang and Lirong Dai. 2015b. The New HOPE Way to Learn Neural Networks. *Proc. of Deep Learning Workshop at ICML 2015*.

Unsupervised Decomposition of a Multi-Author Document Based on Naive-Bayesian Model

Khaled Aldebei **Xiangjian He**
School of Computing and Communications
Faculty of Engineering and IT
University of Technology, Sydney, Australia
Khaled.w.aldebei@student.uts.edu.au
Xiangjian.He@uts.edu.au

Jie Yang
Lab of Pattern Analysis
and Machine Intelligence
Shanghai Jiaotong University
jieyang@sjtu.edu.cn

Abstract

This paper proposes a new unsupervised method for decomposing a multi-author document into authorial components. We assume that we do not know anything about the document and the authors, except the number of the authors of that document. The key idea is to exploit the difference in the posterior probability of the Naive-Bayesian model to increase the precision of the clustering assignment and the accuracy of the classification process of our method. Experimental results show that the proposed method outperforms two state-of-the-art methods.

1 Introduction

The traditional studies on text segmentation, as shown in Choi (2000), Brants et al. (2002), Misra et al. (2009) and Hennig and Labor (2009), focus on dividing the text into signification components such as words, sentences and topics rather than authors. Natural Language Processing techniques (NLP) and various machine learning schemas have been applied for these approaches. Due to the availability of online communication facilities, the cooperation between authors to produce a document becomes much easier. The co-authored documents include Web pages, books, academic papers and blog posts. There are almost no approaches that have concentrated on developing techniques for segmentation of a multi-author document according to the authorship. The existing approaches, as those in Schaalje et al. (2013), Segarra et al. (2014) and Layton et al. (2013) that are most related to our research in this paper, deal with documents written by a single author only. Although the work in Koppel et al. (2011) has considered the segmentation of a document according to multi-authorship, this approach requires manual translations and concordance to be available beforehand. Hence, their method can only be applied on particular types of documents such as Bible books. Akiva and Koppel (2013) investigated this limitation and presented a generic unsupervised method. They evaluated their method using two different types of features. The first one is the occurrence of the 500 most common words in the document. The second one is the synonym set, which is only valid on special types of documents like Bible books. Their method relies on the distance measurement to increase the precision and accuracy of the clustering and classification process. The performance of this method is degraded when the number of authors increases to more than two.

The contributions of this paper are as follows.

- A procedure for segment elicitation is developed and it is applied in the clustering assignment process. It is for the first time to develop such a procedure relying upon the differences in the posterior probabilities.
- A probability indication procedure is developed to improve the accuracy of sentence classification. It selects the significant and trusted sentences from a document and involves them to reclassify all sentences in the document. Our approach does not require any information about the document and the authors other than the number of authors of the document.
- Our proposed method is not restricted to any type of documents. It is still workable even when the topics in a document are not detectable.

The organization of this paper is as follows. Section 2 demonstrates the proposed framework. Section 3 uses an example to clarify our method. Results are conducted in Section 4. Finally, Section 5 presents the conclusion and future work.

Proceedings of the 53rd Annual Meeting of the Association for Computational Linguistics and the 7th International Joint Conference on Natural Language Processing (Short Papers), pages 501–505, Beijing, China, July 26-31, 2015.

2 Proposed Framework

Given a multi-author document written by l authors, it is assumed that every author has written consecutive sequences of sentences, and every sentence is completely written by only one of the l authors. The value of l is pre-defined.

Our approach goes through the following steps:

- *Step 1* Divide the document into segments of fixed length.
- *Step 2* Represent the resulted segments as vectors using an appropriate feature set which can differentiate the writing styles among authors.
- *Step 3* Cluster the resulted vectors into l clusters using an appropriate clustering algorithm targeting on achieving high *recall* rates.
- *Step 4* Re-vectorize the segments using a different feature set to more accurately discriminate the segments in each cluster.
- *Step 5* Apply the "*Segment Elicitation Procedure*" to select the best segments from each cluster to increase the *precision* rates.
- *Step 6* Re-vectorize all selected segments using another feature set that can capture the differences among the writing styles of all sentences in a document.
- *Step 7* Train the classifier using the Naive-Bayesian model.
- *Step 8* Classify each sentence using the learned classifier.
- *Step 9* Apply the "*Probability Indication Procedure*" to increase the *accuracy* of the classification results using five criteria.

To assess the performance of the proposed scheme, we perform our experiments on an artificially merged document. The generation of this merged document begins with randomly choosing an author from an authors list. Then, we pick up the first r previously-unselected sentences from a document of that author, and merge them with the first r previously-unselected sentences from the documents of other randomly selected authors. Keep doing like this until all sentences from all authors' documents are selected. The value of r on each switch is an integer value chosen randomly from a uniform distribution varying from 1 to V.

3 Ezekiel-Job Document as Example

For interpretative intent, we will exploit the bible books of Ezekiel and Job to create a merged document. The book of Ezekiel contains 1,273 sentences and book of Job contains 1,018 sentences. We use this example of a merged document to clarify each step of our proposed framework shown in Section 2. We also use this merged document to work out the values of parameters used in our approach. We set V to be equal to 200. In the merged document, there are 2,291 sentences in total and there are hence 20 transitions from Ezekiel sentences to Job sentences and from Job's to Ezekiel's.

In *Step 1*, we divide the merged document into segments. Each segment has 30 sentences. As a result, we get 77 segments, of which 34 are written by Ezekiel, 27 are written by Job and 16 are mixed. In *Step 2*, we represent each segment using a binary vector that reflects all words that appear at least three times in the document. In *Step 3*, we cluster these segments by using a Gaussian Mixture Model (GMMs) into 2 multivariate Gaussian densities. The GMMs are trained using the iterative Expectation-Maximization (EM) algorithm (Bilmes and others, 1998). We find that all 34 Ezekiel segments are clustered in Cluster 1, and all 27 Job segments are clustered in Cluster 2. Mixed segments are divided equally between the two clusters (Note that, the *recalls* of both cluster are 100%, and the precisions are 81% and 77% in Cluster 1 and Cluster 2, respectively). In *Step 4*, all of the segments in both clusters are re-vectorized using the binary representation of the 1500 most frequently-appeared words in the document.

In the *Step 5*, a Segment Elicitation Procedure is proposed. The key idea is to choose only the segments from a cluster that can best represent the writing style of the cluster. We call these selected segments *vital segments*. The vital segments have the following two features. First, they can represent the expressive style of a specific cluster. Second, they can distinguish the writing style of that cluster from other clusters. Henceforth, we consider all of the segments as labelled, based on the results of the clustering assignment (Step 3). To find the vital segments of each class (noting that, the term 'cluster' is now substituted with 'class'), we consider the differences in the posterior probabilities of each segment according to the other classes. Expressly, for each segment in a class, we compute the differences between the posterior probability of that segment in its class and the maximum posterior probability of that segment in other classes. Then, we select $s\%$ of them which have the biggest differences as vital segments of that class. To prevent the underflow point, we compute the posterior probability by adding the logarithms of probabilities instead of multiplying the probabilities. Furthermore, we assume that the features in the segments are mutually independent. In the Ezekiel-Job document, Cluster 1 is the Ezekiel class and Cluster 2 is the Job class. We set s to be 80, so we get 34 vital segments for the Ezekiel class and 28 vital segments for the Job class. Of the 34 vital segments in Ezekiel class, 30 are truly written by Ezekiel, and of the 28 vital segments in Job class, 25 are truly written by Job. As a result, the precisions of Ezekiel class and Job class are increased to 88.2% and 89.3%, respectively. The vital segments for two classes are used to train the supervised classifier which can best classify each sentence to the correct author's class. Therefore, in *Step 6*, the vital segments are represented in terms of the frequencies of all words that have appeared at least three times in the whole document.

In *Step 7*, the Naive-Bayesian model is applied to learn a classifier. In *Step 8*, this classifier is used to classify the sentences in the merged document to either Ezekiel class or Job class.We find that 93.1% of all sentences of Ezekiel and Job classes are correctly classified.

In (*Step 9*), a probability indication procedure is proposed based on the following five criteria. *First*, any sentence in the document is considered as *trusted sentence* if its posterior probability in its class is greater than its posterior probabilities in all other classes by more than threshold q. Thereupon, every trusted sentence holds its class. *Second*, if the first sentences in the document are not deemed to be trusted sentences, then they are assigned to the same class of the first trusted sentence that follow them. *Third*, if the last sentences in the document are not deemed to be trusted sentences, then they are assigned to the same class of the last trusted sentence that precede them. *Fourth*, if a group of unassigned sentences is located between two trusted sentences which have the same class, then all of the sentences in that group are assigned to the same class of these trusted sentences. *Fifth*, if a group of unassigned sentences is located between two trusted sentences which have different labels, then the best separated point in that group is detected to separate it into two subgroups, left and right subgroups. The left subgroup is assigned to the same label of the last trusted sentence that precede it and the right subgroup is assigned to the same label of the first trusted sentence that follow it. In the Ezekiel-Job document, by setting the value of q to be 5.0, 98.8% of the Ezekiel sentences and 99.1% of the Job sentences are correctly classified. The overall accuracy of all sentences is 99.0%.

4 Results

We use three datasets to test our method and show the adaptability of our method to different types of documents. The first dataset consists of 690 blogs written by Gary Becker and Richard Posner. This dataset containing articles of multiple authors is challenging because it covers a lot of different topics. That means, we cannot depend on the topics to help us distinguish the authors. The second dataset consists of 1,182 *New York Times* articles. These articles have been written by Maureeen Dowd, Gail Collins, Thomas Friedman and Paul Krugman. The third dataset consists of 5 biblical books which are written in Hebrew, a language other than English. These books are written by Isaiah (for Chapters 1-33), Jeremiah, Ezekiel, Job (for Chapters 3-41) and Proverbs. The first 3 are all in the prophetic literature and the other two are in the wisdom literature. In view of this, we conduct our experiments on three different datasets, each dataset has its characteristics which yield us to use it. In our experiments, the merged documents are created in the same way as we have discussed before. We set the value of V to be 200, and the number of authors of these documents to be two, three or four ($l = \{2,3,4\}$). We use the same values of the parameters as we have used in the Ezekiel-Job document.

4.1 Becker-Posner

In the first dataset, each author has written for a lot of different topics, and there have been some topics taken by both authors. Therefore, there is no topic indication to distinguish between the two authors. We have achieved an overall accuracy of 96.6% when testing on this dataset. This result is gratifying in this merged document that has more than 246 transitions between sentences writ-

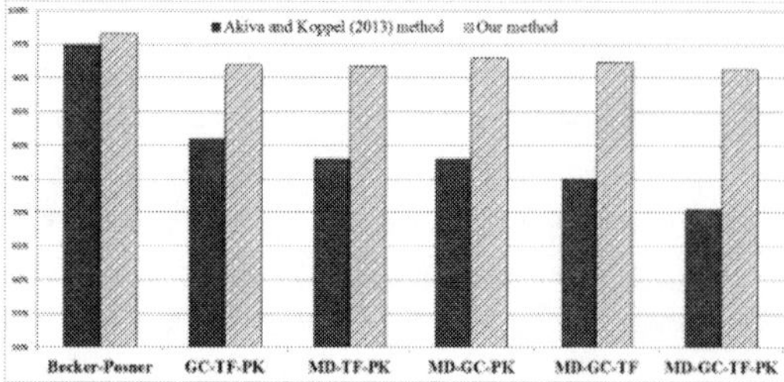

Figure 1: Accuracy comprisons between our method and the method used by Akiva and Koppel (2013) in Becker-Posner document, and in documents created by three or four *New York Times* authors (GC = Gail Collins, PK = Paul Krugman, TF = Thomas Friedman, MD = Maureen Dowd)

ten by the two authors and more than 26,900 sentences. In Figure 1, we show the comparison between our method and the method in Akiva and Koppel (2013).

4.2 *New York Times* Articles

This dataset contains articles written by four authors. First, we test our method using the merged documents created by any pair of the four authors. The results again are noticeable. The classification accuracies range from 93.3% to 96.1%. For comparison,the accuracy can be as low as 88.0% when applying the method in Akiva and Koppel (2013) on some of the merged documents.

To prove that our method can also work well when merged documents written by more than two authors, we have created merged documents written by any three of these four authors and formed four merged documents. We have also created a merged document written by all four *New York Times* authors. Then, we apply our method on these documents. In Figure 1, we show the accuracies of our method for classification on these documents. It is obvious that our method achieves high accuracies even when the documents are written by more than two authors. Furthermore, Figure 1 also compares our results with the results achieved by Akiva and Koppel (2013). It shows that our method has given consistent results and better performance than the ones in Akiva and Koppel (2013).

4.3 Bible Books

In these experiments, we use two literature types of biblical books. We create merged documents written by any pair of authors. The resulted documents may belong to either the same literatures or different literatures.

	Documents	1	2	3	Our method
Different	Eze-Prov	77%	99%	91%	98%
	Jer-Prov	73%	97%	75%	99%
	Jer-Job	88%	98%	93%	98%
	Isa-Job	83%	99%	89%	99%
	Eze-Job	86%	99%	95%	99%
	Isa-Prov	71%	95%	85%	98%
	Overall	***80%***	***98%***	***88%***	***99%***
Same	Jer-Eze	82%	97%	96%	97%
	Isa-Eze	79%	80%	88%	83%
	Job-Prov	85%	94%	82%	95%
	Isa-Jer	72%	67%	83%	71%
	Overall	***80%***	***85%***	***87%***	***87%***

Table 1: Accuracy performance obtained from documents having different literatures or same literatures using the methods of 1- Koppel et al. (2011), 2- Akiva and Koppel (2013)-BinaryCommonWords, 3- Akiva and Koppel (2013)-Synonyms and our method

In Tables 1, we show the comparisons of accuracies of using our method and the methods presented in Koppel et al. (2011), Akiva and Koppel (2013)-BinaryCommonWords and Akiva and Koppel (2013)-Synonyms.

As can be seen, the accuracies using our method in the documents with different literatures are interesting, and have achieved the accuracies of either 99% or 98% and have performed a lot better than the three state-of-the-art methods. Furthermore, the accuracies using our method on the documents with same literature are encouraging, and our method has achieved approximately the same overall accuracy compared with the method in Akiva and Koppel (2013), and have achieved better overall accuracy compared with the methods in Akiva and Koppel (2013) and Koppel et al. (2011).

5 Conclusion and Future Work

In this paper, we have proposed an unsupervised method for decomposing a multi-author document by authorship.

We have tested our method on three datasets, of which every one has its own characteristics. It is clear that our method has achieved a significantly high accuracies in these datasets, even when there is no topic indication to differentiate sentences between authors, and when the number of authors exceeds 2. Our results tested on these datasets have shown significantly better than those using the methods in Koppel et al. (2011) and Akiva and

Koppel (2013). Furthermore, our method can also compete with the method proposed in (Akiva and Koppel, 2013)-Synonyms, which is only valid for Bible documents.

In our research, our aim is to segment classify sentences in a multi-author document according to the sentences' authors. We assume that the number of authors of that document is known. In our future work, we work to automatically determine the number of authors of a multi-author document. Furthermore, we will explore an adaptive learning method to select the optimal value of the threshold q for the probability indication procedure.

References

Navot Akiva and Moshe Koppel. 2013. A generic unsupervised method for decomposing multi-author documents. *Journal of the American Society for Information Science and Technology*, 64(11):2256–2264.

Jeff A Bilmes et al. 1998. A gentle tutorial of the em algorithm and its application to parameter estimation for gaussian mixture and hidden markov models. *International Computer Science Institute*, 4(510):126.

Thorsten Brants, Francine Chen, and Ioannis Tsochantaridis. 2002. Topic-based document segmentation with probabilistic latent semantic analysis. In *Proceedings of the eleventh international conference on Information and knowledge management*, pages 211–218. ACM.

Freddy YY Choi. 2000. Advances in domain independent linear text segmentation. In *Proceedings of the 1st North American chapter of the Association for Computational Linguistics conference*, pages 26–33. Association for Computational Linguistics.

Leonhard Hennig and DAI Labor. 2009. Topic-based multi-document summarization with probabilistic latent semantic analysis. In *RANLP*, pages 144–149.

Moshe Koppel, Navot Akiva, Idan Dershowitz, and Nachum Dershowitz. 2011. Unsupervised decomposition of a document into authorial components. In *Proceedings of the 49th Annual Meeting of the Association for Computational Linguistics: Human Language Technologies-Volume 1*, pages 1356–1364. Association for Computational Linguistics.

Robert Layton, Paul Watters, and Richard Dazeley. 2013. Automated unsupervised authorship analysis using evidence accumulation clustering. *Natural Language Engineering*, 19(01):95–120.

Hemant Misra, François Yvon, Joemon M Jose, and Olivier Cappe. 2009. Text segmentation via topic modeling: an analytical study. In *Proceedings of the 18th ACM conference on Information and knowledge management*, pages 1553–1556. ACM.

G Bruce Schaalje, Natalie J Blades, and Tomohiko Funai. 2013. An open-set size-adjusted bayesian classifier for authorship attribution. *Journal of the American Society for Information Science and Technology*, 64(9):1815–1825.

Santiago Segarra, Mark Eisen, and Alejandro Ribeiro. 2014. Authorship attribution through function word adjacency networks. *arXiv preprint arXiv:1406.4469*.

Extended Topic Model for Word Dependency

Tong Wang[1], Vish Viswanath[2] and Ping Chen[1]
[1]University of Massachusetts Boston, Boston, MA
[2]Harvard School of Public Health, Boston, MA
tongwang0001@gmail.com, Ping.Chen@umb.edu
Vish_Viswanath@dfci.harvard.edu

Abstract

Topic Model such as Latent Dirichlet Allocation(LDA) makes assumption that topic assignment of different words are conditionally independent. In this paper, we propose a new model Extended Global Topic Random Field (EGTRF) to model non-linear dependencies between words. Specifically, we parse sentences into dependency trees and represent them as a graph, and assume the topic assignment of a word is influenced by its adjacent words and distance-2 words. Word similarity information learned from large corpus is incorporated to enhance word topic assignment. Parameters are estimated efficiently by variational inference and experimental results on two datasets show EGTRF achieves lower perplexity and higher log predictive probability.

1 Introduction

Probabilistic topic model such as Latent Dirichlet Allocation(LDA) (Blei et al, 2003) has been widely used for discovering latent topics from document collections by capturing words' co-occuring relation. However, the "bag of words" assumption is employed in most existing topic models, it assumes the order of words can be ignored and topic assignment of each word is conditionally independent given the topic mixture of a document.

To relax the "bag of words" assumption, many extended topic models have been proposed to address the limitation of conditional independence. Wallach (Wallach, 2006) explores a hierarchical generative probabilistic model that incorporates both n-gram statistics and latent topic variables. Gruber (Gruber et al, 2007) models the topics of words in the document as a Markov chain, and assumes all words in the same sentence are more likely to have the same topic. Zhu (Zhu et al, 2010) incorporates Markov dependency between topic assignments of neighboring words, and employs a general structure of the GLM to define a conditional distribution of latent topic assignments over words. Most of the models above are limited to model linear topical dependencies between words, word topical dependencies can also be modeled by a non-linear way. In Syntactic topic models (Boyd-Graber et al, 2009), each word of a sentence is generated by a distribution that combines document-specific topic weights and parse-tree-specific syntactic transitions.

In Global Topic Random Field(GTRF) model (Li et al, 2014), sentences of a document are parsed into dependency trees (Marneffe et al, 2008) (Manning et al, 2014) (Marneffe et al, 2006). They show topics of semantically or syntactically dependent words achieve the highest similarity and are able to provide more useful information in topic modeling, which is also the basic assumption of our model. Then they propose GTRF to model non-linear topical dependencies, word topics are sampled based on graph structure instead of "bag of words" representation, the conditional independence of word topic assignment is thus relaxed.

However, GTRF assumes topic assignment of a word vertex depends on the topic mixture of the document and its neighboring word vertices, ignoring the fact that word vertex can also be influenced by the distance-2 or further word vertices. In this paper, we extend GTRF model and present a novel model Extended Global Topic Random Field (EGTRF) to exploit topical dependency between words. In EGTRF, the topic assignment of a word is assumed to depend on both distance-1 and distance-2 word vertices. An example of a simple document that has two sentences shows in Figure 1. The two sentences are parsed into dependency trees respectively, and then merged into a graph.

Proceedings of the 53rd Annual Meeting of the Association for Computational Linguistics and the 7th International Joint Conference on Natural Language Processing (Short Papers), pages 506–510,
Beijing, China, July 26-31, 2015.

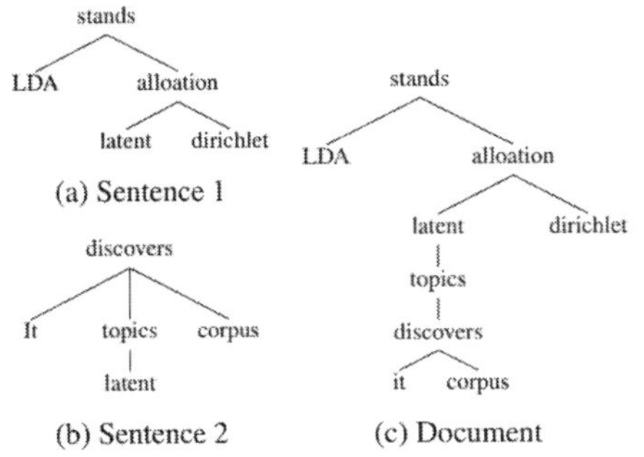

Example document: LDA stands for latent dirichlet allocation. It discovers latent topcis from corpus.

Example word vertex: allocation

Distance-1 word vertics: {stands, latent, dirichlet}

Distance-2 word vertics: {LDA, topics}

Figure 1: Dependency tree example

Some hidden dependency relations can also be extracted by merging dependency trees. For example, word "allocation" has a new distance-2 word "topics" after merging. Therefore, EGTRF can exploit more semantically or syntactically word dependencies. Theoretically, we can also model the distance further than 2, however, it leads to more complicated computation and small increase of performance.

Another advantage of EGTRF is it incorporates word features. The word vector representations are very interesting because the learned vectors explicitly encode many linguistic regularities and patterns (Mikolov et al, 2013). We use the pre-trained model from Google News dataset(about 100 billion words) using word2vec[1] tool to represent each word as a 300-dimensional word vector, and apply normalized word similarity as a confidence score to indicate how possible two word vertices share same topic.

We organized the paper as below: EGTRF is presented in Section 2, variational inference and parameter estimation are derived in Section 3, experiments on two datasets are showed in Section 4, we conclude the paper in Section 5.

2 Extended Global Topic Random Field

In this section, we first present Extended Global Random Field(EGRF) in section 2.1, then show how to model topical dependencies using EGRF in section 2.2. We incorporate word similarity information into model in section 2.3.

[1] https://code.google.com/p/word2vec/

2.1 Extended Global Random Field

After representing document to undirected graph on previous section, we extend Global Random Field and give the definition of Extended Global Random Field to model the graph as below:

Given an undirected graph G, word vertex set is denoted as $W = \{w_i | i = 1, 2, ..n\}$, where w_i is a word vertex, and n is the number of unique words in a document. E_1 is distance-1 edge set, $E_1 = \{(w_i, w_j) | \exists \textit{path between } w_i, w_j \textit{ that length is 1}\}$. E_2 is distance-2 edge set, $E_2 = \{(w_i, w_j) | \exists \textit{path between } w_i, w_j \textit{ that length is 2}\}$. The state(topic assignment) of a word vertex w is generated from $Z = \{z_i | i = 1, 2, ..., k\}$, k is the number of topics.

$$P(G) = f_G(g) = \frac{1}{|E_1| + |E_2|} \prod_{w \in W} f(z_w) \times \left(\sum_{(w'_1, w''_1) \in E_1} f_{(1)}(z_{w'_1}, z_{w''_1}) + \sum_{(w'_2, w''_2) \in E_2} f_{(2)}(z_{w'_2}, z_{w''_2}) \right) \tag{1}$$

$$\begin{aligned} s.t. \quad & 1. f(z) > 0, f_{(1)}(z', z'') > 0, f_{(2)}(z', z'') > 0 \\ & 2. \sum_{z \in Z} f(z) = 1 \\ & 3. \sum_{z', z'' \in Z} f(z') f(z'') f_{(1)}(z', z'') = 1 \\ & 4. \sum_{z', z'' \in Z} f(z') f(z'') f_{(2)}(z', z'') = 1 \end{aligned}$$

In Equation (1), $f(z)$ is the function defined on word vertex, which is a probability measure because of the constraints 1 and 2. $f_{(1)}(z, z')$ and $f_{(2)}(z, z')$ are the function defined on edge set E_1 and E_2. $f_{(1)}$ and $f_{(2)}$ are not necessarily probability measure, however, summing over all possible states of the product of the edge and the linked word pair should equal to 1, which are from constraints 3 and 4. So $f(z')f(z'')f_{(1)}(z', z'')$ and $f(z')f(z'')f_{(2)}(z', z'')$ are probability measure. g is one sample of word topic assignments from graph G. If Equation (1) satisfies all the four constraints, it is easy to verify $P(G)$ is also a probability measure since summing over all possible samples g equals to 1.

We define the random field as in Equation (1) a Extended Global Random Field (EGRF). And EGRF does not have normalization factor, which is much simplier than models with intractable normalizing factor.

2.2 Topic Model Using EGRF

We define Extended Global Topic Random Field based on EGRF. EGTRF is a generative probabilistic model, the basic idea is that documents are represented as mixtures of topics, words are generated depending on the topic mixtures and graph structure of current document. The generative process for word sequence of a document is described as below:

For each document d in corpus D:
  Transform document d into graph.
  Choose $\theta \sim Dir(\alpha)$.
  For each of the n words w_n in d:
    Choose topic $z_n \sim P_{egrf}(z \mid \theta)$,
    Choose word $w_n \sim Multi(\beta_{z_n,w_n})$.

Given Dirichlet prior α, word distribution of topics β, topic mixture of document θ, topic assignments $\mathbf{z}$ and words $\mathbf{w}$. We obtain the marginal distribution of a document:

$$p(\mathbf{w} \mid \alpha, \beta) = \int P(\theta \mid \alpha) \sum_z P_{egrf}(z \mid \theta) \prod_n P(w_n \mid z_{w_n}, \beta) d\theta \quad (2)$$

We can see the marginal distribution is similar to LDA except topic assignment of word is sampled by Extended Global Random Field instead of Multinomial. So the word topic assignment is no longer conditionally independent. According to EGRF described in section 2.1, we define the probability of topic sequence $\mathbf{z}$ as below:

$$P_{egrf}(z \mid \theta) = \frac{1}{\mid E_1 \mid + \mid E_2 \mid} \prod_{w \in V} f(z_w) \times \left(\sum_{(w_1', w_1'') \in E_1} f_{(1)}(z_{w_1'}, z_{w_1''}) + \sum_{(w_2', w_2'') \in E_2} f_{(2)}(z_{w_2'}, z_{w_2''}) \right) \quad (3)$$

$$\text{where } f(z_w) = Multi(z_w \mid \theta) \quad (4)$$

$$f_{(1)}(z_{w_1'}, z_{w_1''}) = \sigma_{z_{w_1'} = z_{w_1''}} \lambda_1 + \sigma_{z_{w_1'} \neq z_{w_1''}} \lambda_2 \quad (5)$$

$$f_{(2)}(z_{w_2'}, z_{w_2''}) = \sigma_{z_{w_2'} = z_{w_2''}} \lambda_3 + \sigma_{z_{w_2'} \neq z_{w_2''}} \lambda_4 \quad (6)$$

σ is an indicator function and equals 1 if the topic assignments of two words on an edge are same. In order to model Equation (3) as an EGRF, it must satisfy all the four constraints in Equation (1). Equation (4) defines word vertex as multinomial distribution, and we assign λ_1, λ_2, λ_3 and λ_4 nonzero values, then it is clear to verify constraint 1 and 2 are satisfied. To satisfy the constraint 3 and 4, combine with (5), (6), we get the relation between λ_1 and λ_2, λ_3 and λ_4.

$$\sum \theta_i^2 \lambda_1 + (1 - \sum \theta_i^2) \lambda_2 = 1 \quad i = 1, 2, ..|E_1| \quad (7)$$

$$\sum \theta_i^2 \lambda_3 + (1 - \sum \theta_i^2) \lambda_4 = 1 \quad i = 1, 2, ..|E_2| \quad (8)$$

Lower λ_2, λ_4 give higher reward to the edge that connects two word vertices with same topic. If (7) and (8) hold true, Equation (3) is an EGRF. And we define the topic model based on EGRF as Extended Global Topic Random Field(EGTRF). If $|E_2| = 0, |E_1| \neq 0$, EGTRF is equivalent to GTRF. If $|E_1| = 0, |E_2| = 0$, EGTRF is equivalent to LDA.

2.3 Word Similarity Information

The *coherent edge* is the edge that the two linked words have same topic. In distance-i edge set, i= $1, 2$. E_{C_i} includes all coherent edges, E_{NC_i} contains all non-coherent edges. Then equation (3) can be represented as below:

$$\begin{aligned} & P_{egrf}(z \mid \theta) \\ &= \frac{1}{\mid E_1 \mid + \mid E_2 \mid} \prod_{w \in V} Multi(z_w \mid \theta) \times \\ & (\mid E_{C_1} \mid \lambda_1 + \mid E_{NC_1} \mid \lambda_2 + \mid E_{C_2} \mid \lambda_3 + \mid E_{NC_2} \mid \lambda_4) \\ &= \frac{\prod_{w \in V} Multi(z_w \mid \theta)}{(\mid E_1 \mid + \mid E_2 \mid) \theta^T \theta} \times (\mid E_{C_1} \mid (1 - \lambda_2) + \mid E_1 \mid \lambda_2 \theta^T \theta + \\ & \mid E_{C_2} \mid (1 - \lambda_4) + \mid E_2 \mid \lambda_4 \theta^T \theta) \end{aligned} \quad (9)$$

From the second line to the third line of Equation (9), we represent λ_1, λ_3 as the function of λ_2, λ_4 based on (7) and (8). The expectation of the number of edges in E_{c_i} can be computed as:

$$E(\mid E_{C_i} \mid) = \sum_{(w_1, w_2) \in E_i} \phi_{w_1}^T \phi_{w_2} S_{w_1, w_2} \quad (10)$$

ϕ is the K dimensional variational multinomial parameters and can be thought as the posterior probability of a word given the topic assignment. S_{w_1,w_2} is the similarity measure between word w_1 and w_2.

As we discussed in section 1, word similarity information S_{w_1,w_2} works as a confidence score to model how likely two words on an edge have same topic. And we make assumption that two words are more likely to have same topic if they have a higher similarity score. To get the similarity score between words, we use word2vec tool to learn the word representation of each word from pre-trained model. The word representations are computed using neural networks, and the learned representations explicitly encode many linguistic regularities

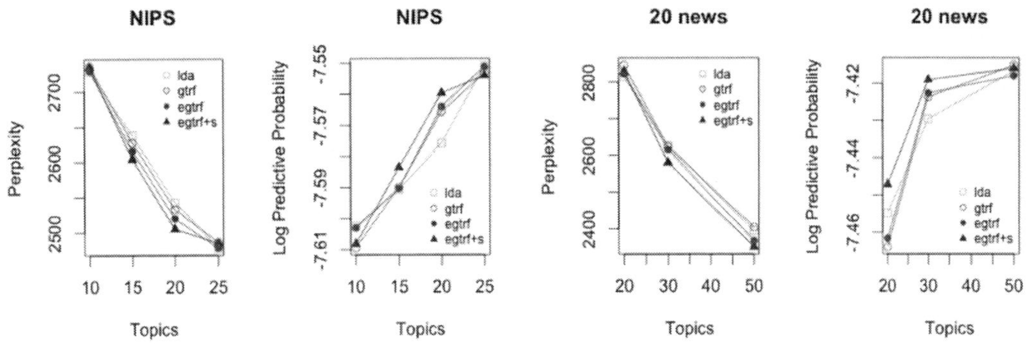

Figure 2: Experimental results on NIPS(left) and 20 news(right) data

and patterns from the corpus. Normalized similarity between word vectors can be regarded as the confidence score of how possible two words have same topic. In this way, knowledge from large corpus other than current document collections is incorporated to guide topic modeling.

3 Posterior Inference and Parameter Estimation

We derive Variational Inference for posterior inference. The variational function q is same to the original LDA paper (Blei et al, 2003). All terms except $P(z|\theta)$ in likelihood function are also same to LDA, Based on Equation (9), we obtain:

$$\begin{aligned} & E_q[\log P_{egrf}(z \mid \theta)] \\ \approx & E_q[\log(\prod_n Multi(z_{w_n} \mid \theta))] + \\ & \frac{1-\lambda_2}{\zeta_1} E_q(\mid E_{C_1} \mid) + \frac{1-\lambda_4}{\zeta_1} E_q(\mid E_{C_2} \mid) + \\ & (\frac{\mid E_1 \mid \lambda_2 + \mid E_2 \mid \lambda_4}{\zeta_1} - \frac{\mid E_1 \mid + \mid E_2 \mid}{\zeta_2}) E_q(\theta^T \theta) + \\ & \log \zeta_1 - \log \zeta_2 \end{aligned} \tag{11}$$

We get the approximation in Equation (11) from Taylor series, where ζ_1 and ζ_2 are Taylor approximation. $E_q(\mid E_{C_i} \mid)$ is obtained directly from (10), $E_q(\theta^T \theta)$ is from the property of Dirichlet distribution. The updating rule of α and β are same to LDA, γ is updated using Newton method since we can not obtain the direct updating rule for γ. ϕ can be approximated as:

$$\begin{aligned} \phi_{w_{n,i}} \propto \beta_{i,v} exp(\Psi(\gamma_i) + \frac{1-\lambda_2}{\zeta_1} \times \sum_{(w_n, w_m) \subset E_1} \phi_{w_{m,i}} S_{m,n} + \\ \frac{1-\lambda_4}{\zeta_1} \times \sum_{(w_n, w_p) \in E_2} \phi_{w_{p,i}} S_{p,n}) \end{aligned} \tag{12}$$

EM algorithm is applied using above updating rules. At E-step, we estimate the best γ and ϕ given current α and β. At M-step, we update new α and β based on obtained γ and ϕ. We run such iterations until convergence.

4 Experiment

In this section we study the empirical performance of EGTRF on two datasets. For each dataset, we remove very short documents, and compute a vocabulary by removing stop words, rare words, frequent words. Eighty percent data are used for training, others for testing.

- *20 News Groups*: After processing, it contains 13706 documents with a vocabulary of 5164 terms.
- *NIPS data* (Globerson et al, 2004): Spanning from 2000 to 2005. After processing, it contains 843 documents with a vocabulary of 6098 terms.

We evaluate how well a model fits the data with held-out perplexity (Blei et al, 2003) and predictive distribution (Hoffman et al, 2013). Lower perplexity, higher log predictive probability indicate better generalization performance. We implement GTRF without adding self defined edges from the original paper, and set $\lambda_2 = 0.2$ to give higher reward to edges from E_1 that the two word vertices have same topic. We set $\lambda_4 = 1.2$ to give lower(even negative) reward to edges from E_2 that the two word vertices have same topic in EGTRF, since the distance-1 words are expected to have greater topical affects than distance-2 words. Word is represented as vector from pre-trained Google News dataset, we use the word vector learned from original corpus when the word does not exist in pre-trained Google News dataset.

We choose 10, 20, 30, 50 topics for 20 news dataset, 10, 15, 20, 25 topics for NIPS dataset. Figure 2 shows the experimental results of four models: lda, gtrf, egtrf(EGTRF without word similarity information), and egtrf+s(EGTRF with word similarity information) on two datasets. The results show EGTRF outperforms LDA and GTRF in general, and EGTRF with word similarity information achieves best performance.

We believe modeling distance-2 word vertices can exploit more semantically or syntactically word dependencies from document, and word similarity information obtained from large corpus can make up the lack of sufficient information from the original corpus. Therefore, adding the influence of distance-2 word vertices and word similarity information can improve performance of topic modeling.

5 Conclusion

In this paper, we extended Global Topic Random Field(GTRF) and proposed a novel topic model Extended Global Topic Random Field(EGTRF) which can model dependency relation between adjacent words and distance-2 words. Word topics are drawed by Extended Global Random Field(EGRF) instead of Multinomial, the conditional independence of word topic assignment is thus relaxed. Word similarity information learned from large corpus is incorporated into the model. Experiments on two datasets show EGTRF achieves better performance than GTRF and LDA, which confirm our assumption that adding topical dependency of distance-2 words and incorporating word similarity information can improve model performance.

References

Amir Globerson, Gal Chechik, Fernando Pereira, Naftali Tishby Euclidean Embedding of Co-occurrence Data. In *Advances in neural information processing systems*. pp. 497-504. 2004.

Amit Gruber, Michal Rosen-Zvi and Yair Wei. Hidden Topic Markov Models. In *Proceedings of the Eleventh International Conference on Artificial Intelligence and Statistic*. pp. 163-170. 2007.

David Blei, Andrew Ng., and Michael Jordan. Latent Dirichlet Allocation. *The Journal of Machine Learning Research*. 3:993-1022, 2003.

Hanna M Wallach. Topic modeling: Beyond bag-of-words. In *International Conference on Machine Learning*. pp. 977-984. ACM, 2006.

Jordan Boyd-Graber and David Blei. Syntactic topic models. In *Neural Information Processing Systems*. pp. 185-192. 2009.

Jun Zhu and Eric P. Xing. Conditional Topic Random Fields. In *Proceedings of the 27th International Conference on Machine Learning*. 2010.

Christopher D. Manning, Mihai Surdeanu, John Bauer, Jenny Finkel, Steven J. Bethard and David McClosky. The Stanford CoreNLP Natural Language Processing Toolkit. In *Proceedings of 52nd Annual Meeting of the Association for Computational Linguistics: System Demonstrations*. pp. 55-60. 2014.

Marie-Catherine de Marneffe, Bill MacCartney, and Christopher D. Manning. Generating typed dependency parses from phrase structure parses. In *Proceedings of LREC*. Vol. 6, No. 2006, pp. 449-454. 2006.

Marie-Catherine de Marneffe, Christopher D. Manning. The Stanford typed dependencies representation. In *COLING 2008 Workshop on Cross-framework and Cross-domain Parser Evaluation*. pp. 1-8. 2008.

Matthew Hoffman, David Blei, Chong Wang, John Paisley Stochastic Variational Inference *The Journal of Machine Learning Research*. 14(1), 1303-1347. 2013.

Tomas Mikolov, Kai Chen, Greg Corrado, and Jeffrey Dean. Efficient Estimation of Word Representations in Vector Space. In *Proceedings of Workshop at ICLR*. arXiv:1301.3781, 2013.

Tomas Mikolov, Ilya Sutskever, Kai Chen, Greg Corrado, and Jeffrey Dean. Distributed Representations of Words and Phrases and their Compositionality. In *Proceedings of NIPS*. pp. 3111-3119. 2013.

Tomas Mikolov, Wen-tau Yih, and Geoffrey Zweig. Linguistic Regularities in Continuous Space Word Representations. In *Proceedings of NAACL HLT*. pp. 746-751, 2013.

Zhixing Li, Siqiang Wen, Juanzi Li, Peng Zhang and Jie Tang. On Modeling Non-linear Topical Dependencies. In *Proceedings of the 31th International Conference on Machine Learning*. pp. 458-466, 2014.

Dependency Recurrent Neural Language Models for Sentence Completion

Piotr Mirowski
Google DeepMind
piotr.mirowski@computer.org

Andreas Vlachos
University College London
a.vlachos@cs.ucl.ac.uk

Abstract

Recent work on language modelling has shifted focus from count-based models to neural models. In these works, the words in each sentence are always considered in a left-to-right order. In this paper we show how we can improve the performance of the recurrent neural network (RNN) language model by incorporating the syntactic dependencies of a sentence, which have the effect of bringing relevant contexts closer to the word being predicted. We evaluate our approach on the Microsoft Research Sentence Completion Challenge and show that the dependency RNN proposed improves over the RNN by about 10 points in accuracy. Furthermore, we achieve results comparable with the state-of-the-art models on this task.

1 Introduction

Language Models (LM) are commonly used to score a sequence of tokens according to its probability of occurring in natural language. They are an essential building block in a variety of applications such as machine translation, speech recognition and grammatical error correction. The standard way of evaluating a language model has been to calculate its perplexity on a large corpus. However, this evaluation assumes the output of the language model to be probabilistic and it has been observed that perplexity does not always correlate with the downstream task performance.

For these reasons, Zweig and Burges (2012) proposed the Sentence Completion Challenge, in which the task is to pick the correct word to complete a sentence out of five candidates. Performance is evaluated by accuracy (how many sentences were completed correctly), thus both probabilistic and non-probabilistic models (e.g. Roark et al. (2007)) can be compared. Recent approaches for this task include both neural and count-based language models (Zweig et al., 2012; Gubbins and Vlachos, 2013; Mnih and Kavukcuoglu, 2013; Mikolov et al., 2013).

Most neural language models consider the tokens in a sentence in the order they appear, and the hidden state representation of the network is typically reset at the beginning of each sentence. In this work we propose a novel neural language model that learns a recurrent neural network (RNN) (Mikolov et al., 2010) on top of the syntactic dependency parse of a sentence. Syntactic dependencies bring relevant contexts closer to the word being predicted, thus enhancing performance as shown by Gubbins and Vlachos (2013) for count-based language models. Our Dependency RNN model is published simultaneously with another model, introduced in Tai et al. (2015), who extend the Long-Short Term Memory (LSTM) architecture to tree-structured network topologies and evaluate it at sentence-level sentiment classification and semantic relatedness tasks, but not as a language model.

Adapting the RNN to use the syntactic dependency structure required to reset and run the network on all the paths in the dependency parse tree of a given sentence, while maintaining a count of how often each token appears in those paths. Furthermore, we explain how we can incorporate the dependency labels as features.

Our results show that the dependency RNN language model proposed outperforms the RNN proposed by Mikolov et al. (2011) by about 10 points in accuracy. Furthermore, it improves upon the count-based dependency language model of Gubbins and Vlachos (2013), while achieving slightly worse than the recent state-of-the-art results by Mnih and Kavukcuoglu (2013). Finally, we make the code and preprocessed data available to facilitate comparisons with future work.

Proceedings of the 53rd Annual Meeting of the Association for Computational Linguistics and the 7th International Joint Conference on Natural Language Processing (Short Papers), pages 511–517,
Beijing, China, July 26-31, 2015.

2 Dependency Recurrent Neural Network

Count-based language models operate by assigning probabilities to sentences by factorizing their likelihood into n-grams. Neural language models further *embed* each word $w(t)$ into a low-dimensional vector representation (denoted by $\mathbf{s}(t)$)[1]. These word representations are learned as the language model is trained (Bengio et al., 2003) and enable to define a word in relation to other words in a metric space.

Recurrent Neural Network Mikolov et al. (2010) suggested the use of Recurrent Neural Networks (RNN) to model long-range dependencies between words as they are not restricted to a fixed context length, like the feedforward neural network (Bengio et al., 2003). The hidden representation $\mathbf{s}(t)$ for the word in position t of the sentence in the RNN follows a first order auto-regressive dynamic (Eq. 1), where $\mathbf{W}$ is the matrix connecting the hidden representation of the previous word $\mathbf{s}(t-1)$ to the current one, $\mathbf{w}(t)$ is the one-hot index of the current word (in a vocabulary of size N words) and $\mathbf{U}$ is the matrix containing the embeddings for all the words in the vocabulary:

$$\mathbf{s}(t) = f\left(\mathbf{W}\mathbf{s}(t-1) + \mathbf{U}\mathbf{w}(t)\right) \quad (1)$$

The nonlinearity f is typically the logistic sigmoid function $f(x) = \frac{1}{1+\exp(-x)}$. At each time step, the RNN generates the word probability vector $\mathbf{y}(t)$ for the next word $\mathbf{w}(t+1)$, using the output word embedding matrix $\mathbf{V}$ and the softmax nonlinearity $g(x_i) = \frac{\exp(x_i)}{\sum_i \exp(x_i)}$:

$$\mathbf{y}(t) = g\left(\mathbf{V}\mathbf{s}(t)\right) \quad (2)$$

RNN with Maximum Entropy Model Mikolov et al. (2011) combined RNNs with a maximum entropy model, essentially adding a matrix that directly connects the input words' n-gram context $\mathbf{w}(t-n+1,\ldots,t)$ to the output word probabilities. In practice, because of the large vocabulary size N, designing such a matrix is computationally prohibitive. Instead, a hash-based implementation is used, where the word context is fed through a hash function h that computes the index $h(\mathbf{w}(t-n+1,\ldots,t))$ of the context words in a one-dimensional array $\mathbf{d}$ of size D (typically, $D = 10^9$). Array $\mathbf{d}$ is trained in the same way as the rest of the RNN model and contributes to the output word probabilities:

$$\mathbf{y}(t) = g\left(\mathbf{V}\mathbf{s}(t) + \mathbf{d}_{h(\mathbf{w}(t-n+1,\ldots,t))}\right) \quad (3)$$

As we show in our experiments, this additional matrix is crucial to a good performance on word completion tasks.

Training RNNs RNNs are trained using maximum likelihood through gradient-based optimization, such as Stochastic Gradient Descent (SGD) with an annealed learning rate λ. The Back-Propagation Through Time (BPTT) variant of SGD enables to sum-up gradients from consecutive time steps before updating the parameters of the RNN and to handle the long-range temporal dependencies in the hidden $\mathbf{s}$ and output $\mathbf{y}$ sequences. The loss function is the cross-entropy between the generated word distribution $\mathbf{y}(t)$ and the target *one-hot* word distribution $\mathbf{w}(t+1)$, and involves the log-likelihood terms $\log y_{w(t+1)}(t)$.

For speed-up, the estimation of the output word probabilities is done using hierarchical softmax outputs, i.e., class-based factorization (Mikolov and Zweig, 2012). Each word w^i is assigned to a class c^i and the corresponding log-likelihood is effectively $\log y_{w^i}(t) = \log y_{c^i}(t) + \log y_{w^j}(t)$, where j is the index of word w^i among words belonging to class c^i. In our experiments, we binned the words found in our training corpus into 250 classes according to frequency, roughly corresponding to the square root of the vocabulary size.

Dependency RNN RNNs are designed to process sequential data by iteratively presenting them with word $\mathbf{w}(t)$ and generating next word's probability distribution $\mathbf{y}(t)$ at each time step. They can be reset at the beginning of a sentence by setting all the values of hidden vector $\mathbf{s}(t)$ to zero.

Dependency parsing (Nivre, 2005) generates, for each sentence (which we note $\{w(t)\}_{t=0}^{T}$), a parse tree with a single root, many leaves and an unique path (also called *unroll*) from the root to each leaf, as illustrated on Figure 1. We now note $\{w_i\}_i$ the set of word tokens appearing in the parse tree of a sentence. The order in the notation derives from the breadth-first traversal of that tree (i.e., the root word is noted w_0). Each of the unrolls can be seen as a different sequence of words

[1] In our notation, we make a distinction between the word token $w(t)$ at position t in the sentence and its one-hot vector representation $\mathbf{w}(t)$. We note w_i the i-th word token on a breadth-first traversal of a dependency parse tree.

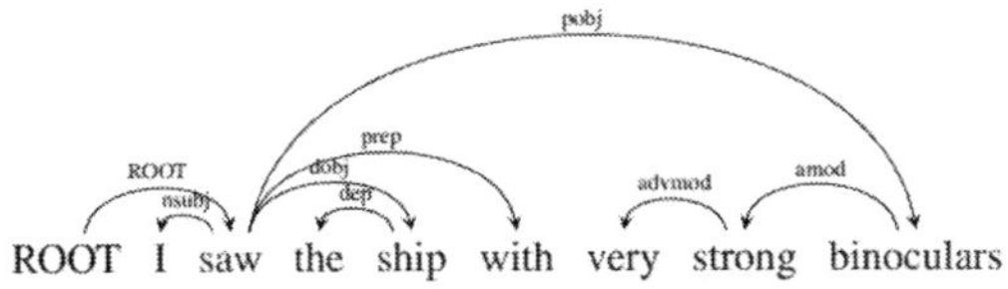

Figure 1: Example dependency tree

$\{w_i\}$, starting from the single root w_0, that are visited when one takes a specific path on the parse tree. We propose a simple transformation to the RNN algorithm so that it can process dependency parse trees. The RNN is reset and independently run on each such unroll. As detailed in the next paragraph, when evaluating the log-probability of the sentence, a word token w_i can appear in multiple unrolls but its log-likelihood is counted only once. During training, and to avoid over-training the network on word tokens that appear in more than one unroll (words near the root appear in more unrolls than those nearer the leaves), each word token w_i is given a weight discount $\alpha_i = \frac{1}{n_i}$, based on the number n_i of unrolls the token appears in. Since the RNN is optimized using SGD and updated at every time-step, the contribution of word token w_i can be discounted by multiplying the learning rate by the discount factor: $\alpha_i \lambda$.

Sentence Probability in Dependency RNN Given a word w_i, let us define the ancestor sequence $A(w_i)$ to be the subsequence of words, taken as a subset from $\{w_k\}_{k=0}^{i-1}$ and describing the path from the root node w_0 to the parent of w_i. For example, in Figure 1, the ancestors $A(\texttt{very})$ of word token `very` are `saw`, `binoculars` and `strong`. Assuming that each word w_i is conditionally independent of the words outside of its ancestor sequence, given its ancestor sequence $A(w_i)$, Gubbins and Vlachos (2013) showed that the probability of a sentence (i.e., the probability of a lexicalized tree S^T given an unlexicalized tree T) could be written as:

$$P[S^T|T] = \prod_{i=1}^{|S|} P[w_i|A(w_i)] \quad (4)$$

This means that the conditional likelihood of a word given its ancestors needs to be counted only once in the calculation of the sentence likelihood, even though each word can appear in multiple unrolls. When modeling a sentence using an RNN, the state $\mathbf{s}_j$ that is used to generate the distribution of words $\mathbf{w}_i$ (where j is the parent of i in the tree), represents the vector embedding of the history of the ancestor words $A(w_i)$. Therefore, we count the term $P[\mathbf{w}_i|\mathbf{s}_j]$ only once when computing the likelihood of the sentence.

3 Labelled Dependency RNN

The model presented so far does not use dependency labels. For this purpose we adapted the context-dependent RNN (Mikolov and Zweig, 2012) to handle them as additional M-dimensional label input features $\mathbf{f}(t)$. These features require a matrix $\mathbf{F}$ that connects label features to word vectors, thus yielding a new dynamical model (Eq. 5) in the RNN, and a matrix $\mathbf{G}$ that connects label features to output word probabilities. The full model becomes as follows:

$$\mathbf{s}(t) = f\left(\mathbf{W}\mathbf{s}(t-1) + \mathbf{U}\mathbf{w}(t) + \mathbf{F}\mathbf{f}(t)\right) \quad (5)$$

$$\mathbf{y}(t) = g\left(\mathbf{V}\mathbf{s}(t) + \mathbf{G}\mathbf{f}(t) + \mathbf{d}_{h(\mathbf{w}_{t-n+1}^t)}\right) \quad (6)$$

On our training dataset, the dependency parsing model found $M = 44$ distinct labels (e.g., *nsubj*, *det* or *prep*). At each time step t, the context word $\mathbf{w}(t)$ is associated a single dependency label $\mathbf{f}(t)$ (a one-hot vector of dimension M).

Let $G(w)$ be the sequence of grammatical relations (dependency tree labels) between successive elements of $(A(w), w)$. The factorization of the sentence likelihood from Eq. 4 becomes:

$$P[S^T|T] = \prod_{i=1}^{|S|} P[w_i|A(w_i), G(w_i)] \quad (7)$$

4 Implementation and Dataset

We modified the Feature-Augmented RNN toolkit[2] and adapted it to handle tree-structured data. Specifically, and instead of being run sequentially on the entire training corpus, the RNN is run on all the word tokens in all unrolls of all the sentences in all the books of the corpus. The RNN is reset at the beginning of each unroll of a sentence. When calculating the log-probability of a sentence, the contribution of each word token is counted only once (and stored in a hash-table specific for that sentence). Once all the unrolls of a sentence are processed, the log-probability of the sentence is the sum of the per-token log-probabilities in that hash-table. We also further

[2]http://research.microsoft.com/en-us/projects/rnn/

enhanced the RNN library by replacing some large matrix multiplication routines by calls to the CBLAS library, thus yielding a two- to three-fold speed-up in the test and training time.[3]

The training corpus consists of 522 19th century novels from Project Gutenberg (Zweig and Burges, 2012). All processing (sentence-splitting, PoS tagging, syntactic parsing) was performed using the Stanford CoreNLP toolkit (Manning et al., 2014). The test set contains 1040 sentences to be completed. Each sentence consists of one ground truth and 4 impostor sentences where a specific word has been replaced with a syntactically correct but semantically incorrect *impostor* word. Dependency trees are generated for each sentence candidate. We split that set into two, using the first 520 sentences in the validation (development) set and the latter 520 sentences in the test set. During training, we start annealing the learning rate λ with decay factor 0.66 as soon as the classification error on the validation set starts to increase.

5 Results

Table 1 shows the accuracy (validation and test sets) obtained using a simple RNN with 50, 100, 200 and 300-dimensional hidden word representation and 250 frequency-based word classes (vocabulary size $N = 72846$ words appearing at least 5 times in the training corpus). One notices that adding the direct word context to target word connections (using the additional matrix described in section 2), enables to jump from a poor performance of about 30% accuracy to about 40% test accuracy, essentially matching the 39% accuracy reported for Good-Turing n-gram language models in Zweig et al. (2012). Modelling 4-grams yields even better results, closer to the 45% accuracy reported for RNNs in (Zweig et al., 2012).[4]

As Table 2 shows, dependency RNNs (depRNN) enable about 10 point word accuracy improvement over sequential RNNs.

The best accuracy achieved by the depRNN on the combined development and test sets used to report results in previous work was 53.5%. The best reported results in the MSR sentence completion challenge have been achieved by Log-BiLinear Models (LBLs) (Mnih and Hinton, 2007), a variant of neural language models with 54.7% to 55.5% accuracy (Mnih and Teh, 2012; Mnih and Kavukcuoglu, 2013). We conjecture that their superior performance might stem from the fact that LBLs, just like n-grams, take into account the order of the words in the context and can thus model higher-order Markovian dynamics than the simple first-order autoregressive dynamics in RNNs. The depRNN proposed ignores the left-to-right word order, thus it is likely that a combination of these approaches will result in even higher accuracies. Gubbins and Vlachos (2013) developed a count-based dependency language model achieving 50% accuracy. Finally, Mikolov et al. (2013) report that they achieved 55.4% accuracy with an ensemble of RNNs, without giving any other details.

Architecture	50h	100h	200h	300h
RNN (dev)	*29.6*	*30.0*	*30.0*	*30.6*
RNN (test)	28.1	30.0	30.4	28.5
RNN+2g (dev)	*29.6*	*28.7*	*29.4*	*29.8*
RNN+2g (test)	29.6	28.7	28.1	30.2
RNN+3g (dev)	*39.2*	*39.4*	*38.8*	*36.5*
RNN+3g (test)	40.8	40.6	40.2	39.8
RNN+4g (dev)	*40.2*	*40.6*	*40.0*	*40.2*
RNN+4g (test)	42.3	41.2	40.4	39.2

Table 1: Accuracy of sequential RNN on the MSR Sentence Completion Challenge.

Architecture	50h	100h	200h
depRNN+3g (dev)	53.3	**54.2**	54.2
depRNN+3g (test)	51.9	**52.7**	51.9
ldepRNN+3g (dev)	48.8	51.5	49.0
ldepRNN+3g (test)	44.8	45.4	47.7
depRNN+4g (dev)	52.7	54.0	52.7
depRNN+4g (test)	48.9	51.3	50.8
ldepRNN+4g (dev)	49.4	50.0	(48.5)
ldepRNN+4g (test)	47.7	51.4	(47.7)

Table 2: Accuracy of (un-)labeled dependency RNN (depRNN and ldepRNN respectively).

6 Discussion

Related work Mirowski et al. (2010) incorporated syntactic information into neural language models using PoS tags as additional input to LBLs but obtained only a small reduction of the word error rate in a speech recognition task. Similarly, Bian et al. (2014) enriched the Continuous Bag-of-

[3]Our code and our preprocessed datasets are available from: `https://github.com/piotrmirowski/DependencyTreeRnn`

[4]The paper did not provide details on the maximum entropy features or on class-based hierarchical softmax).

Words (CBOW) model of Mikolov et al. (2013) by incorporating morphology, PoS tags and entity categories into 600-dimensional word embeddings trained on the Gutenberg dataset, increasing sentence completion accuracy from 41% to 44%. Other work on incorporating syntax into language modeling include Chelba et al. (1997) and Pauls and Klein (2012), however none of these approaches considered neural language models, only count-based ones. Levy and Goldberg (2014) and Zhao et al. (2014) proposed to train neural word embeddings using skip-grams and CBOWs on dependency parse trees, but did not extend their approach to actual language models such as LBL and RNN and did not evaluate the word embeddings on word completion tasks.

Note that we assume that the dependency tree is supplied prior to running the RNN which limits the scope of the Dependency RNN to the scoring of complete sentences, not to next word prediction (unless a dependency tree parse for the sentence to be generated is provided). Nevertheless, it is common in speech recognition and machine translation to use a conventional decoder to produce an N-best list of the most likely candidate sentences and then re-score them with the language model. (Chelba et al., 1997; Pauls and Klein, 2011)

Tai et al. (2015) propose a similar approach to ours, learning Long Short-Term Memory (LSTM) (Hochreiter and Schmidhuber, 1997; Graves, 2012) RNNs on dependency parse tree network topologies. Their architectures is not designed to predict next-word probability distributions, as in a language model, but to classify the input words (sentiment analysis task) or to measure the similarity in hidden representations (semantic relatedness task). Their relative improvement in performance (tree LSTMs vs standard LSTMs) on these two tasks is smaller than ours, probably because the LSTMs are better than RNNs at storing long-term dependencies and thus do not benefit form the word ordering from dependency trees as much as RNNs. In a similar vein to ours, Miceli-Barone and Attardi (2015) simply propose to enhance RNN-based machine translation by permuting the order of the words in the source sentence to match the order of the words in the target sentence, using a source-side dependency parsing.

Limitations of RNNs for word completion Zweig et al. (2012) reported that RNNs achieve lower perplexity than n-grams but do not always outperform them on word completion tasks. As illustrated in Fig. 2, the validation set perplexity (comprising all 5 choices for each sentence) of the RNN keeps decreasing monotonically (once we start annealing the learning rate), whereas the validation accuracy rapidly reaches a plateau and oscillates. Our observation confirms that, once an RNN went through a few training epochs, change in perplexity is no longer a good predictor of change in word accuracy. We presume that the log-likelihood of word distribution is not a training objective crafted for $precision@1$, and that further perplexity reduction happens in the middle and tail of the word distribution.

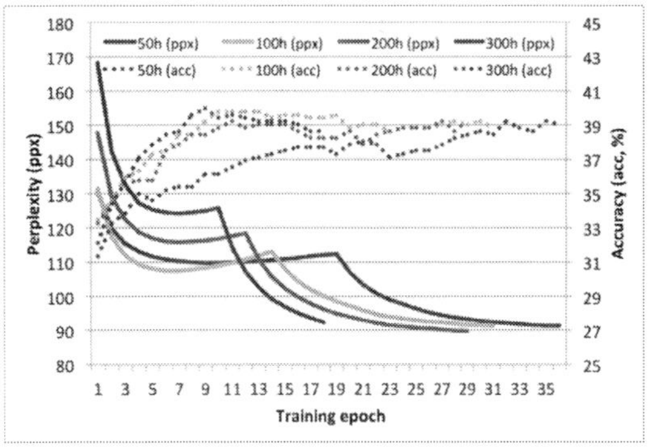

Figure 2: Perplexity vs. accuracy of RNNs

7 Conclusions

In this paper we proposed a novel language model, dependency RNN, which incorporates syntactic dependencies into the RNN formulation. We evaluated its performance on the MSR sentence completion task and showed that it improves over RNN by 10 points in accuracy, while achieving results comparable with the state-of-the-art. Further work will include extending the dependency tree language modeling to Long Short-Term Memory RNNs to handle longer syntactic dependencies.

Acknowledgements

We thank our anonymous reviewers for their valuable feedback. PM also thanks Geoffrey Zweig, Daniel Voinea, Francesco Nidito and Davide di Gennaro for sharing the original Feature-Augmented RNN toolkit on the Microsoft Research website and for insights about that code, as well as Bhaskar Mitra, Milad Shokouhi and Andriy Mnih for enlighting discussions about word embedding and sentence completion.

References

Yoshua Bengio, Réjean Ducharme, Pascal Vincent, and Christian Janvin. 2003. A neural probabilistic language model. *The Journal of Machine Learning Research*, 3:1137–1155.

Jiang Bian, Bin Gao, and Tie-Yan Liu. 2014. Knowledge-powered deep learning for word embedding. In *Machine Learning and Knowledge Discovery in Databases, Lecture Notes in Computer Science*, volume 8724, pages 132–148.

Ciprian Chelba, David Engle, Frederick Jelinek, Victor Jimenez, Sanjeev Khudanpur, Lidia Mangu, Harry Printz, Eric Ristad, Ronald Rosenfeld, Andreas Stolcke, et al. 1997. Structure and performance of a dependency language model. In *Proceedings of Eurospeech*, volume 5, pages 2775–2778.

Alex Graves. 2012. *Supervised Sequence Labelling with Recurrent Neural Networks*. Studies in Computational Intelligence. Springer.

Joseph Gubbins and Andreas Vlachos. 2013. Dependency language models for sentence completion. In *Proceedings of the 2013 Conference on Empirical Methods in Natural Language Processing*.

Sepp Hochreiter and Jurgen Schmidhuber. 1997. Long short-term memory. *Neural Computation*, 9:17351780.

Omer Levy and Yoav Goldberg. 2014. Dependency-based word embeddings. In *Proceedings of the 52nd Annual Meeting of the Association for Computational Linguistics (Volume 2: Short Papers)*, pages 302–308.

Christopher D. Manning, Mihai Surdeanu, John Bauer, Jenny Finkel, Steven J. Bethard, and David McClosky. 2014. The Stanford CoreNLP natural language processing toolkit. In *Proceedings of 52nd Annual Meeting of the Association for Computational Linguistics: System Demonstrations*, pages 55–60.

Antonio Valerio Miceli-Barone and Giuseppe Attardi. 2015. Non-projective dependency-based pre-reordering with recurrent neural network for machine translation. In *The 53rd Annual Meeting of the Association for Computational Linguistics and The 7th International Joint Conference of the Asian Federation of Natural Language Processing*.

Tomas Mikolov and Geoff Zweig. 2012. Context dependent recurrent neural network language model. In *Speech Language Technologies (SLT), 2012 IEEE Workshop on*. IEEE.

Tomas Mikolov, Martin Karafiát, Lukas Burget, Jan Cernockỳ, and Sanjeev Khudanpur. 2010. Recurrent neural network based language model. In *INTERSPEECH 2010, 11th Annual Conference of the International Speech Communication Association, Makuhari, Chiba, Japan, September 26-30, 2010*, pages 1045–1048.

Tomas Mikolov, Anoop Deoras, Daniel Povey, Lukas Burget, and Jan Cernocky. 2011. Strategies for training large scale neural network language models. In *Automatic Speech Recognition and Understanding (ASRU), 2011 IEEE Workshop on*, pages 196–201. IEEE.

Tomas Mikolov, Kai Chen, Greg Corrado, and Jeffrey Dean. 2013. Efficient estimation of word representations in vector space. *arXiv preprint arXiv:1301.3781*.

Piotr Mirowski, Sumit Chopra, Suhrid Balakrishnan, and Srinivas Bangalore. 2010. Feature-rich continuous language models for speech recognition. In *Spoken Language Technology Workshop (SLT), 2010 IEEE*, pages 241–246. IEEE.

Andriy Mnih and Geoffrey Hinton. 2007. Three new graphical models for statistical language modelling. In *Proceedings of the 24th International Conference on Machine Learning*, page 641648.

Andriy Mnih and Koray Kavukcuoglu. 2013. Learning word embeddings efficiently with noise-contrastive estimation. In C.J.C. Burges, L. Bottou, M. Welling, Z. Ghahramani, and K.Q. Weinberger, editors, *Advances in Neural Information Processing Systems 26*, pages 2265–2273. Curran Associates, Inc.

Andriy Mnih and Yee W Teh. 2012. A fast and simple algorithm for training neural probabilistic language models. In *Proceedings of the 29th International Conference on Machine Learning (ICML-12)*, pages 1751–1758.

Joakim Nivre. 2005. Dependency grammar and dependency parsing. *MSI report*, 5133(1959):1–32.

Adam Pauls and Dan Klein. 2011. Faster and Smaller N-Gram Language Models. In *Proceedings of the 49th Annual Meeting of the Association for Computational Linguistics: Human Language Technologies*, pages 258–267. Association for Computational Linguistics.

Adam Pauls and Dan Klein. 2012. Large-scale syntactic language modeling with treelets. In *Proceedings of the 50th Annual Meeting of the Association for Computational Linguistics: Long Papers-Volume 1*, pages 959–968. Association for Computational Linguistics.

Brian Roark, Murat Saraclar, and Michael Collins. 2007. Discriminative n-gram language modeling. *Computer Speech & Language*, 21(2):373 – 392.

Kai Sheng Tai, Richard Socher, and Christopher Manning. 2015. Improved semantic representations from tree-structured long short-term memory networks. In *The 53rd Annual Meeting of the Association for Computational Linguistics and The 7th International Joint Conference of the Asian Federation of Natural Language Processing*.

Yinggong Zhao, Shujian Huang, Xinyu Dai, Jianbing Zhang, and Jiajun Chen. 2014. Learning word embeddings from dependency relations. In *In Proceedings of Asian Language Processing (IALP)*.

Geoffrey Zweig and Christopher J. C. Burges. 2012. A challenge set for advancing language modeling. In *Proceedings of the NAACL-HLT 2012 Workshop: Will We Ever Really Replace the N-gram Model? On the Future of Language Modeling for HLT*, pages 29–36. Association for Computational Linguistics.

Geoffrey Zweig, John C Platt, Christopher Meek, Christopher J. C. Burges, Ainur Yessenalina, and Qiang Liu. 2012. Computational approaches to sentence completion. In *Proceedings of the 50th Annual Meeting of the Association for Computational Linguistics*, pages 601–610.

Point Process Modelling of Rumour Dynamics in Social Media

Michal Lukasik[1], **Trevor Cohn**[2] and **Kalina Bontcheva**[1]
[1]Department of Computer Science,
The University of Sheffield
[2]Department of Computing and Information Systems,
The University of Melbourne
{m.lukasik, k.bontcheva}@shef.ac.uk
t.cohn@unimelb.edu.au

Abstract

Rumours on social media exhibit complex temporal patterns. This paper develops a model of rumour prevalence using a point process, namely a log-Gaussian Cox process, to infer an underlying continuous temporal probabilistic model of post frequencies. To generalize over different rumours, we present a multi-task learning method parametrized by the text in posts which allows data statistics to be shared between groups of similar rumours. Our experiments demonstrate that our model outperforms several strong baseline methods for rumour frequency prediction evaluated on tweets from the 2014 Ferguson riots.

1 Introduction

The ability to model rumour dynamics helps with identifying those, which, if not debunked early, will likely spread very fast. One such example is the false rumour of rioters breaking into McDonald's during the 2011 England riots. An effective early warning system of this kind is of interest to government bodies and news outlets, who struggle with monitoring and verifying social media posts during emergencies and social unrests. Another application of modelling rumour dynamics could be to predict the prevalence of a rumour throughout its lifespan, based on occasional spot checks by journalists.

The challenge comes from the observation that different rumours exhibit different trajectories. Figure 1 shows two example rumours from our dataset (see Section 3): online discussion of rumour #10 quickly drops away, whereas rumour #37 takes a lot longer to die out. Two characteristics can help determine if a rumour will continue to be discussed. One is the dynamics of post occurrences, e.g. if the frequency profile decays quickly, chances are it would not attract further attention. A second factor is text from the posts themselves, where phrases such as *not true*, *unconfirmed*, or *debunk* help users judge veracity and thus limit rumour spread (Zhao et al., 2015).

This paper considers the problem of modelling temporal frequency profiles of rumours by taking into account both the temporal and textual information. Since posts occur at continuous timestamps, and their density is typically a smooth function of time, we base our model on *point processes*, which have been shown to model well such data in epidemiology and conflict mapping (Brix and Diggle, 2001; Zammit-Mangion et al., 2012). This framework models count data in a continuous time through the underlying intensity of a Poisson distribution. The posterior distribution can then be used for several inference problems, e.g. to query the expected count of posts, or to find the probability of a count of posts occurring during an arbitrary time interval. We model frequency profiles using a log-Gaussian Cox process (Møller and Syversveen, 1998), a point process where the log-intensity of the Poisson distribution is modelled via a Gaussian Process (GP). GP is a non-parametric model which allows for powerful modelling of the underlying intensity function.

Modelling the frequency profile of a rumour based on posts is extremely challenging, since many rumours consist of only a small number of posts and exhibit complex patterns. To overcome this difficulty we propose *a multi-task learning approach*, where patterns are correlated across multiple rumours. In this way statistics over a larger training set are shared, enabling more reliable predictions for distant time periods, in which no posts from the target rumour have been observed. We demonstrate how text from observed posts can be used to weight influence across rumours. Using a set of Twitter rumours from the 2014 Ferguson unrest, we demonstrate that our models provide good

Proceedings of the 53rd Annual Meeting of the Association for Computational Linguistics and the 7th International Joint Conference on Natural Language Processing (Short Papers), pages 518–523,
Beijing, China, July 26-31, 2015.

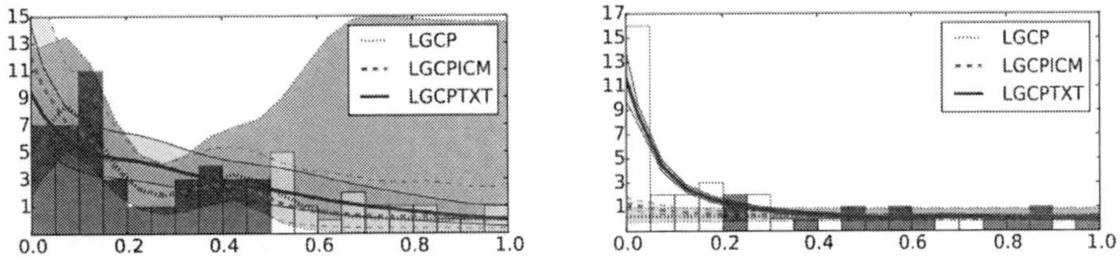

(a) rumour #37

(b) rumour #10

Figure 1: Predicted frequency profiles for example rumours. Black bars denote training intervals, white bars denote test intervals. Dark-coloured lines correspond to mean predictions by the models, light shaded areas denote the 95% confidence interval, $\mu \pm 2\sigma$. This figure is best viewed in colour.

prediction of rumour popularity.

This paper makes the following contributions: 1. Introduces the problem of modelling rumour frequency profiles, and presents a method based on a log-Gaussian Cox process; 2. Incorporates multi-task learning to generalize across disparate rumours; and 3. Demonstrates how incorporating text into multi-task learning improves results.

2 Related Work

There have been several descriptive studies of rumours in social media, e.g. Procter et al. (2013) analyzed rumours in tweets about the 2011 London riots and showed that they follow similar life-cycles. Friggeri et al. (2014) showed how Facebook constitutes a rich source of rumours and conversation threads on the topic. However, none of these studies tried to model rumour dynamics.

The problem of modelling the temporal nature of social media explicitly has received little attention. The work most closely related modelled hash tag frequency time-series in Twitter using GP (Preotiuc-Pietro and Cohn, 2013). It made several simplifications, including discretising time and treating the problem of modelling counts as regression, which are both inappropriate. In contrast we take a more principled approach, using a point process. We use the proposed GP-based method as a baseline to demonstrate the benefit of using our approaches.

The log-Gaussian Cox process has been applied for disease and conflict mapping, e.g. Zammit-Mangion et al. (2012) developed a spatio-temporal model of conflict events in Afghanistan. In contrast here we deal with temporal text data, and model several correlated outputs rather than their single output. Related also is the extensive work done in spatio-temporal modelling of meme spread. One example is application of Hawkes processes (Yang and Zha, 2013), a probabilistic framework for modelling self-excitatory phenomena. However, these models were mainly used for network modelling rather than revealing complex temporal patterns, which may emerge only implicitly, and are more limited in the kinds of temporal patterns that may be represented.

3 Data & Problem

In this section we describe the data and we formalize the problem of modelling rumour popularity.

Data We use the Ferguson rumour data set (Zubiaga et al., 2015), consisting of tweets collected in August and September 2014 during the Ferguson unrest. It contains both source tweets and the conversational threads around these (where available). All source tweets are categorized as rumour vs non-rumour, other tweets from the same thread are assigned automatically as belonging to the same event as the source tweet. Since some rumours have few posts, we consider only those with at least 15 posts in the first hour as rumours of particular interest. This results in 114 rumours consisting of a total of 4098 tweets.

Problem Definition Let us consider a time interval $[0, l]$ of length l=2 hours, a set of n rumours $R = \{E_i\}_{i=1}^n$, where rumour E_i consists of a set of m_i posts $E_i = \{p_j^i\}_{j=1}^{m_i}$. Posts are tuples $p_j^i = (\mathbf{x}_j^i, t_j^i)$, where $\mathbf{x}_j^i$ is text (in our case a bag of words text representation) and t_j^i is a timestamp describing post p_j^i, measured in time elapsed since the first post on rumour E_i.

Posts occur at different timestamps, yielding varying density of posts over time, which we are interested in estimating. To evaluate the predicted density for a given rumour E_i we leave out posts from a set of intervals $T_{te} = \{[s_k^i, e_k^i]\}_{k=1}^{K_i}$ (where s_k^i and e_k^i are respectively start and end points of interval k for rumour i) and estimate performance at predicting counts in them by the trained model.

The problem is considered in supervised settings, where posts on this rumour outside of these intervals form the training set $E_i^{\text{O}} = \{p_j^i : t_j^i \notin \bigcup_{k=1}^{K_i} [s_k^i, e_k^i]\}$. Let the number of elements in E_i^{O} be m_i^{O}. We also consider a domain adaptation setting, where additionally posts from other rumours are observed $R_i^O = R \setminus E_i$.

Two instantiations of this problem formulation are considered. The first is *interpolation*, where the test intervals are not ordered in any particular way. This corresponds to a situation, e.g., when a journalist analyses a rumour during short spot checks, but wants to know the prevalence of the rumour at other times, thus limiting the need for constant attention. The second formulation is that of *extrapolation*, where all observed posts occur before the test intervals. This corresponds to a scenario where the user seeks to predict the future profile of the rumour, e.g., to identify rumours that will attract further attention or wither away.

Although our focus here is on rumours, our model is more widely applicable. For example, one could use it to predict whether an advertisement campaign would be successful or how a political campaign would proceed.

4 Model

We consider a log-Gaussian Cox process (LGCP) (Møller and Syversveen, 1998), a generalization of inhomogeneous Poisson process. In LGCP the intensity function is assumed to be a stochastic process which varies over time. In fact, the intensity function $\lambda(t)$ is modelled using a latent function $f(t)$ sampled from a Gaussian process (Rasmussen and Williams, 2005), such that $\lambda(t) = \exp\left(f(t)\right)$ (exponent ensures positivity). This provides a non-parametric approach to model the intensity function. The intensity function can be automatically learned from the data set and its complexity depends on the data points.

We model the occurrence of posts in a rumour E_i to follow log-Gaussian Cox process (LGCP) with intensity $\lambda_i(t)$, where $\lambda_i(t) = \exp(f_i(t))$. We associate a distinct intensity function with each rumour as they have varying temporal profiles. LGCP models the likelihood that a single tweet occurs at time t in the interval $[s, t]$ for a rumour E_i given the latent function $f_i(t)$ as

$$p(y = 1|f_i) = \exp(f_i(t)) \exp(-\int_s^t \exp(f_i(u))du).$$

Then, the likelihood of posts E_i^{O} in time interval T given a latent function f_i can be obtained as

$$p(E_i^{\text{O}}|f_i) = \exp\left(-\int_{T-T_{te}} \exp\left(f_i(u)\right) du + \sum_{j=1}^{m_i^{\text{O}}} f_i(t_j^i)\right) \quad (1)$$

The likelihood of posts in the rumour data is obtained by taking the product of the likelihoods over individual rumours. The likelihood (1) is commonly approximated by considering subregions of T and assuming constant intensities in sub-regions of T (Møller and Syversveen, 1998; Vanhatalo et al., 2013) to overcome computational difficulties arising due to integration. Following this, we approximate the likelihood as $p(E_i^{\text{O}}|f_i) = \prod_{s=1}^{S} \text{Poisson}(y_s \mid l_s \exp\left(f_i(\dot{t}_s)\right))$. Here, time is divided into S intervals indexed by s, $\dot{t}_s$ is the centre of the sth interval, l_s is the length of the sth interval and y_s is number of tweets posted during this interval.

The latent function f is modelled via a Gaussian process (GP) (Rasmussen and Williams, 2005): $f(t) \sim \mathcal{GP}(m(t), k(t, t'))$, where m is the mean function (equal 0) and k is the kernel specifying how outputs covary as a function of the inputs. We use a Radial Basis Function (RBF) kernel, $k(t, t') = a \exp(-(t - t')^2/l)$, where lengthscale l controls the extent to which nearby points influence one another and a controls the scale of the function.

The distribution of the posterior $p(f_i(t)|E_i^{\text{O}})$ at an arbitrary timestamp t is calculated based on the specified prior and the Poisson likelihood. It is intractable and approximation techniques are required. There exist various methods to deal with calculating the posterior; here we use the Laplace approximation, where the posterior is approximated by a Gaussian distribution based on the first 2 moments. For more details about the model and inference we refer the reader to (Rasmussen and Williams, 2005). The predictive distribution over time t_* is obtained using the approximated posterior. This predictive distribution is then used to obtain the intensity function value at the point t_*:

$$\lambda_i(t_*|E_i^{\text{O}}) = \int \exp\left(f_i(t)\right) p\left(f_i(t)|E_i^{\text{O}}\right) df_i \,.$$

The predictive distribution over counts at a particular time interval of length w with a mid-point t_* for rumour E_i is Poisson distributed with rate $w\lambda_i(t_*|E_i^{\text{O}})$.

Multi-task learning and incorporating text In order to exploit similarities across rumours we propose a multi-task approach where each rumour represents a task. We consider two approaches.

First, we employ a multiple output GP based on the Intrinsic Coregionalization Model (ICM) (Álvarez et al., 2012). It is a method which has been successfully applied to a range of NLP tasks (Beck et al., 2014; Cohn and Specia, 2013). ICM parametrizes the kernel by a matrix representing similarities between pairs of tasks. We expect it to find correlations between rumours exhibiting similar temporal patterns. The kernel takes the form

$$k_{\text{ICM}}((t,i),(t',i')) = k_{time}(t,t')B_{i,i'},$$

where B is a square coregionalization matrix (rank 1, $B = \boldsymbol{\kappa} I + \boldsymbol{v}\boldsymbol{v}^T$), i and i' denote the tasks of the two inputs, k_{time} is a kernel for comparing inputs t and t' (here RBF) and $\boldsymbol{\kappa}$ is a vector of values modulating the extent of each task independence.

In a second approach, we parametrize the inter-task similarity measures by incorporating text of the posts. The full multi-task kernel takes form

$$k_{\text{TXT}}((t,i),(t',i')) = k_{time}(t,t') \times k_{text}\Bigg(\sum_{p_j^i \in E_i^O} \mathbf{x}_j^i, \sum_{p_j^{i'} \in E_{i'}^O} \mathbf{x}_j^{i'}\Bigg).$$

We compare text vectors using cosine similarity, $k_{text}(\mathbf{x},\mathbf{y}) = b + c\frac{\mathbf{x}^T\mathbf{y}}{\|\mathbf{x}\|\|\mathbf{y}\|}$, where the hyperparameters $b > 0$ and $c > 0$ modulate between text similarity and a global constant similarity. We also consider combining both multi-task kernels, yielding $k_{\text{ICM+TXT}} = k_{\text{ICM}} + k_{\text{TXT}}$.

Optimization All hyperparameters are optimized by maximizing the marginal likelihood of the data $L(E_i^O|\theta)$, where $\theta = (a, l, \boldsymbol{\kappa}, \boldsymbol{v}, b, c)$ or a subset thereof, depending on the choice of kernel.

5 Experimental Setup

Evaluation metric We use mean squared error (MSE) to measure the difference between true counts and predicted counts in the test intervals. Since probabilistic models (GP, LGCP) return distributions over possible outputs, we also evaluate them via the log-likelihood (LL) of the true counts under the returned distributions (respectively Gaussian and Poisson distribution).

Baselines We use the following baselines. The first is the Homogenous Poisson Process (HPP) trained on the training set of the rumour. We select its intensity λ using maximum likelihood estimate, which equals to the mean frequency of posts in the training intervals. The second baseline is Gaussian Process (GP) used for predicting hashtag frequencies in Twitter by Preotiuc-Pietro and Cohn (2013). Authors considered various kernels in their experiments, most notably periodic kernels. In our case it is not apparent that rumours exhibit periodic characteristics, as can be seen in Figure 1. We restrict our focus to RBF kernel and leave inspection of other kernels such as periodic ones for both GP and LGCP models for future. The third baseline is to always predict 0 posts in all intervals. The fourth baseline is tailored for the interpolation setting, and uses simple interpolation by averaging over the frequencies of the closest left and right intervals, or the frequency of the closest interval for test intervals on a boundary.

Data preprocessing In our experiments, we consider the first two hours of each rumour lifespan, which we split into 20 evenly spaced intervals. This way, our dataset consists in total of 2280 intervals. We iterate over rumours using a form of folded cross-validation, where in each iteration we exclude some (but not all) time intervals for a single target rumour. The excluded time intervals form the test set: either by selecting half at random (interpolation); or by taking only the second half for testing (extrapolation). To ameliorate the problems of data sparsity, we replace words with their Brown cluster ids, using 1000 clusters acquired on a large scale Twitter corpus (Owoputi et al., 2013).

The mean function for the underlying GP in LGCP methods is assumed to be 0, which results in intensity function to be around 1 in the absence of nearby observations. This prevents our method from predicting 0 counts in these regions. We add 1 to the counts in the intervals to deal with this problem as a preprocessing step. The original counts can be obtained by decrementing 1 from the predicted counts. Instead, one could use a GP with a non-zero mean function and learn the mean function, a more elegant way of approaching this problem, which we leave for future work.

6 Experiments

The left columns of Table 1 report the results for the extrapolation experiments, showing the mean and variance of results across the 114 rumours. According to log likelihood evaluation metric, GP is the worst from the probabilistic ap-

	Extrapolation		Interpolation	
	MSE	LL	MSE	LL
HPP	7.14±10.1⋆	-23.5±10.1⋆	7.66±7.55⋆	-25.8±11.0⋆
GP	4.58±11.0⋆	-34.6±8.78⋆	6.13±6.57⋆	-90.1±198 ⋆
Interpolate	4.90±13.1⋆	-	5.29±6.06⋆	-
0	2.76±7.81⋆	-	7.65±11.0⋆	-
LGCP	3.44±9.99⋆	-15.8±11.6†⋆	6.01±6.29⋆	-21.0±8.77†⋆
LGCP ICM	2.46±7.82†⋆	-14.8±11.2†⋆	8.59±19.9⋆	-20.7±9.87†⋆
LGCP TXT	2.32±7.06†	-14.7±9.12†	3.66±5.67†	-16.9±5.91†
LGCP ICM+TXT	2.31±7.80†	-14.6±10.8†	3.92±5.20†	-16.8±5.34†

Table 1: MSE between the true counts and the predicted counts (lower is better) and predictive log likelihood of the true counts from probabilistic models (higher is better) for test intervals over the 114 Ferguson rumours for extrapolation (left) and interpolation (right) settings, showing mean ± std. dev. Baselines are shown above the line, with LGCP models below. Key: † denotes significantly better than the best baseline; ⋆ denotes significantly worse than LGCP TXT, according to one-sided Wilcoxon signed rank test $p < 0.05$.

proaches. This is due to GP modelling a distribution with continuous support, which is inappropriate for modelling discrete counts. Changing the model from a GP to a better fitting to the modelling temporal count data LGCP gives a big improvement, even when a point estimate of the prediction is considered (MSE). The 0 baseline is very strong, since many rumours have comparatively little discussion in the second hour of their lifespan relative to the first hour. Incorporating information about other rumours helps outperform this method. ICM, TXT and ICM+TXT multi-task learning approaches achieve the best scores and significantly outperform all baselines. TXT turns out to be a good approach to multi-task learning and outperforms ICM. In Figure 1a we show an example rumour frequency profile for the extrapolation setting. TXT makes a lower error than LGCP and LGCPICM, both of which underestimate the counts in the second hour.

Next, we move to the interpolation setting. Unsurprisingly, Interpolate is the strongest baseline, and outperforms the raw LGCP method. Again, HPP and GP are outperformed by LGCP in terms of both MSE and LL. Considering the output distributions (LL) the difference in performance between the Poisson Process based approaches and GP is especially big, demonstrating how well the principled models handle uncertainty in the predictive distributions. As for the multi-task methods, we notice that text is particularly useful, with TXT achieving the highest MSE score out of all considered models. ICM turns out to be not very helpful in this setting. For example, ICM (just as LGCP) does not learn there should be a peak at the beginning of a rumour frequency profile depicted in Figure 1b. TXT manages to make a significantly smaller error by predicting a large posting frequency there. We also found, that for a few rumours ICM made a big error by predicting a high frequency at the start of a rumour lifespan when there was no such peak. We hypothesize ICM performs poorly because it is hard to learn correct correlations between frequency profiles when training intervals do not form continuous segments of significant sizes. ICM manages to learn correlations more properly in extrapolation setting, where the first hour is fully observed.

7 Conclusions

This paper introduced the problem of modelling frequency profiles of rumours in social media. We demonstrated that joint modelling of collective data over multiple rumours using multi-task learning resulted in more accurate models that are able to recognise and predict commonly occurring temporal patterns. We showed how text data from social media posts added important information about similarities between different rumours. Our method is generalizable to problems other than modelling rumour popularity, such as predicting success of advertisement campaigns.

8 Acknowledgments

We would like to thank Srijith P. K. for helpful comments. This work was funded by the PHEME FP7 project (grant No. 611233) and partially supported by the Australian Research Council.

References

Mauricio A. Álvarez, Lorenzo Rosasco, and Neil D. Lawrence. 2012. Kernels for vector-valued functions: A review. *Found. Trends Mach. Learn.*, 4(3):195–266.

The GPy authors. 2012–2015. GPy: A Gaussian process framework in Python. `http://github.com/SheffieldML/GPy`.

Daniel Beck, Trevor Cohn, and Lucia Specia. 2014. Joint emotion analysis via multi-task Gaussian processes. In *Proceedings of the Conference on Empirical Methods in Natural Language Processing*, EMNLP '14, pages 1798–1803.

Anders Brix and Peter J. Diggle. 2001. Spatiotemporal prediction for log-gaussian cox processes. *Journal of the Royal Statistical Society Series B*, 63(4):823–841.

Trevor Cohn and Lucia Specia. 2013. Modelling annotator bias with multi-task Gaussian processes: An application to machine translation quality estimation. In *51st Annual Meeting of the Association for Computational Linguistics*, ACL '13, pages 32–42.

Adrien Friggeri, Lada Adamic, Dean Eckles, and Justin Cheng. 2014. Rumor cascades. In *International AAAI Conference on Weblogs and Social Media*.

Jesper Møller and Anne Randi Syversveen. 1998. Log Gaussian Cox processes. *Scandinavian Journal of Statistics*, pages 451–482.

Olutobi Owoputi, Chris Dyer, Kevin Gimpel, Nathan Schneider, and Noah A. Smith. 2013. Improved part-of-speech tagging for online conversational text with word clusters. In *Proceedings of NAACL*, pages 380–390.

Daniel Preotiuc-Pietro and Trevor Cohn. 2013. A temporal model of text periodicities using Gaussian processes. In *Proceedings of the Conference on Empirical Methods in Natural Language Processing*, EMNLP '13, pages 977–988.

Rob Procter, Jeremy Crump, Susanne Karstedt, Alex Voss, and Marta Cantijoch. 2013. Reading the riots: What were the police doing on twitter? *Policing and society*, 23(4):413–436.

Carl Edward Rasmussen and Christopher K. I. Williams. 2005. *Gaussian Processes for Machine Learning (Adaptive Computation and Machine Learning)*. The MIT Press.

Jarno Vanhatalo, Jaakko Riihimäki, Jouni Hartikainen, Pasi Jylänki, Ville Tolvanen, and Aki Vehtari. 2013. Gpstuff: Bayesian modeling with Gaussian processes. *J. Mach. Learn. Res.*, 14(1):1175–1179.

Shuang-Hong Yang and Hongyuan Zha. 2013. Mixture of mutually exciting processes for viral diffusion. In *ICML (2)*, volume 28 of *JMLR Proceedings*, pages 1–9.

Andrew Zammit-Mangion, Michael Dewar, Visakan Kadirkamanathan, and Guido Sanguinetti. 2012. Point process modelling of the Afghan War Diary. *Proceedings of the National Academy of Sciences of the United States of America*, 109(31):12414–12419.

Zhe Zhao, Paul Resnick, and Qiaozhu Mei. 2015. Early detection of rumors in social media from enquiry posts. In *International World Wide Web Conference Committee (IW3C2)*.

Arkaitz Zubiaga, Maria Liakata, Rob Procter, Kalina Bontcheva, and Peter Tolmie. 2015. Towards detecting rumours in social media. In *AAAI Workshop on AI for Cities*.

Learning Hidden Markov Models with Distributed State Representations for Domain Adaptation

Min Xiao and **Yuhong Guo**
Department of Computer and Information Sciences
Temple University, Philadelphia, PA 19122, USA
{minxiao,yuhong}@temple.edu

Abstract

Recently, a variety of representation learning approaches have been developed in the literature to induce latent generalizable features across two domains. In this paper, we extend the standard hidden Markov models (HMMs) to learn distributed state representations to improve cross-domain prediction performance. We reformulate the HMMs by mapping each discrete hidden state to a distributed representation vector and employ an expectation-maximization algorithm to jointly learn distributed state representations and model parameters. We empirically investigate the proposed model on cross-domain part-of-speech tagging and noun-phrase chunking tasks. The experimental results demonstrate the effectiveness of the distributed HMMs on facilitating domain adaptation.

1 Introduction

Domain adaptation aims to obtain an effective prediction model for a particular target domain where labeled training data is scarce by exploiting labeled data from a related source domain. Domain adaptation is very important in the field of natural language processing (NLP) as it can reduce the expensive manual annotation effort in the target domain. Various NLP tasks have benefited from domain adaptation techniques, including part-of-speech tagging (Blitzer et al., 2006; Huang and Yates, 2010a), chunking (Daumé III, 2007; Huang and Yates, 2009), named entity recognition (Guo et al., 2009; Turian et al., 2010), dependency parsing (Dredze et al., 2007; Sagae and Tsujii, 2007) and semantic role labeling (Dahlmeier and Ng, 2010; Huang and Yates, 2010b).

In a typical domain adaptation scenario of NLP, the source and target domains contain text data of different genres (*e.g.*, newswire vs biomedical (Blitzer et al., 2006)). Under such circumstances, the original lexical features may not perform well in cross-domain learning since different genres of text may use very different vocabularies and produce cross-domain feature distribution divergence and feature sparsity issue. A number of techniques have been developed in the literature to tackle the problem of cross-domain feature divergence and feature sparsity, including clustering based word representation learning methods (Huang and Yates, 2009; Candito et al., 2011), word embedding based representation learning methods (Turian et al., 2010; Hovy et al., 2015) and some other representation learning methods (Blitzer et al., 2006).

In this paper, we extend the standard hidden Markov models (HMMs) to perform distributed state representation learning and induce context-aware distributed word representations for domain adaptation. Instead of learning a single discrete latent state for each observation in a given sentence, we learn a distributed representation vector. We define a state embedding matrix to map each latent state value to a low-dimensional distributed vector and reformulate the three local distributions of HMMs based on the distributed state representations. We then simultaneously learn the state embedding matrix and the model parameters using an expectation-maximization (EM) algorithm. The hidden states of each word in a sentence can be decoded using the standard Viterbi decoding procedure of HMMs, and its distributed representation can be obtained by a simple mapping with the state embedding matrix. We then use the context-aware distributed representations of the words as their augmenting features to perform cross-domain part-of-speech (POS) tagging and noun-phrase (NP) chunking.

The proposed approach is closely related to the clustering based method (Huang and Yates,

Proceedings of the 53rd Annual Meeting of the Association for Computational Linguistics and the 7th International Joint Conference on Natural Language Processing (Short Papers), pages 524–529,
Beijing, China, July 26-31, 2015.

2009) as we both use latent state representations as generalizable features. However, they use standard HMMs to produce discrete hidden state features for each observation word, while we induce distributed state representation vectors. Our distributed HMMs share similarities with the word embedding based method (Hovy et al., 2015), and can be more space-efficient than the standard HMMs. Moreover, our model can incorporate context information into observation feature vectors to perform representation learning in a context-aware manner. The distributed state representations induced by our model hence have larger representing capacities and generalizing capabilities for cross-domain learning than standard HMMs.

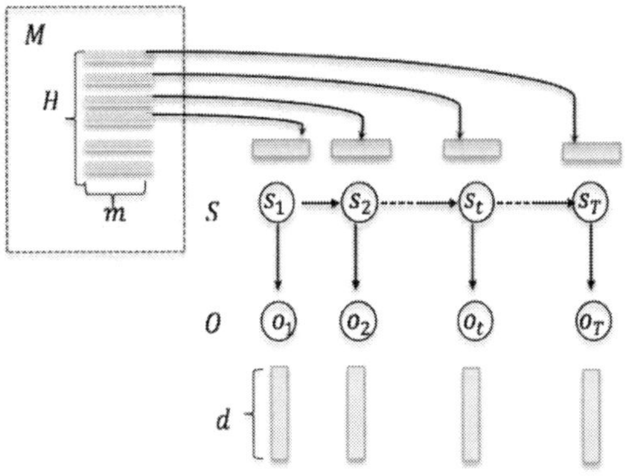

Figure 1: Hidden Markov models with distributed state representations (dHMM).

2 Related Work

A variety of representation learning approaches have been developed in the literature to address NLP domain adaptation problems. The *clustering based word representation learning* methods perform word clustering within the sentence structure and use word cluster indicators as generalizable features to address domain adaptation problems. For example, Huang and Yates (2009) used the discrete hidden state of a word under HMMs as augmenting features for cross-domain POS tagging and NP chunking. Brown clusters (Brown et al., 1992), which was used as latent features for simple in-domain dependency parsing (Koo et al., 2008), has recently been exploited for out-of-domain statistical parsing (Candito et al., 2011).

The *word embedding based representation learning* methods learn a dense real-valued representation vector for each word as latent features for domain adaptation. Turian et al. (2010) empirically studied using word embeddings learned from hierarchical log-bilinear models (Mnih and Geoffrey, 2008) and neural language models (Collobert and Weston, 2008) for cross-domain NER tasks. Hovy et al. (2015) used the word embeddings learned from the Skip-gram Model (SGM) (Mikolov et al., 2013) to develop a POS tagger for Twitter data with labeled newswire training data.

Some other representation learning methods have been developed to tackle NLP cross-domain problems as well. For example, Blitzer et al. (2006) proposed a structural correspondence learning method for POS tagging, which first selects a set of pivot features (occurring frequently in the two domains) and then models the correlations between pivot features and non-pivot features to induce generalizable features.

In terms of performing distributed representation learning for output variables, our proposed model shares similarity with the structured output representation learning approach developed by Srikumar and Manning (2014), which extends the structured support vector machines to simultaneously learn the prediction model and the distributed representations of the output labels. However, the approach in (Srikumar and Manning, 2014) assumes the training labels (i.e., output values) are given and performs learning in the standard supervised in-domain setting, while our proposed distributed HMMs address cross-domain learning problems by performing unsupervised representation learning. There are also a few works that extended standard HMMs in the literature, including the observable operator models (Jaeger, 1999), and the spectral learning method (Stratos et al., 2013). But none of them performs representation learning to address cross-domain adaptation problems.

3 Proposed Model

In this paper, we propose a novel distributed hidden Markov model (dHMM) for representation learning over sequence data. This model extends the hidden Markov models (Rabiner and Juang, 1986) to learn distributed state representations. Similar as HMMs, a dHMM (shown in Figure 1) is a two-layer generative graphical model, which generates a sequence of observations from a sequence of latent state variables using Markov properties. Let $O = \{\mathbf{o}_1, \mathbf{o}_2, \ldots, \mathbf{o}_T\}$ be the sequence of observations with length T, where each observation $\mathbf{o}_t \in \mathbb{R}^d$ is a d-dimensional feature vector. Let $S = \{s_1, s_2, \ldots, s_T\}$ be the sequence of T hidden states, where each hidden state s_t has a discrete state value from a total H hidden states $\mathcal{H} = \{1, 2, \ldots, H\}$. Besides, we assume that there is a low-dimensional distributed representation vector associated with each hidden state. Let $M \in \mathbb{R}^{H \times m}$ be the state embedding matrix where the i-th row $M_{i:}$ denotes the m-dimensional representation vector for the i-th state. Previous works have demonstrated the usefulness of discrete hidden states induced from a HMM on addressing feature sparsity in domain adaptation (Huang and Yates, 2009). However, expressing a semantic word by a single discrete state value is too restrictive, as it has been shown in the literature that words have many different features in a multi-dimensional space where they could be separately characterized as number, POS tag, gender, tense, voice and other aspects (Sag and Wasow, 1999; Huang et al., 2011). Our proposed model aims to overcome this inherent drawback of standard HMMs on learning word representations. Given a set of observation sequences in two domains, the dHMM induces a distributed representation vector with continuous real values for each observation word as generalizable features, which has the capacity of capturing multi-aspect latent characteristics of the word clusters.

3.1 Model Formulation

To build the dHMMs, we reformulate the standard HMMs by defining three main local distributions based on the distributed state representations, i.e., the initial state distribution, the state transition distribution, and the observation emission distribution. Below we introduce them by using Θ to denote the set of parameters involved and using $\mathbf{1}$ to denote a column vector with all 1s.

First we use the following multinomial distribution as the *initial state distribution*,

$$P(s_1; \Theta) = \phi(s_1)^\top \lambda,$$

where $\phi(s_t) \in \{0, 1\}^H$ is a one-hot vector with a single 1 value at its s_t-th entry, and $\lambda \in \mathbb{R}^H$ is the parameter vector such that $\lambda \geq 0$ and $\lambda^\top \mathbf{1} = 1$.

We then define a multinomial logistic regression model for the *state transition distribution*,

$$P(s_{t+1}|s_t; \Theta) = \frac{\exp\left\{\phi(s_{t+1})^\top W M^\top \phi(s_t)\right\}}{Z(s_t; \Theta)}$$

where $W \in \mathbb{R}^{H \times m}$ is the regression parameter matrix and $Z(s_t; \Theta)$ is the normalization term.

Finally, we assume the observation vector is generated from a multivariate Gaussian distribution, i.e., $\mathbf{o}_t \sim \mathcal{N}\left(\phi(s_t)^\top MQ, \sigma I_d\right)$, and use the following model for the *emission distribution*,

$$P(\mathbf{o}_t|s_t; \Theta) = \frac{\exp\left\{\frac{-1}{2\sigma}\kappa(s_t, \mathbf{o}_t)\kappa(s_t, \mathbf{o}_t)^\top\right\}}{(2\pi)^{d/2}\sigma^{d/2}},$$

with $\kappa(s_t, \mathbf{o}_t) = \phi(s_t)^\top MQ - \mathbf{o}_t^\top$, where $Q \in \mathbb{R}^{m \times d}$ and $\sigma \in \mathbb{R}$ are the model parameters. Different from the standard HMMs which have discrete hidden states and discrete observations, the multivariate Gaussian model here generates each observation $\mathbf{o}_t$ as a d-dimensional continuous feature vector. This type of emission distribution provides us the flexibility to incorporate local context information or statistical global information for inducing distributed state representations. For example, we can use the concatenation of the one-hot word vectors within a sliding window around the target word as the observation vector. Moreover, we can also use the globally preprocessed continuous word vectors as the observation vectors, which we will describe later in our experiments.

The standard HMMs (Rabiner and Juang, 1986) use conditional probability tables for the state transition distribution, which grows quadratically with respect to the number of hidden states, and the emission distribution, which grows linearly with respect to the observed vocabulary size that is usually very large in NLP tasks. Instead, the dHMMs can significantly reduce the sizes of these conditional probability tables by introducing the low-dimensional state embedding vectors, and the dHMM is much more efficient in terms of memory storage. In fact, the complexity of dHMMs can be independent of the vocabulary size by using flexible observation features. We represent the dHMM parameter set as $\Theta = \{M \in \mathbb{R}^{H \times m}, W \in \mathbb{R}^{H \times m}, Q \in \mathbb{R}^{m \times d}, \sigma \in \mathbb{R}, \lambda \in [0, 1]^H\}$, where m is a small constant.

3.2 Model Training

Given a data set of N observed sequences $\{O^1, \ldots, O^n, \ldots, O^N\}$, its regularized log-

Table 1: Test performance for cross-domain POS tagging and NP chunking.

Systems	POS Tagging (Accuracy (%))		NP Chunking (F1-score)	
	All Words	OOV Words	All NPs	OOV NPs
Baseline	88.3	67.3	0.86	0.74
SGM (Hovy et al., 2015)	89.0	71.4	0.88	0.78
HMM (Huang and Yates, 2009)	90.5	75.2	0.91	0.85
dHMM	**91.1**	**76.0**	**0.93**	**0.88**

likelihood can be written as follows

$$\mathcal{L}(\Theta) = \sum_n \log P(O^n; \Theta) - \frac{\eta}{2}\mathcal{R}(W, Q, M) \quad (1)$$

where the regularization function is defined with Frobenius norms such as $\mathcal{R}(W, Q, M) = \|W\|_F^2 + \|Q\|_F^2 + \|M\|_F^2$. Moreover, each log-likelihood term has the following lower bound

$$\log P(O^n; \Theta) = \log \sum_{S^n} P(O^n, S^n; \Theta)$$
$$\geq \log P(O^n; \Theta) - \text{KL}(\mathcal{Q}(S^n) || P(S^n | O^n; \Theta)) \quad (2)$$

where $\mathcal{Q}(S^n)$ is any valid distribution over the hidden state variables S^n and KL(.||.) denotes the Kullback-Leibler divergence. Let $\mathcal{F}(\mathcal{Q}, \Theta)$ denote the regularized lower bound function obtained by plugging the lower bound (2) back into the objective function (1). We then perform training by using an expectation-maximization (EM) algorithm (Dempster et al., 1977) that iteratively maximizes $\mathcal{F}(\mathcal{Q}, \Theta)$ to reach a local optimal solution. We first randomly initialize the model parameters while enforcing λ to be in the feasible region ($\lambda \geq 0, \lambda^\top \mathbf{1} = 1$). In the (k+1)-th iteration, given $\{\mathcal{Q}^{(k)}, \Theta^{(k)}\}$, we then sequentially update $\mathcal{Q}$ with an E-step (3) and update Θ with a M-step (4).

$$\mathcal{Q}^{(k+1)} = \arg\max_{\mathcal{Q}} \mathcal{F}(\mathcal{Q}, \Theta^{(k)}) \quad (3)$$

$$\Theta^{(k+1)} = \arg\max_{\Theta} \mathcal{F}(\mathcal{Q}^{(k+1)}, \Theta) \quad (4)$$

3.3 Domain Adaptation with Distributed State Representations

We use all training data from the two domains to train dHMMs for local optimal model parameters $\Theta^* = \{M^*, W^*, Q^*, \sigma^*, \lambda^*\}$. We then infer the latent state sequence $S^* = \{s_1^*, s_2^*, \ldots, s_T^*\}$ using the standard Viterbi algorithm (Rabiner and Juang, 1986) for each labeled source training sentence and each target test sentence. The corresponding distributed state representation vectors can be obtained as $\{M^{*\top}\phi(s_1^*), M^{*\top}\phi(s_2^*), \ldots, M^{*\top}\phi(s_T^*)\}$. We then train a supervised NLP system (*e.g.*, POS tagging or NP chunking) on the labeled source training sentences using the distributed state representations as augmenting input features and perform prediction on the augmented test sentences.

4 Experiments

We conducted experiments on cross-domain part-of-speech (POS) tagging and noun-phrase (NP) chunking tasks. We used the same experimental datasets as in (Huang and Yates, 2009) for cross-domain POS tagging from Wall Street Journal (WSJ) domain (Marcus et al., 1993) to MEDLINE domain (PennBioIE, 2005) and for cross-domain NP chunking from CoNLL shared task dataset (Tjong et al., 2000) to Open American National Corpus (OANC) (Reppen et al., 2005).

4.1 Representation Learning

We first built a unified vocabulary with all the data in the two domains. We then conducted *latent semantic analysis* (LSA) over the sentence-word frequency matrix to get a low-dimensional representation vector for each word. We used a sliding window with size 3 to construct the d-dimensional feature vector ($d = 1500$) for each observation in a given sentence. We used $\eta = 0.5$, set the number of hidden states H to be 80 and the dimensionality $m = 20$. We used all the labeled and unlabeled training data in the two domains to train dHMMs.

4.2 Test Results

We used the induced distributed state representations of each observation as augmenting features to train conditional random fields (CRF) with the CRFSuite package (Okazaki, 2007) on the labeled source sentences and perform prediction on the target test sentences. We compared with the following systems: a *Baseline* system without representation learning, a SGM based word embedding system (Hovy et al., 2015), and a discrete hidden state based clustering system (Huang and Yates, 2009). We used the word id and orthographic features as the baseline features for POS tagging and added POS tags for NP chunking. We reported the POS tagging accuracy for all words and out-of-vocabulary (OOV) words (which appear less than three times in the labeled source training sentences), and NP chunking F1 scores for all NPs and only OOV NPs (whose beginning word is an OOV word) in Table 1.

We can see that the *Baseline* method performs poorly on both tasks especially on the OOV words/NPs, which shows that the original lexical based features are not sufficient to develop a robust POS tagger/NP chunker for the target domain with labeled source training sentences. By using unlabeled training sentences from the two domains, all representation learning approaches increase the cross-domain test performance, especially on the OOV words/NPs. These improvements over the *Baseline* method demonstrate that the induced latent features do alleviate feature sparsity issue across the two domains and help the trained NLP system generalize well in the target domain. Between these representation learning approaches, the proposed distributed state representation learning method outperforms both of the word embedding based and discrete HMM hidden state based systems. This suggests that by learning distributed representations in a context-aware manner, dHMMs can effectively bridge domain divergence.

4.3 Sensitivity Analysis over the Dimensionality of State Embeddings

We also conducted experiments to investigate how does the dimensionality of the distributed state representations, m, in our proposed approach affect cross-domain test performance given a fixed state number $H = 80$. We tested a number of different m values from $\{10, 20, 30, 40\}$ and used the same experimental setting as before for each m value. The POS tagging accuracy on all words of the test sentences and the chunking F1 score on all NPs with different m values are reported in Figure 2. We can see that the performance of both POS tagging and NP chunking has notable improvements with m increasing from 10 to 20. The POS tagging performance improves very slightly from $m = 20$ to $m = 30$ and is very stable from

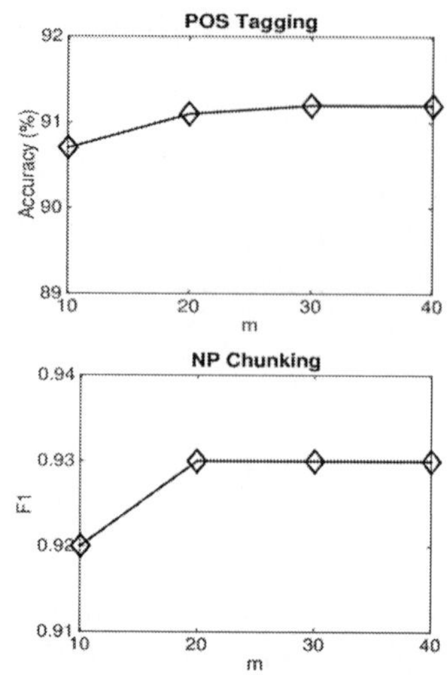

Figure 2: Cross-domain test performance with respect to different dimensionality values (m) of the hidden state representation vectors.

$m = 30$ to $m = 40$. The NP chunking performance is very stable from $m = 20$ to $m = 40$. These results suggest that the distributed state representation vectors only need to have a succinct length to capture useful information. The proposed distributed HMMs are not sensitive to the dimensionality of the state embeddings as long as m reaches a reasonable small value.

5 Conclusion

In this paper, we extended the standard HMMs to learn distributed state representations and facilitate cross-domain sequence predictions. We mapped each state variable to a distributed representation vector and simultaneously learned the state embedding matrix and the model parameters with an EM algorithm. The experimental results on cross-domain POS tagging and NP chunking tasks demonstrated the effectiveness of the proposed approach for domain adaptation. In the future, we plan to apply this approach to other cross-domain prediction tasks such as named entity recognition or semantic role labeling. We also plan to extend our method to learn cross-lingual representations with auxiliary resources such as bilingual dictionaries or parallel sentences.

Acknowledgments

This research was supported in part by NSF grant IIS-1065397.

References

J. Blitzer, R. McDonald, and F. Pereira. 2006. Domain adaptation with structural correspondence learning. In *Proc. of the Conference on Empirical Methods in Natural Language Processing (EMNLP)*.

P. Brown, P. deSouza, R. Mercer, V. Pietra, and J. Lai. 1992. Class-based n-gram models of natural language. *Compututal Linguistics*, 18(4):467–479.

M. Candito, E. Anguiano, and D. Seddah. 2011. A word clustering approach to domain adaptation: Effective parsing of biomedical texts. In *Proc. of the Inter. Conference on Parsing Technologies (IWPT)*.

R. Collobert and J. Weston. 2008. A unified architecture for natural language processing: deep neural networks with multitask learning. In *Proc. of the Inter. Conference on Machine Learning (ICML)*.

D. Dahlmeier and H. Ng. 2010. Domain adaptation for semantic role labeling in the biomedical domain. *Bioinformatics*, 26(8):1098–1104.

H. Daumé III. 2007. Frustratingly easy domain adaptation. In *Proc. of the Annual Meeting of the Association of Computational Linguistics (ACL)*.

A. Dempster, N. Laird, and D. Rubin. 1977. Maximum likelihood from incomplete data via the em algorithm. *Journal of the Royal Statistical Society, Series B*, 39(1):1–38.

M. Dredze, J. Blitzer, P. Talukdar, K. Ganchev, J. Graça, and O. Pereira. 2007. Frustratingly hard domain adaptation for dependency parsing. In *Proc. of CoNLL Shared Task Session of EMNLP-CoNLL*.

H. Guo, H. Zhu, Z. Guo, X. Zhang, X. Wu, and Z. Su. 2009. Domain adaptation with latent semantic association for named entity recognition. In *Proc. of Human Language Technologies: The Annual Conf. of North American Chapter of ACL (HLT-NAACL)*.

D. Hovy, B. Plank, H. Alonso, and A. Søgaard. 2015. Mining for unambiguous instances to adapt pos taggers to new domains. In *Proc. of the Conference of the North American Chapter of ACL (NAACL)*.

F. Huang and A. Yates. 2009. Distributional representations for handling sparsity in supervised sequence-labeling. In *Proc. of the Annual Meeting of the ACL and the IJCNLP of the AFNLP (ACL-AFNLP)*.

F. Huang and A. Yates. 2010a. Exploring representation-learning approaches to domain adaptation. In *Proc. of the Workshop on Domain Adaptation for Natural Language Processing (DANLP)*.

F. Huang and A. Yates. 2010b. Open-domain semantic role labeling by modeling word spans. In *Proc. of the Annual Meeting of ACL (ACL)*.

F. Huang, A. Yates, A. Ahuja, and D. Downey. 2011. Language models as representations for weakly-supervised nlp tasks. In *Proc. of the Conference on Comput. Natural Language Learning (CoNLL)*.

H. Jaeger. 1999. Observable operator models for discrete stochastic time series. *Neural Computation*, 12:1371–1398.

T. Koo, X. Carreras, and M. Collins. 2008. Simple semi-supervised dependency parsing. In *Proc. of the Annual Meeting of the Association for Computational Linguistics (ACL)*.

M. Marcus, M. Marcinkiewicz, and B. Santorini. 1993. Building a large annotated corpus of english: The Penn treebank. *Computational Linguistics*, 19(2):313–330.

T. Mikolov, I. Sutskever, K. Chen, G. Corrado, and J. Dean. 2013. Distributed representations of words and phrases and their compositionality. In *Advances in Neural Information Processing Systems (NIPS)*.

A. Mnih and E. Geoffrey. 2008. A scalable hierarchical distributed language model. In *Advances in Neural Information Processing Systems (NIPS)*.

N. Okazaki. 2007. CRFsuite: a fast implementation of conditional random fields (CRFs). http://www.chokkan.org/software/crfsuite/.

PennBioIE. 2005. Mining the bibliome project. http://bioie.ldc.upenn.edu.

L. Rabiner and B. Juang. 1986. An introduction to hidden Markov models. *IEEE ASSP Magazine*, 3(1):4–16.

R. Reppen, N. Ide, and K. Suderman. 2005. American national corpus (anc) second release. Linguistic Data Consortium.

I. Sag and T. Wasow. 1999. *Syntactic theory : a formal introduction*. CSLI publications.

K. Sagae and J. Tsujii. 2007. Dependency parsing and domain adaptation with lr models and parser ensembles. In *Proc. of CoNLL Shared Task Session of EMNLP-CoNLL*.

V. Srikumar and C. Manning. 2014. Learning distributed representations for structured output prediction. In *Advances in Neural Information Processing Systems (NIPS)*.

K. Stratos, A. Rush, S. Cohen, and M. Collins. 2013. Spectral learning of refinement HMMs. In *Proc. of the Conference on Computational Natural Language Learning (CoNLL)*.

K. Tjong, E. Sang, , and S. Buchholz. 2000. Introduction to the CoNLL-2000 shared task: Chunking. In *Proc. of the Conference on Computational Natural Language Learning (CoNLL)*.

J. Turian, L. Ratinov, and Y. Bengio. 2010. Word representations: a simple and general method for semi-supervised learning. In *Proc. of the Annual Meeting of the Association for Comput. Linguistics (ACL)*.

MT Quality Estimation for Computer-assisted Translation: Does it Really Help?

Marco Turchi, Matteo Negri, Marcello Federico
FBK - Fondazione Bruno Kessler,
Via Sommarive 18, 38123 Trento, Italy
{turchi,negri,federico}@fbk.eu

Abstract

The usefulness of translation quality estimation (QE) to increase productivity in a computer-assisted translation (CAT) framework is a widely held assumption (Specia, 2011; Huang et al., 2014). So far, however, the validity of this assumption has not been yet demonstrated through sound evaluations in realistic settings. To this aim, we report on an evaluation involving professional translators operating with a CAT tool in controlled but natural conditions. Contrastive experiments are carried out by measuring post-editing time differences when: *i)* translation suggestions are presented together with binary quality estimates, and *ii)* the same suggestions are presented without quality indicators. Translators' productivity in the two conditions is analysed in a principled way, accounting for the main factors (*e.g.* differences in translators' behaviour, quality of the suggestions) that directly impact on time measurements. While the general assumption about the usefulness of QE is verified, significance testing results reveal that real productivity gains can be observed only under specific conditions.

1 Introduction

Machine translation (MT) quality estimation aims to automatically predict the expected time (*e.g.* in seconds) or effort (*e.g.* number of editing operations) required to correct machine-translated sentences into publishable translations (Specia et al., 2009; Mehdad et al., 2012; Turchi et al., 2014a; C. de Souza et al., 2015). In principle, the task has a number of practical applications. An intuitive one is speeding-up the work of human translators operating with a CAT tool, a software designed to support and facilitate the translation process by proposing suggestions that can be edited by the user. The idea is that, since the suggestions can be useful (good, hence post-editable) or useless (poor, hence requiring complete re-writing), reliable quality indicators could help to reduce the time spent by the user to decide which action to take (to correct or re-translate).

So far, despite the potential practical benefits, the progress in QE research has not been followed by conclusive results that demonstrate whether the use of quality labels can actually lead to noticeable productivity gains in the CAT framework. To the best of our knowledge, most prior works limit the analysis to the intrinsic evaluation of QE performance on gold-standard data (Callison-Burch et al., 2012; Bojar et al., 2013; Bojar et al., 2014). On-field evaluation is indeed a complex task, as it requires: *i)* the availability of a CAT tool capable to integrate MT QE functionalities, *ii)* professional translators used to MT post-editing, *iii)* a sound evaluation protocol to perform between-subject comparisons,[1] and *iv)* robust analysis techniques to measure statistical significance under variable conditions (*e.g.* differences in users' post-editing behavior).

To bypass these issues, the works more closely related to our investigation resort to controlled and simplified evaluation protocols. For instance, in (Specia, 2011) the impact of QE predictions on translators' productivity is analysed by measuring the number of words that can be post-edited in a fixed amount of time. The evaluation, however, only concentrates on the use of QE to rank MT outputs, and the gains in translation speed are measured against the contrastive condition in which no QE-based ranking mechanism is used. In this artificial scenario, the analysis disregards the relation

[1]Notice that the same sentence cannot be post-edited twice (*e.g.* *with/without* quality labels) by the same translator without introducing a bias in the time measurements.

Proceedings of the 53rd Annual Meeting of the Association for Computational Linguistics and the 7th International Joint Conference on Natural Language Processing (Short Papers), pages 530–535,
Beijing, China, July 26-31, 2015.

between the usefulness of QE and the intrinsic features of the top-ranked translations (*e.g.* sentence length, quality of the MT). More recently, Huang et al. (2014) claimed a 10% productivity increase when translation is supported by the estimates of an adaptive QE model. Their analysis, however, compares a condition in which MT suggestions are presented with confidence labels (the two factors are not decoupled) against the contrastive condition in which no MT suggestion is presented at all. Significance testing, moreover, is not performed.

The remainder of this work describes our on-field evaluation addressing (through objective measurements and robust significance tests) the two key questions:

- *Does QE really help in the CAT scenario?*
- *If yes, under what conditions?*

2 Experimental Setup

One of the key questions in utilising QE in the CAT scenario is how to relay QE information to the user. In our experiments, we evaluate a way of visualising MT quality estimates that is based on a color-coded binary classification (green vs. red) as an alternative to real-valued quality labels. In our context, '*green*' means that post-editing the translation is expected to be faster than translation from scratch, while '*red*' means that post-editing the translation is expected to take longer than translating from scratch.

This decision rests on the assumption that the two-color scheme is more immediate than real-valued scores, which require some interpretation by the user. Analysing the difference between alternative visualisation schemes, however, is certainly an aspect that we want to explore in the future.

2.1 The CAT Framework

To keep the experimental conditions as natural as possible, we analyse the impact of QE labels on translators' productivity in a real CAT environment. To this aim, we use the open-source MateCat tool (Federico et al., 2014), which has been slightly changed in two ways. First, the tool has been adapted to provide only one single translation suggestion (MT output) per segment, instead of the usual three (one MT suggestion plus two Translation Memory matches). Second, each suggestion is presented with a colored flag (green for good, red for bad), which indicates its expected quality and usefulness to the post-editor. In the contrastive condition (no binary QE visualization), grey is used as the neutral and uniform flag color.

2.2 Getting binary quality labels.

The experiment is set up for a between-subject comparison on a single long document as follows.

First, the document is split in two parts. The first part serves as the training portion for a binary quality estimator; the second part is reserved for evaluation. The *training* portion is machine-translated with a state-of-the-art, phrase-based Moses system (Koehn et al., 2007)[2] and post-edited under standard conditions (*i.e.* without visualising QE information) by the same users involved in the testing phase. Based on their post-edits, the raw MT output samples are then labeled as 'good' or 'bad' by considering the HTER (Snover et al., 2006) calculated between raw MT output and its post-edited version.[3] Our labeling criterion follows the empirical findings of (Turchi et al., 2013; Turchi et al., 2014b), which indicate an HTER value of 0.4 as boundary between post-editable (HTER $\leq$ 0.4) and useless suggestions (HTER$>$ 0.4).

Then, to model the subjective concept of quality of different subjects, for of each translator we train a separate binary QE classifier on the labeled samples. For this purpose we use the Scikit-learn implementation of support vector machines (Pedregosa et al., 2011), training our models with the 17 baseline features proposed by Specia et al. (2009). This feature set mainly takes into account the complexity of the source sentence (*e.g.* number of tokens, number of translations per source word) and the fluency of the target translation (*e.g.* language model probabilities). The features are extracted from the data available at prediction time (source text and raw MT output) by using an adapted version (Shah et al., 2014) of the open-source QuEst software (Specia et al., 2013). The SVM parameters are optimized by cross-validation on the training set.

With these classifiers, we finally assign quality flags to the raw segment translations in the *test*

[2]The system was trained with 60M running words from the same domain (Information Technology) of the input document.

[3]HTER measures the minimum edit distance (# word Insertions + Deletions + Substitutions + Shifts / # Reference Words) between the MT output and its manual post-edition.

Average PET (sec/word)	colored 8.086 grey 9.592	$p = 0.33$
% Wins of colored	51.7	$p = 0.039$

Table 1: Comparison (Avg. PET and ranking) between the two testing conditions (*with* and *without* QE labels).

portion of the respective document, which is eventually sent to each post-editor to collect time and productivity measurements.

2.3 Getting post-editing time measurements.

While translating the test portion of the document, each translator is given an even and random distribution of segments labeled according to the test condition (colored flags) and segments labeled according to the baseline, contrastive condition (uniform grey flags). In the distribution of the data, some constraints were identified to ensure the soundness of the evaluation in the two conditions: *i)* each translator must post-edit all the segments of the test portion of the document, *ii)* each translator must post-edit the segments of the test set only once, *iii)* all translators must post-edit the same amount of segments with colored and grey labels. After post-editing, the post-editing times are analysed to assess the impact of the binary coloring scheme on translators' productivity.

3 Results

We applied our procedure on an English user manual (Information Technology domain) to be translated into Italian. Post-editing was performed independently by four professional translators, so that two measurements (post-editing time) for each segment and condition could be collected. Training and and test respectively contained 542 and 847 segments. Half of the 847 test segments were presented with colored QE flags, with a ratio of green to red labels of about 75% 'good' and 25% 'bad'.

3.1 Preliminary analysis

Before addressing our research questions, we performed a preliminary analysis aimed to verify the reliability of our experimental protocol and the consequent findings. Indeed, an inherent risk of presenting post-editors with an unbalanced distribution of colored flags is to incur in unexpected subconscious effects. For instance, green flags could be misinterpreted as a sort of pre-validation, and induce post-editors to spend less time on the corresponding segments (by producing fewer changes). To check this hypothesis we compared the HTER scores obtained in the two conditions (colored vs. grey flags), assuming that noticeable differences would be evidence of unwanted psychological effects. The very close values measured in the two conditions (the average HTER is respectively 23.9 and 24.1) indicate that the professional post-editors involved in the experiment did what they were asked for, by always changing what had to be corrected in the proposed suggestions, independently from the color of the associated flags. In light of this, post-editing time variations in different conditions can be reasonably ascribed to the effect of QE labels on the time spent by the translators to decide whether correcting or re-translating a given suggestion.

3.2 Does QE Really Help?

To analyse the impact of our quality estimates on translators' productivity, we first compared the average post-editing time (PET – seconds per word) under the two conditions (colored vs. grey flags). The results of this rough, global analysis are reported in Table 1, first row. As can be seen, the average PET values indicate a productivity increase of about 1.5 seconds per word when colored flags are provided. Significance tests, however, indicate that such increase is not significant ($p > 0.05$, measured by approximate randomization (Noreen, 1989; Riezler and Maxwell, 2005)).

An analysis of the collected data to better understand these results and the rather high average PET values observed (8 to 9.5 secs. per word) evidenced both a large number of outliers, and a high PET variability across post-editors.[4] To check whether these factors make existing PET differences opaque to our study, we performed further analysis by normalizing the PET of each translator with the *robust z-score* technique (Rousseeuw and Leroy, 1987).[5] The twofold advantage of

[4]We consider as outliers the segments with a PET lower than 0.5 or higher than 30. Segments with unrealistically short post-editing times may not even have been read completely, while very long post-editing times suggest that the post-editor interrupted his/her work or got distracted. The average PET for the four post-editors ranges from 2.266 to 13.783. In total, 48 segments have a PET higher than 30, and 6 segments were post-edited in more than 360 seconds.

[5]For each post-editor, it is computed by removing from

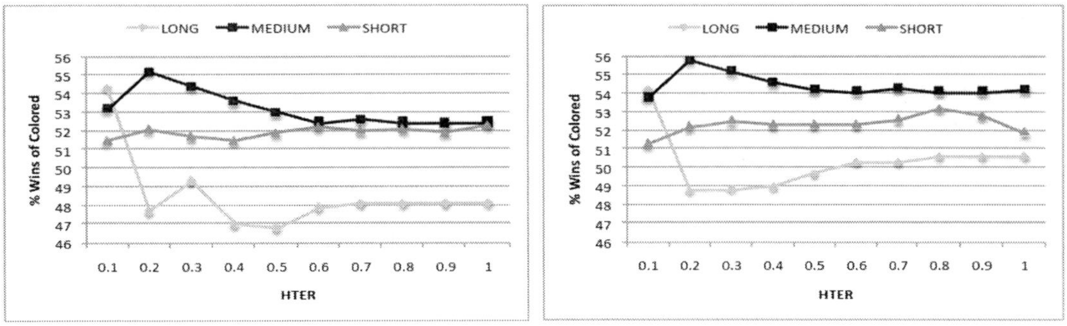

Figure 1: % wins of colored with respect to length and quality of MT output. Left: all pairs. Right: only pairs with correct color predictions.

this method is to mitigate idiosyncratic differences in translators' behavior, and reduce the influence of outliers. To further limit the impact of outliers, we also moved from a comparison based on average PET measurements to a ranking-based method in which we count the number of times the segments presented with colored flags were post-edited faster than those presented with grey flags. For each of the (*PET_colored, PET_grey*) pairs measured for the test segments, the percentage of wins (*i.e.* lower time) of *PET_colored* is calculated. As shown in the second row of Table 1, a small but statistically significant difference between the two conditions indeed exists.

Although the usefulness of QE in the CAT framework seems hence to be verified, the extent of its contribution is rather small (51.7% of wins). This motivates an additional analysis, aimed to verify if such marginal global gains hide larger local productivity improvements under specific conditions.

3.3 Under what Conditions does QE Help?

To address this question, we analysed two important factors that can influence translators' productivity measurements: the length (number of tokens) of the source sentences and the quality (HTER) of the proposed MT suggestions. To this aim, all the (*PET_colored, PET_grey*) pairs were assigned to three bins based on the length of the source sentences: short (length$\leq$5), medium (5<length$\leq$20), and long (length>20). Then, in each bin, ten levels of MT quality were identified (HTER $\leq$ 0.1, 0.2, ..., 1). Finally, for each bin and HTER threshold, we applied the ranking-based method described in the previous section.

The left plot of Figure 1 shows how the "% wins of colored" varies depending on the two factors on all the collected pairs. As can be seen, for MT suggestions of short and medium length the percentage of wins is always above 50%, while its value is systematically lower for the long sentences when HTER>0.1. However, the differences are statistically significant only for medium-length suggestions, and when HTER>0.1. Such condition, in particular when 0.2<HTER$\leq$0.5, seems to represent the ideal situation in which QE labels can actually contribute to speed-up translators' work. Indeed, in terms of PET, the average productivity gain of 0.663 secs. per word measured in the [0.2 − 0.5] HTER interval is statistically significant.

Although our translator-specific binary QE classifiers (see Section 2) have acceptable performance (on average 80% accuracy on the test data for all post-editors),[6] to check the validity of our conclusions we also investigated if, and to what extent, our results are influenced by classification errors. To this aim, we removed from the three bins those pairs that contain a misclassified instance (*i.e.* the pairs in which there is a mismatch between the predicted label and the true HTER measured after post-editing).[7]

The results obtained by applying our ranking-based method to the remaining pairs are shown in the right plot of Figure 1. In this "ideal", error-free scenario the situation slightly changes (unsurprisingly, the "% wins of colored" slightly increases,

the PET of each segment the post-editor median and dividing by the post-editor median absolute deviation (MAD).

[6]Measured by comparing each predicted binary label with the 'true' label obtained applying the 0.4 HTER threshold as a separator between good and bad MT suggestions.

[7]The three bins contained 502, 792, 214 pairs *before* misclassification removal and 339, 604, 160 pairs *after* cleaning.

especially for long suggestions for which we have the highest number of misclassifications), but the overall conclusions remain the same. In particular, the higher percentage of wins is statistically significant only for medium-length suggestions with HTER>0.1 and, in the best case (HTER$\leq$0.2) it is about 56.0%.

4 Conclusion

We presented the results of an on-field evaluation aimed to verify the widely held assumption that QE information can be useful to speed-up MT post-editing in the CAT scenario. Our results suggest that this assumption should be put into perspective. On one side, global PET measurements do not necessarily show statistically significant productivity gains,[8] indicating that the contribution of QE falls below expectations (*our first contribution*). On the other side, an in-depth analysis abstracting from the presence of outliers and the high variability across post-editors, indicates that the usefulness of QE is verified, at least to some extent (*our second contribution*). Indeed, the marginal productivity gains observed with QE at a global level become statistically significant in specific conditions, depending on the length (between 5 and 20 words) of the source sentences and the quality (0.2<HTER$\leq$0.5) of the proposed MT suggestions (*our third contribution*).

Acknowledgements

This work has been partially supported by the EC-funded projects MateCat (FP7 grant agreement no. 287688) and QT21 (H2020 innovation programme, grant agreement no. 645452).

[8]Unless, for instance, robust and non-arbitrary methods to identify and remove outliers are applied.

References

Ondrej Bojar, Christian Buck, Chris Callison-Burch, Christian Federmann, Barry Haddow, Philipp Koehn, Christof Monz, Matt Post, Radu Soricut, and Lucia Specia. 2013. Findings of the 2013 Workshop on Statistical Machine Translation. In *Proceedings of the 8th Workshop on Statistical Machine Translation*, WMT-2013, pages 1–44, Sofia, Bulgaria.

Ondrej Bojar, Christian Buck, Christian Federmann, Barry Haddow, Philipp Koehn, Johannes Leveling, Christof Monz, Pavel Pecina, Matt Post, Herve Saint-Amand, Radu Soricut, Lucia Specia, and Aleš Tamchyna. 2014. Findings of the 2014 workshop on statistical machine translation. In *Proceedings of the Ninth Workshop on Statistical Machine Translation*, pages 12–58, Baltimore, Maryland, USA.

José G. C. de Souza, Matteo Negri, Marco Turchi, and Elisa Ricci. 2015. Online Multitask Learning For Machine Translation Quality Estimation. In *Proceedings of the 53rd Annual Meeting of the Association for Computational Linguistics)*, Beijing, China.

Chris Callison-Burch, Philipp Koehn, Christof Monz, Matt Post, Radu Soricut, and Lucia Specia. 2012. Findings of the 2012 Workshop on Statistical Machine Translation. In *Proceedings of the 7th Workshop on Statistical Machine Translation (WMT'12)*, pages 10–51, Montréal, Canada.

Marcello Federico, Nicola Bertoldi, Mauro Cettolo, Matteo Negri, Marco Turchi, Marco Trombetti, Alessandro Cattelan, Antonio Farina, Domenico Lupinetti, Andrea Martines, Alberto Massidda, Holger Schwenk, Loïc Barrault, Frederic Blain, Philipp Koehn, Christian Buck, and Ulrich Germann. 2014. The MateCat tool. In *Proceedings of COLING 2014, the 25th International Conference on Computational Linguistics: System Demonstrations*, pages 129–132, Dublin, Ireland.

Fei Huang, Jian-Ming Xu, Abraham Ittycheriah, and Salim Roukos. 2014. Adaptive HTER Estimation for Document-Specific MT Post-Editing. In *Proceedings of the 52nd Annual Meeting of the Association for Computational Linguistics (Volume 1: Long Papers)*, pages 861–870, Baltimore, Maryland.

Philipp Koehn, Hieu Hoang, Alexandra Birch, Chris Callison-Burch, Marcello Federico, Nicola Bertoldi, Brooke Cowan, Wade Shen, Christine Moran, Richard Zens, Chris Dyer, Ondřej Bojar, Alexandra Constantin, and Evan Herbst. 2007. Moses: Open Source Toolkit for Statistical Machine Translation. In *Proceedings of the 45th Annual Meeting of the ACL on Interactive Poster and Demonstration Sessions*, pages 177–180, Stroudsburg, PA, USA.

Yashar Mehdad, Matteo Negri, and Marcello Federico. 2012. Match without a Referee: Evaluating MT Adequacy without Reference Translations. In *Proceedings of the Machine Translation Workshop (WMT2012)*, pages 171–180, Montréal, Canada.

Eric W. Noreen. 1989. Computer-intensive methods for testing hypotheses: an introduction. *Wiley Interscience*.

Fabian Pedregosa, Gal Varoquaux, Alexandre Gramfort, Vincent Michel, Bertrand Thirion, Olivier Grisel, Mathieu Blondel, Peter Prettenhofer, Ron Weiss, Vincent Dubourg, Jake Vanderplas, Alexandre Passos, David Cournapeau, Matthieu Brucher, Matthieu Perrot, and douard Duchesnay. 2011. Scikit-learn: Machine Learning in Python. *Journal of Machine Learning Research*, 12:2825–2830.

Stefan Riezler and John T Maxwell. 2005. On some Pitfalls in Automatic Evaluation and Significance Testing for MT. In *Proceedings of the ACL workshop on intrinsic and extrinsic evaluation measures for machine translation and/or summarization*, pages 57–64.

Peter J Rousseeuw and Annick M Leroy. 1987. *Robust regression and outlier detection*, volume 589. John Wiley & Sons.

Kashif Shah, Marco Turchi, and Lucia Specia. 2014. An efficient and user-friendly tool for machine translation quality estimation. In *Proceedings of the Ninth International Conference on Language Resources and Evaluation (LREC'14)*, Reykjavik, Iceland.

Matthew Snover, Bonnie Dorr, Richard Schwartz, Linnea Micciulla, and John Makhoul. 2006. A Study of Translation Edit Rate with Targeted Human Annotation. In *Proceedings of Association for Machine Translation in the Americas*, pages 223–231, Cambridge, Massachusetts, USA.

Lucia Specia, Nicola Cancedda, Marc Dymetman, Marco Turchi, and Nello Cristianini. 2009. Estimating the Sentence-Level Quality of Machine Translation Systems. In *Proceedings of the 13th Annual Conference of the European Association for Machine Translation (EAMT'09)*, pages 28–35, Barcelona, Spain.

Lucia Specia, Kashif Shah, José G.C. de Souza, and Trevor Cohn. 2013. QuEst - A Translation Quality Estimation Framework. In *Proceedings of the 51st Annual Meeting of the Association for Computational Linguistics: System Demonstrations*, ACL-2013, pages 79–84, Sofia, Bulgaria.

Lucia Specia. 2011. Exploiting Objective Annotations for Minimising Translation Post-editing Effort. In *Proceedings of the 15th Conference of the European Association for Machine Translation (EAMT 2011)*, pages 73–80, Leuven, Belgium.

Marco Turchi, Matteo Negri, and Marcello Federico. 2013. Coping with the Subjectivity of Human Judgements in MT Quality Estimation. In *Proceedings of the 8th Workshop on Statistical Machine Translation*, pages 240–251, Sofia, Bulgaria.

Marco Turchi, Antonios Anastasopoulos, José G. C. de Souza, and Matteo Negri. 2014a. Adaptive Quality Estimation for Machine Translation. In *Proceedings of the 52nd Annual Meeting of the Association for Computational Linguistics (Volume 1: Long Papers)*, pages 710–720, Baltimore, Maryland, USA.

Marco Turchi, Matteo Negri, and Marcello Federico. 2014b. Data-driven Annotation of Binary MT Quality Estimation Corpora Based on Human Post-editions. *Machine translation*, 28(3-4):281–308.

Context-Dependent Translation Selection Using Convolutional Neural Network

Baotian Hu[‡] **Zhaopeng Tu**[†*] **Zhengdong Lu**[†] **Hang Li**[†] **Qingcai Chen**[‡]

[‡]Intelligent Computing Research Center, Harbin Institute of Technology Shenzhen Graduate School
baotianchina@gmail.com
qingcai.chen@hitsz.edu.cn

[†]Noah's Ark Lab
Huawei Technologies Co. Ltd.
tu.zhaopeng@huawei.com
lu.zhengdong@huawei.com
hangli.hl@huawei.com

Abstract

We propose a novel method for translation selection in statistical machine translation, in which a convolutional neural network is employed to judge the similarity between a phrase pair in two languages. The specifically designed convolutional architecture encodes not only the semantic similarity of the translation pair, but also the context containing the phrase in the source language. Therefore, our approach is able to capture *context-dependent* semantic similarities of translation pairs. We adopt a curriculum learning strategy to train the model: we classify the training examples into easy, medium, and difficult categories, and gradually build the ability of representing phrases and sentence-level contexts by using training examples from easy to difficult. Experimental results show that our approach significantly outperforms the baseline system by up to 1.4 BLEU points.

1 Introduction

Conventional statistical machine translation (SMT) systems extract and estimate translation pairs based on their surface forms (Koehn et al., 2003), which often fail to capture translation pairs which are grammatically and semantically similar. To alleviate the above problems, several researchers have proposed learning and utilizing semantically similar translation pairs in a continuous space (Gao et al., 2014; Zhang et al., 2014; Cho et al., 2014). The core idea is that the two phrases in a translation pair should share the same semantic meaning and have similar (close) feature vectors in the continuous space.

The above methods, however, *neglect the information of local contexts*, which has been proven to be useful for disambiguating translation candidates during decoding (He et al., 2008; Marton and Resnik, 2008). The matching scores of translation pairs are treated the same, even they are in different contexts. Accordingly, the methods fail to adapt to local contexts and lead to precision issues for specific sentences in different contexts.

To capture useful context information, we propose a convolutional neural network architecture to measure context-dependent semantic similarities between phrase pairs in two languages. For each phrase pair, we use the sentence containing the phrase in source language as the context. With the convolutional neural network, we summarize the information of a phrase pair and its context, and further compute the pair's matching score with a multi-layer perceptron. We discriminately train the model using a curriculum learning strategy. We classify the training examples according to the difficulty level of distinguishing the positive candidate from the negative candidate. Then we train the model to learn the semantic information from *easy* (basic semantic similarities) to *difficult* (context-dependent semantic similarities).

Experimental results on a large-scale translation task show that the context-dependent convolutional matching (CDCM) model improves the performance by up to 1.4 BLEU points over a strong phrase-based SMT system. Moreover, the CDCM model significantly outperforms its context-independent counterpart, proving that it is necessary to incorporate local contexts into SMT.

Contributions. Our key contributions include:

- we introduce a novel CDCM model to capture context-dependent semantic similarities between phrase pairs (Section 2);
- we develop a novel learning algorithm to train the CDCM model using a curriculum learning strategy (Section 3).

* Corresponding author

Proceedings of the 53rd Annual Meeting of the Association for Computational Linguistics and the 7th International Joint Conference on Natural Language Processing (Short Papers), pages 536–541,
Beijing, China, July 26-31, 2015.

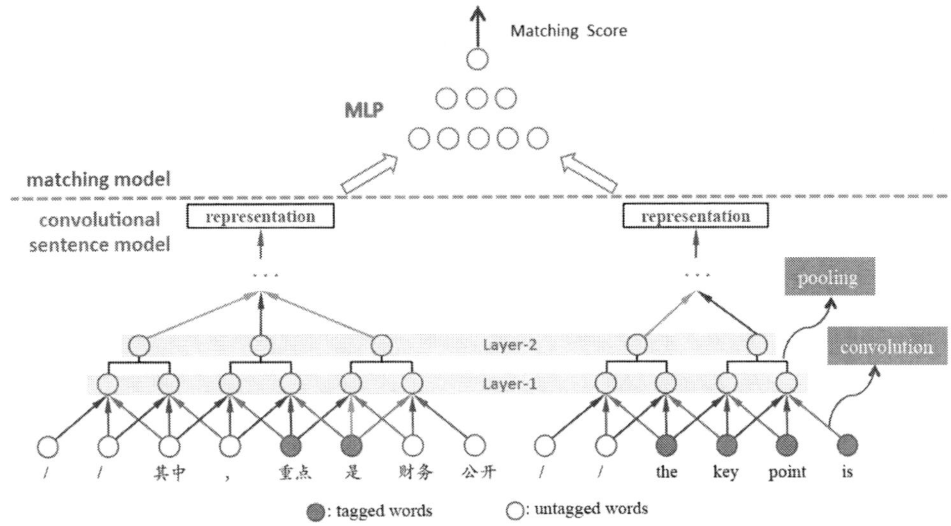

Figure 1: Architecture of the CDCM model. The *convolutional sentence model* (bottom) summarizes the meaning of the tagged sentence and target phrase, and the *matching model* (top) compares the representations using a multi-layer perceptron. "/" indicates all-zero padding turned off by the gating function.

2 Context-Dependent Convolutional Matching Model

The model architecture, shown in Figure 1, is a variant of the convolutional architecture of Hu et al. (2014). It consists of two components:

- *convolutional sentence model* that summarizes the meaning of the source sentence and the target phrase;
- *matching model* that compares the two representations with a multi-layer perceptron (Bengio, 2009).

Let $\hat{e}$ be a target phrase and $\mathbf{f}$ be the source sentence that contains the source phrase aligning to $\hat{e}$. We first project $\mathbf{f}$ and $\hat{e}$ into feature vectors $\mathbf{x}$ and $\mathbf{y}$ via the convolutional sentence model, and then compute the matching score $s(\mathbf{x}, \mathbf{y})$ by the matching model. Finally, the score is introduced into a conventional SMT system as an additional feature.

Convolutional sentence model. As shown in Figure 1, the model takes as input the embeddings of words (trained beforehand elsewhere) in $\mathbf{f}$ and $\hat{e}$. It then iteratively summarizes the meaning of the input through layers of convolution and pooling, until reaching a fixed length vectorial representation in the final layer.

In Layer-1, the convolution layer takes sliding windows on $\mathbf{f}$ and $\hat{e}$ respectively, and models all the possible compositions of neighbouring words. The convolution involves a *filter* to produce a new feature for each possible composition. Given a k-sized sliding window i on $\mathbf{f}$ or $\hat{e}$, for example, the jth convolution unit of the composition of the words is generated by:

$$\mathbf{c}_i^{(1,j)} = g(\hat{\mathbf{c}}_i^{(0)}) \cdot \phi(\mathbf{w}^{(1,j)} \cdot \hat{\mathbf{c}}_i^{(0)} + \mathbf{b}^{(1,j)}) \quad (1)$$

where

- $g(\cdot)$ is the gate function that determines whether to activate $\phi(\cdot)$;
- $\phi(\cdot)$ is a non-linear activation function. In this work, we use ReLu (Dahl et al., 2013) as the activation function;
- $\mathbf{w}^{(1,j)}$ is the parameters for the jth convolution unit on Layer-1, with matrix $\mathbf{W}^{(1)} = [\mathbf{w}^{(1,1)}, \ldots, \mathbf{w}^{(1,J)}]$;
- $\hat{\mathbf{c}}_i^{(0)}$ is a vector constructed by concatenating word vectors in the k-sized sliding widow i;
- $\mathbf{b}^{(1,j)}$ is a bias term, with vector $\mathbf{B}^{(1)} = [\mathbf{b}^{(1,1)}, \ldots, \mathbf{b}^{(1,J)}]$.

To distinguish the phrase pair from its context, we use one additional dimension in word embeddings: 1 for words in the phrase pair and 0 for the others. After transforming words to their tagged embeddings, the convolutional sentence model takes multiple choices of composition using sliding windows in the convolution layer. Note that sliding windows are allowed to cross the boundary of the source phrase to exploit both phrasal and contextual information.

In Layer-2, we apply a local max-pooling in non-overlapping 1×2 windows for every convolution unit

$$\mathbf{c}_i^{(2,j)} = \max\{\mathbf{c}_{2i}^{(1,j)}, \mathbf{c}_{2i+1}^{(1,j)}\} \tag{2}$$

In Layer-3, we perform convolution on output from Layer-2:

$$\mathbf{c}_i^{(3,j)} = g(\hat{\mathbf{c}}_i^{(2)}) \cdot \phi(\mathbf{w}^{(3,j)} \cdot \hat{\mathbf{c}}_i^{(2)} + \mathbf{b}^{(3,j)}) \tag{3}$$

After more convolution and max-pooling operations, we obtain two feature vectors for the source sentence and the target phrase, respectively.

Matching model. The matching score of a source sentence and a target phrase can be measured as the similarity between their feature vectors. Specifically, we use the multi-layer perceptron (MLP), a nonlinear function for similarity, to compute their matching score. First we use one layer to combine their feature vectors to get a hidden state h_c:

$$h_c = \phi(w_c \cdot [\mathbf{x}_{\bar{f}_i} : \mathbf{y}_{\bar{e}_j}] + b_c) \tag{4}$$

Then we get the matching score from the MLP:

$$s(\mathbf{x}, \mathbf{y}) = MLP(h_c) \tag{5}$$

3 Training

We employ a discriminative training strategy with a max-margin objective. Suppose we are given the following triples $(\mathbf{x}, \mathbf{y}^+, \mathbf{y}^-)$ from the oracle, where $\mathbf{x}, \mathbf{y}^+, \mathbf{y}^-$ are the feature vectors for $\mathbf{f}, \hat{e}^+, \hat{e}^-$ respectively. We have the ranking-based loss as objective:

$$L_\Theta(\mathbf{x}, \mathbf{y}^+, \mathbf{y}^-) = \max(0, 1 + s(\mathbf{x}, \mathbf{y}^-) - s(\mathbf{x}, \mathbf{y}^+)) \tag{6}$$

where $s(\mathbf{x}, \mathbf{y})$ is the matching score function defined in Eq. 5, Θ consists of parameters for both the convolutional sentence model and MLP. The model is trained by minimizing the above objective, to encourage the model to assign higher matching scores to positive examples and to assign lower scores to negative examples. We use stochastic gradient descent (SGD) to optimize the model parameters Θ. We train the CDCM model with a curriculum strategy to learn the context-dependent semantic similarity at the phrase level from *easy* (basic semantic similarities between the source and target phrase pair) to *difficult* (context-dependent semantic similarities for the same source phrase in varying contexts).

3.1 Curriculum Training

Curriculum learning, first proposed by Bengio et al. (2009) in machine learning, refers to a sequence of training strategies that start small, learn easier aspects of the task, and then gradually increase the difficulty level. It has been shown that the curriculum learning can benefit the non-convex training by giving rise to improved generalization and faster convergence. The key point is that the training examples are not randomly presented but organized in a meaningful order which illustrates gradually more concepts, and gradually more complex ones.

For each positive example $(\mathbf{f}, \hat{e}^+)$, we have three types of negative examples according to the difficulty level of distinguishing the positive example from them:

- *Easy*: target phrases randomly chosen from the phrase table;
- *Medium*: target phrases extracted from the aligned target sentence for other non-overlap source phrases in the source sentence;
- *Difficult*: target phrases extracted from other candidates for the same source phrase.

We want the CDCM model to learn the following semantic information from easy to difficult:

- the *basic semantic similarity* between the source sentence and target phrase from the *easy* negative examples;
- the *general semantic equivalent* between the source and target phrase pair from the *medium* negative examples;
- the *context-dependent semantic similarities* for the same source phrase in varying contexts from the *difficult* negative examples.

Alg. 1 shows the curriculum training algorithm for the CDCM model. We use different portions of the overall training instances for different curriculums (lines 2-11). For example, we only use the

Algorithm 1 Curriculum training algorithm. Here T denotes the training examples, W the initial word embeddings, η the learning rate in SGD, n the pre-defined number, and t the number of training examples.

```
1: procedure CURRICULUM-TRAINING(T, W)
2:     N_1 ← easy_negative(T)
3:     N_2 ← medium_negative(T)
4:     N_3 ← difficult_negative(T)
5:     T ← N_1
6:     CURRICULUM(T, n · t)                          ▷ CUR. easy
7:     T ← MIX([N_1, N_2])
8:     CURRICULUM(T, n · t)                          ▷ CUR. medium
9:     for step ← 1 . . . n do
10:        T ← MIX([N_1, N_2, N3], step)
11:        CURRICULUM(T, t)                          ▷ CUR. difficult
12: procedure CURRICULUM(T, K)
13:    iterate until reaching a local minima or K iterations
14:    calculate L_Θ for a random instance in T
15:    Θ = Θ − η · ∂L_Θ/∂Θ                          ▷ update parameters
16:    W = W − η · 0.01 · ∂L_Θ/∂W                   ▷ update embeddings
17: procedure MIX(N, s = 0)
18:    len ← length of N
19:    if len < 3 then
20:        T ← sampling with [0.5, 0.5] from N
21:    else
22:        T ← sampling with [1/(s+2), 1/(s+2), s/(s+2)] from N
```

training instances that consist of positive examples and *easy* negative examples in the *easy* curriculum (lines 5-6). For the latter curriculums, we gradually increase the difficulty level of the training instances (lines 7-12).

For each curriculum (lines 12-16), we compute the gradient of the loss objective L_Θ and learn Θ using the SGD algorithm. Note that we meanwhile update the word embeddings to better capture the semantic equivalence across languages during training. If the loss function L_Θ reaches a local minima or the iterations reach the predefined number, we terminate this curriculum.

4 Related Work

Our research builds on previous work in the field of context-dependent rule matching and bilingual phrase representations.

There is a line of work that employs local contexts over discrete representations of words or phrases. For example, He et al. (2008), Liu et al. (2008) and Marton and Resnik (2008) employed within-sentence contexts that consist of discrete words to guide rule matching. Wu et al. (2014) exploited discrete contextual features in the source sentence (e.g. words and part-of-speech tags) to learn better bilingual word embeddings for SMT. In this study, we take into account all the phrase pairs and directly compute phrasal similarities with convolutional representations of the local contexts, integrating the strengths associated with the convolutional neural networks (Collobert and Weston, 2008).

In recent years, there has also been growing interest in bilingual phrase representations that group phrases with a similar meaning across different languages. Based on that translation equivalents share the same semantic meaning, they can supervise each other to learn their semantic phrase embeddings in a continuous space (Gao et al., 2014; Zhang et al., 2014). However, these models focused on capturing semantic similarities between phrase pairs in the global contexts, and neglected the local contexts, thus ignored the useful discriminative information. Alternatively, we integrate the local contexts into our convolutional matching architecture to obtain context-dependent semantic similarities.

Meng et al. (2015) and Zhang (2015) have proposed independently to summary source sentences with convolutional neural networks. However, they both extend the neural network joint model (NNJM) of Devlin et al. (2014) to include the whole source sentence, while we focus on capturing context-dependent semantic similarities of translation pairs.

5 Experiments

5.1 Setup

We carry out our experiments on the NIST Chinese-English translation tasks. Our training data contains 1.5M sentence pairs coming from LDC dataset.[1] We train a 4-gram language model on the Xinhua portion of the GIGAWORD corpus using the SRI Language Toolkit (Stolcke, 2002) with modified Kneser-Ney Smoothing (Kneser and Ney, 1995). We use the 2002 NIST MT evaluation test data as the development data, and the 2004, 2005 NIST MT evaluation test data as the test data. We use minimum error rate training (Och, 2003) to optimize the feature weights. For evaluation, case-insensitive NIST BLEU (Papineni et al., 2002) is used to measure translation performance. We perform a significance test using the *sign-test* approach (Collins et al., 2005).

[1]The corpus includes LDC2002E18, LDC2003E07, LDC2003E14, Hansards portion of LDC2004T07, LDC2004T08 and LDC2005T06.

Models	MT04	MT05	All
Baseline	34.86	33.18	34.40
CICM	35.82^{α}	33.51^{α}	34.95^{α}
$CDCM_1$	35.87^{α}	33.58	35.01^{α}
$CDCM_2$	35.97^{α}	33.80^{α}	35.21^{α}
$CDCM_3$	$36.26^{\alpha\beta}$	$33.94^{\alpha\beta}$	$35.40^{\alpha\beta}$

Table 1: Evaluation of translation quality. $CDCM_k$ denotes the CDCM model trained in the kth curriculum in Alg. 1 (i.e., three levels of curriculum training), CICM denotes its context-independent counterpart, and "All" is the combined test sets. The superscripts α and β indicate statistically significant difference ($p < 0.05$) from Baseline and CICM, respectively.

For training the neural networks, we use 4 convolution layers for source sentences and 3 convolution layers for target phrases. For both of them, 4 pooling layers (pooling size is 2) are used, and all the feature maps are 100. We set the sliding window $k = 3$, and the learning rate $\eta = 0.02$. All the parameters are selected based on the development data. We train the word embeddings using a bilingual strategy similar to Yang et al. (2013), and set the dimension of the word embeddings be 50. To produce high-quality bilingual phrase pairs to train the CDCM model, we perform forced decoding on the bilingual training sentences and collect the used phrase pairs.

5.2 Evaluation of Translation Quality

We have two baseline systems:

- *Baseline*: The baseline system is an open-source system of the phrase-based model – Moses (Koehn et al., 2007) with a set of common features, including translation models, word and phrase penalties, a linear distortion model, a lexicalized reordering model, and a language model.
- CICM (context-*independent* convolutional matching) model: Following the previous works (Gao et al., 2014; Zhang et al., 2014; Cho et al., 2014), we calculate the matching degree of a phrase pair without considering any contextual information. Each unique phrase pair serves as a positive example and a randomly selected target phrase from the phrase table is the corresponding negative example. The matching score is also introduced into Baseline as an additional feature.

Table 1 summaries the results of CDCMs trained from different curriculums. No matter from which curriculum it is trained, the CDCM model significantly improves the translation quality on the overall test data (with gains of 1.0 BLEU points). The best improvement can be up to 1.4 BLEU points on MT04 with the fully trained CDCM. As expected, the translation performance is consistently increased with curriculum growing. This indicates that the CDCM model indeed captures the desirable semantic information by the curriculum learning from easy to difficult.

Comparing with its context-independent counterpart (CICM, Row 2), the CDCM model shows significant improvement on all the test data consistently. We contribute this to the incorporation of useful discriminative information embedded in the local context. In addition, the performance of CICM is comparable with that of $CDCM_1$. This is intuitive, because both of them try to capture the basic semantic similarity between the source and target phrase pair.

One of the hypotheses we tested in the course of this research was disproved. We thought it likely that the *difficult* curriculum ($CDCM_3$ that distinguishs the correct translation from other candidates for a given context) would contribute most to the improvement, since this circumstance is more consistent with the real decoding procedure. This turned out to be false, as shown in Table 1. One possible reason is that the "negative" examples (other candidates for the same source phrase) may share the same semantic meaning with the positive one, thus give a wrong guide in the supervised training. Constructing a reasonable set of negative examples that are more semantically different from the positive one is left for our future work.

6 Conclusion

In this paper, we propose a context-dependent convolutional matching model to capture semantic similarities between phrase pairs that are sensitive to contexts. Experimental results show that our approach significantly improves the translation performance and obtains improvement of 1.0 BLEU scores on the overall test data.

Integrating deep architecture into context-dependent translation selection is a promising way to improve machine translation. In the future, we will try to exploit contextual information at the target side (*e.g.*, partial translations).

Acknowledgments

This work is supported by China National 973 project 2014CB340301. Baotian Hu and Qinghai Chen are supported by National Natural Science Foundation of China 61173075 and 61473101. We thank Junhui Li, and the anonymous reviewers for their insightful comments.

References

Yoshua Bengio, Jérôme Louradour, Ronan Collobert, and Jason Weston. 2009. Curriculum learning. In *ICML 2009*.

Yoshua Bengio. 2009. Learning deep architectures for ai. *Foundations and Trends® in Machine Learning*, 2(1):1–127.

Kyunghyun Cho, Bart van Merrienboer, Caglar Gulcehre, Fethi Bougares, Holger Schwenk, and Yoshua Bengio. 2014. Learning phrase representations using rnn encoder-decoder for statistical machine translation. In *EMNLP 2014*.

M. Collins, P. Koehn, and I. Kučerová. 2005. Clause restructuring for statistical machine translation. In *ACL 2005*.

Ronan Collobert and Jason Weston. 2008. A unified architecture for natural language processing: Deep neural networks with multitask learning. In *ICML 2008*.

George E Dahl, Tara N Sainath, and Geoffrey E Hinton. 2013. Improving deep neural networks for lvcsr using rectified linear units and dropout. In *ICASSP 2013*.

Jacob Devlin, Rabih Zbib, Zhongqiang Huang, Thomas Lamar, Richard Schwartz, and John Makhoul. 2014. Fast and robust neural network joint models for statistical machine translation. In *ACL 2014*.

Jianfeng Gao, Xiaodong He, Wen-tau Yih, and Li Deng. 2014. Learning continuous phrase representations for translation modeling. In *ACL 2014*.

Zhongjun He, Qun Liu, and Shouxun Lin. 2008. Improving statistical machine translation using lexicalized rule selection. In *COLING 2008*.

Baotian Hu, Zhengdong Lu, Hang Li, and Qingcai Chen. 2014. Convolutional neural network architectures for matching natural language sentences. In *NIPS 2014*.

Reinhard Kneser and Hermann Ney. 1995. Improved backing-off for m-gram language modeling. In *ICASSP 1995*.

Philipp Koehn, Franz Josef Och, and Daniel Marcu. 2003. Statistical phrase-based translation. In *NAACL 2003*.

Philipp Koehn, Hieu Hoang, Alexandra Birch, Chris Callison-Burch, Marcello Federico, Nicola Bertoldi, Brooke Cowan, Wade Shen, Christine Moran, Richard Zens, Chris Dyer, Ondrej Bojar, Alexandra Constantin, and Evan Herbst. 2007. Moses: open source toolkit for statistical machine translation. In *ACL 2007*.

Qun Liu, Zhongjun He, Yang Liu, and Shouxun Lin. 2008. Maximum entropy based rule selection model for syntax-based statistical machine translation. In *EMNLP 2008*.

Yuval Marton and Philip Resnik. 2008. Soft syntactic constraints for hierarchical phrased-based translation. In *ACL 2008*.

Fandong Meng, Zhengdong Lu, Mingxuan Wang, Hang Li, Wenbin Jiang, and Qun Liu. 2015. Encoding source language with convolutional neural network for machine translation. In *ACL 2015*.

Franz Josef Och. 2003. Minimum error rate training in statistical machine translation. In *ACL 2003*.

Kishore Papineni, Salim Roukos, Todd Ward, and Wei-Jing Zhu. 2002. Bleu: a method for automatic evaluation of machine translation. In *ACL 2002*.

Andreas Stolcke. 2002. Srilm - an extensible language modeling toolkit. In *Proceedings of Seventh International Conference on Spoken Language Processing*, volume 3, pages 901–904. Citeseer.

Haiyang Wu, Daxiang Dong, Xiaoguang Hu, Dianhai Yu, Wei He, Hua Wu, Haifeng Wang, and Ting Liu. 2014. Improve statistical machine translation with context-sensitive bilingual semantic embedding model. In *EMNLP 2014*.

Nan Yang, Shujie Liu, Mu Li, Ming Zhou, and Nenghai Yu. 2013. Word Alignment Modeling with Context Dependent Deep Neural Network. In *ACL 2013*.

Jiajun Zhang, Shujie Liu, Mu Li, Ming Zhou, and Chengqing Zong. 2014. Bilingually-constrained phrase embeddings for machine translation. In *ACL 2014*.

Jiajun Zhang. 2015. Local translation prediction with global sentence representation. In *IJCAI 2015*.

Learning Word Reorderings for Hierarchical Phrase-based Statistical Machine Translation

Jingyi Zhang[1,2], Masao Utiyama[1], Eiichro Sumita[1], Hai Zhao[3,4]
[1]National Institute of Information and Communications Technology,
3-5Hikaridai, Keihanna Science City, Kyoto 619-0289, Japan
[2]Graduate School of Information Science, Nara Institute of Science and Technology,
Takayama, Ikoma, Nara 630-0192, Japan
[3]Department of Computer Science and Engineering,
Shanghai Jiao Tong University, Shanghai 200240, China
[4]Key Laboratory of Shanghai Education Commission for Intelligent Interaction
and Cognitive Engineering, Shanghai Jiao Tong University, Shanghai 200240, China
jingyizhang/mutiyama/eiichiro.sumita@nict.go.jp
zhaohai@cs.sjtu.edu.cn

Abstract

Statistical models for reordering source words have been used to enhance the hierarchical phrase-based statistical machine translation system. Existing word reordering models learn the reordering for any two source words in a sentence or only for two continuous words. This paper proposes a series of separate sub-models to learn reorderings for word pairs with different distances. Our experiments demonstrate that reordering sub-models for word pairs with distance less than a specific threshold are useful to improve translation quality. Compared with previous work, our method may more effectively and efficiently exploit helpful word reordering information.

1 Introduction

The hierarchical phrase-based model (Chiang, 2005) is capable of capturing rich translation knowledge with the synchronous context-free grammar. But selecting proper translation rules during decoding is a challenge as a huge number of hierarchical rules can be applied to one source sentence.

Chiang (2005) used a log-linear model to compute rule weights with features similar to Pharaoh (Koehn et al., 2003). However, to select appropriate rules, more effective criteria are required. A lot of work has been done for better rule selection. He et al. (2008) and Liu et al. (2008) used maximum entropy approaches to integrate rich contextual information for target side rule selection. Cui et al. (2010) proposed a joint model to select hierarchical rules for both source and target sides.

Hayashi et al. (2010) demonstrated the effectiveness of using word reordering information within hierarchical phrase-based SMT by integrating Tromble and Eisner (2009)'s word reordering model into decoder as a feature, which estimates the probability of any two source words in a sentence being reordered during translating. Feng et al. (2013) proposed a word reordering model to learn reorderings only for continuous words, which reduced computation cost a lot compared with Tromble and Eisner (2009)'s model and still achieved significant reordering improvement over the baseline system.

In this paper, we incorporate word reordering information into hierarchical phrase-based SMT by training a series of separate reordering sub-models for word pairs with different distances. We will demonstrate that the translation performance achieves consistent improvement as more sub-models for longer distance reorderings being integrated, but the improvement levels off quickly. That means sub-models for reordering distance longer than a given threshold do not improve translation quality significantly. Compared with previous models (Tromble and Eisner, 2009; Feng et al., 2013), our method makes full use of helpful word reordering information and also avoids unnecessary computation cost for long distance reorderings. Besides, our reordering model is learned by feed-forward neural network (FNN) for better performance and uses efficient caching strategy to further reduce time cost.

Phrase reordering models have also been integrated into hierarchical phrase-based SMT. Phrase reordering models were originally developed for phrase-based SMT (Koehn et al., 2005; Zens and Ney, 2006; Ni et al., 2009; Li et al., 2014) and

Proceedings of the 53rd Annual Meeting of the Association for Computational Linguistics and the 7th International Joint Conference on Natural Language Processing (Short Papers), pages 542–548,
Beijing, China, July 26-31, 2015.

could not be used in hierarchical phrase-based model directly. Nguyen and Vogel (2013) and Cao et al. (2014) proposed to integrate phrase-based reordering features into hierarchical phrase-based SMT. However, their work limited to learning the reordering of continuous phrases. For short phrases, in extreme cases, when phrase length is one, their model only learned reordering for continuous word pairs like Feng et al. (2013)'s work, while our model can be applied to word pairs with longer distances.

2 Our Approach

Let $e_1^m = e_1, \ldots, e_m$ be a target translation of $f_1^l = f_1, \ldots, f_l$ and A be word alignments between e_1^m and f_1^l, our model estimates the reordering probability of the source sentence as follows:

$$\begin{aligned} &\Pr\left(f_1^l, e_1^m, A\right) \\ &\approx \prod_{n=1}^{N} \prod_{i,j:1\le i<j\le l, j-i=n} \Pr\left(f_1^l, e_1^m, A, i, j\right) \end{aligned} \quad (1)$$

where $\Pr\left(f_1^l, e_1^m, A, i, j\right)$ is the reordering probability of the word pair $\langle f_i, f_j \rangle$ during translating; N is the maximum distance for source word reordering, which is empirically determined by supposing that estimating reorderings longer than N does not improve translation performance any more.

Previous word reordering models (Tromble and Eisner, 2009; Feng et al., 2013) consider the reordering of a source word pair to be reversed or not. When a source word is aligned to several uncontinuous target words, it can be hard to determine if a word pair is reversed or not. They solved this problem by only using one alignment from multiple alignments and ignoring the others. In contrast, our model handles all alignments as shown below.

Suppose that f_i is aligned to π_i ($\pi_i \ge 0$) target words. When $\pi_i > 0$, $\{a_{ik} | 1 \le k \le \pi_i\}$ stands for the positions of target words aligned to f_i. If $\pi_i = 0$ or $\pi_j = 0$, $\Pr\left(f_1^l, e_1^m, A, i, j\right) = 1$, otherwise,

$$\begin{aligned} &\Pr\left(f_1^l, e_1^m, A, i, j\right) \\ &= \prod_{u=1}^{\pi_i} \prod_{v=1}^{\pi_j} \Pr\left(o_{ijuv} | f_{i-3}, \ldots, f_{j+3}, e_{a_{iu}}, e_{a_{jv}}\right) \\ &where \\ &o_{ijuv} = \begin{cases} 0 & (a_{iu} \le a_{jv}) \\ 1 & (a_{iu} > a_{jv}) \end{cases} \end{aligned} \quad (2)$$

We train a series of sub-models,

$$M_1, M_2, \ldots, M_N$$

Algorithm 1 Extract training instances.

Require: A pair of parallel sentence f_1^l and e_1^m with word alignments.
Ensure: Training examples for $M_1, M_2, \ldots, M_N$.
for $i = 1$ to $l-1$ **do**
  for $j = i+1$ to l **do**
    if $j - i \le N$ **then**
      for $u = 1$ to π_i **do**
        for $v = 1$ to π_j **do**
          if $a_{iu} \le a_{jv}$ **then**
            $\left(f_{i-3}, \ldots, f_{j+3}, e_{a_{iu}}, e_{a_{jv}}, 0\right)$ is a negative instance for M_{j-i}
          else
            $\left(f_{i-3}, \ldots, f_{j+3}, e_{a_{iu}}, e_{a_{jv}}, 1\right)$ is a positive instance for M_{j-i}

to learn reorderings for word pairs with different distances. That means, for the word pair $\langle f_i, f_j \rangle$ with distance $j - i = n$, its reordering probability $\Pr\left(o_{ijuv} | f_{i-3}, \ldots, f_{j+3}, e_{a_{iu}}, e_{a_{jv}}\right)$ is estimated by M_n. Different sub-models are trained and integrated into the translation system separately.

Each sub-model M_n is implemented by an FNN, which has the same structure with the neural language model in (Vaswani et al., 2013). The input to M_n is a sequence of $n + 9$ words: $f_{i-3}, \ldots, f_{j+3}, e_{a_{iu}}, e_{a_{jv}}$. The input layer projects each word into a high dimensional vector using a matrix of input word embeddings. Two hidden layers can combine all input data[1]. The output layer has two neurons that give $\Pr\left(o_{ijuv} = 1 | f_{i-3}, \ldots, f_{j+3}, e_{a_{iu}}, e_{a_{jv}}\right)$ and $\Pr\left(o_{ijuv} = 0 | f_{i-3}, \ldots, f_{j+3}, e_{a_{iu}}, e_{a_{jv}}\right)$.

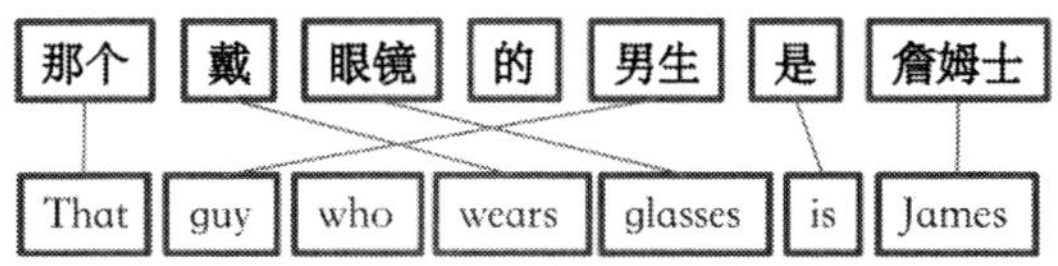

Figure 1: A Chinese-English sentence pair.

The backpropagation algorithm is used to train these reordering sub-models. The training instances for each sub-model are extracted from the word-aligned parallel corpus according to Algorithm 1. For example, the word pair "戴*(wears)* 男生*(guy)*" in Figure 1 will be extracted as a positive instance for M_3. The input of this instance is as follows: "<*s*> <*s*> 那个 戴 眼镜 的 男生 是

[1]If we choose the averaged perceptron algorithm to learn reordering task as used in (Hayashi et al., 2010), we need to artificially select n-gram features, which is not necessary for FNN.

詹姆士 </s> *wears guy*", where <s> and </s> represent the beginning and ending of a sentence. If a word never occurs or only occurs once in training corpus, we replace it with a special symbol <unk>.

3 Integration into the Decoder

In the hierarchical phrase-based model, a translation rule r is like:

$$X \rightarrow \langle \gamma, \alpha, \sim \rangle$$

where X is a nonterminal, γ and α are respectively source and target strings of terminals and nonterminals, and $\sim$ is the alignment between nonterminals and terminals in γ and α.

Each rule has several features and the feature weights are tuned by the minimum error rate training (MERT) algorithm (Och, 2003). To integrate our model into the hierarchical phrase-based translation system, a new feature $score_n(r)$ is added to each rule r for each M_n. The score of this feature is calculated during decoding. Note that these scores are correspondingly calculated for different sub-models M_n and the sub-model weights are tuned separately.

Suppose that r is applied to the input sentence f_1^l, where

- r covers the source span $[f_\varphi, f_\vartheta]$
- γ contains nonterminals $\{X_k | 1 \leq k \leq K\}$
- X_k covers the span $[f_{\varphi_k}, f_{\vartheta_k}]$

Then

$$\begin{aligned} & score_n(r) \\ = & \sum_{\langle i,j\rangle \in S - \bigcup_{k=1}^{K} S_k \wedge j-i=n} \log\left(\Pr\left(f_1^l, e_1^m, A, i, j\right)\right) \\ & where \\ & S : \{\langle i,j\rangle \,|\, \varphi \leq i < j \leq \vartheta\} \\ & S_k : \{\langle i,j\rangle \,|\, \varphi_k \leq i < j \leq \vartheta_k\} \end{aligned}$$

For example, if a rule "X1 X2 男生→ X1 *guy* X2" is applied to the input sentence in Figure 1, then

$$\begin{aligned} & [f_\varphi, f_\vartheta] = [1,5]; [f_{\varphi_1}, f_{\vartheta_1}] = [1,1]; [f_{\varphi_2}, f_{\vartheta_2}] = [2,4] \\ & S - \bigcup_{k=1}^{K} S_k = \left\{ \begin{array}{l} \langle 1,2\rangle, \langle 1,3\rangle, \langle 1,4\rangle, \langle 1,5\rangle, \\ \langle 2,5\rangle, \langle 3,5\rangle, \langle 4,5\rangle \end{array} \right\} \end{aligned}$$

One concern in using target features is the computational efficiency, because reordering probabilities have to be calculated during decoding. So we cache probabilities to reduce the expensive neural network computation in experiments.

4 Experiments

We evaluated the proposed approach for Chinese-to-English (CE) and Japanese-to-English (JE) translation tasks. The official datasets for the patent machine translation task at NTCIR-9 (Goto et al., 2011) were used. The detailed statistics for training, development and test sets are given in Table 1.

			SOURCE	TARGET
CE	TRAINING	#Sents	954K	
		#Words	37.2M	40.4M
		#Vocab	288K	504K
	DEV	#Sents	2K	
	TEST	#Sents	2K	
JE	TRAINING	#Sents	3.14M	
		#Words	118M	104M
		#Vocab	150K	273K
	DEV	#Sents	2K	
	TEST	#Sents	2K	

Table 1: Data sets.

In NTCIR-9, the development and test sets were both provided for CE task while only the test set was provided for the JE task. Therefore, we used the sentences from the NTCIR-8 JE test set as the development set for JE task. The word segmentation was done by BaseSeg (Zhao et al., 2006; Zhao and Kit, 2008; Zhao et al., 2010; Zhao and Kit, 2011; Zhao et al., 2013) for Chinese and Mecab[2] for Japanese.

To learn neural reordering models, the training and development sets were put together to obtain symmetric word alignments using GIZA++ (Och and Ney, 2003) and the *grow-diag-final-and* heuristic (Koehn et al., 2003). The reordering instances extracted from the aligned training and development sets were used as the training and validation data respectively for learning neural reordering models. Neural reordering models were trained by the toolkit NPLM (Vaswani et al., 2013). For CE task, training instances extracted from all the 1M sentence pairs were used to train neural reordering models. For JE task, training instances were from 1M sentence pairs that were randomly selected from all the 3.14M sentence pairs.

We also implemented Hayashi et al. (2010)'s model for comparison. The training instances for their model were extracted from the same sentence pairs as ours.

[2]http://sourceforge.net/projects/mecab/files/

	Base	Hayashi model	M_1^1	M_1^2	M_1^3	M_1^4
CE	32.95	34.25	34.78	35.75	35.97	36.05
JE	30.13	30.70	31.35	32.07	32.40	32.60

(a) BLEU scores

CE	*Base*	Hayashi model	M_1^1	M_1^2	M_1^3
Hayashi model	$\gg$				
M_1^1	$\gg$	$\gg$			
M_1^2	$\gg$	$\gg$	$\gg$		
M_1^3	$\gg$	$\gg$	$\gg$	$>$	
M_1^4	$\gg$	$\gg$	$\gg$	$>$	$-$

JE	*Base*	Hayashi model	M_1^1	M_1^2	M_1^3
Hayashi model	$\gg$				
M_1^1	$\gg$	$\gg$			
M_1^2	$\gg$	$\gg$	$\gg$		
M_1^3	$\gg$	$\gg$	$\gg$	$\gg$	
M_1^4	$\gg$	$\gg$	$\gg$	$\gg$	$-$

(b) Significance test results using bootstrap sampling (Koehn, 2004) w.r.t. BLEU scores. The symbol $\gg$ represents a significant difference at the $p < 0.01$ level; $>$ represents a significant difference at the $p < 0.05$ level; $-$ means not significantly different at $p = 0.05$.

Table 2: Translation results.

For each translation task, the recent version of the Moses hierarchical phrase-based decoder (Koehn et al., 2007) with the training scripts was used as the baseline system *Base*. We used the default parameters for Moses. A 5-gram language model was trained on the target side of the training corpus by IRST LM Toolkit[3] with the improved Kneser-Ney smoothing.

We integrated our reordering models into *Base*. Table 2 gives detailed translation results. "Hayashi model" represents the method of (Hayashi et al., 2010). "M_1^j $(j = 1, 2, 3, 4)$" means that *Base* was augmented with the reordering scores calcuated from a series of sub-models M_1 to M_j.

As shown in Table 2, integrating only M_1, which predicts reordering for two continuous source words, has already given BLEU improvement 1.8% and 1.2% over baseline on CE and JE, respectively. As more sub-models for longer distance reordering being integrated, the translation performance improved consistently, though the improvement leveled off quickly. For CE and JE tasks, M_n with $n \geq 3$ and $n \geq 4$, respectively, cannot give further performance improvement at any significant level.

Why did the improvement level off quickly? In other words, why do long distance reordering models have a much less leverage over translation performance than short ones?

[3]http://hlt.fbk.eu/en/irstlm

Sub-model	M_1	M_2	M_3	M_4
CE	93.9	92.8	92.2	91.2
JE	92.9	91.3	90.1	89.3

(a) Our model

Reordering Distance	1	2	3	4
CE	90.1	88.3	87.0	85.6
JE	85.3	81.9	80.6	78.8

(b) Hayashi model

Table 3: Classification accuracy (%).

First, the prediction accuracy decreases as the reordering distance increasing. Table 3a gives classification accuracies on the validation data for each sub-model. The reason for accuracy decreasing is that the input size of sub-model grows as reordering distance increasing. Namely, long distance reordering needs to consider more complicated context.

Second, we attribute the influence decrease of the longer reordering models to the redundancy of the predictions among different reordering models. For example, in Figure 1, when word pairs "男生(*guy*) 是(*is*)" and "是(*is*) 詹姆士(*James*)" are both predicted to be not reversed, the reordering for "男生(*guy*) 詹姆士(*James*)" can be logically determined to be not reversed without further reordering model prediction. That means, sometimes, a long distance word reordering can be determined by a series of shorter word reordering pairs.

But still, some predictions for longer reordering are useful. For example, the reordering of "戴(*wears*) 男生(*guy*)" cannot be determined when "戴(*wears*) 眼镜(*glasses*)" is predicted to be not reversed and "眼镜(*glasses*) 男生(*guy*)" is reversed. This is the reason why translation performance improves as more sub-models being integrated.

As shown in Table 2, with 4 sub-models being integrated, our model improved baseline system significantly and also outperformed Hayashi model clearly. It is easy to understand, since our model was trained by feed-forward neural network on a high dimensional space and incorporated rich context information, while Hayashi model used the averaged perceptron algorithm and simple features. Table 3b shows the prediction accuracies of Hayashi model. Note that Hayashi model predicts reorderings for all word pairs, but only prediction accuracies for word pairs with distance 4 or less are shown. Compared with Table 3a, the prediction accuracy of our model is much higher than Hayashi model. Actually, FNN is not suitable for Hayashi model since the computation cost for Hayashi model is quite expensive. Using FNN to reorder all word pairs could cost nearly one minute to translate one sentence according to our experiments, while integrating 4 sub-models only cost 10 seconds[4].

Compared with Hayashi model, our model not only speeds up decoding time but also reduces the training time. Training for Hayashi model is much slower since word pairs with all different distances are used as training data. By using separate sub-models, we can train each sub-model one by one and stop when translation performance cannot be improved any more. However, despite of efficiency, one unified model will theoretically have better performance than separate sub-models since separate sub-models do not share training instances and the unified model will suffer less from data sparsity. So, we did some extra experiments and trained a neural network which had the same structure as M_4 to learn reorderings for all word pairs with distance 4 or less, instead of using 4 separate neural networks. A specific word *null* was used since word pairs with distance 1,2,3 do not have enough inputs for M_4. The significance test results showed that translation performance had no significant difference between one unified model and multiple sub-models. This is because the training corpus for our model is quite large, so separate training sets are sufficient for each sub-model to learn the reorderings well. Besides, using neural networks to learn these sub-models on a continuous space can relieve the data sparsity problem to some extent.

Note that if we only integrate M_4 into Base, the translation quality of Base can be improved in our preliminary experiments. But M_4 cannot predict reorderings for word pairs with distance less than 4. So M_1^3 will be still needed for predicting reorderings of word pairs with distance 1,2,3. But after M_1^3 being integrated, M_4 will not be needed due to the redundancy of the predictions among different reordering models.

[4]Note that cache was used in all our experiments to reduce the expensive neural network computation cost and turned out to be very useful. Without caching, integrating 4 sub-models could cost nearly 7 minutes to translate a sentence.

5 Conclusion

In this paper, we propose to enhance hierarchical phrase-based SMT by training a series of separate sub-models to learn reorderings for word pairs with distances less than a specific threshold, based on the experimental fact that longer distance reordering models are not quite helpful for translation quality. Compared with Hayashi et al. (2010)'s work, our model is much more efficient and keeps all helpful word reordering information. Besides, our reordering model is learned by feed-forward neural network and incorporates rich context information for better performance. On both Chinese-to-English and Japanese-to-English translation tasks, the proposed model outperforms the previous model significantly.

Acknowledgments

Masao Utiyama and Hai Zhao are corresponding authors. This work was done when the first author was a master's student at Shanghai Jiao Tong University. Hai Zhao was supported by the National Natural Science Foundation of China under Grants 60903119, 61170114 and 61272248, the National Basic Research Program of China under Grant 2013CB329401, the Science and Technology Commission of Shanghai Municipality under Grant 13511500200, the European Union Seventh Framework Program under Grant 247619, the Cai Yuanpei Program (CSC fund 201304490199, 201304490171), and the art and science interdiscipline funds of Shanghai Jiao Tong University under Grant 14X190040031(14JCRZ04).

References

Hailong Cao, Dongdong Zhang, Mu Li, Ming Zhou, and Tiejun Zhao. 2014. A lexicalized reordering model for hierarchical phrase-based translation. In *Proceedings of COLING 2014, the 25th International Conference on Computational Linguistics: Technical Papers*, pages 1144–1153.

David Chiang. 2005. A hierarchical phrase-based model for statistical machine translation. In *Proceedings of the 43rd Annual Meeting of the Association for Computational Linguistics (ACL'05)*, pages 263–270.

Lei Cui, Dongdong Zhang, Mu Li, Ming Zhou, and Tiejun Zhao. 2010. A joint rule selection model for hierarchical phrase-based translation. In *Proceedings of the ACL 2010 Conference Short Papers*, pages 6–11.

Minwei Feng, Jan-Thorsten Peter, and Hermann Ney. 2013. Advancements in reordering models for statistical machine translation. In *Proceedings of the 51st Annual Meeting of the Association for Computational Linguistics (Volume 1: Long Papers)*, pages 322–332.

Isao Goto, Bin Lu, Ka Po Chow, Eiichiro Sumita, and Benjamin K Tsou. 2011. Overview of the patent machine translation task at the NTCIR-9 workshop. In *Proceedings of The 9th NII Test Collection for IR Systems Workshop Meeting*, pages 559–578.

Katsuhiko Hayashi, Hajime Tsukada, Katsuhito Sudoh, Kevin Duh, and Seiichi Yamamoto. 2010. Hierarchical phrase-based machine translation with word-based reordering model. In *Proceedings of the 23rd International Conference on Computational Linguistics (Coling 2010)*, pages 439–446.

Zhongjun He, Qun Liu, and Shouxun Lin. 2008. Improving statistical machine translation using lexicalized rule selection. In *Proceedings of the 22nd International Conference on Computational Linguistics (Coling 2008)*, pages 321–328.

Philipp Koehn, Franz Josef Och, and Daniel Marcu. 2003. Statistical phrase-based translation. In *Proceedings of the 2003 Conference of the North American Chapter of the Association for Computational Linguistics on Human Language Technology-Volume 1*, pages 48–54.

Philipp Koehn, Amittai Axelrod, Alexandra Birch, Chris Callison-Burch, Miles Osborne, David Talbot, and Michael White. 2005. Edinburgh system description for the 2005 IWSLT speech translation evaluation. In *The International Workshop on Spoken Language Translation*, pages 68–75.

Philipp Koehn, Hieu Hoang, Alexandra Birch, Chris Callison-Burch, Marcello Federico, Nicola Bertoldi, Brooke Cowan, Wade Shen, Christine Moran, Richard Zens, Chris Dyer, Ondrej Bojar, Alexandra Constantin, and Evan Herbst. 2007. Moses: Open source toolkit for statistical machine translation. In *Proceedings of the 45th Annual Meeting of the Association for Computational Linguistics Companion Volume Proceedings of the Demo and Poster Sessions*, pages 177–180.

Philipp Koehn. 2004. Statistical significance tests for machine translation evaluation. In *Proceedings of EMNLP 2004*, pages 388–395.

Peng Li, Yang Liu, Maosong Sun, Tatsuya Izuha, and Dakun Zhang. 2014. A neural reordering model for phrase-based translation. In *Proceedings of COLING 2014, the 25th International Conference on Computational Linguistics: Technical Papers*, pages 1897–1907.

Qun Liu, Zhongjun He, Yang Liu, and Shouxun Lin. 2008. Maximum entropy based rule selection model for syntax-based statistical machine translation. In *Proceedings of the 2008 Conference on Empirical Methods in Natural Language Processing*, pages 89–97.

ThuyLinh Nguyen and Stephan Vogel. 2013. Integrating phrase-based reordering features into a chart-based decoder for machine translation. In *Proceedings of the 51st Annual Meeting of the Association for Computational Linguistics (Volume 1: Long Papers)*, pages 1587–1596.

Yizhao Ni, Craig Saunders, Sandor Szedmak, and Mahesan Niranjan. 2009. Handling phrase reorderings for machine translation. In *Proceedings of the ACL-IJCNLP 2009 Conference Short Papers*, pages 241–244.

Franz Josef Och and Hermann Ney. 2003. A systematic comparison of various statistical alignment models. *Computational linguistics*, 29(1):19–51.

Franz Josef Och. 2003. Minimum error rate training in statistical machine translation. In *Proceedings of the 41st Annual Meeting of the Association for Computational Linguistics*, pages 160–167.

Roy Tromble and Jason Eisner. 2009. Learning linear ordering problems for better translation. In *Proceedings of the 2009 Conference on Empirical Methods in Natural Language Processing*, pages 1007–1016.

Ashish Vaswani, Yinggong Zhao, Victoria Fossum, and David Chiang. 2013. Decoding with large-scale neural language models improves translation. In *Proceedings of the 2013 Conference on Empirical Methods in Natural Language Processing*, pages 1387–1392.

Richard Zens and Hermann Ney. 2006. Discriminative reordering models for statistical machine translation. In *Proceedings on the Workshop on Statistical Machine Translation*, pages 55–63.

Hai Zhao and Chunyu Kit. 2008. Exploiting unlabeled text with different unsupervised segmentation criteria for chinese word segmentation. *Research in Computing Science*, 33:93–104.

Hai Zhao and Chunyu Kit. 2011. Integrating unsupervised and supervised word segmentation: The role of goodness measures. *Information Sciences*, 181(1):163–183.

Hai Zhao, Chang-Ning Huang, and Mu Li. 2006. An improved chinese word segmentation system with conditional random field. In *Proceedings of the Fifth SIGHAN Workshop on Chinese Language Processing*, pages 162–165.

Hai Zhao, Chang-Ning Huang, Mu Li, and Bao-Liang Lu. 2010. A unified character-based tagging framework for chinese word segmentation. *ACM Transactions on Asian Language Information Processing (TALIP)*, 9(2):5.

Hai Zhao, Masao Utiyama, Eiichiro Sumita, and Bao-Liang Lu. 2013. An empirical study on word segmentation for chinese machine translation. In *Computational Linguistics and Intelligent Text Processing*, pages 248–263.

UNRAVEL—A Decipherment Toolkit

Malte Nuhn and **Julian Schamper** and **Hermann Ney**
Human Language Technology and Pattern Recognition
Computer Science Department, RWTH Aachen University, Aachen, Germany
<surname>@cs.rwth-aachen.de

Abstract

In this paper we present the UNRAVEL toolkit: It implements many of the recently published works on decipherment, including decipherment for deterministic ciphers like e.g. the ZODIAC-408 cipher and Part two of the BEALE ciphers, as well as decipherment of probabilistic ciphers and unsupervised training for machine translation. It also includes data and example configuration files so that the previously published experiments are easy to reproduce.

1 Introduction

The idea of applying decipherment techniques to the problem of machine translation has driven research on decipherment in the recent time. Even though the theoretical knowledge has been published in the form of papers there has not been any release of software until now. This made it very difficult to follow upon the recent research and to contribute new ideas. With this publication we want to share our implementation of two important decipherment algorithms: Beam search for deterministic substitution ciphers and beamed EM training for probabilistic ciphers. It is clear that the field of decipherment is still under heavy research and that the true value of this release does not lie in the current implementations themselves, but rather in the opportunity for other researchers to contribute their ideas to the field.

2 Overview

Enciphering a plaintext into a ciphertext can be done using a myriad of encipherment methods. Each of these methods needs its own customized tools and tweaks in order to be deciphered automatically. The goal of UNRAVEL is not to provide a solver for every single encipherment method, but rather to provide reusable tools that can be applied to unsupervised learning for machine translation.

UNRAVEL contains two tools: DET-UNRAVEL for decipherment of deterministic ciphers, and EM-UNRAVEL for EM decipherment for probabilistic substitution ciphers and simple machine translation tasks. A comparison of both tools is given in Table 1.

The code base is implemented in C++11 and uses many publicly available libraries: The GOOGLE-GLOG logging library is used for all logging purposes, the GOOGLE-GFLAGS library is used for providing command line flags, and the GOOGLETEST library is used for unit testing and consistency checks throughout the code base.

Classes for compressed I/O, access to OpenFST (Allauzen et al., 2007), access to KENLM(Heafield, 2011), representing mappings, n-gram counts, vocabularies, lexicons, etc. are shared across the code base.

For building we use the GNU build system. UNRAVEL can be compiled using GCC, ICC, and CLANG on various Linux distributions and on MacOS X. Scripts to download and compile necessary libraries are also included: This makes it easy to install UNRAVEL and its dependencies in different computing environments.

Also, configuration- and data files (if possible from a license point of view) for various experiments (see Section 4.2 and Section 5.2) are distributed. Amongst others this includes setups for the ZODIAC-408 and Part two of the BEALE ciphers (deterministic ciphers), as well as the OPUS corpus and the VERBMOBIL corpus (probabilistic cipher/machine translation).

3 Related Work

We list the most important publications that lead to the implementation of UNRAVEL: Regarding DET-

Proceedings of the 53rd Annual Meeting of the Association for Computational Linguistics and the 7th International Joint Conference on Natural Language Processing (Short Papers), pages 549–553, Beijing, China, July 26-31, 2015.

UNRAVEL, the following literature is relevant: Hart (1994) presents a tree search algorithm for simple substitution ciphers with known word segmentations. The idea of performing a tree search and looking for mappings fulfilling consistency constraints was later adopted to n-gram based decipherment in an A* search approach presented by Corlett and Penn (2010). DET-UNRAVEL implements the beam search approach presented by Nuhn et al. (2013) together with the refinements presented in (Nuhn et al., 2014). The Bayesian approach presented by Ravi and Knight (2011a) to break the ZODIAC-408 cipher is not implemented, but configuration and data to solve the ZODIAC-408 cipher with DET-UNRAVEL is included. Also it is worth noting that Hauer et al. (2014) provided further work towards homophonic decipherment that is not included in UNRAVEL.

The EM training for the decipherment of probabilistic substitution ciphers, as first described by Lee (2002) is implemented in EM-UNRAVEL together with various improvements and extensions: The beam- and preselection search approximations presented by Nuhn and Ney (2014), the context vector based candidate induction presented by Nuhn et al. (2012), as well as training of the simplified machine translation model presented by Ravi and Knight (2011b).

4 Deterministic Ciphers: DET-UNRAVEL

Given an input sequence f_1^N with tokens f_n from a vocabulary V_f and a language model of a target language $p(e_1^N)$ with the target tokens from a target vocabulary V_e, the task is to find a mapping function $\phi : V_f \rightarrow V_e$ so that the language model probability of the decipherment $p(\phi(f_1)\phi(f_2)\ldots\phi(f_N))$ is maximized.

DET-UNRAVEL solves this optimization problem using the beam search approach presented by Nuhn et al. (2013): The main idea is to structure all partial ϕs into a search tree: If a cipher contains $|V_f|$ unique symbols, then the search tree is of height $|V_f|$. At each level a decision about the n-th symbol is made. The leaves of the tree form full hypotheses. Instead of traversing the whole search tree, beam search traverses the tree top to bottom and only keeps the most promising candidates at each level. Table 2 shows the important parameters of the algorithm.

4.1 Implementation Details

During search, our implementation keeps track of all partial hypotheses in two arrays H_s and H_t. We use two different data structures for the hypotheses in H_s and the hypotheses in H_t: H_s contains the full information of the current partial mapping ϕ. The candidates in the array H_t are generated by augmenting hypotheses from the array H_s by just one additional mapping decision $f \rightarrow e$ and thus we use a different data structure for these hypotheses: They contain the current mapping decision $f \rightarrow e$ and a pointer to the parent node in H_s. This saves memory in comparison to storing the complete mapping at every point in time and is faster than storing the mapping as a tree, which would have to be traversed for every score estimation.

The fact that only one additional decision is made during the expansion process is also used when calculating the scores for the new hypothesis: Only the additional terms of the final score for the current partial hypothesis ϕ are added to the predecessor score (i.e. the scheme is $score_{new} = score_{old} + \delta$, where $score_{old}$ is independent of the current decision $f \rightarrow e$).

The now scored hypotheses in H_t (our implementation also includes the improved rest cost es-

Aspect	Deterministic Ciphers: DET-UNRAVEL	Probabilistic Ciphers: EM-UNRAVEL
Search Space	Mappings ϕ	Substitution tables $\{p(f\|e)\}$
Training	Beam search over all ϕ. The order in which the decisions for $\phi(f)$ for each f are made is based on the extension order.	EM-training: In the E-step use beam search to obtain the most probable decipherments e_1^I for a given ciphertext sequence f_1^J. Update $\{p(f\|e)\}$ in M-step.
Decoding	Apply ϕ to cipher text.	Viterbi decoding using final $\{p(f\|e)\}$.
Experiments	ZODIAC-408, pt. two of BEALE ciphers	OPUS, VERBMOBIL

Table 1: Comparison of DET-UNRAVEL and EM-UNRAVEL.

timation as described in (Nuhn et al., 2014)) are pruned using different pruning strategies: Threshold pruning—given the best hypothesis, add a threshold score and prune the hypotheses with scores lower than best hypothesis plus this threshold score—and histogram pruning—which only keeps the best B_{histo} hypothesis at every level of the search tree. Further, the surviving hypotheses are checked whether they fulfill certain constraints $C(\phi)$ like e.g. enforcing 1-to-1 mappings during search.

Those hypotheses in H_t that survived the pruning step and the constraints check are converted to full hypotheses so that they can be stored in H_s. Then, the search continues with the next cardinality.

The order in which decisions about the symbols $f \in V_f$ are made during search (called *extension order*) can be computed using different strategies: We implement a simple *frequency sorting* heuristic, as well as a more advanced strategy that uses *beam search* to find an improved enumeration of $f \in V_f$, as presented in (Nuhn et al., 2014).

Our implementation expands the partial hypotheses in H_s in parallel: The implementation has been tested with up to 128 threads (on a 128 core machine) with parallelization overhead of less than 20%.

4.2 Experiments

The configurations for decoding the ZODIAC-408 cipher as well as Part two of the BEALE ciphers are almost identical: For both setups we use an 8-gram character language model trained on a subset of the English Gigaword corpus (Parker et al., 2011). We obtain n-gram counts (order 2 to 8) from the input ciphers and pass these to DET-UNRAVEL. In both cases we use the improved heuristic together with the improved extension order as presented in (Nuhn et al., 2014).

For the ZODIAC-408, using a beam size $B_{hist} = 26$ yields 52 out of 54 correct mappings. For the Part two of the BEALE ciphers a much larger beam size of $B_{hist} = 10$M yields 157 correct mappings out of 185, resulting in an error rate on the string of 762 symbols is 5.4 %.

5 Probabilistic Ciphers: EM-UNRAVEL

For probabilistic ciphers, the goal is to find a probabilistic substitution table $\{p(f|e)\}$ with normalization constraint $\forall_e \sum_f p(f|e) = 1$. Learning this table is done iteratively using the EM algorithm (Dempster et al., 1977).

Each iteration consists of two steps: Hypothesis generation (E-Step) and retraining the table $\{p(f|e)\}$ using the posterior probability $p_j(e|f_1^J)$ that *any* translation e_1^I of f_1^J has the word e aligned to the source word f_j (M-Step).

From a higher level view, EM-UNRAVEL can be seen as a specialized word based MT decoder that can efficiently generate and organize *all* possible translations in the E-step, and efficiently retrain the model $\{p(f|e)\}$ on *all* these hypotheses in the M-step.

5.1 Implementation Details

In contrast to DET-UNRAVEL, EM-UNRAVEL processes the input corpus sentence by sentence. For each sentence, we build hypotheses e_1^I from left to right, one word at a time:

First, the empty hypothesis is added to a set of currently active partial hypotheses. Then, for each partial hypothesis, a new source word is chosen such that local reordering constraints are fulfilled. For this, a coverage vector (which encodes the words that have already been translated) has to be updated for each hypothesis. Once the current source word to be translated next has been chosen, hypotheses for all possible translations of this source word are generated and scored. After having processed the entire set of partial hypotheses, the set of newly generated hypotheses is

Name	Description
Pruning	
B_{hist}	Histogram pruning. Only the best B_{hist} hypotheses are kept.
B_{thres}	Threshold pruning. Hypotheses with scores S worse than $S_{best} + B_{thres}$, where S_{best} is the score of the best hyptohesis, are pruned.
Constraints	
$C(\phi)$	Substitution constraint. Hypotheses not fulfilling the constraint $C(\phi)$ are discarded from search.
Extension Order	
V_{ext}	Extension order. Enumeration of the vocabulary V_f in which the search tree over all ϕ is visited.
B_{hist}^{ext}	Histogram Pruning for extension order search.
W_n^{ext}	Weight for $n-$gram language model lookahead score.

Table 2: Important parameters of DET-UNRAVEL.

pruned: Here, the partial hypotheses are organized and pruned with respect to their cardinality. For each cardinality, we keep the B_{histo} best scoring hypotheses.

Similarly to DET-UNRAVEL, the previously described expansion and pruning step is implemented using two arrays H_s and H_t. However, in EM-UNRAVEL the partial hypotheses in H_s and H_t use the same data structures since—in contrast to DET-UNRAVEL—recombination of hypotheses is possible.

In the case of large vocabularies it is not feasible to keep track of *all* possible substitutions for a given source word. This step can also be approximated using the preselection technique by Nuhn and Ney (2014): Instead of adding hypotheses for all possible target words, only a small subset of possible successor hypotheses is generated: These are based on the current source word that is to be translated, as well as the current language model state.

Once the search is completed we compute posteriors on the resulting word graph and accumulate those across all sentences in the corpus. Having finished one pass over the corpus, the accumulated posteriors are used to re-estimate $\{p(e|f)\}$ and the next iteration of the EM algorithm begins. Also, with every new parameter table $\{p(e|f)\}$, the Viterbi decoding of the source corpus is computed.

While full EM training is feasible and gives good results for the OPUS corpus, Nuhn et al. (2012) suggest to include a context vector step in between EM iterations for large vocabulary tasks.

Using the Viterbi decoding of the source sequence from the last E-step and the corpus used to train the LM, we create normalized context vectors for each word e and f. The idea is that vectors for words e and f that are translations of each other are similar. For each word $f \in V_f$, a set of candidates $e \in V_e$ can be computed. These candidates are used to initialize a new lexicon, which is further refined using standard EM iterations afterwards.

Both, EM training and the context vector step are implemented in a parallel fashion (running in a single process). Parallelization is done on a sentence level: We successfully used our implementation with up to 128 cores.

Name	Description
Pruning	
B_{hist}	Histogram pruning. Only the best B_{hist} hypotheses are kept.
Preselection Search	
B_{cand}^{lex}	Lexical candidates. Try only the best B_{cand}^{lex} substitutions e for each word f based on $p(f|e)$
B_{cand}^{LM}	LM candidates. Try only the best B_{hist}^{LM} successor words e with respect to the previous hypothesis' LM state.
Translation Model	
W_{jump}	Jump width. Maximum jump size allowed in local reordering.
C_{jump}	Jump cost. Cost for non-monotonic transitions.
C_{ins}	Insertion cost. Cost for insertions of words.
M_{ins}	Maximum number of insertions per sentence.
C_{del}	Deletion cost. Cost for deletions of words.
M_{del}	Maximum number of of deletions per sentence.
Other	
λ_{lex}	Lexical smoothing parameter.
N_{ctx}	Number of candidate translations allowed in lexicon generation in context vector step.

Table 3: Important parameters of EM-UNRAVEL.

5.2 Experiments

We briefly mention experiments on two corpora: The OPUS corpus and the VERBMOBIL corpus.

The OPUS corpus is a subtitle corpus of roughly 100k running words. Here the vocabulary size of the source language (Spanish) is 562 and the target language (English) contains 411 unique words. Using a 3-gram language model UNRAVEL achieves 19.5 % BLEU on this task.

The VERBMOBIL corpus contains roughly 600k running words. The target language vocabulary size is 3,723 (English) and the source language vocabulary size is 5,964 (German). Using a 3-gram language model and the context vector approach, UNRAVEL achieves 15.5 % BLEU.

6 Download and License

UNRAVEL can be downloaded at `www.hltpr.rwth-aachen.de/unravel`. UNRAVEL is distributed under a custom open source license. This includes free usage for noncommercial purposes as long as any changes made to the original software are published under the terms of the same license. The exact formulation is available at the download page for UNRAVEL.

We have chosen to keep this paper independent of actual implementation details such as method- and parameter names. Please consult the README files and comments in UNRAVEL's source code for implementation details.

7 Conclusion

UNRAVEL is a flexible and efficient decipherment toolkit that is freely available to the scientific community. It implements algorithms for solving deterministic and probabilistic substitution ciphers.

We hope that this release sparks more interesting research on decipherment and its applications to machine translation.

References

[Allauzen et al.2007] Cyril Allauzen, Michael Riley, Johan Schalkwyk, Wojciech Skut, and Mehryar Mohri. 2007. Openfst: A general and efficient weighted finite-state transducer library. In Jan Holub and Jan Zdárek, editors, *CIAA*, volume 4783 of *Lecture Notes in Computer Science*, pages 11–23. Springer.

[Corlett and Penn2010] Eric Corlett and Gerald Penn. 2010. An exact A* method for deciphering letter-substitution ciphers. In *Proceedings of the 48th Annual Meeting of the Association for Computational Linguistics (ACL)*, pages 1040–1047, Uppsala, Sweden, July. The Association for Computer Linguistics.

[Dempster et al.1977] Arthur P. Dempster, Nan M. Laird, and Donald B. Rubin. 1977. Maximum likelihood from incomplete data via the EM algorithm. *Journal of the Royal Statistical Society, B*, 39.

[Hart1994] George W Hart. 1994. To decode short cryptograms. *Communications of the ACM*, 37(9):102–108.

[Hauer et al.2014] Bradley Hauer, Ryan Hayward, and Grzegorz Kondrak. 2014. Solving substitution ciphers with combined language models. In *Proceedings of COLING 2014, the 25th International Conference on Computational Linguistics: Technical Papers*, pages 2314–2325. Dublin City University and Association for Computational Linguistics.

[Heafield2011] Kenneth Heafield. 2011. KenLM: Faster and Smaller Language Model Queries. In *Proceedings of the Sixth Workshop on Statistical Machine Translation*, pages 187–197, Edinburgh, Scotland, July. Association for Computational Linguistics.

[Lee2002] Dar-Shyang Lee. 2002. Substitution deciphering based on hmms with applications to compressed document processing. *Pattern Analysis and Machine Intelligence, IEEE Transactions on*, 24(12):1661–1666.

[Nuhn and Ney2014] Malte Nuhn and Hermann Ney. 2014. Em decipherment for large vocabularies. In *Annual Meeting of the Assoc. for Computational Linguistics*, pages 759–764, Baltimore, MD, USA, June.

[Nuhn et al.2012] Malte Nuhn, Arne Mauser, and Hermann Ney. 2012. Deciphering foreign language by combining language models and context vectors. In *Proceedings of the 50th Annual Meeting of the Association for Computational Linguistics (ACL)*, pages 156–164, Jeju, Republic of Korea, July. Association for Computational Linguistics.

[Nuhn et al.2013] Malte Nuhn, Julian Schamper, and Hermann Ney. 2013. Beam search for solving substitution ciphers. In *Annual Meeting of the Assoc. for Computational Linguistics*, pages 1569–1576, Sofia, Bulgaria, August.

[Nuhn et al.2014] Malte Nuhn, Julian Schamper, and Hermann Ney. 2014. Improved decipherment of homophonic ciphers. In *Conference on Empirical Methods in Natural Language Processing*, Doha, Qatar, October.

[Parker et al.2011] Robert Parker, David Graff, Junbo Kong, Ke Chen, and Kazuaki Maeda. 2011. English gigaword fifth edition. Linguistic Data Consortium, Philadelphia.

[Ravi and Knight2011a] Sujith Ravi and Kevin Knight. 2011a. Bayesian inference for Zodiac and other homophonic ciphers. In *Proceedings of the 49th Annual Meeting of the Association for Computational Linguistics (ACL)*, pages 239–247, Portland, Oregon, June. Association for Computational Linguistics.

[Ravi and Knight2011b] Sujith Ravi and Kevin Knight. 2011b. Deciphering foreign language. In *Proceedings of the 49th Annual Meeting of the Association for Computational Linguistics: Human Language Technologies*, pages 12–21, Portland, Oregon, USA, June. Association for Computational Linguistics.

Multi-Pass Decoding With Complex Feature Guidance for Statistical Machine Translation

Benjamin Marie
LIMSI-CNRS, Orsay, France
Lingua et Machina, Le Chesnay, France
benjamin.marie@limsi.fr

Aurélien Max
LIMSI-CNRS, Orsay, France
Univ. Paris Sud, Orsay, France
aurelien.max@limsi.fr

Abstract

In Statistical Machine Translation, some complex features are still difficult to integrate during decoding and usually used through the reranking of the k-best hypotheses produced by the decoder. We propose a translation table partitioning method that exploits the result of this reranking to iteratively guide the decoder in order to produce a new k-best list more relevant to some complex features. We report experiments on two translation domains and two translations directions which yield improvements of up to 1.4 BLEU over the reranking baseline using the same set of complex features. On a practical viewpoint, our approach allows SMT system developers to easily integrate complex features into decoding rather than being limited to their use in one-time k-best list reranking.

1 Introduction

State-of-the-art Phrase-Based Statistical Machine Translation (PBSMT) systems can use a large number of feature functions decomposable into local scores to efficiently evaluate the partial hypotheses built during decoding. However, some feature functions are difficult to integrate into the decoder mainly because they are not easily decomposable, very costly to compute and/or only available after complete hypotheses have been posited. Usually such *complex features* are used through the rescoring and reranking of the k-best translation hypotheses produced by the decoder (Och et al., 2004). Although this reranking pass is performed over the best part of the decoder search space, it is limited by the actual *diversity* expressed in the k-best list. Additionally, reranking being performed on a list generated by a simpler set of features, it may not have access to hypotheses that can best exploit the potential of the complex features used. We describe a translation table partitioning approach that exploits the result of such a reranking to iteratively guide the decoder to produce new hypotheses that are more relevant to the complex features used. To this end, we focus in this work on the simple exploitation of the disagreement between hypotheses ranked best according to the decoder and to our feature-rich decoder. In particular, we seek to provide the next-pass decoder with separate translation tables that either contain bi-phrases that are unique to the decoder's one-best or to the reranker's one-best, in the hope that it will tend, in a soft manner, to *exploit* the preferences expressed by the complex features, and to otherwise *explore* alternative translation choices. Such a comparison is then iteratively repeated, until convergence on a development set between the new pass of the decoder and a reranker trained on the full set of hypotheses generated thus far. On the test data, this procedure thus produces after each iteration a new decoder n-best, as well as an iteration-specific new reranker best hypothesis. We report consistent improvements of translation quality over a strong reranking baseline using the same features on 2 different domains and 2 translation directions.

The remainder of this article is organized as follows: we first briefly review related work (Section 2), then introduce our approach (Section 3), describe our experiments (Section 4), and finally discuss our results and present our future work (Section 5).

2 Related Work

Chen et al. (2008a; 2008b) expand the k-best list of the decoder using three methods. One of them involves re-decodings using models trained on the decoder k-best list to integrate posterior knowledge during the next re-decoding. The new k-best

Proceedings of the 53rd Annual Meeting of the Association for Computational Linguistics and the 7th International Joint Conference on Natural Language Processing (Short Papers), pages 554–559, Beijing, China, July 26-31, 2015.

list produced by the decoder is concatenated to the original one and then reranked with complex features, which yields improvements over a reranking performed on the original k-best list. The reranking pass is done out of the loop and the re-decodings do not exploit the reranking result that used the complex features.

Recently, we proposed a rewriting system that explores in a greedy fashion the neighborhood of the one-best hypothesis found by the reranking pass using complex features, assuming that a better hypothesis can be very close to this seed hypothesis (Marie and Max, 2014). Nevertheless, this rewriting only explores a small search space, limited by the greedy search algorithm that concentrates on individual, local rewritings.

Other works proposed methods to produce more diverse lists of hypotheses by iteratively encouraging the decoder to produce translations that are different from the previous one (Gimpel et al., 2013) or by making small changes to the scoring function to extract k-best lists from other parts of the search space (Devlin and Matsoukas, 2012). Some useful diversity can be obtained as these hypotheses can be combined using SMT system combination or help to better train reranking systems. But in spite of the introduction of more diversity, these methods do not guarantee that eventually lists containing hypotheses that are more relevant to complex features will be obtained.

3 Translation Table Partitioning

3.1 Exploiting the Reranking Pass Result

Because all bi-phrases initially belong to the same translation table, they share their feature weights after tuning. Our main idea is to partition the set of bi-phrases by putting aside, in new translation tables, possibly misused bi-phrases according to the reranking with complex features of the decoder k-best list (`Rerank`). This partitioning gives to subsequent tunings the opportunity to assign more adapted weights to the features of these specific groups of bi-phrases. Intuitively, if the `Rerank` one-best hypothesis is different from that of the initial decoder, the bi-phrases that account for the differences should have received different weights to encourage the decoder to either choose them or instead avoid them.

To achieve the partitioning of the translation table we compare the `Rerank` one-best hypothesis to the decoder one-best and compute their differences. On the one hand, there are n-grams from the decoder one-best hypothesis that are not found any more in the `Rerank` one-best; on the other hand, there are n-grams that only exist in the `Rerank` one-best hypothesis. Since the decoder produces word alignments between the source sentence to translate and its hypotheses, we can extract all the bi-phrases from the translation table that are compatible with these n-grams and their alignments. Each set of bi-phrases extracted from n-grams[1] either appearing (`IN`) or disappearing (`OUT`) in the `Rerank` one-best hypothesis compared to the decoder's, is moved to a specific translation table. Then a new tuning is performed for each relevant partitioning configuration.

The described translation table partioning procedure can be performed iteratively as each new decoding can be followed by `Rerank` on the new k-best list generated. The differences between `Rerank` and the decoder one-bests are extracted anew and put in new translation tables at each iteration.[2] Iterations are performed until no more improvements of the BLEU score are obtained by `Rerank` on a development set. The decoder is re-tuned and `Rerank` is re-trained after each iteration[3] to obtain more specific and updated weights for each old or new translation table. Finally, at test time, the learned weights corresponding to the current iteration are applied.

3.2 Located Tokens

As a token can appear more than once in an input text and in a sentence, and because complex features are computed locally, the source tokens are *located*: an identifier is concatenated to each token to make them unique in the source text to translate. Tokens of source phrases in the translation table are also located, meaning that each bi-phrases is duplicated to cover all located tokens. This procedure allows our approach to differentiate changes between `Moses` and `Rerank` one-best hypotheses at the token level by taking context into ac-

[1] In decoders phrases typically have a fixed maximum length, which corresponds to our maximum value for n.

[2] So, if both types of translation tables are extracted at each iteration, 3 iterations would produce 6 translation tables in addition to the remainder of the initial one. Note that a bi-phrase can in fact be present in more than one translation table after several iterations.

[3] `Rerank` re-training uses only the k-best list of the current iteration. k-bests from different iteration cannot be concatenated as they use a different number of features corresponding to a different number of translation tables.

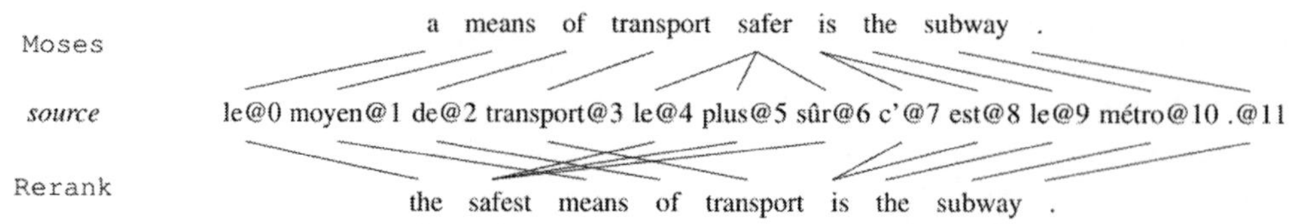

source	OUT	IN
le@0	a	the
le@0 moyen@1	a means	
moyen@1 de@2 transport@3	a means of transport	
le@4 plus@5 sûr@6	safer	safest

Figure 1: Example of IN and OUT translation tables extraction from the n-grams that differ between the Rerank and Moses one-best hypotheses.

count. An example of IN and OUT translation tables extraction with located tokens is presented in Figure 1.

4 Experiments

4.1 Data

We ran experiments on two translation tasks for different domains: the WMT'14 Medical translation task (medical) and the WMT'11 news translation task (news) for the language pair Fr-En on both directions. For both tasks we trained two strong baseline systems using data provided by WMT[4]. Statistics about the training, development and testing data are presented in Table 1.

Tasks	Corpus	Sentences	Tokens (Fr-En)
news	train	12M	383M - 318M
	dev	2,525	73k - 65k
	test	3,003	85k - 74k
medical	train	4.9M	91M - 78M
	dev	500	12k - 10k
	test	1,000	26k - 21k
	in-domain LM		146M - 78M
for both tasks	LM		2.5B - 6B

Table 1: Data used in our experiments.

4.2 MT system

For our experiments we used the Moses phrase-based SMT toolkit (Koehn et al., 2007) with default settings and features, including the five features from the translation table, and kb-mira tuning (Cherry and Foster, 2012). Rerank is trained using kb-mira on the 1,000-best list generated by Moses on the development set with the distinct-nbest parameter to have no duplicates. Testing is also performed on distinct 1,000-best lists. Rerank uses all the decoder features along with the following complex features:

- **MosesNorm**: all decoder features and the Moses score normalized by the hypothesis length
- **NNM**: bilingual and monolingual neural network models with a structured output layer (SOUL) (Le et al., 2012)
- **POSLM**: 6-gram POS language model
- **WPP**: count-based word posterior probability (Ueffing and Ney, 2007)
- **TagRatio**: ratio of translation hypothesis by number of source tokens tagged as: verb, noun or adjective
- **Syntax**: depth, number of nodes and number of unary rules of the syntactic parse normalized by the hypothesis length (Carter and Monz, 2011)
- **IBM1**: IBM1 features (Och et al., 2004; Hildebrand and Vogel, 2008)

Part-of-speech tagging and syntactic parsing were respectively performed with the Stanford Part-of-speech Tagger (Toutanova and Manning, 2000) and the Shift-Reduce parser of Zhu *et al.* (2013). We report the individual performance of each feature set in Table 2 and the Rerank performance when using all feature sets. As expected, the **NNM** feature set brings most of the improvements and attain by itself nearly the BLEU score of Rerank when using all feature sets for the news task with a gain of 1.4 and 1.1 BLEU respectively for En→Fr and Fr→En over the Moses

[4]http://www.statmt.org/wmt14

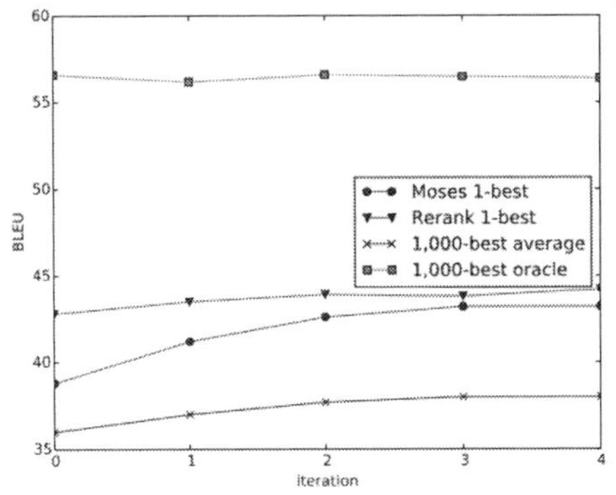

Figure 2: BLEU score evolution over iterations for the `IN` configuration on the test set of the `medical` En→Fr translation task.

baseline. Among the other feature sets, **POSLM** performs well, especially for the `medical` task with an improvement of 0.3 and 0.5 BLEU for En→Fr and Fr→En, respectively.

Some types of our complex features have already been used during decoding, although sometimes for a very important cost (Schwartz et al., 2011). Our feature sets are to be considered only as experimental parameters, as any other feature types usually used during reranking could also be used.

Features	`medical`		`news`	
	En→Fr	Fr→En	En→Fr	Fr→En
`Moses`	38.8	37.1	31.1	28.6
+ **MosesNorm**	38.9	37.2	31.1	28.7
+ **NNM**	41.9	38.9	32.5	29.8
+ **POSLM**	39.2	37.7	31.1	28.9
+ **WPP**	39.1	37.1	31.2	28.6
+ **TagRatio**	38.9	37.3	31.1	28.8
+ **Syntax**	38.8	37.2	31.2	28.9
+ **IBM1**	39.1	37.2	30.9	28.8
`Rerank`	42.8	40.1	32.5	29.9

Table 2: Reranking results for each set of features added individually; `Rerank` uses the full set.

4.3 Results

Table 3 presents our results for different translation table partitioning configurations. For each configuration, results are presented for the last iteration of the multi-pass decoding performed by `Moses` and the reranking of its k-best list by the `Rerank` system using complex features. First, we observe for the baseline systems that `Rerank` outperforms `Moses` for all translation tasks and directions, especially on `medical` with improvements of 3.0 and 4.0 BLEU respectively for Fr→En and En→Fr. These improvements illustrate the strong potential of our set of complex features to provide more accurate scores for translation hypotheses than the set of features used during the initial decoding.

All studied configurations yield improvements with multi-pass `Moses` over the `Moses` baseline, showing the advantage of extracting from the main translation table misused bi-phrases according to a reranking pass done with complex features. As illustrated by Figure 2, the multi-pass decoding quickly reduces the gap in BLEU score between our multi-pass `Moses` and `Rerank` one-best hypotheses. Although the 1,000-best oracle remains at the same level over the iterations, the 1,000-best average score[5] increases by 2 BLEU at the last iteration over the first 1,000-best hypotheses produced by `Moses`, pointing out a strong improvement of the average quality of the 1,000-best hypotheses. However, except for the `IN` configuration on `medical` En→Fr, multi-pass `Moses` does not bring improvements by itself over the `Rerank` baseline. Nevertheless, multi-pass `Moses` coupled with `Rerank` does improve over `Rerank` baseline for all configurations on all translation tasks. These consistent improvements over the `Rerank` baseline demonstrate the ability of our procedure to help the `Moses` decoder to produce k-best lists of better quality which are more suitable to our complex features.

The `IN` configuration, which puts in a translation table all bi-phrases in the one-best hypothesis of `Rerank` that do not belong to the `Moses` one-best hypothesis, performs the best for all translation tasks: multi-pass `Rerank` yields a 1.4 BLEU improvement over the `Rerank` baseline on `medical` En→Fr, and 0.7 BLEU on `news` En→Fr. Improvements are lower, but nonetheless consistent, for the Fr→En direction, with +0.9 and +0.5 BLEU respectively on the `medical` and `news` tasks. The `OUT` configuration yields smaller improvements in comparison, meaning that putting aside (a few) first-ranked bi-phrases downgraded by `Rerank` is less useful in order to produce better k-best lists with `Moses`. Using in the same system both `IN` and

[5]To obtain this average we compute the arithmetic mean of the 1,000-best hypotheses sentence-BLEU scores and select the hypothesis with the closest score to the mean. Once we have selected an hypothesis for each sentence, the BLEU score is computed.

Configuration		medical En→Fr dev	test	# iter.	medical Fr→En dev	test	# iter.	news En→Fr dev	test	# iter.	news Fr→En dev	test	# iter.
baseline	Moses	40.9	38.8	-	41.3	37.1	-	27.1	31.1	-	28.0	28.6	-
	Rerank	43.9	42.8		44.2	40.1		28.5	32.5		29.1	29.9	
OUT	Moses	43.3	41.8	4	43.0	38.7	3	27.9	31.8	1	28.5	29.2	1
	Rerank	45.3	43.8		44.5	40.5		28.5	32.9		29.2	30.3	
IN	Moses	45.1	43.2	4	43.6	39.9	3	28.4	32.4	2	28.6	29.3	2
	Rerank	45.7	**44.2**		45.0	**41.0**		28.8	**33.2**		29.3	**30.4**	
IN and OUT	Moses	44.8	42.4	4	42.8	38.7	3	28.3	32.1	2	28.8	29.2	2
	Rerank	45.3	43.5		44.5	40.6		28.7	32.9		29.3	**30.4**	

Table 3: Results for different translation table partitioning configurations. OUT: configuration with a translation table containing bi-phrases of the Moses 1-best not in the Rerank 1-best. IN: configuration with a translation table containing bi-phrases of the Rerank 1-best not in the Moses 1-best. For all configuration the main translation table is still used but does not contain the extracted bi-phrases.

OUT iteration-specific translation tables ("IN and OUT") yields a performance situated between using IN and OUT separately, but which still consistently improves over the baseline Rerank.

5 Discussion and future work

We have presented a method for guiding a phrase-based decoder with translation tables partitioned on the basis of k-best list reranking making use of complex features. Our results showed consistent improvements in BLEU score over a strong Rerank baseline using the same features. We experimented with a simple criterion for iteratively partitioning the original phrase table of the system, and found that focusing on providing the next iteration decoder with the bi-phrases that were prefered at first rank by Rerank (IN) performed best.[6]

We now intend to study how to better take advantage of the expected characteristics of our IN and OUT tables, possibly by adding more features to our iteration-specific tables, or by exploiting information on bi-phrases computed on the full reranked lists. For our future work, we also plan to study approaches that can enhance the *diversity* in the k-best lists (Chatterjee and Cancedda, 2010; Gimpel et al., 2013) between each iteration of the multi-pass decoding to train a better Rerank after each decoding pass. Another area for improvement lies in the addition of yet more complex features, for instance to allow a better discourse coherence modelling over iterations (Ture et al., 2012; Hardmeier et al., 2012). Going further, we could study the effect of using other hypotheses instead of the Rerank one-best to perform the comparison with the Moses one-best hypothesis. For instance, we can reasonably expect that making this comparison with the output of a rewriting system, such as the one proposed in our previous work (Marie and Max, 2014), could extract more misused and useful bi-phrases on which to base our translation table partitioning since this rewriting system's output is usually better than the Rerank one-best and not in the k-best list of the decoder.

[6]Interestingly, a control experiment showed that using iteration-specific tables yields slightly better performance than fusioning all bi-phrases of a given type in a non iteration-specific table, possibly allowing later tunings to prefer the contents of the most recent, and possibly more reliable tables.

Acknowledgments

The authors would like to thank the anonymous reviewers for their helpful comments, Quoc Khanh Do for his assistance on using SOUL, and Li Gong and Nicolas Pécheux for providing the authors with data used in the experiments. The work of the first author is supported by a CIFRE grant from French ANRT.

References

Simon Carter and Christof Monz. 2011. Syntactic Discriminative Language Model Rerankers for Statistical Machine Translation. *Machine Translation*, 25:317–339.

Samidh Chatterjee and Nicola Cancedda. 2010. Minimum error rate training by sampling the translation lattice. In *Proceedings of EMNLP*, Cambridge, USA.

Boxing Chen, Min Zhang, Aiti Aw, and Haizhou Li. 2008a. Exploiting N-best Hypotheses for SMT Self-

Enhancement. In *Proceedings of ACL, short papers*, Columbus, USA.

Boxing Chen, Min Zhang, Aiti Aw, and Haizhou Li. 2008b. Regenerating Hypotheses for Statistical Machine Translation. In *Proceedings of COLING*, Manchester, UK.

Colin Cherry and George Foster. 2012. Batch Tuning Strategies for Statistical Machine Translation. In *Proceedings of NAACL*, Montréal, Canada.

Jacob Devlin and Spyros Matsoukas. 2012. Trait-based Hypothesis Selection for Machine Translation. In *Proceedings of NAACL*, Montréal, Canada.

Kevin Gimpel, Dhruv Batra, Chris Dyer, Gregory Shakhnarovich, and Virginia Tech. 2013. A Systematic Exploration of Diversity in Machine Translation. In *Proceedings of EMNLP*, Seatlle, USA.

Christian Hardmeier, Joakim Nivre, and Jörg Tiedemann. 2012. Document-wide decoding for phrase-based statistical machine translation. In *Proceedings of EMNLP-CoNLL*, Jeju Island, Korea.

Almut Silja Hildebrand and Stephan Vogel. 2008. Combination of machine translation systems via hypothesis selection from combined n-best lists. In *Proceedings of AMTA*, Honolulu, USA.

Philipp Koehn, Hieu Hoang, Alexandra Birch, Chris Callison-Burch, Marcello Federico, Nicola Bertoldi, Brooke Cowan, Wade Shen, Christine Moran, Richard Zens, Chris Dyer, Ondrej Bojar, Alexandra Constantin, and Evan Herbst. 2007. Moses: Open Source Toolkit for Statistical Machine Translation. In *Proceedings of ACL, demo session*, Prague, Czech Republic.

Hai-Son Le, Alexandre Allauzen, and François Yvon. 2012. Continuous Space Translation Models with Neural Networks. In *Proceedings of NAACL*, Montréal, Canada.

Benjamin Marie and Aurélien Max. 2014. Confidence-based Rewriting of Machine Translation Output. In *Proceedings of EMNLP*, Doha, Qatar.

Franz Josef Och, Daniel Gildea, Sanjeev Khudanpur, Anoop Sarkar, Kenji Yamada, Alex Fraser, Shankar Kumar, Libin Shen, David Smith, Katherine Eng, Viren Jain, Zhen Jin, and Dragomir Radev. 2004. A Smorgasbord of Features for Statistical Machine Translation. In *Proceedings of NAACL*, Boston, USA.

Lane Schwartz, Chris Callison-Burch, William Schuler, and Stephen Wu. 2011. Incremental syntactic language models for phrase-based translation. In *Proceedings of ACL*, Portland, USA.

Kristina Toutanova and Christopher D. Manning. 2000. Enriching the Knowledge Sources Used in a Maximum Entropy Part-of-speech Tagger. In *Proceedings of EMNLP*, Hong Kong.

Ferhan Ture, Douglas W. Oard, and Philip Resnik. 2012. Encouraging consistent translation choices. In *Proceedings of NAACL*, Montréal, Canada.

Nicola Ueffing and Hermann Ney. 2007. Word-Level Confidence Estimation for Machine Translation. *Computational Linguistics*, 33(1):9–40.

Muhua Zhu, Yue Zhang, Wenliang Chen, Min Zhang, and Jingbo Zhu. 2013. Fast and Accurate Shift-Reduce Constituent Parsing. In *Proceedings of ACL*, Sofia, Bulgaria.

What's in a Domain? Analyzing Genre and Topic Differences in Statistical Machine Translation

Marlies van der Wees **Arianna Bisazza** **Wouter Weerkamp**[◊] **Christof Monz**
Informatics Institute
University of Amsterdam
{m.e.vanderwees,a.bisazza,c.monz}@uva.nl
[◊]904Labs, Amsterdam
wouter@904labs.com

Abstract

Domain adaptation is an active field of research in statistical machine translation (SMT), but so far most work has ignored the distinction between the *topic* and *genre* of documents. In this paper we quantify and disentangle the impact of genre and topic differences on translation quality by introducing a new data set that has controlled topic and genre distributions. In addition, we perform a detailed analysis showing that differences across topics only explain to a limited degree translation performance differences across genres, and that genre-specific errors are more attributable to model coverage than to suboptimal scoring of translation candidates.

1 Introduction

Training corpora for statistical machine translation (SMT) are typically collected from a wide variety of sources and therefore have varying textual characteristics such as writing style and vocabulary. The test set, on the other hand, is much smaller and usually more homogeneous. The resulting mismatch between the test data and the majority of the training data can lead to suboptimal translation performance. In such situations, it is beneficial to adapt the translation system to the translation task at hand, which is exactly the challenge of domain adaptation in SMT.

The concept of a *domain*, however, is not unambiguously defined across existing domain adaptation methods. Commonly used interpretations of domains neglect the fact that *topic* and *genre* are two distinct properties of text (Lee and Myaeng, 2002; Stein and Meyer Zu Eissen, 2006). Two texts can discuss a similar topic, but using different styles. Since most work on domain adaptation in SMT uses in-domain and out-of-domain data that differ on both the topic and the genre level, it is unclear whether the proposed solutions address topic or genre differences.

In this work we take a step back and disentangle the concepts topic and genre, then we analyze and quantify their effect on SMT, which we believe is a necessary step towards further improving domain adaptation for SMT. Concretely, we address the following questions:

(i) Can we clarify the ambiguous use of the concept *domain* with regard to adaptation in SMT?

(ii) Which of two intrinsic text properties, topic and genre, presents a larger challenge to SMT?

(iii) To what extent do topic and genre differ with respect to SMT model coverage and observed out-of-vocabulary (OOV) types?

To answer these questions, we introduce a new data set with controlled topic-genre distributions, which we use for an in-depth analysis of the impact of topic and genre differences on SMT.

2 Topic and genre differences in SMT

The definition of a domain varies across work on domain adaptation and is often imprecise. In this work we avoid using this ambiguous term, and instead focus on the text properties topic and genre.

Topic is the general subject of a document. Topics can be determined on multiple levels, ranging from very broad to more detailed. Examples of topics include sports, politics, and science (high-level), or football and tennis (low-level).

Genre is harder to define, as there is no single definition in literature (Swales, 1990; Karlgren,

Proceedings of the 53rd Annual Meeting of the Association for Computational Linguistics and the 7th International Joint Conference on Natural Language Processing (Short Papers), pages 560–566, Beijing, China, July 26-31, 2015.

Topic	Newswire sentence	User-generated sentence
Culture	The 12 contestants competed during a May 3rd Prime before a panel of judges and millions of viewers across the Arab world.	Your program's name is "Arab Idol", which is in English, and you allowed Barwas to participate and represent Iraq while she sings in Kurdish!!!
Economy	Yemen is mulling the establishment of 13 industrial zones across its six planned administrative regions in a bid to stimulate development and create job opportunities.	What development in Yemen are you talking about? We will continue to call for freedom until independence and liberation and the routing of the northern occupation from our lands.

Table 1: English-side samples from the Gen&Topic data set. All pairs of newswire (NW) and user-generated (UG) fragments in the data set discuss the same article and are topically related.

2004). Based on previous definitions, Santini (2004) concludes that the term genre is used as a concept complementary to topic, covering the non-topical text properties function, style, and text type. Like topics, genres can also exhibit different levels of granularity (Lee, 2001). Examples of genres include formal or informal text (high-level), and newswire, editorials, and user-generated text (low-level).

Topic and genre are both intrinsic properties of texts, but most work on domain adaptation uses provenance or subcorpus information to adapt SMT systems to a specific translation task (Foster and Kuhn, 2007; Duh et al., 2010; Bisazza et al., 2011; Sennrich, 2012; Bisazza and Federico, 2012; Haddow and Koehn, 2012, among others). In recent years, some work has explicitly addressed topic adaptation for SMT (Eidelman et al., 2012; Hewavitharana et al., 2013; Hasler et al., 2014a; Hasler et al., 2014c) using latent Dirichlet allocation (Blei et al., 2003). While Hasler et al. (2014b) showed that provenance and topic can serve as complements to each other, the effects of genre and topic on SMT have not been systematically studied.

3 The Gen&Topic benchmark set

To analyze the impact of genre and topic differences in SMT, we need a test set where both dimensions are controlled as much as possible. Unfortunately, currently available and commonly used benchmarks meet this requirement only to a limited degree. For instance, while the NIST OpenMT sets do contain documents drawn from two genres, newswire and web, both genres exhibit a different distribution over topics, i.e., the same topic might not be equally represented across genres, and vice versa.

To overcome this limitation, we introduce a new Arabic-English parallel benchmark set, the Gen&Topic data set, that contains documents with controlled topic and genre distributions. This benchmark set consists of manually translated news articles crawled from the web with their corresponding, manually translated readers' comments and thus comprises the genres *newswire* (NW) and *user-generated* (UG) text. Since each pair of NW and UG documents originates from the same article, we can assume that both documents discuss the same topic, for which labels are provided by the source websites. By including comparable numbers of tokens per genre for each article, we enforce equal topic distributions across the genres. Two examples of NW-UG pairs are shown in Table 1. Note that the selected UG sentences in the Gen&Topic data set are well-formulated comments rather than dialog-oriented content such as SMS or chat messages, which pose substantially larger challenges to SMT than the Gen&Topic comments (van der Wees et al., 2015).

For parameter estimation purposes, we split the

		Genre		
Topic		NW	UG	Total
Culture	segments	654	507	1161
	tokens	15.5K	14.9K	30.4K
Economy	segments	500	578	1078
	tokens	16.0K	15.5K	31.5K
Health	segments	384	319	703
	tokens	9.7K	9.3K	19.1K
Politics	segments	494	646	1140
	tokens	15.8K	15.8K	31.6K
Security	segments	532	826	1358
	tokens	16.1K	15.9K	32.0K
Total	segments	2564	2876	5440
	tokens	73.2K	71.3K	144.5K

Table 2: Statistics of the Arabic-English Gen&Topic data set containing five topics and two genres: newswire (NW) and user-generated (UG) text. Tokens are counted on the Arabic side.

complete benchmark into a development and a test set, such that the development set contains approximately one-third of the data, while ensuring that articles in each set originate from non-overlapping time periods. Table 2 lists the specifications of the complete benchmark, which we make available for download[1].

4 Quantifying the impact of genre and topic differences on SMT

To quantify the impact of multiple genres and topics in a test corpus, we run a series of experiments in which we measure translation quality, model coverage, and observed OOV types.

4.1 Translation quality

We first run a translation experiment on the Gen&Topic test set using our in-house phrase-based SMT system similar to Moses (Koehn et al., 2007). Features include lexicalized reordering, linear distortion with limit 5, and lexical weighting. In addition, we use a 5-gram linearly interpolated language model, trained on 1.6B words with Kneser-Ney smoothing (Chen and Goodman, 1999), that covers all topics and genres contained in the benchmark. We tune our system on the Gen&Topic development set using pairwise ranking optimization (PRO) (Hopkins and May, 2011).

Naturally, performance differences across topics and genres depend on the degree to which both are represented in the parallel training data. To allow for fair comparison, we down-sample our available training data to be as balanced as possible in terms of topics and genres. The resulting system is trained on approximately 200K sentence pairs with 6M source tokens per genre, as much as is available for UG. All data originates from the same web sources as the documents in the benchmark. Our more competitive system (van der Wees et al., 2015) that uses also LDC-distributed data yields slightly higher BLEU scores, but is more favorable for NW than for UG translation tasks. Due to the strict data requirements in terms of topic and genre distributions, as well as the availability of sizable parallel training data, our current experimental set-up covers Arabic-English only.

Table 3 compares BLEU scores (Papineni et al., 2002, 1 reference) of the Gen&Topic data, split down by topics and genres. We observe that translation performance fluctuates much more across genres than across topics: There is a large gap of 3.9 BLEU points between NW and UG, which can be entirely attributed to actual genre differences given the construction of the Gen&Topic data set and the use of down-sampled training data. On the other hand, the gap between different topics is only 0.6 BLEU points on average, and at most 1.1 (between culture and politics). A translation quality gap between genres has also been observed in past OpenMT evaluation campaigns. However, as the NIST benchmarks have not been controlled for topics across genres, it is unclear to what extent this gap can be attributed to genre differences.

	NW	UG	All	
Culture	19.2	17.6	19.3	Avg. diff.: ±0.6
Economy	19.9	15.9	18.9	
Health	19.3	17.7	18.8	
Politics	21.3	13.6	18.2	
Security	19.3	16.2	18.5	
All	19.9	16.0	18.9	
	Avg. diff.: ±3.9			

Table 3: Arabic-to-English BLEU scores on the Gen&Topic test set (1 reference translation) per topic-genre combination. Tuning was done on the complete Gen&Topic development set. Variations in translation quality are represented by average pairwise BLEU score differences.

4.2 Model coverage analysis

Next, to explain the large performance gap between genres, we analyze the phrase lengths within Viterbi translations, source phrase and phrase pair recall, and phrase pair OOV of the Gen&Topic test set (Table 4).

Average source-side phrase length We first compute the average number of source words contained in the phrases that our SMT system uses to produce the 1-best translations for the Gen&Topic test set. One can see that UG is translated with shorter phrases than NW, and that differences between genres are more pronounced than among topics. This difference, in turn, can be due to unreliable translation probabilities but also to the mere lack of translation options in the models. We quantify the impact of the latter by measuring phrase recall on each test portion.

Phrase recall and phrase pair OOV To compute phrase recall, we first automatically word-

[1] `http://ilps.science.uva.nl/resources/gen-topic/`

Gen&Topic portion	BLEU	Avg.phr. length	Source phrase recall 1	2	3	4+	Src-trg phrase pair recall 1	2	3	4+	Phr.pair OOV
NW	19.9	1.45	99.3	81.4	41.8	7.1	73.8	39.4	13.7	1.8	71.5
UG	16.0	1.38	97.2	74.7	36.0	6.3	56.2	28.8	8.7	1.1	76.0
Culture	19.3	1.39	98.2	77.6	36.5	5.3	66.2	35.2	10.7	1.2	74.2
Economy	18.9	1.42	98.4	78.7	39.4	6.5	65.3	33.5	10.9	1.4	73.8
Health	18.8	1.41	98.3	76.6	37.1	5.4	64.5	33.5	11.0	1.2	75.2
Politics	18.2	1.41	98.1	78.6	39.8	7.7	60.8	33.1	11.2	1.5	73.4
Security	18.4	1.42	97.6	77.0	40.2	8.4	62.7	33.3	11.6	1.8	73.3

Table 4: Impact of genre and topic differences on various indicators of SMT model quality.

align the test set and extract from it a set of reference phrase pairs using the same procedure applied to the training data. Then, we count the number of reference phrase pairs whose source side is covered by the translation models (*source phrase recall*) and the number of reference phrase pairs that are fully covered by the translation models (*source-target phrase pair recall*). Formally, we define the set of source-matching phrases as:

$$M^S = \{(\bar{f},\bar{e}) \mid (\bar{f},\cdot) \in P_{test} \wedge (\bar{f},\cdot) \in P_{train}\},$$

where P_d refers to the set of phrase pairs $(\bar{f},\bar{e})$ that can be extracted from corpus d. Source phrase recall R_n^S for phrases of length n is then defined as:

$$R_n^S = \frac{\sum_{(\bar{f},\bar{e})\in M^S \wedge |\bar{f}|=n} c_{test}(\bar{f},\bar{e})}{\sum_{(\bar{f},\bar{e})\in P_{test} \wedge |\bar{f}|=n} c_{test}(\bar{f},\bar{e})}, \quad (1)$$

where $c_{test}(\bar{f},\bar{e})$ denotes the frequency of phrase pair $(\bar{f},\bar{e})$ in the test set. Analogously, we define the set of source-target-matching phrase pairs as:

$$M^{S,T} = \{(\bar{f},\bar{e}) \mid (\bar{f},\bar{e}) \in P_{test} \wedge (\bar{f},\bar{e}) \in P_{train}\}$$

and the source-target phrase pair recall $R_n^{S,T}$ for phrases of length n as:

$$R_n^{S,T} = \frac{\sum_{(\bar{f},\bar{e})\in M^{S,T} \wedge |\bar{f}|=n} c_{test}(\bar{f},\bar{e})}{\sum_{(\bar{f},\bar{e})\in P_{test} \wedge |\bar{f}|=n} c_{test}(\bar{f},\bar{e})}. \quad (2)$$

Finally, we call *phrase pair OOV* the portion of reference phrase pairs that are not covered by the translation models, that is: $1 - \sum_n^N R_n^{S,T}$, where N is the phrase limit used for phrase extraction.

The results of our analysis, broken down by source phrase length, show that source phrase recall is much lower in UG than in NW, while variations among topics are only very small. The stronger impact of genre differences is even more visible on phrase pair recall: for instance, our system knows the correct translation of 73.8% of the single-source-word phrase pairs in the NW genre. In UG this is only 56.2%, despite the equal amounts of training data per genre in our system. These figures suggest that model coverage—both mono- and bilingual—is an important reason for the low SMT quality on UG data.

Most existing approaches to domain adaptation focus on domain-sensitive scoring or selection of existing translation candidates (Matsoukas et al., 2009; Foster et al., 2010; Axelrod et al., 2011; Chen et al., 2013, among others). This strategy is supported by the error analysis of Irvine et al. (2013), who show that scoring errors are more common across domains than errors caused by OOVs, in the source as well as the target language. Across genres however, our results in Table 4 show that both word-level and phrase-level OOVs are a more likely explanation for the performance differences. This stresses the need to address model coverage, for example by paraphrasing (Callison-Burch et al., 2006) or translation synthesis (Irvine and Callison-Burch, 2014).

4.3 Manual OOV analysis

To get a better understanding of the OOVs observed for the genres and topics in the Gen&Topic set, we perform a fine-grained manual analysis[2]. For this analysis a bilingual speaker manually annotated 500 sentences on the source side (equally distributed over genres and topics) to identify the class of each OOV. Annotations are done for top and sub-level classes (e.g., replaced letter, which

[2]Available with the benchmark data at `http://ilps.science.uva.nl/resources/gen-topic/`

Arabic OOV	English translation	Explanation of OOV	Main OOV class
داعش	ISIL	New proper noun	Rare but correct (Rare)
هينسوا	(they) will forget	Dialectal future tense	Dialectal forms (Dial)
يقدسون	(they) revere	Third person plural present tense	Morphological variants (Morph)
توفيرالوظائف	creationofjobs	Missing blank	Spelling errors (Spell)
التطوعيين	volunteeeers	Wrong but understandable spelling	Colloquialisms (Coll)

Table 5: Examples of OOVs observed in the Gen&Topic set with their respective main OOV class.

Gen&Topic	OOV type					
portion	Rare	Dial	Morph	Spel	Coll	Other
NW	77.8	0.0	16.7	5.6	0.0	0.0
UG	9.8	9.0	17.2	42.6	12.3	9.0
Culture	17.4	0.0	17.4	52.2	8.7	4.3
Economy	13.8	0.0	34.5	31.0	13.8	6.9
Health	15.8	10.5	15.8	36.8	10.5	10.5
Politics	25.0	25.0	12.5	25.0	0.0	12.5
Security	23.5	8.8	5.9	41.2	14.7	5.9

Table 6: Error percentages per Gen&Topic portion of main OOV classes, see Table 5 for explanation. Other events include words that are not understandable or occur in the phrase table but only captured in a different context.

is a subclass of spelling errors). In total, we consider 17 subclasses which we group into five main classes, see Table 5 for examples.

Table 6 shows the type level percentages[3] for each main OOV class per genre or topic. When comparing the two *genres*, a number of observations emerge. Firstly, rare but correct words (e.g., proper nouns and technical terms, both regular issues for adaptation in SMT) make up the vast majority of the OOVs in NW, but are relatively infrequent in UG. By contrast, OOVs containing unseen morphological variants are equally common in both genres. Although complex morphology is language-specific, a rare morphological word in Arabic often maps to a rare multi-word phrase in English, resulting in phrase-level OOVs. Next, not entirely surprising, the majority of OOVs in UG are due to spelling errors. Finally, OOVs assigned to the remaining classes are never observed in NW but occasionally occur in UG.

Next, a comparison of the main OOV classes among the various *topics* shows a few notable distributions. Dialectal forms, for example, are rare in all topics except politics, where they are commonly observed in the form of Egyptian future tense. This can be explained by the presence of news articles about elections in Egypt in the Gen&Topic set. Next, while spelling errors are common in all topics, its abundance is most prominent in culture. Most spelling errors concern missing or inserted blanks, suggesting that comments are likely written on mobile devices. Finally, unseen morphological variants are more frequent in economy than in other topics, however with no conclusive explanation.

[3]We also collected token level frequencies which are very similar to the listed type level statistics, except for a small number of repeatedly occurring proper nouns.

5 Conclusions and implications

Despite the fact that domain adaptation is an active field of research in SMT, there is little consensus on what exactly constitutes a domain. By introducing and analyzing a new benchmark with balanced topic and genre distributions, we have shown that earlier findings explaining the differences across topics only explain to a limited degree translation performance differences across genres. Our analysis shows that genre-specific errors are more attributable to model-coverage errors than to suboptimal scoring of existing translation candidates. This suggests that future work on improving SMT across genres needs to investigate approaches that increase model coverage. Our fine-grained manual error analysis at the word level also suggests that source coverage could benefit from text normalization (Bertoldi et al., 2010). Finally, we make both our benchmark and the manual OOV annotations publicly available.

Acknowledgments

This research was funded in part by the Netherlands Organization for Scientific Research (NWO) under project number 639.022.213. We thank Rachel Cotterill, Nigel Dewdney, and the anonymous reviewers for their valuable comments.

References

Amittai Axelrod, Xiaodong He, and Jianfeng Gao. 2011. Domain adaptation via pseudo in-domain data selection. In *Proceedings of the 2011 Conference on Empirical Methods in Natural Language Processing*, pages 355–362.

Nicola Bertoldi, Mauro Cettolo, and Marcello Federico. 2010. Statistical machine translation of texts with misspelled words. In *HLT '10: Human Language Technologies: The 2010 Annual Conference of the North American Chapter of the Association for Computational Linguistics*, pages 412–419.

Arianna Bisazza and Marcello Federico. 2012. Cutting the long tail: Hybrid language models for translation style adaptation. In *Proceedings of the 13th Conference of the European Chapter of the Association for Computational Linguistics*, pages 439–448.

Arianna Bisazza, Nick Ruiz, and Marcello Federico. 2011. Fill-up versus interpolation methods for phrase-based SMT adaptation. In *Proceedings of the 8th International Workshop on Spoken Language Translation*, pages 136–143.

David Blei, Andrew Ng, and Michael Jordan. 2003. Latent dirichlet allocation. *Journal of Machine Learning Research*, 3:993–1022.

Chris Callison-Burch, Philipp Koehn, and Miles Osborne. 2006. Improved statistical machine translation using paraphrases. In *Proceedings of the Human Language Technology Conference of the NAACL, Main Conference*, pages 17–24.

Stanley F. Chen and Joshua Goodman. 1999. An empirical study of smoothing techniques for language modeling. *Computer Speech and Language*, 13(4):359–393.

Boxing Chen, Roland Kuhn, and George Foster. 2013. Vector space model for adaptation in statistical machine translation. In *Proceedings of the 51st Annual Meeting of the Association for Computational Linguistics*, pages 1285–1293.

Kevin Duh, Katsuhito Sudoh, and Hajime Tsukada. 2010. Analysis of translation model adaptation in statistical machine translation. In *Proceedings of the 7th International Workshop on Spoken Language Translation (IWSLT 2010)*, pages 243–250.

Vladimir Eidelman, Jordan Boyd-Graber, and Philip Resnik. 2012. Topic models for dynamic translation model adaptation. In *Proceedings of the 50th Annual Meeting of the Association for Computational Linguistics*, pages 115–119.

George Foster and Roland Kuhn. 2007. Mixture-model adaptation for SMT. In *Proceedings of the Second Workshop on Statistical Machine Translation*, pages 128–135.

George Foster, Cyril Goutte, and Roland Kuhn. 2010. Discriminative instance weighting for domain adaptation in statistical machine translation. In *Proceedings of the 2010 Conference on Empirical Methods in Natural Language Processing*, pages 451–459.

Barry Haddow and Philipp Koehn. 2012. Analysing the effect of out-of-domain data on SMT systems. In *Proceedings of the Seventh Workshop on Statistical Machine Translation*, pages 422–432.

Eva Hasler, Phil Blunsom, Philipp Koehn, and Barry Haddow. 2014a. Dynamic topic adaptation for phrase-based MT. In *Proceedings of the 14th Conference of the European Chapter of The Association for Computational Linguistics*, pages 328–337.

Eva Hasler, Barry Haddow, and Philipp Koehn. 2014b. Combining domain and topic adaptation for SMT. In *Proceedings of the 11th Conference of the Association for Machine Translation in the Americas*, pages 139–151.

Eva Hasler, Barry Haddow, and Philipp Koehn. 2014c. Dynamic topic adaptation for SMT using distributional profiles. In *Proceedings of the Ninth Workshop on Statistical Machine Translation*, pages 445–456.

Sanjika Hewavitharana, Dennis Mehay, Sankaranarayanan Ananthakrishnan, and Prem Natarajan. 2013. Incremental topic-based translation model adaptation for conversational spoken language translation. In *Proceedings of the 51st Annual Meeting of the Association for Computational Linguistics*, pages 697–701.

Mark Hopkins and Jonathan May. 2011. Tuning as ranking. In *Proceedings of the 2011 Conference on Empirical Methods in Natural Language Processing*, pages 1352–1362. Association for Computational Linguistics.

Ann Irvine and Chris Callison-Burch. 2014. Hallucinating phrase translations for low resource MT. In *Proceedings of the Eighteenth Conference on Computational Natural Language Learning*, pages 160–170.

Ann Irvine, John Morgan, Marine Carpuat, Hal Daumé III, and Dragos Stefan Munteanu. 2013. Measuring machine translation errors in new domains. *Transactions of the Association for Computational Linguistics*, 1:429–440.

Jussi Karlgren. 2004. The wheres and whyfores for studying text genre computationally. In *Workshop on Style and Meaning in Language, Art, Music, and Design*.

Philipp Koehn, Hieu Hoang, Alexandra Birch, Chris Callison-Burch, Marcello Federico, Nicola Bertoldi, Brooke Cowan, Wade Shen, Christine Moran, Richard Zens, Chris Dyer, Ondřej Bojar, Alexandra Constantin, and Evan Herbst. 2007. Moses: open source toolkit for statistical machine translation. In

Proceedings of the 45th Annual Meeting of the ACL on Interactive Poster and Demonstration Sessions, pages 177–180.

Yong-Bae Lee and Sung Hyon Myaeng. 2002. Text genre classification with genre-revealing and subject-revealing features. In *Proceedings of the 25th annual international ACM SIGIR conference on Research and development in information retrieval*, pages 145–150.

David Y.W. Lee. 2001. Genres, registers, text types, domains and styles: Clarifying the concepts and navigating a path through the BNC jungle. *Language Learning & Technology*, 5(3):37–72.

Spyros Matsoukas, Antti-Veikko I. Rosti, and Bing Zhang. 2009. Discriminative corpus weight estimation for machine translation. In *Proceedings of the 2009 Conference on Empirical Methods in Natural Language Processing*, pages 708–717.

Kishore Papineni, Salim Roukos, Todd Ward, and Wei-Jing Zhu. 2002. BLEU: a method for automatic evaluation of machine translation. In *Proceedings of the 40th Annual Meeting of the Association for Computational Linguistics*, pages 311–318.

Marina Santini. 2004. State-of-the-art on automatic genre identification. Technical Report ITRI-04-03, Information Technology Research Institute, University of Brighton.

Rico Sennrich. 2012. Perplexity minimization for translation model domain adaptation in statistical machine translation. In *Proceedings of the 13th Conference of the European Chapter of the Association for Computational Linguistics*, pages 539–549.

Benno Stein and Sven Meyer Zu Eissen. 2006. Distinguishing topic from genre. In *Proceedings of the 6th International Conference on Knowledge Management (I-KNOW 06)*, pages 449–456.

John M. Swales. 1990. *Genre Analysis*. Cambridge University Press., Cambridge, UK.

Marlies van der Wees, Arianna Bisazza, and Christof Monz. 2015. Five shades of noise: analyzing machine translation errors in user-generated text. In *Proceedings of the ACL 2015 Workshop on Noisy User-generated Text*.

Learning Cross-lingual Word Embeddings via Matrix Co-factorization

Tianze Shi **Zhiyuan Liu** **Yang Liu** **Maosong Sun**
State Key Laboratory of Intelligent Technology and Systems
Tsinghua National Laboratory for Information Science and Technology
Department of Computer Science and Technology
Tsinghua University, Beijing 100084, China
stz11@mails.tsinghua.edu.cn
{liuzy, liuyang2011, sms}@tsinghua.edu.cn

Abstract

A joint-space model for cross-lingual distributed representations generalizes language-invariant semantic features. In this paper, we present a matrix co-factorization framework for learning cross-lingual word embeddings. We explicitly define monolingual training objectives in the form of matrix decomposition, and induce cross-lingual constraints for simultaneously factorizing monolingual matrices. The cross-lingual constraints can be derived from parallel corpora, with or without word alignments. Empirical results on a task of cross-lingual document classification show that our method is effective to encode cross-lingual knowledge as constraints for cross-lingual word embeddings.

1 Introduction

Word embeddings allow one to represent words in a continuous vector space, which characterizes the lexico-semanic relations among words. In many NLP tasks, they prove to be high-quality features, successful applications of which include language modelling (Bengio et al., 2003), sentiment analysis (Socher et al., 2011) and word sense discrimination (Huang et al., 2012).

Like words having synonyms in the same language, there are also word pairs across languages which share resembling semantic properties. Mikolov et al. (2013a) observed a strong similarity of the geometric arrangements of corresponding concepts between the vector spaces of different languages, and suggested that a cross-lingual mapping between the two vector spaces is technically plausible. In the meantime, the joint-space models for cross-lingual word embeddings are very desirable, as language-invariant semantic features can be generalized to make it easy to transfer models across languages. This is especially important for those low-resource languages, where it allows one to develop accurate word representations of one language by exploiting the abundant textual resources in another language, e.g., English, which has a high resource density. The joint-space models are not only technically plausible, but also useful for cross-lingual model transfer. Further, studies have shown that using cross-lingual correlation can improve the quality of word representations trained solely with monolingual corpora (Faruqui and Dyer, 2014).

Defining a cross-lingual learning objective is crucial at the core of the joint-space model. Hermann and Blunsom (2014) and Chandar A P et al. (2014) tried to calculate parallel sentence (or document) representations and to minimize the differences between the semantically equivalent pairs. These methods are useful in capturing semantic information carried by high-level units (such as phrases and beyond) and usually do not rely on word alignments. However, they suffer from reduced accuracy for representing rare tokens, whose semantic information may not be well generalized. In these cases, finer-grained information at lexical level, such as aligned word pairs, dictionaries, and word translation probabilities, is considered to be helpful.

Kočiský et al. (2014) integrated word aligning process and word embedding in machine translation models. This method makes full use of parallel corpora and produces high-quality word alignments. However, it is unable to exploit the richer monolingual corpora. On the other hand, Zou et al. (2013) and Faruqui and Dyer (2014) learnt word embeddings of different languages in separate spaces with monolingual corpora and projected the embeddings into a joint space, but they can only capture linear transformation.

In this paper, we address the above challenges with a framework of matrix co-factorization. We

Proceedings of the 53rd Annual Meeting of the Association for Computational Linguistics and the 7th International Joint Conference on Natural Language Processing (Short Papers), pages 567–572,
Beijing, China, July 26-31, 2015.

simultaneously learn word embeddings in multiple languages via matrix factorization, with induced constraints to assure cross-lingual semantic relations. It provides the flexibility of constructing learning objectives from separate monolingual and cross-lingual corpora. Intricate relations across languages, rather than simple linear projections, are automatically captured. Additionally, our method is efficient as it learns from global statistics. The cross-lingual constraints can be derived both with or without word alignments, given that there is a valid measure of cross-lingual co-occurrences or similarities.

We test the performance in a task of cross-lingual document classification. Empirical results and a visualization of the joint semantic space demonstrate the validity of our model.

2 Framework

Without loss of generality, here we only consider bilingual embedding learning of the two languages l_1 and l_2. Given monolingual corpora D^{l_i} and sentence-aligned parallel data D^{bi}, our task is to find word embedding matrices of the size $|V^{l_i}| \times d$ where each line corresponds to the embedding of a single word. We also define vocabularies of contexts U^{l_i} and we learn context embedding matrices C^{l_i} of the size $|U^{l_i}| \times d$ at the same time. [1]

These matrices are obtained by simultaneous matrix factorization of the monolingual word-context PMI (point-wise mutual information) matrices M^{l_i}. During monolingual factorization, we put a cross-lingual constraint (cost) on it, ensuring cross-lingual semantic relations. We formalize the global loss function as

$$L_{\text{total}} = \sum_{i \in \{1,2\}} \omega_i \cdot L_{\text{mono}}(W^{l_i}, C^{l_i}) + \omega_c \cdot L_{\text{cross}}(W^{l_1}, C^{l_1}, W^{l_2}, C^{l_2}), \quad (1)$$

where L_{mono} and L_{cross} are the monolingual and cross-lingual objectives respectively. ω_i and ω_c weigh the contribution of the different parts to the total objective. An overview of our algorithm is illustrated in Figure 1.

3 Monolingual Objective

Our monolingual objective follows the GloVe model (Pennington et al., 2014), which learns from global word co-occurrence statistics. For a word-context pair (j, k) in language l_i, we try to

[1] In this paper, we let $U^{l_i} = V^{l_i}$.

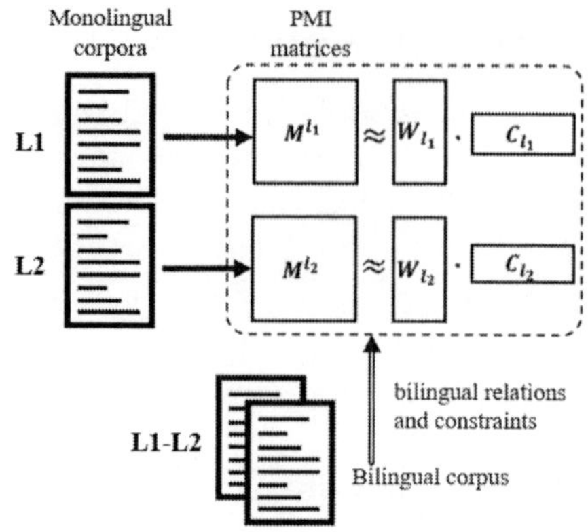

Figure 1: The framework of cross-lingual word embedding via matrix co-factorization.

minimize the difference between the dot product of the embeddings $w_j^{l_i} \cdot c_k^{l_i}$ and their PMI value $M_{jk}^{l_i}$. $M_{jk}^{l_i} = \frac{X_{jk}^{l_i} \cdot \sum_{j,k} X_{jk}^{l_i}}{\sum_j X_{jk}^{l_i} \cdot \sum_k X_{jk}^{l_i}}$, where X^{l_i} is the matrix of word-context co-occurrence counts. As Pennington et al. (2014), we add separate terms $b_{w_j}^{l_i}$, $b_{c_k}^{l_i}$ for each word and context to absorb the effect of any possible word-specific biases. We also add an additional matrix bias b^{l_i} for the ease of sharing embeddings among matrices. The loss function is written as the sum of the weighted square error,

$$L_{\text{mono}}^{l_i} = \sum_{j,k} f(X_{jk}^{l_i}) \left(w_j^{l_i} \cdot c_k^{l_i} + b_{w_j}^{l_i} + b_{c_k}^{l_i} + b^{l_i} - M_{jk}^{l_i} \right)^2, \quad (2)$$

where we choose the same weighting function as the GloVe model to place less confidence on those word-context pairs with rare occurrences,

$$f(x) = \begin{cases} (x/x_{\text{max}})^{\alpha} & \text{if } x < x_{\text{max}} \\ 1 & \text{otherwise} \end{cases}. \quad (3)$$

Notice that we only have to optimize those $X_{jk}^{l_i} \neq 0$, which can be solved efficiently since the matrix of co-occurrence counts is usually sparse.

4 Cross-lingual Objectives

As the most important part in our model, the cross-lingual objective describes the cross-lingual word relations and sets constraints when we factorize monolingual co-occurrence matrices. It can be derived from either cross-lingual co-occurrences or similarities between cross-lingual word pairs.

4.1 Cross-lingual Contexts

The monolingual objective stems from the distributional hypothesis (Harris, 1954) and optimizes words in similar contexts into similar embeddings. It is natural to further extend this idea to define cross-lingual contexts, for which we have multiple choices.

For the definition of cross-lingual contexts, we have multiple choices. A straightforward option is to count all the word co-occurrences in aligned sentence pairs, which is equivalent to a uniform word alignment model adopted by Gouws et al. (2015). For the sentence-aligned bilingual corpus $D^{\text{bi}} = \{(S^{l_1}, S^{l_2})\}$, where each S^{l_i} is a monolingual sentence, we count the co-occurrences as

$$X^{\text{bi}}_{jk} = \sum_{(S^{l_1}, S^{l_2}) \in D^{\text{bi}}} \#(j, S^{l_1}) \times \#(k, S^{l_2}), \quad (4)$$

where X^{bi} is the matrix of cross-lingual co-occurrence counts, and $\#(j, S)$ is a function counting the number of j's in the sequence S. We then use a similar loss function as Equation 2, with the exception that we optimize for the dot products of $w^{l_1}_j \cdot w^{l_2}_k$. This method works without word alignments and we denote it as CLC-WA (Cross-lingual context without word alignments).

We can also leverage word alignments and define CLC+WA (Cross-lingual context with word alignments). The idea is to count those words co-occurring with k as the context of j, where $k \in V^{l_2}$ is the translationally equivalent word of $j \in V^{l_1}$. An example is shown in Figure 2. CLC+WA is expected to contain more precise information than CLC-WA, and we will compare the two definitions in the following experiments.

Once we have counted the co-occurrences, a naïve solution is to concatenate the bilingual vocabularies and perform matrix factorization as a whole. To induce additional flexibility, such as separate weighting, we divide the matrix into three parts. It is also more reasonable to calculate PMI values without mixing the monolingual and bilingual corpora.

4.2 Cross-lingual Similarities

An alternative way to set cross-lingual constraints is to minimize the distances between similar word pairs. Here the semantic similarities can be measured by equivalence in translation, $\text{sim}(j, k)$, which is produced by a machine translation system. In this paper, we use the translation probabilities produced by a machine translation system. Minimizing the distances of related words in the two languages weighted by their similarities gives us the cross-lingual objective

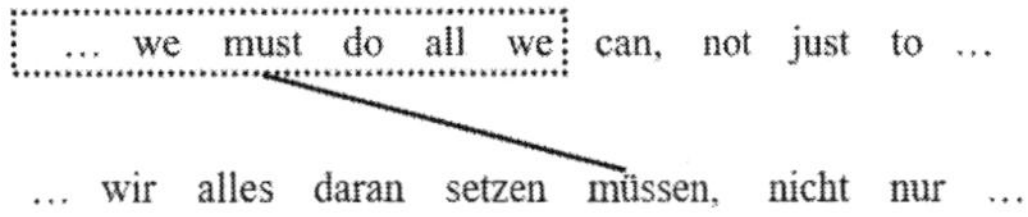

Figure 2: An example of CLC+WA, where we show the cross-lingual context of the German word "müssen" in the dashed box.

Table 1: Accuracy for cross-lingual classification.

Model	en→de	de→en
Machine translation	68.1	67.4
Majority class	46.8	46.8
Klementiev et al.	77.6	71.1
BiCVM	83.7	71.4
BAE	91.8	74.2
BilBOWA	86.5	75.0
CLC-WA	91.3	77.2
CLC+WA	90.0	75.0
CLSim	**92.7**	**80.2**

$$L_{\text{cross}} = \sum_{j \in V^{l_1}, k \in V^{l_2}} \text{sim}(j, k) \cdot \text{distance}(w^{l_1}_j, w^{l_2}_k), \quad (5)$$

where $w^{l_1}_j$ and $w^{l_2}_k$ are the embeddings of j and k in l_1 and l_2 respectively. In this paper, we choose the distance function to be the Euclidean distance, $\text{distance}(w^{l_1}_j, w^{l_2}_k) = ||w^{l_1}_j - w^{l_2}_k||^2$. Notice that similar to the monolingual objective, we may optimize for only those $\text{sim}(j, k) \neq 0$, which is efficient as the matrix of translation probabilities or dictionary is sparse. We call this method CLSim.

5 Experiments

To evaluate the quality of the relatedness between words in different languages, we induce the task of cross-lingual document classification for the English-German language pair, where a classifier is trained in one language and later used to classify documents in another. We exactly replicated the experiment settings of Klementiev et al. (2012).

5.1 Data and Training

For optimizing the monolingual objectives, We used exactly the same subset of RCV1/RCV2 corpora (Lewis et al., 2004) as by Klementiev et al. (2012), which were sampled to balance the number of tokens between languages. Our preprocessing strategy followed Chandar A P et al. (2014), where we lowercased all words, removed punctuations and used the same vocabularies ($|V^{\text{en}}| = 43{,}614$ and $|V^{\text{de}}| = 50{,}110$). When counting

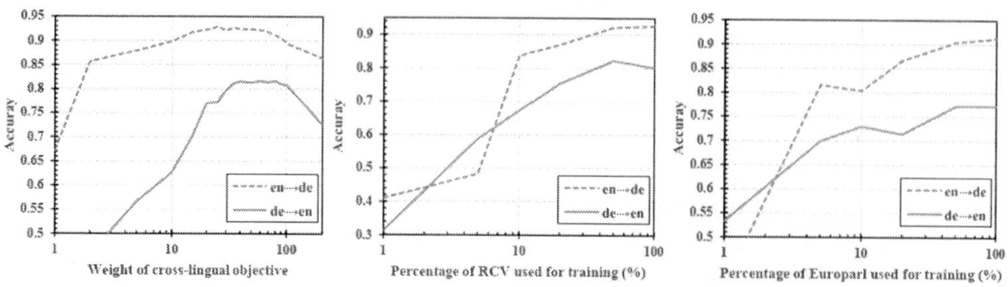

(a) (b) (c)

Figure 3: Cross-lingual document classification accuracy, with (a) varying weighting of cross-lingual objective (b) varying size of training monolingual corpora, and (c) varying size of training bilingual corpus.

word co-occurrences, we use a decreasing weighting function as Pennington et al. (2014), where d-word-apart word pairs contribute $1/d$ to the total count. We used a symmetric window size of 10 words for all our experiments.

The cross-lingual constraints were derived using the English and German sections of the Europarl v7 parallel corpus (Koehn, 2005), which were similarly preprocessed. For CLC+WA and CLSim, we obtained word alignments and translation probabilities with SyMGIZA++ (Junczys-Dowmunt and Szał, 2012). We did not use Europarl for monolingual training.

The documents for classification were randomly selected by Klementiev et al. (2012) from those in RCV1/RCV2 that are assigned to only one single topic among the four: `CCAT` (Corporate/Industrial), `ECAT` (Economics), `GCAT` (Government/Social), and `MCAT` (Markets). 1,000/5,000 documents in each language were used as a train/test set and we kept another 1,000 documents as a development set for hyperparameter tuning. Each document was represented as an idf-weighted average embedding of all its tokens, and a multi-class document classifier was trained for 10 epochs with an averaged perceptron algorithm as by Klementiev et al. (2012). A classifier trained with English documents is used to classify German documents and vice versa.

We trained our models using stochastic gradient descent. We run 50 iterations for all of our experiments and the dimensionality of the embeddings is 40. We set $x_{\max}$ to be 100 for cross-lingual co-occurrences and 30 for monolingual ones, while α is fixed to $3/4$. Other parameters are chosen according to the performance on the development set.

5.2 Results

We present the empirical results on the task of cross-lingual document classification in Table 1, where the performance of our models is compared with some baselines and previous work. The effect of weighting between parts of the total objective and the amount of training data on the quality of the embeddings is demonstrated in Figure 3.

The baseline systems are *Majority class* where test documents are simply classified as the class with the most training samples, and *Machine translation* where a phrased-based machine translation system is used to translate test documents into the same language as the training documents.

We also summarize the classification accuracy reported in some previous work, including Multi-task learning (Klementiev et al., 2012), Bilingual compositional vector model (BiCVM) (Hermann and Blunsom, 2014), Bilingual autoencoder for bags-of-words (BAE) (Chandar A P et al., 2014), and BilBOWA (Gouws et al., 2015). A more recent work of Soyer et al. (2015) developed a compositional approach and reported an accuracy of 90.8% (en→de) and 80.1% (de→en) when using full RCV and Europarl corpora.

Our method outperforms the previous work and we observe improvements when we exploit word translation probabilities (CLSim) over the model without word-level information (CLC-WA). The best result is achieved with CLSim. It is interesting to notice that CLC+WA, which makes use of word alignments in defining cross-lingual contexts, does not provide better performance than CLC-WA. We guess that sentence-level co-occurrence is more suitable for capturing sentence-level semantic relations in the task of document classification.

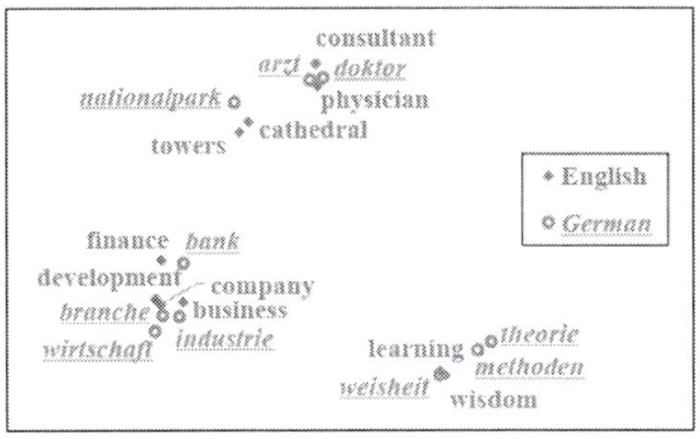

Figure 4: A visualization of the joint vector space.

5.3 Visualization

Figure 4 gives a visualization of some selected words using t-SNE (Van der Maaten and Hinton, 2008) where we observe the topical nature of word embeddings. Regardless of their source languages, words sharing a common topic, e.g. economy, are closely aligned with each other, revealing the semantic validity of the joint vector space.

6 Related Work

Matrix factorization has been successfully applied to learn word representations, which use several low-rank matrices to approximate the original matrix with extracted statistical information, usually word co-occurrence counts or PMI. Singular value decomposition (SVD) (Eckart and Young, 1936), SVD-based latent semantic analysis (LSA) (Landauer et al., 1998), latent semantic indexing (LSI) (Deerwester et al., 1990), and the more recently-proposed global vectors for word representation (GloVe) (Pennington et al., 2014) find their wide applications in the area of NLP and information retrieval (Berry et al., 1995). Additionally, there is evidence that some neural-network-based models, such as Skip-gram (Mikolov et al., 2013b) which exhibits state-of-the-art performance, are also implicitly factorizing a PMI-based matrix (Levy and Goldberg, 2014). The strategy for matrix factorization in this paper, as Pennington et al. (2014), is in a stochastic fashion, which better handles unobserved data and allows one to weigh samples according to their importance and confidence.

Joint matrix factorization allows one to decompose matrices with some correlational constraints. Collective matrix factorization has been developed to handle pairwise relations (Singh and Gordon, 2008). Chang et al. (2013) generalized LSA to Multi-Relational LSA, which constructs a 3-way tensor to combine the multiple relations between words. While matrix factorization is widely used in recommender systems, matrix co-factorization helps to handle multiple aspects of the data and improves in predicting individual decisions (Hong et al., 2013). Multiple sources of information, such as content and linkage, can also be connected with matrix co-factorization to derive high-quality webpage representations (Zhu et al., 2007). The advantage of this approach is that it automatically finds optimal parameters to optimize both single matrix factorization and relational alignments, which avoids manually defining a projection matrix or transfer function. To the best of our knowledge, we are the first to introduce this technique to learn cross-lingual word embeddings.

7 Conclusions

In this paper, we introduced a framework of matrix co-factorization to learn cross-lingual word embeddings. It is capable of capturing the lexico-semantic similarities of different languages in a unified vector space, where the embeddings are jointly learnt instead of projected from separate vector spaces. The overall objective is divided into monolingual parts and a cross-lingual one, which enables one to use different weighting and learning strategies, and to develop models either with or without word alignments. Exploiting global context and similarity information instead of local ones, our proposed models are computationally efficient and effective.

With matrix co-factorization, it allows one to integrate external information, such as syntactic contexts and morphology, which is not discussed in this paper. Its application in statistical machine translation and cross-lingual model transfer remains to be explored. Learning multiple embeddings per word and compositional embeddings with matrix factorization are also interesting future directions.

Acknowledgments

This research is supported by the 973 Program (No. 2014CB340501) and the National Natural Science Foundation of China (NSFC No. 61133012, 61170196 & 61202140). We thank the anonymous reviewers for the valuable comments. We also thank Ivan Titov and Alexandre Klementiev for kindly offering their evaluation package, which allowed us to replicate their experiment settings exactly.

References

Yoshua Bengio, Réjean Ducharme, Pascal Vincent, and Christian Janvin. 2003. A neural probabilistic language model. *JMLR*, 3:1137–1155.

Michael W Berry, Susan T Dumais, and Gavin W O'Brien. 1995. Using linear algebra for intelligent information retrieval. *SIAM review*, 37(4):573–595.

Sarath Chandar A P, Stanislas Lauly, Hugo Larochelle, Mitesh Khapra, Balaraman Ravindran, Vikas C Raykar, and Amrita Saha. 2014. An autoencoder approach to learning bilingual word representations. In *Proceedings of NIPS*, pages 1853–1861.

Kai-Wei Chang, Wen-tau Yih, and Christopher Meek. 2013. Multi-relational latent semantic analysis. In *Proceedings of EMNLP*, pages 1602–1612.

Scott C. Deerwester, Susan T Dumais, Thomas K. Landauer, George W. Furnas, and Richard A. Harshman. 1990. Indexing by latent semantic analysis. *JAsIs*, 41(6):391–407.

Carl Eckart and Gale Young. 1936. The approximation of one matrix by another of lower rank. *Psychometrika*, 1(3):211–218.

Manaal Faruqui and Chris Dyer. 2014. Improving vector space word representations using multilingual correlation. In *Proceedings of EACL*, pages 462–471.

Stephan Gouws, Yoshua Bengio, and Greg Corrado. 2015. Bilbowa: Fast bilingual distributed representations without word alignments. In *ICML*, pages 748–756.

Zellig S Harris. 1954. Distributional structure. *Word*, 10(23):146–162.

Karl Moritz Hermann and Phil Blunsom. 2014. Multilingual models for compositional distributed semantics. In *Proceedings of ACL*, pages 58–68. ACL.

Liangjie Hong, Aziz S Doumith, and Brian D Davison. 2013. Co-factorization machines: modeling user interests and predicting individual decisions in twitter. In *Proceedings of WSDM*, pages 557–566. ACM.

Eric H Huang, Richard Socher, Christopher D Manning, and Andrew Y Ng. 2012. Improving word representations via global context and multiple word prototypes. In *Proceedings of ACL*, pages 873–882. ACL.

Marcin Junczys-Dowmunt and Arkadiusz Szał. 2012. Symgiza++: symmetrized word alignment models for statistical machine translation. In *Security and Intelligent Information Systems*, pages 379–390. Springer.

Alexandre Klementiev, Ivan Titov, and Binod Bhattarai. 2012. Inducing crosslingual distributed representations of words. In *Proceedings of COLING*. ICCL.

Tomáš Kočiský, Karl Moritz Hermann, and Phil Blunsom. 2014. Learning bilingual word representations by marginalizing alignments. In *Proceedings of ACL*, pages 224–229. ACL.

Philipp Koehn. 2005. Europarl: A parallel corpus for statistical machine translation. In *MT summit*, volume 5, pages 79–86.

Thomas K Landauer, Peter W Foltz, and Darrell Laham. 1998. An introduction to latent semantic analysis. *Discourse processes*, 25(2-3):259–284.

Omer Levy and Yoav Goldberg. 2014. Neural word embedding as implicit matrix factorization. In *Proceedings of NIPS*, pages 2177–2185.

David D Lewis, Yiming Yang, Tony G Rose, and Fan Li. 2004. Rcv1: A new benchmark collection for text categorization research. *JMLR*, 5:361–397.

Tomas Mikolov, Quoc V Le, and Ilya Sutskever. 2013a. Exploiting similarities among languages for machine translation. *arXiv:1309.4168*.

Tomas Mikolov, Ilya Sutskever, Kai Chen, Greg S Corrado, and Jeff Dean. 2013b. Distributed representations of words and phrases and their compositionality. In *Proceedings of NIPS*, pages 3111–3119.

Jeffrey Pennington, Richard Socher, and Christopher D Manning. 2014. Glove: Global vectors for word representation. pages 1532–1543.

Ajit P Singh and Geoffrey J Gordon. 2008. Relational learning via collective matrix factorization. In *Proceedings of SIGKDD*, pages 650–658. ACM.

Richard Socher, Jeffrey Pennington, Eric H Huang, Andrew Y Ng, and Christopher D Manning. 2011. Semi-supervised recursive autoencoders for predicting sentiment distributions. In *Proceedings of EMNLP*, pages 151–161. ACL.

Hubert Soyer, Pontus Stenetorp, and Akiko Aizawa. 2015. Leveraging monolingual data for crosslingual compositional word representations. In *Proceedings of ICLR*.

Laurens Van der Maaten and Geoffrey Hinton. 2008. Visualizing data using t-sne. *JMLR*, 9:2579–2605.

Shenghuo Zhu, Kai Yu, Yun Chi, and Yihong Gong. 2007. Combining content and link for classification using matrix factorization. In *Proceedings of SIGIR*, pages 487–494. ACM.

Will Y Zou, Richard Socher, Daniel M Cer, and Christopher D Manning. 2013. Bilingual word embeddings for phrase-based machine translation. In *Proceedings of EMNLP*, pages 1393–1398.

Improving Pivot Translation by Remembering the Pivot

Akiva Miura, Graham Neubig, Sakriani Sakti, Tomoki Toda, Satoshi Nakamura
Graduate School of Information Science
Nara Institute of Science and Technology
8916-5 Takayama-cho, Ikoma-shi, Nara, Japan
{miura.akiba.lr9, neubig, ssakti, tomoki, s-nakamura}@is.naist.jp

Abstract

Pivot translation allows for translation of language pairs with little or no parallel data by introducing a third language for which data exists. In particular, the triangulation method, which translates by combining source-pivot and pivot-target translation models into a source-target model, is known for its high translation accuracy. However, in the conventional triangulation method, information of pivot phrases is forgotten and not used in the translation process. In this paper, we propose a novel approach to *remember* the pivot phrases in the triangulation stage, and use a pivot language model as an additional information source at translation time. Experimental results on the Europarl corpus showed gains of 0.4-1.2 BLEU points in all tested combinations of languages[1].

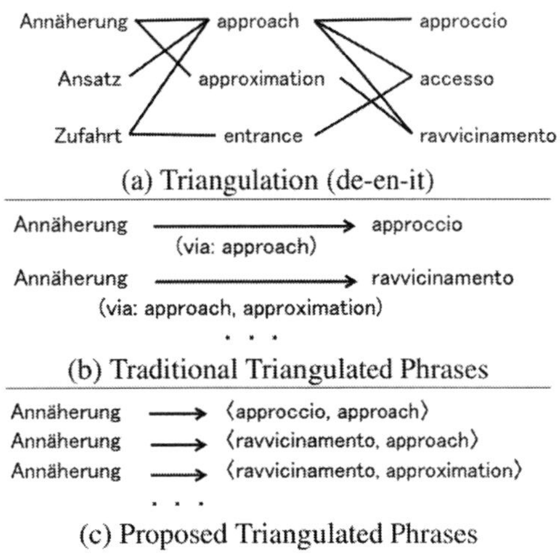

Figure 1: An example of (a) triangulation and the resulting phrases in the (b) traditional method of forgetting pivots and (c) our proposed method of remembering pivots.

1 Introduction

In statistical machine translation (SMT) (Brown et al., 1993), it is known that translation with models trained on larger parallel corpora can achieve greater accuracy (Dyer et al., 2008). Unfortunately, large bilingual corpora are not readily available for many language pairs, particularly those that don't include English. One effective solution to overcome the scarceness of bilingual data is to introduce a pivot language for which parallel data with the source and target languages exists (de Gispert and Mariño, 2006).

Among various methods using pivot languages, the triangulation method (Cohn and Lapata, 2007; Utiyama and Isahara, 2007; Zhu et al., 2014), which translates by combining source-pivot and pivot-target translation models into a source-target model, has been shown to be one of the most effective approaches. However, word sense ambiguity and interlingual differences of word usage cause difficulty in accurately learning correspondences between source and target phrases.

Figure 1 (a) shows an example of three words in German and Italian that each correspond to the English polysemic word "approach." In such a case, finding associated source-target phrase pairs and estimating translation probabilities properly becomes a complicated problem. Furthermore, in the conventional triangulation method, information about pivot phrases that behave as bridges between source and target phrases is lost after learning phrase pairs, as shown in Figure 1 (b).

To overcome these problems, we propose a novel triangulation method that *remembers* the pivot phrase connecting source and target in the records of phrase/rule table, and estimates a joint translation probability from the source to target

[1]Code to replicate the experiments can be found at https://github.com/akivajp/acl2015

Proceedings of the 53rd Annual Meeting of the Association for Computational Linguistics and the 7th International Joint Conference on Natural Language Processing (Short Papers), pages 573–577,
Beijing, China, July 26-31, 2015.

and pivot simultaneously. We show an example in Figure 1 (c). The advantage of this approach is that generally we can obtain rich monolingual resources in pivot languages such as English, and SMT can utilize this additional information to improve the translation quality.

To utilize information about the pivot language at translation time, we train a Multi-Synchronous Context-free Grammar (MSCFG) (Neubig et al., 2015), a generalized extension of synchronous CFGs (SCFGs) (Chiang, 2007), that can generate strings in multiple languages at the same time. To create the MSCFG, we triangulate source-pivot and pivot-target SCFG rule tables not into a single source-target SCFG, but into a source-target-pivot MSCFG rule table that remembers the pivot. During decoding, we use language models over both the target and the pivot to assess the naturalness of the derivation. We perform experiments on pivot translation of Europarl proceedings, which show that our method indeed provide significant gains in accuracy (of up to 1.2 BLEU points), in all combinations of 4 languages with English as a pivot language.

2 Translation Formalisms

2.1 Synchronous Context-free Grammars

First, we cover SCFGs, which are widely used in machine translation, particularly hierarchical phrase-based translation (Hiero; Chiang (2007)).

In SCFGs, the elementary structures are rewrite rules with aligned pairs of right-hand sides:

$$X \rightarrow \langle \overline{s}, \overline{t} \rangle \quad (1)$$

where X is the head of the rewrite rule, and $\overline{s}$ and $\overline{t}$ are both strings of terminals and non-terminals in the source and target side respectively. Each string in the right side tuple has the same number of indexed non-terminals, and identically indexed non-terminals correspond to each-other. For example, a synchronous rule could take the form of:

$$X \rightarrow \langle X_0 \text{ of the } X_1,\ X_1 \text{ 的 } X_0 \rangle . \quad (2)$$

In the SCFG training method proposed by Chiang (2007), SCFG rules are extracted based on parallel sentences and automatically obtained word alignments. Each extracted rule is scored with phrase translation probabilities in both directions $\phi(\overline{s}|\overline{t})$ and $\phi(\overline{t}|\overline{s})$, lexical translation probabilities in both directions $\phi_{lex}(\overline{s}|\overline{t})$ and $\phi_{lex}(\overline{t}|\overline{s})$, a word penalty counting the terminals in $\overline{t}$, and a constant phrase penalty of 1.

At translation time, the decoder searches for the target sentence that maximizes the derivation probability, which is defined as the sum of the scores of the rules used in the derivation, and the log of the language model probability over the target strings. When not considering an LM, it is possible to efficiently find the best translation for an input sentence using the CKY+ algorithm (Chappelier et al., 1998). When using an LM, the expanded search space is further reduced based on a limit on expanded edges, or total states per span, through a procedure such as cube pruning (Chiang, 2007).

2.2 Multi-Synchronous CFGs

MSCFGs (Neubig et al., 2015) are a generalization of SCFGs that are be able to generate sentences in multiple target languages simultaneously. The single target side string $\overline{t}$ in the SCFG production rule is extended to have strings for N target languages:

$$X \rightarrow \langle \overline{s}, \overline{t_1}, ..., \overline{t_N} \rangle . \quad (3)$$

Performing multi-target translation with MSCFGs is quite similar to translating using standard SCFGs, with the exception of the expanded state space caused by having one LM for each target. Neubig et al. (2015) propose a *sequential* search method, that ensures diversity in the primary target search space by first expanding with only primary target LM, then additionally expands the states for other LMs, a strategy we also adopt in this work.

In the standard training method for MSCFGs, the multi-target rewrite rules are extracted from multilingual line-aligned corpora by applying an extended version of the standard SCFG rule extraction method, and scored with features that consider the multiple targets. It should be noted that this training method requires a large amount of line-aligned training data including the source and all target languages. This assumption breaks down when we have little parallel data, and thereby we propose a method to generate MSCFG rules by triangulating 2 SCFG rule tables in the following section.

3 Pivot Translation Methods

Several methods have been proposed for SMT using pivot languages. These include *cascade* methods that consecutively translate from source to pivot then pivot to target (de Gispert and Mariño, 2006), *synthetic data* methods that machine-translate the training data to generate a pseudo-parallel corpus (de Gispert and Mariño, 2006), and *triangulation* methods that obtain a source-target phrase/rule table by merging source-pivot and pivot-target table entries with identical pivot language phrases (Cohn and Lapata, 2007). In particular, the triangulation method is notable for producing higher quality translation results than other pivot methods (Utiyama and Isahara, 2007), so we use it as a base for our work.

3.1 Traditional Triangulation Method

In the triangulation method by Cohn and Lapata (2007), we first train source-pivot and pivot-target rule tables, then create rules:

$$X \rightarrow \langle \overline{s},\ \overline{t} \rangle \tag{4}$$

if there exists a pivot phrase $\overline{p}$ such that the pair $\langle \overline{s}, \overline{p} \rangle$ is in source-pivot table T_{SP} and the pair $\langle \overline{p}, \overline{t} \rangle$ is in pivot-target table T_{PT}. Source-target table T_{ST} is created by calculation of the translation probabilities using phrase translation probabilities $\phi(\cdot)$ and lexical translation probabilities $\phi_{lex}(\cdot)$ for all connected phrases according to the following equations (Cohn and Lapata, 2007):

$$\phi\left(\overline{t}|\overline{s}\right) = \sum_{\overline{p} \in T_{SP} \cap T_{PT}} \phi\left(\overline{t}|\overline{p}\right) \phi\left(\overline{p}|\overline{s}\right), \tag{5}$$

$$\phi\left(\overline{s}|\overline{t}\right) = \sum_{\overline{p} \in T_{SP} \cap T_{PT}} \phi\left(\overline{s}|\overline{p}\right) \phi\left(\overline{p}|\overline{t}\right), \tag{6}$$

$$\phi_{lex}\left(\overline{t}|\overline{s}\right) = \sum_{\overline{p} \in T_{SP} \cap T_{PT}} \phi_{lex}\left(\overline{t}|\overline{p}\right) \phi_{lex}\left(\overline{p}|\overline{s}\right), \tag{7}$$

$$\phi_{lex}\left(\overline{s}|\overline{t}\right) = \sum_{\overline{p} \in T_{SP} \cap T_{PT}} \phi_{lex}\left(\overline{s}|\overline{p}\right) \phi_{lex}\left(\overline{p}|\overline{t}\right). \tag{8}$$

The equations (5)-(8) are based on the memoryless channel model, which assumes $\phi\left(\overline{t}|\overline{p}, \overline{s}\right) = \phi\left(\overline{t}|\overline{p}\right)$ and $\phi\left(\overline{s}|\overline{p}, \overline{t}\right) = \phi\left(\overline{s}|\overline{p}\right)$. Unfortunately, these equations are not accurate due to polysemy and disconnects in the grammar of the languages. As a result, pivot translation is significantly more ambiguous than standard translation.

3.2 Proposed Triangulation Method

To help reduce this ambiguity, our proposed triangulation method remembers the corresponding pivot phrase as additional information to be utilized for disambiguation. Specifically, instead of marginalizing over the pivot phrase $\overline{p}$, we create an MSCFG rule for the tuple of the connected source-target-pivot phrases such as:

$$X \rightarrow \langle \overline{s},\ \overline{t},\ \overline{p} \rangle. \tag{9}$$

The advantage of translation with these rules is that they allow for incorporation of additional features over the pivot sentence such as a strong pivot LM.

In addition to the equations (5)-(8), we also estimate translation probabilities $\phi(\overline{t}, \overline{p}|\overline{s})$, $\phi(\overline{s}|\overline{p}, \overline{t})$ that consider both target and pivot phrases at the same time according to:

$$\phi\left(\overline{t}, \overline{p}|\overline{s}\right) = \phi\left(\overline{t}|\overline{p}\right) \phi\left(\overline{p}|\overline{s}\right), \tag{10}$$

$$\phi\left(\overline{s}|\overline{p}, \overline{t}\right) = \phi\left(\overline{s}|\overline{p}\right). \tag{11}$$

Translation probabilities between source and pivot phrases $\phi(\overline{p}|\overline{s})$, $\phi(\overline{s}|\overline{p})$, $\phi_{lex}(\overline{p}|\overline{s})$, $\phi_{lex}(\overline{s}|\overline{p})$ can also be used directly from the source-pivot rule table. This results in 13 features for each MSCFG rule: 10 translation probabilities, 2 word penalties counting the terminals in $\overline{t}$ and $\overline{p}$, and a constant phrase penalty of 1.

It should be noted that remembering the pivot results in significantly larger rule tables. To save computational resources, several pruning methods are conceivable. Neubig et al. (2015) show that an effective pruning method in the case of a main target T_1 with the help of target T_2 is the T_1-pruning method, namely, using L candidates of $\overline{t_1}$ with the highest translation probability $\phi(\overline{t_1}|\overline{s})$ and selecting $\overline{t_2}$ with highest $\phi(\overline{t_1}, \overline{t_2}|\overline{s})$ for each $\overline{t_1}$. We follow this approach, using the L best $\overline{t}$, and the corresponding 1 best $\overline{p}$.

4 Experiments

4.1 Experimental Setup

We evaluate the proposed triangulation method through pivot translation experiments on the Europarl corpus, which is a multilingual corpus including 21 European languages (Koehn, 2005) widely used in pivot translation work. In our work, we perform translation among German (de), Spanish (es), French (fr) and Italian (it), with English (en) as the pivot language. To prepare the data for these 5 languages, we first use the Gale-Church alignment algorithm (Gale and Church, 1993) to retrieve a multilingual line-aligned corpus of about 900k sentences, then hold out 1,500 sentences each for tuning and test. In our basic

Source	Target	BLEU Score [%]					
		Direct	Cascade	Tri. SCFG (baseline)	Tri. MSCFG -PivotLM	Tri. MSCFG +PivotLM 100k	Tri. MSCFG +PivotLM 2M
de	es	27.10	25.05	25.31	25.38	25.52	† **25.75**
	fr	25.65	23.86	24.12	24.16	24.25	† **24.58**
	it	23.04	20.76	21.27	21.42	† 21.65	‡ **22.29**
es	de	20.11	18.52	18.77	18.97	19.08	† **19.40**
	fr	33.48	27.00	29.54	† 29.87	† 29.91	† **29.95**
	it	27.82	22.57	25.11	25.01	25.18	‡ **25.64**
fr	de	19.69	18.01	18.73	18.77	18.87	† **19.19**
	es	34.36	27.26	30.31	30.53	† 30.73	‡ **31.00**
	it	28.48	22.73	25.31	25.50	† 25.72	‡ **26.22**
it	de	19.09	14.03	17.35	† 17.99	‡ 18.17	‡ **18.52**
	es	31.99	25.64	28.85	28.83	29.01	† **29.31**
	fr	31.39	25.87	28.48	28.40	28.63	† **29.02**

Table 1: Results for each method. Bold indicates the highest BLEU score in pivot translation, and daggers indicate statistically significant gains over Tri. SCFG ($\dagger : p < 0.05, \ddagger : p < 0.01$)

training setup, we use 100k sentences for training both the TMs and the target LMs. We assume that in many situations, a large amount of English monolingual data is readily available and therefore, we train pivot LMs with different data sizes up to 2M sentences.

As a decoder, we use Travatar (Neubig, 2013), and train SCFG TMs with its Hiero extraction code. Translation results are evaluated by BLEU (Papineni et al., 2002) and we tuned to maximize BLEU scores using MERT (Och, 2003). For trained and triangulated TMs, we use T_1 rule pruning with a limit of 20 rules per source rule. For decoding using MSCFG, we adopt the sequential search method.

We evaluate 6 translation methods:

Direct: Translating with a direct SCFG trained on the source-target parallel corpus (not using a pivot language) for comparison.

Cascade: Cascading source-pivot and pivot-target translation systems.

Tri. SCFG: Triangulating source-pivot and pivot-target SCFG TMs into a source-target SCFG TM using the traditional method.

Tri. MSCFG: Triangulating source-pivot and pivot-target SCFG TMs into a source-target-pivot MSCFG TM in our approach. -PivotLM indicates translating without a pivot LM and +PivotLM 100k/2M indicates a pivot LM trained using 100k/2M sentences respectively.

4.2 Experimental Results

The result of experiments using all combinations of pivot translation tasks for 4 languages via English is shown in Table 1. From the results, we can see that the proposed triangulation method considering pivot LMs outperforms the traditional triangulation method for all language pairs, and translation with larger pivot LMs improves the BLEU scores. For all languages, the pivot-remembering triangulation method with the pivot LM trained with 2M sentences achieves the highest score of the pivot translation methods, with gains of 0.4-1.2 BLEU points from the baseline method. This shows that remembering the pivot and using it to disambiguate results is consistently effective in improving translation accuracy.

We can also see that the MSCFG triangulated model without using the pivot LM slightly outperforms the standard SCFG triangulation method for the majority of language pairs. It is conceivable that the additional scores of translation probabilities with pivot phrases are effective features that allow for more accurate rule selection.

Finally, we show an example of a translated sentence for which pivot-side ambiguity is resolved in the proposed triangulation method:

Input (German): ich bedaure , daß es keine gemeinsame annäherung gegeben hat .

Reference (Italian): sono spiacente del mancato approccio comune .

Tri. SCFG: mi rammarico per il fatto che non si ravvicinamento comune . (BLEU+1: 13.84)

Tri. MSCFG+PivotLM 2M:

mi dispiace che non esiste un approccio comune . (BLEU+1: 25.10)
i regret that there is no common approach . (Generated English Sentence)

The derivation uses an MSCFG rule connecting "approccio" to "approach" in the pivot, and we can consider that appropriate selection of English words according to the context contributes to selecting relevant vocabulary in Italian.

5 Conclusion

In this paper, we have proposed a method for pivot translation using triangulation of SCFG rule tables into an MSCFG rule table that remembers the pivot, and performing translation with pivot LMs. In experiments, we found that these models are effective in the case when a strong pivot LM exists. In the future, we plan to explore more refined methods to devising effective intermediate expressions, and improve estimation of probabilities for triangulated rules.

Acknowledgements

The authors thank anonymous reviewers for helpful suggestions. This work was supported in part by the Microsoft CORE project.

References

Peter F. Brown, Vincent J.Della Pietra, Stephen A. Della Pietra, and Robert L. Mercer. 1993. The Mathematics of Statistical Machine Translation: Parameter Estimation. *Computational Linguistics*, 19:263–312.

Jean-Cédric Chappelier, Martin Rajman, et al. 1998. A Generalized CYK Algorithm for Parsing Stochastic CFG. *TAPD*, 98(133-137):5.

David Chiang. 2007. Hierarchical phrase-based translation. *Computational Linguistics*, 33(2):201–228.

Trevor Cohn and Mirella Lapata. 2007. Machine Translation by Triangulation: Making Effective Use of Multi-Parallel Corpora. In *Proc. ACL*, pages 728–735, June.

Adrià de Gispert and José B. Mariño. 2006. Catalan-English Statistical Machine Translation without Parallel Corpus: Bridging through Spanish. In *Proc. of LREC 5th Workshop on Strategies for developing machine translation for minority languages*.

Christopher Dyer, Aaron Cordova, Alex Mont, and Jimmy Lin. 2008. Fast, easy, and cheap: construction of statistical machine translation models with MapReduce. In *Proc. WMT*, pages 199–207.

William A Gale and Kenneth W Church. 1993. A program for aligning sentences in bilingual corpora. *Computational linguistics*, 19(1):75–102.

Philipp Koehn. 2005. Europarl: A parallel corpus for statistical machine translation. In *MT summit*, volume 5, pages 79–86.

Graham Neubig, Philip Arthur, and Kevin Duh. 2015. Multi-Target Machine Translation with Multi-Synchronous Context-free Grammars. In *Proc. NAACL*.

Graham Neubig. 2013. Travatar: A Forest-to-String Machine Translation Engine based on Tree Transducers. In *Proc. ACL Demo Track*, pages 91–96.

Franz Josef Och. 2003. Minimum Error Rate Training in Statistical Machine Translation. In *Proc. ACL*, pages 160–167.

Kishore Papineni, Salim Roukos, Todd Ward, and Wei-Jing Zhu. 2002. BLEU: a method for automatic evaluation of machine translation. In *Proc. ACL*, pages 311–318.

Masao Utiyama and Hitoshi Isahara. 2007. A Comparison of Pivot Methods for Phrase-Based Statistical Machine Translation. In *Proc. NAACL*, pages 484–491.

Xiaoning Zhu, Zhongjun He, Hua Wu, Conghui Zhu, Haifeng Wang, and Tiejun Zhao. 2014. Improving Pivot-Based Statistical Machine Translation by Pivoting the Co-occurrence Count of Phrase Pairs. In *Proc. EMNLP*.

BrailleSUM: A News Summarization System for the Blind and Visually Impaired People

Xiaojun Wan and Yue Hu
Institute of Computer Science and Technology, The MOE Key Laboratory of Computational Linguistics, Peking University, Beijing 100871, China
{wanxiaojun, ayue.hu}@pku.edu.cn

Abstract

In this article, we discuss the challenges of document summarization for the blind and visually impaired people and then propose a new system called BrailleSUM to produce better summaries for the blind and visually impaired people. Our system considers the factor of braille length of each sentence in news articles into the ILP-based summarization method. Evaluation results on a DUC dataset show that BrailleSUM can produce shorter braille summaries than existing methods, meanwhile, it does not sacrifice the content quality of the summaries.

1 Introduction

People with normal vision can read news documents with their eyes conveniently. However, according to WHO's statistics, up to October 2013, 285 million people are estimated to be visually impaired worldwide: 39 million are blind and 246 have low vision. Unfortunately, the large number of blind and visually impaired people cannot directly or conveniently read ordinary news documents like sighted people, and they have to read braille with their fingerprints or special equipments, which brings much more burden to them. Braille is a special system with a set of symbols composed of small rectangular braille cells that contain tiny palpable bumps called raised dots used by the blind and visually impaired. It is traditionally written with embossed paper. Special equipments such as refreshable braille displays and braille embosser have been developed for the blind and visually impaired people to read or print on computers and other electronic supports.

Though some news materials have already been prepared in braille format for the blind people's reading and learning, most daily news documents are written for sighted people, and it is necessary to first translate the news documents into Braille, and then the blind people can read the news with their fingertips. Speech synthesizers are also commonly used for the task (Freitas and Kouroupetroglou, 2008), but the way of reading braille texts is still popular in the daily life of the blind people, especially for the deaf-blind people.

As we know, document summarization is a very useful means for people to quickly read and browse news articles in the big data era. Existing summarization systems focus on content quality and fluency of summaries, and they usually extract several informative and diversified sentences to form a summary with a given length. The summaries are produced for sighted people, but not for the blind and visually impaired people. A text summary can be translated into a braille summary for the blind and visually impaired people's reading, and the length of a braille summary is defined as the number of the braille cells in the summary. It is noteworthy that the shorter the braille summary is, the less burden the blind people have when reading the summary with their fingertips. The burden lies in the fact that reading a braille text by touching each braille cell with fingertips is more difficult and inconvenient than reading a normal text with eyes. So a braille summary is required to be as short as possible, while keeping the content quality and fluency.

In this study, we investigate the task of document summarization for the blind and visually impaired people for the first time. We discuss the major challenges of document summarization for the blind and visually impaired people and then propose a new system called BrailleSUM to produce better summaries for them. Our system considers the factor of braille length of each sentence in news articles into the ILP-based summarization method. Evaluation results on a DUC dataset show that BrailleSUM can produce much shorter braille summaries than existing methods, meanwhile, it does not sacrifice the content quality of the summaries.

2 Related Work

Most previous summarization methods are extraction-based, which directly rank and extract exist-

Proceedings of the 53rd Annual Meeting of the Association for Computational Linguistics and the 7th International Joint Conference on Natural Language Processing (Short Papers), pages 578–582,
Beijing, China, July 26-31, 2015. ©2015 Association for Computational Linguistics

ing sentences in a document set to form a summary. Typical methods include the centroid-based method (Radev et al., 2004), NeATS (Lin and Hovy, 2002), supervised learning based methods (Ouyang et al., 2007; Shen et al., 2007; Schilder and Kondadadi, 2008; Wong et al., 2008), graph-based ranking (Erkan and Radev, 2004; Mihalcea and Tarau, 2005), Integer Linear Programming (Gillick et al., 2008; Gillick and Favre, 2009; Li et al., 2013), and submodular function (Lin and Bilmes, 2010). Moreover, cross-language document summarization has been investigated (Wan et al., 2010), but the task focuses on how to select the translated sentences with good content quality. We can see that all existing summarization systems were proposed for sighted people, but not for the blind and visually impaired people. Document summarization for the blind and visually impaired people has its specialty and is worth exploring.

It has been a long way to help the blind and visually impaired people to browse information as conveniently as ordinary people. Special devices have been developed for achieving this long-term goal (Linvill and Bliss, 1966; Shinohara et al., 1998). After the popularity of Braille, many kinds of braille display devices have been developed for braille reading (Rantala et al., 2009). In addition, most research in this area focused on how to improve accessibility of web information for the blind people (Salampasis et al., 2005; Mahmud et al., 2007; Hadjadj and Burger, 1999).

3 Preliminaries of Braille Grades

Braille is a system of raised dots arranged in cells and it was developed by Louis Braille in the beginning of the 19th century. Braille letters, common punctuation marks, and a few symbols are displayed as raised 6 dot braille cell patterns read by using a fingertip to feel the raised dots. The number and arrangement of these raised dots within a cell distinguish one character from another. For example, the letters "a", "b" and "c" are displayed as ⠁⠃⠉, respectively. Due to the varying needs of braille readers, there are different grades of braille. In this study we adopt grade 2 braille – EBAE (English Braille America Edition). Grade 2 braille was a space-saving alternative to grade 1 braille. In grade 2 braille, a cell can represent a shortened form of a word. Many cell combinations have been created to represent common words, making this the most popular of the grades of braille. There are part-word contractions (e.g. "stand" →⠌⠯, "without" →⠾⠳⠞), which often stand in for common suffixes or prefixes, and whole-word contractions (e.g. "every" → ⠑, "knowledge" →⠅), in which a single cell represents an entire commonly used word. Words may be abbreviated by using a single letter to represent the entire word, using a special symbol to precede either the first or last letter of the word while truncating the rest of the word, using a double-letter contraction such as "bb" or "cc", or removing most or all of the vowels in a word in order to shorten it. A complex system of styles, rules, and usage has been developed for this grade of braille.

4 System Overview

The focus of traditional summarization tasks is how to improve the content quality of a summary with a given length limit, and the content quality of a summary is measured by the overlap between the summary and reference summaries written by annotators. However, document summarization for the blind and visually impaired people is different from traditional summarization tasks. Besides the content quality, the length of a braille summary is a very important factor to be considered, because the number of braille cells in a braille summary have a direct impact on the blind and visually impaired people when they read the summary with their fingertips, and more highly contracted braille is quicker to read, as shown in previous studies such as (Veispak et al., 2012).

Given a document set, our new summarization task aims to produce a braille summary, which are translated from a traditional textual summary with a predefined length (usually measured by the count of words). The braille summary is required to keep the content quality, measured by the content quality of the textual summary. Moreover, the braille length of the summary is required to be as short as possible. The length of a braille summary is defined as the number of the rectangular braille cells in the summary. The shorter the length is, the blind and visually impaired people will spend less time reading the summary with their fingertips and thus the summary is better. For simplicity, we define the braille length of a textual summary as the length of its translated braille summary. For example, the braille length of a text "hello, world!" is 9 since the length of its translated braille text ⠓⠑⠇⠇⠕⠂ ⠸⠺⠖ is 9.

A basic solution to the new summarization task is first applying an existing summarization algorithm (e.g. the most popular ILP-based method) to produce a summary, and then translating the summary into a braille summary, which is called BasicSUM. However, the braille translation is not a simple character-to-block conversion process and there exist various contractions during the translation process, as mentioned in the previous section. Two content-similar sentences may be translated into two braille sentences with totally different lengths due to the different word lengths and conversion contractions. Therefore, our solution is to consider the new factor of braille length of each sentence during the summarization process and produce a summary with shorter braille length while keeping its content quality. In our proposed BrailleSUM system, we incorporate the factor of braille length into the ILP-based summarization framework with a new ILP formulation.

5 ILP-Based Braille Summarization

In this study, we adopt the popular ILP-based summarization framework for addressing the new task of braille summarization. The concept-based ILP method for summarization is introduced by (Gillick et al., 2008; Gillick and Favre, 2009), and its goal is to maximize the sum of the weights of the language concepts (i.e. bigrams) that appear in the summary. The ILP method is very powerful for extractive summarization because it can select important sentences and remove redundancy at the same time. Formally, the ILP method can be represented as below:

$$max \sum_{i=1}^{|B|} c_{b_i} b_i \quad (1)$$

subject to:

$$\sum_{i=1}^{N} l_i s_i \leq L_{max} \quad (2)$$

$$\sum_{i \in B_j} b_i \geq |B_j| s_j, \text{ for } j = 1, \ldots, N \quad (3)$$

$$\sum_{j \in S_i} s_j \geq b_i, \text{ for } i = 1, \ldots, |B| \quad (4)$$

$$b_i, s_j \in \{0,1\}, \forall i, j$$

where:

b_i, s_j are binary variables that indicate the presence of bigram i and sentence j, respectively;

c_{b_i} is the document frequency of bigram b_i;

B is the set of unique bigrams;

B_j is the set of bigrams that sentence j contains.

S_i is the set of sentences that contain bigram i.

N is the count of the sentences;

L_{max} is the maximum word count of the summary, which is set to 250 in the experiments;

l_i is the word count of sentence i.

Constraint (2) ensures that the total length of the selected sentences is limited by the given length limit. Inequalities (3)(4) associate the sentences and bigrams. Constraint (3) ensures that selecting a sentence leads to the selection of all the bigrams it contains, and constraint (4) ensures that selecting a bigram only happens when it is present in at least one of the selected sentences.

The new objective function for braille summarization consists of two parts: the original part reflecting the content quality and the new part reflecting the braille length factor. The function is presented as below and the constraints are the same with (2)(3)(4).

$$max\{(1-\lambda) \sum_{i=1}^{|B|} \frac{c_{b_i} b_i}{C} + \lambda \sum_{j=1}^{N} braille\_ratio_j s_j\} \quad (5)$$

where $C = \sum_{i \in B} c_{b_i}$ is a normalization constant to make the values of the two parts in the equation comparable. $\lambda \in [0, 1]$ is a combination parameter to reflect the different influences of the two parts. $braille\_ratio_j$ is a new factor to reflect the suitability level of sentence j to be selected, which is computed as below:

$$braille\_ratio_j = \frac{l_j}{bl_j} \quad (6)$$

where bl_j is the braille length of sentence j, and it is defined as the number of braille cells in the corresponding braille sentence. l_j is the word count in the original sentence. As mentioned earlier, the number of characters and signs in an English sentence is not equal to the number of the braille cells in the corresponding braille sentence, since grade 2 braille is not based on a simple one-to-one conversion from each character or sign to a braille cell. In this study, we adopt the open-source libbraille[1] tool for converting an English sentence into a braille sentence, and then get the braille length of the sentence. An example English sentence and its corresponding braille sentence are shown below:

Infected feed cannot account for four cases.

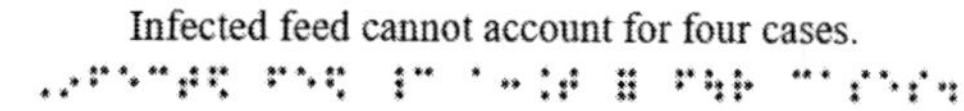

We can see that the number of characters and signs in the English sentence is 38, while the number of braille cells in the braille sentence is 26, and thus the braille length bl_j is 26. We can also simply know that the word count of the sentence l_j is 7. Thus the braille ratio of the sentence is 7/26=0.269. We can see that if a sentence has a larger ratio of its word count to its braille length, then it is more suitable to be selected. Particularly, for two sentences with the same word count, the one with a shorter braille length is preferred. Note that since the sum of l_j for the sentences in a summary is fixed, the sum of bl_j for the sentences should be as small as possible in order to maximize the second part in Equation (5). For the new objective function in Equation (5), the first part ensures the content quality, and the second part tries to make the braille length of the summary as short as possible. The combination of the two

[1] http://libbraille.org/

parts can achieve the two goals of our new summarization task at the same time. If the combination parameter λ is set to 0, then the formulation in (5) is actually the same with (1).

Finally, we solve the above linear programming problem by using the IBM CPLEX optimizer and get the English summary according the value of each variable s_j. The corresponding braille summary can be produced after translation with libbraille.

6 Evaluation

In this study, we used the multi-document summarization task in DUC2006 for evaluation. DUC2006 provided 50 document sets and a summary with a length limit of 250 words was required to be created for each document set. Reference summaries have been provided by NIST annotators. For simplicity, the topic description was ignored in this study. In the experiments, our proposed BrailleSUM system with the new ILP method in Equation (5) was compared with the BasicSUM system with the traditional ILP method in Equation (1). The parameter λ in BrailleSUM is simply set to 1/4 (i.e. 0.25).

Since the aim of our system is reducing the braille length of a summary without sacrificing its content quality, we evaluate the summaries from the following two aspects: First, we evaluate the content quality of the summaries by measuring the content overlap between the summaries and the reference summaries with the ROUGE-1.5.5 toolkit (Lin and Hovy, 2003). In this study, we use three ROUGE recall scores in the experimental results: ROUGE-1 (unigram-based), ROUGE-2 (bigram-based) and ROUGE-SU4 (based on skip bigram with a maximum skip distance of 4). Second, we compute the braille length of each summary by summing the braille lengths of all the sentences in the summary, and then average the lengths across the 50 document sets.

The comparison results on summary content quality and average summary braille length are shown in Table 1. We can see that BrailleSUM and BasicSUM can achieve very similar ROUGE scores, and the score differences are non-significant because the 95% confidence intervals are highly overlapped. The scores of BrailleSUM and BasicSUM are much higher than that of the NIST baseline and the average scores of all participating systems (i.e. AverageDUC). More importantly, BrailleSUM can produce summaries with much shorter braille lengths than BasicSUM, and the braille length reduction is significant. The results demonstrate that BrailleSUM can produce much shorter braille summaries while not sacrificing the summaries' content quality. We can see that the incorporation of the braille length factor into the ILP framework is very effective for addressing the new summarization task.

In order to show the influence of parameter λ in BrailleSUM, we vary λ from 0 to 1, and show the curves of ROUGE-1 and ROUGE-2 scores, and average braille length in Figures 1-3, respectively. We can see that with the increase of λ, the average braille length of the produced summaries is decreasing steadily. The result can be easily explained by that a larger λ means more consideration of the braille length factor. We can also see from the figures that when λ is less than 0.3, the ROUGE scores usually keep steady and do not decline significantly, but when λ is becoming larger, the ROUGE scores decline obviously. The results demonstrate that the content quality factor and the braille length factor need to be balanced with a proper value of λ.

	ROUGE-1	ROUGE-2	ROUGE-SU4	Average Braille Length
BrailleSUM	0.39012 [0.38380-0.39590]	0.09010 [0.08617-0.09396]	0.14009 [0.13665 - 0.14332]	932* ($\triangle bl$=103)
BasicSUM	0.38958 [0.38273-0.39586]	0.09219 [0.08791-0.09614]	0.14011 [0.13691-0.14368]	1035
AverageDUC	0.37250	0.07391	0.12928	-
NIST Baseline	0.30217	0.04947	0.09788	-

Table 1: Comparison results of summary content quality (ROUGE Recall) and average summary braille length. (The 95% confidence interval for each ROUGE score is reported in brackets; Δbl means the reduction of average braille length over BasicSUM; * means the average braille length reduction over BasicSUM is statistically significant with p-value=2.46975E-18 for t-test.)

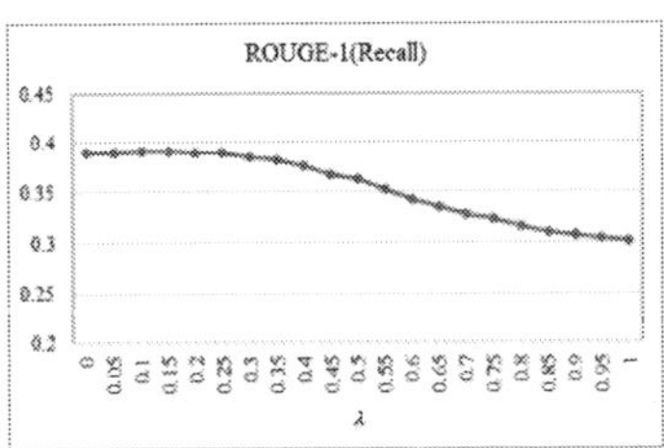

Figure 1. ROUGE-1 vs. λ

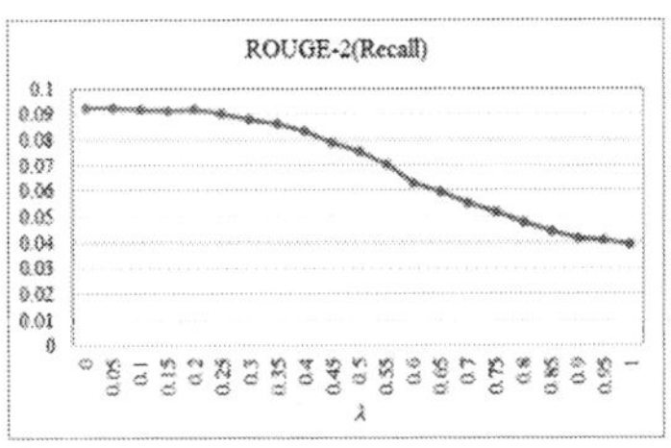

Figure 2. ROUGE-2 vs. λ

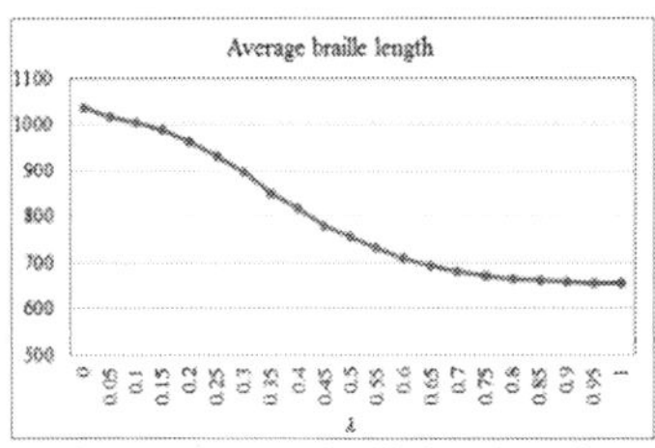

Figure 3. Average braille length vs. λ

Acknowledgments

The work was supported by National Hi-Tech Research and Development Program (863 Program) of China (2015AA015403) and National Natural Science Foundation of China (61170166, 61331011).

References

G. Erkan and D. R. Radev. 2004. LexPageRank: prestige in multi-document text summarization. In *Proceedings of EMNLP-04*.

D. Freitas and G. Kouroupetroglou. 2008. *Speech technologies for blind and low vision persons. Technology and Disability*, 20(2), 135-156.

D. Gillick, B. Favre and D. Hakkani-Tur. 2008. The ICSI summarization system at TAC 2008. In *Proceedings of the Text Understanding Conference*.

D. Gillick and B. Favre. 2009. A scalable global model for summarization. In *Proceedings of the Workshop on Integer Linear Programming for Natural Langauge Processing on NAACL*.

D. Hadjadj and D. Burger. 1999. Braillesurf: An html browser for visually handicapped people. In *Proceedings of Tech. and Persons with Disabilities Conference*, 1999.

C. Li, X. Qian and Y. Liu. 2013. Using supervised bigram-based ILP for extractive summarization. In *Proceedings of ACL* (pp. 1004-1013), 2013.

H. Lin and J. Bilmes. 2010. Multi-document summarization via budgeted maximization of submodular functions. In *Human Language Technologies: The 2010 Annual Conference of the North American Chapter of the Association for Computational Linguistics* (pp. 912-920), 2010.

C.-Y. Lin and E.. H. Hovy. 2002. From single to multi-document summarization: a prototype system and its evaluation. In *Proceedings of ACL-02*.

C.-Y. Lin and E.H. Hovy. 2003. Automatic evaluation of summaries using n-gram co-occurrence statistics. In *Proceedings of HLT-NAACL -03*.

J. G. Linvill and J. C. Bliss. 1966. A direct translation reading aid for the blind. *Proceedings of the IEEE*, 54(1), 40-51, 1966.

J. U. Mahmud, Y. Borodin and I. V. 2007. Ramakrishnan. Csurf: a context-driven non-visual web-browser. In *Proceedings of the 16th international conference on World Wide Web* (pp. 31-40), 2007.

R. Mihalcea and P. Tarau. 2005. A language independent algorithm for single and multiple document summarization. In *Proceedings of IJCNLP-05*.

Y. Ouyang, S. Li, W. Li. 2007. Developing learning strategies for topic-focused summarization. In *Proceedings of CIKM-07*.

D. R. Radev, H. Y. Jing, M. Stys and D. Tam. 2004. Centroid-based summarization of multiple documents. *Information Processing and Management*, 40: 919-938, 2004.

J. Rantala, R. Raisamo, J. Lylykangas, V. Surakka, J. Raisamo, K. Salminen, T. Pakkanen and A. Hippula. 2009. Methods for presenting Braille characters on a mobile device with a touchscreen and tactile feedback. *Haptics, IEEE Transactions on*, 2(1), 28-39, 2009.

M. Salampasis, C. Kouroupetroglou and A. Manitsaris. 2005. Semantically enhanced browsing for blind people in the WWW. In *Proceedings of the sixteenth ACM conference on Hypertext and hypermedia* (pp. 32-34), 2005.

F. Schilder and R. Kondadadi. 2008. FastSum: fast and accurate query-based multi-document summarization. In *Proceedings of ACL-08: HLT*.

C. Shen and T. Li. 2010. Multi-document summarization via the minimum dominating set. In *Proceedings of COLING-10*.

D. Shen, J.-T. Sun, H. Li, Q. Yang, and Z. Chen. 2007. Document summarization using conditional random fields. In *Proceedings of IJCAI-07*.

M. Shinohara, Y. Shimizu and A. Mochizuki. 1998. Three-dimensional tactile display for the blind. *Rehabilitation Engineering, IEEE Transactions on*, 6(3), 249-256, 1998.

A. Veispak, B. Boets and P. Ghesquiere. 2012. Parallel versus Sequential Processing in Print and Braille Reading. *Research in Developmental Disabilities: A Multidisciplinary Journal* 33(6): 2153-2163, 2012.

X. Wan, H. Li and J. Xiao. 2010. Cross-language document summarization based on machine translation quality prediction. In *Proceedings of the 48th Annual Meeting of the Association for Computational Linguistics* (pp. 917-926), 2010.

K.-F. Wong, M. Wu and W. Li. 2008. Extractive summarization using supervised and semisupervised learning. In *Proceedings of COLING-08*.

Automatic Identification of Age-Appropriate Ratings of Song Lyrics

Anggi Maulidyani and Ruli Manurung
Faculty of Computer Science, Universitas Indonesia
Depok 16424, West Java, Indonesia
anggi.maulidyani@ui.ac.id, maruli@cs.ui.ac.id

Abstract

This paper presents a novel task, namely the automatic identification of age-appropriate ratings of a musical track, or album, based on its lyrics. Details are provided regarding the construction of a dataset of lyrics from 12,242 tracks across 1,798 albums along with age-appropriate ratings obtained from various web resources, along with results from various text classification experiments. The best accuracy of 71.02% for classifying albums by age groups is achieved by combining vector space model and psycholinguistic features.

1 Introduction

Media age-appropriateness can be defined as the suitability of the consumption of a media item, e.g. a song, book, film, videogame, etc., by a child of a given age based on norms that are generally agreed upon within a society. Such norms may include behavioral, sociological, psychological, and other factors. Whilst we acknowledge that this is largely a subjective judgment, and that there may be wide variance between very small circles that could be considered demographically homogenous, nevertheless, parents, educators, and policymakers may find such judgments valuable in the process of guiding and supervising the media consumption of children.

This topic is closely related to well-known content rating schemes such as the MPAA film rating system[1], but whereas such schemes are focused more on whether a film contains adult material or not, age-appropriatness can be thought of as being more nuanced, and takes into consideration more factors such as educational value.

One popular resource for such ratings is Common Sense Media[2], a website that provides reviews for various media, with a focus on age appropriateness and learning potential for children.

Whilst acknowledging that such ratings are of interest to many people, the position of this research is neutral towards the efficacy and utility of such ratings: we only seek to ask the question of whether it is possible to automate the identification of these age-appropriateness ratings.

This work focuses on song lyrics. There are many aspects that can contribute to the age-appropriateness of a song, but we believe that by far the most dominant factor is its lyrics. Thus, the approach that is taken to automating the identification of age-appropriatness ratings is to treat it as a supervised text classification task: first, a corpus of song lyrics along with age-appropriateness ratings is constructed, and subsequently this corpus is used to train a model based on various textual features.

To give the reader an idea of this task, Figures 1 to 3 show a sampler of snippets of lyrics[3] from songs along with their age-appropriate ratings according to Common Sense Media. Our goal is to be able to automatically predict the age-appropriate rating given the lyrics of a song in such cases.

Oh, I'm Sammy the snake
And I look like the letter "S"ssss.
Oh, yes.
I'm all wiggly and curvy,
And I look like the letter "S"ssss.
I confess.
(age-appropriate rating: 2)

Figure 1: Snippet of "Sammy the Snake", from Sesame Street Halloween Collection

[1] http://www.mpaa.org/film-ratings

[2] http://www.commonsensemedia.org

[3] All works are copyrighted to their respective owners.

Proceedings of the 53rd Annual Meeting of the Association for Computational Linguistics and the 7th International Joint Conference on Natural Language Processing (Short Papers), pages 583–587,
Beijing, China, July 26-31, 2015.

Do you want to build a snowman?
Come on, let's go and play
I never see you anymore
Come out the door
It's like you've gone away
(age-appropriate rating: 5)

Figure 2: Snippet of "Do you want to build a snowman?", from Frozen Original Motion Picture Soundtrack

You can take everything I have
You can break everything I am
Like I'm made of glass
Like I'm made of paper
Go on and try to tear me down
I will be rising from the ground
Like a skyscraper
Like a skyscraper
(age-appropriate rating: 9)

Figure 3: Snippet of "Skyscraper", from Unbroken - Demi Lovato

In Section 2 we discuss related work, before presenting our work on constructing the corpus (Section 3) and carrying out text classification experiments (Section 4). Finally, we present a tentative summary in Section 5.

2 Related Work

To our knowledge, there is no previous work that has attempted what is described in this paper. There is some thematically related work, such as automatic filtering of pornographic content (Polpinij et al., 2006; Sood et al., 2012; Xiang et al., 2012; Su et al., 2004), but we believe the nature of the task is significantly different such that a different approach is required.

However, text or document classification, the general technique employed in this paper, is a very common task (Manning et al., 2008). In text classification, given a document d, the task is to assign it a class, or label, c, from a fixed, human-defined set of possible classes $C = \{c_1, c_2, \ldots, c_n\}$. In order to achieve this, a training set of *labelled documents* $\langle d, c \rangle$ is given to a *learning algorithm* to learn a classifier that maps documents to classes.

Documents are typically represented as a vector in a high-dimensional space, such as term-document matrices, or results of dimensionality reduction techniques such as Latent Semantic Analysis (Landauer et al., 1998), or more recently, using vector representations of words produced by neural networks (Pennington et al., 2014).

Text classification has many applications, among others spam filtering (Androutsopoulos et al., 2000) and sentiment analysis (Pang and Lee, 2008).

One particular application that could be deemed of relevance with respect to our work is that of readability assessment (Pitler and Nenkova, 2008; Feng et al., 2010), i.e. determining the ease with which a written text can be understood by a reader, since age is certainly a dimension along which readability varies. However, our literature review of this area suggested that the aspects being considered in readability assessment are sufficiently different from the dimensions that seem to be most relevant for media age appropriatness ratings. Following Manurung et al. (2008), we hypothesize that utilizing resources such as the MRC Psycholinguistic Database (Coltheart, 1981) could be valuable in determining age appropriateness, in particular various features such as familiarity, imageability, age-of-acquisition, and concreteness.

3 Corpus Construction

There are three steps in obtaining the data required for our corpus: obtaining album details and age-appropriateness ratings, searching for the track-listing of each album, and obtaining the lyrics for each song. Each step is carried out by querying a different website. To achieve this, a Java application that utilizes the jsoup library[4] was developed.

3.1 Obtaining album details and age-appropriateness ratings

The Common Sense Media website provides reviews for various music albums. The reviews consist of a textual review, the age-appropriate rating for the album, which consists of an integer in the interval [2,17] or the label 'Not For Kids', and metadata about the album such as title, artist, and genre. Aside from that, there are also other annotations such as a quality rating (1-5 stars), and specific aspectual ratings such as positive messages, role models, violence, sex, language, consumerism, drinking, drugs & smoking. The website also allows visitors to contribute user ratings and reviews. In our experiments we only utilize

[4]http://www.jsoup.org

the album metadata and integer indicating the age-appropriate rating.

3.2 Tracklist searching

A tracklist is a list of all the songs, or tracks, contained within an album. From the information previously obtained from Common Sense Media, the next step is to obtain the tracklist of each album. For this we query the MusicBrainz website[5], an open music encyclopedia that makes music metadata available to the public. To obtain the tracklists we employed the advanced query search mode that allows the use of boolean operators. We tried several combinations of queries involving album title, singer, and label information, and it turned out that queries consisting of album title and singer produced the highest recall. When MusicBrainz returns multiple results for a given query, we simply select the first result. For special cases where the tracks on an album are performed by various artists, e.g. a compilation album, or a soundtrack album, it is during this stage that we also extract information regarding the track-specific artist name. Finally, we assume that if the album title contains the string 'CD Single' then it only contains one track and we skip forward to the next step.

3.3 Lyrics searching

For this step, we consulted two websites as the source reference for song lyrics, songlyrics.com and lyricsmode.com. The former is first consulted, and only if it fails to yield any results is the latter consulted. If a track is not found on both websites, we discard it from our data set. Similar to the previous step, we perform a query to obtain results, however during this step the query consists of the song title and singer. Once again, given multiple results we simply choose the first result. In total, we were able to retrieve lyrics from 12,242 songs across 1,798 albums. Table 1 provides an overview of the number of tracks and albums obtained per age rating.

4 Experimentation

Since the constructed data set is imbalanced, we use the SMOTE oversampling technique to overcome this problem (Chawla et al., 2002). This results in a balanced dataset with the same number of samples in each class.

[5]http://www.musicbrainz.org

Group	Age	#Tracks	#Albums
Toddler	2	696	119
	3	130	23
Pre-schooler	4	251	46
	5	204	31
Middle childhood 1	6	281	41
	7	358	71
	8	654	118
Middle childhood 2	9	237	50
	10	1,590	253
	11	580	105
Young teen	12	1,849	253
	13	1,767	242
	14	1,453	177
Teenager	15	653	116
	16	521	64
	17	180	16
Adult	>17	838	73
	Total	12,242	1,798

Table 1: Statistics of the dataset

Once the dataset is complete, classifiers were trained and used to carry out experiment scenarios that vary along several factors. For the class labels, two scenarios are considered: one where each age rating from 2 to 17 and 'Not For Kids' is a separate class, and another where the data is clustered together based on some conventional developmental age groupings[6], i.e. toddlers (ages 2 & 3), preschoolers (ages 4 & 5), middle-childhood 1 (ages 6 to 8), middle-childhood 2 (ages 9 to 11), young-teens (ages 12 to 14), and teenagers (ages 15 to 17), with an additional category for ages beyond 17 using the 'Not For Kids' labelled data.

For the instance data, two scenarios are also considered: one where classification is done on a per-track basis, and one on a per-album basis (i.e. where lyrics from all its constituent tracks are concatenated).

As for the feature representation, three primary variations are considered:

Vector Space Model. This is a baseline method where each word appearing in the dataset becomes a feature, and a vector representing an instance consists of the $tf.idf$ values of all words. Additionally, stemming is first performed on the words, and information gain-based attribute selection is applied.

MRC Psycholinguistic data. For this feature

[6]http://www.cdc.gov/ncbddd/childdevelopment/positiveparenting/

representation, given each distinct word appearing in the lyrics of a track (or album), a lookup is performed on the MRC psycholinguistic database, and if appropriate values exist, they are added to the tally for the familiarity, imageability, age-of-acquisition, and concreteness scores. Thus, an instance is represented by a vector with four real values. The vectors are normalized with respect to the number of words contributing to the values.

GloVe vectors. GloVe[7] is a tool that produces vector representations of words trained on very large corpora (Pennington et al., 2014). It is similar to dimensionality reduction approaches such as latent semantic analysis. For this experiment, the 50-dimensional pre-trained vectors trained on Wikipedia and Gigaword corpora were used.

When combining feature representations, we simply concatenate their vectors.

Finally, for the classification itself, the Weka toolkit is used. Given the ordinal nature of the class labels, classification is carried out via regression (Frank et al., 1998), using the M5P-based classifier (Wang and Witten, 1997). The experiments were run using 4-fold cross validation.

For the initial experiment, only the baseline VSM feature representation was used, and the treatment of class labels and instance granularity was varied. The results can be seen in Table 2, which shows the average accuracy, i.e. the percentage of test instances that were correctly labelled, across 4 folds.

	Age group	Year
Per-track	69.77%	58.58%
Per-album	70.60%	57.15%

Table 2: Initial experiment varying class and instance granularity

For the follow-up experiment, we focus on the task of classifying at the per-album level of granularity, as ultimately this is the level at which the original annotations are obtained. For the class labels, both age groups and separate ages are used. The feature representation was varied ranging from VSM, VSM + MRC, VSM + GloVe, and VSM + GloVe + MRC. The results can be seen in Table 3.

[7] http://nlp.stanford.edu/projects/glove/

Features	Age group	Year
VSM	70.60%	57.15%
VSM + MRC	**71.02%**	56.80%
VSM + GloVe	70.58%	57.68%
VSM + GloVe + MRC	70.47%	**57.85%**

Table 3: Results varying feature representations

5 Discussion & Summary

From the initial experiment, it appears that distinguishing tracks at the level of granularity of specific year/age (e.g. "is this song more appropriate for a 4 or 5 year old?") is very difficult, as indicated by an accuracy of only 57% to 58%. Bear in mind, however, that this is a seventeen-way classification task. Shifting the level of granularity to that of age groups transforms the task into a more feasible one, with an accuracy around the 70% mark. It is surprising to note that the per-track performance is better than the per-album performance when tracks are distinguished by specific age/year rather than age groups. We had initially hypothesized that classifying albums would be a more consistent task given the increased context and evidence available.

As for the various feature representations, we note that the addition of the MRC psycholinguistic features of familiarity, imageability, concreteness, and age-of-acquisition does provide a small accuracy increase in certain cases, as evidenced by the highest accuracy of 71.02% when classifying albums by age group using the VSM + MRC features. The use of the GloVe vectors gives a slight contribution in the case of classifying albums by specific age/year, where the highest accuracy of 57.85% is obtained when combining VSM with both the MRC and GloVe features.

There are many other features and contexts that can also be utilized. For instance, given the metadata of artist, album, and genre, additional information may be extracted from the web, e.g. the artist's biography, general-purpose album reviews, genre tendencies, etc., all of which may contribute to discerning age-appropriateness. Another set of features that can be utilized are readability metrics, as they are often correlated with the age of the reader.

To summarize, this paper has introduced a novel task with clear practical applications in the form of automatically identifying age-appropriate ratings of songs and albums based on lyrics. The work reported is still in its very early stages, nevertheless we believe the findings are of interest to NLP researchers.

Another question that needs to be addressed is what sort of competence and agreement humans achieve on this task. To that end, we plan to conduct a manual annotation experiment involving several human subjects, themselves varied across different age groups, and to measure inter-annotator reliability (Passonneau et al., 2006).

References

Ion Androutsopoulos, John Koutsias, Konstantinos Chandrinos, Georgios Paliouras, and Constantine D. Spyropoulos. 2000. An evaluation of naïve Bayesian anti-spam filtering. In *Proceedings of the workshop on Machine Learning in the New Information Age, 11th European Conference on Machine Learning*, pages 9–17, Barcelona, Spain.

Nitesh V. Chawla, Kevin W. Bowyer, Lawrence O. Hall, and W. Philip Kegelmeyer. 2002. Smote: Synthetic minority over-sampling technique. *J. Artif. Int. Res.*, 16(1):321–357, June.

Max Coltheart. 1981. The MRC psycholinguistic database. *The Quarterly Journal of Experimental Psychology*, 33(4):497–505.

Lijun Feng, Martin Jansche, Matt Huenerfauth, and Noémie Elhadad. 2010. A comparison of features for automatic readability assessment. In *Proceedings of the 23rd International Conference on Computational Linguistics: Posters*, COLING '10, pages 276–284, Stroudsburg, PA, USA. Association for Computational Linguistics.

E. Frank, Y. Wang, S. Inglis, G. Holmes, and I.H. Witten. 1998. Using model trees for classification. *Machine Learning*, 32(1):63–76.

Thomas Landauer, Peter Foltz, and Darrell Laham. 1998. An introduction to latent semantic analysis. *Discourse Processes*, 25:259–284.

Christopher Manning, Prabhakar Raghavan, and Hinrich Schutze. 2008. *Introduction to Information Retrieval*. Cambridge University Press.

Ruli Manurung, Graeme Ritchie, Helen Pain, Annalu Waller, Dave O'Mara, and Rolf Black. 2008. The construction of a pun generator for language skills development. *Applied Artificial Intelligence*, 22(9):841–869.

Bo Pang and Lillian Lee. 2008. Opinion mining and sentiment analysis. *Foundations and trends in information retrieval*, 2(1-2):1–135.

Rebecca Passonneau, Nizar Habash, and Owen Rambow. 2006. Inter-annotator agreement on a multilingual semantic annotation task. In *Proceedings of the Fifth International Conference on Language Resources and Evaluation (LREC 2006)*, Genoa, Italy, May.

Jeffrey Pennington, Richard Socher, and Christopher Manning. 2014. GloVe: Global vectors for word representation. In *Proceedings of the 2014 Conference on Empirical Methods in Natural Language Processing (EMNLP)*, pages 1532–1543. Association for Computational Linguistics.

Emily Pitler and Ani Nenkova. 2008. Revisiting readability: A unified framework for predicting text quality. In *Proceedings of the Conference on Empirical Methods in Natural Language Processing*, EMNLP '08, pages 186–195, Stroudsburg, PA, USA. Association for Computational Linguistics.

J. Polpinij, A. Chotthanom, C. Sibunruang, R. Chamchong, and S. Puangpronpitag. 2006. Content-based text classifiers for pornographic web filtering. In *Systems, Man and Cybernetics, 2006. SMC '06. IEEE International Conference on*, volume 2, pages 1481–1485, Oct.

Sara Owsley Sood, Judd Antin, and Elizabeth F Churchill. 2012. Using crowdsourcing to improve profanity detection. In *AAAI Spring Symposium: Wisdom of the Crowd*.

Gui-yang Su, Jian-hua Li, Ying-hua Ma, and Sheng-hong Li. 2004. Improving the precision of the keyword-matching pornographic text filtering method using a hybrid model. *Journal of Zhejiang University Science*, 5(9):1106–1113.

Y. Wang and I. H. Witten. 1997. Induction of model trees for predicting continuous classes. In *Poster papers of the 9th European Conference on Machine Learning*. Springer.

Guang Xiang, Bin Fan, Ling Wang, Jason Hong, and Carolyn Rose. 2012. Detecting offensive tweets via topical feature discovery over a large scale twitter corpus. In *Proceedings of the 21st ACM International Conference on Information and Knowledge Management*, CIKM '12, pages 1980–1984, New York, NY, USA. ACM.

Ground Truth for Grammatical Error Correction Metrics

Courtney Napoles[1] and **Keisuke Sakaguchi**[1] and **Matt Post**[2] and **Joel Tetreault**[3]
[1]Center for Language and Speech Processing, Johns Hopkins University
[2]Human Language Technology Center of Excellence, Johns Hopkins University
[3]Yahoo Labs

Abstract

How do we know which grammatical error correction (GEC) system is best? A number of metrics have been proposed over the years, each motivated by weaknesses of previous metrics; however, the metrics themselves have not been compared to an empirical gold standard grounded in human judgments. We conducted the first *human evaluation* of GEC system outputs, and show that the rankings produced by metrics such as MaxMatch and I-measure do not correlate well with this ground truth. As a step towards better metrics, we also propose GLEU, a simple variant of BLEU, modified to account for both the source and the reference, and show that it hews much more closely to human judgments.

1 Introduction

Automatic metrics are a critical component for all tasks in natural language processing. For many tasks, such as parsing and part-of-speech tagging, there is a single correct answer, and thus a single metric to compute it. For other tasks, such as machine translation or summarization, there is no effective limit to the size of the set of correct answers. For such tasks, metrics proliferate and compete with each other for the role of the dominant metric. In such cases, an important question to answer is by what means such metrics should be compared. That is, what is the *metric* metric?

The answer is that it should be rooted in the end-use case for the task under consideration. This could be some other metric further downstream of the task, or something simpler like direct human evaluation. This latter approach is the one often taken in machine translation; for example, the organizers of the Workshop on Statistical Machine Translation have long argued that human evaluation is the ultimate ground truth, and have therefore conducted an extensive human evaluation to produce a system ranking, which is then used to compare metrics (Bojar et al., 2014).

Unfortunately, for the subjective task of grammatical error correction (GEC), no such ground truth has ever been established. Instead, the rankings produced by new metrics are justified by their correlation with explicitly-corrected errors in one or more references, and by appeals to intuition for the resulting rankings. However, arguably even more so than for machine translation, the use case for grammatical error correction is human consumption, and therefore, the ground truth ranking should be rooted in human judgments.

We establish a ground truth for GEC by conducting a human evaluation and producing a *human* ranking of the systems entered into the CoNLL-2014 Shared Task on GEC. We find that existing GEC metrics correlate very poorly with the ranking produced by this human evaluation. As a step in the direction of better metrics, we develop the Generalized Language Evaluation Understanding metric (GLEU) inspired by BLEU, which correlates much better with the human ranking than current GEC metrics.[1]

2 Grammatical error correction metrics

GEC is often viewed as a matter of correcting isolated grammatical errors, but is much more complicated, nuanced, and subjective than that. As discussed in Chodorow et al. (2012), there is often no single correction for an error (e.g., whether to correct a subject-verb agreement error by changing the number of the subject or the verb), and errors cover a range of factors including style, register, venue, audience, and usage questions, about

[1]Our code and rankings of the CoNLL-2014 Shared Task system outputs can be downloaded from `github.com/cnap/gec-ranking/`.

Proceedings of the 53rd Annual Meeting of the Association for Computational Linguistics and the 7th International Joint Conference on Natural Language Processing (Short Papers), pages 588–593,
Beijing, China, July 26-31, 2015.

which there can be much disagreement. In addition, errors are not always errors, as can be seen from the existence of different style manuals at newspapers, and questions about the legitimacy of prescriptivist grammar conventions.

Several automatic metrics have been used for evaluating GEC systems. F-score, the harmonic mean of precision and recall, is one of the most commonly used metrics. It was used as an official evaluation metric for several shared tasks (Dale et al., 2012; Dale and Kilgarriff, 2011), where participants were asked to detect and correct closed-class errors (i.e., determiners and prepositions).

One of the issues with F-score is that it fails to capture phrase-level edits. Thus Dahlmeier and Ng (2012) proposed the MaxMatch (M^2) scorer, which calculates the F-score over an edit lattice that captures phrase-level edits. For GEC, M^2 is the standard, having been used to rank error correction systems in the 2013 and 2014 CoNLL shared tasks, where the error types to be corrected were not limited to closed-class errors. (Ng et al., 2013; Ng et al., 2014). M^2 was assessed by comparing its output against that of the official Helping Our Own (HOO) scorer (Dale and Kilgarriff, 2011), itself based on the GNU `wdiff` utility.[2] In other words, it was evaluated under the assumption that evaluating GEC can be reduced to checking whether a set of predefined errors have been changed into a set of associated corrections.

M^2 is not without its own issues. First, phrase-level edits can be gamed because the lattice treats a long phrase deletion as one edit.[3] Second, the F-score does not capture the difference between "no change" and "wrong edits" made by systems. Chodorow et al. (2012) also list other complications arising from using F-score or M^2, depending on the application of GEC.

Considering these problems, Felice and Briscoe (2015) proposed a new metric, I-measure, which is based on accuracy computed by edit distance between the source, reference, and system output. Their results are striking: there is a negative correlation between the M^2 and I-measure scores (Pearson's $r = -0.694$).

A difficulty with all these metrics is that they require detailed annotations of the location and error type of each correction in response to an explicit error annotation scheme. Due to the inherent subjectivity and poor definition of the task, mentioned above, it is difficult for annotators to reliably produce these annotations (Bryant and Ng, 2015). However, this requirement can be relinquished by treating GEC as a text-to-text rewriting task and borrowing metrics from machine translation, as Park and Levy (2011) did with BLEU (Papineni et al., 2002) and METEOR (Lavie and Agarwal, 2007).

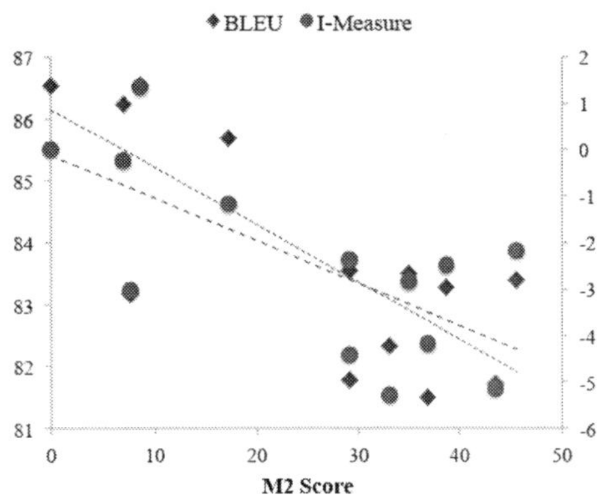

Figure 1: Correlation among M^2, I-measure, and BLEU scores: M^2 score shows negative correlations to other metrics.

As we will show in more detail in Section 5, taking the twelve publicly released system outputs from the CoNLL-2014 Shared Task,[4] we actually find a negative correlation between the M^2 and BLEU scores ($r = -0.772$) and positive correlation between I-measure and BLEU scores ($r = 0.949$) (Figure 1). With the earlier-reported negative correlation between I-measure and M^2, we have a troubling picture: which of these metrics is best? Which one actually captures and rewards the behaviors we would like our systems to report? Despite these many proposed metrics, no prior work has attempted to answer these questions by comparing them to human judgments. We propose to answer these questions by producing a definitive human ranking, against which the rankings of different metrics can be compared.

3 The human ranking

The Workshop on Statistical Machine Translation (WMT) faces the same question each year as part

[2] `http://www.gnu.org/s/wdiff/`

[3] For example, when we put a single character 'X' as system output for each sentence, we obtain $P = 0.27, R = 0.29, M^2 = 0.28$, which would be ranked 6/13 systems in the 2014 CoNLL shared task.

[4] `www.comp.nus.edu.sg/~nlp/conll14st.html`

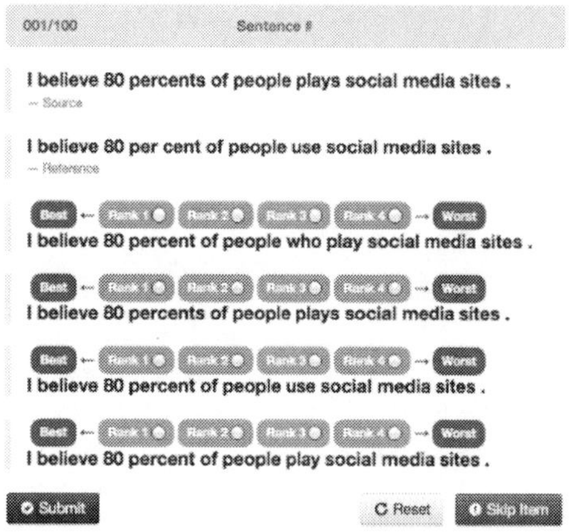

Figure 2: The Appraise evaluation system.

of its metrics shared task. Arguing that humans are the ultimate judge of quality, they gather human judgments and use them to produce a ranking of the systems for each task. Machine translation metrics are then evaluated based on how closely they match this ranking, using Pearson's r (prior to 2014) or Spearman's ρ (2014).

We borrow their approach to conduct a human evaluation. We used Appraise (Federmann, 2012)[5] to collect pairwise judgments among 14 systems: the output of 12 systems entered in the CoNLL-14 Shared Task, plus the source and a reference sentence. Appraise presents the judge with the source and reference sentence[6] and asks her to rank four randomly selected systems from best to worst, ties allowed (Figure 2). The four-way ranking is transformed into a set of pairwise judgments.

We collected data from three native English speakers, resulting in 28,146 pairwise system judgements. Each system's quality was estimated and the total ranking was produced on this dataset using the TrueSkill model (Sakaguchi et al., 2014), as done in WMT 2014. The annotators had strong correlations in terms of the total system ranking and estimated quality, with the reference being ranked at the top (Table 1).

4 Generalized BLEU

Current metrics for GEC rely on references with explicitly labeled error annotations, the type and form of which vary from task to task and can be difficult to convert. Recognizing the inherent ambiguity in the error-correction task, a better metric might be independent of such an annotation scheme and only require corrected references. This is the view of GEC as a generic text-rewriting task, and it is natural to apply standard metrics from machine translation. However, applied off-the-shelf, these metrics yield unintuitive results. For example, BLEU ranks the *source* sentence as second place in the CoNLL-2014 shared task.[7]

The problem is partially due to the subtle but important difference between machine translation and monolingual text-rewriting tasks. In MT, an untranslated word or phrase is almost always an error, but in grammatical error correction, this is not the case. Some, but not all, regions of the source sentence should be changed. This observation motivates a small change to BLEU that computes n-gram precisions over the reference but assigns more weight to n-grams that have been correctly changed from the source. This revised metric, Generalized Language Evaluation Understanding (GLEU), rewards corrections while also correctly crediting unchanged source text.

Recall that BLEU(C, R) (Papineni et al., 2002) is computed as the geometric mean of the modified precision scores of the test sentences C relative to the references R, multiplied by a brevity penalty to control for recall. The precisions are computed over bags of n-grams derived from the candidate translation and the references. Each n-gram in the candidate sentence is "clipped" to the maximum count of that n-gram in any of the references, ensuring that no precision is greater than 1.

Similar to I-measure, which calculates a weighted accuracy of edits, we calculate a weighted precision of n-grams. In our adaptation, we modify the precision calculation to assign extra weight to n-grams present in the candidate that overlap with the reference *but not* the source (the set of n-grams $R \setminus S$). The precision is also penal-

Judges	r	ρ
1 and 2	0.80	0.69
1 and 3	0.73	0.80
2 and 3	0.81	0.71

Table 1: Pearson's r and Spearman's ρ correlations among judges (excluding the reference).

[5] github.com/cfedermann/Appraise

[6] CoNLL-14 has two references. For each sentence, we randomly chose one to present as the answer and one to be among the systems to be ranked.

[7] Of course, it could be the case that the source sentence is actually the second best, but our human evaluation (§5) confirms that this is not the case.

$$p'_n = \frac{\sum_{n\text{-}gram \in C} Count_{R\setminus S}(n\text{-}gram) - \lambda\left(Count_{S\setminus R}(n\text{-}gram)\right) + Count_R(n\text{-}gram)}{\sum_{n\text{-}gram' \in C'} Count_S(n\text{-}gram') + \sum_{n\text{-}gram \in R\setminus S} Count_{R\setminus S}(n\text{-}gram)} \quad (1)$$

ized by a weighted count of n-grams in the candidate that are in the source but not the reference (false negatives, $S \setminus R$). For a correction candidate C with a corresponding source S and reference R, the modified n-gram precision for GLEU(C,R,S) is shown in Equation 1. The weight λ determines by how much incorrectly changed n-grams are penalized. Equations 2–3 describe how the counts are collected given a bag of n-grams B.

$$Count_B(n\text{-}gram) = \sum_{n\text{-}gram' \in B} d(n\text{-}gram, n\text{-}gram') \quad (2)$$

$$d(n\text{-}gram, n\text{-}gram') = \begin{cases} 1 & \text{if } n\text{-}gram = n\text{-}gram' \\ 0 & \text{otherwise} \end{cases} \quad (3)$$

$$\text{BP} = \begin{cases} 1 & \text{if } c > r \\ e^{(1-c/r)} & \text{if } c \leq r \end{cases} \quad (4)$$

$$\text{GLEU}(C, R, S) = \text{BP} \cdot \exp\left(\sum_{n=1}^{N} w_n \log p'_n\right) \quad (5)$$

In our experiments, we used $N = 4$ and $w_n = \frac{1}{N}$, which are standard parameters for MT, the same brevity penalty as BLEU (Equation 4), and report results on $\lambda = \{0.1, 0\}$ ($\text{GLEU}_{0.1}$ and GLEU_0, respectively). For this task, not penalizing false negatives correlates best with human judgments, but the weight can be tuned for different tasks and datasets. GLEU can be easily extended to additionally punish false positives (incorrectly editing grammatical text) as well.

5 Results

The respective system rankings of each metric are presented in Table 2. The human ranking is considerably different from those of most of the metrics, a fact that is also captured in correlation coefficients (Table 3).[8] From the human evaluation, we learn that the source falls near the middle of the rankings, even though the BLEU, I-measure and M^2 rank it among the best or worst systems.

M^2, the metric that has been used for the CoNLL shared tasks, only correlates moderately with human rankings, suggesting that it is not an ideal metric for judging the results of a competition. Even though I-measure perceptively aims to

[8]Pearson's measure assumes the scores are normally distributed, which may not be true here.

Metric	r	ρ
GLEU_0	**0.542**	**0.555**
M^2	0.358	0.429
$\text{GLEU}_{0.1}$	0.200	0.412
I-measure	-0.051	-0.005
BLEU	-0.125	-0.225

Table 3: Correlation of metrics with the human ranking (excluding the reference), as calculated with Pearson's r and Spearman's ρ.

predict whether an output is better or worse than the input, it actually has a slight negative correlation with human rankings. GLEU_0 is the only metric that strongly correlates with the human ranks, and performs closest to the range of human-to-human correlation ($0.73 \leq r \leq 0.81$) GLEU_0 correctly ranks four out of five of the top human-ranked systems at the top of its list, while the other metrics rank at most three of these systems in the top five.

All metrics deviate from the human rankings, which may in part be because automatic metrics equally weight all error types, when some errors may be more tolerable to human judges than others. For example, inserting a missing token is rewarded the same by automatic metrics, whether it is a comma or a verb, while a human would much more strongly prefer the insertion of the latter. An example of system outputs with their automatic scores and human rankings is included in Table 4.

This example illustrates some challenges faced when using automatic metrics to evaluate GEC. The automatic metrics weight all corrections equally and are limited to the gold-standard references provided. Both automatic metrics, M^2 and GLEU, prefer the AMU output in this example, even though it corrects one error and *introduces* another. The human judges rank the UMC output as the best for correcting the main verb even though it ignored the spelling error. The UMC and NTHU sentences both receive $M^2 = 0$ because they make none of the gold-standard edits, even though UMC correctly inserts *be* into the sentence. M^2 does not recognize this since it is in a different location from where the annotators placed it.

Human	BLEU	I-measure	M^2	$GLEU_0$	$GLEU_{0.1}$
CAMB	UFC	UFC	CUUI	CUUI	CUUI
AMU	source	source	CAMB	AMU	AMU
RAC	IITB	IITB	AMU	UFC	CAMB
CUUI	SJTU	SJTU	POST	CAMB	UFC
source	UMC	CUUI	UMC	source	IITB
POST	CUUI	PKU	NTHU	IITB	SJTU
UFC	PKU	AMU	PKU	SJTU	PKU
SJTU	AMU	UMC	RAC	PKU	UMC
IITB	IPN	IPN	SJTU	UMC	NTHU
PKU	NTHU	POST	UFC	NTHU	POST
UMC	CAMB	RAC	IPN	POST	RAC
NTHU	RAC	CAMB	IITB	RAC	IPN
IPN	POST	NTHU	source	IPN	source

Table 2: System outputs scored by different metrics, ranked best to worst.

System	Sentence	Scores
Original sentence	We may in actual fact communicating with a hoax Facebook acccount of a cyber friend , which we assume to be real but in reality , it is a fake account .	–
Reference 1	We may in actual fact **be** communicating with a hoax Facebook acccount of a cyber friend , which we assume to be real but in reality , it is a fake account .	–
Reference 2	We may in actual fact **be** communicating with a **fake** Facebook **account** of **an online** friend , which we assume to be real but , in reality , it is a fake account .	–
UMC	We may **be** in actual fact communicating with a hoax Facebook acccount of a cyber friend , we assume to be real but in reality , it is a fake account .	GLEU = 0.62 M^2 = 0.00 Human rank= 1
AMU	We may in actual fact communicating with a hoax Facebook **account** of a cyber friend , which we assume to be real but in reality , it is a fake **accounts** .	GLEU = 0.64 M^2 = 0.39 Human rank= 2
NTHU	We may of actual fact communicating with a hoax Facebook acccount of a cyber friend , which we **assumed** to be real but in reality , it is a fake account .	GLEU = 0.60 M^2 = 0.00 Human rank= 4

Table 4: Examples of system output (changes are in bold) and the sentence-level scores assigned by different metrics.

However, GLEU awards UMC partial credit for adding the correct unigram, and further assigns all sentences a real score.

6 Summary

As with other metrics used in natural language processing tasks, grammatical error correction metrics must be evaluated against ground truth. The inherent subjectivity in what constitutes a grammatical correction, together with the fact that the use case for grammatically-corrected output is human readers, argue for grounding metric evaluations in a human evaluation, which we produced following procedures established by the Workshop on Statistical Machine Translation. This human ranking shows us that the metric commonly used for GEC is not appropriate, since it does not correlate strongly; newly proposed alternatives fare little better.

Attending to how humans perceive the quality of the sentences, we developed GLEU by making a simple variation to an existing metric. GLEU more closely models human judgments than previous metrics because it rewards correct edits while penalizing ungrammatical edits, while capturing fluency and grammatical constraints by virtue of using n-grams. While this simple modification to BLEU accounts for crucial differences in a monolingual setting, fares well, and could take the place of existing metrics, especially for rapid system development as in machine translation, there is still room for further work as there is a gap in how well it correlates with human judgments.

Most importantly, the results and data from this paper establish a method for objectively evaluating future metric proposals, which is crucial to yearly incremental improvements to the GEC task.

Acknowledgments

We would like to thank Christopher Bryant, Hwee Tou Ng, Mariano Felice, and Ted Briscoe for sharing their research with us pre-publication. We also thank the reviewers and Wei Xu for their valuable feedback, and Benjamin Van Durme for his support.

References

Ondrej Bojar, Christian Buck, Christian Federmann, Barry Haddow, Philipp Koehn, Johannes Leveling, Christof Monz, Pavel Pecina, Matt Post, Herve Saint-Amand, Radu Soricut, Lucia Specia, and Aleš Tamchyna. 2014. Findings of the 2014 Workshop on Statistical Machine Translation. In *Proceedings of the Ninth Workshop on Statistical Machine Translation*, pages 12–58, Baltimore, Maryland, USA, June. Association for Computational Linguistics.

Christopher Bryant and Hwee Tou Ng. 2015. How far are we from fully automatic high quality grammatical error correction? In *Proceedings of the 53rd Annual Meeting of the Association for Computational Linguistics*, Beijing, China, July. Association for Computational Linguistics.

Martin Chodorow, Markus Dickinson, Ross Israel, and Joel Tetreault. 2012. Problems in evaluating grammatical error detection systems. In *Proceedings of COLING 2012*, pages 611–628, Mumbai, India, December. The COLING 2012 Organizing Committee.

Daniel Dahlmeier and Hwee Tou Ng. 2012. Better evaluation for grammatical error correction. In *Proceedings of the 2012 Conference of the North American Chapter of the Association for Computational Linguistics: Human Language Technologies*, pages 568–572. Association for Computational Linguistics, June.

Robert Dale and Adam Kilgarriff. 2011. Helping our own: The HOO 2011 pilot shared task. In *Proceedings of the Generation Challenges Session at the 13th European Workshop on Natural Language Generation*, pages 242–249, Nancy, France, September. Association for Computational Linguistics.

Robert Dale, Ilya Anisimoff, and George Narroway. 2012. HOO 2012: A report on the preposition and determiner error correction shared task. In *Proceedings of the Seventh Workshop on Building Educational Applications Using NLP*, pages 54–62, Montréal, Canada, June. Association for Computational Linguistics.

Christian Federmann. 2012. Appraise: An open-source toolkit for manual evaluation of machine translation output. *The Prague Bulletin of Mathematical Linguistics*, 98:25–35, September.

Mariano Felice and Ted Briscoe. 2015. Towards a standard evaluation method for grammatical error detection and correction. In *Proceedings of the 2015 Conference of the North American Chapter of the Association for Computational Linguistics*, Denver, CO, June. Association for Computational Linguistics.

Alon Lavie and Abhaya Agarwal. 2007. METEOR: An automatic metric for MT evaluation with high levels of correlation with human judgments. In *Proceedings of the Second Workshop on Statistical Machine Translation*, pages 228–231, Prague, Czech Republic, June. Association for Computational Linguistics.

Hwee Tou Ng, Siew Mei Wu, Yuanbin Wu, Christian Hadiwinoto, and Joel Tetreault. 2013. The CoNLL-2013 shared task on grammatical error correction. In *Proceedings of the Seventeenth Conference on Computational Natural Language Learning: Shared Task*, pages 1–12, Sofia, Bulgaria, August. Association for Computational Linguistics.

Hwee Tou Ng, Siew Mei Wu, Ted Briscoe, Christian Hadiwinoto, Raymond Hendy Susanto, and Christopher Bryant. 2014. The CoNLL-2014 shared task on grammatical error correction. In *Proceedings of the Eighteenth Conference on Computational Natural Language Learning: Shared Task*, pages 1–14, Baltimore, Maryland, June. Association for Computational Linguistics.

Kishore Papineni, Salim Roukos, Todd Ward, and Wei-Jing Zhu. 2002. BLEU: A method for automatic evaluation of machine translation. In *Proceedings of 40th Annual Meeting of the Association for Computational Linguistics*, pages 311–318, Philadelphia, Pennsylvania, USA, July. Association for Computational Linguistics.

Y. Albert Park and Roger Levy. 2011. Automated whole sentence grammar correction using a noisy channel model. In *Proceedings of the 49th Annual Meeting of the Association for Computational Linguistics: Human Language Technologies*, pages 934–944, Portland, Oregon, USA, June. Association for Computational Linguistics.

Keisuke Sakaguchi, Matt Post, and Benjamin Van Durme. 2014. Efficient elicitation of annotations for human evaluation of machine translation. In *Proceedings of the Ninth Workshop on Statistical Machine Translation*, pages 1–11, Baltimore, Maryland, USA, June. Association for Computational Linguistics.

Radical Embedding: Delving Deeper to Chinese Radicals

Xinlei Shi, Junjie Zhai, Xudong Yang, Zehua Xie, Chao Liu
Sogou Technology Inc., Beijing, China
{shixinlei, zhaijunjie, yangxudong, xiezehua, liuchao}@sogou-inc.com

Abstract

Languages using Chinese characters are mostly processed at word level. Inspired by recent success of deep learning, we delve deeper to character and radical levels for Chinese language processing. We propose a new deep learning technique, called "radical embedding", with justifications based on Chinese linguistics, and validate its feasibility and utility through a set of three experiments: two in-house standard experiments on short-text categorization (STC) and Chinese word segmentation (CWS), and one in-field experiment on search ranking. We show that radical embedding achieves comparable, and sometimes even better, results than competing methods.

1 Introduction

Chinese is one of the oldest written languages in the world, but it does not attract much attention in top NLP research forums, probably because of its peculiarities and drastic differences from English. There are sentences, words, characters in Chinese, as illustrated in Figure 1. The top row is a Chinese sentence, whose English translation is at the bottom. In between is the pronunciation of the sentence in Chinese, called PinYin, which is a form of Romanian phonetic representation of Chinese, similar to the International Phonetic Alphabet (IPA) for English. Each squared symbol is a distinct Chinese character, and there are no separators between characters calls for Chinese Word Segmentation (CWS) techniques to group adjacent characters into words.

In most current applications (e.g., categorization and recommendation *etc.*), Chinese is

a word a character

Chinese:	今 天/ 天 气/ 真/ 好。
Pinyin:	jīn tiān/ tiān qì/ zhēn/ hǎo。
English:	It is a nice day today.

Figure 1: Illustration of Chinese Language

represented at the word level. Inspired by recent success of delving deep (Szegedy et al., 2014; Zhang and LeCun, 2015; Collobert et al., 2011), an interesting question arises then: *can we delve deeper than word level representation for better Chinese language processing? If the answer is yes, how deep can it be done for fun and for profit?*

Intuitively, the answer should be positive. Nevertheless, each Chinese character is semantically meaningful, thanks to its pictographic root from ancient Chinese as depicted in Figure 2. We could delve deeper by decomposing each character into character radicals.

The right part of Figure 2 illustrates the decomposition. This Chinese character (meaning "morning") is decomposed into 4 radicals that consists of 12 strokes in total. In Chinese linguistics, each Chinese character can be decomposed into no more than four radicals based on a set of preset rules[1]. As depicted by the pictograms in the right part of Figure 2, the 1st radical (and the 3rd that happens to be the same) means "grass", and the 2nd and the 4th mean the "sun" and the "moon", respectively. These four radicals altogether convey the meaning that "the moment when sun arises from the grass while the moon wanes away", which is exactly "morning". On the other hand, it is hard to decipher the semantics of strokes, and radicals are the minimum semantic unit for Chinese. Building deep mod-

[1] http://en.wikipedia.org/wiki/Wubi_method

Proceedings of the 53rd Annual Meeting of the Association for Computational Linguistics and the 7th International Joint Conference on Natural Language Processing (Short Papers), pages 594–598, Beijing, China, July 26-31, 2015.

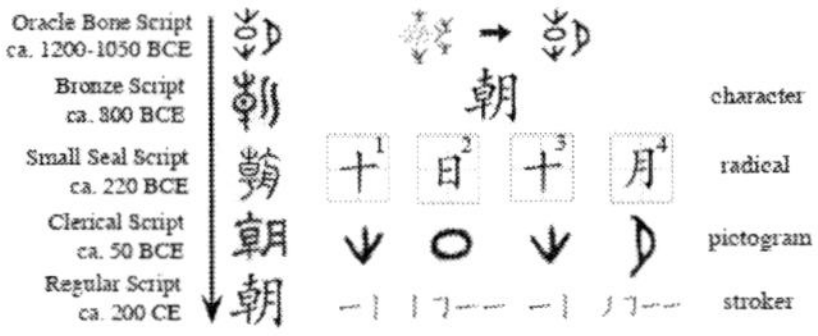

Figure 2: Decomposition of Chinese Character

els from radicals could lead to interesting results.

In sum, this paper makes the following three-fold contributions: (1) we propose a new deep learning technique, called "radical embedding", for Chinese language processing with proper justifications based on Chinese linguistics; (2) we validate the feasibility and utility of radical embedding through a set of three experiments, which include not only two in-house standard experiments on short-text categorization (STC) and Chinese word segmentation (CWS), but an in-field experiment on search ranking as well; (3) this initial success of radical embedding could shed some light on new approaches to better language processing for Chinese and other languages alike.

The rest of this paper is organized as follows. Section 2 presents the radical embedding technique and the accompanying deep neural network components, which are combined and stacked to solve three application problems. Section 3 elaborates on the three applications and reports on the experiment results. With related work briefly discussed in Section 4, Section 5 concludes this study. For clarity, we limit the study to Simplified Chinese in this paper.

2 Deep Networks with Radical Embeddings

This section presents the radical embedding technique, and the accompanying deep neural network components. These components are combined to solve the three applications in Section 3.

Word embedding is a popular technique in NLP (Collobert et al., 2011). It maps words to vectors of real numbers in a relatively low dimensional space. It is shown that the proximity in this numeric space actually embodies algebraic semantic relationship, such as "Queen − Woman + Man ≈ King" (Mikolov et al., 2013). As demonstrated in previous work, this numeric representation of words has led to big improvements in many NLP tasks such as machine translation (Sutskever et al., 2014), question answering (Iyyer et al., 2014) and document ranking (Shen et al., 2014).

	input	output
Convolution	$\boldsymbol{f} \in \mathbb{R}^m$ $\boldsymbol{k} \in \mathbb{R}^n$	$\boldsymbol{y} \in \mathbb{R}^{m+n-1}$ $y_i = \sum_{s=i}^{i+n-1} f_s \cdot k_{s-i}$ $0 \le i \le m-n+1$
Max-pooling	$\boldsymbol{x} \in \mathbb{R}^d$	$y = \max(\boldsymbol{x}) \in \mathbb{R}$
Lookup Table	$\boldsymbol{M} \in \mathbb{R}^{d \times \lvert D \rvert}$ $\boldsymbol{I}_i \in \mathbb{R}^{\lvert D \rvert \times 1}$	$\boldsymbol{v}_i = \boldsymbol{M}\boldsymbol{I}_i \in \mathbb{R}^d$
Tanh	$\boldsymbol{x} \in \mathbb{R}^d$	$\boldsymbol{y} \in \mathbb{R}^d$ $y_i = \frac{e^{x_i}-e^{-x_i}}{e^{x_i}+e^{-x_i}}$ $0 \le i \le d-1$
Linear	$\boldsymbol{x} \in \mathbb{R}^d$	$\boldsymbol{y} = \boldsymbol{x} \in \mathbb{R}^d$
ReLU	$\boldsymbol{x} \in \mathbb{R}^d$	$\boldsymbol{y} \in \mathbb{R}^d$ $y_i = 0 \; if \; x_i \le 0$ $y_i = x_i \; if \; x_i > 0$ $0 \le i \le d-1$
Softmax	$\boldsymbol{x} \in \mathbb{R}^d$	$\boldsymbol{y} \in \mathbb{R}^d$ $y_i = \frac{e^{x_i}}{\sum_{j=1}^{d} e^{x_j}}$ $0 \le i \le d-1$
Concatenate	$\boldsymbol{x}^i \in \mathbb{R}^d$ $0 \le i \le n-1$	$y = (\boldsymbol{x}^0, \boldsymbol{x}^1, ..., \boldsymbol{x}^{n-1})$ $\in \mathbb{R}^{d \times n}$
D: radical vocabulary $\boldsymbol{M}$: a matrix containing $\lvert D \rvert$ columns, each column is a d-dimensional vector represent radical in D. $\boldsymbol{I}_i$: a one hot vector stands for the ith radical in vocabulary		

Table 1: Neural Network Components

Radical embedding is similar to word embedding except that the embedding is at radical level. There are two ways of embedding: CBOW and skip-gram (Mikolov et al., 2013). We here use CBOW for radical embedding because the two methods exhibit few differences, and CBOW is slightly faster in experiments. Specifically, a sequence of Chinese characters is decomposed into a sequence of radicals, to which CBOW is applied. We use the word2vec package (Mikolov et al., 2013) to train radical vectors, and then initialize the lookup table with these radical vectors.

We list the network components in Table 1, which are combined and stacked in Figure 3 to solve different problems in Section 3. Each component is a function, the input column of Table 1 demonstrates input parameters and their dimensions of these functions, the output column shows the formulas and outputs.

3 Applications and Experiments

In this section, we explain how to stack the components in Table 1 to solve three problems: short-text categorization, Chinese word segmentation and search ranking, respectively.

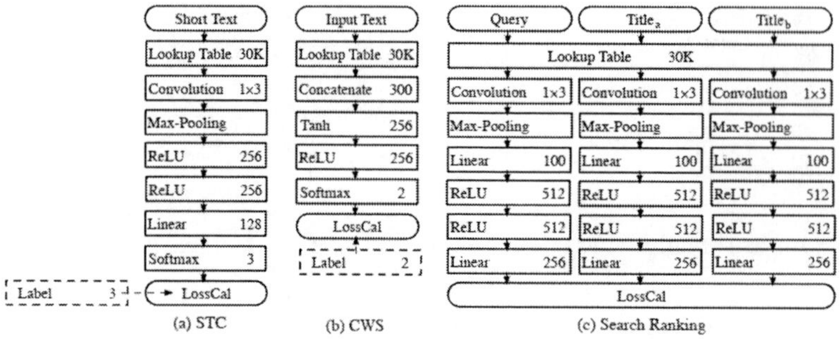

Figure 3: Application Models using Radical Embedding

Accuracy(%)	Competing Methods		Deep Neural Networks with Embedding				
	LR	SVM	wrd	chr	rdc	wrd+rdc	chr+rdc
Finance	93.52	94.06	94.89	**95.85**	94.75	95.70	95.74
Sports	92.40	92.83	95.10	95.01	92.24	95.87	**95.91**
Entertainment	91.72	92.24	94.32	94.77	93.21	**95.11**	94.78
Average	92.55	93.04	94.77	95.21	93.40	**95.56**	95.46

Table 2: Short Text Categorization Results

3.1 Short-Text Categorization

Figure 3(a) presents the network structure of the model for short-text categorization, where the width of each layer is marked out as well. From the top down, a piece of short text, *e.g.*, the title of a URL, is fed into the network, which goes through radical decomposition, table-lookup (*i.e.*, locating the embedding vector corresponding to each radical), convolution, max pooling, two ReLU layers and one fully connected layer, all the way to the final softmax layer, where the loss is calculated against the given label. The standard back-propagation algorithm is used to fine tune all the parameters.

The experiment uses the top-3 categories of the SogouCA and SogouCS news corpus (Wang et al., 2008). 100,000 samples of each category are randomly selected for training and 10,000 for testing. Hyper-parameters for SVM and LR are selected through cross-validation. Table 2 presents the accuracy of different methods, where "wrd", "chr", and "rdc" denote word, character, and radical embedding, respectively. As can be seen, embedding methods outperform competing LR and SVM algorithms uniformly, and the fusion of radicals with words and characters improves both.

3.2 Chinese Word Segmentation

Figure 3(b) presents the CWS network architecture. It uses softmax as well because it essentially classifies whether each character should be a segmentation boundary. The input is firstly decomposed into a radical sequence, on which a sliding window of size 3 is applied to extract features, which are pipelined to downstream levels of the network.

We evaluate the performance using two standard datasets: PKU and MSR, as provided by (Emerson, 2005). The PKU dataset contains 1.1M training words and 104K test words, and the MSR dataset contains 2.37M training words and 107K test words. We use the first 90% sentences for training and the rest 10% sentences for testing. We compare radical embedding with the CRF method[2], FNLM (Mansur et al., 2013) and PSA (Zheng et al., 2013), and present the results in Table 3. Note that no dictionary is used in any of these algorithms.

We see that the radical embedding (RdE) method, as the first attempt to segment words at radical level, actually achieves very competitive results. It outperforms both CRF and FNLM on both datasets, and is comparable with PSA.

[2] `http://crfpp.googlecode.com/svn/trunk/doc/index.html?source=navbar`

Data	Approach	Precision	Recall	F1
PKU	CRF	88.1	86.2	87.1
	FNLM	87.1	87.9	87.5
	PSA	**92.8**	92.0	**92.4**
	RdE	92.6	**92.1**	92.3
MSR	CRF	89.3	87.5	88.4
	FNLM	92.3	92.2	92.2
	PSA	92.9	**93.6**	93.3
	RdE	**93.4**	93.3	**93.3**

Table 3: CWS Result Comparison

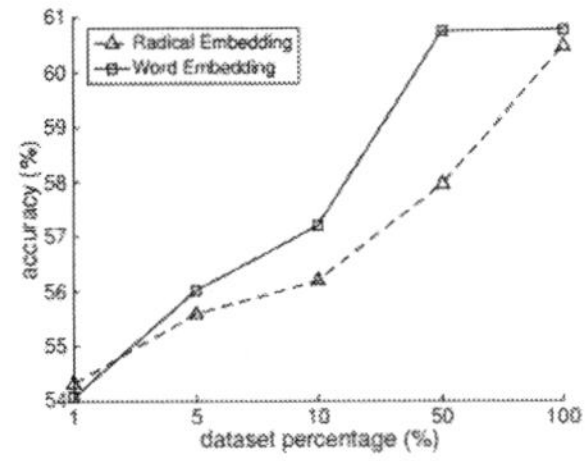

Figure 4: Search Ranking Results

3.3 Web Search Ranking

Finally, we report on an in-field experiment with Web search ranking. Web search leverages many kinds of ranking signals, an important one of which is the preference signals extracted from click-through logs. Given a set of triplets {query, title_a, title_b} discovered from click logs, where the URL title_a is preferred to title_b for the query. The goal of learning is to produce a matching model between query and title that maximally agrees with the preference triplets. This learnt matching model is combined with other signals, *e.g.*, PageRank, BM25F, *etc.* in the general ranking. The deep network model for this task is depicted in Figure 3(c), where each triplet goes through seven layers to compute the loss using Equation (1), where $\boldsymbol{q_i}$, $\boldsymbol{a_i}$, $\boldsymbol{b_i}$ are the output vectors for the query and two titles right before computing the loss. The calculated loss is then back propagated to fine tune all the parameters.

$$\sum_{i=1}^{m} \log\left(1 + \exp\left(-c * \left(\frac{\boldsymbol{q_i^T a_i}}{|\boldsymbol{q_i}||\boldsymbol{a_i}|} - \frac{\boldsymbol{q_i^T b_i}}{|\boldsymbol{q_i}||\boldsymbol{b_i}|}\right)\right)\right) \quad (1)$$

The evaluation is carried out on a proprietary data set provided by a leading Chinese search engine company. It contains 95,640,311 triplets, which involve 14,919,928 distinct queries and 65,125,732 distinct titles. 95,502,506 triplets are used for training, with the rest 137,805 triplets as testing. It is worth noting that the testing triplets are hard cases, mostly involving long queries and short title texts.

Figure 4 presents the results, where we vary the amount of training data to see how the performance varies. The x-axis lists the percentage of training dataset used, and 100% means using the entire training dataset, and the y-axis is the accuracy of the predicted preferences. We see that word embedding is overall superior to radical embedding, but it is interesting to see that word embedding saturates using half of the data, while ranking with radical embedding catches up using the entire dataset, getting very close in accuracy (60.78% vs. 60.47%). Because no more data is available beyond the 95,640,311 triplets, unfortunately we cannot tell if radical embedding would eventually surpass word embedding with more data.

4 Related Work

This paper presents the first piece of work on embedding radicals for fun and for profit, and we are mostly inspired by fellow researchers delving deeper in various domains (Zheng et al., 2013; Zhang and LeCun, 2015; Collobert et al., 2011; Kim, 2014; Johnson and Zhang, 2014; dos Santos and Gatti, 2014). For example, Huang *et al.*'s work (Huang et al., 2013) on DSSM uses letter trigram as the basic representation, which somehow resembles radicals. Zhang and Yann's recent work (Zhang and LeCun, 2015) represents Chinese at PinYin level, thus taking Chinese as a western language. Although working at PinYin level might be a viable approach, using radicals should be more reasonable from a linguistic point of view. Nevertheless, PinYin only represents the pronunciation, which is arguably further away from semantics than radicals.

5 Conclusion

This study presents the first piece of evidence on the feasibility and utility of radical embedding for Chinese language processing. It is inspired by recent success of delving deep in various domains, and roots on the rationale that radicals, as the minimum semantic unit, could be appropriate for deep learning. We demonstrate the utility of radical embedding through two standard in-house and one in-field experiments. While some promising results are obtained, there are still many problems to be explored further, *e.g.*, how to leverage the layout code in radical decomposition that is currently neglected to improve performance. An even more exciting topic could be to train radical, character and word embedding in a unified hierarchical model as they are naturally hierarchical. In sum, we hope this preliminary work could shed some light on new approaches to Chinese language processing and other languages alike.

References

Ronan Collobert, Jason Weston, Léon Bottou, Michael Karlen, Koray Kavukcuoglu, and Pavel P. Kuksa. 2011. Natural language processing (almost) from scratch. *Journal of Machine Learning Research*, 12:2493–2537.

Cícero Nogueira dos Santos and Maira Gatti. 2014. Deep convolutional neural networks for sentiment analysis of short texts. In *25th International Conference on Computational Linguistics, Proceedings of the Conference: Technical Papers*, pages 69–78.

Thomas Emerson. 2005. The second international chinese word segmentation bakeoff. In *Proceedings of the fourth SIGHAN workshop on Chinese language Processing*, volume 133.

Mohit Iyyer, Jordan Boyd-Graber, Leonardo Claudino, Richard Socher, and Hal Daumé III. 2014. A neural network for factoid question answering over paragraphs. In *Proceedings of the 2014 Conference on Empirical Methods in Natural Language Processing*, pages 633–644.

Rie Johnson and Tong Zhang. 2014. Effective use of word order for text categorization with convolutional neural networks. *CoRR*, abs/1412.1058.

Yoon Kim. 2014. Convolutional neural networks for sentence classification. In *Proceedings of the 2014 Conference on Empirical Methods in Natural Language Processing*, pages 1746–1751.

Mairgup Mansur, Wenzhe Pei, and Baobao Chang. 2013. Feature-based neural language model and chinese word segmentation. In *Sixth International Joint Conference on Natural Language Processing, 2013, Nagoya, Japan, October 14-18, 2013*, pages 1271–1277.

Tomas Mikolov, Ilya Sutskever, Kai Chen, Gregory S. Corrado, and Jeffrey Dean. 2013. Distributed representations of words and phrases and their compositionality. In *Advances in Neural Information Processing Systems*, pages 3111–3119.

Yelong Shen, Xiaodong He, Jianfeng Gao, Li Deng, and Gregoire Mesnil. 2014. A latent semantic model with convolutional-pooling structure for information retrieval. In *Proceedings of the 23rd ACM International Conference on Conference on Information and Knowledge Management*, pages 101–110.

Ilya Sutskever, Oriol Vinyals, and Quoc VV Le. 2014. Sequence to sequence learning with neural networks. In *Advances in Neural Information Processing Systems*, pages 3104–3112.

Christian Szegedy, Wei Liu, Yangqing Jia, Pierre Sermanet, Scott Reed, Dragomir Anguelov, Dumitru Erhan, Vincent Vanhoucke, and Andrew Rabinovich. 2014. Going deeper with convolutions. *CoRR*, abs/1409.4842.

Canhui Wang, Min Zhang, Shaoping Ma, and Liyun Ru. 2008. Automatic online news issue construction in web environment. In *Proceedings of the 17th International Conference on World Wide Web*, pages 457–466.

Xiang Zhang and Yann LeCun. 2015. Text understanding from scratch. *CoRR*, abs/1502.01710.

Xiaoqing Zheng, Hanyang Chen, and Tianyu Xu. 2013. Deep learning for chinese word segmentation and POS tagging. In *Proceedings of the 2013 Conference on Empirical Methods in Natural Language Processing*, pages 647–657.

Automatic Detection of Sentence Fragments

Chak Yan Yeung and John Lee
Halliday Centre for Intelligent Applications of Language Studies
Department of Linguistics and Translation
City University of Hong Kong
chak.yeung@my.cityu.edu.hk
jsylee@cityu.edu.hk

Abstract

We present and evaluate a method for automatically detecting sentence fragments in English texts written by non-native speakers. Our method combines syntactic parse tree patterns and parts-of-speech information produced by a tagger to detect this phenomenon. When evaluated on a corpus of authentic learner texts, our best model achieved a precision of 0.84 and a recall of 0.62, a statistically significant improvement over baselines using non-parse features, as well as a popular grammar checker.

1 Introduction

It is challenging to detect and correct sentence-level grammatical errors because it involves automatic syntactic analysis on noisy, learner sentences. Indeed, none of the teams achieved any recall for comma splices in the most recent CoNLL shared task (Ng et al., 2014). Sentence fragments fared hardly better: of the thirteen teams, two scored a recall of 0.25 for correction and another scored 0.2; the rest did not achieve any recall.

Although parser performance degrades on learner text (Foster, 2007), parsers can still be useful for identifying grammatical errors if they produce consistent patterns that indicate these errors. We show that parse tree patterns, automatically derived from training data, significantly improve system performance on detecting sentence fragments.

The rest of the paper is organized as follows. The next section defines the types of sentence fragments treated in this paper. Section 3 reviews related work. Section 4 describes the features used in our model. Section 5 discusses the datasets and section 6 analyzes the experiment results. Our best model significantly outperforms baselines that do not consider syntactic information and a widely used grammar checker.

2 Sentence Fragment

Every English sentence must have a main or independent clause. Most linguists require a clause to contain a subject and a finite verb (Hunt, 1965; Polio, 1997); otherwise, it is considered a sentence fragment. Following Bram (1995), we classify sentence fragments into the following four categories:

No Subject. Fragments that lack a subject,[1] such as "According to the board, is $100."

No finite verb. Fragments that lack a finite verb. These may be a nonfinite verb phrase, or a noun phrase, such as "Mrs. Kern in a show."

No subject and finite verb. Fragments lacking both a subject and a finite verb; a typical example is a prepositional phrase, such as "Up through the ranks."

Subordinate clause. These fragments consist of a stand-alone subordinate clause; the clause typically begins with a relative pronoun or a subordinating conjunction, such as "While they take pains to hide their assets."

3 Related Work

Using parse tree patterns to judge the grammaticality of a sentence is not new. Wong and Dras (2011) exploited probabilistic context-free grammar (PCFG) rules as features for native language identification. In addition to production rules, Post (2011) incorporated parse fragment features computed from derivations of tree substitution grammars. Heilman et al. (2014) used the parse scores and syntactic features to classify the comprehensibility of learner text, though they made no attempt to correct the errors.

In current grammatical error correction systems, parser output is used mainly to locate

[1]Our evaluation data distinguishes between imperatives and fragments. Our automatic classifier, however, makes no such attempt because it would require analysis of the context and significant real-world knowledge.

Proceedings of the 53rd Annual Meeting of the Association for Computational Linguistics and the 7th International Joint Conference on Natural Language Processing (Short Papers), pages 599–603,
Beijing, China, July 26-31, 2015.

relevant information involved in long-distance grammatical constructions (Tetreault et al., 2010; Yoshimoto et al., 2013; Zhang and Wang, 2014). To the best of our knowledge, the only previous work that used distinctive parse patterns to detect specific grammatical errors was concerned with comma splices. Lee et al. (2014) manually identified distinctive production rules which, when used as features in a CRF, significantly improved the precision and recall in locating comma splices in learner text. Our method will similarly leverage parse tree patterns, but with the goal of detecting sentence fragment errors. More importantly, our approach is fully automatic, and can thus potentially be broadly applied on other syntax-related learner errors.

Many commercial systems, such as the Criterion Online Writing Service (Burstein et al., 2004), Grammarly[2], and WhiteSmoke[3], give feedback about sentence fragments. To the best of our knowledge, these systems do not explicitly consider parse tree patterns. The grammar checker embedded in Microsoft Word also gives feedback about sentence fragments, and will serve as one of our baselines.

Aside from the CoNLL-2014 shared task (see Section 1), the only other reported evaluation on detecting or correcting sentence fragments has been performed on Microsoft ESL Assistant and the NTNU Grammar Checker (Chen, 2009). Neither tool detected any of the sentence fragments in the test set.

4 Fragment Detection

We cast the problem of sentence fragment detection as a multiclass classification task. Given a sentence, the system would mark it either as false, if it is not a fragment, or as one of the four fragment categories described in Section 2. Rather than a binary decision on whether a sentence is a fragment, this categorisation provides more useful feedback to the learner, since each of the four fragment categories requires its own correction strategy.

4.1 Models

Baseline Models. We trained three baseline models with features that incorporate an increasing amount of information about sentence structure. The first baseline model was trained on the word trigrams of the sentences, the second model on part-of-speech unigrams, and the third on part-of-speech trigrams. All of these features can be obtained without syntactic parsing. To reduce the number of features, we filtered out the word trigrams that occur less than twenty times and the POS trigrams that occur less than a hundred times in the training data.

Parse Models. Our approach uses parse tree patterns as features. Although any arbitrary subtree structure can potentially serve as a feature, the children of the root of the tree tend to be most salient. These nodes usually denote the syntactic constituents of the sentence, and so often reveal differences between well-formed sentences and fragments. Consider the sentence "While Peter was a good boy.", shown in the parse tree in Figure 1. The child of the root of the tree is SBAR. When the subordinating conjunction "while" is removed to yield a well-formed sentence, the children nodes change accordingly into the expected NP and VP. In contrast, the POS tags, used in the baseline models, tend to remain the same.

We use the label of the root and the trigrams of its children nodes as features, similar to Sjöbergh (2005) and Lin et al. (2011). We also extend our patterns to grandchildren in some cases. When analyzing an ill-formed sentence, the parser can sometimes group words into constituents to which they do not belong, such as forming a VP that does not contain a verb. For example, the phrase "up the hill" was analyzed as a VP in the fragment "A new challenger up the hill" when in fact the sentence is missing a verb. To take into account such misanalyses, we also include the POS tag of the first child of all NP, VP, PP, ADVP, and ADJP as features. The first child is chosen because it often exposes the parsing error, as is the case with the preposition "up" in the purported VP "up the hill" in the above example.

We trained two models for experiments: the "Parse" model used the parser's POS tags and the "Parse + Tag" model used the tags produced by the POS tagger, which was trained on local features and tends to be less affected by ill-formed sentence structures. For example, in the sentence "Certainly was not true.", the word "certainly" was tagged as a plural noun by the parser while the tagger correctly identified it as an adverb. The NP construction in the fragment was encoded as "NP-

[2]www.grammarly.com

[3]www.whitesmoke.com

NNP" in the "Parse" model and "NP-RB" in the "Parse + Tag" model. To reduce the number of features, we filtered out the node trigrams that occur less than ten times in the training data.

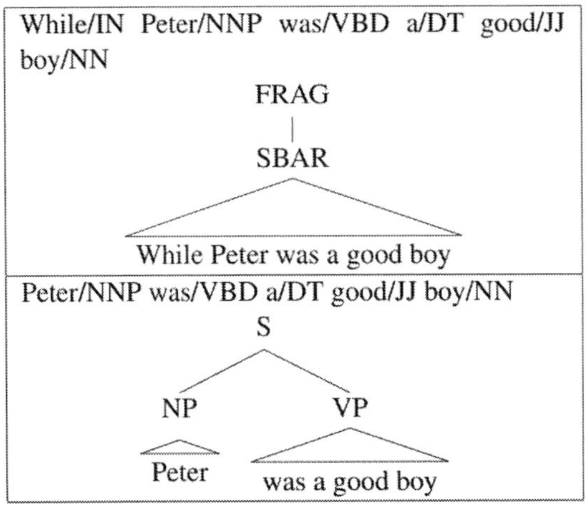

Figure 1: The POS-tagged words and parse trees of the fragment "While Peter was a good boy." and the well-formed sentence "Peter was a good boy.".

5 Data

5.1 Training Data

We automatically produced training data from the New York Times portion of the AQUAINT Corpus of English News Text (Graff, 2002). Similar to Foster and Andersen (2009), we artificially generate fragments that correspond to the four categories (Section 2) by removing different components from well-formed English sentences. For the "no subject" category, the NP immediately under the topmost S was removed. For the "no finite verb" category, we removed the finite verb in the VP immediately under the topmost S. For the "no subject and finite verb" category, we removed both the NP and the finite verb in the VP immediately under the topmost S. For the "subordinate clause" category, we looked for any SBAR in the sentence that is preceded by a comma and consists of an IN child followed by an S. The words under the SBAR are extracted as the fragment. Using this method, we created a total of 60,000 fragments, with 15,000 sentences in each category. Together with the original sentences, our training data consists of 120,000 sentences, half of which are fragments.

5.2 Evaluation Data

Fragment was among the 28 error types introduced in the CoNLL-2014 shared task (Ng et al., 2014), but the test set used in the task only contained 16 such errors and is too small for our purpose. Instead, we evaluated our system on the NUCLE corpus (Dahlmeier et al., 2013), which was used as the training data in the shared task. The error label "SFrag" in the NUCLE corpus was used for sentence fragments in a wider sense than the four categories defined by Bram (1995) (see Section 2). For example, "SFrag" also labels sentences with stylistic issues, such as those beginning with "therefore" or "hence", and sentences that, though well-formed, should be merged with its neighbor, such as "In Singapore, we can see that this problem is occurring. This is so as there is a huge discrepancy in the education levels.".

We asked two human annotators to classify the fragments into the different categories described in Section 2. The kappa was 0.84. Most of the disagreements involved sentences that contain a semi-colon which, when replaced with a comma, would become well-formed. One annotator flagged these cases as fragments while the other did not, considering them to be punctuation errors. Another source of disagreements was whether a sentence should be considered an imperative.

Among the 249 sentences marked as fragments, 86 were classified as one of the Bram (1995) categories by at least one of the annotators. Most of the fragments belong to categories "no finite verb" and "subordinate clause", accounting for 43.0% and 31.4% of the cases respectively. The categories "no subject and finite verb" and "no subject" both account for 12.8% of the cases. We left all errors in the sentences in place so as to reflect our models' performance on authentic learner data.

6 Results

We obtained the POS tags and parse trees of the sentences in our datasets with the Stanford POS tagger (Toutanova et al., 2003) and the Stanford parser (Manning et al., 2014). We used the logistic regression implementation in scikit-learn (Pedregosa et al., 2011) for the maximum entropy models in our experiments. In addition to the three baseline models described in Section 4.1, we computed a fourth baseline using the grammar checker in Microsoft Word 2013 by configuring the checker to capture "Fragments and Run-ons" and "Fragment - stylistic suggestions".

6.1 Fragment detection

We first evaluated the systems' ability to detect fragments. The fragment categories are disregarded in this evaluation and the system's result is considered correct even if its output category does not match the one marked by the annotators. We adopted the metric used in the CoNLL-2014 shared task, $F_{0.5}$, which emphasizes precision twice as much as recall because it is important to minimize false alarms for language learners[4].

The results are shown in Table 1. The "Parse" model achieved a precision of 0.82, a recall of 0.57 and an $F_{0.5}$ of 0.75. Using the POS tags produced by the POS tagger instead of the ones produced by the parser, the "Parse + Tag" model achieved a precision of 0.84, a recall of 0.62 and an $F_{0.5}$ of 0.78, improving upon the results of the "Parse" model and significantly outperforming all four baselines[5].

Most of the false negatives are in the "no finite verb" category and many of them involve fragments with subordinate clauses, such as "The increased of longevity as the elderly are leading longer lives.". In order to create parse trees that fit those of complete sentences, the parser tended to interpret the verbs in the subordinate clauses (e.g., "are" in the above example) as the fragments' main verbs, causing the errors. For false positives, the errors were caused mostly by the presence of introductory phrases. The parse trees of these sentences usually contain a PP or an ADVP immediately under the root, which is a pattern shared by fragments. The system also flagged some imperative sentences as fragments.

System	P/R/$F_{0.5}$
Word Trigrams	0.20/0.03/0.09
POS Tags	0.56/0.33/0.47
POS Trigrams	0.55/0.42/0.52
MS Word	0.80/0.15/0.43
Parse	0.82/0.57/0.75
Parse + Tag	0.84/0.62/0.78

Table 1: System precision, recall and F-measure for fragment detection.

6.2 Fragment classification

For the fragments that the system has correctly identified, we evaluated their classification accuracy[6]. Table 2 shows the confusion matrix of the system's results.

The largest source of error is the system wrongly classifying 'no finite verb" and "subordinate clause" fragments as "no subject and finite verb". Most of these involve fragments that begin with a prepositional phrase, such as "for example", followed by a comma. The annotators treated the prepositional phrase as introductory phrase and focused on the segment after the comma. In contrast, based on the parser output, the system often treated the entire fragment as a PP, which should then belong to "no subject and finite verb". It can be argued that both interpretations are valid. For instance, the fragment "For example, apples and oranges" can be corrected as "For example, apples and oranges are fruits" or, alternatively, "I love fruits, for example, apples and oranges".

→ Expected ↓ System	S	V	SV	C
S	[6]	4	1	1
V	0	[12]	2	0
SV	0	5	[2]	11
C	0	0	0	[9]

Table 2: The confusion matrix of the system for classifying the detected sentence fragments into the categories no subject (S), no finite verb (V), no subject and finite verb (SV) and subordinate clause (C).

7 Conclusion

We have presented a data-driven method for automatically detecting sentence fragments. We have shown that our method, which uses syntactic parse tree patterns and POS tagger output, significantly improves accuracy in detecting fragments in English learner texts.

Acknowledgments

This work was supported in part by a Strategic Research Grant (#7008166) from City University of

[4] $F_{0.5}$ is calculated by $F_{0.5} = (1 + 0.5^2) \times R \times P / (R + 0.5^2 \times P)$ for recall R and precision P.

[5] At $p \leq 0.002$ by McNemar's test.

[6] The grammar checker in Microsoft Word is excluded from this evaluation because it does not provide any correction suggestions for fragments.

Hong Kong.

References

Barli Bram. 1995. *Write Well, Improving Writing Skills*. Kanisius.

Jill Burstein, Martin Chodorow, and Claudia Leacock. 2004. Automated essay evaluation: The Criterion online writing service. *AI Magazine*, 25(3):27.

Hao-Jan Howard Chen. 2009. Evaluating two web-based grammar checkers-Microsoft ESL Assistant and NTNU statistical grammar checker. *Computational Linguistics and Chinese Language Processing*, 14(2):161–180.

Daniel Dahlmeier, Hwee Tou Ng, and Siew Mei Wu. 2013. Building a large annotated corpus of learner english: The NUS Corpus of Learner English. In *Proceedings of the Eighth Workshop on Innovative Use of NLP for Building Educational Applications*, pages 22–31.

Jennifer Foster and Øistein E Andersen. 2009. GenERRate: generating errors for use in grammatical error detection. In *Proceedings of the fourth workshop on innovative use of NLP for building educational applications*, pages 82–90. Association for Computational Linguistics.

Jennifer Foster. 2007. Treebanks gone bad. *International Journal of Document Analysis and Recognition (IJDAR)*, 10(3-4):129–145.

David Graff. 2002. The AQUAINT corpus of English news text. *Linguistic Data Consortium, Philadelphia*.

Michael Heilman, Joel Tetreault, Aoife Cahill, Nitin Madnani, Melissa Lopez, and Matthew Mulholland. 2014. Predicting grammaticality on an ordinal scale. In *Proceedings of ACL-2014*.

Kellogg W Hunt. 1965. Grammatical structures written at three grade levels. NCTE research report no. 3.

John Lee, Chak Yan Yeung, and Martin Chodorow. 2014. Automatic detection of comma splices. In *Proceedings of PACLIC-2014*.

Nay Yee Lin, Khin Mar Soe, and Ni Lar Thein. 2011. Developing a chunk-based grammar checker for translated English sentences. In *Proceedings of PACLIC-2011*, pages 245–254.

Christopher D Manning, Mihai Surdeanu, John Bauer, Jenny Finkel, Steven J Bethard, and David McClosky. 2014. The Stanford CoreNLP natural language processing toolkit. In *Proceedings of 52nd Annual Meeting of the Association for Computational Linguistics: System Demonstrations*, pages 55–60.

Hwee Tou Ng, Siew Mei Wu, Ted Briscoe, Christian Hadiwinoto, Raymond Hendy Susanto, and Christopher Bryant. 2014. The CoNLL-2014 shared task on grammatical error correction. In *Proceedings of the Eighteenth Conference on Computational Natural Language Learning: Shared Task*.

Fabian Pedregosa, Gaël Varoquaux, Alexandre Gramfort, Vincent Michel, Bertrand Thirion, Olivier Grisel, Mathieu Blondel, Peter Prettenhofer, Ron Weiss, Vincent Dubourg, et al. 2011. Scikit-learn: Machine learning in python. *The Journal of Machine Learning Research*, 12:2825–2830.

Charlene G Polio. 1997. Measures of linguistic accuracy in second language writing research. *Language learning*, 47(1):101–143.

Matt Post. 2011. Judging grammaticality with tree substitution grammar derivations. In *Proceedings of the 49th Annual Meeting of the Association for Computational Linguistics: Human Language Technologies: short papers-Volume 2*, pages 217–222. Association for Computational Linguistics.

Jonas Sjöbergh. 2005. Chunking: an unsupervised method to find errors in text. In *Proceedings of the 15th NODALIDA conference*, pages 180–185.

Joel Tetreault, Jennifer Foster, and Martin Chodorow. 2010. Using parse features for preposition selection and error detection. In *Proceedings of ACL-2010*, pages 353–358. Association for Computational Linguistics.

Kristina Toutanova, Dan Klein, Christopher D Manning, and Yoram Singer. 2003. Feature-rich part-of-speech tagging with a cyclic dependency network. In *Proceedings of the 2003 Conference of the North American Chapter of the Association for Computational Linguistics on Human Language Technology-Volume 1*, pages 173–180. Association for Computational Linguistics.

Sze-Meng Jojo Wong and Mark Dras. 2011. Exploiting parse structures for native language identification. In *Proceedings of the Conference on Empirical Methods in Natural Language Processing*, pages 1600–1610. Association for Computational Linguistics.

Ippei Yoshimoto, Tomoya Kose, Kensuke Mitsuzawa, Keisuke Sakaguchi, Tomoya Mizumoto, Yuta Hayashibe, Mamoru Komachi, and Yuji Matsumoto. 2013. NAIST at 2013 CoNLL grammatical error correction shared task. In *Proceedings of the Seventeenth Conference on Computational Natural Language Learning: Shared Task*, volume 26.

Longkai Zhang and Houfeng Wang. 2014. Go climb a dependency tree and correct the grammatical errors. In *Proceedings of EMNLP-2014*.

A Computational Approach to Automatic Prediction of *Drunk-Texting*

Aditya Joshi[1,2,3] **Abhijit Mishra**[1] **Balamurali AR**[4]
Pushpak Bhattacharyya[1] **Mark James Carman**[2]
[1]IIT Bombay, India, [2]Monash University, Australia
[3]IITB-Monash Research Academy, India [4]Aix-Marseille University, France
{adityaj, abhijitmishra, pb}@cse.iitb.ac.in
balamurali.ar@lif.univ-mrs.fr, mark.carman@monash.edu

Abstract

Alcohol abuse may lead to unsociable behavior such as crime, drunk driving, or privacy leaks. We introduce automatic drunk-texting prediction as the task of identifying whether a text was written when under the influence of alcohol. We experiment with tweets labeled using hashtags as distant supervision. Our classifiers use a set of N-gram and stylistic features to detect drunk tweets. Our observations present the first quantitative evidence that text contains signals that can be exploited to detect drunk-texting.

1 Introduction

The ubiquity of communication devices has made social media highly accessible. The content on these media reflects a user's day-to-day activities. This includes content created under the influence of alcohol. In popular culture, this has been referred to as '*drunk-texting*'[1]. In this paper, we introduce automatic 'drunk-texting prediction' as a computational task. Given a tweet, the goal is to automatically identify if it was written by a drunk user. We refer to tweets written under the influence of alcohol as '*drunk tweets*', and the opposite as '*sober tweets*'.

A key challenge is to obtain an annotated dataset. We use hashtag-based supervision so that the authors of the tweets mention if they were drunk at the time of posting a tweet. We create three datasets by using different strategies that are related to the use of hashtags. We then present SVM-based classifiers that use N-gram and stylistic features such as capitalisation, spelling errors, etc. Through our experiments, we make subtle points related to: (a) the *performance of our features*, (b) *how our approach compares against human ability* to detect drunk-texting, (c) *most discriminative stylistic features*, and (d) *an error analysis* that points to future work. To the best of our knowledge, this is a first study that shows the feasibility of text-based analysis for drunk-texting prediction.

[1]Source: http://www.urbandictionary.com

2 Motivation

Past studies show the relation between alcohol abuse and unsociable behaviour such as aggression (Bushman and Cooper, 1990), crime (Carpenter, 2007), suicide attempts (Merrill et al., 1992), drunk driving (Loomis and West, 1958), and risky sexual behaviour (Bryan et al., 2005). Merrill et al. (1992) state that "*those responsible for assessing cases of attempted suicide should be adept at detecting alcohol misuse*". Thus, a drunk-texting prediction system can be used to identify individuals susceptible to these behaviours, or for investigative purposes after an incident.

Drunk-texting may also cause regret. Mail Goggles[2] prompts a user to solve math questions before sending an email on weekend evenings. Some Android applications[3] avoid drunk-texting by blocking outgoing texts at the click of a button. However, to the best of our knowledge, these tools require a user command to begin blocking. An ongoing text-based analysis will be more helpful, especially since it offers a more natural setting by monitoring stream of social media text and not explicitly seeking user input. Thus, automatic drunk-texting prediction will improve systems aimed to avoid regrettable drunk-texting. To the best of our knowledge, ours is the first study that does a quantitative analysis, in terms of prediction of the drunk state by using textual clues.

Several studies have studied linguistic traits associated with emotion expression and mental

[2]http://gmailblog.blogspot.in/2008/10/new-in-labs-stop-sending-mail-you-later.html

[3]https://play.google.com/store/apps/details?id=com.oopsapp

Proceedings of the 53rd Annual Meeting of the Association for Computational Linguistics and the 7th International Joint Conference on Natural Language Processing (Short Papers), pages 604–608,
Beijing, China, July 26-31, 2015.

health issues, suicidal nature, criminal status, etc. (Pennebaker, 1993; Pennebaker, 1997). NLP techniques have been used in the past to address social safety and mental health issues (Resnik et al., 2013).

3 Definition and Challenges

Drunk-texting prediction is the task of classifying a text as drunk or sober. For example, a tweet *'Feeling buzzed. Can't remember how the evening went'* must be predicted as *'drunk'*, whereas, *'Returned from work late today, the traffic was bad'* must be predicted as *'sober'*. The challenges are:

1. **More than topic categorisation**: Drunk-texting prediction is similar to topic categorisation (that is, classification of documents into a set of categories such as *'news'*, *'sports'*, etc.). However, Borrill et al. (1987) show that alcohol abusers have more pronounced emotions, specifically, anger. In this respect, drunk-texting prediction lies at the confluence of topic categorisation and emotion classification.

2. **Identification of labeled examples**: It is difficult to obtain a set of sober tweets. The ideal label can be possibly given only by the author. For example, whether a tweet such as *'I am feeling lonely tonight'* is a drunk tweet is ambiguous. This is similar to sarcasm expressed as an exaggeration (for example, *'This is the best film ever!*), where the context beyond the text needs to be considered.

3. **Precision/Recall trade-off**: The goal that a drunk-texting prediction system must chase depends on the application. An application that identifies potential crimes must work with high precision, since the target population to be monitored will be large. On the other hand, when being used to avoid regrettable drunk-texting, a prediction system must produce high recall in order to ensure that a drunk message does not pass through.

4 Dataset Creation

We use hashtag-based supervision to create our datasets, similar to tasks like emotion classification (Purver and Battersby, 2012). The tweets are downloaded using Twitter API (`https://dev.twitter.com/`). We remove non-Unicode characters, and eliminate tweets that contain hyperlinks[4] and also tweets that are shorter than 6 words in length. Finally, hashtags used to indicate drunk or sober tweets are removed so that they provide labels, but do not act as features. The dataset is available on request. As a result, we create three datasets, each using a different strategy for sober tweets, as follows:

Figure 1: Word cloud for drunk tweets

1. **Dataset 1** (2435 drunk, 762 sober): We collect tweets that are marked as drunk and sober, using hashtags. Tweets containing hashtags #drunk, #drank and #imdrunk are considered to be drunk tweets, while those with #notdrunk, #imnotdrunk and #sober are considered to be sober tweets.

2. **Dataset 2** (2435 drunk, 5644 sober): The drunk tweets are downloaded using drunk hashtags, as above. The list of users who created these tweets is extracted. For the negative class, we download tweets by these users, which do not contain the hashtags that correspond to drunk tweets.

3. **Dataset H** (193 drunk, 317 sober): A separate dataset is created where drunk tweets are downloaded using drunk hashtags, as above. The set of sober tweets is collected using both the approaches above. The resultant is the held-out test set *Dataset-H that contains no tweets in common with Datasets 1 and 2*.

The drunk tweets for Datasets 1 and 2 are the same. Figure 1 shows a word-cloud for these drunk tweets (with stop words and forms of the word *'drunk'* removed), created using

[4]This is a rigid criterion, but we observe that tweets with hyperlinks are likely to be promotional in nature.

Feature	Description
N-gram Features	
Unigram & Bigram (Presence)	Boolean features indicating unigrams and bigrams
Unigram & Bigram (Count)	Real-valued features indicating unigrams and bigrams
Stylistic Features	
LDA unigrams (Presence/Count)	Boolean & real-valued features indicating unigrams from LDA
POS Ratio	Ratios of nouns, adjectives, adverbs in the tweet
#Named Entity Mentions	Number of named entity mentions
#Discourse Connectors	Number of discourse connectors
Spelling errors	Boolean feature indicating presence of spelling mistakes
Repeated characters	Boolean feature indicating whether a character is repeated three times consecutively
Capitalisation	Number of capital letters in the tweet
Length	Number of words
Emoticon (Presence/Count)	Boolean & real-valued features indicating unigrams
Sentiment Ratio	Positive and negative word ratios

Table 1: Our Feature Set for Drunk-texting Prediction

WordItOut[5]. The size of a word indicates its frequency. In addition to topical words such as 'bar', 'bottle' and 'wine', the word-cloud shows sentiment words such as 'love' or 'damn', along with profane words.

Heuristics other than these hashtags could have been used for dataset creation. For example, timestamps were a good option to account for time at which a tweet was posted. However, this could not be used because user's local times was not available, since very few users had geolocation enabled.

5 Feature Design

The complete set of features is shown in Table 1. There are two sets of features: (a) N-gram features, and (b) Stylistic features. We use unigrams and bigrams as N-gram features- considering both presence and count.

Table 1 shows the complete set of stylistic features of our prediction system. POS ratios are a set of features that record the proportion of each POS tag in the dataset (for example, the proportion of nouns/adjectives, etc.). The POS tags and named entity mentions are obtained from NLTK (Bird, 2006). Discourse connectors are identified based on a manually created list. Spelling errors are identified using a spell checker by Aby (2014). The repeated characters feature captures a situation in which a word contains a letter that is repeated three or more times, as in the case of *happpy*. Since drunk-texting is often associated with emotional expression, we also incorporate a set of sentiment-based features. These features include: count/presence of emoticons and sentiment ratio. Sentiment ratio is the proportion of positive and negative words in the tweet. To determine positive and negative words, we use the sentiment lexicon in Wilson et al. (2005). To identify a more refined set of words that correspond to the two classes, we also estimated 20 topics for the dataset by estimating an LDA model (Blei et al., 2003). We then consider top 10 words per topic, for both classes. This results in 400 LDA-specific unigrams that are then used as features.

	A (%)	NP (%)	PP (%)	NR (%)	PR (%)
Dataset 1					
N-gram	**85.5**	72.8	88.8	63.4	92.5
Stylistic	75.6	32.5	76.2	3.2	98.6
All	85.4	71.9	89.1	64.6	91.9
Dataset 2					
N-gram	77.9	82.3	65.5	87.2	56.5
Stylistic	70.3	70.8	56.7	97.9	6.01
All	**78.1**	82.6	65.3	86.9	57.5

Table 2: Performance of our features on Datasets 1 and 2

[5]www.worditout.com

6 Evaluation

Using the two sets of features, we train SVM classifiers (Chang and Lin, 2011)[6]. We show the five-fold cross-validation performance of our features on Datasets 1 and 2, in Section 6.1, and on Dataset H in Section 6.2. Section 6.3 presents an error analysis. *Accuracy, positive/negative precision and positive/negative recall are shown as A, PP/NP and PR/NR respectively. 'Drunk' forms the positive class, while 'Sober' forms the negative class.*

	Top features	
#	**Dataset 1**	**Dataset 2**
1	POS_NOUN	Spelling_error
2	Capitalization	LDA_drinking
3	Spelling_error	POS_NOUN
4	POS_PREPOSITION	Length
5	Length	LDA_tonight
6	LDA_Llife	Sentiment_Ratio
7	POS_VERB	Char_repeat
8	LDA_today	LDA_today
9	POS_ADV	LDA_drunken
10	Sentiment_Ratio	LDA_lmao

Table 3: Top stylistic features for Datasets 1 and 2 obtained using Chi-squared test-based ranking

6.1 Performance for Datasets 1 and 2

Table 2 shows the performance for five-fold cross-validation for Datasets 1 and 2. In case of Dataset 1, we observe that N-gram features achieve an accuracy of 85.5%. We see that our stylistic features alone exhibit degraded performance, with an accuracy of 75.6%, in the case of Dataset 1. Table 3 shows top stylistic features, when trained on the two datasets. Spelling errors, POS ratios for nouns (POS_NOUN)[7], length and sentiment ratios appear in both lists, in addition to LDA-based unigrams. However, negative recall reduces to a mere 3.2%. This degradation implies that our features capture a subset of drunk tweets and that there are properties of drunk tweets that may be more subtle. When both N-gram and stylistic features are used, there is negligible improvement. The accuracy for Dataset 2 increases from 77.9% to 78.1%. Precision/Recall metrics do not change significantly either. The best accuracy of our classifier is 78.1% for all features, and 75.6% for stylistic features. This shows that text-based clues can indeed be used for drunk-texting prediction.

	A1	A2	A3
A1	-	0.42	0.36
A2	0.42	-	0.30
A3	0.36	0.30	-

Table 4: Cohen's Kappa for three annotators (A1-A3)

	A (%)	NP (%)	PP (%)	NR (%)	PR (%)
Annotators	68.8	71.7	61.7	83.9	43.5
Training Dataset	**Our classifiers**				
Dataset 1	47.3	70	40	26	81
Dataset 2	64	70	53	72	50

Table 5: Performance of human evaluators and our classifiers (trained on all features), for Dataset-H as the test set

6.2 Performance for Held-out Dataset H

Using held-out dataset H, we evaluate how our system performs in comparison to humans. Three annotators, A1-A3, mark each tweet in the Dataset H as drunk or sober. Table 4 shows a moderate agreement between our annotators (for example, it is 0.42 for A1 and A2). Table 5 compares our classifier with humans. Our human annotators perform the task with an average accuracy of 68.8%, while our classifier (with all features) trained on Dataset 2 reaches 64%. The classifier trained on Dataset 2 is better than which is trained on Dataset 1.

6.3 Error Analysis

Some categories of errors that occur are:

1. **Incorrect hashtag supervision**: The tweet '*Can't believe I lost my bag last night, literally had everything in! Thanks god the bar man found it*' was marked with'#Drunk'. However, this tweet is not likely to be a drunk tweet, but describes a drunk episode in retrospective. Our classifier predicts it as sober.

[6] We also repeated all experiments for Naïve Bayes. They do not perform as well as SVM, and have poor recall.

[7] POS ratios for nouns, adjectives and adverbs were nearly similar in drunk and sober tweets - with the maximum difference being 0.03%

2. **Seemingly sober tweets**: Human annotators as well as our classifier could not identify whether '*Will you take her on a date? But really she does like you*' was drunk, although the author of the tweet had marked it so. This example also highlights the difficulty of drunk-texting prediction.

3. **Pragmatic difficulty**: The tweet '*National dress of Ireland is one's one vomit.. my family is lovely*' was correctly identified by our human annotators as a drunk tweet. This tweet contains an element of humour and topic change, but our classifier could not capture it.

7 Conclusion & Future Work

In this paper, we introduce automatic drunk-texting prediction as the task of predicting a tweet as drunk or sober. First, we justify the need for drunk-texting prediction as means of identifying risky social behavior arising out of alcohol abuse, and the need to build tools that avoid privacy leaks due to drunk-texting. We then highlight the challenges of drunk-texting prediction: one of the challenges is selection of negative examples (sober tweets). Using hashtag-based supervision, we create three datasets annotated with drunk or sober labels. We then present SVM-based classifiers which use two sets of features: N-gram and stylistic features. Our drunk prediction system obtains a best accuracy of 78.1%. We observe that our stylistic features add negligible value to N-gram features. We use our heldout dataset to compare how our system performs against human annotators. While human annotators achieve an accuracy of 68.8%, our system reaches reasonably close and performs with a best accuracy of 64%.

Our analysis of the task and experimental findings make a case for drunk-texting prediction as a useful and feasible NLP application.

References

Aby. 2014. Aby word processing website, January.

Steven Bird. 2006. Nltk: the natural language toolkit. In *Proceedings of the COLING/ACL on Interactive presentation sessions*, pages 69–72. Association for Computational Linguistics.

David M Blei, Andrew Y Ng, and Michael I Jordan. 2003. Latent dirichlet allocation. *the Journal of machine Learning research*, 3:993–1022.

Josephine A Borrill, Bernard K Rosen, and Angela B Summerfield. 1987. The influence of alcohol on judgement of facial expressions of emotion. *British Journal of Medical Psychology*.

Angela Bryan, Courtney A Rocheleau, Reuben N Robbins, and Kent E Hutchinson. 2005. Condom use among high-risk adolescents: testing the influence of alcohol use on the relationship of cognitive correlates of behavior. *Health Psychology*, 24(2):133.

Brad J Bushman and Harris M Cooper. 1990. Effects of alcohol on human aggression: An intergrative research review. *Psychological bulletin*, 107(3):341.

Christopher Carpenter. 2007. Heavy alcohol use and crime: Evidence from underage drunk-driving laws. *Journal of Law and Economics*, 50(3):539–557.

Chih-Chung Chang and Chih-Jen Lin. 2011. Libsvm: a library for support vector machines. *ACM Transactions on Intelligent Systems and Technology (TIST)*, 2(3):27.

Ted A Loomis and TC West. 1958. The influence of alcohol on automobile driving ability: An experimental study for the evaluation of certain medicological aspects. *Quarterly journal of studies on alcohol*, 19(1):30–46.

John Merrill, GABRIELLE MILKER, John Owens, and Allister Vale. 1992. Alcohol and attempted suicide. *British journal of addiction*, 87(1):83–89.

James W Pennebaker. 1993. Putting stress into words: Health, linguistic, and therapeutic implications. *Behaviour research and therapy*, 31(6):539–548.

James W Pennebaker. 1997. Writing about emotional experiences as a therapeutic process. *Psychological science*, 8(3):162–166.

Matthew Purver and Stuart Battersby. 2012. Experimenting with distant supervision for emotion classification. In *Proceedings of the 13th Conference of the European Chapter of the Association for Computational Linguistics*, pages 482–491. Association for Computational Linguistics.

Philip Resnik, Anderson Garron, and Rebecca Resnik. 2013. Using topic modeling to improve prediction of neuroticism and depression. In *Proceedings of the 2013 Conference on Empirical Methods in Natural*, pages 1348–1353. Association for Computational Linguistics.

Theresa Wilson, Janyce Wiebe, and Paul Hoffmann. 2005. Recognizing contextual polarity in phrase-level sentiment analysis. In *Proceedings of the conference on human language technology and empirical methods in natural language processing*, pages 347–354. Association for Computational Linguistics.

Reducing infrequent-token perplexity via variational corpora

Yusheng Xie[1,#] **Pranjal Daga**[1] **Yu Cheng**[2] **Kunpeng Zhang**[3] **Ankit Agrawal**[1] **Alok Choudhary**[1]

[1] Northwestern University
Evanston, IL USA

[2] IBM Research
Yorktown Heights, NY USA

[3] University of Maryland
College Park, MD USA

yxi389@eecs.northwestern.edu

Abstract

Recurrent neural network (RNN) is recognized as a powerful language model (LM). We investigate deeper into its performance portfolio, which performs well on frequent grammatical patterns but much less so on less frequent terms. Such portfolio is expected and desirable in applications like autocomplete, but is less useful in social content analysis where many creative, unexpected usages occur (e.g., URL insertion). We adapt a generic RNN model and show that, with variational training corpora and epoch unfolding, the model improves its performance for the task of URL insertion suggestions.

1 Introduction

Just 135 most frequent words account for 50% text of the entire Brown corpus (Francis and Kucera, 1979). But over 44% (22,010 out of 49,815) of Brown's vocabulary are *hapax legomena*[1]. The intricate relationship between vocabulary words and their utterance frequency results in some important advancements in natural language processing (NLP). For example, tf-idf results from rules applied to word frequencies in global and local context (Manning and Schütze, 1999). A common preprocessing step for tf-idf is filtering rare words, which is usually justified for two reasons. First, low frequency cutoff promises computational speedup due to Zipf's law (1935). Second, many believe that most NLP and machine learning algorithms demand repetitive patterns and reoccurrences, which are by definition missing in low frequency words.

1.1 Should infrequent words be filtered?

Infrequent words have high probability of becoming frequent as we consider them in a larger context (e.g., *Ishmael*, the protagonist name in *Moby-Dick*, appears merely once in the novel's dialogues but is a highly referenced word in the discussions/critiques around the novel). In many modern NLP applications, context grows constantly: fresh news articles come out on CNN and New York Times everyday; conversations on Twitter are updated in real time. In processing online social media text, it would seem premature to filter words simply due to infrequency, the kind of infrequency that can be eliminated by taking a larger corpus available from the same source.

To further undermine the conventional justification, computational speedup is attenuated in RNN-based LMs (compared to n-gram LMs), thanks to modern GPU architecture. We train a large RNN-LSTM (long short-term memory unit) (Hochreiter and Schmidhuber, 1997) model as our LM on two versions of *Jane Austen's complete works*. Dealing with 33% less vocabulary in the filtered version, the model only gains marginally on running time or memory usage. In Table 1.1, "Filtered corpus" filters out all the hapax legomena in "Full corpus".

	Full corpus	Filtered corpus
corpus length	756,273	751,325
vocab. size	15,125	10,177
running time	1,446 sec	1,224 sec
GPU memory	959 MB	804 MB

Table 1: Filtered corpus gains little in running time or memory usage when using a RNN LM.

Since RNN LMs suffer only small penalty in keeping the full corpus, can we take advantage of this situation to improve the LM?

1.2 Improving performance portfolio of LM

One improvement is LM's performance portfolio. A LM's performance is usually quantified as

[1]Words appear only once in corpus.

Proceedings of the 53rd Annual Meeting of the Association for Computational Linguistics and the 7th International Joint Conference on Natural Language Processing (Short Papers), pages 609–615, Beijing, China, July 26-31, 2015. ©2015 Association for Computational Linguistics

perplexity, which is exponentialized negative log-likelihood in predictions.

For our notation, let V_X denote the vocabulary of words that appear in a text corpus $X = \{x_1, x_2, \ldots\}$. Given a sequence $x_1, x_2, \ldots, x_{m-1}$, where each $x \in V_X$, the LM predicts the next in sequence, $x_m \in V_X$, as a probability distribution over the entire vocabulary V (its prediction denoted as p). If $v_m \in V_X$ is the true token at position m, the model's perplexity at index m is quantified as $\exp(-\ln(p[v_m]))$. The training goal is to minimize average perplexity across X.

However, a deeper look into perplexity beyond corpus-wide average reveals interesting findings. Using the same model setting as for Table 1.1, Figure 1 illustrates the relationship between word-level perplexity and its frequency in corpus. In general, the less frequent a word appears, the more unpredictable it becomes. In Table 1.2, the trained model achieves an average perplexity of 78 on filtered corpus. But also shown in Table 1.2, many common words register with perplexity over 1,000, which means they are practically unpredictable. More details are summarized in Table 1.2. The LM achieves exceptionally low perplexity on words such as *<apostr.>s* (*'s*, the possessive case), *<comma>* (*,* the comma). And these tokens' high frequencies in corpus have promised the model's average performance. Meanwhile, the LM has bafflingly high perplexity on commonplace words such as *read* and *considering*.

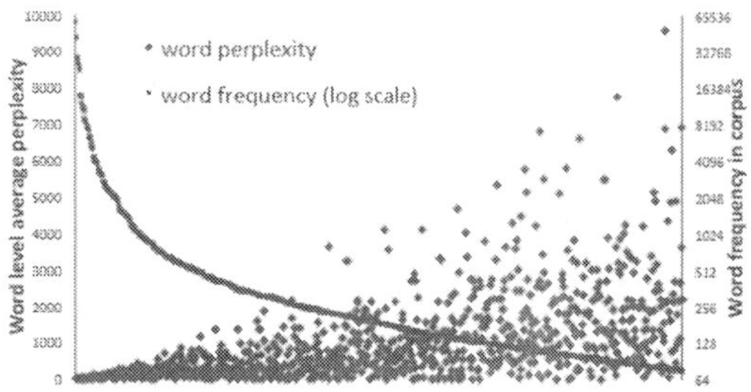

Figure 1: (best viewed in color) We look at word level perplexity with respect to the word frequency in corpus. The less frequent a word appears, the more unpredictable it becomes.

2 Methodology

We describe a novel approach of constructing and utilizing pre-training corpus that eventually reduce LMs's high perplexity on rare tokens. The standard way to utilize a pre-training corpus W is to

Token	Freq.	Perplexity 1	Perplexity 2
corpus avg.	N/A	78	82
<apostr.>s	4,443	1.1	1.1
of	23,046	4.9	5.0
<comma>	57,552	5.2	5.1
been	3,452	5.4	5.7
read	224	3,658	3,999
quiet	108	6,807	6,090
returning	89	7,764	6,268
considering	80	9,573	8,451

Table 2: A close look at RNN-LSTM's perplexity at word level. "Perplexity 1" is model perplexity based on filtered corpus (c.f., Table 1.1) and "Perplexity 2" is based on full corpus.

first train the model on W then fine-tune it on target corpus X. Thanks to availability of text, W can be orders of magnitude larger than X, which makes pre-training on W challenging.

A more efficient way to utilize W is to construct variational corpora based on X and W. In the following subsections, we first describe how replacement tokens are selected from a probability mass function (pmf), which is built from W; then explain how the variational corpora variates with replacement tokens through epochs.

2.1 Learn from pre-training corpus

One way to alleviate the impact from infrequent vocabulary is to expose the model to a larger and overarching pre-training corpus (Erhan et al., 2010), if available. Let W be a larger corpus than X and assume that $V_X \subseteq V_W$. For example, if X is Herman Melville's *Moby-Dick*, W can be Melville's complete works. Further, we use $V_{X,1}$ to denote the subset of V_X that are hapax legonema in corpus X; similarly, $V_{X,n}$ (for $n = 2, 3, \ldots$) denotes the subset of V_X that occur n times in X. Many hapax legomena in $V_{X,1}$ are likely to become more frequent tokens in V_W.

Suppose that $x \in V_{X,1}$. Denoted by ReplacePMF(W, V_W, x) in Algorithm 1, we represent x as a probability mass function (pmf) over $\{x'_1, x'_2, \ldots\}$, where each x'_i is selected from $V_W \cap V_{X,n}$ for $n > 1$ using one of the two methods below. For illustration purpose, suppose the hapax legomenon, x, in question is *matrimonial*:

1) e.g., *matrimony*. Words that have very high literal similarity with x. We measure literal similarity using Jaro-Winkler measure, which is an empirical, weighted measure based on string edit

distance. We set the measure threshold very high (> 0.93), which minimizes false positives as well as captures many hapax legonema due to adv./adj., pl./singular (e.g, *-y/-ily* and *-y/-ies*).

2) e.g., *marital* Words that are direct syno/hyponyms to x in the WordNet (Miller, 1995).

getContextAround(x') function in Algorithm 1 simply extracts symmetric context words from both left and right sides of x'. Although the investigated LM only uses left context in predicting word x', context right of x' is still useful information in general. Given a context word c right of x', the LM can learn x''s predictability over c, which is beneficial to the corpus-wide perplexity reduction.

In practice, we select no more than 5 substitution words from each method above. The probability mass on each x'_i is proportional to its frequency in W and then normalized by softmax: $\text{pmf}(x'_i) = \text{freq}(x'_i)/\sum_{k=1}^{5}\text{freq}(x'_k)$. This substitution can help LMs learn better because we replace the un-trainable $V_{X,1}$ tokens with tokens that can be trained from the larger corpus W. In concept, it is like explaining a new word to school kids by defining it using vocabulary words in their existing knowledge.

2.2 Unfold training epochs

Epoch in machine learning terminology usually means a complete pass of the training dataset. many iterative algorithms take dozens of epochs on the same training data as they update the model's weights with smaller and smaller adjustments through the epochs.

We refer to the the training process proposed in Figure 2 (b) as "variational corpora". Compared to the traditional structure in Figure 2 (a), the main advantage of using variational corpora is the ability to freely adjust the corpus at each version. Effectively, we unfold the training into separate epochs. This allows us to gradually incorporate the replacement tokens without severely distorting the target corpus X, which is the learning goal. In addition, variational corpora can further regularize the training of LM in batch mode (Srivastava et al., 2014).

Algorithm 1 constructs variational corpora $X(s)$ at epoch s. Assuming $X(s+1)$ being available, Algorithm 1 appends snippets, which are sampled from W, into $X(s)$ for the sth epoch. For the last epoch $s = S$, $X(S) = X$. As the epoch number increases, fewer and shorter snippets are appended, which alleviates training stress. By fixing an n value, the algorithm applies to all words in $V_{X,n}$.

In addition, as a regularization trick (Mikolov et al., 2013; Pascanu et al., 2013) , we use a uniform random context window (line 8) when injecting snippets from W into $X(s)$.

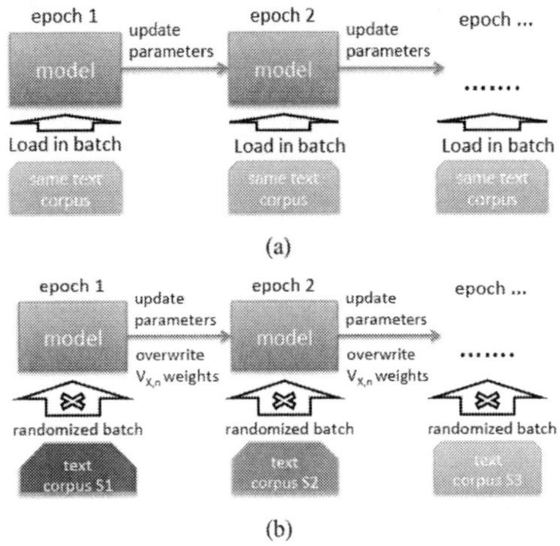

Figure 2: Unfold the training process in units of epochs. (a) Typical flow where model parses the same corpus at each epoch. (b) The proposed training architecture with variational corpora to incorporate the substitution algorithm.

Algorithm 1: Randomly constructs variational corpus at epoch s.

Input: $W, X, V_W, V_X, V_{X,n}, n$, as defined in Section 1.2&2.1,
s, S, current and max epoch number.
Output: $X(s)$, variational corpus at epoch s

```
1  X(s) ← X(s+1)
2  for each x ∈ V_{X,n} do
3      p ← ReplacePMF(W, V_W, x)
4      i ← Dirichlet(p).generate()
5      while i ← X.getNextIdxOf(x) do
6          x' ← i.draw()
7          c ← W.getContextAround(x')
8          c.substr([0, uniformRnd(0, (S−s)/S |c|)])
9          X(s).append(c)
10 return X(s)
```

Freq.	nofilter	3filter	ptw	vc
10	28,542 (668.1)	23,649 (641.2)	27,986 (1,067.2)	**20,994** (950.9)
100	1,180.3 (21.7)	1,158.2 (19.2)	**735.8** (29.8)	755.8 (31.5)
1K	163.2 (12.9)	163.9 (12.2)	138.5 (14.1)	**137.7** (15.7)
5K	47.5 (3.3)	47.2 (3.1)	**40.2** (3.2)	**40.2** (3.3)
10K	16.4 (0.31)	16.7 (0.29)	14.4 (0.42)	**14.1** (0.41)
40K	7.6 (0.09)	7.6 (0.09)	**7.0** (0.09)	**7.0** (0.10)
all tokens	82.1 (2.0)	77.9 (1.9)	**68.6** (2.1)	68.9 (2.1)
GPU memory	959MB	**783MB**	1.8GB	971MB
running time	1,446 sec	**1,181 sec**	9,061 sec	6,960 sec

Table 3: Experiments compare average perplexity produced by the proposed variational corpora approach and other methods on a same test corpus. Bold fonts indicate best. "Freq." indicates the average corpus-frequency (e.g., Freq.=1K means that words in this group, on average, appear 1,000 times in corpus). Perplexity numbers are averaged over 5 runs with standard deviation reported in parentheses. GPU memory usage and running time are also reported for each method.

Err. type	Context before	True token	LM prediction
False neg.	*<unk>, via, <unk>, banana, muffin, chocolate, ___*	URL to a cooking blog	*recipe*
False neg.	*sewing, ideas, <unk>, inspiring, picture, on, ___*	URL to favim.com	*esty*
False neg.	*nike, sports, fashion, <unk>, women, <unk>, ___*	URL to nelly.com	*macy*
False pos.	*new, york, yankees, endless, summer, tee, <unk>, ___*	*shop*	*<url>*
False pos.	*take, a, rest, from, your, #harrodssale, ___*	*shopping*	*<url>*

Table 4: False positives and false negatives predicted by the model in the Pinterest application. The context words preceding to token in questions are provided for easier analysis[3].

3 Experiments

3.1 Perplexity reduction

We validate our method in Table 3 by showing perplexity reduction on infrequent words. We split Jane Austen's novels (0.7 million words) as target corpus X and test corpus, and her contemporaries' novels[4] as pre-training corpus W (2.7 million words). In Table 3, **nofilter** is the unfiltered corpus; **3filter** replaces all tokens in $V_{X,3}$ by *<unk>*; **ptw** performs naive pre-training on W then on X; **vc** performs training with the proposed variational corpora. Our LM implements the RNN training as described in (Zaremba et al., 2014). Table 3 also illustrates the GPU memory usage and running time of the compared methods and shows that **vc** is more efficient than simply **ptw**.

vc has the best performance on low-frequency words by some margin. **ptw** is the best on frequent words because of its access to a large pre-training corpus. But somewhat to our surprise, **ptw** performs badly on low-frequency words, which we reckon is due to the rare words introduced in W: while pre-training on W helps reduce perplexity of words in $V_{X,1}$ but also introduces additional hapax legomena in $V_{W,1} \setminus V_{X,1}$.

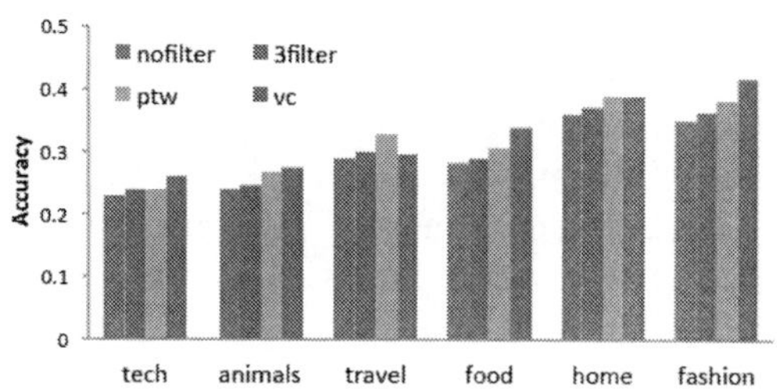

Figure 3: Accuracy of suggested URL positions across different categories of Pinterest captions.

3.2 Locating URLs in Pinterest captions

Beyond evaluations in Table 3. We apply our method to locate URLs in over 400,000 Pinterest captions. Unlike Facebook, Twitter, Pinterest is not a "social hub" but rather an interest-discovery

[3]Favim.com is a website for sharing crafts, creativity ideas. Esty.com is a e-commerce website for trading hand-made crafts. Nelly.com is Scandinavia's largest online fashion store. Macy's a US-based department store. Harrod's is a luxury department store in London.

[4]Dickens and the Bronte sisters

site (Linder et al., 2014; Zhong et al., 2014). To maximally preserve user experience, postings on Pinterest embed URLs in a natural, nonintrusive manner and a very small portion of the posts contain URLs.

In Figure 3, we ask the LM to suggest a position for the URL in the context and verify the suggest with test data in each category. For example, the model is presented with a sequence of tokens: *find, more, top, dresses, at, affordable, prices, <punctuation>, visit,* ___ and is asked to predict if the next token is an URL link. In the given example, plausible tokens after *visit* can be either *<http://macys.com>* or *nearest, Macy, <apostr.>s, store*. The proposed **vc** mechanism outperforms others in 5 of the 6 categories. In Figure 3, accuracy is measured as the percentage of correctly suggested positions. Any prediction next to or close to the correct position is counted as incorrect.

In Table 4, we list some of the false negative and false positive errors made by the LM. Many URLs on Pinterest are e-commerce URLs and the vendors often also have physical stores. So in predicting such e-commerce URLs, some mistakes are "excusable" because the LM is confused whether the upcoming token should be an URL (web store) or the brand name (physical store) (e.g, *http://macys.com* vs. *Macy's*).

4 Related work

Recurrent neural network (RNN) is a type of neural sequence model that have high capacity across various sequence tasks such as language modeling (Bengio et al., 2000), machine translation (Liu et al., 2014), speech recognition (Graves et al., 2013). Like other neural network models (e.g., feed-forward), RNNs can be trained using backpropogation algorithm (Sutskever et al., 2011). Recently, the authors in (Zaremba et al., 2014) successfully apply *dropout*, an effective regularization method for feed-forward neural networks, to RNNs and achieve strong empirical improvements.

Reducing perplexity on text corpus is probably the most demonstrated benchmark for modern language models (n-gram based and neural models alike) (Chelba et al., 2013; Church et al., 2007; Goodman and Gao, 2000; Gao and Zhang, 2002). Based on Zipf's law (Zipf, 1935), a filtered corpus greatly reduces the vocabulary size and computation complexity. Recently, a rigorous study (Kobayashi, 2014) looks at how perplexity can be *manipulated* by simply supplying the model with the same corpus reduced to varying degrees. Kobayashi (2014) describes his study from a macro point of view (i.e., the overall corpus level perplexity). In this work, we present, at word level, the correlation between perplexity and word frequency.

Token rarity is a long-standing issue with n-gram language models (Manning and Schütze, 1999). Katz smoothing (Katz, 1987) and Kneser-Ney based smoothing methods (Teh, 2006) are well known techniques for addressing sparsity in n-gram models. However, they are not directly used to resolve unigram sparsity.

Using word morphology information is another way of dealing with rare tokens (Botha and Blunsom, 2014). By decomposing words into morphemes, the authors in (Botha and Blunsom, 2014) are able to learn representations on the morpheme level and therefore scale the language modeling to unseen words as long as they are made of previously seen morphemes. Shown in their work, this technique works with character-based language in addition to English.

5 Acknowledgements

This work is supported in part by the following grants: NSF awards CCF-1029166, IIS-1343639, and CCF-1409601; DOE award DESC0007456; AFOSR award FA9550-12-1-0458; NIST award 70NANB14H012.

6 Conclusions & future work

This paper investigates the performance portfolio of popular neural language models. We propose a variational training scheme that has the advantage of a large pre-training corpus but without using as much computing resources. On low frequency words, our proposed scheme also outperforms naive pre-training.

In the future, we want to incorporate WordNet knowledge to further reduce perplexity on infrequent words.

References

Yoshua Bengio, Rjean Ducharme, Pascal Vincent, Departement D'informatique Et Recherche Operationnelle, and Centre De Recherche. 2000. A neural probabilistic language model. *Journal of Machine Learning Research*, 3:1137–1155.

Jan A. Botha and Phil Blunsom. 2014. Compositional morphology for word representations and language modelling. In *Proceedings of the 31th International Conference on Machine Learning, ICML 2014, Beijing, China, 21-26 June 2014*, pages 1899–1907.

Ciprian Chelba, Tomas Mikolov, Mike Schuster, Qi Ge, Thorsten Brants, Phillipp Koehn, and Tony Robinson. 2013. One billion word benchmark for measuring progress in statistical language modeling. Technical report, Google.

Kenneth Church, Ted Hart, and Jianfeng Gao. 2007. Compressing trigram language models with golomb coding. In *EMNLP-CoNLL 2007, Proceedings of the 2007 Joint Conference on Empirical Methods in Natural Language Processing and Computational Natural Language Learning, June 28-30, 2007, Prague, Czech Republic*, pages 199–207.

Dumitru Erhan, Yoshua Bengio, Aaron Courville, Pierre-Antoine Manzagol, Pascal Vincent, and Samy Bengio. 2010. Why does unsupervised pre-training help deep learning? *J. Mach. Learn. Res.*, 11:625–660, March.

Nelson Francis and Henry Kucera. 1979. Brown corpus manual. Technical report, Department of Linguistics, Brown University, Providence, Rhode Island, US.

Jianfeng Gao and Min Zhang. 2002. Improving language model size reduction using better pruning criteria. In *Proceedings of the 40th Annual Meeting on Association for Computational Linguistics*, ACL '02, pages 176–182, Stroudsburg, PA, USA. Association for Computational Linguistics.

Joshua Goodman and Jianfeng Gao. 2000. Language model size reduction by pruning and clustering. In *Sixth International Conference on Spoken Language Processing, ICSLP 2000 / INTERSPEECH 2000, Beijing, China, October 16-20, 2000*, pages 110–113.

Alex Graves, Abdel-rahman Mohamed, and Geoffrey E. Hinton. 2013. Speech recognition with deep recurrent neural networks. In *IEEE International Conference on Acoustics, Speech and Signal Processing, ICASSP 2013, Vancouver, BC, Canada, May 26-31, 2013*, pages 6645–6649.

Sepp Hochreiter and Jürgen Schmidhuber. 1997. Long short-term memory. *Neural Comput.*, 9(8):1735–1780, November.

S. Katz. 1987. Estimation of probabilities from sparse data for the language model component of a speech recognizer. *Acoustics, Speech and Signal Processing, IEEE Transactions on*, 35(3):400–401, Mar.

Hayato Kobayashi. 2014. Perplexity on reduced corpora. In *Proceedings of the 52nd Annual Meeting of the Association for Computational Linguistics (Volume 1: Long Papers)*, pages 797–806. Association for Computational Linguistics.

Rhema Linder, Clair Snodgrass, and Andruid Kerne. 2014. Everyday ideation: all of my ideas are on pinterest. In *CHI Conference on Human Factors in Computing Systems, CHI'14, Toronto, ON, Canada - April 26 - May 01, 2014*, pages 2411–2420.

Shujie Liu, Nan Yang, Mu Li, and Ming Zhou. 2014. A recursive recurrent neural network for statistical machine translation. In *Proceedings of the 52nd Annual Meeting of the Association for Computational Linguistics (Volume 1: Long Papers)*, pages 1491–1500, Baltimore, Maryland, June. Association for Computational Linguistics.

Christopher D. Manning and Hinrich Schütze. 1999. *Foundations of Statistical Natural Language Processing*. MIT Press.

Tomas Mikolov, Ilya Sutskever, Kai Chen, Gregory S. Corrado, and Jeffrey Dean. 2013. Distributed representations of words and phrases and their compositionality. In *NIPS*, pages 3111–3119.

George A. Miller. 1995. Wordnet: A lexical database for english. *Commun. ACM*, 38(11):39–41, November.

Razvan Pascanu, Tomas Mikolov, and Yoshua Bengio. 2013. On the difficulty of training recurrent neural networks. In *Proceedings of the 30th International Conference on Machine Learning, ICML 2013, Atlanta, GA, USA, 16-21 June 2013*, pages 1310–1318.

Nitish Srivastava, Geoffrey Hinton, Alex Krizhevsky, Ilya Sutskever, and Ruslan Salakhutdinov. 2014. Dropout: A simple way to prevent neural networks from overfitting. *Journal of Machine Learning Research*, 15:1929–1958.

Ilya Sutskever, James Martens, and Geoffrey Hinton. 2011. Generating text with recurrent neural networks. In Lise Getoor and Tobias Scheffer, editors, *Proceedings of the 28th International Conference on Machine Learning (ICML-11)*, ICML '11, pages 1017–1024, New York, NY, USA, June. ACM.

Yee Whye Teh. 2006. A bayesian interpretation of interpolated kneserney. Technical report.

Wojciech Zaremba, Ilya Sutskever, and Oriol Vinyals. 2014. Recurrent neural network regularization. *arXiv preprint arXiv:1409.2329*.

Changtao Zhong, Mostafa Salehi, Sunil Shah, Marius Cobzarenco, Nishanth Sastry, and Meeyoung Cha. 2014. Social bootstrapping: how pinterest and last.fm social communities benefit by borrowing links from facebook. In *23rd International World Wide Web Conference, WWW '14, Seoul, Republic of Korea, April 7-11, 2014*, pages 305–314.

G.K. Zipf. 1935. *The Psycho-biology of Language: An Introduction to Dynamic Philology*. The MIT paperback series. Houghton Mifflin.

A Hierarchical Knowledge Representation for Expert Finding on Social Media

Yanran Li[1], **Wenjie Li**[1], and **Sujian Li**[2]
[1]Computing Department, Hong Kong Polytechnic University, Hong Kong
[2]Key Laboratory of Computational Linguistics, Peking University, MOE, China
{csyli, cswjli}@comp.polyu.edu.hk
lisujian@pku.edu.cn

Abstract

Expert finding on social media benefits both individuals and commercial services. In this paper, we exploit a 5-level tree representation to model the posts on social media and cast the expert finding problem to the matching problem between the learned user tree and domain tree. We enhance the traditional approximate tree matching algorithm and incorporate word embeddings to improve the matching result. The experiments conducted on Sina Microblog demonstrate the effectiveness of our work.

1 Introduction

Expert finding has been arousing great interests among social media researchers after its successful applications on traditional media like academic publications. As already observed, social media users tend to follow others for professional interests and knowledge (Ramage et al, 2010). This builds the basis for mining expertise and finding experts on social media, which facilitates the services of user recommendation and question-answering, etc.

Despite the demand to access expertise, the challenges of identifying domain experts on social media exist. Social media often contains plenty of noises such as the tags with which users describe themselves. Noises impose the inherent drawback on the feature-based learning methods (Krishnamurthy et al, 2008). Data imbalance and sparseness also limits the performance of the promising latent semantic analysis methods such as the LDA-like topic models (Blei et al, 2003; Ramage et al, 2009). When some topics co-occur more frequently than others, the strict assumption of these topic models cannot be met and consequently many nonsensical topics will be generated (Zhao and Jiang, 2011; Pal et al, 2011; Quercia et al, 2012). Furthermore, not as simple as celebrities, the definition of experts introduces additional difficulties. Experts cannot be simply judged by the number of followers. The knowledge conveyed in what they say is essential. This leads to the failures of the network-based methods (Java et al, 2007; Weng et al, 2010; Pal et al, 2011).

The challenges mentioned above inherently come from insufficient representations. They motivate us to propose a more flexible domain expert finding framework to explore effective representations that are able to tackle the complexity lies in the social media data. The basic idea is as follows. Experts talk about the professional knowledge in their posts and these posts are supposed to contain more domain knowledge than the posts from the other ordinary users. We determine whether or not users are experts on specific domains by matching their professional knowledge and domain knowledge. The key is how to capture such information for both users and domains with the appropriate representation, which is, in our view, the reason why most of previous work fails.

To go beyond the feature-based classification methods and the vector representation inference in expert finding, a potential solution is to incorporate the semantic information for knowledge modeling. We achieve this goal by representing user posts using a hierarchical tree structure to capture correlations among words and topics. To tackle the data sparseness problem, we apply word embeddings to tree-nodes to further enhance semantic representation and to support semantic matching. Expert finding is then cast to the problem of determining the edit distance between the user tree and the domain tree, which is computed with an approximate tree matching algorithm.

The main contribution of this work is to integrate the hierarchical tree representation and structure matching together to profile users' and do-

Proceedings of the 53rd Annual Meeting of the Association for Computational Linguistics and the 7th International Joint Conference on Natural Language Processing (Short Papers), pages 616–622,
Beijing, China, July 26-31, 2015.

mains' knowledge. Using such trees allows us to flexibly incorporate more information into the data representation, such as the relations between latent topics and the semantic similarities between words. The experiments conducted on Sina Microblog demonstrate the effectiveness of the proposed framework and the corresponding methods.

2 Knowledge Representation with Hierarchical Tree

To capture correlations between topics, Pachinko Allocation Model (PAM) (Li and McCallum, 2006) uses a directed acyclic graph (DAG) with leaves representing individual words in the vocabulary and each interior node representing a correlation among its children. In particular, multi-level PAM is capable of revealing interconnection between sub-level nodes by inferencing corresponding super-level nodes. It is a desired property that enables us to capture hierarchical relations among both inner-level and inter-level nodes and thereby enhance the representation of users' posts. More important, the inter-level hierarchy benefits to distribute words from super-level generic topics to sub-level specific topics.

In this work, we exploit a 5-level PAM to learn the hierarchical knowledge representation for each individual user and domain. As shown in Figure 1, the 5-level hierarchy consists of one root topic r, I topics at the second level $X = \{x_1, x_2, \ldots, x_I\}$, J topics at the third level $Y = \{y_1, y_2, \ldots, y_J\}$, K topics at the fourth level $Z = \{z_1, z_2, \ldots, z_K\}$ and words at the bottom. The whole hierarchy is fully connected.

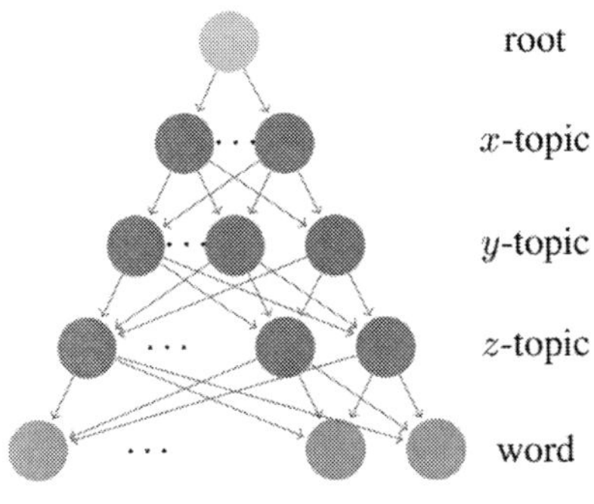

Figure 1: 5-level PAM

Each topic in 5-level PAM is associated with a distribution $g(\cdot)$ over its children. In general, $g(\cdot)$ can be any distribution over discrete variables. Here, we use a set of Dirichlet compound multinomial distributions associated with the root, the second-level and the third-level topics. These distributions are $\{g_r(\alpha)\}$, $\{g_i(\gamma_i)\}_{i=1}^{I}$ and $\{g_i(\delta_j)\}_{j=1}^{J}$. They are used to sample the multinomial distributions θ_x, θ_y and θ_z over the corresponding sub-level topics. As to the fourth-level topics, we use a fixed multinomial distribution $\{\phi_{z_k}\}_{k=1}^{K}$ sampled once for the whole data from a single Dirichlet distribution $g(\beta)$. Figure 2 illustrates the plate notation of this 5-level PAM.

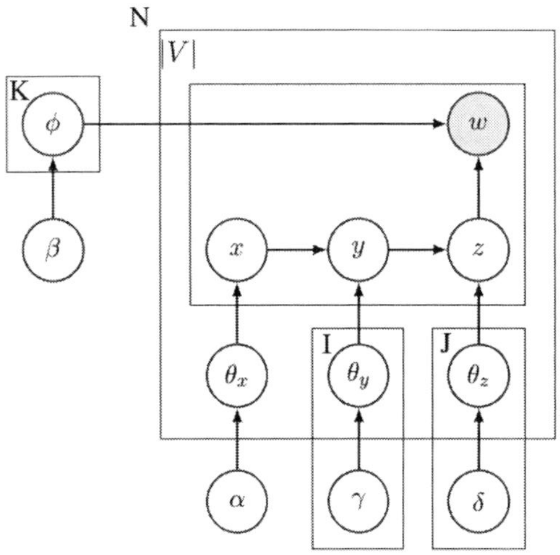

Figure 2: Plate Notation of 5-level PAM

By integrating out the sampled multinomial distributions θ_x, θ_y, θ_z, ϕ and summing over $\mathbf{x}, \mathbf{y}, \mathbf{z}$, we obtain the Gibbs sampling distribution for word $w = w_m$ in document d as:

$$
\begin{aligned}
&P(x_w{=}x_i, y_w{=}y_j, z_w{=}z_k|\mathbf{D}, \mathbf{x}_{-w}, \mathbf{y}_{-w}, \mathbf{z}_{-w}, \alpha, \gamma, \delta, \beta) \\
&\propto P(w, x_w, y_w, z_w|\mathbf{D}_{-w}, \mathbf{x}_{-w}, \mathbf{y}_{-w}, \mathbf{z}_{-w}, \alpha, \gamma, \delta, \beta) \\
&= \frac{P(\mathbf{D}, \mathbf{x}, \mathbf{y}, \mathbf{z}|\alpha, \gamma, \delta, \beta)}{P(\mathbf{D}_{-w}, \mathbf{x}_{-w}, \mathbf{y}_{-w}, \mathbf{z}_{-w}|\alpha, \gamma, \delta, \beta)} \\
&= \frac{n_i^{(d)} + \alpha_i}{n_r^{(d)} + \sum_{i'=1}^{K} \alpha_{i'}} \times \frac{n_{ij}^{(d)} + \gamma_{ij}}{n_i^{(d)} + \sum_{j'=1}^{L} \gamma_{ij'}} \\
&\quad \times \frac{n_{jk}^{(d)} + \delta_{jk}}{n_j^{(d)} + \sum_{k'=1}^{J} \delta_{jk'}} \times \frac{n_{km}^{(d)} + \beta_m}{n_k + \sum_{m'=1}^{n} \beta_{m'}}
\end{aligned}
$$

where $n_r^{(d)}$ is the number of occurrences of the root r in document d, which is equivalent to the number of tokens in the document. $n_i^{(d)}$, $n_{ij}^{(d)}$ and $n_{jk}^{(d)}$ are respectively the number of occurrences of x_i, y_j and z_k sampled from their upper-level topics. n_k is the number of occurrences of the fourth-level topics z_k in the whole dataset and n_{km} is the number of occurrences of word w_m in z_k. $-w$

indicates all observations or topic assignments except word w.

With the fixed Dirichlet parameter α for the root and β as the prior, what's left is to estimate (learn from data) γ and δ to capture the different correlations among topics. To avoid the use of iterative methods which are often computationally extensive, instead we approximate these two Dirichlet parameters using the moment matching algorithm, the same as (Minka, 2000; Casella and Berger, 2001; Shafiei and Milios, 2006). With smoothing techniques, in each iteration of Gibbs sampling we update:

$$mean_{ij} = \frac{1}{N_i + 1} \times \left(\sum_d \frac{n_{ij}^{(d)}}{n_i^{(d)}} + \frac{1}{L} \right)$$

$$var_{ij} = \frac{1}{N_i + 1} \times \left(\sum_d \left(\frac{n_{ij}^{(d)}}{n_i^{(d)}} - mean_{ij}\right)^2 + \left(\frac{1}{L} - mean_{ij}\right)^2 \right)$$

$$m_{ij} = \frac{mean_{ij} \times (1 - mean_{ij})}{var_{ij}} - 1$$

$$\gamma_{ij} = \frac{mean_{ij}}{\exp\left(\frac{\sum_j \log(m_{ij})}{L-1}\right)}$$

where N_i is the number of documents with non-zero counts of super-level topic x_i. Parameter estimation of δ is the same as γ.

3 Expert Finding with Approximate Tree Matching

Once the hierarchical representations of users and domains have been generated, we can determine whether or not a user is an expert on a domain based on their matching degree, which is a problem analogous to tree-to-tree correction using *edit distance* (Selkow, 1977; Shasha and Zhang, 1990; Wagner, 1975; Wagner and Fischer, 1974; Zhang and Shasha, 1989). Given two trees T_1 and T_2, a typical *edit distance*-based correction approach is to transform T_1 to T_2 with a sequence of *editing operations* $S = < s_1, s_2, \ldots, s_k >$ such that $s_k(s_{k-1}(\ldots(s_1(T_1))\ldots)) = T_2$. Each operation is assigned a *cost* $\sigma(s_i)$ that represents the difficulty of making that operation. By summing up the *costs* of all necessary operations, the total cost $\sigma(S) = \sum_{i=1}^{k} \sigma(s_i)$ defines the matching degree of T_1 and T_2.

We assume that an expert could only master a part of professional domain knowledge rather than the whole and thereby revise a traditional approximate tree matching algorithm (Zhang and Shasha, 1989) to calculate the matching degree. This assumption especially makes sense when the domain we are concerned with is quite general. Let T_d and T_u denote the learned domain knowledge tree and the user knowledge tree, we match T_d to the remaining trees resulting from cutting all possible sets of disjoint sub-trees of T_u. We specifically penalize *no cost* if some sub-trees are missing in matching process. We define two types of operations. The *substitution* operations edit the dissimilar words on tree-nodes, while the *insertion* and *deletion* operations perform on tree-structures. Expert finding is then to calculate the minimum matching cost on T_d and T_u. If the cost is smaller than an empirically defined threshold λ_d, we identify user u as an expert on domain d.

To alleviate the sparseness problem caused by direct letter-to-letter matching in tree-node mapping, we embed word embeddings (Bengio et al, 2003) into the substitution operation. We apply the `word2vec` skip-gram model (Mikolov et al, 2013(a); Mikolov et al, 2013(b)) to encode each word in our vocabulary with a probability vector and directly use the similarity generated by `word2vec` as the tree-node similarity. The costs of insertion and deletion operations will be explained in Section 4. Actually all these three costs can be defined in accordance with applicant needs. In brief, by combining both hierarchical representation of tree-structure and word embeddings of tree-nodes, we achieve our goal to enhance semantics.

4 Experiments

The experiments are conducted on 5 domains (i.e., *Beauty Blogger*, *Beauty Doctor*, *Parenting*, *E-Commerce*, and *Data Science*) in Sina Microblog, a Twitter-like microblog in China. To learn PAM, we manually select 40 users in each domain from the official expert lists released by Sina Microblog[1], and crawl all of their posts. In average, there are 113,924 posts in each domain. Notice that the expert lists are not of high quality. We have to do manual verification to filter out noises. For evaluation, we select another 80 users in each domain from the expert list, with 40 verified as experts and the other 40 as non-experts.

Since there is no state-of-art Chinese word embeddings publicly available, we use another Sina

[1] `http://d.weibo.com/1087030002_558_3_2014#`

Table 1: Classification Results

Approach	Precision		Recall		F-Score	
	Macro	Micro	Macro	Micro	Macro	Micro
unigram	0.380	0.484	0.615	0.380	0.469	0.432
bigram	0.435	0.537	0.615	0.435	0.507	0.486
LDA	0.430	0.473	0.540	0.430	0.474	0.451
Twitter-LDA	0.675	0.763	0.680	0.430	0.675	0.451
PAM	**0.720**	**0.818**	**0.720**	**0.720**	**0.714**	**0.769**

Microblog dataset provided by `pennyliang`[2], which contains 25 million posts and nearly 100 million tokens in total, to learn the word embeddings of 50-dimension. We pre-process the data with the `Rwordseg` segmentation package[3] and discard nonsensical words with the `pullword` package[4].

When learning 5-level PAM, we set fixed parameters $\alpha = 0.25$, $\beta = 0.25$ and from top to down, $I = 10$, $J = 20$, $K = 20$ for the number of second, third and fourth levels of topics, respectively. And we initialize γ and δ with 0.25. For tree matching, we define the cost of tree-node *substitution* operation between word a and b as Eq (1). The costs of *insertion* and *deletion* operations for tree-structure matching are `MAX_VALUE`. Here we set `MAX_VALUE` as 100 experimentally. The threshold λ_d used to determine the expert is set to be 12 times of `MAX_VALUE`.

$$\sigma(a \rightarrow b) = \begin{cases} 0, & a = b \\ \text{sim}(a, b), & \text{sim}(a, b) > 0.55 \\ \texttt{MAX\_VALUE}, & otherwise \end{cases} \quad (1)$$

We compare PAM with n-gram (unigram and bigram), LDA (Blei et al, 2003) and Twitter-LDA (Zhao and Jiang, 2011). We set β in LDA and Twitter-LDA to 0.01, γ in Twiitter-LDA to 20. For α, we adopt the commonly used $50/T$ heuristics where the number of topics $T = 50$. To be fair, we all use the tokens after pullword preprocessing as the input to extract features for classification. Following Zhao and Jiang (2011), we train four ℓ_2-regularized logistic regression classifiers using the `LIBLINEAR` package (Fan et al, 2008) on the top 200 unigrams and bigrams ranked according to Chi-squared and 100-dimensional topic vectors induced by LDA and Twitter-LDA, respectively. We also compare our model with/without word embeddings to demonstrate the effectiveness of this semantic enhancement. The results are presented in Table 1.

In general, LDA, Twitter-LDA and PAM outperform unigram and bigram, showing the strength of latent semantic modeling. Within the first two models, Twitter-LDA yields better precisions than LDA because of its ability to overcome the difficulty of modeling short posts on social media. It designs an additional background word distribution to remove the noisy words and assumes that a single post can belong to several topics.

Our 5-level PAM gains observed improvement over Twitter-LDA. We attribute this to the advantages of tree representations over vector feature representations, the effective approximate tree matching algorithm and the complementary word embeddings. As mentioned in Section 1, LDA and other topic models like Twitter-LDA share the same assumption that each topic should be independent with each other. This assumption however is too strict for the real world data. Our tree-like 5-level PAM relaxes such assumption with two additional layers of super-topics modeled with Dirichlet compound multinomial distributions, which is the key to capture topic correlations. Furthermore, by allowing partial matching and incorporating word embeddings, we successfully overcome the sparseness problem.

While macro-averages give equal weight to each domain, micro-averages give equal weight to each user. The significant difference between the macro- and micro- scores in Table 1 is caused by the different nature of 5 domains. In fact, the posts of experts on the domain *E-Commerce* are to some extent noisy and contain lots of words irrelevant to the domain knowledge. Meanwhile, the posts of experts on the domain *Data Science* are less distinguishable. The higher micro-recalls of PAM demonstrate its generalization ability over

[2] `http://chuansong.me/account/pennyjob`
[3] `http://jliblog.com/app/rwordseg`
[4] `http://pullword.com/`

LDA and Twitter-LDA.

5 Conclusion

In this paper, we formulate the expert finding task as a tree matching problem with the hierarchical knowledge representation. The experimental results demonstrate the advantage of using 5-level PAM and semantic enhancement against n-gram models and LDA-like models. To further improve the work, we will incorporate more information to enrich the hierarchical representation in the future.

Acknowledgements

The work described in this paper was supported by the grants from the Research Grants Council of Hong Kong (PolyU 5202/12E and PolyU 152094/14E) and the grants from the National Natural Science Foundation of China (61272291 and 61273278).

References

Eugene Agichtein, Carlos Castillo, Debora Donato, et al. 2008. Finding high-quality content in social media. In *Proc. of WSDM.*

Mohit Bansal, Kevin Gimpel, and Karen Livescu. 2014. Tailoring continuous word representations for dependency parsing. In *Proc. of ACL.*

Yoshua Bengio, Rjean Ducharme, Pascal Vincent, et al. 2003. A neural probabilistic language model. *The Journal of Machine Learning Research,* 3: 1137-1155.

Marc Bernard, Laurent Boyer, et al. 2008. Learning probabilistic models of tree edit distance. *Pattern Recognition,* 41(8): 2611-2629.

David M. Blei, Andrew Y. Ng, and Michael I. Jordan. 2003. Latent Dirichlet Allocation. *The Journal of Machine Learning Research,* 3: 993-1022.

Mohamed Bouguessa, Benot Dumoulin, and Shengrui Wang. 2008. Identifying authoritative actors in question-answering forums: the case of yahoo! answers. In *Proc. of SIGKDD.*

George Casella and Roger L. Berger. 2001. Statistical Inference. *Duxbury Press.*

Danqi Chen and Christopher D. Manning. 2014. A fast and accurate dependency parser using neural networks. In *Proc. of EMNLP,* pages 740750.

Fei Cheng, Kevin Duh, Yuji Matsumoto. 2014. Parsing Chinese Synthetic Words with a Character-based Dependency Model. *LREC.*

Allan M. Collins and M. Ross. Quillian. 1969. Retrieval time from semantic memory. *Journal of Verbal Learning and Verbal Behaviour,* 8: 240247.

Ronan Collobert, Jason Weston, Leon Bottou, et al. 2011. Natural language processing (almost) from scratch. *JMLR,* 12.

Paramveer Dhillon, Dean P Foster, and Lyle H Ungar. 2011. Multi-view learning of word embeddings via cca. In *Advances in Neural Information Processing Systems,* pages 199207.

Rong-En Fan, Kai-Wei Chang, Cho-Jui Hsieh, et al. 2008. LIBLINEAR: A library for large linear classification. *The Journal of Machine Learning Research,* 9: 1871-1874.

Eric H. Huang, Richard Socher, Christopher D. Manning, and Andrew Y. Ng. 2012. Improving Word Representations via Global Context and Multiple Word Prototypes. In *Proc. of ACL.*

Akshay Java, Pranam Kolari, Tim Finin, et al. 2006. Modeling the spread of influence on the blogosphere. In *Proc. of WWW.*

Akshay Java, Xiaodan Song, Tim Finin, and Belle Tseng. 2007. Why we Twitter: Understanding Microblogging Usage and Communities. In *Proc. WebKDD-SNA-KDD.*

Jeffrey Pennington, Richard Socher, and Christopher D. Manning. Glove: Global Vectors for Word Representation. In *Proc. of EMNLP.*

Pawel Jurczyk and Eugene Agichtein. 2007. Discovering authorities in question answer communities by using link analysis. In *Proc. of CIKM.*

David Kempe, Jon Kleinberg, and Eva Tardos. 2003. Maximizing the spread of influence through a social network. In *Proc. of SIGKDD.*

Lingpeng Kong, Nathan Schneider, Swabha Swayamdipta, et al. 2014. A dependency parser for tweets. In *Proc. of EMNLP,* pages 10011012, Doha, Qatar, October.

Balachander Krishnamurthy, Phillipa Gill, and Martin Arlitt. 2008. A few chirps about Twitter. In *Proc. of the first workshop on Online social networks. ACM,* pages 19-24.

Remi Lebret, Jo el Legrand, and Ronan Collobert. 2013. Is deep learning really necessary for word embeddings? In *Proc. of NIPS.*

Omer Levy and Yoav Goldberg. 2014. Dependency-based word embeddings. In *Proc. of ACL.*

Omer Levy, Yoav Goldberg, And Ido Dagan. 2015. Improving Distributional Similarity with Lessons Learned from Word Embeddings. In *Proc. of TACL.*

Wei Li and Andrew McCallum. 2006. Pachinko allocation: DAG-structured mixture models of topic correla-tions. In *Proc. of the 23rd international conference on Machine learning. ACM*, pages 577-584.

Wei Li and Andrew McCallum. 2008. Pachinko allocation: Scalable mixture models of topic correlations. *Journal of Machine Learning Research.*

Shujie Liu, Nan Yang, Mu Li, and Ming Zhou. 2014. A recursive recurrent neural network for statistical machine translation. In *Proc. of ACL*, pages 1491 1500.

Minh-Thang Luong, Richard Socher, and Christopher D. Manning. 2013. Better Word Representations with Recursive Neural Networks for Morphology. In *Proc. of CoNLL.*

George A. Miller. 1995. Wordnet: A lexical database for english. *Communications of the ACM*, 38(11):3941.

Thomas P. Minka. 2000. Estimating a Dirichlet distribution. Technical report, MIT.

Tomas Mikolov, Kai Chen, Greg Corrado, and Jeffrey Dean. 2013(a). Efficient estimation of word representations in vector space. CoRR, abs/1301.3781.

Tomas Mikolov, Ilya Sutskever, Kai Chen, Gregory S. Corrado, and Jeffrey Dean. 2013(b). Distributed representations of words and phrases and their composition-ality. In *Advances in Neural Information Processing Systems*. pages 3111-3119.

Aditya Pal and Joseph A. Konstan. 2010. Expert Identification in Community Question Answering: Exploring Question Selection Bias. In *Proc. of the 19th ACM international conference on Information and knowledge management. ACM*, pages 1505-1508.

Aditya Pal and Scott Counts. 2011. Identifying topical authorities in microblogs. In *Proc. of the fourth ACM international conference on Web search and data mining. ACM*, pages 45-54.

Siyu Qiu, Qing Cui, Jiang Bian, and et al. 2014. Co-learning of Word Representations and Morpheme Representations. In *Proc. of COLING.*

Daniele Quercia, Harry Askham, and Jon Crowcroft. 2012. TweetLDA: supervised topic classification and link prediction in Twitter. In *Proc. of the 4th Annual ACM Web Science Conference. ACM*, pages 247-250.

Daniel Ramage, David Hall, Ramesh Nallapati, and Christopher D. Manning. 2009. Labeled LDA: A supervised topic model for credit attribution in multi-label corpora. In *Proc. of EMNLP.*

Daniel Ramage Susan Dumais, and Dan Liebling. 2010. Characterizing Microblogs with Topic Models. In ICWSM, 5(4): 130-137.

Ana Raposo, Mafalda Mendes, and J. Frederico Marques. 2012. The hierarchical organization of semantic memory: Executive function in the processing of superordinate concepts. *NeuroImage*, 59: 18701878.

Stanley M. Selkow. 1977. The tree-to-tree editing problem. *Information processing letters*, 6(6): 184-186.

Mahdi M. Shafiei and Evangelos E. Milios. 2006. Latent Dirichlet coclustering. In *Proc. of International Conference on Data Mining*, pages 542-551.

Dennis Shasha and Kaizhong Zhang. 1990. Fast algorithms for the unit cost editing distance between trees. *Journal of algorithms*, 11(4): 581-621.

Yaming Sun, Lei Lin, Duyu Tang, and et al. 2014. Radical-enhanced chinese character embedding. *arXiv preprint arXiv:1404.4714.*

Ilya Sutskever, Oriol Vinyals, and Quoc VV Le. 2014. Sequence to sequence learning with neural networks. In *Advances in Neural Information Processing Systems*, pages 31043112.

Jie Tang, Jing Zhang, Limin Yao, et al. 2008. Arnetminer: Extraction and mining of academic social networks. In *Proc. of SIGKDD.*

Duyu Tang, Furu Wei, Nan Yang, et al. 2014. Learning sentiment-specific word embedding for twitter sentiment classification. In *Proc. of ACL.*

Robert A. Wagner. 1975. On the complexity of the extended string-to-string correction problem. In *Proc. of seventh annual ACM symposium on Theory of computing*. pages 218-223. ACM.

Robert A. Wagner and Michael J. Fischer. 1974. The string-to-string correction problem. *Journal of the ACM (JACM)*, 21(1), 168-173.

Wang Ling, Chris Dyer, Alan Black, and Isabel Trancoso. 2015. Two/too simple adaptations of word2vec for syntax problems. In *Proc. of NAACL*, Denver, CO.

Jianshu Weng, Ee Peng Lim, Jing Jiang and Qi He. 2010. Twitterrank: finding topic-sensitive influential twitterers. In *Proc. of WSDM.*

Jason Weston, Antoine Bordes, Oksana Yakhnenko, and Nicolas Usunier. 2013. Connecting language and knowledge bases with embedding models for relation extraction. In *Proc. of Computation and Language.*

Yi Yang and Jacob Eisenstein. 2015. Unsupervised multi-domain adaptation with feature embeddings. In *Proc. of NAACL-HIT.*

Mo Yu and Mark Dredze. 2014. Improving lexical embeddings with semantic knowledge. In *Proc. of ACL.*

Jun Zhang, Mark S. Ackerman, and Lada Adamic. 2007. Expertise networks in online communities: structure and algorithms. In *Proc. of WWW.*

Kaizhong Zhang and Dennis Shasha. 1989. Simple fast algorithms for the editing distance between trees and related problems. *SIAM journal on computing*, 18(6): 1245-1262.

Meishan Zhang, Yue Zhang, Wan Xiang Che, and et al. 2013. Chinese parsing exploiting characters. In *Proc. of ACL*.

Xin Zhao and Jing Jiang. 2011. An empirical comparison of topics in twitter and traditional media. *Singapore Management University School of Information Systems Technical paper series. Retrieved November*, 10: 2011.

Tackling Sparsity, the Achilles Heel of Social Networks: Language Model Smoothing via Social Regularization

Rui Yan[1], **Xiang Li**[1,2], **Mengwen Liu**[3] **and Xiaohua Hu**[3]
[1]Baidu Research, Baidu Inc., Beijing, China
[2]Dept. of Computer Science & Technology, Peking University, Beijing, China
[3]College of Information Science & Technology, Drexel University, Philadelphia, USA
{yanrui02,lixiang32}@baidu.com, {ml943,xh29}@drexel.edu

Abstract

Online social networks nowadays have the worldwide prosperity, as they have revolutionized the way for people to discover, to share, and to diffuse information. Social networks are powerful, yet they still have Achilles Heel: extreme data sparsity. Individual posting documents, (e.g., a microblog less than 140 characters), seem to be too sparse to make a difference under various scenarios, while in fact they are quite different. We propose to tackle this specific weakness of social networks by smoothing the posting document language model based on social regularization. We formulate an optimization framework with a social regularizer. Experimental results on the *Twitter* dataset validate the effectiveness and efficiency of our proposed model.

1 Introduction

Along with Web 2.0 online social networks have revolutionized the way for people to discover, to share and to propagate information via peer-to-peer interactions (Kwak et al., 2010). Although powerful as social networks are, they still suffer from a severe weakness: extreme sparsity. Due to the special characteristics of real-time propagation, the postings on social networks are either officially limited within a limit length (140 characters on Twitter), or generally quite short due to user preference. Given limited text data sampling, a language model estimation usually encounters with zero count problem when facing with data sparsity, which is not reliable. Therefore, *sparsity* is regarded as the Achilles Heel of social networks and now we aim at tackling the bottleneck (Yan et al., 2015).

Statistical language models have attracted much attention in research communities. Till now much

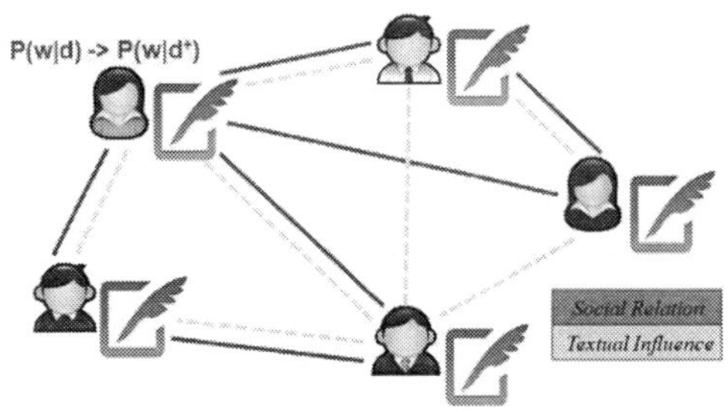

Figure 1: 2 different sources to smooth document language models: texts (colored in yellow) and social contacts (colored in blue). Each piece of texts is authored by a particular social network user.

work on language model smoothing has been investigated based on textual characteristics (Lafferty and Zhai, 2001; Yan et al., 2013; Liu and Croft, 2004; Tao et al., 2006; Lavrenko and Croft, 2001; Song and Croft, 1999). However, for social networks, texts are actually associated with users (as illustrated in Figure 1). We propose that social factors should be utilized as an augmentation to better smooth language models.

Here we propose an optimization framework with regularization for language model smoothing on social networks, using both textual information and the social structure. We believe the social factor is fundamental to smooth language models on social networks. Our framework optimizes the smoothed language model to be closer to social neighbors in the online network, while avoid deviating too much from the original user language models. Our contributions are as follows:

- We have proposed a balanced language model smoothing framework with optimization, using text information with social structure as a regularizer;

- We have investigated an effective and efficient strategy to model the social information among social network users.

Proceedings of the 53rd Annual Meeting of the Association for Computational Linguistics and the 7th International Joint Conference on Natural Language Processing (Short Papers), pages 623–629, Beijing, China, July 26-31, 2015.

We evaluate the effect of our proposed language model smoothing model using datasets from Twitter. Experimental results show that language model smoothing with social regularization is effective and efficient in terms of intrinsic evaluation by perplexity and running time: we show that the Achilles Heel of social networks could be to some extent tackled.

The rest of the paper is organized as follows. We start by reviewing previous works. Then we introduce the language model smoothing with social regularization and its optimization. We describe the experiments and evaluation in the next section and finally draw the conclusions.

2 Related Work

Language models have been paid high attention to during recent years (Ponte and Croft, 1998). Many different ways of language modeling have been proposed to solve different tasks. Better estimation of query language models (Lafferty and Zhai, 2001; Lavrenko and Croft, 2001) and more accurate estimation of document language models (Liu and Croft, 2004; Tao et al., 2006) have long been proved to be of great significance in information retrieval and text mining, etc. Language models are typically implemented based on retrieval models, e.g., text weighting and normalization (Zhai and Lafferty, 2001), but with more elegant mathematical and statistical foundations (Song and Croft, 1999).

There is one problem for language models. Given limited data sampling, a language model estimation sometimes encounters with the zero count problem: the maximum likelihood estimator would assign unseen terms a zero probability, which is not reliable. Language model enrichment is proposed to address this problem, and has been demonstrated to be of great significance (Zhai and Lafferty, 2001; Lafferty and Zhai, 2001).

There are many ways to enrich the original language model. The information of background corpus has been incorporated using linear combination (Ponte and Croft, 1998; Zhai and Lafferty, 2001). In contrast to the simple strategy which smooths all documents with the same background, recently corpus structures have been exploited for more accurate smoothing. The basic idea is to smooth a document language model with the documents similar to the document under consideration through clustering (Liu and Croft, 2004; Tao et al., 2006). Position information has also been used to enrich language model smoothing (Zhao and Yun, 2009; Lv and Zhai, 2009) and has been used in the combination of both enrichment of position and semantic (Yan et al., 2013). Beyond the semantic and/or position related smoothing intuitions, document structure based language model smoothing is another direction to investigate (Duan and Zhai, 2011). Mei *et al.* have proposed to smooth language model utilizing structural adjacency (2008). None of these methods incorporates social factors in language model smoothing.

There is a study in (Lin et al., 2011) which smooths document language models of tweets for topic tracking in online text streams. Basically, it applies general smoothing strategies (e.g., Jelinek-Mercer, Dirichlet, Absolute Discounting, etc.) on the specific tracking task. Social information is incorporated into a factor graph model as features (Huang et al., 2014; Yan et al., 2015). These factor graph model based methods are less efficient so as to better handle *cold-start* situations with little training data. In contrast with these works, we have proposed a language model smoothing framework which incorporates social factors as a regularizer. According to the experimental results, our method is effective with social information and as well much more efficient.

3 Smoothing with Social Regularization

To motivate the model, we briefly discuss the intuitions of proposed language model smoothing. Generally, given a non-smoothed document language model $P(w|d)$, which indicates a word distribution for a term w in document d, we attempt to generate a smoothed language model $P(w|d^+)$ that could better estimate the text contents of a document d as d^+ to avoid zero probabilities for those words not seen in d. Arbitrary assignment of pseudo word counts such as add-λ to every unseen words once was a major improvement for language model smoothing (Chen and Goodman, 1996). However, the purpose of smoothing is to estimate language model more accurately. One of the most useful resources to smooth is the documents similar to d: documents with the larger textual similarity indicate the smaller distance and the better smoothing effects.

Moreover, the author information of the posting documents is easily accessible on social networks. We hence have information related to social factors, which could be used to better estimate the document language model. Through our observation, people are more likely to inherit language habits and usages from their contacts on the social networks. This social factor is important and unique for language model smoothing on social networks. It should be not surprising that smoothing with social factors will be a better optimum. Previously, the pure similarity based smoothing without social factors indicates equal distance for every document from any user on the networks, which is not a fair assumption and presumably leads to a weaker performance.

Yet, with the objective of textual similarity based smoothing with social factors, the smoothed language model might possibly deviate from the original posting documents of a specific user dramatically. It is intuitive that we ought to keep the original representation of document language models of the particular user, and in the meanwhile the postings could be distinguished from one another. Therefore, the combination of the original language model with the social factor as a regularizer ensures the optimum smoothing effects with proper optimization to balance both the textual and social components.

3.1 Problem Formulation

Now we give a formal definition as follows:

Input. Given the entire document set D, and the social network of users U, we aim to smooth the language model of the target document, denoted as $P(w|d_0)$, based on the influence from all other documents d where $\{d|d \in D\}$, and d is authored by $u_d \in U$.

Output. The smoothed language model of $P(w|d_0^+)$ for the original document d_0.

3.2 Methodology Framework

We frame social language smoothing as the interpolation of document representation from the original user and the social factor regularization. Regularization has been cast as an optimization problem in machine learning literature (Zhou and Schölkopf, 2005), and we could form the language model smoothing under this optimization framework. Formally, we propose the smoothing framework for language models with the regularized social factor as follows:

$$O(d_0) = \lambda \sum_{u_{d_i}=u_0} \phi_{d_i} |P(w|d_0^+) - P(w|d_i)|^2 + (1-\lambda) \sum_{u \in U \backslash u_0} \pi_u \sum_{u_{d_j} \neq u_0} \phi_{d_j} |P(w|d_0^+) - P(w|d_j)|^2 \quad (1)$$

where $u_0 = u_{d_0}$, which means the author of d_0 to smooth. Function π_u indicates the social relationship between user u and u_0. Function ϕ_d measures the textual similarity between document d and the document d_0 to smooth. The smoothed document language model is denoted as $P(w|d_0^+)$, and the unsmoothed document language model for d is written as $P(w|d)$.

The objective function of $O(.)$ implement two intuitions: 1) the first component guarantees the smoothed language model would not deviate too much from the language habits of the user of u_0, controlled by the similarity between all the documents from the author of d_0; 2) the second term, namely a harmonic function in semi-supervised learning, incorporating the influence from contacts on the social networks. The framework is general since the functions could be initiated in different instances. Different initiations of functions indicate different features or factors to be taken into account. In this paper, we formulate the textual similarity of ϕ_d, and the social relationship π_u based on the social network dimension. Eventually, we can find the flexibility to extend features and factors in future work.

Firstly, we will define the correlation ϕ_d between document pairs. It is intuitive to measure the relationship among documents based on the textual similarity. In this paper, we utilize the standard cosine metric to measure the similarity between posting document in vector space model representations (Salton et al., 1975). Vector components are set to their *tf.idf* values (Manning et al., 2008). *tf* is the term frequency and *idf* is the inverse document frequency. Next we continue to define the social factor among users.

For π_u, the most intuitive way is to calculate the contacts similarity of the social network users, i.e., friends or followees in common. We first apply the Jaccard distance (Jaccard, 1912; Pang-Ning et al., 2006) on the social contact sets for the two network users (i.e., between u_0 and another particular user u) as follows:

$$\pi_u = \frac{|\{nb(u_0)\} \cap \{nb(u)\}|}{|\{nb(u_0)\} \cup \{nb(u)\}|} \quad (2)$$

#User	#Docs	#Link
9,449,542	364,287,744	596,777,491

Clusters	#Docs	Notes
1. apple	42,528	Tech: apple products
2. nfl	40,340	Sport: American football
3. travel	38,345	General interst

Table 1: Statistics of dataset and topic clusters.

where $\{nb(u)\}$ indicates the set of all neighbor contacts of node u, each of which shares an edge to u.

Now we have finished modeling the language model smoothing with social factors as regularization, and have defined the context correlation between documents and user social relationships. By plugging in Equation (2) into Equation (1), we could compute the smoothed language model of $P(w|d_0^+)$. All the definitions for $\pi(.)$ result in a range which varies from 0 to 1. Particularly, the ego user similarity π_{u0} = 1, which would be a natural and intuitive answer.

4 Experiments and Evaluation

4.1 Datasets and Experimental Setups

Utilizing the data in (Yan et al., 2012), we establish the dataset of microblogs and the corresponding users from 9/29/2012 to 11/30/2012. We use roughly one month as the training set and the rest as testing set. Based on this dataset, we group the posting documents with the same hashtag '#' into clusters as different datasets to evaluate (Lin et al., 2011; Yan et al., 2015; Yan et al., 2011). We manually selected top-3 topics based on popularity (measured in the number of postings within the cluster) and to obtain broad coverage of different types: sports, technology, and general interests, as listed in Table 1.

Pre-processing. Basically, the social network graph can be established from all posting documents and all users. However, the data is noisy. We first pre-filter the pointless babbles (Analytics, 2009) by applying the linguistic quality judgments (e.g., OOV ratio) (Pitler et al., 2010), and then remove inactive users that have less than one follower or followee and remove the users without any linkage to the remaining posting documents. We remove stopwords and URLs, perform stemming, and build the graph after filtering. We establish the language model smoothed with both text information and social factors.

4.2 Algorithms for Comparison

The first baseline is based on the traditional language model: **LM** is the language model without smoothing at all. We include the plain smoothing of **Additive** (also known as Add-δ) smoothing and **Absolute Discounting** decrease the probability of seen words by subtracting a constant (Ney et al., 1995). We also implement several classic strategies smoothed from the whole collection as background information: **Jelinek-Mercer (J-M)** applies a linear interpolation, and **Dirichlet** employs a prior on collection influence (Zhai and Lafferty, 2001; Lafferty and Zhai, 2001).

Beyond these simple heuristics, we also examine a series of semantic based language model smoothing. The most representative two semantic smoothing methods are the Cluster-Based Document Model (**CBDM**) proposed in (Liu and Croft, 2004), and the Document Expansion Language Model (**DELM**) in (Tao et al., 2006). Both methods use semantically similar documents as a smoothing corpus for a particular document. We also include Positional Language Model (**PLM**) proposed in (Lv and Zhai, 2009), which is the state-of-art positional proximity based language smoothing. PLM mainly utilizes positional information without semantic information. We implemented the best reported PLM configuration. We also include the Factor Graph Model (**FGM**) method to make a full comparison with our proposed social regularized smoothing (**SRS**).

4.3 Evaluation Metric

We apply language *perplexity* to evaluate the smoothed language models. The experimental procedure is as follows: given the topic clusters shown in Table 1, we remove the hashtags and compute its *perplexity* with respect to the current topic cluster, defined as a power function:

$$\text{pow}\left[2, -\frac{1}{N}\sum_{w_i \in V} \log P(w_i)\right]$$

Perplexity is actually an entropy based evaluation. In this sense, the lower perplexity within the same topic cluster, the better performance in purity the topic cluster would have.

Topic	#apple	#nfl	#travel
LM	15851	11356	10676
Additive	15195	10035	10342
Absolute	15323	10123	10379
J-M	14115	10011	10185
Dirichlet	13892	9516	10138
PLM	13730	9925	10426
CBDM	12931	9845	9311
DELM	11853	9820	9513
FGM	10788	9539	8408
SRS	11808	9888	9403

Table 2: Perplexity in hashtag clusters.

4.4 Overall Performance

We compare the performance of all methods of language model smoothing on the Twitter datasets. In Table 2 we list the overall results against all baseline methods. We have an average of -7.28% improvement in terms of language perplexity in hashtag topic clusters against all baselines without social information.

The language model without any smoothing strategy performs worst as expected, and once again demonstrates the Achilles Heel of data sparsity on social networks! Simple intuition based methods such as additive smoothing does not help a lot, since it only arbitrarily modifies the given term counts straightforward to avoid zero occurrence, which is proved to be insufficient. Absolute smoothing performs slightly better, due to the idea to incorporate the collection information by term counts. Jelinek-Mercer (J-M) and Dirichlet methods are more useful since they include the information from the whole collection as background language models, but they fail to distinguish documents from documents and use all of them equally into smoothing. PLM offers a strengthened language model smoothing strategy within each posting document based on positions, and smooth the terms outside of the posting document formulating the background collection into a Dirichlet prior. The performance of CBDM and DELM indicates a prominent improvement, and proves that semantic attributes included into the smoothing process really make a difference. Both of the smoothing methods cluster documents, and use the clustered documents as a better background. However, none of these methods has made use of the social factors during the language model smoothing, while both FGM and SRS suggests social factors do have an impact on language model smoothing.

We make a further comparison between FGM and SRS: both are using social information. An interesting phenomenon is that FGM slightly outperforms SRS. The proposed SRS has more efficiency than FGM. It is quite intuitive that FGM is a complicated model based on propagation via linkage while our proposed SRS is a lightweight model using linear combination. Hence SRS is proved to be both effective due to the comparable performance with FGM, and more efficient as the result of simple interpolation.

5 Conclusions

We present a language model smoothing method based on text correlation with social factors as regularization to solve the zero count phenomenon (sparsity!) for short postings on social networks. We smooth the extremely sparse language model based on texts and social connections in optimization. We evaluate the performance of our proposed smoothing method. In general, the social factor is proved to have a meaningful contribution. Our model outperforms all baseline smoothing methods without social information while takes less time to run: the lightweight method balances effectiveness and efficiency best.

Acknowledgments

This work was partially done when the first author was at University of Pennsylvania. We thank all the anonymous reviewers for their valuable and constructive comments in ACL short paper track[1].

References

Pear Analytics. 2009. Twitter study–august 2009. 15.

Stanley F. Chen and Joshua Goodman. 1996. An empirical study of smoothing techniques for language modeling. In *Proceedings of the 34th Annual Meeting on Association for Computational Linguistics*, ACL '96, pages 310–318, Stroudsburg, PA, USA. Association for Computational Linguistics.

Huizhong Duan and Chengxiang Zhai. 2011. Exploiting thread structures to improve smoothing of language models for forum post retrieval. In *Advances in Information Retrieval*, pages 350–361. Springer.

[1]This paper was at first submitted to the ACL long paper track. One reviewer insisted his/her (*perhaps disputable*) opinions and the other two reviewers were outvoted. If interested, we would welcome this reviewer to write emails to us and to discuss his/her *very quick* review offered initially before the author response period.

Yu-Yang Huang, Rui Yan, Tsung-Ting Kuo, and Shou-De Lin. 2014. Enriching cold start personalized language model using social network information. In *Proceedings of the 52nd Annual Meeting on Association for Computational Linguistics*, ACL '14, pages 611–617.

Paul Jaccard. 1912. The distribution of the flora in the alpine zone. *New phytologist*, 11(2):37–50.

Haewoon Kwak, Changhyun Lee, Hosung Park, and Sue Moon. 2010. What is twitter, a social network or a news media? In *Proceedings of the 19th International Conference on World Wide Web*, WWW '10, pages 591–600, New York, NY, USA. ACM.

John Lafferty and Chengxiang Zhai. 2001. Document language models, query models, and risk minimization for information retrieval. In *Proceedings of the 24th Annual International ACM SIGIR Conference on Research and Development in Information Retrieval*, SIGIR '01, pages 111–119, New York, NY, USA. ACM.

Victor Lavrenko and W. Bruce Croft. 2001. Relevance based language models. In *Proceedings of the 24th Annual International ACM SIGIR Conference on Research and Development in Information Retrieval*, SIGIR '01, pages 120–127, New York, NY, USA. ACM.

Jimmy Lin, Rion Snow, and William Morgan. 2011. Smoothing techniques for adaptive online language models: Topic tracking in tweet streams. In *Proceedings of the 17th ACM SIGKDD International Conference on Knowledge Discovery and Data Mining*, KDD '11, pages 422–429, New York, NY, USA. ACM.

Xiaoyong Liu and W. Bruce Croft. 2004. Cluster-based retrieval using language models. In *Proceedings of the 27th Annual International ACM SIGIR Conference on Research and Development in Information Retrieval*, SIGIR '04, pages 186–193, New York, NY, USA. ACM.

Yuanhua Lv and ChengXiang Zhai. 2009. Positional language models for information retrieval. In *Proceedings of the 32Nd International ACM SIGIR Conference on Research and Development in Information Retrieval*, SIGIR '09, pages 299–306, New York, NY, USA. ACM.

Christopher D Manning, Prabhakar Raghavan, and Hinrich Schütze. 2008. *Introduction to information retrieval*, volume 1.

Qiaozhu Mei, Duo Zhang, and ChengXiang Zhai. 2008. A general optimization framework for smoothing language models on graph structures. In *Proceedings of the 31st Annual International ACM SIGIR Conference on Research and Development in Information Retrieval*, SIGIR '08, pages 611–618, New York, NY, USA. ACM.

Hermann Ney, Ute Essen, and Reinhard Kneser. 1995. On the estimation ofsmall'probabilities by leaving-one-out. *Pattern Analysis and Machine Intelligence, IEEE Transactions on*, 17(12):1202–1212.

Tan Pang-Ning, Michael Steinbach, Vipin Kumar, et al. 2006. Introduction to data mining. In *Library of Congress*, page 74.

Emily Pitler, Annie Louis, and Ani Nenkova. 2010. Automatic evaluation of linguistic quality in multi-document summarization. In *Proceedings of the 48th Annual Meeting of the Association for Computational Linguistics*, ACL '10, pages 544–554, Stroudsburg, PA, USA. Association for Computational Linguistics.

Jay M. Ponte and W. Bruce Croft. 1998. A language modeling approach to information retrieval. In *Proceedings of the 21st Annual International ACM SIGIR Conference on Research and Development in Information Retrieval*, SIGIR '98, pages 275–281, New York, NY, USA. ACM.

G. Salton, A. Wong, and C. S. Yang. 1975. A vector space model for automatic indexing. *Commun. ACM*, 18(11):613–620, November.

Fei Song and W. Bruce Croft. 1999. A general language model for information retrieval. In *Proceedings of the Eighth International Conference on Information and Knowledge Management*, CIKM '99, pages 316–321, New York, NY, USA. ACM.

Tao Tao, Xuanhui Wang, Qiaozhu Mei, and ChengXiang Zhai. 2006. Language model information retrieval with document expansion. In *Proceedings of the Main Conference on Human Language Technology Conference of the North American Chapter of the Association of Computational Linguistics*, HLT-NAACL '06, pages 407–414, Stroudsburg, PA, USA. Association for Computational Linguistics.

Rui Yan, Xiaojun Wan, Jahna Otterbacher, Liang Kong, Xiaoming Li, and Yan Zhang. 2011. Evolutionary timeline summarization: A balanced optimization framework via iterative substitution. In *Proceedings of the 34th International ACM SIGIR Conference on Research and Development in Information Retrieval*, SIGIR '11, pages 745–754, New York, NY, USA. ACM.

Rui Yan, Mirella Lapata, and Xiaoming Li. 2012. Tweet recommendation with graph co-ranking. In *Proceedings of the 50th Annual Meeting of the Association for Computational Linguistics: Long Papers - Volume 1*, ACL '12, pages 516–525, Stroudsburg, PA, USA. Association for Computational Linguistics.

Rui Yan, Han Jiang, Mirella Lapata, Shou-De Lin, Xueqiang Lv, and Xiaoming Li. 2013. Semantic v.s. positions: Utilizing balanced proximity in language model smoothing for information retrieval. In

Proceedings of the 6th International Joint Conference on Natural Language Processing, IJCNLP'13, pages 507–515.

Rui Yan, Ian E.H. Yen, Cheng-Te Li, Shiqi Zhao, and Xiaohua Hu. 2015. Tackling the achilles heel of social networks: Influence propagation based language model smoothing. In *Proceedings of the 24th International Conference on World Wide Web*, WWW '15, pages 1318–1328, Republic and Canton of Geneva, Switzerland. International World Wide Web Conferences Steering Committee.

Chengxiang Zhai and John Lafferty. 2001. A study of smoothing methods for language models applied to ad hoc information retrieval. In *Proceedings of the 24th Annual International ACM SIGIR Conference on Research and Development in Information Retrieval*, SIGIR '01, pages 334–342, New York, NY, USA. ACM.

Jinglei Zhao and Yeogirl Yun. 2009. A proximity language model for information retrieval. In *Proceedings of the 32Nd International ACM SIGIR Conference on Research and Development in Information Retrieval*, SIGIR '09, pages 291–298, New York, NY, USA. ACM.

Dengyong Zhou and Bernhard Schölkopf. 2005. Regularization on discrete spaces. In *Pattern Recognition*, pages 361–368. Springer.

Twitter User Geolocation Using a Unified Text and Network Prediction Model

Afshin Rahimi, Trevor Cohn, and **Timothy Baldwin**
Department of Computing and Information Systems
The University of Melbourne
arahimi@student.unimelb.edu.au
{t.cohn,tbaldwin}@unimelb.edu.au

Abstract

We propose a label propagation approach to geolocation prediction based on Modified Adsorption, with two enhancements: (1) the removal of "celebrity" nodes to increase location homophily and boost tractability; and (2) the incorporation of text-based geolocation priors for test users. Experiments over three Twitter benchmark datasets achieve state-of-the-art results, and demonstrate the effectiveness of the enhancements.

1 Introduction

Geolocation of social media users is essential in applications ranging from rapid disaster response (Earle et al., 2010; Ashktorab et al., 2014; Morstatter et al., 2013a) and opinion analysis (Mostafa, 2013; Kirilenko and Stepchenkova, 2014), to recommender systems (Noulas et al., 2012; Schedl and Schnitzer, 2014). Social media platforms like Twitter provide support for users to declare their location manually in their text profile or automatically with GPS-based geotagging. However, the text-based profile locations are noisy and only 1–3% of tweets are geotagged (Cheng et al., 2010; Morstatter et al., 2013b), meaning that geolocation needs to be inferred from other information sources such as the tweet text and network relationships.

User geolocation is the task of inferring the primary (or "home") location of a user from available sources of information, such as text posted by that individual, or network relationships with other individuals (Han et al., 2014). Geolocation models are usually trained on the small set of users whose location is known (e.g. through GPS-based geotagging), and other users are geolocated using the resulting model. These models broadly fall into two categories: text-based and network-based methods. Orthogonally, the geolocation task can be viewed as a regression task over real-valued geographical coordinates, or a classification task over discretised region-based locations.

Most previous research on user geolocation has focused either on text-based classification approaches (Eisenstein et al., 2010; Wing and Baldridge, 2011; Roller et al., 2012; Han et al., 2014) or, to a lesser extent, network-based regression approaches (Jurgens, 2013; Compton et al., 2014; Rahimi et al., 2015). Methods which combine the two, however, are rare.

In this paper, we present our work on Twitter user geolocation using both text and network information. Our contributions are as follows: (1) we propose the use of Modified Adsorption (Talukdar and Crammer, 2009) as a baseline network-based geolocation model, and show that it outperforms previous network-based approaches (Jurgens, 2013; Rahimi et al., 2015); (2) we demonstrate that removing "celebrity" nodes (nodes with high in-degrees) from the network increases geolocation accuracy and dramatically decreases network edge size; and (3) we integrate text-based geolocation priors into Modified Adsorption, and show that our unified geolocation model outperforms both text-only and network-only approaches, and achieves state-of-the-art results over three standard datasets.

2 Related Work

A recent spike in interest on user geolocation over social media data has resulted in the development of a range of approaches to automatic geolocation prediction, based on information sources such as the text of messages, social networks, user profile data, and temporal data. Text-based methods model the geographical bias of language use in social media, and use it to geolocate non-geotagged users. Gazetted expressions (Leidner and Lieberman, 2011) and geographical names (Quercini et

Proceedings of the 53rd Annual Meeting of the Association for Computational Linguistics and the 7th International Joint Conference on Natural Language Processing (Short Papers), pages 630–636,
Beijing, China, July 26-31, 2015.

al., 2010) were used as feature in early work, but were shown to be sparse in coverage. Han et al. (2014) used information-theoretic methods to automatically extract location-indicative words for location classification. Wing and Baldridge (2014) reported that discriminative approaches (based on hierarchical classification over adaptive grids), when optimised properly, are superior to explicit feature selection. Cha et al. (2015) showed that sparse coding can be used to effectively learn a latent representation of tweet text to use in user geolocation. Eisenstein et al. (2010) and Ahmed et al. (2013) proposed topic model-based approaches to geolocation, based on the assumption that words are generated from hidden topics and geographical regions. Similarly, Yuan et al. (2013) used graphical models to jointly learn spatio-temporal topics for users. The advantage of these generative approaches is that they are able to work with the continuous geographical space directly without any pre-discretisation, but they are algorithmically complex and don't scale well to larger datasets. Hulden et al. (2015) used kernel-based methods to smooth linguistic features over very small grid sizes to alleviate data sparseness.

Network-based geolocation models, on the other hand, utilise the fact that social media users interact more with people who live nearby. Jurgens (2013) and Compton et al. (2014) used a Twitter reciprocal mention network, and geolocated users based on the geographical coordinates of their friends, by minimising the weighted distance of a given user to their friends. For a reciprocal mention network to be effective, however, a huge amount of Twitter data is required. Rahimi et al. (2015) showed that this assumption could be relaxed to use an undirected mention network for smaller datasets, and still attain state-of-the-art results. The greatest shortcoming of network-based models is that they completely fail to geolocate users who are not connected to geolocated components of the graph. As shown by Rahimi et al. (2015), geolocation predictions from text can be used as a backoff for disconnected users, but there has been little work that has investigated a more integrated text- and network-based approach to user geolocation.

3 Data

We evaluate our models over three pre-existing geotagged Twitter datasets: (1) GEOTEXT (Eisenstein et al., 2010), (2) TWITTER-US (Roller et al., 2012), and (3) TWITTER-WORLD (Han et al., 2012). In each dataset, users are represented by a single meta-document, generated by concatenating their tweets. The datasets are pre-partitioned into training, development and test sets, and rebuilt from the original version to include mention information. The first two datasets were constructed to contain mostly English messages.

GEOTEXT consists of tweets from 9.5K users: 1895 users are held out for each of development and test data. The primary location of each user is set to the coordinates of their first tweet.

TWITTER-US consists of 449K users, of which 10K users are held out for each of development and test data. The primary location of each user is, once again, set to the coordinates of their first tweet.

TWITTER-WORLD consists of 1.3M users, of which 10000 each are held out for development and test. Unlike the other two datasets, the primary location of users is mapped to the geographic centre of the city where the majority of their tweets were posted.

4 Methods

We use label propagation over an @-mention graph in our models. We use k-d tree descretised adaptive grids as class labels for users and learn a label distribution for each user by label propagation over the @-mention network using labelled nodes as seeds. For k-d tree discretisation, we set the number of users in each region to 50, 2400, 2400 for GEOTEXT, TWITTER-US and TWITTER-WORLD respectively, based on tuning over the development data.

Social Network: We used the @-mention information to build an undirected graph between users. In order to make the inference more tractable, we removed all nodes that were not a member of the training/test set, and connected all pairings of training/test users if there was any path between them (including paths through non training/test users). We call this network a "collapsed network", as illustrated in Figure 1. Note that a celebrity node with n mentions connects $n(n-1)$ nodes in the collapsed network. We experiment with both binary and weighted edge (based on the number of mentions connecting the given users) networks.

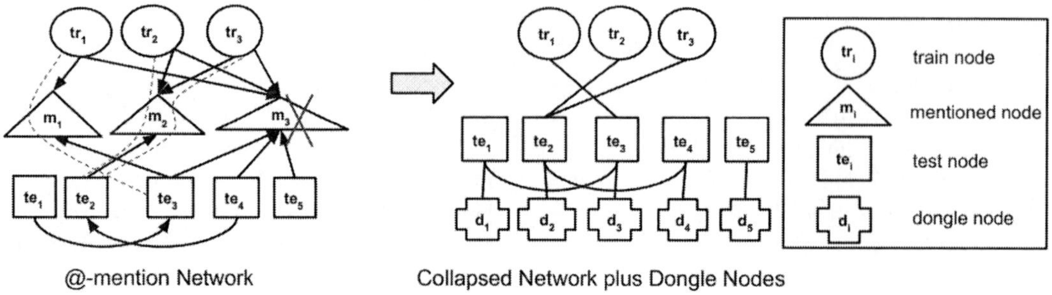

Figure 1: A collapsed network is built from the @-mention network. Each mention is shown by a directed arrow, noting that as it is based exclusively on the tweets from the training and test users, it will always be directed from a training or test user to a mentioned node. All mentioned nodes which are not a member of either training or test users are removed and the corresponding training and test users, previously connected through that node, are connected directly by an edge, as indicated by the dashed lines. Mentioned nodes with more than T unique mentions (celebrities, such as m_3) are removed from the graph. To each test node, a dongle node that carries the label from another learner (here, text-based LR) is added in MADCEL-B-LR and MADCEL-W-LR.

Baseline: Our baseline geolocation model ("MAD-B") is formulated as label propagation over a binary collapsed network, based on Modified Adsorption (Talukdar and Crammer, 2009). It applies to a graph $G = (V, E, W)$ where V is the set of nodes with $|V| = n = n_l + n_u$ (where n_l nodes are labelled and n_u nodes are unlabelled), E is the set of edges, and W is an edge weight matrix. Assume C is the set of labels where $|C| = m$ is the total number of labels. Y is an $n \times m$ matrix storing the training node labels, and $\hat{Y}$ is the estimated label distribution for the nodes. The goal is to estimate $\hat{Y}$ for all nodes (including training nodes) so that the following objective function is minimised:

$$C(\hat{Y}) = \sum_l \left[\mu_1 (Y_l - \hat{Y}_l)^T S (Y_l - \hat{Y}_l) + \mu_2 \hat{Y}_l^T L \hat{Y}_l \right]$$

where μ_1 and μ_2 are hyperparameters;[1] L is the Laplacian of an undirected graph derived from G; and S is a diagonal binary matrix indicating if a node is labelled or not. The first term of the equation forces the labelled nodes to keep their label (prior term), while the second term pulls a node's label toward that of its neighbours (smoothness term). For the first term, the label confidence for training and test users is set to 1.0 and 0.0, respectively. Based on the development data, we set μ_1 and μ_2 to 1.0 and 0.1, respectively, for all the experiments. For TWITTER-US and TWITTER-WORLD, the inference was intractable for the default network, as it was too large.

There are two immediate issues with the baseline graph propagation method: (1) it doesn't scale to large datasets with high edge counts, related to which, it tends to be biased by highly-connected nodes; and (2) it can't predict the geolocation of test users who aren't connected to any training user (MAD-B returns Unknown, which we rewrite with the centre of the map). We redress these two issues as follows.

Celebrity Removal To address the first issue, we target "celebrity" users, i.e. highly-mentioned Twitter users. Edges involving these users often carry little or no geolocation information (e.g. the majority of people who mention Barack Obama don't live in Washington D.C.). Additionally, these users tend to be highly connected to other users and generate a disproportionately high number of edges in the graph, leading in large part to the baseline MAD-B not scaling over large datasets such as TWITTER-US and TWITTER-WORLD. We identify and filter out celebrity nodes simply by assuming that a celebrity is mentioned by more than T users, where T is tuned over development data. Based on tuning over the development

[1] In the base formulation of MAD-B, there is also a regularisation term with weight μ_3, but in all our experiments, we found that the best results were achieved over development data with $\mu_3 = 0$, i.e. with no regularisation; the term is thus omitted from our description.

	GEOTEXT			TWITTER-US			TWITTER-WORLD		
	Acc@161	Mean	Median	Acc@161	Mean	Median	Acc@161	Mean	Median
MAD-B	50	683	146	×××	×××	×××	×××	×××	×××
MADCEL-B	56	609	76	54	709	117	70	936	**0**
MADCEL-W	58	586	60	54	705	116	71	976	**0**
MADCEL-B-LR	57	608	65	**60**	533	**77**	**72**	**786**	**0**
MADCEL-W-LR	**59**	**581**	**57**	**60**	**529**	78	**72**	802	**0**
LR (Rahimi et al., 2015)	38	880	397	50	686	159	63	866	19
LP (Rahimi et al., 2015)	45	676	255	37	747	431	56	1026	79
LP-LR (Rahimi et al., 2015)	50	653	151	50	620	157	59	903	53
Wing and Baldridge (2014) (uniform)	—	—	—	49	703	170	32	1714	490
Wing and Baldridge (2014) (k-d)	—	—	—	48	686	191	31	1669	509
Han et al. (2012)	—	—	—	45	814	260	24	1953	646
Ahmed et al. (2013)	???	???	298	—	—	—	—	—	—
Cha et al. (2015)	???	**581**	425	—	—	—	—	—	—

Table 1: Geolocation results over the three Twitter corpora, comparing baseline Modified Adsorption (MAD-B), with Modified Adsorption with celebrity removal (MADCEL-B and MADCEL-W, over binary and weighted networks, resp.) or celebrity removal plus text priors (MADCEL-B-LR and MADCEL-W-LR, over binary and weighted networks, resp.); the table also includes state-of-the-art results for each dataset ("—" signifies that no results were published for the given dataset; "???" signifies that no results were reported for the given metric; and "×××" signifies that results could not be generated, due to the intractability of the training data).

set of GEOTEXT and TWITTER-US, T was set to 5 and 15 respectively. For TWITTER-WORLD tuning was very resource intensive so T was set to 5 based on GEOTEXT, to make the inference faster. Celebrity removal dramatically reduced the edge count in all three datasets (from 1×10^9 to 5×10^6 for TWITTER-US and from 4×10^{10} to 1×10^7 for TWITTER-WORLD), and made inference tractable for TWITTER-US and TWITTER-WORLD. Jurgens et al. (2015) report that the time complexity of most network-based geolocation methods is $\mathcal{O}(k^2)$ for each node where k is the average number of vertex neighbours. In the case of the collapsed network of TWITTER-WORLD, k is decreased by a factor of 4000 after setting the celebrity threshold T to 5. We apply celebrity removal over both binary ("MADCEL-B") and weighted ("MADCEL-W") networks (using the respective T for each dataset). The effect of celebrity removal over the development set of TWITTER-US is shown in Figure 2 where it dramatically reduces the graph edge size and simultaneously leads to an improvement in the mean error.

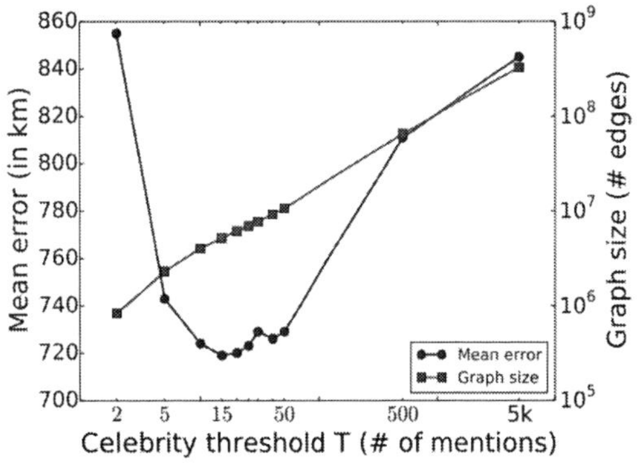

Figure 2: Effect of celebrity removal on geolocation performance and graph size. For each T performance is measured over the development set of TWITTER-US by MADCEL-W.

A Unified Geolocation Model To address the issue of disconnected test users, we incorporate text information into the model by attaching a labelled dongle node to every test node (Zhu and Ghahramani, 2002; Goldberg and Zhu, 2006). The label for the dongle node is based on a text-based l_1 regularised logistic regression model, using the method of Rahimi et al. (2015). The dongle nodes with their corresponding label confidences are added to the seed set, and are treated in the same way as other labelled nodes (i.e. the training nodes). Once again, we experiment with text-based labelled dongle nodes over both binary ("MADCEL-B-LR") and weighted ("MADCEL-W-LR") networks.

5 Evaluation

Following Cheng et al. (2010) and Eisenstein et al. (2010), we evaluate using the mean and median error (in km) over all test users ("Mean" and "Median", resp.), and also accuracy within 161km of the actual location ("Acc@161"). Note that higher numbers are better for Acc@161, but lower numbers are better for mean and median error, with a lower bound of 0 and no (theoretical) upper bound.

To generate a continuous-valued latitude/longitude coordinate for a given user from the k-d tree cell, we use the median coordinates of all training points in the predicted region.

6 Results

Table 1 shows the performance of MAD-B, MADCEL-B, MADCEL-W, MADCEL-B-LR and MADCEL-W-LR over the GEOTEXT, TWITTER-US and TWITTER-WORLD datasets. The results are also compared with prior work on network-based geolocation using label propagation (LP) (Rahimi et al., 2015), text-based classification models (Han et al., 2012; Wing and Baldridge, 2011; Wing and Baldridge, 2014; Rahimi et al., 2015; Cha et al., 2015), text-based graphical models (Ahmed et al., 2013), and network–text hybrid models (LP-LR) (Rahimi et al., 2015).

Our baseline network-based model of MAD-B outperforms the text-based models and also previous network-based models (Jurgens, 2013; Compton et al., 2014; Rahimi et al., 2015). The inference, however, is intractable for TWITTER-US and TWITTER-WORLD due to the size of the network.

Celebrity removal in MADCEL-B and MADCEL-W has a positive effect on geolocation accuracy, and results in a 47% reduction in Median over GEOTEXT. It also makes graph inference over TWITTER-US and TWITTER-WORLD tractable, and results in superior Acc@161 and Median, but slightly inferior Mean, compared to the state-of-the-art results of LR, based on text-based classification (Rahimi et al., 2015).

MADCEL-W (weighted graph) outperforms MADCEL-B (binary graph) over the smaller GEOTEXT dataset where it compensates for the sparsity of network information, but doesn't improve the results for the two larger datasets where network information is denser.

Adding text to the network-based geolocation models in the form of MADCEL-B-LR (binary edges) and MADCEL-W-LR (weighted edges), we achieve state-of-the-art results over all three datasets. The inclusion of text-based priors has the greatest impact on Mean, resulting in an additional 26% and 23% error reduction over TWITTER-US and TWITTER-WORLD, respectively. The reason for this is that it provides a user-specific geolocation prior for (relatively) disconnected users.

7 Conclusions and Future Work

We proposed a label propagation method over adaptive grids based on collapsed @-mention networks using Modified Adsorption, and successfully supplemented the baseline algorithm by: (a) removing "celebrity" nodes (improving the results and also making inference more tractable); and (b) incorporating text-based geolocation priors into the model.

As future work, we plan to use temporal data and also look at improving the text-based geolocation model using sparse coding (Cha et al., 2015). We also plan to investigate more nuanced methods for differentiating between global and local celebrity nodes, to be able to filter out global celebrity nodes but preserve local nodes that can have high geolocation utility.

Acknowledgements

We thank the anonymous reviewers for their insightful comments and valuable suggestions. This work was funded in part by the Australian Research Council.

References

Amr Ahmed, Liangjie Hong, and Alexander J Smola. 2013. Hierarchical geographical modeling of user locations from social media posts. In *Proceedings of the 22nd International Conference on World Wide Web (WWW 2013)*, pages 25–36, Rio de Janeiro, Brazil.

Zahra Ashktorab, Christopher Brown, Manojit Nandi, and Aron Culotta. 2014. Tweedr: Mining Twitter to inform disaster response. In *Proceedings of The 11th International Conference on Information Systems for Crisis Response and Management (ISCRAM 2014)*, pages 354–358, University Park, USA.

Miriam Cha, Youngjune Gwon, and HT Kung. 2015. Twitter geolocation and regional classification via sparse coding. In *Proceedings of the 9th International Conference on Weblogs and Social Media (ICWSM 2015)*, pages 582–585, Oxford, UK.

Zhiyuan Cheng, James Caverlee, and Kyumin Lee. 2010. You are where you tweet: a content-based approach to geo-locating Twitter users. In *Proceedings of the 19th ACM International Conference Information and Knowledge Management (CIKM 2010)*, pages 759–768, Toronto, Canada.

Ryan Compton, David Jurgens, and David Allen. 2014. Geotagging one hundred million twitter accounts with total variation minimization. In *Proceedings of the IEEE International Conference on Big Data (IEEE BigData 2014)*, pages 393–401, Washington DC, USA.

Paul Earle, Michelle Guy, Richard Buckmaster, Chris Ostrum, Scott Horvath, and Amy Vaughan. 2010. OMG earthquake! Can Twitter improve earthquake response? *Seismological Research Letters*, 81(2):246–251.

Jacob Eisenstein, Brendan O'Connor, Noah A Smith, and Eric P Xing. 2010. A latent variable model for geographic lexical variation. In *Proceedings of the 2010 Conference on Empirical Methods in Natural Language Processing (EMNLP 2010)*, pages 1277–1287, Boston, USA.

Andrew B Goldberg and Xiaojin Zhu. 2006. Seeing stars when there aren't many stars: graph-based semi-supervised learning for sentiment categorization. In *Proceedings of the 1st Workshop on Graph Based Methods for Natural Language Processing (TextGraphs 2006)*, pages 45–52, New York, USA.

Bo Han, Paul Cook, and Timothy Baldwin. 2012. Geolocation prediction in social media data by finding location indicative words. In *Proceedings of the 24th International Conference on Computational Linguistics (COLING 2012)*, pages 1045–1062, Mumbai, India.

Bo Han, Paul Cook, and Timothy Baldwin. 2014. Text-based Twitter user geolocation prediction. *Journal of Artificial Intelligence Research*, 49:451–500.

Mans Hulden, Miikka Silfverberg, and Jerid Francom. 2015. Kernel density estimation for text-based geolocation. In *Proceedings of the 29th AAAI Conference on Artificial Intelligence (AAAI-2015)*, pages 145–150, Austin, USA.

David Jurgens, Tyler Finethy, James McCorriston, Yi Tian Xu, and Derek Ruths. 2015. Geolocation prediction in twitter using social networks: A critical analysis and review of current practice. In *Proceedings of the 9th International Conference on Weblogs and Social Media (ICWSM 2015)*, pages 188–197, Oxford, UK.

David Jurgens. 2013. That's what friends are for: Inferring location in online social media platforms based on social relationships. In *Proceedings of the 7th International Conference on Weblogs and Social Media (ICWSM 2013)*, pages 273–282, Boston, USA.

Andrei P Kirilenko and Svetlana O Stepchenkova. 2014. Public microblogging on climate change: One year of Twitter worldwide. *Global Environmental Change*, 26:171–182.

Jochen L Leidner and Michael D Lieberman. 2011. Detecting geographical references in the form of place names and associated spatial natural language. *SIGSPATIAL Special*, 3(2):5–11.

Fred Morstatter, Shamanth Kumar, Huan Liu, and Ross Maciejewski. 2013a. Understanding twitter data with tweetxplorer. In *Proceedings of the 19th ACM SIGKDD International Conference on Knowledge Discovery and Data Mining (SIGKDD 2013)*, pages 1482–1485, Chicago, USA.

Fred Morstatter, Jürgen Pfeffer, Huan Liu, and Kathleen M Carley. 2013b. Is the sample good enough? Comparing data from Twitter's streaming API with Twitter's firehose. In *Proceedings of the 7th International Conference on Weblogs and Social Media (ICWSM 2013)*, pages 400–408, Boston, USA.

Mohamed M Mostafa. 2013. More than words: Social networks text mining for consumer brand sentiments. *Expert Systems with Applications*, 40(10):4241–4251.

Anastasios Noulas, Salvatore Scellato, Neal Lathia, and Cecilia Mascolo. 2012. A random walk around the city: New venue recommendation in location-based social networks. In *Proceedings of the International Conference on Privacy, Security, Risk and Trust and Social Computing (SOCIALCOM-PASSAT 2012)*, pages 144–153, Amsterdam, Netherlands.

Gianluca Quercini, Hanan Samet, Jagan Sankaranarayanan, and Michael D Lieberman. 2010. Determining the spatial reader scopes of news sources using local lexicons. In *Proceedings of the 18th SIGSPATIAL International Conference on Advances in Geographic Information Systems (SIGSPATIAL 2010)*, pages 43–52, New York, USA.

Afshin Rahimi, Duy Vu, Trevor Cohn, and Timothy Baldwin. 2015. Exploiting text and network context for geolocation of social media users. In *Proceedings of the 2015 Conference of the North American Chapter of the Association for Computational Linguistics — Human Language Technologies (NAACL HLT 2015)*, Denver, USA.

Stephen Roller, Michael Speriosu, Sarat Rallapalli, Benjamin Wing, and Jason Baldridge. 2012. Supervised text-based geolocation using language models on an adaptive grid. In *Proceedings of the 2012 Joint Conference on Empirical Methods in Natural*

Language Processing and Computational Natural Language Learning (EMNLP-CONLL 2012), pages 1500–1510, Jeju, Korea.

Markus Schedl and Dominik Schnitzer. 2014. Location-aware music artist recommendation. In *Proceedings of the 20th International Conference on MultiMedia Modeling (MMM 2014)*, pages 205–213, Dublin, Ireland.

Partha Pratim Talukdar and Koby Crammer. 2009. New regularized algorithms for transductive learning. In *Proceedings of the European Conference on Machine Learning (ECML-PKDD 2009)*, pages 442–457, Bled, Slovenia.

Benjamin P Wing and Jason Baldridge. 2011. Simple supervised document geolocation with geodesic grids. In *Proceedings of the 49th Annual Meeting of the Association for Computational Linguistics: Human Language Technologies-Volume 1 (ACL-HLT 2011)*, pages 955–964, Portland, USA.

Benjamin P Wing and Jason Baldridge. 2014. Hierarchical discriminative classification for text-based geolocation. In *Proceedings of the 2014 Conference on Empirical Methods in Natural Language Processing (EMNLP 2014)*, pages 336–348, Doha, Qatar.

Quan Yuan, Gao Cong, Zongyang Ma, Aixin Sun, and Nadia Magnenat Thalmann. 2013. Who, where, when and what: discover spatio-temporal topics for Twitter users. In *Proceedings of the 19th ACM SIGKDD International Conference on Knowledge Discovery and Data Mining (SIGKDD 2013)*, pages 605–613, Chicago, USA.

Xiaojin Zhu and Zoubin Ghahramani. 2002. Learning from labeled and unlabeled data with label propagation. Technical report, Carnegie Mellon University.

Automatic Keyword Extraction on Twitter

Luís Marujo[1,2,3], Wang Ling[1,2,3], Isabel Trancoso[2,3], Chris Dyer[1], Alan W. Black[1], Anatole Gershman[1], David Martins de Matos[2,3], João P. Neto[2,3], and Jaime Carbonell[1]
[1] Language Technologies Institute, Carnegie Mellon University, Pittsburgh, PA, USA
[2] Instituto Superior Técnico, Universidade de Lisboa, Lisbon, Portugal;
[3] INESC-ID, Lisbon, Portugal
{luis.marujo,wang.ling,isabel.trancoso,david.matos,joao.neto}@inesc-id.pt
{cdyer,awb,anatoleg,jgc}@cs.cmu.edu,

Abstract

In this paper, we build a corpus of tweets from Twitter annotated with keywords using crowdsourcing methods. We identify key differences between this domain and the work performed on other domains, such as news, which makes existing approaches for automatic keyword extraction not generalize well on Twitter datasets. These datasets include the small amount of content in each tweet, the frequent usage of lexical variants and the high variance of the cardinality of keywords present in each tweet. We propose methods for addressing these issues, which leads to solid improvements on this dataset for this task.

1 Introduction

Keywords are frequently used in many occasions as indicators of important information contained in documents. These can be used by human readers to search for their desired documents, but also in many Natural Language Processing (NLP) applications, such as Text Summarization (Pal et al., 2013), Text Categorization (Özgür et al., 2005), Information Retrieval (Marujo et al., 2011a; Yang and Nyberg, 2015) and Question Answering (Liu and Nyberg, 2013). Many automatic frameworks for extracting keywords have been proposed (Riloff and Lehnert, 1994; Witten et al., 1999; Turney, 2000; Medelyan et al., 2010; Litvak and Last, 2008). These systems were built for more formal domains, such as news data or Web data, where the content is still produced in a controlled fashion.

The emergence of social media environments, such as Twitter and Facebook, has created a framework for more casual data to be posted online. These messages tend to be shorter than web pages, especially on Twitter, where the content has to be limited to 140 characters. The language is also more casual with many messages containing orthographical errors, slang (e.g., *cday*), abbreviations among domain specific artifacts. In many applications, that existing datasets and models tend to perform significantly worse on these domains, namely in Part-of-Speech (POS) Tagging (Gimpel et al., 2011), Machine Translation (Jelh et al., 2012; Ling et al., 2013), Named Entity Recognition (Ritter et al., 2011; Liu et al., 2013), Information Retrieval (Efron, 2011) and Summarization (Duan et al., 2012; Chang et al., 2013).

As automatic keyword extraction plays an important role in many NLP tasks, building an accurate extractor for the Twitter domain is a valuable asset in many of these applications. In this paper, we propose an automatic keyword extraction system for this end and our contributions are the following ones:

1. Provide a annotated keyword annotated dataset consisting of 1827 tweets. These tweets are obtained from (Gimpel et al., 2011), and also contain POS annotations.

2. Improve a state-of-the-art keyword extraction system (Marujo et al., 2011b; Marujo et al., 2013) for this domain by learning additional features in an unsupervised fashion.

The paper is organized as follows: Section 2 describes the related work; Section 3 presents the annotation process; Section 4 details the architecture of our keyword extraction system; Section 5 presents experiments using our models and we conclude in Section 6.

Proceedings of the 53rd Annual Meeting of the Association for Computational Linguistics and the 7th International Joint Conference on Natural Language Processing (Short Papers), pages 637–643, Beijing, China, July 26-31, 2015.

2 Related Work

Both supervised and unsupervised approaches have been explored to perform key word extraction. Most of the automatic keyword/keyphrase extraction methods proposed for social media data, such as tweets, are unsupervised methods (Wu et al., 2010; Zhao et al., 2011; Bellaachia and Al-Dhelaan, 2012). However, the TF-IDF across different methods remains a strong unsupervised baseline (Hasan and Ng, 2010). These methods include adaptations to the PageRank method (Brin and Page, 1998) including TextRank (Mihalcea and Tarau, 2004), LexRank (Erkan and Radev, 2004), and Topic PageRank (Liu et al., 2010).

Supervised keyword extraction methods formalize this problem as a binary classification problem of two steps (Riloff and Lehnert, 1994; Witten et al., 1999; Turney, 2000; Medelyan et al., 2010; Wang and Li, 2011): candidate generation and filtering of the phrases selected before. MAUI toolkit-indexer (Medelyan et al., 2010), an improved version of the KEA (Witten et al., 1999) toolkit including new set of features and more robust classifier, remains the state-of-the-art system in the news domain (Marujo et al., 2012).

To the best of our knowledge, only (Li et al., 2010) used a supervised keyword extraction framework (based on KEA) with additional features, such as POS tags to performed keyword extraction on Facebook posts. However, at that time Facebook status updates or posts did not contained either hashtags or user mentions. The size of Facebook posts is frequently longer than tweets and has less abbreviations since it is not limited by number of character as in tweets.

3 Dataset

The dataset [1] contains 1827 tweets, which are POS tagged in (Gimpel et al., 2011). We used Amazon Mechanical turk, an crowdsourcing market, to recruit eleven annotators to identify keywords in each tweet. Each annotator highlighted words that he would consider a keyword. No specific instructions about what words can be keywords (e.g., "urls are not keywords"), as we wish to learn what users find important in a tweet. It is also acceptable for tweets to not contain keywords, as some tweets simply do not contain important information (e.g., retweet). The annotations of each annotator are combined by selecting keywords that are chosen by at least three annotators. We also divided the 1827 tweets into 1000 training samples, 327 development samples and 500 test samples, using the splits as in (Gimpel et al., 2011).

[1] The corpus is submitted as supplementary material.

4 Automatic Keyword Extraction

There are many methods that have been proposed for keyword extraction. TF-IDF is one of the simplest approaches for this end (Salton et al., 1975). The k words with the highest TF-IDF value are chosen as keywords, where k is optimized on the development set. This works quite well in text documents, such as news articles, as we wish to find terms that occur frequently within that document, but are not common in the other documents in that domain. However, we found that this approach does not work well in Twitter as tweets tend to be short and generally most terms occur only once, including their keywords. This means that the term frequency component is not very informative as the TF-IDF measure will simply benefit words that rarely occur, as these have a very low inverse document frequency component.

A strong baseline for Automatic Keyword Extraction is the MAUI toolkit-indexer toolkit (Medelyan et al., 2010). The system extracts a list of candidate keywords from a document and trains a decision tree over a large set of hand engineered features, also including TF-IDF, in order to predict the correct keywords on the training set. Once trained, the toolkit extracts a list of keyword candidates from a tweet and returns a ranked list of candidates. The top k keywords are selected as answers. The parameter k is maximized on the development set.

From this point, we present two extensions to the MAUI system to address many challenges found in this domain.

4.1 Unsupervised Feature Extraction

The first problem is the existence of many lexical variants in Twitter (e.g., "cats vs. catz"). While variants tend to have the same meaning as their standardized form, the proposed model does not have this information and will not be able to generalize properly. For instance, if the term "John" is labelled as keyword in the training set, the model would not be able to extract "Jooohn" as keyword as it is in a different word form. One way to address this would be using a normalization system either built using hand engineered rules (Gouws et al., 2011) or trained using labelled data (Han and Baldwin, 2011; Chrupała, 2014). However, these systems are generally limited as these need supervision and cannot scale to new data or data in other languages. Instead, we will used unsupervised methods that leverage large amounts of unannotated data. We used two popular methods for this purpose: Brown Clustering and Continuous Word Vectors.

4.1.1 Brown Clustering

It has been shown in (Owoputi et al., 2013) that Brown clusters are effective for clustering lexical variants. The algorithm attempts to find a clusters distribution to maximize the likelihood of each cluster predicting the next one, under the HMM assumption. Thus, words "yes", "yep" and "yesss" are generally inserted into the same cluster as these tend occur in similar contexts. It also builds an hierarchical structure of clusters. For instance, the clusters 11001 and 11010, share the first three nodes in the hierarchically 110. Sharing more tree nodes tends to translate into better similarity between words within the clusters. Thus, a word a 11001 cluster is simultaneously in clusters 1, 11, 110, 1100 and 11001, and a feature can be extracted for each cluster. In our experiments, we used the dataset with 1,000 Brown clusters made available by Owoputi et al. (Owoputi et al., 2013)[2].

4.1.2 Continuous Word Vectors

Word representations learned from neural language models are another way to learn more generalizable features for words (Collobert et al., 2011; Huang et al., 2012). In these models, a hidden layer is defined that maps words into a continuous vector. The parameters of this hidden layer are estimated by maximizing a goal function, such as the likelihood of each word predicting surrounding words (Mikolov et al., 2013; Ling et al., 2015). In our work, we used the structured skip-ngram goal function proposed in (Ling et al., 2015) and for each word we extracted its respective word vector as features.

4.2 Keyword Length Prediction

The second problem is the high variance in terms of number of keywords per tweet. In larger documents, such as a news article, contain approximately 3-5 keywords, so extracting 3 keywords per document is a reasonable option. However, this would not work in Twitter, since the number of keywords can be arbitrary small. In fact, many tweets contain less than three words, in which case the extractor would simply extract all words as keywords, which would be incorrect. One alternative is to choose a ratio between the number of words and number of keywords. That is, we define the number of keywords in a tweet as the ratio between number of words in the tweet and k, which is maximized on the development set. That is, if we set $k = 3$, then we extract one keyword for every three words.

Finally, a better approach is to learn a model to predict the number of keywords using the training set. Thus, we introduced a model that attempts to predict the number of keywords in each tweet based on a set of features. This is done using linear regression, which extracts a feature set from an input tweet $f_1, ..., f_n$ and returns y, the expected number of keywords in the tweet. As features we selected the number of words in the input tweet with the intuition that the number of keywords tends to depend on the size of the tweet. Furthermore, (2) we count the number of function words and non-function words in the tweet, emphasizing the fact that some types of words tend to contribute more to the number of keywords in the tweet. The same is done for (3) hashtags and at mentions. Finally, (4) we also count the number of words in each cluster using the trained Brown clusters.

5 Experiments

Experiments are performed on the annotated dataset using the train, development and test splits defined in Section 3. As baselines, we reported results using a TF-IDF, the default MAUI toolkit, and our own implementation of (Li et al., 2010) framework. In all cases the IDF component was computed over a collection of 52 million tweets. Results are reported on rows 1 and 2 in Table 1, respectively. The parameter k (column Nr. Keywords) defines the number of keywords extracted for each tweet and is maximized on the development set. Evaluation is performed using F-measure (column F1), where the precision (column P) is defined as the ratio of extracted keywords that are correct and the number of extracted keywords, and the recall (column R) is de-

[2]http://www.ark.cs.cmu.edu/TweetNLP/clusters/50mpaths2

	System	Nr. Keywords	Dev P	Dev R	Dev F1	Test P	Test R	Test F1
1	TF-IDF	15	19.31	83.58	29.97	20.21	85.17	31.16
2	(Li et al., 2010)	4	48.81	50.05	49.42	51.78	50.92	51.35
3	MAUI (Default)	4	51.31	52.47	51.88	53.97	53.15	53.56
4	MAUI (Word Vectors)	4	52.70	53.50	53.10	55.80	54.45	55.12
5	MAUI (Brown)	4	68.08	74.11	70.97	71.95	75.01	73.45
6	MAUI (Brown+Word Vectors)	4	**68.46**	**75.05**	**71.61**	**72.05**	**75.16**	**73.57**
7	MAUI (Trained on News)	4	49.12	49.71	49.41	52.40	51.19	51.79

Table 1: F-measure, precision and recall results on the Twitter keyword dataset using different feature sets.

	Selection	Nr. Keywords	Dev P	Dev R	Dev F1	Test P	Test R	Test F1
1	Fixed	4	68.46	75.05	71.61	72.05	75.16	73.57
2	Ratio	$N//3$	65.70	**82.69**	73.22	69.48	**83.8**	75.97
3	Regression	$y+k$	**67.55**	80.9	**73.62**	71.81	82.55	**76.81**

Table 2: F-measure, precision and recall results on the Twitter keyword dataset using different keyword selection methods.

fined as the ratio between the number of keywords correctly extracted and the total number of keywords in the dataset. We can see that the TF-IDF, which tends to be a strong baseline for keyword/keyphrase extraction (Hasan and Ng, 2010), yields poor results. In fact, the best value for k is 15, which means that the system simply retrieves all words as keywords in order to maximize recall. This is because most keywords only occur once[3], which makes the TF component not very informative. On the other hand, the MAUI baseline performs significantly better, this is because of the usage of many hand engineered features using lists of words and Wikipedia, rather than simply relying on word counts.

Next, we introduce features learnt using an unsupervised setup, namely, word vectors and brown clusters in rows 3 and 4, respectively. These were trained on the same 52 million tweets used for computing the IDF component. Due to the large size of the vocabulary, word types with less than 40 occurrences were removed. We observe that while both features yield improvements over the baseline model in row 2, the improvements obtained using Brown clustering are far more significant. Combining both features yields slightly higher results, reported on row 5. Finally, we also test training the system with all features on an out-of-domain keyword extraction corpus composed by news documents (Marujo et al., 2012). Results are reported on row 6, where we can observe a significant domain mismatch problem between these two domains as results drop significantly.

We explored different methods for choosing the number of keywords to be extracted in Table 2. The simplest way is choosing a fixed number of keywords k and tune this value in the development set. Next, we can also define the number of keywords as the ratio $\frac{N}{k}$, where N is the number of words in the tweet, and k is the parameter that we wish to optimize. Finally, the number of keywords can also be estimated using a linear regressor as $y = f_1 w1, ..., f_n w_n$, where $f_1, ..., f_n$ denote the feature set and $w_1, ..., w_n$ are the parameters of the model trained on the training set. Once the model is trained, the number of keywords selected for each tweet is defined as $y + k$, where k is inserted to adjust y to maximize F-measure on the development set. Results using the best system using Brown clusters and word vectors are described in Table 2. We can observe that defining the number of keywords as a fraction of the number of words in the tweet, yields better results (row 2) yields better overall results than fixing the number of extracted keywords (row 1). Finally, training a predictor for the number of keywords yields further improvements (row 3) over a simple ratio of the

[3]6856 out of 7045 keywords are singletons

number of input words.

6 Conclusions

In this work, we built a corpus of tweets annotated with keywords, which was used to built and evaluate a system to automatically extract keywords on Twitter. A baseline system is defined using existing methods applied to our dataset and improvement significantly using unsupervised feature extraction methods. Furthermore, an additional component to predict the number of keywords in a tweet is also built. In future work, we plan to use the keyword extraction to perform numerous NLP tasks on the Twitter domain, such as Document Summarization.

Acknowledgements

This work was partially supported by Fundação para a Ciência e Tecnologia (FCT) through the grants CMUP-EPB/TIC/0026/2013, SFRH/BD/51157/2010, and the Carnegie Mellon Portugal Program. The authors also wish to thank the anonymous reviewers for their helpful comments.

References

Abdelghani Bellaachia and Mohammed Al-Dhelaan. 2012. Ne-rank: A novel graph-based keyphrase extraction in twitter. In *Proceedings of the The 2012 IEEE/WIC/ACM International Joint Conferences on Web Intelligence and Intelligent Agent Technology - Volume 01*, WI-IAT '12, pages 372–379, Washington, DC, USA. IEEE Computer Society.

Sergey Brin and Lawrence Page. 1998. The anatomy of a large-scale hypertextual Web search engine. *Computer Networks and ISDN Systems*, 30:107–117.

Yi Chang, Xuanhui Wang, Qiaozhu Mei, and Yan Liu. 2013. Towards twitter context summarization with user influence models. In *Proceedings of the Sixth ACM International Conference on Web Search and Data Mining*, WSDM '13, pages 527–536, New York, NY, USA. ACM.

Grzegorz Chrupała. 2014. Normalizing tweets with edit scripts and recurrent neural embeddings. In *Proceedings of the 52nd Annual Meeting of the Association for Computational Linguistics (Volume 2: Short Papers)*, pages 680–686, Baltimore, Maryland, June. Association for Computational Linguistics.

Ronan Collobert, Jason Weston, Léon Bottou, Michael Karlen, Koray Kavukcuoglu, and Pavel Kuksa. 2011. Natural language processing (almost) from scratch. *The Journal of Machine Learning Research*, 12.

Yajuan Duan, Zhumin Chen, Furu Wei, Ming Zhou, and Heung-Yeung Shum. 2012. Twitter topic summarization by ranking tweets using social influence and content quality. In *Proceedings of COLING 2012*, pages 763–780. The COLING 2012 Organizing Committee.

Miles Efron. 2011. Information search and retrieval in microblogs. *J. Am. Soc. Inf. Sci. Technol.*, 62(6):996–1008, June.

Güneş Erkan and Dragomir R. Radev. 2004. LexRank: Graph-based Centrality as Salience in Text Summarization. *Journal of Artificial Intelligence Research*, 22:457–479.

Kevin Gimpel, Nathan Schneider, Brendan O'Connor, Dipanjan Das, Daniel Mills, Jacob Eisenstein, Michael Heilman, Dani Yogatama, Jeffrey Flanigan, and Noah A. Smith. 2011. Part-of-speech tagging for twitter: annotation, features, and experiments. In *Proceedings of the 49th Annual Meeting of the Association for Computational Linguistics: Human Language Technologies: short papers - Volume 2*, HLT '11, Stroudsburg, PA, USA. Association for Computational Linguistics.

Stephan Gouws, Dirk Hovy, and Donald Metzler. 2011. Unsupervised mining of lexical variants from noisy text. In *Proceedings of the First Workshop on Unsupervised Learning in NLP*, EMNLP '11, pages 82–90, Stroudsburg, PA, USA. Association for Computational Linguistics.

Bo Han and Timothy Baldwin. 2011. Lexical normalisation of short text messages: Makn sens a #twitter. In *Proceedings of the 49th Annual Meeting of the Association for Computational Linguistics: Human Language Technologies - Volume 1*, HLT '11, pages 368–378, Stroudsburg, PA, USA. Association for Computational Linguistics.

Kazi Saidul Hasan and Vincent Ng. 2010. V.: Conundrums in unsupervised keyphrase extraction: Making sense of the state-of-the-art. In *In: COLING*, pages 365–373.

Eric H Huang, Richard Socher, Christopher D Manning, and Andrew Y Ng. 2012. Improving word representations via global context and multiple word prototypes. In *Proceedings of the 50th Annual Meeting of the Association for Computational Linguistics: Long Papers-Volume 1*, pages 873–882. Association for Computational Linguistics.

Laura Jehl, Felix Hiebel, and Stefan Riezler. 2012. Twitter translation using translation-based cross-lingual retrieval. In *Proceedings of the Seventh Workshop on Statistical Machine Translation*, Montréal, Canada, June. Association for Computational Linguistics.

Zhenhui Li, Ding Zhou, Yun-Fang Juan, and Jiawei Han. 2010. Keyword extraction for social snippets. In *Proceedings of the 19th International Conference on World Wide Web*, WWW '10, pages 1143–1144, New York, NY, USA. ACM.

Wang Ling, Guang Xiang, Chris Dyer, Alan Black, and Isabel Trancoso. 2013. Microblogs as parallel corpora. In *Proceedings of the 51st Annual Meeting on Association for Computational Linguistics*, ACL '13. Association for Computational Linguistics.

Wang Ling, Chris Dyer, Alan Black, and Isabel Trancoso. 2015. Two/too simple adaptations of word2vec for syntax problems. In *Proceedings of the 2015 Conference of the North American Chapter of the Association for Computational Linguistics: Human Language Technologies*. Association for Computational Linguistics.

Marina Litvak and Mark Last. 2008. Graph-based keyword extraction for single-document summarization. In *Proceedings of the Workshop on Multi-source Multilingual Information Extraction and Summarization*, MMIES '08, pages 17–24, Stroudsburg, PA, USA. Association for Computational Linguistics.

Rui Liu and Eric Nyberg. 2013. A phased ranking model for question answering. In *Proceedings of the 22Nd ACM International Conference on Information & Knowledge Management*, CIKM '13, pages 79–88, New York, NY, USA. ACM.

Zhiyuan Liu, Wenyi Huang, Yabin Zheng, and Maosong Sun. 2010. Automatic keyphrase extraction via topic decomposition. In *Proceedings of the 2010 Conference on Empirical Methods in Natural Language Processing*, EMNLP '10, pages 366–376, Stroudsburg, PA, USA. Association for Computational Linguistics.

Xiaohua Liu, Furu Wei, Shaodian Zhang, and Ming Zhou. 2013. Named entity recognition for tweets. *ACM Transactions on Intelligent Systems and Technology (TIST)*, 4(1):3.

Luís Marujo, Miguel Bugalho, João P. Neto, Anatole Gershman, and Jaime Carbonell. 2011a. Hourly traffic prediction of news stories. In *Proceedings of the 3rd International Workshop on Context- Aware Recommender Systems held as part of the 5th ACM RecSys Conference*, October.

Luís Marujo, Márcio Viveiros, and João P. Neto. 2011b. Keyphrase Cloud Generation of Broadcast News. In *Proceedings of the 12th Annual Conference of the International Speech Communication Association (INTERSPEECH 2011)*. ISCA, September.

Luís Marujo, Anatole Gershman, Jaime Carbonell, Robert Frederking, and João P. Neto. 2012. Supervised topical key phrase extraction of news stories using crowdsourcing, light filtering and co-reference normalization. In *Proceedings of the 8th International Conference on Language Resources and Evaluation (LREC 2012)*.

Luís Marujo, Ricardo Ribeiro, David Martins de Matos, João Paulo Neto, Anatole Gershman, and Jaime G. Carbonell. 2013. Key phrase extraction of lightly filtered broadcast news. In *Proceedings of the 15th International Conference on Text, Speech and Dialogue (TSD)*.

Olena Medelyan, Vye Perrone, and Ian H. Witten. 2010. Subject metadata support powered by maui. In Jane Hunter, Carl Lagoze, C. Lee Giles, and Yuan-Fang Li, editors, *JCDL*, pages 407–408. ACM.

Rada Mihalcea and Paul Tarau. 2004. Textrank: Bringing order into texts. In Dekang Lin and Dekai Wu, editors, *Proceedings of EMNLP 2004*, pages 404–411, Barcelona, Spain, July. Association for Computational Linguistics.

Tomas Mikolov, Ilya Sutskever, Kai Chen, Greg S Corrado, and Jeff Dean. 2013. Distributed representations of words and phrases and their compositionality. In *Advances in Neural Information Processing Systems*, pages 3111–3119.

Olutobi Owoputi, Brendan O'Connor, Chris Dyer, Kevin Gimpel, Nathan Schneider, and Noah A Smith. 2013. Improved part-of-speech tagging for online conversational text with word clusters. In *HLT-NAACL*, pages 380–390.

Arzucan Özgür, Levent Özgür, and Tunga Güngör. 2005. Text categorization with class-based and corpus-based keyword selection. In *Proceedings of the 20th International Conference on Computer and Information Sciences*, ISCIS'05, pages 606–615, Berlin, Heidelberg. Springer-Verlag.

Alok Ranjan Pal, Projjwal Kumar Maiti, and Diganta Saha. 2013. An approach to automatic text summarization using simplified lesk algorithm and wordnet. *International Journal of Control Theory & Computer Modeling*, 3.

Ellen Riloff and Wendy Lehnert. 1994. Information extraction as a basis for high-precision text classification. *ACM Transactions on Information Systems (TOIS)*, 12(3):296–333, July.

Alan Ritter, Sam Clark, Oren Etzioni, et al. 2011. Named entity recognition in tweets: an experimental study. In *Proceedings of the Conference on Empirical Methods in Natural Language Processing*, pages 1524–1534. Association for Computational Linguistics.

G. Salton, A. Wong, and C. S. Yang. 1975. A Vector Space Model for Automatic Indexing. *Communications of the ACM*, 18(11):613–620.

Peter D. Turney. 2000. Learning algorithms for keyphrase extraction. *Information Retrieval*, 2(4):303–336.

Chen Wang and Sujian Li. 2011. Corankbayes: Bayesian learning to rank under the co-training framework and its application in keyphrase extraction. In *Proceedings of the 20th ACM International Conference on Information and Knowledge Management*, CIKM '11, pages 2241–2244, New York, NY, USA. ACM.

Ian H. Witten, Gordon W. Paynter, Eibe Frank, Carl Gutwin, and Craig G. Nevill-Manning. 1999. Kea: practical automatic keyphrase extraction. In *Proceedings of the 4th ACM conference on Digital libraries*, DL '99, pages 254–255, New York, NY, USA. ACM.

Wei Wu, Bin Zhang, and Mari Ostendorf. 2010. Automatic generation of personalized annotation tags for twitter users. In *Human Language Technologies: The 2010 Annual Conference of the North American Chapter of the Association for Computational Linguistics*, HLT '10, pages 689–692, Stroudsburg, PA, USA. Association for Computational Linguistics.

Zi Yang and Eric Nyberg. 2015. Leveraging procedural knowledge base for task-oriented search. In *Proceedings of the 38th international ACM SIGIR conference on Research & development in information retrieval*. ACM.

Wayne Xin Zhao, Jing Jiang, Jing He, Yang Song, Palakorn Achananuparp, Ee-Peng Lim, and Xiaoming Li. 2011. Topical keyphrase extraction from twitter. In *Proceedings of the 49th Annual Meeting of the Association for Computational Linguistics: Human Language Technologies - Volume 1*, HLT '11, pages 379–388, Stroudsburg, PA, USA. Association for Computational Linguistics.

Towards a Contextual Pragmatic Model to Detect Irony in Tweets

Jihen Karoui
IRIT, MIRACL
Toulouse University, Sfax University
karoui@irit.fr

Farah Benamara Zitoune
IRIT, CNRS
Toulouse University
benamara@irit.fr

Véronique Moriceau
LIMSI-CNRS
Univ. Paris-Sud
moriceau@limsi.fr

Nathalie Aussenac-Gilles
IRIT, CNRS
Nathalie.Aussenac-Gilles@irit.fr

Lamia Hadrich Belguith
MIRACL
University of Sfax
l.belguith@fsegs.rnu.tn

Abstract

This paper proposes an approach to capture the pragmatic context needed to infer irony in tweets. We aim to test the validity of two main hypotheses: (1) the presence of negations, as an internal propriety of an utterance, can help to detect the disparity between the literal and the intended meaning of an utterance, (2) a tweet containing an asserted fact of the form $Not(P_1)$ is ironic if and only if one can assess the absurdity of P_1. Our first results are encouraging and show that deriving a pragmatic contextual model is feasible.

1 Motivation

Irony is a complex linguistic phenomenon widely studied in philosophy and linguistics (Grice et al., 1975; Sperber and Wilson, 1981; Utsumi, 1996). Despite theories differ on how to define irony, they all commonly agree that it involves an incongruity between the literal meaning of an utterance and what is expected about the speaker and/or the environment. For many researchers, irony overlaps with a variety of other figurative devices such as satire, parody, and sarcasm (Clark and Gerrig, 1984; Gibbs, 2000). In this paper, we use irony as an umbrella term that covers these devices focusing for the first time on the automatic detection of irony in French tweets.

According to (Grice et al., 1975; Searle, 1979; Attardo, 2000), the search for a non-literal meaning starts when the hearer realizes that the speaker's utterance is context-inappropriate, that is an utterance fails to make sense against the context. For example, the tweet: *"Congratulation #lesbleus for your great match!"* is ironic if the French soccer team has lost the match. An analysis of a corpus of French tweets shows that there are two ways to infer such a context: (a) rely exclusively on the lexical clues internal to the utterance, or (b) combine these clues with an additional pragmatic context external to the utterance. In (a), the speaker intentionally creates an explicit juxtaposition of incompatible actions or words that can either have opposite polarities, or can be semantically unrelated, as in "***The Voice** is more important than **Fukushima** tonight*". Explicit opposition can also arise from an explicit positive/negative contrast between a subjective proposition and a situation that describes an undesirable activity or state. For instance, in "***I love** when my phone **turns the volume down automatically***" the writer assumes that every one expects its cell phone to ring loud enough to be heard. In (b), irony is due to an implicit opposition between a lexicalized proposition P describing an event or state and a pragmatic context external to the utterance in which P is false or is not likely to happen. In other words, the writer asserts or affirms P while he intends to convey P' such that $P' = Not(P)$ or $P' = P$. The irony occurs because the writer believes that/his audience can detect the disparity between P and P' on the basis of contextual knowledge or common background shared with the writer. For example, in "*#Hollande is really a good diplomat #Algeria.*", the writer critics the foreign policy of the French president Hollande in Algeria, whereas in "*The #NSA wiretapped a whole country. No worries for #Belgium: **it is not a whole country.***", the irony occurs because the fact in bold font is not true.

Irony detection is quite a hot topic in the research community also due to its importance for efficient sentiment analysis (Ghosh et al., 2015). Several approaches have been proposed to detect irony casting the problem into a binary classification task relying on a variety of features. Most of them are gleaned from the utterance internal context going from n-grams models, stylistic (punctuation, emoticons, quotations, etc.), to dictionary-based features (sentiment and affect dictionaries, slang languages, etc.). These features have shown to be useful to learn whether a text span is ironic/sarcastic or not (Burfoot and Baldwin, 2009; Davidov et al., 2010; Tsur et al., 2010; Gonzalez-Ibanez et al., 2011; Reyes et al., 2013; Barbieri and Saggion, 2014). However, many authors pointed out the necessity of additional pragmatic features: (Utsumi, 2004) showed that opposition, rhetorical questions and the politeness level are relevant. (Burfoot and Baldwin, 2009) focused on satire detection in newswire articles and introduced the notion of validity which models absurdity by identifying a conjunc-

Proceedings of the 53rd Annual Meeting of the Association for Computational Linguistics and the 7th International Joint Conference on Natural Language Processing (Short Papers), pages 644–650,
Beijing, China, July 26-31, 2015.

tion of named entities present in a given document and queries the web for the conjunction of those entities. (Gonzalez-Ibanez et al., 2011) exploited the common ground between speaker and hearer by looking if a tweet is a reply to another tweet. (Reyes et al., 2013) employed opposition in time (adverbs of time such as *now* and *suddenly*) and context imbalance to estimate the semantic similarity of concepts in a text to each other. (Barbieri and Saggion, 2014) captured the gap between rare and common words as well as the use of common vs. rare synonyms. Finally, (Buschmeier et al., 2014) measured the imbalance between the overall polarity of words in a review and the star-rating. Most of these pragmatic features rely on linguistic aspects of the tweet by using only the text of the tweet. We aim here to go further by proposing a novel computational model able to capture the "outside of the utterance" context needed to infer irony in implicit oppositions.

2 Methodology

An analysis of a corpus of French ironic tweets randomly chosen from various topics shows that more than 62.75% of tweets contain explicit negation markers such as "ne...pas" (not) or negative polarity items like "jamais" (never) or "personne" (nobody). Negation seems thus to be an important clue in ironic statements, at least in French. This rises the following hypotheses: (H1) the presence of negations, as an internal propriety of an utterance, can help to detect the disparity between the literal and the intended meaning of an utterance, and (H2) a tweet containing an asserted fact of the form $Not(P)$ is ironic if and only if one can prove P on the basis of some external common knowledge to the utterance shared by the author and the reader.

To test the validity of the above hypotheses, we propose a novel three-step model involving three successive stages: (1) detect if a tweet is ironic or not relying exclusively on the information internal to the tweet. We use a supervised learning method relying on both state of the art features whose efficiency has been empirically proved and new groups of features. (2) Test this internal context against the "outside of the utterance" context. We design an algorithm that takes the classifier's outputs and corrects the misclassified ironic instances of the form $Not(P)$ by looking for P in reliable external sources of information on the Web, such as Wikipedia or online newspapers. We experiment when labels are given by gold standard annotations and when they are predicted by the classifier. (3) If the literal meaning fails to make sense, i.e. P is found, then the tweet is likely to convey a non-literal meaning.

To this end, we collected a corpus of 6,742 French tweets using the Tweeter API focusing on tweets relative to a set of topics discussed in the media during Spring 2014. Our intuition behind choosing such topics is that a media-friendly topic is more likely to be found in external sources of information. We chose 184 topics split into 9 categories (politics, sport, etc.). For each topic, we selected a set of keywords with and without hashtag: politics (*e.g.* Sarkozy, Hollande, UMP), health (*e.g.* cancer, flu), sport (*e.g.* #Zlatan, #FIFAworldcup), social media (*e.g.* #Facebook, Skype, MSN), artists (*e.g.* Rihanna, Beyoncé), TV shows (*e.g.* TheVoice, XFactor), countries or cities (*e.g.* NorthKorea, Brasil), the Arab Spring (*e.g.* Marzouki, Ben Ali) and some other generic topics (*e.g.* pollution, racism). Then we selected ironic tweets containing the topic keywords, the *#ironie* or *#sarcasme* hashtag and a negation word as well as ironic tweets containing only the topic keywords with *#ironie* or *#sarcasme* hashtag but no negation word. Finally, we selected non ironic tweets that contained either the topic keywords and a negation word, or only the topic keywords. We removed duplicates, retweets and tweets containing pictures which would need to be interpreted to understand the ironic content. Irony hashtags (*#ironie* or *#sarcasme*) are removed from the tweets for the following experiments. To guarantee that tweets with negation words contain true negations, we automatically identified negation usage of a given word using a French syntactic dependency parser[1]. We then designed dedicated rules to correct the parser's decisions if necessary. At the end, we got a total of 4,231 tweets with negation and 2,511 without negation, among them, 30.42% are ironic with negation and 72.36% are non ironic with negation. At the end, we got a total of 4,231 tweets with negation and 2,511 without negation: among them, 30.42% are ironic with negation and 72.36% are non ironic with negation. To capture the effect of negation on our task, we split these tweets in three corpora: tweets with negation only (*NegOnly*), tweets with no negation (*NoNeg*), and a corpus that gathers all the tweets of the previous 2 corpora (*All*). Table 1 shows the repartition of tweets in our corpora.

Corpus	Ironic	Non ironic	TOTAL
NegOnly	470	3,761	**4,231**
NoNeg	1,075	1,436	**2,511**
All	1,545	5,197	**6,742**

Table 1: Tweet repartition.

3 Binary classifier

We experiment with SMO under the Weka toolkit with standard parameters. We also evaluated other learning algorithms (naive bayes, decision trees, logistic regression) but the results were not as good as those obtained with SMO. We have built three classifiers, one for each corpus, namely C_{Neg}, C_{NoNeg}, and C_{All}. Since the number of ironic instances in the first corpus is relatively small, we learn C_{Neg} with 10-cross validation on a balanced subset of 940 tweets. For the second and the last classifiers, we used 80% of the corpus for training

[1]We have used Malt as a syntactic parser.

and 20% for test, with an equal distribution between the ironic (henceforth IR) and non ironic (henceforth NIR) instances[2]. The results presented in this paper have been obtained when training C_{NoNeg} on 1,720 and testing on 430 tweets. C_{All} has been trained on 2,472 tweets (1432 contain negation –404 IR and 1028 NIR) and tested on 618 tweets (360 contain negation – 66 IR and 294 NIR). For each classifier, we represent each tweet with a vector composed of six groups of features. Most of them are state of the art features, others, in italic font are new.

Surface features include tweet length in words (Tsur et al., 2010), the presence or absence of punctuation marks (Gonzalez-Ibanez et al., 2011), words in capital letters (Reyes et al., 2013), interjections (Gonzalez-Ibanez et al., 2011), emoticons (Buschmeier et al., 2014), quotations (Tsur et al., 2010), slang words (Burfoot and Baldwin, 2009), opposition words such as "but" and "although" (Utsumi, 2004), a sequence of exclamation or a sequence of question marks (Carvalho et al., 2009), a combination of both exclamation and question marks (Buschmeier et al., 2014) and finally, *the presence of discourse connectives that do not convey opposition* such as "hence, therefore, as a result" since we assume that non ironic tweets are likely to be more verbose. To implement these features, we rely on manually built French lexicons to deal with interjections, emoticons, slang language, and discourse connectives (Roze et al., 2012).

Sentiment features consist of features that check for the presence of positive/negative opinion words (Reyes and Rosso, 2012) and the number of positive and negative opinion words (Barbieri and Saggion, 2014). We add three new features: *the presence of words that express surprise or astonishment*, and *the presence and the number of neutral opinions*. To get these features we use two lexicons: CASOAR, a French opinion lexicon (Benamara et al., 2014) and EMOTAIX, a publicly available French emotion and affect lexicon.

Sentiment shifter features group checks if a given *tweet contains an opinion word which is in the scope of an intensifier adverb or a modality*.

Shifter features tests if a tweet contains an intensifier (Liebrecht et al., 2013), a negation word (Reyes et al., 2013), or *reporting speech verbs*.

Opposition features are new and check for the presence of specific lexico-syntactic patterns that verify whether a tweet contains a sentiment opposition or an explicit positive/negative contrast between a subjective proposition and an objective one. These features have been partly inspired from (Riloff et al., 2013) who proposed a bootstrapping algorithm to detect sarcastic tweets of the form $[P_+].[P'_{obj}]$ which corresponds to a contrast between positive sentiment and an objective negative situation. We extended this pattern to capture additional types of explicit oppositions. Some of our patterns include: $[Neg(P_+)].[P'_+]$, $[P_-].[P'_+]$, $[Neg(P_+)].[P'_{obj}]$, $[P'_{obj}].[P_-]$. We consider that an opinion expression is under the scope of a negation if it is separated by a maximum of two tokens.

Finally, **internal contextual** deals with the presence/absence of *personal pronouns, topic keywords* and *named entities*, as predicted by the parser's outputs.

For each classifier, we investigated how each group of features contributes to the learning process. We applied to each training set a feature selection algorithm (Chi2 and GainRatio), then trained the classifiers over all relevant features of each group[3]. In all experiments, we used all surface features as baseline. Table 2 presents the result in terms of precision (P), recall (R), macro-averaged F-score (MAF) and accuracy (A). We can see that C_{All} achieves better results. An analysis of the best features combination for each classifier suggests four main conclusions: (1) surface features are primordial for irony detection. This is more salient for *NoNeg*. (2) Negation is an important feature for our task. However, having it alone is not enough to find ironic instances. Indeed, among the 76 misclassified instances in C_{All}, 60% contain negation clues (37 IR and 9 NIR). (3) When negation is concerned, opposition features are among the most productive. (4) Explicit opinion words (i.e sentiment and sentiment shifter) are likely to be used in tweets with no negation. More importantly, these results empirically validate hypothesis (H1), i.e. negation is a good clue to detect irony.

	Ironic (IR)			**Not ironic (NIR)**		
	P	R	F	P	R	F
C_{Neg}	88.9	56.0	68.7	67.9	93.3	78.5
C_{NoNeg}	71.1	65.1	68.0	67.80	73.50	70.50
C_{All}	93.0	81.6	86.9	83.6	93.9	88.4

	Overall Results	
	MAF	A
C_{Neg}	73.6	74.5
C_{NoNeg}	69.2	69.3
C_{All}	87.6	87.7

Table 2: Results for the best features combination.

Error analysis shows that misclassification of ironic instances is mainly due to four factors: presence of similes (ironic comparison)[4], absence of context within the utterance (most frequent case), humor and satire[5], and wrong *#ironie* or *#sarcasme* tags. The absence of context can manifest itself in several ways: (1) there is no pointer that helps to identify the main topic of the tweet, as in "*I've been missing her, damn!*". Even if the topic is present, it is often lexicalized in several collapsed words or funny hashtags (*#baddays, #aprilfoll*),

[2]For C_{NoNeg} and C_{All}, we also tested 10-cross validation with a balanced distribution between the ironic and non-ironic instances but results were not conclusive.

[3]Results with all features are lower.

[4]e.g. "Benzema in the French team is like Sunday. He is of no use.. :D"

[5]*e.g.* "I propose that we send Hollande instead of the space probes on the next comet, it will save time and money ;) #HUMOUR"

which are hard to automatically analyze. (2) The irony is about specific situations (Shelley, 2001). (3) False assertions about hot topics, like in "*Don't worry. Senegal is the world champion soccer*". (4) Oppositions that involve a contradiction between two words that are semantically unrelated, a named entity and a given event (*e.g.* "Tchad and "democratic election"), etc. Case (4) is more frequent in the *NoNeg* corpus.

Knowing that tweets with negation represent 62.75% of our corpus, and given that irony can focus on the negation of a word or a proposition (Haverkate, 1990), we propose to improve the classification of these tweets by identifying the absurdity of their content, following Attardo's relevant inappropriateness model of irony (Attardo, 2000) in which a violation of contextual appropriateness signals ironical intent.

4 Deriving the pragmatic context

The proposed model included two parts: binary classifiers trained with tweet features, and an algorithm that corrects the outputs of the classifiers which are likely to be misclassified. These two phases can be applied successively or together. In this latter case, the algorithm outputs are integrated into the classifiers and the corrected instances are used in the training process of the binary classifier. In this paper, we only present results of the two phases applied successively because it achieved better results.

Our approach is to query Google via its API to check the veracity of tweets with negation that have been classified as non ironic by the binary classifier in order to correct the misclassified tweets (if a tweet saying $Not(P)$ has been classified as non-ironic but P is found online, then we assume that the opposite content is checked so the tweet class is changed into ironic). Let $WordsT$ be the set of words excluding stop words that belong to a tweet t, and let kw be the topic keyword used to collect t. Let $N \subset WordsT$ be the set of negation words of t. The algorithm is as follows:

1. Segment t into a set of sentences S.

2. For each $s \in S$ *such that* $\exists neg \in N$ *and* $neg \in s$*:*

2.1 Remove # and @ symbols, emoticons, and neg*, then extract the set of tokens* $P \subset s$ *that are on the scope of* neg *(in a distance of 2 tokens).*

2.2 Generate a query $Q_1 = P \cup kw$ *and submit it to Google which will return 20 results (title+snippet) or less.*

2.3 Among the returned results, keep only the reliable ones (Wikipedia, online newspapers, web sites that do not contain "blog" or "twitter" in their URL). Then, for each result, if the query keywords are found in the title or in the snippet, then t is considered as ironic. STOP.

3. Generate a second query $Q_2 = (WordsT - N) \cup kw$ *and submit it again to Google and follow the procedure in 2.3. If* Q_2 *is found, then t is considered as ironic. Otherwise, the class predicted by the classifier does not change.*

Let us illustrate our algorithm with the topic *Valls* and the tweet: *#Valls has learnt that Sarkozy was wiretapped in newspapers. Fortunately he is not the interior minister.* The first step leads to two sentences s_1 (*#Valls has learnt that Sarkozy was wiretapped in newspapers.*) and s_2 (***Fortunately he is not the interior minister***). From s_2, we remove the negation word "not", isolate the negation scope $P = \{interior, minister\}$ and generate the query $Q_1 = \{Valls\ interior\ minister\}$. The step 2.3 allows to retrieve the result:

<Title>*Manuel* ***Valls*** *- Wikipedia, the free encyclopedia*</Title>
<Snippet>... *French politician. For the Spanish composer, see Manuel* ***Valls*** *(composer). ....* ***Valls*** *was appointed* ***Minister*** *of the* ***Interior*** *in the Ayrault Cabinet in May 2012.*</Snippet>.

All query keywords were found in this snippet (in bold font), we can then conclude that the tweet is ironic.

We made several experiments to evaluate how the query-based method improves tweet classification. For this purpose, we have applied the method on both corpora *All* and *Neg*: ① A first experiment evaluates the method on tweets with negation classified as NIR but which are ironic according to gold annotations. This experiment represents an ideal case which we try to achieve or improve through other ones. ②: A second experiment consists in applying the method on all tweets with negation that have been classified as NIR by the classifier, no matter if the predicted class is correct or not. Table 3 shows the results for both experiments.

	①		②	
NIR tweets for which:	*All*	*Neg*	*All*	*Neg*
Query applied	37	207	327	644
Results on Google	25	102	166	331
Class changed into IR	5	35	69	178
Classifier Accuracy	87.7	74.46	**87.7**	**74.46**
Query-based Accuracy	**88.51**	**78.19**	78.15	62.98

Table 3: Results for the query-based method.

All scores for the query-based method are statistically significant compared to the classifier's scores ($p\_value < 0,0001$ when calculated with the McNemar's test.). An error analysis shows that 65% of tweets that are still misclassified with this method are tweets for which finding their content online is almost impossible because they are personal tweets or lack internal context. A conclusion that can be drawn is that this method should not be applied on this type of tweets. For this purpose, we made the same experiments only on tweets with different combinations of relevant features. The best results are obtained when the method is applied only on NIR tweets with negation selected via the internal context features, more precisely on tweets which do not contain a personal pronoun and which contain named entities: these results are coherent with the fact that tweets containing personal pronouns and no named entity are likely to relate personal content impossible to validate on the Web (*e.g. I've been missing her, damn! #ironie*). Table 4 shows the results for these experiments. All scores for the query-based method are also statistically significant compared to the classifier's scores.

	①		②	
NIR *tweets for which:*	*All*	*Neg*	*All*	*Neg*
Query applied	0	18	40	18
Results on Google	-	12	17	12
Class changed into IR	-	4	7	4
Classifier Accuracy	87.7	74.46	**87.7**	74.46
Query-based Accuracy	**87.7**	**74.89**	86.57	**74.89**

Table 4: Results when applied on "non-personal" tweets.

For experiment ①, on *All*, the method is not applied because all misclassified tweets contain a personal pronoun and no named entity. The query-based method outperforms the classifier in all cases, except on *All* where results on Google were found for only 42.5% of queries whereas more than 50% of queries found results in all other experiments (maximum is 66.6% in *NegOnly*). Tweets for which no result is found are tweets with named entities but which do not relate an event or a statement (*e.g. AHAHAHAHAHA! NO RESPECT #Legorafi*, where "Legorafi" is a satirical newspaper). To evaluate the task difficulty, two annotators were also asked to label as ironic or not the 50 tweets (40+18) for which the method is applied. The inter-annotator score (Cohen's Kappa) between both annotators is only $\kappa = 0.41$. Among the 12 reclassifications into IR, both annotators disagree with each other for 5 of them. Even if this experiment is not strong enough to lead to a formal conclusion because of the small number of tweets, this tends to show that human beings would not do it better.

It is interesting to note that even if internal context features were not relevant for automatic tweet classification, our results show that they are useful for classification improvement. As shown by ①, the query-based method is more effective when applied on misclassified tweets. We can then consider that using internal contextual features (presence of personal pronouns and named entities) can be a way to automatically detect tweets that are likely to be misclassified.

5 Discussion and conclusions

This paper proposed a model to identify irony in implicit oppositions in French. As far as we know, this is the first work on irony detection in French on Twitter data. Comparing to other languages, our results are very encouraging. For example, sarcasm detection achieved 30% precision in Dutch tweets (Liebrecht et al., 2013) while irony detection in English data resulted in 79% precision (Reyes et al., 2013).

We treat French irony as an overall term that covers other figurative language devices such as sarcasm, humor, etc. This is a first step before moving to a more fine-grained automatic identification of figurative language in French. For interesting discussions on the distinction/similarity between irony and sarcasm hastags, see (Wang, 2013).

One of the main contribution of this study is that the proposed model does not rely only on the lexical clues of a tweet, but also on its pragmatic context. Our intuition is that a tweet containing an asserted fact of the form $Not(P_1)$ is ironic if and only if one can prove P_1 on the basis of some external information. This form of tweets is quite frequent in French (more than 62.75% of our data contain explicit negation words), which suggests two hypotheses: (H1) negation can be a good indicator to detect irony, and (H2) external context can help to detect the absurdity of ironic content.

To validate if negation helps, we built binary classifiers using both state of the art features and new features (explicit and implicit opposition, sentiment shifter, discourse connectives). Overall accuracies were good when the data contain both tweets with negation and no negation but lower when tweets contain only negation or no negation at all. Error analysis show that major errors come from the presence of implicit oppositions, particularly in C_{Neg} and C_{All}. These results empirically validate hypothesis (H1). Negation has been shown to be very helpful in many NLP tasks, such as sentiment analysis (Wiegand et al., 2010). It has also been used as a feature to detect irony (Reyes et al., 2013). However, no one has empirically measured how irony classification behaves in the presence or absence of negation in the data.

To test (H2), we proposed a query-based method that corrects the classifier's outputs in order to retrieve false assertions. Our experiments show that the classification after applying Google searches in reliable web sites significantly improves the classifier accuracy when tested on C_{Neg}. In addition, we show that internal context features are useful to improve classification. These results empirically validate (H2). However, even though the algorithm improves the classifier performance, the number of queries is small which suggests that a much larger dataset is needed. As for negation, querying external source of information has been shown to give an improvement over the basic features for many NLP tasks (for example, in question-answering (Moldovan et al., 2002)). However, as far as we know, this approach has not been used for irony classification.

This study is a first step towards improving irony detection relying on external context. We plan to study other ways to retrieve such a context like the conversation thread.

Acknowledgements

This work was funded by the French National Research Agency (ASFALDA project ANR-12-CORD-023).

References

Salvatore Attardo. 2000. Irony as relevant inappropriateness. *Journal of pragmatics*, 32(6):793–826.

Francesco Barbieri and Horacio Saggion. 2014. Modelling Irony in Twitter: Feature Analysis and Evaluation. In *Proceedings of Language Resources and Evaluation Conference (LREC)*, pages 4258–4264.

Farah Benamara, Véronique Moriceau, and Yvette Yannick Mathieu. 2014. Fine-grained semantic categorization of opinion expressions for consensus detection (Catégorisation sémantique fine des expressions d'opinion pour la détection de consensus) [in French]. In *TALN-RECITAL 2014 Workshop DEFT 2014 : DÉfi Fouille de Textes (DEFT 2014 Workshop: Text Mining Challenge)*, pages 36–44, July.

Clint Burfoot and Clint Baldwin. 2009. Automatic satire detection: Are you having a laugh? In *Proceedings of the ACL-IJCNLP 2009 conference short papers*, pages 161–164. Association for Computational Linguistics.

Konstantin Buschmeier, Philipp Cimiano, and Roman Klinger. 2014. An Impact Analysis of Features in a Classification Approach to Irony Detection in Product Reviews. In *Proceedings of the 5th Workshop on Computational Approaches to Subjectivity, Sentiment and Social Media Analysis*, pages 42–49.

Paula Carvalho, Luís Sarmento, Mário J Silva, and Eugénio De Oliveira. 2009. Clues for detecting irony in user-generated contents: oh...!! it's so easy;-). In *Proceedings of the 1st international CIKM workshop on Topic-sentiment analysis for mass opinion*, pages 53–56. ACM.

Herbert H Clark and Richard J Gerrig. 1984. On the pretense theory of irony. *Journal of Experimental Psychology: General*, 113(1):121–126.

Dmitry Davidov, Oren Tsur, and Ari Rappoport. 2010. Semi-supervised Recognition of Sarcastic Sentences in Twitter and Amazon. In *Proceedings of the Fourteenth Conference on Computational Natural Language Learning*, CoNLL '10, pages 107–116.

Aniruddha Ghosh, Guofu Li, Tony Veale, Paolo Rosso, Ekaterina Shutova, John Barnden, and Antonio Reyes. 2015. Semeval-2015 task 11: Sentiment Analysis of Figurative Language in Twitter. In *Proc. 9th Int. Workshop on Semantic Evaluation (SemEval 2015), Co-located with NAACL*, page 470478. Association for Computational Linguistics.

Raymond W Gibbs. 2000. Irony in talk among friends. *Metaphor and symbol*, 15(1-2):5–27.

Roberto Gonzalez-Ibanez, Smaranda Muresan, and Nina Wacholde. 2011. Identifying sarcasm in Twitter: a closer look. In *Proceedings of the 49th Annual Meeting of the Association for Computational Linguistics: Human Language Technologies: short papers-Volume 2*, pages 581–586. Association for Computational Linguistics.

H Paul Grice, Peter Cole, and Jerry L Morgan. 1975. Syntax and semantics. *Logic and conversation*, 3:41–58.

Henk Haverkate. 1990. A speech act analysis of irony. *Journal of Pragmatics*, 14(1):77 – 109.

Christine Liebrecht, Florian Kunneman, and Bosch Antal van den. 2013. The perfect solution for detecting sarcasm in tweets# not. In *Proceedings of the 4th Workshop on Computational Approaches to Subjectivity, Sentiment and Social Media Analysis*, pages 29–37. New Brunswick, NJ: ACL.

Dan I Moldovan, Sanda M Harabagiu, Roxana Girju, Paul Morarescu, V Finley Lacatusu, Adrian Novischi, Adriana Badulescu, and Orest Bolohan. 2002. LCC Tools for Question Answering. In *TREC*.

Antonio Reyes and Paolo Rosso. 2012. Making objective decisions from subjective data: Detecting irony in customer reviews. *Decision Support Systems*, 53(4):754–760.

Antonio Reyes, Paolo Rosso, and Tony Veale. 2013. A multidimensional approach for detecting irony in twitter. *Language resources and evaluation*, 47(1):239–268.

Ellen Riloff, Ashequl Qadir, Prafulla Surve, Lalindra De Silva, Nathan Gilbert, and Ruihong Huang. 2013. Sarcasm as Contrast between a Positive Sentiment and Negative Situation. In *EMNLP*, pages 704–714.

Charlotte Roze, Laurence Danlos, and Philippe Muller. 2012. Lexconn: A French lexicon of discourse connectives. *Discours, Multidisciplinary Perspectives on Signalling Text Organisation*, 10:(on line).

J. Searle. 1979. *Expression and meaning: Studies in the theory of speech acts*. Cambridge University.

Cameron Shelley. 2001. The bicoherence theory of situational irony. *Cognitive Science*, 25(5):775–818.

Dan Sperber and Deirdre Wilson. 1981. Irony and the use-mention distinction. *Radical pragmatics*, 49:295–318.

Oren Tsur, Dmitry Davidov, and Ari Rappoport. 2010. ICWSM-A Great Catchy Name: Semi-Supervised Recognition of Sarcastic Sentences in Online Product Reviews. In *ICWSM*.

Akira Utsumi. 1996. A unified theory of irony and its computational formalization. In *Proceedings of the 16th conference on Computational linguistics-Volume 2*, pages 962–967. Association for Computational Linguistics.

Akira Utsumi. 2004. Stylistic and contextual effects in irony processing. In *Proceedings of the 26th Annual Meeting of the Cognitive Science Society*, pages 1369–1374.

Po-Ya Angela Wang. 2013. #Irony or #Sarcasm-A Quantitative and Qualitative Study Based on Twitter.

Michael Wiegand, Alexandra Balahur, Benjamin Roth, Dietrich Klakow, and Andrés Montoyo. 2010. A Survey on the Role of Negation in Sentiment Analysis. In *Proceedings of the Workshop on Negation and Speculation in Natural Language Processing*, pages 60–68. Association for Computational Linguistics.

Annotation and Classification of an Email Importance Corpus

Fan Zhang
Computer Science Department
University of Pittsburgh
Pittsburgh, PA 15260
zhangfan@cs.pitt.edu

Kui Xu
Research and Technology Center
Robert Bosch LLC
Palo Alto, CA 94304
Kui.Xu2@us.bosch.com

Abstract

This paper presents an email importance corpus annotated through Amazon Mechanical Turk (AMT). Annotators annotate the email content type and email importance for three levels of hierarchy (senior manager, middle manager and employee). Each email is annotated by 5 turkers. Agreement study shows that the agreed AMT annotations are close to the expert annotations. The annotated dataset demonstrates difference in proportions of content type between different levels. An email importance prediction system is trained on the dataset and identifies the unimportant emails at minimum 0.55 precision with only text-based features.

1 Introduction

It is common that people receive tens or hundreds of emails everyday. Reading and managing all these emails consume significant time and attention. Many efforts have been made to address the email overload problem. There are studies modeling the email importance and the recipients' actions in order to help with the user's interaction with emails (Dabbish and Kraut, 2006; Dabbish et al., 2005). Meanwhile, there are NLP studies on spam message filtering, email intention classification, and priority email selection to reduce the number of emails to read (Schneider, 2003; Cohen et al., 2004; Jeong et al., 2009; Dredze et al., 2009). In our project, we intend to build an email briefing system which extracts and summarizes important email information for the users.

However, we believe there are critical components missing from the current research work. First, to the extent of our knowledge, there is little public email corpus with email importance labeled. Most of the prior works were either based on surveys or private commercial data (Dabbish and Kraut, 2006; Aberdeen et al., 2010). Second, little attention has been paid to study the difference of emails received by people at different levels of hierarchy. Third, most of the prior works chose the user's action to the email (e.g. replies, opens) as the indicator of email importance. However, we argue that the user action does not necessarily indicate the importance of the email. For example, a work-related reminder email can be more important than a regular social greeting email. However, a user is more likely to reply to the later and keep the information of the former in mind. Specifically for the goal of our email briefing system, importance decided upon the user's action is insufficient.

This paper proposes to annotate email importance on the Enron email corpus (Klimt and Yang, 2004). Emails are grouped according to the recipient's levels of hierarchy. The importance of an email is annotated not only according to the user's action but also according to the importance of the information contained in the email. The content type of the emails are also annotated for the email importance study. Section 3 describe the annotation and analysis of the dataset. Section 4 describes our email importance prediction system trained on the annotated corpus.

2 Related work

The most relevant work is the email corpus annotated by Dredze et al. (Dredze et al., 2008a; Dredze et al., 2008b). 2391 emails from inboxes of 4 volunteers were included. Each volunteer manually annotated whether their own emails need to be replied or not. The annotations are reliable as they come from the emails' owners. However, it lacks diversity in the user distribution with only 4 volunteers. Also, whether an email gets response or not does not always indicate its importance. While commercial products such as Gmail Priority Inbox (Aberdeen et al., 2010) has a better cover-

Proceedings of the 53rd Annual Meeting of the Association for Computational Linguistics and the 7th International Joint Conference on Natural Language Processing (Short Papers), pages 651–656,
Beijing, China, July 26-31, 2015.

age of users and decides the importance of emails upon more factors[1], it is unlikely to have their data accessible to public due to user privacy concerns.

The Enron corpus is a public email corpus widely researched (Klimt and Yang, 2004). Lampert et al. (2010) annotated whether an email contains action request or not based on the agreed annotations of three annotators. We followed similar ideas and labeled the email importance and content type with the agreed Amazon Mechanical Turk annotations. Emails are selected from Enron employees at different levels of hierarchy and their importance are labeled according to the importance of their content. While our corpus can be less reliable without the annotations from the emails' real recipients, it is more diverse and has better descriptions of email importance.

3 Data annotation

3.1 Annotation scheme

Annotators are required to select the importance of the email from three levels: *Not important*, *Normal* and *Important*. *Not important* emails contain little useful information and require no action from the recipient. It can be junk emails missed by the spam filter or social greeting emails that do not require response from the recipient. *Important* emails either contain very important information to the recipient or contain urgent issues that require immediate action (e.g. change of meeting time/place). *Normal* emails contain less important information or contain less urgent issues than *Important* emails. For example, emails discussing about plans of social events after work would typically be categorized as *Normal*.

We also annotate the email content type as it reveals the semantic information contained in the emails. There are a variety of email content type definitions (Jabbari et al., 2006; Goldstein et al., 2006; Dabbish et al., 2005). We choose Dabbish et al.'s definition for our work. Eight categories are included: *Action Request*, *Info Request*, *Info Attachment*, *Status Update*, *Scheduling*, *Reminder*, *Social*, and *Other*. While an email can contain more than one type of content, annotators are required to select one primary type.

[1]Including user actions and action time, the user actions not only include the *Reply* action but also includes actions such as *opens*, *manual corrections*, etc.

3.2 Annotation with AMT

Amazon Mechanical Turk is widely used in data annotation (Lawson et al., 2010; Marge et al., 2010). It is typically reliable for simple tasks. Observing the fact that it takes little time for a user to decide an email's importance, we choose AMT to do the annotations and manage to reduce the annotation noise through redundant annotation.

Creamer et al. categorized the employees of the Enron dataset to 4 groups: senior managers, middle managers, traders and employees[2] (Creamer et al., 2009). We hypothesized that the types of emails received by different groups were different and annotated different groups separately. Based on Creamer et al's work, we identified 23 senior managers with a total of 21728 emails, 20 middle managers with 13779 emails and 17 regular employees with 12137 emails. The trader group was not annotated as it was more specific to Enron. For each group, one batch of 750 assignments (email) was released. The emails were randomly selected from all the group members' received emails (to or cc'ed). Turkers were presented with all details available in the Enron dataset, including subject, sender, recipients, cclist, date and the content (with history of forwards and replies). Turkers were required to make their choices as they were in the position.[3] Each assignment was annotated by 5 turkers at the rate of $0.06 per Turker assignment. The email type and the email importance are decided according to the majority votes. If an email has 3 agreed votes or higher, we call this email **agreed**. Table 1 demonstrates the average time per assignment (Time), the effectively hourly rate (Ehr), the number of emails with message type agreed (#TypeAgreed), importance agreed (#ImpoAgreed) and both agreed (#AllAgreed). We find that #AllAgreed is close to #TypeAgreed, which indicates a major overlap between the agreed type annotation and the agreed importance annotation.

3.3 Data discussion

In this paper we focus on the *AllAgreed* emails to mitigate the effects of annotation noise. Table 2 demonstrates the contingency table of the corpus.

[2]Senior managers include CEO, presidents, vice presidents, chief risk officer, chief operating officer and managing directors. The other employees at management level are categorized to middle managers

[3]E.g. instruction of the senior manager batch: Imagine you were the CEO/president/vice president/managing director of the company, categorize the emails into the three categories [Not Important], [Normal], [Important].

Level	Time (s)	Ehr ($)	#All	#TypeAgreed	#ImpoAgreed	#AllAgreed
Senior (23)	40	5.400	750	589	656	574
Middle (20)	33	6.545	750	556	622	550
Employee (17)	31	6.968	750	593	643	586

Table 1: AMT annotation results, notice that #AllAgreed is close to #TypeAgreed

	Act.Req	Info.Req	Info	Status	Schedule	Reminder	Social	Other	All
Senior	60	49	255	**57**	43	4	**68**	38	574
Not	0	0	0	0	0	0	33	30	63
Normal	38	37	231	51	37	4	35	8	441
Important	22	12	24	6	6	0	0	0	70
Middle	82	53	261	22	49	0	37	46	550
Not	0	0	1	0	0	0	10	32	43
Normal	64	47	247	22	49	0	27	14	470
Important	18	6	13	0	0	0	0	0	37
Employee	61	65	326	22	29	1	52	30	586
Not	0	0	1	0	0	0	8	26	35
Normal	43	62	315	22	27	1	44	4	518
Important	18	3	10	0	2	0	0	0	33

Table 2: Contingency table of content type and importance of *AllAgreed* emails; bold indicates the proportions of this category is significantly different between groups ($p<0.05$)

A potential issue of the corpus is that the importance of the email is not decided by the real email recipient. To address this concern, we compared the *AllAgreed* results with the annotations from an expert annotator. 50 emails were randomly selected from *AllAgreed* emails for each level. The annotator was required to check the background of each recipient (e.g. the recipient's position in the company at the time, his/her department information and the projects he/she was involved in if these information were available online) and judge the relationship between the email's contacts before annotation (e.g. if the contact is a family member or a close friend of the recipient). Agreement study shows a Kappa score of 0.7970 for the senior manager level, 0.6420 for the middle manager level and 0.7845 for the employee level. It demonstrates that the agreed Turker annotations are as reliable as well-prepared expert annotations.

We first tested whether the content type proportions were significantly different between different levels of hierarchy. Recipients with more than 20 emails sampled were selected. A vector of content type proportions was built for each recipient on his/her sampled emails. Then we applied multivariate analysis of variance (MANOVA) to test the difference in the means of the vectors between levels[4]. We found that there were significant differences in proportions of status update ($p=0.042$) and social emails ($p=0.035$). This agrees with the impression that the senior managers spend more time on project management and social relationship development. Following the same approach, we tested whether there were significant differences in importance proportions between levels. However, no significant difference was found while we can observe a higher portion of *Important* emails in the *Senior* group in Table 2. In the next section, we further investigate the relationship between content type and message importance using the content type as a baseline feature in email importance prediction.

4 Email importance prediction

In this section we present a preliminary study of automatic email importance prediction. Two baselines are compared, including a *Majority* baseline where the most frequent class is chosen and a *Type* baseline where the only feature used for classification is the email content type.

[4]We cannot use Chi-square to test the difference between groups directly on Table 2 as the emails sampled do not satisfy the independence consumption if they come from the same recipient

Features	Acc	Kappa	P(U)	R(I)
Sr. Mgrs				
Majority	76.83	0	0	0
Type	68.78	37.93	58.76	44.81
Text	76.34	26.96	71.83*	14.67†
Text+Type	78.43	33.80	**75.99***	12.13†
Mgrs				
Majority	85.45	0	0	0
Type	69.81	32.75	50.47	49.80
Text	87.09	26.64	54.67	4.17†
Text+Type	88.55	36.42	63.80*	7.59†
Emp				
Majority	88.39	0	0	0
Type	80.34	38.63	40.21	45.12
Text	88.83	30.98	63.83*	1.67†
Text+Type	89.16	36.71	72.50*	1.67†

Table 3: Results of Experiment 1; * indicates significantly better than the Type baseline; † indicates significantly worse than the Type baseline; bold indicates better than all other methods. With only text-based features, the system achieves at least 54.67 precision in identifying unimportant emails.

Groups	Acc	Kappa	P(U)	R(I)
Sr. Mgrs	77.70	19.24	65.22	10.00
Mgrs	83.27	30.03	61.90	2.70
Emp	83.10	33.89	46.94	33.33

Table 4: Cross-group results of Experiment 2

4.1 Feature extraction

While prior works have pointed out that the social features such as contacting frequency are related to the user's action on emails (Lampert et al., 2010; Dredze et al., 2008a), in this paper we only focus on features that can be extracted from text.

N-gram features Binary unigram features are extracted from the email subject and the email content separately. Stop words are not filtered as they might also hint the email importance.

Part-of-speech tags According to our observation, the work-related emails have more content words than greeting emails. Thus, POS tag features are extracted from the email content, including the total numbers of POS tags in the text and the average numbers of tags in each sentence. [5]

[5]The Part-of-speech (POS) tags are tagged with the Stanford CoreNLP toolkit (Manning et al., 2014; Toutanova et al., 2003), containing 36 POS tags as defined in the Penn Treebank annotation.

Length features We observe that work-related emails tend to be more succinct than unimportant emails such as advertisements. Thus, length features are extracted including the length of the email subject and email content, and the average length of sentences in the email content.

Content features Inspired by prior works (Lampert et al., 2010; Dredze et al., 2008a), features that provide hints of the email content are extracted, including the number of question marks, date information and capitalized words, etc.

4.2 Experiments

We treat our task as a multi-class classification problem. We test classifications within-level and cross-level with only text-based features.

Experiment 1 Each level is tested with 10-fold cross-validation. SVM of the Weka toolkit (Hall et al., 2009) is chosen as the classifier. To address the data imbalance problem, the minority classes of the training data are oversampled with the Weka SMOTE package (Chawla et al., 2002). The parameters of SMOTE are decided according to the class distribution of the training data.

Experiment 2 The classifiers are trained on two levels and tested on the other level. Again, SVM is chosen as the model and SMOTE is used to oversample the training data.

4.3 Evaluation

Kappa[6] and *accuracy* are chosen to evaluate the overall performance in prediction. For our email briefing task specifically, *precision* in unimportant email prediction P(U) (avoid the false recognition of unimportant emails) and *recall* in important email prediction R(I) (cover as many important emails as possible) are evaluated. Paired t-tests are utilized to compare whether there are significant differences in performance ($p < 0.05$).

As demonstrated in Table 3, the text-based features are useful for the prediction of unimportant email classification but not as useful for the recognition of important emails. It also shows that the content type is an important indicator of the email's importance. While the content type is not always accessible in real life settings, the results demonstrate the necessity of extracting semantic information for email importance prediction. In Table 4, precision of unimportant email prediction

[6]The agreement between the system and the majority labels from the Mechanical Turk

is higher on the manager levels but lower on the employee level. This indicates a potential difference of email features between the manager levels and the employee level.

5 Conclusion and future work

In this paper we present an email importance corpus collected through AMT. The dataset focuses on the importance of the information contained in the email instead of the email recipient's action. The content type of the email is also annotated and we find differences in content type proportions between different levels of hierarchy. Experiments demonstrate that the content type is an important indicator of email importance. The system based on only text-based features identifies unimportant emails at minimum 0.5467 precision.

Agreement study shows that the agreed Turker annotations are as good as annotations of well-prepared expert annotators. We plan to increase the size of our dataset through AMT. We expect the dataset to be helpful for studies on email overload problems. Meanwhile, we are aware that the current corpus lacks social and personal information. We believe features regarding such information (e.g. the recipient's email history with the contact, the recipient's personal preference in categorizing emails, etc.) should also be incorporated for importance prediction.

Acknowledgments

We would like to thank Zhe Feng, Doo Soon Kim, Lin Zhao, Sai Sudharsanan and other employees of the Bosch RTC 1.2 group for their helpful feedback, Prof. Diane Litman for her instructions to the first author and all the anonymous reviewers for their suggestions.

This research is supported by the Research and Technology Center of Robert Bosch LLC.

References

Douglas Aberdeen, Ondrej Pacovsky, and Andrew Slater. 2010. The learning behind gmail priority inbox. In *LCCC: NIPS 2010 Workshop on Learning on Cores, Clusters and Clouds*.

Nitesh V Chawla, Kevin W Bowyer, Lawrence O Hall, and W Philip Kegelmeyer. 2002. Smote: synthetic minority over-sampling technique. *Journal of artificial intelligence research*, 16(1):321–357.

William W. Cohen, Vitor R. Carvalho, and Tom M. Mitchell. 2004. Learning to classify email into "speech acts". In Dekang Lin and Dekai Wu, editors, *Proceedings of EMNLP 2004*, pages 309–316, Barcelona, Spain, July. Association for Computational Linguistics.

Germán Creamer, Ryan Rowe, Shlomo Hershkop, and Salvatore J Stolfo. 2009. Segmentation and automated social hierarchy detection through email network analysis. In *Advances in Web Mining and Web Usage Analysis*, pages 40–58. Springer.

Laura A Dabbish and Robert E Kraut. 2006. Email overload at work: an analysis of factors associated with email strain. In *Proceedings of the 2006 20th anniversary conference on Computer supported cooperative work*, pages 431–440. ACM.

Laura A Dabbish, Robert E Kraut, Susan Fussell, and Sara Kiesler. 2005. Understanding email use: predicting action on a message. In *Proceedings of the SIGCHI conference on Human factors in computing systems*, pages 691–700. ACM.

Mark Dredze, Tova Brooks, Josh Carroll, Joshua Magarick, John Blitzer, and Fernando Pereira. 2008a. Intelligent email: reply and attachment prediction. In *Proceedings of the 13th international conference on Intelligent user interfaces*, pages 321–324. ACM.

Mark Dredze, Hanna M Wallach, Danny Puller, Tova Brooks, Josh Carroll, Joshua Magarick, John Blitzer, Fernando Pereira, et al. 2008b. Intelligent email: Aiding users with ai. In *AAAI*, pages 1524–1527.

Mark Dredze, Bill N Schilit, and Peter Norvig. 2009. Suggesting email view filters for triage and search. In *IJCAI*, pages 1414–1419.

Jade Goldstein, Andres Kwasinksi, Paul Kingsbury, Roberta Evans Sabin, and Albert McDowell. 2006. Annotating subsets of the enron email corpus. In *CEAS*. Citeseer.

Mark Hall, Eibe Frank, Geoffrey Holmes, Bernhard Pfahringer, Peter Reutemann, and Ian H Witten. 2009. The weka data mining software: an update. *ACM SIGKDD explorations newsletter*, 11(1):10–18.

Sanaz Jabbari, Ben Allison, David Guthrie, and Louise Guthrie. 2006. Towards the orwellian nightmare: separation of business and personal emails. In *Proceedings of the COLING/ACL on Main conference poster sessions*, pages 407–411. Association for Computational Linguistics.

Minwoo Jeong, Chin-Yew Lin, and Gary Geunbae Lee. 2009. Semi-supervised speech act recognition in emails and forums. In *Proceedings of the 2009 Conference on Empirical Methods in Natural Language Processing: Volume 3-Volume 3*, pages 1250–1259. Association for Computational Linguistics.

Bryan Klimt and Yiming Yang. 2004. The enron corpus: A new dataset for email classification research. In *Machine learning: ECML 2004*, pages 217–226. Springer.

Andrew Lampert, Robert Dale, and Cecile Paris. 2010. Detecting emails containing requests for action. In *Human Language Technologies: The 2010 Annual Conference of the North American Chapter of the Association for Computational Linguistics*, pages 984–992. Association for Computational Linguistics.

Nolan Lawson, Kevin Eustice, Mike Perkowitz, and Meliha Yetisgen-Yildiz. 2010. Annotating large email datasets for named entity recognition with mechanical turk. In *Proceedings of the NAACL HLT 2010 Workshop on Creating Speech and Language Data with Amazon's Mechanical Turk*, pages 71–79. Association for Computational Linguistics.

Christopher D. Manning, Mihai Surdeanu, John Bauer, Jenny Finkel, Steven J. Bethard, and David McClosky. 2014. The Stanford CoreNLP natural language processing toolkit. In *Proceedings of 52nd Annual Meeting of the Association for Computational Linguistics: System Demonstrations*, pages 55–60.

Matthew Marge, Satanjeev Banerjee, and Alexander I Rudnicky. 2010. Using the amazon mechanical turk to transcribe and annotate meeting speech for extractive summarization. In *Proceedings of the NAACL HLT 2010 Workshop on Creating Speech and Language Data with Amazon's Mechanical Turk*, pages 99–107. Association for Computational Linguistics.

Karl-Michael Schneider. 2003. A comparison of event models for naive bayes anti-spam e-mail filtering. In *Proceedings of the tenth conference on European chapter of the Association for Computational Linguistics-Volume 1*, pages 307–314. Association for Computational Linguistics.

Kristina Toutanova, Dan Klein, Christopher D Manning, and Yoram Singer. 2003. Feature-rich part-of-speech tagging with a cyclic dependency network. In *Proceedings of the 2003 Conference of the North American Chapter of the Association for Computational Linguistics on Human Language Technology-Volume 1*, pages 173–180. Association for Computational Linguistics.

Lexical Comparison Between Wikipedia and Twitter Corpora by Using Word Embeddings

Luchen Tan[1], Haotian Zhang[1]*, Charles L.A. Clarke[1], and Mark D. Smucker[2]
[1]David R. Cheriton School of Computer Science, University of Waterloo, Canada
{luchen.tan, haotian.zhang, claclark}@uwaterloo.ca
[2]Department of Management Sciences, University of Waterloo, Canada
mark.smucker@uwaterloo.ca

Abstract

Compared with carefully edited prose, the language of social media is informal in the extreme. The application of NLP techniques in this context may require a better understanding of word usage within social media. In this paper, we compute a word embedding for a corpus of tweets, comparing it to a word embedding for Wikipedia. After learning a transformation of one vector space to the other, and adjusting similarity values according to term frequency, we identify words whose usage differs greatly between the two corpora. For any given word, the set of words closest to it in a particular embedding provides a characterization for that word's usage within the corresponding corpora.

1 Introduction

Users of social media typically employ highly informal language, including slang, acronyms, typos, deliberate misspellings, and interjections (Han and Baldwin, 2011). This heavy use of nonstandard language, as well as the overall level of noise on social media, creates substantial problems when applying standard NLP tools and techniques (Eisenstein, 2013). For example, Kaufmann and Kalita (2010) apply machine translation methods to convert tweets to standard English in an attempt to ameliorate this problem. Similarly, Baldwin et al. (2013) and Han et al. (2012) address this problem by generating corrections for irregularly spelled words in social media.

In this short paper, we continue this line of research, applying word embedding to the problem of translating between the informal English of social media, specifically Twitter, and the formal English of carefully edited texts, such as those found in Wikipedia. Starting with a large collection of tweets and a copy of Wikipedia, we construct word embeddings for both corpora. We then generate a transformation matrix, mapping one vector space into another. After applying a normalization based on term frequency, we use distances in the transformed space as an indicator of differences in word usage between the two corpora. The method identifies differences in usage due to jargon, contractions, abbreviations, hashtags, and the influence of popular culture, as well as other factors. As a method of validation, we examine the overlap in closely related words, showing that distance after transformation and normalization correlates with the degree of overlap.

*Luchen Tan and Haotian Zhang contributed equally to this work.

2 Related Work

Mikolov et al. (2013b) proposed a novel neural network model to train continuous vector representation for words. The high-quality word vectors obtained from large data sets achieve high accuracy in both semantic and syntactic relationships (Goldberg and Levy, 2014).

Some probabilistic similarity measures, based on Kullback-Leibler (KL) divergence (or relative entropy), give an inspection of relative divergence between two probability distributions of corpus (Kullback and Leibler, 1951; Tan and Clarke, 2014). For a given token, KL divergence measures the distribution divergence of this word in different corpora according to its corresponding probability. Intuitively, the value for KL divergence increases as two distributions become more different. Verspoor et al. (2009) found that KL divergence could be applied to analyze text in terms of two characteristics: the magnitude of the differences, and the semantic nature of the characteristic words.

Subašić and Berendt (2011) applied a symmetrical variant of KL divergence, the Jensen-Shannon (JS) divergence (Lin, 1991), to compare various aspects of the corpora such as language

Proceedings of the 53rd Annual Meeting of the Association for Computational Linguistics and the 7th International Joint Conference on Natural Language Processing (Short Papers), pages 657–661,
Beijing, China, July 26-31, 2015.

divergence, headline divergence, named-entity divergence and sentiment divergence. As for the applications derived from above methods, Tang et al. (2011) studied the lexical semantics and sentiment tendency of high frequency terms in each corpus by comparing microblog texts with general articles. Baldwin et al. (2013) analyzed non-standard language on social media in the aspects of lexical variants, acronyms, grammaticality and corpus similarity. Their results revealed that social media text is less grammatical than edited text.

3 Methods of Lexical Comparison

Mikolov et al. (2013a) construct vector spaces for various languages, including English and Spanish, finding that the relative positions of semantically related words are preserved across languages. We adapt this result to explore differences between corpora written in a single language, specifically to explore the contrast between the highly informal language used in English-language social media with the more formal language used in Wikipedia. We assume that there exists a *linear* transformation relationship between the vectors for the most frequent words from each corpus. Working with these frequent terms, we learn a linear projection matrix that maps source to target spaces. We hypothesize that usage of those words appearing far apart after this transformation differs substantially between the two corpora.

Let $a \in \mathbb{R}^{1\times d}$ and $b \in \mathbb{R}^{1\times d}$ be the corresponding source and target word vector representation with dimension d. We construct a source matrix $A = [a_1^T, a_2^T, ..., a_c^T]^T$ and a target matrix $B = [b_1^T, b_2^T, ..., b_c^T]^T$, composed of vector pairs $\{a_i, b_i\}_{i=1}^{c}$, where c is the size of the vocabulary common between the source and target corpora. We order these vectors according to frequency in the target corpus, so that a_i and b_i correspond to the i-th most common word in the target corpus.

These vectors are used to learn a linear transformation matrix $M \in \mathbb{R}^{d\times d}$. Once this transformation matrix M is obtained, we can transform any a_i to $a'_i = a_i M$ in order to approximate b_i. The linear transformation can be depicted as:

$$AM = B \tag{1}$$

Following the solution provided by (Mikolov et al., 2013a), M can be approximately computed by using stochastic gradient descent:

$$\min_M \sum_{i=1}^{n} \parallel a_i M - b_i \parallel^2 \tag{2}$$

where we limit the training process to the top n terms.

After the generation of M, we calculate $a'_i = a_i M$ for each word. For each a_i where $i > n$, we determine the distance between a'_i and b_i:

$$Sim(a'_i, b_i), n \leq i \leq c. \tag{3}$$

Let Z be the set of these words ordered by distance, so that z_j is the word with the j-th greatest distance between the corresponding a' and b vectors. For the experiments reported in this paper, we used cosine distance to calculate this Sim metric.

4 Experiments

In this section, we describe the results of applying our method to Twitter and Wikipedia.

4.1 Experimental Settings

The Wikipedia dataset for our experiments consists of all English Wikipedia articles downloaded from MediaWiki data dumps[1]. The Twitter dataset was collected through the Twitter Streaming API from November 2013 to March 2015. We restricted the dataset to English-language tweets on the basis of the language field contained in each tweet. To obtain distributed word representation for both corpora, we trained word vectors separately by applying the *word2vec*[2] tool, a well-known implementation of word embedding.

Before applying the tool, we cleaned Wikipedia and Twitter corpora. The clean version of Wikipedia retains only normally visible article text on Wikipedia web pages. The Twitter clean version removes HTML code, URLs, user mentions(@), the # symbol of hashtags, and all the retweeted tweets. The sizes of document and vocabulary in both corpora are listed in Table 1.

Corpora	# Documents	# Vocabulary
Wikipedia	3,776,418	7,267,802
Twitter	263,572,856	13,622,411

Table 1: Corpora sizes

[1]https://dumps.wikimedia.org/enwiki/20150304/
[2]https://code.google.com/p/word2vec/

There are two major parameters that affect *word2vec* training quality: the dimensionality of word vectors, and the size of the surrounding words window. We choose 300 for our word vector dimensionality, which is typical for training large dataset with *word2vec*. We choose 10 words for the window, since tweet sentence length is 9.2 ± 6.4 (Baldwin et al., 2013).

4.2 Visualization

In Figure 1, we visualize the vectors of some most common English words by applying principal component analysis (PCA) to the vector spaces. The words "and", "is", "was" and "by" have similar geometric arrangements in Wikipedia and in Twitter, since these common words are not key differentiators for these corpora. On the other hand, the pronouns "I" and "you", are heavily used in Twitter but rarely used in Wikipedia. Despite this difference in term frequency, after transformation, the vectors for these terms appear close together.

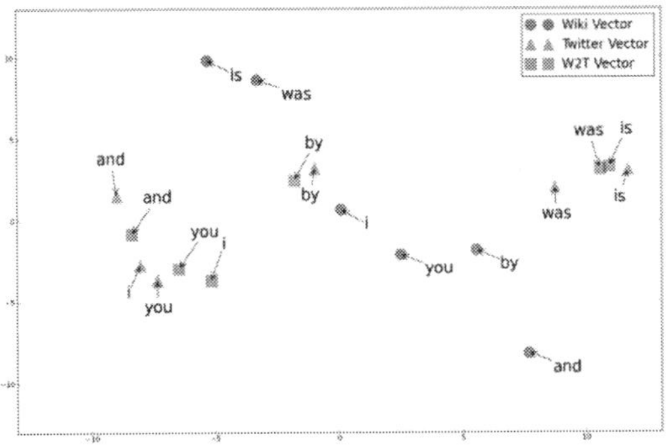

Figure 1: Word representations in Wikipedia, Twitter and transformed vectors after mapping from Wikipedia to Twitter.

4.3 Results

As our primary goal, we hope to demonstrate that our transformation method reflects meaningful lexical usage differences between Wikipedia and Twitter. To train our space transformation matrix, we used the top $n = 1,000$ most frequent words from the 505,121 words that appear in both corpora. The transformation can be either from Twitter to Wikipedia (*T2W*) or the opposite direction *W2T*. We observed that the two transformation matrices are not exactly the same, but they produce similar results. Mikolov et al. (2013c) suggest that a simple vector offset method based on cosine distance was remarkably effective to search both syntactic and semantic similar words. They also report that cosine similarity preformed well, given that the embedding vectors are all normalized to unit norm.

Figure 2 illustrates how *T2W* word vectors are similar to their original word vectors. For the purpose of explaining Figure 2, we define new notation as follows: Let $\mathcal{T}$ and $\mathcal{W}$ be the word sets of Twitter and Wikipedia respectively, and let $\mathcal{C} = \mathcal{T} \cap \mathcal{W}$. Denote the document frequency of a word t in the Twitter corpus as $df(t)$. Sorting the whole set $\mathcal{C}$ by $df(t)$ in an ascending order, we obtain a sequence $\bar{S} = \{c_0, \cdots, c_{m-1}\}$, where $c_i \in \mathcal{C}$; $m = 505,121$; and $df(c_i) \leq df(c_j)$, $\forall i < j$. We partition the sequence $\bar{S}$ into 506 buckets, with a bucket size $b = 1000$. $B_i = \{c_{i*b}, \cdots, c_{(i+1)*b-1}\}$ represents the i-th bucket. We number the curves in Figure 2 from the top to the bottom. The points on the i-th curve demonstrates the cosine similarity of the $(i-1) * 100$-th word in each bucket. From this figure, it is apparent that words with higher frequencies have higher average cosine similarity than those words with lower frequencies. Since our goal is to find words with lower than average similar, we apply the median curve of Figure 2 to adjust word distances.

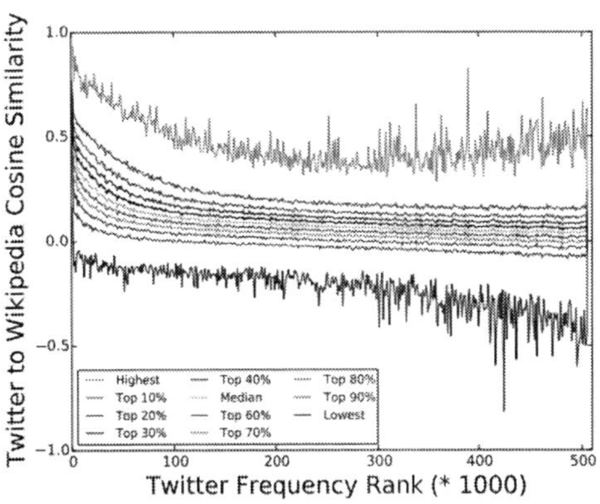

Figure 2: T2W transformated similarity curves.

Defining **adjusted distance** as $D_{adjusted}(t)$ of a given word t, we calculate the cosine distance between t and the median point c_{median} from its corresponding bucket B_i.

$$D_{adjusted}(t) = Sim(c_{median}) - Sim(t) \quad (4)$$

where the index of median point should be $i * b + b/2$. A negative adjusted distance value means the word is more similar than at least half of

Word	Twitter Most Similar	Wikipedia Most Similar
bc	because bcus bcuz cuz cos	bce macedon hellenistic euthydemus ptolemaic
ill	ll imma ima will youll	unwell sick frail fated bedridden
cameron	cam nash followmecam camerons callmecam	gillies duncan mckay mitchell bryce
mentions	unfollow reply respond strangerswelcomed offend	mentions mentioned mentioning reference attested
miss	misss love missss missssss imiss	pageant pageants titlehoder titlehoders pageantopolis
yup	yep yupp yeah yea yepp	chevak yupik gwaii tlingit nunivak
taurus	capricorn sagittarius pisces gemini scorpio	poniatovii scorpio subcompact sagittarius chevette

Table 2: Characteristic Words in Twitter Corpora

words in its bucket. On the other hand, the words that are less similar than at least half of words in their buckets have positive adjusted distance values. The larger an adjusted distance, the less similar the word is between the corpora.

4.4 Examples

Table 2 provides some examples of common words with large adjusted distance, suggesting that their usage in the two corpora are quite different. For each of these words, the example shows the closest terms to that word in the two corpora. In Twitter, "bc" is frequently an abbreviation for "because", while in Wikipedia "bc" is more commonly used as part of dates, e.g. 900 BC. Similarly, in Twitter "ill" is often a misspelling of the contraction "I'll", rather than a synonym for sickness, as in Wikipedia. In Twitter, the most similar words to "cameron" relate to a YouTube personality, whereas in Wikipedia they relate to notable Scotish persons. In Wikipedia, "miss" is related to beauty pageants, while in Twitter it is related to expressions of affection ("I misssss you"). The other examples also have explanations related to popular culture, jargon, slang, and other factors.

5 Validation

To validate our method of comparing lexical distinctions in the two corpora, we employ a ranking similarity measurement. Within a single corpus, the most similar words to a word t can be generated by ranking cosine distance to t. We then determine the overlap between the most similar words to t from Twitter and Wikipedia. The more the two lists overlap, the greater the similarity between the words in the two corpora. Our hypothesis is that larger rank similarity correlates with smaller adjusted distance.

Rank biased overlap (RBO) provides a rank similarity measure designed for comparisons between top-weighted, incomplete and indefinite rankings. Given two ranked lists, A and B, let $A_{1:k}$ and $B_{1:k}$ denote the top k items in A and B (Webber et al., 2010). RBO defines the *overlap* between A and B at depth k as the size of the intersection between these lists at depth k and defines the agreement between A and B at depth k as the overlap divided by the depth. Webber et al. (2010) define RBO as a weighted average of agreement across depths, where the weights decay geometrically with depth, reflecting the requirement for top weighting:

$$RBO = (1-\varphi)\sum_{k=1}^{\infty}\varphi^{k-1}\frac{|A_{1:k}\cap B_{1:k}|}{k} \quad (5)$$

Here, φ is a persistence parameter. As suggested by Webber et al., we set $\varphi = 0.9$. In practice, RBO is computed down to some fixed depth K. We select $K = 50$ for our experiments. For a word t, we compute RBO value between its top 50 similar words in Wikipedia and top 50 similar words in Twitter.

In Figure 3, we validate consistency between results of our space transformation method and RBO. For the top 5,000 terms in the Twitter corpus, we sort them by their adjusted distance value. Due to properties of RBO, there are many zero RBO values. To illustrate the density of these zero overlaps, we smooth our plot by sliding a 100-word window with a step of 10 words. As shown sharply in the figure, RBO and adjusted distance is negatively correlated.

6 Conclusion

This paper analyzed the lexical usage difference between Twitter microblog corpus and Wikipedia corpus. A word-level comparison method based on word embedding is employed to find the characterisic words that particularly discriminating corpora. In future work, we plan to introduce this method to normalize the nonstandard language used in Twitter, applying the methods to problems in search and other areas.

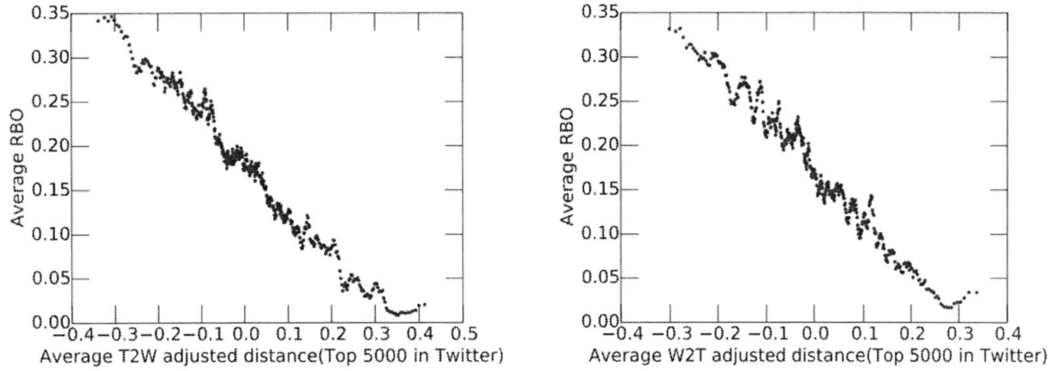

Figure 3: T2W and W2T negative correlation between adjusted distance and RBO.

References

Timothy Baldwin, Paul Cook, Marco Lui, Andrew MacKinlay, and Li Wang. 2013. How noisy social media text, how diffrnt social media sources. In *Proceedings of the Sixth International Joint Conference on Natural Language Processing*, pages 356–364.

Jacob Eisenstein. 2013. What to do about bad language on the internet. In *HLT-NAACL*, pages 359–369.

Yoav Goldberg and Omer Levy. 2014. word2vec explained: deriving mikolov et al.'s negative-sampling word-embedding method. *arXiv preprint arXiv:1402.3722*.

Bo Han and Timothy Baldwin. 2011. Lexical normalisation of short text messages: Makn sens a# twitter. In *Proceedings of the 49th Annual Meeting of the Association for Computational Linguistics: Human Language Technologies-Volume 1*, pages 368–378. Association for Computational Linguistics.

Bo Han, Paul Cook, and Timothy Baldwin. 2012. Automatically constructing a normalisation dictionary for microblogs. In *Proceedings of the 2012 joint conference on empirical methods in natural language processing and computational natural language learning*, pages 421–432. Association for Computational Linguistics.

Max Kaufmann and Jugal Kalita. 2010. Syntactic normalization of twitter messages. In *International conference on natural language processing, Kharagpur, India*.

Solomon Kullback and Richard A Leibler. 1951. On information and sufficiency. *The annals of mathematical statistics*, pages 79–86.

Jianhua Lin. 1991. Divergence measures based on the shannon entropy. *Information Theory, IEEE Transactions on*, 37(1):145–151.

Tomas Mikolov, Quoc V Le, and Ilya Sutskever. 2013a. Exploiting similarities among languages for machine translation. *arXiv preprint arXiv:1309.4168*.

Tomas Mikolov, Ilya Sutskever, Kai Chen, Greg S Corrado, and Jeff Dean. 2013b. Distributed representations of words and phrases and their compositionality. In *Advances in Neural Information Processing Systems*, pages 3111–3119.

Tomas Mikolov, Wen-tau Yih, and Geoffrey Zweig. 2013c. Linguistic regularities in continuous space word representations. In *HLT-NAACL*, pages 746–751.

Ilija Subašić and Bettina Berendt. 2011. Peddling or creating? investigating the role of twitter in news reporting. In *Advances in Information Retrieval*, pages 207–213. Springer.

Luchen Tan and Charles L.A. Clarke. 2014. Succinct queries for linking and tracking news in social media. In *Proceedings of the 23rd ACM International Conference on Conference on Information and Knowledge Management*, CIKM '14, pages 1883–1886, New York, NY, USA. ACM.

Yi-jie Tang, Chang-Ye Li, and Hsin-Hsi Chen. 2011. A comparison between microblog corpus and balanced corpus from linguistic and sentimental perspectives. In *Analyzing Microtext*.

Karin Verspoor, K Bretonnel Cohen, and Lawrence Hunter. 2009. The textual characteristics of traditional and open access scientific journals are similar. *BMC bioinformatics*, 10(1):183.

William Webber, Alistair Moffat, and Justin Zobel. 2010. A similarity measure for indefinite rankings. *ACM Transactions on Information Systems (TOIS)*, 28(4):20.

The Discovery of Natural Typing Annotations: User-produced Potential Chinese Word Delimiters

Dakui Zhang[1], Yu Mao[1], Yang Liu[1], Hanshi Wang[2], Chuyuan Wei[1], Shiping Tang[1]

[1]Beijing Institute of Technology, Beijing, China

[2]Capital Normal University, Beijing, China

{sbirdge,maoyubit,yan9liu,necrostone,weichuyuan}@gmail.com, simontangbit@bit.edu.cn

Abstract

Human labeled corpus is indispensable for the training of supervised word segmenters. However, it is time-consuming and labor-intensive to label corpus manually. During the process of typing Chinese text by Pingyin, people usually need to type "space" or numeric keys to choose the words due to homophones, which can be viewed as a cue for segmentation. We argue that such a process can be used to build a labeled corpus in a more natural way. Thus, in this paper, we investigate Natural Typing Annotations (NTAs) that are potential word delimiters produced by users while typing Chinese. A detailed analysis on over three hundred user-produced texts containing NTAs reveals that high-quality NTAs mostly agree with gold segmentation and, consequently, can be used for improving the performance of supervised word segmentation model in out-of-domain. Experiments show that a classification model combined with a voting mechanism can reliably identify the high-quality NTAs texts that are more readily available labeled corpus. Furthermore, the NTAs might be particularly useful to deal with out-of-vocabulary (OOV) words such as proper names and neo-logisms.

1 Introduction

Unlike English text in which sentences are sequences of words delimited by white spaces, in Chinese text, sentences are usually represented and stored as strings of Chinese characters without similar natural delimiters. To find the basic language units, i.e. words, segmentation is a necessary initial step for Chinese language processing.

Currently most of state-of-the-art methods for Chinese word segmentation (CWS) are based on supervised learning, which depend on large scale annotated corpus. These supervised methods obtain high accuracies on newswire (Xue and Shen, 2003; Zhang and Clark, 2007; Jiang et al., 2009; Zhao et al., 2010; Sun and Xu, 2011). However, manually annotated training data mostly come from the news domain, and the performance can drop severely when the test data shift from newswire to blogs, computer forums, and Internet literature (Liu and Zhang, 2012;).Supervised approaches often have a high requirement on the quality and quantity of annotated corpus, which is always not easy to build. As a result, many previous methods utilize the information of free data which contain limited but useful segmentation information over the Internet, including large-scale unlabeled data, domain-specific lexicons and semi-annotated web pages such as Wikipedia. There has been work on making use of both unlabeled data (Li and Sun, 2009; Sun and Xu, 2011; Wang et al., 2011; Qiu et al., 2014) and Wikipedia (Jiang et al., 2013; Liu et al., 2014;) to improve segmentation. But none of them notice the segmentation information produced by users while typing Chinese.

Chinese is unique due to its logographic writing system. Chinese users cannot directly type in Chinese words using a QWERTY keyboard. Input methods have been proposed to assist users to type in Chinese words (Chen, 1997). Substantial information has been produced, but not recorded and stored during text typing process.

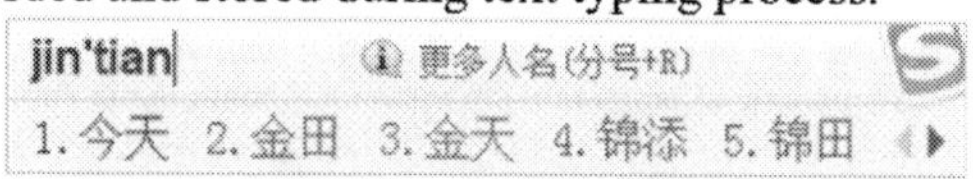

Figure 1: Typical Chinese Pinyin input method (Sogou-Pinyin).

The typical way to type in Chinese words is in a sequential manner (Wang et al., 2001). iRearch (2009) showed that Pinyin input methods have the biggest share of Chinese speakers. We take one of them for example. Suppose users want to type in Chinese word "今天(today)". Firstly, they mentally generate and physically type in corresponding Pinyin "jintian". Then, a Chinese Pinyin input method displays a list of Chinese homophones, as shown in Figure 1. Finally, users visually search the target word from candidates and select numeric key, e.g. '1'-'9'(<NUM#1>-<NUM#9>) or space key (<SPACE>, a shortcut

Proceedings of the 53rd Annual Meeting of the Association for Computational Linguistics and the 7th International Joint Conference on Natural Language Processing (Short Papers), pages 662–667, Beijing, China, July 26-31, 2015. ©2015 Association for Computational Linguistics

for numeric key '1') to get the target word (Zheng et al., 2011). Other Chinese input methods, like Wubi, also take these three steps. Typing English words does not involve the last two steps, which indicates that it is on one side more complicated for Chinese users to type in Chinese words than English, but on the other side more convenient for us to obtain additional information produced by users in typing process. We define numeric keys and the space key as **selection keys** for choosing the target word. For sentence "今天天气不错。(Nice weather today.)", one general sequence with selection keys is like "今天(today)<SPACE>天气(weather)<NUM#2>不错(not bad)<SPACE>。" or "今天 (today) <SPACE>天气不错 (weather is not bad) <SPACE>。" In a certain sense, these user-produced selection keys play a role of word delimiters in a very natural way.

In this paper, we propose the concept of Natural Typing Annotations (NTAs) that are potential word delimiters produced by users while typing Chinese words, and verify that it is plausible to automatically generate labeled data for CWS by exploiting NTAs. According to the principle of statistical sampling, texts with NTAs are gathered from 384 users. Specifically, since the ultimate goal is to exploit NTAs to automatically generate labeled data for word segmentation, the main task is to select high-quality NTAs, which largely overlap with gold segmentation. We do this by 1) training a classifier to distinguish acceptable-quality NTAs from low-quality ones, and then 2) using a voting mechanism to further locate the high-quality NTAs among those identified by the classifier in the first step. Experiments show that Support Vector Machine (SVM) and voting mechanism are effective for this work and the high-quality NTAs texts can be used as the training data for improving the performance of supervised word segmentation model in out-of-domain. In addition, some evidence is provided that user-produced NTAs might be particularly useful to deal with out-of-vocabulary (OOV) words.

In the rest of the paper, we briefly introduce the gold standard and baseline segmenter of our work in section 2, then describe the definition and characteristic of natural typing annotations (NTAs) in section 3, and finally elaborate on the strategy of locating high-quality NTAs texts in section 4.After giving the experimental results and analysis in section 5, we come to the conclusion and the implication of future work.

2 Gold Standard and Baseline segmenter

There are many different standards for word segmentation, and different tasks usually need different standards. The Sighan Bakeoff uses four well-known standards made by four different organizations: Academia Sinica (AS), City University of Hong Kong (CU), Peking University (PKU), and Microsoft Research (MSR). In this study, we take MSR segmentation standard as **gold standard**. Following the work of Zhao et al. (2010) and Sun and Xu (2011), a Conditional Random Fields (CRF) model (Lafferty et al., 2001) is trained with the training corpus of MSR from Sighan Bakeoff-2, to be a baseline segmenter. This general-purpose segmenter is called as **CRF+MSR** in this paper.

3 Natural Typing Annotations Texts

3.1 Formulation

A Chinese sentence is represented as $S = c_1c_2...c_N$ (c_i stands for a Chinese character, N is the length of sentence S). One of the possible sequences with selection keys is defined as $\pi(S) = | c_1...c_{i_1-1} | c_{i_1}...c_{i_2-1} | ... | c_{n_1}...c_N |$.Here, we use the symbol "|" instead of each selection key. "|" is the "**Natural Typing Annotation (NTA)**", which is naturally annotated by users when typing Chinese words. Between the two neighboring "|"s is a **segment**. Then the user-produced $\pi(S) = | segment_1 | segment_2 | ... | segment_M |$ ($M \le N$, M is the number of segments in sentence S) is called as **NTAs text** or **NTAs corpus**.

3.2 Collection of NTAs Texts

We need to collect user-produced NTAs texts independently because there are no similar or alternative open corpora. We posted a public notice on the Internet to gather volunteer participants. For comparison, they were told to type in the same assigned test text while our software recorded the character sequence with NTAs. Two explanations are given as followed. First, to get more users' feedback and keep the significance level of the experiment, we only have 365 Chinese characters in the test text, which contains words with ambiguous meaning, named entities (NEs), neo-logisms and typo-prone words. Even the state-of-the-art segmenters cannot handle this test text very well. Second, according to statistical sampling theory, if we want a 95% confidence interval to have a margin of error less than 5%, the sample size should be no less than 384. Therefore, we randomly accept 384 volunteers to join our typing experiment and get user-produced NTAs texts from them.

3.3 Analysis of Collected NTAs Texts

Users' overall typing habit can be drawn through the analysis of the collected NTAs texts. We firstly focus on segment, because it is the basic unit in our texts. A total of 66,232 segments are obtained from all texts, but only 883 of them are not repeated. Using $Length(seg)$ to represent the length of a segment is easy to get a frequency distribution of different $Length(seg)$ and find that the length of frequent segments is largely concentrated during 1 to 4. The same statistics can be conducted separately with the word segmentation results by gold standard and CRF+MSR. We use relative frequencies to illustrate the overall trend of three results, as shown in Figure 2.

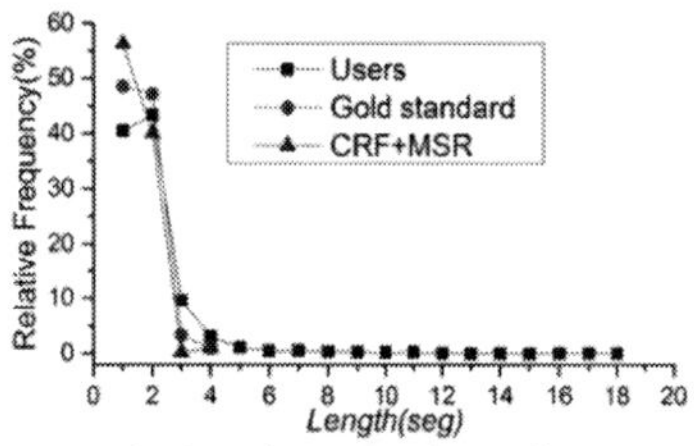

Figure 2: Relative frequencies of segment length from three segmentation.

The results suggest that most Chinese speakers are reluctant to put a long text string into one segment, which is roughly consistent with behavioral economics and psycho-linguistic. Users consciously avoid the mistakes that might be brought by typing in long sequence at a time. Besides, people seldom put illogical sequence of characters into one segment. Taking "主人公严守一把手机给扔了。(The leading character Yan Shouyi has thrown his cellphone away.) " for example, when participants input "给扔了 (have thrown) ", they choose to type in the material as "|给|扔|了|", "|给|扔了|" or "|给扔了|". No one types in the material as "|给扔|了|", because "|给扔|" has no logical meaning in Chinese. Consequently, the constitution of segment is a reflection of natural language logic.

4 High-quality NTAs Texts

4.1 User's Typing Patterns

In this section, we investigate the collected NTAs texts at the sentence level. Direct visual impression is that different users use different typing patterns to input Chinese. S_1 = "不过评价在三星级以上的这几款电脑(However, these several computers are assessed with more than 3 stars) " is taken as an example to explain the different situations. Just as what is shown in the following, $\pi_{gold}(S_1)$ is the gold segmentation of S_1, and others are representative sequences from different users.

$\pi_{gold}(S_1)$ = "|不过|评价|在|三星级|以上|的|这|几|款|电脑|"

$\pi_1(S_1)$ = "|不过|评价|在|三星级|以上|的|这几款|电脑|"

$\pi_2(S_1)$ = "|不过|评价|在|三|星|级|以上|的|这几|款|电脑|"

$\pi_3(S_1)$ = "|不过评价|在|三星级以上|的|这几款电脑|"

$\pi_4(S_1)$ = "|不过评价在三星级以上的|这几款电脑|"

$\pi_5(S_1)$ = "|不|过|评价|在|三|星|级|以|上|的|这|几|款|电|脑|"

We discover three typing patterns of users. The first one is **Discrete Pattern**, where the characters belonging to one segment in the light of gold standard are separated into several segments, such as $\pi_5(S_1)$. The second is **Adhesive Pattern**, which suggests that two or more adjacent individual words by gold standard come together to form one segment, like $\pi_3(S_1)$ and $\pi_4(S_1)$. The third is **Acceptable Pattern**, where user-produced segmentation is largely or exactly the same with the gold standard, such as $\pi_1(S_1)$ and $\pi_2(S_1)$. We find that discrete pattern and adhesive pattern are useless for word segmentation. So we call those NTAs texts that follow acceptable pattern **acceptable-quality NTAs texts**, and others low-quality ones. Furthermore, among acceptable-quality NTAs texts, some of them are more close to gold standard, which is called as **high-quality NTAs texts**. Our strategy is 1) to use a classifier to find all acceptable-quality NTAs texts, and then 2) to further locate the high-quality NTAs texts among those identified by the classifier in the previous step.

4.2 The Classification Approach

Identification of acceptable-quality NTAs texts is a typical binary classification problem. Effective and logical features should be identified to model a classifier. We select the following five features because they are simple but outstanding against other alternatives for this work.

$$Features = \left\{ \begin{array}{l} \text{Len}, \\ \text{SegNum}, \\ \text{SingleSegNum}, \\ \text{MaxConSingleSegNum}, \\ \text{MaxSegLen} \end{array} \right\}$$

Len is the abbreviation for length of a sentence, and **SegNum(SN)** stands for the number of the segments in a sentence. These two features can be used to determine whether the percentage of character number of a sentence and the segment number of a sentence is in a proper range.

SingleSegNum(SSN) stands for the number of the segments whose length equals 1 in a sentence. **MaxConSingleSegNum(MCSSN)** is the maximum number of continuous segments whose length is 1. **MaxSegLen(MSL)** means the length of segment with most characters. These three features can be used to identify whether discrete or adhesive phenomena prevail in a sentence.

4.3 The Voting Mechanism

As the classification approach brings lots of acceptable-quality NTAs texts, voting mechanism is introduced to further locate the high-quality NTAs texts. For a sentence S_i, there possibly exist different user-produced segmentations $\pi_1(S_i)$, $\pi_2(S_i)$, ..., $\pi_k(S_i)$ (k is the total number of these segmentations). If $\pi_j(S_i)$ appears in different users' texts, these texts practically vote for $\pi_j(S_i)$. Different users' texts practically vote for $\pi_j(S_i)$, which appears in these texts. Thus every sentence S_i in a text can get a score:

$$SCORE_{\pi_j(S_i)} = \log_2 count(\pi_j(S_i)) \quad (1)$$

$count(\pi_j(S_i))$ calculates how many users input S_i with segmentation $\pi_j(S_i)$. A text (namely a user) also has a score:

$$SCORE_{text} = \frac{\sum_{\pi_j(S_i)\in text} \log_2 count(\pi_j(S_i))}{num_{\pi_j(S_i)\in text}} \quad (2)$$

$num_{\pi_j(S_i)\in text}$ is the number of sentences in this text.

This score helps us to identify high-quality NTAs texts from all acceptable-quality ones.

5 Experiments

5.1 Identification of High-quality NTAs Texts

In this experiment, we verify the effectiveness of classifier and voting mechanism on locating high-quality NTAs texts from 384 collected ones. You can download part of our collected texts from *https://github.com/dakuiz/NTAs*.

5.1.1 The Classification Experiment

We randomly select 32 NTAs texts that contain 1,089 sentences, and then manually label them to form training set. Taking S_1 mentioned in 4.1 as an example, the manual-labeled training data are shown in table 1. The label 1 and 0 represent acceptable-quality and low-quality NTAs sentence separately.

	Len	SN	SSN	MCSSN	MSL	label
$\pi_1(S_1)$	16	8	2	1	3	1
$\pi_2(S_1)$	16	11	6	3	2	1
$\pi_3(S_1)$	16	5	2	1	5	0
$\pi_4(S_1)$	16	2	0	0	11	0
$\pi_5(S_1)$	16	15	14	12	2	0

Table 1: examples of training data for classifier.

Package of libSVM (Chang and Lin, 2011) is used here. Radial basis function is adopted as the kernel function where gamma value is set to 1/num_features and cost value is 1.

10-fold cross validation is used to validate the results. The 1,089 sentences are partitioned into ten parts randomly. Ten runs are performed with each run using a different part as the testing set. It is conducted ten times and every part should be testing set once. Classification accuracy of the experiment is listed in the table 2.

Num	Accuracy(%)
1	96.33
2	97.22
3	97.25
4	97.25
5	89.91
6	98.17
7	94.50
8	94.59
9	94.55
10	98.11
Average	95.79

Table 2: 10-fold cross validation results.

Since the results indicate the validity of our classification approach, we use this classifier to handle collected NTAs texts. If 85% of sentences in a text are acceptable-quality, we select this text as acceptable-quality NTAs text. Finally, we obtain 211 acceptable-quality NTAs texts from all 384 collected ones.

5.1.2 The Voting Experiment

According to voting mechanism in section 4.3, every acceptable-quality NTAs text can get a score to rank itself. Table3 shows top three high-quality NTAs texts with their user-produced word segmentation results compared with that of CRF+MSR. Because CRF+MSR is a general-purpose segmenter and test data does not come from news wire, its performance drops significantly in out-of-domain.

Table 3 suggests that high-quality NTAs texts are very close to gold standard of word segmentation. To discover the causes of errors, we manually inspected these three texts and found the major error is adhesive phenomenon between simple words. For example, gold segmentation "|这|几|款|" is formed as "|这几款|" by users. This is an error in word segmentation competition, but in some application scenarios, like machine translation, "|这几款|"is better than "|这|几|款|". Similar phenomena shed light on understanding what a "word" really is.

Word segmentation from	p	r	f	r_{oov}
CRF+MSR	90.86	92.02	91.43	50.00
Text#top1	**92.82**	90.19	**91.49**	**100.00**
Text#top2	**91.50**	88.29	89.87	**100.00**
Text#top3	90.38	87.33	88.83	**100.00**

Table 3: Test text word segmentation results from general-purpose segmenter and top 3 texts.

5.2 Effectiveness of High-quality NTAs Corpus on Improving Word Segmentation

It is generally agreed among researchers that users' behavioral patterns maintain consistent over a long period of time (Zhang et al., 2013; Stephane, 2009). In table 3, we listed top 3 high-quality NTAs texts. Users who generated these three NTAs texts are stable sources to provide more well-segmented texts.

To evaluate the effectiveness of high-quality NTAs corpus on building training data for segmenter, we use a web crawler to get 40k Micro-blog (weibo.com) corpus and randomly divided it into 4 equal shares, i.e. A, B, C, T text. The provider of top1 text is invited to retype A text to produce A NTAs text. B and C NTAs texts are separately obtained from other two providers. We use A, B, C NTAs texts as training data to get a CRF segmentation model, which is called as **CRF+NTAs**. Then we train anther CRF segmenter with a combination of A, B, C NTAs texts and the training corpus of MSR from Bakeoff-2, called as **CRF+MSR+NTAs**. We select 1,000 sentences from T text to manually segment by gold standard, and use them to form our test set that contains 6528 characters. The results of the three segmenters on this Micro-blog test set is shown in table 4.

The model directly trained by Micro-blog high-quality NTAs corpus is better than general-purpose segmenter but far from the model trained by the combination of MSR and Micro-blog high-quality NTAs corpus. This is the most compelling evidence to show that high-quality NTAs corpus can be used for improving word segmentation model in out-of-domain.

Word segmentation from	p	r	f
CRF+MSR	88.95	90.63	89.78
CRF+NTAs	**92.38**	89.76	**91.05**
CRF+MSR+NTAs	**96.27**	**94.83**	**95.54**

Table 4: Segmenters' results on test data.

We also find out that the NTAs might be particularly useful to identify OOV words, such as proper names and neo-logisms. If users frequently put some characters in one segment, this segment may be some new word or the new internet slang, such as "白富美(white, rich and pretty) ", "萌萌哒(very cute)", "十动然拒(someone is moved but refuses to become girl/boyfriend)", etc.

6 Conclusion and Future Work

In this paper, we investigate Natural Typing Annotations (NTAs) that are potential word delimiters generated by Chinese speakers while typing Chinese words. The effectiveness of high-quality NTAs corpus on improving word segmentation is evaluated.

Though it is convenient for users to read, sequence of pure characters, namely without any recorded delimiters produced by inputters, loses lots of valuable information, e.g. NTAs. We strongly recommend that NTAs can be recorded in an invisible manner for normal users by dominant text editors, such as MS Word, Notepad, vi, emacs, etc.

In future, we will: 1) collect more NTAs texts from various users; 2) do further work on how to fully leverage NTAs to improve word segmentation; 3) call for dominant text editors to record NTAs.

Acknowledgments

Sincere thanks to the three anonymous reviewers for their thorough reviewing and valuable suggestions! The authors were supported by the National Strategic Basic Research Program ("973" Program) of the Ministry of Science and Technology of China (No. 2012CB720702 and 2013CB329303) and National Science Foundation of China (No. 61303105).

Reference

Chih-Chung Chang, Chih-Jen Lin. 2011. *LIBSVM: A library for support vector machines*. In TIST.

Yuan Chen. 1997.*Chinese Language Processing*. Shanghai Education publishing company.

iRearch.2009. *2009 China Desktop Software Development Research Report.* http://report.iresearch.cn/1290.html.

Wenbin Jiang, Liang Huang, Qun Liu. 2009. *Automatic adaptation of annotation standards: Chinese word segmentation and pos tagging – a case study*. In ACL-AFNLP.

John D. Lafferty, Andrew McCallum, Fernando C. N. Pereira. 2001. *Conditional random fields: Probabilistic models for segmenting and labeling sequence data*. In ICML.

Zhongguo Li, Maosong Sun. 2009. *Punctuation as Implicit Annotations for Chinese Word Segmentation*. Computational Linguistics.

Wenbin Jiang, Meng Sun, Yajuan Lü, Yating Yang, Qun Liu. 2013. *Discriminative Learning with Natural Annotations: Word Segmentation as a Case Study*. In ACL.

Yang Liu, Yue Zhang. 2012. *Unsupervised domain adaptation for joint segmentation and POS-tagging*. In COLING.

Yijia Liu, Yue Zhang, Wanxiang Che, Ting Liu, Fan Wu. 2014. *Domain Adaptation for CRF-based Chinese Word Segmentation using Free Annotations*. In EMNLP.

Xipeng Qiu, ChaoChao Huang, Xuanjing Huang. 2014. *Automatic Corpus Expansion for Chinese Word Segmentation by Exploiting the Redundancy of Web Information*. In COLING.

Weiwei Sun, Jia Xu. 2011. *Enhancing chinese word segmentation using unlabeled data*. In EMNLP.

Lucas Stephane. 2009. *User Behavior Patterns: Gathering, Analysis, Simulation and Prediction*. In HCI.

Jingtao Wang, Shumin Zhai, Hui Su. 2001. *Chinese input with keyboard and eye-tracking: an anatomical study*.In CHI.

Yiou Wang, Jun'ichi Kazama, Yoshimasa Tsuruoka,Wenliang Chen, Yujie Zhang, Kentaro Torisawa. 2011. *Improving chinese word segmentation and pos tagging with semi-supervised methods using large auto-analyzed data*. In IJCNLP.

Nianwen Xue, Libin Shen. 2003. *Chinese word segmentation as lmr tagging*. In SIGHAN.

Chunhong Zhang, Yaxi He, Yang Ji. 2013. *Temporal Pattern of User Behavior in Micro-blog*. In JSW.

Yue Zhang, Stephen Clark. 2007. *Chinese segmentation with a word-based perceptron algorithm*. In ACL.

Hai Zhao, Chang-Ning Huang, Mu Li, Bao-Liang Lu. 2010. *A unified character-based tagging framework for chinese word segmentation*. In ACM.

Yabin Zheng, Lixing Xie, Zhiyuan Liu, Maosong Sun, Yang zhang, Liyun Ru. 2011. *Why Press Backspace? Understanding User Input Behaviors in Chinese Pinyin Input Method*. In ACL.

One Tense per Scene: Predicting Tense in Chinese Conversations

Tao Ge[1,2], **Heng Ji**[3], **Baobao Chang**[1,2], **Zhifang Sui**[1,2]
[1]Key Laboratory of Computational Linguistics, Ministry of Education,
School of EECS, Peking University, Beijing, 100871, China
[2]Collaborative Innovation Center for Language Ability, Xuzhou, Jiangsu, 221009, China
[3]Computer Science Department, Rensselaer Polytechnic Institute, Troy, NY 12180, USA
getao@pku.edu.cn, jih@rpi.edu,
chbb@pku.edu.cn, szf@pku.edu.cn

Abstract

We study the problem of predicting tense in Chinese conversations. The unique challenges include: (1) Chinese verbs do not have explicit lexical or grammatical forms to indicate tense; (2) Tense information is often implicitly hidden outside of the target sentence. To tackle these challenges, we first propose a set of novel sentence-level (local) features using rich linguistic resources and then propose a new hypothesis of "One tense per scene" to incorporate scene-level (global) evidence to enhance the performance. Experimental results demonstrate the power of this hybrid approach, which can serve as a new and promising benchmark.

1 Introduction

In natural languages, tense is important to indicate the time at which an action or event takes place. In some languages such as Chinese, verbs do not have explicit morphological or grammatical forms to indicate their tense information. Therefore, automatic tense prediction is important for both human's deep understanding of these languages as well as downstream natural language processing tasks (e.g., machine translation (Liu et al., 2011)).

In this paper, we concern "semantic" tense (time of the event relative to speech time) as opposed to morphosyntactic tense systems found in many languages. Our goal is to predict the tense (past, present or future) of the main predicate[1] of each sentence in a Chinese conversation, which has never been thoroughly studied before but is extremely important for conversation understanding.

Some recent work (Ye et al., 2006; Xue and Zhang, 2014; Zhang and Xue, 2014) on Chinese tense prediction found that tense in written language can be effectively predicted by some features in local contexts such as aspectual markers (e.g. 着 *(zhe)*, 了 *(le)*, 过 *(guo)*) and time expressions (e.g., 昨天 *(yesterday)*). However, it is much more challenging to predict tense in Chinese conversations and there has not been an effective set of rules to predict Chinese tense so far due to the complexity of language-specific phenomena. Let's look at the examples shown in Table 1.

In general, there are three unique challenges for tense prediction in Chinese conversations:

(1) Informal verbal expressions: sentences in a conversation are often grammatically incorrect, which makes aspectual marker based evidence unreliable. Moreover, sentences in a conversation often omit important sentence components. For example, in conversation 1 in Table 1, "如果*(if)*" which is a very important cue to predict tense of verb "废*(destroy)*" is omitted.

(2) Effects of interactions on tense: In contrast to other genres, conversations are interactive, which may have an effect on tense: in some cases, tense can only be inferred by understanding the interactions. For example, we can see from conversations 2, 3 and 4 in Table 1 that when the second person (你*(you)*) is used as the object of the predicate "告诉*(tell)*", the predicate describes the action during the conversation and thus its tense is present. In contrast, when the third person is used in a sentence, it is unlikely that the tense of the predicate is present because it does not describe an action during the conversation. This challenge is unique to Chinese conversations.

(3) Tense ambiguity in a single sentence: Sentence-level analysis is often inadequate to disambiguate tense. For example, it is impossible to determine whether "告诉*(tell)*" in conversations 3 and 4 in Table 1 is a past action (the speaker already told) or a future action (the speaker hasn't told yet) only based on sentence-level contexts.

[1]The main predicate of a sentence can be considered equal to the root of a dependency parse

Proceedings of the 53rd Annual Meeting of the Association for Computational Linguistics and the 7th International Joint Conference on Natural Language Processing (Short Papers), pages 668–673,
Beijing, China, July 26-31, 2015.

1	a: [如果(if)]你(you)动(touch)我(my)儿子(son)一下(once)，我(I)先(first)废(destroy)了你(you)。(If you touch my son, I'll destroy you.)
2	b: 我(I)告诉(tell)你(you)一声，航班(flight)取消(cancel)了。(I'm telling you: the flight is canceled.)
3	c:你 (you)刚刚 (just now)和他(to him)说(say)什么(what)了？ (What did you say to him just now?) d: 我(I)[刚才(just now)]告诉(tell)他(him)一声，航班(flight)取消(cancel)了。(I told him the flight is canceled.)
4	e: 你(you)要(will)干(do)吗(what)去(go)？ (What are you going to do?) f: 我(I)[要(will)]告诉(tell)他(him)一声，航班(fight)取消(cancel)了。(I'll tell him the flight is canceled.)
5	a: 发生(happen)了什么(what)事情(event)？ (What happened?) b: 我(I)跟吴清(Wu Qing)一起(with) (I was with Wu Qing) b: 我们(We)在(keep)监视(surveilance)一批货(a cargo) (We were keeping surveillance on a cargo...) b: 我们(We)怀疑(suspect)那些(thoses)是(are)偷来的(stolen)文物(antiques) (We suspected those were stolen antiques) b: 那些人(those guys)，突然(suddenly)就走(walk)出来(out)打(beat)我们(us) (Suddenly, all those guys walked out to beat us up!) b: 我(I)要(want)报警(call the police)他们(they)才停手(stop) (They stopped only when I tried to call the police)

Table 1: Five sample conversations that show the challenges in tense prediction in Chinese conversations. a,b,c,d at the beginning of each sentence denote various speakers. The words in square brackets are **omitted content** in the original sentences and the underlined words are main predicates.

In fact, the sentence in conversation 3 omits "刚才*(just now)*" which indicates past tense and the sentence in the conversation 4 omits "要*(will)*" which indicates future tense. If we add the omitted word back to the original sentence, there will not be tense ambiguity.

To tackle the above challenges, we propose to predict tense in Chinese conversations from two views – sentence-level (local) and scene-level (global). We first develop a local classifier with linguistic knowledge and new conversation-specific features (Section 2.1). Then we propose a novel framework to exploit the global contexts of the entire scene to infer tense, based on a new "One tense per scene" hypothesis (Section 2.2). We created a new a benchmark data set[2], which contains 294 conversations (1,857 sentences) and demonstrated the effectiveness of our approach.

ble

2 Method

2.1 Local Predictor

We develop a Maximum Entropy (MaxEnt) classifier (Zhang, 2004) as the local predictor.

Basic features: The unigrams, bigrams and trigrams of a sentence.

Dependency parsing features: We use the Stanford parser (Chen and Manning, 2014) to conduct dependency parsing[3] on the target sentences and use dependency paths associated with the main predicate of a sentence as well as their dependency types as features. By using the parsing features, we can not only find aspectual markers (e.g., "了") but also capture the effect of sentence structures on the tense.

Linguistic knowledge features: We also exploit the following linguistic knowledge from the Grammatical Knowledge-base of Contemporary Chinese (Yu et al., 1998) (also known as GKB):

- Tense of time expressions: GKB lists all common time expressions and their associated tense. For example, GKB can tell us "往年 *(previous years)*" and "中世纪 *(Middle Ages)*" can only be associated with the past tense.

- Function of conjunction words: Some conjunction words may have an effect on tense. For example, the conjunction word "如果*(if)*" indicates a conditional clause and the main predicate of this sentence is likely to be future tense. GKB can tell us the function of common Chinese conjunction words.

Conversation-specific features: As mentioned in Section 1, different person roles being the subject or the object of a predicate may have an effect on the tense in a conversation. We analyze the person roles of the subject and the object of the main predicate and encode them as features, which helps our model understand effects of interactions on tense.

2.2 Global Predictor

As we discussed before, tense ambiguity in a sentence arises from the omissions of sentence components. According to the principle of efficient information transmission (Jaeger and Levy, 2006;

[2]http://nlp.cs.rpi.edu/data/chinesetense.zip

[3]We use CCProcessed dependencies.

Jaeger, 2010) and Gricean Maxims (Grice et al., 1975) in cooperative theory, the omitted elements can be predicted by considering contextual information and the tense can be further disambiguated. In order to better predict tense, we propose a new hypothesis:

One tense per scene: Within a scene, tense in sentences tends to be consistent and coherent.

During a conversation, a speaker/listener can know the tense of a predicate by either a tense indicator in the target sentence or scene-level tense analysis. **A scene** is a subdivision of a conversation in which the time is continuous and the topic is highly coherent and which does not usually involve a change of tense. For example, for the conversation 3 in Table 1, we can learn the scene is about the past from the word "刚刚 *(just now)*" in the first sentence. Therefore, we can exploit this clue to determine the tense of "告诉*(tell)*" as past.

Therefore, when we are not sure which tense of the main predicate in a sentence should be, we can consider the tense of the entire scene. For example, the conversation 5 in Table 1 is about a past scene because the whole conversation is about a past event. For the sentence "我们(We)在(keep)监视(surveillance)一批货(a cargo)" where the tense of the predicate is ambiguous (past tense and present tense are both reasonable), we can exploit the tense of the scene (past) to determine its tense as past.

Global tense prediction

Inspired by the burst detection algorithm proposed by Kleinberg (2003), we use a 3-state automaton sequence model to globally predict tense based on the above hypothesis. In a conversation with n sentences, each sentence is one element in the sequence. The sentence's tense can be seen as the hidden state and the sentence's features are the observation. Formally, we define the tense in the ith sentence as t_i and the observations (i.e., features) in the sentence as o_i. The goal of this model is to output an optimal sequence $\boldsymbol{t}^* = \{t_1^*, t_2^*, ..., t_n^*\}$ that minimizes the cost function defined as follows:

$$Cost(\boldsymbol{t}, \boldsymbol{o}) = \lambda \sum_{i=1}^{n} -lnP(t_i|o_i) + (1-\lambda) \sum_{i=1}^{n-1} \mathbf{1}(t_{i+1} \neq t_i) \quad (1)$$

where $\mathbf{1}(\cdot)$ is an indicator function.

As we can see in (1), the cost function consists of two parts. The first part is the negative log likelihood of the local prediction, allowing the model to incorporate the results from the local predictor. The second part is the cost of tense inconsistency between adjacent sentences, which enables the model to take into account tense consistency in a scene. Finding the optimal sequence is a decoding process, which can be done using Viterbi algorithm in $O(n)$ time. The parameter λ is used for adjusting weights of these two parts. If $\lambda = 1$, the predictor will not consider global tense consistency and thus the optimal sequence $\boldsymbol{t}^*$ will be the same as the output of the local predictor.

Figure 1 shows how the global predictor works for predicting the tense in the conversation 5 in Table 1. The global predictor can correct wrong local predictions, especially less confident ones.

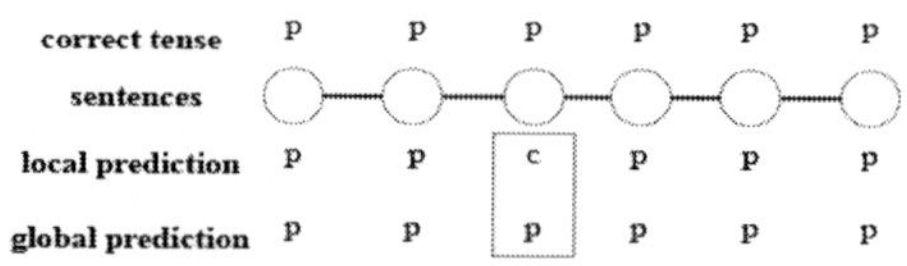

Figure 1: Global tense prediction for the conversation 5 in Table 1.

3 Experiments

3.1 Data and Scoring Metric

To the best of our knowledge, tense prediction in Chinese conversations has never been studied before and there is no existing benchmark for evaluation. We collected 294 conversations (including 1,857 sentences) from 25 popular Chinese movies, dramas and TV shows. Each conversation contains 2-18 sentences. We manually annotate the main predicate and its tense in each sentence. We use ICTCLAS (Zhang et al., 2003) to do word segmentation as preprocessing.

Since tense prediction can be seen as a multi-class classification problem, we use *accuracy* as the metric to evaluate the performance. We randomly split our dataset into three sets: training set (244 conversations), development set (25 conversations) and test set (25 conversations) for evaluation. In evaluation, we ignore imperative sentences and sentences without predicates.

3.2 Experimental Results

We compare our approach with the following baselines:

- Majority: We label every instance with the majority tense (present tense).

- Local predictor with basic features (Local(b))
- Local predictor with basic features + dependency parsing features (Local(b+p))
- Local predictor with basic features + dependency parsing features + linguistic knowledge features (Local(b+p+l))
- Local predictor + all features introduced in Section 2.1 (Local(all))
- Conditional Random Fields (CRFs): We model a conversation as a sequence of sentences and predict tense using CRFs (Lafferty et al., 2001). We implement CRFs using CRFsuite (Okazaki, 2007) with all features introduced in Section 2.1.

Among the baselines, Local(b+p) is the most similar model to the approaches in previous work on Chinese tense prediction in written languages (Ye et al., 2006; Xue, 2008; Liu et al., 2011). Recent work (Zhang and Xue, 2014) used eventuality and modality labels as features that derived from a classifier trained on an annotated corpus. However, the annotated corpus for training the eventuality and modality classifier is not publicly available, we cannot duplicate their approaches.

	Dev	Test
Majority	65.13%	54.01%
Local(b)	69.74%	66.42%
Local(b+p)	70.39%	67.15%
Local(b+p+l)	71.05%	69.34%
Local(all)	71.05%	69.34%
CRFs	69.74%	64.96%
Global	**72.37%**	**72.26%**

Table 2: Tense prediction accuracy.

Table 2 shows the results of various models. For our global predictor, the optimal λ (0.4) is tuned on the development set and used on the test set.

According to Table 2, n-grams and dependency parsing features[4] are useful to predict tense, and linguistic knowledge can further improve the accuracy of tense prediction. However, adding conversation-specific features (interaction features) does not benefit Local(b+p+l). The first reason is that the subject and the object of the predicates in many sentences are omitted, which is common in Chinese conversations. The other reason, also the main reason, is that simply using the person roles of the subject and the object is not sufficient to depict the interaction. For example, the subject and the object of the following sentences have the same person role but have different tenses because "警告(warn)" is the current action of the speaker but "教(teach)" is not. Therefore, to exploit the interaction features of a conversation, we must deeply understand the meanings of action verbs.

我(I)警告(warn)你(you)。 (I'm warning you.)

我(I)教(teach)你(you)。 (I'll teach you.)

The global predictor significantly improves the local predictor's performance (at 95% confidence level according to Wilcoxon Signed-Rank Test), which verifies the effectiveness of "One tense per scene" hypothesis for tense prediction. It is notable that CRFs do not work well on our dataset. The reason is that the transition pattern of tenses in a sequence of sentences is not easy to learn, especially when the size of training data is not very large. In many cases, the tense of a verb in a sentence is determined by features within the sentence, which has nothing to do with tense transition. In these cases, learning tense transition patterns will mislead the model and accordingly affect the performance. In contrast, our global model is more robust because it is based on our "One tense per scene" hypothesis which can be seen as prior linguistic knowledge, thus achieves good performance even when the training data is not sufficient.

3.3 Discussion

There are still many remaining challenges for tense prediction in Chinese conversations:

Omission detection: The biggest challenge for this task is the omission of sentence components. As shown in Table 1, if omitted words can be recovered, it will be less likely to make a wrong prediction.

Word Sense Disambiguation: Some function words which can indicate tense are ambiguous. For example, the function word "要" has many senses. It can mean 将要*(will)*, 想要*(want)* and 需

[4]We also tried adding POS tags to dependency paths but didn't see improvements because POS information has been implicitly indicated by dependency types and thus becomes redundant.

要*(need)*, and also it is sometimes used to present an option. It is difficult for a system to correctly predict tense unless it can disambiguate the sense of such function words:

- 一会儿(later)他(he)要 **(will)**过来 (come)。(He**'ll** come here later.)
- 我 (I)要 **(want)** 吃 (eat) 苹果 (apples)。(I **want** to eat apples)
- 你(you)要**(need)**多多(much)锻炼(exercise) (You **need** to take more exercises.)
- 为什么(why)你(you)要**(opt)**救(save)我(me)? (Why did you save me?)

Verb Tense Preference: Different verbs may have different tense preferences. For example, "以为*(think)*" is often used in the past tense while "认为*(think)*" is usually in the present tense:

- 我(I)以为**(think)**他(he)不会(won't)来(come) (I **thought** he would not come.)
- 我(I)认为**(think)**他(he)不会(won't)来(come) (I **think** he won't come.)

Generic and specific subject/object: Whether the subject/object is generic or specific has an effect on tense. For example, in the sentence "那场(that)战争(war)太(very)残酷(brutal)了", the predicate "残酷(brutal)" is in the past tense while in the sentence "战争(war)太(very)残酷(brutal)了", the predicate "残酷(brutal)" is in the present tense.

4 Related Work

Early work on Chinese tense prediction (Ye et al., 2006; Xue, 2008) modeled this task as a multi-class classification problem and used machine learning approaches to solve the problem. Recent work (Liu et al., 2011; Xue and Zhang, 2014; Zhang and Xue, 2014) studied distant annotation of tense from a bilingual parallel corpus. Among them, Xue and Zhang (2014) and Zhang and Xue (2014) improved tense prediction by using eventuality and modality labels. However, none of the previous work focused on the specific challenge of the tense prediction in oral languages although the dataset used by Liu et al. (2011) includes conversations. In contrast, this paper presents the unique challenges and corresponding solutions to tense prediction in conversations.

5 Conclusions and Future Work

This paper presents the importance and challenges of tense prediction in Chinese conversations and proposes a novel solution to the challenges.

In the future, we plan to further study this problem by focusing on omission detection, verb tense preference from the view of pragmatics, and jointly learning the local and global predictors. In addition, we will study predicting the tense of multiple predicates in a sentence and identifying imperative sentences in a conversation, which is also a challenge of tense prediction.

Acknowledgments

We thank all the anonymous reviewers for their constructive suggestions. We thank Prof. Shiwen Yu and Xun Wang for providing insights from Chinese linguistics. This work is supported by National Key Basic Research Program of China 2014CB340504, NSFC project 61375074, U.S. DARPA Award No. FA8750-13-2-0045 and China Scholarship Council (CSC, No. 201406010174). The contact author of this paper is Zhifang Sui.

References

Danqi Chen and Christopher D Manning. 2014. A fast and accurate dependency parser using neural networks. In *EMNLP*.

H Paul Grice, Peter Cole, and Jerry L Morgan. 1975. Syntax and semantics. *Logic and conversation*, 3:41–58.

TF Jaeger and Roger P Levy. 2006. Speakers optimize information density through syntactic reduction. In *Advances in neural information processing systems*.

T Florian Jaeger. 2010. Redundancy and reduction: Speakers manage syntactic information density. *Cognitive psychology*, 61(1):23–62.

Jon Kleinberg. 2003. Bursty and hierarchical structure in streams. *Data Mining and Knowledge Discovery*, 7(4):373–397.

John Lafferty, Andrew McCallum, and Fernando CN Pereira. 2001. Conditional random fields: Probabilistic models for segmenting and labeling sequence data.

Feifan Liu, Fei Liu, and Yang Liu. 2011. Learning from Chinese-English parallel data for Chinese tense prediction. In *IJCNLP*.

Naoaki Okazaki. 2007. CRFsuite: a fast implementation of conditional random fields (CRFs).

Nianwen Xue and Yuchen Zhang. 2014. Buy one get one free: Distant annotation of Chinese tense, event type, and modality. In *LREC*.

Nianwen Xue. 2008. Automatic inference of the temporal location of situations in Chinese text. In *EMNLP*.

Yang Ye, Victoria Li Fossum, and Steven Abney. 2006. Latent features in automatic tense translation between Chinese and English. In *SIGHAN workshop*.

Shiwen Yu, Xuefeng Zhu, Hui Wang, and Yunyun Zhang. 1998. The grammatical knowledge-base of contemporary Chinese—a complete specification.

Yucheng Zhang and Nianwen Xue. 2014. Automatic inference of the tense of Chinese events using implicit information. In *EMNLP*.

Hua-Ping Zhang, Hong-Kui Yu, De-Yi Xiong, and Qun Liu. 2003. Hhmm-based Chinese lexical analyzer ictclas. In *SIGHAN workshop*.

Le Zhang. 2004. Maximum entropy modeling toolkit for Python and C++.

A Language-Independent Feature Schema for Inflectional Morphology

John Sylak-Glassman*, Christo Kirov*, David Yarowsky, Roger Que****
*Center for Language and Speech Processing
**Department of Computer Science
Johns Hopkins University
Baltimore, MD 21218
jcsg@jhu.edu, ckirov@gmail.com, yarowsky@jhu.edu, query@jhu.edu

Abstract

This paper presents a universal morphological feature schema that represents the finest distinctions in meaning that are expressed by overt, affixal inflectional morphology across languages. This schema is used to universalize data extracted from Wiktionary via a robust multidimensional table parsing algorithm and feature mapping algorithms, yielding 883,965 instantiated paradigms in 352 languages. These data are shown to be effective for training morphological analyzers, yielding significant accuracy gains when applied to Durrett and DeNero's (2013) paradigm learning framework.

1 Introduction

Semantically detailed and typologically-informed morphological analysis that is broadly cross-linguistically applicable and interoperable has the potential to improve many NLP applications, including machine translation (particularly of morphologically rich languages), parsing (Choi et al., 2015; Zeman, 2008; Mikulová et al., 2006), n-gram language models, information extraction, and co-reference resolution.

To do large-scale cross-linguistic analysis and translation, it is necessary to be able to compare the meanings of morphemes using a single, well-defined framework. Haspelmath (2010) notes that while morphological categories will never map with perfect precision across languages and can only be exhaustively defined within a single language, practitioners of linguistic typology have typically recognized that there is sufficient similarity in these categories across languages to do meaningful comparison. For this purpose, Haspelmath (2010) proposes that typologists precisely define dedicated language-independent comparative concepts and identify the presence of these concepts in specific languages. In this spirit, we present a universal morphological feature schema, in which features that have a status akin to those of comparative concepts are used to represent the finest distinctions in meaning that are expressed by inflectional morphology across languages. This schema can in turn be used to universalize morphological data from the world's languages, which allows for direct comparison and translation of morphological material across languages. This greatly increases the amount of data available to morphological analysis tools, since data from any language can be specified in a common format with the same features.

Wiktionary constitutes one of the largest available sources of complete morphological paradigms across diverse languages, with substantial ongoing growth in language and lemma coverage, and hence forms a natural source of data for broadly multilingual supervised learning. Wiktionary paradigm table formats, however, are often complex, nested, 2-3 dimensional structures intended for human readability rather than machine parsing, and are broadly inconsistent across languages and Wiktionary editions. This paper presents an original, robust multidimensional table parsing system that generalizes effectively across these languages, collectively yielding significant gains in supervised morphological paradigm learning in Durrett and DeNero's (2013) framework.

2 Universal Morphological Feature Schema

The purpose of the universal morphological feature schema is to allow any given overt, affixal (non-root) inflectional morpheme in any language to be given a precise, language-independent definition. The schema is composed of a set of features that represent semantic "atoms" that are never decomposed into more finely differentiated meanings in any natural language. This ensures that the meanings of all inflectional morphemes are able to be represented either through single features or through multiple features in combina-

Proceedings of the 53rd Annual Meeting of the Association for Computational Linguistics and the 7th International Joint Conference on Natural Language Processing (Short Papers), pages 674–680,
Beijing, China, July 26-31, 2015.

tion. These features capture only the semantic content of morphemes, but can be integrated into existing frameworks that precisely indicate morpheme form (Sagot and Walther, 2013) or automatically discover it (Dreyer and Eisner, 2011; Hammarström, 2006; Goldsmith, 2001). The fact that the schema is meant to capture only the meanings of overt, non-root affixal morphemes restricts the semantic-conceptual space that must be captured by its features and renders an interlingual approach to representing inflectional morphology feasible.

The universal morphological feature schema is most similar to tagset systematization efforts across multiple languages, such as the Universal Dependencies Project (Choi et al., 2015) and Interset (Zeman, 2008). While these efforts encode similar morphological features to the current schema, their goal is different, namely to systematize pre-existing tagsets, which include lexical and syntactic information, for 30 specific languages. The goal of the schema presented here is to capture the most basic meanings encoded by inflectional morphology across all the world's languages and to define those meanings in a language-independent manner. Because of its wide-scope, our universal morphological feature schema will likely need to include other features and even other dimensions of meaning, for which the authors invite suggestions.

2.1 Construction Methodology

The first step in constructing the universal morphological feature schema was to identify the dimensions of meaning (e.g. case, number, tense, mood, etc.) that are expressed by inflectional morphology in the world's languages. These were identified by surveying the linguistic typology literature on parts of speech and then identifying the kinds of inflectional morphology that are typically associated with each part of speech.

For each dimension, we identified the finest distinctions in meaning made within that dimension by a natural language. Some higher-level 'cover features' representing common cross-linguistic groupings were also included. For example, features such as indicative (IND) and subjunctive (SBJV) represent groupings of basic modality features which occur in multiple languages and show similar usage patterns (Palmer, 2001).

Each dimension has an underlying semantic basis used to define its features. To determine the underlying semantic basis for each dimension, the literature in linguistic typology and in description-oriented linguistic theory was surveyed for explanations of each dimension that offered ways to precisely define the observed features.

2.2 Contents of the Schema

The universal morphological feature schema represents 23 dimensions of meaning with 212 features. Because space limitations preclude a detailed discussion of the semantic basis of each dimension and the definitions of each feature, Table 1 presents each dimension of meaning, the labels of its features, and citations for the main sources for the semantic bases of each dimension. To the extent possible, feature labels conform to the Leipzig Glossing Rules (Comrie et al., 2008) and to the labels in the sources used to define the semantic basis for each dimension of meaning. A substantially expanded exploration and analysis of these dimensions and schema framework may be found in Sylak-Glassman et al. (To appear).

Note that because gender categories are not necessarily defined by semantic criteria and rarely map neatly across languages, this schema treats gender features as open-class.[1]

3 Wiktionary Data Extraction and Mapping

Wiktionary contains a wealth of training data for morphological analysis, most notably inflectional paradigm tables. Since its pages are primarily written by human authors for human readers, and there are no overarching standards for how paradigms should be presented, these tables contain many inconsistencies and are at best semi-structured. Layouts differ depending on the *edition language* in which a word is being defined and within an edition depending on the word's language and part of speech. The textual descriptors used for morphological features are also not systematically defined. These idiosyncrasies cause numerous difficulties for automatic paradigm extraction, but the redundancy of having data presented in multiple ways across different editions gives us an opportunity to arrive at a consensus description of an inflected form, and to fill in gaps when the coverage of one edition diverges from

[1]To limit feature proliferation, the schema encodes gender categories as features that may be shared across languages within a phylogenetic stock or family, in order to capture identical gender category definitions and assignments that result from common ancestry, as may be possible for the 25 historical noun classes in the Bantu stock (Demuth, 2000).

Dimension	*Features*	*Semantic Basis*
Aktionsart	ACCMP, ACH, ACTY, ATEL, DUR, DYN, PCT, SEMEL, STAT, TEL	Cable (2008), Vendler (1957), Comrie (1976a)
Animacy	ANIM, HUM, INAN, NHUM	Yamamoto (1999), Comrie (1989)
Aspect	HAB, IPFV, ITER, PFV, PRF, PROG, PROSP	Klein (1994)
Case	ABL, ABS, ACC, ALL, ANTE, APPRX, APUD, AT, AVR, BEN, CIRC, COM, COMPV, DAT, EQU, ERG, ESS, FRML, GEN, INS, IN, INTER, NOM, NOMS, ON, ONHR, ONVR, POST, PRIV, PROL, PROPR, PROX, PRP, PRT, REM, SUB, TERM, VERS, VOC	Blake (2001), Radkevich (2010)
Comparison	AB, CMPR, EQT, RL, SPRL	Cuzzolin and Lehmann (2004)
Definiteness	DEF, INDEF, NSPEC, SPEC	Lyons (1999)
Deixis	ABV, BEL, DIST, EVEN, MED, NVIS, PROX, REF1, REF2, REM, VIS	Bhat (2004), Bliss and Ritter (2001)
Evidentiality	ASSUM, AUD, DRCT, FH, HRSY, INFER, NFH , NVSEN, QUOT, RPRT, SEN	Aikhenvald (2004)
Finiteness	FIN, NFIN	Binary finite vs. nonfinite
Gender+	BANTU1-23, FEM, MASC, NAKH1-8, NEUT	Corbett (1991)
Info. Structure	FOC, TOP	Lambrecht (1994)
Interrogativity	DECL, INT	Binary declarative vs. interrogative
Mood	ADM, AUNPRP, AUPRP, COND, DEB, IMP, IND, INTEN, IRR, LKLY, OBLIG, OPT, PERM, POT, PURP, REAL, SBJV, SIM	Palmer (2001)
Number	DU, GPAUC, GRPL, INVN, PAUC, PL, SG, TRI	Corbett (2000)
Parts of Speech	ADJ, ADP, ADV, ART, AUX, CLF, COMP, CONJ, DET, INTJ, N, NUM, PART, PRO, V, V.CVB, V.MSDR, V.PTCP	Croft (2000), Haspelmath (1995)
Person	0, 1, 2, 3, 4, EXCL, INCL, OBV, PRX	Conventional person, obviation and clusivity
Polarity	NEG, POS	Binary positive vs. negative
Politeness	AVOID, COL, FOREG, FORM, FORM.ELEV, FORM.HUMB, HIGH, HIGH.ELEV, HIGH.SUPR, INFM, LIT, LOW, POL	Brown and Levinson (1987), Comrie (1976b)
Possession	ALN, NALN, PSSD, PSSPNO+	Type of possession, characteristics of possessor
Switch-Reference	CN-R-MN+, DS, DSADV, LOG, OR, SEQMA, SIMMA, SS, SSADV	Stirling (1993)
Tense	1DAY, FUT, HOD, IMMED, PRS, PST, RCT, RMT	Klein (1994), ?)
Valency	DITR, IMPRS, INTR, TR	Number of verbal arguments from zero to three
Voice	ACFOC, ACT, AGFOC, ANTIP, APPL, BFOC, CAUS, CFOC, DIR, IFOC, INV, LFOC, MID, PASS, PFOC, RECP, REFL	Klaiman (1991)

Table 1: Dimensions of meaning and their features, both sorted alphabetically

that of another.

To make these data available for morphological analysis, we developed a novel multidimensional table parser for Wiktionary to extract inflected forms with their associated descriptors. Although we describe its function in Wiktionary-specific terms, this strategy can be generalized to extract data tuples from any HTML table with correctly marked-up header and content cells. We extracted additional descriptors from HTML headings and table captions, then mapped all descriptors to features in the universal schema.

3.1 Extraction from HTML Tables

In its base form, the table parser takes advantage of HTML's distinction between header and content cells to identify descriptors and potential inflected forms, respectively, in an arbitrary inflection table. Each content cell is matched with the headers immediately up the column, to the left of the row, and in the "corners" located at the row and column intersection of the previous two types of headers. Matching headers are stored in a list ordered by their distance from the content cell. Figure 1 shows an example where *prenais* is assigned the following descriptors:

– Directly up the column: **tu**, **second**, **singular**, **simple**.

– Directly to the left of the row: **imperfect**, **simple tenses**.

– In corners located at the row and column intersection of any headers identified by the previous two methods: **indicative**, **person**.

– Important structured fields found outside the table, including **French** and **Verb**.

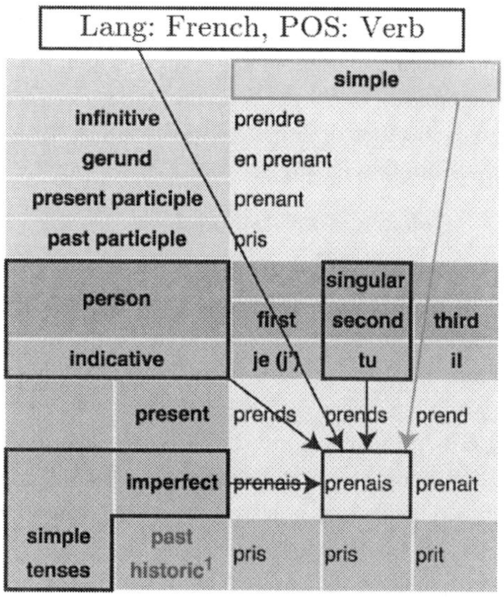

Figure 1: A portion of the English-edition Wiktionary conjugation table for the French verb *prendre* 'take.' The inflected form *prenais* and its row, column, and corner headers are highlighted.

Further, when additional content cells intervene between headers, as they do between **simple** and **singular**, the more distant header is marked as "distal." This labeling is important for proper handling of the column header **simple** in this example: It only applies to the top half of the table, and should be left out of any labeling of the inflected forms in the lower half. This distance information, and a hierarchy of positional precedence, is used in Section 3.4 to discount these and other potentially irrelevant descriptors in the case of conflicts during the subsequent mapping of descriptors to features in the universal schema. In general, the positionally highest ranking header value for each schema dimension are utilized and lower-ranking conflicting values are discarded.

3.2 Extraction from Parenthetical Lists

For some languages, inflected forms are presented inline next to the headword, instead of in a separate table, as shown for the German noun *Haus* 'house':

Haus *n* (*genitive* **Hauses**, *plural* **Häuser**, *diminutive* **Häuschen** *n* or **Häuslein** *n*)

Here, the italic *n* indicates a neuter noun. The inflection data inside the parentheses are extracted as simple tuples containing the lemma, inflected form, and inflectional relationship (e.g. **Haus**, **Häuser**, *plural*).

3.3 Improving Extraction Accuracy

The approach described above is sufficient to parse most Wiktionary data, but a large percentage of Wiktionary inflection tables do not use the correct tags to distinguish between header and content cells, an important component of the parsing procedure. In particular, table authors frequently use only the content cell tag to mark up all of a table's cells, and create "soft" headers with a distinct visual appearance by changing their styling (as with Czech verbs, such as *spadat* 'to be included, fall off'). This is indistinguishable to human viewers, but a naïve parse mistakes the soft headers for inflected forms with no descriptors. Hence we investigated several methods for robustly identifying improperly marked-up table headers and overriding the HTML cell-type tags in a preprocessing step.

Visual identification. Since most of the soft headers on Wiktionary have a distinct background color from the rest of their containing tables, we initially added a rule that treated content cells that defined a background color in HTML or inline CSS as header cells. However, the mere presence of this attribute was not a reliable indicator since some tables, such as those for Latin nouns (e.g. *aqua* 'water'), gave every cell a background color. This caused them to be erroneously considered to consist entirely of headers, resulting in missing data. Other tables used background color for highlighting, as with Faroese nouns (e.g. *vatn* 'water') and the **past historic** row in Figure 1, whose inflected forms were considered to be headers. For these reasons, visual cues were assessed as an unreliable method of identification.

Frequency-based methods. Another, more successful strategy for header discrimination header discrimination utilized the frequency characteristics of cell text, regardless of the cell's type. Although Wiktionary's inflection tables have many different layouts, words with the same language and part of speech pair often share a single template with consistent descriptors. In addition, many simple descriptors, such as **singular**, occur frequently throughout a single edition. Each inflected form, however, can be expected to appear on only a few pages (and in most cases just one). We exploited this tendency by counting the number of pages where each distinct cell text in a Wiktionary edition appeared, and, for each language, manually determined a cutoff point above which any cell with matching text was considered a header. Cells containing only punctuation were excluded from consideration, to avoid problems with dashes that occurred in many tables as a content cell indicating that no such form existed. This strategy surmounted all the problems identified thus far, including both the improper tagging of headers as content cells and the overspecification of background colors.

3.4 Mapping Inflected Forms to Universal Features

Using the results of the frequency-based preprocessing step to the table parsing algorithm, the first two authors manually inspected the list of parsed cells and their frequencies within each language, and then determined both a threshold for inclusion as a header feature (descriptor) and a universal representation for each header feature. When possible header features were above the threshold, but judged not to be contentful, they were not given a universal schema representation.

All inflected forms found by our scrape of Wiktionary were assigned complete universal representation vectors by looking up each of their Wiktionary descriptors using the mapping described in the above paragraph and then concatenating the results. Any conflicts within a dimension were resolved using a positional heuristic that favored descriptors nearer to the inflected form in its original HTML table, with column headings assigned higher precedence than row headings, which had higher precedence to corner headings, based on an empirical assessment of positional accuracy in case of conflict.

Ultimately, the process of extraction and mapping yielded instantiated paradigms for 883,965 unique lemmas across 352 languages (of which 130 had more than 100 lemmas), with each inflected form of the lemma described by a vector of features from the universal morphological feature schema.

4 Seeding Morphological Analyzers

To test the accuracy, consistency, and utility of our Wiktionary extraction and feature mappings, the fully mapped data from the English edition of Wiktionary were used as input to Durrett and DeNero's (2013) morphological paradigm learner. While the results were comparable to those obtained by the hand-tooled and language-specific table parsers of Durrett and DeNero (2013) given an equivalent quantity of training data, the number of language and part of speech combinations which could be subjected to analysis using data from our general-purpose Wiktionary parser and mapping to features in the universal schema was far greater: 123 language-POS pairs (88 distinct languages) versus Durrett and DeNero's 5 pairs (3 languages).[2] In addition, when the available training data were increased from 500 lemmas to the full amount (a number that varied per language but was always > 2000), χ^2 tests demonstrated that the gain in wordform generation accuracy was statistically significant ($p < 0.05$) for 44% (14/32) of the tested language-POS pairs. In the language-POS pairs without significant gains, wordforms were predictable using smaller amounts of data. For example, nearly half (8/18) of the language-POS pairs in this category were nouns in Romance languages, whose pluralization patterns typically involve simply adding /-s/ or some similar variant. Some of the language-POS pairs with significant gains contained multiple inflection classes and/or morpheme altering processes such as vowel harmony, umlaut, or vowel shortening. These linguistic characteristics introduce complexity that reduces the number of exemplars of any given

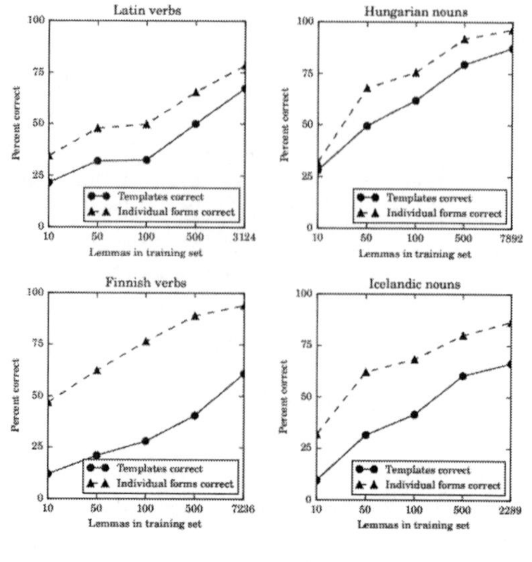

Figure 2: Examples of significant improvements in per-lemma paradigm and wordform generation accuracy with varying amounts of training data

morpheme form, which increases the value of additional data. Figure 2 shows the influence of additional training data on paradigm and wordform generation accuracy for the four languages in which the addition of the full amount of training data provided the most significant improvement (all $p < 0.001$).

5 Conclusion

The proposed universal morphological feature schema incorporates findings from research in linguistic typology to provide a cross-linguistically applicable method of labeling inflectional morphemes according to their meaning. The schema offers many potential benefits for NLP and machine translation by facilitating direct meaning-to-meaning comparison and translation across language pairs. We have also developed original, robust and general multidimensional table parsing and feature mapping algorithms. We then applied these algorithms and universal schema to Wiktionary to generate a significant sharable resource, namely standardized universal feature representations for inflected wordforms from 883,965 instantiated paradigms across 352 languages. We have shown that these data can be used to successfully train morphological analysis tools, and that the increased amount of data available can significantly improve their accuracy.

[2]Language-POS pairs were considered to be suitable for analysis if they possessed 200 or more lemmas that exhibited the maximal paradigm possible.

References

Alexandra Y. Aikhenvald. 2004. *Evidentiality*. Oxford University Press, Oxford.

D. N. Shankara Bhat. 2004. *Pronouns*. Oxford University Press, Oxford.

Balthasar Bickel and Johanna Nichols. 2005. Inclusive-exclusive as person vs. number categories worldwide. In Elena Filimonova, editor, *Clusivity*, pages 49–72. John Benjamins, Philadelphia.

Barry J. Blake. 2001. *Case*. Cambridge University Press, Cambridge, UK, 2nd edition.

Heather Bliss and Elizabeth Ritter. 2001. Developing a database of personal and demonstrative pronoun paradigms: Conceptual and technical challenges. In Steven Bird, Peter Buneman, and Mark Lieberman, editors, *Proceedings of the ICRS Workshop on Linguistic Databases*. Institute for Research in Cognitive Science, Philadelphia.

Penelope Brown and Stephen C. Levinson. 1987. *Politeness: Some Universals in Language Usage*. Studies in Interactional Sociolinguistics. Cambridge University Press, Cambridge, UK.

Seth Cable. 2008. Tense, aspect and Aktionsart. Unpublished handout from "Proseminar on Semantic Theory" for *Theoretical Perspectives on Languages of the Pacific Northwest*. Available at: http://people.umass.edu/scable/PNWSeminar/handouts/Tense/Tense-Background.pdf, Fall.

Shobhana L. Chelliah and Willem J. de Reuse. 2011. *Handbook of Descriptive Linguistic Fieldwork*. Springer, Dordrecht, Netherlands.

Jinho Choi, Marie-Catherine de Marneffe, Tim Dozat, Filip Ginter, Yoav Goldberg, Jan Hajič, Christopher Manning, Ryan McDonald, Joakim Nivre, Slav Petrov, Sampo Pyysalo, Natalia Silveira, Reut Tsarfaty, and Dan Zeman. 2015. Universal Dependencies. Accessible at: http://universaldependencies.github.io/docs/, January.

Bernard Comrie, Martin Haspelmath, and Balthasar Bickel. 2008. The Leipzig Glossing Rules: Conventions for interlinear morpheme-by-morpheme glosses. http://www.eva.mpg.de/lingua/resources/glossing-rules.php, February.

Bernard Comrie. 1976a. *Aspect: An Introduction to the Study of Verbal Aspect and Related Problems*. Cambridge University Press, Cambridge, UK.

Bernard Comrie. 1976b. Linguistic politeness axes: Speaker-addressee, speaker-referent, speaker-bystander. *Pragmatics Microfiche*, 1.7(A3). Department of Linguistics, University of Cambridge.

Bernard Comrie. 1989. *Language Universals and Linguistic Typology*. Basil Blackwell, Oxford, 2nd edition.

Greville G. Corbett. 1991. *Gender*. Cambridge University Press, Cambridge, UK.

Greville G. Corbett. 2000. *Number*. Cambridge University Press, Cambridge, UK.

William Croft. 2000. Parts of speech as language universals and as language-particular categories. In Petra M. Vogel and Bernard Comrie, editors, *Approaches to the Typology of Word Classes*, pages 65–102. Mouton de Gruyter, New York.

Pierluigi Cuzzolin and Christian Lehmann. 2004. Comparison and gradation. In Geert Booij, Christian Lehmann, Joachim Mugdan, and Stavros Skopeteas, editors, *Morphologie. Ein internationales Handbuch zur Flexion und Wortbildung / An International Handbook on Inflection and Word-Formation*, volume 2, pages 1212–1220. Mouton de Gruyter, Berlin.

Katherine Demuth. 2000. Bantu noun classes: Loanword and acquisition evidence of semantic productivity. In G. Senft, editor, *Classification Systems*, pages 270–292. Cambridge University Press, Cambridge, UK.

Markus Dreyer and Jason Eisner. 2011. Discovering morphological paradigms from plain text using a Dirichlet process mixture model. In *Proceedings of EMNLP 2011*, pages 616–627, Edinburgh. Association for Computational Linguistics.

Greg Durrett and John DeNero. 2013. Supervised learning of complete morphological paradigms. In *Proceedings of the 2013 Conference of the North American Chapter of the Association for Computational Linguistics: Human Language Technologies*, pages 1185–1195. Association for Computational Linguistics, Atlanta.

John Goldsmith. 2001. Unsupervised learning of the morphology of natural language. *Computational Linguistics*, 27(2):153–198.

Harald Hammarström. 2006. A naive theory of morphology and an algorithm for extraction. In Richard Wicentowski and Grzegorz Kondrak, editors, *SIGPHON 2006: Proceedings of the 8th Meeting of the ACL Special Interest Group on Computational Phonology*, pages 79–88, New York. Association for Computational Linguistics.

Martin Haspelmath. 1995. The converb as a cross-linguistically valid category. In Martin Haspelmath and Ekkehard König, editors, *Converbs in Cross-Linguistic Perspective: Structure and Meaning of Adverbial Verb Forms – Adverbial Participles, Gerunds*, Empirical Approaches to Language Typology, pages 1–56. Mouton de Gruyter, Berlin.

Martin Haspelmath. 2010. Comparative concepts and descriptive categories in crosslinguistic studies. *Language*, 86(3):663–687, September.

M. H. Klaiman. 1991. *Grammatical Voice*. Cambridge University Press, Cambridge, UK.

Wolfgang Klein. 1994. *Time in Language*. Routledge, New York.

Knud Lambrecht. 1994. *Information Structure and Sentence Form: Topic, Focus and the Mental Representations of Discourse Referents*. Cambridge University Press, Cambridge, UK.

Christopher Lyons. 1999. *Definiteness*. Cambridge University Press, Cambridge.

Marie Mikulová, Alevtina Bémová, Jan Hajič, Eva Hajičová, Jiří Havelka, Veronika Kolářová, Lucie Kučová, Markéta Lopatková, Petr Pajas, Jarmila Panevová, Magda Razímová, Petr Sgall, Jan Štepánek, Zdeňka Urešová, Kateřina Veselá, and Zdeněk Žabokrtský. 2006. Annotation on the tectogrammatical level in the Prague Dependency Treebank: Annotation manual. Technical report, ÚFAL/CKL, Prague. Technical Report TR-2006-30.

Frank R. Palmer. 2001. *Mood and Modality*. Cambridge University Press, Cambridge, UK, 2nd edition.

Nina V. Radkevich. 2010. *On Location: The Structure of Case and Adpositions*. Ph.D. thesis, University of Connecticut, Storrs, CT.

Benoît Sagot and Géraldine Walther. 2013. Implementing a formal model of inflectional morphology. In Cerstin Mahlow and Michael Piotrowski, editors, *Systems and Frameworks for Computational Morphology*, pages 115–134. Springer, Berlin.

Lesley Stirling. 1993. *Switch-Reference and Discourse Representation*. Cambridge Studies in Linguistics. Cambridge University Press, Cambridge, UK.

John Sylak-Glassman, Christo Kirov, Matt Post, Roger Que, and David Yarowsky. To appear. A universal feature schema for rich morphological annotation and fine-grained cross-lingual part-of-speech tagging. In *Proceedings of the Fourth International Workshop on Systems and Frameworks for Computational Morphology*, Communications in Computer and Information Science. Springer-Verlag, Berlin.

Zeno Vendler. 1957. Verbs and times. *The Philosophical Review*, 66(2):143–160, April.

Mutsumi Yamamoto. 1999. *Animacy and Reference*. John Benjamins, Amsterdam.

Daniel Zeman. 2008. Reusable tagset conversion using tagset drivers. In *Proceedings of LREC 2008*, pages 213–218.

Rhetoric Map of an Answer to Compound Queries

Boris Galitsky
Knowledge Trail Inc.
San-Francisco, USA
bgalitsky@hotmail.com

Dmitry Ilvovsky
National Research University Higher School of Economics, Moscow, Russia
dilvovsky@hse.ru

Sergey O. Kuznetsov
National Research University Higher School of Economics, Moscow, Russia
skuznetsov@hse.ru

Abstract

Given a discourse tree for a text as a candidate answer to a compound query, we propose a rule system for valid and invalid occurrence of the query keywords in this tree. To be a valid answer to a query, its keywords need to occur in a chain of elementary discourse unit of this answer so that these units are fully ordered and connected by nucleus – satellite relations. An answer might be invalid if the queries' keywords occur in the answer's satellite discourse units only. We build the rhetoric map of an answer to prevent it from firing by queries whose keywords occur in non-adjacent areas of the Answer Map. We evaluate the improvement of search relevance by filtering out search results not satisfying the proposed rule system, demonstrating a 4% increase of accuracy with respect to the nearest neighbor learning approach which does not use the discourse tree structure.

1 Introduction

Answering compound queries, where its keywords are distributed through text of a candidate answer, is a sophisticated problem requiring deep linguistic analysis. If the query keywords occur in an answer text in a linguistically connected manner, this answer is most likely relevant. This is usually true when all these keywords occur in the same sentence: they should be connected syntactically. For the inter-sentence connections, these keywords need to be connected via anaphora, refer to the same entity or sub-entity, or be linked via rhetoric discourse.

If the query keywords occur in different sentences, there should be linguistic cues for some sort of connections between these occurrences. If there is no connection, then different constraints for an object expressed by a query might be applied to different objects in the answer text, therefore, this answer is perhaps irrelevant. There are following possibilities of such connections.

Anaphora. If two areas of keyword occurrences are connected with anaphoric relation, the answer is most likely relevant.

Communicative actions. If the text contains a dialogue, and some question keywords are in a request and other are in the reply to this request, then these keywords are connected and the answer is relevant. To identify such situation, one needs to find a pair of communicative actions and to confirm that this pair is of request-reply kind.

Rhetoric relations. They indicate the coherence structure of a text (Mann and Thompson, 1988). Rhetoric relations for text can be represented by a Discourse tree (DT) which is a labeled tree. The leaves of this tree correspond to contiguous units for clauses (elementary discourse units, EDU). Adjacent EDUs as well as higher-level (larger) discourse units are organized in a hierarchy by rhetoric relation (e.g., background, attribution). Anti-symmetric relation takes a pair of EDUs: nuclei, which are core parts of the relation, and satellites, the supportive parts of the rhetoric relation.

The most important class of connections we focus in this study is rhetoric. Once an answer text is split into EDUs, and rhetoric relations are established between them, it is possible to establish rules for whether query keywords occurring in text are connected by rhetoric relations (and therefore, this answer is likely relevant) or not connected (and this answer is most likely irrelevant). Hence we use the DT as a base for an ***Answer Map*** of a text: certain sets of nodes in DT correspond to queries so that this text is a valid answer, and certain sets of nodes correspond to an invalid answer. Our definition of the Answer Map follows the methodology of inverse index for search: instead of taking queries and considering all valid answers for it from a set of text,

Proceedings of the 53rd Annual Meeting of the Association for Computational Linguistics and the 7th International Joint Conference on Natural Language Processing (Short Papers), pages 681–686,
Beijing, China, July 26-31, 2015.

we take a text (answer) and consider the totality of valid and invalid queries consisting of the keywords from this text.

Usually, the main clause of a compound query includes the main entity and some of its constraints, and the supplementary clause includes the other constraint. In the most straightforward way, the main clause of a query is mapped into a nucleus and the supplementary clause is mapped into a satellite of RST relation such as *elaboration*. Connection by other RST relation, where a satellite introduces additional constraints for a nucleus, has the same meaning for answer validity. This validity still holds when two EDUs are connected with a symmetric relation such as joint. However, when the images of the main and supplementary clause of the query are satellites of different nucleus, it most likely means that they express constraints for different entities, and therefore constitute an irrelevant answer for this query.

There is a number of recent studies employing RST features for passage re-ranking under question answering (Joty and Moschitti, 2014; Surdeanu et al., 2014). In the former study, the feature space of subtrees of parse trees includes the RST relations to improve question answer accuracy. In the latter project, RST features contributed to the totality of features learned to re-rank the answers. In (Galitsky et al., 2014) rhetoric structure, in particular, was used to broaden the set of parse trees to enrich the feature space by taking into account overall discourse structure of candidate answers. Statistical learning in these studies demonstrated that rhetoric relation can be leveraged for better search relevance. In the current study, we formulate the explicit rules for how a query can be mapped into the answer DT and the relevance of this map can be verified.

2 Example of an Answer Map

Ex. 1. DT including 6 nodes {e1...e6} is shown in Fig 1 (Joty and Moschitti, 2014). Text is split into six EDUs:

[what's more,]e1 [he believes]e2 [seasonal swings in the auto industry this year aren't occurring at the same time in the past,]e3 [because of production and pricing differences]e4 [that are curbing the accuracy of seasonal adjustments]e5] [built into the employment data.]e6

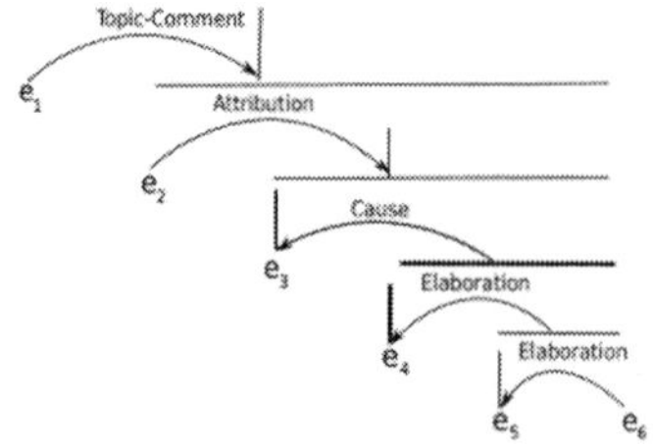

Fig.1. Discourse tree for the Example 1

Horizontal lines indicate text segments; satellites are connected to their nuclei by curved arrows. One can see that this text is a relevant answer to the query

Are seasonal swings in the auto industry due to pricing differences?

but is an irrelevant answer to the query

Are pricing differences built into employment data?

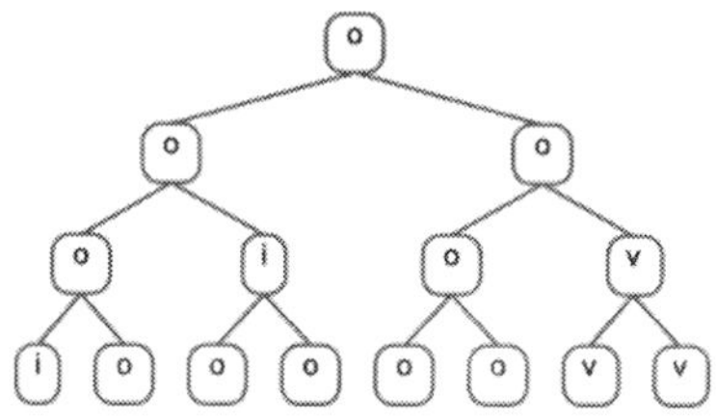

Fig. 2. An Answer Map and its areas for valid and invalid answers

A valid set of nodes of an Answer Map is defined as the one closed under common ancestor relations in a DT. For example, the ***i***-nodes on the bottom-left of DT in Fig. 2 constitute the invalid set, and the ***v***-nodes on the right of DT constitute the valid set.

Ex. 2.

I went to watch a movie because I had nothing else to do. I enjoyed the movie which was about animals finding food in a desert. To feed in a desert environment, zebras run hundreds of miles in search of sources of water.

This answer is valid for the following queries (phrases) since their keywords form ***v***-set:

- enjoy movie watched when nothing else to do
- I went to watch a movie about feeding in desert environment
- I went to watch a movie about zebras run hundreds of miles

- `I went to watch a movie about searching sources of water`

And this text is not a correct answer for the following queries (phrases), since their keywords form *i*-sets:

- `animals find food in desert when have nothing else to do`
- `I had nothing else except finding food in a desert`
- `I had nothing else to do but run hundreds of miles in search of water`
- `finding food in a desert - a good thing to do`

3 Definition and Construction Algorithm

Discourse tree includes directed arcs for anti-symmetric rhetoric relation and undirected arcs for symmetric rhetoric relations such as *joint*, *time sequence*, and others. For two nodes of DT we define its directed common ancestor as a common ancestor node which is connected with these nodes via directed arcs.

The valid set of EDUs which is a result of mapping of a query is closed under common directed ancestor relation: it should contain the set of all directed common ancestor for all EDUs. Hence this constraint is applied for antisymmetric RST relations; query terms can occur in symmetric EDU nodes in an arbitrary way.

To construct an Answer Map from DT, firstly, we need to map keywords and phrases of a query into EDUs of an answer. For each noun phrase for a query, we find one or more EDUs which include noun phrases with the same head noun. Not each keyword has to be mapped, but there should be not more than a single EDU each keyword is mapped under a given mapping. For example, noun phrase from the query `family doing its taxes` is mapped into the EDU `including how individuals and families file their taxes` since they have the same head noun `tax`. If a multiple mapping exists for a query, we need to find at least one valid occurrence to conclude that this query is a valid one for the given map.

For a query Q, if its keywords occur in candidate answer A and the set of EDUs Q_{edu}, then $\text{commonAncestorsDT(A)}(Q_{edu}) \subseteq Q_{edu}$.

For a real-word search system, the enforcement of RST rules occurs at indexing time, since RST parsing is rather slow.

For answer text A, we produce a sequence of texts $A_e < \{\text{A directed common ancestor I}\}$ for all pairs of EDU nodes connected with their parents by directed arcs. Then the match of the set of keyword occurs with the extended index in the regular manner: there is no element A_e for invalid mapping Q to Q_{edu}.

4 Approach Scalability

In terms of search engineering, enforcing of the condition of the Rhetoric Map of an answer requires additional part of the index besides the inverse one. Building this additional index requires enumeration of all maximal sequences of keywords from Rhetoric Map for every document (potential answer A). Once A is determined to be fired by query Q using the regular search index, there should be an entry in Rhetoric Map which is fired by a query formed as a conjunction of terms in Q.

Since application of Rhetoric Map rules occurs via an inverse index, the search time is constant with respect to the size of the overall RM index and size of a given document. The indexing time is significantly higher due to rhetoric parsing, and the size of index is increased approximately by the number of average maximal paths in a DT graph, which is 3-5. Hence although the performance of search will not significantly change, the amount of infrastructure efforts associated with RM technology is substantial.

5 Evaluation

We used the TREC evaluation dataset as a list of topics: http://trec.nist.gov/data/qa/. Given a short factoid question for entity, person, organization, event, etc. such as `#EVENT Pakistan earthquakes of October 2005#` we ran a web search and automatically (using shallow parsing provided by Stanford NLP) extracted compound sentences from search expressions, such as `A massive earthquake struck Pakistan and parts of India and Afghanistan on Saturday morning October 8, 2005. This was the strongest earthquake in the area during the last hundred years.`

Ten to twenty such queries were derived for a topic. Those portions of text were selected with obvious rhetoric relation between the clauses. We then fed Bing Search Engine API such queries and built the Answer Map for each candidate answer. We then ran the Answer Map - based filter. Finally, we manually verify that these filtered answers are relevant to the initial questions and to the queries.

We evaluated improvement of search relevance for compound queries by applying the DT rules. These rules provide Boolean decisions for candidate answers, but we compare them with score-based answer re-ranking based on ML of baseline SVM tree kernel (Moschitti, 2006), discourse-based SVM (Ilvovsky, 2014) and nearest-neighbor Parse Thicket-based approach (Galitsky et al., 2013).

The approach based on SVM tree kernel takes question-answer pairs (also from TREC dataset) and forms the positive set from the correct pairs and negative set from the incorrect pairs. The tree kernel learning (Duffy and Collins, 2002) for the pairs of extended parse trees produces multiple parse trees for each sentence, linking them by discourse relations of anaphora, communicative actions, "same entity" relation and rhetoric relations (Galitsky et al., 2014).

In the Nearest Neighbor approach to question – answer classification one takes the same data of parse trees connected by discourse relations and instead of applying SVM learning to pairs, compare these data for question and answer directly, finding the highest similarity.

To compare the score-based answer re-ranking approaches with the rule-based answer filtering one, we took first 20 Bing answers and classified them as valid (top 10) and invalid (bottom 10) under the former set of approaches and selected up to 10 acceptable (using the original ranking) under the latter approach. Hence the order of these selected set of 10 answers is irrelevant for our evaluation and we measured the percentage of valid answers among them (the focus of evaluation is search precision, not recall).

Answer validity was assessed by Amazon Mechanical Turk. The assessors were asked to choose relevant answers from the randomly sorted list of candidate answers. Table 1 shows the evaluation results.

Table 1. Evaluation results

Filtering method		Baseline Bing search, %	SVM TK learning of QA pairs (baseline improvement), %	SVM TK learning for the pairs for extended parse trees, %	Nearest neighbor for question – answer, %	Answer Map, %
Sources / Query types	Source of discourse information	-	-	Anaphora, same entity, selected discourse relations		Discourse Tree
Clauses connected with *elaboration*		68.3	69.4	73.9	74.6	**79.2**
Clauses connected with *attribution*		67.5	70.1	72.7	75.1	**78.8**
Clauses connected with *summary*		64.9	66.3	70.2	74.0	**78.0**
Clauses in *joint/sequence* relation		64.1	65.2	68.1	72.3	**76.3**
Average		66.2	67.8	71.2	74.0	**78.0**

The top two rows show the answer filtering methods and sources of discourse information. Bottom rows show evaluation results for queries with various rhetoric relations between clauses.

One can observe just a 1.5% improvement by using SVM tree kernel without discourse, further 3.5% improvement by using discourse-enabled SVM tree kernel, and further improvement of 2.8% by using nearest neighbor learning. The latter is still 4% lower than the Answer Map approach, which is the focus of this study. We observe that the baseline search improvement, SVM tree kernel approach has a limited capability of filtering out irrelevant search results in our evaluation settings. Also, the role of discourse information in improving search results for queries with symmetric rhetoric relation between clauses is lower than that of the anti-symmetric relations.

Code and examples are available at code.google.com/p/relevance-based-on-parse-trees/ (package *opennlp.tools.parse_thicket.external_rst*).

6 Discussion and Conclusion

Overall, our evaluation settings are focused on compound queries where most answers correctly belong to the topic of interest in a query and there is usually sufficient number of keywords to assure this. However, in the selected search domain irrelevant answers are those based on foreign entities or mismatched attributes of these entities. Hence augmenting keyword statistics with the structured information of parse trees is not critical to search accuracy improvement. At the same time, discourse information for candidate answers is essential to properly form and interpret the constraints expressed in queries.

Although there has been a substantial advancement in document-level RST parsing, including the rich linguistic features-based of (Feng and Hirst, 2012) and powerful parsing models (Joty et al., 2013), document level discourse analysis has not found a broad range of applications such as search. The most valuable information from DT includes global discourse features and long range structural dependencies between DT constituents.

Despite other studies (Surdeanu et al., 2014) showed that discourse information is beneficial for search via learning, we believe this is the first study demonstrating how Answer Map affects search directly. To be a valid answer for a question, its keywords need to occur in adjacent EDU chain of this answer so that these EDUs are fully ordered and connected by nucleus – satellite relations. Note the difference between the proximity in text as a sequence of words and proximity in DT (Croft et al., 2009). An answer is expected to be invalid if the questions' keywords occur in the answer's satellite EDUs and not in their nucleus EDUs. The purpose of the rhetoric map of an answer is to prevent it from being fired by questions whose keywords occur in non-adjacent areas of this map.

References

S. Joty and A. Moschitti. 2014. Discriminative Reranking of Discourse Parses Using Tree Kernels. Proceedings of the 2014 Conference on Empirical Methods in Natural Language Processing (EMNLP), pages 2049–2060, October 25-29, 2014, Doha, Qatar.

V. Wei Feng and G. Hirst. 2012. Text-level discourse parsing with rich linguistic features. In Proceedings of the 50th Annual Meeting of the Association for Computational Linguistics (ACL-2012), pages 60-68, Jeju, Korea.

P. Jansen, M. Surdeanu, and P. Clark. 2014. Discourse Complements Lexical Semantics for Nonfactoid Answer Reranking. In Proceedings of the 52nd Annual Meeting of the Association for Computational Linguistics (ACL).

S. Joty, G. Carenini, and R. T. Ng. 2012. A Novel Discriminative Framework for Sentence-Level Discourse Analysis. In Proceedings of the 2012 Joint Conference on Empirical Methods in Natural Language Processing and Computational Natural Language Learning, EMNLP-CoNLL'12, pages 904–915, Jeju Island, Korea. Association for Computational Linguistics.

W. Mann, S. Thompson. 1988. Rhetorical Structure Theory: Toward a Functional Theory of Text Organization. Text, 8(3):243–281.

S. Joty, G. Carenini, R. Ng, Y. Mehdad. 2013. Combining Intra- and Multi-sentential Rhetorical Parsing for Document-level Discourse Analysis. In Proceedings of the 51st Annual Meeting of the Association for Computational Linguistics, Sofia, Bulgaria.

B. Galitsky, D. Ilvovsky, S.O. Kuznetsov, F. Strok. 2013. Matching sets of parse trees for answering multi-sentence questions. In Proceedings of the Recent Advances in Natural Language Processing (RANLP), Shoumen, Bulgaria, pages 285–294.

D. Ilvovsky. 2014. Going beyond sentences when applying tree kernels. Proceedings of the Student Research Workshop ACL 2014, pp. 56-63.

B. Galitsky, D. Usikov, S.O. Kuznetsov. 2013. Parse Thicket Representations for Answering Multi-sentence questions. 20th International Conference on Conceptual Structures, ICCS 2013.

B. Galitsky, S.O. Kuznetsov. 2008. Learning communicative actions of conflicting human agents. J. Exp. Theor. Artif. Intell. *20(4): 277-317.*

B. Galitsky. 2012. Machine Learning of Syntactic Parse Trees for Search and Classification of Text. Engineering Application of AI.

A. Moschitti. 2006. Efficient Convolution Kernels for Dependency and Constituent Syntactic Trees. In Proceedings of the 17th European Conference on Machine Learning, Berlin, Germany.

A. Severyn, A. Moschitti. 2012. Structural relationships for large-scale learning of answer re-ranking. SIGIR 2012: 741-750.

A. Severyn, A. Moschitti. 2012. Fast Support Vector Machines for Convolution Tree Kernels. Data Mining Knowledge Discovery 25: 325-357.

M. Collins and N. Duffy. 2002. Convolution kernels for natural language. In Proceedings of NIPS, 625–632.

H. Lee, A. Chang, Y. Peirsman, N. Chambers, Mihai Surdeanu and Dan Jurafsky. 2013. *Deterministic coreference resolution based on entity-centric, precision-ranked rules*. Computational Linguistics 39(4).

B. Croft, D. Metzler, T. Strohman. 2009. Search Engines - Information Retrieval in Practice. Pearson Education. North America.

V. Vapnik. 1995. The Nature of Statistical Learning Theory. – Springer-Verlag.

Thread-Level Information for Comment Classification in Community Question Answering

Alberto Barrón-Cedeño, Simone Filice, Giovanni Da San Martino, Shafiq Joty, Lluís Màrquez, Preslav Nakov, Alessandro Moschitti
Qatar Computing Research Institute, Hamad Bin Khalifa University
{albarron,sfilice,gmartino, sjoty,lmarquez, pnakov,amoschitti}@qf.org.qa

Abstract

Community Question Answering (cQA) is a new application of QA in social contexts (e.g., fora). It presents new interesting challenges and research directions, e.g., exploiting the dependencies between the different comments of a thread to select the best answer for a given question. In this paper, we explored two ways of modeling such dependencies: (*i*) by designing specific features looking globally at the thread; and (*ii*) by applying structure prediction models. We trained and evaluated our models on data from SemEval-2015 Task 3 on Answer Selection in cQA. Our experiments show that: (*i*) the thread-level features consistently improve the performance for a variety of machine learning models, yielding state-of-the-art results; and (*ii*) sequential dependencies between the answer labels captured by structured prediction models are not enough to improve the results, indicating that more information is needed in the joint model.

1 Introduction

Community Question Answering (cQA) is an evolution of a typical QA setting put in a Web forum context, where user interaction is enabled, without much restrictions on who can post and who can answer a question. This is a powerful mechanism, which allows users to freely ask questions and expect some good, honest answers.

Unfortunately, a user has to go through all possible answers and to make sense of them. It is often the case that many answers are only loosely related to the actual question, and some even change the topic. This is especially common for long threads where, as the thread progresses, users start talking to each other, instead of trying to answer the initial question.

This is a real problem, as a question can have hundreds of answers, the vast majority of which would not satisfy the users' information needs. Thus, finding the desired information in a long list of answers might be very time-consuming.

The problem of selecting the relevant text passages (i.e., those containing good answers) has been tackled in QA research, either for non-factoid QA or for passage reranking. Usually, automatic classifiers are applied to the answer passages retrieved by a search engine to derive a relative order; see (Radlinski and Joachims, 2005; Jeon et al., 2005; Shen and Lapata, 2007; Moschitti et al., 2007; Surdeanu et al., 2008; Heilman and Smith, 2010; Wang and Manning, 2010; Severyn and Moschitti, 2012; Yao et al., 2013; Severyn et al., 2013; Severyn and Moschitti, 2013) for detail.

To the best of our knowledge, there is no QA work that effectively identifies good answers based on the selection of the other answers retrieved for a question. This is mainly due to the loose dependencies between the different answer passages in standard QA. In contrast, we postulate that in a cQA setting, the answers from different users in a common thread are strongly interconnected and, thus, a joint answer selection model should be adopted to achieve higher accuracy.

To test our hypothesis about the usefulness of thread-level information, we used a publicly available dataset, recently developed for the SemEval-2015 Task 3 (Nakov et al., 2015). Subtask A in that challenge asks to identify the posts in the answer thread that answer the question *well* vs. those that can be *potentially useful* to the user vs. those that are just *bad or useless*.

We model the thread-level dependencies in two different ways: (*i*) by designing specific features that are able to capture the dependencies between the answers in the same thread; and (*ii*) by exploiting the sequential organization of the output labels for the complete thread.

Proceedings of the 53rd Annual Meeting of the Association for Computational Linguistics and the 7th International Joint Conference on Natural Language Processing (Short Papers), pages 687–693, Beijing, China, July 26-31, 2015.

Q: Can I obtain Driving License my QID is written Employee

A₁ the word employee is a general term that refers to all the staff in your company either the manager, secretary up to the lowest position or whatever positions they have. you are all considered employees of your company.

A₂ your qid should specify what is the actual profession you have. i think for me, your chances to have a drivers license is low.

A₃ dear richard, his asking if he can obtain. means he have the driver license

A₄ Slim chance ...

Figure 1: Simplified example from SemEval-2015 Task 3, English subtask A.

For the latter, we used the usual extensions of Logistic Regression and SVM to linear-chain models such as CRF and SVM^{hmm}.

The results clearly show that the thread-level features are important, providing consistent improvement for all our learning models. In contrast, the linear-chain models fail to exploit the sequential dependencies between nearby answer labels to improve the results significantly: although the labels from the neighboring answers can affect the label of the current answer, this dependency is too loose to have impact on the selection accuracy. In other words, labels should be used together with answers' content to account for stronger and more effective dependencies.

2 The Task

We use the CQA-QL corpus, which was used for Subtask A of SemEval-2015 Task 3 on Answer Selection in cQA. The corpus contains data from the *Qatar Living* forum,[1] and is publicly available on the task's website.[2] The dataset consists of questions and a list of the answers for each question, i.e., the *question-answer thread*. Each question, and also each answer, consists of a short title and a more detailed description. Moreover, there is some meta information associated with both, e.g., ID of the user asking/answering the question, timestamp, question category, etc.

The task asks to determine for each answer in the thread whether it is good, bad, or potentially useful. A simplified example is shown in Figure 1,[3] where answers 2 and 4 are good, answer 1 is potentially useful, and answer 3 is bad.

[1] http://www.qatarliving.com/forum

[2] http://alt.qcri.org/semeval2015/task3/

[3] http://www.qatarliving.com/moving-qatar/posts/can-i-obtain-driving-license-my-qid-written-employee

Below, we start with the original definition of Subtask A, as described above. Then, we switch to a binary classification setting (i.e., identifying *good* vs. *bad* answers), which is much closer to a real cQA application (see Section 4.3).

3 Basic and Thread-Level Features

Subsection 3.1 summarizes the basic features we used to implement the baseline systems. More importantly, Section 3.2 describes the set of thread-level features we designed in order to test our working hypothesis. Below we use the following notation: q is a question posted by user u_q, c is a comment, and C is the comment thread.

3.1 Baseline Features

We measure lexical and syntactic similarity between q and c. We compute the similarity between word n-grams ($n = [1, \ldots, 4]$), after stopword removal, using greedy string tiling (Wise, 1996), longest common subsequences (Allison and Dix, 1986), Jaccard coefficient (Jaccard, 1901), word containment (Lyon et al., 2001), and cosine similarity. We also apply partial tree kernels (Moschitti, 2006) on shallow syntactic trees.

We designed a set of heuristic features that might suggest whether c is *good* or not. Forty-four Boolean features express whether c (*i*) includes URLs or emails (2 feats.); (*ii*) contains the word "yes", "sure", "no", "can", "neither", "okay", and "sorry", as well as symbols '?' and '@' (9 feats.); (*iii*) starts with "yes" (1 feat.); (*iv*) includes a sequence of three or more repeated characters or a word longer than fifteen characters (2 feats.); (*v*) belongs to one of the categories of the forum (*Socialising*, *Life in Qatar*, etc.) (26 feats.); and (*vi*) has been posted by the same u_q, such a comment can include a question (i.e., contain a question mark), and acknowledgement (e.g., contain *thank**, *acknowl**), or none of them (4 feats.). An extra feature captures the length of c (as longer — *good*— comments usually contain detailed information to answer a question).

3.2 Thread-Level Global Features

Comments are organized sequentially according to the time line of the comment thread.[4] Our first four features indicate whether c appears in the proximity of a comment by u_q.

[4] The task organizers report that some comments in the threads were discarded due to disagreement in the annotation process. The extent of discarded comments is unknown.

	P_{ca}	R_{ca}	$F_{1,ca}$	A
Baseline Features				
SVM	52.96	53.14	52.87	67.61
OrdReg	53.33	51.54	51.87	65.38
Baseline+Thread-level Features				
SVM	56.31	56.46	56.33	72.27
OrdReg	57.68	57.04	57.20	72.47
SemEval top three				
JAIST	57.31	57.20	57.19	72.52
HITSZ	57.83	56.82	56.41	68.67
QCRI	54.34	53.57	53.74	70.50

Table 1: Macro-averaged precision, recall, F_1-measure, and accuracy on the multi-class (*good, bad, potential*) setting on the official SemEval-2015 Task 3 test set. The top-2 systems are included for comparison. QCRI refers to our official results, using an older version of our system.

	P	R	F_1	A	$F_{1,ta}$	A_{ta}
Baseline Features						
SVM	70.58	84.45	76.89	74.39	66.52	76.13
SVM^{hmm}	72.57	85.46	78.49	76.37	68.55	77.58
LogReg	65.05	91.27	75.96	70.85	68.84	74.79
CRF_{map}	72.48	86.66	78.94	76.67	67.17	76.55
CRF_{mpm}	71.55	84.25	77.38	75.15	66.54	75.42
Baseline+Thread-level Features						
SVM	75.29	85.26	79.96	78.44	67.65	76.02
SVM^{hmm}	74.84	83.25	78.82	77.43	66.61	77.06
LogReg	73.32	86.56	79.39	77.33	68.10	75.57
CRF_{map}	73.77	85.76	79.31	77.43	66.37	76.08
CRF_{mpm}	74.35	85.46	79.51	77.78	67.36	76.63

Table 2: Performance of the binary (*good* vs. *bad*) classifiers on the official SemEval-2015 Task 3 test dataset. Precision, recall, F_1-measure and accuracy are calculated at the comment level, while $F_{1,ta}$ and A_{ta} are averaged at the thread level.

The assumption is that an acknowledgment or further questions by u_q in the thread could signal a *good* answer. More specifically, they test if among the comments following c there is one by u_q (*i*) containing an acknowledgment, (*ii*) not containing an acknowledgment, (*iii*) containing a question, and, (*iv*) if among the comments preceding c there is one by u_q containing a question. The value of these four features —a propagation of the information captured by some of the heuristics described in Section 3.1— depends on the distance k, in terms of the number of comments, between c and the closest comment by u_q:

$$f(c) = \begin{cases} \max(0,\ 1.1 - (k \cdot 0.1)) \\ 0 \text{ if no comments by } u_q \text{ exist,} \end{cases} \quad (1)$$

that is, the closer the comment to c_q, the higher the value assigned to this feature.

We try to model potential dialogues, which at the end represent *bad* comments, by identifying interlacing comments between two users. Our dialogue features are identifying conversation chains: $u_i \rightarrow \ldots \rightarrow u_j \rightarrow \ldots \rightarrow u_i \rightarrow \ldots \rightarrow [u_j]$. Comments by other users can appear in between the nodes of this "pseudo-conversation" chain. We consider three features: whether a comment is at the beginning, in the middle, or at the end of such a chain. Three more features exist in those cases in which u_q is one of the participants of these pseudo-conversations.

Another Boolean feature for c_{u_i} is set to true if u_i wrote more than one comment in the current thread. Three more features identify the first, the middle and the last comments by u_i. One extra feature counts the total number of comments written by u_i in the thread up to that moment.

Moreover, we empirically observed that the likelihood of some comment being *good* decreases with its position in the thread. Therefore, we also included another real-valued feature: $\max(20, i)/20$, where i represents the position of the comment in the thread.

Finally, we perform a pseudo-ranking of the comments. The relevance of c is computed as its similarity to q (using word n-grams), normalized by the maximum similarity among all the comments in the thread. The resulting relative scores are mapped into three binary features depending on the range they fall at: $[0, 0.2]$, $(0.2, 0.8)$, or $[0.8, 1]$ (intervals resemble the three-class setting and were empirically set on the training data).

4 Experiments

Below we first describe the data we used, then we introduce the experimental setup, and finally we present and discuss the results of our experiments.

4.1 Data

The original CQA-QL corpus (Nakov et al., 2015) consists of 3,229 questions: 2,600 for training, 300 for development, and 329 for testing. The total number of comments is 20,162, with an average of 6.24 comments per question. The class labels for the comments are distributed as follows: 9,941 *good* (49.31%), 2,013 *potential* (9.98%), and 8,208 *bad* (40.71%) comments.

Since a typical answer selection setting only considers correct and incorrect answers, we also experiment with *potential* labelled as *bad*.

	P	R	F_1	A	$F_{1,ta}$	A_{ta}
Baseline Features						
SVM	68.86±1.42	82.34±1.04	74.98±0.73	72.90±1.00	64.56±0.97	75.32±0.40
SVM^{hmm}	70.34±1.57	81.00±1.98	75.28±1.05	73.75±1.56	65.25±1.16	74.68±1.05
LogReg	64.20±1.33	88.54±0.81	74.42±0.80	69.99±0.94	66.00±1.33	73.04±0.96
CRF_{map}	69.11±1.41	80.63±1.76	74.42±1.29	72.66±1.75	63.90±1.71	73.51±0.73
CRF_{mpm}	69.60±1.65	81.17±1.28	74.93±1.19	73.20±1.77	64.53±1.37	74.32±0.92
Baseline+Thread-level Features						
SVM	72.55±0.96	83.39±1.36	77.59±0.95	76.23±1.37	66.41±1.30	76.23±0.45
SVM^{hmm}	73.24±1.66	81.66±1.21	77.21±1.18	76.20±1.81	65.33±1.12	76.43±0.92
LogReg	71.15±0.96	84.44±1.50	77.22±1.07	75.43±1.47	66.57±1.49	75.05±0.70
CRF_{map}	71.27±1.20	83.15±1.81	76.75±1.28	75.14±1.72	65.36±1.45	75.61±0.63
CRF_{mpm}	71.56±1.31	83.34±1.84	77.00±1.35	75.43±1.84	65.57±1.54	75.71±0.71

Table 3: Precision, Recall, F_1, Accuracy computed at the comment level; $F_{1,ta}$ and A_{ta} are averaged at the thread level. Precision, Recall, F_1, $F_{1,ta}$ are computed with respect to the *good* classifier on 5-fold cross-validation (mean±stand. dev.).

4.2 Experimental Setup

Our local classifiers are support vector machines (SVM) with $C = 1$ (Joachims, 1999), logistic regression with a Gaussian prior with variance 10, and logistic ordinal regression (McCullagh, 1980). In order to capture long-range sequential dependencies, we use a second-order SVM^{hmm} (Yu and Joachims, 2008) (with $C = 500$ and $epsilon = 0.01$) and a second-order linear-chain CRF, which considers dependencies between three neighboring labels in a sequence (Lafferty et al., 2001; Cuong et al., 2014). In CRF, we perform two kinds of inference to find the most probable labels for the comments in a sequence. (*i*) We compute the maximum a posterior (MAP) or the (jointly) most probable sequence of labels using the Viterbi algorithm. Specifically, it computes $\mathbf{y}^* = \mathtt{argmax}_{\mathbf{y}_{1:T}} P(\mathbf{y}_{1:T}|\mathbf{x}_{1:T})$, where T is the number of comments in the thread. (*ii*) We use the forward–backward algorithm to find the labels by maximizing (individual) posterior marginals (MPM). More formally, we compute $\hat{\mathbf{y}} = \big(\mathtt{argmax}_{\mathbf{y}_1} P(y_1|\mathbf{x}_{1:T}), \cdots, \mathtt{argmax}_{\mathbf{y}_T} P(y_T|\mathbf{x}_{1:T})\big)$. While MAP yields a globally consistent sequence of labels, MPM can be more robust in many cases; see (Murphy, 2012, p. 613) for details. CRF also uses a Gaussian prior with variance 10.[5]

4.3 Experiment results

In order to compare the quality of our features to the existing state of the art, we performed a first experiment aligned to the multi-class setting of the SemEval 2015 Task 3 competition. Table 1 shows our results on the official test dataset.

As in the competition, the results are macro-averaged at class level. The results of the top 3 systems are reported for comparison: JAIST (Tran et al., 2015), HITSZ (Hou et al., 2015) and QCRI (Nicosia et al., 2015), where the latter refers to our old system that we used for the competition. The two main observations are (*i*) using thread-level features helps significantly; and (*ii*) the ordinal regression model, which captures the idea that *potential* lies between *good* and *bad*, achieves at least as good results as the top system at SemEval, namely JAIST.

For the remaining experiments, we reduce the multi-class problem to a binary one (cf. Section 2). Table 2 shows the results obtained on the official test dataset. Note that ordinal regression is not applicable in this binary setting. The F_1 values for the baseline features suggest that using the labels in the thread sequence yields better performance with SVM^{hmm} and CRF. When thread-level features are used, the models using sequence labels do not outperform SVM and logistic regression anymore. Regarding the two variations of CRF, the posterior marginals maximization is slightly better: maximizing on each comment pays more than on the entire thread.

Since the task consists in identifying *good* answers for a given question, further figures at the question level are necessary, i.e., we compute the target performance measure for all comments of each question and then we average the results over all threads (ta). Table 2 shows such the result using two measures: F_1 and accuracy, i.e., $F_{1,ta}$ and A_{ta}, for which long threads have less impact on the final outcome. The impact of the thread features is not-so-high in terms of these measures, sometimes even negatively affecting some of the models.

[5]Varying regularization strength (variance of the prior) did not make much difference.

Q_{u_1}:	Gymnastic world cup. Does anyone know what time the competition starts today? Thanks	
c_{1,u_2}:	sorry - is this being held here in Doha? If so, I'd love to go. Expat Sueo P.S. Is that a labradoodle in your avatar?	Bad→Bad
c_{2,u_1}:	No actually a Cockapoo! Yes the comp. runs from today until Wednesday at Aspire.	Bad→Bad
c_{3,u_2}:	Thanks for the info - maybe I'll turn up after the TableTop Sale is done and dusted! ES P.S. Cute pup!	Good→Bad

Q_{u_4}:	Good Scissor. Dears, anyone have an idea where to find a good scissor for hair and beard trimming please???	
c_{1,u_5}:	Visit Family food center	Bad→Good
c_{2,u_6}:	Al rawnaq airport road...U'll find all types of scissors there...	Bad→Good
c_{3,u_4}:	Thank you all . . . I will try that.	Bad→Bad

Figure 2: Two real question–comments threads (simplified; ID in CQA-QL: Q770 and Q752). The sub-indexes stand for the position in the thread and the author of the comment. The class label corresponds to the prediction before and after considering thread-level information. The right-hand label matches with the gold one in all the cases.

Cross validation. In order to better understand the mixed results obtained on the single official test set, we performed 5-fold cross validation over the entire dataset. The results are shown in Table 3. When looking at the performance of the different models with the same set of features, no statistically significant differences are observed on F_1 or $F_{1,ta}$ (t-test with confidence level 95%). The sequence of predicted labels in CRF or SVM^{hmm} does not impact the final result. In contrast, an important difference is observed when thread-level features come into play: the performance of all the models improves by approximately two F_1 points absolute, and statistically significant differences are observed for SVM and logistic regression (t-test, 95%). Moreover, while on the test dataset the thread-level features do not always improve $F_{1,ta}$ and A_{ta}, on the 5-fold cross-validation using them is always beneficial: for $F_{1,ta}$ statistically significant difference is observed for SVM only (t-test, 90%).

Qualitative results. In order to get an intuition about the effect of the thread-level features, we show two example comment threads in Figure 2. These comments are classified correctly when thread features are used in the classifier, and incorrectly when only basic features are used.

In the first case (Q_{u_1}), the third comment is classified as *good* by models that only use basic features. In contrast, thanks to the thread-level features, the classifier can consider that there is a dialogue between u_1 and u_2, causing all the comments to be assigned to the correct class: *bad.*

In the second example (Q_{u_4}), the first two comments are classified as *bad* when using the basic features. However, the third comment —written by the same user who asked Q_{u_4}— includes an acknowledgment. The latter is propagated to the previous comments in terms of a thread feature, which indicates that such comments are more likely to be *good* answers. This feature provides the classifier with enough information to properly label the first two comments as *good.*

5 Conclusions

We presented a study on using dependencies between the different answers in the same question thread in the context of answer selection in cQA. Our experiments with different classifiers, features, and experimental conditions, reveal that answer dependencies are helpful to improve results on the task. Such dependencies are best exploited by means of carefully designed thread-level features, whereas sequence label information alone, e.g., used in CRF or SVM^{hmm}, is not effective.

In future work, we plan to (*i*) experiment with more sophisticated thread-level features, as well as with other features that model context in general; (*ii*) try data from other cQA websites, e.g., where dialogue between users is marked explicitly; and finally, (*iii*) integrate sequence, precedence, dependency information with global —thread-level— features in a unified framework.

Acknowledgments

This research is developed by the Arabic Language Technologies (ALT) group at the Qatar Computing Research Institute (QCRI), Hamad Bin Khalifa University, within Qatar Foundation in collaboration with MIT. It is part of the Interactive sYstems for Answer Search (Iyas) project.

References

Lloyd Allison and Trevor Dix. 1986. A bit-string longest-common-subsequence algorithm. *Inf. Process. Lett.*, 23(6):305–310, December.

Nguyen Viet Cuong, Nan Ye, Wee Sun Lee, and Hai Leong Chieu. 2014. Conditional random field with high-order dependencies for sequence labeling and segmentation. *The Journal of Machine Learning Research*, 15(1):981–1009.

Michael Heilman and Noah A. Smith. 2010. Tree edit models for recognizing textual entailments, paraphrases, and answers to questions. In *Proceedings of Human Language Technologies: The 2010 Annual Conference of the North American Chapter of the Association for Computational Linguistics*, HLT '10, pages 1011–1019, Los Angeles, California, USA.

Yongshuai Hou, Cong Tan, Xiaolong Wang, Yaoyun Zhang, Jun Xu, and Qingcai Chen. 2015. HITSZ-ICRC: Exploiting classification approach for answer selection in community question answering. In *Proceedings of the 9th International Workshop on Semantic Evaluation*, SemEval '15, pages 196–202, Denver, Colorado, USA.

Paul Jaccard. 1901. Étude comparative de la distribution florale dans une portion des Alpes et des Jura. *Bulletin del la Société Vaudoise des Sciences Naturelles*, 37:547–579.

Jiwoon Jeon, W. Bruce Croft, and Joon Ho Lee. 2005. Finding similar questions in large question and answer archives. In *Proceedings of the 14th ACM International Conference on Information and Knowledge Management*, CIKM '05, pages 84–90, Bremen, Germany.

Thorsten Joachims. 1999. Making Large-scale Support Vector Machine Learning Practical. In Bernhard Schölkopf, Christopher J. C. Burges, and Alexander J. Smola, editors, *Advances in Kernel Methods*, pages 169–184. MIT Press, Cambridge, Massachusetts, USA.

John Lafferty, Andrew McCallum, and Fernando Pereira. 2001. Conditional random fields: Probabilistic models for segmenting and labeling sequence data. In *Proceedings of the Eighteenth International Conference on Machine Learning*, ICML '01, pages 282–289, San Francisco, California, USA.

Caroline Lyon, James Malcolm, and Bob Dickerson. 2001. Detecting short passages of similar text in large document collections. In *Proceedings of the 2001 Conference on Empirical Methods in Natural Language Processing*, EMNLP '01, pages 118–125, Pittsburgh, Pennsylvania, USA.

Peter McCullagh. 1980. Regression models for ordinal data. *J. Roy. Statist. Soc. B*, 42:109–142.

Alessandro Moschitti, Silvia Quarteroni, Roberto Basili, and Suresh Manandhar. 2007. Exploiting syntactic and shallow semantic kernels for question answer classification. In *Proceedings of the 45th Annual Meeting of the Association of Computational Linguistics*, ACL '07, pages 776–783, Prague, Czech Republic.

Alessandro Moschitti. 2006. Efficient Convolution Kernels for Dependency and Constituent Syntactic Trees. In Johannes Fürnkranz, Tobias Scheffer, and Myra Spiliopoulou, editors, *Machine Learning: ECML 2006*, volume 4212 of *Lecture Notes in Computer Science*, pages 318–329. Springer Berlin Heidelberg.

Kevin Murphy. 2012. *Machine Learning A Probabilistic Perspective*. The MIT Press.

Preslav Nakov, Lluís Màrquez, Walid Magdy, Alessandro Moschitti, Jim Glass, and Bilal Randeree. 2015. SemEval-2015 task 3: Answer selection in community question answering. In *Proceedings of the 9th International Workshop on Semantic Evaluation*, SemEval '15, pages 269–281, Denver, Colorado, USA.

Massimo Nicosia, Simone Filice, Alberto Barrón-Cedeño, Iman Saleh, Hamdy Mubarak, Wei Gao, Preslav Nakov, Giovanni Da San Martino, Alessandro Moschitti, Kareem Darwish, Lluís Màrquez, Shafiq Joty, and Walid Magdy. 2015. QCRI: Answer selection for community question answering - experiments for Arabic and English. In *Proceedings of the 9th International Workshop on Semantic Evaluation*, SemEval '15, pages 203–209, Denver, Colorado, USA.

Filip Radlinski and Thorsten Joachims. 2005. Query chains: Learning to rank from implicit feedback. In *Proceedings of the Eleventh ACM SIGKDD International Conference on Knowledge Discovery in Data Mining*, KDD '05, pages 239–248, Chicago, Illinois, USA.

Aliaksei Severyn and Alessandro Moschitti. 2012. Structural relationships for large-scale learning of answer re-ranking. In *Proceedings of the 35th International ACM SIGIR Conference on Research and Development in Information Retrieval*, SIGIR '12, pages 741–750, Portland, Oregon, USA.

Aliaksei Severyn and Alessandro Moschitti. 2013. Automatic feature engineering for answer selection and extraction. In *Proceedings of the 2013 Conference on Empirical Methods in Natural Language Processing*, EMNLP '13, pages 458–467, Seattle, Washington, USA.

Aliaksei Severyn, Massimo Nicosia, and Alessandro Moschitti. 2013. Learning adaptable patterns for passage reranking. In *Proceedings of the Seventeenth Conference on Computational Natural Language Learning*, CoNLL '13, pages 75–83, Sofia, Bulgaria.

Dan Shen and Mirella Lapata. 2007. Using semantic roles to improve question answering. In *Proceedings of the 2007 Joint Conference on Empirical Methods in Natural Language Processing and Computational Natural Language Learning*, EMNLP-CoNLL '07, pages 12–21, Prague, Czech Republic.

Mihai Surdeanu, Massimiliano Ciaramita, and Hugo Zaragoza. 2008. Learning to rank answers on large online QA collections. In *Proceedings of the 46th Annual Meeting of the Association for Computational Linguistics and the Human Language Technology Conference*, ACL-HLT '08, pages 719–727, Columbus, Ohio, USA.

Quan Hung Tran, Vu Tran, Tu Vu, Minh Nguyen, and Son Bao Pham. 2015. JAIST: Combining multiple features for answer selection in community question answering. In *Proceedings of the 9th International Workshop on Semantic Evaluation*, SemEval '15, pages 215–219, Denver, Colorado, USA.

Mengqiu Wang and Christopher D. Manning. 2010. Probabilistic tree-edit models with structured latent variables for textual entailment and question answering. In *Proceedings of the 23rd International Conference on Computational Linguistics*, COLING '10, pages 1164–1172, Beijing, China.

Michael Wise. 1996. Yap3: Improved detection of similarities in computer program and other texts. In *Proceedings of the Twenty-seventh SIGCSE Technical Symposium on Computer Science Education*, SIGCSE '96, pages 130–134, New York, New York, USA.

Xuchen Yao, Benjamin Van Durme, Chris Callison-Burch, and Peter Clark. 2013. Answer extraction as sequence tagging with tree edit distance. In *Proceedings of the 2013 Conference of the North American Chapter of the Association for Computational Linguistics: Human Language Technologies*, NAACL-HLT '13, pages 858–867.

Chun-Nam Yu and T. Joachims. 2008. Training structural SVMs with kernels using sampled cuts. In *ACM SIGKDD Conference on Knowledge Discovery and Data Mining*, KDD '08, pages 794–802.

Learning Hybrid Representations to Retrieve Semantically Equivalent Questions

Cícero dos Santos[1], Luciano Barbosa[1], Dasha Bogdanova[2], Bianca Zadrozny[1]
[1]IBM Research, 138/146 Av. Pasteur, Rio de Janeiro, Brazil
{cicerons,lucianoa,biancaz}@br.ibm.com
[2]ADAPT centre, School of Computing, Dublin City University, Dublin, Ireland
dbogdanova@computing.dcu.ie

Abstract

Retrieving similar questions in online Q&A community sites is a difficult task because different users may formulate the same question in a variety of ways, using different vocabulary and structure. In this work, we propose a new neural network architecture to perform the task of semantically equivalent question retrieval. The proposed architecture, which we call BOW-CNN, combines a bag-of-words (BOW) representation with a distributed vector representation created by a convolutional neural network (CNN). We perform experiments using data collected from two Stack Exchange communities. Our experimental results evidence that: (1) BOW-CNN is more effective than BOW based information retrieval methods such as TFIDF; (2) BOW-CNN is more robust than the pure CNN for long texts.

1 Introduction

Most Question-answering (Q&A) community sites advise users before posting a new question to search for similar questions. This is not always an easy task because different users may formulate the same question in a variety of ways.

We define two questions as semantically equivalent if they can be adequately answered by the exact same answer. Here is an example of a pair of such questions from Ask Ubuntu community, which is part of the Stack Exchange Q&A community site: (q_1)"*I have downloaded ISO files recently. How do I burn it to a CD or DVD or mount it?*" and (q_2)"*I need to copy the iso file for Ubuntu 12.04 to a CD-R in Win8. How do I do so?*". Retrieving semantically equivalent questions is a challenging task due to two main factors: (1) the same question can be rephrased in many different ways; and (2) two questions may be different but may refer implicitly to a common problem with the same answer. Therefore, traditional similarity measures based on word overlap such as shingling and Jaccard coefficient (Broder, 1997) and its variations (Wu et al., 2011) are not able to capture many cases of semantic equivalence. To capture the semantic relationship between pair of questions, different strategies have been used such as machine translation (Jeon et al., 2005; Xue et al., 2008), knowledge graphs (Zhou et al., 2013) and topic modelling (Cai et al., 2011; Ji et al., 2012).

Recent papers (Kim, 2014; Hu et al., 2014; Yih et al., 2014; dos Santos and Gatti, 2014; Shen et al., 2014) have shown the effectiveness of convolutional neural networks (CNN) for sentence-level analysis of *short texts* in a variety of different natural language processing and information retrieval tasks. This motivated us to investigate CNNs for the task of semantically equivalent question retrieval. However, given the fact that the size of a question in an online community may vary from a single sentence to a detailed problem description with several sentences, it was not clear that the CNN representation would be the most adequate.

In this paper, we propose a hybrid neural network architecture, which we call BOW-CNN. It combines a traditional bag-of-words (BOW) representation with a distributed vector representation created by a CNN, to retrieve semantically equivalent questions. Using a ranking loss function in the training, BOW-CNN learns to represent questions while learning to rank them according to their semantic similarity. We evaluate BOW-CNN over two different Q&A communities in the Stack Exchange site, comparing it against CNN and 6 well-established information retrieval algorithms based on BOW. The results show that our proposed solution outperforms BOW-based information retrieval methods such as the *term frequency - inverse document frequency* (TFIDF) in all evalu-

Proceedings of the 53rd Annual Meeting of the Association for Computational Linguistics and the 7th International Joint Conference on Natural Language Processing (Short Papers), pages 694–699,
Beijing, China, July 26-31, 2015.

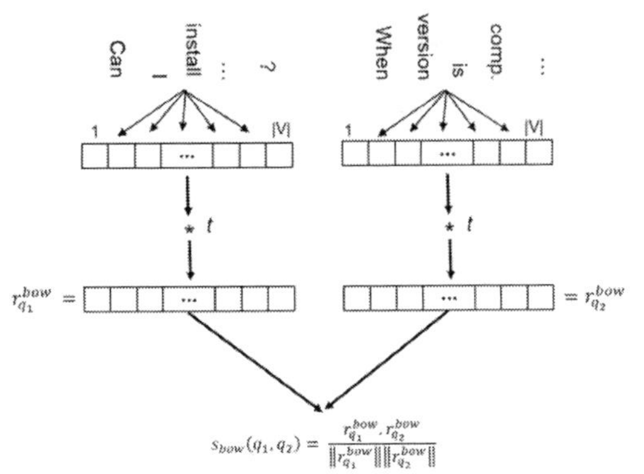

Figure 1: Representing and scoring questions with weighted bag-of-words.

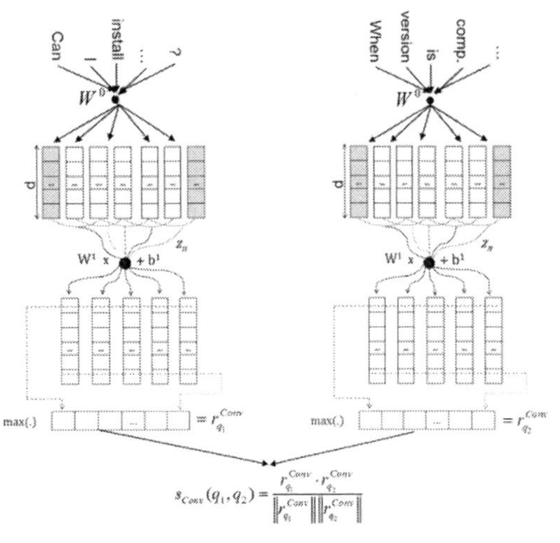

Figure 2: Representing and scoring questions with a convolutional approach.

ated scenarios. Moreover, we were able to show that for short texts (title of the questions), an approach using only CNN obtains the best results, whereas for long texts (title and body of the questions), our hybrid approach (BOW-CNN) is more effective.

2 BOW-CNN

2.1 Feed Forward Processing

The goal of the feed forward processing is to calculate the similarity between a pair of questions (q_1, q_2). To perform this task, each question q follows two parallel paths (BOW and CNN), each one producing a distinct vector representations of q. The BOW path produces a weighted bag-of-words representation of the question, r_q^{bow}, where the weight of each word in the vocabulary V is learned by the neural network. The CNN path, uses a convolutional approach to construct a distributed vector representations, r_q^{conv}, of the question. After producing the BOW and CNN representations for the two input questions, the BOW-CNN computes two partial similarity scores $s_{bow}(q_1, q_2)$, for the CNN representations, and $s_{conv}(q_1, q_2)$, for the BOW representations. Finally, it combines the two partial scores to create the final score $s(q_1, q_2)$.

2.2 BOW Path

The generation of the bag-of-words representation for a given question q is quite straightforward. As detailed in Figure 1, we first create a sparse vector $q^{bow} \in \mathbb{R}^{|V|}$ that contains the frequency in q of each word of the vocabulary. Next, we compute the weighted bag-of-words representation by performing the element-wise vector multiplication:

$$r_q^{bow} = q^{bow} * t \qquad (1)$$

where the vector $t \in \mathbb{R}^{|V|}$, contains a weight for each word in the vocabulary V. The vector t is a parameter to be learned by the network. This is closely related to the TFIDF text representation. In fact, if we fix t to the vector of IDFs, this corresponds to the exact TFIDF representation.

2.3 CNN Path

As detailed in Figure 2, the first layer of the CNN path transforms words into representations that capture syntactic and semantic information about the words. Given a question consisting of N words $q = \{w_1, ..., w_N\}$, every word w_n is converted into a real-valued vector r^{w_n}. Therefore, for each question, the input to the next NN layer is a sequence of real-valued vectors $q^{emb} = \{r^{w_1}, ..., r^{w_N}\}$. Word representations are encoded by column vectors in an embedding matrix $W^0 \in \mathbb{R}^{d \times |V|}$, where V is a fixed-sized vocabulary.

The next step in the CNN path consists in creating distributed vector representations r_{q1}^{conv} and r_{q2}^{conv} from the word embedding sequencies q_1^{emb} and q_2^{emb}. We perform this by using a convolutional layer in the same way as used in (dos Santos and Gatti, 2014) to create sentence-level representations.

More specifically, given a question q_1, the convolutional layer applies a matrix-vector operation to each window of size k of successive windows in $q_1^{emb} = \{r^{w_1}, ..., r^{w_N}\}$. Let us define the vector $z_n \in \mathbb{R}^{dk}$ as the concatenation of a sequence of k word embeddings, centralized in the n-th word:

$$z_n = \left(r^{w_{n-(k-1)/2}}, ..., r^{w_{n+(k-1)/2}}\right)^T$$

The convolutional layer computes the j-th element of the vector $r_{q_1}^{conv} \in \mathbb{R}^{cl_u}$ as follows:

$$[r_{q_1}^{conv}]_j = f\left(\max_{1<n<N}\left[W^1 z_n + b^1\right]_j\right) \quad (2)$$

where $W^1 \in \mathbb{R}^{cl_u \times dk}$ is the weight matrix of the convolutional layer and f is the hyperbolic tangent function. Matrices W^0 and W^1, and the vector b^1 are parameters to be learned. The word embedding size d, the number of convolutional units cl_u, and the size of the word context window k are hyper-parameters to be chosen by the user.

2.4 Question Pair Scoring

After the bag-of-words and convolutional-based representations are generated for the input pair (q_1, q_2), the partial scores are computed as the cosine similarity between the respective vectors:

$$s_{bow}(q_1, q_2) = \frac{r_{q_1}^{bow} . r_{q_2}^{bow}}{\|r_{q_1}^{bow}\| \|r_{q_2}^{bow}\|}$$

$$s_{conv}(q_1, q_2) = \frac{r_{q_1}^{conv} . r_{q_2}^{conv}}{\|r_{q_1}^{conv}\| \|r_{q_2}^{conv}\|}$$

The final score for the input questions (q_1, q_2) is given by the following linear combination

$$s(q_1, q_2) = \beta_1 * s_{bow}(q_1, q_2) + \beta_2 * s_{conv}(q_1, q_2)$$

where β_1 and β_2 are parameters to be learned.

2.5 Training Procedure

Our network is trained by minimizing a ranking loss function over the training set D. The input in each round is two pairs of questions $(q_1, q_2)^+$ and $(q_1, q_x)^-$ where the questions in the first pair are semantically equivalent (positive example), and the ones in the second pair are not (negative example). Let Δ be the difference of their similarity scores, $\Delta = s_\theta(q_1, q_2) - s_\theta(q_1, q_x)$, generated by the network with parameter set θ. As in (Yih et al., 2011), we use a logistic loss over Δ

$$L(\Delta, \theta) = log(1 + exp(-\gamma\Delta))$$

where γ is a scaling factor that magnifies Δ from [-2,2] (in the case of using cosine similarity) to a larger range. This helps to penalize more on the prediction errors. Following (Yih et al., 2011), in our experiments we set γ to 10.

Sampling informative negative examples can have a significant impact in the effectiveness of the learned model. In our experiments, before training, we create 20 pairs of negative examples for each positive pair $(q_1,q_2)^+$. To create a negative example we (1) randomly sample a question q_x that is not semantically equivalent to q_1 or q_2; (2) then create negative pairs $(q_1,q_x)^-$ and $(q_2,q_x)^-$. During training, at each iteration we only use the negative example x that produces the smallest different $s_\theta(q_1, q_2)^+ - s_\theta(q_1, q_x)^-$. Using this strategy, we select more representative negative examples.

We use stochastic gradient descent (SGD) to minimize the loss function with respect to θ. The backpropagation algorithm is used to compute the gradients of the network. In our experiments, BOW-CNN architecture is implemented using Theano (Bergstra et al., 2010).

3 Experimental Setup

3.1 Data

A well-structured source of semantically equivalent questions is the Stack Exchange site. It is composed by multiple Q&A communities, whereby users can ask and answer questions, and vote up and down both questions and answers. Questions are composed by a title and a body. Moderators can mark questions as duplicates, and eventually a question can have multiple duplicates.

For this evaluation, we chose two highly-accessed Q&A communities: Ask Ubuntu and English. They differ in terms of content and size. Whereas Ask Ubuntu has 29510 duplicated questions, English has 6621. We performed experiments using only the title of the questions as well as title + body, which we call *all* for the rest of this section. The average size of a title is very small (about 10 words), which is at least 10 times smaller than the average size of *all* for both datasets. The data was tokenized using the tokenizer available with the Stanford POS Tagger (Toutanova et al., 2003), and all links were replaced by a unique string. For Ask Ubuntu, we did not consider the content inside the tag code, which contains some specific Linux commands or programming code.

For each community, we created training, vali-

Community	Training	Validation	Test
Ask Ubuntu	9802	1991	3800
English	2235	428	816

Table 1: Partition of training, validation and test sets for the experiments.

dation and test sets. In Table 1, we inform the size of each set. The number of instances in the training set corresponds to the number of positive pairs of semantically equivalent questions. The number of instances in the validation and the test sets correspond to the number of questions which are used as queries. All questions in the validation and test set contain at least one duplicated question in the set of all questions. In our experiments, given a query question q, all questions in the Q&A community are evaluated when searching for a duplicate of q.

3.2 Baselines and Neural Network Setup

In order to verify the impact of jointly using BOW and CNN representations, we perform experiments with two NN architectures: the BOW-CNN and the CNN alone, which consists in using only the CNN path of BOW-CNN and, consequently, computing the score for a pair of questions using $s(q_1, q_2) = s_{conv}(q_1, q_2)$.

Additionally, we compare BOW-CNN with six well-established IR algorithms available on the Lucene package (Hatcher et al., 2004). Here we provide a brief overview of them. For further details, we refer the reader to the citation associated with the algorithm.

- **TFIDF** (Manning et al., 2008) uses the traditional Vector Space Model to represent documents as vectors in a high-dimensional space. Each position in the vector represents a word and the weight of words are calculated using TFIDF.
- **BM25** (Robertson and Walker, 1994) is a probabilistic weighting method that takes into consideration term frequency, inverse document frequency and document length. Its has two free parameters: k1 to tune term-frequency saturation; and b to calibrate the document-length normalization.
- **IB** (Clinchant and Gaussier, 2010) uses information-based models to capture the importance of a term by measuring how much its behavior in a document deviates from its behavior in the whole collection.
- **DFR** (Amati and Van Rijsbergen, 2002) is based on divergence from randomness framework. The relevance of a term is measured by the divergence between its actual distribution and the distribution from a random process.
- **LMDirichlet** and **LMJelinekMercer** apply probabilistic language model approaches for retrieval (Zhai and Lafferty, 2004). They differ in the smoothing method: LMDirichlet uses Dirichlet priors and LMJelinekMercer uses the Jelinek-Mercer method.

Param. Name	BOW-CNN	CNN
Word Emb. Size	200	200
Context Winow Size	3	3
Convol. Units	400	1000
Learning Rate	0.01	0.05

Table 2: Neural Network Hyper-Parameters

The word embeddings used in our experiments are initialized by means of unsupervised pre-training. We perform pre-training using the skip-gram NN architecture (Mikolov et al., 2013) available in the `word2vec` tool. We use the English Wikipedia to train word embeddings for experiments with the English dataset. For the AskUbuntu dataset, we use all available AskUbuntu community data to train word embeddings.

The hyper-parameters of the neural networks and the baselines are tuned using the development sets. In Table 2, we show the selected hyper-parameter values. In our experiments, we initialize each element $[t]_i$ of the bag-of-word weight vector t with the IDF of $i-$th word w_i computed over the respective set of questions Q as follows

$$[t]_i = IDF(w_i, Q) = \log \frac{|Q|}{|q \in Q : w_i \in q|}$$

4 Experimental Results

Comparison with Baselines. In Tables 3 and 4, we present the question retrieval performance (Accuracy@k) of different algorithms over the AskUbuntu and English datasets for the *title* and *all* settings, respectively. For both datasets, BOW-CNN outperforms the six IR algorithms for both *title* and *all* settings. For the AskUbuntu *all*, BOW-CNN is four absolute points larger than the

Algorithm	AskUbuntu			English		
	@1	@5	@10	@1	@5	@10
TFIDF	8.3	17.5	22.5	10.0	18.1	21.6
BM25	7.3	17.1	21.8	10.0	18.9	23.2
IB	8.1	18.1	22.6	10.1	18.4	22.7
DFR	7.7	17.8	22.4	10.5	19.0	23.0
LMD	5.6	14.1	19.0	10.9	20.1	24.2
LMJ	8.3	17.5	22.5	10.3	18.5	22.1
CNN	**11.5**	**24.8**	**31.4**	**11.6**	**23.0**	**26.9**
BOW-CNN	10.9	22.6	28.7	11.3	21.4	26.0

Table 3: Question *title* retrieval performance (Accuracy@k) for different algorithms.

Algorithm	AskUbuntu			English		
	@1	@5	@10	@1	@5	@10
TFIDF	16.9	31.3	38.3	25.9	42.0	48.1
BM25	18.2	33.1	39.8	29.4	45.7	52.5
IB	14.9	28.2	34.8	25.4	42.3	48.0
DFR	18.0	32.6	39.2	28.6	45.4	52.5
LMD	13.7	26.8	34.4	23.0	40.2	46.0
LMJ	18.3	33.4	40.7	28.5	45.7	52.3
CNN	20.0	33.8	40.1	17.2	29.6	33.8
BOW-CNN	**22.3**	**39.7**	**46.4**	**30.8**	**47.7**	**54.9**

Table 4: Question *title + body* (*all*) retrieval performance for different algorithms.

best IR baseline (LMJ) in terms of Accuracy@1, which represents an improvement of 21.9%. Since the BOW representation we use is closely related to TFIDF, an important comparison is the performance of BOW-CNN vs. TFIDF. In Tables 3 and 4, we can see that BOW-CNN consistently outperforms the TFIDF model in the two datasets for both cases *title* and *all*. These findings suggest that BOW-CNN is indeed combining the strong semantic representation power conveyed by the convolutional-based representation to, jointly with the BOW representation, construct a more effective model.

Another interesting finding is that CNN outperforms BOW-CNN for short texts (Table 3) and, conversely, BOW-CNN outperforms CNN for long texts (Table 4). This demonstrates that, when dealing with large input texts, BOW-CNN is an effective approach to combine the strengths of convolutional-based representation and BOW.

Impact of Initialization of BOW Weights. In the BOW-CNN experiments whose results are presented in tables 3 and 4 we initialize the elements of the BOW weight vector t with the IDF of each word in V computed over the question set Q. In this section we show some experimental results that indicate the contribution of this initialization.

In Table 5, we present the performance of BOW-CNN for the English dataset when different configurations of the BOW weight vector t are used. The first column of Table 5 indicates the type of initialization, where *ones* means that t is initialized with the value 1 (one) in all positions. The second column informs whether t is allowed to be updated (*Yes*) by the network or not (*No*). The numbers suggest that letting BOW weights free to be updated by the network produces better results than fixing them to IDF values. In addition, using IDF to initialize the BOW weight vector is better than using the same weight (ones) to initialize it. This is expected, since we are injecting a prior knowledge known to be helpful in IR tasks.

t initial	t updated	Title		All	
		@1	@10	@1	@10
IDF	Yes	**11.3**	**26.0**	**30.8**	**54.9**
IDF	No	10.6	25.3	29.7	**54.9**
Ones	Yes	10.7	24.2	26.3	51.2

Table 5: BOW-CNN performance using different methods to initialize the BOW weight vector t.

5 Conclusions

In this paper, we propose a hybrid neural network architecture, BOW-CNN, that combines bag-of-words with distributed vector representations created by a CNN, to retrieve semantically equivalent questions. Our experimental evaluation showed that: our approach outperforms traditional bow approaches; for short texts, a pure CNN obtains the best results, whereas for long texts, BOW-CNN is more effective; and initializing the BOW weight vector with IDF values is beneficial.

Acknowledgments

Dasha Bogdanova's contributions were made during an internship at IBM Research. Her work was partially supported by Science Foundation Ireland through the CNGL Programme (Grant 12/CE/I2267) in the ADAPT Centre (www.adaptcentre.ie) at DCU.

References

Gianni Amati and Cornelis Joost Van Rijsbergen. 2002. Probabilistic models of information retrieval based on measuring the divergence from randomness. *ACM Transactions on Information Systems (TOIS)*, 20(4):357–389.

James Bergstra, Olivier Breuleux, Frédéric Bastien, Pascal Lamblin, Razvan Pascanu, Guillaume Desjardins, Joseph Turian, David Warde-Farley, and Yoshua Bengio. 2010. Theano: a CPU and GPU math expression compiler. In *Proceedings of the Python for Scientific Computing Conference.*

A. Broder. 1997. On the resemblance and containment of documents. In *Proceedings of the Compression and Complexity of Sequences 1997*, SEQUENCES '97, pages 21–, Washington, DC, USA. IEEE Computer Society.

Li Cai, Guangyou Zhou, Kang Liu, and Jun Zhao. 2011. Learning the latent topics for question retrieval in community qa. In *IJCNLP*, volume 11, pages 273–281.

Stéphane Clinchant and Eric Gaussier. 2010. Information-based models for ad hoc ir. In *Proceedings of the 33rd international ACM SIGIR conference on Research and development in information retrieval*, pages 234–241. ACM.

Cícero Nogueira dos Santos and Maíra Gatti. 2014. Deep convolutional neural networks for sentiment analysis of short texts. In *Proceedings of the 25th International Conference on Computational Linguistics (COLING)*, Dublin, Ireland.

Erik Hatcher, Otis Gospodnetic, and Michael McCandless. 2004. Lucene in action.

Baotian Hu, Zhengdong Lu, Hang Li, and Qingcai Chen. 2014. Convolutional neural network architectures for matching natural language sentences. In *Advances in Neural Information Processing Systems 27: Annual Conference on Neural Information Processing Systems 2014, December 8-13 2014, Montreal, Quebec, Canada*, pages 2042–2050.

Jiwoon Jeon, W Bruce Croft, and Joon Ho Lee. 2005. Finding similar questions in large question and answer archives. In *Proceedings of the 14th ACM international conference on Information and knowledge management*, pages 84–90.

Zongcheng Ji, Fei Xu, Bin Wang, and Ben He. 2012. Question-answer topic model for question retrieval in community question answering. In *Proceedings of the 21st ACM international conference on Information and knowledge management*, pages 2471–2474.

Yoon Kim. 2014. Convolutional neural networks for sentence classification. In *Proceedings of the 2014 Conference on Empirical Methods for Natural Language Processing*, pages 1746–1751.

Christopher D Manning, Prabhakar Raghavan, and Hinrich Schütze. 2008. *Introduction to information retrieval*, volume 1. Cambridge university press Cambridge.

Tomas Mikolov, Kai Chen, Greg Corrado, and Jeffrey Dean. 2013. Efficient estimation of word representations in vector space. In *In Proceedings of Workshop at ICLR.*

Stephen E Robertson and Steve Walker. 1994. Some simple effective approximations to the 2-poisson model for probabilistic weighted retrieval. In *Proceedings of the 17th annual international conference on Research and development in information retrieval*, pages 232–241.

Yelong Shen, Xiaodong He, Jianfeng Gao, Li Deng, and Grégoire Mesnil. 2014. A latent semantic model with convolutional-pooling structure for information retrieval. In *Proceedings of the 23rd ACM International Conference on Conference on Information and Knowledge Management*, pages 101–110.

Kristina Toutanova, Dan Klein, Christopher D Manning, and Yoram Singer. 2003. Feature-rich part-of-speech tagging with a cyclic dependency network. In *Proceedings of the North American Chapter of the Association for Computational Linguistics on Human Language Technology*, pages 173–180.

Yan Wu, Qi Zhang, and Xuanjing Huang. 2011. Efficient near-duplicate detection for q&a forum. In *Proceedings of 5th International Joint Conference on Natural Language Processing*, pages 1001–1009, Chiang Mai, Thailand, November. Asian Federation of Natural Language Processing.

Xiaobing Xue, Jiwoon Jeon, and W. Bruce Croft. 2008. Retrieval models for question and answer archives. In *Proceedings of the 31st Annual International ACM SIGIR Conference on Research and Development in Information Retrieval*, SIGIR '08, pages 475–482.

Wen-tau Yih, Kristina Toutanova, John C. Platt, and Christopher Meek. 2011. Learning discriminative projections for text similarity measures. In *Proceedings of the Fifteenth Conference on Computational Natural Language Learning*, CoNLL'11, pages 247–256.

Wen-tau Yih, Xiaodong He, and Christopher Meek. 2014. Semantic parsing for single-relation question answering. In *Proceedings of the 52nd Annual Meeting of the Association for Computational Linguistics (Volume 2: Short Papers)*, pages 643–648. Association for Computational Linguistics.

Chengxiang Zhai and John Lafferty. 2004. A study of smoothing methods for language models applied to information retrieval. *ACM Transactions on Information Systems (TOIS)*, 22(2):179–214.

Guangyou Zhou, Yang Liu, Fang Liu, Daojian Zeng, and Jun Zhao. 2013. Improving question retrieval in community question answering using world knowledge. In *Proceedings of the Twenty-Third international joint conference on Artificial Intelligence*, pages 2239–2245.

Machine Comprehension with Syntax, Frames, and Semantics

Hai Wang Mohit Bansal Kevin Gimpel David McAllester
Toyota Technological Institute at Chicago, Chicago, IL, 60637, USA
{haiwang,mbansal,kgimpel,mcallester}@ttic.edu

Abstract

We demonstrate significant improvement on the MCTest question answering task (Richardson et al., 2013) by augmenting baseline features with features based on syntax, frame semantics, coreference, and word embeddings, and combining them in a max-margin learning framework. We achieve the best results we are aware of on this dataset, outperforming concurrently-published results. These results demonstrate a significant performance gradient for the use of linguistic structure in machine comprehension.

1 Introduction

Recent question answering (QA) systems (Ferrucci et al., 2010; Berant et al., 2013; Bordes et al., 2014) have focused on open-domain factoid questions, relying on knowledge bases like Freebase (Bollacker et al., 2008) or large corpora of unstructured text. While clearly useful, this type of QA may not be the best way to evaluate natural language understanding capability. Due to the redundancy of facts expressed on the web, many questions are answerable with shallow techniques from information extraction (Yao et al., 2014).

There is also recent work on QA based on synthetic text describing events in adventure games (Weston et al., 2015; Sukhbaatar et al., 2015). Synthetic text provides a cleanroom environment for evaluating QA systems, and has spurred development of powerful neural architectures for complex reasoning. However, the formulaic semantics underlying these synthetic texts allows for the construction of perfect rule-based question answering systems, and may not reflect the patterns of natural linguistic expression.

In this paper, we focus on **machine comprehension**, which is QA in which the answer is contained within a provided passage. Several comprehension tasks have been developed, including Remedia (Hirschman et al., 1999), CBC4kids (Breck et al., 2001), and the QA4MRE textual question answering tasks in the CLEF evaluations (Peñas et al., 2011; Peñas et al., 2013; Clark et al., 2012; Bhaskar et al., 2012).

We consider the Machine Comprehension of Text dataset (MCTest; Richardson et al., 2013), a set of human-authored fictional stories with associated multiple-choice questions. Knowledge bases and web corpora are not useful for this task, and answers are typically expressed just once in each story. While simple baselines presented by Richardson et al. answer over 60% of questions correctly, many of the remaining questions require deeper analysis.

In this paper, we explore the use of dependency syntax, frame semantics, word embeddings, and coreference for improving performance on MCTest. Syntax, frame semantics, and coreference are essential for understanding who did what to whom. Word embeddings address variation in word choice between the stories and questions. Our added features achieve the best results we are aware of on this dataset, outperforming concurrently-published results (Narasimhan and Barzilay, 2015; Sachan et al., 2015).

2 Model

We use a simple latent-variable classifier trained with a max-margin criterion. Let P denote the passage, q denote the question of interest, and A denote the set of candidate answers for q, where each $a \in A$ denotes one candidate answer. We want to learn a function $h : (P, q) \rightarrow A$ that, given a passage and a question, outputs a legal $a \in A$. We use a linear model for h that uses a latent variable w to identify the sentence in the passage in which the answer can be found.

Let W denote the set of sentences within the

Proceedings of the 53rd Annual Meeting of the Association for Computational Linguistics and the 7th International Joint Conference on Natural Language Processing (Short Papers), pages 700–706,
Beijing, China, July 26-31, 2015. ©2015 Association for Computational Linguistics

passage, where a particular $w \in W$ denotes one sentence.

Given a feature vector $f(P, w, q, a)$ and a weight vector θ with an entry for each feature, the prediction $\hat{a}$ for a new P and q is given by:

$$\hat{a} = \arg\max_{a \in A} \max_{w \in W} \theta^{\top} f(P, w, q, a)$$

Given triples $\{\langle P^i, q^i, a^i \rangle\}_{i=1}^{n}$, we minimize an ℓ_2-regularized max-margin loss function:

$$\min_{\theta} \lambda ||\theta||^2 + \sum_{i=1}^{n} \Bigg\{ -\max_{w \in W} \theta^{\top} f(P^i, w, q^i, a^i) + \max_{a \in A} \Bigg\{ \max_{w' \in W} \theta^{\top} f(P^i, w', q^i, a) + \Delta(a, a^i) \Bigg\} \Bigg\}$$

where λ is the weight of the ℓ_2 term and $\Delta(a, a^i) = 1$ if $a \neq a^i$ and 0 otherwise. The latent variable w makes the loss function non-convex.

3 Features

We start with two features from Richardson et al. (2013). Our first feature corresponds to their sliding window similarity baseline, which measures weighted word overlap between the bag of words constructed from the question/answer and the bag of words in the window. We call this feature B. The second feature corresponds to their word distance baseline, and is the minimal distance between two word occurrences in the passage that are also contained in the question/answer pair. We call this feature D. Space does not permit a detailed description.

3.1 Frame Semantic Features

Frame semantic parsing (Das et al., 2014) is the problem of extracting frame-specific predicate-argument structures from sentences, where the frames come from an inventory such as FrameNet (Baker et al., 1998). This task can be decomposed into three subproblems: *target identification*, in which frame-evoking predicates are marked; *frame label identification*, in which the evoked frame is selected for each predicate; and *argument identification*, in which arguments to each frame are identified and labeled with a role from the frame. An example output of the SEMAFOR frame semantic parser (Das et al., 2014) is given in Figure 1.

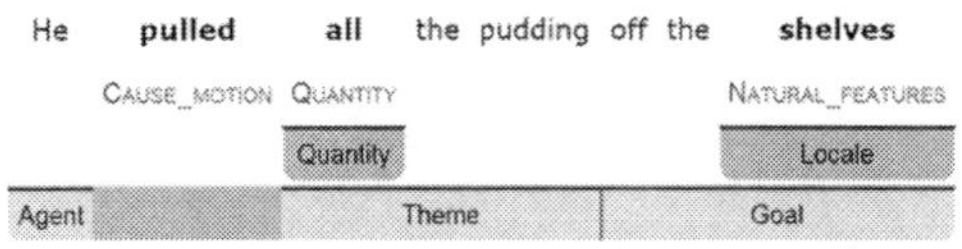

Figure 1: Example output from SEMAFOR.

Three frames are identified. The target words *pulled*, *all*, and *shelves* have respective frame labels CAUSE_MOTION, QUANTITY, and NATURAL_FEATURES. Each frame has its own set of arguments; e.g., the CAUSE_MOTION frame has the labeled *Agent*, *Theme*, and *Goal* arguments. Features from these parses have been shown to be useful for NLP tasks such as slot filling in spoken dialogue systems (Chen et al., 2013). We expect that the passage sentence containing the answer will overlap with the question and correct answer in terms of predicates, frames evoked, and predicted argument labels, and we design features to capture this intuition. Given the frame semantic parse for a sentence, let T be the bag of frame-evoking target words/phrases.[1] We define the bag of frame labels in the parse as F. For each target $t \in T$, there is an associated frame label denoted $F_t \in F$. Let R be the bag of phrases assigned with an argument label in the parse. We denote the bag of argument labels in the parse by L. For each phrase $r \in R$, there is an argument label denoted $L_r \in L$. We define a frame semantic parse as a tuple $\langle T, F, R, L \rangle$. We define six features based on two parsed sentences $\langle T^1, F^1, R^1, L^1 \rangle$ and $\langle T^2, F^2, R^2, L^2 \rangle$:

- f_1: # frame label matches: $|\{\langle s, t \rangle : s \in F^1, t \in F^2, s = t\}|$
- f_2: # argument label matches: $|\{\langle s, t \rangle : s \in L^1, t \in L^2, s = t\}|$.
- f_3: # target matches, ignoring frame labels: $|\{\langle s, t \rangle : s \in T^1, t \in T^2, s = t\}|$.
- f_4: # argument matches, ignoring arg. labels: $|\{\langle s, t \rangle : s \in R^1, t \in R^2, s = t\}|$.
- f_5: # target matches, using frame labels: $|\{\langle s, t \rangle : s \in T^1, t \in T^2, s = t, F^1_s = F^2_t\}|$.
- f_6: # argument matches, using arg. labels: $|\{\langle s, t \rangle : s \in R^1, t \in R^2, s = t, L^1_s = L^2_t\}|$.

We use two versions of each of these six features: one version for the passage sentence w and the question q, and an additional version for w and the candidate answer a.

3.2 Syntactic Features

If two sentences refer to the same event, then it is likely that they have some overlapping dependen-

[1] By *bag*, we mean here a set with possible replicates.

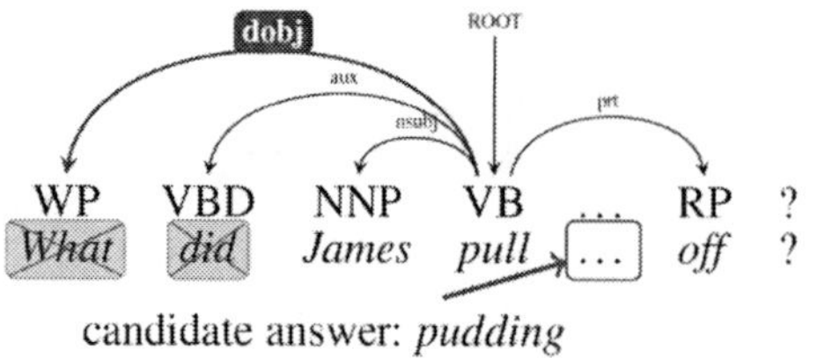

Figure 2: Transforming the question to a statement.

cies. To compare a Q/A pair to a sentence in the passage, we first use rules to transform the question into a statement and insert the candidate answer into the trace position. Our simple rule set is inspired by the rich history of QA research into modeling syntactic transformations between questions and answers (Moschitti et al., 2007; Wang et al., 2007; Heilman and Smith, 2010). Given Stanford dependency tree and part-of-speech (POS) tags for the question, let arc(u, v) be the label of the dependency between child word u and head word v, let $POS(u)$ be the POS tag of u, let c be the *wh*-word in the question, let r be the root word in the question's dependency tree, and let a be the candidate answer. We use the following rules:[2]

- c = *what*, $POS(r)$ = VB, and arc(c, r) = dobj. Insert a after word u where arc(u, r) = nsubj. Delete c and the word after c.
- c = *what*, $POS(r)$ = NN, and arc(c, r) = nsubj. Replace c by a.
- c = *where*, $POS(r)$ = VB, and arc(c, r) = advmod. Delete c and the word after c. If r has a child u such that arc(u, r) = dobj, insert a after u; else, insert a after r and delete r.
- c = *where*, r = *is*, $POS(r)$ = VBZ, and arc(c, r) = advmod. Delete c. Find r's child u such that arc(u, r) = nsubj, move r to be right after u. Insert a after r.
- c = *who*, $POS(r)$ = NN, and arc(c, r) = nsubj. Replace c by a.
- c = *who*, $POS(r) \in$ {VB, VBD}, and arc(c, r) = nsubj. Replace c by a.

We use other rules in addition to those above: change "why x?" to "the reason x is a", and change "how many x", "how much x", or "when x" to "x a".

Given each candidate answer, we attempt to transform the question to a statement using the rules above.[3] An example of the transformation is given in Figure 2. In the parse, *pull* is the root word and *What* is attached as a dobj. This matches the first rule, so we delete *did* and insert the candidate answer *pudding* after *pull*, making the final transformed sentence: *James pull pudding off.*

After this transformation of the question (and a candidate answer) to a statement, we measure its similarity to the sentence in the window using simple dependency-based similarity features. Denoting a dependency as $(u, v, \text{arc}(u, v))$, then two dependencies $(u_1, v_1, \text{arc}(u_1, v_1))$ and $(u_2, v_2, \text{arc}(u_2, v_2))$ match if and only if $u_1 = u_2$, $v_1 = v_2$, and $\text{arc}(u_1, v_1) = \text{arc}(u_2, v_2)$. One feature simply counts the number of dependency matches between the transformed question and the passage sentence. We include three additional count features that each consider a subset of dependencies from the following three categories: (1) $v = r$ and $u = a$; (2) $v = r$ but $u \neq a$; and (3) $v \neq r$. In Figure 2, the triples (*James*, *pull*, nsubj) and (*off*, *pull*, prt) belong to the second category while (*pudding*, *pull*, dobj) belongs to the first.

3.3 Word Embeddings

Word embeddings (Mikolov et al., 2013) represent each word as a low-dimensional vector where the similarity of vectors captures some aspect of semantic similarity of words. They have been used for many tasks, including semantic role labeling (Collobert et al., 2011), named entity recognition (Turian et al., 2010), parsing (Bansal et al., 2014), and for the Facebook QA tasks (Weston et al., 2015; Sukhbaatar et al., 2015). We first define the vector f_w^+ as the vector summation of all words inside sentence w and $f_w^\times$ as the element-wise multiplication of the vectors in w. To define vectors for answer a for question q, we concatenate q and a, then calculate f_{qa}^+ and $f_{qa}^\times$. For the bag-of-words feature B, instead of merely counting matches of the two bags of words, we also use $\cos(f_{qa}^+, f_w^+)$ and $\cos(f_{qa}^\times, f_w^\times)$ as features, where cos is cosine similarity. For syntactic features, where τ_w is the bag of dependencies of w and τ_{qa} is the bag of dependencies for the transformed question for candidate answer a, we use a feature function that returns the following:

$$\sum_{(u,v,\ell)\in\tau_w} \sum_{(u',v',\ell')\in\tau_{qa}} \mathbb{1}_{\ell=\ell'} \cos(u, u') \cos(v, v')$$

[2]There are existing rule-based approaches to transforming *statements* to questions (Heilman, 2011); our rules reverse this process.

[3]If no rule applies, we return 0 for all syntactic features.

where ℓ is short for $\text{arc}(u, v)$.[4]

3.4 Coreference Resolution

Coreference resolution systems aim to identify chains of mentions (within and across sentences) that refer to the same entity. We integrate coreference information into the bag-of-words, frame semantic, and syntactic features. We run a coreference resolution system on each passage, then for these three sets of features, we replace exact string match with a check for membership in the same coreference chain.

When using features augmented by word embeddings or coreference, we create new versions of the features that use the new information, concatenating them with the original features.

4 Experiments

MCTest splits its stories into train, development, and test sets. The original MCtest DEV is too small, to choose the best feature set, we merged the train and development sets in MC160 and MC500 and split them randomly into a 250-story training set (TRAIN) and a 200-story development set (DEV). We optimize the max-margin training criteria on TRAIN and use DEV to tune the regularizer λ and choose the best feature set. We report final performance on the original two test sets (for comparability) from MCTest, named MC160 and MC500.

We use SEMAFOR (Das et al., 2010; Das et al., 2014) for frame semantic parsing and the latest Stanford dependency parser (Chen and Manning, 2014) as our dependency parser. We use the Stanford rule-based system for coreference resolution (Lee et al., 2013). We use the pre-trained 300-dimensional word embeddings downloadable from the `word2vec` site.[5] We denote the frame semantic features by F and the syntactic features by S. We use superscripts ^{w} and ^{c} to indicate the use of embeddings and coreference for a particular feature set. To minimize the loss, we use the `miniFunc` package in MATLAB with LBFGS (Nocedal, 1980; Liu and Nocedal, 1989).

The accuracy of different feature sets on DEV is given in Table 1.[6] The boldface results correspond to the best feature set combination chosen by evaluating on DEV. In this case, the feature dimensionality is 29, which includes 4 bag-of-words features, 1 distance feature, 12 frame semantic features, and with the remaining being syntactic features. After choosing the best feature set on DEV, we then evaluate our system on TEST.

Negations: in preliminary experiments, we found that our system suffered with negation questions, so we developed a simple heuristic to deal with them. We identify a question as negation if it contains "not" or "n't" and does not begin with "how" or "why". If a question is identified as negation, we then negate the final score for each candidate answer.

Features	DEV Accuracy (%)
B + D + F	64.18
B + D + F + S	66.24
B^{wc} + D + F^c + S^{wc}	**69.87**

Table 1: Accuracy on DEV.

The final test results are shown in Table 2. We first compare to results from prior work (Richardson et al., 2013). Their first result uses a sliding window with the bag-of-words feature B described in Sec. 3; this system is called "Baseline 1" (B1). They then add the distance feature D, also described in Sec. 3. The combined system, which uses B and D, is called "Baseline 2" (B2). Their third result adds a rich textual entailment system to B2; it is referred to as B2+RTE.[7] We also compare to concurrently-published results (Narasimhan and Barzilay, 2015; Sachan et al., 2015).

We report accuracies for all questions as well as separately for the two types: those that are answerable with a single sentence from the passage ("Single") and those that require multiple sentences ("Multiple"). We see gains in accuracy of 6% absolute compared to the B2+RTE baseline and also outperform concurrently-published results (Narasimhan and Barzilay, 2015; Sachan et al., 2015). Even though our system only explicitly uses a single sentence from the passage when choosing an answer, we improve baseline accuracy for both single-sentence and multiple-sentence questions. [8]

[4] Similar to the original syntactic features (see end of Section 3.2), we also have 3 additional features for the three subset categories.

[5] `https://code.google.com/p/word2vec/`

[6] All accuracies are computed with tie-breaking partial credit (similar to previous work), i.e., if we have the same score for all four candidate answers, then we get partial credit of 0.25 for this question.

[7] These three results are obtained from files at `http://research.microsoft.com/en-us/um/redmond/projects/mctest/results.html`.

[8] However, we inspected these question annotations and

System		MC160			MC500		
		Single (112)	Multiple (128)	All	Single (272)	Multiple (328)	All
	B1	64.73	56.64	60.41	58.21	56.17	57.09
Richardson et al. (2013)	B2	75.89	60.15	67.50	64.00	57.46	60.43
	B2+RTE	76.78	62.50	69.16	68.01	59.45	63.33
Narasimhan and Barzilay (2015)		82.36	65.23	73.23	68.38	59.90	63.75
Sachan et al. (2015)		-	-	-	67.65	**67.99**	67.83
our system		**84.22**	**67.85**	**75.27**	**72.05**	67.94	**69.94**

Table 2: Accuracy comparison of published results on test sets.

Features	DEV Accuracy (%)
full (B^{wc}+D+F^c+S^{wc})	69.87
− B^{wc} (D + F^c+S^{wc})	58.46
− D (B^{wc}+F^c+S^{wc})	65.89
− B^{wc}, − D (F^c+S^{wc})	54.19
− embeddings (B^c+D+F^c+S^c)	68.28
− coreference (B^w+D+F+S^w)	68.43
− frame semantics (B^{wc}+D+S^{wc})	67.89
− syntax (B^{wc}+D+F^c)	67.64
− negation (B^{wc}+D+F^c+S^{wc})	68.72

Table 3: Ablation study of feature types on the dev set.

We also measure the contribution of each feature set by deleting it from the full feature set. These ablation results are shown in Table 3. We find that frame semantic and syntax features contribute almost equally, and using word embeddings contributes slightly more than coreference information. If we delete the bag-of-words and distance features, then accuracy drops significantly, which suggests that in MCTest, simple surface-level similarity features suffice to answer a large portion of questions.

5 Analysis

Successes To show the effects of different features, we show cases where the full system gives the correct prediction (marked with ∗) but ablating the named features causes the incorrect answer (marked with †) to be predicted:

Ex. 1: effect of embeddings: we find the soft similarity between 'noodle' and 'spaghetti'.

> ***clue:*** *Marsha's favorite dinner was spaghetti.*
> ***q:*** *What is Marsha's noodle made out of?* ∗***A)*** *Spaghetti;* †***C)*** *mom;*

Ex. 2: coreference resolves *She* to *Hannah Harvey*.

> *Hannah Harvey was a ten year old. She lived in New York.* ***q:*** *Where does Hannah Harvey live?* ∗***A)*** *New York;* †***C)*** *Kenya;*

Ex. 4: effect of syntax: by inserting answer **C**, the transformed statement is: *Todd say there's no place like home when he got home from the city.*

> *When his mom asked him about his trip to the city Todd said, "There's no place like home."*
> ***q:*** *What did Todd say when he got home from the city?* †***B)*** *There were so many people in cars;* ∗***C)*** *There's no place like home;*

Errors To give insight into our system's performance and reveal future research directions, we also analyzed the errors made by our system. We found that many required inferential reasoning, counting, set enumeration, multiple sentences, time manipulation, and comparisons. Some randomly sampled examples are given below, with the correct answer starred (∗):

Ex. 1: requires inference across multiple sentences:

> *One day Fritz got a splinter in his foot. Stephen did not believe him. Fritz showed him the picture. Then Stephen believed him.* ***q:*** *What made Stephen believe Fritz?* ∗***A)*** *the picture of the splinter in his foot;* †***C)*** *the picture of the cereal with milk;*

Ex. 2: requires temporal reasoning and world knowledge:

> *Ashley woke up bright and early on Friday morning. Her birthday was only a day away.* ***q:*** *What day of the week was Ashley's birthday?* ∗***A)*** *Saturday;* †***C)*** *Friday;*

Ex. 3: requires comparative reasoning:

> *Tommy has an old bicycle now. He is getting too big for it.* ***q:*** *What's wrong with Tommy's old bicycle?* ∗***B)*** *it's too small;* †***C)*** *it's old;*

6 Conclusion

We proposed several novel features for machine comprehension, including those based on frame semantics, dependency syntax, word embeddings, and coreference resolution. Empirical results demonstrate substantial improvements over several strong baselines, achieving new state-of-the-art results on MCTest. Our error analysis suggests that deeper linguistic analysis and inferential reasoning can yield further improvements on this task.

Acknowledgments

We thank Dekang Lin, Nathan Schneider and the anonymous reviewers for helpful comments.

occasionally found them to be noisy, which may cloud these comparisons.

References

Collin F. Baker, Charles J. Fillmore, and John B. Lowe. 1998. The Berkeley FrameNet project. In *Proceedings of the 17th International Conference on Computational Linguistics-Volume 1*, pages 86–90. Association for Computational Linguistics.

Mohit Bansal, Kevin Gimpel, and Karen Livescu. 2014. Tailoring continuous word representations for dependency parsing. In *Proceedings of the 52nd Annual Meeting of the Association for Computational Linguistics (Volume 2: Short Papers)*, pages 809–815, Baltimore, Maryland, June. Association for Computational Linguistics.

Jonathan Berant, Andrew Chou, Roy Frostig, and Percy Liang. 2013. Semantic parsing on Freebase from question-answer pairs. In *Proceedings of EMNLP*.

Pinaki Bhaskar, Partha Pakray, Somnath Banerjee, Samadrita Banerjee, Sivaji Bandyopadhyay, and Alexander F Gelbukh. 2012. Question answering system for QA4MRE@CLEF 2012. In *CLEF (Online Working Notes/Labs/Workshop)*.

Kurt Bollacker, Colin Evans, Praveen Paritosh, Tim Sturge, and Jamie Taylor. 2008. Freebase: a collaboratively created graph database for structuring human knowledge. In *Proceedings of the 2008 ACM SIGMOD international conference on Management of data*, pages 1247–1250. ACM.

Antoine Bordes, Sumit Chopra, and Jason Weston. 2014. Question answering with subgraph embeddings. In *Proceedings of the 2014 Conference on Empirical Methods in Natural Language Processing (EMNLP)*, pages 615–620, Doha, Qatar, October. Association for Computational Linguistics.

Eric Breck, Marc Light, Gideon S Mann, Ellen Riloff, Brianne Brown, Pranav Anand, Mats Rooth, and Michael Thelen. 2001. Looking under the hood: Tools for diagnosing your question answering engine. In *Proceedings of the workshop on Open-domain question answering-Volume 12*, pages 1–8. Association for Computational Linguistics.

Danqi Chen and Christopher Manning. 2014. A fast and accurate dependency parser using neural networks. In *Proceedings of the 2014 Conference on Empirical Methods in Natural Language Processing (EMNLP)*, pages 740–750, Doha, Qatar, October. Association for Computational Linguistics.

Yun-Nung Chen, William Yang Wang, and Alexander I Rudnicky. 2013. Unsupervised induction and filling of semantic slots for spoken dialogue systems using frame-semantic parsing. In *Automatic Speech Recognition and Understanding (ASRU), 2013 IEEE Workshop on*, pages 120–125. IEEE.

Peter Clark, Philip Harrison, and Xuchen Yao. 2012. An entailment-based approach to the QA4MRE challenge. In *CLEF (Online Working Notes/Labs/Workshop)*.

Ronan Collobert, Jason Weston, Léon Bottou, Michael Karlen, Koray Kavukcuoglu, and Pavel Kuksa. 2011. Natural language processing (almost) from scratch. *J. Mach. Learn. Res.*, 12:2493–2537, November.

Dipanjan Das, Nathan Schneider, Desai Chen, and Noah A. Smith. 2010. Probabilistic frame-semantic parsing. In *Human Language Technologies: The 2010 Annual Conference of the North American Chapter of the Association for Computational Linguistics*, pages 948–956, Los Angeles, California, June. Association for Computational Linguistics.

Dipanjan Das, Desai Chen, André F. T. Martins, Nathan Schneider, and Noah A. Smith. 2014. Frame-semantic parsing. *Computational Linguistics*, 40(1):9–56.

David Ferrucci, Eric Brown, Jennifer Chu-Carroll, James Fan, David Gondek, Aditya A Kalyanpur, Adam Lally, J William Murdock, Eric Nyberg, John Prager, et al. 2010. Building Watson: An overview of the DeepQA project. *AI magazine*, 31(3):59–79.

Michael Heilman and Noah A. Smith. 2010. Tree edit models for recognizing textual entailments, paraphrases, and answers to questions. In *Human Language Technologies: The 2010 Annual Conference of the North American Chapter of the Association for Computational Linguistics*, pages 1011–1019, Los Angeles, California, June. Association for Computational Linguistics.

M. Heilman. 2011. *Automatic factual question generation from text*. Ph.D. thesis, Carnegie Mellon University.

Lynette Hirschman, Marc Light, Eric Breck, and John D Burger. 1999. Deep read: A reading comprehension system. In *Proceedings of the 37th annual meeting of the Association for Computational Linguistics on Computational Linguistics*, pages 325–332. Association for Computational Linguistics.

Heeyoung Lee, Angel Chang, Yves Peirsman, Nathanael Chambers, Mihai Surdeanu, and Dan Jurafsky. 2013. Deterministic coreference resolution based on entity-centric, precision-ranked rules. *Comput. Linguist.*, 39(4):885–916, December.

D. C. Liu and J. Nocedal. 1989. On the limited memory BFGS method for large scale optimization. *Math. Programming*, 45:503–528.

Tomas Mikolov, Ilya Sutskever, Kai Chen, Greg S Corrado, and Jeff Dean. 2013. Distributed representations of words and phrases and their compositionality. In C.J.C. Burges, L. Bottou, M. Welling, Z. Ghahramani, and K.Q. Weinberger, editors, *Advances in Neural Information Processing Systems 26*, pages 3111–3119. Curran Associates, Inc.

Alessandro Moschitti, Silvia Quarteroni, Roberto Basili, and Suresh Manandhar. 2007. Exploiting syntactic and shallow semantic kernels for question answer classification. In *Proceedings of the 45th Annual Meeting of the Association of Computational Linguistics*, pages 776–783, Prague, Czech Republic, June. Association for Computational Linguistics.

Karthik Narasimhan and Regina Barzilay. 2015. Machine comprehension with discourse relations. In *53rd Annual Meeting of the Association for Computational Linguistics*.

Jorge Nocedal. 1980. Updating quasi-newton matrices with limited storage. *Mathematics of Computation*, 35:773–782.

Anselmo Peñas, Eduard H Hovy, Pamela Forner, Álvaro Rodrigo, Richard Sutcliffe, Corina Forascu, and Caroline Sporleder. 2011. Overview of QA4MRE at CLEF 2011: Question answering for machine reading evaluation. In *CLEF (Notebook Papers/Labs/Workshop)*, pages 1–20.

Anselmo Peñas, Eduard Hovy, Pamela Forner, Álvaro Rodrigo, Richard Sutcliffe, and Roser Morante. 2013. QA4MRE 2011-2013: Overview of question answering for machine reading evaluation. In *Information Access Evaluation. Multilinguality, Multimodality, and Visualization*, pages 303–320. Springer.

Matthew Richardson, Christopher J.C. Burges, and Erin Renshaw. 2013. MCTest: A challenge dataset for the open-domain machine comprehension of text. In *Proceedings of the 2013 Conference on Empirical Methods in Natural Language Processing*, pages 193–203, Seattle, Washington, USA, October. Association for Computational Linguistics.

Mrinmaya Sachan, Avinava Dubey, Eric P. Xing, and Matthew Richardson. 2015. Learning answer-entailing structures for machine comprehension. In *53rd Annual Meeting of the Association for Computational Linguistics*.

S. Sukhbaatar, A. Szlam, J. Weston, and R. Fergus. 2015. Weakly supervised memory networks. March.

Joseph Turian, Lev Ratinov, and Yoshua Bengio. 2010. Word representations: A simple and general method for semi-supervised learning. In *Proceedings of the 48th Annual Meeting of the Association for Computational Linguistics*, ACL '10, pages 384–394, Stroudsburg, PA, USA. Association for Computational Linguistics.

M. Wang, N. A. Smith, and T. Mitamura. 2007. What is the Jeopardy model? a quasi-synchronous grammar for QA. In *Proc. of EMNLP-CoNLL*.

Jason Weston, Antoine Bordes, Sumit Chopra, and Tomas Mikolov. 2015. Towards ai-complete question answering: A set of prerequisite toy tasks. April.

X. Yao, J. Berant, and B. Van Durme. 2014. Freebase QA: Information extraction or semantic parsing? In *Workshop on Semantic Parsing*.

A Long Short-Term Memory Model for Answer Sentence Selection in Question Answering

Di Wang and **Eric Nyberg**
Language Technologies Institute
Carnegie Mellon University
Pittsburgh, PA 15213, USA
{diwang,ehn}@cs.cmu.edu

Abstract

In this paper, we present an approach that address the answer sentence selection problem for question answering. The proposed method uses a stacked bidirectional Long-Short Term Memory (BLSTM) network to sequentially read words from question and answer sentences, and then outputs their relevance scores. Unlike prior work, this approach does not require any syntactic parsing or external knowledge resources such as WordNet which may not be available in some domains or languages. The full system is based on a combination of the stacked BLSTM relevance model and keywords matching. The results of our experiments on a public benchmark dataset from TREC show that our system outperforms previous work which requires syntactic features and external knowledge resources.

1 Introduction

A typical architecture of open-domain question answering (QA) systems is composed of three high level major steps: a) question analysis and retrieval of candidate passages; b) ranking and selecting of passages which contain the answer; and optionally c) extracting and verifying the answer (Prager, 2006; Ferrucci, 2012). In this paper, we focus on the answer sentence selection. Being considered as a key subtask of QA, the selection is to identify the answer-bearing sentences from all candidate sentences. The selected sentences should be relevant to and answer the input questions.

The nature of this task is to match not only the words but also the meaning between question and answer sentences. For instance, although both of the following sentences contain keywords "Capriati" and "play", only the first sentence answers the question: "What sport does Jennifer Capriati play?"

Positive Sentence: "Capriati, 19, who has not played competitive *tennis* since November 1994, has been given a wild card to take part in the Paris tournament which starts on February 13."

Negative Sentence: "Capriati also was playing in the U.S. Open semifinals in '91, one year before Davenport won the junior title on those same courts."

Besides its application in the automated factoid QA system, another benefit of the answer sentence selection is that it can be potentially used to predict answer quality in community QA sites. The techniques developed from this task might also be beneficial to the emerging real-time user-oriented QA tasks such as TREC LiveQA. However, user-generated content can be noisy and hard to parse with off-the-shelf NLP tools. Therefore, methods that requires less syntactic features are desirable.

Recently, neural network-based distributed sentence modeling has been found successful in many natural language processing tasks such as word sense disambiguation (McCarthy et al., 2004), discourse parsing (Li et al., 2014), machine translation (Sutskever et al., 2014; Cho et al., 2014), and paraphrase detection (Socher et al., 2011).

In this paper, we present an approach that leverages the power of deep neural network to address the answer sentence selection problem for question answering. Our method employs stacked bidirectional Long Short-Term Memory (BLSTM) to sequentially read the words from question and answer sentences, and then output their relevance scores. The full system, when combined with keywords matching, outperforms previous approaches without using any syntactic parsing or external knowledge resources.

Proceedings of the 53rd Annual Meeting of the Association for Computational Linguistics and the 7th International Joint Conference on Natural Language Processing (Short Papers), pages 707–712, Beijing, China, July 26-31, 2015.

2 Related Work

Prior to this work there were other approaches to address the sentence selection task. The majority of previous approaches focused on syntactic matching between questions and answers. Punyakanok et al. (2004) and Cui et al. (2005) were among the earliest to propose the general tree matching methods based on tree-edit distance. Subsequent to these two papers, the approach in (Wang et al., 2007) use quasi-synchronous grammar to match each pair of question and sentence by their dependency trees. Later, tree kernel function together with a logistic regression model (Heilman and Smith, 2010) or Conditional Random Fields models (Wang and Manning, 2010; Yao et al., 2013) with extracted feature were adopted to learn the associations between question and answer. Recently, discriminative tree-edit features extraction and engineering over parsing trees are automated in (Severyn and Moschitti, 2013).

Besides syntactic approaches, lexical semantic model (Yih et al., 2013) is also used to select answer sentences. This model is to pair semantically related words based on word relations including synonymy/antonymy, hypernymy/hyponymy and general semantic word similarity.

There were also prior efforts in deep learning neural networks to question answering. Yih et al. (2014) focused on answering single-relation factual questions by a semantic similarity model using convolutional neural networks. Bordes et al. (2014) jointly embedded words and knowledge base constituents into same vector space to measure the relevance of question and answer sentences in that space. Iyyer et al. (2014) worked on the quiz bowl task, which is an application of recursive neural networks for factoid question answering over paragraphs. The correct answers are identified from a relatively small fixed set of candidate answers which are in the form of entities instead of sentences.

3 Approach

The goal of this system is to reduce as much as possible the dependency on syntactic features and external resources by leveraging the power of deep recurrent neural network architecture. The proposed network architecture is trained directly on the word sequences of question and answer passages, and is actually not limited to sentences.

3.1 Network Architecture

Recurrent Neural Network RNN is an extension of conventional feed-forward neural network, used to deal with variable-length sequence input. It uses a recurrent hidden state whose activation is dependent on that of the one immediate before. More formally, given an input sequence $x = (x_1, x_2, \dots, x_T)$, a conventional RNN updates the hidden vector sequence $h = (h_1, h_2, \dots, h_T)$ and output vector sequence $y = (y_1, y_2, \dots, y_T)$ from $t = 1$ to T as follows:

$$h_t = \mathcal{H}(W_{xh}x_t + W_{hh}h_{t-1} + b_h) \quad (1)$$

$$y_t = W_{hy}h_t + b_y \quad (2)$$

where the W denotes weight matrices, the b denotes bias vectors and $\mathcal{H}(\cdot)$ is the recurrent hidden layer function.

Long Short-Term Memory (LSTM) Due to the gradient vanishing problem, conventional RNNs is found difficult to be trained to exploit long-range dependencies. In order to mitigate this weak point in conventional RNNs, specially designed activation functions have been introduced. LSTM is one of the earliest attempts and still a popular option to tackle this problem. LSTM cell was originally proposed by Hochreiter and Schmidhuber (1997). Several minor modifications have been made to the original LSTM cell since then. In our approach, we adopted a slightly modified implementation of LSTM in (Graves, 2013).

In the LSTM architecture, there are three gates (input i, forget f and output o), and a cell memory activation vector c. The vector formulas for recurrent hidden layer function $\mathcal{H}$ in this version of LSTM network are implemented as following:

$$i_t = \sigma(W_{xi}x_t + W_{hi}h_{t-1} + b_i) \quad (3)$$

$$f_t = \sigma(W_{xf}x_t + W_{hf}h_{t-1} + b_f) \quad (4)$$

$$c_t = f_t c_{t-1} + i_t \tau(W_{xc}x_t + W_{hc}h_{t-1} + b_c) \quad (5)$$

$$o_t = \sigma(W_{xo}x_t + W_{ho}h_{t-1} + b_o) \quad (6)$$

$$h_t = o_t \theta(c_t) \quad (7)$$

where, τ and θ are the cell input and cell output non-linear activation functions which are stated as $tanh$ in this paper.

LSTM uses input and output gates to control the flow of information through the cell. The input gate should be kept sufficiently active to allow the signals in. Same rule applies to the output gate. The forget gate is used to reset the cell's own state.

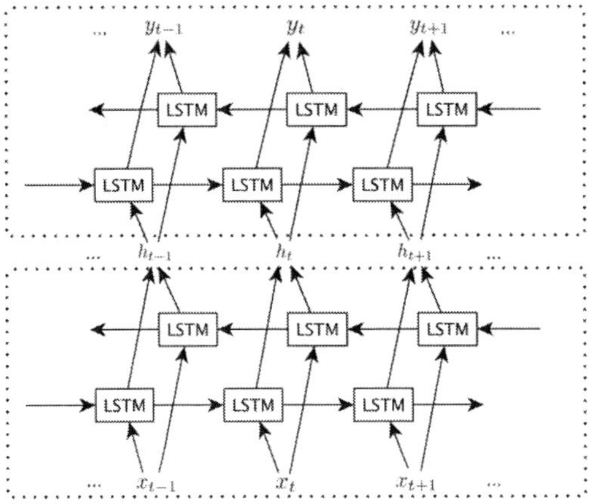

Figure 1: An illustration of a stacked bidirectional LSTM network

In (Graves, 2013), peephole connections are usually used to connect gates to the cell in tasks requiring precise timing and counting of the internal states. In our approach, we don't use peephole connections because the precise timing does not seem to be required.

Bidirectional RNNs Another weak point of conventional RNNs is their utilization of only previous context with no exploitation of future context. Unlike conventional RNNs, bidirectional RNNs utilize both the previous and future context, by processing the data from two directions with two separate hidden layers. One layer processes the input sequence in the forward direction, while the other processes the input in the reverse direction. The output of current time step is then generated by combining both layers' hidden vector $\overrightarrow{h_t}$ and $\overleftarrow{h_t}$ by: $y_t = W_{\overrightarrow{h}y}\overrightarrow{h_t} + W_{\overleftarrow{h}y}\overleftarrow{h_t} + b_y$.

Stacked RNNs In a stacked RNN, the output h_t from the lower layer becomes the input of the upper layer. Through the multi-layer stacked network, it is possible to achieve different levels of abstraction from multiple network layers. There are theoretical supports indicating that a deep, hierarchical model can be more efficient in representing some functions than a shallow one (Bengio, 2009). Empirical performance improvement is also observed in LSTM network compared with the shallow network (Graves et al., 2013).

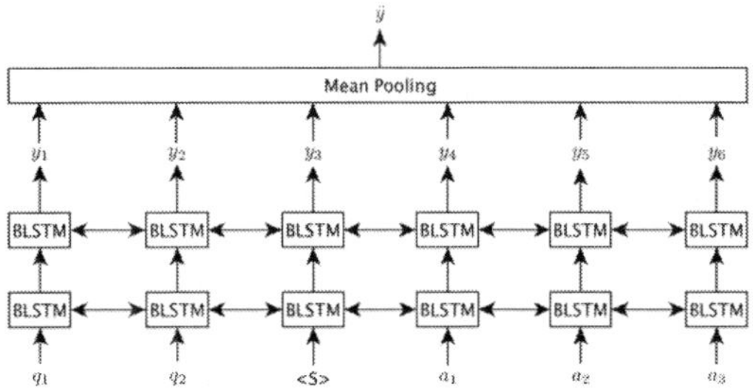

Figure 2: An illustration of our QA sentence relevance model based on stacked BLSTM

3.2 Answer Sentence Selection with Stacked BLSTM

As per analysis in section 3.1, we adopt multilayer stacked bidirectional LSTM RNNs (rather than conventional RNNs) to model the answer sentence selection problem as illustrated in Figure 2. The words of input sentences are first converted to vector representations learned from word2vec tool (Mikolov et al., 2013). In order to differentiate question q and answer a sentences, we insert a special symbol, <S>, after the question sequence. Then, the question and answer sentences word vectors are sequentially read by BLSTM from both directions. In this way, the contextual information across words in both question and answer sentences is modeled by employing temporal recurrence in BLSTM.

Since the LSTM in each direction carries a cell memory while reading the input sequence, it is capable of aggregating the context information and storing it into cell memory vector. For each time step in the BLSTM layer, the hidden vector or the output vector is generated by combining the cell memory vectors from two LSTM of both sides. In other words, all the contextual information across the entire sequence (both question and answer sentences) has been taken into consideration. The final output of each time step is the label indicating whether the candidate answer sentence should be selected as the correct answer sentence for the input question. This objective encourages the BLSTMs to learn a weight matrix that outputs a positive label if there is overlapping context information between two LSTM cell memories. Mean pooling is applied to all time step outputs during the training. During the test phase, we collect mean, sum and max poolings as features.

3.3 Incorporating Keywords Matching

In order to identify the correct candidate answer sentences, it is crucial to match the cardinal numbers and proper nouns with those occurred in the question. However, many cardinal numbers and proper nouns are out of the vocabulary (OOV) of our word embeddings. In addition, some proper nouns' embeddings may bring noise to the matching process. For example, "Japan" and "China" are two words very close in the embedding space. It is critical to discriminate these two proper nouns when matching question and answer sentences. In order to mitigate this weak point of the distributed representations, our full system combined the stacked BLSTM relevance model and exact keywords overlapping baseline by gradient boosted regression tree (GBDT) method (Friedman, 2001).

4 Experiments

Dataset The answer sentence selection dataset used in this paper was created by Wang et al. (2007) based on Text REtrieval Conference (TREC) QA track (8-13) data.[1] Candidate answer sentences were automatically retrieved for each question which is on average associated with 33 candidate sentences. There are two sets of data provided for training. One is the full training set containing 1229 questions that are automatically labeled by matching answer keys' regular expressions.[2] However, the generated labels are noisy and sometimes erroneously mark unrelated sentences as the correct answers solely because those sentences contain answer keys. Wang et al. (2007) also provided one small training set contains 94 questions, which were manually corrected for errors. In our experiments, we use the full training set because it provides significantly more question and answer sentences for learning, even though some of its labels are noisy.

The development and test data sets have 82 and 100 questions, respectively. Following (Wang et al., 2007), candidate answer sentences with over 40 words and questions with only positive or negative candidate answer sentences are removed from evaluation.[3]

Evaluation Metric Following previous works on this task, we also use Mean Average Precision (MAP) and Mean Reciprocal Rank (MRR) as evaluation metrics, which are calculated using the official *trec_eval* evaluation scripts.

Keywords Matching Baseline (BM25) As noted by Yih et al. (2013), counting overlapped keywords, especially when re-weighted by *idf* value of the question word, is a fairly competitive baseline. Following (Yih et al., 2013), our keywords matching baseline also counts the words that occurred in both questions and answer sentences, after excluding stop words and lowering the case. But, instead of the $tf \cdot idf$ formula used in (Yih et al., 2013), word counts are re-weighted by its *idf* value using the Okapi BM25 (Robertson and Walker, 1997) formula (with constants values $K_1 = 1.2$ and $B = 0.75$).

Network Setup The network weights are randomly initialized using a Gaussian distribution ($\mu = 0$ and $\sigma = 0.1$), and the network is trained with the stochastic gradient descent (SGD) with momentum 0.9. We experimented single-layer unidirectional LSTM, single-layer BLSTM, and three-layer stacked BLSTM. Each layer of LSTM and BLSTM has a memory size of 500. We use 300-dimensional vectors that were trained and provided by word2vec tool (Mikolov et al., 2013) using a part of the Google News dataset[4] (around 100 billion tokens) .

5 Results

Table 1 surveys prior results on this task, and places our models in the context of the current state-of-the-art results. Table 2 summarizes the results of our model on the answer selection task. According to Table 1 and 2, our combined system outperforms prior works on MAP and MRR metrics.

As indicated in Table 2, the three-layer stacked BLSTM alone shows better experiment results than single-layer BLSTM and unidirectional

[1] `http://nlp.stanford.edu/mengqiu/data/qg-emnlp07-data.tgz`

[2] Because the original full training dataset is no longer available from the website of the lead author of (Wang et al., 2007), we obtained this data re-released from Yao et al. (2013): `http://cs.jhu.edu/~xuchen/packages/jacana-qa-naacl2013-data-results.tar.bz2`

[3] As mentioned in the footnote 7 of (Yih et al., 2013): *"Among the 72 questions in the test set, 4 of them would always be treated answered incorrectly by the evaluation script used by previous work. This makes the upper bound of both MAP and MRR become 0.9444 instead of 1."* In order to make experiment results comparable with previous works, we also use this experiment setting.

[4] `https://code.google.com/p/word2vec/`

Reference	**MAP**	**MRR**
Yih et al. (2013) – Random	0.3965	0.4929
Wang et al. (2007)	0.6029	0.6852
Heilman and Smith (2010)	0.6091	0.6917
Wang and Manning (2010)	0.5951	0.6951
Yao et al. (2013)	0.6307	0.7477
Severyn and Moschitti (2013)	0.6781	0.7358
Yih et al. (2013) – BDT	0.6940	0.7894
Yih et al. (2013) – LCLR	0.7092	0.7700

Table 1: Overview of prior results on the answer sentence selection task

Features	MAP	MRR
BM25	0.6370	0.7076
Single-Layer LSTM	0.5302	0.5956
Single-Layer BLSTM	0.5636	0.6304
Three-Layer BLSTM	0.5928	0.6721
Three-Layer BLSTM + BM25	**0.7134**	**0.7913**

Table 2: Overview of our results on the answer sentence selection task. Features are keywords matching baseline score (BM25), and pooling values of single-layer unidirectional LSTM (Single-Layer LSTM), single-Layer bidirectional LSTM (Single-Layer BLSTM) and three-Layer stacked BLSTM's (Three-Layer BLSTM) outputs. Gradient boosted regression tree (GBDT) method is used to combine features.

LSTM, and performs comparably to previous systems. In order to mitigate the weak point of the distributed representations previously discussed in section 3.3, we combine the stacked BLSTM outputs with a keywords matching baseline (BM25). Our combined system's results are statistically significantly better than the keywords matching baseline (using the Student's t-test with $p < 0.05$) and outperforms previous state-of-art results.

6 Conclusion

In this paper, we presented an approach to address the answer sentence selection problem for question answering, by a combination of the stacked bidirectional LSTM model and keywords matching. The experiments provide strong evidence that distributed and symbolic representations encode complementary types of knowledge, which are all helpful in identifying answer sentences. Based on the experiment results, we found that our model not only performs better than previous work but most importantly does not require any syntactic features or external resources. In the future, we would like to further evaluate the models presented in this paper for different tasks, such as answer quality prediction in Community QA, recognizing textual entailment, and machine comprehension of text.

References

Yoshua Bengio. 2009. Learning deep architectures for AI. *Foundations and Trends in Machine Learning*, 2(1):1–127. Also published as a book. Now Publishers, 2009.

Antoine Bordes, Sumit Chopra, and Jason Weston. 2014. Question answering with subgraph embeddings. *CoRR*, abs/1406.3676.

Kyunghyun Cho, Bart van Merrienboer, Caglar Gulcehre, Dzmitry Bahdanau, Fethi Bougares, Holger Schwenk, and Yoshua Bengio. 2014. Learning phrase representations using rnn encoder–decoder for statistical machine translation. In *Proceedings of the 2014 Conference on Empirical Methods in Natural Language Processing (EMNLP)*, pages 1724–1734, Doha, Qatar, October. Association for Computational Linguistics.

Hang Cui, Renxu Sun, Keya Li, Min-Yen Kan, and Tat-Seng Chua. 2005. Question answering passage retrieval using dependency relations. In *Proceedings of the 28th Annual International ACM SIGIR Conference on Research and Development in Information Retrieval*, SIGIR '05, pages 400–407, New York, NY, USA. ACM.

David A. Ferrucci. 2012. Introduction to "This is Watson". *IBM Journal of Research and Development*, 56(3):1.

Jerome H. Friedman. 2001. Greedy function approximation: A gradient boosting machine. *The Annals of Statistics*, 29:1189–1232.

Alex Graves, Abdel-rahman Mohamed, and Geoffrey E. Hinton. 2013. Speech recognition with deep recurrent neural networks. In *IEEE International Conference on Acoustics, Speech and Signal Processing, ICASSP 2013, Vancouver, BC, Canada, May 26-31, 2013*, pages 6645–6649.

Alex Graves. 2013. Generating sequences with recurrent neural networks. *CoRR*, abs/1308.0850.

Michael Heilman and Noah A. Smith. 2010. Tree edit models for recognizing textual entailments, paraphrases, and answers to questions. In *Human Language Technologies: The 2010 Annual Conference of the North American Chapter of the Association for Computational Linguistics*, HLT '10, pages 1011–1019, Stroudsburg, PA, USA. Association for Computational Linguistics.

Sepp Hochreiter and Jürgen Schmidhuber. 1997. Long short-term memory. *Neural Comput.*, 9(8):1735–1780, November.

Mohit Iyyer, Jordan Boyd-Graber, Leonardo Claudino, Richard Socher, and Hal Daumé III. 2014. A neural network for factoid question answering over paragraphs. In *Empirical Methods in Natural Language Processing*.

Jiwei Li, Rumeng Li, and Eduard Hovy. 2014. Recursive deep models for discourse parsing. In *Proceedings of Empirical Methods in Natural Language Processing*.

Diana McCarthy, Rob Koeling, Julie Weeds, and John Carroll. 2004. Finding predominant word senses in untagged text. In *Proceedings of the 42nd Annual Meeting on Association for Computational Linguistics*, ACL '04, Stroudsburg, PA, USA. Association for Computational Linguistics.

Tomas Mikolov, Ilya Sutskever, Kai Chen, Greg S Corrado, and Jeff Dean. 2013. Distributed representations of words and phrases and their compositionality. In *Advances in Neural Information Processing Systems*, pages 3111–3119.

John M. Prager. 2006. Open-domain question-answering. *Foundations and Trends in Information Retrieval*, 1(2):91–231.

V. Punyakanok, D. Roth, and W. Yih. 2004. Mapping dependencies trees: An application to question answering. 1.

Stephen E. Robertson and Steve Walker. 1997. On relevance weights with little relevance information. In *Proceedings of the 20th Annual International ACM SIGIR Conference on Research and Development in Information Retrieval*, SIGIR '97, pages 16–24, New York, NY, USA. ACM.

Aliaksei Severyn and Alessandro Moschitti. 2013. Automatic feature engineering for answer selection and extraction. In *Proceedings of the 2013 Conference on Empirical Methods in Natural Language Processing, EMNLP 2013, 18-21 October 2013, Grand Hyatt Seattle, Seattle, Washington, USA, A meeting of SIGDAT, a Special Interest Group of the ACL*, pages 458–467.

Richard Socher, Eric H. Huang, Jeffrey Pennin, Christopher D Manning, and Andrew Y. Ng. 2011. Dynamic pooling and unfolding recursive autoencoders for paraphrase detection. In J. Shawe-Taylor, R.S. Zemel, P.L. Bartlett, F. Pereira, and K.Q. Weinberger, editors, *Advances in Neural Information Processing Systems 24*, pages 801–809. Curran Associates, Inc.

Ilya Sutskever, Oriol Vinyals, and Quoc V. Le. 2014. Sequence to sequence learning with neural networks. In *Proc. NIPS*, Montreal, CA.

Mengqiu Wang and Christopher D. Manning. 2010. Probabilistic tree-edit models with structured latent variables for textual entailment and question answering. In *Proceedings of the 23rd International Conference on Computational Linguistics*, COLING '10, pages 1164–1172, Stroudsburg, PA, USA. Association for Computational Linguistics.

Mengqiu Wang, Noah A. Smith, and Teruko Mitamura. 2007. What is the Jeopardy model? a quasi-synchronous grammar for QA. In *Proceedings of the 2007 Joint Conference on Empirical Methods in Natural Language Processing and Computational Natural Language Learning (EMNLP-CoNLL)*, pages 22–32, Prague, Czech Republic, June. Association for Computational Linguistics.

Xuchen Yao, Benjamin Van Durme, Chris Callison-Burch, and Peter Clark. 2013. Answer extraction as sequence tagging with tree edit distance. In *Proceedings of the 2013 Conference of the North American Chapter of the Association for Computational Linguistics: Human Language Technologies*, pages 858–867. Association for Computational Linguistics.

Wen-tau Yih, Ming-Wei Chang, Christopher Meek, and Andrzej Pastusiak. 2013. Question answering using enhanced lexical semantic models. In *Proceedings of the 51st Annual Meeting of the Association for Computational Linguistics*, pages 1744–1753. Association for Computational Linguistics.

Wen-tau Yih, Xiaodong He, and Christopher Meek. 2014. Semantic parsing for single-relation question answering. In *Proceedings of ACL*. Association for Computational Linguistics.

Answer Sequence Learning with Neural Networks for Answer Selection in Community Question Answering

Xiaoqiang Zhou **Baotian Hu** **Qingcai Chen*** **Buzhou Tang** **Xiaolong Wang**

Intelligent Computing Research Center
Harbin Institute of Technology, Shenzhen Graduate School
{xiaoqiang.jeseph,baotianchina,qingcai.chen,tangbuzhou}@gmail.com
wangxl@insun.hit.edu.cn

Abstract

In this paper, the answer selection problem in community question answering (CQA) is regarded as an answer sequence labeling task, and a novel approach is proposed based on the recurrent architecture for this problem. Our approach applies convolution neural networks (CNNs) to learning the joint representation of question-answer pair firstly, and then uses the joint representation as input of the long short-term memory (LSTM) to learn the answer sequence of a question for labeling the matching quality of each answer. Experiments conducted on the SemEval 2015 CQA dataset shows the effectiveness of our approach.

1 Introduction

Answer selection in community question answering (CQA), which recognizes high-quality responses to obtain useful question-answer pairs, is greatly valuable for knowledge base construction and information retrieval systems. To recognize matching answers for a question, typical approaches model semantic matching between question and answer by exploring various features (Wang et al., 2009a; Shah and Pomerantz, 2010). Some studies exploit syntactic tree structures (Wang et al., 2009b; Moschitti et al., 2007) to measure the semantic matching between question and answer. However, these approaches require high-quality data and various external resources which may be quite difficult to obtain. To take advantage of a large quantity of raw data, deep learning based approaches (Wang et al., 2010; Hu et al., 2013) are proposed to learn the distributed representation of question-answer pair directly. One disadvantage of these approaches lies in that

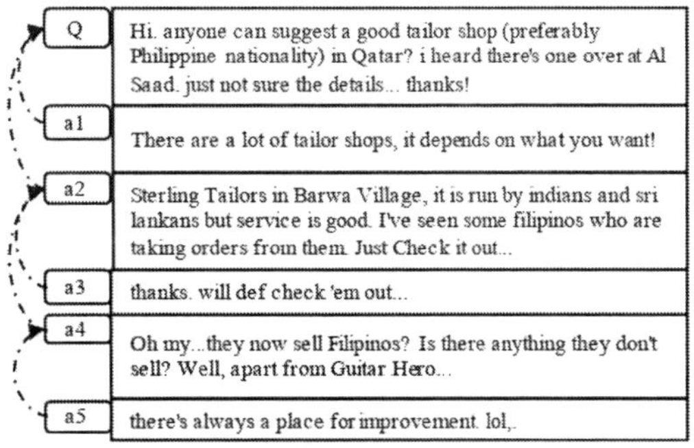

Figure 1: An Example of the Answer Sequence for a Question. The dashed arrows depict the relationships of the answers in the sequence.

semantic correlations embedded in the answer sequence of a question are ignored, while they are very important for answer selection. Figure 1 is a example to show the relationship of answers in the sequence for a given question. Intuitively, other answers of the question are beneficial to judge the quality of the current answer.

Recently, recurrent neural network (RNN), especially Long Short-Term Memory (LSTM) (Hochreiter et al., 2001), has been proved superiority in various tasks (Sutskever et al., 2014; Srivastava et al., 2015) and it models long term and short term information of the sequence. And also, there are some works on using convolutional neural networks (CNNs) to learn the representations of sentence or short text, which achieve state-of-the-art performance on sentiment classification (Kim, 2014) and short text matching (Hu et al., 2014).

In this paper, we address the answer selection problem as a sequence labeling task, which identifies the matching quality of each answer in the answer sequence of a question. Firstly, CNNs are used to learn the joint representation of question answer (QA) pair. Then the learnt joint repre-

* Corresponding author

Proceedings of the 53rd Annual Meeting of the Association for Computational Linguistics and the 7th International Joint Conference on Natural Language Processing (Short Papers), pages 713–718,
Beijing, China, July 26-31, 2015. ©2015 Association for Computational Linguistics

sentations are used as inputs of LSTM to predict the quality (e.g., *Good*, *Bad* and *Potential*) of each answer in the answer sequence. Experiments conducted on the CQA dataset of the answer selection task in SemEval-2015[1] show that the proposed approach outperforms other state-of-the-art approaches.

2 Related Work

Prior studies on answer selection generally treated this challenge as a classification problem via employing machine learning methods, which rely on exploring various features to represent QA pair. Huang et al. (2007) integrated textual features with structural features of forum threads to represent the candidate QA pairs, and used support vector machine (SVM) to classify the candidate pairs. Beyond typical features, Shah and Pomerantz (2010) trained a logistic regression (LR) classifier with user metadata to predict the quality of answers in CQA. Ding et al. (2008) proposed an approach based on conditional random fields (CRF), which can capture contextual features from the answer sequence for the semantic matching between question and answer. Additionally, the translation-based language model was also used for QA matching by transferring the answer to the corresponding question (Jeon et al., 2005; Xue et al., 2008; Zhou et al., 2011). The translation-based methods suffer from the informal words or phrases in Q&A archives, and perform less applicability in new domains.

In contrast to symbolic representation, Wang et al. (2010) proposed a deep belief nets (DBN) based semantic relevance model to learn the distributed representation of QA pair. Recently, the convolutional neural networks (CNNs) based sentence representation models have achieved successes in neural language processing (NLP) tasks. Yu et al. (2014) proposed a convolutional sentence model to identify answer contents of a question from Q&A archives via means of distributed representations. The work in Hu et al. (2014) demonstrated that 2-dimensional convolutional sentence models can represent the hierarchical structures of sentences and capture rich matching patterns between two language objects.

[1]http://alt.qcri.org/semeval2015/task3/

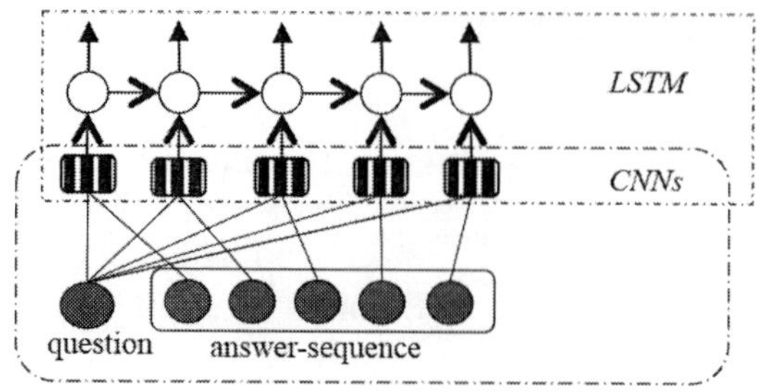

Figure 2: The architecture of R-CNN

3 Approach

We consider the answer selection problem in CQA as a sequence labeling task. To label the matching quality of each answer for a given question, our approach models the semantic links between successive answers, as well as the semantic relevance between question and answer. Figure 2 summarizes the recurrent architecture of our model (R-CNN). The motivation of R-CNN is to learn the useful context to improve the performance of answer selection. The answer sequence is modeled to enrich semantic features.

At each step, our approach uses the pre-trained word embeddings to encode the sentences of QA pair, which then is used as the input vectors of the model. Based on the joint representation of QA pair learned from CNNs, the LSTM is applied in our model for answer sequence learning, which makes a prediction to each answer of the question with softmax function.

3.1 Convolutional Neural Networks for QA Joint Learning

Given a question-answer pair at the step t, we use convolutional neural networks (CNNs) to learn the joint representation p_t for the pair. Figure 3 illustrates the process of QA joint learning, which includes two stages: summarizing the meaning of the question and an answer, and generating the joint representation of QA pair.

To obtain high-level sentence representations of the question and answer, we set 3 hidden layers in two convolutional sentence models respectively. The output of each hidden layer is made up of a set of 2-dimensional arrays called feature map parameters (w_m, b_m). Each feature map is the outcome of one convolutional or pooling filter. Each pooling layer is followed an activation function σ. The output of the mth hidden layer is computed as

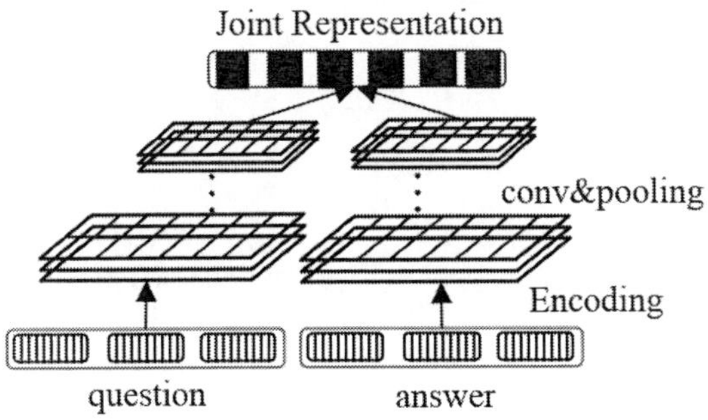

Figure 3: CNNs for QA joint learning

Eq. 1:

$$H_m = \sigma(pool(w_m H_{m-1} + b_m)) \quad (1)$$

Here, H_0 is one real-value matrix after sentence semantic encoding by concatenating the word vectors with sliding windows. It is the input of deep convolution and pooling, which is similar to that of traditional image input.

Finally, we combine the two sentence models by adding an additional layer H_t on the top. The learned joint representation p_t for QA pair is formalized as Eq. 2:

$$p_t = \sigma(w_t H_t + b_t) \quad (2)$$

where σ is an activation function, and the input vector is constructed by concatenating the sentence representations of question and answer.

3.2 LSTM for Answer Sequence Learning

Based on the joint representation of QA pair, the LSTM unit of our model performs answer sequence learning to model semantic links between continuous answers. Unlike the traditional recurrent unit, the LSTM unit modulates the memory at each time step, instead of overwriting the states. The key component of LSTM unit is the memory cell c_t which has a state over time, and the LSTM unit decides to modify and add the memory in the cell via the sigmoidal gates: input gate i_t, forget gate f_t and output gate o_t. The implementation of the LSTM unit in our study is close the one discussed by Graves (2013). Given the joint representation p_t at time t, the memory cell c_t is updated by the input gate's activation i_t and the forget gate's activation f_t. The updating equation is given by Eq. 3:

$$c_t = f_t c_{t-1} + i_t tanh(W_{xc} p_t + W_{hc} h_{t-1} + b_c) \quad (3)$$

Data	#question	#answer	length
training	2600	16541	6.36
development	300	1645	5.48
test	329	1976	6.00
all	3229	21062	6.00

Table 1: Statistics of experimental dataset

The LSTM unit keeps to update the context by discarding the useless context in forget gate f_t and adding new content from input gate i_t. The extents to modulate context for these two gates are computed as Eq. 4 and Eq. 5:

$$i_t = \sigma(W_{xi} p_t + W_{hi} h_{(t-1)} + W_{ci} c_{t-1} + b_i) \quad (4)$$

$$f_t = \sigma(W_{xf} p_t + W_{hf} h_{t-1} + W_{cf} c_{t-1} + b_f) \quad (5)$$

With the updated cell state c_t, the final output from LSTM unit h_t is computed as Eq 6 and Eq 7:

$$o_t = \sigma(W_{xo} p_t + W_{ho} h_{t-1} + W_{co} c_t + b_o) \quad (6)$$

$$h_t = o_t tanh(c_t) \quad (7)$$

Note that (W_*, b_*) is the parameters of LSTM unit, in which W_{cf}, W_{ci} , and W_{co} are diagonal matrices.

According to the output h_t at each time step, our approach estimates the conditional probability of the answer sequence over answer classes, it is given by Eq. 8:

$$P(y_1, ..., y_T | c, p_1, ..., p_{t-1}) = \prod_{t=1}^{T} p(y_t | c, y_1, ..., y_{t-1}) \quad (8)$$

Here, $(y_1, ..., y_T)$ is the corresponding label sequence for the input sequence $(p_1, ..., p_{t-1})$, and the class distribution $p(y_t | c, y_1, ..., .y_{t-1})$ is represented by a softmax function.

4 Experiments

4.1 Experiment Setup

Experimental Dataset: We conduct experiments on the public dataset of the answer selection challenge in SemEval 2015. This dataset consists of three subsets: training, development, and test sets, and contains 3,229 questions with 21,062 answers. The answers falls into three classes: *Good*, *Bad*, and *Potential*, accounting for 51%, 39%, and 10% respectively. The statistics of the dataset are summarized in Table 1, where #question/answer denotes the number of questions/answers, and length stands for the average number of answers for a question.

Competitor Methods: We compare our approach against the following competitor methods:

SVM (Huang et al., 2007): An SVM-based method with bag-of-words (textual features), non-textual features, and features based on topic model (i.e., latent Dirichlet allocation, LDA).

CRF (Ding et al., 2008): A CRF-based method using the same features as the SVM approach.

DBN (Wang et al., 2010): Taking bag-of-words representation, the method applies deep belief nets to learning the distributed representation of QA pair, and predicts the class of answers using a logistic regression classifier on the top layer.

mDBN (Hu et al., 2013): In contrast to DBN, multimodal DBN learns the joint representations of textual features and non-textual features rather than bag-of-words.

CNN: Using word embedding, the CNNs based model in Hu et al. (2014) is used to learn the representations of questions and answers, and a logistic regression classifier is used to predict the class of answers.

Evaluation Metrics: The evaluation metrics include $Macro - precision(P)$, $Macro - recall(R)$, $Macro - F1(F1)$, and $F1$ scores of the individual classes. According to the evaluation results on the development set, all the hyperparameters are optimized on the training set.

Model Architecture and Training Details: The CNNs of our model for QA joint representation learning have 3 hidden layers for modeling question and answer sentence respectively, in which each layer has 100 feature maps for convolution and pooling operators. The window sizes of convolution for each layer are $[1 \times 1, 2 \times 2, 2 \times 2]$, the window sizes of pooling are $[2 \times 2, 2 \times 2, 1 \times 1]$. For the LSTM unit, the size of *input gate* is set to 200, the sizes of *forget gate*, *output gate*, and *memory cell* are all set to 360.

Stochastic gradient descent (SGD) algorithm via back-propagation through time is used to train the model. To prevent serious overfitting, early stopping and dropout (Hinton et al., 2012) are used during the training procedure. The learning rate λ is initialized to be 0.01 and is updated dynamically according to the gradient descent using the ADADELTA method (Zeiler, 2012). The activation functions (σ, γ) in our model adopt the rectified linear unit (ReLU) (Dahl et al., 2013). In addition, the word embeddings for encoding sentences are pre-trained with the unsupervised neural language model (Mikolov et al., 2013) on the Qatar Living data[2].

Methods	P	R	F1
SVM	50.10	54.43	52.14
CRF	53.89	54.26	53.40
DBN	55.22	53.80	54.07
mDBN	56.11	53.95	54.29
CNN	55.33	54.73	54.42
R-CNN	**56.41**	**56.16**	**56.14**

Table 2: Macro-averaged results(%)

4.2 Results and Analysis

Table 2 summarizes the Macro-averaged results. The F1 scores of the individual classes are presented in Table 3.

It is clear to see that the proposed R-CNN approach outperforms the competitor methods over the Macro-averaged metrics as expected from Table 2. The main reason lies in that R-CNN takes advantages of the semantic correlations between successive answers by LSTM, in addition to the semantic relationships between question and answer. The joint representation of QA pair learnt by CNNs also captures richer matching patterns between question and answer than other methods.

It is notable that the methods based on deep learning perform more powerful than SVM and CRF, especially for complicate answers (e.g., *Potential* answers). In contrast, SVM and CRF using a large amount of features perform better for the answers that have obvious tendency (e.g., *Good* and *Bad* answers). The main reason is that the distributed representation learnt from deep learning architecture is able to capture the semantic relationships between question and answer. On the other hand, the feature-engineers in both SVM and CRF suffer from noisy information of CQA and the feature sparse problem for short questions and answers.

[2]http://alt.qcri.org/semeval2015/task3/index.php?id=data-and-tools

Methods	Good	Bad	Potential
SVM	79.78	76.65	0.00
CRF	79.32	75.50	5.38
DBN	76.99	71.33	13.89
mDBN	77.74	70.39	14.74
CNN	76.45	74.77	12.05
R-CNN	77.31	75.88	**15.22**

Table 3: F1 scores for the individual classes(%)

Compared to DBN and mDBN, CNN and R-CNN show their superiority in modeling QA pair. The convolutional sentence models, used in CN-N and R-CNN, can learn the hierarchical structure of language object by deep convolution and pooling operators. In addition, both R-CNN and CNN encode the sentence into one tensor, which makes sure the representation contains more semantic features than the bag-of-words representation in DBN and mDBN.

The improvement achieved by R-CNN over C-NN demonstrates that answer sequence learning is able to improve the performance of the answer selection in CQA. Because modeling the answer sequence can enjoy the advantage of the shared representation between successive answers, and complement the classification features with the learnt useful context from previous answers. Furthermore, memory cell and gates in LSTM unit modify the valuable context to pass onwards by updating the state of RNN during the learning procedure.

The main improvement of R-CNN against with the competitor methods comes from the *Potential* answers, which are much less than other two type of answers. It demonstrates that R-CNN is able to process the unbalance data. In fact, the *Potential* answers are most difficult to identify among the three types of answers as *Potential* is an intermediate category (Màrquez et al., 2015). Nevertheless, R-CNN achieves the highest F1 score of 15.22% on Potential answers. In CQA, Q&A archives usually form one multi-parties conversation when the asker gives feedbacks (e.g., "ok" and "please") to users responses, indicating that the answers of one question are sematic related. Thus, it is easy to understand that R-CNN performs better performance than competitor methods, especially on the recall. The reason is that R-CNN can model semantic correlations between successive answers to learn the context and the long range dependencies in the answer sequence.

5 Conclusions and Future Work

In this paper, we propose an answer sequence learning model R-CNN for the answer selection task by integrating LSTM unit and CNNs. Based on the recurrent architecture of our model, our approach is able to model the semantic link between successive answers, in addition to the semantic relevance between question and answer. Experimental results demonstrate that our approach can learn the useful context from the answer sequence to improve the performance of answer selection in C-QA.

In the future, we plan to explore the methods on training the unbalance data to improve the overall performances of our approach. Based on this work, more research can be conducted on topic recognition and semantic roles labeling for human-human conversations in real-world.

Acknowledgments: This work was supported in part by National 863 Program of China (2015AA015405), NSFCs (National Natural Science Foundation of China) (61402128, 61473101, 61173075 and 61272383). We thank the anonymous reviewers for their insightful comments.

References

George E. Dahl, Tara N. Sainath, and Geoffrey E. Hinton. 2013. Improving deep neural networks for lvcsr using rectified linear units and dropout. In *ICASSP*, pages 8609–8613. IEEE.

Shilin Ding, Gao Cong, Chin yew Lin, and Xiaoyan Zhu. 2008. Using conditional random fields to extract contexts and answers of questions from online forums. In *In Proceedings of ACL-08: HLT*.

Alex Graves. 2013. Generating sequences with recurrent neural networks. *CoRR*, abs/1308.0850.

Geoffrey E. Hinton, Nitish Srivastava, Alex Krizhevsky, Ilya Sutskever, and Ruslan Salakhutdinov. 2012. Improving neural networks by preventing co-adaptation of feature detectors. *CoRR*, abs/1207.0580.

Sepp Hochreiter, Yoshua Bengio, Paolo Frasconi, and Jürgen Schmidhuber. 2001. Gradient flow in recurrent nets: the difficulty of learning long-term dependencies.

Haifeng Hu, Bingquan Liu, Baoxun Wang, Ming Liu, and Xiaolong Wang. 2013. Multimodal dbn for predicting high-quality answers in cqa portals. In *Proceedings of the 51st Annual Meeting of the Association for Computational Linguistics (Volume 2: Short Papers)*, Sofia, Bulgaria, August.

Baotian Hu, Zhengdong Lu, Hang Li, and Qingcai Chen. 2014. Convolutional neural network architectures for matching natural language sentences. In *Advances in Neural Information Processing Systems 27*, pages 2042–2050.

Jizhou Huang, Ming Zhou, and Dan Yang. 2007. Extracting chatbot knowledge from online discussion forums. In *Proceedings of the 20th International Joint Conference on Artifical Intelligence*, IJCAI'07, pages 423–428.

Jiwoon Jeon, W. Bruce Croft, and Joon Ho Lee. 2005. Finding similar questions in large question and answer archives. In *Proceedings of the 14th ACM International Conference on Information and Knowledge Management*, CIKM '05, pages 84–90.

Yoon Kim. 2014. Convolutional neural networks for sentence classification. *CoRR*, abs/1408.5882.

Lluís Màrquez, James Glass, Walid Magdy, Alessandro Moschitti, Preslav Nakov, and Bilal Randeree. 2015. Semeval-2015 task 3: Answer selection in community question answering. In *Proceedings of the 9th International Workshop on Semantic Evaluation (SemEval-2015)*.

Tomas Mikolov, Kai Chen, Greg Corrado, and Jeffrey Dean. 2013. Efficient estimation of word representations in vector space. *CoRR*, abs/1301.3781.

Alessandro Moschitti, Silvia Quarteroni, Roberto Basili, and Suresh Manandhar. 2007. Exploiting syntactic and shallow semantic kernels for question answer classification. In *Proceedings of the 45th Annual Meeting of the Association of Computational Linguistics*, pages 776–783.

Chirag Shah and Jefferey Pomerantz. 2010. Evaluating and predicting answer quality in community qa. In *Proceedings of the 33rd International ACM SIGIR Conference on Research and Development in Information Retrieval*, SIGIR '10, pages 411–418.

Nitish Srivastava, Elman Mansimov, and Ruslan Salakhutdinov. 2015. Unsupervised learning of video representations using lstms. *CoRR*, abs/1502.04681.

Ilya Sutskever, Oriol Vinyals, and Quoc V. Le. 2014. Sequence to sequence learning with neural networks. *CoRR*, abs/1409.3215.

Baoxun Wang, Bingquan Liu, Chengjie Sun, Xiaolong Wang, and Lin Sun. 2009a. Extracting chinese question-answer pairs from online forums. In *IEEE International Conference on Systems, Man, and Cybernetics (SMC)*, pages 1159–1164.

Kai Wang, Zhaoyan Ming, and Tat-Seng Chua. 2009b. A syntactic tree matching approach to finding similar questions in community-based qa services. In *Proceedings of the 32Nd International ACM SIGIR Conference on Research and Development in Information Retrieval*, SIGIR '09, pages 187–194.

Baoxun Wang, Xiaolong Wang, Chengjie Sun, Bingquan Liu, and Lin Sun. 2010. Modeling semantic relevance for question-answer pairs in web social communities. In *Proceedings of the 48th Annual Meeting of the Association for Computational Linguistics*, ACL '10, pages 1230–1238.

Xiaobing Xue, Jiwoon Jeon, and W. Bruce Croft. 2008. Retrieval models for question and answer archives. In *Proceedings of the 31st Annual International ACM SIGIR Conference on Research and Development in Information Retrieval*, SIGIR '08, pages 475–482.

Lei Yu, Karl Moritz Hermann, Phil Blunsom, and Stephen Pulman. 2014. Deep learning for answer sentence selection. *CoRR*, abs/1412.1632.

Matthew D. Zeiler. 2012. ADADELTA: an adaptive learning rate method. *CoRR*, abs/1212.5701.

Guangyou Zhou, Li Cai, Jun Zhao, and Kang Liu. 2011. Phrase-based translation model for question retrieval in community question answer archives. In *Proceedings of the 49th Annual Meeting of the Association for Computational Linguistics: Human Language Technologies - Volume 1*, HLT '11, pages 653–662.

Bilingual Word Embeddings from Non-Parallel Document-Aligned Data Applied to Bilingual Lexicon Induction

Ivan Vulić and Marie-Francine Moens
Department of Computer Science
KU Leuven, Belgium
{ivan.vulic|marie-francine.moens}@cs.kuleuven.be

Abstract

We propose a simple yet effective approach to learning bilingual word embeddings (BWEs) from non-parallel document-aligned data (based on the omnipresent skip-gram model), and its application to bilingual lexicon induction (BLI). We demonstrate the utility of the induced BWEs in the BLI task by reporting on benchmarking BLI datasets for three language pairs: (1) We show that our BWE-based BLI models significantly outperform the MuPTM-based and context-counting models in this setting, and obtain the best reported BLI results for all three tested language pairs; (2) We also show that our BWE-based BLI models outperform other BLI models based on recently proposed BWEs that require parallel data for bilingual training.

1 Introduction

Dense real-valued vectors known as distributed representations of words or *word embeddings* (WEs) (Bengio et al., 2003; Collobert and Weston, 2008; Mikolov et al., 2013a; Pennington et al., 2014) have been introduced recently as part of neural network architectures for statistical language modeling. Recent studies (Levy and Goldberg, 2014; Levy et al., 2015) have showcased a direct link and comparable performance to "more traditional" distributional models (Turney and Pantel, 2010), but the skip-gram model with negative sampling (SGNS) (Mikolov et al., 2013c) is still established as the state-of-the-art word representation model, due to its simplicity, fast training, as well as its solid and robust performance across a wide variety of semantic tasks (Baroni et al., 2014; Levy et al., 2015).

A natural extension of interest from monolingual to multilingual word embeddings has occurred recently (Klementiev et al., 2012; Zou et al., 2013; Mikolov et al., 2013b; Hermann and Blunsom, 2014a; Hermann and Blunsom, 2014b; Gouws et al., 2014; Chandar et al., 2014; Soyer et al., 2015; Luong et al., 2015). When operating in multilingual settings, it is highly desirable to learn embeddings for words denoting similar concepts that are very close in the *shared inter-lingual embedding space* (e.g., the representations for the English word *school* and the Spanish word *escuela* should be very similar). These shared inter-lingual embedding spaces may then be used in a myriad of multilingual natural language processing tasks, such as fundamental tasks of computing cross-lingual and multilingual semantic word similarity and *bilingual lexicon induction (BLI)*, etc. However, all these models critically require at least sentence-aligned parallel data and/or readily-available translation dictionaries to induce *bilingual word embeddings* (BWEs) that are consistent and closely aligned over languages in the same semantic space.

Contributions In this work, we alleviate the requirements: (1) We present the first model that is able to induce bilingual word embeddings from non-parallel data without any other readily available translation resources such as pre-given bilingual lexicons; (2) We demonstrate the utility of BWEs induced by this simple yet effective model in the BLI task from comparable Wikipedia data on benchmarking datasets for three language pairs (Vulić and Moens, 2013b). Our BLI model based on our novel BWEs significantly outperforms a series of strong baselines that reported previous best scores on these datasets in the same learning setting, as well as other BLI models based on recently proposed BWE induction models (Gouws et al., 2014; Chandar et al., 2014). The focus of the work is on learning lexicons from document-aligned comparable corpora (e.g., Wikipedia articles aligned through inter-wiki links).

Proceedings of the 53rd Annual Meeting of the Association for Computational Linguistics and the 7th International Joint Conference on Natural Language Processing (Short Papers), pages 719–725,
Beijing, China, July 26-31, 2015.

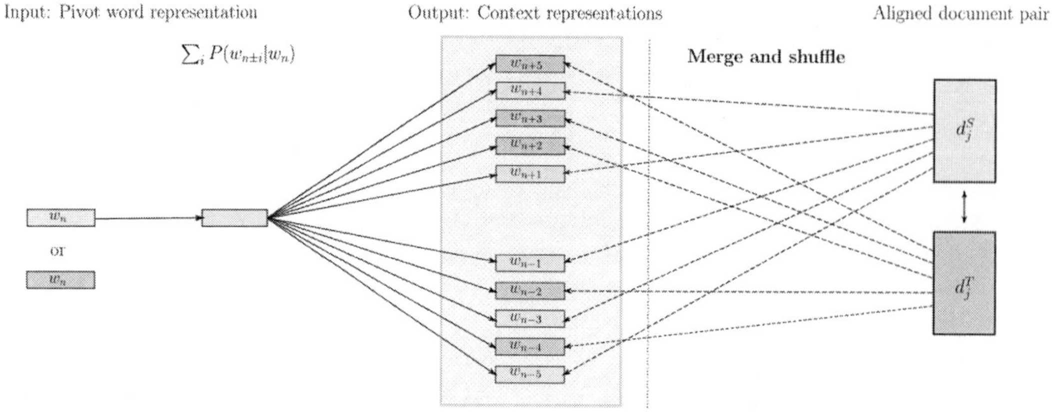

Figure 1: The architecture of our BWE Skip-Gram model for learning bilingual word embeddings from document-aligned comparable data. Source language words and documents are drawn as gray boxes, while target language words and documents are drawn as blue boxes. The right side of the figure (separated by a vertical dashed line) illustrates how a pseudo-bilingual document is constructed from a pair of two aligned documents; two documents are first merged, and then words in the pseudo-bilingual document are randomly shuffled to ensure that both source and target language words occur as context words.

2 Model Architecture

In the following architecture description, we assume that the reader is familiar with the main assumptions and training procedure of SGNS (Mikolov et al., 2013a; Mikolov et al., 2013c). We extend the SGNS model to work with bilingual document-aligned comparable data. An overview of our architecture for learning BWEs from such comparable data is given in fig. 1.

Let us assume that we possess a document-aligned comparable corpus which is defined as $\mathcal{C} = \{d_1, d_2, \ldots, d_N\} = \{(d_1^S, d_1^T), (d_2^S, d_2^T), \ldots, (d_N^S, d_D^T)\}$, where $d_j = (d_j^S, d_j^T)$ denotes a pair of aligned documents in the source language L_S and the target language L_T, respectively, and N is the number of documents in the corpus. V^S and V^T are vocabularies associated with languages L_S and L_T. The goal is to learn word embeddings for all words in both V^S and V^T that will be semantically coherent and closely aligned over languages in a shared cross-lingual word embedding space.

In the first step, we *merge* two documents d_j^S and d_j^T from the aligned document pair d_j into a single "pseudo-bilingual" document d'_j and remove sentence boundaries. Following that, we *randomly shuffle* the newly constructed pseudo-bilingual document. The intuition behind this pre-training completely random shuffling step[1] (see fig. 1) is to assure that each word w, regardless of its actual language, obtains word collocates from both vocabularies. The idea of having bilingual contexts for each pivot word in each pseudo-bilingual document will steer the final model towards constructing a shared inter-lingual embedding space. Since the model depends on the alignment at the document level, in order to ensure the bilingual contexts instead of monolingual contexts, it is intuitive to assume that larger window sizes will lead to better bilingual embeddings. We test this hypothesis and the effect of window size in sect. 4.

The final model called BWE Skip-Gram (BWESG) then relies on the monolingual variant of skip-gram trained on the shuffled pseudo-bilingual documents.[2] The model learns word embeddings for source and target language words that are aligned over the d embedding dimensions and may be represented in the same shared cross-lingual embedding space. The BWESG-based representation of word w, regardless of its actual language, is then a d-dimensional vector: $\vec{w} = [f_1, \ldots, f_k, \ldots, f_d]$, where $f_k \in \mathbb{R}$ denotes the score for the k-th inter-lingual feature within the d-dimensional shared embedding space. Since all words share the embedding space, semantic similarity between words may be computed both

[1] In this paper, we investigate only the random shuffling procedure and show that the model is fairly robust to different outputs of the procedure if the window size is large enough. As one line of future work, we plan to investigate other, more systematic and deterministic shuffling algorithms.

[2] We were also experimenting with GloVe and CBOW, but they were falling behind SGNS on average.

monolingually and across languages. Given w, the most similar word cross-lingually should be its one-to-one translation, and we may use this intuition to induce one-to-one bilingual lexicons from comparable data.

In another interpretation, BWESG actually builds BWEs based on (pseudo-bilingual) document level co-occurrence. The window size parameter then just controls the amount of random data dropout. With larger windows, the model becomes prohibitively computationally expensive, but in sect. 4 we show that the BLI performance flattens out for "reasonably large" windows.

3 Experimental Setup

Training Data We use comparable Wikipedia data introduced in (Vulić and Moens, 2013a; Vulić and Moens, 2013b) available in three language pairs to induce bilingual word embeddings: (i) a collection of 13,696 Spanish-English Wikipedia article pairs (ES-EN), (ii) a collection of 18,898 Italian-English Wikipedia article pairs (IT-EN), and (iii) a collection of 7,612 Dutch-English Wikipedia article pairs (NL-EN). All corpora are theme-aligned comparable corpora, that is, the aligned document pairs discuss similar themes, but are in general not direct translations. Following prior work (Haghighi et al., 2008; Prochasson and Fung, 2011; Vulić and Moens, 2013b), we retain only nouns that occur at least 5 times in the corpus. Lemmatized word forms are recorded when available, and original forms otherwise. TreeTagger (Schmid, 1994) is used for POS tagging and lemmatization. After the preprocessing vocabularies comprise between 7,000 and 13,000 noun types for each language in each language pair. Exactly the same training data and vocabularies are used to induce bilingual lexicons with all other BLI models in comparison.

BWESG Training Setup We have trained the BWESG model with random shuffling on 10 random corpora shuffles for all three training corpora with the following parameters from the `word2vec` package (Mikolov et al., 2013c): stochastic gradient descent with a default learning rate of 0.025, negative sampling with 25 samples, and a subsampling rate of value $1e-4$. All models are trained for 15 epochs. We have varied the number of embedding dimensions: $d = 100, 200, 300$, and have also trained the model with $d = 40$ to be directly comparable to pre-trained state-of-the-art BWEs from (Gouws et al., 2014; Chandar et al., 2014). Moreover, in order to test the effect of window size on final results, we have varied the maximum window size cs from 4 to 60 in steps of 4.[3] Since cosine is used for all similarity computations in the BLI task, we call our new BLI model *BWESG+cos*.

Baseline BLI Models We compare BWESG+cos to a series of state-of-the-art BLI models from document-aligned comparable data:
(1) *BiLDA-BLI* - A BLI model that relies on the induction of latent cross-lingual topics (Mimno et al., 2009) by the bilingual LDA model and represents words as probability distributions over these topics (Vulić et al., 2011).
(2) *Assoc-BLI* - A BLI model that represents words as vectors of association norms (Roller and Schulte im Walde, 2013) over both vocabularies, where these norms are computed using a multilingual topic model (Vulić and Moens, 2013a).
(3) *PPMI+cos* - A standard distributional model for BLI relying on positive pointwise mutual information and cosine similarity (Bullinaria and Levy, 2007). The seed lexicon is bootstrapped using the method from (Peirsman and Padó, 2011; Vulić and Moens, 2013b).

All parameters of the baseline BLI models (i.e., topic models and their settings, the number of dimensions K, feature pruning values, window size) are set to their optimal values according to suggestions in prior work (Steyvers and Griffiths, 2007; Vulić and Moens, 2013a; Vulić and Moens, 2013b; Kiela and Clark, 2014). Due to space constraints, for (much) more details about the baselines we point to the relevant literature (Peirsman and Padó, 2011; Tamura et al., 2012; Vulić and Moens, 2013a; Vulić and Moens, 2013b).

Test Data For each language pair, we evaluate on standard 1,000 ground truth one-to-one translation pairs built for the three language pairs (ES/IT/NL-EN) (Vulić and Moens, 2013a; Vulić and Moens, 2013b). Translation direction is ES/IT/NL → EN.

Evaluation Metrics Since we can build a one-to-one bilingual lexicon by harvesting one-to-one translation pairs, the lexicon qualiy is best reflected in the Acc_1 score, that is, the number of source language (ES/IT/NL) words w_i^S from ground truth translation pairs for which the top ranked word cross-lingually is the correct trans-

[3]We will make all our BWESG BWEs available at: `http://people.cs.kuleuven.be/~ivan.vulic/`

Spanish-English (ES-EN)			Italian-English (IT-EN)			Dutch-English (NL-EN)		
(1) **reina**	(2) **reina**	(3) **reina**	(1) **madre**	(2) **madre**	(3) **madre**	(1) **schilder**	(2) **schilder**	(3) **schilder**
(Spanish)	(English)	(Combined)	(Italian)	(English)	(Combined)	(Dutch)	(English)	(Combined)
rey	*queen(+)*	*queen(+)*	padre	*mother(+)*	*mother(+)*	kunstschilder	*painter(+)*	*painter(+)*
trono	*heir*	rey	moglie	*father*	padre	schilderij	*painting*	kunstschilder
monarca	*throne*	trono	sorella	*sister*	moglie	kunstenaar	*portrait*	*painting*
heredero	*king*	*heir*	figlia	*wife*	*father*	olieverf	*artist*	schilderij
matrimonio	*royal*	*throne*	figlio	*daughter*	sorella	olieverfschilderij	*canvas*	kunstenaar
hijo	*reign*	monarca	fratello	*son*	figlia	schilderen	*impressionist*	*portrait*
reino	*succession*	heredero	casa	*friend*	figlio	frans	*cubism*	olieverf
reinado	*princess*	*king*	amico	*childhood*	*sister*	nederlands	*art*	olieverfschilderij
regencia	*marriage*	matrimonio	marito	*family*	fratello	componist	*poet*	schilderen
duque	*prince*	*royal*	donna	*cousin*	*wife*	beeldhouwer	*drawing*	*artist*

Table 1: Example lists of top 10 semantically similar words for all 3 language pairs obtained using BWESG+cos; $d = 200, cs = 48$; (col 1.) only source language words (ES/IT/NL) are listed while target language words are skipped (monolingual similarity); (2) only target language words (EN) are listed (cross-lingual similarity); (3) words from both languages are listed (multilingual similarity). EN words are given in italic. The correct one-to-one translation for each source word is marked by (+).

lation in the other language (EN) according to the ground truth over the total number of ground truth translation pairs (=*1000*) (Gaussier et al., 2004; Tamura et al., 2012; Vulić and Moens, 2013b).

4 Results and Discussion

Exp 0: Qualitative Analysis Tab. 1 displays top 10 semantically similar words monolingually, across-languages and combined/multilingually for one ES, IT and NL word. The BWESG+cos model is able to find semantically coherent lists of words for all three directions of similarity (i.e., monolingual, cross-lingual, multilingual). In the combined (multilingual) ranked lists, words from both languages are represented as top similar words. This initial qualitative analysis already demonstrates the ability of BWESG to induce a shared cross-lingual embedding space using only document alignments as bilingual signals.

Exp I: BWESG+cos vs. Baseline Models In the first experiment, we test whether our BWESG+cos BLI model produces better results than the baseline BLI models which obtain current state-of-the-art results for BLI from comparable data on these test sets. Tab. 2 summarizes the BLI results.

As the most striking finding, the results reveal superior performance of the BWESG-cos model for BLI which relies on our new framework for inducing bilingual word embeddings over other BLI models relying on previously used bilingual word representations. The relative increase in Acc_1 scores over the best scoring baseline BLI models from comparable data is 19.4% for the ES-EN pair, 6.1% for IT-EN (significant at $p < 0.05$ using McNemar's test) and 65.4% for NL-EN. For large enough values for cs ($cs \geq 20$) (see also fig. 2(a)-2(c)), almost all BWESG+cos models for all language pairs outperform the highest baseline results. We may also observe that the performance of BWESG+cos is fairly stable for all models with larger values for cs ($cs \geq 20$). This finding reveals that even a coarse tuning of these parameters might lead to optimal or near-optimal scores in the BLI task with BWESG+cos.

Pair:	**ES-EN**	**IT-EN**	**NL-EN**
Model	Acc_1	Acc_1	Acc_1
BiLDA-BLI	0.441	0.575	0.237
Assoc-BLI	0.518	0.618	0.236
PPMI+cos	0.577	0.647	0.206
BWESG+cos			
d:100,cs:16	0.617	0.599	0.300
d:100,cs:48	0.667	0.669	0.389
d:200,cs:16	0.613	0.601	0.254
d:200,cs:48	0.685	**0.683**	**0.392**
d:300,cs:16	0.596	0.583	0.224
d:300,cs:48	**0.689**	**0.683**	0.363
d: 40,cs:16	0.558	0.533	0.266
d: 40,cs:48	0.578	0.595	0.308
CHANDAR	0.432	-	-
GOUWS	0.516	0.557	0.575

Table 2: BLI performance for all tested BLI models for ES/IT/NL-EN, with all bilingual word representations except CHANDAR and GOUWS learned from comparable Wikipedia data. The scores for BWESG+cos are computed as post-hoc averages over 10 random shuffles.

Exp II: Shuffling and Window Size Since our BWESG model relies on the pre-training random shuffling procedure, we also test whether the shuffling has significant or rather minor impact on the induction of BWEs and final BLI scores. Therefore, in fig. 2, we present maximum, minimum, and average Acc_1 scores for all three language pairs obtained using 10 different random corpora shuffles with $d = 100, 200, 300$ and varying val-

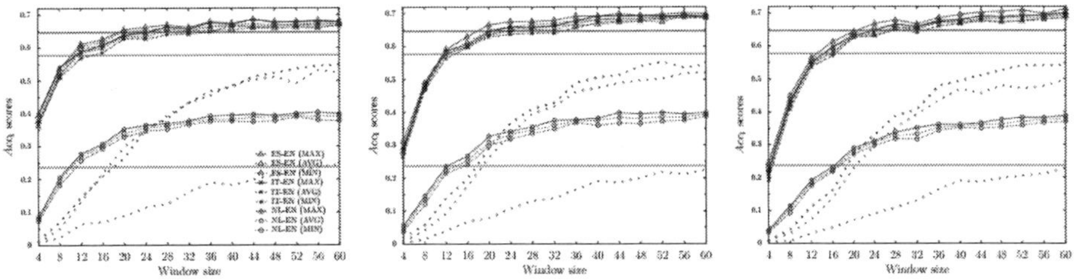

(a) $d = 100$ (b) $d = 200$ (c) $d = 300$

Figure 2: Maximum (MAX), minimum (MIN) and average (AVG) Acc_1 scores with BWESG+cos in the BLI task over 10 different random corpora shuffles for all 3 language pairs, and varying values for parameters cs and d. Solid horizontal lines denote the highest baseline Acc_1 scores for each language pair. NOS (thicker dotted lines) refers to BWESG+cos without random shuffling.

ues for cs. Results reveal that random shuffling affects the overall BLI scores, but the variance of results is minimal and often highly insignificant. It is important to mark that even the minimum Acc_1 scores over these 10 different random shuffles are typically higher than the previous state-of-the-art baseline scores for large enough values for d and cs (compare the results in tab. 2 and fig. 2(a)-2(c)). A comparison with the BWESG model without shuffling (NOS on fig. 2) reveals that shuffling is useful even for larger cs-s.

Exp III: BWESG+cos vs. BWE-Based BLI We also compare our BWESG BLI model with two other models that are most similar to ours in spirit, as they also induce shared cross-lingual word embedding spaces (Chandar et al., 2014; Gouws et al., 2014), proven superior to or on a par with the BLI model from (Mikolov et al., 2013b). We use their pre-trained BWEs (obtained from the authors) and report the BLI scores in tab. 2. To make the comparison fair, we search for translations over the same vocabulary as with all other models. The results clearly reveal that, although both other BWE models critically rely on parallel Europarl data for training, and Gouws et al. (2014) in addition train on entire monolingual Wikipedias in both languages, our simple BWE induction model trained on much smaller amounts of document-aligned non-parallel data produces significantly higher BLI scores for IT-EN and ES-EN with sufficiently large windows.

However, the results for NL-EN with all BLI models from comparable data from tab. 2 are significantly lower than with the GOUWS BWEs. We attribute it to using less (and clearly insufficient) document-aligned training data for NL-EN (i.e., training corpora for ES-EN and IT-EN are almost double or triple the size of training corpora for NL-EN, see sect. 3).

5 Conclusions and Future Work

We have proposed Bilingual Word Embeddings Skip-Gram (BWESG), a simple yet effective model that is able to learn bilingual word embeddings solely on the basis of document-aligned comparable data. We have demonstrated its utility in the task of bilingual lexicon induction from such comparable data, where our new BWESG-based BLI model outperforms state-of-the-art models for BLI from document-aligned comparable data and related BWE induction models.

The low-cost BWEs may be used in other (semantic) tasks besides the ones discussed here, and it would be interesting to experiment with other types of context aggregation and selection beyond random shuffling, and other objective functions. Preliminary studies also demonstrate the utility of the BWEs in monolingual and cross-lingual information retrieval (Vulić and Moens, 2015).

Finally, we may use the knowledge of BWEs obtained by BWESG from document-aligned data to learn bilingual correspondences (e.g., word translation pairs or lists of semantically similar words across languages) which may in turn be used for representation learning from large unaligned multilingual datasets as proposed in (Haghighi et al., 2008; Mikolov et al., 2013b; Vulić and Moens, 2013b). In the long run, this idea may lead to large-scale fully data-driven representation learning models from huge amounts of multilingual data without any "pre-requirement" for parallel data or manually built lexicons.

Acknowledgments

We would like to thank the reviewers for their insightful comments and suggestions. This research has been carried out in the frameworks of the SCATE project (IWT-SBO 130041) and the PARIS project (IWT-SBO 110067).

References

Marco Baroni, Georgiana Dinu, and Germán Kruszewski. 2014. Don't count, predict! A systematic comparison of context-counting vs. context-predicting semantic vectors. In *ACL*, pages 238–247.

Yoshua Bengio, Réjean Ducharme, Pascal Vincent, and Christian Janvin. 2003. A neural probabilistic language model. *Journal of Machine Learning Research*, 3:1137–1155.

John A. Bullinaria and Joseph P. Levy. 2007. Extracting semantic representations from word co-occurrence statistics: A computational study. *Behavior Research Methods*, 39(3):510–526.

Sarath Chandar, Stanislas Lauly, Hugo Larochelle, Mitesh M. Khapra, Balaraman Ravindran, Vikas C. Raykar, and Amrita Saha. 2014. An autoencoder approach to learning bilingual word representations. In *NIPS*, pages 1853–1861.

Ronan Collobert and Jason Weston. 2008. A unified architecture for natural language processing: Deep neural networks with multitask learning. In *ICML*, pages 160–167.

Éric Gaussier, Jean-Michel Renders, Irina Matveeva, Cyril Goutte, and Hervé Déjean. 2004. A geometric view on bilingual lexicon extraction from comparable corpora. In *ACL*, pages 526–533.

Stephan Gouws, Yoshua Bengio, and Greg Corrado. 2014. BilBOWA: Fast bilingual distributed representations without word alignments. *CoRR*, abs/1410.2455.

Aria Haghighi, Percy Liang, Taylor Berg-Kirkpatrick, and Dan Klein. 2008. Learning bilingual lexicons from monolingual corpora. In *ACL*, pages 771–779.

Karl Moritz Hermann and Phil Blunsom. 2014a. Multilingual distributed representations without word alignment. In *ICLR*.

Karl Moritz Hermann and Phil Blunsom. 2014b. Multilingual models for compositional distributed semantics. In *ACL*, pages 58–68.

Douwe Kiela and Stephen Clark. 2014. A systematic study of semantic vector space model parameters. In *CVSC Workshop at EACL*, pages 21–30.

Alexandre Klementiev, Ivan Titov, and Binod Bhattarai. 2012. Inducing crosslingual distributed representations of words. In *COLING*, pages 1459–1474.

Omer Levy and Yoav Goldberg. 2014. Neural word embedding as implicit matrix factorization. In *NIPS*, pages 2177–2185.

Omer Levy, Yoav Goldberg, and Ido Dagan. 2015. Improving distributional similarity with lessons learned from word embeddings. *Transactions of the ACL*, 3:211–225.

Thang Luong, Hieu Pham, and Christopher D. Manning. 2015. Bilingual word representations with monolingual quality in mind. In *Proceedings of the 1st Workshop on Vector Space Modeling for Natural Language Processing*, pages 151–159.

Tomas Mikolov, Kai Chen, Gregory S. Corrado, and Jeffrey Dean. 2013a. Efficient estimation of word representations in vector space. In *ICLR Workshop Papers*.

Tomas Mikolov, Quoc V. Le, and Ilya Sutskever. 2013b. Exploiting similarities among languages for machine translation. *CoRR*, abs/1309.4168.

Tomas Mikolov, Ilya Sutskever, Kai Chen, Gregory S. Corrado, and Jeffrey Dean. 2013c. Distributed representations of words and phrases and their compositionality. In *NIPS*, pages 3111–3119.

David Mimno, Hanna Wallach, Jason Naradowsky, David A. Smith, and Andrew McCallum. 2009. Polylingual topic models. In *EMNLP*, pages 880–889.

Yves Peirsman and Sebastian Padó. 2011. Semantic relations in bilingual lexicons. *ACM Transactions on Speech and Language Processing*, 8(2):article 3.

Jeffrey Pennington, Richard Socher, and Christopher Manning. 2014. GloVe: Global vectors for word representation. In *EMNLP*, pages 1532–1543.

Emmanuel Prochasson and Pascale Fung. 2011. Rare word translation extraction from aligned comparable documents. In *ACL*, pages 1327–1335.

Stephen Roller and Sabine Schulte im Walde. 2013. A multimodal LDA model integrating textual, cognitive and visual modalities. In *EMNLP*, pages 1146–1157.

Helmut Schmid. 1994. Probabilistic part-of-speech tagging using decision trees. In *Proceedings of the International Conference on New Methods in Language Processing*.

Hubert Soyer, Pontus Stenetorp, and Akiko Aizawa. 2015. Leveraging monolingual data for crosslingual compositional word representations. In *ICLR*.

Mark Steyvers and Tom Griffiths. 2007. Probabilistic topic models. *Handbook of Latent Semantic Analysis*, 427(7):424–440.

Akihiro Tamura, Taro Watanabe, and Eiichiro Sumita. 2012. Bilingual lexicon extraction from comparable corpora using label propagation. In *EMNLP*, pages 24–36.

Peter D. Turney and Patrick Pantel. 2010. From frequency to meaning: Vector space models of semantics. *Journal of Artifical Intelligence Research*, 37(1):141–188.

Ivan Vulić and Marie-Francine Moens. 2013a. Cross-lingual semantic similarity of words as the similarity of their semantic word responses. In *NAACL*, pages 106–116.

Ivan Vulić and Marie-Francine Moens. 2013b. A study on bootstrapping bilingual vector spaces from non-parallel data (and nothing else). In *EMNLP*, pages 1613–1624.

Ivan Vulić and Marie-Francine Moens. 2015. Monolingual and cross-lingual information retrieval models based on (bilingual) word embeddings. In *SIGIR*, to appear.

Ivan Vulić, Wim De Smet, and Marie-Francine Moens. 2011. Identifying word translations from comparable corpora using latent topic models. In *ACL*, pages 479–484.

Will Y. Zou, Richard Socher, Daniel Cer, and Christopher D. Manning. 2013. Bilingual word embeddings for phrase-based machine translation. In *EMNLP*, pages 1393–1398.

How Well Do Distributional Models Capture Different Types of Semantic Knowledge?

Dana Rubinstein **Effi Levi** **Roy Schwartz** **Ari Rappoport**
Institute of Computer Science, The Hebrew University
{drubin80,efle,roys02,arir}@cs.huji.ac.il

Abstract

In recent years, distributional models (DMs) have shown great success in representing lexical semantics. In this work we show that the extent to which DMs represent semantic knowledge is highly dependent on the type of knowledge. We pose the task of predicting properties of concrete nouns in a supervised setting, and compare between learning taxonomic properties (e.g., *animacy*) and attributive properties (e.g., *size*, *color*). We employ four state-of-the-art DMs as sources of feature representation for this task, and show that they all yield poor results when tested on attributive properties, achieving no more than an average F-score of 0.37 in the binary property prediction task, compared to 0.73 on taxonomic properties. Our results suggest that the distributional hypothesis may not be equally applicable to all types of semantic information.

1 Introduction

The Distributional Hypothesis states that the meaning of words can be inferred from their linguistic environment (Harris, 1954). This hypothesis lies at the heart of distributional models (DMs), which approximate the meaning of words by considering the statistics of their co-occurrence with other words in the lexicon.

DMs have shown impressive results in many semantic tasks, such as predicting the similarity of two words, grouping words into semantic categories, and solving analogy questions (see Baroni et al. (2014) for a recent survey). They are also used as a source of semantic information by many downstream applications, including syntactic parsing (Socher et al., 2013), image annotation (Klein et al., 2014), and semantic frame identification (Hermann et al., 2014).

However, the empirical success of DMs may not be uniform across the full range of semantic knowledge. It has been argued that DMs can never grasp the full meaning of words, as many aspects of meaning are grounded in the physical world (Andrews et al., 2009). This claim relies chiefly on cognitive theory (Louwerse, 2011), and is somewhat supported in empirical findings (Baroni and Lenci, 2008; Andrews et al., 2009). Moreover, a recent study by (Hill et al., 2014) has shown that DMs may not model word similarity as well as previously believed.

In this work, we seek to further study the capabilities of DMs in capturing semantic information. For our purposes, we assume that the meaning of a word referring to a *concrete object* (henceforth *concept*) is comprised of a list of *properties* (Baroni and Lenci, 2008). For example, the meaning of the concept *an apple* is comprised of such properties as *red, round, edible, a fruit*, etc. We distinguish between *taxonomic* properties (Wu and Barsalou, 2001; McRae et al., 2005), which define the conceptual category that a concept belongs to (e.g. *an apple is a fruit*), and all other types of properties (henceforth referred to as *attributive* properties). In this paper we employ DMs in the task of learning properties of concepts, and show a very large discrepancy in performance between learning taxonomic and attributive properties.

Several previous works addressed semantic property learning, but mostly in terms of automatically extracting salient properties of concepts from raw text (Almuhareb and Poesio, 2005; Barbu, 2008; Baroni and Lenci, 2008; Devereux et al., 2009; Baroni et al., 2010; Kelly, 2013). Baroni and Lenci (2008) is the only work we are aware of that addressed different property types, while utilizing a DM for property extraction. However, their approach is simple, and includes defining the properties of a concept to be the 10 neighboring words of that concept in the DM space.

Proceedings of the 53rd Annual Meeting of the Association for Computational Linguistics and the 7th International Joint Conference on Natural Language Processing (Short Papers), pages 726–730,
Beijing, China, July 26-31, 2015.

In order to determine to what extent properties of concepts are captured by DMs, we define the following task. The goal is to predict, for a given concept, whether it holds a specific property or not (e.g., whether or not the concept *elephant* is considered *large*) . We model this task as a learning problem, in which concepts have a feature representation based on a state-of-the-art DM. A property-predictor is then trained to predict, for any given concept, whether the property applies to it or not (in a binary classification setup), or the strength of affiliation between the property and the concept (in a regression setup). By evaluating the performance of these predictors, we assess the degree to which the property is captured by the DM.

We experiment with four state-of-the-art DMs (Baroni and Lenci, 2010; Mikolov et al., 2013; Levy and Goldberg, 2014; Pennington et al., 2014). Our results show that all DMs, quite successful in many semantic tasks, fail when it comes to predicting attributive properties of concepts. For example, in the classification task, the best performing DM achieves an averaged F-score of only 0.37, contrasted with an average F-score of 0.73 achieved by the same model for taxonomic properties. This result, which may be attributed to an essential difference between taxonomic and attributive properties, demonstrates possible limitations of the distributional hypothesis, at least in terms of the information captured by current state-of-the-art DMs.

2 Learning Semantic Properties of Concepts

The goal of this paper is to gain better understanding of the type of information DMs encode. We do so by evaluating the performance of a predictor trained on a DM-based representation to learn a semantic property. In this section, we describe the proposed learning task, the dataset and the DMs which serve as feature representations.

2.1 Task Description

We model the problem of learning a single semantic property both as a binary classification problem and as a regression problem. The binary setup is simpler, however it may be argued that a regression setup is more appropriate, since the nature of the affiliation between a concept and its properties is not necessarily binary.

Binary Classification. For each property p, we take concepts for which p applies to be positive instances, and concepts for which it does not as negative instances. For example, the property *is loud* is positive for *a trumpet* but negative for *a mouse*. Let $\mathcal{X}$ denote the domain of concepts, and $\mathcal{Y}_p = \{\pm 1\}$ denote the binary label space. Then for each property p we learn a predictor $h_p : \psi(\mathcal{X}) \to \mathcal{Y}_p$, where $\psi(\mathcal{X}) \subseteq \mathbb{R}^n$ is a mapping from the concept domain to some DM space.

Regression. Here we consider the saliency of a property for a concept and regard it as a real-valued measure. For example, *white* is a salient property of *swan*, a less salient property of *house*, and not a property at all of *hammer*. The formal definitions are the same as in the binary classification setup, except that here $\mathcal{Y}_p = \mathbb{R}$.

2.2 The Data

We use the McRae Feature Norms dataset (McRae et al., 2005). This data was collected in a set of experiments, where participants were presented with concepts (concrete nouns only) and were asked to write down properties that describe them. This resulted in a matrix of 541 concepts and 2,526 properties, where each (concept, property) entry holds the number of participants who elicited the property for the concept. This dataset has been widely used in the past as a proxy to the human perceptual representation of concrete objects (Baroni and Lenci, 2008; Barbu, 2008; Devereux et al., 2009; Johns and Jones, 2012).

In the binary classification setting, for each property, we take all concepts for which this property was elicited (by any number of participants)[1] to be positive, and all other concepts to be negative. In the regression setting, we take the $[0, 1]$-scaled number of participants who elicited each property for a concept to be the real-valued measure of its saliency for that concept.

2.3 Distributional Models

We experiment with four state-of-the-art DMs as feature representations for the concept domain. The models differ with respect to their method of generation (neural network or transformed co-occurrence counts) and their consideration of lin-

[1]Due to a pre-defined threshold applied by McRae et al. (2005), only properties mentioned by at least 5 participants are considered positive.

guistic information (using plain text only, morphology, syntax or pattern information).

word2vec. word2vec (*w2v*, Mikolov et al. (2013)) is a neural network model which implements a language model objective. It has reached state-of-the-art results for word similarity, categorization and analogy tasks (Baroni et al., 2014). We use the off-the-shelf 300-dimensional version trained on a corpus of 100B tokens.[2]

GloVe. GloVe (*gv*, Pennington et al. (2014)) is a log bilinear regression model. The authors report state-of-the-art results in word similarity, semantic analogies and NER tasks. We use the off-the-shelf 300-dimensional version trained on a corpus of 840B tokens.[3]

Distributional Memory. The Distributional Memory model (*dm*, Baroni and Lenci (2010)) is a co-occurrence based DM, which admits morphological, structural and pattern information. The authors have shown that it is highly competitive with state-of-the-art co-occurrence models in a range of semantic tasks. We use the off-the-shelf 5K-dimensional version trained on 3B tokens.[4]

Dependency word2vec. The dependency word2vec model (*dep*, Levy and Goldberg (2014)) is a variation of the word2vec model, which takes into account the dependency links between words. The authors have shown that it accurately models word similarity. We use the off-the-shelf 300-dimensional version trained on Wikipedia.[5]

2.4 Experimental Setup

In our experiments, we consider properties which have at least 25 positive instances in the dataset. We then discard attributive properties that clearly correspond to a taxonomic property. For example, the property *has feathers* is no different from the *bird* category, or the property *lives in water* is identical to the *fish* category. The final list consists of 7 taxonomic and 13 attributive properties.[6]

For each property, we learn both a linear SVM classifier in the binary setup, and a linear SVM regressor in the regression setup. For both setups we use the lib-svm package (Chang and Lin, 2011)[7] and follow a 5-fold cross-validation protocol.

In the binary setup, we report F-scores only, as accuracy measures tend to be misleading due to an unbalanced label distribution. In the regression setup, we report Pearson's correlation scores between predicted values and gold standard values.

2.5 Results

Table 1 shows our results in the binary setup (left side) and in the regression setup (right side) for all models. We display average scores separately for taxonomic and attributive properties.

The results for the binary setup show a rather low performance on learning attributive properties, attaining an average F-score of no more than 0.37 (*dep* model). This is emphasized when compared to the average performance on taxonomic properties, which is 0.73 for *dep*, and can be as high as 0.78 (*w2v*). The regression setup shows a similar trend; the average correlation for attributive properties is at most 0.28 (*dep*), compared to 0.59 for taxonomic properties.

While linear Support Vectors are a well-established method for classification and regression, we have attempted the same experiments with several other methods, including K-Nearest-Neighbors and Decision Trees for classification, and simple Least Squares for regression. In all cases, the results were found to be inferior to the ones obtained by the Support Vectors, while maintaining the discrepancy in performance between taxonomic and attributive property learning.

3 Discussion

Our results show that there is a great difference between the performance of DMs when used to predict taxonomic and attributive properties. Concretely, four state-of-the-art DMs fail to predict attributive properties, implying that even if the property information is indicated in text, it is signaled very weakly, at least by means of linguistic regularities captured by current, state-of-the-art DMs.

Our findings are in line with previous work, such as (Baroni and Lenci, 2008), who demonstrated that taxonomic properties are more dominant in text compared to attributive properties. This suggests that the distributional hypothesis may not be equally applicable to all types of semantic information, and in particular, it may be

[2] `code.google.com/p/word2vec/`

[3] `nlp.stanford.edu/projects/glove/`

[4] `clic.cimec.unitn.it/dm/`

[5] `levyomer.wordpress.com/2014/04/25/dependency-based-word-embeddings/`

[6] The average number of positive instances per property is 42 for taxonomic properties and 61 for attributive properties.

[7] `www.csie.ntu.edu.tw/~cjlin/libsvm`

Property		Binary Classification				Regression			
		w2v	gv	dm	dep	w2v	gv	dm	dep
Taxonomic	a bird	0.83	0.86	0.78	0.71	0.63	0.63	0.39	0.57
	a fruit	0.86	0.8	0.72	0.6	0.66	0.69	0.57	0.55
	a mammal	0.71	0.69	0.65	0.73	0.47	0.44	0.46	0.41
	a vegetable	0.74	0.81	0.75	0.7	0.65	0.69	0.54	0.56
	a weapon	0.72	0.64	0.67	0.77	0.61	0.58	0.48	0.58
	an animal	0.8	0.77	0.74	0.82	0.79	0.73	0.51	0.78
	clothing	0.81	0.84	0.64	0.81	0.63	0.69	0.36	0.67
	Average	**0.78**	**0.77**	**0.71**	**0.73**	**0.63**	**0.64**	**0.47**	**0.59**
Attributive	of different colors	0.44	0.41	0.33	0.46	0.36	0.32	0.22	0.38
	is black	0.24	0.2	0.17	0.22	0.09	0.17	0.13	0.15
	is brown	0.28	0.23	0.29	0.33	0.25	0.25	0.16	0.27
	is green	0.4	0.4	0.45	0.44	0.28	0.24	0.28	0.39
	is white	0.19	0.22	0.11	0.2	0.06	0.1	0.06	0.15
	is yellow	0.21	0.14	0.15	0.21	0.12	0.15	0.12	0.23
	is large	0.4	0.41	0.42	0.44	0.39	0.34	0.38	0.33
	is small	0.43	0.4	0.43	0.48	0.29	0.21	0.25	0.31
	is long	0.31	0.24	0.31	0.36	0.24	0.03	0.14	0.27
	is round	0.29	0.3	0.29	0.43	0.22	0.15	0.24	0.28
	is loud	0.35	0.27	0.3	0.36	0.33	0.25	0.15	0.23
	is dangerous	0.45	0.47	0.49	0.5	0.32	0.3	0.25	0.41
	is fast	0.41	0.34	0.29	0.35	0.33	0.32	0.19	0.26
	Average	**0.34**	**0.31**	**0.31**	**0.37**	**0.25**	**0.22**	**0.2**	**0.28**

Table 1: Results for the Property Learning Task. On the left: F-scores for the binary classification task. On the right: Pearson correlation scores for the regression task.

limited with respect to attributive properties.

An interesting observation is found in the relative success of DMs in predicting taxonomic properties. This result, in line with past research, e.g. (Schwartz et al., 2014), may be explained by considering taxonomic properties as a rich aggregate of attributive properties (Baroni and Lenci, 2010). For example, animals usually have legs and mouths, they make sounds, they can be killed, etc. This is contrasted with attributive properties such as *is white*, whose members do not have much in common, other than the property itself. We therefore hypothesize that although attributive properties may be signaled very weakly in text, as our results indicate, their accumulation is sufficient to distinguish concepts that share most of them from concepts that do not.

To demonstrate this, we turned back to the McRae dataset. For each property, we observed the vector of its values across all concepts in the dataset. We then found its 5 nearest neighbors in terms of correlation, and computed the average correlation with these neighbors, denoted c. Next, we compared the averaged c value for taxonomic properties with that of attributive properties. Taxonomic properties show an average c value of 0.62, compared to 0.32 only for attributive properties. This supports our hypothesis that members of taxonomic properties are similar to each other in various aspects, while members of attributive properties are much less so. This finding may provide a partial explanation as to why taxonomic properties are more easily learned compared to attributive properties, as demonstrated in this paper.

To conclude, we have shown that in the context of learning semantic properties, state-of-the-art distributional models perform differently with respect to the type of property learned. Our results serve as a basis for establishing the limitations to the distributional hypothesis. As future work we propose to further investigate the nature of the distributional hypothesis in its manifestation as DMs, possibly by considering a more fine grained distinction between property types. For example, we intend to compare the performance between properties grounded in the physical world, like colors or size, and more abstract properties such as *dangerous* or *cute*.

Acknowledgments

We would like to thank Roi Reichart for his careful reading and helpful comments. This research was funded (in part) by the Intel Collaborative Research Institute for Computational Intelligence (ICRI-CI).

References

Abdulrahman Almuhareb and Massimo Poesio. 2005. Concept learning and categorization from the web. In *Proc. of CogSci*.

Mark Andrews, Gabriella Vigliocco, and David Vinson. 2009. Integrating experiential and distributional data to learn semantic representations. *Psychological review*, 116(3):463.

Eduard Barbu. 2008. Combining methods to learn feature-norm-like concept descriptions. In *Proceedings of the ESSLLI Workshop on Distributional Lexical Semantics*, pages 9–16.

Marco Baroni and Alessandro Lenci. 2008. Concepts and properties in word spaces. *Italian Journal of Linguistics*, 20(1):55–88.

Marco Baroni and Alessandro Lenci. 2010. Distributional memory: A general framework for corpus-based semantics. *Computational Linguistics*, 36(4):673–721.

Marco Baroni, Brian Murphy, Eduard Barbu, and Massimo Poesio. 2010. Strudel: A corpus-based semantic model based on properties and types. *Cognitive Science*, 34(2):222–254.

Marco Baroni, Georgiana Dinu, and Germán Kruszewski. 2014. Dont count, predict! a systematic comparison of context-counting vs. context-predicting semantic vectors. In *Proceedings of the 52nd Annual Meeting of the Association for Computational Linguistics*, volume 1, pages 238–247.

Chih-Chung Chang and Chih-Jen Lin. 2011. LIBSVM: A library for support vector machines. *ACM Transactions on Intelligent Systems and Technology*, 2:27:1–27:27. Software available at `http://www.csie.ntu.edu.tw/~cjlin/libsvm`.

Barry Devereux, Nicholas Pilkington, Thierry Poibeau, and Anna Korhonen. 2009. Towards unrestricted, large-scale acquisition of feature-based conceptual representations from corpus data. *Research on Language and Computation*, 7(2-4):137–170.

Zellig S Harris. 1954. Distributional structure. *Word*.

Karl Moritz Hermann, Dipanjan Das, Jason Weston, and Kuzman Ganchev. 2014. Semantic frame identification with distributed word representations. In *Proceedings of ACL*.

Felix Hill, Roi Reichart, and Anna Korhonen. 2014. Simlex-999: Evaluating semantic models with (genuine) similarity estimation. *arXiv preprint arXiv:1408.3456*.

Brendan T Johns and Michael N Jones. 2012. Perceptual inference through global lexical similarity. *Topics in Cognitive Science*, 4(1):103–120.

Colin Kelly. 2013. Automatic extraction of property norm-like data from large text corpora.

Benjamin Klein, Guy Lev, Gil Sadeh, and Lior Wolf. 2014. Fisher vectors derived from hybrid gaussian-laplacian mixture models for image annotation. *arXiv preprint arXiv:1411.7399*.

Omer Levy and Yoav Goldberg. 2014. Dependencybased word embeddings. In *Proceedings of the 52nd Annual Meeting of the Association for Computational Linguistics*, volume 2, pages 302–308.

Max M Louwerse. 2011. Symbol interdependency in symbolic and embodied cognition. *Topics in Cognitive Science*, 3(2):273–302.

Ken McRae, George S Cree, Mark S Seidenberg, and Chris McNorgan. 2005. Semantic feature production norms for a large set of living and nonliving things. *Behavior research methods*, 37(4):547–559.

Tomas Mikolov, Ilya Sutskever, Kai Chen, Greg S Corrado, and Jeff Dean. 2013. Distributed representations of words and phrases and their compositionality. In *Advances in Neural Information Processing Systems*, pages 3111–3119.

Jeffrey Pennington, Richard Socher, and Christopher D. Manning. 2014. Glove: Global vectors for word representation. In *Proc. of EMNLP*.

Roy Schwartz, Roi Reichart, and Ari Rappoport. 2014. Minimally supervised classification to semantic categories using automatically acquired symmetric patterns. In *Proceedings of COLING 2014, the 25th International Conference on Computational Linguistics: Technical Papers*, pages 1612–1623, Dublin, Ireland, August. Dublin City University and Association for Computational Linguistics.

Richard Socher, John Bauer, Christopher D Manning, and Andrew Y Ng. 2013. Parsing with compositional vector grammars. In *In Proceedings of the ACL conference*. Citeseer.

Ling-Ling Wu and Lawrence W Barsalou. 2001. Grounding concepts in perceptual simulation: I: Evidence from property generation. *Under review http://userwww. service. emory. edu/~ barsalou*.

Low-Rank Tensors for Verbs in Compositional Distributional Semantics

Daniel Fried, Tamara Polajnar, and **Stephen Clark**
University of Cambridge
Computer Laboratory
{df345,tp366,sc609}@cam.ac.uk

Abstract

Several compositional distributional semantic methods use tensors to model multi-way interactions between vectors. Unfortunately, the size of the tensors can make their use impractical in large-scale implementations. In this paper, we investigate whether we can match the performance of full tensors with low-rank approximations that use a fraction of the original number of parameters. We investigate the effect of low-rank tensors on the transitive verb construction where the verb is a third-order tensor. The results show that, while the low-rank tensors require about two orders of magnitude fewer parameters per verb, they achieve performance comparable to, and occasionally surpassing, the unconstrained-rank tensors on sentence similarity and verb disambiguation tasks.

1 Introduction

Distributional semantic methods represent word meanings by their contextual distributions, for example by computing word-context co-ocurrence statistics (Schütze, 1998; Turney and Pantel, 2010) or by learning vector representations for words as part of a context prediction model (Bengio et al., 2003; Collobert et al., 2011; Mikolov et al., 2013). Recent research has also focused on compositional distributional semantics (CDS): combining the distributional representations for words, often in a syntax-driven fashion, to produce distributional representations of phrases and sentences (Mitchell and Lapata, 2008; Baroni and Zamparelli, 2010; Socher et al., 2012; Zanzotto and Dell'Arciprete, 2012).

One method for CDS is the Categorial framework (Coecke et al., 2011; Baroni et al., 2014), where each word is represented by a tensor whose order is determined by the Categorial Grammar type of the word. For example, nouns are an atomic type represented by a vector, and adjectives are matrices that act as functions transforming a noun vector into another noun vector (Baroni and Zamparelli, 2010). A transitive verb is a third-order tensor that takes the noun vectors representing the subject and object and returns a vector in the sentence space (Polajnar et al., 2014).

However, a concrete implementation of the Categorial framework requires setting and storing the values, or parameters, defining these matrices and tensors. These parameters can be quite numerous for even low-dimensional sentence spaces. For example, a third-order tensor for a given transitive verb, mapping two 100-dimensional noun spaces to a 100-dimensional sentence space, would have 100^3 parameters in its full form. All of the more complex types have corresponding tensors of higher order, and therefore a barrier to the practical implementation of this framework is the large number of parameters required to represent an extended vocabulary and a variety of grammatical constructions.

We aim to reduce the size of the models by demonstrating that reduced-rank tensors, which can be represented in a form requiring fewer parameters, can capture the semantics of complex types as well as the full-rank tensors do. We base our experiments on the transitive verb construction for which there are established tasks and datasets (Grefenstette and Sadrzadeh, 2011; Kartsaklis and Sadrzadeh, 2014).

Previous work on the transitive verb construction within the Categorial framework includes a two-step linear-regression method for the construction of the full verb tensors (Grefenstette et al., 2013) and a multi-linear regression method combined with a two-dimensional plausibility space (Polajnar et al., 2014). Polajnar et al. (2014)

Proceedings of the 53rd Annual Meeting of the Association for Computational Linguistics and the 7th International Joint Conference on Natural Language Processing (Short Papers), pages 731–736,
Beijing, China, July 26-31, 2015.

also introduce several alternative ways of reducing the number of tensor parameters by using matrices. The best performing method uses two matrices, one representing the subject-verb interactions and the other the verb-object interactions. Some interaction between the subject and the object is re-introduced through a softmax layer. A similar method is presented in Paperno et al. (2014). Milajevs et al. (2014) use vectors generated by a neural language model to construct verb matrices and several different composition operators to generate the composed subject-verb-object sentence representation.

In this paper, we use tensor rank decomposition (Kolda and Bader, 2009) to represent each verb's tensor as a sum of tensor products of vectors. We learn the component vectors and apply the composition without ever constructing the full tensors and thus we are able to improve on both memory usage and efficiency. This approach follows recent work on using low-rank tensors to parameterize models for dependency parsing (Lei et al., 2014) and semantic role labelling (Lei et al., 2015). Our work applies the same tensor rank decompositions, and similar optimization algorithms, to the task of constructing a syntax-driven model for CDS. Although we focus on the Categorial framework, the low-rank decomposition methods are also applicable to other tensor-based semantic models including Van de Cruys (2010), Smolensky and Legendre (2006), and Blacoe et al. (2013).

2 Model

Tensor Models for Verbs We model each transitive verb as a bilinear function mapping subject and object noun vectors, each of dimensionality N, to a single sentence vector of dimensionality S (Coecke et al., 2011; Maillard et al., 2014) representing the composed subject-verb-object (SVO) triple. Each transitive verb has its own third-order tensor, which defines this bilinear function. Consider a verb V with associated tensor $\mathcal{V} \in \mathbb{R}^{S \times N \times N}$, and vectors $\mathbf{s} \in \mathbb{R}^N$, $\mathbf{o} \in \mathbb{R}^N$ for subject and object nouns, respectively. Then the compositional representation for the subject, verb, and object is a vector $V(\mathbf{s}, \mathbf{o}) \in \mathbb{R}^S$, produced by applying *tensor contraction* (the higher-order analogue of matrix multiplication) to the verb tensor and two noun vectors. The lth component of the vector for the SVO triple is given by

$$V(\mathbf{s}, \mathbf{o})_l = \sum_{j,k} \mathcal{V}_{ljk} \mathbf{o}_k \mathbf{s}_j \qquad (1)$$

We aim to learn distributional vectors $\mathbf{s}$ and $\mathbf{o}$ for subjects and objects, and tensors $\mathcal{V}$ for verbs, such that the output vectors $V(\mathbf{s}, \mathbf{o})$ are distributional representations of the entire SVO triple. While there are several possible definitions of the sentence space (Clark, 2013; Baroni et al., 2014), we follow previous work (Grefenstette et al., 2013) by using a contextual sentence space consisting of content words that occur within the same sentences as the SVO triple.

Low-Rank Tensor Representations Following Lei et al. (2014), we represent each verb's tensor using a low-rank *canonical polyadic (CP) decomposition* to reduce the numbers of parameters that must be learned during training. As a higher-order analogue to singular value decomposition for matrices, CP decomposition factors a tensor into a sum of R tensor products of vectors.[1] Given a third-order tensor $\mathcal{V} \in \mathbb{R}^{S \times N \times N}$, the CP decomposition of $\mathcal{V}$ is:

$$\mathcal{V} = \sum_{r=1}^{R} \mathbf{P}_r \otimes \mathbf{Q}_r \otimes \mathbf{R}_r \qquad (2)$$

where $\mathbf{P} \in \mathbb{R}^{R \times S}, \mathbf{Q} \in \mathbb{R}^{R \times N}, \mathbf{R} \in \mathbb{R}^{R \times N}$ are parameter matrices, $\mathbf{P}_r$ gives the rth row of matrix $\mathbf{P}$, and $\otimes$ is the tensor product.

The smallest R that allows the tensor to be expressed as this sum of outer products is the *rank* of the tensor (Kolda and Bader, 2009). By fixing a value for R that is sufficiently small compared to S and N (forcing the verb tensor to have rank of at most R), and directly learning the parameters of the low-rank approximation using gradient-based optimization, we learn a low-rank tensor requiring fewer parameters without ever having to store the full tensor.

In addition to reducing the number of parameters, representing tensors in this form allows us to formulate the verb tensor's action on noun vectors as matrix multiplication. For a tensor in the form of Eq. (2), the output SVO vector is given by

$$V(\mathbf{s}, \mathbf{o}) = \mathbf{P}^\top (\mathbf{Q}\mathbf{s} \odot \mathbf{R}\mathbf{o}) \qquad (3)$$

where $\odot$ is the elementwise vector product.

[1] However, unlike matrix singular value decomposition, the component vectors in the CP decomposition are not necessarily orthonormal.

3 Training

We train the compositional model for verbs in three steps: extracting transitive verbs and their subject and object nouns from corpus data, producing distributional vectors for the nouns and the SVO triples, and then learning parameters of the verb functions, which map the nouns to the SVO triple vectors.

Corpus Data We extract SVO triples from an October 2013 download of Wikipedia, tokenized using Stanford CoreNLP (Manning et al., 2014), lemmatized with the Morpha lemmatizer (Minnen et al., 2001), and parsed using the C&C parser (Curran et al., 2007). We filter the SVO triples to a set containing 345 distinct verbs: the verbs from our test datasets, along with some additional high-frequency verbs included to produce more representative sentence spaces. For each verb, we selected up to 600 triples which occurred more than once and contained subject and object nouns that occurred at least 100 times (to allow sufficient context to produce a distributional representation for the triple). This resulted in approximately 150,000 SVO triples overall.

Distributional Vectors We produce two types of distributional vectors for nouns and SVO triples using the Wikipedia corpus. Since these methods for producing distributional vectors for the SVO triples require that the triples occur in a corpus of text, the methods are not a replacement for a compositional framework that can produce representations for previously unseen expressions. However, they can be used to generate data to train such a model, as we will describe.

1) Count vectors (SVD): we count the number of times each noun or SVO triple co-occurs with each of the 10,000 most frequent words (excluding stopwords) in the Wikipedia corpus, using sentences as context boundaries. If the verb in the SVO triple is itself a content word, we do not include it as context for the triple. This produces one set of context vectors for nouns and another for SVO triples. We weight entries in these vectors using the t-test weighting scheme (Curran, 2004; Polajnar and Clark, 2014), and then reduce the vectors to 100 dimensions via singular value decomposition (SVD), decomposing the noun vectors and SVO vectors separately.

2) Prediction vectors (PV): we train vector embeddings for nouns and SVO triples by adapting the Paragraph Vector distributed bag of words method of Le and Mikolov (2014), an extension of the skip-gram model of Mikolov et al. (2013). In our experiments, given an SVO triple, the model must predict contextual words sampled from all sentences containing that triple. In the process, the model learns vector embeddings for both the SVO triples and for the words in the sentences such that SVO vectors have a high dot product with their contextual word vectors. While previous work (Milajevs et al., 2014) has used prediction-based vectors for words in a tensor-based CDS model, ours uses prediction-based vectors for both words and phrases to train a tensor regression model.

We learn 100-dimensional vectors for nouns and SVO triples with a modified version of `word2vec`,[2] using the hierarchical sampling method with the default hyperparameters and 20 iterations through the training data.

Training Methods We learn the tensor $\mathcal{V}$ of parameters for a given verb V using multi-linear regression, treating the noun vectors $\mathbf{s}$ and $\mathbf{o}$ as input and the composed SVO triple vector $V(\mathbf{s}, \mathbf{o})$ as the regression output. Let M_V be the number of training instances for V, where the ith instance is a triple of vectors $\left(\mathbf{s}^{(i)}, \mathbf{o}^{(i)}, \mathbf{t}^{(i)}\right)$, which are the distributional vectors for the subject noun, object noun, and the SVO triple, respectively. We aim to learn a verb tensor $\mathcal{V}$ (either in full or in decomposed, low-rank form) that minimizes the mean of the squared residuals between the predicted SVO vectors $V(\mathbf{s}^{(i)}, \mathbf{o}^{(i)})$ and those vectors obtained distributionally from the corpus, $\mathbf{t}^{(i)}$. Specifically, we attempt to minimize the following loss function:

$$L(V) = \frac{1}{M_V} \sum_{i=1}^{M_V} ||V(\mathbf{s}^{(i)}, \mathbf{o}^{(i)}) - \mathbf{t}^{(i)}||_2^2 \quad (4)$$

$V(\mathbf{s}, \mathbf{o})$ is given by Eq. (1) for full tensors, and by Eq. (3) for tensors represented in low-rank form.

In both the low-rank and full-rank tensor learning, we use mini-batch ADADELTA optimization (Zeiler, 2012) up to a maximum of 500 iterations through the training data, which we found to be sufficient for convergence for every verb. Rather than placing a regularization penalty on the tensor parameters, we use early stopping if the loss

[2]`https://groups.google.com/d/msg/word2vec-toolkit/Q49FIrNOQRo/J6KG8mUj45sJ`

increases on a validation set consisting of 10% of the available SVO triples for each verb.

For low-rank tensors, we compare seven different maximal ranks: R=1, 5, 10, 20, 30, 40 and 50. To learn the parameters of the low-rank tensors, we use an alternating optimization method (Kolda and Bader, 2009; Lei et al., 2014): performing gradient descent on one of the parameter matrices (for example $\mathbf{P}$) to minimize the loss function while holding the other two fixed ($\mathbf{Q}$ and $\mathbf{R}$), then repeating for the other parameter matrices in turn. The parameter matrices are randomly initialized.[3]

4 Evaluation

We compare the performance of the low-rank tensors against full tensors on two tasks. Both tasks require the model to rank pairs of sentences each consisting of a subject, transitive verb, and object by the semantic similarity of the sentences in the pair. The gold standard ranking is given by similarity scores provided by human evaluators and the scores are not averaged among the annotators. The model ranking is evaluated against the ranking from the gold standard similarity judgements using Spearman's ρ.

The verb disambiguation task (GS11) (Grefenstette and Sadrzadeh, 2011) involves distinguishing between senses of an ambiguous verb, given subject and object nouns as context. The dataset consists of 200 sentence pairs, where the two sentences in each pair have the same subject and object but differ in the verb. Each of these pairs was ranked by human evaluators on a 1-7 similarity scale so that properly disambiguated pairs (e.g. *author write book – author publish book*) have higher similarity scores than improperly disambiguated pairs (e.g. *author write book – author spell book*).

The transitive sentence similarity dataset (Kartsaklis and Sadrzadeh, 2014) consists of 72 subject-verb-object sentences arranged into 108 sentence pairs. As in GS11, each pair has a gold standard semantic similarity score on a 1-7 scale. For example, the pair *medication achieve result – drug produce effect* has a high similarity rating, while *author write book – delegate buy land* has a low rating. In this dataset, however, the two sentences in each pair have no lexical overlap: neither subjects, objects, nor verbs are shared.

[3]Since the low-rank tensor loss is non-convex, we suspect that parameter initialization may produce better results.

	GS11		KS14		# tensor
	SVD	PV	SVD	PV	params.
Add.	0.13	0.14	**0.55**	**0.56**	–
Mult.	0.13	0.14	0.09	0.27	–
R=1	0.10	0.05	0.18	0.30	300
R=5	0.26	0.30	0.28	0.40	1.5K
R=10	0.29	0.32	0.26	0.45	3K
R=20	0.31	0.34	0.39	0.44	6K
R=30	0.28	0.33	0.32	0.46	9K
R=40	0.32	0.30	0.31	**0.52**	12K
R=50	**0.34**	0.32	**0.42**	0.51	15K
Full	0.29	**0.36**	0.41	**0.52**	1M

Table 1: Model performance on the verb disambiguation (GS11) and sentence similarity (KS14) tasks, given by Spearman's ρ, and the number of parameters needed to represent each verb's tensor. We show the highest tensor result for each task and vector set in bold (and also bold the baseline when it outperforms the tensor method).

5 Results

Table 1 displays correlations between the systems' scores and human SVO similarity judgements on the verb disambiguation (GS11) and sentence similarity (KS14) tasks, for both the count (SVD) and prediction vectors (PV). We also give results for simple composition of word vectors using elementwise addition and multiplication (Mitchell and Lapata, 2008) (using verb vectors produced in the same manner as for nouns). As is consistent with prior work, the tensor-based models are surpassed by vector addition on the KS14 dataset (Milajevs et al., 2014), but perform better than both addition and multiplication on the GS11 dataset.[4]

Unsurprisingly, the rank-1 tensor has lowest performance for both tasks and vector sets, and performance generally increases as we increase the maximal rank R. The full tensor achieves the best, or tied for the best, performance on both tasks when using the PV vectors. However, for the SVD vectors, low-rank tensors surpass the performance of the full-rank tensor for R=40 and R=50

[4]The results in this table are not directly comparable with Milajevs et al. (2014), who compare against *averaged* annotator scores. Comparing against averaged annotator scores, our best result on GS11 is 0.47 for the full-rank tensor with PV vectors, and our best non-addition result on KS14 is 0.68 for the K=40 tensor with PV vectors (the best result is addition with PV vectors, which achieves 0.71). These results exceed the scores reported for tensor-based models by Milajevs et al. (2014).

on GS11, and R=50 on KS14.

On GS11, the SVD and PV vectors have varying but mostly comparable performance, with PV having higher performance on 5 out of 8 models. However, on KS14, the PV vectors have better performance than the SVD vectors for every model by at least 0.05 points, which is consistent with prior work comparing count and predict vectors on these datasets (Milajevs et al., 2014).

The low-rank tensor models are also at least twice as fast to train as the full tensors: on a single core, training a rank-1 tensor takes about 5 seconds for each verb on average, ranks 5-50 each take between 1 and 2 minutes, and the full tensors each take about 4 minutes. Since a separate tensor is trained for each verb, this allows a substantial amount of time to be saved even when using the constrained vocabulary of 345 verbs.

6 Conclusion

We find that low-rank tensors for verbs achieve comparable or better performance than full-rank tensors on both verb disambiguation and sentence similarity tasks, while reducing the number of parameters that must be learned and stored for each verb by at least two orders of magnitude, and cutting training time in half.

While in our experiments the prediction-based vectors outperform the count-based vectors on both tasks for most models, Levy et al. (2015) indicate that tuning hyperparameters of the count-based vectors may be able to produce comparable performance. Regardless, we show that the low-rank tensors are able to achieve performance comparable to the full rank for both types of vectors. This is important for extending the model to many more grammatical types (including those with corresponding tensors of higher order than investigated here) to build a wide-coverage tensor-based semantic system using, for example, the CCG parser of Curran et al. (2007).

Acknowledgments

Daniel Fried is supported by a Churchill Scholarship. Tamara Polajnar is supported by ERC Starting Grant DisCoTex (306920). Stephen Clark is supported by ERC Starting Grant DisCoTex (306920) and EPSRC grant EP/I037512/1. We would like to thank Laura Rimell and the anonymous reviewers for their comments.

References

Marco Baroni and Roberto Zamparelli. 2010. Nouns are vectors, adjectives are matrices: Representing adjective-noun constructions in semantic space. In *Proceedings of the 2010 Conference on Empirical Methods in Natural Language Processing (EMNLP 2010)*, Cambridge, Massachusetts.

Marco Baroni, Raffaela Bernardi, and Roberto Zamparelli. 2014. Frege in space: A program of compositional distributional semantics. *Linguistic Issues in Language Technology*, 9.

Yoshua Bengio, Réjean Ducharme, Pascal Vincent, and Christian Jauvin. 2003. A neural probabilistic language model. *Journal of Machine Learning Research*, (3):1137–1155.

William Blacoe, Elham Kashefi, and Mirella Lapata. 2013. A quantum-theoretic approach to distributional semantics. In *Proceedings of the 2013 Conference of the North American Chapter of the Association for Computational Linguistics: Human Language Technologies (NAACL-HLT 2013)*, Atlanta, Georgia.

Stephen Clark. 2013. Type-driven syntax and semantics for composing meaning vectors. *Quantum Physics and Linguistics: A Compositional, Diagrammatic Discourse*, pages 359–377.

Bob Coecke, Mehrnoosh Sadrzadeh, and Stephen Clark. 2011. Mathematical foundations for a compositional distributional model of meaning. *Linguistic Analysis*, 36(1-4):345–384.

R. Collobert, J. Weston, L. Bottou, M. Karlen, K. Kavukcuoglu, and P. Kuksa. 2011. Natural language processing (almost) from scratch. *Journal of Machine Learning Research*, 12:2493–2537.

James R Curran, Stephen Clark, and Johan Bos. 2007. Linguistically motivated large-scale NLP with C&C and Boxer. In *Proceedings of the Demonstration Session of the 45th Annual Meeting of the Association for Computational Linguistics (ACL 2007)*, Prague, Czech Republic.

James R. Curran. 2004. *From distributional to semantic similarity*. Ph.D. thesis, University of Edinburgh.

Edward Grefenstette and Mehrnoosh Sadrzadeh. 2011. Experimenting with transitive verbs in a DisCoCat. In *Proceedings of the 2011 Workshop on Geometrical Models of Natural Language Semantics (GEMS 2011)*, Edinburgh, Scotland.

Edward Grefenstette, Georgiana Dinu, Yao-Zhong Zhang, Mehrnoosh Sadrzadeh, and Marco Baroni. 2013. Multi-step regression learning for compositional distributional semantics. In *Proceedings of the 10th International Conference on Computational Semantics (IWCS 2013)*, Pottsdam, Germany.

Dimitri Kartsaklis and Mehrnoosh Sadrzadeh. 2014. A study of entanglement in a categorical framework of natural language. In *Proceedings of the 11th Workshop on Quantum Physics and Logic (QPL 2014)*, Kyoto, Japan, June.

Tamara G Kolda and Brett W Bader. 2009. Tensor decompositions and applications. *SIAM Review*, 51(3):455–500.

Quoc V. Le and Tomas Mikolov. 2014. Distributed representations of sentences and documents. In *Proceedings of the 31st International Conference on Machine Learning (ICML 2014)*, Beijing, China.

Tao Lei, Yu Xin, Yuan Zhang, Regina Barzilay, and Tommi Jaakkola. 2014. Low-rank tensors for scoring dependency structures. In *Proceedings of the 52nd Annual Meeting of the Association for Computational Linguistics (ACL 2014)*, Baltimore, Maryland.

Tao Lei, Yuan Zhang, Lluis Marquez, Alessandro Moschitti, and Regina Barzilay. 2015. High-order low-rank tensors for semantic role labeling. In *Proceedings of the 2015 Conference of the North American Chapter of the Association for Computational Linguistics – Human Language Technologies (NAACL-HLT 2015)*, Denver, Colorado.

Omer Levy, Yoav Goldberg, and Ido Dagan. 2015. Improving distributional similarity with lessons learned from word embeddings. *Transactions of the Association for Computational Linguistics*, 3:211–225.

Jean Maillard, Stephen Clark, and Edward Grefenstette. 2014. A type-driven tensor-based semantics for CCG. In *Proceedings of the EACL 2014 Type Theory and Natural Language Semantics Workshop (TTNLS)*, Gothenburg, Sweden.

Christopher D. Manning, Mihai Surdeanu, John Bauer, Jenny Finkel, Steven J. Bethard, and David McClosky. 2014. The Stanford CoreNLP natural language processing toolkit. In *Proceedings of 52nd Annual Meeting of the Association for Computational Linguistics (ACL 2014): System Demonstrations*, pages 55–60, Baltimore, Maryland.

Tomas Mikolov, Ilya Sutskever, Kai Chen, Greg Corrado, and Jeffrey Dean. 2013. Distributed representations of words and phrases and their compositionality. In *Neural Information Processing Systems (NIPS 2013)*.

Dmitrijs Milajevs, Dimitri Kartsaklis, Mehrnoosh Sadrzadeh, and Matthew Purver. 2014. Evaluating neural word representations in tensor-based compositional settings. In *Proceedings of the 2014 Conference on Empirical Methods in Natural Language Processing (EMNLP 2014)*.

Guido Minnen, John Carroll, and Darren Pearce. 2001. Applied morphological processing of English. *Natural Language Engineering*, 7(03):207–223.

Jeff Mitchell and Mirella Lapata. 2008. Vector-based models of semantic composition. In *Proceedings of the 46th Annual Meeting of the Association for Computational Linguistics: Human Language Technologies (ACL-08: HLT)*, Columbus, Ohio.

Denis Paperno, Nghia The Pham, and Marco Baroni. 2014. A practical and linguistically-motivated approach to compositional distributional semantics. In *Proceedings of the 52nd Annual Meeting of the Association for Computational Linguistics (ACL 2014)*, Baltimore, Maryland.

Tamara Polajnar and Stephen Clark. 2014. Improving distributional semantic vectors through context selection and normalisation. In *Proceedings of the 14th Conference of the European Chapter of the Association for Computational Linguistics (EACL 2014)*, Gothenburg, Sweden.

Tamara Polajnar, Luana Fagarasan, and Stephen Clark. 2014. Reducing dimensions of tensors in type-driven distributional semantics. In *Proceedings of the 2014 Conference on Empirical Methods in Natural Language Processing (EMNLP 2014)*, Doha, Qatar.

Hinrich Schütze. 1998. Automatic word sense discrimination. *Computational Linguistics*, 24(1):97–124.

Paul Smolensky and Geraldine Legendre. 2006. *The Harmonic Mind: from neural computation to optimality-theoretic grammar*. MIT Press, Cambridge, MA.

Richard Socher, Brody Huval, Christopher D. Manning, and Andrew Y. Ng. 2012. Semantic Compositionality Through Recursive Matrix-Vector Spaces. In *Proceedings of the 2012 Conference on Empirical Methods in Natural Language Processing and Computational Natural Language Learning (EMNLP-CoNLL 2012)*, Jeju Island, Korea.

Peter D Turney and Patrick Pantel. 2010. From frequency to meaning: Vector space models of semantics. *Journal of Artificial Intelligence Research*, 37(1):141–188.

Tim Van de Cruys. 2010. A non-negative tensor factorization model for selectional preference induction. *Journal of Natural Language Engineering*, 16(4):417–437.

Fabio M Zanzotto and Lorenzo Dell'Arciprete. 2012. Distributed tree kernels. In *Proceedings of the 29th International Conference on Machine Learning (ICML 2012)*, Edinburgh, Scotland.

Matthew D Zeiler. 2012. ADADELTA: an adaptive learning rate method. *arXiv preprint arXiv:1212.5701*.

Constrained Semantic Forests for Improved Discriminative Semantic Parsing

Wei Lu
Information Systems Technology and Design
Singapore University of Technology and Design
luwei@sutd.edu.sg

Abstract

In this paper, we present a model for improved discriminative semantic parsing. The model addresses an important limitation associated with our previous state-of-the-art discriminative semantic parsing model – the *relaxed hybrid tree* model by introducing our *constrained semantic forests*. We show that our model is able to yield new state-of-the-art results on standard datasets even with simpler features. Our system is available for download from http://statnlp.org/research/sp/.

1 Introduction

This paper addresses the problem of parsing natural language sentences into their corresponding semantic representations in the form of formal logical representations. Such a task is also known as *semantic parsing* (Kate and Mooney, 2006; Wong and Mooney, 2007; Lu et al., 2008; Kwiatkowski et al., 2010).

One state-of-the-art model for semantic parsing is our recently introduced *relaxed hybrid tree* model (Lu, 2014), which performs integrated lexicon acquisition and semantic parsing within a single framework utilizing efficient algorithms for training and inference. The model allows natural language phrases to be recursively mapped to semantic units, where certain long-distance dependencies can be captured. It relies on representations called *relaxed hybrid trees* that can jointly represent both the sentences and semantics. The model is essentially discriminative, and allows rich features to be incorporated.

Unfortunately, the relaxed hybrid tree model has an important limitation: it essentially does not allow certain sentence-semantics pairs to be jointly encoded using the proposed relaxed hybrid tree representations. Thus, the model is unable to identify joint representations for certain sentence-semantics pairs during the training process, and is unable to produce desired outputs for certain inputs during the evaluation process. In this work, we propose a solution addressing the above limitation, which makes our model more robust. Through experiments, we demonstrate that our improved discriminative model for semantic parsing, even when simpler features are used, is able to obtain new state-of-the-art results on standard datasets.

2 Related Work

Semantic parsing has recently attracted a significant amount of attention in the community. In this section, we provide a relatively brief discussion of prior work in semantic parsing. The hybrid tree model (Lu et al., 2008) and the Bayesian tree transducer based model (Jones et al., 2012) are generative frameworks, which essentially assume natural language and semantics are jointly generated from an underlying generative process. Such models are efficient, but are limited in their predictive power due to the simple independence assumptions made.

On the other hand, discriminative models are able to exploit arbitrary features and are usually able to give better results. Examples of such models include the WASP system (Wong and Mooney, 2006) which regards the semantic parsing problem as a statistical machine translation problem, the UBL system (Kwiatkowski et al., 2010) which performs CCG-based semantic parsing using a log-linear model, as well as the *relaxed hybrid tree* model (Lu, 2014) which extends the generative hybrid tree model. This extension results in a discriminative model that incorporates rich features and allows long-distance dependencies to be captured. The relaxed hybrid tree model has achieved the state-of-the-art results on standard benchmark datasets across different languages.

Performing semantic parsing under other forms

Proceedings of the 53rd Annual Meeting of the Association for Computational Linguistics and the 7th International Joint Conference on Natural Language Processing (Short Papers), pages 737–742,
Beijing, China, July 26-31, 2015.

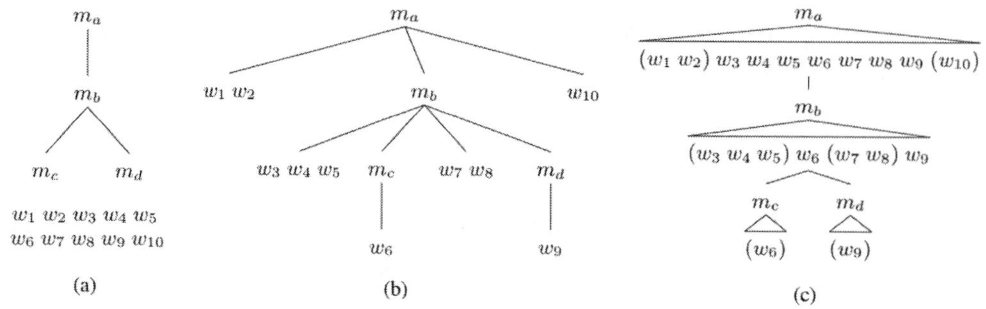

Figure 1: The semantics-sentence pair (a), an example *hybrid tree* (b), and an example *relaxed hybrid tree* (c).

of supervision is also possible. Clarke et al. (2010) proposed a model that learns a semantic parser for answering questions without relying on semantic annotations. Goldwasser et al. (2011) presented a confidence-driven approach to semantic parsing based on self-training. Liang et al. (2013) introduced semantic parsers based on dependency based semantics (DCS) that map sentences into their denotations. In this work, we focus on parsing sentences into their formal semantic representations.

3 Relaxed Hybrid Trees

We briefly discuss our previously proposed *relaxed hybrid tree* model (Lu, 2014) in this section. The model is a discriminative semantic parsing model which extends the generative *hybrid tree* model (Lu et al., 2008). Both systems are publicly available[1].

Let us use $\mathbf{m}$ to denote a complete semantic representation, $\mathbf{n}$ to denote a complete natural language sentence, and $\mathbf{h}$ to denote a complete latent structure that jointly represents both $\mathbf{m}$ and $\mathbf{n}$. The model defines the conditional probability for observing a $(\mathbf{m}, \mathbf{h})$ pair for a given natural language sentence $\mathbf{n}$ using a log-linear approach:

$$P_\Lambda(\mathbf{m}, \mathbf{h}|\mathbf{n}) = \frac{e^{\Lambda \cdot \Phi(\mathbf{n},\mathbf{m},\mathbf{h})}}{\sum_{\mathbf{m}',\mathbf{h}' \in \mathcal{H}(\mathbf{n},\mathbf{m}')} e^{\Lambda \cdot \Phi(\mathbf{n},\mathbf{m}',\mathbf{h}')}} \quad (1)$$

where Λ is the set of parameters (weights of features) used by the model. Figure 1 (a) gives an example sentence-semantics pair. A real example taken from the GeoQuery dataset is shown in Figure 2.

Note that $\mathbf{h}$ is a complete latent structure that jointly represents a natural language sentence and

[1] http://statnlp.org/research/sp/

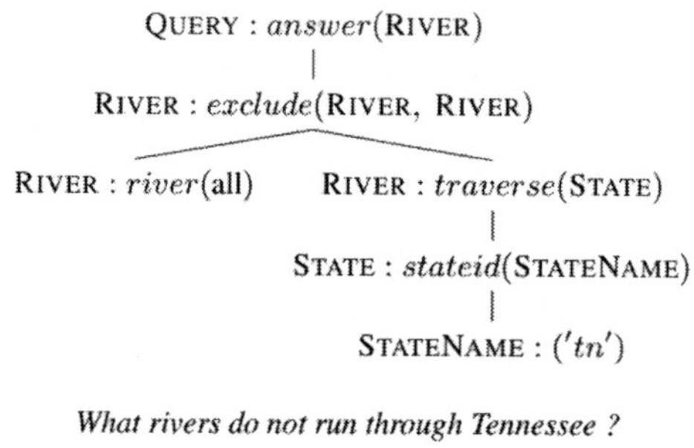

Figure 2: An example tree-structured semantic representation (above) and its corresponding natural language sentence (below).

its corresponding semantic representation. Typically, to limit the space of latent structures, certain assumptions have to be made to $\mathbf{h}$. In our work, we assume that $\mathbf{h}$ must be from a space consisting of *relaxed hybrid tree* structures (Lu, 2014).

The relaxed hybrid trees are analogous to the hybrid trees, which was earlier introduced as a generative framework. One major distinction between these two types of representations is that the relaxed hybrid tree representations are able to capture unbounded long-distance dependencies in a principled way. Such dependencies were unable to be captured by hybrid tree representations largely due to their generative settings. Figure 1 gives an example of a hybrid tree and a relaxed hybrid tree representation encoding the sentence $w_1\ w_2\ w_3\ w_4\ w_5\ w_6\ w_7\ w_8\ w_9\ w_{10}$ and the semantics $m_a(m_b(m_c, m_d))$.

In the hybrid tree structure, each word is strictly associated with a semantic unit. For example the word w_3 is associated with the semantic unit m_b. In the relaxed hybrid tree, however, each word is not only directly associated with exactly one semantic unit m, but also indirectly associated with

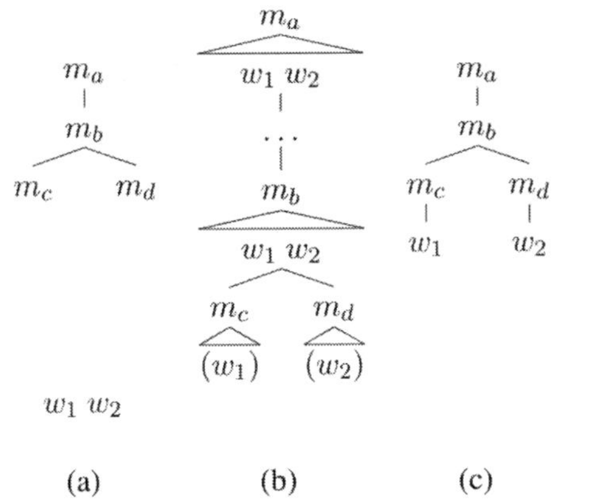

Figure 3: (a) Example semantics-sentence pair that cannot be jointly represented with *relaxed hybrid trees* if pattern **X** is disallowed. (b) Example *relaxed hybrid tree* that consists of an infinite number of nodes when pattern **X** is allowed. (c) Example *hybrid tree* jointly representing both the semantics and the sentence (where pattern **X** is allowed).

all other semantic units that are predecessors of m. For example, the word w_3 now is directly associated with m_b, but is also indirectly associated with m_a. These indirect associations allow the long-distance dependencies to be captured.

Both the hybrid tree and relaxed hybrid tree models define *patterns* at each level of their latent structure which specify how the words and child semantic units are organized at each level. For example, within the semantic unit m_a, we have a pattern **wXw** which states that we first have words that are directly associated with m_a, followed by some words covered by its first child semantic unit, then another sequence of words directly associated with m_a.

3.1 Limitations

One important difference between the hybrid tree representations and the relaxed hybrid tree representations is the exclusion of the pattern **X** in the latter. This ensured relaxed hybrid trees with an infinite number of nodes were not considered (Lu, 2014) when computing the denominator term of Equation 1. In relaxed hybrid tree, $\mathcal{H}(\mathbf{n}, \mathbf{m})$ was implemented as a packed forest representation for exponentially many possible relaxed hybrid trees where pattern **X** was excluded.

By allowing pattern **X**, we allow certain semantic units with no natural language word counterpart to exist in the joint relaxed hybrid tree representation. This may lead to possible relaxed hybrid tree representations consisting of an infinite number of internal nodes (semantic units), as seen in Figure 3 (b). When pattern **X** is allowed, both m_a and m_b are not directly associated with any natural language word, so we are able to further insert arbitrarily many (compatible) semantic units between the two units m_a and m_b while the resulting relaxed hybrid tree remains valid. Therefore we can construct a relaxed hybrid tree representation that contains the given natural language sentence $w_1\ w_2$ with an infinite number of nodes. This issue essentially prevents us from computing the denominator term of Equation 1 since it involves an infinite number of possible $\mathbf{m}'$ and $\mathbf{h}'$.

#Args	Patterns
0	**w**
1	[**w**]**X**[**w**]
2	[**w**]**X**[**w**]**Y**[**w**], [**w**]**Y**[**w**]**X**[**w**]

Table 1: The patterns allowed for our model. [**w**] denotes an optional sequence of natural language words. *E.g.*, [**w**]**X**[**w**] refers to the following 4 patterns: **wX**, **Xw**, **wXw**, and **X** (the pattern excluded by the relaxed hybrid tree model).

To eliminate relaxed hybrid trees consisting of an infinite number of nodes, pattern **X** is disallowed in the relaxed hybrid trees model (Lu, 2014). However, disallowing pattern **X** has led to other issues. Specifically, for certain semantics-sentence pairs, it is not possible to find relaxed hybrid trees that jointly represent them. In the example semantics-sentence pair given in Figure 3 (a), it is not possible to find any relaxed hybrid tree that contains both the sentence and the semantics since each semantic unit which takes one argument must be associated with at least one word. On the other hand, it is still possible to find a hybrid tree representation for both the sentence and the semantics where pattern **X** is allowed (see Figure 3 (c)).

In practice, we can alleviate this issue by extending the lengths of the sentences. For example, we can append the special beginning-of-sentence symbol $\langle s \rangle$ and end-of-sentence symbol $\langle /s \rangle$ to all sentences to increase their lengths, allowing the relaxed hybrid trees to be constructed for certain sentence-semantics pairs with short sentences. However, such an approach does not resolve the theoretical limitation of the model.

4 Constrained Semantic Forests

To address this limitation, we allow pattern $\mathbf{X}$ to be included when building our new discriminative semantic parsing model. However, as mentioned above, doing so will lead to latent structures (relaxed hybrid tree representations) of infinite heights. To resolve such an issue, we instead add an additional constraint – limiting the height of a semantic representation to a fixed constant c, where c is larger than the maximum height of all the trees appearing in the training set.

Table 1 summarizes the list of patterns that our model considers. This is essentially the same as those considered by the hybrid tree model.

Our new objective function is as follows:

$$P_\Lambda(\mathbf{m}, \mathbf{h}|\mathbf{n}) = \frac{e^{\Lambda \cdot \Phi(\mathbf{n},\mathbf{m},\mathbf{h})}}{\sum_{\mathbf{m}' \in \mathcal{M}, \mathbf{h}' \in \mathcal{H}'(\mathbf{n},\mathbf{m}')} e^{\Lambda \cdot \Phi(\mathbf{n},\mathbf{m}',\mathbf{h}')}} \quad (2)$$

where $\mathcal{M}$ refers to the set of all possible semantic trees whose heights are less than or equal to c, and $\mathcal{H}'(\mathbf{n}, \mathbf{m}')$ refers to the set of possible relaxed hybrid tree representations where the pattern $\mathbf{X}$ is allowed.

The main challenge now becomes the computation of the denominator term in Equation 2, as the set $\mathcal{M}$ is still very large. To properly handle all such semantic trees in an efficient way, we introduce a *constrained semantic forest* (CSF) representation of $\mathcal{M}$ here. Such a constrained semantic forest is a packed forest representation of exponentially many possible unique semantic trees, where we set the height of the forest to c. By contrast, it was not possible in our previous relaxed hybrid tree model to introduce such a compact representation over all possible semantic trees. In our previous model's implementation, we directly constructed for each sentence $\mathbf{n}$ a different compact representation over all possible *relaxed hybrid trees* containing $\mathbf{n}$.

Setting the maximum height to c effectively guarantees that all semantic trees contained in the constrained semantic forest have a height no greater than c. We then constructed the (exponentially many) relaxed hybrid tree representations based on the constrained semantic forest $\mathcal{M}$ and each input sentence $\mathbf{n}$. We used a single packed forest representation to represent all such relaxed hybrid tree representations. This allows the computation of the denominator to be performed efficiently using similar dynamic programming algorithms described in (Lu, 2014). Optimization of the model parameters were done by using L-BFGS (Liu and Nocedal, 1989), where the gradients were computed efficiently using an analogous dynamic programming algorithm.

5 Experiments

Our experiments were conducted on the publicly available multilingual GeoQuery dataset. Various previous works on semantic parsing used this dataset for evaluations (Wong and Mooney, 2006; Kate and Mooney, 2006; Lu et al., 2008; Jones et al., 2012). The dataset consists of 880 natural language sentences where each sentence is coupled with a formal tree-structured semantic representation. The early version of this dataset was annotated with English only (Wong and Mooney, 2006; Kate and Mooney, 2006), and Jones et al. (2012) released a version that is annotated with three additional languages: German, Greek and Thai. To make our system directly comparable to previous works, we used the same train/test split used in those works (Jones et al., 2012; Lu, 2014) for evaluation. We also followed the standard approach for evaluating the correctness of an output semantic representation from our system. Specifically, we used a standard script to construct Prolog queries based on the outputs, and used the queries to retrieve answers from the GeoQuery database. Following previous works, we regarded an output semantic representation as correct if and only if it returned the same answers as the gold standard (Jones et al., 2012; Lu, 2014).

The results of our system as well as those of several previous systems are given in Table 2. We compared our system's performance against those of several previous works. The WASP system (Wong and Mooney, 2006) is based on statistical machine translation technique while the HYBRIDTREE+ system (Lu et al., 2008) is based on the generative hybrid tree model augmented with a discriminative re-ranking stage where certain global features are used. UBL-S (Kwiatkowski et al., 2010) is a CCG-based semantic parsing system. TREETRANS (Jones et al., 2012) is the system based on tree transducers. RHT (Lu, 2014) is the discriminative semantic parsing system based on relaxed hybrid trees.

In practice, we set c (the maximum height of a semantic representation) to 20 in our experi-

System	English		Thai		German		Greek	
	Acc.	F	Acc.	F	Acc.	F	Acc.	F
WASP	71.1	77.7	71.4	75.0	65.7	74.9	70.7	78.6
HYBRIDTREE+	76.8	81.0	73.6	76.7	62.1	68.5	69.3	74.6
UBL-S	82.1	82.1	66.4	66.4	75.0	75.0	73.6	73.7
TREETRANS	79.3	79.3	78.2	78.2	74.6	74.6	75.4	75.4
RHT (*all features*)	83.6	83.6	79.3	79.3	74.3	74.3	78.2	78.2
This work	**86.8**	**86.8**	**80.7**	**80.7**	**75.7**	**75.7**	**79.3**	**79.3**

Table 2: Performance of various works across four different languages. Acc.: accuracy percentage, F: F_1-measure percentage.

ments, which we determined based on the heights of the semantic trees that appear in the training data. Results showed that our system consistently yielded higher results than all the previous systems, including our state-of-the-art relaxed hybrid tree system (the full model, when all the features are used), in terms of both accuracy score and F_1-measure. We would like to highlight two potential advantages of our new model over the old RHT model. First, our model is able to handle certain sentence-semantics pairs which could not be handled by RHT during both training and evaluation as discussed in Section 3.1. Second, our model considers the additional pattern $\mathbf{X}$ and therefore has the capability to capture more accurate dependencies between the words and semantic units.

We note that in our experiments we used a small subset of the features used by our relaxed hybrid tree work. Specifically, we did not use any long-distance features, and also did not use any character-level features. As we have mentioned in (Lu, 2014), although the RHT model is able to capture unbounded long-distance dependencies, for certain languages such as German such long-distance features appeared to be detrimental to the performance of the system (Lu, 2014, Table 4). Here in this work, we only used simple unigram features (concatenation of a semantic unit and an individual word that appears directly below that unit in the joint representation), pattern features (concatenation of a semantic unit and the pattern below that unit) as well as transition features (concatenation of two semantic units that form a parent-child relationship) described in (Lu, 2014). While additional features could potentially lead to better results, using simpler features would make our model more compact and more interpretable. We summarized in Table 3 the number of features used in both the previous RHT system and our system across four different languages. It can be seen that our system only required about 2-3% of the features used in the previous system.

System	English	Thai	German	Greek
RHT	2.1×10^6	2.3×10^6	2.7×10^6	2.6×10^6
This work	5.4×10^4	5.2×10^4	7.5×10^4	6.9×10^4

Table 3: Number of features involved for both the RHT system and our new system using constrained semantic forests, across four different languages.

We also note that the training time for our model is longer than that of the relaxed hybrid tree model since the space for $\mathcal{H}'(\mathbf{n}, \mathbf{m}')$ is now much larger than the space for $\mathcal{H}(\mathbf{n}, \mathbf{m}')$. In practice, to make the overall training process faster, we implemented a parallel version of the original RHT algorithm.

6 Conclusion

In this work, we presented an improved discriminative approach to semantic parsing. Our approach does not have the theoretical limitation associated with our previous state-of-the-art approach. We demonstrated through experiments that our new model was able to yield new state-of-the-art results on a standard dataset across four different languages, even though simpler features were used. Since our new model involves simpler features, including unigram features defined over individual semantic unit – word pairs, we believe our new model would aid the joint modeling of both distributional and logical semantics (Lewis and Steedman, 2013) within a single framework. We plan to explore this avenue in the future.

Acknoledgments

The author would like to thank the anonymous reviewers for their helpful comments. This work was supported by SUTD grant SRG ISTD 2013 064 and was partially supported by project 61472191 under the National Natural Science Foundation of China.

References

James Clarke, Dan Goldwasser, Ming-Wei Chang, and Dan Roth. 2010. Driving semantic parsing from the world's response. In *Proc. of CONLL '10*, pages 18–27.

Dan Goldwasser, Roi Reichart, James Clarke, and Dan Roth. 2011. Confidence driven unsupervised semantic parsing. In *Proc. of ACL '11*, pages 1486–1495.

Bevan Keeley Jones, Mark Johnson, and Sharon Goldwater. 2012. Semantic parsing with bayesian tree transducers. In *Proc. of ACL '12*, pages 488–496.

Rohit J. Kate and Raymond J. Mooney. 2006. Using string-kernels for learning semantic parsers. In *Proc. of COLING/ACL*, pages 913–920.

Tom Kwiatkowski, Luke Zettlemoyer, Sharon Goldwater, and Mark Steedman. 2010. Inducing probabilistic ccg grammars from logical form with higher-order unification. In *Proc. EMNLP'10*, pages 1223–1233.

Mike Lewis and Mark Steedman. 2013. Combining distributional and logical semantics. *Transactions of the Association for Computational Linguistics*, 1:179–192.

Percy Liang, Michael I Jordan, and Dan Klein. 2013. Learning dependency-based compositional semantics. *Computational Linguistics*, 39(2):389–446.

D. C. Liu and J. Nocedal. 1989. On the limited memory bfgs method for large scale optimization. *Math. Program.*, 45(3):503–528, December.

Wei Lu, Hwee Tou Ng, Wee Sun Lee, and Luke S. Zettlemoyer. 2008. A generative model for parsing natural language to meaning representations. In *Proc. of EMNLP '08*, pages 783–792.

Wei Lu. 2014. Semantic parsing with relaxed hybrid trees. In *Proc. of EMNLP '14*.

Yuk Wah Wong and Raymond J. Mooney. 2006. Learning for semantic parsing with statistical machine translation. In *Proc. of HLT/NAACL '06*, pages 439–446.

Yuk Wah Wong and Raymond J Mooney. 2007. Learning synchronous grammars for semantic parsing with lambda calculus. In *Proc. of ACL '07*.

Automatic Identification of Rhetorical Questions

Shohini Bhattasali
Dept. of Linguistics
Cornell University
Ithaca, NY, USA

Jeremy Cytryn
Dept. of Computer Science
Cornell University
Ithaca, NY, USA

Elana Feldman
Dept. of Linguistics
Cornell University
Ithaca, NY, USA

Joonsuk Park
Dept. of Computer Science
Cornell University
Ithaca, NY, USA

{sb2295, jmc677, eaf82}@cornell.edu jpark@cs.cornell.edu

Abstract

A question may be asked not only to elicit information, but also to make a statement. Questions serving the latter purpose, called rhetorical questions, are often lexically and syntactically indistinguishable from other types of questions. Still, it is desirable to be able to identify rhetorical questions, as it is relevant for many NLP tasks, including information extraction and text summarization. In this paper, we explore the largely understudied problem of rhetorical question identification. Specifically, we present a simple n-gram based language model to classify rhetorical questions in the Switchboard Dialogue Act Corpus. We find that a special treatment of rhetorical questions which incorporates contextual information achieves the highest performance.

1 Introduction

Rhetorical questions frequently appear in everyday conversations. A rhetorical question is functionally different from other types of questions in that it is expressing a statement, rather than seeking information. Thus, rhetorical questions must be identified to fully capture the meaning of an utterance. This is not an easy task; despite their drastic functional differences, rhetorical questions are formulated like regular questions.

Bhatt (1998) states that in principle, a given question can be interpreted as either an information seeking question or as a rhetorical question and that intonation can be used to identify the interpretation intended by the speaker. For instance, consider the following example:

(1) Did I tell you that writing a dissertation was easy?

Just from reading the text, it is difficult to tell whether the speaker is asking an informational question or whether they are implying that they did not say that writing a dissertation was easy.

However, according to our observation, which forms the basis of this work, there are two cases in which rhetorical questions can be identified solely based on the text. Firstly, certain linguistic cues make a question obviously rhetorical, which can be seen in examples (2) and (3)[1]. Secondly, the context, or neighboring utterances, often reveal the rhetorical nature of the question, as we can see in example (4).

(2) Who ever lifted a finger to help George?

(3) After all, who has any time during the exam period?

(4) Who likes winter? It is always cold and windy and gray and everyone feels miserable all the time.

There has been substantial work in the area of classifying dialog acts, within which rhetorical questions fall. To our knowledge, prior work on dialog act tagging has largely ignored rhetorical questions, and there has not been any previous work specifically addressing rhetorical question identification. Nevertheless, classification of rhetorical questions is crucial and has numerous potential applications, including question-answering, document summarization, author identification, and opinion extraction.

We provide an overview of related work in Section 2, discuss linguistic characteristics of rhetorical questions in Section 3, describe the experimental setup in Section 4, and present and analyze the experiment results in Section 5. We find that, while the majority of the classification relies on features extracted from the question itself, adding

[1]See Section 3 for more details.

Proceedings of the 53rd Annual Meeting of the Association for Computational Linguistics and the 7th International Joint Conference on Natural Language Processing (Short Papers), pages 743–749,
Beijing, China, July 26-31, 2015.

in n-gram features from the context improves the performance. An F_1-score of 53.71% is achieved by adding features extracted from the preceding and subsequent utterances, which is about a 10% improvement from a baseline classifier using only the features from the question itself.

2 Related work

Jurafsky et al. (1997a) and Reithinger and Klesen (1997) used n-gram language modeling on the Switchboard and Verbmobil corpora respectively to classify dialog acts. Grau et al. (2004) uses a Bayesian approach with n-grams to categorize dialog acts. We also employ a similar language model to achieve our results.

Samuel et al. (1999) used transformation-based learning on the Verbmobil corpus over a number of utterance features such as utterance length, speaker turn, and the dialog act tags of adjacent utterances. Stolcke et al. (2000) utilized Hidden Markov Models on the Switchboard corpus and used word order within utterances and the order of dialog acts over utterances. Zechner (2002) worked on automatic summarization of open-domain spoken dialogues i.e., important pieces of information are found in the back and forth of a dialogue that is absent in a written piece.

Webb et al. (2005) used intra-utterance features in the Switchboard corpus and calculated n-grams for each utterance of all dialogue acts. For each n-gram, they computed the maximal predictivity i.e., its highest predictivity value within any dialogue act category. We utilized a similar metric for n-gram selection.

Verbree et al. (2006) constructed their baseline for three different corpora using the performance of the LIT set, as proposed by Samuel (2000). In this approach, they also chose to use a compressed feature set for n-grams and POS n-grams. We chose similar feature sets to classify rhetorical questions.

Our work extends these approaches to dialog act classification by exploring additional features which are specific to rhetorical question identification, such as context n-grams.

3 Features for Identifying Rhetorical Questions

In order to correctly classify rhetorical questions, we theorize that the choice of words in the question itself may be an important indicator of speaker intent. To capture intent in the words themselves, it makes sense to consider a common unigram, while a bigram model will likely capture short phrasal cues. For instance, we might expect the existence of n-grams such as *well* or *you know* to be highly predictive features of the rhetorical nature of the question.

Additionally, some linguistic cues are helpful in identifying rhetorical questions. Strong negative polarity items (NPIs), also referred to as emphatic or even-NPIs in the literature, are considered definitive markers. Some examples are *budge an inch*, *in years*, *give a damn*, *bat an eye*, and *lift a finger* (Giannakidou 1999, van Rooy 2003). Gresillon (1980) notes that a question containing a modal auxiliary, such as *could* or *would*, together with negation tends to be rhetorical. Certain expressions such as *yet* and *after all* can only appear in rhetorical questions (Sadock 1971, Sadock 1974). Again, using common n-grams as features should partially capture the above cues because n-gram segments of strong NPIs should occur more frequently.

We also wanted to incorporate common grammatical sequences found in rhetorical questions. To that end, we can consider part of speech (POS) n-grams to capture common grammatical relations which are predictive.

Similarly, for rhetorical questions, we expect context to be highly predictive for correct classification. For instance, the existence of a question mark in the subsequent utterance when spoken by the questioner, will likely be a weak positive cue, since the speaker may not have been expecting a response. However, the existence of a question mark by a different speaker may not be indicative. This suggests a need to decompose the context-based feature space by speaker. Similarly, phrases uttered prior to the question will likely give rise to a different set of predictive n-grams.

Using these observations, we decided to implement a simple n-gram model incorporating contextual cues to identify rhetorical questions. Specifically, we used unigrams, bigrams, POS bigrams, and POS trigrams of a question and its immediately preceding and following context as feature sets. Based on preliminary results, we did not use trigrams or POS unigrams. POS tags did not capture sufficient contextual information and trigrams were not implemented since the utterances in our dataset were too small to fully utilize them.

Also, to capture the contextual information, we

distinguish three distinct categories - questions, utterances immediately preceding questions, and utterances immediately following questions. In order to capture the effect of a feature if it is used by the same speaker versus a different speaker, we divided the feature space contextual utterances into four disjoint groups: *precedent-same-speaker*, *precedent-different-speaker*, *subsequent-same-speaker*, and *subsequent-different-speaker*. Features in each group are all considered independently.

4 Experimental Setup

4.1 Data

For the experiments, we used the Switchboard Dialog Act Corpus (Godfrey et al. 1992; Jurafsky et al. 1997b), which contains labeled utterances from phone conversations between different pairs of people. We preprocessed the data to contain only the utterances marked as questions (rhetorical or otherwise), as well as the utterances immediately preceding and following the questions. Additionally, connectives like *and* and *but* were marked as *t_con*, the end of conversation was marked as *t_empty*, and laughter was marked as *t_laugh*.

After filtering down to questions, we split the data into 5960 questions in the training set and 2555 questions in the test set. We find the dataset to be highly skewed with only $\frac{128}{2555}$ or 5% of the test instances labeled as rhetorical. Because of this, a classifier that naively labels all questions as non-rhetorical would achieve a 94.99% accuracy. Thus, we chose precision, recall and F_1-measure as more appropriate metrics of our classifier performance. We should note also that our results assume a high level of consistency of the hand annotations from the original taggging of the Switchboard Corpus. However, based on our observation and the strict guidelines followed by annotators as mentioned in Jurafsky et al. (1997a), we are reasonably confident in the reliability of the rhetorical labels.

4.2 Learning Algorithm

We experimented with both Naive Bayes and a Support Vector Machine (SVM) classifiers. Our Naive Bayes classifier was smoothed with an add-alpha Laplacian kernel, where alpha was selected via cross-validation. For our SVM, to account for the highly skewed nature of our dataset, we set the cost-factor based on the ratio of positive (rhetorical) to negative (non-rhetorical) questions in our training set as in Morik et al. (1999). We tuned the trade-off between margin and training error via cross validation over the training set.

In early experiments, Naive Bayes performed comparably to or outperformed SVM because the dimensionality of the feature space was relatively low. However, we found that SVM performed more robustly over the large range and dimensionality of features we employed in the later experiments. Thus, we conducted the main experiments using SVMLite (Joachims 1999).

As the number of parameters is linear in the number of feature sets, an exhaustive search through the space would be intractable. So as to make this feasible, we employ a greedy approach to model selection. We make a naive assumption that parameters of feature sets are independent or codependent on up to one other feature set in the same group. Each pair of codependent feature sets is considered alone while holding other feature sets fixed. Classifier parameters are also assumed to be independent for tuning purposes.

In order to optimize search time without sampling the parameter space too coarsely, we employed an adaptive refinement variant to a traditional grid search. First, we discretely sampled the Cartesian product of dependent parameters sampled at regular geometric or arithmetic intervals between a user-specified minimum and maximum. We then updated minimum and maximum values to center around the highest scoring sample and recursed on the search with the newly downsized span for a fixed recursion depth d. In practice, we choose $k = 4$ and $d = 3$.

4.3 Features

Unigrams, bigrams, POS bigrams, and POS trigrams were extracted from the questions and neighboring utterances as features, based on the analysis in Section 3. Then, feature selection was performed as follows.

For all features sets, we considered both unigram and bigram features. All unigrams and bigrams in the training data are considered as potential candidates for features. For each feature set above, we estimated the maximal predictivity over both rhetorical and non-rhetorical classes, corresponding to using the MLE of $P(c|n)$, where n denotes the n-gram and c is the class. We used these estimates as a score and select the j n-grams with the highest score for each n over each group, regardless of class, where j was selected via 4-fold cross validation.

Each feature was then encoded as a simple occurrence count within its respective group for a given exchange. The highest scoring unigrams and bigrams are as follows: "you", "do", "what", "to", "t_con", "do you", "you know", "going to", "you have", and "well ,".

POS features were computed by running a POS tagger on all exchanges and and then picking the j-best n-grams as described above. For our experiments, we used the maximum entropy treebank POS tagger from the NLTK package (Bird et al. 2009) to compute POS bigrams and trigrams.

Lastly, in order to assess the relative value of question-based and context-based features, we designed the following seven feature sets:

- Question (*baseline*)
- Precedent
- Subsequent
- Question + Precedent
- Question + Subsequent
- Precedent + Subsequent
- Question + Precedent + Subsequent

The question-only feature set serves as our baseline without considering context, whereas the other feature sets serve to test the power of the preceding and following context alone and when paired with features from the question itself.

Feature set	Acc	Pre	Rec	F1	Error 95%
Question	92.41	35.00	60.16	44.25	7.59 ±1.02
Precedent	85.64	12.30	30.47	17.53	14.36 ±1.36
Subsequent	78.98	13.68	60.16	22.29	21.02 ±1.58
Question + Precedent	93.82	41.94	60.94	49.68	6.18 ±0.93
Question + Subsequent	93.27	39.52	**64.84**	49.11	6.73 ±0.97
Precedent + Subsequent	84.93	19.62	**64.84**	30.14	15.07 ±1.38
Question + Precedent + Subsequent	**94.87**	**49.03**	59.38	**53.71**	**5.13± 0.86**

Table 1: Experimental results (%)

AC	PC	Utterance
+	+	X: 'i mean, why not.'
	-	X: 'what are you telling that student?'
-	+	X: '*t_laugh* why don't we do that?'
	-	X: 'who, was in that.'

Table 2: Classification without Context Features (AC: Actual Class, P: Predicted Class. X denotes the speaker)

AC	PC	Utterances
+	+	X: '*t_con* you give them an f on something that doesn't seem that bad to me.' **X: 'what are you telling that student?'** X: 'you're telling them that, hey, you might as well forget it, you know.'
	-	X: 'get homework done,' **X: '*t_con* you know, where do you find the time'.** Y:'well, in the first place it's not your homework,'
-	+	X: 'ha, ha, lots of luck.' **X: 'is she spayed.'** Y: 'yeah'.
	-	Y: '*t_con* it says when the conversation is over just say your good-byes and hang up.' **X: '*t_laugh* why don't we do that?** Y: 'i, guess so.'

Table 3: Classification with Context Features (AC: Actual Class, PC: Predicted Class. X and Y denote the speakers)

5 Results and Analysis

Table 1 shows the performance of the feature sets cross-valided and trained on 5960 questions (with context) in the Switchboard corpus and tested on the 2555 remaining questions.

Our results largely reflect our intuition on the expected utility of our various feature sets. Features in the question group prove by far the most useful single source, while features within the subsequent prove to be more useful than features in the precedent. Somewhat surprisingly however, an F_1-score of 30.14% is achieved by training on contextual features alone while ignoring any cues from the question itself, suggesting the power of context in identifying a question as rhetorical. Additionally, one of the highest scoring bigrams is *you know*, matching our earlier intuitions.

Some examples of the success and failings of our system can be found in Table 2 and 3. For instance, in our question-only feature space, the phrase *what are you telling that student?* was incorrectly classified as non-rhetorical. When the contextual features were added in, the classifier correctly identified it as rhetorical as we might expect. Failure cases of our simple language model based system can be seen for instance in the false positive question *is she spayed* which is interpreted as rhetorical, likely due to the unigram *yeah* in the response.

Overall, we achieve our best results when including both precedent and subsequent context along with the question in our feature space. Thus, our results suggest that incorporating contextual cues from both directly before and after the question itself outperforms classifiers trained on a naive question-only feature space.

5.1 Feature Dimensionality

After model selection via cross validation, our total feature space dimensionality varies between 2914 for the *precedent* only feature set and 16615 for the *question + subsequent* feature set. Distinct n-gram and POS n-gram features are considered for each of same speaker and different speaker for precedents and subsequents so as to capture the distinction between the two. Examining the relative number of features selected for these sub-feature sets also gives a rough idea of the strength of the various cues. For instance, same speaker feature dimensionality tended to be much lower than different speaker feature dimensionality, suggesting that considering context uttered by the respondent is a better cue as to whether the question is rhetorical. Additionally, unigrams and bigrams tend to be more useful features than POS n-grams for the task of rhetorical question identification, or at least considering the less common POS n-grams is not as predictive.

5.2 Evenly Split Distribution

As the highly skewed nature of our data does not allow us to get a good estimate of error rate, we also tested our feature sets on a subsection of the dataset with a 50-50 split between rhetorical and non-rhetorical questions to get a better sense of the accuracy of our classifier. The results can be seen in Table 4. Our classifier achieves an accuracy of 81% when trained on the questions alone and 84% when integrating precedent and subsequent context. Due to the reduced size of the evenly split dataset, performing a McNemar's test with Edwards' correction (Edwards 1948) does not allow us to reject the null hypothesis that the two experiments do not derive from the same distribution with 95% confidence ($\chi^2 = 1.49$ giving a 2-tailed p value of 0.22). However, over the whole skewed dataset, we find $\chi^2 = 30.74$ giving a 2-tailed $p < 0.00001$ so we have reason to believe that with a larger evenly-split dataset integrating context-based features provides a quantifiable advantage.

Feature set	Acc	Pre	Rec	F1	Error 95%
Question	81.25	82.71	78.01	80.29	0.19 ±0.05
Question + Precedent + Subsequent	84.38	88.71	78.01	83.02	0.16 ±0.04

Table 4: Experimental results (%) on evenly distributed data (training set size: 670 & test set size: 288)

6 Conclusions

In this paper, we tackle the largely understudied problem of rhetorical question identification. While the majority of the classification relies on features extracted from the question itself, adding in n-gram features from the context improves the performance. We achieve a 53.71% F_1-score by adding features extracted from the preceding and the subsequent utterances, which is about a 10% improvement from a baseline classifier using only the features from the question itself.

For future work, we would like to employ more complicated features like the sentiment of the context, and dictionary features based on an NPI lexicon. Also, if available, prosodic information like focus, pauses, and intonation may be useful.

7 Acknowledgements

We thank Mary Moroney and Andrea Hummel for helping us identify linguistic characteristics of rhetorical questions and the anonymous reviewers for their thoughtful feedback.

References

Jeremy Ang, Yang Liu, and Elizabeth Shriberg. 2005. Automatic dialog act segmentation and classification in multiparty meetings. In *ICASSP (1)*, pages 1061–1064.

Rajesh Bhatt. 1998. Argument-adjunct asymmetries in rhetorical questions. In *NELS 29*.

Steven Bird, Ewan Klein, and Edward Loper. 2009. *Natural language processing with Python*. O'Reilly Media, Inc.

Allen L. Edwards. 1948. Note on the "correction for continuity" in testing the significance of the difference between correlated proportions. In *Psychometrika*, 13(3):185–187.

Anastasia Giannakidou. 1999. Affective dependencies In *Linguistics and Philosophy*, 22(4): 367–421. Springer

John J. Godfrey, Edward C. Holliman, and Jane McDaniel. 1992. Switchboard: telephone speech corpus for research and development. In *Acoustics, Speech, and Signal Processing, 1992. ICASSP-92., 1992 IEEE International Conference on*, volume 1, pages 517–520 vol.1.

Sergio Grau, Emilio Sanchis, María José Castro, David Vilar. 2004. Dialogue act classification using a Bayesian approach In *9th Conference Speech and Computer*.

Almuth Gresillon. 1980. Zum linguistischen Status rhetorischer Fragen In*Zeitschrift für germanistische Linguistik*, 8(3): 273–289.

Chung-Hye Han. 1998. Deriving the interpretation of rhetorical questions. In *Proceedings of West Coast Conference in Formal Linguistics*, volume 16, pages 237–253. Citeseer.

T. Joachims. 1999. Making large-scale svm learning practical. Advances in kernel methods-support vector learning.

Dan Jurafsky, Rebecca Bates, Noah Coccaro, Rachel Martin, Marie Meteer, Klaus Ries, Elizabeth Shriberg, Andreas Stolcke, Paul Taylor, Carol V. Ess-Dykema, et al. 1997a. Automatic detection of discourse structure for speech recognition and understanding. In *Automatic Speech Recognition and Understanding, 1997. Proceedings., 1997 IEEE Workshop on*, pages 88–95. IEEE.

Dan Jurafsky, Elizabeth Shriberg, and Debra Biasca. 1997b. Switchboard SWBD-DAMSL shallow-discourse-function annotation coders manual. Technical Report Draft 13, University of Colorado, Institute of Cognitive Science.

Simon Keizer, Anton Nijholt, et al. 2002. Dialogue act recognition with bayesian networks for dutch dialogues. In *Proceedings of the 3rd SIGdial workshop on Discourse and dialogue-Volume 2*, pages 88–94. Association for Computational Linguistics.

Katharina Morik, Peter Brockhausen, and T. Joachims. 1999. Combining statistical learning with a knowledge-based approach: a case study in intensive care monitoring. Technical report, Technical Report, SFB 475: Komplexitätsreduktion in Multivariaten Datenstrukturen, Universität Dortmund.

Norbert Reithinger and Martin Klesen. 1997. Dialogue act classification using language models. In *EuroSpeech*. Citeseer.

Jerrold M. Saddock. 1971. Queclaratives In *Seventh Regional Meeting of the Chicago Linguistic Society*, 7: 223–232.

Jerrold M. Saddock. 1974. Toward a linguistic theory of speech acts Academic Press New York

Ken Samuel, Sandra Carberry, and K. Vijay-Shanker. 1999. Automatically selecting useful phrases for dialogue act tagging. *arXiv preprint cs/9906016*.

Ken B. Samuel. 2000. *Discourse learning: an investigation of dialogue act tagging using transformation-based learning*. University of Delaware.

Elizabeth Shriberg, Andreas Stolcke, Dan Jurafsky, Noah Coccaro, Marie Meteer, Rebecca Bates, Paul Taylor, Klaus Ries, Rachel Martin, and Carol Van Ess-Dykema. 1998. Can prosody aid the automatic classification of dialog acts in conversational speech? *Language and speech*, 41(3-4):443–492.

Andreas Stolcke, Klaus Ries, Noah Coccaro, Elizabeth Shriberg, Rebecca Bates, Dan Jurafsky, Paul Taylor, Rachel Martin, Carol Van Ess-Dykema, and Marie Meteer. 2000. Dialogue act modeling for automatic tagging and recognition of conversational speech. *Computational linguistics*, 26(3):339–373.

Robert van Rooy. 2003. Negative polarity items in questions: Strength as relevance In *Journal of Semantics*, 20(3): 239–273. Oxford University Press.

Anand Venkataraman, Andreas Stolcke, and Elizabeth Shriberg. 2002. Automatic dialog act labeling with minimal supervision. In *9th Australian International Conference on Speech Science and Technology, SST 2002*.

Daan Verbree, Rutger Rienks, and Dirk Heylen. 2006. Dialogue-act tagging using smart feature selection; results on multiple corpora. In *Spoken Language Technology Workshop, 2006. IEEE*, pages 70–73. IEEE.

Volker Warnke, Ralf Kompe, Heinrich Niemann, and Elmar Nöth. 1997. Integrated dialog act segmentation and classification using prosodic features and language models. In *EUROSPEECH*.

Nick Webb, Mark Hepple, and Yorik Wilks. 2005. Dialogue act classification based on intra-utterance features. In *Proceedings of the AAAI Workshop on Spoken Language Understanding*. Citeseer.

Klaus Zechner. 2002. Automatic summarization of open-domain multiparty dialogues in diverse genres. *Computational Linguistics*, 28(4):447–485.

Matthias Zimmerman, Yang Liu, Elizabeth Shriberg, and Andreas Stolcke. 2005. A* based joint segentation and classification of dialog acts in multiparty meetings. In *Automatic Speech Recognition and Understanding, 2005 IEEE Workshop on*, pages 215–219. IEEE.

Lifelong Learning for Sentiment Classification

Zhiyuan Chen, Nianzu Ma, Bing Liu
Department of Computer Science
University of Illinois at Chicago
{czyuanacm,jingyima005}@gmail.com, liub@cs.uic.edu

Abstract

This paper proposes a novel lifelong learning (LL) approach to sentiment classification. LL mimics the human continuous learning process, i.e., retaining the knowledge learned from past tasks and use it to help future learning. In this paper, we first discuss LL in general and then LL for sentiment classification in particular. The proposed LL approach adopts a Bayesian optimization framework based on stochastic gradient descent. Our experimental results show that the proposed method outperforms baseline methods significantly, which demonstrates that lifelong learning is a promising research direction.

1 Introduction

Sentiment classification is the task of classifying an opinion document as expressing a positive or negative sentiment. Liu (2012) and Pang and Lee (2008) provided good surveys of the existing research. In this paper, we tackle sentiment classification from a novel angle, *lifelong learning* (LL), or *lifelong machine learning*. This learning paradigm aims to learn as humans do: retaining the learned knowledge from the past and use the knowledge to help future learning (Thrun, 1998, Chen and Liu, 2014b, Silver et al., 2013).

Although many machine learning topics and techniques are related to LL, e.g., lifelong learning (Thrun, 1998, Chen and Liu, 2014b, Silver et al., 2013), transfer learning (Jiang, 2008, Pan and Yang, 2010), multi-task learning (Caruana, 1997), never-ending learning (Carlson et al., 2010), self-taught learning (Raina et al., 2007), and online learning (Bottou, 1998), there is still no unified definition for LL.

Based on the prior work and our research, to build an LL system, we believe that we need to answer the following key questions:

1. What information should be retained from the past learning tasks?
2. What forms of knowledge will be used to help future learning?
3. How does the system obtain the knowledge?
4. How does the system use the knowledge to help future learning?

Motivated by these questions, we present the following definition of *lifelong learning* (LL).

Definition (Lifelong Learning): A learner has performed learning on a sequence of tasks, from 1 to $N-1$. When faced with the Nth task, it uses the knowledge gained in the past $N-1$ tasks to help learning for the Nth task. An LL system thus needs the following four general components:

1. *Past Information Store (PIS)*: It stores the information resulted from the past learning. This may involve sub-stores for information such as (1) the original data used in each past task, (2) intermediate results from the learning of each past task, and (3) the final model or patterns learned from the past task, respectively.
2. *Knowledge Base (KB)*: It stores the knowledge mined or consolidated from PIS (Past Information Store). This requires a knowledge representation scheme suitable for the application.
3. *Knowledge Miner (KM)*. It mines knowledge from PIS (Past Information Store). This mining can be regarded as a meta-learning process because it learns knowledge from information resulted from learning of the past tasks. The knowledge is stored to KB (Knowledge Base).
4. *Knowledge-Based Learner (KBL)*: Given the knowledge in KB, this learner is able to leverage the knowledge and/or some information in PIS for the new task.

Based on this, we can define *lifelong sentiment classification* (LSC):

Definition (Lifelong Sentiment Classification): A learner has performed a sequence of supervised

Proceedings of the 53rd Annual Meeting of the Association for Computational Linguistics and the 7th International Joint Conference on Natural Language Processing (Short Papers), pages 750–756,
Beijing, China, July 26-31, 2015.

sentiment classification tasks, from 1 to $N-1$, where each task consists of a set of training documents with positive and negative polarity labels. Given the Nth task, it uses the knowledge gained in the past $N-1$ tasks to learn a better classifier for the Nth task.

It is useful to note that although many researchers have used transfer learning for supervised sentiment classification, LL is different from the classic transfer learning or domain adaptation (Pan and Yang, 2010). Transfer learning typically uses labeled training data from one (or more) source domain(s) to help learning in the target domain that has little or no labeled data (Aue and Gamon, 2005, Bollegala et al., 2011). It does not use the results of the past learning or knowledge mined from the results of the past learning. Further, transfer learning is usually inferior to traditional supervised learning when the target domain already has good training data. In contrast, our target (or future) domain/task has good training data and we aim to further improve the learning using both the target domain training data and the knowledge gained in past learning. To be consistent with prior research, we treat the classification of one domain as one learning task.

One question is why the past learning tasks can contribute to the target domain classification given that the target domain already has labeled training data. The key reason is that the training data may not be fully representative of the test data due to the *sample selection bias* (Heckman, 1979, Shimodaira, 2000, Zadrozny, 2004). In few real-life applications, the training data are fully representative of the test data. For example, in a sentiment classification application, the test data may contain some sentiment words that are absent in the training data of the target domain, while these sentiment words have appeared in some past domains. So the past domain knowledge can provide the prior polarity information in this situation.

Like most existing sentiment classification papers (Liu, 2012), this paper focuses on binary classification, i.e., positive (+) and negative (−) polarities. But the proposed method is also applicable to multi-class classification. To embed and use the knowledge in building the target domain classifier, we propose a novel optimization method based on the Naïve Bayesian (NB) framework and stochastic gradient descent. The knowledge is incorporated using penalty terms in the optimization formulation. This paper makes three contributions:

1. It proposes a novel lifelong learning approach to sentiment classification, called *lifelong sentiment classification* (LSC).
2. It proposes an optimization method that uses penalty terms to embed the knowledge gained in the past and to deal with domain dependent sentiment words to build a better classifier.
3. It creates a large corpus containing reviews from 20 diverse product domains for extensive evaluation. The experimental results demonstrate the superiority of the proposed method.

2 Related Work

Our work is mainly related to lifelong learning and multi-task learning (Thrun, 1998, Caruana, 1997, Chen and Liu, 2014b, Silver et al., 2013). Existing lifelong learning approaches focused on exploiting invariances (Thrun, 1998) and other types of knowledge (Chen and Liu, 2014b, Chen and Liu, 2014a, Ruvolo and Eaton, 2013) across multiple tasks. Multi-task learning optimizes the learning of multiple related tasks at the same time (Caruana, 1997, Chen et al., 2011, Saha et al., 2011, Zhang et al., 2008). However, these methods are not for sentiment analysis. Also, our naïve Bayesian optimization based LL method is quite different from all these existing techniques.

Our work is also related to transfer learning or domain adaptation (Pan and Yang, 2010). In the sentiment classification context, Aue and Gamon (2005) trained sentiment classifiers for the target domain using various mixes of labeled and unlabeled reviews. Blitzer et al. (2007) proposed to first find some common or pivot features from the source and the target, and then identify correlated features with the pivot features. The final classifier is built using the combined features. Li and Zong (2008) built a meta-classifier (called CLF) using the outputs of each base classifier constructed in each domain. Other works along similar lines include (Andreevskaia and Bergler, 2008, Bollegala et al., 2011, He et al., 2011, Ku et al., 2009, Li et al., 2012, Li et al., 2013, Pan and Yang, 2010, Tan et al., 2007, Wu et al., 2009, Xia and Zong, 2011, Yoshida et al., 2011). Additional details about these and other related works can be found in (Liu, 2012). However, as we discussed in the introduction, these methods do not focus on the ability to accumulate learned knowledge and leverage it in new learning in a lifelong manner.

3 Proposed LSC Technique

3.1 Naïve Bayesian Text Classification

Before presenting the proposed method, we briefly review the Naïve Bayesian (NB) text classification as our method uses it as the foundation.

NB text classification (McCallum and Nigam, 1998) basically computes the conditional probability of each word w given each class c_j (i.e., $P(w|c_j)$) and the prior probability of each class c_j (i.e., $P(c_j)$), which are used to calculate the posterior probability of each class c_j given a test document d (i.e., $P(c_j|d)$). c_j is either positive $(+)$ or negative $(-)$ in our case.

The key parameter $P(w|c_j)$ is computed as:

$$P(w|c_j) = \frac{\lambda + N_{c_j,w}}{\lambda|V| + \sum_{v=1}^{|V|} N_{c_j,v}} \quad (1)$$

where $N_{c_j,w}$ is the frequency of word w in documents of class c_j. $|V|$ is the size of vocabulary V and λ $(0 \leq \lambda \leq 1)$ is used for smoothing.

3.2 Components in LSC

This subsection describes our proposed method corresponding to the proposed LL components.

1. Past Information Store (PIS): In this work, we do not store the original data used in the past learning tasks, but only their results. For each past learning task $\hat{t}$, we store a) $P^{\hat{t}}(w|+)$ and $P^{\hat{t}}(w|-)$ for each word w which are from task $\hat{t}$'s NB classifier (see Eq 1); and b) the number of times that w appears in a positive $(+)$ document $N^{\hat{t}}_{+,w}$ and the number of times that w appears in a negative documents $N^{\hat{t}}_{-,w}$.
2. Knowledge Base (KB): Our knowledge base contains two types of knowledge:
   (a) Document-level knowledge $N^{KB}_{+,w}$ (and $N^{KB}_{-,w}$): number of occurrences of w in the documents of the positive (and negative) class in the past tasks, i.e., $N^{KB}_{+,w} = \sum_{\hat{t}} N^{\hat{t}}_{+,w}$ and $N^{KB}_{-,w} = \sum_{\hat{t}} N^{\hat{t}}_{-,w}$.
   (b) Domain-level knowledge $M^{KB}_{+,w}$ (and $M^{KB}_{-,w}$): number of past tasks in which $P(w|+) > P(w|-)$ (and $P(w|+) < P(w|-)$).
3. Knowledge Miner (KM). Knowledge miner is straightforward as it just performs counting and aggregation of information in PIS to generate knowledge (see 2(a) and 2(b) above).
4. Knowledge-Based Learner (KBL): This learner incorporates knowledge using regularization as penalty terms in our optimization. See the details in 3.4.

3.3 Objective Function

In this subsection, we introduce the objective function used in our method. The key parameters that affect NB classification results are $P(w|c_j)$ which are computed using empirical counts of word w with class c_j, i.e., $N_{c_j,w}$ (Eq. 1). In binary classification, they are $N_{+,w}$ and $N_{-,w}$. This suggests that we can revise these counts appropriately to improve classification. In our optimization, we denote the optimized variables $X_{+,w}$ and $X_{-,w}$ as the number of times that a word w appears in the positive and negative class. We called them *virtual counts* to distinguish them from empirical counts $N_{+,w}$ and $N_{-,w}$. For correct classification, ideally, we should have the posterior probability $P(c_j|d_i) = 1$ for labeled class c_j, and for the other class c_f, we should have $P(c_f|d_i) = 0$. Formally, given a new domain training data D^t, our objective function is:

$$\sum_{i=1}^{|D^t|} \left(P(c_j|d_i) - P(c_f|d_i)\right) \quad (2)$$

Here c_j is the actual labeled class of $d_i \in D^t$. In this paper, we use stochastic gradient descent (SGD) to optimize on the classification of each document $d_i \in D^t$. Due to the space limit, we only show the optimization process for a positive document (the process for a negative document is similar). The objective function under SGD for a positive document is:

$$F_{+,i} = P(+|d_i) - P(-|d_i) \quad (3)$$

To further save space, we omit the derivation steps and give the final derivatives below (See the detailed derivation steps in the separate supplementary note):

$$g(\boldsymbol{X}) = \left(\frac{\lambda|V| + \sum_{v=1}^{|V|} X_{+,v}}{\lambda|V| + \sum_{v=1}^{|V|} X_{-,v}}\right)^{|d_i|} \quad (4)$$

$$\frac{\partial F_{+,i}}{\partial X_{+,u}} = \frac{\frac{n_{u,d_i}}{\lambda+X_{+,u}} + \frac{P(-)}{P(+)} \prod_{w\in d_i} \left(\frac{\lambda+X_{-,w}}{\lambda+X_{+,w}}\right)^{n_{w,d_i}} \times \frac{\partial g}{\partial X_{+,u}}}{1 + \frac{P(-)}{P(+)} \prod_{w\in d_i} \left(\frac{\lambda+X_{-,w}}{\lambda+X_{+,w}}\right)^{n_{w,d_i}} \times g(\boldsymbol{X})} - \frac{n_{u,d_i}}{\lambda + X_{+,u}} \quad (5)$$

$$\frac{\partial F_{+,i}}{\partial X_{-,u}} = \frac{\frac{n_{u,d_i}}{\lambda+X_{-,u}} \times g(\boldsymbol{X}) + \frac{\partial g}{\partial X_{-,u}}}{\frac{P(+)}{P(-)} \prod_{w\in d_i} \left(\frac{\lambda+X_{+,w}}{\lambda+X_{-,w}}\right)^{n_{w,d_i}} + g(\boldsymbol{X})} \quad (6)$$

Alarm Clock	30.51	Flashlight	11.69	Home Theater System	28.84	Projector	20.24
Baby	16.45	GPS	19.50	Jewelry	12.21	Rice Cooker	18.64
Bag	11.97	Gloves	13.76	Keyboard	22.66	Sandal	12.11
Cable Modem	12.53	Graphics Card	14.58	Magazine Subscriptions	26.88	Vacuum	22.07
Dumbbell	16.04	Headphone	20.99	Movies TV	10.86	Video Games	20.93

Table 1: Names of the 20 product domains and the proportion of negative reviews in each domain.

where n_{u,d_i} is the term frequency of word u in document d_i. $\boldsymbol{X}$ denotes all the variables consisting of $X_{+,w}$ and $X_{-,w}$ for each word w. The partial derivatives for a word u, i.e., $\frac{\partial g}{\partial X_{+,u}}$ and $\frac{\partial g}{\partial X_{-,u}}$, are quite straightforward and thus not shown here. $X^0_{+,w} = N^t_{+,w} + N^{KB}_{+,w}$ and $X^0_{-,w} = N^t_{-,w} + N^{KB}_{-,w}$ are served as a reasonable starting point for SGD, where $N^t_{+,w}$ and $N^t_{-,w}$ are the empirical counts of word w and classes $+$ and $-$ from domain D^t, and $N^{KB}_{+,w}$ and $N^{KB}_{-,w}$ are from knowledge KB (Section 3.2). The SGD runs iteratively using the following rules for the positive document d_i until convergence, i.e., when the difference of Eq. 2 for two consecutive iterations is less than $1e-3$ (same for the negative document), where γ is the learning rate:

$$X^l_{+,u} = X^{l-1}_{+,u} - \gamma \frac{\partial F_{+,i}}{\partial X_{+,u}}, X^l_{-,u} = X^{l-1}_{-,u} - \gamma \frac{\partial F_{+,i}}{\partial X_{-,u}}$$

3.4 Exploiting Knowledge via Penalty Terms

The above optimization is able to update the virtual counts for a better classification in the target domain. However, it does not deal with the issue of domain dependent sentiment words, i.e., some words may change the polarity across different domains. Nor does it utilize the domain-level knowledge in the knowledge base KB (Section 3.2). We thus propose to add penalty terms into the optimization to accomplish these.

The intuition here is that if a word w can distinguish classes very well from the target domain training data, we should rely more on the target domain training data in computing counts related to w. So we define a set of words V_T that consists of distinguishable target domain dependent words. A word w belongs to V_T if $P(w|+)$ is much larger or much smaller than $P(w|-)$ in the target domain, i.e., $\frac{P(w|+)}{P(w|-)} \geq \sigma$ or $\frac{P(w|-)}{P(w|+)} \geq \sigma$, where σ is a parameter. Such words are already effective in classification for the target domain, so the virtual counts in optimization should follow the empirical counts ($N^t_{+,w}$ and $N^t_{-,w}$) in the target domain, which are reflected in the L2 regularization penalty term below (α is the regularization coefficient):

$$\frac{1}{2}\alpha \sum_{w \in V_T} \left((X_{+,w} - N^t_{+,w})^2 + (X_{-,w} - N^t_{-,w})^2 \right) \quad (7)$$

To leverage domain-level knowledge (the second type of knowledge in KB in Section 3.2), we want to utilize only those reliable parts of knowledge. The rationale here is that if a word only appears in one or two past domains, the knowledge associated with it is probably not reliable or it is highly specific to those domains. Based on it, we use domain frequency to define the reliability of the domain-level knowledge. For w, if $M^{KB}_{+,w} \geq \tau$ or $M^{KB}_{-,w} \geq \tau$ (τ is a parameter), we regard it as appearing in a reasonable number of domains, making its knowledge reliable. We denote the set of such words as V_S. Then we add the second penalty term as follows:

$$\frac{1}{2}\alpha \sum_{w \in V_S} (X_{+,w} - R_w \times X^0_{+,w})^2 + \frac{1}{2}\alpha \sum_{w \in V_S} (X_{-,w} - (1 - R_w) \times X^0_{-,w})^2 \quad (8)$$

where the ratio R_w is defined as $M^{KB}_{+,w}/(M^{KB}_{+,w} + M^{KB}_{-,w})$. $X^0_{+,w}$ and $X^0_{-,w}$ are the starting points for SGD (Section 3.3). Finally, we revise the partial derivatives in Eqs. 4-6 by adding the corresponding partial derivatives of Eqs. 7 and 8 to them.

4 Experiments

Datasets. We created a large corpus containing reviews from 20 types of diverse products or domains crawled from Amazon.com (i.e., 20 datasets). The names of product domains are listed in Table 1. Each domain contains 1,000 reviews. Following the existing work of other researchers (Blitzer et al., 2007, Pang et al., 2002), we treat reviews with rating > 3 as positive and reviews with rating < 3 as negative. The datasets are publically available at the authors websites.

Natural class distribution: We keep the natural (or skewed) distribution of the positive and negative reviews to experiment with the real-life situation. F1-score is used due to the imbalance.

NB-T	NB-S	NB-ST	SVM-T	SVM-S	SVM-ST	CLF	**LSC**
56.21	57.04	60.61	57.82	57.64	61.05	12.87	**67.00**

Table 2: Natural class distribution: Average F1-score of the negative class over 20 domains. Negative class is the minority class and thus harder to classify.

NB-T	NB-S	NB-ST	SVM-T	SVM-S	SVM-ST	CLF	**LSC**
80.15	77.35	80.85	78.45	78.20	79.40	80.49	**83.34**

Table 3: Balanced class distribution: Average accuracy over 20 domains for each system.

Balanced class distribution: We also created a balance dataset with 200 reviews (100 positive and 100 negative) in each domain dataset. This set is smaller because of the small number of negative reviews in each domain. Accuracy is used for evaluation in this balanced setting.

We used unigram features with no feature selection in classification. We followed (Pang et al., 2002) to deal with negation words. For evaluation, each domain is treated as the target domain with the rest 19 domains as the past domains. All the models are evaluated using 5-fold cross validation.

Baselines. We compare our proposed LSC model with Naïve Bayes (NB), SVM[1], and CLF (Li and Zong, 2008). Note that NB and SVM can only work on a single domain data. To have a comprehensive comparison, they are fed with three types of training data:

a) labeled training data from the target domain only, denoted by NB-T and SVM-T;
b) labeled training data from all past source domains only, denoted by NB-S and SVM-S;
c) merged (labeled) training data from all past domains and the target domain, referred to as NB-ST and SVM-ST.

For LSC, we empirically set $\sigma = 6$ and $\tau = 6$. The learning rate λ and regularization coefficient α are set to 0.1 empirically. λ is set to 1 for (Laplace) smoothing.

Table 2 shows the average F1-scores for the negative class in the natural class distribution, and Table 3 shows the average accuracies in the balanced class distribution. We can clearly see that our proposed model LSC achieves the best performance in both cases. In general, NB-S (and SVM-S) are worse than NB-T (and SVM-T), both of which are worse than NB-ST (and SVM-ST). This shows that simply merging both past domains and the target domain data is slightly beneficial. Note that the average F1-score for the positive class is not shown as all classifiers perform very well because the positive class is the majority class (while our model performs slightly better than the baselines). The improvements of the proposed LSC model over all baselines in both cases are statistically significant using paired t-test ($p < 0.01$ compared to NB-ST and CLF, $p < 0.0001$ compared to the others). In the balanced class setting (Table 3), CLF performs better than NB-T and SVM-T, which is consistent with the results in (Li and Zong, 2008). However, it is still worse than our LSC model.

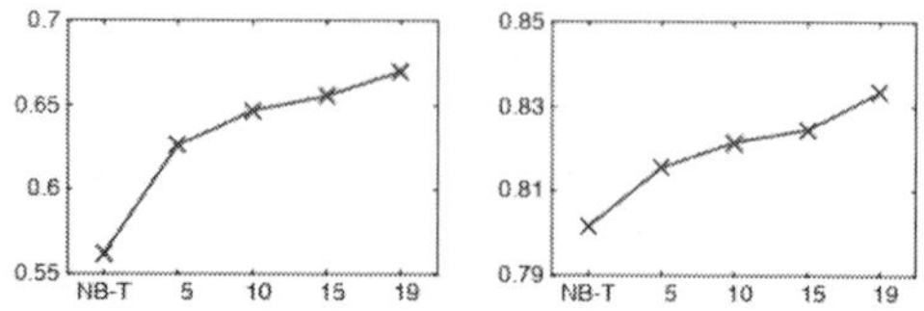

Figure 1: (Left): Negative class F1-score of LSC with #past domains in natural class distribution. (Right): Accuracy of LSC with #past domains in balanced class distribution.

Effects of #Past Domains. Figure 1 shows the effects of our model using different number of past domains. We clearly see that LSC performs better with more past domains, showing it indeed has the ability to accumulate knowledge and use the knowledge to build better classifiers.

5 Conclusions

In this paper, we proposed a lifelong learning approach to sentiment classification using optimization, which is based on stochastic gradient descent in the framework of Bayesian probabilities. Penalty terms are introduced to effectively exploit the knowledge gained from past learning. Our experimental results using 20 diverse product review domains demonstrate the effectiveness of the method. We believe that lifelong learning is a promising direction for building better classifiers.

[1]http://www.csie.ntu.edu.tw/~cjlin/libsvm/

References

Alina Andreevskaia and Sabine Bergler. 2008. When Specialists and Generalists Work Together: Overcoming Domain Dependence in Sentiment Tagging. In *ACL*, pages 290–298.

Anthony Aue and Michael Gamon. 2005. Customizing Sentiment Classifiers to New Domains: A Case Study. In *RANLP*.

John Blitzer, Mark Dredze, and Fernando Pereira. 2007. Biographies, Bollywood, Boom-boxes and Blenders: Domain Adaptation for Sentiment Classification. In *ACL*, pages 440–447.

Danushka Bollegala, David J Weir, and John Carroll. 2011. Using Multiple Sources to Construct a Sentiment Sensitive Thesaurus for Cross-Domain Sentiment Classification. In *ACL HLT*, pages 132–141.

Léon Bottou. 1998. Online algorithms and stochastic approximations. In David Saad, editor, *Online Learning and Neural Networks*. Cambridge University Press, Cambridge, UK. Oct 2012.

Andrew Carlson, Justin Betteridge, and Bryan Kisiel. 2010. Toward an Architecture for Never-Ending Language Learning. In *AAAI*, pages 1306–1313.

Rich Caruana. 1997. Multitask Learning. *Machine learning*, 28(1):41–75.

Zhiyuan Chen and Bing Liu. 2014a. Mining Topics in Documents : Standing on the Shoulders of Big Data. In *KDD*, pages 1116–1125.

Zhiyuan Chen and Bing Liu. 2014b. Topic Modeling using Topics from Many Domains, Lifelong Learning and Big Data. In *ICML*, pages 703–711.

Jianhui Chen, Jiayu Zhou, and Jieping Ye. 2011. Integrating low-rank and group-sparse structures for robust multi-task learning. In *KDD*, pages 42–50.

Yulan He, Chenghua Lin, and Harith Alani. 2011. Automatically Extracting Polarity-Bearing Topics for Cross-Domain Sentiment Classification. In *ACL*, pages 123–131.

James J Heckman. 1979. Sample selection bias as a specification error. *Econometrica: Journal of the econometric society*, pages 153–161.

Jing Jiang. 2008. A literature survey on domain adaptation of statistical classifiers. Technical report.

Lun-Wei Ku, Ting-Hao Huang, and Hsin-Hsi Chen. 2009. Using morphological and syntactic structures for Chinese opinion analysis. In *EMNLP*, pages 1260–1269.

Shoushan Li and Chengqing Zong. 2008. Multi-domain sentiment classification. In *ACL HLT*, pages 257–260.

Fangtao Li, Sinno Jialin Pan, Ou Jin, Qiang Yang, and Xiaoyan Zhu. 2012. Cross-domain Co-extraction of Sentiment and Topic Lexicons. In *ACL*, pages 410–419.

Shoushan Li, Yunxia Xue, Zhongqing Wang, and Guodong Zhou. 2013. Active learning for cross-domain sentiment classification. In *AAAI*, pages 2127–2133.

Bing Liu. 2012. Sentiment Analysis and Opinion Mining. *Synthesis Lectures on Human Language Technologies*, 5(1):1–167.

Sinno Jialin Pan and Qiang Yang. 2010. A Survey on Transfer Learning. *IEEE Trans. Knowl. Data Eng.*, 22(10):1345–1359.

Bo Pang and Lillian Lee. 2008. Opinion mining and sentiment analysis. *Foundations and Trends in Information Retrieval*, 2(1-2):1–135.

Bo Pang, Lillian Lee, and Shivakumar Vaithyanathan. 2002. Thumbs up? Sentiment Classification using Machine Learning Techniques. In *EMNLP*, pages 79–86.

Rajat Raina, Alexis Battle, Honglak Lee, Benjamin Packer, and Andrew Y Ng. 2007. Self-taught Learning : Transfer Learning from Unlabeled Data. In *ICML*, pages 759–766.

Paul Ruvolo and Eric Eaton. 2013. ELLA: An efficient lifelong learning algorithm. In *ICML*, pages 507–515.

Avishek Saha, Piyush Rai, Suresh Venkatasubramanian, and Hal Daume. 2011. Online learning of multiple tasks and their relationships. In *AISTATS*, pages 643–651.

Hidetoshi Shimodaira. 2000. Improving predictive inference under covariate shift by weighting the log-likelihood function. *Journal of statistical planning and inference*, 90(2):227–244.

Daniel L Silver, Qiang Yang, and Lianghao Li. 2013. Lifelong Machine Learning Systems: Beyond Learning Algorithms. In *AAAI Spring Symposium: Lifelong Machine Learning*, pages 49–55.

Songbo Tan, Gaowei Wu, Huifeng Tang, and Xueqi Cheng. 2007. A novel scheme for domain-transfer problem in the context of sentiment analysis. In *CIKM*, pages 979–982.

Sebastian Thrun. 1998. Lifelong Learning Algorithms. In S Thrun and L Pratt, editors, *Learning To Learn*, pages 181–209. Kluwer Academic Publishers.

Qiong Wu, Songbo Tan, and Xueqi Cheng. 2009. Graph Ranking for Sentiment Transfer. In *ACL-IJCNLP*, pages 317–320.

Rui Xia and Chengqing Zong. 2011. A POS-based Ensemble Model for Cross-domain Sentiment Classification. In *IJCNLP*, pages 614–622. Citeseer.

Yasuhisa Yoshida, Tsutomu Hirao, Tomoharu Iwata, Masaaki Nagata, and Yuji Matsumoto. 2011. Transfer Learning for Multiple-Domain Sentiment Analysis-Identifying Domain Dependent/Independent Word Polarity. In *AAAI*, pages 1286–1291.

Bianca Zadrozny. 2004. Learning and evaluating classifiers under sample selection bias. In *ICML*, page 114. ACM.

Jian Zhang, Zoubin Ghahramani, and Yiming Yang. 2008. Flexible latent variable models for multi-task learning. *Machine Learning*, 73(3):221–242.

Harnessing Context Incongruity for Sarcasm Detection

Aditya Joshi[1,2,3] **Vinita Sharma**[1] **Pushpak Bhattacharyya**[1]
[1]IIT Bombay, India, [2]Monash University, Australia
[3]IITB-Monash Research Academy, India
aadi.cse@iitb.ac.in, pb@cse.iitb.ac.in

Abstract

The relationship between context incongruity and sarcasm has been studied in linguistics. We present a computational system that harnesses context incongruity as a basis for sarcasm detection. Our statistical sarcasm classifiers incorporate two kinds of incongruity features: explicit and implicit. We show the benefit of our incongruity features for two text forms - tweets and discussion forum posts. Our system also outperforms two past works (with F-score improvement of 10-20%). We also show how our features can capture inter-sentential incongruity.

1 Introduction

Sarcasm is defined as *'a cutting, often ironic remark intended to express contempt or ridicule'*[1]. Sarcasm detection is the task of predicting a text as sarcastic or non-sarcastic. The past work in sarcasm detection involves rule-based and statistical approaches using: (a) unigrams and pragmatic features (such as emoticons, etc.) (Gonzalez-Ibanez et al., 2011; Carvalho et al., 2009; Barbieri et al., 2014), (b) extraction of common patterns, such as hashtag-based sentiment (Maynard and Greenwood, 2014; Liebrecht et al., 2013), a positive verb being followed by a negative situation (Riloff et al., 2013), or discriminative n-grams (Tsur et al., 2010a; Davidov et al., 2010).

Thus, the past work detects sarcasm with specific indicators. However, we believe that it is time that sarcasm detection is based on well-studied linguistic theories. In this paper, we use one such linguistic theory: **context incongruity**. Although the past work exploits incongruity, it does so piecemeal; we take a more well-rounded view of incongruity and place it center-stage for our work.

[1]Source: The Free Dictionary

The features of our sarcasm detection system are based on two kinds of incongruity: '**explicit**' and '**implicit**'. The contribution of this paper is:

- We present a sarcasm detection system that is grounded on a linguistic theory, the theory of context incongruity in our case. Sarcasm detection research can push the frontiers by taking help of well-studied linguistic theories.
- Our sarcasm detection system outperforms two state-of-art sarcasm detection systems (Riloff et al., 2013; Maynard and Greenwood, 2014). Our system shows an improvement for short 'tweets' as well as long 'discussion forum posts'.
- We introduce inter-sentential incongruity for sarcasm detection, that expands context of a discussion forum post by including the previous post (also known as the 'elicitor' post) in the discussion thread.

Rest of the paper is organized as follows. We first discuss related work in Section 2. We introduce context incongruity in Section 3. Feature design for explicit incongruity is presented in Section 3.1, and that for implicit incongruity is in Section 3.2. We then describe the architecture of our sarcasm detection system in Section 4 and our experimental setup in Section 5. Quantitative evaluation is in Section 6. Inter-sentential sarcasm detection is in Section 7. Section 8 presents the error analysis. Section 9 concludes the paper and points to future directions.

2 Related Work

Sarcasm/irony as a linguistic phenomenon has been extensively studied. According to Wilson (2006), sarcasm arises from situational disparity. The relationship between context incongruity and sarcasm processing (by humans) has been studied in Ivanko and Pexman (2003). Several properties of sarcasm have also been investigated. Campbell

Proceedings of the 53rd Annual Meeting of the Association for Computational Linguistics and the 7th International Joint Conference on Natural Language Processing (Short Papers), pages 757–762,
Beijing, China, July 26-31, 2015.

and Katz (2012) state that sarcasm occurs along different dimensions, namely, failed expectation, pragmatic insincerity, negative tension, presence of a victim and along stylistic components such as emotion words. Eisterhold et al. (2006) observe that sarcasm can be identified based on the statement preceding and following the sarcastic statement. This is particularly true in cases where the incongruity is not expressed within the sarcastic text itself.

Computational detection of sarcasm is a relatively recent area of research. Initial work on sarcasm detection investigates the role of lexical and pragmatic features. Tepperman et al. (2006) present sarcasm recognition in speech using prosodic, spectral (average pitch, pitch slope, *etc.*) and contextual cues (laughter or response to questions). Carvalho et al. (2009) use simple linguistic features like interjection, changed names, *etc.* for irony detection. Davidov et al. (2010) train a sarcasm classifier with syntactic and pattern-based features. Gonzalez-Ibanez et al. (2011) study the role of unigrams and emoticons in sarcasm detection. Liebrecht et al. (2013) use a dataset of Dutch tweets that contain sarcasm-related hashtags and implement a classifier to predict sarcasm. A recent work by **?**) takes the output of sarcasm detection as an input to sentiment classification. They present a rule-based system that uses the pattern: if the sentiment of a tokenized hashtag does not agree with sentiment in rest of the tweet, the tweet is sarcastic, in addition to other rules.

Our approach is architecturally *similar* to Tsur et al. (2010b) who use a semi-supervised pattern acquisition followed by classification. Our feature engineering is based on Riloff et al. (2013) and Ramteke et al. (2013). Riloff et al. (2013) state that *sarcasm is a contrast between positive sentiment word and a negative situation.* They implement a rule-based system that uses phrases of positive verb phrases and negative situations extracted from a corpus of sarcastic tweets. Ramteke et al. (2013) present a novel approach to detect thwarting: the phenomenon where sentiment in major portions of text is reversed by sentiment in smaller, conclusive portions.

3 Context Incongruity

Incongruity is defined as '*the state of being not in agreement, as with principles*'[1]. Context incongruity is a necessary condition for sarcasm (Campbell and Katz, 2012). Ivanko and Pexman (2003) state that the sarcasm processing time (time taken by humans to understand sarcasm) depends on the degree of context incongruity between the statement and the context.

Deriving from this idea, we consider two cases of incongruity in sarcasm that are analogous to two degrees of incongruity. We call them **explicit incongruity** and **implicit incongruity**, where implicit incongruity demands a higher processing time. It must be noted that our system only handles incongruity between the text and common world knowledge (i.e., the knowledge that '*being stranded*' is an undesirable situation, and hence, '*Being stranded in traffic is the best way to start my week*' is a sarcastic statement). This leaves out an example like '*Wow! You are so punctual*' which may be sarcastic depending on situational context.

3.1 Explicit incongruity

Explicit incongruity is overtly expressed through sentiment words of both polarities (as in the case of '*I love being ignored*' where there is a positive word '*love*' and a negative word '*ignored*'). The converse is not true as in the case of '*The movie starts slow but the climax is great*'.

3.2 Implicit Incongruity

An implicit incongruity is covertly expressed through phrases of implied sentiment, as opposed to opposing polar words. Consider the example "*I love this paper so much that I made a doggy bag out of it*". There is no explicit incongruity here: the only polar word is '*love*'. However, the clause '*I made a doggy bag out of it*' has an implied sentiment that is incongruous with the polar word '*love*'.

3.3 Estimating prevalence

We conduct a naïve, automatic evaluation on a dataset of 18,141 sarcastic tweets. As a crude estimate, we consider an explicit incongruity as presence of positive and negative words. Around 11% sarcastic tweets have at least one explicit incongruity. We also manually evaluate 50 sarcastic tweets and observe that 10 have explicit incongruity, while others have implicit incongruity.

4 Architecture

Our system for sarcasm detection augments the feature vector of a tweet with features based on the two types of incongruity. Specifically, we use four kinds of features: (a) **Lexical**, (b) **Pragmatic**, (c) **Implicit congruity**, and (d) **Explicit incongruity** features. Lexical features are unigrams obtained using feature selection techniques such as χ^2 Test and Categorical Proportional Difference. Pragmatic features include emoticons, laughter expressions, punctuation marks and capital words as given by Carvalho et al. (2009). In addition to the two, our system incorporates two kinds of incongruity features, as discussed next. The explicit incongruity features are numeric, qualitative features, while implicit incongruity features are related to implicit phrases.

4.1 Feature Design: Explicit Incongruity

An explicit incongruity giving rise to sarcasm bears resemblance to thwarted expectations (another commonly known challenge to sentiment analysis). Consider this example: '*I love the color. The features are interesting. But a bad battery life ruins it*'. The positive expectation in the first two sentences is thwarted by the last sentence. A similar incongruity is observed in the sarcastic '*My tooth hurts! Yay!*'. The negative word '*hurts*' is incongruous with the positive '*Yay!*'. Hence, our explicit incongruity features are a relevant subset of features from a past system to detect thwarting by Ramteke et al. (2013). These features are:

- Number of sentiment incongruities: The number of times a positive word is followed by a negative word, and vice versa
- Largest positive/negative subsequence: The length of the longest series of contiguous positive/negative words
- Number of positive and negative words
- Lexical Polarity: The polarity based purely on the basis of lexical features, as determined by Lingpipe SA system (Alias-i, 2008). Note that the '*native polarity*' need not be correct. However, a tweet that is strongly positive on the surface is more likely to be sarcastic than a tweet that seems to be negative. This is because sarcasm, by definition, tends to be caustic/hurtful. This also helps against humble bragging. (as in case of the tweet '*so i have to be up at 5am to autograph 7,000 pics of myself? Sounds like just about the worst Wednesday morning I could ever imagine*').

4.2 Feature Design: Implicit Incongruity

We use phrases with implicit sentiment as the implicit incongruity features. These phrases are sentiment-bearing verb and noun phrases, the latter being situations with implied sentiment (e.g. '*getting late for work*'). For this, we modify the algorithm given in Riloff et al. (2013) in two ways: (a) they extract only positive verbs and negative noun situation phrases. We generalize it to both polarities, (b) they remove subsumed phrases (i.e. '*being ignored*' subsumes '*being ignored by a friend*') while we retain both phrases. The benefit of (a) and (b) above was experimentally validated, but is not included in this paper due to limited space.

While they use rule-based algorithms that employ these extracted phrases to detect sarcasm, we include them as implicit incongruity features, in addition to other features. It is possible that the set of extracted situation phrases may contain some phrases without implicit sentiment. We hope that the limited size of the tweet guards against such false positives being too many in number. We add phrases in the two sets as count-based implicit incongruity features.

5 Experimental Setup

We use three datasets to evaluate our system:

1. **Tweet-A (5208 tweets, 4170 sarcastic)**: We download tweets with hashtags *#sarcasm* and *#sarcastic* as sarcastic tweets and *#notsarcasm* and *#notsarcastic* as non-sarcastic, using the Twitter API (`https://dev.twitter.com/`). A similar hashtag-based approach to create a sarcasm-annotated dataset was employed in Gonzalez-Ibanez et al. (2011). As an additional quality check, a rough glance through the tweets is done, and the ones found to be wrong are removed. The hashtags mentioned above are removed from the text so that they act as labels but not as features.
2. **Tweet-B (2278 tweets, 506 sarcastic)**: This dataset was manually labeled for Riloff et al. (2013). Some tweets were unavailable, due to deletion or privacy settings.
3. **Discussion-A (1502 discussion forum posts, 752 sarcastic)**: This dataset is created from the Internet Argument Corpus (Walker et al., 2012) that contains manual annota-

Lexical	
Unigrams	Unigrams in the training corpus
Pragmatic	
Capitalization	Numeric feature indicating presence of capital letters
Emoticons & laughter expressions	Numeric feature indicating presence of emoticons and 'lol's
Punctuation marks	Numeric feature indicating presence of punctuation marks
Implicit Incongruity	
Implicit Sentiment Phrases	Boolean feature indicating phrases extracted from the implicit phrase extraction step
Explicit Incongruity	
#Explicit incongruity	Number of times a word is followed by a word of opposite polarity
Largest positive /negative subsequence	Length of largest series of words with polarity unchanged
#Positive words	Number of positive words
#Negative words	Number of negative words
Lexical Polarity	Polarity of a tweet based on words present

Table 1: Features of our sarcasm detection system

tions for sarcasm. We randomly select 752 sarcastic and 752 non-sarcastic discussion forum posts.

To extract the implicit incongruity features, we run the iterative algorithm described in Section 4.2, on a dataset of 4000 tweets (50% sarcastic) (also created using hashtag-based supervision). The algorithm results in a total of 79 verb phrases and 202 noun phrases. We train our classifiers for different feature combinations, using LibSVM with RBF kernel (Chang and Lin, 2011), and report average 5-fold cross-validation values.

Features	P	R	F
Original Algorithm by Riloff et al. (2013)			
Ordered	0.774	0.098	0.173
Unordered	0.799	0.337	0.474
Our system			
Lexical **(Baseline)**	0.820	0.867	0.842
Lexical+Implicit	0.822	0.887	0.853
Lexical+Explicit	0.807	0.985	0.8871
All features	0.814	0.976	**0.8876**

Table 2: Comparative results for Tweet-A using rule-based algorithm and statistical classifiers using our feature combinations

6 Evaluation

Table 2 shows the performance of our classifiers in terms of Precision (P), Recall (R) and F-score (F), for Tweet-A. The table first reports values from a re-implementation of Riloff et al. (2013)'s two rule-based algorithms: the ordered version predicts a tweet as sarcastic if it has a positive verb phrase followed by a negative situation/noun phrase, while the unordered does so if the two are present in any order. We see that all statistical classifiers surpass the rule-based algorithms. The best F-score obtained is 0.8876 when all four kinds of features are used. This is an **improvement of about 5%** over the baseline, and 40% over the algorithm by Riloff et al. (2013). Table 3 shows that even in the case of the Discussion-A dataset, our features result in an improved performance. The F-score increases from 0.568 to 0.640, **an improvement of about 8%** in case of discussion forum posts, when all features are used.

Features	P	R	F
Lexical **(Baseline)**	0.645	0.508	0.568
Lexical+Explicit	0.698	0.391	0.488
Lexical+Implicit	0.513	0.762	0.581
All features	0.489	0.924	**0.640**

Table 3: Comparative results for Discussion-A using our feature combinations

To confirm that we indeed do better, we compare our system, with their reported values. This is necessary for several reasons. For example, we reimplement their algorithm but do not have

Approach	P	R	F
Riloff et al. (2013) **(best reported)**	0.62	0.44	0.51
Maynard and Greenwood (2014)	0.46	0.38	0.41
Our system (all features)	**0.77**	**0.51**	**0.61**

Table 4: Comparison of our system with two past works, for Tweet-B

access to their exact extracted phrases. Table 4 shows that we achieve a 10% higher F-score than the best reported F-score of Riloff et al. (2013). This value is also 20% higher than our re-implementation of Maynard and Greenwood (2014) that uses their hashtag retokenizer and rule-based algorithm.

7 Incorporating inter-sentential incongruity

Our system performs worse for Discussion-A than Tweet-A/B possibly because of incongruity outside the text. Because of the thread structure of discussion forums, sarcasm in a 'target post' can be identified using the post preceding it (called '*elicitor post*'), similar to human conversation (Eisterhold et al., 2006). For example, '*Wow, you are smart!*' may or may not be sarcastic. If a sarcasm classifier incorporates information from the elicitor post '*I could not finish my assignment*', a correct prediction is possible. Hence, we now explore how our incongruity-based features can help to capture '**inter-sentential incongruity**'. We compute the five explicit incongruity features for a concatenated version of target post and elicitor post (elicitor posts are available for IAC corpus, the source of Discussion-A). The precision rises to **0.705** but the recall falls to 0.274. A possible reason is that only 15% posts have elicitor posts, making the inter-sentential features sparse.

That notwithstanding, our observation shows that **using the inter-sentential context** is an interesting direction for sarcasm detection.

8 Error Analysis

Some common errors made by our system are:

1. **Subjective polarity**: The tweet '*Yay for 3 hour Chem labs*' is tagged by the author as sarcastic, which may not be common perception.
2. **No incongruity within text**: As stated in Section 2, our system does not detect sarcasm where incongruity is expressed outside the text. About 10% misclassified examples that we analyzed, contained such an incongruity.
3. **Incongruity due to numbers**: Our system could not detect incongruity arising due to numbers as in '*Going in to work for 2 hours was totally worth the 35 minute drive.*'.
4. **Dataset granularity**: Some discussion forum posts are marked as sarcastic, but contain non-sarcastic portions, leading to irrelevant features. For example, '*How special, now all you have to do is prove that a glob of cells has rights. I happen to believe that a person's life and the right to life begins at conception*'.
5. **Politeness**: In some cases, implicit incongruity was less evident because of politeness, as in, '*Post all your inside jokes on facebook, I really want to hear about them*'.

9 Conclusion & Future Work

Our paper uses the linguistic relationship between context incongruity and sarcasm as a basis for sarcasm detection. Our sarcasm classifier uses four kinds of features: lexical, pragmatic, explicit incongruity, and implicit incongruity features. We evaluate our system on two text forms: tweets and discussion forum posts. We observe an improvement of 40% over a reported rule-based algorithm, and 5% over the statistical classifier baseline that uses unigrams, in case of tweets. The corresponding improvement in case of discussion forum posts is 8%. Our system also outperforms two past works (Riloff et al., 2013; Maynard and Greenwood, 2014) with 10-20% improvement in F-score. Finally, to improve the performance for discussion forum posts, we introduce a novel approach to use elicitor posts for sarcasm detection. We observe an improvement of 21.6% in precision, when our incongruity features are used to capture inter-sentential incongruity.

Our error analysis points to potential future work such as: (a) role of numbers for sarcasm, and (b) situations with subjective sentiment. We are currently exploring a more robust incorporation of inter-sentential incongruity for sarcasm detection.

References

Alias-i. 2008. Lingpipe natural language toolkit.

Francesco Barbieri, Horacio Saggion, and Francesco Ronzano. 2014. Modelling sarcasm in twitter, a novel approach. *ACL 2014*, page 50.

John D Campbell and Albert N Katz. 2012. Are there necessary conditions for inducing a sense of sarcastic irony? *Discourse Processes*, 49(6):459–480.

Paula Carvalho, Luís Sarmento, Mário J Silva, and Eugénio de Oliveira. 2009. Clues for detecting irony in user-generated contents: oh...!! it's so easy;-). In *Proceedings of the 1st international CIKM workshop on Topic-sentiment analysis for mass opinion*, pages 53–56. ACM.

Chih-Chung Chang and Chih-Jen Lin. 2011. Libsvm: a library for support vector machines. *ACM Transactions on Intelligent Systems and Technology (TIST)*, 2(3):27.

Dmitry Davidov, Oren Tsur, and Ari Rappoport. 2010. Semi-supervised recognition of sarcastic sentences in twitter and amazon. In *Proceedings of the Fourteenth Conference on Computational Natural Language Learning*, pages 107–116. Association for Computational Linguistics.

Jodi Eisterhold, Salvatore Attardo, and Diana Boxer. 2006. Reactions to irony in discourse: Evidence for the least disruption principle. *Journal of Pragmatics*, 38(8):1239–1256.

Roberto Gonzalez-Ibanez, Smaranda Muresan, and Nina Wacholder. 2011. Identifying sarcasm in twitter: a closer look. In *Proceedings of the 49th Annual Meeting of the Association for Computational Linguistics: Human Language Technologies: short papers-Volume 2*, pages 581–586. Association for Computational Linguistics.

Stacey L Ivanko and Penny M Pexman. 2003. Context incongruity and irony processing. *Discourse Processes*, 35(3):241–279.

CC Liebrecht, FA Kunneman, and APJ van den Bosch. 2013. The perfect solution for detecting sarcasm in tweets# not.

Diana Maynard and Mark A Greenwood. 2014. Who cares about sarcastic tweets? investigating the impact of sarcasm on sentiment analysis. In *Proceedings of LREC*.

Ankit Ramteke, Pushpak Bhattacharyya, Akshat Malu, and J Saketha Nath. 2013. Detecting turnarounds in sentiment analysis: Thwarting. In *Proceedings of ACL*.

Ellen Riloff, Ashequl Qadir, Prafulla Surve, Lalindra De Silva, Nathan Gilbert, and Ruihong Huang. 2013. Sarcasm as contrast between a positive sentiment and negative situation. In *Proceedings of the 2013 Conference on Empirical Methods in Natural Language Processing*, pages 704–714. Association for Computational Linguistics.

Joseph Tepperman, David R Traum, and Shrikanth Narayanan. 2006. yeah right : sarcasm recognition for spoken dialogue systems. In *INTERSPEECH*.

Oren Tsur, Dmitry Davidov, and Ari Rappoport. 2010a. Icwsm-a great catchy name: Semi-supervised recognition of sarcastic sentences in online product reviews. In *ICWSM*.

Oren Tsur, Dmitry Davidov, and Ari Rappoport. 2010b. Icwsm-a great catchy name: Semi-supervised recognition of sarcastic sentences in online product reviews. In *ICWSM*.

Marilyn A Walker, Jean E Fox Tree, Pranav Anand, Rob Abbott, and Joseph King. 2012. A corpus for research on deliberation and debate. In *LREC*, pages 812–817.

Deirdre Wilson. 2006. The pragmatics of verbal irony: Echo or pretence? *Lingua*, 116(10):1722–1743.

Emotion Detection in Code-switching Texts via Bilingual and Sentimental Information

Zhongqing Wang[†‡], Sophia Yat Mei Lee[‡], Shoushan Li[†*], and Guodong Zhou[†]
[†]Natural Language Processing Lab, Soochow University, China
[‡]Department of Chinese and Bilingual Studies, The Hong Kong Polytechnic University
{wangzq.antony, sophiaym}@gmail.com,
{lishoushan, gdzhou}@suda.edu.cn

Abstract

Code-switching is commonly used in the free-form text environment, such as social media, and it is especially favored in emotion expressions. Emotions in code-switching texts differ from monolingual texts in that they can be expressed in either monolingual or bilingual forms. In this paper, we first utilize two kinds of knowledge, i.e. *bilingual* and *sentimental* information to bridge the gap between different languages. Moreover, we use a term-document bipartite graph to incorporate both bilingual and sentimental information, and propose a label propagation based approach to learn and predict in the bipartite graph. Empirical studies demonstrate the effectiveness of our proposed approach in detecting emotion in code-switching texts.

1 Introduction

With the rapid development of Web 2.0, emotion analysis in social media has become of great value to market predictions and analysis (Liu et al., 2013; Lee et al., 2014). Previous researches on emotion analysis have mainly focused on emotion expressions in monolingual texts (Chen et al., 2010; Lee et al., 2013a). However, in informal settings such as micro-blogs, emotions are often expressed by a mixture of different natural languages. Such a mixture of language is called code-switching. Specifically, code-switching text is defined as text that contains more than one language (code). It is a common phenomenon in multilingual communities (Auer, 1999; Adel et al., 2013). For instance, [E1-E3] are three examples of code-switching emotional posts containing both Chinese and English words. [E1] expresses the *happiness* emotion through English, and the *anger* emotion in [E2] is expressed through both Chinese and English, while the *fear* emotion in [E3] is expressed through a mixed English-Chinese phrase (hold不住).

[E1] 我们已经自**high**起来了
(*We are already getting* ***hyper*** *ourselves.*)

[E2] 最厌恶的一句话就是“爱情没有先来后到，不被爱的才是第三者”。**shit!**
(*A quote, to my great disgust, is "There's no staking claims in a relationship based on who got there first - the one who isn' t loved is the true third party."* ***Shit!***)

[E3] 这么个划重点法。。。窝们**hold不住**啊！！！
(*The so-called "highlighting"...we* ***can't hold it anymore****.*)

It is more difficult to detect emotions in code-switching texts than in monolingual ones since emotions in code-switching posts can be expressed through one or two languages. Hence, traditional automatic emotion detection methods which simply consider monolingual texts (Liu et al., 2013; Lee et al., 2013a) would not be readily applicable.

The key issue of emotion detection in code-switching texts is to deal with the emotions expressed through different languages. Thus bridging the gap between different languages becomes essential for emotion detection in code-switching texts. A straightforward approach to handle this issue is to translate texts from one language into another. Since Chinese is the dominant language in our data set, a word-by-word statistical machine translation strategy (Zhao et al., 2009) is adopted to translate English words into Chinese. Additionally, as text from micro-blogs is informal,

*Corresponding author

Proceedings of the 53rd Annual Meeting of the Association for Computational Linguistics and the 7th International Joint Conference on Natural Language Processing (Short Papers), pages 763–768,
Beijing, China, July 26-31, 2015.

synonym dictionary and PMI similar based word correlation (Turney, 2002) are used to enhance the language model for machine translation.

In spite of the English-to-Chinese translation, many English and Chinese words are still unconnected. Hence, we use sentiment analysis strategy (Turney, 2002; Li et al., 2013) to extract the polarity of both Chinese and English texts, and then connect words of similar polarity.

Moreover, for propagating label information between the bilingual texts from training data to test data, we use a term-document bipartite graph to incorporate both bilingual and sentimental information and propose a label propagation (Zhu and Ghahramani, 2002) based approach to learn and predict in the graph. Specially, the label information between Chinese and English texts would be propagated through the bipartite graph by word-document relations, bilingual information, and sentiment information. Evaluation of the data set indicates the importance of the task and the effectiveness of our proposed approach.

2 Related Work

Emotion analysis has been a hot research topic in NLP in the last decade. One main group of related studies on this task is about emotion resource construction (Xu et al., 2010; Volkova et al., 2012; Lee et al., 2014). Moreover, emotion classification is one of the most important tasks in emotion analysis, while emotion classification aims to classify text into multiple emotion categories (Chen et al., 2010; Liu et al., 2013). Despite a growing body of research on emotion analysis, little has been done on the analysis of emotion in code-switching due to the complexities of processing two languages at the same time.

Besides, although several research studies have focused on analyzing bilingual (Wan, 2009; Lu et al., 2011; Tang et al., 2014) and code-switching texts (Li and Fung, 2012; Ling et al., 2013; Lignos and Marcus, 2013), none of them has studied the multilingual code-switching issues in emotion detection. This research area is especially crucial when public emotions are mostly expressed in the free-form text on the Internet.

3 Data Collection

We collect our data set from *Weibo.com*, one of the most popular SNS websites in China. We use encoding code for each character in the post to identify the code-switching posts. After removing posts containing noise and advertisements, we extract 4,195 code-switching posts from the dataset for emotion annotation. Five basic emotions are annotated, namely *happiness, sadness, fear, anger* and *surprise* (Lee et al., 2013b). After the annotation process, results show 2,312 posts which include emotions. Moreover, 81.4% of emotional posts are expressed through Chinese. Although there are a few words of English in each post (an average of 3 words per post), 43.5% of emotion posts are caused by English. This statistic indicates that English is of vital importance to emotion expression even in code-switching contexts dominated by Chinese.

The corpora is annotated by two annotators and the inter-annotator agreement calculation shows that the agreement of our annotation is 0.692 in Cohen's Kappa coefficient, which indicates that the quality of the annotation is guaranteed.

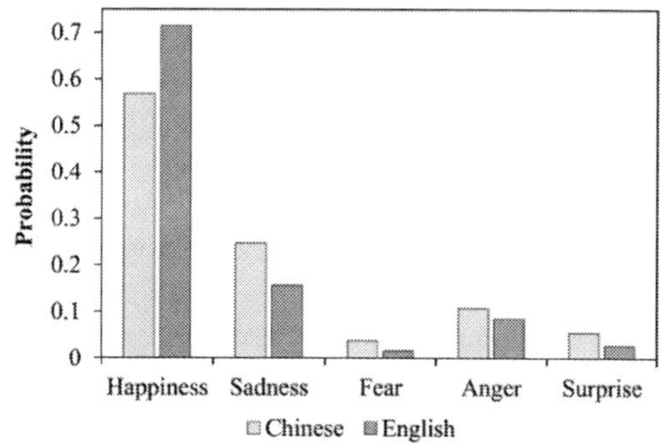

Figure 1: Distribution of Emotions and Languages

The joint distribution between emotions and caused languages is illustrated in Figure 1. The Y-axis of the figure presents the conditional probability of a post expressing the emotion e_i given that l_j is the caused language, $p(e_i|l_j)$.

It is suggested in Figure 2 that: 1) *happiness* occurs more frequently than other emotions; 2) people would like to use English text to express the *happiness* emotion much more than the *sadness* emotion; 3) the distribution of emotions expressed through Chinese and English text are similar.

4 Emotion Detection via Bilingual and Sentiment Information

In this paper, our goal is to predict the emotion label for each unlabeled post. Simply, we only choose those posts with single emotion on our research. We systematically explore both the bilingual and sentimental information to detect emotions in code-switching posts. Moreover, we use a term-document bipartite graph to incorporate these two kinds of information, and propose a Label Propagation (LP) based approach to learn and predict emotion in code-switching texts. In the following subsections, we will discuss these issues one by one.

4.1 Bilingual Information

For using bilingual information, a word-by-word statistical machine translation strategy is adopted to translate words from English into Chinese. For better clarity, a word-based decoding, which adopts a log-linear framework as in (Och and Ney, 2002) with translation model and language model being the only features, is used:

$$P(c|e) = \frac{\exp\left[\sum_{i=1}^{2} \lambda_i h_i(c,e)\right]}{\sum_c \exp\left[\sum_{i=1}^{2} \lambda_i h_i(c,e)\right]} \quad (1)$$

where

$$h_1(c,e) = \log(p_\gamma(c|e)) \quad (2)$$

is the translation model, which is converted from the bilingual lexicon[1], and

$$h_2(c,e) = \log(p_{\theta_{LM}}(c) p_{\theta_{SYN}}(c) p_{\theta_{PMI}}(c)) \quad (3)$$

is the language model, and $p_{\theta_{LM}}(c)$ is the bigram language model which is trained from a large scale *Weibo* data set[2]. As text in micro-blogs is informal, synonym dictionary[3] and PMI based word correlation are used to enhance the language model for machine translation. $p_{\theta_{SYN}}(c)$ denotes the synonym similarity between translated words and the contexts. This is necessary since the sense of translated words and the contexts are expected to be similar; and $p_{\theta_{PMI}}(c)$ presents the PMI similarity between translated words and the contexts, while the PMI score is calculated by the individual and co-occurred hit count between translated words and contexts from the search engine[4] (Turney, 2002). This is to ensure that the translated words are highly associated with the contexts.

[1] *MDBG CC-CEDICT* is adopted as the bilingual lexicon: http://www.mdbg.net/chindict/chindict.php?page=cedict

[2] The large-scale *Weibo* data set contains 2,716,197 posts in total.

[3] *TongYiCiLin* is adopted as the Chinese synonym dictionary: http://www.ltp-cloud.com/

[4] We use *BING.com* as the search engine for PMI: http://www.bing.com/

The candidate target sentences made up of a sequence of the optional target words are ranked by the language model. The output will be generated only if it reaches the maximum probability as follows (Brown et al., 1990; Zhao et al., 2009):

$$c = argmax \prod p(w_c) \quad (4)$$

4.2 Sentimental Information

Sentimental information is very useful in emotion detection (Gao et al., 2013). In this paper, we extract polarity from both Chinese and English texts to ensure text of similar polarity will be connected.

In this paper, both Chinese[5] and English[6] sentimental lexicons are employed to identify candidate opinion expressions by searching the occurrences of negative and positive expressions in text, and predict the polarity of both Chinese and English texts through the word-counting approach (Turney, 2002).

4.3 LP-based Emotion Detection

For the knowledge of bilingual and sentimental information to be well incorporated, we use a term-document bipartite graph to incorporate the information, and propose a label propagation based approach to learn and predict emotion in code-switching texts.

The input of the LP algorithm is a graph describing the relationship between each sample pair in the labeled and test data (Sindhwani and Melville, 2008; Li et al., 2013). In a bipartite graph, the nodes consist of two parts: documents and all terms extracted from the documents. An undirected edge (d_i, w_k) exists if and only if the document d_i contains the term w_k.

Note that, there are four kinds of terms on the graph, i.e., Chinese words, English words, translated Chinese words (bilingual information), and sentimental features. Although Chinese words and English words cannot be connected directly, the label information between Chinese and English words would be propagated through the bipartite graph by word-document relations, bilingual information, and sentiment information. The example of the bipartite graph is illustrated on the Figure 2.

[5] *DUTIR Sentiment Lexicon* is adopted as the Chinese sentiment lexicon: http://ir.dlut.edu.cn/EmotionOntologyDownload.aspx

[6] English sentiment lexicon is utilized from *MPQA Subjectivity Lexicon*: http://mpqa.cs.pitt.edu/lexicons/subj_lexicon/

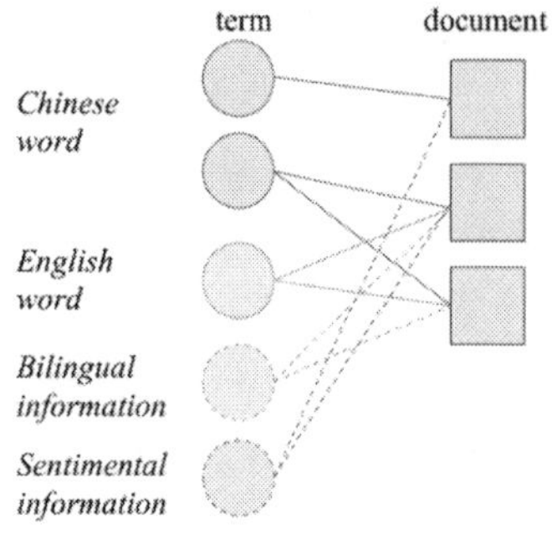

Figure 2: Example of the bipartite graph

When all terms are taken into consideration, we get the transition probability from d_i to d_j as in (5):

$$t_{ij} = \sum_k \frac{x_{ik}}{\sum_k x_{ik}} \cdot \frac{x_{jk}}{\sum_k x_{jk}} \quad (5)$$

where x_{ik} is the frequency of term w_k in document d_i.

After building the document-document transfer matrix through the bipartite graph, we use label propagation algorithm (Zhu and Ghahramani, 2002; Zhou and Kong, 2009) to learn and predict emotions in the graph, in which the probabilities of the labeled data are clamped in each loop using their initial ones and act as a force to propagate their labels to the test data.

5 Experiments

In this section, we first introduce the experimental settings, and then evaluate the performance of our proposed approach for detecting emotions in code-switching texts.

5.1 Experimental Settings

As described in Section 3, the data are collected from *Weibo.com*. We randomly select half of the annotated posts as the training data and another half as the test data. FNLP[7] is used for Chinese word segmentation.

5.2 Experimental Results

Our first group of experiments is to investigate whether our proposed label propagation model with both bilingual and sentimental information can improve emotion detection in code-switching texts. Figure 3 shows the experimental results of different models, where *ME* is the basic Maximum Entropy (ME) classification model[8] in which all Chinese and English words of each post function as a feature, *ME-CN* and *ME-EN* in which only the Chinese or English text of each post function as features, and *BLP-BS*, our proposed LP-based approach which incorporates both bilingual and sentimental information. We adopt F1-Measure (F1.) to measure the performance of each model in the respective emotions.

From Figure 3, we find that the results of *ME-CN* and *ME-EN* are instable. It indicates that only considering one kind of language text is not very effective for predicting emotions in code-switching texts. Moreover, as Chinese and English texts are taken into account collectively with both bilingual and sentimental information, our proposed *BLP-BS* model is significantly better than basic approaches on all the emotions.

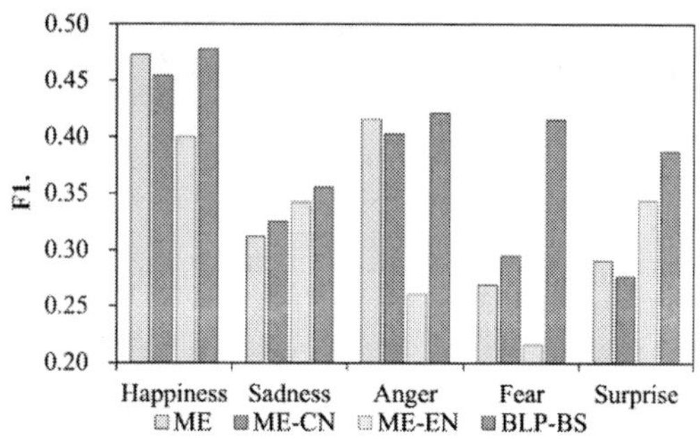

Figure 3: Results of emotion detection

We then analyze the influence of different factors in our proposed approach with average F1-Measure of the five emotions with the results illustrated in Table 1. In the table, *Basic SMT* refers to using basic word-by-word statistical machine translation to help the detection process; *Enhanced SMT* refers to using both synonyms and word correlation to enhance the machine translation process; *Sentiment* refers to using sentimental information to help the detection process; *ME-BS* refers to using the maximum entropy model with both bilingual and sentimental information, and *BLP* refers to the label propagation model in which all of the words in Chinese and English text function as a feature.

From Table 1, it is observed that: 1) sentimental information (*Sentiment*) are effective for predicting emotion in both *ME*-based and *BLP-*

[7] *FNLP (FudanNLP)*, https://github.com/xpqiu/fnlp/

[8] ME algorithm is implemented with the *MALLET Toolkit*, http://mallet.cs.umass.edu

Method	Average F1.
ME	0.354
+Basic SMT	0.354
+Enhanced SMT	0.382
+Sentiment	0.369
ME-BS	0.383
BLP	0.385
+Enhanced SMT	0.392
+Sentiment	0.406
BLP-BS	**0.412**

Table 1: Results of influence on different factors

based models; 2) *Enhanced SMT* outperforms *Basic SMT*, which proves the effectiveness of our enhanced approaches for statistical machine translation; and 3) our proposed approach (*BLP-BS*) outperforms the other approaches. This indicates the complementarity of bilingual and sentimental information on the bipartite graph based label propagation model.

6 Conclusion

In this study, we address a novel task, namely emotion detection in code-switching texts. First, we collect and extract the code-switching posts from *Weibo.com*, which are annotated with emotions. Then, we use both SMT-based bilingual information and sentimental information to bridge the gap between different languages in code-switching texts. Finally, we propose a bipartite graph based label propagation model to effectively incorporate both bilingual and sentimental information for detecting emotion in code-switching texts. Empirical studies demonstrate that our model significantly outperforms several strong baselines.

Our current work assumes the independence of emotions and caused languages. In future work, we would like to explore the relation among emotions and caused languages for detecting the emotion and caused languages collectively.

Acknowledgments

Prof. Deyi Xiong contributed valuable insights and wise counsel on machine translation. Our colleague, Helena Yan Ping Lau, did excellent work on corpus analysis for probing and understanding the problem, and helped us review the paper, offering valuable feedback and helpful leads.

We thank our anonymous reviewers for prudent advice.

The work is funded by an Early Career Scheme (ECS) sponsored by the Research Grants Council of Hong Kong (No. PolyU 5593/13H), and supported by the National Natural Science Foundation of China (No. 61273320, and No. 61375073) and the Key Project of the National Natural Science Foundation of China (No. 61331011).

References

Adel H., N. Vu, and T. Schultz. 2013. Combination of Recurrent Neural Networks and Factored Language Models for Code-Switching Language Modeling. In *Proceedings of ACL-13*.

Auer P. 1999. *Code-Switching in Conversation*. Routledge.

Brown P., J. Cocke, S. Pietra, V. Pietra, F. Jelinek, J. Lafferty, R. Mercer, and P. Roossin. 1990. A Statistical Approach to Machine Translation. *Computational Linguistics*, 16(2):79-85.

Chen Y., S. Lee, S. Li, and C. Huang. 2010. Emotion Cause Detection with Linguistic Constructions. In *Proceeding of COLING-10*.

Gao W., S. Li, S. Lee, G. Zhou, and C. Huang. 2013. Joint Learning on Sentiment and Emotion Classification. In *Proceedings of CIKM-13*.

Lee S., H. Zhang, and C. Huang. 2013a. An Event-Based Emotion Corpus. In *Proceedings of CLSW 2013*.

Lee S., Y. Chen, C. Huang, and S. Li. 2013b. Detecting Emotion Causes with a Linguistic Rule-Based Approach. *Computational Intelligence*, 29(3), 390-416.

Lee S., S. Li, and C. Huang. 2014. Annotating Events in an Emotion Corpus. In *Proceedings of LREC-14*.

Li Y., and P. Fung. 2012. Code-switch Language Model with Inversion Constraints for Mixed Language Speech Recognition. In *Proceedings of COLING-12*.

Li S., Y. Xue, Z. Wang, and G. Zhou. 2013. Active Learning for Cross-domain Sentiment Classification. In *Proceeding of IJCAI-2013*.

Ling W., G. Xiang, C. Dyer, A. Black, and I. Trancoso. 2013. Microblogs as Parallel Corpora. In *Proceedings of ACL-13*.

Lignos C., and M. Marcus. 2013. Toward Web-scale Analysis of Codeswitching. In *Proceedings of Annual Meeting of the Linguistic Society of America*.

Liu H., S. Li, G. Zhou, C. Huang, and P. Li. 2013. Joint Modeling of News Reader's and Comment Writer's Emotions. In *Proceedings of ACL-13*, shorter.

Lu B., C. Tan, C. Cardie and B. Tsou. 2011. Joint Bilingual Sentiment Classification with Unlabeled Parallel Corpora. In *Proceedings of ACL-2011*.

Och F., and H. Ney. 2002. Discriminative Training and Maximum Entropy Models for Statistical Machine Translation. In *Proceedings of ACL-02*.

Quan C., and F. Ren. 2009. Construction of a Blog Emotion Corpus for Chinese Emotional Expression Analysis. In *Proceedings of EMNLP-09*.

Sindhwani V. and P. Melville. 2008. Document-Word Co-Regularization for Semi-supervised Sentiment Analysis. In *Proceedings of ICDM-08*.

Tang X., X. Wan, and X. Zhang. 2014. Cross-Language Context-aware Citation Recommendation in Scientific Articles. In *Proceedings of SIGIR-14*.

Turney P. 2002. Thumbs up or Thumbs down? Semantic Orientation Applied to Unsupervised Classification of comments. In *Proceedings of ACL-02*.

Volkova S., W. Dolan, and T. Wilson. 2012. CLex: A Lexicon for Exploring Color, Concept and Emotion Associations in Language. In *Proceedings of EACL-12*.

Xu G., X. Meng, and H. Wang. 2010. Build Chinese Emotion Lexicons Using A Graph-based Algorithm and Multiple Resources. In *Proceeding of COLING-10*.

Wan X. 2009. Co-Training for Cross-Lingual Sentiment Classification. In *Proceedings of ACL/IJCNLP-09*.

Zhao H., Y. Song, C. Kit, and G. Zhou. 2009. Cross Language Dependency Parsing using a Bilingual Lexicon. In *Proceedings of ACL-09*.

Zhou G. and K. Fang. 2009. Global Learning of Noun Phrase Anaphoricity in Coreference Resolution via Label Propagation. In *Proceedings of EMNLP-2009*.

Zhu X. and Z. Ghahramani. 2002. Learning from Labeled and Unlabeled Data with Label Propagation. *CMU CALD Technical Report*. CMU-CALD-02-107.

Model Adaptation for Personalized Opinion Analysis

Mohammad Al Boni[1], Keira Qi Zhou[1], Hongning Wang[2], and Matthew S. Gerber[1]

[1]Department of Systems and Information Engineering
[2]Department of Computer Science
[1,2]University of Virginia, USA
[1,2]{ma2sm,qz4aq,hw5x,msg8u}@virginia.edu

Abstract

Humans are idiosyncratic and variable: towards the same topic, they might hold different opinions or express the same opinion in various ways. It is hence important to model opinions at the level of individual users; however it is impractical to estimate independent sentiment classification models for each user with limited data. In this paper, we adopt a model-based transfer learning solution – using linear transformations over the parameters of a generic model – for personalized opinion analysis. Extensive experimental results on a large collection of Amazon reviews confirm our method significantly outperformed a user-independent generic opinion model as well as several state-of-the-art transfer learning algorithms.

1 Introduction

The proliferation of user-generated opinionated text data has fueled great interest in opinion analysis (Pang and Lee, 2008; Liu, 2012). Understanding opinions expressed by a population of users has value in a wide spectrum of areas, including social network analysis (Bodendorf and Kaiser, 2009), business intelligence (Gamon et al., 2005), marketing analysis (Jansen et al., 2009), personalized recommendation (Yang et al., 2013) and many more.

Most of the existing opinion analysis research focuses on population-level analyses, i.e., predicting opinions based on models estimated from a collection of users. The underlying assumption is that users are homogeneous in the way they express opinions. Nevertheless, different users may use the same words to express distinct opinions. For example, the word "expensive" tends to be associated with negative sentiment in general, although some users may use it to describe their satisfaction with a product's quality. Failure to recognize this difference across users will inevitably lead to inaccurate understanding of opinions.

However, due to the limited availability of user-specific opinionated data, it is impractical to estimate independent models for each user. In this work, we propose a transfer learning based solution, named LinAdapt, to address this challenge. Instead of estimating independent classifiers for each user, we start from a generic model and adapt it toward individual users based on their own opinionated text data. In particular, our key assumption is that the adaptation can be achieved via a set of linear transformations over the generic model's parameters. When we have sufficient observations for a particular user, the transformations will push the adapted model towards the user's personalized model; otherwise, it will back off to the generic model. Empirical evaluations on a large collection of Amazon reviews verify the effectiveness of the proposed solution: it significantly outperformed a user-independent generic model as well as several state-of-the-art transfer learning algorithms.

Our contribution is two-fold: 1) we enable efficient personalization of opinion analysis via a transfer learning approach, and 2) the proposed solution is general and applicable to any linear model for user opinion analysis.

2 Related Work

Sentiment Analysis refers to the process of identifying subjective information in source materials (Pang and Lee, 2008; Liu, 2012). Typical tasks include: 1) classifying textual documents into positive and negative polarity categories, (Dave et al., 2003; Kim and Hovy, 2004); 2) identifying textual topics and their associated opinions (Wang et al., 2010; Jo and Oh, 2011); and 3) opinion summarization (Hu and Liu, 2004; Ku et al., 2006). Approaches for these tasks focus on population-level opinion analyses, in which one model is shared across all users. Little effort has been devoted to personalized opinion analyses, where each user has a particular model, due to the absence of user-

Proceedings of the 53rd Annual Meeting of the Association for Computational Linguistics and the 7th International Joint Conference on Natural Language Processing (Short Papers), pages 769–774, Beijing, China, July 26-31, 2015.

specific opinion data for model estimation.

Transfer Learning aims to help improve predictive models by using knowledge from different but related problems (Pan and Yang, 2010). In the opinion mining community, transfer learning is used primarily for domain adaptation. Blitzer et al. (2006) proposed structural correspondence learning to identify the correspondences among features between different domains via the concept of pivot features. Pan et al. (2010) propose a spectral feature alignment algorithm to align domain-specific sentiment words from different domains for sentiment categorization. By assuming that users tend to express consistent opinions towards the same topic over time, Guerra et al. (2011) applied instance-based transfer learning for real time sentiment analysis.

Our method is inspired by a personalized ranking model adaptation method developed by Wang et al. (2013). To the best of our knowledge, our work is the first to estimate user-level classifiers for opinion analysis. By adapting a generic opinion classification model for each user, heterogeneity among their expressions of opinions can be captured and it help us understand users' opinions at a finer granularity.

3 Linear Transformation Based Model Adaptation

Given a generic sentiment classification model $y = f^s(x)$, we aim at finding an optimal adapted model $y = f^u(x)$ for user u, such that $f^u(x)$ best captures u's opinion in his/her generated textual documents $D^u = \{x_d, y_d\}_{d=1}^{|D|}$, where x_d is the feature vector for document d, y_d is the sentiment class label (e.g., positive v.s., negative). To achieve so, we assume that such adaptation can be performed via a series of linear transformations on $f^s(x)$'s model parameter w_s. This assumption is general and can be applied to a wide variety of sentiment classifiers, e.g., logistic regression and linear support vector machines, as long as they have a linear core function. Therefore, we name our proposed method as LinAdapt. In this paper, we focus on logistic regression (Pang et al., 2002); but the proposed procedures can be easily adopted for many other classifiers (Wang et al., 2013).

Our global model $y = f^s(x)$ can be written as,

$$P^s(y_d = 1|x_d) = \frac{1}{1 + e^{-w^{s\mathsf{T}} x_d}} \qquad (1)$$

where w^s are the linear coefficients for the corresponding document features.

Standard linear transformations, i.e., scaling, shifting and rotation, can be encoded via a $V \times (V+1)$ matrix A^u for each user u as:

$$\begin{pmatrix} a^u_{g(1)} & c^u_{g(1),12} & c^u_{g(1),13} & 0 & 0 & b^u_{g(1)} \\ c^u_{g(2),21} & a^u_{g(2)} & c^u_{g(2),23} & \cdots & 0 & b^u_{g(2)} \\ c^u_{g(3),31} & c^u_{g(3),32} & a^u_{g(3)} & \ddots & \vdots & b^u_{g(3)} \\ 0 & \cdots & \cdots & \cdots & \ddots & \vdots \\ 0 & 0 & \cdots & \cdots & a^u_{g(V)} & b^u_{g(V)} \end{pmatrix}$$

where V is the total number of features.

However, the above transformation introduces $O(V^2)$ free parameters, which are even more than the number of free parameters required to estimate a new logistic regression model. Following the solution proposed by Wang et al. (2013), we further assume the transformations can be performed in a group-wise manner to reduce the size of parameters in adaptation. The intuition behind this assumption is that features that share similar contributions to the classification model are more likely to be adapted in the same way. Another advantage of feature grouping is that the feedback information will be propagated through the features in the same group while adaptation; hence the features that are not observed in the adaptation data can also be updated properly.

We denote $g(\cdot)$ as the feature grouping function, which maps V original features to K groups, and a^u_k, b^u_k and c^u_k as the scaling, shifting and rotation operations over w^s in group k for user u. In addition, rotation is only performed for the features in the same group, and it is assumed to be symmetric, i.e., $c^u_{k,ij} = c^u_{k,ji}$, where $g(i) = k$ and $g(j) = k$. As a result, the personalized classification model $f^u(x)$ after adaptation can be written as,

$$P^u(y_d = 1|x_d) = \frac{1}{1 + e^{-(A^u \tilde{w}^s)^{\mathsf{T}} x_d}} \qquad (2)$$

where $\tilde{w}^s = (w^s, 1)$ to accommodate the shifting operation.

The optimal transformation matrix A^u for user u can be estimated by maximum likelihood estimation based on user u's own opinionated document collection D^u. To avoid overfitting, we penalize the transformation which increases the discrepancy between the adapted model and global model by the following regularization term,

$$\begin{aligned} R(A^u) = & -\frac{\eta}{2}\sum_{k=1}^{K}(a^u_k - 1)^2 - \frac{\sigma}{2}\sum_{k=1}^{K} b^{u2}_k \\ & -\frac{\epsilon}{2}\sum_{k=1}^{K}\sum_{i,g(i)=k}\sum_{j \neq i, g(j)=k} {c^u_{k,ij}}^2, \end{aligned} \qquad (3)$$

where η, σ and ϵ are trade-off parameters controlling the balance among shifting, scaling and rotation operations in adaptation.

Combining the newly introduced regularization term for A^u and log-likelihood function for logistic regression, we get the following optimization problem to estimate the adaptation parameters,

$$\max_{A^u} L(A^u) = L_{LR}(D^u; P^u) + R(A^u) \quad (4)$$

where $L_{LR}(D^u; P^u)$ is the log-likelihood of logistic regression on collection D^u, and P^u is defined in Eq (2).

Gradient-based method is used to optimize Eq (4), in which the gradient for a_k^u, b_k^u and c_k^u can be calculated as,

$$\frac{\partial L(A^u)}{\partial a_k} = \sum_{d=1}^{D^u} \{y_d[1 - p(y_d|x_d)] \sum_{i,g(i)=k} w_i^s x_{di}\} - \eta(a_k - 1)$$

$$\frac{\partial L(A^u)}{\partial b_k} = \sum_{d=1}^{D^u} \{y_d[1 - p(y_d|x_d)] \sum_{i,g(i)=k} x_{di}\} - \sigma b_k$$

$$\frac{\partial L(A^u)}{\partial c_{k,ij}} = \sum_{d=1}^{D^u} \{y_d[1 - p(y_d|x_d)] w_j^s x_{di}\} - \epsilon c_{k,ij}$$

4 Experiments and Discussion

We performed empirical evaluations of the proposed LinAdapt algorithm on a large collection of product review documents. We compared our approach with several state-of-the-art transfer learning algorithms. In the following, we will first introduce the evaluation corpus and baselines, and then discuss our experimental findings.

4.1 Data Collection and Baselines

We used a corpus of Amazon reviews provided on Stanford SNAP website by McAuley and Leskovec. (2013). We performed simple data preprocessing: 1) annotated the reviews with ratings greater than 3 stars (out of total 5 stars) as positive, and others as negative; 2) removed duplicate reviews; 3) removed reviewers who have more than 1,000 reviews or more than 90% positive or negative reviews; 4) chronologically ordered the reviews in each user. We extracted unigrams and bigrams to construct bag-of-words feature representations for the review documents. Standard stopword removal (Lewis et al., 2004) and Porter stemming (Willett, 2006) were applied. Chi-square and information gain (Yang and Pedersen, 1997) were used for feature selection and the union of the resulting selected features are used in the final controlled vocabulary. The resulting evaluation data set contains 32,930 users, 281,813 positive reviews, and 81,522 negative reviews, where each review is represented with 5,000 text features with TF-IDF as the feature value.

Our first baseline is an instance-based adaptation method (Brighton and Mellish, 2002). The k-nearest neighbors of each testing review document are found from the shared training set for personalized model training. As a result, for each testing case, we are estimating an independent classification model. We denote this method as "ReTrain." The second baseline builds on the model-based adaptation method developed by Geng et al. (2012). For each user, it enforces the adapted model to be close to the global model via an additional L2 regularization when training the personalized model. But the full set of parameters in logistic regression need to estimated during adaptation. We denote this method as "Reg-LR."

In our experiments, all model adaptation is performed in an online fashion: we first applied the up-to-date classification model on the given testing document; evaluated the model's performance with ground-truth; and used the feedback to update the model. Because the class distribution of our evaluation data set is highly skewed (77.5% positive), it is important to evaluate the adapted models' performance on both classes. In the following comparisons, we report the average F-1 measure of both positive and negative classes.

4.2 Comparison of Adaptation Performance

First we need to estimate a global model for adaptation. A typical approach is to collect a portion of historical reviews from each user to construct a shared training corpus (Wang et al., 2013). However, this setting is problematic: it already exploits information from every user and does not reflect the reality that some (new) users might not exist when training the global model. In our experiment, we isolated a group of random users for global model training. In addition, since there are multiple categories in this review collection, such as book, movies, electronics, etc, and each user might discuss various categories, it is infeasible to balance the coverage of different categories in global model training by only selecting the users. As a result, we vary the number of reviews in each domain from the selected training users to estimate the global model. We started with 1000 reviews from the top 5 categories (Movies & TV, Books, Music, Home & Kitchen, and Video Games), then evaluated the global model on 10,000 testing users which consist of three groups: light users with 2 to 10 reviews, medium users with 11 to 50 reviews, and heavy users with 51 to 200 reviews. After each evaluation run, we added an extra 1000 reviews and repeated the training and evaluation.

Table 1: Global model training with varying size of training corpus.

Model	Metric	1000	2000	3000	4000	5000
Global	Pos F1	0.741	0.737	0.738	0.734	0.729
	Neg F1	0.106	0.126	0.125	0.132	**0.159**
LinAdapt	Pos F1	0.694	0.693	0.692	0.694	**0.696**
	Neg F1	0.299	0.299	0.296	0.299	**0.304**

Table 2: Effect of feature grouping in LinAdapt.

Method	Metric	100	200	400	800	1000
Rand	Pos F1	0.691	0.692	0.696	0.686	0.681
	Neg F1	0.295	0.298	0.300	0.322	0.322
SVD	Pos F1	0.691	0.698	0.704	0.697	0.696
	Neg F1	0.298	0.302	0.300	0.322	**0.334**
Cross	Pos F1	**0.701**	**0.702**	**0.705**	**0.700**	0.696
	Neg F1	0.298	0.299	**0.303**	**0.328**	0.331

To understand the effect of global model training in model adaptation, we also included the performance of LinAdapt, which only used shifting and scaling operations and $Cross$ feature grouping method with $k = 400$ (detailed feature grouping method will be discussed in the next experiment). Table 1 shows the performance of the global model and LinAdapt with respect to different training corpus size. We found that the global model converged very quickly with around 5,000 reviews, and this gives the best compromise for both positive and negative classes in both global and adaptaed model. Therefore, we will use this global model for later adaptation experiments.

We then investigated the effect of feature grouping in LinAdapt. We employed the feature grouping methods of SVD and $Cross$ developed by Wang et al. (2013). A random feature grouping method is included to validate the necessity of proper feature grouping. We varied the number of feature groups from 100 to 1000, and evaluated the adapted models using the same 10,000 testing users from the previous experiment. As shown in Table 2, $Cross$ provided the best adaptation performance and random is the worse; a moderate group size balances performance between positive and negative classes. For the remaining experiments, we use the $Cross$ grouping with $k = 400$ in LinAdapt. In this group setting, we found that the average number of features per group is 12.47 while the median is 12, which means that features are normally distributed across different groups.

Next, we investigated the effect of different linear operations in LinAdapt, and compared LinAdapt against the baselines. We started LinAdapt with only the shifting operation, and then included scaling and rotation. To validate the necessity of personalizing sentiment classification models, we also included the global model's performance in Figure 1. In particular, to understand the longitudinal effect of personalized model adaptation, we only used the heavy users (4,021 users) in this experiment. The results indicate that the adapted models outperformed the global model in identifying the negative class; while the global model performs the best in recognizing positive reviews. This is due to the heavily biased class distribution in our collection: global model puts great emphasis on the positive reviews; while the adaptation methods give equal weights to both positive and negative reviews. In particular, in LinAdapt, scaling and shifting operations lead to satisfactory adaptation performance for the negative class with only 15 reviews; while rotation is essential for recognizing the positive class.

To better understand the improvement of model adaptation against the global model in different types of users, we decomposed the performance gain of different adaptation methods. For this experiment, we used all the 10,000 testing users: we used the first 50% of the reviews from each user for adaptation and the rest for testing. Table 3 shows the performance gain of different algorithms under light, medium and heavy users. For the heavy and medium users, which only consist 0.1% and 35% of the total population in our data set, our adaptation model achieved the best improvement against the global model compared with Reg-LR and ReTrain. For the light users, who cover 64.9% of the total population, LinAdapt was able to improve the performance against the global model for the negative class, but Reg-LR and ReTrain had attained higher performance. For the positive class, none of those adaptation methods can improve over the global model although they provide a very close performance (in LinAdapt, the differences are not significant). The significant improvement in negative class prediction from model adaptation is encouraging considering the biased distribution of classes, which results in poor performance in the global model.

The above improved classification performance indicates the adapted model captures the heterogeneity in expressing opinions across users. To verify this, we investigated textual features whose sentiment polarities are most/least frequently updated across users. We computed the variance of the absolute difference between the learned feature weights in LinAdapt and global model. High variance indicates the word's sentiment polarity frequently changes across different users. But there are two reasons for a low variance: first, a rare

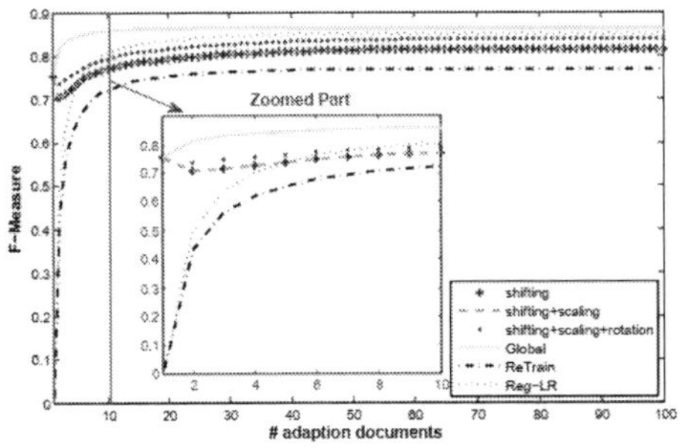

(a) Positive F-1 measure

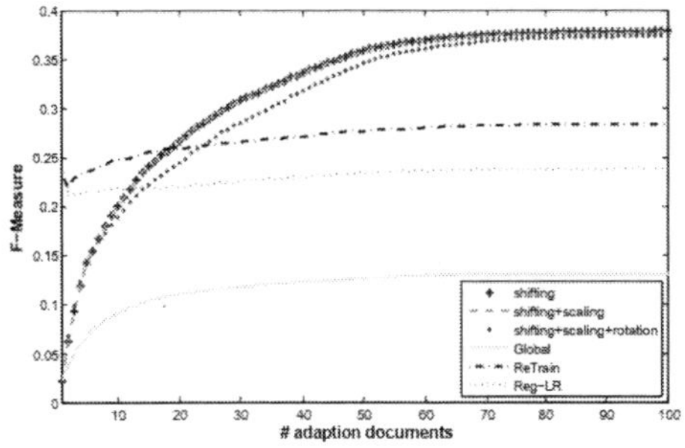

(b) Negative F-1 measure

Figure 1: Online adaptation performance comparisons.

Table 3: User-level performance gain over global model from ReTrain, Reg-LR and LinAdapt.

Method	User Class	Pos F1	Neg F1
ReTrain	Heavy	-0.092	0.155*
	Medium	-0.095	0.235*
	Light	-0.157*	**0.255***
Reg-LR	Heavy	-0.010	0.109*
	Medium	-0.005	0.206*
	Light	-0.060	0.232*
LinAdapt	Heavy	-0.046	**0.248***
	Medium	-0.049	**0.235***
	Light	-0.091	0.117*

* p-value< 0.05 with paired t-test.

Table 4: Top 10 words with the highest and lowest variance of learned polarity in LinAdapt.

Variance	Features		
Highest	waste	good	attempt
	money	return	save
	poor	worst	annoy
Lowest	lover	correct	pure
	care	the product	odd
	sex	evil	less than

word that is not used by many users; second, a word is being used frequently, yet, with the same polarity. We are only interested in the second case. Therefore, for each word, we compute its user frequency (UF), i.e., how many unique users used this word in their reviews. Then, we selected 1000 most popular features by UF, and ranked them according to the variance of learned sentiment polarities. Table 4 shows the top ten features with the highest and lowest polarity variance.

We inspected the learned weights in the adapted models in each user from LinAdapt, and found the words like *waste, poor*, and *good* share the same sentiment polarity as in the global model but different magnitudes; while words like *money, instead*, and *return* are almost neutral in global model, but vary across the personalized models. On the other hand, words such as *care, sex, evil, pure*, and *correct* constantly carry the same sentiment across users. Table 5 shows the detailed range of learned polarity for three typical opinion words in 10,000 users. This result indicates LinAdapt well captures the fact that users express opinions differently even with the same words.

Table 5: Learned sentiment polarity range of three typical words in LinAdapt.

Feature	Range	Global Weight	Used as Positive	Used as Negative
Experience	[-0.231,0.232]	0.002	3348	1503
Good	[-0.170,0.816]	0.032	8438	1088
Money	[-0.439,0.074]	-0.013	646	6238

5 Conclusion and Future Work

In this paper, we developed a transfer learning based solution for personalized opinion mining. Linear transformations of scaling, shifting and rotation are exploited to adapt a global sentiment classification model for each user. Empirical evaluations based on a large collection of opinionated review documents confirm that the proposed method effectively models personal opinions. By analyzing the variance of the learned feature weights, we are able to discover words that hold different polarities across users, which indicates our model captures the fact that users express opinions differently even with the same words. In the future, we plan to further explore this linear transformation based adaptation from different perspectives, e.g., sharing adaptation operations across users or review categories.

6 Acknowledgements

This research was funded in part by grant W911NF-10-2-0051 from the United States Army Research Laboratory. Also, Hongning Wang is partially supported by the Yahoo Academic Career Enhancement Award.

References

John Blitzer, Ryan McDonald, and Fernando Pereira. 2006. Domain adaptation with structural correspondence learning. In *Proceedings of the 2006 conference on empirical methods in natural language processing*, pages 120–128. Association for Computational Linguistics.

Freimut Bodendorf and Carolin Kaiser. 2009. Detecting opinion leaders and trends in online social networks. In *Proceedings of the 2nd ACM workshop on Social web search and mining*, pages 65–68. ACM.

Henry Brighton and Chris Mellish. 2002. Advances in instance selection for instance-based learning algorithms. *Data mining and knowledge discovery*, 6(2):153–172.

Pedro Henrique Calais Guerra, Adriano Veloso, Wagner Meira Jr, and Virgflio Almeida. 2011. From bias to opinion: a transfer-learning approach to real-time sentiment analysis. In *Proceedings of the 17th ACM SIGKDD international conference on Knowledge discovery and data mining*, pages 150–158. ACM.

Kushal Dave, Steve Lawrence, and David M Pennock. 2003. Mining the peanut gallery: Opinion extraction and semantic classification of product reviews. In *Proceedings of the 12th international conference on World Wide Web*, pages 519–528. ACM.

Michael Gamon, Anthony Aue, Simon Corston-Oliver, and Eric Ringger. 2005. Pulse: Mining customer opinions from free text. In *Advances in Intelligent Data Analysis VI*, pages 121–132. Springer.

Bo Geng, Yichen Yang, Chao Xu, and Xian-Sheng Hua. 2012. Ranking model adaptation for domain-specific search. *Knowledge and Data Engineering, IEEE Transactions on*, 24(4):745–758.

Minqing Hu and Bing Liu. 2004. Mining and summarizing customer reviews. In *Proceedings of the tenth ACM SIGKDD international conference on Knowledge discovery and data mining*, pages 168–177. ACM.

Bernard J Jansen, Mimi Zhang, Kate Sobel, and Abdur Chowdury. 2009. Twitter power: Tweets as electronic word of mouth. *Journal of the American society for information science and technology*, 60(11):2169–2188.

Yohan Jo and Alice H Oh. 2011. Aspect and sentiment unification model for online review analysis. In *Proceedings of the fourth ACM international conference on Web search and data mining*, pages 815–824. ACM.

Soo-Min Kim and Eduard Hovy. 2004. Determining the sentiment of opinions. In *Proceedings of the 20th international conference on Computational Linguistics*, page 1367. Association for Computational Linguistics.

Lun-Wei Ku, Yu-Ting Liang, and Hsin-Hsi Chen. 2006. Opinion extraction, summarization and tracking in news and blog corpora. In *AAAI spring symposium: Computational approaches to analyzing weblogs*, volume 100107.

David D Lewis, Yiming Yang, Tony G Rose, and Fan Li. 2004. Smart stopword list.

Bing Liu. 2012. Sentiment analysis and opinion mining. *Synthesis Lectures on Human Language Technologies*, 5(1):1–167.

Julian McAuley and Jure Leskovec. 2013. Hidden factors and hidden topics: understanding rating dimensions with review text. In *Proceedings of the 7th ACM conference on Recommender systems*, pages 165–172. ACM.

Sinno Jialin Pan and Qiang Yang. 2010. A survey on transfer learning. *Knowledge and Data Engineering, IEEE Transactions on*, 22(10):1345–1359.

Sinno Jialin Pan, Xiaochuan Ni, Jian-Tao Sun, Qiang Yang, and Zheng Chen. 2010. Cross-domain sentiment classification via spectral feature alignment. In *Proceedings of the 19th international conference on World wide web*, pages 751–760. ACM.

Bo Pang and Lillian Lee. 2008. Opinion mining and sentiment analysis. *Foundations and trends in information retrieval*, 2(1-2):1–135.

Bo Pang, Lillian Lee, and Shivakumar Vaithyanathan. 2002. Thumbs up?: sentiment classification using machine learning techniques. In *Proceedings of the ACL-02 conference on Empirical methods in natural language processing-Volume 10*, pages 79–86. Association for Computational Linguistics.

Hongning Wang, Yue Lu, and Chengxiang Zhai. 2010. Latent aspect rating analysis on review text data: a rating regression approach. In *Proceedings of the 16th ACM SIGKDD international conference on Knowledge discovery and data mining*, pages 783–792. ACM.

Hongning Wang, Xiaodong He, Ming-Wei Chang, Yang Song, Ryen W White, and Wei Chu. 2013. Personalized ranking model adaptation for web search. In *Proceedings of the 36th international ACM SIGIR conference on Research and development in information retrieval*, pages 323–332. ACM.

Peter Willett. 2006. The porter stemming algorithm: then and now. *Program*, 40(3):219–223.

Yiming Yang and Jan O Pedersen. 1997. A comparative study on feature selection in text categorization. In *ICML*, volume 97, pages 412–420.

Dingqi Yang, Daqing Zhang, Zhiyong Yu, and Zhu Wang. 2013. A sentiment-enhanced personalized location recommendation system. In *Proceedings of the 24th ACM Conference on Hypertext and Social Media*, pages 119–128. ACM.

Linguistic Template Extraction for Recognizing Reader-Emotion and Emotional Resonance Writing Assistance

Yung-Chun Chang[1,2], Cen-Chieh Chen[1,3], Yu-Lun Hsieh[1,3], Chien Chin Chen[2], Wen-Lian Hsu[1*]
[1]Institute of Information Science, Academia Sinica, Taipei, Taiwan
[2]Department of Information Management, National Taiwan University, Taipei, Taiwan
[3]Department of Computer Science, National Chengchi University, Taipei, Taiwan
[1]{changyc,can,morphe,hsu}@iis.sinica.edu.tw, [2]patonchen@ntu.edu.tw

Abstract

In this paper, we propose a flexible principle-based approach (PBA) for reader-emotion classification and writing assistance. PBA is a highly automated process that learns emotion templates from raw texts to characterize an emotion and is comprehensible for humans. These templates are adopted to predict reader-emotion, and may further assist in emotional resonance writing. Results demonstrate that PBA can effectively detect reader-emotions by exploiting the syntactic structures and semantic associations in the context, thus outperforming well-known statistical text classification methods and the state-of-the-art reader-emotion classification method. Moreover, writers are able to create more emotional resonance in articles under the assistance of the generated emotion templates. These templates have been proven to be highly interpretable, which is an attribute that is difficult to accomplish in traditional statistical methods.

1 Introduction

The Internet has rapidly grown into a powerful medium for disseminating information. People can easily share experiences and emotions anytime and anywhere on social media websites. Human feelings can be quickly collected through emotion classification, as these emotions reflect an individual's feelings and experiences toward some subject matters (Turney, 2002; Wilson et al., 2009). Moreover, people can obtain more sponsorship opportunities from manufacturers if their articles about a certain product are able to create more emotional resonance in the readers. Therefore, emotion classification has been attracting more and more attention, e.g., Chen et al. (2010), Purver and Battersby (2012).

Emotion classification aims to predict the emotion categories (e.g., *happy* or *angry*) of the given text (Quan and Ren, 2009; Das and Bandyopadhyay, 2009). There are two aspects of emotions in texts, namely, writer's and reader's emotions. The former concerns the emotion expressed by the writer of the text, and the latter concerns the emotion a reader had after reading it. Recognizing reader-emotion is different and may be even more complex than writer-emotion (Lin et al., 2008; Tang and Chen, 2012). A writer may directly express her emotions through sentiment words. By contrast, reader-emotion possesses a more perplexing nature, as even common words can invoke different types of reader-emotions depending on the reader's personal experiences and knowledge (Lin et al., 2007). For instance, a sentence like "*Kenya survivors describe deadly attack at Garissa University*" is simply stating the facts without any emotion, but may invoke emotions such as *angry* or *worried* in its readers.

In light of this rationale, we propose a principle-based approach (PBA) for reader-emotion classification. It is a highly automated process that integrates various types of knowledge to generate discriminative linguistic templates that can be acknowledged as the essential knowledge for humans to understand different kinds of emotions. PBA recognizes reader-emotions of documents using an alignment algorithm that allows a template to be partially matched through a statistical scoring scheme. Experiments demonstrate that PBA can achieve a better performance than other well-known text categorization methods and the state-of-the-art reader-emotion classification method. Furthermore, we adopt these generated templates to assist in emotional resonance writing. Results show that writers are able to generate more emo-

*Corresponding author

Proceedings of the 53rd Annual Meeting of the Association for Computational Linguistics and the 7th International Joint Conference on Natural Language Processing (Short Papers), pages 775–780,
Beijing, China, July 26-31, 2015.

$$-2log\left[\frac{p(w)^{N(w\wedge E)}(1-p(w))^{N(E)-N(w\wedge E)}p(w)^{N(w\wedge\neg E)}(1-p(w))^{N(\neg E)-N(w\wedge\neg E)}}{p(w|E)^{N(w\wedge E)}(1-p(w|E))^{N(E)-N(w\wedge E)}p(w|\neg E)^{N(w\wedge\neg E)}(1-p(w|\neg E))^{N(\neg E)-N(w\wedge\neg E)}}\right] \quad (1)$$

tional resonance in readers after exploiting these templates, demonstrating the capability of PBA in extracting templates with high interpretability.

2 Extracting Emotion Templates from Raw Text

PBA attempts to construct emotion templates through recognition of crucial elements using a three-layered approach. First, since keywords contain important information, PBA learns reader-emotion specific keywords using an effective feature selection method, log likelihood ratio (LLR) (Manning and Schütze, 1999). It employs Equation (1) to calculate the likelihood of the assumption that the occurrence of a word w in reader-emotion E is not random. In (1), E denotes the set of documents of the reader-emotion in the training data; $N(E)$ and $N(\neg E)$ denote the numbers of documents that do or do not contain this emotion, respectively; and $N(w \wedge E)$ is the number of documents with emotion E and having w. The probabilities $p(w)$, $p(w|E)$, and $p(w|\neg E)$ are estimated using maximum likelihood estimation. A larger LLR value is considered closely associated with an emotion. Words in the training data are ranked by LLR values, and the top 200 are included in our emotion keyword list.

Next, named entities (NEs) have been shown to improve the performance of identifying topics (Bashaddadh and Mohd, 2011). Thus, we utilize Wikipedia to semi-automatically label NEs with their semantic classes, which can be considered as a form of generalization. Wikipedia's category tags are used to label NEs recognized by the Stanford NER[1]. If there are more than one category tag for an NE, we select the most dominant one with the highest number of associated Wikipedia pages. The assumption is that the generality of a tag is indicated by the number of Wikipedia pages that are linked to it. For example, a query "奥巴马 (Obama)" to the Wikipedia would return a page titled "贝拉克.奥巴马 (Barack Obama)". Within this page, there are a number of category tags such as "民主党 (Democratic Party)" and "美国总统 (Presidents of the United States)". Suppose "美国总统 (Presidents of the United States)" has more out-going links, we will label "奥巴马 (Obama)" as "[美国总统] (Presidents of the United States)". We also annotate those NEs not found in Wikipedia with their category tags. In this manner, we can transform plain NEs to a more general class and increase the coverage of each label. Finally, to incorporate richer semantic context, we exploit the Extended HowNet (E-HowNet) (Chen et al., 2005) after the above processes to tag the remaining text with sense labels. Figure 1 illustrates crucial element labeling process. Consider the clause C_n = "奥巴马又代表民主党赢得美国总统选举 (Obama, representing the Democratic Party, won the U.S. Presidential election)". First, "奥巴马 (Obama)" is found in the emotion keyword list and tagged. Then, NEs like "民主党 (Democratic Party)" and "总统选举 (Presidential election)" are recognized and tagged as "{政党 (Party)}" and "{总统选举 (Presidential election)}". Subsequently, other terms such as "代表 (represent)" and "赢得 (won)" are labeled with their corresponding E-HowNet senses. Finally, we obtain the sequence "[奥巴马] : {代表} : {政党} : {得到} : {国家} : {总统选举} ([Obama] : {represents} : {party} : {got} : {country} : {Presidential election})." This three-layered labeling process serves as a generalization of the raw text for capturing crucial elements used in the template generation stage that follows.

The emotion template generation process aims at automatically constructing representative templates consisting of a sequence of crucial elements. We observed that the rank-frequency distribution of the elements follows the Zipf's law (Manning and Schütze, 1999). Thus, we rank the templates according to their frequency, and adopt a dominating set algorithm (Johnson, 1974) to use the top 20% templates to cover the rest. First, we constructed a directed graph $G = \{V, E\}$, in which vertices V contains all crucial element sequences $\{CES_1, \cdots, CES_m\}$ in each emotion, and edges E represent the dominating relations between sequences. If CES_x dominates CES_y, there is an edge $CES_x \rightarrow CES_y$. A

[1]http://nlp.stanford.edu/software/CRF-NER.shtml

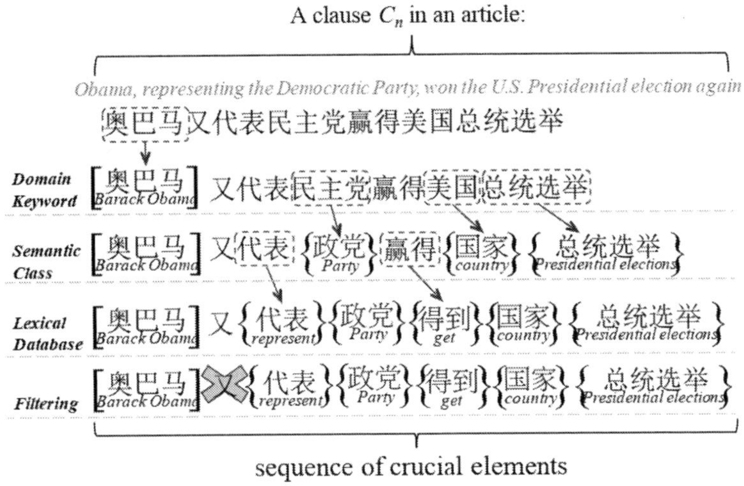

Figure 1: Crucial element labeling process.

dominating relation is defined as follows. 1) Crucial element sequences with high frequency are selected as candidate dominators. 2) Longer sequences dominate shorter ones if their head and tail elements are identical. The intermediate elements are treated as insertions and/or deletions, which can be scored based on their distribution in this emotion during the matching process. Lastly, we preserve top 100 most prominent and distinctive ones from approximately 55,000 sequences based on the dominating rate. This process serves as a kind of dimension reduction and facilitates the execution of our matching algorithm.

3 Template Matching for Inference

We believe that human perception of an emotion is through recognizing important events or semantic contents. For instance, when an article contains strongly correlated words such as "Japan (country)", "Earthquake (disaster)", and "Tsunami (disaster)" simultaneously, it is natural to conclude that this article is more likely to elicit emotions like depressed and worried rather than happy and warm. Following this line of thought, PBA uses an alignment algorithm (Needleman and Wunsch, 1970) to measure the similarity between templates and texts. It enables a single template to match multiple semantically related expressions with appropriate scores. For each clause in a document d_j, we first label crucial elements $CE = \{ce_1, \cdots, ce_n\}$, followed by the matching procedure that compares all sequences in CE from d_j to all emotion templates $ET = \{et_1, \cdots, et_j\}$ in each emotion category, and calculates the scores. Within the alignment matching, a statistical based scoring criterion is used to score insertions, deletions, and substitutions as described below. The emotion e_i with the highest sum of scores defined in (2) is considered as the winner.

$$
\begin{aligned}
&Emotion(d_j) \\
&= \underset{e_i \in E}{\arg\max} \sum_{et_n \in ET_{c_i}, ce_m \in CE_{d_j}} \Delta(et_n, ce_m) \\
&= \sum_k \sum_l \Delta(et_n \cdot sl_k, ce_m \cdot ce_l) \qquad (2)
\end{aligned}
$$

where sl_k and ce_l represent the kth slot of et_n and l^{th} element of ce_m, respectively. Details for scoring matched and unmatched elements are as follows. If $et_n \cdot sl_k$ and $ce_m \cdot ce_l$ are identical, we add a matched score (*MS*) obtained from the LLR value of ce_l if it matches a keyword. Otherwise, the score is determined by multiplying the frequency of the crucial element in category c_i by a normalizing factor $\lambda = 100$, as in (3). On the other hand, an unmatched element is given a score of insertion or deletion. The insertion score (*IS*), defined as (4), can be accounted for by the inversed entropy of this element, which represents the uniqueness or generality of it among categories. And the deletion score (*DS*), defined as (5), is computed from the log frequency of this crucial element in this emotion category.

$$MS(ce_l) = \begin{cases} LLR_{ce_l}, \text{if } ce_l \in \text{keyword} \\ \lambda \frac{f_{ce_l}}{\sum_{i=1}^{m} f_{ce_i}}, \text{otherwise} \end{cases} \quad (3)$$

$$IS(ce_l) = \frac{1}{-\sum_{i=1}^{m} P(ce_{l_{c_i}}) \cdot log_2(P(ce_{l_{c_i}}))} \quad (4)$$

$$DS(ce_l) = log \frac{f_{ce_l}}{\sum_{i=1}^{m} f_{ce_i}} \quad (5)$$

4 Experiments

4.1 Dataset and Setting

We collected a corpus of Chinese news articles from Yahoo! Kimo News[2], in which each article is given votes from readers with emotion tags in eight categories: *angry*, *worried*, *boring*, *happy*, *odd*, *depressing*, *warm*, and *informative*. We consider the voted emotions as the reader's emotion toward the news. Following previous studies such as Lin et al. (2007) and Lin et al. (2008) that used a similar source, we exclude "*informative*" as it is not considered as an emotion category. To ensure the quality of our evaluation, only articles with a clear statistical distinction between the highest vote of emotion and others determined by *t*-test with a 95% confidence level are retained. Finally, 47,285 out of 68,026 articles are kept, and divided into the training set and the test set, each containing 11,681 and 35,604 articles, respectively.

4.2 Reader's Emotion Classification

Several classification methods are implemented and compared. Naïve Bayes (McCallum et al., 1998) serves as the baseline, denoted as *NB*. In addition, a probabilistic graphical model that uses LDA as document representation to train an SVM classifier that determines a document as either relevant or irrelevant (Blei et al., 2003), denotes as *LDA*. Next, an emotion keyword-based model, denoted as *KW*, is trained using SVM to test the effect of our keyword extraction approach. *CF* is the state-of-the-art reader-emotion recognition method that combines various features including bigrams, words, metadata, and emotion category words (Lin et al., 2007). For evaluation, we adopt the accuracy measures as used by Lin et al. (2007), and compute the macro-average (A^M) and micro-average (A^μ). Table 1 shows a comprehensive evaluation of PBA and other methods[3].

[2]https://tw.news.yahoo.com

Emotion	*Accuracy(%)*				
	NB	LDA	KW	CF	PBA
angry	47.00	74.21	79.21	83.71	**87.83**
worried	69.56	**92.83**	81.96	87.50	75.80
boring	75.67	76.21	84.34	87.52	**90.52**
happy	37.90	67.59	80.97	86.27	**88.94**
odd	73.90	**85.40**	77.05	84.25	83.34
depressing	73.76	81.43	85.00	87.70	**92.15**
warm	75.09	87.09	79.59	85.83	**91.91**
A^M	58.11	76.10	80.36	85.80	**86.43**
A^μ	52.78	74.16	80.81	85.70	**88.56**

Table 1: Comparison of the accuracies of five reader-emotion classification systems.

Since *NB* only considers surface word weightings and ignore inter-word relations, it only achieved an accuracy of 58.11%. By contrast, *LDA* includes both keywords and long-distance relations, thus greatly outperforms *NB* with an overall accuracy of 76.10%. It even obtained the highest accuracy of 92.83% for the emotions "*worried*" and "*odd*" among all methods. Notably, *KW* can bring about substantial proficiency in detecting the emotions, which indicates that reader-emotion can be recognized effectively by using only the LLR scores of keywords. Meanwhile, *CF* achieved a satisfactory overall accuracy around 85%, due to the combined lexical feature sets (e.g., character bigrams, word dictionary, and emotion keywords), paired with metadata of the articles. For instance, we found that many sports-related articles invoke the emotion "*happy*". Specifically, 45% of all "*happy*" instances are sports-related, and a sports-related article has a 31% chance of having the emotion tag "*happy*". Hence, the high accuracy of the emotion category "*happy*" could be the result of people's general enthusiasm over sports rather than a particular event. On top of that, PBA can generate distinctive emotion templates to capture variations of similar expressions, thus achieving better outcome. For instance, the template "{国家 country}" : [发生 occur] : [地震 earthquake] : {劫难 disaster}" is generated by PBA

[3]The dictionary required by all methods is constructed by removing stop words according to (Zou et al., 2006), and retaining tokens that make up 90% of the accumulated frequency. As for unseen events, we used the Laplace smoothing in *NB*. *LDA* is implemented using a toolkit (http://nlp.stanford.edu/software/tmt/tmt-0.4/).

for the emotion "*worried*". It is perceivable that this template is relaying information about disastrous earthquakes in a country, and such news often makes readers worry. The ability to yield such emotion-specific, human interpretable templates could account for the outstanding performance of PBA.

4.3 Reader's Emotion Templates Suggestion in Emotional Resonance Writing

This experiment aims at testing the effectiveness of the emotion templates in aiding writers to compose articles with stronger emotional resonance. Here, we only consider coarse-grained emotion categories (i.e., *positive* and *negative*). Thus, fine-grained emotions like *happy*, *warm*, and *odd* are merged into '*positive*', while *angry*, *boring*, *depressing*, and *worried* are merged into '*negative*'. 10 templates for each of the fine-grained emotions are selected, resulting in 30 and 40 templates for the two coarse-grained emotions, respectively. We recruited seven writers to compose two articles that they think will trigger positive and negative emotions without using templates (denoted as *NT*). Then, we asked them to compose two more articles with the aid of templates (denoted as *WT*). Afterwards, all articles are randomly organized into a questionnaire to test the emotional resonance. Subjects are required to perform two tasks: 1) answer 'positive', 'neutral', or 'negative' 2) give a score according to the five-point Likert scale (Likert, 1932) for a given emotion. In the end, 42 effective responses are gathered. For Task 1, the score is defined as the number of matching responses and answers. As for Task 2, the score is the sum of all articles. Higher scores indicate better emotional resonance between writers and readers. Figure 2 shows the sum of scores in Task 1 from all subjects, grouped by writer. As for Task 2, Figure 3 shows the average score across subjects, grouped by writers. In both tasks, we can see that higher scores are obtained after using templates, indicating that emotion templates can indeed assist writers in creating stronger emotional resonance in their composition.

To sum up, results show that PBA can generate emotion templates that not only help machines predict reader's emotion, but also effectively aid writers in creating a stronger emotional resonance with the readers.

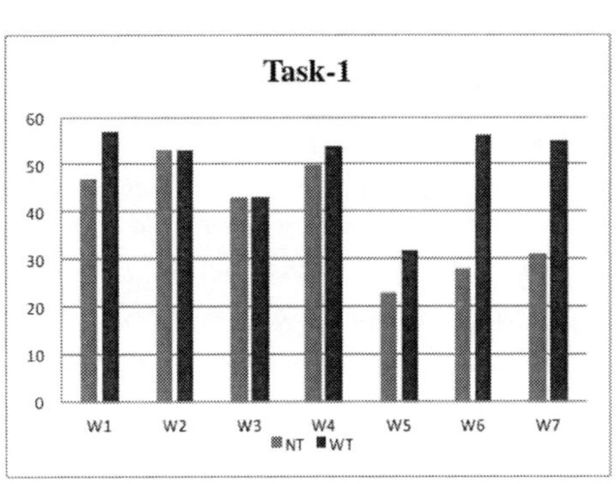

Figure 2: Comparison of the number of correct emotional response before and after utilizing templates.

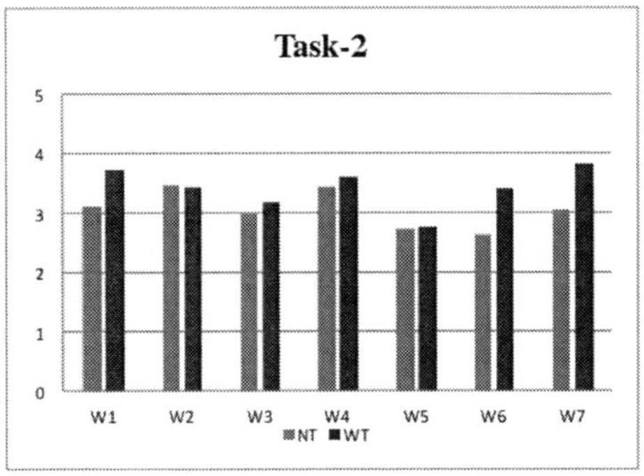

Figure 3: Degree of emotional resonance between writers and readers.

5 Conclusion

In this paper, we present PBA, a flexible, highly automated, and human-interpretable approach for reader-emotion classification. By capturing prominent and representative patterns in texts, PBA can effectively recognize the reader-emotion. Results demonstrate that PBA outperforms other reader-emotion detection methods, and can assist writers in creating higher emotional resonance. In the future, we plan to further refine and employ it to other NLP applications. Also, additional work can be done on combining statistical models into different components of PBA.

Acknowledgments

We are grateful to the anonymous reviewers for their insightful comments. This research was supported by the Ministry of Science and Technology of Taiwan under grant MOST 103-3111-Y-001-027, 103-2221-E-002-106-MY2, and NSC102-3113-P-001-006.

References

Omar Mabrook A Bashaddadh and Masnizah Mohd. 2011. Topic detection and tracking interface with named entities approach. In *Proceedings of the International Conference on Semantic Technology and Information Retrieval (STAIR)*, pages 215–219.

David M Blei, Andrew Y Ng, and Michael I Jordan. 2003. Latent Dirichlet allocation. *Journal of Machine Learning Research*, 3:993–1022.

Keh-Jiann Chen, Shu-Ling Huang, Yueh-Yin Shih, and Yi-Jun Chen. 2005. Extended-HowNet - a representational framework for concepts. In *Proceedings of OntoLex 2005 - Ontologies and Lexical Resources IJCNLP-05 Workshop*.

Ying Chen, Sophia Yat Mei Lee, Shoushan Li, and Chu-Ren Huang. 2010. Emotion cause detection with linguistic constructions. In *Proceedings of the 23rd International Conference on Computational Linguistics*, pages 179–187.

Dipankar Das and Sivaji Bandyopadhyay. 2009. Word to sentence level emotion tagging for bengali blogs. In *Proceedings of the ACL-IJCNLP 2009 Conference*, pages 149–152.

David S. Johnson. 1974. Approximation algorithms for combinatorial problems. *Journal of Computer and System Sciences*, 9(3):256 – 278.

Rensis Likert. 1932. A technique for the measurement of attitudes. *Archives of Psychology*, 140:1–55.

Kevin Hsin-Yih Lin, Changhua Yang, and Hsin-Hsi Chen. 2007. What emotions do news articles trigger in their readers? In *Proceedings of the 30th Annual International ACM SIGIR Conference on Research and Development in Information Retrieval*, pages 733–734.

Kevin Hsin-Yih Lin, Changhua Yang, and Hsin-Hsi Chen. 2008. Emotion classification of online news articles from the reader's perspective. In *Proceedings of the 2008 IEEE/WIC/ACM International Conference on Web Intelligence and Intelligent Agent Technology*, volume 1, pages 220–226.

Christopher D Manning and Hinrich Schütze. 1999. *Foundations of statistical natural language processing*. MIT press.

Andrew McCallum, Kamal Nigam, et al. 1998. A comparison of event models for naive bayes text classification. In *AAAI-98 workshop on learning for text categorization*, volume 752, pages 41–48.

Saul B Needleman and Christian D Wunsch. 1970. A general method applicable to the search for similarities in the amino acid sequence of two proteins. *Journal of Molecular Biology*, 48(3):443–453.

Matthew Purver and Stuart Battersby. 2012. Experimenting with distant supervision for emotion classification. In *Proceedings of the 13th Conference of the European Chapter of the Association for Computational Linguistics*, pages 482–491.

Changqin Quan and Fuji Ren. 2009. Construction of a blog emotion corpus for chinese emotional expression analysis. In *Proceedings of the 2009 Conference on Empirical Methods in Natural Language Processing*, volume 3, pages 1446–1454.

Yi-jie Tang and Hsin-Hsi Chen. 2012. Mining sentiment words from microblogs for predicting writer-reader emotion transition. In *Proceedings of the 8th International Conference on Language Resources and Evaluation (LREC)*, pages 1226–1229.

Peter D Turney. 2002. Thumbs up or thumbs down?: semantic orientation applied to unsupervised classification of reviews. In *Proceedings of the 40th Annual Meeting of the Association for Computational Linguistics*, pages 417–424.

Theresa Wilson, Janyce Wiebe, and Paul Hoffmann. 2009. Recognizing contextual polarity: An exploration of features for phrase-level sentiment analysis. *Computational Linguistics*, 35(3):399–433.

Feng Zou, Fu Lee Wang, Xiaotie Deng, Song Han, and Lu Sheng Wang. 2006. Automatic construction of chinese stop word list. In *Proceedings of the 5th WSEAS International Conference on Applied Computer Science*, pages 1010–1015.

Aspect-Level Cross-lingual Sentiment Classification with Constrained SMT

Patrik Lambert
Universitat Pompeu Fabra, Barcelona, Spain
patrik.lambert@upf.edu

Abstract

Most cross-lingual sentiment classification (CLSC) research so far has been performed at sentence or document level. Aspect-level CLSC, which is more appropriate for many applications, presents the additional difficulty that we consider sub-sentential opinionated units which have to be mapped across languages. In this paper, we extend the possible cross-lingual sentiment analysis settings to aspect-level specific use cases. We propose a method, based on constrained SMT, to transfer opinionated units across languages by preserving their boundaries. We show that cross-language sentiment classifiers built with this method achieve comparable results to monolingual ones, and we compare different cross-lingual settings.

1 Introduction

Sentiment analysis (SA) is the task of analysing opinions, sentiments or emotions expressed towards entities such as products, services, organisations, issues, and the various attributes of these entities (Liu, 2012). The analysis may be performed at the level of a document (blog post, review) or sentence. However, this is not appropriate for many applications because the same document or sentence can contain positive opinions towards specific aspects and negative ones towards other aspects. Thus a finer analysis can be conducted at the level of the aspects of the entities towards which opinions are expressed, identifying for each opinionated unit elements such as its target, polarity and the polar words used to qualify the target.

The two main SA approaches presented in the literature are (i) a machine learning approach, mostly supervised learning with features such as opinion words, dependency information, opinion shifters and quantifiers and (ii) a lexicon-based approach, based on rules involving opinion words and phrases, opinion shifters, contrary clauses (but), etc. Thus in most SA systems we may distinguish three types of resources and text:

TRAIN Resources (collection of training examples, lexicons) used to train the classifier.

TEST Opinions to be analysed.

OUT Outcome of the analysis. It depends on the level of granularity. At the document or sentence level, it is the polarity of each document or sentence. At the aspect level, it may the set of opinion targets with their polarity.

The internet multilingualism and the globalisation of products and services create situations in which these three types of resources are not all in the same language. In these situations, a language transfer is needed at some point to perform the SA analysis or to understand its results, thus called cross-lingual sentiment analysis (CLSA).

Sentences or documents are handy granularity levels for CLSA because the labels are not related to specific tokens and thus are not affected by a language transfer. At the aspect level, labels are attached to a specific opinionated unit formed by a sequence of tokens. When transferring these annotations into another language, the opinionated units in the two languages have thus to be mapped.

This paper is one of the first ones to address CLSA *at aspect level* (see Section 3). It makes the following specific contributions:

(i) an extended definition of CLSA including use cases and settings specific to aspect-level analyses (Section 2);

(ii) a method to perform the language transfer preserving the opinionated unit boundaries. This avoids the need of mapping source and target opinionated units after the language transfer via methods such as word alignment (Section 4);

Proceedings of the 53rd Annual Meeting of the Association for Computational Linguistics and the 7th International Joint Conference on Natural Language Processing (Short Papers), pages 781–787,
Beijing, China, July 26-31, 2015.

The paper also reports (in Section 5) experiments comparing different settings described in Section 2.

2 Use Cases and Settings

We can think of the following use cases for CLSA:

Use case I. There are opinions we want to analyse, but we do not avail of a SA system to perform this analysis. We thus want to predict the polarity of opinions expressed in a language L_{TEST} using a classifier in another language L_{TRAIN}. We can assume that the language L_{OUT} of the analysis outcome[1] is the same as the one of the opinions. In this case, equation 1 applies, yielding CLSA settings a and b as follows (see also Figure 1).

$$L_{TRAIN} \neq L_{TEST}; L_{OUT} = L_{TEST} \quad (1)$$

(a) available training resources are transferred into the test language to build a classifier in the test language.

(b) we translate the test into the language of the classifier, classify the opinions in the test, and then transfer back the analysis outcome into the source language by projecting the labels or/and opinionated units onto the test set.

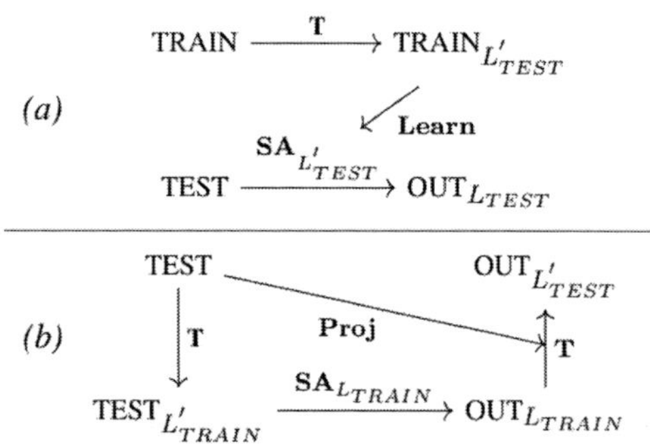

Figure 1: Use case I settings. $\mathbf{SA}$ refers to Sentiment Analisys, $\mathbf{T}$ to Translation, $\mathbf{Proj}$ to Projection and $\mathbf{Learn}$ to Learning, and the prime symbol designs a language into which a set has been automatically translated.

Use case II. We may have training resources in the language of the opinions, but we need the result of the analysis in a different language. Here, the inequality of Eq. 2 applies, yielding CLSA settings c and d as follows (see also Figure 2).

$$L_{OUT} \neq L_{TEST} \quad (2)$$

(c) $L_{TRAIN} = L_{TEST}$; the test opinions are first analysed in their language, then the analysis outcome is transferred into the desired language.

(d) $L_{TRAIN} = L_{OUT}$; the test set is first transferred into the desired outcome language, and the SA is performed in this language.

$$(c) \quad \text{TEST} \xrightarrow{\mathbf{SA}_{L_{TEST}}} \text{OUT}_{L_{TEST}} \xrightarrow{\mathbf{T}} \text{OUT}_{L'_{OUT}}$$

$$(d) \quad \text{TEST} \xrightarrow{\mathbf{T}} \text{TEST}_{L'_{OUT}} \xrightarrow{\mathbf{SA}_{L_{OUT}}} \text{OUT}$$

Figure 2: Use case II settings.

Use case II only makes sense for aspect-level analysis,[2] and to our knowledge, it was not addressed in the literature so far.

Use case III. We want to benefit from data available in several languages, either to have more examples and improve the classifier accuracy, or to have a broader view of the opinions under study.

In this paper we focus on use cases I and II.

3 Related Work

The main CLSC approaches described in the literature are via lexicon transfer, via corpus transfer, via test translation and via joint classification.

In the lexicon transfer approach, a source sentiment lexicon is transferred into the target language and a lexicon-based classifier is build in the target language. Approaches to transfer lexica include machine translation (MT) (Mihalcea et al., 2007), Wordnet (Banea et al., 2011; Hassan et al., 2011; Perez-Rosas et al., 2012), relations between dictionaries represented in graphs (Scheible et al., 2010), or triangulation (Steinberger et al., 2012).

The corpus transfer approach consists of transferring a source training corpus into the target language and building a corpus-based classifier in the target language. Banea et al. (2008) follow this approach, translating an annotated corpus via MT. Balamurali et al. (2012) use linked Wordnets to

[1] As mentioned above, at the aspect level, the outcome of the analysis may be a set of opinion targets with their polarity. It may also be more complex, such as a set of opinion expressions with their respective target, polarity, holder and time (Liu, 2012). The outcome may need to be in another language as the opinions themselves. For example, a company based in China may survey the opinions of their Spanish-speaking customers, and then transfer the SA outcome into Chinese so that their marketing department can understand it.

[2] For document and sentence-level classification, the outcome is a set of polarity labels independent on language.

replace words in training and test corpora by their (language-independent) synset identifiers. Gui et al. (2014) reduce negative transfer in the process of transfer learning. Popat et al. (2013) perform CLSA with clusters as features, bridging target and source language clusters with word alignment.

In the test translation approach, test sentences from the target language are translated into the source language and they are classified using a source language classifier (Bautin et al., 2008).

Work on joint classification includes training a classifier with features from multilingual views (Banea et al., 2010; Xiao and Guo, 2012), co-training (Wan, 2009; Demirtas and Pechenizkiy, 2013), joint learning (Lu et al., 2011), structural correspondence learning (Wei and Pal, 2010; Prettenhofer and Stein, 2010) or mixture models (Meng et al., 2012). Gui et al. (2013) compare several of these approaches.

Brooke et al. (2009) and Balamurali et al. (2013) conclude that at document level, it is cheaper to annotate resources in the target language than building CLSA systems. This may not be true at aspect level, in which the annotation cost is much higher. In any case, when the skills to build such annotated resources are lacking, CLSA may be the only option. In language pairs in which no high-quality MT systems are available, MT may not be an appropriate transfer method (Popat et al., 2013; Balamurali et al., 2012). However, Balahur and Turchi (2014) conclude that MT systems can be used to build sentiment analysis systems that can obtain comparable performances to the one obtained for English.

All this work was performed at sentence or document level. Zhou et al. (2012) and Lin et al. (2014) work at the aspect level, but they focus on cross-lingual aspect extraction. Haas and Versley (2015) use CLSA for individual syntactic nodes, however they need to map target-language and source-language nodes with word alignment.

4 Language Transfer

In aspect-level SA, there may be several opinionated segments in each sentence. When performing a language transfer, each segment in the target language has to be mapped to its corresponding segment in the source language. This may not be an obvious task at all. For example, if a standard MT system is used for language translation, the source opinionated segment may be reordered and split in several parts in the target language. Then the different parts have to be mapped to the original segment with a method such as word alignment, which may introduce errors and may leave some parts without a corresponding segment in the source language. To avoid these problems, we could translate only the opinionated segments, independently of each other. However, the context of these segments, which may be useful for some applications, would then be lost. Furthermore, the translation quality would be worse than when the segments are translated within the whole sentence context.

To solve these problems, we translate the whole sentences but with reordering constraints ensuring that the opinionated segments are preserved during translation. That is, the text between the relevant segment boundaries is not reordered nor mixed with the text outside these boundaries.[3] Thus the text in the target language segment comes only from the corresponding source language segment. We use the Moses statistical MT (SMT) toolkit (Koehn et al., 2007) to perform the translation. In Moses, these reordering constraints are implemented with the `zone` and `wall` tags, as indicated in Figure 3. Moses also allows mark-up to be directly passed to the translation, via the `x` tag. We use this functionality to keep track, via the tags `<ou[id][-label]>` and `</ou[id]>`, of the segment boundaries (`ou` stands for Opinionated Unit), of the opinionated segment identifier (`[id]`) and, for training and evaluation purposes, of the polarity label (`[-label]`). In the example of Figure 3, the id is 1 and the label is P.

5 CLSA experiments

In order to compare CLSA settings *a* and *b* (of use case I), we needed data with opinion annotations at the aspect level, in two different languages and in the same domain. We used the OpeNER[4] opinion corpus,[5] and more specifically the opinion expression and polarity label annotations of the hotel review component, in Spanish and English. We split the data in training (train) and evaluation (test) sets as indicated in Table 1.

The SMT system was trained on freely avail-

[3]However, reordering within the segment text is allowed.

[4]http://www.opener-project.eu/

[5]Described in deliverable D5.42 (page 6) at: http://www.opener-project.eu/project/publications.html. This corpus will be freely available from June 2016 on, and until then can be used for research purposes.

Source: On the other hand `<zone> <x translation="oul-P">x</x> <wall/>` a big advantage `<wall/> <x translation="/oul">x</x> </zone>` of the hostel is its placement
Translation: por otra parte `<oul-P>`una gran ventaja`</oul>` del hostal es su colocación

Figure 3: Source text with reordering constraint mark-up as well as code to pass tags, and its translation.

	Lang	Docs	Words	Op. Units
Train	EN	346	32149	3643
	ES	359	31511	3905
Test	EN	49	4256	496
	ES	50	3733	484

Table 1: Number of documents (Docs), words and opinionated units (Op. Units) in the OpeNER annotated data for English (EN) and Spanish (ES).

able data from the 2013 workshop on Statistical Machine Translation[6] (WMT 2013). We also crawled monolingual data in the hotel booking domain, from booking.com and TripAdvisor.com. From these in-domain data we extracted 100k and 50k word corpora, respectively for data selection and language model (LM) interpolation tuning. We selected the data closest to the domain in the English-Spanish parallel corpora via a cross-entropy-based method (Moore and Lewis, 2010), using the open source XenC tool (Rousseau, 2013). The size of available and selected corpora are indicated in the first 4 rows of Table 2. The LM was an interpolation of LMs trained with the target part of the parallel corpora and with the rest of the Booking and Trip Advisor data (last 2 rows of Table 2). We used Moses Experiment Management System (Koehn, 2010) with all default options to build the SMT system.[7]

Because the common crawl corpus contained English sentences in the Spanish side, we applied an LM-based filter to select only sentence pairs in which the Spanish side was better scored by the Spanish LM than with the English LM, and conversely for the English side.

We conducted supervised sentiment classification experiments for settings a and b of use case I (see Section 2). We trained and evaluated classifiers on the annotated data (Table 1), using as features the tokens (unigrams) within opinion expressions, and SP (Strong Positive), P (Positive), N (Negative) and SN (Strong Negative) as labels. We performed the experiments with the weka toolkit (Hall et al., 2009), using a filter to convert strings into word vectors, and two learning algorithms: SVMs and bagging with Fast Decision Tree Learner as base algorithm.

Figure 4 represents the experiments conducted with the EN test set. A monolingual classifier in English is trained with the EN training set, and evaluated with the EN test set (1 mono). The re-

[6] http://www.statmt.org/wmt13/translation-task.html

[7] We kept selected parallel data of the common crawl corpus for tuning and test. We obtained BLEU scores of 42 and 45 in the English–Spanish and Spanish–English directions.

	Available		Selected	
Corpus	EN	ES	EN	ES
Common Crawl	46.7	49.5	6.7	7.0
Europarl v7	54.6	57.1	1.7	1.7
News Commentary	4.5	5.1	4.5	5.1
UN	321.7	368.6	3.4	3.5
Booking	1.7	2.6	1.7	2.6
Trip Advisor	23.4	4.4	23.4	4.4

Table 2: Size of the available and selected corpora (in million words) in English (EN) and Spanish (ES) used to train the SMT system.

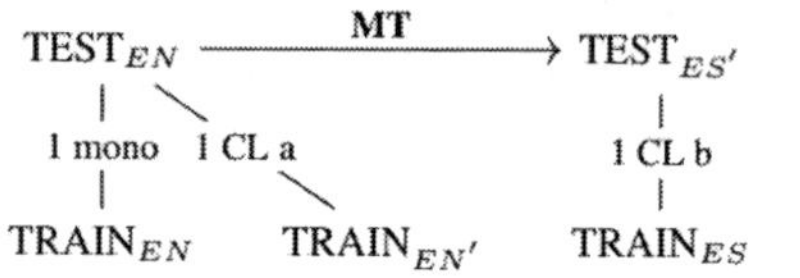

Figure 4: Experiments corresponding to group of rows 1 of Table 3. "mono" refers to monolingual and "CL a" and "CL b" refer to settings a and b of use case I (Sec. 2).

			LM Filter		No Fil
Config	Train	Test	Bag.	SVM	SVM
1 mono	EN	EN	77.2	83.4	83.4
1 CL a	EN′	EN	70.3	75.4	75.8
1 CL b	ES	ES′	73.0	75.8	73.6
2 mono	ES	ES	76.8	81.1	81.1
2 CL a	ES′	ES	66.2	72.5	73.0
2 CL b	EN	EN′	74.5	77.6	76.8

Table 3: Accuracy (in %) achieved by the different systems. LM Filter and No Fil(ter) refer to the presence or not of the LM filter for the common crawl parallel corpus. "Bag." refers to bagging.

sults are reported in the first row of Table 3. To evaluate cross-lingual setting a, the ES training set is translated into English (see Section 4), and an English classifier is trained on the translated data and evaluated on the EN test set (1 CL a). To evaluate setting b, the EN test set is translated into Spanish, and this translated test is used to evaluate a classifier trained on the ES training set (1 CL b). With this very simple classifier, we achieve up to 83.4% accuracy in the monolingual case. With cross-lingual settings, we loose from about 4% to 8% accuracy, and with the higher quality SMT system (LM filter), CL-b setting is slightly better than CL-a.

The same three experiments were conducted for the ES test set (last three rows of Table 3). We achieved an accuracy of 81.1% in the monolingual case. Here the CL-b setting achieved a clearly better accuracy than the CL-a setting (at least 5% more), and only from 2.3% to 3.5% below the monolingual one. Thus with the higher quality SMT system, it is always better to translate the test data (CL-b setting) than the training corpus.

Comparing the SVM classification accuracy in the "LM Filter" and "No Fil" columns, we can see the effect of introducing noise in the MT system. We observe that the results were more affected by the translation of the test (-2.2% and -0.8% accuracy) than the training set (+0.5% accuracy in both cases). This agrees with the intuition than errors in the test directly affect the results and thus may be more harmful than in the training set, where they may hardly affect the results if they represent infrequent examples.

Regarding use case II, setting c implies a translation of the analysis outcome. We can use our method to translate the relevant opinionated units with their predicted label in their test sentence context, and extract the relevant information in the outcome language. In setting d, the test is translated in the same way as in setting b.

6 Conclusions and Perspectives

We extended the possible CLSA settings to aspect-level specific use cases. We proposed a method, based on constrained SMT, to transfer opinionated units across languages by preserving their boundaries. With this method, we built cross-language sentiment classifiers achieving comparable results to monolingual ones (from about 4 to 8% and 2.3 to 3.5% loss in accuracy depending on the language and machine learning algorithm). We observed that improving the MT quality had more impact in settings using a translated test than a translated training corpus. With the higher MT quality system, we achieved better accuracy by translating the test than the training corpus.

As future work, we plan to investigate the exact effect of the reordering constraints in terms of possible translation model phrase pairs and target language model n-grams which may not be used depending on the constraint parameters, in order to find the best configuration.

Acknowledgements

This work has received funding from the Seventh Framework Program of the European Commission through the Intra-European Fellowship (CrossLingMind-2011-300828) Marie Curie Actions. We also acknowledge partners of the OpeNER project, in particular Montse Cuadros, for providing us with the aspect-level annotated data.

References

Alexandra Balahur and Marco Turchi. 2014. Comparative experiments using supervised learning and machine translation for multilingual sentiment analysis. *Computer Speech & Language*, 28(1):56–75.

A.R. Balamurali, Aditya Joshi, and Pushpak Bhattacharyya. 2012. Cross-lingual sentiment analysis for Indian languages using linked wordnets. In *Proc. of the International Conference on Computational Linguistics (COLING)*, pages 73–82, Mumbai, India.

A. R. Balamurali, Mitesh M Khapra, and Pushpak Battacharyya. 2013. Lost in Translation: Viability of Machine Translation for Cross Language Sentiment Analysis. In *Proc. of International Conference on Intelligent Text Processing and Computational Linguistics (CICLing)*, pages 38–49, Samos, Greece.

Carmen Banea, Rada Mihalcea, and Janyce Wiebe. 2008. A bootstrapping method for building subjectivity lexicons for languages with scarce resources. In *Proc. of the International Conference on Linguistic Resources and Evaluation (LREC)*, pages 2764–2767, Marrakech, Morocco, May.

Carmen Banea, Rada Mihalcea, and Janyce Wiebe. 2010. Multilingual subjectivity: Are more languages better? In *Proc. of the International Conference on Computational Linguistics (COLING)*, pages 28–36, Beijing, China.

Carmen Banea, Rada Mihalcea, and Janyce Wiebe. 2011. Multilingual sentiment and subjectivity analysis. In D. M. Bikel and I. Zitouni, editors, *Multilingual Natural Language Applications: From Theory to Practice*. Prentice-Hall.

Mikhail Bautin, Lohit Vijayarenu, and Steven Skiena. 2008. International sentiment analysis for news and blogs. In *Proc. of the International Conference on Weblogs and Social Media*, pages 19–26, Seattle, U.S.A.

Julian Brooke, Milan Tofiloski, and Maite Taboada. 2009. Cross-Linguistic Sentiment Analysis: From English to Spanish. In *Proc. of the International Conference on Recent Advances in Natural Language Processing (RANLP)*, pages 50–54, Borovets, Bulgaria.

Erkin Demirtas and Mykola Pechenizkiy. 2013. Cross-lingual Polarity Detection with Machine Translation. In *Proc. of the International Workshop on Issues of Sentiment Discovery and Opinion Mining - WISDOM '13*, pages 9:1–9:8, Chicago, Illinois, USA. ACM Press.

Lin Gui, Ruifeng Xu, Jun Xu, Li Yuan, Yuanlin Yao, Jiyun Zhou, Qiaoyun Qiu, Shuwei Wang, Kam-fai Wong, and Ricky Cheung. 2013. A Mixed Model for Cross Lingual Opinion Analysis. In *Second CCF Conference, Natural Language Processing and Chinese Computing*, pages 93–104.

Lin Gui, Ruifeng Xu, Qin Lu, Jun Xu, Jian Xu, Bin Liu, and Xiaolong Wang. 2014. Cross-lingual opinion analysis via negative transfer detection. In *Proc. of the Annual Meeting of the Association for Computational Linguistics*, pages 860–865, Baltimore, Maryland.

Michael Haas and Yannick Versley. 2015. Subsentential sentiment on a shoestring: A crosslingual analysis of compositional classification. In *Proc. of the North American Chapter of the Association for Computational Linguistics: Human Language Technologies*, pages 694–704, Denver, Colorado.

Mark Hall, Eibe Frank, Geoffrey Holmes, Bernhard Pfahringer, Peter Reutemann, and Ian H. Witten. 2009. The weka data mining software: An update. *SIGKDD Explorations*, 11(1).

Ahmed Hassan, Amjad AbuJbara, Rahul Jha, and Dragomir Radev. 2011. Identifying the semantic orientation of foreign words. In *Proc. of the Annual Meeting of the Association for Computational Linguistics: Human Language Technologies*, pages 592–597, Portland, Oregon, USA, June.

Philipp Koehn, Hieu Hoang, Alexandra Birch, Chris Callison-Burch, Marcello Federico, Nicola Bertoldi, Brooke Cowan, Wade Shen, Christine Moran, Richard Zens, Chris Dyer, Ondrej Bojar, Alexandra Constantin, and Evan Herbst. 2007. Moses: Open source toolkit for statistical machine translation. In *Proc. of the 45th Annual Meeting of the Association for Computational Linguistics (Demo and Poster Sessions)*, pages 177–180, Prague, Czech Republic, June. Association for Computational Linguistics.

Philipp Koehn. 2010. An experimental management system. *Prague Bulletin of Mathematical Linguistics (PBML)*, (94):87–96.

Zheng Lin, Xiaolong Jin, Xueke Xu, Yuanzhuo Wang, Weiping Wang, and Xueqi Cheng. 2014. A cross-lingual joint aspect/sentiment model for sentiment analysis. In *Proc. of the ACM International Conference on Conference on Information and Knowledge Management*, CIKM '14, pages 1089–1098, Shanghai, China.

Bing Liu. 2012. *Sentiment Analysis and Opinion Mining*. Synthesis Lectures on Human Language Technologies. Morgan & Claypool Publishers.

Bin Lu, Chenhao Tan, Claire Cardie, and Benjamin K. Tsou. 2011. Joint bilingual sentiment classification with unlabeled parallel corpora. In *Proc. of the Annual Meeting of the Association for Computational Linguistics: Human Language Technologies*, pages 320–330, Portland, Oregon, USA.

Xinfan Meng, Furu Wei, Xiaohua Liu, Ming Zhou, Ge Xu, and Houfeng Wang. 2012. Cross-lingual mixture model for sentiment classification. In *Proc. of the Annual Meeting of the Association for Computational Linguistics*, pages 572–581, Jeju Island, Korea.

Rada Mihalcea, Carmen Banea, and Janyce Wiebe. 2007. Learning multilingual subjective language via cross-lingual projections. In *Proc. of the Annual Meeting of the Association for Computational Linguistics*, pages 976–983, Prague, Czech Republic, June.

Robert C. Moore and William Lewis. 2010. Intelligent selection of language model training data. In *Proceedings of the ACL 2010 Conference Short Papers*, pages 220–224, Uppsala, Sweden.

Veronica Perez-Rosas, Carmen Banea, and Rada Mihalcea. 2012. Learning sentiment lexicons in spanish. In *Proc. of the International Conference on Linguistic Resources and Evaluation (LREC)*, pages 3077–3081, Istanbul, Turkey, may.

Kashyap Popat, Balamurali A.R, Pushpak Bhattacharyya, and Gholamreza Haffari. 2013. The haves and the have-nots: Leveraging unlabelled corpora for sentiment analysis. In *Proc. of the Annual Meeting of the Association for Computational Linguistics*, pages 412–422, Sofia, Bulgaria.

Peter Prettenhofer and Benno Stein. 2010. Cross-language text classification using structural correspondence learning. In *Proc. of the Annual Meeting of the Association for Computational Linguistics*, pages 1118–1127, Uppsala, Sweden. Association for Computational Linguistics.

A Rousseau. 2013. XenC: An Open-Source Tool for Data Selection in Natural Language Processing. *Prague Bulletin of Mathematical Linguistics (PBML)*, (100):73–82.

Christian Scheible, Florian Laws, Lukas Michelbacher, and Hinrich Schütze. 2010. Sentiment translation through multi-edge graphs. In *Proc. of the International Conference on Computational Linguistics (COLING)*, pages 1104–1112, Beijing, China, August.

Josef Steinberger, Mohamed Ebrahim, Maud Ehrmann, Ali Hurriyetoglu, Mijail Kabadjov, Polina Lenkova, Ralf Steinberger, Hristo Tanev, Silvia Vázquez, and Vanni Zavarella. 2012. Creating sentiment dictionaries via triangulation. *Decision Support Systems*, 53(4):689 - 694.

Xiaojun Wan. 2009. Co-training for cross-lingual sentiment classification. In *Proceedings of the Joint Conference of the 47th Annual Meeting of the ACL and the 4th International Joint Conference on Natural Language Processing of the AFNLP*, pages 235–243, Suntec, Singapore.

Bin Wei and Christopher Pal. 2010. Cross lingual adaptation: An experiment on sentiment classifications. In *Proc. of the ACL 2010 Conference Short Papers*, pages 258–262, Uppsala, Sweden. Proc. of the Annual Meeting of the Association for Computational Linguistics.

Min Xiao and Yuhong Guo. 2012. Multi-view adaboost for multilingual subjectivity analysis. In *Proc. of the International Conference on Computational Linguistics (COLING)*, pages 2851–2866, Mumbai, India.

Xinjie Zhou, Xiaojun Wan, and Jianguo Xiao. 2012. Cross-Language Opinion Target Extraction in Review Texts. In *IEEE 12th International Conference on Data Mining*, pages 1200–1205, Brussels, Belgium.

Predicting Valence-Arousal Ratings of Words Using a Weighted Graph Method

Liang-Chih Yu[1,3], Jin Wang[2,3,4], K. Robert Lai[2,3] and Xue-jie Zhang[4]
[1]Department of Information Management, Yuan Ze University, Taiwan
[2]Department of Computer Science & Engineering, Yuan Ze University, Taiwan
[3]Innovation Center for Big Data and Digital Convergence Yuan Ze University, Taiwan
[4]School of Information Science and Engineering, Yunnan University, Yunnan, P.R. China
Contact: lcyu@saturn.yzu.edu.tw

Abstract

Compared to the categorical approach that represents affective states as several discrete classes (e.g., positive and negative), the dimensional approach represents affective states as continuous numerical values on multiple dimensions, such as the valence-arousal (VA) space, thus allowing for more fine-grained sentiment analysis. In building dimensional sentiment applications, affective lexicons with valence-arousal ratings are useful resources but are still very rare. Therefore, this study proposes a weighted graph model that considers both the relations of multiple nodes and their similarities as weights to automatically determine the VA ratings of affective words. Experiments on both English and Chinese affective lexicons show that the proposed method yielded a smaller error rate on VA prediction than the linear regression, kernel method, and pagerank algorithm used in previous studies.

1 Introduction

Thanks to the vigorous development of online social network services, anyone can now easily publish and disseminate articles expressing their thoughts and opinions. Sentiment analysis thus has become a useful technique to automatically identify affective information from texts (Pang and Lee, 2008; Calvo and D'Mello, 2010; Liu, 2012; Feldman, 2013). In sentiment analysis, representation of affective states is an essential issue and can be generally divided into categorical and dimensional approaches.

The categorical approach represents affective states as several discrete classes such as binary (positive and negative) and Ekman's six basic emotions (e.g., anger, happiness, fear, sadness, disgust and surprise) (Ekman, 1992). Based on this representation, various techniques have been investigated to develop useful applications such as deceptive opinion spam detection (Li et al., 2014), aspect extraction (Mukherjee and Liu, 2012), cross-lingual portability (Banea et al., 2013; Xu et al., 2015), personalized sentiment analysis (Ren and Wu, 2013; Yu et al., 2009) and viewpoint identification (Qiu and Jiang, 2013). In addition to identifying sentiment classes, an extension has been made to further determine their sentiment strength in terms of a multi-point scale (Taboada et al., 2011; Li et al., 2011; Yu et al., 2013; Wang and Ester, 2014).

The dimensional approach has drawn considerable attention in recent years as it can provide a more fine-grained sentiment analysis. It represents affective states as continuous numerical values on multiple dimensions, such as valence-arousal (VA) space (Russell, 1980), as shown in Figure 1. The valence represents the degree of pleasant and unpleasant (or positive and negative) feelings, and the arousal represents the degree of excitement and calm. Based on such a two-dimensional representation, a common research goal is to determine the degrees of valence and arousal of given texts such that any affective state can be represented as a point in the VA coordinate plane. To accomplish this goal, affective lexicons with valence-arousal ratings are useful resources but few exist. Most existing applications rely on a handcrafted lexicon ANEW (Af-

Proceedings of the 53rd Annual Meeting of the Association for Computational Linguistics and the 7th International Joint Conference on Natural Language Processing (Short Papers), pages 788–793,
Beijing, China, July 26-31, 2015.

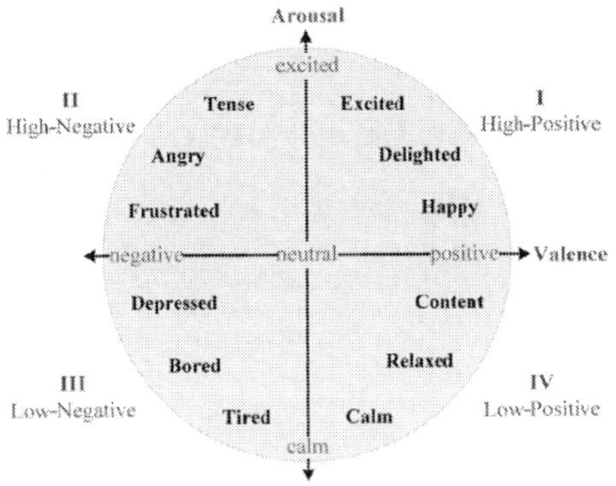

Figure 1. Two-dimensional valence-arousal space.

fective Norms for English Words) (Bradley, 1999) which provides 1,034 English words with ratings in the dimensions of pleasure, arousal and dominance to predict the VA ratings of short and long texts (Paltoglou et al, 2013; Kim et al., 2010). Accordingly, the automatic prediction of VA ratings of affective words is a critical task in building a VA lexicon.

Few studies have sought to predict the VA rating of words using regression-based methods (Wei et al., 2011; Malandrakis et al., 2011). This kind of method usually starts from a set of words with labeled VA ratings (called seeds). The VA rating of an unseen word is then estimated from semantically similar seeds. For instance, Wei et al. (2011) trained a linear regression model for each seed cluster, and then predicted the VA rating of an unseen word using the model of the cluster to which the unseen word belongs. Malandrakis et al. (2011) used a kernel function to combine the similarity between seeds and unseen words into a linear regression model. Instead of estimating VA ratings of words, another direction is to determine the polarity (i.e., positive and negative) of words by applying the label propagation (Rao and Ravichandran, 2009; Hassan et al., 2011) and pagerank (Esuli et al., 2007) on a graph. Based on these methods, the polarity of an unseen word can be determined/ranked through its neighbor nodes (seeds).

Although the pagerank algorithm has been used for polarity ranking, it can still be extended for VA prediction. Therefore, this study extends the idea of pagerank in two aspects. First, we implement pagerank for VA prediction by transforming ranking scores into VA ratings. Second, whereas pagerank assigns an equal weight to the edges connected between an unseen word and its neighbor nodes, we consider their similarities as weights to construct a weighted graph such that neighbor nodes more similar to the unseen word may contribute more to estimate its VA ratings. That is, the proposed weighted graph model considers both the relations of multiple nodes and the similarity weights among them. In experiments, we evaluate the performance of the proposed method against the linear regression, kernel method, and pagerank algorithm on both English and Chinese affective lexicons for VA prediction.

The rest of this paper is organized as follows. Section 2 describes the proposed weighted graph model. Section 3 summarizes the comparative results of different methods for VA prediction. Conclusions are finally drawn in Section 4.

2 Graph Model for VA Prediction

Based on the theory of link analysis, the relations between unseen words and seed words can be considered as a graph, as shown in Figure 2. The valence-arousal ratings of each unseen word can then be predicted through the links connected to the seed words to which it is similar using their similarities as weights. To measure the similarity between words (nodes), we use the word2vec toolkit (Mikolov et al., 2013) provided by Google (http://code.google.com/p/word2vec/).

The formal definition of a graph model is described as follows. Let $G=(V, E)$ be an undirected graph, where V denotes a set of words and E denotes a set of undirected edges. Each edge e in E denotes a relation between word v_i and word v_j in V ($1 \leq i, j \leq n, i \neq j$), representing the similarity between them. For each node v_i, $N(v_i)=\{v_j \mid (v_j, v_i) \in E\}$ denotes the set of its neighbor nodes, representing a set of words to which it is similar. The valence or arousal of v_i, denoted as val_{v_i} or aro_{v_i}, can then be determined by its neighbors, defined as

$$val_{v_i} = (1-\alpha) \cdot val_{v_i} + \alpha \frac{\sum_{v_j \in N(v_i)} Sim(v_i, v_j) \cdot val_{v_j}}{\sum_{v_j \in N(v_i)} Sim(v_i, v_j)}, \tag{1}$$

where α is a decay factor or a confidence level for computation (a constant between 0 and 1), which limits the effect of rank sinks to guarantee convergence to a unique vector. Initially, the valence (or arousal) of each unseen word is assigned to a random value that between 0 and 10. Later, it is iteratively updated using the following formula,

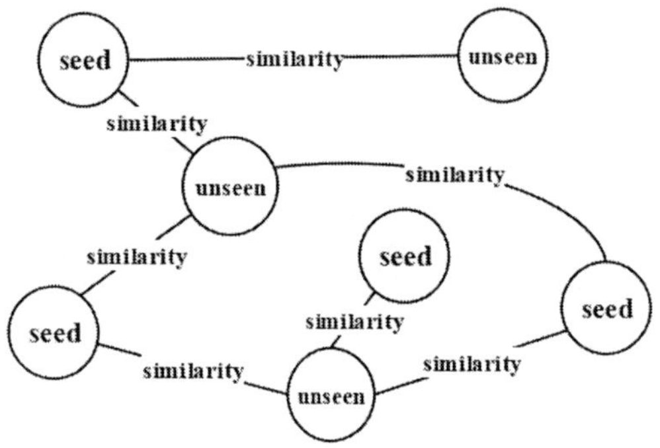

Figure 2. Conceptual diagram of a weighted graph model for VA prediction.

$$val_{v_i}^t = \begin{cases} RandomValue & (t=0) \\ (1-\alpha)\cdot val_{v_i}^{t-1} + \alpha \dfrac{\sum_{v_j \in N(v_i)} Sim(v_i, v_j)\cdot val_{v_j}^{t-1}}{\sum_{v_j \in N(v_i)} Sim(v_i, v_j)} & (t>0) \end{cases} \quad (2)$$

where t denotes the t-th iteration. It is worth noting that the valence (or arousal) of the seed words is a constant in each iterative step. Based on this, the valence (or arousal) of each unseen word is propagated through the graph in multiple iterations until convergence.

To improve the efficiency of the iterative computation, Eq. (2) can be transformed into a matrix notation. Suppose that the vectors,

$$\mathbf{V} = (val_{v_1}, val_{v_1}, \cdots, val_{v_N})^T,$$

$$\mathbf{A} = (aro_{v_1}, aro_{v_1}, \cdots, aro_{v_N})^T$$

are the vectors of the valence-arousal rating of all words (including seed words and unseen words). Matrix

$$\mathbf{S} = \begin{bmatrix} Sim(v_1, v_1) & \cdots & Sim(v_1, v_j) & \cdots & Sim(v_1, v_N) \\ \vdots & & \vdots & & \vdots \\ Sim(v_i, v_1) & \cdots & Sim(v_i, v_j) & \cdots & Sim(v_i, v_N) \\ \vdots & & \vdots & & \vdots \\ Sim(v_N, v_1) & \cdots & Sim(v_N, v_j) & \cdots & Sim(v_N, v_N) \end{bmatrix}$$

is the adjacency matrix of each words, where $Sim(v_i, v_j)$ represents the similarity between words i and j, where i, j=1, 2, ⋯, N, $i \neq j$.

Given two other vectors $\mathbf{I} = (1, 1, \cdots, 1)^T$ and $\mathbf{D} = (d_1, d_2, \cdots, d_N)^T$, where

$$d_i = \begin{cases} \alpha & if \;\; node_i \in \mathbf{cand} \\ 0 & if \;\; node_i \in \mathbf{seed} \end{cases},$$

α is the previously mentioned decay factor. For vectors $\mathbf{A} = (a_1, a_2, \cdots, a_N)^T$ and $\mathbf{B} = (b_1, b_2, \cdots, b_N)^T$, function $\mathcal{M}(\mathbf{A}, \mathbf{B})$ and $\mathcal{D}(\mathbf{A}, \mathbf{B})$ can be defined as

$$\mathcal{M}(\mathbf{A}, \mathbf{B}) = (a_1 \times b_1, a_2 \times b_2, \cdots, a_N \times b_N)^T,$$

$$\mathcal{D}(\mathbf{A}, \mathbf{B}) = (a_1 / b_1, a_2 / b_2, \cdots, a_N / b_N)^T.$$

Then, Eq. (2) can be turned into the following matrix format.

$$\mathbf{V}_t = \mathcal{M}[(\mathbf{I} - \mathbf{D})^T, \mathbf{V}_{t-1}] + \mathcal{M}[\mathbf{D}^T, \mathcal{D}(\mathbf{S}\mathbf{V}_{t-1}, \mathbf{S} \cdot \mathbf{I})],$$

$$\mathbf{A}_t = \mathcal{M}[(\mathbf{I} - \mathbf{D})^T, \mathbf{A}_{t-1}] + \mathcal{M}[\mathbf{D}^T, \mathcal{D}(\mathbf{S}\mathbf{A}_{t-1}, \mathbf{S} \cdot \mathbf{I})] \quad (3)$$

Through the transformation of matrix multiplication, the computation of VA prediction can converge within only a few iterations.

3 Experimental Results

Data. This experiment used two affective lexicons with VA ratings: 1) ANEW which contains 1,034 English affective words (Bradley, 1999) and 2) 162 Chinese affective words (CAW) taken from (Wei et al., 2011). Both lexicons were used for 5-fold cross-validation. That is, for each run, 80% of the words in the lexicons were considered as seeds and the remaining 20% were used as unseen words. The similarities between English words and between Chinese words were calculated using the word2vec toolkit trained with the respective English and Chinese wiki corpora (https://dumps.wikimedia.org/).

Implementation Details. Two regression-based methods were used for comparison: linear regression (Wei et al., 2011) and the kernel method (Malandrakis et al., 2011), along with two graph-based methods: pagerank (Esuli et al., 2007) and the proposed weighted graph model. For both regression-based methods, the similarities and VA ratings of the seed words were used for training, and the VA ratings of an unseen word were predicted by taking as input its similarity to the seeds. In addition, for the kernel method, the linear similarity function was chosen because it yielded top performance. Both graph-based methods used an iterative procedure for VA prediction and required no training. For pagerank, the iterative procedure was implemented using the algorithm presented in (Esuli et al., 2007), which estimates the VA ratings of an unseen word by assigning an equal weight to the edges connected to its neighbor seeds. For the proposed method, the iterative procedure was implemented by considering the word similarity as weights.

Valence	ANEW (English)			CAW (Chinese)		
	RMSE	MAE	MAPE(%)	RMSE	MAE	MAPE(%)
Weighted Graph	1.122	0.812	11.51	1.224	0.904	13.03
PageRank	1.540	1.085	15.69	1.642	1.187	16.84
Kernel	1.926	1.385	19.55	2.028	1.426	20.57
Linear Regression	1.832	1.301	18.61	1.935	1.393	19.66
Arousal	ANEW (English)			CAW (Chinese)		
	RMSE	MAE	MAPE(%)	RMSE	MAE	MAPE(%)
Weighted Graph	1.203	0.894	12.24	1.311	0.966	13.37
PageRank	1.627	1.149	16.48	1.735	1.238	17.51
Kernel	2.007	1.419	20.27	2.118	1.434	21.44
Linear Regression	1.912	1.382	19.33	2.020	1.421	20.46

Table 1. Comparative results of different methods in VA prediction.

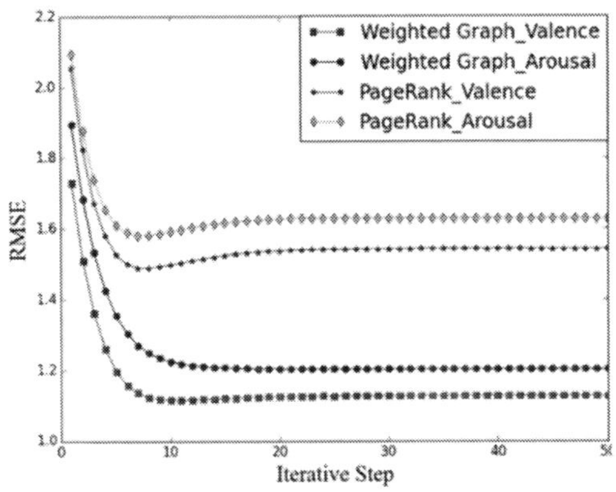

Figure 3. Iterative results of the pagerank algorithm and weighted graph model.

Evaluation Metrics. The prediction performance was evaluated by examining the difference between the predicted values of VA ratings and the corresponding actual values in the ANEW and CAW lexicons. The evaluation metrics included:

- *Root mean square error* (RMSE)

$$RMSE = \sqrt{\sum_{i=1}^{n} (A_i - P_i)^2 / n}$$

- *Mean absolute error* (MAE)

$$MAE = \frac{1}{n} \sum_{i=1}^{n} | A_i - P_i |,$$

- *Mean absolute percentage error* (MAPE)

$$MAPE = \frac{1}{n} \sum_{i=1}^{n} \frac{|A_i - P_i|}{A_i} \times 100\%$$

where A_i is the actual value, P_i is the predicted value, and n is the number of test samples. A lower MAPE, MAE or RMSE value indicates more accurate forecasting performance.

Iterative Results of the Graph-based Methods. Figure 3 uses RMSE as an example to show the iterative results of the pagerank and proposed methods. The results show that the performance of both methods stabilized after around 10 iterations, indicating its efficiency for VA prediction. Another observation is that the ultimate converging result of each word is unrelated to the decay factor and the initial random assignment.

Comparative Results. Table 1 compares the results of the regression-based methods (Linear Regression and Kernel) and graph-based methods (PageRank and Weighted Graph). The performance of PageRank and Weighted Graph was taken from results of the 50th iteration. The results show that both graph-based methods outperformed the regression-based methods for all metrics. For the graph-based methods, the proposed Weighted Graph yielded better MAPE performance than PageRank (around 4%), Kernel (around 8%) and Linear Regression (around 7%) on both the ANEW and CAW corpora. The weighted graph model achieved better performance because it predicted VA ratings by considering both the relations of multiple nodes and the weights between them. For the regression-based methods, both Linear Regression and Kernel achieved similar results. Another observation is that the arousal prediction error is greater than that for the valence prediction, indicating that the arousal dimension is more difficult to predict.

4 Conclusion

This study presents a weighted graph model to predict valence-arousal ratings of words which can be used for lexicon augmentation in the valence and arousal dimensions. Unlike the equal weight used in the traditional pagerank algorithm, the proposed method considers the similarities between words as weights such that the neighbor nodes more similar to the unseen word may contribute more to VA prediction. Experiments on both English and Chinese affective lexicons show that the proposed method yielded a smaller error rate than the pagerank, kernel and linear regression methods. Future work will focus on extending the VA prediction from the word-level to the sentence- and document-levels.

Acknowledgments

This work was supported by the Ministry of Science and Technology, Taiwan, ROC, under Grant No. NSC102-2221-E-155-029-MY3. The authors would like to thank the anonymous reviewers and the area chairs for their constructive comments.

Reference

Carmen Banea, Rada Mihalcea, and Janyce Wiebe. 2013. Porting multilingual subjectivity resources across languages. *IEEE Trans. Affective Computing*, 4(2):211-225.

Margaret M. Bradley and Peter J. Lang. 1999. Affective norms for English words (ANEW): Instruction manual and affective ratings. Technical Report C-1, The Center for Research in Psychophysiology, University of Florida.

Rafael A. Calvo and Sidney D'Mello. 2010. Affect detection: An interdisciplinary review of models, methods, and their applications. *IEEE Trans. Affective Computing*, 1(1): 18-37.

Paul Ekman. 1992. An argument for basic emotions. *Cognition and Emotion*, 6:169-200.

Andrea Esuli and Fabrizio Sebastiani. 2007. Pageranking wordnet synsets: An application to opinion mining. In *Proceedings of the 45th Annual Meeting of the Association for Computational Linguistics (ACL-07)*, pages 424-431.

Ronen Feldman. 2013. Techniques and applications for sentiment analysis. *Communications of the ACM*, 56(4):82-89.

Ahmed Hassan, Amjad Abu-Jbara, Rahul Jha, Dragomir Radev. 2011. Identifying the semantic orientation of foreign words. In *Proceedings of the 49th Annual Meeting of the Association for Computational Linguistics (ACL-11)*, pages 592-597.

Sunghwan Mac Kim, Alessandro Valitutti, and Rafael A. Calvo. 2010. Evaluation of unsupervised emotion models to textual affect recognition. In *Proc. of Workshop on Computational Approaches to Analysis and Generation of Emotion in Text*, pages 62-70.

Fangtao Li, Nathan Liu, Hongwei Jin, Kai Zhao, Qiang Yang, and Xiaoyan Zhu. 2011. Incorporating reviewer and product information for review rating prediction. In *Proceedings of the 22nd International Joint Conference on Artificial Intelligence (IJCAI-11)*, pages 1820-1825.

Jiwei Li, Myle Ott, Claire Cardie, and Eduard Hovy. 2014. Towards a general rule for identifying deceptive opinion spam. In *Proceedings of the 52nd Annual Meeting of the Association for Computational Linguistics (ACL-14)*, pages 1566-1576.

Bing Liu. 2012. Sentiment Analysis and Opinion Mining. Morgan & Claypool, Chicago, IL.

Nikos Malandrakis, Alexandros Potamianos, Iosif Elias, and Shrikanth Narayanan. 2011. Kernel models for affective lexicon creation. In *Proceedings of the 12th Annual Conference of the International Speech Communication Association (Interspeech-11)*, pages 2977-2980.

Tomas Mikolov, Ilya Sutskever, Kai Chen, Greg Corrado, and Jeffrey Dean. 2013. Distributed representations of words and phrases and their compositionality. In *Advances in Neural Information Processing Systems 26 (NIPS-13)*, pages 3111-3119.

Arjun Mukherjee and Bing Liu. 2012. Aspect extraction through semi-supervised modeling. In *Proceedings of the 50th Annual Meeting of the Association for Computational Linguistics (ACL-12)*, pages 339-348.

Georgios Paltoglou, Mathias Theunis, Arvid Kappas, and Mike Thelwall. 2013. Predicting emotional responses to long informal text. *IEEE Trans. Affective Computing*, 4(1):106-115.

Bo Pang and Lillian Lee. 2008. Opinion mining and sentiment analysis. *Foundations and trends in information retrieval*, 2(1-2):1-135.

Minghui Qiu and Jing Jiang. 2013. A latent variable model for viewpoint discovery from threaded forum posts. In *Proceedings of the 2013 Conference of the North American Chapter of the Association for Computational Linguistics: Human Language Technologies (NAACL/HLT-13)*, pages 1031-1040.

Delip Rao and Deepak Ravichandran. 2009. Semi-supervised polarity lexicon induction. In *Proceedings of the 12th Conference of the European Chapter of the Association for Computational Linguistics (EACL-09)*, pages 675–682.

Fuji Ren and Ye Wu. 2013. Predicting user-topic opinions in Twitter with social and topical context. *IEEE Trans. Affective Computing*, 4(4):412-424.

James A. Russell. 1980. A circumplex model of affect. *Journal of personality and social psychology*, 39(6):1161.

Maite Taboada, Julian Brooke, Milan Tofiloski, Kimberly Voll, and Manfred Stede. 2011. Lexicon-based methods for sentiment analysis. *Computational Linguistics*, 37(2):267-307.

Hao Wang and Martin Ester. 2014. A sentiment-aligned topic model for product aspect rating prediction. In *Proceedings of the 2014 Conference on Empirical Methods in Natural Language Processing (EMNLP-14)*, pages 1192-1202.

Wen-Li Wei, Chung-Hsien Wu, and Jen-Chun Lin. 2011. A regression approach to affective rating of Chinese words from ANEW. In *Proc. of Affective Computing and Intelligent Interaction (ACII-11)*, pages 121-131.

Ruifeng Xu, Lin Gui, Jun Xu, Qin Lu, and Kam-Fai Wong. 2015. Cross lingual opinion holder extraction based on multi-kernel SVMs and transfer learning. *World Wide Web*, 18:299-316.

Liang-Chih Yu, Chung-Hsien Wu, and Fong-Lin Jang. 2009. Psychiatric document retrieval using a discourse-aware model. *Artificial Intelligence*, 173(7-8): 817-829.

Liang-Chih Yu, Jheng-Long Wu, Pei-Chann Chang, and Hsuan-Shou Chu. 2013. Using a contextual entropy model to expand emotion words and their intensity for the sentiment classification of stock market news. *Knowledge-based Systems*. 41:89-97.

Multi-domain Dialog State Tracking using Recurrent Neural Networks

Nikola Mrkšić[1,2], Diarmuid Ó Séaghdha[2], Blaise Thomson[2], Milica Gašić[1]
Pei-Hao Su[1], David Vandyke[1], Tsung-Hsien Wen[1] and Steve Young[1]
[1] Department of Engineering, University of Cambridge, UK
[2] VocalIQ Ltd. , Cambridge, UK
{nm480,mg436,phs26,djv27,thw28,sjy}@cam.ac.uk {diarmuid, blaise}@vocaliq.com

Abstract

Dialog state tracking is a key component of many modern dialog systems, most of which are designed with a single, well-defined domain in mind. This paper shows that dialog data drawn from different dialog domains can be used to train a general belief tracking model which can operate across all of these domains, exhibiting superior performance to each of the domain-specific models. We propose a training procedure which uses out-of-domain data to initialise belief tracking models for entirely new domains. This procedure leads to improvements in belief tracking performance regardless of the amount of in-domain data available for training the model.

1 Introduction

Spoken dialog systems allow users to interact with computer applications through a conversational interface. Modern dialog systems are typically designed with a well-defined domain in mind, e.g., restaurant search, travel reservations or shopping for a new laptop. The goal of building open-domain dialog systems capable of conversing about any topic remains far off. In this work, we move towards this goal by showing how to build *dialog state tracking models* which can operate across entirely different domains. The state tracking component of a dialog system is responsible for interpreting the users' utterances and thus updating the system's *belief state*: a probability distribution over all possible states of the dialog. This belief state is used by the system to decide what to do next.

Recurrent Neural Networks (RNNs) are well suited to dialog state tracking, as their ability to capture contextual information allows them to model and label complex dynamic sequences (Graves, 2012). In recent shared tasks, approaches based on these models have shown competitive performance (Henderson et al., 2014d; Henderson et al., 2014c). This approach is particularly well suited to our goal of building open-domain dialog systems, as it does not require handcrafted domain-specific resources for semantic interpretation.

We propose a method for training multi-domain RNN dialog state tracking models. Our hierarchical training procedure first uses all the data available to train a very general belief tracking model. This model learns the most frequent and general dialog features present across the various domains. The general model is then specialised for each domain, learning domain-specific behaviour while retaining the cross-domain dialog patterns learned during the initial training stages. These models show robust performance across all the domains investigated, typically outperforming trackers trained on target-domain data alone. The procedure can also be used to initialise dialog systems for entirely new domains. In the evaluation, we show that such initialisation always improves performance, regardless of the amount of the in-domain training data available. We believe that this work is the first to address the question of multi-domain belief tracking.

2 Related Work

Traditional rule-based approaches to understanding in dialog systems (e.g. Goddeau et al. (1996)) have been superseded by data-driven systems that are more robust and can provide the probabilistic dialog state distributions that are needed by POMDP-based dialog managers. The recent Dialog State Tracking Challenge (DSTC) shared tasks (Williams et al., 2013; Henderson et al., 2014a; Henderson et al., 2014b) saw a variety of novel approaches, including robust sets of hand-crafted rules (Wang and Lemon, 2013), conditional random fields (Lee and Eskenazi, 2013; Lee, 2013; Ren et al., 2013), maximum entropy models (Williams, 2013) and web-style ranking (Williams, 2014).

Proceedings of the 53rd Annual Meeting of the Association for Computational Linguistics and the 7th International Joint Conference on Natural Language Processing (Short Papers), pages 794–799, Beijing, China, July 26-31, 2015.

Henderson et al. (2013; 2014d; 2014c) proposed a belief tracker based on recurrent neural networks. This approach maps directly from the ASR (automatic speech recognition) output to the belief state update, avoiding the use of complex semantic decoders while still attaining state-of-the-art performance. We adopt this RNN framework as the starting point for the work described here.

It is well-known in machine learning that a system trained on data from one domain may not perform as well when deployed in a different domain. Researchers have investigated methods for mitigating this problem, with NLP applications in parsing (McClosky et al., 2006; McClosky et al., 2010), sentiment analysis (Blitzer et al., 2007; Glorot et al., 2011) and many other tasks. There has been a small amount of previous work on domain adaptation for dialog systems. Tur et al. (2007) and Margolis et al. (2010) investigated domain adaptation for dialog act tagging. Walker et al. (2007) trained a sentence planner/generator that adapts to different individuals and domains. In the third DSTC shared task (Henderson et al., 2014b), participants deployed belief trackers trained on a restaurant domain in an expanded version of the same domain, with a richer output space but essentially the same topic. To the best of our knowledge, our work is the first attempt to build a belief tracker capable of operating across disjoint dialog domains.

3 Dialog State Tracking using RNNs

Belief tracking models capture users' goals given their utterances. Goals are represented as sets of constraints expressed by *slot-value* mappings such as [food: *chinese*] or [wifi: *available*]. The set of slots S and the set of values V_s for each slot make up the *ontology* for an application domain.

Our starting point is the RNN framework for belief tracking that was introduced by Henderson et al. (2014d; 2014c). This is a single-hidden-layer recurrent neural network that outputs a distribution over all goal slot-value pairs for each user utterance in a dialog. It also maintains a *memory* vector that stores internal information about the dialog context. The input for each user utterance consists of the ASR hypotheses, the last system action, the current memory vector and the previous belief state. Rather than using a spoken language understanding (SLU) decoder to convert this input into a meaning representation, the system uses the turn input to extract a large number of word n-gram features. These features capture some of the dialog dynamics but are not ideal for sharing information across different slots and domains.

Delexicalised n-gram features overcome this problem by replacing all references to slot names and values with generic symbols. Lexical n-grams such as [want cheap price] and [want Chinese food] map to the same delexicalised feature, represented by [want *tagged-slot-value tagged-slot-name*]. Such features facilitate transfer learning between slots and allow the system to operate on unseen values or entirely new slots. As an example, [want available internet] would be delexicalised to [want *tagged-slot-value tagged-slot-name*] as well, a useful feature even if there is no training data available for the *internet* slot. The delexicalised model learns the belief state update corresponding to this feature from its occurrences across the other slots and domains. Subsequently, it can apply the learned behaviour to slots in entirely new domains.

The system maintains a separate belief state for each slot s, represented by the distribution $\mathbf{p}_s$ over all possible slot values $v \in V_s$. The model input at turn t, $\mathbf{x}^t$, consists of the previous belief state $\mathbf{p}_s^{t-1}$, the previous memory state $\mathbf{m}^{t-1}$, as well as the vectors $\mathbf{f}_l$ and $\mathbf{f}_d$ of lexical and delexicalised features extracted from the turn input[1]. The belief state of each slot s is updated for each of its slot values $v \in V_s$. The RNN memory layer is updated as well. The updates are as follows[2]:

$$\begin{aligned}
\mathbf{x}_v^t &= \mathbf{f}_l^t \oplus \mathbf{f}_d^t \oplus \mathbf{m}^{t-1} \oplus p_v^{t-1} \oplus p_\emptyset^{t-1} \\
g_v^t &= \mathbf{w}_1^s \cdot \sigma\left(\mathbf{W}_0^s \mathbf{x}_v^t + b_0^s\right) + b_1^s \\
p_v^t &= \frac{\exp(g_v^t)}{\exp(g_\emptyset^t) + \sum_{v' \in V} \exp(g_{v'}^t)} \\
\mathbf{m}^t &= \sigma\left(\mathbf{W}_{m_0}^s \mathbf{x}_t + \mathbf{W}_{m_1}^s \mathbf{m}^{t-1}\right)
\end{aligned}$$

where $\oplus$ denotes vector concatenation and $p_\emptyset^t$ is the probability that the user has expressed no constraint up to turn t. Matrices $\mathbf{W}_0^s$, $\mathbf{W}_{m_0}^s$, $\mathbf{W}_{m_1}^s$ and the vector $\mathbf{w}_1^s$ are the RNN weights, and b_0 and b_1 are the hidden and output layer RNN bias terms.

For training, the model is unrolled across turns and trained using backpropagation through time and stochastic gradient descent (Graves, 2012).

[1] Henderson et al.'s work distinguished between three types of features: the delexicalised feature sets $\mathbf{f_s}$ and $\mathbf{f_v}$ are subsumed by our delexicalised feature vector $\mathbf{f}_d$, and the turn input $\mathbf{f}$ corresponds to our lexical feature vector $\mathbf{f}_l$.

[2] The original RNN architecture had a second component which learned mappings from lexical n-grams to specific slot values. In order to move towards domain-independence, we do not use this part of the network.

4 Hierarchical Model Training

Delexicalised features allow transfer learning between slots. We extend this approach to achieve transfer learning between domains: a model trained to talk about hotels should have some success talking about restaurants, or even laptops. If we can incorporate features learned from different domains into a single model, this model should be able to track belief state across all of these domains.

The training procedure starts by performing *shared initialisation*: the RNN parameters of all the slots are tied and all the slot value occurrences are replaced with a single generic tag. These slot-agnostic delexicalised dialogs are then used to train the parameters of the *shared RNN model*.

Extending shared initialisation to training across multiple domains is straightforward. We first delexicalise all slot value occurrences for all slots across the different domains in the training data. This combined (delexicalised) dataset is then used to train the multi-domain shared model.

The shared RNN model is trained with the purpose of extracting a very rich set of lexical and delexicalised features which capture general dialog dynamics. While the features are general, the RNN parameters are not, since not all of the features are equally relevant for different slots. For example, [eat *tagged-slot-value* food] and [near *tagged-slot-value*] are clearly features related to *food* and *area* slots respectively. To ensure that the model learns the relative importance of different features for each of the slots, we train slot specific models for each slot across all the available domains. To train these *slot-specialised* models, the shared RNN's parameters are replicated for each slot and specialised further by performing additional runs of stochastic gradient descent using only the slot-specific (delexicalised) training data.

5 Dialog domains considered

We use the experimental setup of the Dialog State Tracking Challenges. The key metric used to measure the success of belief tracking is *goal accuracy*, which represents the ability of the system to correctly infer users' constraints. We report the *joint goal accuracy*, which represents the marginal test accuracy across all slots in the domain.

We evaluate on data from six domains, varying across topic and geographical location (Table 1). The Cambridge Restaurants data is the data from DSTC 2. The San Francisco Restaurants and Hotels data was collected during the Parlance project (Gašić et al., 2014). The Tourist Information domain is the DSTC 3 dataset: it contains dialogs about hotels, restaurants, pubs and coffee shops.

Dataset / Model	Domain	Train	Test	Slots
Cambridge Rest.	Restaurants	2118	1117	4
SF Restaurants	Restaurants	1608	176	7
Michigan Rest.	Restaurants	845	146	12
All Restaurants	Restaurants	4398	-	23
Tourist Info.	Tourist Info	2039	225	9
SF Hotels	Hotels Info	1086	120	7
R+T+H Model	Mixed	7523	-	39
Laptops	Laptops	900	100	6
R+T+H+L Model	Mixed	8423	-	45

Table 1: datasets used in our experiments

The Michigan Restaurants and Laptops datasets are collections of dialogs sourced using Amazon Mechanical Turk. The Laptops domain contains conversations with users instructed to find laptops with certain characteristics. This domain is substantially different from the other ones, making it particularly useful for assessing the quality of the multi-domain models trained.

We introduce three *combined* datasets used to train increasingly general belief tracking models:

1. *All Restaurants* model: trained using the combined data of all three restaurant domains;
2. R+T+H model: trained on all dialogs related to restaurants, hotels, pubs and coffee shops;
3. R+T+H+L model: the most general model, trained using all the available dialog data.

6 Results

As part of the evaluation, we use the three combinations of our dialog domains to build increasingly *general* belief tracking models. The domain-specific models trained using only data from each of the six dialog domains provide the baseline performance for the three general models.

6.1 Training General Models

Training the shared RNN models is the first step of the training procedure. Table 2 shows the performance of shared models trained using dialogs from the six individual and the three combined domains. The joint accuracies are not comparable between the domains as each of them contains a different number of slots. The *geometric mean* of the six accuracies is calculated to determine how well these models operate across different dialog domains.

Model / Domain	Cam Rest	SF Rest	Mich Rest	Tourist	SF Hotels	Laptops	Geo. Mean
Cambridge Restaurants	75.0	26.2	33.1	48.7	5.5	54.1	31.3
San Francisco Restaurants	66.8	**51.6**	31.5	38.2	17.5	47.4	38.8
Michigan Restaurants	57.9	22.3	64.2	32.6	10.2	45.4	32.8
All Restaurants	75.5	49.6	67.4	48.2	19.8	53.7	48.5
Tourist Information	71.7	27.1	31.5	62.9	10.1	55.7	36.0
San Francisco Hotels	26.2	28.7	27.1	27.9	57.1	25.3	30.6
Rest ∪ Tourist ∪ Hotels (R+T+H)	**76.8**	51.2	**68.7**	**65.0**	**58.8**	48.1	60.7
Laptops	66.9	26.1	32.0	46.2	4.6	74.7	31.0
All Domains (R+T+H+L)	**76.8**	50.8	64.4	63.6	57.8	**76.7**	**64.3**

Table 2: Goal accuracy of shared models trained using different dialog domains (ensembles of 12 models)

The parameters of the three multi-domain models are not slot or even domain specific. Nonetheless, all of them improve over the domain-specific model for all but one of their constituent domains. The R+T+H model outperforms the R+T+H+L model across four domains, showing that the use of laptops-related dialogs decreases performance slightly across other more closely related domains. However, the latter model is much better at balancing its performance across all six domains, achieving the highest geometric mean and still improving over all but one of the domain-specific models.

6.2 Slot-specialising the General Models

Slot specialising the shared model allows the training procedure to learn the relative importance of different delexicalised features for each slot in a given domain. Table 3 shows the effect of slot-specialising shared models across the six dialog domains. Moving down in these tables corresponds to adding more out-of-domain training data and moving right corresponds to slot-specialising the shared model for each slot in the current domain.

Slot-specialisation improved performance in the vast majority of the experiments. All three slot-specialised general models outperformed the RNN model's performance reported in DSTC 2.

6.3 Out of Domain Initialisation

The hierarchical training procedure can exploit the available out-of-domain dialogs to initialise improved shared models for new dialog domains.

In our experiments, we choose one of the domains to act as the *new* domain, and we use a subset of the remaining ones as *out-of-domain* data. The number of in-domain dialogs available for training is increased at each stage of the experiment and used to train and compare the performance of two slot-specialised models. These models slot-specialise from two different shared models. One is trained using in-domain data only, and the other is trained on all the out-of-domain data as well.

The two experiments vary in the degree of similarity between the in-domain and out-of-domain dialogs. In the first experiment, Michigan Restaurants act as the new domain and the remaining R+T+H dialogs are used as out-of-domain data. In the second experiment, Laptops dialogs are the in-domain data and the remaining dialog domains are used to initialise the more general shared model.

Figure 1 shows how the performance of the two differently initialised models improves as additional in-domain dialogs are introduced. In both experiments, the use of out-of-domain data helps to

Model	Cambridge Restaurants		SF Restaurants		Michigan Restaurants	
	Shared Model	Slot-specialised	Shared Model	Slot-specialised	Shared Model	Slot-specialised
Domain Specific	75.0	75.4	51.6	**56.5**	64.2	65.6
All Restaurants	75.5	77.3	49.6	53.6	67.4	65.9
R+T+H	76.8	**77.4**	51.2	54.6	**68.7**	65.8
R+T+H+L	76.8	77.0	50.8	54.1	64.4	66.9
	Tourist Information		**SF Hotels**		**Laptops**	
	Shared Model	Slot-specialised	Shared Model	Slot-specialised	Shared Model	Slot-specialised
Domain Specific	62.9	65.1	57.1	57.4	74.7	78.4
R+T+H	65.0	**67.1**	58.8	60.7	-	-
R+T+H+L	63.6	65.5	57.8	**61.6**	76.7	**78.9**

Table 3: Impact of slot specialisation on performance across the six domains (ensembles of 12 models)

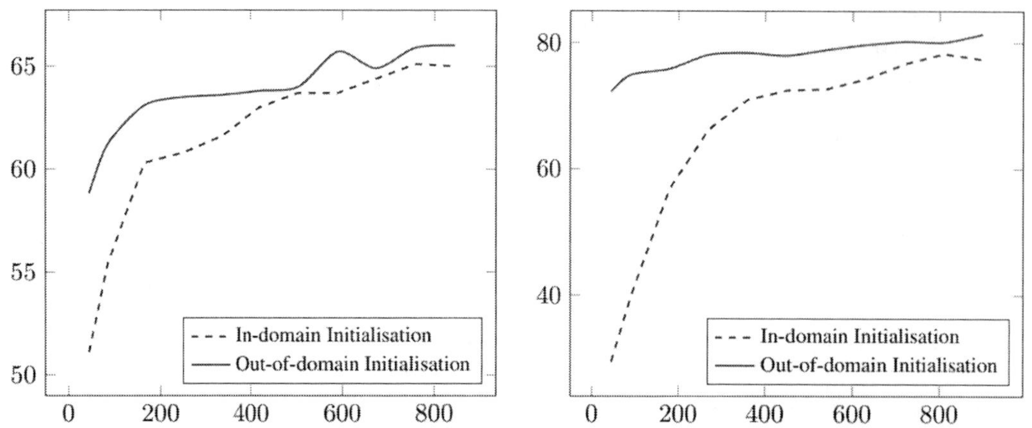

Figure 1: Joint goal accuracy on Michigan Restaurants (left) and the Laptops domain (right) as a function of the number of in-domain training dialogs available to the training procedure (ensembles of four models)

initialise the model to a much better starting point when the in-domain training data set is small. The out-of-domain initialisation consistently improves performance: the joint goal accuracy is improved even when the entire in-domain dataset becomes available to the training procedure.

These results are not surprising in the case of the system trained to talk about Michigan Restaurants. Dialog systems trained to help users find restaurants or hotels should have no trouble finding restaurants in alternative geographies. In line with these expectations, the use of a shared model initialised using R+T+H dialogs results in a model with strong starting performance. As additional restaurants dialogs are revealed to the training procedure, this model shows relatively minor performance gains over the domain-specific one.

The results of the Laptops experiment are even more compelling, as the difference in performance between the differently initialised models becomes larger and more consistent. There are two factors at play here: exposing the training procedure to substantially different out-of-domain dialogs allows it to learn delexicalised features not present in the in-domain training data. These features are applicable to the Laptops domain, as evidenced by the very strong starting performance. As additional in-domain dialogs are introduced, the delexicalised features not present in the out-of-domain data are learned as well, leading to consistent improvements in belief tracking performance.

In the context of these results, it is clear that the out-of-domain training data has the potential to be even more beneficial to tracking performance than data from relatively similar domains. This is especially the case when the available in-domain training datasets are too small to allow the procedure to learn appropriate delexicalised features.

7 Conclusion

We have shown that it is possible to train general belief tracking models capable of talking about many different topics at once. The most general model exhibits robust performance across all domains, outperforming most domain-specific models. This shows that training using diverse dialog domains allows the model to better capture general dialog dynamics applicable to different domains at once.

The proposed hierarchical training procedure can also be used to adapt the general model to new dialog domains, with very small in-domain data sets required for adaptation. This procedure improves tracking performance even when substantial amounts of in-domain data become available.

7.1 Further Work

The suggested domain adaptation procedure requires a small collection of annotated in-domain dialogs to adapt the general model to a new domain. In our future work, we intend to focus on initialising good belief tracking models when no annotated dialogs are available for the new dialog domain.

References

John Blitzer, Mark Dredze, and Fernando Pereira. 2007. Biographies, Bollywood, boom-boxes and blenders: Domain adaptation for sentiment classification. In *Proceedings of ACL*.

Milica Gašić, Dongho Kim, Pirros Tsiakoulis, Catherine Breslin, Matthew Henderson, Martin Szummer, Blaise Thomson, and Steve Young. 2014. Incremental on-line adaptation of POMDP-based dialogue managers to extended domains. In *Proceedings of INTERSPEECH*.

Xavier Glorot, Antoine Bordes, and Yoshua Bengio. 2011. Domain adaptation for large-scale sentiment classification: A deep learning approach. In *Proceedings of ICML*.

D. Goddeau, H. Meng, J. Polifroni, S. Seneff, and S. Busayapongchai. 1996. A form-based dialogue manager for spoken language applications. In *Proceedings of ICSLP*.

Alex Graves. 2012. *Supervised Sequence Labelling with Recurrent Neural Networks*. Springer, Berlin.

Matthew Henderson, Blaise Thomson, and Steve Young. 2013. Deep neural network approach for the Dialog State Tracking Challenge. In *Proceedings of SIGDIAL*.

Matthew Henderson, Blaise Thomson, and Jason D. Wiliams. 2014a. The Second Dialog State Tracking Challenge. In *Proceedings of SIGDIAL*.

Matthew Henderson, Blaise Thomson, and Jason D. Wiliams. 2014b. The Third Dialog State Tracking Challenge. In *Proceedings of IEEE SLT*.

Matthew Henderson, Blaise Thomson, and Steve Young. 2014c. Robust dialog state tracking using delexicalised recurrent neural networks and unsupervised adaptation. In *Proceedings of IEEE SLT*.

Matthew Henderson, Blaise Thomson, and Steve Young. 2014d. Word-based dialog state tracking with recurrent neural networks. In *Proceedings of SIGDIAL*.

Sungjin Lee and Maxine Eskenazi. 2013. Recipe for building robust spoken dialog state trackers: Dialog State Tracking Challenge system description. In *Proceedings of SIGDIAL*.

Sungjin Lee. 2013. Structured discriminative model for dialog state tracking. In *Proceedings of SIGDIAL*.

Anna Margolis, Karen Livescu, and Mari Ostendorf. 2010. Domain adaptation with unlabeled data for dialog act tagging. In *Proceedings of the ACL Workshop on Domain Adaptation*.

David McClosky, Eugene Charniak, and Mark Johnson. 2006. Effective self-training for parsing. In *Proceedings of HLT-NAACL*.

David McClosky, Eugene Charniak, and Mark Johnson. 2010. Automatic domain adaptation for parsing. In *Proceedings of NAACL HLT*.

Hang Ren, Weiqun Xu, Yan Zhang, and Yonghong Yan. 2013. Dialog state tracking using conditional random fields. In *Proceedings of SIGDIAL*.

Gokhan Tur, Umit Guz, and Dilek Hakkani-Tür. 2007. Model adaptation for dialog act tagging. In *Proceedings of IEEE SLT*.

Marilyn Walker, Amanda Stent, François Mairesse, and Rashmi Prasad. 2007. Individual and domain adaptation in sentence planning for dialogue. *Journal of Artificial Intelligence Research*, 30:413–456.

Zhuoran Wang and Oliver Lemon. 2013. A simple and generic belief tracking mechanism for the Dialog State Tracking Challenge: On the believability of observed information. In *Proceedings of SIGDIAL*.

Jason D. Williams, Antoine Raux, Deepak Ramachandran, and Alan W. Black. 2013. The Dialogue State Tracking Challenge. In *Proceedings of SIGDIAL*.

Jason D. Williams. 2013. Multi-domain learning and generalization in dialog state tracking. In *Proceedings of SIGDIAL*.

Jason D. Williams. 2014. Web-style ranking and slu combination for dialog state tracking. In *Proceedings of SIGDIAL*.

Dialogue Management based on Sentence Clustering

Wendong Ge
Institute of Automation,
Chinese Academy of Sciences,
Beijing, China
wendong.ge@ia.ac.cn

Bo Xu
Institute of Automation,
Chinese Academy of Sciences,
Beijing, China
xubo@ia.ac.cn

Abstract

Dialogue Management (DM) is a key issue in Spoken Dialogue System (SDS). Most of the existing studies on DM use Dialogue Act (DA) to represent semantic information of sentence, which might not represent the nuanced meaning sometimes. In this paper, we model DM based on sentence clusters which have more powerful semantic representation ability than DAs. Firstly, sentences are clustered not only based on the internal information such as words and sentence structures, but also based on the external information such as context in dialogue via Recurrent Neural Networks. Additionally, the DM problem is modeled as a Partially Observable Markov Decision Processes (POMDP) with sentence clusters. Finally, experimental results illustrate that the proposed DM scheme is superior to the existing one.

1 Introduction

Dialogue Management (DM) is an important issue in Spoken Dialogue Systems (SDS). (Paek et al., 2008) Most of the existing studies on DM use the abstract semantic representation such as Dialogue Act (DA) to represent the sentence intention. In (Bohus et al., 2009), authors propose a plan-based, task-independent DM framework, called RavenClaw, which isolates the domain-specific aspects of the dialogue control logic from domain-independent conversational skills. (Daubigney et al., 2010) proposes a Kalman Temporal Differences based algorithm to learn efficiently in an off-policy manner a strategy for a large scale dialogue system. In (Emmanuel et al., 2013), authors propose a scheme to utilize a socially-based reward function for reinforcement learning and use it to fit the user adaptation issue for DM. (Young et al., 2013) provides an overview of the current state of the art in the development of POMDP-based spoken dialog systems. (Hao et al., 2014) presents a dialog manager based on a log-linear probabilistic model and uses context-free grammars to impart hierarchical structure to variables and features.

As we know, sentences in human-human dialogues are extremely complicated. The sentences labeled with the same DA might contain different extra meanings. Thus, it is difficult for DA to represent the nuanced meaning of sentence in dialogue. In this paper, we propose a novel DM scheme based on sentence clustering. The contributions of this work are as follows.

- Semantic representation of sentence in dialogue is defined as sentence cluster which could represent more nuanced semantic information than DA. Sentence similarity for clustering is calculated via internal information such as words and sentence structures and external information such as the distributed representation of sentence (vector) from Recurrent Neural Networks (RNN).

- The DM problem is modeled as a POMDP, where state is defined as sequence of sentence clusters, reward is defined as slot-filling efficiency and sentence popularity, and state transition probability is calculated by the prediction model based on RNN, considering historical dialogue information sufficiently.

The rest of this paper is organized as follows. In Section 2, system model is introduced. Section 3 describes sentence clustering and prediction model based on RNN, and Section 4 models the DM problem as a POMDP. Extensive experimental results are provided in Section 5 to illustrate the performance comparison, and Section 6 concludes this study.

Proceedings of the 53rd Annual Meeting of the Association for Computational Linguistics and the 7th International Joint Conference on Natural Language Processing (Short Papers), pages 800–805,
Beijing, China, July 26-31, 2015.

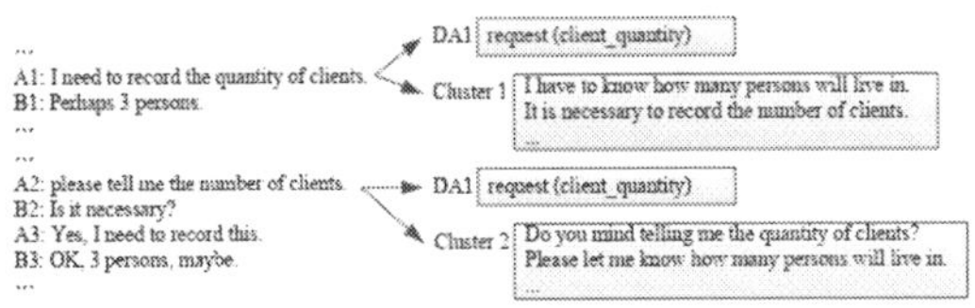

Figure 1: sentence cluster vs. DA

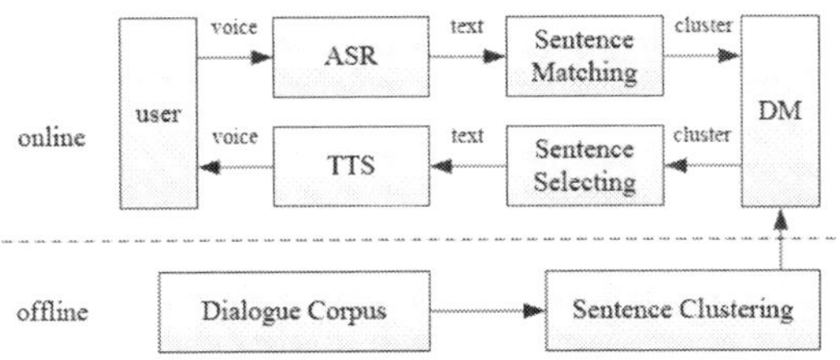

Figure 2: system model

2 System Model

In this paper, we establish a SDS via human-human dialogue corpus, where sentence cluster rather than DA is utilized to represent sentence intention due to its ability of catching finer-grained semantic information. For example, Fig. 1 shows some dialogue segments in hotel reservation. Both A1 and A2 could be labeled with "request (client_quantity)", because the aims of them are requesting the quantity of clients. However, A1 has an extra meaning that it is a necessity for the reception to record the quantity of clients, while A2 not, which might lead to different evolutions of dialogues. Probably, we could add this necessity to the DA corresponding to A1 manually, but it is infeasible for all the sentences to distinguish the fine-grained semantic information by adding abstract symbol to DA. Thus, in this paper, we automatically cluster all the sentences in dialogues, and utilize sentence clusters to represent sentence intentions, which has more powerful capability to capture semantic information.

The SDS based on sentence clustering could be divided into offline stage and online stage, illustrated in Fig. 2.

In offline stage:

Sentence Clustering: The sentence similarity is calculated based on not only internal information such as words and sentence structure, but also external information such as the distributed representation from RNN. And then the sentences in dialogue corpus are clustered into different tiny groups, which will be discussed in section 3.

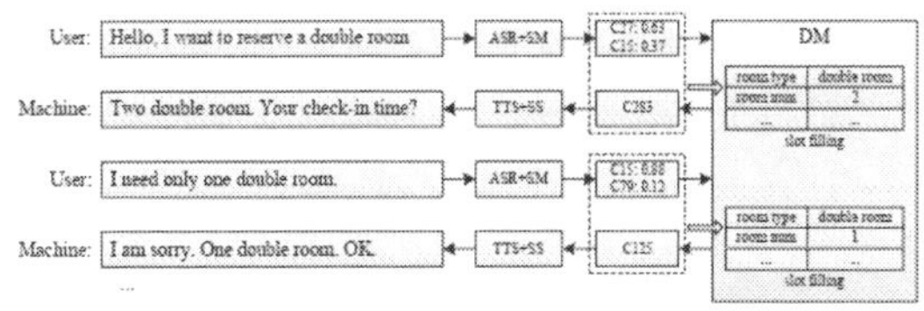

Figure 3: an online example

Dialogue Policy Training: We label the dialogues in corpus with the sentence clusters generated in the previous process. Thus, these labeled dialogues could be utilized to train the optimal dialogue policy with Reinforcement Learning, which will be introduced in section 4.

In online stage:

Automatic Speech Recognition (ASR): When receiving user voice, ASR module transforms it into text (Vinyals et al., 2012). As there might be ambiguity and errors in ASR, it is difficult to obtain the exact text corresponding to the input voice. Thus, the distribution over possible texts is used to represent the result of ASR.

Sentence Matching (SM): the function of SM is to establish a mapping from the distribution over possible texts to the distribution over possible sentence clusters.

DM: Based on the distribution of clusters, DM model updates the belief state in POMDP and selects the optimal action, namely the optimal machine sentence cluster, according to the dialogue policy. The relevant slots are also filled based on the user and machine sentence clusters.

Sentence Selection: This module selects the most appropriate sentence from the output machine sentence cluster according to the user profile such as personality character (Ball et al., 2000).

Text To Speech (TTS): This model transforms the selected sentence text into the output voice as a response (Zen et al., 2007).

Fig. 3 is a human-machine dialogue example in online stage.

3 Sentence Clustering based on RNN

In this section, we cluster the sentences for DM modeling, which might be different from general sentence clustering. Sentence similarity for clustering are calculated from two aspects. Firstly, it is calculated traditionally based on internal information such as words and sentence structures, which is widely researched in (Li et al., 2006) (Achananuparp et al., 2008). (Word embedding

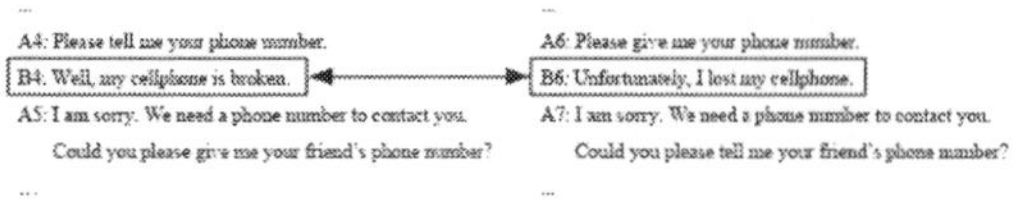

Figure 4: an example of sentence similarity

and sentence parsing might be used for this calculation.) Additionally, for DM-based sentence clustering, the sentences that we intend to put into the same cluster are not only the sentences with similar surface meaning, but also the sentences with similar intention (Semantics or Pragmatics), even if they might be different in surface meaning sometimes. For example, illustrated in Fig. 4, B4 and B6 are different in surface meaning, but they have similar intention, namely he or she might not provide his or her phone number right now. Thus, in the sentence clustering for DM modeling, they should be clustered into the same group. It is difficult to give a high similarity score between B4 and B6 only according to the internal information, but we could observe that the sentences around them in the context are similar. Thus, external information is also important to the sentence clustering for DM. In the following, we will discuss the clustering process.

We denote the sentence cluster set as $\mathscr{C}^k = \left\{c_1^k, c_2^k, \cdots, c_{N_C^k}^k\right\}$, and the dialogue set as $\mathscr{D}^k = \left\{d_1^k, d_2^k, \cdots, d_{N_D^k}^k\right\}$ in the k-th iteration. Thus, the steps of sentence clustering are:

Step 1: Initially, we only utilize the internal information to cluster the sentences via Affinity Propagation (AP) algorithm (Brendan et al., 2007) and denote the clustering result as $\mathscr{C}^0$. If $\mathscr{C}^0$ is used to label the sentences in dialogues, the j-th dialogue could be denoted as a sequence of clusters, namely $d_j^0 = \left\{c_1^0, c_2^0, \cdots, c_{N_j^d}^0\right\}$.

Step 2: In the k-th iteration, we use cluster set $\mathscr{C}^k$ to label dialogue set $\mathscr{D}^k$.

Step 3: We utilize RNN to obtain the distributed representation of sentence, illustrated in Fig. 5. The input of RNN is sentence cluster in each turn, namely c_t^k. The input layer $\mathbf{I}(t)$ is the one-hot representation of c_t^k. (Turian et al., 2010) (The size of $\mathbf{I}(t)$ is equivalent to $\left|\mathscr{C}^k\right|$. There is only one 1 in $\mathbf{I}(t)$ corresponding to the c_t^k position, and other elements are zeros.) $\mathbf{H}(t)$ is defined as the hidden layer. The output layer $\mathbf{O}(t)$ is the distribution over possible c_{t+1}^k, which could be calculated as follow. (Mikolov et al., 2010)

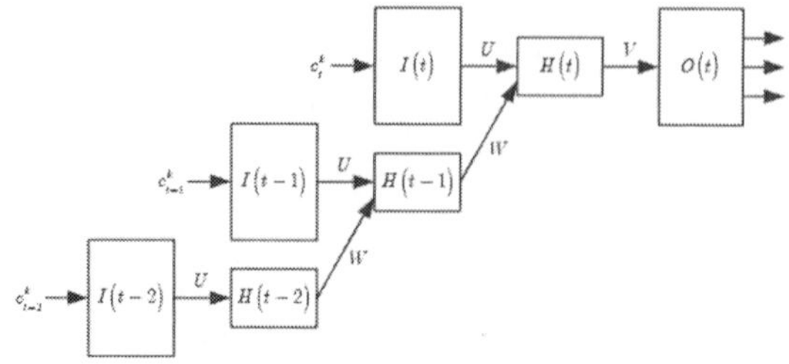

Figure 5: RNN for sentence clustering

$$\begin{cases} \mathbf{H}(t) = f(\mathbf{UI}(t) + \mathbf{WH}(t-1)) \\ \mathbf{O}(t) = g(\mathbf{VH}(t)) \end{cases} \quad (1)$$

where $f(x) = 1/(1+e^{-x})$ and $g(x_i) = e^{x_i} \Big/ \sum_{i=1}^{N_e} e^{x_i}$. The parameters of this RNN could be trained by the Back Propagation Through Time (BPTT) algorithm. (Mikolov, 2012) From RNN, we could obtain two significant results: one is the distributed representation (vectors) of the sentence clusters ($\mathbf{U}$), which is used for sentence clustering; the other is the prediction model for sentence clusters, which is used for DM.

Step 4: we calculate the sentence similarity based on vectors obtained in **Step 3**, and combine it with the sentence similarity from internal information (weighted mean), in order to cluster the set $\mathscr{C}^k$ via AP algorithm, which is denoted as $\mathscr{C}^{k+1}$.

Step 5: $\bar{N}_C = \sum_{i=k-k_{th}+2}^{k+1} N_C^i$ is defined as the average number of clusters in the last k_{th} iteration. If $\sum_{i=k-k_{th}+2}^{k+1} \left|N_C^i - \bar{N}_C\right| < N_{th}$, stop the iteration of clustering, or go to **Step 2**, where N_{th} is the variation threshold of quantity of clusters.

Thus, in the last iteration, we get the cluster set $\mathscr{C}^{\bar{k}} = \left\{c_1^{\bar{k}}, c_2^{\bar{k}}, \cdots, c_{N_C^{\bar{k}}}^{\bar{k}}\right\}$ and prediction model for these sentence clusters. We divide all the sentences in dialogue corpus into the sentence set spoken by customers and the sentence set spoken by customer service representatives, and then utilize $\mathscr{C}^{\bar{k}}$ to label them respectively, which is denoted as $\mathscr{C}^u = \left\{c_1^u, c_2^u, \cdots, c_{N_u}^u\right\}$, namely the clusters of user sentences, and $\mathscr{C}^m = \left\{c_1^m, c_2^m, \cdots, c_{N_m}^m\right\}$, namely the clusters of machine sentences.

4 DM based on Sentence Clustering

The dialogue process mentioned in section 2 could be formulized as follows, illustrated in Fig. 6. It is defined $X = \{x_1, \cdots, x_T\}$ as inner (or exact) sentence cluster corresponding to the user input in each turn, which is unobservable and $x_t \in$

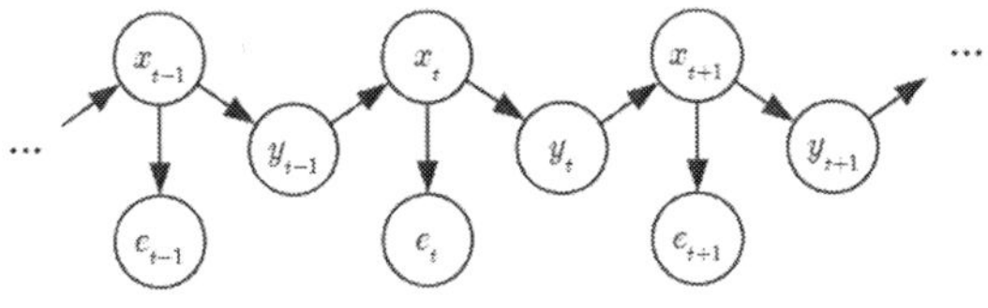

Figure 6: dialogue process

$\mathscr{C}^u$. $E = \{e_1, \cdots, e_T\}$ is defined as the input voice, which is observable to infer x_t in each turn. $Y = \{y_1, \cdots, y_T\}$ is defined as the output cluster of machine, where $y_t \in \mathscr{C}^m$. Thus, the DM problem is to find out the optimal y_t according to $\{e_1, y_1, \cdots, e_t\}$. In the following, the DM problem is modeled as a POMDP.

State in the t-th epoch is defined as the sequence of clusters, namely $s_t = \{x_{t-\tau}, y_{t-\tau}, \cdots, x_{t-1}, y_{t-1}, x_t\}$, where $s_t \in \mathscr{S}$. Action in the t-th epoch is defined as $a_t = y_t$, where $a_t \in \mathscr{A}$. The state transition probability $\Pr\{s_{t+1} | s_t, a_t\}$ could be shown as

$$\begin{aligned}&\Pr\{s_{t+1} | s_t, a_t\} \\ &= \Pr\{x_{t+1} | y_t, x_t, \cdots, y_{t-\tau}, x_{t-\tau}\}\end{aligned} \quad (2)$$

which is calculated by the prediction model based on RNN in section 3.

Observation is defined as $o_t = \{e_{t-\tau}, \cdots, e_t\}$, where $o_t \in \mathscr{O}$. As $\{x_{t-\tau}, \cdots, x_t\}$ in state s_t is unobservable, belief state is defined to represent the distribution over possible states, which is denoted as $b(t) \in \mathscr{B}$. According to (Kaelbling et al., 1998), the belief state updating could be represented as

$$b_{t+1}(s_{t+1}) = \frac{\Pr\{o_{t+1} | s_{t+1}, a_t\} p_{s_{t+1}}}{\Pr\{o_{t+1} | b_t, a_t\}} \quad (3)$$

where $p_{s_{t+1}} = \sum_{s_t \in \mathscr{S}} \Pr\{s_{t+1} | s_t, a_t\} b_t(s_t)$. According to Fig. 5, $\Pr\{o_{t+1} | s_{t+1}, a_t\}$ could be shown as

$$\begin{aligned}&\Pr\{o_{t+1} | s_{t+1}, a_t\} \\ &= \Pr\{o_{t+1} | s_{t+1}\} \\ &= \Pr\{e_{t-\tau+1}, \cdots, e_{t+1} | x_{t-\tau+1}, \cdots, y_t, x_{t+1}\} \\ &= \Pr\{e_{t-\tau+1}, \cdots, e_{t+1} | x_{t-\tau+1}, \cdots, x_{t+1}\} \\ &= \prod_{i=t-\tau+1}^{t+1} \Pr\{e_i | x_i\}\end{aligned} \quad (4)$$

However, it is difficult to obtain the probability $\Pr\{e_t | x_t\}$, as different people have different habits of expression and pronunciation. Fortunately, $\Pr\{x_t | e_t\}$ could be estimated based on ASR and SM. Thus, based on Bayes Rules, we have the following equation.

$$\Pr\{e_i | x_i\} = \frac{\Pr\{x_i | e_i\} \Pr\{e_i\}}{\Pr\{x_i\}} \quad (5)$$

where $\Pr\{x_t\}$ is the prior distribution of x_t and could be counted by corpus. With (4) and (5), (3) could be rewritten as

$$b_{t+1}(s_{t+1}) = \frac{\kappa \cdot p_{s_{t+1}} \cdot \prod_{i=t-\tau+1}^{t+1} \Pr\{x_i | e_i\}}{\prod_{i=t-\tau+1}^{t+1} \Pr\{x_i\}} \quad (6)$$

where

$$\kappa = \prod_{i=t-\tau+1}^{t+1} \Pr\{e_i\} \Big/ \Pr\{o_{t+1} | b_t, a_t\} \quad (7)$$

is a normalization constant.

The reward function is defined as

$$r_t(s_t, a_t, s_{t+1}) = \lambda_f r^f_{(s_t, a_t, s_{t+1})} + \lambda_p r^p_{(s_t, a_t, s_{t+1})} \quad (8)$$

where $\lambda_f + \lambda_p = 1$ and $r_t(s_t, a_t, s_{t+1}) \in \mathscr{R}$. Firstly, $r^f_{(s_t, a_t, s_{t+1})}$ stands for the number of unfilled slots that are filled by the sequence of sentence clusters corresponding to (s_t, a_t, s_{t+1}). This slot-filling process could be achieved by a classifier trained by the dialogues labeled with sentence clusters and slot-filling information. (Inputs are cluster sequences, and outputs are filled slots.) Additionally, $r^p_{(s_t, a_t, s_{t+1})}$ is defined as the normalized quantity of s_{t+1} conditioned by s_t and a_t, which could be counted in corpus and stands for the popularity features of human-human dialogues. Thus, for the belief state, the reward function could be represented as

$$\begin{aligned}r_t(b_t, a_t) = &\sum_{s_{t+1} \in \mathscr{S}} \sum_{s_t \in \mathscr{S}} r_t(s_t, a_t, s_{t+1}) \\ &\cdot \Pr(s_{t+1} | s_t, a_t) b_t(s_t)\end{aligned} \quad (9)$$

Therefore, if we define the policy as a mapping from belief state to action, namely $\zeta \in \mathscr{Z} : \mathscr{B} \to \mathscr{A}$, the POMDP-based DM problem is shown as

$$\begin{aligned}&\max_{\zeta \in \mathscr{S}} E_\zeta \left[\sum_{t=1}^{T} \beta r_t(b_t, a_t)\right] \\ &s.t.\ b_{t+1}(s_{t+1}) = \frac{\kappa \prod_{i=t-\tau+1}^{t+1} \Pr\{x_i | e_i\}}{\prod_{i=t-\tau+1}^{t+1} \Pr\{x_i\}} \\ &\quad \cdot \sum_{s_t \in \mathscr{S}} \Pr\{s_{t+1} | s_t, a_t\} b_t(s_t)\end{aligned} \quad (10)$$

where β is the time discount factor and $0 < \beta < 1$. This problem is a MDP problem with continuous states, which could be solved by the Natural Actor and Critic algorithm (Peters et al., 2008).

5 Experimental Results

In this section, we compare the performances of the proposed Sentence Clustering based Dialogue Management (SCDM) scheme and the existing D-M scheme. The existing scheme is designed according to (Young et al., 2013), where DA is utilized to represent the semantic information of sentence and the dialogue policy is trained via Reinforcement Learning. It is also an extrinsic (or end-to-end) evaluation to compare the semantic representation ability between sentence cluster and DA.

In order to compare the performances of the DM schemes, we collect 171 human-human dialogues in hotel reservation and utilize 100 dialogues of them to establish a SDS. The residual 71 dialogues are used to establish a simulated user for testing (Schatzmann et al., 2006). We define the slots requested from machine to user as "room type", "room quantity", "checkin time", "checkout time", "client name" and "client phone". We also define the slots requested from users to machine as "hotel address = No.95 East St.", "room type set = single room, double room, and deluxe room", "single room price = \$80", "double room price = \$100", "deluxe room price = \$150". The hotel reservation task could be considered as a process of exchanging the slot information between machine and user to some extent.

Fig. 7 illustrates the dialogue turn in the DM schemes, using different training corpus. Here, we vary the size of training corpus from 10 dialogues to 100 dialogues and define average turn as the average dialogue turn cost to complete the task. From this picture, we find out that the SCD-M scheme has lower average turn than the existing scheme, partly because the sentence are automatically clustered into many small groups that could represent more nuanced semantic information than DAs, partly because RNN could estimate next sentence cluster according to the vector in hidden layer that contains abundant historical dialogue information. As the number of sentence clusters is greater than number of DAs, RNN could also solve the scarcity problem and smoothing problem in the predicting process. Additionally, with the increment of training dialogue size, the average turn of dialogue decreases, which ought to be ascribed to the fact that more training data could let SD-S reach more states with more times and increase the accuracy of the parameter estimation in RNN and POMDP. Furthermore, with the increment of training dialogue size, the dialogue turn improvement of the proposed scheme turns less obvious, because the number of new sentence pattern deceases with the training size increment.

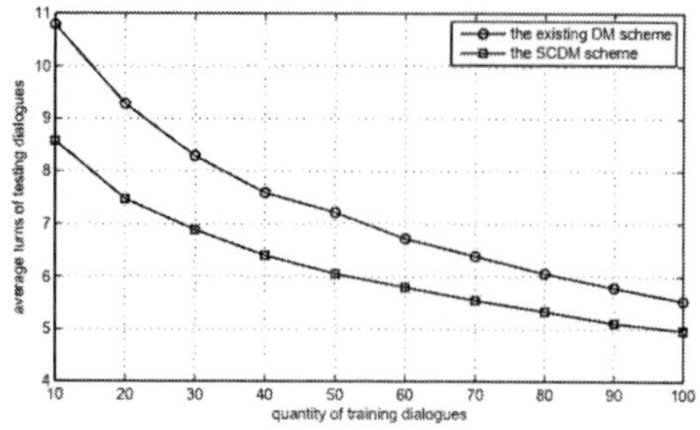

Figure 7: comparison of average turn

6 Conclusion

In this paper, we focused on the DM scheme based on sentence clustering. Firstly, sentence cluster is defined as the semantic representation of sentence in dialogue, which could describe more naunced sentence intention than DA. Secondly, RNN is established for sentence clustering, where sentence similarity is calculated not only based on the internal information such as words and sentence structure, but also based on the external information such as context in dialogue. Thirdly, the DM problem is modeled as a POMDP, where the state is defined as the sequence of sentence clusters and the state transition probability is estimated by RN-N, considering the whole information of historical dialogue. Finally, the experimental results illustrated that the proposed DM scheme is superior to the existing one.

Acknowledgments

This work is supported by the National Program on Key Basic Research Project (973 Program), basic theories and methods of Chinese Language Processing and Deep Computing in Internet environment, multi-lingual Automatic Speech Recognition for complex environments. (No. 2013CB329302)

References

Dan Bohus, Alexander, I. Rudnicky. 2009. The RavenClaw dialog management framework: Architecture and systems *Computer Speech and Language*, vol. 23, pages: 332-361, 2009.

Emmanuel Ferreira, Fabrice Lefvre. 2013. Social signal and user adaptation in reinforcement learning-based dialogue management. *MLIS '13*, Aug, 2013.

Brendan J. Frey, Delbert Dueck. 2007 Clustering by Passing Messages Between Data Points. *Science*, 2007.

Ball, G., Breese, J. 2000. Emotion and personality in a conversational agent. *Embodied conversational agents*, pages: 189-219, 2000.

Zen, H., Nose, T., Yamagishi, J., Sako, S., Masuko, T., Black, A. W., Tokuda, K. 2007 The HMM-based speech synthesis system version 2.0. *In Proc. 6th ISCA Workshop on Speech Synthesis*, Aug, 2007.

Schatzmann, J., Weilhammer, K., Stuttle, M., Young, S. 2006 A survey of statistical user simulation techniques for reinforcement-learning of dialogue management strategies. *The knowledge engineering review*, 21(02), 97-126, 2006.

Turian, J., Ratinov, L., Bengio, Y. 2010 Word representations: a simple and general method for semi-supervised learning. *In Proceedings of the 48th annual meeting of the association for computational linguistics*, Jul, 2010.

Peters, J., Schaal, S. 2008 Natural actor-critic. *Neurocomputinge*, 71(7), 1180-1190, 2008.

Kaelbling, L., Littman, M., and Cassandr, A. 1998 Planning and acting in partially observable stochastic domains. *Artif. Intell.*, vol.101, pages: 99-134, 1998.

Daubigney, L., Geist, M., Pietquin, O. 2012. Off-policy learning in large-scale POMDP-based dialogue systems. *EEE International Conference on Acoustics, Speech and Signal Processing (ICASSP).*, pages: 4989-499, Mar, 2012.

Vinyals, O., Ravuri, S. V., Povey, D. 2012. Revisiting Recurrent Neural Networks for robust ASR. *2012 IEEE International Conference on Acoustics, Speech and Signal Processing (ICASSP)*, 2012.

Achananuparp, P., Hu, X., Shen, X. 2008. The evaluation of sentence similarity measures. *In Data Warehousing and Knowledge Discovery*, pages: 305-316, 2008.

Young, S., Gasic, M., Thomson, B., Williams, J. D. (2013). 2013. Pomdp-based statistical spoken dialog systems: A review. *Proceedings of the IEEE*, 101(5), pages: 1160-1179, 2013.

Mikolov, T. 2012 Statistical language models based on neural networks. *Presentation at Google, Mountain View*, 2012.

Mikolov, T., Karafit, M., Burget, L., Cernocky, J., Khudanpur, S. 2010 Recurrent neural network based language model. *11th Annual Conference of the International Speech Communication Association*, Sep, 2010.

Paek, T., Pieraccini, R. 2008. Automating spoken dialogue management design using machine learning: An industry perspective. *Speech communication*, 50(8), 716-729, 2008.

Hao Tang, Watanabe, S., Marks, T. K., Hershey, J. R. 2014. Log-linear dialog manager. *IEEE International Conference on Acoustics, Speech and Signal Processing (ICASSP)*, May, 2014.

Li Y, McLean D, Bandar Z A, et al. 2006. Sentence similarity based on semantic nets and corpus statistics. *Knowledge and Data Engineering, IEEE Transactions on*, 18(8), 1138-1150, 2006.

Compact Lexicon Selection with Spectral Methods

Young-Bum Kim[†] **Karl Stratos**[‡] **Xiaohu Liu**[†] **Ruhi Sarikaya**[†]

[†]Microsoft Corporation, Redmond, WA
[‡]Columbia University, New York, NY
{ybkim, derekliu, ruhi.sarikaya}@microsoft.com
stratos@cs.columbia.edu

Abstract

In this paper, we introduce the task of selecting compact lexicon from large, noisy gazetteers. This scenario arises often in practice, in particular spoken language understanding (SLU). We propose a simple and effective solution based on matrix decomposition techniques: canonical correlation analysis (CCA) and rank-revealing QR (RRQR) factorization. CCA is first used to derive low-dimensional gazetteer embeddings from domain-specific search logs. Then RRQR is used to find a subset of these embeddings whose span approximates the entire lexicon space. Experiments on slot tagging show that our method yields a small set of lexicon entities with average relative error reduction of $> 50\%$ over randomly selected lexicon.

1 Introduction

Discriminative models trained with large quantities of arbitrary features are a dominant paradigm in spoken language understanding (SLU) (Li et al., 2009; Hillard et al., 2011; Celikyilmaz et al., 2013; Liu and Sarikaya, 2014; Sarikaya et al., 2014; Anastasakos et al., 2014; Xu and Sarikaya, 2014; Celikyilmaz et al., 2015; Kim et al., 2015a; Kim et al., 2015c; Kim et al., 2015b). An important category of these features comes from *entity dictionaries* or *gazetteers*—lists of phrases whose labels are given. For instance, they can be lists of movies, music titles, actors, restaurants, and cities. These features enable SLU models to robustly handle unseen entities at test time.

However, these lists are often massive and very noisy. This is because they are typically obtained automatically by mining the web for recent entries (such as newly launched movie names). Ideally, we would like an SLU model to have access to this vast source of information at deployment. But this is difficult in practice because an SLU model needs to be light-weight to support fast user interaction. It becomes more challenging when we consider multiple domains, languages, and locales.

In this paper, we introduce the task of selecting a small, representative subset of noisy gazetteers that will nevertheless improve model performance nearly as much as the original lexicon. This will allow an SLU model to take full advantage of gazetteer resources at test time without being overwhelmed by their scale.

Our selection method is two steps. First, we gather relevant information for each gazetteer element using domain-specific search logs. Then we perform CCA using this information to derive low-dimensional gazetteer embeddings (Hotelling, 1936). Second, we use a subset selection method based on RRQR to locate gazetteer embeddings whose span approximates the the entire lexicon space (Boutsidis et al., 2009; Kim and Snyder, 2013). We show in slot tagging experiments that the gazetteer elements selected by our method not only preserve the performance of using full lexicon but even improve it in some cases. Compared to random selection, our method achieves average relative error reduction of $> 50\%$.

2 Motivation

We motivate our task by describing the process of lexicon construction. Entity dictionaries are usually automatically mined from the web using resources that provide typed entities. On a regular basis, these dictionaries are automatically updated and accumulated based on local data feeds and knowledge graphs. Local data feeds are generated from various origins (e.g., yellow pages, Yelp). Knowledge graphs such as `www.freebase.com` are resources that define a semantic space of entities (e.g., movie names, per-

Proceedings of the 53rd Annual Meeting of the Association for Computational Linguistics and the 7th International Joint Conference on Natural Language Processing (Short Papers), pages 806–811,
Beijing, China, July 26-31, 2015.

sons, places and organizations) and their relations.

Because of the need to keep dictionaries updated to handle newly emerging entities, lexicon construction is designed to aim for high recall at the expense of precision. Consequently, the resulting gazetteers are noisy. For example, a movie dictionary may contain hundreds of thousands movie names, but many of them are false positives.

While this large base of entities is useful as a whole, it is challenging to take advantage of at test time. This is because we normally cannot afford to consume so much memory when we deploy an SLU model in practice. In the next section, we will describe a way to filter these entities while retaining their overall benefit.

3 Method

3.1 Row subset selection problem

We frame gazetteer element selection as the row subset selection problem. In this framework, we organize n gazetteer elements as matrix $A \in \mathbb{R}^{n \times d}$ whose rows $A_i \in \mathbb{R}^d$ are some representations of the gazetteer members. Given $m \leq n$, let $\mathcal{S}(A, m) := \{B \in \mathbb{R}^{m \times d} : B_i = A_{\pi(i)}\}$ be a set of matrices whose rows are a subset of the rows of A. Note that $|\mathcal{S}(A, m)| = \binom{n}{m}$. Our goal is to select [1]

$$B^* = \operatorname*{arg\,min}_{B \in \mathcal{S}(A,m)} \left|\left|A - AB^+B\right|\right|_F$$

That is, we want B to satisfy range$(B^\top) \approx$ range$(A^\top)$. We can solve for B^* exactly with exhaustive search in $O(n^m)$, but this brute-force approach is clearly not scalable. Instead, we turn to the $O(nd^2)$ algorithm of Boutsidis et al. (2009) which we review below.

3.1.1 RRQR factorization

A key ingredient in the algorithm of Boutsidis et al. (2009) is the use of RRQR factorization. Recall that a (thin) QR factorization of A expresses $A = QR$ where $Q \in \mathbb{R}^{n \times d}$ has orthonormal columns and $R \in \mathbb{R}^{d \times d}$ is an upper triangular matrix. A limitation of QR factorization is that it does not assign a score to each of the d components. This is in contrast to singular value decomposition (SVD) which assigns a score (singular value) indicating the importance of these components.

[1]The Frobenius norm $||M||_F$ is defined as the entry-wise L_2 norm: $\sqrt{\sum_{i,j} m_{ij}^2}$. B^+ is the Moore-Penrose pseudo-inverse of B

Input: d-dimensional gazetteer representations $A \in \mathbb{R}^{n \times d}$, number of gazetteer elements to select $m \leq n$
Output: m rows of A, call $B \in \mathbb{R}^{m \times d}$, such that $\left|\left|A - AB^+B\right|\right|_F$ is small

- Perform SVD on A and let $U \in \mathbb{R}^{d \times m}$ be a matrix whose columns are the left singular vectors corresponding to the largest m singular values.
- Associate a probability p_i with the i-th row of A as follows:

$$p_i := \min\left\{1, \lfloor m \log m \rfloor \frac{||U_i||^2}{m}\right\}$$

- Discard the i-th row of A with probability $1 - p_i$. If kept, the row is multiplied by $1/\sqrt{p_i}$. Let these $O(m \log m)$ rows form the columns of a new matrix $\bar{A} \in \mathbb{R}^{d \times O(m \log m)}$.
- Perform RRQR on $\bar{A}$ to obtain $\bar{A}\Pi = QR$.
- Return the m rows of the original A corresponding to the top m columns of $\bar{A}\Pi$.

Figure 1: Gazetteer selection based on the algorithm of Boutsidis et al. (2009).

RRQR factorization is a less well-known variant of QR that addresses this limitation. Let $\sigma_i(M)$ denote the i-th largest singular value of matrix M. Given A, RRQR jointly finds a permutation matrix $\Pi \in \{0,1\}^{d \times d}$, orthonormal $Q \in \mathbb{R}^{n \times d}$, and upper triangular $R = [R_{11}\ R_{12};\ 0\ R_{22}] \in \mathbb{R}^{d \times d}$ such that

$$A\Pi = Q \begin{bmatrix} R_{11} & R_{12} \\ & R_{22} \end{bmatrix}$$

satisfying $\sigma_k(R_{11}) = O(\sigma_k(A))$ and $\sigma_1(R_{22}) = \Omega(\sigma_{k+1}(A))$ for $k = 1 \ldots d$. Because of this ranking property, RRQR "reveals" the numerical rank of A. Furthermore, the columns of $A\Pi$ are sorted in the order of decreasing importance.

3.1.2 Gazetteer selection algorithm

The algorithm is a two-stage procedure. In the first step, we randomly sample $O(m \log m)$ rows of A with carefully chosen probabilities and scale them to form columns of matrix $\bar{A} \in \mathbb{R}^{d \times O(m \log m)}$. In the second step, we perform RRQR factorization on $\bar{A}$ and collect the gazetteer elements corresponding to the top components given by the RRQR permutation. The algorithm is shown in Figure 1. The first stage involves random sampling and scaling of rows, but it is shown that $\bar{A}$

has $O(m \log m)$ columns with constant probability.

This algorithm has the following optimality guarantee:

Theorem 3.1 (Boutsidis et al. (2009)). *Let $\hat{B} \in \mathbb{R}^{m \times d}$ be the matrix returned by the algorithm in Figure 1. Then with probability at least 0.7,*

$$\left\|A - A\hat{B}^{+}\hat{B}\right\|_F \leq O(m\sqrt{\log m}) \times \min_{\substack{\tilde{A} \in \mathbb{R}^{n \times d}: \\ rank(\tilde{A}) = m}} \left\|A - \tilde{A}\right\|_F$$

In other words, the selected rows are not arbitrarily worse than the best rank-m approximation of A (given by SVD) with high probability.

3.2 Gazetteer embeddings via CCA

In order to perform the selection algorithm in Figure 1, we need a d-dimensional representation for each of n gazetteer elements. We use CCA for its simplicity and generality.

3.2.1 Canonical Correlation Analysis (CCA)

CCA is a general statistical technique that characterizes the linear relationship between a pair of multi-dimensional variables. CCA seeks to find k dimensions (k is a parameter to be specified) in which these variables are maximally correlated.

Let $x_1 \ldots x_n \in \mathbb{R}^d$ and $y_1 \ldots y_n \in \mathbb{R}^{d'}$ be n samples of the two variables. For simplicity, assume that these variables have zero mean. Then CCA computes the following for $i = 1 \ldots k$:

$$\arg\max_{\substack{u_i \in \mathbb{R}^d,\ v_i \in \mathbb{R}^{d'}: \\ u_i^\top u_{i'} = 0\ \forall i' < i \\ v_i^\top v_{i'} = 0\ \forall i' < i}} \frac{\sum_{l=1}^n (u_i^\top x_l)(v_i^\top y_l)}{\sqrt{\sum_{l=1}^n (u_i^\top x_l)^2}\sqrt{\sum_{l=1}^n (v_i^\top y_l)^2}}$$

In other words, each (u_i, v_i) is a pair of projection vectors such that the *correlation* between the projected variables $u_i^\top x_l$ and $v_i^\top y_l$ is maximized, under the constraint that this projection is *uncorrelated* with the previous $i - 1$ projections.

This is a non-convex problem due to the interaction between u_i and v_i. However, a method based on singular value decomposition (SVD) provides an efficient and exact solution to this problem (Hotelling, 1936). The resulting solution $u_1 \ldots u_k \in \mathbb{R}^d$ and $v_1 \ldots v_k \in \mathbb{R}^{d'}$ can be used to project the variables from the original d- and d'-dimensional spaces to a k-dimensional space:

$$x \in \mathbb{R}^d \longrightarrow \bar{x} \in \mathbb{R}^k : \bar{x}_i = u_i^\top x$$
$$y \in \mathbb{R}^{d'} \longrightarrow \bar{y} \in \mathbb{R}^k : \bar{y}_i = v_i^\top y$$

The new k-dimensional representation of each variable now contains information about the other variable. The value of k is usually selected to be much smaller than d or d', so the representation is typically also low-dimensional.

3.2.2 Inducing gazetteer embeddings

We now describe how to use CCA to induce vector representations for gazetteer elements. Using the same notation, let n be the number of elements in the entire gazetteers. Let $x_1 \ldots x_n$ be the original representations of the element samples and $y_1 \ldots y_n$ be the original representations of the associated features in the element.

We employ the following definition for the original representations. Let d be the number of distinct element types and d' be the number of distinct feature types.

- $x_l \in \mathbb{R}^d$ is a zero vector in which the entry corresponding to the element type of the l-th instance is set to 1.
- $y_l \in \mathbb{R}^{d'}$ is a zero vector in which the entries corresponding to features generated by the element are set to 1.

In our case, we want to induce gazetteer (element) embeddings that correlate with the relevant features about gazetteers. For this purpose, we use three types of features: context features, search click log features, and knowledge graph features.

Context features: For each gazetteer element g of domain l, we take sentences from search logs on domain l containing g and extract five words each to the left and the right of the element g in the sentences. For instance, if g = "The Matrix" is a gazetteer element of domain l = "Movie", we collect sentences from movie-specific search logs involving the phrase "The Matrix". Such domain-specific search logs are collected using a pre-trained domain classifier.

Search click log features: Large-scale search engines such as Bing and Google process millions of queries on a daily basis. Together with the search queries, user clicked URLs are also logged anonymously. These click logs have been used for extracting semantic information for various NLP tasks (Kim et al., 2015a; Tseng et al., 2009; Hakkani-Tür et al., 2011). We used the clicked URLs as features to determine the likelihood of an entity being a member of a dictionary. These features are useful because common URLs are shared across different names such as movie, business and music. Table 1 shows the top five most frequently clicked URLs for movies "Furious 7" and "The age of adaline".

Furious 7	The age of adaline
imdb.com	imdb.com
en.wikipedia.org	en.wikipedia.org
furious7.com	youtube.com
rottentomatoes.com	rottentomatoes.com
www.msn.com	movieinsider.com

Table 1: Top clicked URLs of two movies.

One issue with using only click logs is that some entities may not be covered in the query logs since logs are extracted from a limited time frame (e.g. six months). Even the big search engines employ a moving time window for processing and storing search logs. Consequently, click logs are not necessarily good evidence. For example, "apollo thirteen" is a movie name appearing in the movie training data, but it does not appear in search logs. One way to solve the issue of missing logs for entities is to search `bing.com` at real time. Given that the search engine is updated on a daily basis, real-time search can make sure we capture the newest entities. We run live search for all entities no matter if they appear in search logs or not. Each URL returned from the live search is considered to have an additional click.

Knowledge graph features: The graph in `www.freebase.com` contains a large set of tuples in a resource description framework (RDF) defined by W3C. A tuple typically consists of two entities: a subject and an object linked by some relation.

An interesting part of this resource is the entity type defined in the graph for each entity. In the knowledge graph, the "type" relation represents the entity type. Table 2 shows some examples of entities and their relations in the knowledge graph. From the graph, we learn that "Romeo & Juliet" could be a film name or a music album since it has two types: "film.film" and "music.album".

Subject	Relation	Object
Jason Statham	type	film.actor
Jason Statham	type	tv.actor
Jason Statham	type	film.producer
Romeo & Juliet	type	film.film
Romeo & Juliet	type	music.album

Table 2: Entities & relation in the knowledge graph.

4 Experiments

To test the effectiveness of the proposed gazetteer selection method, we conduct slot tagging experiments across a test suite of three domains: Movies, Music and Places, which are very sensitive domains to gazetteer features. The task of slot tagging is to find the correct sequence of tags of words given a user utterance. For example, in Places domain, a user could say "search for home depot in kingsport" and the phrase "home depot" and "kingsport" are tagged with `Place_Name` and `Location` respectively. The data statistics are shown in Table 3. One domain can have various kinds of gazetteers. For example, Places domain has business name, restaurant name, school name and etc. Candidate dictionaries are mined from the web and search logs automatically using basic pattern matching approaches (e.g. entities sharing the same or similar context in queries or documents) and consequently contain significant amount of noise. As the table indicates, the number of elements in total across all the gazetteers (#total gazet elements) in each domain are too large for models to consume.

In all our experiments, we trained conditional random fields (CRFs) (Lafferty et al., 2001) with the following features: (1) n-gram features up to $n = 3$, (2) regular expression features, and (3) Brown clusters (Brown et al., 1992) induced from search logs. With these features, we compare the following methods to demonstrate the importance of adding appropriate gazetteers:

- *NoG*: train without gazetteer features.
- *AllG*: train with all gazetteers.
- *RandG*: train with randomly selected gazetteers.
- *RRQRG*: train with gazetteers selected from RRQR.
- *RankAllG*: train with all ranked gazetteers.

Domains	#labels	#kinds of gazets	#total gazet elements	#training queries	#test queries
Movies	25	21	14,188,527	43,784	12,179
Music	7	13	62,231,869	31,853	8,615
Places	32	31	34,227,612	22,345	6,143

Table 3: Data statistics

Here gazetteer features are activated when a phrase contains an entity in a dictionary. For RandG, we first sample a category of gazetteers uniformly and then choose a lexicon from gazetteers in that category. The results when we use selected gazetteer randomly in whole categories are very low and did not include them here. For selecting gazetteer methods (NoG, RnadG and RRQRG), we select 500,000 elements in total.

	Places	Music	Movies	AVG.
NoG	89.10	81.53	84.78	85.14
AllG	92.11	84.24	88.56	88.30
RRQRG	91.80	83.83	87.41	87.68
RandG	86.20	76.53	77.23	79.99

Table 4: Comparison of models evaluated on three domains. The numbers are F1-scores.

4.1 Results across Domains

First, we evaluate all models across three domains. Note that the both training and test data are collected from the United States. The results are shown in Table 4. Not surprisingly, using all gazetteer features (AllG) boosts the F1 score from 85.14 % to 88.30%, confirming the power of gazetteer features. However, with a random selection of gazetteers, the model does not perform well, only achieving 79.99% F1-score. Interestingly, we see that across all domains our method (RRQRG) fares better than both RandG and NoG, almost reaching the AllG performance with gazetteer size dramatically reduced.

4.2 Results across Locales

In the next experiments, we run experiments across three different locales in Places domain: United Kingdom (GB), Australia (AU), and India (IN). The Places is a very sensitive domain to locales[2]. For example, restaurant names in India are very different from Australia. Here we assume that unlike the previous experiments, the training data is collected from the United States and test data is collected from different locales. We used same training data in the previous experiments and the size of test data is about 5k for each locale. The results are shown in Table 5. Interestingly, the RRQR even outperforms the AllG. This is because some noisy entities are filtered.

[2]Since it is very difficult to create all locale specific training data, gazetteer features are very crucial.

Finally, we show that the proposed method is useful even in all gazetteer scenario (AllG). Using RRQR, we can order entities according to their importance and transform a gazetteer feature into a few ones by binning the entities with their rankings. For example, instead of having one single big business names gazetteer, we can divide them into lexicon with first 1000 entities, 10000 entities and so on. Results using ranked gazetteers are shown in Table 6. We see that the Ranked gazetteers approach (RankAllG) has consistent gains across domains over AllG.

	GB	AU	IN
NoG	87.70	82.20	80.30
AllG	90.12	86.98	89.77
RRQRG	90.18	87.48	90.28
RandG	86.20	65.34	64.20

Table 5: Comparison of models across different locales.

	Places	Music	Movies	AVG.
AllG	92.11	84.24	88.56	88.30
RankAllG	92.78	86.30	89.1	89.40

Table 6: Comparison of models with or without ranked gazetteers. These are evaluated on three domains collected in the United States.

5 Conclusion

We proposed the task of selecting compact lexicons from large and noisy gazetteers. This scenario arises often in practice. We introduced a simple and effective solution based on matrix decomposition techniques: CCA is used to derive low-dimensional gazetteer embeddings and RRQR is used to find a subset of these embeddings. Experiments on slot tagging show that our method yields relative error reduction of $> 50\%$ on average over the random selection method.

References

Tasos Anastasakos, Young-Bum Kim, and Anoop Deoras. 2014. Task specific continuous word representations for mono and multi-lingual spoken language understanding. In *ICASSP*, pages 3246–3250. IEEE.

Christos Boutsidis, Michael W Mahoney, and Petros Drineas. 2009. An improved approximation algorithm for the column subset selection problem. In *Proceedings of the twentieth Annual ACM-SIAM Symposium on Discrete Algorithms*, pages 968–977. Society for Industrial and Applied Mathematics.

Peter F Brown, Peter V Desouza, Robert L Mercer, Vincent J Della Pietra, and Jenifer C Lai. 1992. Class-based n-gram models of natural language. *Computational linguistics*, 18(4):467–479.

Asli Celikyilmaz, Dilek Z Hakkani-Tür, Gökhan Tür, and Ruhi Sarikaya. 2013. Semi-supervised semantic tagging of conversational understanding using markov topic regression. In *ACL (1)*, pages 914–923.

Asli Celikyilmaz, Dilek Hakkani-Tur, Panupong Pasupat, and Ruhi Sarikaya. 2015. Enriching word embeddings using knowledge graph for semantic tagging in conversational dialog systems. AAAI - Association for the Advancement of Artificial Intelligence, January.

Dilek Hakkani-Tür, Gokhan Tur, Larry Heck, Asli Celikyilmaz, Ashley Fidler, Dustin Hillard, Rukmini Iyer, and S. Parthasarathy. 2011. Employing web search query click logs for multi-domain spoken language understanding. IEEE Automatic Speech Recognition and Understanding Workshop, December.

Dustin Hillard, Asli Celikyilmaz, Dilek Z Hakkani-Tür, and Gökhan Tür. 2011. Learning weighted entity lists from web click logs for spoken language understanding. In *INTERSPEECH*, pages 705–708.

Harold Hotelling. 1936. Relations between two sets of variates. *Biometrika*, 28(3/4):321–377.

Young-Bum Kim and Benjamin Snyder. 2013. Optimal data set selection: An application to grapheme-to-phoneme conversion. In *HLT-NAACL*, pages 1196–1205. Association for Computational Linguistics.

Young-Bum Kim, Jeong Minwoo, Karl Startos, and Ruhi Sarikaya. 2015a. Weakly supervised slot tagging with partially labeled sequences from web search click logs. In *HLT-NAACL*, pages 84–92. Association for Computational Linguistics.

Young-Bum Kim, Karl Stratos, and Ruhi Sarikaya. 2015b. Pre-training of hidden-unit crfs. In *ACL*. Association for Computational Linguistics.

Young-Bum Kim, Karl Stratos, Ruhi Sarikaya, and Minwoo Jeong. 2015c. New transfer learning techniques for disparate label sets. In *ACL*. Association for Computational Linguistics.

John Lafferty, Andrew McCallum, and Fernando CN Pereira. 2001. Conditional random fields: Probabilistic models for segmenting and labeling sequence data. In *ICML*, pages 282–289.

Xiao Li, Ye-Yi Wang, and Alex Acero. 2009. Extracting structured information from user queries with semi-supervised conditional random fields. In *Proceedings of the 32nd international ACM SIGIR conference on Research and development in information retrieval*.

Xiaohu Liu and Ruhi Sarikaya. 2014. A discriminative model based entity dictionary weighting approach for spoken language understanding. In *Spoken Language Technology Workshop (SLT)*, pages 195–199. IEEE.

Ruhi Sarikaya, Asli C, Anoop Deoras, and Minwoo Jeong. 2014. Shrinkage based features for slot tagging with conditional random fields. In Proceeding of ISCA - International Speech Communication Association, September.

Huihsin Tseng, Longbin Chen, Fan Li, Ziming Zhuang, Lei Duan, and Belle Tseng. 2009. Mining search engine clickthrough log for matching n-gram features. In *Proceedings of the 2009 Conference on Empirical Methods in Natural Language Processing: Volume 2-Volume 2*, pages 524–533. Association for Computational Linguistics.

Puyang Xu and Ruhi Sarikaya. 2014. Targeted feature dropout for robust slot filling in natural language understanding. In *ISCA - International Speech Communication Association*, September.

The Impact of Listener Gaze on Predicting Reference Resolution

Nikolina Koleva[1] **Martín Villalba**[2] **Maria Staudte**[1] **Alexander Koller**[2]

[1]Embodied Spoken Interaction Group, Saarland University, Saarbrücken, Germany
[2] Department of Linguistics, University of Potsdam, Potsdam, Germany
{nikkol | masta}@coli.uni-saarland.de
{martin.villalba | alexander.koller}@uni-potsdam.de

Abstract

We investigate the impact of listener's gaze on predicting reference resolution in situated interactions. We extend an existing model that predicts to which entity in the environment listeners will resolve a referring expression (RE). Our model makes use of features that capture which objects were looked at and for how long, reflecting listeners' visual behavior. We improve a probabilistic model that considers a basic set of features for monitoring listeners' movements in a virtual environment. Particularly, in complex referential scenes, where more objects next to the target are possible referents, gaze turns out to be beneficial and helps deciphering listeners' intention. We evaluate performance at several prediction times before the listener performs an action, obtaining a highly significant accuracy gain.

1 Introduction

Speakers tend to follow the listener's behavior in order to determine whether their communicated message was received and understood. This phenomenon is known as *grounding*, it is well established in the dialogue literature (Clark, 1996), and it plays an important role in collaborative tasks and goal–oriented conversations. Solving a collaborative task in a shared environment is an effective way of studying the alignment of communication channels (Clark and Krych, 2004; Hanna and Brennan, 2007).

In situated spoken conversations ambiguous linguistic expressions are common, where additional modalities are available. While Gargett et al. (2010) studied instruction giving and following in virtual environments, Brennan et al. (2013) examined pedestrian guidance in outdoor real environments. Both studies investigate the interaction of human interlocutors but neither study exploits listeners' eye movements. In contrast, Koller et al. (2012) designed a task in which a natural language generation (NLG) system gives instructions to a human player in virtual environment whose eye movements were tracked. They outperformed similar systems in both successful reference resolution and listener confusion. Engonopoulos et al. (2013) attempted to predict the resolution of an RE, achieving good performance by combining two probabilistic log–linear models: a *semantic* model P_{sem} that analyzes the semantics of a given instruction, and an *observational* model P_{obs} that inspects the player's behavior. However, they did not include listener's gaze. They observed that the accuracy for P_{obs} reaches its highest point at a relatively late stage in an interaction. Similar observations are reported by Kennington and Schlangen (2014): they compare listener gaze and an incremental update model (IUM) as predictors for the resolution of an RE, noting that gaze is more accurate before the onset of an utterance, whereas the model itself is more accurate afterwards.

In this paper we report on the extension of the P_{obs} model to also consider listener's visual behaviour. More precisely we implement features that encode listener's eye movement patterns and evaluate their performance on a multi–modal data collection. We show that such a model as it takes an additional communication channel provides more accurate predictions especially when dealing with complex scenes. We also expand on concepts from the IUM, by applying the conclusions drawn from its behaviour to a dynamic task with a naturalistic interactive scenario.

2 Problem definition

We address the research question of how to automatically predict an RE resolution, i.e., answering the question of which entity in a virtual environment has been understood by the listener af-

Proceedings of the 53rd Annual Meeting of the Association for Computational Linguistics and the 7th International Joint Conference on Natural Language Processing (Short Papers), pages 812–817,
Beijing, China, July 26-31, 2015.

ter receiving an instruction. While the linguistic material in instructions carries a lot of information, even completely unambiguous descriptions may be misunderstood. A robust NLG system should be capable of detecting misunderstandings and preventing its users from making mistakes.

Language comprehension is mirrored by interlocutors' non verbal behavior, and this can help when decoding the listener's interpretation. Precise automatic estimates may be crucial when developing a real–time NLG system, as such a mechanism would be more robust and capable at avoiding misunderstandings. As mentioned in section 1, Engonopoulos et al. (2013) propose two statistical models to solve that problem: a semantic model P_{sem} based on the linguistic content, and an observation model P_{obs} based on listener behavior features.

More formally, let's assume a system generates an expression r that aims to identify a target object o_t among a set O of possible objects, i.e. those available in the scene view. Given the state of the world s at time point t, and the observed listener's behavior $\sigma(t)$ of the user at time $t \geq t_b$ (where t_b denotes the end of an interaction), we estimated the conditional probability $p(o_p|r, s, \sigma(t))$ that indicates how probable it is that the listener resolved r to o_p. This probability can be also expressed as follows:

$$P(o_p|r, s, \sigma(t)) \propto \frac{P_{sem}(o_p|r, s)P_{obs}(o_p|\sigma(t))}{P(o_p)}$$

Following Engonopoulos et al. (2013) we make the simplifying assumption that the distribution of the probability among the possible targets is uniform and obtain:

$$P(o_p|r, s, \sigma(t)) \propto P_{sem}(o_p|r, s)P_{obs}(o_p|\sigma(t))$$

We expect an NLG system to compute and output an expression that maximizes the probability of o_p. Due to the dynamic nature of our scenarios, we also require the probability value to be updated at certain time intervals throughout an interaction. Tracking the probability changes over time, an NLG system could proactively react to changes in its environment. Henderson and Smith (2007) show that accounting for both fixation location and duration are key to identify a player's focus of attention.

The technical contribution of this paper is to extend the P_{obs} model of Engonopoulos et al. (2013) with gaze features to account for these variables.

3 Episodes and feature functions

The data for our experiment was obtained from the GIVE Challenge (Koller et al., 2010), an interactive task in a 3D virtual environment in which a human player (instruction follower, IF) is navigated through a maze, locating and pressing buttons in a predefined order aiming to unlock a safe. While pressing the wrong button in the sequences doesn't always have negative effects, it can also lead to restarting or losing the game. The IF receives instructions from either another player or an automated system (instruction giver, IG). The IF's behavior was recorded every 200ms, along with the IG's instructions and the state of the virtual world. The result is an interaction corpus comprising over 2500 games and spanning over 340 hours of interactions. These interactions were mainly collected during the GIVE-2 and the GIVE-2.5 challenges. A laboratory study conducted by Staudte et al. (2012) comprises a data collection that contains eye-tracking records for the IF. Although the corpus contains both successful and unsuccessful games, we have decided to consider only the successful ones.

We define an *episode* over this corpus as a typically short sequence of recorded behavior states, beginning with a manipulation instruction generated by the IG and ending with a button press by the IF (at time point t_b). In order to make sure that the recorded button press is a direct response to the IG's instruction, an episode is defined such that it doesn't contain further utterances after the first one. Both the target intended by the IG (o_t) and the one selected by the IF (o_p) were recorded.

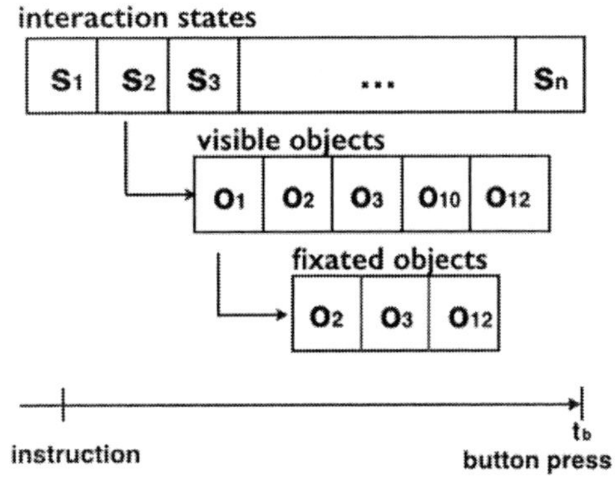

Figure 1: The structure of the interactions.

Figure 1 depicts the structure of an episode when eye-tracking data is available. Each episode can be seen as a sequence of interaction states $(s_1, \ldots, s_n)$, and each state has a set of visible objects $(\{o_1, o_2, o_3, o_{10}, o_{12}\})$. We then compute the subset of fixated objects $(\{o_2, o_3, o_{12}\})$. We update both sets of visible and fixated objects dynamically in each interaction state with respect to the change in visual scene and the corresponding record of the listener's eye movements.

We developed feature functions over these episodes. Along with the episode's data, each function takes two parameters: an object o_p for which the function is evaluated, and a parameter d seconds that defines how much of the episode's data is the feature allowed to analyze. Each feature looks only at the behavior that happens in the time interval $-d$ to 0. Henceforth we refer to the value of a feature function over this interval as its value at time $-d$. The value of a feature function evaluated on episodes with length less than d seconds is undefined.

4 Prediction models

Given an RE uttered by an IG, the *semantic* model P_{sem} estimates the probability for each possible object in the environment to have been understood as the referent, ranks all candidates and selects the most probable one in a current scene. This probability represents the semantics of the utterance, and is evaluated at a single time point immediately after the instruction (e.g. "press the blue button") has been uttered. The model takes into account features that encode the presence or absence of adjectives carrying information about the spatial or color properties (like the adjective "blue"), along with landmarks appearing as post modifiers of the target noun.

In contrast to the semantic model, the *observational* model P_{obs} evaluates the changes in the visual context and player's behavior after an instruction has been received. The estimated probability is updated constantly before an action, as the listener in our task–oriented interactions is constantly in motion, altering the visual context. The model evaluates the distance of the listener position to a potential target, whether it is visible or not, and also how salient an object is in that particular time window.

As we have seen above, eye movements provide useful information indicating language comprehension, and also how to map a semantic representation to an entity in a shared environment. Interlocutors constantly interact with their surrounding and point to specific entities with gestures. Gaze behaviour is also driven by the current state of an interaction. Thus, we extend the basic set of P_{obs} features and implement eye–tracking features that capture gaze information. We call this the *extended observational* model P_{Eobs} and consider the following additional features:

1. *Looked at:* feature counts the number of interaction states in which an object has been fixated at least once during the current episode.

2. *Longest Sequence:* detects the longest continuous sequence of interaction states in which a particular object has been fixated.

3. *Linear Distance:* returns the euclidean distance $dist$ on screen between the gaze cursor and the center of an object.

4. *Inv-Squared Distance:* returns $\frac{1}{1+dist^2}$.

5. *Update Fixated Objects:* expands the list of fixated objects in order to consider the IF's focus of attention. It successively searches in 10 pixel steps and stops as soon as an object is found (the threshold is 100 pixels). This feature evaluates to 1 if the list of fixated objects is been expanded and 0 otherwise.

When training our model at time $-d_{train}$, we generate a feature matrix. Given a training episode, each possible (located in the same room) object o_p is added as a new row, where each column contains the value of a different feature function for o_p over this episode at time $-d_{train}$. Finally, the row based on the target selected by the IF is marked as a positive example. We then train a log-linear model, where the weights assigned to each feature function are learned via optimization with the L-BFGS algorithm. By training our model to correctly predict a target button based only on data observed up until $-d_{train}$ seconds before the actual action t_b, we expect our model to reliably predict which button the user will select. Analogously, we define accuracy at testing time $-d_{test}$ as the percentage of correctly predicted target objects when predicting over episodes at time $-d_{test}$. This pair of training and test parameters is denoted as the tuple (d_{train}, d_{test}).

5 Dataset

We evaluated the performance of our improved model over data collected by Staudte et al. (2012) using the GIVE Challenge platform. Both training and testing were performed over a subset of the data obtained during a collection task involving worlds created by Gargett et al. (2010), designed to provide the task with varying levels of difficulty. This corpus provides recorded eye-tracking data, collected with a remote faceLAB system. In contrast, the evaluation presented by Engonopoulos et al. (2013) uses only games collected for the GIVE 2 and GIVE 2.5 challenges, for which no eye-tracking data is available. Here, we do not investigate the performance of P_{sem} and concentrate on the direct comparison between P_{obs} and P_{Eobs} in order to find out if and when eye–tracking can improve the prediction of an RE resolution.

We further filtered our corpus in order to remove noisy games following Koller et al. (2012), considering only interactions for which the eye-tracker calibration detected inspection of either the target or another button object in at least 75% of all referential scenes in an interaction. The resulting corpus comprises 75 games, for a combined length of 8 hours. We extracted 761 episodes from this corpus, amounting to 47m 58s of recorded interactions, with an average length per episode of 3.78 seconds ($\sigma = 3.03 sec.$). There are 261 episodes shorter than 2 sec., 207 in the 2-4 sec. range, 139 in the 4-6 sec. range, and 154 episodes longer than 6 sec.

6 Evaluation and results

The accuracy of our probabilistic models depends on the parameters (d_{train}, d_{test}). At different stages of an interaction the difficulty to predict an intended target varies as the visual context changes and in particular the number of visible objects. As the weights of the features are optimized at time $-d_{train}$, it would be expected that testing also at time $-d_{test} = -d_{train}$ yields the highest accuracy. However, the difficulty to make a prediction decreases as $t_b - d_{test}$ approaches t_b, i.e. as the player moves towards the intended target. We expect that testing at $-d_{train}$ works best, but we need to be able to update continuously. Thus we also evaluate at other timepoints and test several combinations of the (d_{train}, d_{test}) parameters.

Given the limited amount of eye-tracking data available in our corpus, we replaced the cross-corpora-challenge test setting from the original P_{obs} study with a ten fold cross validation setup. As training and testing were performed over instances of a certain minimum length according to (d_{train}, d_{test}), we first removed all instances with length less than $max(d_{train}, d_{test})$, and then perform the cross validation split. In this way we ensure that the number of instances in the folds are not unbalanced. Moreover, each instance was classified as *easy* or *hard* depending on the number of visible objects at time t_b. An instance was considered *easy* if no more than three objects were visible at that point, or *hard* otherwise. For $-d_{test} = 0$, 59.5% of all instances are considered *hard*, but this proportion decreases as $-d_{test}$ increases. At $-d_{test} = -6$, the number of hard instances amounts to 72.7%.

We evaluated both the original P_{obs} model and the P_{Eobs} model on the same data set. We also calculated accuracy values for each feature function, in order to test whether a single function could outperform P_{obs}. We included as baselines two versions of P_{obs} using only the features *InRoom* and *Visual Salience* proposed by Engonopoulos et al. (2013).

The accuracy results on Figure 2 show our observations for $-6 \leq -d_{train} \leq -2$ and $-d_{train} \leq -d_{test} \leq 0$. The graph shows that P_{Eobs} performs similarly as P_{obs} on the *easy* instances, i.e. the eye-tracking features are not contributing in those scenarios. However, P_{Eobs} shows a consistent improvement on the *hard* instances over P_{obs}.

For each permutation of the training and testing parameters (d_{train}, d_{test}), we obtain a set of episodes that fulfil the length criteria for the given parameters. We apply P_{obs} and P_{Eobs} on the obtained set of instances and measure two corresponding accuracy values. We compared the accuracy values of P_{obs} and P_{Eobs} over all 25 different (d_{train}, d_{test}) pairs, using a paired samples t-test. The test indicated that the P_{Eobs} performance ($M = 83.72$, $SD = 3.56$) is significantly better than the P_{obs} performance ($M = 79.33$, $SD = 3.89$), ($t(24) = 9.51, p < .001, Cohen's\ d = 1.17$). Thus eye-tracking features seem to be particularly helpful for predicting to which entity an RE is resolved in hard scenes.

The results also show a peak in accuracy near the -3 seconds mark. We computed a 2x2 contingency table that contrasts correct and incorrect predictions for P_{obs} and P_{Eobs}, i.e. whether o_i was

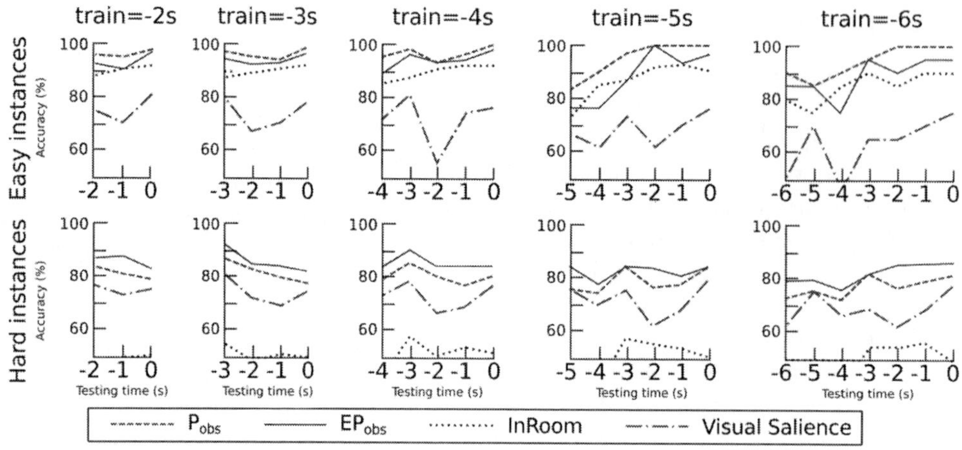

Figure 2: Accuracy as a function of training and testing time.

classified as target object or not. Data for this table was collected from all episode judgements for models trained at times in the $[-6\,sec., -3\,sec.]$ range and tested at -3 seconds. McNemar's test showed that the marginal row and column frequencies are significantly different ($p < 0.05$). This peak is related to the average required time between an utterance and the resulting target manipulation. This result shows that our model is more accurate precisely at points in time when we expect fixations to a target object.

7 Conclusion

In this paper we have shown that listener's gaze is useful by showing that accuracy improves over P_{obs} in the context of predicting the resolution of an RE. In addition, we observed that our model P_{Eobs} proves to be more robust than P_{obs} when the time interval between the prediction $(t_b - d_{test})$ and the button press (t_b) increases, i.e. gaze is especially beneficial in an early stage of an interaction. This approach shows significant accuracy improvement on hard referential scenes where more objects are visible.

We have also established that gaze is particularly useful when combined with some other simple features, as the features that capture listeners visual behaviour are not powerful enough to outperform even the simplest baseline. Gaze only benefits the model when it is added on top of features that capture the visual context, i.e. the current scene.

The most immediate future line of research is the combination of our P_{Eobs} model with the semantic model P_{sem}, in order to test the impact of the extended features in a combined model. If successful, such a model could provide reliable predictions for a significant amount of time before an action takes place. This is of particular importance when it comes to designing a system that automatically generates and online outputs feedback to confirm correct and reject incorrect intentions.

Testing with users in real time is also an area for future research. An implementation of the P_{obs} model is currently in the test phase, and an extension for the P_{Eobs} model would be the immediate next step. The model could be embedded in an NLG system to improve the automatic language generation in such scenarios.

Given that our work refers only to NLG systems, there's no possible analysis of speaker's gaze. However, it may be interesting to ask whether a human IG could benefit from the predictions of P_{Eobs}. We could study whether predictions based on the gaze (mis-)match between both interlocutors are more effective than simply presenting the IF's gaze to the IG and trusting the IG to correctly interpret this data. If such a system proved to be effective, it could point misunderstandings to the IG before either of the participants becomes aware of them.

Acknowledgements

This work was funded by the Cluster of Excellence on "Multimodal Computing and Interaction" of the German Excellence Initiative and the SFB 632 "Information Structure".

References

Susan E. Brennan, Katharina S. Schuhmann, and Karla M. Batres. 2013. Entrainment on the move and in the lab: The walking around corpus. In *Proceedings of the 35th Annual Conference of the Cognitive Science Society*, Berlin, Germany.

Herbert H. Clark and Meredyth A. Krych. 2004. Speaking while monitoring addressees for understanding. *Journal of Memory and Language*, 50(1):62–81, January.

Herbert H. Clark. 1996. *Using Language*. Cambridge University Press, May.

Nikos Engonopoulos, Martín Villalba, Ivan Titov, and Alexander Koller. 2013. Predicting the resolution of referring expressions from user behavior. In *Proceedings of the Conference on Empirical Methods in Natural Language Processing (EMNLP)*, Seattle.

Andrew Gargett, Konstantina Garoufi, Alexander Koller, and Kristina Striegnitz. 2010. The give-2 corpus of giving instructions in virtual environments. In *Proceedings of the Seventh International Conference on Language Resources and Evaluation (LREC'10)*, Valletta, Malta, May. European Language Resources Association (ELRA).

Joy E. Hanna and Susan E. Brennan. 2007. Speakers' eye gaze disambiguates referring expressions early during face-to-face conversation. *Journal of Memory and Language*, 57(4):596–615, November.

John M. Henderson and Tim J. Smith. 2007. How are eye fixation durations controlled during scene viewing? further evidence from a scene onset delay paradigm. *Visual Cognition*, 17(6-7):1055–1082.

Casey Kennington and David Schlangen. 2014. Comparing listener gaze with predictions of an incremental reference resolution model. *RefNet workshop on Psychological and Computational Models of Reference Comprehension and Production.*

Alexander Koller, Kristina Striegnitz, Andrew Gargett, Donna Byron, Justine Cassell, Robert Dale, Johanna Moore, and Jon Oberlander. 2010. Report on the Second NLG Challenge on Generating Instructions in Virtual Environments (GIVE-2). In *Proceedings of the 6th International Natural Language Generation Conference (INLG).*

Alexander Koller, Maria Staudte, Konstantina Garoufi, and Matthew Crocker. 2012. Enhancing referential success by tracking hearer gaze. In *Proceedings of the 13th Annual Meeting of the Special Interest Group on Discourse and Dialogue*, SIGDIAL '12, pages 30–39, Stroudsburg, PA, USA. Association for Computational Linguistics.

Maria Staudte, Alexander Koller, Konstantina Garoufi, and Matthew Crocker. 2012. Using listener gaze to augment speech generation in a virtual 3D environment. In *Proceedings of the 34th Annual Meeting of the Cognitive Science Society (CogSci)*, Sapporo.

A Simultaneous Recognition Framework for the Spoken Language Understanding Module of Intelligent Personal Assistant Software on Smart Phones

Changsu Lee and Youngjoong Ko
Computer Engineering, Dong-A University
840 Hadan 2-dong, Saha-gu,
Busan 604-714 Korea
{blue772001,youngjoong.ko}@gmail.com

Jungyun Seo
Computer Science, Sogang University
Sinsu-dong 1, Mapo-gu
Seoul, 121-742, Korea
seojy@ccs.sogang.ac.kr

Abstract

The intelligent personal assistant software such as the *Apple's Siri* and *Samsung's S-Voice* has been issued these days. This paper introduces a novel Spoken Language Understanding (SLU) module to predict user's intention for determining system actions of the intelligent personal assistant software. The SLU module usually consists of several connected recognition tasks on a pipeline framework, whereas the proposed SLU module simultaneously recognizes four recognition tasks on a recognition framework using Conditional Random Fields (CRF). The four tasks include named entity, speech-act, target and operation recognition. In the experiments, the new simultaneous recognition method achieves the higher performance of 4% and faster speed of about 25% than other method using a pipeline framework. By a significance test, this improvement is considered to be statistically significant as a *p-value* of smaller than 0.05.

1 Introduction

Currently, one of the most issued and promising software is the intelligent personal assistant software such as *Apple's Siri* (Wikipedia, 2011) and *Samsung's S-Voice* (Wikipedia, 2012). This kind of software provides users a natural language user interface to answer questions, make recommendations and perform actions. One of the core modules to develop this software is the Spoken Language Understanding (SLU) module. The SLU module predicts the user's intention of user utterance, and one of the various software actions is selected to provide appropriate information to a user (Wang et al., 2005).

The SLU model of the intelligent personal assistant software has several different aspects from the previous other SLU modules, such as ones of ATIS (Automatic Terminal Information Service) and DARPA (Defense Advanced Research Project Agency) projects, which are based on rule-based methods (Ward et al. 1994; Wang et al. 2001) and statistical methods (Wang et al. 2006; Raymond et al. 2007). Because the SLU module is operated for various applications (Apps) of mobile devices such as weather, transportation, etc., it has to be able to deal with more heterogeneous domains than the ATIS and DARPA projects and it does more detailed analysis for each domain in order to offer users accurate information. In addition, since the SLU module in the previous dialogue systems has a complicated architecture that is composes of many sub-modules, it is difficult for them to be directly applied into the SLU module of intelligent personal assistant software with those many domains for mobile devices. That is, building up a complicated architecture for each domain can make a heavy system and this kind of system is not proper to mobile devices.

In this paper, we propose a new SLU module with a simultaneous recognition framework for the intelligent personal assistant software. The proposed SLU module consists of four components: named entity (NE), speech-act, target and operator recognition. Each component of the proposed SLU module has different recognition unit, e.g. the named entity recognition is based on a morpheme/phrase unit, whereas the target, operator and speech-act are on an utterance unit. To integrate these recognition units into the same unit, we develop a new tag addition approach that represents a user utterance as a tag sequence for an input to CRF (Lafferty et al. 2001).

Proceedings of the 53rd Annual Meeting of the Association for Computational Linguistics and the 7th International Joint Conference on Natural Language Processing (Short Papers), pages 818–822,
Beijing, China, July 26-31, 2015. ©2015 Association for Computational Linguistics

In the experiments, the proposed simultaneous recognition module showed the better performance of 4% than a pipeline module. And it has an additional benefit that it is composed of a simple architecture with only one recognition module so it can be more efficient than other methods with respect to processing time, etc. As a result, the processing time of our system was reduced about 25% when compared to the pipeline system.

The remainder of the paper is organized as the follows. Section 2 describes related work. In the section 3, we define four components of our SLU module for the intelligent personal assistant software. Section 4 introduces our simultaneous recognition framework in detail. Section 5 explains our experimental settings and results. Finally, section 6 draws conclusions.

2 Related Work

The approaches for developing the SLU modules are largely divided into the rule-based methods and the statistical methods. The rule-based modules have typically been implemented via hand-crafted semantic level grammar rules and some robust parsers (Seneff. 1992; Ward et al. 1999). However, these semantic grammar approaches carry a high development cost and they can also lead to fragile operations since users do not typically know what grammatical constructions are supported by the system. An alternative approach is to use some statistical methods to directly map from word strings to the intended meaning structures. Statistical methods are attractive because they can be easily adapted to new conditions using only annotated training data. Statistical methods for SLU have been studied in a Hidden Vector State (HVS) Model (He et al., 2005) and a data-driven statistical models (Miller et al. 1994; Pieraccini et al. 1992; Wang et al. 2006). In addition, Jeong and Lee (2008) proposed a unified probabilistic model (triangular-chain CRF) combining the named entity and dialog-act of SLU. This method achieved the high performance for SLU. But the triangular-chain CRF has a complicated architecture with a modified CRF. And this method was built only to combine the named entity and dialog-act, whereas we need to combine four components. In practical, the triangular-chain CRF showed low performance when combining four components in the experiments. As a result, the proposed SLU module achieved high performance in spite of its simple architecture.

3 Components of the Proposed SLU Module for the Intelligent Personal Assistant Software

Since the SLU module of intelligent personal assistant software needs to determine the actions of Apps of smart phone according to user needs, they require more elaborate user intent analysis. Thus we define four components of the SLU module. An analysis result of our SLU module is shown in Figure 1 as follows:

Utterance : 지금 뉴욕은 얼마나 더워 ?
How hot is it in New York now ?

Named entities : 지금 (now) / Time
뉴욕 (New York) / Location
Target : Temperature_Info
Operator : Lookup
Speech-act : Wh_question

Figure 1: Example of analysis results

Named Entity (NE) recognition: NE recognition extracts keywords from user utterances, such as person, time, location, etc.

Target recognition: target describes the object of system action. In Figure 1, the target is "Temperature_Information." By this recognized target, the software can offer users accurate information.

Operator recognition: operator is to detect one of the various software actions (Lookup, Set, Delete, etc.). In Figure 1, the operator is identified as "Lookup".

Speech-act recognition: speech-act tries to designate a surface level speech-act. "Wh_Question" as speech-act in Figure 1 provides the user's intention of surface level to dialogue systems.

4 Simultaneous Recognition Framework

We assume that four components of our SLU module are correlated with each other. In order to improve the performance and speed of the SLU module, we propose a new framework to simultaneously recognize the four components. But these components have different recognition units; NE has a morpheme/phrase unit and target, operator and speech-act have an utterance unit. A new tag addition method is proposed to solve this problem. Using this method, we can construct a novel simultaneous recognition framework for SLU.

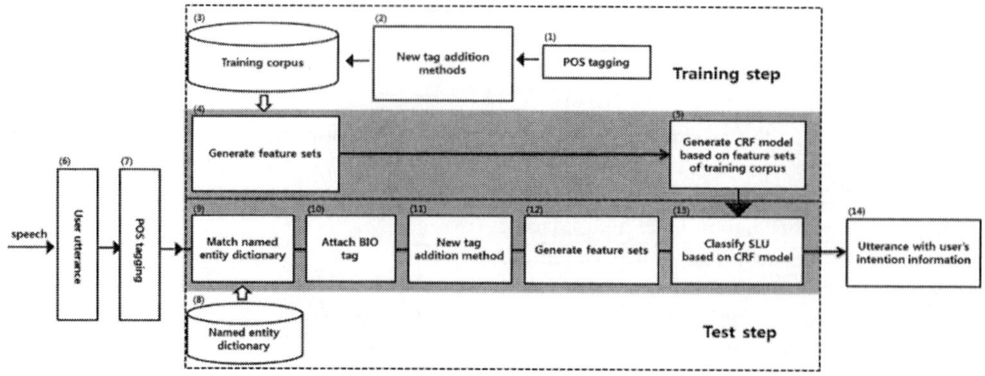

Figure 3: Architecture for the simultaneous recognition framework

4.1 New tag addition method

Target, operator and speech-act are based on an utterance unit. In order to construct a simultaneous recognition framework, we attach pseudo morphemes with target, operator and speech-act tags in front of each user utterance. Using these pseudo morphemes, target, operator and speech-act can utilize the features of NE, and NE can also do target, operator and speech-act information as additional features. Figure 2 shows an example of the new tag addition method.

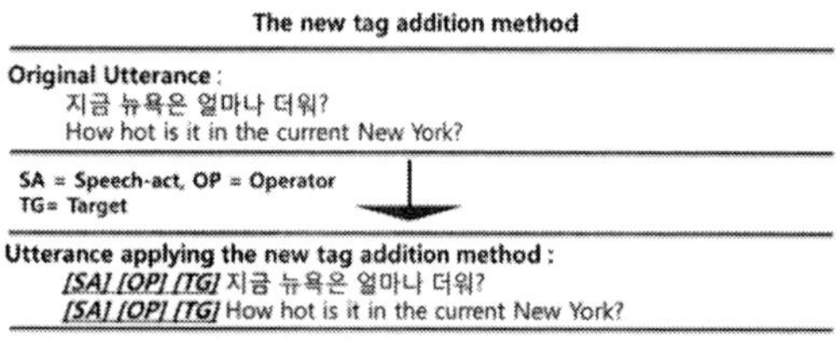

Figure 2: Example of the new tag addition method

4.2 Simultaneous recognition framework

On the simultaneous recognition framework with the new tag addition method, an input utterance is analyzed by a sequential labeling classifier, CRF. It is possible to use all of component labels as additional features in this classification method. We think that this is a main reason why the proposed method improves recognition performances.

Our framework needs only NE dictionary and BIO annotated training corpus; BIO tags were used in (Ramshaw and Marcus. 1995). It is very simple and fast because it can output all of four different SLU results in one classification execution. The architecture of our framework is shown in Figure 3. Our SLU module is widely divided into a training step and a test step.

4.3 Feature Sets

The three feature sets are extracted for SLU: basis features (Lee et al. 2010), NE dictionary features and target/operator/speech-act features. All the basic and NE dictionary features are analyzed based on the morpheme unit.

- **Basis features**

Current lexicon/POS tag information
Based on the position of the current lexicon, lexicon contextual information. window size : -2~2
Based on the position of the current POS tag, POS tag contextual information. window size : -2~2
The words of Korean language can consist of one or more morphemes; - current morpheme position information in a word - current morpheme POS tag/word length information

- **NE dictionary features**

Based on current morpheme, NE tag information matched from NE dictionary

- **Target/operator/speech-act features**

Verb information in the utterance
Lexicon unigram information in the utterance
Lexicon & POS tag bigram information in the utterance
Lexicon & POS tag trigram information in the utterance

5 Experiments

5.1 Experimental settings

The MADS data set (Multi-Applications Dialogues for Smart phones) was constructed and used to develop the SLU modules for the intelligent personal assistant software. The MADS data set was annotated by 8 NEs, 28 targets, 5 operators and 6 speech-act tags. In addition, The MADS data set consists of 1,925 user utterance in 6 domains: *weather, clock, alarm, schedule, exchange and traffic*. The Mallet toolkit was chosen for our CRF model (McCallum. 2002).

All experiments were evaluated by accuracy in the utterance level. When the proposed SLU module generates all the correct labels of NE, target, operator and speech-act of an input utterance, the utterance is considered as correct. The performance of the SLU module is averaged on 5-fold cross validation. In addition, we used the paired *t*-test and Wilcoxon singed rank test to verify statistically significant between our framework and compared baseline framework. The pipeline framework (Moreira et al., 2011) is used a baseline system in our experiments because it is the most common method for multi-domains SLU module.

5.2 Experimental results

Each component of the SLU module is first evaluated by comparison of accuracies between the proposed and baseline frameworks. Figure 4 illustrates the accuracies of each component.

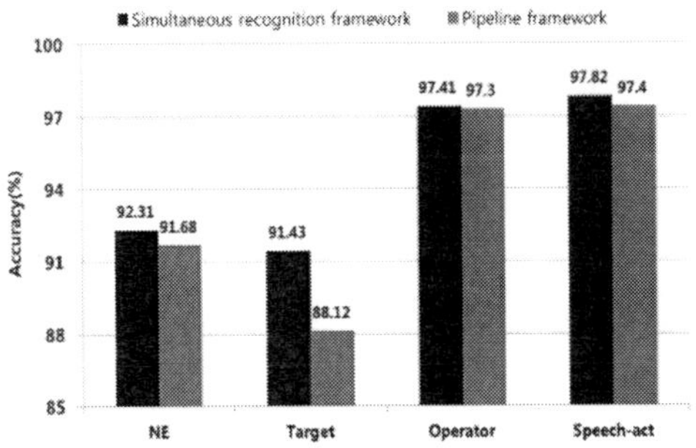

Figure 4: Comparison of the accuracies of each component for SLU

A pipeline framework commonly has some disadvantage that the errors of previous component are propagated to the next components. It can cause a cascade of performance degradation.

Figure 5 shows the accuracies of entire SLU modules in an utterance level.

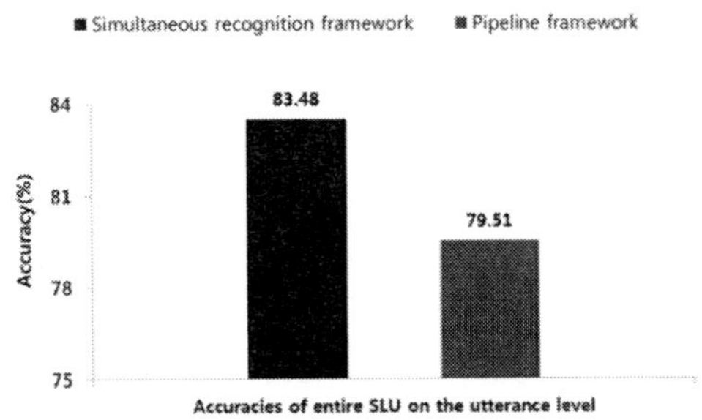

Figure 5: Comparison of accuracies of entire SLU modules on the utterance level

The proposed framework achieved significantly better performance than the baseline framework.

To verify statistically significant on accuracy difference between the proposed and baseline frameworks, we performed significant test using the *t*-test and Wilcoxon singed rank test (Demsar. 2006). Table 1 shows the results of significant test.

p-value < 0.05 (95%)	Our framework *vs.* Pipeline framework
paired t-test	0.00001
Wilcox signed rank test	0.021

Table 1: Results of significant tests

In both of two significance tests, our framework was statistically significantly better than the pipeline framework ($p<0.05$).

In the comparison of processing time, our framework obtained faster processing speed than pipeline framework with about 25% reduction.

Test user utterance (388 utterances)	
Our framework	15 sec.
Pipeline framework	19 sec.

Table 2: Results of processing time comparison

In addition, we tried to compare our module and the triangular-chain CRF (Jeong and Lee, 2008). Table 3 shows the performances when NE and speech-act recognition tasks are combined and all four recognition tasks are combined. As a result, our module outperformed the triangular-chain CRF in both of cases.

	NE+Speech-act	All (four tasks)
Our framework	90.61	83.48
Triangular-chain CRF	87.07	16.4

Table 3: comparison of our module and triangular-chain CRF

6 Conclusions

In this paper, we have presented a novel SLU framework to predict user's intention for determining system actions of the intelligent personal assistant software. The proposed SLU module with a simultaneous recognition framework achieved higher performance and faster processing speed than the existing pipeline system. In addition, our module outperformed other method, the triangular-chain CRF, especially when four components were all analyzed.

Acknowledgement

This research was supported by Basic Science Research Program through the National Research Foundation of Korea (NRF) funded by the Ministry of Education, Science and Technology (No. NRF-2013R1A1A2009937)

References

Janez Demsar. 2006. Statistical comparisons of classifiers over multiple data sets. *Journal of Machine Learning Research, Vol. 7. pp.1–30.*

Yulan He and Steve Young. 2005. Semantic Processing using the Hidden Vector State Model. *Computer Speech and Language, Vol. 19, No. 1, pp. 85-106.*

Minwoo Jeong and Gary-Geunbae Lee, 2008. Triangular-chain conditional random fields. *IEEE Transactions on Audio, Speech, and Language Processing,* Vol. 16, pp. 1287-1302.

John Lafferty, Andrew McCallum and Fernando C.N. Pereira. 2001. Conditional random fields: Probabilistic models for segmenting and labeling sequence data, *In Proceedings of the Eighteenth International Conference on Machine Learning." Morgan Kaufmann Publishers Inc., SanFrancisco, CA, USA, pp. 282-289.*

Changki Lee and Myung-Gil Jang. 2010. Named Entity Recognition with Structural SVMs and Pegasos algorithm. *Korean Journal of Cognitive Science.* Vol. 21. No. 4, 655-667.

Andrew McCallum. 2002. Mallet: A machine learning for language kit, http://mallet.cs.umass.edu.

Scott Miller, Revert Bobrow, Robert Ingria, and Robert Schwartz. 1994. Hidden understanding models of natural language. *In Proceedings of the ACL, Association for Computational Linguistics, pp. 25–32.*

Catarina Moreira, Ana Cristina Mendes, Lu´ısa Coheur and Bruno Martins, 2011. Towards the rapid development of a natural language understanding module. *In Proceedings of 10th international conference on Intelligent virtual agents, pp. 309–315.*

Roberto Pieraccini, Evelyne Tzoukermann, Zakhar Gorelov, Jean-Luc Gauvain, Esther Levin, Chine-Hui Lee and Jay G. Wilpon. 1992. A speech understanding system based on statistical representation of semantics. *In Proceedings of the ICASSP, San Francisco, CA.*

Launce A. Ramshaw and Mitchell P. Marcus. 1995. Text Chunking using Transformation-Based Learning. *In Proceedings of the Third Workshop on Very Large Corpora*, pp. 82-94.

Christian Raymond and Giuseppe Riccardi. 2007. Generative and discriminative algorithms for spoken language understanding. *In Proceedings of the Interspeech, Antwerp, Belgium.*

Stephanie Seneff. 1992. TINA: A Natural Language System for Spoken Language Applications. *Computational Linguistics.*

Ye-Yi Wang. 2001. Robust Spoken Language Understanding in MiPad. *In proceedings of Eurospeech, Aalborg, Denmark.*

Ye-Yi Wang and Alex Acero. 2006. Discriminative models for spoken language understanding. *In Proceedings of the ICSLP, Pittsburgh, PA.*

Ye-Yi Wang, Li Deng and Alex Acero. 2005. Spoken language understanding : an introduction to the statistical framework. *IEEE Signal Processing Magazine 22(5): 16-31.*

Wayne Ward, Bryan Pellom, and Sameer Pradhan. 1999. The CU Communicator System, *IEEE Workshop on ASRU Proc., Keystone, Colorado.*

Wayne Ward and Sunil Issar. 1994. Recent Improvements in the CMU Spoken language Understanding System. *in Human Language Technology Workshop, Plainsboro, New Jersey.*

Wikipedia Contributors. 2011. Siri, Wikipedia, the Free Encyclopedia.

Wikipedia Contributors. 2012. S-Voice, Wikipedia, the Free Encyclopedia.

A Deeper Exploration of the Standard PB-SMT Approach to Text Simplification and its Evaluation

Sanja Štajner[1] and **Hannah Béchara**[1] and **Horacio Saggion**[2]
[1]Research Group in Computational Linguistics, University of Wolverhampton, UK
[2]TALN Research Group, Universitat Pompeu Fabra, Spain
{SanjaStajner,Hanna.Bechara}@wlv.ac.uk, horacio.saggion@upf.edu

Abstract

In the last few years, there has been a growing number of studies addressing the Text Simplification (TS) task as a monolingual machine translation (MT) problem which translates from 'original' to 'simple' language. Motivated by those results, we investigate the influence of quality vs quantity of the training data on the effectiveness of such a MT approach to text simplification. We conduct 40 experiments on the aligned sentences from English Wikipedia and Simple English Wikipedia, controlling for: (1) the similarity between the original and simplified sentences in the training and development datasets, and (2) the sizes of those datasets. The results suggest that in the standard PB-SMT approach to text simplification the quality of the datasets has a greater impact on the system performance. Additionally, we point out several important differences between cross-lingual MT and monolingual MT used in text simplification, and show that BLEU is not a good measure of system performance in text simplification task.

1 Introduction

In the last few years, a growing number of studies have addressed the text simplification (TS) task as a monolingual machine translation (MT) problem of translating sentences from 'original' to 'simple' language. Several studies reported promising results using standard phrase-based statistical machine translation (PB-SMT) for this task (Specia, 2010; Coster and Kauchak, 2011a; Wubben et al., 2012), but made no attempt to explain the reasons behind the success of their systems. Specia (2010) obtained reasonably good results (BLEU = 60.75) despite the small size of the datasets used (4,483 original sentences and their corresponding simplifications). Her results indicated that in this specific monolingual MT task, we do not need such large datasets (as in cross-lingual MT) in order to achieve good results.

At the moment, the scarcity and very limited sizes of the available TS datasets (usually only up to 1,000 sentence pairs) are the main factors which impede the use of data-driven approaches to text simplification for all languages except English (for which English Wikipedia and Simple English Wikipedia offer a large comparable TS dataset). Therefore, in this paper, we decided to investigate several important issues in MT-based text simplification:

1. The impact of the size of the training and development datasets;

2. The impact of the similarity between the original and simplified sentences in the training and development datasets; and

3. The suitability of using the BLEU score for the automatic evaluation of system's performance.

To the best of our knowledge, there have been no studies which address those important questions.

In order to explore the first two issues, we conduct 40 translation experiments using the aligned sentence pairs from the largest existing TS corpus (Wikipedia TS corpus), controlling the training and development datasets for: (1) sentence similarity (in terms of the S-BLEU score), and (2) size. Our results indicate that only the former can influence the MT output significantly. In order to explore the last issue, we test our models on two different test sets and perform human evaluation of the output of several systems.

Proceedings of the 53rd Annual Meeting of the Association for Computational Linguistics and the 7th International Joint Conference on Natural Language Processing (Short Papers), pages 823–828,
Beijing, China, July 26-31, 2015.

2 Related Work

Specia (2010) used the standard PB-SMT model provided by the Moses toolkit (Koehn et al., 2007) to translate from 'original' to 'simple' sentences in Brazilian Portuguese. The dataset contained manual simplifications aimed at people with low literacy levels. The most commonly used simplifications (by human editors) were lexical substitutions and splitting sentences (Gasperin et al., 2009). In terms of the automatic BLEU evaluation (Papineni et al., 2002), the results were reasonably good (BLEU = 60.75) despite the small size of the corpora (4,483 original sentences and their corresponding simplifications). However, the TS system was overcautious in performing simplifications, i.e. the simplifications produced by the systems were closer to the source than to the reference segments (Specia, 2010).

Coster and Kauchak (2011a) used the same approach for English. Additionally, they extended the PB-SMT system by adding phrasal deletion to the probabilistic translation model in order to better cover deletion, which is a frequent phenomenon in TS. The system was trained on 124,000 aligned sentences from English Wikipedia and Simple English Wikipedia. The analysis of the Wikipedia TS corpus (Coster and Kauchak, 2011b) reported that rewordings (1–1 lexical substitutions) are the most common simplification operation (65%). The system with added phrasal deletion achieved the BLEU score of 60.46, while the the standard model without phrasal deletion achieved the BLEU score of 59.87. However, the baseline (BLEU score when the system does not perform any simplification on the original sentence) was 59.37, indicating that the systems often leave the original sentences unchanged. In order to address that problem, Wubben et al. (2012) performed post-hoc reranking on the Moses' output (simplification hypotheses) based on their dissimilarity to the input (original sentences), while at the same time controlling for its adequacy and fluency.

Štajner (2014) applied the same PB-SMT model to two different TS corpora in Spanish, which contained different levels of simplification. The results, which should be regarded only as preliminary as both corpora have fewer than 1,000 sentence pairs, imply that the level of simplification in the training datasets has a greater impact than the size of the datasets on the system's performance.

3 Methodology

We focus on the two TS corpora available for English (Wikipedia and EncBrit) and train a series of translation models on training and development datasets of varying size and quality.

3.1 Corpora

Wikipedia is a comparable TS corpus of 137,000 automatically aligned sentence pairs from English Wikipedia and Simple English Wikipedia[1], previously used by Coster and Kauchak (2011a). We use a small portion of this corpus (240 sentence pairs) to build the first test set (WikiTest), and 88,000 sentence pairs from the remaining sentence pairs to build translation models.

EncBrit is a comparable TS corpus of original sentences from Encyclopedia Britannica and their manually simplified versions for children (Barzilay and Elhadad, 2003).[2] Given its small size (601 sentence pairs) this dataset is not used in the translation experiments. It is only used as the second test set (EncBritTest).

3.2 Experimental Setup

In all experiments, we use the same standard PB-SMT model (Koehn et al., 2007), the GIZA++ implementation of IBM word alignment model 4 (Och and Ney, 2003), and the refinement and phrase-extraction heuristics described further by Koehn *et al.* (2003). We tune the systems using minimum error rate training (MERT) (Och, 2003). For the language model (LM) we use the corpus of 60,000 Simple English Wikipedia articles[3] and build a 3-gram language model with Kneser-Ney smoothing trained with SRILM (Stolcke, 2002). We limit our stack size to 500 hypotheses during decoding.

3.3 Training and development datasets

We tokenise and shuffle the initial dataset of 167,689 aligned sentences from the Wikipedia dataset.[4] Using the simplified sentences as references and the original sentences as hypotheses,

[1] http://www.cs.middlebury.edu/~dkauchak/simplification/

[2] http://www.cs.columbia.edu/~noemie/alignment/

[3] Version 2.0 document-aligned data, available at: http://www.cs.middlebury.edu/~dkauchak/simplification/

[4] Version 2.0 sentence-aligned data, available at: http://www.cs.middlebury.edu/~dkauchak/simplification/

Table 1: Examples of sentences pairs with various S-BLEU scores from the training sets

S-BLEU	Original sentence	Simpler version
0.08	*In women, the larger* mammary glands *within* the breast *produce the milk.*	The breast *contains* mammary glands.
0.38	*Built as a double-track railroad bridge, it* was completed on January 1, 1889, and *went out of service* on May 8, 1974.	*It was built for trains and* was completed on January 1, 1889. *It closed down* on May 8, 1974 *after a bad fire.*
0.55	In 2000, the series *sold its naming rights to* Internet search engine Northern Light *for five seasons, and t*he series was named the Indy Racing Northern Light Series.	In 2000, the series *sponsor became the* Internet search engine Northern Light. *T*he series was named the Indy Racing Northern Light Series.
0.63	*Wildlife which eat acorns as* an important part of their diet*s* include birds, such as jays, pigeons, some ducks, and several species of woodpeckers.	*Creatures that make acorns* an important part of their diet include birds, such as jays, pigeons, some ducks and several species of woodpeckers.
0.77	It was *discovered* by Brett J. Gladman in 2000, and given the *temporary* designation S2000 S 5.	It was *found* by Brett J. Gladman in 2000, and given the designation S2000 S 5.
0.87	Austen was not well known in Russia *and t*he first Russian translation of an Austen novel did not appear until 1967.	Austen was not well known in Russia. *T*he first Russian translation of an Austen novel did not appear until 1967.

we rank each sentence pair by its sentence-wise BLEU (S-BLEU) score and categorise the sentence pairs into eight different sets depending on the interval in which their S-BLEU scores lie ((0, 0.3], (0.3, 0.4], (0.4, 0.5], (0.5, 0.6], (0.6, 0.7], (0.7, 0.8], (0.8, 0.9], (0.9, 1]). With each of the eight sets, we train five translation models, varying the number of sentences used for training and tuning (2,000, 4,000, 6,000, 8,000, and 10,000 for training and 200, 400, 600, 800, and 1,000 for tuning, respectively). That leads to a total of 40 translation models varying by number of sentence pairs and similarity between original and simplified sentences (in terms of the S-BLEU score) in the datasets used for their training and tuning. Several examples of sentence pairs with various S-BLEU scores are presented in Table 1.

3.4 Test datasets

We test our models on two different test sets:

1. The **WikiTest** which contains a total of 240 sentence pairs, with 30 sentence pairs from each of the eight categories with different intervals for the S-BLEU scores ([0,0.3], (0.3,0.4], ... , (0.9,1]);

2. The **EncBritTest** which contains all 601 sentence pairs present in the EncBrit corpus (with an unbalanced number of sentence pairs from each of the eight S-BLEU intervals).

The sizes of both test sets and their BLEU scores (calculated using the original sentences as simplification/translation hypotheses and the corresponding manually simplified sentences as simplification/translation references) are given in Table 2. Note that those BLEU scores can be regarded as the baselines for the translation experiments, as they correspond to the BLEU score obtained when the systems do not perform any changes to the input.

Table 2: Test sets for all translation experiments

Test set	Size	BLEU
WikiTest	240	62.27
EncBritTest	601	12.40

4 Automatic Evaluation

The BLEU scores for all 40 experiments tested on the WikiTest dataset, are presented in Table 3. The baseline BLEU score (when no simplification is performed) for this test set is 62.27 (Table 2). As shown in Table 3, none of the 40 experiments have even reached that baseline. We compare S-BLEU scores for each pair of experiments (240 reference sentences in the test set and their corresponding automatically simplified sentences) using the paired t-test in SPSS in order to check whether the differences in the obtained results are significant. The only results that are significantly lower than the rest are those obtained for the experiments in which the training and development datasets consist only of the sentence pairs with S-BLEU scores between 0 and 0.3. The results sug-

Table 3: BLEU scores on the WikiTest dataset

S-BLEU	Size of the training set				
	2,000	4,000	6,000	8,000	10,000
[0, 0.3]	56.38	56.38	56.15	57.75	57.89
(0.3, 0.4]	60.89	61.35	61.76	61.52	61.37
(0.4, 0.5]	61.27	61.36	61.74	61.55	**62.11**
(0.5, 0.6]	60.96	61.30	61.52	61.77	61.98
(0.6, 0.7]	60.96	61.30	61.60	61.69	61.80
(0.7, 0.8]	61.56	61.38	61.67	61.77	61.89
(0.8, 0.9]	61.54	61.49	61.51	61.57	61.61
(0.9, 1]	61.57	61.57	61.59	61.55	61.55

The rows represent intervals of the S-BLEU scores on the training and development datasets, while the columns represent the number of the sentence pairs used for training. The highest score is presented in bold; the baseline (no simplification performed) is 62.27.

Table 4: BLEU scores on the EncBritTest dataset

S-BLEU	Size of the training set				
	2,000	4,000	6,000	8,000	10,000
[0, 0.3]	13.84	13.84	13.87	13.68	13.59
(0.3, 0.4]	14.05	13.95	14.08	14.06	14.01
(0.4, 0.5]	14.02	14.09	14.17	14.15	14.12
(0.5, 0.6]	14.09	14.22	14.27	14.16	14.13
(0.6, 0.7]	14.25	14.30	14.35	14.35	14.32
(0.7, 0.8]	14.30	14.29	14.30	14.30	14.28
(0.8, 0.9]	14.38	14.40	14.40	14.40	**14.41**
(0.9, 1]	12.71	12.52	12.46	12.39	12.54

The rows represent intervals of the S-BLEU scores on the training and development datasets, while the columns represent the number of the sentence pairs used for training. The highest score is presented in bold; the baseline (no simplification performed) is 12.40.

gest that the sizes of the training and development datasets do not influence the translation results significantly on any type of sentence pairs used.

The results of the experiments tested on EncBritTest (Table 4) again show that the quantity of the training data does not influence system performance. There are no statistically significant differences (measured by the paired t-test on S-BLEU scores on all 601 reference sentences and the corresponding automatic simplifications) among experiments which differ only in the size of the training and development datasets. However, the models trained and tuned on the datasets consisting of the sentence pairs with the highest and the lowest S-BLEU scores ([0,0.3] and (0.9,1]) perform significantly worse than the models trained and tuned on the sentence pairs with S-BLEU scores belonging to other intervals.

5 Human Evaluation

The results presented in Tables 3 and 4 indicate that the BLEU score, in MT-based text simplification, mostly reflects the surface similarity of the original and simplified sentences in the test set and does not give an informative evaluation of the systems. Therefore, we conducted a human assessment of the generated sentences. Following the standard procedure for human evaluation of TS systems used in previous studies (Coster and Kauchak, 2011a; Drndarević et al., 2013; Wubben et al., 2012; Saggion et al., 2015), three human evaluators were asked to assess the generated sentences on a 1–5 scale (where the higher mark always denotes better output) according to three criteria: grammaticality (G), meaning preservation (M), and simplicity (S).

Table 5: Systems used in human evaluation

System	Training size	Dev. size	S-BLEU
S-03-200	2,000	200	[0,0.3]
S-03-1000	10,000	1,000	[0,0.3]
S-06-200	2,000	200	(0.5,0.6]
S-06-1000	10,000	1,000	(0.5,0.6]
S-10-200	2,000	200	[0.9,1]
S-10-1000	10,000	1,000	[0.9,1]

We decided that the same person has to rate all simplified versions of the same original sentence (shown always in a random order), in order to make a fairer comparison among the systems. That decision, however, limited the number of systems we can evaluate. Therefore, we focused only on six out of 40 trained systems (Table 5). Several examples of the automatically simplified sentences and their scores are presented in Table 6.

The results of the human evaluation are given in Table 7. It seems that the use of the sentence pairs with the S-BLEU score between 0.5 and 0.6 leads to the best system performances in terms of grammaticality and meaning preservation, while at the same time improving the simplicity of the sentences.[5] Furthermore, the differences in human scores between the systems differing only in size of the datasets used were not statistically significant. At the same time, the differences in human

[5] The details of the human evaluation and examples can be found in (Štajner, 2015).

Table 6: Outputs of different systems and their human evaluation scores

System	Sentence	G	M	S
Original	Madrid was occupied by French troops during the Napoleonic Wars, and Napoleon's brother Joseph was installed on the throne.	5	/	4
S-03-200	Madrid was occupied by French *his soldiers* during the Napoleonic Wars, and Napoleon's brother Joseph was installed on the throne.	4	4	4
S-03-1000	Madrid was occupied by French troops during the Napoleonic Wars, and Napoleon's brother Joseph was *put* on the throne.	5	5	5
S-10-1000	Madrid was occupied by French troops during the Napoleonic Wars, and Napoleon's brother Joseph was *-RRB-* installed *on them* on the throne.	3	3	3
Original	Although largely of postwar construction, this central area retains its old street pattern, and most of the surviving historical and architectural monuments are located there.	5	/	2
S-03-200/1000	Although largely of postwar construction, this central area retains its old street pattern, and most of the surviving *and architectural historical* monuments are located there.	5	4	3
S-06-1000	Although *mostly* of postwar construction, this central area retains its old street pattern, and most of the surviving historical and architectural monuments are located there.	5	5	2
S-10-200	Although largely of postwar construction, this central area retains its old street pattern, and most of the surviving historical monuments and architectural *are a instead.*	3	3	2
S-10-1000	*As* of *the* postwar construction, *in* this central area *uses* its old street pattern, and most of the *historical monuments and and architectural* are located there.	2	3	2

The columns *G*, *M*, *S* contain the mean value of the human scores for grammaticality, meaning preservation, and simplicity, respectively. Differences to the original versions are shown in italics. Systems which are not presented did not make any changes to these two original sentences.

Table 7: Results of the human evaluation

System	G	M	S
Original	4.85	/	2.60
S-03-200	4.03	3.95	2.57
S-03-1000	4.20	4.03	**2.85**
S-06-200	**4.50**	4.45	2.68
S-06-1000	4.43	**4.48**	2.72
S-10-200	3.25	2.92	2.45
S-10-1000	2.92	2.95	2.53

The mean value of the human scores for grammaticality (*G*), meaning preservation (*M*), and simplicity (*S*). The highest achieved scores (excluding the scores for original sentences) on each aspect (G, M, and S) are presented in bold.

scores between the systems differing only in similarity of the sentence pairs (the interval of the S-BLEU score) used were statistically significant.

6 Conclusions

Recently, there have been several attempts at addressing the TS task as a monolingual translation problem, translating from 'original' to 'simple' sentences. However, they did not try to seek reasons for the success or the failure of their systems.

Our experiments, conducted on 40 different, carefully designed datasets from the largest available sentence-aligned TS corpus (Wikipedia TS corpus), provide valuable insights into how much of an effect the size and the quality of the training data have on the performance of the PB-SMT system which tries to learn to translate from 'original' to 'simple' sentences. The results indicate that using the sentence pairs with low S-BLEU scores for training and tuning of PB-SMT models for TS tend to cause the fluency to deteriorate and even change the meaning of the output. Furthermore, it seems that the sizes of the training and development datasets do not play a significant role in how successful the model is. It appears that carefully selected sentence pairs in the training and development datasets (i.e. sentence pairs with a moderate similarity) lead to best performances of PB-SMT systems regardless of the size of the datasets.

Our results open up new directions for enhancing the current PB-SMT models for TS, indicating that their performance can be significantly improved by carefully filtering sentence pairs used for training and tuning.

Acknowledgements

The research described in this paper was partially funded by the project SKATER-UPF-TALN (TIN2012-38584-C06-03), Ministerio de Economía y Competitividad, Secretaría de Estado de Investigación, Desarrollo e Innovación, Spain, and the project ABLE-TO-INCLUDE (CIP-ICT-PSP-2013-7/621055). Hannah Béchara is supported by the People Programme (Marie Curie Actions) of the European Union's Seventh Framework Programme FP7/2007-2013/ under REA grant agreement no. 31747.

References

Regina Barzilay and Noemie Elhadad. 2003. Sentence alignment for monolingual comparable corpora. In *Proceedings of the Conference on Empirical Methods in Natural Language Processing (EMNLP)*, pages 25–32. Association for Computational Linguistics.

William Coster and David Kauchak. 2011a. Learning to Simplify Sentences Using Wikipedia. In *Proceedings of the 49th Annual Meeting of the Association for Computational Linguistics (ACL)*, pages 1–9. Association for Computational Linguistics.

William Coster and David Kauchak. 2011b. Simple English Wikipedia: a new text simplification task. In *Proceedings of the 49th Annual Meeting of the Association for Computational Linguistics: Human Language Technologies (ACL&HLT)*, pages 665–669. Association for Computational Linguistics.

Biljana Drndarević, Sanja Štajner, Stefan Bott, Susana Bautista, and Horacio Saggion. 2013. Automatic Text Simplication in Spanish: A Comparative Evaluation of Complementing Components. In *Proceedings of the 12th International Conference on Intelligent Text Processing and Computational Linguistics (CICLing)*, volume 7817 of *Lecture Notes in Computer Science*, pages 488–500. Springer Berlin Heidelberg.

Caroline Gasperin, Lucia Specia, Tiago F. Pereira, and Sandra M. Aluísio. 2009. Learning When to Simplify Sentences for Natural Text Simplification. In *Proceedings of the Encontro Nacional de Intelignecia Artificial (ENIA), Bento Gonalves, Brazil*, pages 809–818.

Philipp Koehn, Franz Josef Och, and Daniel Marcu. 2003. Statistical phrase-based translation. In *Proceedings of the Conference of the North American Chapter of the Association for Computational Linguistics on Human Language Technology - Volume 1*, pages 48–54. Association for Computational Linguistics.

Philipp Koehn, Hieu Hoang, Alexandra Birch, Chris Callison-Burch, Marcello Federico, Nicola Bertoldi, Brooke Cowan, Wade Shen, Christine Moran, Richard Zens, Chris Dyer, Ondrej Bojar, Alexandra Constantin, and Evan Herbst. 2007. Moses: Open source toolkit for statistical machine translation. In *Proceedings of the 45th Annual Meeting of the Association for Computational Linguistics (ACL)*. Association for Computational Linguistics.

Franz Josef Och and Hermann Ney. 2003. A systematic comparison of various statistical alignment models. *Computational Linguistics*, 29(1):19–51.

Franz Och. 2003. Minimum Error Rate Training in Statistical Machine Translation. In *Proceedings of the 41st Annual Meeting of the Association for Computational Linguistics (ACL)*, pages 160–167. Association for Computational Linguistics.

Kishore Papineni, Salim Roukos, Todd Ward, and Wei-Jing Zhu. 2002. BLEU: a method for automatic evaluation of machine translation. In *Proceedings of ACL*.

Horacio Saggion, Sanja Štajner, Stefan Bott, Simon Mille, Luz Rello, and Biljana Drndarevic. 2015. Making It Simplext: Implementation and Evaluation of a Text Simplification System for Spanish. *ACM Transactions on Accessible Computing*, 6(4):14:1–14:36.

Lucia Specia. 2010. Translating from complex to simplified sentences. In *Proceedings of the 9th international conference on Computational Processing of the Portuguese Language (PROPOR)*, volume 6001 of *Lecture Notes in Computer Science*, pages 30–39. Springer Berlin Heidelberg.

Andreas Stolcke. 2002. SRILM - an Extensible Language Modeling Toolkit. In *Proceedings of the International Conference on Spoken Language Processing (ICSLP)*, pages 901–904.

Sanja Štajner. 2014. Translating sentences from 'original' to 'simplified' spanish. *Procesamiento del Lenguaje Natural*, 53:61–68.

Sanja Štajner. 2015. *New Data-Driven Approaches to Text Simplification*. Ph.D. thesis, University of Wolverhampton, UK.

Sander Wubben, Antal van den Bosch, and Emiel Krahmer. 2012. Sentence simplification by monolingual machine translation. In *Proceedings of the 50th Annual Meeting of the Association for Computational Linguistics (ACL): Long Papers - Volume 1*, pages 1015–1024. Association for Computational Linguistics.

Learning Summary Prior Representation for Extractive Summarization

Ziqiang Cao[1,2]* Furu Wei[3] Sujian Li[1,2] Wenjie Li[4] Ming Zhou[3] Houfeng Wang[1,2]
[1]Key Laboratory of Computational Linguistics, Peking University, MOE, China
[2]Collaborative Innovation Center for Language Ability, Xuzhou, Jiangsu, China
[3]Microsoft Research, Beijing, China
[4]Computing Department, Hong Kong Polytechnic University, Hong Kong
{ziqiangyeah, lisujian, wanghf}@pku.edu.cn
{furu, mingzhou}@microsoft.com cswjli@comp.polyu.edu.hk

Abstract

In this paper, we propose the concept of summary prior to define how much a sentence is appropriate to be selected into summary without consideration of its context. Different from previous work using manually compiled document-independent features, we develop a novel summary system called PriorSum, which applies the enhanced convolutional neural networks to capture the summary prior features derived from length-variable phrases. Under a regression framework, the learned prior features are concatenated with document-dependent features for sentence ranking. Experiments on the DUC generic summarization benchmarks show that PriorSum can discover different aspects supporting the summary prior and outperform state-of-the-art baselines.

1 Introduction

Sentence ranking, the vital part of extractive summarization, has been extensively investigated. Regardless of ranking models (Osborne, 2002; Galley, 2006; Conroy et al., 2004; Li et al., 2007), feature engineering largely determines the final summarization performance. Features often fall into two types: document-dependent features (e.g., term frequency or position) and document-independent features (e.g., stopword ratio or word polarity). The latter type of features take effects due to the fact that, a sentence can often be judged by itself whether it is appropriate to be included in a summary no matter which document it lies in. Take the following two sentences as an example:

1. Hurricane Emily slammed into Dominica on September 22, causing 3 deaths with its wind gusts up to 110 mph.
2. It was Emily, the hurricane which caused 3 deaths and armed with wind guests up to 110 mph, that slammed into Dominica on Tuesday.

The first sentence describes the major information of a hurricane. With similar meaning, the second sentence uses an emphatic structure and is somewhat verbose. Obviously the first one should be preferred for a news summary. In this paper, we call such fact as summary prior nature[1] and learn document-independent features to reflect it.

In previous summarization systems, though not well-studied, some widely-used sentence ranking features such as the length and the ratio of stopwords, can be seen as attempts to measure the summary prior nature to a certain extent. Notably, Hong and Nenkova (2014) built a state-of-the-art summarization system through making use of advanced document-independent features. However, these document-independent features are usually hand-crafted, difficult to exhaust each aspect of the summary prior nature. Meanwhile, items representing the same feature may contribute differently to a summary. For example, "September 22" and "Tuesday" are both indicators of time, but the latter seldom occurs in a summary due to uncertainty. In addition, to the best of our knowledge, document-independent features beyond word level (e.g., phrases) are seldom involved in current research.

The CTSUM system developed by Wan and Zhang (2014) is the most relevant to ours. It attempted to explore a context-free measure named certainty which is critical to ranking sentences in summarization. To calculate the certainty score, four dictionaries are manually built as features and a corpus is annotated to train the feature weights using Support Vector Regression (SVR). How-

*Contribution during internship at Microsoft Research

[1]In this paper, "summary prior features" and "document-independent features" hold the same meaning.

Proceedings of the 53rd Annual Meeting of the Association for Computational Linguistics and the 7th International Joint Conference on Natural Language Processing (Short Papers), pages 829–833,
Beijing, China, July 26-31, 2015.

ever, a low certainty score does not always represent low quality of being a summary sentence. For example, the sentence below is from a topic about "Korea nuclear issue" in DUC 2004: *Clinton acknowledged that U.S. is not yet certain that the suspicious underground construction project in North Korea is nuclear related.* The underlined phrases greatly reduce the certainty of this sentence according to Wan and Zhang (2014)'s model. But, in fact, this sentence can summarize the government's attitude and is salient enough in the related documents. Thus, in our opinion, certainty can just be viewed as a specific aspect of the summary prior nature.

To this end, we develop a novel summarization system called PriorSum to automatically exploit all possible semantic aspects latent in the summary prior nature. Since the Convolutional Neural Networks (CNNs) have shown promising progress in latent feature representation (Yih et al., 2014; Shen et al., 2014; Zeng et al., 2014), PriorSum applies CNNs with multiple filters to capture a comprehensive set of document-independent features derived from length-variable phrases. Then we adopt a two-stage max-over-time pooling operation to associate these filters since phrases with different lengths may express the same aspect of summary prior. PriorSum generates the document-independent features, and concatenates them with document-dependent ones to work for sentence regression (Section 2.1).

We conduct extensive experiments on the DUC 2001, 2002 and 2004 generic multi-document summarization datasets. The experimental results demonstrate that our model outperforms state-of-the-art extractive summarization approaches. Meanwhile, we analyze the different aspects supporting the summary prior in Section 3.3.

2 Methodology

Our summarization system PriorSum follows the traditional extractive framework (Carbonell and Goldstein, 1998; Li et al., 2007). Specifically, the sentence ranking process scores and ranks the sentences from documents, and then the sentence selection process chooses the top ranked sentences to generate the final summary in accordance with the length constraint and redundancy among the selected sentences.

Sentence ranking aims to measure the saliency score of a sentence with consideration of both document-dependent and document-independent features. In this study, we apply an enhanced version of convolutional neural networks to automatically generate document-independent features according to the summary prior nature. Meanwhile, some document-dependent features are extracted. These two types of features are combined in the sentence regression step.

2.1 Sentence Ranking

PriorSum improves the standard convolutional neural networks (CNNs) to learn the summary prior since CNN is able to learn compressed representation of n-grams effectively and tackle sentences with variable lengths naturally. We first introduce the standard CNNs, based on which we design our improved CNNs for obtaining document-independent features.

The standard CNNs contain a convolution operation over several word embeddings, followed by a pooling operation. Let $v_i \in \mathbb{R}^k$ denote the k-dimensional word embedding of the i_{th} word in the sentence. Assume $v_{i:i+j}$ to be the concatenation of word embeddings $v_i, \cdots, v_{i+j}$. A convolution operation involves a filter $\mathbf{W}_t^h \in \mathbb{R}^{l \times hk}$, which operates on a window of h words to produce a new feature with l dimensions:

$$c_i^h = f(\mathbf{W}_t^h \times v_{i:i+h-1}) \quad (1)$$

where f is a non-linear function and $tanh$ is used like common practice. Here, the bias term is ignored for simplicity. Then $\mathbf{W}_t^h$ is applied to each possible window of h words in the sentence of length N to produce a feature map: $\mathbf{C}^h = [c_1^h, \cdots, c_{N-h+1}^h]$. Next, we adopt the widely-used max-over-time pooling operation (Collobert et al., 2011) to obtain the final features $\hat{c}^h$ from $\mathbf{C}^h$. That is, $\hat{c}^h = \max\{\mathbf{C}^h\}$. The idea behind this pooling operation is to capture the most important features in a feature map.

In the standard CNNs, only the fixed-length windows of words are considered to represent a sentence. As we know, the variable-length phrases composed of a sentence can better express the sentence and disclose its summary prior nature. To make full use of the phrase information, we design an improved version of the standard CNNs, which use multiple filters for different window sizes as well as two max-over-time pooling operations to get the final summary prior representation. Specifically, let $\mathbf{W}_t^1, \cdots, \mathbf{W}_t^m$ be m filters for window sizes from 1 to m, and correspondingly we can obtain m feature maps $\mathbf{C}^1, \cdots, \mathbf{C}^m$. For each feature map $\mathbf{C}^i$, We first adopt a max-over-time pooling operation $max\{\mathbf{C}^i\}$ with the goal of capturing the most salient features from each window size i. Next, a second max-over-time pooling operation is operated on all the windows to acquire the most representative features. To formulate, the document independent features x_p can be generated by:

$$x_p = \max\{\max\{\mathbf{C}^1\}, \cdots, \max\{\mathbf{C}^m\}\}. \quad (2)$$

Kim (2014) also uses filters with varying window sizes for sentence-level classification tasks. However, he reserves all the representations generated by filters to a fully connected output layer. This practice greatly enlarges following parameters and ignores the relation among phrases with different lengths. Hence we use the two-stage max-over-time pooling to associate all these filters.

Besides the features x_p obtained through the CNNs, we also extract several document-dependent features notated as x_e, shown in Table 1. In the end, x_p is combined with x_e to conduct sentence ranking. Here we follow the regression framework of Li et al. (2007). The sentence saliency y is scored by ROUGE-2 (Lin, 2004) (stopwords removed) and the model tries to estimate this saliency.

$$\phi = [x_p, x_e] \quad (3)$$

$$\hat{y} = w_r^T \times \phi \quad (4)$$

where $w_r \in R^{l+|x_e|}$ is the regression weights. We use linear transformation since it is convenient to compare with regression baselines (see Section 3.2).

Feature	Description
POSITION	The position of the sentence.
AVG-TF	The averaged term frequency values of words in the sentence.
AVG-CF	The averaged cluster frequency values of words in the sentence.

Table 1: Extracted document-dependent features.

2.2 Sentence Selection

A summary is obliged to offer both informative and non-redundant content. Here, we employ a simple greedy algorithm to select sentences, similar to the MMR strategy (Carbonell and Goldstein, 1998). Firstly, we remove sentences less than 8 words (as in Erkan and Radev (2004)) and sort the rest in descending order according to the estimated saliency scores. Then, we iteratively dequeue one sentence, and append it to the current summary if it is non-redundant. A sentence is considered non-redundant if it contains more new words compared to the current summary content. We empirically set the cut-off of new word ratio to 0.5.

3 Experiments

3.1 Experiment Setup

In our work, we focus on the generic multi-document summarization task and carry out experiments on DUC 2001 2004 datasets. All the documents are from newswires and grouped into various thematic clusters. The summary length is limited to 100 words (665 bytes for DUC 2004). We use DUC 2003 data as the development set and conduct a 3-fold cross-validation on DUC 2001, 2002 and 2004 datasets with two years of data as training set and one year of data as test set.

We directly use the look-up table of 25-dimensional word embeddings trained by the model of Collobert et al. (2011). These small word embeddings largely reduces model parameters. The dimension l of the hidden document-independent features is experimented in the range of $[1, 40]$, and the window sizes are experimented between 1 and 5. Through parameter experiments on development set, we set $l = 20$ and $m = 3$ for PriorSum. To update the weights W_t^h and w_r, we apply the diagonal variant of AdaGrad with mini-batches (Duchi et al., 2011).

For evaluation, we adopt the widely-used automatic evaluation metric ROUGE (Lin, 2004), and take ROUGE-1 and ROUGE-2 as the main measures.

3.2 Comparison with Baseline Methods

To evaluate the summarization performance of PriorSum, we compare it with the best peer systems (PeerT, Peer26 and Peer65 in Table 2) participating DUC evaluations. We also choose as baselines those state-of-the-art summarization results on DUC (2001, 2002, and 2004) data. To our knowledge, the best reported results on DUC 2001, 2002 and 2004 are from R2N2 (Cao et al., 2015), ClusterCMRW (Wan and Yang, 2008) and REGSUM[2] (Hong and Nenkova, 2014) respectively. R2N2 applies recursive neural networks to learn

[2]REGSUM truncates a summary to 100 words.

feature combination. ClusterCMRW incorporates the cluster-level information into the graph-based ranking algorithm. REGSUM is a word regression approach based on some advanced features such as word polarities (Wiebe et al., 2005) and categories (Tausczik and Pennebaker, 2010). For these three systems, we directly cite their published results, marked with the sign "*" as in Table 2. Meanwhile, LexRank (Erkan and Radev, 2004), a commonly-used graph-based summarization model, is introduced as an extra baseline. Comparing with this baseline can demonstrate the performance level of regression approaches. The baseline StandardCNN means that we adopt the standard CNNS with fixed window size for summary prior representation.

To explore the effects of the learned summary prior representations, we design a baseline system named **Reg_Manual** which adopts manually-compiled document-independent features such as NUMBER (whether number exist), NENTITY (whether named entities exist) and STOPRATIO (the ratio of stopwords). Then we combine these features with document-dependent features in Table 1 and tune the feature weights through LIBLINEAR[3] support vector regression.

From Table 2, we can see that PriorSum can achieve a comparable performance to the state-of-the-art summarization systems R2N2, ClusterCMRW and REGSUM. With respect to baselines, PriorSum significantly[4] outperforms Reg_Manual which uses manually compiled features and the graph-based summarization system LexRank. Meanwhile, PriorSum always enjoys a reasonable increase over StandardCNN, which verifies the effects of the enhanced CNNs. It is noted that StandardCNN can also achieve the state-of-the-art performance, indicating the summary prior representation really works.

3.3 Analysis

In this section, we explore what PriorSum learns according to the summary prior representations. Since the convolution layer follows a linear regression output, we apply a simple strategy to measure how much the learned document-independent features contribute to the saliency estimation. Specifically, for each sentence, we ignore its document-dependent features through setting their values as zeros and then apply a linear transformation using the weight w_r to get a summary prior score x_p. The greater the score, the more possible a sentence is to be included in a summary without context consideration. We analyze what intuitive features are hidden in the summary prior representation.

From Table 3, first we find that high-scored sentences contains more named entities and numbers, which conforms to human intuition. By contrast, the features NENTITY and NUMBER in Reg_Manual hold very small weights, only $2\%, 3\%$ compared with the most significant feature AVG-CF. One possible reason is that named entities or numbers are not independent features. For example, "month + number" is a common timestamp for an event whereas "number + a.m." is over-detailed and seldom appears in a summary. We can also see that low-scored sentences are relatively informal and fail to provide facts, which

Year	System	ROUGE-1	ROUGE-2
2001	PeerT	33.03	7.86
	R2N2*	35.88	7.64
	LexRank	33.43	6.09
	Reg_Manual	34.55	7.18
	StandardCNN	35.19	7.63
	PriorSum	**35.98**	**7.89**
2002	Peer26	35.15	7.64
	ClusterCMRW*	**38.55**	8.65
	LexRank	35.29	7.54
	Reg_Manual	34.81	8.12
	StandardCNN	35.73	8.69
	PriorSum	36.63	**8.97**
2004	Peer65	37.88	9.18
	REGSUM*	38.57	9.75
	LexRank	37.87	8.88
	Reg_Manual	37.05	9.34
	StandardCNN	37.90	9.93
	PriorSum	**38.91**	**10.07**

Table 2: Comparison results (%) on DUC datasets.

high scored	Meanwhile, Yugoslavia's P.M. told an emergency session Monday that the country is faced with war. The rebels ethnic Tutsis, disenchanted members of President Laurent Kabila's army took up arms, creating division among Congo's 400 tribes. The blast killed two assailants, wounded 21 Israelis and prompted Israel to suspend implementation of the peace accord with the Palestinians.
low scored	The greatest need is that many, many of us have been psychologically traumatized, and very, very few are receiving help. Ruben Rivera: An impatient hitter who will chase pitches out of the strike zone. I think we should worry about tuberculosis and the risk to the general population.

Table 3: Example sentences selected by prior scores.

[3] `http://www.csie.ntu.edu.tw/~cjlin/liblinear/`

[4] T-test with p-value ≤ 0.05

are difficult for human to generalize some specific features. For instance, informal sentences seem to have more stopwords but the feature STOPRATIO holds a relatively large positive weight in Reg_Manual.

4 Conclusion and Future Work

This paper proposes a novel summarization system called PriorSum to automatically learn summary prior features for extractive summarization. Experiments on the DUC generic multi-document summarization task show that our proposed method outperforms state-of-the-art approaches. In addition, we demonstrate the dominant sentences discovered by PriorSum, and the results verify that our model can learn different aspects of summary prior.

Acknowledgments

We thank all the anonymous reviewers for their insightful comments. This work was partially supported by National Key Basic Research Program of China (No. 2014CB340504), National Natural Science Foundation of China (No. 61273278 and 61272291), and National Social Science Foundation of China (No: 12&ZD227). The correspondence author of this paper is Sujian Li.

References

Ziqiang Cao, Furu Wei, Li Dong, Sujian Li, and Ming Zhou. 2015. Ranking with recursive neural networks and its application to multi-document summarization. In *AAAI-2015*.

Jaime Carbonell and Jade Goldstein. 1998. The use of mmr, diversity-based reranking for reordering documents and producing summaries. In *Proceedings of SIGIR*, pages 335–336.

Ronan Collobert, Jason Weston, Lon Bottou, Michael Karlen, Koray Kavukcuoglu, and Pavel Kuksa. 2011. Natural language processing (almost) from scratch. *The Journal of Machine Learning Research*, 12:2493–2537.

John M Conroy, Judith D Schlesinger, Jade Goldstein, and Dianne P Oleary. 2004. Left-brain/right-brain multi-document summarization. In *Proceedings of DUC*.

John Duchi, Elad Hazan, and Yoram Singer. 2011. Adaptive subgradient methods for online learning and stochastic optimization. *The Journal of Machine Learning Research*, 12:2121–2159.

Günes Erkan and Dragomir R Radev. 2004. Lexrank: Graph-based lexical centrality as salience in text summarization. *J. Artif. Intell. Res.(JAIR)*, 22(1):457–479.

Michel Galley. 2006. A skip-chain conditional random field for ranking meeting utterances by importance. In *Proceedings of EMNLP*, pages 364–372.

Kai Hong and Ani Nenkova. 2014. Improving the estimation of word importance for news multi-document summarization. In *Proceedings of EACL*.

Yoon Kim. 2014. Convolutional neural networks for sentence classification. *arXiv preprint arXiv:1408.5882*.

Sujian Li, You Ouyang, Wei Wang, and Bin Sun. 2007. Multi-document summarization using support vector regression. In *Proceedings of DUC*.

Chin-Yew Lin. 2004. Rouge: A package for automatic evaluation of summaries. In *Proceedings of the ACL Workshop*, pages 74–81.

Miles Osborne. 2002. Using maximum entropy for sentence extraction. In *Proceedings of ACL Workshop on Automatic Summarization*, pages 1–8.

Yelong Shen, Xiaodong He, Jianfeng Gao, Li Deng, and Grégoire Mesnil. 2014. Learning semantic representations using convolutional neural networks for web search. In *Companion publication of the 23rd international conference on World wide web companion*, pages 373–374.

Yla R Tausczik and James W Pennebaker. 2010. The psychological meaning of words: Liwc and computerized text analysis methods. *Journal of language and social psychology*, 29(1):24–54.

Xiaojun Wan and Jianwu Yang. 2008. Multi-document summarization using cluster-based link analysis. In *Proceedings of SIGIR*, pages 299–306.

Xiaojun Wan and Jianmin Zhang. 2014. Ctsum: extracting more certain summaries for news articles. In *Proceedings of the 37th international ACM SIGIR conference on Research & development in information retrieval*, pages 787–796. ACM.

Janyce Wiebe, Theresa Wilson, and Claire Cardie. 2005. Annotating expressions of opinions and emotions in language. *Language resources and evaluation*, 39(2-3):165–210.

Wen-tau Yih, Xiaodong He, and Christopher Meek. 2014. Semantic parsing for single-relation question answering. In *Proceedings of ACL*.

Daojian Zeng, Kang Liu, Siwei Lai, Guangyou Zhou, and Jun Zhao. 2014. Relation classification via convolutional deep neural network. In *Proceedings of COLING*, pages 2335–2344.

A Methodology for Evaluating Timeline Generation Algorithms based on Deep Semantic Units

Sandro Bauer and Simone Teufel
Computer Laboratory
University of Cambridge
Cambridge, United Kingdom
{sandro.bauer,simone.teufel}@cl.cam.ac.uk

Abstract

Timeline generation is a summarisation task which transforms a narrative, roughly chronological input text into a set of timestamped summary sentences, each expressing an atomic historical event. We present a methodology for evaluating systems which create such timelines, based on a novel corpus consisting of 36 human-created timelines. Our evaluation relies on deep semantic units which we call *historical content units*. An advantage of our approach is that it does not require human annotation of new system summaries.

1 Introduction

A timeline of historical events is a special kind of summary. We define a timeline as a list of textual event descriptions, each paired with a date (see Figure 1). A timeline is different from a standard single- or multi-document summary: Each event description is accompanied by a timestamp, and event descriptions themselves are independent linguistic units which should be understandable on their own. Additionally, a good timeline satisfies conflicting constraints: it should contain only salient events, and the overall time period considered should be covered well by events. Timeline construction is not a new task. It has been performed, for example, in a multi-document summarisation (Chieu and Lee, 2004; Yan et al., 2011; Nguyen et al., 2014) or in a single-document classification context (Chasin et al., 2013).

It is crucial to reliably evaluate algorithms that create such timelines automatically. Of course, any summary can be evaluated by surface methods such as ROUGE (Lin, 2004). But even for traditional summaries, ROUGE-based evaluation has been criticised for being too shallow, and it is even less adequate for timelines, because of their special properties described above.

(...) In the 1997 unrest in Albania the general elections of June 1997 brought the Socialists and their allies to power. President Berisha resigned from his post, and Socialists elected Rexhep Meidani as president of Albania. Albanian Socialist Party Chairman Fatos Nano was elected Prime Minister, (...)

1997	There was unrest in Albania.
June 1997	Fatos Nano was elected Prime Minister.

Figure 1: Extract from a Wikipedia article and two lines of a corresponding timeline.

We therefore opt for a "deep" method which attempts to measure to which degree a system-generated timeline contains semantic units found in gold-standard timelines. Our content units resemble those of van Halteren and Teufel (2003) and Nenkova and Passonneau (2004), but are larger in that they correspond to historical events.

Traditional deep summarisation evaluation is expensive because it involves annotation of gold-standard summaries as well as annotation of each system summary. A major operational advantage of our approach is that we require human annotation only for gold-standard summaries, not for system summaries. After a one-time effort of creating semantic units and mapping them to the original text, the quality of a system's content selection can be evaluated for infinitely many new system summaries for free. Our method is the following:

1. Ask timeline writers to create timelines with a fixed number of date-event pairs.
2. An HCU creator (the first author) transforms these timelines into HCUs, historical content units, which are defined based on semantic overlap between timeline text.
3. We then create a mapping between HCUs and the source text, or more precisely, TimeML events in the source text. This mapping between HCUs and source text allows us to evaluate new systems without a human ever inspecting system output at all.

Proceedings of the 53rd Annual Meeting of the Association for Computational Linguistics and the 7th International Joint Conference on Natural Language Processing (Short Papers), pages 834–839,
Beijing, China, July 26-31, 2015.

HCU 16	
Action	Fatos Nano is elected Prime Minister
Agent	*not given*
Patient	Fatos Nano
Time	June 1997
Location	Albania

Figure 2: HCU for one event from Figure 1

Any summarisation evaluation based on human judgment is inherently subjective, but we restrict this subjectivity in three ways. First, timeline creation (step 1) involves the selection of important content, which is by far the most subjective of the decisions involved in our evaluation method. We therefore ask three independent timeline writers to perform this task. Second, the generation of HCUs (step 2) is prescribed by fixed rules and definitions inspired by the methodology of van Halteren and Teufel (2003). With this method, the timeline writers, not the HCU creators, decide which material is available for creating the HCUs. Third, for the creation of mappings between HCUs and the source text (step 3), which was performed using a different set of detailed guidelines, we report agreement between the first and second author.

In section 2, we explain and contrast our concept of HCUs to existing work. In section 3, we present our new evaluation corpus and explain how we derived it. In section 4, we give details on how system scores for individual HCUs are calculated. In section 5, we analyse agreement of timeline writers on HCUs using two 3-person groups of annotators. We do not present our own algorithm for timeline generation here, but we sanity-check our evaluation methodology for a number of baseline timeline generation algorithms (section 6), where we demonstrate how systems are scored with our method.

2 Historical Content Units

Our event representation is called *Historical Content Unit* (HCU), which is inspired by the Summary Content Units (SCU) used in the pyramid method of Nenkova and Passonneau (2004) (henceforth NP04). Their approach is based on the idea that, due to the inherent subjectivity of summarisation tasks, there is no such thing as a single best gold standard summary. Instead, there are many equally good gold standard summaries. The way to differentiate between a good and a bad system summary is to consider each content unit selected by a system and count how many gold standard summaries it appears in. SCUs that are mentioned by many annotators contribute more to a system's score than less frequently chosen units. We follow this general weighting idea, but our HCUs are more abstract than SCUs, which are tied to a clause in the summary text without any further semantic characterisation by the annotator.

HCUs are more abstract in that they express an event, i.e. a concrete real-world action (*France invades Algeria*) or state change (*Obama becomes president*), while SCUs are more textual, not semantically defined and generally represent a smaller unit of meaning. State descriptions, opinions, wishes, aspirations, intentions and utterances do not constitute events. HCUs normally contain a logical agent (for actions) or a patient (for state changes), plus possibly other semantic roles. The action occurs at a given point in time, not as a continuous (e.g. "species adapt") or regular action ("the sun sets"), and the location of the event has to be delimitable, too (e.g., "in France" is acceptable, but not "on coral reefs"). An example HCU is given in Figure 2. Our HCU definition implies that each historical event is considered equally important. For system evaluation, this means that a system can score at most one point per HCU (exactly one point if it gives a perfect rendition of that HCU). This is different to evaluation based on the SCUs in NP04. Their method of linking words to SCUs may lead to a situation where some events are represented by multiple SCUs, and hence are effectively considered more important than others.

HCU construction proceeds by treating each line in each timeline as a single HCU candidate. If a line contains more than one event (for instance an event plus additional information), we decide what the main event is based on syntactic criteria and discard the additional information. We then have to decide whether two or more surface string descriptions of events by different timeline authors correspond to the same HCU. For this, we follow the method described by van Halteren and Teufel (2003). As long as two event descriptions do not contain conflicting information about an event and as long as their timestamps do not disagree, we can safely assume they refer to the same real-world action and map them to the same HCU, for instance, the two sentences "Nano was elected Prime Minister" and "Party Chairman Nano was elected PM".

This matching process results in a number of

HCUs for a source text, each with associated surface representations by human timeline authors. In the future, these gold standard event realisations could be used to evaluate the surface form of system timelines. This paper, however, is mainly concerned with content selection evaluation.

We now use the number of surface representations available to assign a weight to each HCU (following NP04), and the following formula is used to calculate the total score for a system:

$$score = \frac{\sum_{i \in HCUs} w_i \cdot score_i}{score_{max}}$$

where $score_i$ denotes the individual scores (between 0 and 1) calculated for each HCU i and w_i is the number of annotators whose timeline contains that HCU. $score_{max}$ is the sum of the weighted maximum scores of the n most highly weighted HCUs in the pyramid, where n is the desired timeline length.

3 Corpus construction

To find suitable historical articles for our corpus, we created the intersection of all Wikipedia articles whose title starts with "History of" with the articles in a large collection of timelines described by Bauer et al. (2014). Articles with errors in their Wikitext were removed. We also excluded articles that were incomplete, did not contain narrative text or were not chronologically structured. None of these criteria aim at hand-picking well-written articles or articles that describe well-attested topics. The final set consists of 408 articles. We manually grouped these according to their general topic area (GEO-POLITICAL ENTITY, SCIENCE, ...). From these, we select a set of 11 articles representative in terms of length and subject area. For each of the articles in our corpus, we removed the introductions (which tend to contain a summary of the entire article). We then asked 3 annotators per text[1] to produce a historical digest with a given maximum length determined by the number of verbs in each article (resulting in 25-40 events). For one text, we asked an additional 3 annotators to provide timelines, such that this one text was covered by six annotators. This means that in total, we had 36 combinations of texts and timeline writers.

Our instructions do not tell the timeline writers how content selection (in the source text) and surface realisation (in the timelines produced) should be performed. We merely state that the timeline should strike a balance between mentioning all and only important events and still giving a complete account of the time period covered. Annotators are also told that each line should contain exactly one event and must be given a timestamp.

Our approach brings with it the challenge of deciding when an algorithm operating on the source text has correctly selected an HCU. We assume that individual words in the text – verbs, nominalisations and certain other event-like nouns (such as "war") – are associated with the core action or state change expressed by an HCU and that we or a system can find those. While our methodology does not presuppose any particular event definition or event extraction paradigm, we make use of the TimeML project (Pustejovsky et al., 2003), which has provided a substantial body of work on how to extract events and timestamps in the form of TimeML EVENT and TIMEX instances (cf. the TempEval shared tasks (Verhagen et al., 2007; Verhagen et al., 2010; UzZaman et al., 2013)).

To construct the links between the HCUs we found in the texts (between 32 and 80 per text[2]) and the surface text, we first run a publicly available, recent TimeML-based extraction system, TIPSem-B (Llorens et al., 2010), over our texts. We then manually annotate each HCU with all surface sentences that express the action or state change described by the HCU, and manually decide which TimeML event(s) identified in any such matching sentence express(es) the HCU's content. This results in a 1:n mapping between HCUs and events. For this matching process, we use a detailed set of guidelines. A subset of the 2066 matchings (all matchings for 60 HCUs) was re-annotated independently by the second author; inter-annotator agreement was 87.9%.

Where the TimeML system failed to recognise what we consider to be the correct event anchor, we manually tagged this event anchor, and we provide this information with our corpus. This is because we want our gold standard to be independent of any particular event extraction package.

4 Scoring system

As stated above, the reward a system may receive for a single HCU is capped to one. This is true regardless of how many TimeML events represent-

[1]The annotators recruited included both computational linguists and students in higher education.

[2]We obtain 100 HCUs for the text annotated by 6 humans.

ing the HCU are retrieved by the system. We uphold this principle because we aim to evaluate how many HCUs a system returns, not how many textual elements representing them are retrieved.

Apart from this global constraint, the general principle is to treat the contribution of each individual TimeML event additively. For example, if three events have been found to represent a third of the meaning of the HCU, respectively, and two of them are selected by the system, the total score obtained for this HCU will be $\frac{2}{3}$.

For some pairs of TimeML events, however, this additive paradigm is not the desired behaviour: The TimeML software sometimes tends to mark two very closely related words, e.g. a verb ("start") and its object ("war"), as events. In this case, we do not want these two events, which we consider to be members of an *event group*, to contribute additively (AND); instead, an OR logic is appropriate, meaning that it is irrelevant whether one or both of the participating events are chosen. The human matcher may impose such constraints between multiple events linked to the same HCU.

In general, an event group E is a set which may contain individual events $e_1, e_2, ...$ and further subgroups $E_1, E_2, ...$ of events.

$$E = \{E_1, E_2, ..., E_n, e_1, e_2, ..., e_n\}$$

Each event and subgroup in E is associated with a number $v \in [0, 1]$ that denotes how much the event or subgroup contributes to the total meaning of event group E in context of HCU i; these numbers are set by the human matcher.

The total $score_i$ that a system will receive for an HCU i is calculated using the function $S(i, E)$, where E is an event group that includes all events linked to HCU i by a human:

$$S(i,E) = min(1, \sum_{E_j \in E} v_{E_j} \cdot S(i,E_j) + \sum_{e_j \in E} v_{e_j} \cdot s(i,e_j))$$

$S(i, E_j)$ represents the contribution made by all TimeML events in an event subgroup $E_j \in E$, which is again capped to 1 via the recursive definition of the score function. $s(i, e)$ is a function for an individual event in group E which, if the system to be evaluated has chosen the event, returns one, and zero otherwise:

$$s(i,e) = \begin{cases} 1 & \text{if the system has chosen event } e \\ 0 & \text{otherwise} \end{cases}$$

Note that $S(i, E)$ simplifies to $s(i, e)$ if there is only one event e linked to HCU i (and if $v_e = 1$).

See Figure 3 for an example of an HCU along with all TimeML events in a sentence from the source article and their respective contributions to the HCU's meaning (in brackets). Here, the matcher has decided, according to our guidelines, that "began" fully represents the HCU's meaning, while "recording" only represents half of the meaning. Importantly, a system selecting both these events will still only receive a total score of 1.0 for this HCU since it is capped to that number.

5 Data analysis

While we do not expect perfect agreement for timeline generation, we hope to observe a pyramid form like in NP04; i.e. a situation where few HCUs are chosen by all three annotators, a higher number are chosen by two annotators, and so on. Indeed this was the case for 9 of the documents.

We also investigated how different the gold standard would have been if a different set of three humans had annotated the texts. We asked three further annotators to create historical digests of one text and then considered all possible splits into two groups of three annotators each. For illustration, Tables 1 and 2 represent two examples out of the 10 possible configurations, showing the number of annotators per group that agreed on HCUs. The grey areas in the tables capture cases where the two annotator teams chose an HCU with the same frequency or where the two frequencies differ only by one. Averaged across the 10 splits, 91.9% of all HCUs fall into this area.

Consider cell (#0, #0): These are the cases where all six annotators decided that these events are not worthy of being mentioned in the timeline. Since we do not annotate non-selected HCUs, we can only give an approximation for this number based on the average observed HCU frequency per sentence. We do this since these cases should arguably also contribute posivitely to the agreement. Using these tables, we calculate Krippendorff's α across annotator groups; i.e. each HCU can receive a score between 0 and 3, depending on how many annotators expressed it in their timeline. We use an interval difference function and obtain $\alpha = 0.530$. This is arguably a non-standard use of α; we provide this number to give the reader a rough idea of the agreement across groups.

6 Baseline results

To illustrate our method, we now present the results of a number of baseline algorithms. We only evaluate the systems' choice of events, not the sur-

Action	The Southern Semites began recording their history
Agent	the Southern Semites
Patient	their history
Time	800 BC
Surface text	This **led (0.0)** to **contact (0.0)** with the Phoenicians and from them , the Southern Semites **adopted (0.0)** their writing script in 800 BCE and **began (1.0) recording (0.5)** their history .

Figure 3: Example HCU with links into the surface text (the HCU's location is not given)

		Team 2			
		#0	#1	#2	#3
Team 1	#0	87	19	2	1
	#1	18	15	10	1
	#2	6	8	9	4
	#3	1	0	3	3

Table 1: Best split (94.1% in grey area)

		Team 2			
		#0	#1	#2	#3
Team 1	#0	87	17	6	0
	#1	20	9	6	3
	#2	8	14	5	1
	#3	0	2	6	3

Table 2: Worst split (89.8% in grey area)

face realisation or the timestamps. In the future, a more sophisticated mechanism may be devised which takes these aspects into account as well.

Our algorithms are listed in Table 3. They may select individual TimeML events from the source text (1-6), or entire sentences (7-10); in the latter case, all events in the sentences count as selected. Some of the baselines select events from anywhere in the article (4, 5, 6, 10); others proceed in a round-robin fashion by iteratively selecting one event or sentence per section (1, 1b, 2, 3, 7, 8, 9, "RR"). For the latter methods, in each iteration we can proceed from the top (1, 1b, 7) or the bottom (2, 8) of the section, or we randomly select any event or sentence in the section (3, 9). Choosing the first or the last events of the entire article (5, 6) does not look like a good method, since the timeline needs to cover the entire timespan. Finally, we examine whether selecting only events with a date in the same sentence has any effect; results can only be calculated over 10 articles since one of the articles does not contain enough such events. The result in Table 3 is therefore marked with a star (*). The results of methods that involve randomly selecting items were averaged over 100 runs. In principle, existing systems such as that by Chasin et al. (2013) could also be evaluated with our method, but we do not do this here.

ID	Method	Scores
1	RR, first events in section	0.23
1b	like 1, events with dates only	0.33*
2	RR, last events in section	0.13
3	RR, random events in section	0.13
4	Random events in article	0.11
5	First events in article	0.13
6	Last events in article	0.11
7	RR, first sentences in section	0.22
8	RR, last sentences in section	0.11
9	RR, random sentences in section	0.12
10	Random sentences in article	0.10

Table 3: Baseline results (average pyramid scores); the result with a * is based on 10 articles

Algorithms inspired by the well-established "first n words" baseline for summarisation of newswire articles perform best here too, when applied on a section level (1, 1b, 7). All these algorithms perform significantly better when compared to any of the other algorithms (2-6, 8-10); statistical significance is measured for each pair of algorithms at $\alpha = 0.05$ using the Wilcoxon signed-rank test ($p < 0.05$). This suggests that important events tend to be placed at the beginning of a section. Selecting the first events from the entire article (5) produces worse results than selecting the first events from each section. The best results are obtained when selecting only events with dates in their proximity (1b); however, this result is based only on 10 of the 11 articles, and the difference to algorithm 1 is not significant ($p = 0.1391$).

7 Conclusion

We have introduced a novel methodology for evaluating timeline generation algorithms based on deep semantic content units, including a new corpus of 36 human-written timelines and associated HCUs. Our evaluation focuses on a deeper model of meaning (based on events) rather than n-gram overlap, and provides links between each HCU and the source text. This allows us to subsequently evaluate an unlimited number of system summaries without any further cost, rationalising the evaluation of timeline construction algorithms.

References

Sandro Bauer, Stephen Clark, and Thore Graepel. 2014. Learning to Identify Historical Figures for Timeline Creation from Wikipedia Articles. In Luca Maria Aiello and Daniel A. McFarland, editors, *Social Informatics - SocInfo 2014 International Workshops, Barcelona, Spain, November 11, 2014, Revised Selected Papers*, volume 8852 of *Lecture Notes in Computer Science*, pages 234–243. Springer.

Rachel Chasin, Daryl Woodward, Jeremy Witmer, and Jugal Kalita. 2013. Extracting and Displaying Temporal and Geospatial Entities from Articles on Historical Events. *The Computer Journal*, pages 403–426.

Hai Leong Chieu and Yoong Keok Lee. 2004. Query Based Event Extraction Along a Timeline. In *Proceedings of the 27th Annual International ACM SIGIR Conference on Research and Development in Information Retrieval*, SIGIR '04, pages 425–432, Sheffield, United Kingdom.

Chin-Yew Lin. 2004. ROUGE: A Package for Automatic Evaluation of Summaries. In Stan Szpakowicz Marie-Francine Moens, editor, *Text Summarization Branches Out: Proceedings of the ACL-04 Workshop*, pages 74–81, Barcelona, Spain, July. Association for Computational Linguistics.

Hector Llorens, Estela Saquete, and Borja Navarro. 2010. TIPSem (English and Spanish): Evaluating CRFs and Semantic Roles in TempEval-2. In *Proceedings of the 5th International Workshop on Semantic Evaluation*, SemEval '10, pages 284–291, Los Angeles, California. Association for Computational Linguistics.

Ani Nenkova and Rebecca Passonneau. 2004. Evaluating Content Selection in Summarization: The Pyramid Method. In Daniel Marcu Susan Dumais and Salim Roukos, editors, *HLT-NAACL 2004: Main Proceedings*, pages 145–152, Boston, Massachusetts, USA, May 2 - May 7. Association for Computational Linguistics.

Kiem-Hieu Nguyen, Xavier Tannier, and Véronique Moriceau. 2014. Ranking Multidocument Event Descriptions for Building Thematic Timelines. In *Proceedings of COLING 2014, the 25th International Conference on Computational Linguistics: Technical Papers*, pages 1208–1217, Dublin, Ireland.

James Pustejovsky, José M. Castaño, Robert Ingria, Roser Sauri, Robert J. Gaizauskas, Andrea Setzer, Graham Katz, and Dragomir R. Radev. 2003. TimeML: Robust Specification of Event and Temporal Expressions in Text. In Mark T. Maybury, editor, *New Directions in Question Answering, Papers from 2003 AAAI Spring Symposium, Stanford University, Stanford, CA, USA*, pages 28–34. AAAI Press.

Naushad UzZaman, Hector Llorens, Leon Derczynski, James Allen, Marc Verhagen, and James Pustejovsky. 2013. SemEval-2013 Task 1: TempEval-3: Evaluating Time Expressions, Events, and Temporal Relations. In *Second Joint Conference on Lexical and Computational Semantics (*SEM), Volume 2: Proceedings of the Seventh International Workshop on Semantic Evaluation (SemEval 2013)*, pages 1–9, Atlanta, Georgia, USA.

Hans van Halteren and Simone Teufel. 2003. Examining the Consensus Between Human Summaries: Initial Experiments with Factoid Analysis. In *Proceedings of the HLT-NAACL 03 on Text Summarization Workshop - Volume 5*, HLT-NAACL-DUC '03, pages 57–64, Edmonton, Canada. Association for Computational Linguistics.

Marc Verhagen, Robert Gaizauskas, Frank Schilder, Mark Hepple, Graham Katz, and James Pustejovsky. 2007. SemEval-2007 Task 15: TempEval Temporal Relation Identification. In *Proceedings of the 4th International Workshop on Semantic Evaluations*, SemEval '07, pages 75–80, Prague, Czech Republic. Association for Computational Linguistics.

Marc Verhagen, Roser Sauri, Tommaso Caselli, and James Pustejovsky. 2010. SemEval-2010 Task 13: TempEval-2. In *Proceedings of the 5th International Workshop on Semantic Evaluation*, pages 57–62, Uppsala, Sweden, July. Association for Computational Linguistics.

Rui Yan, Xiaojun Wan, Jahna Otterbacher, Liang Kong, Xiaoming Li, and Yan Zhang. 2011. Evolutionary Timeline Summarization: A Balanced Optimization Framework via Iterative Substitution. In *Proceedings of the 34th International ACM SIGIR Conference on Research and Development in Information Retrieval*, SIGIR '11, pages 745–754, Beijing, China.

Unsupervised extractive summarization via coverage maximization with syntactic and semantic concepts

Natalie Schluter and **Anders Søgaard**
Center for Language Technology
University of Copenhagen
{natschluter,soegaard}@hum.ku.dk

Abstract

Coverage maximization with bigram concepts is a state-of-the-art approach to unsupervised extractive summarization. It has been argued that such concepts are adequate and, in contrast to more linguistic concepts such as named entities or syntactic dependencies, more robust, since they do not rely on automatic processing. In this paper, we show that while this seems to be the case for a commonly used newswire dataset, use of syntactic and semantic concepts leads to significant improvements in performance in other domains.

1 Introduction

State-of-the-art approaches to extractive summarization are based on the notion of coverage maximization (Berg-Kirkpatrick et al., 2011). The assumption is that a good summary is a selection of sentences from the document that contains as many of the important concepts as possible. The importance of concepts is implemented by assigning weights w_i to each concept i with binary variable c_i, yielding the following coverage maximization objective, subject to the appropriate constraints:

$$\sum_{i}^{N} w_i c_i \tag{1}$$

In proposing bigrams as concepts for their system, Gillick and Favre (2009) explain that:

> [c]oncepts could be words, named entities, syntactic subtrees or semantic relations, for example. While deeper semantics make more appealing concepts, their extraction and weighting are much more error-prone. Any error in concept extraction can result in a biased objective function, leading to poor sentence selection. (Gillick and Favre, 2009)

Several authors, e.g., Woodsend and Lapata (2012), and Li et al. (2013), have followed Gillick and Favre (2009) in assuming that bigrams would lead to better practical performance than more syntactic or semantic concepts, even though bigrams serve as only an approximation of these.

In this paper, we revisit this assumption and evaluate the maximum coverage objective for extractive text summarization with syntactic and semantic concepts. Specifically, we replace bigram concepts with new ones based on syntactic dependencies, semantic frames, as well as named entities. We show that using such concepts can lead to significant improvements in text summarization performance outside of the newswire domain. We evaluate coverage maximization incorporating syntactic and semantic concepts across three different domains: newswire, legal judgments, and Wikipedia articles.

2 Concept coverage maximization for extractive summarization

In extractive summarization, the unsupervised version of the task is sometimes set up as that of finding a subset of sentences in a document, within some relatively small budget, that covers as many of the important concepts in the document as possible. In the maximum coverage objective, concepts are considered as independent of each other. Concepts are weighted by the number of times they appear in a document. Moreover, due the NP-hardness of coverage maximization, for an exact solution to the concept coverage optimization problem, we resort to fast solvers for integer linear programming, under some appropriate constraints.

Bigrams. Gillick and Favre (2009) proposed to use bigrams as concepts, and to weight their contribution to the objective function in Equation (1)

Proceedings of the 53rd Annual Meeting of the Association for Computational Linguistics and the 7th International Joint Conference on Natural Language Processing (Short Papers), pages 840–844,
Beijing, China, July 26-31, 2015.

by the frequency with which they occur in the document. Some pre-processing is first carried out to these bigrams: all bigrams consisting uniquely of stop-words are removed from consideration, and each word is stemmed. They also require bigrams to occur with a minimal frequency (cf. Section 3.2).

Named entities. We consider three new types of concepts, all suggested, but subsequently rejected by Gillick and Favre (2009). The first is simply to use named entities, e.g., *Court of Justice of the European Union*, as concepts. This reflects the intuition that persons, organizations, and locations are particularly important for extractive summarization. We use an NER maximum entropy tagger[1] to augment documents with named entities.

Syntactic dependencies. The second type of concept is dependency subtrees. In particular, we extract labeled and unlabeled syntactic dependencies, e.g., DEPENDENCY(walks,John) or SUBJECT(walks,John), from sentences and represent them by such syntactic concepts. We use the Stanford parser[2] to augment documents with syntactic dependencies. As was done for bigrams, each word in the dependency is stemmed. Syntactic dependency-based concepts are intuitively a closer approximation than bigrams to concepts in general.

Semantic frames. The intuition behind our use of frame semantics is that a summary should represent the most central semantic frames (Fillmore, 1982; Fillmore et al., 2003) present in the corresponding document—indeed, we consider these frames to be actual types of concepts. We extract frame names from sentences for a further type of concepts under consideration. We use SEMAFOR[3] to augment documents with semantic frames.

3 Experiments

3.1 Data

In order to investigate the importance of concept types across different domains, we evaluate our systems across three distinct domains, which we refer to as ECHR, TAC08, and WIKIPEDIA.

ECHR consists of judgment-summary pairs scraped from the European Court of Human Rights case-law website, HUDOC[4]. The document-summary pairs were split into training, development and test sets, consisting of 1018, 117, and 138 pairs, respectively. In the training set (pruning sentences of length less than 5), the average document length is 13,184 words or 455 sentences. The average summary length is 806 words or 28 sentences. For both documents and summaries, the average sentence length is 29 words.

TAC08 consists of 48 queries and 2 newswire document sets for each query, each set containing 10 documents. Document sets contain 235 input sentences on average, and the mean sentence length is 25 words. Summaries consist of 4 sentences or 100 words on average.

WIKIPEDIA consists of 992 Wikipedia articles (all labeled "good article"[5]) from a comprehensive dump of English language Wikipedia articles[6]. We use the Wikipedia abstracts (the leading paragraphs before the table of contents) as summaries. The (document,summary) pairs were split into training, development and test sets, consisting of 784, 97, and 111 pairs, respectively. In the training set (pruning sentences of length less than 5), the average document length is around 8918 words or 339 sentences. The average summary length is 335 words or 13 sentences. For both documents and summaries, the average sentence length is around 26 words.

In our main experiments, we use unsupervised summarization techniques, and we only use the training summaries (and not the documents) to determine output summary lengths.

3.2 Baseline and systems

Our baseline is the bigram-based extraction summarization system of Gillick and Favre (2009), `icsisumm`[7]. Their system was originally intended for multi-document update summarization, and summaries are extracted from document sentences that share more than k content words with some query. We follow this approach for the TAC08 data. For ECHR and WIKIPEDIA, the task is single document summarization, and the now irrelevant topic-document intersection preprocessing step is eliminated.

[1] http://www.nltk.org/

[2] http://nlp.stanford.edu/software/lex-parser.shtml

[3] http://www.ark.cs.cmu.edu/SEMAFOR/

[4] http://hudoc.echr.coe.int/

[5] http://en.wikipedia.org/wiki/Wikipedia:Good_articles

[6] https://dumps.wikimedia.org/enwiki/latest/enwiki-latest-pages-articles-multistream.xml.bz2

[7] https://code.google.com/p/icsisumm/

The original system uses the GNU linear programming kit[8] with a time limit of 100 seconds. For all experiments presented in this paper, we double this time limit; we experimented with longer time limits on the development set for the ECHR data, without any performance improvements. Once the summarizer reaches the time limit, a summary is output based on the current feasible solution, whether the solution is optimal or not. Moreover, the current `icsisumm` (v1) distribution prunes sentences shorter than 10 words. We note that we also tried replacing `glpk` by `gurobi`[9], for which no time limit was necessary, but found poorer results on the development set of the ECHR data.

The original system takes several important input parameters.

1. **Summary length,** for TAC08, is specified by the TAC 2008 conference guidelines as 100 words. For WIKIPEDIA and ECHR, we have access to training sets which gave an average summary length of around 335 and 805 words respectively, which we take as the standard output summary length.

2. **Concept count cut-off** is the minimum frequency of concepts from the document (set) that qualifies them for consideration in coverage maximization. For bigrams of the original system on TAC08, there are two types of document sets: 'A' and 'B'. For 'A' type documents, Gillick and Favre (2009) set this threshold to 3 and for 'B' type documents, they set this to 4. For WIKIPEDIA and ECHR, we take the bigram threshold to be 4. In our extension of the system to other concepts, we do not use any threshold.

3. **First concept weighting:** in multi-document summarization, there is the possibility for repeated sentences. Concepts from first-encountered sentences may be weighted higher: these concept counts from first-encountered sentences are doubled for 'B' documents and remain unchanged for 'A' documents in the original system on TAC08. For other concepts, we do not alter frequencies in this manner, which is justified by the task change to single-document summarization.

4. **Query-sentence intersection threshold,** is set to 1 for 'A' documents and 0 to 'B' documents in the original system on TAC08. This threshold is only for the update summarization task and therefore does not concern ECHR and WIKIPEDIA.

In addition to our baseline, we consider five single-concept systems using (a) named entities, (b) labeled dependencies, (c) unlabeled dependencies, (d) semantic frame names, and (e) semantic frame dependencies, as well as the five systems combining each of these new concept types with bigrams. For the combination of these new concepts with bigrams, we extend the objective function to maximise in, Equation (1), into two sums—one for bigram concepts and the other for the new concept type—with their relative importance controlled by a parameter α. N_1 and N_2 are the number of bigram and other concept types occurring with the permitted threshold frequency in the document, relatively. Given that we are carrying out unsupervised summarization, rather than tune α, we set $\alpha = 0.5$, so the concepts are considered in their totality (i.e., $N_1 + N_2$ concepts together) with no explicit favouring of one over the other that does not naturally fall out of concept frequency.

$$(1-\alpha)\sum_{i}^{N_1} w_i \texttt{bigram}_i + \alpha \sum_{j}^{N_2} w_j \texttt{new\_concept}_j$$

3.3 Results

We evaluate output summaries using ROUGE-1, ROUGE-2, and ROUGE-SU4 (Lin, 2004), with no stemming and retaining all stopwords. These measures have been shown to correlate best with human judgments in general, but among the automatic measures, ROUGE-1 and ROUGE-2 also correlate best with the Pyramid (Nenkova and Passonneau, 2004; Nenkova et al., 2007) and Responsiveness manual metrics (Louis and Nenkova, 2009). Moreover, ROUGE-1 has been shown to best reflect human-automatic summary comparisons (Owczarzak et al., 2012).

For single concept systems, the results are shown in Table 1, and concept combination system results are given in Table 2.

We first note that our runs of the current distribution of `icsisumm` yield significantly worse ROUGE-2 results than reported in (Gillick and Favre, 2009) (see Table 1, BIGRAMS): 0.081 compared to 0.110 respectively.

[8] http://www.gnu.org/software/glpk/
[9] http://www.gurobi.com/

On the TAC08 data, we observe no improvements over the baseline BIGRAM system for any ROUGE metric here. Hence, Gillick and Favre (2009) were right in their assumption that syntactic and semantic concepts would not lead to performance improvements, when restricting ourselves to this dataset. However, when we change domain to the legal judgments or Wikipedia articles, using syntactic and semantic concepts leads to significant gains across all the ROUGE metrics.

For ECHR, replacing bigrams by frame names (FRAME) results in an increase of +0.1 in ROUGE-1, +0.031 in ROUGE-2 and +0.046 in ROUGE-SU4. We note that FrameNet 1.5 covers the legal domain quite well, which may explain why these concepts are particularly useful for the ECHR dataset. However, labeled (LDEP) and unlabeled (UDEP) dependencies also significantly outperform the baseline.

For WIKIPEDIA, replacing bigrams by labeled or unlabeled syntactic dependencies results in significant improvements: an increase of +0.088 for ROUGE-1, +0.015 for ROUGE-2, and +0.03 for ROUGE-SU4. Interestingly, the NER system also yields significantly better performance over the baseline, which may reflect the nature of Wikipedia articles, often being about historical figures, famous places, organizations, etc.

We observe in Table 2, that for concept combination systems as well, ROUGE scores on TAC08 do not indicate any improvement in performance. However, best ROUGE-1 scores are produced for both ECHR and WIKIPEDIA data with systems that incorporate semantic frame names. For WIKIPEDIA, best ROUGE-2 and ROUGE-SU4 scores incorporate named-entity information.

4 Related work

Most researchers have used bigrams as concepts in coverage maximization-based approaches to unsupervised extractive summarization. Filatova and Hatzivassiloglou (2004), however,use relations between named entities as concepts in extractive summarization. They use slightly different extraction algorithms, but their work is similar in spirit to ours. Nishikawa et al. (2010), also, use opinions – tuples of targets, aspects, and polarity – as concepts in opinion summarization. In early work on summarization, Silber and McCoy (2000) used WordNet synsets as concepts. Kitajima and Kobayashi (2011) replace words by syntactic dependencies in the Maximal Marginal Relevance Multidocument measure first proposed by Goldstein et al. (2000) for evaluating the importance of sentences in query-based extractive summarization, yielding improvements for their Japanese newswire dataset.

ECHR			
concept	R-1 (95% conf.)	R-2 (95% conf.)	R-SU4 (95% conf.)
BIGRAMS	0.544 (0.528-0.562)	0.204 (0.195-0.215)	0.266 (0.257-0.277)
NER	0.549 (0.534-0.564)	0.184 (0.174-0.193)	0.254 (0.244-0.264)
LDEP	0.609 (0.597-0.621)	0.225 (0.217-0.235)	0.293 (0.285-0.302)
UDEP	0.612 (0.6-0.626)	0.227 (0.218-0.238)	0.295 (0.287-0.305)
FRAMES	**0.643** (0.63-0.657)	**0.235** (0.224-0.248)	**0.312** (0.302-0.323)
TAC08			
concept	R-1 (95% conf.)	R-2 (95% conf.)	R-SU4 (95% conf.)
BIGRAMS	**0.35** (0.34-0.36)	**0.081** (0.073-0.089)	**0.119** (0.113-0.126)
NER	0.307 (0.297-0.317)	0.054 (0.049-0.06)	0.093 (0.089-0.099)
LDEP	0.335 (0.325-0.346)	0.072 (0.065-0.08)	0.109 (0.103-0.116)
UDEP	**0.342** (0.331-0.353)	**0.075** (0.067-0.083)	**0.113** (0.106-0.12)
FRAMES	0.301 (0.292-0.31)	0.048 (0.042-0.053)	0.089 (0.085-0.094)
WIKIPEDIA			
concept	R-1 (95% conf.)	R-2 (95% conf.)	R-SU4 (95% conf.)
BIGRAMS	0.391 (0.364-0.415)	0.103 (0.094-0.113)	0.152 (0.134-0.163)
NER	**0.473** (0.46-0.487)	**0.114** (0.105-0.123)	**0.178** (0.169-0.186)
LDEP	**0.478** (0.461-0.495)	**0.116** (0.107-0.125)	**0.179** (0.169-0.188)
UDEP	**0.479** (0.462-0.497)	**0.118** (0.109-0.128)	**0.18** (0.17-0.189)
FRAMES	**0.476** (0.461-0.494)	**0.102** (0.094-0.112)	**0.172** (0.164-0.182)

Table 1: Single concept results on ECHR, TAC08, and WIKIPEDIA.

5 Conclusions

This paper challenges the assumption that bigrams make better concepts for unsupervised extractive summarization than syntactic and semantic concepts relying on automatic processing. We show that using concepts relying on syntactic dependencies or semantic frames instead of bigrams leads to significant performance improvements of coverage maximization summarization across domains.

References

Taylor Berg-Kirkpatrick, Dan Gillick, and Dan Klein. 2011. Jointly learning to extract and compress. In *Proc of ACL*, Portland, OR, USA.

ECHR			
concept	R-1 (95% conf.)	R-2 (95% conf.)	R-SU4 (95% conf.)
NER	0.605	0.228	0.093
	(0.595-0.616)	(0.22- 0.237)	(0.288-0.303)
LDEP	0.614	0.235	0.301
	(0.597-0.632)	(0.225-0.246)	(0.29-0.312)
UDEP	0.62	0.237	0.304
	(0.605-0.634)	(0.227-0.247)	(0.294-0.313)
FRAMES	**0.65**	**0.251**	**0.322**
	(0.638-0.662)	(0.24-0.262)	(0.313-0.333)

TAC08			
concept	R-1 (95% conf.)	R-2 (95% conf.)	R-SU4 (95% conf.)
NER	0.35	0.082	0.119
	(0.339-0.361)	(0.074-0.09)	(0.112-0.126)
LDEP	0.345	0.08	0.117
	(0.334-0.355)	(0.072-0.088)	(0.11-0.124)
UDEP	0.347	0.08	0.12
	(0.336-0.358)	(0.072-0.088)	(0.11-0.125)
FRAMES	0.344	0.078	0.115
	(0.334-0.354)	(0.071-0.086)	(0.11-0.122)

WIKIPEDIA			
concept	R-1 (95% conf.)	R-2 (95% conf.)	R-SU4 (95% conf.)
NER	**0.496**	**0.136**	**0.195**
	(0.483-0.51)	(0.127-0.146)	(0.187-0.204)
LDEP	**0.495**	**0.132**	**0.192**
	(0.479-0.511)	(0.122-0.141)	(0.183-0.202)
UDEP	0.493	0.13	0.18
	(0.478-0.511)	(0.121-0.14)	(0.181-0.199)
FRAMES	**0.497**	0.124	0.187
	(0.482-0.513)	(0.114-0.133)	(0.179-0.197)

Table 2: Results for systems combining bigrams with new concepts, on ECHR, TAC08 and WIKIPEDIA.

Elena Filatova and Vasileios Hatzivassiloglou. 2004. Event-based extractive summarization. In *ACL Workshop on Text Summarization Branches Out*.

Charles J. Fillmore, Christopher. R. Johnson, and Miriam R. L. Petruck. 2003. Background to framenet. *International Journal of Lexicography*, 16.

Charles J. Fillmore, 1982. *Linguistics in the Morning Calm*, chapter Frame Semantics, pages 111–137. Hanshin Publishing Co., Seoul, South Korea.

Dan Gillick and Benoit Favre. 2009. A scalable global model for summarization. In *Proc of ILP*, pages 10–18.

Jade Goldstein, Vibhu Mittal, Jaime Carbonell, and Mark Kantrowitz. 2000. Multi-document summarization by sentence extraction. In *Proc of the ANLP/NAACL Workshop on Automatic Summarization*, pages 40–48.

Risa Kitajima and Ichiro Kobayashi. 2011. A latent topic extracting method based on events in a document and its application. In *Proc of ACL-HLT Student Session*, pages 30–35, Portland, OR, USA.

Chen Li, Xian Qian, and Yang Liu. 2013. Using supervised bigram-based ilp for extractive summarization. In *Proc of ACL*, Sofia, Bulgaria.

Chin-Yew Lin. 2004. Rouge: A package for automatic evaluation of summaries. In *Proc of WAS*, Barcelona, Spain.

Annie Louis and Ani Nenkova. 2009. Automatically evaluation content selection in summarization without human models. In *Proc of EMNLP*, pages 306–314, Singapore.

Ani Nenkova and Rebecca Passonneau. 2004. Evaluating content selection in summarization: The pyramid method. In *Proc. of HLT-NAACL*.

Ani Nenkova, Rebecca Passonneau, and Kathleen McKeown. 2007. The pyramid method:incorporating human content selection variation in summarization evaluation. *ACM Transactions on Speech and Language Processing*, 4.

Hitoshi Nishikawa, Takaaki Hasegawa, Yoshihiro Matsuo, and Genichiro Kikui. 2010. Opinion summarization with integer linear programming formulation for sentence extraction and ordering. In *COLING*.

Karolina Owczarzak, John M. Conroy, Hoa Trang Dang, and Ani Nenkova. 2012. An assessment of the accuracy of automatic evaluation in summarization. In *Proc of the Workshop on Evaluation Metrics and System Comparison for Automatic Summarization*, pages 1–9, Montréal, Canada.

H. Gregory Silber and Kathleen McCoy. 2000. An efficient text summarizer using lexical chains. In *INLG*.

Kristian Woodsend and Mirella Lapata. 2012. Multiple aspect summarization using integer linear programming. In *Proc of EMNLP/CoNLL*, pages 233–243, Jeju Island, Korea.

Low Resource Dependency Parsing: Cross-lingual Parameter Sharing in a Neural Network Parser

Long Duong,[12] **Trevor Cohn,**[1] **Steven Bird,**[1] and **Paul Cook**[3]
[1]Department of Computing and Information Systems, University of Melbourne
[2]National ICT Australia, Victoria Research Laboratory
[3]Faculty of Computer Science, University of New Brunswick
lduong@student.unimelb.edu.au {t.cohn,sbird}@unimelb.edu.au paul.cook@unb.ca

Abstract

Training a high-accuracy dependency parser requires a large treebank. However, these are costly and time-consuming to build. We propose a learning method that needs less data, based on the observation that there are underlying shared structures across languages. We exploit cues from a different source language in order to guide the learning process. Our model saves at least half of the annotation effort to reach the same accuracy compared with using the purely supervised method.

1 Introduction

Dependency parsing is a crucial component of many natural language processing systems, for tasks such as text classification (Özgür and Güngör, 2010), statistical machine translation (Xu et al., 2009), relation extraction (Bunescu and Mooney, 2005), and question answering (Cui et al., 2005). Supervised approaches to dependency parsing have been successful for languages where relatively large treebanks are available (McDonald et al., 2005). However, for many languages, annotated treebanks are not available. They are costly to create, requiring careful design, testing and subsequent refinement of annotation guidelines, along with assessment and management of annotator quality (Böhmová et al., 2001). The Universal Treebank Annotation Guidelines aim at providing unified annotation for many languages enabling cross-lingual comparison (Nivre et al., 2015). This project provides a starting point for developing a treebank for resource-poor languages. However, a mature parser requires a large treebank for training, and this is still extremely costly to create. Instead, we present a method that exploits shared structure across languages to achieve a more accurate parser. Structural information from the source resource-rich language is incorporated as a prior in the supervised training of a resource-poor target language parser using a small treebank. When compared with a supervised model, the gain is as high as 8.7%[1] on average when trained on just 1,000 tokens. As we add more training data, the gains persist, though they are more modest. Even at 15,000 tokens we observe a 2.9% improvement.

There are two main approaches for building dependency parsers for resource-poor languages: delexicalized parsing and projection (Täckström et al., 2013). The delexicalized approach was proposed by Zeman et al. (2008). A parser is built without any lexical features, and trained on a treebank in a resource-rich source language. It is then applied directly to parse sentences in the target resource-poor languages. Delexicalized parsing relies on the fact that identical part-of-speech (POS) inventories are highly informative of dependency relations, enough to make up for cross-lingual syntactic divergence.

In contrast, projection approaches use parallel data to project source language dependency relations to the target language (Hwa et al., 2005). McDonald et al. (2011) and Ma and Xia (2014) exploit both delexicalized parsing and parallel data. They use parallel data to constrain the model which is usually initialized by the English delexicalized parser.

In summary, existing work generally starts with a delexicalized parser and uses parallel data to improve it. In this paper, we start with a source language parser and refine it with help from dependency annotations instead of parallel data. This choice means our method can be applied in cases where linguists are dependency-annotating small amounts of field data, such as in Karuk, a nearly-extinct language of Northwest California (Garrett et al., 2013).

[1]We use absolute values herein.

Proceedings of the 53rd Annual Meeting of the Association for Computational Linguistics and the 7th International Joint Conference on Natural Language Processing (Short Papers), pages 845–850,
Beijing, China, July 26-31, 2015.

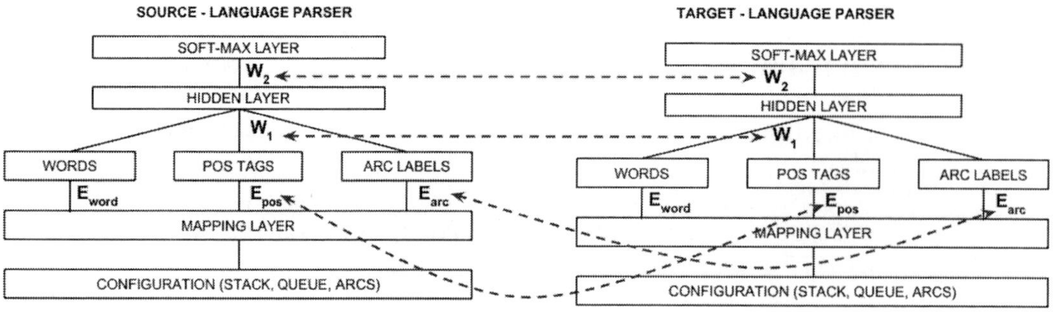

Figure 1: Neural Network Parser Architecture from Chen and Manning (2014) (left). Our model (left and right) with soft parameter sharing between the source and target language shown with dashed lines.

2 Supervised Neural Network Parser

In this section we review the parsing model which we use for both the source language and target language parsers. It is based on the work of Chen and Manning (2014). This parser can take advantage of target language monolingual data through word embeddings, data which is usually available for resource-poor languages. Chen and Manning's parser also achieved state-of-the-art monolingual parsing performance. They built a transition-based dependency parser (Nivre, 2006) using a neural-network. The neural network classifier decides which transition is applied for each configuration.

The architecture of the parser is illustrated in Figure 1 (left), where each layer is fully connected to the layer above. For each configuration, the selected list of words, POS tags and labels from the Stack, Queue and Arcs are extracted. Each word, POS or label is mapped to a low-dimension vector representation (embedding) through the Mapping Layer. This layer simply concatenates the embeddings which are then fed into a two-layer neural network classifier to predict the next parsing action. The set of parameters for the model is $E_{word}, E_{pos}, E_{labels}$ for the mapping layer, W_1 for the cubic hidden layer and W_2 for the softmax output layer.

3 Cross-lingual parser

Our model takes advantage of underlying structure shared between languages. Given the source language parsing structure as in Figure 1 (left), the set of parameters E_{word} will be different for the target language parser shown in Figure 1 (right) but we hypothesize that E_{pos}, E_{arc}, W_1 and W_2 can be shared as indicated with dashed lines. In particular we expect this to be the case when languages use the same POS tagset and arc label sets, as we presume herein. This assumption is motivated by the development of unified annotation for many languages (Nivre et al., 2015; Petrov et al., 2012; McDonald et al., 2013).

To allow parameter sharing between languages we could jointly train the parser on the source and target language simultaneously. However, we leave this for future work. Here we take an alternative approach, namely regularization in a similar vein to Duong et al. (2014). First we train a lexicalized neural network parser on the source resource-rich language (English), as described in Section 2. The learned parameters are $E^{en}_{word}, E^{en}_{pos}, E^{en}_{arc}, W^{en}_1, W^{en}_2$. Second, we incorporate English parameters as a prior for the target language training. This is straightforward when we use the same architecture, such as a neural network parser, for the target language. All we need to do is modify the learning objective function so that it includes the regularization part. However, we don't want to regularize the part related to E^{en}_{word} since it will be very different between source and target language. Letting $W_1 = (W_1^{word}, W_1^{pos}, W_1^{arc})$, the learning objective over training data $\mathcal{D} = \{x^{(i)}, y^{(i)}\}_{i=1}^{N}$, becomes:[2]

$$\mathcal{L} = \sum_{i=1}^{N} \log P(y^{(i)}|x^{(i)}) - \frac{\lambda_1}{2}\Big[\|W_1^{pos} - W_1^{en:pos}\|_F^2 + \|W_1^{arc} - W_1^{en:arc}\|_F^2 + \|W_2 - W_2^{en}\|_F^2\Big] - \frac{\lambda_2}{2}\Big[\|E_{pos} - E^{en}_{pos}\|_F^2 + \|E_{arc} - E^{en}_{arc}\|_F^2\Big] \qquad (1)$$

This is applicable where we use the same POS

[2]All other parameters, i.e. W_1^{word} and E_{word}, are regularized using a zero-mean Gaussian regularization term, with weight $\lambda = 10^{-8}$, as was done in the original paper.

	Train	Dev	Test	Total
cs	1173.3	159.3	173.9	1506.5
de	269.6	12.4	16.6	298.6
en	204.6	25.1	25.1	254.8
es	382.4	41.7	8.5	432.6
fi	162.7	9.2	9.1	181.0
fr	354.7	38.9	7.1	400.7
ga	16.7	3.2	3.8	23.7
hu	20.8	3.0	2.7	26.5
it	194.1	10.5	10.2	214.8
sv	66.6	9.8	20.4	96.8

Table 1: Number of tokens ($\times$ 1,000) for each language in the Universal Dependency Treebank collection.

tagset and arc label annotation for the source and target language. The same POS tagset is required so that the source language parser has similar structure with the target language parser. The requirement of same arc label annotation is mainly needed for evaluation using the Labelled Attachment Score (LAS).[3] We fit two separate regularization sensitivity parameters, λ_1 and λ_2, since they correspond to different parts of the model. λ_1 is used for the shared (universal) part, while λ_2 is used for the language specific parts. Together λ_1 and λ_2 control the contribution of the source language parser towards the target resource-poor model. In the extreme case where λ_1 and λ_2 are large, the target model parameters are tied to the source model, except for the word embeddings E_{word}. In the opposite case, where they are small, the target language parser is similar to the purely supervised model. We expect that the best values fall between these extremes. We use stochastic gradient descent to optimize this objective function with respect to $W_1, W_2, E_{word}, E_{pos}, E_{arc}$.

4 Experiments

In this part we want to see how much our cross-lingual model helps to improve the supervised model, for various data sizes.

4.1 Dataset

We experimented with the Universal Dependency Treebank collection V1.0 (Nivre et al., 2015) which contains treebanks for 10 languages.[4] These treebanks have many desirable properties for our model: the dependency types and coarse POS are the same across languages. This removes the need for mapping the source and target language tagsets to a common tagset. Moreover, the dependency types are also common across languages allowing LAS evaluation. Table 1 shows the dataset size of each language in the collection. Some languages have over $400k$ tokens such as *cs*, *fr* and *es*, meanwhile, *hu* and *ga* have only around $25k$ tokens.

4.2 Monolingual Word Embeddings

We initialize the target language word embeddings E_{word} of our neural network cross-lingual model with pre-trained embeddings. This is an advantage since we can incorporate monolingual data which is usually available for resource-poor languages. We collect monolingual data for each language from the Machine Translation Workshop (WMT) data,[5] Europarl (Koehn, 2005) and EU Bookshop Corpus (Skadiņš et al., 2014). The size of monolingual data also varies significantly. There are languages such as English and German with more than 400 million words, whereas, Irish only has 4 million. We use the skip-gram model from `word2vec` to induce 50-dimension word embeddings (Mikolov et al., 2013).

4.3 Coarse vs Fine-Grain POS

Our model uses the source language parser as the prior for the target language parser. The requirement is that the source and target should use the same POS tagset. It is clear that information will be lost when using the coarser shared-POS tagset. Here, we simply want to quantify this loss. We run the supervised neural network parser on the coarse-grained Universal POS (UPOS) tagset, and the language-specific fine-grained POS tagset for languages where both are available in the Universal Dependency Treebank.[6] Table 2 shows the average LAS for coarse- and fine-grained POS tagsets with various data sizes. For the smaller dataset, using the coarse-grained POS tagset performed better. Even when we used all the data, the coarse-grained POS tagset still performed reasonably well, approaching the performance obtained using the fine-grained POS tagset. Thus, the choice of the coarse-grained Universal POS tagset

[3] However, same arc-label set also informs some information about the structure.

[4] Czech (cs), German (de), English (en), Spanish (es), Finnish (fi), French (fr), Irish (ga), Hungarian (hu), Italian (it), Swedish (sv)

[5] `http://www.statmt.org/wmt14/`

[6] Czech, English, Finnish, Irish, Italian, and Swedish

Tokens	Coarse UPOS	Fine POS
1k	46.8	42.3
3k	54.3	52.4
5k	56.9	55.8
10k	59.9	59.8
15k	61.5	61.4
All	74.7	75.2

Table 2: Average LAS for supervised learning using the modified version of the Universal POS tagset and the fine-grained POS tagset across various training data sizes.

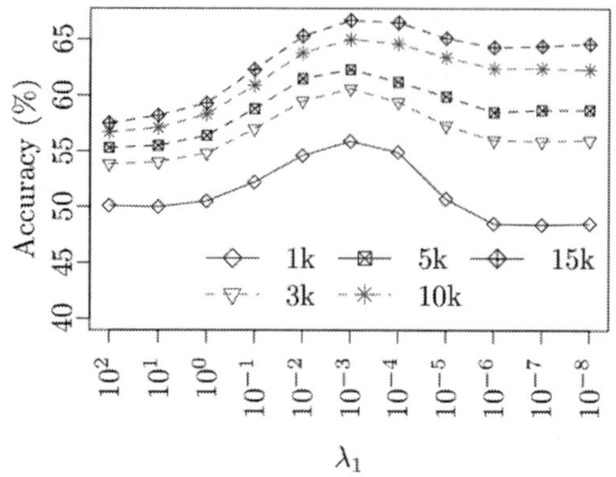

Figure 2: Sensitivity of regularization parameter λ_1 against the average LAS measured on all 9 languages (except English) on the development set for various data sizes (tokens)

instead of the original POS tagset is relevant, given that we assume there will only be a small treebank in the target language. Moreover, even when we have a bigger treebank, using the UPOS tagset does not hurt the performance much.[7]

4.4 Tuning regularization sensitivity

As shown in equation 1, λ_1 and λ_2 control the contribution of the source language parser toward the target language parser. We tune these parameters separately using development data. Firstly, we tune λ_1 by fixing $\lambda_2 = 0.1$. The reason for choosing such a large value of 0.1 is that we expect the POS and arc label embeddings to be fairly similar across languages. Figure 2 shows the average LAS for all 9 languages (except English) on different data sizes using different values of λ_1. We observed that $\lambda_1 = 0.001$ gives the optimum value on the development data consistently across different data sizes. We compare the performance at two extreme values of λ_1. For small data size, at 1k tokens, $\lambda_1 = 100$ is better than when $\lambda_1 = 10^{-8}$. This shows that when trained using a small data set, the source language parser is more accurate than the supervised model. However, at 3k tokens, the supervised model is starting to perform better.

We now fix $\lambda_1 = 0.001$ to tune λ_2 in the same range as λ_1. However, the average LAS didn't change much for different values of λ_2. It appears that λ_2 has very little effect on parsing accuracy. This is understandable since λ_2 affects only a small number of parameters (POS and arc embeddings). Thus, we choose $\lambda_1 = 0.001$ and $\lambda_2 = 0.1$ for our experiments.

[7]This is because UPOS generalizes better, and when aggregating with lexical information, it has similar distinguishing power compared with the fine-grained POS tagset.

4.5 Learning Curve

We choose English as our source language to build different target parsers for each language in the Universal Dependency Treebank collection. We train the supervised neural network parser as mentioned in Section 2 on the Universal Dependency English treebank using UPOS tagset. The UAS and LAS for the English parser is 85.2% and 82.9% respectively, when evaluated on the English test set. We use the English parser as the prior for our cross-lingual model, as described in Section 3. Figure 3 shows the learning curve for both the supervised neural network parser and our cross-lingual model with respect to our implemention of McDonald et al.'s (2011) delexicalized parser, i.e. their basic model which uses no parallel data and no target language supervision. Overall, both the supervised model and the cross-lingual model are much better than this baseline. For small data sizes, our cross-lingual model is superior when compared with the supervised model, giving as much as an 8.7% improvement. This improvement lessens as the size of training data increases. This is to be expected, because the supervised model becomes stronger as the size of training data increases, while the contribution of the source language parser is reduced. However, at 15k tokens we still observed a 2.9% average improvement, demonstrating the robustness of our cross-lingual model. Using our model also reduced the standard deviation ranges on each data point from 12% to 7%.

Using our cross-lingual model can save the annotation effort that is required in order to reach

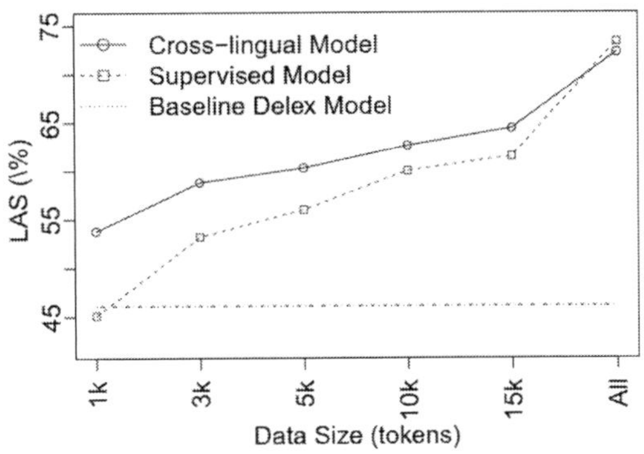

Figure 3: Learning curve for cross-lingual model and supervised model with respect to the baseline delexicalized parser from McDonald et al. (2011): the x-axis is the size of data (number of tokens); the y-axis is the average LAS measured on 9 languages (except English).

the same accuracy compared with the supervised model. For example, we only need 1k tokens in order to surpass the supervised model performance on 3k tokens, and we only need 5k tokens to match the supervised model trained on 10k tokens. The error rate reduction is from 15.8% down to 6.5% for training data sizes from 1k to 15k tokens. However, when we use all the training data, the supervised model is slightly better.

5 Conclusions

Thanks to the availability of the Universal Dependency Treebank, creating a treebank for a target resource-poor language has becoming easier. This fact motivates the work reported here, where we assume that only a tiny treebank is available in the target language. We tried to make the most out of the target language treebank by incorporating a source-language parser as a prior in learning a neural network parser. Our results show that we can achieve a more accurate parser using the same training data. In future work, we would like to investigate joint training on the source and target languages.

Acknowledgments

This work was supported by the University of Melbourne and National ICT Australia (NICTA). Trevor Cohn is the recipient of an Australian Research Council Future Fellowship (project number FT130101105).

References

Alena Böhmová, Jan Hajič, Eva Hajičová, and Barbora Hladká. 2001. The Prague Dependency Treebank: A Three-Level Annotation Scenario. In Anne Abeillé, editor, *Treebanks: Building and Using Syntactically Annotated Corpora*, pages 103–127. Kluwer Academic Publishers.

Razvan C. Bunescu and Raymond J. Mooney. 2005. A shortest path dependency kernel for relation extraction. In *Proceedings of the Conference on Human Language Technology and Empirical Methods in Natural Language Processing*, HLT '05, pages 724–731, Stroudsburg, PA, USA. ACL.

Danqi Chen and Christopher Manning. 2014. A fast and accurate dependency parser using neural networks. In *Proceedings of the 2014 Conference on Empirical Methods in Natural Language Processing (EMNLP)*, pages 740–750, Doha, Qatar. ACL.

Hang Cui, Renxu Sun, Keya Li, Min-Yen Kan, and Tat-Seng Chua. 2005. Question answering passage retrieval using dependency relations. In *Proceedings of the 28th Annual International ACM SIGIR Conference on Research and Development in Information Retrieval*, SIGIR '05, pages 400–407, New York, NY, USA. ACM.

Long Duong, Trevor Cohn, Karin Verspoor, Steven Bird, and Paul Cook. 2014. What can we get from 1000 tokens? a case study of multilingual pos tagging for resource-poor languages. In *Proceedings of the 2014 Conference on Empirical Methods in Natural Language Processing (EMNLP)*, pages 886–897, Doha, Qatar. ACL.

Andrew Garrett, Clare Sandy, Erik Maier, Line Mikkelsen, and Patrick Davidson. 2013. Developing the Karuk Treebank. Fieldwork Forum, Department of Linguistics, UC Berkeley.

Rebecca Hwa, Philip Resnik, Amy Weinberg, Clara Cabezas, and Okan Kolak. 2005. Bootstrapping parsers via syntactic projection across parallel texts. *Natural Language Engineering*, 11:311–325.

Philipp Koehn. 2005. Europarl: A Parallel Corpus for Statistical Machine Translation. In *Proceedings of the Tenth Machine Translation Summit (MT Summit X)*, pages 79–86, Phuket, Thailand.

Xuezhe Ma and Fei Xia. 2014. Unsupervised dependency parsing with transferring distribution via parallel guidance and entropy regularization. In *Proceedings of the 52nd Annual Meeting of the Association for Computational Linguistics (Volume 1: Long Papers)*, pages 1337–1348. Association for Computational Linguistics.

Ryan McDonald, Koby Crammer, and Fernando Pereira. 2005. Online large-margin training of dependency parsers. In *Proceedings of the 43rd Annual Meeting on Association for Computational Linguistics*, ACL '05, pages 91–98, Stroudsburg, PA, USA. ACL.

Ryan McDonald, Slav Petrov, and Keith Hall. 2011. Multi-source transfer of delexicalized dependency parsers. In *Proceedings of the Conference on Empirical Methods in Natural Language Processing*, EMNLP '11, pages 62–72.

Ryan McDonald, Joakim Nivre, Yvonne Quirmbach-Brundage, Yoav Goldberg, Dipanjan Das, Kuzman Ganchev, Keith Hall, Slav Petrov, Hao Zhang, Oscar Täckström, Claudia Bedini, Núria Bertomeu Castelló, and Jungmee Lee. 2013. Universal dependency annotation for multilingual parsing. In *Proceedings of the 51st Annual Meeting of the Association for Computational Linguistics (Volume 2: Short Papers)*, pages 92–97, Sofia, Bulgaria. ACL.

Tomas Mikolov, Ilya Sutskever, Kai Chen, Greg S. Corrado, and Jeff Dean. 2013. Distributed representations of words and phrases and their compositionality. In C.j.c. Burges, L. Bottou, M. Welling, Z. Ghahramani, and K.q. Weinberger, editors, *Advances in Neural Information Processing Systems 26*, pages 3111–3119.

Joakim Nivre, Cristina Bosco, Jinho Choi, Marie-Catherine de Marneffe, Timothy Dozat, Richárd Farkas, Jennifer Foster, Filip Ginter, Yoav Goldberg, Jan Hajič, Jenna Kanerva, Veronika Laippala, Alessandro Lenci, Teresa Lynn, Christopher Manning, Ryan McDonald, Anna Missilä, Simonetta Montemagni, Slav Petrov, Sampo Pyysalo, Natalia Silveira, Maria Simi, Aaron Smith, Reut Tsarfaty, Veronika Vincze, and Daniel Zeman. 2015. Universal dependencies 1.0.

Joakim Nivre. 2006. *Inductive Dependency Parsing (Text, Speech and Language Technology)*. Springer-Verlag New York, Inc., Secaucus, NJ, USA.

Levent Özgür and Tunga Güngör. 2010. Text classification with the support of pruned dependency patterns. *Pattern Recognition Letters*, 31(12):1598–1607.

Slav Petrov, Dipanjan Das, and Ryan McDonald. 2012. A universal part-of-speech tagset. In *Proceedings of the Eighth International Conference on Language Resources and Evaluation (LREC'12)*, Istanbul, Turkey.

Raivis Skadiņš, Jörg Tiedemann, Roberts Rozis, and Daiga Deksne. 2014. Billions of parallel words for free: Building and using the eu bookshop corpus. In *Proceedings of the 9th International Conference on Language Resources and Evaluation (LREC-2014)*, Reykjavik, Iceland. European Language Resources Association (ELRA).

Oscar Täckström, Ryan McDonald, and Joakim Nivre. 2013. Target language adaptation of discriminative transfer parsers. In *Proceedings of the 2013 Conference of the North American Chapter of the Association for Computational Linguistics: Human Language Technologies*, pages 1061–1071, Atlanta, Georgia. ACL.

Peng Xu, Jaeho Kang, Michael Ringgaard, and Franz Och. 2009. Using a dependency parser to improve smt for subject-object-verb languages. In *Proceedings of Human Language Technologies: The 2009 Annual Conference of the North American Chapter of the Association for Computational Linguistics*, pages 245–253, Boulder, Colorado. ACL.

Daniel Zeman, Univerzita Karlova, and Philip Resnik. 2008. Cross-language parser adaptation between related languages. In *In IJCNLP-08 Workshop on NLP for Less Privileged Languages*, pages 35–42.

Semantic Structure Analysis of Noun Phrases using Abstract Meaning Representation

Yuichiro Sawai **Hiroyuki Shindo** **Yuji Matsumoto**
Graduate School of Information Science
Nara Institute of Science and Technology
8916-5 Takayama, Ikoma, Nara, 630-0192, Japan
{sawai.yuichiro.sn0,shindo,matsu}@is.naist.jp

Abstract

We propose a method for semantic structure analysis of noun phrases using Abstract Meaning Representation (AMR). AMR is a graph representation for the meaning of a sentence, in which noun phrases (NPs) are manually annotated with internal structure and semantic relations. We extract NPs from the AMR corpus and construct a data set of NP semantic structures. We also propose a transition-based algorithm which jointly identifies both the nodes in a semantic structure tree and semantic relations between them. Compared to the baseline, our method improves the performance of NP semantic structure analysis by 2.7 points, while further incorporating external dictionary boosts the performance by 7.1 points.

1 Introduction

Semantic structure analysis of noun phrases (NPs) is an important research topic, which is beneficial for various NLP tasks, such as machine translation and question answering (Nakov and Hearst, 2013; Nakov, 2013). Among the previous works on NP analysis are internal NP structure analysis (Vadas and Curran, 2007; Vadas and Curran, 2008), noun-noun relation analysis of noun compounds (Girju et al., 2005; Tratz and Hovy, 2010; Kim and Baldwin, 2013), and predicate-argument analysis of noun compounds (Lapata, 2002).

The goal of internal NP structure analysis is to assign bracket information inside an NP (e.g., *(lung cancer) deaths* indicates that the phrase *lung cancer* modifies the head *deaths*). In noun-noun relation analysis, the goal is to assign one of the predefined semantic relations to a noun compound consisting of two nouns (e.g., assigning a relation *purpose* to a noun compound *cooking pot*, meaning that *pot* is used for *cooking*). On the other hand, in predicate-argument analysis, the goal is to decide whether the modifier noun is the subject or the object of the head noun (e.g., *car* is the object of *love* in *car lover*, while *child* is the subject of *behave* in *child behavior*).

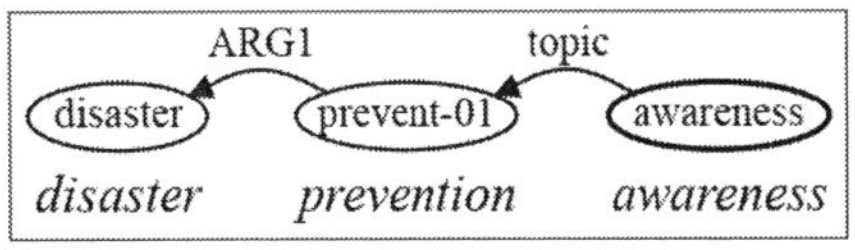

Figure 1: *disaster prevention awareness* in AMR. Predicate-argument relation *ARG1*, noun-noun relation *topic*, and internal structure *(disaster prevention) awareness* are expressed.

Previous NP researches have mainly focused on these different subproblems of NP analysis using different data sets, rather than targeting general NPs simultaneously. However, these subproblems of NP analysis tend to be highly intertwined when processing texts. For the purpose of tackling the task of combined NP analysis, we make use of the Abstract Meaning Representation (AMR) corpus.

AMR is a formalism of sentence semantic structure by directed, acyclic, and rooted graphs, in which semantic relations such as predicate-argument relations and noun-noun relations are expressed. In this paper, we extract substructures corresponding to NPs (shown in Figure 1) from the AMR Bank[1], and create a data set of NP semantic structures. In general, AMR substructures are graphs. However, since we found out that NPs mostly form trees rather than graphs in the AMR Bank, we can assume that AMR substructures corresponding to NPs are trees. Thus, we define our task as predicting the AMR tree structure, given a sequence of words in an NP.

The previous method for AMR parsing takes a

[1] http://amr.isi.edu/

Proceedings of the 53rd Annual Meeting of the Association for Computational Linguistics and the 7th International Joint Conference on Natural Language Processing (Short Papers), pages 851–856,
Beijing, China, July 26-31, 2015.

Train	Dev	Test
3504	463	398

Table 1: Statistics of the extracted NP data

two-step approach: first identifying distinct concepts (nodes) in the AMR graph, then defining the dependency relations between those concepts (Flanigan et al., 2014). In the concept identification step, unlike POS tagging, one word is sometimes assigned with more than one concept, and the number of possible concepts is far more than the number of possible parts-of-speech. As the concept identification accuracy remains low, such a pipeline method suffers from error propagation, thus resulting in a suboptimal AMR parsing performance.

To solve this problem, we extend a transition-based dependency parsing algorithm, and propose a novel algorithm which jointly identifies the concepts and the relations in AMR trees. Compared to the baseline, our method improves the performance of AMR analysis of NP semantic structures by 2.7 points, and using an external dictionary further boosts the performance by 7.1 points.

2 Abstract Meaning Representation

2.1 Extraction of NPs

We extract substructures (subtrees) corresponding to NPs from the AMR Bank (LDC2014T12). In the AMR Bank, there is no alignment between the words and the concepts (nodes) in the AMR graphs. We obtain this alignment by using the rule-based alignment tool by Flanigan et al. (2014). Then, we use the Stanford Parser (Klein and Manning, 2003) to obtain constituency trees, and extract NPs that contain more than one noun and are not included by another NP. We exclude NPs that contain named entities, because they would require various kinds of manually crafted rules for each type of named entity. We also exclude NPs that contain possessive pronouns or conjunctions, which prove problematic for the alignment tool. Table 1 shows the statistics of the extracted NP data.

2.2 Previous Method for AMR Analysis

We adopt the method proposed by Flanigan et al. (2014) as our baseline, which is a two-step pipeline method of concept identification step and

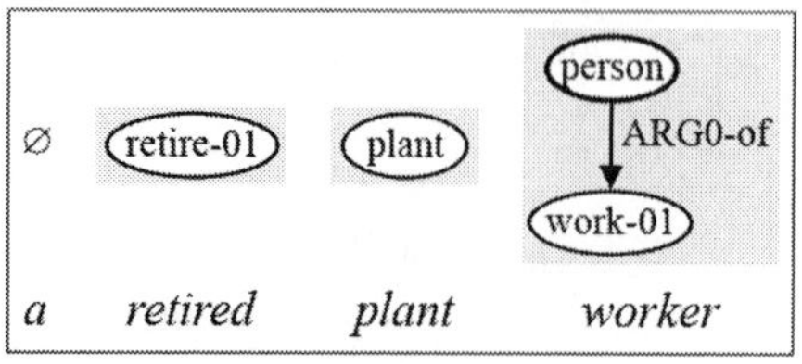

Figure 2: Concept identification step of (Flanigan et al., 2014) for *a retired plant worker*. ∅ denotes an empty concept.

relation identification step. Their method is designed for parsing sentences into AMR, but here, we use this method for parsing NPs.

In their method, concept identification is formulated as a sequence labeling problem (Janssen and Limnios, 1999) and solved by the Viterbi algorithm. Spans of words in the input sentence are labeled with concept subgraphs. Figure 2 illustrates the concept identification step for an NP *a retired plant worker*.

After the concepts have been identified, these concepts are fixed, and the dependency relations between them are identified by an algorithm that finds the maximum spanning connected subgraph (Chu and Liu, 1965), which is similar to the maximum spanning tree (MST) algorithm used for dependency parsing (McDonald et al., 2005).

They report that using gold concepts yields much better performance, implying that joint identification of concepts and relations can be helpful.

3 Proposed Method

In this paper, we propose a novel approach for mapping the word sequence in an NP to an AMR tree, where the concepts (nodes) corresponding to the words and the dependency relations between those concepts must be identified. We extend the arc-standard algorithm by Nivre (2004) for AMR parsing, and propose a transition-based algorithm which jointly identifies concepts and dependency

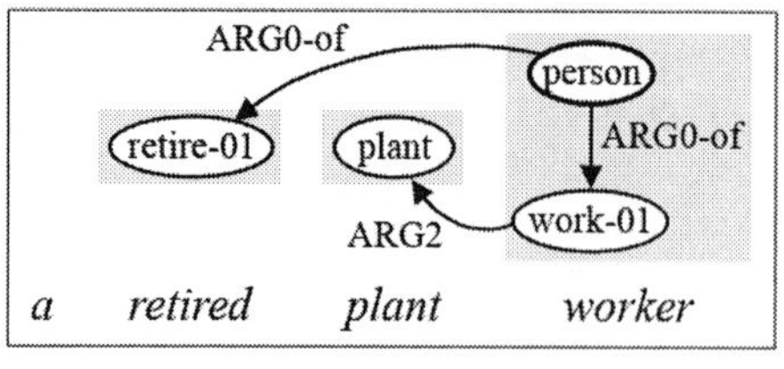

Figure 4: *a retired plant worker* in AMR

	Previous action	σ_1	σ_0	β	R
0	(initial state)			[a retired plant worker]	∅
1	SHIFT(EMPTY(a))		∅	[retired plant worker]	∅
2	EMPTY-REDUCE			[retired plant worker]	∅
3	SHIFT(DICT$_{\text{PRED}}$(retired))		retire-01	[plant worker]	∅
4	SHIFT(LEMMA(plant))	retire-01	plant	[worker]	∅
5	SHIFT(KNOWN(worker))	plant	person ↓ARG0-of work-01	[ ]	∅
6	LEFT-REDUCE(ARG2, n_{child})	retire-01	person ↓ARG0-of work-01	[ ]	{(work-01) $\xrightarrow{\text{ARG2}}$ (plant)}
7	LEFT-REDUCE(ARG0-of, n_{root})		person ↓ARG0-of work-01	[ ]	{(work-01) $\xrightarrow{\text{ARG2}}$ (plant), (person) $\xrightarrow{\text{ARG0-of}}$ (retire-01)}

Figure 3: Derivation of an AMR tree for *a retired plant worker* (σ_0 and σ_1 denote the top and the second top of the stack, respectively.)

Action	Current state	Next state
SHIFT($c(w_i)$)	$(\sigma, [w_i\|\beta], R)$	$([\sigma\|c(w_i)], \beta, R)$
LEFT-REDUCE(r, n)	$([\sigma\|c_i\|c_j], \beta, R)$	$([\sigma\|c_j], \beta, R \cup \{n_{\text{root}}(c_i) \xleftarrow{r} n(c_j)\})$
RIGHT-REDUCE(r, n)	$([\sigma\|c_i\|c_j], \beta, R)$	$([\sigma\|c_i], \beta, R \cup \{n(c_i) \xrightarrow{r} n_{\text{root}}(c_j)\})$
EMPTY-REDUCE	$([\sigma\|\phi], \beta, R)$	(σ, β, R)

Table 2: Definitions of the actions

relations. Our algorithm is similar to (Hatori et al., 2011), in which they perform POS tagging and dependency parsing jointly by assigning a POS tag to a word when performing SHIFT, but differs in that, unlike POS tagging, one word is sometimes assigned with more than one concept. In our algorithm, the input words are stored in the buffer and the identified concepts are stored in the stack. SHIFT identifies a concept subtree associated with the top word in the buffer. REDUCE identifies the dependency relation between the top two concept subtrees in the stack. Figure 3 illustrates the process of deriving an AMR tree for *a retired plant worker*, and Figure 4 shows the resulting AMR tree.

Table 2 shows the definition of each action and state transition. A state is a triple (σ, β, R), where σ is a stack of identified concept subtrees, β is a buffer of words, and R is a set of identified relations. SHIFT($c(w_i)$) extracts the top word w_i in the buffer, generates a concept subtree $c(w_i)$ from w_i, and pushes $c(w_i)$ onto the stack. The concept subtree $c(w_i)$ is generated from w_i by using one of the rules defined in Table 3. LEFT-REDUCE(r, n) pops the top two subtrees c_i, c_j from the stack, identifies the relation r between the root $n_{\text{root}}(c_i)$ of c_i and the node $n(c_j)$ in c_j, adds r to R, and pushes c_j back onto the stack. Here, n denotes a mapping from a subtree to its specific node, which allows for attachment to an arbitrary concept in a subtree. Since the sizes of the subtrees were at most two in our data set, $n \in \{n_{\text{root}}, n_{\text{child}}\}$, where n_{root} is a mapping from a subtree to its root, and n_{child} is a mapping from a subtree to the direct child of its root. RIGHT-REDUCE(r, n) is defined in the same manner. EMPTY-REDUCE removes an empty subtree ∅ at the top of the stack. EMPTY-REDUCE is always performed immediately after SHIFT(∅) generates an empty subtree ∅. In the initial state, the stack σ is empty, the buffer β contains all the words in the NP, and the set of the identified relations R is empty. In the terminal state, the buffer β is empty and the stack σ contains only one subtree. The resulting AMR tree is obtained by connecting all the subtrees generated by the SHIFT actions with all the relations in R.

The previous method could not generate unseen concepts in the training data, leading to low recall in concept identification. In contrast, our method defines five rules (Table 3), three of which

Rule	Concept subtree to generate	Example of subtree generation
EMPTY	an empty concept subtree ∅	fighters → ∅
KNOWN	a subtree aligning to the word in the training data	fighters → (person) $\xrightarrow{\text{ARG0-of}}$ (fight-01) | ...
LEMMA	a subtree with the lemma of the word as the only concept	fighters → (fighter)
DICT$_{\text{PRED}}$	a subtree with a predicate form of the word as the only concept	fighters → (fight-01) | (fight-02) | ...
DICT$_{\text{NOUN}}$	a subtree with a noun form of the word as the only concept	fighters → (fight)

Table 3: Rules for generating a concept subtree (Vertical lines indicate multiple candidate subtrees.)

(LEMMA, DICT$_{\text{PRED}}$, and DICT$_{\text{NOUN}}$) allow for generation of unseen concepts from any word.

3.1 Features

The feature set $\phi(s, a)$ for the current state s and the next action a is the direct product (all-vs-all combinations from each set) of the feature set $\phi_{state}(s)$ for the current state and the feature set $\phi_{action}(s, a)$ for the next action.

$$\phi(s, a) = \phi_{state}(s) \times \phi_{action}(s, a)$$

$\phi_{state}(s)$ is the union of the feature sets defined in Table 4, where $w(c)$ denotes the word from which the subtree c was generated.

Table 5 shows the feature set $\phi_{action}((\sigma, [w_i|\beta], R), a)$ for each action a, where $rule(w_i, c)$ is a function that returns the rule which generated the subtree c from the top word w_i in the buffer. In order to allow different SHIFT actions and different LEFT-RIGHT/REDUCE actions to partially share features, Table 5 defines features of different granularities for each action. For example, although SHIFT((run-01)) and SHIFT((sleep-01)) are different actions, they share the features "S", "S"∘"DICT$_{\text{PRED}}$" because they share the generation rule DICT$_{\text{PRED}}$.

Name	Definition
LEM	$\{w(\sigma_1).\text{lem}, w(\sigma_0).\text{lem}, \beta_0.\text{lem},$ $w(\sigma_1).\text{lem} \circ w(\sigma_0).\text{lem}, w(\sigma_0).\text{lem} \circ \beta_0.\text{lem}\}$
SUF	$\{w(\sigma_1).\text{suf}, w(\sigma_0).\text{suf}, \beta_0.\text{suf},$ $w(\sigma_1).\text{suf} \circ w(\sigma_0).\text{suf}, w(\sigma_0).\text{suf} \circ \beta_0.\text{suf}\}$
POS	$\{w(\sigma_1).\text{pos}, w(\sigma_0).\text{pos}, \beta_0.\text{pos},$ $w(\sigma_1).\text{pos} \circ w(\sigma_0).\text{pos}, w(\sigma_0).\text{pos} \circ \beta_0.\text{pos}\}$
DEP	$\{w(\sigma_1).\text{dep}, w(\sigma_0).\text{dep}, \beta_0.\text{dep},$ $w(\sigma_1).\text{dep} \circ w(\sigma_0).\text{dep}, w(\sigma_0).\text{dep} \circ \beta_0.\text{dep}\}$
HEAD	$\{w(\sigma_1).\text{off}, w(\sigma_0).\text{off}, \beta_0.\text{off},$ $w(\sigma_1).\text{off} \circ w(\sigma_0).\text{off}, w(\sigma_0).\text{off} \circ \beta_0.\text{off}\}$
ROOT	$\{n_{\text{root}}(\sigma_1), n_{\text{root}}(\sigma_0), n_{\text{root}}(\sigma_1) \circ n_{\text{root}}(\sigma_0)\}$
MID	all words between $w(\sigma_1)$ and $w(\sigma_0)$ ∪ all words between $w(\sigma_0)$ and β_0

Table 4: Feature sets for the state (.lem is the lemma, .suf is the prefix of length 3, .pos is the part-of-speech, .dep is the dependency label to the parent word, .off is the offset to the parent word, and ∘ denotes concatenation of features.)

Action a	$\phi_{action}((\sigma, [w_i\|\beta], R), a)$
SHIFT(c)	{"S", "S" ∘ $rule(w_i, c)$, "S" ∘ $rule(w_i, c) \circ c$}
LEFT-REDUCE(r, n)	{"L-R", "L-R"∘r, "L-R"∘r∘n}
RIGHT-REDUCE(r, n)	{"R-R", "R-R"∘r, "R-R"∘r∘n}
EMPTY-REDUCE	{"E-R"}

Table 5: Feature sets for the action

4 Experiments

We conduct an experiment using our NP data set (Table 1). We use the implementation [2] of (Flanigan et al., 2014) as our baseline. For the baseline, we use the features of the default settings.

The method by Flanigan et al. (2014) can only generate the concepts that appear in the training data. On the other hand, our method can generate concepts that do not appear in the training data using the concept generation rules LEMMA, DICT$_{\text{PRED}}$, and DICT$_{\text{NOUN}}$ in Table 3. For a fair comparison, first, we only use the rules EMPTY and KNOWN. Then, we add the rule LEMMA, which can generate a concept of the lemma of the word. Finally, we add the rules DICT$_{\text{PRED}}$ and DICT$_{\text{NOUN}}$. These two rules need conversion from nouns and adjectives to their verb and noun forms, For this conversion, we use CatVar v2.1 (Habash and Dorr, 2003), which lists categorial variations of words (such as verb *run* for noun *runner*). We also use definitions of the predicates from PropBank (Palmer et al., 2005), which AMR tries to reuse as much as possible, and impose constraints that the defined predicates can only have semantic relations consistent with the definition.

During the training, we use the max-violation perceptron (Huang et al., 2012) with beam size 8 and average the parameters. During the testing, we also perform beam search with beam size 8.

Table 6 shows the overall performance on NP semantic structure analysis. We evaluate the performance using the Smatch score (Cai and Knight,

[2] `https://github.com/jflanigan/jamr`

Method	P	R	F_1
(Flanigan et al., 2014)	75.5	61.1	67.5
Our method (EMPTY/KNOWN)	78.0	63.8	70.2
Our method+LEMMA	75.7	75.2	75.4
Our method+LEMMA/DICT	77.3	77.3	77.3

Table 6: Performance on NP semantic structure analysis

Method	P	R	F_1
(Flanigan et al., 2014)	88.4	71.4	79.0
Our method (EMPTY/KNOWN)	88.9	72.2	79.7
Our method+LEMMA	84.8	84.2	84.5
Our method+LEMMA/DICT	85.8	85.6	85.7

Table 7: Performance on concept identification

2013), which reports precision, recall, and F_1-score for overlaps of nodes, edges, and roots in semantic structure graphs. Compared to the baseline, our method improves both the precision and recall, resulting in an increasing of F_1-score by 2.7 points. When we add the LEMMA rule, the recall increases by 11.4 points because the LEMMA rule can generate concepts that do not appear in the training data, resulting in a further increase of F_1-score by 5.2 points. Finally, when we add the DICT rules, the F_1-score improves further by 1.9 points.

Table 7 shows the performance on concept identification. We report precision, recall, and F_1-score against the correct set of concepts. For each condition, we observe the same tendency in performance increases as Table 6. Thus, we conclude that our method improves both the concept identification and relation identification performances.

5 Conclusion

In this paper, we used Abstract Meaning Representation (AMR) for semantic structure analysis of noun compounds (NPs). We extracted substructures corresponding to NPs from the AMR Bank, and created a data set of NP semantic structures. Then, we proposed a novel method which jointly identifies concepts (nodes) and dependency relations in AMR trees. We confirmed that our method improves the performance on NP semantic structure analysis, and that incorporating an external dictionary further boosts the performance.

Acknowledgements

This work was supported by JSPS KAKENHI Grant Number 15K16053, 26240035.

References

Shu Cai and Kevin Knight. 2013. Smatch: An evaluation metric for semantic feature structures. pages 748–752.

Y.J. Chu and T.H. Liu. 1965. On the shortest arborescence of a directed graph. *Science Sinica*, 14:1396–1400.

Jeffrey Flanigan, Sam Thomson, Jaime Carbonell, Chris Dyer, and Noah A. Smith. 2014. A discriminative graph-based parser for the Abstract Meaning Representation. In *Proceedings of the 52nd Annual Meeting of the Association for Computational Linguistics*, pages 1426–1436.

Roxana Girju, Dan Moldovan, Marta Tatu, and Daniel Antohe. 2005. On the semantics of noun compounds. *Computer Speech and Language*, 19:479–496.

Nizar Habash and Bonnie Dorr. 2003. A categorial variation database for English. In *Proceedings of the 2003 Human Language Technology Conference of the North American Chapter of the Association for Computational Linguistics*, pages 17–23.

Jun Hatori, Takuya Matsuzaki, Yusuke Miyao, and Jun'ichi Tsujii. 2011. Incremental joint POS tagging and dependency parsing in Chinese. In *Proceedings of the 5th International Joint Conference on Natural Language Processing*, pages 1216–1224.

Liang Huang, Suphan Fayong, and Yang Guo. 2012. Structured perceptron with inexact search. In *Proceedings of the 2012 Conference of the North American Chapter of the Association for Computational Linguistics: Human Language Technologies*, pages 142–151.

Jacques Janssen and Nikolaos Limnios. 1999. *Semi-Markov models and applications*. Springer, October.

Su Nam Kim and Timothy Baldwin. 2013. A lexical semantic approach to interpreting and bracketing English noun compounds. *Natural Language Engineering*, 19(3):385–407.

Dan Klein and Christopher D. Manning. 2003. Accurate unlexicalized parsing. In *Proceedings of the 41st Annual Meeting on Association for Computational Linguistics*, pages 423–430.

Maria Lapata. 2002. The disambiguation of nominalizations. *Computational Linguistics*, 28(3):357–388.

Ryan McDonald, Fernando Pereira, Kiril Ribarov, and Jan Hajič. 2005. Non-projective dependency parsing using spanning tree algorithms. In *Proceedings of Human Language Technology Conference and Conference on Empirical Methods in Natural Language Processing (HLT/EMNLP)*, pages 523–530.

Preslav I. Nakov and Marti A. Hearst. 2013. Semantic interpretation of noun compounds using verbal and other paraphrases. *ACM Transactions on Speech and Language Processing*, 10(3):1–51.

Preslav Nakov. 2013. On the interpretation of noun compounds: Syntax, semantics, and entailment. *Natural Language Engineering*, 19(1):291–330.

Joakim Nivre. 2004. Incrementality in deterministic dependency parsing. In *Proceedings of the Workshop on Incremental Parsing: Bringing Engineering and Cognition Together*, pages 50–57.

Martha Palmer, Daniel Gildea, and Paul Kingsbury. 2005. The Proposition Bank: An annotated corpus of semantic roles. *Computational Linguistics*, 31(1):71–106.

Stephen Tratz and Eduard Hovy. 2010. A taxonomy, dataset, and classifier for automatic noun compound interpretation. In *Proceedings of the 48th Annual Meeting of the Association for Computational Linguistics*, pages 678–687.

David Vadas and James R. Curran. 2007. Adding noun phrase structure to the penn treebank. In *Proceedings of the 45th Annual Meeting of the Association for Computational Linguistics*, pages 240–247.

David Vadas and James R. Curran. 2008. Parsing noun phrase structure with CCG. In *Proceedings of the 46th Annual Meeting of the Association for Computational Linguistics: Human Language Technologies*, pages 335–343.

Boosting Transition-based AMR Parsing with Refined Actions and Auxiliary Analyzers

Chuan Wang
Brandeis University
cwang24@brandeis.edu

Nianwen Xue
Brandeis University
xuen@brandeis.edu

Sameer Pradhan
Boulder Language Technologies
pradhan@bltek.com

Abstract

We report improved AMR parsing results by adding a new action to a transition-based AMR parser to infer abstract concepts and by incorporating richer features produced by auxiliary analyzers such as a semantic role labeler and a coreference resolver. We report final AMR parsing results that show an improvement of 7% absolute in F_1 score over the best previously reported result. Our parser is available at: `https://github.com/Juicechuan/AMRParsing`

1 Introduction

AMR parsing is the task of taking a sentence as input and producing as output an Abstract Meaning Representation (AMR) that is a rooted, directed, edge-labeled and leaf-labeled graph that is used to represent the meaning of a sentence (Banarescu et al., 2013). AMR parsing has drawn an increasing amount of attention recently. The first published AMR parser, JAMR (Flanigan et al., 2014), performs AMR parsing in two stages: concept identification and relation identification. Flanigan et al. (2014) treat concept identification as a sequence labeling task and utilize a semi-Markov model to map spans of words in a sentence to concept graph fragments. For relation identification, they adopt graph-based techniques similar to those used in dependency parsing (McDonald et al., 2005). Instead of finding maximum spanning trees (MST) over words, they propose an algorithm that finds the maximum spanning connected subgraph (MSCG) over concept fragments identified in the first stage.

A competitive alternative to the MSCG approach is transition-based AMR parsing. Our previous work (Wang et al., 2015) describes a transition-based system that also involves two stages. In the first step, an input sentence is parsed into a dependency tree with a dependency parser. In the second step, the transition-based AMR parser transforms the dependency tree into an AMR graph by performing a series of actions. Note that the dependency parser used in the first step can be any off-the-shelf dependency parser and does not have to trained on the same data set as used in the second step.

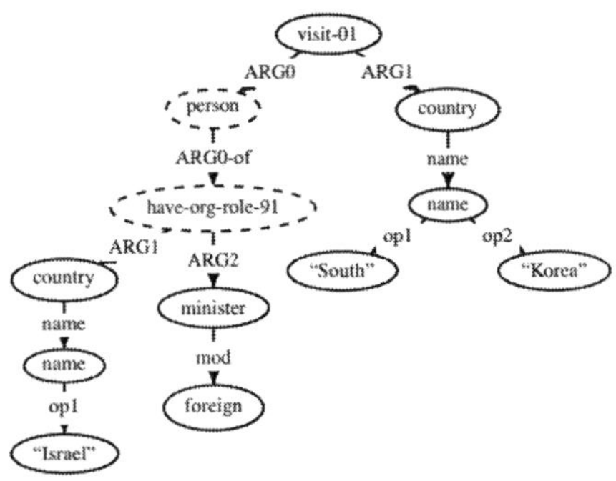

Figure 1: An example showing abstract concept `have-org-role-91` for the sentence "Israel foreign minister visits South Korea."

Unlike a dependency parse where each leaf node corresponds to a word in a sentence and there is an inherent alignment between the words in a sentence and the leaf nodes in the parse tree, the alignment between the word tokens in a sentence and the concepts in an AMR graph is non-trivial. Both JAMR and our transition-based parser rely on a heuristics based aligner that can align the words in a sentence and concepts in its AMR with a 90% F_1 score, but there are some concepts in the AMR that cannot be aligned to any word in a sentence.

This is illustrated in Figure 1 where the concept `have-org-role-91` is not aligned to any word or word sequence. We refer to these concepts as **abstract** concepts, and existing AMR parsers do not have a systematic way of inferring such abstract concepts.

Proceedings of the 53rd Annual Meeting of the Association for Computational Linguistics and the 7th International Joint Conference on Natural Language Processing (Short Papers), pages 857–862,
Beijing, China, July 26-31, 2015.

Current AMR parsers are in their early stages of development, and their features are not yet fully developed. For example, the AMR makes heavy use of the framesets and semantic role labels used in the Proposition Bank (Palmer et al., 2005), and it would seem that information produced by a semantic role labeling system trained on the PropBank can be used as features to improve the AMR parsing accuracy. Similarly, since AMR represents limited within-sentence coreference, coreference information produced by an off-the-shelf coreference system should benefit the AMR parser as well.

In this paper, we describe an extension to our transition-based AMR parser (Wang et al., 2015) by adding a new action to infer the abstract concepts in an AMR, and new features derived from an off-the-shelf semantic role labeling system (Pradhan et al., 2004) and coreference system (Lee et al., 2013). We also experimented with adding Brown clusters as features to the AMR parser. Additionally, we experimented with using different syntactic parsers in the first stage. Following our previous work, we use the averaged perceptron algorithm (Collins, 2002) to train the parameters of the model and use the greedy parsing strategy during decoding to determine the best action sequence to apply for each training instance. Our results show that (i) the transition-based AMR parser is very stable across the different parsers used in the first stage, (ii) adding the new action significantly improves the parser performance, and (iii) semantic role information is beneficial to AMR parsing when used as features, while the Brown clusters do not make a difference and coreference information slightly hurts the AMR parsing performance.

The rest of the paper is organized as follows. In Section 2 we briefly describe the transition-based parser, and in Section 3 we describe our extensions. We report experimental results in Section 4 and conclude the paper in Section 5.

2 Transition-based AMR Parser

The transition-based parser first uses a dependency parser to parse an input sentence, and then performs a limited number of highly general actions to transform the dependency tree to an AMR graph. The transition actions are briefly described below but due to the limited space, we cannot describe the full details of these actions, and the reader is referred to our previous work (Wang et al., 2015) for detailed descriptions of these actions:

- NEXT-EDGE-l_r (ned): Assign the current edge with edge label l_r and go to next edge.
- SWAP-l_r (sw): Swap the current edge, make the current dependent as the new head, and assign edge label l_r to the swapped edge.
- REATTACH$_k$-l_r (reat): Reattach current dependent to node k and assign edge label l_r.
- REPLACE-HEAD (rph): Replace current head node with current dependent node.
- REENTRANCE$_k$-l_r (reen): Add another head node k to current dependent and assign label l_r to edge between k and current dependent.
- MERGE (mrg): Merge two nodes connected by the edge into one node.

From each node in the dependency tree, the parser performs the following 2 actions:

- NEXT-NODE-l_c (nnd): Assign the current node with concept label l_c and go to next node.
- DELETE-NODE (dnd): Delete the current node and all edges associated with current node.

Crucially, none of these actions can infer the types of abstract concepts illustrated in Figure 1. And this serves as our baseline parser.

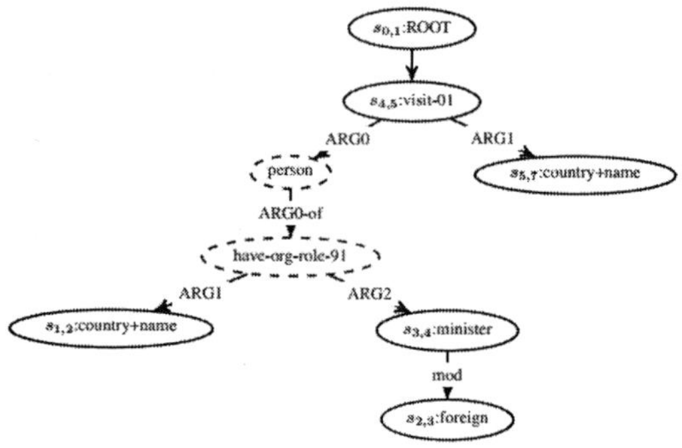

Figure 2: Enhanced Span Graph for AMR in Figure 1, "Israel foreign minister visits South Korea." $s_{x,y}$ corresponds to sentence span (x, y).

3 Parser Extensions

3.1 Inferring Abstract Concepts

We previously create the learning target by representing an AMR graph as a **Span Graph**, where each AMR concept is annotated with the text span of the word or the (contiguous) word sequence it is aligned to. However, abstract concepts that are not aligned to any word or word sequence are simply ignored and are unreachable during training. To address this, we construct the span graph by keeping the abstract concepts as they are in the AMR graph, as illustrated in Figure 2.

In order to predict these abstract concepts, we design an INFER-l_c action that is applied in the following way: when the parser visits an node in dependency tree, it inserts an abstract node with concept label l_c right between the current node and its parent. For example in Figure 3, after applying action INFER-`have-org-role-91` on node *minister*, the abstract concept is recovered and subsequent actions can be applied to transform the subgraph to its correct AMR.

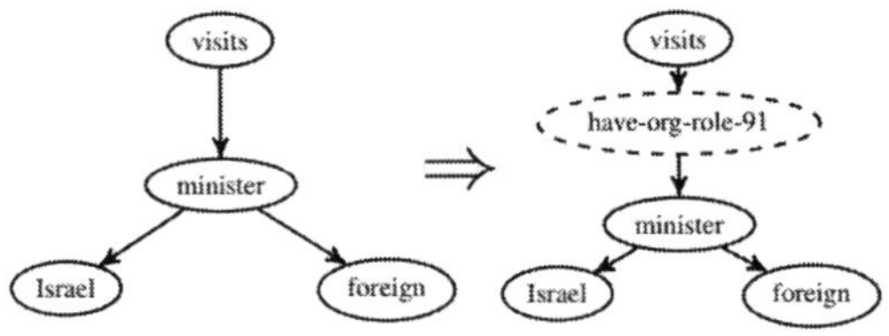

Figure 3: INFER-`have-org-role-91` action

3.2 Feature Enrichment

In our previous work, we only use simple lexical features and structural features. We extend the feature set to include (i) features generated by a semantic role labeling system—ASSERT (Pradhan et al., 2004), including a frameset disambiguator trained using a word sense disambiguation system—IMS (Zhong and Ng, 2010) and a coreference system (Lee et al., 2013) and (ii) features generated using semi-supervised word clusters (Turian et al., 2010; Koo et al., 2008).

Coreference features Coreference is typically represented as a chain of mentions realized as noun phrases or pronouns. AMR, on the other hand, represents coreference as re-entrance and uses one concept to represent all co-referring entities. To use the coreference information to inform AMR parsing actions, we design the following two features: 1) SHARE_DEPENDENT. When applying REENTRANCE$_k$-l_r action on edge (a, b), we check whether the corresponding head node k of a candidate concept has any dependent node that co-refers with current dependent b. 2) DEPENDENT_LABEL. If SHARE_DEPENDENT is true for head node k and assuming k's dependent m co-refers with the current dependent, the value of this feature is set to the dependency label between k and m.

For example, for the partial graph shown in Figure 4, when examining edge $(wants, boy)$, we may consider REENTRANCE$_{believe}$-ARG1 as one of the candidate actions. The candidate head $believe$ has dependent him which is co-referred with current dependent boy, therefore the value of feature SHARE_DEPENDENT is set to true for this candidate action. Also the value of feature DEPENDENT_LABEL is dobj given the dependency label between $(believe, him)$.

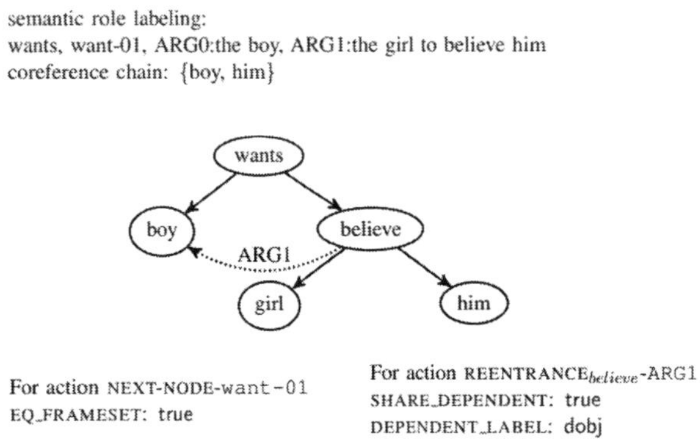

Figure 4: An example of coreference feature and semantic role labeling feature in partial parsing graph of sentence,"The boy wants the girl to believe him."

Semantic role labeling features We use the following semantic role labeling features: 1) EQ_FRAMESET. For action that predicts the concept label (NEXT-NODE-l_c), we check whether the candidate concept label l_c matches the frameset predicted by the semantic role labeler. For example, for partial graph in Figure 4, when we examine node $wants$, one of the candidate actions would be NEXT-NODE-`want-01`. Since the candidate concept label `want-01` is equal to node $wants$'s frameset `want-01` as predicted by the semantic role labeler, the value of feature EQ_FRAMESET is set to true. 2) IS_ARGUMENT. For actions that predicts the edge label, we check whether the semantic role labeler predicts that the current dependent is an argument of the current head. Note that the arguments in semantic role labeler output are non-terminals which corresponds to a sentence span. Here we simply take the head word in the sentence span as the argument.

Word Clusters For the semi-supervised word cluster feature, we use Brown clusters, more specifically, 1000 classes word cluster trained by Turian et al. (2010). We use prefixes of lengths 4,6,10,20 of the word's bit-string as features.

4 Experiments

We first tune and evaluate our system on the newswire section of LDC2013E117 dataset. Then we show our parser's performance on the recent LDC2014T12 dataset.

4.1 Experiments on LDC2013E117

We first conduct our experiments on the newswire section of AMR annotation corpus (LDC2013E117). The train/dev/test split of dataset is 4.0K/2.1K/2.1K, which is identical to the settings of JAMR. We evaluate our parser with Smatch v2.0 (Cai and Knight, 2013) on all the experiments.

System	P	R	F_1
Charniak (ON)	**.67**	**.64**	**.65**
Charniak	.66	.62	.64
Stanford	.64	.62	.63
Malt	.65	.61	.63
Turbo	.65	.61	.63

Table 1: AMR parsing performance on development set using different syntactic parsers.

System	P	R	F_1
Charniak (ON)	.67	.64	.65
+INFER	.71	.67	.69
+INFER+BROWN	.71	.68	.69
+INFER+BROWN+SRL	**.72**	**.69**	**.71**
+INFER+BROWN+SRL+COREF	.72	.69	.70

Table 2: AMR parsing performance on the development set.

4.1.1 Impact of different syntactic parsers

We experimented with four different parsers: the Stanford parser (Manning et al., 2014), the Charniak parser (Charniak and Johnson, 2005) (Its phrase structure output is converted to dependency structure using the Stanford CoreNLP converter), the Malt Parser (Nivre et al., 2006), and the Turbo Parser (Martins et al., 2013). All the parsers we used are trained on the 02-22 sections of the Penn Treebank, except for CHARNIAK(ON), which is trained on the OntoNotes corpus (Hovy et al., 2006) on the training and development partitions used by Pradhan et al. (2013) after excluding a few documents that overlapped with the AMR corpus[1]. All the different dependency trees are then used as input to our baseline system and we evaluate AMR parsing performance on the development set.

From Table 1, we can see that the performance of the baseline transition-based system remains very stable when different dependency parsers used are trained on same data set. However, the Charniak parser that is trained on a much larger and more diverse dataset (CHARNIAK (ON)) yields the best overall AMR parsing performance. Subsequent experiments are all based on this version of the Charniak parser.

4.1.2 Impact of parser extensions

In Table 2 we present results from extending the transition-based AMR parser. All experiments are conducted on the development set. From Table 2, we can see that the INFER action yields a 4 point improvement in F_1 score over the CHARNIAK(ON) system. Adding Brown clusters improves the recall by 1 point, but the F_1 score remains unchanged. Adding semantic role features on top of the Brown clusters leads to an improvement of another 2 points in F_1 score, and gives us the best result. Adding coreference features actually slightly hurts the performance.

4.1.3 Final Result on Test Set

We evaluate the best model we get from §4.1 on the test set, as shown in Table 3. For comparison purposes, we also include results of all published parsers on the same dataset: the updated version of JAMR, the old version of JAMR (Flanigan et al., 2014), the Stanford AMR parser (Werling et al., 2015), the SHRG-based AMR parser (Peng et al., 2015) and our baseline parser (Wang et al., 2015).

[1]Documents in the AMR corpus have some overlap with the documents in the OntoNotes corpus. We excluded these documents (which are primarily from Xinhua newswirte) from the training data while retraining the Charniak parser, ASSERT semantic role labeler, and IMS frameset disambiguation tool). The full list of overlapping documents is available at http://cemantix.org/ontonotes/ontonotes-amr-document-overlap.txt

System	P	R	F_1
Our system	**.71**	**.69**	**.70**
JAMR (GitHub)[2]	.69	.58	.63
JAMR (Flanigan et al., 2014)	.66	.52	.58
Stanford	.66	.59	.62
SHRG-based	.59	.58	.58
Wang et al. (2015)	.64	.62	.63

Table 3: AMR parsing performance on the news wire test set of LDC2013E117.

From Table 3 we can see that our parser has significant improvement over all the other parsers and outperforms the previous best parser by 7% points in Smatch score.

4.2 Experiments on LDC2014T12

In this section, we conduct experiments on the AMR annotation release 1.0 (LDC2014T12), which contains 13,051 AMRs from newswire, weblogs and web discussion forums. We use the training/development/test split recommended in the release: 10,312 sentences for training, 1,368 sentences for development and 1,371 sentences for testing. We re-train the parser on the LDC2014T12 training set with the best parser configuration given in §4.1, and test the parser on the test set. The result is shown in Table 4. For comparison purposes, we also include the results of the updated version of JAMR and our baseline parser in (Wang et al., 2015) which are also trained on the same dataset. There is a significant drop-off in performance compared with the results on the LDC2013E117 test set for all the parsers, but our parser outperforms the other parsers by a similar margin on both test sets.

System	P	R	F
Our system	**.70**	**.62**	**.66**
Wang et al. (2015)	.63	.56	.59
JAMR (GitHub)	.64	.53	.58

Table 4: AMR parsing performance on the full test set of LDC2014T12.

We also evaluate our parser on the newswire section of LDC2014T12 dataset. Table 5 compares the performance of JAMR, the Stanford AMR parser and our system on the same dataset.

[2]This is the updated JAMR from https://github.com/jflanigan/jamr

System	P	R	F
Our system	**.72**	**.67**	**.70**
Stanford	.67	.58	.62
JAMR (GitHub)	.67	.53	.59

Table 5: AMR parsing performance on newswire section of LDC2014T12 test set

And our system still outperforms the other parsers by a similar margin.

5 Conclusion

We presented extensions to a transition-based AMR parser that leads to an improvement of 7% in absolute F_1 score over the best previously published results. The extensions include designing a new action to infer abstract concepts and training the parser with additional semantic role labeling and coreference based features.

Acknowledgments

We want to thank the anonymous reviewers for their suggestions.. This work was partially supported by the National Science Foundation via Grant No.0910532 entitled Richer Representations for Machine Translation. All views expressed in this paper are those of the authors and do not necessarily represent the view of the National Science Foundation.

References

Laura Banarescu, Claire Bonial, Shu Cai, Madalina Georgescu, Kira Griffitt, Ulf Hermjakob, Kevin Knight, Philipp Koehn, Martha Palmer, and Nathan Schneider. 2013. Abstract meaning representation for sembanking. In *Proceedings of the 7th Linguistic Annotation Workshop and Interoperability with Discourse*, pages 178–186. Association for Computational Linguistics.

Shu Cai and Kevin Knight. 2013. Smatch: an evaluation metric for semantic feature structures. In *Proceedings of the 51st Annual Meeting of the Association for Computational Linguistics (Volume 2: Short Papers)*, pages 748–752. Association for Computational Linguistics.

Eugene Charniak and Mark Johnson. 2005. Coarse-to-fine n-best parsing and maxent discriminative reranking. In *Proceedings of the 43rd Annual Meeting on Association for Computational Linguistics*, ACL '05, pages 173–180, Stroudsburg, PA, USA. Association for Computational Linguistics.

Michael Collins. 2002. Discriminative training methods for hidden markov models: Theory and experiments with perceptron algorithms. In *Proceedings of the ACL-02 conference on Empirical methods in natural language processing-Volume 10*, pages 1–8. Association for Computational Linguistics.

Jeffrey Flanigan, Sam Thomson, Jaime Carbonell, Chris Dyer, and Noah A. Smith. 2014. A discriminative graph-based parser for the abstract meaning representation. In *Proceedings of the 52nd Annual Meeting of the Association for Computational Linguistics (Volume 1: Long Papers)*, pages 1426–1436, Baltimore, Maryland, June. Association for Computational Linguistics.

Eduard Hovy, Mitchell Marcus, Martha Palmer, Lance Ramshaw, and Ralph Weischedel. 2006. Ontonotes: the 90% solution. In *Proceedings of the human language technology conference of the NAACL, Companion Volume: Short Papers*, pages 57–60. Association for Computational Linguistics.

Terry Koo, Xavier Carreras, and Michael Collins. 2008. Simple semi-supervised dependency parsing. *ACL-08: HLT*, page 595.

Heeyoung Lee, Angel Chang, Yves Peirsman, Nathanael Chambers, Mihai Surdeanu, and Dan Jurafsky. 2013. Deterministic coreference resolution based on entity-centric, precision-ranked rules. *Computational Linguistics*, 39(4):885–916.

Christopher D. Manning, Mihai Surdeanu, John Bauer, Jenny Finkel, Steven J. Bethard, and David McClosky. 2014. The Stanford CoreNLP natural language processing toolkit. In *Proceedings of 52nd Annual Meeting of the Association for Computational Linguistics: System Demonstrations*, pages 55–60.

Andre Martins, Miguel Almeida, and Noah A. Smith. 2013. Turning on the turbo: Fast third-order non-projective turbo parsers. In *Proceedings of the 51st Annual Meeting of the Association for Computational Linguistics (Volume 2: Short Papers)*, pages 617–622, Sofia, Bulgaria, August. Association for Computational Linguistics.

Ryan McDonald, Fernando Pereira, Kiril Ribarov, and Jan Hajič. 2005. Non-projective dependency parsing using spanning tree algorithms. In *Proceedings of the Conference on Human Language Technology and Empirical Methods in Natural Language Processing*, HLT '05, pages 523–530, Stroudsburg, PA, USA. Association for Computational Linguistics.

Joakim Nivre, Johan Hall, and Jens Nilsson. 2006. Maltparser: A data-driven parser-generator for dependency parsing. In *Proceedings of LREC*, volume 6, pages 2216–2219.

Martha Palmer, Daniel Gildea, and Paul Kingsbury. 2005. The proposition bank: An annotated corpus of semantic roles. *Computational linguistics*, 31(1):71–106.

Xiaochang Peng, Linfeng Song, and Daniel Gildea. 2015. A synchronous hyperedge replacement grammar based approach for AMR parsing. In *Proceedings of the Nineteenth Conference on Computational Natural Language Learning*.

Sameer Pradhan, Wayne Ward, Kadri Hacioglu, James Martin, and Dan Jurafsky. 2004. Shallow semantic parsing using support vector machines. In *Proceedings of the Human Language Technology Conference/North American chapter of the Association of Computational Linguistics (HLT/NAACL)*, Boston, MA, May.

Sameer Pradhan, Alessandro Moschitti, Nianwen Xue, Hwee Tou Ng, Anders Björkelund, Olga Uryupina, Yuchen Zhang, and Zhi Zhong. 2013. Towards robust linguistic analysis using OntoNotes. In *Proceedings of the Seventeenth Conference on Computational Natural Language Learning*, pages 143–152, Sofia, Bulgaria, August.

Joseph Turian, Lev Ratinov, and Yoshua Bengio. 2010. Word representations: a simple and general method for semi-supervised learning. In *Proceedings of the 48th annual meeting of the association for computational linguistics*, pages 384–394. Association for Computational Linguistics.

Chuan Wang, Nianwen Xue, and Sameer Pradhan. 2015. A transition-based algorithm for AMR parsing. In *North American Association for Computational Linguistics*, Denver, Colorado.

Keenon Werling, Gabor Angeli, Melvin Johnson Premkumar, and Christopher D. Manning. 2015. Robust subgraph generation improves abstract meaning representation parsing. In *ACL*.

Zhi Zhong and Hwee Tou Ng. 2010. It makes sense: A wide-coverage word sense disambiguation system for free text. In *Proceedings of the ACL 2010 System Demonstrations*, pages 78–83, Uppsala, Sweden.

Generative Incremental Dependency Parsing with Neural Networks

Jan Buys[1] and **Phil Blunsom**[1,2]
[1]Department of Computer Science, University of Oxford [2]Google DeepMind
{jan.buys,phil.blunsom}@cs.ox.ac.uk

Abstract

We propose a neural network model for scalable generative transition-based dependency parsing. A probability distribution over both sentences and transition sequences is parameterised by a feed-forward neural network. The model surpasses the accuracy and speed of previous generative dependency parsers, reaching 91.1% UAS. Perplexity results show a strong improvement over n-gram language models, opening the way to the efficient integration of syntax into neural models for language generation.

1 Introduction

Transition-based dependency parsers that perform incremental local inference with a discriminative classifier offer an appealing trade-off between speed and accuracy (Nivre, 2008; Zhang and Nivre, 2011; Choi and Mccallum, 2013). Recently neural network transition-based dependency parsers have been shown to give state-of-the-art performance (Chen and Manning, 2014; Dyer et al., 2015; Weiss et al., 2015). However, the downstream integration of syntactic structure in language understanding and generation tasks is often done heuristically.

Neural networks have also been shown to be powerful generative models for language modelling (Bengio et al., 2003; Mikolov et al., 2010) and machine translation (Kalchbrenner and Blunsom, 2013; Devlin et al., 2014; Sutskever et al., 2014). However, currently these models lack awareness of syntax, which limits their ability to include longer-distance dependencies even when potentially unbounded contexts are used.

In this paper we propose a generative model for incremental parsing that offers an efficient way to incorporate syntactic information into a generative model. It relies on the strength of neural networks to overcome sparsity in the long conditioning contexts required for an accurate model, while also offering a principled approach to learn dependency-based word representations (Levy and Goldberg, 2014; Bansal et al., 2014).

Generative models for graph-based dependency parsing (Eisner, 1996; Wallach et al., 2008) are much less accurate than their discriminative counterparts. Syntactic language models based on PCFGs (Roark, 2001; Charniak, 2001) and incremental parsing (Chelba and Jelinek, 2000; Emami and Jelinek, 2005) have been proposed for speech recognition and machine translation. However, these models are also limited in either scalability, expressiveness, or both. A generative transition-based dependency parser based on recurrent neural networks (Titov and Henderson, 2007) obtains high accuracy, but training and decoding is prohibitively expensive.

We perform efficient linear-time decoding with a particle filtering-based beam-search method where derivations after pruned after every word generation and the beam size depends on the uncertainty in the model (Buys and Blunsom, 2015).

The model obtains 91.1% UAS on the WSJ, which is 0.2% UAS better than the previous highest accuracy generative dependency parser (Titov and Henderson, 2007), while also being much more efficient. As a language model its perplexity reaches 111.8, a 23% reduction over an n-gram baseline, when combining supervised training with unsupervised fine-tuning. Finally, we find that the model is able to generate sentences that display both local and syntactic coherence.

Proceedings of the 53rd Annual Meeting of the Association for Computational Linguistics and the 7th International Joint Conference on Natural Language Processing (Short Papers), pages 863–869,
Beijing, China, July 26-31, 2015.

2 Generative Transition-based Parsing

Our parsing model is based on transition-based arc-standard projective dependency parsing (Nivre and Scholz, 2004). The generative formulation is similar to previous generative transition-based parsers (Titov and Henderson, 2007; Cohen et al., 2011; Buys and Blunsom, 2015), and also related to the joint tagging and parsing model of Bohnet and Nivre (2012).

The model predicts a sequence of parsing transitions: A shift transition generates a word (and its POS tag), while a reduce transition adds an arc (i, l, j), where i is the head node, j the dependent and l is the dependency label.

The joint probability distribution over a sentence with words $\boldsymbol{w}_{1:n}$, tags $\boldsymbol{t}_{1:n}$ and a transition sequence $\boldsymbol{a}_{1:2n}$ is defined as

$$\prod_{i=1}^{n} \Big(p(t_i|\boldsymbol{h}_{m_i}) p(w_i|t_i, \boldsymbol{h}_{m_i}) \prod_{j=m_i+1}^{m_{i+1}} p(a_j|\boldsymbol{h}_j) \Big),$$

where m_i is the number of transitions that have been performed when (t_i, w_i) is shifted and $\boldsymbol{h}_j$ is the conditioning context at the jth transition.

A parser configuration (σ, β, A) for sentence $\boldsymbol{s}$ consists of a stack σ of indices in $\boldsymbol{s}$, an index β to the next word to be generated, and a set of arcs A. The stack elements are referred to as $\sigma_1, \ldots, \sigma_{|\sigma|}$, where σ_1 is the top element. For any node a, $lc_1(a)$ refers to the leftmost child of a in A, and $rc_1(a)$ to its rightmost child. A root node is added to the beginning of the sentence, and the head word of the sentence (we assume there is only one) is the dependent of the root.

The initial configuration is $([], 0, \emptyset)$, while A terminal configuration is reached when $\beta > |\boldsymbol{s}|$ and $|\sigma| = 1$.

The transition types are shift, left-arc and right-arc. *Shift* generates the next word of the sentence and pushes it on the stack. *Left-arc* adds an arc (σ_1, l, σ_2) and removes σ_2 from the stack. *Right-arc* adds (σ_2, l, σ_1) and pops σ_1.

The parsing strategy adds arcs bottom-up. In a valid transition sequence the last transition is a right-arc from the root to the head word, and the root node is not involved in any other dependencies. We use an oracle to extract transition sequences from the training data: The oracle prefers reduce over shift transitions when both may lead to a valid derivation.

Order	Elements
1	$\sigma_1, \sigma_2, \sigma_3, \sigma_4$
2	$lc_1(\sigma_1), rc_1(\sigma_1), lc_1(\sigma_2), rc_1(\sigma_2)$ $lc_2(\sigma_1), rc_2(\sigma_1), lc_2(\sigma_2), rc_2(\sigma_2)$
3	$lc_1(lc_1(\sigma_1)), rc_1(rc_1(\sigma_1))$ $lc_1(lc_1(\sigma_2)), rc_1(rc_1(\sigma_2))$

Table 1: Conditioning context elements for neural network input: First, second and third order dependencies are used.

3 Neural Network Model

Our probability model is based on neural network language models with distributed representations (Bengio et al., 2003; Mnih and Hinton, 2007), as well as feed-forward neural network models for transition-based dependency parsing (Chen and Manning, 2014; Weiss et al., 2015). We estimate the distributions $p(t_i|\boldsymbol{h}_i)$, $p(w_i|t_i, \boldsymbol{h}_i)$ and $p(a_j|\boldsymbol{h}_j)$ with neural networks with shared input and hidden layers but separate output layers.

The templates for the conditioning context used are defined in Table 1. In the templates we obtain sentence indexes, which are then mapped to the corresponding words, tags and labels (for the dependencies of 2nd and 3rd order elements). The neural network allows us to include a large number of elements without suffering from sparsity.

In the input layer we make use of additive representations (Botha and Blunsom, 2014) so that for each word input position i we can include the word type, tag and other features, and learn input representations for each of these. Each context feature f has an input representation $\mathbf{q}_f \in \mathbb{R}^D$. The composite representation is computed as $\mathbf{q}_i = \sum_{f \in \mu(w_i)} \mathbf{q}_f$, where $\mu(w_i)$ are the word features. The hidden layer is then defined as

$$\phi(\boldsymbol{h}) = g(\sum_{j=1}^{L} \mathbf{C}_j \mathbf{q}_{h_j}),$$

where $\mathbf{C}_j \in \mathbb{R}^{D \times D}$ are transformation matrices defined for each position in sequence $\boldsymbol{h}$, $L = |\boldsymbol{h}|$ and g is a (usually non-linear) activation function applied element-wise. The matrices $\mathbf{C}_j$ can be approximated to be diagonal to reduce the number of model parameters and speed up the model by avoiding expensive matrix multiplications.

For the output layer predicting the next transition a, the hidden layer is mapped with a scoring function

$$\chi(a, \boldsymbol{h}) = \mathbf{k}_a^T \phi(\boldsymbol{h}) + e_a,$$

where $\mathbf{k}_a$ is the transition output representation and e_a is the bias weight. The score is normalised with the soft-max function:

$$p(a|\boldsymbol{h}) = \frac{\exp(\chi(a, \boldsymbol{h}))}{\sum_{a' \in A} \exp(\chi(a', \boldsymbol{h}))}.$$

The output layer for predicting the next tag has a similar form, using the scoring function

$$\tau(t, \boldsymbol{h}) = \mathbf{t}_t^T \phi(\boldsymbol{h}) + o_t$$

for tag representation $\mathbf{t}_t$ and bias o_t.

The probability $p(w|t, \boldsymbol{h})$ can be estimated similarly. However, to reduce the computational cost of normalising over the entire vocabulary, we factorize the probability as $P(w|\boldsymbol{h}) = P(c|t, \boldsymbol{h})P(w|c, t, \boldsymbol{h})$, where $c = c(w)$ is the unique class of word w. For each c, let $\Gamma(c)$ be the set of words in that class. The vocabulary is clustered into approximately $\sqrt{|V|}$ classes using Brown clustering (Brown et al., 1992), reducing the number of items to sum over in the normalisation factor from $O(|V|)$ to $O(\sqrt{|V|})$. Class-based factorization has been shown to be an effective strategy in normalizing neural language models (Baltescu and Blunsom, 2015),

The class prediction score is defined as $\psi(c, \boldsymbol{h}) = \mathbf{s}_c^T \phi(\boldsymbol{h}) + d_c$, where $\mathbf{s}_c \in \mathbb{R}^D$ is the output weight vector for class c and d_c is the class bias weight. The output layer then consists of a softmax function for $p(c|\boldsymbol{h})$ and another softmax for the word prediction

$$p(w|c, \boldsymbol{h}) = \frac{\exp(\Phi(w, \boldsymbol{h}))}{\sum_{w' \in \Gamma(c)} \exp(\Phi(w', \boldsymbol{h}))},$$

where $\Phi(w, \boldsymbol{h}) = \mathbf{r}_w^T \phi(\boldsymbol{h}) + b_w$ is the word scoring function with output word representation $\mathbf{r}_w$ and bias weight b_w.

The model is trained with minibatch stochastic gradient descent (SGD) with Adagrad (Duchi et al., 2011) and L2 regularisation, to minimise the negative log likelihood of the joint distribution over parsed training sentences. For our experiments we train the model while the training objective improves, and choose the parameters of the iteration with the best development set accuracy (early stopping). The model obtains high accuracy with only a few training iterations.

4 Decoding

Beam-search decoders for transition-based parsing (Zhang and Clark, 2008) keep a beam of partial derivations, advancing each derivation by one transition at a time. When the size of the beam exceeds a set threshold, the lowest-scoring derivations are removed. However, in an incremental generative model we need to compare derivations with the same number of words shifted, rather than transitions performed. To let the decoding time remain linear, we also need to bound the total number of reduce transitions that can be performed over all derivations between two shift transitions.

To achieve this, we use a decoding method recently proposed for generative incremental parsing (Buys and Blunsom, 2015) based on particle filtering (Doucet et al., 2001), a sequential Monte Carlo sampling method.

In the algorithm, a fixed number of particles are divided among the partial derivations in the beam. Suppose i words have been shifted in all the derivations on the beam. To predict the next transition from derivation d_j, its particles are divided according to $p(a|\boldsymbol{h})$. In practice, adding only shift and the most likely reduce transition leads to almost no accuracy loss. After all the derivations have been advanced to shift word $i+1$, a selection step is performed: The number of particles of each derivation is redistributed according to its probability, weighted by its current number of particles. Some derivations may be assigned 0 particles, in which case they are removed.

The particle filtering method lets the beam size depend of the uncertainty of the model, somewhat similar to Choi and Mccallum (2013), while fixing the total number of particles constrains the decoding time to be linear. The particle filter also allow us to sample outputs, and to marginalise over the syntax when generating.

5 Experiments

We evaluate our model for parsing and language modelling on the English Penn Treebank (Marcus et al., 1993) WSJ parsing setup[1]. Constituency trees are converted to projective CoNLL syntactic dependencies (Johansson and Nugues, 2007) with the LTH converter[2]. For some experiments

[1] Training on sections 02-21, development on section 22, and testing on section 23.

[2] http://nlp.cs.lth.se/software/treebank_converter/

Activation	UAS	LAS
linear	88.40	86.48
rectifier	89.99	88.31
tanh	90.91	89.22
sigmoid	91.48	89.94

Table 2: Parsing accuracies using different neural network activation functions.

Model	UAS	LAS
Wallach et al. (2008)	85.7	-
Titov and Henderson (2007)	90.93	89.42
NN-GenDP	**91.11**	**89.41**
Chen and Manning (2014)	92.0	90.7

Table 3: Parsing accuracies for dependency parsers on the WSJ test set, CoNLL dependencies.

we also use the Stanford dependency representation (De Marneffe and Manning, 2008) (SD)[3].

Our neural network implementation is partly based on the OxLM neural language modelling framework (Baltescu et al., 2014). The model parameters are initialised randomly by drawing from a Gaussian distribution with mean 0 and variance 0.1, except for the bias weights, which are initialised by the unigram distributions of their output. We use minibatches of size 128, the L2 regularization parameter is 10, and the word representation and hidden layer of size is 256. The Adagrad learning rate is initialised to 0.05.

POS tags for the development and test sets are obtained with the Stanford POS tagger (Toutanova et al., 2003), with 97.5% test set accuracy. Words that occur only once in the training data are treated as unknown words. Unknown words are replaced by tokens representing morphological surface features (based on capitalization, numbers, punctuation and common suffixes) similar to those used in the implementation of generative constituency parsers (Klein and Manning, 2003).

5.1 Parsing results

We report unlabelled attachment score (UAS) and labelled attachment score (LAS) in our results, excluding punctuation. On the development set, we consider the effect of the choice of activation function (Table 2), finding that a sigmoid activation (logistic function) performs best, following by `tanh`. Under our training setup the model can obtain up to 91.0 UAS after only 1 training iteration, thereby performing pure online learning.

We found that including third order dependencies in the conditioning context performs just 0.1% UAS better than including only first and second order dependencies. Including additional elements does not improve performance further. The model can obtain 91.18 UAS, 89.02 LAS when trained only on words, not POS tags. Dependency parsers that do not use distributed representations tend to rely much more on the tags.

Test set results comparing generative dependency parsers are given in Table 3 (our model is refered to as NN-GenDP). The graph-based generative baseline (Wallach et al., 2008), parameterised by Pitman-Yor Processes, is quite weak. Our model outperforms the generative model of Titov and Henderson (2007), which we retrained on our dataset, by 0.2%, despite that model being able to condition on arbitrary-sized contexts. The decoding speed of our model is around 20 sentences per second, against less than 1 sentence per second for Titov and Henderson's model. Using diagonal transformation matrices further increases our model's speed, but reduces parsing accuracy.

On the Stanford dependency representation our model obtains 90.63% UAS, 88.27% LAS. Although this performance is promising, it is still below the discriminative neural network models of Dyer et al. (2015) and Weiss et al. (2015), who obtained 93.1% UAS and 94.0% UAS respectively.

5.2 Language modelling

We also evaluate our parser as a language model, on the same WSJ data used for the parsing evaluation[4]. We perform unlabelled parsing, as experiments show that including labels in the conditioning context has a very small impact on performance. Neither do we use POS tags, as they are too expensive to predict in language generation applications.

Perplexity results on the WSJ are given in Table 4. As baselines we report results on modified Knesser-Ney (Kneser and Ney, 1995) and neural network 5-gram models. For our dependency-based language models we report perplexities based on the most likely parse found by the decoder, which gives an upper bound on the true

[3]Converted with version 3.4.1 of the Stanford parser, available at http::/nlp.stanford.edu/software/lex-parser.shtml.

[4]However instead of using multiple unknown word classes, we replace all numbers by 0 and have a single unknown word token.

the u.s. union board said revenue rose 11 % to $ NUM million , or $ NUM a share .
mr. bush has UNK-ed a plan to buy the company for $ NUM to NUM million , or $ NUM a share .
the plan was UNK-ed by the board 's decision to sell its $ NUM million UNK loan loan funds .
in stocks coming months , china 's NUM shares rose 10 cents to $ NUM million , or $ NUM a share .
in the case , mr. bush said it will sell the company business UNK concern to buy the company .
it was NUM common shares in addition , with $ NUM million , or $ NUM a share , according to mr. bush .
in the first quarter , 1989 shares closed yesterday at $ NUM , mr. bush has increased the plan .
last year 's retrenchment price index index rose 11 cents to $ NUM million , or $ NUM million is asked .
last year earlier , net income rose 11 million % to $ NUM million , or 91 cents a share .
the u.s. union has UNK-ed $ NUM million , or 22 cents a share , in 1990 , payable nov. 9 .

Table 5: Sentences of length 20 or greater generated by the neural generative dependency model.

Model	Perplexity
KN 5-gram	145.7
NN 5-gram	142.5
NN-GenDP	**132.2**
NN-GenDP + unsup	**111.8**

Table 4: WSJ Language modelling test results. We compare our model, with and without unsupervised tuning, to n-gram baselines.

value of the model perplexity.

First we only perform standard supervised training with the model - this already leads to an improvement of 10 perplexity points over the neural n-gram model. Second we consider a training setup where we first perform 5 supervised iterations, and then perform unsupervised training, treating the transition sequence as latent. For each minibatch parse trees are sampled with a particle filter. This approach further improves the perplexity to 111.8, a 23% reduction relative to the Knesser-Ney model.

The unsupervised training stage lets the parsing accuracy fall from 91.48 to 89.49 UAS. We postulate that the model is learning to make small adjustments to favour of parsing structures that explain the data better than the annotated parse trees, leading to the improvement in perplexity.

To test the scalability of our model, we also trained it on a larger unannotated corpus – a subset (of around 7 million words) of the billion word language modeling benchmark dataset (Chelba et al., 2013). After training the model on the WSJ, we parsed the unannotated data with the model, and continued to train on the obtained parses. We observed a small increase in perplexity, from 203.5 for a neural n-gram model to 200.7 for the generative dependency model. We expect larger improvements when training on more data and with more sophisticated inference.

To evaluate our generative model qualitatively, we perform unconstrained generation of sentences (and parse trees) from the model, and found that sentences display a higher degree of syntactic coherence than sentences generated by an n-gram model. See Table 5 for examples generated by the model. The highest-scoring sentences of length 20 or more are given, from 1000 samples generated. Note that the generation includes unknown word tokens (here NUM, UNK and UNK-ed are used).

6 Conclusion

We presented an incremental generative dependency parser that can obtain accuracies competitive with discriminative models. The same model can be applied as an efficient syntactic language model, and for future work it should be integrated into language generation tasks such as machine translation.

Acknowledgements

We acknowledge the financial support of the Oxford Clarendon Fund and the Skye Foundation.

References

Paul Baltescu and Phil Blunsom. 2015. Pragmatic neural language modelling in machine translation. In *Proceedings of NAACL-HTL*, pages 820–829.

Paul Baltescu, Phil Blunsom, and Hieu Hoang. 2014. Oxlm: A neural language modelling framework for machine translation. *The Prague Bulletin of Mathematical Linguistics*, 102(1):81–92, October.

Mohit Bansal, Kevin Gimpel, and Karen Livescu. 2014. Tailoring continuous word representations for dependency parsing. In *Proceedings of the ACL*.

Yoshua Bengio, Réjean Ducharme, Pascal Vincent, and Christian Janvin. 2003. A neural probabilistic language model. *Journal of Machine Learning Research*, 3:1137–1155.

Bernd Bohnet and Joakim Nivre. 2012. A transition-based system for joint part-of-speech tagging and labeled non-projective dependency parsing. In *Proceedings of EMNLP-CONLL*, pages 1455–1465.

Jan A. Botha and Phil Blunsom. 2014. Compositional morphology for word representations and language modelling. In *Proceedings of the 31st International Conference on Machine Learning (ICML)*.

Peter F. Brown, Peter V. deSouza, Robert L. Mercer, Vincent J. Della Pietra, and Jenifer C. Lai. 1992. Class-based n-gram models of natural language. *Computational Linguistics*, 18(4):467–479.

Jan Buys and Phil Blunsom. 2015. A Bayesian model for generative transition-based dependency parsing. *arXiv preprint arXiv:1506.04334*.

Eugene Charniak. 2001. Immediate-head parsing for language models. In *Proceedings of ACL*, pages 124–131. Association for Computational Linguistics.

Ciprian Chelba and Frederick Jelinek. 2000. Structured language modeling. *Computer Speech & Language*, 14(4):283–332.

Ciprian Chelba, Tomas Mikolov, Mike Schuster, Qi Ge, Thorsten Brants, Phillipp Koehn, and Tony Robinson. 2013. One billion word benchmark for measuring progress in statistical language modeling. Technical report, Google.

Danqi Chen and Christopher D Manning. 2014. A fast and accurate dependency parser using neural networks. In *Proceedings of EMNLP*.

Jinho D. Choi and Andrew Mccallum. 2013. Transition-based dependency parsing with selectional branching. In *Proceedings of ACL*.

Shay B. Cohen, Carlos Gómez-Rodríguez, and Giorgio Satta. 2011. Exact inference for generative probabilistic non-projective dependency parsing. In *Proceedings of EMNLP*, pages 1234–1245.

Marie-Catherine De Marneffe and Christopher D Manning. 2008. The Stanford typed dependencies representation. In *Coling 2008: Proceedings of the workshop on Cross-Framework and Cross-Domain Parser Evaluation*, pages 1–8.

Jacob Devlin, Rabih Zbib, Zhongqiang Huang, Thomas Lamar, Richard Schwartz, and John Makhoul. 2014. Fast and robust neural network joint models for statistical machine translation. In *Proceedings of ACL*, pages 1370–1380.

Arnaud Doucet, Nando De Freitas, and Neil Gordon. 2001. *Sequential Monte Carlo methods in practice*. Springer.

John Duchi, Elad Hazan, and Yoram Singer. 2011. Adaptive subgradient methods for online learning and stochastic optimization. *Joural of Machine Learning Research*, 12:2121–2159.

Chris Dyer, Miguel Ballesteros, Wang Ling, Austin Matthews, and Noah A. Smith. 2015. Transition-based dependency parsing with stack long short-term memory. In *Proceedings of ACL 2015*.

Jason Eisner. 1996. Three new probabilistic models for dependency parsing: An exploration. In *Proceedings of COLING*, pages 340–345.

Ahmad Emami and Frederick Jelinek. 2005. A neural syntactic language model. *Machine Learning*, 60(1-3):195–227.

Richard Johansson and Pierre Nugues. 2007. Extended constituent-to-dependency conversion for English. In *16th Nordic Conference of Computational Linguistics*, pages 105–112, Tartu, Estonia.

Nal Kalchbrenner and Phil Blunsom. 2013. Recurrent continuous translation models. In *Proceedings of EMNLP*, pages 1700–1709.

Dan Klein and Christopher D. Manning. 2003. Accurate unlexicalized parsing. In *Proceedings of ACL*, pages 423–430.

Reinhard Kneser and Hermann Ney. 1995. Improved backing-off for m-gram language modeling. In *ICASSP*, volume 1, pages 181–184. IEEE.

Omer Levy and Yoav Goldberg. 2014. Dependency-based word embeddings. In *Proceedings of ACL: Short Papers*.

Mitchell P. Marcus, Beatrice Santorini, and Mary Ann Marcinkiewicz. 1993. Building a large annotated corpus of English: The Penn Treebank. *Computational Linguistics*, 19(2):313–330.

Tomas Mikolov, Martin Karafiát, Lukas Burget, Jan Cernocký, and Sanjeev Khudanpur. 2010. Recurrent neural network based language model. In *INTERSPEECH*, pages 1045–1048.

Andriy Mnih and Geoffrey Hinton. 2007. Three new graphical models for statistical language modelling. In *Proceedings of the 24th International Conference on Machine learning*, pages 641–648.

Joakim Nivre and Mario Scholz. 2004. Deterministic dependency parsing of English text. In *Proceedings of COLING*.

Joakim Nivre. 2008. Algorithms for deterministic incremental dependency parsing. *Computational Linguistics*, 34(4):513–553.

Brian Roark. 2001. Probabilistic top-down parsing and language modeling. *Computational linguistics*, 27(2):249–276.

Ilya Sutskever, Oriol Vinyals, and Quoc VV Le. 2014. Sequence to sequence learning with neural networks. In *Advances in Neural Information Processing Systems*, pages 3104–3112.

Ivan Titov and James Henderson. 2007. A latent variable model for generative dependency parsing. In *Proceedings of the Tenth International Conference on Parsing Technologies*, pages 144–155.

Kristina Toutanova, Dan Klein, Christopher D. Manning, and Yoram Singer. 2003. Feature-rich part-of-speech tagging with a cyclic dependency network. In *Proceedings of HLT-NAACL*, pages 173–180.

Hanna M Wallach, Charles Sutton, and Andrew McCallum. 2008. Bayesian modeling of dependency trees using hierarchical Pitman-Yor priors. In *ICML Workshop on Prior Knowledge for Text and Language Processing*.

David Weiss, Chris Alberti, Michael Collins, and Slav Petrov. 2015. Structured training for neural network transition-based parsing. In *Proceedings of ACL 2015*.

Yue Zhang and Stephen Clark. 2008. A tale of two parsers: Investigating and combining graph-based and transition-based dependency parsing. In *Proceedings of EMNLP*, pages 562–571.

Yue Zhang and Joakim Nivre. 2011. Transition-based dependency parsing with rich non-local features. In *Proceedings of ACL-HLT: Short papers*, pages 188–193.

Labeled Grammar Induction with Minimal Supervision

Yonatan Bisk **Christos Christodoulopoulos** **Julia Hockenmaier**
Department of Computer Science
The University of Illinois at Urbana-Champaign
201 N. Goodwin Ave, Urbana, IL 61801
{bisk1, christod, juliahmr}@illinois.edu

Abstract

Nearly all work in unsupervised grammar induction aims to induce unlabeled dependency trees from gold part-of-speech-tagged text. These clean linguistic classes provide a very important, though unrealistic, inductive bias. Conversely, induced clusters are very noisy. We show here, for the first time, that very limited human supervision (three frequent words per cluster) may be required to induce *labeled* dependencies from automatically induced word clusters.

1 Introduction

Despite significant progress on inducing part-of-speech (POS) tags from raw text (Christodoulopoulos et al., 2010; Blunsom and Cohn, 2011) and a small number of notable exceptions (Seginer, 2007; Spitkovsky et al., 2011; Christodoulopoulos et al., 2012), most approaches to grammar induction or unsupervised parsing (Klein and Manning, 2004; Spitkovsky et al., 2013; Blunsom and Cohn, 2010) are based on the assumption that gold POS tags are available to the induction system. Although most approaches treat these POS tags as arbitrary, if relatively clean, clusters, it has also been shown that the linguistic knowledge implicit in these tags can be exploited in a more explicit fashion (Naseem et al., 2010). The presence of POS tags is also essential for approaches that aim to return richer structures than the standard unlabeled dependencies. Boonkwan and Steedman (2011) train a parser that uses a semi-automatically constructed Combinatory Categorial Grammar (CCG, Steedman (2000)) lexicon for POS tags, while Bisk and Hockenmaier (2012; 2013) show that CCG lexicons can be induced automatically if POS tags are used to identify nouns and verbs. However, assuming clean POS tags is highly unrealistic for most scenarios in which one would wish to use an otherwise unsupervised parser.

In this paper we demonstrate that the simple "universal" knowledge of Bisk and Hockenmaier (2013) can be easily applied to induced clusters given a small number of words labeled as *noun*, *verb* or *other*, and that this small amount of knowledge is sufficient to produce labeled syntactic structures from raw text, something that has not yet been proposed in the literature. Specifically, we will provide a labeled evaluation of induced CCG parsers against the English (Hockenmaier and Steedman, 2007) and Chinese (Tse, 2013) CCGbanks. To provide a direct comparison to the dependency induction literature, we will also provide an unlabeled evaluation on the 10 dependency corpora that were used for the task of grammar induction from raw text in the PASCAL Challenge on Grammar Induction (Gelling et al., 2012).

The system of Christodoulopoulos et al. (2012) was the only participant competing in the PASCAL Challenge that operated over raw text (instead of gold POS tags). However, their approach did not outperform the six baseline systems provided. These baselines were two versions of the DMV model (Klein and Manning, 2004; Gillenwater et al., 2011) run on varying numbers of induced Brown clusters (described in section 2.1). We will therefore compare against these baselines in our evaluation.

Outside of the shared task, Spitkovsky et al. (2011) demonstrated impressive performance using Brown clusters but did not provide evaluation

Proceedings of the 53rd Annual Meeting of the Association for Computational Linguistics and the 7th International Joint Conference on Natural Language Processing (Short Papers), pages 870–876, Beijing, China, July 26-31, 2015.

for languages other than English.

The system we propose here will use a coarse-grained labeling comprised of three classes, which makes it substantially simpler than traditional tagsets, and uses far fewer labeled tokens than is customary for weakly-supervised approaches (Haghighi and Klein, 2006; Garrette et al., 2015).

2 Our Models

Our goal in this work will be to produce labeled dependencies from raw text. Our approach is based on the HDP-CCG parser of Bisk and Hockenmaier (2015) with their extensions to capture lexicalization and punctuation, which, to our knowledge, is the only unsupervised approach to produce labeled dependencies. It first induces a CCG from POS-tagged text, and then estimates a model based on Hierarchical Dirichlet Processes (Teh et al., 2006) over the induced parse forests. The HDP model uses a hyperparameter which controls the amount of smoothing to the base measure of the HDP. Setting this value will prove important when moving between datasets of drastically different sizes.

The induction algorithm assumes that a) verbs may be predicates (with category S), b) verbs can take nouns (with category N) or sentences as arguments (leading to categories of the form S|N, (S|N)|N, (S|N)|S etc.), c) any word can act as a modifier, i.e. have a category of the form X|X if it is adjacent to a word with category X or X|Y, and d) modifiers X|X can take nouns or sentences as arguments ((X|X)|N). Our contribution in this paper will be to show that we can replace the gold POS tags used by Bisk and Hockenmaier (2013) with automatically induced word clusters, and then use very minimal supervision to identify noun and verb clusters.

2.1 Inducing Word Clusters

We will evaluate three clustering approaches:

Brown Clusters Brown clusters (Brown et al., 1992) assign each word to a single cluster using an aglomerative clustering that maximizes the probability of the corpus under a bigram class conditional model. We use Liang's implementation[1].

BMMM The Bayesian Multinomial Mixture Model[2] (BMMM, Christodoulopoulos et al. 2011) is also a hard clustering system, but has the ability to incorporate multiple types of features either at a token level (e.g. ± 1 context word) or at a type level (e.g. morphology features derived from the Morfessor system (Creutz and Lagus, 2006)). The combination of these features allows BMMM to better capture morphosyntactic information.

Bigram HMM We also evaluate unsupervised bigram HMMs, since the soft clustering they provide may be advantageous over the hard Brown and BMMM clusters. But it is known that unsupervised HMMs may not find good POS tags (Johnson, 2007), and in future work, more sophisticated models (e.g. Blunsom and Cohn (2011)), might outperform the systems we use here.

In all cases, we assume that we can identify punctuation marks, which are moved to their own cluster and ignored for the purposes of tagging and parsing evaluation.

2.2 Identifying Noun and Verb Clusters

To induce CCGs from induced clusters, we need to label them as $\{noun, verb, other\}$. This needs to be done judiciously; providing every cluster the *verb* label, for example, leads to the model identifying prepositions as the main sentential predicates.

We demonstrate here that labeling three frequent words per cluster is sufficient to outperform state-of-the-art performance on grammar induction from raw text in many languages. We emulate having a native speaker annotate words for us by using the universal tagset (Petrov et al., 2012) as our source of labels for the most frequent three words per cluster (we map the tags NOUN, NUM, PRON to *noun*, VERB to *verb*, and all others to *other*). The final labeling is a majority vote, where each word type contributes a vote for each label it can take (see Table 4 for some examples). This approach could easily be scaled to allow more words per cluster to vote. But we will see that three per cluster is sufficient to label most tokens correctly.

3 Experimental Setup

We will focus first on producing CCG labeled predicate-argument dependencies for English and Chinese and will then apply our best settings to produce a comparison with the tree structures of the languages of the PASCAL Shared Task. All languages will be trained on sentences of up to length 20 (not counting punctuation). All cluster induction algorithms are treated as black boxes

[1]https://github.com/percyliang/brown-cluster

[2]https://github.com/christos-c/bmmm

and run over the complete datasets in advance. This alleviates having to handle tagging of unknown words.

To provide an intuition for the performance of the induced word clusters, we provide two standard metrics for unsupervised tagging:

Many-to-one (M-1) A commonly used measure, M-1 relies on mapping each cluster to the most common POS tag of its words. However, M-1 can be easily inflated by inducing more clusters.

V-Measure Proposed by Rosenberg and Hirschberg (2007), V-Measure (VM) measures the information-theoretic distance between two clusterings and has been shown to be robust to the number of induced clusters (Christodoulopoulos et al., 2010). Both of these metrics are known to be highly dependent on the gold annotation standards they are compared against, and may not correlate with downstream performance at parsing.

Of more immediate relevance to our task is the ability to accurately identify nouns and verbs:

Noun, Verb, and Other Recall We measure the (token-based) recall of our three-way labeling scheme of clusters as *noun/verb/other* against the universal POS tags of each token.

4 Experiment 1: CCG-based Evaluation

Experimental Setup For our primary experiments, we train and test our systems on the English and Chinese CCGbanks, and report directed labeled F1 (LF1) and undirected unlabeled F1 (UF1) over CCG dependencies (Clark et al., 2002). For the labeled evaluation, we follow the simplification of CCGbank categories proposed by Bisk and Hockenmaier (2015): for English to remove morphosyntactic features, map NP to N and change VP modifiers (S\NP)|(S\NP) to sentential modifiers (S|S); for Chinese we map both M and QP to N. In the CCG literature, UF1 is commonly used because undirected dependencies do not penalize argument vs. adjunct distinctions, e.g. for prepositional phrases. For this reason we will include UF1 in the final test set evaluation (Table 2).

We use the published train/dev/test splits, using the dev set for choosing a cluster induction algorithm, and then present final performance on the test data. We induce 36 tags for English and 37 for Chinese to match the number of tags present in the treebanks (excluding symbol and punctuation tags).

		Tagging		Labeling			Parsing	
		M-1	VM	N	V	O	LF1	Gold
English	Brown	62.4	56.3	**85.6**	59.4	81.2	23.3	
	BMMM	**66.8**	**58.7**	81.0	**81.2**	**82.7**	**26.6**	38.8
	HMM	51.1	41.7	76.3	63.3	**82.6**	25.8	
Chinese	Brown	**66.0**	**50.1**	88.9	28.6	**91.3**	10.2	
	BMMM	64.8	50.0	**94.4**	**48.7**	87.0	**10.5**	16.6
	HMM	46.3	30.8	68.0	44.6	76.7	3.13	

Table 1: Tagging evaluation (M-1, VM, N/V/O Recall) and directed labeled CCG-Dependency performance (LF1) as compared to the use of gold POS tags (Gold) for three clustering algorithms.

Results Table 1 presents the parsing and tagging development results on the two CCG corpora. In terms of tagging performance, we can see that the two hard clustering systems significantly outperform the HMM, but the relative performance of Brown and BMMM is mixed.

More importantly, we see that, at least for English, despite clear differences in tagging performance, the parsing results (LF1) are much more similar. In Chinese, we see that the performance of the two hard clustering systems is almost identical, again, not representative of the differences in the tagging scores. The N/V/O recall scores in both languages are equally poor predictors of parsing performance. However, these scores show that having only three labeled tokens per class is sufficient to capture most of the necessary distinctions for the HDP-CCG. All of this confirms the observations of Headden et al. (2008) that POS tagging metrics are not correlated with parsing performance. However, since BMMM seems to have a slight overall advantage, we will be using it as our clustering system for the remaining experiments.

Since the goal of this work was to produce labeled syntactic structures, we also wanted to evaluate our performance against that of the HDP-CCG system that uses gold-standard POS tags. As we can see in the last two columns of our development results in Table 1 and in the final test results of Table 2, our system is within 2/3 of the labeled performance of the gold-POS-based HDP-CCG[3].

Figure 1 shows an example labeled syntactic structure induced by the model. We can see the system successfully learns to attach the final

[3]To put this result into its full perspective, the LF1 performance of a supervised CCG system (Hockenmaier and Steedman, 2002), HWDep model, trained on the same length-20 dataset and tested on the simplified CCGbank test set is 80.3.

	This	Gold
English	26.0 / 51.1	37.1 / 64.9
Chinese	10.3 / 33.5	15.6 / 39.8

Table 2: CCG parsing performance (LF1/UF1) on the test set with and without gold tags.

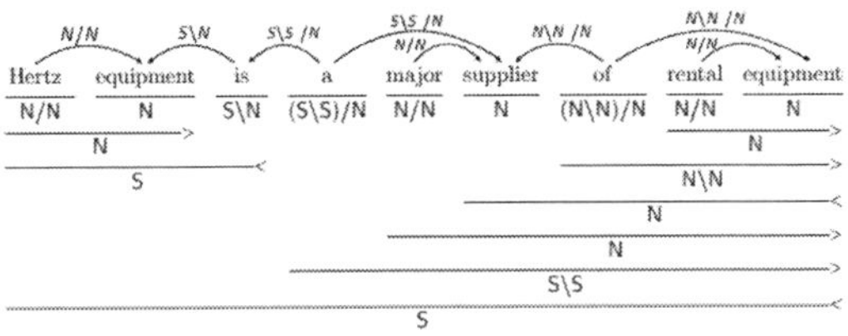

Figure 1: A sample derivation from the WSJ Section 22 demonstrating the system is learning most of the correct categories of CCGbank but has incorrectly analyzed the determiner as a preposition.

prepositional phrase, but mistakes the verb for intransitive and treats the determiner *a* as a preposition. The labeled and undirected recall for this parse are 5/8 and 7/8 respectively.

5 Experiment 2: PASCAL Shared Task

Experimental Setup During the PASCAL shared task, participants were encouraged to train over the complete union of the data splits. We do the same here, use the dev set for choosing a HDP-CCG hyperparameter, and then present final results for comparison on the test section. We vary the hyperparamter for this evaluation because the datasets fluctuate dramatically in size from 9K to 700K tokens on sentences up to length 20. Rather than match all of the tagsets, we simply induce 49 (excluding punctuation) classes for every language. The actual tagsets vary from 20 to 304 tags (median 39, mean 78).

Results We now present results for the 10 corpora of the PASCAL shared task (evaluated on all sentence lengths). Table 3 presents the test performance for each language with the best hyperparameter chosen from the set $\{100, 1000, 2500\}$. Also included are the best published results from the joint tag/dependency induction shared task (ST) as well as the results from Bisk and Hockenmaier (2013), the only existing numbers for multilingual CCG induction (BH) with gold part-of-speech tags. Note that the systems in ST do not have access to any gold-standard POS tags, whereas our system has access to the gold tags for

	VM	N / V / O	This	ST	@15	BH
Czech_{2500}	42	86 / 67 / 67	9.49	**33.2**	12.2	50.7
English_{2500}	59	87 / 76 / 85	**43.8**	24.4	51.6	62.9
CHILDES_{2500}	68	84 / 97 / 89	**47.2**	42.2	47.5	73.3
Portuguese_{2500}	55	88 / 81 / 69	**55.5**	31.7	55.8	70.5
Dutch_{1000}	50	81 / 81 / 82	**39.9**	33.7	43.8	54.4
Basque_{1000}	52	2 / 78 / 95	**31.1**	28.7	35.2	45.0
Swedish_{1000}	50	89 / 74 / 85	**45.8**	28.2	52.9	66.9
Slovene_{1000}	50	83 / 75 / 79	18.5	**19.2**	23.6	46.4
Danish_{100}	59	95 / 79 / 82	16.1	**31.9**	17.8	58.5
Arabic_{100}	51	85 / 76 / 90	34.5	**44.4**	43.7	65.1
Average	54	78 / 78 / 82	**34.2**	31.8	38.4	59.4

Table 3: Tagging VM and N/V/O Recall alongside Directed Accuracy for our approach and the best shared task baseline. Additionally, we provide results for length 15 to compare to previously published results ([ST]: Best of the PASCAL joint tag/dependency induction shared task systems; [BH]: Bisk and Hockenmaier (2013).

the three most frequent words of each cluster.

The languages are sorted by the number of non-punctuation tokens in sentences of up to length 20. Despite our average performance (34.2) being slightly higher than the shared task (31.8), the st. deviation is substantial ($\sigma = 15.2$ vs $\sigma_{ST} = 7.5$). It seems apparent from the results that while data sparsity may play a role in affecting performance, the more linguistically interesting thread appears to be morphology. Czech is perhaps a prime example, as it has twice the data of the next largest language (700K tokens vs 336K in English), but our approach still performs poorly.

Finally, while we saw that the hard clustering systems outperformed the HMM for our experiments, this is perhaps best explained by analyzing the average number of gold fine-grained tags per lexical type in each of the corpora. We found, counterintuitively, that the "difficult" languages had lower average number of tags per type (1.01 for Czech, 1.03 for Arabic) than English (1.17) which was the most ambiguous. This is likely due to morphology distinguishing otherwise ambiguous lemmas.

6 Cluster Analysis

In Table 4, we present the three most frequent words from several clusters produced by the BMMM for English and Chinese. We also provide a *noun/verb/other* label for each of the words in the list. One can clearly see that there are many ambiguous cases where having three labels voting

English	Labels	Chinese	Chinese gloss	Labels
shares, sales, business	N, N, N	同时, 政治, 生产	simultaneously, politics, production	O, N, N
the, its, their	O, N, N	进行, 举行, 开始	advance, hold, begin	V, V, V
other, interest, chief	O, N, O	在, 有, 对	in, have, for	O, V, O
of, in, on	O, O, O	中国, 台湾, 美国	China, Taiwan, USA	N, N, N
up, expected, made	O, V, V	也, 将, 就	also, will, then	O, O, O
be, make, sell	V, V, V	大, 多,高	big, many, high	O, N, O *
offer, issue, work	N, N, N *	是, 希望, 代表	is, desire, representative	V, V, N

Table 4: The top three words in BMMM clusters with their *noun/verb/other* labels. In two cases (marked with *) all three of the most frequent words also occurred as a verb at least one third of the time.

on the class label proves a beneficial signal. We have also marked two classes with * to draw the reader's attention to a fully *noun* cluster in English and an *other* cluster in Chinese which are highly ambiguous. Specifically, in both of these cases the frequent words also occur frequently as verbs, providing additional motivation for a better soft-clustering algorithm in future work.

How to most effectively use seed knowledge and annotation is still an open question. Approaches range from labeling frequent words like the work of Garrette and Baldridge (2013) to the recently introduced active learning approach of Stratos and Collins (2015). In this work, we were able to demonstrate high noun and verb recall with the use of a very small set of labeled words because they correspond to an existing clustering. In contrast, we found that labeling even the 1000 most frequent words led to very few clusters being correctly identified; e.g. in English, using the 1000 most frequent words results in identifying 2 *verb* and 5 *noun* clusters, compared to our method's 9 *verb* and 16 *noun* clusters. This is because the most frequent words tend to be clustered in a few very large clusters resulting in low coverage.

Stratos and Collins (2015) demonstrated, similarly, that using a POS tagger's confidence score to find ambiguous classes can lead to a highly effective adaptive learning procedure, which strategically labels very few words for a very highly accurate system. Our results align with this research, leading us to believe that this paradigm of guided minimal supervision is a fruitful direction for future work.

7 Conclusions

In this paper, we have produced the first labeled syntactic structures from raw text. There remains a noticeable performance gap due to the use of induced clusters in lieu of gold tags. Based on our final PASCAL results, there are several languages where our performance greatly exceeds the currently published results, but equally many where we fall short. It also appears to be the case that this problem correlates with morphology (e.g. Arabic, Danish, Slovene, Basque, Czech) and some of the lowest performing intrinsic evaluations of the clustering and N/V/O labeling (Czech and Basque).

In principle, the BMMM is taking morphological information into account, as it is provided with the automatically produced suffixes of Morfessor. Unfortunately, its treatment of them simply as features from a "black box" appears to be too naive for our purposes. Properly modeling the relationship between prefixes, stems and suffixes both within the tag induction and parsing framework is likely necessary for a high performing system.

Moving forward, additional raw text for training, as well as enriching the clustering with induced syntactic information (Christodoulopoulos et al., 2012) may close this gap.

8 Acknowledgments

We want to thank Dan Roth and Cynthia Fisher for their insight on the task. Additionally, we would like to thank the anonymous reviewers for their useful questions and comments. This material is based upon work supported by the National Science Foundation under Grants No. 1053856, 1205627, 1405883, by the National Institutes of Health under Grant HD054448, and by DARPA under agreement number FA8750-13-2-0008. Any opinions, findings, and conclusions or recommendations expressed in this material are those of the author(s) and do not necessarily reflect the views of the National Science Foundation, the National Institutes of Health, DARPA or the U.S. Government.

References

Yonatan Bisk and Julia Hockenmaier. 2012. Simple Robust Grammar Induction with Combinatory Categorial Grammars. In *Proceedings of the Twenty-Sixth Conference on Artificial Intelligence (AAAI-12)*, pages 1643–1649, Toronto, Canada, July.

Yonatan Bisk and Julia Hockenmaier. 2013. An HDP Model for Inducing Combinatory Categorial Grammars. *Transactions of the Association for Computational Linguistics*, pages 75–88.

Yonatan Bisk and Julia Hockenmaier. 2015. Probing the linguistic strengths and limitations of unsupervised grammar induction. In *Proceedings of the 53rd Annual Meeting of the Association for Computational Linguistics*.

Phil Blunsom and Trevor Cohn. 2010. Unsupervised Induction of Tree Substitution Grammars for Dependency Parsing. *Proceedings of the 2010 Conference on Empirical Methods of Natural Language Processing*, pages 1204–1213, October.

Phil Blunsom and Trevor Cohn. 2011. A hierarchical pitman-yor process hmm for unsupervised part of speech induction. In *Proceedings of the 49th Annual Meeting of the Association for Computational Linguistics: Human Language Technologies*, pages 865–874, Portland, Oregon, USA, June.

Prachya Boonkwan and Mark Steedman. 2011. Grammar Induction from Text Using Small Syntactic Prototypes. In *Proceedings of 5th International Joint Conference on Natural Language Processing*, pages 438–446, Chiang Mai, Thailand, November.

Peter F Brown, Peter V deSouza, Robert L Mercer, Vincent J Della Pietra, and Jenifer C Lai. 1992. Class-Based n-gram Models of Natural Language. *Computational Linguistics*, 18.

Christos Christodoulopoulos, Sharon Goldwater, and Mark Steedman. 2010. Two decades of unsupervised PoS induction: How far have we come? In *Proceedings of EMNLP*, pages 575–584.

Christos Christodoulopoulos, Sharon Goldwater, and Mark Steedman. 2011. A Bayesian Mixture Model for Part-of-Speech Induction Using Multiple Features. In *Proceedings of the 2011 Conference on Empirical Methods in Natural Language Processing*, Edinburgh, Scotland, UK., July.

Christos Christodoulopoulos, Sharon Goldwater, and Mark Steedman. 2012. Turning the pipeline into a loop: iterated unsupervised dependency parsing and PoS induction. In *WILS '12: Proceedings of the NAACL-HLT Workshop on the Induction of Linguistic Structure*, June.

Stephen Clark, Julia Hockenmaier, and Mark Steedman. 2002. Building deep dependency structures using a wide-coverage ccg parser. In *Proceedings of 40th Annual Meeting of the Association for Computational Linguistics*, pages 327–334, Philadelphia, Pennsylvania, USA, July.

Mathias Creutz and Krista Lagus. 2006. Morfessor in the Morpho challenge. In *Proceedings of the PASCAL Challenge Workshop on Unsupervised Segmentation of Words into Morphemes*, pages 12–17.

Dan Garrette and Jason Baldridge. 2013. Learning a Part-of-Speech Tagger from Two Hours of Annotation. In *Proceedings of the 2013 Conference of the North American Chapter of the Association for Computational Linguistics: Human Language Technologies*, pages 138–147, Atlanta, Georgia, June.

Dan Garrette, Chris Dyer, Jason Baldridge, and Noah A Smith. 2015. Weakly-Supervised Grammar-Informed Bayesian CCG Parser Learning. In *Proceedings of the Association for the Advancement of Artificial Intelligence*.

Douwe Gelling, Trevor Cohn, Phil Blunsom, and João V Graca. 2012. The PASCAL Challenge on Grammar Induction. In *NAACL HLT Workshop on Induction of Linguistic Structure*, pages 64–80, Montréal, Canada, June.

Jennifer Gillenwater, Kuzman Ganchev, João V Graca, Fernando Pereira, and Ben Taskar. 2011. Posterior Sparsity in Unsupervised Dependency Parsing. *The Journal of Machine Learning Research*, 12:455–490, February.

Aria Haghighi and Dan Klein. 2006. Prototype-Driven Grammar Induction. In *Association for Computational Linguistics*, pages 881–888, Morristown, NJ, USA.

William P. Headden, III, David McClosky, and Eugene Charniak. 2008. Evaluating unsupervised part-of-speech tagging for grammar induction. In *Proceedings of the 22Nd International Conference on Computational Linguistics - Volume 1*, COLING '08, pages 329–336, Stroudsburg, PA, USA.

Julia Hockenmaier and Mark Steedman. 2002. Generative models for statistical parsing with combinatory categorial grammar. In *Proceedings of 40th Annual Meeting of the Association for Computational Linguistics*, pages 335–342, Philadelphia, Pennsylvania, USA, July.

Julia Hockenmaier and Mark Steedman. 2007. CCGbank: A Corpus of CCG Derivations and Dependency Structures Extracted from the Penn Treebank. *Computational Linguistics*, 33:355–396, September.

Mark Johnson. 2007. Why doesn't EM find good HMM POS-taggers. In *Proceedings of the 2007 Joint Conference on Empirical Methods in Natural Language Processing and Computational Natural Language Learning (EMNLP-CoNLL)*, January.

Dan Klein and Christopher D Manning. 2004. Corpus-Based Induction of Syntactic Structure: Models of Dependency and Constituency. In *Proceedings of the 42nd Meeting of the Association for Computational Linguistics (ACL'04), Main Volume*, pages 478–485, Barcelona, Spain, July.

Tahira Naseem, Harr Chen, Regina Barzilay, and Mark Johnson. 2010. Using universal linguistic knowledge to guide grammar induction. In *Proceedings of the 2010 Conference on Empirical Methods in Natural Language Processing*, pages 1234–1244, Cambridge, MA, October.

Slav Petrov, Dipanjan Das, and Ryan McDonald. 2012. A Universal Part-of-Speech Tagset. In *Proceedings of the Eighth International Conference on Language Resources and Evaluation (LREC-2012)*, pages 2089–2096, Istanbul, Turkey, May.

Andrew Rosenberg and Julia Hirschberg. 2007. V-measure: A conditional entropy-based external cluster evaluation measure. In *Proceedings of the 2007 Joint Conference on Empirical Methods in Natural Language Processing and Computational Natural Language Learning (EMNLP-CoNLL)*, pages 410–420, Prague, Czech Republic, June.

Yoav Seginer. 2007. Fast Unsupervised Incremental Parsing. In *Proceedings of the 45th Annual Meeting of the Association of Computational Linguistics*, pages 384–391, Prague, Czech Republic, June.

Valentin I Spitkovsky, Hiyan Alshawi, Angel X Chang, and Daniel Jurafsky. 2011. Unsupervised Dependency Parsing without Gold Part-of-Speech Tags. In *Proceedings of the 2011 Conference on Empirical Methods in Natural Language Processing*, pages 1281–1290, Edinburgh, Scotland, UK., July.

Valentin I Spitkovsky, Hiyan Alshawi, and Daniel Jurafsky. 2013. Breaking Out of Local Optima with Count Transforms and Model Recombination: A Study in Grammar Induction. In *Empirical Methods in Natural Language Processing*.

Mark Steedman. 2000. *The Syntactic Process*. The MIT Press, September.

Karl Stratos and Michael Collins. 2015. Simple semi-supervised pos tagging. In *Proceedings of the 1st Workshop on Vector Space Modeling for Natural Language Processing*, pages 79–87, Denver, Colorado, June.

Yee-Whye Teh, Michael I Jordan, Matthew J Beal, and David M Blei. 2006. Hierarchical Dirichlet Processes. *Journal of the American Statistical Association*, 101(476):1566–1581.

Daniel Tse. 2013. *Chinese CCGBank: Deep Derivations and Dependencies for Chinese CCG Parsing*. Ph.D. thesis, The University of Sydney.

On the Importance of Ezafe Construction in Persian Parsing

Alireza Nourian⋆, Mohammad Sadegh Rasooli☾, Mohsen Imany⋆, and Heshaam Faili□

⋆Department of Computer Engineering, Iran University of Science and Technlogy, Tehran, Iran
{nourian,m_imany}@comp.iust.ac.ir
☾ Department of Computer Science, Columbia University, New York, NY, USA
rasooli@cs.columbia.edu
□School of Electrical and Computer Engineering, University of Tehran, Tehran, Iran
hfaili@ut.ac.ir

Abstract

Ezafe construction is an idiosyncratic phenomenon in the Persian language. It is a good indicator for phrase boundaries and dependency relations but mostly does not appear in the text. In this paper, we show that adding information about Ezafe construction can give 4.6% relative improvement in dependency parsing and 9% relative improvement in shallow parsing. For evaluation purposes, Ezafe tags are manually annotated in the Persian dependency treebank. Furthermore, to be able to conduct experiments on shallow parsing, we develop a dependency to shallow phrase structure convertor based on the Persian dependencies.

1 Introduction

There have been many studies on improving syntactic parsing methods for natural languages. Although most of the parsing methods are language-independent, we may still require some language specific knowledge for improving performance. Besides many studies on parsing morphologically rich languages (Seddah et al., 2013; Seeker and Kuhn, 2013), syntactic parsing for the Persian language is not yet noticeably explored. Concretely speaking, there are some recent work on dependency parsing for Persian (Seraji et al., 2012; Ghayoomi, 2012; Khallash et al., 2013) and very few studies on shallow parsing (Kian et al., 2009).

The main focus of this paper is on the usefulness of Ezafe construction in Persian syntactic processing. Ezafe is an unstressed vowel -e that occurs at the end of some words (-ye in some specific occasions) that links together elements belonging to a single constituent (Ghomeshi, 1997). It often approximately corresponds in usage to the English preposition "of" (Abrahams, 2004). In the following example, the first word has an Ezafe vowel:

$$\begin{cases} montazer_e & Ab \\ waiting_{Ezafe} & water \end{cases} \quad waiting\ for\ water$$

This is an idiosyncratic construction that appears in the Persian language with Perso-Arabic script. This construction is similar to Idafa construction in Arabic and construct state in Hebrew (Habash, 2010). It is mostly used for showing a possessive marker, adjective of a noun or connecting parts of a name (i.e. first and last name) or title. As a general statement, Ezafe occurs between any two items that have some sort of connection (Ghomeshi, 1997). Ezafe vowel is attached to the head noun and to the modifiers that follow it: attributive nouns, adjectival and prepositional phrases (Samvelian, 2006). As depicted in Figure 1, this construction is very useful for disambiguating syntactic structures. The main issue here is that Ezafe rarely appears in the written text. This relies on the fact that Persian is written in Perso-Arabic script and vowels are mostly not written.

There are few studies (Noferesti and Shamsfard, 2014; Asghari et al., 2014) on automatically finding Ezafe construction. In this work, we modify the part of speech tagset for the Persian words. This is done by adding an indicator of Ezafe to each part of speech (POS) tag and then train a supervised tagger on the modified tags. We show that having this modified tagset can both improve dependency parsing and shallow parsing (chunking). We achieve 12.8% and 4.6% relative error reduction in dependency parsing with gold and auto-

Proceedings of the 53rd Annual Meeting of the Association for Computational Linguistics and the 7th International Joint Conference on Natural Language Processing (Short Papers), pages 877–882,
Beijing, China, July 26-31, 2015.

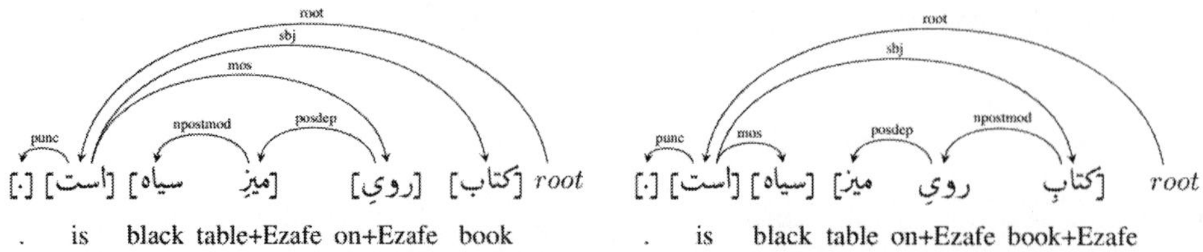

(a) First reading: The book is on the black table.

(b) Second reading: The book on the table is black.

Figure 1: This figure shows two different readings for the same sentence with different Ezafe constructions. As shown in the trees, Ezafe affects both phrase boundaries and dependency relations.

matic POS tags. We also achieve 31% and 9% relative error reduction in shallow parsing with gold and automatic POS tags.

Our work is not only restricted to the effect of Ezafe in parsing, but as a byproduct, we create an open-source rule-based dependency to chunk converter for the Persian language. We have also manually tagged all words in the Persian dependency treebank (Rasooli et al., 2013) with 99.6% annotator agreement. This dataset is available for research purposes.[1]

The main contributions of this paper are: 1) showing the usefulness of Ezafe construction on dependency parsing and chunking, 2) developing a statistical chunker for the Persian language, 3) enriching the Persian treebank with manual Ezafe tags. The remainder of this paper is organized as the following: we describe our approach and data preparation in §2 and then conduct experiments in §3. Error analysis and conclusion are made in §4 and §5.

2 Data Preparation

We define a simple procedure to include the information about Ezafe construction in our data. Concretely, we attach the Ezafe indicator to the tags and train a POS tagger on the new tagset. This idea is very similar to that of (Asghari et al., 2014). Thanks to the presence of Ezafe feature in the Peykare corpus (Bijankhan et al., 2011), we can easily train a POS tagger on the new tagset. We use the developed tagger to tag the dependency treebank. Peykare corpus has approximately ten million tokens and can give us a very accurate POS tagger even with the finer-grained Ezafe tags. We try this idea on two different tasks: dependency parsing and shallow parsing.

[1] `http://dadegan.ir/catalog/ezafe`

2.1 Chunking Data Preparation

Unfortunately there is no standard chunking data for the Persian language. To compensate for this, we define the following rules to convert a dependency tree (based on Dadegan treebank dependencies (Rasooli et al., 2013)) to a shallow phrase structure:

- We initialize every node (word) as a separate chunk; e.g. verb creates a VP.
- If a node has a head or dependent belonging to a chunk (without any gap), attach that node to the same chunk.
- If a node is a preposition/postposition, attach it to its next/previous dependent and create a PP.
- A node with a dependency relation "non-verbal element", "verb particle", or "enclitic non-verbal element" belongs to the same VP as its head.
- If a node is a particle, subordinating clause, coordinating conjunction, or punctuation, we should not create an independent chunk for it.
- If a node is a "noun post modifier" or "Ezafe dependent", attach it to its parent chunk.
- If a node is a "conjunction of a noun" or "conjunction of an adjective" and has a sibling with either "Ezafe dependent" or "noun post-modifier" dependency relation, it should have the same chunk as its parent.
- If a node with pseudo-sentence POS has an adverbial dependency with its parent, it creates an ADVP and otherwise a VP.

Implementation of the above rules is available in the Hazm toolkit.[2] There are some minor exceptions in the above rules that are handled manually in the toolkit.

3 Experiments

In this section we describe our experiments on Ezafe tagging, parsing and also adding manual Ezafe tags to the Persian dependency treebank.

3.1 Automatic Ezafe Tagging

As mentioned in §2, we attach Ezafe feature indicator to the tags and train a POS tagger on the new tagset. We use Wapiti tagger (Lavergne et al., 2010) to train a standard trigram CRF sequence tagger model with standard transition features and the following emission features: word form of the current, previous and next word, combination of the current word and next word, combination of the current word and previous word, prefixes and suffixes up to length 3, indicator of punctuation and number (digit) for the current, previous and next word. The tagger has an accuracy of 98.71% with the original tagset and 97.33% with the modified tagset.

3.2 Gold Standard Ezafe Tags

The Persian dependency treebank does not provide gold Ezafe tags. In order to evaluate the effect of gold Ezafe tags, we try to manually annotate Ezafe in the treebank. This is done by six annotators where all of them are native speakers and linguists. The inter-annotator agreement of a small portion of the data (one thousand sentences) is 99.6%. Our manual investigation shows that almost half of the disagreements was because of the mistakes and not because of the complicated structure. Table 1 shows the statistics about the presence of Ezafe tag for each specific POS.

3.3 Chunking

We use Wapiti tagger (Lavergne et al., 2010) to train a standard CRF tagger with IOB tags for phrase chunking. The features include third order transition features and emission features of word form and POS for the current word, previous word and the word before it, the next word and the word after it. As shown in Table 2 and 3, our intuition holds for both gold and automatic tags. We observe that using Ezafe on gold tags, gives

[2]https://github.com/sobhe/hazm

Tag	Freq.	Relative Freq.	Ezafe %
N	190048	39.24%	34.22%
PREP	56376	11.64%	12.04%
ADJ	35902	7.41%	17.45%
PRENUM	6018	1.24%	1.21%
IDEN	835	0.17%	5.03%
POSNUM	560	0.12%	30.71%
other	194572	40.18%	00.10%

Table 1: Statistics about Ezafe for each POS tag in the Persian dependency treebank.

us better performance compared to using coarse-grained POS tags and also fine-grained POS tags (FPOS) provided by the dependency treebank annotators. The tagset in Peykare corpus is very different from the treebank. Because of this inconsistency, we could not reproduce the results with automatic FPOS tags trained on Peykare corpus. Our experiments on training solely on the treebank FPOS tags do not give us a reliable FPOS tagger and this leads to very low parsing accuracy. Therefore we do not conduct experiments with automatic FPOS tags. Table 3 shows the results with automatic tags. As shown in the table, using the the Ezafe tagset improves the chunking accuracy.

Tagset	Precision	Recall	F-Measure
POS	91.98%	90.37%	91.17%
FPOS	92.37%	90.92%	91.64%
POSe	**93.88%**	**93.97%**	**93.92%**

Table 2: Chunking results on the Persian dependency treebank test data with gold POS tags. FPOS refers to the fine-grained POS tags in the Persian dependency treebank and POSe is the modified Ezafe-enriched tagset.

Tagset	Tag Acc.	Precision	Recall	F-Measure
POS	98.71%	89.44%	88.02%	88.72%
POSe	97.33%	**90.42%**	**89.13%**	**89.77%**

Table 3: Chunking results on the Persian dependency treebank test data with automatic POS tags.

3.4 Dependency Parsing

Similar to the chunking experiments, we provide two sets of experiments to validate our hypothesis about the importance of Ezafe construction. We

Tagset	MaltParser		YaraParser		TurboParser	
	LAS	UAS	LAS	UAS	LAS	UAS
POS	88.13%	90.69%	88.60%	91.17%	89.88%	92.25%
FPOS	88.46%	91.01%	89.02%	91.56%	89.98%	92.30%
POSe	**89.12%**	**91.64%**	**89.91%**	**92.42%**	**90.85%**	**93.24%**

Table 4: Dependency Parsing results on the test data with different gold standard tagsets. UAS is the unlabeled attachment score and LAS is the labeled attachment score.

Tagset	Tag acc.	MaltParser		YaraParser		TurboParser	
		LAS	UAS	LAS	UAS	LAS	UAS
POS tagger	98.71%	85.34%	88.80%	85.90%	89.43%	87.28%	90.59%
POSe tagger	97.33%	**85.74%**	**89.24%**	**86.35%**	**89.86%**	**87.73%**	**91.02%**

Table 5: Dependency Parsing results on the test data with different automatic tagsets.

use three different off-the-shelf parsers: 1) Malt parser v1.8 (Nivre et al., 2007), 2) Yara parser v0.2 (Rasooli and Tetreault, 2015), and 3) Turbo parser v2.2 (Martins et al., 2013). We train Malt with Covington non-projective algorithm (Covington, 1990) after optimizing it with Malt optimizer (Ballesteros and Nivre, 2012), Yara with the default settings (64 beam) and 10 training epochs and Turbo with its default settings. The main reason for picking these three parsers is that we want to see the effect of Ezafe construction on a greedy parser (Malt), beam parser (Yara), and a graph-based parser (Turbo). As shown in Table 4 and 5, the parsing accuracy is improved across all different parsers by using the Ezafe tagset.

4 Error Analysis

In this section we provide some error analysis for showing the effectiveness of our approach.

Effect on the common POS tags Our investigation on the development data shows that the dependency attachment accuracy is improved by 6.5% for adjectives and 6.2% for nouns. This is consistent with our intuition because Ezafe construction mostly occurs in nouns and adjectives. It is worth noting that for some tags such as determiners the Ezafe construction does not help.

Ezafe indicator as a feature We try to use Ezafe as an independent feature in Malt parser. This is done by adding the indicator in the feature column in CoNLL dependency format. We then use Malt optimizer (Ballesteros and Nivre, 2012) to find the optimized feature setting. We see that adding this feature gives us the same accuracy improvement as having the modified tagset. This shows that we do not really need to have a parser that uses extra features to add Ezafe information.

Manual data investigation We randomly picked some sentences from the development data and observed the same effect as we could expect from adding Ezafe to the tagset: the main gain is on those sentences where the presence/absence of Ezafe construction is crucial for making correct decisions by the parser. For example, in the following sub-sentence, the word چین means "China" but the dependency parser without knowing Ezafe tag, confused it with the other meaning: "ruffle" and created a "non-verbal element" (light verb) dependency with the verb, instead of making it an Ezafe dependent to the previous word (سواحل).

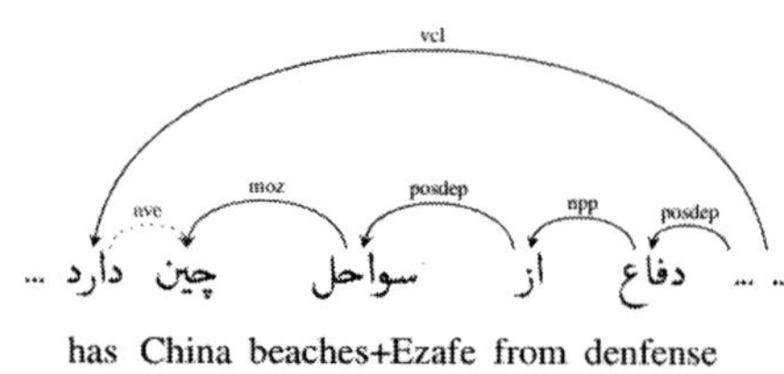

Effect on the training data size For investigating the benefit of Ezafe construction, we train Malt parser on different data sizes starting from 50% of the original size. This trend is depicted in Figure 2. The interesting fact is that we can leverage Ezafe construction and use only 70% of the training data while reaching the accuracy of the original part of speech tagset trained on the whole data.

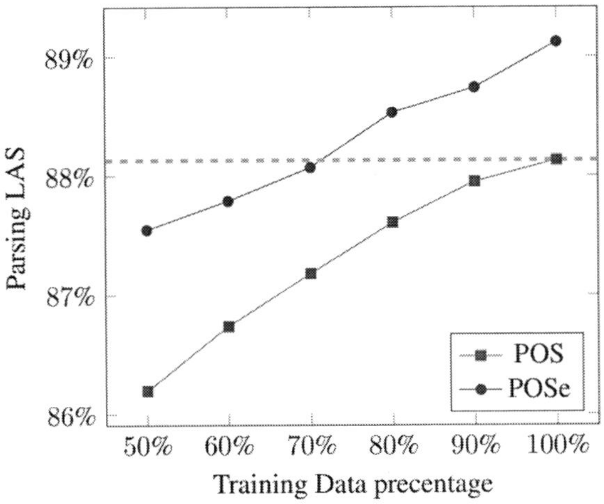

Figure 2: Trend on the data size and accuracy. As shown by the horizontal dashed line, Ezafe tags can improve over standard tags while having approximately 70% of the data.

5 Conclusion

In this paper we showed the effectiveness of Ezafe construction as a robust feature for syntactic parsing in Persian. One interesting direction for further research would be to show the effect of this feature in other natural language processing tasks.

Acknowledgement

We thank Computer Research Center of Islamic Sciences (CRCIS) for supporting us on corpus annotation. We thank Parinaz Dadras, Saeedeh Ghadrdoost-Nakhchi, Manouchehr Kouhestani, Mostafa Mahdavi, Azadeh Mirzaei, Neda Poormorteza-Khameneh, Morteza Rezaei-Sharifabadi and Salimeh Zamani for helping us on annotation and the three anonymous reviewers for their helpful comments.

References

Simin Abrahams. 2004. *Modern Persian: a coursebook*. Routledge.

Habibollah Asghari, Jalal Maleki, and Heshaam Faili. 2014. A probabilistic approach to persian ezafe recognition. In *Proceedings of the 14th Conference of the European Chapter of the Association for Computational Linguistics*, pages 138–142, Gothenburg, Sweden, April. Association for Computational Linguistics.

Miguel Ballesteros and Joakim Nivre. 2012. Maltoptimizer: A system for maltparser optimization. In *Proceedings of the Eighth International Conference on Language Resources and Evaluation*, pages 2757–2763, Istanbul, Turkey, May. European Language Resources Association (ELRA).

Mahmood Bijankhan, Javad Sheykhzadegan, Mohammad Bahrani, and Masood Ghayoomi. 2011. Lessons from building a Persian written corpus: Peykare. *Language Resources and Evaluation*, 45:143–164.

Michael A Covington. 1990. Parsing discontinuous constituents in dependency grammar. *Computational Linguistics*, 16(4):234–236.

Masood Ghayoomi. 2012. Word clustering for Persian statistical parsing. In *Advances in Natural Language Processing*, pages 126–137. Springer.

Jila Ghomeshi. 1997. Non-projecting nouns and the ezafe: Construction in Persian. *Natural Language & Linguistic Theory*, 15(4):729–788.

Nizar Y Habash. 2010. Introduction to Arabic natural language processing. *Synthesis Lectures on Human Language Technologies*, 3(1):1–187.

Mojtaba Khallash, Ali Hadian, and Behrouz Minaei-Bidgoli. 2013. An empirical study on the effect of morphological and lexical features in Persian dependency parsing. In *Proceedings of the Fourth Workshop on Statistical Parsing of Morphologically-Rich Languages*, pages 97–107, Seattle, Washington, USA, October. Association for Computational Linguistics.

Soheila Kian, Tara Akhavan, and Mehrnoush Shamsfard. 2009. Developing a Persian chunker using a hybrid approach. In *International Multiconference on Computer Science and Information Technology, 2009. IMCSIT'09*, pages 227–234. IEEE.

Thomas Lavergne, Olivier Cappé, and François Yvon. 2010. Practical very large scale CRFs. In *Proceedings the 48th Annual Meeting of the Association for Computational Linguistics (ACL)*, pages 504–513. Association for Computational Linguistics, July.

André F. T. Martins, Miguel Almeida, and Noah A. Smith. 2013. Turning on the turbo: Fast third-order non-projective turbo parsers. pages 617–622.

Joakim Nivre, Johan Hall, Jens Nilsson, Atanas Chanev, Gülsen Eryigit, Sandra Kübler, Svetoslav Marinov, and Erwin Marsi. 2007. Maltparser: A language-independent system for data-driven dependency parsing. *Natural Language Engineering*, 13(02):95–135.

Samira Noferesti and Mehrnoush Shamsfard. 2014. A hybrid algorithm for recognizing the position of ezafe constructions in Persian texts. *International Journal of Interactive Multimedia and Artificial Intelligence*, 2(6):17–25.

Mohammad Sadegh Rasooli and Joel Tetreault. 2015. Yara parser: A fast and accurate dependency parser. *arXiv preprint arXiv:1503.06733*.

Mohammad Sadegh Rasooli, Manouchehr Kouhestani, and Amirsaeid Moloodi. 2013. Development of a Persian syntactic dependency treebank. In *Proceedings of the 2013 Conference of the North American Chapter of the Association for Computational Linguistics: Human Language Technologies*, pages 306–314.

Pollet Samvelian. 2006. When morphology does better than syntax: the Ezafe construction in Persian. *Ms., Université de Paris*, (1997):1–54.

Djamé Seddah, Reut Tsarfaty, Sandra Kübler, Marie Candito, Jinho D. Choi, Richard Farkas, Jennifer Foster, Iakes Goenaga, Koldo Gojenola, Yoav Goldberg, Spence Green, Nizar Habash, Marco Kuhlmann, Wolfgang Maier, Joakim Nivre, Adam Przepiorkowski, Ryan Roth, Wolfgang Seeker, Yannick Versley, Veronika Vincze, Marcin Wolinski, Alina Wroblewska, and Eric Villemonte de la Clergerie. 2013. Overview of the SPMRL 2013 shared task : Cross-framework evaluation of parsing morphologically rich languages. *Proceedings of the Fourth Workshop on Statistical Parsing of Morphologically Rich Languages*, (October):146–182.

Wolfgang Seeker and Jonas Kuhn. 2013. Morphological and syntactic case in statistical dependency parsing. *Computational Linguistics*, 39(1):23–55.

Mojgan Seraji, Beáta Megyesi, and Joakim Nivre. 2012. Dependency parsers for Persian. In *Proceedings of the 10th Workshop on Asian Language Resources*, pages 35–44, Mumbai, India, December. The COLING 2012 Organizing Committee.

Author Index